WITHDRAWN

AMERICAN NATIONAL BIOGRAPHY

AMERICAN
NATIONAL BIOGRAPHY

Published under the auspices of the
AMERICAN COUNCIL OF LEARNED SOCIETIES

General Editors

John A. Garraty

Mark C. Carnes

VOLUME 20

OXFORD UNIVERSITY PRESS

New York   1999   Oxford

OXFORD UNIVERSITY PRESS

Oxford   New York
Athens Auckland Bangkok Bogotá
Buenos Aires Calcutta Cape Town Chennai
Dar es Salaam Delhi Florence Hong Kong Istanbul
Karachi Kuala Lumpur Madrid Melbourne Mexico City
Mumbai Nairobi Paris São Paulo Singapore
Taipei Tokyo Toronto Warsaw
and associated companies in
Berlin   Ibadan

Published by Oxford University Press, Inc.,
198 Madison Avenue, New York, New York 10016
http://www.oup-usa.org

Funding for this publication was provided in part by
the Andrew W. Mellon Foundation, the Rockefeller Foundation,
and the National Endowment for the Humanities,
a federal agency.

Library of Congress Cataloging-in-Publication Data

American national biography / general editors, John A. Garraty, Mark C. Carnes
p.   cm.
"Published under the auspices of the American Council of Learned Societies."
Includes bibliographical references and index.
1. United States—Biography—Dictionaries. I. Garraty, John Arthur,
1920– .   II. Carnes, Mark C. (Mark Christopher), 1950–   .
III. American Council of Learned Societies.
CT213.A68   1998   98-20826   920.073—dc21   CIP
ISBN 0-19-520635-5 (set)
ISBN 0-19-512799-4 (vol. 20)

Printing (last digit): 9 8 7 6 5 4 3 2 1

Printed in the United States of America
on acid-free paper

American national biography

S

CONTINUED

SIMMS, Florence (17 Apr. 1873–6 Jan. 1923), Christian social reformer and Young Women's Christian Association (YWCA) leader, was born Daisy Florence Simms in Rushville, Indiana, the daughter of Michael M. Simms, a farmer and "homespun philosopher," and Jane Amanda Taylor, a devout Methodist. As a child, she performed well in school and exhibited a flair for public speaking, winning several elocution competitions. Encouraged by her father, she attended DePauw University on a scholarship and graduated in 1895 with a bachelor of philosophy degree.

Although Simms joined the Kappa Alpha Theta sorority, she was too outgoing and independent to confine her friendships only to her sorority sisters. Temperance and women's rights commanded her interest during her college years, and through the campus branch of the YWCA she was able to apply her deeply felt religious convictions to the pursuit of those interests. She sincerely believed in the message of Christ and the place it should have in daily life. Even the temptations of college life could not dissuade her from her strict Methodist view of Christianity. When competing social and religious obligations conflicted, Simms followed the religious demands.

The college women of DePauw recognized Simms as a champion of women's rights. Her eloquence, humor, and intelligence in pleading the cause of women prompted the American Committee of the YWCA in Chicago to offer her an appointment to the staff upon her graduation.

For the next two years Simms traveled to colleges and universities in the upper Mississippi Valley. Her purpose was twofold, to bring to women students the ideal of the Christian life and to organize and revitalize branches of the YWCA. Her success in this mission was aided by the fact that she believed in her message. With persuasive oratory, the statuesque redhead with "flashing" grey eyes established 278 college branches with 12,000 members during her period of service.

After Chicago, Simms spent two years in Portland, Maine, and another two years in Binghamton, New York. With each new appointment, she performed "especially good work" and was praised for being "an energetic worker" who possessed "marked executive ability." In 1902 the YWCA promoted her to executive secretary of the Michigan State Committee. In 1904 she became cosecretary of the Industrial Department of the American Committee. For the remainder of her life, Florence Simms would be vitally concerned with the conditions of women in industry.

When Simms first became secretary of the Industrial Department, she still believed that simply bringing the message of Christianity to the women in the mills and factories would produce for them the "abundant life." Gradually, however, it became clear to her that women needed more in their lives than the gospel. Her contact with industrial workers opened her eyes to the severe conditions under which they labored: long hours, low wages, unemployment, child labor, unsafe work areas, and difficulty in organizing. Over time, Simms's religious conservatism metamorphosed, and she became a staunch religious liberal, living the social gospel in defense of working women, not only through the YWCA but also in cooperation with the Consumer's League, the National Women's Trade Union League, the Social Service Commission of the Federal Council of Churches, and the American Association for Labor Legislation. Simms realized that perfection of the individual could only be achieved through perfection of society.

In 1906 the American Committee of the YWCA and the International Committee merged to form the National Board of the YWCA. Simms moved to the headquarters in New York City, where she was promoted to secretary of the National Board Industrial Department, a position she held until her death.

Shortly after her appointment to the National Board, Simms was chosen to chair an international commission to study the place of the YWCA in social and industrial life. Based on her report presented at the 1910 international meeting in Berlin, Germany, the YWCA passed resolutions committing the association to education and support of legislation to regulate hours and wages for industrial women. For the first time, the National YWCA advocated active participation in the field of women's rights.

At the 1920 convention, at Simms's urging, the National Board recommended a "Social Ideals" platform of sixteen items designed to ameliorate the conditions of women and children in the workplace. Although "inhuman" conditions shocked many women, others were equally shocked over the "Social Ideals." One National Board member went so far as to obliquely accuse Simms of radical socialism. Undaunted by this personal attack, Simms addressed the convention and spoke with fervor of Christian social principles and what the YWCA should be doing to further legislation aimed at working women. After two days' debate, all of the recommendations were unanimously accepted.

For her last two years, Simms traveled extensively to industrial departments of the YWCA throughout the United States, urging them to recognize that their strength lay in educating women about the labor movement. Only through education would working women learn of the power of collective action in attaining their rights. The religious individualism of Simms's early years had completely disappeared, to be

1

replaced by her concern for the whole society of industrial women.

In the fall of 1922 Simms developed problems with her throat, which were manifested as a bad cough and difficulty in speaking. She disregarded her doctor's advice to rest and continued to work her regular schedule. On a Christmas visit with her parents in Mattoon, Illinois, she underwent mastoid surgery and did not recover. Simms had never married.

Through her involvement in the YWCA, Simms converted from a Christian conservative to a social gospel activist. The Industrial Department of the YWCA, in turn, provided an innovative way for this Christian social reformer to reach immigrant and working women. Her belief that all women, working in concert, could effect the kingdom of God on earth set the YWCA on a path of social reform that has not wavered.

• Some of Simms's papers are in the YWCA archives at the National Headquarters in New York City and in the YWCA Papers, Smith College. Biographies include Richard Roberts, *Florence Simms* (1926), and Marion O. Robinson, *Eight Women of the YWCA* (1966). See Mary Van Kleeck, "Florence Simms," *Woman's Press* (Apr. 1923), for a contemporary account, along with obituaries in the *New York Times*, 7 Jan. 1923, and the *Mattoon (Ill.) Daily Journal Gazette*, 6 and 8 Jan. 1923.

PATRICIA AUSTIN DiSABATINO

SIMMS, William Elliott (2 Jan. 1822–25 June 1898), lawyer and congressman, was born near Cynthiana, Kentucky, the son of William Marmaduke Simms, a farmer, and Julia Shropshire. His mother died when Simms was quite young. In 1840 his brother died and his father was in poor health, so he took over the family farm. After his father died in 1844, Simms entered Transylvania University to study law and graduated in 1846. He practiced in Paris, Bourbon County, Kentucky, which remained his residence for the rest of his life. Simms must have been a man of some wealth, for he was reported as owning seven slaves in the 1860 census.

The Mexican War began shortly after Simms moved to Paris, and in 1847 he raised a company of volunteers for the Third Kentucky Regiment of Infantry and was selected as captain. After the war he ran as a Democrat for the Kentucky House of Representatives and won, serving in 1849. He returned to his law practice with notable success, but he also continued his interest in politics. In 1857 he became editor of the *Kentucky State Flag*, a paper that supported the positions of the Democratic party and secession.

Simms is significant primarily for his political activity just before and during the Civil War. A Democratic candidate for Congress in 1859, he waged a bitter campaign that culminated in the threat of a duel with former Know Nothing and bitter anti-secessionist Garrett Davis, but the adversaries settled their differences before blood was shed. Simms won election, defeating John Marshall Harlan by a mere sixty votes. He served in the Thirty-sixth Congress, 1859–1861, taking a

strong prosouthern stand on the issues of the day. He claimed in February 1861 that the Republican party had chosen "to inaugurate civil war" for the purpose of "enforcing the laws" and "the overthrow of slavery." His opinions on the nature of the Union were too extreme for most of his constituents, however, and although he was renominated by the Democrats, he lost a special election in June 1861 to John J. Crittenden, who ran as a Unionist and received 8,272 votes to Simms's 5,706. Simms urged secession if the government attempted to coerce any state to remain in the Union. In his postwar amnesty petition to President Andrew Johnson he explained that he had believed "that the cause of the South was just—that it was the cause of constitutional liberty and free government."

In September 1861 he, John C. Breckinridge, and other leading Kentuckians with Confederate sympathies broke with the Union and with the established government of Kentucky, which remained loyal to the Union. Simms entered the Confederate army and was assigned to raising and organizing troops. After the Russellville convention established a pro-Confederate provisional government, 18–20 November 1861, and passed an ordinance of secession, Simms resigned his colonelcy and became a lieutenant colonel. In command of the First Battalion of Kentucky Cavalry, he saw action with General Humphrey Marshall (1812–1872) in Kentucky and western Virginia. The provisional government of Kentucky appointed him commissioner to the Confederate government to negotiate admission into the Confederacy. Simms addressed the Provisional Congress on 9 December 1861, and Kentucky was formally admitted to the Confederacy the following day. On 3 January 1862 the provisional legislature selected him senator in the permanent Confederate Congress. He served in this role from the opening day of the First Congress, 18 February 1862, to the final adjournment of the Second Congress, 18 March 1865, having been reelected by the provisional government of Kentucky in 1864.

Simms favored drastic action to ensure Confederate victory. He opposed the system of substitution in the original Confederate conscription laws; he also favored a broad construction of the Confederate constitution and believed the war power was "unlimited." He thought the Confederate government had the constitutional power to seize the railroads, and by the end of the war he was willing to take the drastic step of recruiting blacks for the Confederate army. He even proposed that Confederate president Jefferson Davis take the field and lead the armies himself, although toward the end he supported changes in the Confederate command system because he became disillusioned with Davis's leadership. As he confessed after the war, he had "advocated and voted for any measure . . . which he believed would honorably contribute to the ability and power of the Government to maintain the position of Independence it had assumed."

After the war Simms applied for pardon and received it from President Johnson in December 1865. Uncomfortable with the change in affairs, however,

Simms moved to Virginia for a short time and then to Canada. He returned to Kentucky in January 1866, withdrew from politics, and devoted the remaining thirty-two years of his life to agriculture, becoming one of the wealthiest men in the country. He was married in 1866 to Lucy Blythe, and they had three children. He died in Paris, Kentucky.

Simms was not a particularly outstanding figure, but he is a good example of the border state mentality in the Confederacy. He was far more willing than deep south congressmen to grant the Confederate government sweeping powers if it would help win the war, and he always had the comfort of knowing that, since Kentucky was under Union control, his constituents would not be affected by the actions of the Confederate government. His behavior in the postwar period is also typical, showing at first resignation at the turn of events then acceptance and achievement in another field.

• Like many former Confederates, Simms explained himself in his postwar amnesty petition to President Johnson, which is found in Case Files of Applications from Former Confederates for Presidential Pardons (Amnesty Papers), 1865–1867, Record Group 94, Records of the Adjutant General's Office, 1780–1917, National Archives Microfilm Publication M-1003. The best brief sketches of Simms are in John E. Kleber, ed., *The Kentucky Encyclopedia* (1992), and in *The Biographical Encyclopedia of Kentucky of the Dead and Living Men of the Nineteenth Century* (1878), although Lewis Collins and Richard H. Collins, *History of Kentucky* (2 vols., 1874), is also useful. The most significant portions of Simms's political career are covered by the *Congressional Globe* for the Thirty-sixth U.S. Congress; the *Journal of the Congress of the Confederate States of America, 1861–1865*, vols. 2–4, 58th Cong., 2d sess., 1904–1905, S. Doc. 234; and the "Proceedings of the . . . Confederate Congress" [title varies], *Southern Historical Society Papers*, vols. 44–52 (1923–1959). Brief sketches of Simms's career are found in the *Biographical Directory of the American Congress 1774–1989* (1989), which, however, contains inaccuracies; Stewart Sifakis, *Who Was Who in the Civil War* (1988); Jon L. Wakelyn, *Biographical Dictionary of the Confederacy* (1977); and Ezra J. Warner and W. Buck Yearns, *Biographical Register of the Confederate Congress* (1975).

RICHARD E. BERINGER

SIMMS, William Gilmore (17 Apr. 1806–11 June 1870), author, was born in Charleston, South Carolina, the son of William Gilmore Simms, a merchant, and Harriet Ann Augusta Singleton. When Simms was not yet two, his mother died in childbirth (the baby dying also); and his disconsolate father, calling Charleston "a place of tombs," left the city, eventually settling in Mississippi, where he acquired a plantation and remained for the rest of his life (Trent, p. 4). The young Simms was reared in Charleston by his maternal grandmother, Jane Miller Singleton Gates, who told him stories of Indians, pirates, the colonial era, and the American Revolution, thereby stimulating his imagination and furnishing him with a vast fund of material on which he would draw for his writing.

Simms claimed that his formal education was "almost wholly nominal & was wretchedly neglected": he attended the city schools for four years and the College of Charleston for two (*Letters*, vol. 1, p. 161). The family's financial circumstances were modest, and Simms's grandmother took him out of school when he was twelve in order to apprentice him to an apothecary, apparently hoping to prepare him for a career in medicine. Somewhat later he studied law and practiced briefly as an attorney. But his literary ambitions were already manifest: during boyhood he had become, as he told a correspondent, "an insatiate reader" who "soon emptied all the bookcases" of his friends and also a productive young writer who penned odes, sonnets, sketches, and tragedies (*Letters*, vol. 1, p. 161).

Encouraging Simms's inclination toward authorship were two long trips he made in the mid-1820s to see his father in Mississippi when it was still Indian and pioneer territory. He and his father explored the wild and primitive region by horseback, sometimes going several hundred miles west of the Mississippi. Though his father urged him to remain in Mississippi, Simms was already engaged to Anna Malcolm Giles, a Charleston woman he had known for some years; and, returning to South Carolina, he married her in 1826 (ill since youth, she died in 1832, leaving him a single daughter to rear).

Simms's upbringing and travels exposed him to two great historic regions of the South: the Tidewater, with its strong sense of tradition and the past, and the Gulf South, or Old Southwestern frontier, in its pioneer and settlement stages. His knowledge of these regions, amplified by reading and by further travel in the Gulf South and the Appalachian mountains, sinewed his best work and formed the basis for his view of southern culture. His experiences are reflected in his poetry, histories, biographies, and essays, and they gave rise to the two major branches of his fiction: historical romances, tales, and short novels set in the low country that trace its development from the seventeenth century through the Revolution and the antebellum era, and novels and tales set in the Old Southwest or the Appalachian mountains portraying adventure, crime, and comedy in the backwoods. From these branches derive the three major groups of his novels: the revolutionary war, border, and mountain romances.

In 1825–1826, Simms joined other young Charlestonians in editing a weekly journal, the *Album*; in the late 1820s and in the early 1830s he edited or helped to edit the *Southern Literary Gazette*, the *Cosmopolitan*, and the *Charleston City Gazette*. An ardent "Southron," he hoped that the journals would provide appropriate outlets for the literary productions of his fellow southerners. But because contributions were slow to come in he was forced to fill the pages of the journals with much of his own early fiction and verse, an activity that marks the beginning of his career as a professional author. He collected some of his poetry in several volumes, among them *Lyrical and Other Poems* and *The Vision of Cortes*, issued near the end of the 1820s.

In the 1830s—encouraged by the success of Walter Scott in England and James Fenimore Cooper in the United States—Simms moved confidently into the field of long fiction, particularly historical fiction, which has formed the lasting basis for his literary reputation. His first three novels, *Guy Rivers* (1834), *The Yemassee* (1835), and *The Partisan* (1835), garnered tremendous acclaim. Reviewers insisted that his fiction equalled or surpassed Cooper's, observed that his name guaranteed the quality of his books, and announced that his reputation was permanently established. Spurred by this praise, during the decade Simms published several additional novels—*Mellichampe* (1836), *Richard Hurdis* (1838), *Pelayo* (1838), and *The Damsel of Darien* (1839)—as well as three collections of short fiction, a pamphlet on slavery, and a substantial volume of poetry, *Southern Passages and Pictures* (1839). Virtually all of these volumes were issued by important northern houses. Beginning in the 1830s and continuing until the Civil War, Simms went north almost every year to see his publishers and superintend his publishing interests, becoming in effect a Knickerbocker author, well known and influential in city social and literary circles (Trent, p. 72). In 1836 he wed Chevillette Eliza Roach, the daughter of a wealthy South Carolina planter, and settled with her upon one of the family plantations, "Woodlands." He and Chevillette enjoyed a life of extremely happy domesticity for nearly thirty years, during which time they had fourteen children, only five of whom lived to adulthood.

Throughout the 1830s and the 1840s Simms was also making valuable literary and political friends—William Cullen Bryant, Herman Melville, Washington Irving, and others in the North; Nathaniel Beverley Tucker, James Henry Hammond, John Pendleton Kennedy, and many others in the South. In the middle 1840s he served in the state legislature and narrowly lost the race for lieutenant governor in 1846. Tirelessly promoting southern literature, from the 1840s onward he befriended dozens of established or aspiring authors, among them Edgar Allan Poe, Henry Timrod, John Esten Cooke (1830–1886), and Paul Hamilton Hayne.

But even as Simms's political and literary influence was growing, his literary prospects were beginning to decline. The severe financial recession known as the panic of 1837, whose effects lasted well into the 1840s, made the publication of costly two-volume novels such as his and Cooper's economically unprofitable. Further harming the sales of long fiction were the spread of cheap paper-bound books and the appearance of "mammoth weekly" newspapers whose publishers pirated the work of popular British writers.

Thus, at a time when Simms might naturally have continued to cultivate his reputation as a novelist by mining the veins of long fiction he had opened in the previous decade, he was forced away from his major field into a welter of miscellaneous work. Early in the 1840s he brought out four novels—*Border Beagles* (1840), *The Kinsmen* (1841; later retitled *The Scout*), *Confession* (1841), and *Beauchampe* (1842). When these sold poorly, he devoted the remainder of the decade to history, biography, short novels, tales, and poetry, producing an astonishing total of twenty-nine books. Particularly noteworthy among these were *The History of South Carolina* (1840); two volumes of literary criticism titled *Views and Reviews in American Literature, History and Fiction* (1845); and a remarkable collection of short fiction, *The Wigwam and the Cabin* (1845), depicting life in the colonial low country and the nineteenth-century backwoods South. In addition to this immense amount of writing, Simms somehow found time to edit two influential periodicals, the *Magnolia* and the *Southern and Western Monthly Magazine and Review*, popularly known as "Simms's Magazine." And from 1849 through 1854 he served as editor of the *Southern Quarterly Review*, for which he secured contributions from some of the best-known southern writers of the era.

By 1850 the book market had sufficiently recovered for Simms to resume the writing of novels, and he published some of his best works, including *Woodcraft* (1854), *The Forayers* (1855), *Eutaw* (1856), and *The Cassique of Kiawah* (1859). He also brought out several short novels, the most notable perhaps an urbane comedy of plantation manners called *The Golden Christmas* (1852) and an impressive two-volume collection of his poetry entitled *Poems Descriptive, Dramatic, Legendary and Contemplative* (1853).

Midway through the decade, however, Simms's personal circumstances took an unfortunate turn. During an extended lecture tour of the North in 1856, he offended audiences through uncomplimentary references to northern politicians and strident praise of South Carolina that carried distinct political overtones. Surprised by hostile reviews in northern newspapers, he canceled the rest of the tour, donated what he had earned to public charities, and returned to Woodlands. During the remainder of the 1850s plantation responsibilities and such family tragedies as the deaths of several young children (including two sons on the same day in 1858) hampered his ability to write. Further hampering it were the increasing debts at Woodlands that forced him into "clearing lands, making compost, cutting diches, making fences, building houses, [and] giving physic" instead of composing literature (*Letters*, vol. 4, p. 112).

Simms's personal difficulties multiplied during the 1860s; in fact, by the end of the decade, he told a correspondent that he felt he had "been tried in all the furnaces of affliction" (*Letters*, vol. 5, p. 174). In 1861 he lost a son and daughter; then in 1863 his wife died suddenly, leaving him with several children to rear. Woodlands burned twice during the Civil War, destroying Simms's magnificent library of more than 10,000 volumes.

Helping to deflect Simms's attention from these losses was his wholehearted involvement in the Confederate cause. Long an advocate of slavery and secession, he revealed his skill as a military tactician in letters of the early 1860s, which are filled with plans for firing on the forts in the Charleston harbor, reinforcing defenses with iron, and seizing Union vessels in the bay. The war also found a place in his other writing: he treated it in poetry, in the framing story of his backwoods novel *Paddy McGann* (serialized 1863), in the graphic, vigorous *Sack and Destruction of the City of Columbia, S.C.* (1865), and in the anthology *War Poetry of the South* (1866) that he compiled and edited. Inevitably, however, the conflict—which interrupted Simms's negotiations with northern publishers and hurt the sales of his books—damaged a career already harmed by sectional politics and economic recession.

After the war Simms resumed his annual visits to the North; and in the autumn of 1868, desperately trying to support his family, he took contracts for three books to be written at the same time. One of these volumes, never completed, was apparently to deal with the colonial era. For the other two, which were serialized late in the 1860s, as well as several shorter works, he turned for material to the Appalachian mountains—the only important region of the South he had not yet fully treated in his fiction. Little known until the 1970s, the novels based on his travels in the mountains in the 1840s, *The Cub of the Panther* and *Voltmeier* (both serialized in 1869), are noteworthy for their combination of realism and folklore, their biting social commentary, and their humor. And the two fine tall tales likewise deriving from his mountain trip, "How Sharp Snaffles Got His Capital and Wife" and "Bald-Head Bill Bauldy," put Simms into the first rank of nineteenth-century southern backwoods humorists. But the enormous load of writing strained Simms's health severely. He wrote a friend that he had confined himself to his desk for "nearly 9 months, without walking a mile in a week, riding but twice and absent from work but half a day on each of these occasions. The consequence was that I finished two of the books & broke down on the third. . . . I have been forbidden the studio, & do little beyond my correspondence which, at all times has been very exacting" (*Letters*, vol. 5, p. 282). Exhausted by this work, and suffering from an undiagnosed disease that was probably cancer, he died in Charleston, surrounded by the surviving members of his family.

A widely read writer with a national and even an international reputation, Simms was enormously influential as author and cultural spokesman throughout the antebellum era. But ultimately the story of his life and career is a tragic story, and thus far the extent of the tragedy—its effect on his writing and his posthumous reputation—has not been fully understood or explored. He began his career as the most promising of southern writers, with "brilliant prospects . . . opening before him"; he concluded it an ill, careworn old man "living quite obscurely, whether at home or abroad," "drearily drudging at the desk," and striving "simply to procure the wherewithal of life for my children" (*Southern Literary Journal* 1 [1835]: 284; *Letters*, vol. 5, pp. 213, 201). An extremely productive

author with a fine comic imagination, he worked hastily, and much of his work is uneven in quality. But his best writing, including *Woodcraft*, *The Golden Christmas*, "Sharp Snaffles," and "Bill Bauldy," is firm, direct, bold, and moving, made memorable by clever social satire or sprightly dialect humor. Unjustly obscuring his considerable attainment in letters were factors over which he had no control—the recession of 1837, which forced him away from his major field, long fiction; the deleterious effects of the Civil War upon the sale of his books; and the lack of regard after the war for antebellum southern literature, especially that espousing proslavery sentiments.

Simms's great importance, for his century and thereafter, lies—as one of his most perceptive contemporaries saw—in his extraordinary ability to reflect "the moral and intellectual attributes that distinguish the spirit and temper of Southern civilization." In his writing, he "announces its opinions, illustrates its ideas, embodies its passions and prejudices, and betrays those delicate shades of thought, feeling, and conduct, that go to form the character, and stamp the individuality of a people" (*De Bow's Review* 29 [1860]: 708). Many of the elements—its concern with history, its evocation of era and region, its attention to concrete, particularized details, and its emphasis upon the art of telling a good story—are anticipated in the work of William Gilmore Simms.

• Simms's most important papers, including personal memoranda and manuscripts of unpublished works, are in the Charles Carroll Simms Collection at the South Caroliniana Library, University of South Carolina. The most valuable single source for the study of the author is *The Letters of William Gilmore Simms*, ed. Mary C. Simms Oliphant, Alfred Taylor Odell, and T. C. Duncan Eaves (6 vols., 1952–1982). The two full-length biographies of Simms are William P. Trent, *William Gilmore Simms* (1892), inaccurate in many of its facts and badly dated in its judgments, and John C. Guilds, *Simms: A Literary Life* (1992), the authorized and authoritative treatment. Critical studies include J. V. Ridgely, *William Gilmore Simms* (1962); several essays on Simms collected in C. Hugh Holman, *The Roots of Southern Writing* (1972); the articles appearing in John C. Guilds, ed., *"Long Years of Neglect": The Work and Reputation of William Gilmore Simms* (1988); and Mary Ann Wimsatt, *The Major Fiction of William Gilmore Simms* (1989). The most significant treatments of Simms's poetry are by James E. Kibler, Jr., *The Poetry of William Gilmore Simms: An Introduction and Bibliography* (1979) and *Selected Poems of William Gilmore Simms* (1990), which contains a lengthy introduction. A useful survey of Simms's extensive work as a critic may be found in Edd Winfield Parks, *William Gilmore Simms as Literary Critic* (1961). Bibliographies of Simms's work include Keen Butterworth, "William Gilmore Simms," in *First Printings of American Authors: Contributions toward Descriptive Checklists*, ed. Matthew J. Bruccoli and C. E. Frazer Clark, Jr., vol. 1 (1977). A valuable bibliography of secondary sources is Keen Butterworth and James E. Kibler, Jr., eds., *William Gilmore Simms: A Reference Guide* (1980). Several important articles address particular aspects of Simms's career. John C. Guilds has studied Simms's work as editor: see, for instance, "Simms's First Magazine: *The Al-*

bum," *Studies in Bibliography* (1956): 169–83; "William Gilmore Simms and the *Southern Literary Gazette*," *Studies in Bibliography* 21 (1969): 59–92; and "Simms as Editor and Prophet: The Flowering and Early Death of the Southern *Magnolia*," *Southern Literary Journal* 4 (1972): 69–92. Miriam J. Shillingsburg has analyzed Simms's late writing in "From Notes to Novel: Simms's Creative Method," *Southern Literary Journal* 5 (1972): 89–107, and "Simms's Last Novel, *The Cub of the Panther*," *Southern Literary Journal* 17 (1985): 108–19.

MARY ANN WIMSATT

SIMMS, Willie (16 Jan. 1870–26 Feb. 1927), jockey and trainer, was born William Simms in Augusta, Georgia, the son of former slaves. Enticed by racing silks as a boy, he ran away from home to become a jockey. He worked for C. H. Pettingill's stable in New York for two years, until trainer Con Leighton "discovered" him riding in Clifton, New Jersey, in 1887–1888.

For Simms's first important race, Leighton assigned him to ride the two-year-old Banquet, a 20–1 underdog, in the 1889 Expectation Stakes. Banquet defeated both the favorite, Bellisarius, ridden by Edward "Snapper" Garrison, and Banquet's preferred stablemate, Chaos. Later, at Monmouth Park in New Jersey, Simms guided Chaos, now a 30–1 underdog, to victory over favored Banquet. Freelancing in 1891, Simms enjoyed great success at Saratoga. In 1892 P. J. Dwyer hired Simms, who won the Champion Stakes aboard Lamplighter. After signing with the Rancocas Stable later in 1892, Simms rode Dobbins in the famous 1893 dead-heat match race with the record money-earner Domino.

In 1895 Simms signed with M. F. Dwyer, who sent him to England for four months. Simms's "American" riding style, which featured extremely short stirrups, a whip, and spurs, was different from that of the English jockeys. The English ridiculed him and his high seat as "the monkey on a stick." In April he became the first American riding an American-owned and -trained horse to win an English race when he finished first in the Crawford Plate at Newmarket on Richard Croker's Eau Gallie. He later had an easy win riding Banquet at Newmarket.

Although Simms achieved some success, English jockeys did not initially copy his more efficient riding style. Two years later, after Ted Sloan won twenty races in England riding in the same fashion, the English switched to the more efficient style.

Simms won the Kentucky Derby on Ben Brush (1896) and Plaudit (1898), the Preakness on Sly Fox (1898), and the Belmont Stakes on Comanche (1893) and Henry of Navarre (1894). His other major stakes wins included the 1895 Champagne Stakes and the 1897 Suburban Handicap on Ben Brush, the 1893 Ladies' Handicap on Naptha, and the Lawrence Realization on Daily America (1893) and Dobbins (1894). Simms earned $20,000 in 1895 and, investing it well, became one of America's wealthiest jockeys. In his career in the United States, he rode 1,173 winners (25 percent) in 4,701 races, placed second 951 times, and finished third 763 times. On three different occasions he won five out of six races in a day. After retiring as a rider in 1902, he trained horses until 1924.

Simms, a bachelor, died of pneumonia in Asbury Park, New Jersey. Characterized in the *Thoroughbred Record* as one of the best jockeys in America in 1895, he was known for his "most excellent judgement, especially on horses that require a lot of coaxing and placing. He had beautiful hands and is especially quick and clever in an emergency." In 1977 he was inducted into the National Museum of Racing Hall of Fame.

• Biographical sketches of Simms are in *The Blood Horse* 103 (8 Aug. 1977): 3,548, and Fred Burlew's letter to the Hall of Fame Nominating Committee, June 1985, Keeneland Library, Lexington, Ky. See also John P. Davis, *The American Negro Reference Book* (1966); *Illustrated Sporting News*, 23 May 1908, p. 7; George Lambton, *Men and Horses I Have Known* (1924); *Thoroughbred Record* 41 (1895): 87, 171, 279, 362; Marjorie R. Weber, "Negro Jockeys: Kentucky Derby Winners" (unpublished MS, Keeneland Library, Lexington); and Lyman Horace Weeks, ed., *The American Turf* (1898). Obituaries appear in the *New York Times*, 1 Mar. 1927, and the *Thoroughbred Record*, 5 Mar. 1927.

STEVEN P. SAVAGE

SIMON, Kate (5 Jan. 1912–4 Feb. 1990), writer, was born Kaila Grobsmith in Warsaw, Poland, the daughter of Jacob Grobsmith, a skilled shoemaker, and Lina Babicz, a corsetiere. Braving wartime travel to save the life of her ailing young son, Lina Grobsmith along with her two children came to the United States in 1916 by steerage, joining her husband who had arrived three years earlier.

Now called Kate, the young Simon spent much of her Bronx childhood in city parks tending her sickly brother or watching the carriage of her much younger sister, but she also managed to spend hours each week at the local public library. Early exhibiting multiple talents, she was soon accomplished at the piano, making her father dream of becoming rich from her concert career. Reacting to her father's tyrannical ways, she refused to practice on the new piano he purchased for her, and he retaliated by insisting that she attend high school for only a year to prepare herself for a job. But even he could not buck the letter from her commercial high school, signed by the principal as well as her English and German teachers, stating with authority that she belonged in James Monroe High school. Her essay on the Bronx's street cries, ballads, and game songs won her a special place in the "collective eye" of the English department of her new school.

Finding adolescence a "rebirth struggle" that she could not wage under her father's roof, Simon left home. At first living with neighbors, she kept in contact with her mother while supporting herself by giving piano lessons to six- and seven-year-olds and teaching English to old immigrant women. Feeling "skinless and unprotected," she became at fourteen a mother's helper and later a live-in baby sitter for an intellectually stimulating couple who, along with her high school English teachers, had faith that "the rattling handful of mosaic bits called Kate . . . would sometime join each other smoothly" (*A Wider World*, p. 65).

At Hunter College, Simon held varied jobs while living in damp cellars and cold lofts and skipped meals to buy movie tickets or an occasional drink at a famous bar. With other English majors, she determined to avoid the "withering and staling" fate of immigrant women, patterning herself instead on the daring women portrayed in literature and on Edna St. Vincent Millay and other "burners of candles at both ends." Before she graduated from Hunter in 1935, Simon began living with Stanley F. Goldman (called Steve in *Etchings in an Hourglass*, p. 63), a young medical doctor who later was the father of her only child and whom she considered her husband, even though they were not legally married. He died from multiple brain tumors in 1942, and their daughter, suffering in the late stages of a similar disease, committed suicide in 1954. While making her living in the publishing field, Simon developed as a writer by rewriting, editing, and reviewing other people's work and met Robert Simon, a publisher, whom she married in 1947 and divorced in 1960.

Kate Simon's first book, *New York Places and Pleasures: An Uncommon Guidebook* (1959), became a bestseller. It was a celebration of her beloved city, and her claims for it help explain why "the little dreams stay at home and the big ones come to New York" (p. 25). Like her subsequent guides—including ones to Mexico (1960), Paris (1967), London (1968), Italy (1970), Rome (1972), and England (1974)—it was for travelers bent on "possessing" a place, not merely seeing it. Reviewers commended Simon's taste and urbane style. Few readers realized that she achieved her sparkling prose by "condensing, condensing, condensing," because for her writing was revision. Simon had the genius, the distinguished historian J. H. Plumb declared, to make the guidebook "a brilliant work of art." In numerous magazine articles and in interviews, Simon advised travelers. "*Go slow,*" she said when interviewed for *Contemporary Authors* in 1986. "If you have the time for eight countries, take five. If you're rushed to take five, take three" (pp. 409, 413).

Simon's *Fifth Avenue: A Very Social History* (1978) captures that famous avenue when those living in its mansions controlled the world's purse strings. Called a mix of "elaborate architectural commentary" and "unauthorized biography," the book preserves with vitality demolished buildings and forgotten lives without romanticizing times "when hotel advertisements still carried the legend 'No Jews, no dogs'" (p. 310). Similar to *Fifth Avenue* in its blending of past lives with buildings and scenic locales is Simon's *A Renaissance Tapestry: The Gonzaga of Mantua* (1988). Her last book to be published in her lifetime, it depicts life in Mantua (the site of Italy's first tapestry industry) during plague times and good times from the early fourteenth century to the early eighteenth century. Even more ostentatious than their Fifth Avenue counterparts, the ruling Gonzaga family collected jewels, dwarfs, and paintings. Among the artistic giants it employed were Leonardo da Vinci, Titian, and Peter Paul Rubens.

Between 1965 and 1988 Simon frequently contributed articles to the *New York Times*, *Vogue*, *Harper's*, *National Geographic*, *Harper's Bazaar*, *Saturday Review*, *Holiday*, and *Travel and Leisure*. Her three memoirs have become autobiographical classics. "Few people in our time," novelist Doris Grumbach observed in the *New York Times*, "have so keenly remembered, and so frankly recounted in print, the vagaries, defeats, successes and losses of a gallant and independent life" (19 Aug. 1990). Free from sentimental nostalgia and rich with accounts of immigrant experiences, *Bronx Primitive: Portraits in a Childhood* (1982) vividly describes Simon's childhood. *A Wider World: Portraits in an Adolescence* (1986) recounts in an unpretentious style her coming of age during the Great Depression and exhibits "her aristocratic disdain for cant, her frank worldliness" (Robert Pinsky, *New York Times*, 23 Feb. 1986). *Etchings in an Hourglass* (1990), the account of Simon's adult life in this trilogy, was written when Simon knew she was dying. Like memory, these moving narratives are not chronological but random. In this final book, she recalls chance encounters, lovers, and affairs she cannot forget. At seventeen Simon had promised herself that she "would experience everything," and, before her death of cancer at her home in New York City, she declared, "it has pretty much all happened" (*New York Times*, 19 Aug. 1990).

• Simon's papers are in the Archives and Special Collections of Hunter College, City University of New York. See *Contemporary Authors*, vol. 127, pp. 409–14, for citations to periodicals containing biographical and critical information on Simon, as well as an interview with her and a long synopsis of her writing career with frequent quotes from the reviews of her books. For a personal view of Simon, see Florence Howe, "Memories of Kate Simon: Dazzling without Show," *Women's Studies Quarterly* 18 (1990): 153–58. An obituary is in the *New York Times*, 5 Feb. 1990.

OLIVE HOOGENBOOM

SIMON, Norton Winfred (5 Feb. 1907–2 June 1993), business executive and art collector, was born in Portland, Oregon, the son of Myer Simon, a department store owner, and Lillian Glickman. After receiving his early education in his hometown, he completed high school in San Francisco, where he moved in 1921 with his father and two sisters following his mother's death and the collapse of his father's business. He began his business career while he was still in high school, wholesaling paper products. He relocated to Los Angeles at age sixteen and joined an export concern. In 1923 he entered the University of California at Berkeley but dropped out after only a few weeks.

Still only sixteen years of age, Simon returned to Los Angeles to work for an export company. By investing a portion of his salary in the then-booming stock market, he was able to start his own steel distribution firm, the Los Angeles Steel Products Company, in 1927. He continued to invest in the stock market. Effective at hedging his portfolio, he emerged from the crash of 1929 not only solvent but $35,000 richer for his efforts. His next business move came in 1931, when he invested $7,000 in Gold Brands, Incorporated, an orange juice bottler in Fullerton, California, that was in bankruptcy. Simon wasted little time effecting a turnaround. He changed the company's name to Val Vita Foods in 1932, broadened its product to include tomatoes, switched from bottles to less-expensive cans, and set up his own can manufacturing process to reduce costs still further. He also attempted to expand his firm's market share by undercutting the competition, and the results soon proved the wisdom of his efforts. Sales rose from $43,000 in 1931 to an astounding $9 million by 1940, and Simon had found the source of his fortune. In 1933 he married Lucille Ellis; the couple had two sons.

Never content to rest on his laurels, Simon began to acquire stock in the Hunt Brothers Packing Company in 1941. Based in San Francisco, Hunt had been a leading producer of processed foods in the area since 1890. In what came to be his standard method of operation, Simon sold Val Vita to Hunt for $3 million and then invested the proceeds in additional Hunt stock. By 1944 he had gained control of Hunt, which he renamed Hunt Food and Industries. Other changes soon followed. During what he termed the "unblocking" of the firm, Simon mechanized production lines, streamlined operations, revamped the company's accounting system, and reduced the number of can sizes offered to the public. In addition, he plunged heavily into advertising while attempting to market tomato sauce nationwide, a first. Simon spent $1.5 million on outdoor and magazine advertising in 1947, and in the following year he doubled that figure. He sponsored a full-color ad in *Life* magazine each week and ran ads in five additional national magazines. He spent heavily on plant expansion and modernization at Hunt, implementing a plan to invest $7 million in manufacturing facilities by 1950. His work paid off. Hunt sales, which had stood at $14 million in 1942, rose to over $48 million by 1946 and to over $100 million a year by the mid-1950s.

As sales continued to increase at Hunt, Simon kept 9.5 percent of his company's assets available for investment in other corporations. Over the course of the next two decades he purchased $34.2 million worth of stocks that later achieved a market value of $39 million. An innovator of the so-called "hostile takeover," Simon, as the era's leading corporate "raider," focused his attentions on potentially profitable firms whose stocks were both widely held and undervalued because of poor management. Once formulated, his strategy remained largely unchanged. After quietly buying small amounts of stock in an enterprise, he investigated its potential. If the company held promise of future profits, Simon would typically acquire 10 percent of its outstanding stock and then demand a place on its board of directors. Despite hostile reactions from management, Simon became successful by convincing shareholders that he had their best interests at heart.

He obtained support from an unlikely source—the firm's workers—by offering them relatively benevolent employment practices.

Throughout the late 1940s and the 1950s Simon and his methods were enormously successful. He began investing in the Ohio Match Company in 1944 and by 1946 was its president. After modernizing that firm, Simon oversaw an increase in its sales from $9 million to $24 million within ten years. He consolidated several holdings to create the United Can & Glass Company in 1950, which by 1955 enjoyed sales of $35 million a year. In the early 1950s he took an interest in McCall Corporation and in 1956 owned a third of its stock. With its board under his control, Simon instituted major changes. He terminated both *Blue Book* and *Better Living* magazines, spent lavishly to upgrade *McCall's Magazine*, and acquired the *Saturday Review* for $3 million in 1960. Again his efforts paid off. By 1965 circulation had increased by 60 percent and corporate earnings had risen an amazing 550 percent.

Not all of Simon's ventures proved equally successful, however. His 1964 attempt to take over Wheeling Steel Corporation created so much ill will in the company and within the steel industry that he was eventually forced to sell in 1967 at a loss of $700,000. Also in 1964 he launched a bid to acquire American Broadcasting Company-Paramount Theaters Incorporated, but that attempt collapsed when ABC convinced International Telephone & Telegraph to purchase enough shares to thwart him. In the same period Simon settled for a 34 percent share in Canada Dry Corporation and also failed in a bid to acquire Swift and Company. Always restless and easily bored with day-to-day management duties, he relinquished the presidency of Hunt in 1964, becoming chairman of the firm's finance committee. In 1968 Simon combined all his holdings into a new enterprise, Norton Simon, Incorporated. He then shocked many when he resigned the following year and named David Mahoney, who had served as Canada Dry's president since 1966, as his successor.

Simon devoted his later years to his massive art collection. Having begun his acquisitions in 1954, when he bought a Gauguin, a Pissarro, and a Bonnard for his Los Angeles home, he became, in his own words, "hooked." As shrewd in his art purchases as he was in business, his collection totaled 12,000 pieces by the late 1980s and was appraised at $750 million. As did his business dealings, his art collecting occasionally attracted unwanted attention. Simon interrupted the bidding process at a 1965 auction in London when he accused the auctioneer of slighting his bid for Rembrandt's *Titus* and favoring the bid of a local collector. After an extensive argument, bidding resumed, and Simon emerged with the painting, for which he paid over $2.2 million. In the early 1970s he purchased the *Shivapuram Nataraja*, a tenth-century bronze idol, for over $1 million, only to face the ire of the Indian government, which claimed that the item was stolen. Although Simon later acknowledged that the 44-inch bronze had been smuggled, he claimed not to know if it had been stolen. The controversy was settled when Simon agreed to return the artifact after ten years.

Controversy aside, Simon made welcome contributions to the art community. He began refurbishing the Pasadena Art Museum in California in 1974, eventually purchasing and renaming the facility the Norton Simon Museum. He also, through the Norton Simon Foundation, enabled museums throughout the world to borrow portions of his collection. Increasingly reclusive in his later years, he divorced his first wife in 1970, the same year he made an abortive run for the U.S. Senate. A year later he married actress Jennifer Jones; they had no children. Stricken with Guillain-Barré syndrome, he spent the last ten years of his life in a wheelchair. He died at his home in the Bel Air section of Los Angeles.

Controversial in both his business career and his art collecting, Simon left a solid legacy of achievement in both fields. While many found much to dislike in his business methods, those methods had a lasting impact on the international business scene.

• Simon's papers have not been located. He received extensive coverage throughout his career in publications such as *Time, Business Week, Newsweek, Forbes,* and *Fortune.* See especially "Food: Tin Can King," *Time,* 8 Oct. 1945, pp. 86–88; Spencer Davidson, "Management: The Corporate Cézanne," 4 June 1965, pp. 74–80; "Management: Keeping the Company Reins in the Owners' Hands," *Business Week,* 13 Apr. 1957, pp. 173–82; and Carol J. Loomis, "Companies: Incredible Shrinking Norton Simon," *Fortune,* 7 Mar. 1983, pp. 86–90. Simon is also a subject of Milton Moskowitz et al., *Everybody's Business* (1980). His former protégé David Mahoney and Richard Conarroe produced *Confessions of a Street-Smart Manager* (1988), which mentions many of Simon's later dealings. An obituary is in the *New York Times,* 4 June 1993.

EDWARD L. LACH, JR.

SIMON, Richard Leo (6 Mar. 1899–29 July 1960), publisher, was born in New York City, the son of Leo Leopold Simon, a wholesale milliner, and Anna Mayer. Early in life he became a pianist and organist. He was educated at the Ethical Culture School and then enrolled at Columbia University. His education was interrupted in 1918 by World War I when he served as a second lieutenant in the infantry, stationed at Plattsburgh, New York. He returned to Columbia, graduated in 1920, and then worked briefly for a sugar-importing company. A job selling pianos led him into publishing. During a sales call on Max Lincoln Schuster, the editor of a motor trade magazine, the two young men discussed their mutual interest in French novelist Romain Rolland and discovered that they were both Columbia graduates. Schuster suggested that Simon seek employment with publishers Boni and Liveright. In 1921 Simon was hired to sell their books on commission, and a year later he was their sales manager.

In 1924 Simon and Schuster formed their own publishing firm. With $4,000 or so in savings and pledges from friends they rented an office and determined from the outset to unite their exemplary literary standards and their driving ambition to make money. Simon had an aunt so addicted to crossword puzzles that she wished there were whole books of them. Seeing possibilities, Simon and his partner persuaded the puzzle editors of the *New York World* to assemble *The Cross-Word Puzzle Book,* issued in 1924 and the first in the world. An instant success, it was quickly followed by two more; by year's end, sales totaled 375,000 copies and netted the firm $100,000. Scores of such puzzle books followed over the next decades.

From the outset Simon and Schuster (S&S) published a combination of serious books and commercial blockbusters, all flamboyantly advertised. They shrewdly guessed which topics the public would prefer and commissioned authors to write on those topics. They conducted opinion polls to test possible ideas, leading to what Simon called "planned publishing." In 1924 they issued not only Don C. Seitz's *Joseph Pulitzer: His Life & Letters* but also books on common-sense investing and on how to play tennis. In 1926 Simon published his own translation of Arthur Schnitzler's *None but the Brave.* Emanuel Haldeman-Julius, the Girard, Kansas, publisher of five-cent and ten-cent books, persuaded S&S to issue in a single volume his eleven little books by Will Durant on eminent philosophers. Durant rewrote them as *The Story of Philosophy* (1926), which was enormously popular worldwide. Schnitzler and Durant remained with S&S, to their mutual betterment. In 1934 Simon married Andrea Louise Heinemann, his secretary; the couple had four children, including singer-songwriter Carly Simon.

By 1934 the firm had published 251 titles, of which 32 were best sellers or close to that category, selling 3,000,000 copies in all. Representative titles are Franz Werfel's *Verdi: A Novel of the Opera* (1925), Ernest Dimnet's *The Art of Thinking* (1928), Robert L. Ripley's *Believe It or Not!* (1929), Felix Salten's *Bambi* (1929), and Leon Trotsky's *History of the Russian Revolution* (3 vols., 1932). Leon Shimkin, who joined the firm in 1924 as a bookkeeper and later became a partner, persuaded his associates to publish Dale Carnegie's phenomenal success, *How to Win Friends and Influence People* (1936), and J. K. Lasser's *How to Make Out Your Income Tax* (1939). These were the best moneymakers of S&S's many "How to" titles, for which Simon used his wizardry to produce, advertise, and distribute profitably. However, all was not smooth sailing. Some authors proved unsatisfactory, and these were dropped ruthlessly. Moreover, both *Trader Horn* (1927), Alfred Aloysius Horn's African adventures, and *The Cradle of the Deep* (1929), Joan Lowell's story of spending the first sixteen years of her life at sea, proved to be fraudulent. The firm was embarrassed, spoofs were rushed into print by rival publishers, and Simon even had a brief nervous breakdown.

In 1936 S&S launched their highly regarded series of Inner Sanctum Mysteries, the title being based on Simon's *Publishers Weekly* column, "From the Inner Sanctum" (1926–1935). In 1939, after other firms lost money trying to market paperback books, Simon, his two partners, and Robert Fair de Graff founded Pocket Books—and quickly made millions. S&S's other successes were their "Treasury" books, including innovative four-color art volumes, a Gilbert and Sullivan coffee-table item, and anthologies of great letters, hymns, speeches, and reporting. In 1942 came the Little Golden Books series for children, selling well over 2 million its first year and 300 million by 1950. In 1943 S&S established a profitable book club with the backing of Sears, Roebuck and Company. During World War II Simon was chairman of the board of the Council on Books in Wartime and was partly responsible for massive shipments of books to the armed services overseas. His main commercial problem during the war was the paper shortage. Nevertheless, in 1945 S&S published *A History of Western Philosophy* by Bertrand Russell, and in 1946, *My Three Years with Eisenhower* by Harry C. Butcher. On the lighter side of production over the years were items featuring Walt Kelly's "Pogo" and the creations of James Thurber and Charles Addams. In the 1950s S&S continued to cater to escapist readers with novelty and stunt items, even as they published serious authors such as Clarence Darrow, Harold L. Ickes, Nikos Kazantzakis, J. Robert Oppenheimer, and Norbert Wiener.

In 1957, while S&S was issuing an average of three books a week, Simon had two heart attacks, resigned from the firm, and sold his stock to Schuster and Shimkin. Simon was never merely a workaholic sales genius. He pursued several hobbies with characteristic gusto, combining some of them with his commercial interests. He loved music passionately all his life and published *Beethoven's 32 Sonatas for the Pianoforte*, edited by Artur Schnabel (1935). He was an expert bridge player and published Charles Henry Goren's popular *Point Count Bidding in Contract Bridge* (1949). He enjoyed golf, was a competent amateur photographer, and wrote and published *Miniature Photography, from One Amateur to Another* (1937). He was a member of the Riverdale Camera Club as well as New York City's Dutch Treat Club and Artists and Writers Golf Association. He was still keeping alive an ambition to found a new publishing company when he died at his country home in North Stamford, Connecticut.

• The enormous Richard L. Simon Papers, including correspondence, memos, manuscripts of writings, legal and financial correspondence, and miscellaneous items, are at Columbia University. Some other papers concerning Simon are in the libraries at Knox College, Galesburg, Ill., and at East Carolina University, Greenville, N.C. Bennett Cerf, in "Trade Winds," *Saturday Review*, 10 Sept. 1960, p. 6, praised his friend Simon as always forthright. Summaries of Simon's career are in Charles A. Madison, *Book Publishing in America* (1966); Kenneth C. Davis, *Two-Bit Culture: The Paperbacking of America* (1984); and John Tebbel, *Between Covers: The Rise and Transformation of Book Publishing in America* (1987). Alice Payne Hackett, *70 Years of Best Sellers: 1895–1965* (1967), lists numerous Simon and Schuster publications. An obituary is in the *New York Times*, 30 July 1960.
ROBERT L. GALE

SIMONDS, Ossian Cole (11 Nov. 1855–20 Nov. 1931), landscape gardener, was born in Grand Rapids, Michigan, the son of Joel A. Simonds and Harriet Newell Garfield, farmers. Simonds intended to become an engineer and studied civil engineering at the University of Michigan in Ann Arbor. During his last two years, he became fascinated by lectures in architecture given by William Le Baron Jenney, who was organizing a program in architecture at the university at the time. Before Simonds was to graduate, however, the architecture program was discontinued, and in 1878 he completed his degree in civil engineering. Following a short stint at surveying work in western Michigan, he went to work for Jenney's office in Chicago, still intending to pursue architecture as a career. Sometime around 1880, Simonds joined with William Holabird, also from Jenney's office, to form the architectural firm of Holabird & Simonds, which later became Holabird, Simonds, & Roche with the addition of Martin Roche.

In 1881 Simonds married Martha Elnora Rumsey of Grand Rapids, Michigan, and together they had six children. The family maintained a home in the Buena Park neighborhood of Chicago and a summer home near Fennville, Michigan, on land that Simonds had surveyed shortly after graduating from the university.

Before leaving Jenney's office, Simonds began work on the enlargement of a lagoon in Graceland Cemetery and became fascinated with the prospect of landscape design. At the urging of Bryan Lathrop, who served as president of the board of managers of Graceland Cemetery and was active in the parks movement in Chicago, Simonds became superintendent of Graceland Cemetery in 1881. With Lathrop's support, Simonds revamped the cemetery as a naturalistic garden following a style promoted by Adolph Strauch, whose work at Spring Grove Cemetery in Cincinnati Simonds deeply admired. Through his own work at Graceland, Simonds became widely known as a landscape gardener and the nation's foremost authority on "rural" cemetery design. These cemeteries were so named because of the desire to have places of burial located at a distance from urban centers and to have the grounds designed to be places of beauty, reflecting the character of the rural countryside. He served as superintendent until 1898 and thereafter as a member of the board of managers and as landscape gardener.

In 1903 Simonds formed O. C. Simonds & Company, building an extensive practice that included numerous parks and park systems, residences, college campuses, and cemeteries throughout the Middle West. After J. Roy West joined the firm in 1918, it became known as Simonds & West. Simonds advocated a style of design that emphasized local landforms and native plantings and was often associated with Jens Jensen and Walter Burley Griffin as an initiator of the "prairie style" of landscape gardening. Simonds, however, was not keen on labeling his designs as a prairie style or restricting his work to the Middle West. He instead argued that his work was developed in response to local features and was an attempt to encourage people to appreciate natural beauty. Besides his design work for Graceland Cemetery in Chicago, Simonds's notable projects include the extension of Lincoln Park north of Diversey Parkway in Chicago; Fort Sheridan in Highland Park, Illinois; the Morton Arboretum in Lisle, Illinois; Frick Park in Pittsburgh, Pennsylvania; Washington Park in Springfield, Illinois; various parks in Dixon and Quincy, Illinois; Palmer Park and Subdivision in Detroit, Michigan; Nichols Arboretum in Ann Arbor, Michigan; Sinnissippi Farm, the estate of governor Frank O. Lowden in Oregon, Illinois; and the estate of Anton G. Hodenpyl on Long Island, New York. At the time of his death in Chicago, Simonds was said to have worked in every state of the continental United States.

Simonds was one of the founding members of the American Society of Landscape Architects and served as its president in 1913. He was also active in groups such as the American Civic Association, the Western Society of Engineers, the Association of American Cemetery Superintendents (president, 1895–1896), the Chicago City Club, and the Cliff Dwellers (Chicago). In 1900 he was awarded a silver medal by the Paris exposition and a gold medal by the Architectural League in 1925.

Simonds wrote extensively on the art of landscape gardening, and perhaps the best record of his philosophy is his book *Landscape Gardening*, published in 1920. He advocated direct study of nature as a model for design and hoped to inspire attitudes of conservation through his work. In 1908 he began teaching courses in landscape design at the University of Michigan and helped to establish the design program there. Most of the early professors came from Simonds's office, and in 1929 Simonds was awarded an honorary M.A. degree from the university. The citation for Simonds's honorary degree included the following testament to his work: "A staunch defender of the natural charm of the American landscape, sensitive to its beauty and skillful in the means of creating it, he has found joy and service in awakening civic ideals which express themselves in the development of city plans and parks. A better heritage for later days no man can leave." He remains highly regarded as a founder of the landscape design profession in the United States and a pioneer in an ecologically oriented approach to design.

• There is no extensive collection of Simonds's papers. Graceland Cemetery in Chicago has limited records. Archives at the Morton Arboretum in Lisle, Ill., include miscellaneous plans, photographs, and some letters, while collections at the Department of Landscape Architecture at Iowa State University in Ames contain several of Simonds's plans. In addition to *Landscape Gardening* (1920), Simonds wrote extensively on various aspects of landscape design, including "A Few Words from a Landscape Gardener," *Park and Cemetery*, July 1895, pp. 74–76; "Landscape Design in Public Parks," *Park and Cemetery*, June 1909, pp. 50–52; and "Nature as the Great Teacher in Landscape Gardening," *Landscape Architecture*, Jan. 1932, pp. 100–8. For Simonds's own discussion of his work at Graceland and on cemeteries in general, the best sources are "Graceland at Chicago," *American Landscape Architect*, Jan. 1932, pp. 12–17, and "Notes on Graceland," *American Landscape Architect*, May 1930, pp. 8–9. For another viewpoint of Graceland, see Wilhelm Miller, "An American Idea in Landscape Art," *Country Life in America*, Sept. 1903, pp. 349–50. For Simonds's thoughts on residential design, see his series "Home Grounds," *House Beautiful*, Mar. 1899, pp. 169–72; Apr. 1899, pp. 214–18; May 1899, pp. 275–79; June 1899, pp. 25–30; and Sept. 1899, pp. 178–86; or his article "Country Life Near Chicago," *House Beautiful*, Apr. 1902, pp. 337–41.

Wilhelm Miller featured Simonds's work in many articles, including "How to Multiply Your Grounds by Four," *Country Life in America*, 1 Aug. 1912, pp. 34–36; "A Series of Outdoor Salons," *Country Life in America*, Apr. 1914, pp. 39–40; and "What Is the Matter with Our Water Gardens," *Country Life in America*, 15 June 1912, pp. 23–26, 54. For Miller's discussion of the "prairie style" and Simonds's work, see two circulars from the Agriculture Experiment Station, University of Illinois, Urbana, *The "Illinois Way" of Beautifying the Farm* (1914) and *The Prairie Spirit in Landscape Gardening* (1915), as well as "The Prairie Style of Landscape Architecture," *Architectural Record* 40 (Dec. 1916): 590–92. Mara Gelbloom provides a contemporary view of Simonds's contribution to the "prairie style" in "Ossian Simonds: Prairie Spirit in Landscape Gardening," *Prairie School Review* 12, no. 2 (1975): 5–18. Robert Grese discusses the relation of Simonds to the work of Jens Jensen in *Jens Jensen: Maker of Natural Parks and Gardens* (1992), and Julia Sniderman provides an overview of Simonds's contributions to the Chicago parks in "Bringing the Prairie Vision into Focus," *Prairie in the City: Naturalism in Chicago's Parks, 1870–1940* (1991). For a view of Simonds's contributions to ecologically oriented design, see Ervin Zube, "The Advance of Ecology," *Landscape Architecture*, Mar.-Apr. 1986, pp. 58–67; Dave Egan, "Historical Initiatives in Ecological Restoration," *Restoration & Management Notes* 8 (Winter 1990): 83–90; and Robert Grese, "Historical Perspectives on Designing with Nature," in *The Proceedings of the First Annual Conference of the Society for Ecological Restoration*, ed. H. Glenn Hughes and Thomas M. Bonnicksen (1990). Grese also provides a brief overview of Simonds's career in "Ossian Cole Simonds," *American Landscape Architecture*, ed. William H. Tishler (1989). Obituaries are in *Park and Cemetery*, Dec. 1931, pp. 301–2; *American Landscape Architect*, Dec. 1931, p. 17; and *Civic Comment*, Nov.-Dec. 1931, p. 24.

ROBERT E. GRESE

SIMONS, Algie Martin (9 Oct. 1870–11 Mar. 1950), Marxist theoretician and editor, was born in North Freedom, Wisconsin, near Baraboo, the son of Horace Buttoph Simons and Linda Blackman, farmers. Simons worked his way through the University of Wisconsin, where he was a student of historian Frederick Jackson Turner and economist Richard T. Ely. Drawn to the emerging social sciences and to their practical application to society's ills, he wrote his senior thesis on railroad monopolies and gave a graduation address on organized religion and social issues.

Entering social work, in 1895 Simons was appointed a fellow at the University of Cincinnati's Settlement House, where he served as an investigator determining applicant eligibility for support. That same year he moved to Chicago, where he worked for its Bureau of Charities. Living at Hull House and then at the University of Chicago Settlement House, he was assigned to the stockyards neighborhood, where he supervised social workers. He wrote a study of the meat-packing industry, focusing on unemployment, which he published in the *American Journal of Sociology* and as a short piece called *Packingtown*, which was an influence on writer Upton Sinclair's thinking. By 1897 he had become disillusioned with investigative charity and joined the Socialist Labor Party.

Simons married his high school sweetheart, May Wood, in 1897; they had two children. Together they became increasingly prominent socialist activists over the next twenty years. Simons edited the party newspaper, the *People*, until he broke with party leader Daniel DeLeon over his authoritarianism and his policy of dual unionism. In 1899 Simons left social services and became a full-time editor of the weekly *Workers' Call*. In 1900, after the accidental death of the Simonses' eighteen-month-old son, the couple spent six months in England, France, and Belgium, where they met major leaders of international socialism. Thereafter Simons maintained contacts with many of those leaders and translated and published several of their works. In 1901 Simons became one of the founders of the Socialist Party of America. By then he was a leading figure in the Chicago branch of the party and the editor of the most influential American socialist periodical, the *International Socialist Review*. With its publisher, Charles H. Kerr, Simons was responsible for the publication of the widely circulated series the Pocket Library of Socialism. He also campaigned for public office as a socialist, undertook party speaking tours, developed a curriculum for its study groups, taught at the socialistic Ruskin College in Glen Elyn, Illinois, and wrote and published articles and books on socialism.

Simons's major significance rests on his work on the *Review* from 1900 to 1908. As its first editor, his main goal was to introduce his readers to the classics of scientific socialism, using the pages of the journal to conduct discussions with an already committed readership. In addition, he sought to undermine any remaining links to the utopianism that had been a feature of nineteenth-century American socialism, and he tried to shape Socialist party policy so that it remained ideologically orthodox while at the same time placing Marxism in an American context and idiom. However, within a few years he became a revisionist socialist, breaking with his earlier views, which helped lead to his dismissal from the editorship by Kerr. During this time he authored volumes such as *The American Farmer* (1902) and *Class Struggles in America* (1903). His writings introduced the public to a Marxist interpretation of American history. In other editing stints, Simons worked for a number of mostly short run socialist newspapers in the Midwest, such as the *Chicago Daily Socialist* and *Coming Nation* as well as the durable *Appeal to Reason* and the *Milwaukee Leader*, and nonsocialist publications such as the *Independent* and the *World Today*.

As a high-ranking party official and a candidate for public office, Simons tried especially to shape party policy toward the working class, both farmers and urban workers. He was one of the few party leaders to define farmers as workers, and he tried to develop a party program for that segment of the working class. Only in 1912 was he able to convince a party convention to establish an agricultural plank, one which eschewed confiscation and collectivization of land in favor of a policy of taxation on absentee landowners and the promotion of cooperatives. His views on party outreach to the urban proletariat were framed by a contempt for the craft-union-based American Federation of Labor. Seeking a connection to the masses of unorganized workers, he was a founding member of the Industrial Workers of the World but broke with the IWW within a year over the role of his old antagonist, DeLeon. He became convinced of the value of a labor party patterned after the English example, but when his ideas became known, he was denounced and never again elected to a high office within the party.

Simons moved his wife and daughter to Milwaukee in 1913 when he joined the staff of Victor Berger's *Milwaukee Leader*. With the onset of World War I, the Anglophile Simons found himself increasingly uncomfortable in German Milwaukee and in the Socialist party, both of which he believed to be sympathetic to the Central Powers. He favored American intervention on behalf of the Allied side, and in 1917 he was expelled from the Socialist party over the issue of the war. He then worked for the Wisconsin Loyalty League and organized prowar socialists into the Social Democratic League. Toward the end of the war he accepted President Woodrow Wilson's appointment to lead the American Socialist and Labor Mission to Europe, where it met with social democratic leaders on behalf of American peace and postwar initiatives. Retiring from his political commitments, Simons devoted his energies to scientific management and personnel policies, finally specializing in the issue of medical insurance for the American Medical Association. He died in New Martinsville, West Virginia, as a result of an automobile accident.

Simons was a significant figure in the Socialist Party of America in its most dynamic era. As an editor, a writer, and a political leader, he was at the center of many of its major controversies, and his own progression from orthodox to revisionist Marxist represented a not unusual path, as did his departure from the party during World War I.

• The collected papers of A. M. Simons and May Wood Simons are at the State Historical Society of Wisconsin. In addition, other collections located there have his correspondence, as does the Milwaukee County Historical Society and Duke University Library's Socialist Party of America Collection. His published work can be found by perusing issues of the early *International Socialist Review*. A biography of Simons is Karl Kreuter and Gretchen Kreuter, *An American Dissenter: The Life of Algie Martin Simons, 1870–1950* (1969). An article of interest is William A. Glaser, "Algie Martin Simons and Marxism in America," *Mississippi Valley Historical Review* 41 (1954): 419–34. An obituary is in the *New York Times*, 12 Mar. 1950.

SALLY M. MILLER

SIMONS, Henry Calvert (9 Oct. 1899–19 June 1946), economist, was born in Virden, Illinois, the son of Henry Calvert Simons, a lawyer, and Mollie Willis Sims. After completing his undergraduate education at the University of Michigan, Simons taught economics at the University of Iowa from 1920 to 1927, during which time he also pursued graduate studies at Columbia University and at the University of Chicago. He joined Chicago's economics faculty in 1927, eventually becoming the first professor of economics at that institution's law school.

Simons was one of the fathers of the Chicago School of Economics, and he served on Chicago's faculty until his death. During this period, he influenced notable students, such as Aaron Director, Milton Friedman, and George J. Stigler, and served with a nucleus of notable professors that included Frank Knight and Jacob Viner. Simons offered detailed prescriptions for several major policy issues in economics. He believed that resources should be allocated by market forces, that economic fluctuations should be controlled by a stable monetary program, and that income inequality should be lessened by progressive taxation of personal income.

Simons's contribution to the field of economics must be viewed in the context of his times. His writings first appeared during the Great Depression. Central planning, New Deal nostrums, and Keynesian economics were becoming the conventional wisdom, with economic stagnation commonly taken as evidence of capitalism's defects. Simons stood outside the interventionist mainstream of the period. He also stood outside the special-interest economics of reactionary conservatism. He was a classical liberal (he liked the term libertarian) whose ideas most forcefully appeared in his 1934 tract, *A Positive Program for Laissez-Faire.* Here Simons wrote that "*the great enemy of democracy is monopoly in all its forms*" (emphasis in original).

Monopoly, to Simons, embraced large corporations and entrenched labor unions. He was a relentless critic of both. He favored trust-busting of a radical sort: limiting the size of a corporation in its primary market and its ability to own stock in other corporations. His "Some Reflections on Syndicalism" (*Journal of Political Economy* 52 [1994]: 1–25) became a classic unraveling of the then-popular view that labor unions serve the poor and stand in opposition to large corporations. In *A Positive Program* Simons warned: "[If] the state undertakes to tolerate (instead of destroying) such organizations and to regulate their regulations, it will have assumed tasks and responsibilities incompatible with its enduring in a democratic form."

Simons "positive program" differed starkly from the social blueprints of large-state interventionists and zero-state libertarians. He supported laissez-faire, but maintained that government intervention was necessary "to maintain the kind of legal and institutional framework within which competition can function effectively as an agency of control." Simons argued against direct government intervention in determining prices and wages, whether by subsidy, protection, or decree. Establishing prices, he believed, was the job of market forces.

Simons was one of the few economists to embrace the normally divergent fields of competition policy and monetary policy. Indeed, he is best known among economists for his contributions to monetary theory and policy. However, Simons did not see the two fields as disparate. The bridge linking the two was flexible prices. Flexible prices, to Simons, meant prices that were not set by government edict or by firms with monopoly power (or, in the case of the price of labor services, determined by powerful labor unions). Prices that were flexible would respond to changing demand and supply conditions, thereby eliminating the problem of surpluses and shortages in individual markets; promoting competition, in Simons's view, would keep prices in line with costs. The government, then, could focus attention on macroeconomic policies affecting aggregate employment and price levels.

While Simons did not eschew the use of fiscal policy as a policy lever, it was the lever of monetary policy with which his name is identified. During the time of his writing, the Keynesian influence had reduced the importance assigned to monetary policy as a policy vehicle. Simons believed this to be a mistake. It was not until the 1960s that the economics profession returned to Simons's view that a nation's monetary policy powerfully affected an economy's employment level and rate of economic growth.

Simons's monetary policy had two distinct components. The first, and less influential, was his plan to eliminate fractional reserve banking and substitute a 100 percent banking scheme. Because banks in the United States were required to maintain only a fractional reserve, they could have liabilities in the form of demand deposits far in excess of their reserves. Simons believed the private banking system's ability to create deposits or debt instruments made economic stability less likely because monetary aggregates such as cash reserves and velocity would fluctuate more in response to swings in business confidence.

Simons's proposal for 100 percent reserve banking was never adopted. Far more influential was the second element of Simons's program for monetary reform. He maintained that, just as the government should set the "rules of the game" to keep markets competitive, the government should set rules that would stabilize the monetary system. Simons wavered as to what monetary variable the government was to stabilize: the supply of money or the overall price level. Whichever, the government was to bind itself to a stable monetary rule by assuming full control of the money supply. If price levels were escalating, the government should retire currency (largely by tax increases); declining price levels were to be bolstered by currency expansions (accomplished by tax reductions).

Simons believed that reductions in economic power would improve economic efficiency, enhance economic growth, and help maintain a democratic society. His concern about concentrated economic power also extended to inequalities of income. He was a strong supporter of the progressive personal income tax. Unlike some individuals who call themselves libertarians, Simons placed high value on equality as well as individual liberty. His tax policy was carefully developed, and at root called for the taxation of all personal income at the same rate, regardless of its source. The resources spent by individuals on lobbyists, accountants, and attorneys to transform income from more to less heavily taxed categories would be unnecessary. Under Simons's regime, there would be no separate taxation of business firms.

Simons was a gifted writer but not a public speaker. He would rather talk with students at Handley's, a 55th Street Chicago tavern, than address a large audience. A dapper dresser, but sardonic by nature, he preferred billiards at the University of Chicago's Quadrangle Club to direct participation in university or national politics.

Simons's more radical policy proposals have not secured wide favor. Economists generally have not supported his call for the nationalization of public utilities, limitations on corporate advertising, the federal chartering of corporations, wide-scale dissolution of large corporations, 100 percent reserve banking, and a tax policy footed only on progressive income taxation. In fact, by 1945, Simons's concern about the power of large corporations had waned, though not his concern about labor unions.

Simons married Marjorie Kimball Powell in 1941 and they had one child. He died in Chicago five years later of a sleeping pill overdose. Simons did not live to see the future stature of the Chicago School as it flourished under the next generation of economists, some of whom were his students. Nor did he witness the vindication of his writings on the importance of stable monetary policy and his warning about the problems of government as the promoter of monopoly in labor and product markets.

• Simons's papers are held at the University of Chicago. Much of his published work and a complete bibliography are contained in his *Economic Policy for a Free Society* (1948). A description of these holdings can be found in Clara Ann Bowler, "The Papers of Henry C. Simons," *Journal of Law & Economics* 17, no. 1 (1974): 7–11. Simons's books on taxation are *Personal Income Taxation: The Definition of Income as a Problem of Fiscal Policy* (1938) and *Federal Tax Reform* (1943, published posthumously in 1950). A biographical article is George J. Stigler, "Henry Calvert Simons," *Journal of Law & Economics* 17, no. 1 (1974): 1–5. Assessments of his contributions include William Breit and Roger L. Ransom's chapter on Simons in *The Academic Scribblers* (1982); John Davenport, "The Testament of Henry Simons," *Fortune*, Sept. 1946, pp. 116–19; Bradford J. De Long, "In Defense of Henry Simons' Standing as a Classical Liberal," *Cato Journal* 9 (1990): 601–18; Milton Friedman, "The Monetary Theory and Policy of Henry Simons," *Journal of Law & Economics* 10 (1967): 1–13; Wilber G. Katz, "Economics and the Study of Law: The Contribution of Henry C. Simons," *University of Chicago Law Review* 14 (1946): 1–4; and Herbert Stein's entries on Henry Simons in *International Encyclopedia of the Social Sciences* 14 (1968): 260–62 and *The New Palgrave* 4 (1987): 333–35. For a scholarly account of the Chicago School and Simons's role, see Melvin W. Reder, "Chicago Economics: Permanence and Change," *Journal of Economic Literature* 20 (1982): 1–38. An obituary is H. G. Lewis, "Henry Calvert Simons," *American Economic Review* 36 (1946): 668–69.

KENNETH G. ELZINGA

SIMONS, Minot (24 Sept. 1868–25 May 1941), clergyman, was born in Manchester, New Hampshire, the son of Langdon Simons and Sarah Frances Shepard. He was educated at Harvard, where he completed undergraduate work in 1891 and received master of arts and bachelor of sacred theology degrees in 1894. In December 1894 Simons married Helen Louise Savage, daughter of the prominent Unitarian minister Minot Judson Savage; they had one child.

In 1895 Simons was ordained to the Unitarian ministry and accepted a pastorate in Billerica, Massachusetts. From 1900 to 1919 he was minister of the First Unitarian Church in Cleveland, Ohio. During this period he also served as preacher for Western Reserve University. In 1919 he became secretary of the Church Extension Department for the American Unitarian Association. From 1923 until his death, he led All Souls Unitarian Church in New York City.

It was from this New York City pulpit that Simons attained his greatest prominence as an advocate for liberal Christianity and for social causes. His goal as a preacher, he said, was "to bring to a congregation the elements of a modern theistic philosophy in terms that the layman can use to create his own religious philosophy with which to face the religious problems which today beset him theoretically and practically" (*Modern Theism*, p. v). Simons's well-crafted sermons were filled with practical applications and embellished with illustrations drawn as often from classical and nineteenth-century literature as from the Bible. This was consistent with his understanding that religion was based on experience rather than scriptural or ecclesiastical authority. Revelation was "a natural process of the unfolding of God's truth as the human mind grows in understanding." The Bible recorded this advance, but "the Word of God is not contained between the two covers of a book." "Our proclamation is," he declared, "trust in your own mind and heart with a faith that is your own" (*Working Faiths*, pp. 42, 44, 131).

Simons was confident that religion and modern thought were compatible, and he implored liberal intellectuals to stay within the churches rather than yield the field to fundamentalism. At the same time, he also warned against the secular alternative, humanism. Although he valued it for its affirmation of the "sacredness in human life" and for its commitment to service, humanism was not enough. Instead, Simons advocated "Humanism plus"—a religion committed to humanitarian reform and grounded in theism. Simons believed that recent scientific work, particularly astronomy and Albert Einstein's physics, had strengthened the notion of a spirit-infused universe by undercutting the earlier Newtonian mechanical conception. The more scientists were driven to theory and symbolic language in their effort to explain reality, the more Simons considered that they confirmed idealism. This meant a world that was created and sustained by a "Cosmic Mind" or "Cosmic Intention" that was personal, immanent in all things, purposeful, and compassionate with the human predicament. Simons thought and spoke frequently in evolutionary terms. Ethical qualities like courage, prudence, thrift, cooperation, and self-sacrifice had "survival value," which meant that "in the development of the inner life, natural selection has played some part" (*Modern Theism*, p. 180). Simons adamantly rejected the orthodox cycle of Fall, Atonement, and Redemption. The world was "undeveloped," not lost, and education, not salvation, was the appropriate description of human need.

Simons followed a Jesus divested of myth and unique divinity. Jesus' sinlessness was a "mere dogma," which, if believed, removed all ethical significance from the gospel story. For Simons, "moral harmony" was "established only at the cost of moral effort and struggle," a principle that applied equally to Jesus and all humans (*Modern Theism*, pp. 83–84). Jesus' character emerged throughout the gospel account until, by the end, he had become "morally and spiritually invincible." His "self-sacrifice" had continuing appeal because he died for "spiritual principles" that were immortal, that is, were significant beyond the moment. In this sense, Jesus "lived and died as an immortal" (*Modern Theism*, pp. 102–3) and testified to the immortality of the human spirit—a belief made credible more by its historical survival than by any dogma about the bodily resurrection. Simons invited his congregation to leave such dogma to those helped by it.

Simons's theism was active and social. "The only effective goodness is the goodness done," he said in a 1925 sermon. From his Cleveland pulpit, he supported the Progressive movement's reform agenda. Both in Cleveland and New York City he took leadership roles in community charities. He was equally active in educational matters. From 1912 to 1928 he was a trustee of the Meadville Theological School. A devoted supporter of Harvard University, he was active in alumni affairs and a member of the board of preachers, 1912–1913, and of the board of overseers, 1932–1938. He was also a trustee of Phillips Exeter Academy and of the Hackley School in Tarrytown, New York.

Over the length of his career, his sermons touched on nearly every current topic. A 1927 series considered the implications of new gender roles; marriage was now a partnership of "two distinct, co-equal individuals," and childrearing could no longer be based on an outmoded "sentimental idealizing of women." Although he considered Prohibition an unenforceable mistake, he hesitated to urge repeal without an alternate policy in place. Always an advocate of cooperation among the churches, he was particularly offended by attacks on presidential candidate Alfred E. Smith's Catholicism in 1928.

Throughout the 1920s he used his pulpit to warn against the "selfish and lawless extravagance" of the wealthy. Unrestrained individualism was "as much

out of date in sociology as special creation in biology" (*Modern Theism*, p. 203). He complained that the churches overemphasized otherworldly salvation to the detriment of service in this world. Trying to get souls into heaven was always a "poor business"; it was better "to get heaven into this world." Simons also spoke forcefully on international issues. Unlike many liberals, he did not become a pacifist after World War I, although he favored the World Court and treaties outlawing war. He was quick to oppose Nazism. He considered the Munich Accords of 1938 dangerously naive, and in 1939 he urged repeal of the Neutrality Act. During 1940 he became an ardent advocate of aid to Britain. At his death, in New York City, he was hailed as an "early champion of national defense."

Simons was not an original thinker in theology, but he was an effective popularizer who, especially by his preaching, demonstrated in his day the continuing power of the urban pulpit to mold opinion. Consistently throughout his career, Simon used his voice to promote a combination of liberal Christianity and social commitment.

• Simons published three books of collected sermons—*Vexed Questions* (1913), *Working Faiths* (1914), and *A Modern Theism* (1931)—as well as occasional pamphlets and tracts. Synopses of his sermons appeared regularly in the *New York Times* from 1923 to 1940. An obituary is in the *New York Times*, 26 May 1941.

CHARLES D. CASHDOLLAR

SIMONSON, Lee (26 June 1888–23 Jan. 1967), theater set designer and critic, was born in New York City, the son of Saul Simonson and Augusta Goldenberg. Inspired by the paintings of Maxfield Parrish, Simonson decided on an art career at the age of ten and in high school sold illustrations to *Good Housekeeping*. After graduation in 1908 from Harvard, where he studied playwriting under George Pierce Baker and helped found the Harvard Dramatic Club, Simonson prepared for a career as a mural painter at the Academie Julien in Paris, often meeting with other artists at the home of Leo and Gertrude Stein. He also viewed the innovative designs of Serge Diaghilev at the Ballet Russe in Paris and of Max Reinhardt at the Kunstlertheater in Munich.

Simonson returned to the United States in 1912, and in 1915 Philip Moeller invited him to design his first show, Leonid Andreiev's *Love of One's Neighbor*, for the newly formed Washington Square Players. This began a prolific 24-year period during which Simonson designed as many as seven shows a year, interrupted only by a stint as lieutenant in the Corps of Interpreters during World War I. In 1919 Simonson joined Moeller as one of six founders of the Theatre Guild, a self-styled "art theater" that sought to bring innovative drama by American and European playwrights to New York audiences. His first show for the new organization was John Masefield's *The Faithful*. Simonson not only designed many other Guild shows but helped select the plays to be staged, especially the

European plays he saw while overseas on Guild business.

Simonson has been grouped with Robert Edmond Jones and others as part of the "New Stagecraft" movement, a break from the prevalent realism of the modern stage, inspired by such Europeans as Adolphe Appia and Edward Gordon Craig. However, in his own writings—especially his influential 1932 study of theater design, *The Stage Is Set*—Simonson attacked Craig as a false messiah, promoting instead the design theories of Appia and the Duke of Saxe Meiningen. Despite his art training and his passion for color, Simonson's own pragmatic methods and principles were closer to an architect's than to a painter's. Using a method that has become standard, Simonson would first devise a floor plan so the scenery could direct the actors' movements and accommodate necessary changes of locale; only then would he address specific issues of decor, color, and lighting. Because Simonson rarely began with scenic renderings and usually avoided them altogether, his designs are mostly available through production photographs.

Two major playwrights whose work Simonson shaped for American audiences were George Bernard Shaw and Eugene O'Neill. Simonson credited Shaw's *Candida* and *Man and Superman* for first inspiring his passion for drama; he designed five Shaw plays for the Theatre Guild, *Heartbreak House* (1920), *Back to Methusaleh* (1922), *The Devil's Disciple* (1923), *Arms and the Man* (1925), and *The Apple Cart* (1930). Simonson's sets for three of O'Neill's plays received more praise than the playwright's work. His spectacular powerhouse in *Dynamo* (1929) and the stark crucifixion imagery in *Days without End* (1934) managed to upstage the plays themselves, while his three-part framework for *Marco Millions* (1928) created a scenic unity that was lacking in the script.

Simonson's other important designs for Theatre Guild productions included Ferenc Molnar's *Liliom* (1921), Karel Capek's *R.U.R.*, Georg Kaiser's *From Morn to Midnight*, Leonid Andreiev's *He Who Gets Slapped* (1922), Elmer Rice's *The Adding Machine* (1923), Ernst Toller's *Man and Masses* (1924), and Franz Werfel's *Goat Song* and *Juarez and Maximillian* (1926). He also designed Herbert Biberman's *Roar China* and Philip Barry's *Hotel Universe* (both in 1930), Pearl Buck's *The Good Earth* (1932), S. N. Behrman's *End of Summer* and Robert Sherwood's *Idiot's Delight* (both in 1936), and Jean Giradoux's *Amphytrion 38* (1938).

In spite of Simonson's largely architectonic method, he was also proficient in the arts of lighting and costuming. Calling the lighting switchboard the "nerve center of a modern stage," Simonson drew on his painter's sensibility to use lighting as a "second brush" for creating various intensities of color and depth, especially on smaller stages. As a costume designer he tried to obtain a thorough grasp of garment making; during his travels in Europe he often purchased old pattern books, courtiers' costumes, and even the clothes of peasants he met. He would study these while devising costumes for the stage; in 1937 he donated his collection to the Metropolitan Museum of Art, helping to found its Museum of Costume Art. In 1932 Simonson designed costumes for *La Pas D'Acier*, a ballet with music by Prokofiev, and in 1937 he designed both settings and costumes for Balanchine's *Apollon Musagete*, Tchaikovsky's *Swan Lake*, and *Voices of Spring*, with music by Johann Strauss. In addition to ballet, Simonson fashioned the sets for the Metropolitan Opera's 1947 production of Wagner's *Ring of the Niebelungen*.

Behind the scenes Simonson worked for the arts in various capacities. His art criticism, collected in the 1927 volume *Minor Prophecies*, continued to appear into the 1940s, and he arranged numerous shows for art museums, including the International Theater Exhibition of 1934 at the Museum of Modern Art. In 1939 and 1940 he applied his expertise in theater architecture as consultant to new playhouses at the University of Wisconsin, the University of Indiana, and Hunter College. He also worked occasionally as an interior designer and decorator, wrote articles on decoration, fashion, and cooking, and even tried his hand at poetry with the forgettable 1946 volume *Untended Groves*. In 1950 he published *The Art of Scene Design*, a textbook for novices that summarized the important innovations Simonson contributed to the ideas and practices of American stage design.

Simonson was married twice. He had one daughter with his first wife, Helen Strauss, whom he married in 1916 and divorced in 1926; in 1927 he married Theatre Guild designer Carolyn Hancock, with whom he had one son and one daughter. He died in Yonkers, New York.

• The Lee Simonson Papers, which include approximately 100 drawings, designs, blueprints, and photographs, are housed in the Harvard Theatre Collection. Aside from his own *Part of a Lifetime: Drawings and Designs, 1919–1940* (1943), a full assessment of Simonson's work is Orville K. Larson, *Scene Design in the American Theatre: From 1915 to 1960* (1989). See also Norris Houghton, "The Designer Sets the Stage: Lee Simonson," and Ronald H. Wainscott, *Staging O'Neill: The Experimental Years, 1920–1934* (1988). Other important sources include Lawrence Langner, *The Magic Curtain* (1951); Roy S. Waldau, *Vintage Years of the Theatre Guild, 1928–1939* (1972); Walter Prichard Eaton, *The Theatre Guild: The First Ten Years* (1929); and Mordecai Gorelick, *New Theatres for Old* (1940). A complete list of Simonson's productions is included in Thomas J. Mikotowicz, ed., *Theatrical Designers: An International Biographical Dictionary* (1992). An obituary is in the *New York Times*, 24 Jan. 1967.

KURT EISEN

SIMPSON, Albert Benjamin (15 Dec. 1843–29 Oct. 1919), founder of the Christian and Missionary Alliance, was born in Bayview, Prince Edward Island, Canada, the son of James Simpson and Jane Clark, farmers. The family moved to a farm near Chatham, Ontario, when Simpson was three years old. He had a strict Presbyterian upbringing. With the help of his mother, who enjoyed reading English classics much more than farm chores, he developed an imaginative and visionary outlook and a love of language and literature. His father's reading was largely limited to daily doses of Richard Baxter's *The Saints' Everlasting Rest* and Philip Doddridge's *The Rise and Progress of Religion in the Soul*. Simpson is said to have committed himself to the gospel ministry upon reading a missionary biography at the age of nine. Another book, *Gospel Mystery of Sanctification*, by Walter Marshall, is described as having led him to personal conversion.

Simpson completed high school and was mentored by tutors, then taught school for a time before entering Knox College in Toronto in 1861. He graduated in 1865 and was invited to become the minister of a prestigious Presbyterian church in Hamilton, Ontario. He preached his first sermon there on Sunday, 11 September 1865. The following day, on Monday, he was ordained, and on Tuesday he married Margaret Henry. The couple had nine children, five of whom survived to adulthood.

After eight years in Hamilton, during which time his congregation grew steadily, Simpson accepted a call in December 1873 to become minister of the prosperous Chestnut Street Presbyterian Church in Louisville, Kentucky. It was there that his evangelistic zeal became apparent. Under his leadership the church spearheaded a series of revival meetings held in a public auditorium. A visiting evangelist urged the assembled masses to make their peace with God. Reconciliatory efforts also helped to ease tensions left over from the Civil War. A new and much larger church building also emerged from these initiatives.

During his ministry in Louisville, Simpson felt increasingly that gospel outreach should be world oriented, and as a result he became more interested in missionary work and how it could be promoted through the printed page. In 1880 he moved to New York City to become minister of the Thirteenth Street Presbyterian Church in Manhattan. An early biographer states that the chief reason for the change was Simpson's desire to begin publishing an illustrated missionary periodical. Within two months of his arrival in New York, copies of *The Gospel in All Lands* were being distributed. Within two years he had established a training school for missionaries, which eventually became Nyack (N.Y.) College.

As he did in Louisville, Simpson put a great priority in beckoning the unchurched. He personally ventured into the streets to extend the message, and people from all walks of life responded. When it came time to receive some of the poorer individuals into membership, however, church officials balked.

Simpson left the church in November 1881 and later recalled that "the parting was most friendly." He also forsook his Presbyterian ordination, citing differences over infant baptism (he had come to oppose it) and "divine healing," which he promoted in ways some clergy found excessive. Along with his growing missionary impulse, he developed new understandings of the Bible that included provision, in some cases, for supernatural recovery from physical and mental illnesses. He also evolved into an exponent of a doctrine of sanctification that included "a second work of grace" subsequent to that of personal salvation.

Although Simpson never expressed any intent to start a new denomination, that is what eventually happened. Two weeks after resigning his Presbyterian parish he met with a group of people to discuss the spiritual needs of the city. A few days later, around a stove in a nearby dance hall, those "in sympathy with an aggressive spiritual movement" assembled again to confer and pray. Only seven other people were there with Simpson.

Under his persuasive leadership, however, momentum built rapidly. A new congregation came into being, and a wide variety of interdenominational ministries were developed. These included relief work in disadvantaged neighborhoods, support for overseas missionary endeavors, and production of literature. Associations were formed to coordinate domestic and foreign interests with branches begun in other localities. These came together in 1887 in what was called the Christian and Missionary Alliance, which over the years was gradually recognized as a denomination. By 1996 it embraced more than 16,500 churches in some fifty-six countries with a total constituency of about 2,500,000.

Simpson served as president of the Christian and Missionary Alliance for the remainder of his life. He died at his home in Nyack, New York.

• The bulk of Simpson materials is in the national office of the Christian and Missionary Alliance, Colorado Springs, Colo. Some materials are at Nyack College, Nyack, N.Y., and at Christian Publications, Inc., Camp Hill, Pa. Biographies of Simpson are A. E. Thompson, *The Life of A. B. Simpson* (1920; rev. ed., 1960), and A. W. Tozer, *Wingspread: Albert B. Simpson, a Study in Spiritual Altitude* (1943). An obituary is in the *New York Times*, 30 Oct. 1919.

DAVID E. KUCHARSKY

SIMPSON, Edmund Shaw (1784–31 July 1848), actor and theater manager, was born in England to a merchant family and was educated to follow into the family business. He decided to pursue an acting career, encouraged in this pursuit by his friend Thomas Hilson. Simpson made his debut in Towcester, Northamptonshire, in May 1806 as Baron Steinford in *The Stranger* and as Fainwould in *Raising the Wind*. He later played in Buckingham, Dover, Margate, Brighton, and Dublin. Simpson emigrated to the United States in October 1809, accompanied by Mrs. Mason (later Mrs. Entwisle). Both had been engaged by the theater enterprise of Thomas A. Cooper and Stephen Price, and they opened at the Park Theatre in New York; Simpson played Harry Dornton in *The Road to Ruin* and Frank Heartall in *The Soldier's Daughter*, opposite Mrs. Mason's Widow Cheerly.

Simpson was praised in *Rambler's Magazine* (Nov. 1809) for his "form well proportioned, delicate though manly—a face regular, intelligent and interesting—his voice, modulant and sonorous—his gestures graceful, and his motions easy." Indeed, "his face and figure exactly harmonized with the sentiments he uttered [and] with just as much freedom as is perfectly graceful, and as much spirit as is consistent with decorum." Simpson's abilities were also recognized by Cooper and Price, who appointed him stage manager at the Park the following year. In 1812 he was made acting manager, and after Cooper's departure he became Price's full partner. In 1820 Simpson married Julia Elizabeth Jones, an actress.

From 1822 to 1827 Simpson and Price also controled the Walnut Street Theatre in Philadelphia in absentia, and they hired Joe Cowell, an English actor engaged at the Park Theatre, to manage the day-to-day operations. Cowell described Simpson as "a blunt, plain man . . . without either warmth or ceremony . . . but [with] the most amiable expression of countenance" (Cowell, p. 58). Simpson's dedication to the theater is also noted by Cowell, who wrote, "Simpson . . . was the most industrious man I ever knew; he generally played in every piece that there was any necessity for his appearing in, whether in his line or not, greatly to his own disadvantage, for in a certain range of characters he was excellent. For six days in the week he was scarcely out of the theatre; but on Sunday, it must be a very urgent point of business that would induce him even to write a letter" (Cowell, p. 59).

Simpson's success as actor and manager, however, began to turn sour in December 1827, when during a performance of *Faustus* a large piece of the set collapsed, laming him for life. The following April Simpson advertised to sell his interest in the theater, but he ended up remaining in charge, despite the evidence of sliding fortunes. By 1833 he had effectively retired from acting, appearing only in benefit performances.

The real-estate bust and subsequent economic depression of the late 1830s devastated Simpson's overextended land investments, and he never fully recovered financially. At the Park Theatre Simpson began to emphasize drama over music, possibly inspired by the success of the English actress Ellen Tree's performances. But popular tastes were swinging the other way, and the theater began to lose its steady audience. Price's death in 1840 left Simpson in sole charge of the fading theater. Simpson's last stage appearance was in late 1841 as Dazzle in Boucicault's *London Assurance*, with Henry Placide as Sir Harcourt Courtly and Charlotte Cushman as Lady Gay Spanker.

During the late 1840s the Park's fortunes diminished, and the length of its season was shortened to two-thirds of what it had been ten years earlier. Even reduced prices and occasional hits such as *Les Danseuses Viennoises* could not turn the tide, and in June 1848 Simpson sold control of the theater to Thomas S. Hamblin for a small annuity of $1,500. Simpson died in New York City only a few weeks later.

On his retirement, Simpson was recognized by the New York City broadside *Albion* (10 June 1848) for his contribution to American theater, and the paper's critic admonished the community for ignoring him in his plight. The writer credited Simpson with raising the level of American theater standards by introducing so many eminent English and European performers. He also focused on Simpson's introduction of "musical compositions of high and refined cast" (p. 284), in particular the wildly popular Italian opera brought to New York by the renowned Garcia company, which first appeared at Simpson's Park Theatre. Despite the *Albion* critic's urging, it was only after Simpson's death that the public acknowledged their appreciation; an official proclamation and a series of theater benefit performances raised several thousand dollars for the grieving family.

• For a detailed analysis of the theaters under Simpson's control, see Weldon Durham, *American Theatre Companies*, vol. 1 (1986), pp. 396–405 (Park Street), 524–27 (Walnut Street). Personal contemporary observations are related in Joseph Cowell, *Thirty Years Passed among the Players of England and America* (1844); and Francis Wemyss, *Twenty-Six Years of the Life of an Actor and Manager* (1847). See also William Dunlap, *A History of the American Theatre and Anecdotes of the Principal Actors* (1832; repr. 1963), pp. 269–71; T. Allston Brown, *History of the American Stage* (1870; repr. 1969), pp. 335–36; Lillian Hall, *Catalogue of Dramatic Portraits in the Theatre Collection of the Harvard College Library*, pp. 70–71; Joseph Ireland, *Records of the New York Stage, from 1750 to 1860* (2 vols., 1866–1867); and George C. D. Odell, *Annals of the New York Stage* (15 vols., 1927–1949). Obituaries are in the *Evening Post*, 1 Aug. 1848, and the *Albion*, 5 Aug. 1848.

GLEN NICHOLS

SIMPSON, George Gaylord (16 June 1902–6 Oct. 1984), paleontologist, was born in Chicago, Illinois, the son of Joseph A. Simpson, a lawyer, and Helen J. Kinney. While Simpson was still an infant, his parents moved from Chicago to Cheyenne, Wyoming, to Denver, where he attended the local public schools. He enrolled at the University of Colorado at Boulder in 1918 with vague ambitions to become a writer until he took a course in geology. He was immediately converted to the world of rocks and fossils, transferring to Yale University in his senior year (1922) when he learned that Yale was the leading institution for paleontology. Simpson received his Ph.B. in 1923 and remained at Yale for his Ph.D. in paleontology. In 1923 he married Lydia Pedroja, with whom he had four children.

In his first year as a graduate student, Simpson discovered in the basement of Yale's Peabody Museum a large collection of primitive mammals from Mesozoic Age rocks of the American West. Although Simpson was initially dissuaded from studying these fossils because they were too important for a beginner, they eventually provided him with the core materials for his doctoral dissertation on American Mesozoic mammals, which he completed in 1926. Simpson then went on to the British Museum (natural history) in London for a year of postdoctoral research on similar British and Continental fossil specimens.

Upon his return from England in the fall of 1927, Simpson joined the scientific staff of the American Museum of Natural History in New York City as assistant curator of fossil vertebrates. Simpson continued his fossil mammal studies in the South American strata of Patagonia, which had yielded an unusual and important fauna evolving in isolation from the rest of the world during the long time that South America was an island continent in the Cenozoic Age, when mammals diversified and assumed their modern appearance. Simpson's first book, *Attending Marvels* (1934), is a combination of travel journal and popular science of his first expedition to Patagonia.

By 1932 Simpson and his wife were separated; they eventually divorced in 1938. During his last year of graduate work at Yale, Simpson had chanced to encounter Anne Roe, his childhood friend from Denver, who was working for her doctorate in psychology at Columbia University. After his (and her own) divorce, Simpson and Roe married in 1938 and spent the rest of that year and part of the next doing field work in Venezuela. A distinguished psychologist in her own right, Roe was a source of great intellectual and emotional support for the rest of Simpson's life, including raising three of his four daughters, whose full custody he obtained in his divorce.

In the late 1930s and early 1940s Simpson continued studying fossil mammals, with his research beginning to address more theoretical evolutionary issues. In 1939 he published *Quantitative Zoology* in collaboration with Roe, and by the end of 1942, just before Simpson joined the U.S. Army, he completed two book-length manuscripts, *Tempo and Mode in Evolution* (1944) and *Principles of Classification and a Classification of Mammals* (1945).

In *Tempo and Mode in Evolution*, his most significant book, Simpson argued that Darwinian natural selection operating on inherited variation within species, as observed by laboratory geneticists and field naturalists, provided a parsimonious interpretation of the adaptations, specializations, and extinctions observed by the paleontologists among their fossils. Consequently, there was no need to rely on inherent, metaphysical mechanisms popular with most contemporary paleontologists to explain rates and patterns of evolution. *Tempo and Mode in Evolution* thus joined a half-dozen other books of that era that formed the foundation for what came to be known as the modern evolutionary synthesis, "synthesis" because the new theory of evolution came from a number of disciplines—genetics, ecology, anatomy, field biology, and botany as well as paleontology.

By the spring of 1943, Simpson was a captain in military intelligence with the Allied Forces Command led by General Dwight D. Eisenhower, first in North Africa and then, with the subsequent invasions in the summer of 1943, in Sicily and Italy. In late 1944 Simpson was shipped home with a severe case of hepatitis, the rank of major, and two Bronze Stars.

Simpson returned to the American Museum and in 1945 became chairman of the new Department of Geology and Paleontology; he also accepted appointment as professor of vertebrate paleontology at Columbia University. In 1949 he published *The Meaning of Evolution*, a popular account of modern evolutionary theory as seen from the point of view of the fossil evidence. The book, which was subsequently translated into ten languages and sold some half-million copies, spread the modern principles of organic evolution among the educated public.

In 1953 Simpson published another semitechnical volume, *Evolution and Geography*, which outlined the principles for explaining the distributions of land animals, especially mammals, in the geologic past. It contradicted the claims made by Alfred Wegener, the German scientist who asserted that drifting continents carried land animals far and wide from their original distribution. Instead, Simpson cogently argued that the natural means of animal and plant dispersal over the huge intervals of geologic time would achieve the same patterns of distribution on continents that did not move. Simpson was eventually converted to the new theory of plate tectonics when geophysical data from the ocean floors in the 1960s provided convincing evidence that new seafloor was created at midocean ridges and moved outward, carrying the continents—and often their resident floras and faunas—with them.

In the summer of 1956 Simpson made another South American expedition, this time to the headwaters of the Amazon in westernmost Brazil. Near the end of the trip in late August, while camp was being cleared, a felled tree dropped on Simpson, badly breaking his lower right leg. After a painful trip back downriver, Simpson reached the hospital a week later in New York City. He resisted all advice to have the leg amputated, undergoing twelve separate operations, and finally recovered the use of the leg, although it always pained him, and he remained somewhat lame.

In 1958 Simpson resigned the chairmanship of the Department of Geology and Paleontology at the American Museum and in 1959 accepted an appointment as Alexander Agassiz Professor at Harvard's Museum of Comparative Zoology. That same year also marked the centennial of Darwin's *On the Origin of Species*, which brought Simpson, once again, into the public limelight as one of the leading evolutionary theorists. Simpson always had a special interest in Darwin, because Darwin represented for Simpson the quintessential liberator of the human spirit who sought answers to the puzzle of human existence without recourse to supernatural explanations. Simpson's reading of Darwin reinforced his own predilection for a materialistic, positivistic view of the world.

Shortly after Simpson joined Harvard, his wife Anne Roe was also appointed to a full professorship in the school of education. They thus became the first married couple to receive professorial appointments at Harvard. In 1964 Simpson published his favorite book, *This View of Life*, a collection of his essays on various evolutionary themes, including the role of Darwin, the nature of historical biology, the problem of apparent purpose in living nature, and speculations about cosmic evolution and the human evolutionary future.

In 1967 Simpson and Roe moved to Tucson where they had earlier bought a house in preparation for their retirement. He was given an appointment at the University of Arizona, which involved some teaching at first but later evolved to weekly luncheon meetings with a few students and faculty. Over the next fifteen years Simpson continued to publish books—on South American mammals, penguins, Darwin, fossils, and the history of life—collections of essays and his autobiography.

Acknowledgment of Simpson's important contributions to paleontology and evolutionary biology is indicated by his election to the two premier scientific bodies in the United States, the American Philosophical Society (1936) and the National Academy of Sciences (1941), and by his invitation to become a foreign member of the Royal Society of London (1958). He served as president of the Society of Vertebrate Paleontology (1942), the Society for the Study of Evolution (1946), the American Society of Mammalogists (1962), the Society for Systematic Zoology (1962), and the American Society of Zoologists (1964). He received the National Medal of Science from President Lyndon Johnson in 1966 and more than a dozen other medals and prizes from international scientific societies and organizations.

George Gaylord Simpson was not an easy man to know. Even to colleagues with whom he worked closely he seemed reserved, often aloof, extremely guarded about his private life, and capable of sharp critical comment. He did not make friends at all easily, and those whom he referred as "good friends" in his autobiography were surprised to be so considered. In the last years of his life, Simpson's world had shrunk perceptibly. Except for immediate family and a few loyal colleagues, he became a lonely, somewhat testy man, living out his days working and writing in professional isolation. His health gradually declined, and in summer 1984 he was suffering the aftereffects of a serious attack of pneumonia that he had earlier contracted on a South Pacific cruise. His condition worsened over the summer, and he died in Tucson. His remains were privately cremated and later dispersed in the Arizona desert.

• Simpson's papers are in the archives of the American Philosophical Society, Philadelphia, and the Department of Vertebrate Paleontology, American Museum of Natural History, New York City. Simpson wrote a short autobiographical memoir, "The Compleat Paleontologist?" published in *Annual Reviews of Earth and Planetary Science* (1976), followed by a full autobiography, *Concession to the Improbable* (1978). Additional information can be found in L. F. Laporte, ed., *Simple Curiosity: Letters from George Gaylord Simpson to His Family, 1921–1970* (1987), which also provides an annotated bibliography of forty of Simpson's major publications. Simpson's complete bibliography from 1925 to 1971 is included at the end of a brief biographical essay by M. K. Hecht and others in *Evolutionary Biology* 6 (1972): 1–29. See also L. F. Laporte, "George G. Simpson, Paleontology, and the Expansion of Biology," in *The Expansion of American Biology* (1991). An obituary is in the *New York Times*, 8 Oct. 1984, and memorials were written by S. J. Gould in the journal *Evolution* 39 (1985); L. F. Laporte in *American Philosophical Society Yearbook, 1984* (1985); E. C. Olson in Geological Society of America, *Memorials*, vol. 16 (1986); and H. B. Whittington, *Biographical Memoirs of the Royal Society of London* (1986).

LÉO F. LAPORTE

SIMPSON, Jerry (31 Mar. 1842–23 Oct. 1905), U.S. representative, was born in Westmoreland County, New Brunswick, Canada, the son of Joseph Simpson, a sailor and sawmill owner, and his wife, whose maiden name was Washburn (given name unknown). In 1848 the family moved to Oneida County, New York, where Jerry received a brief and rudimentary education in public schools. Beginning in 1852 the Simpsons moved to a series of towns near the Great Lakes in both Canada and the United States. At fourteen Simpson left home to work on lake freighters for twenty-three years, first as a cook, then a sailor, and ultimately as a ship captain. In 1861 he enlisted in the Twelfth Illinois Infantry but was mustered out after three months, suffering from the poor health that plagued his life. In 1870 he married Jane Cape; they had two children.

After a preliminary visit in 1878, in 1879 Simpson moved his family to Kansas, where he first farmed and operated a sawmill near Holton and then, in 1884, started a cattle ranch near Medicine Lodge. The terrible winter of 1886 destroyed this venture and left Simpson heavily in debt. He undertook a variety of small business ventures and gained appointment as marshal of Medicine Lodge, but Simpson increasingly turned his attention to politics. He had previously been a Republican, but in Kansas he was attracted to the oppositional politics and reform principles of single-taxers, Greenbackers, and other third parties. He twice ran unsuccessfully for the state legislature, as a Greenbacker in 1886 and as the Union Labor candidate in 1888.

When the state was thereafter engulfed in agricultural depression, these traditional reform elements merged with the expansive Farmers' Alliance to form the new People's party in 1890, and Simpson was chosen its nominee for Congress from southwestern Kansas. His sharp wit and folksy political style enabled him to convey the Populist message of economic and political reform to his largely rural audiences. A misguided Republican attempt to ridicule that style led to Simpson's famous nickname of "Sockless Jerry," which he quickly turned to his political advantage. "There are lots of farmers in Kansas today," he sharply observed, "who are stockingless and almost clothingless, they and their wives and children. They don't go that way because they want to, I assure you. They would be pleased to wear white shirts and silk socks and broadcloth, and if they ever get one-half of the privileges from this government that the capitalists have got they will be able to" (Clanton, p. 268).

With Democratic support, Simpson was elected to Congress in 1890, 1892, and 1896; he was narrowly defeated in 1894 and 1898. In Congress he was the floor leader of the Populist House delegation but introduced few bills and generally limited his speaking to the repartee in which he was unequalled. His most important service came in 1897–1898, when he provided the major parliamentary opposition to Speaker Thomas B. Reed and persistently attempted to limit what he saw as steps toward militarism and imperialism.

Politically, Simpson was a leader of the fusion wing of the People's party, recognizing that he needed Democratic support to carry his own district and convinced that Democratic-Populist cooperation could also achieve national power. He was an influential advocate of the Populist nomination of Democratic presidential candidate William Jennings Bryan in 1896 and repeatedly urged Populists to vote for other Democrats as well. To make fusion attractive to the more conservative Democrats, moreover, he frequently attempted to narrow the Populist reform platform and to frustrate the party's more radical legislative objectives. These tactics to promote fusion (and himself) often infuriated other Populists, sometimes splintered the party, and provoked great personal resentments.

Following his 1898 defeat for a fourth term in Congress, from May 1899 to September 1900 Simpson published a newspaper entitled *Jerry Simpson's Bayonet* (Wichita) to both attack his opponents and maintain his political visibility. After failing in 1900 to gain party backing for a bid for the U.S. Senate, he withdrew from active involvement in politics. He sold cattle for a while in Wichita and in 1902 moved to Roswell, New Mexico, where he resumed ranching and became a land agent for the Santa Fe Railroad Company, which he had earlier assailed as a grasping monopoly. His health continuing to deteriorate, he returned to Kansas in 1905 and died in Wichita.

Simpson left behind both devoted admirers and bitter enemies but no political organization, legislative achievements, or written work. He was essentially an agitator whose brilliant political skills enabled him to articulate what he called the "profound popular passion" of the Populist movement (Franks, p. ii). This important accomplishment brought attention to new political ideas and, as his former Republican opponents acknowledged at his death, helped frame the issues for the Progressive Era.

• Annie L. Diggs, *The Story of Jerry Simpson* (1908), is an uncritical biography by a fellow Kansas Populist. At the opposite extreme is Karel D. Bicha, "Jerry Simpson: Populist without Principle," *Journal of American History* 54 (Sept. 1967): 291–306, a hostile and sometimes misleading account. More useful are two theses, Charles K. Franks, "Jerry Simpson, A Kansas Populist" (master's thesis, Northwestern Univ., 1940), and Myron C. Scott, "A Congressman and His Constituents: Jerry Simpson and the Big Seventh" (master's thesis, Fort Hays Kansas State College, 1959). For Simpson's congressional career, see Peter H. Argersinger, "No Rights on This Floor: Third Parties and the Institutionalization of Congress," *Journal of Interdisciplinary History* 22 (Spring 1992): 655–90. See also O. Gene Clanton, *Kansas Populism, Ideas and Men* (1969), and Argersinger, *Populism and Politics: William Alfred Peffer and the People's Party* (1974).
PETER H. ARGERSINGER

SIMPSON, Matthew (21 June 1811–18 June 1884), Methodist bishop and orator, was born in Cadiz, Ohio, the son of James Simpson, a manufacturer and storekeeper, and Sarah Tingley. While growing up in western Pennsylvania, Simpson had little formal schooling, but he read widely and acquired knowledge of history, mathematics, literature, and religion under the tutelage of his uncle Matthew Simpson. As a boy, Simpson helped his family in the manufacturing of weaver's reeds. He learned about the law by attending the county court with another uncle who was clerk. A third uncle published a weekly newspaper; by assisting him, Simpson learned much about publishing and the world beyond Cadiz. At age fifteen, he helped his uncle Matthew teach at a private academy. Two years later he attended Madison College in Uniontown, Pennsylvania, for two months before returning to Cadiz. In 1830, desiring a more stable career, Simpson began the study of medicine under a local doctor; three years later he qualified to practice on his own.

After only eight months as a physician, Simpson decided that God wanted him to be a preacher. In 1834 the Pittsburgh Conference of the Methodist Episcopal church admitted him on a trial basis and assigned him to the Cadiz circuit. In November 1835 he married Ellen Verner. They had seven children. After three years of preaching in eastern Ohio and western Pennsylvania, Simpson became professor of natural science at Allegheny College, a Methodist school in Williamsport, Pennsylvania. Having taught at the college for less than six months, he was named vice president of the institution as well. In 1839 Indiana Asbury University (now DePauw University) in Greencastle, Indiana, elected him president. While there, Simpson's reputation as a powerful and eloquent orator began to spread across Indiana.

In 1843 the Indiana Annual Conference honored Simpson by electing him to lead its delegation to the 1844 General Conference. When the General Conference met in New York City, agitation over slavery led the body to adopt a Plan of Separation, which divided American Methodism into northern and southern churches. At the 1848 General Conference in Pittsburgh, Simpson, again leading the Indiana delegation, authored a resolution declaring that because southern Methodists had violated the Plan of Separation, it was "null and void." The General Conference adopted the resolution, and outraged southern Methodists successfully appealed to the civil courts for their share of joint properties. When the conference elected him editor of the *Western Christian Advocate*, he resigned from Indiana Asbury University, and moved to Cincinnati, Ohio.

Through the columns of the *Western Christian Advocate*, Simpson repeatedly denounced the institution of slavery, which he blamed for dividing American Methodism. His opposition to the Fugitive Slave Act of 1850 gave him a national reputation as an antislavery spokesman. The 1852 General Conference in Boston elected him as one of its bishops. In 1857 he served as the denomination's fraternal delegate to the English

Wesleyan Conference in Liverpool and to the Evangelical Alliance meeting in Berlin, Germany. Garrett Theological Seminary in Evanston, Illinois, elected him president in 1859, but his popularity as a speaker and duties as a bishop left him little time to devote to the school.

During the Civil War Simpson used his considerable oratorical skills in supporting the Union cause. He united religious and national imagery in a powerful appeal for the war effort: "We will take our glorious flag—the flag of our country—and nail it just below the cross! There let it wave, as it waved of old. Around it let us gather: first Christ's, and then our country's."

In addition to meeting his responsibilities as bishop, Simpson spoke at meetings to raise funds for the U.S. Christian Commission and the U.S. Sanitary Commission. In 1863 he moved to Philadelphia, Pennsylvania, where Methodist laymen had given him a home. During the war President Abraham Lincoln as well as Secretary of War Edwin M. Stanton and other members of the cabinet sought Simpson's counsel. Simpson used his influence, with limited success, to advocate the appointment of more Methodists to government offices. Although invited to direct the Freedmen's Bureau, Simpson declined, citing "ecclesiastical obligations." During the latter half of the war he pursued the religious reconstruction of the South, seizing southern Methodist churches under orders from the War Department and sending missionaries into the South to organize "loyal" Methodist churches. After Lincoln's assassination in April 1865, Simpson delivered a stirring funeral oration both in Washington, D.C., and at the graveside in Springfield, Illinois, ending his tribute to the slain president: "Hero, Martyr, Friend, farewell!"

Expecting Andrew Johnson to pursue a stern policy toward the South in Reconstruction, Simpson was disappointed by Lincoln's successor, who seemed far too conciliatory toward southern rebels and insisted on the return of southern Methodist church properties. When Radical Republicans impeached Johnson, Simpson openly supported their efforts. He remained politically influential long after the Civil War and enjoyed personal friendships with Presidents Ulysses S. Grant and Rutherford B. Hayes.

Within the Methodist Episcopal church, Simpson advocated the admission of lay delegates to Methodist governing bodies, a reform that was successful in 1870. During the 1870s he became a historian for the denomination, writing *A Hundred Years of Methodism* (1876) and editing the *Cyclopaedia of Methodism* (1878). Once more representing northern American Methodists, Simpson delivered the opening sermon at the first Ecumenical Methodist Conference in London, England, in 1881. Three years later Simpson, as the senior bishop of the Methodist Episcopal church, presided over his last General Conference, held in Philadelphia. Shortly after the close of the conference, he died in Philadelphia.

Simpson's oratorical skills in inspiring northern audiences, his position as bishop in the large and growing Methodist Episcopal church, and his access to political leaders propelled him to national prominence during the sectional crises of the mid-nineteenth century. He united religious zeal and patriotic fervor into vital support for the Union war effort and for Radical Reconstruction. Within the church he was a progressive bishop open to reform and an advocate of Methodist unity.

• The Matthew Simpson Papers in the Library of Congress contain his manuscript autobiography and journal, extensive correspondence, manuscript sermons, and other materials. The DePauw University Archives contain his academic papers as president of the university from 1839 to 1848. The Historical Society of the Eastern Pennsylvania Annual Conference, United Methodist church, has a collection of 1,060 letters written to Simpson between 1834 and 1884, which is held at Old St. George's Church in Philadelphia. The latter two collections have been microfilmed. Simpson's published writings include numerous editorials in the *Western Christian Advocate* between 1848 and 1852. In addition to his historical works, he authored *Lectures on Preaching, Delivered before the Theological Department of Yale College* (1879). Shortly after Simpson's death, George R. Crooks edited a collection of his sermons, which was published as Matthew Simpson, *Sermons* (1885). Crooks also produced the first biography of Simpson, *The Life of Bishop Matthew Simpson, of the Methodist Episcopal Church* (1890), which includes portions of Simpson's manuscript autobiography and journal. Ezra M. Wood, *The Peerless Orator: The Rev. Matthew Simpson* (1909), and Clarence T. Wilson, *Matthew Simpson, Patriot, Preacher, Prophet* (1929), are celebratory biographies. Robert D. Clark, *The Life of Matthew Simpson* (1956), is the best scholarly treatment of Simpson's life and significance.

DANIEL W. STOWELL

SIMPSON, Wallis Warfield (19 June 1896–24 Apr. 1986), duchess of Windsor, was born at Blue Ridge Summit, Pennsylvania, the daughter of Teakle Wallis Warfield, a bank clerk, and Alice Montague. The Warfields and Montagues were both old, reputable Baltimore, Maryland, families, but the two families did not get along. Within five months of her birth, Wallis's father died of tuberculosis, leaving her mother essentially penniless. As a result, Wallis Warfield grew up in genteel poverty; however, with the help of her father's older brother Solomon Warfield, a man of considerable wealth, Wallis was able to attend a finishing school, Oldfields, in Baltimore. There are no indications that she had any intellectual pretensions. Like many young women of her day, her main goal in life was marriage.

In 1916 Wallis married Earl Winfield Spencer, Jr., an aviator pilot and junior officer in the U.S. Navy. In time Spencer proved to be an alcoholic and often became violent when drunk. The marriage was disastrous for Wallis, and she left her husband in 1920 intending to divorce him, a course of action that neither her mother nor her uncle Solomon could approve. They both urged Wallis to try to make the marriage work, and she did. Despite several attempted reconciliations, by 1925 it was clear that the marriage was a failure, and Wallis was determined to obtain a divorce. She was advised to seek it in Virginia, where she would have to reside for a year; she moved to Warrenton, and on 10 December 1927 she was granted the divorce.

It was during that year-long wait that a school friend from her Oldfield days, Mary Kirk Raffray, introduced Wallis to Ernest Aldrich Simpson, a married man whose marriage was in difficulties. Simpson was the son of a British father and an American mother, Harvard educated (he did not take a degree), and a great Anglophile, and he had enlisted in the Cold Stream Guards in the first World War. His father had established a ship brokerage, Simpson, Spence & Young, with offices in London and New York. At the time of his meeting Wallis, Ernest was in charge of the New York office, although he soon moved to the London one. After a relatively brief courtship Wallis agreed to marry Ernest, and they were married at the Chelsea Registry Office in London, England, on 21 July 1928. There is nothing to suggest that Wallis was passionately in love with this man, but he was cultivated and interested in the arts, and, because his shipping business was relatively prosperous, he represented more security for Wallis than she had known before. They took up residence in London, first in a rented house at 12 Upper Berkeley Street and a year later in a flat at No. 5 Byranston Court. Initially Wallis Simpson's existence in London was a bit lonely, but her husband's sister gradually introduced her to a social set, mostly comprising Americans, and Wallis gained a reputation as a fine hostess.

An old acquaintance of Wallis Simpson's, Benjamin Thaw, had become first secretary at the American embassy in London and had married Consuelo Morgan of the famous Morgan sisters. Thaw introduced Simpson to his sister-in-law, Thelma Morgan Furness, who was married to Viscount Marmaduke Furness, owner of the Furness-Withy Shipping Lines. By late 1930 Thelma Furness had become a mistress of Edward, prince of Wales, and she introduced Simpson to the prince on 10 January 1931 at her country house, "Burrough Court," near Melton Mowbray, Leicestershire. Wallis does not seem to have made any great impression on the prince on this occasion, but it was also at Thelma Furness's suggestion that Simpson was presented at court before King George V and Queen Mary on 10 June 1931. It was not long after this event that Wallis and Ernest Simpson began seeing a great deal of the prince, being invited on numerous occasions to his country residence near Windsor, Fort Belvedere, and the prince in turn being a frequent dinner guest at 5 Byranston Court.

In March 1933 Wallis Simpson paid her first visit to Fort Belvedere on her own, at the prince's invitation. By the beginning of February 1934 she had effectively replaced Thelma Furness in the prince of Wales's affections, and in the course of that year Simpson came to be accepted in English high society, the prince representing the pinnacle of that society.

According to Philip Ziegler, Edward's "official" biographer, from the early 1920s the prince had been involved in countless affairs, most of them fleeting, but late in the 1920s he began serious relationships, first with Freda Dudley Ward, then with Thelma Furness, and subsequently with Wallis Simpson, all married women. This development was most disconcerting to his father, King George V. But by early 1935 it became apparent that Edward's attachment to Mrs. Simpson (as she was known formally and to the public) was more serious than anything in his life. The royal family and "the establishment" in England were aghast. This twice-married American woman was totally unsuitable as a prospective partner for the heir to the throne.

On 20 January 1936 George V died, and on 21 January 1936 the accession of Edward as king was proclaimed. In one sense Wallis Simpson's position rose higher than ever. By early spring, however, the news began to spread within the establishment that plans were afoot for Simpson to divorce her husband. Ernest Simpson went through a ritual act of adultery in July, and the solicitor hired by Wallis got the petition for divorce down for the Assizes to be held at Ipswich in Suffolk in October. On 27 October 1936 she was granted a decree nisi from her second husband. This event triggered a great crisis in the political establishment. The prime minister, Stanley Baldwin, along with Cosmo Lang, the archbishop of Canterbury, primate of the Church of England, of which the king was governor, opposed Edward's intentions to marry Wallis Simpson in six months, as soon as her divorce became final. This would have occurred only weeks before the king's coronation, which was scheduled for 12 May 1937. Simpson was considered totally unacceptable as a candidate to be queen of England, not only by the establishment in England but also in the dominions within the British Empire, most notably in Canada. As a result, Edward abdicated the throne on 11 December 1936.

Following the abdication, his successor, King George VI, created Edward duke of Windsor, and with his marriage to Wallis in France on 3 June 1937 she became the duchess of Windsor. By Letters Patent the duke was permitted to be addressed as "His Royal Highness," although the address "Her Royal Highness" was specifically denied to the duchess. She was addressed as "Her Grace," a fact that rankled the Windsors for the rest of their lives.

From the moment of the abdication, which shook the monarchy to its foundations, the royal family and establishment firmly rejected the Windsors and made it quite clear that they would never be welcome to live in England again. As a result, they were left for the rest of their days to pursue a nomadic though leisurely existence, with the exception of the years of World War II when the duke was given a post as governor general of the Bahamas.

Because Edward had given up the throne for her, the duchess saw her role during their married life as one of providing a royal surrounding, a royal court without the throne, for her husband. She used her abilities as an interior decorator and provided a remarkable dining table wherever they traveled, which was mostly in France, in Paris and at "The Mill" southwest of Paris, with lengthy sojourns in the United States.

It is doubtful whether the duchess felt any more passion for Edward upon their marriage than she had felt for Ernest Simpson when she married him. Edward on the other hand regarded her with an adoration that never abated to the end of his life. In her own way the duchess probably did come to love him in later years, but it is also clear that she was always the dominant partner in the marriage.

With the duke of Windsor's death on 28 May 1972 the duchess's life was transformed. She initially went into seclusion, although she seems to have resumed a limited social life. For the last eight years of her life her health steadily deteriorated, and she was confined to her house in Paris until her death there.

• Michael Bloch's works contain the most important primary sources in print, letters by the duke and duchess of Windsor; see *Wallis and Edward: Letters 1931–1937* (1986), *The Secret File of the Duke of Windsor: The Private Papers 1937–1972* (1988), and *The Duke of Windsor's War* (1982). Simpson's memoirs, published as *The Heart Has Its Reasons* (1956), and those of the duke of Windsor, *A King's Story* (1947), must be read with caution. Most of what has been written on Wallis Simpson is unreliable, much of it simply gossip and a minefield for the historian. J. Bryan III and Charles Murphy, *The Windsor Story* (1979), provides information not to be found anywhere else, but not everything presented there is to be accepted uncritically. Philip Ziegler discusses Simpson reliably in *King Edward VIII* (1991). Michael Thornton, *Royal Feud* (1985), presents some interesting views on the royal family's attitude toward Simpson before and after the abdication. Suzy Menkes provides some insights into the lifestyle of the Windsors after the Second World War in *The Windsor Style* (1987). Obituaries of Simpson are in the *Times* (London) and the *New York Times*, both 25 Apr. 1986.

CARL ERICSON

SIMPSON, William Hood (19 May 1888–15 Aug. 1980), U.S. Army general, was born in Weatherford, Texas, the son of Edward J. Simpson, a rancher, and Elizabeth Amelia Hood. Inspired by stories of his father's and his uncle's service in Nathan Bedford Forrest's cavalry during the Civil War, Hood chose by age ten to make the military his career. He passed the admissions test for the U.S. Military Academy well before he graduated from high school, and when he entered West Point in June 1905, only one month past his seventeenth birthday, he was the youngest in his class. Dubbed "Cheerful Charlie" and "Greaser" from his Texas origins—the latter nickname following him throughout his career—the popular Simpson played second-team football, and his military talent won him the rank of cadet lieutenant. No academic star, however, he graduated third from the bottom in the class of 1909.

Simpson's early career assignments were typical for a junior officer at that time. Commissioned a second lieutenant of infantry, he spent 1910 through mid-1912 leading a unit of the Sixth Infantry Regiment against the Moros on Mindanao. He was transferred to the Presidio in San Francisco in July 1912 and then to Texas in 1914, when tensions with Mexico caused a buildup of U.S. troops along the Rio Grande. After serving in San Francisco for most of 1915, Simpson returned to Texas in 1916, when General John J. Pershing launched his punitive expedition to capture Pancho Villa. He was promoted to first lieutenant in July 1916 for leading the advance guard across the Rio Grande.

In May 1917, one month after the United States entered World War I, Simpson became a captain and was assigned as aide-de-camp to General George Bell, Jr., commander of the Thirty-third Division. After accompanying Bell on a tour of the French battlefront, he helped devise a stateside divisional training program based on their observations. Once his division deployed in France in May 1918, Simpson served primarily as a staff officer, winning a Silver Star for his work in the Meuse-Argonne campaign. He received promotions to the temporary ranks of major in June 1918 and lieutenant colonel in November 1918 before becoming division chief of staff at the young age of thirty. With the demobilization of 1919, Simpson reverted to his prewar captaincy until he was promoted to the permanent rank of major in June 1920.

In 1921 Simpson married Ruth Webber Krakauer, a recent widow he had first met during his West Point years. They had no children of their own, but Ruth's two children joined the Simpson household. The family followed Simpson through a challenging, but not unusual, series of assignments in the afterwar years. From 1921 through 1923 he served in Washington at the Office of the Chief of Infantry. He graduated from the Infantry Advanced Course at Fort Benning in 1924 and was named a distinguished graduate of the Command and General Staff School in 1925. Putting his earlier academic problems behind him, he developed into a genuine student of his profession, taking Robert E. Lee and Thomas "Stonewall" Jackson as his military idols. After his stint at the Command and General Staff School, Simpson returned to troop command with a battalion of the Twelfth Infantry Regiment, then graduated from the Army War College in the class of 1928. For the next four years he served in the Intelligence Branch of the General Staff, and from 1932 until 1936 he headed the Reserve Officers Training Corps (ROTC) detachment at Pomona College. Promoted to lieutenant colonel in October 1934, he became a colonel in September 1938 while an instructor at the Army War College.

After World War II began, Simpson's star rose rapidly. He took command of the Ninth Infantry Regiment in August 1940 and in October was promoted to the temporary rank of brigadier general and assistant commander of the Second Infantry Division. From April through October 1941, with the temporary rank of major general, he commanded Camp Wolters in Texas, a training base for new recruits. In October 1941 he took command of the Thirty-fifth Division and accompanied it to California after Pearl Harbor to provide reinforcements in the event of a Japanese invasion of the Pacific Coast. After that fear subsided, Simpson's wartime efforts through mid-1944 focused on the stateside training of troops for overseas duty. He always stressed the importance of good morale to combat efficiency, and in addition to weapons training, he took special pains to make sure that sufficient numbers of trained medics and chaplains went with his men.

In May 1944 Simpson finally went to England to organize what became the Ninth Army, a unit that would include many of the troops he had trained in the United States. As part of General Omar N. Bradley's Twelfth Army Group, the Ninth Army first saw action in the successful capture of the French port of Brest in September 1944. In the fall of that year the Ninth Army was among the first Allied troops to break through the Siegfried Line; Simpson himself won a Bronze Star for his work in the capture of Aachen. Although not known for rapid movement—Simpson was devoted to detailed planning before his men were committed to action—the Ninth Army won Bradley's respect for its fighting ability and was assigned the toughest missions. Simpson proved to be one of the few senior American generals who could work with British field marshall Bernard Montgomery; on occasion, as in the Battle of the Bulge in December 1944, the Ninth Army operated under Montgomery's immediate control with few problems. As the Allies moved toward the German border, Montgomery refused to allow any move that undermined his own plans or that gave the Americans too much credit. However, Simpson's men finally crossed the Rhine on 24 March 1945 and on 1 April made contact with General Courtney Hodges's First Army to complete an encirclement of the Ruhr industrial area and the capture of over 300,000 German troops. Simpson's soldiers were the first American or British troops to cross the Elbe River on 12 April 1945.

After the defeat of Germany, Japan's imminent surrender made the Ninth Army's transfer to the Pacific unnecessary. Simpson took command of the Second Army in the United States until he retired in November 1946. In July 1954 he was promoted to full general on the retired list.

Living in San Antonio after his retirement, Simpson became a vice president of the Alamo National Bank and helped raise funds for hospital construction and other civic causes in Texas. A strong anti-Communist during the Cold War years of the 1950s and early 1960s, he spoke frequently to veterans and civic organizations to decry the lack of patriotism and self-sacrifice he felt he saw in the American youth of the Vietnam era. In 1971 his wife of fifty years died, and in 1978 Simpson married Catherine Berman. Simpson died in San Antonio and was buried in Arlington National Cemetery.

Simpson was often called "a soldier's soldier." He claimed that his command philosophy was "Never send an infantryman where you can send an artillery shell," a sentiment his men appreciated. General Dwight D. Eisenhower summed up Simpson's military ability best: "If Simpson ever made a mistake as an army commander, it never came to my attention. . . . Alert, intelligent and professionally capable, he was the type of leader that American soldiers deserve."

• A substantial collection of Simpson's papers is at the U.S. Army Military History Institute, Carlisle Barracks, Pa. He is the subject of Thomas R. Stone, "He Had the Guts to Say No: A Military Biography of William Hood Simpson" (Ph.D. diss., Rice Univ., 1975), which had the active cooperation of Simpson himself. See also Russell Weigley, *Eisenhower's Lieutenants* (1981); Omar N. Bradley and Clay Blair, *A General's Life* (1983); and U.S. Army, *Conquer: The Story of the Ninth Army, 1944–1945* (1947). Informative obituaries are in the *New York Times*, 17 Aug. 1980, and *Assembly* 40 (Mar. 1982): 116–17.

CAROL REARDON

SIMS, J. Marion (25 Jan. 1813–12 Nov. 1883), pioneer gynecologist, was born James Marion Sims in Lancaster, South Carolina, the son of John Sims, a farmer and hotel keeper, and Mahala Mackey. He was educated at South Carolina College, where he received a B.A. in 1832. He decided to enter medicine and began by apprenticing to a local doctor, Churchill Jones. After attending lectures at the Medical College of Charleston, he obtained his medical diploma at Jefferson Medical College in Philadelphia in 1835. Sims launched his practice in Mount Meigs, Alabama, and in 1836 married Eliza Theresa Jones. In 1849 the couple settled with their extended family in Montgomery, Alabama. They had at least five children.

In Alabama, Sims established his reputation as a skillful surgeon. Acting primarily as a plantation physician, he became known for operations on club feet, cleft palates, and crossed eyes and soon had one of the largest surgical practices in Alabama. He might have made general surgery his career, but following an unfortunate, well-publicized incident in which he misdiagnosed a lockjaw case he redirected his medical energies.

In 1845 Sims turned his attention to the female reproductive tract and, behind his office at home, built a small hospital for women. There he began to experiment with vesico-vaginal fistula repair—the operation that made his name and that was the cornerstone in establishing gynecology's status in the United States as a separate discipline. This heretofore unsuccessful procedure was designed to close lesions in the wall between the bladder and the vagina—lesions often inflicted during childbirth. Toward that end, he developed the vaginal speculum, an instrument associated with Sims. This device, which separated the vaginal walls, facilitated internal visualization and provided surgical access to the fistula. By 1849 Sims was making progress with his fistula repairs and continuing to improve his equipment and techniques. One of his chief innovations was the application of silver sutures instead of silk. Silver did not cause infections as silk did, and thus wounds healed better.

In order to develop this operation, however, Sims had used captive patients. All of his early experimental surgeries were performed on slave women placed in his custody because of their inability to work. Over the course of four years, Sims executed approximately forty operations for fistula repair, mainly on three slaves, Anarcha, Betsey, and Lucy.

Although Sims found Alabama conducive to his surgery, the climate was destroying his health. To recover from bouts of malaria and dysentery, he visited numerous resorts and finally, in 1853, moved his family to New York City. This was an ambitious transition, and Sims struggled to establish a practice in a city where he was little known. Gynecology was not recognized as a valid specialty, and Sims lacked social and professional connections. Nevertheless, he set out to found a special hospital for women, an enterprise that brought him into conflict with the majority of the medical establishment. Sims persisted and garnered support from the city's philanthropic women. He managed, in 1855, to open a small institution where he performed gynecological procedures on charity cases. These operations drew attention, enabling him to secure a charter for the Woman's Hospital of the State of New York in 1857.

Having gained a foothold in New York, Sims began to travel abroad. In 1861 he visited Dublin, Belfast, Edinburgh, London, and Paris. In Edinburgh he was impressed by the skill of the eminent surgeon James Syme; in London he performed surgery at one of Britain's first hospitals for women, the Samaritan, an institution headed by the renowned gynecologist Thomas Spencer Wells. In Paris, Sims was a remarkable success, surprising his audience by completing a complex vesico-vaginal fistula repair. This brought him to the attention of European surgeons and aristocrats, and he began receiving invitations to demonstrate his surgical prowess throughout much of northern Europe.

On returning to New York in December 1861, Sims found that the Civil War prevented many of his wealthier southern patients from making the journey north. His deep Confederate sympathies, combined with financial decline, prompted Sims and his family to retreat to Paris. There his reputation guaranteed abundant work and income. His patients included the duchess of Hamilton and Napoleon III's empress. During this period, he wrote his classic *Clinical Notes on Uterine Surgery* (1866), a textbook that placed Sims on the forefront of gynecological thought and practice.

Now internationally famous, Sims spent the rest of his life in the gynecological limelight of the United States and Europe, dividing his time among New York, Paris, and London. He was chief surgeon in 1870 in the Anglo-American Ambulance Corps, which served the French army in the Franco-Prussian War. He returned to the New York Woman's Hospital in 1872 but fought with its administrators and resigned from the board of surgeons two years later. He nevertheless was elected president of the American Medical Association in 1876. Such an appointment attested to Sims's personal success and, as well, to the widespread acceptance of the new specialty of gynecology. In recognition of his prime role in establishing his discipline's existence, the American Gynecological Society elected him president in 1880.

While Sims was in poor health and could have retired, he continued to travel extensively. Despite a severe bout of pneumonia in the winter of 1881, he traveled to Europe in early 1882 and stayed, mostly in Paris, until August 1883. Returning to New York, he continued to see patients until his death there.

Sims's life was controversial. On the one hand, he pioneered in gynecological surgery and founded America's first women's hospital. On the other, he experimented on slaves and developed his techniques on the poor. He maintained that the slaves were willing collaborators in this work; unfortunately the women—who submitted to repeated operations without anesthesia or antiseptics—left no account. Sims, who was a confirmed, slave-owning southerner, never openly acknowledged that his experimental surgery was ethically questionable. Moreover, as a medical entrepreneur, he was confident that self-interest coincided with the greater good being served by advancing gynecological surgery in the United States and abroad.

• Among Sims's more noteworthy works is *Silver Sutures in Surgery* (1858). Sims's autobiography, edited by his son H. Marion Sims, is *The Story of My Life* (1884); it was republished in 1968 with a new preface by C. Lee Buxton. Sims's life and career are discussed in Deborah Kuhn McGregor, *Sexual Surgery and the Origins of Gynecology: J. Marion Sims, His Hospital, and His Patients* (1990); James Pratt Marr, *Pioneer Surgeons of the Woman's Hospital: The Lives of Sims, Emmet, Peaslee, and Thomas* (1957); and Seale Harris, *Woman's Surgeon: The Life Story of J. Marion Sims* (1950). An obituary is in the *New York Times*, 14 Nov. 1883.

JANE ELIOT SEWELL

SIMS, William Sowden (15 Oct. 1858–28 Sept. 1936), naval officer, was born in Port Hope, Ontario, Canada, the son of Alfred William Sims, an American railroad engineer, and Adelaide Sowden. The family moved to Orbisonia, Pennsylvania, in 1872, and in 1876 young Sims was appointed to the U.S. Naval Academy. Poorly prepared and an indifferent student, Sims graduated in the middle of the class of 1880, receiving his commission after the standard two-year cruise. He spent the following decade in typical peacetime service, seeing conflict only in 1885 while helping to suppress the Panamanian revolution. After nine years at sea and one in Paris learning French, Sims taught navigation to naval cadets and wrote a widely used text on the subject. During his next tour as intelligence officer, Sims wrote such voluminous reports on the Sino-Japanese War that he developed a disabling writer's cramp. As naval attaché to Paris, Madrid, and St. Petersburg (1896–1898), Sims again sent volumes of information to the eager assistant navy secretary, Theodore Roosevelt (1858–1919), who fast became an ally, promoter, and protector. During the

Spanish-American War (1898), Sims developed an intelligence ring to report on Spanish preparation and fleet movements.

After the war and back at sea, Sims made a study of the flaws in naval construction and gunnery, remarking of the nation's newest ship, "The *Kentucky* is not a battleship at all. She is the worst crime on naval construction ever perpetrated by the white race" (Morison, p. 80). He risked court-martial by circumventing his immediate superiors and writing directly to President Roosevelt to complain of the poor gun sighting and of "the extreme danger of the present very inefficient condition of the navy, considered as a fighting force" (Morison, p. 103). Roosevelt responded by appointing Lieutenant Commander Sims inspector of target practice (1902–1909), a position in which he achieved unprecedented success and in which he also served as the president's naval aide (1907–1909). In 1905 Sims, later described by his son-in-law biographer as "Tall, erect, [and] beautifully proportioned" (Morison, p. 53), married Anne Hitchcock, the daughter of Roosevelt's secretary of the interior. The couple raised five children.

In 1906 Sims encouraged his classmate and ally, Lieutenant Commander Homer Poundstone, to submit a proposal for an all-big-gun battleship to replace those armed with mixed-caliber weapon systems. Sims advocated for this "dreadnought," which even the esteemed Admiral A. T. Mahan thought represented too great a concentration of power and potential loss. Sims won, and the navy started building these behemoths. In the following several years Sims repeatedly rankled navy leadership, provoking an investigation of its flawed battleship construction and assaulting the navy's bureaucratic system three times, each time unsuccessfully. Although his bureaucratic reform efforts failed, gun sighting and firing did improve remarkably under his tutelage. Outgoing president Roosevelt rewarded Sims with command of the battleship *Minnesota*, though still only a commander.

In England with the *Minnesota* in 1910, Sims spoke at London's Guildhall, apparently promising "every man, every drop of blood, every ship, and every dollar" should Britain ever need the United States's support against a foreign threat. President William Howard Taft reprimanded Sims and disavowed the speech. Again chastised but not checked, newly promoted Captain Sims moved to the Naval War College, first as a student and then an instructor (1911–1913). He was then given command of the Atlantic Destroyer Flotilla, which he deemed a "war college afloat" for its educational potential and for which he designed highly effective new tactical maneuver doctrines. His innovations were once again rewarded, this time with command of the newest battleship, the *Nevada*, in 1915.

Early in 1917 Rear Admiral Sims was appointed to the presidency of the Naval War College. Barely setting foot in Newport, Sims was dispatched in early April 1917 on a secret mission to establish liaison with the British Royal Navy. Soon after, Congress declared war, and temporary Admiral (four stars) Sims took command of all U.S. naval forces operating in European waters (serving from June 1917 to March 1919) and started calling immediately for less battleship construction, more destroyers, and the establishment of a convoy system. Sims was one of the first to understand that his beloved American battleships would have no more effect on the war's outcome than had those of the Royal Navy; instead, he called for small ships that could maintain the logistical supply line against the fearsome U-boat menace. By late 1917 the total Allied shipping losses had hit a staggering 350,000 tons a month. The convoy system and the various other antisubmarine warfare efforts that evolved early in 1918 brought monthly losses down to 250,000 tons in June 1918, and by October they stood at a more tolerable 112,427 tons.

With the close of the war, Sims's fertile mind turned to its lessons. In 1919 Navy Secretary Josephus Daniels published his tentative list of all wartime medal winners, and Sims pounced on the occasion to remonstrate publicly against all that he saw as arbitrary and wrongheaded in the Daniels secretaryship. The medals were only the excuse for Sims's attack on Daniels's allegedly haphazard and politicized administration of the navy's war efforts. Once again his allegations led to a congressional investigation but failed to change the naval bureaucracy. The chief of naval operations remained weakly subordinate to his political superior—a blow to many naval professionals who had hoped that the service would be run by its ranking officer instead of by a politician. Despite the acrimony, Sims emerged unharmed and returned to the presidency of the War College. There he educated young officers, argued for reform, and wrote *Victory at Sea* (1920) with Burton Hendrick, winning the Pulitzer Prize for history in 1921. Retiring in 1922, Sims actively pursued his interests in naval reform and history in Boston, where he died.

• The complete Sims collection is in the Library of Congress. Elting E. Morison (who had married Sims's third daughter) wrote *Admiral Sims and the Modern American Navy* (1942), which provides an exhaustive account of the life and times of Sims as well as a complete primary-source bibliography. See also Josephus Daniels, *The Wilson Era: Years of War and After, 1917–1923* (1946). Also useful are Kenneth J. Hagan, *This People's Navy: The Making of American Sea Power* (1991); David F. Trask, *Captains and Cabinets: Anglo-American Naval Relations, 1917–1918* (1972); and Robert O'Connell, *Sacred Vessels: The Cult of the Battleship and the Rise of the U.S. Navy* (1991).

MARK RUSSELL SHULMAN

SIMS, Zoot (29 Oct. 1925–23 Mar. 1985), jazz tenor saxophonist, was born John Haley Sims in Inglewood, California, the son of Pete Sims and Kate Haley. His parents, whose full first names are unknown, were a veteran vaudeville team. Sims began his musical career at age ten after being recruited along with his two older brothers for a grade school band in Hawthorne, California. A self-taught musician who learned from recordings, he played clarinet for three years before his mother bought him his first Conn tenor saxophone.

Sims entered high school in 1939, but impatient to begin his professional career, he lasted only one year before leaving to join Ken Baker's band in Los Angeles in 1940. (It was during his tenure with Baker that he acquired the nickname "Zoot.") With this fledgling start (the first job with Baker stranded the entire band in Phoenix, Ariz.), Sims embarked on a performing career during the 1940s in bands led by Bobby Sherwood, Sonny Dunham, Bob Astor, Sid Catlett, Benny Goodman, and, after two years of service during World War II, Benny Goodman again and then Woody Herman.

As an original member of Herman's "Four Brothers" saxophone section from 1947 until 1949, Sims, along with Serge Chaloff, Stan Getz, and Herbie Steward, pioneered the use of harmonized bebop lines and a tenor lead—a concept no doubt inspired by the influential saxophonist Lester Young.

After leaving Herman, Sims found himself unemployed in New York for long stretches before he joined Stan Kenton's orchestra in 1953 for a six-month tour. A return to California following the tour produced little opportunity for work, and Sims turned to painting houses for about a year and a half before joining Gerry Mulligan's sextet in New York in 1956. The following year he and fellow tenor saxophonist Al Cohn, whom he first met in Woody Herman's band in 1948, formed a band together—a performing partnership that lasted for nearly thirty years. Few instrumentalists (especially two tenor saxophonists) have found so satisfying a musical relationship. Their regular appearances at the Half Note, south of Greenwich Village, beginning in 1959 provided a perfect setting for club jazz in an informal atmosphere—an environment that Sims preferred to any other venue. "I really didn't get into the studio scene . . . my life is really in nightclubs. That's my life and it has been pretty good," he told a *Down Beat* interviewer (2 Dec. 1976).

Another of Sims's successful associations was his intermittent membership in various Benny Goodman orchestras and small groups. Following his initial tour with Goodman in 1943, during which he performed on the soundtrack of the Hollywood film *Sweet and Lowdown*, Sims became a periodic member of Goodman's bands for the next thirty years, completing a number of national tours as well as three tours of Europe with Goodman in 1950, 1958, and 1972, and a tour of Australia in 1973. A veteran sideman, Sims also toured with the Birdland All Stars (spring 1957), with Jazz at Carnegie Hall (fall 1958), after which he remained in Europe for several months, and with Norman Granz's Jazz at the Philharmonic tour of the United States and Europe in 1967.

The 1960s were perhaps the most difficult years for Sims—as they were for virtually all mainstream jazz musicians. The dramatic rise of saxophonists Sonny Rollins, and later John Coltrane and Ornette Coleman during the late 1950s, only heightened Sims's tendency toward critical self-scrutiny. For a time he began to perceive his conservative leanings as a disadvantage and to doubt his effectiveness as a jazz musician. It took a period of adjustment before he found his stride as a confident, straight-ahead player. Nothing is known of his first marriage, but his second (highly successful) marriage to journalist Louise Ault in 1970 provided the stability he needed for the final chapter of his professional life, but bouts with chronic alcoholism during the 1970s and the discovery of cancer in the summer of 1984 signaled the end of what had been a tenacious if not celebrated career. During a period when he was undergoing radiation treatments, his health judged too fragile to allow an operation, he died in New York City.

Unaffected by the multitude of new jazz styles and developments he encountered during his forty-year career, Sims stubbornly pursued the path of a mainstream jazz performer through the 1950s, 1960s, and 1970s. Thus, his tenacity and ability as an accomplished improviser was often overlooked as critics tended to group him together with other white, post–World War II tenor saxophonists. Even his initial stylistic indebtedness to Lester Young was misunderstood, for in reality, Sims was first inspired by Ben Webster, Coleman Hawkins, Chu Berry, and Sam Donahue before focusing on Young in 1943. Contemporaries generally regarded him more as a skilled player than a significant innovator among jazz saxophonists, but he was nevertheless a savvy assimilator of styles, always managing to absorb important information from others while not surrendering his own individuality under their influence.

Sims is well represented on recordings, both under his own name (perhaps as many as fifty albums), and as a sideman or partner with Woody Herman, Gerry Mulligan, Al Cohn, Pepper Adams, Bucky Pizzarelli, Joe Venuti, Quincy Jones, Oscar Peterson, Count Basie, Jimmy Rowles, and many others.

• Printed articles about Sims began to appear in popular jazz journals soon after his initial success with the Woody Herman band. An introductory sketch on his early days in New York is Barbara Hodgkins, "Zoot," *Metronome*, Dec. 1950, pp. 16, 20. Ira Gitler gives his impressions on first meeting Sims and his impact on the jazz of the 1950s in "The Colorful World of Zoot Sims," *Down Beat*, 13 Apr. 1961, pp. 20–23. Sims's initial encounters with Benny Goodman and Woody Herman are related in Burt Korall, "Settled Life Suits Zoot," *Melody Maker*, 16 Feb. 1974, p. 56. Two interviews that provide information on Sims's activities in the 1970s and 1980s are Michael Bourne, "Zoot Sims: Elemental Elegance," *Down Beat*, 2 Dec. 1976, pp. 13, 34–35; and Bob Rusch, "Zoot Sims," *Cadence*, Nov. 1984, pp. 5–10. A good summary of Sims's career as well as an insight into his domestic life can be found in Whitney Balliett, "Zoot and Louise," *New Yorker*, 12 May 1986, pp. 112–16 (repr. in *American Musicians: Fifty-six Portraits in Jazz* [1986], pp. 273–82). The most complete discography of his recorded work has been done by Arne Astrup, *The John Haley Sims Discography* (1983).

CHARLES BLANCQ

SINCLAIR, Harry Ford (6 July 1876–10 Nov. 1956), oil producer, was born in Wheeling, West Virginia, the son of John Sinclair, a pharmacist, and Phoebe Simmons. In 1882 the family moved to Independence, Kansas, where Sinclair attended public schools. In 1897–1898 he studied pharmacy at the University of Kansas, and after receiving a certificate in 1898, he went home to take over his father's drugstore. By 1901 Sinclair had lost the business. Shortly thereafter he began a new career in the oil industry of Kansas and Oklahoma, selling lumber for oil derricks and buying and selling oil leases. His entrepreneurial flair attracted the support of financiers such as Chicago meat packer J. M. Cudahy, for whom he obtained drilling rights on the farms and ranches of Southeast Kansas. In 1903 Sinclair married Elizabeth Farrell; they had two children.

In 1904 a drilling syndicate Sinclair had organized in Kiowa, Oklahoma, netted him $100,000, enabling him to become an independent producer. He brought in his first well on 25 July 1905 in the Indian Territory. By 1912 he was involved in sixty-two venture companies, owned eight drilling rigs, and with his brother controlled a Tulsa bank. In addition, he formed a partnership with Patrick J. White, a former oil field supply man. When White & Sinclair sold its producing properties in January 1916, Sinclair moved toward realizing his vision of an "integrated" company that would produce, refine, transport, and market oil and its products. He bought the refinery and properties of John T. Milliken & Associates and of his former employer, the Cudahy Refinery Company of Chanute, Kansas. To these he added his own producing properties and leases and purchased more undeveloped property. The result was the Sinclair Oil and Refining Corporation, founded on 1 May 1916.

The new company promptly invested in the construction of two new refineries in the Midwest and an eight-inch pipeline from Drumright, Oklahoma, to East Chicago. After the completion of the refineries, Sinclair's research chief, E. W. Isom, developed a thermal cracking method to produce more gasoline from crude oil than the industry average. The company prospered and gradually created an extensive sales and retail distribution network in the northern part of the United States east of the Rockies. In 1919 this company merged with the Sinclair Gulf Corporation, which Sinclair had founded in 1917 to take over oil fields in Mexico and the Southwest, forming the Sinclair Consolidated Oil Corporation.

During World War I, Sinclair contributed to the war effort as a member of the Committee on Raw Materials, Minerals and Metals of the Council of National Defense. But he became much better known for his involvement in the Teapot Dome oil scandals of the 1920s. In 1922 he formed a separate company, the Mammoth Oil Company, to lease the naval oil reserve at Teapot Dome, Wyoming. In 1923 Congress found evidence that the lease, as made by Secretary of the Interior Albert B. Fall, had been obtained corruptly. In 1924 the government began a civil suit against Sinclair to cancel the lease and was finally successful when the U.S. Supreme Court invalidated the lease in 1927. In 1928 Sinclair was acquitted of a charge of conspiracy to defraud the U.S. government, but he served six and a half months in jail in 1929 for contempt of court for having jurors "shadowed," and for contempt of the U.S. Senate for refusing to answer some of the questions asked by an investigating committee.

After his release from jail, Sinclair returned to his job as chairman of the board of the Sinclair Consolidated Oil Corporation. At the beginning of the Great Depression, he sold half of his pipeline system, together with its 50 percent interest in the Sinclair Crude Oil Purchasing Company, to Standard Oil Company (Ind.) for $72.5 million. He also raised another $35 million through the sale of a new common-stock issue. With these funds he retired pressing bank notes and began the acquisition of companies in financial trouble. His first purchase was the Pierce Petroleum Corporation, an important retailer in the southern states. In 1932 he acquired the assets of the Prairie Oil & Gas Company and the Prairie Pipe Line Company, and a few months later he acquired the Rio Grande Oil Company, which produced crude oil and marketed in California. In addition, in 1936 he helped salvage the bankrupt Richfield Oil Company of California. Under Sinclair's ownership, Richfield became one of the leading integrated petroleum companies on the West Coast.

During the second half of the 1930s, Sinclair embarked on a five-part business strategy that placed his principal company in a strong position during World War II. First, he sold its European marketing subsidiaries and hence was not directly affected by the German occupation of Europe. Second, he anticipated the wartime necessity for 100-octane gasoline with research into alkylation and polymerization processes, begun in 1937. Third, he increased oil exploration in Venezuela and discovered a major new field there. Fourth, he enhanced his tanker fleet with ten fast, new vessels, which were delivered in 1941 and 1942. Last, he built a new pipeline linking Marcus Hook with the Ohio River with spurs to Baltimore and Washington, D.C. This line enabled Sinclair to reach civilian markets when other transport was requisitioned by the military.

During World II Sinclair Consolidated Oil Corporation was among the leading oil companies in the number of war plants constructed. More specifically, the company's contributions to the war effort included a supply of 100-octane fuel for the U.S. Air Force, the manufacture of military oils and greases, a butadiene plant to provide raw materials for synthetic rubber, the production of fuel oil for the navy, and the delivery of regular grade gasoline for military and government use. Sinclair served as a member of the Petroleum Industry War Council from 1942 through 1945.

After World War II, in response to a huge increase in the civilian demand for oil, Sinclair undertook a $90 million renovation program. He also abandoned unprofitable markets, including those in five southern states, and greatly reduced his company's operations in sparsely settled areas. Instead, Sinclair expanded operations in the rapidly growing suburbs and along strategic highways. For a time the company built 600 new service stations per annum.

In 1949 Sinclair retired and moved to Pasadena, California. At the time of his retirement, the Sinclair Oil Corporation was valued at $700 million and had retail outlets in areas covering 85 percent of the population of the United States. Sinclair died in Pasadena.

In addition to his oil interests, Sinclair owned the famous Rancocas racing stable in New Jersey as a hobby until the early 1930s, and he owned a share of the St. Louis Browns baseball club. Sinclair was one of the most important independent oil men during the first half of the twentieth century. He survived the Teapot Dome scandal of the 1920s to regain his position as one of the most respected business leaders in the United States.

• P. C. Spencer, *Oil—and Independence!: The Story of the Sinclair Oil Corporation* (1957), is an account of Sinclair's career in the oil business. See also the autobiography of one of Sinclair's contemporaries, William L. Connelly, *The Oil Business As I Saw It; Half a Century with Sinclair* (1954). M. R. Werner and J. Starr, *The Teapot Dome Scandal* (1959), covers Sinclair's involvement in the naval oil reserve scandal. Sinclair Oil Corporation, *A Great Name in Oil: Sinclair through Fifty Years* (1966), is a business history of Sinclair's principal company. Obituaries are in the *New York Times*, 11 Nov. 1956; *Time*, 19 Nov. 1956; and *Newsweek*, 19 Nov. 1956.

RICHARD A. HAWKINS

SINCLAIR, Isabella McHutcheson (c. 1840–1890), author and illustrator, was born near Stirling, Scotland. William McHutcheson and Isabella Phelps are believed to be her parents, and her father was employed by the Inland Revenue Service. He is thought to have been the brother of Elizabeth McHutcheson Sinclair, the matriarch who bought the Hawaiian island of Niihau with her sons in 1864. The William McHutcheson family migrated in 1861 from Scotland to Canterbury, New Zealand, probably to live near the family of Elizabeth Sinclair (widowed in 1846), who had originally settled at Pigeon Bay in 1843. Private tutoring offered Isabella McHutcheson a gentlewoman's education and developed her early-recognized artistic abilities. She was well versed in the lore of the Maoris and understood their knowledge of flowering New Zealand plants.

At twenty-five Isabella accepted the proposal of marriage from her cousin Francis "Frank" Sinclair, who had moved to Hawaii in 1863 with his widowed mother Elizabeth Sinclair and other relatives, all of whom had settled on their newly purchased Hawaiian island of Niihau. The newlyweds joined the large Sinclair family home at Kiekie, Niihau, and later, Isabella and Frank built their own home at Makaweli, Kauai. Here they looked after the family property and business interests on that island, and Isabella freely explored the plant life of the Waimea and Olokele regions, comparing them to the New Zealand species she knew so well.

Collecting numerous specimens on both Kauai and Niihau, Sinclair set about to preserve them through painting a series of watercolors and then identifying each flowering specimen with its Hawaiian name, botanical name, natural habitat, and blossoming period. She compiled these materials into a large folio-size book, *Indigenous Flowers of the Hawaiian Islands* (1885), the first book featuring color plates of Hawaiian flowers and plants. She was assisted in plant identification by Dr. Joseph D. Hooker, director of the Royal Botanical Gardens at Kew, England, who sent her the correct scientific name for each of the flowering plants she had sent as specimens. (In 1884–1885 Sinclair and her husband journeyed to England, where she met with Hooker, who rechecked her plants' scientific names before the publication of the book.) She was also assisted by the native Hawaiian community, who appreciated her work and added to her botanical knowledge. Isabella acknowledged the community's interest and assistance in the book's dedication: "To the Hawaiian Chiefs and People who have been most appreciative friends, and most lenient critics, this work is affectionately inscribed."

Elderly Hawaiians had been most helpful to Sinclair. She wrote in her introduction: "It is from old people—and few of them—that any reliable information can be obtained, regarding plants which have their habitat far from the abodes of the people of the present generation." Young Hawaiians had lost the ability to recognize the flora Sinclair sought to preserve in her paintings and text. Older Hawaiians were able to give her different names for her plant specimens, depending on the region, but she was able to trace reliable information on each specimen through the "similarity of story and folklore associated with each; and many and graceful are these myths, handed down from generation to generation, seemingly from very ancient times."

Sinclair trained herself as an anthropologist and ethnographer as well as a botanist, as indicated by her description of the *ie ie* (a climbing vine): "Its Maori name is Kiekie—one of the many proofs of the close association of the Maori and Hawaiian races. . . . A species of the ieie is found in New Zealand. There the inflorescence is considered by the natives quite a delicacy." For Sinclair it was "very interesting to find varieties almost precisely similar under such different conditions of climate and in latitudes so far apart." Her plant descriptions were both scientific and artistic, as in her description of the *ohia-lehua* (a tree or shrub with a tufted blossoming red flower):

On the high table-land of Kauai, about 4,000 feet above the sea, a great deal of the lehua is merely a low shrub a few feet in height, but by no means less beautiful than in the lower country. Indeed the flowers seem to increase in brilliancy in proportion as they are found above sea level. . . . The blossoms are loaded with honey, which is the favorite food of the lovely *olokele*, a small bird with brilliant scarlet plumage. Few sights in the Hawaiian Islands realize one's dreams for the tropics so fully, as a lehua in full bloom, with olokeles flittering from flower to flower, the birds only distinguishable from the blossoms by their quick graceful movements. (p. 2)

The book's publication earned Sinclair fame both as an artist and ecology-minded preservationist. Her introduction to the book discussed her concerns for the endangered species she had painted and revealed the local Hawaiian names for the plants, their habitats, and the plants' eroding or destructive agents. She worried that many of the plants were becoming extinct because of the changes made by civilization to their natural habitats. Sinclair was a careful researcher and had consulted the proper scientific sources for her information about the plant habitats and features. Her book was well received and was reviewed in the *Journal of Botany* by editor James Britten, who praised the book for its scientific plant descriptions of Hawaii's flowering plants, which at the time were imperfectly known and of wide interest to naturalists worldwide.

Sinclair's private life appears to have been very happy, although she and her husband had no children. Her nieces remembered Aunt Isabella as someone "always full of fun" who "taught us new games" that included Scottish flings. Her husband was a businessman as well as a scholar, writing numerous books on ballads and poems of the Pacific, memories of living and traveling in the Pacific region, and fiction dealing with Oceana and Hawaii. After Isabella's death in California, where she was working on another book, Frank Sinclair married her widowed sister Wilhelmina McHutcheson and, after selling his interests in Hawaii to his nephews, moved to England.

On the island of Kauai at Kokee Museum, the delicate pictures Isabella Sinclair had painted of Hawaii's most beautiful flowering plants can still be seen as treasured pieces of nineteenth-century Hawaiiana.

• The archives of the Alexander Turnbull Library, Wellington, New Zealand, include material on the Sinclair family. The watercolor plates that Isabella Sinclair made for her *Indigenous Flowers of the Hawaiian Islands* are on display in the Kokee Museum, Kauai, Hawaii. Copies of her book are at the Kokee Museum and in the Hawaii-Pacific Collection of Hamilton Library, University of Hawaii in Honolulu. Additional papers and information can be found in the Kauai Museum, Hawaii. James Britten's review of Sinclair's book is in the *Journal of Botany* 24 (1886): 27. See also Harold St. John's detailed review of her book in *Pacific Science* 8 (Apr. 1954): 140–46. G. H. Scholefield, ed., *A Dictionary of New Zealand Biography* (1940) provides family background.

BARBARA BENNETT PETERSON

SINCLAIR, Upton (20 Sept. 1878–25 Nov. 1968), novelist, reformer, and politician, was born Upton Beall Sinclair, Jr., in Baltimore, Maryland, the son of Upton Beall Sinclair, Sr., a wholesale liquor salesman, and Priscilla Harden. Sinclair's father was irresponsible and alcoholic and left the boy's care to his mother, who encouraged him to read. In 1886 or 1887 the family moved to New York City, where in 1889 Sinclair attended public school classes for the first time. During the next two years he completed eight elementary grades and in 1892 enrolled in the City College of New York. In 1894 he began to sell jokes and puzzles to children's periodicals and a year later was selling stories to juvenile magazines to support himself. He graduated from City College with a B.A. in 1897, abandoned an ambition to become a lawyer, and enrolled in graduate school at Columbia University, all the while writing almost a hundred "half-dime" novels for Street and Smith, America's leading pulp-fiction publisher. Attracted to courses in music, contemporary politics, and poetry, especially that of Percy Bysshe Shelley, Sinclair decided to become an influential man of letters. In May 1900 he left Columbia without a graduate degree, rented a cabin for three months in southern Quebec, and wrote an idealistic novel, *Springtime and Harvest*. In October of that year he married Meta H. Fuller in New York.

Unable to find a publisher for his novel, Sinclair borrowed money from an uncle and issued it himself in 1901, but he barely recouped his expenses. Republished commercially as *King Midas* (1901), the novel still failed. Its message, that beauty and poetry in a marriage are more important than mere sex, deluded and later embarrassed Sinclair, the birth of whose one child in 1901 also displeased him. In 1902 he joined the Socialist party. A year later he moved with his family to the countryside just outside Princeton, New Jersey. His next published novel, *The Journal of Arthur Stirling* (1903), a "spiritual autobiography," was billed by him as the diary of a real-life poet who committed suicide in New York, but the hoax was soon exposed. In 1903 Sinclair also published *Prince Hagen*, a novel about a Nibelung who with access to secret gold opposes his greed to Wall Street's. Its message is that humanity's ills cross political and religious lines and can be eradicated only by an idealistic worship of beauty. The failure of these novels reinforced Sinclair's belief in secular socialism, which he found more acceptable than Christian capitalism as a solution to human woes. Millionaire-socialist George D. Herron subsidized Sinclair while he wrote *Manassas: A Novel of the War* (1904), a well-researched novel combining history and politics. Its hero, Allan Montague, meets John Brown, Jefferson Davis, Frederick Douglass, Abraham Lincoln, and other Civil War–era figures and is indoctrinated into the neo-abolitionist socialism by a German refugee soldier. Although better than Sinclair's earlier novels, *Manassas* sold just as poorly.

In 1904 Sinclair published several articles in *Appeal to Reason*, a populist-socialist weekly, whose editor challenged him to follow his account of nineteenth-century "chattel slaves" in *Manassas* with a novel about twentieth-century "wage slaves." With that purpose in mind, Sinclair went to Chicago to observe the business practices of the beef trust. There greedy capitalist owners of slaughterhouses and meat factories paid farmers and ranchers low prices for livestock and held down workers' wages; they condoned crooked foremen, permitted unspeakably unsanitary conditions, loaned their own refrigerated cars to the railroads, and demanded special freight rates, all the while corrupting city politicians. Appalled, Sinclair returned to New Jersey and started a novel based on what he saw, *The Jungle*, which the *Appeal* serialized beginning in February 1905. That summer he and his friend Jack London and several other socialists in New York City founded the Intercollegiate Socialist Society (later called the League for Industrial Democracy), which attracted important liberal Americans. Sinclair resumed writing *The Jungle* and, after finding a publisher (Doubleday, Page) for the book, completed the last third of the manuscript.

The Jungle narrates the miseries of Jurgis Rudkus, a Lithuanian immigrant who works in the stockyards. After marrying and having a son, he is injured and loses his job. Taking to drink, he attacks a man who has led Rudkus's wife into prostitution to support the family; the assault results in his being jailed. When Rudkus's wife dies and their son drowns, he returns to work and is injured again, turns to crime, scabs during a strike, chances to attend a socialist meeting, and finds secular salvation in working toward a socialistic utopia. Sinclair's plot, apart from brilliantly dramatizing poor people's communal life, including an occasional picnic and vivid marriage ceremonies, is less significant than his horrifying depiction of working conditions in the meat-packing industry. Slaughtering techniques were dangerous; cattle were processed even when diseased; dangerous chemicals were carelessly used; floors ran with blood and human and rat waste; and human mutilations, blood poisoning, and other injuries and illnesses were common. Published in February 1906, *The Jungle* was internationally influential; a British edition and seventeen translations soon followed. President Theodore Roosevelt invited Sinclair to lunch in the White House and in June signed the Pure Food and Drug Act and the Meat Inspection Act—for which Sinclair's book was primarily responsible. Despite the passage of the act, *The Jungle* induced thousands of Americans to become vegetarians for decades thereafter. (Adding to its impact, the novel was made into a movie eight years after its publication.) The rest of Sinclair's long life, though fascinating and varied, was in a sense anticlimactic.

In October 1906 Sinclair used most of his $30,000 in *Jungle* royalties to build Helicon Colony, a communal living venture, in Englewood, New Jersey, but a fire destroyed the establishment four months later. His immense popularity enabled Sinclair to pour out books, though rarely with much financial gain. *A Captain of Industry*, a novel finished in 1903 but published in 1906, features a money-corrupted industrialist swept off his yacht, drowned, and mangled by an inimical nature. *The Industrialist Republic* (1907) foolishly projects America's happy turn to socialism under President William Randolph Hearst beginning in 1913. Another novel published in 1907 but written some years before, *The Overman*, was inspired by Sinclair's reading of Friedrich Nietzsche's *Thus Spake Zarathustra* in German. It features a self-contained genius who lives on a desert island and composes in his head tragically ecstatic music. Two more novels were published in 1908: *Metropolis* castigates New York's high society; *The Moneychangers* portrays the fiscal chicanery of a "hero" patterned on J. P. Morgan.

From 1908 to 1914 Sinclair restlessly moved about, enjoyed California, flirted with single-tax theorists in Alabama and Delaware, checked into clinics in Michigan more than once for depression, visited Europe and met fellow socialists (including George Bernard Shaw), sought publicity at every turn, and wrote essays on capitalism, dieting, marriage, education, tourism, and pacifism. His prolific output of books did not abate, even as the circumstances of his personal life changed. His novel of 1910, *Samuel the Seeker*, ridicules capitalists and churchmen and praises socialism. In 1912, after having embarrassingly fictionalized his childhood and marriage in *Love's Pilgrimage* (1911), he divorced his wife for promiscuity long tolerated. A year later he married Mary Craig Kimbrough (with whom he did not have children). Soon after the marriage, he published the novel *Damaged Goods* (1913), which depicts the dangers of venereal disease. Two other novels, *Sylvia* (1913) and *Sylvia's Marriage* (1914), are based on events in his new wife's earlier life.

Sinclair's social conscience continued to find new causes to pursue. In 1914, to support the coal miners' bloody strike in Ludlow, Colorado, Sinclair had himself arrested for picketing outside the New York offices of John D. Rockefeller, Jr., who controlled the mines and who later praised Sinclair for his courage and beneficial influence. (Rockefeller went to Ludlow, visited miners, danced with their wives, recognized the union, and helped improve working conditions.) Three years later, now living in California, Sinclair published *King Coal*, a muckraking, pro-union novel based on the "coal war," but it also sold poorly, for by this time the war in Europe was a more absorbing concern. In that same year, 1917, the former advocate of pacifism resigned from the Socialist party to protest its nonintervention policy. But Sinclair did not renounce his liberal impulses, as illustrated by his cogent, anticonservative letters to President Woodrow Wilson concerning American shipping, censorship, the treatment of conscientious objectors, and Russia's future. During the war Sinclair corresponded with and personally helped many oppressed fellow liberals, including Eugene V. Debs, Max Eastman, Michael Gold, and John Reed, whether he agreed precisely with their opinions or not. To argue his position he produced his own quickly insolvent magazine, *Upton Sinclair's* (1918–1919).

Between 1918 and 1928 Sinclair published seventeen books. Six were iconoclastic, nonfiction works focusing on the continued ills of America and constituted what he called his "Dead Hand" series, the hand being capitalism, a strangling influence on one American liberty after another. *The Profits of Religion: An Essay in Economic Interpretation* (1918) castigates churches as moneymaking, politicized predators; its partial validity is lost by excessive stress on Catholic "plotting" and Jewish "Shylocks." *The Brass Check* (1919) deplores procapitalistic editorial censorship in the press. *The Goose-Step* (1923) describes the commercializing of American higher education, and *The Goslings* (1924) examines the same process affecting grade school and high school education. *Mammonart* (1925) theorizes that through the ages most artists have served their respective economic establishments. *Money Writes! A Study of American Literature* (1927) criticizes recent writers for not being politically radical. Sinclair published these books, often disfigured by socialistic propagandizing and highly personal rantings, at his own expense; some were also picked up by commercial firms. All six were influential, and *The Brass Check* became a bestseller. Of his five novels during these years, only *Oil!* (1927) and *Boston* (2 vols., 1928) are of enduring value. *Oil!* deals in general with the California petroleum business and in particular with the 1924 Teapot Dome scandal during President Warren Harding's administration. The book sold better after it was banned in Boston for incidentally mentioning birth control. (Margaret Sanger, the controversial advocate of family planning, was one of Sinclair's close friends.) *Boston* was inspired by the 1927 executions of Nicola Sacco and Bartolomeo Vanzetti, the Italian immigrant anarchists convicted of a 1920 payroll robbery and murder in Braintree, Massachusetts, but whose guilt seemed to many not at all certain. The case outraged American liberals and resulted in many poems, plays, short stories, and novels, of which *Boston* is among the very best. To prepare for it, Sinclair interviewed Vanzetti—and judged him to be innocent. He placed the two Italian prisoners at the center of a sprawling work involving Bostonians of several social and financial levels and rebuked the entire conservative establishment.

In the 1930s Sinclair the writer faltered: his *Mental Radio* (1930) concerns mental telepathy, while in *The Wet Parade* (1931) he praises Prohibition. Sinclair the politician came to the fore. In 1933 he published *I, Governor of California, and How I Ended Poverty* to advance his 1934 gubernatorial bid as a Democratic candidate with EPIC—End Poverty in California—as his battle cry. He campaigned vigorously, in part by making effective radio broadcasts. But his opponent smeared him as a free-love communist, and he lost, although many of his left-wing suggestions, including state ownership of certain industries to ameliorate statewide unemployment, earned him almost 44 percent of the slightly more than 2 million votes cast and influenced President Franklin D. Roosevelt's federal policies. As usual, Sinclair quickly sought to justify his political position in both fiction and nonfiction. Three novels of this period are notable: *The Flivver King* (1937), attacking Henry Ford's antiunion policies; *No Pasaran!* (1937), featuring an American fighting with the Loyalists in the Spanish Civil War; and *Little Steel* (1938), rebuking the big steel companies' hatred of labor unions.

Now followed the Lanny Budd series of eleven novels, for which—along with *The Jungle*, *Oil!*, and *Boston*—Sinclair will be remembered the longest. The Budd titles are *World's End* (1940, a Literary Guild selection), *Between Two Worlds* (1941), *Dragon's Teeth* (1942, a 1943 Pulitzer Prize winner), *Wide Is the Gate* (1943), *Presidential Agent* (1944), *Dragon Harvest* (1945), *A World to Win* (1946, a bestseller), *Presidential Mission* (1947), *One Clear Call* (1948), *O, Shepherd, Speak!* (1949), and *The Return of Lanny Budd* (1953). This monumental series, totaling 7,014 pages, vivifies contemporary history, in exciting narrative form, from 1913 to the beginning of the Cold War in 1949 and beyond, through the eyes of one observer, who is also a participant. Sinclair did not plan a sequel when he introduced in *World's End* Lanny Budd, the illegitimate son of a rich American munitions maker and an internationally famous beauty. But over the years Budd evolved into an art dealer, Roosevelt's secret agent, and a smooth lover. Like Allan Montague of *Manassas*, Budd encounters many historical figures of his time, among them Isadora Duncan, Albert Einstein, Hermann Goering, Adolf Hitler, Mao Tse-tung (Mao Zedong), Marshal Pétain, George Bernard Shaw, Joseph Stalin, Lincoln Steffens, Woodrow Wilson, and Sir Basil Zaharoff. Sinclair researched his topics with great diligence. He even wrote a thousand or more letters to important persons with specific queries, received many detailed answers, and was also aided by unsolicited correspondents. The result may have been fodder for adverse critics, one of whom said that Budd combined the traits of d'Artagnan (the fourth Musketeer), Sherlock Holmes, the British dandy Beau Brummell, the actor Douglas Fairbanks, the philosopher Herbert Spencer, and Casanova. Millions of readers, however, enjoyably learned their history from the Lanny Budd series, which was also relished by such discerning readers as President Lyndon B. Johnson's wife, Lady Bird, and Hugh Sidey, Washington correspondent for *Time*, both of whom freely admitted as much. Sinclair's romantic hope, though not his realistic expectation, was that his Lanny Budd series, corny but coherent, as one reviewer put it, would encourage the masses to espouse socialism without the taint of communism. Always antifascist, Sinclair was also never a communist, although for decades he was friendly with and supported many communists and preferred many of their beliefs to those of capitalists—even after he grew aware of Stalin's atrocities. The final Lanny Budd volume, however, reflects a shift to anticommunism and to a measured pro-American position.

The last decade of Sinclair's life was marked by a slowing of his literary production, many accolades, and changes in his personal affairs. He updated *American Outpost*, his 1932 autobiography, with *My Lifetime in Letters* (1960) and *The Autobiography of Upton Sinclair* (1962), the latter a frank, rollicking work. In 1959 his wife Mary Craig Sinclair published her autobiography, *Southern Belle*, mostly about her childhood but also often lauding Sinclair. She died two years later, and the following year Sinclair married Mary "May" Elizabeth Willis, a great-grandmother, age seventy-nine. May predeceased him by three years. Optimistic and exuberant to swarms of admirers, Sinclair died in a nursing home near Bound Brook, New Jersey.

During his long, productive life Sinclair was a rebellious literary and political voice for progressive movements, a muckraker whose realistic fiction prompted legislative action, a candidate for important political office seeking radical change to improve the lot of capitalism's victims, and the author of a multivolume novel the effect of which was to teach history to millions of readers unwilling to tackle their history straight. His direct and easy style, often lapsing into the quick and shallow, appeals to such readers. Above all Sinclair sought to lessen the ever dangerous gap between the wealthy and those ground down by poverty in his native land, which he loved enough to want it to be more humane.

• Sinclair's voluminous papers are in at least eighty-five repositories. The bulk is in the Lilly Library at Indiana University. Other sizable collections are at Stanford University, the Bancroft Library of the University of California at Berkeley, the Houghton Library at Harvard University, and the Henry W. and Albert A. Berg Collection of English and American Literature at the New York Public Library. Ronald Gottesman, *Upton Sinclair: An Annotated Checklist* (1973), contains a chronological list of 2,259 published works by Sinclair. See also Gottesman and Charles L. P. Silet, *The Literary Manuscripts of Upton Sinclair* (1972), which locates Sinclair's letters in thirty-eight institutions. Reliable biographical and critical works are Floyd Dell, *Upton Sinclair: A Study in Social Protest* (1927; repr. 1970); Leon Harris, *Upton Sinclair: American Rebel* (1975); Jon A. Yoder, *Upton Sinclair* (1975); William A. Bloodworth, Jr., *Upton Sinclair* (1977); and R. N. Mookerjee, *Art for Social Justice: The Major Novels of Upton Sinclair* (1988). Alfred Kazin, *On Native Grounds: An Interpretation of American Prose Literature* (1942), and Walter B. Rideout, *The Radical Novel in the United States, 1900–1954: Some Interrelations of Literature and Society* (1956; repr. 1982), place Sinclair's protest fiction in context. Abraham Blinderman, ed., *Critics on Upton Sinclair: Readings in Literary Criticism* (1975), assembles numerous reviews and essays, with stress on *The Jungle*. An obituary is in the *New York Times*, 26 Nov. 1968.

ROBERT L. GALE

SINEY, John (31 July 1831–16 Apr. 1880), coal miner and labor reformer, was born in Bornos, County Queens, Ireland, the son of Patrick Siney and Catherine (maiden name unknown), tenant farmers. After their potato crop failed in 1835 the family was evicted from their homestead and moved to Wigan, Lancashire, England, when Siney was five years old. Two years later he took a job as bobbin boy in a cotton mill and for the next nine years worked at various mills in the area. At about age sixteen he was apprenticed as a brick maker; he later organized the Brickmakers' Association of Wigan, serving seven terms as president.

In his late twenties Siney married Mary Hennessey, but their life together was cut short when she died in 1862, just two years after the birth of their daughter.

Leaving the child with his widowed mother Siney journeyed to the United States in 1863, settling in St. Clair, Schuylkill County, Pennsylvania, a coal mining town in the anthracite region where other Wigan emigrants had found work. With the nation embroiled in the Civil War and the Union army in need of men and coal, Siney easily secured employment as a laborer and then a miner. In June 1864 he participated in a successful strike to raise wages.

After the war the market for anthracite collapsed, and operators slashed wages 25 to 35 percent. But when they tried to reduce wages again in 1868, Siney and his coworkers at the Eagle colliery called a strike. Renting a hall to serve as headquarters and raising funds to support the strikers' families, Siney made a name for himself as an organizer and speaker; he held the men together throughout the successful six-week struggle. Buoyed by this small victory—wages were not reduced—Siney joined with fifteen other miners to form the Workingmen's Benevolent Association of St. Clair (WBA), a labor organization that collected dues, paid sickness and death benefits, and provided weekly support in case of strikes. Later that summer he was elected president of the WBA.

Local labor leaders had been trying to organize anthracite miners since the 1840s, but they had been stymied by employer hostility, ethnic divisions among the miners, and regional economic competition that usually resulted in low prices for coal and low wages for miners. Siney recognized the weakness of an isolated union under these circumstances and set out to expand the local union at once. In July 1868 he chaired a meeting that led to the formation of the WBA of Schuylkill County (later the Miners' and Laborers' Benevolent Association), which represented 20,000 miners in twenty-two districts. As president and chairman of the executive board, a paid position that he held until 1874, Siney was able to work full time at the job. Because he was convinced that wages would rise only when miners worked together to control production, he called on anthracite miners throughout the state to suspend work on 10 May 1869. Although miners in the northern region refused to cooperate, after a three-week suspension Siney and a joint committee of Schuylkill County miners and operators negotiated a sliding-scale wage formula that stabilized the industry in that county until 1874.

Disappointed that miners had placed regional loyalties above class cooperation in this struggle, Siney turned his attention to labor politics, lobbying for improved mine-safety laws and urging wage earners to establish and support independent labor parties. In 1871 he helped organize a labor party in Schuylkill County, and the following year he chaired the founding convention of the national Labor Reform party in Columbus, Ohio. He also began publishing the *Workingman*, a four-page weekly labor paper, in 1873 but gave it up within a year to labor journalist C. Ben Johnson, who published it until it folded in 1876.

Around this time bituminous miners in the Midwest were anxious to form a national union, and in 1873

Siney and four other miners' leaders issued a call for a convention to meet in Youngstown, Ohio, in October. With Siney presiding as permanent chairman, forty-two delegates from five states launched the Miners' National Association (MNA), an industrial union open to men of all trades who worked in and around coal and metal mines throughout the United States. Adopting a constitution that endorsed shorter working hours, improved safety laws, and arbitration to resolve industrial disputes, the MNA also promised to pay weekly benefits to members engaged in properly authorized strikes.

Siney moved to Cleveland in 1874 to serve as MNA president (taking a cut in salary to do so), but he faced serious problems almost immediately. In the first place his own union, the Miners' and Laborers' Benevolent Association, refused to affiliate with the MNA, since the new union, which charged lower initiation fees, also offered fewer benefits. At the same time, a nationwide economic depression had slowed industry significantly, and mine operators all over the country were reducing wage rates. Determined to avoid strikes that he believed could not be won, Siney counseled MNA unions to accept reductions and organize secretly to build up their strength. But his members rejected this cautious advice, calling strikes and demanding strike-payments regardless of the organization's financial condition. By 1875, when the MNA treasury was almost bankrupt, Siney proposed that union members invest in a cooperative mining scheme, in order to escape the wage system entirely. The plan fell through, however, and the union disbanded.

Siney returned to Schuylkill County in 1876 where he tried to make a new life for himself. Purchasing a tavern and working as a truck farmer, he married Margaret Behan; two years later, in 1878, they welcomed the birth of a son. Siney also remained active in politics, supporting the antimonopoly Greenback party, which favored paper currency and the recognition of labor rights. He served as president (1875) and vice president (1878) of the national Independent or Greenback party and helped to organize a local Greenback-Labor party in Schuylkill County. He never regained his place with the miners, however, who blamed their economic decline on his conservative union leadership, and he died there a broken man, a victim of miners' consumption, better known today as black lung.

Like many early union-builders, Siney was revered only after his death for his pioneering efforts to promote labor-management conciliation and for his vision of a national, industrial union for mine workers. In 1887 the Miners' and Mine Laborers' Amalgamated Association, which had been founded in 1883, raised funds to erect a public monument in his honor in St. Clair; it was dedicated on 1 November 1888. His co-worker in the WBA, John Parker, spoke of Siney's frustrations that day. "I have seen him when he could have cried that he should be so misrepresented by those for whom he had but one thought—their ad-

vancement, and who had no gratitude or faith." Ultimately Siney's legacy was a symbolic one, for his memory inspired union leaders for years to come. As one United Mine Workers' spokesman put it in 1915, John Siney "laid the foundation for the larger things we have gained in our struggle to achieve the better things of life."

• Although Siney's correspondence was apparently destroyed, early issues of the WBA's official paper, the *Anthracite Monitor*, are available at the Pennsylvania State University Labor Collection, University Park. Details of Siney's life and career can be found in Edward Pinkowski, *John Siney, The Miners' Martyr* (1963), and in Charles Edward Killeen, "John Siney: The Pioneer in American Industrial Unionism and Industrial Government" (Ph.D. diss., Univ. of Wisconsin, 1942). Biographical information can also be found in "American Labor Portraits #3," *Workingman's Advocate*, 22 Nov. 1873, p. 1, and in Terence V. Powderly, "A Man and a Stone," *United Mine Workers' Journal*, 11 May 1916, pp. 6–7; 18 May 1916, pp. 8, 25; 25 May 1916, pp. 8, 25. Obituaries are in the *Shenandoah Herald*, 17 Apr. 1880, and the *National Labor Tribune*, 24 Apr. 1880.

GRACE PALLADINO

SINGER, Isaac Bashevis (21 Nov. 1904–24 July 1991), writer, was born Icek-Hersz Zinger in Leoncin, Poland, the son of Pinchas Mendl Zinger, a Hasidic rabbi, and Bathsheva Zylberman, a daughter of the rabbi of Bilgoray. His date of birth is sometimes given as 14 July; Singer himself said he had "two birthdays" and never admitted which one was correct. His family moved in 1907 to Radzymin and then in 1908 to Warsaw where his father became the rabbi of Krochmalna Street. Singer was educated in the local *cheders*, or religious primary schools, and then under his father's tutelage. In his father's rabbinical court, or *Beth Din*, he learned about talmudic law, ritual observances, and domestic problems, all governed by religion. Contrary to his parents' wishes that he concern himself only with religious study, he also began a secular education. A voracious reader, he read modern science, politics, economics, and fiction.

When the German army occupied Poland in 1915, many in the city, particularly in the Jewish ghetto, suffered from famine and epidemics. Partly to escape the extreme conditions and partly out of a concern for her father's health, Bathsheba Singer left Warsaw in 1917, taking Isaac and her younger son Moishe with her to Bilgoray. In the next four years Singer studied the Talmud in the Turisk study house founded by his grandfather. Even more than in the Warsaw ghetto, Singer came in contact with what he termed the "old Jewishness," the way of life in a Jewish shtetl. "Time seemed to flow backward. I lived Jewish history," he wrote in *In My Father's Court*. However, even in this small village, the modern world was intruding as Polish Jews displaced by the war moved to Bilgoray. Singer found friends among them and continued his secular education by reading in Yiddish many European authors, including Strindberg, Chekhov, and Spinoza. He also studied modern Hebrew, which, to his mother's dismay, he taught to young men and women in private homes, and he began writing poems and stories for publication in a local Yiddish newspaper.

In 1921, feeling stifled in Bilgoray, Singer returned to Warsaw and at his father's insistence studied for one year at the Tachkemoni Rabbinical Seminary. However, he was not interested in becoming a rabbi, and his studies did not distract him from his poverty and loneliness. He returned to Bilgoray and teaching Hebrew but, unable to support himself, he joined his family in nearby Dzikow where his father was now the rabbi. In 1923 his older brother, Israel Joshua, offered him a job as proofreader on the staff of *Literarishe Bletter*, a Yiddish literary magazine. Singer was glad to be back in Warsaw, although he was still poor and lonely. He spent much of his free time either at the Yiddish Writer's Club, where he met writer Aaron Zeitlin who encouraged the shy Singer in his literary ambitions, or at the library, where he continued his voracious reading in philosophy, psychology, science, and the occult. Soon, Singer began supplementing his income by translating German novels into Yiddish for the *Radio*, a Warsaw newspaper. Some were popular suspense novels that he had to convert to a Polish setting with Jewish characters, but he also translated more serious works like Thomas Mann's *The Magic Mountain* and Erich Maria Remarque's *All Quiet on the Western Front*.

Singer's goal, however, was to become a writer of fiction in Yiddish, and in 1927 he published his first short story, "Oyf der Elter" (In old age) in *Literarishe Bletter* under the pseudonym Tse. Later that year he published two more stories, this time under the name Isaac Bashevis, derived from his mother's name, to distinguish himself from his brother whose writing had already earned him an international reputation.

During this time Singer met and fell in love with a woman he called Runya. Although they were never married by a rabbi, Singer spoke of her as his wife. She bore him his only child in 1929, the same year that his father died. The couple lived together intermittently for several years. Most of their quarrels were on the subject of politics: Runya was a Communist but Singer decidedly was not. Her outspoken activities led to several arrests, and Singer himself spent one day in jail, an experience that confirmed his dislike of politics.

In 1932 Zeitlin founded the Yiddish literary journal *Globus*, with Singer as coeditor. Singer published several of his stories in the magazine and, in installments in 1933, his first novel, *Satan in Goray*. (The novel was published in book form in Warsaw in 1935.) Beginning in 1934 Singer also wrote for *Parizer Haint*, a Paris Yiddish newspaper, and he began selling stories to the *Jewish Daily Forward*, a Yiddish newspaper in New York, through his brother, who had emigrated to the United States. In 1935, assisted by his brother, Singer came to New York. (Runya and their son moved to the Soviet Union and later to Palestine; Singer did not see his son again until 1955.) He worked as a freelance journalist for the *Forward*, using the pen names I. Warshawsky and D. Segal. His second novel, *The Sinning Messiah*, which he had started writing in Poland, was serialized in the *Forward* in 1935–1936 in the United States, in the *Varshanahaint* in Warsaw, and in *Paiser Haint* in Paris. For the next several years Singer wrote only a few articles and sketches. His move to America and the distressing situation of the Jews in Eastern Europe had left him feeling isolated and cast adrift. Since he firmly believed that "literature is completely connected with one's origin, with one's roots" (Burgin, p. 61), his feeling of being lost made it impossible for him to write fiction.

In 1937 Singer met and fell in love with Anna Haimann Wasserman, a German immigrant. They married in 1940. Anna worked first in a factory and then as a salesclerk to help support them, and Singer finally felt as though he had a real home. He began publishing stories again in 1943, the year he became a U.S. citizen. The following year Singer's brother Israel died of a heart attack. He considered losing his brother "the greatest misfortune of my entire life. He was my father, my teacher. I never really recovered from this blow" (Kresh, p. 176). Yet the death seemed to act as a catalyst for Singer to develop his powers as a writer. For his subject matter, he returned to the world of his childhood. As he described it, "I said to myself, 'Warsaw has just been destroyed. No one will ever see the Warsaw I knew. Let me write about it'" (Burgin, p. 73). The result was his first family novel, *The Family Moskat*, serialized in the *Forward* during the next three years and published in both Yiddish and English in 1950. Singer followed this trend of serializing his novels first in the *Forward* for the rest of his career. (After the war Singer learned that his mother and younger brother had been taken by the Nazis to Kazakhstan by cattle car and had frozen to death; his sister, Hinde Esther, who had married and moved to England, died in 1954.)

Singer caught American readers' attention with *The Family Moskat*. When his short story "Gimpl tam" was translated by Saul Bellow as "Gimpel the Fool" and published in *Partisan Review* in 1953, Singer achieved a critical breakthrough, and his work began to be available to a wide audience. Although he continued to write for the *Forward* for the rest of his life (he moved from freelance to staff writer in the early 1940s), he began publishing his stories and essays in mainstream periodicals such as the *New Yorker*, *Harper's*, *Partisan Review*, *Commentary*, and *Esquire*. He always wrote in Yiddish; when asked why he wrote in a language that was dying, he said, "I felt that Yiddish and the Jewish people were important for me and that if I wanted to be a real writer I would have to write about them . . . and to stay with my language" (Burgin, p. 62). Most of his work was translated into English either by Singer himself or in collaboration with him. In 1957 his first collection of short stories, *Gimpel the Fool and Other Stories*, was published in English. With the publication in English of his second short story collection, *The Spinoza of Market Street* (1961), Singer came to be recognized as one of the great short story writers. In 1962 he was included in the Modern Language Association's bibliography of scholarly publications, an indication that academics were taking note of his work.

As his reputation grew, Singer was invited to lecture at colleges and universities. In spite of his shyness—of which in another context Singer had noted, "It has been my experience that shy persons are sometimes unusually bold" (Kresh, p. 77)—he found that he enjoyed lecturing and traveling. He accepted positions as writer-in-residence at several universities, including Oberlin (1966), the University of California (1967), and Bard College (1974–1975), teaching literature and creative writing. He received many honors for his writing, including election to the National Institute of Arts and Letters in 1964; three Newbery Awards for his collections of stories for children in 1966, 1967, and 1969; four volumes of stories named an American Library Association Notable (1967, 1969, 1972, 1976); two National Book Awards (1970, 1974); the American Academy and Institute of Arts and Letters Gold Medal (1989); and in 1978 the Nobel Prize for literature.

Singer continued to write and publish until his death in Surfside, Florida. In an interview with Richard Burgin, he said, "Literature is not enriched by a man who is all the time looking into himself, but by a writer who looks into other people" (p. 2). Singer looked deeply into others and recreated a world that humanity had allowed to be destroyed, a world populated by Jews firmly rooted in the shtetls of Poland and by Jewish immigrants in America haunted by the lives left behind in Poland. His was sometimes a supernatural world where his Jewish characters lived side by side with ghosts, dybbuks, witches, and demons. Singer stated in his Nobel speech that the writer "must be an entertainer of the spirit" because there is "no excuse for tedious literature that does not intrigue the reader, uplift his spirit, give him the joy and escape that true art always grants" (Kresh, p. 411). He did that, and in the doing he kept alive a world that otherwise could have slipped away.

• Singer published his autobiography in four volumes: *In My Father's Court* (1966), *A Little Boy in Search of God* (1976), *A Young Man in Search of Love* (1978), and *Lost in America* (1981). His best-known novels include *The Magician of Lublin* (1960), *The Slave* (1962), *Enemies, a Love Story* (1972), and *Shosha* (1978). Singer's collections of widely acclaimed stories include *Zlateh the Goat and Other Stories* (1966), *When Schlemiel Went to Warsaw and Other Stories* (1968), *A Crown of Feathers* (1973), and *Yentl the Yeshiva Boy* (1984). Grace Farrell collected a number of interviews with Singer in *Isaac Bashevis Singer: Conversations* (1992); see also Richard Burgin, *Conversations with Isaac Bashevis Singer* (1985). Paul Kresh, *Isaac Bashevis Singer: The Magician of West 86th Street* (1979), is an excellent biography. For critical discussions of his work see Grace Farrell Lee, *From Exile to Redemption: The Fiction of Isaac Bashevis Singer* (1987), and Irving Malin, ed., *Critical Views of Isaac Bashevis Singer* (1969). Joseph Epstein, "Our Debt to I. B. Singer," *Commentary*, Nov. 1991, offers a look back at Singer's career after his death. An obituary is in the *New York Times*, 25 July 1991.

ALTHEA E. RHODES

SINGER, Isaac Merritt (27 Oct. 1811–23 July 1875), inventor and manufacturer, was born in Pittstown or in nearby Schaghticoke, New York, the son of Adam Singer, a cooper, and Ruth Benson. Singer's father emigrated from Germany in the late 1760s and shortened the family name from Reisinger soon after his arrival in the United States. Isaac was the couple's youngest child. In 1821 his parents divorced, and his father remarried shortly thereafter.

Singer led a nomadic and often chaotic life. Unhappy at home and unable to get along with his stepmother, at age twelve he moved to Rochester, New York, to live with an older brother. Isaac Singer stayed there for seven years working at odd jobs, including a four-month stint as an apprentice machinist. He also picked up a few years of formal schooling between jobs, but his later success was based far more on talent than training. As a mechanic, Singer was adept enough to teach himself the craft on the job. As an inventor, he was blessed with an intuitive ability to "see" how machines could be built to carry out a given task. But as a businessman, Singer was hampered by his nearly indecipherable spelling and grammar, although he was an avid and wide-ranging reader his entire adult life.

Singer's life hit a major turning point when he discovered the theater at age nineteen; it remained one of his greatest loves throughout his life. For the next nineteen years Singer traveled the country working as an actor or advance man when he could and as a laborer, mechanic, or cabinetmaker when theater jobs were scarce. He used the surnames "Merritt" and "Mathews" as well as Singer during these years.

Singer never prospered as an actor. His first brush with material success came in 1839 when, while working for his brother who was a contractor on the Lockport and Illinois Canal, he invented a rock-drilling machine. He sold the patent for $2,000 and used the money to finance his own theater company, the Merritt Players, which traveled the Midwest performing Shakespearean and temperance dramas. The troupe, made up primarily of Singer, his mistress, and their four children, hovered near the edge of profitability until 1844 when it collapsed in Fredricksburg, Ohio.

Singer returned to the life of a mechanic. Now looking for fortune after his failure at fame, Singer returned to invention. He developed a machine for carving metal or wood type. His efforts to perfect and market his invention, which he patented in 1849, took the Singers first to Pittsburgh and then to New York City.

In New York Singer obtained the backing of A. B. Taylor & Company to build his carving machine. The only model was destroyed in a boiler explosion at Taylor's shop shortly after its completion in 1850. Singer's search for new partners brought him to George Zieber, a book publisher and seller who had been impressed by Singer's machine. Zieber borrowed enough to finance another machine and a move to Boston, then a publishing center. In Boston, Singer and Zieber rented space from Orson Phelps, who had been commissioned to manufacture Lerow & Blodgett sewing machines.

Singer's type-carving machine worked but had no buyers, so in desperation he turned to the sewing machine. Within twelve hours of inspecting his first machine Singer discovered its defects and came up with a new and unique design to correct them. Eleven days later he completed a working model to be made and marketed by I. M. Singer & Company, as the partnership of Singer, Phelps, and Zieber was called. Singer's patent was granted in 1851.

His machine was not the first, but it was the best. Elias Howe, Jr., had patented a semireliable machine in 1846, and a host of others had followed him into the field before Singer arrived. Few entered the business after Singer because the superiority of his machine and the efficiency of his firm discouraged competition.

In business and in his personal life Singer was often ruthless and occasionally unscrupulous. Contrary to his partnership agreement, Singer patented the sewing machine in his name only. He hounded Phelps and another partner, Barzillan Ransom, out of the business to increase his own profits. In 1851 he tricked Zieber into selling his interest for a mere $6,000 by convincing the then seriously ill Zieber that he would soon be dead and should therefore settle his affairs for the sake of his family. Singer actually knew nothing of his partner's condition, and Zieber recovered completely.

Singer pushed his partners and employees vigorously but lacked the skill or interest to direct the firm's day-to-day operations. The man most responsible for making the I. M. Singer Company into a multinational corporation was Edward Clark. Singer brought Clark, a lawyer, into the firm as a partner in 1851 to deal with the patent-infringement suits that threatened the survival of all sewing machine makers. Clark became the chief architect of the patent pool that ended the "sewing machine war" in 1856 and left Singer one of the dominant firms in the industry.

As the company prospered Singer took less interest in the business and more in enjoying his fortune and fame. His personal affairs were complex. He had married Catherine Maria Haley in 1830, and they had two children before he abandoned her and established another family with Mary Ann Sponsler in the mid-1830s. Singer and Sponsler had ten children, two of whom died in infancy. Shortly after moving to New York City in 1849 Singer established two more families. The first, under the name of Merritt, was with Mary Eastwood Walters; they had one child. The second, with Mary McGonigal, was under the name of Mathews and produced five children. Singer's growing fame made it difficult to keep his families separate, and in 1860 his divorce from Haley and a chance meeting by Sponsler and McGonigal set off a series of private crises and public scandals that led Singer to take refuge in Europe. There he met Isabella Boyer, whom he married in 1863; they had six children.

Singer, who had been dividing his time between Europe and the United States since 1860, retired from any active participation in the company in 1863 and moved permanently to Europe in 1867. In his later years Singer lived the life of a rich, respectable, and eccentric country gentleman surrounded by some of the twenty-four children from his five families. He died at his estate near Torquay, Devonshire, England. He left a fortune in excess of $13 million and was recognized worldwide as the inventor of the first practical sewing machine.

• The records of the I. M. Singer Co. can be found at the Wisconsin State Historical Society in Madison. For a well-researched and highly readable biography of Singer and his times see Ruth Brandon, *A Capitalist Romance: Singer and the Sewing Machine* (1977). Peter Lyon, "Isaac Singer and His Wonderful Sewing Machine," *American Heritage* (Oct. 1958), is a good brief summary of Singer's career and personal life. Andrew B. Jack, "The Channels of Distribution for an Innovation: The Sewing Machine in America, 1860–1865," *Explorations in Entrepreneurial History* 9 (1956–1957): 113–41, focuses on the early years of the I. M. Singer Co.

THOMAS S. DICKE

SINGER, Isidore (10 Nov. 1859–20 Feb. 1939), managing editor of the *Jewish Encyclopedia*, was born in Mährisch-Weisskirchen, Moravia, the son of Joseph Singer and Charlotte Eysler, merchants. Singer studied history, philosophy, and ancient languages at the Universities of Vienna and Berlin, earning his Ph.D. from the former in 1884. He also studied at the rabbinical seminary in Vienna and at the Hochschule für die Wissenschaft des Judentums in Berlin. During these years, Singer became deeply cognizant of the seriousness of rising anti-Semitism in Europe. He tried to combat it through education, writing several pieces on anti-Semitism. While living in Paris in 1893, Singer responded to Edouard Drumont's anti-Semitic *La Libre Parole* by launching a short-lived biweekly journal entitled *La Vrai Parole*.

As an outgrowth of his resolve to counter anti-Semitism, Singer first developed his idea for a Jewish encyclopedia. After trying unsuccessfully to launch this work in Europe, Singer came to New York in 1895. He convinced the Funk & Wagnalls Company to publish the encyclopedia and devoted his full efforts from 1898 to 1905 to realizing this dream. The *Jewish Encyclopedia* (1901–1905) was the first comprehensive collection of all the available material pertaining to the Jews—their history, literature, philosophy, ritual, sociology, and biography. Singer hoped that the work would combat anti-Semitism by presenting accurate, impartial material. Yet the *Jewish Encyclopedia* accomplished more. The work marked the culmination of a century of scholarly activity that began with the struggle for Jewish emancipation in Europe. Moreover, the encyclopedia became a stimulus for twentieth-century research in Judaica, for it symbolized the emergence of Jewish scholarship in America. It was often referred to as "Singer's encyclopedia," and this association secured his fame for posterity.

A controversial figure from the start, Singer had trouble garnering support for his project from American Jewish leaders. They doubted the extent of Singer's commitment to and understanding of Judaism, and Funk & Wagnalls soon came to feel these concerns as well. Singer was pressured into sharing his vision with world-renowned scholars and rabbis through the creation of a *Jewish Encyclopedia* editorial board. This action, though it diminished Singer's control, enabled the encyclopedia to become a first-rate authoritative work. Several hundred scholars from around the world contributed entries to the twelve-volume encyclopedia. The *Jewish Encyclopedia* was highly praised by both the Jewish and the general public; it quickly became the standard against which subsequent reference works on Judaica were measured.

American Jewish leaders were particularly disturbed by Singer's views on Judaism. Singer urged Jews to discard the remaining ceremonial vestiges of their "disintegrating religion." Although Isaac Funk was attracted by Singer's universalistic views, they were held in check in order to secure the support of Jewish scholars for the project. After the publication of the encyclopedia, Singer furthered his ideas of universal religion by becoming the literary editor of the Amos Society, a monotheistic world league. Many of his ideas were incorporated into his *A Religion of Truth, Justice and Peace: A Challenge to Church and Synagogue to Lead in the Realization of the Social and Peace Gospel of the Hebrew Prophets* (1924).

After the publication of the encyclopedia, Singer worked on numerous projects, most of which were never realized. He tried unsuccessfully to build on the reputation of the encyclopedia by launching several projects that would highlight the Jews' contributions to the world. Singer also sought to exploit the increased interest in encyclopedias by trying to publish them in other fields, such as transportation, that still lacked them. He did edit the seven-volume *International Insurance Encyclopedia* (1910). He had plans to issue multivolume works of both Hebrew and Slavonic classics and succeeded in serving as chief of the board of translators for the twenty-volume *German Classics: Masterpieces of German Literature Translated into English* (1913–1914).

Singer married Virginie Charrat in 1888, and they had three children, but little else is known of Singer's personal life. He was an energetic visionary, constantly brimming with new ideas, ever eager to realize them. Yet his volatile personality often undermined his success. The diversification of Singer's energies to non-Jewish subjects in the years after the *Jewish Encyclopedia* surely stemmed from the growing friction between him and the leadership of the American Jewish community. Difficult and stubborn at times, Singer often criticized his most loyal supporters. Yet it was just this obstinacy and persistence that proved crucial to the successful completion of his most treasured accomplishment, the *Jewish Encyclopedia*. He died in New York.

• Isidore Singer's papers and correspondence are in the American Jewish Archives, Cincinnati. Singer's account of his experiences on the *Jewish Encyclopedia* is found in "Chips from the Workshop of a Jewish Encyclopedist," *Hebrew Union College Monthly* 9 (Jan. 1923): 15–21, (Feb. 1923): 11–16, (Mar. 1923): 8–13. Other works by Singer include "The Attitude of the Jews toward Jesus," *North American Review* 191 (Jan. 1910): 128–34; *A Bird's-Eye View of the Condition of the Jews in Past and Present* (1905); *Der Juden: Kampf ums Recht* (The Jews: Struggle for justice) (1902); "Die jüdische Renaissance in Amerika" (The Jewish renaissance in America), *Popular-wissenschaftliche Monatsblätter* 22 (1902): 73–79, 105–11, 125–31; "Professor Schechter's Message to the Jews of America," *New Era* 5 (Oct. 1904): 480–91; *Russia at the Bar of the American People* (1904); *Social Justice* (1923); and *Theology at the Crossroads* (1928). The most complete information on Singer's life and views is found in Shuly Rubin Schwartz, *The Emergence of Jewish Scholarship in America* (1991). Biographical information can also be found in Reuven Brainin, "Isidore Singer" (Hebrew), *Ha-Dor*, 12 Sept. 1901, and Ben-Zion Eisenstadt, *Hakhme Yisra'el be-Amerikah* (Jewish scholars in America) (1903). There is no full-scale biography.

SHULY RUBIN SCHWARTZ

SINGER, Israel Joshua (30 Nov. 1893–10 Feb. 1944), Yiddish writer, was born Yisroel Yehoshua Zinger in Bilgoray, Poland, the son of Pinchas Mendl Zinger, a rabbi and author of rabbinic commentaries, and Basheva Zylberman. He received a traditional Jewish religious education in the small towns in which his father taught before the family moved to Warsaw. At the same time, Singer secretly read secular books and turned to painting, leaving his home at age eighteen to live in a Warsaw artist's atelier. For several years he painted, worked as an unskilled laborer and as a proofreader, and in 1916 began writing short stories.

Singer traveled widely in Poland and the Soviet Union. He lived in Kiev after the Russian Revolution and, in 1920, went to Moscow and was disappointed to find that the Soviet Yiddish cultural figures he esteemed found his literary concerns to be too "bourgeois." While in Kiev he married Genya Kupfershtock in 1918; they had two sons, one of whom died young. He returned to live in Warsaw in 1921, and his literary career was launched in earnest two years later when Abraham Cahan, the powerful editor of the New York Yiddish daily, the *Forverts*, read his story "Perl" (Pearls) and republished it. Under his own name and the pseudonym G. Kuper, Singer became a correspondent for the *Forverts*, sending essays, sketches, and stories from his travels in Galicia, Poland, and the Soviet Union.

In Warsaw, in addition to two novels, numerous essays, and criticism, Singer published two collections of stories, *Perl* (Pearls) (1922) and *Af fremder erd* (On foreign ground) (1925); two plays, *Erdvey* (Earth pangs) (1922) and *Savinkov* (1933); and a volume of travelogues, *Nay rusland* (New Russia) (1928). Singer's first novel, *Shtol un Ayzn* (1927; *Blood Harvest* [1935] and *Steel and Iron* [1969]), was not well received by Yiddish critics, who objected to its loosely constructed plot and to Singer's attack on socialism. Partly in response to these reviews and what he saw as the fractious nature of Yiddish culture, he claimed in a 1928 letter to the Warsaw press that "under present conditions there is, unfortunately, no room for the Yiddish writer." In this famous letter he renounced Yiddish literature only to return within four years with his critically acclaimed novel, *Yoshe Kalb* (1932). Raising questions about Jewish and individual identity, the novel also examined what home and exile might mean for contemporary Jews. His first trip to the United States in 1932 was occasioned by Maurice Schwartz's extraordinarily successful theatrical adaptation of *Yoshe Kalb*.

In late 1933, when Singer emigrated from Poland to the United States, he had already established a significant literary reputation on both continents. In the ten years of his life in America, Singer was equally productive. He published the expansive family sagas for which he is perhaps best known: *Di brider Ashkenazi* (1936; *The Brothers Ashkenazi* [1936 and 1980]) and *Di mishpokhe Karnovski* (1943; *The Family Carnovsky* [1969]). *The Brothers Ashkenazi* traces the development of the major industrial city of Lodz, Poland, as seen through the troubled lives of twin boys who unsuccessfully seek to control its economic development. In *The Family Carnovsky*, Singer follows three generations of a family who move from Poland to Germany to the United States as each generation responds to the Enlightenment, modern secular culture, and, finally, the rise of Nazism. Another novel, *Khaver Nakhmen* (Comrade Nakhman) (1938; *East of Eden* [1939]), and a volume of stories titled *Friling* (Spring) (1937) met with less critical success. His memoir, *Fun a velt vos iz nishto mer* (1946; *Of a World That Is No More* [1970]), collected from the pages of the *Forverts*, appeared posthumously. In it, he described the people and places of his early years and the conflicting religious sensibilities of his mother's rationalism and his father's mystical zeal. Another posthumous volume titled *Dertseylungen* (Stories) appeared in 1949. Most of Singer's stories remain untranslated; some were collected and published in English by Maurice Samuel in *The River Breaks Up* (1938). In addition to the adaptation of *Yoshe Kalb* for the Yiddish stage, *Di brider Ashkenazi* was performed in 1938, *Khaver Nakhmen* in 1939, and *Di mishpokhe Karnovski* in 1943.

Singer's stories are not at all nostalgic about Eastern European Jewry in the decades before its destruction, or sentimental about the new American possibilities to which many of his characters turn. They offer an extraordinary contemporary view of Jewish culture at a crossroads leading in a number of directions. Traditional religious life, art, Zionism, socialism, secularism, or Yiddish culturalism are all explored and found wanting by his characters. En route, his fiction compels readers to confront the central political and cultural upheavals of Jewish life between the two world wars and on two continents.

By the time Singer suddenly died of a heart attack in New York City, he had become a controversial and renowned writer, one of the most popular Yiddish authors of the twentieth century. In subsequent decades, his prominence was eclipsed by that of his younger brother, the prolific writer Isaac Bashevis Singer.

Their older sister, Esther Singer Kreitman, also wrote short stories and novels.

• Collections of Singer's papers and manuscripts are at the YIVO Institute for Jewish Research in New York City and the National Library at Hebrew University in Jerusalem. Much of the critical assessment of Singer's fiction is in Yiddish, written by significant contemporaries such as Abraham Cahan, Nakhmen Mayzl, Shmuel Niger, Y. Rapaport, Melekh Ravitch, and Aaron Zeitlin. In addition to English-language reviews of each of the novels as they appeared in translation, there are important considerations of Singer in Irving Howe, "The Other Singer," *Commentary* 31, no. 3 (1966): 76–82, and Sander L. Gilman, "Madness and Racial Theory in I. J. Singer's *The Family Carnovsky*," *Modern Judaism* 1 (1981): 90–100. Comparisons of Singer and his brother have also appeared in English, most notably in Clive Sinclair, *The Brothers Singer* (1983). For a bibliography of primary and secondary materials and a comprehensive consideration of Singer's work in its Yiddish, European, and American contexts, see Anita Norich, *The Homeless Imagination in the Fiction of Israel Joshua Singer* (1991).

ANITA NORICH

SINGLETON, Benjamin (15 Aug. 1809–1892), black nationalist and land promoter known as "Pap," was born into slavery in Nashville, Tennessee. Little is known about the first six decades of his life. In his old age Singleton reminisced that his master had sold him to buyers as far away as Alabama and Mississippi several times, but that each time he had escaped and returned to Nashville. Tiring of this treatment, he ran away to Windsor, Ontario, and shortly thereafter moved to Detroit. There he quietly opened a boardinghouse for escaped slaves and supported himself by scavenging. In 1865 he came home to Edgefield, Tennessee, across the Cumberland River from Nashville, and supported himself as a cabinetmaker and carpenter.

Although Singleton loved Tennessee, he did not see this state in the post–Civil War era as a hospitable place for African Americans. Since coffin making was part of his work, he witnessed firsthand the aftermath of the appalling murders of African Americans by white vigilantes: "Julia Haven; I made the outside box and her coffin, in Smith County, Tennessee. And another young lady I know, about my color, they committed an outrage on her and then shot her, and I helped myself to make the outside box (Senate Report 693, vol. III, pp. 382–83). Already Singleton dreamed that he and other African Americans would possess their own land, so that they could be independent of whites, but the high price of land in Tennessee made large-scale purchases of land impractical. He observed that "the whites had the land and the sense, and the blacks had nothing but their freedom" (Athearn, p. 228).

Although Singleton stated that he was a Ulysses S. Grant Republican, African Americans were never able to win a significant political role in the reconstruction of Tennessee, and he was less interested in politics than in economics. Nourishing his dream of black landownership, he increasingly focused on locations outside the state. His attention was drawn to Kansas, John Brown's former state and the locus of much land settlement since Congress had passed the Homestead Act in 1862. He envisioned the establishment of communities of African Americans who had left the South for the free soil of Kansas.

He made his first scouting expedition to Kansas in 1873 and found that "it was a good country." Along with several friends, he formed the Edgefield Real Estate and Homestead Association to encourage African Americans' purchase and settlement of land outside the South. Singleton printed and widely distributed fliers that advertised Kansas land, mailing them to African Americans in every southern state. As a result of his promotional activities, hundreds of African Americans in Kentucky and Tennessee decided to move to Kansas in 1877 and 1878. At least four black Kansas communities founded during this time, in Cherokee, Graham, Lyons, and Morris counties, owed their origins largely to his efforts. Singleton himself lived for most of 1879–1880 in the colony of Dunlap in Morris County. In addition, some Tennessee migrants settled in Kansas cities such as Topeka, where the African-American community became known as "Tennessee Town." Singleton seems to have made little money from his land promotion, but that was not his aim. He saw himself as a prophet who was fulfilling God's plans rather than as a businessman. "I have had open air interviews with the living spirit of God for my people," he stated, "and we are going to leave the South."

In 1879 approximately 20,000 destitute African Americans left Mississippi, Louisiana, and Texas to settle in Kansas. Although Singleton's fliers had circulated in these states, the fresh wave of "Exodusters" seems not to have been occasioned by his publicity but by political repression and economic hardship in the states they left and by millenarian hopes for their destination. These new migrants suffered much hardship in Kansas, too, as they struggled to find work. A national controversy erupted over the reasons for the exodus, with Democrats accusing Republicans of encouraging the migration for political gain. Singleton excoriated black leaders such as Frederick Douglass who spoke out in opposition to the exodus. He felt that after many years of receiving patronage from their white friends, middle-class black men like Douglass "think they must judge things from where they stand, when the fact is the possum is lower down the tree—down nigh to the roots." He appeared in 1880 as a witness before a committee of the U.S. Senate that was investigating the exodus. Unshaken by the Democrats' cross-examination, he garnered much publicity for his claim that he was the "whole cause" of the Kansas migration. His claim was in fact greatly exaggerated, but he nevertheless won fame as "the Moses of the Colored Exodus." By late 1880, however, he no longer advocated African-American migration to Kansas, arguing that the state could not absorb any more impoverished immigrants. Still, after the initial hardships of relocation, many of the migrants achieved some success and preferred their new home to the South.

Singleton lived most of the remaining years of his life in the Tennessee Town neighborhood of Topeka, where he settled in 1880. He founded and actively supported a number of short-lived political associations, including the United Colored Links, an organization that sought race unity in order to build up factories and other industries controlled by African Americans, and to fashion a coalition with white workers through the Greenbacker party. In the mid-1880s he actively supported a proposal by Bishop Henry McNeal Turner of the AME church that African Americans should return to Africa and build up industry and governments there. This plan, in Singleton's words, would enable "the sons and daughters of Ham [to] return to their God-given inheritance, and Ethiopia [to] regain her ancient renown." African Americans, he said, would find that their needs could only be met by a separate black nation. Unlike his successful promotion of Kansas migration, Singleton was never able to instigate migration of African Americans to Africa. After years of poor health, he died in St. Louis.

Against all odds, Singleton was able to achieve part of his dreams. A black nationalist who attempted to provide African Americans with economic independence, he was able to foster the establishment of several all-black communities in Kansas through his exceptionally strong sense of a God-given mission. He fell short of his goal of true freedom for his people, as a lack of money and the strength of racial prejudice proved to be too much to overcome.

• The scrapbook in which Singleton kept his press clippings has been preserved in the manuscript collection of the Kansas State Historical Society, Topeka. The fullest account of his life can be found in Nell Irvin Painter, *Exodusters: Black Migration to Kansas after Reconstruction* (1977). Singleton's opinions on a variety of contemporary issues can be found in Robert Athearn, *In Search of Canaan: Black Migration to Kansas, 1879–1880* (1978). Arna Bontemps and Jack Conroy, *They Seek a City* (1945), provides the context for the Senate hearing in which Singleton gained prominence. The early years of his longest-lived colony are chronicled in Kenneth Marvin Hamilton, "The Origins and Early Promotion of Nicodemus: A Pre-Exodus, All-Black Town," *Kansas History* 5 (1982): 220–42.

STEPHEN W. ANGELL

SINGLETON, Zutty (14 May 1898–14 July 1975), jazz drummer, was born Arthur James Singleton in Bunkie, Louisiana. (No information on his parents is available.) Singleton was given his nickname—a Creole term meaning cute—during his earliest years. As a child, he moved with his family to New Orleans, where he grew up and attended public school.

An uncle, Willie "Bontin" Bontemps, a banjoist-guitarist, encouraged Singleton's childhood interest in the rich musical life of New Orleans. Singleton first performed on drums (1915–1916) with Steve Lewis's band and with another band led by John Robichaux. A U.S. Navy hitch came during World War I. Following his discharge (probably in 1919), Singleton played with groups led by such well-known local figures as

Papa Celestin and Big Eye Louis Nelson, performed with the Tuxedo and Maple Leaf marching brass bands, and was leader of his own group.

Around this time he became close friends with trumpeter Louis Armstrong. (One chronicler tells of Armstrong rejecting an attractive offer to play in New York City unless Singleton was hired, too.) Late in 1921 Singleton joined Armstrong in Fate Marable's Mississippi riverboat band. Singleton was associated with Marable for nearly two years, markedly improving his technique and musical knowledge by playing the band's relatively complex written arrangements each night. He performed on Marable's sole recording, "Frankie and Johnny," in 1924.

From 1923 until 1925 Singleton moved between New Orleans and St. Louis, playing mostly with Robichaux's theater orchestra in his hometown and with Charlie Creath's band upriver. The date of Singleton's marriage is uncertain, but probably around this time he became engaged to, or married, pianist Marge Creath, the bandleader's sister; they remained husband and wife for more than four decades. (He had at least one daughter.)

In 1925 Singleton moved to Chicago, which was a thriving jazz center. He first replaced drummer Baby Dodds in Vernon Roulette's band, performed in 1927 with other groups, and played with the great clarinetist Jimmie Noone at the Nest. From Noone's trio he moved to Clarence Jones's band, where he joined Armstrong. For a short spell he was in a small group with Armstrong and pianist Earl Hines, and in 1928 he and Armstrong shifted over to Carroll Dickerson's band.

The recordings that Singleton made with Armstrong's Hot Five and Hot Seven in 1928 sealed his fame in jazz history. On 27 and 28 June he recorded six sides with Armstrong and Hines (plus clarinet, trombone, and banjo), including the jazz classics "West End Blues" and "Sugar Foot Strut." On 29 June and 5 July Armstrong made three more recordings with Singleton, and five months later they cut ten more numbers. At the December 1928 sessions Singleton found that he could compensate for primitive recording techniques by placing a microphone under the snare and playing brushes to capture a fuller drum effect. Each Armstrong recording can be singled out for some Singleton highlight, but generally his cymbal work, snare accents, and effortless drive keyed the soloists he accompanied to greater melodic variety and swing.

By age thirty, Singleton was recognized by musicians as one of the two pioneers of jazz drumming. The other, accurately described by critics as the father of jazz drums, was Baby Dodds, who established his name and inimitable style first. Dodds's basic drumming approach was dense and heavy, a hand-to-hand, rudimentary technique. Some critics speak of his "tempestuous," "savage" "jungle" rhythms. He used bells, woodblocks, whistles, etc., for maximum coloristic effects. He invariably played the snare with wooden drumsticks, never brushes, and his backing of soloists was moderately complex and polyrhythmic.

Singleton's style was far different. He discarded the novelty devices that Dodds freely employed. He integrated the ride and hi-hat cymbals into his overall playing. And, most noticeably, he used an evenly spaced, steady beat (in those days $2/4$) throughout each tune. To attain rhythmic and sonic variety, he explored off-beats and accents that he could meld into a constant, pulsating flow. Singleton's approach, rather than Dodds's, pointed to the direction that mainstream jazz drumming would take in the years ahead.

Less well recognized are Singleton's innovations, evidenced when he played with Noone in Chicago. Singleton devised and developed the chorus-long jazz drum solo there. His solos added flair and variety to a jazz trio's playing, and they avoided nonmusical, crowd-catering displays. Typically, Singleton structured a solo around a song's melodic phrasing: in effect, a theme-and-variation approach.

During the 1930s Singleton worked and recorded with a who's who of jazz instrumentalists and singers. Early in the decade he played with Fats Waller at Connie's Inn in New York. He also worked with Duke Ellington alumni Bubber Miley and Otto Hardwicke, with trumpeter Tommy Ladnier, and in Chicago with Carroll Dickerson at the Grand Terrace and with his own groups at the Three Deuces, the New Deal Club, and the Flagship. From September 1936 through November 1938 he performed in New York with trumpeter Roy Eldridge, with Mezz Mezzrow, and at Nick's with Sidney Bechet. Then, until early 1943, Singleton led his own trio or sextet at Nick's, the Village Vanguard, Kelly's Stable, and Jimmy Ryan's; often he used trumpeter Sidney De Paris.

Singleton's move to Los Angeles in April 1943 marked a major transition in his professional career. Although he frequently performed in local jazz clubs, his steady income came from film studio jobs and as a featured regular on Orson Welles's weekly radio broadcast. Singleton was seen on-screen in two feature films, *Stormy Weather* (1943) and *New Orleans* (1946).

Singleton's recording colleagues in the 1930s and 1940s included pianists Waller, Joe Sullivan, Art Hodes, and Jelly Roll Morton (at some of Morton's final sessions); reedmen Bechet, Pee Wee Russell, Edmond Hall, Joe Marsala, and Buster Bailey; brass players Jack Teagarden, Red Allen, and Wingy Manone; and others such as Lionel Hampton, Slim Gaillard, and Mildred Bailey.

Singleton's career as a vital jazz performer was concentrated in his first two playing decades. He always remained a thoroughgoing professional, but from the 1940s until the end of his playing days he was basically repeating high points of his jazz life. With the postwar Dixieland revival he found ready work in New York at Nick's, the Stuyvesant Casino, and the Metropole Café on Broadway, where he led a group in 1959. In the 1960s he worked for long stretches at Jimmy Ryan's, and he appeared at several festivals.

In 1970 Singleton suffered a stroke that left him unable to maintain a full-time musical schedule. He died in New York City.

Many critics contend that Singleton's playing directly influenced Gene Krupa, Ray Bauduc, Sid Catlett, and George Wettling. Although other drummers who generally followed his stylistic path were more technically skilled and imaginative, Singleton's achievements as one of the leading early jazzmen will last as long as the sounds of the Armstrong Hot Five and Hot Seven recordings can be heard.

• Details of Singleton's career and discussions of his playing can be found in virtually any standard jazz reference work. Among the reliable and sometimes insightful brief studies and sketches are those in Leonard Feather, *The Encyclopedia of Jazz* (1960); Barry Kernfeld, ed., *The New Grove Dictionary of Jazz* (1988); John Chilton, *Who's Who of Jazz*, rev. ed. (1985); Len Lyons and Don Perlo, *Jazz Portraits: The Lives and Music of the Jazz Masters* (1989); Whitney Balliett, *Such Sweet Thunder* (1966); and Gunther Schuller, *Early Jazz: Its Roots and Musical Development* (1968). Any number of articles and book chapters are available on the Armstrong recordings of 1928. An obituary is in the *New York Times*, 15 July 1975.

ROBERT MIRANDON

SINKLER, William H., Jr. (24 Dec. 1906–22 Sept. 1960), surgeon, was born in Summerville, South Carolina, the son of William H. Sinkler, Sr., a teacher, and a mother whose name is unrecorded. After completing his early education, Sinkler attended Haines Normal Institute in Augusta, Georgia, graduating in 1924. He then entered Lincoln University in Oxford, Pennsylvania, where he received an A.B. in 1928. Active in campus life and an excellent student, he decided on a career in medicine. He enrolled at the Howard University Medical School in Washington, D.C., and continued to experience academic success. Elected a member of Kappa Pi honorary society, he received his M.D. degree in 1932.

After his graduation from Howard, Sinkler moved to St. Louis, Missouri, where he successively completed one year as a junior intern (1932–1933), one year as an assistant resident (1933–1934), and two years as a resident surgeon—an internship and residency—at City Hospital No. 2. From its opening in November 1919, City Hospital No. 2 had served as a source of treatment for indigent African-American patients and was one of the few locations in the country where African-American medical school graduates could pursue postgraduate medical instruction and training. Sinkler made an early impression on the surgical profession by performing a delicate operation on a patient who had sustained a stab wound in his heart. At a time when few heart operations were being performed by any surgeons (white or black), this procedure brought Sinkler to the attention of his peers nationwide.

In 1936 Sinkler established a private surgical practice in St. Louis, and in the following year he married Blanche Vashon, the daughter of a prominent local family; the couple had one son. In 1938 Sinkler was appointed a consultant in chest surgery at Koch Hospital in St. Louis by Ralph Thompson, the city hospital commissioner. Sinkler was the first African-American surgeon to hold such a post, and he was successful enough to merit appointment as medical director and associate chief of staff at nearby Homer G. Phillips Hospital (HGPH) in 1941. Replacing Henry E. Hampton in the post, Sinkler assumed responsibility for patient medical care, physician training, and the supervision of attending physicians at the recently opened (1937) facility, which had been created to replace City Hospital No. 2—which had proved inadequate to the needs of the African-American community.

Having received the unanimous endorsement of his peers at the Mound City Medical Forum at the time of his appointment, Sinkler soon made his presence felt at Phillips, and within two years of its opening the hospital was accepting nearly half of the African-American graduates of U.S. medical schools for postgraduate training. While committed to excellence in HGPH's training programs and to the African-American physicians who participated in them, patient care at the extremely busy facility was not neglected; Sinkler made sure that those under him treated all patients, whether indigent or not, with the same degree of dignity and professionalism. Working with his chief of surgery, Robert Elman (who was white), Sinkler went beyond the walls of HGPH, helping to develop postgraduate medical training for African-American surgeons at institutions outside the St. Louis area. His most notable success in this area came in 1941, when (with several colleagues) he successfully obtained Rosenwald Foundation grants that enabled several promising young surgeons to obtain advanced specialized training elsewhere.

During his nearly twenty years (1941–1960) of service to Homer G. Phillips Hospital, Sinkler influenced in some manner more than one-third of the black physicians receiving postgraduate medical training in the United States. As chief of surgery after Elman's death in 1956, he served as a model for young African Americans who aspired to a career in medicine. Sinkler was one of the first black members of the American College of Surgeons (1948) and in the following year became a member of the International College of Surgeons as well. He was the first black surgeon appointed to the faculty and the surgical service at the Washington University School of Medicine in St. Louis (serving from 1950 to 1960) and the first to operate at St. Louis's Cardinal Glennon Children's Hospital, the Barnes Hospital (Washington University), and the Jewish Hospital of St. Louis.

Sinkler received numerous awards as a result of his achievements. In 1953 he received the Insignia of the Haitian National Order for his work with Haitian physicians (several of whom received training at Phillips), and he received the Distinguished Alumni Award from Howard University in 1959. While he actively participated in numerous professional societies, including the Missouri Medical Society, the Mound City

Medical Society, the St. Louis Medical Society, and the American Medical Association, he was most active with National Medical Association, serving as vice chairman of its surgical section from 1941 to 1949 and as chairman of the section in 1950. He also published numerous scholarly articles throughout his career, which appeared in the *American Journal of Surgery*, the *Archives of Surgery*, and the *Journal of the National Medical Association*. Sinkler died of heart disease in St. Louis, Missouri.

William Sinkler was instrumental in the development of Homer Phillips Hospital as a training ground for aspiring physicians and surgeons. Although the hospital eventually closed in 1979, his influence on the training of countless African-American medical professionals remains as solid testimony to his role as a pioneering African-American surgeon and educator.

• Sinkler's papers have not been located. Among his published articles were "Etiology of Acute Abdominal Pain," *Journal of the National Medical Association* 32 (1940): 97–99; "Challenge of Medicine in the Future," *Journal of the National Medical Association* 37 (1945): 198–200; "Paget's Disease of the Male Breast" (with T. J. Cooper), *American Journal of Surgery* 98 (1959): 623–24; and "The Value of Peripheral Arteriography in Assessing Acute Vascular Injuries" (with A. D. Spencer), *Archives of Surgery* 80 (1960): 300–304. Secondary information on Sinkler is scarce; aside from an uncredited article, "Sinkler Receives Honorary Degree," *Journal of the National Medical Association* 47, no. 2 (Mar. 1955), the best source is Frank O. Richards's article in *A Century of Black Surgeons: The U.S.A. Experience*, vol. 1, ed. Claude H. Organ, Jr., and Margaret M. Kosiba (1987). Obituaries are in the *Journal of the National Medical Association* 52, no. 6 (Nov. 1960): 455, and the *Journal of the American Medical Association* 175, no. 2 (Jan. 1961): 147.

EDWARD L. LACH, JR.
FRANK O. RICHARDS

SINNOTT, Edmund Ware (5 Feb. 1888–6 Jan. 1968), botanist, was born in Cambridge, Massachusetts, the son of Charles Peter Sinnott, a normal school science teacher, and Jessie Elvira Smith. He attended public schools in Bridgewater, Massachusetts, and then entered Harvard University, from which he received an A.B. in 1908, an A.M. in botany in 1910, and a Ph.D. in botany in 1913. At Harvard, his principal mentor was plant morphologist Edward Charles Jeffrey, under whose guidance Sinnott was able to publish a number of papers in comparative anatomy of the higher plants; for one of these, he received the Bowdoin Medal in 1910. During his graduate years, he was also able to make a trip to Australia as a Sheldon Fellow with plant morphologist and anatomist Arthur J. Eames; the two spent the period 1910–1911 collecting plant specimens, particularly of the *Coniferae*. Sinnott's doctoral dissertation, "Reproductive Structures in the Podocarpineae" (*Annals of Botany* 27 [1913]: 39–82), helped determine the classification position of these plants.

After graduate school Sinnott taught at the Harvard Forestry School and at the Bussey Institute at Harvard; he also did research and published several papers with plant anatomist Irving W. Bailey. In 1915 Sinnott joined the faculty of Connecticut Agricultural College (now the University of Connecticut at Storrs) as professor of botany and genetics. He remained there until 1928, when he was appointed professor and chairman of the botany department at Barnard College, Columbia University. In 1940 Sinnott became Sterling Professor and, until 1950, chairman of the botany department at Yale University. At Yale, he was also director of the Marsh Botanical Garden (1940–1950), director of the Sheffield Scientific School (1945–1956), and dean of the graduate school (1945–1956). He married Mabel Haskell Shaw in 1916; they had three children.

As a researcher, Sinnott's principal work was the study of how developmental factors—environmental and genetic—determine and influence plant form. In his earlier professional papers he emphasized, in a traditional way, the evolutionary history of the angiosperms and their distribution, but from 1916, he entered the field of genetic analysis with studies of the family Cucurbitaceae (the gourds and squashes). His articles from Connecticut showed that form in this family is directly dependent on the laws of Mendelian inheritance. His was the most extensive genetic analysis of form in a plant organ during that period. In another area of research, Sinnott, along with Albert F. Blakeslee, studied the genetics of *Datura*, a genus of the Solanaceae family. By discovering the influence of specific chromosomes on the structure of its flower stalk, they were able to introduce a new method for studying the genetics of form.

With further research into the origin of traits of form and size, Sinnott brought together concepts of plant histology, genetics, and morphogenesis. He investigated the cellular basis of shape differences in the growth of a fruit, showing that there is development along a precise curve that is unaffected by the manner of growth itself (either increase in cell size or in cell number). This work established the basic relationships between cells and organs in plants and demonstrated how genes can exercise control differently in different species. Sinnott summed up much of this work in *Plant Morphogenesis* (1960) and in *The Problem of Organic Form* (1963). In addition to these works, Sinnott coauthored two important textbooks, *Botany: Principles and Problems* (1923) and *Principles of Genetics* (1925), with L. C. Dunn, and he wrote about 120 scientific papers.

Outside of the laboratory and the botanical garden, Sinnott participated in a large range of activities. He was editor of the *American Journal of Botany*; a trustee of *Biological Abstracts*, of the New York Botanical Garden, of Boyce Thompson Institute for Plant Research; and consulting editor for McGraw-Hill publications in the agricultural and botanical sciences. He also served as president of the Torrey Botanical Club, the American Association for the Advancement of Science, the Botanical Society of America, and the American Society of Naturalists and was a member of the National Academy of Sciences and the American Philosophical

Society. A fellow of the American Academy of Arts and Sciences, he received several honorary degrees and was elected to Phi Beta Kappa and Sigma Xi. He retired from Yale in 1956.

In his later years, Sinnott, having concluded that analysis could not fully explain morphogenesis, concerned himself with larger questions, such as the nature of biological organization itself. He urged his colleagues to go beyond purely mechanical explanations in biology and search for new questions that would provoke new answers. He believed that the biological activities that constitute life are not mechanical but can be found in the nature of living material itself. He elaborated his ideas in a number of popular books, including *Cell and Psyche* (1950), *The Biology of the Spirit* (1956), and *Matter, Mind, and Man* (1957). One of his themes was that everything human was biologically based and that biology could serve as a link between science and religion and philosophy. He also sought to establish the humanistic nature of science and to describe its role in American culture.

Sinnott's contributions to American science were exceptional: he helped to change the direction of inquiry in morphology and was one of the principal researchers in the problem of organic form. He believed that the basic problem of biology was the subject matter of morphogenesis, and he educated two generations of students in this subject. An outstanding teacher, author, and university administrator and an important spokesman for the achievements of American science, he was one of the few scientists of his day to believe that science should not be isolated from other regions of thought and ideas. He died in New Haven.

• Sinnott's correspondence and other papers are in the Archives and Manuscripts Division of Sterling Memorial Library, Yale University. Other sources of biographical data are Albert F. Blakeslee, "Edmund Ware Sinnott," *Scientific Monthly* 66, no. 1 (1948): 5–8; an obituary by K. S. Wilson in *Plant Science Bulletin* 14, no. 1 (1968): 6–7; and Frans A. Stafleu, *Taxonomic Literature*, vol. 5 (1985), pp. 617–18. An obituary by George S. Avery in the *Bulletin of the Torrey Botanical Club* 95 (1968): 647–52, contains a portrait and a complete bibliography. Also see National Academy of Sciences, *Biographical Memoirs* 54 (1983): 350–72.

ROBERT F. ERICKSON

SIPLE, Paul Allman (18 Dec. 1908–25 Nov. 1968), Antarctic explorer and scientist, was born in Montpelier, Ohio, the son of Clyde L. Siple, an electric plant employee, and Fannie Hope Allman, a schoolteacher. He grew up in Erie, Pennsylvania, where he attended high school. In 1923 he achieved the rank of eagle scout in the Boy Scouts of America (BSA). When Commander Richard E. Byrd decided to include a scout on his 1928 Antarctic expedition, more than 60,000 young men applied. BSA executives and Byrd selected Siple from a group of six outstanding finalists.

Initially Byrd did not intend to include Siple in the wintering party, but the young scout had other ideas. His hard work aboard ship and initiative at the Little America base impressed Byrd. Siple became an expedition dog driver and biologist, performing his duties in an exemplary manner. After returning home in 1930, he gained national recognition with his book, *A Boy Scout with Byrd* (1931), and a second book, *Exploring at Home* (1932).

Siple earned his bachelor's degree in biology from Allegheny College in 1932. From 1933 to 1935 he served as chief biologist on the second Byrd Antarctic Expedition. This time he planned Byrd's Advance Base 100 miles south of Little America and led an exploring party eastward into Marie Byrd Land. Siple's party made important geological and biological discoveries in this previously unexplored area. Siple attempted to bring forty penguins to the United States, but only eleven survived the voyage. After the second expedition, Siple continued his education at Clark University, where he obtained his doctorate in geography. He married Ruth I. Johannesmeyer in 1936; they had three daughters.

In 1939 he rejoined Byrd for the United States Antarctic Service Expedition (USASE). Having started as a novice in Antarctica eleven years before, he now became leader at Little America III (West Base). Under Siple's direction, the expedition discovered new territory in Marie Byrd Land and explored new areas of the Ross Ice Shelf. During this expedition, he developed windchill charts for measuring the effect of wind and cold on humans.

During World War II, Siple served in the U.S. Army Quartermaster Corps developing clothing for both polar and tropical climates. He returned to Antarctica in 1946–1947, with Operation Highjump, as technical adviser to Admiral Byrd. He also served as military geographer to the army general staff and continued his work on military clothing.

Antarctic duties again summoned Dr. Siple for Operation Deepfreeze, 1955–1956 and the International Geophysical Year (IGY), 1957–1958. The most important U.S. IGY scientific base would be built at the South Pole. Dr. Siple had reservations about the logistical problems and divided civilian-military command structure for such a base. Approaching the age of fifty, he preferred to stay at home in Alexandria, Virginia, with his wife and young daughters. In a fateful meeting with Admiral Byrd, his old leader insisted that Siple should command the South Pole base. Siple reluctantly accepted the assignment.

As scientific leader, Siple did his utmost to make the South Pole station a success. Building and supplying the base proved to be a logistical nightmare. Some important supplies and equipment never arrived. Bone-chilling cold and the 9,000-foot altitude made physical work exhausting and painful. The scientific leader did far more than his share of the labor, despite being the oldest member of the party. He lost forty pounds during this period. In his introduction to *90° South*, Lieutenant John Tuck, the military commander, wrote, "On any task, especially an unpopular one, he was first on the job and last to leave it. In the long and arduous process of digging the 1,000-foot tunnel to the seismometer pit his shovel was invariably the first set in motion and the last set down. In the snow mine also, Paul logged more hours' work than anyone else."

The first men to winter at the South Pole faced additional challenges. The temperature plummeted below −100 degrees Fahrenheit after the sun had disappeared for the winter. Siple and Tuck faced daily challenges to operate the base, collect the scientific data, and maintain harmony among the eighteen isolated men, who were relative strangers.

Scientific work included observation of the inland weather and the ionosphere and studies of the snow at various levels below the surface. Even uncontaminated snow from the bottom of the mine contained spores and pollen. Indoor attempts to grow vegetables failed. The men participated in various physical and psychological testing in their unique environment. They also tested their clothing and equipment in extremely low temperatures. On 23 September 1958 the sun returned, but the temperature did not rise above −40 degrees Fahrenheit until November 13. The base experienced 169 consecutive days at −40 degrees or colder. New incoming flights brought replacement personnel, supplies, and written accounts of Admiral Byrd's death. Siple finally departed on 30 November, exactly one year after his arrival.

After returning from his South Pole assignment, Siple wrote an account of his experiences and returned to his duties with the army. In 1961 he traveled to India and Australia, and from 1963 to 1966 he served in Canberra, Australia, as scientific attaché for the U.S. State Department. While in Australia he suffered a stroke that may have resulted from his strenuous South Polar work. He and his family returned to the United States. After a period of rehabilitation, he resumed his army duties part-time. He died at his office in Alexandria from a heart attack, just five days short of the tenth anniversary of his return from the South Pole.

Siple's fame as "Byrd's boy scout" overshadowed his scientific achievements on Byrd's second expedition and his leadership at Little America III from 1939 to 1941. Before 1958, no one knew if human beings could survive a winter at the South Pole. Siple played the key role in the success of the South Pole base. Few, if any, could have matched his expertise, leadership, physical effort, and dedication to the project. His six expeditions cumulatively constitute a record for the most time in Antarctica.

Siple's windchill index is used internationally in polar work and even for daily weather broadcasts. His work in developing polar clothing has prevented many deaths and injuries in cold climates. Among his many accolades were the Silver Buffalo from the BSA and the Hubbard Medal from the National Geographical Society. He served as president of the American Polar Society, the Association of American Geographers, and the Antarctican Society.

• Siple's papers are in the National Archives; in the Paul A. Siple Family Collection (1831–1968), Arlington, Va.; and in the possession of Ruth Siple, Alexandria, Va. Besides the works mentioned in the text, Siple wrote *Scout to Explorer* (1936), *Adaptations of the Explorer to the Climate of Antarctica* (1939), *Army Observers' Report of Operation Highjump: Task Force 68, U.S. Navy* (1947), and *90° South: The Story of the American South Pole Conquest* (1959). His articles include "Ornithology of the Second Byrd Antarctic Expedition," *Auk* 54 (1937): 147–60; "Geographical Exploration from Little America III" and "General Principles Governing Selection of Clothing for Cold Climates," *Reports on Scientific Results of the USASE 1939–1941* (1945), pp. 23–60 and 200–234, respectively; "We Are Living at the South Pole," *National Geographic*, July 1957, pp. 5–34; and "Man's First Winter at the South Pole," *National Geographic*, April 1958, pp. 439–78. Numerous other sources provide insights into Siple's work and character. Richard E. Byrd, *Little America* (1930) and *Discovery* (1935), describe Byrd's first two antarctic expeditions. Eugene Rodgers used Siple's 1928–1930 diary in his *Beyond the Barrier* (1990). *Reports on Scientific Results of the USASE 1939–1941* (1945) is a collection of articles by members of Little America III and East Base. Charles Passel describes his work at Little America III with Siple in *Ice: The Antarctic Diary of Charles F. Passel* (1995). Walter Sullivan, *Assault on the Unknown* (1961), provides information about the South Pole base in relation to the IGY. Ruth Siple orally provided data about her husband's last years. Obituaries are in the *New York Times*, 26 Nov. 1968, and the *Polar Times*, Dec. 1968.

TED HECKATHORN

SIRICA, John Joseph (19 Mar. 1904–14 Aug. 1992), federal judge, was born in Waterbury, Connecticut, the son of Ferdinand Sirica, a barber, and Rose Zinno, a grocery store manager. Sirica became a lawyer at the urging of his parents, who lived in many different parts of the United States during Sirica's youth in a struggle to make a living. Lacking any college training, Sirica found law school difficult and dropped out twice before graduating from Georgetown University's law school in 1926. Sirica supported himself during law school by teaching boxing and went to Miami after his graduation to resume his boxing career because he expected to fail the bar exam. Returning to Washington after he was admitted to the bar, he joined a small firm specializing in criminal law when he was turned down for jobs by the city's larger firms.

From 1930 to 1934 Sirica served as an assistant U.S. attorney. He started his own practice in 1934, and in 1949 he became a partner at a prominent Washington law firm, Hogan & Hartson, where he served as chief trial counsel and remained until he became a federal judge eight years later. In 1944 Sirica served as general counsel to the House Select Committee to Investigate the Federal Communications Commission.

Having received his position as a U.S. attorney through connections in the Republican party, Sirica was active in Republican politics until he became a judge. He served as a member of the Republican committee in the District of Columbia and was regularly available for sundry services to the party. During several presidential campaigns, Sirica toured various states to give speeches on behalf of the Republican candidate, mostly before Italian-American audiences.

In 1952 he married Lucile M. Camalier; the couple would have two daughters and one son.

Largely as a reward for his services to the Republican party, Sirica became a judge of the U.S. District Court for the District of Columbia in April 1957. In April 1971, on the basis of seniority, he became chief judge. Despite his long record of service, Sirica never would have achieved national fame if he had not presided over the trials of the defendants in the cases involving the 1972 burglary of the Democratic National Committee headquarters in the Watergate complex in Washington.

In his capacity as chief judge, Sirica assigned the Watergate case to himself because he believed that a Republican would be less vulnerable to allegations of partisanship. At the first trial in early 1973, the jury convicted several persons in connection with the burglary. Suspicious that more prominent persons might have been involved in the burglary, Sirica meted out stiff preliminary sentences but indicated that defendants who cooperated with a Senate investigation might receive leniency.

In March 1973 James McCord, a convicted Watergate defendant who had served as security coordinator for President Richard Nixon's 1972 reelection campaign, sent a letter to Sirica alleging that some of his codefendants had perjured themselves at the trial and had been offered payments in return for promises to refrain from implicating others. McCord's letter provided a major impetus for the investigations conducted by the Senate and the U.S. Justice Department's special prosecutor's office.

In July 1973 Sirica granted the special prosecutor's request for a subpoena directing Nixon to produce tapes of nine White House conversations relevant to the prosecutor's investigations. When Nixon invoked the claim of executive privilege and refused to turn over the tapes, Sirica issued a stern judicial opinion ordering Nixon to provide a cause why he could not produce them. In October 1973, after the U.S. Court of Appeals upheld Sirica's order, Nixon released edited transcripts of some of the tapes that indicated that his complicity was greater than was generally supposed. Meanwhile, Sirica directed a long grand jury investigation that ended in March 1974 with the indictment of several prominent Nixon administration officials, including former attorney general John Mitchell and several of Nixon's close aides. The grand jury also named Nixon as an unindicted coconspirator in the coverup of the Watergate investigation.

In May 1974 Sirica approved the special prosecutor's request for tapes of sixty-four more White House conversations. Nixon refused to turn over anything beyond edited transcripts of the tapes until the Supreme Court, in a landmark decision in July 1974, rejected his claims of executive privilege and ordered him to release the tapes to the special prosecutor. Nixon then surrendered the tapes, which implicated him in the coverup of the Watergate investigation and led to his resignation in August 1974 in the face of imminent impeachment.

After Nixon's resignation, Sirica presided over the trials of several top Nixon administration officials, including Mitchell, who were convicted and sent to prison for their role in covering up the Watergate investigation. In an autobiography published several years later, Sirica expressed disappointment that President Gerald R. Ford had precluded any trial of Nixon by granting the former president a full pardon. Although Sirica believed that the conviction of so many of Nixon's aides and the resignation of Nixon vindicated the integrity of the Constitution and the American legal system, he feared that Nixon's avoidance of criminal prosecution created the unfortunate perception that the president was beyond the full reach of the law.

In his book about the Watergate trials, Sirica stated, "The judiciary, standing above politics as the enforcer and arbiter of our laws, was the critical branch of government in the resolution of the Watergate crisis. And it is our faith and trust in the law, our devotion to the notion that ours should be a government of laws and not men, that saved us from this scandal" (p. 301).

Sirica's vigorous role in investigating the Watergate burglary and facilitating the prosecution of persons responsible for the burglary and its coverup was widely credited for ensuring that formidable political forces did not thwart justice. His courage in seeking the truth and his personal modesty transformed him into a folk hero, and he received a wide array of honors, including designation as *Time* magazine's "Man of the Year" for 1973. Sirica, who often questioned witnesses from the bench and participated in other aspects of fact-finding, was sometimes criticized, however, for taking a more active role than was customary for trial judges of his era. Sirica explained later that he "had no intention of sitting on the bench like a nincompoop and watching the parade go by" (p. 127). Federal procedural rules were changed, expressly permitting judges to question witnesses.

Sirica stepped down as chief judge in March 1974 when he reached the mandatory retirement age of seventy, but he remained active as a judge on senior status until 1986. He died in Washington, D.C.

• Sirica's personal papers are in the Manuscript Division of the Library of Congress, although access to them is restricted. Sirica published one book, *To Set the Record Straight: The Break-in, the Tapes, the Conspirators, the Pardon* (1979), an account of the Watergate trial that includes an autobiographical prologue. Sirica's role as a Watergate judge is the subject of David William Guard, *John Sirica and the Crisis of Watergate, 1972–1975* (Ph.D. thesis, Michigan State Univ., 1995). An obituary is in the *New York Times*, 15 Aug. 1992.

WILLIAM G. ROSS

SIRINGO, Charles Angelo (7 Feb. 1855–18 Oct. 1928), cowboy, detective, and author, was born on Matagorda Peninsula, in Texas, the son of an Italian immigrant (first name unavailable) and Irish-born Bridgit White, farmers. His mother was widowed in 1856, married a drunkard named Carrier in 1868, lived with and then without him in Lebanon, Illinois, and next moved to St. Louis. Siringo had no schooling during the Civil

War years in Texas, became a cowboy at age eleven, ran cattle for an employer named Faldien, worked at odd jobs in Lebanon (1868–1869), and was a bellhop for a year in a St. Louis hotel. After a fight with another employee he made his way to New Orleans, where he was befriended by a childless couple who sent him to school until a near-fatal knife fight, which he won, caused him to decamp for Texas in 1871.

An adventurous life followed. Siringo was a cowboy for Abel H. "Shanghai" Pierce (1871), a Texas rancher, trailing stray cattle, rounding up mavericks, and branding them for Pierce's Rancho Grande, in Wharton County. When Shanghai and his brother Jonathan sold to Allen, Pool, and Company, Siringo worked for that firm until he was caught starting his own illegal herd with strays that were technically his bosses' property. He signed on at W. B. Grimes's ranch in Matagorda County, Texas, where he handled scattered horse herds. He skinned frozen cattle with a neighbor (1873–1874), was hired by the Muckleroy brothers to drive cattle up the Chisholm Trail to Kansas in 1874, and carried passengers and food inland by wagon from the port of Indianola, Texas. That failing, he hit the Chisholm Trail again for Grimes in 1876 and 1877. Soon after the Lincoln County War, in New Mexico (1878), Siringo met Billy the Kid in the Texas Panhandle. Siringo cofounded and worked for the LX Ranch in the Panhandle until 1883. That year he married Mamie Lloyd in Caldwell, Kansas, bought a store there, and sold cigars, ice cream, and oysters.

Siringo wrote the first autobiography by a cowboy ever published, *A Texas Cow Boy . . .* (1885). In 1886 he became a detective for the Pinkerton's National Detective Agency, in Chicago and on ranges out of a Denver office. During his tenure as a Pinkerton, he had numerous adventures detailed in later books. Four assignments were especially dramatic. First, during the 1886 trial of the eight Haymarket "anarchists" accused of killing seven policemen, Siringo was ordered to spy on their friends and to determine whether their defense attorneys were tampering with the jury. Siringo rationalized by saying that he favored stamping out anarchy; later, however, he wrote that the prosecution had fixed the jury. Second, in 1887 Siringo went to Archuleta County, Colorado, where conflict had broken out between American residents and Mexican sheep ranchers. Siringo joined the Mexicans, learned their plans, and reported them to fraudulently elected white officials. Third, he infiltrated the labor union of silver and lead miners in Coeur d'Alene, Idaho, and reported their plans to the mine owners (1891–1892). At first sympathetic with the miners, he soon concluded that their leaders were anarchists and spied on them effectively. When violence and sabotage led to the arrest of eighteen union leaders, Siringo's testimony helped convict them. Fourth, Siringo performed bodyguard duty in 1906 and 1907 during the trial in Boise, Idaho, of William "Big Bill" Haywood, a Western Federation of Miners official accused of murder. Siringo boasted that following the not-guilty verdict he foiled a plot to kill Clarence Darrow, Haywood's chief counsel. Siringo accepted other dangerous assignments, often under cover, to find missing persons, track bank and train robbers, chase rustlers, and investigate crimes such as arson, kidnapping, and murder.

Siringo's marital career was quite varied. The death of his wife Mamie in 1889 left Siringo with their five-year-old daughter. In 1893 he married Lillie Thomas of Denver; the two had a son in 1896 but separated amiably soon thereafter. (He named his son Lee Roy because that was his own favorite alias.) Siringo married a woman named Grace in 1907 in Oregon (probably in Prineville); she left the "Sunny Slope Ranch," his home in Santa Fe, six months later and divorced him in 1909. In 1913 he married a widow named Ellen Partain of Blessing, Texas; she left the Sunny Slope after only two months and divorced him later the same year.

Just before his third marriage, Siringo resigned from the Pinkertons and began raising cattle, chickens, and pigeons at his ranch. He also freelanced as a detective, once more chasing rustlers, ore thieves, and bank robbers. He was a ranger for the Cattle Sanitary Board of New Mexico, operating out of Carrizozo and pursuing rustlers and horse thieves (1916–1918). He wrote and published *A Cowboy Detective: A True Story of Twenty-Two Years with a World-Famous Detective Agency* (1912), containing thinly veiled details that disturbed Pinkerton attorneys. *Two Evil Isms* (1915), though much shorter, was even more alarming, as is made clear by its subtitle: *Pinkertonism and Anarchism. By a Cowboy Detective Who Knows, as He Spent Twenty-Two Years in the Inner Circle of Pinkerton's National Detective Agency.* In 1919 he published *A Lone Star Cowboy* and *A Song Companion to a Lone Star Cowboy* and followed these works a year later with his *History of "Billy the Kid."* In 1922, ill with pleurisy, he moved to California, first living in San Diego with his married daughter, then in Los Angeles, and at last in Hollywood. He was hired to play an old cowboy in a western movie in 1924. A year later he met the famous western actor William S. Hart, who hired him as a consultant for *Tumbleweeds*, perhaps Hart's best film. Siringo's last publication was *Riata and Spurs* (1927), in which he partly combined reworked material from earlier books. He died in Hollywood.

Of Siringo's seven books, the three most important are *A Texas Cow Boy, Two Evil Isms*, and *History of "Billy the Kid."* In thirty rollicking chapters, the 1885 version of *A Texas Cow Boy* discusses Siringo's boyhood; his early cowpunching; his labors in Texas and along the Chisholm Trail; his pursuit of thieves; his weeks among Comanche, Pawnee, and Cheyenne Indians; the exploits of Billy the Kid; a "love scrape" with a Mexican teenager; and the beginnings of his life as a merchant. Siringo begins his book with disarming candor: "My excuse for writing this book is money—and lots of it." The narrative that follows is straightforward, simple, and mostly factual; Siringo comes across as alternately callow, boastful, and cunning, and seemingly as unaware of his own obvious courage as he is of the historical value of his report. For a revised edition the next year, he included a vivid addendum detailing cattle-business risks and profits. *A Texas Cow Boy*, often reprinted, sold hundreds of thousands of copies.

Two Evil Isms was more daring than *A Cowboy Detective* because it braved the wrath of the Pinkerton Detective Agency, as his *Cowboy Detective* had not. Whereas Siringo had disguised, albeit thinly, the names of the agency and certain of its more infamous personnel in the earlier work, he identified them in *Two Evil Isms*. Siringo also revised the account of his undercover spying against the striking miners in Coeur d'Alene to show sympathy to the men he had previously called homicidal anarchists. He even detailed the Pinkerton practices of corrupting policemen and politicians, kidnapping would-be witnesses, bribing juries, and ordering murders. The well-financed Pinkerton Agency easily persuaded a judge to prepare an injunction on the grounds that Siringo was violating his signed contract pledging not to reveal agency secrets and was actually jeopardizing agency efficiency. The court seized all available copies of *Two Evil Isms* and delivered them to the agency for destruction. As a result, the first edition is a collector's item.

History of "Billy the Kid," though partly based on the prejudiced account published in 1882 by Billy's killer, Pat Garrett, is highly readable and retains some historical value. Siringo led a crew in pursuit of Billy for stealing cattle in the Panhandle (1880) and sent trackers from his own crew to help Garrett, but he still sympathized with Billy to a degree since both shared similar backgrounds. Siringo was such a popular author that his account of Billy helped spread and color the notorious gunman's legend.

Charles Siringo is now regarded as a usually authentic source of information on one of the most colorful periods in western American history—especially with respect to the daily lives of cowboys, miners, and criminals, and their pursuers.

• Siringo's papers, preserved by his son, were burned by renters of the Siringo house in Altadena, Calif., in 1935 or soon thereafter. Early biographical studies are Charles D. Peavey, *Charles A. Siringo: A Texas Picaro* (1967), and Orlan Sawey, *Charles A. Siringo* (1981). More exhaustively researched is Ben E. Pingenot, *Siringo* (1989), which includes a thorough primary and secondary bibliography. James D. Horan, *Desperate Men: Revelations from the Sealed Pinkerton Files* (1949; rev. and enl. ed., 1962), contains an absorbing narrative of Siringo's work in tracking train robbers. Robert Wayne Smith, *The Coeur d'Alene Mining War of 1892: A Case Study of an Industrial Dispute* (1961), portrays Siringo as a treacherous spy. Douglas Branch, *The Cowboy and His Interpreters* (1926), places Siringo's writings in the field of cowboy literature. Eugene Manlove Rhodes, "He'll Make a Hand!" *Sunset Magazine*, June 1927, pp. 23, 89–91, by a fellow cowboy-writer, includes an interview with Siringo and a summary of his legendary feats. Ramon F. Adams not only in his *A Fitting Death for Billy the Kid* (1960) but also in his *Burrs under the Saddle: A Second Look at Books and Histories of the West* (1964) identifies errors in Siringo's account of Billy. Obituaries are in the *Fort Worth Star-Telegram*, 20 Oct. 1928, and the *Houston Post-Dispatch*, 21 Oct. 1928.

ROBERT L. GALE

SISLER, George Harold (24 Mar. 1893–26 Mar. 1973), baseball player and manager, was born in Manchester, Ohio, the son of Cassius Sisler and Mary Whipple. Both parents were athletes. Sisler's athletic prowess was apparent early, and in high school he was a successful pitcher. Without his parents' approval, he signed a contract with the Akron Champs of the Ohio-Pennsylvania League, a farm club of the Columbus Senators of the American Association. Then, however, he chose to go into college ball, without having played for Akron or having accepted money from the contract. After refusing baseball scholarships from the University of Pennsylvania and Western Reserve, he attended the University of Michigan, where he reputedly won 50 games and lost none.

Michigan's manager was the former major league catcher Branch Rickey; when Rickey became a scout with the St. Louis Browns of the American League, he recommended Sisler to owner Robert Hedges. After graduating with a bachelor's degree in mechanical engineering, Sisler signed with St. Louis. But Barney Dreyfus of the Pittsburgh Pirates purchased his early contract from Columbus and claimed him. The National Commission decided the controversy in favor of the Browns. Dreyfus never forgave Cincinnati Reds president Garry Herrmann, who chaired the commission.

Sisler compiled an inclusive 5–6 won-lost record with St. Louis in 1915–1916, including 2–1 and 1–0 victories over the Washington Senators' Walter Johnson. But management soon realized that Sisler, a great hitter, would be more valuable as an everyday player. The Browns had suffered a glaring weakness at first base since sending Tommy Jones to the Detroit Tigers in 1909. Although struggling initially, Sisler showed the raw talent and physical dexterity that enabled him to set the standard for grace and poise at his position.

The addition of other stars, including Ken Williams, "Baby Doll" Jacobson, Johnny Tobin, and Urban Shocker, enabled the Browns to become legitimate American League pennant contenders. In 1920 Sisler batted .407 and registered 257 hits, a long-standing major league record. In 1922 the Browns battled the Yankees to the last weekend, falling a game short of the franchise's first pennant. Although injured down the stretch, Sisler enjoyed an extraordinary year, hitting .420 and compiling a 41-game hitting streak, a record at the time. His 18 doubles and his 134 runs scored, as well as his 51 stolen bases, 246 hits, and .420 average, all led the American League that season. He won the league's most valuable player award.

Sisler missed the following season because of severe sinusitis that perilously affected his eyesight. When he returned in 1924, he reluctantly agreed to manage the club and still play first base. His $25,000 salary was the highest ever paid a Browns player up to that time. In 1926 the Browns fell to seventh place. Sisler hit only .290, his lowest mark since 1915. He resigned as manager with a composite 218–241 mark (.475) but continued to play first base.

The Browns sold Sisler to the Washington Senators of the American League in December 1927 for $25,000. The Senators shipped him the next May to the Boston Braves of the National League, where he played from 1928 to 1930. Sisler finished his career with a .340 lifetime batting mark, sharing fifteenth place with Lou Gehrig on the all-time list. He later signed with his mentor Branch Rickey as a scout and batting instructor for the Brooklyn Dodgers in 1943 and from 1946 to 1950, and followed Rickey, ironically, to the Pittsburgh Pirates from 1951 to 1966.

Sisler neither drank nor smoked. After seeing him play at Boston's Fenway Park during Prohibition, comedian W. C. Fields, who had no aversion to alcohol, invited Sisler to his dressing room after his show. When Sisler refused his offer of a drink, the bulbous-nosed humorist quipped, "Oh well, not even the perfect ballplayer can have everything!"

In 1915 he married his college sweetheart, Kathleen Holznagle. They had four children; all three of their sons were connected with professional baseball. Dick Sisler and Dave Sisler played in the major leagues; George Sisler, Jr., served as the general manager of the Rochester Red Wings of the International League and later became league president.

In 1939 George Sisler was inducted into the National Baseball Hall of Fame, along with other legendary greats Babe Ruth, Connie Mack, Walter Johnson, and Ty Cobb. The St. Louis Browns Historical Society made him the first inductee into its Hall of Fame in 1985. He died in Richmond Heights, a suburb of St. Louis, Missouri.

• The National Baseball Hall of Fame Library, Cooperstown, N.Y., has a file on Sisler. For biographical profiles, see David L. Porter, ed., *Biographical Dictionary of American Sports: Baseball* (1987); Bill Borst, *Ables to Zoldak*, vol. 3 (1991); Bob Broeg, *Super Stars of Baseball* (1971); John P. Carmichael, *My Greatest Day in Baseball* (1951); Paul Greenwell, "The 1922 Browns-Yankees Pennant Race," *Baseball Research Journal* 6 (1977): 68–73; Gene Karst and Martin Jones, *Who's Who in Professional Baseball* (1973); Ronald Liebman, "George Sisler the Pitcher," *Baseball Research Journal* 8 (1979): 94–98; Lowell Reidenbaugh, *Cooperstown: Where Baseball's Legends Live Forever* (1983); Ira L. Smith, *Baseball's Famous First Basemen* (1956); and Mike Shatzkin, ed., *The Ball Players* (1990). An obituary is in the *New York Times*, 27 Mar. 1973.

WILLIAM A. BORST

SISSLE, Noble (10 July 1889–17 Dec. 1975), popular songwriter and bandleader, was born Noble Lee Sissle in Indianapolis, Indiana, the son of George Andrew Sissle, a Methodist minister, and Martha Angeline Scott, a public school teacher and juvenile probation officer. Sissle was a boy soprano in church and school choirs, and from 1906, after the family moved to Cleveland, he was the tenor soloist in the Central High School glee club. He began singing professionally in 1908 with the Edward Thomas Male Quartet, which performed on the Chataqua circuit. Having interrupted his schooling for various work, he graduated at the age of twenty-one in 1911. After touring with Hann's Jubilee Singers, he briefly rejoined his family to move back to Indianapolis after his father's death in 1913. He spent one semester at De Pauw University in Greencastle, Indiana, before transferring to Butler University in Indianapolis in January 1914. Concurrently he worked as a singer and dancer and in 1915 formed his first orchestra.

Quitting the university, Sissle initiated a songwriting partnership with pianist Eubie Blake in May 1915 in Baltimore. Their first song, "It's All Your Fault," with Sissle and Eddie Nelson supplying lyrics in collaboration with Blake's music, was premiered by Sophie Tucker. From 1915 to 1916 he sang with society dance bands under Bob Young and James Reese Europe and then worked in a duo with Blake. After rejoining Europe in New York in September 1916, Sissle became a drum major in Europe's 369th U.S. Infantry band, which toured France in 1918. Having achieved the rank of lieutenant, he returned to the United States early the next year, recorded "Jazzola" as vocalist with the Europe group, and remained with the band until Europe was murdered in May 1919.

Sissle then began working in vaudeville with Blake, touring for three years on the prestigious Keith circuit as the Dixie Duo. In this setting they refused to act as ragged, ignorant Negroes in blackface and instead appeared as they really were: elegant, witty sophisticates; but they still had to tolerate the many aspects of racism built into the vaudeville life. Sissle married the widow Harriett Toye (maiden name unknown) in 1919 or 1920.

In collaboration with the comedy team of (Flournoy E.) Miller and (Aubrey) Lyles, Sissle and Blake wrote the musical comedy *Shuffle Along*, which opened at the Sixty-third Street Theatre in New York on 23 May 1921. In its run of 504 performances *Shuffle Along* offered opportunities for the young Josephine Baker, Paul Robeson, and Florence Mills, it helped popularize jazz dancing, and it introduced the songs "Love Will Find a Way" and "I'm Just Wild about Harry." Sissle and Blake were admitted to the American Society of Composers, Authors and Publishers (ASCAP) in 1922, and royalties from "I'm Just Wild about Harry" alone would provide the two men with a secure income for the rest of their lives. From summer 1922 through 1923 *Shuffle Along* toured nationally with three companies working concurrently. Independent of *Shuffle Along*, Sissle and Blake coauthored the hit song "You Were Meant for Me" for Noël Coward and Gertrude Lawrence's show, *London Calling*, in 1923.

Sissle and Blake's second show, *In Bamville*, opened in Rochester, New York, in March 1924 and, renamed *The Chocolate Dandies*, in New York City on 1 September 1924. At some point during this year, reed player Sidney Bechet and trumpeter Joe Smith performed in the show. *Chocolate Dandies* was well received, but it lost money because of the extravagance of the production, and the show closed in May 1925.

Sissle and Blake returned to American vaudeville for a few months and then in September 1925 sailed with their wives to Europe to spend eight months as a vaudeville duo, performing mainly in London but also touring as far as Dublin before they returned home via Paris. Sissle alone went to Paris in summer 1927 to attend an American Legion Convention, and that fall he performed in England in a duo with composer and pianist Harry Revel serving in Blake's stead. During a stand-in in June 1928 at Les Ambassadeurs club in Paris as the intermission act for Fred Waring's Pennsylvanians, Waring declined to extend his contract, and Sissle was suddenly made a bandleader, beginning 5 July 1928. He wired back home for musicians, including alto saxophonist Otto Hardwick, and he hired Bechet and trumpeter Johnny Dunn, who were already in Paris. Of this period, John Chilton writes, "Sissle adopted a style of leadership—blending traits of a sternish uncle, a jovial headmaster and a conscientious sergeant major—that was to remain constant throughout his career. . . . He always kept a close watch on business matters and on the behavior of his musicians . . . those who worked with him for any length of time regarded him with affection" (pp. 80–81).

In September 1928 the vaudeville duo was reactivated, initially with Revel in Britain and Ireland and then with Sam Ross late in 1928 and Barrie Mills in early 1929. During a brief return to New York in March and April 1929, Sissle organized a new band for the upcoming season at Les Ambassadeurs. Among the band members for the first few weeks at Les Ambassadeurs in May was trumpeter Bubber Miley, then in the decline of his career after having left Duke Ellington.

Clarinetist Buster Bailey, violinist Juice Wilson, and trumpeters Arthur Briggs and Tommy Ladnier were among Sissle's sidemen during further residencies in Europe, extending to 1 December 1930. At an engagement at Ciro's in London during this month, one of Sissle's fans, the prince of Wales (the future King Edward VIII) reportedly sat in on drums. After returning to New York later that month, Briggs and Ladnier were joined by Bechet for Sissle's debut at the Rockland Palace on 24 December.

Bechet, in what was evidently the most stable and happy affiliation of his career, served as Sissle's featured instrumentalist throughout the 1930s. The orchestra held residencies in major American cities and once again at Les Ambassadeurs (May to June 1931). It began recording—although the recordings are of little significance beyond the contributions of Sissle's jazz soloists, particularly Bechet—and that same year it broadcast nationally on the CBS radio network during the first of several residencies at the Park Central Hotel in New York.

In 1932 Sissle was reunited with Blake and Miller—Lyles having died that year—to write *Shuffle Along of 1933*. While touring, the show failed in Los Angeles, stranding, among others, pianist Nat (not yet "King") Cole. Sissle reorganized his orchestra and returned to the Park Central Hotel in 1933. After an engagement at the Lafayette Theater in May 1934, Sissle held a residency for six months at the French Casino in Chica-

go, with Billy Banks and Lavaida Carter added to the group as singers. After performing in New York at the Casino Theater beginning 25 December 1934 and then at the Supper Club of the Ziegfeld Theater, Sissle's group toured extensively from 1935 to 1938. The young Lena Horne replaced Carter and soon thereafter served as singer and conductor for performances in Cincinnati in June 1935, when Sissle and Banks were in an auto accident in which Sissle's skull was fractured. Less than two months later, at the Ritz-Carlton ballroom in Boston, Sissle resumed his position as conductor.

From December 1938, shortly after Bechet left the band, through May 1942, Sissle worked at Billy Rose's Diamond Horseshoe in New York City. During this period he married Ethel Harrison and they had two children; details of his previous divorce are unknown. Disbanding, Sissle then performed in theatrical tours in support of the war effort, including a United Service Organizations tour to Italy in 1945, during which he offered an updated version of *Shuffle Along*. He reorganized an orchestra and returned to the Diamond Horseshoe from 1945 till about 1950.

Sissle helped to create a Negro Actors' Guild and was elected its first president. He also was elected to the honorary post of mayor of Harlem in 1950. In the meantime, Harry Truman's dramatic election to the presidency had spurred a revival of "I'm Just Wild about Harry," which was used as a campaign song, and as a consequence Sissle and Blake were somewhat rediscovered. Yet another updated *Shuffle Along* followed in 1952, this time with the producers (not Sissle and Blake) having rewritten the show so badly that it failed immediately. During rehearsals Sissle was injured in a fall into the orchestra pit, and this caused some permanent discomfort. In the last decades of his life, Sissle concentrated on managing his music publishing company. He also ran a nightclub and occasionally performed as a bandleader and entertainer until 1963. In 1975, five years after moving to Tampa, Florida, he died in his home there.

Sissle was only of minor importance for his involvement in jazz. His significance rather was in opening up new chapters in the history of African Americans in vaudeville performance, songwriting, and musical theater, especially in his pioneering role as coauthor of the Broadway show *Shuffle Along*.

• The principal source, *Reminiscing with Sissle and Blake* (1973), is by Robert Kimball and William Bolcom, who annotate a magnificent collection of photos, handbills, and clippings, and also provide extensive details of compositions and recordings. See also Buddy Howard, "Noble Sissle International Star," *Down Beat*, 1 Oct. 1942, p. 21; John R. T. Davies, "Eubie Blake: His Life and Times, Part 2: Blake and Noble Sissle," *Storyville* 2 (Oct.–Nov. 1966): 12–13, 27; Gene Fernett, *Swing Out: Great Negro Jazz Bands* (1970), pp. 45–48; Albert McCarthy, *Big Band Jazz* (1974), p. 296; Peter Carr, "Travellin' Man: The Story of Demas Dean," *Storyville* 72 (Aug.–Sept. 1977): 207–25; Howard Rye, "Visiting Firemen, 7: Eubie Blake & Noble Sissle," *Storyville* 105

(Feb.–Mar. 1983): 89–95; and John Chilton, *Sidney Bechet: The Wizard of Jazz* (1987). An obituary is in the *New York Times*, 18 Dec. 1975.

BARRY KERNFELD

SISSON, Jack (1743?–1821), soldier, was also known as Tack Sisson, Guy Watson, or Prince. He was one of those African-American patriots whose lives were allowed by their contemporaries to become shrouded in obscurity. Little record exists of his whereabouts, activities, or circumstances before or after the exploit for which he is noted—the July 1777 abduction of Brigadier General Richard Prescott, commander of the redcoat garrison at Newport, Rhode Island. Sisson was among the forty volunteers Lieutenant Colonel William Barton raised from his regiment with the intention of seizing a British officer of sufficient rank that he might be exchanged for the captured American general Charles Lee. Some accounts suggest Sisson was Barton's servant. Sisson steered one of the whaleboats that made their way with muffled oars from Tiverton, Rhode Island, toward Prescott's lodgings at the Overing House near Newport. Escaping the attention of British ships, the force landed on the night of 9–10 July and overpowered a sentry outside Prescott's quarters. Finding the door to the British general's room locked, the short but powerfully built Sisson, it was said, butted it twice with his head, breaking open a panel and allowing the latch to be lifted from the inside. Prescott, dressed in not much more than his nightshirt, was spirited away without anyone being killed or even a shot fired. His capture led eventually to the release of General Lee.

The American press celebrated the exploit, one of the solitary bits of good news that patriots received in those dismal months. A ballad circulated at the time placed Sisson at the center of events, though it did not accord him the respect his contribution merited or even call him by his proper name:

> A tawney son of Afric's race
> Them through the ravine led,
> And entering then the Overing house,
> They found him in his bed
>
> But to get in they had no means
> Except poor Cuffee's head,
> Who beat the door down, then rushed in
> And seized him in his bed.
>
> Stop, let me put my breeches on,
> The general then did pray.
> Your breeches, massa, I will take,
> For dress we cannot stay.
> (Kaplan, p. 58)

It is unclear to what extent the emphasis on Sisson's use of his skull as a battering ram partook of a longstanding penchant among many white Americans for making lame jests about the imagined hardness of black people's heads.

In the wake of Prescott's capture, Barton was promoted to colonel, while Sisson enlisted in the Rhode Island First Regiment, which recruited approximately 200 black soldiers, both slave and free. What Sisson did after the war is unclear, but he reportedly celebrated holidays by appearing on parade grounds in his old uniform. Some sources describe him as unhappy that his role in the capture of Prescott was not better known. On 3 November 1821 the *Providence Gazette* reported the death of Sisson, "aged about 78 years," in Plymouth, Massachusetts. Even though he has become an elusive figure, Sisson stands as an emblem of black people's contributions to American freedom through those long decades during which few of them could partake fully of its benefits or could even win from many of their white contemporaries a decent respect for their efforts.

• Sisson is briefly mentioned in Sidney Kaplan and Emma Nogrady Kaplan, *The Black Presence in the Era of the American Revolution*, rev. ed. (1989); Catherine Williams, *Biographies of Revolutionary Heroes* (1839); Benjamin Quarles, *The Negro in the American Revolution* (1961); and Leonard Falkner, "Captor of the Barefoot General," *American Heritage* 11 (Aug. 1960): 29–31, 98–100.

PATRICK G. WILLIAMS

SISTER ANTHONY. *See* Anthony.

SISTER SAINT MARY MAGDALEN. *See* Healy, Eliza.

SITTING BULL (c. 1831–15 Dec. 1890), Sioux chief, was born Tatanka Yotanka, probably on the Grand River in present-day South Dakota, the son of Sitting Bull and Her-Holy-Door. His father bore the name Sitting Bull, which connotes a buffalo bull of great strength and endurance planted solidly on his haunches to fight to the death, until his son became a warrior at age fourteen, at which time he gave his name to the boy and took the name Jumping Bull. His father died in battle with Crow warriors in 1859, but his mother lived with him until her death in 1884.

A member of the Hunkpapa tribe, one of seven tribes of the Teton or Western Sioux, or the Lakota, who inhabited the Plains between the Missouri River and the Bighorn Mountains, Sitting Bull achieved renown in early manhood both as an accomplished buffalo hunter and as a warrior in raids against Crow, Assiniboine, Flathead, and other tribal enemies. His war record brought him many honors as well as high rank in prestigious men's societies, and in 1857 he was designated a war chief of the Hunkpapas.

Sitting Bull also became a holy man, one of a select few who had mastered the sacred powers of the natural world and the ceremonies that influenced human wellbeing. Many times he danced the various orders of the Sun Dance and sacrificed his flesh in token to Wakantanka. Unlike most holy men, whose rites and devotions solicited benefit for individuals, Sitting Bull nearly always sought the welfare of his tribe. By middle age he was widely admired by his people as an exemplar of the four cardinal virtues of the Tetons: bravery, fortitude, generosity, and wisdom.

Sitting Bull had at least five wives throughout his lifetime. The first died in childbirth in the early 1850s. He expelled his second wife, Snow-on-Her, from his lodge in 1865, and his third wife, Red Woman, died about 1870. He married two sisters in 1872, Seen-by-Her-Nation and Four Times. He greatly loved children and had at least nine, including two pairs of twins. In addition, he had two stepsons, an adopted son, and an adopted brother.

In the 1840s and 1850s the Hunkpapas gained material benefit from white culture mainly through barter at the trading post of Fort Pierre on the Missouri River. Traders played a vital role in Sioux life and were not generally viewed as a threat. Sitting Bull even worked for a time for the traders at Fort Berthold. However, with the arrival of government agents, travelers, and especially soldiers to the upper Missouri, conflict developed between whites and Hunkpapas.

Sitting Bull first battled U.S. soldiers during the early 1860s, when shock waves from the Minnesota Sioux uprising of 1862 spilled into the Dakota Territory, and gold seekers followed the Missouri River corridor to the new mines in western Montana. He probably fought the armies of both Generals Henry Hastings Sibley and Alfred Sully in their campaigns of 1863, and he is known to have played a leading part in clashes between Sully and the Tetons in 1864 at Killdeer Mountain and the Badlands. After the army built forts on the upper Missouri, Sitting Bull led a sustained offensive to expel the soldiers from his lands. Besides raids on Forts Rice, Buford, and Totten, he fought against military columns campaigning against the Sioux in Powder River Country in 1865.

These hostilities coincided with a growing division within the Teton tribes as the federal government concluded treaties and established agencies where the Indians could obtain rations and other goods. Gradually one faction became attached to the agencies while the other continued to follow the buffalo herds and shun association with whites. Sitting Bull never signed a treaty, and after the crucial Treaty of 1868, establishing the Great Sioux Reservation, he emerged as the most prominent leader of the nontreaty or hunting bands, usually called "hostiles."

The nontreaty bands, made up of portions of all the Teton tribes, numbered about 3,000 and lived year-round west of the Great Sioux Reservation in the Powder, Tongue, and Yellowstone valleys. About 1869 some members staged a great ceremony in which Sitting Bull was designated head chief of all the nontreaty bands. Although the office had never before existed and was probably not supported by a majority, Sitting Bull's leadership over the next seven years was so effective that he functioned as a head chief de facto if not de jure.

In 1871 Sitting Bull called off the offensive against the army posts on the upper Missouri and thereafter adopted a defensive strategy. Henceforth, the hunting bands would fight only when they were attacked or their territory was invaded. With the support of the Oglala war leader Crazy Horse, in 1872 and 1873 the hunting bands battled military commands escorting workers of the Northern Pacific Railroad, whose route pierced the heart of the buffalo ranges claimed by the hunting bands.

These Sioux did not oppose the expedition of 1874 headed by Lieutenant Colonel George A. Custer that penetrated the Black Hills, indisputably part of the Great Sioux Reservation, and discovered gold. The ensuing gold rush, however, led to a severe political problem for the government. Efforts to persuade the agency chiefs to cede the Black Hills were thwarted by Sitting Bull and his followers. To counter this influence, the government ordered the "hostiles" to abandon the chase and settle on the reservation, resulting in the Sioux War of 1876.

U.S. military strategy featured three offensive columns converging on the Yellowstone country. The Indians did not foresee war until soldiers attacked a village on the Powder River in March. Thereafter, under Sitting Bull's leadership, the scattered camps coalesced for self-defense and were joined by many comrades from the agencies. Sitting Bull fought at the battle of the Rosebud against General George Crook's forces on 17 June 1876 and in the battle of the Little Bighorn on 25 June, in which his warriors wiped out Custer and five companies of his regiment. Sitting Bull would be seen by whites everywhere as the mastermind who trapped Custer and inflicted the memorable disaster. However, Indians did not fight as disciplined units under the command of a particular chief, and, as a senior chief, Sitting Bull actually fought only in the opening phases, when the women and children were directly threatened.

The Little Bighorn so shocked Americans that heavy reinforcements poured into the war theater. Sitting Bull fought at Slim Buttes on 9 September, then spent the winter trying to elude the columns of Colonel Nelson A. Miles. Finally, in April 1877, he led a small following across the boundary into Canada, where the refugee bands ultimately numbered more than 2,000. He got along well with the North-West Mounted Police. Diminishing buffalo, however, caused defections and finally left him isolated with only a handful of starving followers. He surrendered to the U.S. Army at Fort Buford, Dakota Territory, on 20 July 1881.

After nearly two years as a prisoner of war at Fort Randall, Sitting Bull and his small band settled at the Standing Rock agency. Here he tried to take up the life of a farmer while also resisting the "civilization" programs of the government, and in 1888–1889 he opposed the cession of parts of the Great Sioux Reservation to the United States. He and the equally strong-minded agent, James McLaughlin, feuded for seven years. For one season during this time Sitting Bull traveled with Buffalo Bill's "Wild West" in Canada and the United States.

In 1890 the Ghost Dance religion swept the Sioux reservations. It prescribed beliefs and rituals intended to renew the earth and expel the whites. Although some observers doubted that Sitting Bull truly believed its tenets, he assumed the role of apostle of the new religion at Standing Rock. After disorders at the other Sioux agencies led the president to send in the army, orders were issued for Sitting Bull's arrest. McLaughlin assigned the task to Indian police, who on 15 December 1890 attempted to make the arrest. The chief's followers resisted, and in the exchange of fire, the police shot and killed Sitting Bull.

Sitting Bull's significance lies in his role as the leading nontreaty chief who led the Teton tribes in their resistance to white invasion of the northern Plains. Both in offensive and defensive modes, he was highly effective as a military and political leader. He also possessed qualities that made him, in the perception of his people, the ideal Lakota. Today his name symbolizes the Native American's fight for land and freedom.

• There are numerous popular but unreliable biographies of Sitting Bull, mainly drawn from the standard authority of many years, Stanley Vestal [Walter S. Campbell], *Sitting Bull, Champion of the Sioux* (1932; rev. ed., with a foreword by Raymond J. DeMallie, 1989). Campbell's extensive research materials, most importantly interviews with Sitting Bull's relatives and associates, are in the Walter S. Campbell Collection at the University of Oklahoma Library. Drawing heavily on Campbell's research but differing significantly from his biography is Robert M. Utley, *The Lance and the Shield: Sitting Bull and His Times* (1993).

ROBERT M. UTLEY

SITTLER, Joseph Andrew, Jr. (26 Sept. 1904–28 Dec. 1987), Lutheran theologian, was born in Upper Sandusky, Ohio, the son of the Reverend Pastor Joseph A. Sittler and Minnie Vieth. The congregation served by Sittler's father was made up largely of people descended from German immigrants. A German Lutheran ethos, marked by love for hymnody and an accent on preaching, shaped the environment for the future theologian. In 1927 Sittler graduated from the Lutheran church–related Wittenberg University in Springfield, Ohio, and continued in an associated institution, Hamma Divinity School, also in Springfield, where he gained the Bachelor of Divinity degree en route to ordination in 1930. His first charge was Messiah Lutheran Church in Cleveland Heights, Ohio, where he served as minister from 1930 to 1943.

After lecturing part-time at Oberlin College in 1942, Sittler served from 1943 to 1957 as professor of systematic theology at Chicago Lutheran Theological Seminary in Maywood, Illinois. This school was eventually to merge into the Lutheran School of Theology at Chicago, and Sittler ended his career in an active emeritus post there. Thus his teaching career began and ended in the setting of his denomination, while during his middle years he served the interdenominational movement for church unity.

The Federated Theological Faculty, a coalescence of seminaries and divinity schools located at and near the University of Chicago, appointed Sittler to a chair in theology in 1957. When this federation dissolved, he remained to teach at one of its components, the Divinity School of the university, most of whose alumni went on to become college and university teachers. Sittler was thus poised between the worlds of church and academy. Most people in his position made a choice: either to serve as a theologian who interpreted the language of the believing community to the church or as a professor of religious studies who addressed the people in scholarly disciplines of the university without being mindful of the interests of the church. Sittler refused to make such a choice. He took the risk of trying to blend two sets of languages into one theological voice and thus to transcend conventional constraints of discipline and intended audiences. He chose to make a theological issue of his poise and did bridge the communities more successfully than most of his colleagues.

From 1951 to 1966 Sittler was a member of the Faith and Order Commission of the World Council of Churches, then the most prestigious and productive Protestant-Orthodox theological forum. A specialist in the theology of the ecumenical movement, Sittler provoked considerable controversy when he delivered a major address at the Third Assembly of the World Council of Churches at New Delhi in 1961. The Protestant and Eastern Orthodox church leaders there were accustomed to hearing Lutherans focus on the grace of God in Jesus Christ. The scheme of divine revelation and redemption was in that case directed entirely to the salvation of the sinner. Sittler surprised the council members by connecting this rescuing grace of God with the theme of "nature" and "creation." In the code language of Lutheran and ecumenical thought, this meant that he concentrated on the relation of God to ecology, the environment, science, and the cosmos—all legitimate themes in historic Christian thought, but much neglected before 1961. This dual vision of a God who creates and sustains the cosmos and who saves humans in the midst of it (more than from it, as ascetical theologies would have it) characterized Sittler's thought for the rest of his career and made him a pioneer in devotion to environmental theology.

Sittler was an anomaly among academic theologians because he never earned a Doctor of Philosophy degree (though he shared this status with Reinhold Niebuhr, his most-noted contemporary in theology). Given his interest in fusing churchly and academic language and the themes of nature and grace in a time of ever-increasing specialization in theology, he tended to be seen as part maverick, part pioneer, part seer. A highly literate theologian and master rhetorician, he also chose to direct his energies to articulating formal theology for broad publics. This concentration became manifest at a time when preaching was often treated as a merely practical task, not a subject for reflection. Informed by his careful reading of literature, including both the classics and modern writers such as Joseph Conrad, Herman Melville, and Henry Adams, he became an exemplar to two generations of preachers. His literacy especially commended him to campus chaplains and student congregations in North America, to whom he tirelessly gave his energies.

Much of that exemplarity resulted from his itinerancy: he was frequently on the road as lecturer, preacher, and consultant. Not a prolific author, Sittler thus made his influence felt through his rhetoric—he was one of the most eloquent preachers of his day—and by personal influence on ministers who took part in continuing education conferences and retreats that he led. Typical of these occasions was the Lyman Beecher lectureship at Yale, which he filled in 1959. In 1951 Sittler served as president of the American Theological Society.

Sittler did publish a number of brief but notable volumes, beginning with *The Doctrine of the Word in the Structure of Lutheran Theology* (1948). The book created a stir among Lutherans in the United States, because it appeared at a time when several Lutheran bodies were discussing merger. One faction advocated a scholastic view of scriptural authority, accenting its inerrancy. Inerrancy was a favorite theme of fundamentalists in Protestantism and scholastic conservatives in Lutheranism. Its advocates argued that all assertions of fact in the Bible—even of geographical, historical, or scientific character—could not contain "error." The other element, led by people like Sittler, promoted a "dynamic" approach, in which the spoken Word of God was seen as more important than devotion to the text of the printed Bible. In his book, Sittler showed that he had been influenced by twentieth-century Scandinavian and German research into the thought of Martin Luther. Sittler denounced the scholastics and biblical literalists in the interest of this dynamic approach. Sittler's kind of thought came to prevail, and inerrancy was excluded from formulations in the mergers of church bodies that eventually became the Evangelical Lutheran Church in America. Its leaders considered him a pacesetter who helped make the merger possible, however controversial his contributions were at first.

Ten years later Sittler published *The Structure of Christian Ethics* (1958), which applied the dynamic notion of the Word of God to moral action and systems. *The Ecology of Faith* (1961) followed three years later. It was a collection of essays that stressed the location and context of believers in respect to the preacher, the culture, and the natural environment. Devoted to the role of imagination in preaching, this book also showed Sittler criticizing the "maceration of the minister." Sittler became associated with the school of critics who bewailed the waste of energies that resulted when ministers attempted to respond to too many administrative demands. Later Sittler books were collections of sermons, essays, and in *Gravity and Grace* (ed. Linda-Marie Delloff, 1986), short paragraphs, often aphoristic in character.

In 1939 he married Helen Jeanne Seitz, a church composer and organist of some note; they had six children. During years in which Jeanne suffered from a debilitating illness, Sittler, though having lost most of his eyesight and hearing, cared for her lovingly, even while keeping a busy travel and postretirement teaching and consulting schedule, until his own death in Hyde Park, a suburb of Chicago.

The leadership of the successive Lutheran bodies to which he belonged—their names kept changing because of mergers—took pride in Sittler. They found him too controversial during times of delicate merger negotiations and paraded him at ecumenical gatherings and in secular settings more than in the settings of Lutheran church life. He liked to quote Franklin Clark Fry, the influential president of the Lutheran Church in America, as saying, "We use you, but only for export." This "export" use made Sittler far better known than most Lutherans had been; they were just coming out of isolation into the mainstream of Christian thought during Sittler's years. It also made possible the extension of his influence during the period when American Protestants were trying once again to connect, as Sittler did, the classic themes of divine creation of nature and divine redemption of the human.

• The Sittler papers are in the Jesuit-Krauss-McCormick Library at the Lutheran School of Theology at Chicago. In addition to the volumes mentioned in the text, Sittler published *The Anguish of Preaching* (1966), *The Care of the Earth and Other University Sermons* (1964), *Essays on Nature and Grace* (1972), and *Grace Notes and Other Fragments*, ed. Robert Herhold and Linda-Marie Delloff (1981). A bibliography of his writings to 1964 appears in Philip J. Hefner, ed., *The Scope of Grace: Essays on Nature and Grace in Honor of Joseph Sittler* (1964). He was also honored with a special issue of *The Journal of Religion* 54, no. 2 (1974), where more of his themes were developed.

MARTIN E. MARTY

SIX, Robert Forman (25 June 1907–6 Oct. 1986), airline executive, was born in Stockton, California, the son of Clarence Logan Six, a pioneering plastic surgeon, and Genevieve Peters. Six's father wanted him to become a physician; Robert had hoped to attend the U.S. Naval Academy. Six proved an indifferent student, however, and dropped out of St. Mary's High School in Oakland at the end of his sophomore year. Six's parents died within three years of each other while he was still a teenager.

A restless young man, Six spent time as a factory worker, merchant seaman, and bill collector. Inspired by Charles A. Lindbergh's solo transatlantic flight in 1927, Six began to take flying lessons in his spare time. After securing a pilot's license in 1929, he used part of his inheritance to purchase a single-engine Travelair biplane. Under the name of Valley Flying Service, Six flew charter and scenic flights in the San Francisco Bay area until the depression brought the business to an end.

Six spent nearly three years abroad, traveling in China, Spain, and France. Returning to the United States, he became a delivery truck driver for the *San Francisco Chronicle*. In August 1934 he married Henriette Erhart Ruggles, daughter of William H. Erhart, chairman of the board of Charles Pfizer & Company, a leading pharmaceutical firm. They had no children.

The aviation business continued to attract Six. In 1935 he joined with a friend, Monty Mouton, to form a distributing company for Beechcraft airplanes on the West Coast. The following year he persuaded his father-in-law to spend $90,000 for a 40 percent interest in Varney Air Transport. Erhart gave Six the voting rights to his stock.

Owned by Louis H. Mueller, Varney Air Transport held a government contract to fly the mail between El Paso, Texas, and Pueblo, Colorado (later extended to Denver). In 1936 Six went to work for the tiny company, which he renamed—somewhat grandiloquently—Continental Air Lines on 1 July 1937. The following February he became president of Continental, which operated six small airplanes over 624 route-miles.

Continental made only slow progress in the years before the United States entered World War II. In September 1942, Six joined the U.S. Army Air Force as a captain. He spent two years with the Air Transport Command and saw service in the Pacific. Rising to the rank of lieutenant colonel, he received a medical discharge in 1944 after suffering a minor cerebral hemorrhage.

Continental remained a regional air carrier following the end of the war. The Civil Aeronautics Board (CAB), which tightly controlled the nation's airline route structure, favored the larger carriers in awarding new routes. A frustrated Six could only focus on enhancing Continental's efficiency and profitability while waiting for the CAB to give the smaller airlines the opportunity to expand.

Six's marriage ended in divorce in 1952. The following year he married Ethel Merman, a star of Broadway musicals. This union lasted until 1960. Again divorced, Six married Audrey Meadows, a prominent television actress, in August 1961.

The turning point in Continental's history came in 1955 when the CAB granted it authority to fly from Chicago to Los Angeles via Kansas City and Denver. Six seized the opportunity and borrowed $64 million to purchase new aircraft. At a time when the airline had a net worth of only $5.5 million, Six had bet the airline's future on his ability to generate traffic to pay off the large debt. "We could easily have gone broke," he later admitted.

Through a combination of marketing innovations that emphasized service and stringent cost-control measures, Continental prospered. By 1963 the airline served thirty-six cities on a 7,000-mile route through nine states. It boasted the lowest jet operating costs in the industry. With an industry-high daily aircraft utilization of thirteen hours, Continental could make a profit by filling 42 percent of its passenger seats when other airlines needed over 50 percent.

"A tall hulking man of 55," a *New York Times* profile described Six in 1963, "a disarming combination of derring-do and cafe society, he is a blunt, tough airline executive." A connoisseur of fine wines and collector of modern French paintings, Six also enjoyed playing musical chairs on horseback and practicing fast draws with a six-gun. His consuming passion, however, was his airline. "You saw him everywhere," an associate once commented, "in the tire shop, in the hostess division." No aspect of the airline's operation escaped his attention, from selection of aircraft to the shade of paint on ramp equipment.

Six also was ambitious. Having made the transition from a regional to a national airline, Continental reached out to Asia in the 1960s. In 1964 Six signed what proved to be a lucrative contract with the U.S. Air Force's Military Airlift Command for charter service to Southeast Asia. The following year he formed a subsidiary in Laos—Continental Air Services—that carried cargo and personnel for the U.S. Agency for International Development and other government departments. In 1967 Six secured a five-year agreement to provide air service for the Trust Territories of the Pacific Islands. President Richard M. Nixon thwarted Six's plans for commercial routes across the Pacific when he overturned a decision by President Lyndon B. Johnson in favor of Continental, which Nixon considered to be politically inspired. But the airline did receive authority to fly to Hawaii in 1969.

Six's Pacific dreams became reality in the 1970s when Continental secured routes to Taiwan, Australia, and New Zealand. At the same time passage of the Airline Deregulation Act in October 1978 created a new competitive environment in which Continental fared poorly. No longer the cost-efficient leader it was in the 1960s, Continental now had the highest-paid aircrews in the industry. Following a series of heavy financial losses, Continental was taken over by Frank A. Lorenzo's Texas Air Corporation in July 1982. Although Lorenzo retained the Continental name, little else remained the same.

Six never officially retired, although he gave up the presidency of the airline in 1976. No doubt the fate of Continental troubled him deeply in his final years. He died in Beverly Hills, California.

• Six delivered a Newcomen Society lecture on the early years of his airline, which was published as a pamphlet: *Continental Airlines: A Story of Growth* (1959). Robert J. Serling, *Maverick: The Story of Robert Six and Continental Airlines* (1974), is an informative if uncritical (and premature) biography. A more balanced treatment of the man and his airline can be found in R. E. G. Davies, *Rebels and Reformers of the Airways* (1987) and *Continental Airlines: The First Fifty Years, 1934–1984* (1985). Michael Murphy, *The Airline That Pride Almost Bought* (1986), deals with the collapse of Six's dream. An obituary is in the *New York Times*, 7 Oct. 1986.

WILLIAM M. LEARY

SIZER, Nelson (21 May 1812–18 Oct. 1897), phrenologist, was born in Chester, Massachusetts, the son of Fletcher Sizer, a mechanic, and Lydia Bassett. At fourteen he worked in a woolen mill, becoming its manager three years later. Subsequently he was a carpenter and then partner in a paper mill, and he also contributed articles to the local press. In 1832, when Johann Gaspar Spurzheim lectured on phrenology in

Boston, Sizer was deeply impressed with the new so-called science of mind. In 1833 he married Lucinda Maria Phelps, with whom he had two children. She died in 1839, and in that year he abandoned paper manufacturing to devote himself to phrenology.

A visit in 1839 to Orson Fowler's phrenological office in Philadelphia intensified Sizer's interest. He believed that the Fowler firm's *American Phrenological Journal* was "the organ of a great cause," and as Fowler agent he solicited subscribers for the periodical. Sizer enthusiastically accepted the tenets of phrenology: since the brain was the organ of the mind and shaped the skull, there was an observable concomitance between the mind—talents, character, and temperament—and the shape of the head; consequently, an examination of the head would reveal the nature of the mind. A phrenological examination included measurement of the head and tactile study of the areas of the skull occupied by the various organs or faculties (for example, amativeness, ideality, acquisitiveness, combativeness). The organs were sized from one (very small) to seven (very large), and the subject's nature was thus ascertained with seemingly scientific exactitude.

In 1841 Sizer, joined with phrenologist Phineas Lyman Buell, lectured on phrenology and making character analyses in the field. In 1843, on the basis of phrenological selection, he married a widow, Sarah Hale Remington, with whom he had one child. Sizer continued on his own as a phrenological examiner until 1849 when he joined the staff of Fowlers and Wells in New York as resident phrenological examiner.

Sizer was a perceptive character analyst, observing that "some men's minds are like great broad-axes; not very sharp, but they have a tremendous amount of power and breadth; another mind is like the lynx,—pointed & keen." The temperance reformer Frances E. Willard described his vocabulary as "boundless, its pictorial quality exhaustless, and his anecdotes many and apt." Among his earliest subjects was Horace Mann. In 1858 he examined John Brown (1800–1859) of Osawatomie. Others who sat for his phrenological readings included New York governor Samuel J. Tilden, sculptor Harriet Hosmer, editors Cyrus Curtis and Edward Bok, and poet Ella Wheeler Wilcox. Estimates indicate that by the mid-1890s Sizer performed between 200,000 and 300,000 professional examinations, some of which were recorded by an attendant shorthand reporter.

In 1849 the American Phrenological Society was established, and Sizer delivered the first lecture, the "History, Progress, and Prospects of Phrenology." Between 1854 and 1856 he served as supervisor of a branch office established by the Fowler firm in Philadelphia, where examinations were made, books were sold, and evening classes in practical phrenology were taught. Sizer resumed his work in the New York office in 1856, writing for and, with firm member Samuel R. Wells, editing the *Phrenological Journal*, managing lectures, and making examinations. When the firm heads

toured the United States and Canada in 1858, the office was placed in Sizer's charge.

Sizer was active in the American Institute of Phrenology, founded in April 1866 to promote phrenological science, collect casts and busts, and teach phrenology. After the death of Samuel Wells in 1875 Sizer was in charge of the phrenological cabinet besides continuing as chief examiner. The Fowler and Wells Company was incorporated in February 1884 with Sizer as vice president. Three years later the firm launched a quarterly series, the Human Nature Library, concerned with the study of body and mind and edited by Sizer and *Phrenological Journal* editor Henry S. Drayton. For this Sizer contributed the first number, *Self-Reliance*.

For nearly a half-century, until his death in Brooklyn, Sizer was a member of the best-known phrenological firm in the United States, serving for much of that time as its chief examiner. His numerous analyses, articulated in salty language and anecdotal style, helped popularize phrenology and promote the causes it espoused, especially vocational guidance and marriage counseling. He related the pseudoscience successfully to the life of the times and helped shape it into a practical instrument for analyzing human behavior.

• Sizer letters are in the Fowler Family Papers in the Collection of Regional History in Cornell University Library and in the John Brown Papers in the Ohio Historical Society. His analysis of Moncure Daniel Conway is preserved in Special Collections, Columbia University Library, and his analysis of S. M. Blackstock is in the Manuscript Division of Syracuse University Library. Sizer's publications include *How to Teach According to Temperament and Mental Development* (1877); the autobiographical *Forty Years in Phrenology* (1882); *The Royal Road to Wealth* (1882); *Heads and Faces and How to Study Them* (1885), with Henry S. Drayton; *The Value of Phrenology* (1894); and *How to Study Strangers by Temperament, Face, and Head* (1895), a sequel to *Heads and Faces*. Details of Sizer's life and career are found in John D. Davies, *Phrenology Fad and Science: A 19th-Century American Crusade* (1955); Lillian Hubbard Holch, *Sizer Genealogy: A History of Antonio de Zocieur Who Changed His Name to Anthony Sizer* (1941); and Madeleine B. Stern, *Heads and Headlines: The Phrenological Fowlers* (1971). See also Stern, *A Phrenological Dictionary of Nineteenth-Century Americans* (1982). Death notices are in the *New York Daily Tribune* and the *New York Times*, both 19 Oct. 1897.

MADELEINE B. STERN

SKENANDOA (c. 1706–11 Mar. 1816), Oneida war chief, was, according to tradition, of Conestoga (Susquehannock) birth and adopted into the Wolf clan of the Oneida. His parents' names and birthplace are unknown. The birth date assigned for Skenandoa is based on estimates of his age late in his life and may well be inaccurate, possibly too early by a decade or two. In 1760 he led fourteen Oneida warriors as part of the Iroquois forces that accompanied Sir Jeffery Amherst's expedition against the French at Montreal in the final phase of the French and Indian War in North America. His wife's name and marriage date are unknown, but it is known that his wife was a strong

Christian from as early as 1770. His daughter Margaret married the rising Mohawk chief Joseph Brant in 1765. Margaret died in 1771, after bearing two children.

The Connecticut-born missionary Samuel Kirkland came to enjoy tremendous influence among the Oneida in general and with Skenandoa in particular. Kirkland began his labors among the Oneida in 1766. With the outbreak of the American Revolution, Kirkland's influence led the Oneida and a portion of the Tuscarora to actively fight in support of the rebellious colonists.

When other members of the Iroquois Confederacy, principally the Mohawk, Cayuga, and Seneca nations, entered the conflict on the side of the Crown in 1777, Skenandoa provided intelligence to the American garrison at Fort Stanwix (now Rome, N.Y.) of motives and actions of the British and their allies. After American forces under General John Sullivan laid waste to the Seneca and Cayuga towns in 1779, Skenandoa was one of four pro-American emissaries who traveled on snowshoes carrying a message to the Iroquois refugee population at Fort Niagara in February 1780 urging the pro-British Iroquois to withdraw from the conflict. The pro-British Iroquois refused to accept the wampum belts brought by Skenandoa and the other emissaries. British Indian Superintendent Guy Johnson threw the four into Fort Niagara's prison, where one died. Skenandoa and the others were kept in the windowless jail until they agreed to serve the British cause in July 1780. That summer Skenandoa accompanied the expedition of Joseph Brant, which burned the chief Oneida village, including Skenandoa's frame house and the church where Kirkland had preached.

After the American Revolution the Oneida, despite their military record fighting beside the Americans during the war, were subject to the same intense pressure to sell their lands that the pro-British Iroquois experienced. Skenandoa's name appears on many of the land surrenders made to New York State. The Oneida became severely divided, and Skenandoa became a vocal leader of the Christian party. The nature of divisiveness among the Oneida at this time is indicated by the refusal of Skenandoa's children and grandchildren to embrace Christianity despite the fact that Skenandoa and his wife had professed Christianity for decades. Most Oneidas were nominal Christians, but active participation waxed and waned throughout Kirkland's ministry. Teachings of prophets from several Iroquois communities led to a revival of traditional religious practices after 1800. This revival probably did not attract a majority of Oneidas, however. It was not until 1804 that Skenandoa's only surviving son, Thomas Skenandoa, became a Christian.

Recurrent themes in the journals of the missionary Kirkland are Skenandoa's depression over violent conflict among his people and Skenandoa's continual lectures in favor of temperance. In 1799 Kirkland described him as "almost the *soul* of the Village" and "a man of good sense, ready invention & quick wit, not an eloquent speaker, but good Counsellor" (Kirkland, p. 315). In 1806 Kirkland noted "an affectionate address" made by Skenandoa to those assembled for worship. "He is now become nearly blind, & but just able to walk to the Church, with the help of a guide. He spoke like a dying Father to his Children" (Kirkland, p. 416).

Skenandoa lived another ten years, but on his death near Oneida Castle (Oneida, N.Y.) he was buried at his request beside Samuel Kirkland, who died in 1808. The missionary and the convert, whose lives had been intertwined for half a century, lie next to each other in graves on the grounds of Hamilton College in Clinton, New York.

• Only brief biographies of Skenandoa have been published. An essential source is Samuel Kirkland, *The Journals of Samuel Kirkland*, ed. Walter Pilkington (1980). On the Oneida and the revolutionary war, see Barbara Graymont, *The Iroquois in the American Revolution* (1972), and her chapter in Jack Campisi and Laurence M. Hauptman, eds., *The Oneida Indian Experience* (1988).

THOMAS S. ABLER

SKENE, Alexander Johnston Chalmers (17 June 1837–4 July 1900), gynecologist and professor of medicine, was born in Fyvie, Aberdeenshire, Scotland, the son of Johnston Skene and Jean McConachie. He was educated in local schools and then attended King's College in Aberdeen (now part of the university) before emigrating to North America at the age of nineteen. He studied medicine in Toronto, Ontario, Canada, in 1860, and at the University of Michigan in 1861 and 1862; he then went to New York and earned his M.D. degree from the Long Island College Hospital Medical School, Brooklyn, in 1863. Immediately afterward, during the Civil War, Skene served for a year in South Carolina as an assistant surgeon with the Union volunteer corps. He later renewed his military connections when, in 1884 and 1885, he was surgeon on the staff of the commander of the New York State National Guard.

In 1864 Skene began his practice in gynecology and obstetrics in Brooklyn and was appointed an adjunct professor at the Long Island College Hospital Medical School, with which he was connected until his death. In 1872 he became professor of gynecology, and from 1886 to 1893 he served as dean of the faculty; from 1893 to 1900 he was president of the school. Between 1883 and 1886 Skene also taught gynecology at the medical school of New York Post-Graduate Hospital, and over the years he was a consulting physician at several other hospitals. In addition to his own extensive practice, he established a large private sanitarium in Brooklyn in 1884; in the last year of his life, he was planning to open a free hospital, to be known as Skene's Hospital for Self-Supporting Women.

Considered one of the foremost gynecologists of his day, Skene derived his international reputation from his skills as diagnostician and teacher, as well as from his contributions to the medical literature and his innovations. In 1880, for example, he discovered the paraurethral glands now known as Skene's glands, or tubercles; he also devised several surgical procedures and instruments, including (in 1897) a hemostatic forceps. A pioneer in many ways, Skene was at the same time conservative about resorting to hysterectomy or ovariectomy; his diagnoses were based on careful evaluation of the patient's total condition.

Skene's medical writings include *Diseases of the Bladder and Urethra in Women* (1878); the very influential *Treatise on the Diseases of Women, for the Use of Students and Practitioners* (1888, 3d ed., rev., 1898); *Education and Culture as Related to the Health and Disease of Women* (1889); *Medical Gynecology: A Treatise on the Diseases of Women from the Standpoint of the Physician* (1895); and *Electro-Haemostasis in Operative Surgery* (1899). A contributor of many articles to the medical journals, he also served as an editor of the *American Medical Digest* (1884–1889) and of the *New York Gynaecological and Obstetrical Journal* (1891–1900).

Skene also found time to write a novel, *True to Themselves: A Psychological Study* (1897). Another avocation, to which he enthusiastically devoted himself during his few leisure hours, was sculpture; his portrait busts in marble were considered quite able.

Skene played an active role in several medical associations. At his inauguration as president of the Kings County Medical Society (1874–1875), he gave an address on "The Relationship of Medical Societies to Progress in Science." He was a founding member of the American Gynecological Society (president, 1886–1887) and of the International Congress of Gynecology and Obstetrics in Geneva (honorary president, 1896). He belonged to the New York Obstetrical Society (president, 1877–1879) and was a corresponding member of medical bodies in Paris, Leipzig, Brussels, Edinburgh, and London.

Skene was married to Annette Wilhelmine Lillian Van der Wegen, a native of Brussels; they had no children of their own but adopted a daughter. Despite a heart condition he continued his rigorous work schedule to the end; he died suddenly at his Catskill Mountains summer home in Highmount, New York.

• Material on Skene and some of his articles are available in the medical library of Long Island College Hospital. The Library of Congress also has a collection of his medical papers. Obituaries are in the *New York Times*, 6 July 1900, and the *Brooklyn Daily Eagle*, 5 and 9 July 1900.

ELEANOR F. WEDGE

SKENE, Philip (9 Jan. 1725–9 June 1810), British officer and Loyalist, was born in London, England, the son of James Skene, a Jacobite, and Mary Anne (maiden name unknown). Raised by an uncle who was a military man, Philip Skene was exposed early in life to the British army. During 1741 he became an ensign and fought in Europe in that decade. He participated in the suppression of the Jacobite invasion of Scotland and was severely wounded at the battle of Culloden (16 Apr. 1746). Afterward, he took part in more European battles and rose to lieutenant in 1750. During January of that year he wed Katharine Heyden. Their marriage would produce three children.

The French and Indian War (1756–1763) brought Skene, who was promoted to captain in 1757, to America and to the more northerly parts of New York. In the unsuccessful British campaign against the French fort of Ticonderoga (July 1758), he was wounded again. When the British occupied Ticonderoga in 1759, Skene, displaying great personal courage, managed to prevent the explosion of the fort's gunpowder supply, which the French had deliberately sabotaged. His courage brought him the rank of major. He then participated in the successful British invasion of Cuba and in 1762 was named provost marshal of Havana.

However, Skene had seemingly lost interest in a military career and eventually, in 1769, sold his army commission. During 1759 he had become desirous of obtaining land in the New York colony at Wood Creek, near Lake Champlain. British general Sir Jeffrey Amherst strongly supported Skene's request, and he started developing the area. When Skene returned to New York in 1763, he brought with him 270 veterans of the Cuban campaign, who wished to settle at Wood Creek as his tenants. In 1765 he received from London some 25,000 acres at the site, which became known as Skenesborough (now Whitehall). The colonial government gave him still more land. By the American Revolution, the Skenes had amassed over 50,000 acres. As a prominent landholder in New York, Philip Skene received positions commensurate with his status. In 1768 he was made a militia colonel, and during 1772 he became a judge in Charlotte County.

Skene sought still another office, the lieutenant governorship of two British posts near his lands, Ticonderoga, and its neighbor on Lake Champlain, Crown Point. To obtain this position (and its £200 salary), he journeyed to Britain during 1774. Successful in his quest in January 1775, he was unfortunate enough to return to America after fighting had begun. In June 1775 his ship docked at Philadelphia and the Continental Congress immediately arrested him. He was sent as a prisoner to Hartford, Connecticut, and remained there until September 1776 when he was exchanged. He soon left British-occupied New York City for England, where he learned of General John Burgoyne's planned invasion in 1777 of northern New York. Skene promptly sailed to Canada to do everything he could to help.

Burgoyne welcomed Skene's assistance, and his advice was taken to heart by the general. Skene reinforced Burgoyne's mistaken belief that most New Yorkers were Loyalists. Skene helped guide the army through northern New York after the British capture of Ticonderoga (6 July 1777). The invading army encamped at Skenesborough for awhile, as that settlement could provide enough forage for the invaders. While at Skenesborough, Burgoyne instructed Skene to warn nearby Vermonters to return to their former allegiance to secure protection from pro-British Indians. On 15 July 1777 several hundred intimidated Vermonters listened to Skene and accepted the offer.

Burgoyne found another task for Skene. He was to accompany Lieutenant Colonel Friedrich Baum on a foray to Bennington, Vermont, and recruit Loyalists along the way. Skene took seriously everyone who claimed to be a Loyalist, but some of these supposed Tories were merely seeking information for the patriots. When, on 16 August 1777 Baum's men were attacked by patriot soldiers, Skene fought bravely. He managed to elude capture after this disastrous British defeat and rejoined Burgoyne's army.

When Burgoyne surrendered in October 1777, Skene became a patriot prisoner again. As he was never exchanged, he could not take any further actions against the revolutionaries. He returned to Britain during 1778. In 1779 Skene and his son, Andrew Philip Skene, were attainted by New York State and lost their extensive landholdings.

In 1784 Philip Skene tried to trick the New Yorkers into thinking that he was repentant. He probably hoped to regain Skenesborough, but he was also planning to undercut the American confederation by luring Vermont back to the British. Nothing came of any of his schemes as he remained in England until his death.

• Skene letters are at the New York State Library, Albany. Additional items are in the Philip Schuyler Papers and the Emmet Collection at the New York Public Library, which also has Skene's claim for compensation in the Loyalist Transcripts, vol. 45. John Pell, "Philip Skene of Skenesborough," *Quarterly Journal of the New York State Historical Association* 9 (1928): 27–44, reprints many Skene documents. The only biography is Doris Begor Morton, *Philip Skene of Skenesborough* (1959).

PHILIP RANLET

SKIBINE, George (30 Jan. 1920–14 Jan. 1981), ballet dancer, choreographer, and company director, was born Iurii Borisovich Skibin in Yasnaya Polyana, Russia, the son of Boris Skibin, an actor and dancer, and Vera Hobe. Two years after George's birth, the Skibines immigrated to Paris. Boris Skibine became a member of Serge Diaghilev's famed Ballets Russes in 1923, and young George, known as Youra, was indoctrinated into the world of ballet. He was educated at the Lycée Albert de Mun and was fascinated by science. By the age of sixteen, however, he began to study ballet, working first with his father and then with two great Russian émigrée ballerinas, Olga Preobrajenska and Lubov Egorova, and ex-Bolshoi Ballet star Alexandre Volinine.

Skibine danced in Paris in a variety of places, including the Tabarin Music Hall (the Bal Tabarin), where he often performed Russian character dances, and the Paris Ballet de la Jeunesse, where he performed in 1937. The following year the Russian ballet master and choreographer Léonide Massine saw the young Skibine at the Tabarin and recruited him as a member of René Blum's Ballets Russes de Monte Car-lo. He appeared in the company's 1938–1939 seasons, making his debut with the company in the role of the Stag in Massine's ballet *Seventh Symphony* (1938). Skibine accompanied the troupe on its American tour in the fall of 1938 and danced with the company for two seasons in Monte Carlo. He essayed roles in Massine's *Gaîté Parisienne* (1938) and *Le Beau Danube* (restaged for the company in 1933), and he performed various roles in the classical ballet repertory.

In 1940 the Ballets Russes, then under the direction of Colonel de Basil, toured Australia, where Skibine danced his first major role, in Igor Schwezoff's *The Eternal Circle* (1940). Skibine soon became known for his qualities as a *danseur noble*; his elegant bearing, virtuosic technique, dramatic intensity, and natural charm became the hallmarks of his stage presence. He performed assorted roles in Michel Fokine's *Carnaval* (1910), *Petrouchka* (1911), and *Polovtsian Dances* (1909), and he danced classical roles and pas de deux. Skibine left the Ballets Russes following its Australian tour and joined Ballet Theatre (later American Ballet Theatre) in New York, with which he again worked with Massine and Fokine and created the title role in Massine's *Aleko* (1942). The ballet, based on Aleksandr Pushkin's poem "Gypsies," about a young man who joins a gypsy tribe to find love and adventure, enabled Skibine to display his fine character dancing, romantic appearance, and dramatic ability. He danced a variety of principal roles in the classical ballet repertoire, including Siegfried in *Swan Lake* (act 2), Colas in Bronislava Nijinska's version of *La Fille Mal Gardée* (1940), and the Poet in Fokine's *Les Sylphides* (1909).

Skibine joined the U.S. Army in 1942 and served with the Office of Strategic Services in the counterintelligence division. For his service he was awarded the Bronze Star and became a naturalized American citizen. After World War II the impresario Sol Hurok persuaded Skibine to return to dancing. Accordingly, he joined the ballet company formed by the British ballet stars Alicia Markova and Anton Dolin, touring Central America and Mexico with them in 1945–1946. He then danced briefly with the Original Ballet Russe. In the summer of 1947 Skibine became a *premier danseur étoile* of the newly formed Grand Ballet du Marquis de Cuevas; he remained with that company until 1956.

Skibine's years with the de Cuevas Ballet were among the most fruitful of his career. He married the American ballerina Marjorie Tallchief in 1947; they had twin sons. Tallchief, who with her sister Maria had trained with Bronislava Nijinska, was a dancer with an exceptional bravura technique and a vibrant personality. She and Skibine formed a dynamic partnership both on and off the stage. Their performances in Nijinska ballets—*Les Biches* (1924, first presented by the de Cuevas Ballet in 1950), *Les Noces* (1923), *Brahms Variations* (1944), and *Pictures at an Exhibition* (1944)—were especially memorable. In George Balanchine's *La Sonnambula* (1946), a darkly romantic story of clandestine love and suppressed desire, Tallchief and Skibine created a sensation in the roles of the

Sleepwalker and the Poet. They were also invited to perform as guest artists with Ruth Page's Chicago Opera Ballet in 1956 and 1957.

Skibine choreographed his first work, *Tragédie à Vérone* (1950), for the de Cuevas company. Also for the company was his *Annabel Lee* (1951), based on the poem by Edgar Allan Poe. The latter, primarily a long pas de deux for Tallchief and Skibine, was considered successful as an evocation of mood. His other choreographic efforts for de Cuevas include *Prisoner of the Caucasus* (1951), *L'Ange Gris* (1953), and *Le Retour* (1954). *Idylle* (1954), to a score by François Serrette, was among Skibine's most popular works of this period. A charming story of a little white mare courted by a black stallion and a flashy circus horse, the fable was interpreted by Skibine in a witty and stylish manner.

After nearly ten years with the de Cuevas company, Skibine and Tallchief joined the Paris Opera Ballet, she as a *première danseuse étoile* and he as both *premier danseur* and choreographer. In late 1958 Skibine became ballet master of that company, on the retirement of the sometimes controversial and always flamboyant Russian dancer-choreographer Serge Lifar. During his tenure at the Opera, which lasted until 1962, Skibine created more than a dozen works, including *Concerto* for the Opéra-Comique (1958, inspired by Sean O'Casey's play *Red Roses for Me*), *Isoline* (1958), *Les Fâcheuses Rencontres* (1959), *Metamorphoses* (1961), and *Pastorale* (1961). His best-known work, and the one most often revived, originally created for the Opera in 1959, was his interpretation of *Daphnis and Chloe*, which he choreographed to the original Ravel score. The ballet's lavish sets, by the Russian painter Marc Chagall, were widely praised and served to highlight Skibine's passionate adagios for the ballet's principal characters. The French government later honored his tenure at the Opera by naming him a Chevalier in the Ordre des Artes et Lettres in 1967.

Following his tenure at the Paris Opera, Skibine was chosen in 1964 by the heiress Rebekah Harkness to serve as artistic director of her new company, the Harkness Ballet, based in New York. Skibine endeavored to create a versatile American ballet company with a varied repertory. The company made its debut in Cannes in February 1965, performing a repertory that included August Bournonville's *Napoli* (1842), Alvin Ailey's *Feast of Ashes* (1962), and Skibine's *Daphnis and Chloe*. Skibine left the Harkness Ballet in 1966 and became a freelance choreographer, mounting works for a variety of companies, including those of the Paris Opera and the Teatro Colón in Buenos Aires, Argentina.

In 1969 Skibine was invited to become artistic director of a small regional ballet company in Dallas, Texas. Through his skill and guidance the company grew steadily, eventually becoming the widely recognized Dallas Ballet. In his role as artistic director, which he retained until his death, Skibine was sensitive to the individual creativity of each dancer. He worked to create a company with a vital, ensemble spirit, commissioning works from such contemporary American cho-

reographers as Peter Anastos, Stuart Hodes, and John Clifford. Renowned as a dancer for his elegance, nobility, intelligence, and virtuosity, and admired as a director and choreographer, Skibine passed on his years of experience, knowledge, and understanding to the next generation of dancers, teachers, and choreographers. He died in Dallas.

• The chief repositories of materials documenting the career of Skibine are the Dance Collection of the New York Public Library for the Performing Arts, Lincoln Center, and the Dance Archive of the Dallas Public Library. For an overview of Skibine's career, see Peter Anastos, "A Conversation with George Skibine," *Ballet Review* (Spring 1982): 68–97. Additional assessments of his work as a dancer include John Percival, "Accent on the Male: 8—George Skibine," *Dance and Dancers* (Jan. 1959): 15–17; and Sonia Roberts, "Interview with George Skibine," *Ballet Today* (Nov. 1957): 9. A brief discussion of his early career and his ballets *Annabel Lee*, *L'Ange Gris*, and *Idylle* is included in the section on Skibine in Cyril Beaumont, *Ballets Past and Present* (1955).

SHELLEY CELIA BERG

SKIDMORE, Louis (8 Apr. 1897–27 Sept. 1962), architect, was born in Lawrenceburg, Indiana, the son of Edgar Hiram Skidmore, a railroad engineer, and Matilda Matheus. After two years at the Bradley Polytechnic Institute (now Bradley University) in Peoria, Illinois, Skidmore received a degree in 1917. He then briefly taught manual training in Findlay, Ohio, before becoming a sergeant in the Sixteenth Areo Construction Company of the U.S. Army. Serving in England from 1918 to 1919, he helped build airports for the Allied Expeditionary Force. Following the war, Skidmore worked for a year in the Cincinnati firm of Kruckmeyer and Strong before beginning formal training in architecture at the Massachusetts Institute of Technology. Upon graduation in 1924 he entered the Boston architectural firm of Maginnis and Walsh. Winning the Rotch Traveling Fellowship in 1926, he traveled for three years throughout most of Western Europe, Egypt, and Asia Minor, studying at the American Academy in Rome and the École des Beaux-Arts in Paris. Known for his drafting skills, Skidmore was asked in 1928 to execute measured drawings for Samuel Chamberlain's *Tudor Homes of England* (1929). In Paris he met Eloise Owings, whom he married in 1930. They had two sons.

In the spring of 1929 Skidmore met in Paris with Raymond Hood, who was coordinating the early planning stages of the 1933 Chicago Exposition, "A Century of Progress." Skidmore was enlisted to help prepare the presentation drawings for the fair's general plan. Within a year he became the fair's chief of design, responsible for organizing the design, construction, and demolition of more than 500 exhibits. Adept at coordinating talent while attending to business concerns, Skidmore rose to the occasion in the Chicago tradition of Daniel H. Burnham, who said, "Make no little plans." Despite depression-era scarcity, Skidmore produced an impressive display of modern architecture. The functionalist designs, economy of construction, and innovative use of materials encapsulated a variety of American and European modernist approaches to design.

In 1936 Skidmore formed a partnership with his brother-in-law Nathaniel A. Owings, who had overseen the planning of concessions for the fair. Three years later they were joined by structural engineer John O. Merrill. From the beginning Skidmore, Owings and Merrill (SOM) sought to provide complete professional services in the fields of architecture, design, planning, and engineering. Following closely the modernist paradigm that good buildings foster good society, SOM favored a functionalist approach that catered to the needs of the building's future inhabitants. Such pragmatism made SOM popular among clients, and the partners quickly prospered.

As early as 1937 Skidmore decentralized operations by opening a branch office in New York to secure a commission with the American Radiator Company. Using to advantage contacts made in Chicago, particularly with Robert Moses and Howard Heinz, Skidmore also consulted on designs for the 1939 New York World's Fair, winning commissions for the Westinghouse Building, the Venezuelan Pavilion, and the Gas Exhibits Building, which consequently led to larger projects such as the Fort Hamilton Veterans' Hospital (1939).

In the 1940s the firm took on numerous government projects related to housing, particularly in connection with national defense. Experimentation in low-cost prefabricated housing was succeeded by the monumental commission to design and build the community of Oak Ridge, Tennessee, a covert town for scientists engaged in the Manhattan Project. SOM's early fair experience aided greatly in solving logistical and organizational problems. To meet the diverse demands of town planning, land surveying, utilities, and the design of housing and community facilities for 75,000 inhabitants, the office staff was expanded to nearly 500 by 1946. The experience established the organizational framework that would allow SOM to undertake the extensive and varied commissions that would increasingly come their way following the war.

Driven by high volume and organized on the principle of group practice, in which independently functioning teams were assembled to carry a project from design to construction, SOM set the standard for the large-scale corporate practice of architecture. Autonomous offices would eventually open around the nation and in Europe. Although this success was not won by one man, Skidmore's ability to obtain commissions, organize operations, and motivate designers cannot be overestimated. His New York office handled the bulk of the firm's earliest work as well as the most prestigious clients. His gifted staff—including J. Walter Severinghaus, Robert W. Cutler, William S. Brown, and, most notably, designer Gordon Bunshaft—transformed the radical European modernism of the early twentieth century into the image of the contemporary corporation. Lever House, built on New York's Fifth Avenue in 1952, established a new precedent in skyscraper design that quickly became the preferred style of commercial and government institutions. True to the canons of the international style, Lever House is a pure geometric composition—a vertical slab on a horizontal base—composed of tinted blue glass and shiny stainless steel. A model of the building was the featured display in the Museum of Modern Art's 1950 retrospective of SOM, the museum's first exhibition ever devoted to an architectural firm rather than an individual.

In the early 1950s SOM produced many of their trademark buildings, including Manufacturers Hanover Trust in New York (1953–1954) and Connecticut General Life Insurance in Bloomfield, Connecticut (1954–1957). Modernist machines in the city and landscape, respectively, the structures have the careful detailing, modern materials, and ordered designs typical of the firm's output. Also characteristic is the integration of contemporaneous paintings, sculptures, and decorative arts into interiors and landscaping. The last design with which Skidmore was associated as an active partner was that for the U.S. Air Force Academy in Colorado Springs, Colorado (1954–1964). He retired in 1955, remaining a consulting partner until his death in Winter Haven, Florida.

Skidmore's contribution to architecture was as a businessman, salesman, and organizer of the first full-service architectural firm. From his planning factory issued forth the paradigm of the twentieth-century office building. Recognized by his peers in 1957, Skidmore was awarded the coveted Gold Medal of the American Institute of Architects, which praised him for pioneering new paths in a new technology.

• A collection of Skidmore's papers is in the Library of Congress. For discussions of the firm's early history see Ernst Danz, *Architecture of Skidmore, Owings and Merrill, 1950–1962* (1963), and Christopher Woodward, *Skidmore, Owings and Merrill* (1970). Nathaniel Owings, *The Spaces in Between: An Architect's Journey* (1973), provides a more personal account of Skidmore, as does the Art Institute of Chicago, *Oral History of Gordon Bunshaft* (1990).

LISA A. TORRANCE

SKILLIN, John (1745–? Jan. 1800), and **Simeon Skillin, Jr.** (1756–1806), woodcarvers, were born in Boston, Massachusetts, the sons of Simeon Skillin, Sr., a woodcarver, and Ruth Philips. John, Simeon, and their brother Samuel apprenticed in the workshop that their father had established in 1738. One of their father's earliest patrons was John Erving, a wealthy merchant with important political and mercantile connections, who was also responsible for outfitting the vessels of the Massachusetts navy. With his support, the elder Simeon's reputation as a carver of ships' figures spread throughout coastal Massachusetts. In 1766 he was given the commission to carve the first known public monument in New England, a bust of William Pitt, made for the Sons of Liberty in Dedham, Massachusetts, in honor of the repeal of the Stamp Act. Although his work was held in high esteem, no known piece can be traced to his hand.

When the revolutionary war began, John Skillin had taken his father's place as master carver of the shop. As the colonies scrambled to create a navy, John and Simeon Skillin received several important commissions, including a head of Minerva for the brig *Hazard* (1777), a vessel destined for the ill-fated Penobscot Expedition to dislodge British naval forces of the coast of what is now Maine. During the British occupation of Boston, John found employment with Nathaniel Shaw, Jr., of New London, Connecticut, naval agent for the Continental Congress, for whom he carved the figurehead and sternboard of the *Confederacy*, one of the first ships of the Continental navy. Drawings of the ship made for the British Royal Admiralty at the time of its capture in 1781, now in Greenwich, England, are rare documentations of the sculptural iconography on eighteenth-century American ships.

In 1782 John and Simeon Skillin were given the prestigious commission to do the extensive carvings on the 74-gun ship *America*, presented to the French government with John Paul Jones as its commander. The greatest homage to John's talent as a shipcarver, however, came in 1797, when William Rush of Philadelphia recommended him for the carving of the figurehead and sternboard for the famed *Constitution*, one of the first frigates of the U.S. Navy.

Once independence was achieved, American merchant ships were free to travel to ports throughout the world, where they became symbols of American commercial prowess. New England merchants knew that these ships would "bare the Inspection of the Most Critical Eye, both as to Construction and Workmanship," and they expected the Skillins to embellish their merchant ships as they had their warships. A drawing signed "S. Skillin," in the New York Public Library, shows the extensive carving Simeon designed for the sternboard of the *Massachusetts*, the largest merchant vessel built in America at the time of its launching in 1789.

In 1788 the citizens of Boston celebrated the ratification of the Constitution and, a year later, the triumphal entry of George Washington into the city. On both occasions, John Skillin was given the honor of leading the city's carvers in the processions of artisans. He undoubtedly was responsible for the carvings on the triumphal arch, designed by architect Charles Bulfinch, which greeted the president as he was led to the State House. In the years following, Bulfinch called on the Skillin workshop on several occasions to embellish his neoclassical buildings. In 1794–1795 the Skillin shop decorated both the interior and exterior of the Federal Street Theater. In 1797 they carved the Corinthian capitals, pilaster caps, and modillions for Bulfinch's Massachusetts State House as well as the pinecone that tops the dome. The capitals and caps were removed and replaced with metal reproductions in 1960; two pilaster caps are now owned by the Society for the Preservation of New England Antiquities in Boston, and a capital is in the Museum of Fine Arts, Boston. Simeon, Jr., continued to work for Bulfinch

after John's death. He and his assistants made the Corinthian capitals for the New North Church (1802–1804), the only Bulfinch church in existence with the original capitals still intact.

Members of the Skillin workshop were also responsible for figurative sculpture on Boston's public buildings. In 1793 they carved a figure of *Mercury* (Bostonian Society) to top the newly constructed post office on State Street. Praising the workmanship of the Skillins, a reporter for the *Columbian Centinel* described the figure as seen springing from a globe, carrying his caduceus and a letter directed to Thomas Russell, the merchant responsible for the new building. A nineteenth-century historian credited the Skillins with the figures of Hope and Justice that stood atop the second customhouse on State Street, and are now at the H. F. du Pont Winterthur Museum.

With huge profits from the China trade, New England merchants sought the most fashionable items for their estates, in emulation of the British gentry. The Skillins provided them with emblematic busts and figures to sit atop pieces of furniture, doors, and mantelpieces; to rest on pedestals; and to stand in garden groves. Only a few of these pieces have survived; the best documented are those made for Elias Haskett Derby of Salem. Derby, one of the first American merchants to send his ships around the world, was also one of the earliest patrons of the shop; in 1782 he had ready ordered two "Mehogoney Bustos" for a casepiece of furniture. In 1791 he asked John and Simeon to carve three mahogany figures to top a chest-on-chest made by Stephen Badlam (Yale University Art Gallery). This elaborate group consists of two reclining female figures representing Peace and Plenty, which flank a standing female figure carrying the attributes of Liberty, Victory, and Virtue, a tribute to the new nation.

In 1793 Derby ordered several garden figures for his farm in Danvers, Massachusetts, four of which are listed in an extant bill—a gardener, a shepherdess, a figure of Plenty, and a hermit. All except the hermit have survived in various states of repair. The *Gardener* (Danvers Historical Society) and his mate *Plenty* (Peabody Museum, Salem), represented by a milkmaid, were placed atop a summer house designed and built by Samuel McIntire. The *Shepherdess* (Peabody Museum), now called *Pomona* because she carries a cornucopia, is dressed in fashionable attire and is an excellent example of the vivacious quality that exists in the best work of the Skillin shop.

Several works created in the Skillin shop remain undocumented. They can, however, be attributed to the carvers because of their close resemblance to the Derby figures. John and Simeon can be credited with the carved molds used to cast the twelve figures that embellish the Joseph Pope Orrery (Houghton Library, Harvard University). This gear-driven model of the solar system rests in a mahogany and glass case on which were placed full-length brass portraits of Governor James Bowdoin and Benjamin Franklin, and busts of Sir Isaac Newton, each reproduced four times.

Bowdoin, a scientist and friend of Franklin, was responsible for Harvard's purchase of this orrery in 1789. Other works that closely resemble the Derby pieces include *Angel Gabriel*, made for the first Congregational Church in Royalston, Massachusetts, and a bust of Apollo, now in the New York State Historical Association in Cooperstown.

Tax records confirm that John and Simeon each worked with an apprentice or journeyman. In the late 1780s a nephew named Samuel Skillin assisted Simeon. When Samuel opened his own shop in the early 1790s, Simeon took Jonathan Burton as his assistant. Burton left for the West Indies in 1798, and Isaac Fowle took his place. Edmund Raymond worked for John and stayed in the shop after his master's death to assist Simeon. Because of the number of carvers in the shop, there are many variations in quality of workmanship—even in documented works. Some of the carved work is soft and fluid, while other carvings are sharp and brisk. Heads, in general, are full cheeked, with pert mouths, slightly curved noses, straight lower lids under the eyes, and lively hair. Stances are spritely, although figures are often long waisted and slightly disjointed. Some figures are fleshier with softer rounded folds in their dress. Good examples of this work can be seen in a mahogany allegorical figure, one of a pair that topped a desk and bookcase (Metropolitan Museum of Art); a figure of Plenty, which was used as an overdoor (private collection); and a bust of Apollo in the Assembly House in Salem.

John married Ann Fowle in 1768. After she died in 1795, he married Mary Fowle. Upon his sudden death in Boston, his obituary stated that he left a widow and "young family to lament." However, it cannot be ascertained how many children he actually had. Simeon, Jr., married Margaret Cazneau in 1780 and had no children. When his brother died, Simeon continued to run the shop and became a member of the Charitable Mechanic Association, an organization for artisans in Boston, in 1803. He died in Boston.

• Documents on extant work of John and Simeon Skillin can be found in the Derby papers, Essex Institute, Salem; bills for the Massachusetts State House are in the Massachusetts Archives; bills for the Federal Street Theater are in the Boston Public Library; records on the ship *Massachusetts* are in the Hudson papers in the New York Public Library; and bills for the USS *Constitution* are in the Massachusetts Historical Society. A rare contemporary mention of the work of John Skillin and of his death is given in *The Diary of William Bentley, D.D.* (4 vols., 1905–1914). The first to identify a body of work that can be attributed to the Skillin shop was Mabel Swan, "A Revised Estimate of McIntire," *Antiques*, Dec. 1931, pp. 338–43. The Skillins are also discussed in Pauline Pinckney, *American Figureheads and Their Carvers* (1940); M. V. Brewington, *Shipcarvers of North America* (1962); Wayne Craven, *Sculpture in America* (1968; repr. 1984); and Sylvia Leistyna Lahvis, "Icons of American Trade: The Skillin Workshop and the Language of Spectacle," *Winterthur Portfolio* 27 (Winter 1992): 213–33. The most recent information on the Badlam chest-on-chest can be found in Gerald Ward, *American Case Furniture in the Mabel Brady Garvan and Other Collections at Yale University* (1989). For the most recent and comprehensive study of the Skillin workshop, see Lahvis, "The Skillin Workshop: The Emblematic Image in Federal Boston" (Ph.D. diss., Univ. of Delaware, 1990).

SYLVIA LEISTYNA LAHVIS

SKINNER, B. F. (20 Mar. 1904–18 Aug. 1990), psychologist, was born Burrhus Frederic Skinner in Susquehanna, Pennsylvania, the son of William Arthur Skinner, an attorney, and Grace Madge Burrhus. He developed an early interest in literature and displayed a knack for constructing mechanical toys and gadgets. As a teenager, he read extensively in the works of Francis Bacon and Charles Darwin, two figures who greatly influenced his later thought. Majoring in English language and literature at Hamilton College, in Clinton, New York (1922–1926), he wrote for the campus literary magazine, studied biology, and engaged in collegiate pranks. During his senior year, an encouraging letter from Robert Frost led him to spend an unhappy year after graduation trying to write a novel. Following the "Dark Year," Skinner went to New York City, where he worked in a bookstore and led a bohemian life. For a time he considered pursuing graduate work in English, but he discovered behaviorism through Bertrand Russell's endorsement of John B. Watson's *Behaviorism* in the literary magazine *Dial*. After reading two of Watson's books and Ivan Pavlov's *Conditioned Reflexes*, Skinner realized that what intrigued him about literature was its descriptions of human behavior. Convinced by a friend that "science is the art of the twentieth century," he decided to undertake graduate work in psychology, even though he had never had a course in the subject.

After enrolling at Harvard University in 1928, Skinner found that his behaviorist leanings put him at odds with the department's orthodoxy, typified by the departmental chair, E. G. Boring. Skinner had liked Watson's "campaigning style" and became the department's enfant terrible, promoting the behaviorist viewpoint in collaboration with fellow graduate student Fred Keller, who later became his disciple. Working largely without supervision, Skinner pursued experimental research on animal behavior in the physiology laboratory of William J. Crozier, whose idiosyncratic approach stressed the behavior of the whole organism and the need to control behavior in order to understand it. There Skinner put his manual skills to use in devising the series of apparatuses that led to the construction of the famous Skinner box and the cumulative recorder, a device that displayed moment-by-moment changes in the behavior of a single organism. At Harvard, Skinner also encountered Percy Bridgman's 1927 book on operationism and the works of Ernst Mach, whose strict positivism reinforced Skinner's Baconian predilection toward careful inductive method and instilled an aversion to hypothetical constructs not grounded in direct observation.

After receiving his Ph.D. in 1931, Skinner remained at Harvard as a member of Harvard's Society of Fellows, continuing his research in Crozier's laboratory. In a series of papers in the 1930s, he drew the important distinction between *respondent* behavior, or Pavlovian conditioned reflexes that are elicited by antecedent stimuli, and *operant* behavior, which is governed by the consequences it produces by virtue of its acting on the environment. Those consequences could either reduce the likelihood of the response recurring (punishment) or increase its likelihood (reinforcement). This bare-bones conceptual framework was published along with a wealth of experimental data in *The Behavior of Organisms* (1938). Although the phenomena of reinforcement and punishment had been studied previously by E. L. Thorndike and others, Skinner's book was notable for its demonstrations of orderly functional relations between behavior and environment as well as for its rejection of speculation about both the physiological mechanisms of behavior and its possible mental causes. In effect, the book established the behavior of intact organisms as a lawful scientific domain in its own right, and it became the model of later research in the Skinnerian tradition.

In 1936 Skinner was appointed instructor of psychology at the University of Minnesota. That fall he married Yvonne Blue, a recent graduate of the University of Chicago who shared his interest in literature and the theater. During World War II he developed a missile-guidance system that used the precise visual skills of pigeons to direct missiles to their targets. Although the system was never implemented, it led to a refined understanding of the technique of behavioral shaping, in which novel behaviors are produced by reinforcing successive approximations to the desired response. The missile-guidance project also convinced Skinner of the feasibility of engineering behavior to precise specifications, and he began to speak of the prospects for a "behavioral technology." With a Baconian eye toward applying science to the betterment of the human condition, Skinner conceived a fictional community designed on operant principles, publishing an account in 1948 as the utopian novel *Walden Two*. The community was characterized by its small scale, harmony with the natural environment, avoidance of needless consumption, and the use of positive reinforcement rather than punishment to produce desirable behavior in its members. In response to critics who found the deliberate design of a culture a frightening prospect, Skinner defended his proposals by holding that all behavior is controlled anyway and that to avoid scientific control was to leave the control to accidental factors.

Meanwhile, the growing notoriety that *Walden Two* brought Skinner was enhanced by his excursion into domestic engineering. To simplify the care of the Skinners' second child, Deborah, he constructed a sound-attenuating, glass-walled "Baby Tender" (or "Air Crib"), which became a subject of attention in the popular media. Although little more than a climate-controlled crib, the device was confused in the public mind with the Skinner box that was becoming widely used in animal experimentation. For decades he was dogged by persistent rumors that Deborah had become mentally ill and committed suicide; in fact she

became a successful artist and writer, while her sister Julie became a professor of educational psychology.

After chairing the psychology department at Indiana University for three years, Skinner returned to Harvard in 1948. In 1953 he published *Science and Human Behavior*, a textbook on operant psychology and its implications for social reform. While attending Father's Day at his daughters' school in 1953, Skinner was disturbed by the inefficiency and imprecision of the teaching methods used. Again putting his mechanical skills to use, he devised a series of teaching machines that used shaping and other operant methods to build repertoires of knowledge in various fields. Later he extended the techniques of programmed instruction to textbook format.

From 1956 to 1962 Skinner's views on education, behavioral technology, and human nature were aired in a well-known series of debates with the humanistic psychologist Carl Rogers. In 1957 he published (with Charles Ferster) *Schedules of Reinforcement*, a careful analysis of how behavior is governed by contingencies of reinforcement, and the long-awaited *Verbal Behavior*, an inductive classification of types of utterances based on their functional controlling properties. Though sharply criticized in a famous review by the linguist and left-wing social critic Noam Chomsky, *Verbal Behavior* stimulated behaviorist research on language as well as applications to language learning in subnormal populations.

When Clark Hull's highly theoretical version of behaviorism fell out of favor during the 1950s, Skinner's operant psychology, with its pragmatic, atheoretical orientation, became an influential movement in American psychology. Centers of graduate training at Harvard, Columbia, Indiana University, and elsewhere produced operant psychologists who went on to apply Skinnerian methods to psychotherapy, psychopharmacology, education, and the management of businesses, prisons, and mental hospitals. The movement soon established its own professional societies and journals. In part because its use of single-subject research designs and its uncompromising adoption of deterministic philosophical assumptions, the movement remained largely insulated from mainstream psychology. Though hard-line operant psychologists were sometimes viewed as a cultlike faction, the movement's influence on American psychology grew through the 1960s, and its techniques of behavior modification came into widespread use.

With the growth of social criticism and interest in alternative lifestyles during the 1960s, sales of *Walden Two* rose sharply (eventually reaching millions of copies), and Skinner's own efforts turned increasingly from laboratory work to popular and philosophical writings. In response to public concern over problems of war, pollution, and overpopulation, Skinner again posed the solution of a designed culture in which efficient, nondestructive conduct was behaviorally engineered. Perceiving that resistance to cultural engineering lay in misguided political theories of human freedom, Skinner published *Beyond Freedom and Dig-*

nity in 1971. There he criticized the theory of "autonomous man," arguing that science had shown humans to be causally determined products of their genetic and environmental histories. Although the theory of "autonomous man" had served a useful function in helping people to resist the punishing sanctions of poorly designed governments, it would become obsolete in a culture whose members were controlled through positive reinforcement. At the same time, the dignity associated with heroism and individual achievement would give way to an understanding that socially beneficial behaviors are a function of good environments rather than good people; likewise, the blame for bad behavior would be assigned to unfavorable environments, which could then be redesigned. Only through science-based cultural engineering, Skinner urged, could serious social problems be solved and the collective aims of the democratic West be realized.

Beyond Freedom and Dignity provoked a strong critical reaction. Noam Chomsky likened Skinner's views to nazism, the philosopher Karl Popper called Skinner "an enemy of freedom and of democracy" who advocated a "behaviorist dictatorship," and Vice President Spiro Agnew attacked Skinner as a dangerous radical bent on undermining American values. As the book rose on the bestseller charts, Skinner began to appear on talk shows and was featured on the cover of *Time* magazine. In 1972 the American Humanist Association named him the "Humanist of the Year" for his devotion to human problems and his critiques of religious and political institutions. By 1975 one survey showed him to be the best-known American scientist among college students, outranking the likes of Margaret Mead and Jonas Salk.

Although Skinner's public exposure peaked in the 1970s, he remained active from his retirement in 1974 until his death. His later writings were devoted to problems of cultural design, criticism of the cognitive movement in psychology, and the parallels between natural selection in biology and the selection of behavior by the environment in individual learning. Only days before his death in Cambridge, Massachusetts, he delivered a sharp critique of cognitive psychology to an audience of several thousand psychologists.

Despite his unbending adherence to scientific determinism in human affairs and his strident critique of entrenched traditions, Skinner himself was widely regarded as a gentle, cultured, and literate figure. He was a competent classical pianist and a published poet who enjoyed friendships with such literati as I. A. Richards and James Agee; even his ideological opponents frequently found themselves disarmed by his friendly demeanor and subtle humor. In many ways, he was a modern relic of the Enlightenment faith in human perfectibility through rational social engineering, and his proposals for applying behavioral technology to society brought him large measures of both notoriety and adulation. His views forced Americans to confront the deeply rooted tensions between their scientific faith in technological solutions and their political faith in the ideals of freedom and autonomy. Although he never succeeded in persuading the public to resolve that tension in favor of science, the methods of behavioral change that arose from his work made their way into numerous spheres of life.

Skinner has been described as "a psychologist with the soul of an engineer," and toward the end of his life he stated that he wished to be remembered as a social inventor. Although his life was guided by a Baconian faith in the powers of science to ameliorate the human condition, he grew pessimistic in his later years about the prospects for the emergence of cultural practices that would ensure human survival in the face of social and environmental problems, believing that behavioral science had emerged too late in human history to overturn the prescientific conceptions of human nature that stood in the way of its implementation.

• Skinner's papers are in the Harvard University Archives. Bibliographies appear in *Behaviorism* 5, no. 1 (1977): 99–110, and A. Charles Catania and Stevan Harnad, eds., *The Selection of Behavior: The Operant Behaviorism of B. F. Skinner* (1988), which also reprints a number of his most important journal articles. Skinner's three-volume autobiography comprises *Particulars of My Life* (1976), *The Shaping of a Behaviorist* (1979), and *A Matter of Consequences* (1983). Excerpts from his intellectual diary are in *Notebooks*, ed. Robert Epstein (1980), and the longest of the Skinner-Rogers debates is in Howard Kirschenbaum and Valerie L. Henderson, eds., *Carl Rogers: Dialogues* (1989).

Major works by Skinner include *The Technology of Teaching* (1968); *Contingencies of Reinforcement* (1969); *Cumulative Record* (1959); *About Behaviorism* (1974); *Reflections on Behaviorism and Society* (1978); and *Upon Further Reflection* (1987). His crucial papers formulating the operant concept in the 1930s are reprinted in *Cumulative Record*.

The best biography of Skinner is Daniel W. Bjork, *B. F. Skinner: A Life* (1993). General works on Skinner include Daniel W. Bjork, *B. F. Skinner: A Life* (1993); Richard I. Evans, *B. F. Skinner: The Man and His Ideas* (1968); Robert L. Geiser, *Behavior Mod and the Managed Society* (1976); and Robert D. Nye, *The Legacy of B. F. Skinner* (1992). For wide-ranging critical discussions, see John Harvey Wheeler, ed., *Beyond the Punitive Society* (1973), and Sohan Modgil and Celia Modgil, eds., *B. F. Skinner: Consensus and Controversy* (1987). See also Laurence D. Smith, *Behaviorism and Logical Positivism* (1986), on Skinner's philosophical roots and his relation to other behaviorists, and Paul T. Sagal, *Skinner's Philosophy* (1981), on Skinner as an Enlightenment figure. Notable critiques of Skinner are in Noam Chomsky, "Review of Skinner's *Verbal Behavior*," *Language* 35 (1959): 26–58; "The Case against B. F. Skinner," *New York Review of Books*, 27 Dec. 1971, pp. 18–24; Tibor Machan, *The Pseudoscience of B. F. Skinner* (1974); and Robert W. Proctor and Daniel J. Weeks, *The Goal of B. F. Skinner and Behavior Analysis* (1990). For obituaries, see the *New York Times*, 20 Aug. 1990; Fred S. Keller, "Burrhus Frederic Skinner (1904–1990)," *Journal of the History of the Behavioral Sciences* 27 (1991): 3–6; and John A. Nevin, "Burrhus Frederic Skinner: 1904–1990," *American Journal of Psychology* 105 (1992): 613–19.

LAURENCE D. SMITH

SKINNER, Clarence Russell (23 Mar. 1881–27 Aug. 1949), Universalist minister and theological professor, was born in Brooklyn, New York, the son of Charles

Montgomery Skinner, editor of the *Brooklyn Eagle*, and Ada Blanchard. He went to St. Lawrence University in Canton, New York, graduating in 1904. There he became a member of Phi Beta Kappa. Although he had not trained for the ministry, he became an assistant that same year to the Reverend Dr. Frank Oliver Hall, minister of the Church of the Divine Paternity (Universalist) in New York City. The next year he was ordained, and later he took graduate work at Columbia, Harvard, and the Boston School of Social Workers. Meadville Theological School gave him a D.D. in 1926. His alma mater gave him an M.A. in 1910 and a D.D. in 1933.

In 1906 Skinner was called to the Universalist church in Mount Vernon, New York. That same year he married Clara L. Ayres; they had no children. While at Mount Vernon he assisted the Mount Vernon Society in building a new Universalist church and became involved in settlement house work in New York City. During those years he helped organize the New York clergy into a group that eventually became the Church Peace Union. In 1910 he moved to Grace Universalist Church in Lowell, Massachusetts. He was appointed assistant professor of applied Christianity at Crane Theological School, Tufts College (now University) in 1914. As a staunch pacifist he experienced years of controversy on the Tufts campus during both world wars, standing his ground quietly but effectively.

Within his denomination Skinner became active in the Social Gospel movement and was the chief author of the "Declaration of Social Principles" adopted by the Universalists in 1917. This was the first official expression of denominational social policy. It affirmed social goals in the economic, social, moral, and spiritual realms and clearly was modeled on the Social Creed of the Federal Council of Churches. In 1920 he organized the Community Church of Boston. He continued as "leader," not minister, of this church until 1936, all the while carrying out his teaching duties at Tufts. In 1933 he was appointed dean of the theological school and served until his retirement in 1945. Tufts awarded him an honorary Litt.D. that year. He died in Stamford, Connecticut.

Skinner was a passionate believer in social justice for all peoples. As a dedicated and enthusiastic teacher, his intense idealism magnetized and inspired the many students he taught and the hundreds of people he reached through his sermons and books and articles. His style, one critic has pointed out, was essentially homiletical: "full of aphorisms but short on sustained analysis and surprisingly weak when analysis is attempted" (uncited quote in Miller, p. 500).

The real strength and depth of the man lay in his vision, his faith in people, and his understanding that the power of religion is in its inclusiveness—its "universalism." There was always a strong undercurrent of mysticism in Skinner that influenced both his theology and his sociology. Indeed, he regarded mysticism as the heart of religion. For him a unifying vision was the essence of religious experience. This was what he reached for in his concept of the unities and the universals as spelled out in his prose poems and in his book *A Religion for Greatness* (1945). The thrust of his message was toward a restructuring of thought, of worship, and of the church in terms of present needs and opportunities. He has accurately been described as "the most influential Universalist minister of his generation."

Skinner's influence continued beyond his death. The Unitarian Universalist Association's award for the most significant sermon of social concern, given annually since 1958, was named for him, as was the building housing the denomination's Beacon Press. Even though some of Skinner's views dealt with issues limited to his time, much in his thinking has remained pertinent to later generations. For this reason his writings have been reprinted and are still cited as an inspiration.

• The papers of Clarence Skinner, including letters and correspondence, book manuscripts, articles, addresses, biographical material, and photographs, are in the archives of the Harvard Divinity School Library. His other principal books are *The Social Implications of Universalism* (1915), *Liberalism Faces the Future* (1937), *Human Nature and the Nature of Evil* (1939), and *Worship and the Well Ordered Life* (1955). With Alfred S. Cole he wrote a biography of John Murray, *Hell's Ramparts Fell* (1941). A full bibliography of his other writings can be found in the Universalist Historical Society *Annual Journal* 5 (1964–1965): 66–77. Extensive coverage of his life and work can be found in Russell Miller, *The Larger Hope*, vol. 2 (1985). An obituary is in the *New York Times*, 28 Aug. 1949.

CARL SEABURG

SKINNER, Constance Lindsay (7 Dec. 1877–27 Mar. 1939), poet, novelist, and historian, was born Constance Annie Skinner in Quesnal, British Columbia, Canada, the daughter of Robert James Skinner, a factor for the Hudson Bay Company, and Annie Lindsay. In Quesnal, an isolated fur-trading post northeast of Vancouver, Constance played with Native American children; these early experiences influenced her writing, particularly her poetry. The Skinners lived in a large cedar house, 500 miles from the railroad, so Constance was tutored by her parents from their extensive library. She loved to read and often ran off into the forest to peruse the books that fascinated her. When Constance was fourteen, the family moved to Vancouver, where she attended a private school, her only formal education.

Constance Skinner wrote her first story at age five and her first novel at eleven; while a schoolgirl in Vancouver, she wrote the libretto and score for a three-act children's operetta, which was produced to raise money for charity. At sixteen she was contributing editorials and political features to the *Vancouver Evening World*; two years later she applied, by letter, for employment with a Los Angeles, California, newspaper. In spite of her youth, she was given the position, writing feature stories for the *Los Angeles Times* and the *San Francisco Examiner*. Later she moved to Chicago,

Illinois, and supported her mother and herself through her journalistic efforts. In her twenties she became a literary critic for the *New York Herald Tribune* and moved to New York City.

In New York in 1917 Skinner's play, *Good Morning, Rosamonde!* from her novel of the same name published the same year, opened to mixed critical reviews; three earlier plays had been produced in California and on tour. Neither journalism nor dramatic writing, however, was to become Skinner's main interest. She studied American history, researching the advancing of the frontiers and the development of the country. *Pioneers of the Old Southwest: A Chronicle of the Dark and Bloody Ground* (1919) and *Adventurers of Oregon* (1920) were published as part of the Chronicles of America series, edited by Allen Johnson. Although originally published for adults, both books became required reading in many American high schools. *Beavers, Kings and Cabins* (1933), a history of the fur trade, was a tribute to her father. His letters and notes were sources of Indian lore, as were the writings and art of some American Indians, including Chief Standing Bear of the Lakotas. Historian Frederick Jackson Turner corresponded with Skinner, assisting her with her research.

During this same period Skinner wrote adventure stories for *Boys' Life*, the Boy Scout magazine, and *American Girl*, the Girl Scout magazine. *Silent Scot: Frontier Scout* and *Becky Landers: Frontier Warrior* appeared as serials in these magazines before being published as books in 1926. Several of her stories and novels featured girls as central characters and most had frontier settings. The *Saturday Review of Literature* said of *Becky Landers*, "We cannot think of a better book to put into the hands of girls just entering, or already in, their teens." *Silent Scot* and other books were based on actual events. By 1934 she had written eleven books for children. Reviewing *Red Willows* (1929), set in British Columbia, the *New York Herald Tribune* spoke of the quality of her prose and reminded its readers that "Miss Skinner is a poet of unusual distinction."

It is for her work as a poet that Skinner is best known in Canada. She received awards from *Poetry*, the London *Bookman*, and *Lyric West* for poems published in those magazines. Some of her poems, dramatic monologues drawn from the experience, particularly the female experience, of the Squamish Indians of British Columbia, were collected in *Songs of the Coast Dwellers* (1930). Some of these poems were later included in *The Book of Canadian Poetry* (1948). In response to a young man dying of tuberculosis who had praised her poetry she wrote: "Pure poetry flows from our moments of spiritual splendor, it frees us from the shackles of . . . microscopic thinking." She related her love for that "vast wild northern beauty, . . . symbolical of strength, joy and freedom," and said that her writing flowed from that. "Beauty restores the soul, and the soul mends the body," she told him.

A large woman who usually wore bright-colored dresses, many chains of beads and bracelets, and large hats, Skinner was striking in appearance and strong willed, yet warm and friendly. She encouraged many young writers, giving freely of her time and often providing financial aid. An active member of the Women's National Book Association (WNBA), Skinner helped found the *Bookwoman*, a WNBA publication. She was also a member of the Poetry Society of America, the Author's Club (New York), and the Champlain Society of Canada. She was a fellow of the American Geographical Society and the Royal Geographical Society of England. She numbered among her friends Jack London and the Canadian poet and critic Florence Randall Livesay.

When in 1935 Rinehart and Farrar accepted Skinner's idea for a series of books telling the history of America and its peoples through the stories of its rivers, she became one of the first women to hold a major editorial position in American adult book publishing. She chose the rivers and the folk tales to be included, asking that the writing be literary as well as historical. She planned to write the story of the Missouri River herself but did not live long enough to complete the project. Six books were published before her death, and the title pages of the remaining books of the series state that it had been "planned and started by Constance Lindsay Skinner." In 1961 the series was published in a young readers edition, which would surely have pleased her.

Unmarried "from inclination," as she said, and from being too busy to marry, Skinner lived alone, concentrating on her work while seeing few people. Among those few was Helen Hoke, a children's editor, who became a close friend and protégé during Skinner's last two years. Hoke was the last person to speak to her, by telephone, the evening before her death from complications following influenza.

Skinner was found dead in her New York City apartment, sitting in a straight-back chair in which she had been correcting the galleys of Carl Carmer's *The Hudson*. She left neither a will nor records of any relatives, so friends arranged nondenominational services. In 1940 the Women's National Book Association established the Constance Lindsay Skinner Award to be given to "women who have made an exceptional contribution to books and, through books, to society"—a fitting tribute to a woman who had contributed so much herself.

• The most complete and accurate biographical information on Skinner can be found in Ann Heidbreder Eastman, ed., *Constance Lindsay Skinner: Author and Editor, Sketches of Her Life and Character, with a Checklist of Her Writings and the "Rivers of America" Series* (1980). Short biographies are in many reference books; one of the best is Anne Commire et al., eds., *Yesterday's Authors of Books for Children: From Early Times to 1960* (1977). See also May Lamberton Becker, ed., *Golden Tales of Canada* (1938), and Clara Thomas, *Canadian Novelists* (1946). Informative articles include Jean West Maury, "From a Fur-Trading Post to New York: Constance Lindsay Skinner's Progress from Her Earliest Days in British Columbia," *Boston Evening Transcript*, 6 May 1933. Obituaries are in the *New York Times*, 28 Mar. 1939, *Publishers Weekly*, 1 Apr. 1939, *Library Journal*, 15 Apr. 1939, and *Wilson Library Bulletin*, May 1939.

BLANCHE COX CLEGG

SKINNER, Cornelia Otis (30 May 1901–9 July 1979), author and actress, was born in Chicago, Illinois, the daughter of Otis Skinner, a matinee idol, and Maud Durbin, an actress. After Skinner's mother retired from acting in 1906, the family moved to Bryn Mawr, Pennsylvania, where Otis Skinner resided when he was not performing. In 1920 Skinner left Bryn Mawr College during her sophomore year to study in Paris. She attended the Sorbonne and studied acting at the Comédie Francaise and the Jacques Copeau School. Returning to the United States, Skinner landed her first dramatic role in the stage adaptation of Blasco-Ibanez's *Blood and Sand* (1921), which starred her father. Roles in *Will Shakespeare* (1923), *Tweedles* (1923), *The Wild Wescotts* (1923), *In His Arms* (1924), and *White Collars* (1925) followed.

Skinner's first play, *Captain Fury*, which she wrote for her father, was produced in 1925, and she began writing and performing monologues that combined wry humor and keen observation. She toured in these productions and made her first London appearance at the St. James in 1929. Drawing on her interest in history, she wrote and enacted one-woman shows that presented a variety of characters: *The Wives of Henry VIII* (1931), *The Empress Eugenie* (1932), *The Loves of Charles II* (1933), and *The Mansion on the Hudson* (1935). Her adaptation of Margaret Ayer Barnes's novel *Edna, His Wife* played to receptive audiences in London in 1937 and in its 1938 U.S. tour. During World War II she traveled for the American Theatre Wing, presenting her monologues to members of the armed services; she combined a series of character sketches for the London stage in 1949.

The versatile Skinner succeeded in more traditional theater as well. She received critical acclaim for her starring role in George Bernard Shaw's *Candida* in its 1937 London production and 1939 U.S. tour. After seeing her performance, Shaw cabled, "Excellent—greatest." She responded, "Undeserving such praise." Shaw wired, "Meant the play." Skinner rejoined, "So did I." Her other important roles included Angelica in *Love for Love* (1940), Emily Hazen in Lillian Hellman's *The Searching Wind* (1944), and Mrs. Erlynne in *Lady Windermere's Fan* (1946).

Skinner married Alden S. Blodget in 1928; the couple had one child. She drew on her life as actress, writer, wife, mother, and citizen of Long Island and New York City to write poetry and essays for magazines such as *Ladies' Home Journal*, *New Yorker*, *Reader's Digest*, *Theatre Arts Monthly*, and *Vogue*. Dodd, Mead and Company published collections of these essays as *Tiny Garments* (1932), *Excuse It, Please!* (1936), *Dithers and Jitters* (1938), and *Soap behind the Ears* (1941). *That's Me All Over* (1948), with drawings by Constantin Alajálov, reprinted selections from these volumes. Later volumes—*Nuts in May* (1950), *Bottoms Up!*

(1955), and *The Ape in Me* (1959), also illustrated by Alajálov—continue this personal focus, employing self-deprecating humor and subtle intelligence. Skinner's memoirs, *Family Circle* (1948) and *Happy Family* (1950), reflect on her career and that of her father.

Skinner's most acclaimed personal writing is *Our Hearts Were Young and Gay* (1942), an amusing account of a trip to Paris with her friend Emily Kimbrough in the 1920s. Kimbrough collaborated in the writing of the book, and Alajálov did the illustrations. A bestseller for eight weeks, *Our Hearts* sold more than a million copies and received critical praise as well. The account of the women's uninformed and unexpected responses to such peculiarities as bed bugs and brothels provides an arresting combination of naïveté and sophistication. The movie version was produced in 1944, and Jean Kerr adapted it for the stage in 1948.

Skinner also excelled in collaborative playwriting. She created and acted the fourteen characters in *Paris '90* (1952), for which Kay Swift wrote music and lyrics. In 1958 Skinner and Samuel Taylor wrote *The Pleasure of His Company*; she played the role of Katherine Dougherty.

After touring in *Pleasure* in 1960, Skinner retired from the stage but continued to write. In 1962 she published *Elegant Wits and Grand Horizontals*, which developed earlier material from *Paris '90*. She also wrote highly commended biographies of Sarah Bernhardt, *Madame Sarah* (1967), and of Howard Lindsay and Russell Crouse, *Life with Lindsay and Crouse* (1976).

Skinner died in New York City. She held honorary degrees from numerous colleges and universities. The French minister of National Education named her Officier de Academie in 1953, and she received the Barter Theatre Award in 1952.

• Letters form Skinner are in the William Glasgow Bruce Carson Collection at Washington University Library and in the Hazel Ida Kirk Collection at the Andover-Harvard Theological Library of Harvard University Divinity School. A recorded interview with Mimi Benzel is in the Special Collections at the University of Wyoming Library. Obituaries are in the *New York Times*, *Chicago Tribune*, and *Washington Post*, all 10 July 1979.

MARILYN ROBERSON ELKINS

SKINNER, John Stuart (22 Feb. 1788–21 Mar. 1851), publisher and editor, was born in Calvert County, Maryland, the son of Frederick Skinner, a planter, and Bettie Stuart. Educated in local schools and at Charlotte Hall Academy, from which he graduated in 1806, Skinner began studying law. Making his home at Annapolis, he served as a reading clerk for the legislature and was admitted to the Maryland bar in 1809. In 1812 he married Elizabeth Glenn Davies, with whom he would have three sons.

Skinner first entered public life as a government official. At the beginning of the War of 1812 President James Madison appointed him inspector of European mail and agent for prisoners of war. Moving from Annapolis to Baltimore in 1813, he was commissioned the next year as a purser in the navy. In this role he was conducting negotiations aboard an enemy man-of-war on the night of 13 September 1814, when the British bombardment of Fort McHenry began; detained overnight along with colleague Francis Scott Key, Skinner was also present the next day at Key's writing of "The Star Spangled Banner." Later he arranged to have the manuscript printed. After the war he served in the postal service for most of the rest of his life, acting as Baltimore postmaster from 1816 to 1837 and as third assistant postmaster general from 1841 to 1845. Though effective in his national duties, he lost his position in Washington, D.C., with the advent of the James Polk administration.

Skinner built a reputation for himself as a writer and editor devoted to agricultural and sporting affairs. Concerned from his childhood with the often shoddy farming practices of his native state and region, he established what became the first regularly published agricultural paper in the United States, *American Farmer*. From its first issue on 2 April 1819, the four-page weekly covered improved agricultural methods and rural life in general; fair schedules and reports from independent agricultural organizations were included along with recommendations about new farm machinery, fertilization, and horticulture. Skinner gathered much of the material in *American Farmer* through his concurrent positions as corresponding secretary of the Maryland Agricultural Society, manager of the Maryland Association for the Improvement of the Breed of Horses, and secretary of the Maryland Society for Internal Improvement. He corresponded with leaders of similar organizations in other states, incorporating their insights into his magazine. He also got advice from dignitaries such as Thomas Jefferson, James Madison, and the French general and hero of the American Revolution the marquis de Lafayette.

American Farmer covered hunting, angling, and—especially—horse racing. In 1825 Skinner expanded his attention to these activities by adding the "Sporting Olio," thereby creating the nation's first regular magazine section devoted to sports. Borrowing heavily from British publications and practices, Skinner explained rules and etiquette, encouraged greater participation in sport, and introduced new sports. Fox hunting and horse racing remained his favorites, however, and by September 1829 his interest in the latter led Skinner to create a new periodical, the *American Turf Register and Sporting Magazine*. At first primarily intended to encourage the systematic breeding of thoroughbreds, this monthly magazine increasingly focused on horse racing and on outdoor sports in general. Burdened by the demands of his successful new effort—as well as by a new position as corresponding secretary of the Maryland Jockey Club—Skinner sold his *American Farmer* in 1830, although he remained an occasional contributor. The *Register* became his primary focus, and he developed it with specifics on race results and pedigrees and also with advice encouraging Americans to participate in the athletic revolution already begun by the

English. At least six rival sports magazines sprang up during 1826–1835, most of which blatantly copied Skinner's style and format. In fact, Skinner maintained close friendships with the editors of two of these publications and encouraged the development of sports journalism across the country.

After selling the *Register* in 1835, Skinner shifted his attention to government duties for most of the next five years, though he also made time to edit the magazine of the newly formed American Silk Society. After losing his position as Baltimore postmaster, however, he for two years returned—full time—to the editorship of his original magazine (which he again named *American Farmer*—it had been known as *Farmer and Gardener* since his departure). His appointment in Washington under the William Henry Harrison–John Tyler administration required his complete attention, but after 1845 he again immersed himself in journalism, this time in New York—at the invitation of Horace Greeley, publisher of the *New York Tribune*—as the editor of the *Farmers' Library and Monthly Journal of Agriculture*. His new publication featured fine engravings, reprints of the best foreign agricultural articles, and news of farming techniques and inventions.

The publication proved too technical to attract a large general audience, however, and when Skinner's contract with Greeley expired in 1848, he moved to Philadelphia to pursue an independent course. With the help of his son Frederick, he established a new monthly of his own, *The Plough, the Loom, and the Anvil*, which took its title from his favorite maxim on the relationship of agriculture and industry: "The plough profits by the successes of the anvil and the loom." Though this publication clearly focused on agriculture again, Skinner's interests in his later years remained broad, as evident in the popular sports writing found in his book *The Dog and the Sportsman* (1845). He continued writing and editing until his death of head injuries sustained in an accidental fall during a visit to friends in Baltimore.

At the time of his death Skinner had been inducted as an honorary member of virtually every American and European agricultural society. His contribution to agricultural journalism is unquestionable; yet it is perhaps his contribution to sports journalism that is more impressive and enduring. While agriculture was an essential and necessary part of American life during his time, the significance of sport was still an unsettled question in the national mind. In those years when play first became as important as work to the young nation, Skinner filled a void in popular culture and earned himself the title of "father of American sports journalism."

• Skinner's papers are at the Maryland Historical Society; the University of Virginia, Charlottesville; Cornell University, Ithaca, N.Y.; and the National Sporting Library, Middleburg, Va. The most extensive study is Jack Berryman, "John Stuart Skinner and Early American Sports Journalism, 1819–35" (Ph.D. diss., Univ. of Maryland, 1976). Harold Pinkett, "The *American Farmer*, a Pioneer Agricultural Journal, 1819–1834," *Agricultural History* 24 (July 1950): 146–51, clearly focuses on Skinner's role in the beginnings of agricultural journalism. More general biographical information is in Ben Perley Poore, "Biographical Sketch of John Stuart Skinner," *The Plough, the Loom, and the Anvil* 7 (July 1854): 1–20, and Harry Worcester Smith, *A Sporting Family of the Old South: With Which Is Included Reminiscences of an Old Sportsman by Frederick Gustavus Skinner* (1936). An obituary is in the *Baltimore Clipper*, 22 Mar. 1851.

W. FARRELL O'GORMAN

SKINNER, Otis (28 June 1858–4 Jan. 1942), actor-manager, was born in Cambridge, Massachusetts, the son of Charles Augustus Skinner, a Universalist minister, and Cornelia Bartholomew. His adolescent years were spent in Hartford, Connecticut, where he did poorly in school and left at age sixteen to become a warehouse clerk and editor of a free weekly paper. The defining event in his early life was a visit to a New York City theater to see *The Hunchback of Notre Dame*. From then on, he was enthralled by the stage.

After some amateur dramatics in Hartford, Skinner obtained a letter of introduction from his father's friend P. T. Barnum and on the strength of it was hired in 1877 to play small parts at a minor theater in Philadelphia. He played ninety-two parts in his first professional season, starting out as Jim, an elderly black man, in *Woodleigh*. The following season he moved on to the resident stock company that supported visiting stars at Philadelphia's Walnut Street Theatre. Performing, rehearsing, and learning lines occupied him day and night. "But what a school it was!" he wrote in his autobiography, *Footlights and Spotlights* (1924). "I learned my art crudely, roughly, but by leaps and bounds, driven by necessity to an intuitive grasp of character and the way to express it."

Skinner first appeared in a New York production in 1879 and the following year was hired by Edwin Booth for a two-month season. The next fifteen years brought Skinner work in prominent companies, playing more and more substantial roles. He appeared in dramas with Lawrence Barrett (1881–1884) and in fashionable comedies with the Augustin Daly company (1884–1889). In 1889 a conflict with Daly led him to join a touring company headed by Booth and Helena Modjeska. He traveled to England in 1890 to play Romeo in a production of *Romeo and Juliet*; then he rejoined Modjeska and toured in her company until 1894, playing leads. His rise as an actor can be traced through his changing roles in *Macbeth*: in 1880, with Booth, he had one scene as the Wounded Soldier; with Booth and Modjeska in 1889, he was the vengeful MacDuff; and finally with Modjeska on the road in the 1890s, he played the title role of Macbeth to her Lady Macbeth.

By 1894 Skinner was a completely trained actor, painstaking in technique and ever intent on giving a perfect performance. He went out on his own as a touring star, assembling a company of actors. Among them was actress Maud Durbin, whom he married in 1895. In his years of touring he played varying kinds of roles, both leads and character parts. Two plays in

his repertoire were written in collaboration with his brother Charles: *The King's Jester* and *Villon the Vagabond*. Both were historical romances, much in vogue at the time, and indicate the type of play in which Skinner, an actor in the grand romantic tradition, would find his career's greatest successes. Lovable rascals from the exotic, romantic past, swaggerers who used their wits and cunning to sweep aside all difficulties were the roles that his following—his autobiography calls them "my clientele"—wanted him to play.

Apart from appearing on Broadway opposite stage star Joseph Jefferson in *The Rivals* (1898), Skinner stayed on tour. He was better known to national audiences than in New York City, which had become the hub of theatrical activity and fame. In 1900 he opened there in his own dramatized version of a Robert Louis Stevenson story, *Prince Otto*. His performance in this play and in a 1901 revival of George H. Boker's *Francesca da Rimini* that he brought to New York won him critical praise. In 1902 he had a daughter, Cornelia Otis Skinner, later an actress, monologist, and writer.

By 1904 Skinner had realized that the increasingly commercial American theater necessitated his giving up the old system of touring in a repertory of plays. His future lay in creating a Broadway success and taking it on the road. That year he disbanded his company and went under the management of Charles Frohman, a leading New York producer and a power in the Theatrical Syndicate that controlled theaters nationwide. As one of Frohman's stable of stars, he consolidated his Broadway status in several plays.

Then in 1907 Frohman had a French play loosely adapted by one of his playwrights as *The Honor of the Family*. It showed how a swaggering ex-soldier in post-Napoleonic France overcame the schemes of conniving relatives by rascally wit and bluster. Frohman offered the lead role to Skinner, and it became one of the actor's most memorable roles. It also served as evidence that the audience knows best. Although he had conceived of the role of Philippe Bridau as a serious one, the reaction of an out-of-town audience showed him otherwise. His entrance at the end of act one was brief but forceful, ending with a threat and the crash of his swagger cane onto a table. He later recalled, "A yell of laughter went up from the audience and my blood froze. 'My God! They think I'm funny!' I had thought it a serious part. Instead, I found I was a comedian. But I didn't know it until the audience told me." After that, "bit by bit, and performance by performance," he revised his performance to make it a "serio-comic" role (*Theatre*, Apr. 1922).

Skinner's greatest success was yet to come. In *Kismet* (1911), a classic of romantic drama, he played the rascally, clever beggar Hajj, who goes from rags to riches to rags again in a single day, marrying his daughter to the young Caliph and murdering the evil Grand Vizier along the way. It ran a year in New York and three years on the road. The part, which Skinner's daughter writes was "longer than Hamlet and more strenuous than d'Artagnan," was taxing to a man now in his fifties and left him exhausted. In 1913, while on the road, he had to be operated on for "a virulent mastoid" that brought him near death.

Back in New York before a final year touring *Kismet*, Skinner found theatrical tastes shifting away from his grand style, which playwright George Middleton later would describe as "flamboyant and scene-filling, like rich claret running over everything." The public now wanted realism. In a *Harper's Weekly* article (11 Oct. 1913), Skinner expressed his hope that "the pendulum of the stage fashion" would swing back again. The public's interest in theater was being overtaken by growing fascination with motion pictures. In *The Silent Voice* (1914) Skinner tried to accommodate both developments. He played a modern role as deaf Montgomery Starr, who lip-reads his neighbors' troubles while they pass by his window and comes to their aid; filmed episodes projected on a screen show what Starr sees while the character's thoughts are spoken by Skinner as asides. The play did not succeed.

Two solid successes came to Skinner in his remaining years as a stage star. The role of a gentle, merry Italian in the romantic comedy *Mr. Antonio* carried him through the seasons of 1916–1918. He was also well received as bullfighter Juan Gallardo, ensnared by a siren, in *Blood and Sand* (1921). In addition, he appeared in a silent movie version of *Kismet* (1920).

Thereafter Skinner's acting was mainly limited to appearing in revivals and Shakespearean productions with limited runs. His last Broadway appearance was as a shrewd centenarian who reorders his family in *A Hundred Years Old* (1929). In a talking picture version of *Kismet* (1930) a reviewer found him "venerable" but "vigorous and effective" (*New York Times*, 31 Oct. 1930). Skinner, faithful to the stage, deplored in several articles the "art" of the movies. In semiretirement from acting, he published his autobiography in 1924, numerous magazine articles, and three more books: *Mad Folk of the Theatre* (1928); *One Man in His Time* (1938), an edition of a strolling player's memoirs; and *The Last Tragedian* (1939), a selection of Edwin Booth's letters. He died in New York City.

It must be said, as George Philip Birnbaum does, that Skinner "never appeared in an American play of lasting value, and he won most of his twentieth-century successes in old-fashioned romantic costume dramas." His place in theatrical history is as a leading exponent of the grand romantic style of acting popular from the late nineteenth century to World War I. He lived through three generations of theatrical change: from the stock company era he moved into the age of touring productions of Broadway hits, and he endured into a cinema-shadowed era of theatrical realism. Through it all he remained the complete professional as an actor, one who knew his strengths and his "clientele," played some 325 parts, wrote or co-wrote some of the works in which he appeared, starred in and managed a traveling company for years, and directed thirty-three of his plays.

• Otis Skinner's papers are in the Harvard Theatre Collection. Materials on his life and career are in the Billy Rose Theatre Collection at the New York Public Library for the Performing Arts, Lincoln Center. The fullest biographical source is his autobiography, *Footlights and Spotlights*; further views are in Cornelia Otis Skinner, *Family Circle* (1948). John Mason Brown's essay on Skinner's art is in his *Upstage* (1930). George Middleton's richly descriptive summary of Skinner's acting style is in *These Things Are Mine* (1947). Articles by and about Skinner are listed in Stephen Archer, *American Actors and Actresses: A Guide to Information Sources* (1983). Portraits and production photographs are in Daniel C. Blum, *Great Stars of the American Stage* (1952), *A Pictorial History of the American Theatre* (1960), and *A Pictorial History of the Silent Screen* (1953). Obituaries are in the *New York Times* and the *New York Herald Tribune*, both 5 Jan. 1942, and in *Variety*, 14 Jan. 1942.

WILLIAM STEPHENSON

SKLAR, George (31 May 1908–15 May 1988), playwright, novelist, and screenwriter, was born in Meriden, Connecticut, the son of Ezak Sklar and Bertha Marshak, the owners of a sporting-goods store. From high school in Meriden, Sklar entered Yale, where he took part in the student Dramatic Association as a writer and actor. After election to Phi Beta Kappa and graduation in 1929, he remained at Yale for two years to study playwriting in the School of Drama under George Pierce Baker.

In 1931 Sklar and Albert Maltz, a friend who also had studied with Baker, wrote *Merry-Go-Round*, a melodrama of corruption in big city politics. After a brief run at the Provincetown Playhouse in the spring of 1932, it was moved to Broadway, although only with difficulty. Mayor James J. Walker's administration, itself corrupt, made a bumbling effort to suppress it. Favorable reviews led to Hollywood offers for the authors and a film version, *Afraid to Talk*, released late in 1932.

After a brief period at the studios, Sklar came back to New York in 1933, as did Maltz. On their return, both writers were asked to join the executive board of the Theater Union, a new production unit dedicated to staging plays on social issues as viewed from a liberal-to-left perspective. In its short life from 1933 to 1937, this company offered even plays. The first was Sklar and Maltz's *Peace on Earth*, an antiwar tragedy. The next was *Stevedore* by Sklar and Paul Peters (1934), a revised version of a play written earlier by Peters. A suspenseful melodrama of a clash between black dockworkers and the white establishment in New Orleans, this work was the longest-running Theater Union production. It went on tour in the United States and was produced in London with a cast headed by Paul Robeson. The company had hoped to produce *Parade*, a revue with sketches mostly by Sklar and Peters, but, lacking the means, let the authors turn it over to the prestigious Theater Guild. It opened in 1935 to poor notices.

Also in 1935 Sklar along with seventy other writers signed the call for the first meeting of the American Writers' Congress, which was held in April. This meeting led to the formation of the League of American Writers, and organization whose members represented a spectrum of political views from the center to the far left. In the same year Sklar married Miriam Blecher, a dancer and choreographer who was active in social-minded dance troupes that, like the Theater Union, were a product of the Great Depression. The couple had three children.

With his three early successes, Sklar attracted the attention of major figures in mainstream theater as well as the burgeoning off-Broadway theater. In 1935 he was invited to serve on the advisory board of the Federal Theater Project, a nationwide network of producing units created to provide jobs for unemployed theater personnel, and in the following year he was elected to the executive committee of the Dramatists' Guild. In New York the Federal Theater's last production was Sklar's *Life and Death of an American*, a work tracing the hard life of the first (fictional) child of the twentieth century from his birth to his death from the bullet of a strikebreaking policeman. The play was in its second month when the Federal Theater was shut down by Congress in June 1939. Soon afterward Sklar returned to Hollywood. Los Angeles became his permanent home.

Although Sklar worked on scripts for major studios, he received few screen credits. He was not happy with his film work and took little interest in the social life of the film colony apart from gatherings of persons who, like himself, espoused leftist political causes. In 1947, seeking relief from screenwriting, he collaborated with Vera Caspary on a dramatic adaptation of her novel *Laura*, which had been filmed successfully in 1944. This was his last play to be staged in New York. Also in 1947 he published his first novel, *The Two Worlds of Johnny Truro*.

In 1951 at a hearing of the House Un-American Activities Committee, then investigating alleged Communist infiltration of Hollywood, Sklar was named by an informant as a sometime member of the Communist party. Sklar himself was never called before the committee and refused either to confirm or deny the charge. As a result, he was blacklisted by the studios. No longer employable as a screenwriter, he confined his attention to fiction and produced three more novels, *The Promising Young Men* (1951), *The Housewarming* (1953), and *The Identity of Dr. Frazier* (1961). Reviews ranged from respectful to enthusiastic, but the novels generated only modest income and because of the blacklist could not be bought for filming. Sklar's wife became the family's breadwinner as a teacher of dance. She continued to teach until 1977, two years before her death.

In 1966 Sklar returned to writing for the stage with *And People All Around*, a work based on the murder two years before of three young civil-rights workers in Mississippi. The play was produced to good notices in some forty university and community theaters. In 1967 it was staged by the Bristol Old Vic. Sklar's last play to be produced, *Brown Pelican* (1972), dealt with the urgent need to protect the earth's physical environment. This too was staged by troupes across the nation.

Sklar endured with an even temper the hardships created by the blacklist. A soft-spoken man, he possessed a fund of amusing and informative anecdotes about the theater of the depression and enjoyed sharing them. His hobby was listening to jazz, and he took pride in his massive collection of jazz recordings. He died in Los Angeles.

• Sklar's manuscripts and other papers are in the collection of Boston University. The New York Performing Arts Library has a slim file of clippings on his career and a file on each of his plays. Information on his family life and later career has been provided for this essay by his son, Zachary Sklar. For a detailed account of Sklar's theatrical activities in the 1930s, see Malcolm Goldstein, *The Political Stage: Drama and Theater of the Great Depression* (1974). On Sklar's politics and the blacklist, see Victor S. Navasky, *Naming Names* (1980), and Larry Ceplair and Steven Englund, *Inquisition in Hollywood: Politics in the Film Community, 1930–1960* (1980). An obituary is in the *New York Times*, 18 May 1988.

MALCOLM GOLDSTEIN

SKOURAS, Spyros Panagiotes (28 Mar. 1893–16 Aug. 1971), motion picture executive, was born near Skourahorion, Greece, the son of Panagiotes Skouras, a sheepherder; his mother's name is unknown. At fifteen, Skouras studied for the priesthood in Petras while working as a printer's devil and later as an office boy. In 1910 he emigrated to the United States, where he joined his older brother Charles in St. Louis. Skouras took a job as a busboy at the Planters Hotel. His sixteen-hour day began at the hotel before dawn, and at 4:00 P.M. he left for night school, where he studied English, accounting, commercial law, and shorthand. After two years at Jones Commercial College, he studied business at Benton College of Law. Pooling their earnings, the two brothers sent for their younger brother, George, and by 1914 the three of them had saved $3,000, which they invested, along with $1,000 from another partner, in an 800-seat motion picture theater in St. Louis, the Olympia. Much of their success as exhibitors resulted from their highly publicized concern for their customers' comfort and enjoyment, or, as one observer put it, their ability to create "an atmosphere of warm solicitude." By the end of 1914 the three brothers were able to buy out their partner and purchase two other theaters. In 1917 Skouras enlisted in the U.S. Army, but the war ended before he was commissioned, and in 1919 he returned to St. Louis. By 1926 the three brothers owned thirty-seven theaters in the St. Louis area as well as theaters in Kansas City and Indianapolis, which they managed in an association with Paramount's Publix theater chain. At a cost of $6 million the Skourases had also built a seventeen-story, air-conditioned office tower, which boasted St. Louis's premier movie palace, the Ambassador Theater. In 1920 Skouras married Saroulia Bruiglia, whom he had met at Jones Commercial College; they had five children.

In 1925 Skouras became a board member and trustee of First National Pictures, and four years later Warner Bros. purchased the chain and named Skouras general manager of all Warner theaters. In 1931 he left Warner Bros. for a similar job with Paramount, managing its theaters in New York, New Jersey, Delaware, Maryland, the District of Columbia, Virginia, West Virginia, and Ohio. In 1932 Skouras left Paramount for Fox, where he became head of its Metropolitan Theatres in New York. Within twelve months he transformed Metropolitan's $1 million-a-year loss into a $200,000 profit. Together with his brothers, Skouras took over administration of Wesco Corporation, Fox's West Coast theater chain. The chain was then in receivership, but within a year Skouras transformed it into a profit-making operation. By 1942 Wesco consisted of 563 theaters and was celebrated as "one of the outstandingly successful theatre operations in the country" (*Current Biography*). In 1942 Skouras became president of Twentieth Century–Fox, a position he held for twenty years. In 1933 his brother Charles became president of National Theaters, Fox's theater chain, while George eventually headed United Artists Theaters and in the 1950s played a role in developing the Todd-AO wide-screen process.

During World War II Skouras was head of Greek War Relief Association, raising more than $30 million to provide food, medicine, and other supplies to more than three million besieged Greeks. After the war he continued his involvement with the recovery of Greece through the American Overseas Aid–United National Appeal.

Skouras was instrumental in Twentieth Century–Fox's production of a number of film projects with religious themes, including *The Song of Bernadette* (1943), *The Keys of the Kingdom* (1944), and *The Robe* (1953). Pet projects included the studio's film noir semidocumentary dramas such as *The House on 92nd St.* (1945) and *Call Northside 777* (1948).

Skouras pushed Twentieth Century–Fox to invest in new technologies for exhibiting film. In the late 1940s the studio became involved in the research and development of a new Swiss invention known as Eidophor, a large-screen color television projection system designed for theater use.

His chief success in the innovation of exhibition technology was the development of CinemaScope, an anamorphic wide-screen process that quickly became a new industry standard, inspiring other major studios to devise similar processes, such as Panascope, Warnerscope, and Superscope. CinemaScope was based on the optical principles developed decades earlier by a French scientist, Henri Chrétien, and on stereo magnetic sound, which had been used in the Cinerama process (c. 1952). The CinemaScope camera lens squeezed a wide angle of view onto normal 35mm film; in the theater, a similar lens unsqueezed the compressed image, projecting it onto a screen that was originally 2.55 but later 2.35 times as wide as it was high. CinemaScope was designed, in part, to satisfy the needs of exhibitors for a new, affordable technology that could lure moviegoers away from other leisure-time pursuits and back into theaters. Introduced with *The Robe* in September 1953, CinemaScope revital-

ized the studio, whose profits dramatically increased during the next year, from $4.8 million to $8 million.

In 1962, under pressure from stockholders and the studio's board of directors, Skouras resigned as president of Twentieth Century–Fox after unprecedented losses of more than $35 million over the previous two years. The bulk of the losses resulted from the celebrated overexpenditures on *Cleopatra* (1963), a project that Skouras had approved; the film's budget more than doubled from an original $15 million. At the same time, Skouras was criticized for spending more than $20 million on the still-experimental Eidophor process, which was never successfully used. In addition, problems with actress Marilyn Monroe during the shooting of her last (unreleased) picture, *Something's Gotta Give* (1962), led to her firing and the film's cancellation, incurring losses of more than $2 million. Skouras was replaced by the longtime head of production at Twentieth Century–Fox, Darryl F. Zanuck. During the last decade of his life, Skouras increased his long-standing involvement in the shipping business, serving as chairman of the board of the Prudential-Grace Lines, Inc., and as a board director of Admiralty Enterprises. He died in Mamaroneck, New York.

As president of Twentieth Century–Fox, Skouras became one of the industry's most prominent champions of the motion picture exhibitor. After 1948, when the U.S. Supreme Court ordered the studios to divest themselves of their theater holdings, he sought to bridge the newly created gap between producer-distributors and exhibitors. According to *Time*, he "dealt directly with people in a manner that could make even a small hick-town exhibitor think he was God." His chief contribution to the industry—the development of CinemaScope—grew out of his appreciation of the power of movies as a theatrical experience for spectators and his efforts to make that experience as enjoyable and memorable as possible.

• Information about Skouras can be found in Glendon Allvine, *The Greatest Fox of Them All* (1969); Robert Coughlan, "Spyros Skouras and His Wonderful CinemaScope," *Life*, 20 July 1953; *Current Biography* (1943); Carlo Curti, *Skouras, King of Fox Studios* (1967); Douglas Gomery, "The Skouras Brothers: Bringing Movies to St. Louis and Beyond," *Marquee* 16, no. 1 (1984); and Aubrey Solomon, *Twentieth Century–Fox: A Corporate and Financial History* (1988). An obituary is in the *New York Times*, 17 Aug. 1971.

JOHN BELTON

SLADE, Joseph Alfred (1829 or 1830–10 Mar. 1864), reputed "bad man," was born in Carlyle, Illinois, the son of Charles W. Slade, a founder of Carlyle, an Illinois assemblyman, and a U.S. congressman, and Mary Kane. Little is known about Slade's childhood or education. In May 1847 he joined the volunteer army and served in the Mexican War, primarily as a teamster, detailed to protect the supply lines to the Santa Fe Trail. Honorably discharged on 16 October 1848, he soon obtained a veteran's land warrant for 160 acres and returned to Carlyle. From there he fled west, possibly to California, after killing a man with a rock in 1849. The deed may have been justified, for when he returned to Carlyle for a visit in the spring of 1863, he was not arrested.

In the late 1850s, Slade was in the employ of Russell, Majors & Waddell as a freighter and wagon-train boss and gained a considerable reputation as a cool and fearless fighter. When that firm established a passenger and mail service in the autumn of 1859 under the name of the Central Overland California and Pike's Peak Express Company, Slade replaced Jules Beni at the Julesburg station in the northeastern corner of Colorado and was charged to bring peace to the stagecoach divisions stretching along the southern border of present-day Wyoming. With gun and rope, he moved vigorously against Indian predators, horse thieves, and highwaymen and in so doing became involved in a feud with Jules Beni, who once caught Slade unarmed and unaware and riddled him with bullets and buckshot. Slade recovered, swore vengeance, and eventually trapped Beni. One legend has it that he tied him to a corral snubbing-post and slowly shot him to death in a most cruel manner, although there are discrepancies and disputes about virtually every aspect of this celebrated incident. It is a fact, however, that Slade cut off Beni's ears and carried them to the day of his own death.

When Russell, Majors & Waddell became insolvent in 1862, Ben Holladay, who took over some of its operations, continued to employ Slade but moved him to division headquarters at Virginia Dale in northern Colorado. Slade's indulgence in liquor increased, and he became a dangerous hell-raiser. After U.S. Army authorities complained about his destructive spree at Fort Halleck, located at the foot of the Medicine Bow Mountains, Holladay fired him near the end of 1862.

Slade and Maria Virginia (his wife either by formal ceremony or common law) and an Indian boy who lived with them moved to the Fort Bridger area in southwestern Wyoming, where Slade engaged in the freighting business on his own. From there he followed the gold rush to Virginia City, Montana, arriving in June 1863. He acquired mining claims, established two ranches—Ravenswood and Spring Dale—in Madison County, and engaged in freighting. He might have prospered had he not again succumbed to drunken rowdyism, shooting up saloons and stores and terrifying the citizenry of Virginia City and nearby towns. But he did not commit murder or theft and often made restitution for his destructiveness. A final spree during which he defied the People's Court and threatened the judge was his undoing. Vigilantes at Virginia City and the nearby mining camp of Nevada hanged Slade. His widow put his body in alcohol in a zinc coffin and buried him in Salt Lake City.

So ended the career of one of the West's gunmen. Reputedly he had claimed twenty-six lives, but he had never robbed or stolen and had risked his life many times so that passengers, supplies, and mails might travel in safety. The Montana editor of the *Madisonian* (quoted by McClernan, p. 7) noted that five years after

the hanging of Jack Slade, "another gunman, 'Wild Bill' Hickok, who had gone down in history as a great peacemaker and marshal, was known as 'the Slade of western Kansas.'"

"Jack" Slade's army discharge papers described him as five feet, six inches tall, with dark complexion, black eyes, and light hair. Mark Twain, who met him at the Rocky Ridge station, east of South Pass, noted that he was "rather broad across the cheek bones" with lips "peculiarly thin and straight" and "the most gentlemanly appearing, quiet and affable officer" he had found along the road.

• John B. McClernan, *Slade's Wells Fargo Colt* (1977), best documents Slade's career and includes a good bibliography. Lew L. Callaway, "Joseph Alfred Slade: Killer or Victim?," *Montana: The Magazine of Western History* 3 (1953): 4–34, gives details about the violent episodes, real and legendary. In *Roughing It* (1872), Mark Twain devoted two chapters to Slade, one recounting his meeting and reaction to Slade on the overland stage, and the second quoting Thomas J. Dimsdale's description of the arrest and execution of Slade in his *The Vigilantes of Montana* (1866).

MARY LEE SPENCE

SLATER, Duke (19 Dec. 1898–15 Aug. 1966), football player and judge, was born Frederick Wayman Slater in Normal, Illinois, the son of the Reverend George W. Slater, Jr., and Letha Jones. As a minister in the African Methodist Episcopal church, Slater's father moved around so frequently that as a boy he was left to live for long periods with his grandparents in Chicago. During these visits he recalled playing "prairie" football, a pick-up form of the game, at Racine Avenue and Sixty-first Street, the neighborhood from which would spring his future team, the Chicago Cardinals. His old friends speculated that Slater received his nickname because of a mongrel dog named Duke, which he owned as a boy.

In 1913 his father accepted a position in Clinton, Iowa, where Slater attended high school and played football. When he asked his parents to buy him a helmet and a pair of football shoes, neither of which were supplied by the Clinton team, he was told that they could only afford one of the items. Slater chose the shoes; he subsequently played without a helmet through his career in high school, college, and the pros. After a spectacular four years as a tackle at Clinton High School, the 6'2", 210-pound Slater enrolled at the University of Iowa. Because so many able-bodied athletes were at war in 1918, Slater was allowed to compete as a freshman and almost immediately established himself as one of the nation's best college linemen. He was selected by an Iowa newspaper to the Iowa all-state college team in 1918 as well as in each of his three succeeding varsity years. In 1919 Slater was named by Walter Camp as a third team tackle on his prestigious All-America team. Slater was one of only a score of African Americans playing football at major white colleges in the postwar years. He was occasionally harassed by fans or singled out for extra rough play, but he seldom responded to the offenses. Because of his size, strength, and agility, Slater was usually double-teamed and occasionally triple-teamed. Herbert "Fritz" Crisler, a former Michigan player and later a famed coach, who played against Slater in 1919 and 1920, remarked that "Duke Slater was the best tackle I ever played against. I tried to block him throughout my college career but never once did I impede his progress to the ball carrier" (*Chicago Tribune*, 16 Aug. 1966).

In 1921, the year he graduated, Slater led Iowa to its most successful season to that point. The Hawkeyes were undefeated (7–0), won the Western Conference (Big Ten) championship, and defeated a highly regarded Notre Dame team that had not suffered a loss in three seasons. Slater considered the 10–7 victory over Notre Dame his greatest day in sports. After the season, he was named second team tackle on Walter Camp's All-America team but was selected first team All-America tackle on several other teams, including those picked by Walter Eckersall, the International News Service, and Walter Trumbull for the *New York Herald*.

After graduation Slater joined the Rock Island Independents of the recently renamed National Football League. With the exception of the three games in 1922 when he was loaned out to the Milwaukee Badgers who were coached by his friend Fritz Pollard, Slater played for Rock Island in the NFL from 1922–1925. He did not get a full chance to showcase his awesome talent because the Independents were mainly an NFL "road team." These road teams played a limited schedule against other NFL teams, were not serious contenders for the league championship, and played all or most of their games on the road. During the early 1920s when there were usually less than a half-dozen African Americans in the NFL, black players such as Dick Hudson, Jay Mayo "Ink" Williams, and Sol Butler found it easier to find employment with road teams.

Slater continued to play with Rock Island after it joined the recently created American Football League, founded in 1926 by Harold "Red" Grange and his business partner Charles C. Pyle. When the Rock Island franchise folded in early November, Slater was signed by the Chicago Cardinals of the NFL. He played the remainder of his career (1926–1931) with the Cardinals and established himself as one of the league's best tackles. He made unofficial all-NFL teams as tackle three times, in 1927, 1928, and 1929. In 1927 and 1929, he was the only African-American player in the league. Grange, who played with the rival Chicago Bears after the demise of the AFL, considered Slater the greatest tackle of all time. Among his many thrills in the NFL, Slater rated as the most memorable the Cardinals Thanksgiving Day 1929 40–7 victory over the Chicago Bears in which Ernie Nevers scored all forty points.

While playing pro football, Slater attended law school in the off-season at the University of Iowa. He married Edda Searcy in 1926; they had no children. Slater received his law degree in 1928, was admitted to

the Iowa bar the same year, and the Illinois bar the following year. After he retired from pro football in 1931, he opened a law practice in Chicago. In 1934 Slater was director of athletics and football coach at Douglass High School in Oklahoma City, but he returned to Chicago the following year and became involved in Democratic politics. After spending thirteen years in various governmental positions, including assistant corporate counsel for Chicago and assistant commissioner of the Illinois Commerce Commission, he was elected to the Chicago Municipal Court in 1948. Slater was only the third African American elected to that court in more than forty years. He was later advanced to the Superior Court and the Circuit Court. Among his many honors, Slater is in the College Football Hall of Fame. He was still a judge at the time of his death in Chicago.

• A clipping file on Slater is in the Professional Football Hall of Fame in Canton, Ohio. For a brief review of his college career, see Ocania Chalk, *Black College Sport* (1976). On his NFL years, see David S. Neft and Richard M. Cohen, *The Sports Encyclopedia: Pro Football, the Early Years* (1987), and Mike Rathet and Don R. Smith, *Their Deeds and Dogged Faith* (1984). See also John O'Donnell, "Sports Chat," (Davenport) *Times-Democrat*, 16 Aug. 1966, and Leighton Housh, "Fair Play," (Des Moines) *Register*, 4 Sept. 1966. An obituary is in the *Chicago Tribune*, 16 Aug. 1966.

JOHN M. CARROLL

SLATER, John Clarke (22 Dec. 1900–25 July 1976), physicist, was born in Oak Park, Illinois, the son of John R. Slater, a journalist, and Katherine Chapin. The family moved to Rochester, New York, when Slater's father became a professor of English at the University of Rochester in 1905. After graduating from East Rochester High School in 1917, Slater completed a bachelor of science degree in physics at the University of Rochester in 1920. He studied physics at Harvard University and earned a master's degree in 1922 and a doctorate in 1923. Under the supervision of Percy Williams Bridgman, Slater investigated the compressibility of the alkali halides at high temperatures. As he completed his doctoral studies, however, his interests turned to theoretical physics, especially quantum mechanics. Slater pursued this new interest in the major physics laboratories of Cambridge, England, and Copenhagen, Denmark, as a recipient of Harvard's Scandinavian and Sheldon Travelling Fellowships from 1923 to 1924. At Cambridge, he developed a quantum theory of radiation, maintaining that light quanta were guided by the classical radiation fields. In Copenhagen, he shared these ideas with Niels Bohr, the father of modern atomic structure, who immediately appreciated Slater's ideas and, in 1924, published four papers with him that established the quantum theory of radiation.

Upon his return to the United States, Slater joined the physics faculty at Harvard University as an instructor in 1924. He became an assistant professor in 1926 and an associate professor in 1929. Slater's research initially concentrated on atomic spectra theory, investigating particularly how quantum mechanics could be extended from Bohr's theory to multielectron systems. Just as he was about to complete a paper on the equivalence of classical Poisson brackets with quantum mechanical communicators in 1926, he learned that Paul Dirac, of Great Britain, had just published a paper on a closely related topic. In 1927 Slater found himself again in competition with Dirac in reaching a complete understanding of the emission and absorption of radiation. At that time, he switched the focus of his study from dynamic to stationary states of matter. Slater decided to investigate the binding energy of the helium molecule, since Bohr's theory of atomic structure failed to explain the behavior of simple electron systems, such as the helium and hydrogen molecules. Through trial and error, he arrived at an approximate wave function for the helium molecule, using a line of reasoning quantitatively similar to Hartree's self-consistent-field method. Slater's solution to the helium problem led to an understanding of the repulsive interaction between two helium atoms, a problem that—as a graduate student in 1923—he had believed to be irresolvable within the paradigm of classical electrostatic interaction.

Slater's investigation of simple electron systems led him to develop determinants, known as Slater's determinants, to explain single-electron spin-orbital functions. By studying hydrogen, he showed how Hartree's self-consistent-field approach for several multielectron systems also explained the similarity of alkalis to hydrogen, and how Hartree's single-electron eigenvalues were approximations of ionization energies. In applying Hartree's single-electron eigenvalues, as well as Heisenberg and Dirac's ideas of wave function symmetry and antisymmetry, to the three-electron lithium atom, Slater demonstrated that a determinant of one-electron spin-orbital function automatically satisfied Pauli's exclusion principle. He refined his ideas of determinants, applying them to crystalline solids, as a Guggenheim fellow in Leipzig, Germany, from 1929 to 1930.

In 1930 Slater became the head of the physics department at the Massachusetts Institute of Technology (MIT). In addition to reorganizing both the undergraduate and graduate programs, he increased the size of the department, enhancing both the national and international prestige of the department. With his colleague Nathaniel H. Frank, Slater reworked the courses and started writing a series of textbooks, an endeavor that he continued for the duration of his academic career. In addition to administrative duties, he continued to conduct research, and his interests shifted from atomic structure to the structure of molecules and solids, especially energy bands in metals, the structure of alloys and insulating crystals, and superconductivity. In 1937 he introduced the augmented plane-wave method for calculating energy bands in crystals, in which solutions of the Schrödinger equation in spherically symmetrical potentials about the lattice sites are matched with the plane-wave solutions of a constant potential in the interstitial regions.

During World War II Slater became part of the Radiation Laboratory at MIT, which was established to develop microwave radar. He worked on magnetrons, a variety of diode vacuum tubes, the operation of which was then poorly understood. Within a few weeks he had worked out a general theory of magnetrons, using methods analogous to the calculation of a self-consistent field in an atom. His theory formed the basis of most subsequent advances in magnetron design. In 1941 Slater transferred to the Bell Telephone Laboratories, where he continued both experimental and theoretical work on magnetrons until 1945. After World War II he transformed the Radiation Laboratory into the peacetime Research Laboratory of Electronics and established the Laboratory of Nuclear Science and Engineering at MIT.

At this time Slater returned to the study of molecular and solid-state theory. In 1951 he developed a simplification of the Hartree-Fock self-consistent-field method, later known as the X method. This method facilitated the calculation of correlation or exchange energies, which is particularly difficult to handle in self-consistent-field computations. In 1950 Slater organized a small research group called the Solid State and Molecular Theory Group to put the quantum theory of atoms, molecules, and solids on a quantitative basis as rapidly as possible. Slater stressed the importance of the Hartree-Fock method, particularly the X method, for calculating electronic structure. At this time, his research was aided by computers. The greatest activity in the study of atoms came in the 1950s and 1960s with extensive Hartree-Fock equations. Work on molecules, however, progressed slowly because of the greater difficulties in computation, but increasing computational skill and more powerful computers enabled them to construct more realistic wave functions, and by the early 1960s work had been done on diatomic molecules, water, and methane. Calculations of the electronic structure of solids were the most difficult. The early attempts neglected self-consistency; they gave reasonably good results for energy bands but were unsatisfactory in other respects. By 1965 the methods were made self-consistent.

After his retirement from MIT in 1966, Slater joined the Quantum Theory Project set up by Per-Olov Lowdin at the University of Florida. With Lowdin and others, Slater extended and refined the methods he had developed in the 1950s and 1960s, using increasingly powerful computer programs. The properties calculated included compressibility of solids, magnetic properties of ferromagnetic and antiferromagnetic materials, and binding energies and magnetic properties of polyatomic molecules. Unlike many of the young American physicists trained in the 1920s who turned to nuclear physics, many as a result of working on the development of nuclear weapons during World War II, Slater focused instead on theoretical physics and promoted that course of investigation in the United States. Under his leadership at MIT, the United States became the leader in that aspect of physical research as well as nuclear physics. Slater died at Sanibel Island, Florida.

• Slater's personal papers, a major collection, are in the library of the American Philosophical Society, Philadelphia, Pa. The universities with which he was associated have biographical files on Slater. His books include *Introduction to Theoretical Physics*, with N. H. Frank (1933); *Introduction to Chemical Physics* (1939); *Microwave Transmission* (1942); *Mechanics*, with Frank (1947); *Quantum Theory of Matter* (1951; 2d ed., 1968); *Modern Physics* (1955); *Quantum Theory of Atomic Structure* (2 vols., 1960); *Quantum Theory of Molecules and Solids* (4 vols., 1963–1974); and *Solid-State and Molecular Theory: A Scientific Biography* (1975), among others. For additional biographical information see Katherine R. Sopka, *Quantum Physics in America, 1920–1935* (1980). Obituaries are in *Physics Today* 29 (Oct. 1976): 88–89, and the *New York Times*, 27 July 1976.

ADAM R. HORNBUCKLE

SLATER, John Fox (4 Mar. 1815–7 May 1884), textile manufacturer and philanthropist, was born in Slatersville, Rhode Island, the son of John Slater, a successful cotton manufacturer who established the company town of Slatersville, and Ruth Bucklin. Slatersville was sited by John Slater in 1805, two years after he migrated to the United States, at age twenty-seven, from Derbyshire, England, bringing with him a knowledge of the latest in cotton textile technology. John joined his older brother Samuel Slater, the reputed "father of the American textile industry," and two Quaker merchant-capitalist partners in constructing the nation's most modern yarn-spinning mill. Newly married, John moved to the village to manage operations. The Slatersville mills were run in an authoritarian, paternalistic manner. John and Ruth Slater, devout Congregationalists, commanded church and Sunday school attendance and forbade the use of spirits. John Fox, the elder of two sons, was reared in this rural, religious environment. Through his mid-teen years, he received a superior education in private academies in Connecticut and Massachusetts.

In 1831, at age sixteen, John Fox was given supervisory responsibilities in operating a cotton mill at Jewett City, Connecticut, which had been acquired by his father and uncle Samuel in 1823 and conveyed to his father eight years later. By 1834, with his father aging, John Fox Slater was placed in full charge of the Jewett City facilities as well as a smaller mill at Hopeville, Connecticut.

In 1840 Slater decided to make Norwich, Connecticut, his base of operations. In 1844 he married Marianna "Mary" Lanman Hubbard of that city and there constructed a Greek-revival style home; the couple eventually had two children.

Following his father's death in 1843, John and his brother William acquired the family's extensive business interests and until 1872 operated under a partnership arrangement, styled J. and W. Slater, with William managing the Slatersville properties and John the Jewett City facilities. John Fox Slater proceeded to make significant improvements to his mills, replacing the initial wooden structure with a larger brick building. In 1859 he substantially increased mill housing. The capacity of his mills grew steadily, from ninety looms in 1853 to 449 looms in 1884. By 1865 he was identified as Norwich's wealthiest citizen, with an annual income of $104,269, more than twice that of the city's next two most affluent residents.

In 1869 Slater joined a number of entrepreneurs in building a mill at a virgin site just outside Norwich. In a company town named Taftville, the Ponemah mill, completed in 1871, was the largest single structure for cotton manufacturing in the nation. Housing for 1,500 employees was constructed on a hillside overlooking the mill, and an entire mill village was established. Slater was named president of the enterprise. In 1872 the Slater partnership was dissolved, with John Fox Slater becoming solely responsible for both the Jewett City and Ponemah mills operations, while William continued to manage the Slatersville properties.

Over the years, Slater became financially involved in a wide range of business enterprises. He became an investor and director of Washburn & Moen Manufacturing Company of Worcester, Massachusetts, Pacific Mills of Lawrence, Massachusetts, and American Screw Company of Providence, Rhode Island. He was named a director of the Norwich and New London Steamship Company and served as a director of three railroads, the Norwich and Worcester, the Joliet and Chicago, and the Chicago and Alton, which named the town of Slater, Missouri, after him.

In Norwich he became a director of the Norwich Fire Insurance Company and the Norwich City Gas Company. He was a major contributor to a host of civic charities, especially those dealing with education. For a quarter-century he served as trustee of the Norwich Free Academy, and he was a longtime member and major contributor to the Park Congregational Church. In 1862 Slater built a mansion on a nine-acre lot, with a conservatory in the rear. When he and his wife later separated, Slater built Mary Slater a substantial brick home in 1876. Widely traveled, with a taste for art, reserved and unostentatious, and described by a contemporary as "a delightful and resourceful conversationalist" on a wide spectrum of issues, Slater gained the respect and admiration of leading men of affairs throughout the nation.

Feeling a deep sense of responsibility for his wealth, as he grew older Slater pondered how best to begin disposing some of it usefully during his lifetime. In 1882, on the occasion of his sixty-seventh birthday, Slater informed the press that ten distinguished Americans had agreed to administer a fund amounting to $1 million that he was making available, the purpose of which would be "the uplifting of the lately emancipated population of the Southern States and their posterity by conferring on them the blessings of a Christian education." The aid was justified, he stated, "in view of the prevailing ignorance, which exists by no fault of their own." The enhanced education, designed to make them "good men and good citizens," would also be "for the sake of our common country," in which the freedmen had recently been granted political rights.

Slater designated former U.S. president Rutherford B. Hayes to head the fund. Other trustees included Chief Justice of the Supreme Court Morrison R. Waite, William E. Dodge, cofounder of Phelps–Dodge Corporation, Daniel C. Gilman, president of Johns Hopkins University, and Alfred A. Colquitt, governor of. Georgia. Chartered in New York State as the John F. Slater Fund on 1 May 1882, the corporation was given the power to invest the principal amount and distribute the proceeds periodically at the trustees' discretion, with no restrictions. Slater did request that priority be given to the training of teachers. The first allocation, made in 1882–1883, was $16,250 for scholarships to twelve schools that provided instruction in trades and manual occupations. In 1937 the Slater fund was one of three foundations merged to form the Southern Educational Foundation of Atlanta, Georgia. As of the late twentieth century, the foundation was still in existence. Congress in 1883 passed a resolution thanking Slater and in 1886 appropriated a sum of $1,000 to strike a gold medal, which was presented posthumously to his son. Slater died in Norwich.

• A full-length biography of John Fox Slater has yet to be published. Considerable biographical information, however, is contained in William R. Bagnall, *The Textile Industries of the United States* (1893), reprinted by Augustus M. Kelley (1971). S. H. Howe, "A Brief Memoir of the Life of John F. Slater of Norwich, Connecticut, 1815 to 1884" (1894), quotes contemporary sources regarding Slater's character and personality. The Otis Library in Norwich carries issues of the city's newspaper, the *Norwich Bulletin*, and the *Norwich Heritage Trust Newsletter*, valuable for information on both Slater and the Slater fund. See especially the obituary in the *Bulletin*, 8 May 1884, and articles in the 6 June 1965 and 13 Sept. 1987 issues. An essay on the Slater family in the *Norwich Heritage Trust Newsletter* (May 1987) contains information not found elsewhere. Barbara M. Tucker, *Samuel Slater and the Origins of the American Textile Industry, 1790–1860* (1984), provides an excellent overview of the industry in the antebellum period. David J. Jeremy, *Transatlantic Industrial Revolution: The Diffusion of Textile Technologies between Britain and America, 1790–1830s* (1981), describes mill technology at the time Slater launched his business career as well as information on his father and uncle and the town of Slatersville. Steve Dunwell, *The Run of the Mill* (1978), is useful on the rise and decline of the Rhode Island and Connecticut mill centers developed by the Slater family.

JACK BLICKSILVER

SLATER, Samuel (9 June 1768–20 Apr. 1835), cotton manufacturer, was born in Belper, Derbyshire, England, the son of William Slater, an independent farmer and timber merchant, and Elizabeth Fox. Slater spent his youth in Derbyshire, home to the world's first water-powered textile mills. He had a common school education and favored writing and arithmetic. At age fourteen Slater went to work for Jedediah Strutt, a friend of his father's and the former partner of Richard Arkwright, the man who in 1771 had produced the first water-powered spinning frame. After his father died, Slater signed his own indenture papers on 8 January 1783 and became Strutt's apprentice for six years at his new mill in nearby Milford, where he rose to the position of overseer. After his apprenticeship he worked for Strutt as a salaried supervisor for several months, thereby improving his comprehensive knowledge of Strutt's factories and the Arkwright spinning system.

Lured by rumors and newspaper advertisements of bounties offered for mechanical expertise by American state legislatures, Slater took ship in London for New York. The emigration of textile mechanics and exportation of related technology from England was illegal at the time, so Slater carried only his indenture certificate as evidence of his profession.

On 18 November 1789 Slater arrived in New York, but soon he sailed to Rhode Island to meet Moses Brown, who was known to be searching for mechanics familiar with Arkwright's machines, and who had already collected some inoperative replicas of Arkwright machines at Pawtuckett. On 5 April 1790 Slater contracted with William Almy and Smith Brown to begin a water-powered cotton-spinning mill. In return for one-half the net profits and one-half ownership of the machinery, Slater agreed to build machines "similar to those used in England, for the like purposes."

Slater's friend and chief biographer, George S. White, who has influenced most subsequent accounts, emphasized that Slater worked without written plans or diagrams and "without the aid of anyone who had ever seen such machinery." In reality, Slater was assisted by skilled ironworkers and woodworkers in salvaging parts from and possibly rebuilding one of Moses Brown's inoperative machines. Within months he had produced America's first cotton yarn spun by waterpower. On 20 December 1790 Slater and his partners began operating three carding and roving machines and two spinning frames with seventy-two spindles in a converted fulling mill.

In 1791 Slater married Hannah Wilkinson, with whose family he had boarded since arriving in Pawtuckett. Together they would raise six boys—one other son and two daughters died in infancy—before Hannah died of consumption in 1812. She is credited with discovering cotton sewing thread in 1793, when she spun together two strands of the yarn produced by Slater's mill and found the result stronger than the conventional linen sewing thread.

Almy, Brown, and Slater moved their machinery to a new, two-and-a-half story building in 1793, creating what became known as the "Old Slater Mill." Slater then formed Samuel Slater & Co. with his in-laws and opened a second factory, "the White Mill," in Rehoboth, Massachusetts, in 1798. He continually struggled to find laborers during these early years, first attempting to replicate Strutt's apprenticeship method and a system of contract child laborers. Slater established a Sunday school as Strutt had done and offered firm and fair discipline in his mills, yet he still had to overcome the poor reputation that English textile laborers had in the United States. In addition, he vied with parents over the control of their children who worked for him. Slater's solution, in addition to adopting elements of Strutt's and Arkwright's management practices, was to use a family system of labor, whereby children tended his machines while their fathers worked for the company in more traditionally accepted occupations. Slater's system provided a model for many of his competitors.

In 1807 Almy, Brown, Slater, and Slater's brother John opened a third mill on the South Branch of the Blackstone River. Slater earlier had invited his brother, who had a working knowledge of Derbyshire's new Crompton spinning mule, to join him in America. The mill community they created became known as Slatersville, Rhode Island, and may have been the first planned factory village in the United States.

War came in 1812 and initially helped the nascent textile industry, though it ultimately would confirm Slater's long-held fears about overproduction. The wartime prosperity and reduction of imports encouraged expansion, such as Slater's "Green Mill" at Oxford, Massachusetts, a town that later became Webster, named so by Slater out of admiration for Daniel Webster. Well established, experienced, and financially diversified, Slater, unlike many other mill owners, survived the postwar deluge of cheap English textiles.

The Slater family and businesses continued to grow. In 1817 he married Esther Parkinson, the widow of a friend. They had no children. He, his sons, and in-laws expanded their milling ventures. In 1827 at Providence, Rhode Island, Slater built one of the nation's earliest steam cotton mills. Though careful in his own enterprises, Slater weathered the depression of 1829 with the huge burden of having endorsed too many younger entrepreneurs for a combined total of $300,000 debt. By 1835 Slater rebounded. He had founded, purchased, or partially owned sixteen firms, thirteen of which were textile mills. That same year, Slater died at home in Webster, Massachusetts.

In 1833 President Andrew Jackson, having toured the Old Slater Mill, visited Slater at his house: "I understand you taught us how to spin, so as to rival Great Britain in her manufactures; you set all these thousands of spindles to work." Slater replied, "Yes sir, I suppose that I gave out the psalm, and they have been singing to the tune ever since."

Although he is no longer heroized as the man from whose head sprang the American textile industry, he was a central figure in its birth. He was responsible both for advancing the transfer of crucial technology and, perhaps more important, for developing the necessary managerial practices.

• The first and most influential chronicle of Slater's life is George Savage White, *Memoir of Samuel Slater, The Father of American Manufactures, Connected with a History of the Rise and Progress of the Cotton Manufacture in England and America, with Remarks on the Moral Influence of Manufactories in the United States* (1836). Other standard works include William R. Bagnall, *Samuel Slater and the Early Development of the Cotton Manufacture in the United States* (1890), and Frederick Lewis Lewton, "Samuel Slater and the Oldest Cotton Machinery in America," in the *Annual Report of the Board of Regents of the Smithsonian Institution . . . 1926* (1926). See also Barbara M. Tucker, *Samuel Slater and the Origins of the American Textile Industry, 1790–1860* (1984), and Jonathan Prude, *The Coming of Industrial Order: Town and Factory Life in Rural Massachusetts, 1810–1860* (1983), on his contribution to industrial organization and principles of management, and James L. Conrad, Jr., "The Evolution of Industrial Capitalism in Rhode Island, 1790–1830: Almy, the Browns, and the Slaters" (Ph.D. diss., Univ. of Connecticut, 1973), and Gary B. Kulik, "The Beginnings of the Industrial Revolution in America: Pawtuckett, Rhode Island, 1672–1829" (Ph.D. diss., Brown Univ., 1980), on his impact on New England's artisan economy and early factory workers. Also useful is Paul E. Rivard, *Samuel Slater: A Short Interpretive Essay on Samuel Slater's Role in the Birth of the American Textile Industry* (1974).

JOHN R. DICHTL

SLATTERY, Charles Lewis (9 Dec. 1867–12 Mar. 1930), Episcopal bishop, was born in Pittsburgh, Pennsylvania, the son of George Sidney Leffingwell Slattery, an Episcopal priest, and Emma McClellan Hall. His father died in 1872, and the family then moved to Brunswick, Maine. He received his B.A. summa cum laude in 1891 from Harvard, where he studied classics and philosophy, and his B.D. in 1894 from the Episcopal Theological School, Cambridge, Massachusetts. On 20 June 1894 Bishop William Lawrence of Massachusetts ordained him deacon, and he began his ministry as master of Groton School, also teaching Greek, and serving St. Andrew's Church in Ayer, Massachusetts, as minister-in-charge. Bishop Lawrence ordained him priest on 8 June 1895.

From 1896 to 1907 Slattery was dean of the Cathedral of Our Merciful Saviour in Faribault, Minnesota, the first cathedral in the Episcopal church. As dean of the cathedral Slattery worked with the bishop in supervising clergy in mission work, designing a full range of liturgical services, and in managing a program of pastoral care and social action. While at Faribault he was a lecturer at the Seabury Divinity School (1905–1907). He also represented the diocese of Minnesota on the standing committee and in the general convention. In 1907 he became rector of Christ Church in Springfield, Massachusetts, succeeding John Cotton Brooks, the brother of Phillips Brooks. He remained at Christ Church until 1910 and in 1909–1910 was a lecturer at the Berkeley Divinity School, Middletown, Connecticut. In 1909 he was elected professor of ecclesiastical history at the General Theological Seminary, New York City, but declined because of his commitment to the parochial ministry.

From 1910 to 1922 Slattery was rector of Grace Church, New York City, where he succeeded William Reed Huntington, who had been rector from 1883 to 1909. As a result of Slattery's preaching and his effective administration of the parish, Grace Church increased its membership, added $1 million to the parish endowment, and contributed more than $400,000 (the largest sum given by any parish) to the church pension fund, which began operation on 1 March 1917. While at Grace Church he served on the standing committee of the diocese of New York.

Slattery was a clerical deputy to the general conventions of 1907, 1919, 1922, and 1925. In this capacity he served on both the Hymnal Commission and the Church War Commission. He was chairman of the Commission for the Revision and Enrichment of the Book of Common Prayer. The work of this commission resulted in the 1928 prayer book. Slattery was an overseer of Harvard College, a trustee of Boston University and Brooks School (Andover), president of the Board of Trustees of Wellesley College, and director of the Wellesley Conference for Church Workers. He also served as general chairman of the church congress. He delivered the Paddock Lectures at the General Theological Seminary in 1911–1912 and the West Lectures at Stanford University in 1915.

On 4 May 1922 Slattery was elected bishop coadjutor of Massachusetts and was consecrated at Trinity Church, Boston, on 31 October 1922 by Bishop William Lawrence of Massachusetts. In 1923 he married Sarah Lawrence, daughter of Bishop Lawrence; they had no children. Bishop Lawrence retired on 1 June 1927, and Slattery succeeded him as the eighth bishop of Massachusetts, a position he held for less than three years. He died in Boston after a brief illness.

Slattery was a prolific writer who could craft theological books for a popular audience. Several of his books grew out of his instruction of confirmation classes; others treated practical dimensions of the Christian life, such as the technique of prayer and how to prepare for Holy Communion. He was especially adept at writing biographies, among them, *Felix Reville Brunot, 1820–1898, a Civilian in the War for the Union, President of the First Board of Indian Commissioners* (1901), a study of the man who served as his surrogate father during his childhood in Maine; *Edward Lincoln Atkinson, 1865–1902* (1904), a Harvard friend; *Alexander Viets Griswold Allen* (1911), his teacher at seminary; *David Hummel Greer, 1841–1908, Eighth Bishop of New York* (1921), Slattery's bishop while he was at Grace Church, New York; and *William Austin Smith, a Sketch* (1925), a friend. All of his biographies were of close friends.

A Broad churchman committed to the ecumenical movement, Slattery was concerned that Christian doctrine not be interpreted in a narrow, exclusive way, and he was open to the new insights of science and biblical criticism. Possibly his major contribution to the church was his work on the revision of the Episcopal prayer book.

• Most of Slattery's papers are in the archives of the diocese of Massachusetts in Boston and in the archives of the Episcopal church, Austin, Tex. His major published works are *The Master of the Word, a Study of Christ* (1906), *Life beyond Life, a Study of Immortality* (1907), *The Historic Ministry and the Present Christ, an Appeal for Unity* (1908), *Present-day Preaching* (1910), *The Authority of Religious Experience* (1912), *The Light Within, a Study of the Holy Spirit* (1915), *Why Men Pray* (1916), *The Gift of Immortality, a Study in Responsibility* (1916), *A Churchman's Reading, an Essay for Laymen* (1917), *Certain American Faces: Sketches from Life* (1918), *With God in the War* (1918), *The Holy Communion* (1918), *How to Pray, a Study of the Lord's Prayer* (1920), *The Ministry* (1921), *Prayers for Private and Family Use* (1922), *Holy Communion, What It Means and How to Prepare for It* (1922), *The Spirit of France, as Told in Forty-two Sonnets* (1923), *Bible Lessons for the Sunday Mornings of the Christian Year* (1925), *The Words from His Throne, a Study of the Cross* (1927), *In Time of Sorrow, a Book of Consolation* (1927), and *Following Christ* (1928). The only significant study of his life and work is Howard Chandler Robbins, *Charles Lewis Slattery* (1931).

DONALD S. ARMENTROUT

SLATTERY, John Richard (16 July 1851–6 Mar. 1926), priest and attorney, was born in New York City, the son of James Slattery, a contractor, and Margaret Sbreel, Irish immigrants. His father rose from laborer to entrepreneur during the 1860s in partnership with his brothers Patrick and John. Their construction business depended heavily on municipal contracts for roads and parks and hence on political patronage. The Slatterys invested their contracting profits in real estate. They attended St. Paul's parish at Fifty-ninth Street and Ninth Avenue, where John made the acquaintance of Isaac Hecker and the Paulist fathers.

John Slattery was educated in New York public schools and at the College of the City of New York. In 1865 he entered St. Charles College in Ellicott City, Maryland, to study for the priesthood for the Archdiocese of New York. A recurring eye problem caused him to leave the next year. In 1871 he entered Columbia College School of Law. In 1872 he heard Bishop Herbert Vaughan, founder of the English Foreign Mission Society, preach at St. Paul's on the need for missionaries to African Americans. Shortly before graduation, after witnessing a parade of African Americans on a New York street, he made a seemingly sudden and unexpected decision to devote his life to their evangelization. In January 1873 he entered the seminary for the English Foreign Mission Society at Mill Hill, London, England.

Ordained to the priesthood on 17 March 1877, Slattery returned to the United States that October. He served as pastor of St. Francis Xavier Church in Baltimore, as U.S. provincial for Mill Hill (1878–1883), as missionary in the Richmond area (1884–1887), and as rector of St. Joseph's Seminary in Baltimore (1888–1902). He founded the seminary and Epiphany Apostolic College to train priests for the African-American mission. In 1892, with the approval of Cardinal Gibbons of Baltimore and Vaughan, Slattery arranged for five priests to separate from Mill Hill to form St. Joseph's Society of the Sacred Heart (the Josephites) to work exclusively among African Americans. From 1892 to 1903 he served as first superior general of the Josephites.

Slattery published more than thirty articles, many in the Paulists' *Catholic World*, and was recognized as the leading Catholic spokesperson on the race question. Against the rising "scientific" racism of the day, he defended the full human dignity of African Americans. "The negro, then," he declared before the World Parliament of Religions in Chicago in 1893, "is of the race of Adam, created by the same God, redeemed by the same Saviour and destined to the same heaven as the white man" (Barrows, p. 1104). He was convinced that the Catholic mission to African Americans would not succeed without black priests. At a time when solidifying racial segregation patterns kept Catholic institutions of higher learning closed to black students, Slattery integrated Josephite seminaries and, with the cooperation of the Sulpicians, St. Mary's Seminary in Baltimore. The first two African-American Catholic priests ordained in the United States, the Josephites Charles Randolph Uncles and John Henry Dorsey, were educated in these institutions. At Montgomery, Alabama, in 1901, Slattery opened a training college for black catechists modeled on Booker T. Washington's Tuskegee Institute. By 1904 it had fifty-five students.

During the 1890s Slattery belonged to the "Americanist" party among Catholic bishops and clergy. Their liberal reform movement suffered a major setback in 1899 with Pope Leo XIII's apostolic letter, *Testem Benevolentiae*, addressed to Cardinal Gibbons. In the pope's censure of "Americanism," with its warning against introducing a certain false liberty into the church, Slattery read "the condemnation of all my ideas" ("Biographie," ch. XIV, p. 13). This, combined with disillusionment over racism in the church and lack of support for Josephite work, sent Slattery into a period of spiritual desolation. He became a "pawn of doubt" ("Biographie," ch. XVI, p. 12). Struggling to see beneath ecclesiastical politics some glimpse of divine reality, he studied theologian John Henry Newman, modernist biblical scholar Alfred Loisy, and historian of dogma Adolph von Harnack. He publicly voiced his doubts on 22 June 1902 in a controversial sermon at John Henry Dorsey's first mass.

Taking refuge in Europe, Slattery spent the fall semester learning German in Berlin, where he met Harnack. In November 1902 he was named superior emeritus of the Josephites, effectively ending his work as a missionary. He spent the academic year 1903–1904 at the University of Berlin studying law, political economy, and sociology. In June 1904 he informed the Josephites that he would formally retire. His father died in 1905, leaving him a considerable inheritance. By this time Slattery had concluded that Catholicism could never be reconciled with political liberty and science. He no longer believed that God worked through the church. On 15 June 1906, in an Anglican church in London, he married 25-year-old Adele Wingate of St. Louis; the couple had no children. The following September, in the columns of the *Independent*, he renounced both the church and the priesthood.

For the next six years Slattery associated with an international group of liberal Christians that included Albert Houtin and Paul Sabatier. Splitting his time between Europe and the United States, he wrote and translated religious polemics. In 1909 he returned to Columbia College School of Law. By 1912 he had completed, in collaboration with Houtin, his unpublished autobiography. He lived the last fourteen years of his life in apparently self-imposed obscurity. New York City remained his chief residence, but he traveled frequently, especially in Europe. On 16 April 1915 he was admitted to the practice of law in the state of California. He died in Monte Carlo, Monaco, where he is buried. Most of his nearly $1.3 million estate was left to his wife and, after her death in 1956, to the New York Public Library. Among the names of the benefactors for 1948–1958, John R. Slattery's appears in gilded letters on a column in the library's main foyer.

Slattery is a key figure in African-American Catholic history. His pioneering efforts for the evangelization and full inclusion of African Americans in the life of the Catholic church, especially his advocacy of black Catholic clergy, were damaged by his resignation as well as by the system of racial segregation taking shape in places where Josephites worked. But his vision was institutionalized in the Josephites, who, after the civil rights gains of the 1960s, were positioned to assume a leadership role in the development of African-American Catholicism in the United States. Slattery's modernist struggles illumine the late Victorian crisis of belief brought on by scientific challenges to traditional forms of Christianity.

• Slattery's papers to c. 1904 are at the Josephite Archives, 1130 North Calvert Street, Baltimore. His unpublished autobiography (c. 1912), titled "Biographie de J. R. Slattery," is in the Papiers Houtin at the Bibliothèque Nationale, Paris, France. Representative Slattery published writings include "The Catholic Negro's Complaint," *Catholic World* 52 (Dec. 1890): 347–53; "The Catholic Church and the Negro Race," *The World's Parliament of Religions*, ed. J. H. Barrows (1893), pp. 1104–6; "A Root Trouble in Catholicism," *Independent* 55 (Mar. 1903): 662–65; "The Workings of Modernism," *American Journal of Theology* 13 (Oct. 1909): 555–74. On Slattery's work among African Americans, see Stephen J. Ochs, *Desegregating the Altar: The Josephites and the Struggle for Black Priests, 1871–1960* (1990). On Slattery and modernism, see R. Scott Appleby, *"Church and Age Unite!" The Modernist Impulse in American Catholicism* (1992). A substantial account of a surrogate court's decision on the probate of his will is in the *New York Times*, 14 June 1928.

WILLIAM L. PORTIER

SLEDD, Andrew (7 Nov. 1870–16 Mar. 1939), educator and clergyman, was born in Lynchburg, Virginia, the son of Robert Newton Sledd and Frances Carey. In his home and early schooling Sledd was grounded in the post–Civil War nostalgia for the Old South and in the hard-line orthodoxy of Jim Crowism. His father, a minister in the Methodist Episcopal Church, South, who held appointments in larger urban parishes in Virginia, was known for his rigid views on race.

The younger Sledd received both his B.A. and M.A. from Randolph-Macon College, Ashland, Virginia, in 1894. After teaching a year at Randolph-Macon Academy in Bedford, Virginia, he entered Harvard, where he was awarded an A.M. in Greek in 1896. He earned a Ph.D. in Latin from Yale in 1903.

Sledd's views about race were shaken when he interrupted his undergraduate course for a year to teach in rural Mississippi and Arkansas, where he confronted firsthand the brutal treatment of blacks and the appalling deficiencies of the South's educational system. It was his two years at Harvard, however, that began, in his words, "the work of broadening of my views and sympathies and liberalizing my whole mode of thought" ("Autobiography," p. 298).

After a brief term as teaching fellow at Vanderbilt University, Sledd went in 1898 to Methodist-sponsored Emory College at Oxford, Georgia, to become professor of Latin. Though the youngest member of the faculty, he pressed for curriculum reform and higher academic standards, for adoption of an elective system, and for the introduction of intercollegiate athletics. Here he was licensed as a local preacher in the Methodist church, but he was critical of the "flamboyant religiosity" of the campus. His advocacy of northern innovations was not welcomed by his colleagues.

In 1899 Sledd married Annie Florence Candler, daughter of Bishop Warren Akin Candler, who was president of Emory when Sledd was employed. After leaving the presidency Candler remained intimately involved in affairs of the college and, later, Emory University in Atlanta. Though supportive in other respects, the bishop did not approve of his son-in-law's liberalism. The Sledds had eight children.

Sledd was assiduous in building his department and in both scholarly and polemical writing. His publication in the latter category revealed the passion for reform that would shape his agenda for the early part of his career. In his view the South's fundamental problem was educational. He considered problems of poverty, racism, and political heresy as superficial.

It was, however, Sledd's challenge of southern racial orthodoxy that occasioned his resignation from the Emory faculty. Having witnessed a savage lynching en route to his home from Atlanta, he published in the *Atlantic Monthly* in July 1902 an article titled "The Negro: Another View." Though conservative from a later perspective, in the charged atmosphere of the South of 1902 the author's views were subversive. He wrote of the inalienable rights of black people, defended equality before the law, and condemned the barbaric practice of lynching and the ideology of white supremacy that fostered it. Popular anger exploded, and when Sledd offered his resignation, President James E. Dickey and the trustees eagerly accepted it.

Declining invitations from other institutions, Sledd entered Yale to pursue his doctorate and returned to the South with a "new impulse . . . to scholarship and independence" ("Autobiography," p. 331). In the fall of 1903 he began an appointment as professor of Greek at Southern University (later Birmingham-Southern College) in Greensboro, Alabama.

In 1904 Sledd was elected president of the University of Florida. In five years there he upgraded the faculty, reformed the curriculum, restored student discipline, and effected the relocation of the school from Lake City to Gainesville. However, his achievements came in the face of unremitting political interference and bitter conflict over the removal to Gainesville. In 1909 he submitted his resignation.

In 1910 Sledd returned to Southern University, this time as president; his four years there brought to a close the first part of his career. In 1914 he accepted appointment as professor of Greek and New Testament literature in the school of theology in Atlanta, which would become a division of the new Emory University chartered in 1915. The refocusing of Sledd's career was consistent with his long-held objective of a liberated intellectual life in the South. He believed that reactionary religion, supported by misuse of the Bible, stood in the way of that objective.

The remainder of Sledd's years were devoted to introducing southerners to the new critical scholarship then coming to the fore in biblical studies. He is not remembered for original contributions to biblical scholarship, and his own views were less radical than those of some other scholars. (He accepted, for example, traditional assignments of authorship of certain books of the New Testament.) Some of his students, however, would rank among the leaders of critical New Testament scholarship in the succeeding generation. One scholar wrote of his exposure to Sledd's person: "I began to understand how humane culture, rigorous scholarship and vital piety could fit together in a single mind and heart, and how they could complement each other" (Matthews, p. 250). Because Sledd continued to hold liberal views on race, some of his graduates would play a significant role in freeing Southern Methodism from inherited rigidities in both religion and race.

The reach of his influence extended farther through his students who became editors, teachers, and writers. He himself wrote comments on biblical material studied in Sunday school classes throughout the denomination. His skill in bringing results of biblical scholarship to the laity was evidenced in two popular commentaries, *St. Mark's Life of Jesus* (1927) and *His Witnesses: A Study of the Book of Acts* (1935), and in a historical study, *The Bibles of the Churches* (1930). He was a popular preacher at church conferences and in the seminary chapel.

Sledd held his ground under severe attack during a surge of fundamentalism in the church in the 1920s. His critical approach to scripture was offensive to biblical literalists, and at one point he confronted threats of a heresy trial. His survival may have been due in part to the quiet efforts of conservative Bishop Candler, who had proposed his son-in-law as the first member of the new seminary faculty. In his last years Sledd was embarrassed by financial reverses that diverted energy from his scholarly work. He died in Decatur, Georgia, where he made his home.

• Sledd's papers are in the University Archives, University of Florida, Gainesville. Correspondence with and concerning

Sledd is in the Warren A. Candler Papers, Special Collections, Robert W. Woodruff Library, Emory University, Atlanta, Ga. Terry Lee Matthews, "The Emergence of a Prophet: Andrew Sledd and the 'Sledd Affair' of 1902" (Ph.D. diss., Duke Univ., 1989), has a full bibliography of Sledd's writings and related materials. Appended to the Matthews dissertation, pp. 279–358, is the edited text of Sledd's manuscript, "The Autobiography of a Southern Schoolmaster." (Citations from the "Autobiography" follow pagination of the text in Matthews.) Albert E. Barnett, *Andrew Sledd— His Life and Work* (n.d.), is by one of Sledd's students. See also Arthur W. Wainwright's biographical sketch in Charles E. Cole, ed., *Something More Than Human* (1986), pp. 213–27; Raymond H. Firth, "The Life of Andrew Sledd" (B.D. thesis, Candler School of Theology, Emory Univ., 1940); Henry Y. Warnock, "Andrew Sledd, Southern Methodists, and the Negro: A Case History," *Journal of Southern History* 31 (1965): 251–71; and Ralph E. Reed, Jr., "Emory College and the Sledd Affair of 1902: A Case Study in Southern Honor and Racial Attitudes," *Georgia Historical Quarterly* 72 (1988): 463–92. An obituary is in the *Journal of the Alabama Annual Conference, the Methodist Church* (1939).

JAMES W. MAY

SLEMP, Campbell Bascom (4 Sept. 1870–7 Aug. 1943), congressman and presidential secretary, was born in Turkey Cove, Lee County, Virginia, the son of Campbell Slemp, a businessman and congressman, and Nannie Cawood. He attended local public schools. After graduating from the Virginia Military Institute in 1891, he studied law at the University of Virginia. Slemp helped with his family's business interests and, beginning in 1900, taught mathematics as an adjunct professor at the Virginia Military Institute, resigning when he was admitted to the Virginia bar in 1901. His law practice at Big Stone Gap, Virginia, was connected principally with coal lands in Virginia and Kentucky.

From his father, a former Confederate colonel who had served in the Virginia state legislature, Slemp acquired an interest in politics. In 1905 he became chairman of the Virginia Republican State Committee. On 17 December 1907 he was elected to the U.S. House of Representatives from the Ninth Virginia District to fill the vacancy occasioned by the death of his father, who had held the congressional seat since 1903. Slemp won seven consecutive terms and served in Congress until 1923. In 1908 Slemp endorsed the presidential aspirations of Secretary of War William Howard Taft and lined up the Virginia delegates for him at the Republican National Convention in Chicago. Throughout the course of the campaign, Slemp kept in close touch with Taft concerning political matters.

Slemp loyally supported Taft's administration. In 1909, amid the controversy surrounding tariff reform, Slemp defended the principle of protection for all manufacturing interests and all producers of raw materials. Placing his Republicanism above his own personal interests, he reluctantly voted for the reduced duties of the Payne Tariff Bill as passed by the House, hoping that the Senate would add protective amendments. In the end, he endorsed the Payne-Aldrich Tariff of 1909. His voting record was consistently with the conservative wing of the Republican party, and in 1910 supported Republican Speaker Joseph G. Cannon in his battle against progressive Republicans, who sought to restrict the Speaker's powers. Angered by former president Theodore Roosevelt's "Bull Moose" party in 1912, Slemp staunchly supported Taft over Roosevelt for the Republican presidential nomination and a second term as president.

In 1920 Slemp was among the leaders of the Republican campaign to crack the Democratic Solid South for Senator Warren G. Harding, the party's presidential standard-bearer, and he managed the first southern Republican headquarters in Washington. On election day, Harding carried the Border States of Maryland, West Virginia, Tennessee, and Missouri. Delighted with Harding's landslide victory, Slemp celebrated the Republican restoration after eight years of Democrat Woodrow Wilson in the White House and advocated a reduced federal bureaucracy with more authority given to the states. He had been a member of the Republican National Committee since 1918, but he declined to seek reelection to his House seat in 1922, preferring to concentrate his activity on his professional and business life.

On 4 September 1923, one month after Harding's death, President Calvin Coolidge, acting on the strong recommendations of party leaders, selected Slemp to be his presidential secretary. In this capacity, Slemp acted as the president's liaison with Congress and the Republican National Committee, assisted with patronage matters, and protected Coolidge from outsiders demanding to see the president. Ordinarily people wanting to confer with Coolidge went through Slemp, who functioned as the president's conciliator with various groups and handled much of the party's politics for him. Without question Slemp was Coolidge's right-hand man.

While vacationing in Palm Beach, Florida, in December 1923, Slemp met former secretary of the interior Albert B. Fall, who was implicated in the Teapot Dome scandal that had engulfed the Harding administration. On 25 February 1924 Slemp testified before the Senate Oil Investigating Committee that it was a happenstance without meaning. He further claimed that his sojourn was for his health, not a presidential mission, and Coolidge remained untouched by the scandals.

Slemp probably played his greatest political role in June 1924 at the Republican National Convention in Cleveland, where he was among the top political operatives who orchestrated Coolidge's presidential nomination. Coordinating the activities, Slemp was able to swing the southern delegates to the president. As Coolidge's campaign manager for the southern states, he traveled widely during the canvass, met with state leaders, oversaw many campaign details, and contributed to the president's smooth victory in November. On 4 March 1925, the day of Coolidge's inauguration to a full term as president, Slemp resigned his position as secretary to the president. Possibly disappointed that he was not offered a cabinet portfolio, he nevertheless continued to admire Coolidge.

Slemp subsequently opened a private law practice in Washington and represented a Chicago law firm there. In 1926 he published *The Mind of the President*, in which he, with commentary, compiled and edited some of Coolidge's views on public questions. He contended that Coolidge had been the most potent constructive force of the day in domestic matters, observing that the presidency was a test of character and wisdom. He added that no amount of political manipulation could ever take the place of personal probity, sound principles, and clear action. Slemp confessed, however, that Coolidge was somewhat of an enigma to the public because on many occasions he had expressed no opinion.

Although he never again sought political office, Slemp remained active in party matters and civic affairs. He was a member of the Republican National Committee until 1932. In 1927 he was instrumental in founding the Institute of Public Affairs at the University of Virginia at Charlottesville. The next year, when Coolidge chose not to seek another term, Slemp backed Secretary of Commerce Herbert Hoover for the presidency and worked diligently at the Republican National Convention in Kansas City for the support of southern delegates. In 1931 President Hoover appointed Slemp American commissioner general at the French Colonial Exposition in Paris.

Slemp remained active in law and business affairs during the Great Depression. He believed that President Franklin D. Roosevelt's program would restore prosperity, and in May 1941 he commended Roosevelt for his policy of aiding England in its war against Germany. A lifelong bachelor, Slemp spent his last years helping to establish a museum of colonial frontier life in Virginia in honor of his sister, Janie Slemp Newman, who had served as his official hostess during his Washington days. While on his way home to Virginia from a Florida resort, Slemp died in Knoxville, Tennessee.

Slemp was one of the most forceful figures on the Virginia political scene, leading the state Republican party for thirty years. A courtly southern gentleman, he built a political machine based on federal patronage while making a fortune from the timber and coal resources of southwestern Virginia. From his entrenched citadel in Virginia, the "Sage of Turkey Cove" sought to increase Republican power throughout the South. His removal from national politics after 1925 did not lessen his influence on Virginia patronage, and he kept himself informed on national events and issues affecting the Republican party.

• Slemp's papers are at the University of Virginia Library in Charlottesville. Correspondence and other papers relating to his term as secretary to the president are in the Calvin Coolidge Papers in the Manuscripts Division of the Library of Congress. His speeches are in the *Congressional Record* from 1907 to 1923. See also *Selected Addresses of C. Bascom Slemp*, ed. J. Frederick Essary (1938). A major work on Slemp is Guy B. Hathorn, "The Political Career of C. Bascom Slemp" (Ph.D. diss., Duke Univ., 1950). Additional material is in William Allen White, *A Puritan in Babylon* (1938), and Donald R. McCoy, *Calvin Coolidge: The Quiet President* (1967). Obituaries are in the *New York Times*, *Washington Post*, *Richmond News-Leader*, and *Richmond Times-Dispatch*, 8 Aug. 1943.

LEONARD SCHLUP

SLESINGER, Tess (16 July 1905–21 Feb. 1945), fiction and film writer, was born Theresa Slesinger in New York City, the daughter of Anthony Slesinger, a garment manufacturer, and Augusta Singer, a social welfare worker and, later, a lay psychoanalyst. Slesinger was raised in a highly assimilated third-generation Jewish family. She attended Swarthmore College (1923–1925) and Columbia University School of Journalism (B.Litt., 1927), where she studied writing under novelist Dorothy Scarborough.

Between 1927 and 1930 Slesinger regularly reviewed books for the *New York Evening Post* and other publications. In 1930 she published her first short story, "Mother to Dinner," in the *Menorah Journal* and between then and 1936 published twenty-two short stories in mainstream and literary magazines. Some of these stories use stream of consciousness to probe the psychological dimensions of personal relationships. Others explore the ways in which gender, class, race, work, or politics impinge on personality, and others emphasize the connections between individual and social life. Notable examples are "White on Black" (*American Mercury*, 1930), a study of racial discrimination in a progressive private school, and "Missis Flinders" (*Story Magazine*, 1932), the first story depicting abortion and its aftermath to appear in an American general circulation magazine. It later became the last chapter of *The Unpossessed* and was reprinted in the tenth anniversary issue of *Story* (May–June 1941), which highlighted ten of the nearly 1,000 stories published in the magazine during the previous decade.

Slesinger's 1934 novel, *The Unpossessed*, originated in the *Menorah Journal* circle and in Slesinger's marriage in 1927 to Herbert Sidney Solow, which ended in divorce in 1932 after Solow insisted that Slesinger have an abortion for political and economic reasons. (Slesinger and Solow had no children.) Solow, a political journalist, was assistant editor of the *Menorah Journal*, which was begun in 1915 to encourage a Jewish humanism in America but moved to the left by the early years of the depression. Through Solow, Slesinger became part of a young left-wing group surrounding the editor, Elliot Cohen, later founder of *Commentary*. The *Journal* coterie has since been identified as the earliest source of the highly influential New York literary left. Among its members was Lionel Trilling, who later wrote an ambiguous interpretation of Slesinger as a woman writer and a spokesperson for the 1930s.

The first and one of the few depression-era novels to treat radical urban intellectuals, *The Unpossessed* is a modernist satire of the Old Left written from a feminist perspective (its female characters decry both the "Bohemian train of fast living" and the seat they have been assigned on that train), and it questions the separation between private and political life as well as the place and purpose of the intellectual in a time of rapid historical change. The novel was widely and mostly favorably reviewed and saw four printings within a month as well as a British edition. *The Unpossessed* was politically controversial because it both derided and sympathized with radical intellectuals. Liberal reviewers saw it as "a credit to her honesty that the book does not end with a wishful red [i.e., communist] sunrise on the immediate horizon" (Ferner Nuhn, *Nation*, 23 May 1941), while reviewers for radical publications criticized Slesinger for failing "to give a disciplined [political] orientation to the intellectual whose need for it she makes so palpable" (Philip Rahv, *New Masses*, 29 May 1934).

In 1935, after publishing the collection *Time: The Present*, which contained about half her stories and was praised for its breadth of human sympathy and skillful experimental writing, Slesinger set out for the West Coast to begin a new career as a screenwriter. Brought to Hollywood to coauthor the script for the 1937 film version of Pearl Buck's *The Good Earth* (1931), which set the standard for multimillion dollar films under producer Irving Thalberg, Slesinger authored or coauthored scripts for seven films that were produced and for numerous others that were "shelved."

Between 1940 and 1945 she often worked in collaboration with her second husband, Frank Davis (married in 1936; two children), a former producer who consciously left management for labor when he joined Slesinger to form a successful screenwriting team.

In addition to *The Good Earth*, which won several Academy Awards, Slesinger wrote the script for *Girls' School* (1938). The film was derived from her novella, "The Answer on the Magnolia Tree," which was based on Slesinger's experience teaching creative writing at Briarcliff Manor in Briarcliff, New York, from 1933 to 1934. Her other films include *Dance, Girl, Dance* (1940), directed by Dorothy Arzner, one of Hollywood's few female studio directors, and *A Tree Grows in Brooklyn* (1945), director Elia Kazan's first film, based on the popular novel by Betty Smith.

In Hollywood, Slesinger, who in New York had picketed to support labor organizing among white-collar workers in publishing, helped establish the Screen Writers Guild (founded by John Howard Lawson in 1933), the first film-industry union, whose founding was bitterly opposed by the producers but vindicated in one of the first decisions by the National Labor Relations Board (1938). Through monetary contributions, petitions, and public actions, she also supported the freeing of Thomas Mooney, the release of the Scottsboro Boys, the fighting of the Abraham Lincoln Brigade in the Spanish Civil War, the Hollywood Anti-Nazi League, and the League of Women Shoppers. She served on the executive board of the Motion Picture Guild, which encouraged the production of liberal and progressive films.

Slesinger was about to return to the full-time writing of fiction when she died in Los Angeles of carcinoma of the tonsils. She left fragments of a serious Hollywood novel that explores connections between personal life and social action in the context of work, politics, and heterosexual relations in the filmmaking industry.

In the 1930s Slesinger was read either as a witness to or a satirist of left-wing politics. By the 1960s she was seen as the writer of books "around which a fresh image of the American literary Thirties will have to be constituted" (Robert M. Adams, *New York Review of Books*, 20 Oct. 1966), an image that would have to acknowledge but go beyond the period's political and literary disagreements. Current assessments emphasize Slesinger's foreshadowing of the second wave of feminism because of her ability to depict politics and sexual politics together, thereby producing an unusually complex picture of both.

• Slesinger's manuscript materials remain in private hands. *The Unpossessed* was reprinted in 1966 with an afterword by Lionel Trilling and in 1984 with an introduction by Alice Kessler-Harris and Paul Lauter and an afterword by Janet Sharistanian. Her selected stories were reprinted under the title *On Being Told That Her Second Husband Has Taken His First Lover and Other Stories* in 1971, 1975, and 1990. The screenplay of *The Good Earth* was published in John Gassner, ed., *Twenty Best Film Plays* (1943). See also Shirley Biagi, "Forgive Me for Dying," *Antioch Review* 35 (1977): 2–3; Sharistanian, "Tess Slesinger's Hollywood Sketches," *Michigan Quarterly Review* 18 (1979): 3; Sharistanian, "Tess Slesinger's 'Young Wife,'" *Helicon Nine: The Journal of Women's Arts and Letters*, no. 16 (1986); Alan M. Wald, *The New York Intellectuals: The Rise and Decline of the Anti-Stalinist Left from the 1930s to the 1980s* (1987); Paula Rabinowitz, *Labor and Desire: Women's Revolutionary Fiction in Depression America* (1991); Philip Abbott, "Are Three Generations of Radicals Enough?: Self-Critique in the Novels of Tess Slesinger, Mary McCarthy, and Marge Piercy," *Review of Politics* 53 (1991): 4; and Harvey Teres, *Renewing the Left: Politics, Imagination, and the New York Intellectuals, 1930–1970* (1996). Obituaries are in the *New York Times*, 22 Feb. 1945, and *Variety*, 28 Feb. 1945.

JANET SHARISTANIAN

SLICHTER, Sumner Huber (8 Jan. 1892–27 Sept. 1959), economist and industrial relations expert, was born in Madison, Wisconsin, the son of Charles Sumner Slichter, a mathematics professor and dean of the graduate school, and Mary Louise Byrne. After a year at the University of Munich in 1910, Slichter returned to Wisconsin to study labor problems with John R. Commons, receiving his A.B. in 1913 and his M.A. in 1914. Through Commons's assistance, he obtained his first professional job, a position with the Research Division of the U.S. Commission on Industrial Relations (CIR, 1913–1915). He then earned a doctorate at the University of Chicago (1918), writing a dissertation under the direction of labor economist Harry A. Millis. Published as *The Turnover of Factory Labor* (1919), it offered an analysis of data collected by William M. Leiserson and other staffers at the CIR.

In June 1918 Slichter enlisted in the U.S. Army Field Artillery and that month also married Ada Pence; they had two sons. Although he received a commission as a second lieutenant in December 1918, he returned to civilian life. Despite a slight speech impediment, which he eventually mastered, he began a forty-year academic career with an instructorship at Princeton during the 1919–1920 academic year.

Slichter was an economist who acted not only as an interpreter of the emerging mass-production industrial order but as an adviser and policy maker steering the development of that political economy. During his tenure at the CIR, he tackled the controversial issue of financial control over the nation's core industries. In a painstaking examination of transportation, industrial, and public utility firms, he found that six financial groups controlled or dominated companies with a total capitalization of $21 billion and 31 percent of the U.S. workforce.

Known for his keen intellect and boundless energy, Slichter made significant contributions to both economic forecasting and labor economics. While at Cornell University in the 1920s (assistant professor, 1920–1925; professor, 1925–1930), he commenced a lengthy study of trade unionism and shop rules—a study that entailed three years of fieldwork (1925–1926, 1927–1928, 1929–1930) subsidized by the Brookings Institution. It was the successful experiments he found in labor-management cooperation in established industries—especially those in the shops of the Baltimore and Ohio and Canadian National railroads, in the men's clothing industry, and in the Cleveland, Ohio, women's garment industry—that fascinated him and shaped his views of New Deal industrial relations. The research, published in 1941 as *Union Policies and Industrial Management*, was a pioneering study that viewed collective bargaining as a mechanism for establishing "industrial jurisprudence"—the creation of a body of common law in industry that would guarantee workers' rights and curtail the arbitrary decision making of management—in an economy shaped by conditions that varied from industry to industry.

Slichter's move to the Harvard School of Business Administration in 1930 and the collapse of the American economy proved to be major stimuli to his scholarship. He wrote continuously on the problems of unemployment, business cycles, and government intervention in the economy during the depression decade. He criticized the Franklin D. Roosevelt administration for failing to encourage business enterprise, charging that the government never understood the private sector's needs, especially the need for new sources of venture capital. Throughout his association with the school, he taught courses on "The Problems of Industrial Relations" and "Problems of Economic Balance." In 1935 he joined the department of economics and, upon its creation, the Littauer School of Public Administration. In 1940 he led the effort to establish the Harvard Trade Union Program for the education of union representatives. For a decade of efforts, the university appointed him Lamont University Professor, the first Harvard faculty member to hold this rank. In 1941 he served as president of the American Economic Association.

Slichter embraced opinions unpopular in New Deal liberal circles during the war years. Counter to such stagnation theory advocates as Alvin Hansen, he believed that the U.S. economy had not reached maturity by the 1930s and would not slip back into depression after World War II. By the late 1930s he also thought that unions were part of the power structure and had to be regulated just like corporations. Indeed, he asserted that the rapid rise of trade unionism from 1933 to 1948 had transformed the United States into a "laboristic" society in which employees, rather than employers, exerted the greater influence on social life. As an adviser to Massachusetts state government, he opposed granting state employees the right to strike.

The postwar economic boom, with its apparent social stability, confirmed Slichter's optimism and his position as one of the nation's most influential economic forecasters. He explored the inherent contradiction between price stability and full employment, believing that progress brought gradual increases in the price level. During this period, the transformation in U.S. industrial relations profoundly shaped his views on labor. By the time of his death in Boston, Massachusetts, he had perceived that the challenges of trade unionism had improved management. In his perspective, industrial relations in the United States had become an effort in managerial problem solving, rather than a process of industrial jurisprudence.

Never an avowed theorist, Slichter practiced theoretically informed historical economics. While he rejected elaborate system building or dogmatic theories, he avidly applied economic theory to problems and tested principles against his evidence. Slichter was one of the principal contributors to a diverse nationwide effort, conducted by government and academic institutions, to add systematically to America's economic knowledge.

• Slichter's papers for the post-1930 period are in the Harvard University Archives. In addition to his 1919 and 1941 studies, Slichter wrote *Modern Economic Society* (1931), *Present Savings and Postwar Markets* (1943), *Trade Unions in a Free Society* (1947), *The American Economy: Its Problems and Prospects* (1948), and *What's Ahead for American Business?* (1951). For his life and career, see the introduction to John T. Dunlop, ed., *Potentials of the American Economy* (1961), which has a bibliography of Slichter's works; and Mark H. Ingram, *Charles Sumner Slichter: The Golden Vector* (1972). An obituary is in the *New York Times*, 29 Sept. 1959.

CLARENCE E. WUNDERLIN

SLIDELL, John (1793–29 July 1871), U.S. senator and Confederate diplomat, was born in New York City, the son of John Slidell, a merchant and banker, and Margery Mackenzie. Slidell grew up amid the affluence of New York's thriving mercantile community. After graduating from Columbia College in 1810, he spent several years in Europe working for a New York mercantile firm. He returned to New York, passed the bar examination, and pursued a bachelor's carefree existence that involved him in a duel with an outraged husband. Sobered by this scandal, he sought his future in New Orleans.

Taking advantage of his New York connections and his legal and commercial expertise, Slidell built a fortune and established a sound reputation at the bar and within the New Orleans business community. In 1835 he married Marie Mathilde Deslonde, a young woman from a distinguished Gallic family. They had a son, two daughters, and possibly another daughter. The marriage brought him an entry into the city's clannish French community.

Disappointment characterized Slidell's early political career. Defeated for Congress on the Andrew Jackson ticket in 1828, he received a patronage post as district attorney of New Orleans in 1829. He lost that position when he ran afoul of Martin Gordon, the Democratic party chieftain in Louisiana. Gordon's influence deprived Slidell of a diplomatic posting in 1833, and the Louisiana legislature rejected his bid for a seat in the U.S. Senate in 1834 and in 1836. From 1843 to 1845 he served in the U.S. House of Representatives, where he advocated "a tariff for revenue only," supporting sugar duties but opposing those on cotton. He presented a resolution to remit the $1,000 fine levied against Jackson in 1815 after Jackson was found guilty of contempt of court as a result of his arrest under martial law of U.S. Attorney John Dick in New Orleans at the end of the War of 1812. Slidell's resolution of 25 March 1844 called for increased state control over the judiciary. He took a constructive interest in naval affairs, championed a constitutional amendment for the direct election of the president, and supported a measure calling for the use of civil law in the federal courts in Louisiana.

Slidell came to national notice when, in the 1844 presidential election, he applied his genius for organization and his fertile imagination to carrying Louisiana for James K. Polk. Subsequently, he received appointment as commissioner to Mexico with a mission to adjust the Texas boundary and to purchase New Mexico and California—objectives beyond diplomacy and soon to be won in war.

Slidell persisted in efforts to organize Louisiana's Democracy. In 1848 the object of his ambitions, a seat in the U.S. Senate, once again eluded him and went instead to his rival for Democratic leadership in the state, Pierre Soulé. When Soulé abandoned his seat in the Senate in 1853, the legislature selected Slidell as his replacement, and the Democratic organization that Slidell had carefully built backed his election to a full senatorial term in 1856.

Slidell had few oratorical gifts, and he seldom took the Senate floor. He was most persuasive with individuals and small groups in relaxed, intimate surroundings. A constructive legislator, Slidell supported measures that promised to benefit Louisiana, the South, and the nation. He promoted bills that encouraged filibustering. He authored a bill to purchase Cuba and disapproved the Clayton-Bulwer Treaty, and he took a lively interest in developing the railroad system of the country. He advocated the admission of Kansas under the Lecompton constitution, and he became the watchdog of the U.S. Treasury, consistently opposing unjustifiable expenditures. Finally, he proposed a resolution to remove the injunction of secrecy covering Senate action on nominations submitted for confirmation.

Above all else, Slidell was a masterful politician and an important source of influence and power during a critical period in the nation's history. He had actively supported the nomination of his friend and confidant James Buchanan as the Democratic presidential nominee since 1848. The capstone of his power in Louisiana and in the nation came when, with assistance from Slidell, Buchanan won the nomination and went on to carry the presidential election of 1856. Thereafter, federal patronage in Louisiana and in the nation came within Slidell's bestowal—power that he effectively used to woo, to reward, and to chastise political friends and foes.

In Louisiana during Buchanan's term, Slidell deprived the opposition of political substance and reigned supreme. In the nation his voice directed presidential appointments and designated patronage recipients. He headed the movement to strip leading northern Democrat Stephen Douglas of power and influence. Slidell's hostility to Douglas was rooted in Louisiana politics. Soulé had long supported Douglas as the Democratic presidential candidate, and a Douglas presidency would have deprived Slidell of power and patronage in the state. Slidell led those who were implacably opposed to Douglas at the Charleston convention in 1860, and while he did not want to see the Democratic party split, he was unwilling to accept Douglas as the nominee. Slidell had always been a Unionist, and not until the Republican victory in 1860 did he reluctantly surrender his allegiance to the Union. He led the immediate secessionists and Louisiana out of the Union in 1861.

Slidell was a logical choice to represent the Confederacy in France. When on 8 November 1861 U.S. naval forces removed Slidell and James Mason from the British mail steamer *Trent* and detained them at Fort Warren, a tense diplomatic situation developed. Eventually the Confederate diplomats were allowed to proceed to their missions. In France Slidell served as Confederate commissioner to the Court of Napoleon III. Confederate sympathizers, Napoleon III, and government officials gave Slidell a warm reception, and he moved freely in the inner circles of power in that country. Slidell was an accomplished diplomat in Confederate service, and he attempted innovative plans to provide the Confederate navy with vessels built in French shipyards, to use cotton as collateral to acquire public or private loans, and to secure French recognition of the Confederacy. That he was unsuccessful had more to do with the international temper of the times, especially the relationship between Great Britain and France (Napoleon was unwilling to act alone in supporting the Confederacy completely, and he held to the Anglo alliance in which the British and French had agreed to act in concert concerning the American war), rather than lack of skill or imagination on his part.

With the defeat of the Confederacy, Slidell and his family continued to reside in Paris, and they frequently visited England. He did not seek pardon, and Andrew Johnson did not respond to his request to visit Louisiana in 1866. Slidell died in Cowes, England.

• Like many Confederate exiles, Slidell's surviving papers are few. The most extensive letter collection is in the Buchanan papers in the Pennsylvania Historical Society Library; copies of this collection are also available at Hill Memorial Library, Louisiana State University Archives, in Baton Rouge. The James M. Mason Papers in the Library of Congress contain Slidell letters, and the Morse-Wederstrandt collection at Tulane University in New Orleans also contains significant letters. A biography is Louis Sears, *John Slidell* (1925). Joseph Tregle, "The Political Apprenticeship of John Slidell," *Journal of Southern History* 26 (1960): 57–70, provides an excellent account of Slidell's early career. James K. Greer, *Louisiana Politics, 1845–1861* (1930), gives important information on Slidell's command of the Democracy in La. A. J. Diket, *Senator John Slidell and the Community He Represented in Washington 1853–1861* (1982), contains important information. For an account of Slidell's determined efforts to ruin Douglas see Diket, "John Slidell and the 'Chicago Incident' of 1858," *Louisiana History* 5 (1964): 369–86; and *The Letters of Stephen A. Douglas*, ed. Robert Johannsen (1961). Slidell's diplomatic career is discussed in Beckles Willson, *Slidell and the Confederates in Paris* (1932); Frank L. Owsley, *King Cotton Diplomacy* (1931); S. F. Bemis, ed., *American Secretaries of State and Their Diplomacy*, vol. 5 (1928); John Bigelow, *France and the Confederate Navy* (1888); Lynn Case and Warren Spencer, *The United States and France: Civil War Diplomacy* (1970); and Gordon Warren, *Fountain of Discontent: The "Trent" Affair and Freedom of the Seas* (1981). An obituary is in the *New Orleans Daily Picayune*, 1 Aug. 1871.

CAROLYN E. DE LATTE

SLIPHER, Vesto Melvin (11 Nov. 1875–8 Nov. 1969), astronomer, was born near Mulberry, Indiana, the son of Daniel Clark Slipher and Hannah App, farmers. After graduating from high school, Slipher taught at a small country school near Frankfort, Indiana, until 1897, when he entered Indiana University. He received an A.B. in mechanics and astronomy in 1901, later earning an A.M. (1903) and Ph.D. (1909) in astronomy from the university.

As an undergraduate Slipher studied with astronomer Wilbur Cogshall, who had recently joined the Indiana faculty from the Lowell Observatory in Flagstaff, Arizona. Through Cogshall's influence, Slipher joined the observatory in 1901, soon proving himself a valuable member of the facility's staff. He balanced his observatory duties with various returns to Indiana for graduate study. While on one of these trips in 1904, he married Emma Rosalie Munger of Frankfort. The couple returned to Flagstaff, where they had two children.

Slipher's early work at the Lowell Observatory focused on planetary astronomy. Percival Lowell had founded his facility in 1894 to investigate the possibility of life on Mars, soon expanding his research to other planets. Slipher's first assignment was to study the planets with a new spectrograph attached to the 24-inch refractor. He successfully measured the rotation periods of Mars, Jupiter, Saturn, and Uranus, but his primary task involved the planet Venus. Astronomers had offered various estimates of the planet's period, ranging from twenty-four hours to approximately 225 days. By March 1903 Slipher had recorded spectrograms that indicated a long rotation period, but he refused to provide a specific estimate because of uncertainties in the data. Radar observations sixty years later showed that the planet's rotation period was 243 days. Slipher also attempted a spectrographic analysis of the Martian atmosphere to determine the presence of water vapor and oxygen, but the photographic plates of the time proved inadequate to the task.

Although he continued to pursue Lowell's research agenda, Slipher also employed the observatory's spectrographic equipment to study the radial velocities of stars. Slipher's stellar research led to his first professional publication, a 1902 article in *Astronomical Journal* discussing the variable velocity of the star Zeta Herculis. His work also led to a major discovery by 1909, when he observed several sharp spectral lines in otherwise blurry spectra of single and double stars. This discovery supported the noted astronomer Jacobus C. Kapteyn's theory that interstellar gas would produce spectral lines distinguishable from those of stars. Slipher also showed that interstellar dust existed when his 1912 spectrographic studies of the Pleiades nebula indicated that it was shining solely by reflected starlight.

Slipher's most significant contribution to astronomy, however, was his spectrographic investigation of spiral nebulae. These phenomena remained the focus of a major debate within the profession. Many astronomers accepted the explanation that they were "island universes" consisting of large aggregates of stars beyond the Milky Way. Others argued that these phenomena represented planetary systems in the early stages of development. Recognizing the value of the latter explanation to his work on extraterrestrial life, Lowell directed Slipher to undertake a study of these nebulae to determine if their spectrographic characteristics were similar to those of the Earth's solar system. Slipher soon realized that the existing spectrograph was unsuitable for this new research and began to assemble a small instrument from parts on hand. His task was made more complicated by Lowell's decision to assign the new 40-inch reflecting telescope to planetary work, including the search for a trans-Neptunian planet. The Lowell refractor and Slipher's fabricated spectrograph thus represented a less than optimal combination and delayed serious observations until the early fall of 1912.

Slipher's work with the new equipment, however, quickly led to a remarkable discovery. During late 1912 he recorded several exposures of the Andromeda galaxy (M31), which were detailed enough to allow the comparison of the galaxy's spectral lines with those of laboratory spectra. The Doppler shift of these lines enabled Slipher to calculate the radial velocity of the galaxy. By February 1913 he had determined that M31 was traveling at approximately 300 kilometers per second in the direction of Earth. Radial velocities of some 1,200 stars had previously been calculated, but they were less than one-third the velocity Slipher found for Andromeda. He confirmed this unexpected discovery the following April by similarly analyzing the spectrum of a nebula in Virgo, finding a large shift toward the red end of the spectrum that indicated a velocity of nearly 1,000 kilometers per second away from Earth.

Over the next decade Slipher continued his observations of nebular velocities, ultimately recording those of forty-one nebulae, almost all of which were receding from the Earth. These determinations provided Dutch theorist Willem de Sitter with valuable support for his theory of an expanding universe and ultimately led to Edwin Hubble's development of the velocity-distance relationship in 1929. Hubble combined Slipher's velocity measurements with his own determination of nebular distances to show that the two parameters were proportional to each other (v=Hd). The discovery of this relationship provided important support for both the island universe and expanding universe concepts.

Another contribution from Slipher's nebular research proved more controversial. By 1917 he had collected spectrographic evidence that several spiral nebulae were rotating like winding springs, with rotational velocities of a few hundred kilometers per second. Slipher's findings clashed with the earlier work of noted astronomer Adriaan van Maanen, who had compared photographs of nebulae taken a few years apart and determined that the spiral arms were unwinding. More than a simple clash of observed results, the two competing views had a significant implication. If photographs taken at relatively short intervals showed internal motion along the arms, nebular distances could not be sufficiently great to support the island universe concept. Preferring to avoid controversy, Slipher remained quiet, but astronomers continued to investigate this phenomenon for nearly two decades. By the mid-1930s they had discovered systematic errors in van Maanen's measurements, which led even van Maanen to reject his earlier conclusions. Slipher's research and the island universe explanation of spiral nebulae had received important confirmation.

The initial skepticism concerning Slipher's research provides insight concerning his place in his profession. His association with the Lowell Observatory carried with it his colleagues' continued doubts about the facility. Lowell's attempts to prove the habitability of Mars had led to his professional ostracism that, to some extent, carried over to the observatory and its staff. Slipher's personality also helps to explain his lack of immediate recognition. A quiet and reserved individual, he rarely attended professional meetings and was cautious about announcing research results until they were confirmed to his satisfaction. Most of his more than 100 publications were essentially observational reports with very little speculation or interpretation.

In addition to his research pursuits, Slipher was heavily involved in the administration of the Lowell Observatory. Appointed assistant director in 1915, he assumed the post of acting director following Lowell's death the following year. He remained in this position until he became director in 1926. Slipher's nebular work suffered from his increased administrative duties, but the observatory's 24-inch refractor also proved inadequate for further investigations. This research passed to astronomers with access to larger telescopes, such as the 100-inch Hooker telescope on Mount Wilson in California. Slipher nonetheless directed the Lowell facility toward significant achievements in astronomy, leading eclipse expeditions to Kansas (1918) and Mexico (1923) and, after 1927, directing the search for a trans-Neptunian planet. This program ultimately led to Clyde Tombaugh's discovery of Pluto in 1930. Slipher also served in administrative capacities in national and international organizations. During the late 1920s he served as president of the Commission on Nebulae of the International Astronomical Union. In this position he coordinated the collection and distribution of information during a crucial period in astronomers' investigation of these phenomena. He later served as vice president of the American Astronomical Society (1931) and of the American Association for the Advancement of Science (1933).

Slipher was also active in community affairs in Flagstaff. He was a member and later chairman of the school board and assisted in the foundation of the Museum of Northern Arizona and served on its board of directors. He engaged in business activity as well, owning various ranch and rental properties and operating a furniture store. He retired as director of the observatory in 1954, after which he remained moderately active in community and observatory affairs. He died in Flagstaff.

Slipher's contributions to astronomy were recognized by his colleagues in various ways. Among the more significant awards he received were the Lalande Prize of the Paris Academy of Sciences (1919), the Henry Draper Medal of the National Academy of Sciences (1933), the Gold Medal of the Royal Astronomical Society (1933), and the Bruce Medal of the Astronomical Society of the Pacific (1935). He was elected to membership in the National Academy of Sciences, the American Academy of Arts and Sciences, and the American Philosophical Society. As both a researcher and an administrator, Slipher contributed significantly to astronomy during an important period in the development of the discipline.

• Slipher's papers are in the Lowell Observatory Archives, Flagstaff, Ariz. His most important published works include "The Spectrum of Mars," *Astrophysical Journal* 28 (1908): 397–404, "Spectrographic Observations of Nebulae," *Popular Astronomy* 23 (1915): 21–24, "Nebulae," *Proceedings of the American Philosophical Society* 56 (1917): 403–10, "Spectrographic Studies of the Planets," *Monthly Notices of the Royal Astronomical Society* 93 (1933): 657–68, and "The Trans-Neptunian Planet Search," *Proceedings of the American Philosophi-

cal Society 79 (1938): 435–40. A survey of Slipher's career, which includes a complete bibliography of his publications, is William Graves Hoyt, "Vesto Melvin Slipher," National Academy of Sciences, *Biographical Memoirs* 52 (1980): 411–49. For Slipher's role in astronomy, see also Norriss S. Hetherington, "The Measurement of Radial Velocities of Spiral Nebulae," *Isis* 62 (1971): 309–13; Hetherington, "The Simultaneous 'Discovery' of Internal Motions in Spiral Nebulae," *Journal for the History of Astronomy* 6 (1975): 115–25; Robert W. Smith, "The Origins of the Velocity-Distance Relation," *Journal for the History of Astronomy* 10 (1979): 133–65; Richard Berendzen et al., *Man Discovers the Galaxies* (1976); and Smith, *The Expanding Universe* (1982). An obituary is in *Publications of the Astronomical Society of the Pacific* 81 (1969): 922–23.

GEORGE E. WEBB

SLOAN, Alfred Pritchard, Jr. (23 May 1875–17 Feb. 1966), industrialist and philanthropist, was born in New Haven, Connecticut, the son of Alfred Pritchard Sloan, a coffee and tea importer, and Katherine Mead. The oldest of five children, Sloan grew up in a comfortable upper-middle-class home in which he was encouraged to develop his considerable intelligence. His family moved to Brooklyn, New York, when he was ten years old. He began studying mechanics and engineering at the Brooklyn Polytechnic Institute a year later. Sloan subsequently matriculated at the Massachusetts Institute of Technology. A self-confessed "grind," he completed an electrical engineering program in just three years and was the youngest graduate in the class of 1895.

With his father's help, Sloan found employment as a draftsman at the Hyatt Roller Bearing Company in Harrison, New Jersey, at a salary of $50 a month. Although Hyatt sold a good product, the firm was poorly managed. Sloan was anxious to marry his college sweetheart, Irene Jackson of Boston, so he looked for a more lucrative business opportunity. In early 1897 he formed a partnership with William Wood, a naval engineer who had invented an electrical refrigerator. The two men established their Hygienic Refrigerator Company in Manhattan and received contracts to install refrigeration machinery in nearby hotels. Now confident about his prospects, Sloan married Jackson that September. Their marriage endured until her death in 1956; they had no children.

In 1898 mechanical failures and the death of his partner forced Sloan to liquidate the refrigerator company. Once again his father intervened on his behalf. Alfred Sloan, Sr., and an associate purchased the Hyatt Roller Bearing Company for $5,000 and put Alfred, Jr., in charge. As general manager, the younger Sloan poured himself into the job. For the remainder of his life Sloan seemed to live for his work. He developed no hobbies, read very little, and seldom traveled for pleasure.

At the turn of the century Sloan found a growing market for Hyatt's bearings among midwestern automobile manufacturers. Soon his company was supplying the Ford Motor Company, Oldsmobile, and Weston-Mott, an axle-maker that sold to the Cadillac,

Buick, and Maxwell Motor companies. By 1916 Hyatt's annual sales topped $20 million. To better manage the firm's increasingly diverse business, Sloan developed a multidivisional structure. Hyatt's sprawling factory complex was located in Harrison, while the headquarters and sales and engineering staffs of its machinery division occupied offices in Newark. The company's automotive sales and engineering offices were in Detroit and its tractor division in Chicago.

In 1916 William C. Durant, founder of the General Motors Corporation (GM), purchased Hyatt for $13.5 million, adding it to United Motors, an automotive parts-making conglomerate. The sale of Hyatt made Sloan, Sr., a millionaire. Sloan, Jr., received a large block of United's stock and was appointed the new company's president. He then moved quickly to rationalize United's structure, institute uniform accounting procedures, and centralize control of finances and marketing in his office. In 1918 United Motors was incorporated into General Motors as part of Durant's frantic wartime expansion program. Sloan, Jr., became a GM vice president and a member of the corporation's executive committee.

Sloan was quickly alienated by Durant's intuitive managerial style and GM's extremely decentralized structure. He was contemplating resignation when a financial crisis forced Durant to leave GM in 1920. The du Pont family, which had been buying General Motors stock since 1917, took control of the troubled corporation. A reluctant Pierre S. du Pont became interim president of General Motors, and Sloan was named his principal assistant. Sloan had been secretly working on a plan to completely restructure GM operations, and now he was in a position to implement it.

Between 1921 and 1925 Sloan directed a managerial revolution at General Motors. His famous "Organization Study" became the blueprint for establishing two tiers of authority within the vast corporation. Senior officers working with their own staffs in the central offices formed the executive and finance committees, which had full responsibility for planning, allocation of resources, accounting policies, and finances. At the same time, more than forty manufacturing operations were organized into five operating groups. Within these groups each manufacturing division became a semiautonomous unit responsible for designing, producing, selling, and marketing its own products. Interdivisional relations committees were established to coordinate purchasing, sales, and other functions. This sophisticated multidivisional structure permitted Sloan to control the total performance of General Motors without stifling initiative among the operating units. It also reflected his own managerial style. Never one to simply give orders, Sloan insisted on detailed presentations of facts and consensus-building committee discussions before making policy decisions.

In 1923 Sloan took over the presidency of General Motors from du Pont. He continued his reforms, standardizing accounting procedures and developing a sophisticated system of consumer surveys, including gathering statistics on the preferences of first-time car buyers versus those buying replacement cars. The system was used to forecast demand and adjust inventory, labor, credit, and price policies. Sloan also perfected General Motors' automotive product line, creating a series of noncompeting car divisions, each aimed at a distinct income bracket—from low-priced Chevrolet to high-priced Cadillac—in the overall automotive marketplace. To constantly stimulate demand among a public increasingly made up of replacement car buyers, Sloan had GM designers emphasize body styling, color, and trimwork, and they constantly invented new accessories. This shift in emphasis culminated in the annual model change, which became standard policy in the industry in the 1930s.

By 1928 General Motors had replaced Ford as the undisputed leader of the American automobile industry. The world's largest, most profitable industrial enterprise, GM also became the most studied corporation in the country. General Motors continued to increase its market share and make profits during the Great Depression, a record that earned Sloan new accolades. However, during the GM sitdown strike in early 1937, Sloan's reputation suffered when he was publicly rebuked by President Franklin D. Roosevelt for refusing to bargain with the new United Automobile Workers union (UAW). After the strike was settled, Sloan allowed William Knudsen, the GM vice president who had actually negotiated with the union, to become the company's president. But Sloan retained real power, serving as both chief executive officer and chairman of the board. He subsequently directed GM's conversion to war production in 1941–1942 and its rapid reconversion to civilian production in 1945–1946. During the reconversion period, Sloan successfully resisted the UAW's attempt to expand its role in GM decision making by accepting a 114-day strike rather than opening the corporation's books as the union demanded.

Sloan retired as General Motors' CEO in 1946, and he stepped down as chairman of the board in 1956. Meanwhile, he continued to work full time managing the Alfred P. Sloan Foundation. He had established the foundation in December 1937 after the Treasury Department reported that Sloan had avoided paying $1.9 million in taxes. By 1966 Sloan and his wife (until her death) had endowed the foundation with more than $300 million. During Sloan's lifetime grants from the foundation were used to establish the Sloan-Kettering Institute for Cancer Research, the School of Industrial Management at MIT, and the funds for basic research in the physical sciences at MIT and the California Institute of Technology. He died in New York City.

Twentieth-century American industrial capitalism carried the imprint of Alfred P. Sloan, Jr.'s work. Sloan's methods of organizing vast enterprises and selling consumer technology remained essential to big business. But what became "Sloanism" also became the object of intense public scrutiny. Since the 1960s consumer and environmental activists condemned Sloan's marketing philosophy as "planned obsoles-cence" and the basis for America's "throwaway economy." Numerous critics have also depicted General Motors as the best example of an overmanaged, overly bureaucratic business in the United States. Undoubtedly, this criticism has merit, but it is equally true that Sloan's business policies were a principal foundation of the greatest period of prosperity in American history.

• Sloan's first autobiography, *Adventures of a White Collar Man* (1941), provides insight into his personal life and personality; his second autobiography, *My Years with General Motors* (1963), is much more a technocratic career summary. Paul F. Douglass, *Six upon the World: Towards an American Culture for an Industrial Age* (1954), contains a valuable biography of Sloan. See also Alfred D. Chandler, Jr., *Strategy and Structure: Chapters in the History of the Industrial Enterprise* (1962); Ed Cray, *Chrome Colossus: General Motors and Its Times* (1980); and James J. Flink, *The Automobile Age* (1988). An obituary is in the *New York Times*, 18 Feb. 1966.

RONALD EDSFORTH

SLOAN, Harold Paul (12 Dec. 1881–22 May 1961), Methodist minister, editor, and author, was born in Westfield, New Jersey, the son of Theodore Reber Sloan, an artist, and Miriam B. Hickman. He was raised in a pietistic Methodist home by parents who were Sunday school teachers; his mother was the daughter of a Methodist clergyman. At age fourteen he joined the Methodist Episcopal church. He attended the University of Pennsylvania for two years and in 1902 entered Drew Theological Seminary in Madison, New Jersey. In 1904 he was ordained a deacon and continued his studies at Crozier Theological Seminary in Chester, Pennsylvania, until 1906, when he was ordained an elder. He then returned to Drew, where he received a B.D. in 1908. He married Ethel Beatrice Buckwalter in 1909; they had two children.

During the first twenty years of his ministry, Sloan served National Park, Atco, West Creek, South River, New Brunswick, Red Bank, and Bridgeton charges, all in New Jersey. In 1924 he was appointed to the Haddonfield Methodist Church, which in the ten years of his pastorate became the largest Methodist congregation in New Jersey. From 1934 to 1936 he was district superintendent of the Camden district. The 1936 General Conference elected him editor of the *New York Christian Advocate*, a post he filled until 1941. From 1942 to 1953 he was pastor of the Wharton Memorial Methodist Church, Philadelphia, Pennsylvania, and thereafter a conference evangelist until his death. Within his home conference he served on the review committee for Sunday school literature and the ministerial course of training. For thirty years he taught the Auditorium Bible Class at Ocean Grove, New Jersey, and served as a trustee of the association. He was elected a delegate to the 1921 Ecumenical Methodist Conference, which met in London, and in 1934 ministered as an exchange preacher in England.

Conservative in theology, Sloan became a major figure in the fundamentalist-modernist debate between 1916 to 1932, particularly within Methodism. First elected a delegate to the General Conference of 1920, and to every subsequent one until elected editor in 1936, he was a forceful spokesman for what he called "historic Christianity." His review of denominational literature convinced him that the essentials of the Christian faith contained in the constitution of the church, the *Discipline*, *Twenty-five Articles of Religion*, and the sermons of John Wesley were being eroded. At the 1920 General Conference there were petitions from thirty annual conferences seeking an investigation and revision of the materials in the ministerial course of study. By 1928 an initiative to examine the teachings in theological schools failed, but a proposal to revise the *Articles of Religion* was also defeated. In 1932 an effort to remove the *Articles of Religion* from the constitution of the Methodist Episcopal church and place them in an appendix of the *Discipline* was narrowly defeated.

Throughout this controversy, Sloan was not a doctrinaire fundamentalist, though he was so labeled. His purpose was to maintain the supernatural dimensions of the Christian faith as expressed in the basic documents of the church. He opposed liberal theology and its humanistic reconstruction of the Christian faith that eliminated or minimized the divinity of Jesus and the need for human redemption. On the other hand, he accepted the so-called higher criticism of biblical scholarship, did not reject evolution, and had little concern over premillennialism (a doctrine that the second coming of Christ will usher in a millennium of peace and virtue), all of which were controversial to fundamentalists. With the emergence of neo-orthodoxy after 1932, Sloan believed a return to historic Christianity was under way. Thereafter, he increasingly focused on the dangers of Nazism and communism and their threat to Christianity and democracy.

The published record of his brand of conservatism is evident in *Historic Christianity* (1922), in the magazine *Call to Colors* (later titled *The Essentialist*, 1925–1932), *The Christ of the Ages* (1928), *The Apostles' Creed* (1930), and *Personality and the Fact of Christ* (1933). Nine additional books of his were published reaffirming a conservative theological position among Methodists. By championing this cause, he is credited with making a major contribution to the reunification of Methodism, North and South, into the Methodist church in 1939. He lectured at Boston University School of Theology, Drew Theological Seminary, and Garrett Theological Seminary throughout his career. He died in Trenton, New Jersey.

• The Harold Paul Sloan Papers are in the United Methodist History and Archives Commission, Drew University, Madison, N.J. In addition to the works cited above, Sloan published *The Child and the Church* (1916), *The Case of Methodism against Modernism* (1929), *He Is Risen* (1942), *One Gospel for One World* (1946), *Eternal Life* (1948), *Faith Is the Victory* (1950), *Jesus Christ Is Lord* (1955), *The Heavenly Vision* (1958), *Christian Choice in Basic Truth* (1959); his "Science and Religion" (1960) is unpublished. William B. Lewis, "The Role of Harold Paul Sloan and the Methodist League of Faith and Life in the Fundamentalist-Modernist Controversy of the Methodist Episcopal Church" (Ph.D. diss., Vanderbilt Univ., 1963), and Floyd T. Cunningham, "The Christian Faith Personally Given: Divergent Trends in Twentieth Century American Methodist Thought" (Ph.D. diss., Johns Hopkins Univ., 1983), are valuable. Floyd T. Cunningham, "Harold Sloan and Methodist Essentials," *Asbury Theological Journal* 42, no. 1 (Spring 1987): 65–76, summarizes Sloan's theology.

FREDERICK V. MILLS, SR.

SLOAN, John (2 Aug. 1871–7 Sept. 1951), realist painter and printmaker, was born John French Sloan in Lock Haven, Pennsylvania, the son of James Dixon Sloan, an occasional salesman, and Henrietta Ireland, an English teacher at a local girls' school. He grew up in a modest home with his two sisters Elizabeth and Marianna, the latter of whom also became an artist. His well-educated maternal extended family provided the children with opportunities to develop their intellectual and artistic interests. Mrs. Sloan shouldered the responsibility of raising the children during her husband's long absences owing to his job as a traveling salesman, teaching them to read even before they began their formal education. As a child Sloan became familiar with the works of William Hogarth, Thomas Rowlandson, and many other artists in the library of his great-uncle, the inventor Alexander Priestley.

When he was not working Sloan's father tinkered around the house; a skilled craftsman, he often invented gadgets and copied paintings, but he was a poor businessman. For years he floundered unsuccessfully, trying to find a suitable occupation to support his family; however, the Sloans eventually lost their home and moved to Philadelphia. Young John Sloan abandoned his plan to become a dentist and quit high school at sixteen to help support his family. At first, Sloan worked briefly in an unsatisfactory job as an errand boy in a low firm. Then, in April 1888, he took a job first at Porter and Coates, a company dealing in books and fine prints, and later at A. Edward Newton, a similar establishment, where he designed calendars and sold his own small etchings. During this time, he had taught himself to etch using *The Etcher's Handbook* by Philip Gilbert Hamerton.

Sloan's formal art training was sparse and interspersed with his daily work routine. In 1890 he attended drawing classes at night at the Spring Garden Institute. A year later he worked independently as an advertising artist in his own small studio, and by 1892 he was hired as a newspaper artist by the *Philadelphia Inquirer*. During this period he took classes with Thomas Anshutz at the Pennsylvania Academy of the Fine Arts. However, it was through another teacher that Sloan met the artist Robert Henri, who first encouraged him to become a painter. Sloan joined Henri's circle of friends, artist-reporters such as William Glackens, George Luks, and Everett Shinn, who later constituted part of the "Eight," a group that later expanded into what was popularly known as the "Ashcan School."

In 1894 Sloan received his first public recognition as a poster designer in the Chicago magazines *Inland Printer* and *Chapbook*, a great honor for one so young. For a brief period that year, he was the art editor for a Philadelphia-based "little" magazine, *Moods*. A year later, he left his job at the *Inquirer* for a position at the *Philadelphia Press*, where he became well known for his elaborate, colored art nouveau–styled picture puzzles and his comic-strip riddles, which were to become his only steady source of income during his early years as a New York artist. While in Philadelphia, Sloan began to build his reputation as a story and book illustrator, first contributing to Stephen Crane's *Great Battles of the World* in 1900 and then beginning the task of creating fifty-four drawings and fifty-three etchings for the deluxe edition of Charles Paul de Kock's novels (1902–1905).

In 1901 Sloan married Anna M. Wall, whom he had met and courted in Philadelphia. Nicknamed Dolly because of her small size, she supported her husband's ambitions to become an artist and gave him the courage he needed to join his Philadelphia artist friends in New York City in 1904. It was in New York that the "Eight" was formed, led by Henri and including Glackens, Shinn, Luks, Ernest Lawson, Maurice Prendergast, Arthur B. Davies, and Sloan. Similar to their nineteenth-century predecessors Winslow Homer and Thomas Eakins, these artists preferred representational realism over the aestheticism of James McNeil Whistler and William Merritt Chase. Before the 1913 Armory Show, the first major exhibition of European modernism in America, the "Eight" distinguished themselves as a revolutionary force that resisted the entrenched hierarchy of the National Academy of Design in New York. Emphasizing direct observation and individual response, these artists sought to create an authentic American art from everyday life. Along the way, they rejected the modernist theories of abstract form espoused by Alfred Stieglitz and his circle at Gallery "291."

While Sloan began painting and etching city scenes in Philadelphia, he is best known for his images of New York at the turn of the twentieth century. Between 1905 and 1906 he produced a very fine series of ten etchings titled *New York City Life*. These scenes, including *The Show Case*, *Fun, One Cent* and *Turning Out the Light*, captured the freshness and immediacy of daily life, and they attest to Sloan's sharp wit and optimistic view of humanity. While these etchings received critical acclaim, the American Water Color Society pronounced four of the images unduly "vulgar" for public presentation, after having invited Sloan to participate in their exhibition of April 1906.

Later paintings such as *Hairdresser's Window*, *The Haymarket*, and *Election Night* (all 1907), further demonstrate Sloan's astute powers of observation and his sympathetic understanding of his subjects. Taking a keen interest in the spectacle of the modern city, Sloan depicts people of all ages strolling, shopping, and surveying their surroundings and each other. While some critics found Sloan's lower-class subject matter exciting, others, accustomed to more genteel themes, found it disturbing. Hostile critics charged that his paintings, like others of the "Eight," were "vulgar" and crudely finished and that they lacked the beauty of academic painting. Although Sloan received honorable mention for his painting *The Coffee Line* from the Eighth International of the Carnegie Institute in 1905, he was very discouraged during these early years of his career because he found no buyers for his work.

Sloan participated in several pioneer exhibitions, including The Eight at the MacBeth Gallery (1908), the Exhibition of Independent Artists on West Thirty-fifth Street (1910), and the Armory Show at Lexington and Twenty-fifth Streets (1913). These major shows were attempts by avant-garde artists to expand exhibition opportunities in America beyond the scope of the National Academy. Sloan entered two paintings and five etchings in the Armory Show, and that year marked the sale of a painting, *Nude, Green Scarf*, to collector and personal friend Albert C. Barnes. He was granted a one-man exhibition at Gertrude Vanderbilt Whitney's studio in 1916.

Following Henri's example and John Ruskin's theories, Sloan searched the city for inspiration and found it in the working-class people around him. Despite his concern for the plight of his subjects and the fact that he was troubled by the signs of injustice that he saw around him, Sloan attempted to keep social and political ideologies from filtering into his art. He made strict distinctions between his commercial work and the paintings and etchings that he did for exhibition in galleries and museums, referring only to the latter as "art." Nonetheless, he remained politically progressive, joining the Socialist party in 1910. During this period (1910–1915) both he and his wife became active participants in labor demonstrations and party politics. He even ran unsuccessfully as the Socialist party candidate for the New York State Assembly from 1910 through 1912.

In 1912 Sloan assumed the position of art editor of *The Masses*, a revolutionary magazine with socialist leanings, which addressed working-class issues. Sloan produced innovative magazine layouts and provocative drawings during his term as art editor. However, on the eve of World War I, Sloan became disillusioned with the ability of the Socialist party to make a real difference in workers' lives, and in 1914 he withdrew from both the party and his work on *The Masses*. He finally resigned from *The Masses* in 1916, following a dispute regarding the political content of the magazine's artwork.

Between 1914 and 1918 Sloan spent his summers at Gloucester, Massachusetts, where he painted many brilliantly dynamic landscapes for which today he is seldom recognized. He taught art classes there in the summer of 1916, and in the fall he began teaching at the Art Students League in New York, where he served as president in 1931, resigning from the league in 1932. He began teaching there again regularly in 1935 and remained an energetic instructor until his resignation in 1938. Known for his sharp tongue and incisive criticism, students, among them Alexander Calder, David Smith, Reginald Marsh, and Barnett Newman, respected him.

In 1917 Sloan had a one-man show at Kraushaar's in New York, a gallery with which he maintained a life-long connection. One year later he was named president of the Society of Independent Artists, a position that he held until his death.

In 1920 the Sloans bought a house in Santa Fe, New Mexico. This house became their second home in the summer months, while the couple involved themselves in community affairs focusing on Native-American culture. For many years Sloan served as illustrator for the *New Mexico Quarterly* and presided over several local cultural foundations, including the Exposition of Indian Tribal Arts, the Santa Fe Painters and Sculptors, and the New Mexico Alliance for the Arts.

The 1920s marked a significant change in the nature of Sloan's art. He became preoccupied with structure and form, an interest that began to develop slowly after seeing the European modernist paintings in the 1913 Armory Show. In 1928 Sloan abandoned the painting technique that he learned from his mentor Henri—the fresh application of opaque colors based on the Maratta color system. Instead, he adopted the old master techniques of Titian and Peter Paul Rubens, which he learned by looking at the late nudes of Auguste Renoir. This method consisted of opaque underpainting in tempera with layers of oil glazes applied on top. During this period, except for his New Mexico landscapes, Sloan concentrated on female nude figures. In 1929 he superimposed graphic line work and crosshatching over the painted figures in order to better realize the form and to create a signature style. He also distorted both figure and space, experimenting with different types of perspective. Viewers, accustomed to Sloan's early works and familiar with his competence as a draftsman, were perplexed by the awkwardness and disturbing quality of the later nudes, even though the surfaces are beautifully rendered. Most viewers did not place them within the sphere of postimpressionism, which would preclude interpreting distortion as ineptitude. To Sloan's dismay, viewers failed to recognize the significance of these later works.

While experimenting with new painting techniques, Sloan carried on his work as a printmaker. In 1936 he exhibited one hundred etchings at the Whitney Museum, and he mounted an etching retrospective at Kraushaar's the following year. Also in 1937 he produced sixteen prints illustrating Somerset Maugham's novel *Of Human Bondage*. Sloan continued to exhibit regularly throughout the 1930s and participated in the 1937 Whitney exhibition, New York Realists: 1900–1914, which featured the early city scenes for which he was known and praised.

In 1939 Sloan wrote a treatise entitled *Gist of Art*, which spelled out the principles of and motivations behind his art. Here, Sloan discusses his struggle to go beyond the painted surface in order to communicate a deeper reality about life. The book was prepared with the assistance of his student and friend Helen Farr, whose class notes, memories, and collected remarks from other students formed the basis of the text. This document, encompassing techniques of art making as well as Sloan's personal vision of the world, stands as a testament to a dedicated artist and teacher.

In May 1943 Dolly Sloan died of a heart attack. Barely one year later Sloan married Farr, whom he had met at the Art Students League in the 1920s. With his own health restored after three operations to clear his gall duct between 1938 and 1943, he began working with his usual enthusiasm. In 1950 he was awarded a gold medal for painting by American Academy of Arts and Letters.

While preparing for a major retrospective at the Whitney Museum, Sloan and his wife spent the summer of 1951 in Hanover, New Hampshire. Sloan's doctors discouraged his usual trip to Santa Fe because of the potential effect of the altitude on the now almost eighty-year-old artist. Sloan died later that summer in Hanover. The curator of the Whitney Museum, Lloyd Goodrich, characterized the artist in the 1952 retrospective exhibition catalog: "In his green old age, Sloan with his leonine mass of gray hair, his indomitable face, his keen eyes, and his sharp tongue, was one of the legendary characters of the art world." Indeed, his urban scenes endure as major documents in American art and social history.

• The John Sloan Archives are at the Delaware Art Museum, Wilmington. Sloan's diary (1906–1912) is published as *John Sloan's New York Scene* (1965). Biographical information is in John Loughery, *John Sloan: Painter and Rebel* (1995); Van Wyck Brooks, *A Painter's Life* (1955); Lloyd Goodrich, *John Sloan, 1871–1951* (1952), an exhibition catalog for the Whitney Museum of American Art; and David W. Scott and E. John Bullard, *John Sloan, 1871–1951* (1971), an exhibition catalog for the National Gallery of Art. For information on Sloan's work see Rowland Elzea, *John Sloan's Oil Paintings: A Catalogue Raisonné* (1991), and Peter Morse, *John Sloan's Prints: A Catalogue Raisonné of Etchings, Lithographs, and Posters* (1969). See also Janice M. Coco, "Re-viewing John Sloan's Images of Women," *Oxford Art Journal* 21, no. 2 (1998); Patricia Hills, "John Sloan's Images of Working-Class Women: A Case Study of the Roles and Interrelationships of Politics, Personality, and Patrons in the Development of Sloan's Art, 1905–16," *Prospects* 5 (1980): 157–96; and Rebecca Zurier et al., *Metropolitan Lives: The Ashcan Artists and Their New York* (1995), an exhibition catalog for the National Museum of American Art.

JANICE MARIE COCO

SLOAN, Matthew Scott (5 Sept. 1881–14 June 1945), utility and railroad executive, was born in Mobile, Alabama, the son of Matthew Scott Sloan, the chief of the city fire department, and Mary Elizabeth Scott. Details of his early education are sketchy. He entered Alabama Polytechnic Institute (now Auburn University) at the age of fourteen and received a B.S. in 1901 and an M.S. in 1902 in electrical engineering. Following graduation, he briefly served as the manager of an electric light plant in Dothan, Alabama, and then he worked for a streetcar company in Nashville, Tennessee. Later in 1902 he moved north and began an apprenticeship in the railway motor testing department of the General Electric Company (GE) in Schenectady, New York. At GE, Sloan advanced steadily through the ranks and became supervisor of turbine installations by 1906. Returning to his native state, he went to work for a GE subsidiary, the Electric Bond and Share Company, which operated a number of utilities nationwide, as the chief engineer and assistant to the president of the Birmingham Railway Light and Power Company. In 1911 he married Lottie Everard Lane; they had one daughter.

In 1914 Sloan moved to New Orleans, where he served as vice president and general manager of another Electric Bond firm, the New Orleans Railway and Light Company. From there he returned to New York in 1917 as assistant to the vice president and general manager of the New York Edison Company. His new employer was one of four subsidiaries of the Consolidated Gas Company, the powerful if incredibly inefficient distributor of electrical power throughout New York City. While Sloan deplored the political patronage and corruption that controlled company hiring and operations, he could do little in his initial position. Upon becoming the president of Brooklyn Edison, another subsidiary, in 1929, however, Sloan sprang into action. Following the lead of such industry pioneers as Samuel Insull of Chicago and Alex Dow in Detroit, he initiated a massive modernization program at Brooklyn Edison. He built a huge 600,000 horsepower steam generating plant in the borough, which dramatically lowered production costs and enabled the company to better service its subscribers, whose number rose from 150,000 to more than 750,000 during his presidency. Although he cut rates several times, Sloan also presided over a period of increasing revenues, which rose from $8.5 million to $48 million during his tenure. A firm believer in good public relations, he also streamlined internal operations to provide better and more efficient customer service.

Following the 1928 consolidation of New York's utilities, which later became known as Con Edison, Sloan became the president of New York Edison Company and its affiliates. In attempting to reform citywide utility service in the manner of Brooklyn, he faced powerful obstacles. The system's infrastructure was a shambles. While Manhattan under New York Edison was divided between 25-cycle alternating current and 3-wire direct current, the Bronx under the same firm was served by a 4-phase alternating current. Another affiliate, United Electric Power & Light, served both Manhattan and the Bronx with a variety of alternating current phases whose frequency matched that of Brooklyn's while its voltage differed. Although Sloan's initial pleas for uniformity gained acceptance in the face of the city's clear need for electricity to service its rapidly expanding subway system, still greater obstacles, economic and political, lay in his path.

The advent of the Great Depression in late 1929 was Sloan's first setback. Declining sales and therefore declining revenues made internal improvements difficult and exacerbated an already growing difficulty in raising outside capital for the proposed projects in the chaotic financial markets. Labor contract problems only made matters worse, but the final straw came in the form of political resistance. In the corrupt political atmosphere exemplified by such figures as Mayor Jimmy Walker, Sloan made many enemies at Tammany Hall, the city's Democratic political machine, by insisting on competence over political expediency. Resistance to his initiatives sprang up at every turn, and by late 1931 his position at New York Edison was untenable. Company directors demanded his resignation early in 1932.

Sloan remained in New York City following his untimely departure from New York Edison, and for two years he served as co-chair with Standard Oil Company president Walter C. Teagle of the "share-the-work" movement. In 1934 he undertook the last great task of his career, the attempted salvation of the Missouri-Kansas-Texas Railroad. Known familiarly as the "Katy," the road presented Sloan with many of the same problems that he had encountered in New York. Its infrastructure was in ruins, and running any railroad presented problems enough in the depths of the depression. Nevertheless Sloan, who became president and chairman of the board of the line in 1934, set about his task with characteristic vigor. Matters grew worse before they got better as company stock sold for twenty-five cents a share during the 1938 recession, but Sloan managed to nurse the road through the 1930s. The advent of World War II, with its increase in traffic, saved the Katy and a number of other roads. By 1944 the line produced a profit of $6.1 million.

Once again, however, Sloan generated enemies. His insistence on putting company profits back into the line over dividend payments aroused the anger of a powerful minority stockholder, and a bitter proxy battle ensued. Sloan died in New York City in the midst of the fight, having never relocated his residence after leaving New York Edison.

Sloan's career serves as a cautionary tale for business leaders everywhere. Energy, foresight, and a burning desire for efficiency took him far in the business world yet could not save him when institutions and circumstances conspired against him. He does deserve recognition, however, for his role in the creation of Con Edison and for his stabilization of the Katy, a line that many had given up for dead.

• Sloan's papers have apparently not survived. His career at New York Edison receives attention in Frederick L. Collins, *Consolidated Gas of New York: A History* (1934), while his efforts to revive the Katy are covered in V. V. Masterson, *The Katy Railroad and the Last Frontier* (1952). An obituary is in the *New York Times*, 15 June 1945.

EDWARD L. LACH, JR.

SLOAN, Samuel (25 Dec. 1817–22 Sept. 1907), railroad president, was born in Lisburn, County Lisburn, Ireland, the son of William Sloan and Elizabeth Simpson. His family immigrated to the United States when

Sloan was a year old, and they settled in New York City. Sloan attended Columbia College Preparatory School until the age of fourteen, when he left school to support his family following his father's death. He worked for a local merchant for two years and then took a job with the linen-importing firm of McBride & Company in 1831. He served his new employer in a variety of capacities, and in 1844 he became a partner of the firm. Also in 1844 he married Margaret Elmendorf; they had six children.

Sloan relocated to Brooklyn, New York, in 1844. While continuing in the import business, he added the duties of county supervisor for Kings County (Brooklyn) in 1852. At about this time he took note of the investment potential of the newly emerging railroad industry and began investing heavily in railroad stocks. He was elected to the board of directors of the Hudson River Railroad (later a part of the New York Central system) in 1855 and later that year became president of the line. Sloan also served as president of the Long Island College Hospital and briefly entered politics as a Democrat, serving in the New York State Senate for one term (1856–1858).

A hands-on railroad president, Sloan set out to learn the business from top to bottom. He visited and spoke with men in all the various company positions, and he reputedly knew every man in the firm. He aggressively improved the road's physical condition. In an age when many railroad operators were only concerned with immediate profits at the expense of both shareholders and the public, Sloan insisted on providing the best service possible. He upgraded the line's roadbed, installed heavier rails, and implemented telegraph service on operating trains. Investors soon recognized the value of these improvements, and Hudson River stock prices rose from $17 a share to $140 a share during his presidency. Like other railroaders, Sloan apparently benefited from the inflation generated by the Civil War that reduced the burdens of lines carrying heavy debt loads. Founded in a daring attempt to wrestle freight traffic along the Hudson River from steamboat shipping lines, the Hudson River Railroad soon attracted the attention of Cornelius Vanderbilt. Vanderbilt had owned stock in the line as early as 1861 and acquired complete control by the end of 1865. Interested in the line as a complimentary route to the New York & Harlem Railroad, of which he had become president in 1863, Vanderbilt installed his son William Vanderbilt as vice president of the Hudson in 1865. Although Vanderbilt offered Sloan the presidency of the New York & Harlem in 1865, Sloan doubted that he could work alongside the ambitious Vanderbilt and resigned as president of the Hudson River Railroad that year.

Sloan quickly rebounded from this setback to serve from 1865 to 1867 as commissioner of the Trunk Lines Association for the Middle Atlantic States, a group that sought to bring order to the chaotic rate structures and operating schedules of the day. Nevertheless, he longed to run his own road. His next opportunity came with a directorship of the Delaware, Lackawanna & Western Railroad secured in 1864 through the efforts of a close friend, Moses Taylor, the president of New York's National City Bank. Sloan became the president of the Lackawanna, as it was popularly known, in 1867. The line had long been known as a "coal road," one of several small lines that ran through and divided Pennsylvania's anthracite coal mining region. Although the railroad was successful, Sloan had a much larger vision for the line. He wanted to expand it into a general freight handler, which would reduce the line's dependency on coal shipments while increasing overall traffic.

Sloan's position offered a variety of challenges. The competing area lines operated in a climate of cutthroat competition, with rate reductions and shipper rebates common practices. Although Sloan managed to negotiate a rate agreement among the competitors in 1870, the victory was short-lived. By 1876 the truce lay in shambles, and two of Sloan's largest rivals, the Philadelphia & Reading and the New Jersey Central, slid into bankruptcy. The Lackawanna operated at a competitive disadvantage against both the New York Central and the Pennsylvania railroads, and its problems were not fully solved until the line amicably joined the trunk line pool in 1884. As did most of his peers during the period, Sloan opposed labor unions and the right of workers to strike.

In the midst of attempting to restore sanity to railroad shipping rates, Sloan faced another massive problem with the Lackawanna's physical plant. The line used an old, six-foot track gauge, while the rest of the railroad world had adopted a standard gauge of four feet, eight and one-half inches in width. Changing the system meant modifying the rails at enormous cost and modifying the line's rolling stock as well. Sloan remained undaunted. After sending his work crews out to lay a third rail at the proper distance on his existing tracks, he in 1876 closed the entire line over a weekend, and within twenty-four hours the line was again operational. Although the transaction cost the Lackawanna over $1.25 million, it proved to be the wisest of investments. The company's stock shot up from 30 to 94 almost overnight, and with the regauging completed, the Lackawanna was able to extend its lines both northward and westward. Gaining an entrance into Buffalo, New York, and the trade from the Great Lakes was particularly valuable. From 1881 to 1890 coal traffic increased by 32 percent, and general freight shipping increased by 160 percent. The line even experienced an 88 percent increase in its passenger traffic. All this newfound prosperity paid off for the Lackawanna's stockholders, who received a yearly dividend of 7 percent between 1885 and 1905.

Possessing few outside interests beyond the business world, Sloan also served as president of a number of other railroad lines, including the Watertown & Ogdensburg in upstate New York, the International & Great Northern in Texas, the Pere Marquette in Michigan, and Indiana's Fort Wayne & Jackson. His least successful experience was running the Michigan Central Railroad, a line that had suffered greatly in the wake of the panic of 1873. The Michigan Central had long been of interest to stock speculators. Sloan gained the presidency of the line in 1877 at the instigation of his friend Taylor, whose bank held the largest number of stock shares. Unfortunately for Sloan, William Vanderbilt and Jay Gould also held a large block of shares. Vanderbilt acquired influence over a sufficient number of proxies to control the line, and he replaced Sloan as president in 1878.

Sloan was a director of a number of other firms, including the Bank of Metropole; the Bank of the Manhattan Trust Company; National City Bank; New York Mutual Gas; Seamans Bank for Savings; Western Union Telegraph Company; Consolidated Gas; Queens Insurance Company of America; Mt. Hope Mineral; the Farmers' Loan & Trust; the Texas & Pacific Railway; the Oswego & Syracuse Railroad; the Utica, Chenango & Susquehanna Valley; the Louisville, New Albany & Chicago Railroad; the Missouri Pacific Railway; the Wabash Railroad; the Green Bay, Winona & St. Paul Railway; the Mechanics Bank; and the National Security Company. Sloan resigned as president of the Lackawanna in 1899 but remained chairman of the board until his death in Garrison, New York.

Sloan was one of the major railroad builders of the late nineteenth century. Although not as well known as several of his contemporaries, his solid work in upgrading the Lackawanna merits attention, as does his leadership of more than a dozen smaller lines.

• Sloan's papers are divided between the Michigan Central Railroad Archives in Detroit, Mich., and the Erastus Corning Papers at the Albany Institute of History and Art in Albany, N.Y. Good secondary sources on his life and career are Jules I. Bogen, *The Anthracite Railroads* (1927); Robert J. Casey and W. A. S. Douglas, *The Lackawanna Story* (1951); and Joseph Rankin Duryee, *The Story of Samuel and Margaret Sloan* (1927). Obituaries are in the *New York Evening Post* and the *New York Tribune*, 23 Sept. 1907.

EDWARD L. LACH, JR.

SLOAN, Samuel T. (7 Mar. 1815–19 July 1884), architect and author, was born at Beaver Dam, Pennsylvania, the son of William Sloan, a carpenter, and Mary Kirkwood. The Sloans were a large clan of Presbyterian Irish, most of whom were in the building trades, so in 1821, at the age of six, Samuel was sent to Lancaster, Pennsylvania, for his schooling and carpenter's apprenticeship. In 1833 he rejoined his family, who had moved to Hamilton Village, a western suburb of Philadelphia. There Sloan found work, first on the construction of the Eastern State Penitentiary and then at the Department for the Insane of the Pennsylvania Hospital. He was employed at the Department of the Insane from 1834 until completion of the hospital in 1841, becoming superintendent of work in 1838. The training he received at the penitentiary and the Department for the Insane was invaluable to his later career as an institutional architect.

Also invaluable was his association, while superintendent of work at the department, with young Dr. Thomas S. Kirkbride, who later became the foremost alienist (as psychiatrists were then called) in the United States. As a result of their professional friendship, Kirkbride turned to Sloan for architectural services in 1852 when the doctor was proposing a radical change in the design of hospitals for the insane. The success of his "Kirkbride Plan" (a linked series of long wards separated by treatment pavilions) resulted in the lifelong collaboration of Kirkbride and Sloan. At the time of the architect's death he had designed thirty-two hospitals based on the "Kirkbride Plan," in every state of the Union.

Kirkbride was also responsible for Sloan's evolution from carpenter to architect over the decade of the 1840s, making his extensive library available to the young man and encouraging him to study. In the same decade Sloan married Mary Pennell, from another large family of builders and contractors, and the first of their three children was born. In 1849 he received his first architectural commission, the "Public Buildings" (courthouse and jail) of Delaware County, Pennsylvania. With the courthouse, Sloan established his design for a building type, ten of which he was to erect before his death.

In the ten years from 1852 to 1862, Sloan reached the height of his professional success. He became the chosen architect of Philadelphia's rising industrial and entrepreneurial elite. For them he built mansions, commercial buildings, speculative housing, even entire resort communities, like that at Riverton, New Jersey. Because of their political influence, he became the leading public school architect in Pennsylvania. His design for primary and secondary schools, known as the "Sloan Plan," was published by the state as a guide for school construction throughout Pennsylvania and received international acclaim. The "Sloan Plan" was unique in its attention to generous circulation, which would promote rapid evacuation of the buildings in case of fire, and in the use of sliding or folding partitions that could divide a large assembly space into small classrooms. Unfortunately, the "Plan" was fifty years ahead of contemporary teaching methods, and it was discarded as soon as Sloan's political friends were out of office.

In 1852 Sloan issued *The Model Architect*, a collection of unusually thorough drawings (plans, elevations, sections, details, and perspectives) together with explanatory descriptions of the designs and short essays on every aspect of architectural practice. This "pattern book" was an immediate and lasting success with the upper middle class, at which it was aimed, and went through four official editions, the last being issued in 1873. By that date Sloan had published four additional pattern books as well as the first American architectural periodical, the *Architectural Review*, and the *American Builders Journal*. The first issue of the *Review* came out in 1868 and was hailed by the newly reorganized American Institute of Architects, of which Sloan was a fellow. However, the animosity of Philadelphia architects, stemming from their suspicion of Sloan's business methods, destroyed the confidence of the profession in the *Journal*, and its last issues appeared in 1870.

From his professional debut in 1849 until the financial panic of 1857–1858, Sloan was among the most active architects in the nation. He received commissions for Protestant churches in all the states between Pennsylvania and Alabama. His design for the Second Masonic Temple in Philadelphia (1853) initiated a national career in the design of civic buildings. At the very end of the decade (1858) Sloan received the commission for what is today his best-known work, "Longwood," the huge octagonal, "oriental" villa for Dr. Haller Nutt, a wealthy cotton planter of Natchez, Mississippi. The house, left unfinished when its Philadelphia workmen fled because of the Civil War, survives today very much as it was at Nutt's death in 1864.

In 1860 Sloan was accused of conspiracy and malpractice for trying to influence the award of the commission for the "New Public Buildings of the City of Philadelphia" (new City Hall). The ensuing scandal, broadcast in Philadelphia's newspapers, was to shadow the remainder of his life in the city. Although he was thereafter to design important buildings in eastern Pennsylvania and New Jersey (the main building of Swathmore College, the Seminary of St. Charels Borromeo at Overbrook, two hospitals for the insane, and several public schools), because of professional distrust Sloan was never again the preeminent architect he had been in the 1850s. In an attempt to offset this distrust, Sloan took several partners, the most important of whom was the young Quaker architect Addison Hutton, who had been a draftsman in Sloan's office from 1859 to 1861. Sloan's final effort to recover professional standing in Pennsylvania was his two entries in the competition for the buildings of the Centennial Exhibition of 1875. Both entries received second place. Feeling that he would always be discriminated against locally, Sloan moved his office to Raleigh, North Carolina, where he remained until his death. In North Carolina he executed four more private schools, several buildings for the University of North Carolina, the State Exhibition Buildings and the Governor's Mansion in Raleigh (the latter with his last associate, Gustavus Adolphus Bauer), and a large hospital for the insane in Morganton.

Samuel Sloan died in Raleigh and was later interred in Mount Moriah Cemetery, Kingsessing, Philadelphia. His considerable accomplishments as an architect and publisher, and his many contributions to the architectural profession in the United States, were largely forgotten within a decade of his death. Sloan was a typical transitional figure, being at once both functionally advanced and stylistically conservative. Much of his inventive programming was ahead of its time, while his visual expressions were eclectic and determined by the enthusiasm of his clients. In essence, he was a "commercial" architect, but as such he rendered a great service to the practitioners who followed him.

• The letters of Samuel Sloan to Dr. Haller Nutt in the two collections of Nutt papers at the Duke University Library, Durham, N.C., and at the Henry E. Huntington Library, San Marino, Calif., provide insight into the man's personality and working methods. This is strengthened by the letters of Addison Hutton in the Hutton papers, Quaker Collection, Haverford College Library, Haverford, Penn. The primary source for Sloan's designs are his own publications: *The Model Architect* (2 vols., 1852); *City and Suburban Architecture* (1859); *Sloan's Constructive Architecture* (1859); and *Sloan's Homestead Architecture* (1861). Thomas S. Kirkbride, *Hospitals for the Insane*, 2d ed. (1880), is the primary documentation of the Sloan-Kirkbride collaboration and gives the particulars of the "Kirkbride Plan." The only modern assessment of Sloan, together with a catalog of his work, is Harold N. Cooledge, Jr., *Samuel Sloan, Architect of Philadelphia, 1815–1884* (1986).

HAROLD N. COOLEDGE, JR.

SLOAN, Tod (10 Aug. 1874–21 Dec. 1933), jockey, was born James Forman Sloan at Bunker Hill, near Kokomo, Indiana, the son of Samuel Sloan and Martha (maiden name unknown). His father, a psychologically scarred Civil War veteran who had a barbershop and real estate business, was unable to care for his children. Soon after Tod's mother died when he was five, the family disintegrated. The diminutive "Toad" was adopted by Dan and Lib Blauser, but they could not tame the lad, who was not well behaved and indifferent to his public school studies. He ran away at age thirteen and thereafter was on his own. He worked in gas and oil wells, cleaned out stables and saloons, and assisted aeronaut "Professor" A. L. Talbot, who made balloon ascensions at county fairs. He then worked with older brother Cassius, a jockey in St. Louis, Missouri, as a stable boy and apprentice jockey. Tod seemed a natural jockey at 4'8" and 80 pounds, but he had been scared of horses as a child and struggled to ride well. He was reputedly extremely kind to animals, and supposedly he could make any horse run fast by whispering in its ear and stroking its mane.

Sloan's first break came in 1894, when trainer Charlie Hanlon taught him to study horses and built up his confidence. Later that year in San Francisco, Sloan began perfecting a new style of riding he had seen Harry Griffin employ, in which the jockey lay along the neck and shoulders of his horse. The classic style then was for the rider to sit far back in the saddle, his back erect, with long stirrups and long rein. The new technique became known as the American seat, or the "monkey on a stick." It was probably first employed by black stable hands and introduced at the track by Snapper Garrison. Sloan popularized the style in California and then at the leading eastern tracks. He found this technique comfortable since he had unusually short legs and rode in a crouch high on the horse's neck, with short stirrups and short rein, looking down over the animal's head. This gave him more control over his mounts, cut wind resistance, and better distributed the jockey's weight.

In 1895 Sloan became a favorite on the West Coast of the renowned plunger Pittsburgh Phil, and thereafter signed up with the leading eastern racing stables. Sloan won 29.9 percent of his 442 races the following year, 37.1 percent of 369 events in 1897, and then 166 of his 362 starts, or 45.9 percent, in 1898. That year he won five races in one day three times in England and twice in America. He became the principal rider for William C. Whitney, owner of the preeminent American stable for whom sloan won several notable stakes events, including the 1900 Futurity. He was said to have been the first jockey to demand and receive a percentage of the purse in addition to the regular riding fee.

In 1897 Sloan went to England, the international center of the turf, at the encouragement of American horseman James R. Keene, who wanted Sloan to ride for him. Sloan won 20 of 53 races that autumn and 43 of 78 the following autumn, and he became a favorite of the leading stable owners. In 1899 he won a record 108 times out of 345 contests (31.3 percent), including a victory in the prestigious £1,000 Oaks, and placed in 103 races. Sloan was the leading winner in 1900, taking nearly 27 percent of his races. He even rode for the prince of Wales, whose agent gave Sloan a £6,000 retainer at the end of 1900.

Sloan's presence greatly boosted the American invasion of the British turf, and by 1900 the careers of English jockeys were in jeopardy. His success was first greeted with derision for his racing style, but that style was soon adapted by English jockeys, marking the end of the classic English riding style. American riders had several advantages, including the American seat; familiarity with starting gates, just introduced in Great Britain in 1897; and the customary style of racing to the front and holding leads. They left the British jockeys, who were accustomed to waiting races, in their wake. However, the Americans were unfamiliar with idiosyncratic British race courses that had their own unique designs, unlike American dirt tracks that were basically identical.

Like several other American jockeys, Sloan was frequently suspended both because he gambled and because he associated with gamblers, who had followed him from America and often gave him gifts following betting coups. He bet heavily on horses he rode, which was customary in the United States but not in Great Britain. He got into trouble following a second place with Codoman in the Cambridgeshire Stakes at the end of the 1900 season, when he was sent off by the Stewards for betting on the race. His efforts at social climbing, exuberant self-confidence, and occasional boorish behavior irritated the English racing elite. Consequently, the Newmarket Jockey Club intimated that he need not apply for a new license in 1900, without giving any formal reasons. The press presumed that this was because his betting and other actions were considered detrimental to the turf. The decision destroyed Sloan's career because all the major tracks around the world followed the lead of the English Jockey Club. However, Sloan was permitted to own and train horses, work them out at the track, and make wagers. The historian John Dizikes speculated that the

action was taken following the coronation of Edward VII so the Crown would be dissociated from the American jockey, as well as serving as an impetus to reform the English turf by ridding itself of "unwholesome" American gamblers and jockeys. Most contemporary observers felt his punishment was far greater than any malfeasance he might have committed.

Sloan was renowned for his lifestyle and social climbing. He associated with royalty and such noted personalities as Lillian Russell and Diamond Jim Brady. He spent money freely, lived in the finest hotels, and was famed for his vanity—he had a 38-trunk wardrobe. He was married and divorced from actresses Julia Sanderson (1907–1913) and Elizabeth Saxon Malone (1920–1927). He had one daughter with his second wife.

Sloan tried for years to regain his license and wrote a 1915 autobiography to vindicate himself. He traveled extensively between London, Paris, and New York and lived a profligate life, spending much of his $300,000 career earnings and ending up broke. In the mid-1910s he worked in New York as a bookmaker, vaudevillian, and manager of a billiard parlor owned by the baseball manager John J. McGraw. In the 1920s he sold real estate in San Diego, California, and had bit parts in the movies. Sloan spent his last five years living on the kindness of friends. He died in Los Angeles, California.

Sloan was one of the last representatives of the rugged individualistic sportsman, as sport became increasingly rationalized and complex. A leading sportsman and celebrity, he provided the inspiration for Ernest Hemingway's short story "My Old Man." An innovative jockey who had a great sense of pace, Sloan revolutionized racing by his style of riding and his daring practice of forcing matches by leading from start to finish rather than setting back in the pack and waiting for a final sprint to win. Sloan was elected to the National Museum of Racing Hall of Fame in 1955 and to the Jockey Hall of Fame in 1956.

• Sloan published an autobiography in London in collaboration with sports writer A. Dick Luckman, *Tod Sloan by Himself* (1915), in which he tried to justify his career and lifestyle in hopes of regaining his jockey license. For an excellent brief biography of Sloan, see John Dizikes, "Tod Sloan: Fairy Tales and Nightmares," *Arete: The Journal of Sport Literature* 1 no. 2 (Spring 1984): 95–112. See also William H. P. Robertson, *The History of Thoroughbred Racing in America* (1964). Obituaries are in the *New York Times* and the *Times* (London), both 22 Dec. 1933.

STEVEN A. RIESS

SLOANE, Isabel Cleves Dodge (26 Feb. 1896–9 Mar. 1962), race horse and dog owner and breeder, was born in Detroit, Michigan, the daughter of John Francis Dodge, an auto manufacturer, and Ivy S. Hawkins. Sloane attended the Liggett School in Grosse Point, Michigan, from which she graduated in 1913. Her father died in 1920 and she inherited $7 million of his

$40 million estate, which was divided among her four siblings. On 28 February 1921 she married securities broker George Sloane.

In 1923 Sloane and her husband started Brookmeade Stable in Locust Valley, New York, where they owned an estate. Sloane did not ride horses herself; she played tennis and golf, fished for salmon, and shot grouse. However, she once commented to the *New York Times* (16 Sept. 1934), in one of her rare interviews, "I'd always liked horses; [they] interested me. I thought it would be amusing to own one and have it run for me. We picked up a [steeplechase] horse named Skyscraper [II] on sale, and he made me a fan for life by winning his first important start, the Manley in Maryland [in 1924]." Among her best known steeplechasers were National Anthem, Delhi Dan, Fleettown, Greek Flag, and His Boots, the latter being the Grand National winner in 1949 and 1953.

In 1925 Brooms became the first thoroughbred stakes winner to carry the white silks with the royal blue cross sashes of Brookmeade Stable when he won the prestigious Hopeful Stakes. By 1927 Sloane focused more on flat racing than on the jumpers. Arthur White of Middleburg, Virginia, a lifelong friend and confidant, handled her steeplechase division until shortly before her death.

After Sloane and her husband, who were childless, divorced in 1929, she purchased land in Upperville, Virginia. There she established Brookmeade Stud for breeding race horses. She also purchased a house overlooking the golf course in Saratoga, New York, where her horses competed at the historic track during August. Originally Sloane developed her racing stock by purchasing her runners at yearling sales and then retiring them to stud in Virginia at the end of their racing careers. After several years of building up her stock and selective breeding, she produced some notable winners, among them Sailor, Sword Dancer (top money earner and Horse of the Year in 1959) and Bowl of Flowers (champion two-year-old filly in 1960). The success of Brookmeade helped revive Virginia's horse breeding industry.

In 1932 Sloane purchased Cavalcade for a paltry $1,200 at the Saratoga yearling sales. By 1934 the colt developed into a multiple stakes winner, with six victories including the Chesapeake Stakes (in which Cavalcade set a new track record) and the Kentucky, American, and Detroit derbies. When Cavalcade won the Kentucky Derby, the usually dignified and sedate Sloane screamed wildly, calling it "the greatest thrill of my life." She later named her Saratoga stable area Cavalcade Park in honor of her big winner. The success of Cavalcade and other two and three-year-olds, including Preakness winner High Quest, placed Brookmeade as the top money-winning stable for 1934, making Sloane the first woman to outearn all other thoroughbred owners in a given year. In only her tenth season of racing, Sloane's horses won 49 races and earned over $250,000. She topped the list of money won by leading owners again in 1950 and in 1959.

Sloane enjoyed betting on the races, except for the big races in which her horses ran. She made it a rule not to bet "because I'm much too interested in the race even to think about betting." Otherwise, she "bet small sums, because the interesting thing about betting to me is not the amount of money you can make. It's whether or not you can finish ahead of the bookmakers for the day" (*New York Times*, 16 Sept. 1934).

At the stable Sloane was a "hands-on" owner who made all major decisions regarding the purchasing, breeding, and racing of her horses. Sloane employed first Robert A. Smith, then Preston Burch, and finally Burch's son Elliott Burch to train her race horses. During the height of Brookmeade Stable's prominence on the racing circuit, Sloane kept 85 horses in training, with entries in nearly every major stakes race.

Sloane generally shied away from high society and its trappings to devote her energies to the kennels and stables, although she occasionally hosted extravagant parties at track clubhouses. In her characteristic bluntness, Sloane, who was a conservative dresser, once sent a butler back to the telephone to respond to a society editor's inquiry about what she would wear to the races the next day: "I have delivered your message to Mrs. Sloane and Mrs. Sloane wishes me to say to the person telephoning, 'Who the hell cares?!'"During World War II she helped raise money at race tracks for the war effort and played a role in both the American Women's Voluntary Services and its salvage bureau.

In addition to the racing stable Sloane devoted herself to breeding pedigree show dogs, a pursuit that began when she and her husband started kennels in Syosset, New York. Under the management of Frank Brumby, later a respected show judge, Brookmeade Kennels specialized in breeding and showing medium-sized and miniature schnauzers and basset hounds. She imported from Germany and England the finest bloodlines of these two breeds, considered to be her greatest contribution to purebred dog fancy in the United States. Sloane's first award-winning schnauzer was Champion Fred Gamundia, judged best in show at Westbury in 1925 and best of breed in 40 more shows. Brookmeade Kennels also introduced the basset hound to America. In 1928 Sloane's Walhampton Grappler took best in breed in bassets and Champion Harno vom Schoenblick won best in breed in schnauzers at the Westminster Kennel Club show. A keen business woman, Sloane sold off an entire season's 22 yearlings for $142,800 in 1952 when she discovered the kennels were more financially successful than the stable. Thereafter she operated Brookmeade on a reduced scale.

Sloane died unexpectedly following intestinal surgery in West Palm Beach, Florida. The horses of Brookmeade Stable and Brookmeade Stud were sold at a dispersal sale. During her lifetime Sloane was known, along with Helen Hay Whitney, as "the first lady of racing." Through her success in horse racing and dog breeding, she has remained one of the most noteworthy sportswomen in America.

• Sloane's personal papers apparently are not extant. John Hervey, *Racing in America, 1922–1936* (1937), details the early impact and influence of Brookmeade Stable on thoroughbred racing. An Aug. 1927 article about Brookmeade Kennels was reprinted as "America's Great Kennels of the Past," *Pure-Bred Dogs American Kennel Gazette*, June 1965. Obituaries are in the *New York Herald Tribune* and the *New York Times*, both 11 Mar. 1962.

SUSAN HAMBURGER

SLOAT, John Drake (26 July 1781–28 Nov. 1867), naval officer, was born at Sloatsburg, Rockland County, New York, the son of John Sloat, a revolutionary war soldier who was killed accidentally by a sentry before John Drake was born, and Ruth Drake, reportedly descended from Sir Francis Drake. John Drake's mother died in his infancy, and he was raised by his maternal grandparents.

In the midst of growing tensions between the United States and France, Sloat was appointed a midshipman on 20 February 1800, serving on the *President* under Commodore Thomas Truxtun. When Thomas Jefferson became president in March 1801, differences with France subsided, the navy was reduced, and Sloat was discharged on 21 May.

Sloat became a merchant seaman, eventually rising to captain. With the proceeds from an inheritance from a grandfather, he bought and commanded his own vessel. On the renewal of hostilities between France and Britain, Sloat, like many other Americans engaged in maritime trade with Europe, suffered economic loss. The United States entered the conflict in 1812, and Sloat returned to naval service as sailing master of the frigate *United States*. He was promised that he would be promoted expeditiously to the appropriate rank as if his service had not been interrupted. Sloat was wounded in the ship's engagement with the *Macedonian* in October 1812. The *United States* was blockaded in New London for the remainder of the war. During the blockade, Sloat was promoted to lieutenant on 24 July 1813, and he married Abby Gordon that year. The couple would have three children.

When the War of 1812 ended in 1815, Sloat secured a furlough and returned to the merchant service. He sailed to France as captain of the *Transit*. He soon returned to the navy and on 4 June 1816 was assigned to the New York Navy Yard, transferring to the Portsmouth Navy Yard in New Hampshire on 9 March 1820. Sea duty followed in 1821, first on the *Washington*, and later that same year he sailed the Pacific coasts of Latin America as first lieutenant on the *Franklin*, Commodore Charles Stewart commanding. On 30 September 1822 Sloat was transferred to the *Congress* under Commodore James Biddle, whose station was South America.

On 12 December 1823 Sloat was named captain of the *Grampus*, his first command. He was ordered to Africa to suppress the slave trade thence to Puerto Rico, where he collaborated with local authorities in combating piracy. He was instrumental in the capture of the notorious Cofrecinas and his crew.

Sloat was promoted on 21 March 1826 to master commandant. Named commander of the *St. Louis* on 15 October 1828, he cruised the Pacific for three years, repeatedly visiting Latin American ports. Sloat was promoted to the rank of captain on 9 February 1839 and was assigned the following year to head the Portsmouth Navy Yard in New Hampshire, where he remained for three years.

Amid deteriorating relations between the United States and Mexico over the Texas question and American designs on the Mexican province of California, Sloat on 27 August 1844 was named commander of the Pacific Squadron, succeeding Commodore Francis Dallas. Now Sloat would carry the title of commodore, signifying command of a squadron. On 2 October 1845, aboard his flagship *Savannah* at Honolulu, Sloat received orders from George Bancroft, secretary of the navy, dated 24 June 1845. The commodore was instructed to maintain friendly relations with Mexicans and avoid any hint of aggression, but in the event of a Mexican declaration of war against the United States, he was to seize the port of San Francisco and occupy or blockade other Mexican ports as his force permitted.

The fleet sailed from Honolulu on 12 October 1845 and arrived at Mazatlán on Mexico's west coast on 18 November. In February Archibald Gillespie, a secret agent of President James K. Polk carrying a dispatch for U.S. consul Thomas O. Larkin in Monterey, arrived in Mazatlán. The dispatch appointed Larkin a confidential agent of the President and instructed him to try to influence Californians to separate from Mexico and apply for a peaceful association with the United States. Gillespie would have notified Sloat of the war preparations he had seen during his trek across Mexico. On 17 May Sloat received an unconfirmed report of hostilities on the Rio Grande. He sent a secret message to Consul Larkin, telling him that he was preparing to sail for California and asking Larkin to be ready to advise him on his arrival.

However, Sloat did not sail and has been faulted for his inaction at this point. His detractors point out that if he had sailed promptly, he would have prevented the turmoil that resulted from the Bear Flag uprising by Americans in California. Sloat knew nothing of that movement, but he was aware of the rash act of his predecessor, Commodore Thomas ap Catesby Jones, who, with orders similar to his own, had seized Monterey in 1842, only to find to his embarrassment that there was no war.

On 7 June Sloat received a reliable report that hostilities had begun north of the Rio Grande and that the U.S. Navy had blockaded the Gulf Coast of Mexico. The Pacific Fleet set sail and arrived in Monterey on 1 July 1846. Sloat conferred with Larkin, and together they drafted a proclamation. On 7 July a force was landed, the American flag was raised, and the proclamation was read. Sloat came not as the enemy of the Californians, said the proclamation, but as "their best friend." Californians were invited to American citizenship, they would be treated fairly, and their property was secure. Unfortunately, Sloat's benevolent policy would be reversed by his successor.

With the Stars and Stripes flying throughout California, Sloat, in ill health, turned over his command to Commodore Robert F. Stockton on 23 July and on 29 July departed in the *Levant* for the East via Panama. Reaching Washington in November, he was lauded by Secretary Bancroft for operations in California.

Sloat commanded the Norfolk Navy Yard from 19 January 1848 to 1 February 1851. Following his appointment on 17 January 1852 as senior member of a board to locate a navy yard in California, Sloat returned to California. Mare Island was designated on his recommendation, and he took part in planning for the new yard. Placed on the retired list on 27 September 1855, Sloat advised the Navy Department during the Civil War. He was promoted to commodore when the official rank was created in 1862 and to rear admiral on 6 August 1866. He died at his home at Staten Island and is buried in Greenwood Cemetery, Brooklyn.

Sloat is best remembered for his role in the American conquest of California. While he was early faulted for indecisiveness and vacillation, it soon became evident that his benign policy toward the Californians was right for the times. Sloat described himself with some justification as a friend of California, a liberator who would protect Californians from the oppression of Mexico. Commodore Stockton, his successor, would be conqueror, and his ill-conceived harsh policies antagonized Mexican Californians, eventually pushing them to rebellion.

• A scholarly biography of Sloat has yet to be published. Edwin A. Sherman, *The Life of the Late Rear Admiral John Drake Sloat* (1902), and Peter T. Conmy, "John Drake Sloat, Commodore United States Navy, Apostle of the American Occupation of California" (1941), an unpublished document at the Bancroft Library, University of California, Berkeley, are uncritical biographical sketches. The latter appears the more reliable. A brief volume published on the fifty-year anniversary of the conquest commemorates Sloat's part: James Layton et al., *History of the Celebration of the Fiftieth Anniversary of the Taking Possession of California & Raising of the American Flag at Monterey, California, by Commodore John Drake Sloat, USN, July 7, 1846* (1896). Sloat's role in California is best covered in Neal Harlow, *California Conquered: War and Peace on the Pacific, 1846–1850* (1982). Obituaries are in *New York Tribune*, 29 Nov. 1867, and the *Army and Navy Journal*, 7 Mar. 1868. Sloat was senior honorary member of the Society of California Pioneers; a resolution commenting on his place in the society and in California affairs, adopted by the society on 3 Feb. 1868, is in the Society of California Pioneers archives.

HARLAN HAGUE

SLOCUM, Frances (4 Mar. 1773–9 Mar. 1847), Indian captive, was born in Warwick, Rhode Island, the daughter of Jonathan Slocum and Ruth Tripp, farmers. Her Quaker parents moved a year after her birth to present-day Scranton, Pennsylvania, and then later to Wilkes-Barre. Slocum was captured shortly after the July 1778 Wyoming Massacre in the Wyoming Valley of Pennsylvania, in which Indians and British loyalists attacked and killed American settlers. Slocum was snatched in retaliation—it is said—for a brother (even though a Quaker) serving in the battle against the Indians. In her captivity she met a goodly number of similar people who had been snatched.

Tearful when first seized, Slocum received gentle treatment that won her over to the Native-American way of life. Tuck-Horse, a Delaware leader, took her under his special protection. Either he personally adopted her, or more probably he convinced an older, childless couple to raise her. Slocum received the name Weletawash, the name of a recently buried child of the adoptive parents. Since the older couple knew some English and seemed to have rather successfully interacted with whites before, it is not surprising that Slocum accepted their authority and moved back and forth with them through the Niagara, Northern Ohio, Detroit, and northern Wabash River areas. Although she spoke some English with her new father, she soon forgot her first name.

In the years after Frances Slocum's capture, Ruth Slocum urged her sons to find her missing daughter. In 1789, at age fifty-nine, Ruth Slocum took a difficult and dangerous frontier trip to Athens, Pennsylvania, where a number of Indian captives had been brought, but Frances was not among them. Various brothers spent several summers between 1784 and 1826 riding from Indian village to Indian village seeking information on Frances's whereabouts, but they did not find her.

While her family searched for her, Slocum was assimilated into the Indian tribe that had captured her, and eventually she married an Indian. Her first marriage turned out badly, however, and she left her husband and returned to her Indian father and mother. Sometime later, her adoptive family found a wounded war leader, Shepoconah, of the Miamis, on a small battlefield. While nursing Shepoconah back to health, Frances fell in love with him. They married and went to live among his people, first near Fort Wayne and then at Osage Village at the mouth of the Mississinewa River. Eventually they had four children. Slocum's strength, pluck, and ability to ride any horse soon earned her the new name Maconaquah (young female bear). When Shepoconah became deaf, he gave up his leadership and retired with Slocum to an area five miles distant.

Late in her life, Slocum's existence was discovered by her American family only through an unlikely sequence of events. Her fear that Americans would force her from her Indian family had caused her to keep her history to herself. However, finding herself quite ill and expecting to die shortly, Slocum decided at last to tell her story to George Ewing, a wealthy trader. Although she asked him not to tell her story to anyone until after her death, he sent a letter dated 20 January 1835 to Lancaster, Pennsylvania, asking for help in finding relatives. After two years an editor of a local newspaper published it. In August 1837 two brothers and a sister learned of her existence and immediately traveled to Peru, Indiana, where their sister was living.

When they discovered that Maconaquah had one finger cut off at the first joint, the result of a childhood mishap, the Slocums knew their search was over. Frances, however, initially greeted them with reserve. Taken aback, the Slocums thought, "Great God! Is this unfeeling, indifferent, old woman, a veritable Indian, my sister?" (Stephens, p. 47). Gradually, though, Frances was reassured by their sincerity and became friendly. When her brother Joseph came a second time accompanied by his two daughters, Frances grew quite warm. With the appearance shortly before her death of a nephew and his wife with their young daughter, who bore a strong resemblance to Frances, the Slocums and Frances's Indian family were emotionally united.

Shepoconah, because of his important status as a tribe leader, had received generous allotments of land from the U.S. government, and when the Slocum family later found Frances they were impressed with her wealth. Around 1833 Shepoconah died, but, like many of the Miami elite, Frances was still able to acquire a section of land in the 1838 treaty that required most Miamis to retire west of the Mississippi. After the treaty of 1840, however, she was forced to turn to her American relatives to get a congressional petition that allowed her to continue to receive annuity payments without moving west.

As soon as the Slocums found Frances, to her consternation they immediately began to record her stories. The younger Slocum women made extensive diary notations when they visited her. Numerous newspapers printed letters describing Frances and her history. While she was still alive, John Todd told her story with a Eurocentric emphasis that was typical of the times; his book was titled *The Lost Sister of Wyoming* (1842). The unique personal experience of the "White Rose of the Miami" immediately intrigued Americans.

Frances Slocum died in the house she had shared with her husband near Peru, Indiana. After her death her pious nephew saw that she was given a Christian burial, but Slocum told her daughter to place a pole with a white flag on her grave so that the Great Spirit would find her. The old white woman of the Miamis was surely not Frances Slocum, but Maconaquah.

In 1900 a monument was erected in Slocum's honor, and some 3,000 people attended the unveiling. The inscription read, "She became a stranger to her brethren, and an alien to her mother's children, through her captivity." A Pennsylvania paper stated that the stealing of the child and the search for her, which lasted for half a century, form the most interesting romance and, next to the Wyoming Massacre, the historic event of the Wyoming Valley. More perceptively, local Indiana historian J. H. Stephens stressed in 1896 "the tenacity with which she clung to her adopted people." Her life exemplifies the perceptions of colonial thinkers who noted that many whites became Indians, but no Indians accepted white culture.

• Family tradition as reported by a son-in-law and a grandson, along with apt quotations from primary sources, enlivens the long account found in John H. Stephens, *History of Miami County* (1896). In some ways, the most perceptive analysis of the primary documents is found in Charles E. Slocum, *History of Francis Slocum* (1908), a short book written by a family member and historian. Otho Winger, *The Lost Sister among the Miamis* (1936), is a long account by a historian well versed in Miami history. The rich history of Native Americans in the Mississinewa River area receives full treatment in Winger, *The Frances Slocum Trail* (1933). Her personal history and the larger Miami history are both described in Jacob Piatt Dunn, *True Indian Stories* (1909). Much traditional Miami and Maconaquah family lore is given in Clarence Godfroy, *Miami Indian Stories* (1961).

LEROY V. EID

SLOCUM, Henry Warner (24 Sept. 1826–14 Apr. 1894), soldier and lawyer, was born in the village of Delphi, Onondaga County, New York, the son of Matthew B. Slocum, a businessman, and Mary Ostrander. Slocum received his early education at Cazenovia Seminary and at the State Normal School in Albany. He entered the U.S. Military Academy in 1848, where he roomed with Philip Sheridan. In 1852 Slocum graduated seventh in his class of forty-three and was commissioned a second lieutenant in the First Artillery. He was assigned to duty with his regiment in Florida, where it was active in maintaining the peace with the Seminole Indians. He was subsequently posted to garrison duty in 1853 at Fort Moultrie, South Carolina. While stationed at the fort, Slocum received a furlough to return to New York and wed Clara Rice in 1854. They had four children. He occupied his idle time in garrison duty by reading law under B. C. Presley, who later was elected to the supreme court of South Carolina. Slocum tired of garrison duty and resigned on 31 October 1856 to return to Onondaga County, where he opened a law practice in Syracuse. He was appointed county treasurer soon after and in 1859 was elected to the state legislature.

When the Civil War broke out, Slocum immediately offered his services to New York state and was appointed colonel of the Twenty-seventh New York Infantry. At the battle of Bull Run (Manassas), he was severely wounded in the left thigh and was disabled for two months. On 9 August 1861 he was promoted to brigadier general of volunteers and placed in command of a brigade in William B. Franklin's division of the Army of the Potomac. When Franklin was promoted to command of the Sixth Corps early in the 1862 Virginia peninsula campaign, Slocum was advanced to division command. He was an exacting disciplinarian and an efficient administrator. Fitz-John Porter deemed Slocum's division during the Virginia peninsula campaign to be "one of the best divisions in the army." At Gaines' Mill, Slocum's prompt march to cross the Chickahominy and reinforce Porter's soldiers helped avert disaster for the Union forces. On 4 July 1862 Slocum received promotion to major general of volunteers. Following the withdrawal from the peninsula, Slocum's division helped cover the Union retreat after the defeat at Second Manassas. His division then accompanied the army into Maryland. At the battle of South Mountain, Slocum's command stormed Crampton's Pass in what Franklin called "the completest victory gained up to that time by any part of the Army of the Potomac." Several days later, Slocum participated in the battle of Antietam. His conspicuous performance in the campaigns of 1861 and 1862 was recognized by promotion to command of the Twelfth Army Corps in October 1862. The corps participated in the Fredericksburg campaign but did not actually fight in the battle. At Chancellorsville, Slocum temporarily commanded the Fifth, Eleventh, and Twelfth corps. Following Thomas "Stonewall" Jackson's successful flank attack, Slocum was instrumental in organizing a defense that checked the Confederate onslaught. On the first day of the battle of Gettysburg, Slocum was unusually dilatory in marching to the battlefield, even though his corps was within six miles of the field by noon. On the second and third day of the battle, he was placed in command of the right wing of the army on Culp's Hill, including his own Twelfth Corps and elements of the First, Sixth, and Eleventh corps. During George G. Meade's council on the night of 2 July, when asked whether the army should stay and hold its position or retire, Slocum uttered the famous terse response, "Stay and fight it out."

In September 1863 Slocum and his Twelfth Corps were ordered west to the relief of the Army of the Cumberland at Chattanooga. Slocum's corps and the Eleventh Corps were placed under the command of General Joseph Hooker. Slocum had no respect for Hooker as an officer after his dismal performance at Chancellorsville or as a gentleman, and he tendered his resignation to President Abraham Lincoln. His resignation was not accepted, but Slocum was relieved and posted to duty guarding the Nashville and Chattanooga Railroad. In April 1864 he was assigned to command the District of Vicksburg, which was rife with corruption. Slocum performed his duty in this position so effectively that, when an effort was made to transfer him to an active field command in Georgia, General Ulysses S. Grant prevented it.

On 30 July 1863 Slocum was assigned to command of the Twentieth Corps, which included the divisions of his old Twelfth Corps. He joined his command on 26 August in front of Atlanta, and on 2 September his troops were the first to enter the city. Slocum occupied Atlanta for ten weeks. He carried out William T. Sherman's harsh orders in regard to the city and its civilian population, but he took no enjoyment from the South's suffering. He wrote to his wife, "I wish for humanity's sake that this sad war could be brought to a close. While laboring to make it successful, I shall do all in my power to mitigate its horrors."

On the march through Georgia to the sea and north through the Carolinas, Slocum assumed command of the left wing of Sherman's army. At the battle of Bentonville, 19 March 1865, Slocum's army bore nearly the entire burden of the battle. A member of Sherman's staff wrote afterward that the Confederate attack at Bentonville was unexpected, "but Slocum was more than equal to the necessities of the hour, and his success justified General Sherman's selection of him as the commander of the Left Wing of the army."

Following the end of the war, Slocum was assigned to command the important Department of Mississippi, with headquarters at Vicksburg. One of his most significant actions in this command was to disband the Mississippi state militia, which was being used to prevent blacks from exercising their new rights as citizens. On 28 September 1865 Slocum resigned from the army to return to Syracuse. He ran as a Democrat for secretary of state for New York but was defeated by Francis C. Barlow. In 1866 he and his wife moved to Brooklyn, where he opened a law practice. Slocum was nominated to run for Congress and as a presidential elector in 1868. Elected to both offices, in 1870 he won reelection to Congress. He took particular interest in affairs concerning the military and veterans. In 1876 he was selected to be commissioner of public works in Brooklyn. He resigned before his term expired and traveled to Europe with his family in 1880. In 1882 he was elected again to Congress and served until March 1885. During the postwar years, Slocum remained active in veterans' affairs, and he served on the New York Monuments Commission for the Battlefield of Gettysburg until his death in New York City.

Slocum was an accomplished soldier and administrator and a selfless patriot to his country and state. A former member of his wartime staff wrote of him after his death: "In all the sterling qualities that go to make up a man, I have seldom met the equal or superior of Major-General Henry W. Slocum. Firm and resolute of purpose, yet with so much modesty, so little of self-assertion; so faithful in the performance of whatever he believed to be his duty; so independent in his speech and conduct, whatever might be the future result."

• Slocum's unpublished correspondence concerning his performance and that of his corps at Gettysburg is in the Samuel P. Bates Collection, Pennsylvania Historical and Museum Commission, and the John B. Bachelder Papers, New Hampshire Historical Society. Slocum's brief recollections are published in the *Syracuse Courier*, 2 Apr. 1879. Charles E. Slocum, *The Life and Services of Major General Henry Warner Slocum* (1913), is an uncritical but nevertheless informative biography of the general. Also see New York Monuments Commission, *In Memoriam: Henry Warner Slocum 1826–1894* (1904), which includes a biography of Slocum, a history of the corps that served under his command, and the reports and dedication ceremonies associated with his equestrian monument at Gettysburg. Slocum's military record can be found in G. W. Cullum, *Biographical Register of the Officers and Graduates of the United States Military Academy* (1891). For his military operations in the Civil War and select correspondence see U.S. War Department, *The War of the Rebellion: A Compilation of the Official Records of the Union and Confederate Armies* (128 vols., 1880–1901); Milo Quaife, *From the Cannon's Mouth: The Civil War Letters of General Alpheus S. Williams* (1959); and William T. Sherman, *Memoirs of General William T. Sherman*, vol. 2 (1875). For Slocum's family history, refer to Charles E. Slocum, *History of* the Slocums, Slocumbs, and Slocombs of America, vol. 1 (1882) and vol. 2 (1908). An obituary is in the Brooklyn Daily Eagle, 16 Apr. 1894.

D. SCOTT HARTWIG

SLOCUM, Joshua (20 Feb. 1844–Nov. 1909?), circumnavigator, shipbuilder, and author, was born in Wilmot Township, Nova Scotia, Canada, the son of John Slocombe, a farmer and bootmaker, and Sarah Jane Southern. Slocum attended school only until age ten, when he was set to work to earn his keep. He left home permanently after the death of his mother when he was sixteen, working as a deep-water sailor. From that time on his life, for better and for worse, was defined by the sea.

His first command (in 1869, the same year he became a U.S. citizen) was of a coastwise schooner between Seattle and San Francisco, after which he commanded the bark *Washington*, sailing to Sydney, Australia, in 1870. In Sydney in 1871 he married Virginia Albertina Walker, an American. The well-matched couple spent most of the next thirteen years together at sea, accompanied, ultimately, by their four children, until Virginia died in 1884.

During those years Slocum captained several large ships, carrying various cargos mostly to Pacific ports. His last command was the bark *Aquidneck*, which he also owned. Not only a sailor and navigator, Slocum built the hull of an eighty-ton steamer in Subic Bay, the Philippines. Though he was paid for the job with a small schooner, the money he was promised never materialized—the first of several financial disappointments.

In 1886, in Boston, Slocum married his cousin Henrietta "Hettie" Miller Elliott. Their wedding trip on the *Aquidneck* (with two of his children along) included a mutiny, in which the captain shot two men, killing one, and it ended in disaster when the uninsured ship stranded in Brazil and was a total loss. Saving what he could from the wreck, Slocum built by hand a 35-foot "canoe," rigged it with sails sewed by Hettie, named it *Liberdade* because of its being launched on the day Brazil's slaves were freed, and sailed it 5,500 miles to Washington, D.C. That was the end of Hettie's seafaring.

It was also the end of Joshua Slocum's career as a merchant captain. He was a wind sailor, and the age of sail was almost over—too few sailing ships, too many captains. Slocum, who despite his lack of formal education had read widely, turned to authorship, publishing *The Voyage of the Liberdade* in 1890 but not realizing a profit. Odd jobs took up the next few years.

In 1892 an acquaintance gave him the decrepit hulk of a 37-foot oyster sloop named *Spray*. Slocum, who had said that "next in attractiveness, after seafaring, came ship-building," rebuilt it himself. When he launched it, he thought it "sat on the water like a swan." Once more he had a vessel—but not an occupation. In 1893 he was commissioned to deliver the iron gunboat *Destroyer*, built by John Ericsson (designer of the Civil War *Monitor*), to naval authorities in Brazil.

He brought the vessel into Bahia, turning it over to Brazilians who, for uncertain reasons, soon sank it. Once again, Slocum received no money for the job. Hoping to benefit somehow from the misadventure, he published *Voyage of the Destroyer from New York to Brazil* in 1894. It was well reviewed in Boston but earned him nothing.

Ultimately Slocum decided on what he thought would be a gratifying and remunerative endeavor: to take the *Spray* around the world, alone. On 24 April 1895 he left Boston on his solo voyage, reportedly with only $1.50 in his pocket. Other less-than-ideal conditions included the absence of a chronometer (for calculations of longitude)—considered essential in his day. Altering his intended track according to local conditions (such as the threat of piracy in the Mediterranean), Captain Slocum sailed across the Atlantic to Gibraltar and then recrossed it, entering the Pacific through the Strait of Magellan. He traversed the South Pacific to Australia, sailed through the Coral Sea and the Indian Ocean, rounded the Cape of Good Hope, and crossing the Atlantic for the third time, returned to the United States after 46,000 miles under wind power on 27 June 1898, having accomplished the world's first single-handed circumnavigation. *Sailing Alone around the World* (serialized in 1899–1900 and then published as a book in 1900) is the justly admired record of his seamanship, character, and navigational skill, a classic of nautical literature.

Readers remember Slocum's delirium off the Azores, in which he saw the pilot of Columbus's *Pinta* steering the *Spray*; they recall his protecting himself from Fuegians by sprinkling the deck with carpet tacks and writing, "Now, it is well known that one cannot step on a tack without saying something about it." Such dry wit is a prominent feature of his writing, as in his encounter with an American warship at sea after the Spanish-American War had broken out. The *Spray* signaled, "Let us keep together for mutual protection." And in the minds of most readers must linger the captain's repeated expressions of love and admiration for his vessel: "There the *Spray* rode, now like a bird on the crest of a wave, and now like a waif deep down in the hollow between seas; and so she drove on."

With proceeds from the book and from lecturing about his experiences, Slocum bought a house on Martha's Vineyard in 1902. It was no doubt what Hettie wanted, but Joshua was not happy. Clearly ill at ease, he began making solitary trips in the *Spray* to spend winters in the Caribbean. Returning from the first of these, he stopped to lecture at Riverton, New Jersey, where he was arrested on a charge of raping a twelve-year-old girl. Though rape was medically disproved and the charge was ultimately reduced to one of indecency, Slocum, insisting he had no memory of the incident, did spend more than a month in jail. Not long after his release after a plea of no contest, he was delivering a rare orchid from the Caribbean to a cordial President Theodore Roosevelt.

Finally, at age sixty-five, the captain conceived another extraordinary plan: he would sail the *Spray* to South America, up the Orinoco and Rio Negro to the still unknown source of the Amazon, down the Amazon to the sea and to New England again. The *Spray*, according to some observers, was in bad repair and the captain negligent. Whether those were contributing factors or not, the weather was stormy when he left, and Captain Slocum and his boat were never seen again. He was finally declared by a court to have officially died the day he set sail, 14 November 1909.

• Letters and consular dispatches related to the *Aquidneck* events are in the National Archives; other letters are in various hands, including the Smithsonian Institution. Walter Teller, *The Voyages of Joshua Slocum* (1956), collects Slocum's writings and provides a detailed introduction to each, along with other information. The best biography of Slocum is Teller's *Joshua Slocum* (1971), which is the last of his several books on or including the captain. Slocum's son Victor wrote *Capt. Joshua Slocum: The Life and Voyages of America's Best Known Sailor* (1950). The literary connection between Slocum and Henry David Thoreau is the subject of Dennis Berthold, "Deeper Soundings: The Presence of *Walden* in Joshua Slocum's *Sailing Alone around the World*," in *Literature and Lore of the Sea*, ed. Patricia Ann Carlson (1986). Another treatment from a literary perspective is Bert Bender, "Joshua Slocum and the Reality of Solitude," *American Transcendental Quarterly* 6 (1992): 59–71.

HASKELL SPRINGER

SLONIMSKY, Nicolas (27 Apr. 1894–25 Dec. 1995), musicologist, conductor, and composer, was born Nikolai Leonidovich Slonimsky (the name is also given as Slonimski) in St. Petersburg, Russia, the son of Leonid Slonimsky, a prominent Russian scholar and writer, and Faina Vengerova. His paternal grandfather was the highly respected Hebrew scholar and scientist, Haim Selig Slonimsky. Determined to excel in all endeavors, and especially music, he received his first piano lessons at age six from his mother's sister, the renowned pianist Isabelle Vengerova. He later enrolled in the St. Petersburg Conservatory, where from 1913 to 1918 he studied harmony and orchestration with Vasili Kalafati and Maximilian Steinberg, both of whom had studied under Nikolai Rimsky-Korsakov. Leaving St. Petersburg following the outbreak of the Revolution, he first went to Kiev, where he worked as a rehearsal pianist at the Kiev Opera and, in 1919, took composition lessons with Reinhold Glière; then, for a brief period in 1920, he was in Yalta, working as a piano accompanist instructor at the Yalta Conservatory. He then toured Europe, eventually settling in Paris, where he served as secretary and rehearsal pianist to Serge Koussevitzky. In 1923 he immigrated to the United States, becoming a coach in the opera department of the Eastman School of Music in Rochester, New York, where he also studied composition with Salim Palmgren and conducting with Albert Coates. In 1925 he rejoined Koussevitzky, who was

then conductor of the Boston Symphony Orchestra, but Koussevitzky found him resistant to authority and fired him two years later.

After leaving Koussevitzky, Slonimsky taught theory at the Malkin and Boston conservatories; he also served as conductor of the Pierian Sodality at Harvard University (1929–1932) as well as the Apollo Chorus (1928–1930). Desiring to present modern musical compositions, in 1927 he organized the Chamber Orchestra of Boston and over the next seven years introduced audiences to the works of Charles Ives, Edgar Varèse, and Henry Cowell, among others. From 1927 to 1941 Slonimsky published articles about music in the *Boston Evening Transcript*; he also wrote articles for the *Christian Science Monitor*, and in the 1950s he compiled a column of musical anecdotes for the monthly music magazine *Étude*. He became a naturalized citizen in 1931 and that same year married Dorothy Adlow, an art critic for the *Christian Science Monitor*; they would have one child, a daughter named Electra.

After returning from a lengthy European tour sponsored by the Pan-American Association of Composers in 1932, Slonimsky conducted concerts of modern American, Cuban, and Mexican music with the Los Angeles Philharmonic (1932) and at the Hollywood Bowl (1933). However, whereas these performances received a positive reception when they were presented in Paris, Berlin, and Budapest, they so disturbed the American audiences that Slonimsky's conducting contract was not renewed. In 1962–1963, under the auspices of the U.S. State Department's Office of Cultural Exchange, he went on an extensive lecture tour, traveling to Russia, Poland, Yugoslavia, Bulgaria, Romania, Greece, and Israel. After his return he taught variegated music subjects at the University of California, Los Angeles, from 1964 to 1967. He received a Guggenheim Fellowship in 1987 and in 1991 was inducted as an honorary member of the American Academy and Institute of Arts and Letters.

Slonimsky's musical style was best suited to miniature forms, such as *Studies in Black and White*, a study in counterpoint for piano (1928; orchestrated as *Piccolo Divertimento*, in Los Angeles on 17 Oct. 1983); *Gravestones*, a song cycle for voice and piano using actual tombstone inscriptions as its text (1945); and *Minitudes*, a collection of fifty quirky, mathematically inspired piano pieces (1971–1977). In addition to *My Toy Balloon* (1942), an orchestral work based on a Brazilian song that incorporates, as a part of its instrumentation, 100 colored balloons to be exploded at the climax, Slonimsky composed the whimsical *Möbius Strip-Tease*, a perpetual vocal canon (similar to a round) notated on a Möbius band (a strip of paper or other material joined at both ends) to be revolved around the singer's head. He also wrote the earliest-known commercial jingles using for text actual advertisements from the *Saturday Evening Post*; these include *Make This a Day of Pepsodent*, *No More Shiny Nose*, and *Children Cry for Castoria* (all 1925), which because of protests from the product sponsors, remained unpublished for more than sixty years. Just as iconoclastic, however scholarly, was his *Thesaurus of Scales and Melodic Patterns* (1947), an inventory of all conceivable tonal combinations, including the incredible "Grandmother Chord," which comprises twelve different tones and eleven different intervals.

Slonimsky found his most prominent niche as a musicologist specializing in musical lexicography. He published *Music since 1900*, a valuable chronology of musical events (1937; 5th ed., rev., 1994), and participated in the production of two standard reference works, the *International Cyclopedia of Music and Musicians* (4th–8th eds., 1946–1958) and *Baker's Biographical Dictionary of Musicians* (5th–8th eds., 1958–1992), as well as *The Concise Baker's Biographical Dictionary of Musicians* (1988). He also translated Boris de Schloezer's biography of Russian composer Alexander Scriabin from the original Russian (1987) and produced a lively compendium of articles titled *Lectionary of Music* (1988). In addition, he compiled the now-classic *Lexicon of Musical Invective*, a random assortment of historical reviews, most of them negative, of musical works composed since Beethoven's time that are now thought of as masterpieces (1953). Also notable was his "Sex and the Music Librarian," a humorous paper that elicited great outbursts of laughter when it was delivered, by proxy, at a symposium of the Music Library Association held in February 1968. Slonimsky's death in Los Angeles—four months shy of his 102d birthday—brought to a close one of the most varied careers in twentieth-century musical history.

• Collections of Slonimsky's papers and personal materials are at the Library of Congress. Slonimsky's other writings include *Music of Latin America* (1945; Spanish ed., 1947); *The Road to Music*, a collection of his articles in the *Christian Science Monitor* (1947); and *A Thing or Two about Music*, a collection of historical anecdotes (1948). For a collection of his writings see *Nicolas Slonimsky: The First Hundred Years*, ed. R. Kostelanetz (1994). Slonimsky's autobiography, which he began in 1978 with a working title of *Failed Wunderkind* (subtitled: *Rueful Autopsy*), was published in 1988 as *Perfect Pitch*. Slonimsky's life was the subject of a two-part profile by L. Weschler in the *New Yorker*, 17 and 24 Nov. 1986. Obituaries are in the *New York Times* and the *Los Angeles Times*, both 27 Dec. 1995.

LAURA KUHN

SLOSSON, Edwin Emery (7 June 1865–15 Oct. 1929), chemist and journalist, was born in the frontier town of Albany (now Sabetha), Kansas, the son of William Butler Slosson, a merchant, and Achsa Louise Lilly, a former schoolteacher. Slosson earned a B.S. in 1890 and an M.S. in 1892 at the University of Kansas, where the breadth of his interests prompted the faculty to elect him to both Sigma Xi and Phi Beta Kappa. In 1891 he married May Gorsline Preston, the first woman to obtain a Ph.D. from Cornell University (1880). They had two children, one of whom, Preston W. Slosson, became a well-known historian at the University of Michigan.

Slosson accepted a position in 1891 at the newly founded University of Wyoming, where for the next twelve years he taught all the chemistry courses and introduced the study of experimental psychology. During the same period he also served as chemist of the Wyoming Agricultural Experiment Station, and his studies of Wyoming coal, petroleum, soils, and food products were published in its bulletin. Slosson is said to be the first to use the bomb calorimeter to determine the fuel value of packaged cereals. During summers he studied organic chemistry with Julius Stieglitz and John Nef at the University of Chicago, receiving his doctorate in 1902. Appointed state chemist in 1903, he helped secure passage of Wyoming's pure food law.

Slosson also enjoyed success as a writer, publishing occasional essays on both scientific and nonscientific topics in the *Independent*, a respected New York magazine affiliated with his church, the Congregationalists. A summer job with the *Independent* in 1903 led to the offer of a full-time position as its literary editor. Dropping a huge research project on the chemistry of odors, he moved his family to New York City in 1904 to embark on a new career as a journalist. Slosson helped transform the *Independent* from a small-circulation denominational weekly to a secular weekly with over 100,000 readers. He wrote from three to six thousand words a week on foreign affairs, literature, education, and science and was one of the first to write serious reviews of motion pictures. His frank, fearless style earned him a reputation as the "Wild West editor." His first major literary success was a series of articles on "Great American Universities," which was published as a book in 1910. This was followed by a series of interviews with twelve leading intellectuals, which was published as *Major Prophets of Today* (1914) and *Six Major Prophets* (1917). From 1912 to 1920 he taught courses on physical science for journalists at the Pulitzer School of Journalism at Columbia University.

During World War I—popularly known as the "Chemists' War"—Slosson authored a series of articles that explained in lay terms how synthetic organic chemistry was revolutionizing industry, agriculture, medicine, and warfare. The resulting volume, *Creative Chemistry* (1919), became a classic in the popularization of science. With the help of the Chemical Foundation, an organization established by the Wilson administration in 1919 to promote the growth of domestic chemical manufacturing, Slosson's book became a bestseller. The Foundation chose *Creative Chemistry* as the centerpiece of its campaign to win public support for the fledgling American organic chemical industry, and by 1937 it had distributed 143,000 copies free or at cost to members of Congress, businessmen, editors, schools, and other groups.

Creative Chemistry and a brief volume called *Easy Lessons in Einstein* (1920) won national fame for Slosson and made him the natural choice to lead Science Service, a nonprofit institution for the popularization of science, which was founded by newspaper magnate E. W. Scripps in 1920. As director of Science Service in Washington, D.C., from 1921 until his death, Slosson became the nation's preeminent science popularizer. He was in constant demand as a public lecturer, and he wrote hundreds of the articles that Science Service sold to newspapers and published in its magazine, *Science News-Letter* (later *Science News*). His essays were collected and published in *Chats on Science* (1924), *Keeping Up with Science* (1924), *Sermons of a Chemist* (1925), and *Short Talks on Science* (1930), but none of these books equaled the impact of *Creative Chemistry*. Rather, his most important contribution during this period was raising the standards of science reporting in the daily press and training writers for the emerging profession of science journalism.

Although something of a modern "Renaissance man" (at his death, Rollins College in Florida was planning to name him "Professor of Things in General"), Slosson firmly believed in the superiority of science to literary and other forms of knowledge. His tireless crusade to spread science to the masses was motivated in part by his belief that World War I had unleashed a rising tide of irrationalism and superstition. A passionate defender of the common man, he nevertheless feared racial as well as cultural degeneration and became a supporter of eugenic ideas. The pessimism of his later years led one writer to call him "the gloomy dean of America." He died in Washington, D.C.

• There is no one collection of Slosson's papers, but useful material may be found in the following locations: Biographical Files, University of Wyoming Library; William E. Ritter Papers, Bancroft Library, University of California–Berkeley; Science Service Records, Smithsonian Institution Archives; and the corporate records of Science Service, Washington, D.C. The most complete biography is Preston W. Slosson, "Edwin E. Slosson, Pioneer," in Edwin E. Slosson, *A Number of Things*, (1930). See also David J. Rhees, "A New Voice for Science: Science Service under Edwin E. Slosson, 1921–1929" (M.A. thesis, Univ. of North Carolina, 1979), and Ronald C. Tobey, *The American Ideology of National Science, 1919–1930* (1971). Obituaries are in the *New York Times*, 21 Oct. 1929; *Book League Monthly*, Dec. 1929; *Journal of Chemical Education*, Dec. 1929; *Journal of the Washington Academy of Sciences*, 4 Nov. 1929; and the *Washington Post*, 16 and 17 Oct. 1929.

DAVID J. RHEES

SLOWE, Lucy Diggs (4 July 1885–21 Oct. 1937), educator and club organizer, was born in Berryville, Virginia, the daughter of Henry Slowe and Fannie Porter. Orphaned by the age of six, Slowe was raised by her aunt, Martha Slowe Price in Lexington, Virginia, until the family moved to Baltimore, Maryland, when Slowe was thirteen. In 1904 she finished second in her class at the Colored High School in Baltimore, and she entered Howard University in Washington, D.C., that same year. While enrolled at Howard, Slowe did well in her studies and became involved in many extracurricular activities, including the founding of Alpha Kappa Alpha, the first sorority for African-American women in the nation.

After receiving her B.A. from Howard University in 1908, Slowe became an English teacher at Baltimore Colored High School. She completed an M.A. in English at Columbia University in 1915 and then taught in a Washington, D.C., high school. In 1919 the first junior high school for African Americans was established in Washington, D.C., and Slowe was appointed principal.

Slowe's administrative leadership and her success as an educator resulted in her being appointed in 1922 as the dean of women at Howard University, a position she held until her death. She was the first African-American woman to serve as a dean at Howard. She also served as associate professor of English while dean at Howard. Influenced by noted women student personnel scholars such as Esther Lloyd-Jones at Teachers College at Columbia University and Thyrsa Amos of the University of Pittsburgh, Slowe pioneered this field on the historically black college campuses. While at Howard Slowe worked to ensure that the position of dean of women there and at other black colleges would be as respected as administrative jobs filled by men. She pushed to increase this position to one that was concerned with women's education as a whole. Slowe was selected in her senior year at Howard to be a chaperone for other female students on downtown shopping trips. While most black colleges expected deans of women to continue such appointments, Slowe frequently spoke out against such expectations. She stated, "when a college woman cannot be trusted to go shopping without a chaperone, she is not likely to develop powers of leadership."

Slowe's continued advocacy for leadership development of African-American women college students also included becoming the first president of the National Association of College Women (NACW) in 1923. The NACW was an organization of African-American women college graduates of accredited liberal arts colleges and universities. The organization was in part based on the white American Association of University Women. However, under Slowe's leadership, the NACW focused its activities on raising the standards of colleges where African-American women were present, improving the conditions of black women faculty, and encouraging advanced scholarship among African-American women. Slowe also hoped to make the organization a "center of guidance, encouragement and information" to African-American high school women.

In furthering the cause of the NACW, Slowe researched the status of women on black college campuses. Her findings, which were published in 1933 in the *Journal of Negro Education*, showed that African-American women were not trained to be leaders in their course work, campus activities, or interaction with faculty. A primary goal of the NACW was to encourage the hiring of well-trained deans of women at black colleges. By 1929 the number of women deans and advisers to women on black campuses had grown. Slowe then established, as a part of the NACW, the National Association of Deans of Women and Advisors to Girls in Negro Schools. In 1935, as the number of Deans of Women's positions increased further, the group retained its original name and became an independent organization.

Slowe was active in a range of organizations in addition to the NACW and the National Association of Deans of Women and Advisors to Girls in Negro Schools. In 1935, with Mary McLeod Bethune, Slowe helped begin the National Council of Negro Women, an umbrella group of national African-American women's clubs. Slowe also served as the group's first executive secretary. Slowe was actively involved with the National YWCA and the Women's International League for Peace and Freedom. In addition, she served on the advisory board of the National Youth Administration and was a member of the predominantly white National Association of Deans of Women.

Outside of her professional activities, Slowe was a prize-winning tennis player. During a time when few African Americans competed against whites, she won seventeen tennis cups. Slowe also sang in the choirs at the St. Francis Catholic Church and at the Madison Street Presbyterian Church in Baltimore, where she was a member. From 1922 until her death, at her home in Washington, D.C., Slowe had as her companion and housemate Mary Burrill, who was well known in the city as a teacher and playwright.

Throughout her career, Slowe encouraged African-American women students to prepare themselves not only for leadership within the African-American communities but throughout the world. As one of the earliest black female administrators in higher education, she was an untiring advocate for the presence of African-American women in similar positions. She was active on this behalf in both African-American and interracial organizations.

• The Lucy Diggs Slowe Papers are housed at the Moorland-Spingarn Collection at Howard University, Washington, D.C. Information concerning the National Association of College Women and the National Association of Deans of Women and Advisors to Girls in Negro Schools as well as photographs of Slowe are found in the Slowe papers. An excellent account of Slowe's career is given in an article by Karen Anderson, "Brickbats and Roses: Lucy Diggs Slowe, 1883–1937," in *Lone Voyagers: Academic Women in Coeducational Institutions, 1870–1937,* ed. Geraldine Jonçich Clifford (1989).

LINDA M. PERKINS

SMALL, Albion Woodbury (11 May 1854–24 Mar. 1926), sociologist, was born in Buckfield, Maine, the son of Rev. Albion Keith Parris Small, a Baptist minister, and Thankful Lincoln Woodbury. Small grew up in a strict and intensely religious household. He took these standards for granted and did not rebel against them. Indeed, he followed in his father's footsteps in training for the ministry, and his family's moral standards ultimately shaped Small's vision of sociology as an ethical science.

Small was educated in Maine, graduating from Colby University (now Colby College) in Waterville, Maine, in 1876. At Colby Small became interested in German thought—an interest that influenced both his personal and professional lives and his practice of sociology. After graduating from Colby Small attended his father's alma mater, Newton Theological Seminary (Massachusetts), to train for the Baptist ministry. He graduated in 1879 but was never ordained. Instead Small went abroad to pursue graduate study in the social sciences. His introduction to German thought at Colby was decisive in his choice to study first at the University of Berlin (1879–1880) and then at the University of Leipzig (1880–1881).

Small met and married Valeria von Massow in Germany in 1881; they had one child. Later that year, without completing his graduate study, Small returned with Valeria to the United States to accept a position teaching history and political economy at Colby. In his biography of Small, George Christakes reports that these were not considered "proper college subjects" by some of Small's colleagues; as a result, Small's teaching load was restricted. The advantage of this for Small was that he had a great deal of time available for reading in these fields and in the developing field of sociology.

In 1888, on sabbatical from Colby, Small attended Johns Hopkins University and earned a Ph.D. in history (no sociology graduate programs then existed in the United States). In 1889, at the age of thirty-five, Small returned to Colby to assume the presidency of the college. He replaced the traditional course in moral philosophy taught by the president with a course on sociology—one of the first three sociology courses in the nation. In conjunction with this course, Small privately published a textbook, *Introduction to a Science of Society* (1890), consisting mostly of extracts from German social thinkers and philosophers.

In 1892 Small was persuaded to leave Colby by William Rainey Harper, who was then selecting distinguished faculty for a new university in Chicago. In turn Small persuaded Harper to create a department of social science (consisting of sociology and anthropology) at the new University of Chicago—the first sociology department in the United States. Small spent the rest of his career at Chicago as a member of the faculty and in various administrative positions, including department head (1892–1926), dean of the College of Liberal Arts (beginning in 1892), and dean of the Graduate School of Arts, Literature, and Science (1905–1926).

Most of Small's writing was published while he was at Chicago. In 1894 he published (with his student and colleague George E. Vincent) *An Introduction to the Study of Society,* the first sociology textbook intended for a wide audience. The following year Small founded the *American Journal of Sociology,* the first sociology journal in the United States. As a frequent author in and the chief editor of the journal until 1926, Small's influence on the field of sociology was extensive.

Three ideas are central to Small's written work. First, he delineated the unique subject matter of sociology as "the part which the group factor has played, the part which the group factor is playing, in different areas of human experience" (*The Origins of Sociology*, 1924). Small ranked this among his most important achievements. In a letter to his friend and former student Edward Cary Hayes, Small wrote, "If my name is anywhere extant at that time, I hope it will have a tag attached with the memorandum 'he had something to do with laying the individualistic superstition' [to rest]" (Odum, p. 184).

Second, Small articulated sociology's method by insisting on the scientific and empirical basis of sociology. In *General Sociology* (1905) Small wrote, "The same logical methods which have arrived at these generalizations [in biology, chemistry and physics] make irresistibly toward the conviction that coherence and unity of knowledge about human experience demand *a science of men in their associational processes.* Many of these processes have long been studied in detail, but study of them in their correlation is . . . the work of a distinct order of science, with a peculiar object of attention . . . *sociology*" (p. 8).

Finally, Small emphasized that the goal of sociology is to provide the theoretical and scientific basis for social reform. He rejected the Social Darwinist views of Spencer, Sumner, and others in which social change could be left to natural evolution. Instead Small proposed sociology, and later social science, as the basis for controlled, progressive social reform. In *The Meaning of Social Science* (1910), Small described "councils of scientists"—modern philosopher-kings—who would "represent the greatest possible number of human interests." Though he later tempered these assertions, he never doubted that the "primary and chief function of science is to act as all men's proxy in finding out all that can be known about what sort of world this is, and what we can do in it to make life most worth living" (1910).

Small's tenure at Chicago was marked by many other achievements. He served as president of the American Sociological Society and the Institute International de Sociologie de Paris. Small also brought to Chicago sociologists now well known, including William I. Thomas, Robert Park, and Ernest Burgess. Small died in Chicago.

In an issue of the *American Journal of Sociology* (July 1926) devoted to Small after his death, his contemporary Harry Elmer Barnes offered an estimate of Small's place in American sociology: "[A]mong the first generation of our sociologists Small's place in advancing the subject matter of sociology is second only to that of Ward and Giddings, while in promoting the professional and academic standing of the subject he was without any close rival." Small's vision of sociology as a scientific enterprise aiming at the betterment of human society together with the institutional bases he established for carrying out this mission indelibly mark his preeminent place in the discipline.

• The papers of Albion Small are located at the University of Chicago. These are incomplete, however, partly because of a fire that destroyed many of the pre-1904 papers. Smaller collections can be found in the archives of Andover-Newton

Theological Seminary, Colby College, and Johns Hopkins University. Other major works by Small include *Adam Smith and Modern Society* (1907), *The Cameralists* (1909), *Origins of Sociology* (1924), and a novel, *Between Eras: From Capitalism to Democracy* (1913). Small also published over 100 articles; most can be found in the *American Journal of Sociology* (1895–1925). Two fine analyses of Small's career and ideas are George Christakes, *Albion W. Small* (1978), and Vernon K. Dibble, *The Legacy of Albion Small* (1975). Both works also contain concise biographies, and Christakes's contains an extensive bibliography and an essay on twentieth-century assessments of Small. The essay by Small's student Edward Cary Hayes, "Albion Woodbury Small," in *American Masters of Social Science*, ed. Howard W. Odum (1927), provides a contemporary assessment, as do the following articles in the *American Journal of Sociology*: T. W. Goodspeed, "Albion Woodbury Small," 32 (1926): 1–14; Harry Elmer Barnes, "The Place of Albion Woodbury Small in Modern Sociology," 32 (1926): 15–44; and Annie Marion MacLean, "Albion Woodbury Small: An Appreciation," 32 (1926): 45–48. Ernest Becker, *The Lost Science of Man* (1971), offers an encomium. An obituary is in the *Chicago Daily Tribune*, 25 Mar. 1926.

CHERYL LAZ

SMALLS, Robert (5 Apr. 1839–23 Feb. 1915), congressman, was born in Beaufort, South Carolina, the son of an unknown white man and Lydia, a slave woman who worked as a house servant for the John McKee family in Beaufort. Descendants of Smalls believed that his father was John McKee, who died when Robert was young. The McKee family sent Robert to live with their relatives in Charleston, where he worked for wages that he turned over to his master. Smalls apparently taught himself the rudiments of reading and writing during this period. Later he attended school for three months, and as an adult he hired tutors. In 1856 Smalls married Hannah Jones, a slave who worked as a hotel maid. They had three children, one of whom died of smallpox. The couple lived apart from their owners, to whom they sent most of their income.

In 1861 Smalls began working as a deckhand on the *Planter*, a steamer that operated out of Charleston Harbor. By 1862 he was the craft's pilot. He knew the locations of Confederate armaments in the channels and on shore, and he knew of the U.S. Navy fleet anchored just outside Charleston Harbor. When he learned of the Federal occupation of Beaufort, Smalls determined with several other slave sailors to guide the *Planter* to Union waters. Secretly loading their families on board, the men rushed the vessel out of Charleston Harbor under cover of darkness and surrendered it to the U.S. Navy. Congress awarded Smalls and his aides monetary compensation for liberating the *Planter* from Confederate hands. From occupied Beaufort, Smalls piloted the vessel, now outfitted as a troop transport, around the Sea Islands, carrying messages, supplies, and men for the Union army. He always maintained that eventually he was commissioned as a captain, but his papers were lost, and after the war he had difficulty proving his service when he tried to obtain a pension. He piloted other ships as well, including the ironclad *Keokuk* in an unsuccessful assault on the city of Charleston.

During the war Smalls and his family traveled to the North to elicit popular sympathy for the slaves' plight and to attest to the service ex-slaves might perform if the Federal government would allow them the opportunity. Smalls began a store for freedpeople in Beaufort and, at the war's end, bought his former owner's house, where he resided until his death, for unpaid taxes. By 1870 Smalls had $6,000 in real estate and $1,000 in personal property.

Smalls entered politics as a delegate to South Carolina's constitutional convention of 1868 and in the same year won election as a Republican to the state's general assembly. He served in that body until 1875, first as a representative and later as a state senator. In 1874 Smalls was elected congressman from South Carolina's Fifth District, which included Beaufort. During his second congressional term in 1877, a South Carolina jury convicted him of accepting a bribe while he served in the state senate. Smalls had chaired the Printing Committee, which parceled out the state's printing. Evidence suggested that a leading printer bribed Smalls in return for state business. The judge sentenced Smalls to three years in the state penitentiary at hard labor. Smalls protested his innocence and appealed, losing before the state supreme court. He appealed to the U.S. Supreme Court, but before the case could be resolved the Democratic governor, William D. Simpson, pardoned him in exchange for a federal agreement to drop an investigation into the Democrats' violation of election laws.

With his conviction blighting his reputation and the Democratic paramilitary group known as the Red Shirts terrorizing his constituents, Smalls lost a third bid for Congress in 1878. He ran again in 1880 but lost in an election characterized by fraud on the part of the Democrats. This time Smalls contested the result, and the House awarded him the seat. In 1882 he failed to receive his party's nomination after Democrats redistricted Beaufort into the Seventh District. When the victorious Republican died in office in 1884, however, Smalls was elected to serve the remainder of the term, and he won reelection to another term later in the year. He lost the seat permanently in 1886, as Democrats threw out ballots with impunity and extralegal violence kept black voters from the polls.

Hannah Smalls died in 1883, and Robert married Annie Wigg in 1890. They had one son before her death in 1895. Effectively excluded from local politics by the Democrats' electoral fraud and the state's disfranchisement of African Americans in 1895, Smalls remained active in the Republican party at the national level. Those contacts gained him appointment as collector of customs for the Port of Beaufort in 1889, a post he lost with the Democratic national victory of 1892. He regained the office in 1898 with the return of a national Republican administration. He served until 1913, despite growing lily-white sentiment in the Republican party and the difficulties of discharging his duties in now-segregated Beaufort. Beset by several grave illnesses, Smalls died there, disillusioned by the reversal of the African-American political gains for which he had worked in Reconstruction.

• No single collection of Smalls's private or public papers exists, but his letters and documents are in other collections, notably the Frederick Douglass and Carter Godwin Woodson collections at the Library of Congress and the Governor Wade Hampton Collection at the South Carolina Department of Archives and History. His public career is documented in records of the South Carolina General Assembly, the U.S. House of Representatives, and the Veterans Administration at the National Archives. Two scholarly biographies provide documentation on Smalls's life, Okon Edet Uya, *From Slavery to Political Service: Robert Smalls, 1839–1915* (1971), and Edward A. Miller, Jr., *Gullah Statesman: Robert Smalls from Slavery to Congress, 1839–1915* (1995). Smalls was the subject of numerous biographical sketches during his lifetime, including William H. Quick, *Negro Stars in All Ages of the World* (1890), and William Johnson Simmons, *Men of Mark: Eminent, Progressive and Rising* (1887). One of the early scholarly articles on Smalls is Carter Godwin Woodson, "Robert Smalls and His Descendants," *Negro History Bulletin* 11 (Nov. 1947): 27–33. A biography for the general reader and young adult is Dorothy Sterling, *Captain of the "Planter": The Story of Robert Smalls* (1958). The *Planter* escape is told in Louise Meriwether, *The Freedom Ship of Robert Smalls* (1971). Biographical information and context for Smalls's political career is in Thomas Cleveland Holt, *Black over White: Negro Political Leadership in South Carolina during Reconstruction* (1977); Howard N. Rabinowitz, ed., *Southern Black Leaders of the Reconstruction Era* (1982); George Brown Tindall, *South Carolina Negroes, 1877–1900* (1952); Joel Williamson, *After Slavery: The Negro in South Carolina during Reconstruction, 1861–1877* (1965); and Idus A. Newby, *Black Carolinians: A History of Blacks in South Carolina from 1895 to 1968* (1973).

GLENDA E. GILMORE

SMALLWOOD, William (1732–14 Feb. 1792), officeholder and soldier, was born in Charles County, Maryland, probably on his father's estate, "Smallwood's Retreat," on Mattawoman Creek. He was the son of Bayne Smallwood, a prominent planter and delegate to the lower house of the Maryland General Assembly, and Priscilla Heabard (Heaberd). Smallwood was educated in England at Kendall and Eaton, and served in the Seven Years' War upon his return to Maryland. His political career began in 1761, when he was elected to the lower house of the General Assembly. He represented Charles County in the House of Delegates until 1774, and served on the Arms and Ammunition Committee during most of his years in the assembly. Locally, Smallwood served as a Charles County justice in 1762, and from 1770 to 1773, and was a member of the vestry of Durham Parish Anglican church from 1775 to 1776.

During the events leading to the Revolution, Smallwood firmly supported the patriot cause. In 1769 he joined the Maryland Non-Importation Association to protest the Townshend Acts. In 1774 he became a member of the Charles County Committee of Observation, and in 1775 he signed the Association of Freemen of Maryland, an oath of loyalty to the patriot cause.

In June 1774, Smallwood represented Charles County in the first of nine extralegal conventions called by patriot leaders to coordinate resistance against British policies. In January 1776, the convention commissioned Smallwood a colonel and authorized him to raise troops for what became the First Maryland Regiment. Smallwood complained to the convention shortly after his appointment that the allowance of hunting shirts, but no "spatterdashes," or leggings, for his troops was unsatisfactory, as he wished the regiment to appear "respectable" and "formidable" to the enemy.

In June 1776, Smallwood led nine companies of Maryland troops to tender their services to Congress in Philadelphia. Congress ordered Smallwood and his men to reinforce General George Washington's army in New York. The Maryland battalion became part of a brigade commanded by William Alexander, self-styled Lord Stirling. In August 1776, while Smallwood was absent attending a court-martial, about 400 of his men participated in the crucial battle of Long Island. Smallwood's troops under the command of Major Mordecai Gist successfully held a far superior British force long enough to enable the American army to escape across Gowanus Creek to safety on Manhattan Island.

Although Smallwood lost more than 250 men at the battle of Long Island, the remnants of the regiment continued to distinguish themselves. At White Plains in October 1776, Smallwood's men were among the last Americans to leave the field of battle, and Smallwood was wounded twice.

In October 1776, Congress promoted Smallwood to brigadier general and ordered him back to Maryland to recover from his wounds and to raise more troops. While he was there, Congress ordered Maryland to suppress an insurrection of Loyalists in Somerset and Worcester counties on Maryland's Eastern Shore. Smallwood headed a hastily assembled expeditionary force of militia and regular troops, and by early March 1777 he had established his headquarters in Somerset County.

Smallwood soon had twelve Loyalist leaders in custody. Despite this success, he discovered that disaffection among the citizens of the lower Eastern Shore remained widespread.

Smallwood was ordered to rejoin the Continental army in April 1777, but was soon recalled to Maryland to command militia troops raised to counter a rumored British invasion of Baltimore. When the attack failed to materialize, Washington ordered Smallwood and his militia to harass the British army marching on Philadelphia. The militia performed poorly, especially at the battle of Germantown in October 1777. Smallwood complained of the militia's "disorder & licentiousness," adding that their lack of discipline would "ever render them contemptible in the field." After the British occupied Philadelphia in late September, Washington again put Smallwood in command of the Maryland Continentals, ordering them to Wilmington

for the winter to protect the American army's southern flank.

In 1779–1780, Smallwood was in charge of surveillance on the Chesapeake Bay. In 1780, he was ordered to South Carolina to serve under Baron de Kalb (Johann Kalb) in General Horatio Gates's southern campaign. Smallwood had often complained about the preference in rank that Congress accorded foreign-born officers, but his problem in South Carolina was not de Kalb but the ineptitude of General Gates. At the battle of Camden in August 1780, Gates's blundering resulted in a rout of the American forces and in de Kalb's death. A total disaster was averted only because of the bravery of the Maryland and Delaware troops.

For a few weeks after Camden, Smallwood commanded the southern army. Congress expressed its thanks to Smallwood by promoting him to major general, making him the highest-ranking Maryland officer in the army. After his promotion, Smallwood's immediate superior officer was Baron von Steuben, and once again Smallwood protested having to serve under a "foreigner." Nathanael Greene, the new commander of the Southern Department, solved the problem by ordering Smallwood back to Maryland to raise new recruits and supplies for the army, tasks at which he excelled.

Smallwood set about the task of raising men and supplies with his accustomed vigor. At this late stage of the war, there were few recruits filled with patriotic fervor. Smallwood turned to the lower classes for recruits: the sons of tenant farmers, common laborers, and recently freed indentured servants. Supplies too were scarce, as farmers were increasingly reluctant to accept potentially worthless paper in payment. Nevertheless, Smallwood's persistence enabled him to raise and equip a regiment of more than 300 men.

Smallwood's military career was marred by his frequent complaints about his treatment by military and civilian superiors. He most often directed his opprobrium at Congress, which he believed failed adequately to recognize Maryland's—and thereby his own—contributions. One of his fellow officers from Maryland, Otho Holland Williams, faulted Smallwood's behavior during the war, criticizing his "low ambition" and the "meanness of his resentments."

Smallwood resigned his commission in November 1783, and returned to his Charles County plantation. He eventually owned over 5,000 acres in Maryland and Virginia and a number of slaves. He cofounded the Society of the Cincinnati in Maryland and served as its first president.

In 1784, Smallwood was elected one of the state's representatives to the U.S. Congress, but he declined to serve. The following year, the Maryland General Assembly elected Smallwood to the first of three consecutive one-year terms as governor of Maryland. During his first two terms, the state suffered through the effects of the postwar economic depression and a divisive battle in the General Assembly over whether to pass a paper money bill to ease the burden on debtors. During his last year as governor, the Maryland convention met in Annapolis to consider ratification of the proposed U.S. Constitution. Smallwood may have had reservations about the proposed Constitution, but he did not use his office to oppose it. Maryland easily ratified the proposed Constitution in April 1788.

Smallwood assumed his last public office in 1791, when Maryland's senate electors chose him to serve a five-year term as one of the fifteen members of the upper house of the state assembly. Smallwood's fellow senators elected him president of that body, a position he held until his death.

William Smallwood never married. He died on his plantation, "Smallwood's Retreat." The heirs to his large but heavily indebted estate were his only surviving sister and several nieces and nephews.

• No collection of William Smallwood's papers exists, but much of his public career can be traced in the Maryland State Papers at the Maryland State Archives in Annapolis. No full biography of Smallwood has been written, but a good brief treatment is Ross M. Kimmel, *In Perspective; William Smallwood* (1976). His family history and public career are outlined in the Smallwood sketch in Edward C. Papenfuse et al., *A Biographical Dictionary of the Maryland Legislature, 1635–1789* (2 vols., 1979–1985), 2:741–42. For his recruiting efforts late in the war, see Edward C. Papenfuse and Gregory A. Stiverson, "General Smallwood's Recruits: The Peacetime Career of the Revolutionary War Private," *William and Mary Quarterly*, 3d ser., 30 (Jan. 1973): 117–32.

GREGORY A. STIVERSON

SMART, David Archibald (4 Oct. 1892–16 Oct. 1952), publisher, was born in Omaha, Nebraska, the son of Louis Smart, a barber and musician, and Mary Aronson. The family soon moved to Chicago, Illinois. Smart dropped out of the Crane Technical High School after two years to sell hats. In 1911 he began selling advertising for the *Chicago Tribune*. He was so successful that Colonel Robert Rutherford McCormick, the *Tribune*'s owner, put him on salary. This salary was lower than his commission income; so Smart started an advertising agency of his own.

During World War I Smart was a field artillery soldier with the U.S. Army in France and was slightly wounded. After the war, he returned to the United States to become a commodities speculator. He made $750,000 in sugar but lost $700,000 in other ventures. In 1921 he established the David A. Smart Publishing Company, naming his brother Alfred Smart secretary-treasurer. Smart's habit of taking orders for booklets, calendars, and other small advertising items before producing them resulted in his outdoing traditional competitors. He and a partner, William Hobart Weintraub, founded a trade magazine, the *National Men's Wear Salesman*, and an illustrated stylebook, the *Gentleman's Quarterly*, which resembled a clothing catalog. Smart hired Arnold Gingrich away from the Kuppenheimer clothing company, where he was a skillful advertising copywriter. Gingrich began a long association with Smart as an editor of his several ventures.

In 1931 Smart and his associates founded *Apparel Arts*. The success of this trade periodical showed that there was an untapped market for a men's fashion magazine. His *Esquire* was the result, beginning as a quarterly in Chicago in October 1933. Its success was assured when Weintraub showed a dummy of it to owners of menswear stores and obtained advance orders for 100,000 copies at fifty cents each. Gingrich soon assembled pieces by George Ade, Nicholas Murray Butler, John Dos Passos, Douglas Fairbanks, Jr., F. Scott Fitzgerald, Dashiell Hammett, Ernest Hemingway, Bobby Jones, and Gene Tunney. Especially appealing were color cartoons by E. Simms Campbell and George Petty, whose long-limbed "Petty Girl" became a standard feature. Smart made himself president and chairman of Esquire, Inc.

In January 1934 *Esquire* became a monthly, with the pop-eyed, white-mustached "Esky" as its cartoon mascot on the cover. Profits in 1936 totaled $115,802.82. By 1936 circulation reached 550,000. The magazine sent shock waves through the industry with "Latins Are Lousy Lovers" (Oct. 1936), an anonymously published essay by Helen Norden (later Helen Lawrenson), a former *Vanity Fair* editor. Outraged, the Cuban government banned *Esquire*. The drawing power of Hemingway's regular column in *Esquire* was so great that Smart paid him $1,000, double the customary story price, for "The Snows of Kilimanjaro" (Aug. 1936). Furthermore, when *Esquire* stock went public in 1937, he gave Hemingway a thousand shares. By then, circulation of *Esquire* stood at 675,000. It aimed its appeal at professional men under forty-five years of age, with a desire for good times, good clothes, good drink, and occasional trips abroad.

Smart founded *Coronet* in 1936 without Weintraub, their friendship having cooled. Smart became president and chairman of Esquire-Coronet, Inc. *Coronet*, pocket-sized and free of ads, featured beautiful illustrations, included prose pieces, and was never intended to turn a profit. While Smart was on a two-day visit to Paris in 1937 for unsuccessful acupuncture treatment for persistent migraine headaches, he met Efstratios Eleftheriades. E. Tèriade, as he was known professionally in France, was a Greek-born art critic and editor of *Minotaure*, an art journal in Paris that had lost its sponsor in 1936. Smart, with characteristic impetuous generosity, bought it for $1,000 and had Tèriade publish it in Paris. Gingrich suggested a new name for the journal, *Verve*, which Tèriade edited brilliantly beginning in December 1937. The first issue, now a collector's item, with a cover "specially composed" by Tèriade's friend Henri Matisse, included essays by André Gide, Dos Passos, and André Malraux, unpublished letters by Paul Cézanne, photographs, and breathtaking color and gilt plates. In 1939 Smart stopped financing *Verve*, and Tèriade quit publishing it when the Germans seized Paris in 1940.

In April 1938 Smart launched *Ken: The Insider's World* with the help of Jay Cooke Allen, a foreign correspondent from the *Chicago Tribune*. *Ken* (meaning "knowledge," as in "beyond his ken") was a newsmagazine, biweekly and then weekly, and combined photographs and controversial articles. An essay by a prostitute and another on the Spanish Civil War caused the Catholic church to boycott it in 1939. Its inconsistent editorial policy, first criticizing General Francisco Franco's pro-fascist policies and praising his communist enemies and then reversing this position, also alienated advertisers. *Ken* lost $400,000 and after sixteen months ceased publication. By 1940 the circulation for *Coronet* had fallen to a third of its 250,000 high. Smart transferred Oscar Dystel from his *Esquire* staff to edit *Coronet*. In 1941 Smart and his brother were indicted for manipulating some 200,000 shares of stock in their Esquire-Coronet enterprise. Sensing defeat in court, they pleaded *nolo contendere*, were fined $10,000 each, and were sentenced to two-year prison terms (suspended). Meanwhile, Dystel was making *Coronet* less artistic but so popular that by 1947, the first year it accepted advertisements, its circulation of more than 2 million outdid that of *Esquire* itself.

Smart's two main hobbies were photography and rose culture. Putting the former to use in 1940, he organized Coronet Instructional Films, which produced educational movies in a studio in Glenview, Illinois, a suburb just northwest of Chicago where Smart lived. During World War II the U.S. Navy made use of facilities of Smart's company to produce training films. In 1942 Smart, long a handsome ladies' man, married Edna Gabrielle Richards, a fashion model whose professional name was Gaby Duré and whom he had known for seven years. The flamboyant couple had no children.

In 1943 the U.S. Post Office Department threatened to withdraw second-class mailing privileges from both *Esquire* and *Coronet*, alleging that neither magazine provided the public with useful information or had any artistic, literary, or scientific merit, but that both were lascivious and obscene, not least because of Alberto Vargas's foldout drawings of pretty girls for *Esquire*. This despite their popularity with wartime servicemen. If the magazines had been obliged to pay first-class postage, the extra expense would have come to half a million dollars annually and would probably have spelled their doom. Supported by owners of similarly endangered publications, Smart went to court and won his case after a unanimous Supreme Court decision.

When World War II ended, Gingrich began a seven-year retirement in Switzerland, and Smart rather foolishly appointed himself both editor and publisher of both *Esquire* and *Coronet*. The enormous Christmas 1946 *Esquire* issue, its biggest ever, had 352 pages. However, both magazines lacked focus even as sales increased. In 1949 Smart bought Ideal Pictures Corporation. In 1950 he moved to New York City and rented office space on Madison Avenue. In 1951 he was devastated by the sudden death of his brother Alfred, after which he gave his still younger brother, John Smart, greater company responsibilities. In August 1952 Gingrich returned from Europe, began to work for *Flair* magazine in New York, saw Smart again, and promptly returned to *Esquire*. Smart did not live to see the magazine's revival. He died a few days after surgery in a Chicago hospital for the removal of an intestinal polyp. He was a debonair, mercurial, chance-taking publisher whose behavior, generosity, and successes were legendary in the turbulent decades of the 1930s and 1940s.

• Some *Esquire* and Arnold Gingrich papers are in the Michigan Historical Collections, University of Michigan. The best source of information on Smart is Arnold Gingrich, *Nothing but People: The Early Days at "Esquire," A Personal History, 1928–1958* (1971). Henry F. Pringle, "Sex, Esq.," *Scribner's Magazine*, Mar. 1938, pp. 33–39, 88, says that the early *Esquire* succeeded because it was an "unholy combination of erudition and sex." Helen Lawrenson, *Stranger at the Party: A Memoir* (1975), evokes the heady times of the magazine-publishing world of the 1930s and 1940s. Herman Baron, *Author Index to Esquire, 1933–1973* (1976), demonstrates the immense range of talent published in the first 481 issues of *Esquire*. Russell Miller, *Bunny: The Real Story of "Playboy"* (1984), discusses *Playboy* magazine publisher Hugh Hefner's time spent working as a copyeditor for Smart in the late 1940s. Carol Polsgrove, *It Wasn't Pretty, Folks, but Didn't We Have Fun?: "Esquire" in the Sixties* (1995), deals tangentially with Smart. Michel Anthonioz, *"Verve": The Ultimate Review of Art and Literature (1937–1960)* (1987), includes an informative introduction and excellent illustrations. Obituaries are in the *Chicago Daily Tribune* and the *New York Times*, both 17 Oct. 1952.

ROBERT L. GALE

SMART, James Henry (30 June 1841–21 Feb. 1900), educator, was born in Center Harbor, New Hampshire, the son of William Hutchings Smart, a physician, and Nancy Farrington. Smart's father, at one time a high school teacher, had become a successful physician in Center Harbor, where he educated his children at home. In 1847 the family moved to Concord, New Hampshire, so the children could attend good schools. In 1853, at the age of twelve, James started high school in Concord, but that same year he heard a lecture about self-sufficiency that convinced him to drop out of school and get a job. He continued his studies in the evenings under the guidance of his father and older brother. From that time on, James was economically independent.

For the next five years Smart held jobs in various areas of business with the intention of pursuing business as a profession. After unsuccessful attempts in Boston, he returned to Concord High School in 1858. Within six months he was hired temporarily at the school to teach a class in math and another in reading when the principal was absent. In 1859 Smart taught in Sanborton, New Hampshire, where, in the custom of the era, he boarded 'round and received $15 per month for ten weeks. Thereafter he returned to Concord to finish high school.

In the spring of 1860 Smart began a year of teaching the upper level classes at a village school in Laconia, New Hampshire, and the following two years he taught in Claremont, New Hampshire. His reputation as an excellent teacher grew. He was active in the state teachers association, and in 1862 he was appointed associate editor of the New Hampshire *Journal of Education*, published in Manchester.

In the spring of 1863 Smart was invited to take charge of a ward school in Toledo, Ohio, and in June of that year he was promoted to head the intermediate department of the high school. The local paper praised him for the order and discipline he brought to the institution. In 1864 he published a small book related to physical education and health, *A Manual of Free Gymnastic and Dumbbell Exercises.*

In 1865, when Smart was not quite twenty-five years old, he was hired by the Board of School Trustees of Fort Wayne, Indiana, to fill the superintendent's position. He was charged with bringing order, efficiency, and discipline to a public school system that was alleged to be overcrowded, understaffed, and poorly managed. In his ten years as superintendent he built a high school and numerous elementary schools; reduced the number of grades from twenty-eight to fourteen; set guidelines for students and teachers; incorporated strict attendance policies; brought in special teachers of music, drawing, painting, reading, and writing; and started a normal school, one of the first in the Midwest, to train teachers. In this last endeavor he was assisted by Mary H. Swan, the first principal of the Fort Wayne Normal School in 1867. Smart married Swan in 1870; they had two children.

While in Fort Wayne, Smart became well known for his energy, his organizational skill, his diplomacy, and his broad interest in illiteracy and moral education. As superintendent he was a member of the Indiana State Board of Education, a position he held for the next twenty-seven years. He was elected president of the Indiana State Teachers Association in 1873, and that year he also represented the United States in Vienna at the World's Exposition.

In March 1874 Smart was elected superintendent of public instruction for the state of Indiana, a position he held for a precedent-setting time, three two-year terms. He distinguished his office by his diplomacy in dealing with the highly contested county superintendency law of 1873, which brought greater state control over rural schooling by empowering county superintendents at the expense of local township trustees. Smart also won acclaim for his detailed annual reports, his national recognition as a leader among the state school superintendents presenting school exhibits at the Philadelphia Centennial Exposition of 1876, and his presidency of the National Education Association in 1880–1881. His writings during this period include *The Indiana Schools and the Men Who Have Worked in Them* (1876); *Books and Reading for the Young* (1880), a reprint from his annual report as state superintendent; and *The Best System of Schools for a State* (1880).

After Smart's terms as state superintendent, he worked as the statewide agent for the publishing firm of D. Appleton & Company. In December 1882 he was elected a trustee of Indiana University, but he resigned in January 1883, when he was chosen president of Purdue University, Indiana's struggling, nine-year-old land-grant university in West Lafayette.

As Purdue's fifth president, Smart inherited a university that was torn by faculty strife, lack of direction, and diminished financial support. The previous administration had offended alumni and legislators by banning Greek fraternities, and state funding was not renewed. In his first years as president Smart diplomatically healed broken relationships with the legislature and among the faculty, renewed and stabilized public and private contributions, created the School of Pharmacy, expanded the size of the student body and faculty, constructed new buildings, and built the engineering schools into the most esteemed in the country, propelling Purdue on its road to excellence in engineering. Smart transported a steam locomotive to campus to serve as a lab as well as a symbol of the university's technological focus. In 1893 he built a state-of-the-art engineering building, Heavilon Hall, which was destroyed by fire only four days after it was dedicated in January 1894. He had the building refunded and rebuilt by September of that same year. In 1895 Smart initiated the Western Conference for college athletics, which in 1912 became the Big Ten Conference.

Smart's high energy and intense devotion to organizational tasks were legendary, but by 1894 his health began to fail. He died in West Lafayette after leading Purdue for seventeen years. His death was attributed to neurasthenia.

Smart is remembered as an educator with great administrative and organizational talent combined with a vision of public education at all levels, a vision that paralleled that of the most progressive educators of his day. This self-educated man set norms of excellence in his many educational roles, from district schoolteacher to city schoolteacher, from city superintendent to state superintendent, from state university president to member of numerous state, national, and international forums. His vision, talent, diplomacy, and energy helped transform and reform an array of educational arenas.

• Some of Smart's papers from his Purdue years are in Special Collections, Purdue University Libraries, West Lafayette, Ind. His writings also include *Commentary on the School Law of Indiana* (1881) and *Teachers' Institutes,* Circulars of Information of the Bureau of Education, no. 2-1885 (1885). Arlene Argerbright wrote about "The Educational Career of James H. Smart," *Old-Fort News* 4, nos. 1–3 (Nov. 1939): 4–12; and Robert W. Topping covered "James H. Smart's Glory Years" in *A Century and Beyond, The History of Purdue University* (1988). An obituary is in the *Indianapolis News,* 22 Feb. 1900.

KATHLEEN A. MURPHEY

SMEDLEY, Agnes (23 Feb. 1892–6 May 1950), journalist and author, was born in Campground, Sullivan County, Missouri, the daughter of Charles Smedley, an itinerant miner, and Sarah Ralls, a boardinghouse operator and washerwoman. The family was supported primarily by a prostitute aunt; Charles Smedley was more interested in get-rich-quick schemes than in holding a steady job. The family shuttled between towns in Missouri and Colorado when Charles Smedley would obtain new employment. Agnes Smedley went to work after school as a domestic helper at age fourteen and later quit school in 1907 to take in work as a washerwoman.

Smedley was determined to continue her education; in 1908 she left home and went to New Mexico as a schoolteacher. Her mother died the next year, and she took a job as a secretary, then as a sales agent, at a Denver magazine. In 1911 she studied at Tempe Normal School in Arizona for a year, where she met Ernest "Walfred" Brundin. She moved with him to California, and the two were married in 1912, despite the fact that she had spoken out against marriage for years. Smedley was terrified of having children and the restrictions they would put on her freedom; convinced she would relive her parents' lives, she had two abortions while married to Brundin. They were divorced in 1916.

Smedley moved to New York City in that year, where she attended classes part time at New York University and worked as a secretary for Lajpat Rai, an Indian Nationalist leader. She became active in the Indian movement for independence and was also involved in Margaret Sanger's birth control movement. She served as a secretary, then as associate editor on the magazine the *Birth Control Review*. Because of her association with the Indian movement she was arrested in 1918 as a violator of the Espionage Act, supposedly a member of a group plotting rebellions in India. She spent a few weeks in prison, though the charges were later dropped.

In 1920 Smedley moved to Berlin and became more deeply involved in Indian activism. She moved in with Virendranath "Chatto" Chattopadhyaya, another Indian Nationalist leader, who became her common-law husband; they had no children. Throughout her life her mental state reflected itself in her physical state; she resented not being treated as an equal by Chatto and his Indian companions and suffered severe depression and a nervous breakdown. As treatment Smedley began psychoanalysis, and she also enrolled at the University of Berlin. She wrote articles championing the Indian cause for the *Nation, Die Frau,* and other publications. She realized living with Chatto was not helping her depression, and she left him in 1925. While vacationing and recuperating with a friend in Denmark, she began the first draft of her first book, *Daughter of Earth* (1929), a mostly autobiographical account and an attempt by Smedley to cleanse her life of past unhappinesses. Back in Berlin she soon became involved again in a favorite cause and helped found Germany's first public birth control clinic in 1928.

For both political and personal reasons Smedley decided to go to China in 1928 as a journalist for the German *Frankfurter Zeitung*. While in Shanghai she met many communist supporters and befriended prominent writer Lu Xun (Hsün). She found she identified with the Chinese communists, especially lower-class women, because they reminded her so vividly of her own underprivileged, downtrodden childhood. She wrote articles and, later, books that championed the communist fight against Nationalist government leader Chiang Kai-shek. She later also reported for the *Manchester Guardian, New Masses,* and the *New Republic*. In 1933 she went for a rest to the U.S.S.R., where she was disillusioned with Soviet communism. She visited the United States in 1934 and the same year returned to China, where she continued to write. In December 1936 she was in Xi'an (Sian) when Chiang Kai-shek was kidnapped by communist rebels, and Smedley issued daily radio reports on the situation until the beginning of 1937. Hers was the only news coming out of Xi'an at the time, and she gained national prominence for her reports. She then went to Yan'an (Yenan), Mao Zedong's headquarters. Her first impression of him was that he was "aloof and spiritually isolated." There she promoted hygiene—specifically an anti-rat crusade, supported by Mao—and dancing for exercise and stress relief.

Many of the women in Yan'an had survived the Long March fleeing from Chiang Kai-shek and resented Smedley's urging them against behaving subserviently and vilifying their lack of strength in their marriages. Mao's wife, He Zizhen, hit Smedley at one point and accused her of creating problems in their marriage, specifically, introducing him to another woman. Smedley was advised to leave Yan'an because of these conflicts. When the Sino-Japanese War started later that year, she devoted herself to the war effort and traveled with the Eighth Route Army (the Red Army division in the united war against Japan) in the Shaanxi (Shansi) province. Her experiences and impressions are documented in *China Fights Back: An American Woman with the Eighth Route Army* (1938; repr. 1977).

In 1938 Smedley went to Hankou (Han Kow) and raised funds for the Chinese Red Cross. Later that year, when Hankou fell to the Japanese, she left town to travel with the Communist New Fourth Army until 1940 and intermittently continued her fundraising efforts. While with them, she attempted to adopt a young Chinese boy. He refused, telling her he would go fight for China and when the war was over he would return and let her adopt him. She fell ill around that time and went to Hong Kong for treatment.

Smedley needed additional medical care and returned to the United States in 1941. There she toured and lectured about her experiences in China and stayed with various friends while continuing to write. In 1943 she went to live in the Yaddo artists' colony in upstate New York with contemporaries such as Katherine Anne Porter and Carson McCullers. The Cold War atmosphere of the country made her less marketable as a lecturer and journalist, and her political opposites labeled her a communist. The Federal Bureau of Investigation began to investigate her activities as a suspected communist, and in 1949 the U.S. Army released a report labeling her as a Soviet spy. She disagreed in a press release and told the army to waive their immunity and she would sue them for libel. The report was retracted, but she remained a difficult sell.

Smedley chose not to appear in public events with some of her friends for fear they would suffer from guilt by association; other friends outright rejected her.

In 1950 she decided to return to China. En route she was so ill that she had an operation in England to remove two-thirds of her stomach because of an ulcer. She died the following day in Oxford, England. Her ashes are buried in a suburb of Babaoshan, China, in the Cemetery for Revolutionaries.

Smedley was a passionate, high-strung woman who poured all her energy into the causes she supported, often at the cost of her health. She wrote prolifically, though with a narrow viewpoint, about the Chinese communist cause. Smedley also ardently championed a woman's right to remain unmarried and not have children. While not a sophisticated writer, her contacts with the Chinese Communist party allowed her access to information and incidents that she might not otherwise have known or seen.

• For a complete biography of Smedley, see Janice R. MacKinnon and Stephen R. MacKinnon, *Agnes Smedley: The Life and Times of an American Radical* (1987). Smedley's books are mostly autobiographical and provide insight into her travels and experiences in China. See *Chinese Destinies: Sketches of Present-Day China* (1933; repr. 1977). Her *Battle Hymn of China* (1943; repr. 1984 as *China Correspondent*) was written while at Yaddo about the Sino-Japanese conflict. See also her *Portraits of Chinese Women in Revolution*, comp. and ed. Janice R. MacKinnon and Stephen R. MacKinnon (1976). Obituaries appear in *Time* and *Newsweek*, both 7 May 1950, and the *New York Times*, 9 May 1950.

SHANE SPEER

SMIBERT, John (24 Mar. 1688–2 Apr. 1751), portrait painter, was born in Edinburgh, Scotland, the son of John Smibert, a litster (dyer of wool), and Alison Bell. Smibert attended the local parish grammar school and at the age of fourteen was apprenticed to Walter Melville, a decorative house painter and plasterer. As an apprentice, Smibert worked on painted designs and raised decorative plaster ceilings for the homes of Edinburgh's wealthy citizens.

In 1709, at the end of his apprenticeship, Smibert traveled to London, England, where, according to some records, he worked as a coach painter. He soon moved on to copying Old Master and other paintings for picture dealers, a somewhat lucrative field as well as one closer to the "fine arts." In 1714 Smibert joined the school conducted by Sir James Thornhill, the first formal art academy in London, which had been formed only three years earlier. The primary activity at the academy was drawing, and one of the directors was the noted portrait painter Godfrey Kneller.

Smibert returned to Edinburgh in 1716 to capitalize on his exotic (in comparison to his Scottish contemporaries) London academic training. He had little financial success, however, until he received the patronage of Sir Francis Grant (Lord Cullen). Smibert completed portraits of five members of Grant's family beginning with Anne Hamilton (c. 1717, Grant's daughter-in-law). With Smibert's skills passing the test, Grant soon commissioned a large group portrait, *Sir Francis Grant and His Family* (1718). During this time in Edinburgh, Smibert painted a few landscapes, though none have survived. He also struck up a friendship with Allan Ramsay, a noted Scottish poet. Smibert painted two portraits of the poet, one of which was later engraved for the frontispiece of Ramsay's collected works (1728).

Though he was moderately successful in Edinburgh, Smibert, even with his novel academic training, faced competition from more established portrait painters such as William Aikman. In 1719, with an eye toward increasing his knowledge of Italian masters and advancing his career, Smibert traveled to Italy. After brief stops in London and Paris, he arrived in Florence on 19 November 1719. In Italy, Smibert copied Old Masters and created an occasional commissioned portrait. In 1720, while still in Florence, Smibert first made the acquaintance of George Berkeley, a philosopher and Anglican prelate. Smibert completed the first of his portraits of Berkeley around 1722. After a few months in Rome, Smibert returned to London in early 1722.

Smibert set up a studio and residence in the Strand, a convenient, yet less-than-fashionable area for a portrait painter to reside. Capitalizing on acquaintances he made with English travelers in Italy, Smibert received portrait commissions from a number of them (such as Colonel James Otway, whose portrait he completed in 1724). However, Smibert still was unable to compete with the top portrait painters in London for commissions. His clients were primarily wealthy merchants, lawyers, and other professionals. Few of them were from the nobility. Most of his work was for bust or three-quarter-length portraits, which brought in lower prices than full-length pictures. In London, Smibert joined the Rose and Crown Club, an artists' social club that met regularly at a tavern near Covent Garden. In 1725 Smibert moved to Covent Garden, then the center of London's artistic community, where his residence and studio was next to the King's Arms tavern. In the same year he moved to Covent Garden, Smibert joined the Society of Antiquaries to further his possibility of gaining patronage.

Though his move to Covent Garden had increased the number of wealthy patrons seeking his talents, his income did not keep up with his mounting costs. To supplement his income, Smibert painted miniatures, though none from his London period have survived. George Berkeley renewed his friendship with Smibert in 1726 and sat for a second portrait (1726). Planning a college in Bermuda, Berkeley used Smibert's Covent Garden residence as his headquarters. Though 1727 saw Smibert painting more portraits than ever, his economic situation remained grim, as full payment for many of the portraits was not forthcoming.

With the plans for his college in Bermuda moving swiftly along, Berkeley invited Smibert to join the project as director of the college's painting academy. Smibert accepted, and he, Berkeley, and four others departed from England in late 1728. The entourage landed in Newport, Rhode Island, on 27 January 1729. Berkeley planned to use Newport as a base of operations while awaiting the final funding for the college in Bermuda. After several months in Newport, Smibert traveled to nearby Boston for what he thought would be a few days' visit. Finding Boston hospitable and Berkeley's Bermuda plans becoming uncertain, Smibert set up a residence and studio in the North End. Here, his copies of the Italian and Dutch masters and casts of classical sculpture captivated the population. Mather Byles, a young nephew of Boston's Congregational leader Cotton Mather, was so impressed with the contents of Smibert's studio that he composed a long poem, "To Mr. Smibert on the Sight of His Pictures," that was published in newspapers in Philadelphia and London.

Though his first portraits completed in Boston were of Francis Brinley and his family (who were Anglicans), it was after his portrait of Judge Samuel Sewall, an important member of Boston's Congregationalist leadership, that commissions began to flood his studio. During the course of the next five years, Smibert painted nearly one hundred portraits, a number far outstripping the total portrait output of the colonies to that time.

Smibert's greatest work in the New World, however, was planned before he left England. John Wainwright, an admirer of Berkeley, commissioned Smibert to create a large painting honoring Berkeley and his Utopian expedition. This painting, now known as *The Bermuda Group*, is composed of three-quarter-length portraits of Berkeley; his wife, Anne Forster; his young son, Henry; Mrs. Berkeley's traveling companion, Miss Handcock; Wainwright; John James; and Richard Dalton. Smibert, in his only known self-portrait, appears in the rear of the composition. Smibert worked on the painting for more than two years, completing the work in circa 1731. The painting was never sent to Wainwright in England, possibly because of the failure of Berkeley's Bermuda plan, and it remained in Smibert's studio.

Shortly before completing *The Bermuda Group*, Smibert married Mary Williams in 1730; the couple had four children. Throughout the 1730s Smibert actively depicted Boston's religious, mercantile, and political leaders. In around 1734 he opened a small shop, where he sold artists' supplies, mezzotints, and framed Italian, Dutch, and English prints. An active Presbyterian while in England, Smibert embraced the Congregational faith while in Boston. In 1737 he was one of the founding members of West Church, the city's newest congregation.

Though he had traveled extensively in Europe during his youth, Smibert made only one excursion in the colonies. In 1740 he made a tour of Philadelphia and New York; during this trip he began a number of portraits that he later completed in Boston.

In 1740 Smibert also turned his hand to architecture. A longtime friend of Boston merchant Peter Faneuil (whose portrait Smibert painted on at least four

times) commissioned Smibert to design a public market. Faneuil Hall (1742), the first public market in a colonial city, quickly became a Boston landmark. Evidence also points to Smibert having designed the Holden Chapel (1742) for Harvard College.

The battle of Louisburg between the French and British in May 1744 resulted in a victory for the British and a number of portrait commissions for Smibert. A full-length portrait of Governor William Shirley (1746, now unlocated) as well as portraits of Sir Peter Warren (1746) and Sir William Pepperrell (1746) were completed. Smibert's portrait of Sir Richard Spry (1746), another hero of Louisburg, is his last known work. During this time, Smibert was being treated by the Boston physician Dr. William Clark for an unknown illness.

Though he appears to have ceased his portrait work, in a letter from 1749 Smibert mentions that he has been "diverting my self with somethings in the Landskip way" (quoted in Saunders, p. 259). The only located Smibert landscape, however, is his *View of Boston* (c. 1738–1740).

Described by Horace Walpole (*Anecdotes of Painting in England* [1826–1828]) as "a silent, modest man, who abhorred the finesse of some of his profession" (quoted in Frank W. Bayley's *Five Colonial Artists of New England* [1929], p. 339), Smibert died in Boston and was interred in the Granary burying ground. As one of the founders of American portraiture, Smibert's works, particularly *The Bermuda Group*, influenced the generation of artists immediately following him, most notably Robert Feke and John Greenwood. Though Smibert brought with him a European style, art historian Alan Burroughs has noted, "He was an American, not by accident, but by assimilation and choice" (p. 121). After his death Smibert's studio remained almost entirely intact. Containing both his own portrait work as well as his copies after European masters, the studio became a pilgrimage site for generations of American artists including John Singleton Copley and Charles Willson Peale. Smibert's *Cardinal Guido Bentivoglio* (a copy after Van Dyck, c. 1719–1720), was later owned by John Trumbull.

• Works are in the collections of the Scottish National Portrait Gallery; the Wadsworth Atheneum, Hartford, Conn.; the Yale Center for British Art, New Haven, Conn.; Bowdoin College Museum of Art, Bowdoin, Maine; Metropolitan Museum of Art, New York City; the Boston Atheneum; the Massachusetts Historical Society, Boston, Mass.; and the National Galleries of Scotland and Ireland. There is no major collection of Smibert's papers. Small amounts of correspondence are held by the National Archives of Scotland, the Newport (R.I.) Historical Society, the British Museum, the Archives of American Art (Smithsonian Institution), the British Library, and the Boston Public Library. Smibert's notebook, in which he recorded more than twenty-six years of commissions, is held by the Public Records Office in London. The notebook has been reprinted as *The Notebook of John Smibert* (1969). A biography and catalog of works is Richard H. Saunder, *John Smibert: Colonial America's First Portrait Painter* (1995), which greatly expands on *John Smibert, Painter* (1950), by Henry Wilder Foote. The notebooks of George Vertue, which have been published as *Notebooks* in many volumes (1930–1955), offer contemporary comments on Smibert's life and career. See also the Yale University Art Gallery exhibition catalog, *The Smibert Tradition* (1949); Theodore Bolton, "John Smibert: Notes and a Catalogue," *Fine Arts* (Aug. 1933): 11–15, 39–42; and Alan Burroughs, "Notes on Smibert's Development," *Art in America* 30, no. 2 (Apr. 1942): 109–21. Obituaries are in the *Boston News-Letter*, 4 Apr. 1751, and the *Boston Gazette*, 9 Apr. 1751.

MARTIN R. KALFATOVIC

SMILIE, John (16 Sept. 1742–29 Dec. 1812), revolutionary, Antifederalist, and congressman, was born in county Down, Ireland, the son of Thomas Smilie. His mother's name is unknown. In 1760 he immigrated to Lancaster County, Pennsylvania, where he attended public schools and engaged in self-education. Smilie married Jane Porter; they had three children. He supported himself and his family as a farmer.

Smilie strongly favored independence from Britain and was active in the revolutionary war from 1776 to 1777. He served as a private in the militia of Lancaster County Associators and participated in various political committees. A member of the Lancaster County Committee of Safety, he was a delegate to the Pennsylvania Provincial Conference of 18 June 1775 and of 18–24 June 1776. The 1776 Provincial Conference, which met at Carpenters Hall in Philadelphia, adopted a resolution supportive of "a vote in Congress declaring the United colonies free and independent States." This body also called for the convention of delegates who wrote the 1776 Pennsylvania constitution. In state politics, Smilie was a "radical," strongly supportive of the democratic values and institutions in the Pennsylvania constitution. This constitution placed virtually all governmental power in the hands of a unicameral legislature elected by manhood suffrage. The judiciary was subservient to the legislature, and executive functions were handled by the Supreme Executive Council, which eliminated the office of governor. The twelve-member council, consisting of a member from each county plus Philadelphia, was elected for three-year terms by the freemen. Smilie was elected to the Pennsylvania General Assembly in 1778 and 1779. During this period he supported adoption of the 1780 law providing for the gradual abolition of slavery in Pennsylvania. Near the end of the Revolution, Smilie moved to Westmoreland County, Pennsylvania, where he resided for the rest of his life. The part of Westmoreland where he lived was annexed to Fayette County in 1783.

After migrating to western Pennsylvania, Smilie was chosen to represent Westmoreland County as a delegate in the Pennsylvania Council of Censors, 1783–1784. The Council of Censors, elected by the freemen every seven years, had authority to examine the workings of the state government and make recommendations for amending the constitution by a two-thirds vote. The council also conducted a census of taxable population in order to reapportion representation in the unicameral legislature. Smilie vigorously defended the constitution of 1776 against Republicans who wished to amend it. Republicans desired repeal of the test acts, recharter of the Bank of North America, and strengthening of the central government by revising the Articles of Confederation. Smilie and other Constitutionalists favored test acts requiring every voter and officeholder to swear they would not "do any act . . . prejudicial or injurious to the constitution," opposed the Bank of North America, and wanted state sovereignty. Smilie led the successful effort to retain the unicameral legislature and the Supreme Executive Council provided in the Pennsylvania constitution of 1776.

Smilie served in the state house of representatives from 1784 to 1786 as one of the first delegates from Fayette County. In 1785 he battled against the Bank of North America, supporting revocation of the bank's charter. From April to June 1786, under the name "Atticus," he wrote four essays in the *Pennsylvania Packet and Daily Advertiser* (25 Apr., 8 May, 22 May, and 28 June) against the recharter of the Bank of North America. He opposed the bank because he saw it as a monopoly, he feared foreign influence in the bank, and he was concerned that the bank would exert undue influence on legislation and dictate to the assembly. Most of all he thought the bank threatened the republican ideal of equality.

On 2 November 1786 Smilie was elected to a term on the Supreme Executive Council from Fayette County. During this term, he was elected by the voters in Fayette County to the 1787 Pennsylvania ratification convention, where he was one of the three leading opponents of the proposed U.S. Constitution. With Robert Whitehill and William Findley, he condemned the plan as too much of a "consolidation" of power. It shifted too many powers to the central government, threatened to undermine the sovereignty of the states, and provided too little protection of citizens' liberties. He voted against ratification, favored Whitehill's list of proposed amendments to the Constitution, and signed the "Dissent of the Minority." Whitehill's proposed amendments included such items as freedom of conscience, liberty in matters of religion, trial by jury, rights of the accused, and protection against excessive bail or cruel punishments. Smilie also promoted freedom of speech and the press and sought limitation of central government power with protection of state sovereignty. Smilie, Findley, and Whitehill kept up their opposition to the Constitution even after it was ratified in Pennsylvania on 14 December 1787, but they also led the struggle from 1787 to 1791 to amend it with a bill of rights. During this period, Smilie attended the Harrisburg Convention of 1788, which aimed to recall Pennsylvania's ratification and promote a bill of rights.

Smilie was one of the three leading rural political leaders in Pennsylvania in the 1780s, along with Findley and Whitehill. Smilie's views on constitutional government changed over the course of the late colonial period to the early Republic, adjusting to public opinion changes in Pennsylvania and nationally from

1776 to 1788. At the state level he strongly defended the 1776 constitution but then served as a delegate to the state constitutional convention of 1789–1790, which radically transformed the state's system of government. The Supreme Executive Council was replaced by a governor, who held an executive veto. The 1790 constitution ended the unicameral assembly and established a bicameral legislature. In addition, the judiciary became independent of the legislature and served for life on good behavior. Smilie signed the 1790 Constitution, thus indicating his approval of the changes. Findley chaired the convention committee that wrote the plan, but Whitehill refused to sign it because it was too undemocratic. Elected to the state senate in 1790, Smilie strongly opposed the federal excise tax on whiskey in 1791 as despotic and unfair in a free society. He attended large public meetings in opposition to the excise at Redstone on 17 July 1791 and in Pittsburgh on 21–22 August 1792. George Clymer reported to Alexander Hamilton on 10 October 1792 that Smilie and Albert Gallatin were the leaders of the antiexcise movement in Fayette County. Smilie was considered a participant in the Whiskey Rebellion of 1794 in western Pennsylvania, but little evidence of his direct involvement exists. His son, Robert Smilie, was arrested and tried but released in the aftermath of the affair.

Though Smilie had opposed the U.S. Constitution, he later held office for many years in the Congress it created. He resigned from the state senate in 1792, when he was elected to the U.S. House of Representatives. He served in the Third Congress, 4 March 1793–3 March 1795. Between 1795 and 1799 he served in the state house of representatives from Fayette County. As a Jeffersonian Republican, he was elected to the Sixth through the Twelfth Congresses (4 Mar. 1799–3 Mar. 1813), and in 1796 he was a presidential elector. During part of his time in the House of Representatives, Smilie served as chairman of the Foreign Relations Committee. He voted with the Jeffersonian Republican majority in the Pennsylvania delegation in 80 percent of the votes he cast in Congress. He voted for nonimportation in 1806 and the embargo of 1807, saying the embargo and laws to enforce it were necessary to protect "our valuable national rights." He condemned the attack of the HMS *Leopard* on the USS *Chesapeake* on 22 June 1807, asserting that "wherever our armed ships are, there is our jurisdiction" and that the attack required "immediate retaliation." Smilie also voted for Macon's Bill #2 (which reopened trade with Britain and France), the April 1812 embargo, and the declaration of war on 18 June 1812. He was elected to Congress again in November 1812 but died in Washington, D.C., shortly afterward.

• Smilie's speeches opposing the Constitution in the Pa. ratification convention of 1787 are in Merrill Jensen, ed., *Ratification of the Constitution by the States: Pennsylvania* (1976). Smilie's role in the House of Representatives is followed in *The Debates and Proceedings in the Congress of the United States (1834–1856)* (1967). See Edward G. Everett, "John Smilie in Pennsylvania Politics" (M.A. thesis, Univ. of Pittsburgh, 1948); Everett, "John Smilie, Forgotten Champion of Early Western Pennsylvania," *Western Pennsylvania Historical Magazine* 33 (1950): 77–89; and Rodger C. Henderson, "John Smilie, Antifederalism, and the 'Dissent of the Minority', 1787–1788," *Western Pennsylvania Historical Magazine* 71 (1988): 235–61. An obituary is in the *Pittsburgh Mercury*, 14 Jan. 1813.

RODGER C. HENDERSON

SMILLIE, George Henry (29 Dec. 1840–10 Nov. 1921), landscape painter, was born in New York City, the son of the noted engraver James Smillie and Catherine van Valckenburg. Smillie's career was closely linked with that of his brother, James David Smillie, with whom he traveled to gather material for his paintings. Unlike his older brother, however, George Smillie was primarily a painter, making only a few excursions into printmaking. His works in oil and watercolor were based upon in situ drawings of exquisite sensitivity.

Although born into a family of artists, Smillie was first employed by a gas pipe manufacturing firm, apparently in some clerical capacity. He stayed there for about a year; then around 1860–1861 he entered the studio of the painter James McDougal Hart. He could not have been a raw beginner, for the next year, 1862, he exhibited two paintings at the National Academy of Design in New York City. From the age of twenty-two to the end of his life he supported himself by the sale of his works, supplemented by a little private teaching.

Smillie's brother, James David Smillie, returned from a tour of Europe in 1862 determined to give up commercial work in favor of fine art. The two young men shared adjacent studio rooms in Manhattan in winter, traveling in the summer to the Catskills, the Berkshire mountains of Massachusetts, and rural Pennsylvania. The brothers traveled and worked together, often helping each other prepare paintings for exhibit. Each had private pupils, and if one fell ill, the other took the students into his studio. Smillie sketched views that he developed into paintings during the winter months. His works quickly brought recognition. He was elected an associate of the National Academy in 1864, when he was twenty-four years old and had been painting professionally for less than three years.

Smillie's subject matter followed a familiar pattern. As taste for the nearby subjects like the Catskills faded, he and his brother began to travel farther and to seek wilder views. Smillie first painted the White Mountains in 1867, first visited the Adirondacks in 1868 (where he and his brother camped out on the Ausable Lakes), and traveled to the far West in the summer of 1871, visiting San Francisco, Yosemite, and the Rocky Mountains. Smillie's highly emotional impressions of the Rockies were published in *Appleton's Journal* in 1872. He wrote of Gray's Peak: "As we made one turn in the trail, we caught the first sight of our objective peak. . . . Crag and dizzy height rose one upon the other, till hid by the dazzling mantle of perpetual snow." From the peak he looked out at the landscape: "Deep, deep through that mysterious gloom came dim glimpses of the South Park. . . . On one side black clouds swept down into an unfathomable gulf, while just beyond rose majestic snowcaps radiant in the noonday sun." The article was illustrated by engravings after some of the many oils and watercolors he painted on the trip.

Smillie's placid landscapes fell from style, contributing to his declining sales in the 1870s. After a serious breakdown, he returned to prominence in 1879 when he sent to the National Academy *Goat Pasture*, a somber painting executed with much more vigorous brushwork than his previous works (unlocated; a study is in a private collection). That same year the American Water-Color Society elected him treasurer. The award of such offices constituted recognition of artistic merit.

Smillie soon added rich colors to his new, freer style. His paintings from 1880 onward are lively mood pieces rather than meticulous descriptions of specific sites. Often the foreground is an open plane, so that surface is stressed rather than perspective. However, his apparent impressionistic vision is still based upon careful observation; preliminary drawings are always precise and accurate. A trip to France and England in 1884 enabled Smillie to see the works of French Barbizon painters, but records of the trip show that he spent most of his time with American expatriate artists. The impressionists are never mentioned.

Smillie married Helen "Nellie" Sheldon Jacobs in 1881. A talented artist herself, she had been a student at the Cooper Union in New York City before she entered Smillie's brother's studio. She continued to paint—largely exquisite floral still lifes—despite the birth of three sons. The Smillie family lived in New York City; in Ridgefield, Connecticut; and, eventually, in a house in Lawrence Park, Bronxville, New York, one of the first planned artists' communities in the United States. In this period Smillie painted some of his finest works, such as *Light and Shadow along the Shore* (1885–1887, Union League Club, Philadelphia, Pa.), a large, almost abstract depiction of the Massachusetts coast near Marblehead, and *Springtime in Westchester* (1912, Joslyn Art Museum, Nebr.), a work in Smillie's last style that has a warmer palette and less austere appearance than *Light and Shadow*. He also lectured on art at local clubs and libraries and contributed short articles on composition and expression to the local newspapers.

After his brother's death in 1909, Smillie finished some of James's canvases and assembled paintings and prints for a memorial exhibition in 1910 at the Century Club in New York City. *The Rise of the River* (Montclair Art Museum, N.J.) was begun by James in 1901 and completed by George in 1915. Both artists signed the painting. Smillie died in Bronxville.

• A brief unpublished autobiography is in *Autobiographies of Modern Artists* (c. 1910), Stevens Collection, Archives of American Art. He is referred to repeatedly in his brother's diaries, also in the Archives of American Art. Little has been written about Smillie; he is frequently mentioned in discussions of his father's and his brother's work. Toward the end of his life Smillie frequently contributed essays on art to New York City newspapers. His angry reaction to the Armory show appeared in the *New York Evening Sun*, 4 Apr. 1913. Smillie published "From Denver to Gray's Peak," an account of his Western journeys, in *Appletons' Journal* 7, no. 154 (9 Mar. 1872). His works were reproduced in the *Art Journal*, *Harper's Weekly*, and catalogs of the American Water-Color Society between 1879 and 1883. His painting *East Hampton Meadows* is illustrated in Ronald G. Pisano, *Long Island Landscape Painting 1820–1920* (1985). Other paintings are included in the catalogs of the Metropolitan Museum of New York and the Union League Club of Philadelphia. See also Brucia Witthoft, "George Smillie: The Life of an Artist," *American Art Review* 5, no. 1 (Summer 1992): 120–45, and Loretta Hoagland, *Lawrence Park. Bronxville's Turn-of-the-Century Art Colony* (1994).

BRUCIA WITTHOFT

SMILLIE, James (23 Nov. 1807–4 Dec. 1885), pictorial engraver, was born in Edinburgh, Scotland, the son of David Smillie, a jeweler and mineralogist, and Elizabeth Cumming. James Smillie's father was a skilled craftsman but an irresponsible businessman. In 1815, offered a chance to voyage to the Faro Islands, David Smillie left his shop in the hands of his brother-in-law and departed. The business failed, the family was reduced to poverty, and James's brief formal schooling came to an end. In 1817 the Smillies moved to Portobello. The rural atmosphere had an important influence on young James, who remembered it with pleasure all his life, leading him to settle later in life in quiet Poughkeepsie, New York. When the family returned to Edinburgh, young James was apprenticed to a silver engraver, James Johnston, where he began to draw but learned little of his future trade.

David Smillie moved his family to Quebec in 1821, joining a brother. Injured in a fall on shipboard, the father was unable to support his family, and young James worked in a bakery making mutton pies. In the baker's back room he taught himself to engrave on copper, producing a few visiting cards and inscribed rings. His copies of English prints brought him to the attention of Lord Dalhousie, the governor of Quebec, who was instrumental in helping him sail for London to further his skills as a pictorial engraver. In Smillie's autobiography, *A Pilgrimage*, he recorded the conflict he felt between his happy anticipation of the trip and the knowledge that his father lay dying and his family was living in poverty.

Smillie arrived in London knowing no one. None of the engravers there would take him on; an interview with the elderly John Landseer foundered over the famed engraver's deafness. Smillie continued on to Scotland, where he learned of his father's death. He entered the Edinburgh shop of Andrew Wilson, according to the autobiography "a man of very moderate talents as an engraver but he was good and kind."

In 1828 Smillie returned to Quebec, his brief apprenticeship leaving him more skilled in his art than anyone else in that city. He engraved fifteen views for the Reverend George Bourne's *Picture of Quebec*. Discovering that no Canadian printer could publish his images, he made his first trip to New York City, where in 1829 a competent printer was easily found. This was the first of several short trips to the United States that preceded his settling in New York.

The event that led to Smillie's career in America was his meeting with Robert W. Weir, the American painter and later professor of drawing at the U.S. Military Academy at West Point. In 1830 Weir invited Smillie to engrave his latest painting, *The Convent Gate*, and offered him a room in the attic of his Manhattan home as a place to work. Through Weir, Smillie met Asher B. Durand, whose subsequent fame as a painter has obscured his importance as a pictorial and bank-note engraver. Smillie successfully engraved a second work by Weir, *The Ruins of Old Fort Putnam*, for Durand's projected *American Landscape*. After a brief, homesick return to Quebec, Smillie returned to Manhattan, sent for his mother and sisters, and worked on engraving Bourne's *Views of New York*.

In 1831 Smillie became a partner of George W. Hatch, the first of several alliances with various commercial engravers. Until the 1870s private firms designed and printed the bank notes that were circulated as currency, and designs for monies were among the most lucrative if not the most interesting work of the engraver. Smillie's first engraving after Thomas Cole, a copper plate depicting *The Garden of Eden* (1831), was of far greater artistic importance.

Smillie was elected an associate of the National Academy of Design in 1832. The same year he married Catharine (or Katharine) Van Valkenburgh of Lexington, New York. Their long and happy marriage yielded seven children: James David Smillie and George Henry Smillie became professional artists, William Main Smillie became a skilled letter engraver, and Charles Francis Smillie became a fine amateur photographer. The family lived in Manhattan during these years, and Smillie had so much work that he sent off to Scotland for a journeyman assistant, Robert Hinshelwood. Smillie was responsible for all the engravings for the *New York Mirror* and produced illustrations for numerous books and magazines, including *Graham's Magazine*, the *Token* (Boston), and various religious tracts. In 1840 he became a partner in the bank-note firm of Rawdon, Wright, and Hatch, expanding the company's activities to include pictorial engraving.

Smillie's engraved bank notes were the mainstay of his income, but his interest lay in more complex pictorial commissions. His beautiful small landscapes after Durand, Casilear, and others appeared in numerous periodicals. More important—and, for the artist, more challenging—were the large engravings after Thomas Cole's four allegorical paintings, *The Voyage of Life*, commissioned by their owner, educator Gorham D. Abbott. Smillie first engraved *Youth* for the American Art-Union in 1848. The engraving was markedly popular, and, after the set of paintings passed into Abbott's possession, Smillie recut *Youth* and engraved *Childhood* (1853), *Manhood* (1855), and *Old Age* (1856) on plates measuring 15 by 23 inches. Perhaps influenced by the success of *Youth*, the National Academy elected Smillie to full membership effective in 1852.

In 1857 Smillie contracted with the *Lady's Repository*, a Methodist periodical published in Cincinnati, to provide engravings after contemporary paintings of his choice. He greatly enjoyed the artistic liberty this gave him but found that the pay did not compensate him for the amount of work involved. Therefore, in 1861 he accepted an offer from the new American Bank-Note Engraving Company to work for them for a salary of $2,500 plus stock, beginning a long association that ended only when he died.

Smillie and his oldest son James David spent much of 1862 in Europe. Shortly after his return he undertook his last major commission, the engraving of Albert Bierstadt's *The Rocky Mountains*. Smillie spent more than three years engraving Bierstadt's very large painting (now in the Metropolitan Museum of Art, it measures 73½ by 120¾ inches) on a steel plate 17 by 28 inches in size. A series of trial proofs in the New York Public Library attests to the complex and meticulous techniques of a perfectionist. The work combines line engraving, etching, and aquatint to make texture serve all the functions that color provided in Bierstadt's original. Despite our present appreciation of the work, Smillie found the Bierstadt commission frustrating. He thought the plate lacked finish, as the painting was taken to England before he could look at it sufficiently. In his autobiography Smillie wrote, "I gave up [that is, turned over to Bierstadt] my plate completely disgusted. . . . after two full years of incessant labor, I had the mortification of leaving it in a condition that, every time I look upon it I am filled with a thousand regrets" (*A Pilgrimage*, p. 94). It was this disappointment that convinced him he had no future as a pictorial engraver: "I had had my last chance and that had proved a failure" (p. 94).

Smillie moved to Poughkeepsie, in New York, in 1874, setting up a studio in his house, where he continued to engrave the small and less-demanding vignettes for the American Bank-Note Company on a freelance basis. Failing health gradually reduced his activity. His last work, an engraving after Rosa Bonheur's *Family of Lions*, was completed after his death by his son James David. He died at home in Poughkeepsie.

Smillie's work displayed the highest technical and artistic standards in steel engraving. His pictures served an important function in disseminating knowledge of the works of contemporary artists into homes of modest means, providing the middle classes with the characteristic engraved images that decorated the formal parlor and stairwell in the nineteenth-century home.

• A copy of Smillie's holograph autobiography is in the Archives of American Art, Smithsonian Institution, Washington, D.C. The early sections, dealing with Scotland and Canada, are published in Mary Macaulay Allodi and Rosemarie

L. Tovell, *An Engraver's Pilgrimage: James Smillie in Quebec, 1821–1830* (1989). Several accounts of Smillie's life and work as a bank-note engraver are in periodicals dealing with commercial engraving, among them Thomas Morris's four-part "James Smillie" in the 1944 *Essay-Proof Journal*, no. 2: 67–74, no. 3: 133–41, no. 4: 199–207, and no. 5: 19–25; and Glenn B. Smedley, "The Smillie Family: American Engravers and Painters," *Numismatist* 71 (July 1958): 771–80. Smillie is listed in David McNeely Stauffer, *American Engravers* (1907; repr. 1964). An outline of the development of the bank-note industry can be found in Robert Noxon Toppan, *100 Years of Bank-Note Engraving in the United States* (1896). Paul D. Schweizer, "'So Exquisite a Transcript': James Smillie's Engravings after Cole's *Voyage of Life*," pt. 1, *Imprint* 11, no. 2 (Autumn 1986): 2–13; pt. 2, *Imprint* 12, no. 1 (Spring 1987): 13–24, deals with a major commission, as does Brucia Witthoft, "The History of James Smillie's Engraving after Albert Bierstadt's *The Rocky Mountains*," *American Art Journal* 19, no. 2 (1987): 40–51. There are many references to James Smillie in the unpublished diary of his son James David Smillie in the Archives of American Art.

BRUCIA WITTHOFT

SMILLIE, James David (16 Jan. 1833–14 Sept. 1909), etcher, engraver, and painter, was born in New York City, the son of James Smillie, an engraver, and Catharine (or Katharine) Van Valkenburgh. He learned printmaking techniques in early childhood: his first attempt at etching, carefully preserved by his father, dates to his seventh year. He worked as his father's assistant in his teens but seems to have had ambitions beyond reproductive engraving (based on paintings) from an early age. He prepared several drawings for his father's engravings of Greenwood Cemetery (1847) and first exhibited a drawing, *The Washington Monument*, at the National Academy when he was twenty. He first appears in the employee records of the American Bank-Note Company in 1859. A trip to Europe in 1862 inspired him with the determination to become a painter rather than a commercial artist.

Smillie continued to engrave pictorial vignettes for the bank-note industry for many years, but after 1862 he worked primarily as a painter, sharing a studio with his younger brother George Henry Smillie in Manhattan. The brothers spent their summers gathering material for landscapes depicting the Berkshires, the Catskills, and eventually the White Mountains and the Far West. The finished works were prepared in the studio during the winter for exhibition at the National Academy of Design and elsewhere. Smillie was elected an associate of the academy in 1865 and a full member in 1876.

Smillie never attended formal classes in art and acquired his technical knowledge haphazardly. Undoubtedly his acquaintance with prominent artists like illustrator Felix O. C. Darley and landscapist John William Casilaer, both of whom made the transition from commercial to fine art, helped him acquire both the skills and the self-confidence to concentrate on fine arts. His close relationship with George led to a friendly competition from which both brothers benefited. In addition to the sale of works in oil and watercolor, both took private pupils and taught sketching and

painting. Commercial engraving provided more than half of James David's income, however, until well into the 1870s.

Smillie's trip to the Far West in 1871 provided material for a decade of paintings. A fine writer, he was the only artist to write his own text for an article in *Picturesque America*, William Cullen Bryant's great celebration of the American landscape published in 1872–1874. Smillie wrote "The Yosemite Falls" and drew the designs for both that chapter and "St. Lawrence and the Saguenay."

Smillie's work as an arts administrator occupied much of his time in mid-career. He headed the watercolor committee for the exhibition at the Philadelphia Centennial of 1876, frequently served on the hanging committee for the National Academy's annual exhibits, and served that organization as treasurer for several terms. He also held offices in the American Water Color Society. His most important contribution to the organization of the arts, however, was his central role in founding in 1877 the first professional fine-arts printmaking society in the United States, the New-York Etching Club.

The "etching revival," which first appeared in France and England in the mid-nineteenth century, reached America after the Civil War. A few pioneers had used the medium, and Smillie had tried to found a group in 1870, but there was so little response that the attempt foundered. By 1877 interest in the medium had grown. Sixteen artists showed up for a first meeting at Smillie's studio. Here his expertise as an engraver and printer was a vital asset to the success of the etching movement. For some of those attending, this was their first look at the medium. Smillie ground a small plate, Sanford R. Gifford drew on it, and Leroy Yale printed it. By the end of the evening the enthusiastic group had elected officers, and the etching revival was under way.

Smillie married Anna "Annie" Clinch Cook in 1881. Cook came from a wealthy family, and so the artist no longer needed to support himself; major expenses, such as the purchase of a house in Manhattan and the building of an elegant summer residence in Montrose, Pennsylvania, were paid for by his wife. His income from prints and paintings, which had been adequate for a bachelor, had never been on the scale needed to maintain a place in New York society.

In the 1880s and 1890s Smillie devoted most of his artistic activity to printmaking. Three-quarters of his etchings date from these two decades. He was an incessant experimenter, using a great variety of aquatint tones, exploring mezzotint, and even trying out a new substance—celluloid—for etching plates. The subjects of his reproductive etchings included works by Jonathan Eastman Johnson, Lawrence Alma-Tadema, and Daniel Huntington. His original etchings include landscapes, genre scenes, and experimental floral images. Views of "Yo-Semite" were based on his western trip of 1871. A trip to Europe in 1893 yielded etchings of scenes in France and northern Italy. In 1894 he taught the first classes in etching ever offered at the

National Academy, where Ernest Roth and Maurice Sterne were among his students.

His wife's untimely death from pneumonia in 1895 was a devastating blow from which Smillie never fully recovered. He was left alone to bring up their two young sons. Shortly before his wife's death Smillie had agreed to purchase a studio in Sniffen Court, 156 East Thirty-sixth Street, a former stable celebrated as an early example of Romanesque revival architecture. He also built a summer cottage on land he had long owned in the Adirondack Mountains of New York. Despite bouts of depression he continued to produce a small number of etchings and paintings and to volunteer as an officer or administrator for arts organizations. When the New York Public Library moved to its new building on Fifth Avenue, he helped design the print storage areas.

Toward the end of his life he cataloged his collection of his and his father's prints, including many trial proofs, for the New York Public Library. This invaluable collection of study materials is marked with a small monogram stamp. The orderly habits of mind that he had learned from his father enabled him to leave an invaluable body of documentation about the life and works of nineteenth-century printmakers. The year after Smillie's death in New York City, his brother George organized a memorial exhibition at the Century Association that displayed the breadth and quality of his life's work.

• Smillie's diaries, 1865–1909, consisting of forty-five small leather-bound volumes, are the primary source for information about the events of his life. They belong to the Archives of American Art and are available on Archives of American Art microfilm rolls 2849–53. A typescript essay, Rena van Scoten, "James David Smillie, the Artist" (1947), with added notes by Dana A. Watrous, is in the Susquehanna County Historical Society and Free Library, Montrose, Pa. Smillie's own essays on etching were published in various catalogs of the New-York Etching Club between 1882 and 1893. His description of Yosemite appeared in *Picturesque America*, ed. William Cullen Bryant (2 vols., 1872–1874). Published works on the artist include the Century Association, *Some Works by James David Smillie, N.A.* (1910; catalog of the memorial exhibition); and Rona Schneider, "The Career of James David Smillie (1833–1909) as Revealed in His Diaries," *American Art Journal* 16, no. 1 (Winter 1984): 4–33. Brucia Witthoft, *The Fine-Arts Etchings of James David Smillie, 1833–1909: A Catalogue Raisonné* (1992), includes an extensive bibliography. Smillie's works were frequently discussed in nineteenth-century art periodicals such as the *Studio* (American ed.), 12 Jan. 1884, pp. 140–41. Patricia Mandel, "A Look at the New-York Etching Club 1877–1894," *Imprint* 4, no. 1 (Apr. 1979): 31–36, describes Smillie's role in the formation of that organization. J. R. W. Hitchcock, Frederick Keppel, Ernest Knaufft, and Sylvester Rosa Koehler included his prints in a number of etching portfolios issued in the 1880s; Koehler wrote an appreciation of Smillie's work in "The Works of American Etchers. 12. James David Smillie," *American Art Review* 1, no. 12 (Oct. 1888): 524–25. Obituaries are in the *New York Times*, 15 Sept. 1909, and *American Art News*, 20 Sept. 1909.

BRUCIA WITTHOFT

SMILLIE, Ralph (8 July 1887–16 Feb. 1960), civil engineer, was born in Montrose, Pennsylvania, the son of James David Smillie, an artist, and Anna C. Cook. He received his B.A. from Yale University in 1909 and his B.S. in civil engineering from Columbia University in 1912. In 1915 he was granted an M.S. from Yale.

Smillie started his career as a resident engineer in charge of steel plate construction and various other assignments for the New York City subway system and then worked for the navy during World War I. In 1919 he became assistant engineer of design for the Holland Tunnel. He worked on this project for nearly a decade, rising to the post of engineer of design by the time the tunnel was opened in 1927. In 1929 he became transit engineer for the city of Newark, New Jersey. Smillie married Grace Cooley; they had three children.

At its inception in 1919, the Holland Tunnel was the world's first vehicular highway to be constructed under a river. Smillie joined a team with a formidable task—to design a tunnel under the Hudson River, connecting New York City and Hoboken, New Jersey. Two gigantic cast-iron tubes, each nearly two miles in length, had to be constructed through the silt, sand, gravel, and rock sixty feet below the mean low tide line of the Hudson. Throughout their length, the air needed to be changed minute by minute to avoid the buildup of lethal carbon monoxide gas. From the outset, it was this problem of ventilation that posed the most difficult engineering challenge, requiring an innovative combination of scientific principles and experimental techniques.

Previously, tunnel ventilation had been effected by the simple process of forcing air in at one portal and out through the other, but using that method in the Holland tubes would have resulted in very high wind velocity. Instead, the Holland team developed an elaborate ventilating plant housed in four shafts, five stories high, constructed on top of caissons sunk on either side of the Hudson. From these shafts, powerful blower fans forced fresh air into the tunnel through flues in the lower part of the roadway, while exhaust fans drew noxious air from ducts in the ceiling; the air in the active tunnel was completely changed every minute and a quarter. The expertise acquired by Smillie on this project made him one of the nation's foremost tunnel experts during the middle decades of the twentieth century.

Shortly after the Holland Tunnel opened to traffic in 1927, and while the George Washington Bridge was still under construction (it opened in 1932), it became apparent to city planners that a third highway linking New York City and New Jersey would be necessary to accommodate the increase in vehicular traffic across the Hudson. Smillie was chosen as chief of design for the original twin-tubes of the Lincoln Tunnel, construction of which started in 1934. Smillie's design skills stamped the character of the new tunnel, located seven miles south of the George Washington Bridge and three miles north of the Holland Tunnel. It quickly became the center of cross-river traffic within the greater New York City metropolitan area. Although in general the design of the Lincoln Tunnel followed some principles developed for the Holland Tunnel—which, in Smillie's view "served as a valuable laboratory and proving ground where many new features were tested under actual operating conditions before being incorporated in the design of the Lincoln Tunnel" (Smillie [1937]: 551)—Smillie developed a number of new methods of construction. These concerned, most notably, increased diameter of the tubes and wider roadways, more effective waterproofing material used in surfacing for roadways and walls, the use of glass tile for ceilings, and improvements in ventilation to deal more effectively with traffic jams or fire. The first, or south, tube was opened in 1937, but the north bore was not put into service until 1945, its construction having been delayed by World War II. Smillie was reengaged by the Port Authority to oversee the construction of the third Lincoln tube; when it went into service in May 1957, it represented the first major postwar breakthrough in ameliorating the New York–New Jersey traffic bottleneck.

In 1945 Smillie was appointed chief engineer for New York's Triborough Bridge and Tunnel Authority. His main project during the next five years was overseeing the construction of the Brooklyn-Battery Tunnel connecting Brooklyn with Manhattan, which, at more than 9,100 feet, was to be one of the longest vehicular tunnels in the United States. Other projects he supervised included the Sumner Vehicular Tunnel under Boston harbor; the Bankhead Vehicular Tunnel under the Mobile River at Mobile, Alabama; seven vehicular rock tunnels under the Allegheny Mountains for the Pennsylvania Turnpike; and the Washburn Vehicular Tunnel at Houston, Texas. He was also a consulting engineer on a large number of other tunnels and depressed highway projects in the United States, as well as several in Canada and Venezuela.

A partner in Smillie and Griffin, a consulting engineering firm, Smillie was a member of the American Society of Civil Engineers. A soft-spoken man, he was known affectionately and respectfully by his subordinates and workers as "Lemondrop." At the time of his death at Mountainside Hospital, Montclair, New Jersey, Smillie was widely regarded as a leading figure in the field of tunnel design, both in the United States and internationally.

• Smillie offered an informative account, "Design Features of the Lincoln Tunnel," *Civil Engineering* 7 (Aug. 1937): 547–51. O. H. Ammann, chief engineer of the Port of New York Authority, wrote a companion piece in the same journal, "Planning the Lincoln Tunnel under the Hudson: General Conception and Development of Vehicular Tube Connection to New York City," 7 (June 1937): 387–91. The significance of the Holland Tunnel, particularly with respect to the problems overcome in its construction, is examined in Marion T. Colley, "A Highway under the Hudson: A Great New Bridge Built under a River," *World's Work* 54 (1927): 554–62. Major sources on Smillie's career are articles in the *New York Times* during the 1940s and 1950s. An obituary is in the *New York Times*, 17 Feb. 1960.

MARTIN FICHMAN

SMITH, Al. (1873–1944). *See* Smith, Alfred E.

SMITH, Al (2 Mar. 1902–24 Nov. 1986), cartoonist, was born Albert Schmidt in Brooklyn, New York, the son of Henry Schmidt and Josephine Dice. After attending public schools, he started in newspapering as a copy boy for the *New York Sun*, leaving within a year for the *New York World*, where he followed the traditional apprenticeship route from copy boy to cartoonist: first, he was permitted to assist other cartoonists, then he drew an occasional fill-in cartoon, and eventually he graduated to his own regular cartoon. *From 9 to 5*, a panel cartoon about office life, was syndicated by the *World* until the newspaper folded in 1931. United Feature Syndicate continued the feature for a short time, but when it ceased, Smith freelanced, doing artwork for various clients, including the Works Progress Administration and John Wheeler's Bell Syndicate. In 1932 Wheeler and cartoonist Bud Fisher approached Smith about ghosting Fisher's celebrated comic strip, *Mutt and Jeff* (which had been written and drawn for the previous fourteen years by Ed Mack).

Smith conducted the classic strip without much interference from the flamboyant and heavy-drinking Fisher, and he soon revamped it to suit his own comedic sensibilities. Mutt became less a racetrack tout and sporting enthusiast and more a paterfamilias and breadwinner. The habitual gambler was thoroughly domesticated, and the strip focused on his frustrations as husband and father, with occasional forays into various entrepreneurial schemes. In these schemes, the lanky Mutt was usually joined by the diminutive Jeff, whose dim-witted but entirely innocent bumbling inevitably upset Mutt's plans, leaving them both as broke as ever. When not working with Mutt in some enterprise, Jeff went happily on his way, blundering through life in his own uniquely demented fashion (which often proved to be the sanest). Smith's penchant for humorous animal antics yielded a secondary strip, *Cicero's Cat* (about the cat that belonged to Mutt's son), in a feature that ran at the top of the *Mutt and Jeff* Sunday page. After Fisher's death in 1954, Smith was permitted to sign his own name to the strip, which he continued to do until he retired in 1981, having produced the feature over four times longer than its creator did.

Smith's graphic style was more polished than that of his several ghostly predecessors on the strip, but he nonetheless preserved the turn-of-the-century feel of the visuals. By the end of the 1930s, the faces and anatomy of his cast had crystallized into static doodles, stylized approximations of human appearance, embellished by the crosshatching and shading techniques of the earlier era.

Smith married Erna Anna Strasser in 1921, as he launched into his cartooning career; they had three children. In 1950 he inaugurated his own feature syndicate, the Smith Service, to provide comic strips and cartoons to weekly newspapers. For this purpose, Smith produced two features, *Rural Delivery* and *Re-*

member When. Other similarly folksy offerings included *Down Main Street* by Joe Dennett and *Pops* by George Wolfe.

Active in the National Cartoonists Society, Smith held several offices (treasurer for nine years) before being elected president (1967–1969). In 1968 his NCS colleagues awarded him the organization's trophy for the year's best humor strip for *Mutt and Jeff*. He died in Rutland, Vermont.

• Although Al Smith is associated with one of the medium's most historic creations, his association began after *Mutt and Jeff* had made its signal contribution to the medium by establishing the daily "strip" format, and Smith's connection was anonymous for the earliest portion of his tenure on the feature when the strip was still famous. Perhaps for these reasons, his name is barely mentioned in most histories of the medium. His life and career receive their due only in Maurice Horn's often error-laden *World Encyclopedia of Comics* (1976).

ROBERT C. HARVEY

SMITH, Alban Gilpin (22 Mar. 1795–5 Aug. 1861), physician and medical educator, was born near Wilmington, Delaware, the son of Samuel Smith and Lydia Gilpin. Little is known of his parents, who, after brief residencies elsewhere, from 1797 permanently resided in Philadelphia.

Smith's formal schooling was obtained at Westtown, Pennsylvania, from January 1809 until April 1810. This precluded his being present at Dr. Ephraim McDowell's now famous ovariotomy in Danville, Kentucky, on 25 December 1809, when McDowell first successfully opened the abdominal (peritoneal) cavity and removed a large ovarian tumor. Identifying Smith's lack of education, the vituperous Daniel Drake, M.D., observed in a *Western Journal of Medical and Physical Sciences* editorial, "[Smith] is profoundly ignorant of the grammar and orthography of his mother tongue" (11, no. 41 [1837], p. 164).

After completing his apprenticeship (date unknown), Smith's whereabouts are undetermined until 27 September 1815, when having begun to practice medicine in Port Tobacco, Maryland, he requested transfer of his membership in the South Philadelphia (Quaker) Monthly Meeting to the Alexandria (Va.) Monthly Meeting (granted 21 Dec. 1815). In Port Tobacco, he met and married in 1817 Taliaferro H. Middleton, who was not a member of the Society of Friends. This alliance resulted in Alban's removal from the Alexandria Monthly Meeting in April 1818. Three of the couple's seven children lived to maturity.

Smith left his medical practice in 1821 to further his medical education in Philadelphia. His choice of private medical lectures conducted by the Quaker physician Joseph Parrish at the Philadelphia Alms House had several advantages. The lectures were less expensive than attending the university, they were conducted in the summer months, didactic lectures were supplemented by clinical cases in Parrish's extensive practice, and surgical operations could be observed in the hospital.

In 1822 Smith returned to Danville to practice until 1826 as a partner with his former preceptor, McDowell. Practicing with this widely known surgeon and lithotomist, Smith had opportunity to cultivate his surgical skills, performing the third successful ovariotomy in the world in May 1823. Around 1827 he performed the first documented laminectomy (removing portions of the vertebrae) for treatment of fracture of the spine with paralysis below the shoulders. Although full function did not return to the patient's extremities, Smith's operation demonstrated that fractured vertebrae could be surgically exposed even if treatment of the injured spinal cord was not yet understood. Smith received an academic appointment in 1823 as professor of chemistry at Centre College in Danville.

In mid-1829, Smith traveled to Paris to study Jean Civiale's technique of crushing stones in the bladder without subjecting the patient to the more hazardous surgical procedure of "cutting for stone." Returning to the United States in December 1830, he stopped in Philadelphia to visit family and chanced to meet Daniel Drake, physician and editor of the *Western Journal of Medical and Physical Sciences*, who requested him to comment on Civiale's instruments and techniques for his journal. Smith complied with the request in a letter dated 2 December 1830, which was published in the *Journal* the following year. Soon after his return to Danville, Smith performed the first lithotrity—the crushing of a bladder stone with an instrument, requiring no surgical incision—in the western country.

Seeking greater opportunity for exercising his surgical skills, Smith in 1831 moved to Louisville, Kentucky, where he was soon appointed to the surgical staff of Louisville's public hospital, the only such hospital in Kentucky. While in Danville, Smith had inquired unsuccessfully about establishing a medical department at Centre College. In the larger city of Louisville, Smith was able to obtain a charter in 1833 for the Louisville Medical Institute, naming himself and eight other local physicians as incorporators. Modifications of the charter were made in 1835 and 1836 that finally designated a lay board of managers who were empowered to select a medical faculty and to operate the school. This board ultimately gathered the necessary funds to launch the new institute in 1837.

Discouraged by the delays encountered with the first charter, Smith in 1833 accepted an appointment as professor of surgery at the Medical College of Ohio in Cincinnati. Soon after his arrival, a polemical history of the institution, attributed to Smith but unsigned, was published serially and then as a pamphlet extra of the *Cincinnati Whig and Commercial Intelligencer* (1835). After several more years in an unfavorable medico-political climate, having been accused of causing the Medical College of Ohio to deteriorate, he accepted an appointment in 1837 to the chair of surgery in the College of Physicians and Surgeons of the University of the State of New York in New York City. During his residence in Cincinnati, Smith became a member of an informal group of young artists whose talents he recognized and whose development he encouraged over a decade or more, even after leaving Ohio. Smith, apparently a developing miniaturist while in Cincinnati, became an able painter and provided illustrations for one of his texts.

Later in 1837 Smith resigned his appointment at the College of Physicians and Surgeons after only two sessions, thereafter continuing private surgical practice in New York City. Soon after his resignation, Smith petitioned the Legislature of the State of New York, then convened in its sixty-second session, to change his surname to Goldsmith, for reasons that are unknown. The petition was granted in 1839. After the death of his wife, Goldsmith in 1845 married Ann Higby.

Smith was a multitalented individual whose professional attainments were confined to the fringe of greatness. While in addition to his achievements as a surgeon and anatomist, he obtained the first charter for the Louisville Medical Institute in 1833, he became too impatient to remain in Louisville to effect the necessary revisions of charters before the school could convene its first class four years later. After leaving the faculty of the College of Physicians and Surgeons, he focused his attentions on genito-urinary surgery, developing a successful specialty practice and publishing two small books: *Lithotripsy of the Breaking of Stone in the Bladder* (1843) and *Diseases of the Genito-Urinary Organs* (1857). He continued to practice until his death, in Barrytown, New York.

• Smith's five extant letters in the Hiram Powers Papers in the Cincinnati Historical Society are related to art and artists rather than medicine. His contributions to surgery appearing in *North American Medical and Surgical Journal* 1 (1826): 30–38, and 8 (1829): 94–97 are reviewed in S. D. Gross, *Report on Kentucky Surgery, Read Before the Kentucky State Medical Society, at Its Annual Meeting at Louisville, October 20, 1852* (1853), pp. 16, 74, and 106. The original charter of the Louisville Medical Institute appears in *Acts Passed at the First Session of the Forty-First General Assembly for the Commonwealth of Kentucky* (1833), pp. 300–1. A summary of his life and work appears in Eugene H. Conner, "Alban Gilpin Smith (Alban Goldsmith), M.D." *Journal of the History of Medicine and Allied Sciences* 32 (1977): 205–10. An obituary is in the *(Rondout, N.Y.) Courier*, 8 Aug. 1861.

EUGENE H. CONNER

SMITH, Alexander (28 Jan. 1874–20 Apr. 1930), professional golfer, was born in Carnoustie, Scotland, the son of John Smith, a golf course greenkeeper, and Johann Robertson. Smith, commonly known as Alex, was one of five brothers who became golf professionals, the others being Willie, George, Jimmy, and Macdonald. Following a basic education, he became an apprentice blacksmith and acquired skills that led naturally into clubmaking. Golf did not come easily to Smith, but his game began to improve in the mid-1890s, and he served as the professional at Luton and St. Neots golf clubs. By 1895 Smith married Jessie Maiden, with whom he had two children. He returned to Carnoustie in 1897 as foreman of Bob Simpson's clubmaking shop. After several victories in local competitions, he left for the United States in 1898 with four professionals from St. Andrews to join the staff at Washington Park Golf Club in Chicago. He was said to be the first of an estimated three hundred "men of Carnoustie" who soon came to occupy positions as golf professionals throughout the world.

In the early days of American golf, tournaments had small purses, and the frequent practice of "syndicating"—splitting winnings with at least one other golfer to ensure that expenses would be covered—limited the financial attraction of competitive careers. Professionals therefore used tournaments primarily as a means to attract more lucrative exhibition matches and to gain better positions at the proliferating number of country clubs where their skills as clubmakers and teachers were in great demand. Smith amassed many victories on the irregular tournament circuit that sprang up throughout the country. Haphazard recordkeeping and reporting were often unreliable, but among his most notable titles were two Western opens—the country's second most prestigious championship (1903, 1906), four Metropolitan opens (1905, 1909, 1910, 1913), three Eastern Professional Golfers Association championships (1906, 1909, 1911), three California opens before 1907 (dates unknown), and at least two Florida championships (1907, 1911).

Smith's most significant performances, however, came in the U.S. Open. He finished second in 1898 and in 1901, when he lost a playoff, 85–86, to fellow Scot and eventual four-time U.S. Open champion Willie Anderson, at the fiendishly penal Myopia Hunt Club in South Hamilton, Massachusetts, after firing the tournament's low score of 80 in the final round. He then finished fourth in 1903 and second in 1905 (despite a severe attack of malaria). He broke through with a victory in 1906 at Onwentsia in Lake Forest, Illinois, thus matching the triumph of his brother Willie in 1899 and making them the first and, as of the late 1990s, the only brothers to win the U.S. Open. Smith's four-round total of 295, including a remarkable closing round of 75 in a driving rainstorm, marked the first time that 300 had been broken in the championship and was seven shots better than runner-up Willie Smith's score. Strong third-place showings in 1908 (when Willie Smith lost a playoff for the title) and 1909 followed. In 1910 Smith was tied with his youngest brother, Macdonald, and Johnny McDermott at 298 after the four rounds at Philadelphia Cricket Club. He won the playoff with a 71, besting McDermott's 75 and Macdonald Smith's 77. Smith's prize was $300 and a gold medal. He again finished third in 1912. In 1921 when he was approaching age fifty, he tied for fifth with the new, eighteen-year-old star Bobby Jones, demonstrating that the high scores of the early golfers were more a reflection of the primitive courses and equipment with which they had to contend than a true measure of their ability.

These impressive showings enabled Smith to move from Washington Park in Chicago to some of the country's most exclusive clubs, including the Nassau Country Club in Glen Cove, New York, in 1901, Wykagyl in New Rochelle, New York, in 1909, and

Shenecossett in New London, Connecticut, in 1920. Beginning in 1925 he split his professional duties between Shenecossett and the new Westchester Biltmore Country Club at Rye, New York, during the summers, and he switched his winter affiliation from Florida's Belleair Country Club, near Tampa, to the Miami Biltmore. His continued success in tournaments also meant frequent exhibition matches for sizable stakes and often a share of the gallery's winning bets. As early as 1899 the Atchison, Topeka and Santa Fe Railroad sent Alex and his brother Willie to California to play a series of matches that helped popularize the game in that state and was the first organized professional tour in the United States. In the most memorable exhibition match, he and his brother Macdonald handed the legendary British golfers Harry Vardon and Ted Ray their only defeat of a 41-match tour of the United States in 1913. That same year, Smith captained a team of five American pros who took on a French team in Versailles in the first international match for a U.S. team.

Tournament glory brought other benefits. Smith's first U.S. Open victory led to publication of *Lessons in Golf* (1907), one of the earliest and most successful of a growing number of golf instruction books. The book solidified his reputation as the nation's foremost teacher. In 1952 golfer Gene Sarazen called Smith the greatest golf teacher he had seen. When a former PGA president asked Smith if he was not the greatest, Smith modestly replied, "I don't think I'm great, but I know I'm good." He was especially noted for spotting the essential flaws in a golfer's swing and for tailoring his instruction to that person's physical capabilities. His own struggle to master the game no doubt contributed to his skill as a teacher.

Smith's reputation was both justified and furthered by his students' achievements. Jerome Travers won the 1915 U.S. Open and four U.S. amateur championships, and Glenna Collett (later Vare), "the female Bobby Jones," won an unmatched six U.S. Women's amateurs. Smith also tutored Walter Hagen, winner of eleven British, U.S., and PGA championships.

Easygoing and gregarious, Smith was popular not only with students but with fellow professionals, including his closest friend, the dour Willie Anderson. He took defeat well and victory with graciousness. As he and his competitor went from bunker to bunker during one horrendous round at the 1905 British Open, for example, he reassured the gallery, "Never mind, we're getting a lot of practice." Like most professionals of his generation, he played fast, and his advice on putting further endeared him to fans—"miss 'em quick." A sturdy 5'9" and 170 pounds and blessed with huge hands and muscular forearms, he was one of the longest drivers of his day, although, like most golfers on the bumpy greens of the time, an erratic putter.

Smith died in a Baltimore sanatorium after a long illness. His wife, who had died in 1908, was a sister of two other prominent Carnoustie golf professionals who had a significant impact on early American golf. They were the noted player and teacher James Maiden, and his brother, Stewart Maiden, mentor to Bobby Jones. Together with the Maidens, Willie Anderson, Willie Dunn, Willie Park, and his own brothers, Smith was part of a remarkable generation of transplanted Scotsmen who introduced golf to America's social elite and dominated the country's professional tournaments into the twentieth century's second decade.

None of these other golfers, however, could match Smith's combined success as a teacher and player. As a sign of the high regard in which he was held, his friends endowed the Alex Smith Memorial Medal in 1931 to be awarded to the low qualifier in the PGA Championship. In 1940 he was among the first twelve players selected for the PGA Hall of Fame.

• Smith's papers have not been collected. Fifteen of his championship medals (four others having been stolen) were presented by his brother Macdonald to the Carnoustie Golf Club in 1931. No comprehensive treatment of Smith's life and career has been published, but his *Lessons in Golf* (1907), although partially ghostwritten, accurately presents his teaching philosophy, and the foreword provides a good introduction to his early years. Further information on his golf-related activities in Scotland, his tournament record, and his club positions can be found in Stewart Hackney, *Carnoustie Links: Courses and Players* (1989). Howard Rabinowitz, "Alex Smith and the Early Days of American Golf," *Golf Journal*, Oct. 1994, pp. 17–19, is the most accurate brief sketch. For Smith's place as a teacher, see Herb Graffis, "Golf's Greatest Teacher—Who?" *Golfing*, Apr. 1952, pp. 18–19, 29–30. For Smith and his contemporaries, see Herbert Warren Wind, *The Story of American Golf: Its Champions and Its Championships* (1956). A generally reliable obituary appears in the *New York Times*, 22 Apr. 1930.

HOWARD N. RABINOWITZ

SMITH, Alfred E. (30 Dec. 1873–4 Oct. 1944), politician, was born Alfred Emanuel Smith in New York City, the son of a truckman and Union army veteran who passed his full name to his son and Catherine Mulvehill, a factory worker and shopkeeper. In his political career "Al" Smith, as he was commonly known, was to be the symbolic spokesman of the nation's city dwellers of stock that Anglo-Americans have considered immigrant. For this role he had, most clearly on his mother's side, an appropriate ancestry; she was the daughter of Irish immigrants. The noncommittal but normally English "Smith" obscures his father's European origins, about which little is known. One scholar suggests Italian forebears. Enemies of Al Smith, probably trying to sever him from the Irish, spread rumors that the father had changed his name from "Schmidt." Al Smith, at any rate, is remembered as Irish American and a product of New York City's multiethnic culture.

Smith's childhood was neither bone poor nor comfortably middle class. As the driver of a horse-drawn truck, the elder Smith was a laborer but operated with something of the independence of a businessman; one account labels him a "boss truckman." His death in 1886 put further financial strain on the family. The Lower East Side neighborhood was at once poor and stable, its gritty respectability safe in the stern but kindly keeping of Smith's Roman Catholic church. He was for a time an altar boy, and his years of education, which extended through the eighth grade, were at St. James's parochial school. He was also notable for his love of animals, which would continue in his adult life, and a will to surround himself with a disorder of pets. His mother was employed in an umbrella factory, took home extra work at night, and later operated a neighborhood store. Al held a series of jobs, including a later-legendary employment at the Fulton Fish Market. For under two years, beginning at the age of nineteen, he did work there that included hauling fish for his employer and estimating the size of the day's catch.

Smith's early ambitions were for a profession akin to politics. An amiable show-off, he was attracted to the theater, but among the institutions and folkways that made Smith's environment secure was Tammany Hall. He joined the local Tammany organization, momentarily dissident from the larger body. Before long he was a regular in the political circle of Tom Foley, a saloon keeper as was typical of bosses, and he gained a reputation for public speaking. To strict reformers, the moral certainties of Catholicism and the manipulative ways of ethnic politics would have seemed antithetical. But to a youth at ease with his surroundings, the two must have appeared natural components of a well-conducted world, as natural as his later compound of a spotlessly Catholic sexual morality and a lawbreaking laxity about alcohol. In 1900 he married Catherine Dunn; it was an inseparable, lifelong union that produced five children.

Smith's first political job was as an investigator under the city's commissioner of jurors. If his daughter Emily Smith Warner's explanation is accurate, he got the job in a Byzantine world of New York City politics. Another sponsor, having participated in the local rebellion against the machine, had an entrée into the anti-Tammany administration that took office in 1895. Smith later became a loyal member of Tammany, and Foley made him its successful candidate for a seat in the state assembly.

In 1904 Smith took his place in the Albany assembly, a position he held until 1915, secured by yearly election. As a freshman he made no mark on the process of governance, nor did he cut a large figure in the next term. But he soon revealed that he was more than a political hack. Membership in a committee investigating dirty dealing among insurance companies contributed to sharpening his social conscience. Increasingly he mastered the technicalities of legislation, being successful also in getting along with both Democratic and Republican members. He introduced bills representing the substantive needs of the public, among them a measure requiring air brakes on trains. In time he came under the wing of Charles F. Murphy, the citywide boss of Tammany. Then, on 26 March 1911, a fire in the Triangle Shirtwaist factory in lower Manhattan, an enterprise especially employing immigrant women, killed 146 workers. That disaster, followed by widespread political protest against what stood revealed as the minimal safety conditions in the state's factories, more than any other event turned Smith into a major progressive figure.

A state factory commission included Smith, by then majority leader of the assembly, as its vice chairman. The chairman was his fellow Democrat Robert F. Wagner, Sr. Smith was a relentless investigator, and he introduced bills recommended by the commission providing for safety and for the health of women and children employees. In January 1913 he took up the office of Speaker of the assembly. He continued to press for welfare legislation, including a bill for the support of widows and their children. Like many progressive legislators and institutions in a nation increasingly convinced of the efficacy of expertise, the Triangle commission consulted nonpolitical experts on social conditions. Smith became an associate of such figures as Frances Perkins and the future Belle Moskowitz, who would later become one of his closest advisers.

After resigning from the assembly, Smith served in the state's constitutional convention of 1915, distinguishing himself in a successful assault on an amendment that would have deprived the state government of the ability to pass social legislation. That year Tammany nominated him for the oddly prestigious office of sheriff of New York County, a position that had little to do with normal police work. He won the citywide election. Next came his election in 1917 to the presidency of New York City's board of aldermen. In 1918 he was Murphy's choice for the Democratic gubernatorial nomination. This meant moving for the first time beyond his constituency in the city, selling himself to upstate Democratic leaders and voters, and then, after his success in the primary, appealing to the state as a whole in a contest against the Republican incumbent. It was a landslide in the city that delivered him a narrow victory in that race.

Smith's first term in the governor's mansion, which began in January 1919, was distinguished by his appointment of a commission for the reconstruction of the state government. A historian has described his recommendations as reflecting one of the several impulses in progressivism: the belief in efficient government, fit for social legislation, as opposed to the progressive impulse toward the total submission of government to democratic processes. Advocates of centralization argued that putting governance in the hands of a strong administration ultimately responsible to the popular will would be more democratic in the long run than mincing government into a clutter of elective offices. In any event, Smith was committing himself to a vision of administration at odds with the small-scale democracy of ward politics.

Smith's first term is memorable also for a bruising fight with William Randolph Hearst, who accused Smith of representing the milk interest and permitting a rise in the price of that commodity. Failing to show up at a public meeting at which Smith demolished the accusation, Hearst emerged with his political hopes weakened and his hostilities inflamed. The governor, departing from what folklore would have expected of a devout and culturally conservative ethnic Catholic, went visibly though unsuccessfully to the defense of five elected socialists, who were refused their seats by the state assembly, and otherwise opposed repressive measures offered in the legislature in this time of antiradical hysteria.

In the Democratic National Convention of 1920, Smith was New York's favorite-son presidential candidate: a gesture, but a measure of his political stature. In that Republican year, he suffered his first defeat in a popular vote, losing his effort for reelection to the governorship though running ahead of the Democratic presidential candidate James M. Cox.

Out of office and thinking his political life at an end, Smith received an appointment from President Woodrow Wilson to the National Board of Indian Commissioners, and Republican governor Nathan L. Miller placed him on the Port of New York Authority. Smith worked with an organization pressing for a restructuring of the state government in accordance with the plan prepared by the commission he had appointed in 1919. He served as chairman of the United States Trucking Corporation, also directing private businesses. His candidacy for the party's 1922 gubernatorial nomination squelched Hearst's powerful bid, and he won both the nomination and the election, along with two succeeding two-year terms.

One scholar of the period has seen Smith's administrations as an anticipation of the New Deal; another has pointed to him as bringing into mainline politics the immigrant groups whom more traditional leaders had failed to recognize. He continued the progressive practice of calling in experts: social and settlement-house workers and others outside of electoral politics who could comment on economic and social questions. Especially notable, and again contrary to expectations for an ethnic Catholic traditionalist, was the number of women to whom he turned for advice. Among his achievements were the restriction of weekly working hours for women and children, a program for the elimination of railroad grade crossings, a steep increase in funding for public education, and a scheme of cooperation between government and business in the provision of low-cost housing. He continued to guide an extensive reorganization of the state government. He is best remembered, however, for the turmoil that attended two defeats: for his party's presidential nomination in 1924 and for the presidency itself four years later.

The 1924 Democratic National Convention, held in New York City's Madison Square Garden, was the first to be carried widely by radio. Generations of Americans with some knowledge of political and social history are familiar with its richly symbolic presentation of the cultural conflicts of the twenties. In the countryside, in the small towns of the South, Midwest, and elsewhere, and among Americans of long native ancestry in the cities, hostility to the social manners of urban ethnic communities expressed itself in a prohibitionist identification of immigrants with alcohol, a Protestant fundamentalist abhorrence of the Roman Catholicism of the Irish and more recent immigrant groups, and suspicion of big cities as places of political corruption and moral decay.

That common representation oversimplifies the complexity of political alignments in the 1920s. That Thomas James Walsh, who presided over the convention, was Irish, Catholic, dry, and a senator from the rural western states of Montana is only the most conspicuous example of its limitations. The Ku Klux Klan, champion of nativism, racism, Prohibition, and anti-Catholicism, was shunned by the more respectable opponents of Smith. Often overlooked, too, is that elements of progressivism were quite consistent with the sternly religious morality of William Jennings Bryan and his following. William Gibbs McAdoo, the candidate of the forces loyal to Bryan who were arrayed against Smith, denounced New York City (of which he had long been a resident) as the seat of arrogant wealth, a progressive sentiment fully consonant with a moral conservative's repugnance at the private vices of sensuousness and selfishness. Recent scholarship has pointed up the close connections between progressivism and Prohibition and, especially later in the decade, between conservatism and opposition to the Eighteenth Amendment. By the end of the twenties a significant portion of the conservative and wealthy business community would be lending support to repeal of that amendment for inviting other kinds of federal intervention into the economy and society and for eliminating alcohol as a source of revenue alternative to the graduated income tax. That Smith as late as 1924 had not broken with his commitment to essentially progressive policies at the same time that he opposed Prohibition complicates the political story of the times, as does Walsh in his different way.

For a placement of Smith within the political strife of the times, however, the customary view of the cultural divisions in the Democratic party will do. He was Catholic, of Irish ancestry, and an urbanite nurtured in the most famous of urban machines. His signing in 1923 of a bill repealing a law enforcing Prohibition defined him as a major figure in the fight against the Eighteenth Amendment. New York City supporters of Smith acted the part of urban toughs, jeering the inland McAdoo forces from the galleries, and so the balloting went on for over a hundred countings. In the end, the withdrawal of both candidates opened the way for the nomination of John William Davis on the 103d ballot. He was a lawyer for big business but with some progressive credentials, a plain and solid choice destined for defeat at the hands of Calvin Coolidge.

Smith was nonetheless a leading contender for his party's presidential nomination for 1928. His problem, like that of any other politician with a strong identity, whether regional, social, or ideological, was that whatever might draw one constituency—in Smith's case the big-city ethnic communities—risks repelling others.

Smith's position on Prohibition, for example, was both an asset and a liability, a liability compounded by suppositions that he not only opposed Prohibition but violated it. His religion gave him major trouble. He was not prepared to hedge on any point of faith or practice. A suggestion that his Catholicism might put him at odds with the country's civic institutions and its tradition of separation of church from state would turn him impatient, apparently uncomprehending. In March 1927 Ellery Sedgwick, editor of the *Atlantic Monthly*, sent him the proofs of an open letter by Charles C. Marshall, about to be published, challenging Smith on the question of whether the teachings of his religion were compatible with the nation's Constitution and liberties. Smith's reply in the May issue was the work of his Jewish friend and adviser Joseph M. Proskauer, Father Francis P. Duffy, well known as a chaplain in the First World War, and Smith himself, with the approval of Patrick Cardinal Hayes. It was a careful argument. In response to Marshall's charge that Catholicism preached the supremacy of the church over the civil state, it cited prominent members of the American Catholic hierarchy and clergy who had endorsed religious liberty and the autonomy of the nation's secular law. It pointed to Smith's record of dispassionate service to all elements in his state, and in the face of what had been much narrow indoctrination within Catholic schooling, Smith's statement denied that parochial schooling taught religious intolerance. But neither this nor any subsequent utterances on Smith's part could have stilled the question.

Another threat to Smith's fortunes had to do with the subtleties of personal manner. Other twentieth-century presidents have had sharp regional personalities that did not clash with a national identification: the Vermont Yankee Coolidge, the down-home Missourian Harry S. Truman, the assertive Texan Lyndon Johnson, the proudly Arkansan William Clinton. Smith's New York City ways gnawed at popular nerves. New York evokes more outside hostility than Vermont or Missouri, but Smith—his New York accent grating over the radio waves—worsened the problem with his air of mocking puzzlement about the staid customs of the hinterland.

None of this was enough to deny Smith the national party's choice. The convention was carefully orchestrated. In a priceless millisecond in American political history, Tammany delegates earnestly joined in a demonstration on behalf of the nation's beleaguered farmers. Franklin D. Roosevelt gave the nominating speech for Smith and dubbed him "the happy warrior." Smith won on the first ballot. For balance the convention selected as his running mate a southern dry, Senator Joseph T. Robinson of Arkansas.

The election was as ugly as the convention had been harmonious. The stiffly correct Republican candidate Herbert Hoover (1874–1964) did not participate in the trashing of Smith for his faith, but preachers, religious publications, and pamphlets savaged the candidate and his church. The previously uninformed could enlighten themselves, for example, with the knowledge that the church had purchased high ground on which artillery could be trained on the federal government. Beside the tracks of the train that was to carry Smith to Oklahoma City, the crosses of the Klan burned. In his campaigning, Smith tried to discuss what he conceived to be substantial issues, among them water power, Republican scandals and fiscal policy, Prohibition, and aid to farmers, that last a topic imperfectly covered in Tammany ward meetings. The religious issue persisted.

It is puzzling not so much that Smith did not find a way to surmount the political obstacle of his religion—there was no way—but that he was so surprised that it was an obstacle. He seemed startled to find that his church was considered authoritarian and shocked to encounter widespread anti-Catholicism in a country then stoutly Protestant in much of its folk culture. Perhaps the stereotype of the savvy city politico never really fitted Smith. He had won elections in a Democratic city under the protection of the Democratic organization and had gone on to the governor's office with the city to back him. It was as a legislator, an administrator, an investigator of social conditions, and a seeker of experts who knew about them that he had excelled. His progressivism was less of the direct-democracy kind than of the brand that trusted to the dry methods and virtues of trained inquiry.

There was another circumstance that Smith and his campaign staff under the direction of the wealthy businessman John J. Raskob could not have overcome. The Republicans were widely associated with the real or apparent prosperity of the moment, and they had nominated a remarkably attractive candidate: humanitarian, engineer, brilliant administrator, the embodiment of much that was most promising in this age of technological and, so it seemed, business triumph. Hoover took more than 58 percent of the popular ballot, winning 444 electoral votes to Smith's 87.

Largely unnoticed at the time was a fact about the election that has been credited with foreshadowing the politics of the New Deal, as Smith's gubernatorial programs had foreshadowed its policies. In addition to nearly doubling the size of the popular Democratic presidential vote over that of 1924, Smith had won the total vote of the country's twelve biggest cities. His 38,000-vote margin was minuscule, but compared to the Republican urban pluralities of the previous two elections, it was an anticipation of the triumphant Democratic coalition of future years, of which the big cities and their ethnic and working-class residents were to be a major element.

Out of office, Smith became a big businessman, notably as president of the Empire State Building, then still under construction. He was now a close friend of Raskob. As the election of 1932 approached, the two were settling into the conservative wing of the Democratic party, agreeing also that the party should openly oppose Prohibition—an opposition by then much in favor among business conservatives. Roosevelt, now governor of New York State, was in the liberal wing of the Democracy, continuing in Albany a progressivism that had once defined Smith. In a Jefferson Day speech in April 1932, Smith delivered a conservative's warning against stirring up class warfare in time of depression. At the Democratic National Convention, Smith received substantial support for several ballots but remained a distant competitor to Roosevelt. In the election itself, he supported the nominee.

Smith's office-seeking career was now over. Nor, it turned out, was there any place for him in the national administration. Soon he became a spokesman for the Liberty League, formed to oppose the New Deal as a threat to freedom. Democrats in the organization worked in 1936 to prevent Roosevelt's renomination. On 26 January Smith, in a nationwide radio address, denounced the New Deal for setting class against class, providing for the arbitrary bureaucratic disposition of the country's resources, and threatening the Constitution. In the presidential campaign Smith supported Alfred E. Landon, Roosevelt's Republican opponent. Four years later he backed Wendell Willkie.

What had happened to the one-time champion of social and labor legislation in New York State who became the opponent of what looks much like a national counterpart to his policies? Smith had customarily revealed a taste for frugality in the state government over which he presided, and the New Deal quickly acquired a reputation for spending. By the 1930s he may also have been distinguishing between the realm of the states and that of the federal government, favoring for the one a scope of intervention into the economy inappropriate to the other. Suspicion of Roosevelt after a time of uneasy association may have additionally affected his view. But as to whether Smith, in his own mind, had changed or was simply opposed on particular grounds to the specific content of the New Deal, no conclusive evidence remains. At least one disagreement with Roosevelt's policy is consonant with Smith's upbringing in a city of immigrants, his recoil from the red-baiting intolerance of 1919 and the ethnic and religious intolerance of 1928, and his form of progressivism demonstrating a concern not only for efficiency but also for the relief of suffering: he disapproved of the president's refusal to urge that immigrant laws be softened for the admission of Jewish refugees from Nazism.

By the time of Smith's death in New York City, the nation's lower east sides were no longer remote corners of American life. With his assistance, they had become major components of the national Democratic politics he had turned to opposing.

• A small collection of Smith papers is at the New York State Library in Albany. For additional biographical information see Richard O'Connor, *The First Hurrah: A Biography of Alfred E. Smith* (1956); Emily Smith Warner, *The Happy Warrior: A Biography of My Father, Alfred E. Smith* (1956); Oscar Handlin, *Al Smith and His America* (1958); and Paula Eldot, *Governor Alfred E. Smith: The Politician as Reformer* (1983). See also David Burner, *The Politics of Provincialism: The Democratic Party in Transition, 1918–1936* (1968).

DAVID BURNER

SMITH, Alfred Holland (26 Apr. 1863–8 Mar. 1924), railroad executive, was born in Cleveland, Ohio, the son of William Smith and Charlotte Holland. In 1879,

after his father's death, Smith had to abandon his desire to attend college to help support his mother and four siblings. He found employment with the Lake Shore and Michigan Southern Railroad (LSMS) as a messenger in its Cleveland office. After being promoted to clerk, Smith requested a transfer to a construction crew and began working on the LSMS's Michigan Division. He helped his foreman file company reports that caught the attention of superiors, precipitating his rapid advance to construction gang foreman. In September 1885 he married Maude Emery; they had one child.

Smith continued to rise within the LSMS, a subsidiary of the New York Central Railroad. In 1890 the company appointed Smith superintendent of its Kalamazoo Division. Smith continued to advance within the LSMS, being promoted to progressively larger divisions until 1902, when he was made general superintendent and transferred to the New York Central and Hudson River Railroad. In 1906 he became vice president and general manager, and in 1913 senior vice president with jurisdiction over all roads and all departments of the Central. In January 1914 he ascended to the presidency of the New York Central Lines, which carried nearly 12 percent of the total freight tonnage hauled in the United States. Smith presided over the Central during an extremely trying decade. American railroads had to deal with the increased demands placed on them by World War I, federalization and the return to private control of the railroad properties, postwar depression, and the Shopmen's Strike of 1922.

During World War I Smith resigned from the New York Central to serve as regional director of the eastern railroads in the U.S. Railroad Administration, where his managerial skills were severely tested. When he assumed his new post in January 1918 the nation was in the midst of a severe transportation crisis, which greatly hindered its ability to aid France and Great Britain. A harsh winter, coupled with an uncoordinated system of unloading freight cars, had brought rail traffic, and consequently supply-laden ships bound for Europe, to a near standstill. Smith quickly abolished the government's priority shipping scheme and established an efficient system of unloading much-needed freight on the eastern seaboard. Smith's accomplishments may have passed relatively unnoticed by the general public, but government and railroad officials were quick to recognize his invaluable contribution.

Smith resumed his position as president of the New York Central in June 1919 and oversaw the road's transition back to private control. Largely owing to Smith's foresight, the Central emerged from the war in somewhat better condition than most other roads. As soon as the war began, but before wartime inflation struck the economy, Smith ordered new locomotives, passenger cars, and freight cars, saving the road millions of dollars and better equipping it to handle the extraordinary demands placed on it by the war. The large purchase equipped the Central with relatively better rolling stock immediately after the war.

In the postwar period, as president of one of the largest carriers in the nation, Smith had little choice but to become involved in the Association of Railroad Executives, a group created to counter the growing political organization and acumen of organized railroad labor. He did not, however, take a leadership role in the new organization, preferring to concentrate on improving the Central.

Smith took great interest in increasing locomotive power and improving freight handling methods at a time when most of his peers scoffed at the idea. He ordered the mechanical division to build the "super-locomotive," which became the most powerful engine of its day. The new locomotive, the "8,000," was capable of pulling a train weighing more than 9,000 tons. Smith was one of a handful of railway executives to experiment with container transportation—steel boxes that could be readily transferred from freight cars to trucks. Another important contribution by Smith was construction of a bridge across the Hudson River south of Albany, New York, which permitted Central trains to bypass the city's famous bottleneck. The Central named the bridge for Smith after his death. In addition to his duties on the Central, Smith served on numerous boards of directors of construction, gas, electric light, street railway, and finance companies.

Smith died when he was thrown from his horse while riding in New York City's Central Park. The horse came to a sudden stop and Smith lost his balance; he died instantly. Press accounts of Smith's life and tenure at the Central note that despite his age and the travails of running one of the largest roads in the country for nearly a decade, he remained exceptionally vigorous.

Smith's capabilities and vast knowledge of every aspect of the railroad industry were widely recognized by his contemporaries. His determined leadership guided the New York Central through an extremely difficult decade. Accounts of his career contain numerous stories of his business acumen, especially his ability to identify ways to cut business costs.

• Most of the New York Central's corporate records were destroyed prior to its merger with the Pennsylvania Railroad in 1968, but scanty references to Smith can be found in the Pennsylvania records at the Hagley Museum. Syracuse University also has a small collection of Central records. The best sources are contemporary articles that appeared in the trade and popular journals. Edward Hungerford, "Who Are the Railways?" *Colliers*, 2 June 1923, and "Are Railroad Presidents Worth Their Salaries?" *Literary Digest*, 27 Jan. 1923, discuss his business savvy and accomplishments. An obituary is in the *New York Times*, 9 Mar. 1924.

JON R. HUIBREGTSE

SMITH, Amanda Berry (23 Jan. 1837–24 Feb. 1915), evangelist, missionary, and reformer, was born in Long Green, Maryland, the daughter of Samuel Berry and Mariam Matthews, slaves on neighboring farms. By laboring day and night, Samuel Berry earned enough to buy his freedom and that of his wife and children, including Amanda. By 1850 the family had moved to a farm in York County, Pennsylvania. Their home was a station on the Underground Railroad.

Samuel and Mariam Berry stressed the value of education and hard work. Taught at home, Amanda learned to read by age eight; later she briefly attended a local school in which white students were given priority. At age thirteen she entered household service, living with a series of white employers in Maryland and Pennsylvania. She married Calvin M. Devine in 1854 but soon regretted his lack of piety and his indulgence in alcohol. After a period of fasting and earnest prayer, she experienced conversion in 1856 and envisioned a life devoted to evangelism. Devine enlisted in the Union army in 1862 and died fighting in the Civil War. They had two children, but only one reached adulthood.

Amanda moved to Philadelphia and by 1864 had married James Henry Smith, a coachman who was an ordained deacon in the African Methodist Episcopal (AME) Church. He later reneged on his prenuptial promise that he would undertake active ministry, and his unkindness and religious skepticism seemed to hinder her spiritual growth. She continued working as a domestic and taking in laundry. Their three children died young.

Close but not always harmonious ties with other devout women introduced Amanda Smith to the Holiness movement that swept nineteenth-century Protestantism. Advocates of Holiness urged believers, regardless of sex, race, social status, or church affiliation, to testify publicly about their spiritual experience. Irresistibly drawn to the movement's controversial tenet that entire sanctification—purification from intentional sin—was attainable by faith, she fervently sought this transformative blessing. In 1865 the Smiths moved to New York City, where James found work, but three years later Amanda declined to accompany him when he relocated again to take a well-paid position. During a Methodist church service in September 1868, she "felt the touch of God from the crown of my head to the soles of my feet." Walking home, she shouted praises and sang with joy at being sanctified, "married to Jesus" (*Autobiography* [1893; 1987], pp. 77, 81).

Smith expanded her religious activities after James died in 1869, supporting herself and her surviving child during midnight hours at the washtub and ironing table. By her own testimony she wrestled with fears and temptations presented by Satan; she constantly prayed to learn God's will for her by interpreting randomly-chosen Bible verses, dreams, and internal voices. In 1870 she determined to trust providence and went to work full-time organizing groups for testimony and spiritual nurturance, praying with the sick, and singing and preaching at camp meetings and urban revivals. Participating in national Holiness camp meetings enlarged her network of friends. Although she periodically encountered resistance to female preachers, clergymen of various denominations invited her to address large racially-mixed and all-white audiences. Her own AME Church, like most denominations, withheld ordination from women, and Smith did not press for institutional authorization or financial support. Confident that God had ordained her, she accepted individuals' donations and hospitality. She was the most widely known of the nineteenth century's black women itinerant preachers.

In 1878 Smith felt called to England, Ireland, and Scotland to participate in temperance revivals and Holiness conventions. After traveling on the European continent in 1879, she proceeded overland to India. There she worked with James M. Thoburn, Methodist Episcopal bishop of India, who had previously observed her in the United States. Thoburn affirmed, "I have never known anyone who could draw and hold so large an audience as Mrs. Smith" (*Autobiography*, p. vi). In 1882 she went to west Africa to help "civilize" the natives and to cultivate mainstream Protestant values among black Americans who had immigrated to Liberia. Cooperating with Baptists, Congregationalists, and Presbyterians in potentially competitive situations, she proselytized, promoted temperance and Western-style education, and started a Christian school for boys.

Returning to the United States in 1890, Smith resumed preaching and activism despite her failing health. With her own savings and supporters' contributions she founded a home for black orphans in Harvey, Illinois. It opened in 1899 and was later named the Amanda Smith Industrial School for Girls, operating until it burned in 1918. Exhausted by years of fundraising, Smith retired in 1912 to Sebring, Florida, where she died in a home a donor had built for her.

The careers of Amanda Smith and contemporary women evangelicals and reformers reinforced the proposition, unwelcome in some quarters, that females could function without male control. The black Methodist Episcopal clergyman Marshall W. Taylor portrayed Smith as an exemplar of their race's progress and "a Christian of the highest type," unmatched by any living person, black or white (*Life* [1886], pp. 57–58).

Smith's *Autobiography* is valuable to scholars of black women's writing and to historians of the Holiness, temperance, and foreign missions movements; the roles of women in the Methodist Episcopal and AME churches; and blacks' experiences and perspectives during the Reconstruction era and ensuing decades of heightened interracial tension. Smith's description and interpretation of conditions in Liberia and Sierra Leone reflect certain Anglo-American views of "heathen darkness" and "superstitions" (pp. 346, 451), but she firmly rejected the assumption that black people were inferior. General readers will find this book a circumstantial, often engaging account of the joys and rigors of a life committed to improvement.

• Entries from Smith's journal are incorporated in *An Autobiography: The Story of the Lord's Dealings with Mrs. Amanda Smith, the Colored Evangelist* (1893, repr. 1987, 1988). See also Marshall W. Taylor, *The Life, Travels, Labors, and Helpers of Mrs. Amanda Smith, the Famous Negro Missionary Evangelist* (1886); and M. H. Cadbury, *The Life of Amanda Smith* (1916), which sketches her later years. Jean M. Humez examines the *Autobiography* in "'My Spirit Eye': Some Functions of Spiritual and Visionary Experience in the Lives of Five Black Women Preachers, 1810–1880," in *Women and the Structure of Society*, ed. Barbara J. Harris and JoAnn K. McNamara (1984), pp. 129–43.

On women's roles in evangelism, see Nancy Hardesty et al., "Women in the Holiness Movement: Feminism in the Evangelical Tradition," in *Women of Spirit: Female Leadership in the Jewish and Christian Traditions*, ed. Rosemary Ruether and Eleanor McLaughlin (1979), pp. 225–54; David W. Wills, "Womanhood and Domesticity in the A.M.E. Tradition: The Influence of Daniel Alexander Payne," in *Black Apostles at Home and Abroad: Afro-Americans and the Christian Mission from the Revolution to Reconstruction*, ed. David W. Wills and Richard Newman (1982), pp. 133–46; Jualynne E. Dodson, "Introduction" to the reprint edition of Smith's *Autobiography* (1988); and Sylvia M. Jacobs, "Afro-American Women Missionaries Confront the African Way of Life," in *Women in Africa and the African Diaspora*, ed. Rosalyn Terborg-Penn et al. (1987), pp. 121–32.

MARY DE JONG

SMITH, Andrew Jackson (28 Apr. 1815–30 Jan. 1897), soldier, was born in Bucks County, Pennsylvania, the son of Samuel Smith, a farmer. His mother's name is unknown. Graduating from the U.S. Military Academy at West Point in 1838, he was commissioned second lieutenant in the First Dragoons. Until the Civil War he served with that regiment at various posts throughout the West and also in the Mexican War. He was promoted to first lieutenant in 1845 and captain two years later, in the midst of the Mexican War. He was married to Ann Mason Simpson of St. Louis.

The outbreak of the Civil War found Smith in California. He was quickly promoted to major (13 May 1861) and on 2 October was commissioned colonel of the Second California Cavalry. Having aided in the organization of the regiment, he resigned on 3 November 1861 and made his way east, eventually taking the position of chief of cavalry to General Henry W. Halleck. In the spring of 1862 Smith was commissioned brigadier general of volunteers. In this capacity he served throughout Halleck's Corinth campaign, which ended in May 1862 with the Union occupation of that key rail junction. He then commanded an infantry division in Kentucky and Tennessee. In December 1862 he commanded one of General William T. Sherman's divisions in the unsuccessful attack on Chickasaw Bayou. Sherman's forces were reorganized the following month, and when they moved against Fort Hindman (Arkansas Post), Smith commanded one of the divisions of General John McClernand's XIII Corps. He continued in this command throughout the Vicksburg campaign, which culminated in the capture of that Confederate stronghold with its garrison on 4 July 1863.

When political general Nathaniel P. Banks led an expedition up the Red River in Louisiana in the spring of 1864, he succeeded in obtaining orders to borrow troops from Sherman's Army of the Tennessee. These turned out to be two divisions of the XVI Corps and one of the XVII Corps, with Smith placed in charge of the entire Army of the Tennessee detachment. Under Banks's bumbling leadership, the expedition turned out to be a miserable failure. On several occasions only the presence of Smith, with his cool, steady competence—and ten thousand or so tough, confident veteran troops—saved Banks and his expedition from complete disaster. This was particularly the case on 9 April 1864. The day before, the rest of Banks's army had been soundly whipped at Mansfield, Louisiana. During the night it had fallen back in more or less disorder on the solid support of Smith's troops posted at Pleasant Hill. On the afternoon of the ninth, the jubilant rebels, now substantially reinforced, arrived in pursuit and immediately launched a furious assault. Smith's men received the onslaught and then hurled it back with a vigorous counterattack. Though slightly outnumbered, Smith inflicted greater casualties on the enemy than he sustained himself. To the enormous disgust of Smith and his men, the thoroughly cowed Banks chose to continue the retreat rather than follow up Smith's hard-won victory. Banks did at least give credit where it was due, telling Smith, "You have saved the army." Smith was brevetted for his performance at Pleasant Hill.

Returned from the Red River expedition, Smith was promoted to major general of volunteers and, at about the same time, to the regular army rank of lieutenant colonel of the Fifth Cavalry. His next assignment was to neutralize Confederate cavalry raider Nathan Bedford Forrest. Sherman, now battling his way toward Atlanta, was anxious to have Forrest removed as a threat to his supply lines. The several officers he had already dispatched for this purpose had had their reputations (and sometimes their commands) destroyed by Forrest. On 5 July 1864 Smith set out from Memphis. He conducted his expedition with such skill and cunning that Forrest's own scouts, looking for an opening to strike, had to admit that he kept "his column well closed up, his wagon train well protected, and his flanks covered in an admirable manner." When Forrest finally did strike on 14 July, he found Smith well posted at Tupelo, Mississippi. There Smith administered one of the few outright defeats Forrest ever suffered, even wounding the hard-riding Confederate commander in the bargain. For this service, Smith was brevetted a regular army brigadier general. Later that summer Smith led another sweep into Mississippi, and while this expedition failed to make contact with Forrest, it did help to keep him off Sherman's supply lines. In September Confederate general Sterling Price led a cavalry raid into Missouri. Union Missouri commander William S. Rosecrans requested and received the assignment of Smith's veteran divisions, who then spent several weeks vainly chasing Price's gray-clad riders. When Confederate general John B. Hood moved north that November to invade Middle Tennessee, Smith took the XVI Corps to join

General George H. Thomas in opposing Hood. On both days of the battle of Nashville (15–16 Dec. 1864), Smith led his corps successfully in action. On the second day he helped to take the key Confederate position at Shy's Hill. In the closing days of the war, Smith and his command took part in operations against Mobile, Alabama.

After the war, Smith was brevetted major general in the regular army for his wartime services. Naturally, however, he served in his regular rank of lieutenant colonel. In 1866 he became colonel of the new Seventh U.S. Cavalry. In 1869 he resigned and became postmaster in St. Louis. In 1889 he was added to the army's retired list as a colonel. He commanded a brigade of Missouri militia during the strikes of 1877 and was auditor of St. Louis from 1877 to 1889. He died in St. Louis.

• For further information on Smith see Shelby Foote, *The Civil War: A Narrative* (3 vols., 1958–1974); E. B. Long and Barbara Long, *The Civil War Day by Day: An Almanac, 1861–1865* (1971); U.S. War Department, *The War of the Rebellion: A Compilation of the Official Records of the Union and Confederate Armies* (128 vols., 1880–1901); and Ezra J. Warner, *Generals in Blue: The Lives of the Union Commanders* (1964).

STEVEN E. WOODWORTH

SMITH, Arthur. *See* Smith, Fiddlin' Arthur.

SMITH, Arthur Henderson (18 July 1845–31 Aug. 1932), missionary, was born in Vernon, Connecticut, the son of Albert Smith, a Congregational minister, and Sarah Tappan Stoddard. He grew up in the Midwest. He attended Beloit College in Wisconsin, graduating in 1870; there, in April 1864, he met Henry Dwight Porter, who became a lifelong friend. The two served together as Abraham Lincoln's "100 Days Men" in the Civil War and attended Union Theological Seminary and the College of Physicians and Surgeons (1870–1871) together. Under the American Board of Commissioners for Foreign Missions, they sailed to China in 1872 to serve jointly at the Tientsin station. In 1871 Smith married Emma Jane Dickinson.

Smith became interested in Shantung Province at the urging of a Chinese enquirer who wanted a mission station located in his village of P'angchiachuang, En Hsien. Visiting the province during the famine of 1878, Smith recognized the opportunities it offered even while he doled out famine relief funds. In 1880 the Smith and Porter families moved to P'angchiachuang and opened a new mission station there. In this rural community, where Smith served for twenty-five years, the missionaries opened schools and a hospital. Both men were early advocates of mission self-support and advocated the transfer of mission work to Chinese Christians.

Smith was the author of numerous works on China. His first book, *The Proverbs and Common Sayings of the Chinese* (1888), was scholarly and well received, but an extensive revision of it was lost in the Boxer uprising.

Smith's more popular books appealed to vast audiences and gained him an international reputation. These publications include *Chinese Characteristics* (1890), which was translated into French, German, Japanese, and Chinese; *Village Life in China* (1899); the two-volume *China in Convulsion* (1901), about the Boxer movement; and *The Uplift of China* (1907), which sold 180,000 copies in the English edition alone. He was also a frequent contributor to the *Chinese Recorder* and the *North China Daily News*, first publishing parts of his books in both periodicals.

Described by colleagues as keen-minded, Smith was known as a paradox, always stating the worst side of an issue first. Some considered him a cynic, but he was more of a satirist. His penetrating observations of both the Chinese and his fellow countrymen along with his wit and literary abilities frequently produced descriptions that many found far too true for comfort.

Living in Shantung, Smith early recognized the dangers the Boxers posed but was unable to convince diplomats in Peking (Beijing) that the threats to foreigners were real. Caught in Peking when the worst Boxer violence erupted in 1900, he and his wife were first housed with the other missionaries at the Methodist Mission and then moved to the legation quarter, where they endured the siege. When recalled to the United States several years later to work on fundraising for the American Board of Commissioners for Foreign Missions, he met with President Theodore Roosevelt and suggested the remission of the Boxer indemnity money to China. Although ridiculed at first, the idea was typical of Smith's far-ranging worldview and dedication to the Chinese people. With Roosevelt's support, the plan was approved by the U.S. Congress, and the Chinese decided to use the indemnity money for education. As a result Tsing Hua University was founded, and many hundreds of Chinese journeyed to the United States to pursue an education, which had a profound influence on the future relations between the two countries.

Upon his return to China Smith was appointed missionary at large by the American Board of Commissioners for Foreign Missions and worked continuously for the cooperation and union of Christian mission work throughout the country. He was the American chairman of the 1907 Centenary Missionary Conference held in Shanghai. In 1908 the Smiths moved to the mission station in Tungchou, Shantung, where Arthur Smith became a weekly speaker at the North China American School, whose students called him "Uncle Ming." In 1910 he served as a China delegate to the Edinburgh missionary conference.

During this period of his life, Smith traveled extensively in China, working first with the 1907 conference's China Continuation Committee and then for the creation of the National Christian Council of China, which was established in 1922 to coordinate Christian work in China nationally. His wife died in 1926. After 1926 Smith lived in retirement in Claremont, California, where he died.

• In addition to the works already mentioned, Smith published *Rex Christus: An Outline Study of China* (1903), *China and America Today* (1907), and *A Manual for Young Missionaries to China* (1918). For further information see *Yearbook of the Congregational and Christian Churches* (1932). Obituaries are in the *Chinese Recorder*, Dec. 1932; the Shanghai *North China Herald*, 21 Sept. 1932; and the *New York Times*, 2 Sept. 1932.

KATHLEEN L. LODWICK

SMITH, Ashbel (13 Aug. 1805–21 Jan. 1886), surgeon general and secretary of state of the Republic of Texas, physician, and businessman, was born in Hartford, Connecticut, the son of Moses Smith, Jr., a hatmaker, and Phoebe Adams. Smith attended the Hartford public schools, and in 1823 he entered Yale, where he was a member of Phi Beta Kappa and received both his B.A. and M.A. by the end of his first year. To pay college debts he taught school in Salisbury, North Carolina, between 1824 and 1826, then returned to the North to study medicine. After receiving his medical degree from Yale in 1828, he established a practice in Salisbury.

In 1831 he left North Carolina to study surgery for one year in Paris, where he attended lectures by many of the French founders of modern medicine. At the same time he immersed himself in the life of Paris, becoming friends with Americans such as James Fenimore Cooper and Samuel F. B. Morse and prominent Frenchmen such as the Marquis de Lafayette. At Neckar Hospital during an 1832 Asiatic cholera epidemic, Smith wrote a well-received pamphlet on cholera based on his experiences and established his reputation as an expert on the disease.

Returning to the United States, Smith resumed his medical practice at Salisbury in 1832, but at the same time he invested in land and slaves. He purchased a part interest in the *Western Carolinian* and edited it. As editor, the Democrat Smith supported nullification, strongly opposing the federal tariff and the policies of President Andrew Jackson. His editorial duties introduced Smith to politics, which became for him an enduring passion. While at Salisbury he was baptized as an Episcopalian and began to attend that church, although theologically he was a freethinker.

In 1836 friends encouraged Smith to go to Texas and support its fight for independence. Smith went, but by the time he arrived in 1837, the revolution had ended. Shortly after he reached Texas, however, he met Sam Houston, president of the republic, who appointed him surgeon general of the Texas army. After serving for one year, Smith returned to private medical practice and became a permanent resident of Texas. He purchased land near Houston that became his "Evergreen" plantation.

Smith was unable, however, to stay away from politics, and he soon returned to government and began a career of distinguished service to the republic. He was a commissioner to the Comanches in 1838. He was minister to England and France between 1842 and 1844. In 1845 republic president Anson Jones named

Smith secretary of state, and he negotiated the Smith-Cuevas Treaty with Mexico, which secured Mexican recognition of Texas independence and paved the way for a more secure existence for the republic. Smith's efforts to establish a permanent, independent republic ended, however, when the United States annexed Texas in 1845.

After 1845 Smith played a less visible role in the public affairs of the state of Texas but continued his versatile career. In 1846, with the outbreak of the Mexican-American War, Smith joined the Texas Volunteers as a physician, although an attack of fever prevented him from seeing battle. However, his business interests thrived. At Evergreen Smith experimented with alternatives to cotton and established himself as a successful sugar planter and sheep rancher. He became a business partner with Gail Borden and in 1851 promoted Borden's meat biscuits at the London Industrial Exposition, which he attended as a commissioner from Texas. Smith also speculated in Texas land and promoted railroads.

Smith seldom practiced medicine but was active in early efforts to professionalize medical practice in the state. He was one of the founders in 1848 of the Medical and Surgical Society of Galveston, one of the first professional organizations in Texas, and played a prominent role in organizing the Texas Medical Association in 1853. He was also active in educational activities, serving on the board of visitors of West Point in 1848 and promoting public education in Texas.

Out of office, Smith remained active in Democratic party politics, both at the state and national levels. He was a major proponent of state aid to railroad construction. He also encouraged the development of common schools. In the sectional crisis of the 1850s, Smith backed his party in its strong assertion of states' rights and favored secession. In 1855 he served one term in the state legislature, where he supported both railroad and educational legislation.

At the outbreak of the Civil War, Smith organized the Bayland Guards, which ultimately became part of the Second Texas Volunteer Infantry. He led his company at Shiloh, where he was severely wounded. While recovering from his wounds he was elected lieutenant colonel of the regiment and commanded it at the battle of Farmington. He was absent on a recruiting mission to Texas during the battle of Corinth, where the regiment's colonel was killed, and when he returned to the regiment he was named its colonel. He led his unit at Vicksburg and was captured there. After being paroled and returning to Texas, Smith retained command of his regiment, although he was detailed on a variety of missions within the state. At war's end he was serving as commander of the defenses of Galveston, and Texas governor Pendleton Murrah sent him to New Orleans as a commissioner to negotiate a surrender.

In 1865 Smith took the oath of amnesty. Although excluded by law from holding office, in 1866 he ran for the Texas House of Representatives, was elected, and was allowed to take his seat. Smith played a major role in the session as chairman of the Committee on Federal Relations, leading the legislature's rejection of the proposed Fourteenth Amendment to the U.S. Constitution. Thereafter, Smith remained a strong opponent of Congressional Reconstruction and, after 1870, the Republican administration of Governor Edmund J. Davis. Although Smith did not actively seek public office, he was engaged in Democratic party politics for the remainder of his life, consulting with party figures throughout the state and attending national party conventions in 1868 and 1872. He served one more term in the state legislature, after being elected in 1878.

Even though he was deeply involved in politics, Smith devoted a great deal of attention to his business ventures and many other interests. On his plantation he experimented with growing grapes and making wine. In 1873 he helped organize the Texas Medical College and Hospital at Galveston and was on its board of trustees. The same year he helped organize the Texas Veterans Association, composed of Texas Republic veterans. In 1876 he served as a judge at the International Exhibition in Philadelphia, and that same year he was appointed to the commission that established the first state university for blacks, the Agricultural and Mechanical College for Colored Youths, later Prairie View A & M. In 1881 Governor Oran M. Roberts named him to the first board of regents of the University of Texas and Smith personally supervised the hiring of its first faculty. As a regent he was instrumental in having the medical branch of the state university located at Galveston. Never married, Smith died at Evergreen and was buried in the state cemetery at Austin.

• Ashbel Smith's personal papers are located at the American History Center, University of Texas at Austin. The most significant modern study of Smith is Elizabeth Silverthorne, *Ashbel Smith of Texas, Pioneer, Patriot, Statesman, 1805–1886* (1982). For additional insights, see James H. M'Neilly, "Col. Ashbel Smith," *Confederate Veteran* 27 (1919): 463–65, and Chauncey D. Leake, "Ashbel Smith, M.D., 1805–1886: Pioneer Educator in Texas," *Yale Journal of Biology and Medicine* 20 (1949): 225–32.

CARL H. MONEYHON

SMITH, Benjamin Mosby (30 June 1811–14 Mar. 1893), minister and educator, was born in Powhatan County, Virginia, the son of Josiah Smith, a tobacco planter, and Judith Micheau Mosby. In 1819 Josiah Smith's death left Benjamin fatherless. Like other planter sons, Benjamin was educated by hired tutors, at a school on the plantation, and at various neighborhood "old field" schools. In 1825 Smith entered Presbyterian Hampden-Sydney College, where he was active in one of the college's two debating societies, the Union Society. In September 1829 he shared the college's highest graduating honors with one of his classmates.

On graduation from Hampden-Sydney, Smith began a lifelong career as an educator. At age eighteen he was hired as the sole teacher at the Milton Male Academy, in Caswell County, North Carolina, near the Virginia border. At Milton Smith's religious faith blossomed, and in 1832 he entered the Union Theological Seminary, then located at Hampden-Sydney (later in Richmond). Graduating in 1834, Smith was elected to the Union faculty as a tutor. Licensed by the West Hanover Presbytery in 1834, he was ordained in 1835, while still on the Union faculty. During the following year, he served as a supply, or temporary, minister for the Guinea Church, near Hampden-Sydney. Out of what one contemporary described as his desire to "extend his opportunities for study," Smith in 1836 resigned his Union position and traveled and studied in Europe. During 1836–1837 he attended the University of Halle, where he studied under the German theologian and Pietist scholar Friedrich A. G. Tholuck; he spent the last portion of that year at the University of Berlin.

On his return from Europe in 1837 Smith received a call to become the pastor of the Danville, Virginia, Presbyterian church. While at Danville, in 1838 he first met Mary Moore Morrison, daughter of a Shenandoah Valley Presbyterian minister. Married in 1838, the couple would have six surviving children. In 1840 Smith was called to a pastorate in the Shenandoah Valley, in Augusta County's Tinkling Springs and Waynesboro Church; this was followed by a pastorate at the Staunton, Virginia, Presbyterian church beginning in 1845. In 1853 Smith took leave from the Staunton pastorate to serve as secretary of the board of publications of the Presbyterian church in Philadelphia. Maintaining his residence in Staunton, Smith traveled extensively and served in this position for only a few months.

In 1854 he was recalled to Union Theological Seminary as a professor of Oriental literature, and he held that position for the next thirty-five years—declining offers from prominent pulpits around the country—until his retirement at age seventy-eight. At Union Smith published, among other works, *Family Religion* (1859), *A Commentary on the Psalms and Proverbs* (1859), *The Poetical Books of the Holy Scriptures* (1867), and *Questions on the Gospels* (1868), along with a number of sermons.

Smith was widely admired by Union faculty and students. One colleague described him as a "man of great versatility of gifts, varied knowledge, broad reading, eminent practical wisdom and common sense, with a mind of unusual breadth and vigor, and a warm, loving, and sympathetic nature." According to another observer, Smith was "one of the most eminent ministers of the Presbyterian Church" who "exercised wide influence all over the country, both South and North." A fixture on the Union faculty, Smith was instrumental in securing the outside financial support that enabled the seminary to survive the devastating effects of the Civil War. He also served as co-pastor (along with the well-known Presbyterian divine Robert Louis Dabney) of the College Church at Hampden-Sydney from 1858 to 1874. During his years at Union, Smith accelerated his participation in denominational affairs. In 1876 he was elected moderator of the General Assembly of the Presbyterian Church in the United States, the southern Presbyterian church.

Fused with Smith's Presbyterianism was an intense interest in education. In Staunton, Smith helped to found the Augusta Female Seminary (later Mary Baldwin College) in 1842; he was also a supporter and trustee of Washington (later Washington and Lee) College. But his most significant contributions outside of the church occurred in public education. While a student in Germany in 1836–1837, he made a study of the Prussian school system. At the request of Virginia governor David Campbell, in late 1838 Smith composed a widely read report that contrasted the Prussian system with Virginia's weak and decentralized system of schools. In 1841 Smith spoke before a convention held in Lexington, Virginia, that recommended the creation of a new common school system; he participated in statewide educational conventions in 1841 and 1845. Smith was also active in the Educational Association of Virginia, which had been founded in Petersburg in 1863, and he served as the leading spokesman for white school reformers in the commonwealth. In 1870, after the establishment of the new Reconstruction era public school system, Smith was named as one of the first twelve county superintendents in the commonwealth, assigned to the Prince Edward County schools. He held that position until 1882, when the Readjusters took power and fired most of the commonwealth's school superintendents.

An avid exerciser—Smith walked two miles a day—he was in good health when he retired from the Union faculty in 1889. In his retirement he continued to act as the seminary librarian and to dabble in denominational affairs. He also enjoyed frequent visits with his sons, daughters, sons-in-law (all of the sons-in-law were Presbyterian ministers), and his sixteen grandchildren. In declining health, he lived his last years with his daughter in Petersburg, Virginia. As his family sang favorite hymns on his deathbed, in what the attending doctor described as the "most beautiful death I have ever seen," Smith died in Petersburg, Virginia.

• There is a small collection of materials relating to Smith's life at the Department of History (Montreat), Presbyterian Church USA in Montreat, N.C. An indispensable primary source for Smith's life is his diary (1836–1890), the original of which is part of the Records of the Presbytery of Lexington, Union Theological Seminary Library, Richmond, Va. Smith's grandson, Francis R. Flournoy, has written the most complete biography, *Benjamin Mosby Smith, 1811–1893* (1947). On the background to Smith's involvement in public education, consult William A. Maddox, *The Free School Idea in Virginia before the Civil War* (1918), and William A. Link, *A Hard Country and a Lonely Place: Schooling, Society, and Reform in Rural Virginia, 1870–1920* (1986). For other biographical information, see Alfred Nevin, ed., *Encyclopedia of the Presbyterian Church in the United States* (1884), pp. 833–34; *Minutes of the Synod of Virginia* (1893), pp. 266–68; *Southern Presbyterian*, 23 Mar. 1893; Joseph DuPuy Eggleston, Jr., "Reminiscences of the 'Hill': The Professors of Hampden-Sidney, Va.," *Christian Observer*, 16 Aug. 1899;

and *General Catalogue of the Trustees, Officers, Professors, and Alumni of the Union Theological Seminary in Virginia, 1807–1924* (1924).

WILLIAM A. LINK

SMITH, Bessie (15 Apr. 1894–26 Sept. 1937), blues singer, was born in Chattanooga, Tennessee, the daughter of William Smith, a part-time Baptist preacher, and Laura (maiden name unknown). She was one of seven children. The parents died when Smith was eight. An older sister, Viola, raised the children who were still at home in what Smith later referred to as a "little ramshackle cabin." (According to the journalist George Hoefer, however, Smith was brought up by a grandmother of another future jazz-woman, Lovie Austin.) At about age nine she began singing on Chattanooga's Ninth Street for pennies, accompanied by her brother Andrew on guitar. When another brother, Clarence, joined Moses Stokes' Traveling Show (based in Chattanooga's Ivory Theater), he arranged an audition for her. While still in her teens, she joined the troupe, working primarily as a dancer. In 1912 blues singer Ma Rainey, who had come through Chattanooga while on tour with Fat Chappell's Rabbit Foot Minstrels, heard Smith sing and invited her to join the show. Later that same year, she also toured briefly as a chorus line member in Irvin C. Miller's tent show, *Glorying the Brownskin Girl*.

In 1913 Smith played at the "81" Theater in Atlanta and in the following year teamed with Buzzin' Burton to work as a singer/dancer in *Park's Big Revue* at the Dixie Theater, also in Atlanta. A few years later she began performing with several minstrel and vaudeville shows, including the Pete Werley Florida Cotton Blossoms Minstrel Show and the Silas Green Minstrel Show. She also teamed with Hazel Green to perform in 1918 at the Douglas Gilmore Theater in Baltimore, Maryland, and starred in her own revue, *Liberty Belles* (1918–1919), as a singer, dancer, and male impersonator. Around 1920 Smith married Earl Love, who died in 1922. It is not known if the couple had children. During the early 1920s she performed throughout the South and the East Coast, including club dates in and around Atlantic City, where she performed with Charles Johnson's Band and Charley Taylor's Band. Having gradually acquired a substantial following, in 1921 she cut a recording test for Black Swan Records (the only record company owned at the time by African Americans) and for Emerson, where she recorded the piece "Sister Kate" with clarinetist Sidney Bechet. Neither company signed her on. In 1922 Smith moved to Philadelphia, where she worked at Horan's Madhouse Club (1920–1923), the Standard Theater with her own band (beginning 1921), and the Dunbar Theater with Bechet in the musical comedy *How Come* (1923). Frank Walker of Columbia Records, having heard Smith sing in Selma, Alabama, sent pianist Clarence Williams to bring her to New York City for a recording session. Columbia signed her on in 1923.

Also in 1923 she married Jack Gee, a night watchman she had met while performing at Horan's Madhouse Club in Philadelphia. (She also officially adopted a co-worker's son, whom they named Jack Gee, Jr., in 1926; however, with her divorce in 1929 from Jack, Sr., she lost custody of the young boy.) Shortly after the release of her first recording, *Down-Hearted Blues* (1923), she returned to Atlanta's "81" Theater. Her first night there was so successful that her performance on the following evening was broadcast live on radio. Smith brought an emotional intensity to the stage. She incorporated broad phrasing, had a wide singing range, and was considered to have excellent intonation and creative grasp of the blue note inflections. She quickly gained respect among musicians and audiences alike and her album sold over two million copies during its first year. Her income, reported at $2,000 per week, established Smith as the most successful African-American performing artist of the time, and she became known as the "Empress of the Blues," as she was billed on her tours.

During the next ten years, Smith recorded a total of 180 songs, recording with such music greats as James P. Johnson, Coleman Hawkins, and various members of Fletcher Henderson's Band, including Louis Armstrong, Charlie Green, Joe Smith, and Tommy Ladnier. In 1928, however, her popularity began to diminish. Possible explanations for this include the fading of the blues era; audiences' desire for something "new"; the popularity of radio and film (in which Smith was only remotely involved); and Smith's drinking habits. Although in 1929 she appeared in the film *St. Louis Blues* and in the Broadway show Pansy, her performance opportunities were becoming more limited, probably in part because of the Depression. She managed to get secondary roles as a singer on vaudeville tours (with some she was expected to sell cigarettes between acts), and she did not record again until John Hammond brought her back into the studio in 1933. The Hammond session was designed to appease the increasing European jazz audiences and featured white musicians Jack Teagarden and Benny Goodman. Smith, acutely aware of the changing times, specifically asked that "pop" tunes such as "Do Your Duty" and "Take Me for a Buggy Ride" be included on the album. The album, however, failed to succeed as Hammond had hoped. Smith then moved from Philadelphia to New York City.

In 1934 Smith toured theaters in the South with the *Hot From Harlem* revue, and performed with Ida Cox in *Fan Waves* revue at the Apollo Theater and with Don Redman's Orchestra at the Harlem Opera House, both in New York City. Still performing in New York, in 1935 she worked the *Blackbirds* revue at the Cotton Club and in 1936 performed in both the *Stars Over Broadway* revue at Connie's Inn and the *League of Rhythm* revue at the Apollo. In 1937 she began a tour with the *Broadway Rastas* revue, working once again in theaters in the South.

On 26 September 1937, with Richard Morgan at the wheel, her car collided with a truck, parked without lights on the roadside at Coahoma, Mississippi, just south of Memphis. Because of her skin color, she was refused admission in nearby hospitals and therefore had to be taken to an African-American hospital in Clarksdale, Mississippi—over 200 miles from the accident site. Never regaining consciousness, she died eight and a half hours after the time of the accident due to internal injuries and loss of blood. The controversy surrounding her lack of medical treatment because of her race mythicized her death and interested journalists to the point that she earned more column inches in the white press in death than she ever had during her life.

Beginning about a decade after Smith's death, memorials began appearing in various forms, commemorating her work as a blues singer. These include a Bessie Smith Memorial Concert that was held in New York City's Town Hall in 1948; the Edward Albee show *Death of Bessie Smith* that was produced in 1959, opening in West Berlin, Germany, in 1960, and in New York City in 1961; a short film, *Bessie Smith*, released in 1968; and a musical revue, *Me and Bessie*, starring Linda Hopkins, that played the Ambassador Theater in New York City from 1975 to 1976, followed by tours elsewhere. In 1967 Smith was posthumously given the *Down Beat* magazine International Jazz Critics Hall of Fame Award. In 1979 the Columbia record series "The World's Greatest Blues Singer: Bessie Smith" won the Grand Prix du Disque at the Montreux Jazz Festival in Switzerland.

Bessie Smith was buried at the Mount Lawn Cemetery, Sharon Hill, Pennsylvania, in an unmarked grave. In 1970, two women, singer Janis Joplin and Juanita Green (who had cleaned the Smith home as a child and later became president of the North Philadelphia chapter of the NAACP), shared the costs of the headstone. Erected thirty-three years after her death, it reads, "The greatest blues singer in the world will never stop singing."

• For more biographical information, see Chris Albertson, *Bessie: Empress of the Blues* (1972); Paul Oliver, *Bessie Smith* (1959); Carman Moore, *Somebody's Angel Child* (1969); and Elaine Feinstein, *Bessie Smith* (1985). See also George Hoefer's article in *Down Beat*, 16 June 1950. For a critical analysis of her recordings, see Edward Brooks, *The Bessie Smith Companion: A Critical and Detailed Appreciation of the Recordings* (1982). About the controversy surrounding her death, see Edward Albee, *The Zoo Story: The Death of Bessie Smith* (1960). Useful secondary sources include Walter Bruyninckx, *Sixty Years of Recorded Jazz, 1917–1977* (1980), pp. S468–76; Sheldon Harris, *Blues Who's Who: A Biographical Dictionary of Blues Singers* (1979), pp. 462–64; Daphne Duval Harrison, *Black Pearls: Blues Queens of the 1920s* (1988); Paul Oliver, *The Story of the Blues* (1969); Sally Placksin, *American Women in Jazz: 1990 to the Present* (1982), pp. 16–21; and Gunther Schuller, *Early Jazz: Its Roots and Musical Development* (1968), p. 226.

NANETTE DE JONG

SMITH, Betty (15 Dec. 1896–17 Jan. 1972), novelist and playwright, was born Elizabeth Wehner in Brooklyn, New York, the child of John Wehner and Catherine Hummel, German immigrants. There is some discrepancy, however, in her birth date; the Library of Congress lists it as 1904, but the date on her tombstone is 1896. Her father died when Betty was very young, and her mother remarried an Irish immigrant, Michael Keogh. The hardships and triumphs of her early years form the basis of her best-known work, *A Tree Grows in Brooklyn* (1943), where Francie Nolan looks up at the "green umbrellas" of the tree shading her tenement fire escape and dreams.

Shy and serious, Betty was an avid reader and an excellent student, hungry for experience beyond the Brooklyn streets, but her formal education ended after the eighth grade. She was forced to go to work to help support her family, taking on a series of factory, office, and retailing jobs. In June 1924 she married a Brooklyn native, George H. E. Smith, who was a law student at the University of Michigan. For the first time she was able to continue her education as a "special student" attending English and drama classes and developing a lifelong love of the theater. In 1930 she won the Avery Hopwood Award of $1,000 for playwriting, and that year the Smiths moved to New Haven, Connecticut, with their two small daughters. Until 1934 Smith studied at the Yale Drama School under George P. Baker, Walter P. Eaton, and John Mason Brown. Involved in Federal Theater projects, she moved to Chapel Hill, North Carolina, arriving with her children and a box of play scripts to begin a career as a playwright. She had been separated from her husband for several years, and in 1938 her marriage ended in divorce.

As part of a flourishing theater community and the recipient of Rockefeller and Dramatists Guild fellowships in playwriting, Smith compiled, edited, and wrote a wide variety of plays during the 1930s and studied with Frederick Koch and dramatist Paul Green at the University of North Carolina. In addition, she spent an hour every day creating a kind of fictional diary, the story of a young girl's encounters with junk dealers and shop owners on the streets of Brooklyn. On 31 December 1942 she mailed off more than a thousand pages to Harper and Bros., where the editors trimmed some six hundred pages and published it as *A Tree Grows in Brooklyn*. A runaway bestseller, it sold 300,000 copies in six weeks, achieving wide critical acclaim for its meticulous descriptions of immigrant life. By the author's death, it had been translated into sixteen languages and had sold over six million copies in thirty-seven hardcover printings.

In August 1943, the same month that her novel appeared, Smith married Joseph Piper Jones, assistant editor of the *Chapel Hill Weekly*. Theirs was a wartime romance—he had joined the army and was stationed at Norfolk at the time of their wedding. After the war they lived in Chapel Hill and shared mutual interests in writing, birdwatching, and gardening. Smith planted an ailanthus in their yard to remind her of the inspiration for her first novel: "There's a tree that grows in Brooklyn. Some people call it the Tree of Heaven. No matter where its seed falls, it makes a tree which struggles to reach the sky. It grows in boarded-up lots and out of cellar gratings. It is the only tree that grows out of cement."

During this decade Smith enjoyed her celebrity status, daily answered her fan mail—one-fifth of which began, "Dear Francie"—and noted, "The thrill of someone's asking for my autograph never wears off." Describing her appearance at this time, a *Saturday Review* interviewer commented: "She's petite, has a low, relaxed voice, dark hair, gray eyes, and, because 'it looks more prosperous' (her words), a year-round tan." She was paid $55,000 for the movie rights to her novel. Released in 1945, the film was directed by Elia Kazan and starred Peggy Ann Garner, Dorothy McGuire, Joan Blondell, Lloyd Nolan, and James Dunn, who won an Academy Award for best supporting actor, in the role of Francie's father. Two years later, the novel was adapted for a radio series, and in 1951 a successful musical version was produced at the Alvin Theater in New York City.

Smith's second bestseller, *Tomorrow Will Be Better* (1948), was praised for its honest portrayal of young Margy Shannon, who survives poverty and a loveless marriage without losing her sense of hope. The novel's often dark tone perhaps presaged the end of Smith's second marriage in divorce three years later. In 1952, after an automobile accident, Smith began *Maggie-Now*, another saga of Irish-American Brooklyn, which won the 1958 Sir Walter Raleigh Award, given by the Historical Book Club of Greensboro, North Carolina.

In 1957 Smith married Robert Finch, a fellow playwright and close friend for twenty years, who collaborated with her on such projects as the prizewinning one-act play "Western Star." The subjects of her plays varied from historical and biblical drama to slapstick comedy. In 1958 she helped edit *A Treasury of Non-Royalty One-Act Plays.* In her preface to an earlier collection of similar plays, she writes, "The drama is a community art," and she participated in the most productive years of the national little theater movement. Her play *Durham Station* was shown on Durham station WTVD in 1961, sponsored by the North Carolina Centennial Commission.

Smith's last novel, *Joy in the Morning* (1963), written after Finch's untimely death in 1959, re-created the early years of her first marriage at the University of Michigan. Later, she commented, "As I wrote, I realized to my delight that the book was more than a novel of college life. It was the anatomy of a marriage: the story of victory over odds." The protagonist, Annie McGairy, is reminiscent of a grown-up Francie as she faces the difficulties of married student life with humor and spirit. In 1965 MGM's film version of the novel premiered in Chapel Hill, starring Yvette Mimieux and Richard Chamberlain.

Until her death in Shelton, Connecticut, Smith participated actively in the life of her community, reaching out to people around her, especially young writers. She took her responsibility as a writer seriously, blending naturalism with an optimistic outlook to create characters who showed determination, loyalty, independence, and the capacity to love. She described

the ordinary happenings of ordinary people, explaining, "I loved the people I was writing about." These ordinary characters survive in her fiction.

• The Betty Smith Papers are in the Southern Historical Collection, University of North Carolina Library, Chapel Hill. In addition, numerous plays by Smith and articles by and about her are in the North Carolina Collection at the University of North Carolina Library. There is no full-length biography, but the *Dictionary of Literary Biography Yearbook* for 1982 contains a critical-biographical study, with illustrations and a bibliography. An interview by Robert Van Gelder appears in *Vogue* (April 1949), and Blanche H. Gelfant's comments on *A Tree Grows in Brooklyn* are included in Susan M. Squier, ed., *Women Writers and the City* (1984). Obituaries are in the *New York Times*, 18 Jan. 1972; *Washington Post*, 19 Jan. 1972; *Newsweek*, 30 Jan. 1972; and *Time*, 31 Jan. 1972.

HARRIET L. KING

SMITH, Bruce (23 May 1892–18 Sept. 1955), criminologist and police department consultant, was born in Brooklyn, New York, the son of Clarence B. Smith, a banker and real estate promoter, and Jessie Annin. After graduating from high school in Brooklyn, he studied at Wesleyan University but was such a vocal critic of compulsory chapel attendance that he was expelled in 1913 during his senior year. He entered Columbia University and graduated in 1914 with a B.A. He married Mary Belle Rowell in 1915; they had two children. Smith earned his M.A. and LL.B. at Columbia in 1916 but never took the bar examination. While a student, he worked at the New York Bureau of Municipal Research, located at Columbia and under the direction of Charles Austin Beard, a professor of politics there and later a distinguished historian. He persuaded Smith to study aspects of government, especially public administration and city finance. In 1916 the Bureau of Municipal Research (soon renamed the Institute of Public Administration) dispatched Smith to Harrisburg, Pennsylvania, to systematize records of complaints received by the police. He did so in three weeks.

When the United States entered World War I, Smith trained as a pilot in the Signal Corps and went to France in August 1918. Although he was never in combat, his hearing was permanently impaired by noise from airplane engine exhausts. In 1919 he returned to the bureau, becoming manager in 1921. In 1923 he was invited to New Orleans to recommend improvements in its police department. His recommendations led to increased police mobility and better detective work. In 1926 he studied the police in St. Louis, Missouri. In 1928, in the first of several trips abroad, he observed police techniques in Belgium, England, France, and Germany and concluded that the United States had unique problems because law-enforcement agencies operated on federal, state, and local levels and because states defined crimes differently. He recommended nationwide definitions of seven major crimes—homicide, rape, aggravated assault, robbery, burglary, auto theft, and larceny. In 1929–1930 he and a team of assistants surveyed Chicago's

6,712-man police force for eighteen months and found it so mired in poor training and procedures, corruption, and low morale that he recommended, though unsuccessfully, a total replacement. His accepted suggestions led to more economical use of personnel, a doubling of the number of officers on patrol, and at the same time a reduction in total strength.

Smith was a member of the executive board of the American Institute of Criminal Law and Criminology (1930–1942) and a member of several New York State commissions to administer justice and propose revisions of laws. As his reputation grew, he was invited to conduct police surveys in more cities, ultimately examining fifty or so departments in eighteen states and in several foreign countries. He regularly advocated streamlining administration, eliminating inefficient use of manpower, rooting out corruption, and compiling and reporting crime figures more honestly. From 1938 to 1955 he sat on the Committee on Police Training and Merit Systems of the American Bar Association and briefly served as chairman of that committee (1943–1944).

In late December 1941, the U.S. Army asked Smith to consult on making the U.S. Army Air Force efficient. He suggested assigning 350 desk colonels to field duty. He served as acting director of the Institute of Public Administration in 1940; he later served as acting director (1941–1946, 1950–1952) and director (1954–1955). In 1951–1953, with a fifteen-man staff and an $85,000 budget, he analyzed the New York police force and found it poorly organized and replete with an undeserved, clannish pride. A few of his recommendations, such as prohibiting police from guarding private payrolls and maintaining vehicles better, were accepted but little else was adopted from what he called his "most complex" report. Members of the Patrolmen's Benevolent Association publicly reviled and privately praised him. In 1954–1955 he advised the U.S. Department of the Treasury and the Commission on Intergovernmental Relations.

When Smith was invited to reexamine police departments in various cities, he too often saw inadequate improvement and concluded that individual locales must actively want reform to get and keep it. In addition, he always felt that, regardless of effective police work, "wickedness," as he called it, in violence-prone America would always be rampant. In fact he half-admired the bravery and ingenuity of American criminals and elevated them, perhaps with tongue in cheek, over their insipid European counterparts.

In 1954 Smith returned to England to replace an old sloop he owned with a new yacht. For years he had enjoyed fishing in Canada and sailing the waters off Long Island. He also wanted to observe police administration in England once more. He made friends with Colonel Sir Frank Brook, former Inspector of Constabulary for England and Wales, who regarded Smith as peerless in his knowledge of all aspects of police work. Smith had little time to enjoy his yacht, because he suffered a fatal heart attack at Southampton, New York.

Smith was a prolific writer. In addition to articles published in several encyclopedias, including the *Britannica* and the *Americana*, and in professional police journals, he published several books, three of which are of special significance. *The State Police: Organization and Administration* (1925) studies state police forces and discusses matters of jurisdiction, administrative powers and limitations, pay, welfare of rank-and-file officers, assignments of patrol units, investigative methods, identification of offenders, and crime prevention. *Rural Crime Control* (1933), written under the auspices of the Bureau of Social Hygiene, concerns methods of law enforcement at the levels of sheriff, constable, coroner, and justice of the peace and treats the relationship of county and state law-enforcement officers. Reviewers praised the work as a challenge to public inertia in the face of rural crime growth. *Police Systems in the United States* (1940; rev. and enl., 1949) describes public police agencies—federal, state, and local—often with severe criticism and suggestions for improvement, including nationwide networking to control criminal activities and make speedier arrests. It also discusses problems stemming from the public's desire to control police organizations, personnel, leadership, and matériel. Reviewers defined this publication as an indispensable guidebook. Although never a policeman, Smith was a proud member of the International Association of Chiefs of Police and was lauded "a cop's cop."

• Papers of Smith are in the Institute of Public Administration, New York City. In 1954 he edited *New Goals in Police Management*. Part of his work was reprinted in *Urban Police: Selected Surveys* (1971). Robert Schlapen, "Not Like Taking the Waters," *New Yorker*, 27 Feb. 1954, is a valuable biographical essay. Orlando Winfield Wilson, "Bruce Smith," *Journal of Criminal Law, Criminology and Police Science* 47 (July–Aug. 1956): 235–37, is a brief sketch. An obituary is in the *New York Times*, 19 Sept. 1955.

ROBERT L. GALE

SMITH, Caleb Blood (16 Apr. 1808–7 Jan. 1864), lawyer, congressman, and secretary of the interior, was born in Boston, Massachusetts; his parents' names are unknown. When he was six years old, he moved with his parents to Cincinnati, Ohio. This city of ten thousand was on its way to becoming the "Queen City of the West," and Smith formed much of his lifelong thinking while living there. During 1825 and 1826 he attended Miami University at Oxford, Ohio. He did not graduate but returned briefly to Cincinnati and then left Ohio for Connersville, Indiana, to study law with Oliver H. Smith. Caleb Smith was admitted to the bar at Connersville in 1828. He rose quickly in his profession and was "remarkably fluent, rapid, and eloquent before the jury" (Bailey, p. 214). In 1831 Smith married Elizabeth B. Walton; they had three children.

While practicing law on the local circuit, Smith entered politics. After he ran unsuccessfully for the Indiana House of Representatives in 1831, he purchased the local *Political Clarion*, changed its name to the *Indiana Sentinel*, and made the newspaper a lively organ for Whig sentiment. Smith published and edited the paper jointly with Matthew R. Hull for two years, then left it in Hull's hands.

Smith was elected to the Indiana house in 1833 and reelected in 1834, 1835, and 1836. In the sessions of 1835–1836 and 1836–1837, he was speaker of the house. Internal improvements were the primary business of the legislature. Better roads, canals, and railroads were a major focus of Whig policy in Indiana, as they were in other Midwestern states seeking markets for their farm products and lower costs for importing manufactured goods. Many improvement projects were enacted under Smith's leadership; during 1837 and 1838, Smith was one of three fund commissioners, who collected assets and adjusted debts when projects were jeopardized by the panic of 1837. This was not a job to enhance his popularity, but Smith was elected to a fifth term in 1839, and during the 1840–1841 term he served as chairman of the Committee on Canals.

Smith moved toward national politics as a Whig elector in 1840, campaigning enthusiastically in Indiana, where William Henry Harrison easily won over Democrat Martin Van Buren. Seeking to go to Washington himself, Smith entered the 1841 three-way race for the Twenty-seventh Congress and lost; however, he was one of only two Whigs elected from Indiana to the Twenty-eighth and Twenty-ninth Congresses, and in 1847 he was the sole Whig returned to Washington from Indiana. In the Twenty-ninth Congress, Smith served on the Committee on Foreign Affairs; in the Thirtieth Congress, he was chairman of the Committee on Territories.

Smith opposed the Mexican War, with some risk to his political future; however, he represented a safe Whig district. He began speaking out on the issue with President James K. Polk's 11 May 1846 request for permission to enroll volunteers in a war begun, the president contended, by Mexican hostilities. Some Whigs joined the Democrats in supporting the president; some adamantly denounced the war and refused to vote for the men and supplies sought by the administration; and the moderate Whigs, including Smith, took a less simplistic position. They blamed the president for an unnecessary and unconstitutional war, yet they maintained that the men sent to fight it must be supported and supplied.

Smith consistently opposed the war with Mexico, contending that it was a consequence of the policy of annexing Texas, and he noted with pride that Whig leaders had warned of this. He regarded the administration as a southern one and thought its war would result in the acquisition of new territory into which to extend slavery. Smith offered a novel solution to this problem: the territory seized from Mexico should be kept out of the Union.

Although his antiwar stand may have cost Smith the Speakership of the House of Representatives (he lost in the Whig caucus to Massachusetts Whig Robert C. Winthrop), he continued to denounce the war and its consequences throughout his last term. Refusing another nomination, he left Congress in 1849 after four terms.

In the 1848 presidential election, the Whig candidate was General Zachary Taylor, who commanded the military force President Polk had ordered to the Rio Grande River against Mexico. Smith supported Taylor, hoping to become postmaster general in the new administration. Instead, Taylor appointed him to a board of commissioners to investigate American claims against Mexico stemming from the war.

In 1851 Smith returned to his boyhood home of Cincinnati to practice law. He also became president of the Cincinnati and Chicago Railroad, which proved a disastrous venture. Like many other railroads, it suffered financial difficulties because of inept management, construction expenses, and political pressures that resulted in unwise routes.

By the time of the 1856 presidential election, Smith had joined the many northern Whigs who went into the new Republican party when the old Whig organization broke apart; he supported John C. Frémont. In 1859 Smith moved to Indianapolis, resumed law practice there, and became an important Indiana Republican.

Smith was chairman of the Indiana delegation that went uncommitted to the 1860 Republican convention in Chicago. There, he was active in the selection of Abraham Lincoln as the party's presidential candidate and was asked to second Lincoln's nomination. When the vote for the nominee was called, the Indianans solidly backed Lincoln. Later, David Davis, Lincoln's manager at the convention, reminded the president-elect that the Indianans "could not have been got as a unit" without the services of Smith (Donald, p. 265).

After the convention, Smith was one of the notification committee members who went down to Springfield to congratulate the nominee. He subsequently campaigned throughout Indiana, and that state's electoral votes went to Lincoln. When President Lincoln formed his cabinet, he appointed Smith secretary of the interior. Some historians say the appointment was payment of "a debt to Indiana for early support" of Lincoln's nomination (McPherson, p. 260). Some, including Kenneth M. Stamp, contend it was the result of a promise to Smith made, without Lincoln's knowledge, by David Davis at Chicago; others, including David Herbert Donald, refute this charge. But many agree that Indiana's crucial support, and therefore Smith's, was thus rewarded.

Prior to assuming his cabinet post, Smith was appointed a member of the National Peace Conference, which convened in Washington on 4 February 1861 to seek ways of preventing civil war. Compromise was not Smith's way, however, and he opposed all concessions to the South.

The work of the Interior Department was not greatly affected by the war, and Smith seemed to lack enthusiasm for his cabinet post. He felt that the president made all the important decisions. Mark E. Neely, Jr., noted, "His only important influence on administration policy stemmed from his zeal for colonization" and returning freed slaves to Africa, and he opposed using blacks as soldiers in the Union army. Because Lincoln knew Smith favored colonization (and because other cabinet members didn't want the assignment), he put Smith in charge of a short-lived project to develop a colony for American freedmen on the Chiriqui Lagoon in New Granada (now Panama). Smith was opposed to Lincoln's emancipation proposals, but this became irrelevant when, in December 1862, he resigned from the cabinet. Lincoln appointed him U.S. judge for the Indiana District. Smith's health was poor, and he had served little more than a year when he was stricken at his office in the courthouse in Indianapolis and died later the same day.

• The Caleb B. Smith Papers are at the Library of Congress. Louis J. Bailey, "Caleb Blood Smith," *Indiana Magazine of History* 29 (Sept. 1933): 213–39, adequately treats Smith as no profound thinker but a skilled orator and cites important primary sources. *Biographical and Genealogical History of Wayne, Fayette, Union and Franklin Counties, Indiana*, vol. 1 (1899), includes a good summary of Smith's life. Willard L. King, *Lincoln's Campaign Manager: David Davis* (1960), is useful on the cabinet appointment. See also Burton J. Hendrick, *Lincoln's War Cabinet* (1946); James M. McPherson, *Battle Cry of Freedom: The Civil War Era* (1988); David Herbert Donald, *Lincoln* (1995); and Kenneth M. Stampp, *Indiana Politics during the Civil War* (1949; repr. 1978). W. W. Thornton, "United States District Court for the District of Indiana," in *Biographical Sketches and Review of the Bench and Bar of Indiana* (1895), places Judge Smith in context as a jurist. Numerous citations of primary sources and essential details on Smith's view of the Mexican War are in Hal W. Bochin, "Caleb B. Smith's Opposition to the Mexican War," *Indiana Magazine of History* 69 (June 1973): 95–114. Mark E. Neely, Jr., "Lincoln and the Mexican War," *Civil War History* 24 (Mar. 1978): 5–24, compares Smith's and Lincoln's views; in the *Abraham Lincoln Encyclopedia* (1982), Neely provides an objective overview of Smith and his cabinet appointment. An obituary is in the *New York Times*, 8 Jan. 1864, and an "Order of Condolence" by the president is in the *New York Times*, 17 Jan. 1864.

SYLVIA B. LARSON

SMITH, C. Aubrey (21 July 1863–20 Dec. 1948), actor, was born Charles Aubrey Smith in London, England, the son of Charles John Smith, a surgeon, and Sarah Ann Clode. After schooling at Charterhouse, he studied at St. John's College, Cambridge University, gaining distinction as an amateur cricket player. Following his graduation in 1884, he captained the Sussex cricket team and later led English teams on tour in Australia and South Africa. He found employment as well, first as a math "crammer," tutoring young men preparing for military entrance exams, and then on the London Stock Exchange.

While in Australia with the English cricket team in 1887, Smith was encouraged by a theatrical manager to take up acting professionally. When Smith said he knew nothing of stage acting, he recalled in an interview, the manager replied, "That's all right—you don't have to. . . . All you have to do is be natural" (*New York Herald Tribune*, 22 July 1934). The manag-

er had seen, as did audiences the rest of Smith's life, that he was a natural physical type to play British aristocrats, men of title, and military officers. He was 6′3″ with an erect posture and booming voice. All his facial features were commanding: a jutting chin, a beak of a nose, and fierce-looking eyes under heavy eyebrows. He also sported a thick, bristling mustache. He embodied the popular idea of how defenders of the British empire's honor should look. If a role had a sentimental scene, his stern visage could melt into tenderness, and his blue eyes twinkle with warmth.

Following work with Australian stock companies, Smith in 1892 began acting in England with a provincial stock company located in Hastings. He soon became a skilled professional. By 1894 he was playing the male lead in a touring production of *The Second Mrs. Tanqueray*. He made his London debut in 1895 in *The Notorious Mrs. Ebbsmith*. Over the next few years, acting in the companies of Fred Terry, Sir John Hare, and Sir George Alexander, he appeared in London and on tour in Britain and the United States. Two outstanding roles at this time, both in 1896, were Black Michael in *The Prisoner of Zenda* and Frederick in *As You Like It*. In 1896 he married Isabel Mary Wood; the couple had one daughter.

Apart from two interludes when he managed London theaters, the St. James (1898–1900) and the Comedy (1924), Smith spent the rest of his long life playing to type in somewhere around 150 productions, going back and forth between Britain and the United States, and between stage and screen. He performed in leading roles opposite most of the great stars of the era. He appeared with Sir Johnston Forbes-Robertson in *The Light That Failed* (London, 1903) and toured with that actor in the United States in 1903–1904, both in that play and in *Hamlet*. In the latter, "That sound and virile actor, Mr. C. Aubrey Smith . . . was cast for the Ghost, and later Fortinbras, carrying both parts with distinction" (*New York Times*, 8 Mar. 1904).

Smith's appearances in London were regularly interspersed with productions in the United States. Returning to the New York stage in 1907, he had a great personal success in *The Morals of Marcus*, playing the title role of Sir Marcus Ordeyne opposite Marie Doro. He toured this country again in 1909 with Grace George, appearing in *A Woman's Way* and *The Best People*. In 1911 he was on Broadway once more with Billie Burke in *The Runaway*. In 1914–1915 he toured the United States with Margaret Illington in *The Lie*. While in New York he appeared in two silent films, *Builder of Bridges* (1915) and *The Witching Hour* (1916). In 1916 he starred in the successful London production of *Daddy Long-Legs*. He returned to filmmaking in Britain in *Red Pottage* (1918).

The same pattern of stage appearances on both sides of the Atlantic continued for Smith in the years after World War I. He began the 1920s in various London productions, notably those of *Pygmalion* (1920), *Polly with a Past* (1921), *A Bill of Divorcement* (1921), and *Mr. Pim Passes By* (1922). He was equally successful in New York appearances opposite Minnie Maddern

Fiske in *Mary, Mary Quite Contrary* (1923) and Ethel Barrymore in *The Constant Wife* (1926). Following the latter play's long run, he took the title role in the Broadway production of *The Bachelor Father* (1928) and repeated its success in London in 1929. He also acted in British silent films steadily throughout the decade. In *The Way to Treat a Woman* (1930) he made his final appearance on the London stage.

Metro-Goldwyn-Mayer's film version of *The Bachelor Father* (1931) moved Smith easily into talking pictures and life in Hollywood. Now in his late sixties, he also made a smooth transition from roles as a leading man to substantial character roles. He remained in demand to portray stalwart, commanding men, usually British, in dozens of top Hollywood productions during the 1930s, from *Queen Christina* (1933) and *The House of Rothschild* (1934) to *Little Lord Fauntleroy* (1936), *The Prisoner of Zenda* (1937), and *Kidnapped* (1939). Perhaps the epitome of his many portrayals of a soldier of empire and symbol of British honor, who nevertheless can show a humorous and ironic side to his character, is found in *The Four Feathers* (1939). He was a leader of the colony of British actors regularly appearing in Hollywood films during that period and reportedly remained completely British in his ways—tweeds or cricket blazer, pipe, tea and the *Times* of London daily, and cricket at least once a week. He was created a commander of the British Empire by George VI in 1938. Yet he was content to live in Beverly Hills at his home named "The Round Corner," a reference to his style of bowling in cricket. He told an interviewer that a visit to England a few years previously had shown him too many changes in familiar landscapes and "at the clubs, the chairs which had always held so many familiar faces—they were empty. It was very disheartening" (*New York Times*, 10 Apr. 1938).

Smith returned to the New York stage one more time at the age of seventy-eight in the comedy *Spring Again* (1941). He was warmly received by the public and critics, though the reviewer for the *New York Herald Tribune* found it "not easy to think of [Smith] as the son of an American general of Civil War days [when he has] been for so long the favorite British commander in chief of all of us. . . . [or as the] son of any one save possibly of some ancient chieftain of Britain who had warred against Julius Caesar" (11 Nov. 1941). Otherwise he remained a film actor for the rest of his life, in such productions as *Rebecca* (1940) and *The White Cliffs of Dover* (1944). A knighthood came to him in 1944, and he was thereafter styled Sir Aubrey Smith. Becoming increasingly deaf in later years, he continued to act by reading lips on the set. His final film appearance was in *Little Women*, released in 1949. He died at his home in Beverly Hills, California.

• Materials on his life and career are in the Billy Rose Theatre Collection at the New York Public Library for the Performing Arts, Lincoln Center. A biography of Smith is David Rayvern Allen, *Sir Aubrey* (1982). A list of film appearances is in James Robert Parish, *Hollywood Character Actors* (1978). See also Sheridan Morley, *Tales from the Hollywood Raj: The British, the Movies, and Tinseltown* (1983). Articles on his life and career are "Cricket Won for Wellington and Smith Too," *New York Herald Tribune* (22 July 1934), and Bosley Crowther, "Britannia and Mr. Smith," *New York Times* (10 Apr. 1938). Obituaries are in the *New York Times* and *New York Herald Tribune*, both 21 Dec. 1948, and *Variety*, 22 Dec. 1948.

WILLIAM STEPHENSON

SMITH, Chard Powers (1 Nov. 1894–31 Oct. 1977), writer, was born in Watertown, New York, the son of Edward North Smith, a lawyer and judge of the New York Supreme Court, and Alice Lamon. Smith earned a B.A. from Yale in 1916. Between 1917 and 1920 he served in the U.S. Army Field Artillery. He attended the Army Staff College in Langres, France, and attained the rank of captain. Smith received his LL.B. from Harvard in 1921 and did graduate study at Oxford University during the summer of that year. In 1924 he returned to Harvard for further graduate study in English and, many years later, earned an M.A. in history at Columbia in 1949. Smith married Olive Carey Macdonald in 1921, but she died early in 1924 while they were in Italy; they had no children. In 1929 he married Marion Antoinette Chester; they had two children. After a divorce in 1957, Smith married Eunice Waters Clark, a professor of French; they had no children.

Although trained as a lawyer, Smith practiced this profession only briefly. He was a law clerk for the firm of Hubbell, Taylor, Goodwin, and Moser (1921–1922), and he later served part time as a justice of the peace in Cornwall, Connecticut (1936–1947). Upon the recommendation of John Erskine (1879–1951), then president of the Poetry Society of America, Smith was invited to the MacDowell Colony in July 1924. He had already published a few poems in literary magazines, and the MacDowell experience, which allowed him to establish a friendship with Edwin Arlington Robinson, confirmed Smith's desire to be a poet. Subsequent volumes of poetry include *Along the Wind* (1925), *Lost Address* (1928), *The Quest of Pan* (1930), *Hamilton: A Poetic Drama* (1930), and *Prelude to Man* (1936). This final work is an epic treatment of evolution; it reflects Smith's intense interest in paleontology, an area in which he did field work for the American Museum of Natural History.

Smith received considerably more recognition as a writer when he turned to historical fiction. In 1939 he published *Artillery of Time*, a long novel set in upstate New York in the years before the Civil War. Well-received by critics, the book was frequently described as a northern counterpart of *Gone with the Wind*. Intended as the first of a series of novels, *Artillery of Time* emphasizes the moral confusion and decline resulting from the decay of agrarian values. A second novel in the series, *Ladies Day* (1941), focuses on the country's urban and industrial development in the last decades of the nineteenth century. The book's title refers to charitable projects carried on mostly by women—a contrast with the prevailing selfishness and materialism of the day. The outbreak of World War II diverted Smith from this historical series. He published instead a short novel entitled *Turn of the Dial* (1943). This book satirizes radio advertising and shows how Hitler and Goebbels adopted techniques of American public relations for their own propaganda purposes. Also in 1943 Smith published *He's in the Artillery Now*, a patriotic treatment of the American war effort.

Several of Smith's books also display his interest in literary criticism and education. In 1932 he published *Pattern and Variation in Poetry*, an attempt to formulate laws of poetic form and content by studying over 2,000 poems. *Annals of the Poets, Their Private Lives and Personalities* (1935) was a scientific inquiry into the nature of the poetic temperament. Smith was a lecturer on poetry and history at Northwestern University (1937) and the University of Kansas (1950), and in 1948 he arranged a private printing of his *Treatise on Elementary Education*.

After World War II, Smith again concentrated primarily on historical writing. *The Housatonic: Puritan River* (1946) was a bestselling volume in the Rivers of America series. It provided a geologic, cultural, and commercial history of the entire river valley from its origin in the Berkshire Mountains to Long Island Sound. *Yankees and God* (1954) offered an even more comprehensive history of New England culture. *Where the Light Falls* (1965) began as a brief memoir but turned into a detailed biography of Robinson, a friend of Smith's from 1924 until 1935. Shortly before his death (in a nursing home in Williamstown, Mass.), Smith was at work on an autobiography and a history of the "Lost Generation."

Remarkable for the wide range of his interests and publications, Smith progressed from writing lyric works of self-expression to historical fiction heavy with social commentary to cultural history and biography. The critic Harry Warfel comments that Smith "devoted his life to the search for moral and religious absolutes, and to the restatement of them in contemporary idiom." A devout Quaker for much of his life, Smith not only declared his theological bias in writing history but went on to affirm, "The world needs our prophecy" (*Yankees and God*).

• A significant collection of Smith's manuscripts and letters is in the Beinecke Library at Yale. Several other university libraries (including Harvard, Brown, Syracuse, and the State University of New York at Buffalo) have additional holdings. Harry Warfel, *American Novelists of Today* (1951), includes a brief but useful analysis of Smith's writing. For basic biographical information an obituary is in the *New York Times*, 3 Nov. 1977.

ALBERT E. WILHELM

SMITH, Charles Alphonso (28 May 1864–13 June 1924), professor of English and author, was born in Greensboro, North Carolina, the son of J. Henry Smith, a pastor of the Presbyterian church, and his second wife, Mary Kelly Watson. A boyhood friend of William Sydney Porter (later known as O. Henry), C. Alphonso Smith grew up in the South of the Reconstruction, attending the Greensboro public schools. He received an A.B. and an A.M. from Davidson College in 1884 and 1887, respectively, and, following graduation, taught school in the small North Carolina towns of Sanford, Princeton, and Selma. In 1889 Smith left to study at Johns Hopkins University, where he also worked for the next three years as an instructor of English.

He received his Ph.D. from Johns Hopkins in 1893 after writing his doctoral dissertation, "The Order of Words in Anglo-Saxon Prose." He then went to Louisiana State University as professor of English language and literature from 1893 to 1902. During this time he wrote two books, *Repetition and Parallelism in English Verse* (1894) and *An Old English Grammar* (1896). These would be followed in later years by various articles, a series of grammars for school use, and more books. He established his reputation for the study of language with works such as *An English-German Conversation Book* (1902), *Studies in English Syntax* (1906), *The American Short Story* (1912), *Keynote Studies in Keynote Books of the Bible* (1919), and *New Words Self-Defined* (1919). From 1897 to 1899 he served as president of the central division of the Modern Language Association. Smith was influential in developing scholarly study of regional literature by serving from 1907 to 1923 as editor in chief of the seventeen-volume series Library of Southern Literature.

In 1902 Smith went to the University of North Carolina, where he remained until 1909. He started as a professor of English and soon after arriving at Chapel Hill became the first dean of its graduate department. From 1907 to 1909 he was also head of the English department. As founder and editor of the university-sponsored journal *Studies in Philology*, Smith was influential in fostering graduate scholarship at the University of North Carolina. In 1908 he married Susie McGee Heck of Raleigh; they had three children.

In 1909 he left the University of North Carolina for the University of Virginia, where he was the first Edgar Allan Poe Professor of English and gained renown for his inspired teaching in the humanities and for bringing scholarly attention to America's indigenous literature of authors such as Washington Irving, Nathaniel Hawthorne, James Fenimore Cooper, and Edgar Allan Poe. In 1910 Smith went on leave to the University of Berlin, Germany, as Roosevelt Professor of American History and Institutions. He returned to Virginia the following year, where he remained until 1917 and gained a reputation as "one of the ablest lecturers" in the university's history (Virginius Dabney, *Mr. Jefferson's University* [1981], p. 50). After the move to Virginia, Smith wrote his most widely circulated and most characteristic book, *What Can Literature Do for Me?* (1913), in which he presented a lively case for the popularization of the humanities, what he called "applied literature," to be made part of the "life and experience of as many men and women as possible" (Barr, p. 13). That was followed in 1916 by the major literary work of his career, the *O. Henry Biography*.

While at Virginia he also founded the Virginia Folk-Lore Society in 1913, which, under his leadership, brought together a rich collection of genuine folk ballads and which Stringfellow Barr described as "in the long run the activity for which he may be best remembered." This collection was posthumously published in 1929 as *Traditional Ballads of Virginia*.

Smith left Virginia in 1917 to head the English department at the U.S. Naval Academy at Annapolis, where he gained distinction for his pioneering commitment to making the study and appreciation of literature integral to the education of future naval officers. At Annapolis he taught and continued his literary and editorial activities until stricken by a sudden illness in 1924. He died in Annapolis. Although Smith achieved respect in his field as a scholar, he was best remembered after his death for his belief that American literature was the embodiment of our national spirit, a belief that he imparted zealously to his students throughout his life. He helped to expand the notion of literature by calling attention to dimensions such as folklore, the richness of slang and colloquial language, and the contribution of local and regional authors. This role as impassioned expounder and interpreter of literature for students and readers at all levels characterized his teaching, writing, and editing over several decades.

• There is no known repository of Smith papers. C. Alphonso Smith, *Southern Literary Studies* (1927), contains a bibliography of Smith's published works and an extensive biographical sketch by F. Stringfellow Barr. The reader is directed also to the *Biographical Dictionary of American Educators*. Brief obituaries of Smith are in the *New York Times* and the *Greensboro Daily News*, both 14 June 1924.

JOHN R. THELIN
SHARON THELIN-BLACKBURN

SMITH, Charles Emory (18 Feb. 1842–19 Jan. 1908), newspaper owner and politician, was born in Mansfield, Connecticut, the son of Emory Boutelle Smith, a silk manufacturer, and Avrilla Topliff Royce. At the age of seven, he moved with his parents to Albany, New York. Smith qualified to enter Union College of Schenectady, New York, as a junior in 1859; he graduated in June 1861. During his college years he pursued his twin lifetime interests by writing for and editing the *University Review* and leading the college Republican party organization.

Smith initially played an active part in the Civil War by serving on the staff of General John Rathbone in Albany, where volunteer regiments were assembled. For unknown reasons Smith resigned in 1862 and spent the remainder of the war teaching in Albany Academy and continuing his newspaper career. As early as 1858 he had written articles for the *Albany Evening Transcript* and the *Express*. From 1865 to 1870 he was an editor of the *Express*. In 1870 Smith purchased an interest in the *Albany Journal*, a prominent Republican newspaper in New York State, four years later becoming the paper's editor in chief until 1880, when he split with his fellow owners over various mat-

ters. In 1863 he married Ella Huntley; they had no children.

During the 1860s Smith began his lifelong involvement in Republican party affairs. On the New York State level he served as secretary to Governor Reuben Fenton (1865–1869) but then switched to Roscoe Conkling's faction of the party. After being a delegate in 1872 to the New York Republican Convention, Smith was a delegate in 1876 at the first of his eight national Republican conventions.

Based on his experience at the state level on the Committee on Resolutions, at the 1876 convention in Cincinnati Smith was appointed to the National Committee on Resolutions. Thanks to his industry and fluid pen, for the next quarter-century he helped draft Republican presidential platforms. In this task Smith was an architect, diligently crafting the party's views as formulated by others. His prominence in both the newspaper profession and Republican politics in this period led to several honors. In 1874 he was president of the New York State Press Association. The Republican state legislature appointed him a regent of the University of New York in 1879, and Union College made him a trustee in 1881.

Seizing the opportunity to move to a larger city and to acquire a more influential newspaper, Smith became editor in chief of the *Philadelphia Press* in 1880 and shortly thereafter purchased a controlling share of the paper. He remained a part of the newspaper's operations until his death. Under his lead, the *Press*, which had lost readership and influence in the 1870s, once again became the principal Republican paper in Pennsylvania. In the *Press* Smith consistently supported national Republican views, favoring protective tariffs, the gold standard, and after 1898 expansionism. On the local level he endorsed various educational, health, and municipal reforms. He became active in the Republican politics of his newly adopted state while continuing his role at the national level, for example, campaigning vigorously for presidential candidates James A. Garfield; James G. Blaine, a longtime friend and the man who introduced him to William McKinley; and Benjamin Harrison (1833–1901).

On 14 February 1890 Smith received his reward for these services, when he was unexpectedly appointed the U.S. minister to Russia, where he resided until mid-1892. A major issue during his tenure was the treatment in the Russian empire of American Jews specifically and Russian Jews in general. Although he was unfairly seen by Jewish circles in the United States as unsympathetic to the Jewish plight, Smith by means of several memoranda, which remained unknown to the American public at the time, informed the Russian authorities of the State Department's concern. He was also involved in the distribution of American aid to the famine victims of 1892. Later Smith wrote two insightful articles on the new czar, Nicholas II, and the revolution of 1905.

Smith reached the height of his national prominence when President McKinley on 21 April 1898 appointed him postmaster general, replacing James A. Gray. As postmaster general Smith completed the system of rural free delivery and created mail service to Cuba, Puerto Rico, and the Philippines. While personally honest, Smith allowed the postal service to flourish as a source of patronage under the direction of Mark Hanna. In the Spanish-American War and the ensuing debate over American territorial acquisitions, Smith confined himself to the position of observer, although he did order the confiscation of antiwar literature sent to American soldiers by Edward Atkinson of the Anti-Imperialist League. Smith often accompanied McKinley, whom he served as more of a friend than an adviser, on his numerous travels around the country, including the fatal trip to Buffalo in September 1901.

On 15 January 1902 Smith resigned as postmaster general so that the new president, Theodore Roosevelt (1858–1919), could appoint his own candidate to this politically sensitive position. Smith devoted the rest of his life to the *Press* and battles with the Republican governor of Pennsylvania, Samuel W. Pennypacker, over what Smith deemed to be attempts to limit freedom of the press. After the death of his first wife in the early 1900s, Smith married Henrietta Nichols in October 1907; they had no children. A few months later, Smith died suddenly in Philadelphia.

Throughout his career Smith was an effective and entertaining orator, as evidenced by his frequently being called on to speak at public occasions. He once said, "I loved politics as an accessory to the newspaper and the newspaper has been my sole ambition." A genial person and good companion, Smith thoroughly enjoyed his newspaper work and activity with the Republican party but made no lasting impression in either area.

• Smith left no known collection of papers, and no biographical study exists. His own writings are mainly confined to articles and editorials in several Albany newspapers and, especially, the *Philadelphia Press*. A number of his addresses were published in pamphlet form. His two articles on Russia are "A Young Czar and His Advisers," *North American Review* 160 (1895): 21–28, and "The Internal Situation in Russia," *Annals of the American Academy of Political and Social Sciences* 26 (July 1905): 89–95. See also Charles Morris, ed., *Makers of Philadelphia* (1894); S. W. Pennypacker, *The Autobiography of a Pennsylvanian* (1918); Lewis Gould, *The Presidency of William McKinley* (1980); and Gary Best, *To Free a People: American Jewish Leaders and the Jewish Problem in Eastern Europe, 1890–1914* (1982). Detailed obituaries are in the *New York Times* and the *Philadelphia Press*, 20 Jan. 1908.

JAMES A. MALLOY, JR.

SMITH, Charles Ferguson (24 Apr. 1807–25 Apr. 1862), soldier, was born in Philadelphia, Pennsylvania, the son of Samuel Blair Smith, an army surgeon, and Mary Ferguson. Attending the U.S. Military Academy, he graduated in 1825, ranking nineteenth in a class of thirty-seven, and was commissioned a second lieutenant of artillery. Four years later he returned to West Point and commenced thirteen years of service there, first as an instructor, then as an adjutant to the superintendent, and finally as commandant of cadets. He made quite an impression on several of the cadets, notably Ulysses S. Grant. He was promoted to first lieutenant in 1832 and to captain in 1838. In 1840 Smith married Fanny Mactier; the couple had three children.

Smith saw extensive action in the Mexican-American War, commanding battalions of light infantry under the command of both Zachary Taylor and Winfield Scott, and distinguishing himself in battle. He saw action at Palo Alto, Resaca de la Palma, Monterrey, Contreras, and Churubusco, and later he commanded the police guard in Mexico City. Despite the fact that he won brevets to major, lieutenant colonel, and colonel as a result of the conflict, not until 1854 did he gain promotion to major. The following year he was elevated to the rank of lieutenant colonel. In 1856 he led an exploring expedition up the Red River in Minnesota, and the next year he participated in the campaign against the Mormons in Utah. In 1860 he headed the Department of Utah. In 1861, when the Civil War broke out, he headed the Department of Washington for a short period of time before finding himself reassigned to recruiting duty in New York. Some Republicans, mistaking his stiff, professional demeanor and skepticism toward politicians for a lack of enthusiasm, questioned his commitment to the Union cause and delayed his advancement. Not even George B. McClellan could secure his services. Finally on 31 August Smith received a commission as a brigadier general with orders to report to John C. Frémont for assignment. Placed in command of the garrison at recently occupied Paducah, Kentucky, as head of the District of Western Kentucky, Smith worked beside his former student Grant at Cairo, Illinois. It took Grant some time to get used to the fact that he outranked his old idol. Once more Smith, accused of being too lenient in his treatment of secessionist civilians, fended off charges that he was less than loyal to the Union, and his superior officers, including Grant, who eventually became Smith's immediate superior, rose to his defense.

In January 1862 Smith, as part of a feint, took a small force and a few gunboats up the Tennessee River to the Kentucky-Tennessee border, where the Confederates were erecting Forts Henry and Heiman. A dozen miles to the east, on the Cumberland River, was Fort Donelson. Smith reported back to Grant that Donelson was vulnerable, and Grant finally succeeded in gaining approval to attack the Confederate defenses. Forts Henry and Heiman fell on 6 February 1862. Smith commanded one of Grant's three divisions that then marched on Donelson, taking up position on the left. On 15 February the Confederates launched an attack against Grant's right flank, and Grant ordered Smith to counterattack. Urging his men forward, Smith shouted: "Come on, you volunteers, come on. This is your chance. You volunteered to be killed for love of your country and now you can be." The resulting gains so severely compromised the Confederate position that the Confederates were compelled to surrender. When Grant showed him Confederate commander Simon Buckner's request for terms, Smith reportedly growled, "No terms to the damned Rebels!" Grant's rephrasing of it, "No terms except unconditional and immediate surrender can be accepted," made him a household hero and earned him the sobriquet "Unconditional Surrender" Grant (Catton, pp. 170, 175). As recognition for his service, Smith won promotion to major general of volunteers the following month.

When Henry W. Halleck, dissatisfied with irregularities in the administration of Grant's command, ordered Grant to remain at Fort Henry, Smith took charge in March 1862 of a force moving up the Tennessee River to the Mississippi border and occupied Pittsburg Landing. Just as Grant prepared to resume command in the field, Smith injured his right leg jumping into a yawl. Infection set in, confining Smith to bed, and he died, presumably in Savannah, Tennessee, two and a half weeks after the battle of Shiloh. In a statement reflecting both great respect for Smith and some confusion over chronology, William T. Sherman remarked years later, "Had C. F. Smith lived, Grant would have disappeared to history after Fort Donelson."

• Smith's papers are in private hands. The best accounts of his Civil War career are in Bruce Catton, *Grant Moves South* (1960), and Kenneth P. Williams, *Lincoln Finds a General*, vol. 3 (1956).

BROOKS D. SIMPSON

SMITH, Charles Henry (15 June 1826–24 Aug. 1903), humorist, was born in Lawrenceville, Georgia, the son of Asahel Reid Smith and Caroline Ann Maguire. One of ten children, he attended the Gwinnet County Manual Labor Institute and clerked in his father's store. In 1844 he entered Franklin College (later the University of Georgia), but he left in 1847, before completing his degree, when his father's illness forced him to return home and manage the family store. Smith married sixteen-year-old Mary Octavia Hutchins in 1849; they eventually had thirteen children. After briefly studying law, Smith was admitted to the bar and became a lawyer traveling for the Georgia Circuit Court. Moving his growing family to Rome, Georgia, in 1851, he formed a law partnership with John W. H. Underwood. A respected member of the Rome community, Smith became clerk of the city council in 1852 and city alderman in 1861.

When the Civil War began, Smith enlisted as a private in the Rome Light Guards. In April 1861 he sent a letter signed "Bill Arp" to the *Southern Confederacy*, a Rome, Georgia, newspaper. It was the first of more than 2,000 humorous letters, most of which appeared first in southern newspapers, that he published between 1861 and 1903. Addressed to Abraham Lincoln ("Abe Linkhorn") and supposedly written by an almost illiterate Georgia cracker named Bill Arp, it appeared shortly after the taking of Harpers Ferry by Union forces. The letter pokes fun at Lincoln with a tone of mock indignation: how dare an insignificant politician from Illinois call southerners rebels and command them to lay down their arms and disperse!

In July 1861 Smith joined the Eighth Georgia Regiment, which he served as a supply commissioner with the rank of major. Arp's second letter to Lincoln appeared in January 1862, his third and fourth such letters in December of the same year. For the most part, Smith's Bill Arp maintains a tone of skeptical inquiry, satirizing such subjects as high taxes, corrupt officials, and draft dodgers. These dialect letters are quite unlike those of George Washington Harris's Sut Lovingood, which attack Lincoln and all Yankees in a vicious manner. Smith was reelected a Rome city alderman in 1863, and the following year he was made a first lieutenant in the Forrest Light Artillery Company. He again became city alderman in 1864 and also was appointed a judge advocate in Macon, Georgia. Setting up a store in Rome in 1865, Smith was soon elected to the Georgia senate.

When he first wrote for the newspapers, Smith was clearly influenced by Charles Farrar Browne, creator of "Artemus Ward." Bill Arp's initial letters to Lincoln are reminiscent of Ward's earlier interviews with Lincoln and Jefferson Davis. At the beginning of their writing careers, both Smith and Browne relied on pulverized grammar and misspelling for comic effect. Neither could avoid puns. Much of Smith's pun play is derived from mispronunciation, as in Arp's "Abe Linkhorn" or "Mack C. Million." Arp also joined Ward in misquoting classical authors. Misquotation combined with mispronunciation to produce comic redundancy, the piling of one comic touch on top of another. Smith, like Browne, frequently ridiculed belles lettres and pompous oratory. In time, however, both writers toned down their characters, perhaps in order to appeal to wider audiences.

Smith's greatest popularity among his contemporaries and his most lasting fame came from the Bill Arp letters he wrote during and at the conclusion of the Civil War. His *Bill Arp, So Called: A Side Show of the Southern Side of the War*, which contains the four letters to Lincoln and other wartime sketches, was published in New York in 1866 and became an immediate success. The main object of Smith's satire was the North and its conduct of the war. According to Arp, the actions of Yankee soldiers were frequently despicable, and northern versions of accomplishments by the Union army often were exaggerated. Yet Arp's letters made it clear that southerners were never unanimously behind the Confederacy. He attacked those who mismanaged or did not support the war. Shirkers and draft dodgers came in for criticism from Arp's pen, as did the fluctuations of Confederate money, the currency bill, and the suspension of habeas corpus. In speculating on a Union victory toward the war's end, he usually became defiant, thus foreshadowing southern attitudes during Reconstruction. Smith's view of the war mellowed with time, and he came to see, for example, that not all Union soldiers had been villains.

Between 1867 and 1877 Smith, a staunch and unreconciled Democrat, spent much of his time on politics, serving as mayor of Rome in 1867 and four terms as city alderman. Arp's letters of the Reconstruction period were the most bitter Smith ever wrote. Many of them appeared in *Bill Arp's Peace Papers* (1873) but were not published in later collections of Arp letters. In various letters of the late 1860s and early 1870s, Arp approved President Andrew Johnson's efforts to implement Lincoln's policy of moderation toward the South, attacked former governor Joseph Brown when he counseled compromise with the Reconstructionists of Georgia, revealed bitter feelings toward the "black Republicans," and deplored the political scandals of the Grant administration. As Smith made clear through Arp: "I'm not rekonsiled. I thought I was, but I ain't. I've been trying to make peace, and make friends, ever since the confounded old war was over but, it won't do" (*Peace Papers*, p. 201).

By 1873–1874, Smith's last year as a Rome alderman, he was apparently losing interest in politics. In 1877 Smith gave up the law, storekeeping, and politics to become a farmer. He supplemented his negligible farm income by lecturing and contributing Arp letters to the *Atlanta Constitution*. The character of Smith's post-1877 letters is different from that of the earlier ones. Less satirical and more sentimental, they reveal a certain political disengagement. The "new" Arp is an industrious, good-humored farmer who chats about his family, farm life, friends, and social conditions in Georgia. Now a genial, homely philosopher, he advocates reconciliation between North and South. Smith died in Cartersville, Georgia.

With Bill Arp, Smith joined the ranks of a new breed of literary comedians produced by the Civil War—including Henry Wheeler Shaw ("Josh Billings"), David Ross Locke ("Petroleum V. Nasby"), and Charles Farrar Browne ("Artemus Ward")—who capitalized on caricatures, tortured dialects of illiterate individuals, and comic misquotations and misspellings. Smith's Bill Arp is best remembered as a simple and strong Georgia cracker whose letters provide a unique record of the hopes and frustrations, the successes and failures of the common southerner during the Civil War, Reconstruction, and the Gilded Age.

• Additional works by Smith include *Bill Arp's Scrapbook; Humor and Philosophy* (1884), *The Farm and the Fireside: Sketches of Domestic Life in War and Peace* (1891), and *Bill Arp: From the Uncivil War to Date, 1861–1903* (1903). The last of those volumes is the most complete collection of Bill Arp letters.
Biographical information and critical materials dealing with Smith's life and works can be found in Anne M. Christie, "Charles Henry Smith: 'Bill Arp': A Biographical and Critical Study of a Nineteenth-Century Georgia Humorist, Politician, Homely Philosopher" (Ph.D. diss., Univ. of Chicago, 1952); James E. Ginther, "Charles Henry Smith, Alias 'Bill Arp'," *Georgia Review* 4 (Winter 1950): 313–21, and "Charles Henry Smith, the Creator of Bill Arp," *Mark Twain Journal* 10 (Summer 1955): 11–12, 23–24; Anne M. Christie, "Civil War Humor: Bill Arp," *Civil War History* 2 (Sept. 1956): 103–19; Jay B. Hubbell, *The South in American Literature, 1607–1900* (1954), pp. 683–86; Wade H. Hall, "A Study of Southern Humor, 1865–1913," (Ph.D. diss., Univ. of Illinois, 1961); and James C. Austin, *Bill Arp* (1969).
L. MOODY SIMMS, JR.

SMITH, Charles Perrin (5 Jan. 1819–27 Jan. 1883), editor and politician, was born in Philadelphia, the son of George Wishart Smith, a native of Virginia who had moved north after the family fortune had been lost in the Revolution, and Hannah Carpenter Ellet, a Quaker from Salem in southwestern New Jersey. His father died when Smith was two years old, and his mother remarried.

Smith spent his childhood and young manhood in Salem. On finishing school at fifteen, he started working for the local Whig newspaper, the Salem *Freeman's Banner*. He did well at his job, and by the time he was twenty-one he was able, with a small inheritance, to buy the paper. At the same time he became chief editor. Holding the reins for eleven years, between 1840 and 1851, the most important change he made was in the paper's name, which became the *National Standard*. Three years after buying the *Freeman's Banner*, in 1843, Smith married Hester A. Driver; they had four children.

Aside from journalism, Smith's major interest in his Salem years was politics. A staunch Whig, he ran for township and county offices with mixed success. He was elected to the county Board of Chosen Freeholders in 1848 but lost the Salem County surrogacy the same year. Six years later he was elected to the New Jersey Senate. He conducted his campaign in opposition to a local railroad project being taken over by the Joint Companies, the politically powerful corporation, usually allied with the Democrats, that held a governmentally sanctioned monopoly on railroad and canal transportation between Philadelphia and New York. His stance was good Whig politics and was sound from a regional point of view, since the monopoly allegedly thwarted railroad development in the southern part of the state.

After serving one term in the senate, Smith was appointed clerk of the New Jersey Supreme Court in 1857, a reward for his loyalty to the governor in a patronage dispute. With an income derived from fees for various court services, the clerkship was perhaps the most lucrative sinecure in the state. There is no way to determine Smith's annual income precisely, but it was probably in the $25,000 to $50,000 range, and there was a tacit understanding that, since the appointment was a reward for service to his party, he should return a certain portion to the party organization. At any rate, Smith held the clerkship for fifteen years, causing him to move permanently from Salem to Trenton.

Another political landmark in Smith's life came in 1859, when he was placed on the state Executive Committee of the United Opposition party, a coalition of the factions that emerged after the collapse of the New Jersey Whigs. By 1860 the United Opposition was secure enough to be called the Republican party. Smith served on the state Executive Committee until 1871, often as chairman. His tenure on the committee was stormy, particularly after 1865, when his leadership was challenged by an opposing faction led by Alexander G. Cattell and George M. Robeson, post–Civil War newcomers to New Jersey politics. This power struggle over patronage grew increasingly bitter as time went on; Smith, as a member of the "old guard," had his back to the wall and finally resigned in disgust.

Smith played an active role on the home front during the Civil War. An ardent supporter of the Union, he was the governor's special agent in facilitating troop movements across the state and seeing that New Jersey soldiers were well equipped. Occasionally his duties took him to Washington, where he conferred with Secretary of War Edwin M. Stanton. He kept up enthusiasm for the war effort in Trenton by celebrating all Union victories and forming the Trenton Artillery, a volunteer unit composed of the young men of the city. He was also one of the founders of the Union League of Trenton, which, along with Union Leagues in other cities, encouraged prominent business and professional leaders to support Abraham Lincoln's policies.

Smith retired from politics in 1872, presumably because there was no place for him in a party dominated by his enemies. His tenure as clerk of the supreme court had made him extremely wealthy, and one may speculate that he was unpopular with many New Jersey Republican leaders, who suspected he was keeping too large a portion of the clerkship fees for himself. In any event, his way of life was that of a rich man. His house at 178 West State Street he described as "palatial," containing many expensive pieces of statuary, mirrors, silk curtains, and ornate candelabra. From time to time he gave lavish receptions for over one hundred state officials, at which the best in food and drink was served to the strains of orchestral music. His wealth also enabled him and his family to take two lengthy trips to Europe.

Smith's primary occupation during retirement was writing his reminiscences. If it were not for them, he would most likely be forgotten today. They provide an inside look at many aspects of mid-nineteenth-century politics in New Jersey, especially the "nuts and bolts" of gubernatorial appointments and factional infighting within the Whig and Republican parties, that cannot be obtained from perusal of contemporary newspapers or the limited manuscript collections for the period. Smith never explained his reason for writing, but clearly he did not intend publication, as his remarks about people and events are uninhibited and biased. What comes across most clearly in the reminiscences is his tremendous ego, for he believed that he played a decisive role in all the doings in which he was involved. Issues apparently meant little to him; what mattered was getting the right people in elective or appointive office.

Smith died in Trenton. There had been little in his world outside of politics, and even his immediate family seems to have been subordinate to his professional work.

• Smith's manuscript reminiscences are in the New Jersey State Library, Trenton. The only other major source on Smith is Hermann K. Platt, ed., *Charles Perrin Smith: New Jersey Political Reminiscences, 1828–1882* (1965). There are few secondary sources on New Jersey politics in the mid-nineteenth century. Charles M. Knapp, *New Jersey Politics in the Period of the Civil War and Reconstruction* (1924), is generally dated in its interpretation and too reliant on Smith for the war era.

HERMANN K. PLATT

SMITH, Chloethiel Woodard (2 Feb. 1910–30 Dec. 1992), architect and city planner, was born in Peoria, Illinois. Her parents' names and details of her childhood are unknown. In 1932 she earned her bachelor's degree in architecture with honors from the University of Oregon. One year later she received a master's degree in architecture in city planning from Washington University in St. Louis, Missouri. She then spent two years working for architectural firms in Portland, Oregon; Seattle, Washington; and New York City before moving to Washington, D.C., in 1935 as chief of research and planning for the Federal Housing Administration, where she worked until 1939. In 1940 she married Bromley K. Smith, a foreign service officer. They had two children.

Her husband's work provided Smith with opportunities and outlets for her creativity she probably would not have otherwise experienced. For example, in Montreal, where her husband was posted from 1940 to 1941, Smith organized City for Living, an exhibition about the planning of Montreal. In La Paz, Bolivia, from 1942 to 1945 she became involved with the architectural profession in South America, a connection she maintained throughout her career. While living in Bolivia, she taught architecture at the University San Andres in La Paz, wrote numerous articles for newspapers, gave lectures, and analyzed the master plan for Quito, Ecuador.

In 1944 Smith was awarded a Guggenheim fellowship to travel throughout South America to study and survey contemporary architecture. Although her original intention of writing a book about her findings was never realized, she turned her South American experience into a valuable contribution toward understanding the spread of International Style architecture beyond the confines of Europe. She published three important articles, a two-part series in *Architectural Forum* (Nov. 1946 and Feb. 1947) and an essay in the 1949 issue of the *Architect's Yearbook*, presenting the recent developments in South American architecture as objectively as possible. She chose to position South American architecture within its sociopolitical context and to focus on its positive qualities instead of belittling it for its reliance on European precedent.

Smith's own architectural star began to rise in the 1950s with her work on the redevelopment of southwest Washington. She also designed the American Embassy Chancery and Residence in Asunción, Paraguay, in 1959 and the Channel Waterfront Master Plan in Washington, D.C., in 1960. In 1963 she established her own firm, Chloethiel Woodard Smith and Associates. Her projects include the Capitol Park Apartments (1965–1967), designed in partnership with Nicholas Satterlee, and Harbour Square (1966). Designed to provide housing for 4,000 people, Capitol Park consists of five high-rise apartment blocks elevated one story above the ground and a series of row houses clustered around courts. The combination of more traditional forms (row houses) with a modern structure (the high rise) denotes a sensitivity on the part of the architect toward the needs of the inhabitants, a characteristic of Smith's work. Harbour Square is a residential design of 450 units and follows the same pattern of integrating modern and traditional forms, including incorporation of seven historic houses that existed on the site.

Among Smith's well-known and highly praised projects outside Washington is LaClede Township in St. Louis (1966–1967). LaClede is an urban renewal project designed to give its residents a living environment with which they could identify: wood-frame houses of two and three stories. Another aspect of LaClede's planning that demonstrates Smith's sensitivity toward the occupants was the inclusion of stores, recreational facilities, and a pub. These services were provided as a means of making the inhabitants feel comfortable, not ostracized, living in a housing project. In 1968 she designed, the Harcourt, Brace and World Store and Executive Offices in New York.

Smith enjoyed a long and successful career (she retired in 1982) because she was committed to finding solutions to architectural and urban-planning problems that would result in a design that was both humane and attractive. Her colleagues honored her contribution to twentieth-century American architecture by electing her a fellow of the American Institute of Architects in 1960. As a student at the University of Oregon, Smith began a lifelong correspondence with Lewis Mumford. His influence on her is seen in Capitol Park and LaClede. As her career advanced, Smith never lost her delight in the simple task of putting black lines on clean tracing paper, but her pleasure was given an extra dimension when these drawn lines were transformed into three-dimensional structures.

• Smith's papers and drawings are divided between the American Institute of Architects Archives and the Prints and Drawings Collection of the Octagon Museum, American Architectural Foundation, Washington, D.C. The personal, and often revealing, letters she wrote to Lewis Mumford between 1932 and 1982 are in the Special Collections of the Van Pelt Library at the University of Pennsylvania. Although she was a major figure in the post–World War II shaping of Washington, D.C., Smith and her work have not received widespread attention. Beginning in the mid-1950s a number of significant articles, among them Ellen Perry Berkeley, "LaClede Town: The Most Vital Town in Town," *Architectural Forum* 129 (Nov. 1968), were devoted to her designs. In 1979 Anne-Imelda Radice featured Smith's work in the exhibition Two on Two at the Octagon: Design for the Urban Environment and provided a chronological survey in the accompanying catalog. One of the more comprehensive examinations of Smith's career is Jayne L. Doud, "Chloethiel Woodard Smith, FAIA: Washington's Urban Gem" (M.A. thesis, Univ. of Oregon, 1994).

LORETTA LORANCE

SMITH, Chris (12 Oct. 1879–4 Oct. 1949), songwriter and vaudevillian, was born in Charleston, South Carolina, the son of Henry Mirtry, a shoemaker, and Clara Smith (maiden name Browne). Although the 1880 U.S. census shows his first name as Christopher, he was commonly known as Chris Smith. Little is known about his personal life. He was married and had at least two children (both daughters), but other specifics are not known.

A baker by trade, Smith learned to play the piano and guitar by himself and showed much interest in and took part in local entertainment. He left Charleston with his friend Elmer Bowman to join a medicine show while they were "still in short pants," as he told Edward B. Marks. Smith and Bowman went to New York sometime in the 1890s and formed a vaudeville act billed as Smith Bowman. Smith began to publish songs in the late 1890s, and his "Good Morning Carrie!" (1901), written with Bowman, can be considered his first major hit.

In the late 1890s and the 1900s Smith was an important member of the community of black entertainers in New York, at that time the center of the black entertainment world, through the conjuncture of the flowering of black theatricals, the development of the popular music publishing business, and the growing popularity of ragtime music. Smith was closely affiliated with Gotham-Attucks Music Co., the first black-owned publishing house. Gotham-Attucks represented many songwriters and performers who were central figures of the black musical comedies, including Will Marion Cook, Bert Williams, R. C. "Cecil Mack" McPherson, Alex Rogers, Will Tyers, James Reese Europe, Tom Lemonier, James T. Brymn, Henry S. Creamer, and Ford Dabney, with many of whom Smith was also associated. With Cecil Mack, the head of the firm, Smith formed a successful songwriting team, scoring hits such as "He's a Cousin of Mine" (1906). Smith was also a close associate of Bert Williams, supplying many songs throughout Williams's career. Several of Smith's songs were featured in the Williams and Walker show *Bandanna Land* (1908). During this period Smith's songs were also popularized by white stars such as May Irwin and Marie Cahill.

From early on, Smith was acquainted with the firm of Jos. W. Stern & Co., which was the major publisher of Smith's songs throughout most of his career. Edward B. Marks, the cofounder of the firm, indicated in his autobiography that he had known Smith since 1895 and praised the longevity of Smith as a successful songwriter.

Many of Smith's works during the early period of his career were ragtime songs, a new genre of popular song introduced to the mainstream in the late 1890s. Ragtime songs were noted for their vigorous syncopation, considered an African-American quality and often called "colored rhythm." This kind of song played an important role in the development of black musical comedies and in the prosperity of Jos. W. Stern and other Tin Pan Alley publishers in the 1900s. Smith's songs were also noted for their combination of rhythmic vitality, interesting, often unusual harmonies, and felicitous lyrics.

In the 1910s Smith was active in vaudeville, teaming with George Cooper and with Billy B. Johnson. In 1913 Smith produced his most famous song, "Ballin' the Jack," whose popularity can be understood in the context of the modern dance movement of the early 1910s. This song is noted for Smith's use of ingenious harmonies and for James (or Jim) Burris's lyrics describing dance steps, and it was later revived on many occasions, including the 1942 motion picture *For Me and My Gal*, starring Judy Garland and Gene Kelly, and *On the Riviera* (1951), starring Danny Kaye.

In the early 1920s Smith was engaged in the realm of private entertainment as well as in songwriting. According to the trumpeter Rex Stewart, Smith belonged to the Clef Club cliques, which "were the aristocracy . . . the bigwigs who played Miami Beach, Piping Rock, Bar Harbor and all the other posh resorts where society gathered to follow the sun." At this time Smith was associated with some important blues and jazz musicians of the day, such as Perry Bradford, Mamie Smith, Clarence Williams, and W. C. Handy. Smith also collaborated with the comedian Jimmy Durante.

Although Smith was a prolific songwriter until the mid-1920s, he did not become a member of the American Society of Composers, Authors and Publishers (ASCAP) until 1931. In the 1930s and 1940s the number of Smith's new compositions declined, but he continued writing songs until his death in New York City.

Smith is representative of the generation of black musicians who entered the entertainment field in New York around the turn of the century. They wrote songs in a distinctly black musical idiom and led successful careers in both songwriting and performing. Most of his collaborators came from the same pool of black talent and included Elmer Bowman, Cecil Mack, Harry Brown, Billy B. Johnson, John Larkins, James Burris, Tim Brymn, and Henry Troy, many of whom provided lyrics to Smith's melodies.

Well-known works other than those mentioned above are "I Ain't Poor No More" (1899), "Shame on You" (1904), "All In, Down and Out" (1906), "He's a Cousin of Mine" (1906), "Down among the Sugar Cane" (1908), "You're in the Right Church but the Wrong Pew" (1908), "There's a Big Cry Baby in the Moon" (1909), "Come after Breakfast" (1909), "Constantly" (1910), "Honky Tonky Monkey Rag" (1911), "Beans, Beans, Beans" (1912), "I've Got My Habits On" (1921), "Cake Walking Babies from Home" (1924), and "Of All the Wrongs You've Done to Me" (1924).

Another important aspect of Smith as a songwriter was the fact that he opposed the use of the derogatory term *coon* in the popular songs of the late 1890s. Ac-

cording to Tom Fletcher, a black entertainer and one of Smith's close associates, Smith's refusal to use the term in the song "Good Morning Carrie!" started the turn away from "coon songs" around the turn of the century.

• The most thorough treatment of the subject to date is Eunmi Shim, *Chris Smith and the Ragtime Song* (1993). Two autobiographies, Tom Fletcher's *100 Years of the Negro in Show Business* (1984) and Edward B. Marks's *They All Sang: From Tony Pastor to Rudy Vallee* (1934), are important because they were written by firsthand witnesses of Smith's activities. In addition to short biographical entries in the standard secondary sources, references to Smith can be found in Maxwell Marcuse, *Tin Pan Alley in Gaslight* (1959), and David A. Jasen, *Tin Pan Alley* (1988). An obituary is in the *New York Amsterdam News*, 8 Oct. 1949.

EUNMI SHIM

SMITH, Clara (1894–2 Feb. 1935), blues and vaudeville singer, was born in Spartanburg, South Carolina. Nothing is known of her parents and childhood. In about 1910 she began touring the South in vaudeville. Probably in 1920 she joined the new Theater Owners' Booking Association circuit, in which context guitarist Lonnie Johnson recalled working with Clara and Mamie Smith (no relation) in New Orleans. He said Clara was "a lovely piano player and a lovely singer" (Oliver, *Conversations*, p. 135).

In 1923 Smith came to New York to sing in Harlem clubs and to begin a recording career that stretched to 1932; she became the most frequently recorded classic blues singer after Bessie Smith (also no relation). Discs from 1923 include "I Never Miss the Sunshine," "Awful Moanin' Blues" (documenting her nickname, "Queen of the Moaners"), and "Kansas City Man Blues." In 1924 she recorded "Good Looking Papa Blues," "Mean Papa, Turn in Your Key," "Texas Moaner Blues," "Freight Train Blues," and "Death Letter Blues." That same year she opened the Clara Smith Theatrical Club in New York while resuming her extensive touring. Visits to the West Coast reportedly extended into 1925, and she performed in Nashville, although she also worked at a theater in Harlem and recorded regularly in New York that year. Cornetist Louis Armstrong was among her accompanists on "Nobody Knows the Way I Feel 'Dis Mornin'," "Shipwrecked Blues" (a morbidly chilling account of drowning and one of the earliest examples of a twelve-bar blues consistently in a minor key), and "My John Blues." Further sessions from 1925 include "My Two-Timing Papa" and two uninspired duets with Bessie Smith. Later that year these Columbia Records blues stars became drunk at a party and got into a fistfight, with Bessie severely beating Clara; this fight ended their friendship and collaborations.

In 1926 Smith married Charles "Two-Side" Wesley, a manager in the Negro baseball leagues; no children are mentioned in biographies or her obituary. Her recordings from that year include "Whip It to a Jelly," "Salty Dog," "My Brand New Papa," and two gospel songs. She had her own Clara Smith Revue at the Lincoln Theater in 1927, and she continued working in Harlem theater revues until 1931. She recorded "Jelly Look What You Done Done," "Gin Mill Blues," and "Got My Mind on That Thing" (all 1928); "It's Tight Like That" and "Papa I Don't Need You Now" (both 1929); and two vaudeville vocal duets with Lonnie Johnson, "You Had Too Much" and "Don't Wear It Out," these last under the pseudonym Violet Green (1930).

Smith sang with Charlie Johnson's Paradise Band at the Harlem Opera House in 1931 and that year appeared in the African-American cowboy show *Trouble on the Ranch* in Philadelphia. She worked in Cleveland from around 1931 to 1932 before returning to New York, where she joined drummer Paul Barbarin at the Strollers Club in about 1934. She also worked for six months at Orchestra Gardens in Detroit. Smith had just returned to Detroit from further performances in Cleveland when she suffered heart trouble. Hospitalized for eleven days, she died of a heart attack. By the time of her death she was evidently separated from her husband, who could not be located.

Smith's singing straddled vaudeville and down-home blues styles. Her voice was slightly raspy. Moaning blue notes abounded, as for example in the session with Armstrong, but she enunciated lyrics clearly, using a southern African-American pronunciation. In her first years of recording Smith favored lugubrious blues and vaudeville songs, but it may be obvious from titles listed above that she later followed a fashion for perky, risqué songs.

Smith was the subject of one of the finest contemporary descriptions of classic blues singing, written by Carl Van Vechten: "As she comes upon the stage through folds of electric blue hangings at the back, she is wrapped in a black evening cloak bordered with white fur. . . . Clara begins to sing:

> *All day long I'm worried;*
> *All day long I'm blue;*
> *I'm so awfully lonesome,*
> *I don' know what to do;*
> *So I ask yo', doctor,*
> *See if yo' kin fin'*
> *Somethin' in yo' satchel*
> *To pacify my min'.*
> *Doctor! Doctor!*
> (Her tones become poignantly pathetic; tears roll down her cheeks.)
> *Write me a prescription fo' duh Blues*
> *Duh mean ole Blues.*

. . . Her voice is powerful or melancholy, by turn. It tears the blood from one's heart" (pp. 106–8).

• For more information on Clara Smith see Carl Van Vechten, "Negro 'Blues' Singers: An Appreciation of Three Coloured Artists Who Excel in an Unusual and Native Medium," *Vanity Fair*, Mar. 1926, pp. 67, 106, 108; Paul Oliver, "'Clara Voce': A Study in Neglect," *Jazz Monthly* 4 (1958): 2–5, 24; Oliver, *Conversation with the Blues* (1965); Ronald Clifford Foreman, Jr., "Jazz and Race Records, 1920–1932: Their Origins and Their Significance for the Record Industry and Society" (Ph.D. diss., Univ. of Illinois, 1968); Robert M. W. Dixon and John Godrich, *Recording the Blues* (1970); Derrick Stewart-Baxter, *Ma Rainey and the Classic Blues Singers* (1970); and Chris Albertson, *Bessie: Empress of the Blues* (1972). See also Sheldon Harris, *Blues Who's Who: A Biographical Dictionary of Blues Singers* (1979); Edward Brooks, *The Bessie Smith Companion: A Critical and Detailed Appreciation of the Recordings* (1982); Sally Placksin, *American Women in Jazz, 1900 to the Present: Their Words, Lives, and Music* (1982); Doug Seroff, "Blues Itineraries: Clara Smith on the Road," *Whiskey, Women, and . . .*, no. 12–13 (1983): 58; Eric Townley, "The Forgotten Ones: Clara Smith," *Jazz Journal International* 38 (July 1985): 16–17; and Daphne Duval Harrison, "'Classic' Blues and Women Singers," in *The Blackwell Guide to Blues Records*, ed. Oliver (1989; rev. as *The Blackwell Guide to Recorded Blues* [1991]). An obituary is in the *Chicago Defender*, 9 Feb. 1935.

BARRY KERNFELD

SMITH, Cotton Ed. *See* Smith, Ellison DuRant.

SMITH, Cyrus Rowlett (9 Sept. 1899–4 Apr. 1990), airline executive, was born in Minerva, Texas, the son of Roy Edgerton Smith, a laborer, and Marion Burck. Early in life Cyrus became known as "C. R.," a nickname he favored throughout his career. The impoverished Smith family moved frequently, as C. R.'s father won and lost jobs all over Texas and Louisiana. After settling in Amarillo, the elder Smith left the house one day and vanished, leaving his wife, nine-year-old C. R., and six younger brothers and sisters to fend for themselves. Fortunately, Marion Smith had some education; she found a teaching job and took in boarders; she became politically active and held several appointive posts, including supervisor of the state census. C. R. added to the meager family funds by working as an office boy for a wealthy cattle rancher. During these years, he developed a deep appreciation for western legends and lore, an affinity he maintained all his life.

As a young man Smith held jobs as a bookkeeper before graduating in 1924 from the University of Texas with a degree in business. He worked as an accountant for various firms, including Southern Air Transport, after one of his employers had bought it. Smith learned to fly and stayed on as an officer in what became American Airways. By 1934 the administration of Franklin D. Roosevelt had forced the reorganization of the airline industry to break up monopolistic arrangements. Smith became president of a new entity, American Airlines, based on its predecessor's main routes.

Later in 1934 Smith married Elizabeth L. Manget, with whom he had a son, but the marriage soon ended. The airline business totally consumed Smith's time; although Smith and his son were later reconciled, the evolution of American Airlines completely occupied him for the whole of his adult life, and he never remarried. He was determined to keep American not only the biggest airline in the United States but also to make it an international industry leader. Moreover, Smith was committed to the airline industry itself and to the increase of public confidence in air travel. In the depression era, when there was intense competition with railroads for a shrunken travel market, he felt that it was imperative to improve the airlines' image of reliability and safety.

Smith modernized American's fleet with the fourteen-passenger Douglas DC-2s, but he wanted a bigger plane. He finally convinced Douglas to build a new design to carry twenty-one passengers, but the manufacturer needed financial guarantees, and American Airlines did not have the necessary $4 million. Smith headed to Washington, D.C., for a conference with an old acquaintance from Texas, Jesse Jones. As head of the Reconstruction Finance Corporation, Jones had the sort of money Smith needed. Such a loan not only would keep American in the air, Smith argued, but also boost the aircraft industry and its suppliers of radio equipment, tires, upholstery, electrical equipment, and so on. Smith got a total loan of $4.5 million to launch the Douglas Sleeper Transport, eventually labeled the DC-3.

Although the DC-3 became a standard aircraft for every major airline in the United States and amassed an enviable safety record, the public still harbored strong fears about airline safety. Smith faced the issue head-on in 1937, composing the first draft of a letter that eventually appeared in the most widely read periodicals of the era. As a full-page advertisement, the text asked, "Why dodge this question: afraid to fly?" The copy went on to state that every form of transportation carried elements of risk but emphasized that airline travel was certainly not unsafe and commented on stringent safety procedures. For an industry that had been reluctant to address the safety issues, the ad was a bombshell. The ad campaign, while making it clear American was doing a good job, was also an effort to boost the airlines as a whole—a typical Smith approach.

In the late 1930s Smith decided to move American's headquarters from Chicago to New York City. At Chicago's Midway Airport, the airline chafed under increasing city fees and other constraints of urban growth. New York's La Guardia Field presented an opportunity to move in as one of the first tenants of the nation's largest and newest airport at the time, with a choice of favorable hangar space, terminal gates, and offices. During the move to New York, Smith relied more and more on Carlene Roberts, the college-educated young woman whom he had hired as a secretary but who quickly became an administrative assistant. In planning for the physical resettlement of some 800 employees and their families from Chicago to New York, Roberts orchestrated it all, also publishing a 100-page brochure on New York residential areas, including data on bus schedules, schools, churches, and bowling alleys.

In the early 1940s, when American established a Washington office to deal with burgeoning bureaucratic issues, Smith promoted Roberts to head it. In an industry traditionally dominated by males, she continued to work effectively, and Smith continued to acknowledge her abilities with successive promotions. In 1951 he promoted her to a vice-president's chair, making Roberts the first woman among the major airlines to reach that status. For that era, Smith and Roberts had carried off a small revolution.

During World War II Smith took a leave of absence from American Airlines in 1942 to become chief of operations for the Air Transport Command (ATC). Planes and crews for the ATC were drafted from the various airline fleets in the United States and augmented by a massive war production effort. Holding the rank of colonel, Smith pioneered direct routes to Europe across the challenging North Atlantic rather than relying totally on the longer but safer routes across the South Atlantic between South America and Africa.

Having proved the feasibility of a North Atlantic Service, the ATC soon launched dozens of similar ferry and cargo flights. By the summer of 1945 the ATC had concluded some 7,000 transatlantic missions, averaging nearly 500 flights per month. While American Airlines' own crews and others honed their skills over the Atlantic waters, Pacific Coast routes north to Alaska proved particularly challenging, and Northwest Airlines crews picked up the task of initiating pilots unaccustomed to the rigors of arctic flying. Other routes stretched into the South Pacific. The ATC also operated a string of maintenance bases around the globe, from the frozen wastes of Iceland to the steamy jungles of India. In the summer of 1945 Smith left the Air Force with the rank of major general and numerous commendations.

The postwar years brought rapid change in the air travel industry. Smith committed tens of millions of dollars for new equipment on American's expanding route system, acquiring pressurized Convair CV-240 twin-engine transports for short hauls and Douglas DC-6 four-engine airliners for longer routes and prestigious transcontinental service. This rapid expansion, complex new airliners, snowballing maintenance costs, long-range planning, and multiplying numbers of personnel created an unusually complex set of financial controls for American and other airlines in what was still a young industry. Smith acknowledged his own weakness in the intricacies of this new environment and went outside the industry to hire a new vice president and financial officer, William J. Hogan, an experienced controller and executive from Firestone Tire and Rubber.

Slowly, the airlines began to develop more sophistication in finance and marketing. Although there had been collaboration in co-location of ticket offices in New York before the war, the 1930s-vintage airline facility at Forty-second Street and Park Avenue became outmoded after 1945. Acting on their own, Smith and Hogan bought several parcels of real estate near the Queens Midtown Tunnel, the main link to La Guardia Field and the proposed Idlewild Airport. With some subtle arm twisting by Smith, other airlines joined American to set up the East Side Airlines Terminal. American, Eastern, TWA, United, and Pan Am each held 15 percent of the stock; smaller shares were taken by Allegheny, Braniff, Capital, Colonial, Mohawk, National, Northeast, and Northwest. It was a good example of Smith's industrywide concern. American benefited, to be sure, but so did the other carriers. The terminal opened in 1953, and its success prompted a similar West Side Airlines Terminal only two years later.

With Hogan in financial command, American introduced several innovative marketing programs in the postwar decades. Discounted weekend fares were promoted in the late 1940s, a scheme soon followed by other airlines. To compete with nonscheduled airlines that began offering group travel at bargain-basement prices, American also became a leader in offering coach-class service and lower fares. As a means of reaching nationwide markets, Smith supported American Airlines ads in a variety of popular magazines, launched flashy theme campaigns like "Royal Coachman" flights complete with trumpeters in eighteenth-century costumes, and encouraged other similar promotions. One of the most successful was the American-sponsored "Music 'til Dawn" radio programs, which ran coast-to-coast in the 1950s and 1960s and won a Peabody Award for excellence.

Still, Smith felt that reliable, fast, comfortable service remained the major commitment. Staying abreast of other major airlines, American's first jet airliners were ordered in the late 1950s, a commitment to equipment that was paralleled by the airline's decision to establish an elaborate college for its stewardesses to ensure high standards of cabin service in a highly competitive travel industry. During the 1960s Smith led the industry when he issued a contract to IBM for an advanced computer reservations system that cut reservation processing from 45 minutes to several seconds.

Smith retired in 1968, spent several months as secretary of commerce for the Lyndon Johnson administration that same year, and then joined the investment firm of Lazard Frères and Company. In the meantime American's fortunes had soured, leading Smith to return briefly for a six-month term in 1973–1974. His success in cutting costs and raising morale smoothed the way for a qualified successor.

Smith died in Bethesda, Maryland, following sixteen years of retirement involving aviation activities. As one of the airline pioneers who successfully bridged the transition from fabric-covered twin-engine planes to multiengine jet airliners, Smith not only made his mark on his own company but played a progressive role in the airline industry's evolution as the nation's principal passenger travel network. Many American Airlines personnel went on to leadership in other airlines; American's office in Washington, D.C., was often the center of industry action involving federal legislation; effective marketing and consistent safety in the industry owed a debt to Smith. Honors from the Aviation Hall of Fame, Travel Hall of Fame, Business Hall of Fame, and similar groups all attested to the singular lifetime focus on his profession and to his success as a major airline pioneer.

• A collection of Smith papers is at the C. R. Smith Museum, which was established by American Airlines at the Dallas–Fort Worth airport. Robert J. Serling, *Eagle: The History of American Airlines* (1985), contains a wealth of anecdotal material about C. R. Smith. See also Jack Alexander, "Just Call Me C. R.," *Saturday Evening Post*, 1 Feb. 1941, pp. 9–11. Smith's role in American Airlines' rise to prominence is summarized in *"A. A." American Airlines—Since 1926* (1954), printed for the Newcomen Society in North America. Because American Airlines became such a powerhouse in domestic air transport, it represents a consistent theme in R. E. G. Davies, *Airlines of the United States since 1914* (1982), and Henry Ladd Smith, *Airways: The History of Commercial Aviation in the United States* (1942). An obituary is in the *New York Times*, 5 Apr. 1990.

ROGER E. BILSTEIN

SMITH, Daniel (17 Oct. 1748–16 June 1818), revolutionary soldier, statesman, and surveyor, was born near Aquia Creek in Stafford County, Virginia, the son of Henry Smith and Sarah Crosby. The eldest of twelve children, he attended the College of William and Mary and then studied both law and medicine. However, he also learned the use of surveying instruments while still a teenager, and the demand for frontier surveys kept him occupied principally in that profession for most of his life.

In June 1773 he married Sarah Michie of Albemarle County, Virginia (or possibly Maryland's Eastern Shore); they had one son and one daughter. That same year they moved to Augusta, where he became deputy county surveyor. In 1774 he commanded a company of local men and fought marauding Indians. Three years later, during the Revolution, he helped form a militia company and participated in a number of engagements in Virginia and North Carolina, including Guilford Courthouse and Kings Mountain.

After the Revolution Smith resumed his career as a surveyor and, for a brief time, practiced law. He soon made plans to move westward to the Cumberland Valley, and in 1783 he settled with his family and slaves on 3,140 acres of land on Drake's Creek, northeast of Nashville near what is now Hendersonville, Tennessee. He quickly constructed a log home but soon began work on a home of Tennessee limestone, which he called "Rock Castle" and which took him ten years to complete.

Smith immediately entered into the political activities of the Nashville area, and public service became an important interest for the rest of his life. He was appointed a member of the quarterly court of the newly created county of Davidson even before he arrived from Virginia, and at the first meeting he was named county surveyor. In 1786, Davidson County was partitioned and Smith's property was located in the newly created Sumner County to the northeast. He was elected chairman of the county court. A few months later, he was appointed brigadier general of the entire Cumberland area.

In 1790 the Watauga and Cumberland settlements, comprising North Carolina's western land claims, became a U.S. territory, and Smith was appointed by

President George Washington as territorial secretary under Governor William Blount. He served in this capacity for the full six years of the territory's existence, exercising broad powers that included acting as governor in Blount's not infrequent absences. Smith also became a leader in the movement for statehood, which culminated in Tennessee's admission as the sixteenth state in 1796. He was one of five representatives from Sumner County summoned to Knoxville by Governor Blount in January 1796 to help draft a constitution for the new state. In the convention he played a significant role, serving as president pro tem and writing much of the bill of rights that was included in the basic document. Smith often is credited with having exercised influential leadership in persuading other delegates to accept "Tennessee" as the name of the new state.

Shortly before Tennessee was admitted, Smith drafted a map of the Tennessee country based upon his extensive surveys. Widely heralded when published, it was the best map of the territory until others were constructed in the early 1800s. In 1793 he wrote *A Short Description of the Tennassee Government* based upon his frontier experiences while surveying and establishing boundary lines. Always interested in education, Smith, at one time or another, was a trustee of Davidson Academy in Nashville, Blount College in Knoxville, and Greene College in Tusculum.

Smith was appointed to the U.S. Senate in 1798 when Andrew Jackson suddenly resigned, but he held it for only a few months until legislators elected a successor. He was chosen again for the Senate as a Republican in 1805—this time for a full six-year term—but he resigned in 1809 because of ill health. His major interest while in the Senate was Indian affairs, although he also was a careful observer of the increasingly deteriorating relations with both France and England and the threats imposed by Aaron Burr to the southwest. While in Washington, he kept up a steady correspondence with the prominent men of the time, including Governor John Sevier, Andrew Jackson, and James Robertson, as well as with members of his own family. He died at Rock Castle.

• Smith papers are held at the Tennessee Library and Archives, and Smith's "Survey Book" is in a collection at the University of Chicago. For information on Smith, see Walter T. Durham, *Daniel Smith: Frontier Statesman* (1976); Kenneth D. McKellar, *Tennessee Senators As Seen By One of Their Successors* (1942); "Rock Castle," *American Historical Magazine*, Oct. 1900, pp. 291–95; and "Papers of General Daniel Smith," *American Historical Magazine*, July 1901, pp. 213–45. An obituary is in the *Nashville Clarion*, 23 June 1818.

ROBERT E. CORLEW

SMITH, David (9 Mar. 1906–23 May 1965), sculptor, was born David Roland Smith in Decatur, Indiana, the son of Harvey Martin Smith, a telephone engineer and erstwhile inventor, and Golda Stoler. Smith's early years were spent in Decatur. In 1921, when his father became manager of the Paulding Telephone Company, Smith moved with his family to Paulding, Ohio. At seventeen he took a correspondence course in cartooning from the Cleveland Art School. After completing high school in 1924, he enrolled at Ohio University in Athens, where he took art courses for two semesters. During the following summer Smith found employment as a welder and riveter at the Studebaker automobile plant in South Bend, Indiana. These skills would later be put to use in his construction of sculpture from industrial metals. In September 1925 he enrolled as a special student at Notre Dame University but attended only a few weeks before resuming his employment with Studebaker, this time in the banking branch.

Studebaker Finance Department transferred Smith to the Morris Plan Bank in Washington, D.C., in 1926. While living in the northwest area of the District of Columbia, Smith attended two poetry classes at George Washington University. In September 1926 he was reassigned to the Industrial Acceptance Corporation in New York City. That same fall he met Dorothy Dehner, a painter attending the Art Students League. Smith began evening classes there late in 1926. By the following September he became a full-time student at the league, studying with John Sloan, Kimon Nicolaides, and Jan Matulka until 1931.

In December 1927 Smith married Dehner. They had no children. After a number of odd jobs, including positions as a seaman on oil tankers, Smith began to draw illustrations for sports journals and design layouts for *Tennis* magazine. In 1929 the Smiths purchased a farm in Bolton Landing, New York, a resort community bordering Lake George in the Adirondack Mountains, and began to spend summers there. In 1931 they spent eight months in the Virgin Islands, where Smith painted, took photographs, and experimented with constructions of wood, wire, and pieces of coral.

Smith's first constructions of metal were made in 1933, after his purchase of a welding outfit and oxyacetylene torch. Always ambitious and determined to make his art, he rented studio space at a machine shop in Brooklyn, the Terminal Iron Works, while supporting himself as an adviser for the Temporary Emergency Relief Administration. In 1935 Smith took his first trip to Europe. He spent a month in Paris, where John Graham introduced him to modernists and Smith made etchings at Stanley William Hayter's Atelier 17. He spent the winter months in Greece, followed by a three-week tour through the Soviet Union in 1936. Beginning in 1937 Smith worked for two years for the Works Progress Administration. That year he joined the American Abstract Artists and began exhibiting with the group. Smith's sculpture at this time included the *Medals for Dishonor* (1938–1940), cast bronze reliefs about ten inches in diameter that were motivated by his reaction to the Spanish civil war and the rise of Nazi Germany. These fifteen medals, with dozens of related sketches, include scenes of brutality and political machinations. Smith combined imagery of violence from the ancient world with his anti-Fascist responses to contemporary events to form a complex iconographic scheme. His other sculpture of the late

1930s is indicative of his active experimentation with materials and methods. *Head* (1938; Museum of Modern Art, New York), for example, is welded of cast iron and steel elements that make an openwork silhouette of a face reminiscent of Pablo Picasso's abstract studies of the figure in the same decade.

After 1938 Smith welded industrial metals into nonobjective works that feature polychrome surfaces. He also modeled in wax for bronze casting, constructs in balsa, and later carved stone. His abstract construction in painted steel was included in the 1939 New York World's Fair. In the late 1930s he was active with the Artists' Union and various leftist groups. As the political climate changed in New York, Smith retreated to full-time residence in Bolton Landing. By the spring of 1940 he and his wife had moved to their Adirondack Mountain retreat and were permanent residents there for more than a decade. Finding alternative war service, Smith worked for the American Locomotive Company assembling tanks and locomotives. When he was disqualified from serving in the military in 1944 after being examined by military physicians, he returned to Bolton Landing and made welded constructions that comment on the destructive forces of World War II. *Royal Bird* (1948; Walker Art Center) is among a number of bird images of the 1940s, in which Smith used the skeleton of a predatory creature from the American Museum of Natural History as a source but developed a symbolic content that relates to the time of its creation.

Throughout the 1940s Smith favored allusive glyphs rather than outright imagery. These glyphic elements are combined into a complex but obscure iconography. Frequently a linear structure joins the glyphs in an open composition reminiscent of the surrealist sculptor Alberto Giacometti. Such works as *Reliquary House* (1945; private collection) and *Royal Incubator* (1949; private collection) can be linked to various images from the ancient or medieval period, but for Smith they assumed a personal resonance.

In 1948 Smith began teaching part-time at Sarah Lawrence College. By 1950 he was beginning to receive some critical recognition. He was awarded a Guggenheim Foundation Fellowship and began to sell his work. In 1952 his marriage ended in a divorce, and the next year he married Jean Freas. They had two daughters before divorcing in 1961. During the 1950s Smith continued teaching part-time. In 1954–1955 he was a visiting professor in fine arts at Indiana University, and the following year he taught at the University of Mississippi in Oxford for one semester.

The proportions of Smith's welded constructions changed to larger than human scale totems. Some featured recycled machine parts, while others were constructed of sheets of steel and aluminum. Beginning with the Agricola series of 1951 and continuing with the Tanktotems of the mid-1950s, he installed his sculptures in the fields surrounding his farmhouse and studio in Bolton Landing. An example is *Tanktotem I* (1952; Art Institute of Chicago), a welded steel personage more than seven feet high that "stands" on spindly legs and seems to gesture with an attached machine part that resembles a shield.

By the end of the 1950s Smith was recognized as one of the leading American artists of his generation. He represented the United States at the Sao Paulo Bienal and at the Venice Biennale on two occasions and was included in the Second Documenta Exhibition in Kassel, Germany. During the early 1960s he continued to work simultaneously on a number of series: the Zigs, Circles, Voltri-Boltons, Wagons, and Cubi. During the final years of his life, Smith explored in large-scale welded sculptures some of the formal issues that characterize his entire production: relationship of volume to planarity and the fusion of painting, drawing, and sculpture. Polychrome sculpture continued to interest him, and many of his sculptures were brightly painted steel. Sculptures of singular interest are the Voltris, which were constructed in a fever pitch of activity during a month of 1962 spent in Voltri, Italy. The twenty-seven sculptures he created in thirty days were installed in an amphitheater at the Fourth Festival of Two Worlds in Spoleto. Welded sculptures from the 1960s, including the Voltris, the Voltri-Bolton series (twenty-five constructions from machine parts shipped from Voltri), and the Voltons are among Smith's crowning achievements as direct metal constructions. In February 1965 he was appointed to the National Council on the Arts. He died three months later, following an accident in his truck near Bennington, Vermont. After Smith's death, Clement Greenberg became the immediate custodian of his art since Smith's daughters were minors. Greenberg, who abhorred Smith's polychrome sculpture, allowed the works to deteriorate in the fields at Bolton Landing so that the removal of paint could be justified. Many works survive as flat, unmodulated steel or aluminum surfaces, where originally Smith had painted the industrial metals or burnished the surfaces.

• Smith's papers, including letters, catalogs, and newspaper clippings, are in the Archives of American Art, Smithsonian Institution, Washington, D.C. Statements by the artist about his work are in *David Smith by David Smith*, ed. Cleve Gray (1968). For documentary materials, see Garnett McCoy, ed., *David Smith* (1973), and Rosalind E. Krauss, *The Sculpture of David Smith: A Catalogue Raisonné* (1977). See also monographs by Krauss, *Terminal Iron Works: The Sculpture of David Smith* (1971), and Karen Wilkin, *David Smith* (1984). An obituary is in the *New York Times*, 25 May 1965.

JOAN MARTER

SMITH, David Eugene (21 Jan. 1860–29 July 1944), teacher and historian of mathematics, was born in Cortland, New York, the son of Abram P. Smith, a lawyer and county judge, and Mary Elizabeth Bronson. Smith's scholarly learning began with lessons in Greek and Latin from his mother, who died when he was twelve. After attending the State Normal School in Cortland, he studied art and classical languages, including Hebrew, at Syracuse University, where he obtained a bachelor's degree in 1881 and a master's degree in 1884.

Under the influence of his father in Cortland, Smith also prepared for the profession of law and was admitted to the bar in 1884. That same year, however, he abandoned this direction to teach mathematics at the Normal School in Cortland. While teaching he earned a doctorate in art history from Syracuse in 1887, the same year he married Fanny Taylor of Cortland. He moved in 1891 to the Michigan State Normal School in Ypsilanti and developed what a later colleague at Columbia University, Clifford B. Upton, described as the first genuinely professional course for training teachers of secondary mathematics in the United States. His first publications, consisting of reviews of books in mathematics and in history of mathematics, appeared from this time.

After receiving a master of pedagogics at the Normal School in 1898, Smith returned to his home state to fill the position of principal of the New York State Normal School in Brockport. While there his *The Teaching of Elementary Mathematics* (1900) appeared as part of a series of books for teachers edited by Nicholas Murray Butler, who became president of Columbia University in 1901. That same year Smith became a professor of mathematics in Teachers College at Columbia, where he stayed until his retirement in 1926.

The move to Columbia marked the beginning of a number of professional activities for Smith: in 1902 he became librarian of the American Mathematical Society and associate editor of its *Bulletin* (both positions held until 1920) and mathematics editor of the *International Encyclopedia* (until 1916). The society housed its library at that time at Columbia University, and Smith made extensive additions to it. Also, before the First World War he traveled to Europe and the Far East and acquired materials for his own library that were to make it one of the premier historical mathematical collections in the country.

In 1908 Smith became active in the International Commission on the Teaching of Mathematics, holding the positions of vice president (1908–1920), president (1928–1932), and honorary president (thereafter). The commission was appointed at the Fourth International Congress of Mathematicians in 1908 to report on the teaching being done in mathematics at all levels of education. Together with other American members, such as William F. Osgood and John Wesley A. Young, Smith published reports that had a wide influence in the United States. The commission was also a means of sharing ideas between the United States and Europe.

In 1915 the Mathematical Association of America was founded for those interested in the teaching of collegiate mathematics, and Smith was elected president for the 1920–1921 term. In 1922 he was elected a vice president of the research-oriented American Mathematical Society, and in 1923, when the society became incorporated, he was a member of its first board of trustees. Having participated in organizations supporting mathematics and the teaching of mathematics, Smith felt the need for a group that supported what had become his main interest, the history of mathe-

matics. His efforts led to the formation in 1924 of the History of Science Society; he served as its president in 1927.

In demand as a speaker, Smith was especially effective with high school audiences on the subject of the history of mathematics and on book collecting in that field. At a tribute to Smith in 1936 the historian Raymond Clare Archibald credited Smith in large part for the fact that courses in the history of mathematics were then offered at nearly 160 U.S. institutions. Smith's first wife having died in 1928, in 1940 he married Eva May Luse. (Both marriages were childless.)

Two of Smith's most authoritative works in the field have continued to be useful: *A Source Book in Mathematics* (1929) and *History of Mathematics* (1925), each in two volumes. Smith also wrote fifteen biographies of mathematicians for the *Dictionary of American Biography* (1928–1935). Some of his books he wrote under the pseudonym David Dunham. According to his friend W. D. Reeve, Smith's *Number Stories of Long Ago* (1951) originated from stories he told nightly to children during his summer vacations explaining how and why the ancients created numbers. In 1933 the government of Iran presented Smith with a medal honoring him for his translation of the *Rubáiyát of Omar Khayyám*.

During his travels Smith collected mathematical manuscripts, instruments, and portraits of mathematicians, as well as books, from all periods and many countries, both for himself and for George Plimpton of Ginn and Company, Smith's publisher. The two collectors agreed not to duplicate each other in their collecting. Smith's doctoral student Lao Genevra Simons recounted how, on a trip in 1907 to Japan, Smith had obtained every mathematical book he could find. On another occasion he purchased from W. J. C. Miller, editor of the British journal *Educational Review*, an autograph collection of mathematical letters. This collection is presumably the source of the letters from such famous British mathematicians as J. J. Sylvester, Arthur Cayley, and William Kingdon Clifford that now are a part of the Smith collection. Smith's history books, especially the two already cited, are generously illustrated from sources in the Smith and Plimpton collections. Smith died at his home in New York City.

Through his collecting, teaching, and publishing, Smith was a major influence in establishing the history of mathematics as both an intellectual discipline and as a profession in the United States.

• The D. E. Smith Papers and the Smith and Plimpton collections are in the Butler Library, Columbia University. "Dinner in Honor of Professor David Eugene Smith," *Mathematics Teacher* 19 (May 1926): 259–81, contains the proceedings of Smith's retirement dinner, for which Clifford B. Upton was toastmaster; speeches are included by his doctoral student Lao G. Simons and by George Plimpton, C. J. Keyser, and others. The first volume of *Osiris*, a journal devoted to the history of science, includes a tribute to Smith, "Dedication to David Eugene Smith," by its editor, George Sarton (1936): 5–8, plus a 562-item bibliography of Smith's nontextbook writings by Bertha M. Frick (pp. 9–78), and a portrait of Smith (frontispiece). Brief biographical articles are Raymond C. Archibald, "Bibliograhia de Mathematicis XIII," *Scripta Mathematica* 4 (Apr. 1936): 176–88; William David Reeve, "David Eugene Smith," *Mathematics Teacher* 37 (Oct. 1944): 278–79; and William Benjamin Fite, "David Eugene Smith," *American Mathematical Monthly* 52 (May 1945): 237–38. An obituary by Simons is in *Bulletin of the American Mathematical Society* 51 (Jan. 1945): 40–50.

ALBERT C. LEWIS

SMITH, Edgar Fahs (23 May 1854–3 May 1928), chemist and educator, was born in his father's gristmill at King's Mill, near York, Pennsylvania, the son of Gibson Smith, a miller, and Susan Elizabeth Fahs. The family soon moved to York, where the father became a fairly prosperous grain, wood, and coal merchant; he died suddenly of pneumonia in middle age, leaving a sizable estate. After early education at the local private school and at home, Smith attended the York Country Academy (1867–1872). Here he acquired a fondness for the classics and the humanities that he never lost. While at the academy he taught Latin for two years to the younger boys, and he ran a short-lived magazine. He also served as a compositor and proofreader at a local publishing house.

Smith intended to enter Yale University to major in chemistry to become a physician, but he was so advanced in his studies that he was able to be admitted as a junior at Pennsylvania College at Gettysburg (now Gettysburg College) in 1872. He majored in chemistry and mineralogy under Samuel Philip Sadtler, who convinced him to become a chemist and to study under Friedrich Wöhler at the University of Göttingen in Germany. After receiving his B.S. from Pennsylvania College in 1874, Smith spent two years at Göttingen, receiving his A.M. and Ph.D. in 1876. In 1879 he married Margie A. Gruel of Gettysburg; they had no children.

Smith served as instructor in analytical chemistry and assistant to Frederick Augustus Genth at the University of Pennsylvania (1876–1881). He was named Asa Packer Professor of Chemistry at Muhlenberg College, Allentown, Pennsylvania (1881–1883); professor of chemistry at Wittenberg College, Springfield, Ohio (1883–1888); and finally professor of analytical chemistry (1888–1907) and chemistry department chair (1892–1920), Blanchard Professor of Chemistry (1907–1920), and professor emeritus (1920–1928) at the University of Pennsylvania. At Pennsylvania, Smith, a devoutly religious man, kept in his office desk drawer a Bible and *Daily Prayers for Moravian Households*, from which he read every day. While he was vice provost (1898–1911) and provost (1911–1920) of the university, he conducted daily quarter-hour chapel services for a group of present and former students. On the campus, in sight of the Harrison Laboratory that he planned and in which he labored for many years, a statue of him was erected during his lifetime. After his death, the annual Edgar Fahs Smith Memorial Lecture was established. He wrote 169 research articles and authored or edited twelve books on general, inorganic, and organic chemistry and electrochemistry.

Between 1883 and 1918 Smith directed the research of eighty-seven doctoral students. His earliest research was in the field of organic chemistry. His doctoral research involved the trisubstituted benzol compounds and the action of chlorine on benzyl trichloride. After 1889 his interest in the organic field waned, and he returned to it only to direct an occasional dissertation. His most important contributions were in electrochemistry, in which he began to publish in 1879, becoming a recognized leader. He devised new methods of analysis, separation, and determination. In 1901 he introduced the rotating anode, which, with the use of high current densities and high voltage, greatly reduced the time required for electroanalysis and led to its broader application in research and industry.

Smith's discovery of new processes of analytical separation and the preparation of many elements and compounds in exceptional purity led him and his students to determine more precisely the atomic weights of eighteen elements, about one-fifth of all then known. They analyzed silver, cadmium, mercury, palladium, chlorine, and bromine by electrolytic methods; molybdenum, vanadium, antimony, nitrogen, arsenic, selenium, and fluorine by methods based on the volatilization of certain constituents in an anhydrous hydrogen chloride current; and tantalum, niobium, tungsten, scandium, and boron by various other methods. Smith and his students also investigated a class of substances known as complex inorganic acids (now called heteropoly acids) and their salts, proving that many of those previously regarded as mixtures of isomorphs were actually distinct chemical compounds. He revised the chemical understanding of naturally occurring silicates. Among the numerous complex inorganic acids and salts that he prepared and whose relationships he elucidated were those containing the elements aluminum, arsenic, bismuth, manganese, molybdenum, phosphorus, platinum, silicon, thorium, tin, titanium, tungsten, vanadium, and zirconium. He also investigated compounds of rarer elements, such as beryllium, cesium, germanium, indium, rhodium, rubidium, ruthenium, and thallium.

Smith was also the most prominent historian of chemistry, particularly of American chemistry, in his time. This interest probably resulted from his love of books, which he began collecting as a youth. Smith's widow presented his private collection of books, portraits, autographed letters, and memorabilia of famous chemists, probably the finest of its kind in the United States, to the University of Pennsylvania. During the 1870s, after his course of lectures on the subject bored his students, he adopted a biographical approach that fascinated students and made them aware of the neglected human element in chemistry. After his retirement, he continued to teach this course. In 1922, with Charles Albert Browne, he founded an American Chemical Society Section of the History of Chemistry, which became a division in 1927. He also was involved in founding the ACS Division of Chemical Education.

Smith was active in city, state, and national affairs, both inside and outside science. He was three times president of the American Chemical Society (1895, 1921, and 1922) and president of the American Philosophical Society (1902–1908) and the History of Science Society (1928). He was elected a member of the National Academy of Sciences (1898) and an officer of the Legion of Honor of France (1923). He received the Franklin Institute's Elliott Cresson Medal (1914), Columbia University's Chandler Medal (1922), and the Priestley Medal, the ACS's highest award (1926). He was appointed to the Jury of Awards, Chicago Exposition (1893); U.S. Assay Commission (1895, 1901–1905); and the board of technical advisers at the disarmament conference (1921) and chair of the international committee on poison gas and high explosives. He served in the Electoral College for Pennsylvania (1917; president, 1925), the Commission for Revision of Constitution of Pennsylvania (1919), and the state College and University Council (1911–1920) and Council of Education (1920–1922). For the Carnegie Institution he was adviser in Chemistry (1902), research associate (1915, 1918–1924), and for the Carnegie Foundation, trustee (1914–1920); he was president of the Wistar Institute of Anatomy and Biology (1917–1922). He died in Philadelphia.

An unassuming, approachable, sympathetic, genial person, Smith was an excellent conversationalist and in great demand as a lecturer and public speaker. He desired money only for the benefit of others, particularly for the University of Pennsylvania. Although some of his research projects—such as those on tungsten, used in incandescent lamp filaments—possessed large potential commercial applications and profits, he never applied for any patents. Smith was a leading pioneer in electrochemistry and the history of American chemistry.

Smith's historical works include *Chemistry in America: Chapters from the History of the Science in the United States* (1914; repr. 1972), *The Life of Robert Hare, an American Chemist (1781–1858)* (1917), and *Old Chemistries* (1927); on the history of chemistry he also wrote four more books, thirty-two articles, and twenty-eight brochures. On electrochemistry, he wrote *Electrochemical Analysis* (6 eds., 1890–1918; German, 1893, 1903; French, 1900) and *Elements of Electrochemistry* (1913, 1917), which were standard texts.

• Biographies of Smith include Francis X. Dercom et al., *Memorial Service for Edgar Fahs Smith* (1928); Charles A. Browne, "Edgar Fahs Smith, 1854–1928," *Journal of Chemical Education* 5 (1928): 656–63; Walter T. Taggart, "Edgar Fahs Smith," *Science* 68 (6 July 1928): 6–8; Marston T. Bogert, "Edgar Fahs Smith—Chemist," *Science* 69 (1929): 557–65; a sketch in *American Chemists and Chemical Engineers*, ed. Wyndham D. Miles (1976), pp. 445–46; and George H. Meeker, "Biographical Memoir of Edgar Fahs Smith, 1854–1928," National Academy of Sciences, *Biographical Memoirs*, 17 (1936): 103–49, with complete bibliography. The "Edgar Fahs Smith Memorial Number" of the *Journal of Chemical Education* 9, no. 4 (Apr. 1932): 607–705, contains a number of articles on Smith. Eva V. Armstrong, "Foreword," *Chymia* 1 (1948): i–xiv, discusses Smith and the Edgar Fahs Smith Memorial Collection; Herbert S. Klickstein, "Edgar Fahs Smith—His Contributions to the History of Chemistry," *Chymia* 5 (1959): 11–30, contains a bibliography of publications and unpublished manuscripts by and about Smith and his collection. An account of Smith at Göttingen is "Some Experiences of Dr. Edgar Fahs Smith as a Student under Wöhler" (as recorded by William McPherson), *Journal of Chemical Education* 5 (1928): 1554–57.

GEORGE B. KAUFFMAN

SMITH, Edmund Kirby (16 May 1824–28 Mar. 1893), soldier and educator, was born in St. Augustine, Florida, the son of Joseph Lee Smith, a lawyer, soldier, and judge, and Frances Kirby. Both of the future Confederate general's parents were originally from Connecticut. In childhood the precocious lad, who was known as "Ned" or "Ted," was tutored by his older sister Frances Smith. Smith's father was compelled to resign his federal judgeship in 1832 as a result of political pressures, and family finances grew increasingly strained. The decision was eventually made to prepare Smith for a career in the army, and he was sent to a private academy in Alexandria, Virginia, where he stayed from 1836 to 1841.

Smith entered West Point in 1841. Nicknamed "Seminole" by his fellow students, he grew increasingly unhappy at the academy and contemplated resigning, in part because of strained relations between his parents and in part because of illness. His academic standing slipped, but he managed to graduate twenty-fifth in his class of forty-one in 1845. The authorities initially planned to deny him a commission because of his nearsightedness, but his instructor and members of the academic board rallied to his support. Appointed a brevet second lieutenant in the Fifth Infantry, Smith was sent to Mexico. He distinguished himself during the Mexican War, winning brevets as first lieutenant and captain for his actions at Contreras and Cerro Gordo.

In 1849, after a brief stay at Jefferson Barracks, Missouri, Smith returned to West Point as an instructor in mathematics and remained there three years. In 1852 he rejoined his old regiment, then stationed along the Mexican border. Though he had no formal training in the subject, he served for a time as botanist to the Mexican Boundary Commission while protecting the civilian commissioners with his dragoons. In 1855 Smith was transferred to the Second Cavalry at Jefferson Barracks, then moved with his unit into the Red River country, where he spent much of his time in pursuit of Comanche Indian bands. Following a lengthy leave of absence in Florida, Smith sailed to Europe in May 1858 for a tour of the Continent. He returned in the fall of that year and resumed his duties on the Great Plains. Wounded in the thigh during action against the Comanches in late May 1859, he quickly recovered. During the next several years he also established a ranch on the Colorado River in Texas.

Serving at Camp Colorado, Texas, when Texas held its secession convention at the beginning of February 1861, a deeply conflicted Smith at first refused to surrender the Federal property under his command, including arms and equipment belonging to his men. Following further negotiations, he and his troops, with their weapons and equipment, evacuated the post to avoid hostilities and moved out for Fort Mason, Texas.

Shortly thereafter, in March 1861, Smith was promoted to the rank of major, but he resigned almost immediately when Florida seceded from the Union. He was commissioned a lieutenant-colonel in the Confederate army and spent some time in Lynchburg, Virginia, mustering in a number of new regiments. At about this time he assumed the surname of Kirby Smith to distinguish himself from the other Smiths in the Confederate service. He did not consider Kirby part of his family name, though that name became standard practice within his family after his death. Late in May 1861 Smith went to Harpers Ferry, where he served for a time under General J. E. Johnston in the Shenandoah Valley. Appointed a brigadier general on 17 June 1861, Smith followed Johnston to Manassas, where his timely appearance with his brigade during the first battle of Bull Run (First Manassas) on 21 July 1861 helped bring about a Confederate victory. Smith was badly wounded at the beginning of the attack, which was successfully pressed by a subordinate. Smith was praised by many as the "Blücher of Bull Run," a reference to the Prussian general of that name, Gebhard Leberecht von Blücher, whose arrival on the field of Waterloo in 1815 led to Napoleon's defeat there. Some of Smith's critics have suggested that this adulation went to his head and gave him an exaggerated impression of his own importance. He felt that the timing of his unit's arrival on the field had been critical to victory, but he never at any time said anything to detract from the vital role played that day by General Thomas J. "Stonewall" Jackson. Later that year Smith married Cassie Selden; the couple had eleven children.

Promoted to major general in October 1861, Smith was placed in command of a division in the Army of Northern Virginia. In February 1862 he was selected as commander of the Department of East Tennessee, with headquarters in Knoxville. His task there was daunting in that many residents of the region were loyal to the Union. Smith and his superior, General Braxton Bragg, developed a plan that entailed retaking Cumberland Gap from the Federal troops, defeating Don Carlos Buell, the Union commander in the area, and then pushing Union forces out of Central Tennessee. Finally they would move into Kentucky. In the months that followed, Smith and Bragg, thinking that Confederate sympathizers in Tennessee and Kentucky could be persuaded to rally to them and the southern cause, marched and countermarched through parts of both states, trying to turn the better-supported Union position without success. The hoped-for backing by the civilian population did not materialize. Smith did destroy a poorly trained force of Union troops at Richmond, Kentucky (30 Aug. 1862), and occupied Lexington (2 Sept. 1862), but beyond this the campaign accomplished little. Smith was criticized by some for failure to cooperate more closely with Bragg. For his part, Smith felt that Bragg had not been sufficiently aggressive in dealing with Union troops during the campaign.

In January 1863 Smith was named commander of the Army of the Southwest. On 9 February 1863 he was placed in charge of the entire Trans-Mississippi Department, embracing the three states of Texas, Louisiana, and Arkansas. On 7 March 1863 Smith, headquartered at Shreveport, assumed command of all Confederate forces west of the Mississippi River, some 30,000 troops stretching from west central Arkansas to the Rio Grande. His strength rose to about 43,000 by the early months of 1865. Once Vicksburg fell in July 1863, however, he was effectively cut off from the rest of the Confederacy by the Union navy. Though Smith, a devout Episcopalian, gave serious thought to leaving the army and entering the ministry in late 1863, he was promoted to full general in February 1864 and remained at his post.

Smith led a successful defense of his command against a poorly planned Federal army and naval advance up the Red River toward Shreveport from early March to mid-May 1864. In a pivotal battle fought on 8 April, troops fighting under an able subordinate, Major General Richard Taylor, defeated Union major general Nathaniel Banks at Mansfield, Louisiana. Though the Union commander managed to win a victory at Pleasant Hill, Louisiana, the next day, he was obliged to continue his retreat, thus ending the Union threat.

In July 1863 President Jefferson Davis granted Smith "any assumption of authority which may be necessary" within his department. Despite Smith's best efforts, the maintenance of morale in "Kirby Smithdom," as the Trans-Mississippi Department was frequently described, became increasingly difficult because of poor communications with the Confederate capital at Richmond and a lack of fiscal resources. Smith was criticized for not doing more to support the war effort east of the Mississippi, but Union control of the river after 1863 rendered that virtually impossible. Smith was an able commander but an overextended administrator who, in his isolated circumstances, attempted to provide civil as well as military leadership within his jurisdiction, though a vocal minority found him wanting in both spheres. At no time did he interfere with the actions of the civil authorities unless these impeded his military initiatives. His efforts to break the Union blockade through a military thrust into Mexico and to secure foreign, principally French, assistance for his department were not notably successful. Despite his best efforts, he was never able to completely satisfy his superiors in Richmond, who were largely out of touch with the realities of his situation. During his two-year tenure, Smith created a number of general officers to fulfill his local requirements, some of whom were approved by President

Davis, while others were not. Ultimately, the devaluation of the Confederate currency and insuperable logistical difficulties rendered Smith's situation untenable. With the collapse of the Confederacy in the spring of 1865, Smith was obliged to capitulate to Union general E. R. S. Canby in Galveston, Texas, on 26 May, 1865.

After living briefly in Mexico and in Cuba, Smith returned to the United States and attempted to enter business in Kentucky. His brief presidencies of the Accident Insurance Company of Louisville and of the Atlantic and Pacific Telegraph Company there were unsuccessful. For a short time he operated a school in New Castle, Kentucky, that was destroyed by fire in 1868. From 1870 to 1875 he directed the Academic Department and preparatory school at the University of Nashville (later George Peabody College for Teachers). In 1875 he became professor of mathematics at the University of the South in Sewanee, Tennessee, a post he held to the end of his life. He was considered an excellent teacher but not a notable scholar. He died in Sewanee.

• The Edmund Kirby Smith Papers in the Southern Historical Collection of the University of North Carolina, Chapel Hill, are valuable for family information extending back to the revolutionary war period. Smith's own correspondence with his family, particularly his mother and his wife, are in this material. Several smaller collections are in the Archives of the University of the South and in the P. G. T. Beauregard, Bradley Johnson, and Clement C. Clay papers at Duke University are also helpful. Other useful collections with a bearing on Smith's administration of the Trans-Mississippi Department include the papers of Governor Thomas O. Moore, Louisiana State University, and Governors Francis R. Lubbock and Pendleton Murrah at the Texas State Archives. The papers of Thomas C. Reynolds, a consistent supporter of Smith who acted as Confederate "governor" of Mo., are in the Manuscripts Division at the Library of Congress. Significant materials are in *The War of the Rebellion: A Compilation of the Official Records of the Union and Confederate Armies* (128 vols., 1880–1901) and in *The Official Records of the Union and Confederate Navies in the War of the Rebellion* (30 vols., 1894–1922). Smith wrote little about his wartime experiences except for his "Defense of the Red River" in *Battles and Leaders of the Civil War*, vol. 4, ed. Robert U. Johnson and Clarence C. Buel (1888), in which he emphatically refuted allegations that he sought to profit from the illicit sale of cotton during the Red River campaign. One critical view of Smith's efforts is Thomas L. Snead, "The Conquest of Arkansas," in *Battles and Leaders*, vol. 3. Richard Taylor, *Destruction and Reconstruction: Personal Experiences of the Late War* (1879), contains bitter criticisms of Smith that mar an otherwise excellent and balanced memoir. The standard biography is Joseph Howard Parks, *General Edmund Kirby Smith CSA* (1954). Robert L. Kirby, *Kirby Smith's Confederacy: The Trans-Mississippi South, 1863–1865* (1972), is an important study. An older work, Arthur Howard Noll, *General Kirby-Smith* (1907), is less useful. See also Emma J. Blackwood, ed., *To Mexico with Scott: Letters of Captain E. Kirby Smith to His Wife* (1917), and a volume completed by his wife, Cassie Selden Kirby Smith, in 1901 and later published by a daughter, Nina Kirby-Smith Buck, as *All's Fair in Love and War; or, The Story of How a Virginia Belle Won a Confederate Colonel* (1945).

KEIR B. STERLING

SMITH, Elias (17 June 1769–29 June 1846), minister, religious journalist and polemicist, and botanical doctor, was born in Lyme, Connecticut, the son of Stephen Smith and Irene Ransom. Like many New England farm families in search of adequate land during this period, Stephen Smith and his family moved in 1782 to the Vermont frontier near Woodstock. As formal schooling was a luxury that few could afford, the adolescent Elias received an education largely through a course of self-study with the assistance of his uncle Elisha Ransom, a Baptist preacher in Woodstock. Smith began teaching in a local school at the age of nineteen, but he was preoccupied by spiritual matters that had begun with a vision of God followed by conversion in 1785. Smith was especially perplexed about baptism, which had been a point of contention in the family because his father was a Separate Baptist and his mother a Separate Congregationalist. He finally decided in 1789 to be baptized and join the Baptist church in Woodstock.

Many in Woodstock encouraged Smith to become a preacher, but he resisted out of feelings of inadequacy concerning his spiritual and educational qualifications even though he was an avid reader of the Bible and various theological works. With the encouragement of Baptist preachers, Smith did eventually sense a divine call to the ministry and began to preach in 1790. Soon after he left his teaching and his family in Woodstock to become an itinerant Baptist minister in the northern Connecticut River valley and throughout New Hampshire. Almost immediately, Smith found himself on a trajectory that quickly led him away from the humble and itinerant life of a rural Baptist preacher. Smith was ordained in 1792, became the regular preacher of the Baptist church in Salisbury, New Hampshire, from 1793 to 1798, and finally settled in 1798 as the installed minister of the Baptist church in Woburn, Massachusetts, a fashionable town outside of Boston that afforded him the opportunity to associate with the influential Boston Baptist ministers Samuel Stillman and Thomas Baldwin.

Troubled, however, by his comfortable circumstances, Smith concluded that he and the Baptists had departed from the plain but vibrant gospel message by adopting practices and doctrines that were contrary to a straightforward reading of the Bible. Neither the pastors who were salaried, settled, and distinguished by their black clerical garb nor their learned Calvinistic theology—nor even the worship of the Trinity—was biblical and thus acceptable to Smith. He decided to quit the Woburn church in 1801 and henceforth to reject all church polities, doctrines, practices, and even denominational names not found in the New Testament, which alone would safeguard the evangelical piety and revivalism that he knew on the Vermont frontier. After a brief but unsuccessful business venture, Smith moved to Portsmouth, New Hampshire, where in 1803 he began the "Church of Christ" as a protest against the upward mobility and increasing formalism of New England Baptists and as a restoration of the primitive and evangelically vibrant church of the New Testament. This congregation became the catalyst for the Christian Connection that spread throughout New England and the mid-Atlantic states under the leadership of Smith and fellow evangelist and reformer Abner Jones.

Smith devoted his life to a quest for "gospel liberty," which he understood to be the recovery of a pure Christianity unencumbered by the contingencies of history that had implications for broader societal concerns such as communications, politics, and medicine. Through itinerant preaching, travels, and inexpensive pamphlets and newspapers, including his most significant magazine, the *Herald of Gospel Liberty*, Smith proclaimed a theology of human ability and freedom, Jeffersonian Republican politics, anticlerical polemics, calls for religious disestablishment, and the practice of Thomsonian or botanical medicine, a family-based medicine that he adopted in 1817 in direct challenge to the specialization of the medical profession. Although Smith was derided as unstable by his critics for his multiple and seemingly unrelated interests, his attacks on the prerogatives of the established clergy, Federalist politicians, and regular doctors exemplified a consistent ideal that common people can and should take charge of the most important areas of their own lives.

Smith's bases of operations in the Christian Connection were variously located in Philadelphia, Portsmouth, and Portland, Maine, until in 1816 when he moved his large family to Boston to devote most of his remaining years to practicing botanic medicine. About the same time, Smith also decided to join the Universalists because he concluded that the doctrine of universal salvation was consistent with his democratic ideology, though he later vacillated between the Universalists and the Christian Connection. Smith had six children with his first wife, Mary Burleigh of Newmarket, New Hampshire, whom he had married in 1793. After she died in 1814, Smith married Rachel Thurber of Providence, Rhode Island, later that year. Smith died in Lynn, Massachusetts, largely a forgotten person.

Both the Christian Connection, which merged with the Congregationalists in 1931, and the Universalists have been ambivalent about Smith because of his divided loyalties. But Elias Smith remains an important representative of the religious and democratic ferment and iconoclasm of a turbulent period in the early republic. In his life one can see the beginnings of the democratic populism, primitivist or restorationist impulse, religious experimentation, and elevation of religious experience and private judgment that have since played a large role in American religion and culture.

• Smith was a prolific writer of pamphlets and short treatises, in addition to his journalistic efforts, which include the *Christian's Magazine, Reviewer, and Religious Intelligencer* (1805–1808), the *Herald of Gospel Liberty* (1808–1817), *Herald of Life and Immortality* (1819–1820), and the *Morning Star and City Watchman* (1827–1829). His anti-Federalist and anticler-ical views are found in the four-part series titled *The Clergyman's Looking-Glass* (1803–1804), *The Whole World Governed by a Jew* (1805), and *The History of Anti-Christ* (1811). His religious primitivism is captured well in *Articles of Faith and Church Building* (1802), *A Sermon on New Testament Baptism* (1807), and *The New Testament Dictionary* (1812), and his medical views can be found in *The People's Book* (1836) and *The American Physician and Family Assistant* (1832). In addition to composing hymns and publishing hymnbooks such as *A Collection of Hymns, for the Use of Christians* (1804), Smith produced two editions of an autobiography titled *The Life, Conversion, Preaching, Travels, and Sufferings of Elias Smith* (1816, 1840).

For secondary studies of Smith, see Timothy E. Fulop, "Elias Smith and the Quest for Gospel Liberty: Popular Religion and Democratic Radicalism in Early Nineteenth-Century New England" (Ph.D. diss., Princeton Univ., 1992), and Michael G. Kenny, *The Perfect Law of Liberty: Elias Smith and the Providential History of America* (1994). Nathan O. Hatch, *The Democratization of American Christianity* (1989), offers a general discussion of the religiously volatile period of the early republic.

TIMOTHY E. FULOP

SMITH, Elihu Hubbard (4 Sept. 1771–19 Sept. 1798), medical practitioner, man of letters, and founder of the first national American medical journal, was born in Litchfield, Connecticut, the son of Reuben Smith, a physician, and Abigail Hubbard. Smith entered Yale College at the age of eleven and received a B.A. in 1786. He spent an additional year in academic study under Timothy Dwight (who later became president of Yale) at the Academy at Greenfield Hill in Fairfield, Connecticut. He then returned to Litchfield to work as an apprentice in his father's apothecary shop. At the same time he began the study of medicine along with five other young men under the preceptorship of Dr. Daniel Sheldon. In late 1790 he went to Philadelphia and attended lectures given by the noted physician Benjamin Rush at the Medical College of Philadelphia. When the classes ended in February 1791, Smith had reached the end of his formal medical education. He never received a medical degree. Then just twenty years of age, he was ineligible to be certified as a physician since the minimum age in Pennsylvania for certification was twenty-four.

Smith remained nevertheless in Philadelphia, attempting to be a writer. He published some twenty-one poems, nine sonnets, nine odes, two fragments, and a long piece titled "Laura and Mary" in the *Gazette of the United States* under the pen name of "Ella." He returned to Connecticut in late 1791 and tried to establish a medical practice in Wethersfield without much success. Returning to his home in Litchfield, he completed a major project of editing and publishing *American Poems, Selected and Original, Volume I* (1793), which is generally considered to be the first anthology of American verse.

In September 1793, Smith moved to New York City, where he spent the remainder of his short life. He took over the medical practice of a Dr. Miller, which afforded him a modest livelihood. In January 1794 he began gratuitous medical service in the City

Dispensary. Shortly after his arrival in New York, Smith became involved in the Manumission Society, whose members included Noah Webster, John Jay, and Alexander Hamilton. The principal activity of the society was the maintenance of a school for the children of slaves. (Although a precise number of African-American slaves in New York during Smith's time is not known, it was probably significant. As late as the 1850 census there were close to 14,000 blacks in New York City of which close to 90 percent were slaves.) In May 1794 he became a trustee of the school and worked vigorously in its behalf until his death. At the same time he worked on a volume of poetry and began revising a three-act opera, *Edwin and Angelina*. His practice grew, albeit slowly. According to James E. Cronin, the editor of Smith's diary, however, "Smith emerged from the winter of 1794 in a thoroughly unhappy state of mind. . . . Perhaps in an effort to analyze himself—something he frequently tried—he began in July 1794 to write a history of his life" (*The Diary of Elihu Hubbard Smith*, p. 14). The extant manuscript begins with volume three; the first entry is dated 4 September 1795. Volumes one and two are missing, probably destroyed by Smith himself. The final entry was written four days before his death. This remarkable document, chronicling the life and times of Smith contains lengthy sketches of personal encounters with such notables as Alexander Hamilton, John Adams, and General Thaddeus Kosciusko; commentaries on new books and plays; and copies of his correspondence with physicians, politicians, and other notables.

Throughout 1795 Smith was busily engaged with the Manumission Society, attempting to put together the second volume of *American Poems*, revising his opera (music composed by Victor Pelissier), and attending to his practice. In early 1796 Smith began to formulate an idea for a national medical journal. In mid-November Smith, together with Drs. Edward Miller and Samuel Latham Mitchill, was ready to launch the *Medical Repository*, and he prepared a circular addressed to the "Physicians of the United States" soliciting their input. Smith's aim was "to obtain an accurate & annual account of those general diseases which reign, in each season, over every part of the United States" (*Diary*, p. 205). In a letter of 10 August 1797, he reports that the first number of the *Medical Repository* was published. It consisted of some 100 pages and sold for fifty cents. The quarterly journal was a successful publication for twenty-seven years (1797–1824). It was the first national medical journal in the United States. According to James Thacher in his *American Medical Biography; or, Memoirs of Eminent Physicians Who Have Flourished in America* (1828), Smith's contributions to the *Medical Repository* were the history of the plagues of Athens; a case of mania successfully treated with mercury; observations of pestilential fever on the island of Grenada; the natural history of the elk; and accounts of pestilential fevers in the Athenian, Carthaginian, and Roman armies in and around Syracuse.

With the launching of the journal, Smith turned more and more of his attention to science and medicine but did not abandon his theatrical interests and his poetry writing and publishing. His diary reveals that he continued work on his opera throughout the year and finally saw *Edwin and Angelina; or, The "Banditti"* (1795) performed on 19 December 1796. According to Cronin, "[The opera] was a complete failure. . . . From first to last it was bad theater. . . . Despite all of its faults, however, the responsibility for the failure of the piece should probably rest on Pelissier, the composer" (*Diary*, p. 273). Smith seems to have taken the failure well. He wrote, "They [the audience] heard the Piece with as much attention as could be desired; with more than I expected; & tho' they bestowed but little applause, bestowed as much of that as I expected. It went off, on the whole, tolerably well" (*Diary*, p. 273).

In 1796 the governors of the New York Hospital named him a physician to the institution. He served the hospital until his death. He continued to read modern literature and ancient history and to compose verse. He maintained a wide correspondence, gave his time freely to philanthropic causes, and indulged in music and theater. In September 1798 with Edward Miller, Smith experimented with the effects of ether some fifty years before Horace Wells introduced it as an anesthetic. In the same year, he edited an American edition of Erasmus Darwin's *Botanic Garden*, appending a poetic prefix lauding the author's work. The prefix was so highly regarded that it was retained in the 1806 second American edition of the work. Smith never married, but his circle of friends, both men and women, was extensive. He was a friend to prominent Federalist lawyer and politician Uriah Tracy, a confidant of statesman Alexander Hamilton and lexicographer Noah Webster, and a student and correspondent of Benjamin Rush. In spite of these many accomplishments, Smith was introspective, self-doubting, and often self-critical. Typical is an entry in his diary of August 1796: "Altho' I am exceedingly weak & irresolute, as every page of my Journal evinces, yet I am ready, at times, to believe that strength is certainly, tho' slowly, acquired" (*Diary*, p. 198).

On 15 September 1798 (the last entry in his *Diary*) he noted "a day of great fatigue of body, & still greater distress of mind" (p. 464). Yellow fever once again raged in New York City. He too had contracted the disease. Within twenty-four hours he was gravely ill and was taken by Drs. Mitchill and Miller, his attending physicians and close associates, to the home of his friend Horace Miller in New York City, where in spite of their ministrations he died four days later. He is buried in the cemetery of the Presbyterian Church on Wall Street in New York City.

Smith's many accomplishments attest to his intelligence, energy, and equal interest in the arts and sciences. In his brief twenty-seven years, Smith founded a successful medical journal and contributed numerous articles to it, particularly on fevers; edited and published the first anthology of American verse; wrote an opera in three acts; and compiled a history of the American elk. A drama in five acts entitled *Andre*, which was produced in New York in 1798, is attributed to him.

• The principal source of information is *The Diary of Elihu Hubbard Smith (1771–1798)*, ed. James E. Cronin (1973). Short biographies can also be found in Howard A. Kelly and Walter L. Burrage, eds., *American Medical Biographies* (1920); James Thacher, *American Medical Biography; or, Memoirs of Eminent Physicians Who Have Flourished in America* (1828; repr. 1967); and Franklin B. Dexter, *Biographical Sketches of the Graduates of Yale College with Annals of the College History* (6 vols., 1885–1912). A more recent article regarding Smith and the *Medical Repository* can be found in S. W. Lowenthal, "Dr. Elihu Hubbard Smith and the Beginning of Medical Communication among Physicians in America," *Connecticut Medicine* 60 (Oct. 1996): 613–16.

STANLEY L. BLOCK

SMITH, Elizabeth Oakes (8 Aug. 1806–15 Nov. 1893), author and lecturer, was born Elizabeth Oakes Prince near North Yarmouth, Maine, the daughter of David Cushing Prince, part owner of a trading ship, and Sophia Blanchard. Elizabeth exhibited a remarkable intelligence at an early age. When she was two years old, she insisted that she be allowed to accompany her sister to school, where she learned how to read. While still a child, she taught Sunday school and tutored her male cousins in their college courses. She yearned for a college education to prepare her for a career as a teacher, but her mother denied her request, saying, "No daughter of mine is going to be a schoolma'am." Smith regretted her lack of formal education for the rest of her life. This early disappointment shaped her career as a lecturer and campaigner for women's rights.

Following the custom of the Puritan faith they practiced, Smith's mother arranged an early marriage for her. On 6 March 1823 Elizabeth Prince married Seba Smith, editor and part owner of the *Eastern Argus* in Portland, Maine. Although they began their married life as virtual strangers, the Smiths shared many interests, including writing and social reform. But Smith's desire to write had to be subordinated to the needs of her household, which included servants, apprentices, and, eventually, four sons. Smith always struggled to resolve the tension between her family and her career, a tension she attributed to the differences between men's and women's opportunities. When friends offered her comfort because she had no daughters, she admitted in her autobiography that "I was secretly glad not to add to the number of human beings who must be from necessity curtailed of so much that was desirable in life; who must be arrested, abridged, engulfed in the tasteless actual."

Although "the tasteless actual" often intruded, Smith carved enough time out of her busy family life to continue her studies. She rose early every day to read and write, eager to develop her mind. But it was her family's financial trouble that thrust her into a literary career. In the late 1830s her husband lost most of the family's money on a bad investment, and the Smiths had to leave their home in Portland. In the winter of 1839 they landed in New York City, where Smith began her career as a writer and lecturer.

While her husband looked for work as an editor, Smith began to write essays, hoping to help support her family. By 1840 she was a regular contributor to several prominent publications, including *Godey's Lady's Book* and the *Ladies' Companion*. In 1842 the *Southern Literary Messenger* published her poem "The Sinless Child," establishing her reputation as a writer. Smith contributed regularly to popular annuals and gift books, and her collections of poetry went through several editions. She also published fiction for children and adults. Although she never felt she earned enough from her writing, she remained an important contributor to her family's finances for many years.

In 1849 Smith launched a series of articles for Horace Greeley's *New York Tribune* titled "Woman and Her Needs." The response from readers was overwhelming, and she began to attend women's rights conventions, serving as a speaker and committee member. By 1851 she had secured a position on the Lyceum circuit, a popular series of lectures that traveled across the country. Smith believed herself to be the first woman to appear on a Lyceum tour, at a time when it was considered bad taste for a woman to air her opinions on a public stage. She spoke for abolition and prison reform, but her favorite topic was women's rights. These words from her autobiography probably approximate the message of her lectures: "It is useless to talk about the sphere of woman. The measure of capacity is the measure of sphere to either man or woman. I do not strike at the root of any social harmonies. I leave the fireside intact. . . . But I see there are thousands capable of a sphere beyond the fireside, and, being thus qualified, they hold a commission from God himself to go out into this broader field."

Smith's interest in women's rights and other reform movements influenced her writing. In 1854 she published two novels, *Bertha and Lily* and *The Newsboy*, which reflect her political convictions. A feminist novel, *Bertha and Lily* tells the story of an independent woman who refuses to be limited by societal expectations. *The Newsboy*, published anonymously, explores the plight of the poverty-stricken young men who sold papers on street corners in the city. Her novels did not enjoy much critical success, but they were popular among reform-minded people. Smith's career also influenced her religious beliefs. She often had felt herself to be in conflict with Puritanism's stricter tenets, even as she drew strength and courage from them. After her column "Woman and Her Needs" became popular, she gradually broke with Puritanism and began to explore other religions, including Unitarianism and Catholicism.

The years after the Civil War were hard ones for the Smiths. As Democrats they opposed the war and so experienced several conflicts with the wartime government in New York. Smith also endured a string of private tragedies: one son succumbed to yellow fever in 1865, her husband died in 1868, and another son drowned in 1869. Her family responsibilities and her grief kept her from her career for many years. In 1874 she moved to Hollywood, North Carolina, to live with her oldest son Appleton and his family. There she started a Temperance League and a Sunday school and began lecturing, but she never was able to command widespread attention again. In 1877, at the age of seventy-one, she became pastor of the Independent Church of Canastota, New York. She kept that post for only one year, returning to live with her son Alvin and his family in Patchogue, Long Island. By 1884 she was unable to support herself and worried that she was a burden to her family. On 2 September 1887 she wrote in her diary, "My life has come to an end of purpose." She died in Hollywood, North Carolina.

As a novelist, essayist, and Lyceum lecturer, Elizabeth Oakes Smith helped to popularize the goals of the women's rights and temperance movements. Her life illustrates the struggle faced by many middle-class women in the nineteenth century who sought to combine individual ambition with religious faith and family responsibilities.

• Smith's papers are held at the New York Public Library and the Alderman Library at the University of Virginia. Her autobiography is at the New York Public Library; it was excerpted in *Selections from the Autobiography of Elizabeth Oakes Smith*, ed. Mary Alice Wyman (1924). In addition to her work mentioned above, see also *The Western Captive* (1842); *The Sinless Child and Other Poems* (1843); *The Poetical Writings of Elizabeth Oakes Smith* (1846); and *Old New York; or, Democracy in 1689* (1853). Wynola L. Richards, "A Review of the Life and Writings of Elizabeth Oakes Smith: Feminist, Author, and Lecturer, 1806–1893" (Ph.D. diss., Ball State Univ., 1981), offers the most complete assessment of Smith's work and contains a comprehensive bibliography.

LAURA CRAWLEY

SMITH, Ellison DuRant (1 Aug. 1864–17 Nov. 1944), U.S. senator, was born near Lynchburg, Sumter (now Lee) County, South Carolina, the son of William Hawkins Smith, a Methodist Episcopal minister, and Mary Isabella McLeod. Smith was raised on the family's cotton plantation, which retained many of its antebellum characteristics. In 1886 Smith enrolled at Wofford College, a Methodist school in Spartanburg, South Carolina, where he excelled in debate, science, and literature and from which he received an A.B. in 1889.

Soon after graduation, Smith returned home to manage the 2,000-acre farm. In 1892 he married Martha Cornelia Moorer, who died the following year after giving birth to their first child. Smith remarried in 1906 to Annie Brunson Farley; they had four children.

Smith's political career began in 1896 when he was elected to the South Carolina legislature. Although identified with the Bourbon establishment, he accepted many Populist precepts during this decade of rural unrest and was influenced by that movement's agrarianism for the rest of his life. He was reelected in 1898 but chose not to seek a third two-year term, and in 1901 he made an unsuccessful bid for a seat in the U.S. Congress. Smith became renowned for his efforts on behalf of cotton producers, and in 1905 he was one of the principal organizers of the Southern Cotton Association. The organization was short-lived, but it established Smith's reputation as an impressive orator and unsurpassed defender of cotton, earning him his famous moniker "Cotton Ed."

Smith was elected to the U.S. Senate in 1908. This campaign, which established a winning style that served him well in five subsequent races, was described thirty years later for the readers of *Collier's* in "He's for Cotton." Cotton Ed typically made his appearance in a rural farm town in "a spring wagon drawn by a pair of the slickest mules in the county. On the wagon was a bale of cotton; on the bale sat a bristling man of thirty-nine with a fierce handle-bar mustache that quivered happily at each cheer from the crowd." In his lapel Smith "wore a cotton boll . . . and as he stepped from the wagon he stroked the white-tipped bud and said lovingly but loudly: 'My sweetheart, my sweetheart—others may forget you, but you will always be my sweetheart.'" After shaking the hand of "every farmer he could reach," Cotton Ed "mounted a platform and rushed into a roaring, ripping political speech."

Smith is remembered for championing white supremacy and the poll tax and for opposing federal antilynching laws, but he was identified with the Progressives during his early years in Washington. Senator Smith opposed high tariffs and attacked Wall Street, favored more antitrust legislation and restrictive immigration laws, advocated measures to make the national currency more elastic, and supported federal programs that promised to aid the rural South, such as swampland reclamation and "good roads." During the 1910s, Smith opposed submission of the woman suffrage amendment, as did the senior senator from South Carolina, Benjamin "Pitchfork Ben" Tillman, but supported Woodrow Wilson's New Freedom, coauthored the Cotton Futures Act, and was frequently identified as a La Follette reformer.

Cotton Ed's progressive tendencies in matters other than race relations continued through the 1920s. He was a founding member of the congressional "agricultural bloc," which emerged in response to the farm crisis of 1920, and he supported most of this group's initiatives, including its drive for federal money to combat the menacing boll weevil. A latecomer to the movement for the McNary-Haugen two-price plan for supporting farm commodities, Cotton Ed was an early backer of the Muscle Shoals development for the production of electricity and nitrates (for munitions and farm fertilizers) and was a member of the "Norris group" that sought public development of the Tennessee Valley in the late 1920s. Thwarted by the administration of Herbert Hoover, this group saw its efforts come to fruition when Franklin D. Roosevelt signed legislation creating the Tennessee Valley Authority on 18 May 1933.

In addition to the presidency, Democrats controlled both houses of Congress after 1933. This meant that Smith could finally assume the chairmanship of the

Senate Committee on Agriculture and Forestry, but relations soon soured with the administration. Smith opposed the nomination of Rexford Tugwell as under secretary of agriculture and grew "tired of being dictated to . . . by window-sill agriculturists" who, he asserted, did "not know a cotton stalk from a Jimson weed." Cotton Ed favored the price-support policies of the first Agricultural Adjustment Act but objected to its stringent crop controls. In many other policy areas he resisted New Deal usurpation of state and local authority and was soon recognized as one of Roosevelt's bitterest critics. In Philadelphia in 1936, Cotton Ed walked out of his party's national convention when a black minister was asked to deliver the invocation. Smith had upset the president to such an extent by 1938 that he became a target of Roosevelt's futile attempt to purge conservative Democrats from the Democratic party.

During his final term, Smith opposed Roosevelt's preparedness program and lost touch with his constituents. As a result, he failed in his bid for a seventh Democratic nomination in August 1944; three months later he died at his lifelong plantation home. A "master on the stump" and "one of the most colorful" political figures of his generation, a "symbol of a vanished South" who "decorated his [Senate] speeches by 'pings' at a spittoon ten feet away" (*Time*, 7 Aug. 1944, p. 18), Smith failed to see that his time had passed.

A consistent champion of a basic agrarian philosophy, Smith attracted considerable attention to the plight of farmers during an era of revolutionary change. He was "tenacious" but "neither fertile nor original in political imagination," wrote historian Selden K. Smith; his support of agrarian causes was important, but the ideas and leadership came from others. Thus, while Smith built a moderately successful record during his first four terms, he authored little legislation, and his legacy—one of racial prejudice and obstructionism—arose largely from his final, hapless decade.

• Senator E. D. Smith's congressional papers were destroyed, and there is no known collection of private papers or personal correspondence. His political career and remarks on various issues must be traced through the newspapers and the *Congressional Record*. Selden K. Smith, "Ellison DuRant Smith: A Southern Progressive, 1909–1929" (Ph.D. diss., Univ. of South Carolina, 1970), and Daniel W. Hollis, "'Cotton Ed Smith'—Showman or Statesman?" *South Carolina Historical Magazine* 71 (Oct. 1970): 235–56, have given his life and career scholarly attention, but a full-scale biography has not been produced. Of interest also are the writings of John A. Rice, a nephew of Smith: *I Came Out of the Eighteenth Century* (1942) and "Grandmother Smith's Plantation," part 1, *Harper's Magazine*, Nov. 1938, pp. 572–82, and part 2, Dec. 1938, pp. 88–96. See also the biographical sketch by S. K. Smith in the *Encyclopedia of Southern History*, ed. David C. Roller and Robert W. Twyman (1979), p. 1119; Robert McCormick, "He's for Cotton: The Senatorial Career of Cotton Ed," *Collier's: The National Weekly*, 23 Apr. 1938, pp. 48, 52; William Allen White, "Storming the Citadel: Capture of the Outworks of the Senate by the Insurgents Significant of Greater Change," *American Magazine*, Sept. 1911, pp. 570–75; Beverly Smith, "F.D.R., Here I Come," *American Magazine*, Jan. 1939, pp. 20–21, 145–47; and Theodore Saloutos, "The Southern Cotton Association, 1905–1908," *Journal of Southern History* 13 (Nov. 1947): 492–510. Obituaries are in the *New York Times* and the *Washington Post*, 18 Nov. 1944.
VIRGIL W. DEAN

SMITH, Emma Hale (10 July 1804–30 Apr. 1879), humanitarian, was born at Harmony Township (now Oakland), Pennsylvania, the daughter of Isaac Hale and Elizabeth Lewis. Isaac was a farmer and hunter, and Elizabeth kept an inn or tavern in their large farmhouse. Working beside her mother and three sisters, Emma acquired business and social skills she would later use to support her own family, first by taking in boarders, and later by operating two hotels. From her mother, she also learned to use medicinal herbs and home remedies in caring for the sick.

Emma had a typical frontier education. Most likely, her mother taught her and the other Hale children to read. At age nine she attended school in Harmony's first log schoolhouse, and sometime in her teens she had a year of finishing school. She emerged from her Pennsylvania youth with a written fluency that became evident in her late correspondence. She possessed a quick wit and self-confidence. Described as fine looking, smart, and a good singer, Emma stood about five feet nine inches tall, with refined features, hazel eyes, and dark brown hair. She was an excellent horsewoman, exhibited warm hospitality, possessed a sense of humor, and would become an effective leader.

In November 1825 Joseph Smith, Jr., came from Manchester (near Palmyra), New York, to board at the Hale's home. He and several other men had been hired by Josiah Stowell, a friend of Emma's family, to dig for treasures that Stowell believed were buried on his land. Emma and Joseph became attracted to each other, but Isaac Hale, who objected to the treasure-hunting enterprise, twice refused to give his permission for them to marry. Consequently, they eloped to South Bainbridge, New York, and were married there on 18 January 1827. Unwilling to face her father's wrath, the newlyweds traveled to Joseph's parents' farm 130 miles north, where they lived for about a year.

Acting on visions that led him to ancient records, Joseph Smith, Jr., dictated the manuscript for the *Book of Mormon* from the records, while Emma, among others, acted as scribe. In upstate New York on 6 April 1830 he founded the Church of Christ, now known as the Church of Jesus Christ of Latter-day Saints (LDS or Mormon, with world headquarters in Salt Lake City, Utah), becoming its first prophet and president. Mormon doctrine is based on the Bible, Book of Mormon, and Doctrine and Covenants, all considered scripture. Doctrines of the church include baptism for the dead by proxy, marriage for eternity, continuing revelation from God, and adherence to a health code that prohibits the use of tobacco, liquor, and hot caffeine drinks. Emma was baptized into the church on 28 June 1830. The following month, Joseph pronounced a revelation that designated her as an "Elect Lady," admonished her to be a support and comfort to her husband, and commissioned her to compile the first hymnal for the church (Doctrine and Covenants, section 25). The hymnal was published in 1835. During her seventeen years of marriage to Joseph, Smith experienced persecution and mob violence through five states (New York, Pennsylvania, Ohio, Missouri, and Illinois) as opposition to the new religion grew among members of other churches, politicians, and those suspicious of Mormon beliefs.

During those same years Smith gave birth to nine children and adopted twins. Several babies died at birth or as small children: Alvin (1828) died in Harmony, Pennsylvania; twins Thaddeus and Louisa (1830) died in Kirtland, Ohio; an adopted year-old twin, also named Joseph (1831–1832), succumbed to measles after exposure to the freezing air the night a mob tarred and feathered Emma's husband in Hiram, Ohio; Don Carlos (1840–1841) perished of malaria at age fourteen months and an unnamed son died in 1842, both at Nauvoo, Illinois. Frederick Granger Williams Smith (1836–1862) died at age twenty-six of an unidentified illness. Only Julia Murcock Smith (the other adopted twin, 1831–1880), Joseph Smith III (1832–1914), Alexander Hale Smith (1838–1909), and David Hyrum Smith (1844–1904) outlived their mother.

Throughout her adult life, Smith opened her home to friends, strangers, destitute converts, homeless widows, and orphaned children. During the Mormons' first summer in Nauvoo, she moved her own family into a tent and turned their home into a hospital so she could care for members of the malaria-stricken community. Smith's peers elected her president of the first LDS women's organization in 1842: the Nauvoo Female Relief Society. Under her leadership the society gave aid and comfort to the poor, the widows, and the suffering, provided jobs for women, and raised money to help build the Nauvoo temple. (In 1991 the LDS Church Relief Society membership totaled over three million women in 135 countries.) Joseph Smith also admonished the society to watch over the morals of the community. This charge, which Smith and other women took seriously, soon became problematic.

Two years earlier in 1840, Joseph had secretly introduced the doctrine and practice of plural marriage to a select group of his followers. At first Smith did not know that her husband was marrying additional wives. When she did find out, she struggled over acceptance of the doctrine. After consenting to his marriage to at least four other women, she finally rejected the practice outright, then used the Female Relief Society forum to speak against it. The suspension of the society in 1844 is attributed to Smith's opposition to polygamy and her use of the organization to fight it.

A mob murdered Joseph Smith, Jr., in Carthage, Illinois, on 27 June 1844. Smith gave birth to their last son five months later. In the early months of 1846 the main body of the church left Nauvoo to find a new place of refuge, first along the Iowa-Nebraska border,

then the following year in the Rocky Mountains. Smith refused to go. She opposed the doctrine of plural marriage and did not support Brigham Young's ascension to church leadership. Neither did she choose to follow any of the leaders of the many Mormon splinter groups formed by other Mormons who chose not to go west. Smith fled Nauvoo in September 1846 as anti-Mormon forces entered the city. She and her children traveled north by riverboat to Fulton, Illinois. They returned to Nauvoo when it became safe the following spring. There she raised her family, supporting them by running a hotel as she did earlier. She also cared for Joseph's mother, Lucy Mack Smith, who died in Smith's home in 1856.

On 23 December 1847 Smith married one of the new citizens of Nauvoo, a non-Mormon named Lewis C. Bidamon. This marriage lasted until Emma's death thirty-two years later.

Sometime between Joseph's death and the adulthood of her sons, Smith began to either ignore or deny that her husband ever had plural wives. Eventually a number of Joseph Smith's followers who had not gone west and who had become disillusioned with leaders of the various splinter groups formed the Reorganized Church of Jesus Christ of Latter Day Saints (RLDS). In December 1856 representatives of this faith visited Smith and solicited her help in persuading her eldest son, Joseph Smith III, to lead their church. She told them they would have to ask him themselves. Young Joseph Smith at first refused them, but in the spring of 1860, after nearly four years of reflection, he acquiesced.

On 6 April 1860 Smith accompanied her son to Amboy, Illinois, where Joseph Smith III presented himself to the congregation for confirmation of his position as prophet and president of the RLDS church. In his first address to the congregation, he denounced polygamy as a tenet of the RLDS faith and denied his father's involvement in it. At the same meeting, the congregation also accepted Emma Smith into full fellowship by virtue of her original baptism and commissioned her to compile a new hymnal.

For the next 136 years (until 1996) Smith's descendants would lead the RLDS church (world headquarters are in Independence, Missouri). All three of her sons, Joseph, Alexander, and David, eventually traveled to Utah on missions for their church. David, a sensitive and talented poet, would spend the last years of his life in a mental institution. Smith called the illness of her youngest son her "greatest trouble." Smith never renounced her faith, but she did claim to have been Joseph Smith's only wife. She did not live to see the Utah church officially ban plural marriages in 1890 (any LDS church member who advocates or practices polygamy is now excommunicated), but her opposition to it contributed to the century-long controversy in both LDS and RLDS churches about its origin and practice. She died in Nauvoo, Illinois, in 1879.

As a result of her decision not to go west with the main body of the church her husband founded and her refusal to accept polygamy, Brigham Young condemned Emma Smith from the pulpit, and she was virtually written out of official LDS church histories for a hundred years after her death. Today she is honored among members of both LDS and RLDS churches as a leader of women, a compassionate caretaker, a devoted wife and mother, and a significant player in the history of Mormonism.

• The library and archives of the RLDS church in Independence, Mo., have Emma Smith and Lewis C. Bidamon Collections as well as the papers of Smith's sons Alexander Hale Smith, David Hyrum Smith, and Joseph Smith III. The LDS Church Archives in Salt Lake City has two different sets of Emma Smith Bidamon and Lewis C. Bidamon Papers in the Marcia Vogel and Nancy Kalk Collections; it also holds the David Hyrum Smith Papers and the Joseph Smith, Jr., Collection. The Marriott Library at the University of Utah has other manuscript sources on Smith, and the Henry E. Huntington Library in San Marino, Calif., has a collection of Emma Smith Bidamon and Lewis C. Bidamon Papers. A complete assessment of Smith's life is Linda King Newell and Valeen Tippetts Avery, *Mormon Enigma: Emma Hale Smith* (1984; rev. ed., 1994). See also Donna Hill, *Joseph Smith: The First Mormon* (1977); Lucy Mack Smith, *Biographical Sketches of Joseph Smith the Prophet and His Progenitors for Many Years* (1853; repr. 1958); Valeen Tippetts Avery, "Last Years of the Prophet's Wife: Emma Hale Smith Bidamon and the Establishment of the Reorganized Church of Jesus Christ of Latter Day Saints" (M.A. thesis, Northern Arizona Univ., 1981); Raymond T. Bailey, "Emma Hale, Wife of the Prophet Joseph Smith" (M.A. thesis, Brigham Young Univ., 1952); and Robert D. Hutchins, "Joseph Smith III, Moderate Mormon" (M.A. thesis, Brigham Young Univ., 1977).

LINDA KING NEWELL

SMITH, Erwin Frink (21 Jan. 1854–6 Apr. 1927), plant pathologist, was born at Gilberts Mills, New York, the son of Rancellor King Smith, a tanner and shoemaker, and Louisa Frink. In 1870 his father bought eighty acres of land for a farm in Michigan, to which the family moved in March of that year. Because Smith helped with the farm work, he did not graduate from the Ionia, Michigan, high school until 1880. Michigan was then undergoing deforestation, and the flora were interesting and rich. Smith became friends with Charles F. Wheeler, the village druggist and postmaster, and Volney M. Spalding of the University of Michigan at Ann Arbor. Smith wrote that Wheeler "showed me how to study flowering plants . . . and was my companion on a thousand delightful rambles" and that Spalding "taught me how to study parasitic fungi and where to find the literature." In 1881 he and Wheeler published the *Catalogue of the Phaenogamous and Vascular Cryptogamous Plants of Michigan*, which described 1,634 species and was well received.

Smith worked his way through college, eventually receiving his B.S. from the University of Michigan in 1886; three years later the university awarded him the Sc.D. One summer he worked as a guard at the Ionia State Reformatory, returning the following year as one of the keepers. These posts enabled him to read on a diversity of topics. Early in 1882 the editor and publisher of the *School Moderator* assigned Smith respon-

sibility of the "Scientific and Sanitary" section of that publication, to which Smith made contributions on topics ranging from cheap aquaria to meteoric fossils. In June of the same year Smith was hired as a correspondence clerk at the Michigan State Board of Health and moved to Lansing.

After graduating from college, Smith became temporary assistant to E. L. Scribner in the mycological section of the recently established Division of Vegetable Pathology at the U.S. Department of Agriculture, where he worked for the rest of his life. Smith was assigned the problem of peach yellows, a disease then rampant in Delaware and Maryland. After a detailed investigation, he demonstrated that the disease could be transmitted by bud-grafting, but he failed to show that leaf hoppers were the vector or to find a causal agent. The concept of viruses in plants, which Smith would help establish, had yet to emerge.

While retaining an interest in peach yellows, peach rosette, and "little peach," Smith turned his attention to potato blight and vine mildew. From 1894 to 1910 he studied *Fusarium* problems in melons, cotton, potatoes, and other crops. His paper "The Fungous Infestation of Agricultural Crops in the United States," which stemmed from this research, stimulated others to develop highly resistant strains of the crop plants he discussed.

Smith's fame rests on his pioneering studies of bacterial diseases of plants, which he began in the 1890s and continued until his death. The inspiration to investigate this topic was Thomas J. Burrill and Joseph C. Arthur's study of pear blight. Smith first investigated bacterial wilt of cucurbits and published a description of the disease in 1893 but did not identify the causal pathogen until 1895. Smith subsequently published detailed accounts of brown rot of tomato (1896), black rot of cabbage and other crucifers (1897), bean blight (1898), and bacterial wilt of maize (1898), all still recognized as important diseases. He presented these and other results in three quarto volumes of *Bacteria in Relation to Plant Diseases* (1905, 1911, 1914), the third volume of which includes a history of bacterial diseases of plants. A fourth volume was planned but never completed. In 1920 Smith published a textbook, *An Introduction to Bacterial Diseases of Plants*, lavishly illustrated with his own photographs.

In 1897 Alfred Fischer of Leipzig published *Vorlesungen über Bakterien*, in which he categorically stated that bacteria do not cause disease in plants. Smith replied in the *Centralblatt für Bakteriologie*, providing groundbreaking evidence of the bacterial origin of plant disease. In the end Fischer was silenced. In the early 1900s Smith acquired a lifelong interest in crown gall in plants, and through his writings on the subject he offered much rather inconclusive speculation on a possible relation of the crown gall organism to cancer in humans.

Smith's personal appearance was striking. As a young man he had a full black beard. With age the beard turned white, but his hair became only streaked with gray. He avoided alcohol and did not smoke. As he grew older, he reduced his meals to two a day and preferred to walk; only toward the end of his life did he use a car to take him to his laboratory. He had a working knowledge of French and German (publishing in both languages), as well as Italian. A story is told that before visiting Italy he asked in a Boston bookstore to be shown all the books it had on that country and purchased thirty to add to his well-stocked library, on which he never stinted money. He appreciated music, collected vases, and was a member of the Arts Club of Washington. He married twice. In 1893 he wed Charlotte May Buffett. After her death in 1906, he published privately a book of sonnets and other poems, *For Her Friends and Mine* (1915), in her memory. In 1914 he married Ruth Warren. There were no children by either marriage.

Smith welcomed foreign students to his laboratory and was unusual in the opportunities he gave women to do research, both in his own laboratory and at the USDA. The following notation from his diary (5 Mar. 1927), a month before his death, gives a sense of the many projects undertaken by female researchers:

Miss Fawcett has interesting studies of distilled water well along. Agnes Quirk and Miss Brown are working on crowngall oxidation phenomena. Miss Brown has a note with two plates on sweet pea fascination due to *Bact. tumefaciens* in *Phytopathology*. Miss Elliot has written a paper on stripe disease of oats. Miss Hedges is working on diseases of beans. Miss Bryan on several things—one of which is Aplanobacter on tomato. Lucia McCulloch is working on bulb diseases. Miss Cash on miscellaneous things. Miss Fox the same. I am trying to complete the illustrations for my Ithaca paper. (Rogers, P. 651)

Smith died in Washington, D.C.

• The results of Smith's investigations into peach yellows and peach rosette are in *Bulletin of the U.S. Department of Agriculture, Botany Division, Section of Plant Pathology* (1888), and *Bulletin of the U.S. Department of Agriculture, Division of Vegetable Pathology* (1891). His paper on fungal infestation of American agricultural crops is in *Scientific American* 48 (1899): 19981–82. The English translation of his controversy with Alfred Fischer is C. L. Campbell, trans., *Phytopathological Classics*, vol. 13 (1981). Smith's address in 1927 to the International Congress of Plant Science, "Fifty Years of Plant Pathology," is illustrated by portraits of more than 275 plant pathologists and mycologists and was published posthumously in *Proceedings of the International Congress of Plant Science* 1 (1929): 13–46. The standard account of Smith's life is A. D. Rogers III, *Erwin Frink Smith: A Story of North American Plant Pathology* (1952). Other useful accounts of his life are E. W. Brander, *Science* 66 (1927): 383–85; L. R. Jones and F. V. Rand, *Journal of Bacteriology* 15 (1983): 21–27; F. V. Rand, *Mycologia* 20 (1928): 181–88; G. P. Clinton, *Proceedings of the American Academy of Arts and Sciences* 70 (1936): 575–78; and C. L. Campbell, *Annual Review of Phytopathology* 21 (1975): 467–68. An obituary notice with a bibliography (1881–1926) is in *Phytopathology* 17 (1927): 675–88.

G. C. AINSWORTH

SMITH, Fiddlin' Arthur (10 Apr. 1898–28 Feb. 1971), musician and composer, was born in the hamlet of Bold Springs, Humphries County, about forty miles west of Nashville, Tennessee, the son of William Calvin Smith, a farmer. His mother's name is unknown. Family stories recall Smith trying to play the fiddle when he was as young as five; the West Tennessee area, where he grew up, was rich in a distinctive fiddling tradition that eventually produced other nationally known musicians like Howdy Forrester and Paul Warren. Smith grew up playing for rural dances in the area, eventually marrying (in 1914) a young woman named Nettie (maiden name unknown), who played guitar for him. The couple had eight children. His fiddling continued to develop under the influence of a local musician named Grady Stringer.

To help support his growing clan, Smith took a job for the North Carolina and St. Louis Railroad, known informally as "the Dixie Line." The job required constant travel, and for much of the time Smith lived in railroad cars, practicing his fiddle to while away the nights. Soon he encountered a fellow Dixie Line employee, Harry Stone, who was starting to work at the new Nashville radio station, WSM. Impressed, Stone arranged for Smith to start playing on a new show the station was starting, the Grand Ole Opry. Smith made his debut there in December 1927. It would signal a tenure that would last some twelve years and would win Smith nationwide fame.

At first his act was billed as "Arthur and Homer Smith" and featured just his fiddle and a guitar accompaniment by his cousin Homer. About 1930 he was paired with the McGee Brothers, Sam and Kirk, who had been performing with popular banjo player Uncle Dave Macon; this trio, which combined three of the most dazzling instrumentalists in the field of early country music, soon became known as the Dixieliners. Though they did not actually record together until the 1950s, the band became the most popular on the Opry and toured widely throughout the South. When Smith made his first commercial records in January 1935, it was with another Opry act, the Delmore Brothers, and for the RCA Victor subsidiary Bluebird. In the next five years he would record some fifty-two sides with the Delmores or other pickup bands and would often play backup for the Delmores on their records. Many of Smith's best-known records were fiddle tunes, including his "Blackberry Blossom" (1935), "Red Apple Rag" (1935), "Lost Train Blues" (1935), "Fiddler's Dream" (1935), "Goofus" (1935), "Dickson County Blues" (1936), and "Florida Blues" (1937). However, the Delmores, skillful composers themselves, encouraged Smith to also begin singing and to write new songs, and soon he had crafted vocal hits like "There's More Pretty Girls Than One" (1936), "Chittlin' Cookin' Time in Cheatham County" (1936), "Pig in the Pen" (1937), "Walking in My Sleep" (1937), "Beautiful Brown Eyes" (1937), and "Kilby Jail" (c. 1937). During the 1930s the records that he and the Delmores made were the bestselling of any artists on the Opry.

In 1938 the Delmore Brothers left the Opry, and Smith joined another WSM band, Jack Shook and His Missouri Mountaineers, and then Herald Goodman and the Tennessee Valley Boys. Both of these bands had a smooth, western flavor to them, and Smith became adept at this newer, jazzier style. From 1940 to 1946 he traveled restlessly around the South, playing for short times for Zeke Phillips in Birmingham, the Bailes Brothers in West Virginia, the York Brothers, and on the radio program "Saddle Mountain Round-Up" in Dallas. In 1945 he traveled to the West Coast, where he was featured with cowboy star Jimmy Wakeley both on radio and in films. During this time he helped to popularize "Orange Blossom Special" at big showrooms in Las Vegas.

Tired and cynical, he returned to Tennessee in the early 1950s and tried to retire from music. In 1957, though, he was rediscovered by Mike Seeger and introduced to fans of the folk music revival. He and the McGees were reunited, and they traveled widely to folk festivals, including the prestigious one at Newport, Rhode Island. Several new LP albums were made (two for Folkways, one for Starday), and younger bluegrass fiddlers began adapting the Smith style and tunes to bluegrass music. But the years of hard living and hard drinking had taken their toll, and in the late 1960s Smith's health began to fail. He made his last public appearance at Bill Monroe's Bean Blossom Festival in 1969. He died in Louisville, Kentucky. A two-LP set of his best work from the 1930s was issued by County Records in 1978.

• The most detailed account of Smith's career is "The Odyssey of Arthur Smith," in Charles K. Wolfe, *The Devil's Box: Masters of Southern Fiddling* (1996). He is discussed at length in Alton Delmore's autobiography, *Truth Is Stranger Than Publicity*, rev. ed., ed. Wolfe (1995). A complete discography of the Smith recordings is found in the periodical *Devil's Box* 11, no. 4 (1978).

CHARLES K. WOLFE

SMITH, Francis Henney (18 Oct. 1812–21 Mar. 1890), military officer and educator, was born in Norfolk, Virginia, the son of Francis Smith, a merchant, and Ann Marsden. Smith graduated from the U.S. Military Academy at West Point, New York, in 1833 and was commissioned a second lieutenant in the artillery. After a year of garrison duty at various posts, he became an assistant professor of geography, history, and ethics at the academy. In 1834 he married Sarah Henderson, with whom he had seven children. In 1836 Smith resigned his commission and accepted the professorship of mathematics at Hampden-Sydney College in Virginia. Hampden-Sydney awarded him an M.A. degree in 1838.

In June 1839 Smith was recommissioned as a major and, with the support of Claudius Crozet, a former professor of engineering at West Point and at the time chief engineer of Virginia, was appointed the first superintendent and professor of mathematics of the newly formed Virginia Military Institute (VMI) at Lexington, Virginia. The institute opened on 11 November 1839 with one other instructor and twenty-eight cadets. For the next fifty years (1839–1889) Smith devoted himself to directing the affairs of VMI. He emphasized a utilitarian rather than classical approach to education (offering more scientific courses than was the norm) and established a military system of organization and discipline based on the West Point model. In 1846 Smith introduced at VMI the first course in industrial chemistry in the South.

The Virginia legislature's annual appropriation of $6,000 in support of VMI was insufficient to enable Smith to adopt in full the West Point course of instruction as he had planned. Consequently, he soon established a system of instructional exchange with neighboring Washington College (now Washington and Lee University), an arrangement that lasted until 1846. In spite of efforts at cooperation, relations with Washington College and other segments of the Lexington community were at times strained. Washington College and VMI had to compete for students and benefactions. The establishment of a commissary angered local merchants. Lexington Presbyterians resented Smith's leadership in founding an Episcopal church and accused him of sectarian bias in the administration of the institute. Local sentiment began to soften in 1849, however, when the legislature contemplated moving the institute to another location. The threat of VMI's moving was enough to cause local merchants and others to back away from continued criticism, and the institute was not moved.

Under Smith's capable leadership, and with increased state appropriations, VMI expanded significantly in the 1850s, adding buildings and faculty and increasing enrollment. In 1858 Smith spent six months in Europe inspecting scientific schools. Upon his return he published *Special Report of the Superintendent of the Virginia Military Institute: Scientific Education in Europe* (1859) in which he recommended that VMI increase its scientific offerings.

Smith's plans for VMI were interrupted by the Civil War. Under orders from Governor Henry A. Wise (1806–1876), he served as the commanding officer at the execution of John Brown (1800–1859) in December 1859. Soon after, he was appointed by newly elected Governor John Letcher to a special commission empowered to purchase armament for the state. He was named to the governor's three-member advisory board and, bestowed with the rank of major general of the Virginia Volunteers, was placed in command of Craney Island near Norfolk in 1861. Although the institute closed when VMI cadets were called into active service at the outbreak of the war, it was revived in January 1862 with Smith still in charge as superintendent. In June 1864 VMI was burned by Union forces, but by January 1865 instruction was resumed in Richmond. Classes were once more suspended in April following the evacuation of Richmond and General Robert E. Lee's surrender, but by October Smith managed to reopen the badly damaged institute in Lexington. As Smith began the process of rebuilding and reorganizing VMI, he and the faculty agreed to contribute one-third of their authorized salaries as security for bonds issued in the amount of $50,000. VMI was fully restored by 1870, and in 1884 the bonded debt was assumed by the legislature. In 1879 Smith was invited to speak at the West Point annual reunion, the first time that a Confederate officer had been recognized at the academy since the Civil War.

Smith retired as superintendent on 31 December 1889. He died in Lexington. A deeply religious man, Smith has been memorialized in a bronze statue on the VMI grounds depicting his practice of presenting every graduate with a Bible along with his diploma. He published a variety of books on subjects ranging from mathematics to educational reform. Several of his addresses have been published as well.

• Some pieces of correspondence involving Francis Henney Smith are catalogued in several collections housed in the Manuscripts Division of the University of Virginia Library. Two books by Smith are autobiographical in character: *West Point Fifty Years Ago* (1879) and *The Virginia Military Institute: Its Building and Rebuilding* (published posthumously in 1912). Smith receives extensive treatment in William Couper, *One Hundred Years at V.M.I.*, vols. 1, 2, and 3 (1939). Jennings C. Wise, *The Military History of the Virginia Military Institute from 1839 to 1865* (1915), and Henry A. Wise, *Drawing Out the Man: The VMI Story* (1978), also are useful sources. Of some help are Jennings C. Wise, *Sunrise of the Virginia Military Institute as a School of Arms: Spawn of the Cincinnati* (1958); R. Ernest Dupuy, *Men of West Point: The First 150 Years of the United States Military Academy* (1951); Sidney Forman, *West Point: A History of the United States Military Academy* (1950); and Herbert C. Bradshaw, *History of Hampden-Sydney College* vol. 1 (1976). See also James I. Robertson, "The Council of Three: Advisors to Governor 'Honest John' Letcher," *Virginia Cavalcade* 26 (4 Mar. 1977): 176–83. Obituaries are in the *Richmond Dispatch*, 22 Mar. 1890, and the *Rockbridge County News*, 27 Mar. 1890.

JENNINGS L. WAGONER, JR.

SMITH, Francis Hopkinson (23 Oct. 1838–7 Apr. 1915), mechanical engineer, writer, and artist, was born in Baltimore, Maryland, the son of Francis Smith, a musician, mathematician, and philosopher, and Susan Teakle. Smith was reared in the genteel society of old Baltimore, where he studied for entrance to Princeton University. Smith's family suffered economic ruin, however, and he never attended college. Before the Civil War he held jobs in a hardware store and an ironworks. Around 1858 he moved to New York City, where, after some training with a partner named James Symington, he set up an engineering firm. Over the years he increasingly complemented this enterprise with his work in the fine arts and as a speaker. He was usually thought of, and perhaps thought of himself, as a southern gentleman. In 1866 Smith married Josephine Van Deventer of Astoria, New York. They had two children.

Among Smith's major feats as an engineer were the government seawall around Governor's Island; another at Tompkinsville, Staten Island; the Block Island Breakwater; and the foundation of Bedloe's Island for Bartholdi's Statue of Liberty (1885–1886). His own favorite work was Race Rock Lighthouse (1871–1879), eight miles at sea off New London, Connecticut.

Smith also studied painting with the artist Alfred Jacob Miller. He became a member of the prestigious Tile Club in New York. Other members included painters such as Edwin Austin Abbey, Elihu Vedder, and William Merritt Chase. Smith traveled frequently to various parts of the world, sketching, painting, and taking notes (see, e.g., *Well-Worn Roads of Spain, Holland, and Italy* [1886] and *A White Umbrella in Mexico* [1889]). He referred to "my romantic life," getting to know people by going into the streets and sketching scenes while sitting under his artist's umbrella. Smith wrote and illustrated many books describing the places he had traveled, including *Gondola Days* (1897), *Venice of To-Day* (1897), *Charcoals of New and Old New York* (1912), *In Thackeray's London* (1913), and *In Dickens' London* (1914).

"Night in Venice," in *Gondola Days*, exemplifies Smith's technique of creating atmosphere and his almost musical facility with language: "A night of ghostly gondolas, chasing specks of stars in dim canals; of soft melodies broken by softer laughter; of tinkling mandolins, white shoulders, and tell-tale cigarettes. . . . No pen can give this beauty, no brush its color, no tongue its delight." With "pen," "brush," and "tongue," he refers to his own varied talents.

Smith's artist's eye for detail of color, texture, and proportion led to his creating brilliant imagery in fiction also. His travel sketches complemented his fiction style, and his close observations of people helped him produce fine fictional characterizations. Examples are in his books of short stories: *A Day at Laguerre's and Other Days* (1892), *The Other Fellow* (1899), *At Close Range* (1905), and *The Wood Fire in No. 3* (1905). His stories stress atmosphere. It is for his novels, however, that Smith has been taken most seriously, as a bestseller in his lifetime and as a premodern writer whose works mark the end of the genteel era in the fine arts in America.

A contemporary, John S. Patton, described Smith as "of medium height, active, with iron-gray hair, close cropped, and gray moustaches, looking, at the first glance, like a prosperous French man of affairs." Smith's friend and fellow novelist Thomas Nelson Page spoke of him as possessing a bundle of qualities—always young, independent yet readily friendly, distinguished, witty, cheerful, optimistic, modest in his popularity, painstaking as a writer. He was often an advocate of liberal causes. For example, he forbade the exhibition of his pictures in Paris because of the Dreyfus case.

There is a pronounced autobiographical element in much of Smith's fiction. And dramatist Augustus Thomas noticed that "women in his treatment were always objects of romance to be protected." Literary historian Arthur Hobson Quinn remarks on Smith's constant revisions and of how, before writing *The Tides of Barnegat* (1906), he "went to Barnegat Light . . . and lived among the life-saving crew to gain the atmosphere." In the preface to the posthumously published novel *Enoch Crane* (1916), his son noted that Smith thought of his fictional characters as real persons: "It was my father's practise, in planning a novel, first to prepare a most complete synopsis from beginning to end—never proceeding with the actual writing of the book until he had laid out the characters and action of the story—chapter by chapter."

Probably the best liked of Smith's novels was his first, *Colonel Carter of Cartersville* (1891), about a conservative Virginia gentleman, stranded in New York, who tells after-dinner stories. Featured are pictures of happy Old South blacks and benevolent masters. The book was illustrated by Edward W. Kemble and the author. One of the stories, "One-Legged Goose," illustrates Smith's humor and his use of dialect in telling a tale: "Dem was high times. . . . Git up in de mawnin' an' look out ober de lawn, an' yer come fo'teen or fifteen couples ob de fustest quality folks, all on horseback ridin' in de gate. . . . Old marsa an' missis out on de po'ch, an' de little pickaninnies runnin' from de quarters. . . ." In a footnote Smith wrote, "This story . . . I have told for so many years and to so many people, and with such varied amplifications, that I have long since persuaded myself that [it is] my own. . . . [But] I know [it] is as old as the 'Decameron.'" A sentimental sequel, *Colonel Carter's Christmas*, appeared in 1903.

Smith's next triumph was *Tom Grogan* (1896), a novel about blackmail, arson, and attempted murder—as well as labor strife—on the New York waterfront. The wife of a stevedore who dies becomes the "Tom" running the deceased husband's business in secret. She is an extremely strong character, strong of both body and spirit. Like *Tom Grogan, Caleb West, Master Diver* (1898) in part exploits Smith's engineering expertise. First serialized in the *Atlantic Monthly* in 1897–1898, *Caleb West* was also issued, in 1899, in a "special edition limited to one hundred thousand copies." In 1902 *The Fortunes of Oliver Horn* continued Smith's high reputation and large sales. It is a more noticeably autobiographical novel, which Quinn calls a "romantic-idealistic" story. Then, in 1906, Smith published perhaps his best-written novel, *The Tides of Barnegat*. Here he deals with family problems, including divorce. Although tragedy strikes Barnegat, a New Jersey fishing community, the selfless heroine and the book's secondary characters come to a happy ending.

The chapter "The Surprise," from *Peter* (1908), one of Smith's late novels, illustrates his style in description and dialogue. There he writes:

It was wonderful how young he looked, and how happy he was, and how spry his step, as the two turned into William Street and so on to the cheap little French restaurant with its sanded floor, little tables for two and four, with their tiny pots of mustard and flagons of oil and red vinegar—this last, the "left-overs" of countless bottles of Bordeaux—to say nothing of the great piles of French bread weighing down a shelf beside the proprietor's desk, racked up like cordwood, and all the same color, length and thickness. . . . "And now, I have got a surprise for you, Uncle Peter," cried Jack, smothering his eagerness as best he could. The old fellow held up his hand, reached for the shabby, dust-begrimed

bottle, that had been sound asleep under the sidewalk for years; filled Jack's glass, then his own; settled himself in his chair and said with a dry smile: "If it's something startling, Jack, wait until we drink this," and he lifted the slender rim to his lips. "If it's something delightful, you can spring it now."

Smith's is a most readable, word-painting kind of fiction.

Scribner's published a ten-volume Beacon Edition of Smith's works around 1903, revised and augmented, with illustrations and high-quality paper and bindings. The illustrators included Howard Chandler Christy, whose works perfectly complement Smith's. This edition was increased to twelve volumes around 1906.

Between 1902 and 1915 Scribner's also issued, in high compliment to the author, a twenty-three volume edition, *The Novels, Stories and Sketches of F. Hopkinson Smith*. Many illustrations—by various hands—are in color, and here a reader can see Smith's own impressionistic drawings wonderfully reproduced.

Smith received many honors for his work in the fine arts: a bronze medal at the Buffalo Exposition in 1901, a silver medal from the Charleston Exposition in 1902, and gold medals from the Philadelphia Art Club in 1902 and from the American Art Society in 1902. In Augustus Thomas's published tribute to Smith, he called him "an artist . . . of living," who remains "notable for his expression . . . as measured by his own emotions." His was the "ability to transmute the ordinary into the beautiful." Smith died in New York.

Smith left a heritage of engineering feats that provide safer and greater access to the waters around New York City, along with his fine starlike design for the base of the Statue of Liberty. He exemplifies in his travel sketches and in his paintings and illustrations the rare renaissance mind and person of letters of his era. His fiction is still rewarding reading, and his career shows how a writer of enormous fame can fade into obscurity as times and tastes change.

• The main repositories of Smith's manuscripts are the Beinecke Library, Yale University, and the Alderman Library, University of Virginia. Major published works not mentioned above are *Old Lines in New Black and White* (1855), *A Book of the Tile Club* (1890), *American Illustrators* (1892), *A Gentleman Vagabond, and Some Others* (1895), *The Under Dog* (1903), *The Veiled Lady* (1907), *The Romance of an Old-Fashioned Gentleman* (1907), *Forty Minutes Late* (1909), and *The Arm Chair at the Inn* (1912). There is no major biography. For critical assessment of Smith and his work, see Horace Spencer Fiske, *Provincial Types in American Fiction; Theodore Hornberger* (1903); "The Effect of Painting on the Fiction of F. Hopkinson Smith," *University of Texas Studies in English* 23 (1943): 162–92, and "Painters and Painting in the Writings of F. Hopkinson Smith," *American Literature* 16 (1944): 1–10; H. W. Mabie, "Hopkinson Smith and His Work," *Book Buyer* 25 (1902): 17–20; Thomas Nelson Page, "Francis Hopkinson Smith," *Scribner's*, Sept. 1915, pp. 305–13; Arthur Hobson Quinn, *American Fiction: An Historical and Critical Survey* (1936); Courtland Y. White III, "Francis Hopkinson Smith" (Ph.D. diss., Univ. of Pennsylvania, 1932); and G. Willets, "F. Hopkinson Smith in Three Professions," *Are-*

na 22 (1899): 68–70. See also Augustus Thomas, *Commemorative Tribute to Francis Hopkinson Smith* (1922). Obituaries are in *American Art News*, 13 Apr. 1915, and the *New York Times*, 8 Apr. 1915.

WILLIAM K. BOTTORFF

SMITH, Francis Marion (2 Feb. 1846–27 Aug. 1931), mining and railroad entrepreneur, was born in Richmond, Wisconsin, the son of Henry Grovier Smith and Charlotte Paul, farmers. After completing grade school in Richmond, Smith attended high school in nearby Milton and Allen's Grove. He worked on the farm until he reached the age of twenty-one, when he succumbed to the lure of the West. In 1867 he traveled to Montana Territory, where he tried prospecting and both placer and hard-rock mining. Unimpressed with the return, he resumed his travels, working at various jobs until he reached western Nevada, where he became a restaurateur. After a few months he decided that prospecting was more interesting, and for the next five years he followed various mineral rushes in the region.

Smith was cutting wood for a borax-concentrating plant at Columbus, Nevada, when he discovered unusually rich deposits of ulexite, a borate of soda, at a high-desert, normally dry lake called Teel's Marsh in 1872. He had at last made his strike. After he staked and recorded his claims, he convinced his older brother Julius Paul Smith to join him in creating the firm of Smith Brothers, producers of borax. He arranged for the refining and sales aspects of the business to be handled by William T. Coleman and Company of San Francisco and New York. Smith married Mary Rebecca Thompson Wright in 1875. They eventually made their home at "Arbor Villa," an estate in Oakland, California. Childless themselves, they provided a home to several foster children.

Smith Brothers did well enough that Frank Smith was able to purchase other borax properties in Nevada and California, including the Pacific Borax Company and the famous Harmony works in Death Valley. With an eye to the future, he acquired large underground bodies of borate of calcium, another source of borax known as colemanite, in the Greenwater Range to the east of Death Valley and in the Calico Mountains near Barstow, California. Eventually he also purchased all of Coleman's borax interests.

Smith combined his acquisitions into a single concern, the Pacific Coast Borax Company, in 1890. He became president of the company and also its major stockholder. As the world's largest producer of the mineral, Smith earned the nickname "Borax," of which he was justifiably proud. Pacific Coast Borax became part of a larger corporation, Borax Consolidated, Limited, in 1899. Created to merge Smith's borax interests with those of Richard C. Baker, an English producer, Borax Consolidated also reflected Smith's growing interest in the acquisition of borax deposits worldwide. Smith owned a majority of the new company's voting stock.

In addition to locating and acquiring new sources of borax, developing better methods of refining borax ores, and creating markets for the finished product, Smith also had to deal with serious transportation problems, because the best sources of borax were found in sparsely populated, almost inaccessible deserts. While conveying borates from the mines to the refinery, he experimented with pack animals, long teams of twenty or more mules pulling specially built wagons, steam tractors, and railroads. Although the colorful twenty-mule teams used to haul borates from Death Valley to the railroad at Mojave, California, became Pacific Coast Borax's well-known trademark, the solution to his transportation problem proved to be railroads.

Smith's first line was the short, narrow-gauge Borate & Daggett Railroad. Completed in 1898, it connected colemanite mines in the Calico Mountains with the main line of the Santa Fe Railway at Daggett. Although the line was only eight miles long, it was very successful. After the success of the Borate & Daggett, Smith built two much longer desert railways, the Tonopah & Tidewater Railroad, completed in 1907, and the Death Valley Railroad, the first stage of which was finished in 1914. Both were designed primarily to facilitate the transportation of borax ores. Smith's wife died in 1905. He married Evelyn Kate Ellis in 1907; they had four children.

Smith's most ambitious and extensive railroad project was his Key Route. Centered on the east side of San Francisco Bay, it was intended to be a comprehensive urban and interurban transportation system for Oakland and nearby cities and towns. Utilizing transbay ferries, it also served San Francisco. Smith had begun acquiring essential East Bay railroads in the early 1890s, and in 1912 he consolidated them into the San Francisco–Oakland Terminal Railways Company. Worth an estimated $30.5 million, it operated 245 miles of track and carried nearly 100 million passengers per year.

Like many others, Smith financed a significant share of his growing financial empire with short-term debt. He developed cash flow problems in 1913, and, on the advice of his bankers, gave up his interest in the Key Route, Borax Consolidated, and several other concerns in order to satisfy creditors. For the first time in more than forty years, "Borax" Smith was not in the borax business.

Although he had lost millions, Smith was far from impoverished. He maintained his interest in a number of properties, including the West End Consolidated Mining Company, a silver-mining concern with operations in Tonopah, Nevada. Smith successfully used it to rebuild his fortune and to get back into borax. By 1926, when he resigned the presidency of West End Consolidated, he was president of West End Chemical Company, a leading producer of borax that was growing rapidly. At age eighty he had once again become a major contender in the borax industry.

Accustomed to strenuous physical and mental activity, Smith realized he could no longer effectively lead

West End Chemical when his health began to fail. He retired in 1928 and died three years later in Oakland.

In addition to philanthropic activities, such as donating land for parks and funding a trust to maintain homes for orphaned girls, Smith served as a Republican presidential elector in 1904 and 1908. Despite such endeavors, he is best known as the world's leading borax industrialist of his day and a major railroad entrepreneur.

• The standard biography of Smith is George H. Hildebrand, *Borax Pioneer: Francis Marion Smith* (1982). For an account of the borax industry and Smith's role in it, see Norman J. Travis and E. John Cocks, *The Tincal Trail: A History of Borax* (1984). The stories of Smith's three desert borax railroads are told in David F. Myrick, *Railroads of Nevada and Eastern California*, vol. 2: *The Southern Roads* (1963), while his involvement with the Key Route is chronicled in Harre W. Demoro, *The Key Route: Transbay Commuting by Train and Ferry*, pt. 1 (1985). Obituaries are in the *Oakland Tribune*, 27 Aug. 1931, and the *San Francisco Chronicle*, 28 Aug. 1931.

DELMER G. ROSS

SMITH, Fred Burton (24 Dec. 1865–4 Sept. 1936), YMCA leader and reformer, was born in Lone Tree, Iowa, the son of Robert Ames Smith and Endora Dinwiddie, farmers. He briefly attended Hiatt's Academy, Williams Business College, and the State University of Iowa, all in Iowa City, the last because he was recruited to play baseball. When his family moved to the Dakota Territory in 1882, his formal education ended. In 1886 Smith married Minnie (Mary) Agnes Colvin; they had five children.

After working as a clerk in a store and as a salesman for farm machinery, Smith began twenty-five years of ministry with the YMCA in 1888. His decision to work as secretary of the Sioux Falls, Dakota Territory, YMCA resulted from his conversion experience in 1885 at a small country Congregationalist church near his home in 1885. In 1891 Smith moved to Dubuque, Iowa, to serve as a YMCA secretary and in 1896 went to Chicago to engage in evangelistic work for the organization. By the 1890s the Y had begun to emphasize social services and recreational facilities, but evangelism continued to be one of its major activities. During the Spanish-American War Smith organized preaching missions among troops in southern camps and honed his own skills by speaking to soldiers at evangelistic meetings.

When the war ended Smith became the head of the Religious Work Department of the International Committee of the YMCA, a position he held for sixteen years. He administered programs in Bible study, missionary education, and youth ministry but devoted himself primarily to evangelism. His commanding voice, physical stature, straightforward message, and extraordinary energy (he traveled an average of 50,000 miles a year, often giving one major address a day) made him North America's greatest lay evangelist during the early twentieth century. Hundreds of thousands of men filled auditoriums to hear him, and many of them responded to his appeals.

Searching for a "more complete gospel," Smith read the books of Josiah Strong, Washington Gladden, Walter Rauschenbusch, and other proponents of the Social Gospel. In an attempt to combine the messages of evangelism and social reform, he organized a series of fifty meetings in congregations, factories, and schools in Cleveland in 1909. The following year he worked with the brotherhoods of various Protestant denominations and the International Sunday School Association to plan a continentwide campaign to evangelize men and involve them in the work of the church. Smith helped to recruit a central committee and four teams of specialists for the "Men and Religion Forward" movement and served as its national campaign leader. The specialists spent eight months surveying social conditions in ninety major North American cities and served as the principal speakers for the movement, which consisted primarily of eight days of meetings held in more than seventy cities between September 1911 and April 1912. These seminars and services, which attracted almost 1.5 million people, emphasized evangelism, social reform, boys' work, missions, and Bible study. Many prominent Progressives—including Jane Addams, William Jennings Bryan, and Booker T. Washington—addressed its concluding congress in New York City in April 1912; their speeches and the movement's findings were published in seven volumes as *The Men and Religion Messages* (1912). The crusade sparked investigation, discussion, and concrete efforts to improve social conditions in many cities. Smith was indispensable to the movement's success in the United States, and from December 1912 to September 1913 he led a team that spread its message from London to Sidney and many cities in between.

In 1914 Smith resigned his position with the YMCA, primarily because of the organization's unwillingness to pursue the broad social ministry that characterized the movement. For the next ten years he worked as assistant to T. Frank Manville, Sr., president of the Johns-Manville Company, whom Smith had met while raising funds for the YMCA. This job allowed him the freedom to travel and speak widely. He chaired a commission of the Federal Council of Churches (an interdenominational agency established by thirty-three denominations in 1908), which worked to organize state and local federations. During World War I Smith spoke to troops in mobilization camps across the country, urging them to adhere to traditional moral values. After the death of his first wife, he married Lillian Eberenz, his personal secretary, in 1917.

During the 1920s Smith concentrated on promoting the peace movement and the enforcement of Prohibition. His experience with soldiers in the United States and France and the destructiveness of the Great War convinced Smith that "the whole process [of war] was anti-Christian" and "debasing to everybody" and that, therefore, preventing future wars was "the supreme

Christian task" (*I Remember*, pp. 121–22). From 1925 until the end of his life Smith chaired the American branch of the World Alliance for International Friendship through the Churches. He published *On the Trail of the Peacemakers* (1922) and *Must We Have War?* (1929) and gave addresses in scores of countries on the reduction of armaments and international cooperation. He advocated stricter enforcement of Prohibition as head of the Citizens Committee of One Thousand for Law Enforcement and as editor of *Law vs. Lawlessness* (1924), a volume of essays on Prohibition.

In addition to his leadership in evangelism, pacifism, and Prohibition, Smith was involved with a variety of religious and humanitarian groups. He was a fellow of the American Geographical Society and actively participated in Republican politics, attending every national convention except one from 1884 until 1936. He served as moderator of the National Council of Congregational Churches in 1929–1931 and on the denomination's executive committee from 1931 to 1936. In recognition of his many accomplishments Smith was awarded the Christian Herald Distinguished Service Award in 1929. He died at his home in White Plains, New York.

In his own day Smith was recognized as "the epitome of . . . forthright and commanding lay leadership" (*Christian Century*, 16 Sept. 1936) and as a "born promoter" who taught businessmen "the joy of Christian stewardship" (*Christian Century*, 14 Oct. 1936). The *New York Times* obituary (5 Sept. 1936) declared that "his booming platform voice and fiery words, his splendid physique and tireless energy all made him an effective campaigner for the causes which he espoused."

• The primary source for Smith's life and convictions is his autobiography, *I Remember* (1936). In addition to the books mentioned in the text above, Smith also wrote *Men Wanted* (1911), *A Man's Religion* (1913), and *Observations in France* (1918). For his work with the YMCA, see C. Howard Hopkins, *History of the Y.M.C.A. in North America* (1951). The role he played in the Men and Religion Forward movement is discussed in Gary Scott Smith, "The Men and Religion Forward Movement of 1911–12: New Perspectives on Evangelical Social Concern and the Relationship between Christianity and Progressivism," *Westminster Theological Journal* 49 (1987): 91–118; Gail Bederman, "'The Women Have Had Charge of the Church Long Enough': The Men and Religion Forward Movement of 1911–1912 and the Masculinization of Middle-class Protestantism," *American Quarterly* 41 (Sept. 1989): 432–65; and "Religious Forward Movement Will Girdle the World," *New York Times*, 4 June 1911.

GARY SCOTT SMITH

SMITH, Fred M. (31 May 1888–23 Feb. 1946), physician and researcher, was born in Yale, Illinois, the son of John Alfred Smith and Sarah Ellen Newlin, farmers. Smith graduated from the University of Chicago in 1913 and then attended medical school at Rush Medical College. After receiving an M.D. in 1914, Smith did his house-staff training at the Presbyterian Hospital in Chicago. There he was known as a hard worker, often choosing to study medicine while his compatriots played poker or pool. After a brief stint in the U.S. Army Medical Corps as first lieutenant in 1918–1919, Smith returned to Rush Medical College. In 1924 he moved to the State University of Iowa to serve as professor and head of the Department of Theory and Practice of Medicine, a position he held until his death. Smith married Helen Louise Bushee in 1917; they had three children.

Smith's major contribution to medical knowledge stemmed from his work with the electrocardiogram, an instrument invented in 1902 that recorded electrical currents associated with the heart beat. Most of the early clinical work on the electrocardiogram, conducted in England, had focused on use of the machine to evaluate people with abnormal cardiac rhythms. Smith's role came in helping to demonstrate the utility of the electrocardiogram for evaluation of people whose cardiac rhythm was normal but who suffered from heart disease nonetheless. Such people might complain of symptoms directly referable to the heart, such as chest pain or chest pressure, or they might complain of symptoms that seemed to be naturally attributable to other organs, such as nausea or vomiting. All of these symptoms could result from heart disease but often from a form of heart disease in which the person's cardiac rhythm remained regular and normal. For them, the electrocardiogram could be a particularly important diagnostic tool.

After returning to Chicago at the end of the First World War, Smith started to work with James Herrick, a prominent Chicago physician who had been given an electrocardiogram machine by a private donor. Smith did a series of experiments in which he ligated the coronary arteries—the blood vessels that supply oxygen to the heart—of several dogs. He demonstrated that this ligation led to characteristic changes in the electrocardiogram tracing. Soon after Smith demonstrated the changes in the dog, Herrick demonstrated similar changes in human beings, a finding that helped to define the disease entity of myocardial infarction, or heart attack. This disease was soon recognized as a major cause of morbidity and mortality in the United States. We now conceptualize myocardial infarction as being caused by death of some part of the heart, usually resulting from an insufficient supply of oxygen from the coronary arteries. The work of Smith and Herrick was important in defining the disease as a specific entity and attracting attention to its widespread clinical significance. Following the appearance of their publications, myocardial infarction started to be reported far more often as a cause of death.

The serious nature of Smith's early attention to clinical investigation is demonstrated by the fact that in 1919 Smith had half of his yearly salary ($600) provided to pursue research in heart disease, an unusually generous amount of research support at the time. Smith studied at University College in London with Sir Thomas Lewis, then one of the leading electrocardiogram researchers in the world. Lewis had transformed the ECG machine from what had been an obscure laboratory tool in 1908 into a widely recognized device by around 1922. Smith's association with Lewis in a well-equipped laboratory at University College doubtless gave him a sense of the value (and enjoyment) of medical experimentation.

During his twenty-two years as head of the Department of Medicine at the State University of Iowa, Smith served in several national leadership roles. He was the editor of the *American Heart Journal*, one of the key journals that helped to define the new specialty of cardiology in the United States. He also served as president of the American Society for Clinical Investigation and was a charter member of the Central Society for Clinical Investigation, two organizations that encouraged their members to advance medical knowledge through scientific investigations. As chair of his department at Iowa, Smith participated in a major departmental reorganization in 1927–1928, in which a schoolwide controversy caused the resignation of many key faculty members. Smith managed to retain some members of his department and to recruit others, and he assembled a group of internists who would later make important contributions to the state of medical knowledge. In order to promote original research, Smith encouraged his faculty to travel, because he felt that it was important for them to participate in the national communities of scientists that were being created, and he went to great lengths to enable them to attend professional meetings. At Iowa, Smith also continued his own studies of the effects of coronary artery disease treatments, including diet and drugs such as theophylline. In 1941 he suffered his first attack of coronary artery disease, the disease he had studied. A few years later he had a recurrence and died in Iowa City.

• There are no known collections of Smith papers. His seminal work on the electrocardiogram is "The Ligation of Coronary Arteries with Electrocardiographic Study," *Archives of Internal Medicine* 22 (1918): 8–27. (As was typical of the period, Smith's mentor, James Herrick, is not a coauthor but is simply thanked in the acknowledgements.) The salary support for Smith and his work with Sir Thomas Lewis are documented in letters from Herrick to Oliver Ormsby, 21 Nov. 1919, and Lewis to Herrick, 10 Nov. 1923, in the Special Collections of Regenstein Library at the University of Chicago. Smith's house-staff behavior is observed in James Herrick, *Memories of Eighty Years* (1949), pp. 245–46. A biographical sketch of Smith and a description of the department under his leadership are in Walter L. Bierring, *A History of the Department of Internal Medicine, State University of Iowa, College of Medicine, 1870–1958* (1958), pp. 63–78. For a general discussion of the context of Smith's early ECG work, see Joel D. Howell, "Early Perceptions of the Electrocardiogram: From Arrhythmia to Infarction," *Bulletin of the History of Medicine* 58 (1984): 83–98. A biographical notice by Charles F. Wooley is in the *Journal of Laboratory and Clinical Medicine* 108 (Dec. 1986): 635–36.

JOEL D. HOWELL

SMITH, George (10 Feb. 1808–7 Oct. 1899), financier, was born at Millhill, Old Deer Parish, Aberdeenshire, Scotland, the son of James Smith and Catharine An-

derson. He received his early education at the parish school and a private school in Udney. At age fifteen he went to Marishcal College in Aberdeen, staying two years, and then spent three years as a "Medical pupil." Finding he had weak eyes, he turned to rental farming, but it did not suit him. At age twenty-five he sailed for the United States, arriving in New York on 1 August 1833.

Smith carried letters of introduction to leading banking houses in New York City but found no openings. He pushed west, spent the winter in Buffalo, New York, and then moved on to Chicago, Illinois. He arrived just in time to participate in frenzied land speculation in Chicago—between 1830 and 1836 land prices went up sixtyfold—and then, in 1835 and 1836, speculated on land along the Lake Michigan shore as far north as Sheybogan, Wisconsin, well north of Milwaukee.

Smith had a good sense of what lands would become valuable and was a tough, shrewd bargainer, so with only limited capital he was successful. More important, he recognized the pressing need of the rapidly growing economy around Chicago for capital, a need that would become dramatically more urgent when Andrew Jackson's Specie Circular went into effect on 15 August 1836, requiring that purchases of public land be made in specie. Good coin would be at a premium. In July 1836 Smith left Chicago for Aberdeen, intent on raising the capital needed to provide that money.

In Scotland, Smith's cousin Alexander Anderson had emerged as a leading promoter. Already well established as a lawyer, Anderson in 1836 launched two joint-stock companies—one for insurance, one for banking—whose stock sold briskly. Anderson soon organized the Illinois Investment Company as a vehicle to raise funds for Smith to invest in Chicago and the Upper Midwest; within a month of its first advertisement in Aberdeen's *Weekly Journal* on 1 February 1837, it had sold three-quarters of its capital stock. With two other Scots, Smith left within a week. On 1 May 1837 the new company opened for business in Chicago. Although it was at first a success, paying a healthy dividend, its affairs were soon in disarray; after many a delay and disappointment, it was wound up in 1852, most of its investors having lost money.

In the meantime, in early 1839 Smith created a second joint-stock company, the Wisconsin Marine and Fire Insurance Company. Because Jackson Democrats, often deeply hostile to banks, dominated legislatures in the Midwest, no traditional bank could secure a charter. Yet the rapidly developing commercial economy of the region desperately needed a useable money. All sorts of extralegal currencies had already emerged; some companies issued script, while small tradesmen offered "tickets of credit" for change. None had good reputations, and none could be converted to specie except at a frightful discount. Smith recognized this need for a reliable currency and resolved to meet it by opening a bank, by stealth. The new company's charter specifically denied it banking privileges but did permit it to "receive money on deposit, and loan the same." From its inception Smith used certificates of deposit issued by the Wisconsin company as currency—although no evidence suggests that the company ever accepted deposits. Its certificates were issued in overwhelming numbers in the name of a single clerk.

Smith had two models from which to work. The Chicago Marine and Fire Insurance Company had responded to the panic of 1837 by issuing large-denomination certificates of deposit, which had then circulated as money. In Scotland, banking had been especially innovative, issuing fully redeemable notes in small denominations and creating a network of branches to serve small communities; among the leaders in this process was Anderson's North of Scotland Bank. The certificates of deposit that Wisconsin Marine and Fire Insurance issued were payable to the bearer and fully redeemable in specie on demand, either at company offices in Milwaukee or at a Chicago agency. To assure acceptance of the certificates, Smith declared he had "the means of taking up its whole circulation at a moment's notice, either in Illinois funds or Eastern exchange"—which indeed he could, with more than $175,000 to cover $29,000 in certificates. In 1846 he underlined the credibility of "George Smith's notes" by pledging publicly his entire private fortune to support redemption. Smith assured wide use of his certificates by using them in all his own myriad transactions. Given the absence of other acceptable money—legal or extralegal—and Smith's credibility, his certificates were soon the preferred money of the Upper Midwest. By 1851 he had $1.47 million in circulation in six states, with redemption offices in Galena, St. Louis, Detroit, and Cincinnati. The certificates could also be redeemed at numerous banking offices throughout the country and in Europe.

Because Smith operated beyond any effective state control, he was under constant attack; but attempts to repeal his charter in Wisconsin failed, lawsuits were dismissed, and neither state enacted laws to charter traditional banks and thus create competitors. Finally, in 1851 Illinois voters approved a referendum permitting charters, and within days the first charter went to Chicago's Marine Bank. Smith withstood the new competition until 1853, when the legislature simply outlawed extralegal note issue. Smith then sold Wisconsin Marine and Fire to his longtime partner Alexander Mitchell, who converted it to a bank. But he fought back with a new strategy; he bought chartered banks in areas that had lax supervision and required no reserves. In 1852 he took control of the Bank of America, chartered in Washington, D.C., then bought two banks in Georgia.

Chicago's bankers detested Smith's Georgia notes, which competed successfully with their own for use in the local economy. They spread rumors that he was about to fail and organized massive runs on his banks; once they presented for redemption more than $2 million in notes over four months, and on another occasion they collected every note they could and dispatched a courier to present them in Atlanta. But Smith withstood all attacks. His notes were so popular that Chicago merchants publicly declared they would accept them at full value; he was so rich that he easily redeemed with specie every note presented. In 1854, with ten incorporated banks operating in Chicago, his notes still accounted for roughly 75 percent of circulating currency.

By 1856 Smith's special role had run its course; legal banks were offering increasing competition, and both Wisconsin and Illinois were mounting new legal attacks on his issues. In 1857 he told his Chicago cashier, "This making of money grows tiresome. I shall quit." He did. Smith rapidly reduced the notes in circulation, returning to Britain in 1858. He returned to America only twice, in 1860 and 1866, to arrange his affairs and establish an agency to manage his interests. Smith had been elected a member of London's Reform Club in 1851; he became a permanent resident there in 1861 and bought two castles in Scotland. Smith had never married, and while he checked on his business affairs almost daily, he lived quietly. He died in London and was buried next to his sister in Elgin. He left an enormous estate, valued at $42 million in New York and perhaps another $50 million in Britain; his estate dues bought the British navy a new dreadnought.

Smith was described as a forbidding figure, carefully groomed, with an aristocratic bearing—one of the few in Chicago who insistently wore "a silk hat and a white shirt." Interminably absorbed in business, he took little interest in politics, and his service on the boards of area railroads was perfunctory. Yet what he accomplished had remarkable impact on the economic development of the Upper Midwest. Smith's money was the preferred medium of exchange for nearly fifteen years; without it, the region's economic growth simply would not have achieved the dimensions that it did. An editorial in the *Chicago Democrat* offers a testimonial to that significance. Noting that no one had had the capital, boldness, or ability to deal with the financial collapse brought on by the panic of 1857, a crisis that left more than 500 Chicago businesses bankrupt, the *Democrat* declared, "If George Smith were here," he would not have hesitated to put a million or more in Atlanta money into circulation, perhaps preventing "a very severe financial revulsion. . . . Were he here today, he could do more to restore confidence in the community than any other man."

• The best source on Smith's life and career is Alice E. Smith, *George Smith's Money: A Scottish Investor in America* (1964), which includes a good bibliographical essay. Smith naturally gets significant attention in histories of banking in the period; see, for example, Bray Hammond, *Banks and Politics in America from the Revolution to the Civil War* (1957); F. Cyril James, *The Growth of Chicago Banks* (2 vols., 1938); and Andrew Russel and Francis Murray Huston, *Financing an Empire* (1926).

FRED CARSTENSEN

SMITH, George Albert (4 Apr. 1870–4 Apr. 1951), president of the Church of Jesus Christ of Latter-day Saints, was born in Salt Lake City, Utah, the son of

John Henry Smith, a high-ranking Mormon official, and Sarah Farr. At age thirteen Smith received an unsolicited blessing under the hands of Zebedee Coltirn, a Mormon patriarch, who foretold Smith's apostleship and declared that "none" in his father's family would "exceed" his future position. This statement was incredibly powerful given that his father was then serving as one of the church's twelve apostles; his grandfather, George A. Smith, had been a counselor to Brigham Young; and Joseph Smith, founder of the church, was his grandfather's cousin.

In 1883, when his father was sent on a proselytizing mission to Great Britain for two and a half years, Smith, as the oldest boy in his family, was required to help provide for his family. He received his secondary schooling at Brigham Young Academy and the University of Deseret (now the University of Utah). He did not graduate. He also worked briefly for the Zion's Cooperative Mercantile Institution (ZCMI) as a wholesaler, then he worked as a farm implement salesman. In 1888, while working on a railroad surveying crew, Smith permanently damaged his sight as a result of sun glare. The handicap made it impossible for him to continue work on the crew or to return to school. He later studied law through correspondence courses.

Smith spent a short time as a recruiter for the Young Men's Mutual Improvement Association (YMMIA), the youth ancillary, but he quit when he was asked to serve a two-year proselytizing mission in the South. Before leaving, he married Lucy Emily Woodruff in 1892. They had three children. Smith served as mission secretary while in Tennessee, and it was his duty to supervise the mission during two protracted periods of absence by the mission president. He returned to Salt Lake City in 1894.

Smith maintained a keen interest in politics and was one of the sixteen organizers of the Utah Republican party. He actively supported William McKinley for president in 1896 and in 1898 secured an appointment as receiver of public monies and special disbursing agent for the U.S. Land Office. The appointment was renewed in 1902 by President Theodore Roosevelt, and Smith held the position through 1906. Smith was encouraged to run for Congress in 1902, but he declined. He was called, in 1903, to be one of the church's twelve apostles during a general conference at the church. Smith was not present at the conference, nor had he been notified in advance of the decision to make him an apostle. When a neighbor rushed to his house during the session and informed him of the announcement, Smith was certain she was mistaken. She brought back the news that no mistake had been made.

Smith spent much of his long tenure as an apostle directing programs for youth, beginning in 1904 when he became a board member of the YMMIA. Smith's poor eyesight gave him empathy for the difficulties faced by the blind, and he devoted much of his time to seeking solutions to related problems. In 1904 he became vice president of the Society for Aid of the Sightless in Utah, and in 1933 he served as president. He later brought about the first publication of the Book of Mormon in braille and facilitated the building of a blind center in Salt Lake City in 1937. In 1904 Smith actively campaigned for several political candidates, including Theodore Roosevelt.

In 1909 Smith's active schedule was brought to an abrupt halt by the onset of a disease, initially diagnosed as la grippe, whose symptoms included general weakness and nervousness. He spent several years convalescing and was not again able to take on the full responsibilities of his office for any length of time until 1913. The possibility of renewed poor health was a constant reality Smith faced for the remainder of his life, a threat that forced him to monitor his rest and diet and to limit his work pace. During his long period of convalescence, Smith was given to much reflection. His "creed" of compassion and understanding for the poor and underprivileged sustained him through times of sickness and health.

In 1919 Smith became an executive board member of the Salt Lake scouting council and was elected to the National Executive Council of the Boy Scouts of America in 1931. He received numerous awards, including boy scouting's two highest, the Silver Beaver and the Silver Buffalo. Smith served as president of the European mission from 1919 to 1920, residing in Great Britain but traveling throughout the Continent. When church president Heber J. Grant issued the calling, he promised Smith blessings of health if he would accept. In addition to supervising proselytizing missionaries and serving as the ecclesiastical leader for many members of the church, Smith during this time edited the *Millennial Star*, a European Mormon periodical. In the aftermath of World War I, Smith also worked to rebuild the missionary force and restore relations between the church and the governments of European nations.

Following Smith's return to Salt Lake City, he became the general superintendent of the YMMIA, a post he held from 1921 to 1935. He promoted a churchwide basketball tournament and dance festival and created programs for older youth that were later modeled by the Boy Scouts of America. In 1930 Smith became the founding president of the Utah Pioneer Trails and Landmarks Association, a nondenominational organization devoted to placing historical markers on sites relevant to the exploration and settling of Utah. During Smith's tenure, the association placed more than 100 plaques on sites scattered throughout the western United States. Smith's crowning achievement as president of the association was the 1947 unveiling of the This is the Place Monument in the mouth of Salt Lake City's Emigration Canyon on the centennial anniversary of Young's arrival in the valley.

Smith had a hand in other projects of historical significance, including the erection of monuments at Joseph Smith's and Young's birthplaces, both in Vermont, and the placement of a statue of Young in the U.S. Capitol. He was also responsible for or influential in the church's acquisition of a number of key historical sites. He personally negotiated the purchases, both in New York, of the Joseph Smith family farm and of the Hill Cumorah, believed by Mormons to be the burial site of the ancient plates from which the Book of Mormon was translated.

Always interested in technological developments that facilitated spreading the church's teachings, Smith participated in the first Mormon preaching by radio in 1922. Having taken his first flight in 1920, he encouraged church leaders to travel by airplane from the early years of commercial aviation, and he promoted the growth of the airline industry through word and deed. He was a member of the board of directors of Western Air Express (later Western Airplanes) from 1942 until he died.

Upon the death of Grant in 1945, Smith, who had been the senior apostle since 1943, succeeded to the presidency. His administration was marked by an emphasis on missionary work, including a postwar renewal of the missionary force; diplomacy, especially in relations with other denominations; programs for the youth, including a continued emphasis on scouting for boys and the church's Bee Hive program for girls; and relations with Native Americans. In terms of both membership and number of buildings, the church grew at an unprecedented rate while Smith was president. He gave his final public address, appropriately, to the congregation to which he had belonged since 1918. He died at home in Salt Lake City.

Those who knew Smith most commonly described him as a man of love and kindness with no regard to personal station. His lifelong habit of discussing his beliefs with fellow travelers during journeys of any type converted many to Mormonism over the course of his lifetime, and his genteel manner won numerous friends both for himself and for the church he led. In so doing, he forged many strong bonds.

• Smith's writings, journals, scrapbooks, and other papers are in the J. Willard Marriott Library at the University of Utah and the historical archives of the Church of Jesus Christ of Latter-day Saints. A topical assortment of Smith's religious writings and discourses are in Robert McIntosh and Susan McIntosh, eds., *The Teachings of George Albert Smith* (1996). The most complete assessments of Smith's life are Francis M. Gibbons, *George Albert Smith: Kind and Caring Christian, Prophet of God* (1990), and the treatment of Smith in Merlo J. Pusey, *Builders of a Kingdom* (1981). An informative obituary is in the *Deseret News*, 5 Apr. 1951.

BRUCE GELDER

SMITH, George Otis (22 Feb. 1871–10 Jan. 1944), geologist and federal administrator, was born in Hodgdon, Aroostock County, Maine, the son of Joseph Otis Smith, a Civil War veteran and newspaper publisher, and Emma Mayo. In 1878 Joseph Smith founded the *Somerset Independent Reporter* in Skowhegan, Maine. Young George helped his father and also edited his campus newspaper at Colby College, in Waterville, Maine, before forsaking journalism for geology. Encouraged by Colby geology professor William Bayley, Smith earned a bachelor's degree in 1893. Then, after the first of three successive summers spent with U.S.

Geological Survey (USGS) field parties in Michigan and Washington, Smith began graduate studies at Johns Hopkins University under William B. Clark, Edward B. Mathews, G. K. Gilbert, and Bailey Willis. In 1896 Colby awarded Smith a master's degree; that same year he completed a doctoral dissertation on the geology of Maine's Fox Islands and was appointed an assistant geologist with the USGS. He also married Grace Maud Coburn, a Colby classmate; they had five children, of whom one daughter did not survive infancy. Smith's marriage brought him additional experience and wealth, since he helped to manage the Coburn family's extensive land and timber interests in Maine and the Midwest.

As a full-time member of the USGS Geologic Branch, Smith conducted field work in northwestern Washington. For the *Geologic Atlas of the United States*, he helped to map four reconnaissance-scale quadrangles in the Cascade Mountains and adjacent areas, while studying the region's coals, igneous rocks, metallic ores, physiography, and water resources. Smith also helped to investigate the Tintic mining district in Utah. In 1903, two years after being promoted geologist, Smith was reassigned to join and then to lead geologic work in New England. He also mapped and studied the geology, minerals, and water resources of the Kennebec, Penobscot, and Perry basins in Maine.

In 1906 the Geologic Branch shifted Smith from directing field operations to program management as chief of the Section of Petrography; he was also detailed to head a subgroup analyzing USGS business methods. His report drew the attention of Commissioner of Corporations James R. Garfield. When USGS director Charles D. Walcott resigned, Garfield, the new secretary of the interior, recommended that Smith replace him. Smith became acting director on 1 May 1907; the Senate confirmed his appointment early the following December. Reflecting the growth of graduate education in America, Smith was the USGS's first director with a Ph.D., but also the first who was not a member of the National Academy of Sciences. Except for a year's leave of absence during 1922–1923 to chair the U.S. Coal Commission, Smith served continuously as USGS director for twenty-three years, by far the longest tenure of any of the post's twelve incumbents through 1997. Although he was a conservative Republican, Smith's view of the USGS as an objective and apolitical finder and presenter of scientific facts made him equally acceptable to one Democrat and five Republican presidents and their nine secretaries of the interior. His standing with Garfield and other Progressive conservationists in both parties fell somewhat when, for reasons of ethics and policy, he supported Garfield's successor Richard Ballinger in his dispute during 1909–1911 with Garfield's friend and fellow reformer Gifford Pinchot, chief of the U.S. Forest Service. Like Ballinger, Smith strictly construed the law; he held that public lands could not be reserved or assessed without specific legislative or executive authority.

While Smith led the USGS, the agency's total funds rose from $1,868,000 to $4,197,000. Acquiring increased nonfederal funds enabled the USGS to enlarge its staff from 840 to 1,127 employees to accomplish the expanded data-gathering and mapping, but it reduced the USGS's control over programs and decreased their research content. During Smith's directorate the USGS faced major challenges: informed classification of the public lands and their resources to aid wise management; World War I; the postwar energy crisis; and the advent of the Great Depression.

After Smith overestimated the nation's independence from foreign sources of metals and fuels in 1914, USGS geologists inventoried U.S. minerals and explored successfully at home and in Latin America for manganese, potash, and other critical materials. They also assessed the naval petroleum reserves and began continuous studies of volcanoes and their hazards. Smith joined Woodrow Wilson's Advisory Committee on Coal Production, published *The Strategy of Minerals: A Study of the Mineral Factor in the World Position of America in War and Peace* (1919), and became a member of the National Research Council's Division of Government Relations. USGS personnel also compiled, under Smith's direction, a *World Atlas of Commercial Geology*—one volume each on water powers and the distribution of mineral resources—in time to aid the peacemakers at Versailles. Smith predicted a shortage of natural gas and suggested that government support business in searches for new sources overseas.

As director, Smith concentrated on continuing his predecessor Walcott's efforts to make USGS science more useful to the public, but unlike Walcott, Smith did not try to develop research components in his applied programs. He directed the agency away from its previously nationwide operations toward a conservation-oriented business policy for managing the public domain. Smith, who defined "conservation" as the efficient, maximum, and purposeful use or reservation of natural resources for public and private good, changed the USGS method of classifying the public domain from its original scientific basis to a presale classification of public lands and their resources. Smith deemphasized USGS investigations of mineral resources to aid industry, for which his agency had been founded in 1879. He also destroyed its healthy balance of basic and applied work. Smith's policies ensured support from the USGS's political and other constituencies, but reduced research and low salaries led many of the agency's scientists, engineers, and managers to seek employment elsewhere.

To accomplish the USGS's new mission, Smith in December 1908 established a Land-Classification Board within the Geologic Branch. The board's responsibilities increased dramatically as congresses and presidents withdrew phosphate lands, established naval petroleum and oil-shale reserves, authorized enlarged and stock-raising homesteads, promoted the leasing and mining of coal, phosphate, oil, oil shale, gas, and sodium, and provided for surveys to develop and conserve energy from water power.

In his early years as director, Smith advocated and helped to found the policy that withdrew from entry the public oil lands. He strove to preserve the nation's petroleum resources to avoid waste and overproduction and to ensure adequate supplies for military and civilian use, while also supporting stable prices, fair salaries, and sensible profits for industry. Smith emerged safely from the Harding administration's oil-lands scandals and became one of Calvin Coolidge's leading experts on power derived from supplies of domestic and foreign mineral fuels and water. He also served as the new president's chief proponent of reasonable conservation. In 1924 Smith chaired the president's Commission on Oil Reserves, which formulated a conservation-storage policy for the four naval petroleum reserves. Smith also led (1924–1931) the technical-advisory commission of the Federal Oil Conservation Board, and he represented the Interior Department at the first World Power Conference in London.

For Smith, effective conservation required talented engineering. He greatly admired Coolidge's successor Herbert Hoover, a USGS veteran, successful mining engineer, and former member of the Oil Conservation Board. In 1929, at Hoover's request, Smith helped to complete the unitization of commercial oil fields in California, gathered evidence for an interstate oil compact, and accompanied the U.S. delegation to the World Engineering Congress in Tokyo. The next year Hoover nominated Smith to lead the Federal Power Commission (FPC), with which the USGS had cooperated closely since the FPC's founding in 1920. As FPC chairman Smith favored privately rather than publicly regulated power, a view that imperiled his appointment. The Senate withdrew its consent to Smith's nomination, but the Supreme Court finally sustained Hoover's choice in May 1932. Franklin Roosevelt, Hoover's successor, asked for and accepted Smith's resignation on 31 October 1933.

During Smith's three decades in Washington, D.C., he advocated to industrial, political, and scientific audiences plain speaking, plain writing, and plain geology. He actively participated in the Cosmos Club, the National Geographic Society, the National Press Club, Phi Beta Kappa, and other organizations. He also served as president of the Geological Society of Washington (1909), the Metropolitan Washington's YMCA (1909–1922), and the American Institute of Mining and Metallurgical Engineers (1928–1929). Smith received an LL.D. in 1920 from Colby, on whose board of trustees he had served since 1903, and Sc.D. degrees from the Case School of Applied Technology (1914) and the Colorado School of Mines (1928). The University of Chicago also numbered him among its trustees. The American Geographical Society awarded him its C. P. Daly Gold Medal in 1920. Smith Knob, in the Directors Range portion of Antarctica's Thiel Mountains, honors his achievements in public service. Smith retired to Skowhegan, where he continued to be active in charitable works, conservation, education, the power industry, and the Baptist Church. He died in Augusta, Maine.

• The National Archives and Records Administration, College Park, Md., holds Smith's official papers from his federal service in Record Groups 51 (Keep Commission), 57 (Geological Survey, including the President's Commission on Oil Reserves), 138 (Federal Power Commission), and 232 (Federal Oil Conservation Board). Smith's extensive private papers (1906–1934) are at the University of Wyoming's American Heritage Center, Laramie; the University of Washington, Seattle, holds additional letters. The Smith Collection at Colby College has his printed publications but contains no manuscript documents. *U.S. Geological Survey Bulletin* 746 (1923): 958–60, 823 (1931): 564–65, and 937 (1944): 865 list Smith's principal publications through 1933; these data also are available on CD-ROM as part of the American Geological Institute's "GeoRef" online bibliographical database. Brief memorials by colleagues include Edson S. Bastin, *Economic Geology* 39 (1944): 247; Carroll E. Dobbin, *Bulletin of the American Association of American Geologists* 28 (1944): 683–86; and Thomas A. Rickard, *Mining and Metallurgy* 25 (1944): 191. A lengthier memoir and bibliography is Philip S. Smith, *Proceedings of the Geological Society of America for 1944* (1945): 309–29. Mary C. Rabbitt, *Minerals, Lands, and Geology for the Common Defence and General Welfare*, vol. 2: *1879–1904*, and vol. 3: *1904–1939* (1980, 1986), contain an internal but more critical view of Smith's career in a wider context. For external analysis of his USGS directorate see Thomas G. Manning, "George Otis Smith as Fourth Director of the U.S. Geological Survey," in *Two Hundred Years of Geology in America*, ed. Cecil J. Schneer (1979). An evaluation of Smith's efforts to secure oil conservation is Gene M. Gressley, "GOS, Petroleum, Politics, and the West," in *The Twentieth-Century American West: A Potpourri* (1977).

CLIFFORD M. NELSON

SMITH, George Washington (c. 1820–18 Feb. 1899), dancer, ballet master, and choreographer, was born in Philadelphia, Pennsylvania, but otherwise his early life is obscure. Smith recalled that he made his dance debut in 1832. He gradually gained a reputation in Philadelphia's theaters as an entr'acte dancer who specialized in flatfoot and clog dancing. He was first featured in the *Public Ledger* in May 1840: "Mr. G. SMITH, for the first time will dance a HORNPIPE" at a firemen's benefit.

Smith apparently had had no ballet training whatsoever when the celebrated Fanny Elssler came to Philadelphia in June 1840. Her partner, James Sylvain, taught ballet to Smith and also coached him in dramatic interpretation of harlequin roles. Smith was invited to join the company, although the dates of his engagement are unknown. Contrary to the historian Lillian Moore's published account, Smith did not go to Cuba with the company but instead in 1859 joined the Ronzani troupe. This suggests that he was attached to Elssler's troupe for as few as seven months from the fall of 1841 to January 1842 (when Sylvain left for Europe and Elssler for Cuba). According to Smith's son Joseph, his father briefly substituted for Sylvain as Elssler's partner, although by 15 January she had hired Jules Martin, formerly attached to the Paris Opéra, to play opposite her.

Despite its short duration, the experience was a life-changing one for Smith. He quit clog dancing in order to develop his skills in ballet. If he returned, however briefly, to this genre, he Frenchified the title to *pas de sabots*, just as his sailor's hornpipe was transformed into the *pas de matelot*. It is indicative of his admiration for the great ballerina that he named his daughter, Fanny Elssler Smith, after her. Certainly his expertise and lifelong interest in Spanish dancing dated from this point. He performed most of the Spanish dances from Elssler's repertory such as the *Bolero*, *El Jaleo de Jerez*, and so on, and achieved such a level of competence that he could ably partner the Spaniard Pepita Soto throughout her American tour.

In contrast, he never mounted any of the great Romantic ballet classics that Elssler performed in the United States, which might indicate that his lack of ballet training precluded his learning them at that point. He evidently continued to study dance, since by 1846 he was proficient enough to partner America's prima ballerina, Mary Ann Lee, in three famous ballets that she had brought back from Paris: *La Jolie fille du Gand*; the American premiere of the first authentic staging of *Giselle*; and *La Fille du Danube*.

Smith's repertory was representative of the mix of ballet genres popular in his lifetime. In all, Smith danced in fifteen of the most famous ballets from the Paris Opéra repertory, such as *La Esmeralda*, and even more of the lesser known ballet-pantomimes. He appeared in at least fifteen character or national dances, as they were termed at that time, including the *pas russe*, *pas styrienne*, *La Savoyard*, *Cracovienne*, a polka called *La Taquenette*, and so forth. He did not limit himself to heroic roles but also played several comical pieces, especially early in his career. He danced in seven different operas, including *William Tell*, *Le Dieu et la bayadère*, *Gustav III*, *Semiramide*, and *Un ballo in maschera*. While opera was his favorite art form, Smith was not above choreographing ballets for P. T. Barnum's circus or dancing as Lola Montez's partner on her American tour. Toward the end of his career spectacles proved extremely popular, and Smith choreographed *The Little Tycoon*, *1492*, and a version of that famous ancestor of Broadway musicals, *The Black Crook*.

Smith partnered practically every well-known ballerina who toured throughout the United States, including some American-born ones. Besides Mary Ann Lee, there were several American dancers who formed part of the Elssler ensemble: the Vallee sisters from Philadelphia and Julia Turnbull. The latter sparked a riot at the Bowery Theatre in New York when Smith, for unknown reasons, refused to dance a polka with her and expressed a preference for a foreign ballerina, Giovanna Ciocca. The crowd quieted down only after Smith apologized publicly and performed the *Polka nationale* as American flags waved in the background. He danced with many Italian ballerinas, including Ciocca, Giuseppina Morlacchi, and Annetta Galletti, some of whom had trained under the illustrious Carlo Blasis at La Scala. He also performed with several

French dancers, including Louise Ducy-Barre and Mlle Lamoureux. He worked closely with several male dancers who visited the United States: James Sylvain, his teacher; Jules Martin; Gaetano Neri; and the extraordinary dancer-teacher Leon Espinosa.

Smith's convent-educated wife, Mary Coffee, whom he married in 1854, disapproved of the theater as a career for their ten children. Their son Joseph Smith waited until her death to make his theatrical debut. His early training from his father served him well in musical comedy appearances for Florenz Ziegfeld. He claimed to have invented the Turkey Trot and introduced Apache dancing to Broadway.

Praised in the *Spirit of the Times* newspaper as a worthy and urbane gentleman who "gained the esteem of all who [came] into contact with him," this modest man made the most of the scarce resources available and found full employment as a *danseur noble* in times hardly conducive to such an enterprise. Photographs reveal him to have been a dancer with good posture, muscular legs posed in perfect turnout, and a handlebar moustache of almost comical proportions. His lengthy career spanned almost the entire nineteenth century and enabled him to hand on to his ballet pupils some of the poetry of the Romantic style during the dark days when spectacles became blatant leg shows. "Le grand Smith," as he was sometimes called, continued to teach in Philadelphia until his death there. Smith is considered to be America's first *danseur noble* due to the many leading ballet roles that he played and ballerinas whom he partnered over the course of his lengthy 67-year career.

• George Washington Smith's daughter Carrie Smith owned a notebook, dated 1848, that contained notes for Smith's choreography. Whereabouts of the notebook is unknown. An 1884 interview with Smith, conducted by a Philadelphia newspaper, can be found in *Philadelphia Press* (1884), *American Theatre Scrapbook*, vol. 4, at the New York Public Library for the Performing Arts, Theatre Division. Smith's son Joseph was the subject of "The Story of a Harlequin," *Saturday Evening Post*, 30 May 1914, in which he recalls details of his father training him for the stage. For biographical information, see Lillian Moore, "George Washington Smith," in *Chronicles of the American Dance*, ed. Paul Magriel (1948), pp. 139–88. A description of Smith's choreographic notebooks, as well as reproductions of several pages, can be found in Moore's article.

MAUREEN NEEDHAM

SMITH, Gerald Birney (3 May 1868–2 Apr. 1929), Baptist theologian and educator, was born in Middlefield, Massachusetts, the son of Metcalf John Smith and Harriet Louise Eldredge. He graduated from Brown University in 1891 (A.B.), then taught Latin at Oberlin Academy in 1891–1892 and mathematics and foreign languages at Worcester (Mass.) Academy from 1892 to 1895. He married Inez Michener in 1894; they had one son. In 1895 he entered Union Theological Seminary in New York City and graduated in the joint program with Columbia University in 1898 (M.A. Columbia, B.D. Union). Smith received a travel fellowship and studied in Europe at the Universities of Berlin, Marburg, and Paris from 1898 to 1900. In 1900 Smith began his long and distinguished career at the University of Chicago, where he moved through the ranks to full professor of Christian theology in the Divinity School. In 1902 he was ordained to the Christian ministry at the Hyde Park Baptist Church in Chicago.

Throughout his career, Smith struggled to divorce religious values from coercive dogma. Much influenced by theologians Wilhelm Herrmann and William Newton Clarke, he saw religious experience as the primary source for Christian theology. This led him to urge theologians to draw on the social sciences and the study of history: he desired to discover the historical background of the Bible, particularly the teachings of the historical Jesus, as a guide for theological judgments.

Smith also felt that the modern world required a new interpretation of Christian values that was grounded in the application of the scientific method to the study of scripture, ethics, and theology. In an influential lecture in 1903, he advocated a new "practical theology" that would shift attention to current social problems by showing how religious beliefs had functioned in their original social settings.

In 1912 Smith delivered the Nathaniel W. Taylor Lectures at Yale Divinity School. Published in 1913 as *Social Idealism and the Changing Theology: A Study of the Ethical Aspects of Christian Doctrine*, the lectures advocated a reconstruction of theology in view of ethical evolution in the West. Rejecting traditional Catholic and Protestant concepts of doctrine and authority, he urged that ethical norms and human experience serve as warrants for modern theologians.

Smith declined to write his own systematic theology. Instead, he urged his students to develop critical methods for a "constructive theology" that would replace systematic and dogmatic approaches by relying on insights drawn from human experience. Further, he saw a struggle between ecclesiastical ethics and the moral challenges of the modern world. The glory of true Christianity, he wrote in 1912, was in its ethical character: "That which was inherently unbelievable or immoral cannot be made sacred by the Church" (*Social Idealism*, p. xvii). Nothing could be more foreign to this age, for instance, than the idea of a catastrophic end to the world as prophesied in the New Testament.

Smith was a member of the second generation of the Chicago School of Christian thought that transformed a significant segment of liberal Protestant thought. With fellow Chicago professors Shailer Mathews and Shirley Jackson Case, he tried to redirect the education of ministers. Changes in the churches and the society, he wrote, demanded greater sensitivity to scientific methods. Practical theology would enable students to formulate Christian truth in ways valuable for life. He believed historical and sociological approaches to doctrine would discern the deeper values in Scripture, church history, and contemporary human experience. He rejected any claims for the "finality of Christianity as the exclusive way to religious truth." A prolific scholar, he also edited the *American Journal of Theology* from 1909 to 1920 and the *Journal of Religion* from 1921 to 1926.

In June 1920 Charles H. Fountain, a Baptist fundamentalist from Plainfield, New Jersey, attacked Smith's *Social Idealism and the Changing Theology* before the Committee on Denominational Schools of the Northern Baptist Convention. The charges were not taken seriously, but Fountain reprinted them in a pamphlet titled *Charges of Teaching False Doctrine* (1922). He objected that Smith seemed to deny the possibility of miracles, to dismiss as "magic" the Apostle Paul's view of the Lord's Supper, and to minimize the differences between Christianity and other religions.

A frequent target of fundamentalist adversaries, Smith always insisted, as in his speech at the opening of classes at the Divinity School in 1922, that he stood in an "evangelical" tradition. He claimed that evangelicals—from the sixteenth-century Protestant reformers to the Pietists and the revivalists—had always emphasized Christian experience. It was they, not theological dogmatists, who had expanded world missions. Smith saw himself as joining them in "winning the world to Christ," not "conquering the world in the name of Christ." He said that the true spirit of evangelical Christianity was to promote genuine Christian experience, not adherence to some doctrinal system.

Smith defined a liberal as "one who valued experience as a criterion of the verification of religious life more than doctrine." When he criticized doctrines by analyzing the meaning of such ideas as God and salvation, he troubled traditionalists; but, like Social Gospel advocate Walter Rauschenbusch, Smith believed that the goal of Christianity should be the Christianization of the social order, so that all who directed society would embody the spirit of service and religious aspirations found in Christianity at its best. In *The Principles of Christian Living: A Handbook of Christian Ethics* (1924), he sought to apply his view of Christian ethics to issues of family, wealth, recreation, politics, and industry. For him, Christianity was a religion of joy that should prompt lawyers, politicians, and professionals to adopt optimistic principles of social reform.

Smith was active in his church and community. He was a deacon at Hyde Park Baptist Church and the chairman of the board of the University of Chicago Settlement. He sponsored a history of Middlefield, Massachusetts, and served as an adviser to the Religious Education Association. At the university, he served as the chair of the University Orchestral Association. Smith died suddenly of food poisoning while on a motor trip in Dayton, Ohio. Mathews said of him that "few men in America have touched so many minds and freed them from prejudice and bigotry without arousing scorn and cynicism" (*Baptist*, 27 Apr. 1929).

• In addition to the works mentioned above, see Smith's *Practical Theology: A Neglected Field in Theological Education* (1903); *A Guide to the Study of the Christian Religion* (ed., 1916); *A Dictionary of Religion and Ethics* (ed. with Mathews, 1921); "The Spirit of Evangelical Christianity," *Journal of Religion* 2, no. 6 (Nov. 1922): 624–34; *A Christian Test of Christianity* (n.d.); *Jesus' Way of Living* (1926); *Religious Thought in the Last Quarter Century* (ed., 1927); and "The Problem of Authority in Protestantism," *Crozer Quarterly* 5, no. 4 (Oct. 1928): 396–412. For information about his career see "The Professor and the Fundamentalist," *Christian Century* (11 Nov. 1926): 1392–93. Obituaries are in the *Baptist*, 13 Apr. 1929.

WILLIAM H. BRACKNEY

SMITH, Gerald Lyman Kenneth (27 Feb. 1898–15 Apr. 1976), minister, publisher, and political crusader, was born in Pardeeville, Wisconsin, the son of Lyman Z. Smith, a farmer and traveling salesman, and Sarah Henthorn, a schoolteacher. Raised in poverty in small towns in Wisconsin, Smith graduated from Viroqua High School, where he won prizes for track and oratory.

Smith attended Valparaiso University and, graduating in 1918, became a minister, preaching at Footville, Soldiers Grove, and Beloit, Wisconsin, following in the footsteps of his father and grandfather, who were part-time ministers in the same denomination, the Christian (Disciples of Christ) church. On 22 June 1922 he married Elna M. Sorenson. Smith's success as a fund-raiser and his oratorical talents drew praise from his congregants, and he was called to larger churches in Illinois and Indiana.

For the sake of his wife's health—she had contracted tuberculosis—Smith relocated in the South. A few months before the stock market crash in 1929, he accepted a position as minister of the Kings Highway Christian Church in Shreveport, Louisiana. Once again he excelled as a fund-raiser, nearly doubled the church's membership, and was a leader in civic activities. After U.S. Senator Huey P. Long saved the homes of some of his congregants from foreclosure, Smith became his friend and supporter. In 1933 he became involved in a dispute with his church about his political activities with Long and resigned under the threat of being fired.

Following a short association with William Dudley Pelley, a militant anti-Semite who modeled his organization on Germany's Nazi party, Smith became a political organizer for Long. From early 1934 until Long's death on 10 September 1935, he was national organizer for the senator's Share Our Wealth Society, which advocated the confiscation and redistribution of the incomes of millionaires. After Long's assassination, Smith preached the funeral oration to 100,000 mourners.

Smith left Louisiana early in 1936 in search of a new movement. He spoke at a presidential rally for Governor Eugene Talmadge of Georgia, but after a Talmadge candidacy failed to materialize, he joined the movement of Dr. Francis E. Townsend, a California physician who advocated generous retirement pensions as a means of helping the elderly and increasing purchasing power to end the Great Depression. Smith and Townsend then joined Father Charles E. Coughlin, the "radio priest," to create the Union party, which ran North Dakota Congressman William Lemke for president. Lemke, however, polled only 891,858 votes and failed to carry any states.

Smith settled in Detroit, where he befriended Henry Ford and delivered radio speeches heard throughout the Midwest, founding the America First party and the Christian Nationalist Crusade. In 1942 he began publishing *The Cross and the Flag* and entered the race for U.S. senator, but he finished a distant third.

In the 1940s and 1950s Smith traveled the nation delivering anti-Semitic speeches and drawing large crowds, operating from home bases in St. Louis and Tulsa. He also wrote voluminously, publishing pamphlets and short books, most of them attacking Jews, communists, and liberal ideas. He ran for president as the candidate of his own Christian Nationalist party in 1944, 1948, and 1956, but he polled only a few thousand votes each time.

In the 1950s Smith turned increasingly to writing. In addition to *The Cross and the Flag*, which he published until his death, he wrote a newsletter for selected followers, who sent donations that enabled him to become a millionaire. Smith condemned integration of the races, water flouridation, and the welfare state. *The Cross and the Flag* averaged about 25,000 subscribers, and through speeches, tracts, and radio broadcasts Smith reached hundreds of thousands more. He combined devout Christian fundamentalism and reactionary politics, growing increasingly extreme as he aged. In 1953 he moved his headquarters to Los Angeles, where he had attracted large crowds.

Smith's following declined in the late 1950s, but in 1964 he launched a new career as a religious entrepreneur by constructing a seven-story statue of Jesus, the Christ of the Ozarks, in the mountain community of Eureka Springs, Arkansas. He added a Bible museum and a Christian art gallery and in 1968 began staging a Passion play in an amphitheater; the production became the largest outdoor pageant in the United States. His projects brought Smith a new burst of publicity, a degree of respectability, and revived the economy of the Ozark town.

Smith died in Los Angeles and was buried in Eureka Springs at the foot of the Christ of the Ozarks. His will specified that most of his assets be turned over to a foundation to perpetuate his religious activities in Eureka Springs. Smith's widow became head of the foundation. His survivors also included an adopted son, Gerald L. K. Smith, Jr.

Smith was one of the foremost orators of his generation, an emotional speaker who filled stadiums in the 1930s and 1940s, and he pioneered in the mass dissemination of propaganda that combined religion and politics. H. L. Mencken considered him the best public speaker he had ever heard. Smith's message, however, was bigoted, and his legacy is as a preacher of hate. "To have the power to touch men's hearts with glory or with bigotry, and to choose the latter, is a saddening thing," the Arkansas *Gazette* concluded his obituary.

• Smith's papers are in the Bentley Historical Library of the University of Michigan. He wrote an autobiography, *Besieged Patriot* (1978). The chief biography is Glen Jeansonne, *Gerald L. K. Smith: Minister of Hate* (1988). See also Leo P. Ribuffo, *The Old Christian Right: The Protestant Far Right From the Great Depression to the Cold War* (1983). David H. Bennett's *Demagogues in the Depression: American Radicals and the Union Party, 1932–1936* (1969) has an excellent account of Smith's participation in the Union party campaign. George Thayer's *The Farther Shores of Politics: The American Political Fringe Today* (1967) has a chapter on Smith. His obituary appeared in the Arkansas *Gazette*, 24 Apr. 1976.

GLEN JEANSONNE

SMITH, Gerrit (6 Mar. 1797–28 Dec. 1874), land speculator and abolitionist, was born in Utica, New York, the son of Peter Smith, a land speculator, and Elizabeth Livingston. Smith resided practically his entire life in Peterboro, Madison County, New York, where his father operated a land speculation business. A former partner of John Jacob Astor (1763–1848), the wealthy fur trader, the elder Smith acquired more than a quarter million acres of undeveloped land scattered across the states of New York, Vermont, Michigan, and Virginia. Gerrit's mother was from one of the state's leading families and was related to two other wealthy and powerful local clans, the Schuylers and the Van Rensselaers. Smith graduated as valedictorian from Hamilton College in 1818. He married Weltha Ann Backus, daughter of that college's president, in January 1819, but she died seven months later. In 1822 Smith married Ann Carroll Fitzhugh from Rochester, New York. They were the parents of four children.

In the 1820s Smith took over management of the vast land holdings of his increasingly erratic father. The Smith family fortune was threatened by the nationwide financial depression of the late 1830s, but Gerrit ultimately survived the crisis richer than ever. In the 1840s and 1850s his annual income from his landholdings and investments in banking and railroads typically exceeded $60,000.

Smith's great fortune allowed him to become one of the leading philanthropists of the early nineteenth century. Although he was antisectarian in his personal religious beliefs, Smith gave generously to the American Bible Society, the American Tract Society, and the American Sunday School Union. He also devoted much of his time and fortune to assisting numerous reform movements popular in upstate New York's famous "Burned-Over District" during the 1830s, 1840s, and 1850s. Smith became a leader and major financial sponsor of state and national organizations promoting temperance, prison reform, international peace, and land reform. He also supported his wife's and daughter Elizabeth's active participation in the women's rights movement.

The cause that captured the greatest portion of Smith's attention was the campaign to end slavery. At first Smith supported efforts to colonize slaves in Africa, but in 1835 he joined the more militant abolitionist movement that demanded immediate emancipation of the slaves. He also supported self-improvement efforts of northern free blacks as a means of combating pervasive racial prejudice. He distributed thousands of acres of unimproved land in upstate New York to poor black families to help them become economically independent. Smith initially believed that the abolitionist mission was exclusively one of moral suasion: to "publish the truth about slavery."

Following a series of fissures in the antislavery movement in the early 1840s, however, Smith became affiliated with the abolitionists' independent political arm, the Liberty party. Smith and the Liberty party called for an immediate abolition of slavery wherever constitutionally possible and for the repeal of all racially discriminatory legislation. In the early and mid-1840s he traveled across the North to stump for Liberty party candidates. When most Liberty party leaders agreed to merge with more moderate antislavery factions to form the Free Soil party in 1848, Smith balked at what he regarded as abandonment of the abolitionist commitment to immediate emancipation. Instead, he became the leader of a small faction of uncompromising political abolitionists who nominated him for president of the United States in 1848, 1856, and 1860. Under Smith's leadership the reorganized Liberty party pledged itself to battle not only slavery but also "wars, tariffs, the traffic in intoxicating drinks, land monopolies, and secret societies." In 1852 a coalition of abolitionists and more moderate antislavery voters elected Smith to Congress. However, he experienced considerable frustration in promoting his abolitionist program in Washington. He was especially disappointed when Congress passed the Kansas-Nebraska Act (1854), which repealed the Missouri Compromise's ban on slavery in the former Louisiana Purchase territories. Private expressions of that frustration belied his public explanation for resigning his congressional seat in August 1854, citing the "pressure of my far too extensive private business."

Smith's growing despair concerning the failure of political antislavery tactics converted him into a proponent of violent abolitionist tactics by the mid-1850s. In 1851 he played a prominent part in the mob that stormed a police station in Syracuse, New York, and freed the escaped slave Jerry McHenry. Smith donated an estimated $16,000 to the free-state movement in Kansas, which frequently employed armed means to resist efforts to establish slavery there. It was through his contacts with the Kansas free-state guerrillas that Smith drew close to the militant abolitionist John Brown (1800–1859). Although he publicly denied it, Smith gave warm encouragement and financial assistance to Brown's attempt to incite a large-scale slave insurrection at Harpers Ferry, Virginia, in 1859. Guilt over the failure of Brown's raid and fear of possible arrest as a co-conspirator caused Smith to commit himself to the Utica State Lunatic Asylum. Smith's treatment, under the direction of pioneer psychiatrist John P. Gray, consisted of rest, isolation from stimulation, special diet, and administration of various sedatives. His symptoms comport with the modern diagnosis of a bipolar disorder, better known as manic-depressive behavior. After eight weeks of hospitalization at the Utica asylum, Smith was released.

In his final years Smith's psychological stability apparently returned, and he resumed his business and reform activity. During the Civil War, he supported the Republican party but frequently criticized its lukewarm enthusiasm for emancipation and black rights. In the late 1860s Smith participated in efforts to found a national prohibition party but soon returned to the Republican fold. He also continued to attend reform conventions and to donate large sums to favorite charities and causes, including world peace and women's rights, until his death in New York City.

• The Gerrit Smith Papers are located at the George Arents Research Library, Syracuse University. The only scholarly biography of Smith is Ralph Volney Harlow, *Gerrit Smith: Philanthropist and Reformer* (1939). Some additional factual information on Smith's life can be found in Octavius Brooks Frothingham, *Gerrit Smith: A Biography* (1878), and Charles A. Hammond, *Gerrit Smith: The Story of a Noble Life* (1908).
JOHN R. McKIVIGAN

SMITH, Gilbert Morgan (6 Jan. 1885–11 July 1959), botanist and educator, was born in Beloit, Wisconsin, the son of Erastus Gilbert Smith, a professor of chemistry at Beloit College, and Elizabeth Maria Mayher, a graduate of Mt. Holyoke College. Smith attended public schools in Beloit and showed more interest in schoolboy pranks than in academic pursuits. After two undistinguished years at Beloit College's academy, he entered Williston Academy in Easthampton, Massachusetts, where he first demonstrated an aptitude for the sciences. With an interest in biology and chemistry, Smith entered Beloit College and graduated with a bachelor of science degree in 1907, achieving membership in Phi Beta Kappa. He then served as a high school teacher in Stoughton, Wisconsin, before entering graduate school at the University of Wisconsin in Madison.

Smith already had an interest in algae, stimulated by studying Friedrich Oltmanns's *Morphologie und Biologie der Algen* to improve his command of German. He was an assistant in botany at Wisconsin between 1909 and 1910. From 1910 to 1911 he was an instructor at Pomona College in California before returning to graduate studies at Wisconsin. He was an instructor at Wisconsin in 1911 and graduated with a Ph.D. in 1913. During this period he began isolating and documenting the morphology and life cycles of diverse algae. He married Helen Pfuderer in 1913; they had no children.

After graduating Smith remained at the University of Wisconsin. From 1914 to 1917 he spent his summers studying planktonic algae from the numerous lakes of Wisconsin. In 1915 he was promoted to assistant professor and in 1917 to associate professor. In 1920, after publishing the first part of *The Phytoplankton of the Inland Waters of Wisconsin*, he traveled to Europe to study more algae, especially desmids. The second volume was published in 1924; the acclaimed two-part monograph was the first to contain descriptions and figures of all the planktonic algae for any region. In the same year Smith published, with five Wisconsin colleagues, *A Textbook of General Botany*, an undergraduate text that remained popular through five editions. He continued his field investigations in North America, discovering and describing many new genera and species of algae, and summarized his work in the reference book *The Fresh-water Algae of the United States* (1933).

In 1923 Smith visited Stanford University for one academic quarter; in 1925 he accepted an invitation to become professor of botany there. For his teaching assignments at Stanford he developed lectures on the cryptogamic plants—algae and other plants such as mosses and ferns—that formed the basis for his two-volume reference work *Cryptogamic Botany* (1938). He spent his summers teaching at the Hopkins Marine Station, doing research published as *Marine Algae of the Monterey Peninsula, California* (1944).

With completion of this major work, Smith returned to his early interest in the life cycles of isolated algae. He focused on the soil alga *Chlamydomonas*, later used as a genetic model, and demonstrated mating activities in more than a dozen species. His most important result was the identification of crocetin, a hormonal substance that even in low concentration stimulated sexual reproduction of these algae. In 1947 Smith was a member of a research team investigating the effects of an atomic test on the flora and fauna of Bikini Island. He examined marine algae found at increasing distances from the center of the blast.

After retiring from Stanford in 1950, Smith remained active in editing, speaking, research, and writing. In particular he continued his research on the hormones controlling *Chlamydomonas* mating; unpublished results are in his notebooks at the Stanford Library. Smith and his wife used their leisure to travel for both study and pleasure through the South Pacific, Asia, Africa, and South America. Smith died in Palo Alto, California.

Smith was elected to membership in the National Academy of Sciences in 1948. He was a member of the American Academy of Arts and Sciences, Beta Theta Pi, and Sigma Xi. He served as vice president (1942) and president (1944) of the Botanical Society of America and received its gold medal, designating him one of fifty outstanding botanists of the twentieth century. He was the president of the American Microscopical Society (1928), vice president of the American Association for the Advancement of Science (1941), first president of the Phycological Society of America (1947), and vice president of the Western Society of Naturalists (1954). He was a delegate to the Seventh Science Congress (1949), the Seventh International Botanical Congress at Stockholm (1950), and honorary president of the Phycology Section at the Eighth International Botanical Congress in Paris (1954). Appreciative colleagues named at least eight species, one variety, and four genera of algae in his honor.

Although Smith considered himself a morphologist, he is remembered for the diversity of his contributions to phycology, the study of algae. His research ranged from detailed developmental and reproductive studies on isolated cultures to extensive surveys of both marine and freshwater algae. Smith, a meticulous researcher and dedicated teacher, is best known for his five influential reference works and textbooks. These books, exceptional in their clarity and completeness, trained a generation of North American botanists.

• The Stanford University Library holds Smith's manuscripts, notes, and reprints. The Farlow Herbarium at Harvard University has his correspondence with W. G. Farlow, and the Gray Herbarium at Harvard has other correspondence. A biographical sketch is in National Academy of Sciences, *Biographical Memoirs* 36 (1962): 289–313. An obituary is in the *New York Times*, 14 July 1959.

PAULA DePRIEST

SMITH, Giles Alexander (29 Sept. 1829–5 Nov. 1876), soldier, was born in Jefferson County, New York, the son of Cyrus Smith and Laura Wales, occupations unknown. In his late teens he moved to London, Ohio, where in 1850 he married Martha McLain; the number of their children, if any, is unknown. Smith worked in the dry goods business in Cincinnati and, after 1856, in Bloomington, Illinois. From 1859 until the outbreak of the Civil War he managed two hotels in Bloomington. In June 1861, two months after the firing on Fort Sumter, he traveled to Missouri, where his older brother, Colonel Morgan L. Smith, was raising an infantry regiment. Giles Smith was promptly elected captain of Company D, Eighth Missouri Volunteers, a unit composed primarily of Illinoisans.

Despite his lack of military experience, Smith showed an aptitude for training volunteer troops and leading them in action. He impressed superiors and subordinates alike with his quiet competence and lack of ostentation. Wholly lacking in self-promotion, Smith allowed his performance in camp and field to speak for him. When assigned a mission, he would accomplish it to the utmost of his ability and with a minimum of supervision. He was also a stern disciplinarian, intolerant of soldiers who violated the property of civilians.

In Smith's first battle, Fort Donelson, 15 February 1862, the Eighth Missouri retook defenses lost by other troops, captured the battle flags of three Confederate regiments, and maintained its position despite being hard-pressed throughout the engagement. Smith received "great credit for his coolness and the condition in which he held his men during the fight." The regiment saw limited action at Shiloh, but it played a conspicuous role during the subsequent advance on Corinth, Mississippi. After the 17 May action at Russell's House, Smith's immediate superior lauded his "judgment and courage," as well as his versatility: "Captain Smith is capable of filling any position in the army."

A month after Corinth, Smith won his eagles, replacing his brother in command of the Eighth Missouri. By year's end he was leading the First Brigade, Second Division, in Major General William T. Sherman's Thirteenth Army Corps. Smith's new command comprised not only four volunteer regiments but also one regiment of regular infantry—a rarity for a nonprofessional soldier and testimony to the caliber of his leadership. Prevented by a poor position from playing a major role in the 29 December fighting at Chickasaw Bluffs, Smith's brigade was in the thick of action the following month during the capture of Arkansas Post. In that fight he suffered a slight wound after having his horse shot from beneath him. His contribution to victory persuaded Sherman to recommend him for a brigadier's star.

In March 1863, during the early stages of the Vicksburg campaign, Smith led a portion of his brigade to the relief of five ironclad gunboats under Acting Rear Admiral David Dixon Porter, surrounded by Confederate troops near the confluence of Deer Creek and Rolling Fork near Yazoo City, Mississippi. Several weeks later Smith accompanied Major General Ulysses S. Grant's army in overland operations below Vicksburg. His brigade performed admirably at Raymond (16 May), as well as the following day along the Big Black River, where it captured a sizable force of the enemy. Until Vicksburg's surrender on 4 July, Smith's brigade took a conspicuous part in the arduous, debilitating siege operations.

During the Chattanooga campaign Smith, who had been promoted to brigadier general of volunteers to rank from 4 August 1863, continued his distinguished service. On 24 November his enlarged brigade spearheaded Sherman's offensive down the Tennessee River, seizing rebel pickets on the south bank and covering the crossing of his brother's Second Division, Fifteenth Corps. Later that day, during the assault against Missionary Ridge, Smith was forced to the rear with a severe wound.

Smith recovered sufficiently to take an active role in the Atlanta campaign, winning notice at Resaca (15 May 1864), Dallas (26 May), and Kennesaw Mountain (27 June). Late in July he received command of the Fourth Division, Seventeenth Corps, which held the extreme left of Sherman's line outside Atlanta. His command launched a successful assault on 21 July that ensured the capture of Leggett's Hill, but on the following day, during the battle of Atlanta, it was gouged out of its entrenchments when overwhelmed by a three-sided attack. Smith's command also performed ably at Ezra Church on 28 July and at Jonesboro on 31 August. For gallantry in action at Jonesboro, he was recommended for a second star.

During the March to the Sea, Smith's division encountered minimal opposition; its only sustained action came on 22 November along the Oconee River, when Georgia state troops failed to prevent it from burning a strategic railroad bridge. Upon reaching Savannah in late December, its commander proudly reported his troops as having "marched 300 miles, and

thoroughly destroyed twenty-four miles and a half of railroad track." They wrecked dozens of additional miles of communications during the Carolinas campaign, by which time Smith was a brevet major general of volunteers. His division also had the honor of securing and occupying Fayetteville, North Carolina, a strategic point on Sherman's northward trek, 11 March 1865.

On 29 May, one month after General Joseph E. Johnston's surrender ended the Carolinas campaign, Smith was detached from Sherman's armies. At the order of General in Chief Grant, he was assigned to command a division in the Twenty-fifth Corps, the only army corps in U.S. history to be composed entirely of black troops. During the second week in June, Smith's new command was transported from Fort Monroe, Virginia, to the lower Rio Grande. For the next year and a half the division served near Brownsville and Brazos Santiago, Texas, building works, performing constabulatory duties, and making demonstrations to impress the French forces that had occupied Mexico in violation of the Monroe Doctrine. In November 1865, in belated recognition of his services in the field, Smith was elevated to the full rank of major general of volunteers.

Smith served on the Mexican border until early 1866, when he resigned his commission. Having refused the position of colonel of cavalry in the regular service, Smith went home to Bloomington, Illinois, and reentered the dry goods trade. In 1866 he helped found the Society of the Army of the Tennessee and served as one of its vice presidents. In 1869, a year after an unsuccessful congressional bid, he was appointed by President Grant second assistant postmaster general. He served for only three years before failing health forced him to resign. Smith moved to San Jose, California, in 1874 in a futile attempt to overcome advancing consumption, returning to Bloomington two months before his death there.

Although sometimes overshadowed by his brother, another highly capable leader who usually held higher rank, Giles Smith was an outstanding example of a nonprofessional soldier equal to the demands of high command in wartime. Throughout the war he held the confidence of demanding superiors, such as Grant and Sherman, and he never let them down; thus they entrusted him with critical elements of their campaign plans from Vicksburg through the Carolinas campaign. An indication of Smith's value was the fact that at the close of the fighting around Atlanta his command had been reduced by casualties to 50 percent of its precampaign strength but continued to be regarded by many observers as the most capable division in the Army of the Tennessee.

• No body of Smith's papers is known to exist. His Civil War service is traceable in *The War of the Rebellion: A Compilation of the Official Records of the Union and Confederate Armies* (128 vols., 1880–1901). After-action reports of the many battles and campaigns in which he participated are to be found in ser. 1, vols. 17 (pt. 1), 24 (pts. 1–2), 32 (pt. 1), 38 (pt. 3), 44,

47 (pt. 3), and 48 (pt. 2). Smith's service in 1863–1865 is covered in some detail in William T. Sherman, *Memoirs of Gen. W. T. Sherman* (1875), as well as in two Sherman biographies, B. H. Liddell Hart, *Sherman: Soldier, Realist, American* (1929, repr. 1958), and Lloyd Lewis, *Sherman: Fighting Prophet* (1932). Other sources in which Smith is mentioned prominently include Edwin C. Bearss, *The Vicksburg Campaign* (1985–1986); Albert Castel, *Decision in the West: The Atlanta Campaign of 1864* (1992); and John M. Gibson, *Those 163 Days: A Southern Account of Sherman's March from Atlanta to Raleigh* (1961). Informative obituaries can be found in the *St. Louis Globe-Democrat*, 6 Nov. 1876, as well as in the *Report of the Proceedings of the Society of the Army of the Tennessee . . . Eleventh Annual Meeting* (1885).

EDWARD G. LONGACRE

SMITH, Gustavus Woodson (1 Jan. 1822–24 June 1896), soldier, was born in Georgetown, Kentucky, the son of Byrd Smith and Sarah Hatcher Woodson, farmers. He spent his childhood on the family farm and entered the U.S. Military Academy at West Point in 1838. He graduated eighth of fifty-six members in the class of 1842 and was commissioned as a second lieutenant in the Corps of Engineers. His first assignment as assistant engineer at New London, Connecticut, involved the construction of coastal fortifications. In October 1844 he married Lucretia Bassett; they had no children. From 1844 to 1846 Smith served as acting assistant professor of engineering at West Point.

In March 1846 Congress authorized recruitment of a company of engineer soldiers in the regular army. In addition to providing engineering support to the army, the company would provide troop-leading experience to engineer officers, the best West Pointers who would later provide most general officers during the Civil War. Captain Alexander J. Swift became the first commander of the engineer company, after studying in France at the military school in Metz. Swift selected Smith as senior lieutenant and George B. McClellan as junior lieutenant. The company soon joined the invasion of Mexico, and Captain Swift fell ill as soon as they reached the Rio Grande in October 1846. Actual command of the company fell to Lieutenant Smith for the entire war.

Lieutenant Smith and the engineer company distinguished themselves. General David E. Twiggs reported that, "Whenever his legitimate duties with the pick and spade were performed, he always solicited permission to join in the advance of the storming party with his muskets, in which position his gallantry and that of his officers and men, was conspicuously displayed." In 1854 General Winfield Scott wrote that he had never known so frequently and highly distinguished a junior officer; Smith received brevet promotions to first lieutenant and captain for bravery at the battles of Cerro Gordo and Contreras. General Scott requested a third brevet to major, but the president and secretary of war overruled the promotion because "no Second Lieutenant could be allowed to hold three brevets at once, no matter what his merits or services."

At the end of the war Smith returned to West Point as principal assistant professor of engineering, serving there until December 1854. The professor of engineering, Dennis H. Mahan, played a dominant role in instilling professionalism in the officer corps in the years before the Civil War.

Resigning from the army at the end of 1854, Smith engaged in a number of endeavors before the Civil War. The story later circulated that he had resigned to join in the filibustering expedition to Cuba led by John A. Quitman, but Quitman's Cuban involvement had ended several years earlier. In New Orleans he supervised repairs to the mint and construction of a marine hospital for the Treasury Department. He served as chief engineer of the Trenton (N.J.) Iron Company in 1856. In 1857–1858 he acted as agent for London bankers examining land grants for railroads in Iowa. Smith became street commissioner of New York City in 1858 and actively worked in the Democratic party.

In April 1861, just before the attack on Fort Sumter, Smith suffered an attack of paralysis. After several months as an invalid, he headed south for medical reasons. Learning that Federal authorities had ordered his arrest as a disloyal person, Smith went to Richmond and on 19 September received appointment as a major general. His later publications on the Civil War (*Confederate War Papers*, 1884, and *The Battle of Seven Pines*, 1891) pressed his claims that he had not been appreciated as a Confederate general and that he had not conspired against the United States during his tenure as New York City's street commissioner. He commanded a corps of Joseph E. Johnson's Army of the Potomac through the Peninsular Campaign. When Johnson was wounded at the Battle of Seven Pines on 31 May 1862, Smith commanded the army until Robert E. Lee arrived the next day. Another attack of paralysis overcame Smith on 2 June. Returning to duty in August, Smith had lost the confidence of Lee and President Jefferson Davis. He commanded three divisions on Lee's right flank, supervised defenses of Richmond and North Carolina, and spent three days as interim secretary of war in November 1862. Angered that junior officers (including James Longstreet) had been promoted over him to lieutenant general, Smith complained bitterly. Ironically, Longstreet had been angered at Smith's initial promotion to major general, but Longstreet's reasoned letter of complaint had gotten him a quick promotion.

When Jefferson Davis refused to provide what Smith considered a suitable position, Smith resigned in February 1863 and moved to Georgia to become president of the Etowah Manufacturing and Mining Company and aide-de-camp to the governor. He supervised fortifications and was elected major general in the Georgia militia. Smith's militia provided some of the most inspired defense against Sherman's march to the sea, especially along the Chattahoochee River and in the battle for Savannah. Smith surrendered his remaining troops at Macon, Georgia, on 20 April 1865.

Paroled in 1866, Smith became general manager of the South Western Iron Company in Chattanooga. In 1870 he published *Notes on Life Insurance* and became the first insurance commissioner of the state of Kentucky, a post he held until 1876. In 1876 he moved to New York City and engaged in private business until 1883, when failing health forced his retirement. During retirement he published a number of articles and books, including *Generals J. E. Johnston and G. T. Beauregard at Manassas* (1892) and *Company "A," Corps of Engineers . . . in the Mexican War* (1896). He died in New York City.

Douglas S. Freeman characterized Smith as "possessed of a sensitive pomposity that offset his administrative ability and colored curiously his willingness to assume responsibility." Smith's valor as an engineer troop leader during the Mexican War was unquestioned, and business associates admired his integrity and high standards.

• Smith's own writings recount his version of events during the Civil War and most books on the Civil War mention him. The most complete contemporary obituary of Smith, written by C. Seaforth Stewart, is in the West Point *Annual Report of the Association of Graduates* for 1897.

PETER L. GUTH

SMITH, H. Allen (19 Dec. 1906–24 Feb. 1976), journalist and author, was born Harry Allen Smith in McLeansboro, Illinois, the son of Henry Arthur Smith and Adeline Allen (professions unknown). Smith's childhood was full of transitions. The family moved to Decatur, Illinois, in 1913, then to Defiance, Ohio, in 1919, and to Huntington, Indiana, in 1922, always remaining close to the general area of southern Illinois between the Mississippi and Ohio rivers. The area, commonly called "Little Egypt," was a geographical location that figured prominently in his later writing.

After completing the eighth grade, mostly in Catholic parochial schools, Smith forsook formal education and engaged in a number of menial jobs. In 1922, when he was fifteen, a sister's suitor helped him obtain a $3-a-week job as a proofreader on the *Huntington Press*. Eventually he became a reporter on the newspaper and the creator of a series of humorous columns, purportedly written by "Miss Ella Vator." His mother suggested that he adopt the byline H. Allen Smith to distinguish him from other Smiths.

In 1924 Smith wrote "Stranded on the Davenport," an imaginative and ribald essay that found its way into the hands of some girls at the local high school. The author was arrested and convicted by the local justice of the peace for writing and distributing a "lewd, licentious, obscene, and lascivious, tale." He was fined $22.50, ordered to read the Scriptures, and ostracized by his neighbors. As a result, he soon moved to Jeffersonville, Indiana, where he worked on the *Jeffersonville Bulletin* for a short time. He then found work at the *Evening Post and Times* in Louisville, Kentucky. This pattern of moving from newspaper to newspaper continued from the mid-1920s until 1941. When he was nineteen Smith became the editor of the *Seabring* (Fla.) *American*. While there he met Nelle Mae Simpson, a graduate of the University of Missouri school of

journalism and society editor of the newspaper. When the *American* folded in 1926, he became a boat-caulker and then moved to Texas, where he sold town directories. Subsequently, he took a job with the *Tulsa* (Okla.) *Tribune*. Shortly after Smith arrived in Tulsa, Nelle joined him, and the two were married in early 1927. They had two children.

In the meantime, Smith joined the staff of the *Denver Morning Post* as a reporter. His sojourn in Denver turned out to be an important one in his literary career; on the advice of his colleagues, generally well-educated and well-read young men, he overcame the deficiencies in his education by reading H. G. Wells's *Outline of History*, Charles Dickens, Plutarch, Anatole France, and H. L. Mencken's *The American Language* and *Prejudices*. Mencken became his literary idol.

After two years the itinerant writer decided to try his luck in New York City. He sent his wife and children to Nelle's family home in Missouri until he got established, after which time they joined him in New York. He had arrived there in September 1929 with $10 in his pocket, and he was glad to obtain a position as rewrite man for the United Press. This work proved valuable in the development of his style; he wrote between thirty and fifty stories daily on subjects ranging from christenings to stockholders' meetings, murders, and lawsuits. Soon, however, he was writing bylined features and refining his humor. He left the United Press in 1934, and in 1936, after brief stints doing public relations for radio and film companies, he took a job with the New York *World-Telegram*. Smith soon became a featured interviewer for the newspaper as well as the writer of humorous articles on "Major and Minor Celebrities, Human Oddities, and Ordinary Mortals." Among his interview subjects were Marlene Dietrich, Gary Cooper, Vivien Leigh, and the strippers Gypsy Rose Lee and Kay Fears.

Smith's first book was *Robert Gair*, a commissioned biography of a Brooklyn manufacturer of paper bags who was a pioneer in the development of the pasteboard carton. Published in 1939, this "spirited and informal" volume was written while the author was employed at the *World-Telegram*, as were his next two works. *Mr. Klein's Kampf* (1940), which was written in thirteen days, is a humorous novel spoofing Adolf Hitler through the character Orson Klein, an actor who could make himself look like der Fuhrer.

Low Man on the Totem Pole (1941), however, made Smith's literary reputation. This collection of childhood reminiscences and accounts of people whom he had interviewed was introduced by comedian Fred Allen. Calling the author "the screwball's Boswell," Allen wrote that "Smith never knows where his next screwball is coming from. The world is his laboratory, the human race his clinic, the nearest disciple of mono-mania's story his immediate concern. He will walk twenty miles to hear a cliche—and frequently does." Allen went on to say that "if Smith were an Indian he would be low man on any totem pole," a quote that an editor at the Doubleday publishing house proposed as the book's title. The book immediately became a bestseller, and the expression "low man on a totem pole" entered the American idiom.

Based on the successful reception of *Low Man on the Totem Pole*, Smith agreed to write a daily column called "The Totem Pole" for the United Features Syndicate, although he abandoned the column after six months in April 1942 because he believed that the shortage of newsprint brought about by World War II would result in newspapers discarding some of their newer features. In 1941 he left the *World Telegram*. Beginning in February of the following year he acted as master of ceremonies on the weekly radio network program "Swop Nite," a position that he left after ten weeks due to an argument over money. From this point onward he devoted his time to nonjournalistic writing.

Smith's *Life in a Putty Knife Factory* (1943) is another anthology of tales and interviews that became very popular. In fact, Paramount Studios invited Smith to Hollywood as a screenwriter, a practice that had been common with East Coast humorists from the 1930s onward. Although the writer remained in Hollywood for only eight months, he managed to gather enough material to write *Lost in the Horse Latitudes* (1944), a collection of humorous retellings of his experiences in "the land of the false eyelash and the flying custard pie."

In 1946 Smith published *Rhubarb*, a story about a "large, irascible and very rich cat that inherits one million dollars and a baseball team." His most popular novel, *Rhubarb* was translated into a popular film in 1951. The Smith family moved to Mount Kisko, New York, in 1947, the same year that he published *Lo, the Former Egyptian*, a collection of stories about his southern Illinois birthplace. In *Larks in the Popcorn*, published in 1948, he detailed his struggles in Westchester County to raise watermelons, strawberries, and popcorn only to find that poison ivy and wasps in his new home diverted his attention considerably. *Son of Rhubarb* (1967) and *The View from Chibo* (1971) followed.

At this time Smith was also writing for a number of popular magazines: *Cosmopolitan*, *Playboy*, *Family Weekly*, *True*, *Reader's Digest*, *Saturday Review*, and *Variety* among them (Elton Miles has listed a total of 196 articles published by Smith through 1972). In 1952 he wrote *Smith's London Journal*, a travel book about his visit to England in which he included the first American publication of an essay written by Mark Twain that had appeared in a British book in 1907. In 1962 Smith's autobiography, *To Hell in a Handbasket*, appeared. Although he indicates in the concluding chapter that he intends a sequel to bring the reader up to date from the point at which he ends this volume (through his years as a newspaper man), the promised sequel was never published.

In 1967, having grown tired of New York's urban sprawl, which was encroaching on Mount Kisko, Smith moved to Alpine, Texas, where he would live until he suffered a fatal heart attack in San Francisco while on a research trip.

A successful journalist, Smith was even more successful as "A fellow who realizes, first, that he is no better than anybody else, and second that nobody else is either," which is how he defined a humorist. For a considerable period of time Smith was as popular as his friends James Thurber and Robert Benchley. While some critics objected to his unrestrained, bawdy humor, the public accepted his work to the extent that between 1941 and 1946 his books sold approximately 1.4 million copies. His easygoing style, which showed up in a loose and disjointed structure and conversational tone, combined with his Dickensian eye for detail and easy facility in creating characterizations that he used to lambast pomposity and other human failings. Smith wrote in his autobiography that he thought of himself as "a reporter with a humorist slant. I am funny only in the sense that the world is funny." Some critics called him a midwestern humorist in the tradition of Mark Twain, Booth Tarkington, Damon Runyon, Ring Lardner, and others such as Davy Crockett, Finley Peter Dunne, and George Ade. Other critics viewed Smith's penchant for tall tales, cussing, suggestive stories, and the use of dialect as representative of the literary tradition known as the humor of the old Southwest. However he is categorized, Smith was an important humorist during the third quarter of the twentieth century.

• The majority of Smith's papers are in the Special Collections Division of the Morris Library at Southern Illinois University at Carbondale. Included are photographs and three chapters of Elton E. Miles's unpublished biography. Additional material and Smith's more than 2,000-volume personal library are housed at Sul Ross State University in Alpine, Tex.

Other books written by Smith include *Low and Inside* (1949) and *Three Men on Third* (1951), both were written with Ira Lepouce Smith; *People Named Smith* (1950); and *We Went Thataway* (1949), another of his travel books. There was also a satire on western movies, *Mr. Zip* (1952), and Smith's "American masterpiece of satire," *The Age of the Tail* (the premise being that all babies born after 22 September 1957 have tails), and the *The Rebel Yell* (1954). Collections of children's prose and verse, *Write Me a Poem, Baby* (1956) and *Don't Get Personal with a Chicken* (1959), were followed by *The Pig in the Barbershop* (1958), *Let the Crabgrass Grow* (1960), *Waikiki Beachnik* (1960), *How to Write without Knowing Nothing* (1961), *A Short History of Fingers and Other State Papers* (1963), *Two-thirds of a Coconut Tree* (1963), *Buskin' with H. Allen Smith* (1968), *With a Great Chili Confrontation* (1969), *Low Man Writes Again* (1973), and *Return of the Virginian* (1974).

Little scholarly writing has been devoted to Smith. Critical sources include Gregory Curtis, "The Dream House of H. Allen Smith," *Texas Monthly*, Feb. 1976; Bergen Evans's introduction to the anthology *The World, the Flesh, and H. Allen Smith* (1954); Malcolm Hayward's entry on Smith in the *Encyclopedia of American Humorists*, ed. Steven H. Gale (1980); Elton Miles, ed., introduction to *The Best of H. Allen Smith* (1972); Merle Miller, "Mr. Smith, and Not So Funny," *Saturday Review of Literature*, 3 Aug. 1946, p. 19; and Joe Nawrozki, "Humor Was Serious Stuff for Smith," *Baltimore News-American*, 29 Feb. 1976. Robert Van Gelder's "An Interview with Mr. H. Allen Smith" is in the *New York*

Times Book Review, 24 Aug. 1941, pp. 2, 22. Obituaries are in the *New York Times*, 25 Feb. 1976, the *Washington Post*, 26 Feb. 1976, and *Publishers Weekly*, 22 Mar. 1976, among other print sources.

STEVEN H. GALE

SMITH, Hannah Whitall (7 Feb. 1832–1 May 1911), author and evangelist, was born in Philadelphia, Pennsylvania, the daughter of birthright Quakers John Mickle Whitall, a glass manufacturer, and Mary Tatum. An idyllic home life and an incessant quest for spiritual truth and experiential religion marked her youth and shaped all of her life thereafter. The first-born child in a prominent Friends family, her persistent vivacity and curiosity made her a lifelong leader within an influential circle of family and friends. A basic education in the Friends' schools in the Philadelphia area whetted her appetite for higher education at a time when society in general gave her little encouragement.

Hannah married Quaker Robert Pearsall Smith in June 1851. Marriage and the birth of her first child followed by six more children brought an end to her plans for further education in spite of her husband's strong affirmation of her goals. Only three of their seven children lived into adulthood: Mary Logan Whitall (1864), wife first of Frank Costelloe, Irish barrister and member of Parliament, and later married to art historian Bernard Berenson; Logan Pearsall (1865), Oxford professor and creator of the literary genre trivia; and Alys Pearsall (1867), first wife of Bertrand Russell.

Just as he had with her educational dreams, Smith's husband fully sympathized with her quest for spiritual fulfillment and religious service. Both professed experiences of personal spiritual conversion in the religious revival of 1857–1858. Serious doctrinal schisms in Quakerism in the first half of the nineteenth century and the negative response of much of the Philadelphia Yearly Meeting of Friends to the New American revival movements led both Smith and her husband to resign their membership in the Society of Friends in 1859.

Throughout the two decades of her evangelistic period, Smith never joined any other church, but eventually rejoined the Friends through the Baltimore (Md.) Yearly Meeting. In the interim of her evangelistic ministry, her spiritual affinities lay most strongly with Methodism and its doctrines of assurance of salvation and the entire sanctification of the Christian life. She had been introduced to Methodist holiness teaching during the Civil War by Methodist workers of the Millville, New Jersey, Whithall-Tatum glass factory managed by her husband. Both she and her husband testified to experiencing the Methodist "second blessing" of perfection in love at the first national holiness camp meetings, which became the centers for Methodist promotion of Christian holiness at the war's end. Their personal enthusiasm and social prominence made them, although lay persons, much sought after speakers within a growing network of revival services and summer camp meetings, sponsored by the area's churches and developing social agencies such as the Young Men's Christian Associations.

Smith expanded her holiness/higher-life ministry through writing books and publishing numerous articles for the religious periodicals that supported the holiness revival. The circulation of *The Record of a Happy Life: Being Memorials of Franklin Whitall Smith* (1873) in England and Europe brought their message of victorious Christian living to the attention of evangelical leaders there. This account of the life, spirituality, and untimely death of her son Franklin Whitall, while a student at Princeton, helped to prepare the way for a surge of holiness evangelism in England and across Europe. Princeton theologian Benjamin B. Warfield, a critic of the movement, called it the most unusual Christian evangelistic activity since the time of the Apostles.

In 1874 Smith joined her husband in England where he had become deeply involved in a series of seemingly spontaneous and dramatic ecumenical holiness renewal meetings where clergy and lay persons of the Church of England and the free churches gathered to hear the Smiths' message of Christian consecration and sanctification by faith, not works. The culmination of these meetings for the promotion of holiness in the churches was the Brighton Convention in May 1875, when more than 8,000 clergy and laypeople from England and Europe met for ten days of teaching and worship. Evangelist Dwight L. Moody judged the Brighton meeting to be one of the most critical Christian meetings ever to be held. The English Keswick movement and the German Fellowship movement brought the revival's influence to the established and free churches of England and the Continent. The most popular sessions of the Brighton Convention were those where Smith preached her practical secrets of the happy Christian life to audiences of five thousand or more, mostly clergymen who theologically rejected the right of a woman to preach. She became known as "the angel of the churches."

Smith's book, *The Christian's Secret of a Happy Life* (1859), which outlined her theme of daily Christian victory by faith and the power of the Holy Spirit, rapidly established itself as one of the classics of Christian devotional literature. In the first hundred years after its initial publication, *The Christian's Secret* went through more than thirty different English editions besides numerous foreign language editions. After reading the book, philosopher William James wrote to Hannah that if he were a Christian, he would like to be one of that sort. At least seventeen other books followed over her lifetime, most of them concerned with Christian living and devotion; in others she outlined her views on motherhood and recorded family biography.

Smith's husband's fall from grace following rumors of moral and doctrinal deviance, which spread immediately after the success of the Brighton Convention in 1875, ended their evangelistic ministry in England. Although Smith admitted to the tendency toward looseness of doctrinal statements, both she and her husband denied any actual moral lapses. Even though upon their return to America they found the rumored failures had not diminished their opportunities for ministry there, the events effectively ended their American revivalist ministry as well. Her husband never recovered from these affronts, but Smith turned her attention to her family and reform movements such as the Women's Christian Temperance Union (WCTU) with the same verve and vigor that had always characterized her revivalism. She served as one of the first presidents of the Pennsylvania state chapter of the union and later became the first national superintendent of its evangelistic arm. A lifelong friend and supporter of Frances Willard, Smith was instrumental in placing her in the presidency of the movement and was a regular speaker at its national conventions.

Smith's reform interest continued when the family moved to England in 1888 after the birth of daughter Mary's first child there in 1887. Smith and her daughter Alys were instrumental in working with Willard of the WCTU and Lady Somerset, leader of the British temperance movement, in creating an international women's temperance union. She supported the temperance movement's broader concerns for woman suffrage. Always in good health until the last few years of her life Smith maintained a full schedule speaking on behalf of English reform concerns of the late nineteenth century from women's rights to animal rights. Over the same period she was a frequent speaker in Quaker and other churches, advocating evangelical religion as well as political and social issues. Confinement to a wheelchair in her later years did not completely quash her reformist activism; she had her granddaughter wheel her to the House of Parliament when a vote on woman suffrage was to be taken. Smith died at Iffly Place at her son Logan's home near Oxford, England.

• The largest collection of Smith and Whitall family papers and memorabilia is in the library of Indiana University, Bloomington. Papers and letters concerning Smith's revivalism, religious writings, and correspondence with Frances Willard and WCTU activities are in the library of Asbury Theological Seminary, Wilmore, Ky. The Asbury collection is described and illustrated in *The Asbury Seminarian* 38, no. 2 (Spring 1983). The Library of Congress holds some letters in the Logan Pearsall Smith Collection.

Smith's great-granddaughter Barbara Strachey (Halpern)'s *Remarkable Relations: The Story of the Pearsall Smith Family* (1980) provides a comprehensive family history and a complete bibliography of Smith's writings and the numerous other published resources related to her life. Especially useful among these are Smith's autobiography, *The Unselfishness of God and How I Discovered It* (1903); *A Religious Rebel: Selected Letters of Hannah Whitall Smith* (1949), edited by her son Logan Pearsall Smith; her granddaughter Ray Strachey's *A Quaker Grandmother* (1914); and Robert A. Parker's *The Transatlantic Smiths* (1959).

The period of the Smith's higher-life evangelism that produced her devotional classic, *The Christian's Secret* (1875),

and brought her international fame is outlined and analyzed in Benjamin B. Warfield, *Perfectionism* (1934), and Melvin E. Dieter, *The Holiness Revival of the Nineteenth Century* (1996).

MELVIN E. DIETER

SMITH, Harold Dewey (6 June 1898–23 Jan. 1947), public administrator, was born near Haven, Kansas, the son of James William Smith and Miranda Ebling, wheat farmers. Smith worked his way through high school, joined the navy during World War I, and then enrolled in the University of Kansas. He graduated in 1922 with a bachelor's degree in engineering. He had briefly contemplated going to China as a missionary, but his political science professor persuaded him to pursue a career in government service instead. Therefore, in 1923 Smith accepted a graduate assistantship in the new public administration program at the University of Michigan, completing his master's degree there in 1925. The following year Smith married Lillian Mayer; they had five children, four of whom survived childhood.

Smith first worked as a city reformer with the Detroit Bureau of Government Research and next served as a consultant for the League of Kansas Municipalities. When the Michigan Municipal League was founded in 1928, Smith became its director. As head of that organization until 1937, he edited the *Michigan Municipal Review*, wrote city charters, improved municipal purchasing systems, and advised city officials on economy and efficiency measures. He also brought municipal administration and university expertise closer together, especially after he became, in 1934, chief of the University of Michigan's Bureau of Government. In 1937 Governor Frank Murphy, who earlier as mayor of Detroit had relied on Smith's counsel, appointed Smith Michigan budget director. Murphy wanted Smith to streamline and modernize the budgeting and accounting practices of the state, which Smith proceeded to do.

Smith's achievements as Murphy's budget director brought him to Franklin D. Roosevelt's attention. In April 1939 the president signed the Reorganization Act, granting him limited authority to reconfigure the executive branch. Among the changes Roosevelt desired was the creation of a more effective Budget Bureau, headed by a professional administrator rather than a partisan politician. Presidential adviser Louis Brownlow and Governor Murphy recommended Smith. In April Roosevelt called Smith to Washington and offered him the job. When Smith hesitated, saying he still had bridges to burn in Michigan, Roosevelt handed him a match and commanded, "Burn them."

As federal budget director Smith, with Brownlow and several others, drafted the reorganization plan that Roosevelt accepted in September 1939. The plan established the Executive Office of the President, with the Budget Bureau as the principal agency within it. The bureau coordinated and compiled the budget, predicted its effects on the economy, and supervised all government expenditures, and under Smith's leadership it took on a host of additional responsibilities.

Every bill passed by Congress was analyzed by the bureau, which recommended either the president's signature or veto. All proposals from the executive branch to Congress had to clear the Budget Bureau first, and the bureau drafted Roosevelt's executive orders. Indeed, the bureau often influenced Roosevelt to create wartime agencies, delegate power, and shift bureaus among departments in and out of Washington to increase efficiency. During the war years, the bureau acted as the president's principal staff. As its importance grew, so did its ranks, from 50 employees in 1939 to more than 500 in 1946.

Smith's key role in the administration arose from more than the powers of the bureau he headed. Roosevelt's speech writer Robert E. Sherwood observed that there was "no one whose judgment and integrity and downright common sense the President trusted more completely" than Smith's (Sherwood, p. 72). Roosevelt depended on the deliberate, meticulous, scrupulously nonpartisan Smith to mediate quarrels between warring cabinet heads; fire nonperforming officials, something the president could never manage to do; and trim wasteful, extravagant budgetary requests from departments.

Smith saw as his primary function securing the greatest possible economy and efficiency in the conduct of the government. However, he was also sensitive to the social impact of budgetary and fiscal policies. With mixed success, he urged Roosevelt and Congress during World War II to take stronger anti-inflation measures, including larger tax increases, income tax withholding from pay checks, price and wage controls, and compulsory savings plans. He did not hold balanced budgets sacred, believing federal spending and taxing should be used to moderate business cycles. On the other hand, he differed with those who refused to worry about huge deficits "because we owe the money to ourselves." When asked to characterize his politics, Smith said he was "an independent Republican with Socialist leanings who frequently votes Democratic."

Smith continued as budget director under Harry S. Truman, resigning in June 1946 to become vice president of the International Bank for Reconstruction and Development (World Bank). In his letter of resignation to President Truman, Smith explained that his "keen interest in the international field" and the excellent salary induced him to take the position. He added, "had this opportunity not arisen it would only have been a short time until existing limitations on the salaries of public officials would have forced me out of the Federal Government." While presiding over greater federal expenditures between 1941 and 1946 than the government had made in total from 1789 to 1941, Smith earned $10,000 a year.

When Eugene Meyer, head of the World Bank, quit in December 1946, Smith stepped in as acting director. One month later Smith suffered a fatal heart attack at his farm near Culpeper, Virginia. His skill in public administration and courage in resisting unreasonable budgetary requests enabled the U.S. government during World War II to function with greater effectiveness and economy.

• The Harold Dewey Smith Papers are in the Franklin D. Roosevelt Library at Hyde Park, N.Y. Smith appears often in the oral histories of other members of the Roosevelt administration in the Columbia University Oral History Collection (COHO), especially the Reminiscences of Bernard L. Gladieux and the Reminiscences of Claude R. Wickard. Smith wrote one book, *The Management of Your Government* (1945). His many articles include "The Bureau of the Budget," *Public Administration Review* (Winter 1941): 106–13; "Our 300-Billion-Dollar Headache," *American Magazine*, June 1945, pp. 42–43, 114–17; "Trifles that Smother the President," *American Magazine*, June 1946, pp. 23, 121–26; and "Government Must Have and Pay for Good Men," *New York Times Magazine*, 14 July 1946, pp. 9, 34–36. Smith's roles in the 1939 reorganization of the executive branch and his wartime leadership of the Budget Bureau are discussed in James MacGregor Burns, *Roosevelt: The Soldier of Freedom, 1940–1945* (1970), Robert E. Sherwood, *Roosevelt and Hopkins* (1948), Louis Brownlow, *A Passion for Anonymity* (1958), and Richard Polenberg, *Reorganizing Roosevelt's Government, 1936–1939* (1966). Biographical information and thoughtful evaluation of Smith's career and importance are in two obituary articles, Brownlow, "Harold D. Smith," *American Political Science Review* (May 1947): 327–30; and Paul H. Appleby, "Harold D. Smith—Public Administrator," *Public Administration Review* (Spring 1947): 77–81. Another obituary is in the *New York Times*, 24 Jan. 1947.

BARBARA BLUMBERG

SMITH, Harry Clay (28 Jan. 1863–10 Dec. 1941), newspaper editor and politician, was born in Clarksburg, West Virginia, the son of John Smith and Sarah (maiden name unknown), occupations unknown. Accompanied by his sister and widowed mother, he came to Cleveland in 1866 and remained there for the rest of his life. A self-taught cornet player, Smith played in several bands while attending high school. After graduating in 1883 he and three friends established the *Cleveland Gazette*. Smith, who remained a lifelong bachelor, soon bought out his partners and became sole proprietor and editor. The first significant African-American newspaper in the city, the *Gazette* was published weekly by Smith until his death, when the newspaper went out of existence. Known for its militant editorial stance on racial issues, the *Gazette* circulated widely throughout Ohio before World War I. After 1917 its influence steadily declined as a result of competition from other African-American newspapers in Cleveland.

Smith was one of the most eloquent, most consistently militant race leaders of his era. Throughout his career, he used the *Gazette* as a forum to attack segregation and racial discrimination in all its forms. He continually urged blacks to use political pressure, legal action, or boycotts in the struggle against racism. Smith was a leader in the successful campaign to end segregated schools in Ohio in 1887. He was a founding member of the Afro-American League in 1890 and was one of the first to criticize Booker T. Washington when, in his famous Atlanta Cotton Exposition address of 1895, the headmaster of Tuskegee Institute seemed to accept the validity of racial segregation in the South.

Smith entered Republican politics in 1885 when, in return for the editor's support of Joseph B. Foraker for governor, Smith was appointed deputy state inspector of oils, a patronage position he held for four years. He was elected three times to the Ohio General Assembly, serving during 1894–1898 and 1900–1902. In the state legislature, Smith became known as a vigorous advocate of civil rights legislation. He was one of the main sponsors of the Ohio Civil Rights Act of 1894, which prohibited discrimination in public accommodations, and the Anti–Mob Violence Act of 1896, one of the first state antilynching laws.

In the late 1890s Smith gradually became alienated from the mainstream of the Republican party as well as from other, more conservative African-American politicians in the state. Though formally remaining in the party, Smith grew increasingly independent and sometimes refused to support Republican candidates—an unusual position for an African-American editor at that time. In 1908 the *Gazette* urged blacks to vote for "anyone but [William Howard] Taft," primarily in protest against Theodore Roosevelt's summary dismissal, two years before, of a black regiment in Brownsville, Texas, on unproven charges of rioting.

Smith had participated actively in the anti-Bookerite Niagara Movement of 1905 and was named to the National Association for the Advancement of Colored People's select Committee of One Hundred soon after that organization was established in 1910. In 1912 he led an unsuccessful battle against the establishment of the Phillis Wheatley Association, a facility for homeless African-American girls, calling it a "jim crow hotel." From 1915 to 1917 he led a campaign to block the showing of the racist film *The Birth of a Nation* in Cleveland. When white mobs attacked black residents of Chicago and other cities during World War I, Smith urged blacks to arm themselves and retaliate if necessary. He was subsequently investigated by the young J. Edgar Hoover, who in his 1919 Justice Department report on black radicalism labeled the editorial stand of the *Gazette* "vicious."

By the time of the "Great Migration" of African Americans to northern industrial centers (1916–1919), Smith was one of a dwindling group of black leaders who adamantly refused to distinguish between segregation undertaken by the state and self-segregation by private organizations founded by and on behalf of African Americans. Perhaps because as a young man Smith had studied and worked alongside whites on a basis of equality, he strongly opposed the trend toward self-help and racial solidarity that was becoming popular among other black leaders at the time. During the decade following World War I he opposed the creation of a separate black YMCA and vehemently attacked a proposal, which failed largely for lack of funds, to build a private hospital in Cleveland primarily for African Americans. Occasionally, Smith urged blacks to support black businesses, but this was virtually the only exception to a lifelong opposition to racial separatism of any kind. African Americans, the editor stated in 1914, should "be trying to wipe out color-lines, rather than be trying to multiply them."

In the early 1920s the administrations of Warren G. Harding and Calvin Coolidge angered Smith because of their military occupation of Haiti and refusal to end the segregation of African Americans in some departments of the federal government. In 1924 Smith opposed Coolidge and set up an Independent Colored Voters League to support Robert La Follette, the Progressive party presidential candidate. At the local and state level, too, Smith grew dissatisfied with the Republican party's declining interest in civil rights and its failure to support more blacks for public office. In 1921 he ran unsuccessfully for city council as an independent against Thomas Fleming, the only African-American member of the council at that time but a supporter of the city's dominant white machine. Smith also campaigned for the Republican nomination for secretary of state in 1920 and governor in 1922, 1924, 1926, and 1928. He received few votes but broke new ground by being the first African American to seek statewide office in Ohio. In the late 1920s and early 1930s Smith encouraged black insurgency in the local Republican party, but unlike most African Americans in the North he did not shift his allegiance from the Republican to the Democratic party during the depression. Franklin D. Roosevelt's failure to deal with segregation and lynching in the South kept Smith within the Republican fold for the remainder of his life. For Smith, racial issues had always taken precedence over economic ones.

Philosophically and personally, Smith had much in common with William Monroe Trotter, the editor of another African-American weekly, the Boston *Guardian*. Both men were uncompromising integrationists who refused to change with the times, and after World War I both found themselves increasingly relegated to the role of the principled but ineffective gadfly. Like Trotter, Smith was prone to personalize the struggle for racial equality. A rugged individualist who owned his own business, he was often reluctant to cooperate with other black leaders or organizations. Smith supported the formation of the NAACP, for example, but had little to do with the local Cleveland branch of the association, even when it supported his positions. Ironically, the same maverick traits that made Smith outspoken in the struggle for racial equality also restricted his ability to advance his own principles. He died in Cleveland.

• No collections of papers by Smith are known to exist. The most complete record of his views may be found in the editorials of the *Cleveland Gazette*, which were written by Smith. The best sources on his early life are the brief sketches in William J. Simmons, *Men of Mark: Eminent, Progressive, and Rising* (1887), and I. Garland Penn, *The Afro-American Press and Its Editors* (1891). Smith's career is discussed extensively in Russell H. Davis, *Black Americans in Cleveland* (1972), and Kenneth L. Kusmer, *A Ghetto Takes Shape: Black Cleveland,*

1870–1930 (1976). See also August Meier, *Negro Thought in America, 1880–1915* (1963), which places Smith in a national context.

KENNETH L. KUSMER

SMITH, Harry Pratt (18 Feb. 1895–12 Apr. 1972), pathologist and medical educator, was born in Johnson County, Iowa, the son of Walter Z. Smith and Estella M. Pratt, homestead farmers. He spent his boyhood on a farm near Gotebo, Oklahoma. He attended the University of California at Berkeley, receiving an A.B. in 1916, an M.S. in 1918, and an M.D. in 1921. In 1917 he met George H. Whipple, director of the George William Hooper Foundation for Medical Research at the University of California Medical School in San Francisco, and was appointed the same year a student fellow there. Besides participating in clinical activities, Smith conducted research on blood volume determinations; his findings were published in the *American Journal of Physiology* and earned him a reputation for quantitative experimental work.

After Smith's graduation from medical school, Johns Hopkins University appointed him assistant and then instructor in pathology. Prior to his appointment at Hopkins, he had conducted studies with A. Elmer Belt, H. R. Arnold, and E. Beatrice Carrier (later Seegal), at Long Lake in the Sierra Nevada of California, on high-altitude changes in blood volume. His early work demonstrated that an expanded blood volume at high altitudes was the result of an increase in red blood cell and hemoglobin volumes; this early work presaged later studies by others on erythropoietin. In 1923 Smith was awarded a one-year fellowship by the National Research Council and conducted chemical research at Columbia University and in Europe. After the fellowship, Whipple, who was now dean of the medical school at the University of Rochester, offered Smith a position there as an associate professor.

In 1930 the University of Iowa appointed Smith professor and chairman in the pathology department. He collected a group of students and fellows to study blood coagulation, including Kenneth M. Brinkhous, Edwin Theodore Mertz, Charles A. Owen, Jr., Walter Seegers, and Emory D. Warner. The Iowa group was one of the first modern American groups to conduct research on blood coagulation. Smith's approach to coagulation was quantitative and practical, not theoretical: the Iowa group did not propose a theoretical scheme to explain blood clotting but instead undertook the purification and quantifying of known clotting factors from blood. The first factor purified to homogeneity was the clotting enzyme thrombin, along with its inactive precursor prothrombin. Smith's group developed a two-stage assay to measure accurately and reproducibly the amount of prothrombin in blood. The Iowa group was also responsible for identifying the importance of vitamin K in various bleeding disorders. Although Smith's group of researchers did not discover a new clotting factor, they did describe the presence of a cofactor in blood responsible for the anticoagulant action of heparin. Heparin cofactor was later identified as antithrombin III, according to Seeger's nomenclature. In 1941 Smith received the Ward Burdick Award from the American Society of Clinical Pathologists for his work in blood coagulation. With World War II the Iowa clotting group disbanded; its members received academic posts around the country and continued to develop programs in blood coagulation.

In 1945 Smith was appointed the Delafield Professor and chair of pathology at Columbia University's College of Physicians and Surgeons. During his tenure at Columbia he was also head of the Presbyterian Hospital's pathology service. He initially continued research in blood coagulation at Columbia but shortly turned his attention to administrative and committee duties.

In 1960 Smith retired from Columbia to become archivist and librarian for the American Society of Clinical Pathologists in Chicago, where he was involved in the development of information systems using computers. He also served as president of the society (1957–1958) and was given its Distinguished Service Award (1968). In 1974 the society inaugurated a memorial lectureship and the H. P. Smith Award in his honor. The following year, he left his post at the society and became associated with the pathology department at the University of Missouri.

During the latter part of his career Smith was often a consultant on the legislative activities of the American Medical Association. He was active in a number of other societies, including the College of American Pathology, Association of Pathology and Bacteriology, Federation of the American Societies for Experimental Biology and Medicine, and Physiology Society. He was also a member of the American Society for Experimental Pathology and served as its secretary-treasurer (1940–1942) and president (1948). He died in Columbia, Missouri.

Smith never married. His legacy was his research and the students he taught and placed in influential academic positions. Of Smith's impact on American pathology, Brinkhous wrote, "His earlier experiences in teaching, in science, and in the administrative problems in academia made him unusually well qualified for his role in helping upgrade clinical pathology to a major medical specialty undergirded by a firm scientific basis" (p. 608). As for Smith's personal attributes: "In spite of his attainments, he was a modest and almost shy individual. He was sensitive and generous, and would often give credit to colleagues rather than take personal credit" (p. 608).

• The Harry Pratt Smith Collection is housed at the Augustus C. Long Health Sciences Library, Columbia University, N.Y.; another significant collection of Smith material is at the College of American Pathologists, Northfield, Ill. For biographical information on Smith, see Kenneth M. Brinkhous, "Harry P. Smith (1895–1972)," *American Journal of Clinical Pathology* 63 (1975): 605–8; Charles A. Owen, Jr., "H. P. Smith's Place in the History of Blood Coagulation," *American*

Journal of Clinical Pathology 81 (1984): 424–26; and George W. Corner, *George Hoyt Whipple and His Friends: The Life-Story of a Nobel Prize Pathologist* (1963).

JAMES A. MARCUM

SMITH, Henry Boynton (21 Nov. 1815–7 Feb. 1877), theologian, was born in Portland, Maine, the son of Henry Smith, a merchant, and Arixene Southgate, and grew up in a well-to-do Unitarian home. At Bowdoin College he underwent a conversion experience that led him to identify with New England Calvinism. After graduating in 1834 he studied theology a year each at Andover Theological Seminary and at Bangor Theological Seminary. He then tutored for a year at Bowdoin and spent three years studying philosophy, theology, and church history at Halle and Berlin. In 1842, after teaching again at Bowdoin he was ordained in the Congregational ministry at West Amesbury, Massachusetts, where he served a congregation until 1847. In 1843 he married Elizabeth Lee Allen, with whom he had four children. From 1847 to 1850 he was professor of philosophy at Amherst College.

The major phase of his career began in 1850 when he moved to Union Theological Seminary in New York City, where he served as professor of church history until 1855 and then as professor of systematic theology until his resignation, due to ill health, in 1874. Union was a seminary of the New School Presbyterian church, to which Smith transferred his ministerial credentials. In 1863 he was chosen as moderator of the General Assembly of the New School denomination and during the succeeding years was the leading figure promoting the New School's reunion with the Old School Presbyterian church, which was consummated in 1869. In 1859 he founded the *American Theological Review*, which he edited under its various titles until 1874. He died in New York City.

Smith's reputation as one of the leading American academics of his day rested mainly on his original and engaging work as a teacher and essayist. Converted to Calvinism in an era marked by intense theological debates, Smith was renowned for his mediating positions and conciliatory temper. He was an admirer of Jonathan Edwards (1703–1758), but his traditionalist Calvinism was tempered by a romantic spirit, which he developed in Germany under the influence of the pietist theologian Friedrich August Gottreu Tholuck of Halle. Rather than emphasizing, as did the contending American Calvinists, either the sovereignty of God or a system of morality as the organizing principle of theology, Smith emphasized the incarnation of Christ as a mediating principle. The Christian affirmation of the infinite God entering history, he believed, was the key to resolving the contentions between faith and modern philosophy and to seeing how natural historical development could contain divine meaning. Smith thus anticipated some themes in the liberal Protestantism of the next generation, but he did so within the framework of a moderate Edwardsean orthodoxy and a traditional view of the inspiration and authority of Scripture. Accordingly his work suffered the fate of many mediators: in the fierce debates over theological liberalism in the next era he was considered too conservative by the liberals and too moderate by the conservatives.

• Elizabeth L. Smith, ed., *Henry Boynton Smith: His Life and Work* (1881), and Lewis F. Stearns, *Henry Boynton Smith* (1892), contain considerable correspondence of Smith as well as other biographical information. Besides translations, Smith published his *History of the Church of Christ in Chronological Tables* (1859), mainly charts. His *Apologetics* (1882), *Introduction to Christian Theology* (1883), and *System of Christian Theology* (1884) were compiled by William S. Karr from his lectures. Secondary works about Smith include William K. B. Stoever, "Henry Boynton Smith and the German Theology of History," *Union Seminary Quarterly Review* 24 (Fall 1968): 69–89; Richard A. Muller, "Henry Boynton Smith: Christocentric Theologian," *Journal of Presbyterian History* 61 (Winter 1983): 429–44; John R. Wiers, "Henry B. Smith, Theologian of New School Presbyterianism," in *Pressing toward the Mark*, ed. Charles G. Dennison and Richard C. Gamble (1986), pp. 183–99; and George M. Marsden, *The Evangelical Mind and the New School Presbyterian Experience* (1970).

GEORGE M. MARSDEN

SMITH, Henry Nash (29 Sept. 1906–6 June 1986), literary critic and historian, was born in Dallas, Texas, the son of Loyd Bond Smith, an accountant, and Elizabeth Nash. He took to reading at an early age and gained broad exposure to the classics through a Harvard-educated uncle's library. British and American writers appealed to him the most, and he entered Southern Methodist University at age sixteen to study literature. After graduation in 1926 he moved on to Harvard for a year of graduate study.

On his return to Texas in 1927 Smith taught English literature at Southern Methodist and became involved in the production of the *Southwest Review*, a regional literary quarterly. Working with editor John H. McGinnis, as well as writers such as J. Frank Dobie, Howard Mumford Jones, and Mary Austin, Smith found a forum for exploring his ideas about the Southwest and literature and a venue for gaining writing experience. Those associated with the *Review* believed that the Southwest possessed a distinctive culture but also one with links to broader American and British literary traditions. They were particularly intent on distinguishing southwestern culture and writing from that of the South, which was then exemplified by the southern agrarians, a group of writers headed by Allen Tate who promoted values associated with an agrarian ideology and emphasis on regionalism. In addition to contributing articles and writing book reviews, Smith served as both associate editor and editor at various times between 1927 and 1937. Also, while at Southern Methodist, Smith married Elinor Lucas. They would eventually have three children.

While Smith was teaching at Southern Methodist, James Conant Bryant, president of Harvard, created an American civilization program and appointed Howard Mumford Jones as its head. The interdisciplinary nature of this program as well as his previous association with Jones lured Smith back to Harvard, where he pursued a doctorate in literature and history under the tutelage of Jones and Frederick Meek, Harvard's historian of the West.

After receiving his degree in 1940 he again returned to Southern Methodist University but remained only a year before accepting appointment as professor of history and literature at the University of Texas in Austin. Encountering political problems while at Texas he took leaves in 1945 and 1946 to teach at Harvard and do research in the Huntington Library. In 1947 he moved to the University of Minnesota to become part of its fledgling American studies program.

While at Minnesota Smith published *Virgin Land: The American West as Symbol and Myth* (1950), an expanded version of his Harvard dissertation (encompassing ten years of additional research and writing) and what would become his most widely known book. Smith acknowledged that his interest in southwestern culture and interdisciplinary aims grew into *Virgin Land*. As he stated, "I simply followed out, if you like, some exploration of my own identity as a Texan, a Southwesterner with no ties to the East" and "tr[ied] to place myself within the total framework of the whole American cultural history" (Forrey, p. 191). In this study he explored myths associated with the West and analyzed them both in terms of their social, political, and economic contexts and in terms of the American values and beliefs they expressed. He identified three patterns for the most common myths: belief in a Northwest Passage to the Far East; belief in western mountain men as heirs of James Fenimore Cooper's "Leatherstocking"; and the perception of the West as the "garden of the world." Smith noted the presence of these mythological themes in many forms of written expression from scholarly tracts to dime novels and claimed that, while often not truly reflective of reality, they influenced the historical development of the West. Portrayals of the West as a lush green space, for example, while contradicted by the relatively barren plains and deserts, drew people to move there. Smith also pointed out that adherence to these myths by scholars such as Frederick Jackson Turner ignored social and economic realities and limited interpretations of America's past. By bringing social and economic issues to the forefront, he also challenged the "safety valve" theory, which asserted that the open spaces of the West gave Americans alternatives to laboring in factories and crowded cities in the East and thus solved social tensions inherent in industrialization. The book was widely reviewed and praised by both historians and literary scholars. Historian Richard Hofstadter noted the book's "structural complexity" and "profound scholarship" and called it "one of those seminal books that grow more capacious the more the reader brings to them" (Hofstader, *American Quarterly* 2 [1950]: 279). It was awarded the Bancroft Prize from Columbia University and the American Historical Association's John H. Dunning Prize in United States History.

In 1953 Smith accepted a position on the faculty at the University of California, Berkeley, and an editorship of the Mark Twain Papers. He shifted away from American studies, and while there he chaired the English department from 1957 to 1961 and was president of the Modern Language Association in the 1968–1969 academic year. His work on the Twain papers is highly regarded, especially that on the Mark Twain–William Dean Howells correspondence. His interest in interdisciplinary methodologies continued in the attention he paid to the influence of historical context on writers such as Mark Twain in *Mark Twain: The Development of a Writer* (1962) and Herman Melville, Walt Whitman, and Nathaniel Hawthorne in *Democracy and the Novel: Popular Resistance to Classic American Writers* (1978). Smith retired from Berkeley in 1974 but continued to study and write. He died twelve years later in an automobile accident in Nevada.

During his career as a scholar, Smith frequently took stands supporting academic freedom. At Southern Methodist University he was almost fired for arranging publication of an early William Faulkner short story that was considered obscene by the head of the English department. His later departure from Texas took place in the context of political conflicts, and at the request of students he made a public statement of his views. In the late 1940s, at Minnesota, he wrote in defense of the right of faculty to join the Communist party without losing their jobs, and later, at Berkeley, he protested loyalty oath requirements for faculty and mediated free speech movement controversies.

Henry Nash Smith trained many American studies, literature, and history scholars who have become influential in their fields. His most important legacy, though, is *Virgin Land*. Although criticized on many fronts, including its failure to consider Native Americans and women, *Virgin Land* remains a landmark work in American studies and the historiography of the West. This innovative monograph brought new attention to studies of the West and introduced methodologies that would establish models for future work in American studies. Smith's methods of examining myths and symbols for meanings they may have in relation to the formation of culture gained adherents as well as critics and for a short time shaped some studies. Longer lasting results came from the interdisciplinary nature of Smith's approach, which utilized as sources elements of literary criticism, sociology, history, anthropology, analysis of rhetorical strategies, and diverse literatures (including scholarly works, advertising tracts, travel accounts, political speeches and writings, and dime novels).

• Smith's papers, comprising more than eight linear feet of correspondence, personal papers, and published and unpublished writings and research, are at the Bancroft Library at the University of California in Berkeley. Biographical material dealing with Smith can be found in Robert Forrey, "Interviews on American Studies: Henry Nash Smith," *Amerikastudien/American Studies* 22 (1977): 190–97, and Richard Bridgman, "The American Studies of Henry Nash Smith," *American Scholar* 56 (Spring 1987): 259–68. Two biographical articles and a bibliography of Smith's publications can be found in Beverly Voloshin, ed., *American Literature, Culture and Ideology: Essays in Memory of Henry Nash Smith* (1990).

KATHRYN WAGNILD FULLER

SMITH, Henry Preserved (23 Oct. 1847–26 Feb. 1927), clergyman and professor of biblical literature and the history of religions, was born in Troy, Ohio, the son of Preserved Smith, a businessman, and Lucy Mayo. After attending Marietta College (1864–1866), Smith graduated from Amherst College (B.A., 1869) and Lane Theological Seminary in Cincinnati (B.D., 1872). He was licensed to preach by the Presbyterian church in 1871. After studying at the University of Berlin (1872–1874), he was ordained in 1875 by the Presbytery of Dayton. He was married to Anna Macneale in 1877; they had four children, of whom two survived to adulthood. After teaching church history (1874–1875) and Hebrew (1875–1876) at Lane, Smith studied modern biblical criticism under Franz Delitzsch at the University of Leipzig (1876–1877) in preparation to teach Old Testament literature. Between 1877 and 1893 he was a professor of Old Testament at Lane.

By temperament and training Smith was theologically conservative and thus initially reluctant to promote the critical study of Scripture, preferring to approach the text from a grammatical and expository point of view that bypassed embarrassing questions about authorship, sources, and historical accuracy raised by the new higher criticism. Intellectual honesty, however, gradually led him to acknowledge the inadequacy of traditional views of the Bible. In 1882 he published a rather cautious defense of Julius Wellhausen's critical treatment of the Old Testament his *Geschichte Israels*. There, Smith acknowledges the composite character of the Pentateuch and of the writings attributed to Isaiah, and he notes irreconcilable discrepancies between the historical accounts given in Kings and Chronicles. He also argues that the historical character of the biblical texts requires the interpreter of Scripture to adhere to the same principles that govern the analysis of noncanonical literature. Yet a basically evangelical perspective is reflected in Smith's fairly cautious way of engaging in literary-historical criticism: for instance, he continues to believe in miracles and refuses to reject biblical accounts of miraculous phenomena a priori. As early as 1882 some conservatives raised questions about Smith's orthodoxy. The crisis was postponed, however, for a decade.

On 20 January 1891, Charles Augustus Briggs, biblical scholar at Union Theological Seminary in New York City and prominent spokesman for the critical view of Scripture, recently appointed to the Edward Robinson chair in biblical theology, delivered an inaugural address defending biblical criticism in ways that traditionalists in the Presbytery of New York found offensive. Smith's vigorous defense of Briggs at the General Assembly of 1891 so inflamed conservatives in the Presbytery of Cincinnati that they brought charges of heresy against him for denying the verbal inspiration and inerrancy of the Bible.

At his trial, which began on 14 November 1892, Smith contended that the theory of verbal inspiration was neither required by the Westminster Confession nor supported by an honest scientific analysis of the text. By a vote of 31 to 26, the presbytery convicted Smith of heresy, and on 13 December 1892 it suspended him from the Presbyterian ministry. An appeal to the Synod of Ohio was rejected on 13 October 1893. A further appeal to the General Assembly of 1894 hinged on the question of whether a belief in the inerrancy of the lost original autographs of Scripture should be required for ministerial status. Criticizing the conservatives' preoccupation with the autographs, Smith sought to demonstrate that the inerrantists required far more than the historic Reformed confessions had affirmed. By a vote of 396 to 102 the General Assembly rejected his appeal.

By January 1893 Smith's position at Lane was clearly untenable, and he tendered his resignation. Until January 1898 he held no official position either in church or in academe: he devoted these years to research and writing before becoming associate pastor and professor of biblical literature at Amherst College (1898–1906). In 1899 Smith was ordained by the Hampshire Association to the ministry of the Congregational church. From 1907 to 1913 he taught Old Testament literature and the history of religions at Meadville Theological Seminary in western Pennsylvania.

Smith's *Old Testament History* (1903) reflects his debt to the modern biblical critics. In it he argues that the biblical texts contain abundant evidence of adaptations to changing circumstances (as seen in redactions and interpolations). He calls for selectivity in the use of biblical sources and for a frank recognition that only varying degrees of probability could be accorded to factual claims made in the Bible. Biblical "histories," he stresses, are not historical in the modern sense of that word; their aim was not to provide an objective description of past events but rather to make some moral or theological point. Smith also presents Hebrew religion in the context of other religious beliefs and practices in the ancient Near East (noting, for instance, that the biblical account of the Flood was clearly modeled after an earlier Babylonian myth).

A comparative, contextual methodology also shapes his treatment of the Bible in *The Religion of Israel* (1914). Here Smith argues for a "historico-genetic" treatment of Scripture: he views the Bible not as a static deposit but as a living, adapting, evolving organism bearing the indelible imprint of political, social, and economic changes within the environment that produced it. A cautious, moderate approach is evident in his warning against too great a skepticism concerning the historical value of the biblical text; at the same time, he does not hesitate to recognize the presence of mythological elements in the biblical narratives.

In 1913 Smith became chief librarian at Union Theological Seminary, where he served until his retirement in 1925. He died two years later in Pough-keepsie, New York. Smith played a pivotal role in introducing modern methods of biblical study to an American audience, and his work influenced several generations of American scholars. Both by words and by example, his defense of freedom in scholarly inquiry marked a significant chapter in the struggle for liberty of conscience in American religion.

• Smith's cautious early defense of the biblical higher criticism is summarized in "Critical Theories of Julius Wellhausen," *Presbyterian Review* 3 (Apr. 1882): 357–88. Other important works include *Inspiration and Inerrancy* (1893), *The Bible and Islam* (1897), *A Critical and Exegetical Commentary on the Books of Samuel* (1899), *Essays in Biblical Interpretation* (1921), and his autobiography, *The Heretic's Defense* (1921). A sympathetic review of Smith's contributions as a scholar and as a teacher is found in Julius A. Bewer, "Henry Preserved Smith," *American Journal of Semitic Languages and Literatures* 43 (July 1927): 249–54. For an analysis of the Smith case in the context of the evolution of Presbyterian responses to modernity, see Lefferts A. Loetscher, *The Broadening Church* (1954), pp. 63–68. An obituary is in the *New York Times*, 27 Feb. 1927.

JOHN L. FARTHING

SMITH, Hezekiah (21 Apr. 1737–24 Jan. 1805), Baptist clergyman and missionary, was born in Hempstead, Long Island, New York, the son of Peter Smith and Rebecca Nichols, probably farmers. The family soon moved to Morris County, New Jersey, where in February 1756 Hezekiah repudiated the family's Church of England affiliation to receive baptism at the hands of Baptist minister John Gano. Experiencing a call to preach himself, Smith enrolled at the first Baptist academy founded in the colonies, directed by the Reverend Isaac Eaton in Hopewell, New Jersey. After three years of study, he entered the College of New Jersey (now Princeton University) as a sophomore; he graduated in 1762.

Inspired to spread the word, within a year Smith traveled more than 4,000 miles and preached 173 sermons, besides "exhortations and expositions" too numerous to record, in a journey southward (*Journal*, 27 Sept. 1764). Ordained on 20 September 1763, he ministered to the First Baptist Church of Charleston, South Carolina, before moving to the small town of Cashaway in the Pee Dee region. Slaveowners and future Regulators comprised significant portions of his audiences.

Returning north in 1764, Smith assisted his friend James Manning in founding the College of Rhode Island (now Brown University). He served as one of twelve fellows of the college from 1765 until his death forty years later and raised £4,000 for it through his letters and future speaking trips to the South. In 1765 he began preaching to New England's first Baptist congregation outside Boston, in Haverhill, Massachusetts, and in November 1766 he was installed as pastor, a position he held for the rest of his life. In 1771 he married Hephzibah Kimball of Boxford, a wealthy woman. Smith did not see a conflict between God and

mammon: he owned several stores, a farm, an orchard, land in New Hampshire, and at least one slave, and he traveled in a chaise. Four of his six children survived to adulthood.

Smith worked indefatigably for the Baptists for all his adult life. In 1767 he was instrumental in organizing the Warren Association, which sought to preserve church discipline among New England Baptists. With Isaac Backus, to whom he is usually ranked second as a formative force in the development of the Baptist denomination, he petitioned and lobbied consistently for the separation of church and state. One of the first to volunteer as an army chaplain when the Revolution broke out, he remained with George Washington's army until 1780 and preached the sermon on the execution of British spy John André. In the later years of his life, he undertook at least one extended missionary journey a year, preaching about 150 sermons per year. He spoke in each of the original thirteen states and to Congregational, Presbyterian, and Episcopal as well as Baptist congregations. An observer noted that his powerful sermons "caused my very soul to tremble." Only a paralytic stroke a week before his death in Haverhill ended his labors.

Smith embodied the transformation of the Baptists from a sect of mostly poor folk to a respectable Protestant denomination. He was both an itinerant missionary and a pastor of a settled flock. Like many Baptists, he won favor for his enthusiastic support of the Revolution, and through his own schoolteaching and support of the College of Rhode Island he powerfully advocated an educated ministry. Smith's lifework also illustrates that faith was by no means sleeping between the First Great Awakening (1740s) and the Second (c. 1800).

• Smith's unpublished manuscripts are at the Andover-Newton Theological Seminary, Newton, Mass., and the Haverhill Public Library. Smith's extensive journal, vols. 1–11 at the Library of Congress and vol. 12 at the Massachusetts Historical Society, has been prepared with a biographical introduction by John D. Broome (master's thesis, Louisiana State Univ., 1973). See also James McLaughlin, *Princetonians 1748–1768* (1976), pp. 411–13, Reuben A. Guild, *Chaplain Smith and the Baptists: or, Life, Journals, Letters and Addresses of the Rev. Hezekiah Smith* (1885), and William G. McLoughlin, *New England Dissent, 1630–1833: The Baptists and the Separation of Church and State* (2 vols., 1971).

WILLIAM PENCAK

SMITH, Hilda Jane Worthington (1888–13 Mar. 1984), educator and government official, was born in New York City, the daughter of a well connected and established family. Smith received her education at private schools and at Bryn Mawr College, where she obtained an M.A. As part of her volunteer fieldwork, she worked with community suffrage groups and factory women at a Philadelphia settlement house.

In the 1920s and 1930s Smith became a leading representative of workers' education. At Bryn Mawr, Smith received the opportunity to head a pioneering project in women workers' education. Bryn Mawr president Martha Carey Thomas selected Smith for the position of college dean in 1919 and asked her to lead the Bryn Mawr summer school for women workers in 1921. From 1921 to 1936 Smith ran a summer program for about 100 women factory workers with support from the Women's Trade Union League (WTUL) and the Young Women's Christian Association; other schools soon copied the program. Smith believed that workers' education programs would have a positive effect "on the whole pattern of our national life in government and in politics, directing national planning along democratic lines for the benefit of all" (Kornbluh, p. 22).

Smith's interest in workers' education and its benefits for a democratic society got her involved with the New Deal, in which she soon played an important role. In 1933, after an interview with Harry Hopkins, Smith was offered a job with the Federal Emergency Relief Administration. Smith began her new job on 25 September 1933 as specialist in workers' education. In 1934 Smith initiated teacher training programs in the Emergency Education Program (EEP) of the Works Progress Administration (WPA) under the direction of Hopkins. The EEP began with six weeks of residential training for instructors and later allocated funds for state-based programs. In the spring of 1935 about 45,000 men and women were enrolled in 1,800 EEP classes, taught by 480 teachers in 570 communities. Lasting until 1942, the EEP often just barely survived opposition from other government agencies, critics of the New Deal, and parts of the labor movement.

Smith's approach to workers' education as preparation for citizenship meshed well with New Deal policy goals. But Smith also gained influence within the New Deal because of the background she shared with Eleanor Roosevelt and because of a larger network of progressive women reformers of which she was part, including Rose Schneiderman of the WTUL and the National Recovery Administration Labor Advisory Board; Grace Abbot, chief of the U.S. Children's Bureau; Secretary of Labor Frances Perkins; Mary Dewson, Democratic women's activist and member of the Social Security Board; and Marian Dickerman, Democratic party activist and educator. Moreover, Smith, Eleanor Roosevelt, Secretary Perkins, and Hopkins all had roots in the Settlement House movement of the Progressive era.

Among the most crucial problems Smith faced while running the EEP was the recruiting of suitable instructors for the workers' education programs, which prompted her to expand the EEP by including teacher training programs. Probably among Smith's most valuable contribution to the EEP, teacher education nonetheless suffered from problems of its own. Since funding for the trainees depended on eligibility, the teacher training programs deteriorated into relief programs, with trainees being often unsuitable for the job. Only in 1935, when a nationwide WPA teacher training program got under way, did the program begin to conform more closely to Smith's ideals.

After 1935 Smith's efforts faced increasing obstacles. The New Deal's critics gained ground, which led to cutbacks in programs. Smith's attempt to transform the EEP into a permanent effort at workers' education and teacher training came to naught when a bill for a four-year experiment failed to pass Congress in 1937. In 1939 the administration reorganized several New Deal programs. Florence Kerr, who had doubts about the value of Smith's teacher training and workers' education programs, became her supervisor. Kerr soon began cutting Smith's staff, and the EEP was redesigned as the Workers' Service Program, with less emphasis on education as preparation for citizenship. On 2 May 1942 the EEP was terminated when it was merged with the WPA War Services Division. Smith herself was relegated to a peripheral role, and her tenure with the WPA ended in September of that year.

Over the next eight years Smith labored for a federally funded Labor Extension Service, modeled on the Agricultural Extension Service and her earlier attempt to create a permanent workers' education program. In 1945, as part of a larger coalition of labor educators, university staff, and union leaders, Smith helped to form the National Committee for the Extension of Labor Education, which she also headed. The committee drafted the Labor Extension Act, which would have provided for federal funding for university and college-based labor education. However, the bill failed to pass Congress in 1950. From 1965 to 1972 Smith worked as an analyst for the Office of Economic Opportunity. She retired in 1972. She died in Washington, D.C. She never married.

• Smith's papers are located in the Franklin D. Roosevelt Library and the Schlesinger Library. Smith wrote extensively on workers' education. She wrote a book on workers' education for women at Bryn Mawr, *Women Workers at the Bryn Mawr Summer School* (1929), but most of her writings appeared in article form. The best account of her life can be found in Joyce L. Kornbluh, *A New Deal for Workers' Education: The Workers' Service Program, 1933–1942* (1987), which also served as the primary source for the above account. On Smith's role in the New Deal, see Susan Ware, *Beyond Suffrage: Women in the New Deal* (1981). A short biographical sketch is in Theodore Brameld, ed., *Workers' Education in the United States*, Fifth Yearbook of the John Dewey Society (1941). For an obituary, see the *New York Times*, 14 Mar. 1984.

THOMAS WINTER

SMITH, Hilton (27 Feb. 1912–18 Nov. 1983), baseball pitcher, nicknamed Smitty, was born Hilton Lee Smith in Giddings, Texas, the son of John Smith, a schoolteacher, and Mattie Smith. After attending Prairie View A&M College for two years, the hard-throwing right-hander started his baseball career with the Austin Senators in 1933. That same year he married Louise Humphrey, with whom he had two children, both sons. In 1934 Smith joined the Monroe (La.) Monarchs of the Negro Southern League, before touring with the Bismarck (N.D.) team in 1935 and 1936. While pitching for the Bismarck club, he compiled a

5–0 record in the highly regarded National Baseball Congress Semi-Pro Tournament held in Wichita, Kansas. His perfect performance at the National Baseball Congress tournament prompted a contract from the Kansas City Monarchs, whom he joined in 1936. The next year, Smith pitched a no-hit, shutout game against the Chicago American Giants, striking out six batters, walking one, and allowing only two balls to be hit out of the infield, in a 4–0 Monarch victory.

Smith led the Negro League in wins for five seasons (1938–1942), more than any other pitcher in league history, and during the 1941 season he never lost a game. John "Buck" O'Neil, a teammate and manager of Smith's, recalled, "Hilton Smith was unbeatable there for a spell, from 1938 to 1942. Unbeatable! He had more natural stuff, a good rising fastball and an excellent curveball with good control. My land! He would have been a 20-game winner in the major leagues with the stuff he had. We played against an all-star team the year Stan Musial came up in 1941. Satchel Paige and Bob Feller pitched three innings. Musial hit a home run off Satchel on the roof of that stadium. But Musial and Johnny Mize said they'd never seen a curveball like Hilton's curveball."

When the Brooklyn Dodgers signed Jackie Robinson to a major league contract in 1945, Smith was thirty-three years old. Although Smith entertained offers from major league clubs, he refused to take a pay cut to start in minor league baseball. As one of the premier pitchers in the Negro League, Smith was drawing a top salary of $800 a month, twice the amount he was being offered to play in a league very cautiously beginning to integrate. Smith retired from the Monarchs in 1948. But, a year later, at the age of 37, he joined the integrated semi-pro Fulda team from Minnesota. On opening day, Smith struck out twelve batters and won the game with a triple, with two runners on base, in the ninth inning.

Smith pitched in seven Negro League East-West all-star games; only Leon Day pitched in more (nine). As an all-star, Smith also was second in most innings pitched, with 19, and second in most strikeouts, with 13. In postseason play, Smith won a game in the 1942 Negro World Series and another in the 1946 series, compiling an ERA of 1.29. Based on statistics compiled by the Society for American Baseball Research, he completed his Negro League career with 72 wins against only 32 losses. He ranks third in highest strikeouts per innings ratio, behind Satchel Paige, also of the Monarchs, and Leon Day of the Newark Eagles.

Smith played winter ball with equal success. In two seasons in Cuba (1937–1938 and 1939–1940) he compiled a 10–5 record. While in Venezuela, he won eight and lost five games for the league-leading Vargas club. Proof of his overall effectiveness is evident in exhibition games against white major league teams, where Smith fashioned a 6–1 won-lost record. In 1946, as a member of the Satchel Paige All-Stars, he beat the Bob Feller All-Stars, 3–2.

After completing his baseball career, Smith coached major league hopefuls in the young adult Casey Sten-gel League for fifteen years, while working at the Sheffield Steel (later called Amco Steel) plant in Kansas City, Missouri. Until his death, he also scouted for the Chicago Cubs of the National League. He was active in his Baptist church and helped supervise a Boy Scout troop. Smith died in Kansas City.

In 1993 the Negro Leagues Baseball Museum in Kansas City, Missouri, conducted a survey, polling Negro League veterans to determine the greatest players in the league's history and how they should be ranked. Among pitchers, Smith finished with the third highest number of votes behind Paige and Day. Recognition by his peers only partially served to bring Smith out of the shadow of his teammate Paige. When asked about Paige's overwhelming popularity in comparison to his own, Smith simply replied, "When Paige got the publicity, we all ate good." Nevertheless, many players considered Smith the better pitcher because of the variety of his pitches and his superb control. Known generally for his fastball, he was in his day most famous for his curveball. He deserves to be in the National Baseball Hall of Fame in Cooperstown, New York.

• Entries on Smith are in David Porter, ed., *Biographical Dictionary of American Sports* (1987), and James A. Riley, *The Biographical Encyclopedia of the Negro Baseball Leagues* (1994). Smith is mentioned in John B. Holway, *Voices from the Great Black Baseball Leagues* (1975). Accounts of the no-hit game by Smith are taken from the *Kansas City Call*, 21 May 1937. Comments by teammate Buck O'Neil come from a 1992 interview. Seasonal statistics are from Dick Clark and Larry Lester, *The Negro Leagues Book* (1994). The all-time all-star survey was conducted by Larry Lester, research director for the Negro Leagues Baseball Museum, in 1993. Personal history was obtained from an interview with DeMorris "Mickey" Smith in 1995. An obituary appears in the *Kansas City Star*, 20 Nov. 1983.

LARRY LESTER

SMITH, Hoke (2 Sept. 1855–27 Nov. 1931), political leader, was born Michael Hoke Smith in Newton, North Carolina, the son of Hildreth Hosea (or Hosea Hildreth) Smith, an educator from New England, and Mary Brent Hoke, a member of a prominent North Carolina family. Hoke Smith grew up in Chapel Hill, where his father taught Greek and Latin as well as modern foreign languages at the University of North Carolina, and in Lincolnton, North Carolina, where the elder Smith operated a private school for several years. In 1872 the Smith family moved to Atlanta, Georgia. The younger Smith had relatively little formal education, but he profited from his father's tutelage. In May 1872 he began to read law in the offices of a local firm and was admitted to the bar before his eighteenth birthday. A devoted family man, in 1883 Smith married Marion McHenry "Birdie" Cobb, the daughter of General Thomas R. R. Cobb; they had four children.

Smith gradually made a place for himself in Atlanta, and by the early 1880s his practice was well established. A large man and a forceful advocate before juries, he was especially successful in representing clients with claims against railroads. The *American Law Review* called him "the damage lawyer of Georgia par excellence." Meanwhile, Smith took an active part in civic affairs, promoting the city and serving on the Atlanta Board of Education. In politics he was a supporter of Governor John B. Gordon and a champion of Grover Cleveland. Henry W. Grady, editor of the Atlanta *Constitution*, both inspired and challenged Smith, who decided in 1887 to acquire his own newspaper, the Atlanta *Journal*. Smith used the *Journal* to promote Cleveland and tariff reform. His spirited support of Cleveland in 1892 led to his appointment as secretary of the Interior.

Smith's tenure as secretary—from 6 March 1893 to 1 September 1896—was creditable but hardly distinguished. The Georgian was criticized, sometimes unfairly, for violating the civil service rules in his appointments, for rejecting the pension claims of Union veterans, and for favoring railroad companies in land-grant cases. However, he brought enthusiasm and vigor to his task and demonstrated administrative ability in handling many of his far-flung responsibilities. He became the foremost spokesman for the Cleveland administration in his home state. When the advocates of free silver and agrarian reform swept to victory in the South and William Jennings Bryan won the Democratic presidential nomination in July 1896, Smith resigned from the cabinet because of his decision to support Bryan and free silver.

Smith became a political exile for the next decade. Meanwhile, he plunged back into his law practice, which continued to flourish. He was reelected to the Atlanta Board of Education in 1897 and later became its president. He participated in the Southern Educational Movement and became a trustee of the Peabody Education Fund. Smith's longtime advocacy of more stringent railroad regulation and his work for reform of public education brought him back into the political limelight. In June 1905 he announced his candidacy for governor on a reform platform. Seeking the endorsement of the Populist leader Thomas E. Watson, Smith agreed to push for the disfranchisement of the state's African Americans. Over the next year, the Atlantan waged a vigorous campaign, emphasizing disfranchisement and railroad regulation. He won an overwhelming victory in the Democratic primary of 1906, receiving more popular votes than the combined total of his four opponents.

Smith was denied reelection in 1908 by Joseph M. Brown, but two years later he narrowly defeated Brown in a bitter rematch that perpetuated the division among the state's Democrats on the basis of Smith's reforms and the personalities and ambitions of factional leaders. Soon after resuming the governorship in 1911, Smith was elected by the general assembly to fill a vacancy in the U.S. Senate. As governor (1907–1909, 1911), Smith had guided a number of progressive measures through the state legislature: a comprehensive railroad regulation law that reorganized the railroad commission and broadened its juris-

diction; statewide prohibition of alcoholic beverages; abolition of the convict lease system; an antilobbying statute and the outlawing of free railroad passes; and a measure reorganizing the state's public schools. Smith, a racial paternalist and an advocate of improved race relations in earlier years, also orchestrated the disfranchisement of black Georgians by amending the state constitution.

Smith was one of the first prominent leaders to endorse the presidential candidacy of Woodrow Wilson, and his political faction worked for Wilson's nomination in 1912. Like most southern congressmen, he gave staunch support to Wilson's New Freedom legislation. Smith was an ardent advocate of federal appropriations for agricultural and educational advances. As chairman of the Committee on Education and Labor during the years 1913–1919, he sponsored and steered to passage in the Senate the Smith-Lever Act (1914), which provided for a national system of agricultural extension through the land-grant colleges, and the Smith-Hughes Act (1917), which introduced a program of agricultural, industrial, and domestic arts instruction in the nation's secondary schools.

The senator was easily reelected in 1914, but the First World War and factional politics strained Smith's relations with President Wilson and weakened his influence and effectiveness. One disruptive episode was an economic crisis in the southern cotton belt, precipitated by the onset of the war, and the demands made by Smith and other Dixie congressmen for federal relief. Smith voted for most of Wilson's wartime legislation, although he spoke out against what he considered a concentration of authority in the executive branch and an erosion of congressional power. He criticized Wilson's League of Nations and voted for the Lodge reservations to the Treaty of Versailles. He was soundly defeated in his bid for reelection in 1920.

After his defeat, Smith opened an office in Washington that specialized in claims against federal agencies. His first wife died in 1919, and Smith married Mazie Crawford in 1924. In 1925 the former senator returned to Atlanta, where he spent the rest of his life amid the surroundings he loved so well. He died in Atlanta.

An urban man imbued with the Atlanta spirit, Smith envisioned a New South based on industrialization, economic diversification, and social stability. He represented his region's "uptown" leadership, which helps to explain his continuing efforts to authenticate his rural credentials. His support of railroad regulation, the development of public education, and agricultural innovation made him Georgia's preeminent progressive and an influential senator in the Wilson era. His opposition to the power wielded by railroads, his effort to abolish Georgia's county-unit system, and his resistance to the rule of seniority in the Senate marked him as a democratic leader. On the other hand, he supported an antiblack democracy, and his leadership of the disfranchisement movement in Georgia was both demagogic and opportunistic. Finally, his leadership was a catalyst in the creation of Georgia's Democratic bifactionalism early in the twentieth century.

• The most important collection of Smith papers is in the University of Georgia library. The papers of Thomas E. Watson, a valuable collateral collection, are part of the Southern Historical Collection, University of North Carolina at Chapel Hill. Dewey W. Grantham, *Hoke Smith and the Politics of the New South* (1958), is a comprehensive biography. Ted Carageorge, "An Evaluation of Hoke Smith and Thomas E. Watson as Georgia Reformers" (Ph.D. diss., Univ. of Georgia, 1963), is a useful comparative study. For other works that throw light on Smith, see C. Vann Woodward, *Tom Watson: Agrarian Rebel* (1938); Numan V. Bartley, *The Creation of Modern Georgia* (1983); and William M. Gabard, "Joseph Mackey Brown: A Study in Conservatism" (Ph.D. diss., Tulane Univ., 1963). An obituary and other information are in the Atlanta *Journal*, 27–29 Nov. 1931.

DEWEY W. GRANTHAM

SMITH, Holland McTyeire (20 Apr. 1882–12 Jan. 1967), Marine Corps officer, was born at Seale, Alabama, the son of John Wesley Smith and Cornelia Elizabeth McTyeire. Like his father, Smith intended to pursue a legal career and graduated from Alabama Polytechnic Institute (now Auburn University) in 1901 before obtaining his law degree from the University of Alabama in 1903. Smith was admitted to the bar and practiced two years in Montgomery before seeking a second lieutenant's commission in the U.S. Marine Corps in March 1905. In 1909 he married Ada Wilkinson; they had one child. Smith subsequently saw duty in the Philippines (1906–1908; 1912–1914), Panama 1909–1910, and the Dominican Republican, 1916–1917. He was promoted to captain shortly before sailing to France in June 1917, commanding a machine gun company of the Fifth Marines. However, upon arrival, Smith became the first Marine officer ever selected to attend the Army General Staff College at Langres. Following graduation he served as adjutant of the Fourth Marine Brigade and in July 1918 took a post as staff officer with I Corps, First Army. In this capacity Smith fought with distinction at the battles of Aisne-Marne, St.-Mihiel, Oise, and Meuse-Argonne and received the Croix de Guerre. He ended the war with the rank of major and attached to the staff of the Third Army. Following a tour of occupation duty at Koblenz, Germany, Smith returned home in March 1919.

Smith graduated from the Naval War College, Newport, Rhode Island, in 1921 and joined the Office of Naval Operations. He also became the first marine officer appointed to the Joint Army-Navy Planning Committee between 1921 and 1923. Smith functioned as chief of staff with the marine brigade in Haiti between 1924 and 1925 and two years later was stationed at the marine barracks in Philadelphia. As colonel he became commander of the marine barracks in Washington, D.C., between 1931 and 1934. Smith was chief of staff in the Department of the Pacific from 1935 to 1937 and then, as brigadier general, assumed control of the Division of Operations and Training from 1938 to 1939. He became assistant to General Thomas Holcomb, commandant of the corps, in April 1939 and focused on developing new techniques and equipment, especially landing craft and amphibious tractors. Five months later he took charge of the First Marine Brigade at Guantánamo, Cuba, and thoroughly trained it in the new methods. Smith rose to major general in February 1941, and his brigade was expanded to form the First Marine Division. This force, in concert with various army and navy elements, became part of the Amphibious Force, Atlantic Fleet, under Admiral R. Kelly Turner.

Smith was actively deployed and served with distinction throughout World War II. For several months following Pearl Harbor, he was responsible for training army and marine units in amphibious warfare. In September 1942 his headquarters relocated to the West Coast, where it was redesignated the V Amphibious Corps. In June 1943 Smith was directed to take charge of this force, consisting of the Second and Fourth Marine Divisions, and blazed a trail of glory across the Central Pacific. In the fall of 1943 Smith and Admiral Chester W. Nimitz attacked and captured Makin and Tarawa atolls in the Gilbert Islands. Tarawa was a particularly stiff engagement, in which the Americans sustained heavy losses, and Smith's insistence on deploying additional amphibious tractors probably saved the battle. In January 1944 Kwajalein and Eniwetok fell to the V Corps, followed in June by the Mariana atolls of Saipan, Tinian, and Guam. At Saipan Smith became embroiled in an acrimonious controversy for relieving army general Ralph Smith for lack of aggressive tactics. This episode engendered bitter feelings on both sides and threatened to jeopardize interservice cooperation, but nonetheless Smith was promoted to lieutenant general in August 1944 and was appointed commander of the newly created Fleet Marine Force. In February 1945 he personally led troops ashore at Iwo Jima, one of the most grueling battles in Marine Corps history. In spite of heavy casualties and fanatical resistance, the island was secured in twenty-six days. In July 1945 Smith assumed control of the Marine Training and Replacement Command at San Diego and left the Pacific theater of operations. Among his numerous wartime awards were the Distinguished Service Medal and three gold stars.

Smith retired in August 1946, having become the third marine officer to achieve four star status. He settled in La Jolla, California, and penned a controversial autobiography, *Coral and Brass* (1948), which is highly opinionated and critical of his contemporaries. Smith died in San Diego and is commemorated by Camp H. M. Smith, Fleet Marine Force Headquarters, Pearl Harbor, Hawaii.

In his long career, Smith made indelible contributions to the refinement of amphibious warfare and to the cause of victory in the Pacific. Before 1939 the Marine Corps possessed little in the manner of training in these procedures and completely lacked modern equipment. Tenacious and combative, Smith argued with superiors over the issues of tactics, landing craft, naval gunfire, and air support and argued strenuously for an aggressive, hard-hitting strategy. His advice, if strongly presented, was seldom wrong. Smith's ferocity in training, in battle, and in consultation garnered him the appellation "Howlin Mad." He did, however, lay the groundwork for successful landing operations in Europe as well as the Pacific and is rightfully regarded as the father of modern amphibious warfare.

• Smith's official correspondence is in Record Group 407, National Archives. Large collections of personal papers are at the Marine Corps Museum, Quantico, Va., the Marine Corps Historical Center, Washington Navy Yard, D.C., and the Auburn University Library. Regarding his dismissal of General Smith, consult the Charles G. Nast Papers, U.S. Army Military History Institute, Carlisle Barracks, Pa. Two biographical treatments are Norman V. Cooper, "The Military Career of General Holland M. Smith" (Ph.D. diss., Univ. of Alabama, 1974); and Norman V. Cooper, *A Fighting General: The Biography of Holland McTyeire "Howlin' Mad" Smith* (1987). His wartime accomplishments are amply covered in Frank O. Hough et al., *History of U.S. Marine Corps Operations in World War II* (5 vols., 1956–1971); Jeter A. Isley and Philip A. Crowl, *The U.S. Marines and Amphibious War* (1951); Harry A. Gailey, *Howlin' Mad vs. the Army: Conflict in Command, Saipan, 1944* (1986); and Edmund G. Love, "Smith vs. Smith," *Infantry Journal* 63 (1948): 3–13.

JOHN C. FREDRIKSEN

SMITH, Homer William (2 Jan. 1895–25 Mar. 1962), physiologist and science popularizer, was born in Denver, Colorado, the son of Albert C. Smith and Margaret E. Jones. His mother died when he was almost seven. Smith grew up in Cripple Creek, Colorado, but returned to Denver to finish his high school education after the death of his father around 1911. A chemistry book had sparked his lifelong fascination with science, which he studied at the University of Denver (A.B., 1917). His military service was spent partly in the laboratory of E. K. Marshall investigating the biological effects of mustard gas, after which he did postgraduate research with William H. Howell at Johns Hopkins (D.Sc., 1921). After two years in the Eli Lilly laboratories, he went to Harvard on a National Research Council Fellowship to work with Walter B. Cannon. In 1925 Smith was appointed chair of the Department of Physiology at the University of Virginia School of Medicine. Three years later he moved to the New York University School of Medicine as professor of physiology and director of the physiological laboratories.

By the time Smith went to New York, his research interests had focused on the kidney, and from the 1930s his laboratory was widely recognized as a mecca of renal physiology. His own contributions to elucidating the functions of the kidney in health and disease were fundamental. Independently of, but at about the same time as A. N. Richards, Smith showed that the inert sugar inulin is excreted by the kidneys and that it is neither absorbed nor further excreted as it passes through the renal tubules after being filtered by the kidney's glomeruli. Inulin thus provided a handy tool for the quantitative assessment of the glomerular filtration rate (GFR), and Smith and his colleagues undertook basic studies in the ways in which the kidney "clears" a large number of waste products, including creatinine, urea, and sodium. This work led to important clinical tests to assess both normal and abnormal kidney function and helped to provide the scientific basis for modern diuretics. A parallel series of investigations helped to reveal the role of the kidneys in the regulation of blood pressure and the development of hypertension.

Although not himself medically trained, Smith had many medical collaborators, and he encouraged close ties between his department and clinical ones in the medical school. Some 175 associates passed through his department, including many leading nephrologists and renal physiologists. His major synthetic monograph, *The Kidney: Structure and Function in Health and Disease* (1951), long remained a bible in the field. At the same time, Smith approached his research primarily as a biologist. He was deeply interested in the evolution of the kidney, and his studies of the African lungfish (*Protopterus aethiopicus*), from 1928, provided important clues about the evolutionary history of the organ. He summarized this research in a successful philosophical novel, *Kamongo: The Lungfish and the Padre* (1932), and returned to the same theme in a popular monograph, *From Fish to Philosopher* (1953). *Man and His Gods* (1952), a historical and philosophical account of man's place in nature, is imbued with Smith's religious agnosticism and faith in the possibilities of scientific rationality to improve the lot of human beings on earth. His scientific and popular writings were equally distinguished by their clarity of style and elegance of expression.

A childhood stutter had reinforced Smith's natural reserve, and though he lost the stutter and became a popular public speaker, he remained an intensely private individual who hated pomp and sentiment. He inspired awe and, at a distance, affection. His first marriage, in 1921, to Carlotta Smith (no previous relation) ended in divorce in 1948. A second marriage, to Margaret Wilson (1949), produced his only child and brought much happiness until Margaret's accidental death in 1960. Smith retired from NYU in 1961 and died shortly thereafter at his home in New York City.

• Monographs by Smith not mentioned above include *The End of Illusion* (1935), *The Physiology of the Kidney* (1937), and *Principles of Renal Physiology* (1956). A complete bibliography of his publications is in Herbert Chasis and William Goldring, eds., *Homer William Smith: His Scientific and Literary Achievements* (1965). This contains a generous selection of scientific and popular writing, biographical material, and a short memoir of Smith, by Robert F. Pitts, which is reprinted, with bibliography, in National Academy of Sciences, *Biographical Memoirs* 39 (1967): 445–70. A more recent assessment is Elmer Bendiner, "Homer Smith: 'Master of All Things Renal,'" *Hospital Practice* 17 (1982): 145–83. An obituary is in the *New York Times*, 26 Mar. 1962.

W. F. BYNUM

SMITH, Howard Worth (2 Feb. 1883–3 Oct. 1976), U.S. congressman, was born in Broad Run, Virginia, the son of William Worth Smith and Lucinda Lewis, farmers. Howard Smith was born in a slave-built plantation home called "Cedar Hill" in the Shenandoah valley. All his life, he embraced the values that were commonplace among whites in the Old Dominion—white supremacy, limited government, and self-reliance. He gravitated toward public service as his mother and congressman cousin, John F. Rixey, tutored him in the ways of politics. He earned his law degree in 1903 from the University of Virginia, the most well connected school in the state. He then practiced law and invested in real estate in Alexandria and moved quickly into local political circles. As an organization Democrat, he easily won election or appointment as city councilman, commonwealth's attorney, corporation court judge, and circuit court judge. This was the start of a sixty-year political career. In 1930 Smith gained Virginia's Eighth District congressional seat by finessing the Prohibition issue; he promised to uphold the nation's laws, which included Prohibition, but he also claimed that a "permanent and satisfactory" answer to alcohol consumption demanded an "open mind and free hand." His position permitted him to avoid antagonizing voters on both sides of the controversy.

Throughout his life, the serious-minded Smith was preoccupied with work first and his family second. He married Lillian Violett Proctor in 1913, and they had two children. She died in the flu epidemic of 1919, and four years later the forty-year-old Smith took a second wife, Ann Corcoran, the young nanny then looking after his children.

"Judge Smith," as he preferred to be addressed, first gained notoriety as a member of the House Rules Committee. This committee was intended to serve as a "traffic cop" for the majority party, expediting bills approved by standing committees to the floor of the House. By the late 1930s a rebellious Smith joined the nascent conservative coalition of southern Democrats and northern Republicans in resisting Franklin D. Roosevelt's New Deal programs, particularly those favoring workers and organized labor. Smith's opposition prompted the president and the unions to seek the Virginian's ouster in the 1938 Democratic primary campaign.

Smith survived that purge attempt and, like most southern Democrats, became an unremitting foe of foreign radicals, the "labor dictatorship," "race mixing," and domestic spending generally. He won congressional support for three major bills. The Alien Registration Act of 1940, commonly known as the Smith Act, outlawed the advocacy of violence against the U.S. government and led to roundups of Communists. During World War II, Smith tried to thwart "insurrectionary" strikes in defense industries through the Smith-Connally Wartime Labor Disputes Act (among other provisions, the act required unions to give a thirty-day strike notice). He also wrote the "open shop" provision of the Taft-Hartley Act of 1947,

making mandatory union membership unnecessary for industrial employment.

Smith opposed many bills that provided federal monies or granted rights to groups he regarded as threatening or undeserving. To stand in the way of these allegedly unconstitutional measures, he marshaled the conservative coalition of one hundred House members in an often brilliant fashion, organizing the amending process to dilute the bills, making sure his supporters were present for the votes, and using procedural motions to delay or derail debate. He also worked with allies in the Senate, especially Virginia senator Harry F. Byrd, Sr.

Smith reached the zenith of his power as chairman of the House Rules Committee (1955–1966). He used the committee's blanket authority and byzantine procedures to block measures that would have increased public housing, Social Security coverage, black civil rights, and minimum wages. His control of Congress was so complete that sometimes he could personally order changes in a bill before it left his committee.

Smith's power began to wane in the early 1960s, when Democratic liberals with urban constituencies pressured Speaker Sam Rayburn to break the conservative logjam. After John F. Kennedy was elected president, Rayburn orchestrated a heavyweight fight that enlarged the Rules Committee and changed its procedures. The net result was that Smith became a mere "traffic cop," a role that he had always despised.

One sign of Smith's diminished power came with the Civil Rights Act of 1964. In a maneuver that backfired, he attempted to kill the bill by tacking on an amendment barring sex discrimination in the hope that liberals could not simultaneously swallow racial and gender equality. When the entire bill passed, Smith became, in effect, a midwife of the modern feminist movement.

With the liberal tide at floodstage, the 83-year-old Smith faced the electorate once again in a 1966 party primary. He had long been insulated from political changes in his district, thanks to its rural configuration and the poll tax that depressed voter turnout. When the district was redrawn and the poll tax was abolished, he was defeated by the groups he had consistently opposed—blacks, union members, and federal government workers. Smith died at home in Alexandria.

Smith's importance is threefold. His far-reaching Smith Act encouraged attacks on radicals. His extraordinary manipulation of Congress weakened, delayed, or killed the onrush of civil rights and social welfare legislation in the twentieth century; and his sex discrimination amendment unwittingly granted women legal equality. Speaker Carl Albert concluded, "He may not have stopped the flow of federal involvement in human affairs in his day and generation, but he certainly slowed it down."

• Smith's papers are in the University of Virginia. Additional Smith correspondence can be found in the Virginia State Library, the Earl Gregg Swem Library of the College of William and Mary in Williamsburg, the presidential libraries from Hoover to Ford, the U.S. Department of Justice in Washington, the Sam Rayburn Library in Bonham, Tex., the Dallas Historical Society, and the Boston University Library, among other places. His autobiographical account of his early life is *Our Paternal Hearth* (1976). See also Bruce J. Dierenfield, *Keeper of the Rules: Congressman Howard W. Smith of Virginia* (1987). An obituary is in the *New York Times*, 4 Oct. 1976.

BRUCE J. DIERENFIELD

SMITH, Israel (6 Apr. 1759–2 Dec. 1810), congressman, senator, and governor, was born in Suffield, Connecticut, the son of Anna Kent and Daniel Smith, innkeepers. During his childhood the family moved from Connecticut to the small village of Rupert in Bennington County, Vermont. His parents, deeply religious and strong believers in the worth of education, sacrificed to send him to Yale College, where he received a baccalaureate degree in 1781. His older brother Noah, who was later to become prominent in Vermont politics, preceded him, graduating from Yale in 1778. A lawyer, Noah established a practice in Bennington, where he took in Israel as an apprentice.

In 1783 Smith gained admission to the Vermont bar and set up an independent practice in Rupert. That year he married Abiah Douglass; they had one son. During the following years he became active in politics, representing Rupert in the general assembly in 1785 and again from 1788 to 1790. He made a favorable impression on his legislative peers, who in 1789 appointed him as one of seven commissioners to the joint Vermont–New York Boundary Commission, which settled the contested boundary between the two states. Smith played a major role in working out a compromise that ended the bloody rivalry between settlers in the disputed region and was designated as one of the group's principal intermediaries to communicate with New York governor George Clinton. Having served successfully as commissioner, Smith was elected to the state convention, which in January 1791 assented to and adopted the Constitution of the United States—the necessary first step in gaining Vermont's admission into the Union.

In the hope of improving his fortune, Smith moved to the larger town of Rutland in 1791, where in addition to practicing law he engaged in farming. That year he was elected to the U.S. House of Representatives, where he served from 17 October 1791 to 3 March 1797. Unlike most of his fellow New England congressmen, Smith aligned himself with the Jeffersonian Republicans rather than the Federalists. During his first two terms, when party lines were only beginning to form, he voted independently of any political faction. But by 1795, when he supported the unsuccessful effort of House Republicans to block Jay's Treaty by refusing to appropriate funds to carry the unpopular treaty into effect, he was clearly on the Republican side politically. Smith's opposition to Jay's Treaty angered many of his constituents, as a result of which he lost his bid for reelection in 1797.

Returning home to Rutland in the spring of 1797, Smith resumed his law practice. In the fall he was elected to another term in the state legislature, where the Republican majority promptly elected him as the chief justice of the state supreme court. Although he fulfilled the demands of that office competently and commanded respect as a jurist, the position of chief justice was an important political plum that was snatched from Smith in 1798 when a new Federalist legislative majority elected one of their own to the office. With the election of Thomas Jefferson to the presidency in 1800, however, Republicans regained control of the Vermont legislature, and they promptly elected Smith to his former position on the supreme court. Smith, however, declined the position, deciding instead to run for governor. He was defeated by the popular Federalist incumbent, Isaac Tichenor. As a consolation prize, Smith was elected to his old seat in the House and served until 1803, when he was elected to the Senate. He served in the Senate until October 1807, when he resigned to accept the governorship of Vermont after Republicans had finally succeeded in breaking the Federalist monopoly on that office. Smith's career in Congress was undistinguished. He was attentive to legislative details and worked effectively in party harness, but he never played a leadership role in either house.

Smith served only a single one-year term as governor. In his inaugural address he advocated several progressive measures, but he lacked both the money and the time to implement them. He urged the legislature to appropriate funds for the construction of new prisons to replace the miserably filthy and unhealthy structures then in use. He also urged the state to substitute imprisonment at hard labor for corporal punishment. To promote education and economic progress, he recommended that the state establish schools for the education of poor children who could not otherwise afford an education and that the state supervise the construction and maintenance of highways. Although Smith did manage to establish the Vermont State Prison during his governorship, most of the programs were too costly for tight-fisted Vermont farmers, who decided in 1808 that they preferred Smith's more frugal Federalist predecessor, whom they returned to office in 1808. Smith remained a trustee of Middlebury College, which he had served for many years. His political defeat was accompanied by a rapid decline in his health, especially his mental health. His death in Rutland soon thereafter deprived Vermont Republicans of one of their most popular political leaders.

• The only surviving collection of Smith's papers, located at the University of Vermont at Burlington, consists of two letters. Short biographical sketches can be found in the *Biographical Directory of the American Congresses* (1928); Robert Sobel and John W. Raine, eds., *Biographical Directory of the Governors of the United States, 1789–1978* (4 vols., 1978); Franklin Bowditch Dexter, *Biographical Sketches of Yale College, with Annals of the College History*, vol. 4 (1907); and Prentiss C. Dodge, comp. and ed., *Encyclopedia of Vermont*

Biography (1912). Miscellaneous information can be found in *Records of the Governor and Council of the State of Vermont*, vol. 5 (1877), and Benjamin H. Hall, *History of Eastern Vermont* (1858).

CHARLES D. LOWERY

SMITH, Jabbo (24 Dec. 1908–16 Jan. 1991), jazz trumpeter, trombonist, and singer, was born Cladys Smith in Pembroke, Georgia, and was given his unusual name to complement that of an infant cousin, Gladys. His father (name unknown) was a barber, and his mother, Ida (maiden name unknown), ultimately became a schoolteacher. After her husband's death in 1912, Ida Smith moved to Savannah, Georgia, and in 1914 she placed Cladys in the Jenkins Orphanage Home in Charleston, South Carolina. After two years of musical tutelage, in 1918 he was assigned to play cornet in one of the orphanage's several brass bands. In 1922, while touring with the band in Jacksonville, Cladys ran away and played for three months in Eagle Eye Shields's jazz band before he was caught and returned to the orphanage. After a few more instances of rebelliousness, in 1924 Rev. Jenkins expelled him from the home. Smith moved to Philadelphia and worked in Harry Marsh's band for three months, during which time his fellow bandsmen, amused by the name of an Indian character in a William S. Hart movie, started calling him "Jabbo."

After leaving Marsh, Smith went to Atlantic City, where he worked for one month with another Jenkins alumnus, trumpeter Gus Aiken. He played with pianist Charlie Johnson from the fall of 1925 through January 1928, working extended residencies in Harlem and occasional college dances before leaving over a salary dispute. He also participated in two recording sessions with Johnson, and on one freelance date with Duke Ellington he took Bubber Miley's place as soloist on "What Can a Poor Fellow Do?" and "Black and Tan Fantasy." Between February and November 1928 he played with Fats Waller and Garvin Bushell in James P. Johnson's pit band for *Keep Shufflin'*, leaving when the murder of the revue's backer, gambler Arnold Rothstein, forced the show's cancellation during a Midwest tour. Smith remained in Chicago and joined Charlie Elgar's orchestra at the Dreamland Ballroom.

Between January and August 1929, Smith recorded a brilliant series of small band performances under his own name for Brunswick, all the while working through 1930 as the "house" trumpeter at the Sunset Café, where he played in a succession of different orchestras, including those of Carroll Dickerson, Sammy Stewart, Earl Hines, Dave Peyton, Tiny Parham, and Jimmy Bell. At the same time, he also worked at the Vendôme Theater with Erskine Tate and the Dreamland with Elgar and led his own six-piece band at My Cellar. Throughout this period Smith was one of the most highly regarded trumpeters in Chicago, considered by some to be the equal of Louis Armstrong, and on the basis of his recordings, his reputation among musicians spread even beyond the Midwest. However, his quick rise to prominence coupled with a lack of maturity led to a cocky self-assurance marked by heavy drinking and unreliability. In late 1930 Smith moved to Milwaukee, but he continued to travel back and forth between the two cities, going from one band to another. As a result of his increased irresponsibility and failure to live up to his earlier promise, he went unrecorded for five years and dropped into almost total obscurity. In 1936 he signed a two-year contract with the Claude Hopkins Orchestra, then on tour from its regular stand at the Roseland Ballroom in New York City.

In the spring of 1939 he started rehearsing with Sidney Bechet's new group, and when Bechet decided to move on he turned the leadership over to Smith, who then secured a job for the band at the Midway Inn at the New York World's Fair. After the fair closed in 1940, Smith disbanded the group and, over the next four years, played in a variety of groups at the Alcazar in Newark, New Jersey. In 1944 he rejoined Hopkins briefly and then a year later settled in Milwaukee, where he worked as both a sideman and leader of his own sextet. Trying to maintain a stable life after his 1948 marriage, he started working days in a drug store, and in 1955, with the end of a long engagement at the Flame Bar, he took a job with the Avis Rent-A-Car Company, where he worked full-time for the next thirteen years. Smith remained relatively inactive musically until early 1961, when local jazz record collectors learned of his whereabouts and urged him to return to music. He appeared in a concert staged by the Milwaukee Jazz Society in June and started working again locally and in Chicago. Smith's embouchure, though, was in poor shape for lack of practice as well as dental problems, but he was still able to sing and play trombone, an instrument he had learned as a child at the Jenkins Orphanage.

He played trombone and piano and sang occasionally in the late 1960s and early 1970s, and he appeared at the Breda Jazz Festival in Holland in 1971 and 1972. In 1975 he was voted into the Jazz Hall of Fame at the Newport–New York Jazz Festival, and in 1977 he appeared in London and once again at Breda. Later that year he played at New Orleans's Preservation Hall, an engagement that led to his joining the company of *One Mo' Time*. The show opened in New York City at the Village Gate in October 1979 with Smith playing trumpet in Orange Kellin's small jazz band and singing two of his own numbers onstage. In 1981 he suffered the first of three strokes but recuperated sufficiently to return to the show after a brief layoff. In March 1982 he played ten concerts in France, Italy, and Switzerland with the Hot Antic Jazz Band, but following that tour he suffered his second stroke, recovering in time to play at the Nice Jazz Festival in 1982 and again at Breda. By the next year he could no longer play, but he performed as a singer both in Europe and at several New York City clubs. In 1986, on the strangest booking of his career, he appeared with avant-garde trumpeter Don Cherry at Jazzfest Berlin. Although almost completely blind as a result of his strokes, he continued to sing and write songs until his death at home in New York.

During his peak in the late 1920s, Jabbo Smith was considered by many musicians to be Louis Armstrong's only serious competition. Although he can be heard to good advantage on the records he made with Charlie Johnson, Duke Ellington, and the Louisiana Sugar Babes (the recording name of James P. Johnson's *Keep Shufflin'* band), it is on the twenty sides he made in 1929 as leader of Jabbo Smith's Rhythm Aces that his astonishing gifts can most be appreciated. Designed by Brunswick to compete with the highly successful OKeh records by Louis Armstrong's Hot Five and Hot Seven, this series presented Smith with a challenge his talent and ego could not resist. All but one of the titles were released promptly, but despite the high regard in which fellow jazz musicians held such remarkable performances as "Jazz Battle," "Take Your Time," "Sweet 'n Low Blues," "Take Me to the River," "Ace of Rhythm," "Sau-Sha Stomp," "Decatur Street Tutti," and "Lina Blues," they failed to bring the success hoped for, most likely because of poor promotion and distribution by Brunswick. Smith and clarinetist Omer Simeon were at their best on such brightly paced original themes as "Jazz Battle" and "Ace of Rhythm," where, in a series of increasingly heated solos and ensembles, they played with a crackling excitement rarely heard on records before. Typically, the trumpeter's pyrotechnics were met head on by Simeon's sharply articulated, blues-intoned clarinet to a breathtaking effect of unrelieved intensity. But with the onset of the depression, while the public could still respond to Armstrong's proven talent and charisma, it could not also support the efforts of an ambitious contender, however gifted.

Smith's incendiary tone, range, technical fluency, and imaginative phrasing contained the seeds that would later emerge fully grown in the playing of Roy Eldridge and Dizzy Gillespie. But for all of these virtues, he lacked Armstrong's deeply moving vibrato, breadth of tone, and sense of structure, not to mention his inventiveness and originality. However, Smith's singing, as is evidenced on many of these sides, was almost on a par with the master's. Unfortunately, this promising artist never again achieved the high plateau he set in 1929, and when he recorded as leader in 1938, after nearly a decade of obscurity, his playing, although technically polished, was so devoid of creativity that some believed it the work of a different musician. Smith regained some of his earlier powers, though, for a final series of recordings in the late 1970s and early 1980s.

• Transcribed interview material can be found in the notes to LP sets on *Melodeon* (1965) and *Jazz Art* (1984), as well as in the oral history archives of the Institute of Jazz Studies at Rutgers University. The best analytical examination of Smith's trumpet style is Gunther Schuller, *Early Jazz: Its Roots and Musical Development* (1968), while details on his early working associations are chronicled in Albert McCarthy, *Big Band Jazz* (1974). For information on his formative years, see John Chilton, *A Jazz Nursery: The Story of the Jen-*

kins' *Orphanage Bands of Charleston, South Carolina* (1980). Full chapter articles based equally on personal interviews, research, and critiques are in Whitney Balliett, *Jelly Roll, Jabbo, and Fats* (1983; repr. in Balliett's *American Musicians* [1986]), and Chip Deffaa, *Voices of the Jazz Age* (1990; repr. 1992). Complete discographical information is in Brian Rust, *Jazz Records: 1897–1942* (1982), and Walter Bruyninckx, *Traditional Jazz Discography: 1897–1988* (6 vols., 1988–1989) and *Swing Discography: 1920–1988* (12 vols., 1988–1989). An obituary is in the *New York Times*, 18 Jan. 1991.

JACK SOHMER

SMITH, James (1737–1814), soldier and author, was born in Franklin County, Pennsylvania. Little is known of his parents and early life. Apparently he received no formal education, but he did learn a great deal about woodlore and life on the frontier. At the age of eighteen he was captured by American Indians while laboring to clear a road in western Pennsylvania and was adopted into one of their tribes. For four years he traveled with them through the old Northwest, then he managed to escape. Returning to his birthplace, he settled into a life of farming. In 1763 he married Anne Wilson, with whom he had seven children before she died twenty years later. He also became an active military campaigner, serving off and on from 1763 to 1769 as commander of the "Black Boys," a self-appointed group of irregulars that protected white settlements in his region from Indian depredations. In 1764 he joined Henry Bouquet's expedition against the Ohio Indians as a lieutenant. With a group of comrades he explored eastern Kentucky and Tennessee in 1766 and 1767, being among the first Europeans to enter that part of the world.

In about 1768 or 1769 Smith and his family moved to Jacob's Creek, in what later would be Bedford, then Westmoreland County, Pennsylvania. There he became an important citizen, serving in 1771 on the board of commissioners of Bedford County, then in the same body for Westmoreland County two years later. During Dunmore's War in 1774, he saw duty as captain of a ranging company. At the outbreak of the revolutionary war in 1775 he was appointed a major in the Associated Battalion of Westmoreland County. In 1776 he became a member of the Westmoreland County convention and in the same year was elected to a two-year term in the newly organized Pennsylvania Assembly. Resuming his military career in 1777, he was put in command of a scouting party in New Jersey. Later he was commissioned colonel and commander of Pennsylvania militiamen fighting American Indians on that state's frontier. After the war Smith settled once more into his home in western Pennsylvania and in 1785 married Margaret Rodgers Irvin, a widow; they had no children. During the summer of that year he lived in Kentucky, adjusting land claims. Three years later he moved with his new wife to Cane Ridge, near Paris, Kentucky. Immediately he was elected a member of the Danville convention to discuss separation of the District of Kentucky from Virginia. When Kentucky achieved statehood in 1792, he attended the constitutional convention to draft a new basic law for the commonwealth and over the next several years represented Bourbon County in the legislature.

In his sixties Smith manifested sides of his personality and abilities that had not been obvious before. In 1799 he wrote *An Account of the Remarkable Occurrences in the Life and Travels of Col. James Smith, during His Captivity with the Indians . . .* , which was published by John Bradford in Lexington, Kentucky. This book, which spread Smith's fame far and wide, was an account of his earlier adventures among the Indians. Since its appearance it has gone through numerous reprintings and has been used extensively by historians writing about early frontier life in Ohio. In 1812 Smith drew extensively on his earlier work to compose *A Treatise on the Mode and Manner of Indian War, Their Tactics, Discipline and Encampments.* Smith also became interested in religion. Having always been of a quiet and contemplative bent (despite his earlier warlike and political proclivities), he had long been a member of the Presbyterian church. Now, for a time, he fell under the sway of Barton W. Stone, leader of New Light Presbyterians who broke off from the main church after the Great Revival at Cane Ridge. Soon, however, he returned to the Presbyterian church, whereupon he received licensure to conduct missionary activity among the Indians of Ohio and Tennessee. To this duty he devoted the major part of his remaining life, save for a short time when his attention was diverted toward the Shakers. His son James Smith, it seems, had moved his family to a Shaker community near Lebanon, Ohio, and had prevailed on his father, whose second wife had died in 1800, to join the sect for a season. Smith developed an immediate aversion to the Shakers and in 1810 wrote two scathing pamphlets against them, *Remarkable Occurrences Lately Discovered among the People Called Shakers; of a Treasonous and Barbarous Nature; or Shakerism Developed* and *Shakerism Detected; Their Erroneous and Treasonous Proceedings . . . Exposed to Public View.* Except for the aggravation he felt when Richard McNemar, a Shaker leader, responded bluntly to his screeds, Smith lived the remainder of his days with his family in calm religious study and meditation. He died in Washington County, Kentucky.

• There are two biographies of Smith, Neil H. Swanson, *The First Rebel . . . A Biography of Colonel James Smith . . .* (1937), and Wilbur S. Nye, *James Smith: Early Cumberland Valley Patriot* (1969). Useful biographical sketches are in the 1834 and 1870 editions of *An Account of the Remarkable Occurrences in the Life and Travels of Col. James Smith, during His Captivity with the Indians . . .* Background information is in Lewis Collins, *History of Kentucky* (3 vols., 1891), and John Newton Boucher, *History of Westmoreland County, Pennsylvania* (1906). Smith's analysis of American-Indian warfare is ably critiqued by Leroy V. Eid in "'Their Rules of War': The Validity of James Smith's Summary of Indian Woodland War," *Register of the Kentucky Historical Society* 86 (1988): 4–23.

PAUL DAVID NELSON

SMITH, James (1771–12 June 1841), physician, was born in Elkton, Cecil County, Maryland, the son of Martha and David Smith, an attorney and register of wills of the county. After graduating from Dickinson College in Carlisle, Pennsylvania, in 1792, Smith attended lectures in medicine at the University of Pennsylvania but did not take a medical degree. He had begun to practice medicine in Baltimore when, in 1797, yellow fever broke out, and he was assigned by the city's board of health to a temporary hospital erected for the care of victims. On the return of the fever three years later, when 1,197 deaths were recorded, Smith opened his own house to patients. In the epidemic of 1819–1820 he advocated sanitary measures to combat the disease.

In Baltimore, Smith was a founder of the City General Dispensary in 1801 and a founder of the Beneficial Society for Prevention of Hydrophobia in 1814. A member of the Maryland Medical and Chirurgical Faculty, he was the organization's treasurer from 1811 to 1817. In both yellow fever and smallpox epidemics he was often at odds with the board of health.

Smith's career was indissolubly linked with the treatment and prevention of smallpox. He was among the first American doctors to learn and make use of Edward Jenner's discovery (1798) that vaccination with cowpox, in place of inoculation with smallpox, was a preventive of the latter disease. In Baltimore, Dr. John Crawford received some of the vaccine in 1800; the next year a second supply was received and was given to Smith, who on 1 May 1801 inoculated a young inmate of the City Almshouse, where Smith was an attending physician. In an account of his first ten or twelve cases published in the *Federal Gazette and Baltimore Daily Advertiser*, 3 and 5 December 1801, Smith concluded that the cowpox "is an effectual and certain preventative" of the smallPox."

In March 1802, with the approval and support of the city's mayor, trustees of the poor, and a large number of physicians, Smith organized a vaccine institute (or clinic) in Baltimore. Operated from his own house, at his expense and with charitable gifts, the clinic provided vaccination to the poor. Smith spread word of the value of vaccination through newspapers and enlisted Baltimore physicians in the cause: during one period fifty-eight doctors offered free vaccinations to the poor and paid twenty-five cents to each child who presented proof of successful vaccination. When smallpox broke out again in Baltimore in 1810, a Vaccine, or Jennerian, Society was formed to raise funds to expand the work of the institute; it was reorganized in 1812 with Smith as secretary. In the same year he sent a sample of his vaccine to England, where Jenner pronounced it genuine.

The obvious benefits of vaccination led Smith to petition the Maryland legislature to create a vaccine institute for the state, with himself as its director; the law passed in 1809, but with inadequate funding. Smith next turned to the federal government, and on 27 February 1813 a National Vaccine Institute was established by act of Congress, and Smith was named national vaccine agent. The institute's obligation was to preserve a supply of vaccine and to distribute it to physicians and other citizens who asked for it. No salary was attached to the position, but the vaccine agent charged for the vaccine and was allowed to frank letters and packages dealing with smallpox and vaccination. An unusual element of Smith's plan was the premise that intelligent laymen could perform vaccinations simply by following the printed instructions that accompanied each batch of vaccine mailed out.

With the authority that these appointments bestowed—Smith was also vaccine agent for Virginia after 1814—he supplied vaccine to physicians, medical societies, postmasters, the army and navy, and even to the West Indies and South America. He also helped personally in coping with smallpox when it broke out in Baltimore and several Maryland counties after 1810. In the four years after 1812 there was not one death from smallpox in Baltimore (Cordell, p. 678). Smith oversaw twenty agents nationwide, who were estimated to have vaccinated 100,000 persons. In 1816 and 1818 he asked Congress, without success, to extend and strengthen the vaccine institute.

In 1820–1821 two events occurred that brought about Smith's dismissal as vaccine agent and the abolition of the National Vaccine Institute. First, the startling realization that vaccination, contrary to widely held belief, did not confer permanent immunity was forced on advocates of vaccination when a Baltimore citizen contracted smallpox some time after he had been vaccinated. Confidence in the vaccine institute and its agent was badly shaken, and some physicians briefly resumed the old practice of inoculation. The second episode was a tragic accident in North Carolina. A physician in Tarboro received inexplicably a package of smallpox scabs instead of genuine vaccine matter. Not knowing the difference, the local doctor performed inoculations with the result that smallpox became epidemic and several persons died. Smith was removed as national vaccine agent on 10 April 1822, and the act establishing the vaccine institute was repealed on 4 May. Although some physicians had been critical of the institute because it seemed to establish a monopoly in Smith's favor, two of his strongest defenders in the national House of Representatives were themselves physicians.

The Baltimore Vaccine Society was reorganized once again, and for a dozen years Smith continued to vaccinate. But he devoted much time and thought to seeking an explanation of the Tarboro incident and to vindicating his conduct. In 1822 he issued a small periodical called *The Vaccine Inquirer*, which reprinted many of his public letters and other statements. On 10 July 1822 he received a patent for his improved method of transmitting vaccine through the post (moistening the vaccine crust and grating it on small pieces of glass or ivory, to which it would adhere when dry so that it might be mailed). In 1828 he addressed an *Appeal to the Citizens of Baltimore in His Own Vindication*.

Although the funds of the National Vaccine Institute ran out in 1823, local vaccine institutes and societies, already established in various states and cities, continued to operate. Like Smith, these organizations recognized that vaccination had to be general if smallpox was to be eliminated and that government support and authority were required if the poor were to be vaccinated. None of them proposed, however, as had Smith, that the operation be performed by laymen.

Smith had married in 1801 a Miss Caldwell of Baltimore. Their children were vaccinated in infancy. One son was named Edward Jenner, and two sons and a daughter were exposed to smallpox in 1819 to demonstrate the efficacy of vaccination. Smith died in Pikesville, Baltimore County, Maryland, where in 1814 he had bought land and named the settlement for General Zebulon Pike.

• *The Vaccine Inquirer* (1822) contains some biographical data on Smith as well as material for the history of the national program for vaccination. His other publications, many ephemeral, are listed in Robert B. Austin, *Early American Medical Imprints . . . 1668–1820* (1961). The legislative history of the National Vaccine Institute may be followed in the several volumes of the *Annals of Congress*. Smith's account of his first cases, published in a Baltimore newspaper in 1801, was reprinted in *Americanische Annalen der Arzneykunde, Naturgeschichte, Chemie und Physik* 1 (1802): 161–63; and his published offer (1812) to examine vaccine scabs to determine if vaccination had been successful was reprinted in *Edinburgh Medical and Surgical Journal* 8 (1812): 382–83. Smith's patent, signed by President James Madison, is in the Medical and Chirurgical Faculty of Maryland, Baltimore. The fullest biographical sketch is Whitfield J. Bell, Jr., "Dr. James Smith and the Public Encouragement for Vaccination for Smallpox," *Annals of Medical History*, 3d ser., 2 (1940): 500–17. See also Everett S. Brown, "An Early American Experiment in Socialized Medicine," *Michigan Alumnus Quarterly Review* 57 (1951): 226–34; Eugene F. Cordell, *The Medical Annals of Maryland, 1799–1899* (1903); and John R. Quinan, *Medical Annals of Baltimore* (1884), pp. 155–56.

WHITFIELD J. BELL, JR.

SMITH, James Allen (5 May 1860–30 Jan. 1924), political scientist, was born in Pleasant Hill, Missouri, the son of Isaac James Smith and Naomi Holloway, slaveholding agriculturalists. Raised in a border state during the bitter days of the Civil War and Reconstruction, Smith developed a lifelong interest in politics and economics and cultivated an interest in the single-tax theories of economic reformer Henry George, author of *Progress and Poverty*. Graduating from the University of Missouri in 1886, Smith took a law degree the following year and practiced in Kansas City until 1890 but eventually concluded that a legal career "did not offer a suitable opportunity for one who was mainly interested in political and economic reforms." In November of that year he married Doris J. Lehmann of Kansas City; she recognized his discontent with the limitations of a legal career, appreciated his scholarly ambitions, and urged him to undertake graduate education in the social sciences. Enrolling in the University of Michigan in 1890, Smith studied under Henry Carter Adams and wrote his doctoral dissertation on the theoretical foundations of money, refuting many of the basic contentions held by advocates of the gold standard. Although some members of the Michigan faculty vigorously opposed his thesis, Smith defended it skillfully enough to receive his Ph.D. degree in 1894 and to earn an appointment to Marietta College the following year.

The publication of his dissertation, retitled "The Multiple Money Standard," in the March 1896 issue of the *Annuals of the American Academy of Political and Social Science*, created such a furor during that volatile election year that Smith was fired from his academic position, ostensibly on the grounds of economic retrenchment. The resultant notoriety, however, made Smith a celebrity among reformers, progressives, and populists, leading, in 1897, to his appointment as a professor of political science at the University of Washington. He held that position for the remainder of his life, doubling as dean of the graduate school between 1909 and 1920.

In 1907 Smith published his most widely celebrated book, *The Spirit of American Government*, in which he severely criticized various "undemocratic" characteristics of the American polity, especially the system of checks and balances, the lack of responsibility and policy coherence among political parties, and the tendency of judicial review to degenerate into "judge-made law that usurped the prerogatives of popularly elected legislations in the service of vested interests." His analyses invoked favorable commentary from such prominent liberal publicists and politicians of the Progressive Era as Robert M. La Follette, Sr., Theodore Roosevelt, Lincoln Steffens, Samuel S. McClure, Charles McCarthy, Walter Weyl, and Frederick C. Howe but so outraged conservatives that calls for his dismissal became commonplace.

Increasingly active in politics and public affairs, Smith frequently wrote articles for the journals of municipal reform organizations and functioned as a leading figure in the movement to reform Seattle city government and politics. In 1912 he refused the gubernatorial nomination of the Washington State Progressive party and, ten years later, turned down an offer to run for the U.S. Senate. Beset by a deteriorating heart condition, Smith also rejected overtures to become a university administrator and resigned as graduate dean of the University of Washington in 1920. For the remainder of his life, he taught political science and worked diligently on the research and writing of *The Growth and Decadence of Constitutional Government*, a book that was completed, posthumously, by his daughter, Elfreda Allen Smith, in 1930.

Growth and Decadence protested the growing centralization of administration in the federal government, attacked the modern state as a dominating influence that undermined popular control, and pled for increased initiative and authority on the part of local government. In contrast to his thesis in *The Spirit of American Government*, Smith argued that "individual liberty" was more important than democracy and that "public opinion" was a more effective tool than political reform. World War I, the Treaty of Versailles, American rejection of the League of Nations, the Red Scare, the apparent failure of Progressive Era efforts at democratization, and the capture of the federal government by probusiness Republicans had forced an "agonizing reappraisal" of many of Smith's basic views. Big business had displaced political conservation as the chief villain, and his faith in the ultimate political wisdom of "the people" had been severely shaken. In a 1923 letter Smith wrote that he preferred "to wait until the local public is educated to the need of political action, than to get immediate results by transferring the power to act to the central government" (Smith papers; quoted in Goldman, p. 210).

J. Allen Smith is most celebrated for the influence that he exercised over the large number of his students who became public servants or educators and for his pioneering efforts in the economic interpretation of American politics that also informed the writings of Charles Beard, Irving Fisher, Vernon Louis Parrington, Richard Hofstadter, Merrill Jensen, and other scholars. He remained an active member of the University of Washington faculty until his death in Seattle. Parrington, his closest friend, called Smith a "scholar, teacher, democrat, gentleman" and "another pioneer figure, who applied to the abstract theorizings of political science the economic realities that underlie and determine them."

• Smith's papers are at the University of Washington in Seattle. The best sources on Smith, besides his own works, are introductions by Cushing Strout to the 1965 edition of *The Spirit of American Government* and by Vernon Louis Parrington to *The Growth and Decadence of Constitutional Government* (1930). The tension between scholar and activist within Smith is examined in Eric F. Goldman, "J. Allen Smith: The Reformer and His Dilemma," *Pacific Northwest Quarterly* 35 (1944): 195–214. The most complete treatments of Smith's career are in Thomas C. McClintock, "J. Allen Smith and the Progressive Movement: A Study in Intellectual History" (Ph.D. diss., Univ. of Washington, 1959), and in his article "J. Allen Smith: A Pacific Northwest Progressive," *Pacific Northwest Quarterly* 53 (1962): 49–59. Obituaries are in the Seattle *Daily Times*, 30 Jan. 1924, and the *New York Times*, 31 Jan. 1924.

JOHN D. BUENKER

SMITH, James Francis (28 Jan. 1859–29 June 1928), colonial administrator and judge, was born in San Francisco, California, the son of Patrick Smith (occupation unknown) and Ann (maiden name unknown). Smith graduated from Santa Clara College in 1878, attended Hastings Law School, and was admitted to the bar in 1881. In 1885 he married Lillie A. Dunnigan; the couple had at least one child.

In the Spanish-American War of 1898 Smith commanded the First California Volunteers in the Philippines. On 13 August Smith's regiment stormed Manila. In January 1899 Smith served on an American commission that held a series of five meetings with the representatives of Emilio Aguinaldo, president of the Philippine Republic, to try to adjust political claims and avoid hostilities. The talks came to naught, and on

4 February 1899 the Philippine-American War began. In the initial encounters Smith's volunteers broke through the Filipino lines. One American general reported that Smith demonstrated "the very best qualities of a volunteer officer" (Blount, p. 194). He was commended for gallantry and promoted to brigadier general.

In March 1899 Smith was sent to Negros, a province that did not join Aguinaldo's resistance movement, and in April he became military commander of the Visayas. In July Smith became military governor of Negros. A tactful administrator, he convinced potential revolutionaries to cooperate with the Americans.

In October 1900 Smith became customs collector at Manila where he introduced "order and integrity into that long graft- and dispute-ridden institution" (Gleeck, p. 76). In June 1901 he became an associate justice of the Supreme Court of the Philippines, a post he particularly enjoyed. In January 1903 he reluctantly left the court to join the Philippine Commission and served as secretary of public instruction. Under Smith's leadership, David Prescott Barrows, director of education for the Philippines, ran the educational system on a day-to-day basis. Barrows attempted to inculcate Jeffersonian values into Filipino students and to establish a basis by which ordinary people could resist the oppression that he felt was inherent in the *caciquismo* system of rural tenant-landlord relationships characterized by mutual obligations and dependence. Smith generally supported Barrows, although he came to want more "industrial" education (manual and vocational education) in the curriculum than Barrows thought wise.

In September 1906 Smith became governor general, and his reputation as a sensitive administrator persisted. Shortly after he took office he spared two resistance leaders who had been sentenced to death. Smith also showed understanding of the *pulajanes*, members of a religious sect, the followers of a local "pope," whom most Americans dismissed as bandits. Smith realized that these uplanders had been treated unjustly and were therefore susceptible to religious fanaticism. In his first annual report he wrote, "Education and just treatment will make out of the pulahan a good citizen" (*Report of the Philippine Commission, 1907*, vol. 1, p. 87).

Smith agreed with the first civil governor, William Howard Taft, that American retention of the islands should be indefinite. He felt that the Philippines had no way to defend itself and that Filipinos lacked political experience. He never belittled the people's intelligence, however, and took pride that under his administration the number of Filipinos who passed the civil service examination steadily increased.

As governor general, Smith had a reputation for candor and often clashed with the press and with Commissioner (later governor general) W. Cameron Forbes. He publicly acknowledged that racial tension was increasing in the islands. Concerned about charges that Americans wanted to exploit the islands, Smith made few concessions to potential investors. Similarly,

he had serious doubts about the Payne Bill passed in 1909 by the U.S. Congress, which he thought treated Philippine products unfairly and would reduce the islands' revenues.

In 1907 the first Philippine Assembly was elected. Smith supported the Partido Nacional Progresista, a continuation of the Partido Federalista, which had been established with American encouragement. In the elections, however, the Partido Nacionalista, formally dedicated to immediate independence, soundly defeated the Progresistas. Smith worked reasonably well with his political opponents in the assembly but pointed to provincial and municipal elections to show that "conservative and moderate views" still held sway among the populace at large (*Report of the Philippine Commission, 1908*, vol. 1, p. 63).

Attracted to the City Beautiful movement of the late nineteenth and early twentieth century, Smith succeeded in acquiring land for parks in Manila. He also experimented with different kinds of street paving and provided for a sensible way to build roads and bridges by allowing provinces to double the *cedula* (a poll tax inherited from the Spanish).

Smith's Roman Catholic faith helped him relate to Filipinos, but Protestant missionaries, who had objected to his appointment, often looked upon him with suspicion. Protestants felt that there was more religious persecution when Smith was governor general and alleged that he promoted gambling. The charges were unjustified. As a later governor general wrote, Smith was "always more than scrupulous of his duties and responsibilities in the public service" (Forbes, p. 88).

In 1909 Smith, who much preferred legal work to administration, asked President-elect Taft to relieve him of his post and, if possible, give him a judicial appointment in the United States. In 1910 Taft appointed him associate judge of the Court of Customs Appeals in Washington, D.C., where he served contentedly and with distinction until his death in Washington, D.C.

• The small collection of Smith papers in the Washington State Historical Society contains materials related primarily to Smith's military and political career in the Philippines. There is little about family genealogy. Many of Smith's papers relating to his early life were lost in the San Francisco fire of 1906. Smith's own writings are limited to official reports and court decisions. There are no biographies. The most complete account is in Louis E. Gleeck, Jr., *The American Governors-General and High Commissioners in the Philippines: Proconsuls, Nation-Builders and Politicians* (1986). Important contemporary works that discuss Smith include David Prescott Barrows, *The History of the Philippines* (1926); James H. Blount, *The American Occupation of the Philippines, 1898–1912* (1912); W. Cameron Forbes, *The Philippine Islands* (1945); James A. LeRoy, *The Americans in the Philippines: A History of the Conquest and the First Years of Occupation* (1914); and Dean C. Worcester, *The Philippines Past and Present* (1914). Smith's approach to Philippine education and his relations with the Philippine Assembly are discussed in Glenn A. May, *Social Engineering in the Philippines: The Aims, Execution, and Impact of American Colonial Policy,*

1900–1913 (1980). Smith's relations with the Protestant missionaries are traced in Kenton J. Clymer, *Protestant Missionaries in the Philippines, 1898–1916: An Inquiry into the American Colonial Mentality* (1986). The most complete obituary is in the Washington *Evening Star*, 30 June 1928.

KENTON J. CLYMER

SMITH, James McCune (18 Apr. 1813–17 Nov. 1865), abolitionist and physician, was born in New York City, the son of slaves. All that is known of his parents is that his mother was, in his words, "a self-emancipated bond-woman." His own liberty came on 4 July 1827, when the Emancipation Act of the state of New York officially freed its remaining slaves. Smith was fourteen at the time, a student at the Charles C. Andrews African Free School No. 2, and he described that day as a "real full-souled, full-voiced shouting for joy" that brought him from "the gloom of midnight" into "the joyful light of day." He graduated with honors from the African Free School but was denied admission to Columbia College and Geneva, New York, medical schools because of his race. With assistance from black minister Peter Williams, Jr., he entered the University of Glasgow, Scotland, in 1832 and earned the degrees of B.A. (1835), M.A. (1836), and M.D. (1837). He returned to the United States in 1838 as the first professionally trained black physician in the country.

Smith resettled in New York City, in 1838 or 1839 married Malvina Barnet, with whom he had five children, and established himself as a successful physician. He set up practice in Manhattan as a surgeon and general practitioner for both blacks and whites, became the staff physician for the New York Colored Orphan Asylum, and opened a pharmacy on West Broadway, one of the first in the country owned by a black.

Smith's activities as a radical abolitionist and reformer, however, secured his reputation as one of the leading black intellectuals of the antebellum era. As soon as he returned to the United States, he became an active member of the American Anti-Slavery Society, which sought immediate abolition by convincing slaveholders through moral persuasion to renounce the sin of slavery and emancipate their slaves. By the late 1840s he had abandoned the policies of nonresistance and nonvoting set forth by William Lloyd Garrison and his followers in the society. Instead, Smith favored political abolitionism, which interpreted the U.S. Constitution as an antislavery document and advocated political and ultimately violent intervention to end slavery. In 1846 Smith championed the campaign for unrestricted black suffrage in New York State; that same year he became an associate and good friend of Gerrit Smith, a wealthy white abolitionist and philanthropist, and served as one of three black administrators for his friend's donation of roughly fifty acres apiece to some 3,000 New York blacks on a vast tract of land in the Adirondacks. He became affiliated with the Liberty party in the late 1840s, which was devoted to immediate and unconditional emancipation, unre-

stricted suffrage for all men and women, and land reform. In 1855 he helped found the New York City Abolition Society, which was organized, as he put it, "to Abolish Slavery by means of the Constitution; *or otherwise*," by which he meant violent intervention in the event that peaceful efforts failed (though there is no indication that he resorted to violence). When the Radical Abolition party, the successor to the Liberty party, nominated him for New York secretary of state in 1857, he became the first black in the country to run for a political office.

In his writings Smith was a central force in helping to shape and give direction to the black abolition movement. He contributed frequently to the *Weekly Anglo-African* and the *Anglo-African Magazine* and wrote a semiregular column for *Frederick Douglass' Paper* under the pseudonym "Communipaw," an Indian name that referred to a charmed and honored settlement in Jersey City, New Jersey, where blacks had played an important historic role. He also wrote the introduction to Frederick Douglass's 1855 autobiography, *My Bondage My Freedom*, and he often expressed his wish that Douglass relocate his paper from Rochester to New York City. Douglass considered Smith the "foremost" black leader who had influenced his reform vision.

Smith's writings focused primarily on black education and self-help, citizenship, and the fight against racism; these themes represented for him the most effective means through which to end slavery and effect full legal and civil rights. He was a lifelong opponent of attempts among whites to colonize blacks in Liberia and elsewhere and a harsh critic of black nationalists who, beginning in the 1850s, encouraged emigration to Haiti and West Africa rather than continue to fight for citizenship and equal rights. Although he defended integration, he also encouraged blacks to establish their own presses, initiatives, and organizations. "It is emphatically our battle," he wrote in 1855. "Others may aid and assist if they will, but the moving power rests with us." His embrace of black self-reliance in the late 1840s paralleled his departure from the doctrines of Garrison and the American Anti-Slavery Society, which largely ignored black oppression in the North—even among abolitionists—by focusing on the evils of slavery in the South. Black education in particular, he concluded, led directly to self-reliance and moral uplift, and these values in turn provided the most powerful critique against racism. He called the schoolhouse the "great caste abolisher" and vowed to "fling whatever I have into the cause of colored children, that they may be better and more thoroughly taught than their parents are."

The racist belief in the innate inferiority of blacks was for Smith the single greatest and most insidious obstacle to equality. In 1846 he became despondent over the racial "hate deeper than I had imagined" among the vast majority of whites. Fourteen years later he continued to lament that "our white countrymen do not know us"; "they are strangers to our characters, ignorant of our capacity, oblivious to our history." He hoped his own distinguished career and writings would serve as both a role model for uneducated blacks and a powerful rebuttal against racist attacks. As a black physician he was uniquely suited to combat the pseudoscientific theories of innate black inferiority. In two important and brilliantly argued essays—"Civilization" (1844) and "On the Fourteenth Query of Thomas Jefferson's Notes on Virginia" (1859)—he incorporated his extensive knowledge of biology and anatomy to directly refute scientific arguments of the innate inferiority of blacks.

The driving force behind Smith's reform vision and sustained hope for equality was his supreme "confidence in God, that firm reliance in the saving power of the Redeemer's Love." Much like other radical abolitionists such as Douglass and Gerrit Smith, he viewed the abolition movement and the Civil War in millennialist terms; slavery and black oppression were the most egregious of a plethora of sins ranging from tobacco and alcohol to apathy and laziness that needed to be abolished in order to pave the way for a sacred society governed by "Bible Politics," as he envisioned God's eventual reign on earth. He strove to follow his savior's example by embracing the doctrine of "equal love to all mankind" and at the same time remaining humble before him. He likened himself to "a coral insect . . . loving to work beneath the tide in a superstructure, that some day when the labourer is long dead and forgotten, may rear itself above the waves and afford rest and habitation for the creatures of his Good, Good Father of All." Following his death in Williamsburg, New York, from heart failure, his writings and memories remained a powerful source of inspiration, "rest and habitation" to future generations of reformers.

• The best source on Smith's career and worldview is David W. Blight's excellent essay, "In Search of Learning, Liberty, and Self Definition: James McCune Smith and the Ordeal of the Antebellum Black Intellectual," *Afro-Americans in New York Life and History* 9, no. 2 (July 1985): 7–25, which contains in the footnotes the most complete listing of Smith's published writings, correspondence, and secondary references. C. Peter Ripley, ed., *The Black Abolitionist Papers*, vols. 3–5 (1991), includes a number of Smith's letters and excellent reference notes and is another important source. The Gerrit Smith Papers, housed in the George Arents Research Library at Syracuse University and widely distributed on microfilm, include thirty letters from James McCune Smith to Gerrit Smith that contain valuable information. *Frederick Douglass' Paper* contains more essays by Smith than any other contemporary publication. *Anglo-African Magazine, Volume I—1859* has been reprinted by Arno Press (1968) and includes four important essays by Smith: "Civilization, Its Dependence on Physical Circumstances"; "The German Invasion"; "Citizenship"; and "On the Fourteenth Query of Thomas Jefferson's Notes on Virginia." Smith also wrote the introduction to Henry Highland Garnet, *A Memorial Discourse* (1865).

JOHN STAUFFER

SMITH, Jedediah Strong (6 Jan. 1799?–27 May 1831), fur trader and explorer, was born (some say on 24 June 1798) in Bainbridge, Chenango County, New York,

the son of Jedediah Smith, probably a farmer and possibly a part-time tailor. His mother's name is unrecorded. Raised and educated in elementary schools in Pennsylvania and Ohio, young Smith became a clerk on a Lake Erie trading vessel. In 1822 he joined the fur-trading venture of General William H. Ashley and Andrew Henry heading up the Missouri River to the mouth of the Yellowstone. He not only survived the debacle of Ashley's defeat by the "Rees" (Arikara Indians) in 1823 but also distinguished himself in the fight. A natural leader, he found and opened up new beaver trapping grounds south of the Yellowstone River. In 1824, with his close friend, Tom "Broken Hand" Fitzpatrick, he located South Pass, the gateway to the Far West. This natural, easy pass through the Wind River Range of Wyoming's Rocky Mountains was probably traversed by John Jacob Astor's "Astorians," returning from the Pacific Coast in October 1812, but it remained unknown to other European and American trappers and settlers until Smith used it.

Smith was badly mauled and scarred for life by a grizzly bear near Powder River but went on to become Ashley's business partner, dropping down to St. Louis in 1825 with 9,000 pounds of beaver pelts. At Great Salt Lake in 1826, Ashley sold his firm to his most promising lieutenants, Smith, David E. Jackson, and William Sublette.

Smith was considered one of the greatest mountain men, comparable to Fitzpatrick, Jim Bridger, Kit Carson, and Captain Joe Walker. He was not illiterate like Bridger, Carson, Caleb "Old" Greenwood, and the mulatto Jim Beckwourth. He profited from a good common-school education and was almost unique among his irreligious peers in that he was a Bible-toting Christian. The clean-shaven, six-foot Methodist did not smoke or swear and drank in moderation. More important, he was the most intelligent and well read of the American fur men, a diarist, and a mapmaker as well as a first-rate explorer. Smith never married or, apparently, formed a relationship with an Indian woman, as did some of his companions in the Far West.

Smith's major exploring feats, after his discovery of the key South Pass route through the Rockies, occurred during expeditions of 1826–1829. He left Cache Valley, Utah, with seventeen men in August 1826 and made the first successful traverse of the Mojave Desert by Anglo-Americans, reaching California in November. He had failed to find the fabled Buenaventura River, a stream reputedly flowing unobstructed from the Rocky Mountains to the Pacific near San Francisco, because like the Northwest Passage, it did not exist.

Smith was well received by Padre José Sánchez at Mission San Gabriel, but Governor José M. Echeandiá was inclined to imprison him as a trespasser without *pasaporte*. But an influential Boston shipmaster in California interceded in Smith's behalf. The governor granted him permission to remain, but only till he could retrace his steps eastward. Though Smith had planned a look at the Hudson's Bay Company's

Columbia River fur country, reported to be as rich as the Rockies, he heeded Echeandía's orders and prepared to return to Great Salt Lake and the annual rendezvous, where trappers met their suppliers and fur buyers. After one false start, with just two men, Smith ascended either the Stanislaus or the American rivers, the latter named for him and his followers by the *Californios*. After negotiating the High Sierra, Smith, the first white man to pass over the range, and his party had to cross the Nevada-Utah desert via the precarious lifeline of the Humboldt River. Smith thereby became the first American to explore the Great Basin. He and his companions nearly starved, although they ate at least one of their horses.

After resting for less than a fortnight at the Bear Lake rendezvous, Smith led eighteen reinforcements for his party back to California, following his original westward route. He was surprised by Mojave Indians on 18 August 1827 when his company was split in half while crossing the Colorado River. The Mojaves killed ten of his men and looted his camp. With the survivors, Smith pushed on to San Gabriel Mission and then rejoined his original party, now in bad shape. But, after Smith signed a bond, a reluctant, still-suspicious Governor Echeandía let the interloper purchase food and supplies with which to recross the Sierra to American territory. But instead, after wintering in the Sacramento Valley, Smith led his men up the Sacramento River, believed by some to be the legendary Buenaventura, to become the first American to cross the Siskiyou Mountains from Mexican California into Oregon Territory. He got as far as the Umpqua River when he was again surprised by hostiles. On 14 July 1828 Umpquas, or Kelawatsets, massacred the entire party save Smith and three of his men. Dr. John McLoughlin, chief factor at the Hudson's Bay Company post of Fort Vancouver, rescued some of the Americans' property and cared for the survivors till Smith could take them to the rendezvous at Pierre's Hole in March 1829.

Smith's trapping company was successful, but in 1830 he and his partners sold out at the Popo Agie River annual rendezvous. The company was bought by Bridger and four other mountain men, who named it the Rocky Mountain Fur Company. Smith gave up the fur business and entered the Santa Fe trade with a wagon train. In May 1831 he was ahead of his party, alone, searching for water when he was lanced to death by Comanches at a spring (perhaps present-day Fargo Springs) near the Cimarron River in Southwest Kansas.

Besides being the effective discoverer of South Pass, Smith added greatly to Americans' knowledge of the Mojave Desert, the Great Basin, California, and Oregon. Partisans of his peers, such as Captain Joe Walker, have criticized him for carelessly letting his guard down not once but three times, with two resulting massacres and his own violent death. They point out that a more careful trapper, George Yount, lived on to pioneer settlement in California's Napa Valley and died in bed at age seventy-one. Still, as an explorer,

Jed Smith was possibly rivaled only by his Canadian counterpart, Peter Skene Ogden.

• Smith family papers are at the Bancroft Library of the University of California, Berkeley, and at the University of the Pacific, Stockton, Calif., but virtually all original manuscripts of importance on Jed Smith himself have been published in books or journal articles. Among the best sources are Dale Morgan, *Jedediah Smith and the Opening of the West* (1953); Maurice Sullivan, *Travels of Jedediah Smith* (1924) and *Jedediah Smith, Trader and Trail Breaker* (1936); Alson J. Smith, *Men against the Mountain* (1956); and Harrison C. Dale, *The Ashley-Smith Expeditions* (1918).

RICHARD H. DILLON

SMITH, Jeremiah (29 Nov. 1759–21 Sept. 1842), member of Congress, fourth governor of New Hampshire, and chief justice of New Hampshire, was born at Peterborough, New Hampshire, the son of William Smith, a justice of the peace, and Elizabeth Morison, both farmers. Smith's father was a member of the Provincial Congress in 1774. Smith did not have much early formal education. He entered Harvard in 1777, stayed two years, and, after serving briefly in the American Revolution, graduated from Queens College (now Rutgers) in 1780. Having determined to enter the law, Smith spent several years teaching in Massachusetts and New Hampshire and studying law alone. He was admitted to the bar at Amherst in Hillsborough County, New Hampshire, in 1786 and spent the remainder of his life in the law in New Hampshire. Rapidly becoming prominent in public life, Smith served as selectman in Peterborough and its representative in the general assembly, 1788–1790; member of the 1791 New Hampshire constitutional convention, where he helped draft the judiciary article; member of a special committee for collecting and codifying the law of New Hampshire, 1792; and Federalist member of Congress, 1790–1797.

In 1797 Smith retired from Congress to become U.S. attorney for the New Hampshire district and moved to Exeter. In that same year he married Eliza Ross of Maryland, with whom he had five children. Appointed probate judge for Rockingham County in 1800, Smith improved that branch of New Hampshire law and gathered materials for a treatise on the subject titled "An Essay on the Law of Descent and of Last Wills and Testaments." On 20 February 1801 President John Adams appointed him to one of the new federal circuit court judgeships created by the Judiciary Act of 1801. His tenure was brief because the Repeal Act of 1802 canceled those judgeships. Before assuming that post, he had studied fourteen hours a day for three months and thereafter spoke of that preparation time as the beginning of his legal education. On 17 May 1802 he became chief justice of New Hampshire and worked hard for the next seven years to modernize and systematize New Hampshire law. He resigned the chief justiceship in 1809 to serve one term as governor and then resumed his law practice.

Politics and the law were closely intertwined in Smith's life. Stalwart federalism had played an important, if secondary, role in his judicial appointments and in his election as New Hampshire's fourth governor. After an electoral victory in 1813, New Hampshire Federalists radically reorganized the state's courts, throwing out all the existing judges and making all judges subject to removal through impeachment and by the governor and council when asked by the legislature. Smith had profound objections to this judicial reorganization—he had lost his federal judgeship through just such a change—but his party loyalty caused him to accept appointment as chief justice in 1813 and to hold court until 1816 when victorious New Hampshire Republicans brought another wave of judicial reform.

The Republican victory in 1816 also brought to a boil the simmering political and sectarian feud known as the Dartmouth College case, in which Smith along with Jeremiah Mason and Daniel Webster represented the college trustees in their effort to stop a state takeover of the institution. Smith, like Mason, was a powerful shaper of the trustees' argument that the charter of Dartmouth College was a grant establishing a private corporation, a private right that the state could not deprive without due process of law, a judicial inquiry into the reasonableness of the deprivation. Webster used Smith's and Mason's arguments as the basis for his successful argument before the Supreme Court of the United States in 1819. Smith's argument is reported in Timothy Farrar's *Report of the Case of the Trustees of Dartmouth College against William H. Woodward* (1819).

In 1820 Smith retired from practice and became president of the branch of the Bank of the United States at Exeter; he also served as treasurer at Phillips Exeter Academy, 1828–1842. He retained his legendary humor and maintained his reputation as an extraordinary conversationalist and master of repartee. After the death of his wife, he married Elizabeth Hale of Dover, New Hampshire, in 1831; they had one child. In 1842 Smith moved to Dover, where he died.

Smith's reputation and place in history rest squarely on his prowess as a state judge and judicial reformer. His opinions were distinguished by painstaking legal research, and he was one of the pioneers of reform of the bench in New Hampshire. He was to the bench what Mason had been to the bar of New Hampshire. As a lawyer Smith fit well with the "giants" of Rockingham County. William Plumer, Jr., called Smith "the Menelaus, with a touch of the Thersites humor" to Mason's Agememnon (Peabody, p. 179). Lawyer Smith pointed his arguments more to the court than to the jury and worked to persuade the courts to clarify and standardize New Hampshire law and practice. He was, for example, one of the first and most successful advocates of judicial review in New Hampshire. Then, after election to the court in 1802, Smith brought to the New Hampshire judiciary the same quality of argument and attention to forms that distinguished giants of the Rockingham County bar.

New Hampshire chief justice Charles Doe, in *Lisbon v. Lyman* (1870), noted that "Chief Justice Smith, who found the law of New Hampshire in practice and administration, a chaos, and who left it comparatively an organized and scientific system," had provided the state with judicial labors of "inestimable" value.

• The best collection of Smith papers is in J. H. Morison, *Life of the Honorable Jeremiah Smith, LL.D.* (1845). Morison was the custodian of Smith's papers at his death and from them produced his memoir. Morison's *Life* also contains Smith's probate treatise. There were no official court records published for New Hampshire prior to 1816. Smith's careful record of the cases that came before him, however, is in Jeremiah Smith, Jr., *Decisions of the Superior and Supreme Courts of N.H., from 1801 to 1809 and from 1813 to 1816. Selected from the Manuscript Reports of the Late Jeremiah Smith, Chief Justice of Those Courts with Extracts from Judge Smith's Manuscript Treatise on Probate Law* (1879). Charles Henry Bell, *Bench and Bar of New Hampshire* (1894), offers a full biographical treatment. William Plumer, Jr., *Life of William Plumer*, ed. A. P. Peabody (1857; repr. 1969), gives a full but not always accurate discussion of Smith and the other personalities of the Rockingham County bar. See also Lynn W. Turner, *William Plumer of New Hampshire, 1759–1850* (1962). For Smith's argument in the *Dartmouth College* case, see Francis N. Stites, *Private Interest and Public Gain: The Dartmouth College Case, 1819* (1972). An obituary is in the *Boston Daily Advertiser*, 21 Sept. 1842.

FRANCIS N. STITES

SMITH, Job Lewis (15 Oct. 1827–9 June 1897), pediatrician, was born in Spafford Township, Onondaga County, New York, the son of Lewis Smith, a farmer and local politician, and Chloe Benson. He completed his secondary education at Homer (N.Y.) Academy, where he apparently developed an interest in botany, particularly the curative properties of plants. This interest, coupled with the influence of his older brother Stephen (who eventually became a prominent surgeon), led to his decision to pursue a medical career. After receiving his B.A. from Yale University in 1849, he studied medicine as an intern to Caleb Green of Homer and two doctors named Goodyear and Hyde, of Cortlandt, New York, while attending Buffalo Medical School. While a medical student, he attracted the attention of Austin Flint, the noted physiologist. In 1852, as a result of Flint's influence, Smith became an intern in the Buffalo Hospital of the Sisters of Charity. The next year he enrolled in New York City's College of Physicians and Surgeons, receiving his M.D. in 1853.

Later that year, after a brief stint as curator and consulting physician of New York's Nursery and Child's Hospital, Smith opened a general medical practice in one of the city's less affluent neighborhoods. He often provided his services without charge for those who could not otherwise afford medical care. He soon came into contact with a number of children who suffered from a variety of illnesses, many of which afflicted only the young, and he began to take a particular interest in their treatment. Although he continued to practice general medicine until his death, he devoted increasing amounts of his time to studying and treating childhood diseases and medical conditions, eventually becoming one of the most knowledgeable pediatricians in the United States.

In 1858 Smith married Mary Anne Hannah, with whom he would have seven children. That same year he established a children's clinic at the Northwestern Dispensary, with which he remained affiliated for the next ten years. In 1860 he became the attending physician in charge of infants and sick children at Charity Hospital, and in 1869 he was appointed attending physician at the city's Infant Asylum. He also wrote *A Treatise on the Diseases of Infancy and Childhood* (1869), one of the first works devoted to this topic by an American author; in it he strongly advocated the use of preventive medicine to preserve the health of children. The book became a standard reference work among physicians and nurses who treated children, and by 1896 it had gone through eight editions, each incorporating the latest findings in pediatric medicine.

In 1871 Smith became a professor of morbid anatomy at Bellevue Hospital Medical College, having served briefly as a lecturer on that topic ten years earlier, but he resigned the next year. He returned to the college in 1876 as a clinical professor of childhood diseases and served in this capacity for the next twenty years. His most important research work during this period included a study of scarlatinal nephritis, a kidney disease associated with scarlet fever, and tetanus neonatorum, a tetanus infection that occurs in newborns as a result of an infected navel.

In 1884 Smith and William Perry Watson founded *Archives of Pediatrics*, the first American medical journal devoted to the diagnosis and treatment of childhood diseases. That same year he played an instrumental role in establishing a section of pediatrics in the New York Academy of Medicine. In 1887 he served as president of the pediatric section of the Ninth International Medical Congress. Shortly after the congress adjourned, several physicians who had participated in the section's activities met in New York City to discuss the creation of a professional medical organization devoted to pediatrics. Smith was elected temporary chairman of the meeting, which resulted in the formation of the American Pediatric Society (APS) the following year; in 1890 he served as its second president. In 1896 he retired from the college but continued to practice privately until his death in New York City.

Smith's role as a practitioner, author, educator, editor, and organizer established his reputation as one of the pioneers in American pediatrics. With the exception of Abraham Jacobi, no other single individual contributed more to the establishment of pediatrics as a separate branch of medical practice.

• Smith's role as a pioneer in pediatrics is discussed in Francis R. Packard, *History of Medicine in the United States* (repr. 1963). Biographical memoirs published after Smith's death include Eliot Ellsworth, "Memorial to Job Lewis Smith," New York Academy of Medicine, *Transactions*, 2d ser., 13 (1897): 220, and J. Shrady, "Memoir of J. Lewis Smith," New York State Medical Association, *Transactions* 14 (1897): 524. An obituary is in the *New York Times*, 10 June 1897.

CHARLES W. CAREY, JR.

SMITH, Joe (28 June 1902–2 Dec. 1937), jazz cornetist and trumpeter, was born Joseph E. (or C.) Smith in Ripley, Ohio, the son of Luke Smith, a Cincinnati brass band leader from whom he received his first tutelage. Nothing is known of his mother, but all six of his brothers also studied trumpet, the most well known being Russell Smith, who later played lead trumpet with Fletcher Henderson and other top swing bands. During his teens Joe played with local bands and left town with a traveling show, but after becoming stranded in Pittsburgh he returned home. Around 1920 he went to New York and worked with drummer Kaiser Marshall in a dance hall on Forty-eighth Street, following which he returned to Pittsburgh for local jobs. In January 1922 he went to Chicago to join Fletcher Henderson's Black Swan Jazz Masters and then toured with Ethel Waters. He recorded a session with Waters in May 1922. After concluding the tour in July, he replaced Bubber Miley in Mamie Smith's Jazz Hounds. It was in this group that he first played with Coleman Hawkins, later an important fellow sideman in Henderson's orchestra. While with Mamie Smith, he toured the Loew's theater circuit in Canada and as far west as California but left her act in New York in early 1923 to work locally with Billy Paige's Broadway Syncopators and do freelance recording dates. In March 1924 he toured as musical director and featured soloist with Noble Sissle and Eubie Blake's *In Bamville* revue, which in September opened in New York at the Colonial Theater as *The Chocolate Dandies*. Not wishing to travel again, Smith left the show in November, and from that time until April 1925 he worked in New York venues accompanying blackface comedian Johnny Hudgins, another Sissle and Blake star.

In the spring of 1922 Smith began recording blues accompaniments for Ethel Waters, Mamie Smith, Ma Rainey, Alberta Hunter, and Bessie Smith, as well as a host of other lesser-known singers. As was true of most New York–based trumpeters of the early 1920s, Smith was under the influence of Johnny Dunn, but to his credit he quickly abandoned Dunn's staccato attack and raggy phrasing and instead adopted a more relaxed rhythmic flow with a broad, expressive tone and acquired an ear for melodic nuance. He is especially winning on Waters's "Tell 'Em about Me" and "Smile!" and at his best on almost all of Bessie Smith's titles, most notably "Weeping Willow," "The Bye Bye Blues," "The Yellow Dog Blues," "At the Christmas Ball," "Money Blues," "Baby Doll," "Young Woman's Blues," "Alexander's Ragtime Band," and "There'll Be a Hot Time in the Old Town Tonight." On these records, Smith defines his conception of blues accompaniment as being something quite different from that of Louis Armstrong, who was equally prolific in this capacity and with many of the same artists. Where Armstrong by the sheer force of his own surging creativity tended to outshine rather than support the singers he was hired to accompany, Smith, with his plaintive, burnished tone, complemented their lines with linking phrases, often to compellingly poignant effect. Not only did he play with much less vibrato and timbral drama than Armstrong, but he also avoided the upper register in which Armstrong excelled. Where Armstrong was the epitome of raw, unfettered, blues-based expression, Smith was spare, refined, and polished. Indeed, it was most likely these qualities and the contrast they afforded her own passionate style that accounted for the preference shown him by Bessie Smith.

In mid-April 1925 Smith replaced Howard Scott in Fletcher Henderson's brass section, and for the next seven months he played alongside Armstrong both at the Roseland Ballroom and in the recording studios. His most characteristic early playing with the band is heard on "Memphis Bound," "What-Cha-Call-'Em Blues," and "TNT," where his alternating solo spots with Armstrong clearly demonstrate the marked stylistic differences between the two. Following Armstrong's return to Chicago in early November, Smith stepped to the fore more frequently on numbers such as "The Stampede," "Fidgety Feet," "Sensation," "Variety Stomp," and "The St. Louis Blues." Throughout Smith's tenure with the band, Henderson and arranger Don Redman used his pure-toned, lyrical style as a contrast to the hotter, earthier approaches of Armstrong and, after his departure, Rex Stewart, Tommy Ladnier, and Bobby Stark. But Smith also possessed a talent for mimicry, so it is not surprising to observe his direct nod to Armstrong on Bessie Smith's May 1926 "Hard Driving Papa" and "Lost Your Head Blues" and to Bix Beiderbecke, a much closer stylistic model, on Henderson's January 1927 "Ain't She Sweet."

In late September 1928 Smith and his brother Russell left Henderson to join Allie Ross's Plantation Orchestra in the touring company of Lew Leslie's famous *Blackbirds of 1928*. In late June 1929 Smith and Kaiser Marshall appeared in a James P. Johnson–led band in the Bessie Smith film, *St. Louis Blues*. In the summer Smith joined the Detroit-based McKinney's Cotton Pickers and first appeared on record with them in November, when he soloed on "Gee, Ain't I Good to You" and "The Way I Feel Today." Between January and July 1930 his expansive tone, both muted and open, was documented on "Words Can't Express," "If I Could Be with You One Hour Tonight," "Travelin' All Alone," and "Okay Baby." (Although long attributed to Smith, the muted solo on "I Want a Little Girl" was actually the work of George "Buddy" Lee, a recent addition to the band.) Unlike the role he enjoyed on the blues records or with Henderson, on the Cotton Pickers' arrangements Smith was rarely given fully improvised solos, his parts largely being restricted to straight exposition of the melodies, albeit enhanced by his expressive handling of the plunger mute.

In late 1930, while the band was on tour in New England, Smith, long a heavy drinker, chose to drive Kaiser Marshall's car to an engagement in Bridgeport instead of riding with the others on the band bus. With the band's valet and saxman/singer George "Fathead" Thomas as passengers, Smith reportedly drove so recklessly that the car went off the road and crashed in a ditch. Although Smith escaped unhurt and the band-boy survived numerous fractures, Thomas was critically injured and died a few days later, a tragedy that only exacerbated the remorseful Smith's already severe drinking problem. In the words of banjoist/singer Dave Wilborn, "Joe brooded over Fathead's death, and drank continually from then on. He quickly slipped downhill and eventually lost his mind."

Following the accident, Smith left the Cotton Pickers and joined Marshall's band in Boston, but he returned in August 1931 and recorded one short but characteristic solo that September on "Wrap Your Troubles in Dreams." By this time, though, his behavior had become increasingly erratic and unreliable, and he left the band on New Year's Eve. In early 1932 he moved to Kansas City, where he may have worked for a while with Bennie Moten. In February 1933 he was playing with Clarence Love's band at El Torreon Ballroom, but he was so ill that when Fletcher Henderson happened to see him while on tour he convinced Smith to return to New York, the hope being that he would regain his health and ultimately rejoin the band. However, this proved in vain, for not only was Smith suffering from acute alcoholism but he was also mentally unstable. He was placed in a sanatorium on Long Island, but after further deterioration he was transferred to Bellevue Hospital in New York, where he died of paresis, an advanced stage of syphilis. There is no record of marriage or children.

Unlike Armstrong, Beiderbecke, and Bubber Miley, the three most influential stylists of the 1920s, Smith did not attract legions of disciples. His artistry lay not so much in creativity or innovation as in his establishment of an alternate temperament with which to play blues and, by extension, ballads. It has been said that he was probably the first "cool" jazz trumpeter, preceding Miles Davis by some twenty-five years, but that claim ignores the contemporaneous presence and influence of Beiderbecke and Red Nichols, who were each admired and widely emulated by both black and white jazzmen of the 1920s. But neither of these were bluesmen, and Smith was an anomaly within a mainstream established by King Oliver, Armstrong, and Miley. He was also a remarkable synthesist, whose greater sensitivity enabled him to break away completely from the rhythmically restrictive mold of Johnny Dunn and develop a tone that soon became the envy of many. Although Smith did not leave any direct stylistic descendants, the influence of his wistful tone and economical phrasing can be heard in the playing of Buck Clayton, Bill Coleman, Frankie Newton, and Doc Cheatham.

• The best discussions of Smith's style and that of his first influence, Johnny Dunn, are in Gunther Schuller, *Early Jazz* (1968), but the most detailed sources of information on Smith's career are Walter C. Allen, *Hendersonia: The Music of Fletcher Henderson and His Musicians: A Bio-Discography* (1973), and John Chilton, *McKinney's Music: A Bio-Discography of McKinney's Cotton Pickers* (1978). Reminiscences of Smith's contemporaries are in Nat Shapiro and Nat Hentoff, eds., *Hear Me Talkin' to Ya* (1955); Stanley Dance, *The World of Swing* (1974); Rex Stewart, *Boy Meets Horn* (1991); and

Bill Coleman, *Trumpet Story* (1990). Supplementary information regarding Smith's activities with Mamie Smith's Jazz Hounds and the Henderson and McKinney orchestras is in John Chilton, *The Song of the Hawk: The Life and Recordings of Coleman Hawkins* (1990). Complete discographical listings are in Brian Rust, *Jazz Records: 1897–1942* (1982), as well as in the Allen and Chilton bio-discographies cited above.

JACK SOHMER

SMITH, John (1580–21 June 1631), colonial governor, promoter, and historian, was born in Willoughby by Alford in Lincolnshire, the son of George Smith, a yeoman, and Alice Rickard. His earliest schooling may have been under Francis Marbury, father of Anne Hutchinson, who was schoolmaster in Alford. Toward the end of his life Smith published an autobiography, one of the first examples of the modern genre, which he titled *The True Travels, Adventures, and Observations of Captaine John Smith* (1630). Although the order and dating of events in his early life recounted there do not correspond to dates that can be established independently, the shape of his early career seems clear. His first patron was Lord Willoughby of Eresby, his father's landlord. He was apprenticed in 1595 to Thomas Sendall, a merchant in King's Lynn, having already formed a resolution to "get beyond the Sea." After his father's death the next year (Smith wrote that his father had died when he was thirteen), he left his apprenticeship because Sendall refused to send him abroad.

Smith traveled to France, where he "first began to learne the life of a Souldier." He wrote that he went to Europe initially as escort to young Peregrine Bertie, son of Lord Willoughby, and that he decided to stay in France. But, as Bertie did not receive a license to travel until 1599 and Smith by his own account served as a soldier with an English company in France and the Low Countries for "three or foure yeeres," it is unclear how the Bertie commission fits into the story. On leaving the Continent he went to Scotland futilely seeking the life of a courtier. Then he returned to his English home and studied to prepare himself for the life of a knight.

Soon, "desirous to see more of the world," he decided to "trie his fortune against the Turkes, both lamenting and repenting to have seene so many Christians slaughter one another." In late 1600, after adventures in the Mediterranean and in Italy, he signed on with Austrian forces fighting the Turkish Empire. He was promoted to the rank of captain before being captured in Transylvania. He escaped from captivity in Turkey and traveled via Russia through Europe to Morocco before returning to England in the winter of 1604–1605.

Smith was selected by the newly formed Virginia Company of London in 1606 to be one of the governing council in Virginia, the only person chosen because of his experience. He sailed with the contingent that settled Jamestown in May 1607. He spent much of the first year exploring, one venture ending with his capture in December 1607. His captors were clients of Powhatan, who was in the process of creating an "empire" of client tribes around the Chesapeake. As a captive for about three weeks, Smith was shown to several villages and finally met Powhatan himself. He was subjected to what was probably an adoption ceremony, in which Powhatan's daughter, Pocahontas, played a crucial role; Smith thought she had rescued him from death. Powhatan informed Smith that he was now a werowance, or subchief, under him.

Smith devoted the summer of 1608 to exploration of Chesapeake Bay. He had an excellent eye for important detail and a highly developed ability to understand relationships; from his experience exploring and trading for corn he produced an important report on the Virginia Algonquian Indians. His ethnographical account has gained in stature as modern archaeological research has confirmed elements of it. From his notes he also supervised the engraving of the highly accurate map included in his book describing the land and its people, *A Map of Virginia* (1612). Part 2 of *A Map of Virginia*, focusing primarily on the colony and its development, was published separately as *The Proceedings of the English Colonie in Virginia* (1612). Smith carefully supervised publication of these and his subsequent books; an earlier work had been badly edited and published in garbled form in London as *A True Relation of Such Occurrences and Accidents of Note As Hath Hapned in Virginia* (1608) while he was still in America. Smith, like others involved in new enterprises, understood the importance of print technology and was determined to use it effectively.

While Smith explored, the colony's leadership was mowed down by disease and crippled by poor planning. On his return in September 1608 he was elected president of the council, effectively governor of Virginia. Smith, having observed Indian practice, dispersed the colonists to live off the land in small groups away from the river. He forced all colonists, even the gentlemen and "tufftafety humorists," into productive activity, digging wells and building sound fortifications. The death rate from disease dropped dramatically during his administration.

Smith was particularly proud of the respectful, wary relationship he established with the "great emperor" Powhatan; he argued that only an experienced military man could gain the respect of such a leader and approach him on terms of equality. All colonial leaders, Smith among them, believed that the English must always dominate in their relationships with Indians; the only possible alternative was Indian domination of the settlers. Thus he followed a policy of intimidation which, he argued, increased Powhatan's respect for him. He contrasted his success with the spectacle of Captain Christopher Newport's humiliating failures in Indian relations. Newport, the admiral of Virginia Company supply fleets, was always in command when he was in the colony; Smith claimed that he had to repair damaged American respect for the English after Newport left.

The Virginia Company sent out a new administration under their renewed charter of 1609. Since the proposed leaders were shipwrecked on Bermuda and prevented from arriving in Virginia, Smith initially refused to give up command. He decided to return to England in October 1609 after he was severely burned by the accidental explosion of his powder bag as he traveled in a canoe. Back in England he became a critic of the Virginia Company for failing to put strong leaders in control and then trusting them to govern wisely. He argued that the settlers' attention had been diverted from the primary necessity of building strong colonial foundations to premature and fruitless searches for precious minerals and other commodities offering quick and easy returns. He was also harshly critical of the quality of the gentlemen the company had chosen for command. The Virginia Company was uninterested in what he had to say, and it may have been opposition from leading members that caused him to publish his *Map of Virginia* in Oxford rather than London.

Smith now turned his attention to the land north of Virginia. Norembega, as it was called, had been seen as barren and inhospitable since the failure of the western merchants' Virginia settlement at Sagadahoc in Maine in 1607. In 1614 Smith, backed by west-country merchants, made a brief voyage to New England and published a tract promoting that region, *A Description of New England* (1616), which included a map decorated with an inset portrait of Smith. The backdrop for this promotion was popular knowledge of the high death rate in Virginia and of that region's enervating heat. Smith coined the name New England, a brilliant propaganda ploy implicitly arguing that colonists in the north, unlike those in Virginia, could live a recognizably English life in a familiar setting. The primacy of New England as a focus of English colonization, supported by statistical information about the fishing industry, was reaffirmed in his *New Englands Trials* (1620; 2d ed., 1622). Despite his promotional activity and the plans he outlined, he was unable to get the backing to found a new colony in the north with himself in command.

Smith spent the last fifteen years of his life writing to promote a coherent theory of empire and analyzing the colonial record. Although he is best known as the man of action who stepped in to force the disoriented Jamestown colonists to save themselves, his contribution as historian and theorist was extremely important. In 1624 he published his large *Generall Historie of Virginia, New-England, and the Summer Isles*, just at the time that the royal government was pursuing the quo warranto proceedings that resulted in the revocation of the Virginia Company's charter. Like all promoters, Smith borrowed heavily from the work of other writers in compiling his history, but he differed from others in that he had firsthand experience of the difficulties of creating a colonial society. He reshaped every work he used to fit his own argument on the meaning of the colonial experience. Moreover he was the only participant-writer who treated all of English America as a coherent venture.

Against the backdrop of the Virginia Company's failure, and building on his previous work, Smith enunciated a new vision of colonization in his *Generall Historie* and in his final and most philosophical book, *Advertisements for the Unexperienced Planters of New England, or Anywhere* (1631). He argued that the English effort had suffered from inadequate leadership and unrealistic, poorly conceived goals. Because aims had not been intelligently delineated, the wrong kinds of people had been sent; those who had gone to America had spent their time foolishly. Smith was the first experienced theorist to argue that North America had riches to offer Europe, but that these would come only when people were prepared to emigrate and to produce commodities through their own hard work. Riches would come from humble commodities, fish and agricultural products, not from easily obtained and high-value goods. Land should be offered to all comers with secure tenures, which alone would lure the right kind of settlers. Only a society built on such foundations would be truly English; had the hopes of early promoters been realized, they would have produced perversions of England. Smith was contemptuous of tobacco, already emerging as the chief commodity of Virginia and argued that it was not an appropriate crop on which to build a society.

Smith placed his hopes on New England. In fact, though they did not acknowledge it, the Puritans of Plymouth Colony and Massachusetts Bay designed their colonies on the lines Smith indicated, a fact he pointed out in his *Advertisements*. But, as he wrote, they were not willing to offer him a place in their plans.

Between the *Generall Historie* and the *Advertisements*, Smith published several other books. He produced two books on seamanship, *An Accidence or the Path-way to Experience: Necessary for All Young Seamen* (1626) and *A Sea Grammar* (1627), both mostly glossaries of terms taken from other books. His autobiography, as well as telling the story of his early life, brought the history of the colonies up to date from the end of the *Generall Historie*. John Smith is buried in London, his place of death unknown.

Most of what we know about John Smith's life comes from his own writing. His accounts of his young manhood and his exploits in Virginia were judged by nineteenth-century scholars to be too extraordinary and internally inconsistent to be true. This assessment was shared by Henry Adams, who employed newly developed techniques of textual criticism. Partly because his own role was magnified as he retold his stories in successive works, Smith was put down as a braggart whose accounts were not to be trusted. In the latter half of the twentieth century, however, scholars established the authenticity of his work, demonstrating that the people and events of which he wrote, adjusting for Smith's rendition of names in unfamiliar languages, can be identified. His account of adventures in the wars against the Turks has made him an important source for that poorly documented period in eastern European history just as ethnohistorical and archaeological work in American history has enhanced scholarly estimation of his achievement.

• John Smith's writings are collected in *The Complete Works of Captain John Smith*, ed. Philip L. Barbour (3 vols., 1986), which includes an extensive bibliography. *Captain John Smith: A Select Edition of His Writings*, ed. Karen Ordahl Kupperman (1988), is selected from the texts prepared by Barbour. The best modern biography is Philip L. Barbour, *The Three Worlds of Captain John Smith* (1964); the introduction to Barbour's edition of Smith's works presents information discovered since 1964. See also Alden Vaughan, *American Genesis: Captain John Smith and the Founding of Virginia* (1975). The literary aspects of Smith's work are the subject of Everett Emerson, *Captain John Smith* (1971). On Smith's reputation for truthfulness see Laura Polanyi Striker and Bradford Smith, "The Rehabilitation of Captain John Smith," *Journal of Southern History* 28 (1962): 474–81, and Bradford Smith, *Captain John Smith: His Life and Legend* (1953), with an appendix by Laura Polanyi Striker.

KAREN ORDAHL KUPPERMAN

SMITH, John (c. 1735–30 July 1824), minister, merchant, and U.S. senator, was born in Virginia. Nothing is known about his parents, and very little is known about his early life. Smith appeared in the new settlement of Columbia (just east of Cincinnati) in May 1790. He had traveled from the forks of the Cheat River in what is now West Virginia, where he had been a Baptist minister. Apparently, he had had no education, was relatively poor, and was looking to improve the situation of his household. Described by contemporaries as large, handsome, and dark complected, he had as his only assets a talent for public speaking and a winning personality that expertly balanced seriousness and gregariousness. But they were enough to win the confidence of a small Baptist congregation who engaged him as their pastor. In 1791 Smith established his wife, Elizabeth Mason Hickman, and seven children in Columbia. With characteristic enthusiasm, the new preacher went to work to spread the gospel: he helped to design and construct the first Protestant church in the region in 1793, ordained other men as Baptist preachers, and led in the formation of the Miami Baptist Association in 1797.

The next year Smith gave up his ministry, although he remained a devout Baptist. The primary reason for this shift was the economic success that followed in part from his popularity as a preacher. Smith was a land speculator, but the foundation of his fortune was commerce. Taking advantage of the fact that Cincinnati was the military headquarters of the Northwest Territory, he got into the business of supplying the troops who were stationed at Fort Washington in the 1790s. Soon he was the operator of two dry goods stores and a partner in two grain mills on the Little Miami River. In his role as a merchant, Smith developed connections with important men throughout the Ohio and Mississippi valleys as well as in the army and the federal government. By 1796 Smith owned a $2,600 estate and was one of the wealthiest men in the Cincinnati area.

In the late 1790s, the minister-merchant turned his attention toward politics. Like many entrepreneurs, Smith was eager to replace the territorial government with a state government more responsive to local interests. In 1798 he was elected to the first meeting of the territorial legislature and emerged as a leader of the opposition to territorial governor Arthur St. Clair. Smith was adamantly pro-statehood, even when Congress angered residents of the Cincinnati area by dividing the Northwest Territory in two in 1800 and making Chillicothe the capital of the eastern part. Smith remained popular, however, and was elected to the Ohio constitutional convention in 1802. The next spring his constancy in support of statehood and his alliance with leading figures in the Scioto Valley paid off when he was chosen to be one of Ohio's first two senators.

In Washington, Smith was better known as a lobbyist for and expert on western interests than as a prominent member of the Senate. President Thomas Jefferson twice called upon him for information about Louisiana, which was appropriate because Smith was developing commercial and speculative interests in both Louisiana and West Florida. In addition, he continued to obtain contracts to supply the army in the West and participated in several land schemes. Without question, Smith was one of the most important and powerful men in Trans-Appalachia. No wonder, then, that Vice President Aaron Burr (1756–1836) made a point of cultivating his friendship.

The former vice president visited Cincinnati in May 1805 and spent several days at Smith's new home in Terrace Park discussing plans for building a canal around the Falls of the Ohio at Louisville. Burr was interested in much more than this. He wanted to lead an expedition against the northeastern regions of the Spanish empire, with or without the cooperation of the United States. Smith was interested in working with Burr, but he had no desire to encourage western secession. Why would a man as affluent and successful as Smith have wanted to risk everything he had built on such a vague and uncertain adventure? Clearly, he was eager to supply Burr's proposed expedition—that was his business, after all, and besides, he thought war with Spain imminent—but he wanted no part of treason. Although Burr stayed with Smith while he was in Cincinnati in September 1806, the senator was increasingly nervous about the relationship. Later that fall, a worried Smith demanded an explanation from Burr and got what he thought was a satisfactory answer. He backed away entirely when he heard rumors of Burr's arrest while on a business trip in Kentucky. In December 1806 Smith strongly supported the efforts of local and state officials to break up the activities of Burr's associates in the Ohio Valley. The senator then conducted several flatboats full of military supplies to New Orleans, after which he traveled to Washington to take his seat in the Senate in January 1807.

Meanwhile, Smith's well-known association with the now notorious Burr was causing him no end of trouble. Encouraged by political opponents from Cincinnati, the Ohio General Assembly demanded his resignation. He refused. In late summer a grand jury in

Richmond, Virginia, indicted him. Escorted from the Mississippi Territory, where he had voluntarily surrendered, to Cincinnati, he was released when word arrived that the charges had been dropped because of the acquittal of Burr. Smith's problems were just beginning, however. In November the Senate denied him his seat pending an investigation of his conduct. After an April 1808 trial, senators voted 19 to 10 for expulsion, short of the two-thirds majority required. Angry but realistic, Smith resigned on 25 April 1808.

With his reputation in ruins, Smith could no longer get the credit he needed to carry on his business. Former friends demanded immediate payment of his debts, and he soon lost almost all of his many land and commercial holdings. In the summer of 1810 Smith and his wife left Cincinnati for the Louisiana Territory to start over on some land he owned there. They ended up in St. Francisville, where his wife and a son died. With "no money and scarcely bread to eat," the former senator ended his life (in St. Francisville) with nothing more than he had had when he first arrived in the Northwest Territory in 1790.

• The Smith papers in the Cincinnati Historical Society deal mainly with the Burr conspiracy. A valuable source is *Report of the Committee Appointed to Inquire into the Facts relating to the Conduct of John Smith, a Senator of the United States from the State of Ohio, as an Alleged Associate of Aaron Burr* (1808). The best account of Smith's life is Robert W. Wilhelmy, "Senator John Smith and the Aaron Burr Conspiracy," *Cincinnati Historical Society Bulletin* 28 (1970): 38–60. See also Thomas Perkins Abernethy, *The Burr Conspiracy* (1954); Andrew R. L. Cayton, *The Frontier Republic: Ideology and Politics in the Ohio Country, 1780–1825* (1986); and Isaac Joslin Cox, *The West Florida Controversy: 1798–1813* (1918).

ANDREW CAYTON

SMITH, John Bernhard (21 Nov. 1858–12 Mar. 1912), entomologist, was born in New York City, the son of John Smith, a cabinetmaker, and Elizabeth Scheuerman. Smith attended local grammar schools and became a law office clerk. Admitted to the bar in 1879, he was a junior law partner until 1884. In 1886 he married Marie von Meske; they had two children.

With no scientific training, Smith became interested in insects through the Brooklyn Entomological Society. He was quoted as saying that "a fly on the wall is more interesting than a [law] case in hand." His first entomological scientific note appeared in 1881. For his taxonomic activities in entomological societies of several eastern cities, Smith was recognized by C. V. Riley, the pioneer entomologist in the U.S. Department of Agriculture, and in 1884 he was hired by the department as a special agent. Leaving the practice of law, Smith worked on identifying and controlling insects on hops and cranberries from 1884 to 1886. In 1886 he became assistant curator of insects at the U.S. National Museum. Smith resigned from this position in 1889 and accepted a position as entomologist for the New Jersey State Agricultural College Experiment Station and as professor of entomology at Rutgers College in New Brunswick. In 1894 he became the state entomol-

ogist for the New Jersey Board of Agriculture. He occupied these posts until his death.

Smith's work as a lawyer and then as a taxonomist and economic entomologist prepared him for the scientific, technological, and legislative aspects of dealing with insects. In New Jersey he surveyed statewide insect activity and field-tested to help manage insect populations on crops and animals. Smith's *Annual Report of 1890* describes many tests to reduce insect populations. He used the results to address farmers, to prepare informational material, to teach classes, and to aid in carrying on extensive public service correspondence. According to his 1895 *Report*, he wrote 1,017 pages of letters to the public that year, and in 1896 the number was 1,415. Over the course of his career Smith authored fifty-four articles and two books. Many publications reflect his continuing interest in taxonomy, despite his primary work in the economic and health aspects of entomology. His personal insect collection was large and contained 30,000 specimens of *Noctuidae* (owlet moths).

Smith recognized New Jersey as the "kitchen garden," where many native and imported crops and animals were raised to feed city markets. In his 1890 *Report* he asserted that insect pest problems in New Jersey would not amount to a "knockout effect" produced by a single pest, such as the devastation of wheat by the Hessian fly in the West. Rather, there would be many pests inflicting damage on a multiplicity of crops. Smith's approach to entomology entailed constant surveillance and adjustment of control measures to meet each situation.

Smith first described mosquitoes as a statewide problem in his 1901 *Report*, which details many species, identifies locations, and proposes a survey and a plan of action. Smith envisioned not extermination but rather "intelligent activity to reduce populations along well-developed lines," requiring legislative action and financial support. That same year L. O. Howard, chief of the Bureau of Entomology in Washington, D.C., spoke in South Orange, New Jersey, on mosquito control and supported a government program to reduce the mosquito population in New Jersey (efforts at mosquito control also began at this time on Long Island).

Smith prepared a survey questionnaire that he and station director Edward Voorhees sent to 458 municipalities, asking about the local mosquito situation. He furnished the recipients with vials to procure specimens for his identification of problem species. Results of the survey and Smith's strong convictions prompted the station and its supporters to press successfully for an act of the legislature to begin Smith's program in early 1902. Major supporters were the State Board of Health, the State Medical Society, the State Sanitary Association, and the Newark Board of Health. The bill empowered the station to investigate and report on mosquitoes, including life histories, breeding locations, and societal effects relating to diseases, injuries to agricultural workers, and sanitation. Although Governor Franklin Murphy signed the bill, no money was appropriated for action, so the governor furnished the station with $1,000 from his emergency funds.

Smith's approaches to mosquito control in inland areas were not unique, but he was the first to recognize the migration up to forty miles inland of the coastal salt marsh species *Aedes sollicitans*. Such migration overwhelmed towns' efforts to control local breeding species and highlighted the necessity for county and state protection programs. Smith and town officials mapped salt marshes and began ditching them to permit the flow of tides to bear predatory fish, which destroy mosquito larval forms. By 1904 Smith's report on the mosquitoes of New Jersey and their control had greatly stimulated public interest across the United States. Early on, municipalities in New Jersey paid for most of the ditching under Smith's direction. Later, the station/county programs were supplemented with more state and county money. By 1912 more than forty thousand acres of salt marshes from Hudson County (opposite New York City) to Barnegat (southern New Jersey) had been treated with five million feet of ditching.

Smith's crowning achievement, the County Mosquito Commission Law, was signed by Governor Woodrow Wilson just nine days after Smith's death. Under this legislation New Jersey, through the Agricultural Experiment Station, controlled all funds and activity statewide for a control program that continued with little change for more than sixty years, reducing mosquito infestation, protecting health, and allowing economic development. Malaria had caused 481 deaths in New Jersey in 1881. By 1912 the number was reduced to about 400 cases and 14 deaths attributed to malaria each year. By 1941 there were no cases reported. During World War II the disease resurged, but thereafter no outbreaks occurred until 1991, when two cases were reported.

Smith traveled twice to Europe. In 1900 he visited agricultural research stations in Germany, Holland, and Austria-Hungary over a ten-week period. On his second trip, in 1910, he traveled to Holland, Belgium, and Germany to investigate agricultural pests and mosquito control measures. While there Smith observed the value of mandatory plant nursery inspection for insects and diseases. He had earlier used his law background to ensure the passage in 1898 of legislation in New Jersey that called for mandatory nursery inspection. During his 1910 trip Smith investigated the swamp plant *Azolla* for an antimosquito effect but determined that it was not applicable for New Jersey marshes.

Smith was active in at least fourteen scientific societies, including the Canadian Entomological Society, the American Entomological Society, and the New York Entomological Society. He died of Bright's disease at home in New Brunswick.

• Some of Smith's papers are located in the Rutgers University Alexander Library archives, which contain a file on his activities at the New Jersey State Agricultural College Experiment Station. For a listing of his entomological works see the *Proceedings of the Staten Island Association of Arts and Sciences*, vol. 4, pts. 1–2 (Oct. 1911–May 1912). A complete report of Smith's field research and public activity is included in the annual reports of the Entomology Department at the Agricultural Experiment Station (1889–1912). Carl R. Woodward and Ingrid N. Waller, *The New Jersey Agricultural Experiment Station* (1932), chronicles his activity closely. Herbert Osborn, *Brief History of Entomology* (1952), describes Smith's personality. L. O. Howard, *Mosquitoes, How They Live . . .* (1901), is an early source of data on mosquitoes in which Smith is quoted. David L. Cowen, *Medicine and Health in New Jersey: A History* (1964), reports Smith's work in glowing terms.

LELAND G. MERRILL

SMITH, John Cotton (12 Feb. 1765–7 Dec. 1845), Connecticut governor, was born in Sharon, Connecticut, the son of the Reverend Cotton Mather Smith and Temperance Worthington Gale. He graduated from Yale in 1783 and studied law in the office of John Canfield of Sharon. He remained in his native town after his admittance to the bar in 1786, perhaps because the death of Canfield provided the opportunity for a successful legal practice in that community. In 1786 he married Margaret Everton of Amenia, New York, and the couple had one child.

Smith served in the May 1793 session of the Connecticut General Assembly and for ten consecutive terms between May 1796 and October 1800. He was chosen clerk of the lower house, the second ranking position in that body, in October 1798, a position to which he was reelected the next two sessions. His peers twice elected him Speaker in 1800, but he resigned after his second election to fill a vacancy in the U.S. House of Representatives. He remained in Congress for six years, where he served as chair of the Committee on Claims. Despite belonging to the Federalist minority, Smith was widely respected and frequently presided as chair when the House acted as a committee of the whole. He considered himself a Federalist of the George Washington and John Jay school and condemned the "scourge" of the French Revolution as the consequence of a "combination long since formed in Europe, by infidels and Atheists, to root out and effectually destroy religion and civil government" (Andrews, pp. 23–24).

Smith resigned from Congress in July 1806 to care for his elderly father and intended to devote himself to farming and literary pursuits. The freemen of Sharon, however, elected him to the lower house for every legislative session between October 1806 and May 1809. Smith was again chosen Speaker in October 1807, May 1808, and October 1808.

By the time Smith returned to Connecticut's political arena, the state was politically divided between a predominant Federalist majority and an aggressive Republican minority. He was Speaker when the Federalist legislature passed resolutions in November 1808 condemning the Embargo Act, a December 1807 action of Congress that prohibited all foreign trade, as "unnecessary and grievous" (*Public Records* 14, p. 124) and ruled that the Republican protest could not be made part of the official records. He also presided at a special February 1809 session of the general assembly convened to denounce the Embargo Act and the administration of Thomas Jefferson. In May 1809 Smith was one of four new Federalists elected to the state's twelve-man upper house. That October the general assembly appointed him to the superior court.

A split in Connecticut's ruling establishment, between older, more religious Federalists and younger, more sectarian ones, soon provided Smith with opportunities for further political advancement. In 1811 Lieutenant Governor Roger Griswold, a Federalist, defeated incumbent John Treadwell in the gubernatorial election with Republican support. Smith, who had polled 1,719 votes for lieutenant governor, was chosen for that position by the general assembly, in part perhaps because he was president of the Connecticut Bible Society and his selection would placate Congregational supporters of Treadwell. On the death of Griswold on 25 October 1812, the general assembly chose Smith governor, and he was reelected every year until 1817.

Griswold was gravely ill at the outbreak of the War of 1812, so the lieutenant governor performed many of the governor's official duties prior to his death, including issuing orders to activate a portion of the militia to defend the state's unprotected seacoast and endorsing his refusal to place Connecticut militia under federal control. Like most Connecticut Federalists, Smith opposed the most unpopular war in U.S. history prior to the Vietnam conflict. He praised Connecticut congressman John Davenport in December 1812 for "resisting every measure calculated *directly & solely* to augment the means of carrying on this iniquitous war" but criticized him for opposing the navy appropriation. "I do consider a navy as the most natural defence of this country . . . and full as necessary *for the preservation of peace* as for the prosecution of war" (*Smith Papers* 7, p. 17). The governor was both captain general and commander in chief of the Connecticut militia and, despite numerous conflicts with federal authorities over the control of state troops and supplies for the militia, was indefatigable in his efforts to defend the state from invasion, protect the coastal communities from British raids, and properly feed and supply the militia. As he stated in an address to the general assembly in October 1813: "The government of Connecticut, the last to invite hostilities, should be the first to repel aggression. In my view, it was not a time to inquire into the character of our enemy, or the causes which made him such, when our territory was invaded, and our citizens were demanding protection; and when no inconsiderable portion of our gallant navy was exposed, within our own waters, to instant capture or destruction" (quoted in Andrews, p. 304).

Smith was not a delegate to the Hartford Convention, a meeting of antiwar Federalists that convened in December 1814 to consider New England's proper relationship with the Union, but supported its conclusions, which included six proposed amendments to the Constitution, and he appointed two delegates from the state to travel to Washington, D.C., to urge their adoption. The Hartford Convention, tarred by Republicans as a disunionist gathering, together with the refusal of the Federalist upper house in 1815 to support an appropriation for the Episcopalian bishop's fund, paved the way for the defeat of Smith and the collapse of Connecticut Federalism. Republicans and disgruntled Episcopalians formed the Toleration party in 1816, which advocated disestablishment of the Congregational church and a new constitution to replace the Charter of 1662. Former Federalist secretary of the treasury Oliver Wolcott, Jr., defeated Smith by a vote of 13,655 to 13,119 in 1817, and the following year the new party took control of the upper house.

John Cotton Smith retired to his 1,000-acre farm in Sharon and never again stood for public office. He devoted his remaining twenty-eight years to benevolent activities, religious studies, and the causes of antislavery and orthography. Smith was first president of the Connecticut Bible Society, president of the American Board of Commissioners for Foreign Missions (1826–1841), president of the American Bible Society (1831–1845), first president of the Litchfield County Temperance Society, and one of many vice presidents of the American Colonization Society. He was also a founding member of the Connecticut Academy of Arts and Sciences, member of the Massachusetts and Connecticut historical societies, and in 1836 was elected to the Royal Society of Northern Antiquaries of Copenhagen. Like many of those active in benevolent causes, Smith supported the Whig party. He opposed the policies of the Andrew Jackson and Martin Van Buren administrations, considered Daniel Webster America's greatest statesman since Alexander Hamilton, and condemned the proposed annexation of Texas as designed to perpetuate slavery. Smith considered slavery "a national evil" and hoped for its end through compensated emancipation, although he opposed the "intemperate conduct of [William Lloyd] Garrison and his abettors" (Andrews, p. 133). He was also devoted to maintaining the purity of the English language and opposed Noah Webster's deletions of *u* from words like honour and neighbour in the name of orthography. He died in Sharon.

Smith was, in the words of his earliest biographer, "a thorough-going old-school man in his views of politics, theology, and language" (Andrews, p. vi). As the last Federalist governor of Connecticut, Smith is properly viewed as representing the end of an era, an era of rule by a Federalist elite under terms of the state's ancient charter.

• The John Cotton Smith Papers are located at the Connecticut Historical Society in Hartford. Selections from his papers covering the period between October 1811 and June 1817 have been published as vols. 25–31 of the *Collections of the Connecticut Historical Society* (1948–1967). The only work that provides any detail about his life is the Reverend William W. Andrews, *The Correspondence and Miscellanies of the Hon. John Cotton Smith . . .* (1847). Aside from this book, the best overview of Smith is in Franklin Bowditch Dexter, *Biographical Sketches of the Graduates of Yale College*, vol. 4 (1907), pp.

307–10. Further information about Smith can be found in vols. 8–15 of Charles J. Hoadley et al., *The Public Records of the State of Connecticut* (15 vols., 1894–1981). A major secondary work covering the period is the dated Richard J. Purcell, *Connecticut in Transition: 1775–1818*, first published in 1918. Two unpublished sources, Norman L. Stamps, "Political Parties in Connecticut, 1789–1819" (Ph.D. diss., Yale Univ., 1950), and Edmund B. Thomas, Jr., "Politics in the Land of Steady Habits: Connecticut's First Political Party System, 1789–1820" (Ph.D. diss., Clark Univ., 1972), do not break any new ground. Only John H. Chatfield, "'Already We Are a Fallen People': The Politics and Ideology of Connecticut Federalism, 1797–1812" (Ph.D. diss., Columbia Univ., 1988), has studied Connecticut Federalism from the post-Vietnam perspective, and his work provides a clearer understanding of Smith and Connecticut politics in the early nineteenth century than any previous works.

BRUCE P. STARK

SMITH, John Lawrence (16 or 17 Dec. 1818–12 Oct. 1883), chemist, mineralogist, and physician, was born near Charleston, South Carolina, the son of Benjamin Smith, a wealthy merchant; his mother's name is unknown. At a very young age, even before he could read, John Lawrence Smith demonstrated precocity in mathematics. After attending private schools and receiving a classical education at the College of Charleston, in 1835 he entered the University of Virginia, where he concentrated on science, mathematics, and engineering. Returning to Charleston in 1837, he worked for one year on a Charleston-to-Cincinnati railroad engineering project before entering the Medical College of Charleston and completing requirements for his M.D. degree in 1840. He studied in Europe for several years with Justus Liebig (who inspired him to focus his research efforts on chemistry), J. B. Dumas, Matthieu Joseph Bonaventure Orfila, and Élie de Beaumont. Also at this time he initiated a lifelong association with Benjamin Silliman, Jr.

In 1844 Smith returned to Charleston, where he established a medical practice, gave lectures, and pursued his scholarly research interests. In 1846 he and S. D. Sinkler cofounded the *Southern Journal of Medicine and Pharmacy* (which later became the *Charleston Medical Journal and Review*). He also served as an assayer for gold mined in the southern gold belt and did extensive soil research and analysis. His reports on the effects of soils and meteorological conditions upon cotton culture attracted the attention of Secretary of State James Buchanan, who appointed him in 1846 to an agricultural advisory commission requested by Turkey's Sultan Abdul Mecid. After arriving in Turkey and evaluating the commission's directives, Smith decided that the project was unsound; however, at the request of the Turkish government he agreed to stay and serve as a mining engineer. He spent the next few years investigating Turkey's natural resources. His most significant work there was the discovery of emery deposits that enabled Turkey to break a Greek monopoly and drastically lower world prices. In addition, his account of the mineral associations of emery led to the discovery and development of deposits in Massachusetts and North Carolina.

Returning to the United States in 1850 after a brief sojourn in Paris, Smith spent the next two years in New Orleans studying and lecturing. He held a titular professorship in chemistry at the embryonic University of Louisiana, an institution he described as existing "on paper only." In 1852 he was appointed professor of chemistry at the University of Virginia, where he continued to pursue his research on American minerals. During his tenure, he and his assistant, George Brush, recorded the results of their work relating to the chemistry of minerals; these documents were later published as a series of papers in the *American Journal of Science*. (Brush went on to a distinguished career in mineralogy at Yale University, working in collaboration with James Dwight Dana.)

Smith married Sarah Julia Guthrie of Louisville, Kentucky, on 24 June 1852. They had no children. In 1853 Smith moved to Washington, D.C., where he worked and lectured at the Smithsonian Institution. In 1854 he joined the staff of the University of Louisville as professor of medical chemistry and toxicology, succeeding his longtime friend and colleague Benjamin Silliman, Jr. In 1866 Smith was sufficiently secure financially to resign from his teaching position and pursue independent investigations of meteorites, an area of science that had fascinated him for many years. His *Memoir on Meteorites*, published in 1883, discusses meteoritic origins, relating them to volcanic eruptions on the moon. At the end of his life he had accumulated one of the finest collections of meteoritic stones in America—approximately 2,500 pounds of material representing 250 falls. To ensure that it would be preserved intact, he sold the entire collection to Harvard University shortly before his death. In 1884, with an endowment equal to the amount paid by Harvard for the collection, Smith's wife established the National Academy of Sciences J. Lawrence Smith Medal for Researches in Meteoric Bodies.

Among Smith's most important contributions are his studies and writings on phosphatic marls in the Charleston area; his discoveries in Turkey of significant coal, chrome, and emery; and his work with George Brush in precisely determining the chemical and physical character of numerous American minerals. Other notable contributions include the inverted microscope (which facilitated manipulation of objects and protected the lenses from chemical vapors) that he invented in Paris in 1850; his significant additions to the literature, including 145 scientific papers; and his phenomenal collection of meteoritic specimens. His contributions to his field were international in scope, as evidenced by decorations of honor awarded him by Turkey, France, and Russia. He also gave of his time and talents to a number of professional associations, including the American Association for the Advancement of Science, the National Academy of Sciences, and the Academy of Sciences of the Institute of France.

Smith died in Louisville, Kentucky. During his years in Louisville, in addition to his scientific pursuits he had served as president of the Louisville Gas Works and worked with Edward R. Squibb, who later founded the E. R. Squibb Company, a major firm in the pharmaceutical and chemical manufacturing industry. He also founded and generously supported the Baptist Orphanage of Louisville.

• *Mineralogy and Chemistry* (1873) is a collection of 145 papers written by Smith; it was reprinted as *Original Researches in Mineralogy and Chemistry by Professor J. Lawrence Smith,* ed. J. B. Marvin (1884), which includes a list of Smith's publications and biographical sketches by Marvin, Benjamin Silliman, Jr., and Middleton Brown. Biographical information can be found in Joseph Benson Marvin, "Smith, John Lawrence, 1818–1883," in *American Medical Biographies* (1920), pp. 1071–72, and a biographical sketch in *Popular Science Monthly,* Dec. 1874, pp. 233–35. Published memorials include an obituary in the *American Journal of Science,* 3d ser., 26 (1883): 414–15; Benjamin Silliman, Jr.'s memoir of Smith, which includes a portrait, in National Academy of Sciences, *Biographical Memoirs* 2 (1886): 219–37; the *Year Book* of the City of Charleston, S.C., for 1883 (1884); and the American Association for the Advancement of Science, *Proceedings* 48 (1899). Obituaries appear in the *Louisville (Ky.) Courier-Journal* and the *New York Times,* both 13 Oct. 1883.

RALPH L. LANGENHEIM, JR.

SMITH, John Walter (20 July 1900–3 May 1972), railroad executive, was born in Baltimore, Maryland, the son of James Goldfinch Smith and Christina Reifschneider. Like most of his colleagues who occupied railway presidential suites after the mid-twentieth century, Smith was a college graduate, having earned a B.S. in civil engineering from the University of Maryland in 1921. Three years later Smith took a job with the Seaboard Air Line Railroad (SAL), where he worked for a year as an engineering inspector of construction work. He was then posted to the road's maintenance-of-way department, where he was responsible for maintaining the company's track, roadbed, drainage, bridges, signals, and wayside structures. He remained with that department for seven years, until he was appointed division engineer with responsibility for all engineering on a specific section of the road. In 1936 he moved to the operating and engineering department, where he came into daily contact for the first time with the executives charged with the company's operations.

Smith's new post was a difficult one, for his railway had gone into receivership in 1930 and remained there during World War II. Wartime traffic demands on the financially precarious SAL were terrific, and the railroad's lack of centralized traffic signals caused a number of disastrous collisions. Smith's technical talents, however, caught the eye of Legh Powell, Jr., the road's receiver throughout its bankruptcy, who named Smith assistant chief engineer and assistant general superintendent in 1944. Smith performed his new duties admirably for two years, and when the SAL emerged from receivership and Powell became president of the reorganized line, he named Smith as his personal as-

sistant. Smith's staff responsibilities increased in 1950, when he was named vice president for administration. Two years later, when Powell became chairman of the board, he named his protégé as his successor.

Smith inherited a railroad that was a marginal property competing against the Atlantic Coast Line (ACL) and trucks for Florida's perishable produce transport. A cautious technician rather than an innovator, Smith attacked his road's problems by upgrading its facilities, installing centralized traffic control (CTC) on its main lines, and by heavy spending to buy all diesel locomotives. He also undertook a modest expansion program by merging with a subsidiary line, the Macon, Dublin & Savannah, in 1958 and purchasing the stock of the Gainesville Midland Railroad a year later.

Despite all the improvements Smith made on the SAL, he realized he was barely holding his own. The road was in the black, but by the mid-1950s it was slowly losing its profitable citrus and peach traffic from Florida to trucks and what was left of its passenger business to automobiles and airplanes. Smith believed that no matter how much capital he invested in improvements or how hard he worked to achieve internal corporate economies, he could not reverse his company's slow decline. Over on the competing ACL, Thomas Rice was reaching the same conclusion, and in 1958 the two men began exploratory merger talks. The congressional hearings that year on conditions in the rail industry demonstrated that the government was not going to ease its tight regulatory policies, and this knowledge accelerated the merger talks. By 1960 Smith and Rice had worked out the details; they took their proposal to the Interstate Commerce Commission (ICC) for hearings in 1961.

Smith's plans led the ICC to establish new precedents that would affect later mergers, most notably the ill-fated Penn Central. Smith and Rice maintained that the ICC should allow two profitable, competing roads to merge, arguing that both were earning less than a fair rate of return on their assets. They also argued, against ICC precedent, that although the merger would decrease competition within the railroad industry, they needed their combined resources to compete with other means of transportation, namely trucks. The ICC agreed and in December 1963 gave its approval for the merger. The combined company brought together resources valued at more than $1 billion, and combined gross revenues totaled $400 million a year. Smith had created a huge company; the Seaboard Coast Line (SCL) operated 9,624 miles of track, making it the seventh longest railway in the country, while its revenues were the eighth highest in the nation. The SCL owned 1,000 diesel locomotives and 62,000 freight cars, one of the country's largest fleets.

Smith was past retirement age at the time of the merger, while Rice was twelve years his junior, so Smith became chairman of the board and Rice took over daily operations. Smith retained his position until 1971, when he turned it over to Rice, but he kept his seat on the board until his death.

The rather serious looking Smith married Mary Elizabeth Apple in 1926; they had two children. Smith took the social side of his corporate responsibilities seriously and belonged to an array of private clubs that stretched from New York City to Florida. Throughout the later part of his career he sat on a large number of outside boards, mostly railroads affiliated with his road or terminal companies in which the SAL held an interest. He was also a director of State Planters Bank of Commerce & Trusts and was a trustee of the Richmond Memorial Hospital in Richmond, Virginia. Even after he rose to the executive suite, he maintained his affiliations with professional organizations such as the American Railway Engineering Association and the National Defense Transportation Association. Smith died in Richmond, where he had lived most of his life.

Smith's career was typical of many twentieth-century railroad executives. Technically trained, he took a job with a railway and stayed with it for his entire working life, rising through the ranks until he came to the attention of a mentor who groomed him for an executive office. Smith, however, brought to the SAL's presidency adroit managerial skills and an outlook that rose above parochial corporate interests, which enabled him to rebuild his railway and negotiate a favorable and friendly merger that enabled it to survive the intense competition.

• For personal information on Smith, consult *Who Was Who in Railroading* (1954) and *Who Was Who in America* (1969–1973). For an overview of the SAL's history see Richard E. Prince, *Seaboard Air Line Railway* (1969). For details on the SAL and ACL merger, see the *New York Times*, 1 July 1967.

JAMES A. WARD

SMITH, Joseph (30 Mar. 1790–17 Jan. 1877), naval officer, was born in Hanover, Massachusetts, the son of Albert Smith and Anne Lentham Eels. Smith entered the navy as a midshipman in 1809 and was commissioned a lieutenant in 1813. In the War of 1812 he was first lieutenant aboard the brig *Eagle* on 11 September 1814 in the battle of Lake Champlain, where he was wounded. He then served aboard the *Constellation* in the Mediterranean Squadron, 1815–1816, and cooperated in the capture of several vessels during the Algerine War. In 1818 he married Harriet Bryant; they had four children.

Over the next two decades Smith alternated between service in the Mediterranean Squadron and service at the Boston Navy Yard. He served aboard the *Guerriere*, 1828–1831, and as commander of the *Ohio*, the flagship of the squadron, 1838–1840. In 1845, with the rank of captain, Smith commanded the Mediterranean Squadron, with the *Cumberland* as his flagship.

In 1846 Smith was appointed chief of the Bureau of Yards and Docks. In 1855 he was placed on the retired list, and he retired in 1861. However, he continued in the service for several years. In August 1861 President Abraham Lincoln appointed Smith, as chief of the Bureau of Yards and Docks, to the board that chose the

design for the *Monitor*. Smith worked with designer and inventor John Ericsson, who built the ironclad in the remarkably short time of about three months. Secretary of War Gideon Welles credited Smith more than any other person in the Navy Department for the success of the revolutionary ship.

During the Civil War, Smith's son, Lieutenant Joseph Bryant Smith, commanded the *Congress*, which surrendered after being burned by the Confederate ironclad *Virginia*, the former *Merrimack*, on 8 March 1862. On hearing the news, Captain Smith concluded that his son must have been killed, or the ship would not have surrendered. He was correct. The *Monitor* arrived in Hampton Roads later on the day of the destruction of the *Congress*. The next day the *Monitor* engaged the *Virginia*, which had returned to destroy the rest of the Union fleet there. After the famous battle between the two ironclads on 9 March 1862, which resulted in the *Virginia* withdrawing, Smith was promoted to the rank of admiral on 16 July 1862. Now well into his seventies, he remained as chief of the Bureau of Yards and Docks through 1869 and then served as president of the Retiring Board, 1870–1871. He died in Washington, D.C.

Smith is remembered partly for his active longevity, as he continued to make contributions to his service after age eighty. However, his lasting fame derived from another consideration. The *Monitor-Virginia* battle received close attention from contemporaries and continued to do so for historians. The battle was often assessed as having a revolutionary effect upon naval ship design. As a consequence of the interest in minute details of that encounter, Smith is remembered for the apparently ironic justice in the fact that the *Monitor*, the construction of which took place on his watch as bureau chief, defeated the ship that a day before had killed his son.

• Sources on Smith include William Cogar, *Dictionary of Admirals of the U.S. Navy* (1989).

RODNEY P. CARLISLE

SMITH, Joseph (23 Dec. 1805–27 June 1844), founder of the Church of Jesus Christ of Latter-day Saints, known as the Mormon church, was born in Sharon, Windsor County, Vermont, the son of Joseph Smith, Sr., and Lucy Mack, farmers. Joseph Smith was notable among religious figures for claiming to receive revelations and to translate ancient religious texts. Mormons consider these writings, published as the Doctrine and Covenants and the Book of Mormon, as scripture on par with the Bible and think of Smith as a prophet in the biblical tradition. Smith did not consider himself to be either a reformer or the founder of a new religion. In his own eyes, he was restoring the Christian gospel as taught by Jesus and the first apostles. Nothing in Joseph Smith's background prepared him to write scriptures or to head a religious movement. His parents were poor New England farmers who began life with a farm in Tunbridge, Vermont, but lost it in 1803 after a commercial venture failed.

When Joseph Smith, Jr., was born two years later, the Smith family lived on a farm rented from a relative. In 1816 they migrated to Palmyra, New York, and in 1818 purchased 100 acres in Farmington (later Manchester) a few miles south of Palmyra village. For the first time in fourteen years they owned land of their own.

Lucy and Joseph Smith, Sr., had drifted to the margins of New England congregationalism by the time they married in 1796. She was deeply religious but went unbaptized until adulthood, rarely attending meetings. Joseph, Sr., was suspicious of the clergy and of professing Christians. When Lucy joined the Presbyterian church around 1819, Joseph, Sr., refused to attend. His dreams, recorded in detail by his wife, revealed a yearning for redemption and a frustration at not finding it. Along with his neighbors he searched for buried treasure, a common practice among poor New Englanders at that time. These ventures often blended quests for religious enlightenment with the exercise of magical power. He was seeking something that he could not find. Joseph Smith, Jr., was heir to the yearnings and uncertainties of his parents. He was troubled by the inability of his family to agree on a church when evangelical preaching seemed to demand a decision. At age fourteen, according to his account, he prayed to know which church was right. Two beings of indescribable "brightness and glory" appeared to him, introducing themselves as the Father and the Son. Smith said they forgave his sins and told him to join none of the churches because none of them was right. Latter-day Saints now speak of this event as the First Vision, but at the time it made little impression on the people around Smith, who easily dismissed the visions of a young boy. Ministers, believing that revelation ended with the Bible, disparaged his story and left him to his own devices, more alienated than ever from established Christianity.

From that time to the end of his life, Smith recorded visions and revelations that seemed fabulous to most of his contemporaries but attracted a growing number of believers. In September 1823 he prayed again for direction and received another revelation. According to Smith, an angel who called himself Moroni appeared at his bedside and told him about a record of prophecy from ancient America. Smith was instructed to obtain the record and translate it in preparation for the restoration of Israel and the return of Christ. Moroni, the last of the prophets purported to have written in this record, allegedly said it was engraved on gold plates buried in a hill not far from the Smiths' house. Going there the next day, Smith reportedly found the plates in a stone box and saw Moroni again. The angel told him not to take the plates but to return the next year. For four years Smith went back to the hill on the same day and, according to his account, finally on 22 September 1827 took home the gold plates.

In the interim his ideas about the gold plates underwent a change. He had assisted his father in some treasure-seeking expeditions, among them a search for supposed Spanish treasure near Harmony in northern Pennsylvania. He later reported that on his first trip to see the plates thoughts of their worth crossed his mind, but the angel rebuked him and warned him against the money diggers and thoughts of profit. By the time he obtained the plates in 1827, he had come to focus on their contents and to put aside considerations of their value as gold. While digging for treasure in Harmony, Smith met Emma Hale at the house where he was staying, and an attraction developed between them. She was tall, slender, and dark-haired. He stood over six feet with broad chest and shoulders, light brown hair, and blue eyes. Emma's father was not happy with the match. He had little use for a young man who dug for treasure and claimed to have revelations. Joseph continued to see Emma and married her in 1827 in spite of her father's objections.

For the next two years Smith dictated what he said was a translation of the plates, his words taken down by Emma and then Martin Harris, a prosperous Palmyra farmer, and Oliver Cowdery, a schoolteacher. The Smiths lived in a small house on the Hale's farm in Harmony and later moved to a house in Fayette, New York, belonging to the Whitmer family, who had heard about Smith from Oliver Cowdery. The translation went slowly because of work on the farm and other interruptions until the spring of 1829, when, between April and June, the bulk of the work was accomplished. During the translation Smith permitted no one to see the plates, but in June 1829, according to Harris, Cowdery, and one of the Whitmers, the angel Moroni appeared and showed them the plates, and Smith showed them to eight of his family and close friends. In March 1830 the translation was published as the Book of Mormon.

The undertaking was remarkable in many respects and enough to strain the credulity even of Smith's closest friends. He said the angel provided him with interpreters (Urim and Thummim), "two seer stones set in silver bows" fastened to a "breast plate," to assist him in translation, a claim that scarcely made Smith's account more credible. The entire story could have been dismissed as the fabrication of an overwrought imagination if not for the 500 pages of printed text that Smith produced. The townspeople considered the book a fraud and refused to buy it. The printer undertook to publish it only because Martin Harris provided financial backing. The book purports to be a scriptural history of the people of ancient America. It was named for the prophet Mormon, who is thought by the Saints to have written the story of his people in the fourth century after Christ. Followers believe that Mormon drew on the records of prophets who had written the history of their own times, beginning with Nephi who migrated to the western hemisphere from Jerusalem about 600 B.C. These prophets taught the Christian gospel and prophesied the coming of Christ to America as well as to Palestine. Mormon wrote that the purpose of the book was to convince its readers that Jesus was Christ and God. The message was especially directed to the remaining descendants of the people in the Book of Mormon, who the Mormons assumed included the American Indians.

Smith collected enough believers by the time the Book of Mormon was published to form a church. On 6 April 1830, at the Whitmer's house in Fayette, he organized the Church of Christ, with himself and Oliver Cowdery as first and second elders. Smith was also given the titles of seer, translator, and prophet. The church set his life on a new course. Until then he had been a young man claiming a divine gift and a mission to translate a book. After 1830 he became the prophetic leader of a people.

He claimed to lead the church, as he had translated the Book of Mormon, by direct revelation. He received scores of revelations dealing with trivial details of administration and cosmic visions of the life hereafter. Among the first was a command to take the Book of Mormon to the Indian tribes being settled along the frontier in western Missouri. In September and October of 1830 four missionaries set out, reaching their destination in midwinter. They preached to the Indians and enjoyed some small success before government agents stopped them, fearing that the presence of Christian preachers would jeopardize the fragile peace with the tribes.

Byproducts of this journey turned out to be even more significant than the mission to the Indians. En route the missionaries stopped in Kirtland, Ohio, and made more converts in a few weeks than Smith had assembled in a year. Smith's claims to restore the authority and spiritual gifts of early Christianity appealed to people confused by competing religious discriminations. Some of these new members visited him in New York, and by the end of 1830 Smith received a revelation directing the entire church to move to Ohio. Kirtland was regarded as a temporary location because of another outcome of the Missouri mission. The Book of Mormon had spoken of the construction of a New Jerusalem where all converts were to gather and form a new society called Zion in preparation for the Second Coming of Christ. Revelations had indicated that Zion was to be somewhere in the West, and in the summer of 1831 Smith and other leading figures in the church traveled to Missouri, where he received a revelation designating the exact site for the New Jerusalem near Independence in Jackson County. For the next five or six years church efforts focused on the organization of Zion. While Smith continued to live in Ohio, his ultimate aim was to direct new converts to Missouri where the New Jerusalem was to rise. But the plans for Zion quickly ran into trouble. The people of Jackson County were unhappy at the prospect of Mormons inundating their society and in the fall of 1833 drove them out of the county. The next spring Smith organized a private army called Zion's Camp, which proved to be unsuccessful in its attempt to reinstate his followers on their property. For a few years the Mormons remained in Clay County across the Missouri River from Independence, until the Missouri government agreed to open a new area for them, organized as Caldwell County in north central Missouri. For the time being,

church members were required to suspend their hopes for the establishment of Zion at the site of the New Jerusalem.

In Kirtland Smith continued to plan for Zion. He rounded out the organization of the leadership structure, appointing twelve apostles as second in command to himself, sent missionaries throughout the United States and to England, and saw to the construction of a temple in Kirtland, which was dedicated in 1836. Revelations continued to come to him, among them "the Word of Wisdom" cautioning the Mormons (by then known as Latter-day Saints) to avoid tobacco and liquor. He claimed to be visited by ancient prophets, who restored their authority to him, and by Christ himself. Smith also made plans for the Kirtland economy. In Zion property was to be redistributed to people according to their needs, and their surplus each year was to be returned to a common treasury. Although this system had to be abandoned because of the expulsion from Jackson County, Smith had become accustomed to reordering many aspects of ordinary life along religious lines. In Kirtland he organized a bank as part of a broad economic program. Undercapitalization doomed it from the start, and the panic of 1837 sealed its fate. The bank's collapse hurt many of the investors and depositors, and they blamed Smith. The opposition rose to such a pitch that he felt his life was in danger. He and other church leaders fled Kirtland for Missouri in early 1838.

Smith had plans for another temple in Caldwell County at the Mormon settlement of Far West, Missouri, but these ambitions were never realized. Enmity toward the Saints was building once again and broke out in violence at an election in August. The concentration of Mormons in the area had allowed them to dominate voting results, arousing the wrath of other citizens. A bizarre sect could be tolerated in small numbers, but not when they threatened to control all local political offices. In the summer and fall of 1838, pitched battles broke out between the Missourians and the Mormons, claiming lives on both sides. Governor Lilburn Boggs issued an order for the Mormons to leave the state or face extermination. On 31 October 1838 Smith and other leaders were arrested and imprisoned awaiting trial while the Saints fled eastward to Illinois in search of refuge. Languishing in jail for the next five months, Smith had time to contemplate the course of his life to that point. He had always anguished over the state of his own soul; his first prayer for guidance had included a plea to know his standing with God. When traveling he would seek seclusion in the woods to "give vent to all the feelings of my heart in meditation and prayer." In 1839 he was less worried about his sins than the suffering of himself and his people. Why had God permitted the wicked to separate the Prophet from his people and to drive the Saints from the state? In letters from prison he told his people that their sufferings gave them experience and to remember that Christ had suffered more than any human. The Saints were not to use authority unjustly themselves, but to lead only "by long-suffering, by

gentleness and meekness, and by love unfeigned."
The Missouri officials allowed Smith to escape his captors in April 1839, and he joined his followers clustered along the banks of the Mississippi near Quincy,
Illinois. They were poor, suffering from fever, and uncertain about the future. Ill himself, Smith made efforts to obtain land and eventually arranged for plots at
Commerce, Illinois, and across the river in Iowa.
From this low point the Mormons began to rebuild
their society.

Late in 1839 Smith went to Washington to seek redress from the federal government for the loss of property in Missouri. Denied by President Martin Van
Buren, Smith asked the Illinois legislature to charter a
new city to be called Nauvoo where the Mormons
would have control of all the agencies of government.
Within the legal walls provided by the charter, he
hoped once more to erect a Zion. From Nauvoo Smith
launched a renewed missionary effort, and converts
soon came flooding in from all over the United States
and parts of Europe, especially Great Britain. He organized a female Relief Society and laid plans for another temple. In 1841 he began to teach the doctrine of
eternal marriage, including the idea of plural marriage, which he himself practiced. In the temple, faithful Saints would be endowed with a deeper knowledge
of the gospel and be sealed as husband and wife for
eternity. Living Saints could also be baptized for persons who had died without hearing the gospel of
Christ. In March 1844 he organized a Council of Fifty
composed of leading Mormons and a few sympathetic
non-Mormons to manage the political affairs of the
kingdom. All this was more than some of the Saints
could accept. Doctrines such as plural marriage went
so far beyond conventional Christian teaching, not to
mention the bounds of Victorian propriety, that an influential small group came to believe that Smith had
betrayed his divine calling. They joined forces with
anti-Mormons in surrounding towns who were jealous
of the Mormon's growing political influence. The fears
of his enemies were only confirmed when Smith announced his candidacy for the presidency in the spring
of 1844 and sent missionaries throughout the country
to campaign on his behalf. His candidacy meant that
Mormons were no longer wooed by Whigs and Democrats, which had made them enemies to whichever
party they did not support, and Smith may have believed that, with divine assistance, he could be elected
as a preliminary step toward a millennial kingdom.

In April 1844 dissenters in Nauvoo organized a reform church and published a newspaper, the *Nauvoo
Expositor*, to expose Smith's errors. The Nauvoo City
Council, with Smith presiding as mayor, determined
that the *Expositor* was a threat to the peace of the community and a public nuisance. As mayor, Smith was
authorized to close the paper and did, which ignited
the opposition. On 12 June Smith was charged with
inciting a riot for destruction of the press. He ultimately submitted to arrest and was taken to Carthage, the
nearby county seat, under the governor's protection.
As he left for Carthage, Smith had premonitions of his

own death, which proved to be accurate. On 27 June
1844, while he awaited a hearing, a mob with black-
ened faces stormed the jail, killing him and his brother
Hyrum. The mob fled, fearing reprisal from the Mormons, who did not retaliate. The bodies were returned
the next day to Nauvoo, where 10,000 Latter-day
Saints gathered to mourn the loss of their prophet.
Four of his eleven children (two adopted) were living,
and a fifth was to be born to Emma Smith four months
later.

Joseph Smith was, in the technical sense, a charismatic leader; he exercised authority by virtue of a perceived divine gift. But the movement he began did not
rest solely on the strength of his personality. Soon after
his death, Brigham Young, as president of the
Twelve Apostles and a stalwart friend and defender of
Smith, assumed leadership of the church and in 1846
led the Saints west in search of a new place to build
Zion. Through the Mormon church Smith's influence
continues to be felt. His followers to this day accept
the Book of Mormon and the collection of his revelations in the Doctrine and Covenants as divine writings
and honor him as a leader, Christian teacher, and
prophet.

• The papers of Joseph Smith, located in the Church Archives, Salt Lake City, Utah, are being edited by Dean C.
Jessee, who published *The Personal Writings of Joseph Smith*
in 1984 and the first volume of the *Papers* in 1989 and the
second in 1992. Lucy Mack Smith narrated reminiscences
later published as *Biographical Sketches of Joseph Smith the
Prophet* (1853). The best complete biography is Donna Hill,
Joseph Smith, the First Mormon (1977). See also Fawn M.
Brodie, *No Man Knows My History* (1945), for a critical view
by a disaffected Mormon, and Richard L. Bushman, *Joseph
Smith and the Beginnings of Mormonism* (1984), for a sympathetic account.

RICHARD L. BUSHMAN

SMITH, Joseph, III (6 Nov. 1832–10 Dec. 1914), Mormon religious leader, was born in Kirtland, Ohio, the
son of Joseph Smith, Jr., the founder of the Church of
Jesus Christ of Latter-day Saints, and Emma Hale.
When he was a boy the Smith family moved from
place to place in the American Midwest as the Mormons—as members of the new sect often were called—
sought a spiritual and literal haven for their unique
religious ideals. He lived in Far West, Missouri, in
1838–1839 but went to Illinois when the Mormons
were expelled from the state. In the spring of 1839
some 5,000 Mormons began settling on the Mississippi River about fifty miles north of Quincy at a place
they named Nauvoo.

The rapid and sustained growth of Nauvoo as a
Mormon stronghold in the early 1840s elicited a great
deal of animosity in the community, as did the Mormons' esoteric religious beliefs. Joseph Smith, Jr., was
arrested and while incarcerated in the Hancock County Jail at Carthage, Illinois, lynched on 27 June 1844.
After his death, Mormonism split into several factions,
each with leaders vying for control of the institution.

The largest group, led by Brigham Young, journeyed overland to the Great Basin in 1846–1847. This group was remarkably successful in making unique Mormon religious doctrine square with secular authority and establishing a Mormon theocratic kingdom based at Salt Lake City.

Not all, or even most, of the early Mormons accepted the leadership of Brigham Young and Rocky Mountain Mormonism. One who refused to do so was Joseph Smith III, the eldest son of the church's founder, who grew to maturity in a largely deserted Nauvoo following the exodus of Young's group. After a series of personal crises, in 1860 Smith was ordained president of the Reorganized Church of Jesus Christ of Latter Day Saints, which in time became the second-largest faction of a Mormon movement that had splintered into at least fifteen factions in the 1844–1846 period, with more than 25,000 members by 1900. Smith presided over that church until his death.

As president of the Reorganized Church, Smith grappled with his father's legacy and developed positions at odds with those of the Utah Mormons. He tried to chart a course between the extreme Mormonism that Brigham Young had embraced and more socially acceptable American Christianity. One crucial question was whether Mormons should establish communities separate from non-Mormons. He actively opposed doing so until his mother, who had also joined the Reorganized Church, died in 1879, and he remained hesitant about separating from larger society thereafter. His mother had argued that earlier gatherings of Mormons had ensured conflict, and she had urged her son not to repeat her husband's mistake. Smith called for the church to be involved in the affairs of the world with the hope that they would assist in changing it. "Strife and contention, with disobedience," he chided in 1868, "are sure fruit that the gospel, with great witness, had not wrought in us the work of peace, and without peace in our heart we predict that *no perfectness will come in Zion.*"

In keeping with his emphasis on integration, Smith reversed the early Mormons' policy of political and military organization. Unlike his father, Smith refused to endorse candidates, make political speeches for or against anything but accepted moral issues, and refrained from discussing political parties and candidates in any public forum. He wrote in the church newspaper in 1876 that "no subject is of less importance to the Saints than politics." Smith emphasized caution as he sought to demonstrate a bipartisan spirit and an apolitical posture.

Smith also drew lessons about military issues from his early Mormon experiences. The establishment early on of a 5,000-man Mormon militia force, known as the Nauvoo Legion, had agitated other residents of western Illinois in the mid-1840s. As a boy Smith participated in the children's unit of the Legion, practicing martial tactics with wooden swords and toy rifles. Smith said he enjoyed and benefited from these experiences, but he questioned the unit's warlike stance. "Looking back along the pathway," he wrote in his memoirs, "I feel it was a pity that such a [martial] spirit crept in among them, however, and a still greater one that the leading minds of the church partook of it."

Smith essentially rejected the standard Mormon idea of a political kingdom of God brought about by a unification of church and state. He recognized, as did few others of his movement, that unlike the portion of the church that had followed Brigham Young to the refuge of the Great Basin, the Reorganized Church lived in the middle of the United States and so had to conform, both for its own identity apart from the Utah Mormons and to ensure that the problems associated with early Mormonism were not repeated. The Utah Mormons, ensconced in their Rocky Mountain hideaway, were able to defer an accommodation with the larger American society until near the turn of the twentieth century.

From a theological perspective, the Reorganized Church under Smith's leadership also rejected or modified many of the more controversial religious ideas that were developed and promulgated in early Mormonism. These included speculations about the nature of eternity, the multiplicity of gods, the possibility of progression to godhood, celestial and plural marriage, baptism for the dead, and other ideas associated with Mormon temple endowments. A few of them were simply considered quaint by non-Mormons, such as baptism for the dead; others, such as plural marriage, aroused volatile emotions and became rallying points for opposition to the movement.

Smith recognized the difficulties these doctrines presented for the church both in terms of theological compatibility and external pressure. Smith's opposition to plural marriage was a principal case in point. His inaugural address, given when he accepted leadership of the Reorganized Church on 6 April 1860, encapsulated most of his central ideas on the subject. In it he denounced the practice of plural marriage, which had been adopted by Brigham Young's movement as well as by some other Mormon-oriented organizations, and he declared unequivocally that those involved in it were doing so without divine authority. Indeed, Smith concluded, God explicitly opposed these practices. He commented that some had charged his father with teaching and practicing plural marriage, but that did not square with what he remembered of his father, and he always denied, as he had been taught by Emma Smith, that his father had originated the practice and that it had been officially sanctioned by the church. Smith spent the rest of his life trying, unsuccessfully, to clear his father's name of any hint of polygamy.

In addition to opposing polygamy on doctrinal grounds, Smith became involved in the political antipolygamy crusade in the latter decades of the nineteenth century. He was a vocal advocate of legislation to prohibit plural marriage, and as the son of the Mormon prophet he held a special place in the effort. At one point in the early 1880s Smith was even considered a serious contender to be appointed to territorial governor of Utah because he would enforce enthusiastically the antipolygamy laws. When the Utah Mormon leader Wilford Woodruff announced in 1890 that the church would no longer countenance the performance of plural marriages, Smith was overjoyed. It was, for him, a vindication of his efforts since becoming president of the Reorganized Church.

Smith inaugurated a vigorous missionary program to "rescue" those Latter-day Saints enmeshed in what members of the Reorganized Church believed was the "evil practice" of polygamy. Simplistically, they believed that all the Reorganized Church had to do to convert these people was to offer an alternative, pointing out the errors of plural marriage and the illegitimacy of Young's leadership. Smith sent the first Reorganization mission to Utah in 1863 with the express mission of teaching the residents of the great conspiracy by the Apostles and to call them to affiliate with his church. Thereafter the Reorganization maintained a missionary effort in Utah for the purpose of showing the errors of the Mormon leadership. In addition to missionary contact, the Reorganized Church published and distributed hundreds of tracts, pamphlets, magazine articles, and books designed to show the evil designs of Young. To the chagrin of the Reorganization's leadership, none of these efforts were particularly effective.

In his fifty-four years as head of the Reorganized Church, Smith helped it grow from a membership of only a few hundred to almost 70,000 at the time of his death. Smith steered the Reorganized Church down a middle path that emulated a moderate Mormon theology. He took a variety of paths, and it took him a number of years to accomplish his task, but over time Smith directed the church into the formal adoption of his doctrinal beliefs. The theological consensus that Smith forged held sway until the 1960s, when the Reorganized Church turned toward an even greater identification with mainstream Protestantism.

Smith had married Emmeline Griswold in 1856. They had five children, two of whom died in infancy. Emmeline died in 1869 after a protracted illness. Smith then married Bertha Madison in 1869 in Plano, Illinois. They had nine children, two of whom lived only a few hours. Bertha died in 1896 after being thrown from a carriage. Smith then married for a third time in 1898, to Ada Rachel Clark of Waldemar, Ontario. They had three sons. Smith died at his home in Independence, Missouri. He passed his presidential office on to his oldest living son, Frederick Madison Smith.

• The Joseph Smith III Papers at the Library-Archives of the Reorganized Church of Jesus Christ of Latter Day Saints, Independence, MO., contain information on virtually every aspect of Smith's life and career. These materials are described in Daniel T. Muir, "Sources for Studies in the Life of Joseph Smith III," *Courage: A Journal of History, Thought, and Action* 1 (Dec. 1970): 93–101. Additional information on Joseph Smith III can be found in various collections held by the Archives of the Church of Jesus Christ of Latter-day Saints, Salt Lake City, Utah; the Restoration History Manuscript Collection, Graceland College, Lamoni, Iowa; and the Utah State Historical Society, Salt Lake City. Smith's autobiography was serialized in the Reorganized Church's magazine, *Saints' Herald*, between 1934 and 1937. These recollections were printed in facsimile form as *The Memoirs of President Joseph Smith (1832–1914)*, ed. Richard P. Howard (1979). An earlier condensation of these memoirs appeared as Bertha Audentia Anderson Hulmes, ed., *Joseph Smith III and the Restoration* (1952). Two published biographies are by Roger D. Launius, *Joseph Smith III: Pragmatic Prophet* (1988) and *Joseph Smith III and the Creation of the Reorganized Church* (1990).

ROGER D. LAUNIUS

SMITH, Joseph Fielding (13 Nov. 1838–19 Nov. 1918), sixth president of the Church of Jesus Christ of Latter-day Saints, was born in Far West, Missouri, the son of Hyrum Smith, patriarch to the church and counselor and brother to Joseph Smith (1805–1844), the founder of Mormonism, and Mary Fielding, a British convert and Utah pioneer. In his early years Smith lived in constant fear of harm or death, as civil war raged in Missouri between the older settlers from southern states and Mormons from the North and Canada. At the time of Smith's birth, Missouri officials had imprisoned his father in Richmond, charging him and others with treason for defending Mormons against attacks by mobs and the state militia. As a baby Smith nearly suffocated when a mob headed by Samuel Bogart, a Protestant minister bent on killing the Mormons or expelling them from Missouri, raided his mother's house, overturned his crib, and buried him under the bedding. After being driven from Missouri with his family and the other Mormons, five-year-old Smith was living in Nauvoo, Illinois, when members of a local militia unit murdered his father and uncle in a jail at Carthage where they also had been charged with treason. The militiamen apparently acted in an effort to destroy Mormon power in the state.

Living in a single-parent home with a mother who was often sick herself, young Smith assumed responsibilities far beyond his years. At age nine, after the Mormons had been expelled from Nauvoo, he drove a team of oxen from Omaha to Salt Lake City. After the death of his mother following a lingering illness in 1852, he moved into the household of George A. Smith, a member of the Council of the Twelve Apostles and later a counselor to Brigham Young in the LDS church's First Presidency (the president and two counselors who are the principal governing authority of the church). Possessing a hot temper, Smith ran into trouble with schoolteachers. Expelled from school for misbehavior, he was sent at age fifteen by Brigham Young on a proselyting mission to Hawaii (then the Sandwich Islands) for the LDS church. Enjoying a remarkable facility for the language, Smith remained in the islands for four years. Later he served on three missions to England (1860–1863, 1874–1875, and 1877) and on a second mission to Hawaii (1864).

After returning from his first Hawaiian mission Smith served in the Utah militia, which was then opposing the 1858 U.S. expedition headed by Albert Sidney Johnston that was sent to quell a supposed rebellion among the Mormons and to escort Governor Alfred Cumming to Utah. Following the Utah War, he married a cousin, Levira Annette Clark Smith, in 1859; they had no children. Divorced from her in 1868, he also married five other women: Julina Lambson (1866; thirteen children), Sarah Ellen Richards (1868; eleven children), Edna Lambson (1871; ten children), Alice Ann Kimball (1883; seven children), and Mary Taylor Schwartz (1884; seven children). Smith's polygamous marriages made him a target of federal marshals during the antipolygamy prosecutions of the 1880s, and in late 1884 he left for Hawaii, where he remained through mid-1887.

Called as an apostle and counselor to Brigham Young in 1866, he became a member of the Council of the Twelve Apostles in 1867. John Taylor chose him as his second counselor in 1880, and he continued to serve as a counselor in the First Presidency until his call as president of the LDS church in 1901. During his presidency, which lasted until his death, Smith helped the Latter-day Saints achieve a degree of respectability in American society. Following the public disclosures during hearings on the seating of Senator Reed Smoot that Mormons had entered plural marriages after the Manifesto of 1890 had promised an end to such practices, Smith issued in April 1904 a proclamation that threatened church discipline for anyone who did so in the future. Smith and his associates followed in 1909 and 1911 with additional measures that led to the disciplining of two members of the Council of the Twelve Apostles and numerous other lower-level officials who insisted on entering into new polygamous marriages or encouraging others to do so. In an effort to achieve a favorable public reception, the church organized a bureau of information and promoted the publication of articles favorable to Mormons in the national press. In addition, Mormon leaders ingratiated themselves with the national Republican party leadership in order to take advantage of Republican political power in the West.

Fiscally, Smith promoted the rationalization of church finances. By 1907, as a result of austere budgetary measures that had been instituted by his predecessor Lorenzo Snow and continued by Smith, the church had extinguished a heavy burden of debt. In addition, by establishing regular budgetary procedures, Smith placed the church on a sound fiscal footing. Also, by promoting internal administrative reorganization in the church he increased central and priesthood control over auxiliary organizations such as the women's Relief Society, the Primary Association (an organization for young children), and the Young Men's and Young Women's Mutual Improvement Associations (educational and recreational organizations for young adults) that previously had operated independently. Smith also promoted certain types of welfare and morality reform in Utah. In 1916 he inaugurated a committee that coordinated church efforts to influence the community to deal with such diverse problems as prostitution, housing for young women living away from home, dance standards, social standards, playground construction, supplying nutritional food to poor children, juvenile delinquency, venereal disease, and motion picture censorship.

During the nineteenth century church members had held many disparate views on the nature of human beings, God, Christ, and the Holy Ghost. As president, Smith facilitated the formulation of church doctrine on these questions by authorizing members of the Council of the Twelve Apostles to write treatises on these questions and by securing approval from the First Presidency and the Council, the church's principal governing bodies, on statements defining these doctrines. In addition, he facilitated the development of important church doctrines related to the redemption of dead people who during their lifetimes had not had the opportunity to hear the gospel or accept Jesus Christ as their savior. On this question Smith received a personal revelation shortly before his death, which the Council of the Twelve Apostles accepted as authoritative and which spelled out the role of Christ and others in teaching the gospel in the postearth existence.

During Smith's administration the question of prohibition became an extremely important issue in the United States. Before 1900 the church had been lax in enforcing dietary regulations, first proposed by Joseph Smith, that counseled Mormons to refrain from the use of tobacco, coffee, tea, and alcohol. Under Smith, however, the church began to insist that members adhere to these rules in order to gain admission into the temples—the church's most holy places—and to hold responsible positions in church leadership.

• The papers of Joseph F. Smith are housed in the archives of the Church of Jesus Christ of Latter-day Saints in Salt Lake City. A collection of his writings was published posthumously as *Gospel Doctrine: Selections from the Sermons and Writings of Joseph F. Smith* (1919). His son Joseph Fielding Smith wrote a biography, *The Life of Joseph F. Smith . . .* (1938). Another biography is Francis M. Gibbons, *Joseph F. Smith: Patriarch and Preacher, Prophet of God* (1948). Secondary sources include Hyrum M. Smith and Scott G. Kenney, *From Prophet to Son: Advice of Joseph F. Smith to His Missionary Sons* (1981), and Thomas G. Alexander, *Mormonism in Transition: A History of the Latter-Day Saints, 1890–1930* (1986). An obituary is in the *Deseret Evening News*, 19 Nov. 1918.

THOMAS G. ALEXANDER

SMITH, Joseph Fielding (19 July 1876–2 July 1972), historian and tenth president of The Church of Jesus Christ of Latter-day Saints, was born in Salt Lake City, Utah, the son of Joseph F. Smith, the church's sixth president, and Julina Lambson. He attended the LDS University (what might be thought of today as a junior college). Although he received no formal university degree, Smith assembled an extensive library during his lifetime and was an avid reader. In 1898 Smith married Louie E. Shurtliff; they had two daughters. After little more than a year of marriage, he was called to serve for two years at his own expense as a missionary in Great Britain; his wife remained in Salt

Lake City. Upon completing his missionary service he took a job in the Mormon church historian's office. In 1906 he was appointed as assistant church historian. The following year his first wife died, and in November 1908 Smith married Ethel G. Reynolds; they had nine children. After the death of his second wife, in 1938 Smith married Jessie Ella Evans; they had no children.

Smith served most of his adult life as a member of the governing councils of the Mormon church. In April 1910 he was ordained by his father (then church president) as one of the Quorum of the Twelve Apostles. For sixty years Smith served as a member of the Twelve, traveling around the world and teaching and supervising local church units. Smith's assignment as an apostle was the context that gave impact to his other work as historian, genealogist, and author.

In 1921 Smith became the church historian, having direct supervision of the church's historical department. The Mormon church has always placed great emphasis on keeping a faithful organizational history, and Smith felt he had a personal connection and a sense of continuity with the church's history. Born when Brigham Young was president, he personally knew all the men who succeeded Young including John Taylor, Wilford Woodruff, and Lorenzo Snow, as well as his own father. Smith's keen desire to remain true to the church's founders and teachings was energized by his family's experience with persecution. His great uncle Joseph Smith, the church's founder, and his grandfather Hyrum Smith were shot by a mob in Carthage, Illinois; when Smith was eight, his father and mother left him and his siblings in Salt Lake City and went to Hawaii for two years to avoid the federal marshals who were seeking to arrest and imprison polygamous church leaders. Much of Smith's professional life was devoted to maintaining what he considered an accurate record of historical continuity in both fact and doctrine from the founding days of the church until his death.

Complementary to Smith's work as the church historian were his assignments in developing and managing the Mormon church's archive of genealogy and family history. Accurate genealogical records are of primary religious significance to Mormons who perform religious ceremonies (including "eternal" marriage) for both living members of the church and for the dead. Beginning in 1907 Smith was appointed secretary of the Genealogical Society of Utah; later he served as a board member and as the first editor of the society's *Genealogical and Historical Magazine*, he later became the vice president of the society and in 1934 was made its president. In 1909 he made an extensive trip to major genealogical libraries in the eastern United States, returning with valuable ideas that helped establish the Mormon church's genealogical and family history library which has now grown to a world preeminence. Smith supervised the religious worship in the historic Salt Lake Temple, acting as a counselor to two temple presidents from 1919 until 1935 and as the temple's president from 1945 to 1949.

Smith's twenty-five published works are perhaps his most significant legacy to the Mormon church. His two volumes of family history are *Asahel Smith of Topsfield, Massachusetts, with Some Account of the Smith Family* (1903) and a biography of his father, *The Life of Joseph F. Smith* (1938). His works related to Mormon Church history include *Essentials in Church History* (1922) and the two-volume *Church History and Modern Revelation* (1953). His theological writings, some eighteen works dealing with theology, scriptural commentary, and gospel doctrine, have become part of what might be considered the core of Mormon orthodoxy. Examples include *Teachings of the Prophet Joseph Smith* (1938) a doctrinal summary of the original seven-volume church history prepared under the church founder's direction. *Man: His Origin and Destiny* (1954) argues for the divine origin of humans and proposes the view that life on earth is part of a premortally developed God-directed eternal plan, not the process of a random evolutionary accident. The three-volume compilation titled *Doctrines of Salvation* (1954, 1955, 1956) covers such topics as the Godhead, Christ as the Savior, the Atonement; and the significance of the Book of Mormon. The five volumes of *Answers to Gospel Questions* (1954, 1958, 1960, 1963, 1966) were put together by Smith's son Joseph, from a series of articles written by Smith in the church's official magazine, the *Improvement Era*, as well as from thousands of letters written by church members asking for clarification on practices ranging from drinking caffeinated cola and playing games of chance (he discouraged both), to shopping on Sunday (he favored passing a civil law prohibiting commerce on Sunday). Several of Smith's published works were used as teaching manuals for the church's programs of instruction.

In 1965 he was appointed a counselor in the First Presidency, the primary directive board of the church. In 1971, at the death of President David O. McKay, Smith was ordained prophet and tenth president of the church. He served in this capacity until his death in Salt Lake City.

• Basic biographical sources are Doyle L. Green, ed., *Our Leaders* (1951); Joseph F. McConkie, *True and Faithful* (1971); and Joseph Fielding Smith, Jr., and John J. Stewart, *The Life of Joseph Fielding Smith* (1972). An obituary is in the *New York Times*, 3 July 1972.

J. CRAIG PEERY

SMITH, Joshua Bowen (1813–5 July 1879), abolitionist, was born in Coatesville, Pennsylvania. Little is known of his childhood except that he obtained an education in the local public schools through the influence and financial support of a wealthy Quaker woman.

Smith moved to Boston in 1836 and found employment as a headwaiter at the Mount Washington House. Over the following decade, while serving tables, he made the acquaintance of Francis G. Shaw, Charles Sumner, and other notable whites on the periphery of the antislavery movement. Many of these men became his lifelong friends. Smith also worked briefly as a personal servant for the Shaw family, then joined the staff of Henry L. W. Thacker, a local black caterer. In 1849 Smith opened his own catering establishment. Over the next twenty-five years he developed a successful business and gained a sizable personal fortune by serving gatherings of the local elite, as well as catering various functions at Harvard College, antislavery bazaars, and commemorations of the Emancipation Proclamation. He gained a reputation among Bostonians as "the prince of caterers."

In the 1840s Smith emerged as an important figure in the local abolitionist crusade. Through his friendships with Shaw and Sumner he became a close acquaintance and ally of William Lloyd Garrison, George Luther Stearns, Theodore Parker, and other prominent abolitionists; he remained a devoted follower of Garrison for nearly three decades. He regularly attended and sometimes chaired antislavery gatherings in Boston's African-American community. And he actively participated in the struggle to end segregation in the city's public school system. But Smith expended the bulk of his energies in aiding and protecting fugitive slaves who reached Boston. After the arrest in 1842 of George Latimer, a slave from Virginia, Smith helped found and served as vice president of the New England Freedom Association, an all-black organization devoted to providing runaway slaves with food, clothing, shelter, transportation, and legal aid. Some of the actions taken by the Freedom Association were not only illegal but occasionally violent; nevertheless, Smith viewed them as legitimate antislavery work. When the interracial Boston Committee of Vigilance was formed in 1846, he became a vocal member of its executive committee. He served briefly as the committee's agent, interviewing and arranging assistance for fugitives who came to the members' attention.

After passage of the Fugitive Slave Act of 1850, which created a federal apparatus for the capture and return of runaway bondsmen, Smith encouraged Boston's blacks to resist the efforts of slave hunters and federal agents to enforce the law. He urged slaves in the city to purchase revolvers and, if necessary, to use them to prevent their recapture. He pressed local free blacks to protect the fugitives in their midst. At one antislavery gathering, speaking from the pulpit of Boston's African Meeting House, he brandished a bowie knife and a pistol, declared his intent to wield them to protect runaways, and demonstrated the proper method for their use. Smith became an active member of the newly created Boston Vigilance Committee (the successor to the Committee of Vigilance in 1850), personally feeding, clothing, and transporting to Canada several slaves who reached Boston. He even used his catering business to further these efforts. While catering he could keep a watchful eye on the movements of slave hunters in the city, and he could also provide temporary employment to a number of runaways. Smith refused to cater an affair for Senator Daniel Webster of Massachusetts, protesting Webster's vocal support of the act.

Smith welcomed the coming of the Civil War, seeing in it an opportunity to overthrow the institution of slavery. In 1861 he was selected by Governor John Andrew as the caterer for the Twelfth Massachusetts Regiment, the first volunteer unit raised in the state during the war. Because of his devotion to the Union cause in the conflict, he agreed to perform the task for a lower price than that charged by other Boston caterers. During the ninety-three days the regiment trained in Boston prior to leaving for the South, he furnished daily rations for the officers and enlisted men. His expenditures amounted to $40,378. This proved to be Smith's financial undoing. The governor initially refused to pay the bill, citing inadequate legislative appropriations for the purpose. Although the catering bills of all other units were paid by the state, Smith received only $23,760.80, and then only after the federal government made funds available to the state for that purpose. He petitioned the state for payment of the balance several times before his death, but the debt remained unpaid. Despite personal frugality and keen business skills, he never recovered his lost fortune.

Even with his precarious finances, Smith remained an important figure in Boston's African-American community after the war. Well respected by local whites, he was selected in 1867 as the first black member of St. Andrew's Lodge of Freemasons of Massachusetts. A Republican party stalwart, he represented Cambridge in the Massachusetts Senate in 1873 and 1874 and was one of the few blacks to attend national party conventions during that time. Smith died at his Cambridgeport residence after an illness of several months. He was survived by his wife, Emiline (maiden name unknown); their only child, a daughter, had preceded him in death. Hundreds of leading Bostonians turned out to pay their respects at his funeral. At his death his generosity became even more apparent: he left debts some thirty times greater than the value of his estate, in large part on account of his unpaid expenditures for the Twelfth Massachusetts Regiment and decades of contributions to the abolitionist cause.

• Many documents relevant to Smith's work in the abolitionist crusade can be found in the 1836 to 1865 issues of the *Liberator* (Boston). A brief biography of Smith is in C. Peter Ripley et al., eds., *The Black Abolitionist Papers*, vol. 3 (1991). His efforts to aid and protect fugitive slaves are discussed in James Oliver Horton and Lois E. Horton, *Black Bostonians: Family Life and Community Struggle in the Antebellum North* (1979); Irving H. Bartlett, "Abolitionists, Fugitives, and Imposters in Boston, 1846–1847," *New England Quarterly* 55 (1982): 97–110; and the Treasurer's Account Book of the Boston Vigilance Committee to Assist Fugitive Slaves, in the Siebert collection at Harvard University. Smith's service to the Twelfth Massachusetts Regiment is mentioned in Benjamin F. Cook, *History of the 12th Massachusetts Volunteers* (1882). Obituaries are in the *Boston Evening Transcript*, 7 and 8 July 1879, and the *Boston Evening Traveler*, 8 July 1879.

ROY E. FINKENBINE

SMITH, Judson (28 June 1837–29 June 1906), missionary secretary and educator, was born in the Berkshire hills in Middlefield, Massachusetts, the son of Samuel Smith and Lucina Metcalf, farmers. The family had been in Massachusetts since 1637 when Matthew Smith settled at Woburn. Smith attended Oberlin College for three years, graduated from Amherst College in 1859, and after a year at Union Theological Seminary, New York, graduated from Oberlin Theological Seminary in 1863. In Oberlin he tutored Latin and Greek at the college, from 1862 to 1864, then he taught mental and moral philosophy and mathematics at Williston Seminary in Massachusetts, 1864–1866. Smith married Jerusha Augusta Bushnell of Hartford, Ohio, in 1865; they had at least four children.

In 1866 Smith became professor of Latin at Oberlin College, and in October of that year he was ordained a Congregational minister. Four years later he became professor of ecclesiastical history at the Oberlin Seminary, holding that post until 1884. He also lectured on modern history, 1875–1884, and taught history at Lake Erie Seminary, Painesville, Ohio, 1879–1884. He published *Lectures in Church History and the History of Doctrine* and *Lectures in Modern History*, both in 1881. Beginning in 1871 he was for thirteen years president of the Oberlin board of education.

An influential adviser to students, Smith was instrumental in the development of a mission to Shansi province in China, to be staffed by volunteers from Oberlin serving under the auspices of the American Board of Commissioners for Foreign Missions. The Shansi Mission was organized in 1881, and an Oberlin-Shansi program continued through the next century. The Oberlin missionaries, together with all other missionaries in Shansi, were massacred in the Boxer uprising of 1900. Meanwhile, Smith had become a foreign secretary of the American board, with responsibility for China as well as Africa, Western and Central Turkey, and the Pacific Islands. He held this post until his death. He traveled in Turkey in 1888 and led a group to inspect missions in China in 1898.

Smith's educational background prepared him for an influential role given the fast developing emphasis on educational missions at the turn of the century. He also encouraged the development of social service as an aspect of missions. A man of impressive bearing and great enthusiasm, he played a major role in the movement toward ecumenical cooperation in missions. In 1888 he attended the General Conference on Missions in London, and he helped organize the Ecumenical Conference on Foreign Missions at New York in 1900. As chairman of its general committee, he told the conference that the record of missions was "more thrilling and more significant than any epic which man has produced."

Smith's ideas are expressed in his numerous contributions to the American board's magazine, the *Missionary Herald*, and in the annual reports of the American board. Most of these reports from 1884 to 1897 contain a major statement by Smith. His first, in 1884, is titled "The Historical Argument for Christian Missions" and expounds his favorite theme that the expansion and influence of Christianity is the major force in the progress of civilization. Drawing on his experience of teaching modern history he argues that the spread of the Christian faith produces "a *new manhood*" and from this regeneration of individuals "every other blessing which man anywhere requires will follow." In linking Christianity and civilization Smith came close to affirming the expanding imperialism of Western nations, then in its heyday. He rejoiced that Christianity was coming to be the dominant religion of the world, not only numerically but in the sense that the leading powers, Germany, England, and the United States "are all of them Christian states, their life permeated with Christian thought and sentiment, their history and institutions and policy controlled by Christian ideas."

Smith was chairman of the trustees of Mt. Holyoke College during its evolution from seminary to college; he was also a trustee of Oberlin and of Williston Seminary. He lectured on missions at Oberlin and Hartford Seminaries and was associate editor of *Bibliotheca Sacra*. He died at his home in Roxbury, Massachusetts.

• Smith's life and career are sketched in *Amherst College Biographical Record* (1927), and F. F. Goodsell, *They Lived Their Faith* (1961), pp. 272–74. The *Report of the Ecumenical Missionary Conference on Foreign Missions* (1900), and the American Board of Commissioners for Foreign Missions, *Annual Reports* (1884–1906), reflect his thought. An obituary is in the *Missionary Herald* 102 (Aug. 1906): 365–68.

DAVID M. STOWE

SMITH, Julia (25 Jan. 1911–8 Apr. 1989), pianist and composer, was born in Denton, Texas. No information is available regarding Smith's parents. She spent all of her childhood and early adult life in Texas. At an early age she began to study with Harold von Mickwitz at the Institute of Musical Art in Dallas, Texas. In 1930 she received her B.A. in music from North Texas State University. She moved to New York to enter the Juilliard School of Music, where she studied composition with Rubin Goldmark and Frederick Jacobi and piano with Carl Friedberg. After a short time at the Juilliard School, she began further study at New York University, and in 1933 she received her M.A. in music from the university, where she had studied with Marion Bauer, Vincent Jones, and Virgil Thomson. Smith completed requirements for the Ph.D. at New York University in 1952. In 1938 she married Oscar A. Vielehr, an engineer and inventor.

Smith began her teaching career as a music theory professor at the Juilliard School of Music (1940–1942). From 1941 to 1945 she was the founder and head of the Department of Music Education at the Julius Hartt College of Music at the University of Hartford in Connecticut. In 1944 she began a two-year term as a faculty member at the New Britain State Teacher's College in Connecticut. Throughout the remainder of her life she continued to teach theory and composition, she gave private piano instruction, and she wrote works of pedagogy such as the three-volume *String Method*. An authority on twentieth-century composers and literature, she often lectured on contemporary music and musicians. Her outstanding book, *Aaron Copland, His Work and Contribution to American Music* (1955), won her recognition as one of the leading authorities on the works of Copland. In 1963 she published her second major biography, *Master Pianist: The Career and Teaching of Carl Friedberg*, and was also named one of the ten leading women composers by the National Council of Women of the United States.

As the recipient of two Martha Baird Rockefeller grants (1971 and 1976), Smith's reputation as a composer soared. She received numerous requests for commissioned works and was much in demand to participate in composers' forums and clinics. Her compositions included orchestral works, operas, piano and vocal solos and duets, and organ, choral, band, and chamber works. Her style contains much variety, especially in harmonic language, which ranges from diatonicism to atonality. Especially prominent in her harmonic structures are added tones and chord clusters. Her melodies also demonstrate Smith's versatility: some are mildly disjunct, or jagged, while others are drawn from (or are actual restatements of) traditional American and American Indian melodies.

The "American quality" in her works appeals to both performers and audiences and adds to her acclaim as one of the leading American women composers. Many of her works are musical portraits of aspects of American history. Two of her operas and many choral works, such as *Our Heritage* (1959) and *Remember the Alamo* (1964), for band, optional narrator, and chorus, are unique, musical presentations of historical events.

American Dance Suite (1935) is a delightful piano duet, which includes four movements closely related to American folk tunes: "One Morning in May," "Lost My Partner," "Negro Lullaby," and "Chicken Reel." *American Indian Dances*, for two pianos, and the opera *Cynthia Parker* (1940) are based on authentic American Indian melodies. The melodies for these two works were chosen from Natalie Curtis's *The Indians' Book*, a collection of traditional melodies of the Hopi (of northeastern Arizona), the Wabanaki, the Pueblo, and the Dakota Indians.

Smith's works were performed by major organizations and orchestras, including the Columbia Broadcasting System Symphony, conducted by Howard Barlow and Bernard Herrmann, the WOR Symphony, conducted by Alfred Wallenstein, the Orchestrette of New York, the New York Philharmonic "Pops," the Columbia University Orchestra, and many others in the United States and abroad. Her six operas have been performed by companies such as the Fort Worth Opera Association, the Syracuse Opera Theater, and many college and university opera workshops.

In 1971 Smith received the first of two Ford Foundation recording-publication grants, making possible the recording of her *Quartet for Strings* (1964), performed by the Kohon Quartet. The quartet was included in the album *Four American Composers* on the Desto record label. The second grant was awarded in 1976 for the recording of *Highlights from "Daisy"* on the Orion label. *Daisy*, a two-act opera, had been commissioned in 1971 by the Greater Miami Opera Association and the Girl Scout Council of Tropical Florida to celebrate the sixtieth anniversary of the Girl Scouts of America. The opera, based on the life of the Girl Scouts' founder, Juliette Gordon Low, was premiered on 3 and 4 November 1973 in Miami. Later the opera played an important role in celebrations of America's bicentennial and other historic events. Another opera, *The Gooseherd and the Goblin* (1947), had been commissioned by the Hartt College of Music and was performed frequently by the Hartt College Opera Workshop. Smith's other operas, all of which have been performed, are *The Stranger of Manzano* (1947), a one-act opera, *Cockcrow* (1954), a one-act opera, and *The Shepherdess and the Chimneysweep* (1967), a Christmas opera in one act.

From 1970 Smith's involvement with the National Federation of Music Clubs had a major impact on the programs of the federation. Many of her compositions were included in the Parade of American Music and the American Women Composers' programs presented annually by music clubs. In 1970 the National Federation of Music Clubs published the first *Directory of American Women Composers*, compiled and edited by Smith. She served as the chair for both the American Women Composers Association and the Decade of Music, sponsored by the National Federation of Music Clubs in the 1970s to promote the exposure of women composers and conductors. Her "Invocation" for solo voice and piano is the official invocation of the National Federation of Music Clubs.

Smith continually promoted other performers and composers. In 1972–1973 she was responsible for two thirteen-week series of radio broadcasts featuring forty-six American composers, twenty-two of whom were women. She owned and managed Mowbray Music Publishers, which provided publishing opportunities for herself and other composers. As a concert pianist, she presented new keyboard works and familiarized audiences with contemporary musicians. Her life was dedicated to teaching, performing, and writing with particular emphasis on American music and musicians.

• A few of Smith's music manuscripts are in the Music Library at Texas Christian University, Fort Worth. An interview with Smith, broadcast on 3 Dec. 1978, is preserved on tape in the Voice of America Music Library Collection at the Library of Congress. A brief biography is included in Christine Ammer's *Unsung: A History of Women in American Music* (1980). See also the prefaces to her musical scores. Her available works, originally published by Mowbray Music, are distributed by Theodore Presser Company. A complete list of her published works and limited biographical data may be obtained through the American Society of Composers, Authors, and Publishers.

LINDA P. SHIPLEY

SMITH, Julia Evelina (27 May 1792–6 Mar. 1886), and **Abby Hadassah Smith** (1 June 1797–23 July 1878), suffragists and translators, were born in Eastbury and Glastonbury, Connecticut, the daughters of Zephaniah Hollister Smith, a pastor and attorney, and Hannah Hadassah Hickok, a linguist, astronomer, poet, and gentlewoman farmer. Born into a family of educated parents who refused to be bound by the contemporary constraints of the nineteenth century placed on women's opportunities to learn, both girls were given access to the study of mathematics, music, astronomy, languages, philosophy, and politics. They were sent to the only available private classes for women of the day, and Julia was hired by Emma Willard (founder of the Troy Female Seminary in Troy, N.Y.) during the 1820s to teach French and mathematics to young women of the caliber of Elizabeth Cady Stanton, whose tenure at the seminary came later in 1831.

For most of their lives the two sisters lived with their parents and three elder sisters at the family farm in Glastonbury. Julia's diary lists multiple daily chores, reading circles, and social gatherings as the primary substance of their existence. After Zephaniah died in 1836, Hannah and the five sisters managed the farm and continued to sell farm products to provide income. Money had been available to the family from Zephaniah's law practice and the abundant sale of farm goods. The fact that the family was financially comfortable ultimately brought Julia and Abby into conflict with the Glastonbury authorities.

Exposed not only to the cultural dimensions of the affluent life, the women were also caught up in, and involved with, the contemporary issues that dominated both church and community. The girls' father was trained at Yale University as a pastor and came to forsake Congregationalism in order to embrace Sandemanianism, a Protestant creed that had made its way from Scotland to Connecticut in the 1760s via Robert Sandeman. The Smith family provided William Lloyd Garrison a tree stump from which to preach when, in the 1830s, the local church establishment closed its doors to the abolitionist preacher long before abolition was a popular cause.

The Smiths not only made their home a place from which to espouse the gospel but a literary enclave that ultimately produced an entire translation of the Bible. Roused to a deep and personal study of the Bible by Sandemanianism and the millennial messages of eschatological doom preached by those such as William Miller, Julia single-handedly translated every word of both testaments from the Hebrew (self-taught at the age of fifty-five) and from the Greek and Latin (learned as a child). The result of Julia's seven-year effort (1847–1854) was to produce some ten thousand single-spaced, handwritten pages of translations currently held by the Connecticut Historical Society in Hartford, but privately kept in storage in the Smith home in Glastonbury for years until it became needed for publication by the sisters.

The published version of Julia's Bible translation might never have become a reality had not Abby protested the double-billing and increase of the tax bills with which she and Julia were presented in 1869. When the sisters pressed the local tax office for more details, they learned that the town "fathers" had need of money to pay bills. As a solution to the problem, an arbitrary assessment had been made to increase the property tax on the Smith farm and the property of two widows who lived in town in order to secure the needed funds. The Smiths eventually petitioned the town to have permission to pay interest on their outstanding tax bill, which they were hard pressed to meet, living on limited income from basic farming. The town refused the petition and instead authorized the tax collector to seize the Smith property, which could then be sold at auction to pay the taxes owed.

It became apparent that if the Smith sisters, now in their seventies, did not fight the injustice of taxation without representation, their entire life holdings might be seized while they remained legally helpless to stop the process. The sisters made use of an interested and sympathetic press and a newly emerging women's rights movement to fight their case. Abby, in particular, became something of a cause célèbre among suffragists and others for her articulate, intelligent, and clever statements. Many men in Glastonbury, the state of Connecticut, and the federal government honestly believed that women should have no say regarding assessment, taxation, and seizure of property. Most especially aggravating to the sisters was the seizure of their prized Alderney cows, which not only provided food and income for them but a type of companionship as well. The press made much of a farcical parade led by the tax collector as he marched the cows to a neighbor's farm for auction, with the Smith sisters and local townspeople following diligently behind!

Greatly distressed to discover the contempt in which they were held by people with whom they had lived and shared most of their lives, and disappointed in a system that they had helped to change by endorsing the vote for black men, the sisters decided to remove Julia's Bible translation manuscript from obscurity in 1875 to prove women's intellectual capabilities. Julia edited and redacted thousands of pages of translation, and the sisters contracted with the American Publishing Company of Hartford, Connecticut, to publish *The Holy Bible: Containing the Old and New Testaments; Translated Literally from the Original Tongues*, in 1876 at their own expense of $4,000. One thousand copies were published at eleven hundred pages each. Their motivation was not to make money on the project (the Bibles sold for $2.50 apiece) but rather partially to defray their tax bills (which were growing ever larger) and primarily to prove that "a woman can do more than any man has ever done." When asked why they were investing their money in a Bible rather than directly in the fight against taxation without representation, Julia and Abby wrote:

God governs the world by moral means; and no logic can be plainer, no truth can be clearer, than, if it be wrong to take a man's property without his consent, [it] must be equally wrong to take a woman's property without her consent; and the men therefore, must take it from her on the ground that her intellect is not as strong as theirs. . . . Now there is no learning that is so much respected by the whole world . . . as knowledge of the most ancient languages, in which the Bible was written. . . . And here is a woman, with no motive but the love of doing it . . . [who] has gone further, alone, in translating these languages, than any man has ever gone, and without any of his help, and *no law of the land gives her any protection.* (*Abby Smith and Her Cows*, pp. 57–58)

Julia and Abby Smith undertook their publishing efforts in order to prove a point, not to make a profit. The stress of the three trials necessary to finally establish that the Smith sisters had been wrongfully treated by the state of Connecticut and the town of Glastonbury took its toll and may have hastened Abby's death. The first trial had been decided in the Smith sisters' favor, the second trial (the collector's appeal) was decided against them, and the third trial finally found in their favor. No tax bill was ever paid on the Glastonbury property until Julia later married, and her husband paid the bill presented to him rather than be taken to jail as the party responsible for his wife's debts.

After Abby's death in 1878 in her home in Glastonbury, Julia went on to speak, write, publish, and in her eighty-seventh year (1879) to marry the prominent judge and author Amos Andrew Parker from New Hampshire. That union was believed by many to be Julia's ruination and a betrayal of the women's rights movement of which she had become a part. Some felt that she had soiled her previously untarnished image as a successful single woman, and others were horrified by her insensitivity to family members to whom she had reneged on promises of future inheritance of her property. After she died in Parkville, Connecticut, a request was found in her Bible that she be buried under her maiden name.

The artistic, literary, and political contributions of the entire Smith family deserve consideration, but it is Abby Hadassah and Julia Evelina to whom credit should go for creatively and persistently challenging the status quo that constituted American life in the nineteenth century. Julia's translation of the entire Bible was no small accomplishment, earning the acclaim of the female intelligentsia and kudos from Professor Young, who taught Hebrew at Harvard University and who is recorded as having personally said to Julia, "I am astonished that you could get the translation so correct without consulting some learned man" (Francis Ellen Burr, "Obituary," *Hartford Times*, 8 Mar. 1886). Abby's fierce determination and honest articulation before the men of the community, the law courts, and the U.S. Senate in 1875 served as a model for many who came to be inspired by her public demonstration of courage and strength in the face of injustice. Together, the Smith sisters were formidable as they fought to conquer ignorance by the use of their own intelligence and the protection of the American justice system.

What demands our attention about these two nineteenth-century women is their tenacity in the face of adversity and their genius in the use of the pen as a weapon of defense. Refusing to be unfairly manipulated by either men or men's laws, they used the power of the press, the power of the women's lobby, and the power of religious zeal to fight their battles. They left a legacy of written materials that demonstrate not only their intellectual acumen but a detailed record of the political turmoil that characterized nineteenth-century America. Their contributions reveal the grit of a pioneering American spirit that refused to permit injustice to triumph and demonstrated that gender has nothing whatever to do with the ability to think, speak, and act effectively.

• The best primary sources are at the Historical Society of Glastonbury, Conn., and the Connecticut Historical Society and the Connecticut State Library, both in Hartford. Copies of the Smith Bible translation (1876), along with diaries, letters, and Julia Smith's important publication, *Abby Smith and Her Cows with a Report of the Law Case Decided Contrary to Law* (1877), may be found at these locations. An extensive listing of periodicals that recorded the political meanderings of the Smith Sisters' case is in Susan J. Shaw, *A Religious History of Julia Evelina Smith's 1876 Translation of the Holy Bible, Doing More Than Any Man Has Ever Done* (1993), which also offers a categorized bibliography. See also Pamela Cartledge, "Seven Cows on the Auction Block: Abby and Julia Smith's Fight for Enfranchisement of Women," *Connecticut Historical Society Bulletin* 52 (Winter 1987): 15–43; Kathleen Housley, "'The Letter Kills but the Spirit Gives Life': Julia Smith's Translation of the Bible," *New England Quarterly* 61 (Dec. 1988): 555–68; and Elizabeth Speare, "Abby, Julia and the Cows," *American Heritage* 8 (June 1957): 54–57, 96.

SUSAN J. SHAW

SMITH, Kate (1 May 1907–17 June 1986), singer and radio and television personality, was born Kathryn Elizabeth Smith in Washington, D.C., the daughter of William Smith, a news dealer, and Charlotte Yarnell Hanby. Singing and dancing as a youngster, she won many amateur contests even before she was in high school. She graduated from Business High School in Washington in 1923. She attended the George Washington School of Nursing for nine months before deciding to be an entertainer.

In 1926 Smith was discovered by playwright-actor-lyricist Eddie Dowling and given a part as a comic buffoon who sang and danced the Charleston in his new Broadway musical comedy, *Honeymoon Lane.* In 1928 she starred, in blackface, in a revival of the Vincent Youmans musical *Hit the Deck*, in which she sang "Hallelujah," the big hit of that show. In 1930 she had a starring role in the George White musical comedy *Flying High*, with Bert Lahr and Oscar Shaw. Again she was the comic foil. A vice president of the Columbia Phonograph Company named Ted Collins chanced to attend this show. Taken by Smith's rich, rangy contralto voice, he became her personal manager "on a handshake" and gave her her start in radio. The partnership endured until Collins's death in 1964.

Smith went on the air for the Columbia Broadcasting System (CBS) 26 April 1931, becoming an immediate success in a quarter-hour singing program. In July Mayor Jimmy Walker crowned her Queen of the Air. Her theme song, "When the Moon Comes Over the Mountain," became a major hit. Her opening was a simple "Hello everybody," and her closing was "Thanks for list'nin' and goodbye folks." Her trademarks were her "just folks" manner and a hearty laugh. She starred at the Palace Theatre for a record-breaking eleven weeks in 1931. Smith had a cameo role in the 1932 Paramount motion picture, *The Big Broadcast* and starred in another Paramount film, *Hello Everybody!*, later that year, with costar Randolph Scott.

In October 1933 Smith was invited to sing with the Philadelphia Orchestra for a fundraiser. Conductor Leopold Stokowski was astounded to learn that she had never had a singing lesson. He advised her, "God gave you that voice. Don't let anyone change it." She said she thanked God every day for that voice.

In autumn 1933 Smith's vaudeville show, "Kate Smith's Swanee Revue," took to the road, playing coast-to-coast for eight months. In 1934–1935 she headlined the Hudson New Star Revue, a weekly prime-time half-hour radio series sponsored by Hudson-Terraplane motor cars. She broadcast for the Atlantic & Pacific Tea Company (A&P) from 1935 to 1937, with a weekly prime-time variety hour beginning in September 1936. This became "The Kate Smith Hour," one of the most popular musical-variety hours in radio for a decade.

Smith was a humanitarian, visiting the sick and crippled in hospitals, performing at benefits, aiding the down-and-out during the depression, raising money for drought relief, and working for the National Recovery Administration and the American Red Cross. During the Korean War she arranged for people in the service to send messages home through her television show.

During the 1930s Smith was repeatedly named most popular "girl" singer in polls. She is associated with such songs as "When Your Lover Has Gone" (1931), "It Was So Beautiful" (1932), "Moon Song" (1933), "I Only Have Eyes for You" (1934), and "These Foolish Things Remind Me of You" (1936), all powerful ballads with impressive high notes. She introduced more than six hundred songs on the radio. Because Ted Collins selected nearly all of the songs for her to sing, he was courted by songwriters and music publishers along Tin Pan Alley. She recorded some 580 songs during a period of forty-seven years. She recorded for Columbia (1926–1932 and 1940–1946), RCA Victor (1937–1939 and 1963–1968), Brunswick (1933), Decca (1934), Capitol (1954), Kapp (1958), Tops (1959), and Atlantic (1973). More than twenty of her records sold more than a million copies, including a live Carnegie Hall concert album in 1963 and three religious albums.

In 1938 Ted Collins asked Irving Berlin to compose a new patriotic anthem for Smith to introduce on her Armistice Eve program. The result was "God Bless America." It became her, and Berlin's, most important song and made Smith a symbol of patriotism. She sang it on the home front throughout World War II, and the song became a staple at all of her live concerts, always evoking a standing ovation. In the 1943 Warner Brothers all-Irving Berlin picture, *This Is the Army*, Smith had a cameo role recreating the radio introduction of "God Bless America." All proceeds from her performances of this song went to the Boy Scouts and Girl Scouts of America. In 1938 she also began her popular noontime program, "Kate Smith Speaks," in which she commented on events of the day, new books, plays, and movies, gave editorial opinions, and recited essays about motherhood, the seasons, and folks doing good deeds. This program ranked first among daytime listeners for several seasons and lasted thirteen years.

During World War II Smith was at the height of her popularity, repeatedly named one of the three most beloved and important women of America. Her ability to sell defense bonds was unequaled by any other celebrity. Through her legendary radio marathons she is credited with the sale of more than $600 million in war bonds. She helped popularize such wartime hits as "I Don't Want to Walk Without You," "The White Cliffs of Dover," "Blues in the Night," "One Dozen Roses," "Rose O'Day," "Comin' In on a Wing and a Prayer," "I'll Be Seeing You," and "I'll Walk Alone."

The "Kate Smith Hour" was the first daytime television program of any significance, aired live each weekday from 1950 to 1954. Like Smith's weekly radio hour, it featured her singing as well as a variety of acts from ventriloquists to dancing dogs to vaudeville stars. Ted Collins interviewed names in the news on his "Cracker Barrel" segment. In 1951–1952 she also hosted the television prime-time "Kate Smith Evening Hour" for the National Broadcasting Company (NBC). She curtailed her activities after Collins suffered a severe heart attack early in 1956, although she did appear on "The Ed Sullivan Show" twenty times, hosted a combined commentary/recorded music series on Mutual radio in 1958, and had a weekly musical television series on CBS in 1960.

After Collins's death in May 1964, Smith vowed she would not sing again, but she changed her mind late that summer, saying "Ted would have wanted me to go on singing." She converted from her mother's Presbyterian faith to Catholicism. She was seen frequently on television shows hosted by Andy Williams, Dean Martin, Jack Paar, the Smothers Brothers, Jim Nabors, and Tony Orlando and in a number of live concerts. In 1972 (for two weeks) and 1973 (for two weeks) she appeared at John Ascuaga's Nugget casino in Sparks, Nevada, the largest in the Reno area.

In 1973 Smith was asked to sing "God Bless America" at a Philadelphia Flyers' hockey season opener. The playing of her record had coincided with the team's victory on a number of occasions. She sang the song on the ice before critical games, spurring them to victory each time, including two Stanley Cups. This performance marked a resurgence of her popularity in the last years of her fifty-year career. The Flyers had a bronze statue of her erected outside the Spectrum arena. She was also named grand marshal of the Tournament of Roses Parade in Pasadena, California, in the 1976 bicentennial celebration. Smith enjoyed summers at her vacation home at Lake Placid, New York, for forty years. She died of diabetes and circulatory ailments in Raleigh, North Carolina.

A physically large woman blessed with a powerful vocal gift, Smith received countless awards over the years, including the American Guild of Variety Artists' Entertainer of the Year Award in 1973 and the Medal of Freedom, presented by President Ronald Reagan in 1982.

• Kate Smith published two autobiographies, *Living in a Great Big Way* (1938) and *Upon My Lips a Song* (1960). She also wrote a children's book, *Stories of Annabelle* (1951), and a cookbook, *Kate Smith's "Company's Coming" Cookbook* (1958). A psychological analysis of the Kate Smith radio war bond marathon on 21 Sept. 1943 was made by Columbia University and published as Robert K. Merton's *Mass Persuasion: The Psychology of a War Bond Drive* (1946). See also an objective biography, Richard K. Hayes, *Kate Smith: When the Moon Came Over the Mountain* (1995), and Michael R. Pitts, comp., *Kate Smith: a Bio-Bibliography* (1988). An obituary is in the *New York Times*, 18 June 1986.

RICHARD K. HAYES

SMITH, Kirby Flower (6 Dec. 1862–6 Dec. 1918), classicist, was born in Pawlet, Vermont, the son of Henry H. Smith and Julia M. Flower. He received his A.B. from the University of Vermont in 1884 and his LL.D. there in 1910. The favorite student of Basil Lanneau Gildersleeve, whom he called variously "teacher, friend, and foster-father," Smith received his Ph.D. from the Johns Hopkins University in 1889. He stayed on at Johns Hopkins as instructor of Latin in 1889, becoming associate (1892), associate professor (1893), and ultimately its first professor of Latin in 1902. Smith was an anchor of the classics program and mainstay of the *American Journal of Philology*, contributing six articles and twenty-seven reviews. In addition, he wrote a number of articles for popular literary journals on the Roman poets Propertius, Ovid, and Martial, as well as on the value of classics in American culture. A selection of these articles, published posthumously as *Martial, the Epigrammatist and Other Essays* (1920), shows a remarkable range of knowledge extending to English, French, and Italian literature, evident from his first article, on the werewolf in literature, to his commentary on Tibullus. Indeed, he seems rarely to have written on the same subject or author twice, and his knowledge was always conveyed with a wit and facility that often obscured the depth and exactness of his scholarship.

Smith was one of the few American Latinists in an era dominated by majestic Hellenists like William Watson Goodwin, Gildersleeve, Paul Shorey, and Herbert Weir Smyth. His *Elegies of Albius Tibullus* (1913) is one of the first and greatest full-scale commentaries on a Latin author by an American. There had been no modern full-scale commentary on Tibullus in any language when Smith was commissioned to produce a school text. In a remarkably short time he produced a work comprising 343 pages of commentary on only forty-eight pages of poems. The commentary both explicated Tibullus' poetry and placed it in the context of first-century B.C. Roman poetry. Although he was obliged to reduce his introduction drastically (to just over ninety pages) and to eliminate histories of the text and an apparatus criticus, this weakness is more than offset by the strength of his remarks on the later tradition and the imitation of Tibullus by later authors. Indeed, one could compose a history of the Greek and Latin elegy from the information contained in the notes. The work displays the great depth of learning and independence from fashion and dogma that marks the best scholarship of any age. The volume was particularly well received in Europe, was reprinted in Germany, and is likely to remain the standard commentary into the twenty-first century.

He devoted his career to teaching at Johns Hopkins, taking leave only once, to be acting director of the School of Classical Studies at the American Academy in Rome (1914–1915). He married Charlotte Rogers in 1893; they had a son and a daughter. The Tibullus volume indicated the maturity of a significant career that promised further great contributions, but Smith's sudden and early death from a heart attack at his home in Baltimore deprived the study of Latin poetry in this country of one of its most learned and sensitive practitioners.

• There is a small collection of Smith's letters in the Manuscripts Collection at the Milton S. Eisenhower Library, Johns Hopkins University. Smith's journal publications include "An Historical Study of the Werwolf in Literature," *PMLA* 9, no. 1 (1894): 1–42; "Some Irregular Forms of the Elegiac Distich," *American Journal of Philology* 22 (1901): 165–94; "The Sources of Ben Jonson's 'Still to be Neat,'" *American Journal of Philology* 29 (1908): 133–55; "Marston's Malcontent," *American Journal of Philology* 37 (1916): 318–24, 487; "Propertius: A Modern Lover in the Augustan Age," *Sewanee Review* 25 (1917): 20–39; "Martial, the Epigrammatist" *Sewanee Review* 26 (1918): 1–27; and "The Poet Ovid," *Studies in Philology* 15 (1918): 307–32. *Martial, the Epigrammatist* (cited in the text) contains an autobiographical essay, "Some Boyhood Reminiscences of a Country Town." See obituaries by B. L. Gildersleeve in the *American Journal of Philology* 40 (1919): 110–11 and by Wilfred P. Mustard in *Classical Philology* 14 (1919): 95–96.

WARD W. BRIGGS

SMITH, Lillian Eugenia (12 Dec. 1897–28 Sept. 1966), essayist, novelist, and social critic, was born in Jasper, Florida, the daughter of Anne Hester Simpson and Calvin Warren Smith, a prominent businessman and civic leader. The relative economic and social security of her childhood, richly re-created in her *Memory of a Large Christmas* (1962), ended abruptly in 1915 when her father lost his turpentine mills in Jasper and moved the family to their summer home in the mountains near Clayton, Georgia. Facing economic hardship for the first time, Smith worked her way through one year at Piedmont College, taught in small mountain schools, and helped her family manage a hotel before she was able to pursue her professional interest in music at the Peabody Conservatory in Baltimore, Maryland. A self-described bohemian and rebel, Smith took another step outside the prescribed role of southern white ladyhood in 1922 when she accepted a three-year position teaching music in a Methodist girls' school in Huchow, China. Her dreams of a career in music, however, ended when her parents' poor health necessitated her return to Clayton to assume responsibility for the family's business, Laurel Falls Camp.

Under her directorship from 1925 to 1948, the popular and innovative summer camp for girls was known for its curriculum in the arts, music, dance, and modern psychology. Through her work with Laurel Falls campers and counselors Smith began to examine systematically her culture's attitudes about race, gender, and sexuality. There, also, she met Paula Snelling, a native of Pinehurst, Georgia, with whom she developed the lifelong relationship that nurtured and sustained her writing career. With an M.A. in psychology and literature from Columbia University, Snelling shared Smith's intellectual interests in people and ideas. Through their discussions about literature Smith began to redirect her creative expression from music to writing. Although Smith never acknowledged publicly the intimate nature of her relationship with Snelling, closeted sexual relationships between women figure significantly in her fiction, and in her writing she frequently attacked her society's rigid and repressive attitudes toward sexuality.

From 1936 to 1945 Smith and Snelling coedited a small literary magazine, first called *Pseudopodia*, then *North Georgia Review*, and finally *South Today*. Criticizing those who romanticized the Old South while ignoring the region's poverty and social inequities and publishing and reviewing the works of blacks and whites, women and men, the magazine quickly became known as a forum for liberal ideas in the region.

With the publication of her novel *Strange Fruit* in 1944, Smith found herself the famous and then infamous author of a record-breaking bestseller. Selling at the rate of 25,000 to 30,000 copies a week even before it was banned in Boston, the interracial love story set in the post–World War I South of Smith's youth sold a million copies in hardcover and more than 3 million copies during her lifetime. It was also translated into fifteen languages and was made into a Broadway play. In the years immediately following the publication of *Strange Fruit*, Smith was in demand as a speaker on popular radio programs, at numerous colleges, and before many religious and interracial groups. Her letters and essays appeared in national publications such as the *New York Times*, the *New Republic*, and the *Nation*; from October 1948 to September 1949 she wrote a weekly column for the Chicago *Defender*.

While *Strange Fruit* brought Smith international acclaim as a writer and social critic, *Killers of the Dream* (1949) affronted too many southerners—including powerful moderates—to be financially or critically successful. Written confessionally and autobiographically, combining personal memoir, allegory, and direct social commentary, the work effectively psychoanalyzed the South's rigid commitment to racial segregation like no other. Its subject matter and innovative style were met with hostility or deliberate silence by both the literary establishment and the general public of Cold War America. After an initial run of 30,000 copies, sales dropped dramatically; when critics and reviewers refused to accord it notice, Smith felt effectively silenced.

Smith wrote more philosophically in *The Journey* (1954) and *One Hour* (1959), demonstrating that her concerns extended beyond race relations in the American South to include all aspects of human relationships in the modern world. In *The Journey*, a spiritual autobiography completed while she recuperated from her first bout with cancer, Smith found the true measure of the human spirit in the individual's creative response to ordeal. After two young white boys set fire to her home in November 1955, destroying her personal belongings, thousands of valuable letters, and unpublished manuscripts, Smith returned to fiction to address her own questions about why her ideas about social change and human relationships were so strongly resisted. *One Hour* brilliantly depicts the destructive effects of mass hysteria and censorship associated with the McCarthy era while probing the dynamics of personal relationships of white, upper-middle-class intellectuals. Smith focused in particular on the power of unacknowledged fears associated with taboo sexual relationships.

In whatever genre she wrote, Smith refused to separate the seemingly conflicting roles of artist and activist. She was deeply respected and sought after by those who actively worked for justice in the South, from the National Association for the Advancement of Colored People and the Southern Conference for Human Welfare in the late 1930s and early 1940s, to the Americans for Democratic Action in the late 1940s and 1950s, and the Congress of Racial Equality and the Student Nonviolent Coordinating Committee in the 1960s. Hailing *Brown v. Board of Education of Topeka* as "every child's Magna Carta" in a letter to the *New York Times* (6 June 1954), she wrote *Now Is the Time* (1955), urging support for the Supreme Court's school desegregation ruling. As interpreter and clarifier for the movement, in her last book, *Our Faces, Our Words* (1964), Smith portrayed the inner conflicts of civil rights activists and, as she stated in the dedication, "the complexities and difficulties of creating new kinds of human relationships with one's fast changing world."

While challenging her culture's fundamental assumptions about race, class, gender, and sexuality, Lillian Smith chose to remain in her north Georgia mountain home to write her books and live her life. There also she was buried, among the remains of Laurel Falls Camp, after battling cancer for thirteen years. In 1968 the Smith family and the Southern Regional Council established the Lillian Smith Book Awards for outstanding writing about the South.

• The two major collections of Smith's papers are at the University of Florida and the University of Georgia. Since her death three additional volumes of her work have been published: *From the Mountain*, ed. Helen White and Redding S. Sugg, Jr. (1972) which includes articles from her magazine; *The Winner Names the Age*, ed. Michelle Cliff, with a preface by Paula Snelling (1978), a collection of her speeches and essays; and *How Am I to Be Heard? Letters of Lillian Smith*, ed. Margaret Rose Gladney (1993). Two book-length biographies are Louise Blackwell and Frances Clay, *Lillian Smith* (1971), and Anne C. Loveland, *Lillian Smith: A Southerner Confronting the South* (1986). For a comparative assessment of Smith's contributions as a southern woman writer, especially in *Killers of the Dream*, see Will Brantley, *Feminine Sense in Southern Memoir* (1993).

MARGARET ROSE GLADNEY

SMITH, Lloyd Pearsall (6 Feb. 1822–2 July 1886), librarian, publisher, and editor, was born in Philadelphia, Pennsylvania, the son of John Jay Smith, a librarian, and Rachel Collins Pearsall. Following graduation from Haverford College at age fifteen, Smith became a bookkeeper and an accountant in the counting house of Waln & Leaming. In 1844 he married Hannah E. Jones, with whom he later adopted a daughter. While still at Waln & Leaming, Smith began publishing, among other works, *Smith's Weekly Volume* (successor to *Waldie's Select Circulating Library*), a periodical that was edited by his father and continued until 1846.

In 1849 Smith became assistant librarian of the Library Company of Philadelphia, where his father was then librarian. The Library Company, although open to the public, was an important private library, founded in 1731 by a junto that included Benjamin Franklin. As the library grew, it incorporated the library of James Logan in the 1790s and included extensive collections of rare Americana. Logan's will gave to his descendants preference for the appointment of "hereditary librarian" of the Logonian library and in 1851 Smith succeeded his father as librarian, a position he held for the remainder of his life. One of his first projects in the new post was to issue the third volume of the *Catalogue of the Books Belonging to the Library Company of Philadelphia* (1856), which included his copious index. He also initiated a card catalog in 1857 that may well have been the first in the country. By 1876 the library consisted of more than 100,000 volumes.

One of the few interruptions in Smith's library career came in 1863, when the Confederate forces invaded Pennsylvania. Smith closed the library and enlisted in a volunteer regiment, taking part in the battle of Gettysburg. Other war work included collecting money for the relief of East Tennessee patriots who had remained loyal to the Union and publishing the report of a commission sent to investigate conditions there.

Smith's interests varied widely. George M. Abbot, his assistant at the library for nearly twenty-five years, wrote that Smith was "consumed by an insatiable thirst for knowledge and [was] interested in a wide range of subjects." For example, in 1865 he reviewed the first volume of *Histoire de Jules César*, which he later published as a pamphlet titled *Remarks on the Apology for Imperial Usurpation Contained in Napoleon's Life of Caesar*. During 1868–1869 he served as the first editor of *Lippincott's Magazine* and published Anthony Trollope's *Vicar of Bullhampton* and Robert Dale Owen's *Beyond the Breakers*, among other works. Libraries, however, were not forgotten. In 1876 Smith became one of the original associate editors of *American Library Journal*. One of the founding members of the American Library Association, he hosted the first organizing conference in Philadelphia in October 1876. Smith also later read a paper titled *Symbolism and Science* in 1885 before the Germantown Science and Art Club. That same year he published *A Bibliography of That Ancient and Honourable Order, the Society of the Cincinnati*.

The article that Smith contributed to the 1876 landmark volume, *Public Libraries in the United States of America*, issued by the U.S. Bureau of Education, on "Public Libraries of Philadelphia" (pp. 952–77), contains something of his attitude toward change: "Rotation in office has not yet invaded this venerable institution [the Library Company]. It has happened more than once in its history that directors have held office for over fifty years and during the last ninety years there have been only four librarians and five secretaries." In his tribute to Smith shortly after his sudden death, William F. Poole wrote, "His mind had a mediaeval tinge which led him to take delight in the monkish Latin of the middle ages. . . . He believed in what is old, rather than what is new, and in this respect was a typical Philadelphian."

Nevertheless, Smith was best known for his knowledge of library management practices, and his addresses to the American Library Association were remembered for their practical insights. At the first American conference of librarians in 1853, Smith had presented a paper describing his classified index to the Library Company's catalog. Another paper delivered and published in 1882, titled "On the Classification of Books," again described the library's unique system— one that is still in use at the library. Although his library classification was considered by S. Austin Allibone and H. J. Dennis to be one of the best then in existence, Smith became a supporter of Melvil Dewey after hearing Dewey describe his own system at an American Library Association annual conference.

Not a public librarian himself, Smith was nonetheless an energetic promoter of the public library movement. He wrote in the July 1881 *Library Journal*: "The present is an opportune time for Pennsylvania to act, and no better way of celebrating the two-hundredth anniversary of the landing of William Penn could be found than to establish a free public library in the city of Philadelphia." Even though he thought that books should be kept safely in locked cabinets, Smith believed in providing the best service possible to library patrons. If library visitors were treated as gentlemen, he asserted, they would behave as guests in a gentleman's house. Smith died in Philadelphia.

• Brief biographical information concerning Smith appears in several works, the most helpful of which are George M. Abbot, *A Short History of the Library Company of Philadelphia* (1913); Abbot, "Some Recollections of Lloyd P. Smith," *Library Journal* 12 (1887): 545–46; and Austin K. Gray, *Benjamin Franklin's Library: A Short Account of the Library Company of Philadelphia, 1731–1931* (1937). Edward G. Holley, *Raking the Historical Coals: The ALA Scrapbook of 1876* (1967), contains information not found elsewhere. See also J. T. Scharf and Thompson Wescott, *History of Philadelphia* (1884); Samuel Swett Green, *The Public Library Movement in the United States, 1853–1893* (1913); and the *Biographical Catalog of the Matriculates of Haverford College* (1922). An obituary is in the *Philadelphia Public Ledger*, 3 July 1886.

DONALD G. DAVIS, JR.
JEANNETTE WOODWARD

SMITH, Logan Pearsall (18 Oct. 1865–2 Mar. 1946), essayist, philologist, and critic, was born Lloyd Logan Pearsall Smith in Millville, New Jersey, the son of Robert Pearsall Smith, a wealthy partner in the family glass-bottle factory, and Hannah Tatum Whitall. Both parents were Quakers but later became influential revivalist preachers and tract writers. In 1868 the family moved to Philadelphia and in 1872 vacationed in England. Smith's education was sporadic but excellent: he attended the Friends' William Penn Charter School, Philadelphia (1880–1881), Haverford College (1881–1884), and Harvard University (1884–1885). In 1885, when he was a guest at his older sister Mary's wedding ceremony in Oxford, England, he resolved to take classes there eventually. After a year of study at Berlin University and an unhappy year in the family business, he persuaded his father in 1887 to give him enough money so that he could live simply and never have to work again. His father settled $25,000 on him, and he entered Balliol College, Oxford, in 1888. That same year his family moved permanently to a country house outside London, where visitors included William James, George Santayana, George Bernard Shaw, and Beatrice and Sidney Webb. Smith studied with Benjamin Jowett, Oxford's eminent professor of Greek, and graduated with a B.A. from Oxford in 1891.

Smith lived in Paris from 1891 to 1895, associated with painter James Abbott McNeill Whistler, and traveled, after which he established permanent residences in England. In 1895 he published six unimportant short stories in a book titled *The Youth of Parnassus*. During 1896–1899 he traveled in Italy. With his sister Mary and her future husband, art critic Bernard Berenson, he produced a review titled *The Golden Urn* and printed it privately in Fiesole (1897–1898). In 1898, following the death of his father, Smith's mother began living with him.

Having published several of his own tiny aphoristic essays in *The Golden Urn*, Smith gathered them together in 1902, added more, and privately issued *Trivia*, the first of four such collections. Later titles are *More Trivia* (1922), *Afterthoughts* (1931), *All Trivia* (1933), and *Last Words* (1933). By these compact, beautifully styled, often ironic "pieces of moral prose," as he called them, Smith remains best known. Epigrammatic and ironic, they say much in little, and range from simple and sweet to cynical and even quietly enraged. They generally show his amusement at life's puzzles, occasionally invite dissent, and tend to remain in the reader's memory. One ends thus: "Is it Hope, or is it not rather Vanity, that I love the best?"

Combining scholarly reading, steady composition, and association with innumerable friends—young and old—Smith published *The Life and Letters of Sir Henry Wotton* (2 vols., 1907) and *The English Language* (1912). His Wotton work, still considered definitive, begins with a life of the seventeenth-century diplomat and poet, then presents his letters, with erudite annotations and many touches of humor. *The English Language* is a concise history of English—its origins, foreign infusions, and stream of neologisms—and includes essays on language and history and on language and thought. In 1911 Smith's mother died, and his sister Alys, separated from her husband, philosopher Bertrand Russell, began to live with Smith, who never married.

The poet Robert Bridges was so fascinated by Smith's philological studies that he, Smith, and a few others in 1913 inaugurated the Society for Pure English. That same year Smith became a naturalized British subject; a year later, having lived in various country places, he moved permanently with Alys to London, where he became known as "the sage of Chelsea." Amid other writings, he published five anthology-like volumes—concerning English prose (1919), John Donne's sermons (1919), George Santayana (1920), English aphorisms (1928), and Jeremy Taylor (1930), all with extensive bibliographies. He also wrote *Four Words: Romantic, Originality, Creative, Genius* (1924) and then *Words and Idioms* (1925), which incorporates *Four Words*. Calling the word *romantic* adventuresome in England and abroad, *originality* great and modern, *creative* important, and *genius* portentous, he traces the words' histories expertly and wittily. *Words and Idioms* treats sea terms, popular sayings, and figurative expressions, relating them where possible to common occupations and rustic sports.

One of Smith's finest works is *On Reading Shakespeare* (1933). Demonstrating a thorough and controlled mastery of his subject, he begins by archly saying why one should avoid Shakespeare, then reveals his utter devotion to Shakespeare both as poet and as dramatist. He introduces numerous quotations cannily, discusses them lucidly, and comments on critics (especially Samuel Taylor Coleridge, his favorite). His *Reperusals and Re-collections* (1936) is a collection of nineteen essays on authors and their works. He combines authority and warmth and is especially striking when he focuses on Jane Austen, Montaigne, and Walter Pater. Smith's most notable publishing success was *Unforgotten Years* (1939), his endearing and surprisingly popular autobiography. Organized chronologically, the work is livened by anecdotes concerning his many illustrious friends (notably Matthew Arnold, Henry James, Edith Wharton, and Walt Whitman); it contains a chapter on the challenges and joys of manuscript hunting and another in defense of expatriates. His last book, the short work *Milton and His Modern Critics* (1940), deftly excoriates T. S. Eliot, Ezra Pound, and their followers for not appreciating Milton's diction, syntax, and intent.

In his last years, Smith continued to travel when health permitted, influenced many brilliant younger people, including art historian Kenneth Clark, literary critics Cyril Connolly and Desmond MacCarthy, writer Rose Macaulay, and historian Hugh Trevor-Roper, wrote scores of letters to them and others, developed symptoms of manic depression (especially severe in lonely winters), survived the Nazi blitz without leaving London, and lived to know that his *Trivia* books, many of his critical insights, and his autobiography had achieved enduring celebrity. Smith died in his London home.

• Most of Smith's voluminous papers are in the Library of Congress, Washington, D.C., and at Temple University, Philadelphia. Many of the others are in libraries at the University of Southern California, Harvard University, Kent State University, the New York Public Library, the University of Texas at San Antonio, and Yale University. Standard biographies are Robert Gathorne-Hardy, *Recollections of Logan Pearsall Smith: The Story of a Friendship* (1950), and the introduction by John Russell, ed., *A Portrait of Logan Pearsall Smith, Drawn from His Letters and Diaries* (1950); both Gathorne-Hardy and Russell were Smith's close companions. *A Chime of Words: The Letters of Logan Pearsall Smith*, ed. Edwin Tribble (1984), contains a succinct biography. Edmund Wilson, *The Bit between My Teeth: A Literary Chronicle of 1950–1965* (1965), includes a sharp critical essay on Smith, pp. 114–30. An obituary is in the *New York Times*, 3 Mar. 1946.

ROBERT L. GALE

SMITH, Lucy Harth (24 Jan. 1888–20 Sept. 1955), racial activist and educator, was born in Roanoke, Virginia, the daughter of Daniel Washington Harth, Jr., a minister and lawyer, and Rachel Emma Brockington. In 1904 she attended the normal department of the Hampton Institute in Virginia, completing both the high school and college courses in four years. Subsequently, she accepted an elementary school teaching post in Roanoke. Two years later, following her marriage to Paul Smith, a school administrator, she left the labor force; the couple had five children.

In 1917 the family relocated to Lexington, Kentucky, where Paul Smith became principal of the Booker T. Washington Elementary School. The next year Lucy Harth Smith returned to public education, serving as teacher and assistant principal alongside her husband. In 1932 she graduated magna cum laude

from Kentucky State College, in Frankfort, Kentucky. After her husband transferred to another local school in 1935, Smith assumed the principalship of the Booker T. Washington Elementary School, a position she held for twenty years.

Like many college-educated black women with families, Smith forged a distinguished career of public service while raising her children. In 1943 she completed her formal education, earning a master's degree in education from the University of Cincinnati. In her thesis she investigated the career of the noted African-American scholar and inventor George Washington Carver.

Smith actually pursued two careers: racial activist and educator. An active clubwoman, Smith served as president of the Kentucky Association of Colored Women and chaired the executive board of the National Association of Colored Women's Clubs. Through her work with these organizations and with the public schools, Smith addressed the problems of black children in a segregated society.

In the spirit of Progressivism, Smith was a persistent advocate of the right of black children to equal access not only to education but also to recreation and good health. In 1944 Smith organized and secured private funding for a summer Health Camp for Colored Children in central Kentucky. The Community Chest of Lexington later supported this endeavor. Smith also was a member of the Governor's Committee on Youth and Children.

Smith made major contributions as an educator through her work as a public school administrator and as an active member of various professional associations and through her activities as a curriculum reformer. Although principalships at the elementary level became somewhat more common for white women in the post–World War II era, relatively few women of any color held administrative posts in the 1930s and 1940s. Principals were accorded great honor in black communities, for persons of either gender. Thus Smith occupied a significant position among African Americans in Lexington.

Smith was active in professional organizations at both the national and local levels. She served as a regional vice president and trustee of the American Teachers Association and held the presidency of the Lexington Teachers Association. She also became the first woman president of the Kentucky Negro Education Association.

For thirty years, from 1925 to 1955, Smith was numbered among the most dedicated members of the Association for the Study of Negro History and Life. In its obituary, the association's *Journal of Negro History* (Apr. 1956) described Smith as "a perennial figure at the association's annual meeting." Smith's role was both administrative and scholarly. As a long-time member of the executive committee, she participated in policy-making decisions, and as a historian, she chaired numerous paper sessions.

Smith's most notable contribution to the association remains her persistent and compelling advocacy of the inclusion of black history in the curriculum of the public schools. In an address at the annual meeting in November 1933, she concluded that both whites and blacks benefited from the introduction of black history into the curriculum. She believed that an accurate recounting of African-American history would not only alter the attitudes of thoughtful whites but would also inspire great pride within black students (*Journal of Negro History*, Jan. 1934). During the darkest days of the Second World War, at the association's annual meeting in November 1942, Smith's lecture concluded that through exemplary military participation and support of the war, African Americans in the United States belonged in the "front ranks as citizens" (*Journal of Negro History*, Jan. 1943). Smith died in Lexington, Kentucky.

Although Smith did not enjoy unquestioned success as a racial activist and educator, she remains a significant figure because she numbered among a minority of college-educated African-American women who were unafraid to speak out and to take action to enhance opportunities for African-American children in the South. In its account of her career and involvement with the association, the *Journal of Negro History* (Apr. 1956) ranked Smith with the inimitable Mary McLeod Bethune, stating, "Where [Bethune] built institutions, Lucy Harth Smith became a crusader in inspiring colored people to look to their past for sources of hope in the achievements and contributions of Negroes to civilization and history."

Smith received numerous honors for her work. The *Louisville Defender*, an African-American newspaper, included her among the most outstanding black Kentuckians. The Kentucky Human Rights Commission named her in 1973 to its Gallery of Great Black Kentuckians. In 1974 the Kentucky Education Association honored her service by inaugurating the Lucy Harth Smith–Atwood S. Wilson Award for Civil and Human Rights in Education.

• For a detailed record of Lucy Harth Smith's views on the inclusion of black history in the public school curriculum, the importance of African-American role models, and the role of African Americans as citizens, see "Proceedings of the Annual Meeting of the Association for the Study of Negro Life and History," *Journal of Negro History*, 1928–1955. An obituary, including a biographical sketch, is in *Journal of Negro History* 41 (Apr. 1956): 177–78.

CAROLYN TERRY BASHAW

SMITH, Macdonald (18 Mar. 1890–31 Aug. 1949), golfer, was born in Carnoustie, Scotland, the son of John Smith, a golf course greenkeeper, and Johann Robertson. At age eighteen Smith came to the United States and worked for his brother George at the Claremont Golf Club and the Hotel Del Monte in California.

Although Smith won more than fifty tournaments worldwide, he is remembered primarily for being the best golfer never to have won a "major" championship (U.S. Open, British Open, Masters, or Professional Golfers Association title). He came closest to victory in his first U.S. Open at the Philadelphia Cricket Club in 1910, when he tied for first with his brother Alex and Johnny McDermott. Smith shot a 77 in the playoff, trailing McDermott's 75 and Alex's 71.

In 1912 Smith won the Western Open, the era's third most important tournament. In 1913 he filled in for his brother Alex at Wykagyl in New York's Westchester County and tied for fourth in his second U.S. Open. Following the championship, he and Alex handed Harry Vardon and Ted Ray their only defeat during the legendary Englishmen's 41-match tour of the United States. Vardon subsequently called Smith the best golfer he had seen in America.

During a one-year stint at Oakmont outside Pittsburgh in 1914, Smith won the Metropolitan Open (his record score of 278 stood until 1940). But after a successful season on the fledgling Professional Golfers Association Tour in 1916, he mysteriously vanished from the tournament scene.

Information about Smith for the next few years remains sketchy and is often contradictory. He evidently spent some winters working as one of Alex's clubmakers in Florida and served briefly as the professional at the San Jose Country Club in California. Sources disagree over whether he served with the U.S. Army in France or in the coast artillery during World War I, but he incurred a hearing loss that contributed to one of his nicknames—the Silent Scot. By 1919 he was working at the Union Iron Works shipyard in San Francisco. Heavy drinking apparently took a toll on his nerves and helped account for his absence from tournament golf.

Smith reemerged from his self-imposed exile in March 1920 in a local competition at Lincoln Park Golf Club, where he shot a second-round 64. Joe Adleman of the Wright & Ditson Sporting Goods Company sent him to the following week's Southern California Open, in which he finished a close second. The next month Smith became the pro at San Francisco's Olympic Golf Club. But he did not enjoy the everyday responsibilities of a club pro. Time devoted to golf lessons limited his playing to state tournaments and exhibitions. He left Olympic during 1921 and opened an immediately successful golf school in San Francisco.

Smith's marriage in 1922 to Louise Cahill Harvey, a "well-known society woman of San Francisco and prominent Christian Scientist," turned his life around. Thirteen years his senior and entering her third marriage, she helped him control his drinking and financed his return to major tournament golf. Smith ranked among the top twenty-five players on the PGA Tour in 1923, sharing nineteenth place in his first U.S. Open since 1915. He recorded his first win in the 1924 California Open.

During the following years Smith made one of the great career comebacks in professional sports. He earned twenty-three more tour victories, his last coming in 1936 at the age of forty-six in the Seattle Open. His most important wins included two more Western Opens (1925, 1933); the North and South Open (1925); four Los Angeles Opens (1928, 1929, 1932,

1934), the tour's first event with a purse of $10,000; the Canadian Open (1926); and two more Metropolitan Opens (in 1926 when he shot 66 in a third 18-hole playoff to defeat Gene Sarazen and in 1931). His best years came with four victories in 1925 and five in 1926.

But Smith remained more famous for his defeats than his triumphs. In 1925 he led the British Open at Prestwick, Scotland, by five strokes going into the final round. An enthusiastic crowd of at least 15,000 turned out to see the native Scot they called "Mac-Smith" win. The golf course could not handle such a throng, as his loving but unruly gallery cost him the championship. His 82, ten strokes over par, dropped him to fourth place, three strokes behind Jim Barnes. Former British Open champion George Duncan concluded, "I don't think anybody could have got 78 [the highest score that would have still won] playing against that crowd." Nevertheless, a similar collapse at Carnoustie in 1931 produced a 5-6-5 finish, when even par 3-4-5 would have beat Tommy Armour.

On other occasions Smith fell just short after valiant efforts to overcome large leads. In the British Open he finished third in 1923, two strokes back of Arthur Havers, and third in 1924, three strokes behind Walter Hagen. In 1932 a closing round 70 gave him second place, five strokes behind Gene Sarazen. Even at age forty-six in the 1936 U.S. Open, he produced a final round 70, bettered only by winner Tony Manero's 67, to move from nineteenth to fourth place.

Smith's most historic failures, however, came during Bobby Jones's Grand Slam year of 1930, when Smith finished second to Jones by two strokes in both the British and U.S. opens held at Hoylake (near Liverpool) and Interlachen (in a suburb of Minneapolis. Smith's final round of 70 at the U.S. Open was five strokes better than Jones's score. Another 75 by Jones in the last round of the British Open made him vulnerable once again to a Smith charge, but Smith's brilliant 71 still fell short.

Golf professionals and sportswriters of that time agreed that Smith's game exhibited no weaknesses and that he possessed the ideal temperament for the sport. Above all, they lauded his long, flowing swing with its distinct pause at the top and the seemingly effortless result that left no divot. Tommy Armour called Smith the "stylist of all stylists," adding, "He treats the grass of a golf course as though it were an altar cloth." After almost seventy years of watching the game's greats, Harvey Penick, one of golf's master teachers, concluded in 1992 that "the prettiest swing I ever saw belonged to Macdonald Smith."

Smith's successful comeback led to a position at the Lakeville Club on Long Island, New York, from 1924 until 1930. But Smith found other ways to capitalize on his fame. In 1932 he severely cut back his tournament schedule and moved to Nashville, Tennessee, to design and promote hickory-shafted "Macdonald Smith Hand Made Golf Clubs." Hickory's popularity had declined after steel shafts had been approved for tournament play by the U.S. Golf Association in 1926. Although Smith occasionally experimented with steel

toward the end of his career, he remained a hickory man. Indeed, he remained the only golfer in the 1935 British Open still using hickories. Smith's dedication to tradition, further revealed in a preference for well-tailored plus fours in an age of long pants, and his solid, nonflashy golf game earned him a second nickname, "Old Carnoustie."

After the hickory venture failed, Smith moved in 1935 to the Oakmont Country Club in Glendale, California, where he made clubs and gave lessons to members and numerous professionals. Ill health forced him to abandon plans both for a last-ditch effort at the British Open in 1937 and for continuing his temporarily revived tournament play at the end of the 1938 season. He died of a heart attack in Glendale. In 1954 he was inducted into the PGA Golf Hall of Fame.

Authorities variously ascribed Smith's failure to win a "major" to bad luck, drinking, or an inability to deal with pressure. But he lost major championships during his frequent periods of sobriety, and, whether during drinking episodes or sober, he often came from behind or held leads to win other important championships with much more money at stake. Moreover, during the first three decades of the twentieth century, the Western and Metropolitan opens *were* majors. His opportunities to win the modern majors also were more limited than is commonly acknowledged. The Masters, not fully accorded the status of a major until the 1950s, was not played until late in Smith's career. He tied for seventh in the first Masters in 1934, the only one he entered. His deep disappointment over his loss at Prestwick in 1925 led to boycott the 1926, 1927, and 1928 British Opens when he stood at the peak of his powers and would have ranked among the favorites. And alone among the great golfers of his or any other era, he never sought to qualify for the PGA, evidently because he disliked match play. Yet Smith's unfortunate failure to capture an arbitrarily defined major rather than his numerous victories and flawless swing guaranteed him a prominent place in golf history.

• No Smith papers have been collected. Twenty-eight of his tournament medals are on display at Carnoustie Golf Club. Smith comes alive in Tommy Armour's affectionate portrait, "Penshots of the Masters," *American Golfer*, July 1935, pp. 12, 48. Herbert Warren Wind, *The Story of American Golf: Its Champions and Its Championships* (1956), and Bernard Darwin, *Golf between Two Wars* (1944), thoughtfully analyze his play. Al Barkow's *The History of the PGA Tour* (1989) has the most detailed statistical information about his career from 1916 on. Stewart Hackney, *Carnoustie Links: Courses and Players* (1989), and the *San Francisco Chronicle*, 25 Aug. 1922, contain valuable information about his family and early life. For the impact of his drinking on his career, see Charles Price, "The Pro Who Drank Too Much," *Golf Digest*, May 1991, pp. 184–89. Detailed obituaries are in the *New York Times* and *Los Angeles Times*, both 1 Sept. 1949. Unfortunately, all of these sources contain serious errors and omissions. Two efforts at correcting the record are Howard N. Rabinowitz, "Macdonald Smith: The Golf Great Who Couldn't Win a Major," *Golfiana*, no. 2, 1994, pp. 29–33, and Howard Rabinowitz, "Death by Love at Prestwick," *Golf Journal*, July 1994, pp. 36–38.

HOWARD N. RABINOWITZ

SMITH, Mamie (26 May 1883–30 Oct. 1946?), blues and vaudeville singer and film actress, was born Mamie Robinson in Cincinnati, Ohio. Nothing is known of her parents. At the age of ten she toured with a white act, the Four Dancing Mitchells. She danced in J. Homer Tutt and Salem Tutt-Whitney's The Smart Set Company in 1912 and then left the tour the next year to sing in Harlem clubs and theaters. Around this time she married William "Smitty" Smith, a singing waiter who died in 1928. At the Lincoln Theater in 1918 she starred in Perry Bradford's musical review *Made in Harlem*, in which she sang "Harlem Blues."

In 1920 Bradford persuaded a New York recording company, OKeh, to take a chance recording Smith, despite racist threats of a boycott. In February she recorded his songs "That Thing Called Love" and "You Can't Keep a Good Man Down," accompanied by a white band; this disc was not immediately released because of an industrywide patent dispute. In August, with a hastily organized African-American band that came to be known as her Jazz Hounds, Smith recorded "It's Right Here for You" and "Crazy Blues." The latter tune, a retitled version of "Harlem Blues," sold spectacularly well. Further female blues singers were sought after and recorded, and a new marketing category, "race records," was under way in the industry.

Bradford organized a touring Jazz Hounds band. Trumpeter Johnny Dunn and reed player Garvin Bushell were among Smith's accompanists in 1920. Trumpeter Bubber Miley replaced Dunn, perhaps early in 1921. Tenor saxophonist Coleman Hawkins joined that summer, as Bradford placed Smith on the Theater Owner's Booking Association circuit and continued directing recording sessions. Immensely popular, Smith made huge earnings in royalties (reportedly nearly $100,000) and performance fees (often more than $1,000 per week), enabling her to purchase a lavishly furnished house on 130th Street. Dan Burley reported, "There were servants, cars, and all the luxuries that would go with being the highest paid Negro star of that day" (24 Feb. 1940, p. 20). She bought a building on St. Nicholas Place, which she later lost in the stock market crash, and another home in Jamaica, New York.

Because of Bradford's financial and touring disputes with Smith's second husband, Sam Gardner, and her boyfriend and band manager, Ocey (or Ocie) Wilson, Smith's contract was sold to a white manager, Maurice Fulchner, and Bradford left OKeh for the Columbia label to work with singer Edith Wilson. Later, Burley writes, "Mister Bradford came to serve a summons on the blues queen on account of certain 'misunderstandings' having to do with his songs. Reports are that Mr. Bradford jumped roofs for a block and a half after Mamie got her gun" (9 Mar. 1940).

Late in 1922 Smith recorded "I Ain't Gonna Give Nobody None o' This Jelly-Roll" and "The Darktown Flappers' Ball." She continued to tour nationally with her Jazz Hounds. Hawkins remained with her until 1923, and in that year he may have worked alongside reed player Sidney Bechet with Smith at the Garden of Joy in New York. Featured in her own shows, Smith performed in theaters through the 1920s and into the 1930s. Among her recordings were "Goin' Crazy with the Blues," "What Have I Done?" (both from 1926), and "Jenny's Ball" (1931).

In 1929 Smith married a Mr. Goldberg (given name unknown), one of the brothers who managed and owned the Seven Eleven troupe in which she performed. No account of her marriage mentions children. She appeared in the film short *Jailhouse Blues* (1929) and costarred in *Fireworks of 1930*, a short-lived revue written and performed by Fats Waller and James P. Johnson. She worked with pianist and singer Fats Pichon's band from 1932 to 1934 and toured Europe around 1936, at which time she also led her Beale Street Boys at the Town Casino in New York. At some point in the 1930s she sang with Andy Kirk's big band.

Smith starred in a series of low-budget African-American films: *Paradise in Harlem* (1940) with Lucky Millinder's big band, *Mystery in Swing* (1940), *Murder on Lenox Avenue* and *Sunday Sinners* (both 1941), and the soundie (a film short for video juke boxes) *Because I Love You* (c. 1942), again with Millinder. She last sang in a concert at the Lido Ballroom in New York in August 1944. Confined to Harlem Hospital during a long illness, she died in New York.

Among classic female blues and vaudeville singers, Smith is celebrated more as a racial pioneer than as a great performer. Bushell recalled that "Mamie was a very fine-looking lady, had a nice personality, and was a bit higher cultured than a lot of the singers. She wasn't a low, gutbucket type of singer that they were wanting on records. . . . She usually had a husband who was a big bruiser, taking all her money" (p. 22). Derrick Stewart-Baxter writes that "her voice lacked the richness of the truly great women artists who were to follow her into the recording studios. . . . Seldom was she really involved in what she was singing, and at times she lapsed into the sentimental. . . . There may appear to be an outward toughness, but occasionally the marshmallow at the roots comes to the surface" (p. 10).

But Smith unquestionably had a special stage presence. Singer Victoria Spivey recalled seeing her for the first time:

Miss Smith walked on that stage and I could not breathe for a minute. She threw those big sparkling eyes on us with that lovely smile showing those pearly teeth with a diamond the size of one of her teeth. Then I looked at her dress. Nothing but sequins and rhinestones, plus a velvet cape with fur on it. We all went wild. And then she sang—she tore the house apart. Between numbers while the band was playing she would make a complete change in about a minute, and was back in record time for her next selection. Her full voice filled the entire auditorium without the use of mikes like we use today. That was singing the blues! I was really inspired and kept plugging to become a singer. (quoted in Stewart-Baxter, p. 16)

This talent comes across reasonably well in the late-career film roles, where Smith repeatedly steals the show, acting and singing in a manner that seems refreshingly natural and comfortable by comparison with and in spite of her consistently mediocre associates.

• For further information on Smith see Dan Burley, "'Crazy Blues' and the Woman Who Sold 'em," *Amsterdam News*, 17 Feb. 1940, cont. as "The 'Crazy Blues,'" 24 Feb. 1940, 3 Mar. 1940, 9 Mar. 1940; Leonard Kunstadt and Bob Colton, "Mamie Smith: First Lady of the Blues," *Record Research* 31 (Nov. 1960): 7; Samuel B. Charters and Kunstadt, *Jazz: A History of the New York Scene* (1962; repr. 1981); Perry Bradford, *Born with the Blues: Perry Bradford's Own Story: The True Story of the Pioneering Blues Singers and Musicians in the Early Days of Jazz* (1965); Ronald Clifford Foreman, Jr., "Jazz and Race Records, 1920–1932: Their Origins and Their Significance for the Record Industry and Society" (Ph.D. diss., Univ. of Illinois, 1968); Robert M. W. Dixon and John Godrich, *Recording the Blues* (1970); and Derrick Stewart-Baxter, *Ma Rainey and the Classic Blues Singers* (1970). Entries on Smith are in Sheldon Harris, *Blues Who's Who: A Biographical Dictionary of Blues Singers* (1979); Sally Placksin, *American Women in Jazz, 1900 to the Present: Their Words, Lives, and Music* (1982); and John Chilton, *Who's Who of Jazz: Storyville to Swing Street*, 4th ed. (1985). See also Chilton, *Sidney Bechet: The Wizard of Jazz* (1987); Garvin Bushell and Mark Tucker, *Jazz from the Beginning* (1988); and Laurie Wright, *"Fats" in Fact* (1992).

BARRY KERNFELD

SMITH, Margaret Bayard (20 Feb. 1778–7 June 1844), author and society leader, was born on a farm near Swede's Ford on the Schuylkill River in Pennsylvania, the daughter of John Bubenheim Bayard, a merchant, and Margaret Hodge. The family had moved from Philadelphia just before the city was occupied by the British. A revolutionary war leader, Bayard had commanded a regiment in the battles of Princeton, Brandywine, and Germantown and spent part of the winter of 1777–1778 with George Washington at Valley Forge.

Margaret's childhood was far from stable. Growing up in a family of eleven children, she lost both her mother and stepmother at an early age, and her father married for a third time. After the family moved to New Brunswick, New Jersey, in 1788, she enrolled at the Moravian school in Bethlehem, Pennsylvania. By the time she went to live with a brother in Philadelphia at the age of thirteen, she had become an avid reader, especially of romantic novels. She soon returned to New Brunswick to live with her sister Jane and brother-in-law Andrew Kirkpatrick, a lawyer, who took it upon themselves to educate her. Under their guidance she began reading serious works such as the Gospels, the plays of Sophocles, and James Bruce's *Travels to*

Discover the Source of the Nile (1790), besides continuing to read novels.

In 1797 Margaret became engaged to her second cousin, Samuel Harrison Smith, editor of the Jeffersonian *New World* in Philadelphia, then the national capital. They married in 1800, and the lives of the young couple were immediately linked with the history of the young nation when presidential candidate Thomas Jefferson asked Smith to establish a newspaper in Washington, D.C., after the government moved there in November. The Smiths reached Washington on 3 October and made their home on Capitol Hill. The first issue of the *National Intelligencer* appeared on 31 October, the day before President John Adams (1735–1826) first occupied the White House and less than three weeks before Congress first met in the Capitol. In the fall election Jefferson defeated Adams but tied with Aaron Burr (1756–1836) in the electoral college, and it was not until 17 February 1801 that the House of Representatives elected Jefferson president.

Meanwhile, Margaret Smith settled into a demanding life style. Even though she had servants, she baked bread, cooked meals, nursed her husband during his frequent illnesses, and cared for their four children. In the mornings, she often visited with women friends such as Dolley Madison and Hannah Gallatin, wife of Secretary of the Treasury Albert Gallatin. Later in the day came teas, card parties, dinner parties, and other events that enlivened social life in the capital. Her friendliness and sympathy, her skill at whist and chess, and her intelligent, lively conversation made her a popular, influential leader of society. She found the poet Joel Barlow a place to stay in the city, talked with the elder Robert Owen, a Welsh socialist and philanthropist, about his reform plans, and hosted a tea party for British writer Harriet Martineau. Both devoted supporters of Thomas Jefferson, she and her husband often dined with the president and exchanged visits with Jefferson at Monticello and at their summer residence near present-day Catholic University. Despite being loyal Jeffersonians and later Whigs, however, the Smiths entertained leaders from all parties.

The Smiths' financial interests shifted from journalism to banking in 1809 and 1810 when Samuel became president of the Bank of Washington and sold the *National Intelligencer*. In 1828, when he became president of the Washington branch of the Bank of the United States, the family moved to a fashionable home near Lafayette Square. Both deeply interested in civic improvements, Margaret became a founder of a female orphanage, and Samuel helped establish the city library and other institutions.

As the children grew older, Margaret Smith began a career as an author, bringing a combination of romanticism and morality to her work. In her first novel, *A Winter in Washington; or, Memoirs of the Seymour Family* (1824), she drew on her own experiences, promising to scatter "the flowers which adorn the surface of life" before the reader. In *What Is Gentility?: A Moral*

Tale (1828), she sought to "demonstrate that *gentility* is independent of birth, wealth, or condition." She also contributed to *Godey's Lady's Book*, publishing a description of presidential inaugurations, several short stories, and another moral tale, "Who Is Happy?" (1839). In addition, she wrote for the *Southern Literary Messenger, Peter Parley's Annual*, the *National Intelligencer*, and the *National Portrait Gallery of Distinguished Americans* (1834–1839). A skillful writer and delightful storyteller, she was one of a number of successful women authors in the early Republic, including Sarah Josepha Hale, Caroline Gilman, Eliza Leslie, and Catharine Sedgwick.

Margaret Smith's most influential writing was contained in her notebooks and in her letters to members of her family, excerpts of which appeared in 1906 in *The First Forty Years of Washington Society*, edited by Gaillard Hunt. A rich source for historians, these writings reflect her fears that Jacksonian Democracy would destroy the Jeffersonian customs and values she embraced. She was alarmed by party politics and the spoils system, and she could not accept Peggy Eaton, a tavernkeeper's daughter who, as the second wife of Secretary of War John H. Eaton, was rejected by Washington society, leading to the disruption of Andrew Jackson's cabinet. Her descriptions of Jefferson, the burning of Washington, and the inauguration of Jackson are classics. The deaths of Smith and her husband in Washington in consecutive years, along with those of others in their group, marked the passing of an era.

• A large collection of the papers of Margaret Smith is at the Library of Congress, which also houses the papers of Samuel Harrison Smith in the Jonathan Bayard Smith family papers. The role of the Smiths in the early history of Washington is carefully examined in Constance M. Green, *Washington: Village and Capital, 1800–1878* (1962), and Wilhelmus B. Bryan, *A History of the National Capital*, vol. 1 (1914). For the Bayard family, see James G. Wilson, "Col. John Bayard and the Bayard Family of America," *New York Genealogical and Biographical Record* 16 (1885): 49–72, and Morton Borden, *The Federalism of James A. Bayard* (1955). Smith's early life is described in Frank Van Der Linden, *The Turning Point: Jefferson's Battle for the Presidency* (1962).

DONALD B. COLE

SMITH, Margaret Chase (14 Dec. 1897–29 May 1995), U.S. congresswoman and senator, was born Margaret Madeline Chase in Skowhegan, Maine, the daughter of George Emery Chase, a barber, and Carrie Murray. After graduating in 1916 from Skowhegan High School she taught briefly in local schools. Between 1917 and 1930 she worked as a switchboard operator for the telephone company, spent nine years in the circulation, advertising, and editorial departments of the community's weekly *Independent-Reporter*, and managed the office of a woolen textile mill. She also served during 1925–1927 as president of the Maine state federation of business and professional women's clubs.

In 1930 Margaret Chase married Clyde Harold Smith, a state highway commissioner, Skowhegan town selectman, former state legislator, and co-owner of the local newspaper, who was twenty-one years her senior. They had no children. He was elected in 1936 and 1938 as a Republican to the U.S. Congress, and she helped manage his office. In April 1940 he suffered a heart attack, and before he died he urged Maine voters to choose his "partner in public life" as his successor. In a special election they did so, and she took her seat in June 1940. She gained reelection in 1940, 1942, 1944, and 1946. In 1948 she decided to run for an open seat in the U.S. Senate. She won that year and again in 1954, 1960, and 1966, but in 1972, at the age of seventy-four, she lost a bid for a fifth term to Democratic congressman William D. Hathaway.

Thus from 1940 until 1973 Smith represented Maine in Congress as a Republican. The "Lady from Maine" became known for her expertise on military matters, her courage and independence, and the single red rose she wore each day. She was the first woman to serve in the Senate as a Republican, the first woman to gain a Senate seat without first being appointed to it, and the first woman to be elected to both houses of Congress. She was mentioned as a possible vice presidential candidate in 1952 and 1956, and in 1964 she entered the New Hampshire presidential primary. When she gained nomination for the presidency at the Republican National Convention in 1964, she was the first woman to do so by a major party.

Perhaps Smith's finest moment took place on the floor of the Senate early in her tenure there. Having supported all major Cold War initiatives, both at home and abroad, she started out friendly with Wisconsin's Republican senator Joseph R. McCarthy. She finally concluded that, having failed to supply the evidence he kept promising, he had gone too far in his red-baiting charges of communists in the federal government. On 1 June 1950, introducing a statement also supported by six other senators, she gave a speech—she subsequently called it her "Declaration of Conscience"—that perhaps no other senator would have dared to make. She declared that "the greatest deliberative body in the world . . . has . . . been debased to the level of a forum of hate and character assassination sheltered by the shield of congressional immunity. . . . Freedom of speech . . . has been so abused by some that it is not exercised by others. . . . The nation sorely needs a Republican victory. But I don't want to see the Republican Party ride to political victory on the four horsemen of calumny—fear, ignorance, bigotry, and smear." Her public criticism earned her McCarthy's enmity, and the Wisconsin senator eventually endorsed a Republican alternative designed to defeat her bid for reelection in 1954. But when she won that primary five-to-one she demonstrated that McCarthy was not unstoppable. In July 1954, in the wake of the U.S. Army–McCarthy hearings, she and her colleagues censured McCarthy and ended his effectiveness as a playmaker in American politics.

Committed to military preparedness and an interventionist in foreign affairs, Smith played leading roles, both substantive and symbolic, on military matters throughout her career. In 1940, beginning with her first important vote in Congress, she went against the majority of her party to support the Selective Service Act. She went on in 1941 to support the extension of that act as well as enactment of Lend Lease, a measure designed to supply Great Britain and the Soviet Union in their fight against Adolph Hitler's Germany. In 1943 she joined the House Naval Affairs Committee. As a member of that committee during World War II, she once donned coveralls and rode to Boston on a U.S. Navy destroyer that had been built in Bath, Maine, and she also toured the Pacific theater of war. In 1947 she joined the new House Armed Services Committee and became a subcommittee chair. In the 1950s she was a lieutenant colonel in the U.S. Air Force Reserve. Her work in support of a strong defense, from her first year in Congress, gave her a constituency that reached far beyond Maine's borders. It also brought so much defense spending to her state that she once said in a campaign statement, "Maine is just one big air base."

Smith insisted, "I am not a feminist," though, newly elected to the Senate, she pledged herself "women's Senator at Large" (Wallace, p. 89). She embodied the mid-twentieth-century quest for an expanded public role for women and once remarked, "What is woman's place? Everywhere." She effectively exploited her long-term electoral success and her national visibility in Congress by taking leadership, particularly in the 1940s, on matters of equalizing women's access to wartime defense jobs and then to the military itself. In her maiden speech in Congress she argued for public nurseries and day-care centers. Her crowning legislative victory came with the enactment in June 1948 of the Women's Armed Forces Integration Act, an outcome that Smith was instrumental in achieving. Thus in the same summer that President Harry Truman issued an executive order directing the racial desegregation of the armed services, Smith's legislative efforts reduced the exclusion of and discrimination against women in the military.

Smith was a fixture in the Senate in many ways. Hip surgery in August 1968 brought an end to her unbroken string of 2,941 roll call votes. A moderate Republican on domestic issues, she voted in favor of civil rights legislation and federal aid to education. Late in her tenure in the Senate she was the ranking Republican on the Senate Armed Services Committee as well as the second ranking Republican member of the Aeronautical and Space Committee and the third ranking Republican on the Appropriations Committee, and she chaired the Senate Republican Conference during her final term. She challenged anyone who seemed to merit challenge. She criticized President John F. Kennedy for being insufficiently prepared to use nuclear weapons, a stance that she thought weakened the nation in its rivalry with the Soviet Union. When, during the 1960s, she caught Defense Secretary Robert S. McNamara in a falsehood about a shipyard closing, she asked him: "If I can't trust you on the little lies, sir, how will I ever believe

you on the big ones?" Her concern in 1950 with "the attempted repression by extreme Rightists" became by 1970 an equivalent concern with "the anarchism of the extreme Leftists" (Lewis, ed., p. 430), which she denounced in a second "Declaration of Conscience" on the twentieth anniversary of the first one.

Though she never attended college, Smith received ninety-five honorary degrees, and she lectured on college campuses under the auspices of the Woodrow Wilson National Fellowship Foundation (1973–1977). In 1989 George Bush awarded her the Presidential Medal of Freedom. One biographer, Patricia Ward Wallace, has termed her "the most influential woman in the history of American politics." She died at her home in Skowhegan.

• Smith's papers are at the Margaret Chase Smith Library Center in Skowhegan, Maine. The center is described in *Architectural Record* 173 (Mar. 1985): 112–13. William L. Lewis, Jr., her close friend and administrative assistant, edited *Declaration of Conscience* (1972), a collection of her speeches and writings, and the *Boston Globe* published an interview with her on 9 Apr. 1991. Book-length studies include Frank Graham, *Margaret Chase Smith: Woman of Courage* (1964); Dennis Morrison, *Woman of Conscience: Senator Margaret Chase Smith of Maine* (1994); and Patricia Ward Wallace, *Politics of Conscience: A Biography of Margaret Chase Smith* (1995). Smith is one of the subjects of Rhodri Jeffreys-Jones, *Changing Differences: Women and the Shaping of American Foreign Policy, 1917–1994* (1995). A specialized study of her effectiveness is Janann Sherman, "'They Either Need These Women or They Do Not': Margaret Chase Smith and the Fight for Regular Status for Women in the Military," *Journal of Military History* 54 (Jan. 1990): 47–78. Obituaries are in the *Boston Globe*, the *New York Times*, the *Los Angeles Times*, and the *Washington Post*, all on 30 May 1995.

PETER WALLENSTEIN

SMITH, Margaret Gladys (10 Feb. 1896–1 May 1970), pathologist, was born in Carnegie, Pennsylvania, the daughter of William Smith, a machine shop foreman; Smith's mother's name was not recorded in any of her archival papers.

Smith completed a bachelor's degree at Mount Holyoke College in 1918, then studied medicine at Johns Hopkins University. She earned a medical degree in 1922 and remained at Johns Hopkins initially as an assistant in pathology. During the 1920s she was promoted to instructor and associate in pathology on the Johns Hopkins faculty.

In 1929 Smith moved to St. Louis, Missouri, where she was employed by the Washington University School of Medicine as an assistant professor in pathology. As a faculty member at Washington University, Smith pursued pioneering research on infectious diseases, especially in children. Her work in pediatric pathology resulted in watershed medical discoveries crucial in combating epidemics, including the 1933 encephalitis epidemic.

Smith is credited with being the first person to isolate the St. Louis encephalitis virus. She described how the immunity against this virus could be transferred to suckling mice through foster mothers' milk in "Isolation of St. Louis Encephalitis Virus during Inter and Epidemic Periods" (with H. McCordock and E. Moore, *Proceedings of the Society for Experimental Biology and Medicine* 37 [1937]: 288–90). With colleague S. A. Luse, she also isolated the salivary gland virus. Smith conducted research on this virus throughout her career, writing "Propagation in Tissue Cultures of a Cytopathogenic Virus from Human Salivary Gland Virus Disease" in 1956. (*Proceedings of the Society for Experimental Biology and Medicine* 92: 424–30), which aided research to control the often-fatal virus's spread.

Smith also was the first person to propagate the herpes simplex virus in a mouse. In 1941 she published "Isolation of the Virus of Herpes Simplex and the Demonstration of Intranuclear Inclusions in a Case of Acute Encephalitis" (with Edwin H. Lennette and Harold R. Reames, *American Journal of Pathology* 17: 55–68). She also was the first researcher to discover the cytomegetic inclusion disease virus.

Smith published approximately seventy articles, reflecting her work on the pathology of infectious diseases encountered in St. Louis hospitals, in periodicals such as the *American Journal of Pathology, Proceedings of the Society for Experimental Biology and Medicine,* and *Journal of Experimental Medicine.* She and Washington University pathology professor John M. Kissane prepared the thousand-page *Pathology of Infancy and Childhood* (1967), which was considered one of the most thorough, accurate, and up-to-date works of its kind; after her death, Kissane issued an expanded second edition in 1975.

Smith was known for her research in pediatric pathology. She evaluated the behavior of cells in the tissues and fluids of infants and children afflicted with diseases ranging from measles to encephalitis, analyzing autopsy samples to try to understand the diseases in order to control future outbreaks and prevent epidemics. She observed patients in the St. Louis Children's Hospital and compiled case studies and pursued laboratory research to isolate and identify etiological agents causing diseases so that preventive measures and effective treatments could be developed.

Smith was a member of the American Association of Pathologists and Bacteriologists. Recognized for her accomplishments, she was one of only five women in her time promoted to the rank of full professor at Washington University; she attained this position in 1957. Her honors included being named one of the *St. Louis Globe-Democrat*'s Women of Achievement in 1959. Washington University presented her with a faculty citation at the 1964 Founders Day ceremonies. Smith was guest speaker at the 1964 dedication of the Toronto, Canada, Children's Research Center.

Smith retired from Washington University School of Medicine in 1964 but retained professional contact as a professor emeritus and lecturer in pathology. She died at her Webster Groves home, outside of St. Louis. She had never married.

• Smith donated her personal papers, which include an interesting collection of lecture and laboratory notes, correspondence, and case studies about her research in pediatric pathology as well as her notebooks and other memorabilia, to the Washington University School of Medicine Library's Archives. Among Smith's works is, with Marshall G. Seibel, "Tumors of Islands of Langerhans and Hypoglycemia," *American Journal of Pathology* 7 (1931): 723–39. Secondary sources include Esmond R. Long, "History of the American Association of Pathologists and Bacteriologists," bound as a supplement in the *American Journal of Pathology* 77 (Oct. 1974): 1s–218s. An obituary is in *Journal of the American Medical Association* 214 (5 Oct. 1970): 159.

ELIZABETH D. SCHAFER

SMITH, Melancton (7 May 1744–29 July 1798), merchant, lawyer, and political leader, was born in Jamaica, Long Island (now Queens County, N.Y., and the Borough of Queens, New York City), the son of Samuel Smith and Elizabeth Bayles, farmers. Schooled at home, at an early age he became a store clerk in Poughkeepsie, Dutchess County, New York, then the most rapidly expanding region of the state. By the 1770s, known for his seriousness and wide reading, he had become a prosperous merchant and owner of many properties throughout the county (which included today's Putnam County).

As the revolutionary crisis with Great Britain intensified, Smith was elected in 1775 one of ten Dutchess County delegates to New York's First Provincial Congress. Almost immediately, he became involved in military affairs, although he never saw battle. He helped raise a line regiment in the county and organized the county's first militia company, whose principal duty was control of the region's Loyalists. He was appointed the unit's captain, and for his effectiveness the state's Committee for Detecting Conspiracies in 1776 named Smith commander of all such New York companies and assigned him the rank of major. A year later the committee also appointed him one of three New York State commissioners for detecting and subduing Loyalist conspiracies. That same year he commenced his lifelong political challenge to the state's landlord aristocracy, symbolized by such families as the Livingstons, Schuylers, and Van Rensselaers, by defeating Philip Livingston to become Dutchess County sheriff, a post he held for two years.

Smith had become deeply knowledgeable about the affairs of internal enemies because of his dual civil and military positions. He had also profited from government contracting, as purchasing agent for the state and through service as aide to the U.S. commissary general. As a result, Smith was able to accumulate confiscated Loyalist estates in New York City and elsewhere, lands on the Chenango River and at the site of present-day Plattsburgh, and revolutionary soldiers' land claims. He thus extended his landholdings more widely and, like many who profited from their political connections, emerged from the war a wealthy man. In 1782 George Washington made use of Smith's wartime experience by appointing him to a commission to resolve disputes between the Continental army and its contractors. When a New York City court, moved by the arguments of Alexander Hamilton in the 1784 case of *Rutgers v. Waddington*, nullified a state statute that both allowed suits by those whose properties had been seized by the occupying British and prohibited a defense on the part of those who seized them on the grounds that they were following military orders, Smith, already a known opponent of Hamilton, led protests against and wrote a pamphlet assailing the court's decision.

In 1784 Smith moved to New York City, where he continued his mercantile activities, took up the practice of law, and intensified his political activities. He had become a close adviser and confidant of Governor George Clinton and was thus associated with Clinton's powerful faction. Nevertheless, Smith, who was widely regarded for his engaging manner and whose appeal was enhanced by his physical height, maintained cordial relations with those whose positions he from time to time opposed. In 1785 the Clinton-controlled state assembly elected Smith to the first of three annual terms in the Confederation Congress. He distinguished himself particularly by his contributions to the provisions and passage of the Land Ordinance of 1785 and the Northwest Ordinance of 1787. He led a successful effort in debates over the land ordinance to expunge a provision that would have restricted religious freedom in the old Northwest Territory. He was also a member of the committee that prepared the final draft of the great Northwest Ordinance for the governance of American territories not yet admitted to statehood.

Smith played his most significant historical role as a participant in debates over ratification of the Constitution of 1787. After the Constitution was made public in September 1787, he helped lead its Antifederalist opponents in New York State and helped set up the Antifederalist committee in New York City. Although conclusive evidence is lacking, Smith was probably author of the celebrated *Letters from the Federal Farmer*, a pamphlet published in October 1787 and widely reprinted and distributed thereafter throughout the nation. Characterized as "the single most important Antifederalist publication in New York, and probably the entire country" (Schechter, p. 71), the *Letters* were also acknowledged to be the "most plausible" Antifederalist attacks on the Constitution by no less a contemporary Federalist authority than Hamilton, writing as "Publius" in *Federalist 68*. In April 1788, shortly before the state ratification convention opened in Poughkeepsie, Smith, as "A Plebeian," also published *An Address to the People of the State of New-York*. In both of these works, he arraigned the broad powers granted to the proposed government and urged amendments to it. While acknowledging that "a federal government of some sort is necessary" (Jensen, p. 19), he declared that the constitution was "not calculated equally to preserve the rights of all orders of men in the community" (Jensen, p. 19). He also argued that the powers of the new government were too great, that it would "make the states one consolidated government" (Jen-

sen, p. 24), that a free government could not exist over so large an expanse of territory, and that the absence of a bill of rights threatened people's liberty. While all of these had become conventional Antifederalist arguments, Smith's statement lent them unusual cogency and force.

In the spring of 1788 Smith sought membership—from both New York City, his residence, and Dutchess County, where he remained a major property-holder—in the Poughkeepsie convention called to ratify the Constitution in New York State. Losing in the overwhelmingly Federalist city (where he also simultaneously lost election to the state assembly), Smith was elected from the Antifederalist upstate county of his youth. There, however, he met criticism from those, probably Federalists, who argued that residency alone and not property qualified someone for convention membership. As it was, Smith was the only Antifederalist delegate at the Poughkeepsie convention who lived in New York City.

At the start of the convention, Antifederalists outnumbered Federalists 46 to 19. Along with John Lansing, Jr., and Robert Yates, Smith led the Antifederalist opposition against such potent, conservative, Federalist supporters of the Constitution as Hamilton, John Jay, and Chancellor Robert R. Livingston, Jr. Enunciating the democratic philosophy for which he was widely known, he opposed the Constitution because the "great" who support it and who will fill the new Congress "do not feel for the poor and middling class [and] consider themselves above the common people." A government closer to the people and "a representative body, composed principally of respectable yeomanry, is the best possible security to liberty" (Young, pp. 104–5). Yet while he long held off the powerful arguments of the Federalists, circumstances external to the convention began to weaken the Antifederalists' position there. New Hampshire and then Virginia became the ninth and tenth states to ratify the Constitution, thus, under provisions of the new Constitution, making the new government effective. Fears of New York's isolation outside the reconstituted government began to take hold. Also, Antifederalists in other states, such as Massachusetts, had agreed to ratify with proposed amendments after being assured by Federalists that a bill of rights would be considered in the first federal Congress and in the hope that they might succeed in calling a second constitutional convention. Moreover, Smith concluded that New York could not make ratification conditional on the passage of amendments, as others were urging, because he believed that the Confederation Congress, of which he was still a member, would refuse to recognize New York's ratification on those terms.

So, while retaining his conviction, which he held into the 1790s, that the Constitution was "radically defective" (DePauw, p. 242), Smith nevertheless became convinced that New York could no longer wisely withhold its ratification. Breaking with other, "non-adopting" Antifederalists, some of whom never forgave him, Smith led a successful compromise effort to ratify the Constitution unconditionally and yet to couple ratification with a letter from the convention to Congress requesting that a second constitutional convention be called. This compromise narrowly secured New York's ratification by a vote of 30 to 27, after twelve "adopting" Antifederalists, including a number from Dutchess County, whom Smith carried with him, voted in the affirmative. Thus, with only Rhode Island and North Carolina remaining outside the new government, the Constitution was allowed to go into effect. In changing his position, Smith cast what was arguably the nation's most weighty vote in favor of ratification of the Constitution of 1787.

Returning to the Confederation Congress, where he kept the most complete record of debates over the new Constitution, Smith led an unsuccessful effort to have Congress submit the Constitution to the states accompanied by a resolution stating that the Philadelphia Convention had exceeded its authority. In elections to the first federal Congress, he worked for the choice of those favoring a second convention. Yet, his hopes that, under Article V of the Constitution, two-thirds of the states would call for a second convention were also thwarted. He was probably the author of letters signed "A Federal Republican," which argued this position in New York newspapers in late 1788 and early 1789, as well as many other pseudonymous works of the time.

Despite his grave misgivings about the new government, like most other original opponents Smith gradually committed himself to it, in part no doubt from the increase in value, as a result of the federal government's assumption of state revolutionary war debts, of the New York State bonds he had purchased in the 1780s. Despite his split with most Clintonians over ratification, a position that may have cost him nomination to seats in the new House and Senate and probably permanently damaged his political career, Smith retained ties to his Clintonian brethren. After failing to be elected to the state assembly in 1790 (as he would again in 1792), he won a seat in the assembly in 1791, was chosen a "sachem" of Tammany Hall in 1792, and actively backed Clinton for the governorship and vice presidency that year. His involvement in organizing a New York reception for Edmond Genet, the French ambassador, in 1793 and his membership in the New York Democratic Society in 1794 are evidence that Smith had moved into the camp soon identified with the Democratic-Republican party and Thomas Jefferson by the mid-1790s.

While pursuing his political career, Smith continued his mercantile activities and in 1789 became first president of the New York Society for Encouraging Manufacturing. He also involved himself in early reform efforts, distinguishing himself as one of few former Antifederalists and moderate Democrats to do so. He was a founder of the New York Dispensary, vice president of the antislavery New York Manumission Society, and member, among many organizations, of the Society for the Relief of Distressed Debtors, the Humane Society, and the Emigrant Aid Society. He

died in New York City, a victim of a yellow fever epidemic.

Smith was among the most influential of the "new men" of the Revolution—those who, starting in humble circumstances (and in his case in a region controlled by powerful, conservative landlords), used their native talents during the crises of the revolutionary era to gain wealth, authority, and fame, often adopting the popular, democratic politics that complemented the nation's growing middle-class acquisitiveness. Smith's way was eased by his congenial personality and unwavering character, both of which earned him the respect and affection even of those whom he opposed. In deciding to vote in favor of the Constitution, when to do otherwise might have jeopardized the prospects of the new government and the interests of his native state, he achieved lasting significance.

• The principal collection of Smith's manuscripts is housed in the New York State Library, Albany. Two works that feature Smith prominently are Staughton Lynd, *Anti-Federalism in Dutchess County, New York* (1962), and Alfred F. Young, *The Democratic Republicans of New York: The Origins, 1763–1797* (1967). On Smith's role in the contest over ratification, see Linda Grant DePauw, *The Eleventh Pillar: New York State and the Federal Constitution* (1966), Stephen L. Schechter, ed., *The Reluctant Pillar: New York and the Adoption of the Federal Constitution* (1985), and Robin Brooks, "Alexander Hamilton, Melancton Smith, and the Ratification of the Constitution in New York," *William and Mary Quarterly*, 3d ser., 24 (July 1967): 339–58. For "highly probable" evidence that Smith wrote the *Letters from the Federal Farmer*, see Robert H. Webking, "Melancton Smith and the *Letters from the Federal Farmer*," *William and Mary Quarterly*, 3d ser., 44 (July 1987): 510–28. The *Letters* are most conveniently available in Merrill Jensen et al., *The Documentary History of the Ratification of the Constitution* 14 (1983): 14–54. Smith's record of the final debates in the Confederation Congress are discussed in Julius Goebel, Jr., "Melancton Smith's Minutes of Debates on the New Constitution," *Columbia University Law Review* 64 (Jan. 1964): 26–43. Robin Brooks, "Melancton Smith: New York Anti-Federalist, 1744–1798" (Ph.D. diss., Univ. of Rochester, 1964), is the best biography of Smith.

JAMES M. BANNER, JR.

SMITH, Melancton (24 May 1810–19 July 1893), naval officer, was born in New York City, the son of Melancton Smith, a colonel during the War of 1812, and Cornelia Haring. Smith began his naval career on 1 March 1826 with a three-year tour of duty in the Pacific. He then attended the naval school in New York, becoming a passed midshipman in April 1832. He next alternated cruises in the West Indies with shore duty in New York. Smith was promoted to lieutenant in 1837, and the same year he married Mary Jackson Jones. He was involved in the Seminole War during 1839 and 1840.

During the 1840s and 1850s Smith served in a wide variety of settings. He was on Mediterranean service from 1841 until 1843 and with the *Vandalia* in U.S. waters from 1844 until 1846. During the war with Mexico, Smith performed logistical and administrative duties as the executive officer of the Pensacola

Navy Yard. He returned to the Mediterranean on the *Constitution* from 1848 until 1851. In 1855 he was promoted to commander and served aboard the *Potomac* for a few months. Between 1855 and 1861 Smith was engaged in shore duties.

Smith began the Civil War with an assignment at the mouth of the Mississippi as skipper of the *Massachusetts*. On 9 July 1861 the *Massachusetts* shelled the Confederate guns on Ship Island, and he engaged the Confederate ship *Florida* on 19 October 1861. These actions earned him the navy's praise for efficiency. In 1862 Smith was skipper of the side-wheeler *Mississippi* with Admiral David G. Farragut, operating against New Orleans. He battled the Confederate ram *Manassas* while running the forts below New Orleans on the night of 23–24 April 1862. The *Mississippi* was the third ship of Farragut's first division to run the forts. The ram picked the *Mississippi* as a chief target and managed to inflict a rip seven feet long in the Union vessel's hull. But Smith skillfully battled back, using his guns to good effect. The *Manassas* was run aground and heavily damaged by two broadsides from the *Mississippi*'s guns. With a growing reputation for combat proficiency, Smith was promoted to captain in 1862.

On 14 March 1863 Smith attempted to press the *Mississippi* north of Port Hudson. Confederate guns there badly damaged the ship when it ran aground, and Smith was forced to abandon it and set it on fire. He and the crew escaped by floating down the river in the *Mississippi*'s small boats. This incident and Smith's coolness under fire made a lifelong impression on Smith's young executive officer, George Dewey. Dewey described the cigar-chomping Smith as a determined, fearless leader and a tenacious fighter who inspired respect and admiration. Dewey noted that smoking seemed to be Smith's only vice and pictured his commander lighting each cigar off the butt of the previous one. Smith was variously described as a temperate, intensely serious, and religious man of little humor. His record clearly points to his superiors' recognition of his skills and fighting qualities.

Smith's next ship was the *Monongahela*, to which he was assigned in 1863. During this period, Admiral Farragut spoke of Smith's competence and value to the navy, hoping the navy would recognize Smith's value to the service. Later Smith was given command of the *Onodaga*. He was involved in the less than successful attempt to destroy the Confederate ram *Albemarle* in Albemarle Sound, near the mouth of the Roanoke River, in June 1864. Unfortunately, Smith's force consisted of a few wooden gunboats, hardly a match for the ram, but he did force the *Albemarle* up the Roanoke. The navy recognized the difficulties and congratulated Smith on doing well with what he had. Later he commanded the *Wabash* in Admiral David Dixon Porter's fleet assaulting Fort Fisher, North Carolina. Porter praised Smith for his masterful handling of the *Wabash* during the bombardment of Fort Fisher both in December 1864 and in January 1865.

After the Civil War, in 1866, Smith was promoted to commodore and served as the chief of the Bureau of Equipment and Recruiting. In 1870 he was promoted to rear admiral and commanded the New York Naval Yard. He retired on 24 May 1871 and became governor of the Philadelphia Naval Asylum, serving during 1871–1872. Eight years after his wife's death in 1885, Smith died in Green Bay, Wisconsin. His chief contribution was in setting an example of aggressive and persistent offensive action in combat.

• Smith's career is traced in L. R. Hamersly, *The Records of Living Officers of the U.S. Navy and Marine Corps*, 4th ed. (1890). Admiral George Dewey provides an excellent description of Smith in his *Autobiography of George Dewey, Admiral of the Navy* (1916). Smith's obituary is in the *Army and Navy Journal*, 22 July 1893, and the *New York Tribune*, 21 July 1893.

ROD PASCHALL

SMITH, Meriwether (1730–24 Jan. 1794), revolutionary patriot, legislator, and congressman, was born at "Bathurst," Essex County, Virginia, the son of Francis Smith, a planter and legislator, and Lucy Meriwether. He was born into the elite of Virginia on both sides of his family. His maternal grandfather, Launcelot Bathurst, was a patentee of nearly 8,000 acres of land in New Kent County, while his father, who mentioned sixty-three slaves in his will, was a vestryman and justice of the peace and was elected to the Virginia House of Burgesses from Essex four times (1752–1758). Meriwether Smith followed this tradition of political involvement just as Virginia was assuming a leading role in the movement toward the Revolution. About 1760 he married Alice Lee Clarke; they had two children before Alice died. A signer of the Westmoreland Association against the Stamp Act in 1766, Smith was elected to the Virginia House of Burgesses from Essex in 1768 and in 1769 was a member of the illegal assembly of burgesses at Raleigh Tavern in Williamsburg that framed the association with other colonies to boycott British imports. In 1769 he married Elizabeth Daingerfield; they had two children.

By 1774 Smith was playing a significant part in the revolutionary movement in Virginia. A member of the Essex County Committee of Safety and the House of Burgesses, he participated in the conventions of 1775 and 1776, where John Augustine Washington classed him as one of the five best speakers in the important convention of 1776. Smith submitted a draft resolution on 15 May 1776 calling for the dissolution of royal government and for a committee to prepare a declaration of rights and a plan of government. His position was more advanced than an alternative resolution proposed by Patrick Henry, who wanted the colonies to act in unison, hopefully with foreign aid, before making a decisive break. The convention agreed to a compromise worked by Edmund Pendleton that asked Congress to declare independence but retained verbatim Smith's other two proposals. Smith was named second to the committee to prepare a constitution and a bill of rights. He apparently submitted a draft of a constitution, but the final product was primarily the work of George Mason.

Smith was a member of the Virginia House of Delegates in 1776, 1778, 1781–1782, 1785, and 1788 and was elected to the Continental Congress in 1778. He arrived in Congress at a time when partisan politics were particularly intense as a result of the pressures brought to bear by the recently concluded alliance with France and the collateral Arthur Lee–Silas Deane imbroglio. He entered that fray as an implacable foe of the Lee interest, which, aligned with the New England delegations and Pennsylvania radicals, had become personae non grata with France and its minister to the United States, Conrad Alexandre Gerard. In this controversy, which involved the terms that the United States would insist upon as a condition for peace as well as the status of American obligations to France for its early assistance in the war, Smith was an outspoken supporter of the French position, which constrained American peace objectives. His participation in debates on these issues earned him the enmity of the Lees and the gratitude of Gerard, who called him "un de nos amis les plus zélés" (John J. Meng, *Despatches and Instructions of Conrad Alexandre Gerard* [1939], p. 564). Smith's support of the French interest may have had to do with a desire he expressed to Governor Thomas Jefferson for a post abroad, presumably in France.

The charge against Deane, U.S. minister in Paris, by Arthur Lee in Paris and Richard Henry Lee in Congress was that Deane and his mercantile associates were profiting from French aid to the United States. It was an indictment that had particular force in a republican revolution against old world corruption as Smith, a merchant as well as a planter, soon discovered. Coincidentally with his reelection to Congress on 18 June 1779, the Virginia House of Delegates, urged on by the Lee interest, passed a resolution requiring delegates to Congress to take an oath not to engage in foreign or domestic commerce. Protesting that he was free from guilt but that to take the oath would deprive him of a significant source of income, Smith declined to serve. He also became involved in a controversy with the legislature over his accounts while in Congress. He was vindicated in some measure by his reelection to Congress for a third time in 1780, after which he served from February to September 1781.

While in Congress Smith aligned with proponents of national authority, such as Robert Morris and James Madison, but when the issue of national versus states rights acquired more clarity during the remainder of the 1780s, he became an outspoken advocate of state sovereignty. During that time he held state office on the Council of State (1782–1785) and in the House of Delegates (1785 and 1788). He was a leading opponent of the Annapolis Convention to coordinate interstate trade, and though elected a delegate to that body, he refused to serve. Not a member of the federal convention of 1787, he participated in the Virginia ratifying convention as an active Antifederalist, organizing a

Virginia caucus that acted in concert with the Federal Republican Committee of New York. He warned the freeholders of Essex that the Constitution "in the present Dress . . . is a wolf in Sheep's clothing, that will seek & find opportunity to devour us" (Kukla, p. 295). He may have feared a national government that would force collection of English debts, for, according to Edmund Randolph's sources, Smith had "made over the whole of his property for a british [*sic*] debt" (William M. E. Rachal, ed., *Papers of James Madison* [1975], vol. 9, p. 373). His opposition to the Constitution did not dissuade him from seeking, unsuccessfully, a seat in the first House of Representatives nor from petitioning George Washington, again unsuccessfully, for a post in the new federal government.

Some of his contemporaries expected that Smith would become governor. An Essex County compatriot, George McCall, had noted in 1779 that "as he is in great reputation it is imagined he will [be] Governor of Virginia soon" (Joseph S. Ewing, ed., "The Correspondence of Archibald McCall and George McCall, 1779–1783," *Virginia Magazine of History and Biography* 73, p. 347). It is probable that Smith's volatile personality and oft-noted eccentricities, such as being a noted violinist, which engendered the nickname "Fiddlehead," precluded his rising to higher office than he held. He apparently was admirably suited to open a revolution but was less capable of carrying it forth, even though in 1781 he offered a plan of finance to the Continental Congress and a plan of departments for Virginia, neither of which was adopted. He died at "Marigold," Essex County.

• Few documents relating to Smith's private life exist. Some of Smith's letters are in the Library of Congress and in the Smith papers at the Virginia State Library. Most of his letters are in Paul H. Smith et al., eds., *Letters of Delegates to Congress, 1774–1789* (1976–). The genealogy of the Smith family is in *William and Mary College Quarterly*, 1st ser., 6 (1897–1898): 41–52; and *Genealogies of Virginia Families from Tyler's Quarterly . . .*, vol. 3 (1981). For Smith's role in the convention of 1776 see Hugh Blair Grigsby, *The Virginia Convention of 1776* (1855), and John E. Selby, *The Revolution in Virginia* (1988). For his role in the politics of the Continental Congress see H. James Henderson, *Party Politics in the Continental Congress* (1974). His antifederalism is noted in Jon Kukla, "A Spectrum of Sentiments . . . 1787–1788," *Virginia Magazine of History and Biography* 96, no. 3 (July 1988). 294–95. James B. Slaughter, *Settlers, Southerners, Americans: The History of Essex County, Virginia* (1985), puts Smith in the context of Essex County. See also Emory L. Carlton, "Col. Meriwether Smith and His Times, 1730–1794," *Essex County Historical Society Bulletin* 21 (1982): 1–5.

H. JAMES HENDERSON

SMITH, Michael J. *See* Challenger Shuttle Crew.

SMITH, Morgan Lewis (8 Mar. 1821–28 Dec. 1874), Union general, was born in the small Oswego County town of Mexico, New York, the son of Cyrus Smith and Laura Wales, farmers. He was the elder brother of Giles A. Smith, who also became a prominent Union general. At the age of twenty-one, Smith left his family's home in Jefferson County, New York, and settled first in Meadville, Pennsylvania, then in New Albany, Indiana, where he taught school for two years. In 1845 he entered the U.S. Army under the assumed name of Martin L. Sanford (the reason for the false name is unknown) and served for five years, during which time he rose to the rank of sergeant and served as a drill instructor at the recruit depot in Newport, Kentucky. From 1850 until the outbreak of the Civil War in 1861, he worked as a riverboatman on the Mississippi and Ohio rivers.

At the outbreak of hostilities between the states, Smith helped to recruit a regiment of men from the wharfs in St. Louis and was named colonel of the Eighth Missouri Volunteer Infantry on 4 July 1861. In short order he turned this rowdy bunch of ruffians into a crack regiment that became noted for its discipline and fighting ability. On 1 February 1862 Smith was placed in command of a brigade. Two weeks later he led his command into battle at Fort Donelson on the Cumberland River in Tennessee. In a furious battle that raged throughout the day on 15 February, Smith handled his brigade with consummate skill and earned the praise of his superiors. General Lew Wallace wrote of Smith in his official report:

I have reserved for the last the mention of that officer whose mention I must confess gives me most pleasure—Col. Morgan L. Smith. . . . Words cannot do justice to his courage and coolness. All through the conflict I could see him ride to and fro, and could hear his voice, clear as a bugle's, and as long as I heard it I knew the regiments were safe and their victory sure. Promotion has been frequently promised him; if it does not come now Missouri will fail to recognize and honor her bravest soldier.

Two months later, on 7 April Smith led his brigade in the second day of fighting at the bloody battle of Shiloh and again earned the praise of his division commander. Wallace reported that Smith's conduct "was beyond the praise of words" and to him belongs "the highest honors of victory." During the advance on Corinth, Smith's brigade captured a key position at Russell's House on 17 May. His action won mention in the report of General William T. Sherman, who wrote that Smith "conducted the advance of his brigade handsomely. . . . I leave to him the full credit of conducting the advance and of carrying the position at Russell's." For his service, Smith was awarded the star of a brigadier general of volunteers on 16 July 1862 and was elevated to division command on 12 November 1862.

Smith's division served in Tennessee and in the operations in northern Mississippi but saw little action. His first test as a division commander came during Sherman's expedition against Vicksburg. Moving down the Mississippi River from Memphis, Sherman's force ascended the Yazoo River, north of Vicksburg, and disembarked near the mouth of Chickasaw Bayou. On 28 December, while making a personal reconnaissance along Chickasaw Bayou, Smith was wounded in the hip by a Confederate sharpshooter and was carried to the rear. Sherman lamented the loss of Smith in his official report and noted that the wound "lost to me one of my best and most daring leaders, and to the United States the service of a practical soldier and enthusiastic patriot." Sherman emphasized, "I cannot exaggerate the loss to me personally and officially of General Morgan L. Smith at that critical moment." Incapacitated from the wound, Smith went on sick leave and did not return to duty until 6 October 1863.

Sherman anxiously awaited Smith's return to duty. He wrote to the assistant adjutant general, General John Rawlins, "I want Morgan L. Smith to have his old division." In accordance with Sherman's wishes, Smith led his division in the operations around Chattanooga and distinguished himself in the assault on Missionary Ridge. Afterward his division moved to the relief of a Union garrison in Knoxville that was besieged by Confederate general James Longstreet. From 25 January to 5 February 1864 he conducted a successful expedition from Scottsborough, Alabama, to Rome, Georgia, during which his men destroyed an important niter works at Rawlingsville, Alabama. Smith served with distinction during the Atlanta campaign, during which he temporarily commanded a corps. General John Logan recommended Smith for promotion, citing his "meritorious service" during the campaign for Atlanta.

Physically weakened and his old wound inflamed by the rigors of the campaign, Smith was relieved from field command at his own request and went on sick leave from 17 August to 27 September 1864. On return to duty, he was placed in command of the District of Vicksburg, where he remained until the war's end. During his tenure at Vicksburg, the steamer *Sultana* was overloaded with Federal prisoners released from Andersonville and Cahaba prisons. Although informed that too many men were being loaded on the boat, Smith failed to investigate the reports, and the *Sultana*, with a legal carrying capacity of 376, left Vicksburg with more than 2,400 soldiers aboard. Three days later, the *Sultana*'s boilers exploded under the strain, and more than 1,800 soldiers perished in the cold water of the Mississippi River. Although the investigation into the *Sultana* disaster never produced charges against Smith, his reputation was tarnished, and he never received the long coveted promotion to major general.

Smith resigned from the army on 12 July 1865 and remained in Vicksburg. On 18 December 1866 Smith, then forty-six years of age, married Louise Genella, who was only twenty. The couple had two daughters. Named U.S. consul to the Sandwich Islands by Andrew Johnson, Smith served in Honolulu for about two years. On his return from the Pacific, he declined the governorship of the Colorado Territory. For a brief period during the administration of President Ulysses S. Grant, Smith served as the second assistant postmaster general. He resigned his post and contracted with the government to carry mail on routes throughout the Northwest, West, and the South.

In December 1874 a series of stories appeared in the newspapers concerning an ongoing investigation by the Ways and Means Committee of the House of Representatives into bribes offered government officials by the Pacific Mail Steamship Company. Smith was accused of accepting a $50,000 bribe in exchange for the company receiving a government contract worth $500,000. During the course of the investigation, Smith mysteriously died in Jersey City, New Jersey. The *New York Times* reported on 30 December 1874, "Yesterday morning Gen. M. L. Smith was found dead in his bed at Taylor's Hotel." The St. Louis *Post Dispatch* also reported his death, and a story on 2 January 1875 read, "It is said that [Smith] has been very excited for some time past, in consequence of his name having been connected with some expositions in relations to mail contracts, and it is even intimated that he may have committed suicide." Smith was buried in Arlington National Cemetery.

Regardless of the circumstances surrounding his death, Smith's service during the Civil War was a record of leadership, devotion to duty, and courage on the field of battle. He was a solid and reliable officer on whom superiors could depend and in whom the common soldier placed his trust.

• For additional information on Smith see *The War of the Rebellion: A Compilation of the Official Records of the Union and Confederate Armies*, 1st ser., vols. 7, 10, 17, 30, 38 (128 vols., 1880–1901); Ezra J. Warner, *Generals in Blue* (1964); Stewart Sifakis, *Who Was Who in the Union* (1988); Robert U. Johnson and Clarence C. Buel, eds., *Battles and Leaders of the Civil War* (4 vols., 1888); and the U.S. Pension Records Office. Obituaries are in the (Washington, D.C.) *Evening Star*, the *Washington Chronicle*, and the (Washington, D.C.) *National Republican*, all 30 Dec. 1874, and the *New York Times*, 31 Dec. 1874.

TERRENCE J. WINSCHEL

SMITH, Nathan (12? Sept. 1762–26 Jan. 1829), physician, surgeon, and medical educator, was born in Rehoboth, Massachusetts, the son of John Smith, a farmer, and his second wife Elizabeth Ide Hills, a sometime midwife. The family moved to Chester, Vermont, when Nathan was age nine; his father, active in town affairs, died less than three years later, leaving Nathan and three older siblings to be raised by their mother. Little is known of Smith's life in Chester, though he is said to have spent time as a teacher in the village school despite having only a modest home-schooling himself.

In 1784 Smith decided he wanted to become a doctor, a decision inspired by an encounter with Josiah Goodhue, a surgeon who visited Chester to perform an amputation. When Goodhue needed assistance, Smith stepped forward with what turned out to be characteristic self-assurance and performed "the trying task without flinching" (Cushing, p. 10). At Goodhue's urging, Smith undertook to improve his education with help from the Reverend Samuel Whiting in Rockingham, Vermont. After a few months under Whiting's tutelage, Smith spent three years as Goodhue's apprentice in Putney, Vermont.

Smith then set up practice in Cornish, New Hampshire, in 1787. How Smith is said to have responded to a prank locals endeavored to play on him hints at the accuracy of his subsequent reputation for diligence and shrewdness. Summoned to the tavern to treat a patient with a broken leg, Smith found the "patient" was a goose. With a straight face, he "examined the broken limb, prepared his splints, reduced the fracture, and bound it up in the most scientific manner." He also sent a bill to the hapless tavern keeper—and "suddenly found himself famous" (Child, p. 335).

Despite a rapidly developing and busy practice, Smith was well aware of gaps in his education. Determined to improve his skill as a physician, he attended the department of medicine at Harvard University; there he studied with John Warren, Benjamin Waterhouse, and Aaron Dexter. In 1790 he earned his M.B. (converted to M.D. in 1811), becoming the fifth graduate of Harvard's fledgling medical school. His graduation paper, "On the Causes and Effects of Spasm in Fevers," though published in the *Massachusetts Magazine* (Jan. 1791), made no great contribution to medical science.

Smith returned to his practice in Cornish, where his first apprentice, Lyman Spalding, had cared for patients in his absence. There in 1791 Smith married Elizabeth Chase, daughter of revolutionary war hero General Jonathan Chase. She died, childless, within two years. Smith then married her younger half sister, Sarah Hall Chase, in 1794; they had ten children.

Eager to raise the low estate of the medical profession, Smith concluded that the apprenticeship system common at the time did not constitute adequate education. He knew that not all prospective doctors could afford to travel to Philadelphia, New York, or Boston, where the country's only medical schools were located. He dreamed of establishing a medical school "to rear up for the . . . interior of New England a race of better educated, more enlightened, and more skilful physicians and surgeons" (Allen, p. 10). Smith wanted for his pupils a library, a laboratory, and opportunities to do dissections, and he concluded that affiliation with an institution of higher learning would facilitate providing these assets. His 1796 proposal to the Board of Trust at nearby Dartmouth that he, a relatively inexperienced country physician, be appointed professor of medicine at the college was stunningly bold. The Board of Trust hesitated; Smith pronounced himself ready to do whatever was needed to satisfy their concerns. Armed with a supportive letter from the college's president, John Wheelock, Smith traveled to Glasgow, Edinburgh, and London. Nine months abroad increased both his knowledge and his self-confidence but left him in financial difficulty (a condition he endured most of his life).

On his return from England Smith put in only a brief appearance in Cornish before going to Hanover. There, in the autumn of 1797, he gave the inaugural set of lectures at Dartmouth Medical School—although it took the Board of Trust another year officially to approve his "medical department" and appoint him professor. Apart from assistance rendered by Spalding in teaching chemistry the first two years, Smith was the lone member of the Dartmouth medical faculty for more than a decade. Though not quite the task that it would be today, teaching all the courses—anatomy, surgery, the "theory and practice of physic [internal medicine]," chemistry, and "materia medica [what amounted to primitive pharmacology]"—was an impressive feat even then. Smith also had a large practice, with patients in widely scattered places (his account books mention towns fifty miles apart); he clearly had unusual dedication and stamina.

In May 1810 Smith wrote his former student and close friend George Cheyne Shattuck that he had decided to leave Hanover. He was frustrated by a variety of difficulties: a heavy teaching load, institutional politics, and ongoing financial problems (aggravated then by the construction of a handsome and sturdy building, which stood until 1963, to house the medical school). He was further distressed by the growing public agitation over dissections; some of his students had been bound over to court for grave-robbing incidents, and the anatomy department was always at risk for riots and raids. These factors, combined with the appeal of a challenge, took Smith to New Haven in 1813, where his prestige and presence helped establish and ensure the success of the Medical Institute of Yale College. Made Yale's first "Professor of the Theory and Practice of Physic, Surgery and Obstetrics," Smith remained on its faculty until his death.

In 1821 Smith's reputation as a physician and a surgeon, coupled with his experience as a medical educator, led Bowdoin College in Maine and the University of Vermont to seek his advice and assistance in forming medical schools. He played a sufficiently active role to qualify as a founder of those two medical schools as well as of that in New Haven (in Hanover he is rightly credited as the sole founder). Bowdoin and Vermont subsequently claimed Smith as a faculty member, and he offered a course of lectures at each institution several times from 1821 to 1825. Yale, however, having allowed Smith to accept a return appointment at Dartmouth for one term in 1816 and having permitted him to rush from his Yale lectures to teach at Bowdoin, Vermont, or both, finally asked him to drop other affiliations. He was "by far the most distinguished member of the first faculty of the Yale Medical School" (William H. Welch, in E. Smith), and Yale seems to have wanted exclusive claim on his services. From 1825 Smith lectured only at Yale.

As a physician, Smith was sought after for his diagnostic skills (much was made of this by students and colleagues alike). Smith's letters and the notes students took during his lectures illustrate his conservative approach to medicine, as both practitioner and teacher. A strong believer in the healing power of nature, he was disdainful of those who relied on theory while ignoring the evidence of practical experience.

Welch said that Smith was "possessed . . . of the true spirit and method of scientific inquiry."

As a surgeon, Smith was much in demand. When he successfully performed an ovariotomy in 1821, it appears he did so without knowing that Ephraim McDowell had pioneered the procedure several years before. He made a major assault on blindness in New England by operating on dozens of patients with cataracts: "Doct. Smith has performed the operation of Couching [surgical displacement of the damaged lens] five times within these six weeks. They report to him from all parts of the Country" (A. Boyd to W. Boyd, 26 Nov. 1826). He also invented a device for extracting coins from the esophagus and a new splint for treating fractures of the femur; he devised improved procedures for dealing with amputation stumps, harelip, imperforate anus, and osteomyelitis. His most famous patient with the latter disease was the young Joseph Smith (no relation), founder of the Church of Latter Day Saints.

As a medical writer, Smith left disappointingly little, though his edition of Philip Wilson Philip's *Treatise on Febrile Diseases* (2d American ed., 1813) includes signed notes by Smith that give strong hints of his own practice of medicine. His best work was the *Practical Essay on Typhous [typhoid] Fever* published in 1824. Smith's precise clinical description of the disease, his recommended treatments, and his insight that this was a self-limiting disease entity in its own right (different from other fevers) led Sir William Osler, seventy-five years later, to pay it tribute: "Try" he said, "to have a copy of Nathan Smith's 'A Practical Essay on Typhous Fever' (1824) to hand any young physician who asks for something good & fresh on typhoid fever" (*Aequanimitas*, 3d ed., pp. 302–3). Smith's son Nathan Ryno Smith reprinted several of his father's essays posthumously in *Medical and Surgical Memoirs* (1831); especially noteworthy is his "Observations on Necrosis [osteomyelitis]."

Smith manifested a remarkably modern view of medicine, including a prescient understanding of the importance of a medical school whose primary mission was to train rural physicians to care for rural patients. His place in history was perhaps best summed up by his Yale colleague Jonathan Knight, who said Smith's students filled New England "with a race of young, enterprising, intelligent physicians, who all justly looked up to Dr. Smith as their friend and professional father" (Knight, pp. 10–11). Some of those students taught and practiced far beyond New England as well, and Smith became one of the most influential physicians in the nation.

• Letters and papers connected with Smith (including student lecture notes) are chiefly in the Yale and Dartmouth archives; the Countway Library at Harvard and the Massachusetts Historical Society also have relevant materials. *Improve, Perfect, & Perpetuate: Dr. Nathan Smith and Early American Medical Education* (1998), by Oliver S. Hayward and Constance E. Putnam, significantly expands on the story told by Emily A. Smith, in *Life and Letters of Nathan Smith* (1914). Also helpful are Oliver P. Hubbard, *Dartmouth Medical Col-*

lege and *Nathan Smith: An Historical Discourse* (1879); Gilman Kimball, "Biographical Sketch of Dr. Nathan Smith," *Gynecological Transactions* 8 (1883): 27–42; and Harvey Cushing, *The Medical Career . . . Containing a Tribute to Dr. Nathan Smith* (1929). Information on Smith in Cornish can be found in William H. Child, *History of the Town of Cornish . . .* (repr. 1975).

Numerous articles (especially by Oliver S. Hayward) on Smith have appeared throughout the twentieth century. See, e.g., Hayward, "Nathan Smith's Medical Practice or Dogmatism versus Patient Inquiry," *Bulletin of the History of Medicine* 36, no. 3 (May–June 1962): 260–67; LeRoy S. Wirthlin, "Nathan Smith: Surgical Consultant to Joseph Smith," *Brigham Young University Studies* 17, no. 3 (Spring 1977): 319–37; Gordon A. Donaldson, "The First All-New England Surgeon," *American Journal of Surgery* 135, no. 4 (Apr. 1978): 471–79; A. W. Oughterson, "Nathan Smith and Typhoid Fever," *Yale Journal of Biology & Medicine* 12, no. 2 (Dec. 1939): 122–36; and John R. Paul, "Nathan Smith and Typhoid Fever," *Yale Journal of Biology & Medicine* 2, no. 3 (June 1930): 169–81. Important eulogies include William Allen, *Address Occasioned by the Death of Nathan Smith, M.D.* (1829), and Jonathan Knight, *An Eulogium on Nathan Smith, M.D.* (1829).

CONSTANCE E. PUTNAM

SMITH, Oliver Hampton (23 Oct. 1794–19 Mar. 1859), attorney, congressman, and U.S. senator, was born in Bucks County, Pennsylvania, the son of Thomas Smith and Letitia (maiden name unknown), occupations unknown. A devoted family of Quakers, the Smiths claimed ancestry in America dating to the founding of Pennsylvania in the 1680s. After fragmentary elementary schooling, young Oliver decided to carry his fortunes, and his limited resources, westward to Rising Sun, Indiana. He read law in Lawrenceburg and prepared to assume his role among the itinerant practitioners on the frontier. Admitted to the bar in 1820, Smith opened practice in Versailles and moved shortly after to Connorsville. In 1821 he married Mary Bramfield, also a Quaker; they had three children. By the following year he had built sufficient reputation to win election to the Indiana assembly.

Despite little experience as an attorney, Smith found himself appointed chairman of the Indiana House Judiciary Committee. Climbing rapidly amid the hurly-burly of frontier politics, he left the legislature to accept gubernatorial appointment as prosecuting attorney for the Third Judicial District. With a chance to reconcile public duty with his private Quaker ethos, Smith gained notoriety for winning convictions of four local toughs charged with murdering several American-Indian tribesmen.

Prior to the emergence of a clearly-defined second party system, candidates for office announced themselves independently but often pinned their ambitions to the personal appeal of a leading national figure. In Indiana of the mid-1820s, the choice broke down to the followers of Andrew Jackson versus those of Henry Clay. Smith gained a seat in Congress as a "Clay man" in 1826, defeating a fellow Clay supporter, Judge John Test, in the state's third district. In the House, one of the central issues of the day quickly re-

vealed Smith's philosophical as well as political aversion for the Jackson crowd: Indian policy. Again suggesting his basic Quaker outlook, he advocated humane treatment of Native Americans from his post on the House Indian Affairs Committee. Opposed to removal of the Chickasaws and Choctaws from their native lands, Smith delivered on 19 February 1828 the most impassioned floor speech of his congressional career. "This government is bound, by every tie of humanity, justice, morality, and religion, to do all in her power to save the wreck of this people," he implored. On subjects of less moral import, Smith evinced compelling sectional interest; he joined fellow northwesterners in pushing for extension of the Cumberland Road. Urging some colleagues to put aside "constitutional scruples" on the limits of congressional powers, he envisioned the road as "one of the strongest links in the chain of interest that draws this Union together." Meanwhile, political tides in Indiana turned against Smith; his bid for reelection collapsed under the organized Jacksonian surge of 1828.

With Jackson in the White House, Smith retired to his Indiana farm and law practice, but he remained prominent in state politics. In that arena, the newly formed Whig party gained control of both houses of the legislature by 1836. With his election to the U.S. Senate in 1836 over Governor Noah Noble, Ratliff Boon, and the incumbent Democrat William Hendricks, Smith's political influence at the national level reached its crest. At that time he was the lone Whig senator from the Northwest. Serving on the militia and judiciary committees and, finally, as chairman of the Senate committee on public lands, the Hoosier lawyer impressed colleagues with his forensic skills and keen intellect. In his first Senate speech, on 21 September 1837 he voiced strong opposition to the Sub-Treasury Bill and appealed for restoration of a national bank. He generally supported Clay's efforts for protective tariffs and federally promoted internal improvements. On other matters, Smith followed his section and, occasionally, his conscience. As a Whig, he urged distribution of land proceeds among the western states; as a westerner, revision of land policy to benefit actual settlers as opposed to absentee speculators; as a Quaker, prevention of any further westward spread of slavery. Smith expressed no public affinity for abolitionists, however, and regarded their radical tactics as "the worst possible course to attain the object they have in view." Also, despite general sympathy for preemption—the legal validation of squatters' claims to federal lands—he voted against the Preemption Bill of 1838 in an apparent act of political loyalty to Clay.

In the dramatic Whig nomination sweepstakes of 1840, Smith faced an awkward dilemma: whether to back party chief Henry Clay or the Indiana favorite William Henry Harrison. While Clay of Kentucky remained the intellectual preference of early supporters of the party, Harrison brought a populist dimension akin to Jackson's former appeal that now seemed indispensable for presidential victory. Smith personally favored Clay, but political reality dictated his public decision. "On that class who joined us under the Harrison flag we can not rely, should you be the candidate," he declared in a soul-wrenching letter to the Kentuckian in September 1839. Without Harrison to lead them, Smith expected the Whigs to lose Indiana to the incumbent Martin Van Buren and to rival Democrats in state elections. Finally winning both the nomination and the 1840 election, Harrison carried Indiana, where Whig gubernatorial candidate Samuel Bigger and a large majority of Whig party designates for the state legislature also triumphed.

When the Indiana legislature gave his seat to the Democrat Edward A. Hannegan in January 1843, Smith turned from the affairs of party to the market revolution going on back home in Indianapolis, where he finally settled. In the aftermath of the panic of 1837, with canal companies technologically obsolete and in bankruptcy, Smith joined the railroad investors. Political connections made him a sensible choice as first president of the Indianapolis and Bellefontaine Railroad, which built the first line from the state capitol to Evansville.

Smith died in Indianapolis, leaving behind his *Recollections of a Congressional Life* (1834) and *Early Indiana Trials: Sketches, Reminiscences* (1858), a valuable collection of memoirs, letters, and vignettes written late in life for the *Indianapolis Daily Journal*.

• With the Smith papers mostly scattered, the best sources on his career remain his *Recollections, Early Indiana Trials*, and the record of his activities kept in Gales and Seaton, comps., *Register of Debates in Congress, 1825–1837* (29 vols., 1825–1837), and the *Congressional Globe* (46 vols., 1834–1873). For valuable Indiana background, see R. Carlyle Buley, *The Old Northwest: Pioneer Period, 1815–1840* (2 vols., 1951). Obituaries are in the *Indianapolis Daily Journal*, 21 Mar. 1859, and the *Lafayette Daily Journal*, 22 Mar. 1859.

JOHN R. VAN ATTA

SMITH, Paul Joseph (30 Oct. 1906–25 Jan. 1985), composer, was born in Calumet, Michigan, the son of Joseph Smith, a college professor; his mother's name is unknown. Joseph Smith instilled in his children the importance of music and began teaching Paul various instruments at an early age, including piano, violin, and several brass instruments. The family moved to Caldwell, Idaho, where Smith's father had taken a professorship at the University of Idaho. Smith continued music lessons from his father and other instructors from the college throughout high school. In 1924 Smith received a Juilliard Scholarship to study music at the Bush Conservatory in Chicago, Illinois. He received his B.A., majoring in piano, in 1928. After graduation Smith made extra money giving violin concerts; he took a job teaching music at Elmhurst College in Elmhurst, Indiana, and he also taught at York High School in Elmhurst. In 1930 Smith returned to school to earn his general teaching credentials with an A.B. in English from the University of California at Los Angeles.

In 1930 Smith was hired by Walt Disney Studios as an arranger and composer, working primarily on background orchestrations when Disney Studios began expanding their musical staff. Smith's first big success with Disney came in 1937 with the animated feature *Snow White and the Seven Dwarfs*. Smith's background score for the film contributed greatly to its overall success and earned him his first Academy Award nomination. In his discussion of the music in the film, David Tietyen describes how Smith built the mood of danger and suspense when the huntsman has been ordered to kill Snow White "with muted French horns to symbolize the approaching huntsman," how the music then grows "frantic and builds to a whirlwind finish" during Snow White's escape, followed by a "light, spring-like melody" as the woodland animals approach her (p. 39). *Snow White* was such a success that Walt Disney Studios continued to create full-length feature animated films.

The next major Disney project for Smith was *Pinocchio*, released in 1940. Smith wrote the background score in collaboration with Leigh Harline and Ned Washington. The key to the success of a background score is the suggestion and reinforcement of the mood being created on screen. For example, Smith explained that "the old-world quality of Geppetto's life was caught by the tinkle of the music boxes. The quaintness of the village was tonally fixed by the themes of set, long-ago rhythms. The whale and the fishing scenes were scored in distinctly modern tonality, to suggest eeriness" (Tietyen, p. 60). The trio of background composers won an Academy Award for their score of *Pinocchio*. Smith followed *Pinocchio* with his collaboration with Charles Wolcott on *Bambi* (1942), followed by *Victory through Air Power* (1942), a propaganda film that used live action and animation. Collaborating with Edward Plumb and Oliver Wallace, Smith earned his third Academy Award nomination for this score.

According to Smith, "occasionally you really fall in love with a film. In my case it was *Cinderella*" (Tietyen, p. 35), released by Disney in 1950. Smith collaborated once more on the musical score with Oliver Wallace and garnered his fourth Academy Award nomination. Smith also contributed the song "So This Is Love" to the film. In 1954 Disney released its first live-action film, *20,000 Leagues under the Sea*, with the musical score by Smith. According to Tietyen, Smith "developed an eerie underwater effect that stands out today as a unique means of achieving this mood" (p. 113). To create this effect Smith explained that he "used a combination of low strings and woodwinds, piano, harp, gong, and . . . an orchestra bass marimba that could reach the lowest F on the piano. Together they provide the perfect underwater effect" (p. 113). Smith received three more Academy Award nominations for best score for *Three Caballeros*, *The Song of the South*, and *Perri*.

Perri was an extension of Disney's *True-Life Adventure* series, the studio's biggest success in the late 1940s and 1950s. Smith composed the orchestrations for nearly the entire series and critics believe the background scores were a key component to the success of the series. Thirteen films in the series were produced, with Smith winning Academy Awards for *Beaver Valley* (1950), *Nature's Half Acre* (1951), *The Living Desert* (1953), and *The Vanishing Prairie* (1954). The challenge for Smith in the *True-Life* series was to create characters from the live animals with music (rather than dialogue) and to create a score based on a fully edited film—matching the score to the film took patience and timing. *Time*'s review of *Beaver Valley* praised Smith's score as a "miracle of synchronization and human comment" (18 Feb. 1952, p. 3), and *Newsweek* commented that with "Smith's eloquent background music, the entire cast, which includes also crickets, tree frogs, and a goggle-eyed great blue heron, become tragic, comical, and often near-human personalities" (7 Jan. 1952, p. 26). "I found animal and nature films a joy to work on," Smith said, " . . . it provided an opportunity and setting for me to use my classical training in new and imaginative ways" (Tietyen, p. 69). In addition to the *True-Life* series, Smith also wrote the music for more than seventy Disney short films. Smith continued to write for Disney until he retired in 1964, including writing the scores for *Pollyanna* (1960), *The Parent Trap* (1961), and *The Three Lives of Thomasina* (1964). Smith died in Glendale, California.

Music has always been a successful part of Disney film production, and Paul Smith's award-winning orchestrations were an integral part of that success. Smith drew upon his experience on his early animated films to create memorable scores in his greatest success—the *True-Life Adventure* series. Nominated for a total of eleven Academy Awards, and winning five times, Smith's innovative scores contributed greatly to the development of the music written for film.

• While no personal papers of Paul Smith exist, information and an analysis of Smith's career with Walt Disney Studios is in David Tietyen's *The Musical World of Walt Disney* (1990). Additional information is found in the Walt Disney Studios' Archive Department. Smith's obituary is in the *New York Times* and the *Chicago Tribune*, both 30 Jan. 1985, and *Variety*, 6 Feb. 1985.

MELISSA VICKERY-BAREFORD

SMITH, Persifor Frazer (16 Nov. 1798–17 May 1858), soldier, was born in Philadelphia, Pennsylvania, the son of Jonathan Smith and Mary Anne Frazer. He attended the College of New Jersey (now Princeton University) and received a bachelor's degree at age seventeen. Smith read law with Charles Chauncey and in 1819 moved to New Orleans, Louisiana, where he was admitted to the bar. He married Frances Jeanette Bureau in 1822; they had one child. Smith developed an intense interest in military affairs and read several military manuals while practicing law. He obtained a commission in the state militia and received command first of a company and later of a battalion. Smith allied himself with the Whig party, and in 1835 Governor Edward Douglass White (1795–1847) appointed him adjutant general over a Democratic party rival.

At the outbreak of the Second Seminole War in January 1836, General Edmund Pendleton Gaines, commander of the U.S. Army's Western Department, passed through New Orleans and asked White to raise a regiment of volunteers to go to Florida. Smith took an active role in raising money to equip the volunteers. By 3 February the regiment had completed its organization, and White named Smith as its commander. The Louisiana troops reached Fort Brooke, near present-day Tampa, on 10 February. There Gaines formed a force with the intention of relieving Fort King, which he believed to be surrounded by American Indians. Smith's men accompanied Gaines's column as it marched from the fort on 13 February. They reached Fort King on the twenty-second to find it in no danger. Four days later, Gaines began his return to Fort Brooke. The force met resistance in trying to cross the Withlacoochee River on 28 February and was besieged by the Indians for six days. Smith led the right column of General Winfield Scott's force during a campaign into this same area 24 March–5 April. Smith's regiment conducted a campaign on the Peace River from 10 to 25 April but did not engage the enemy. Their term of service having expired, the Louisianans left for New Orleans on 1 May.

In response to another call for volunteers, Smith led 600 men back to Florida in September 1837. The next month, they participated in General Thomas Sidney Jesup's campaign in southern Florida. Jesup entrusted Smith with a march into the area between the Caloosahatchee River and Cape Sable. The Louisianans fought in a couple of skirmishes and captured 243 prisoners. In December 1837 and January 1838, Smith commanded a column of Louisiana, Pennsylvania, and New York volunteers in cooperation with a larger force led by Colonel Zachary Taylor. Smith had the responsibility of covering the area west of Lake Okeechobee and preventing any Seminoles from escaping toward the north. Smith's troops were successful, and at the end of the campaign, he returned to New Orleans.

Smith resumed his law practice as well as his position as adjutant general of the state militia. He was elected as judge of the city court of Lafayette (now part of New Orleans) and later became judge for Jefferson Parish. Governor André Bienvenu Roman reappointed Smith adjutant general in early 1839. Later that year, Smith helped organize an artillery company, which became the nucleus for the famous Washington Artillery of New Orleans. A new Democratic governor, Alexandre Mouton, took office in 1843 and replaced Smith as adjutant general. Smith soon became colonel of the Washington Regiment in the militia.

When the Mexican War began, General Taylor requested that Governor Isaac Johnson raise four regiments of infantry and recommended that Johnson place Smith in command of them. Smith received a commission as brigadier general of Louisiana volunteers on 15 May 1846. His troops reached the Rio Grande and reinforced the small garrison at Barita. On 27 May Smith became colonel of the Regiment of

Mounted Rifles. The enlistments of the Louisiana brigade expired before they saw action, but Smith remained with Taylor's army. He was given command of the Second Brigade of General William Jenkins Worth's division, and his brigade led the army's march toward Monterrey. In the battle there on 21 September, he led his men in an attack on Fort Soldada, which they captured in a few minutes. Smith commanded the troops of the division that occupied the city's citadel four days later. He was breveted as brigadier general to date from 23 September for meritorious and gallant conduct in the battle. Joining General Scott's army in its campaign against Veracruz, Smith received command of the First Brigade of General David Emanuel Twiggs's division. His men fought a small engagement near Vergara during the siege of the city. In the battle of Contreras on 20 August, Smith assumed command of three brigades and led an attack on the rear of the Mexican position. The assault lasted only seventeen minutes and resulted in the rout of the enemy soldiers. Smith also distinguished himself in the attack at Chapultepec on 13 September. For those two actions, he received a brevet as major general to date from 20 August. Smith served on the armistice commission, as military governor of Mexico City, and as commander at Veracruz prior to the evacuation of U.S. troops.

Smith commanded the Pacific Division from 1849 to 1850, dealing with the turmoil from the gold rush and problems between white settlers and the local American Indians as well as establishing several new forts, including one at San Diego. As commander of the Department of Texas from 1850 to 1856, he continued to establish new forts and put down Indian uprisings in New Mexico Territory. From 1856 to 1858 Smith attempted, without much success, to help keep the peace in Kansas and resisted calls by the opposing sides for large-scale employment of troops. He received a commission as brigadier general on 30 December 1856. His first wife died in 1852, and he married Anne Monica Millard Armstrong in 1854, becoming stepfather to future Confederate general Frank Crawford Armstrong. Assigned to head the Department of Utah in April 1858, Smith established his headquarters at Fort Leavenworth, Kansas. He died there the next month and was buried in Laurel Hill Cemetery in Philadelphia.

Though not widely known today as a military leader, Smith enjoyed the admiration and respect of his contemporaries. A courageous, intelligent, and bold soldier, he acquitted himself exceptionally well and deserves more credit for his successes on the battlefields of the Seminole and Mexican wars.

• Miscellaneous correspondence and papers of Smith are in the Pennsylvania State Teachers College Library and the Historical Society of Pennsylvania. A biography of Smith has yet to be published. For his service in the Second Seminole War see Canter Brown, Jr., "Persifor F. Smith, the Louisiana Volunteers, and Florida's Second Seminole War," *Louisiana History* 30 (1993): 389–410; John K. Mahon, *History of the Second Seminole War, 1835–1842* (1967); and John T. Sprague,

The Origin, Progress, and Conclusion of the Florida War (1848). The best sources for Smith's activities in Mexico are Justin H. Smith, *The War with Mexico* (2 vols., 1919), and Nathan C. Brooks, *A Complete History of the Mexican War* (1849; repr. 1965). Contemporary assessments of Smith and accounts of his military career can be found in Dabney H. Maury, *Recollections of a Virginian in the Mexican, Indian, and Civil Wars* (1894); William B. Lane, "The 'Regiment of Mounted Riflemen'; or, From Puebla to the City of Mexico," *United Service* 14 (1895): 301–13; and (author unknown), "Recollections of the Rifles," *Southern Literary Messenger* 33 (1861): 371–80. See Evans J. Casso, *Louisiana Legacy: A History of the State National Guard* (1976), for a brief account of Smith's role as adjutant general of Louisiana. An obituary is in the New Orleans *Daily Picayune*, 20 May 1858.

ARTHUR W. BERGERON, JR.

SMITH, Peter (6 Feb. 1753–31 Dec. 1815), itinerant doctor and preacher, was born probably in New Jersey, the son of Hezekiah Smith, an "Indian doctor," and Sarah (maiden name unknown). The family tradition that he studied at the College of New Jersey (Princeton) cannot be documented. He laid claim to "a slight classical education," and his basic medical knowledge came from the "practice and experience" he had learned under his father. He was practicing medicine in New Jersey as early as 1777, for he reported having inoculated about 130 people for smallpox in the winter of that year. He sought out medical men as he traveled, and although he credited many friends in the profession for adding to his knowledge, he believed that "nature had made him a physician" and that "he was somehow providentially prevented" from becoming a regular practitioner. He was, however, acquainted with the writings of Benjamin Rush and John Brown, and the influence of Brunonianism is quite evident in his writings. (Brunonianism maintained that diseases arose from either an excess or deficiency of excitement and were to be treated with sedatives or stimulants.) He was also acquainted with the more popularly oriented writings of Nicholas Culpeper, Simon-André Tissot, and William Buchan.

In 1776 Smith married Catherine Stout in New Jersey. They had twelve children. In 1780 the family left New Jersey for some fourteen years of moving about before finally settling down in Ohio. From New Jersey, the Smiths traveled to Pennsylvania, Virginia, North and South Carolina, Georgia, and Kentucky. Smith, a devout Baptist and itinerant preacher, referred to himself as a "minister of the Gospel." His hopes to settle first in Georgia and then in Kentucky were dashed by his strong antislavery principles. In Ohio, where the family settled at Duck Creek and finally at Donnel's Creek, Smith farmed, preached in the churches of the area, and doctored his neighbors.

Smith is best known for *The Indian Doctor's Dispensatory, Being Father Smith's Advice Respecting Diseases and Their Cure; Consisting of Prescriptions for Many Complaints; and a Description of Medicines, Simple and Compound, Showing Their Virtues and How to Apply Them*. The book, consisting of more than 100 pages, was printed in Cincinnati in 1813 and is said to be the first medical book printed west of the Alleghenies. It was intended as a domestic medicine manual and contains practical advice drawn from various doctors, from testimonials, and from his own experiences. In addition, Smith offered an account of his medical theories and a rationalization of his medical practice. He agreed with John Brown that there were only two kinds of diseases, and he departed from Benjamin Rush in concluding that the latter used calomel too much. (Calomel, mercurous chloride, was a powerful cathartic and a mainstay of Rush's "heroic" practice of medicine. Smith was an early critic of this dangerous therapeutic approach.) The main portion of the book, arranged by numbered prescriptions (ninety) and interspersed with directions specifying which prescriptions, by number, were to be used for described symptoms, was intended to benefit his family and friends and "especially the citizens of the western parts of the United States of America."

Smith called himself an "Indian doctor" because he had "incidentally obtained a knowledge of many of the simples used by the Indians, but chiefly because [he] obtained [his] knowledge in the same way as the Indians do." Although his remedies were largely roots and herbs, there is a good deal of evidence of ideas and usages—venesection and vaccination, for example—he could have picked up only from an acquaintance with regular medical practice. Although Smith considered the book "rather a clergyman's book," in 1813 he sent a copy to the committee overseeing the Boylston Medical Prize (under the aegis of the Massachusetts Medical Society and Harvard University), soliciting its publication in the East. The committee found it composed "principally of inert popular recipes . . . and by no means calculated to advance the interests of medical science." In 1828 Constantine Rafinesque, in his *Medical Flora*, described Smith's work as "a guide for Empirics, some medical facts; but it is difficult to ascertain to what species they apply, no descriptions nor figures, nor correct names are given." Yet, although it is impossible to determine how widely the book was circulated, the fact that three different issues of it were printed in 1813 suggests that it gained some popularity. John Uri Lloyd, noted plant chemist and pharmaceutical manufacturer, in his introduction to the 1901 reprint of the *Dispensatory* in the *Bulletin of the Lloyd Library*, recalled that during his boyhood in Kentucky, Peter Smith was a familiar name and that the name "lingers yet about Western domestic medicine." Smith died at Donnel's Creek.

• An autobiographical sketch of Smith in his *Indian Doctor's Dispensatory* deals mainly with his medical experiences. His grandson, Joseph W. Kiefer, in his *Slavery and Four Years of War*, vol. 2 (1900), includes biographical sketches of Smith and his descendants. Kiefer made use of John Uri Lloyd's "Dr. Peter Smith and His Dispensatory," which appeared in the *American Journal of Pharmacy* 70 (Jan. 1898), pp. 1–9. This was essentially repeated as a preface to the reproduction of the *Indian Doctor's Dispensatory* that was issued as no. 2 of the *Bulletin of the Lloyd Library* (1901), pp. 3–6. Lloyd gave some attention to the medical and pharmaceutical contents of the *Dispensatory*, as did O. Juettner in "Peter Smith, the Indian Doctor, an Historical Sketch," *Ohio State Medical Journal* 11 (1915): 98–99. Smith's letter to the Boylston committee is in the Francis A. Countway Library in Boston. Richard A. Wolfe has described it in "A Footnote to the Publication of Peter Smith's Indian Doctor's Dispensatory (Cincinnati, 1813)," *Harvard Library Bulletin* 27 (1979): 202–22. Robert G. Hayman describes the three 1813 issues in "Addendum to Shaw and Shoemaker: Smith's Indian Doctor's Dispensatory," *Papers of the Bibliographical Society of America* 63 (1969): 126–28.

DAVID L. COWEN

SMITH, Peter (15 Nov. 1768–14 Apr. 1837), land speculator, fur trader, and entrepreneur, was born near Tappan, New York, the son of Gerrit P. Smith and Wyntje Lent, the descendants of strongly religious seventeenth-century Dutch immigrants. Smith's temporal life began well enough. He was in his mid-teens when he accepted his first job clerking for Abraham Herring, a New York City merchant. Smith soon demonstrated his entrepreneurial spirit and a belief in his inherent abilities by opening his own shop, selling books, school and library provisions, canes, and snuffboxes from 1785 until 1788. He also sold theatrical supplies in response to his interest in acting, which he suppressed because of the religious scruples he held throughout his life.

Eager for more than a career in trade, Smith capitalized on his meeting with John Jacob Astor. Although the exact date of their meeting is unknown, it is likely that they met during Smith's New York venture. By 1789, drawn together by a common interest in drama and strict religious convictions, the two had begun a lifelong friendship. That year Smith opened the first general store in Utica, New York (formerly Old Fort Schuyler, Herkimer County), trading supplies and merchandise with the Indians and trappers for grain, furs (including muskrat, marten, and bear cub), and skins. Smith and Astor used the store for their headquarters when they entered the first of their joint business enterprises: trading with the Indians for furs, which they allegedly sold for a 1,000 percent profit in England and Europe. This was the pair's only formal partnership, and it lasted little more than a year. After the partnership was dissolved, Astor and Smith continued to trade in furs until 1795 and even participated in some scattered dealings as late as 1799. Despite Astor's financial accounts, which referred to the increasingly poor quality of the furs, the positive impact of the partnership on Smith's future business dealings was undiminished.

By late 1793, with the fur trade dying, Smith and Astor needed to supplement the meager takings from that enterprise and began the first of their joint forays into land speculation. This intermittent business relationship lasted until Smith's death. Smith was not content to wait until his speculations gave him security and social status in New York society. The socially grasping elite regarded land dealing as essential and as a desirable lifestyle and worthy interest for all classes. Smith's new career and his business shrewdness led him in 1792 to marry Elizabeth Livingston of the powerful and influential Livingston family of New York. They had six children, including a son named Gerrit, who became an abolitionist and social reformer.

From the outset, Smith demonstrated a respect for the Indians in his speculations that manifested itself in fair dealings with the local tribes. His experience with the trading store had reinforced the importance of maintaining a friendly and honest alliance with the native landholders: the Indians had been eager to deal with Smith and Astor and even carried the goods themselves to assist the new traders. Smith's rapport with the Indians soon helped him achieve his first major success in land speculations. In 1794 he persuaded the Oneida tribe to lease him a large tract of land covering part of the Oneida and Onondaga counties. Within a year, the state formalized a treaty with the Indians and established proprietorship over the land. With his title to the land formally recognized by the state, Smith's speculative acumen was validated; he indulged his developing ego by choosing the name "Peterboro" for the collection of lesser dwellings that grew up around his new house, "Homestead," and by naming the town "Smithfield."

Also in 1794, at nearly the same time as the start of his land dealings with the Oneida, Smith began a venture with Astor and William Laight to buy the land known as the Charlotte River and Byrnes Patents in the Mohawk Valley that stands out in sharp contrast. These tracts had formerly been owned by William Johnson, who before the revolution had given a number of settlers, or "associates," the right to the land under the letters patent. Smith and his partners were unaware of the competing claims and were unable to sell the land; they were forced to resort to threatening the rival claimants through newspaper advertisements. The matter was not settled until 1802, when Smith, rather than either Astor or the heirs of the recently deceased Laight, took the initiative and proposed a compromise scheme of compensation that was acceptable to all parties—if the land could be sold.

The final resolution of the Mohawk Valley land deal sheds light on the nature and dichotomy of the Smith-Astor friendship. Much of the property did not sell, and in 1827 Smith, who had been administering the property for approximately thirty years without reward, presented an estimate of the value of the unsold land to Astor and indicated that he was due something for his efforts. The next year Astor rebuked Smith for his presumption. Although Astor usually agreed with Smith, the older and more experienced Laight's influence in this venture extended far beyond the grave and the normally agreeable Astor denied his friend just recognition. Smith often appeared to hold the upper hand in his relationship with Astor, who wrote him letters expressing concern for his health and urging him to accept the bounties of life. In this case, however, Astor and Laight had used Smith's talents without compensation, while leading him to believe mistakenly that he was an equal partner in the venture. By 1829 harmony was restored when Smith bought out Astor, who in turn lent Smith the money to buy out the Laight heirs.

Prior to the Mohawk Valley dealings, Smith was still unsatisfied with his new wealth and had begun a series of purchases that had resulted in his holding over 1 million acres, dispersed throughout New York. Astor often recognized Smith's ability to identify opportunities, but Smith himself never took advantage of those chances. After his first wife's death, Smith developed a morbid disposition and became preoccupied with religion. As if to clear the way for a future alone, Smith transferred his business interests to his son Gerrit in 1819 but kept a liquid capital asset base of $125,000. Financially secure and freed from family cares, Smith diversified his business interests into agriculture, the manufacture of scarce grindstones, and the management of a glass factory.

Smith's new ventures resulted in a brief period of happiness. In 1820 he married the English-born Sarah Pogson from Charleston, South Carolina. Their subsequent separation after the failure of their childless and acrimonious marriage, the failed land deal with Astor and Laight, and similar perceived slights caused Smith to retreat even further into paranoia. His disturbed state of mind was founded on his conviction that he had forsaken appropriate religious activities for worldly success. In an attempt to regain his self-respect, Smith proposed giving part of the Mohawk Valley land to converted Jews, and he distributed numerous religious tracts. Before sinking into a depression, Smith had led the way in county politics. He served as Herkimer County's first sheriff and was the initial first judge of Madison County. Smith was also an officer of the New York Tract Society.

Smith was doomed to live and be remembered in the shadows of others, whether it was his son Gerrit or his more acclaimed business associates. He died an embittered man, despite his enviable business astuteness and the love and care of his friends and first wife; he could never accept the happiness that his family could give him. Smith died alone in his house in Schenectady, New York, leaving his entire estate—most of it in land and estimated at a potential value of $400,000—to Gerrit, who found it difficult to raise money using the land as collateral because only a small proportion was productive.

• Most of the Smith family papers are held at the Syracuse University Library in the Gerrit Smith Miller Collection. Smith's career is addressed in Kenneth Wiggins Porter, *John Jacob Astor, Business Man* (2 vols., 1931); Ruth L. Higgins, *Expansion in New York with Especial Reference to the Eighteenth Century* (1931); and Thomas Elliot Norton, *The Fur Trade in Colonial New York, 1686–1776* (1974). See also William Wyckoff, *The Developer's Frontier: The Making of the Western New York Landscape* (1988), and Cynthia A. Kierner, *Traders and Gentlefolk: The Livingstons of New York, 1675–1790* (1992).

RICHARD GROVES

SMITH, Pine Top (11 June 1904–15 Mar. 1929), boogie-woogie pianist and singer, was born Clarence Smith in Troy, Alabama, the son of Sam Smith and Molly (maiden name unknown). His nickname, spelled as Pine Top or Pinetop, came from a boyhood game of hanging a wire from treetop to treetop and talking through tin cans, as if the wire were a telephone line. From 1918 to 1920 Smith lived in Birmingham, where he taught himself to play the piano. He moved to Pittsburgh in 1920 and from that home base toured as a pianist and tap dancer in various revues, mainly with lesser-known entertainers but also with Ma Rainey. While back in Pittsburgh he met Sarah Horton, whom he married in 1924; they had two children.

At the suggestion of pianist Charles "Cow Cow" Davenport, Smith moved to Chicago in the summer of 1928. His family followed soon after. He played at parties and successfully auditioned for J. Mayo Williams, producer for Brunswick Records. From December 1928 to March 1929 he made a series of solo recordings, singing, speaking over music, and playing vaudeville songs and boogie-woogie blues. (On a few pieces Williams added his own voice, in conversation with Smith.) Eight titles were released posthumously, including "I'm Sober Now," "Now I Ain't Got Nothin' at All," and two versions each of "Pine Top's Blues" and "Pine Top's Boogie Woogie." An innocent bystander during a fight at a party at a Masonic lodge in Chicago, Smith was killed by a stray bullet.

The precise origins of boogie-woogie piano playing will never be known. Certainly Jimmy Yancey developed the style well ahead of Smith, and Meade Lux Lewis recorded a version of "Honky Tonk Train Blues" a year before Smith's first session. Nonetheless, "Pine Top's Boogie Woogie" is the landmark recording in the popularization of the style, and as such it—perhaps more than any other piece—provided a foundation on which rhythm-and-blues and rock-and-roll were built. Both takes of this title feature a reiterated, rollicking left-hand bass line that traces out the blues progression and right-hand melodies made from brief and catchy blues phrases, trills, and repeated syncopated chording (after the manner of the "Charleston" rhythm). Also in each take Smith gives joyful instructions to dancers, including colorful stops and starts that give the performance a special energy absent from many subsequent boogie-woogie pieces of unvarying rhythmic character. During the national craze for boogie-woogie music in the late 1930s, "Pine Top's Boogie Woogie" was re-created numerous times in versions as diverse as pianist Albert Ammons's solo tribute and Deane Kincaide's big band arrangement for the Tommy Dorsey orchestra. In thus serving as a template for the boogie-woogie style and subsequent stylistic developments, it was an immensely influential piece.

• Biographies and details of Smith's early death appear in Sharon A. Pease, " 'I Saw Pinetop Spit Blood': The Life and Death of Clarence Smith, Creator of Boogie Woogie," *Down Beat*, 1 Oct. 1939, pp. 4, 18, 23, continued in the magazine's next issue as "Will Pinetop's Sons Be Great Like Their Dad?: Clarence and Eugene Smith Today Play Boogie-Woogie with the Best of Them," 15 Oct. 1939, p. 4. See also Bob Hall and Richard Noblett, "The Birth of the Boogie," *Blues Unlimited* 133 (Jan.–Feb. 1979): 10–11; Francis Smith, "I Saw Pine Top Spit Blood, or How Pinetop Smith DIDN'T Die," *Blues Unlimited* 139 (Autumn 1980): 34; and Sheldon Harris, *Blues Who's Who: A Biographical Dictionary of Blues Singers* (1979). For divergent assessments of Smith's stature in the field, compare William Russell, "Boogie Woogie," in *Jazzmen: The Story of Hot Jazz Told in the Lives of the Men Who Created It*, ed. Frederic Ramsey, Jr., and Charles Edward Smith (1939; repr. 1977), pp. 187–88, and Max Harrison, "Boogie Woogie," in *Jazz*, ed. Nat Hentoff and Albert J. McCarthy (1959), pp. 133–34.

BARRY KERNFELD

SMITH, Red (25 Sept. 1905–15 Jan. 1982), sportswriter, was born Walter Wellesley Smith in Green Bay, Wisconsin, the son of Walter Philip Smith, a dealer in wholesale produce and retail groceries, and Ida Richardson. A good and diligent student, Smith skipped the third grade and graduated from East High School in Green Bay in 1922, having won his school's annual essay contest with a humorous look at the school's debating team. Because the family did not have enough money to send him to college right away, Smith took a job as a filing clerk at a hardware company.

In 1923 Smith entered the University of Notre Dame in South Bend, Indiana, as a journalism major, already wanting to become a newspaperman. As a freshman he did an uneventful stint as a reporter for the school's newspaper, but by his junior year he was editing Notre Dame's annual, the *Dome*. Smith professed to have been influenced most by his journalism professor, who impressed upon him a reporter's crucial task of factual accuracy, the attractions of a simple and straightforward writing style, and the need to look beyond one's natural areas of interest.

In 1927 Smith completed his liberal arts education and graduated cum laude. That same year he was hired as a general assignment reporter by the *Milwaukee Sentinel*. In 1928, selling himself somewhat inaccurately as an experienced, versatile newspaperman, he moved to the *St. Louis Star* after learning that this paper needed copyreaders. One of the more significant attractions of the St. Louis job was the higher pay: $40 a week, compared to $24 at the *Sentinel*. Shortly after arriving at the *Star*, Smith joined the paper's sports department. In 1929, reporting from the St. Louis Browns spring training camp, he also earned his first byline: W. W. Smith.

Also in 1929 Smith met Webster College student Catherine M. "Kay" Cody, whom he married on 11 February 1933. The couple had two children. Around this time Smith also became active in the newly organized American Newspaper Guild.

In 1934 Smith changed jobs at the paper (known as the *Star-Times* after a merger with the *St. Louis Times*) to become a rewrite man, one of a staff of two. During this time there were days, he recalled later, that he almost literally wrote the entire paper. The rewrite job, Smith and others claimed, helped him solidify his writing style, avoid clichés, and develop a sharp eye for detail.

In 1936 Smith took a job as a sportswriter at the *Philadelphia Record*. It paid $60 a week, five dollars more than at the *Star-Times*; more important, he became closer to New York City, in his eyes the heart of the world of writing. Later, Smith emphasized that at the time he was not committed to making a career exclusively as a sports reporter. But sports would remain his department for the rest of his life. Smith's favorite sports were racing, football, baseball, boxing, and fishing; the latter was the only sporting activity he personally engaged in. One other trademark became institutionalized upon his arrival at the *Record*: After Kay vetoed her redheaded husband's first byline ("Walt Smith"), all parties accepted the paper's second try: "Red." In 1939 the *Record* gave Red Smith a full-time column.

Although now a sportswriter, Smith occasionally ventured into other areas. Covering the Philadelphia Athletics' spring training in Mexico City in 1937, he interviewed the exiled Bolshevik Leon Trotsky. The story was written in Smith's light, ironic style, as illustrated in the following passage, beginning with Trotsky speaking. "'I still do harm. My writings, my books, what I say, they penetrate into Russia. I do harm.' Harm. He says it like a small boy insisting 'I'm tough. I carry matches'" (*Reader*, p. 170). Later in his career, Smith would also cover the 1956 and 1968 national political conventions for the *New York Herald Tribune* and the Publishers-Hall Newspaper Syndicate, respectively.

Although insisting at various times during his life that he never wanted to be anything but "a newspaper stiff" (*The American Spectator*, p. 25; *Contemporary Authors*, p. 510), his ambitions stretched further. When in 1944 he sold his first piece (a sports-related story) to *The Saturday Evening Post*, he was elated as well as boastful at what he saw, probably only half-jokingly, as his newly acquired immortality.

Although not yet too old to serve, Smith chose not to enlist when the U.S. entered World War II in 1941. Often questioning the purpose of watching and participating in sports he continued to cover sports anyway because, as he put it later, there was "some morale value to games" (*Holtzman*, p. 255).

Smith's ultimate ambition as a newspaper reporter, a job in New York, became a reality in August 1945 when sports editor Stanley Woodward invited him to the *New York Herald Tribune*. His hiring showed that he had become one of the nation's more prominent sportswriters. Within four months Smith had his own column, forever after citing, as well as adhering to, Woodward's suggestion to write about "the smell of the cabbage cooking in the corridors" (*Writer's Digest*, p. 23).

Smith's arrival in New York inaugurated his glory years as a sports columnist and writer, which would last until the folding of the *Herald Tribune* in 1966. Although Smith would make a strong comeback at the *New York Times* during the 1970s and early 1980s—winning a Pulitzer Prize in 1976—his prestige and influence were highest between 1945 and 1966.

During these first postwar decades Smith fully developed his trademark style, while the impact of his craft had not yet been diminished by the advent of television. Meanwhile, Smith's column made an appearance in Ernest Hemingway's novel *Across the River and into the Trees*, and Smith's national stature increased thanks to the *Herald Tribune*'s syndicate. After the death of Grantland Rice in 1954, Smith's columns were syndicated to more papers than those of any other sportswriter.

Rather than traditional reports or commentaries, Smith's columns were often like short stories. What made them stand out was their phrasing, the product of a most creative, literate, and humorous mind. Although loving the carefree lifestyle that came with his job, Smith was very serious about his writing, often likening it to doing hard labor at the typewriter. It would produce gems like the following from 1947, a description of a college basketball player's physique: "He measures one-half inch less than seven feet from end to end and he looks and moves more like an institution than a man, with agonizing deliberation and great grinding of gears" (*Reader*, p. 198).

The years after the *Herald Tribune*'s disappearance were somewhat of a struggle for Smith. After the paper's successor, the *World Journal Tribune*, lasted only one year, he did not have a permanent base in the newspaper world other than the Publishers-Hall Newspaper Syndicate, which continued to distribute his work.

By the time the *Times* began to run Smith's work in the 1970s (starting 15 Nov. 1971) his choice of topics had begun to change. Helped along by the twin impact of a politically turbulent time and changes in his family life (after the death of his wife Kay in 1967, Smith had married Phyllis Warner Weiss in 1968), Smith was writing more about sports as part of the larger world, paying more attention to the business of sports.

He would, as his tendency had been all along, side with those who in his eyes were the underdogs in the sports world. He also employed his trademark sharp wit against what he saw as bad judgment and/or poor taste, especially on the part of officials, team owners, and administrators. When in 1972 officials failed to interrupt the Olympic games during a terrorist attack on Israeli quarters, Smith wrote: "The men who run the Olympics are not evil men. Their shocking lack of awareness can't be due to callousness. It has to be stupidity" (*Reader*, p. 43).

Although in failing health in the late 1970s due to cancer, Smith insisted on continuing to write, so long as the *Times* cared to keep him or until someone would tell him he had lost his touch. But in late 1981 he agreed to cut back from four to three columns per week. The first piece in the new regimen, appearing on 11 January 1982, would be the last of his career. Smith died four days later of heart failure, after a short hospital stay in Stamford, Connecticut.

Shortly after Smith's death, a colleague at the *Times*, Dave Anderson, wrote: "Red Smith was, quite simply, the best sportswriter. Put the emphasis on writer" (*Friends*, p. vii). The acknowledgment, just like the numerous awards Smith received throughout his career, was both deserved and discerning.

In spite of his considerable prestige, Smith remained modest about his accomplishments. This was partly because he believed the praise he received to be exaggerated, partly because he rarely saw sports as anything more than entertainment. Sportswriting, he believed, mainly served to have the game entertain the public a second time around. This is not to say that Smith believed this entertainment to be irrelevant. Neither did he think that his craft should be taken lightly by its practitioners. He frequently warned aspiring sportswriters to go into the profession out of love for the newspaper business, not out of love for sports, and that, unless they wanted to be bad citizens and poor sportswriters, they should be involved in the wider world of which sports was only a small part. This view reflected his own career, which had always been more about being a newspaperman than a sportswriter. It was a combination of his professional ethic and pure literary ability that made Smith one of the best read and most respected sportswriters of the mid-twentieth century.

• Smith's papers are in the Notre Dame Archives, University of Notre Dame. Much of Smith's work was published in book form: *Out of the Red* (1950); *Red Smith's Sports Annual, 1961* (1961); *Red Smith on Fishing* (1963); *Strawberries in Wintertime* (1974); *Press Box: Red Smith's Favorite Sports Stories* (1976); *To Absent Friends* (1982); and *The Red Smith Reader* (1982). Smith also published *Terry and Bunky Play Football*, with Richard Mark Fishel (1945), and edited *The Saturday Evening Post Sports Stories* (1949). He also wrote a revealing article, "My Press-Box Memoirs," *Esquire*, Oct. 1975. Indispensable for Smith's life and career is Ira Berkow, *Red: A Biography of Red Smith* (1986). Helpful also are interviews with Jerome Holtzman, *No Cheering in the Press Box* (1973); John L. Kern, "Red Smith in the Final Innings," *Writer's Digest*, June 1982; James Grant, "Just a Newspaper Stiff," *The American Spectator*, Nov. 1977; and Jane Leavy, "Red, He Juggled for Us," *Village Voice*, 20 Nov. 1978. Also insightful are Wilfrid Sheed, "Reds," *New York Review of Books*, 23 Sept. 1982; Donald Hall, "First a Writer, then a Sportsman," *New York Times Book Review*, 18 July 1982; and Frank Deford, "It's a Quarter of a Century Overdue, but at Last Red Smith Has a Pulitzer," *Sports Illustrated*, 7 June 1976. See also *Contemporary Authors* (1979), vols. 77–80. An obituary is in the *New York Times*, 16 and 17 Jan. 1982.

RUUD VAN DIJK

SMITH, Relliford Stillmon (30 Nov. 1889–28 June 1965), physician, was born in Americus, Georgia, the son of Dennis Smith, a laborer, and Mollie Daniels. Smith came from a poor family, and he worked hard during his youth at a variety of menial jobs, including service industry employee, domestic, office worker, and railroad employee, to help support himself and his parents. He received his elementary and secondary education at the Americus Institute, then in 1906 he began studies at Shaw University in Raleigh, North Carolina, where he earned a B.S. in 1910. During the

summers he worked as a bookkeeper and a butcher in the city markets of Americus. He attended Leonard Medical College of Shaw University from 1910 to 1914 and received an M.D. in 1914 from the University of West Tennessee College of Medicine and Surgery. He earned a graduate degree at Meharry Medical College in 1916. While in graduate school, he worked during the summers as a Pullman porter and a steamboat waiter. Smith began the general practice of medicine in 1916 in Americus, Georgia, after he passed medical licensing examinations in Georgia, South Carolina, Maryland, and the District of Columbia. In 1918 he entered the U.S. Army Medical Corps, and from 1918 to 1919 he served as assistant regimental surgeon, New Receiving Camp Infirmary, Camp Wheeler, Georgia. After an honorable discharge, he established a medical practice in Macon. In 1920 he married Gertrude Savage. They had children, but the exact number is unknown.

Smith was keenly aware of the value of graduate training for physicians, especially black physicians, who because of racial barriers were restricted to a black world. Throughout his career he took advanced graduate courses whenever possible, including numerous sessions at the Medical College of Georgia, Grady Hospital of Emory University Medical School, the Mayo Clinic in Rochester, Minnesota, Howard University School of Medicine, and Johns Hopkins University School of Medicine. In taking courses with public health significance, he became personally acquainted in 1938 with U.S. Surgeon General Thomas A. Parran and Assistant Surgeon General R. A. Vonderlear. Through these relationships Smith convinced the U.S. Public Health Service to grant modest stipends, beginning in the summer of 1938, to each black physician who attended the Howard University medical school postgraduate course in venereal diseases. Without this aid, many black physicians would not have been able to afford to attend the sessions.

Smith served as a local medical examiner for the Guaranty Life Insurance Company (1919–1965) and was a member of that company's board of directors for more than twenty years. He overcame repressive racial and financial barriers to gain local, state, and national recognition as an excellent medical practitioner, an effective advocate for medical improvement, and a reliable civil rights spokesman for black physicians. For example, the annual medical seminars hosted by the Medical College of Georgia, which Smith attended for seventeen consecutive years, permitted black physicians to attend but would not give them certificates verifying their presence or the courses they had taken. Smith made this an issue, and the university changed its policy. Beginning in 1935 any physician, black or white, who attended any of those seminars received a certificate.

Smith actively participated in many civic and professional organizations, including the Macon Academy of Medicine, Dentistry, and Pharmacy, which he served as president; the Georgia State Medical Association of Physicians and Pharmacists; the John Andrew

Clinic, Tuskegee Institute; the Macon County Academy of Medicine and Surgery, serving as president; and the Tremont Baptist Church. In spite of an excellent reputation, extraordinary medical preparation and knowledge, and recognition by the U.S. Public Health Service, Smith was not permitted to join the "whites only" Bibb County Medical Society. Fifty-one years after being awarded a medical degree, when racial barriers were finally dropped in 1965, the Bibb County Medical Society invited Smith to join.

Smith for many years served the National Medical Association (NMA) in almost every capacity possible. He was the fifty-eighth president of the organization, vice president, vice speaker of the house of delegates, six-year member of the board of trustees, three-year chairman of the budget committee of the board, six-year member of the judicial counsel and for three years its chairman, and a 24-year member of the house of delegates. Because of his excellent sense of organization, his ability as a team player, and his hard work, Smith was considered one of the NMA's best presidents.

Smith's first wife died in 1946, and in 1947 he married Cynthiabelle Blacke Gordon. They had no children. He died in Washington, D.C.

Smith lived during a difficult time in American history. All around him were the pervasive strictures and proscriptions of race, which reduced his cultural interactions and professional opportunities to a small fraction of what they could have otherwise been. No written record exists that illuminates the fears, anger, and frustrations that living in such a cultural milieu may have engendered in him. The record that does exist shows the noteworthy achievements of a modest man who wanted to bring the benefits of medical knowledge to a greater number of people, especially those who, like him, had been walled off by a system designed to frustrate their efforts to claim a better life. Undoubtedly he improved the practice of medicine.

• For a biographical sketch see Vivian Ovelton Sammon, *Blacks in Science and Medicine* (1990). For a summary of his professional life see "The President Elect," *Journal of the National Medical Association* 49 (Nov. 1957): 419–20. For an assessment of him by colleagues see W. Montague Cobb, "Relliford Stillmon Smith, M.D. 1889–1965," *Journal of the National Medical Association* 58 (Mar. 1966): 145–47.

BILLY SCOTT

SMITH, Richard (22 Mar. 1735–17 Sept. 1803), lawyer, diarist, and member of the Continental Congress, was born in Burlington, New Jersey, the son of Richard Smith, a Quaker merchant and member of the colonial assembly, and Abigail Smith. Richard Smith's older brother Samuel Smith was the treasurer and secretary of the council of New Jersey and a noted historian of the colony and state. Richard Smith received his schooling from tutors and at a Quaker school. As a young adult he studied law with Joseph Galloway in Philadelphia, Pennsylvania. In about 1760 he was admitted to the bar in New Jersey and held office in Burlington as either recorder of the town or clerk of the county. In 1762 he married Elizabeth Rodman, with whom he had five children. Smith later served as a member of the New Jersey Assembly.

In 1768, as a result of the Treaty of Fort Stanwix, by which representatives of the Iroquois Confederacy ceded a 69,000-acre tract of land between the Susquehanna and Mohawk rivers in central New York (now the southern part of Otsego County), Smith and a group of other speculators received large portions of land. With Robert Wells and several other associates, Smith visited the tract in 1769. He kept a detailed journal of the trip, including observations on the people and geography of the valleys of the Hudson, Mohawk, Susquehanna, and Delaware rivers. He was especially attentive to the quality of the soil and the timber, the extent of settlement, prices for land and for goods, and the diversity of wildlife. Between 1769 and 1783 Smith visited the area three more times and helped promote settlement there. In 1773 he built a house, called "Smith Hall," on his part of the tract, which comprised 4,000 acres on both sides of the Otsdawa Creek in what is now the town of Laurens.

In 1774 Smith was elected as one of five delegates from New Jersey to the First Continental Congress. He was reelected twice and served in Congress until 1776. During this time he kept an unusually detailed diary of the workings of the Congress, covering the proceedings from 12 September to 1 October 1775 and from 12 December 1775 to 30 March 1776. His diary is generally considered one of the richest sources on the Continental Congress and contains several pieces of information not available in any other record of the proceedings.

Possibly because of Burlington's largely Loyalist population, Smith was one of the more conservative members of the Congress. He signed the conciliatory "olive branch" petition to King George III in 1775 and never openly favored complete independence from Great Britain. Less than a month before the signing of the Declaration of Independence, Smith, citing poor health, resigned from Congress. He was quickly replaced by a delegation that was far more sympathetic to the cause of independence. In the fall of 1776 Smith was elected New Jersey's state treasurer. He resigned from that position early the following year and spent the rest of his life in retirement.

In 1790 Smith moved from New Jersey and made his permanent home in Smith Hall, where he lived until 1799. During this time his son, Richard R. Smith, became the first sheriff of the new Otsego County, New York. In 1799 the elder Smith moved to Philadelphia. He died in Natchez, Mississippi, while making a tour of the Mississippi delta in 1803.

Smith's fame is based on two remarkable writings, the journals he kept while touring New York's major river valleys and serving in the Continental Congress. Both documents remain vital for the study of colonial New York and the coming of the American Revolution.

• The journal Smith kept while traveling in present-day Otsego County was edited with a useful but brief biographical foreword by F. W. Halsey, *A Tour of Four Great Rivers* (1906). Smith's diary of the Continental Congress is in the Library of Congress. It was published, along with a biographical sketch, "The Diary of Richard Smith in the Continental Congress, 1775–1776," in the *American Historical Review* 1 (Jan. and Apr. 1896). R. M. Smith, *The Burlington Smiths* (1877), contains useful information on Smith's family background.

THADDEUS RUSSELL

SMITH, Richard Penn (13 Mar. 1799–12 Aug. 1854), lawyer and playwright, was born in Philadelphia, the son of William Moore Smith and Ann Rudulph. Smith's father, an attorney, enjoyed writing poetry, and he did his best to raise his son to appreciate the literary arts. As a teenager Smith studied at John Johnson's school at Huntingdon, Pennsylvania. In 1818 he returned to Philadelphia to study law in the law office of William Rawle. He was admitted to the bar three years later.

About 1821 Smith began making literary contributions to the *Union*. A series of moral literary essays entitled *The Plagiary* was published, and in 1822 he wrote a biography of Francis Hopkinson for John Sanderson's *Biography of the Signers of the Declaration of Independence*. In late 1822 he bought the Philadelphia newspaper the *Aurora*, later merging it with the *Franklin Gazette* in 1824. But after he grew weary of editorial responsibilities, he sold the paper in 1827 and resumed his law practice.

Although Smith devoted a great deal of time to practicing law, he never lost interest in writing. Greatly attracted to theater, he tried his hand at writing dramas. Between 1825 and 1835 he wrote twenty plays. The fact that fifteen of these works were produced attests to the popularity of his theatrical endeavors. As a dramatist, Smith was more an adaptor than an innovator. He relied a great deal on foreign models; for example, five of his twenty plays were inspired by French sources. During this period of literary and political nationalism, Smith crafted his adaptations in such a way that his foreign characters expressed American democratic ideals, thus appealing to an American audience.

His first dramatic compositions, although never acted, were *The Pelican* (1825), a farce, and *The Divorce* (1825), a romantic comedy. The latter play, based in part on Thomas Dekker's *The Honest Whore*, was later produced as *The Deformed* in 1830. His first acted play, *Quite Correct*, was staged at the Chestnut Street Theater on 27 May 1828. This comedy owes its existence to an English story by Theodore Hook and a French comedy *L'Hôtel garni* by Désaugiers and Gentil. In 1829 Smith made use of American history in his *The Eighth of January*, a melodramatic portrayal of the battle of New Orleans. The play, an adaptation of *Le Maréchal de Luxembourg* (1812) by Frédéric and Boirie, celebrates Jackson's victory at New Orleans and his victory in the presidential election of 1828. The Chestnut Street Theater audience applauded the drama's

central message: "popular" government was better than "upper-class" rule. Smith wrote two additional plays dealing with American history: *William Penn* (1829), which was acted but not printed, and *The Triumph at Plattsburg* (1830).

Smith's most successful play was the tragedy *Caius Marius*, produced in 1831. Written for Edwin Forrest, the play employs a Roman setting to express an American notion: democracy must defeat oligarchy. Quite popular with critics and audiences, the play (like others by Smith) has not survived in manuscript, owing, in part, to Forrest's insistence that, to prevent rival companies from producing them, plays intended for Forrest's use not be published. Although frequently weak in the areas of plot and characterization, Smith's plays represent the work of a playwright who experimented with numerous dramatic forms including romantic comedy and tragedy, historical plays, melodrama, and farce. His works were quite popular and drew praise from both critics and audiences.

Smith also wrote a novel, *The Forsaken* (1831), a few tales, and some poetry. Some scholars believe that Smith penned the 1836 *Col. Crockett's Exploits and Adventures in Texas*, a work allegedly written by Davy Crockett prior to his death at the Alamo. More than 10,000 readers in the United States purchased copies of this popular work, and the book also did well in England when it was published there in 1837.

Smith married twice. He wed his first wife, Elinor Matilda Blodget, a cousin, in 1823. They had five children, only one surviving to maturity. After his wife's death in 1834, Smith in 1836 married Isabella Stratton Knisell, and the couple had five children. In 1839 Smith and his second wife hosted a dinner party at which William Evans Burton introduced Edgar Allan Poe to Philadelphia's affluent citizens. For the most part, Smith spent the last eighteen years of his life enjoying retirement. He died at his home outside Philadelphia.

• The Historical Society of Pennsylvania in Philadelphia houses a large collection of Smith's papers. Some biographical information appears in H. W. Smith, ed., *The Miscellaneous Works of the Late Richard Penn Smith* (1856), and B. W. McCullough, *The Life and Writings of Richard Penn Smith* (1917). See also Arthur Hobson Quinn, *A History of the American Drama from the Beginning to the Civil War* (1923). An obituary is in the Philadelphia *Daily Pennsylvanian*, 14 Aug. 1854.

MICHAEL L. BURDUCK

SMITH, Robert (14 Jan. 1722–11 Feb. 1777), architect and carpenter, was born in Lugton, Midlothian, Scotland, the son of John Smith, a baxter or baker, and Martha Lawrie. The Smiths were poor tenants of the duchess of Buccleuch, whose family was prominent in the region southeast of Edinburgh. It is not known where Smith served his apprenticeship. He seems to have arrived in Philadelphia by late 1748, just a few months after the death of Scottish architect William Adam by whom he could have been trained, and after a possible stay in London. But whatever his technical background may have been, Smith's advanced abilities as a designer and builder quickly put him at the forefront of his trades. By the following spring, Smith had become chief carpenter for Pennsylvania governor James Hamilton in the completion of his great country house called "Bush Hill" (1749–1751) northwest of the city. In February 1749 Smith was selected to design and erect with fellow carpenter Gunning Bedford the Second Presbyterian Church (1750–1752) at Third and Arch Streets. This significant departure from local church architecture was noted by Benjamin Franklin as a "capacious and very elegant Meeting-house." From that point forward, Smith received commissions to design and/or build most of the principal structures erected in rapidly expanding Philadelphia. He married Esther Jones in December 1749; they had five children.

Between 1750 and 1775 Smith provided plans for eight more churches in the greater Philadelphia area, three of which he also helped to construct. In these structures he incorporated a roof system of long-span trusses introduced from English pattern books that made possible column-free auditoriums accommodating large congregations. Of his nine ecclesiastical works, Zion Lutheran Church (1766–1769) at Fourth and Cherry Streets was acclaimed as the largest house of worship in British North America. It was also one of the most richly ornamented and finished churches undertaken by Smith. The soaring steeple at Christ Church (1753–1754), designed and erected by Smith, was much admired, as was St. Peter's Church (1758–1761) on Society Hill. Both of these works remain in well-preserved condition. Smith's other city church commissions included St. Paul's (1760–1761) and Third Presbyterian, known as "Old Pine" (1767–1768), as well as a steeple added to the Second Presbyterian Church (1762–1763).

Smith undertook a large volume of work on public buildings, including the College of Philadelphia (later the University of Pennsylvania) at its campus on Fourth Street below Arch Street. His projects there included remodeling an existing meeting house to accommodate classrooms and lecture halls (1750–1755) as well as erecting a three-story dormitory (1762–1763) and a residence for the provost (1774–1776). Among Smith's other public commissions were the east wing of the Pennsylvania Hospital (1755–1756), the "Bettering House" or public alms and work house (1766–1767), Carpenters' Hall (1770–1774), and the Walnut Street Prison (1773–1774), a huge brick-vaulted, fireproof structure that faced the State House yard.

Private houses for the affluent as well as the working class also constituted a significant part of Smith's business, including a mansion (1764–1765) for Benjamin Franklin, located in a courtyard off Market Street. In 1771 Smith acquired the whole tract of land fronting on the north side of Spruce Street from Fourth to Fifth Streets. The parcel was divided into seventeen smaller lots, and several brick houses were built by him, his son John, and his carpenter son-in-law William Williams. He also erected five new houses on Second Street, along with some stores (1773–1774). Through his membership in the Carpenters' Company, he was often called on to measure and evaluate the finished work of other craftsmen in order to settle accounts.

In the field of what was later called structural engineering, Smith was a pioneer. In 1769 he presented to the Pennsylvania Assembly a model and plan for an arched truss, multiple-span covered bridge to carry Market Street westward over the Schuylkill River. Unfortunately, the assembly tabled the proposal. His advanced designs for long-span truss roof systems incorporated innovative uses of iron straps and bolts that improved the performance of British design prototypes.

Besides such extensive work in his home city, Smith designed Nassau Hall (1754–1756)—one of the largest American buildings of its day—and the President's House (1757–1758) at Princeton. Other commissions included the Hospital for the Mad & Insane (1771) at Williamsburg, Virginia, known later as the Eastern State Hospital. He also provided plans for Christ Church (1769) in Shrewsbury, New Jersey; a new stone Presbyterian meeting house (1769) at Carlisle, Pennsylvania; St. Peter's Church (1771) in Freehold, New Jersey; and quite probably the preliminary designs for Rhode Island College (1770), now Brown University in Providence.

Smith materially supported American independence. At the time of his death in Philadelphia, he was involved in the construction of military barracks at Billingsport, New Jersey, and was working with Benjamin Franklin on wartime defenses along the Delaware River. His sunken timber chevaux-de-frises effectively delayed the occupation of Philadelphia by the British as their ships could not pass the blockade. He left behind real property and other personal assets appraised at the sizable sum of £10,642. Smith was a member of the St. Andrew's Society (1752), the Masonic Lodge (c. 1752), and the American Philosophical Society (1768) and owned a public house.

An obituary in the *Pennsylvania Evening Post* (13 Feb. 1777) commented that "by the death of this worthy and ingenious man, the public have sustained a very heavy loss. . . . Several public buildings in this city, and its environs, are ornaments of his great abilities." The drawings of Robert Smith were still valued highly enough in 1795 for a selection of them to be displayed in an exhibition held that year by the Columbianum or American Academy of Painting, Sculpture and Architecture, the first American school of the arts founded the year before. Yet only two rough drawings from Smith's hand have survived. Owen Biddle, author of *The Young Carpenters' Assistant* published in Philadelphia in 1805, noted the design of the Christ Church steeple "for the justness of its proportions, simplicity and symmetry of its parts equal if not superior in beauty to any Steeple of the spire kind, either in Europe or America." No other individual so fully influenced the physical appearance of what was then the largest city in colonial North America.

• Smith's career has been discussed in several articles, the most informative of which are Charles E. Peterson, "Robert Smith, Philadelphia Builder-Architect: From Dalkeith to Princeton," in *Scotland and America in the Age of Enlightenment*, ed. Richard B. Sher and Jeffrey R. Smitten (1990), pp. 275–99; Charles E. Peterson, "Notes on Robert Smith, Architect of Carpenters' Hall," in *Historic Philadelphia from the Founding until the Early Nineteenth Century*, ed. Luther P. Eisenhart, issued as vol. 43, pt. 1, of the Transactions of the American Philosophical Society (1953), pp. 119–23; and Charles E. Peterson, "Philadelphia Carpentry According to Palladio," in *Building by the Book 3*, ed. Mario di Valmarana (1990), pp. 1–39. See also Francis James Dallett, "The Family of Mrs. Robert Smith," in *Pennsylvania Genealogical Magazine*, vol. 33 (1984), pp. 307–23, and Beatrice B. Garvan, "Robert Smith (1722–1777)," in *Philadelphia: Three Centuries of American Art* (1976), pp. 31–32.

CHARLES E. PETERSON

SMITH, Robert (14 Aug. 1732–28 Oct. 1801), the first Episcopal bishop of South Carolina, was born in Worstead, Norfolk County, England, the son of Stephen Smith, a herdsman, and Hannah Press. Smith was admitted to Gonville and Caius College at Cambridge University as a sizar on 30 June 1749. He received a B.A. in 1754 and was ordained as a priest by the bishop of Ely on 21 December 1756.

Assisted by his patron, William Mason, a member of Parliament, Smith received an offer to become assistant rector of St. Philip's Parish in Charles Town, South Carolina. He accepted and arrived in the colony on 3 November 1757. St. Philip's Church was an impressive brick structure with an eighty-foot steeple and at that time the only Anglican church in Charles Town. Its Sunday services often attracted more than 500 people. When his predecessor resigned in February 1759, Smith became the rector. A few months later, he married Elizabeth Paget, a wealthy heiress possessed of "Brabant Plantation," which covered 3,600 acres in nearby St. Thomas Parish. Still in his twenties, Smith was in a position to become a leading figure in the genteel society of low-country South Carolina.

Smith quickly won the respect and affection of both his parishioners and his fellow clergymen, often giving temporary service in nearby parishes and aiding their incumbents in other ways. Without official status, he functioned as a leader among the twenty or so clergymen in the colony. He was a founding member of the Society for the Relief of the Widows and Orphans of the Clergy of the Church of England that was organized in Charles Town in 1762. In addition to his clerical duties at St. Philip's, he also supervised the Charles Town Negro School, an Anglican institution that had been founded in 1743 and continued in operation until 1768, when its slave teacher was unable to continue his duties.

In 1768 Smith returned to England because of illness and remained until 1770. His first wife died the following year, leaving him her property. Three years later he married Sarah Shubrick, who died in 1779, survived by a daughter. At a later date, he married Anna Maria Tilghman of Maryland, who bore him four children.

During the American Revolution, Smith distinguished himself as a partisan of the American cause. Only a quarter of the Anglican clergymen in South Carolina were loyal to the mother country, but one of them created a sensation in August 1774 by giving a sermon that belittled democratic politics and the colonial point of view. By contrast, Smith delivered a patriotic sermon in St. Philip's on 17 February 1775 that was attended by the colonial assembly and the revolutionary committee and for which he received the formal thanks of the assembly. During the siege of Charles Town in 1780, Smith continued to use his pulpit in support of the American effort, and he also served as a common soldier with a musket on his shoulder. When the city fell, he was among the local leaders exiled to Philadelphia. During the next few years, he served St. Paul's Parish on the eastern shore of Maryland on a temporary basis and also functioned as the first chaplain general of the Southern Department of the Continental army, a position that led to his later membership in the Society of the Cincinnati.

Returning to South Carolina in 1783, Smith took up his duties at St. Philip's, which had lost its public support and responsibilities when the Church of England was disestablished in 1778. Adjusting to the new circumstances, he opened a successful academy in the rectory. In 1785 Smith was one of a distinguished group of trustees who hoped to create the College of Charleston, and the following year he became president of the board. He also loaned the college money to assist it in renovating suitable buildings. In 1789 Smith was awarded a doctor of divinity degree by the University of Pennsylvania. That same year, the sixty pupils in his school became the first students of the College of Charleston, and Smith became its principal, or chief academic official, a position he held until 1 January 1798.

Smith also played an important role in the organization of the Protestant Episcopal church, an activity complicated by the fact that the South Carolina laity were accustomed to controlling their own church and deeply suspicious of episcopal authority. The South Carolina Episcopal Convention elected Smith to attend the national convention in 1785 but also chose four prominent laymen to go with him. Unable to attend that year, he was at the convention in 1786 and opposed the efforts of Bishop Samuel Seabury (1729–1796), who had been elected by the Connecticut clergy and ordained by Scottish bishops, to exercise control over the nascent church as a whole. Later, however, Smith helped to bring about a reconciliation with Seabury that united Episcopalians in the Protestant Episcopal church, an organization that gave considerable power to the laity. Smith's own elevation to the episcopate came about in part because the South Carolina convention opposed the veto power granted to the House of Bishops in the general convention. Fearing that they might be forced to leave the national organization, the Carolinians wanted their own bishop so that he could ordain new clergymen. The state convention nominated Robert Smith as a candidate for bishop on 10 February 1795, and he was consecrated at Christ Church in Philadelphia on 13 September of that year.

Bishop Smith exemplified the practical piety of the Church of England and its close relationship with the upper class. He was an important religious leader in South Carolina for more than three decades, an outstanding Anglican clerical patriot, a founder of the Protestant Episcopal church, the first bishop of South Carolina, and a major figure in the creation of the College of Charleston. He died in Charleston and was buried in St. Philip's Cemetery.

• The most complete account of Robert Smith's life is Albert S. Thomas, "Robert Smith: First Bishop of South Carolina," *Historical Magazine of the Protestant Episcopal Church* 15 (1946): 15–29. Still useful is Frederick Dalcho, *An Historical Account of the Protestant Episcopal Church in South Carolina. . . .* (1820), which also contains the journals of the state conventions. See also S. Charles Bolton, *Southern Anglicanism: The Church of England in Colonial South Carolina* (1982); J. H. Easterby, *A History of the College of Charleston* (1935); Frederick V. Mills, Sr., *Bishops by Ballot: An Eighteenth-Century Ecclesiastical Revolution* (1978); and John Venn, *Biographical History of Gonville and Caius College* (1897).

S. CHARLES BOLTON

SMITH, Robert (3 Nov. 1757–26 Nov. 1842), U.S. secretary of state and secretary of the navy, was born in Carlisle, Pennsylvania, the son of John Smith, a merchant, and Mary Buchanan. When he was two, he moved with his family to Baltimore. During the Revolution he served briefly in the Continental army as a private, seeing action at Brandywine, but he graduated from the College of New Jersey (now Princeton University) with the class of 1781. After the war he studied law in Baltimore and was admitted to the bar. Baltimore emerged in these years as an important American port, and Smith took up the practice of admiralty law, aided by good family connections. In 1790 he married Margaret Smith. The couple had eight children.

Like his brother, General Samuel Smith (1752–1839), Robert Smith became active in local and state politics, enjoying a reputation for energy and amiability. He enthusiastically supported ratification of the Constitution and was a presidential elector in 1788. Between 1789 and 1800 he served several terms in the Maryland House of Delegates and was a member of the state senate from 1793 to 1795. He sat on the Baltimore City Council from 1798 to 1801 and was offered, but rejected, a seat on the state supreme court.

Smith seems to have been slower than his brother to shed his Federalist allegiances, but with the election of Thomas Jefferson as president in 1800 his career in national politics began. Jefferson offered the post of secretary of the navy to Samuel Smith, already a power to be reckoned with in the Republican party, but Samuel Smith refused to serve on anything but a temporary basis. Jefferson's bias against the navy disinclined others from taking the post, and after several rejections Jefferson actually joked with his secretary of the Treasury, Albert Gallatin, that he thought he might have to advertise for a secretary. After four months of searching, Jefferson finally offered the post to Robert Smith, who accepted. Smith served in the Navy Department from 27 July 1801 to 7 March 1809, though with a curious interlude in 1805. Shortly before Jefferson's second inauguration Smith asked if he might have the post of attorney general, recently vacated by Levi Lincoln. Jefferson agreed and at the same time nominated Jacob Crowninshield of Massachusetts to replace Smith at the Navy Department. The Senate confirmed both men, but then, to Jefferson's surprise, Crowninshield turned the job down. Smith gracefully agreed to stay on as secretary of the navy and for a short time also served as attorney general until replaced by John Breckinridge. In the confusion of events Smith was never actually reconfirmed as secretary.

On cordial terms with Jefferson and possessing considerable skills at organization, Smith was able to serve the nation well as secretary of the navy despite being faced with some difficult dilemmas. For reasons of economy, Jefferson and Gallatin were anxious to reduce the size of the navy, yet the depredations of North African states on shipping seemingly made it necessary for the United States to float a considerable naval presence in the Mediterranean. Though he once insisted to Jefferson that he had no taste for department details, Smith in fact ably handled an enormous amount of them, ranging from buying whiskey (instead of rum) for frigates to the dispatch of ships during the war with Tripoli. Indeed, it was with the Mediterranean operations against the Barbary corsairs that Smith made his most important contributions. Through his efforts the department was able to establish and maintain a fairly complex logistical network that allowed U.S. vessels to stay on station, eventually forcing the Tripolitans to make peace.

In the aftermath of the Tripolitan War, Jefferson and Gallatin again looked to naval reduction, despite the maritime disruptions occasioned by the Napoleonic wars. The president ordered the laying up of large vessels and advocated the building of small gunboats as an inexpensive means of coastal defense. Smith opposed the policy and tended to agree with the naval establishment in finding the "Jeffs," as the boats were often called, puny and pitiful. Still, he remained discreetly mute, as the efforts he made on the navy's behalf had already antagonized Gallatin. Smith similarly disliked but cooperated in the imposition of the embargo in 1807. Ironically, the gunboats that he had opposed became useful in enforcing it.

After the inauguration of James Madison in 1809, Smith again found himself holding a cabinet post for which he had not been the first choice. Madison had wished to appoint Gallatin secretary of state, but Gallatin's enemies, including Samuel Smith, opposed his appointment. Unwilling to alienate the Smiths, Madison instead appointed Robert Smith secretary of state, leaving Gallatin as secretary of the Treasury. The arrangement would prove most unhappy.

Smith quickly forged a seemingly auspicious agreement with David Erskine, Britain's minister in Washington, by which England would end the wartime restrictions it had imposed on American commerce with Europe and the United States would lift its retaliatory prohibition on trade with Britain. However, British officials repudiated the agreement, insisting Erskine had exceeded his instructions, and the minister's successor seemed little disposed to make a similar arrangement. Madison thereafter grasped at Napoleon Bonaparte's vague assurances that he would end France's interference with American trade and subsequently reimposed a ban on trade with England. Smith resisted so quick an embrace of French blandishments and began making indiscreet comments at the expense of the administration—sometimes to representatives of foreign governments. In the meantime the Smiths' bickering with Gallatin had escalated to the point that Gallatin was making poorly supported charges that the brothers had misused official funds while Robert was secretary of the navy. Gallatin eventually threatened to resign, forcing Madison to choose between Smith and him. Madison, a former secretary of state who had frequently felt himself obliged to compose or rewrite Smith's official communications, had little difficulty in making the choice. He called Smith to the White House in March 1811 and chided him both for criticizing the administration and for alleged inefficiency in the performance of his duties. The president insisted Smith resign, offering him, in place of the State Department, a diplomatic posting in Russia. After some hesitation, Smith declined and returned to Baltimore. Madison appointed James Monroe in his stead, which allowed the president to craft a politically useful reconciliation with his fellow Virginian.

Bitter, Smith in June 1811 published *Address to the People of the United States*, in which he stressed and, contemporaries and some historians contended, exaggerated his opposition to the administration's tilt toward France. He also accused Madison of financial improprieties while secretary of state. This intemperate attack further soured Smith's political fortunes. As Henry B. Adams ungenerously concluded, "Never again did this genial gentleman sun himself in the rays of Executive power, or recover the smallest share of influence."

Back in Baltimore, Smith resumed the practice of law, participated in a variety of agricultural and religious organizations, including the American Bible Society, and managed his extensive investments and landholdings. He also taught law at the University of Maryland and from 1813 to 1815 served as the school's figurehead provost. He died in Baltimore.

• A small collection of Robert Smith Papers is at the Maryland Historical Society in Baltimore, and some material is in the Samuel Smith Papers at the University of Virginia library. Official communications are in the Records of the Department of State and Records of the Office of the Secretary of the Navy at the National Archives. See also the volumes of *American State Papers* (1832–1861) devoted to foreign relations and naval affairs. A brief biography of Smith is in Richard Harrison, *Princetonians 1776–1783: A Biographical Dictionary* (1981). The best sources for Smith as secretary of the navy are Frank L. Owsley, "Robert Smith," in *American Secretaries of the Navy*, vol. 1, ed. Paolo E. Coletta (1980), and Charles O. Paullin, "Naval Administration under Secretaries of the Navy Smith, Hamilton and Jones, 1801–1814," U.S. Naval Institute, *Proceedings* 32 (1906): 1289–1328. His tenure as secretary of state is discussed at length in the essay by Charles Tansill in *The American Secretaries of State and Their Diplomacy*, vol. 3, ed. S. F. Bemis (1927).

WILLIAM M. FOWLER, JR.

SMITH, Robert Sidney (13 Feb. 1877–20 Oct. 1935), cartoonist, known as Sidney Smith, was born in Bloomington, Illinois, the son of Thomas H. Smith, a dentist, and Frances A. Shafer. His father hoped he would become a dentist, but Smith, who had sold some drawings to the *Bloomington Sunday Eye* while in high school, wanted to be an artist. He left Illinois Wesleyan University before completing his first year and went on a one-man lecture tour, illustrating humorous chalk talks at Sunday schools and saloons throughout the Midwest and beyond. After a year or so of this itinerant life, usually riding the rods under freight trains to get from one engagement to the next, Smith found a position in the art department of the *Indianapolis News*, and soon he was head of the department.

Like many newspapermen at the time, Smith moved around, taking jobs at a succession of papers in Philadelphia, Pittsburgh, and Toledo. While at the *Toledo News-Bee*, he developed his first continuing comic character, a goat named Buck Nix, who first appeared on the sports page in an "ear" (a box on either side of the section's first-page heading) from which he delivered a daily wisecrack. When Smith went to the *Chicago Examiner* in 1908, he took the goat with him. When he joined the staff of the *Chicago Tribune* three years later, the goat emerged once more, this time as Old Doc Yak in a comic strip of that name. In 1917 Smith started on the road to fame and fortune with *The Gumps*, the first of a series of celebrated comic strips nurtured by Joseph Medill Patterson, co-owner (with his cousin Robert McCormick) of the *Tribune*.

In conceiving the strip, Patterson harkened back to the novels he had written as a young man under the influence of Theodore Dreiser's social realism. The strip would focus humorously on an average lower middle-class family, whose aspirations and adventures would mirror the ordinary ambitions and appetites of the *Tribune*'s readers as Patterson imagined them to be. In christening this family, Patterson employed a slightly derisive term he and his sister had applied as children to loudmouth adults. In Andy Gump's case, the name was a self-fulfilling prophecy. Patterson picked Smith to do *The Gumps*, and he turned out to be an inspired choice. Launching the new strip on 12 February 1917, he quickly warmed to his task and was soon soaping his stories with every sudsy bubble of melodrama he could lay his pen to, but the people remained unequivocally ordinary people.

"I wanted everyday things to happen to them," Smith said in an interview in *American Magazine*. "I was not so much concerned about making them terribly funny, but I did want them to be *true*. I thought I'd get what I wanted if I could draw something which a wife would read and hand to her husband with the remark, 'There, that's *you!*'" The people with whom Smith wanted readers to identify were husband Andy and wife Min and son Chester (about eight years old). Although undistinguished in social status, the bald, long-nosed Andy Gump was a distinctive physical specimen: he had an elongated neck and no chin. Later the cast expanded to include a fabulously wealthy uncle from Australia named Bim, whose fortune Andy hoped Chester would inherit.

The Gumps was not only the first comic strip to emphasize the events of ordinary daily living, it was the first comic strip to carry a narrative forward from day to day in a seriously suspenseful way. Other early strips had burlesqued the serial genre with outrageously comic cliffhangers, but the Gumps took themselves in earnest. The continuity was at first largely thematic: a week's strips would all deal with the same subject. Andy has mother-in-law troubles for days on end, goes fishing on his vacation, and rails in endless monologue against the minor evils and irritations of the world, particularly those that festered in the middle-class mind, such as taxes, waste in government, the rising cost of living, and women's fashions. Then in February 1921, Uncle Bim falls into the clutches of the Widow Zander, a gold-digging matron whose marital intentions for Bim threaten Andy's hopes, and the strip began a strong narrative that continued from day to day, each day's installment necessarily ending suspensefully with the implicit question, What will happen next?

By then, the popularity of *The Gumps* was manifest on every hand. People requested the *Chicago Tribune* at newsstands by calling for "the Gump paper"; the Board of Trade in Minneapolis suspended operations for a few minutes during the busiest part of the day in order to give brokers a chance to read the early editions of the afternoon paper, where they could find out if Bim escaped the Widow Zander. (He did.) Suspenseful continuity as a device for attracting and holding an audience was convincingly established. In recognition of the strip's value as a circulation-building feature, in 1922 Smith was given a million-dollar contract—$100,000 a year for ten years.

Smith's sketchy and crosshatched artwork was crude by the standards of the next generation of comic strips, but his hasey style suited the often seamy ambience of his stories with their melodramatic plots, bathetic perils, and purple prose. Assisted by artist Stanley Link and writer Blair Walliser, Smith played on his readers' addiction mercilessly. He milked the numerous crises in the strip for every last dribble of suspense, often slowing narrative progress for days to prolong the agony of anticipation. One of his most popular characters, Mary Gold, took more than a week to die in 1929. It was another first for Smith; Gold was the first major comic strip character to die. And her death precipitated a deluge of protest by mail and telephone, an overwhelming reaction that testified to the popularity of the comics with an authority difficult to dispute.

The characters were extensively merchandised as toys and games and novelties, and Universal produced several silent two-reelers of *The Gumps* between 1923 and 1928. The immense popularity of *The Gumps* helped establish the Chicago Tribune Syndicate when out-of-town papers began requesting to buy the strip for their readers.

Smith enjoyed his role as the first million-dollar cartoonist. A brazen playboy, he bought a spacious estate at Lake Geneva, Wisconsin (where he hosted an annual summer party for hundreds of guests), maintained an elaborate wardrobe, and drove an expensive, powerful automobile. Proud of his physique, he exercised regularly, swimming, running, and boxing. He married twice: first to Gertrude C. Craddock (with whom he had two children), then to Kathryn Imogen Eulette. He died tragically early in the morning the day after signing a new three-year contract for $150,000 a year. Driving to his farm in Shirland, Illinois, after an all-night celebratory party at Lake Geneva, Smith collided head-on with another auto. Smith was killed instantly; the other driver recovered. *The Gumps* was continued by Gus Edson until 1959.

• The most complete biography of Smith appears in the introductory matter of *Sidney Smith's The Gumps*, ed. Herb Galewitz (1974). Other details are in William E. Berchtold, "Men of Comics," *New Outlook*, Apr. 1935, pp. 38–39; "Sidney Smith and His 'Gumps'," an interview by Neil M. Clark, *American Magazine*, Mar. 1923, pp. 18–20, 72, 74, 76, 78; Stephen Becker, *Comic Art in America* (1959); and obituaries in *Newsweek*, 2 Nov. 1935, and the *New York Times* and the *Chicago Tribune*, 21 Oct. 1935. Two early collections of his popular comic strip were published, *Book of the Gumps* (1918) and *Andy Gump: His Life Story* (1924).

ROBERT C. HARVEY

SMITH, Samuel (13 Dec. 1720–13 July 1776), historian and colonial official, was born in Burlington, New Jersey, the son of Richard Smith, an assemblyman and merchant, and Abigail Rapier. The Smiths were a Yorkshire Quaker family, one of whom, Samuel's great-uncle John, had been granted an original town lot in Burlington by the London Proprietors. As a young man Samuel was associated for a time with his father in the West India Company and lived in Philadelphia as well as Burlington. He settled in Burlington in the family town house and his nearby estate, "Hickory Grove." In 1741 he married Jane Kirkbride; the couple had four children.

Educated privately, Smith early developed a lifelong interest in colonial history. He collected over many years original letters and documents, which together form the nucleus of his pioneering study *The History of the Colony of Nova-Caesaria, or New Jersey*

... *to the Year 1721* ... (1765). The title employed the ancient name of the English Channel Isle of Jersey, "Caesar's Isle" or "Caesaria," as used by Charles II in his grant to George Carteret from the Isle of Jersey and John Berkeley in 1664. Smith's collected material on Pennsylvania was used in *A History of Pennsylvania* by Robert Proud (1797–1798). Smith's material was published separately in 1913.

"An early example of the historian-activist" (Prince, p. 163), Smith "filled some of the most important public offices in the Province of New Jersey" (Sharp ed., p. vi). He was a member, and for a period secretary, of the King's Council. He was one of three commissioners who took charge of official seals for New Jersey documents during the absence in 1768 of Governor William Franklin. He later served as treasurer of West Jersey. He also is credited with originating efforts that led to the colonizing of New Jersey Indians at a settlement in Burlington County named Brotherton, the "first white-endowed Indian community" (Prince, p. 167). In 1757 Smith wrote a constitution for the "New Jersey Society for helping the Indians" and donated twenty pounds to the cause. In his *History of New Jersey* he describes the approximately three thousand acres of Brotherton encompassing a cedar swamp and saw mill as well as land suitable for hunting and fishing. Any persons except Indians caught cutting timber on the tract were to be fined forty shillings per tree. The entire tract was to be held "in trust for the use of the Indian natives who have or do reside in this colony south of Rariton, and their successors for ever" (p. 483). Efforts by the government and dedicated supporters such as Presbyterian John Brainard, superintendent of Brotherton, failed to keep the settlement going, however. According to historian Richard P. McCormick, by 1801 the last of the Lenape tribe had migrated to northern New York.

Smith is matter-of-fact in describing his history: "To a collection principally intended to consist of a plain state of facts, much need not be premised;" "nothing is aim'd at, more than a fair and candid representation" (preface, pp. xiii, xiv), but over the years the book's reputation has grown steadily. McCormick has called it "a remarkable work, still worthy of study" (p. 176), which "commands respect even today" (p. 101). As Carl E. Prince has written, Smith's history was a "political tract for the times. It provided a reformer's manual to guide the white man in dealing with the Indians and a political lesson in the pitfalls of English hegemony over the American colonies" (p. 176).

Smith's summary of complaints about royal governor Lord Cornbury's "underhand artifice" in dealing with the West Jersey assembly in 1708 presents a good example of what was his growing disaffection with English colonial rule: "That they [assemblymen] found it a great charge to the country, that juries and evidences were brought from remote parts of the province, to the supreme courts at Burlington and Amboy; that it was a great grievance that the practice of the law was so precarious, that innocent persons were prosecuted upon informations, and actions brought against several of the queen's [Queen Anne's] subjects, in which the gentlemen licensed to practise the law, were afraid to appear for them" (p. 350).

A keen eye for the details of nature and of Indian life animates many passages in Smith's history, for example, the following anecdote based on an incident that took place near Crosswicks in 1748:

An Indian hunting, discovered a large buck feeding, creeping to shoot, he heard something among the bushes, presently saw a panther with his eyes so intent on the buck, that he did not perceive him: the Indian watching his motions, observed, that while the buck had his head down to feed, the panther crept, but when he held it up, lay snug; he at last got unperceiv'd, within about twenty feet, and then making a desperate leap, fixed his talons in the buck's neck; after he had nearly kill'd him, he would cease for a minute, give a watchful look round, and then fall to shaking again; having done his work, and about to draw the carcass to a heap of leaves for future service, the Indian shot, and got both. (P. 503)

Rattlesnakes are often mentioned:

The rattle-snake, as the country settles thick, are but little known; many old inhabitants have never seen them alive: the mischief they have yet done, is inconsiderable, their power and opportunities considered: This is remarkable; they have an astonishing charm in their eyes; the venom of their bite is perhaps without comparison; yet their power is happily circumscribed in a way the most effectual, that is, by not having a will to mischief equal to the means, otherwise there would, in some places, scarcely have been any living among them. (Pp. 503–4)

One of the many previously unpublished documents in Smith's history is a letter from newly arrived John Crips to friend Henry Stacy, sent from Burlington in 1677, in which Crips writes: "Here is a good land enough lies void, would serve many thousands of families: and we think if they cannot live here, they can hardly live in any place in the world. . . . But for the country, in short, I like it very well; and I do believe, that this river of Delaware is as good a river as most in the world: It exceeds the river of Thames by many degrees" (p. 104).

Despite its obvious identification with the era and mindset of its author, Smith's history is nonetheless a valuable reference and source. Smith lived long enough to become aware of the signing of the Declaration of Independence in nearby Philadelphia. He died nine days later in Burlington. His history thus provides a useful record of colonial life as well as events leading up to the Revolution.

• Personal papers of Samuel Smith are in the manuscripts collection of the New Jersey Historical Society, Newark, and in the New Jersey Room of Alexander Library at Rutgers University. Smith's *The History of the Colony of Nova-Caesaria, or New-Jersey: Containing an Account of Its First Settlement, Progressive Improvements, the Original and Present Constitution, and Other Events, to the Year 1721. With Some*

Particulars Since; and a Short View of Its Present State was printed and sold by James Parker in Burlington and by David Hall in Philadelphia in 1765; the reprint edition, published by William S. Sharp (1877), contains a two-page biography of Smith by his great-nephew John Jay Smith. Also see Carl E. Prince, "Samuel Smith's *History of Nova-Caesaria*," in *The Colonial Legacy*, vol. 2, *Some Eighteenth-Century Commentators*, ed. Lawrence H. Leder (1971). Among biographical sketches is that by William E. Schermerhorn in *The History of Burlington* (1927). R. Morris Smith, *The Burlington Smiths, a Family History* (1877), contains useful information. Many histories of New Jersey mention Smith's book, such as Richard P. McCormick's *New Jersey from Colony to State, 1609–1789*, rev. ed. (1981).

DORA JEAN ASHE

SMITH, Samuel (27 July 1752–22 Apr. 1839), soldier and politician, was born in Carlisle, Pennsylvania, the son of John Smith, a successful merchant, and Mary Buchanan. The family relocated to Baltimore in 1760, and their personal wealth enabled Smith to attend private academies in Elkton, Maryland, and Newark, Delaware. Intent upon a commercial career, the young man was apprenticed in his father's firm both in America and England, and he spent several years traveling abroad.

Following the onset of the American Revolution, Smith returned and received a captain's commission in Colonel William Smallwood's Maryland regiment. He fought conspicuously at White Plains, Valley Forge, Brandywine, and Monmouth, rising to lieutenant colonel by 1777. In this capacity Smith distinguished himself in the defense of Fort Mifflin on the lower bank of the Delaware River. Commencing 24 October and for seven weeks thereafter, his garrison withstood the bombardment of a British naval squadron, thereby delaying an advance upon Philadelphia. Smith was wounded and evacuated on 10 November, but his heroic stand tied down British reinforcements that might have otherwise assisted General John Burgoyne at Saratoga; Burgoyne, deprived of such assistance, was forced to capitulate. For his efforts Smith received the Thanks of Congress and a sword from his native state. The following year he married Margaret Spear; they had eleven children. In 1779 Smith resigned his commission and returned to Baltimore to spend the balance of the war managing a privateer fleet.

Throughout the 1780s, Smith resumed his mercantile career; having made a fortune through land speculation, he became one of Baltimore's wealthiest citizens. He also maintained close ties to the Maryland militia and in 1791 commanded a detachment sent to quell the so-called Whisky Rebellion in western Pennsylvania. That same year Smith parlayed his wealth and prestige into an effective political campaign and gained election into the Maryland House of Delegates. In 1792 he further capitalized on his popularity by being elected to the U.S. House of Representatives for four consecutive terms. Nominally a Federalist, Smith broke with that party over the terms of the 1794 Jay Treaty, which required American assumption of British prerevolutionary debts in exchange for possession of northwestern posts. He thereupon struck up a liaison with the nascent Jeffersonian Republicans. With consummate skill, Smith welded together a political machine based upon his militia connections, local political societies, and influential friends among Baltimore's commercial elite. After 1798 his economic and political fortunes were secure.

Smith held Thomas Jefferson in high regard and campaigned vigorously on his behalf in 1800. When Jefferson and Burr gained identical numbers of electoral votes, the election passed to the House of Representatives, where Smith brokered a settlement giving the election to Jefferson. Consequently, he was appointed as the acting secretary of the navy and directed initial moves against the Tripolitan pirates. Smith served only a few months before using his influence to help his brother Robert, another Maryland politician, to become the official secretary. Smith then ran successfully for the U.S. Senate in 1803, serving two consecutive terms and, as a result of his rhetorical and legislative skill, functioning as president pro tempore. Smith was regarded as a Republican stalwart who supported Jefferson in difficult votes, such as the passage of the Embargo Act. However, he grew increasingly disillusioned by the foreign policies orchestrated by Secretary of State James Madison, and the latter's election to the presidency in 1809 only increased this estrangement.

Madison's ascension triggered a deliberate and dramatic shift in Smith's political outlook and behavior. Coming as he did from the commercial wing of the Republican party, he stridently opposed the president's southern, agrarian-based priorities. Furthermore, the two men harbored serious disagreements over international relations. Smith, an ardent nationalist, favored strong resistance to maritime harassment by England and France, while Madison preferred varying degrees of commercial restrictions. The president also believed that Smith and his brother Robert, whom he had appointed secretary of state, headed a cabal within Republican ranks to derail his policies. Open rupture occurred in 1810, when Madison dismissed Smith's brother from his cabinet and actively labored to defeat Smith's reelection to the Senate. Smith countered by tying up important legislation, such as the financial measures of Secretary of the Treasury Albert Gallatin, Macon's Bill No. 1, and the declaration of war against Great Britain. Antipathy between the two leaders and their respective factions split the Republican party and nearly paralyzed national policy.

The onset of the War of 1812 did little to improve relations between Smith and the president. Though stripped of patronage, Smith nonetheless retained his popularity with Maryland voters, as well as command of the Third Militia Division. Smith was present at the August 1814 debacle of Bladensburg, whereby a small British force routed a larger force of American militia and burned the capital, but he managed to extricate his men in good order and no stigma was attached to his command. Smith subsequently organized the defenses of Baltimore against a combined British land

and naval assault the following month. His troops closely engaged enemy forces under General Robert Ross at North Point on 11 September 1814 and, while driven back, prevented the enemy from storming the city. The death of Ross and the ensuing British withdrawal accorded Smith the status of national hero, and he was widely feted.

In 1816 Smith resumed his political career by winning three consecutive terms to the U.S. House of Representatives. He capped this success in 1822 by returning to the Senate, and he handily won reelection. In 1833 Smith concluded four decades of public service by resigning, although he continued on as the commander of militia forces. In 1835 he was called upon to restore order in the wake of rioting occasioned by the Maryland Bank failure, and, following the resignation of Jesse Hunt, he was elected mayor of Baltimore by popular acclamation. Smith easily won reelection and remained at city hall for an additional three years. He died in Baltimore following his second and final retirement.

Smith is remembered as one of Maryland's most popular and enduring politicians and an important personality of the early Republic. Regardless of party affiliation, he displayed considerable independence and did not always vote along strict ideological lines. His experience as a merchant induced him to support Federalist, defense-oriented legislation that led to programs like expansion of the navy, while his determined stand against the repressive Alien and Sedition Acts elevated him to the leadership ranks of the Republican party. Smith's longtime feud with Madison gave his political role a divisive quality, especially during the War of 1812, but his victory at Baltimore did much to revive national spirit and the flagging reputation of the American militia.

• Smith's manuscripts are in the Samuel Smith Papers and the William Tappan Collection at the Library of Congress Manuscripts Division; the Samuel Smith Letterbooks at the Maryland Historical Society; the State Papers at the Maryland State Archives, Annapolis; and the Samuel Smith Papers at the University of Virginia Library, Charlottesville. Smaller collections are at the Manuscript Library, Columbia University; the New England Historical and Genealogical Society, Boston; the Rosenbach Museum, Philadelphia; the Clements Library at the University of Michigan; and the Eisenhower Library at Johns Hopkins University. For biographical studies consult John S. Pancake, *Samuel Smith and the Politics of Business* (1971), and Frank Cassell, *Merchant Congressman in the Young Republic* (1971). Details on Smith's military career are amply covered in Walter Lord, *The Dawn's Early Light* (1972); Neil H. Swanson, *The Perilous Fight* (1945); and Joseph E. Whitehorne, *The Battle for Baltimore* (1997).

JOHN C. FREDRIKSEN

SMITH, Samuel Francis (21 Oct. 1808–16 Nov. 1895), editor, Baptist clergyman, and author, was born in Boston, Massachusetts, the son of Samuel Smith and Sarah Bryant. Young Smith was educated at both the Eliot School and the Boston Latin School, where he received the distinguished Franklin medal in 1825. At Harvard College, Smith became part of the famous class of 1829, which also included Oliver Wendell Holmes and James Freeman Clarke. Smith himself is commemorated in the reunion poem by Holmes titled "The Boys" with the lines:

> And there's a nice youngster of excellent pith:
> Fate tried to conceal him by naming him Smith!
> But he shouted a song for the brave and the free-
> Just read on his medal, "My Country, of Thee!"

During this period, Smith helped support his education by translating from the German *Conversations-Lexicon* a great number of articles for the *Encyclopedia Americana*, edited by Francis Leiber.

After finishing at Harvard, Smith entered Andover Theological Seminary, graduating in 1832. While studying at Andover, Smith was asked by his friend Lowell Mason, an early proponent of common school music education, either to translate the lyrics of some German songbooks into English or to supply new lyrics for the tunes. One such song, at the time unknown to Smith as the tune to the British anthem "God Save the King," was the basis of what became one of the most famous of American national hymns: "My Country, 'Tis of Thee." Originally five stanzas, the third was eventually removed to leave the four stanzas known today. Written in thirty minutes and stored away in a desk drawer for months before it was finally sent to Mason, the song was premiered on 4 July 1831 at a children's celebration in the Park Street Church of Boston. First published by Mason in *The Choir* (1832), it was published again four years later in *The Boston Academy* under its most widely known title, "America."

After graduating from Andover, Smith spent one year in Boston as an editor of the *Baptist Missionary Magazine*, which was created primarily to assist the work of pioneering Baptist missionary Adoniram Judson in Burma. Smith was then ordained on 12 February 1834 as the pastor of the First Baptist Church of Waterville, Maine. At the same time, he became a professor of modern languages at Waterville College (now Colby University), a position he held for eight years. In September of that year, Smith also married Mary White, the granddaughter of Dr. Hezekiah Smith, a chaplain during the revolutionary war and a friend of George Washington. Together they had six children, one of whom was Daniel Appleton White Smith, who later served as a missionary to Burma and as president of the Karen Baptist Theological Seminary in Rangoon.

In January 1842 Smith became the pastor of the First Baptist Church of Newton Center, Massachusetts, as well as the editor of the *Christian Review*, a quarterly publication that he directed until 1848. On 30 June 1854 he resigned his pastorate at Newton Center to become the editorial secretary of the American Baptist Missionary Union, a position he held for fifteen years. From 1875 to 1880, Smith traveled widely, visiting missionary stations in France, Spain, Italy,

Austria, Turkey, Greece, Sweden, Denmark, Burma, India, and Ceylon.

Through these varied career changes, Smith never ceased his literary ventures. His prose works include *Life of the Rev. Joseph Grafton* (1849), *Missionary Sketches* (1879), *History of Newton, Mass.* (1880), and *Rambles in Mission Fields* (1883), the last based on his missionary tours through Europe and India. His poetic works, none ever as widely known as "My Country, 'Tis of Thee," include the missionary hymn "The Morning Light Is Breaking" (1832), which was inspired by Judson's work in Burma, and "The Lone Star" (1868), which is commonly thought to have single-handedly saved the Telugu mission in Nellore, India. His works also include three collections of hymnology, both original and translated, including *Lyric Gems* (1843), *Rock of Ages* (1866), and *The Psalmist* (1843), with Baron Stow. *The Psalmist* became the standard Baptist hymnal for the next thirty years. His poetry was also collected in 1895 and appropriately entitled *Poems of Home and Country*.

In April 1895 the city of Boston held a public celebration to honor Smith for the writing of "America," which had by that time become a staple of hymnals and patriotic ceremonies. A bell tower was also erected in his honor at the First Baptist Church of Newton Center. Smith died on his way to Boston to fulfill a preaching commitment. Though his poetry and prose are little read today, Smith's remains secure in the words that are often considered the second national anthem of the United States:

> My country! 'tis of thee,
> Sweet land of liberty,
> Of thee I sing;
> Land where my fathers died;
> Land of the Pilgrim's pride;
> From ev'ry mountainside
> Let freedom ring.

• A few of Smith's papers are in the Library of Congress. Autobiographical information dealing with Smith is in *Poems of Home and Country* (1895). Biographical information is in Albert Edward Bailey, *The Gospel in Hymns: Backgrounds and Interpretations* (1950); Louis F. Benson, *Studies in Familiar Hymns*, vol. 1 (1903); Clint Bonner, *A Hymn Is Born* (1952); H. S. Burrage, *Baptist Hymn Writers and Their Hymns* (1888); William J. Reynolds, *Hymns of Our Faith* (1964); Reynolds, *Companion to Baptist Hymnal* (1976); and H. K. Rowe, *Tercentenary History of Newton* (1930). An obituary is in the *Boston Transcript*, 18 Nov. 1895.

P. KEITH GAMMONS

SMITH, Samuel Harrison (1772–1 Nov. 1845), journalist and banker, was born in Philadelphia, Pennsylvania, the son of Jonathan Smith, a merchant, and Susannah Bayard. Smith's father changed his legal name to Jonathan Bayard Smith after marriage. Smith was educated in Philadelphia schools and earned a B.A. (1787) and an M.A. (1790) from the University of Pennsylvania.

In 1791 Smith opened a printing business in Philadelphia and became involved with the publication of the *American Universal Magazine*, a literary publication that lasted two years. On 15 August 1796 he founded the *New World*, a single-sheet newspaper published twice daily, which warmly supported Jeffersonian principles. Smith ceased publishing the newspaper on 16 August 1797. In September 1797 he purchased the *Independent Gazetteer*, a Republican newspaper edited by the elder Joseph Gales, who taught Smith shorthand. On 16 November 1797 Smith renamed the paper the *Universal Gazette*. He was a moderate Republican, which was reflected in the tone of the *Universal Gazette*, a marked contrast to the vitriolic Republican and Federalist newspapers of the time. Smith married his cousin, Margaret Bayard of Philadelphia, in 1800; they had four children.

Smith first came to the attention of Thomas Jefferson in 1797 when he tied for first prize for the best essay, awarded by the American Philosophical Society, of which Jefferson was president. His essay on a system of education and a plan for free public schools was later published as *Remarks on Education* (1798). Smith afterward served as secretary of the society. In 1800 Smith moved the *Universal Gazette* from Philadelphia to Washington, D.C., upon the invitation of Jefferson. It became the weekly edition of his new venture, the tri-weekly *National Intelligencer and Washington Advertiser*, which first appeared on 31 October 1800. The move was a gamble. He risked leaving the profitable Philadelphia market in hopes that Jefferson would win the presidency, and he would receive a large share of the government's printing business. When the election was thrown to the House of Representatives, Smith had to wait until February 1801 to find out if his gamble paid off.

The *National Intelligencer* became the organ of the Jefferson administration. Smith had an unbounded admiration for the president, and he firmly advocated every measure Jefferson proposed. The paper received the lion's share of government printing contracts and as much as one-half of the congressional printing during Jefferson's two terms. It is difficult to estimate how much he actually earned, but between 1801 and 1805 Smith was paid $8,000 by the State Department alone. This was at a time when printers' wages averaged about ten dollars a week.

The *Intelligencer's* usually calm, even-handed editorials led to Federalists and Republicans alike labeling it, "Silky-Milky Smith's National Smoothing-Plane." However, Smith was not beyond raising the ire of Federalists. In June 1801 the circuit court for the District of Columbia ordered that he be tried for libel after he editorialized that Federalist judges were not impartial. However, a grand jury refused to indict him. He continued to assail the Federalist domination of the judiciary and joined the effort to impeach Supreme Court Associate Justice Salmon Chase in 1805.

Smith's reporting of the proceedings in Congress during the first decade of the nineteenth century is his legacy to history. These reports, published in long columns of small type in the *Intelligencer*, made the newspaper the most important source of Washington news for papers around the country, regardless of political affiliation. In the *Intelligencer*'s first years, Smith covered Congress himself and had to struggle for his right to do so. In December 1800 he requested a seat inside the rail of the House chamber, but Federalists barred his admission. He was forced to sit in the gallery, where it was difficult to hear or to obtain the news from the clerk. He was admitted to the floor in the next session of Congress, after Republican victories in the election of 1800, but he was not given access to the floor of the Senate until January 1802. Later, Smith's reports of the proceedings were included in the *Annals of Congress* (42 vols., 1834, 1849–1856), which was a record of Congress for the years 1789–1824.

By the time Jefferson left office in 1809, Smith seemed to have lost his zeal for political journalism. He had conducted the *Intelligencer* virtually alone, except for the mechanical and production duties, for nearly a decade. Besides reporting on Congress, he wrote other news for the paper, selected stories from the exchanges, and handled all the advertising and billing. In 1807 Smith was looking for a buyer. The elder Gales persuaded Smith to hire his son as a reporter. In 1809 young Joseph Gales became Smith's partner, and on 31 August 1810 Gales assumed full ownership of the newspaper.

Smith entered banking and public service in his remaining years. He was appointed director of the Bank of Washington in 1809 and served as president for nearly a decade beginning in 1810. In July 1813 he was appointed the first commissioner of revenue for the Treasury Department; then he served a short term as Secretary of the Treasury in 1814. Between 1828 and 1836 he was president of the Washington branch of the Second United States Bank. He also was treasurer of the Washington Monument Society and a public school trustee, and he helped to negotiate the purchase of Jefferson's library for the Library of Congress. He died in Washington, D.C. Smith's major contribution to American history was his founding of the *National Intelligencer*, the most important political newspaper of the nineteenth century, in which he reported the debates in Congress at a time when no official records of debates were kept.

• Smith's papers, his wife's diary, and her papers are in the Library of Congress. The best scholarly work on Smith's journalism is William E. Ames, *A History of the National Intelligencer* (1972). Constance McLaughlin Green, *Washington: Village and Capital, 1800–1878*, vol. 1 (1962), is a good contextual study. Margaret Bayard Smith's *The First Forty Years of Washington Society*, ed. Gaillard Hunt (1906), is also highly useful. A good discussion of the *Intelligencer*'s role as government organ is Culver H. Smith, *The Press, Politics, and Patronage: The American Government's Use of Newspapers, 1789–1875* (1977).

JOSEPH P. McKERNS

SMITH, Samuel Stanhope (15 Mar. 1751–21 Aug. 1819), clergyman and college president, was born in Pequea, Pennsylvania, the son of Robert Smith, a Presbyterian clergyman, and Elizabeth Blair. After beginning his education at the age of six in an academy operated by his father, Smith's progress in the study of Latin and Greek was such that he was admitted to the junior class at the College of New Jersey (now Princeton University) when he was sixteen. There Smith excelled in mathematics, which heightened his appreciation of the natural sciences, and developed an intellectual curiosity that he retained to the end of his life.

Following his graduation with an A.B. in 1769, Smith returned to Pequea and taught in his father's academy. He also maintained a course of independent study in literature and theology before returning to Princeton in 1771, where he took a tutor's position and continued to study theology under college president John Witherspoon. Smith remained at the school until 1773, when he received his license to preach from the New Castle Presbytery. Shortly thereafter he developed tuberculosis and decided for the sake of his health to abandon academia. Ordained by Presbyterians in 1774, he removed to the western portion of Virginia, where, following in his father's footsteps, he undertook missionary work. He also served as a pastor at churches in Brierly and Cumberland and was a notable success in the pulpit.

The Presbytery of Hanover, which was in the process of founding its own college, persuaded Smith in 1774 to supervise the institution if adequate funds were raised to begin construction. The anticipated funds in hand, construction of the new Prince Edward Academy began in February 1775. The school, soon renamed Hampden-Sydney Academy (now College), was founded with the dual goals of providing educational opportunity for local Presbyterians and promoting piety. Under Smith, the college grew and prospered despite the difficulties caused by the revolutionary war, its relatively nondenominational nature proving attractive (although founded at the behest of the Presbyterian church, students faced no denominational restrictions, and a majority of the trustees were members of the Episcopal church). Smith married Ann Witherspoon, the daughter of Princeton's president, in 1775; they had nine children.

At the suggestion of his father-in-law, Smith returned to Princeton in December 1779. After turning over the leadership of Hampden-Sydney to his brother John, Smith assumed his Princeton position as professor of moral philosophy at a time when the college was in dire straits. Revolutionary warfare had been heavy in the area, and Nassau Hall (the main building) had suffered not only occupation (by both armies) but had also been shelled by the American troops prior to the British retreat to New Brunswick. The library was gone, funds were depleted, and even the famous Rittenhouse orrery (a mechanical device built to illustrate the rotation of the planets within the solar system) had been damaged. President Witherspoon's service in the Continental Congress from 1776 until 1779 and again in 1781–1782 left Smith with much of the responsibility for reviving the college. Often advancing funds from his own pocket, Smith acquired for the college a few books and worked towards making Nassau Hall at least partly suitable for instructional use.

Smith's duties at Princeton continued to multiply; he served as clerk of the board of trustees from 1781 to 1795 and as college treasurer. In 1783 he assumed the additional duties of professor of theology and in 1786 was rewarded for his efforts on behalf of the college by being named its vice president. Smith was elected to the American Philosophical Society in that same year, before which he read his *Essay on the Causes of the Variety of Complexion and Figure in the Human Species* (1787). In this work, one of the first attempts to fit evolutionary concepts to mankind, Smith argued that the great physical differences between the races were the result of minute inherited characteristics that had been amplified over time as a result of variations in climate, social mores, and lifestyles. The work represented one of the first attempts to reconcile empirical science and revealed religion, and served to establish Smith's reputation as a philosopher.

Following the death in 1794 of his father-in-law, Smith was unanimously elected by the college trustees to replace Witherspoon in May 1795. With the school still in desperate need of funds, Smith appealed to the state legislature, which provided £600 per year for three years with the stipulation that non-Presbyterians also serve on the board of trustees. Perhaps his greatest contribution to Princeton's future was his 1795 appointment of John Maclean as the first-ever undergraduate instructor in chemistry and the natural sciences in the United States (the subject had previously been taught only in medical schools). Smith later expanded scientific instruction by creating a special nondegree program that offered instruction in various scientific subjects in combination with the belles-lettres. Although the program was discontinued (plagued by resistance on the part of the trustees) in 1809 after a ten-year trial, Smith's early experimentation foreshadowed the later development of undergraduate instruction in the sciences.

The college's growth and recovery from the ravages of the revolutionary war came to an abrupt end on 6 March 1802 when a fire gutted Nassau Hall. Although the case was never proven, a few students were subsequently suspended by the trustees on suspicion of arson without any real evidence. The incident served to set the students against the trustees, with Smith placed squarely in the middle. Smith's relationship with the trustees was never solid; he tended to ignore their complaints concerning his emphasis on scientific instruction as well as their concern over his occasionally unorthodox theology (he had, for instance once stated in a lecture that there was no natural law against polygamy).

With the trustees assuming an ever-increasing presence in the maintenance of undergraduate discipline, the students, having been denied any role in their government, grew increasingly restive. In March 1807 full-fledged riots broke out, with the result that 125 students were suspended. Although fifty-five of them were later readmitted, the incident further damaged

Princeton's reputation. The student body, having grown in previous years, declined in number, as did the faculty. Smith's health, never robust, continued to decline under the strain, and he resigned from the presidency (under some pressure from the trustees) in 1812. His remaining years were spent in revising his written works, which included *Lectures on the Evidences of the Christian Religion* (1809), *Lectures on the Subjects of Moral and Political Philosophy* (2 vols., 1812), and *Principles of Natural and Revealed Religion* (1815). He died in Baltimore, Maryland.

An educator ahead of his time, Smith did not witness the full impact of his scholarly and administrative innovations. Instead, caught between reactionary trustees and the rebellious student body of postrevolutionary America, Smith saw most of his work at Princeton destroyed during his lifetime. He nevertheless deserves recognition as a pioneer in both scientific higher education and in the attempt to reconcile science and religion.

• A small collection of Smith material is in the archives of Princeton University. Good secondary sources of information on his life and career include Thomas Jefferson Wertenbaker, *Princeton, 1746–1896* (1946), and Samuel Holt Monk, "Samuel Stanhope Smith: Friend of Rational Liberty," in *The Lives of Eighteen from Princeton*, ed. Willard Thorpe (1946). Older sources include V. L. Collins, *Princeton* (1914), and John Maclean, *History of the College of New Jersey*, vol. 2 (1877).

EDWARD L. LACH

SMITH, Seba (14 Sept. 1792–28 July 1868), newspaper editor and creator of the comic figure Jack Downing, was born in Buckfield, Maine, the son of Seba Smith and Apphia Stevens, farmers. His "Down East" rural boyhood led to schoolteaching and three years at Bowdoin, which he entered as a sophomore in 1815; he graduated at the head of his class in 1818 and was a member of its most prominent literary society. After briefly teaching school and traveling to repair his weak health, in 1819 he began a career in newspapers and journals as assistant editor of the *Portland* (Maine) *Eastern Argus*. In 1823 he married Elizabeth Oakes Prince, a strong-willed seventeen-year-old who was to make her own reputation as a writer and speaker on the rights of women, eclipsing her husband in the 1850s and 1860s; they had four sons.

In 1830, after founding two papers, the *Family Reader*, a weekly miscellany, and the *Portland Courier*, a political paper that was the first daily paper published north and east of Boston, Smith achieved national recognition for his letters to the *Courier* under the name "Jack Downing." Downing was a green, country bumpkin who made comic points out of misunderstanding the partisan bickering of the Maine legislature convening in Portland. *The Life and Writings of Major Jack Downing of Downingville* appeared in 1833 while Smith was embroiled in proving his authorship of the Downing works against the claims of Charles Augustus Davis of New York, the most successful of many imitators and expropriators of the

Downing style and name. The book, a burlesque campaign biography highlighting the absurdity of partisan politics, was instantly successful, boasting in the preface that "it will tell folks more about politics, and how to get offices, than ever they knew before in all their lives; and what is the best ont, it will be pretty likely to get me in to be President." Of competitor Davis, at the *New York Daily Advertiser*, Downing observed, "he that will print his letters and put *my* name to 'em, I think would steal a sheep."

With the exception of the Jack Downing papers, Smith's career is typical of struggling author-editors of the pre–Civil War period. He probably thought less of the Downing letters than he should have and had higher hopes for his more formal writings than they merited. He began the *Downing Gazette*, a weekly political record, on 4 July 1834, but by 15 January 1836, he had written Jack Downing's obituary. Shortly afterward in 1837, Smith lost his interest in the *Portland Courier* through bad land speculations. Moving to New York in 1839, that same year he wrote comic letters for the *New York Mirror*, which became *John Smith's Letters with "Picters" to Match*. He and his wife both produced miscellaneous writings for magazines and gift books during this period. In 1841 he published an ambitious lyrical epic titled *Powhatan; A Metrical Romance*, a turgid formal presentation of the John Smith–Pocahontas legend in rhyme, which although drawing largely unmerited critical praise but scant sales was lambasted by the poet Edgar Allan Poe.

From 1843 through 1845 Smith edited the *Rover*, and also in 1845 he edited the *New York Citizen and American Republican*. In 1840 a short series of Downing letters appeared in the *New York New World*, and in 1844, Downing letters helped set the nativist tone of *Bunker Hill*, a political weekly backed by James Harper, mayor of New York City; however, the vernacular tone of the letters moderated the harshness of the nativist position. In 1845 *May-Day in New York*, containing various sketches and comic pieces, and *Dewdrops of the Nineteenth Century*, a giftbook, both edited by Smith, were modest offerings. Smith's last series of Downing letters appeared in the Washington, D.C., *National Intelligencer* from July 1847 through January 1856; about a third of the letters published in the first year satirized James K. Polk's orchestration of the Mexican-American War. During the same period Smith published *The New Elements of Geometry* (1850), which he vastly overrated as a contribution to the theory and teaching of mathematics, and *'Way Down East; or Portraitures of Yankee Life* (1854), in which he collected some of his best Yankee local tales.

His attempt in 1852 to found a comic paper, *The Budget*, failed within the year, as did most attempts to found comic papers in the period. In the late 1850s he edited various magazines, including the *United States Magazine* and the *United States Journal*, both from 1854 through 1858, which merged into *Emerson's United States Magazine and Putnam's Monthly* in 1857–1858, as well as *The Great Republic* in 1859. At the end of his writing career he published *My Thirty Years Out of the Senate* (1859), a collection of the best of the Downing letters, leaning heavily on those of the later and earlier periods and omitting those from the *Downing Gazette* in the 1840s, which he claimed had been burned in a fire, but which he may have felt were too partisan. Increasingly deaf, he retired to Patchogue, Long Island, in 1860 and died there.

Contemporary critics of the Jack Downing letters were most intrigued by the genuine Yankee dialect and type, with its homely metaphors, money sense, cracker-barrel pragmatism, and shrewdly political patriotism. Downing was usually considered not a burlesque but instead a genuinely truthful reflection of the mores of Yankeedom. A variety of pieces show more of the Yankee character and dialect than overt political commentary, and Smith valued Downing most for his authentic Yankee traits. Jack Downing insouciantly represented self-interested entrepreneurial Yankee republicanism, a prose competitor of the Brother Jonathan and Uncle Sam representations of an uncouth and naive "go-ahead" Yankee nation. At the outset of the letters, Downing manifests some diffidence as a country boy whose exposure to history is largely through hearing his grandfather, old Mr. Zebedee Downing, retelling how "Gineral" Gates won the "fatigue of Burgwine" to his neighbor Mr. Johnson, who sits affably drinking pint after pint of applejack (cider-fermented brandy), until both elderly Yankees retire with a mellow glow. Smith's sketches of Yankee life, *'Way Down East*, expands on these humorously realistic depictions of country life, bringing together gentler and less idiomatic tales and sketches reflecting Smith's nostalgia for the family values developed through good and bad times rather than the harsher self-interest of political spoilsmanship.

Jack Downing as a rustic figure in politics adhered to staunchly conservative principles. Loitering in Portland because "ax handles don't fetch nothing," his homey distress over legislative behavior reveals Smith's distaste for partisanship, as when he laments that poor Mr. Roberts was turned out of his seat by partisan politics in the legislature although "there was a number of seats empty. But they would have it so, and the poor man had to go and stand up in the lobby." Originally neither Democratic Republican (Jacksonite) nor National Republican (anti-Jackson), Downing soon became an office seeker whose doings satirized the excesses of Jacksonian spoilsmanship, a corruption of the apolitical "party of the people" to which Downing claimed he adhered and in which he saw himself enrolled. Northerners like Jack Downing backed Jackson's antinullification stance, however, and Downing reached his peak of popularity in the spring of 1833 when he helped an ailing President Jackson in Philadelphia by reaching his arm underneath Jackson's and shaking hands with well wishers for him. Davis's pirated Jack Downing continued to write Whig letters vehemently through the 1830s, but Smith's original Jack never became as crassly mercenary as the Downing figures created by his competitors. For the remainder of the decade Jack Downing was a national phenomenon, represented on sheet music, in stage plays, and throughout the regional newspapers.

Resurrecting Jack in the 1840s, Smith showed him more of a proponent of native Americanism, which Whigs like Smith adopted in defense against European influences, the Pope, and the growing antislavery movement. In a later series in the 1850s, Uncle Joshua is persuaded to help elect General Pierce when the major cajoles him, "You needn't be at all afraid of the Free-Soilers, Uncle; they ain't so stiff as you think for, and they are as anxious to get the offices as anybody, and will work as hard for 'em." Smith, however, had deep reservations about expansionism as a threat to national stability. Downing remains glad to hobnob with and advise presidents and legislators who seem more confused about how to run their state and country than is the green countryman, but he persistently satirizes their partisanship. *My Thirty Years Out of the Senate* collected his letters under a title that burlesqued the autobiography of Thomas Hart Benton, chronicling his opposition to the Bank of the United States and his support of President Polk in the war against Mexico.

Seba Smith's Downing figure was a presence so marked that it was recopied nationwide in papers of the day, becoming a Whig tool for stronger attacks on Jacksonian Democrats in the late 1830s and early 1840s than Smith himself cared to write, for Smith's vernacular localism remained as important to him as partisan politics. The rapid expansion of print journalism, however, elevated the pragmatic figure onto a significant national platform where his conservative Yankee vision of America brought him a popularity that inspired later Yankee figures such as Sam Slick and Hosea Biglow but overshadowed Smith's other work. Probably the most popular literary characterization of nineteenth-century America, Jack Downing assures Smith's place in American literature. Smith, despite his creation of a truly national Yankee American archetype, was in virtual eclipse as a writer at the time of his death.

• The University of Virginia has the largest holdings of Smith's manuscripts and letters, with only scattered materials reported elsewhere, including Bowdoin and the New York Public Library. A valuable analytic biography is Milton Rickels and Patricia Rickels, *Seba Smith* (1977), which provides a full study of Smith and the Downing letters as Yankee mythic material, advancing the work done by Mary Alice Wyman in *Two American Pioneers: Seba Smith and Elizabeth Oakes Smith* (1927). Cameron Nickels, *The New England Tradition of Native American Humor* (1993), offers definitive coverage of the career of Jack Downing as an American literary phenomenon. Dennis Royot, *L'humour Américain: Des puritains aux yankees* (1980), and Walter Blair and Hamlin Hill, *America's Humor from Poor Richard to Doonesbury* (1978), should also be consulted. A compact selection of Downing letters appears in Blair's *Native American Humor* (1937; repr. 1960), with an introductory survey placing Downing in the American tradition and a helpful bibliography; a chapter in Blair's *Horse Sense in American Humor* (1942) also analyzes Downing as a literary character. "The Pumpkin Freshet" from *'Way Down East* has been reprinted in David E. E. Sloane, ed., *The Literary Humor of the Urban Northeast: 1830–1890* (1983).

DAVID E. E. SLOANE

SMITH, Sidney. *See* Smith, Robert Sidney.

SMITH, Solomon Franklin (20 Apr. 1801–14 Feb. 1869), actor and pioneer theatrical manager, was born in Norwich, New York, the son of Levi Smith and Hannah Holland, farmers. Smith, known as Sol Smith or "Old Sol," spent his early years in a log cabin in Solon, Courtland County, New York. At a very early age he worked on a nearby farm. When he was twelve, Smith walked 300 miles to Boston, where he worked in an older brother's store, then clerked at an Albany, New York, store. He devoted much leisure time to reading Shakespeare and attending the local theater, where Smith became acquainted with the notable Drake theatrical family, who helped him gain free admittance to the theater. Caught up in all things theatrical, Smith pursued the Drake family after they left Albany in hopes of joining their company, but they refused him, and he returned home. Later his brothers decided to move to Cincinnati, but Smith missed connections and ended up floating down to Pittsburgh and eventually on to Ohio. For a time, he was a printer's apprentice, then a foreman for a newspaper.

In the summer of 1820, Smith found the Drake family again and managed to make his professional debut with their company playing at least six different parts in *Pizzaro* in Vincennes, Indiana. As an actor, throughout his career, he excelled in low comedy parts. He then returned to Cincinnati, became a prompter for a theatrical company managed by the Collins and Jones company, and studied law. At the close of the 1821–1822 season, Smith married Martha Therese Mathews, a gifted singer and tolerable actress. They had six children, two of whom, Mark and Sol, Jr., also became actors. Temporarily abandoning the theater, Smith, given liberal credit, became a Cincinnati newspaper owner, publishing the *Independent Press and Freedom Advocate*. This venture lasted very briefly, as he sold the paper and on an impulse bought out Collins and Jones. Thus, in 1823, though acting occasionally, Smith began his theatrical management career in earnest.

For the 1823 season, Smith's company played at Cincinnati's Globe Theater. After a disastrous season, the company disbanded, and Smith and his wife toured for some time giving musical concerts. Arriving in New York City in 1824, Smith hoped to make his debut there but was rebuffed by the manager of the Chatham Theater. It was not until the summer of 1827 that Smith realized some success. He joined James H. Caldwell—who would become his theatrical management rival—in St. Louis, Missouri, playing a three-month season in a converted salt house; in the fall of that year, Smith and his wife made their first appearances in New Orleans. In 1832 the Smiths first ventured to Mobile, Alabama, a move that proved to be so successful that it became the start of future theatrical operations in that city.

In 1835 Smith partnered with Noah M. Ludlow, with whom he virtually controlled the theatrical world of the West and South for eighteen years. They were, arguably, the most powerful theatrical partnership in the country. Their influence was enormous, not only because they could lure stars from the East to the then far reaches of the country but because they also were noted for fair and honest business practices, unlike some other managers of this period. Many times they were without funds to pay performers, resorting to promissory notes. But they always paid them off in time. It was also in 1835 that Smith finally made his New York City debut playing the role of Mr. Mawworm in *The Hypocrite* with an engagement at the Park Theater, alternating with the Walnut Street Theater in Philadelphia. The roles of Mr. Mawworm and Old Delph in *Family Jars* became Smith's favorites throughout his career.

The partnership of Ludlow and Smith opened the first genuine theater west of the Mississippi in 1837 in St. Louis. This operation would last until 1851, and the firm dissolved in 1853 after managing theaters in St. Louis, New Orleans, and Mobile. The financial status of the management team fluctuated wildly. The year 1845 culminated a series of financially dismal seasons. The normally placid Smith felt so much pressure that he retired temporarily to practice law during the summer months. The next year, however, brought renewed prosperity, allowing the partners to refurbish their New Orleans theater. Their best year was 1848, but their fortunes declined thereafter until the firm dissolved. The 1849 season, beset by a cholera epidemic and the great St. Louis fire, was disastrous; 1850 proved little better, and, except for a few bright spots in 1851, their financial situation deteriorated until the end of their operations in St. Louis and New Orleans.

Smith was known as Old Sol, both as a tribute to his playing old men's parts while still in his twenties and for his sunny disposition, which stood in contrast with that of his dour and rather stiff partner. Fittingly, Smith was a friend of another ebullient personage, the showman P. T. Barnum. Smith's partnership with Ludlow is one of the more interesting in theatrical history. It lasted despite vast personality differences and serious financial disagreements. Ludlow, by his own admission, was not a very good businessman. Smith, on the other hand, was obsessed with financial matters and debts in particular. Had it not been for chronic financial problems, Smith would have dissolved the partnership on various occasions. Smith's business sense rescued the firm from disaster many times. On one occasion he had to pay off a husband-and-wife team with land.

From 1835 until the firm's 1853 demise, Smith and Ludlow were responsible for bringing live theater to an area that was bursting with energy and filled with newcomers from the East eager for entertainment. They brought to their theater contemporary stars such as Junius B. Booth, William Charles Macready, E. L. Davenport, and Charles and Ellen Kean to appear in the latest and most popular plays as well as Shakespearean fare. In return, Smith and Ludlow provided future stars such as Joseph Jefferson III and Julia Dean early training as apprentices in frontier theaters before attempting the eastern stages.

In retirement from his theatrical career, Smith practiced law periodically and in 1861 was elected to the State Convention of Missouri. His vote helped to keep Missouri in the Union. He died suddenly in St. Louis. Smith's first wife had died in 1838, and he married Elizabeth Pugsley the following year. They had three children.

• Smith's letters, diaries, notes, and other records are in the Missouri Historical Society in St. Louis. The best source on his life is his *Theatrical Management in the West and South for Thirty Years* (1868). W. G. B. Carson, *The Theater on the Frontier* (1932; repr. 1965) and *Managers in Distress* (1949), along with Larry E. Grisvard, *The Final Years: The Ludlow and Smith Theatrical Firm in St. Louis, 1845–1851* (Ph.D. diss., Ohio State Univ., 1965), are important sources. Also see Noah M. Ludlow, *Dramatic Life as I Found It* (1880; repr. 1966). An obituary is in the *Missouri Republican*, 15 Feb. 1869.

LARRY E. GRISVARD

SMITH, Sophia (27 Aug. 1796–12 June 1870), founder of Smith College, was born in Hatfield, Massachusetts, the daughter of Joseph Smith and Lois White, farmers. Joseph Smith, a highly respected citizen of the village, prospered to the extent of leaving, at the time of his death in 1836, $10,000 to each of his surviving four children.

Sophia Smith was afforded the opportunities for education available in her time, instruction for girls after the hours devoted to boys at the Hatfield Academy and instruction at home in the ambience of a cultivated New England family. Pious and thoughtful, she read the Bible daily and lived by its teaching. She early sought guidance from her pastor, the Reverend Joseph Lyman, and in her later years continued to consult his successor in the Hatfield church, the Reverend John M. Greene.

The details of Smith's life are unrecorded. She was less robust than her three brothers and three sisters and more dependent, a condition greatly enhanced when, at the age of forty, she became deaf and by 1850 so handicapped that she heard only with the one hearing aid available at that time, a tin trumpet.

With the death in 1859 of her sister Harriet, who had succeeded their mother in the active concerns of the Smith household, and in 1861 the sudden death of her brother Austin, who left her a large bequest, Sophia, the final representative of an important village family, was overwhelmed with her responsibilities and her fortune. She sought help in prayer and in frequent consultations, particularly and repeatedly with Reverend Greene.

Her journal, which Greene suggested, and in which Smith wrote intermittently during the last six years of her life, reveals her loneliness, her sense of duty, and her prayers for divine guidance. She records only briefly the events of her life: trips to Saratoga, Andover, Washington, D.C., and Newport and visits from friends, often prolonged, and welcomed in her loneliness. She reports reading sermons; biographies, notably of Mary Lyon and other women; history; and letters. Although it was an area of concern and prolonged discussion, she does not comment on plans for a women's college or other bequests. She built a fine house beside the modest Smith farmhouse on Main Street and furnished it elegantly in the taste of the 1860s. She undertook the great task of making a new will to assure the proper distribution of a large inheritance.

Because her bequests involved public institutions, they demanded profound consideration. She consulted the best authorities. Among her first proposals was the founding of a college for women. It was firmly opposed by her advisers—educators and businessmen who thought the idea to be so impractical as to be irresponsible. Her will dated July 1861 provided $75,000 for an academy in Hatfield, $50,000 for Amherst College, and the remainder to found a school for deaf-mutes. In May 1862 the funds for Amherst College were excised and moved to provide for a public library in Hatfield. In 1868 the endowment by John Clarke of a school for the deaf in Northampton prompted another change.

Developments in advanced education for women (coeducation in some universities, the founding of Vassar College) now supported Smith's wish to leave the remainder of her fortune to endow a college for women. A new will dated 11 July 1868 provided a plan for a women's college in Hatfield. After concerted persuasion by all of her advisers, a final will signed on 8 March 1870 (executed 12 April 1870) relocated her college to Northampton.

Smith's collaboration with Reverend Greene was so constant, and his contribution to the plans for a college for women so substantive, that it is difficult to assess the originality and independence of her thinking. Greene was firmly persuaded that advanced education for women was essential to the future of the church and of the family. Smith firmly felt the injustice of unequal education for women and regretted her own lack of opportunities. She stoutly rejected what she did not approve. He says repeatedly that he put *her* wishes into words.

Their plan when it emerged was for an ideal college for women, insisting on the standards of higher education practiced in the best colleges for men and meeting the objections of conventional fears and prejudices. It was a courageous commitment, a testimony to female capabilities, intellectual and physical, and to the integrity of femininity. Smith died in Hatfield, her will providing a capable board of trustees who brought Smith College to foundation.

• Smith's journal and letters as well as John M. Greene's journal, narrative, and letters are in the Smith College Archives. Among the items of interest are Smith's last will and testament, which was published in L. Clark Seelye, *The Early History of Smith College* (1923); *Addresses at the Inauguration of Rev. L. Clark Seelye as President of Smith College* (1875); *The Centennial of the Birth of Sophia Smith* (1896); and *Celebration of the Quarter-Centenary of Smith College* (1900). See also John M. Greene, "The Early History of Smith College," (Northampton) *Hampshire Gazette*, 31 July 1891 to 12 Apr. 1893; Daniel White Wells and Reuben Field Wells, *A History of Hatfield, Massachusetts* (1910); Elizabeth Deering Hanscom and Helen French Greene, *Sophia Smith and the Beginnings of Smith College* (1925); Gladys Wookey Davis, *Miss Sophia's Legacy* (1950); Hallie Flanagan Davis and Brenden Dowell, eds., *Heritage: A Play in Honor of the 75th Anniversary of the Founding of Smith College* (1953); and Quentin Quesnell, "Whatever Happened to Sophia Smith?," *Smith Alumnae Quarterly* 86 (Spring 1995): 16–20.

ELEANOR TERRY LINCOLN

SMITH, Stephen (1795?–14 Nov. 1873), businessman and minister, was born near Harrisburg, Dauphin County, Pennsylvania, the son of an unknown father and Nancy Smith (maiden name unknown), a Cochran family servant. On 10 July 1801 Thomas Boude, a former revolutionary war officer from Columbia, Lancaster County, Pennsylvania, purchased the boy's indenture. As Smith grew to manhood, he proved so able that Boude eventually made him manager of his entire lumber business.

On 3 January 1816 Smith borrowed $50 to purchase his freedom from Boude. Later that year Smith married Harriet Lee, a domestic servant in the Jonathan Mifflin home. They had no children. Free of his indenture, Smith entered the lumber business for himself, while his wife ran an oyster house. In 1820 his one-and-a-half lots were valued at $300. Thirteen years later, he owned six houses and lots worth $3,000, stocks and bonds of equal value, "a pleasure carriage," a horse, and a cow. His lumberyard became one of the largest on the Susquehanna River. This success aroused the envy of some whites; an anonymous hate letter in 1835 accused him of inflating property prices with his excessive bids.

When the race riots of 1834–1835 broke out in Columbia, Smith's place of business was a target. Windows were broken, his desk rifled, and papers scattered. His property and life in jeopardy, Smith offered his holdings for sale, but after six months with no takers, he withdrew his offer. His financial strength enabled him to weather the 1837 bank panic. With his business partner, William Whipper, a relative and an equally astute merchant, Smith's Columbia investments included $9,000 in a bridge company and $18,000 in a bank. Moving to Philadelphia in 1842, he increased his holdings of houses, lots, stocks, and bonds and expanded his lumber and coal business. By 1849 Smith and Whipper had an inventory of "several thousand bushels of coal," over two million feet of lumber, "and twenty-two of the finest merchantmen cars running on the railroad from Columbia to Philadelphia and Baltimore" (Worner, p. 185). When his partnership with Whipper ended, his wife's nephew, Ulysses B. Vidal, joined him in the coal business.

Smith's business dealings were not his sole occupation. In 1832 he purchased a church building in Columbia and founded the Mount Zion African Methodist Episcopal (AME) Church. Six years later he was ordained an AME minister.

Early on, Smith turned his talents to race rights and reform. He was a well-known participant in the Underground Railroad; Whipper told William Still that it was known "far down in the slave region, that Smith & Whipper, the negro lumber merchants, were engaged in secreting fugitive slaves" (Still, p. 739). Smith opposed the colonization movement and supported the early strivings of Whipper's American Moral Reform Society in 1834–1835. A frequent but not addicted convention goer and mass-meeting participant, he fought for the abolition of slavery, the removal of "white" from the state constitution, and the integration of Philadelphia's railway cars. Smith supported the temperance movement and was an officer in a number of black organizations, including the Odd Fellows, Social, Civil, and Statistical Association; the Grand Tabernacle of the Independent Order of Brothers and Sisters of Love and Charity; and the Union League Association. He hosted John Brown for a week in 1858 and, along with James Wormley and Henry Highland Garnet, had a leadership role in the movement to erect a Lincoln memorial monument.

An occasional victim of white persecution, he had also earned the respect of many whites and worked with them in his business and charitable endeavors. His race views were unequivocal but moderate. In 1855 he was aware "that the colored people of the city of Philadelphia could not obtain [an] opportunity to learn mechanical trades. But," he added, "wherever a colored man understood a trade, he was sustained in Philadelphia" (Foner and Lewis, vol. 1, p. 262). As time went on, Smith became more pessimistic. He discouraged black attempts to integrate the Philadelphia railway cars because he doubted such attempts would receive the support of the city's white citizens.

During the Civil War, though a member of Bethel AME Church, Smith served for a year or so as pastor in charge of the Zion AME Mission Church. He worked with Bethel's committee to collect food, clothing, and money for contrabands in Washington, D.C. He helped to organize one meeting and chaired a second at which Frederick Douglass spoke, urging black recruits for the army and equal rights for all men and women. A short-term trustee of Wilberforce University, he headed a committee to raise funds for that institution.

After Appomattox, Smith continued his business and church activities. Not assigned a parish, he occasionally preached and frequently spoke ("in his usual animated and forcible style") in and around the city. He and his wife regularly summered in Cape May. His major charitable interest centered on a home for the elderly and the Olive Cemetery. He bought the cemetery at a forced auction for payment of debts and rejoiced when in 1863 the state supreme court resolved a seven-year-old management dispute in his favor. The next year Smith and some white Quakers established the Philadelphia Home for the Aged and Infirm. In

1870 a new building was dedicated, a gift of Stephen and Harriet Smith. By bequest the Smiths endowed the home with almost $250,000.

Beyond this, his denomination, including Bethel Church, benefited from his continuing generosity and special gifts. He built the Zion AME Mission church in 1857 and contributed to the establishment of an AME church in Cape May. With nine others, Smith put up $1,000 to buy the vacated Institute for Colored Youth building and convert it into a meeting hall with stores for black retailers.

As an individual, Smith was quiet but stubborn. In 1856 he chastised the *Christian Recorder* editor, Jabez Campbell, for criticizing an AME General Conference ruling, asserting that the editor should "vindicate her [the church's] acts, defend her organization, discipline and laws." Be patient, he urged; "try them, and if they do not suit, repeal them" (*Christian Recorder*, 4 Mar. 1856). Five years later, AME district conference settled another dispute between the two men in Smith's favor. At the 1864 general conference, some Bethel members protested his seat for unstated reasons but their claim was denied. Early in 1873 Wilberforce University's president, Bishop Daniel Payne, stung by rumors of Smith's lack of confidence in him, published an offer to resign if Smith would endow the institution with a $100,000 gift. Smith's terse response praised Payne "as a man of learning and a Christian gentleman," but questioned his abilities to manage finances (*Christian Recorder*, 6 Mar. 1873).

This was probably Smith's last public statement before illness incapacitated him. After his death in Philadelphia, Pennsylvania, he was praised as "the ablest financier and the wealthiest man among the colored people," and "one of the best-known colored citizens of Philadelphia" (*New National Era*, 4 Dec. 1873; *Philadelphia Public Ledger*, 15 Nov. 1873). Smith's life was a rags-to-riches saga, unique in the nineteenth-century black community. He tried to live his Christian creed, courageously patient under persecution, moderate in materialism, and sensitive to the less fortunate.

• The most comprehensive account is William F. Worner, "The Columbia Race Riots," *Lancaster County Historical Society Papers* 26, no. 8 (Oct. 1922): 175–87. The federal censuses of 1850, 1860, and 1870 cite basic data, except for inaccurate ages of Stephen and Harriet Smith. William Still, *The Underground Rail Road* (1872), focuses on William Whipper with useful references to Smith. Carl Oblinger, "In Recognition of Their Prominence . . . ," *Journal of the Lancaster County Historical Society* 72, no. 2 (Easter 1968): 65–83, and Thomas P. Slaughter, *Bloody Dawn: The Christiana Riot and Racial Violence in the Antebellum North* (1991), fill in some Lancaster County details. Benjamin Quarles's two books, *Black Abolitionists* (1969) and *Allies for Freedom: Blacks and John Brown* (1974), connect Smith to the antislavery movement and John Brown. Philip S. Foner and George Walker, eds., *Proceedings of the Black State Conventions, 1840–1865*, vol. 1 (1979), and idem *Proceedings of the Black National and State Conventions, 1865–1900*, vol. 1 (1986), track Smith's participation in conventions. The first volume of Philip S. Foner and Ronald L. Lewis's *The Black Worker to 1869*

(1978), follows Smith's sporadic involvement with labor. *The Christian Recorder*, 1854–1856, 1861–1873, has frequent references to Smith and his activities. Obituaries are in the *New National Era*, 4 Dec. 1873, the *Philadelphia Public Ledger*, 15 Nov. 1873, and the *Philadelphia Inquirer*, 19 Nov. 1873.

LESLIE H. FISHEL, JR.

SMITH, Stephen (19 Feb. 1823–26 Aug. 1922), surgeon and sanitarian, was born near Skaneateles, New York, the son of Lewis Smith, a farmer, county sheriff, and member of the New York State Assembly, and Chloe Benson. Smith's father died when Stephen was six years old, leaving his mother to manage a farm and to raise five children. A sickly child who attended school sporadically, Smith was largely self-educated until he attended the Cortland Academy in Homer, New York, when he was in his early twenties. While his fragile constitution exempted him from most physical work, it did not interfere with his longevity and did result in more time for reading and learning, providing a firm basis for his later extensive literary work.

One of his teachers at the Cortland Academy, prominent local physician Caleb Green, stimulated his student's interest in biology and medicine. After a brief stint as a grade-school teacher, Smith began to study medicine in Green's office in 1846, at the relatively advanced age of twenty-three. In the following year he attended classes at the nearby Geneva Medical College, where his fellow student was Elizabeth Blackwell, who in 1849 became the first woman to earn a regular medical degree in the United States. In 1848 Smith enrolled at the Buffalo Medical College and became an apprentice to Dr. Frank H. Hamilton, a leader in orthopedic surgery. In Buffalo, Smith also served as a house pupil in the Hospital of the Sisters of Charity. Early in 1850 Smith moved to New York City, where the next year he was awarded an M.D. by the College of Physicians and Surgeons. From 1850 to 1852 he served a two-year tour of duty as a house physician to Bellevue Hospital, thus beginning a career in New York City as a surgeon, author, editor, and social reformer that would span nearly seventy years. When he began his long association with Bellevue, it was just in its transition from an almshouse to a general hospital.

While at Bellevue Hospital as a house physician and then as attending physician, Smith observed the large numbers of patients with fevers coming from overcrowded and unsanitary tenements, thus setting in motion his long and strenuous efforts to achieve sanitary reform. In a retrospective account, *The City That Was* (1911), Smith described in graphic terms how he became so involved in public health work.

After he had completed his internship at Bellevue, in 1852, Smith was put in charge of tents on Blackwell's Island in the East River erected to house patients with typhus fever. He noticed that many of these patients came from a single tenement on East Twenty-second Street. A visit to the building revealed "an extreme state of dilapidation generally; the doors and windows were broken; the cellar was partly filled with filthy sewage; the floors were littered with decomposing straw, which the occupants used for bedding; every available place, from cellar to garret was crowded with immigrants—men, women, and children. The whole establishment was reeking with filth and the atmosphere was heavy with the sickening odor of the deadly typhus, which reigned supreme in every room" (*The City That Was*, pp. 35–36).

Smith tracked down the owner of this fever nest, as he called it, who responded only when Smith threatened to expose his tenement in the newspapers. The public health laws of the city were then so ineffective that no civic action was possible. Smith thus enlisted in the battle for sanitary reform in New York, begun a decade or more earlier by physicians such as John H. Griscom but not successful until the 1866 creation of a Metropolitan Board of Health.

While at Bellevue, Smith also began his literary career, when in 1853, on the strength of two long review articles in the *New York Journal of Medicine*, he was asked to join the journal's editorial staff. He served as assistant editor from 1853 to 1857, when he became editor, and from 1860 when the journal merged with the newly established weekly *American Medical Times*, Smith served as its editor until it ceased publication in 1864. His weekly editorials about issues in public health, medical education, regulation of practice, and the medical needs of the Union army reached a wide audience. Smith published a collection of fifty-eight of these editorials in *Doctor in Medicine* (1872). The editorials reveal Smith as a thoughtful observer, always ready to suggest needed changes and improvements, whether in laws, social conditions, or practices.

Much of Smith's general medical writing read like sermons. He was consistent, however, in his preaching for improvement in all areas of medicine and civic life. He became involved not only in medical and public health issues, but also in temperance, eugenics, and tree planting to improve the environment and quality of the air. His extensive historical writing, particularly in the history of surgery, was imbued with the idea of progress; he would describe one discovery or new surgical technique after another, dwelling on their successes. The tone of his writing was quite characteristic of his time. He well understood that his own professional career spanned several epochs, and he was aware of the great changes he witnessed, but he did not fully understand these changes because they had so little relevance to his own work. He began his medical studies in the year anesthesia was introduced, helped to establish antiseptic surgery at Bellevue, and watched the germ theory change the understanding of much of the disease of his time.

Throughout his long professional career Smith played leading roles in several fields. In his primary medical specialty of surgery, and especially in what later would be called orthopedics, Smith taught at the Bellevue Hospital Medical College from its founding in 1861 until 1872. He was an active member of the hospital's surgical staff from 1854 to 1896. Early in the Civil War he compiled a well-illustrated pocket manual, *Handbook of Surgical Operations* (1862), for use by surgeons in the field. It was widely distributed to the Union army surgeons and was copied and issued anonymously by the Confederates. Smith is credited with devising an improved method for amputation below the knee, in which he revised the placing of the incision so that the resulting scar would receive much less pressure from an artificial leg. He also wrote *Operative Surgery*, a large textbook of surgery published in two editions, 1879 and 1886. He had married Lucy Culver around 1857; they had five children.

While serving as the editor of the *American Medical Times*, Smith frequently wrote and spoke about the need for sanitary reforms in New York City. In 1865 he organized and directed a large-scale sanitary survey of the city, carried out by young dispensary physicians. He summarized their findings in testimony before the state legislature on behalf of a Metropolitan Board of Health to be composed of experts rather than mere political appointees. Such a board came into existence in 1866. Creation of this Metropolitan Board of Health had several broad implications for the health of the public. As the first comprehensive legislation of its kind, it served as a model for other cities and for state health departments. It helped to make sanitary science a respectable specialty of medicine and of engineering, thereby fostering new careers and changing the image of what medicine could accomplish. Smith acted as one of the commissioners from 1868 to 1875. In 1872 Smith and a small group of sanitarians founded the American Public Health Association (APHA), for which he served as its first president from 1872 to 1874. Smith also worked with the APHA to establish a National Board of Health, and in 1879 President Rutherford B. Hayes appointed Smith to the National Board of Health, on which Smith served on the executive committee throughout its four-year existence.

Growing quite naturally out of his work in surgery—which was increasingly being performed in hospitals under antiseptic conditions such as Smith had helped foster at Bellevue—and his concerns for a more sanitary civic environment, was Smith's interest in hospital design and construction. Influenced profoundly by the work of Florence Nightingale in England (Smith and his wife had named their third child, in 1859, after her), Smith provided a design for a pavilion-style hospital in New York for the Trustees of the Roosevelt Hospital in 1866. In 1875 he was asked by the Trustees of the Johns Hopkins Hospital to provide one of the five plans for that new venture in Baltimore.

In the 1880s Smith became increasingly involved in public charities work, particularly in care for the mentally ill. As New York State's commissioner on lunacy from 1882 until 1888, he was responsible for conditions in the large state hospitals. He was instrumental in improving their nursing services and in shifting responsibility for care of the mentally ill from county poorhouses, usually inadequately funded, to the responsibility of the state. His work culminated in the State Care Act of 1890. He served as a commissioner of the New York State Board of Charities from 1888 to 1918.

Smith continued to write and to speak publicly well into his nineties. By the time of his death, in Montour Falls, New York, many of the reforms he had championed, such as antisepsis in surgery, nursing schools, better care for the mentally ill, and professional rather than political health departments, had become commonplace.

• There are no significant manuscript collections of Smith papers. He wrote extensively about his own work. See especially *Doctor in Medicine* (1872; repr. 1972); *The City That Was* (1911; repr. 1972); *Who Is Insane* (1916), and "Random Recollections of a Long Medical Life," *Medical Record* 79 (1911): 891–97. See also, John Duffy, *A History of Public Health in New York City, 1625–1966* (2 vols., 1968–1974); Mazyck P. Ravenel, ed., *A Half Century of Public Health* (1921); and G. H. Brieger, "Sanitary Reform in New York City: Stephen Smith and the Passage of the Metropolitan Health Bill," *Bulletin of the History of Medicine* 40 (1966): 407–29. An obituary is in the *New York Times*, 27 Aug. 1922.

GERT H. BRIEGER

SMITH, Stuff (13 Aug. 1909–25 Sept. 1967), jazz violinist, singer, and comedian, was born Leroy Gordon Smith in Portsmouth, Ohio, the son of Cornelius T. Smith, a barber and musician, and Anna Lee Redman, a schoolteacher. Smith's birth certificate gives 13 August, but he celebrated his birthday on 14 August, for reasons unknown (perhaps superstition); also, he was known to many as Hezekiah (or by the nickname Hez), but this name is not on the certificate.

Smith was raised in Massilon, Ohio, from age nine, by which time he was playing in his father's band. His father wanted him to follow his sister Helen, who studied classical violin at Oberlin Conservatory, but Smith heard Joe Venuti and Eddie Lang perform locally and was smitten by jazz. Around 1925 he won a musical scholarship to Johnson C. Smith University in Charlotte, North Carolina, but he never graduated. In 1926 and 1927 he toured with Aunt Jemima's Revue, at which time he acquired his nickname through his habit of calling someone "Stuff" if he could not remember a name. Smith's first wife, a dancer whose name is unknown, had died in childbirth. He married Marion Armeta Harris around 1927. They had one child.

By this time Smith was becoming familiar with Louis Armstrong's recordings, which he felt provided a much greater influence than Venuti's comparatively lightweight work. Smith joined Alphonso Trent's orchestra in Lexington, Kentucky, late in 1927 for southwestern and midwestern tours. He served as the orchestra's conductor and master of ceremonies, thereby developing skills that would later bring him stardom in New York City. Leaving Trent in Davenport, Iowa, in 1928, Smith went to New York, where he joined Jelly Roll Morton, but after two weeks he left because Morton's band played too loudly for the violin to be heard. Smith traveled to Little Rock, Arkansas, to rejoin Trent and to contribute solos to Trent's few recordings, including "Nightmare" and

"Black and Blue Rhapsody" (5 Dec. 1928). He remained with Trent until 1930, touring Canada and the Northeast and making his recording debut as a solo vocalist on "After You've Gone" (Mar. 1930).

With the birth of his son, Smith left Trent to spend several years with his family in Buffalo, New York. There he formed a group that included trumpeter Peanuts Holland from Trent's band, tenor saxophonist Joe Thomas (Joseph Vankert), and later trumpeter Jonah Jones. In January 1936 Smith formed what immediately became an extremely popular sextet at the Onyx Club in New York, where he began using an amplified violin. Together with the leader, the sextet featured Jones and drummer Cozy Cole. They played swing tunes and novelties, well represented on record by "I'se a Muggin'," "After You've Gone," "You'se a Viper," "Old Joe's Hittin' the Jug," and "Knock, Knock, Who's There?" (all from 1936).

Smith's great admirer, Danish baron Timme Rosencrantz, reports: "Often at the Onyx, after the music started, he would tell risqué stories over the microphone. There was one about Adam and Eve in the Garden of Eden, that used to make the management panic. I've seen him stop in the middle of a solo when a young and beautiful woman entered the room and point out to the audience the woman's anatomical qualities" (Barnett and Løgager, p. 56). Together with this verbal outrageousness, Smith's acclaimed sextet presented childlike vocal melodies married to Harlem jazz talk and other silly lyrics (including some wonderfully awful puns in knock-knock jokes); Cole's swinging drumming; Jones's swinging and melodically lyrical trumpet playing in the Armstrong mold; and most significantly, Smith's always swinging and sometimes delightfully weird violin improvisations.

While at the height of his fame at the Onyx, Smith, billed with Billie Holiday, became jealous of her emerging popularity and in a well-publicized incident succeeded in having her fired; later in life they resolved their difficulties, becoming friends and sometimes working together.

Pianist Clyde Hart had joined the sextet by the time that Smith recorded "Upstairs" in May 1937. That month the group traveled to Hollywood to perform in the musical *52nd Street*, but they were excluded from the film because they violated their contract by taking an engagement at the Famous Door in Hollywood from the summer of 1937 to early 1938. Around March 1938 Smith went bankrupt, disbanded, and briefly joined Holland's orchestra in Buffalo. By May Smith had re-formed his band, which worked steadily into 1942, mainly in New York and Chicago. Smith's group in 1942 included former members of Fats Waller's band; they fired the leader "when his eccentricity went beyond reason" (Barnett, p. 90). Smith divorced his wife around 1940. He married Helen Rogers in the early 1940s; they had no children.

In the spring of 1943 Smith formed a trio with pianist Jimmy Jones and string bassist John Levy, and after performing in Chicago and making national radio broadcasts the trio went to New York in September 1944 for recordings and a tenure at the Onyx through the spring of 1945. Pianists Erroll Garner and Billy Taylor each briefly followed Jones in the trio. Over the next decade Smith led lesser-known groups based in Chicago but ranging on occasion from coast to coast. He recorded with trumpeter Dizzy Gillespie's sextet in 1951 and with keyboard player Sun Ra sometime before 1953. Divorced again in 1950, Smith married Arlene Janzig about 1955; they had no children.

Smith's career was revived in the mid-1950s by a series of excellent recordings for Norman Granz. These albums include *Ella Fitzgerald Sings the Duke Ellington Song Book* (1956), Nat King Cole's *After Midnight* (1956), Smith's own *Have Violin, Will Swing* and *Stuff Smith* and, with violinist Stephane Grappelli, *Violins No End* (all from 1957). He toured Europe in the spring of 1957 with Granz's Jazz at the Philharmonic, but he did not complete the tour because of illness. He performed several times on the television series "Art Ford's Jazz Party" in 1958. Recording for Granz again, he made the album *Cat on a Hot Fiddle* in 1959. Settling for a time in Los Angeles, he performed regularly, including appearances at the Monterey Jazz Festival in 1961 and 1962.

Smith played at the Royal Tahitian Room in Ontario, California, from 1963 to 1964. He returned to New York to perform with pianist Joe Bushkin's group at the Embers, but illness ended this affiliation. Early in 1965 he left his wife and settled in Copenhagen, where he found his playing in great demand. He underwent a serious operation in Paris in mid-August; a doctor described Smith as a "medical museum," a consequence of decades of wild and careless living. Nonetheless he immediately resumed playing. He had an illegitimate child with Margaret Fossum Poulsen, but in his final year Smith lived with Eva Løgager. He made the renowned album *Violin Summit* at a jam session with violinists Svend Asmussen, Grappelli, and Jean-Luc Ponty at a concert in Basel, Switzerland, on 30 September 1966. He recorded the album *Black Violin* in Germany the next year. Still touring Europe extensively, Smith died while in Munich.

Even at his peak in the 1930s Smith did not routinely depart from the norms of jazz swing soloing, but whenever he wished he could invent melodies offering a then-unknown level of dissonant pitch selection and dissonant intonation in relationship to blues and pop harmonies, as if the free jazz era had suddenly been unleashed a quarter century too soon. This type of playing may be heard not only on 1936 novelty tunes such as "You'se a Viper" and "Old Joe's Hittin' the Jug" but also in as sedate a setting as "My Blue Heaven" (recorded in 1939). Speaking of their trio of 1943, Jimmy Jones said, "Stuff's a strange guy, you know. He wants to play what he wants to play. Cut out from the melody, depart from the chords. It's a wrong note, maybe, but Stuff makes it right, and we had to make it right with him. . . . I got so I knew his moods, his harmonic tricks, when he would suddenly switch tempo or change key" (interview with Barry Ulanov, repr. in Barnett, p. 109). Because of this melodic impetuous-ness, as well as his raucous approach to tone quality (including explorations of amplified sound) and vibrato, and his hard-driving sense of swing rhythm, Smith is regarded as one of the greatest jazz violinists.

• The definitive source on Stuff Smith is Anthony Barnett, *Desert Sands: The Recordings & Performances of Stuff Smith: An Annotated Discography & Biographical Source Book* (1995), which includes a comprehensive bibliography; a detailed interview with Arlene Smith; a fully annotated catalog of recordings arranged chronologically with extensive biographical information interspersed; and numerous illustrations, including birth certificate, photos, and musical examples. Disjunct autobiographical material appears in Stuff Smith, *Pure at Heart*, ed. Barnett and Eva Løgager (1991). Interviews include Valerie Wilmer, "Stuff Smith: The Genius of Jazz Violin," *Jazz Beat* 2 (June 1965): 16–17; Jacques Pescheux, "Stuff Smith," *Bulletin du Hot Club de France* 150 (Sept. 1965): 2–4; and Stanley Dance, *The World of Swing* (1974; repr. 1979), pp. 176–83 (framed by interviews with Jonah Jones and Cole). See also Arnold Shaw, *The Street That Never Slept* (1971; repr. as *52nd Street: The Street of Jazz*, 1977), pp. 82–95; Dan Morgenstern, "Jazz Fiddle," *Down Beat*, 9 Feb. 1967, pp. 16–19, 38; and René Balagri, "Stuff Smith: le violent du violon," *Jazz*, Feb. 1970, pp. 34–37, 51. Matt Glaser and Stephane Grappelli, *Jazz Violin* (1981), pp. 15–16, 39–45, includes description and musical notation of Smith's improvising. See also Mary Lee Hester, "Hot Stuff!" *Mississippi Rag* 11 (Apr. 1984): 8–9. An obituary is in the *New York Times*, 2 Oct. 1967.

BARRY KERNFELD

SMITH, Theobald (31 July 1859–10 Dec. 1934), microbiologist and comparative pathologist, was born in Albany, New York, the son of German immigrants Phillip Schmitt, a tailor, and Theresa Kexel. Smith spoke German at home and became an accomplished pianist, both talents that profoundly eased his later life. He married Lilian Hillyer Egleston in 1888; they had three children.

After completing both undergraduate and doctoral degrees in biology at Cornell University, Smith entered Albany Medical College in 1881 and graduated at the head of his class two years later. His Cornell mentor and lifetime correspondent, the microscopist Simon H. Gage, soon recommended Smith as laboratory aide to Daniel E. Salmon, then chief of the veterinary division of the U.S. Department of Agriculture. Later in 1883 Congress established the Bureau of Animal Industry, with the authority to investigate and control infectious animal diseases that threatened livestock and poultry markets. Smith was transferred to the BAI to begin the research that launched his scientific career, and in 1891 he was made chief of the Division of Pathology. In collaboration with Salmon and F. L. Kilborne, Smith undertook an early study of artificially induced immunity and published several reports that eventually resolved a heated controversy by validating crucial differences between hog cholera and swine plague.

Smith's single most celebrated discovery was the demonstration, with Kilborne, of the role of a tick in transmitting the parasite that caused Texas Cattle Fever. Their "Investigations into the Nature, Causation and Prevention of Texas or Southern Cattle Fever" (*Special Report on the Cause and Prevention of Swine Plague* [1891]) was the first indisputable account of a blood-sucking arthropod vector carrying a protozoan infection and made it possible to control a lethal and costly disease among livestock. This breakthrough coincided with the discovery of the mosquito as the vector of a blood-borne parasite in malaria.

What began in 1884 as an apprenticeship (at BAI) for a promising young man without significant knowledge of microbiology eventually became oppressive and frustrating employment for a creative, rigorous, and ambitious scientist. In a letter to Simon Gage, Smith called microbiology "a busy, pushing, expanding field," and complained that his mind resembled "a sausage machine . . . constantly ejecting contents to make room for fresh material." Although he applauded research that could be directed to practical ends, he protested that "the Government is not a place for those who have ideas of their own to air" (Letters of 2 Sept. 1890 and 27 Mar. 1891, Simon H. Gage Papers, Cornell Univ. Archives).

His reputation established, Smith moved to more promising terrain in 1895 when he accepted the position of assistant professor of zoology at Harvard University, whose president, Charles William Eliot, calculated, incorrectly, that Smith could rescue the university's faltering veterinary school. With an appointment at Harvard Medical School, Smith settled into his own laboratory and a family home in Jamaica Plain, on grounds also occupied by Harvard's School of Applied Science. Within the year Eliot offered the Massachusetts Board of Health space on the site for laboratories and stables to produce diphtheria antitoxin and smallpox vaccine. In an associated agreement, Smith, now Fabyan Professor of Comparative Pathology at the Medical School, was concurrently appointed director of the state laboratories.

Apparently undeterred by multiple duties and the storms that surrounded the state's venture into competition with pharmaceutical firms, Smith guided the Department of Comparative Pathology for two decades while he retained responsibilities in public health. His letters to Gage took a new turn as he explained "that there is as much pure gold of science to be gathered in the working out of problems applicable to the every-day life of the individual and the State as in other kinds of inquiry aimed much higher" (Letter of 10 May 1897, Gage papers). Much of his laboratory research on the organisms that cause bovine and human tuberculosis and on the immunological properties of smallpox vaccine, diphtheria and tetanus antitoxin, bore directly on public health. Smith reconfigured his civic profile as he lectured and published extensively on the broader implications of mutual dependence between human host and microorganism in health and disease. At the International Congress of Arts and Science held during the St. Louis Universal Exposition (1904), Smith explained that the "social and industrial movement of the human race is continually leading to disturbances of equilibrium in nature, one of whose direct or indirect manifestations is augmentation of disease," and that it was "the true function of medical science to discover . . . those compensatory movements which will counterbalance the temporary ill-effects of . . . human progress" ("Some Problems in the Life History of Pathogenic Microorganisms," *Science* 22 [1904]: 817–32). Smith was the logical choice among his peers to head the new Rockefeller Institute for Medical Research in 1901 but refused the honor, tempering his decision by serving on the board of scientific directors.

Smith left Harvard and the Massachusetts Public Health Laboratories in 1914, when the Rockefeller Institute established a Division of Animal Pathology that became an essentially autonomous research center in Princeton, New Jersey. As division director (emeritus after 1929) he attended to design and construction of the laboratories, recruited the scientific staff and guided the course of investigations with which the institute became identified. Returning to problems that had interested him early in his career, Smith collaborated with younger colleagues to determine the obscure transmission of turkey blackhead and to develop effective bacterial vaccines against infection. Once again, Smith's scientific inquiries flourished as he typically was stimulated to fundamental research in parasitology and immunology by practical problems raised by the transmission of animal diseases. He continued to work in his laboratory and on the board of scientific advisors after retiring as director of the laboratories. Smith died in a New York City hospital after a brief illness.

Smith was elected president of the Society of American Bacteriologists (1903), the National Tuberculosis Association (1926), and the Congress of Physicians and Surgeons (1928); received numerous honorary degrees and awards in the United States and abroad, including membership in the Royal Society of London; and was invited to deliver distinguished lectures, many of them later published.

Celebrated among his contemporaries as the leading comparative pathologist of his time, Smith was famous for his exceptional technical ingenuity, scientific insight, and personal modesty. According to his younger colleague Hans Zinsser, Smith possessed "intellectual vitality" that permitted him to "roam widely," "pick up threads here and there as they appeared in the patterns of his daily work," and follow a problem until he established a principle or devised a tool that "others could reliably employ" (Zinsser, p. 269). Smith frequently emphasized the intimate connection between laboratory experiment and practice in his research, in effect giving credit to the constrained circumstances under which he often worked rather than lamenting their limitations. In an understated self-appraisal he described his work simply as the "study of the causes of infectious disease and a search for their control," but his prodigious research record reveals a magnificent grasp of bacteriological and immunological knowledge gleaned from experimental studies of the microorganisms responsible for many animal and human diseases. In a letter published posthumously he cited the importance of opportunity in his career, urged young scientists to think of research "as an adventure rather than the result of a logical process," and advised them that "prolonged thinking" was necessary but not always productive (*Journal of Bacteriology* [1934]: 19).

Once Smith had established his scientific credentials he voiced an intellectual and moral authority that extended beyond the confines of his laboratory, often framing his research findings to show how the struggle to conquer infection might encourage the emergence of new diseases and how unusual epidemics might encourage the persistent opportunism of parasites under all conditions. In lectures directed to students preparing for careers in medicine Smith proposed that a half-century of progress in biology and medicine required a new perspective on the potential of scientific knowledge: "We cannot return to nature . . . for such a course would destroy civilization. We cannot fly in the face of nature continually for this practice would lead to heavier burdens and eventually to catastrophe. An eclectic course steering carefully as we go along . . . seems to be the proper choice" (*Parasitism and Disease* [1934], pp. 169–70).

• Smith's scientific and personal papers are not in the public domain, but some correspondence is in the Simon H. Gage Papers at the Cornell University Archives, Ithaca, N.Y. Hans Zinsser, "Biographical Memoir of Theobald Smith, 1859–1934," National Academy of Sciences, *Biographical Memoirs* 17 (1936): 261–303, includes a list of Smith's scientific publications. A more recent biographical article in the *Dictionary of Scientific Biography* by the bacteriologist Claude E. Dolman provides a technically informed and highly readable intellectual history of Smith's lasting contributions to biomedical science and a eulogy on his character. The detailed bibliographic note includes brief reference to manuscript collections that include Smith correspondence and secondary literature. For other historical vignettes, see Claude E. Dolman, "Texas Cattle Fever: A Commemorative Tribute to Theobald Smith," *Clio Medica* 4 (1969): 1–31, and Barbara Gutmann Rosenkrantz, *Public Health and the State: Changing Views in Massachusetts, 1842–1936* (1972), pp. 115–26. Obituaries include E. G. Conklin, *Proceedings of the American Philosophical Society* 75 (1935): 333–35, and E. B. McKinley, *Science* 82 (1935): 575–86.

BARBARA GUTMANN ROSENKRANTZ

SMITH, Theodate Louise (9 Apr. 1859–16 Feb. 1914), psychologist, was born in Hallowell, Maine, the daughter of Thomas Smith and Philomel Hall. She attended Smith College, where she earned a B.A. in 1882 and an M.A. in 1884. For a decade after her graduation from Smith she was employed as a teacher, first in Gardiner, Maine, and then in two private high schools for girls, Brooklyn Heights Seminary in New York and Mount Vernon Seminary in Washington, D.C.

Part of the first cohort of women in the United States to be granted admission to graduate work on an equal basis with men, Smith studied psychology at

Yale University from 1893 to 1895 under the direction of E. W. Scripture. She spent the following academic year at Clark University in Worcester, Massachusetts, which was still officially closed to women, carrying out experiments on the relationship of motor activity to memory. Her work at Clark was made possible through special arrangements and with the support of the head of the psychology laboratory, E. C. Sanford, and it formed the basis of the Ph.D. dissertation that she wrote to earn her doctorate at Yale in 1896. She then returned to Mount Vernon Seminary, where she taught from 1896 to 1898. In 1902 she began to work as a research assistant to G. Stanley Hall, professor of psychology and president of Clark University. She occupied this position until 1909, when she was appointed lecturer and librarian at the newly established Children's Institute at Clark, where she remained until her premature death.

Smith's graduate education and career in psychology brought together two important strands of the emerging discipline in the late nineteenth and early twentieth centuries. One of these was Wundtian experimental psychology imported from Germany, which emphasized carefully controlled laboratory studies of sensation and perception in which highly trained adult observers provided introspective reports of their experiences. The other was the child study movement promoted in the United States by G. Stanley Hall, which advocated basing educational practice on the scientific study of child development. E. W. Scripture had come to Yale in 1892 after earning his Ph.D. with Wilhelm Wundt at Leipzig and working with Hall for one year at Clark. Smith's graduate work under Scripture reflected her adviser's twin interests in experimentation and pedagogy and, more specifically, in the scientific study of the child's mind and its implications for educational practice. In an article that reported the results of her dissertation research, Smith wrote that pedagogy rightfully looked to psychology for aid and that providing that aid was the means by which psychology would gain its practical justification.

In 1902, when Smith began her job as research assistant to Hall, child study as an organized movement was beginning to pass from the American educational scene. Yet, the first decade of the twentieth century was a particularly prolific period for Hall's pronouncements about transforming education in light of observations of the child's nature. Smith, as Hall's research assistant, was involved in the organization of vast numbers of such observations, which were collected by parents and teachers through use of the questionnaire method. In 1903 she published an article that defended the use of the questionnaire method, which by that time had been in use at Clark for nine years. Smith claimed that the questionnaire method had brought the practical value of psychology to the attention of the child study movement by demonstrating how it could be applied to real life problems. Her stance signaled a striking departure from the experimental approach that she had followed earlier in her dissertation research, and it would characterize her published work for the remainder of her career.

While she was at Clark, Smith contributed steadily to the psychological literature on childhood, using the results of questionnaires to publish papers on affection, daydreaming, and obstinacy and obedience. In addition, she coauthored papers with Hall on the paired topics of showing off and bashfulness and curiosity and interest. She also became involved in child study and child welfare at the international level, attending and reporting on the Berlin Congress for Child Study in 1906. Other works that reflect these concerns are a 1911 article and a 1912 book on the theory and methods used in Maria Montessori's "houses of childhood" in Italy and a 1912 report on European institutions for the protection of motherhood and the prevention of infant mortality. Her work was cut short by her sudden death, attributed to a diabetic coma, in Worcester.

Although Smith never married, and was not herself a mother, she was remembered by Hall as "a thorough scholar, an expert in child welfare" and someone "whose devotion to the study of children was only surpassed by her love for the individual children of her acquaintance." Smith's most notable contribution was an outgrowth of her international involvement in child study and child welfare: toward the end of her life she became widely recognized as an interpreter for the American audience of the Montessori system of education.

• A list of Smith's publications is included in the *Cumulative Author Index to the Psychological Index 1894–1935 and Psychological Abstracts 1927–1958*. A biographical sketch of Smith can be found in Elizabeth Scarborough and Laurel Furumoto, *Untold Lives: The First Generation of American Women Psychologists* (1987). An obituary is in the *Pedagogical Seminary* 21 (1914): 160.

LAUREL FURUMOTO

SMITH, Thomas Adams (12 Aug. 1781–25 June 1844), army officer, was born in Essex County, Virginia, the son of Francis Smith and Lucy Wilkinson. His father, a property owner, relocated the family to Wilkes County, Georgia, shortly after the Revolution. From there Smith joined the army as a second lieutenant of artillery on 15 December 1803. He served on the staff of General James Wilkinson throughout the old Southwest and on 31 December 1805 became a first lieutenant. In 1807 Wilkinson dispatched Smith from New Orleans to Washington, D.C., to secretly convey news of Aaron Burr's conspiracy. Also in 1807 he married Cynthia Berry, the sister of Hugh Lawson White; the union produced eight children. Smith subsequently transferred to the newly created Regiment of Riflemen on 3 May 1808. Through deft political maneuvering he became colonel of the regiment on 6 July 1812, over the head of Major John Fuller. In this capacity Smith was employed in the so-called Patriot War, a clandestine attempt to annex East Florida from Spain. Chronically short of men, he conducted an unsuccessful siege of St. Augustine in the face of mounting attacks by Creek and Seminole Indians. When the rebellion collapsed, American troops were withdrawn, and Smith transferred north to participate in the War of 1812.

Throughout the summer of 1813, Smith conducted recruiting activity in Tennessee. He soon after joined the Northwestern Army of General William Henry Harrison and also briefly commanded the garrison at strategic Sackets Harbor, New York. On 4 January 1814 Smith was one of six young officers elevated to brigadier general, and he took post with General George Izard's Right Division at Plattsburgh, New York. Such was Smith's fighting reputation that Izard directed him to command the advance guard at Champlain Village. In late August 1814 Smith's brigade accompanied Izard on his controversial march from Plattsburgh to the Niagara frontier. When little fighting materialized, he obtained a furlough and spent the closing weeks of the war with his family in Tennessee.

Smith was retained in the peacetime establishment as colonel of the Regiment of Riflemen with a brevet rank of brigadier general. In September 1815 he assumed command of the Ninth Military District, with headquarters at Bellefountaine near St. Louis. The Ninth Military District was an enormous expanse incorporating the Illinois and Missouri territories. The following spring he ascended the Mississippi River with several companies of riflemen to confront the Fox Indians. War was averted, but as a precaution Smith established Fort Armstrong on Rock Island and Fort Edwards on the Des Moines River. Arriving at Prairie du Chien, Wisconsin Territory, he ordered construction of another important post, Fort Crawford. Smith subsequently supervised military surveys of the Arkansas River region in concert with the noted explorer Major Stephen H. Long. Smith resigned his commission and returned to civilian life on 10 November 1818. The following year Fort Smith, Arkansas Territory, was christened in his honor.

On 1 November 1818 Smith accepted President James Monroe's offer to serve as receiver of public monies at Franklin, Missouri. He functioned there until 1826 and then retired to private life in Saline County, Missouri. Though closely connected to national figures like William Harris Crawford and Thomas Hart Benton, Smith consistently declined political office and spent the remainder of his life pursuing agricultural interests. His plantation, "Experiment," became a model of scientific management and a popular resort for visiting dignitaries. Smith died there as one of Missouri's wealthiest and most respected citizens.

In an age of military incompetence, Smith was an active and enterprising soldier. He joined the military in a period of Jeffersonian cutbacks, rose to command an elite regiment, and campaigned with distinction from Florida to Canada. His skillful administration of the Ninth Military District and conscientious management of public monies demonstrated his efficiency and integrity. Though overshadowed by great contemporaries like Henry Atkinson and Henry Leavenworth, Smith made significant contributions to the early stages of western exploration and expansion.

• Smith's manuscripts are at the State Historical Society of Missouri, Columbia. For published correspondence consult T. Frederick Davis, ed., "United States Troops in Spanish East Florida, 1812–1813," *Florida Historical Quarterly* 9 (July-Oct. 1930): 3–23, 96–116, 135–55, 279–98; and Clarence E. Carter, ed., *Territorial Papers of the United States*, vol. 15 (1948). See also W. Edwin Hemphill, ed., *The Papers of John C. Calhoun*, vols. 4 and 5 (1969). For details on his military activities see Rembert W. Patrick, *Florida Fiasco* (1954), Bruce E. Mahan, *Old Fort Crawford and the Frontier* (1926), and John C. Fredriksen, "Green Coats and Glory: The United States Regiment of Riflemen, 1808–1821," *Military Collector and Historian, Commemorative War of 1812 Issue* (1996). Finally, family information is contained in W. B. Napton, *Past and Present of Saline County, Missouri* (1910), pp. 318–24; and C. W. Coleman, "Genealogy of the Smith Family of Essex County, Virginia," *William and Mary Quarterly* 6 (July 1897): 41–53.

JOHN C. FREDRIKSEN

SMITH, Thorne (27 Mar. 1891–20 June 1934), author and screenwriter, was born James Thorne Smith, Jr., at the U.S. Naval Academy in Annapolis, Maryland, the son of Commodore James Thorne Smith, who later commanded the Port of New York during World War I. His mother's name is unknown. Smith attended the Locust Dale Academy in Virginia, followed by St. Luke's School in Wayne, Pennsylvania. Upon completing his secondary education he studied at Dartmouth College from 1910 to 1912 but left before earning a degree. He began work at an advertising agency in New York and during the following years became acquainted with the artistic and literary circles of Greenwich Village. When the United States entered World War I, Smith enlisted in the navy and rose to the rank of boatswain's mate. While in the navy he edited *Broadside*, a service newspaper. His humorous sketches featuring the mishaps and misfortunes of Biltmore Oswald were later collected and published in *Biltmore Oswald: The Diary of a Hapless Recruit* (1918), followed quickly by *Out o' Luck: Biltmore Oswald Very Much at Sea* (1919). After the war Smith returned to New York and his career in advertising. In 1919 he also published his only collection of poems, *Haunts and By-Paths*. While working in New York he married Celia Sullivan around 1921, and they had two daughters.

Smith's career as an author of comic novels was firmly established in 1926 with the publication of *Topper: An Improbable Adventure*. Introducing the character Cosmo Topper, a staid banker, bored by the routines of his life, the novel records how complicated Topper's life becomes when the ghosts of George and Marion Kerby haunt him. *Topper: An Improbable Adventure*, the most successful of Smith's works, has sold more than 2.5 million copies since publication. Other comic, and at times ribald, gems soon followed, including *The Stray Lamb* (1929) and *Did She Fall?* (1930). *The Night Life of the Gods* (1931) depicts the unrestrainable debauchery of the gods of classical mythology that is unleashed when statues in the Metropolitan Museum of Art are brought to life. That same year Smith published *Turnabout*, a gender-bender novel of manners in which Tim and Sally Willows, husband and wife, exchange bodies and experience how the other lives; Tim's improbable pregnancy brings the novel to its climax. Smith continued his rapid production of manuscripts, publishing *The Bishop's Jaegers* in 1932, the year he also brought back Cosmo Topper in *Topper Takes a Trip*. In 1933 he produced *Rain in the Doorway* and *Skin and Bones*.

In 1933 Smith also traveled to Hollywood to write dialogue for Metro-Goldwyn-Mayer. His own novels became the basis for a number of screenplays. *Night Life of the Gods* appeared in 1935, directed by Lowell Sherman for Universal Studios. *Topper*, starring Cary Grant, Roland Young, and Constance Bennett, was filmed in 1937, directed by Norman MacLeod for MGM. This was followed by *Topper Takes a Trip* (1939) and *Topper Returns* (1941), both produced for United Artists.

While vacationing with his family in Sarasota, Florida, Smith died suddenly of a heart attack. At the time of his death he left an unfinished manuscript, which was completed by Norman Matson and published as *The Passionate Witch* (1941). This novel became the basis for a popular film, *I Married a Witch* (1942), featuring Veronica Lake and Fredric March; Smith is also credited as coauthor with Matson of *Bats in the Belfry* (1943), a sequel.

Smith died at the height of his creative productivity, and one can only speculate as to the additional contributions to humor and fantasy fiction he would have made. Though few people now recognize the name Thorne Smith, his character Topper has secured a place in popular culture, appearing in an eponymous television series from 1953 to 1956, as well as a television remake of the feature film *Topper* in 1979.

• Additional works by Smith include *Dreams' End* (1927), *Lazy Bear Lane* (1931), and *The Glorious Pool* (1934). A critical evaluation is Keith Neilson, "Thorne Smith," in *Supernatural Fiction Writers: Fantasy and Horror*, vol. 2, ed. E. F. Bleiler (1985). A bibliographical review is George H. Scheetz and Rodney N. Henshaw, "Thorne Smith," *Bulletin of Bibliography* 41 (1984): 25–37. Smith is the subject of Howard S. Jitomir, "Forgotten Excellence: A Study of Thorne Smith's Humor" (Ph.D. diss., St. John's Univ., 1983). An obituary is in the *New York Times*, 22 June 1934.

MELISSA MCFARLAND PENNELL

SMITH, Tony (23 Sept. 1912–26 Dec. 1980), sculptor, was born Anthony Peter Smith in South Orange, New Jersey, the son of Peter Anthony Smith, a chairman of the A. P. Smith Company, a waterworks factory, and Josephine McCabe. Afflicted with tuberculosis when he was around four years old, Smith spent his early childhood isolated in a one-room, prefabricated house on his family property. He later attended Fordham College in New York City in spring 1930 and Georgetown University in Washington, D.C., in 1931–1932. Around 1932 Smith operated a used bookstore in

Newark, New Jersey. Between 1933 and 1936 he worked for the family business as a toolmaker, draftsman, and purchasing agent. At night he studied drawing and painting at the Art Students League in New York City with European modernists George Grosz and Vaclav Vytlacil and the American George Bridgman.

Smith's decision in 1937 to become an architect led him to enroll in the progressive New Bauhaus school in Chicago established by László Moholy-Nagy (1937–1938). In the fall of 1938 Smith worked as a bricklayer at Frank Lloyd Wright's Suntop Home project in Ardmore, Pennsylvania; he eventually became clerk-of-the-works there. Smith also did construction estimates for Wright's Usonian houses and helped build the Armstrong home in Ogden Dunes, Indiana.

Smith returned home to New Jersey in November 1940. From 1940 through the mid-1960s he was an independent architectural designer, completing at least twenty building projects and envisioning many others. While his earliest designs reflected Wright's influence, his plans of the later 1940s and early 1950s revealed a strong interest in Le Corbusier and Mies van der Rohe.

Smith met the actress and singer Jane Brotherton in 1943; they were married that year in California. In summer 1945 he returned to the East Coast and built a painting studio in Provincetown, Massachusetts, for his friend Fritz Bultman. He moved to New York City in the fall and the next year began teaching at New York University's School of Education, where he remained until 1950, as well as at Hartley House, a neighborhood settlement house (1946–1952). From 1950 to 1953 he taught at Cooper Union; in 1951–1952 and again in 1957–1958 at Pratt Institute; at Bennington College from 1958 to 1961; at Hunter College from 1962 to 1974 and in 1979–1980; and at Princeton University from 1975 to 1978.

In the late 1940s Smith developed close friendships with abstract expressionist artists, especially Jackson Pollock, Mark Rothko, and Barnett Newman. Smith built a home on Long Island for the painter Theodore Stamos (1951) and a painting studio and guest house for the influential art dealer Betty Parsons (1959–1961).

Smith lived in Germany from 1953 to 1955, joining his wife, who was performing opera there; they also traveled to France, Italy, and Spain. The *Louisenberg* paintings made during this period were based on a framework of circles set into a rectilinear grid, merging organic form with a rational framework. These modular compositions marked a significant stage in Smith's development.

The Smiths' first child, Chiara ("Kiki"), was born in Nuremberg in 1954. Twins Beatrice and Seton were born shortly after the couple returned to the United States in 1955. The Smiths settled in New Jersey, where he returned to teaching and continued to develop architectural projects. *Throne* (1956), Smith's first "named" piece, evolved from an exercise that he had assigned to a design class at Pratt. But it was not until

1961, while recovering from a serious auto accident, that he focused on making sculptural forms by taping together small, handmade paper tetrahedral modules. These models were enlarged by assistants into full-scale plywood mock-ups and then painted with thick black paint (the kind usually used for the undercoating of cars) to approximate the look of sheet steel. A typical example is *The Snake Is Out* from 1962, now in the National Gallery of Art in Washington, D.C. Also in 1962, Smith used a commercial fabricator to realize his first metal sculpture, *The Black Box* (National Gallery of Canada, Ottawa). Rooted in geometric abstraction, Smith's sculptural "presences" also reflected his interest in architecture (primitive and modern) as well as in science, the space-frame engineering of Alexander Graham Bell, and mathematics. Titles were often inspired by literary sources, especially James Joyce's *Finnegans Wake*, for example, *Gracehoper* (1972, Detroit Institute of Arts).

Smith was fifty-two when his sculpture was first publicly exhibited in a group show, *Black, White and Gray*, curated by Samuel Wagstaff, Jr., in 1964 at the Wadsworth Atheneum in Hartford, Connecticut. This exhibition was among the first to present the artists of the burgeoning minimalist movement, whose work was generally based on unitary, rational, geometric modules. Two years later, Wagstaff and Samuel Adams Green organized two concurrent one-man shows of Smith's work, at the Wadsworth Atheneum and at the Institute of Contemporary Art of the University of Pennsylvania in Philadelphia. In October 1967, appearing on the cover of *Time* magazine, Smith was described as the "Master of the Monumentalists." Smith's large, architecturally scaled, geometric objects were associated by critics with the minimalist movement, although Smith's development had been independent of the younger artists of that group. Smith's aesthetic was closer to that of the abstract expressionist artists, who were his friends and contemporaries.

Smith initially articulated his artistic goals—to discover an underlying, unifying aesthetic in American culture—during the last two years of World War II. His ideas were stimulated by literary masters (e.g., Henry David Thoreau, Walt Whitman, and Joyce), philosophers (Nietzsche and Lao Tse), and religious tracts, while his imagery was affected by the vitalist sciences of D'Arcy Thompson (*On Growth and Form* [1917]) and Jay Hambidge (*The Elements of Dynamic Symmetry* [1926; repr. 1967]).

In the 1960s Smith explained that his "presences" were conceived as elements in an invisible space lattice that joined the world we see with the microscopic world we cannot see. The sculptures were designed in a system in which solids and voids have equal physical substance. Smith's interview with Samuel Wagstaff, "Talking with Tony Smith," published in *Artforum* (Dec. 1966), was a significant influence on the artists of the 1960s. His recollection of a night ride on the unfinished New Jersey Turnpike was particularly important, as it was simultaneously decried by the critic Michael Fried in his seminal essay "Art and Objecthood"

(*Artforum*, June 1967) and embraced by the avant-garde, including the Earthwork artist Robert Smithson. Fried objected to Smith's elevation of experience to the status of art, while Smithson was captivated by Smith's aestheticization of the contemporary no-man's land.

Smith received numerous awards, including the American Institute of Architects Fine Arts Medal in 1971; he was elected to the American Institute of Arts and Letters in 1979. He died in New York City. Smith's career defies simple categorization; he was unique in his ability to absorb the past and create work that has retained its feeling for the present.

• Tony Smith's papers are part of the privately held Tony Smith Estate in New York City. A lengthy interview by Paul Cummings with Smith is in the Archives of American Art. Smith's important published writings include the preface and catalog entries in *Tony Smith: Two Exhibitions of Sculpture* (1966), his statement on "Die" in *Art Now: New York* 1 (Nov. 1969), unpaginated, and the "Project for a Parking Lot," *Design Quarterly* 78/79 (1970): 64–66. Informative interviews are by Elayne H. Varian, "Tony Smith," in the Finch College *Schemata 7* exhibition catalog (1967); Renée Sabatello Neu in the *Tony Smith* Museum of Modern Art circulating exhibition brochure (1968); Lucy Lippard, "The New Work: More Points on the Lattice," in *Tony Smith: Recent Sculpture*, Knoedler Gallery exhibition catalog (1971), and "Tony Smith: Talk about Sculpture," *Art News* 7 (Apr. 1971): 48–49, 68, 71–72. A number of Smith's statements and interviews are reprinted in Gregory Battcock, ed., *Minimal Art: A Critical Anthology* (1968). The first important profile of Smith was written by the artist Scott Burton, "Old Master at the New Frontier," *Art News* 65 (Dec. 1966): 52–55, 68–70. See also articles by Lippard, "The Ineluctable Modality of the Visible," *Art International* 11 (Summer 1967): 24–26, and "Escalation in Washington," *Art International* 12 (Jan. 1968): 42–66, and her monograph *Tony Smith* (1972). An obituary is in the *New York Times*, 27 Dec. 1980.

JOAN H. PACHNER

SMITH, Trixie (1895–21 Sept. 1943), blues and vaudeville singer, was born in Atlanta, Georgia. Nothing is known of her parents and childhood. Having studied at Selma University in Alabama, she came to New York City around 1915 to perform in clubs and theaters. She was at the New Standard Theater in Philadelphia in 1916, and she toured on the Theater Owners' Booking Association circuit, probably in 1920 and 1921.

While performing at Harlem's Lincoln Theater and recording for the Black Swan label from 1921 to 1923, Smith furthered her fame by entering and winning a blues contest at the Manhattan Casino on 20 January 1922. Her recordings included "Trixie's Blues" (1921?; by some accounts she recorded it after winning the contest) and two titles accompanied by cornetist Louis Armstrong in 1925, "The World's Jazz Crazy and So Am I" and "Railroad Blues." In 1932 she appeared in the film *The Black King*. She continued working as a singer and actress in New York until 1933 and then on national tours until 1935. As the New Orleans jazz revival was just beginning to get under way, she had an opportunity to record an outstanding session with reed player Sidney Bechet's group in 1938, including "My Daddy Rocks Me." Smith made one further title, "No Good Man," with a jazz trio in 1939. She died in New York City.

Although little is known of Smith's life, she is remembered for her few recordings, which document her stature as one of the best classic blues and vaudeville singers. In her early work Smith's voice is high-pitched and penetrating. On some titles she seems uncomfortable singing blues. But "Railroad Blues" is dramatic and convincing, and it shows a fully idiomatic command of sliding blue notes. She articulates lyrics clearly yet retains some African-American English pronunciation. Thus her historical place among African-American singers is midway between those who attempted to assimilate completely into the mainstream of American popular song, like Ethel Waters, and those who upheld rural southern traditions, like Ma Rainey, whose pronunciation could verge on the indecipherable.

By the time of her 1938 recordings with Bechet, Smith's voice remains as penetrating as it did when it sounded more girlish, but it has acquired a full-bodied timbre. Whether this change reflects her physical maturity or whether it stems from a dozen or so years of improvement in recording fidelity is hard to determine. It may be that vastly better microphones captured what had perhaps been there in her voice all along. Perhaps a far more significant development is represented by an excerpt from the lyrics of "My Daddy Rocks Me," the two-sided (i.e., six-minute-long) 78-rpm record from the session with Bechet:

My daddy rocks me, with one steady roll.
There's no slippin' when he once takes hold.
. . . .
I looked at the clock, and the clock struck ten.
I said, "Gloooooory, Aaaamen."
He kept rockin' with one steady roll.
. . . .
I looked at the clock, and the clock struck eleven.
I said, "Now daddy, ain't we in heaven!"
He kept rockin' with one steady roll.

Through her extroverted and heavy manner of delivering this irreverent blend of sex and religion, Smith claims her place in a path leading from risqué African-American cabaret singing of the 1920s to soul music of the 1950s and 1960s.

• Scattered references to Trixie Smith can be found in a variety of sources: Ronald Clifford Foreman, Jr., "Jazz and Race Records, 1920–1932: Their Origins and Their Significance for the Record Industry and Society" (Ph.D. diss., Univ. of Ill., 1968); Robert M. W. Dixon and John Godrich, *Recording the Blues* (1970); Derrick Stewart-Baxter: *Ma Rainey and the Classic Blues Singers* (1970), p. 81; Sheldon Harris, *Blues Who's Who: A Biographical Dictionary of Blues Singers* (1979); Daphne Duval Harrison, *Black Pearls: Blues Queens of the 1920s* (1988), p. 244; Harrison, "'Classic' Blues and Women

Singers," in *The Blackwell Guide to Blues Records*, ed. Paul Oliver (1989; rev. as *The Blackwell Guide to Recorded Blues*, 1991), pp. 95–97.

BARRY KERNFELD

SMITH, Truman (27 Nov. 1791–3 May 1884), lawyer and congressman, was born in Roxbury, Connecticut, the son of Phineas Smith and Deborah Ann Judson, farmers. He was the nephew of Nathan Smith, a U.S. senator, and Nathaniel Smith, a U.S. representative. Tutored by the Reverend Daniel Parker, he entered Yale College and graduated in 1815. He then studied at the Litchfield Law School, where his uncles had matriculated, and in 1818 he began to practice his profession.

With an agreeable, direct manner and an imposing physique, Smith soon attracted enough clients to his Litchfield law office to become financially secure. He was elected to the Connecticut legislature in 1831, 1832, and 1834. In 1932 he married Maria Cook; they had a son and two daughters. One daughter married Orville H. Platt, a U.S. senator for twenty-six years. Maria Smith died in April 1849.

Elected as a Whig to Congress in 1838, Smith served in that body from 1839 to 1843 and from 1845 to 1849 as an antislavery Conscience Whig, declining to be a candidate in 1842 for the intervening term. In 1844 he was a Whig presidential elector, and in 1848, as a Connecticut delegate to the Whig National Convention at Philadelphia, he supported the party's presidential nominee, Zachary Taylor. Smith served as the Whig national chairman during the ensuing campaign.

Refusing Taylor's offer of secretary of the interior, Smith instead accepted election by his state legislature to the U.S. Senate, where he served from 4 March 1849 until his resignation for financial reasons on 24 May 1854. As a senator during the transition from the dominance of John C. Calhoun, Henry Clay, and Daniel Webster to that of Jefferson Davis, Stephen A. Douglas, and William H. Seward he was not of the first rank. However, he was a reliable supporter of conservative, high-tariff, pro-business doctrines and measures of Daniel Webster's New England section of the Whig party.

In 1850 he married Mary A. Dickinson; they had six sons. Practicing law in New York City from 1854 until his retirement in the autumn of 1872, he commuted from Stamford in Fairfield County, Connecticut. In July 1862, owing to the influence of his former Senate colleague, Secretary of State Seward, Smith was appointed as a judge of the mixed court of international arbitration, which was created by the treaty of 1862 with Great Britain for the final suppression of the slave trade. He was afterward selected as a judge of the court of claims, handling disputes growing out of the Civil War. He remained a judge until 1870. In 1873, at age eighty-one, Smith won a U.S. Supreme Court decision invalidating corporate claims of contractual immunities from negligence lawsuits. He died at his Stamford home.

• The largest collection of Smith's correspondence is at the Connecticut Historical Society, Hartford, scattered among the papers of his contemporaries. Approximately twenty-eight items are at the Litchfield Historical Society. There are also letters from Smith in the papers of Henry S. Samford at the Gen. Samford Memorial Library, Samford, Fla., and in the Thomas Corwin, Abraham Lincoln, William Seward, and Gideon Welles collections at the Library of Congress.

NORMAN B. FERRIS

SMITH, Uriah (2 May 1832–6 Mar. 1903), writer and editor, was born in West Wilton, New Hampshire, the son of Samuel Smith, a highway and bridge contractor, and Rebekah Spalding, a poet. At age four Smith developed an ulcer on his left leg that led to amputation above the knee. This condition in turn contributed to a sedentary life. In 1844 he was baptized into adventism, adopting William Miller's teaching that Christ would physically return that year. After the "Great Disappointment" of 22 October 1844, the last date for Christ's coming adopted by most Millerites, Smith lost interest in religion. At age sixteen he entered Phillips Exeter Academy, from which he graduated in 1851.

That same year, Smith's mother became a sabbatarian adventist, one of a small group of Miller's followers who had adopted Saturday as their day of worship, influencing Uriah to accept her belief in 1851. Smith then declined an invitation to teach at Mount Vernon Academy, New Hampshire, in 1853, going instead to the *Advent Review and Sabbath Herald*, the sabbatarian adventist journal published by James White in Rochester, New York, where Smith operated a hand press.

Smith, who had long held literary ambitions, wrote a 35,000-word epic poem, "The Warning Voice of Time and Prophecy," which the *Review* published serially in 1853. Two years later he became editor of the paper when White moved to Battle Creek, Michigan. Smith, meanwhile, also served as proofreader, business manager, and bookkeeper, and in ensuing years he alternated with White as editor. In 1857 Smith married Harriet Newall Stevens; they had four sons and one daughter.

Suffering from overwork, in 1869 Smith took a leave of absence from the *Review*, which was now the official paper of the Seventh-day Adventist (SDA) church, organized in 1863. After a few months of working as an engraver, Smith returned to the *Review* in 1870 as an associate editor, becoming editor again later that year. Disagreement with White, however, led to Smith's departure in 1873, and for six months he worked as an engraver in Grand Rapids, Michigan. Returning to the *Review* that same year, he alternated with White and others as editor or associate editor until his death.

In addition to his editorial work, Smith served the SDA church in various capacities. In 1861 he became treasurer of the Seventh-day Adventist Publishing Association, the young denomination's first legal entity, which was organized approximately one year before the first state conference of churches and two years before establishment of the General Conference of Seventh-day Adventists. In 1863 he was elected president of the Michigan Conference of Seventh-day Adventists. Ordained to the SDA ministry in 1874, he served as treasurer of the General Conference of Seventh-day Adventists in 1876–1877 and filled several noncontinuous terms as secretary of the General Conference between 1863 and 1888. From 1875 to 1882 he taught the Bible at Battle Creek College, the first SDA college. In 1881 he became chair of the board of trustees but resigned the following year because of conflict over curricular and discipline policies. He also assisted in editing the evangelistic paper, the *Signs of the Times*, beginning in 1874. He traveled to Europe, where he spoke to SDA groups, and the Middle East in 1894.

Despite his influential position among Seventh-day Adventists, Smith held sometimes controversial theological views. Like many early Adventists he rejected the doctrine of the Trinity, regarding Christ as a created being and the Holy Spirit as a divine influence. He continued to hold these opinions even after SDAs moved to trinitarianism in the 1890s. He sometimes questioned the authority of the statements of Ellen G. White, wife of James White and a founder of the church, whose counsels were accepted as divinely inspired by most church members. Smith distinguished between White's "testimonies," which he regarded as human in nature, and her "visions," which he believed were of divine origin. At times he rejected her counsel to him, particularly between 1888 and 1901 when his rather legalistic approach to religion conflicted with a new emphasis on righteousness by faith among SDAs, but he appears to have become more reconciled with the prophetess during the last two years of his life.

In his editorials Smith advocated the strict separation of church and state, opposed Sunday laws, which included the closing of businesses and the prohibition of labor on Sundays, advocated noncombatancy for church members during the Civil War, and objected to SDAs seeking political office. Many of his articles for the *Review* eventually appeared as books, the most important of which were *Thoughts, Critical and Practical on the Book of Revelation* (1867) and *Thoughts, Critical and Practical on the Book of Daniel* (1873), which extended Miller's historicist approach to biblical prophecy. In 1882 these books were combined into one volume, *Daniel and Revelation*, which became the first SDA subscription book. He presented the case for Ellen White's divine inspiration in *The Visions of Mrs. E. G. White* (1868). In *The United States in the Light of Prophecy* (1872) Smith argued that ecclesiastical influence would cause the United States to pass a general Sunday law. He rejected "natural" immortality in favor of "conditional" immortality to be given to the saved at Christ's second coming in *The State of the Dead and the Destiny of the Wicked* (1873). *Looking to Jesus* (1898) examined the meaning of Jesus in terms of the Old Testament sanctuary service. Several of his books appeared in revised and expanded editions under new titles.

In addition to his religious activities, Smith was also an inventor, acquiring a total of at least nine patents, two of which became commercially profitable. In 1863 he developed an artificial leg that bent all the way back at the knee. Twelve years later he introduced a school desk on which the seat could be raised or lowered by standing or sitting. Union School Furniture Company in Battle Creek manufactured this desk until 1891. Smith died in Battle Creek.

• Smith's papers are in the Mark L. Bovee Collection at the Seventh-day Adventist Heritage Center, Andrews University, Berrien Springs, Mich. A biography of Smith is Eugene F. Durand's topically organized *Yours in the Blessed Hope, Uriah Smith* (1986). *The Seventh-day Adventist Encyclopedia,* Commentary Reference Series, vol. 10 (1966; rev. ed., 1976), contains articles on both the *Review and Herald* and Uriah Smith. Further information may be found in Richard W. Schwarz, *Lightbearers to the Remnant* (1979), and Gary Land, ed., *Adventism in America: A History* (1976). An obituary is in the *Advent Review and Sabbath Herald,* 10 Mar. 1903, pp. 3–7.

GARY LAND

SMITH, Venture (1729?–19 Sept. 1805), slave, entrepreneur, and autobiographer, also known as Broteer Venture, was born in Dukandarra, Guinea, the eldest child of Saungm Furro, a prince. His mother, whose name is unknown, was the first of his polygynist father's three wives; she took five-year-old Broteer and her two younger children with her when she left her husband to protest his marrying the third wife without her consent. After traveling for five days over about 140 miles, she left Broteer with a farmer before returning to the country where she was born. This farmer treated Broteer like a son, employing him for a year as a shepherd, until the boy was sent for by his father. Returning to Dukandarra, Broteer found his mother and father reconciled.

This domestic peace was soon interrupted, however, by the sudden invasion of a hostile army, instigated and equipped by Europeans. Although Broteer's father paid tribute, the entire community was forced to flee for their safety. The family's hiding place was soon discovered, and Broteer watched as his father fought and eventually was tortured to death. Broteer and his other family members were taken captive. Young Broteer worked as a servant to the leader of the army's scouting party, carrying his gun, as well as food, cooking supplies, and a 25-pound stone for grinding corn. He also participated in raids on other African nations as the army made its way to the continent's west coast. Taken prisoner yet again when another army defeated his captors, Broteer and his companions were offered in sale to a slave ship from Rhode Island, commanded by Captain Collingwood and his first mate, Thomas Mumford. Broteer was purchased for four gallons of rum and a piece of calico by the ship's steward, Robertson Mumford. Mumford called him "Venture," the latter recalls in his autobiography, *A Narrative of the Life and Adventures of Venture* (1798), "on account of his having purchased me with his own private venture." The ship sailed first to Barbados; of the slaves who survived a devastating shipboard small pox epidemic, all but four were sold there. Venture was among those who sailed on to Rhode Island, where he began life as an American slave at eight years of age.

Venture worked as a household servant at his master's residence on Fisher's Island, carding wool and pounding corn under constant threat of punishment. His master was often away from home, and Venture frequently was subject to the whims of Mumford's son James, who once hung Venture on a cattle gallows for an hour. At age twenty-two Venture married Margaret ("Meg," maiden name unknown), also the slave of his master, with whom he would eventually have four children. After participating in an abortive escape attempt and returning to his master, Venture was sold to Thomas Stanton and moved to Stonington Point, Connecticut; Stanton bought Venture's wife and baby daughter one and a half years later. After repeated beatings by Stanton and his family, Venture was first pawned to Daniel Edwards, Esq., as a cupbearer and waiter and then sold to Colonel Smith at age thirty-one. Having saved a substantial sum of money by shining shoes, fishing, raising and selling vegetables, and doing other odd jobs, Venture purchased his freedom from Smith and adopted the latter's surname as his own.

By the time he was forty-six years old, Smith had purchased his entire family. As a free man he engaged in numerous business ventures, from selling watermelon to cutting wood to running a shipping business. In his memoir he claims to have repeatedly loaned money to both blacks and whites, only to be defaulted on by those who took "advantage of my ignorance of numbers." At age forty-seven Smith moved with his family to East Haddam, Connecticut, where he nursed his daughter until her death. He composed and published his memoirs at age sixty-nine with an anonymous amanuensis-editor and amassed 100 acres of land and three houses. He died in East Haddam or Haddam Neck, Connecticut.

Venture Smith is best known for his *Narrative,* a Franklinesque account of his life, which was reprinted at least three times in the century after his death. Smith's classic slave narrative provides a rare glimpse of the African component of the slave trade and a critical look at slavery in the eighteenth century. Perhaps most important is Smith's portrait of himself as an African-American self-made man. In it he records not only his participation in but also his disillusionment with the American Dream.

• The primary source of information about Venture Smith's life is his *Narrative,* which is discussed in William L. Andrews, *To Tell a Free Story: The First Century of Afro-American Autobiography, 1760–1865* (1986), and Marion Wilson Starling, *The Slave Narrative: Its Place in American History,* 2d ed. (1988).

JEANNINE DELOMBARD

SMITH, Walter Bedell (5 Oct. 1895–9 Aug. 1961), military officer, ambassador, and government official, was born in Indianapolis, Indiana, the son of William

Long Smith and Ida Francis Bedell, who earned a comfortable living as silk buyers. A relative had fought in every American war since the Revolution, and all that Bedell, as he was called from childhood, ever wanted to be was an army officer. An exceptionally bright but indifferent student who trained as a machinist at vocational high school, he lacked the influence to secure an appointment to West Point. The day he turned sixteen, therefore, Smith enlisted in the Indiana National Guard. Within a year he was made company sergeant, and in 1916 he accompanied the expedition to Mexico.

After the United States entered the First World War, Smith's company commander recommended him for officer training school at Fort Benjamin Harrison in Indiana. Smith married Mary Eleanor (Nory) Cline in 1917; they had no children. Commissioned as a second lieutenant, he was deployed to France in May 1918 and almost immediately saw action along the Marne, where he was wounded. Following his recovery he was assigned to the War Department Bureau of Military Intelligence. Thus began a succession of staff positions that would demonstrate Smith's managerial skills.

Smith was promoted to first lieutenant during World War I, and with the passage of the National Defense Act of 1920 he received a regular army commission at the same rank. Following an assignment to the Bureau of the Budget, in 1929 he was detailed to the Philippines, where he received his promotion to captain. Advancement in the army was slow during the depression era, but fortuitously for Smith his next assignment brought him to the Infantry School at Fort Benning, Georgia. There he impressed Major Omar N. Bradley and General George C. Marshall. At their urging he remained at Fort Benning as an instructor until entering the 1934–1935 class of the Command and General Staff School at Fort Leavenworth, Kansas. He graduated 39th out of 120, a performance sufficient for him to receive an appointment, after another stint at the Infantry School, to the Army War College in Washington, D.C.

After graduation Smith returned to Fort Benning, but shortly thereafter a vacancy opened in the secretariat of the War Department General Staff. Bradley recommended Smith, and Marshall, then the Army chief of staff, concurred. Smith's appointment as assistant secretary in 1939 was a boon to his career. Promoted to major, he earned Marshall's trust and confidence by exhibiting loyalty, competence, and a willingness to make decisions. These would become his trademark attributes. In 1941 he was promoted to lieutenant colonel and colonel in rapid succession, and Marshall made him secretary of the General Staff. Then, following the creation of the Joint Chiefs of Staff after Pearl Harbor, Marshall made Smith chief of its secretariat. When the British and Americans established the Combined Chiefs of Staff, Smith became head of that secretariat as well. As a brigadier general, he coordinated the flow of information between Marshall, the Navy

Department, Secretary of War Henry Stimson, the White House, and the British.

In these capacities Smith demonstrated not only his managerial talent, but an ability to work harmoniously with the British. Accordingly, when Dwight D. Eisenhower left for London to assume command of the European theater of operations, he requested that Smith accompany him as his chief of staff. Marshall, who had come to rely heavily on his key staff officer, reluctantly acceded. Promoted to major general following his arrival in London in September 1942, Smith began a relationship with Eisenhower that equalled the one he had established with Marshall. Ike and Beetle, as they were popularly known, blended perfectly. In contrast to Eisenhower's congenial disposition and conciliatory demeanor, Smith was abrupt and an authoritarian taskmaster. Granted absolute control over staff management, Smith maintained lines of authority and oversaw all headquarters operations with an iron fist. He also drafted directives and served as Eisenhower's sounding board and confidant. Smith's intensity caused him to develop a painful ulcer, which exacerbated his irascible personality. But he got the job done, and by doing so allowed Eisenhower to concentrate on strategy and encouraging—or restraining—his commanders in the field.

Smith was with Eisenhower throughout World War II and wrote about it in *Eisenhower's Six Great Decisions: Europe 1944–1945* (1956). He helped to plan and execute the invasions of North Africa, Italy, and France, and was the first person Eisenhower turned to for advice when weather threatened to postpone D-day. More important, he served as the commander in chief's troubleshooter and lightning rod. As conflicting views precipitated crises in the grand alliance, Eisenhower charged Smith with personally intervening with both political and military leaders. Secure because he enjoyed the confidence of Franklin Roosevelt, Churchill, and Marshall, he succeeded admirably, forging strong relationships with Eisenhower's principal subordinates, the many feathers he ruffled notwithstanding. As Eisenhower's representative he also played a pivotal role in the 1943 Italian surrender and, a year later, Roosevelt's decision to recognize Charles DeGaulle's provisional government of France.

Although Smith began 1944 with a promotion to lieutenant general, the year would prove the most taxing yet. In preparation for the cross-channel invasion, he spent the early months setting up SHAEF (Supreme Headquarters, Allied Expeditionary Force), at Bushy Park in England. Following the landing and breakout, he would establish a headquarters at Versailles and then another at Reims. While retaining responsibility for these enormous operations, he became increasingly involved in strategic decision making, especially after Eisenhower assumed field command in September 1944. Eisenhower would decide the outlines of strategy and leave it to Smith to work out the details, prepare the orders, explain the rationale, and oversee implementation. Thus he shared Ike's headache over Field Marshall Bernard Law Montgomery, whose egomania and contempt for his American colleagues taxed the combined command to its limit. Smith supported Eisenhower in the broad front versus narrow thrust controversy, and he encouraged his chief to be less conciliatory. After the failure of MARKET-GARDEN, the Montgomery-planned airborne assault through Holland, the allies crossed the Rhine. Despite pressure to race the Soviets to Berlin, Eisenhower decided to halt the advance at the Elbe. Although he would later change his mind, Smith supported him. Eisenhower delegated to his chief of staff the responsibility for negotiating the terms of the German surrender. Although he approached his responsibilities narrowly and never received the glory of the men of action, his role was no less vital. The quintessential organization man, by the end of World War II he epitomized the bureaucrat's contribution to the modern U.S. military establishment.

Smith's permanent rank at the end of the war was lieutenant general. Because his ambition was to be army chief of staff, he was disappointed. Having shown a deft diplomatic touch toward the British and French, and associated intimately with Eisenhower, in 1946 he was appointed ambassador to the Soviet Union. He served until 1949, during which time relations with Moscow turned icy. Smith became an ardent cold warrior. In his 1949 memoir *My Three Years in Moscow*, he argued that the conflict was irreconcilable and required a firm policy of containment to thwart the Soviets' inherent expansionism.

Smith returned to the United States in March 1949 to take command of the First Army on Governor's Island, New York. This appointment assured his receipt of his fourth star, but it suggested he was not in line for army chief of staff. In September 1950 he accepted Truman's offer to become CIA director, a position he had turned down twice previously. He laid the foundation for the fledgling agency's rapid growth in the 1950s by restructuring its organization to increase the director's authority and tightening its internal security. He was unenthusiastic about covert operations, however, and he did little to improve its intelligence gathering or analysis capabilities.

After being elected president in 1952, Eisenhower appointed Smith undersecretary of state, both to bring him into the administration and oblige Secretary of State John Foster Dulles's desire that his brother Allen become CIA director. Smith's role remains obscure. Dulles was proprietary about his authority, and Eisenhower feared appearing unduly influenced by the military. The president's respect for and trust in Smith was undiminished, nevertheless; Eisenhower knew he could count on his former chief of staff to handle delicate situations. Smith, consequently, operated in the shadows. He orchestrated the early months of the CIA's 1954 operation in Guatemala, and he succeeded Dulles as the chief U.S. delegate to the Geneva Conference of 1954 which dealt with issues regarding both Korea and Indochina. There, probably with private instructions from Eisenhower, he conducted convoluted talks with the Soviets and smoothed over differences with the British. The July accords that divided Vietnam at the seventeenth parallel were hardly satisfactory from the administration's perspective, but owing largely to Smith's efforts they were, as he told the press on his return, the "best that could be expected in the circumstances."

Frustrated by playing second fiddle to Dulles, Smith resigned in October 1954. For more than four decades he had served his country. From now on he served on the boards of various corporations. He died in Washington, D.C., and left behind a sizable fortune. What he wanted, nevertheless, was to have been army chief of staff.

Walter Bedell Smith was the consummate staff officer, and as such he epitomized the maturation of the U.S. Army. In his capacities as ambassador to the Soviet Union, CIA director, and undersecretary of state, moreover, he played a vital if often inconspicuous role in the evolving Cold War. His history in the most fundamental sense paralleled that of the United States as it emerged from the depression and World War II as an international superpower.

• Smith's papers, on deposit at the Dwight D. Eisenhower Library, in Abilene, Kansas, are skimpy and unilluminating. Of more value are Eisenhower's papers at that library. The published *Papers of Dwight David Eisenhower* (1970–1984), especially volumes 1–11, should also be consulted, as should the forthcoming volumes on 1953–1954. There is also material in the George C. Marshall papers at the Marshall Library in Lexington, Virginia, and the Modern Military Division of the National Archives in Washington, D.C. Ludwell Montague, *General Walter Bedell Smith as Director of Central Intelligence, October 1950–February 1953* (1992), is the official history of Smith's tenure, originally published internally by the CIA in 1971. The only biography of Smith, which focuses almost exclusively on World War II, is D. K. R. Crosswell, *The Chief of Staff: The Military Career of General Walter Bedell Smith* (1991). A front-page obituary is in the *New York Times*, 10 Aug. 1961.

RICHARD H. IMMERMAN

SMITH, William (8 Oct. 1697–22 Nov. 1769), lawyer and justice, was born in Newport-Pagnell, Buckinghamshire, England, the son of Thomas Smith, a tallow chandler, and Susanna Odell. The family, including four sons and two daughters, emigrated to New York in 1715, perhaps on the same ship that carried James Alexander, who would later become a close associate of William Smith. In England Smith received a liberal education; once in America he earned an undergraduate degree from Yale in 1719 and a master's degree by 1722. Religion and languages were among Smith's loves, and as a young man he considered becoming a minister. He was fluent in Hebrew, Latin, and Greek. Smith was at Yale during unsettled times, the rector and chief tutor resigning from the school in 1722 after embracing episcopacy. A Presbyterian, he was named junior tutor that year and remained until 1724, at which time he declined the rector's chair. That same year he returned to New York City, where he was admitted to the bar, but his interest in education would continue his entire life. In 1727 he married Mary Het, daughter of the Huguenot merchant René Het and his wife, Blanche Du Bois. They had fifteen children, of whom fourteen survived to adulthood.

Smith would prove to be one of New York's premier lawyers and trainers of lawyers. One of a very few college-educated men in the province, aside from ministers, he was admitted to Gray's Inn of the Inns of Court in 1727, although it appears that he never actually attended. He began his career just as New York was restricting those who could practice law. From 1730 to 1745 he was one of only seven allowed to appear before the New York Mayor's Court. In 1729 he and six others formed an association that supervised legal education and by requiring a seven-year apprenticeship professionalized the bar. Their knowledge of the law and access to New York's most powerful appointed and elected officials made them arguably the most influential citizens in the province. One result of this control was to restrict access to the profession just as it became both respected and lucrative.

Eighteenth-century New York politics was famous for its factionalism. These factions, more concerned with power and personality than with ideology, would come to be known as the Livingstons and the DeLanceys, after the two families most influential in them. They would contest for the patronage perquisites of succeeding New York governors, the winners gaining council seats and supreme court judgeships, the losers making life miserable for the governors caught in the middle. Smith became firmly entrenched with James Alexander, the Morrises, and the Livingstons. The cornerstone of their position seems to have been protection of local interests against the prerogative, although they were committed to the empire. In 1733 Smith and Alexander sided with Councillor Rip Van Dam against Governor William Cosby's claim to all of his salary when Van Dam acted as governor. In the process they argued not about salaries but about the legality of the supreme court sitting as a court of exchequer. This case brought them the support of Chief Justice Lewis Morris but the enmity not only of the governor but of Justices James DeLancey and Frederick Philipse. These divisions would persist.

Perhaps Smith's most famous case involved the printer John Peter Zenger. Smith and Alexander were the force and often the authors behind the *New York Weekly Journal* that the immigrant Zenger printed. This opposition newspaper attacked Governor Cosby until Zenger was jailed for seditious libel. Smith and Alexander chose to pursue a deeper legal principle, arguing that DeLancey and Philipse, the supreme court justices, had been appointed illegally since their commissions were at pleasure, not for good behavior. For this attack they were disbarred. Zenger was defended by Andrew Hamilton of Philadelphia, arguably the most famous attorney of the time. Smith and Alexander took their own case to the assembly and two years later were readmitted to the bar.

If Smith seemed to argue against expanding the rights of the Crown, he was by no means opposed to Britain's authority and often served the king's interest, especially when that reinforced his own views or prejudices. In 1737, attempting to set aside the election of Adolph Philipse to the general assembly, he questioned the franchise of New York's few Jews. In an impassioned speech Smith, according to his son, "so pathetically described the bloody tragedy at Mount Calvary that a member cried out with agony and in tears beseeching him to desist. . . . Many others wept; the unfortunate Israelites were content to lose their votes, could they escape with their lives" (Smith, Jr., vol. 2, p. 34). Smith was also one of the king's prosecutors of black slaves following the "Negro plot" of 1741. In the process he helped secure the conviction of John Ury, accused of being a Roman Catholic priest and suspect for that even though his part in the slave conspiracy was never demonstrated or even argued.

While Smith secured most of his considerable fortune from his law practice, he also attempted to augment his income in the ways open to well-connected and privileged New Yorkers. In 1732 he was one of those, including Cadwallader Colden, James Alexander, the Morrises, and Francis Harrison, who tried to monopolize the Oblong Patent, New York's foremost available land at the time. The attempt failed when Harrison turned on the group and joined their competitors. Smith also held public offices, which if not lucrative in their own right, gave him insider knowledge and contacts. In 1751 Governor George Clinton named him attorney general, a position he held temporarily until someone with better contacts in England secured the post. In 1753 Clinton named him to the royal Council, a position he held until 1767 when he resigned in favor of his son William Jr. As a member of the council he represented New York in 1754 at the Albany Congress. He was one of those who drew up and supported the Albany Plan of Union. That same year he served as a commissioner to settle the boundary between New York and Massachusetts. In 1760 Lieutenant Governor Cadwallader Colden offered him the chief justiceship of the supreme court, but only at pleasure, a position Smith had gone on record as opposing and so declined. Still, three years later he was willing to compromise these principles and accept one of the other two supreme court justiceships, which he held until his death.

While much of Smith's energy went into the practice of law, he was also one of New York's foremost legal educators. In an era when professionals learned their craft through apprenticeships, he helped train the brightest lawyers of the next generation, including his son William Jr., William Livingston, and John Moran Scott. He also maintained one of New York's larger private libraries. At his death he owned over 1,600 volumes, of which more than one-quarter were law books. These were available to his students.

Smith was also a more general promoter of education. In 1732 he, Alexander, and some of the Morrises persuaded the general assembly to establish a free school teaching Latin, Greek, and mathematics. His contributions to higher education had a more religious thrust. In 1746 he helped draw up and was named a trustee for the Presbyterian College of New Jersey (later Princeton University). He was subsequently named in the 1748 charter and remained a trustee all his life. He was also one of those initially interested in establishing New York's King's College (later Columbia University). However, when it was taken over by the Anglican establishment he protested, and his three protégés, son William Jr., Livingston, and Scott, led the battle against it in the *Independent Reflector*. On a less formal level, Smith was also a founder and trustee of the New York Society Library, a subscription library.

William Smith married twice. Two of his sons by his first marriage married into the Livingston family, and four became attorneys. His youngest son, Joshua Hett Smith, was suspected in the treason of Benedict Arnold. His first wife died in 1754. In 1761 he married Elizabeth Scott Williams, daughter of the Reverend Thomas Scott of Norwich, England, a noted biblical scholar, and widow of Yale's fourth rector, the Reverend Elisha Williams. A middle-aged woman by the time of their marriage, she was in no way connected to New York's social or political elite. Instead she was a writer of psalms and was also known for her intelligence, learning, and piety. They had no children. William Smith died in New York City.

• William Smith's papers are in the New-York Historical Society. His only published work seems to be *Mr. Smith's Opinion Humbly Offered in General Assembly of the Colony of New York* (1734). There is no full-length biography of Smith. Biographical sketches occur in William Smith, Jr., *The History of the Province of New-York*, ed. Michael Kammen (2 vols., 1972); Franklin Bowditch Dexter, *Biographical Sketches of the Graduates of Yale College* (1885); and Maturin L. Delafield, "William Smith," *Magazine of American History* 6 (1881): 264–82. For Smith's legal interests see Paul Hamlin, *Legal Education in Colonial New York* (1939), and Richard B. Morris, "The New York City Mayor's Court," in *Courts and Law in Early New York: Selected Essays*, ed. Leo Hershkowitz and Milton M. Klein (1978). More general information on New York's politics can be found in Patricia U. Bonomi, *A Factious People* (1971); Stanley Nider Katz, *Newcastle's New York* (1968); and Milton M. Klein, *The Politics of Diversity* (1974). Smith's role as prosecuting attorney in the New York Conspiracy is found in Daniel Horsmanden, *The New York Conspiracy*, ed. Thomas J. Davis (1971). Smith's part in the founding of Princeton is noted in *Memorial Book of the Sesquicentennial Celebration of the Founding of the College of New Jersey* (1898). Smith's association with the New York Society Library is found in Austin Baxter Keep, *History of the New York Society Library* (1908; repr. 1972).

JESSICA KROSS

SMITH, William (7 Sept. 1727–14 May 1803), clergyman and educator, was born in Aberdeen, Scotland, the son of Scottish Episcopal parents Thomas Smith and Elizabeth Duncan. He attended Aberdeen University from 1743 to 1747 but left, without taking a degree, to teach, first in Scotland and then in 1751 as a tutor in the home of Josiah Martin on Long Island, New York. He became involved in the political controversy over the founding of King's College and thereby became a protégé of the Anglican patriarch in America, the Reverend Samuel Johnson. He wrote an essay on education entitled *A General Idea of the College of Mirania* (1753), which impressed Benjamin Franklin, who secured his appointment as a tutor at the Academy of Philadelphia. Franklin furthermore supported Smith's reorganization of the school in 1756 into the College of Philadelphia, with Smith as provost. In 1754, to strengthen his qualifications to head an academic institution, Smith took Anglican orders. In 1758 Smith married Rebecca Moore; the couple had seven children.

The trustees of the College of Philadelphia—Franklin among them—inadvertently led Smith into the labyrinth of Pennsylvania politics by suggesting that he ingratiate himself with Proprietor Thomas Penn. Smith did so with a vengeance, publishing *A Brief State of the Province of Pennsylvania* (1755), which castigated the Quakers for their opposition to military preparations against the French. In 1756 Smith quarreled openly with Franklin over whether the militia should be under popular (that is, Franklin's party) or proprietary control. Franklin's supporters called Smith "the infernal prince of darkness and father of lies," whose writings were "the vomitings of an infamous hireling." Smith retorted that Franklin's "chief aim is to imprint his own corrupt notions of government upon the minds of the people." In 1757 he printed an attack—written by a supporter of the propietary government—on the military preparedness policy of the Pennsylvania assembly. The assembly jailed Smith for violating its privileges. Smith's defense, aided by an opinion by a New York lawyer, probably William Smith, Jr., anticipated habeas corpus and separation of powers doctrines later vindicated by the American Revolution.

Unlike his harshly polemical political role in Pennsylvania politics, his career as an Anglican clergyman displayed qualities of tact and sensitivity—probably reflections of his ecclesiastical ambition. Though a partisan advocate of Anglican control of King's College in 1751, he welcomed Protestant dissenters to the College of Philadelphia. By the time the storm broke in the 1760s over proposals to appoint an American bishop, Smith pushed behind the scenes for the alternative step of an administrative commissary for Anglican clergy in Pennsylvania and New Jersey. Suspicious that Smith hoped to secure that position for himself, the New Jersey clergy rebuffed the proposal. Stung by their criticism, Smith belatedly entered the fray with a series of articles in the *Pennsylvania Gazette* denying that there was anything sinister in the campaign for an American episcopate and accusing dissenters of scurrilous hostility to the Church of England. In 1780 he thwarted Samuel Seabury's high church party within the Episcopal church over issues of liturgy, lay participation in church governance, and ordination. He presided over the convention in 1780 that created the new diocese of Maryland but, though elected its first bishop, was never consecrated because of unproven rumors of public drunkenness.

Though obscured by Smith's political disputes and ecclesiastical ambition, his educational leadership was intellectually and institutionally significant. Smith proposed that college education inculcate religious faith by denying religion a place in the curriculum. Instead, instructors should "breathe *innocence*, *purity*, and *truth*." Teachers should seize "proper opportunities of dropping seeds of goodness" in students' hearts. The College of Philadelphia eschewed any sectarian identity apart from Smith's conducting of Anglican worship and extracurricular discussions of the Bible and religion. Required readings and recitations presented a deist view of the universe and a wide spectrum of eighteenth-century writings on ethics. Students also read Samuel von Pufendorf's Lutheran view of natural law and diplomacy, Francis Hutcheson on moral philosophy, the English Unitarian, Richard Cumberland, and the Swiss legal reformer, Burlamaqui.

During the Stamp Act crisis, Smith privately condemned the measure and publicly praised those who defended colonial liberty without "descending into licentiousness." In 1775 his *Sermon on the Present Situation of Colonial Affairs* offered an elaborate model for imperial reconciliation based on "terms upon which this country can be perpetually united to the parent state." His sermon on 20 July 1775, the national day of prayer and fasting designated by Congress, condemned "turbulent desires," "secret views of fostering party strife," and "impatience with lawful government." Walking a narrow line between allegiance to the Crown and support for moderate libertarian protest, Smith expressed views held by many Philadelphians who were averse to revolutionary upheaval. When Thomas Paine's *Common Sense* demanded independence and radical political transformation in early 1776, Smith replied under the pseudonym "Cato" with an appeal for caution based on colonial self-interest. Suspecting Smith of disaffection from the American cause, the Pennsylvania legislature dissolved the College of Philadelphia in 1779.

During the 1780s, Smith founded Washington College in Maryland, raised funds from wealthy planters, recruited a distinguished faculty, and instituted a curriculum modeled on his Philadelphia experience but wholly nondenominational. He returned to Philadelphia in 1789, when the state resurrected the College of Philadelphia as the new University of Pennsylvania. He was passed over for president and not even offered a faculty position—not as a penalty for his ambivalent patriotism during the Revolution but because the trustees were averse to strong educational and institutional leadership. Though quarrelsome and slovenly, he was an influential and affecting teacher who taught many distinguished students—among them Jacob Duché, Benjamin West, and Francis Hopkinson. Smith died in Philadelphia.

Smith has rightly been called "complicated . . . at the same time one of the most loathsome and most respected men in eighteenth-century America." He was the kind of erudite opportunist who flourished in colonial society. His palpable ambition was both impressive and pathetic. His tolerant approach to education, low church ecclesiology, and desire that the Anglican/ Episcopal church elevate American culture reflected his appreciation of American pluralism. His frenetic political activity, land speculation, and fundraising revealed his understanding of the economics of higher education. His vision of higher education informed by Protestant intellectuality and enlightenment rationalism was as thoughtful as Thomas Jefferson's or John Witherspoon's. His Whiggish Loyalism—his defense of colonial liberty and critique of republican innovation—was an intellectually consistent and candid contribution to the revolutionary debate.

• The standard biography is Albert F. Gegenheimer, *William Smith* (1943), and the major primary sources are Smith's *Selected Sermons* (1803), and Horace W. Smith, ed., *Life and Correspondence* (1869). Three articles in the *Historical Magazine of the Protestant Episcopal Church* revise the traditional view that Smith was at best a trimmer and at worst professionally self-destructive: Bruce R. Lively (1969), Guy F. Goodfellow (1982), and William A. Clebsch (1983). Also see William D. Andrews, "William Smith and the Rising Glory of America," *Early American Literature* 8, no. 1 (Spring 1973): 33–42; Ralph Ketcham, "Benjamin Franklin and William Smith," *Pennsylvania Magazine of History and Biography* 88, no. 2 (Apr. 1964): 142–63; Arthur P. Middleton, "William Smith: Godfather and First President of St. John's College," *Maryland Historical Magazine* 84 (Fall 1989): 235–41; and James Warnock, "Thomas Bradbury Chandler and William Smith: Diversity within Colonial Anglicanism," *Anglican and Episcopal History* 57, no. 3 (Sept. 1988): 272–97. On Smith in the Revolution, see Robert M. Calhoon, *The Loyalists in Revolutionary America* (1973) and *The Loyalist Perception and Other Essays* (1989); and on his role in shaping the Episcopal church in the United States, see Bruce E. Steiner, *Samuel Seabury* (1971).

ROBERT M. CALHOON

SMITH, William (1754–6 Apr. 1821), Episcopal clergyman, was born probably in Aberdeen, Scotland, but no information about his parents exists. He likely attended the University of Aberdeen. He came to the United States in 1785 as an ordained priest in the Scottish Non-Juring Episcopal church, but the dates of his ordination to the diaconate or the priesthood are unknown. He married Magdalen Milne, and they had several children. After his arrival in Pennsylvania, Smith served from January until July 1785 as minister at Trinity Church, Oxford, and at All Saints, Pequestan. He then became rector of Stepney Parish, Maryland, where he remained until 1787. From 7 July 1787 until 28 January 1790 Smith was the rector of St. Paul's Church, Narragansett, Rhode Island, where he was able to rejuvenate a rather depressed congregation. He then served as rector of Trinity Church, Newport, Rhode Island, until 12 April 1797. While at

Newport he and another clergyman led in the organization of the diocese of Rhode Island on 18 November 1790, and Smith preached the convention sermon.

When Smith resigned as rector of St. Paul's Church in Newport, he became the rector of St. Paul's Church, Norwalk, Connecticut, where he remained until 1800. While at Norwalk he preached the sermon at the consecration of Abraham Jarvis as the second bishop of Connecticut on 18 October 1797 at Trinity Church, New Haven. In his sermon, entitled *A Discourse before the Ecclesiastical Convention of the State of Connecticut; Assembled There to Witness the Consecrating of the Rt. Rev. Abraham Jarvis to the Episcopal Chair of Said State; and to Recognize Him as Their Ecclesiastical Superior* (1797), he affirmed that only ordinations performed by a bishop in the historic episcopate were valid, therefore presbyterian ordinations were invalid. For a presbyter to preach at the consecration of a bishop was highly unusual in the Episcopal church. The Reverend Samuel Blatchford, minister of the Congregational church in Bridgeport, took offense at Smith's sermon and responded to it with *The Validity of Presbyterian Ordination Maintained, in a Letter to the Rev. William Smith, D.D.* (1798). Smith replied with *Dr. Smith's Answer to Mr. Blatchford's Letter* (1798). Smith's position in this controversy represented the High Church views of the Non-Jurors and identified him as one who believed in the necessity of episcopacy for valid ordinations.

Sometime in 1800 Smith's Norwalk congregation decided that his tenure should be for one year, renewable each year should the congregation so decide. This change with regard to the permanency of his placement angered Smith, and he resigned. He then went to New York City, where he opened a grammar school and gained a reputation as a teacher.

On 4 June 1794 the diocese of Connecticut appointed a committee to consider the founding of an Episcopal academy, which was not only to be a preparatory school but a "college and a nursery of theological learning." This school was America's first junior college and the Episcopal church's first theological seminary, but it never became a full college. In April 1802 Smith became the school's second principal. He was not successful as a principal and was forced to resign on 5 June 1806. He returned to New York City, where he again taught school. Some time later Smith moved back to Connecticut, where he did supply work at Milford and West Haven but never again had a permanent ecclesiastical position.

Around 1800 a general musical illiteracy existed among Episcopalians. This situation usually only improved when the rector had some appreciation of music or had a competent choir master. While at St. Paul's in Norwalk, Smith, who was a music composer, awakened in his people "a taste for more fluent and attractive melody" (Selleck, p. 66). He influenced the development of church music in the Episcopal church in 1809 when he published *The Churchman's Choral Companion to His Prayer Book.* One historian noted: "Poor as it was, it took an upward step when the general taste was appallingly low. It included an essay on correct chanting, and an amazing collection of chants, anthems, responses, and other selections" (Burr, p. 244). Presiding bishop William White gave chanting a lukewarm endorsement, and the bishops approved the anthems but did not endorse the book as a whole. In 1814 Smith published another important book on church music, *The Reasonableness of Setting Forth the Most Worthy Praise of Almighty God, According to the Usage of the Primitive Church; With Historical Views of the Nature, Origin, and Progress of Metre Psalmody,* which criticized the practice of singing metrical psalms and argued for chanting.

Possibly Smith's greatest contribution was writing "Office of Institution of Ministers." The *Book of Common Prayer,* which was issued in 1789, did not have an office for the induction or institution of ministers to be used when a rector began serving a church. The diocesan convention of Connecticut in 1799 considered this a serious deficiency and requested that Smith prepare a form of service. The diocesan convention adopted his office and sent it on in 1804 to the General Convention, which approved it. The 1808 General Convention made some slight alterations and included it in the *Book of Common Prayer,* where it has remained with modifications. In 1808 the title of the service was changed from "Induction" to "Institution," since induction meant the act in which a cleric was vested with the temporalities of a living, and institution meant the act of committing to his or her charge the care of souls.

Smith, frequently confused with another William Smith (1727–1803), who was also an Episcopal priest, was a leader in organizing the diocese of Rhode Island, was a talented musician and composer, and made a significant contribution to the *Book of Common Prayer.* Although he was not a successful school principal, he was an accomplished teacher. Smith died in New York City.

• A few of Smith's papers are in the Archives of the Diocese of Connecticut in Hartford. Among his other publications are *Consolation from Homar, an Hermit of the East* (1789) and *The Convict's Visitor; or, Penitential Offices, Consisting of Prayers, Lessons, and Meditations; with Suitable Devotions before, and at the Time of Execution* (1791). His work is mentioned in E. Edwards Beardsley, *The History of the Episcopal Church in Connecticut* (2 vols., 1865–1868); Nelson R. Burr, *The Story of the Diocese of Connecticut: A New Branch of the Vine* (1962); George C. Mason, *Annals of Trinity Church, Newport, Rhode Island* (2 vols., 1890–1894); Charles M. Selleck, *Address at the Centenary of St. Paul's Church, Norwalk, Connecticut* (1886); and Wilkins Updike, *A History of the Episcopal Church in Narragansett, Rhode Island* (3 vols., 1847).

DONALD S. ARMENTROUT

SMITH, William (1762–26 June 1840), U.S. senator, apparently was born in North Carolina, somewhere near its border with South Carolina. The identity of his parents and circumstances of his family are unclear, but he was raised in York District in the South Carolina upcountry and was educated at the Mount Sion Collegiate Institute in Winnsboro. He later admitted to having been a wayward youth. In 1781 Smith married fourteen-year-old Margaret Duff; the couple had one daughter. He read law in Charleston and by the late 1780s was practicing in York District. Evidently he prospered, accumulating large tracts in the region. By 1810 he owned seventy-one slaves.

In the meantime, Smith entered politics. He represented York in the South Carolina House of Representatives in 1796–1797 and was elected to the state senate in 1803. He served three consecutive terms there, presiding over the body from 1806 to 1808. He resigned upon being elected judge of the Court of General Sessions and Common Pleas in June 1808. He sat on that court for eight years but in 1816 was elected to the U.S. Senate, both to fill a vacancy and to serve the subsequent full term. He chaired the Senate Committee on the Judiciary from 1819 to 1823.

Senator Smith proved himself to be a combative and uncompromising exponent of states' rights. In advance of many of his fellow Carolinians, he denounced federal funding of internal improvements, protective tariffs, and a broad construction of the Constitution that might accord the national government expansive powers to pursue the "general welfare." This inevitably put him at odds with the, at that point, considerably more nationally minded secretary of war, John C. Calhoun. The ideological difference was exacerbated by personal rivalry, the sharp-tongued and prickly Smith doubtlessly chafed by the reputation and influence his fellow South Carolinian had won at home and in Washington. Within South Carolina, Smith gathered about him a circle of states' rights and strict construction militants who came to be known as "the Radicals."

While Smith's most noted role in South Carolina's history is as leader of an anti-Calhoun faction, his most significant moment in the U.S. Senate came in 1820, during the debates over Missouri's admission to the Union. He pronounced a remarkably straightforward proslavery doctrine, helping to lay the groundwork for the later, and by no means universal, shift among white southerners from the defense of their peculiar institution as a necessary evil to one claiming it to be a positive good. Repudiating Jeffersonian ambivalence, Smith told his colleagues that slavery was sanctioned by historical and biblical precedent and was, in fact, a boon to those subject to its patriarchal controls. "No class of laboring people in any country upon the globe . . . are better clothed, better fed, or are more cheerful, or labor less."

Carolinians were not ready to honor their proslavery prophet, however. Smith's support of the presidential aspirations of the more ideologically compatible Georgian, Secretary of the Treasury William Crawford, over those of native son Calhoun did not sit well with many. Rather than return him for a second full term, the legislature in 1822 replaced Senator Smith with the more nationalistic Robert Y. Hayne, a low-country ally of Calhoun. Yet Smith's career quickly rebounded. As South Carolinians became increasingly convinced that protective tariffs were undermining their

agricultural economy and grew increasingly anxious over the intrusion of the slavery issue into national politics, Smith's adamant insistence on minimizing the powers and resources of the federal government was more enthusiastically embraced. He returned to the state house of representatives in 1824 and was able the following year to induce passage of resolutions denouncing the protective tariff and federal internal improvements as unconstitutional. In November 1826—with Crawford ill, out of the picture, and thus no longer an impediment to Smith's prospects—the legislature, albeit by a very narrow margin, returned Smith to the Senate to fill a vacancy.

The course of Smith's career in his second term presents a striking contrast to those of formerly nationalistic opponents like Calhoun, Hayne, and George McDuffie. Smith yielded to no one in his denunciation of the tariff, internal improvements, and the threat a national majority might present to South Carolina's distinct interests, but he would not endorse the doctrine increasingly wielded by many of the erstwhile nationalists—nullification. Smith apparently felt that states' claims that they might abrogate federal laws they deemed unconstitutional could not be sanctioned by a strict reading of the Constitution. His almost reflexive suspicion of Calhoun and all his works probably also soured him on the movement. Contemporary critics saw personal interest of another sort in Smith's opposition to nullification. Through the preceding decade, he had become increasingly involved in cotton and sugar planting in Alabama and Louisiana. Opponents charged that his zeal to defend South Carolina's faltering economy had diminished, because most of his property interests were now outside the state and as a sugar planter he actually profited from tariff protection. By 1830 Smith found himself outflanked by Calhounite nullifiers, and his own faction split over the question of calling a convention to deliberate on the tariff. He was defeated for reelection that year by Stephen Miller, formerly a "Radical" ally.

Smith again represented York in the state senate the following year and remained prominent among nullification's opponents. The nullifiers' most formidable enemy, President Andrew Jackson, twice offered him a place on the U.S. Supreme Court. He had, in 1828, received Georgia's electoral votes for vice president and in 1836 received Virginia's for the same office. Yet, after his 1830 defeat, the Smith faction ceased to be a major force in state politics. About 1832 Smith moved to Louisiana and shortly thereafter to Huntsville, Alabama. He was elected in 1836 to the Alabama House of Representatives, where he served until his death in Huntsville.

Smith's proslavery arguments and states' rights militance would eventually become the common currency of southern radicalism. But less than optimum timing and his own combativeness and inflexibility prevented Smith from exercising as much influence in regional politics as his prescience might have warranted.

• A small collection of Smith's political correspondence is in the South Caroliniana Library, University of South Carolina, Columbia, and some nonpolitical papers are in the Sondley and Smith Family Collection, Southern Historical Collection, University of North Carolina at Chapel Hill. A vivid discussion of Smith's role in S.C. politics is in William W. Freehling, *Prelude to Civil War: The Nullification Controversy in South Carolina, 1816–1836* (1966). Also helpful is Lacy Ford, *Origins of Southern Radicalism: The South Carolina Upcountry, 1800–1860* (1988). For the impressions of contemporaries, see John B. O'Neall, *Biographical Sketches of the Bench and Bar of South Carolina*, vol. 1 (1859). For additional information, see Caroline Smith, "Jacksonian Conservative: The Later Years of William Smith, 1826–1840" (Ph.D. diss., Auburn Univ., 1977), and N. Louise Bailey et al., *Biographical Directory of the South Carolina Senate, 1776–1985* (1986).

PATRICK G. WILLIAMS

SMITH, William (6 Sept. 1797–18 May 1887), governor of Virginia and Confederate general, was born at his family home, "Marengo," in King George County, Virginia, the son of Caleb Smith and Mary Anne Waugh Smith, farmers. As a youth he attended private academies in Virginia and Connecticut. He completed his education by studying law in the offices of attorneys in Fredericksburg and Warrenton, Virginia, and Baltimore, Maryland. Smith began residing and practicing law in Culpeper, Virginia, in 1818, a profession he would follow for the rest of his life when he was not serving in political or military offices. He married Elizabeth H. Bell in 1821, and they had eleven children, three of whom died in infancy.

Energetic, ambitious, and exuberant, Smith established in 1827 a mail-coach business in Virginia and in 1834 extended it from Washington, D.C., to Georgia and added steamboat mail service from Washington to Baltimore, Norfolk, Pensacola, and Galveston, building a small empire within a few years. His frequent billings to the federal Post Office Department for additional services earned him the sobriquet "Extra Billy," a nickname that followed him throughout his life. A devoted follower of Andrew Jackson and the Democratic party, Smith's ambitions carried him into politics, where he proved to be a talented stump speaker. He was elected to the Virginia Senate in 1836 and was reelected to a second term. He followed service in Richmond with one term in the U.S. House of Representatives (1841–1843) but lost a bid for reelection when his district was gerrymandered by the Whig-dominated state legislature.

Smith then moved from Richmond to Warrenton, Fauquier County, Virginia, and remained deeply involved in Democratic party politics, campaigning energetically and effectively for James K. Polk in 1844. As a reward for helping to carry Virginia for Polk, the Democrats in the state general assembly elected him governor (1 Jan. 1846–1 Jan. 1849). He showed considerable initiative and talent as chief executive. He virtually forced the general assembly to provide Virginia troops and supplies for the Mexican War, successfully led a campaign to provide wider (though still limited) public education for Virginia children, and

nudged the state toward a more ambitious program of internal improvements, especially state support for railroads penetrating into the Ohio River valley and the Deep South. He was unsuccessful in his bid to expel from Virginia all free blacks, whom he considered "a dreadful menace." He strongly recommended a constitutional convention to reapportion and redistrict the state to give more political power to the growing population in western Virginia, an idea that came to fruition in 1851, shortly after his governorship.

In order to reestablish his financial strength after his stay in the governor's mansion, in 1849 Smith followed two of his sons to California, then in the excitement of the gold rush. He practiced law and speculated in real estate in San Francisco, rose quickly to prominence within the state Democratic party, served as presiding officer of the California Democratic Convention in 1852, and even received some support in the state legislature for a U.S. Senate seat. Smith was more interested in Virginia affairs, however, and his financial success in the West enabled him to return to Virginia in late 1852. Less than a year later he was elected to the U.S. House of Representatives, where he served four terms (1853–1861), during which he supported the Gadsden Purchase and the Kansas-Nebraska Act and opposed homestead bills and federal land grants to railroad companies. His strong attachment to southern rights and the Democratic party and his aggressive personality (leading at one point to a fistfight in the House) marked Smith as a staunch Democrat, and he faithfully supported John C. Breckinridge for the presidency in 1860. He showed unusual moderation early in the secession crisis, urging Virginia and other Upper-South states to remain in the Union. President Abraham Lincoln's call for troops to suppress the insurrection tipped Smith toward secession, and he immediately offered his services to the Confederacy.

Appointed colonel of the Forty-ninth Virginia Infantry Regiment in 1861, Smith again brought his colorful personality and natural leadership abilities into play. A popular and bold officer, he was wounded five times in the early battles of the eastern theater, severely at Antietam. Although promoted to brigadier general and then brevet major general in 1863, his inexperience in military operations was manifest, and he was eventually relegated to service as a recruiting officer. Still popular among the voters, Smith was elected to the Confederate Congress (1861–1862) and moved back and forth between congress (where he usually supported President Jefferson Davis's measures for a vigorous war effort) and his command with the army, though he resigned from the congress before the term expired.

Reelected to the governorship in May 1863, Smith served in that office during the painful latter days of the Confederacy (Jan. 1864–May 1865). He again showed amazing energy and initiative, raising large numbers of troops to defend Richmond, purchasing blockade runners to bring supplies to the civilian population, providing clothing and foodstuffs for the home folk, and strongly supporting President Davis. Smith even campaigned for the use of black troops in the Confederate army several months before the Confederate Congress adopted that measure. When General Robert E. Lee's army evacuated Richmond in April 1865, Governor Smith moved the state offices to Danville and tried to arouse Virginians for guerrilla warfare against Union occupation forces. Civilian longing for peace, the collapse of other Confederate armies, and President Andrew Johnson's appointment of Francis H. Pierpont as the legitimate governor of Virginia convinced Smith to surrender on 8 June.

After the war Smith aligned himself with the Conservative party, opposing measures to lift blacks to equality and political participation. When he was in his late seventies, still vital and energetic, he served one term in the Virginia House of Delegates (1875–1877), where he resisted early attempts to scale down the public debt. His wife died soon after his retirement from the legislature, and he spent his last years as an innovative farmer at "Monterosa," his estate near Warrenton in northern Virginia, where he died.

Smith was a natural leader in the new mass politics of the mid-nineteenth century. He was popular with the common voters, and was a strong proponent of southern Jacksonian democracy. At the same time, he demonstrated significant abilities as a state legislator, governor, and congressman.

• The bulk of Smith's personal papers have not been preserved. Some useful letters from Smith are available in the Jefferson Davis Papers (Duke Univ. Library), the William C. Rives Papers (Library of Congress), and the E. M. Law Papers (Univ. of North Carolina Library). Smith's official correspondence for both terms as governor is in the William Smith Executive Papers (Virginia State Library and Archives). The most useful source of primary documents is John W. Bell, ed., *Memoirs of Governor William Smith of Virginia* (1891), a revealing collection of reminiscences, correspondence, official documents, and obituaries. The fullest account of Smith's life is Alvin A. Fahrner, "The Public Career of William 'Extra Billy' Smith" (Ph.D. diss., Univ. of North Carolina, 1953). The best short treatment is Fahrner, "William 'Extra Billy' Smith: Governor in Two Wars," in *The Governors of Virginia, 1860–1978*, ed. Edward Younger et al. (1982). An obituary is in the *Richmond Dispatch*, 21 May 1887.

RICHARD LOWE

SMITH, William Farrar (17 Feb. 1824–28 Feb. 1903), Civil War general, was born in St. Albans, Vermont, the son of Ashbel Smith (occupation unknown) and Sarah Butler. Through his uncle, a U.S. congressman, Smith obtained an appointment to the U.S. Military Academy at West Point in 1841. He graduated fourth in his class of forty-one in 1845 and was commissioned a brevet second lieutenant in the Corps of Topographical Engineers. While attending the academy he was given the nickname "Baldy" by his classmates. Following graduation Smith was assigned to a surveying party on Lake Erie. The next year he returned to West Point and began teaching mathematics, where he re-

mained for three years. During 1849 Smith worked in Texas and Arizona Territory establishing the new boundary with Mexico.

Starting in 1852 Smith spent the next two years in Florida surveying a canal across the peninsula. When he was reassigned to Texas in 1855, he contracted malaria, which caused him to suffer from headaches and depression throughout the rest of his life. Because of his malaria, after returning to West Point to teach mathematics, he was forced to relinquish his duties. Smith was then assigned to the lighthouse district located in Detroit, becoming the assistant secretary of the Lighthouse Board in 1856. He served as the engineer secretary of the board from 1859 to 1861 and was also promoted to captain in 1859. In April 1861 he married Sarah Ward Lyon; they had five children.

At the outbreak of the Civil War, Smith was commissioned colonel of the Third Vermont Volunteers; he fought at First Bull Run (First Manassas) on the staff of General Irvin McDowell. On 13 August 1861 he was promoted to brigadier general of volunteers and given command of the Second Division, VI Corps, Army of the Potomac. Participating in the Peninsula campaign of spring 1862, he led his command in the battle of Williamsburg and later in the Seven Days' battles around Richmond. For his services protecting the crossing of White Oak Swamp, he was brevetted lieutenant colonel in the regular army in June. A month later (4 July) he became a major general of volunteers and was brevetted colonel in the regular army for his service at the battle of Antietam.

After General Ambrose E. Burnside's disaster at Fredericksburg on 13 December 1862, Smith and General William B. Franklin wrote a letter to President Abraham Lincoln criticizing their superior's forthcoming campaign plans. This indiscretion, along with Smith's friendship with General George B. McClellan (1826–1885), resulted in the loss of his corps command and promotion. The Senate refused to accept his nomination for major generalship on 4 March 1863, and he reverted to the rank of brigadier general.

Assigned to lesser commands in Pennsylvania and West Virginia, he was in October 1863 sent to Chattanooga, where General William Rosecrans's troops were besieged by a Confederate army under Braxton Bragg. As chief engineer of the Department of the Cumberland, Smith's mission was to relieve Rosecrans's starving army by reopening a supply line to Bridgeport, Alabama, and bringing in commissary supplies and forage. Using his engineering skills, Smith was helpful in opening the famous "cracker line," winning praise from Generals Ulysses S. Grant, William T. Sherman, and George H. Thomas. The cracker line was a route by which rations, like hardtack, were brought to the Union army via the Tennessee River then overland from Brown's Ferry. For his contribution to the victory at Chattanooga, he was reappointed major general to rank from 9 March 1864, which the Senate confirmed. Although Smith was given the credit for this operation, later his detractors claimed it was "opened by the execution of a plan for recovering Lookout Valley devised by General Rose-crans."

When General Grant came east in March 1864 as overall Federal commander, he brought General Smith and gave him command of the XVIII Corps in General Benjamin F. Butler's Army of the James. Smith did not think well of Butler and said that his commander was "as helpless as a child on the field of battle and as visionary as an opium eater in council." Shortly after his arrival, the XVIII Corps participated in the ill-fated Bermuda Hundred campaign. Because of his bickering with General Butler and his lack of co-operation with the other corps commander, General Quincy Gillmore, Smith's performance in this move-ment on Richmond was lackluster at best.

Smith's corps was next attached to the Army of the Potomac and took part in the battle of Cold Harbor near Richmond. Here he took time to criticize the leadership of his superior, General George G. Meade, to Grant. This action would help the commanding general with his decision to relieve Smith over Butler the next month. On 15 June 1864 Smith led his corps in the first assault on the city of Petersburg. Although his initial attack was successful, his hesitation to press on allowed the Confederates to reentrench their lines and hold the city for another nine and a half months. A month later, on 19 July, Grant relieved him of the XVIII Corps command.

Locating in New York, in November 1864 Smith was sent to New Orleans to investigate the military de-partment administration headquartered there. Al-though he discovered corruption throughout the pre-vious administrations, little was done with his findings. Smith was brevetted brigadier general and major general, U.S. Army, on 13 March 1865 for dis-tinguished services at Chattanooga and in the Virginia campaign of 1864. He resigned his volunteer commis-sion on 4 November 1865 and his commission of major of engineers on 7 March 1867.

Following the war, Smith became president of the International Ocean Telegraph Company, which laid and operated a cable from Jacksonville, Florida, to La Habana, Cuba. In 1873 he sold his interests in the company at a substantial profit. For the next two years he and his family resided in Europe, mainly in Great Britain.

By 1875, facing financial problems, Smith was forced to return to work. He served as a police com-missioner for New York City and, for a period, was president of the board. He resigned in 1881. Through a former army associate, General Horatio G. Wright, chief of engineers, Smith was appointed as a govern-ment agent, supervising the river and harbor works on the peninsula between the Chesapeake and Delaware bays.

In 1889 Congress placed Smith on the retired list as major, and he received his retirement pay while still holding his civil job. He retired from all work in 1901. Smith spent the last ten years of his life in Philadel-phia, where he died.

Contemporaries differed in their evaluations of Smith. Grant remarked that he was "obstinate" and "likely to condemn whatever is not suggested by him-self." On the other hand, General James H. Wilson said he was "direct and vigorous in his methods, and confident of the rectitude of his purposes, he never hesitated to give his views to such as he believed to be entitled to them, without reference to whether they would be well received or not."

• Smith's manuscript collection is in the Vermont Historical Society at Montpelier. It has been edited by Herbert M. Schiller, *Autobiography of Major General William F. Smith, 1861–1864* (1990). Smith himself wrote numerous articles for *Battles and Leaders of the Civil War*, ed. Robert Underwood Johnson and Clarence Clough Buel (4 vols., 1884–1887). He also wrote *Military Operations around Chattanooga* (1886), *The Relief of the Army of the Cumberland* (1891), and *From Chattanooga to Petersburg under Generals Grant and Butler* (1893). Biographies include James H. Wilson, *Life and Serv-ices of William Farrar Smith* (1904), and Stephen N. Siciliano, "Major General William Farrar Smith: Critic of Defeat and Engineer of Victory" (Ph.D. diss., College of William and Mary, 1984). A brief sketch of his life is in Ezra J. Warner, *Generals in Blue* (1964).

CHRIS CALKINS

SMITH, William Henry (4 Dec. 1806–17 Jan. 1872), ac-tor and theater manager, was born William Henry Sedley in Montgomreyshire, Wales. The identity of his parents is uncertain, but it is believed he was the son of a British army officer. At the age of fourteen he ran away from home and joined a troupe of itinerant players, using the name Smith onstage thereafter. Smith adapted to the theater quickly and for the next seven years toured the English provinces with several companies. In 1822 he began to appear regularly as a "walking gentleman" (essentially a bit player) at the Theatre Royal in Lancaster. By the 1820s English ac-tors had found in the United States a wealth of theatri-cal possibilities, and Smith was no exception. After receiving an invitation to appear at the Walnut Street Theatre in Philadelphia, he sailed for America in 1827. Smith made his debut that June as Jeremy Did-dler in *Raising the Wind* and soon after as Lothair in *Adelgitha*. He spent the year as a member of the Wal-nut Street company before moving to Boston, where he became a member of the company at the Tremont Theatre. Smith also acted at the Chatham Street Thea-tre in New York City and at the National Theatre in Washington, D.C.

In November 1840 Smith went to New York City, where he played supporting roles for fellow English-man Junius Brutus Booth. His roles during this en-gagement included Edgar in *King Lear*, Laertes in *Hamlet*, Gratiano in *Merchant of Venice*, and Mark An-tony in *Julius Caesar*. By this time Smith was also showing skills as a stage manager, and in 1843 the Bos-ton Museum and Gallery of Fine Art hired Smith to help organize a new stock company to be housed at the museum. The management hoped to use the museum as a facade that would allow "respectable" people to attend the theater. On 25 October 1943 the "corps dramatique" of the Boston Museum presented its first production, *Little Pickle*.

The next year Smith presented *The Drunkard; or, The Fallen Saved*. There is some question as to Smith's authorship of the play. Some sources claim that the Reverend John Pierpont wrote the play, with one reviewer claiming Pierpont was the pen name used by Smith. Whatever the original source, Smith adapted and revised the play. As the 1830s and 1840s saw the demand for Prohibition laws increase, "temperance plays," which reinforced the idea of the drunkard as a weak and worthless man, became popular. *The Drunkard* became the most successful of these temperance plays.

The Drunkard opened at the Boston Museum on 12 February 1844 with Smith in the title role. Capitalizing on the Prohibitionist movement, Smith offered the play unsupported by the traditional musical acts and farcical pieces. With these traditionally theatrical aspects removed, he billed the play as a "moral drama" or "moral lecture" and drew an audience that typically did not attend the theater. People flocked to the show in such numbers that it secured the financial future of the museum. The play ran for 140 performances—an unprecedented number at the time—and over the next decade it had record runs at other theaters as well as with touring companies. It is estimated that between 1844 and 1878 *The Drunkard* was performed in at least 450 various theaters. *The Drunkard* differed from most other temperance plays, which ceased to be performed when the movement died. Still performed, *The Drunkard* opened at the Los Angeles Theatre Mart in 1933 and ran there for twenty years. A musical version of the play, with music and lyrics by pop star Barry Manilow, was produced on Broadway in 1970.

Smith remained at the Boston Museum as an actor and stage manager for sixteen years. A contemporary historian said that Smith, "as stage-director, has no equal in this city, and to his efforts may be attributed a large portion of the success of the Museum" (Clapp, p. 470). While at the Boston Museum, Smith married Sarah Lapsley Riddle, an esteemed actress; the couple had a son and a daughter, who became an actress. After leaving the museum in 1859, Smith returned to itinerant work, often in his dual role of actor and stage manager, and the details of his life at this time are sketchy. His wife died in 1861, and Smith appeared at a benefit for his daughter on 6 May 1865 at the Winter Garden in New York City. Smith played David Deans to his daughter's Jeanie Deans in Dion Boucicault's *Heart of the Midlothian*. In his later years Smith managed the California Theatre in San Francisco. He married again, but all that is known of Smith's second wife is that her name was Lucy and that she survived him. Smith died in San Francisco.

As an actor Smith played many roles, and, although principally known as a comedian, he also excelled in tragic parts. His friend Joseph Cowell admitted that "in his day [he] was considered the best fop and light comedian on the continent" (*Thirty Years*, p. 81). William Winter called his acting of tragic roles "significant with thought and purpose, and warm with emotion" (*Brief Chronicles*, pt. 3 [1890], p. 272). As a stage manager Smith was well known for his discipline. According to actor William Warren, Smith "knew every in and out of his business, and his discipline was perfection. . . . He was never exacting, but everyone knew by instinct that he, and he only, was the ruling spirit" (*Boston Herald*, 11 July 1893).

As the author of *The Drunkard*, Smith played an important role in the history of the United States. While it may have been Smith's intention to capitalize on the Prohibition movement to generate ticket revenue, the result was a play that became a propaganda tool that reflected the growing antialcohol sentiment of the time. *The Drunkard*'s success helped to keep more than one theater solvent during a time when theatergoing was often frowned on by conservatives, and it remained a standard of melodrama more than 150 years later.

• Sources of information on Smith's life include Joseph Cowell, *Thirty Years Passed among the Players in England and America* (1844); William W. Clapp, *A Record of the Boston Stage* (1853); Claire McGlinchee, *The First Decade of the Boston Museum* (1940); and Bruce A. McConachie, *Melodramatic Formations: American Theatre and Society, 1820–1870* (1992). Obituaries are in the *San Francisco Morning Bull*, 19 Jan. 1872, and the *New York Times*, 20 Jan. 1872.

MELISSA VICKERY-BAREFORD

SMITH, William Henry (1 Dec. 1833–27 July 1896), journalist and political adviser, was born in Austerlitz, New York, the son of William DeForest Smith, a seller of wagons and carriages and a farmer, and Almira Gott. In 1835 Smith moved with his parents to Homer, Ohio. There he later became the secretary of a branch of the Underground Railroad for runaway slaves, which ran through the southern part of Union County. After graduating from Green Mount Seminary, a Quaker school near Richmond, Indiana, he worked for a year as a tutor.

In early 1855 the Cincinnati *Type of the Times* published Smith's article condemning the Know Nothing movement, and after further contributions he moved to Cincinnati in May to become its associate editor. He soon became acquainted with Rutherford B. Hayes, whom he met at a "Free Soilers" meeting at which Hayes presided. In 1855 Smith married Emma Reynolds; they had three children. In October Smith, who knew shorthand and strongly supported the women's movement, was a secretary of the national convention of women's rights advocates held in Cincinnati.

In early 1858 Smith joined the staff of the *Cincinnati Commercial* as its Columbus correspondent, where his hostility to the Democrats led to his expulsion from the floor of the state house of representatives. Early the next year he began working for the *Cincinnati Gazette*, and that June he gave a glowing, partisan report on the orderly Republican state convention. That same month he first met Whitelaw Reid, a newspaperman who would be his lifelong friend.

During the Civil War, Smith campaigned vigorously in the 1863 Ohio gubernatorial campaign for John Brough, a War Democrat who was running on the Union ticket to defeat Clement L. Vallandigham, a Peace Democrat who had counseled resistance to the draft and whom President Abraham Lincoln had banished beyond Union lines. When Brough won, Smith became his private secretary, and the next year he was elected secretary of state for Ohio, serving from 1865 to 1868. In that office, Smith helped raise and supply Ohio regiments and collected and cataloged documents pertaining to the history of Ohio. In 1868 he resigned to edit a new paper, the *Cincinnati Chronicle*, but in 1869 he moved to Chicago to become the general manager of the Western Associated Press.

Smith was instrumental in promoting the political career of Hayes. At the close of the Civil War, while Hayes was still in the Union army, Smith pushed him for Congress, urging him to get "a furlough to take the stump." Smith shrewdly published Hayes's response that an officer who "would abandon his post to electioneer for a seat in Congress ought to be scalped," and Hayes triumphed (Hoogenboom, p. 171). Later, Smith was the first person to suggest seriously that Hayes run for governor of Ohio, an office to which he was elected three times. After winning the Republican nomination for president in 1876, Hayes gratefully told Smith, "Your sagacity in this matter . . . is beyond that of any other friend" (Hoogenboom, p. 265). When the election that followed was disputed, Smith orchestrated negotiations between Republican newspapermen and southern Democrats to secure the election for Hayes, but the "bargains" that were struck had little effect on the rulings by Speaker of the House Samuel J. Randall and the Democratic votes that ended the stalemate. Although Hayes did not have much faith in those negotiations, Smith kept him informed. He was with Hayes, already en route to Washington, when he learned that the disputed election had been decided in his favor and that he indeed would be inaugurated.

Eager to keep Smith by his side, Hayes urged him to be his private secretary; but Smith, reluctant to leave the Western Associated Press, declined. The Western Associated Press had been formed in 1861 (and chartered in 1865) by leading western newspapers to cover local news and to place these papers on a more equal footing with papers belonging to the New York Associated Press. Smith increased the number of words each major newspaper received from his service from 8,000 to 20,000; erased its $18,000 debt, maintaining a $100,000 surplus; and secured from Western Union the first leased wire for transmitting news in the Middle West. But he tailored his job to fit his partisan purposes. When the election of 1876 was in dispute, Smith would not permit the Western Associated Press to carry reports of Democratic protest meetings in Ohio, Indiana, and Virginia.

Hayes appointed Smith collector of the port of Chicago. A good administrator, he remained with the Western Associated Press and performed both of his jobs with skill. Reputedly a reformer, he was actually an efficient spoils politician who had to be badgered to introduce reform practices in the Chicago Customhouse. He was identified with reform because he attacked undervaluations at the New York Customhouse—which put Chicago at a disadvantage when importing directly—at the same time that Hayes was striving to initiate changes that would make the New York Customhouse a showcase for civil service reform. Despite their differences on reform, Smith and Hayes throughout his administration discussed appointments and "public affairs . . . with great freedom" (Hoogenboom, p. 410). "You are so near me," Hayes cautioned him, "that whatever you may say will be considered as coming from me" (Gray, p. 160). Hayes's order that civil servants not engage in political management did not stop Smith from reporting to Treasury Secretary John Sherman on "reliable Sherman men" as far off as New Orleans in his vain attempt to secure the presidential nomination. Nevertheless, when Hayes left the presidency he told Smith, "You were at the cradle and you have followed the hearse 'of this ambitious life.' . . . No man ever had a more sincere, a more judicious, and a more unselfish friend" (Hoogenboom, p. 467).

Smith was fascinated by both past and present politics. Recognizing that as the Ohio secretary of state he had arranged and preserved the records of the Northwest Territory, the Ohio legislature in February 1881 asked him to edit the papers of Arthur St. Clair, the first governor of that territory and the president of the Continental Congress. By the next year Smith had completed this task and published St. Clair's papers in two volumes, which were called by the *Nation* "a well-digested edition . . . classified chronologically by subjects, and provided with a serviceable index" (Gray, p. 195).

When in 1883 the Western Associated Press and the New York Associated Press agreed to operate under a joint executive committee, Smith moved to New York City to be its first general manager. Almost immediately he introduced the typewriter to receive news reports and began replacing telegraph operators in large cities with newspapermen. During these years, ending with his retirement in 1892, he increased the number of reporters in Asia and Eastern Europe; he sent reporters to Brazil and Chile; he enlarged the Associated Press's Washington staff; and he made his "organization the greatest news-collecting and distributing agency in the world" (Williams, 1914, p. 424).

A serious blot on Smith's career during these years, however, was the secret purchase of a controlling interest in the rival United Press by Smith and fellow Associated Press insiders (including Reid of the *New York Tribune* and Charles A. Dana of the *New York Sun*) and their contract arrangements between the two agencies in 1885 and 1888 that enabled the understaffed United Press to receive most of its news from the Associated Press. In effect the latter subsidized the former, making the insider's secret investment in the United Press enormously profitable while diminishing the profits of the Associated Press. Smith defended the arrangement, declaring it had protected members of the Associated Press against competing newspapers and saved them money. But members of the Western Associated Press were so enraged that after an investigation in 1891 they terminated their agreement with the New York Associated Press and reorganized as the Associated Press of Illinois.

While living in New York, Smith worked with Reid to refine the crude mechanical typesetting machine developed by Otto Mergenthaler of Baltimore, Maryland. Working with him, they produced the first successful linotype machine (which Reid began using on 3 June 1886) and organized a company to manufacture it. Reid insisted that Smith's "tact and patience in treating with difficult people" had made this venture productive (Reid, p. xv).

Shortly before Hayes died in 1893, Smith agreed to write his biography but turned first to the background that defined much of Hayes's life. *A Political History of Slavery* (1903), a two-volume work, was substantially finished when Smith died in Lake Forest, Illinois, while letters and papers for the Hayes biography had been merely sorted and arranged. Smith's son-in-law Charles R. Williams continued Smith's work on the Hayes biography, and Smith's son Delavan Smith saw the slavery volumes through press. In that revisionist work, Smith portrayed the abolitionists of New England as a small extremist group, voicing insults and slogans, that had stolen the glory of ending slavery while the successful antislavery force—the one that spoke for a majority and deserved to be remembered—was the Free Soilers of Ohio, Indiana, and Illinois. Smith was, as Hayes had recorded, "an able writer, a most capable man of affairs, a wise public man . . . with an industry and perseverance rarely equalled" (Williams, *Diary and Letters*, vol. 4, p. 357).

• Smith's papers are at the Ohio Historical Society in Columbus and the William Henry Smith Memorial Library of the Indiana Historical Society in Indianapolis. There are also numerous Smith letters at the Hayes Presidential Center in Fremont, Ohio. He is mentioned often in Charles Richard Williams, ed., *Diary and Letters of Rutherford B. Hayes* (5 vols., 1922–1926). The best single source of Smith is Edgar Laughlin Gray, "The Career of William Henry Smith, Politician-Journalist" (Ph.D. diss., Ohio State Univ., 1951). Other helpful biographical sources are Charles Richard Williams, *The Life of Rutherford Birchard Hayes*, vol. 2 (1914), and Whitelaw Reid's introduction to William Henry Smith's *A Political History of Slavery* (2 vols., 1903). See also Ari Hoogenboom, *Rutherford B. Hayes: Warrior and President* (1995). Obituaries are in the *Chicago Daily Tribune*, the *New York Tribune*, and the *New York Times*, 28 July 1896.

OLIVE HOOGENBOOM

SMITH, William Loughton (2 Oct. 1758–19 Dec. 1812), congressman, diplomat, and essayist, was born in Charles Town (later Charleston), South Carolina, the son of Benjamin Smith, a wealthy merchant and colonial legislator, and Anne Loughton. He was educated by private tutors in London and Geneva and

studied law at the Inns of Court (Middle Temple) in England from 1779 to 1782. He remained aloof from events in America during the Revolution and did not return from Europe until 21 November 1783.

Upon returning to South Carolina, Smith sought admission to the state bar, which he was granted in January 1784. During the next five years he amassed a small fortune (around £19,000) as an attorney for Charleston's British merchant community. In 1786 he married Charlotte Izard, whose father, Ralph Izard, was South Carolina's wealthiest planter; they had two children. His marriage entrenched him more firmly in the state's social elite.

In 1784–1786 Smith successively won election to the South Carolina House of Representatives, the state Privy Council, and the office of Warden of the City of Charleston. During his four years in the state legislature (1785–1789), Smith represented the interests of the merchant and planter communities to which he belonged. He opposed the strong debtor-relief measures that the legislature passed in the mid-1780s, and he supported a temporary ban on slave imports in the interest of redressing South Carolina's unfavorable balance of trade. Like the rest of the state's coastal elite, Smith endorsed the federal Constitution of 1787 and voted in favor of it at the state ratifying convention the following May.

In November 1788 Smith stood for election to the U.S. House of Representatives from the district of Charleston. He easily defeated his two opponents, Alexander Gillon and David Ramsay, but the following spring Ramsay asked Congress to reject Smith's credentials on the grounds that he was not an American citizen since he had returned to America only five years earlier. Smith replied that he was a citizen of South Carolina by virtue of birth and parentage, and future rival James Madison supported Smith's case in the ensuing debate. On 22 May 1789 the House voted to accept Smith's credentials, and the South Carolinian took his seat in the first federal Congress.

During his five terms in the House, Smith became a leading member of the Federalist party and a consistent advocate of South Carolina's interests—as he perceived them. In February 1790 he issued a fiery denunciation of the Quakers for bringing antislavery memorials before the House, arguing that Congress had no constitutional right to even consider such petitions. He actively supported Alexander Hamilton's assumption proposal, which provided for the transfer of state war debts to the federal government. The measure relieved South Carolina of much of its $5.5 million public debt and enriched the state's creditors—including Smith, whose family had loaned more than £20,000 to the state government during the war. (Smith's political opponents later charged him with speculating in federal debt certificates during the assumption debate, a charge Smith flatly denied.) In 1791 he supported and helped organize Hamilton's Bank of the United States, which he hoped would provide capital for southern canal and road construction and in which he was an early stockholder.

While Smith's support for Hamilton's economic program was based on personal and regional interest, it also made him one of the treasury secretary's strongest allies in Congress. Conversely, Smith's alliance with Hamilton made him an opponent of Madison and Thomas Jefferson, especially regarding commercial policy. In 1789 and 1794 Madison proposed that Congress subject British shipping to discriminatory tariff rates until the British government opened West Indian markets to American trade. Smith opposed both proposals, and during the 1794 debate he delivered a long and detailed speech (prepared with considerable assistance from Hamilton) arguing that discrimination would hurt American trade far more than it would British and that commercial policy ought to be kept separate from political goals. In 1795–1796, for similar reasons, Smith supported Jay's Treaty, which among other provisions prohibited commercial discrimination against British shipping for ten years.

Smith's pro-British sympathies stemmed in part from his educational background, family ties, and business connections. But his attitude toward Britain was also based on his apprehension of American economic and military weakness. He believed that the United States should "temporize [with the British] until we gain more Strength & can bite as well as shew our teeth" (Smith to Edward Rutledge, 11 Nov. 1791). However, Smith's pro-British posture won him the enmity of a majority of South Carolina's citizens, and in 1794 and 1795 Charleston crowds burned him in effigy. These attacks merely hardened Smith's opinions and increased his devotion to the Federalist cause.

In 1796 Smith wrote a series of satirical articles titled *The Pretensions of Thomas Jefferson to the Presidency Examined*, published under the nom de plume of "Phocion" (a common Federalist sobriquet). He also actively campaigned for the Adams-Pinckney "ticket" in that year's presidential election. In July 1797, after serving briefly as the chairman of the House Ways and Means Committee, Smith was appointed as the minister to Portugal by President John Adams. It proved to be a marginal post, and during his four years in Lisbon Smith did little more than entertain guests and assist American envoys to the Barbary States with their negotiations. In 1799 Adams appointed Smith as the minister to the Ottoman Empire, but this mission was suspended in October, and Smith remained at his earlier station.

After his dismissal by President Jefferson in June 1801, Smith spent two years traveling in Europe and then returned to Charleston. After his first wife's death in 1792, he married Charlotte Wragg, the daughter of former Loyalist William Wragg, in 1805; they had two children. Smith ran for election to Congress in 1804, 1806, and 1808, but the South Carolina Federalist party had collapsed during his absence and he lost each time. In 1806 he wrote a new series of "Phocion" articles attacking the nonimportation policies and anti-British stance of the Republican Congress. Smith spent the final years of his life investing in private canal companies and managing the plantation that he had acquired through his second marriage. He died in Charleston shortly after the outbreak of America's second war with Britain.

• Smith's papers are held by a number of libraries and historical societies, including the Library of Congress; Duke University Library; the Henry E. Huntington Library, San Marino, Calif.; the Rosenbach Foundation, Philadelphia, Pa.; the South Carolina Historical Society; the South Caroliniana Library at the University of South Carolina; and the William L. Clements Library of the University of Michigan. The Timothy Pickering Papers at the Massachusetts Historical Society in Boston contain Smith's diplomatic correspondence. His congressional speeches can be found in Joseph Gales and William Seaton, comps., *The Annals of Congress* (1834–1856). Smith's publications include *A Comparative View of the Constitutions of the Several States with Each Other, & with That of the United States* (1796), and a compilation of the "Phocion" essays of 1806, *The Numbers of Phocion* (1806). The best modern biography is George C. Rogers, *The Evolution of a Federalist: William Loughton Smith of Charleston* (1962). On politics and society in contemporary South Carolina see Jerome Nadelhaft, *The Disorders of War: The Revolution in South Carolina* (1981), and Rachel Klein, *The Unification of a Slave State* (1990). A detailed account of national politics, diplomacy, and ideology in the 1790s and of Smith's place therein can be found in Stanley Elkins and Eric McKitrick, *The Age of Federalism* (1993).

DAVID A. NICHOLS

SMITH, William Stephens (8 Nov. 1755–10 June 1816), revolutionary war officer and congressman, was born in New York City, the son of John Smith, a prosperous merchant, and Margaret Stephens, the daughter of John Stephens, a British army officer. After graduating from the College of New Jersey (Princeton) in 1774, Smith studied law with Samuel Jones in New York City. When the war theater shifted from Boston to New York in summer 1776, Smith joined the Continental army as a major and aide-de-camp to General John Sullivan; he was commissioned on 15 August 1776. At the battle of Long Island, Smith was captured but escaped and crossed the East River to Manhattan in the same boat as George Washington. With Sullivan a prisoner of war, Smith became aide-de-camp to General Nathanael Greene. At the battle of Harlem Heights he was among those of Greene's troops who came into action late, and he was wounded. As Washington's army retreated from Manhattan with the British in pursuit, Smith and six enlisted men destroyed the bridge between Throgs' Neck and the mainland, thus preventing Howe from outflanking the American army. Smith fought at the battle of White Plains and accompanied the army as it retreated across New Jersey. For gallantry in general at Trenton he was promoted to lieutenant colonel (1 Jan. 1777) in William Raymond Lee's Additional Continental Regiment. Smith was acting commander of this regiment from 24 January 1778 to 29 April 1779. He was then transferred to Oliver Spencer's Additional Continental Regiment (which from 1777 to mid-1778 had been called the Fifth New Jersey Regiment).

At the battle of Monmouth (28 June 1778) Smith was in the thick of the action three times. He was present at Sullivan's unsuccessful siege of Newport, Rhode Island, 24 July–31 August 1778. In Spencer's regiment, Smith accompanied Sullivan's army in the campaign of May–November 1779 against the Iroquois Indians in western New York. Smith fought at the battle of Springfield, New Jersey (23 June 1780), the last major engagement in the North. From 1 January to July 1781 Smith served as adjutant and inspector to General Lafayette; then as aide-de-camp to Washington, 6 July 1781–23 December 1783. For a while in 1782, at Dobbs Ferry, New York, he was acting commissary general of prisoners. Smith was present at the siege of Yorktown. As acting officer of the day on 25 November 1783, he supervised the evacuation of New York City by the British.

In 1785 Smith became secretary to the American legation in England, headed by John Adams as U.S. minister. While residing in London, Smith courted for two years Abigail "Nabby" Amelia Adams, daughter of John Adams. They were married in London in 1786 and would eventually have three children. During his diplomatic tenure in England, Smith served on missions to Spain and Portugal and for several months in 1785 toured Europe with Francisco de Miranda, the Venezuelan revolutionist.

The Smiths returned to America in 1788 and settled in Jamaica (in the present borough of Queens, New York City). President Washington appointed Smith the U.S. marshal of the district of New York on 26 September 1789. Two years later Smith received a federal appointment as supervisor of the revenue for New York.

Smith became an active land speculator on his own and as an agent for a syndicate of English investors. On behalf of his English backers he purchased five townships (150,000 acres) in the present counties of Madison and Chenango and the town of Sherburne, lands in upstate New York recently opened for settlement by an Indian treaty. In 1790 and 1792–1793 he resided in England for the purpose of selling these lands.

In 1795 Smith purchased a tract of land along the East River (between present Fifty-eighth and Sixty-second Streets in New York City) and began construction of a mansion, a replication of Washington's "Mount Vernon," but because of financial insolvency the project was abandoned.

Smith's only forte was military ability, and he hoped to be named brigadier general and adjutant general for the army that was to be raised during the French crisis of 1797–1799. President John Adams submitted the nomination of his son-in-law to this post, only to have the Senate reject it, owing to the strenuous opposition of Secretary of State Timothy Pickering and several senators, largely on grounds that Smith was bankrupt and a speculator. The Senate on 19 June 1798 confirmed all of Adams's military nominations except Smith's. Smith, however, did accept a lieutenant colonelcy of an infantry regiment and briefly spent time in

camp before the war mobilization ceased. On 24 June 1800 Adams appointed Smith the surveyor of customs for the port of New York.

In 1806 Smith and his nineteen-year-old son, William Steuben Smith, became involved in Francisco de Miranda's quixotic venture to free Venezuela from Spanish rule. Smith chartered a ship for Miranda and contributed toward the expense of raising men and supplies for the expedition, which set out from New York in February 1806. The younger Smith, dropping out of Columbia College, accompanied the little force of rebels as a lieutenant. The venture met its end with an encounter with a Spanish vessel. Though Miranda escaped, Lieutenant Smith did not, and almost wound up being executed. When William Stephens Smith's role in the Miranda affair became public, President Thomas Jefferson dismissed him from his customs post. From April to July 1806 Smith stood trial in federal circuit court for "high misdemeanor," accused of "setting on foot, or providing means for, a military expedition against a nation with which the United States is at peace." With his defense counsel intimating that Jefferson, James Madison, and other federal officials had knowledge of the Miranda scheme but did nothing, Smith was acquitted.

Smith was impoverished because of his reckless speculative activities and financial failures. Several ships that he had invested in during the late 1790s were seized by privateers. After he died, it was discovered that his estate had an indebtedness of $200,000.

Smith and his wife moved to Lebanon (near Hamilton) in upstate New York in 1808 to a small tract of land owned by Smith and his brothers. There he devoted himself to farming. Abigail Adams tried to secure him a military appointment at the outset of the War of 1812, but Secretary of War James Monroe would not approve. In December 1812 Smith was elected to the U.S. House of Representatives as a Federalist from the district of Madison and Herkimer Counties. In Congress he fought successfully against expansion of army manpower because of the cost. It appeared that Smith won reelection in 1814, but his opponent, Westel Willoughby, challenged the returns. With his old nemesis Timothy Pickering at the head of the House of Representatives elections committee, the decision went for Willoughby. On 13 December 1815 Smith relinquished his congressional seat. Suffering from gout and a liver ailment, Smith died six months later at Lebanon and was buried in a plot that he did not own in the town of Sherburne.

While Smith was affable and a brave soldier, especially in later life he had a reputation for being weak-minded, greedy, vain, and pompous. John Adams considered this family member a disappointment and an embarrassment.

• Correspondence and materials relating to William Stephens Smith are found in the Adams papers, Massachusetts Historical Society, and the George Washington Papers, Library of Congress, both in microfilm editions. For a dual biography, more enthusiastic than substantial, see Katherine M. Roof,

Colonel William Smith and Lady: The Romance of Washington's Aide and Young Abigail Adams (1929). A solid, brief biography is Marcius D. Raymond, "Colonel William Stephens Smith," *New York Genealogical and Historical Record* 25, no. 4 (1894): 153–61. Smith's involvement with Miranda is in William S. Robertson, *The Life of Miranda* (2 vols., 1929). Works on John Adams and the Adams family yield much information on Smith's activities and character; particularly useful of these are Phyllis L. Levin, *Abigail Adams: A Biography* (1987); Page Smith, *John Adams* (2 vols., 1962); and Paul C. Nagel, *Descent from Glory: Four Generations of the John Adams Family* (1983). A death notice is in the *New-York Evening Post*, 17 June 1816.

HARRY M. WARD

SMITH, William Waugh (12 Mar. 1845–29 Nov. 1912), educator, was born in Warrenton, Fauquier County, Virginia, the son of Richard M. Smith and Ellen Blackwell. Smith's father owned a private school in Warrenton, real estate worth $17,000, and five adult slaves. Smith attended his father's school, and when the elder Smith moved to Alexandria, Virginia, to work with Benjamin Hallowell in his Quaker Academy, William continued his education there. Smith enlisted in the Confederate army at age sixteen in 1862 and was shot three times (one bullet being stopped by a book) during the war.

After the war he worked for his father's newspaper, the Richmond *Enquirer*, until 1867, when he entered the University of Virginia. In 1868, when his father became professor of chemistry at Randolph-Macon College in Ashland, Virginia, William followed him and matriculated there. The following year he married Ella Jones. In 1871 he received a master's degree from Randolph-Macon for taking a heavier load of courses and achieving a higher grade point average than was required for the baccalaureate. He then served for several years as associate principal of Bethel Academy in Warrenton under his uncle Major Albert Smith. His first wife died in 1873, and in 1875 he married Marian Love Howison; he had no children by either marriage. In 1877 Smith returned to Randolph-Macon College as professor of philosophy, reportedly taking a decrease in salary, and became professor of Greek and Latin in 1882. He was unpopular with the students, who viewed him as a martinet and a meddler. In 1885–1886 Smith volunteered to lead a fundraising campaign that collected $43,000. This success led the board of trustees to elect him president of the college in 1886. Smith proved a brilliant choice who, while confounding his student critics by his democratic and considerate manner, became a major innovator in education by creating the centrally owned, statewide Randolph-Macon System of two colleges and three preparatory schools.

Virginia in the late nineteenth century suffered from both a poor and a small secondary educational system, which produced too few graduates for the relatively large numbers of colleges. None of these colleges admitted women. Although Smith was not the first president at Randolph-Macon to see the need for more and better-trained high school students, and for higher ed-

ucation for women, his energies aroused local financial support that led to the opening of Randolph-Macon Academy in present-day Bedford, Virginia (1890), and a second Randolph-Macon Academy in Front Royal, Virginia (1892). He persuaded the business leaders of these towns that schools would bring in more revenue than hotels. His crowning achievement was the establishment in 1893 of Randolph-Macon Woman's College in Lynchburg, Virginia, where he officiated as president. An existing preparatory school, the Danville Female Institute, was admitted to the Randolph-Macon System in 1897. The preparatory schools were to act as feeders to the colleges. A single board of trustees controlled the system, but each school was separately funded and managed.

Smith's accomplishments rested upon his philosophy that it was "easier to do a big thing than a little thing." Contemporaries (such as his cousin Robert E. Blackwell, president of Randolph-Macon College from 1902 to 1938, and the Reverend W. W. Lear) commented on his "prophetic foresight" coupled with his "great powers of concentration," "his physical energy and eagerness," his capacity to keep "his whole being under the perfect command of his will." He enjoyed playing games and showing children magic tricks and even the scars from his wounds; according to Blackwell, "The boy never died in him." His love of sports led him in 1887 to institute a requirement for graduation of physical education (calisthenics). In the pursuit of raising funds for the schools he ignored his own finances and even his own health. He gave occasional sermons and was a leader in the Virginia Anti-Saloon League, participating in a successful local-option prohibition movement and in the successful effort to stop freight trains on Sunday.

The board made Smith chancellor of the system in 1897, a post he held concurrently with the presidency of the woman's college until his death (upon which the chancellorship was abolished). By that time, he had raised the endowment of the woman's college to $317,000. The quality of the college grew so rapidly that in 1907 the prestigious Carnegie Foundation for the Advancement of Teaching agreed to offer pensions to its faculty; it was the only college in the South so honored. Despite Smith's pious Methodism, he agreed to the foundation's stipulation of a formal statement that no trustees or faculty members were required to be members of the Methodist Episcopal Church, South. Although no requirement of Methodist affiliation had existed formally, in fact all of the trustees were Methodists, and half were ministers. The foundation expected not only a formal statement but also the membership of non-Methodists on the board. The proposed agreement was bitterly and persistently attacked by the Reverend James Cannon, Jr. (1864–1944), Methodist editor of the *Baltimore and Richmond Christian Advocate*. Although Smith and the trustees in 1911 declined the Carnegie pensions because of Cannon's pressure, the controversy over the church's claim to legal ownership of the system plagued Smith until his death and continued until

1914, when a state court found that the college was legally independent of the church. After suffering from Bright's disease and a railroad handcar injury, which he received in 1911 while en route to a Methodist conference, Smith died in Lynchburg, Virginia. Some contemporaries thought that the struggle with Cannon had "hounded" him to death.

• The principal source for Smith's administration is Randolph-Macon College, Board of Trustees, Minutes, which are located at the college in Ashland, Va. The Blackwell Papers (also at Randolph-Macon College) contain personal reminiscences of Smith by his cousin Robert Emory Blackwell, much of which Blackwell published in "Dr. William Smith: A Portrait," Randolph-Macon Woman's College Alumnae Bulletin 24 (Apr. 1931): 9–31. The archives of Randolph-Macon Woman's College in Lynchburg, Va., has a small collection of Smith's papers and articles. The position of the two sides in the ownership controversy can be found in Randolph-Macon College, Board of Trustees, The Randolph-Macon System: Its Relation to the Church and to the Carnegie Foundation (1908), which contains many primary documents. Smith wrote two books: Outlines of Psychology (1884) and A Parallel Syntax Chart of Latin, Greek, German, and French (1882). See also Roberta D. Cornelius, The History of Randolph-Macon Woman's College (1951); Richard Irby, History of Randolph-Macon College, Virginia [1898]; and James Edward Scanlon, Randolph-Macon College: A Southern History (1983). An obituary is in the Richmond Times-Dispatch, 30 Nov. 1912.

JAMES EDWARD SCANLON

SMITH, Willie "the Lion" (25 Nov. 1897–18 Apr. 1973), jazz pianist, was born William Henry Joseph Bonaparte Bertholoff in Goshen, New York, the son of Ida Oliver, a domestic worker, and Frank Bertholoff. In 1900 Ida expelled Frank from the household; he died the next year, and she married John Smith, who took the family to Newark, New Jersey, where he worked as a meat-wagon driver and later a mechanic. Willie attended Newark High School, where he excelled as an athlete.

Having begun to play the family's home organ by ear, Smith received lessons from his mother, a church pianist and organist. He worked for tips as a dancer but preferred piano and, after winning an upright piano in a contest, devoted himself to it, practicing pop songs and ragtime. From around 1911 he entertained in saloons in Newark. Although his music was informed by his background in the African-American Baptist church, Smith had been befriended by a Jewish family and had embraced Judaism, learning Hebrew as a child and taking the bar mitzvah at age thirteen; later in life he served as a cantor at a synagogue in Harlem.

In the summers of 1915 and 1916 Smith worked in saloons in Atlantic City, New Jersey, initially as a replacement for Eubie Blake. He also began playing professionally in New York City. Pianist Arthur Eck taught Smith to read music, and in exchange Smith improved Eck's improvisatory skills. At age nineteen Smith married Blanche Howard Merrill, a pianist (not the vaudeville songwriter of the same name); they sep-

arated after one year. Smith enlisted in the army in November 1916 and the following July was sent to France, where he played bass drum in Lieutenant Tim Brymn's Regimental Band and where, by one account, his energy as a gunner earned him his nickname, the Lion (Artie Shaw, however, attributed the nickname to the growls that Smith vocalized while playing piano). Late in 1919 Smith was discharged and returned to New York City. Reunited with his lifelong friend James P. Johnson, whom he had met in 1914, and soon joined by their younger colleague Fats Waller, he became a pioneer and a virtuoso in a new jazz style that came to be known as stride piano, a swinging and sometimes improvised offshoot of classic ragtime that features irregular patterns in which the left hand "strides" between the instrument's bass range and mid-range.

Smith performed at Leroy's in Harlem in 1919 and 1920. In August 1920 he organized and performed in the band that accompanied singer Mamie Smith on the historic recording "Crazy Blues." Its success touched off a craze for "classic blues" (female African-American blues and vaudeville singers with jazz bands), and it established a new marketing category that soon acquired the name "race records." As a member of the Holiday in Dixieland troupe, Smith performed in New York in April 1922 and then set out on a brief tour. In 1923, while working in Chicago, he heard some of the great New Orleans jazz musicians.

Back in Harlem by year's end, Smith performed at the Garden of Joy and then at the Capitol Palace, where future jazz soloists Bubber Miley and Jimmy Harrison sat in with the band. Many nights after the Capitol Palace closed, he went to the Rhythm Club, where the house band was led by Sidney Bechet and where emerging giants of jazz came to improvise. Smith took over the leadership and hired soprano saxophonist Johnny Hodges when Bechet left in the spring of 1925. When the Rhythm Club moved, Smith stayed at the same location, now renamed the Hoofers' Club, and he changed the format from an open jam session to a tightly organized quartet that included C-melody saxophonist Benny Carter. Smith played and acted in the drama Four Walls at the John Golden Theater on Fifty-eighth Street in New York City beginning in September 1927. When after 144 performances the show moved to Chicago, he, as usual, chose to stay in New York.

Throughout the mid- to late 1920s, Smith, Johnson, and Waller were in constant demand as solo pianists at rent parties in Harlem. Although the three friends were energetic to excess and lived wild lives, Smith, like Johnson (and unlike Waller), was nonetheless concerned with meticulous show-business mannerisms and a stylishly elegant and orderly presentation: a fine suit, a derby hat, and a cigar were fixtures of his appearance. He was intelligent, inquisitive, and opinionated, and (anticipating the 1960s) he was sensitive to good and bad "vibrations," which would determine his involvement in a given situation.

Smith spent about two years in the early 1930s at another Harlem club, Pods' and Jerry's (officially the Catagonia Club but known by the owners' nick-names). He discouraged sitting in, after the chaos of the Rhythm Club, but he made exceptions for talents of the likes of Bechet and young Artie Shaw; Shaw played without pay for the experience of performing with Smith. At Pods' and Jerry's he met his future wife, then a married woman, Jennie Williams, also known as "Silvertop" or "Jane"; her maiden name, details of the marriage, and the number of their children, if any, are unknown.

Smith began working steadily for Joe Helbock on Fifty-second Street, and with the end of Prohibition in 1933, Helbock made the venue into a legitimate night-club, the Onyx. Smith worked as intermission pianist at the nearby Famous Door from 1934 to 1935. During these years he recorded and broadcast with Eva Taylor in Clarence Williams's band. He may be heard as a soloist on "Somebody Stole My Gal" from a session on 3 October 1934 by a group of Williams's musicians recording under the name of the Alabama Jug Band. Also during this period Smith commenced formal studies with pianist Hans Steinke, and he began to write pieces exhibiting an amalgam of jazz, blues, and European influences.

In 1935, with personnel drawn from Williams's circle, Smith made his first recordings as a leader, including his composition "Echo of Spring." After further sessions of his own in 1937, he agreed to a recording contract with the musically ponderous organist Milt Herth, an association he detested. In January 1938 he recorded two more compositions, "Passionette" and "Morning Air," in a duo with drummer O'Neil Spencer; these are firmly based in the irregularly leaping and swinging patterns of stride and thus exhibit Smith's usual approach to performance. For the Commodore label in January 1939 he made his most famous recordings: fourteen unaccompanied titles comprising popular songs and his own compositions, including "Concentratin'," "Fading Star," "Sneakaway," and "Finger Buster," as well as versions of some previously recorded pieces. The fourteen recordings summarize his two-fold approach, alternately centered in the mainstream of the flamboyant stride piano tradition and exploring a sensitive twist on that tradition. In the best known of these, titled "Echoes of Spring" for the Commodore session (rather than "Echo of Spring"), his exuberant style is modified by a delicacy hinting at turn-of-the-century French piano impressionism and by a simple, repeated, loping accompanimental figure that perhaps owes more to boogie woogie piano than to the complexities of stride. The Tommy Dorsey and Artie Shaw orchestras performed arrangements of Smith's compositions in the 1940s, thereby bringing him a somewhat greater audience, although he was never famous outside of the jazz world.

Smith worked in a trio with Bechet in the spring of 1939. In November, as members of the Haitian Orchestra, they recorded an odd session of arranged merengues, rhumbas, and Haitian melodies, notable for pioneering the concept of Caribbean jazz but not for the result. In 1940 he accompanied blues singer Joe Turner, but unfortunately this pairing was a mismatch: Smith's musically florid and emotionally fluffy blues playing is temperamentally unsuited to Turner's raw style. In 1941 he recorded with Bechet's New Orleans Feetwarmers.

In the 1940s Smith worked at the Man About Town Club on Fifty-first Street and in dixieland bands in Lower Manhattan, including the Pied Piper, where in 1944 he served as the pianist in trumpeter Max Kaminsky's band while also engaging in legendary solo contests with the intermission pianist, his friend James Johnson. Smith also made regular trips to perform in Toronto. Hard living finally took its toll, and he ceased working temporarily. He returned to performing to tour Europe and North Africa from December 1949 through February 1950 and recorded for the Royal Jazz label in Paris. By this time he had arthritis in his fingers, and it slowly worsened over the years, but only the expert and cranky listener will find fault with these performances. His career continued unabated, and he recorded new versions of the Commodore solos for Royal Jazz in December 1950. Despite the strong compositional element in his own pieces, the re-creations are substantially different from the originals of 1939. His dramatic, texturally thick, bent-for-hell readings of several of the popular songs, including "Stormy Weather," "Tea for Two," and "Between the Devil and the Deep Blue Sea," demonstrate the sort of playing that must have given the competition fits.

During the 1950s Smith worked regularly at the Central Plaza, and the film *Jazz Dance* captures him there in 1954. He hated the crass tastelessness of the music (the band was notorious for playing loudly and without regard for the sensitive aspects of musical taste), but he stayed at the Central Plaza until 1958. In the spring of that year he appeared in the third show ("Ragtime") of the television series "The Subject Is Jazz." Smith ceased performing in nightclubs and turned instead to colleges, country clubs, festivals, benefit concerts, and other less demanding work. He toured and recorded again in Europe in 1965 and 1966. In the spring of 1969 he was filmed playing in New York for the French documentary *L'Aventure du jazz* (1970). He died in New York City.

Smith was one of the most formidably talented stride pianists. Although not an innovator of the stature of Johnson, Waller, and Art Tatum, he was a central figure for a half century in the development and subsequent international dissemination of stride and related early jazz styles.

• Smith's autobiography, *Music on My Mind* (1964; repr. 1975), written with George Hoefer's assistance, is among the most entertaining and informative in jazz literature. Hoefer also inserts surveys of Harlem nightlife and descriptions of Smith's style. Further recollections are in Artie Shaw's autobiography, *The Trouble with Cinderella* (1952; repr. 1979), pp. 223–28. Details of Smith's association with Bechet are collected in John Chilton, *Sidney Bechet: The Wizard of Jazz* (1987). Johnny Simmen describes Smith's own recordings and also recordings of "Some Piano Compositions of Willie 'the Lion' Smith Played by Other Musicians" in *Storyville*, no. 44 (1972–1973): 44–51, and no. 45 (1973): 98–108. Leonard Feather surveys his career and supplies a partial musical score of "Echo(es) of Spring" in "Piano Giants of Jazz: Willie 'the Lion' Smith," *Contemporary Keyboard* 3 (Oct. 1977): 55. A serialized catalog of recordings and films is John Collinson, "Willie 'the Lion' Smith," *Storyville*, no. 132 (1 Dec. 1987): 211–12; no. 133 (1 Mar. 1988): 27–28; no. 134 (1 June 1988): 63–66; no. 135 (1 Sept. 1988): 94–98; no. 136 (1 Dec. 1988): 147–51; no. 137 (1 Mar. 1989): 192–94; and no. 138 (1 June 1989): 205–8. An obituary is in the *New York Times*, 19 Apr. 1973.

BARRY KERNFELD

SMITH, Winchell (5 Apr. 1871?–10 June 1933), director and playwright, was born William Brown Smith, Jr., in Hartford, Connecticut, the son of William Brown Smith, a flour, grain, and feed merchant, and Virginia Thrall. Smith's father was a nephew of abolitionist John Brown. Educated in the Hartford public schools, Winchell Smith entered his father's business at an early age. Rejecting plans for a college education, he decided on a career in the theater and enrolled in Franklin Haven Sargent's Lyceum Theatre School of Acting in New York City (the forerunner of the American Academy of Dramatic Art). After completing his training in 1892, Smith found sporadic employment as both an actor and a stage manager. He married Grace Furbush Spencer of Troy, New York, in December 1895. The couple had no children.

Smith's first New York stage role was as the telegraph operator in *Secret Service* (1896) with William Gillette, followed by a London production of the play in 1897. Other London appearances included those in *Sue* and *Too Much Johnson* in 1898, *Arizona* and *All on Account of Eliza* in 1902. From acting he turned to producing and with Arnold Daly introduced George Bernard Shaw's *Candida*, *The Man of Destiny*, *You Never Can Tell*, *How She Lied to Her Husband*, *John Bull's Other Island*, and *Mrs. Warren's Profession* to the United States from 1903 to 1906. In 1906 Smith collaborated with Byron Ongley in a dramatization of George Barr McCutcheon's *Brewster's Millions*. Other collaborations of note were *Polly of the Circus* (1907) with Margaret Mayo and *Via Wireless* (1908) with Paul Armstrong. With Victor Mapes he wrote *My Little Friend* (1913), *The New Henrietta* (1913), and *The Boomerang* (1915). His first original play without a collaborator was *The Fortune Hunter* (1909). This was followed by *Love among the Lions* (1910), adapted from the F. Anstey novel, and *The Only Son* (1911). As a play doctor he completely revised actor John E. Hazzard's crudely written *Turn to the Right* (1916) for producer John Golden.

The height of Smith's success came with his association with actor Frank Bacon in *Lightnin'* (1918). The play ran for over three years, with 1,291 performances on Broadway, breaking all records for an American

production up to that time. Its good fortune was due largely to the remarkable acting of Bacon as "Lightnin' Bill Jones," a loveable ne'er-do-well who drinks to excess and has a delightful gift of exaggeration. *Thank You* (1921), a farce-melodrama, written and directed in collaboration with Tom Cushing, reveals how a minister, through the efforts of his niece, acquires a substantial financial living and an endowment for his parish. In 1925 Smith and George Abbott wrote *A Holy Terror*, a John Golden production with Abbott as director and leading man. *The Zoo* (1927), written with Michael Arlen, proved to be a dismal failure.

Smith was one of the more skilled and proficient directors in the American theater of his time. Perhaps one of the reasons for his success was his empathy with actors and his ability to make them interpret his characters as he wished. In his autobiography George Abbott writes that Smith's greatest quality and interest was "in what went on behind the footlights." As a director, he was always "crystal clear." A pleasant, soft-spoken man who never lost his boyish simplicity or Yankee twang, Smith was well liked by both his theatrical colleagues and his Connecticut neighbors. In addition to being a shrewd showman, Smith was also one of the most astute play doctors of the period. Throughout his career Smith rarely wrote plays alone, perhaps because his collaborative efforts were consistently so successful. In *Matinee Tomorrow*, Ward Morehouse quotes Smith as saying, "I've had about thirty productions since *Brewster's Millions* but I've really written one play. That Play was *The Fortune Hunter* and I wrote it because I wanted to." The plays on which he worked were typically comedies in the American tradition, with broad effects, brisk dialogue, and sentimental endings, enhanced by a subtlety lacking in the older melodramas of the American stage.

By 1930 he conceded that his playwriting career was at an end, because, as he revealed to Morehouse, "The theater's gone on ahead of me. I'm still stage struck, and I always will be, but I'm out of date." The director-playwright bade official farewell to the theater with his staging of Paul Osborn's *The Vinegar Tree* (1930), a comedy that gave Mary Boland one of the best roles of her stage career. In retirement, Smith spent his days developing and maintaining his country estate and spending winters in the south of France. At the time of his death in his Mill Stream home near Farmington, Connecticut, he left an estate estimated at a $1.5 million—a share of which was bequeathed as a trust fund to the Lambs Club for the care of actors and playwrights in financial need.

• Walter Prichard Eaton, *Plays and Players* (1916), Margaret G. Mayorga, *A Short History of the American Drama* (1932), and Arthur Hobson Quinn, *A History of the American Drama from the Civil War to the Present Day*, vol. 2 (1927), are standard sources. For personal and professional insights see Ward Morehouse, *Matinee Tomorrow* (1949), and George Abbott, *Mister Abbott* (1963). See also articles in the *Christian Science Monitor*, 26 Sept. 1916, the *New York Times*, 26 Mar., 19 Nov., and 10 Dec. 1916, and the *Hartford Courant*, 19

Apr. 1931. Obituaries are in the *New York Times* and the *Hartford Courant*, both 11 June 1933, and *Publishers Weekly*, 17 June 1933.

LOUIS A. RACHOW

SMITH, Zilpha Drew (25 Jan. 1852?–12 Oct. 1926), social worker, was born in Pembroke, Massachusetts, the daughter of Silvanus Smith, a carpenter and sail maker, and Judith Winsor McLauthlin. Soon after Smith was born, she moved with her family to Boston, where her father opened a shipyard. From her earliest days Smith was exposed to social concerns, since her parents supported a wide range of reform causes, including abolition, temperance, and woman suffrage. She attended Girls' High and Normal School in Boston, graduating in 1868, after which she found work as a telegrapher. A few years later she took on the task of revising the index of the Suffolk County Probate Court. She also worked as a volunteer, helping to care for the victims of a devastating fire in 1872 and for families left destitute by the panic of 1873.

In 1879 Smith became registrar of the Boston Associated Charities, a new organization established to coordinate the activities and records of the city's several private social agencies. "Organized charity" would be adopted in many American cities during the years that followed, but Boston was one of the first to embrace this approach to social welfare. According to its teachings, casual handouts did the poor more harm than good. Instead, each family seeking relief should be thoroughly investigated to ascertain the root causes of its poverty. The specific needs could then be addressed—in most cases not by financial assistance, but by guidance from a volunteer "friendly visitor," who would help the family members out of their poverty by showing them how to live more orderly and productive lives. This system, it was believed, would eradicate pauperism and also help to break down the growing hostility between classes in the industrial city.

So as to pool information and ensure that no family received aid from more than one agency, all cases within a given city were to be registered in a central file. Smith's initial task was to maintain the central register, or confidential exchange, of Boston Associated Charities. However, her job soon expanded to include the responsibilities of general secretary, and she was given that title in 1886. Her agency became widely known as an exemplar of the new organized charity. Explaining its success, Smith said: "The difference is that somebody . . . has the power of organization and does that work. That is the secret of it all."

Smith presided over a large staff of paid and volunteer workers. The paid employees made the initial investigations, performed much of the administrative work, and provided professional consultation to the volunteers. But it was the volunteers, Smith believed, who constituted the heart of the agency program. She thought that as these "friendly visitors" established personal relationships with the people they served, their cultured approach to life and their high values would prove contagious, inspiring their clients to abandon the bad habits that had brought them to poverty.

Few agencies recruited as many volunteer workers as Smith's, or dedicated so much care to training them. She explained, "You have not only to learn the characters of the poor, but of all your visitors." It was a mistake, Smith observed, to assume that "good visitors are born good visitors; certainly most of the good visitors in any group are *made*." Among other things, she encouraged her professional and volunteer staff to talk regularly with each other; this practice helped lay the groundwork for the later development of casework supervision. Smith's methods were widely adopted; in 1898, for instance, when the New York Charity Organization Society (COS) held its first Summer School in Applied Philanthropy for friendly visitors, lectures by Smith and her protegée, Mary Richmond of the Baltimore COS, dominated the curriculum.

Smith also devoted much attention to the training of her paid workers, taking them through the necessary steps of investigation and treatment and instructing them on the history of social welfare all the way back to Elizabethan Poor Law. In 1888 she helped organize the Monday Evening Club, a forum where social workers could meet regularly for professional discussions. Speaking to the National Conference of Social Work in later years, she recommended that any town with more than twelve paid social workers should organize such a club. Smith devoted considerable thought to analyzing the work performed by her professional staff, and a paper she presented at the 1901 National Conference of Social Work is considered one of the earliest expositions of casework method, although she did not use that term. (Smith herself defined the social worker's job simply as "leaving no stone unturned to find the trouble that drags a person down.") Pursuing another kind of social analysis, she also carried out statistical studies; in 1901, for instance, she presented a pioneering report on child-support needs among 247 deserted families on her agency's roster.

After resigning from the Associated Charities in 1903, Smith moved to the new Boston School of Social Work, which she had helped persuade Harvard University and Simmons College to establish. Besides serving as associate director, she organized a series of classes in which students learned about social work methods by studying actual case records. A demanding teacher, Smith brought to her academic work the same qualities of organization and rigorous precision that had distinguished her social work career. By this time she had established herself as a mentor to charity workers in many cities; as one example of her influence, Richmond's widely read textbook, *Social Diagnosis* (1917), was inspired by Smith's 1908 lecture at the New York School of Philanthropy, "Methods Common to Social Investigation." Smith's style was austere and somewhat reserved, but she was a devoted friend to intimates like Richmond, and during her time away from work she took active pleasure in music, drama, and the New England countryside. She retired from teaching in 1918 and died in Boston some years later.

The investigative side of organized charity has often been criticized as intrusive and judgmental, but Smith always maintained that its principal purpose was to get the fullest possible understanding of a client's situation. "The possibility of imposture," she wrote, "is not so much to be guarded against as the constant danger [of] misunderstanding the real needs of a family." Her views on the causes of poverty lost credibility as the depression swept away the jobs and savings of so many hard-working families, but her thoughtful analysis of how casework is done and how it can be taught represented a significant contribution to the theory and practice of American social welfare.

• Smith's papers are in the Simmons College Archives, Boston. Correspondence with her also appears in the papers of Mary Richmond at Columbia University, New York City. Smith's 1901 paper appeared as a book, *Methods of Social Investigation* (1908). Articles by her appear in the following annual *Proceedings* of the National Conference of Charities and Correction: 1884, pp. 69–72; 1887, pp. 156–62; 1888, pp. 120–30; 1892, pp. 445–49; 1901, pp. 284–89; and 1915, pp. 622–26. See also Frank J. Bruno, *Trends in Social Work, 1874–1956* (1957); Roy Lubove, *The Professional Altruist* (1965); Walter I. Trattner, *From Poor Law to Welfare State: A History of Social Welfare in America,* 3d ed. (1984); Frank Dekker Watson, *The Charity Organization Society Movement in the United States* (1922); Stanley Wenocur and Michael Reisch, *From Charity to Enterprise: The Development of American Social Work in a Market Economy* (1989), and the Simmons School of Social Work alumnae magazine, *Social Worker,* Aug. 1945.

SANDRA OPDYCKE

SMITHSON, Robert Irving (2 Jan. 1938–20 July 1973), artist and art theorist, was born in Passaic, New Jersey, the son of Irving Smithson, the vice president of a mortgage loan firm, and Susan Duke. Smithson grew up in Rutherford and Clifton, New Jersey. His pediatrician was the poet William Carlos Williams. Smithson's love for art, combined with a fascination for natural history, first materialized in childhood drawings and paper constructions of dinosaurs inspired by his visits to the Museum of Natural History in New York City. In 1953, while a junior at Clifton High School, he won a scholarship to the Art Students League in New York City. He obtained time off from high school to spend afternoons and evenings at the League training as a painter and draftsman. He also studied on Saturdays in the studio of the social-realist painter Isaac Soyer. In 1956 he attended the Brooklyn Museum School on scholarship. Following graduation from high school he enlisted in the army reserves, for which he briefly served as artist in residence. After an honorable discharge in 1957 and a hitchhiking trip with friends around the United States and parts of Mexico, he located in New York City and resumed a career in art.

Smithson's paintings of the late 1950s show the influence of abstract expressionism, the predominant artistic movement in New York City at that time. He in-

corporated religious, mythical, and science-fictional characters, derived from classical literature and futuristic novels, into expressionistically rendered paintings and collages. At age nineteen he had his first solo exhibition of paintings at a New York City gallery (Artists Gallery, 1959).

Smithson had a passion for reading, especially science books and science fiction, that would effectively determine the nature of all his art. Around 1962 his fascination with natural science led him to abandon painting for sculptural forms. For an exhibition during this transitional period he prepared rows of labeled jars containing biological specimens.

In the mid-1960s Smithson met artists who were rejecting abstract expressionism and experimenting with ideas leading to minimalism, performance art, process art, and conceptual art. In 1963 he married artist Nancy Holt; they had no children. The couple's friends and colleagues included Carl Andre, Dan Flavin, Michael Heizer, Eva Hesse, Donald Judd, Howard Junker, Sol LeWitt, Lucy Lippard, Robert Morris, and Brigid Polk. In 1966 Smithson joined the Dwan Gallery run by Virginia Dwan, who was instrumental in the promotion of the minimalism and earthworks movements.

Also in 1966 Smithson published the first of his many articles that were to appear in the most influential critically oriented art magazines of the 1960s. In one of his articles, "Entropy and the New Monuments" (*Artforum* 4, no. 10 [June 1966]: 26–31), he theorized a connection between minimalist sculpture and entropy, the second law of thermodynamics: "In a rather round-about way, many of [today's] artists have provided a visible analog for the Second Law of Thermodynamics, which extrapolates the range of entropy by telling us energy is more easily lost than obtained, and that in the ultimate future the whole universe will burn out and be transformed into an all-encompassing sameness." Smithson believed that the pure geometric surfaces of minimalist sculpture simulated magnified matter in a state of arrested motion.

In his own approach to minimalism, Smithson applied mathematical formulas to geological structure to create sculptures—made of glass and highly finished metals—that suggested crystalline growth patterns and stratification. Smithson deviated from pure minimalism, however, when he reached out to the natural environment for art materials. He collected rocks and debris from areas laid waste by industries or natural disasters and displayed them in galleries within sets of geometric containers. The sets were accompanied by photographs and maps of the sites of origin that were cropped in corresponding configurations. These arrangements, called nonsites (e.g., *Nonsite, Line of Wreckage, Bayonne, New Jersey,* 1968), explored dialectical relationships between gallery display, map, and disrupted site.

For some of his nonsites Smithson simply piled loose soil and rocks on and in front of mirrors. He liked to work with mirrors as sculptural material, particularly for their capacity to virtually limit, expand,

and distort the natural world. Some of his mirror projects exemplified the trend of the late 1960s toward the divorce of art from the traditional exhibition and marketing establishments. A trip to the Yucatán Peninsula in 1969 yielded *Incidents of Mirror-Travel in the Yucatan*, an extra-gallery project for which Smithson variously arranged a dozen or more twelve-square-inch mirrors in nine successive landscape settings, photographed them, and then dismantled them. The finished work (published in *Artforum* 8, no. 1 [Sept. 1969]: 28–33) comprises photographs of the mirrors at each site, Smithson's descriptions of the reflected terrain and sunlight, and his personal meditations on Mayan deities and the timelessness of the Yucatán landscape.

In his continuing preoccupation with entropy, Smithson buried part of an old woodshed on the campus of Kent State University, Kent, Ohio, with twenty truckloads of earth, the weight of which fractured the interior center beam. *Partially Buried Woodshed* (1970) is maintained in its collapsed condition by Kent State according to Smithson's specifications.

Smithson began formulating his ideas for earthworks as early as 1966, when he was hired as "artist consultant" for the new Dallas–Fort Worth Regional Airport. Drawing from his airport experiences, he published suggestions for earthen artworks designed to be viewed from the air ("Towards the Development of an Air Terminal Site," *Artforum* 5, no. 10 [June 1967]: 36–40). He and several colleagues went on to build large-scale, site-specific sculptures using indigenous materials. In further writings Smithson advocated the use of earthworks in reclamation projects for mining and other landscape-devastating enterprises. However, he was not a true ecologist: his evolving concern was to use earth art to point to environmental degradation as a form of entropy.

His best-known earth project is *The Spiral Jetty* (1970), a 1500-foot-long, 15-foot-wide spiral made of local volcanic rock, soil, and salt. The jetty coils into the red water of the Great Salt Lake at Rozel Point, Utah, near an abandoned oil-drilling operation. A film of the jetty's construction (*Spiral Jetty*, 1970) was scripted by Smithson to emphasize the primordial and cosmological connotations of the spiral, a form he chose because of its frequent occurrence in natural phenomena. The jetty has been mostly underwater since its construction due to rises in the lake level, but in drought years it has briefly appeared above the surface, thickly encrusted with salt crystals that, as Smithson knew, also generated in spirals.

Another earthwork employing the spiral, as well as the materials from a spoiled site, is Smithson's two-part *Broken Circle/Spiral Hill* (1971), built on an abandoned sand quarry near Emmen, Holland. The circle, half solid and half water and approximately 140 feet in diameter, was formed from the sand in the quarry pool. An earthen hill, defined by a broad spiraling pathway, sits on an embankment above the circle. The quarry with earthwork is preserved as a park by the people of Emmen.

Smithson was killed while just in the planning stages of *Amarillo Ramp* (1973), a 150-foot-long, curved earthen ramp located in a desert lake on a ranch near Amarillo, Texas. The small plane in which he was riding crashed during an aerial inspection of the site. In memory of her husband, Nancy Holt completed the ramp with the help of friends.

Smithson, in his short but extraordinary career, expanded the contexts and definitions of sculpture to include its integral and dialectical relationships to the natural landscape. His theories and examples helped establish the earthworks movement of the late 1960s and early 1970s and influenced the general proliferation of environmental art in the late twentieth century.

• A collection of Smithson's papers including exhibition catalogs, lists, reproductions, checks, and financial information are in the Manuscript Collection of the Archives of American Art. During his life Smithson had dozens of solo exhibitions, and his art was featured in most of the influential environmental and minimalist art exhibitions of the late 1960s and early 1970s, including *Primary Structures* (Jewish Museum, New York, 1966), *Earthworks* (Dwan Gallery, New York City, 1968), and *Earth Art* (Andrew Dickson White Museum, Cornell University, Ithaca, N.Y., 1969). Notable posthumous retrospective exhibitions featuring Smithson's two-dimensional art include *Robert Smithson: Drawings* (New York Cultural Center, 1974), with accompanying catalog; and *Robert Smithson Unearthed* (Miriam and Ira D. Wallach Art Gallery, Columbia University, 1991), with book by Eugenie Tsai, *Robert Smithson Unearthed: Drawings, Collages, Writings* (1991). Photographs by Smithson used to document his environmental projects and his writings were the subject of *Robert Smithson: Photo Works* (Los Angeles County Museum of Art, 1993), catalog by Robert A. Sobieszek, *Robert Smithson: Photo Works* (1993). Smithson's sculptures and earthworks are fully discussed in Robert Hobbs, *Robert Smithson: Sculpture* (1981), which includes a comprehensive annotated bibliography and an extensive chronology. A compilation of his published and unpublished writings and interviews can be found in Nancy Holt, ed., *The Writings of Robert Smithson* (1979). The entire May 1978 issue of *Arts Magazine* was devoted to Smithson. Obituaries are in *Newsweek*, 6 Aug. 1973; the *New York Times*, 12 Aug. 1973; and *Arts Magazine*, Sept./Oct. 1973.

PATRICIA A. FAIRCHILD

SMOHALLA (c. 1815–1895), prophet of the Shahaptian-speaking Wanapam tribe, lived near Priest Rapids along the Columbia River in present-day Washington State. He was born about the same time that the North West Company established a trading post on the Columbia River below Priest Rapids. Little is known of his parentage, but he is reputed to have descended from a line of prophets. He emerged as a spiritual leader of nearly 2,000 "renegades" along the Columbia and its environs who resisted federal attempts to relocate them to reservations and followed ancient patterns of hunting, fishing, and gathering. He strongly influenced the neighboring Palouses, a Shahaptian people of the lower Snake River, and through them the Nez Percé reservation of young Chief Joseph's band. Seeking to avoid confinement on the Nez Percé reservation of west-central Idaho, and wishing to practice the traditionalism enunciated by Smohalla, these people fled from U.S. troops in 1877 but were captured in Montana and incarcerated in the Indian Territory in present-day Oklahoma before returning to the Pacific Northwest on orders from the U.S. government. Although he was not involved in the Ghost Dance movement, he influenced tribes far beyond the Columbia River region, such as the Paiutes of Nevada, whose prophet Wovoka (Jack Wilson) was directly associated with the second Ghost Dance movement around 1890. The link between Smohalla and Wovoka is thought to have occurred in the hop fields of Oregon where Wovoka came to work the harvests.

Smohalla based his credentials as a prophet on his claim that he had been "resurrected" after a three-day "death" and "journey to heaven." Reportedly, after he was severely beaten by traditionalist Chief Moses of the Sinkiuse tribe to the north, he wandered in exile, during which time he experienced prophetic visions. However, no substantial proof exists that such a fight occurred, although animosity remained between him and the followers of Moses.

Smohalla prophesied that in a millennial period God would resurrect all Indians and eliminate white encroachers on their lands, allowing Indians to reinherit the earth. He maintained his hold on his followers by exhibiting repeated trances and by making solar predictions based on information he obtained from a white man's almanac. Aware of the white threat to their lands, his followers were especially concerned after several tribes ceded their lands in the 1885 Walla Walla treaty. They were also alarmed by the devastating effects of various epidemics such as smallpox, which reduced Wanapam numbers from over 1,000 in the early nineteenth century to around 300 scarcely a half century later. Another important aspect of Smohalla's credo was that Indians should engage in "natural" work, accepting the bounty offered them by the Great Spirit and the Earth Mother. Activities such as tilling the soil he condemned as "unnatural" and damaging to the face of the Earth Mother. Like other Indians, he believed that the great 1872 earthquake signified the Earth Mother's displeasure with her people for their sins and for allowing white encroachment on their lands.

That Smohalla regarded the earth as deity did not preclude his use of borrowed Christian creedal and ceremonial elements in his Washani religion and its *washat* dance, which incorporated chanting and gender grouping as found in both native and Roman Catholic worship. The number seven was considered sacred in the *washat*, as were the beating drums used by him and his followers for worship and not for war.

Smohalla was able to practice his religion in relative isolation partly because his desert homeland was unattractive to whites, although fishing and gathering areas long used by the Wanapam were soon appropriated. Their homeland became an island surrounded by three Indian reservations, the nearest, the Yakima, whose agents tried unsuccessfully to force Smohalla and his followers to relocate within its confines.

Avoiding reservation life, Smohalla remained true to his principles until his death, which ironically occurred during a visit to the Yakima Reservation he had sought for so long to avoid. His Washani heritage is perpetuated today among several tribes in the Seven Drum ritual and in the observance of ancient First Root ceremonials. In commemoration of his regard for the earth, Smohalla was inducted into Washington State's Centennial Hall of Honor in 1989.

• For further information, see Eli Huggins, "Smohalla, the Prophet of Priest Rapids," *Overland Monthly*, 5 (Feb. 1981): 208–15; Eugene S. Hunn, *Nch'i-Wána, "The Big River": Mid-Columbia Indians and Their Land* (1990); Junius Wilson MacMurray, "The 'Dreamers' of the Columbia River Valley in 'Washington Territory,'" *Transactions of the Albany Institute*, 11 (1887): 241–48; James Mooney, "The Ghost Dance Religion and the Sioux Outbreak of 1890," in *Fourteenth Annual Report of the Bureau of American Ethnology, to the Secretary of the Smithsonian Institution, 1892–93, part 2* (1896); Click Relander, *Drummers and Dreamers* (1956); Robert H. Ruby and John A. Brown, *Dreamer-Prophets of the Columbia Plateau: Smohalla and Skolaskin* (1989); and Leslie Spier, *The Prophet Dance of the Northwest and Its Derivatives: The Source of the Ghost Dance* (1935).

ROBERT H. RUBY

SMOOT, Reed Owen (10 Jan. 1862–9 Feb. 1941), senator and Mormon apostle, was born in Salt Lake City, Utah, the son of Abraham Owen Smoot, a businessman and politician, and Anne Kirstene Morrison. Smoot's father had joined the Church of Jesus Christ of Latter-day Saints (Mormon) in Kentucky and moved with the church to Illinois and then on to Utah in 1847. Abraham Smoot was a polygamist, and Reed was the third child of the fifth wife, a convert from Norway. Anne Morrison Smoot influenced all her children to have faith, be industrious, and practice prudence. Abraham Smoot was mayor of Salt Lake City for ten years and then moved south to Provo, where he served in that same office for twelve years. Abraham served simultaneously as the president of the Mormon church's Utah Stake, which covered all of Utah County.

Young Reed Smoot attended Latter-day Saints–owned schools in Provo and graduated from Brigham Young Academy in 1879 at the age of seventeen. Smoot's rise to church and civic leadership was spectacular, in part because he avoided normal participation in church activities and his missionary service to Great Britain was limited to ten months instead of the usual two years. In 1884 he married Alpha Mae Eldredge, daughter of Horace S. Eldredge, a highly successful Salt Lake City businessman and a Mormon leader. The marriage provided some capital, which rapidly increased under the astute management of the young Provo financier. The Smoots had six children, but Smoot's wife was frequently ill; from 1920 until her death in 1928 she was an invalid. Through the entire marriage of forty-four years she was a devoted wife and mother and provided a valuable home atmosphere—one that furnished the necessary relaxation from Smoot's varied labor. In July 1930 Smoot married Alice Taylor Sheets; they had no children.

During his years of limited church activity, Smoot remained a believer in the doctrines and did not drift away. He was somewhat indifferent, being too absorbed in making money to become actively committed. However, his church career began seriously in 1895, when he was selected as a counselor to the Utah Stake presidency. From that point on he became intensely devoted to the church, to its membership, leadership, and theology. Religion became the primary concern of his life. Five years later, in 1900, he was named as one of the Council of Twelve Apostles, and he remained a member until his death. He spent the last few years of his life as the senior member of the quorum, which meant he was a step removed from the presidency of the church.

Smoot's father was a rabid Kentucky-born Democrat. Smoot studied the issues of 1884 by analyzing the Blaine-Cleveland campaign as reported by New York newspapers. Just as his father had converted to Mormonism, Smoot converted to the Republican party. Smoot helped found the Republican club in Utah even though his father was horrified.

The election of Smoot to the U.S. Senate by the Utah legislature in 1903 surprised many people. Smoot had never sought office before that election, and he was reelected by the legislature in 1908. Following the passage of the Seventeenth Amendment, Utah's voters reelected Smoot in 1914, 1920, and 1926. Smoot's greatest political battle concerned a three-year Senate debate over whether or not to seat the Utah Republican. In actuality, Mormonism stood on trial, and finally President Theodore Roosevelt intervened and helped obtain a favorable vote. The main two issues concerned polygamy, which the church had abandoned in 1890, and loyalty to the United States.

Smoot served in the Senate during very controversial and demanding times. Although most westerners despised Theodore Roosevelt's conservative policies, Smoot fought hard for the Forest Service, the creation of the Bureau of Reclamation, and setting aside mineral lands. Part of Smoot's protectionism stand of the 1920s was based on his attempts to protect American agriculture and business from foreign competition.

Smoot remained very active in foreign policy. He opposed Woodrow Wilson's policies in Mexico in 1913–1914 and felt that the United States should prepare more rapidly after World War I began. In both cases Smoot ran contrary to the prevailing views of his state and his church. However, he definitely took a political gamble by joining Henry Cabot Lodge's reservationist group regarding the League of Nations. Once again, Smoot, by supporting a form of the League of Nations, was in direct opposition to Mormon church president Heber J. Grant. Smoot feared the growth of federal involvement and earned the nickname of "Watchdog of the Treasury" because of his vigilance in seeking executive branch reorganization. Every spending project underwent close scrutiny from Smoot and his staff.

Senator Smoot's three major beliefs were Mormonism, Americanism, and protectionism. He consistently fought for tariff protection, beginning with Payne-Aldrich and ending with Smoot-Hawley. The Utahan believed that every American product, agriculture or manufacturing, deserved protection. When the Democrats forced through the Underwood Tariff in Wilson's first administration, he fought valiantly against lowering rates. Smoot, ever the financier, kept close watch as exports declined and imports increased; however, World War I reversed this trend. After backing the Fordney-McCumber Tariff of the early 1920s, he pushed through the Smoot-Hawley Tariff in 1930 during the Great Depression. This controversial legislation is traditionally viewed as contributing to a decline of trade; however, Smoot's experience on the World War I Debt Funding Commission convinced him that the United States had to be protected first and foremost. He believed that economic self-reliance would push the country out of the depression. Smoot used his close relations with Presidents William Howard Taft, Warren G. Harding, Calvin Coolidge, and Herbert Hoover as well as Andrew Mellon, the secretary of treasury during the 1920s. Indeed Smoot voted for Harding during the tumultuous 1920 Republican convention.

The Democratic landslide of 1932 included Smoot as one of its victims. After thirty years, Smoot returned to Salt Lake City as a full-time apostle. The New Deal tortured his soul with astronomical deficit, and his critics continued to heap scorn on his legacy, the Smoot-Hawley Tariff. Later in the decade, when a historian said that he would like to write about him, Smoot replied, "Hell, who wants to read about me?" The former senator died while on vacation in St. Petersburg, Florida.

• Smoot's extensive personal papers are at Brigham Young University in Provo, Utah. Reed Smoot, *Beware the Wolf: The Democratic Evolution* (1928), illustrates the senator's thinking during the 1920s. The best biography is Milton R. Merrill, *Reed Smoot, Apostle in Politics* (1990). Frank A. Jonas, "Utah: The Different State," in *Politics of the American West*, ed. Jonas (1968), is very good on his contributions. Charles M. Morris, *Honorable Reed Smoot: Senior United States Senator from Utah* (1914), is very good on his early career. Obituaries are in the *Salt Lake City Tribune* and *Deseret News*, both 10 Feb. 1941, and the *New York Times*, 11 Feb. 1941.

F. ROSS PETERSON

SMYTH, Alexander (14 Sep. 1767–17 Apr. 1830), lawyer, soldier, and congressman, was born on Rathlin Island, County Antrim, twelve miles off the northern coast of Ireland, the son of the Reverend Adam Smyth. His mother's name is unknown. In 1775 his father relocated the family to Botetourt County, Virginia, where he served as rector of the Episcopal parish. Smyth read law and in 1787 was appointed deputy clerk of Botetourt County. He passed the bar in 1789, moved to Wythe County, and married Nancy Binkley in 1791. The couple had four children. A vigorous orator, Smyth entered politics and was elected to the Virginia House of Delegates in 1792, 1796, 1801–1802, and 1804–1808. Success and a mercurial disposition garnered him powerful enemies, however. Foremost among these was John Preston of Wythe County, with whom Smyth dueled in 1795. The confrontation proved bloodless, but the two men and their respective families remained staunch political adversaries.

A devout Jeffersonian, Smyth enjoyed considerable influence in local Republican party affairs, and in 1808 he was elected to the state senate. On 8 July of that year he forsook politics to accept President Thomas Jefferson's invitation to serve as colonel of the newly formed U.S. Rifle Regiment. Ironically William Duane of Philadelphia, another Republican appointee competing for political laurels, served as lieutenant colonel in the same unit. Despite a reputation for bombast, Smyth rendered effective military service, and in 1811 President James Madison's secretary of war, William Eustis, approached him to compile a new system of military discipline to replace the venerated *Blue Book* of Baron Von Steuben. Smyth complied by writing *Regulations for the Field Exercises, Manoeuvres and Conduct of Infantry of the United States*, which became the army's first official drill manual in thirty years. This abridgment of the French 1791 *Reglement*, though much criticized by men like Duane, was adopted on 3 March 1812, the first of a series of French manuals that would dominate American military tactics until the Civil War. Its adoption, however, came too late to influence early battles of the War of 1812.

The onset of hostilities briefly boosted Smyth's military fortunes, and on 14 July 1812 he became inspector general with the rank of brigadier general. Officially, his role was to oversee the training and organization of troops from the capital, but Smyth demanded and received a field command. He assumed control of an army brigade stationed at Buffalo, New York, and here repeatedly quarrelled with his superior, General Stephen Van Rensselaer of the militia. When that officer attempted to invade Niagara at Queenston Heights on 13 October 1812, Smyth refused to assist him. The resulting debacle forced Van Rensselaer to resign and on 24 October Smyth advanced to theater commander. For a month he did little but march his troops and issue bombastic declarations about the impending conquest of Canada. On 28 November a crossing was attempted at Fort Erie, but a shortage of boats hampered operations and it was cancelled. Smyth repeated the effort on 1 December but the ill-equipped, badly disciplined state of his army resulted in another ineffective crossing. When mutinous soldiers threatened his physical safety, the militia was disbanded and the army retired to winter quarters. Militia General Peter Buell Porter, disgusted by Smyth's performance, publicly accused him of cowardice, and the two men subsequently fought a bloodless duel. On 3 March 1813 Congress unceremoniously struck Smyth from the army rolls and the important office of inspector general, which he had discredited by his behavior, disappeared with him.

Smyth's reputation survived his military disgrace, and in 1816 he resumed his political career in Wythe County. In 1816 he became a member of the Board of Public Works and the following year was elected to Congress as representative. Smyth served intermittently over the next thirteen years; as chairman of the House Committee on Military Affairs he argued against reductions in the peacetime establishment. He also explained his religious convictions in a tract titled *An Explanation of the Apocalypse or Revelation of St. John* (1825). Smyth died in Washington, D.C.

Alexander Smyth was a complicated, headstrong individual and not the tragicomic buffoon portrayed in many history books. His ability as a Republican politician was genuine, and he enjoyed trust and confidence at the highest levels of the Republican party. Unfortunately, Smyth's talent did not extend beyond politics and could not sustain his lofty military ambitions. General Winfield Scott, a fellow Virginian and lawyer, considered him intelligent and well read but temperamentally unsuited for command. Ultimately, Smyth overcame his reputation for bombast and staged an impressive political comeback. For seventeen years he served his county, state, and country in a variety of elected positions, and while in Congress he wielded his influence on behalf of the military that had so scorned him.

• A number of manuscripts by and about Smyth are located at the Virginia Historical Society. Insight into his political views can be gauged by reading Alexander Smyth, *Speeches Delivered by Alexander Smyth in the House of Delegates* (1811). For printed correspondence consult Mack H. Sturgill, "Letters from Wythe County Court House, Virginia," *Wythe County Historical Review* 24 (July 1983): 10–18, and Frank H. Severance, "The Case of Brigadier General Alexander Smyth as Shown by His Writings," *Buffalo Historical Society Publications* 18 (1914): 213–55. A brief character sketch is T. N. Parmalee, "Recollections of an Old Stager," *Harper's Magazine* 49 (June 1874): 115–16. See also Walter R. Chitwood, "The Duels of Alexander Smyth," *Wythe County Historical Review* 7 (July 1974): 7–15. For Smyth's role in the War of 1812, see David A. Clary and Joseph W. A. Whitehorne, *The Inspectors General of the United States Army, 1777–1903* (1987), "Reminiscences of the Late War," *Army and Navy Chronicle* 1 (Feb. 1835): 59–60, Donald E. Graves, "Dry Books of Tactics," *Military Collector and Historian* 38 (Summer 1986): 51–60, and Theodore J. Crackle, "The Battle of Queenston Heights, 13 October 1813," in *America's First Battles, 1776–1965*, ed. Charles E. Heller and William A. Sofft (1986), pp. 33–56.

JOHN C. FREDRIKSEN

SMYTH, Henry Dewolf (1 May 1898–11 Sept. 1986), physicist, was born in Clinton, New York, the son of Charles Henry Smyth, Jr., a geology professor, and Ruth Anne Phelps. The family moved to Princeton, New Jersey, in 1905 when Smyth's father became professor at the university. Smyth studied physics and mathematics at Princeton and received his B.S. in 1918. Until the end of World War I, he worked at the

Aberdeen Proving Grounds, where the U.S. Army developed and tested new weapons and vehicles, and in the chemical warfare laboratory in Washington, D.C. He then pursued an independent research project with the Princeton physicist Karl Taylor Compton until 1919. He returned to Princeton and completed his M.S. and Ph.D., both in physics, in 1920 and 1921, respectively. As a National Research Council Fellow in 1921, Smyth studied under Ernest Rutherford at the Cavendish Laboratory in Cambridge, England. He returned to Princeton in 1923 with a Cambridge doctorate and became an instructor in 1924, an assistant professor in 1925, and an associate professor in 1929. He spent 1931–1932 in Germany at the University of Göttingen. In 1936 Princeton University made him a professor. That same year he married Mary DeConingh; the couple had no children.

Smyth's primary research interests between 1919 and 1935 were the study of the ionization of gases by electron impact, positive ray analysis, molecular structure, and atomic energy. But the advances of John Cockcroft, Ernest Walton, and Ernest O. Lawrence in particle accelerators and James Chadwick's discovery of the neutron in 1934 persuaded Smyth to shift to nuclear physics.

In 1935 Smyth became the chairman of Princeton's physics department, and his administrative duties took precedence over his research. He devoted much effort to reorganizing the large introductory physics course. Understanding the importance of integrating teaching and research, he introduced the extensive use of lecture demonstrations. To this end, he published *Matter, Motion and Electricity* in 1939. Co-written with Charles W. Ufford, it was later praised as "perhaps the first beginning text that attempted to cover the most recent physics in addition to the classical material" (*Physics Today*, p. 98).

In 1940 Smyth began working as a member of the Uranium Committee, a subcommittee of the National Defense Research Committee (NDRC). Its purpose was to explore the possibility of producing an atomic chain reaction using a uranium-graphite system with the goal of creating a weapon to be used in war. The NDRC was established in June of that year "to direct, coordinate, and carry out a national program of military research and development" (Jones, p. 26). In June 1941 President Franklin Roosevelt established the Office of Scientific Research and Development (OSRD) to mobilize American scientists for war and made the NDRC one of its subordinate agencies. The Committee on Uranium, somewhat enlarged, remained under the NDRC but was renamed the Section on Uranium. Smyth worked in the Uranium Section's Power Production and Theoretical subsections.

In June 1942 Roosevelt directed the Army Corps of Engineers to construct an atomic bomb. The OSRD was responsible for scientific research and pilot plant experimentation to produce the fissionable materials for use in the atomic bombs. In December 1941 Smyth and E. O. Lawrence suggested that large-scale electromagnetic methods could possibly separate uranium isotopes. By 1943 their method produced the first significant amounts of U-235, the isotope essential to maintain a successful chain reaction. In 1943–1944 Smyth was assistant director of, and later consultant to, the Metallurgical Laboratory at the University of Chicago. Between 1943 and 1945, he served as consultant to the Manhattan Engineer District, which produced the atomic bomb. His responsibilities included overseeing the research at the Metallurgical Laboratory and acting as liaison between the laboratory and E. I. Du Pont de Nemours and Company, which was constructing the plutonium production plant in Hanford, Washington.

In spring of 1944, Smyth suggested the need for an official report on the scientific and administrative operations of the atomic bomb project. In April 1944 the director of the project, Lieutenant General Leslie R. Groves, asked Smyth to proceed with the report, which Groves saw would have the added benefit of delineating what information could be made public and what should remain classified. Smyth's *Atomic Energy for Military Purposes*, which became the official government report on the project, was released on 12 August 1945, shortly after the bombings of Hiroshima and Nagasaki. Popularly known as the "Smyth Report," it was the first source of information on the atomic bomb project for many Americans. It detailed which avenues of research had been explored, what difficulties arose, and how they were addressed, as well as describing the complex administration of the project. The report was subsequently published in September 1945 by Princeton University Press and sold more than 160,000 copies. The document itself was placed in the public domain, in accordance with Smyth's belief that "the ultimate responsibility for our nation's policy rests on its citizens and they can discharge such responsibilities wisely only if they are informed" (p. vi).

Although the Smyth Report was primarily an account of the atomic bomb project, in its preface and general summary Smyth poses the questions that atomic development raises for the public and the world. He wrote "the possible uses of nuclear energy are not all destructive. The second direction in which technical development can be expected is along the paths of peace. . . . [Such] development raises many questions that must be answered in the near future. . . . These questions are not technical questions; they are political and social questions, and the answers given to them may affect all mankind for generations" (pp. 224–27). After 1945, his speeches and articles addressed the relation of science to government and to society, and the historical development of atomic energy, its potential uses in peacetime, and the need for international control of future atomic energy development.

Smyth continued to chair Princeton's understaffed physics department during the war. Between 1945 and 1949, he persisted in his efforts to strengthen the department, having been named the Joseph Henry Professor of Physics in 1946. He relinquished the chair in 1950.

In May 1949 President Harry S. Truman appointed Smyth to a two-year term on the U.S. Atomic Energy Commission (AEC), established to promote U.S. research in nuclear energy and to plan U.S. development of nuclear power during peacetime. Smyth was the only member of the AEC with a scientific background. Truman appointed Smyth to a full five-year term on the AEC in 1951. While on the AEC, Smyth played important roles as a dissenter in two historic controversies, the decision to develop the hydrogen bomb and the J. Robert Oppenheimer security clearance case.

Before 1949, the AEC, though aware of the possibility of a fusion or hydrogen bomb, had decided not to proceed with a full-scale development or crash program. In August 1949 the public pressure caused by the Soviet Union's atomic bomb detonation forced the AEC to reevaluate its decision. The AEC requested the opinion of the General Advisory Committee (GAC), which consisted of nine scientists and engineers, with physicist J. Robert Oppenheimer as chairman. The GAC unanimously opposed a crash program. The AEC submitted to President Truman the GAC's recommendation and the opinions of each of the five AEC members; Smyth was one of three commissioners who also opposed a crash program. They considered it unnecessary in peacetime and hoped that a slower pace would permit public discussion of the international control of atomic weapons. Despite GAC and AEC opposition, on 31 January 1950 Truman announced that the AEC would continue to direct work on atomic weapons, including the development of the hydrogen bomb.

In 1953, during the height of the McCarthy era, Lewis Strauss, chairman of the AEC, expressed doubts about the loyalty of Oppenheimer, who had headed the team that assembled and exploded the first atomic bomb, and urged President Dwight D. Eisenhower to restrict Oppenheimer's access to secret information. After these restrictions were affirmed by the Personnel Security Board, Oppenheimer requested immediate consideration of his case by the Atomic Energy Commission. The AEC's security clearance hearing resulted in a four-to-one vote against his reinstatement; Commissioners Lewis L. Strauss, Thomas E. Murray, Eugene M. Zuckert, and Joseph Campbell voted to revoke his clearance on account of "defects of character." Smyth alone dissented from this opinion. He argued that the "defects" were trivial, if not contrived, and that Oppenheimer's contributions to the atomic energy program were far greater than any potential security risk he was alleged to pose. At Smyth's memorial service, the physicist I. I. Rabi noted this dissent as Smyth's finest hour: "One thinks of a supreme moment in a person's life when he stood against odds and did the right thing. That was Harry Smyth's fortune and Harry Smyth's greatness" (Smyth Papers, Series VIb). Smyth voluntarily resigned from the Atomic Energy Commission in 1954.

Smyth then returned to Princeton, where he became chairman of the Board of Scientific and Engineering Research, known after May 1959 as the University Research Board and charged with developing policies and practices related to federal support of research. Among other projects, the board oversaw the development of the Plasma Physics Laboratory and the cyclotron laboratory. Smyth retired from Princeton in 1966.

In 1961 President John F. Kennedy appointed Smyth the U.S. Representative to the International Atomic Energy Agency (IAEA), a position with ambassadorial rank. The IAEA was established in 1957 under the aegis of the United Nations to accelerate and enlarge the contribution of atomic energy to peacetime purposes and to establish a system of safeguards in order to prevent the possible diversion of nuclear material to military use. At this agency, Smyth contributed to the development of international nuclear safeguards, including the Nonproliferation Treaty in 1970. Glenn Seaborg, the chairman of the U.S. Atomic Energy Commission, noted that "Harry Smyth played a key role in the realization of the nonproliferation treaty, one of the two most important arms control agreements ever achieved. Harry's personal diplomacy, sincerity and commitment were paramount in the accomplishment" (Smyth Papers, Series VIb). Smyth's work with the IAEA ended with his mandatory retirement in 1970.

In 1972 the American Nuclear Society and the Atomic Industrial Forum jointly awarded Smyth the first "nuclear statesmanship" award, naming it in his honor. The award cited his "outstanding services to the people of the world in developing and guiding the uses of atomic energy in constructive channels." Smyth died in Princeton, New Jersey, having played a significant role in determining the direction of U.S. atomic energy development through his contributions as scientist, instructor, policy maker, and administrator.

• The Henry DeWolf Smyth Papers are at the American Philosophical Society Library in Philadelphia, Pa.; this extensive collection documents all aspects of his career, includes several drafts of *Atomic Energy for Military Purposes* and his dissenting opinion in the Oppenheimer case, and contains a bibliography of Smyth's publications and speeches. A biographical sketch is Bill Forbush, "Henry DeWolf Smyth," dated 7 June 1982 in the Smyth papers. For discussion of the atomic bomb project, consult Vincent C. Jones, *Manhattan: The Army and the Atomic Bomb* (1985), and Richard Rhodes, *The Making of the Atomic Bomb* (1986). Richard Rhodes, *Dark Sun* (1995), is an excellent account of the hydrogen bomb project. For information on the Oppenheimer security clearance trial, see Charles P. Curtis, *The Oppenheimer Case* (1955), and Joseph Alsop and Stewart Alsop, *We Accuse!* (1954). An obituary is by Robert H. Dicke et al. in *Physics Today*, May 1989, pp. 96–98.

TIMOTHY T. WILSON

SMYTH, Herbert Weir (8 Aug. 1857–16 July 1937), classicist, was born in Wilmington, Delaware, the son of Clement Biddle Smyth, an iron manufacturer, and

Sarah Sellers. His Quaker family sent their precocious fifteen-year-old son to Swarthmore College, from which he graduated first in the class of 1876. In his eighteenth year, Smyth read Alexander Pope's version of the *Iliad* and determined to read the original. With only one year of Greek he went to Harvard and read Aeschylus with W. W. Goodwin, the man he would eventually succeed as Eliot Professor of Greek. His career would be defined by the interest in Aeschylus nurtured by Goodwin and his study of Greek dialects with the comparative philologist August Fick. After graduating in 1878 Smyth taught in a school in Newport, Rhode Island, for one year and then sailed for Germany. In Leipzig (1879–1880) he studied under the comparative philologists Georg Curtius, Friedrich Karl Brugmann, and Ernst Windisch. In Göttingen (1881–1883), a training ground for three earlier Eliot Professors (Edward Everett, Cornelius Felton, and Goodwin), he studied Greek dialects with Fick and literature with Hans Dilthey. He received a Ph.D. in 1884 with a dissertation on the diphthong EI.

Smyth began his career at Williams College, where he was instructor in classics, German, and Sanskrit from 1883 to 1885, when he was called to Johns Hopkins University by Basil L. Gildersleeve. In 1887 he married Eleanor Adt of Baltimore; the couple had four children. At Johns Hopkins Smyth instituted the first course in this country devoted to Greek dialects and extended his own research. The standard work on dialects (by Fick's teacher Heinrich Ludolf Ahrens) did not deal with Ionic. By the time he became professor of Greek at Bryn Mawr in 1886, he had begun to gather the fruits of his investigation and teaching into a series of articles that culminated in *The Sounds and Inflections of the Greek Dialects: Ionic* (1894), the first complete study of that dialect and a book so learned that Gildersleeve declared himself incompetent to review it. Like Goodwin's *Syntax of the Moods and Tenses of the Greek Verb* (1860), it is a monumental work of scientific American scholarship written by a scholar under the age of forty. Smyth researched independently both the literary remains of Ionic (excluding Homer), especially lyric poetry, and the epigraphical evidence to set out the relation of Ionic phonology and morphology to the other Greek dialects. This minutely detailed work of nearly 670 pages was to be the first of a series, but Smyth never published subsequent volumes.

Rather, he pursued the lyric poetry he had so extensively analyzed for dialect. His *Greek Melic Poets* (1900) was dedicated to Gildersleeve, whose *Pindar* (1885) it complemented. The commentary features parallels from a range of poetic sources for, in the words of C. N. Jackson, "It was his desire . . . to show not so much imitation or coincidence as 'the natural expression of the language of poetry in all ages.'" This book was well received in Europe, and Smyth's sphere of activity began to broaden both literally and figuratively. He was professor of Greek at the American School of Classical Studies at Athens in 1899–1900, and in 1901 he was called to Harvard, first as professor of Greek (1901–1902), then as Eliot Professor (1902–1925). He now broadened his research from the linguistic to the interpretive. Though Smyth published a number of papers on language and meter in the poets, he attempted to reveal the soul of Greek literature chiefly through Aeschylus. His paper "Greek Language and Its Relation to the Psychology of the Ancient Greeks," delivered at the St. Louis Exposition in 1904, treated how language structures and vocabulary reveal ranges and qualities of intellect and emotion. His American Philological Association presidential address, "Aspects of Greek Conservatism," defined the tension in Greek life between restless investigation and experimentation within a context of tradition. To *Harvard Essays on Classical Subjects*, he contributed an edited volume, "Greek Conceptions of Immortality from Homer to Plato," which illuminated the influence of superstition and reason in the development of Greek religion. He wrote a comprehensive (though incomplete) catalog of the manuscripts of Aeschylus around 1912, which he did not publish for twenty years ("Catalogue of the Manuscripts of Aeschylus," *Harvard Studies in Classical Philology* 44 [1933]: 1–62). In 1922 he published the first volume of his masterful Loeb edition of Aeschylus, the second in 1926, and in between gave memorable Sather Lectures at the University of California at Berkeley, published as *Aeschylean Tragedy* (1924). His Loebs established sensible texts of an author with many textual difficulties and offered a noble prose translation that has made them among the best of the series. His Sathers are a methodical drama-by-drama study of the ruin that befalls the Aeschylean hero, its consequences for his family and state, and the presiding justice of Zeus that transforms tragic events to greater significance.

Smyth edited the twenty volumes of his Greek Series for Colleges and Schools for the American Book Company, to which he contributed *A Greek Grammar for Schools and Colleges* (1916), followed by the larger *A Greek Grammar for Colleges* (1920). A reviewer said of the latter that it was like "Goodwin's two books, *Greek Grammar* and *Greek Moods and Tenses*, and Munro's *Homeric Grammar* all in one." It remains the most comprehensive Greek grammar ever written by an American. He served the American Philological Association as secretary-treasurer and editor of the association's *Transactions and Proceedings* for fifteen years (1889–1904), and as president (1904–1905). The classics library at Harvard bears his name.

Smyth was one of the four legendary American classicists with Gildersleeve, Goodwin, and Paul Shorey, all trained in German philological methods and capable of exquisite literary judgment and expression. His colleagues recalled that "he was among the best, if not the best teacher of the Classics that Harvard had ever seen" (transcription from Faculty Minute, Harvard Archives). He mastered the skills of epigraphical, paleographical, linguistic, and grammatical inquiry, but always put these in the service of literary understanding. Like the figure of Aeschylus, he was majestic and even hoary in aspect but often evidenced enormous human sensitivity and lyrical expression.

• Smyth's papers, including his diary of his Harvard student years and his correspondence (mostly with his parents), 1876–1928, are at the Harvard University Archives. There is, as for many of his guild, no full-length biography. The best sources are the memorials of his various colleagues. The fullest is by Carl Newell Jackson in *Harvard Studies in Classical Philology* 49 (1938): 1–21, with full bibliography. See also the Harvard Faculty Minute written at his death in 1937 by E. K. Rand, J. H. Finley, W. C. Greene, and Rand's notice in the *Yearbook of the American Philosophical Society* (1937).

WARD W. BRIGGS

SMYTH, Newman (25 June 1843–6 Jan. 1925), clergyman, was born Samuel Phillips Newman Smyth in Brunswick, Maine, the son of William Smyth, a mathematician at Bowdoin College, and Harriet Porter Coffin. At the age of twelve he was enrolled in Phillips Academy (Andover), and at sixteen he matriculated at Bowdoin College (B.A., 1863; M.A., 1866). During the final months of the Civil War, he served as a first lieutenant with the Sixteenth Maine Volunteers in the Army of the Potomac near Petersburg, Virginia.

Even in his youth Smyth's perspective was marked by an appetite for the down-to-earth, a taste for concrete reality, and a tendency to be suspicious of abstractions not grounded in the lived reality of the mundane world. His experience on the battlefield nourished these tendencies, which were reflected in the pragmatic thrust of his work as a pastor-theologian. Smyth's openness to modern science and his emphasis on the social dimensions of Christian morality expressed a sensibility that was at once realistic and pragmatic.

Smyth graduated from Andover Theological Seminary in 1867 and was ordained to the ministry of the Congregational church in 1868. He married Anna Marston Ayer in 1871, and they had four children. During his years at Andover, Smyth became disillusioned with the faculty's "orthodoxism," a Calvinism grounded in the theology of Jonathan Edwards (1703–1758), seen especially in the dogmatic orthodoxy of Edwards Amasa Park, who resisted the introduction of modern biblical criticism at Andover. Smyth embraced the inductive methods of modern science, which contrasted sharply with Park's more deductive approach. The generous, ecumenical thrust of Smyth's thought made him impatient with the narrow polemicism of Calvinist orthodoxy. His studies in Berlin and Halle (1869–1870) introduced him to the religious thought of Friedrich Tholuck and Isaac Dorner. Smyth discovered the most advanced developments in German critical theology (especially in biblical scholarship), which he wholeheartedly embraced and introduced to his American audience. The liberalism of Friedrich Ernst Daniel Schleiermacher, emphasizing profound affective experience rather than rational proofs for a divine presence in the world, became an important resource for Smith's theological work.

In 1881, with Park's retirement from the Abbot Chair in Christian Theology, the trustees of Andover selected Smyth to fill the vacancy, but Park campaigned against the appointment. Resistance from the seminary's board of visitors prompted Smyth to withdraw his name from consideration. The ostensible reason for opposition to the appointment was an objection to Smyth's pedagogical style, but the deeper reason for the board's resistance was his theological stance, especially his unconventional eschatology. Following Dorner and his own older brother, Egbert C. Smyth, a professor of church history at Andover, Smyth argued that "future probation" rather than eternal damnation awaits those who die without hearing the gospel: the justice of God implies that all people will have an opportunity to accept the gospel, after death if not before. Some conservatives feared that such a view would diminish incentives for missions. In addition, Smyth's historicism disturbed the defenders of orthodoxy. He believed that religious ideas and institutions can be grasped only in their sociohistorical development; since religion is the product of a historical evolution, nothing in Christianity can be understood apart from its history.

Despite attacks on his orthodoxy, Smyth enjoyed a long and successful ministry at Mission Chapel, Providence, Rhode Island (1867–1869); First Congregational Church, Bangor, Maine (1870–1875); First Presbyterian Church, Quincy, Illinois (1876–1882); and Center Church (First Congregational), New Haven, Connecticut (1882–1907, pastor emeritus, 1908–1925). He was a popular preacher; his sermons were noted for their thoughtful content, elegant style, and sincerity of presentation rather than for charisma or spellbinding oratory. He developed his theology of responsiveness to the modern world in a pastoral context. Especially during his years in New Haven, serving as pastor to a community exposed to the intellectual currents emanating from Yale, Smyth articulated a perspective designed to address the religious concerns of an intellectually sophisticated laity. Elements of modernism reflecting the Yale ambience of Smyth's thought include a liberal optimism about the possibilities of human progress, an evolutionary view of history (including the history of religion), and a deep sense of the continuity between nature and culture, spirit and matter, faith and reason, science and religion.

Smyth's perspective came to be known as "evangelical liberalism" or "the new theology." It was marked by an openness to science, especially modern biology and historical-literary criticism. Smyth's writings bear witness to an optimism, grounded in his sense of God's immanence in nature and history, about progress in human and cosmic evolution and about the possibility of a fruitful synthesis between traditional faith and modern science. Smyth's intention was to remain open to scientific perspectives without simply abandoning traditional belief in a supernatural context for natural processes. He sought to show that the basis of supernaturalism is found not in texts or creeds but in the life of the universe itself: the direction of cosmic and organic evolution implies a purposeful, intelligent, compassionate energy directing the universe toward a fulfillment foreshadowed most clearly in Jesus of Nazareth. Smyth spent many hours in the biological laboratories at Yale, hammering out his theology with a Bible in one hand and a microscope in the other. He cultivated "a sympathetic rapport" between faith and reason, matter and spirit, science and religion, the natural and the divine.

In his later years, Smyth was increasingly active in the ecumenical movement. He saw the church evolving toward a higher perfection, in which the historic divisions of Christianity would be overcome in "a grander catholicism." He looked to Roman Catholic modernism as a model for the future development of a progressive, ecumenical Protestantism. His typically liberal optimism about the future led him to anticipate success in the ecumenical dialogue, and his pragmatic activism prompted him to become involved in projects fostering contact between separated communions. In 1913 he chaired a delegation that visited nonconforming churches in England to promote a World Conference of Christian Faith and Order, and from 1915 onward he was a member of the Commission of Comity, Federation, and Unity of the National Council of Congregational Churches. He died in New Haven.

Smyth promoted dialogue rather than confrontation between ancient faith and modern culture; he sought a synthesis between religious vision and scientific discovery. His effectiveness in combining the roles of pastor and theologian made him a major voice in the intellectual life of American Protestantism at the turn of the century.

• Smyth's publications include *The Religious Feeling* (1877); *Old Faiths in New Light* (1878); *The Orthodox Theology of Today* (1881); "Orthodox Rationalism," *Princeton Review* 9 (May 1882): 294–312; *Dorner on the Future State* (1883); *The Reality of Faith* (1884); *Christian Facts and Forces* (1887); *Christian Ethics* (1892); *The Place of Death in Evolution* (1897); *Through Science to Faith* (1902); *Passing Protestantism and Coming Catholicism* (1908); *Modern Belief in Immortality* (1910); *Constructive Natural Theology* (1913); *The Meaning of Personal Life* (1916); *Approaches toward Church Unity*, with Williston Walker (1919); *A Story of Church Unity* (1923); and *Recollections and Reflections* (1926), published posthumously. For an appreciation of Smyth's importance in the transition from nineteenth-century orthodoxy, see John W. Buckham, *Progressive Religious Thought in America* (1919). For an analysis of Smyth's modernist view of Scripture, see John L. Farthing, "Ecumenical Hermeneutics: Newman Smyth and the Bible," *American Journal of Theology and Philosophy* 11, no. 3 (Sept. 1990): 215–32. A comprehensive exposition with a complete bibliography is in Bryan Glynn Gentle, "The Natural Theology of Newman Smyth: A Study of a Response of Late Nineteenth-Century New England Calvinism to Darwinian Evolutionary Science" (Ph.D. diss., Duke Univ., 1976). Smyth's obituary is in the *New York Times*, 7 Jan. 1925.

JOHN L. FARTHING

SMYTH, Thomas (14 June 1808–20 Aug. 1873), Presbyterian clergyman and author, was born in Belfast, Ireland, the son of Samuel Smyth, a merchant and manufacturer, and Ann Magee. His father was prosperous during the early part of Thomas's life but lost a substantial part of his wealth in an economic depression in 1825. Thomas attended the Academic Institution of Belfast, and after graduating from Belfast College with honors in 1829, he entered Highbury College in London. In 1830 he moved with his parents to the United States and entered the senior class of Princeton Theological Seminary. The next year he was called to be the supply pastor to the Second Presbyterian Church in Charleston, South Carolina. In 1832 he married Margaret Milligan Adger, a member of his congregation and daughter of James Adger, one of Charleston's wealthiest merchants. In December 1834 Smyth became the regular pastor at Second Presbyterian, a position he held until 1870, when, upon his resignation, he was made honorary pastor.

From the moment of Smyth's arrival in Charleston in 1831, at the height of the nullification controversy, he was caught up in the growing storm that finally broke over Fort Sumter and the nation. He believed that a moderate, reasonable approach to slavery was the only way to save the Union. In Charleston, however, he was accused of being an abolitionist, and in Britain he was challenged by antislavery forces. In his *Unity of the Human Races* (1850), Smyth defended the full humanity of Africans and their past civilizations against the scorn of Louis Agassiz and his southern supporters. With his associates John Adger and John Girardeau, Smyth helped develop a paternalistic program for slaves built around the Zion Presbyterian Church. Despite the strenuous opposition of many whites in Charleston, the program attempted modest reforms of slavery.

Smyth belonged to a circle of old school Presbyterian scholars associated with Princeton Theological Seminary and the Presbyterian Theological Seminary in Columbia, South Carolina. They shared theological and social perspectives that had been largely shaped by Protestant Scholasticism, Scottish Common Sense Realism, and a social status closely linked with conservative elements in American society. They understood truth to be propositional and believed in a nonextremist approach: with regard to knowledge, between rationalists and romantics; with regard to ethics, asking not what one's conscience demands but what is one's present allotted sphere and task; and with regard to politics, between those on one extreme or the other who would divide the Union.

Smyth had a zeal for collecting books and for writing. His early work was directed against what he regarded as the extreme claims of the English clergyman John Henry Newman and the Oxford movement. For these efforts he was awarded in 1843 an honorary doctor of divinity degree by the College of New Jersey in Princeton. Much of his 20,000-volume library went to Columbia Theological Seminary in 1859. The ten volumes of his *Complete Works* plus his autobiography reveal the degree of his involvement in contemporary controversies. After the outbreak of the Civil War at

Fort Sumter, Smyth became a bitter supporter of the southern cause. He died in Charleston.

• Letters and papers of Smyth are in the Presbyterian Historical Foundation, Montreat, N.C.; in the Manuscript Collection of the South Caroliniana Library, University of South Carolina; and in the South Carolina Historical Society, Charleston. His autobiography is *Autobiographical Notes, Letters, and Reflections*, edited by his granddaughter Louisa Cheves Stoney (1914). His published works are collected in *Complete Works of the Rev. Thomas Smyth, D.D.*, ed. J. Wm. Flynn (10 vols., 1908–1912). See also T. Erskine Clarke, "Thomas Smyth: Moderate of the Old South" (Th.D. diss., Union Theological Seminary, 1970); and H. Alexander White, *Southern Presbyterian Leaders* (1911). An obituary is in the Charleston, S.C., *News and Courier*, 21 Aug. 1873.

T. ERSKINE CLARKE

SNAKE (fl. 1774–1812), Shawnee warrior and diplomat, was also known as Blacksnake and Captain Snake. His Indian name has been rendered as Pataso, Petazo, Peteasua, Patasua, and Ptasua. The name "Snake" was held by at least two Shawnee leaders of the period. Disentangling references to the different individuals is difficult, but the more famous Captain Snake should not be confused with the younger Shemenetoo, or Big Snake, who signed the treaties of Greenville (1814), Spring Wells (1815), and the Miami (1817) and who emigrated from Ohio to territory west of the Mississippi, where he died in the later 1830s. Captain Snake was a notable figure in frontier war and politics during the last quarter of the eighteenth century and evidently died at Wapakoneta on the Auglaize River, Ohio, about 1813.

Snake first appears in records just before the revolutionary war. During "Dunmore's War" (1774), when the Shawnees resisted Virginian expansion, a force of militia destroyed "Snakes' Town" on the Muskingum (Ohio), and its occupants and those of other Shawnee villages on that river fell back to the Scioto. In the Revolution the Shawnees assisted the British to attack American settlements in Kentucky, Pennsylvania, and Virginia, and in 1779 Snake was described as one of their most militant warriors. After American counterattacks against Shawnee villages north of the Ohio in 1779 and 1780, Snake spoke to the British, the Iroquois, and the Lakes Indians at Detroit in April 1781, soliciting greater support. The Indians were promised an advanced British depot at Upper Sandusky. During the ensuing summer Snake assisted the British to remove a party of Moravian Indians from the Tuscarawas River in Ohio to bring them under greater control.

In June 1782, 500 American militia under Colonel William Crawford struck at the Wyandots and Delawares of Upper Sandusky but were intercepted short of their target by the local Indians and a party of British rangers under William Caldwell. Fighting resumed the following day, 5 June, when the stalemate was broken by the arrival of Snake and 140 Shawnees. Crawford's force was routed with a loss of some fifty men killed or captured. After the battle Snake requested the British commandant at Detroit to permit Caldwell's rangers to remain in the Indian country. This suggestion reaped rewards the following August, when Caldwell's volunteers played an important role in the severe defeat of a Kentuckian army at Blue Licks, an engagement that Snake and most of the Shawnees themselves missed.

At the end of the revolutionary war Snake represented the Shawnees at a council at Detroit in July 1783, in which he listened to British explanations of their failure to protect Indian allies in the peace treaty. He supported other Shawnees in refusing to acknowledge American claims to Indian lands north of the Ohio, requested British aid in resisting the incursions, and was hostile to the treaty at Fort Finney (1786), in which American commissioners bullied a number of Shawnee chiefs into ceding southern and eastern Ohio. The treaty was soon repudiated, and full-scale warfare broke out. After the destruction of Shawnee villages about the headwaters of the Great Miami in 1786, Snake and others of his tribe established new towns with the Miamis at the junction of the Maumee, St. Marys, and St. Joseph rivers in present-day Indiana. Snake's village was described as being a short distance above Miamitown, the focus of the complex.

The Shawnees launched raids into Kentucky and on immigrant traffic on the Ohio, and in the summer of 1787 Snake helped arrange an exchange of prisoners with the Kentuckians at Limestone, surrendering one of his captives of the previous year, John Kinsella. The following March he led Shawnee, Cherokee, and Mingo warriors to stifle the flow of white settlers and travelers on the Ohio, capturing four boats and considerable plunder near the mouth of the Big Miami. In March 1790 he repeated the exploit, capturing two boats, dry goods valued at £1,200, and cash and other commodities. Snake's raids were important influences on the decision of the United States to send General Josiah Harmar's army against the Indian towns in 1790. Snake's town was probably among those burnt by Harmar in October, but he likely helped Blue Jacket and Little Turtle organize the force that eventually defeated the Americans and threw them back in disorder.

Snake's diplomatic talents were put to use in the Shawnees' efforts to build an intertribal confederacy capable, with British assistance, of withstanding U.S. expansion into Ohio. In September 1789 he was at Buffalo Creek, near Niagara, New York, urging the Iroquois League to support the confederacy. The following August he addressed a multitribal council at the Wyandot village of Brownstown on the Detroit River, Michigan. After a meeting of the confederacy at the junction of the Maumee and Auglaize ("the Glaize") in October 1792, in which terms for a peace conference with the United States were decided, it was Snake, among others, who approached the British to facilitate the arrangements.

In 1792 Snake established a new town on the Maumee, below the Glaize, but it was abandoned and destroyed in 1794 when the U.S. Army under Anthony

Wayne marched on the hostile tribes. Retiring to the lower Maumee, provisioned by the British, Snake apparently also lost his mother, who was buried between the Glaize and the foot of the Maumee rapids. Despite the defeat of the Indian confederacy at Fallen Timbers in August 1794, Snake does not seem to have supported the peace initiatives and was not a signatory to the treaty of Greenville that ended the war in 1795.

Little is known about Snake's later years. Eventually he settled with other Shawnees at Wapakoneta, on the Auglaize, and there supported Black Hoof's attempts to develop the Shawnee economy in line with advice from the American government and the Society of Friends. In 1805 the Shawnee prophet Tenskwatawa and his abler brother, Tecumseh, returned to Ohio from Indiana Territory and tried to draw support from the established chiefs to an intertribal community espousing traditional values and a rejection of white influences. During the rivalry between the Black Hoof and Tenskwatawa factions, Snake supported the former and in 1807 was accused by Tenskwatawa of witchcraft, a charge that incited Indians to attempt his assassination. Nevertheless, during this period Snake strove to maintain good relations between the whites and all Shawnees and in June 1807 was present when the Tenskwatawa and Black Hoof parties came to some kind of a reconciliation in a council at Springfield, Ohio.

Snake attended a council at the British Fort Malden (Amherstburg) in July 1808. In April 1809 he joined other Wapakoneta leaders in protesting the deductions made from treaty annuities and in desiring the continuance of Quaker assistance for the tribe's development plan. The date of Snake's death is unknown. He was alive in December 1812, when he grieved for the death of his cousin James Logan, but his failure to sign the Greenville treaty of July 1814 suggests he died about 1813. He lingered in the memories of both Indians and whites in Ohio. Oliver M. Spencer remembered him as "a plain, grave chief of sage appearance," and others spoke of a tall, thin "good-hearted" man, a formidable adversary, but kind to prisoners.

• Lyman C. Draper attempted to collate references to Snake (Draper MSS, State Historical Society of Wisconsin, Madison, series BB, vol. 1, pp. 80–81), but both he and apparently some of his informants (John Johnston to Draper, 21 Aug. 1847, Draper MSS, series YY, vol. 11, p. 30) confused Snake with Shemenetoo and perhaps other Shawnee individuals. References to Snake are scattered and often ambiguous. For example, the statement made by Matthew Elliot to Alexander McKee, 29 Mar. 1795, in the Indian Affairs papers, Record Group 10, Public Archives of Canada, Ottawa, 9:8895–96, could be taken to mean that Snake had died in 1794. Printed references include Reuben G. Thwaites and Louise P. Kellogg, eds., *Documentary History of Dunmore's War* (1905), p. 154; Louise P. Kellogg, ed., *Frontier Advance on the Upper Ohio* (1916), pp. 245, 259; Gayle Thornbrough, ed., *Outpost on the Wabash* (1957), pp. 80–81; Milo H. Quaife, ed., "Henry Hay's Journal . . . ," *Proceedings of the State Historical Society of Wisconsin* 62 (1915): 208–61; William H. Smith, ed., *The St. Clair Papers*, vol. 2 (1881), pp. 143–44; *The Indian Captivity of O. M. Spencer* (1917); and Gayle Thornbrough, ed., *Letter Book of the Indian Agency at Fort Wayne* (1961), pp. 45–48. Useful secondary references may be found in Erminie Wheeler Voegelin and Helen Hornbeck Tanner, *Indians of Ohio and Indiana Prior to 1795* (2 vols., 1974), and Dan L. Thrapp, *Encyclopaedia of Frontier Biography*, vol. 4, *Supplemental Volume* (1994).

JOHN SUGDEN

SNEDDEN, David Samuel (19 Nov. 1868–1 Dec. 1951), education theorist, was born in the Kelso valley of Kern County, California, the son of Samuel Snedden, a gold miner turned rancher, and Anna O'Keefe. When David was ten the family moved to the Lockwood valley of Ventura County to escape recurring problems of drought and overgrazing. When a teacher came to the valley in 1884 David assisted in the construction of a log schoolhouse. Until then his mother had been the only teacher of her three children. With a few McGuffey readers, *Pilgrim's Progress*, *The Vicar of Wakefield*, and occasional copies of the *Pacific Rural Press*, David already had the equivalent of an elementary education. For the next three years his teachers prepared him for admission to the newly organized St. Vincent's College (presently Loyola-Marymount) of Los Angeles. There, rejecting the highly popular commercial course, Snedden received an A.B. in the classics in 1890. He later earned an M.A. from St. Vincent's. He found work as a rural schoolmaster, first in Ventura County, then in Fillmore, and finally as principal-teacher in Santa Paula. By then he was quite sure he wanted to be a teacher and enrolled in Leland Stanford Jr. University in the fall of 1895, graduating with an A.B. degree in 1897. Education and economics were his fields of concentration. He went to Paso Robles as principal of the high school with some classroom teaching and as superintendent of schools.

In 1898 David Snedden married Genevra Sisson, whom he had met at Stanford where she was a student of primary education under child-study specialist Earl Barnes. They had three children. In 1900 Snedden left for Columbia University to pursue a master's degree. Before leaving he delivered an address, "Education for the Rank and File," to the Stanford chapter of Phi Beta Kappa. It became the basis for Snedden's life's work. In it he argued that a socially efficient education had to be implemented by the doctrines of social control to provide an optimum total education for America's large and growing workforce. Education, he argued, should go beyond the mere skills of the workplace to include all of daily life to which the whole program of the school must contribute. In the years ahead he would work to perfect this ideal.

At Columbia Snedden worked under Franklin Giddings, Edward L. Thorndike, Frank McMurry, and his adviser, Samuel Train Dutton. He completed the master's degree within the year and returned to California, where in the spring of 1901 he assumed the duties of an assistant professor in education at Stanford University. In 1905, after learning that his future at Stanford without a Ph.D. was insecure, he returned to Columbia. He completed the degree in one year under

Edward T. Devine, leader of New York's social work movement. In his dissertation, "Administration and Educational Work of America's Juvenile Reform Schools," Snedden argued that reform schools, which used techniques of social control, provided a total program calculated to train students to function in society—education for social efficiency—and as such were worthy subjects of study by school professionals.

In March 1906 Snedden was offered the position at Columbia of adjunct professor of educational administration on more favorable terms than those at Stanford. There, for the next three and a half years he began the production of a steady stream of books and articles detailing a program of educational reorganization based on sociological analysis that promised optimum competence in one's life's work. In the course of his career he produced twenty-four books and over 230 articles, most in the area of applied educational sociology, but it was his *Toward Better Education* (1931) that he considered his most complete exposition of the subject.

In 1909 Frederick Perry Fish, chairman of the Massachusetts State Board of Education, asked Snedden to become the state's first commissioner to manage a newly created dual system of vocational schools and high schools. Snedden brought with him Charles Prosser, a former student who in 1912 would become the general secretary of the National Society for the Promotion of Industrial Education. Prosser served Snedden as his deputy commissioner for vocational education. William Orr, a former science teacher and a man who would introduce the "modern" subjects of science and the social studies, became Snedden's deputy commissioner for high schools. Snedden devoted himself to a heavy schedule of writing, speaking, and developing a specialized function for each of the state's various normal schools.

In 1916 Snedden returned to Columbia and a newly created chair in educational sociology. There he refined his theories for a reorganization in cultural, recreational, vocational, and moral education that would prepare an individual for a role of optimum efficiency in society. He dismissed from consideration the "elite," the 10 percent who were college-bound, who were being adequately served by existing institutions. For the "rank and file," "differentiation to destination" would begin in the elementary school but was most important at the high school level. All class content would be reorganized into "lotments" of learning—approximately sixty hours of work toward a specific objective—made up of "paths," a Welsh word for "little pieces," and organized into "strands" that could be identified with various life activities. To provide vocational efficiency Snedden wanted a separate school for each vocation that would be closely tied to the workplace and where teaching could proceed under factory-like conditions. By way of example he suggested special schools for coal-cutting, jewelry salesmanship, tailoring, stationary engine tending, and locomotive engine driving.

A report sponsored by the National Education Association titled *Cardinal Principles of Secondary Education* (1918), which took educational reform in an entirely different direction from that of David Snedden, was, from the outset, almost universally accepted by educators. Its purpose was to bring students destined for different roles in life together in a single, comprehensive high school on the premise that the best preparation for life was also the best preparation for college. All subjects were to contribute to the same "seven aims," which to Snedden could result only in "herd-like" uniformity. He considered the aims too general, and he argued for more specific objectives based on a sociological analysis of vocational and nonvocational subjects that targeted specific career destinations.

In 1935 Snedden retired from Columbia University and returned to a redwood house in the shadow of Stanford University that he had left thirty years before. From there, where he later died, he joined the annual cattle drives of the Snedden Land and Cattle Company until well into his eighties.

• Details of Snedden's early life and a fascinating account of pioneer life in California are in Genevra Sisson Snedden, *Mountain Cattle and Frontier People* (1947), and David Snedden, *Recollections of Over Half a Century Spent in Educational Work* (1949). Both were privately printed. Snedden's address, "Education for the Rank and File," was published in the *Stanford Alumnus* 1 (June 1900): 185–90. See Snedden's "The Cardinal Principles of Secondary Education," *School and Society*, 3 May 1919, and "High School Reorganization—Some Practical Next Steps," *Educational Administration and Supervision* 8 (Feb. 1922): 80–98, for his opposition to the comprehensive high school and his advocacy of "real vocational education." See also Snedden's "Jr. High School Offerings," *School and Society*, 13 Dec. 1924; "Planning Curriculum Research," *School and Society*, 29 Aug. 1925, 5 Sept. 1925, and 12 Sept. 1925; and "New Aims in Education," *Teachers College Record* 29 (Feb. 1928): 397–403, for his proposed organization of instruction into paths, lotments, and strands of learning. Walter H. Drost, *David Snedden and Education for Social Efficiency* (1967), is a detailed presentation of Snedden's professional career.

WALTER H. DROST

SNELL, Bertrand Hollis (9 Dec. 1870–2 Feb. 1958), businessman and U.S. representative, was born in Colton, New York, the son of Hollis Snell, a lumberman, and Flora E. Kimball. After graduating from Amherst College in 1894, he labored as a bookkeeper and lumberjack. He became a successful entrepeneur in the paper mill business, lumbering, cheese making, and other ventures. In 1903 he married Sara Louise Merrick; they had two daughters.

Elected in 1915 to the House of Representatives from upstate New York's Thirty-first district, Snell, a Republican, served in Congress until he retired in 1939. He was intensely loyal to the regular Republican leaders, only deviating from this fidelity when constituent interests were at stake. Early in his congressional service he offered a bill to make the St. Lawrence River more navigable, which he pursued unsuccessfully for the rest of his days in Congress. When the St. Lawrence Seaway finally came to fruition during the Dwight D. Eisenhower administration, one of its locks was named after Snell. According to his biographer, Louis A. Barone, Snell, throughout his congressional career, generally opposed federal regulatory interference in the private sector and big spending programs.

In 1923 Snell became chairman of the important House Rules Committee. This position gave him great power in Congress and the Republican party, because he was in a position to frame legislation and legislative strategy. When Nicolas Longworth ascended to the Speakership and John Q. Tilson became majority floor leader in 1925, they, along with Snell, effectively controlled in concert the House of Representatives.

Snell's first job as chairman of the Rules Committee was to fend off a challenge by insurgent Republicans and Democrats to ease restrictions on discharge petitions. Snell helped fashion a compromise that allowed regular Republican leaders a modicum of control.

When Longworth became Speaker in 1925, the Old Guard reestablished its dominance in the lower chamber. In this, the regular Republicans were aided by Snell's Rules Committee in restricting Democrats and insurgent Republicans from interfering with President Calvin Coolidge's program of spending cuts and tax reduction. To Democrats' complaints that Snell was too restrictive with the rules, the New Yorker responded that the opposition would undoubtedly do the same if and when they came back to power in the House—which they did. During these years Snell also played a role as a go-between for Congress and his college friend from Amherst, President Coolidge. This was not always a popular job, especially when differences arose between the president and Congress.

Snell backed Herbert Hoover for the 1928 GOP presidential nomination, albeit somewhat unenthusiastically. He would have preferred for Coolidge to run for another term. Snell's relations with the engineer president soured slightly when Hoover tried unsuccessfully to seize the initiative in New York patronage.

Snell's dream of eventually becoming Speaker was dashed with the onset of the Great Depression. In the wake of the 1930 midterm elections, the Republicans lost control of the House. After Longworth died in April 1931, Tilson and Snell tusseled for the job of minority leader. Despite being favored by the president, Tilson lost the race to Snell, who appealed to both the Old Guard and to the insurgents. Tilson was too closely associated with the increasingly unpopular Hoover, and Snell had made some concessions to the progressive Republicans.

With Hoover's defeat and the advent of the New Deal, Snell spent the rest of his days in Congress fighting the liberal programs of Franklin D. Roosevelt. His initial reaction to the New Deal was one of cautious but critical cooperation. Snell, in the midst of the economic crisis, supported some early measures of the New Deal, such as the 1933 Emergency Banking Act and the National Economy Act, but he came out in cautious, conservative opposition to most of the president's program. He opposed the Agricultural Adjustment Act, the Thomas amendment favoring inflation, the Reciprocal Trade Agreements Act, and other early New Deal measures.

During the Court-packing battle of 1937, Snell agreed with Senate GOP leaders to allow the now mammoth Democratic majority to fight amongst themselves, which they did, sinking the plan. The so-called Roosevelt recession of 1937 also encouraged Snell and other conservatives to step up their resistance to the New Deal. In late 1937 Snell introduced legislation for a tax cut. During the special session of Congress in the same year, Republicans and southern Democrats combined to recommit Roosevelt's Fair Labor Standards Bill, although it was enacted in the next session.

In 1938 Snell and the GOP minority successfully opposed Roosevelt's original executive branch reorganization plan. The midterm elections that year were a triumph for the GOP, narrowing the partisan gap in Congress. However, because of declining eyesight and hearing and his belief that the Republicans would not retake the House in the near future, Snell decided to retire. After his retirement in 1939, he became publisher of the *Potsdam Courier-Freedom*, which he had bought five years earlier. His life ended in Potsdam, New York.

• Snell's manuscript collection can be found at the Frederick Crumb Library, State University of New York at Potsdam. Useful information on Snell is in Louis A. Barone, "Republican House Minority Leader Bertrand H. Snell and the Coming of the New Deal, 1931–1939" (Ph.D. diss., State Univ. of New York at Buffalo, 1969); Jordan A. Schwarz, *The Interregnum of Despair: Hoover, Congress, and the Depression* (1970); George B. Galloway, *History of the House of Representatives*, 2d ed., rev. Sidney Wise (1976); and memorial addresses in the *Congressional Record*, 85th Cong., 2d sess., 1958, 104, pt. 2: 1549–52. An obituary is in the *New York Times*, 3 Feb. 1958.

TRACY S. UEBELHOR

SNELLING, Josiah (1782–20 Aug. 1828), soldier, was born in Boston, Massachusetts. Nothing is known of his parents. His actions as a youth and his education are uncertain too, but his later career suggests that he had whatever experiences the local schools provided. His military career began in 1803 when he became the first sergeant of a Massachusetts militia company. A year later he married Elizabeth Bell, who died shortly after the birth of their son (date unknown). After moving up to the rank of lieutenant, he resigned his militia commission, and on 3 May 1808 he joined the U.S. Army. For the rest of his life he remained on active duty. He entered the army as a first lieutenant in the Fourth Infantry then being formed as a part of President Thomas Jefferson's response to ongoing difficulties with the British and the French. On 12 June 1809 he was promoted to captain, and he retained that rank through early 1814. During the period of growing tension between the United States and Great Britain, American fears that the British might instigate an Indian war south of the Great Lakes brought a buildup of troops in that region. Snelling served there and fought against the Indians in the battle of Tippecanoe in November 1811, and soon after war was declared in 1812 his unit moved to Detroit. During July and August 1812 he participated in the fighting in Upper Canada, being brevetted a major for distinguished service at the battle of Brownstown there. At Detroit in August 1812 he married Abigail Hunt, the daughter of one of his fellow officers. Together they had four children. When the British threatened Detroit he was one of the officers who urged General William Hull not to surrender but in vain. The forces at Detroit capitulated, and the prisoners were taken to Montreal. By early 1813 Snelling had been exchanged, and during the rest of the year he served as an inspector general on the staff of General George Izzard in New York. On 21 February 1814 he was promoted to lieutenant colonel and assigned to the Fourth Rifle Regiment while he continued to serve as an inspector general in the Niagara campaign.

In the postwar army reduction of 1815 he retained his rank as a lieutenant colonel and was transferred to the Sixth Infantry then being re-formed in New York. For the next three years he served with that unit at Plattsburgh. Then, in 1819 he became colonel of the Fifth Infantry. That assignment brought him to the Mississippi Valley as part of Secretary of War John C. Calhoun's plans to extend the American military presence into the Mississippi and Missouri river valleys to impress the Indians there and to deter the operations of British fur traders from Canada. During the summer of 1819 troops from the Fifth Infantry traveled north up the Mississippi River to establish what would become Fort Snelling at the confluence of that stream and the Minnesota River. The next year Colonel Snelling moved to the post, where he spent most of the rest of his military career.

There he had to oversee relations between whites and local Indians as well as try to keep peace between perpetually raiding bands of Ojibwa and Sioux in the region. While doing that, he supervised the building of the fort for the next several years. In 1825 the War Department named the fort in Snelling's honor. In 1827 he led troops south to Fort Crawford at Prairie du Chien, Wisconsin, as part of General Henry Atkinson's campaign to frighten belligerent groups of Winnebago warriors nearby to keep peace. Later that same year the Fifth Infantry moved south to St. Louis, and the Snellings traveled south with the regiment. In 1828 the colonel took a leave to retrieve one of his daughters then finishing school in Washington, D.C. Shortly after he got to the city, the girl died, and a few weeks later Snelling himself died suddenly of a "seizure" in Washington.

His career mirrored those of many army officers of that day. He entered the service with no formal military training, learning army usages on the job. He proved to be brave and resourceful in combat, but most of his attention focused on routine military matters such as moving troops, building fortifications, and supervising frontier Indian affairs. His contemporary reputation was that of a hard-drinking, hard-driving but supportive officer, and the infantrymen under his command called him "the Prairie hen," supposedly because of his thinning red hair. Although he had few illusions, he claimed to be satisfied by his career. When asked about his military life, he wrote, "I entered the army a subaltern, almost eighteen years ago. From obscurity I have passed through every grade to the command of a regiment. . . . I have obtained my rank in the ordinary course of promotion . . . and I really flatter myself that I still possess the confidence of the government, and the respect of those who serve with and under me" (Hansen, p. 219).

• Snelling left no substantial collection of personal papers, but one diary remains in private hands. His official correspondence is located in several record groups of military records at the National Archives and to a lesser degree in the papers of the Office of Indian Affairs at the same location. For a general discussion of the era and location of his service, see Roger L. Nichols, *General Henry Atkinson: A Western Military Career* (1965). Marcus L. Hansen, *Old Fort Snelling* (1918), and Bruce E. Mahon, *Old Fort Crawford and the Frontier* (1926), follow much of the local activity in the upper Mississippi Valley during the decade after the War of 1812. For Snelling's actions during the 1812 Detroit campaign, see Alec R. Gilpin, *The War of 1812 in the Old Northwest* (1958).

ROGER L. NICHOLS

SNELLING, William Joseph (26 Dec. 1804–24 Dec. 1848), author and journalist, was born in Boston, Massachusetts, the son of Josiah Snelling, an army officer, and Elizabeth Bell. After the death of his mother in 1810, William lived with relatives while attending classical school near Boston; at fourteen, he entered West Point but left after only two years.

After leaving West Point, Snelling gravitated westward toward his father's outpost at Fort Anthony (later renamed Fort Snelling) near present-day St. Paul, Minnesota. After spending a winter among the Dakota Indians, he arrived at the fort in 1821 and for the next five years led an adventuresome life as fur trader and explorer. His knowledge of the Dakota's habits and language evidently made him useful as an interpreter; he took an active part, for example, in mediating outbursts of tribal warfare between the Chippewa, Dakota, and Winnebago tribes. Snelling married a French woman, Dionice Fournier, in 1826, but she died the following year.

Returning to Boston after the death of his father in 1828, Snelling embarked on a career as a journalist and writer. During the next few years, he issued several volumes of travel and adventure tales for children under the pseudonym Solomon Bell. He also became a regular contributor to a variety of newspapers and magazines: from 1828 to 1848, he wrote for and/or edited the *New England Magazine, New England Galaxy, North American Review, Boston Herald, Boston Book, Token,* and *American Monthly.*

A man of passionate and forceful opinions, Snelling's blunt writing in the cause of social reform won him both admirers and enemies. Above all, he was not a man to be ignored. The verse satire, *Truth: A New Year's Gift for Scribblers* (1831) is a witty and bold commentary on the state of American letters in the early nineteenth century. Anticipating James Russell Lowell's *A Fable for Critics* by seventeen years, *Truth* excoriates contemporary poetasters who, in Snelling's opinion, reveal more pomposity and ego in their works than talent. Using his position as editor of the *New England Galaxy*, Snelling next launched a newspaper campaign to rid Boston of gambling. When his zeal resulted in a libel suit, Snelling collected his editorials into a pamphlet entitled "Expose of the Vice of Gaming" (1833), the sale of which went to defray his legal expenses. Later, Snelling's four-month experience in jail on a charge of drunkenness led him to undertake prison reform as well. In 1837 he published "The Rat-Trap; or Cogitations of a Convict in the House of Correction," a long and rambling essay descrying the appalling conditions of prison life.

While significant, Snelling's efforts as a journalist and reformer are secondary to his contributions to American literature as a writer of fiction. Though immersed in his journalistic work, Snelling also spent his early years in Boston writing short stories based on his experiences on the frontier. *Tales of the Northwest; or, Sketches of Indian Life and Character*, a collection of ten such stories, appeared in 1830; several others, such as "Te Zahpahtah" and "The Last of the Iron Hearts," were published separately. Snelling also composed two narrative poems, "The Snow Shoe" and "The Birth of Thunder," on the same theme. In addition, a number of unsigned works, such as "The Fortunes of Mendokaycheenah" and "Shoankah Shahpah," are most likely Snelling's.

Snelling stated his purpose in writing tales of the old Northwest in several prefaces to his works. Keenly aware that the Native-American way of life on the plains was already in danger of vanishing, he wished to capture it as a record for posterity. More important, Snelling was incensed with what he considered the inadequate or stereotyped portrayals of Indians in the works of his contemporaries. "[We] beg leave to assure our readers," he wrote in "The Last of the Iron Hearts," "that the Indian is not the ferocious brute of Hubbard and Mather, or the brilliant, romantic, half-French, half-Celtic Mohegan and Yemassee created by Symmes and Cooper." Rather, Snelling insisted in his preface to *Tales*, one "must live, emphatically, *live*, with Indians; share with them their lodges, their food, and their blankets, for years, before he can comprehend their ideas, or enter into their feelings."

Claiming the authority of his eight-year experience on the frontier, Snelling wrote stories aimed at a "truthful" portrayal of the Indian. What he succeeded in creating are engaging and vigorous tales based on Native-American life and legend as well as stories of the cultural conflict resulting from the early white settlements on the frontier. "Weenokhenchah Wandeeteekah," for example, derives from the Indian legend of a tragic "lover's leap"; "Charles Hess" is based on a factual account of an explorer whose family was slain in a Dakota raid; and "The Bois Brule" details the reception of a half-breed by both white and Native American cultures.

Snelling's stories often suffer from lack of unity and, despite his stated goal of objectivity, lapse at times into sentimentality and didacticism. At his best, however, he succeeds in exploring his characters' motivations with considerable psychological depth while exhibiting an economy of style and attention to detail. Well received in his own time, Snelling's tales have consistently merited praise; Fred Lewis Pattee's *Development of the American Short Story* (1923), for example, states that "his Indian stories are undoubtedly the best written during the early period."

Snelling's personal life in his later years can be briefly summarized. He married his second wife, Mary Leaverett, on an unknown date in Boston; she died in 1837. He married Lucy Jordan in 1838; this union produced three children, the last of which was born eight months after his death. Snelling died of apoplexy, or "congestion of the brain," in Chelsea, Massachusetts.

Although once best known, even infamous, for the satiric poem *Truth*, Snelling's reputation today rests on his stories of frontier life. He was one of the earliest to call for and make attempts at realism in fiction. He was also the first to portray in literature the life of the plains Indians in what is now the upper Midwest; for this reason, his work remains of interest to ethnographers as well. Finally, he was among the first American writers (along with Washington Irving and Nathaniel Hawthorne) to produce a collection of short stories.

• Biographical information about Snelling is available in Allen E. Woodall, "William Joseph Snelling, 1804–1848: A Review of His Life and Writings" (Ph.D. diss., Univ. of Pittsburgh, 1932) and "William Joseph Snelling and the Early Northwest," *Minnesota History* 10 (1929): 367–85. Also informative is the introduction to *Tales of the Northwest* (1936) by John T. Flanagan. For Snelling's reputation as a critic, see Flanagan, "William Joseph Snelling, Forgotten Critic," *Philological Quarterly* 16 (1937): 367–93, and Elizabeth Evans, "William Joseph Snelling: Still a Forgotten Critic," *Markham Review* 5 (1975): 15–20. Snelling's frontier tales receive critical attention in William J. Scheick, "The Half-Breed in Snelling's *Tales of the Northwest*," *Old Northwest* 2 (1976): 141–51; Flanagan, "William Joseph Snelling's Western Narratives," *Minnesota History* 17 (1936): 437–43; and Todd Gray Willy, "Antipode to Cooper: Rhetoric and Reality in William Joseph Snelling's 'The Bois Brule,'" *Studies in American Fiction* 8 (1980): 69–79.

MARY R. REICHARDT

SNETHEN, Nicholas (15 Nov. 1769–30 May 1845), clergyman and founder of the Methodist Protestant church, was born in Fresh Pond (now Glen Cove), Long Island, New York, the son of Barak Snethen, a farmer, miller, and shipper, and Ann Weeks. Barak Snethen was of Welsh descent and served as an officer in the British colonial army before taking up farming, work that Nicholas shared during his early years.

Nicholas attended a country school, and his mother also instructed him in the Book of Common Prayer of the Church of England. In 1790 the family moved to Staten Island, New York, where Snethen was active in the Episcopal church and was converted under the preaching of Richard Channing Moore, who later became bishop of Virginia. In 1791 the family moved to Belleville, New Jersey, where he became active in the Methodist Episcopal church.

Persuaded that he had been called to preach, Snethen entered the itinerant ministry of the Methodist Episcopal church in September 1794 and was appointed to circuits in Connecticut, Vermont, and Maine. Five years later he was assigned to Charleston, South Carolina, and was ordained elder in 1800. In testimony to the high regard in which he was held by his ministerial colleagues, he was elected secretary of the 1800 General Conference, the chief legislative body of the church. From 1800 until 1806 he was appointed to churches in Baltimore and New York City, and he served as traveling companion to Bishop Francis Asbury, who referred to him as his "silver trumpet" because of Snethen's pleasant and melodious voice. He married Susannah Hood Worthington in 1804 and through the marriage became the owner of a farm and slaves. They had six children.

From 1806 until 1809 Snethen left the itinerant ministry to manage the farm, although he occasionally preached in the area and held a camp meeting on his property in August 1807. He resumed the itinerancy, and between 1809 and 1814 he served churches in Baltimore and Fells Point, Maryland; Georgetown, District of Columbia; Alexandria, Virginia; and Frederick, Maryland. During his pastorate in Georgetown he served as chaplain of the U.S. House of Representatives. Snethen again left the itineracy in 1814, returning to his farm. He became interested in politics for the next three years and unsuccessfully ran for Congress as a Federalist in 1816. During this period he became more convinced that laypeople should have a greater official voice and influence in the life of the Methodist Episcopal church and that the authority and power of bishops in the church should be limited, views he had held as early as 1812. In 1821 he was invited to become a regular contributor to the *Wesleyan Repository*, a paper that promoted reform views, including lay representation at both the annual and general conferences of the Methodist Episcopal church. His articles were later collected and published as *Snethen on Lay Representation: Essays on Lay Representation and Church Government* (1835). When *Mutual Rights* succeeded the *Wesleyan Repository* as the principal publication of the Reformers, Snethen became a frequent contributor. Among his major writings are *A Discourse on the Death of the Rev. Francis Asbury* (1816), *Lectures on Preaching* (1822), *Lectures on Biblical Subjects* (1836), and *Sermons* (1846). In 1828 he drafted the critical petition to introduce reforms to the General Conference. Snethen considered himself thoroughly traditional and Wesleyan in his theology. He was convinced that the power that had evolved in the

Methodist episcopacy and the absence of an official voice for laypeople in the affairs of the church were neither Wesleyan nor in the best interests of the church. When his petition lost he joined those Reformers who met in Baltimore in 1828 to establish the Methodist Protestant church. He was influential in drafting its articles of association and devoted the rest of his life to supporting the new church.

In 1829 financial difficulties forced Snethen to sell the Maryland farm, free his slaves, and move his family to Sullivan County, Indiana. Later he moved to Louisville; Cincinnati; and Zanesville, Ohio, where he served pastorates. In 1834 Snethen was elected president of the General Conference and was also chosen co-editor of *Mutual Rights and Methodist Protestant*, the denomination's official publication. He was the head of two educational institutions begun by the Methodist Protestant church, both of which failed because of inadequate finances, one in New York City, established in 1836, and the other a manual labor college in Lawrenceburg, Indiana, which he supervised from 1837 until 1839. In 1843 he was named president of a proposed school to train men for the ministry that was to be situated in Iowa City, Iowa, and called Snethen Seminary. However, before the school could open, Snethen died at the home of his daughter in Princeton, Indiana.

Snethen was an outstanding leader of early American Methodism. He was an effective preacher, editor, writer, educator, and administrator and one of the most important founders of the Methodist Protestant church.

• Biographical information is in Harlan L. Feeman, *Francis Asbury's Silver Trumpet: Nicholas Snethen: Non-Partisan Church Statesman and Preacher of the Gospel, 1769–1845* (1950), T. H. Colhouer, *Sketches of the Founders of the Methodist Protestant Church* (1880), and A. H. Bassett, *A Concise History of the Methodist Protestant Church from Its Origin with Biographical Sketches* (1877).

CHARLES YRIGOYEN, JR.

SNOW, Edgar Parks (19 July 1905–15 Feb. 1972), journalist, was born in Kansas City, Missouri, the son of Anna Edelman and James Edgar Snow, a printer. After working for a time in the Kansas fields, as a teenager Snow bummed his way across the country. Years later he often reminisced about the allure of the Pacific Ocean, which he viewed for the first time when he traveled the country, and the real-life social dramas he witnessed riding the rails.

In 1928, after brief stints at the University of Missouri journalism school and an advertising job in New York City, Snow decided to bum his way around the world. Shortly after landing in Shanghai, he accepted a temporary job on the *China Weekly Review*, edited by a University of Missouri graduate. He stayed on when offered the chance to see the country as a reporter. In 1930 Snow became a correspondent for the newly created Consolidated Press Association, which gave him freedom to trek from South China to Burma and then on to India.

Though interested in adventure at first, Snow was soon drawn to China's political struggles. He disliked foreign settlements and other manifestations of imperialism and looked for solutions to age-old Chinese inequities. Snow's first book, *Far Eastern Front* (1933), chronicled the beginnings of Japanese encroachment in China. Snow had picked up basic Chinese language skills during his early years in China, and in the mid-1930s translated a collection of fictional short stories by Chinese writers. At the time, *Living China* (1937) offered Western readers a unique opportunity to read Lu Xun, Ding Ling, and other leftist writers.

During the early 1930s Snow's by-line became familiar in major newspapers and magazines back home, but in 1936 he moved to the front ranks of American journalists. That year he slipped through the Nationalist government's blockade of the Chinese Communists, who for nearly a decade had dwelt obscurely in the countryside. Snow became the first Western reporter to interview Mao Zedong, Zhou Enlai, and other Chinese Communist leaders. He returned with the sensational news that Mao and his followers were not mere "Red bandits," as Chiang Kai-shek had labeled them, but dedicated revolutionaries advocating sweeping domestic reforms and eager to resist Japanese aggression. Snow's reports were news not only to the outside world but also to the Chinese themselves, many of whom joined the Chinese Communists after reading Chinese-language versions of Snow's book-length report, *Red Star Over China* (1937), which has remained a primary source on the early Chinese Communist movement.

After returning to the United States in 1941, Snow accepted one of the most prestigious jobs in American journalism, foreign correspondent for the influential *Saturday Evening Post*. He covered the Soviet Union and parts of Europe during World War II. Although his insights were not on a par with his China reporting, he correctly forecast the Soviet Union's postwar foreign policy in Central Europe and Asia. Working in Asia after the war, Snow covered Indian independence and predicted the likelihood of protracted war in Vietnam.

Americans' fear of communism, nurtured by the Communists' takeover of China, changed the direction of Snow's career. The conservative *Post* wanted to maintain its relationship with Snow but, in the face of intense criticism of his reporting on the Communists in the 1930s, urged him to write on less controversial topics. Unwilling to bend, Snow and the *Post* editors decided to end their formal relationship in 1951, although Snow continued to write occasional articles for the *Post* for several years. By the mid-1950s he had almost no magazine or newspaper outlets for his work.

The decline of his career coincided with increased personal responsibilities. His 1932 marriage to American Helen Foster had worked while they were in China; they shared many of the same concerns about the country. Under the name Nym Wales, she, too, wrote

about contemporary politics and, after the Japanese seized control of China's coast, the two of them helped start Indusco, a Chinese industrial cooperative movement in the interior. Back in the United States in the 1940s, though, the childless marriage disintegrated. Snow received a divorce in 1949 and the same year married actress Lois Wheeler; they had two children.

During the 1950s Snow turned down invitations to visit China. In addition to difficulty securing State Department approval, he would not let the Communists pay his way and he could find no American financial backing. But when an invitation came for a trip in 1960, *Look* and his publisher Random House agreed to cover his costs and interceded with the government in Washington. Snow became the first American reporter with prior experience in the country to visit Communist China, and his access made him suspect among Americans. In the absence of formal Sino-American diplomatic or commercial ties, Snow tried to counter what he believed was a distorted U.S. picture of China by explaining at length the communist point of view. *Look* published only one of the three articles they had commissioned Snow to write, and his book, *Red China Today: The Other Side of the River* (1961), was as vilified in the United States as *Red Star* had been lauded. Snow, who had relocated his family to Switzerland while he was in China, decided to stay in Europe where he was considerably more popular.

During the 1960s Snow wrote strong articles against American involvement in the Vietnam conflict and continued to visit China. His 1964 visit was the last by an American reporter before the Cultural Revolution; in 1970, he was the first American reporter to return. On that final trip, during the traditional 1 October celebration of the founding of the People's Republic of China, Mao brought Snow to stand with him at Beijing's T'ien An Men Gate, a gesture meant to signal Chinese willingness to improve relations with the United States.

In the 1960s Sino-American rapprochement, plus growing disillusionment with the war in Vietnam, brought Snow a measure of renewed popularity among Americans. He did not, however, realize his ambitions to resettle in the United States nor was he able to accompany the reporters covering President Richard Nixon's landmark visit to China in 1972. Sixty-two hours before Nixon's plane left the United States, Snow died in Switzerland.

• The University of Missouri at Kansas City houses a collection of Edgar Snow's papers. Additional materials can be found in the Nym Wales Papers at the Hoover Institution on War, Revolution, and Peace at Stanford University. Snow frequently included details about himself in his books, which in addition to those mentioned previously include *The Battle for Asia* (1941), *People on Our Side* (1944), *Pattern of Soviet Power* (1945), *Stalin Must Have Peace* (1947), and *The Long Revolution* (1972). His one thoroughly autobiographical account is *Journey to the Beginning* (1958), which recounts his early career. Helen Foster Snow discusses Snow in her autobiography, *My China Years* (1984). His widow, Lois Wheeler Snow, wrote an account of his last days, when the Chinese sent a medical delegation to attend him in Switzerland, *A Death with Dignity* (1974). Robert M. Farnsworth provides biographical information in a collection of Snow's early reports, *Edgar Snow's Journey South of the Clouds* (1991). A full treatment of Snow's life is found in John Maxwell Hamilton's *Edgar Snow: A Biography* (1988), which also includes references to literature on Snow. Obituaries are in the *New York Times*, 16 Feb. 1972, and *Time*, 23 Feb. 1972.

JOHN MAXWELL HAMILTON

SNOW, Edwin Miller (8 May 1820–22 Dec. 1888), physician and public health official, was born in Pomfret, Vermont, the son of Nathan Snow and Rhoda Miller. After preparing for college at Kimball Union Academy in Meredith, New Hampshire, and the New Hampton (N.H.) Literary and Theological Institution, he entered Brown University in 1840. After an absence of a year because of illness, he graduated in 1845 with an A.B. degree and later was awarded an A.M.

Snow spent two years teaching school while also studying medicine in the office of W. P. Buck in Manchester, New Hampshire. In 1849 he received the M.D. degree from the College of Physicians and Surgeons of Columbia University in New York City. He began practice in Holyoke, Massachusetts, but after a year he moved to Providence, Rhode Island. In 1850, he married Anna E. W. Pike; the couple had five children.

Snow gained national prominence following the great cholera epidemic of 1854 in Providence, in which he investigated about 150 cases. There was no health authority in the city, so he personally undertook action to curb the epidemic. He drew up a report sharply criticizing the city's complete lack of sanitary precautions and recommended measures to deal with the problem. Convinced by Snow's arguments, the city undertook drastic sanitary reforms, including broad authority over quarantine, vaccination, and scavenging. Quarantine had to do with detecting Asiatic cholera and smallpox on ships entering the harbor and the isolation of cases of domestic origin; vaccination at that time was exclusively for smallpox, and "scavenging" was garbage collecting and street cleaning. Snow also wrote papers on the control of smallpox and Asiatic cholera, on the keeping of swine in the city, and on the adulteration of milk. He was probably the first health officer to coordinate all these functions. Other cities began to follow Snow's precepts. Although based on the miasmatic rather than the germ theory of contagion, his concepts of sanitation were forward-looking, as were his extensive statistical studies. The reforms in Providence became effective a decade before New York City adopted its great reforms, which were acknowledged to be based on Snow's concepts.

In 1856 Providence established a permanent city health department, and Snow was appointed superintendent of health, becoming America's first professional city medical health officer. He held the position for more than thirty years, almost to the exclusion of private practice.

During his career Snow became interested in preventive medicine and published many reports, emphasizing vital and social statistics that contributed to understanding its principles. Even before establishing the health department, the city had provided for the registration of vital statistics, and in addition to his tenure as superintendent of health, Snow was appointed city registrar. He used the statistics available to him in formulating his policies and in his published papers.

Between 1857 and 1860 four national quarantine and sanitary conventions were held. Snow helped organize all four of these meetings, which stimulated interest in systematizing public health work in accordance with his precepts. Of the seventy-three persons who met in Philadelphia in 1857, only Snow and one other were actual health officers. They devoted their time at the meetings mainly to drafting flexible, humane, and uniform quarantine procedures. Snow was one of a small group who insisted on broadening the scope of the meetings to include sanitary matters other than quarantine. Just before adjournment of the first convention, the delegates passed Snow's resolution calling for accurate registration of vital statistics in every state and city.

At the second convention, Snow was asked to prepare a thorough report on registration for the guidance of all American health workers. He labored over the report for two years and presented it at the fourth convention in Boston; it was published in 1860 as *Report on Registration*. The Civil War interrupted the quarantine and sanitary conventions, but interest was renewed after the war. New York City's famous health reforms were carried out in 1866.

Interest in an organization of sanitarians was revived, and Snow was one of a small group who met in 1872 to form the American Public Health Association; Snow was elected vice president. The meeting in Boston in 1876 was the high point of Snow's career. Now risen to the presidency, he read the presidential address. He emphasized that the sanitary movement in the United States had made an encouraging start, but that it was still far from reaching maturity, both in accumulating vital statistics and in basic sanitary improvements to reduce disease in the cities. The American Public Health Association gave status to the professionalization of health officers, to recognition of public health as a medical discipline, and to the establishment of several schools of public health.

Despite his keen insights and important contributions, Snow never accepted the germ theory of disease, the work of Lister, Koch, and Pasteur not having reached his understanding before his death.

In addition to his health superintendency, Snow was also state prison inspector, a member of the state board of charities and correction (1869–1872), and chairman of the board of cattle inspectors. In 1872 he was state delegate to the International Statistical Congress in St. Petersburg. He was a member of the American Statistical Association and supervisor for the district of Rhode Island in the U.S. census of 1880.

He was a member of the American Medical Association and the American Academy of Medicine, secretary of the Providence Medical Association, secretary (1852–1855) and president (1876–1877) of the Rhode Island Medical Society, a trustee of Brown University (1876–1888), and a member of the Providence Common Council (1855). In the Civil War he was Inspector of Hospitals for the U.S. Sanitary Commission and visited military hospitals in Philadelphia and the field hospitals of the Army of the Potomac. He was consulting physician at Rhode Island Hospital.

In 1884 the offices of registrar and superintendent of health were separated. Snow retained the office of registrar until his death, while Charles Value Chapin became superintendent of health.

Snow died in Providence. Despite his significant contributions to the science of public health, history has cast him in the shadow of Chapin, his friend and talented successor. James H. Cassedy, the biographer of both Snow and Chapin, wrote, "Chapin would take on the job of defining the whole pattern of principles and duties for the American health officer of the twentieth century in terms of the momentous findings of bacteriology. But it was Snow who had set the pattern for the American health officer of the last half of the nineteenth century."

• A well-annotated biographical article is James H. Cassedy, "Edwin Miller Snow, an Important American Public Health Pioneer," *Bulletin of the History of Medicine* 35 (1961): 156. The entry for the class of 1845 in *Historical Catalogue of Brown University 1764–1894* (1895), p. 149, includes Snow's obituary, with lists of his offices and publications. His colleague Chapin contributed a memoir, "Edwin Miller Snow, M.D.," *Transactions of the Rhode Island Medical Society* 4 (1889): 91–96.

SEEBERT J. GOLDOWSKY

SNOW, Eliza Roxcy (21 Jan. 1804–5 Dec. 1887), Mormon women's leader and writer, was born in Becket, Massachusetts, the daughter of Oliver Snow, a farmer, and Rosetta Pettibone. Reared from age two in the Ohio frontier town of Mantua, she excelled in the common schools she attended but lacked opportunity for higher education. Of literary bent, she began in 1826 publishing poetry under various pseudonyms—"Narcissa," "Pocahontas," and "Tullia" among them—in Ohio newspapers. She assisted her father, a county official, as his secretary. Her early training "to the kitchen" also included the domestic duties required of children. Tailoring and weaving straw hats were her specialties.

Eliza was the third of her family to join the Church of Jesus Christ of Latter-day Saints, founded by Joseph Smith (1805–1844), after Smith's 1831 removal from New York to Kirtland, Ohio, thirty miles north of the Snow farm. Baptized in 1835, she became schoolmistress to the Smith children in Kirtland, and most of her family followed her there. In 1838 they relocated with the Mormons near Independence, Missouri; then, after continued persecution there, they removed to Illinois, where the Mormons established the town of Nauvoo. There, Snow assisted in the founding of the Female Relief Society of Nauvoo in 1842. That same year, though the practice of polygamy was essentially kept secret, she married Joseph Smith as his fifth plural wife.

After Smith's death in 1844, she married his successor, Brigham Young. As one of his wives, she developed what she later termed the "noble independence" necessary for a woman whose husband is often absent. She traveled with the Latter-day Saints to Utah, arriving there, penniless, in 1847, Young having returned for the winter to Nebraska. She comments in her diary that in trading the making of a cap for soap, "I begin again to be a woman of property." She eventually joined Young's large family in the spacious Lion House, one among the fourteen other wives who lived there.

After the arrival of her brother Lorenzo Snow and his family to Salt Lake City in 1848, she founded with him the Polysophical Society, a short-lived but significant gathering of the cultural elite of the burgeoning wilderness community. Also at this time she prepared her poetry for publication in two volumes as *Poems: Religious, Historical, and Political*. One volume was published in 1856 by the church's Liverpool publishing house; the other, its manuscript initially misplaced, was not published until 1877 in Salt Lake City. In the 1850s a contemporary critic described her as "a very talented woman, but outrageously bigoted" and saw her and her intimates as "the nuclei for all the female intellect at Salt Lake." What from outside of Mormon circles at the time appeared as bigotry, in hindsight suggests a strongly authoritarian acceptance of church doctrine and organizational dicta.

Although the Nauvoo-founded Relief Society experienced a grass-roots revival in the 1850s, Snow was not significant in its activities until 1866, when Young, now church president, assigned her to reorganize the women's groups in each congregation of the church. The Female Relief Society in Utah was immediately successful and extensive, and Snow served as its general president until her death.

The society owed its rebirth to the women's potential for economic contribution to the community, as perceived by Young, but in Snow's hands its spiritual intent remained uppermost. The pentecostal practices that arose in Nauvoo continued, albeit somewhat abated, in the women's meetings, and the charitable work and "home industry" efforts took second place. The purpose of the society, Snow asserted, was not only to succor the poor, but also to save souls. Her own reputation as "prophetess" arose from this aspect of her ministry. With like-minded companions she traveled from community to community to address local women and direct them in their organizations.

Work among youth followed. Snow served as counselor to the president of the Retrenchment Society, the purpose of which was to encourage frugality, modesty, and home industry among the women and girls. It lasted into the early twentieth century and led to the founding of the Mutual Improvement Association.

The Primary Association, for the religious education of children, founded under her direction, still functions in Latter-day Saint congregations. From 1872 to 1914 Mormon women published the *Woman's Exponent*, a semimonthly journal Snow fostered. Under her direction various "home industry" programs were instituted: silk manufacture, the building of local Relief Society halls for use as meeting rooms and mercantile outlets, a program of storing grain against famine, and nurses' training classes. In celebration of the 1876 U.S. centennial, Mormon women not only sent a display of their crafts to Philadelphia, but also mounted their own Territorial Fair in Utah. When the fair concluded, the items displayed became the initial inventory for the Women's Commission Store, which Snow directed for several years afterward.

In 1882, Snow, at age seventy-eight, directed the founding of the Relief Society–sponsored Deseret Hospital, staffed, supported, and patronized by women. Plagued by financial difficulties, however, the hospital survived her by only four years.

Through the twenty years of her public life, Snow carried on an active literary career. Besides her poetry, she wrote instructional materials for the primary and Sunday schools, compiled hymns, and collected and published as *Correspondence of the Palestine Tourists* (1875) the descriptive letters of her colleagues on an 1872–1873 junket to Britain, continental Europe, and the eastern Mediterranean.

Her most significant prose work was the 1884 *Biography and Family Record of Lorenzo Snow*, tracing her brother's ascent to leadership of the Mormons. After her death, he would become their fifth president. The affection of each for the other is significant, and in public responsibilities, as in personal attributes, they mirrored each other's achievements. Each contributed not only organizationally, but doctrinally to Mormon thought. Eliza's 1845 hymn, now sung as "O My Father," teaches of the existence of divine parents, a Heavenly Mother as well as a Heavenly Father. Mormon doctrine retains the concept.

Her public rhetoric, however, revealed Snow's greatest talent. In small groups or large congregations she preached the essential equality of women and men and their shared responsibilities. Speaking in 1870 before several thousand of her Mormon sisters, she roused them to political action in protesting congressional action against their practice of polygamy. Having found their public voice, the women made use of the franchise granted them in Utah Territory that same year. In 1887, the year of Snow's death, however, an antipolygamy Congress disfranchised practicing Mormons and all Utah women. Her female followers thereafter campaigned vigorously for the return of their voting privilege, and won it in the state constitution, written and ratified in 1895.

Remembered now mainly for her poetry and doctrinal writings, Snow was viewed by her contemporaries in nineteenth-century Utah as the first lady of the Latter-day Saints, the "captain of Utah's woman-host." Before she died, the Relief Society had grown to include more than 300 branches in the American West, Britain, Europe, and Hawaii. As a plural wife of Utah governor and Mormon church president Brigham Young, she influenced ecclesiastical policy toward women, at the same time encouraging women to support church-directed programs. Childless, she was praised as a "mother in Israel," a term that acknowledged not only her lifetime of service, but the spiritual quality of her contribution. "True greatness," she is reported to have said, "is merely usefulness."

• Snow's extant diaries for 1842–1844 are in the Church Archives, Historical Department, Church of Jesus Christ of Latter-day Saints, Salt Lake City, and, for 1846–1849, in the Henry E. Huntington Library, San Marino, Calif. A brief unpublished autobiography is in the Bancroft Library, Berkeley. Correspondence to and from Snow and records of her organizational activities are scattered throughout various collections in the Latter-day Saints Church Archives. A popular biography is Keith Terry and Ann Terry, *Eliza* (1981). More recent is Maureen Ursenbach Beecher, *Eliza and Her Sisters* (1991). An obituary is in *Deseret News*, 5 Dec. 1887.

MAUREEN URSENBACH BEECHER

SNOW, Jessie Baker (26 May 1868–16 June 1947), civil engineer, was born in Nantucket, Massachusetts, the son of Charles Earle Snow and Emily Jane Carpenter. His father operated a packet schooner and later became a merchant. Jessie Snow graduated in 1889 from Union College in Schenectady, New York, with a bachelor's degree in civil engineering. He immediately spent a few months in a field position working in Goshen and Long Island City, New York, surveying and estimating costs for sewage and drainage works. He then returned to Nantucket to open a private practice in which he designed and built the town's first horse-drawn streetcar and began work on a sanitation system that was only partially constructed. From the beginning Snow's career benefited from the enormous expansion of American cities and towns at the end of the nineteenth century.

Until the turn of the century Snow worked on a variety of municipal works projects in numerous cities. In 1891 he moved to West Superior, Wisconsin, to practice as a land surveyor. A bout of typhoid fever sent him home to recuperate; he then spent a year constructing street railways and surveying land subdivisions in North Tonawanda, New York. In 1893 he and T. W. Barrally formed the municipal engineering firm of Barrally & Snow, which acted as city engineer for both North Tonawanda and nearby Tonawanda. The firm designed and constructed sewers, brick and macadam pavements, eight miles of electric street railway, bridges, culverts, and extensions to the water system, including new intake piers in the Niagara River. After five years Snow terminated the partnership and became resident engineer on waterworks and sewer construction projects in five towns in New York, Pennsylvania, and Ohio. In 1902, based on his experience constructing ten miles of single track for the Jamestown, Chatauqua and Lake Erie Railroad, he was appointed chief engineer for two other railway companies. He secured rights of way and constructed railways between South Amboy and Red Bank, New Jersey, for the Jersey City Transit Company and between Avondale, Pennsylvania, and Brandywine, Delaware, for the West Chester, Kennett and Wilmington Electric Railway. During 1904 he again superintended a wide variety of public works projects, including a railroad at Occoquan, Virginia; a waterworks improvement at Bellaire and Portsmouth, Ohio; a power development project at Walling, Tennessee; and surveys for New York City.

During these peripatetic years, Snow married twice. In 1894 he wed Eleanor Curtis Harmon in Schenectady, New York. They had a daughter and a son before she died. In 1903 he married May Purdy, with whom he had one son.

In 1905 Snow first undertook the type of tunneling engineering work for which he later became a recognized expert. He worked until 1910 for the Pennsylvania, New York and Long Island Railroad Company (later the Pennsylvania Tunnel and Terminal Railway), first as inspector, then as first assistant to the engineer in charge. Using the technique of construction under compressed-air conditions, the engineers constructed a railroad tube under the North River to connect Manhattan, New York, and Jersey City, New Jersey. Compressed air permitted excavation under the water table until mechanical supports could be installed, but it sometimes afflicted workers with "the bends," a hazard more commonly faced by divers from the high pressure experienced in deep water. Snow then applied this experience to the reconstruction in 1910 of Hausen Lake Dam near Helena, Montana, for the Foundation Company of New York City. In 1911 he served as engineer for the Canada Syndicate Ltd. of Montreal, Canada, surveying and designing large hydroelectric projects.

In 1914 Snow returned to tunnel engineering and to New York City, joining the Public Service Commission as resident engineer. Before he retired in 1945 he was associated with the construction of five rapid transit tunnels in New York City. Between 1914 and 1919 he worked on two tunnels to Brooklyn, from Old Slip–Clark Street and from Fourteenth Street. From 1919 to 1921 he served as principal assistant to the chief engineer of the New York–New Jersey Interstate Commission, which planned the Holland Tunnel. In 1921 he became tunnel engineer for the Board of Estimate and Apportionment of New York City. When the Board of Transportation was created in 1924, Snow was appointed one of its engineers. Promoted to division engineer in 1925, he acted as chief engineer in 1933 before his appointment to the position the following year. During his tenure as chief, he oversaw the expansion and improvement of the city's subway system. He designed and built new subway lines, maintained the network of lines, and razed elevated lines. During this time he also served as a consultant to the New York City Tunnel Authority on the construction of two vehicular tunnels, the Queens-Midtown tunnel

from 1936 to 1939 and the Brooklyn-Battery tunnel from 1940 to 1943.

Snow's experience proved so valuable that the city extended his employment several times after the mandatory retirement age of seventy. To argue for one of these extensions, Board of Transportation chair John H. Delaney wrote in 1940 that Snow's service was "as nearly indispensable at this time as any person's service can be" (*New York Times*, 18 June 1947). That year several New York City rapid transit lines were consolidated, and Snow became chief engineer of the entire system. Regarded as one of the world's foremost experts in subway engineering, he is credited with several technical advances in the field of subaqueous tunnel construction. He improved the design of the cast-iron rings that bound tunnels by adding a third and intermediate rib perpendicular to the tunnel. This stiffened the tunnels, allowing for the construction of larger rings and therefore wider tunnels. He also junctioned river shields, the steel framework that supported excavation, in earth instead of rock. One noteworthy feat of engineering involved raising the bottom of a portion of the East River to allow for the construction of two Queens-Midtown tunnels while still providing enough earth and stone to cover and protect the tunnels. Snow worked almost until his death in Great Neck, New York.

• Archival materials relating to Snow's tunnel engineering are located in the James Forgie Collection at the Smithsonian Institution. (Forgie was a prominent consulting tunnel engineer who worked in the New York City area at the same time as Snow.) Obituaries are in the *New York Times*, 18 June 1947, and *Transactions of the American Society of Civil Engineers* 113 (1948): 1550–55.

HELEN M. ROZWADOWSKI

SNOW, Lorenzo (3 Apr. 1814–10 Oct. 1901), fifth president of the Mormon Church, was born in Mantua, Ohio, the son of Oliver Snow and Rosetta L. Pettibone. Lorenzo spent his childhood in Portage County, Ohio, and he received his academic training in Ravenna, Ohio. He entered Oberlin College in Amherst, Ohio, in 1835, but left in 1836 to investigate schools in the East. En route he visited his sister Eliza in Kirtland, Ohio. Eliza was a member of the newly founded Mormon church, and she introduced her brother to Joseph Smith, the prophet of the church. Snow embraced the church's teachings and was baptized. He briefly attended a Hebrew school in Kirtland before serving the proselytizing missions in Ohio (1837), Kentucky, Illinois, and Missouri (1838), and England (1840), where he visited with Queen Victoria and presented her with a Book of Mormon.

After his mission Snow returned to the church's new settlement in Nauvoo, Illinois. There he helped to form the Nauvoo Legion, the largest armed militia in Illinois, and he became a captain in the legion. In the spring of 1844 he joined the campaign effort to elect Smith as president of the United States. Smith's murder in June 1844 ended these efforts, and Snow returned to Nauvoo to assist the church members in their westward exodus. Adhering to the church doctrine of plural marriage, he married Harriet Amelia Squires and Charlotte Squires in 1844. In 1845 he married Hannah Goddard and Mary Ann Goddard. Later wives included Sarah Ann Prichard (1845), Elanor Houtz (1848), Caroline Horton (1853), Mary Elizabeth Houtz (1857), Phoebe Amelia Woodruff (1859), and Sarah Minnie Jensen (1871). He had forty-two children.

In February 1846 Snow led a group of pioneers across the frozen Mississippi River into Iowa. He continued to lead the company, which constituted the main body of the Mormons, across the plains. Snow was delayed on the trek by illness, and he did not reach the Salt Lake Valley until 1848. In 1849 he was called to be an apostle and was ordained a member of the Quorum of the Twelve by Mormon leader Brigham Young. Snow helped to organize the Perpetual Emigration Fund to assist in the moving of Mormons living in Europe to the Utah Territory. In 1850 he was elected as a senator of the provisional state of Deseret. Between 1850 and 1852 Snow served on a church mission to Europe, during which he translated the Book of Mormon into Italian and established missionary work in Switzerland.

In 1852 Snow organized the Polysophical Society in Salt Lake City to "cultivate a taste for culture and literature among the saints." The following year he presided over the colonization of Brigham City, Utah. In 1864 he accompanied Joseph F. Smith and Ezra T. Benson, two church apostles, on a mission to the Sandwich Isles in Hawaii, where he nearly died in a boating accident. He returned to Brigham City in 1865 and organized the Brigham City Mercantile and Manufacturing Association.

Between 1872 and 1882 Snow served as president of the Utah Territorial Legislature. He then served as a counselor to church president Brigham Young between 1873 and 1877. A controversy ensued between the church and federal government over the legality of polygamy. In 1882 Congress passed the Edmunds-Tucker Act, which made polygamy unlawful. In 1885 Snow and others were arrested for "unlawful cohabitation." He served an eleven-month sentence between March 1886 and February 1887. His case was reversed by the Supreme Court on 8 February 1887, and he was released from prison. In 1889 Snow became president of the Quorum of the Twelve, and in 1893 he became the first president of the Salt Lake Temple, which was completed that year after forty years of construction. In 1898, at age eighty-four, Snow became the fifth president of the Church of Jesus Christ of Latter-day Saints, after the death of Wilford Woodruff.

Snow is best known for his success in alleviating church debt. Under the Edmunds-Tucker Act many church properties were confiscated, causing hardship for the church and its members. Snow's retrenchment plan consolidated debts into a bond, stopped borrowing for investments, and sold controlling interests in many businesses. In 1899 he initiated a drive to reem-phasize the law of tithing by visiting several Utah settlements. The retrenchment plan was primarily responsible for restoring church solvency. Snow's work set a pattern for church financial management that continued throughout subsequent church administrations. The church also saw the first calling of women to missionary service under Snow's administration. In 1898 Harriet Nye, the wife of E. H. Nye, president of the California mission, was commissioned as a missionary. Snow's primary contribution to Mormon principles was the doctrine of eternal progression, which espoused, "As man now is, God once was; as God now is, man may become." Snow died in Salt Lake City.

• Personal papers are in the Lorenzo Snow Diary, LDS Church Archives, Salt Lake City, Utah. For information on Snow, see Francis M. Gibbons, *Lorenzo Snow: Spiritual Giant, Prophet of God* (1982); Thomas C. Romney, *The Life of Lorenzo Snow* (1955); and Richard S. Van Wagoner and Stephen C. Walker, *A Book of Mormons* (1982). An obituary is in the *Deseret Evening News*, 10 Oct. 1901.

EDWARD E. ADAMS

SNOW, Wilbert (6 Apr. 1884–28 Sept. 1977), college professor, poet, and politician, was born Charles Wilbert Snow on White Head Island, St. George, Maine, the son of Forrest Alwin Snow, a coast guardsman, and Katherine Frances Quinn, the Canadian-born daughter of Irish immigrants. When he was seven the family moved to Spruce Head on the mainland so that four of the six children could attend the village school. Before attending high school in Thomaston, Maine, Snow worked for three years as a lobsterman, deepening his acquaintance with the tasks and rhythms of the coastal life that were to figure in his poetry. After high school he worked in a stone quarry. Fired for trying to organize the laborers there, he taught for two short periods in rural schools. Seeing in both settings the plight of people who worked hard and faced retirement with no pensions and little savings motivated Snow to improve social conditions through political action.

With some scholarship assistance, Snow worked his way through Bowdoin College, graduating in 1907 as a member of Phi Beta Kappa and the first recipient of the Longfellow Fellowship for further study. Given a one-year replacement appointment at New York University as an English instructor and debating coach, he enrolled concurrently as a graduate student in English at Columbia University. He returned to Bowdoin on a temporary appointment (1908–1909) and was next at Williams College (1909–1910). He would have taught at Miami University in Ohio the following year, with his recently completed master's degree (1910) from Columbia in hand, but before classes began the new president asked him to leave: he regarded Snow as a "boat-rocker" who "talk[ed] too plainly with undergraduates about politics and religion," according to Snow's autobiography, *Codline's Child* (p. 130). This "humiliating defeat" left Snow free to accept the most unlikely assignment of his long career, that of Eskimo teacher and reindeer agent in Alaska (1911–1912). He taught in the school in Council City on the Seward peninsula and administered a faltering program in which herders were to teach the natives the breeding and training of reindeer.

After this exhilarating adventure, Snow returned to campus life, first at the University of Utah (1913–1915), where he was dismissed for protesting against what he regarded as unjust dismissals of faculty members. He was next at Indiana University (1916–1918), where for the first time he did not have to teach argumentation and coach debating. He left late in the first year to join the U.S. Army; he served in the field artillery from April 1917 to late November 1918, when he was discharged as a first lieutenant. For a brief period in 1918–1919 he was acting professor of English at Reed College. He returned to Indiana University as an assistant professor and remained there until 1921, when he joined the English faculty of Wesleyan University in Middletown, Connecticut, at the same rank. In 1922 he married Jeannette Simmons, a social worker, with whom he had five children. At Wesleyan he advanced to associate professor in 1926 and to professor in 1929, the position he held until his retirement in 1952.

A lack of a Ph.D. was a hindrance, but Snow published in national magazines and gained recognition as a poet. Reviewing his first book, *Maine Coast* (1923), Harriet Monroe observed that "although Mr. Snow may be in the school [of Robert Frost] . . . , he has his own eye and mind and voice, and he is telling his own story" (*Poetry*, Oct. 1923). His second collection, *The Inner Harbor* (1926), was likewise successful. Concerning his third book, *Down East* (1932), Snow wrote, "To my great relief, the reviewers this time ceased saying that my verse was an echo of Frost" (*Codline's Child*, p. 365). By 1932 Snow's years as a self-described "academic tramp" were long over. A liberal Democratic party stalwart and active school board member, Snow also helped found the Connecticut Association of Boards of Education and was its president in 1940.

Well known throughout the state because of his active campaigning for candidates and causes, Snow was elected lieutenant governor of Connecticut in 1944. In 1946 he ran for governor against Republican James L. McConaughy, the president of Wesleyan University. Snow lost by a vote of 371,852 to 276,335, but when incumbent Raymond E. Baldwin resigned late in 1946 to fill a vacancy in the U.S. Senate, Snow succeeded him and served as governor from 27 December 1946 to 8 January 1947. Failing to win the Democratic nomination for the U.S. Senate race in 1950, he limited his public activity to efforts to improve education and helped establish a local community college. About his withdrawal from active politics, Snow wrote, "Poetry still held first place in my life and always would. So I left the hustings with few regrets" (*Codline's Child*, p. 455).

When Snow's *Collected Poems* appeared, one reviewer wrote, "His range is impressive, from the long story in verse to the brief lyric of a single image. In all, he sustains the form strictly, surely. One is aware of his force and his fine feeling. The vigor of his plain-spoken awareness of life comes through directly" (*Commonweal*, 8 May 1964). Snow was not just a regional poet: his *Sonnets to Steve*, in memory of his son who died at fifteen, won the *Saturday Review of Literature* poetry prize in 1957. But he is mainly perceived as one, as in David Perkins's noting that "Snow's poems convincingly express his love for the country along Maine's Penobscot Bay" (*A History of Modern Poetry* [1976], p. 387).

In 1951–1952 Snow was special lecturer on American literature and culture for the State Department and spoke to various audiences in Europe and Asia. He was a visiting professor at Spelman College and Morehouse College in Atlanta in 1953–1954. At its fortieth reunion, the Wesleyan class of 1927 voted that its alumni contribution be given to Snow to use for research and clerical help in writing his autobiography. *Codline's Child: The Autobiography of Wilbert Snow*, published on his ninetieth birthday in 1974, is a richly detailed and frank account of his extraordinary life, which included friendship with Robert Frost, Carl Sandburg, Vachel Lindsay, Wallace Stevens, and many other poets.

In retirement Snow continued to maintain his many friendships and interests and to write poetry. In good health to the last day of his life, he died suddenly in his summer cottage on Spruce Head Island, Maine. Senator Abraham Ribicoff of Connecticut, speaking in memory of Snow on the floor of the U.S. Senate in 1977, called him "gentle, wise, and humane . . . one of those rare human beings who lived his life absolutely free of vanity, a man who did not have a pretentious bone in his body."

• The Wesleyan University Archives contain large quantities of Snow's papers, including his correspondence with Robert Frost and Charles Olson. In addition to his books mentioned above, he also published *Maine Tides* (1940). *The Collected Poems of Wilbert Snow* was published in 1963 with a second edition in 1973. An article in the *Hartford (Conn.) Courant*, 30 Sept. 1977, discusses the years after the publication of Snow's autobiography. A concise article on Snow is in the *Biographical Directory of the Governors of the United States, 1789–1978*, vol. 1. For an appreciation by one of Snow's former students, the poet George P. Morrill, see "So Long, Bill: The Passing of a True Original," *Wesleyan University Alumnus* 62 (Fall/Winter 1977): 20–21. Obituaries are in the *New York Times* and the *Middletown (Conn.) Press*, 29 Sept. 1977.

VINCENT FREIMARCK

SNOW, William Freeman (13 July 1874–12 June 1950), public health administrator, was born in Quincy, Illinois, the son of William Snow, a small merchant, and Emily Streeter. As a young boy he moved with his family to Biggs, California, where his father opened a general store. After completing his secondary education, he matriculated at Stanford University, where he received his B.A. in chemistry (1896) and his M.A. in physiology (1897). He then enrolled in San Francisco's Cooper Medical College. In 1899 he married Blanche Malvina Boring, with whom he would have two children.

While at Cooper, Snow became concerned about the medical and health care of his fellow students and cofounded the Students' Guild, one of the first student health organizations in the United States. After receiving his M.D. in 1900, he obtained a position at Stanford as director of student health services and opened a private practice in Palo Alto. In 1901 he went to Johns Hopkins University to conduct postgraduate research in ophthalmology, but he returned to Stanford in 1902 as an assistant professor of hygiene. In 1903 he was promoted to associate professor and also became a deputy county health officer and voluntary epidemiologist for the state board of health.

Snow's growing interest in public health led him to convert an old railroad passenger car into a mobile health exhibit that he and his students accompanied on its journeys across the state to educate Californians about preventing the spread of disease. So successful were his efforts at promoting public health education that in 1909, the same year he was promoted to professor of hygiene and public health, he was also appointed secretary and executive officer of the state board of health.

That same year Snow became part of the movement spearheaded by Prince A. Morrow, founder of what became known as the American Federation for Sex Hygiene (AFSH), against the spread of venereal diseases. Because these diseases were closely linked in the public mind with illicit sex, particularly prostitution, their discussion was taboo in polite society, and many Americans lived in virtual ignorance of their existence. By cofounding the California Association for the Study and Prevention of Syphilis and Gonococcus Infections, Snow played an instrumental role in making California the first state to require that the contraction of a venereal disease be reported to state health officials. In 1910 he became an active member of Morrow's society, and three years later he helped to merge the AFSH with the American Vigilance Association (AVA) to form the American Social Hygiene Association (ASHA).

In 1914 Snow moved to New York City to become ASHA's first general secretary. His greatest challenge involved reconciling the former members of the two parent organizations: while AFSH had regarded the venereal disease epidemic as a medical problem, AVA had seen it as a moral problem. Much heated debate surrounded proposals for government-dispensed chemical prophylaxes and inspection of prostitutes because these methods were seen by many as compounding rather than solving the problem. Snow understood that controlling venereal diseases involved both medicine and morals, and he attacked the problem on both fronts. He oversaw ASHA programs to distribute educational leaflets and urged the media to break their silence regarding venereal diseases. He also worked to limit prostitution by educating the general public and by pressuring the federal government. Because many Americans believed that men possessed much stronger sexual drives than women and that masturbation caused insanity, they tolerated prostitution as a "necessary evil." Under Snow's leadership ASHA collected accurate figures and publicized case studies concerning the traffic in women and children that prostitution stimulated, portraying prostitution as a sordid business that enriched madams, pimps, and corrupt local officials while exploiting innocent victims. The society also urged the federal government to ban prostitution from the environs of military bases and encampments and to educate servicemen about venereal diseases.

During World War I Snow served in the U.S. Army Medical Corps as a lieutenant colonel. He was sent to France to protect American service personnel against venereal diseases by implementing programs to educate and treat servicemen, repress prostitution, and provide alternate forms of recreation. He also served as secretary of the Council of National Defense's General Medical Board, chair of its Committee on Civilian Cooperation in Combating Venereal Diseases, and chair of the executive committee of the U.S. Interdepartmental Social Hygiene Board.

In 1920 Snow resigned from Stanford, having been on leave for eleven years, and returned to Johns Hopkins as a lecturer in hygiene. In 1928 he became a lecturer in health education at Columbia University. Between 1930 and 1936 he also taught preventive medicine at New York University. Meanwhile, he continued to campaign against the spread of syphilis and gonorrhea by writing *The Venereal Diseases: Their Medical, Nursing, and Community Aspects* (1924) and by pushing for sex education in public schools. Although he resigned as ASHA's general director in 1938, the same year that the federal Venereal Disease Control Act was signed into law, he continued to play an active role in the campaign against venereal diseases by serving as chair of ASHA's executive committee in 1940, chair of its board of directors in 1944, and president of the International Union against the Venereal Diseases from 1946 to 1950.

Snow served as president of the Association of State and Provincial Boards of Health (1912–1913) and of the National Health Council (1927–1934). He was editor of the *Journal of Social Hygiene* (1914–1919), chair of the League of Nations' Committee to Study Traffic in Women and Children (1924–1928), and special consultant to the U.S. Public Health Service (1936–1950). He was awarded a knighthood in the French Legion of Honor in 1921, the Spanish Order of Isabella the Catholic in 1926, and ASHA's first William Freeman Snow Medal. He died in Bangor, Maine.

Snow contributed to the advance of American society by guiding the social hygiene movement for more than twenty years. His efforts contributed significantly to the drastic reduction of venereal diseases and organized prostitution.

• A brief biography of Snow is Charles Walter Clarke, "William F. Snow: Great and Good Man," in Clarke's *Taboo: The Story of the Pioneers of Social Hygiene* (1961), pp. 70–85. The Dec. 1937 and Dec. 1950 special issues of the *Journal of Social Hygiene* also contain much biographical information on him.

CHARLES W. CAREY, JR.

SNOWDEN, Elmer (10 Sept. or 9 Oct. 1900–14 May 1973), banjo, guitar, and sax player, was born in Baltimore, Maryland (parents' names unavailable from the public record, and exact birth date varies depending on source). In 1915 he began his career in his hometown playing a New Orleans–derived jazz with pianist-composer-leader Eubie Blake and later with pianist Gertie Wells, to whom he was married for several years during the early 1920s. By 1921 he had migrated to nearby Washington, D.C., where he jobbed with Louis Thomas and Claude Hopkins and his own eight-piece group, which played alternately with Duke Ellington's trio. (Snowden appears to have played banjo with Ellington's group earlier, from 1919 to 1920, but this is not reported conclusively.) Snowden's Washington band included Sonny Greer, drums, Arthur Whetsol, trumpet, and Otto Hardwick, sax; the three would later be long-term members of the Ellington orchestra.

Bolstered by the belief that singer-pianist-raconteur Fats Waller was to join the group as featured artist, Snowden and band moved their operation to New York City in 1923. The Waller association proved to be a false start, but a serendipitous happy ending was that in 1924 Ellington joined the band on piano, "replacing" the no-show Waller. This began an arrangement wherein Snowden was nominal leader (financial matters, managerial details), while Ellington was responsible for conducting rehearsals, planning music, and "setting moods" (which probably meant just "counting off" the beat for each number) during performances. At this time the band's name was changed to the Washingtonians in recognition of their geographical past. Key members of the Snowden/Ellington group were Bubber Miley, trumpet (who replaced Whetsol), Charlie Irvis, trombone (soon to be replaced by Tricky Sam Nanton), Hardwick, reeds, Fred Guy, banjo and guitar, and Greer, drums. From 1923 until 1927 the band was nominally based in the Hollywood Club (renamed the Kentucky Club in 1924) at Forty-ninth and Broadway.

The Snowden/Ellington co-op connection reached an ignominious end in early 1927 when members of this talented family discovered that their business representative (Snowden) had on occasion cut himself a disproportionate share of the collective proceeds. (After Snowden's departure in December 1927, Ellington enlarged the band, now called The Duke Ellington Orchestra, to begin his historic appearances at the famed Cotton Club in Harlem.)

Snowden was reported by his contemporaries to have been an exceptional banjo player, an instrument whose time in the jazz world had, alas, run out. He also possessed a keen nose for other talents, and his New York network gave him entrée to some of the hottest jazz talent of the Prohibition era. During the late twenties and early thirties he led groups operating in Harlem and Greenwich Village through which passed names destined to play momentous roles in their art's history. At one time he could boast as many as five bands working under his imprimatur in the New York City area. In an impressive succession, his sidemen included Bill "Count" Basie (whom he reputedly fired), Hopkins, Jimmie Lunceford, Chick Webb, Benny Carter, Fats Waller, Roy Eldridge, and Sid Catlett. Snowden and this array of jazz giants played dates at the "in" clubs: the City, the Hot Feet, the Bamville, the Nest, and Small's Paradise. At the Nest, during the 1930s, Snowden's group featured cornetist Rex Stewart, who would later achieve artist status with the Ellington orchestra. During the band's tenure at Small's, during 1930–1931, its lineup included Catlett, Gus Aiken, Dickie Wells, Al Sears, and Hardwick. At this venue Eldridge, on trumpet, had replaced Stewart. The last-named roster was the band featured in a 1932 Warner Bros. film short, provocatively titled *Smash Your Baggage*.

Snowden's career as a performer and leader did not prosper on schedule. In addition to the gradual replacement of banjos by guitars in bands' rhythm sections, he encountered legal difficulties in the early 1930s with the New York City Musicians' Union. The circumstances were serious enough to lead to his expulsion from Local 802 of the American Federation of Musicians for eight years. This direct professional barrier, added to the difficulties musicians commonly experience in their club-to-club, date-by-date existences, soured him on the performing life of New York. He thus moved to Philadelphia in 1933 to teach banjo, mandolin, and reed instruments, maintaining only modest professional status as a part-time performer and leader. During the two decades of 1940 to 1960, after settling his union problems, he occasionally led small groups for limited engagements in clubs in Canada and the northeastern United States. These sorties were sandwiched between short runs in New York City at Jimmy Ryan's and the Metropole.

In 1963 Snowden moved once again, this time with high hopes for a new start, to Berkeley, California, replacing the steel strings on his old banjo with the gut of a guitar. He played the Monterey Jazz Festival that summer with an unlikely yet smashingly successful quartet consisting of oldtimers Darnell Howard and Pops Foster and the young bebop drummer Tony Williams. That success behind him, he took a job at the Berkeley School of Music, teaching there for three years and playing night dates around the Bay Area with trombonist Turk Murphy. Before returning for good to the East Coast, he led his own groups at the Cabale in Berkeley and at the Coffee House in San Francisco; he even joined a European jazz tour in 1967, then returned to his adopted hometown of Philadelphia, where he died. His last big public performance took place at the fledgling Newport Jazz Festival in 1968.

Ralph Gleason tells a touching story in his *Celebrating the Duke* (1975) about a kind of last roundup meeting between Snowden and Ellington in 1963 (shortly after the Monterey Festival, where both had played but on different days). The meeting took place between sets in Ellington's dressing room in San Francisco's Basin Street West, many years after the two aging pros had last seen each other. Gleason says that

the two of them, Duke, the piano player who went on to the heights of show business success, and Snowden, the man who gave him his first job and had gone down steadily ever since, just radiated love and delight at seeing each other. For an hour they sat there, Duke on the cot and Snowden on the chair, and reminisced. "Remember the night . . . ?" "How did such and such go?" "What ever happened to . . . ?" It was a magic moment and I felt privileged to be present as they played the game of Remember When, each trying to catch the other out by bringing up an old nickname or the title of a song neither one of them had played for forty years.

• Snowden figures prominently in an essay in Stanley Dance's *The World of Swing* (1974) and to a lesser degree in Barry Ulanov's *Duke Ellington* (1946). Aside from these short yet revealing vignettes, Snowden has not been the focus of many jazz chronicles, nor have the recordings on which he played been rereleased. He was a competent artist (although perhaps a bit incompetent as a wheeler-dealer entrepreneur) who got caught in the middle of a stylistic shift, from the banjo-grounded repertory of early ensemble jazz to the guitar-lyricism of the swing band era. A discography of his playing, assembled by B. Demeusy, can be found in *Jazz Journal* 16 (1963): 15.

WILLIAM THOMSON

SNOWDEN, James Ross (9 Dec. 1809–21 Mar. 1878), ninth director of the United States Mint, was born in Chester, Pennsylvania, the son of Reverend Nathaniel Randolph Snowden, the curator of Dickinson College, and Sarah Gustine. Snowden attended Dickinson College, a grammar school in Carlisle, Pennsylvania, where his father taught. Later, after studying law, Snowden filled various political posts, including deputy attorney general of Venango County; Democratic member, later Speaker, of the Pennsylvania House of Representatives; and state treasurer. In 1848 he married Susan Engle Patterson, the daughter of General Robert Patterson (no relation to the two Robert Pattersons who were the fourth and sixth mint directors); they had five children. In 1848 he was also appointed treasurer of the United States Mint. He resigned in 1850 to return to the private practice of law. In June 1853 the director of the mint died unexpectedly and Snowden was appointed in his place.

The increased output of gold in California meant that silver had risen in value relative to gold, and Gresham's law (that when monetary instruments tariffed at the same rate are perceived to have different intrinsic values, then the more intrinsically valuable coins are hoarded and the less intrinsically valuable coins are circulated) operated; silver vanished from circulation, replaced by gold and paper. Snowden oversaw the introduction of a three-cent piece with less silver content, which he later named the "trime." Copper prices also rose, so Snowden reduced the size of the cent and eliminated the half cent.

The status of Spanish and Spanish colonial silver as legal tender in the United States ended at the same time, and much of the country's silver was replaced with copper-nickel coins that were not legal tender. In the autumn of 1857, seasonal strains combined with a longer-term shortage of silver to cause a panic, affecting Britain and Northern Europe as well as the United States. In a December 1857 pamphlet, "A Measure Proposed to Secure to the People a Safe Treasury and a Sound Currency," Snowden suggested that the United States mobilize the frozen metal assets by issuing certificates against gold deposits.

Abuses were rife at the mint. Mint officials made fantasy pieces (coins of unusual design struck solely for presentation to dignitaries or for sale to collectors) and coins with phony dates (such as the 1804 dollar) to sell to collectors. A chief offender was Franklin Peale, who manipulated assay ratios to cheat depositors of gold, sabotaged machinery proposed by people who were not members of the mint's inner circle, spent public monies on private scientific experiments, and was running his own private medal business. Snowden fired Peale, but would not break fully with the mint's establishment, composed primarily of Presbyterians who wanted to hire only fellow Presbyterians or members of certain families. Snowden began to put together a collection of Washington medals for the mint's cabinet and had various fantasy pieces and restrikes made to exchange with collectors. This included fantasy half dimes without "UNITED STATES" on the reverse. Snowden ordered the engraving of a new reverse die for the 1804 fantasy dollar. Unfortunately the mint's night watchman began to strike 1804 dollars on his own. Snowden discovered the scandal, seized the dies, and transferred them to his private vault. It is telling that Snowden stopped the abuses only when scandal forced him to act.

In 1860 "A Description of Ancient and Modern Coins in the Cabinet Collection at the Mint of the United States" was published under Snowden's name. The text, however, was actually written by the curator, George Bull, and the assistant assayer, William Ewing Dubois. "A Description of the Medals of Washington," Snowden's own work, appeared the following year; it also contains much useful information about early mint practices, such as the name of the model for Liberty on early United States coins (Anne Willing Bingham). Snowden assembled the collection with more eagerness than scholarship, so there are some outrageous fakes (for example, the George Washington half cent). In 1859 Snowden's fellow officers at the mint had a medal struck in his honor. It was engraved by Anthony Paquet.

In 1861 Snowden lost his job as director of the mint and became prothonotary of the Pennsylvania Supreme Court. In 1864 he published *Coins of the Bible, and Its Money Terms*. It is a capable work, although it repeats many errors common at the time, such as attributing the coinage of silver shekels to the Maccabees. In March 1867 Snowden delivered a biographical sketch of the life of the Cornplanter, chief of the Senecas, when the memorial to Cornplanter was unveiled. This was published as "An Historical Sketch of Gy-ant-wa-chia, the Cornplanter, and of the Six Nations of Indians." In November 1869 he delivered a paper before the Numismatic and Antiquarian Society of Philadelphia entitled "International Coinage" (published in *Lippincott's Magazine* two months later), discussing the proposal of the Paris Convention of 1867 in favor of an international coinage. Snowden argued that the idea of an international coinage was less attractive than proponents thought but that if it were put into effect, the United States gold dollar should be adopted as its basis because the dollar was the most sensible system then existing—a view based more on chauvinism than on logic.

In politics, Snowden remained a traditional antebellum northern Democrat. The following passage from his diary, dated 2 April 1864, is characteristic of his views:

Did not go to the President's house, nor to his levee. The latter was, I am informed, but poorly attended. *Negroes in uniform were admitted!!* Alas, the days of Jackson, Polk, Pierce and other great men have for a time departed, with Webster, Clay, Wright, Benton, King and others gone. There seems to be no one to take their places. Nothing can save the country from destruction but a return to democratic men and measures with the rights of the states protected, and the Constitution rigidly adhered to and enforced.

A devout Presbyterian, Snowden attended church twice a day on Sunday. He died in Hulmeville, Bucks County, Pennsylvania.

Snowden presided over numerous innovations as director of the mint: the change from the large cent to the small cent, the redemption of the old Spanish and Spanish colonial silver, and a huge influx of gold from California. So far as maintaining mint production is concerned, he seems to have been a capable manager. He took some steps to end the widespread abuses and crookedness at the mint but did not have the character to clean it up entirely. He also committed some offenses himself, such as ordering the creation of fantasy half dimes and the engraving of a new reverse die for the 1804 dollar.

• Some of Snowden's correspondence is in the Historical Society of Pennsylvania, as are two of his diaries (covering the years 1825 and 1864–1865) and the diaries of his father. For background on Snowden's political career, see Charles McCool Snyder, *The Jacksonian Heritage: Pennsylvania Politics 1833–1848* (1958); Snowden is mentioned twice. The best account of Snowden's career at the mint is an article by Robert W. Julian, "Master of the Mint: James Snowden Enriched Our Numismatic Heritage," *COINage* 25 (July 1989): 116, 118. For further appraisals of his career at the mint, see Don Taxay, *The U.S. Mint and Coinage. An Illustrated History from 1776 to the Present* (1966); Walter Breen, *Walter Breen's Complete Encyclopedia of U.S. and Colonial Coins* (1988); and Eric P. Newman and Kenneth E. Bressett, *The Fantastic 1804 Dollar* (1962). Breen, "Semiofficial Restrikes of the Philadelphia Mint," *Numismatist* 66 (Oct. 1953): 1038–39, documents Snowden's involvement in the large-scale production of restrikes. On the Snowden medal of 1859, see Robert W. Julian in *Medals of the United States Mint: The First Century 1792–1892*, ed. N. Neil Harris (1977), p. 180; the medal depicted there is not an original but a modern striking by the mint, made from new dies.

JOHN M. KLEEBERG

SNYDER, John Wesley (21 June 1895–8 Oct. 1985), banker, federal administrator, and secretary of the Treasury, was born in Jonesboro, Arkansas, the son of Jerre Hartwell Snyder, a druggist, and Ellen Hatcher. He graduated from Jonesboro High School in 1914 and attended Vanderbilt University, seeking a degree in electrical engineering. Because of financial hardship, he left Vanderbilt in 1915 to work for his uncle, Judge E. A. Rolfe, in Forrest City, Arkansas.

With U.S. involvement in World War I, Snyder attended officers training camp at Fort Logan H. Roots, Arkansas, from May to August 1917 and was then commissioned a second lieutenant in the field artillery. He was assigned to the Fifty-seventh Field Artillery Brigade staff in France and the army of occupation. In June 1919 he returned to the United States, accepting a position with the First National Bank of Forrest City. In 1920 he married Evlyn Cook; they had one child.

During the 1920s Snyder worked with several banks in Missouri and Arkansas. In 1930 he was appointed to the Insolvent Division of the Office of the Comptroller of Currency. He was the receiver of several national banks in the St. Louis area and was responsible for reorganizing or liquidating them. In 1937 he was appointed manager of the St. Louis office of the Reconstruction Finance Corporation (RFC). Three years later Snyder accepted an appointment to help set up the Defense Plant Corporation (DPC). During his tenure as head of the DPC, between $7 and $11 billion (sources vary) was committed to finance defense plants. In 1943 he returned to the First National Bank of St. Louis as executive vice president.

No person wielded more influence on Snyder's public career than Harry S. Truman, whom Snyder first met at Fort Riley, Kansas, in 1928. That relationship matured during the 1930s. In 1940 Snyder served as a key fundraiser in Truman's reelection campaign to the U.S. Senate. In 1944 he accompanied Truman to the Democratic National Convention. Although Truman disavowed any interest in his party's nomination for vice president, Snyder, without Truman's knowledge, privately worked to help secure this nomination for Truman.

When President Franklin D. Roosevelt died on 12 April 1945, Snyder was in Mexico negotiating a standard exchange rate for the peso. Truman called Snyder shortly thereafter and asked him to return to

Washington immediately. Snyder sacrificed his future in banking to accept Truman's offer of the post of federal loan administrator in April 1945. During Snyder's ten weeks in office, Congress authorized him to merge defense subsidiaries into the RFC and start selling properties to private industries.

On 23 July 1945 Truman promoted Snyder to director of the Office of War Mobilization and Reconversion. Snyder steered the GI Bill through Congress and in June 1946 reported that the nation had largely converted to a peacetime economy without creating massive unemployment. Exhibiting his respect for Snyder's abilities, Truman nominated him as secretary of the Treasury. The Senate confirmed his nomination in June 1946.

Snyder served Truman as a friend and a conservative adviser. During 1946–1947 he opposed the extension of price controls, much of the president's 21-point postwar domestic program, Truman's request for authority to establish fact-finding boards to investigate labor disputes, and Truman's veto of the Taft-Hartley Act in 1947. He could argue heatedly with the president over difficult policy decisions but always supported whatever decision Truman made.

Snyder's first task as Treasury secretary was the reorganization of the department for peacetime operations. He developed a work simplification program, which reduced Treasury personnel by 16 percent and instituted the first uniform accounting system for the federal government. He created the payroll savings plan to reduce the volatility of Treasury securities by encouraging individuals to buy savings bonds. He eliminated currency issues above the $500 denomination to make illegal transactions more difficult, and he was the force behind the Federal Reserve Accord of 1951, which helped slow the rise of interest rates. He appointed Georgia Neese Clark treasurer of the United States, and she became the first woman to hold that position.

Snyder believed that deficit spending created inflation. Consequently, he opposed tax cuts until the budget was balanced. His fiscal conservatism ensured balanced budgets from 1947 to 1949, which enabled the administration to reduce the national debt by about $15 billion. In 1948 he pushed for a tax cut as well as tax reform measures. Given the importance of foreign aid to the Truman administration's containment policy, Snyder helped develop programs to rebuild Germany and Japan and contributed to the drafting of the Marshall Plan and the Truman Doctrine. During his tenure the Treasury Department became a leader in international banking. However, his proposals to reorganize the Bureau of Internal Revenue confronted the Treasury secretary with a major scandal.

In 1950 rumors began to circulate in the press that corruption was rampant within the Bureau of Internal Revenue, and Congress soon began investigations. Eventually almost 200 employees were fired, more than one-third for taking bribes. Snyder took advantage of the scandal to reform the bureau. His major

change eliminated political patronage and created new positions, which were filled through the civil service. Snyder spent the last ten months of his term implementing these reforms.

Snyder served on the North Atlantic Treaty Organization Council from 1949 to 1953, and he was joint chair of the first meeting of the World Bank and International Monetary Fund in September 1946. He served as the U.S. governor of both organizations while at the Treasury Department and became a U.S. adviser to both in 1953.

After leaving the Treasury Department in 1953, Snyder accepted a position as president of the Overland Corporation of Toledo, Ohio. Leaving that position in 1966, he remained on the Overland board of directors and also served as an adviser to the Treasury Department until 1976. He helped found in 1975 the Harry S. Truman Scholarship Foundation, which funds undergraduate and graduate students preparing for careers in public service. He served as chair of the Georgetown University Library Associates from its founding in 1975 until his death and was on the Board of Regents of Georgetown University from 1964 until 1973, serving as its chair in 1970–1971. In 1980 he retired to Seabrook Island, South Carolina, where he died.

A lifelong Democrat, Snyder reluctantly accepted government service. While contemporary critics considered Snyder merely adequate, Truman believed him an excellent Treasury secretary, and he was an influential member of the Truman administration.

• Snyder's papers and an oral history are in the Harry S. Truman Library. See also Donald R. McCoy, *The Presidency of Harry S. Truman* (1984), and Richard Lawrence Miller, *Truman: The Rise to Power* (1986). Obituaries are in the *New York Times* and the *Washington Post*, both 9 Oct. 1985.

RICK D. MEDLIN

SNYDER, Simon (5 Nov. 1759–9 Nov. 1819), governor of Pennsylvania, was born in Lancaster, Pennsylvania, the son of Anthony Snyder (Anton Schneider), a poor mechanic, and Maria Elizabeth Knippenburg Kraemer. When his father, who had emigrated from the Palatinate to America in 1758, died in 1774, Snyder apprenticed himself for four years to a tanner in York, Pennsylvania. Lacking a formal education, he attended night school taught by a Quaker and spent his leisure time in study. A man of deep piety, he became a member of the Moravian church. In 1784, at a time of depression and economic hardship, he established himself as a storekeeper and mill owner in Selin's Grove (now Selinsgrove), Northumberland County, in North Central Pennsylvania. He earned a reputation for being a clever and successful businessman and acquired a small fortune. Also serving his neighbors as a scrivener, he was soon held in high esteem and became popular in the community. He was married three times, in 1790 to Elizabeth Michael, who died in

1794; in 1796 to Catherine Antes, who died in 1810; and to Mary Slough Scott in 1814. He had two children in his first marriage and five in his second.

Snyder began his career in public life as a justice of the peace and judge of the Court of Common Pleas of Northumberland County. In 1789–1790 he participated in the deliberations of the constitutional convention in Philadelphia that adjusted the Pennsylvania revolutionary government to the new federal system. Representing the radical Republican elements of the backcountry, who attracted national attention during the "Whiskey Rebellion" of 1794 with their refusal to pay taxes and their rhetoric against the mercantile interests of the coastal cities, he served in the Pennsylvania Assembly (house of representatives) from 1797 to 1807. In 1802 he was elected Speaker, a position he held for three terms (1804, 1805, and 1807) until he retired. As a leader of the Radical party and in accordance with his democratic convictions, he fought to restrict the executive powers of the governor as well as the competencies of the judiciary. Among other reform measures, he successfully sponsored the so-called hundred dollar act, which, to discourage litigation except in serious cases, allowed justices of the peace or arbitrators to deal with civil suits concerning issues of less than $100.

Snyder's rising popularity induced the antijudiciary Republicans (or Duane-Leib wing, which called for a revision of the state constitution) to nominate him for governor in 1805. Although vigorously supported by the major newspaper of his party, the *Republican Argus* of Northumberland, he lost to the incumbent, Governor Thomas McKean, whose faction joined forces with the Federalists. Back in the legislature, Snyder's attempt to impeach the governor on several grounds, including nepotism and the use of a facsimile stamp to sign bills, also failed. However, in 1808, when McKean's third term ended, Snyder won the gubernatorial race as a candidate for the Jeffersonian Republicans. Being first in line of a number of so-called Dutch governors (i.e., governors of German origin or ancestry), he was reelected by clear majorities in 1811 and 1814. These victories attested to the growing strength of the agrarian backcountry in relation to the more commercial eastern counties and cities.

Inspired by Thomas Jefferson's simplicity, Snyder at first changed the style of government, for example, by sending his messages to the legislature in writing instead of delivering them in person. Besides advocating reform measures, such as making public education more accessible, mitigating the law for debt imprisonment, and abolishing the death penalty, he pushed for a program of internal improvements. In monetary affairs he transferred Jefferson's antipathy against a national bank to the state level by attacking state banks as instruments of the "privileged orders" and speculators. The assembly nevertheless established the banks over his veto.

His strong states' rights position brought him into conflict with the federal government when, in 1809, he called out the state militia to prevent a federal court from enforcing its decision in the Olmstead case, a dispute between the state and federal government over the prize money of a captured vessel. In the end, however, he accepted under protest the authority of the federal government. During the war against Great Britain from 1812 to 1814, he actively supported the political and military course followed by the James Madison administration.

When he left the governorship in December 1817, Snyder was elected to the state senate. After serving for several months, he died at his home in Selinsgrove. Snyder County, Pennsylvania, was named after him.

Snyder's career is remarkable insofar as he rose to the highest position in the state of Pennsylvania without having a brilliant military or legal record. Modest and reliable, sometimes rigid and stubborn, with strong convictions and a sense of duty, he personified the virtues and limits of the "backcountry democracy" in the early national period. By his example he undoubtedly helped to raise the political consciousness and assertiveness of his predominantly agrarian constituency.

• Primary sources are included in the Military Manuscript Collection, the Hiester Family Papers, and the Snyder Family Collection, all located at the Pennsylvania State Archives. Published sources include "Autobiographical Notes by Simon Snyder," *Pennsylvania Magazine of History and Biography* 4 (1880): 248–49, and "Papers of Governor Simon Snyder," *Pennsylvania Archives*, 4th ser., 4 (1900): 657–965. Written from a family perspective is M. K. Snyder, *Life of Governor Simon Snyder* (1888). Snyder is also mentioned in J. B. Linn, *Annals of Buffalo Valley, Pa.* (1877), and in W. G. Wagenseller, comp., *Snyder County Annals*, vol. 1 (1919). Valuable information about party politics of the time is contained in J. H. Peeling, "Governor McKean and the Pennsylvania Jacobins," *Pennsylvania Magazine of History and Biography* 54 (1930): 320–54. Also informative is Sandford W. Higginbotham, *The Keystone in the Democratic Arch: Pennsylvania Politics 1800–1816* (1952).

JÜRGEN HEIDEKING

SOBEL, Janet (30 May 1894–11 Nov. 1968), painter, was born Jennie Lechovsky in Ekaterinoslav, a village outside of Kiev, Ukraine, the daughter of Bernard Lechovsky and Fanny Kahn. Her mother was a midwife, but little is known about her father, who was killed in a pogrom. Janet's widowed mother immigrated with her two sons and daughter to the United States in 1908. At Ellis Island, officials gave them the surname "Wilson." In 1910, at the age of sixteen, Janet married Russian immigrant Max Sobel, an engraver and goldsmith, with whom she had five children. Until 1947, they lived for the most part in Brooklyn. Though she had little formal education, Sobel was literate in Russian, Yiddish, and English. She studied the Bible and the writings of Plato, and she spoke philosophically about her art.

In 1937, after a rather conventional life as a housewife, mother, and grandmother, and with no formal art training, Sobel suddenly took up painting. Her impetus came from her teenage son Sol, who was taking art classes at the Educational Alliance in New York. After she colored and scribbled over some of Sol's drawings, he gave her paintbrushes and materials.

Beginning in a naive style, Sobel progressed in 1943 to crowded compositions that grew increasingly abstract throughout 1944 and 1945, taking on an allover pattern. She painted decorative and colorful representational scenes, like Grandma Moses, who also took up painting in her later years, but in addition Sobel started using radical new techniques of dripping paint in abstract compositions. She also used automatist techniques that allowed her free imagination to rein. She created dripped woven skeins of layered lacquer enamel and oil paint in her rapidly executed compositions (see *Milky Way*, 1945, enamel on canvas; and *Untitled*, c. 1946, oil and enamel on composition board, both in the collection of the Museum of Modern Art). In *Art News* in January 1946, one reviewer described her work as seeming to be "compounded of marble, mother-of-pearl, multi-colored spider webs, and a spatter of milk." Sobel also painted enameled whirling and calligraphic figures on glass in a style approximating the automatic writing technique of the surrealist André Masson and drew with wax crayons on paper. While living in Brighton Beach, Brooklyn, Sobel selected unusual materials for her art: sand, shells, mirrors, shingles, envelopes, boxes, and scraps of paper. She also decorated ceramic vessels. Her husband ran a costume jewelry business and provided some of her materials, like enamel paint. In 1953, after his death, she served as the vice president and a director of the business, helping to coordinate the design and color of new lines of jewelry.

After her son wrote letters on her behalf and introduced her work to some of the major figures in the New York art world, Sobel's talents were recognized and she achieved fame relatively early in her painting career. One of her earliest admirers was Max Ernst, who showed her works to his erstwhile wife Peggy Guggenheim, director of the Art of This Century Gallery in New York.

After exhibiting at the Arts Club of Chicago and the Brooklyn Museum, Sobel had her first one-woman show at the Puma Gallery in New York in 1944. The accompanying catalog, *Janet Sobel*, featured a foreword by the American philosopher and educator John Dewey, whom she had met in Key West, Florida, in 1941. Singling out Sobel's "youthful spontaneity" and "brooding maternal wholeness," Dewey claimed that her work was "extraordinarily free from imitativeness and from self-consciousness and pretense. One can believe that to an unusual degree her forms and colors well up from a subconsciousness that is richly stored with sensitive impressions received directly from contact with nature, impressions which have been reorganized in figures in which color and form are happily wed." Sobel included a naked Dewey among a frieze-like crowd of people surrounded by flowering lilac trees in her colorful oil painting *Spring Festival* (1942, privately owned).

According to Sobel, another one of her figural paintings from the early 1940s, *Chronicle of Our Elders* (privately owned), a large oil on canvas that depicts the persecution of "great men who have devoted themselves to truth," like Moses and Christ, also features Hitler lingering in the shadows. Sobel identified Hitler as "not only anti-Jew and anti-Christ, but a betrayer of all humanity" (WCBS radio transcript, 1946).

Although sometimes identified as a "primitive," Sobel called herself a surrealist. In December 1946, when host Bill Leonard interviewed her on the WCBS radio program, "This Is New York," he introduced her as "one of America's most talked-about surrealist painters, thereby reversing the usual amateur-turned-professional story." The critic and collector Sidney Janis, author of *They Taught Themselves: American Primitive Painters of the 20th Century* (1942), showed Sobel's works at the Mortimer Brandt Gallery in New York in the 1944 exhibition Abstract and Surrealist Art in America. Janis's book of the same title reproduced in color one of Sobel's "all-over" paintings entitled *Music* (1944, duco on canvas, privately owned; formerly collection of Peggy Guggenheim). This work was inspired by Shostakovich's Seventh Symphony.

In 1945 the David Porter Gallery in Washington, D.C., organized two exhibitions of Sobel's work. One, called The Women, an exhibition of thirty artists including Leonora Carrington, Kay Sage, and Charmion von Wiegand, traveled to the Art of This Century Gallery. In the catalog that accompanied Sobel's solo exhibition at the Art of This Century Gallery in 1946, Janis described Sobel's technique as a "metamorphosis" that was "filled with unconscious surrealist phantasy." He added that "unexpected color transpositions and self-invented methods for applying pigment are uncanny plastic weapons in Mrs. Sobel's hands." Sobel painted in an unconventional way, lying on her abdomen on the living-room floor.

Sobel's early abstract work anticipated Jackson Pollock's allover drip style. Pollock had seen her work at the Brandt Gallery and the Art of This Century Gallery. Clement Greenberg, the art critic who championed abstract expressionism, recalled, "Pollock (and I myself) admired these pictures rather furtively. . . . The effect—and it was the first really 'all-over' one that I had seen, since [Mark] Tobey's show came months later—was strangely pleasing. Later on, Pollock admitted that these pictures had made an impression on him" (Greenberg, p. 218).

During the remaining years of her life, Sobel progressed from her early primitive surrealism to abstract swirling forms. Many of her figurative works could be called "outsider art." William Rubin, who would become the chief curator of the Collection of Painting and Sculpture at the Museum of Modern Art in 1969, "rediscovered" Sobel, discussing her work in an article on Jackson Pollock in the April 1967 issue of *Artforum*. In 1947 Sobel moved from Brooklyn to Plainfield, New Jersey, where she lived until her death in 1968, leaving behind a largely undiscovered body of work.

As a grandmother who practiced art late in life, Sobel broke the stereotype of the avant-garde artist. In tandem with discussions of her artistic talent and pioneering role in dripping paint, the contemporary press described her role as a housewife surrounded by kids. She served her roast chicken, gefilte fish, and chicken soup to visitors that included luminaries like André Breton, the founder of surrealism; Peggy Guggenheim; Dewey; Janis; Ernst; and Ernst's son Jimmy. Breton and the Ernsts played chess with the Sobel family.

In 1946 Janis had prophesied that Sobel would probably be known as one of the important surrealist artists, and he compared her work to that of the leaders of surrealism, Ernst and Masson. The fame that she first achieved in the 1940s did not last beyond her lifetime. Her inclusion in an exhibition in 1989 at Rutgers University that explored the lesser-known small-scale works created by painters of the New York School partially resurrected her reputation. Sobel's work is in the permanent collections of the Pennsylvania Academy of Fine Arts, Philadelphia, and the Museum of Modern Art.

• For useful quotes from Sobel, see "Critics Acclaim Boro Grandmother as Top Flight Surrealist Painter," *Brooklyn (N.Y.) Eagle*, 10 Nov. 1946. For historical discussions of Sobel's work, see Clement Greenberg, "'American-Type' Painting" (written in 1955; rev. 1958) in *Art and Culture* (1961), and the catalog by Jeffrey Wechsler for the Rutgers University exhibition, *Abstract Expressionism: Other Dimensions* (1989). An obituary is in the *Plainfield (N.J.) Courier-News*, 12 Nov. 1968.

DEBORAH A. GOLDBERG

SOBELOFF, Simon E. (3 Dec. 1894–11 July 1973), federal appellate judge, was born in Baltimore, Maryland, the son of Russian Jewish immigrants, Jacob Harry Sobeloff, an upholsterer, and Mary Kaplan. At age twelve Sobeloff went to work as a clerk in the law office of William F. Broening. During the 1907 mayoralty campaign, Sobeloff delivered speeches for the Republican candidate, and his efforts won him an appointment as a page in the House of Representatives. Sobeloff attended Loyola College in Baltimore in 1911–1912 and graduated from the University of Maryland School of Law in 1915. While still in law school, he clerked for the chief judge of the Supreme Bench of Baltimore, Morris Ames Soper. Sobeloff was admitted to the bar in 1914 and began private practice. He married Irene Ehrlich in 1918; the couple had two children.

A progressive reformer and active Republican, Sobeloff served as assistant city solicitor of Baltimore from 1919 to 1923 and deputy city solicitor from 1927 to 1931. He advocated a minimum wage, argued in court against higher fares for the local transit system, fought for legislation that required new standards for meat inspection, and headed an antinoise committee. After the crash of 1929, he drafted and campaigned for a state unemployment insurance plan and headed Baltimore's Municipal Commission on Stabilization of Unemployment.

In 1931 President Herbert Hoover appointed Sobeloff U.S. attorney for the District of Maryland. He prosecuted major bootleggers but refused to prosecute minor offenders. He also cracked down on federal law enforcement officers who went beyond the bounds of the law to enforce Prohibition and reined in overzealous censors. When customs officials seized copies of Aristophanes' *Lysistrata* and Dr. Marie Stopes's *Wise Parenthood*, Sobeloff ordered them to release the books.

Amid an outpouring of praise for his performance in the job, Sobeloff resigned as U.S. attorney in 1934 in order to return to private practice, but he continued to play a significant role in public policy. He remained on the unemployment commission and served as labor arbitrator for the garment industry in Baltimore. An outspoken opponent of racial discrimination, Sobeloff testified before Congress in support of a federal antilynching law in 1934. The following year, Judge Eugene O'Dunne appointed him to investigate the failure of the Baltimore Trust Company, the largest banking institution south of Philadelphia. H. L. Mencken praised Sobeloff's report for having "all the compelling plausibility of a demonstration in geometry and all the racy charm of *The Gilded Age*."

When Sobeloff's close friend Theodore Roosevelt McKeldin won election as mayor of Baltimore in 1943, he named Sobeloff city solicitor. During World War II Sobeloff defended the right of aliens to become citizens without undue obstruction and became a leading voice for slum clearance and public housing. After the war Sobeloff stood alone on Baltimore's Board of Estimates in defending the right of the Socialist Labor party to give speeches on a street corner that was traditionally used for religious gatherings on Sundays.

After Democrats won the 1947 city elections, the new mayor prevailed on Sobeloff to remain as city solicitor. Sobeloff stayed on but resigned later that year to return again to private practice; however, he continued to serve as counsel to the Baltimore Housing Authority and as a legal consultant to the mayor. He became a leading opponent of Maryland's antisubversive law, and his continued advocacy of public housing led to the passage of urban renewal legislation in 1944.

Sobeloff actively supported McKeldin's successful race for governor in 1950, after which he functioned as "first minister" in McKeldin's kitchen cabinet. Upon taking office, McKeldin appointed Sobeloff to head a commission to review the operations of state government. In April 1952 McKeldin and Sobeloff went to Paris to urge General Dwight Eisenhower to challenge Robert Taft for the Republican nomination. That summer, Sobeloff wrote the speech with which McKeldin nominated Eisenhower at the Republican convention.

Sobeloff was as well known for his legal craftsmanship as for his reformist politics. In December 1952 McKeldin appointed Sobeloff chief judge of the Maryland Court of Appeals, the state's highest court. In

January 1954 Eisenhower appointed Sobeloff solicitor general of the United States. Sobeloff argued the government's case regarding the implementation of *Brown v. Board of Education* in 1955. Although the Supreme Court's decision generally followed the government's proposals, it did not include the government's suggestion of a ninety-day limit for school districts to propose an acceptable desegregation plan.

Sobeloff split with the administration over the issue of internal security. He overruled attorneys who wanted to appeal a district judge's dismissal of the indictment of Owen Lattimore, who had been ousted from the State Department on charges of disloyalty. Sobeloff came into direct conflict with the administration over the case of John P. Peters, a professor of medicine at Yale who was dismissed as a consultant to the government under the Loyalty Program. Skeptical about the evidence against Peters and unhappy with the fact that neither Peters nor the Loyalty Board knew the identity of some of his accusers, Sobeloff proposed that the government confess error. When the administration decided to press the case, Sobeloff refused to argue the government's position. Instead, Assistant Attorney General Warren E. Burger argued for the government and lost.

Eisenhower nominated Sobeloff to the Fourth Circuit Court of Appeals in 1955, but southern Democrats, led by Olin Johnston of South Carolina, mounted a determined effort to reject him because of his outspoken opposition to segregation. They managed to prevent action on the nomination until Congress adjourned. Eisenhower resubmitted the nomination in 1956. After a long and bitter confirmation battle, Sobeloff took his seat on the Fourth Circuit and became its chief judge in 1958. During his seventeen-year tenure, his opinions broke new ground in criminal justice reform, legislative reapportionment, and civil rights. Under his leadership, the Fourth Circuit won a reputation as one of the most liberal appellate courts in the nation.

Sobeloff was known not only for his impressive legal learning, but for his erudition in areas far removed from the law. His legal prose was clear, forceful, and laced with wit. His concern for the underprivileged underlay his judicial activism. He led the Fourth Circuit away from the view that the U.S. Supreme Court had mandated desegregation, not integration, and toward a more active defense of civil rights for black Americans. Sobeloff's last opinion in a civil rights case was a dissent in *Swann v. Charlotte-Mecklenburg* (1970), in which he voted to uphold the first use of court-ordered busing to achieve integration. The Supreme Court adopted his position the following year.

Sobeloff took qualified retirement at the end of 1970 but continued to hear a full load of cases. He died in Baltimore.

• Sobeloff's papers are in the Library of Congress. His writings include "From McNaughten to Durham and Beyond—A Discussion of Insanity and the Criminal Law," *Maryland Law Review* 15 (1955): 93–109; "The Sentence of the Court: Should There Be Appellate Review?" *American Bar Association Journal* 41 (1955): 13–17; and "Federalism and Individual Liberties—Can We Have Both?" *Washington University Law Quarterly* (1965): 296–310. There is no full-length biography, but see Michael S. Mayer, *Simon E. Sobeloff* (1980). Consult also Abel J. Merrill, "Biographical Sketch," *Maryland Law Review* 34 (1974): 491; Sanford Jay Rosen, "Judge Sobeloff's Public School Race Decisions," *Maryland Law Review* 34 (1974): 498; and Arnold M. Weiner, "Judge Sobeloff's Influence on Criminal Reform," *Maryland Law Review* 34 (1974): 532. Sobeloff's role in cases that concern the right of the criminally accused to counsel is discussed in Daniel John Meador, *Preludes to Gideon* (1967). Information on Sobeloff's early civil rights decisions may be found in J. W. Peltason, *Fifty-eight Lonely Men: Southern Federal Judges and School Desegregation* (1961). Sobeloff's role in *Swann v. Charlotte-Mecklenburg* is discussed in Bernard Schwartz, *Swann's Way: The School Busing Case and the Supreme Court* (1986). For information on Sobeloff's role in *Brown II*, see Michael S. Mayer, "With Much Deliberation and Some Speed: Eisenhower and the *Brown* Decision," *Journal of Southern History* 52, no. 1 (1986): 43–76. Also see Mayer, "Eisenhower and the Southern Federal Judiciary: The Sobeloff Nomination," in *Reexamining the Eisenhower Presidency*, ed. Shirley Anne Warshaw (1993).

MICHAEL S. MAYER

SOBOLEWSKI, Edward (1 Oct. 1804–17 May 1872), conductor, composer, and violinist, was born Johann Friedrich Eduard Sobolewski in Königsberg, East Prussia (now Kaliningrad, Russia), the son of Johann Sobolewski, an oboe player and soldier, and Amalia Louisa Corittkin. His early education included study with Königsberg musicians such as Friedrich Dorn, organist Wilhelm Jensen, composer and conductor Friedrich Selter, and August Gotthold, the director of the Frederick College. At age sixteen he was first violinist in Zander's Quartet, a group established in 1791. He studied composition with Carl Friederich Zelter in Berlin and Carl Maria von Weber in Dresden (1821–1824). In 1830 he became director of music at the theater in Königsberg and became the cantor of the Altstädtische Kirche in 1835. When the Philharmonische Gesellschaft was founded in 1838, Sobolewski was selected as the conductor. He also conducted the chorus of the Academy of Music (from 1843). He served as music critic of the *Ostpreussische Zeitung* and, using the pseudonym J. Feski, as correspondent for the *Neue Zeitschrift für Musik*. He moved to Bremen in 1854 to become music director of the theater there. During this time, he published several pamphlets including *Reaktionäre Briefe* (1854), *Oper, nicht Drama* (1857), *Debatten über Musik* (1957), and *Das Geheimniss der nuesten Schule der Musik* (1859). His opera *Komala* was premiered in Bremen in 1857 and was produced the next year in Weimar under the aegis of Franz Liszt.

In May 1859 Sobolewski left Bremen, immigrating to the United States and settling in Milwaukee the following July. With the help of the Musical Society there, his opera *Mohega, die Blume des Waldes*, which has an American Indian theme and is set during the revolutionary war, was performed on 11 October and 1 November 1859; it is perhaps the first opera on an

American revolutionary war subject. He founded and conducted the first and last concerts of the Milwaukee Philharmonic Society Orchestra in February and April 1860. In June 1860 he moved to St. Louis, where he was engaged as the conductor of the Philharmonic Society. Sobolewski conducted forty concerts during his six years in that post, and he introduced many works of the classical and romantic periods (though few of his own compositions) to St. Louis audiences. In 1866 he resigned in order to devote himself to teaching and composition. From 1869 to 1872 he was professor of vocal music at Bonham's Female Seminary. Sobolewski was married three times. He and his first wife were married around 1831 and had three children; he also had three children with his second wife, Auguste Bertha Minona Dorn, whom he married in 1839; and with his third wife, Bertha von Kleist, he had six children. He died of an apoplectic stroke in St. Louis, Missouri.

Only a few of Sobolewski's works composed in the United States were ever published; most of these were vocal and choral works. The songs, in particular, are of some artistic merit. Robert Schumann admired some of Sobolewski's works but found them deficient in overall planning. Sobolewski, a skilled linguist, mastered five languages. A number of his articles were published in the *Journal of Speculative Philosophy*, including "A Dialogue on Music" (1867), "The New School of Music" (1868), "Mendelssohn" (1872), and "Robert Schumann" (1874).

Besides the opera *Mohega, die Blume des Waldes*, his stage works include *Imogen* (1832); *Velleda* (1835); *Salvator Rosa* (1848); *The Veiled Prophet of Khorassan* (1850); and *An die Freude* (1859), a melodrama. His choral compositions include "Evenings in Greece," "Oh, Fly with Me," "Take Hence the Bowl," "Summer Songs," "Caravan Song," "When Love Is Kind," "Welcome Sweet Bird," "Cupid's Lottery," and four Part-Songs (1871–1872). Some of his published songs for voice and piano are "I Wept As I Lay Dreaming" (1861); "Loving Shepherd" (1864), with organ; "Thoughts of Thee" (1870); "I Arise from Dreams of Thee" (1870); "Sweet Memories of Thee" (1870); "Love's Philosophy" (1870–1871); and "Youth Never Comes Again" (1871); plus the unpublished "Hail Columbia" and "Blow Bugle Blow." He composed an overture on "The Star Spangled Banner" (1860). Other works include *The Awakening of Lazarus* (1837) and *John the Baptist* (1839), both oratorios; *The Saviour*, *The Prophesy*, and *Holy Night* (all 1840); *The First Elements of Vocal Instruction* (1841); *Heaven and Earth* (after Byron, 1845); *South and North: A Tone Painting in the Form of a Choral Symphony* (1845); Piano Trio in E Major (1846); *A Song as Traitor* (1848), an opera; and *Ziska von Kelch* (1851).

• An early discussion of Sobolewski is included in O. Burckhardt's *Der Musikverein von Milwaukee* (1900) and E. E. Hipsher's *American Opera* (1927); his Milwaukee career is treated in J. J. Schlicher, "The Milwaukee Musical Society in Time of Stress," *Wisconsin Magazine of History* 27 (1943–1944): 178. Coverage of Sobolewski in St. Louis appeared in Ernst C. Krohn's "A Century of Missouri Music," *Missouri Historical Review* 7 (1923): 130, and "Some Notes on the Philharmonic Orchestra and Related Amateur Orchestras in St. Louis," *Bulletin of the Missouri Historical Society*, n.s., 4 (1948): 169, both reprinted in *Missouri Music* (1971); and in Thomas B. Sherman, "St. Louis," in *Musical U.S.A.*, ed. Quaintance Eaton (1949). Richard E. Mueller's *A Century of the Symphony* (1979) and Katherine Gladney Wells's *Symphony and Song: The Saint Louis Symphony Orchestra* (1980) give later overviews. Robert T. Laudon's outstanding, detailed discussion of Sobolewski's life and works, "Eduard Sobolewski, Frontier Kapellmeister: From Königsberg to St. Louis," is in *Musical Quarterly* 73, no. 1 (Nov. 1989): 94–118. Obituaries are in the *St. Louis Missouri Republican*, 18, 19, 20 May 1872; and the *Impressario*, June 1872.

JAMES M. BURK

SODERBERG, C. Richard (3 Feb. 1895–17 Oct. 1979), mechanical engineer and educator, was born Carl Richard Soderberg in Ulvöhamn, Sweden, the son of Jonas Axel Soderberg, a fisherman, and Johanna Cristina Nordquist. Soderberg grew up in a village of about thirty families on a remote Baltic island in northern Sweden. He expected to operate a fishing boat in summer and make cans for his father's canning operation in winter, but an inspiring teacher introduced him to the world of books, and a private tutor prepared him for university exams. In 1912 he was admitted to the Tekniska Elementarskolan in Härnösand. He finished the four-year course in three years and entered the Chalmers Institute of Technology in Göteborg, Sweden.

While attending Chalmers, Soderberg also gained some practical engineering experience in a Göteborg shipyard as a student apprentice. More importantly, he was intrigued by new American shipbuilding techniques being developed during World War I. He served his military obligation beginning in 1915. He graduated from Chalmers in the spring of 1919, tied for first in his class and winner of the school's Ericsson Medal as its best student.

Soderberg then decided to emigrate. He applied for and won an American Scandinavian Foundation fellowship that enabled him to attend a university in the United States. Accepted at the Massachusetts Institute of Technology (MIT), he began studies in naval architecture, although he later expressed disappointment in the institute's intellectual atmosphere. Perhaps to compensate, Soderberg also sought admission to the University of Michigan as a special student, intending to use the school's towing tank and work with a noted professor. He was in Ann Arbor from January through April 1920 and planned a thesis on "The Influence of the Middle Body on the Resistance of Long Ships." When MIT would not accept this project, he designed a ship for the Great Lakes and earned his bachelor's degree in 1920. At about the same time, he met Sigrid Kristina Lofstedt, whom he married in May 1921; the couple later had two children.

Because of poor employment prospects in Sweden, the fellowship sponsor urged recipients to look for jobs in America. Soderberg became a hull designer for the New York Shipbuilding Corporation in Camden, New Jersey, in 1920, before moving to East Pittsburgh, Pennsylvania, in 1922 to join Westinghouse Electric and Manufacturing Corporation as a development engineer. He was assigned to design heavy electrical equipment, first traction motors and then turbine generators. Westinghouse was just discovering that vibration and other dynamic forces in its increasingly large and heavy electrical equipment were causing occasional failures, and older rules of thumb used by designers proved inadequate to cope with the challenges. Soderberg was included in an effort at Westinghouse to solve these difficulties with a more theoretical and mathematically rigorous approach to design and problem solving. Russian-born Stephen Timoshenko, Westinghouse's chief engineer, developed a unique internal training and lecture course to introduce the company's young engineers to theoretical mechanics, and the European-trained Soderberg fit in well. This venture helped to introduce a style of engineering into the United States that became widespread after World War II.

Soderberg had become a U.S. citizen in 1927, but in 1928 he was invited to take charge of the design of turbine generators for the Swedish General Electric Company (ASEA). Despite a counteroffer from Westinghouse, he left to work for ASEA, expecting to stay for two years. After he found the Swedish company's plans incomplete, he returned to the United States in 1930 with offers from both Westinghouse and General Electric. He again chose Westinghouse, where he was given more responsibility in the design of large electrical machinery, and in 1931 he became the chief design engineer for large steam turbines at the company's South Philadelphia plant. He helped develop high-temperature, high-pressure turbines for power and propulsion, but the plant sold only one large unit during the depth of the Great Depression.

By 1938, Soderberg was uncomfortable with changes in management attitudes at Westinghouse and accepted an offer to teach mechanical engineering at MIT. He was quickly recognized as a marvelous teacher who stressed professional conduct. He had marvelous rapport with students and brought to the classroom his extensive design experience in ships and heavy equipment. He also was concerned with fundamental principles, including the strength of materials and the dynamic behavior of moving machinery. His primary teaching responsibility was theoretical mechanics, a subject that Soderberg always tied to problem solving in the real world. To that end, he retained close contacts with industry through long-lasting consulting relationships with such firms as ASEA and STAL-LAVAL (Svenska Turbinfabriks Aktiebolaget Ljungstrom and deLaval Turbine Company). The latter connection developed after a trip to Sweden in 1939.

During World War II Soderberg worked on several government-sponsored projects. He played a small part in the Manhattan Project but spent more time doing research for the navy's Bureau of Ships, conducting a study of torpedo propulsion at Columbia University. His primary work, however, centered on the new field of gas turbines, the main focus of his research and consulting after 1940. He worked especially with Pratt & Whitney Aircraft Company and United Aircraft on turbo-jet and aircraft problems; in 1944 he joined the National Advisory Committee on Aeronautics special committee on jet propulsion. Soderberg also explored the development of a gas turbine engine for ships with the Elliott Company. Such efforts as these over the course of his career led to eighteen patents and the publication of more than fifty papers.

Soderberg's arrival at MIT also coincided with major changes in the institute's approach to engineering education. In the 1930s it moved toward a more theoretical and scientific approach to the training of engineers. Soderberg, fully comfortable with this European style, was soon drawn into administrative chores. He first served as chair of the mechanical engineering department's graduate committee; over time he grew concerned about restoring the reputation of the department, which had dropped. He sought to remedy this decline after 1947, when he became head of the mechanical and aeronautical engineering departments. By the end of his term in 1954, the department's reputation had been refurbished.

Soderberg also played a role in larger developments at the institute. Beginning in 1946, he served on the Committee on Educational Survey, which in 1949 released a report that helped to reshape MIT. Usually known as the Lewis Committee Report, it suggested that the institute find ways to blend theory and practice for engineering students, as well as to include more work in the humanities; it also called for strengthening graduate programs and developing interdisciplinary work. Each of these areas was stressed in the postwar development of MIT and most other American engineering schools.

Soderberg was able to help implement these ideas when he became dean of engineering in May 1954. He later recalled spending five years in intense and "very challenging" academic administration. Academic politics at MIT were quite complex, and Soderberg noted later that deans were not the key figures in the academic hierarchy. Even so, during his five-year term MIT strengthened its leading reputation in engineering education. Soderberg also played a major role in developing a successful grant proposal to the Ford Foundation that supported new initiatives in engineering education while maintaining the traditional strengths of the school. Moreover, Soderberg continued his personal work in the area of turbomachinery, despite his administrative burdens, although he gradually restricted his consulting work to two clients—Pratt & Whitney in Connecticut and STAL-LAVAL in Sweden. For Pratt & Whitney, he contributed substantially to the development of the JT-3 and J-57 engines, the latter of which powered the B-52 bomber and became the forerunner of the engine used on the Boeing 707. He also was deeply involved in National Academy of

Sciences, Air Force, and National Advisory Committee on Aeronautics committees.

In 1959 Soderberg was named Institute Professor; he retired as Institute Emeritus Professor only a year later. He maintained some involvement with MIT in the 1960s, most notably as temporary head of mechanical engineering and naval architecture from 1965 to 1967. His main responsibility was to divide these programs into two separate departments; he was especially involved in the search for a new head for naval architecture. He pushed that program to expand and broaden its interests to include marine transportation other than ships. After 1960 Soderberg devoted most of his time to outside activities, including committee work for the National Academy of Sciences and preparation of studies for the University of Pennsylvania and Michigan State. He also was involved in the activities of the American Society for Engineering Education and was an adviser for the U.S. Military Academy at West Point.

Soderberg was a splendid example of a type of engineer that appeared in the United States after 1920, comfortable with rigorous mathematical analysis yet ever cognizant that engineering was about solving real problems and producing practical, working designs. He conveyed this balance through his teaching, research, and consulting; he authored forty-five scholarly papers and took out eighteen patents between 1935 and 1950. Not surprisingly, Soderberg received numerous awards, including certificates of appreciation from the army and navy in 1948 and the Exceptional Service Award of the U.S. Air Force in 1955. He won prizes from the Society of Naval Architects and Marine Engineers (1944), the American Society of Swedish Engineers (1952), the American Society of Mechanical Engineers (1960), and the Swedish Royal Academy of Engineering (1968). He was a member of many professional organizations, including such prestigious elective groups as the National Academy of Science, the National Academy of Engineering, and the Royal Order of the North Star in Sweden. He died in Cambridge, Massachusetts.

• Much information about Soderberg can be found in the Institute Archives and Special Collections of the Massachusetts Institute of Technology, which hold fifty boxes of his personal and professional papers from 1914 to 1979 (Soderberg Papers, MC 23); the official records from his term as dean of engineering (School of Engineering, Office of the Dean, AC-12); and an oral interview conducted in 1975 and 1976 (MC 393). Also available is a typescript copy of a memoir Soderberg prepared, entitled *My Life*. His most important articles include a series of six articles, "The Vibration Problem in Engineering," *Electric Journal* (Jan. 1924–Feb. 1926), and, with Ronald B. Smith and Ashton T. Scott, "A Marine Gas Turbine Plant," *Transactions of the Society of Naval Architects and Marine Engineers* 53 (1945). See also a sketch in National Academy of Sciences, *Memorial Tributes* 2 (1984): 267–71.

BRUCE E. SEELY

SOGLOW, Otto (23 Dec. 1900–3 Apr. 1975), cartoonist, was born in the Yorkville district of New York City, the son of a house painter and a cook, whose names are unknown. He completed a year at Stuyvesant High School and then, deferring a dream of becoming an actor, took a succession of odd jobs—packer, shipping clerk, dishwasher, and errand boy. Following World War I, he enrolled in the Art Students League, after which he pursued a career as a freelance commercial artist, doing illustrations for magazines. In 1925 Soglow joined the art staff at the *New York World* where he produced a series of satiric comic strips for about a year; he also continued to freelance, contributing comic drawings to *Life*, *Judge*, the *New Yorker*, *Collier's*, and other leading magazines. In 1928 he married Anna Rosen; they had one child.

One of the cartoons he drew for the *New Yorker* in the early 1930s featured a diminutive monarch, and Soglow was asked to produce a series of cartoons about the "little king" for the magazine. The popularity of the character led to a syndication contract with King Features, which launched *The Little King* on 9 September 1934 as a Sunday-only comic strip. *The Little King* is notable for the utter simplicity of Soglow's drawing style and for the title character's humility and ingenuity—and silence. Soglow's drawings are minimalist art, diagrams. The body of the Little King, a short fat fellow, is the simplest of circles. The humor of the feature is built on contrast: instead of behaving like a crowned head of state, the Little King acts like an ordinary citizen. When he leaves his castle because it is about to be besieged, he pauses on his way out to leave a note for the milkman. He is often more mischievous youth than reigning monarch; he is not above indulging in a juvenile prank. He confers knighthood upon a courtier but afterward holds out his palm so that the new knight can pay him a fee. He throws out the first ball to begin the baseball season; when the ball goes over the fence and breaks a window in a nearby house, the Little King runs away like any neighborhood kid. When the royal dishwasher quits, leaving behind an enormous stack of dirty dishes, the Little King tackles the problem by putting on his swimsuit and taking the entire stack of dishes with him into the swimming pool.

The simple plots of these gags work because they unfold in pantomime. The Little King never speaks; others in the strip might say a few words occasionally in order to clarify a situation leading to the punchline, but the King is forever mute. With little or no verbiage to prepare us for what is coming, we must rely entirely on the pictures. The visuals "narrate" the "story" one plot increment at a time, keeping us in suspense about what the King is up to until we reach the final panel where the "mystery" is revealed, the surprise and/or the King's inventiveness provoking our laughter.

In addition to producing *The Little King*, Soglow did *Sentinel Louie*, another Sunday pantomime strip, for several years in the 1930s and 1940s. He drew gag cartoons for magazines and regularly illustrated columns and features in such periodicals as the *Saturday Evening Post*; he also did drawings for various books. *The Little King* was discontinued shortly before Soglow died in his New York City apartment. A founder of the National Cartoonists Society in 1946, Soglow earned his niche in the history of cartooning by producing the first long-running syndicated strip to feature pantomimic action.

• Apart from syndicate press releases, there is no biographical information about Otto Soglow. *The Little King* is discussed briefly in the standard histories of the medium, *Comic Art in America* by Stephen Becker (1959) and *The Comics* by Coulton Waugh (1947). Soglow produced several books of cartoons: *Pretty Pictures* (1931), *Everything's Rosy* (1932), *The Little King* (1933), and, with D. Plotkin, *Wasn't the Depression Terrible?* (1934). An obituary is in the *New York Times*, 4 Apr. 1975.

ROBERT C. HARVEY

SOILAND, Albert (5 May 1873–16 May 1946), pioneer radiation oncologist, was born in Stavanger, Norway, the son of Edward Soiland, a ship captain, and Axeline Christine Halvorson. His father died when Albert was only three, and his mother remarried in 1883. Shortly thereafter, at age ten, Soiland moved with his new family to Chicago, Illinois, where he attended high school, became a U.S. citizen in 1895, and in that same year registered at the Chicago College of Physicians and Surgeons. There Soiland was guided by physician W. G. Terry in the study of medicine and became intrigued by the recent discovery of X-rays by a German physicist, Wilhelm Röntgen. In 1896, using Röntgen's technique, the first malignant tumor was successfully irradiated in the United States, in Chicago. In an effort to further the technology in the United States, Soiland assisted Terry in building a coil X-ray generator for the college.

When Soiland became ill with tuberculosis, he decided to move to a warmer climate and chose Los Angeles, California, where he continued his studies at the University of Southern California and graduated with an M.D. in 1900. After a short stint as a surgeon at a saw mill in Louisiana, Soiland returned to Los Angeles and set up practice in Hollywood. There he met Dagfine Berner Swendsen, also a native Norwegian, whom he married in 1902; they had no children.

Soiland continued to follow closely new developments in radiation and its medical applications, including the discovery of radium and its subsequent production and use for the treatment of cancer. Because he noticed that there was increasing interest in the use of X-rays in many California hospitals, he decided to open an independent office to concentrate on the study and practice of radiology alone. The use of X-rays as a medical tool was not readily accepted by many serious medical practitioners. They felt instead that X-rays were a new form of photography that did not have a legitimate medical use. Soiland disagreed and set out to disprove this commonly held notion.

After organizing the first Department of Radiology at the University of Southern California Medical College in 1904, where he served both as a professor and chairman, Soiland traveled to Europe and there bought his own radium to treat skin cancer. He then dedicated himself to the study of radiology, establishing the Albert Soiland Radiological Clinic in Los Angeles in 1910. His concentration was on radiodiagnostics, or using radiation to locate and diagnose disease.

With the onset of World War I, Soiland, who was an avid seaman and sailor, was appointed a lieutenant, M.R.C., U.S. Navy. He did not go to sea but instead was responsible for coordinating radiologic work for naval hospitals in San Francisco, San Diego, and Los Angeles. During this time he founded the Pacific Coast Röntgen-ray Society (1915) and co-founded the Western Röntgen-ray Society (1913), which would later become the Radiological Society of North America (RSNA). He became president of the RSNA in 1919 and was commissioned lieutenant commander of the U.S. Navy following the war's end.

During the war years significant strides were made in the use of radiation for curing, as opposed to treating, cancer. Soiland sold his diagnostic practice and began to practice radiotherapy exclusively. Among the first Americans to do so, he and his associates were devoted to therapeutic radiology and kept informative, lifelong records on their cancer patients. They also experimented with "superradiation," or the use of high voltages to irradiate cancerous tissue.

In 1923 Soiland made his most significant contribution to radiation oncology, the founding of the American College of Radiology in Chicago. In founding this college, he strove to develop an organization, devoted to the study and application of radiology, that would provide a platform for its members to share information. He also sought recognition from the ranks of the medical profession and hoped to discredit false practitioners.

Soiland led a movement that was Key to the formation of the college when he prevented the governor of California from signing a bill that would certify lay "radiographers" to use X-rays "and other photographic means" to diagnose disease. He anticipated that such certification would perpetuate the idea that radiology was a form of photography, and thus that its practitioners need not be medically trained professionals. During a meeting of the American Medical Association in June 1923, Soiland presented a resolution that radiology be recognized as an integral part of medicine and that the AMA establish an authoritative branch dedicated solely to radiology. On the same day, he proposed a constitution and bylaws for such a body, the American College of Radiology. The vote was unanimous; the bill was defeated, and the college born.

When the First International Congress of Radiology was held in London in 1926, Soiland presented a paper on breast cancer. At the Third International Congress in Paris (1929), he was asked to head the delegation and also presented the American College of Radiology Gold Medal to the codiscoverer of radium, Marie Curie.

Soiland continued his research in radiotherapy by experimenting with the use of high-voltage radiation on cancer patients in the early 1930s. The high rate of success persuaded him to acquire a sophisticated, 600

Kilovolt unit to continue his trials. He was one of the first radiotherapists in the world able to treat cancer patients with a supervoltage unit, a procedure that remained in use throughout the twentieth century.

In 1936 the board of chancellors at the American College of Radiology officially praised Soiland's work, stating that the radiologists of America owed him their lasting gratitude for his efforts to further the interests of radiology. He continued to work to that end until his death.

Soiland and his wife, whom he affectionately called "Fink," enjoyed sailing throughout their lives. In 1946, while the two of them were on a voyage to Norway, Soiland suffered a heart attack and died.

Soiland is remembered as an elegant man, whose character was a blend of the adventurous roots of his homeland and the generosity and independent spirit of his adopted nation. His tireless efforts to make radiology a legitimate part of American medicine, in his quiet but persistent manner, earned him distinction and the respect of his fellow radiologists.

• Soiland's trials with supervoltage X-rays are recorded in his work "Experimental Clinical Research with X-Ray Voltages above 500 Kv.," *Radiology* 20 (1933): 99–102. His experiences at sea are covered in his own book, *The Viking Goes to Sea* (1924). Biographical accounts are, by Juan A. del Regato, *Radiation Oncologists* (1995) and "Albert Soiland and the Early Development of Therapeutic Radiology in the United States," *International Journal of Radiation Oncology and Biological Physics* 9 (1983): 243–53.

JUAN A. DEL REGATO

SOLDAN, Frank Louis (20 Oct. 1842–27 Mar. 1908), educator, was born in Frankfurt am Main, Germany, the son of Johann Justin Soldan and Caroline Elssman, and was educated in Frankfurt. In 1862 he married Ottilie Bernhard; they had one daughter. He traveled to the United States in 1863 with his wife, spent a few months in New York, and arrived in St. Louis with a contract to teach in a private German-English school. In 1864 he was appointed principal of the school, and in 1868 he accepted a position teaching modern languages in St. Louis Central High School, beginning a lifelong career in public education.

Soldan's steady rise in the school system was aided by his early involvement in the city's large German community and in William Torrey Harris's St. Louis Philosophical Society, which discussed readings in German philosophy. Harris, superintendent of St. Louis Public Schools from 1868 to 1880, became Soldan's mentor, urging him to translate Georg Hegel's work for the society's *Journal of Speculative Philosophy* and to present his essays to the society. Soldan studied English with another important educator, Calvin M. Woodward, who established the Washington University Manual Training School and periodically served on the board of education from the 1870s to the 1910s. Woodward's support as a member of the board was crucial in the late 1890s, when Soldan pursued significant reforms as St. Louis's superintendent of public instruction.

In 1870 Harris appointed Soldan assistant superintendent of public schools in charge of German instruction. In 1871 Soldan became principal of the city's normal school, which was joined in 1887 with the city's white high school. He continued as chief administrator until 1895. Meanwhile, his national reputation grew. At meetings of the National Education Association (NEA) he spoke on such topics as the school's dual role of imparting knowledge and helping children form habits of hard work, the importance of the continual self-improvement of teachers, German school curriculum and organization, and the uses of folklore to teach children ethics and morality. He served as the NEA's president in 1885. He was invited by South Carolina educators to help establish the state's first normal school in 1880, which led to the reestablishment of the University of South Carolina and for which he received the LL.D.

Soldan's most important work was his service as St. Louis's superintendent of public instruction (1895–1908). He voraciously read philosophy, literature, and political theory, incorporating ideas from his reading and the Hegelian idealism of the Philosophical Society into his administration of schools. Among the ideas he used to frame his leadership was the importance of the relationship between schools and democratic communities. Manual training, for example, was introduced to all children in particular grades to help them connect knowledge with action and to understand the role of work in a democratic society. Teacher training was another theme, which he based on the centrality of teachers to instructional quality; he introduced uniform requirements for employment, raised the quality of normal school education and training, and increased teachers' salaries. His early published essays on the teaching of German and mathematics and on problems in science contributed to his intellectual standing in the school community. His published writings on Hegel, J. F. Herbart, and other German philosophers, encouraged by Harris, also gained him recognition among St. Louis's cultural elite and, over time, among the national intelligentsia who followed the St. Louis Hegelians and the politics of public school leadership.

Soldan participated in devising a new organization for the board of education, which, with "efficiency" as its goal, abolished ward elections to the board, established citywide elections, and concentrated power in the office of the superintendent and his appointed assistants. Soldan assumed from the board of education responsibility for hiring and firing teachers. With Woodward's assistance he lobbied to increase city taxes for the schools and persuaded the board to introduce new instructional programs. Innovations included revising the curriculum in all grades in consultation with teachers; broadening the teaching of history to incorporate Europe as well as the United States and the use of the literature of folklore; extending the teaching of history into the elementary grades and the high schools; expanding the teaching of geography beyond memorization to instruction using map reading, globes, and slides; enriching reading material used in teaching reading, writing, and oral expression; and offering a larger number of topics in natural science classes.

His autocratic powers as superintendent notwithstanding, Soldan fiercely believed in democratic schools to expose students to a common curriculum of reading, writing, and arithmetic. This belief was supported by a Herbartian commitment to providing a general education, rich in literary culture and the arts and directed toward the development of character, within the communal life of the school. As St. Louis grew into a major metropolis populated by immigrants working in its varied industrial economy, Soldan's commitment manifested itself in efforts to reduce the dropout rates of the city's children and provide them with means to become responsible citizens. Woodward worked with him to establish manual training classes for all pupils and to build two additional white high schools, offering manual training programs to hold students beyond the eighth grade. He and Woodward began their manual training effort in 1898 by building on a decade-long experimental, privately funded, after-school program in L'Ouverture, a black elementary school. Soldan's initial publicly financed endeavor offered woodworking for boys and cooking for girls in the seventh and eighth grades. Both black and white students benefited from the vocational program as it expanded. After the turn of the century the program helped keep black and white students in school beyond their enrollment period.

Soldan's career ended suddenly when he collapsed and died on his way to a board of education meeting in St. Louis. During his superintendency, students continuing beyond elementary school increased from 40 to 60 percent, the number of city high schools doubled, teachers' salaries were raised periodically, and free textbooks became available to all students. To commemorate his work, the city named a high school after him.

• Letters from Soldan are in the William Torrey Harris Papers in the St. Louis Historical Society, which also holds other items about Soldan. The annual reports of the superintendent and the St. Louis Board of Education from 1894 through 1908—as well as Soldan's *Grube's Method* (1881), essays in the *Journal of Speculative Philosophy*, and his posthumously published collection, *The Century and the School and Other Educational Essays* (1912)—reveal his thinking. Brief chronologies and descriptions are in the *Missouri Historical Review* 15 (1920–1921); William Hyde and Howard L. Conrad, eds., *Encyclopedia of the History of St. Louis*, vol. 4 (1899); J. M. Greenwood, "F. Louis Soldan," *Educational Review* 25 (May 1903): 517–19; "Public School Leaders," *Outlook*, 22 July 1905, p. 739; "'Boss' Soldan," *Mirror*, 6 May 1897, p. 1; and "Soldan's System," *Mirror*, 13 May 1897, p. 1. See also Charles M. Dye, "Calvin Woodward, Manual Training and the Saint Louis Public Schools," *Missouri Historical Society Bulletin* 31 (1974–1975): 111–35. Ben Blewitt published two useful obituaries; see the *National Education Association Journal of Proceedings and Addresses of the Forty-sixth Annual Meeting* (1908), pp. 492–98, and the *Fifty-fourth Annual Re-*

port of the Board of Education of the City of St. Louis (1909), pp. 18–71. Also informative is the notice in *Educational Review* 35 (May 1908): 527.

MARY ANN DZUBACK

SOLIS-COHEN, Jacob da Silva (28 Feb. 1838–22 Dec. 1927), physician and pioneer laryngologist, was born in New York City, the son of Myer David Cohen and Judith Simiah da Silva Solis. In 1840 the family moved to Philadelphia, where, twenty years later, Solis-Cohen received an M.D. from the University of Pennsylvania School of Medicine. He began his medical residency in 1861 at Old Blockley in Philadelphia but resigned the same year to enlist as a private in the Union army at the outbreak of the Civil War. He was soon commissioned as a lieutenant in the infantry and later appointed as assistant surgeon in the Twenty-sixth Regiment of the Pennsylvania Volunteers. He served the regiment in Joseph Hooker's brigade, first during the defense of Washington and then at Bladensburg.

Solis-Cohen recalled in a 1918 address to the American Laryngological Association that, since he had "passed a few months in the army, I thought it would be a good thing to get some experience in the navy, too, before the war ended." After presenting his credentials to the Medical Examining Board, Solis-Cohen was admitted in September 1861 to the navy, where he was appointed acting assistant surgeon. In this capacity Solis-Cohen accompanied Samuel F. DuPont's expedition to Port Royal and later served in the South Atlantic blockade squadron. During this time he served aboard the USS *Florida*, USS *Stettin*, and USS *Vermont*. After Solis-Cohen's resignation from naval duties in January 1864, the surgeon general of the United States recommended his appointment as visiting surgeon in two Philadelphia military hospitals. Following a brief stint in New York, in 1866 Solis-Cohen returned to Philadelphia to establish a private practice.

Following the treatment of a patient with a throat disease, Solis-Cohen devoted much time to perfecting his use of the laryngoscope, a new diagnostic tool of the time. He instituted and delivered the first systematic course of laryngology lectures in America in 1866 at the Philadelphia School of Anatomy. He devoted much of his practice and teaching during the next sixty-one years to diseases of the nose, throat, and larynx and became recognized for his proficiency in the use of a laryngeal mirror as a diagnostic aid. In 1867 the American Medical Association appointed Solis-Cohen chair of a committee to investigate medical treatment by means of gas inhalation, a position that resulted in his first publication, *Inhalation in the Treatment of Disease—Its Therapeutics and Practice* (1867). That same year Solis-Cohen performed the world's first successful laryngotomy (opening of the larynx) in an effort to remove a cancerous tumor. The Jefferson Medical College appointed Solis-Cohen lecturer in laryngoscopy and diseases of the chest in 1869, and in 1872 he published *Diseases of the Throat and Nasal Passages*, about which Solomon R. Kagan claimed, "No book has ever had a greater influence in disseminating a wide and thorough knowledge of laryngology." Solis-Cohen married Miriam Binswanger in 1875; they had nine children.

In 1883 Solis-Cohen was appointed honorary professor of laryngology at Jefferson Medical College and elected professor of diseases of the throat and chest at the Philadelphia Polyclinic and College for Graduates in Medicine, an institution that he had helped found. He additionally served on the medical and surgical staffs of German Hospital, Home for Consumptives, Northern Dispensary, Jewish Hospital, and St. Mary's Hospital, all in Philadelphia, and was consulting physician for the State Hospital for the Insane in Norristown, Pennsylvania.

Solis-Cohen published thirteen books and more than one hundred articles in the growing specialty of laryngology, drawing on the numerous case studies he attended. He devised and adapted many methods and treatments to lessen the dangers of operative laryngology. His efforts as an organizer and leader in this specialty are evident in his contributions as a founder of the American Laryngeal Association (1878), cofounder and editor of *Archives of Laryngology* (1880–1882), and longtime editor of the laryngological section of *American Journal for Medical Sciences*. In a posthumous tribute in the 1928 *Memorials* of the *Transactions of the American Laryngological Association*, Solis-Cohen's colleagues recalled the "integrity and purity of his purpose, the undaunted courage which sustained him, the calm serenity with which he met every decree of fate," and they recognized his "broad and philosophical mind and, above all, a spirit of tolerance, of kindliness and of devotion to the interests of those about him and to the world at large which placed him among the leaders of his time—well named the Nestor of American Laryngology." In more general service to his profession, he served as president of both the Northern Medical Association (1875) and the Philadelphia County Medical Society (1887–1888), vice president of the Pathological Society of Philadelphia, and treasurer of the Congress of American Physicians and Surgeons. He also wrote a health primer, *The Throat and the Voice* (1879), for a lay audience.

Solis-Cohen also pursued an active lifelong interest in the sciences in general. He lectured in physiology at the Wagner Institute of Science in Philadelphia from 1866 to 1868 and delivered lectures on light and acoustics at the Franklin Institute in Philadelphia in 1870 and the Stevens Institute of Technology in Hoboken in 1871. At meetings of the Academy of Natural Sciences, Solis-Cohen supported Darwinian evolutionary theory and demonstrated Faber's "talking machine," a machine capable of mechanically reproducing the sounds of the human voice. In addition to receiving honorary degrees from Jefferson Medical College and Temple University, he was a member of several honorary groups and service organizations.

In his spare time Solis-Cohen could often be found playing one of a number of musical instruments or horseback riding, his favorite pastime. Active within the Jewish community, Solis-Cohen was a founder of the Hebrew Education Society and participated in services first at the Mikve Israel Synagogue and, later, the Beth-El-Emeth Synagogue. He died in Philadelphia, where he received a traditional Jewish funeral service with military honors of the Loyal Legion.

Solis-Cohen continues to be remembered in the way his colleague, D. Bryson Delavan, once recognized him—the "father of the literature of laryngology in America and of organized instruction in the art."

• There is no known repository of Solis-Cohen papers. Solomon R. Kagan provides the most complete assessment of him together with a complete bibliography of his writings in "Jacob da Silva Solis-Cohen (1838–1927)," *Medical Life* 44 (1937): 291–311. Kagan further addresses Solis-Cohen in *Jewish Contributions to Medicine in America from Colonial Times to the Present* (1939) and *Leaders of Medicine: Biographical Sketches of Outstanding American and European Physicians* (1941). For a synopsis of his surgical achievements, see Louis H. Clerf, "Jacob da Silva Solis-Cohen, M.D.: Pioneer Laryngologist," *Annals of Otology, Rhinology and Laryngology* 81 (1972): 599–602. See Henry Samuel Morais's works, *Eminent Israelites of the Nineteenth Century* (1880) and *The Jews of Philadelphia* (1894), for a discussion of Solis-Cohen's Judaic practice.

PHILIP K. WILSON

SOLIS-COHEN, Solomon (1 Sept. 1857–12 July 1948), physician, Jewish leader, and journalist, was born in Philadelphia, Pennsylvania, the son of Meyer Cohen, a merchant, and Judith Solis. His mother insisted when she married that her name was too important to disappear, hence the name Solis-Cohen. As a boy Solomon attended Mikveh Israel, the fourth-oldest synagogue in America. There he was tutored by his beloved rabbi, Sabato Morais. His intense interest in liberal Orthodox Judaism never wavered throughout his life.

The precocious Solis-Cohen attended Central High School in Philadelphia, a school for academically talented boys. He graduated with honors in 1872 at age fifteen. Upon graduating, he worked as a bookkeeper and part-time journalist. He was a founder of Jewish periodicals. After joining the Young Men's Hebrew Association (YMHA) in 1875, he started a journal, the *Association Review*, a monthly for which he was contributing editor.

In 1879 Solis-Cohen met with Philadelphia and New York friends to establish a 26-page not-for-profit weekly titled the *American Hebrew*. Its purpose was to "disseminate the truth and morality inspired by Israel, to spread the knowledge of Judaic principles and Hebrew literature and to champion the brethren of our faith." Its other motive was to counteract what he and his friends considered the excesses of the Reform Jewish movement. What disturbed the *American Hebrew* staff was the Reform platform abandoning the kosher laws, the use of Hebrew in services, the skullcap and prayer shawl, and the belief that Jews were a people as well as a religious group. Solomon wrote editorials explaining Jewish holidays and commentaries on the Bible and the Talmud. He also included translations of medieval Hebrew poets and original poetry. These poems emphasized Jewish values and the meaning of prayers.

After 1882 immigration from eastern Europe rose dramatically. The American Jewish community became very heterogeneous, reflecting the influx of Jews from the Austro-Hungarian and Russian empires. Those new immigrants published many newspapers and journals, which often mirrored their socialist, atheistic, and anti-Zionist views. The affluent German-Jewish and American-Jewish communities used the *American Hebrew* as a forum for opposing views.

After a short vocation as a Hebrew teacher in the city's only all-day Jewish parochial school, Solis-Cohen was persuaded by his brother Jacob, a famous Civil War surgeon, to become a physician. Solis-Cohen graduated from Jefferson Medical College in 1883. He joined the college's faculty and in 1902 was made professor of clinical medicine. In 1885 he married Emily Grace Nathan de Solis, his first cousin and one of the few Jews accepted as a member of the Daughters of the American Revolution; they had four children.

Probably the most important institution fathered by Solis-Cohen was the Jewish Publication Society (JPS), an organization headquartered in Philadelphia. He saw a need for an enlightened and cultivated Jewry. This meant reading Jewish source material in English by writers who were committed Jews. This was to offset the publication of those sources in Hebrew, a language most Jews could not read, or publications that had a Christological bias. Solis-Cohen, along with his close associates Mayer Sulzberger and Cyrus Adler, drafted in 1888 a constitution for the JPS. The physician-scholar served on the Publication Committee until his death sixty years later. He also served on the subcommittee for Jewish classics. At age seventy-seven, Solis-Cohen published his translation of a medieval Spanish-Jewish bard, *The Selected Poems of Ibn Ezra*.

Solis-Cohen had a major part in the founding of the Conservative Jewish religious movement. He drafted the Jewish Theological Association's constitution and presided over a meeting that led to the founding of the Jewish Theological Seminary (JTS) in 1886. The JTS's purpose was to attract the masses of East European Jews as well as others who could not relate to the untraditional practices of Reform Judaism, yet who viewed the strictly Orthodox as too old worldly and un-Americanized. The seminary would produce rabbis fluent in English, giving English sermons, using mainly Hebrew prayers, advocating kosher laws and the skullcap and prayer shawl, and favoring a homeland in Palestine. Solis-Cohen used his influence with prominent German-Jewish friends such as the wealthy Jacob Schiff to financially support the new seminary. The doctor was also most influential in procuring Solomon Schechter, a world-renowned scholar residing in London, to become president of the JTS in 1902. In 1913 twenty-two Conservative synagogues formed a national organization, United Synagogues of America.

Solis-Cohen drafted their constitution. At about the same time the JTS was in the drafting stage, the physician helped form the nondenominational Gratz College, the school for the training of Hebrew religious teachers.

Solis-Cohen's accomplishments in the medical world gave him an international reputation. From 1887 to 1927 he was physician to the Philadelphia General, Jewish, and Jefferson hospitals of Philadelphia. He was a prolific writer and editor. He edited the *Polyclinic* from 1894 to 1899 and *American Medicine* from 1901 to 1905. He published *Essentials in Diagnosis* (1892) in collaboration with A. Eshner and a textbook, *Pharmacotherapeutics, Materia and Drug Action*, with Thomas S. Githens.

Solis-Cohen was a staunch supporter of the science of pharmacy. He wrote editorials on the dangers of nostrums in various journals and was against patent medicine quackery. For example, in 1892 his paper in the *Alumni Report of the Philadelphia College of Pharmacy and Science* condemns nostrum traffic. In 1902 he edited *A System of Physiologic Therapeutics*. His dictum was, "The right drug at the right time in the right dose will do the right thing."

Solis-Cohen was president of the Philadelphia County Medical Society in 1898 and 1899. He led the fight to filter and sanitize Philadelphia water, an effort that by 1908 led to the virtual end of typhoid fever in the city. As the nineteenth century turned to the twentieth, Solis-Cohen helped initiate the National Tuberculosis Foundation and used his membership as a platform to attack slums and sweatshop conditions and to advocate the need for the government to protect workers.

Solis-Cohen was a strong advocate of drugs to treat diseases. While recognizing the value of fresh air and sunshine to help cure tuberculosis, he was among the first to successfully treat that disease with drugs. He was also a specialist in identification and treatment of nervous blood vessel disorders. As early as 1894 he published in the *American Journal of Medical Science* the first comprehensive study on vasomotor-ataxia (a nervous condition affecting the blood vessels). He later wrote medical papers on disorders of the nervous system. A prodigious writer, he authored 650 medical articles with the emphasis on drugs and medical preparations and their use in treatment of disease.

Solis-Cohen was a member of the Committee of Revision of U.S. Pharmacopoeia (lists of drugs, descriptions of tests for identity, purity, and strength and formulas for making preparations). He edited eleven volumes of the *U.S. Pharmacopoeia* in 1911, which included 2,000 pages of his own analysis of the treatment of diseases.

Solis-Cohen served on the Philadelphia School Board from 1925 to 1943. He initiated the practice of inoculating schoolchildren against diphtheria, promoted a free milk and lunch program, and supported a high school for academically talented girls. Soon after his death in his son's Elkins Park home, an elementary school was named for him.

Solis-Cohen spent ten hours a day working in his regular medical practice; in his free time, he wrote articles advancing his profession. A renaissance man, he translated and wrote poetry and attended civic meetings to improve the lives of Philadelphia citizens, particularly schoolchildren. In addition, he forged national Jewish religious institutions—seminaries, colleges, and publication societies—"to save souls and be the arsenal of the Jewish spirit."

• The most extensive and comprehensive source of information on Solis-Cohen are his papers, located in the Archives of the National Museum of American Jewish History in Philadelphia. Another rich vein of information is Edward Coleman, comp., *Judaism and Science* (1940), which contains Solis-Cohen's addresses, essays, and poems. It also has a bibliography of his writings. Other sources giving an overview of the physician-scholars's life are Murray Friedman, *When Philadelphia Was the Capital of Jewish America* (1993); the *Jewish Exponent*, 9 Sept. 1927; and the *Philadelphia Public Ledger*, 1 Sept. 1939. Solis-Cohen's journalistic and Jewish institutional building career is described in William Langfield, *Fifty Year Chronicle of the YMHA* (1928); the *Jewish Exponent*, 7 Oct. 1921; the *American Hebrew*, 27 Nov. 1912; the *American Hebrew*, 21 June 1918; Moshe Davis, *The Emergence of Conservative Judaism* (1963); Diane King, "Jewish Education in Philadelphia," in *Jewish Life in Philadelphia, 1830–1940*, ed. Murray Friedman (1986); and Jonathan Sarna, *The Jewish Publication Society* (1989). An obituary is in the *New York Times*, 13 July 1948.

PHILIP ROSEN

SOLMSEN, Friedrich Heinrich Rudolph (4 Feb. 1904–30 Jan. 1989), classical philologist, was born in Bonn, Germany, the son of Felix Solmsen, a renowned Indo-European philologist, and Lily Brach. His father died by his own hand when Friedrich was only seven, leaving his mother to raise him on her own. He studied classical philology at Bonn (1922), Heidelberg (1924), and Berlin, where he received his Ph.D. in 1928. It was during his Berlin years that he came into contact with two titanic figures of German classical scholarship: Ulrich von Wilamowitz-Moellendorff and Werner Jaeger. But it was Jaeger, Wilamowitz's successor and the driving force behind Berlin's rejuvenated classics department in the Weimar period, who ultimately most influenced Solmsen's work, especially through his book *Aristoteles* (1923). Solmsen's Berlin dissertation, *Die aristotelische Methodenlehre und die spätplatonische Akademie* (1928), and his monograph *Die Entwicklung der aristotelischen Logik und Rhetorik*, published in Jaeger's monograph series, Neue philologische Untersuchungen (1929), may be seen as a product of that inspiration. Solmsen also published, in this series, *Antiphonstudien* (1931), a study that has remained a standard work on Antiphon to this day. Almost uniquely it treats authoritatively in one volume the philosophical, rhetorical, and forensic legacy of the Athenian orator. Solmsen's interest in Aristotle, and indeed, in all ancient Greek philosophy, continued even into his final year, in which he published articles on the Greek atomists.

On receipt of the Ph.D., Solmsen was appointed assistant at Berlin and began teaching in 1929. In 1932 he married one of his students, Lieselotte Salzer, in Karlsruhe; the marriage was childless. Years later she would joke about their first meeting: "On the day I met Friedrich, there entered his life two perennial pains: myself and gout." Solmsen had begun suffering from this affliction in 1931, and it plagued him for the rest of his life. Only a year after his marriage, however, an even greater event radically altered their lives. In 1933 the Nazis, on racial grounds, removed him from his post. The form agreeing to his firing was signed by his Latin professor, Eduard Norden, himself a Jew. A career in Germany an impossibility, the Solmsens moved to England, settling in Cambridge, where Solmsen obtained a research grant at Trinity College. Although he received a second Ph.D. in 1936, there was no permanent position available in England at the time. So in 1937 the Solmsens, now penniless, emigrated to the United States (their travel expenses paid by the donations of American classicists), where Solmsen had been offered a post as professor of philosophy at Olivet College, a private college in Michigan. He taught at Olivet until 1940, when he secured an appointment at Cornell.

Beginning as an assistant professor, Solmsen became full professor within seven years and served as chairman of the Department of Classics from 1953 until 1962. During his years at Cornell, Solmsen taught both undergraduate and graduate courses and produced an array of books and articles that impress by their exacting scholarship and broad scope. His books *Plato's Theology* (1942), *Hesiod and Aeschylus* (1949), and *Aristotle's System of the Physical World* (1960), all of which were printed in the series Cornell Studies in Classical Philology, secured his reputation as a serious scholar, while his numerous articles and reviews, collected in *Kleine Schriften* (3 vols., 1968–1982), attest to a breadth of interest that ran nearly the gamut of classical literature. His scholarship did not go unnoticed. He received a Guggenheim Fellowship (1947–1948), and a Fulbright professorship at Frankfurt and Kiel (1958–1959), and he accepted an appointment as Herbert F. Johnson Visiting Professor at the University of Wisconsin-Madison (1960–1961). His stay at Madison turned out to be the beginning of the next phase of his career.

In 1962 he accepted a position at Madison in the Institute for Research in the Humanities. This was followed by his tenure there as Moses Slaughter Professor of Classical Studies, an appointment he held from 1964 until his retirement in 1974. Just as his career at Cornell was distinguished by numerous honors, so too was his career at Madison. In 1965 he accepted a second Fulbright professorship, this time at St. Andrews; he was visiting professor at Heidelberg in the summer of 1968; and in 1970 he was visiting professor at Swarthmore College, and in 1972 at Yale. He was elected to the Royal Dutch Academy, the American Philosophical Society, the British Academy, the American Academy of Arts and Sciences, and was made an honorary member of the Society for the Promotion of Hellenic Studies. His scholarly output continued unabated, and he produced during this period his most important work, a critical edition of Hesiod for the Oxford Classical Text series, published in 1970. Solmsen provided more exact collations of the ancient manuscripts, set deletions on a more scientific basis, and incorporated work on the text since the last critical edition of 1902. For this he won the Charles A. Goodwin Award of Merit of the American Philological Association in 1972. His edition remains authoritative.

Although Solmsen retired from the University of Wisconsin in 1974, his prolific career continued. The Solmsens moved from Madison to Chapel Hill, North Carolina, where Solmsen quickly formed ties with the Department of Classics at the University of North Carolina that lasted until his death. As emeritus professor there he continued teaching and writing. In 1975 he published *Intellectual Experiments of the Greek Enlightenment* and in 1979 *Isis among the Greeks and Romans*, a product of his year as Martin Classical Lecturer at Oberlin (1978).

Solmsen was one of some twenty refugee scholars of the 1930s whose contributions invigorated American classics. His rigorous training in the German classical tradition made him almost unique in his easy familiarity with the vast range of Greek and, to a lesser extent, Latin literature. His work is remarkable because he treated ably broad aspects of Greek philosophical thought but as well—this was the legacy of his father—was extraordinarily competent in details of language and meter. He wrote on Hesiod's thought but also edited the authoritative modern Greek text of Hesiod. He based his work on careful scrutiny of original sources, not on English translations. Few today possess such expertise. He died in Chapel Hill.

• Solmsen's papers are at the Department of Classics at the University of North Carolina, Chapel Hill. For Solmsen's reminiscences of his Berlin years, see "Wilamowitz in His Last Ten Years," *Greek, Roman and Byzantine Studies* 20 (1979): 89–122, and "Classical Scholarship in Berlin between the Wars," *Greek, Roman and Byzantine Studies* 30 (1989) 117–40. For his removal from Berlin, see William M. Calder III, "Studies in the Modern History of Classical Scholarship," *Antiqua* 27 (1984), p. 71. There are loyal necrologies by Helen F. North in *Gnomon* 61 (1989): 757–59, and in Ward W. Briggs, Jr., ed., *Biographical Dictionary of North American Classicists* (1994), pp. 604–6.

JOHN P. HARRIS

SOLOMON, Hannah Greenebaum (14 Jan. 1858–8 Dec. 1942), social welfare activist, was born in Chicago, Illinois, daughter of German-Jewish immigrants Sarah Speigel and Michael Greenebaum, a tinsmith and dealer in tinware. She was educated in Chicago public schools and by private tutors. In Hannah's words, her "father, always progressive, believed that girls as well as boys, should be given educational advantages."

Hannah wanted her education in secular and religious subjects to continue into adulthood and yearned to use her knowledge and religious inspiration to do

"practical good." In 1876 she moved closer to these goals when she and her sister were the first Jewish women admitted to membership in the Chicago Women's Club, an organization devoted to literary studies and "good works." In 1879 Hannah married Henry Solomon, a prosperous merchant, and for more than a decade her "life was exceedingly full of household tasks," her time and energy mostly taken up with the roles of wife and mother of three children. But she remained involved in Chicago's most prominent Jewish organizations, including Temple Sinai.

In 1890 Hannah Solomon was asked by two prominent Chicago women to organize a Jewish Women's Congress for the upcoming World's Columbian Exposition. By 1892 she was so encouraged by positive responses to her work for the congress that she determined to build a permanent national organization of Jewish women. At the meetings of the congress in 1893, almost one hundred Jewish women, representing twenty-nine cities, resolved to meet regularly as the National Council of Jewish Women (NCJW). They pledged to study Judaism and Jewish history and to apply the knowledge gained to the improvement of Jewish education and social reform. And they elected Solomon president.

Through her work with the Chicago Women's Club, Solomon had helped create an emergency workroom for needy women during the depression of 1893–1894, and as head of the NCJW she introduced this idea to the council as well. In response to the multiple needs of new Jewish immigrants from Eastern Europe, Solomon worked effectively with American institutions like the Chicago Women's Club and Hull House, but in 1897 she also created the Bureau of Personal Service, an institution to be staffed and administered by Jewish women. The bureau, which Solomon chaired for thirteen years, investigated the financial needs of immigrants for the Women's Loan Society, studied tenement conditions for industrial reports, directed parents with "troubled" children to the appropriate agencies, and cooperated regularly with the settlement houses.

Members of the Chicago chapter of the NCJW, which Solomon had helped begin in 1893, were also largely responsible for the establishment of a separate juvenile court. These women, guided by Solomon, began as inexperienced volunteers, but soon became expert in the field of judicial procedures and juvenile delinquency. Several became unpaid probation officers of the court. The Chicago chapter also created a Sabbath School for girls because the traditional Talmud Torahs did not provide religious education for young women.

Hannah Solomon and other prosperous German-Jewish women from Chicago, including Sadie American, Esther Loeb Kohn, and Rosa Sonneschein, viewed their participation in Jewish social service as a way to define acceptable behavior for women and as a way to achieve equal social status with Gentile club women. They also saw their work as a religious duty—*tikkun olam*—an obligation to repair or improve the

SOMERS • 365

world. In addition they viewed the tasks of "uplift" and "social housekeeping" as a privilege and responsibility of their class. Because her husband was supportive of her work and a prosperous businessman and her family was prominent in Jewish and civic affairs, Solomon was content to remain a volunteer activist, never accepting a salary.

At the 1896 convention of the NCJW, Solomon, an adherent of Reform Judaism, was challenged by a number of Orthodox women who questioned her role as leader and model because she failed to consecrate the Sabbath according to the Orthodox mode. Solomon, connecting her social welfare activism with her identity as a Jew, responded with the statement: "I consecrate every day of the week." She was reelected president.

Challenges to Solomon's views came from other voices as well. In the *American Jewess*, Rosa Sonneschein, the editor of the magazine, ascribed the NCJW's relatively low membership (3,000) to the lack of a central idea or goal. And between 1896 and 1899 she advanced the idea that Zionism could generate genuine excitement among American Jewish women and rejuvenate the NCJW. Hannah Solomon and most other women in the organization did not agree. They believed that the social work projects within their own communities took precedence over work for, or in, Palestine. But also as "good Americans" fearful of charges of "dual loyalty," they were worried about any "nationalist" idea that might appear to dilute their commitment to the United States.

Solomon was also devoted to the cause of woman suffrage and to equality for women within Judaism. In addition to her work with the Bureau of Personal Services and the NCJW, she represented the NCJW on the Council of Women of the United States and became its treasurer in 1899. In 1904 she and Susan B. Anthony were sent as the council's delegates to the convention of the International Council of Women in Berlin. In 1905 she declined reelection as president of the NCJW and devoted herself, the only woman on the board, to the work of the Associated Jewish Charities of Chicago and to the Park Ridge School for Girls, an institution for rehabilitation that had grown out of the Illinois Industrial School for Girls of which Solomon had been president.

In 1942, when she was working on her autobiography, shortly before she died in Chicago, Solomon wrote perceptively about her lifelong participation in movements to improve social conditions: "The motivation for the enterprises and activities in which I have engaged has come, it seems to me, from the Biblical injunction, 'to do justly and to love mercy,' and through the Jewish concept of universal brotherhood."

• Solomon's reports and miscellaneous writings can be found in the *Proceedings of the National Council of Jewish Women* (1897–1923), *The Papers of the Jewish Woman's Congress* (1894), and the papers of the NCJW at the American Jewish Historical Society in Waltham, Mass. Her autobiography, *Fabric of My Life* (1946), is indispensable. Useful secondary sources include Charlotte Baum et al., *The Jewish Woman in America* (1976); Jacob Rader Marcus, *The American Jewish Woman, 1654–1980: A Documentary History* (1981); June Sochen, *Consecrate Every Day: The Public Lives of Jewish American Women, 1880–1980* (1981); and Faith Rogow, *"Gone to Another Meeting": The National Council of Jewish Women, 1893–1993* (1993). An obituary is in the *New York Times*, 9 Dec. 1942.

GERALD SORIN

SOMERS, Richard (15 Sept. 1778–4 Sept. 1804), naval officer, was born on Somers Point, Great Egg Harbor, New Jersey, the son of Richard Somers, a militia colonel and judge, and Sophia Stilwell. He attended school in Philadelphia, where his family resided during the Revolution, and also at an academy in Burlington, New Jersey. He never married. When his father died in October 1794, Somers entered the coastal shipping trade between Philadelphia and New York, gaining experience at sea in a number of small vessels. On 30 April 1798 he entered the U.S. Navy as a midshipman and was assigned duty on the frigate *United States*, forty-four guns, Captain John Barry commanding. He sailed from Philadelphia on 7 July on a voyage to Cape Cod and along the Atlantic Coast to the West Indies in search of French warships and trading vessels during America's undeclared war with France. He returned to Philadelphia on 19 September but shortly thereafter sailed again in the *United States* on convoy duty to Havana. Repeating this voyage a number of times over the next few months, he earned the confidence of Captain Barry, who recommended him to Benjamin Stoddert, secretary of the navy, for promotion to third lieutenant. Stoddert, pronouncing Somers "well qualified" and deserving, gave his support, and on 21 May 1799 Somers received his promotion. He sailed on 3 November from Newport, Rhode Island, on the *United States* for France with peace commissioners on board, but his ship ran into foul weather, was badly damaged, and had to put in at Corunna, Spain. Returning to the United States in early April 1800, the *United States* had to undergo extensive repairs for the remainder of the year at Philadelphia, and Somers and the other officers lived in a boardinghouse.

At the conclusion of the war with France in early 1801, Somers was retained on the active navy list in the peacetime establishment. On 30 July he was ordered to the frigate *Boston*, twenty-eight guns, Captain Daniel McNeill commanding, at Boston. In October he sailed on the *Boston* for Bordeaux, France, to deliver Chancellor Robert Livingston, newly appointed American minister to France, to his destination. Somers then proceeded with the *Boston* to the Mediterranean and joined an American squadron under the command of Captain Richard Dale that was warring against Tripoli, Algeria, and Tunis. In the fall of 1802, without having accomplished much, his ship returned home with the squadron. Early the following year Somers was appointed commander of the schooner *Nautilus*, twelve guns, fitting out in Boston as part of a seven-ship squadron under Commodore Edward Preble to blockade and chastise Tripoli. On 14 August 1803 Somers sailed with Preble and by 19 October was anchored at Gibraltar with the other ships of the squadron except for the *Philadelphia* and the *Vixen*, which were already on station at Tripoli. Preble's ships cleared Gibraltar on 14 November, sailing to join the two vessels, but the commodore learned en route that the *Philadelphia* had run aground and had been captured. Thereupon, he proceeded with his squadron to Syracuse. In February 1804 Somers assisted his friend, Lieutenant Stephen Decatur, Jr., in Decatur's daring raid into Tripoli Harbor to burn the *Constitution*. A month later Somers sailed the *Nautilus* to Messina for extensive repairs after a serious collision with the *Siren*.

Somers was joined at Messina on 26 May by Preble, who was angry that his naval blockade of Tripoli was not working. Concocting a plan for a violent and direct assault on Tripoli by gunboats, Preble secured six of these small vessels from the naval commandant of Naples, manned them with crewmen from the *Nautilus* and volunteer Neapolitan seamen, and appointed Somers commander of the little flotilla. Over the next six weeks Preble gathered together at Syracuse a powerful naval force consisting of two frigates, a schooner, two bomb ketches, and Somers's gunboats and sailed for Tripoli on 13 July. Reaching his objective on 25 July, Preble divided his gunboats into two divisions, one commanded by Somers, the other by Decatur. On 3 August Somers and Decatur attacked the enemy, and although Decatur's division did most of the fighting because contrary winds and currents kept Somers on the sidelines, Somers did assist in destroying an enemy battery. Taking part in three more attacks during August, Somers performed bravely, on one occasion losing a gunboat, and was promoted captain. Nevertheless, he and his colleagues could not breach Tripoli's defenses. Finally, in early September Preble decided as a last resort to try a desperate gamble: to load the ketch *Intrepid* with five tons of black powder, scores of artillery and mortar shells, and huge quantities of inflammable materials, then slip it into the harbor near a key fortress and blow it up.

Somers, perhaps hoping to emulate his friend Decatur's earlier exploit, volunteered to command this foolhardy venture, which under optimal circumstances would allow him and his crew a scant fifteen minutes to clear the danger zone. On 1 September he endeavored to sail the *Intrepid* into the harbor but was forced to withdraw when the wind shifted against him. The following day he had to postpone another trial when Preble ordered his entire squadron to carry out one last general assault with Somers commanding his gunboats. At last, on the evening of 4 September Somers was ready for another attempt with the *Intrepid*. Escorted by three warships to the entrance of the harbor, he proceeded from there on his own. After a time his fellows on the escort ships heard two enemy alarm guns sound from the fortress followed by ten minutes of total silence. Suddenly the *Intrepid*, without having reached its position, was ripped by a huge explosion that killed everyone on board without doing any damage to the enemy. Although it was impossible to know what had happened, Somers's friends asserted that he had deliberately blown up his ship to avoid its capture. No bodies were recovered. On 3 March 1805 Congress voted a Resolution of Condolence for those who had perished, and over the years several ships of the navy have been named for Somers.

• Published documents relating to Somers's role in the undeclared war with France and in the Barbary Wars are in Dudley Knox, ed., *Naval Documents Related to the Quasi-War between the United States and France, 1797–1801* (7 vols., 1935–1938) and *Naval Documents Related to the United States Wars with the Barbary Powers* (6 vols., 1939–1944). Short biographical sketches are in James Fenimore Cooper, *Lives of Distinguished American Naval Officers* (1846); Molly Elliot Seawell, *Decatur and Somers* (1894) and *Twelve Naval Captains, Being a Record of Certain Americans Who Made Themselves Immortal* (1897); and Edna Miriam Hooper, comp., *Richard Somers, 1778–1804: Master Commandant of the United States Navy . . .* (1933). His relations with important colleagues are discussed in Irving Anthony, *Decatur* (1931); Charles L. Lewis, *The Romantic Decatur* (1937); and Christopher McKee, *Edward Preble: A Naval Biography* (1972). For his roles in the wars with France and the Barbary states, see Gardner W. Allen, *Our Naval War with France* (1909) and *Our Navy and the Barbary Corsairs* (1905); Glenn Tucker, *Dawn like Thunder: The Barbary Wars and the Birth of the U.S. Navy* (1963); Howard P. Nash, *The Forgotten Wars: The Role of the U.S. Navy in the Quasi-War with France and the Barbary Wars, 1798–1805* (1968); and William M. Fowler, Jr., *Jack Tars and Commodores: The American Navy, 1783–1815* (1984).

PAUL DAVID NELSON

SOMERVELL, Brehon Burke (9 May 1892–13 Feb. 1955), army general, was born in Little Rock, Arkansas, the son of William Taylor Somervell, a physician, and Mary S. Burke, a schoolteacher. Brehon spent most of his childhood and youth in Washington, D.C., where his parents opened a private school in 1906. Somervell entered the U.S. Military Academy in 1910 and graduated sixth in a class of 107 in 1914. His high academic performance earned him a commission in the Corps of Engineers.

During World War I Somervell served in France with the American Expeditionary Force. As an engineer he was involved initially in construction projects, but late in the war he secured the position of G-3 (operations officer) in the Eighty-ninth Division. He attained the temporary rank of lieutenant colonel but reverted to captain in the postwar demobilization. In 1919 he married Anna Purnell; they had three children.

In the period between the world wars Somervell supervised a number of major engineering projects and held several key administrative positions. He became known as an ambitious, aggressive, hard-working officer who often violated standard procedures in securing resources—he placed success ahead of method and often encroached on the authority of others—but always got positive results. Nevertheless, advancement in rank came slowly in the stagnant interwar army. Somervell's promotion to major came in 1920 and to lieutenant colonel in 1935. From 1936 to 1940 he served as head of the Works Progress Administration (WPA) for New York City. Although only a lieutenant colonel, he attained national prominence and attracted the favorable attention of the Franklin D. Roosevelt administration for his capable if sometimes controversial management of WPA programs. With the onset of prewar mobilization in 1940, Somervell left the WPA to head the Construction Division of the Quartermaster Corps. In this capacity he was responsible for building camps and establishing munitions factories for the burgeoning army. He also played a major role in the design and early construction of the Pentagon Building. In January 1941 Somervell was promoted from lieutenant colonel to brigadier general, skipping the rank of colonel. In November 1941 he was named the assistant chief of staff for logistics (G-4) on the War Department General Staff. His promotion to major general came in January 1942, the month following Japan's attack on Pearl Harbor.

On 9 March 1942 an executive order reorganized the army under three superagencies: Army Ground Forces, which raised and trained combat units; Army Air Forces, which became a semi-independent air arm; and Services of Supply, which centralized many of the army's administrative, procurement, and supply activities under one head. Somervell, who helped draft the reorganization, was promoted to lieutenant general and named to command Services of Supply (later Army Service Forces or ASF). Among the agencies collected into ASF were the Quartermaster Corps, Chemical Warfare Service, Signal Corps, Corps of Engineers, Ordnance Department, Medical Corps, and Transportation Corps.

As the chief of ASF, Somervell participated in the formulation of national and coalition strategy. ASF then translated strategic plans into requirements for procurement, supply, and transportation and awarded contracts to secure the needed matériel and services. ASF coordinated the shipping of men and matériel to camps within the United States and to overseas theaters. It also supervised logistical operations within the combat theaters. During World War II ASF awarded more than 600,000 major contracts and procured over $69 billion worth of war matériel. By the war's end ASF comprised over one million servicemen and women. As head of this massive organization, Somervell was the army's chief representative in the competition for resources. He clashed repeatedly with other agencies and service branches as he fought to secure the army's interests and sought to preserve and expand ASF's prerogatives.

Somervell employed two noteworthy management tools to direct the ASF juggernaut. The first of these was an organization known as the Control Division, a feedback agency staffed by management experts that maintained constant vigil over the organization's progress to uncover and correct any organizational deficiencies. The second was a planning document called the Army Supply Program, which was a long-term forecast of the army's procurement requirements, as determined by national strategy. While not unique to Somervell, these and other management techniques marked him as an administrative innovator.

Somervell's first wife died in 1942, and in 1943 he married Louise Hampton Wartmann. They had no children. Somervell retired from the army in 1946, wearing the four stars of a full general, and made his home in Ocala, Florida. Later that year he embarked upon a second career as president of Koppers Company, a position he retained until shortly before his death. Somervell died in Ocala and was buried in Arlington National Cemetery.

General George C. Marshall, the army's chief of staff during World War II, held Somervell in high regard for his ability to perform monumental tasks and was willing to overlook his penchant for antagonizing others. "What he did was a miracle," said Marshall in a postwar interview. The U.S. Army in World War II was probably the best-supplied army that had ever gone to war. Much of the credit for that accomplishment goes to Somervell, who provided the "sinews of war" for a military effort that literally spanned the globe.

• Somervell's papers are at the U.S. Army Military History Institute in Carlisle, Pa. An essential source is John Kennedy Ohl, *Supplying the Troops: General Somervell and American Logistics in WWII* (1994). Two volumes in the army's official history of World War II deal extensively with Somervell's contributions: Robert W. Coakley and Richard M. Leighton, *Global Logistics and Strategy, 1940–1943* (1955), and Leighton and Coakley, *Global Logistics and Strategy, 1943–1945* (1968). An obituary is in the *New York Times*, 14 Feb. 1955.

CHRISTOPHER R. GABEL

SOMERVILLE, Nellie Nugent (25 Sept. 1863–28 July 1952), suffrage organizer and legislator, was born Eleanor Fulkerson Nugent, in Greenville, Mississippi, the daughter of William Lewis Nugent, a lawyer, and Eleanor Fulkerson Smith. She was born with a deformed right hand, and her parents feared she would not survive; however, apparently most people who knew Somerville in her adult years were not even aware of her defective hand. Her mother died when Nellie was two years old. She was raised primarily by her grandmother S. Myra Smith until 1870, when she moved with her father from Greenville to Jackson. There he practiced law, became well known and wealthy, married again, and had another family.

Somerville's intellectual abilities were recognized early on. She was sent to Whitworth College in Brookhaven, Mississippi, and in 1880 graduated with an A.B. degree from Martha Washington College in Abingdon, Virginia. Choosing to return to Greenville, live with her grandmother, and become a tutor rather than to read law in her father's Jackson office, in 1885 she married Robert Somerville, a civil engineer from Virginia who had come to the Mississippi Delta to work in flood control. The couple made their home in

Greenville. They had four children. Robert Somerville, a conservative, quiet man, was patient with his wife's activism, though he probably never completely understood it. He died in 1925.

Like many other southern women, Somerville's early experiences with organizations were fostered in the church. Her first office was that of district secretary for Women's Foreign Missions of the Methodist Episcopal Church South. Through the years she held other church offices and wrote in church publications advocating a more equal role for women in church affairs. She is said to have been "set wild" by a motion at a board of missions meeting to turn the group's hard-earned dollars over to the bishops to spend.

As a staunch Methodist, she followed in the tradition of social action for which John Wesley had called. She joined the Woman's Christian Temperance Union, first organized in Mississippi in 1883 by Frances Willard. Somerville was president of the Greenville WCTU in 1894–1895 and state corresponding secretary in 1895–1896. As such she tackled the open saloons in Greenville and the subsequent mixing of liquor and gunpowder that made the town's streets unsafe by day or night. It became increasingly clear to her, however, as it did to other women working for progressive social change, that they must have the vote. Thus, following the WCTU convention of 1897, thirty-three suffragists from towns across Mississippi organized the Mississippi Woman Suffrage Association with Somerville as president. "Seeing then the close inseparable connection between moral questions and political questions," she said in a presidential address, "women have very naturally come to desire a share in the settlement of these questions."

From that time until the ratification of the Nineteenth Amendment in 1920, Somerville used her talents as an organizer, writer, and speaker in the cause of votes for women. She also used her secure social position to make suffrage for women socially acceptable in Mississippi. In a newsletter written as one of her first acts as state president, she warned members that the public expected "unpleasant aggressiveness" from suffrage sympathizers and urged them to "endeavor to disappoint such expectations." She worked to involve men in the suffrage movement and hoped that through reason the men of the Mississippi legislature could be persuaded to pass a state suffrage amendment. Another way women could prove their worthiness to vote, she reasoned, was to take positive action in public affairs through the channels that were available to them. "Service" became a keynote. Under Somerville's leadership, the Greenville suffrage group took the name of the Civic Improvement Club. By petitioning the city council, it brought about substantial improvements in the quality of life in Greenville, such as garbage pickup, inspectors for restaurants, no spitting laws, and an antituberculosis campaign that resulted in Greenville's acquisition of the first community health nurse employed in Mississippi. Somerville personally traveled to a number of public schools with a tuberculosis exhibit from the Delta Fair, lecturing teachers and students.

Somerville was active on the state, regional, and national suffrage fronts, too, often traveling to Jackson to lobby for a suffrage amendment or to participate in hearings before the legislature. Some of her speaking tours to county fairs are described in her manuscript "History of Mississippi Woman Suffrage Association, 1897–1919." She volunteered to edit the Greenville Democrat-Times "Woman's Page" without pay and was allowed to put in suffrage articles, which the paper reprinted for her at cost. "In that way I very nearly filled a small steamer trunk with literature. . . . Some of the leaflets were: 'Are Women Too Good to Vote?' 'Who Takes Care of Mississippi Women?' 'Women Voters Keepers at Home,' and 'The Mothers Right to Her Children.'" Somerville also aided the suffrage cause in Mississippi by persuading the national suffrage leader Dr. Anna Howard Shaw to come to Greenville and speak. Outside the state, Somerville was elected treasurer of the Southern States Woman Suffrage Conference and in 1915 second vice president of the National Woman Suffrage Association.

With the beginning of World War I, Somerville turned to chairing the Women's Patriot Committee and writing a series of articles, "Mobilizing the Women," in the Democrat-Times. Suffrage efforts were not neglected, however, and Somerville's disappointment must have been keen when in 1920 the Mississippi House soundly defeated the Nineteenth Amendment after it had been ratified nationally.

Somerville next turned her attention toward educating the state's women for citizenship through speeches and articles and toward holding office herself. She announced her intention to run for the state legislature in the state newspaper for women, the Woman Voter, in 1923: "My life and character are an open book before the people of this country. I am a law abiding God-fearing Christian woman. This I have been for many years and this I shall continue to be." She won that election, becoming Mississippi's first female representative, a position she held until 1927, when she did not run for reelection. She was extremely effective as a legislator, serving as chairwoman of the Committee on Eleemosynary Institutions and bringing about important improvements at the hospital for the insane. She also successfully sponsored the bill that established Delta State Teachers College in Cleveland, where she moved in 1931.

Somerville spent almost every summer of her life from 1887 on at the Monteagle Sunday School Assembly, the "Chautauqua of the South," in Monteagle, Tennessee. She owned a cottage there and was intermittently a member of the board of trustees.

In her later years, Somerville continued to speak, write, and manage her property, proving to be an astute businesswoman. Always interested in history, she was a founder of the Washington County Historical Society and later became active in the Daughters of the American Revolution (DAR). Her attention turned increasingly to conservative causes, such as states' rights, opposition to the merging of the northern and southern branches of the Methodist church, national defense, and anticommunism. She died in Ruleville, Mississippi.

Somerville was the fourth woman named to Mississippi's Hall of Fame. "Nellie Nugent Somerville was always ahead of her times," one of her colleagues wrote. "She was out in front, but she was alone only in her thinking, for her heart reached out to those around her, rich and poor, black and white. She will always remain one of the great women of her generation" (Polly Graham Babcock, "Nellie Nugent Somerville—Recollections," Princeton, N.J., 31 July 1957). A powerful speaker, organizer, and politician, Somerville was remarkable in being able to act successfully in opposition to so many of the constraints placed on southern women in her time. She persuaded others to follow her in defying stereotypes of woman's place and demonstrated unequivocally that "woman's place is in the world."

• The Somerville papers are in the Arthur and Elizabeth Schlesinger Library on the History of Women in America at Radcliffe College, Cambridge, Mass.; the Department of Archives and History in Jackson, Miss., has duplicates of many of the documents. Joanne Hawks, "Like Mother, Like Daughter," *Journal of Mississippi History* 45 (May 1983): 116–23, traces the similarities in the careers of Somerville and her daughter Lucy Somerville Howorth. Rebecca Hood-Adams, "Nellie Nugent Somerville: 1 Woman, 1 Vote," Jackson *Clarion-Ledger*, 7 Mar. 1989, was published in a series "honoring women who shaped Mississippi." The civil war letters of William Nugent to his wife are published in *My Dear Nellie* (1977), ed. William M. Cash and Lucy Somerville Howorth. A key background article is A. Elizabeth Taylor, "The Woman Suffrage Movement in Mississippi, 1890–1920," *Journal of Mississippi History* 30 (Feb. 1968): 1–34. Mary Louise Meredith, "The Mississippi Woman's Rights Movement, 1889–1923" (master's thesis, Delta State Univ., 1974), has detailed information about Somerville's role in the state suffrage movement. An obituary is in the Cleveland (Miss.) *Bolivar Commercial*, 1 Aug. 1952.

DOROTHY SHAWHAN

SOMMERS, Tish (8 Sept. 1914–18 Oct. 1985), organizer of the Displaced Homemaker Network and cofounder of the Older Women's League, was born Letitia Innes in Cambria, California, the daughter of Murray Innes, a mining engineer, and Catherine "Kate" Dorsch, a homemaker, later a salesperson. In her childhood in the Sierra Madre Mountains and in San Francisco, Sommers experienced both affluence and near poverty. After her parents were divorced in 1926 she, her mother, and two brothers experienced financial and emotional hardships. With the help of wealthy relatives, however, she was able to study dance in Germany with well-known modern dancer Mary Wigman from 1933 to 1936. This experience exposed her to the consequences of racism and anti-Semitism and to the dangers of the Nazi programs.

When Sommers returned to California, she attended the University of California at Los Angeles, joined the Communist party (in 1936), and was a youth worker through the 1940s. She married radical writer Sidney Burke in 1938; their childless marriage ended in divorce in 1943. She was a dancer and choreographer at UCLA and performed with the Lester Horton dance group in Los Angeles. During the 1940s she organized professional dancers in Hollywood and established the Pan American Dance Troupe in East Los Angeles, where she worked with a racially and culturally integrated youth group. She was also the Southern California youth group leader for the Henry Wallace presidential campaign in 1948.

In 1949 she married labor organizer Joe Sommers. In 1950–1951 she was the last youth director for the Progressive party in New York City. During the 1950s, living in New York, Birmingham, Alabama, and then Wisconsin, Tish Sommers focused on raising their adopted son, Bill. In the mid-1960s she returned to community organizing as a volunteer coordinator for a poverty program in Seattle. By 1971 she was divorced and living in a collective home in Berkeley, where she produced *The Not-So-Helpless Female* (1973), her manual on organizing, and established (with Ruth McElhinney) the Women's Action Training Center in Oakland to focus on employment issues for women. In 1971, as a board member of the National Organization for Women, she embarked on her second major career, focused on issues affecting older women. She chaired NOW's Task Force on Older Women for seven years and developed a national network that served as the base for the Alliance for Displaced Homemakers. During the mid-1970s Sommers and recently widowed Laurie Shields started the Displaced Homemakers Network, a national grass roots network that focused on legislative and political support for women who in midlife found themselves divorced or widowed with few economic resources or labor market skills. California and other state and national legislation was passed in support of displaced homemakers, primarily through the establishment of hundreds of job training and counseling centers that were coordinated loosely through the Displaced Homemakers Network, Inc., in Washington, D.C.

By 1978 Sommers and Shields were ready to move on to broader issues affecting older women. Their next efforts were educational, through the nonprofit Older Women's League Education Fund (OWLEF), which they founded in 1980 and which distributed Gray Papers on social security, health care, pensions, and welfare. Sommers also spoke to feminist groups across the country reenvisioning images of aging: "I look forward to the time when we can merchandise a cosmetic line to make youth look older—a special crow's foot pencil, the silver bleaches, the stick to make those delicious brown spots on the hands, eyeliner under the eye for that sexy mature look. Let the young ones eat their hearts out!" (Huckle, p. 13). After the laughter, she talked about how lower incomes left women with lower-level pensions; how the impact of no-fault divorce left women with little hope for earning a good living; and how limited access to health care made a cruel mockery of the concept of "golden years."

The political climate was changing in the late 1970s. Some age activists felt that organizations ignored women; some older women felt marginalized in feminist groups. Sommers was well known for her visionary enthusiasm and crisp articulation of issues; Shields was the consummate politician, uniting women across the country. One colleague called them "the cool yogurt and spicy beans of the women's movement." With the help of the Western Gerontological Association and many allies, they organized a regional conference on women's issues to prepare for the White House Conference on Aging in 1981. At the end of the regional conference the Older Women's League was founded, with 300 charter members. Within two years there were more than seventy chapters and nearly 5,000 members. Grass roots chapters focused on access to health care insurance, social security reform, and pension rights. Membership, nearly 20,000 in 1995, was primarily middle class and white, though OWL sponsored conferences on older black women and had elected African-American and Hispanic women to its board by the mid-1990s. The national office in Washington, D.C., coordinated local chapters, provided educational materials on a range of older women's issues, and provided expert testimony before congressional committees.

As their final contributions to OWL's political agenda, Sommers and Shields used their experiences with Sommers's terminal cancer to build an awareness of death and dying in the posthumously published *Women Take Care: The Consequences of Caregiving in Today's Society* (1987). And the last campaign Sommers designed took as its slogan "health care is a right, not a privilege," one that later was taken up by many health care advocates. She died at her home in Oakland, California. Sommers was a political activist throughout her life. She made "displaced homemaker" a national byword and gave impetus to an organized focus on older women's issues. Her work was in the mainstream of revived feminist activism at the end of the twentieth century.

• Sommers's papers, including OWLEF and other publications, congressional testimony, photographs, and materials on the women's movement and aging issues as well as correspondence, are in the Special Collections, Love Library, San Diego State University. Patricia Huckle, *Tish Sommers, Activist, and the Founding of the Older Women's League* (1991), and Kathleen Kautzer, "Moving against the Stream: An Organizational Study of the Older Women's League" (Ph.D. diss., Brandeis Univ., 1988), are important sources. See also Laurie Shields, *Displaced Homemakers: Organizing for a New Life* (1981). National attention was first drawn to the displaced homemaker issue through Cynthia Gorney, "The Discarding of Ms. Hill," *Ladies Home Journal*, 21 Feb. 1976, and to the Older Women's League in a series of *New York Times* articles by Judy Klemesrud, 13 Oct. 1980, 24 Feb. 1981, 1 Dec. 1981, 2 Dec. 1981, and 5 Dec. 1981. Obituaries are in the *Los Angeles Times* and the *New York Times*, both 19 Oct. 1985.

PATRICIA HUCKLE

SONNEBORN, Tracy Morton (19 Oct. 1905–26 Jan. 1981), zoologist, was born in Baltimore, the son of Lee Sonneborn, a businessman, and Daisy Bamberger. Sonneborn was raised in a traditional Jewish family and educated in Baltimore City Schools. As a youth, Sonneborn exhibited a strong love of nature and desire to understand the universe and had considered becoming a rabbi. When religion failed to completely satisfy his thirst for knowledge, he turned to philosophy, classical literature, and music, interests he maintained throughout his life.

At the age of seventeen Sonneborn followed in his older brother's footsteps and enrolled in the B.A. program at The Johns Hopkins University. He originally intended to pursue a career in English, but, chancing to take an introductory level course in biology, he discovered the niche he was searching for. Sonneborn switched the focus of his studies to biology and earned his B.A. in 1925. He continued to study at Johns Hopkins under the direction of Herbert Spencer Jennings, who was then the Henry Walters Professor of Zoology and director of the zoological laboratory, and received a Ph.D. in zoology in 1928. Jennings recommended that his students select one organism to study in depth, reasoning that through the knowledge gleaned from this one organism, students could begin to solve the mysteries of biology. Sonneborn adopted Jenning's philosophy and spent his career specializing in the study of the one-celled paramecium.

Sonneborn remained at Johns Hopkins until 1939, refining his research skills as a postdoctoral student and research assistant. In 1937 he made the first major discovery of his career while working one evening in his laboratory. Scientists had long been puzzled by the mating patterns exhibited by paramecia, seemingly governed by no particular order. At times the organisms would multiply by dividing without mating, while at other times they would mate. The tiny creatures each contain two nuclei in spite of their one-cell status. Scientists observed within the paramecium one large and one small nucleus, which divided as the paramecium itself divided. The two new paramecia formed by the division each contained a small and large nucleus. When the creatures were successfully mated, however, the large nucleus disappeared completely and only the small divided. The parts of the small nucleus were shared by the mating paramecia, and the nuclei reformed as they had been after the organisms separated. Further confusing researchers, paramecia that were not mating exhibited characteristics similar to those mating when their large nucleus sometimes disappeared and the small nuclei divided. Two large and two small nuclei would then form at opposite ends of the cell, which would subsequently divide. For several years Sonneborn observed that mating would occur after periods of endomixis, or nuclear changes within the single cell. Sonneborn surmised that the existence of sex differences in the paramecium was determined by the genes contained within the paramecium's nucleus. He theorized that biologists had failed to consistently make paramecia mate when brought together because they were unknowingly bringing together animals of the same sex. That evening in 1937 the pieces of the puzzle came together for Sonneborn, and he was able to concretely establish and identify mating types in paramecia and effectively mate them by using logical processes of elimination. Excited, Sonneborn is said by his friend and former student Richard Siegel to have raced about the empty halls of the biological building at Johns Hopkins searching for someone to share his discovery with. The only person he found was an elderly and bewildered janitor, who accompanied him back to the laboratory for a demonstration of his findings. After his discovery was formally unveiled, Sonneborn soon became known as the founder of the modern genetics of the protozoa. The discovery unlocked the rich potential of the paramecium for the study of genetics in both one-celled and many-celled organisms. Sonneborn's discovery was an essential stepping stone leading to a deeper scientific understanding of the study, characteristics, and control of genetics and heredity.

In 1939 Sonneborn joined the faculty of Indiana University as an associate professor of zoology. He was promoted to professor of zoology in 1943 and remained at Indiana University for the rest of his career. He continued to make substantial contributions to the field of genetic research, including discovering a method of control cell heredity, extending gene theory to include one-celled organisms, showing non-genetic inheritance for the first time, and showing that non-nuclear cell parts could be used effectively to determine their own heredity and show evidence of the effects of how non-genetic characteristics implement genetic effects. As a professor, Sonneborn was extremely dedicated and well loved by his students. He held Friday evening seminars in his home and sometimes gave his research prize funds to his students to further their research. His style of teaching was to provide guidance and the sharing of observations when needed and, when his assistance was not needed, to respect the student's solitude. He was responsible for guiding the doctoral research of more than thirty-six students during his career. Sonneborn's teaching style earned him the Lieber Memorial Teaching Award in 1967 and the Brown Derby Teaching Award in 1971. From 1963 to 1964 Sonneborn served as acting chairman of Indiana University's Division of Biological Sciences, and in 1976 he was named distinguished professor emeritus.

Sonneborn was the recipient of numerous awards and honors, including several honorary doctoral degrees. He was a co-winner of the Newcomb-Cleveland Prize of the American Association for the Advancement of Science in 1946 and was awarded the Kimber Genetics Award of the National Academy of Sciences in 1959 and the Mendel Centennial Medal of the Czechoslovakian Academy of Sciences in 1965. He was president of the American Society of Naturalists in 1949, the American Society of Zoologists in 1956, the Genetics Society of America in 1949, and the American Institute of the Biological Sciences in 1960–1961,

and he was inducted into the National Academy of Sciences in 1946. Sonneborn was also a member of numerous other societies, including the American Philosophical Society, the Academy of Arts and Sciences, American Society of Cell Biology, French Society of Protozoology, Genetics Society of Japan, Royal Society of London, American Association for the Advancement of Science, Sigma Xi, and Phi Beta Kappa. Sonneborn authored many articles on topics relating to his genetic research with paramecia and edited *The Control of Human Heredity and Evolution* (1965).

Sonneborn married Ruth Bamberger of Baltimore in 1929; they had two sons. Sonneborn died in Bloomington, Indiana.

• A reference file of newspaper articles and a bibliography of Sonneborn's publications is available in the Department of Special Collections and Archives, Milton S. Eisenhower Library, The Johns Hopkins University. Most of this material deals with the early years of Sonneborn's career at Johns Hopkins. The University Archives of Indiana University also maintains biographical reference materials about Sonneborn, and some of his correspondence is in the A. H. Sturtevant Papers at the California Institute of Technology, Pasadena. A biographical account is, by John R. Preer, Jr., in the National Academy of Sciences, *Biographical Memoirs* 69 (1996): 269–92. See also G. H. Beale's sketch in *Biographical Memoirs of Fellows of the Royal Society* 28 (1982): 537–74. An obituary is by former student Richard Siegel, "In Memoriam: Tracy M. Sonneborn (1905–1981), A Personal Panegyric," *Journal of Protozoology* 28, no. 2 (May 1981): 143.

JENNIFER ALLAIN RALLO

SONNECK, Oscar George Theodore (6 Oct. 1873–30 Oct. 1928), music bibliographer, librarian, and editor, was born in Lafayette (now Jersey City), New Jersey, the son of George C. Sonneck, a civil engineer, and Julia Meyne. His father died while Oscar was still an infant, and his mother took him with her to Germany, where she had accepted a domestic position in Frankfurt-am-Main. His primary education took place at Kiel's Gelehrtenschule, and he attended Gymnasium at Frankfurt. After a brief sojourn at the University of Heidelberg, he took up residence at the University of Munich, where he stayed until 1897. His musical education included the study of piano (with James Kwast), composition and orchestration (with Iwan Knorr) in Frankfurt; composition and musicology (with Melchior Ernest Sachs) in Munich; and conducting at the Sondershausen Conservatory under Carl Schröder. During his formative years he displayed a decidedly artistic disposition, composing and publishing a number of songs and piano pieces during the late 1890s and even putting out two volumes of poetry in German in 1895 and 1898.

Sonneck returned to the United States in 1899 and began a project that reflected the first flowering of his scholarly talents. Though he had shown previous curiosity about fairly obscure European composers, once he landed on American shores he developed an intense interest in the musical culture of the United States that was to distinguish him for the rest of his life. His early articles included "Benjamin Franklin's Relation to Music," published in 1900, and contributions to German periodicals that covered topics such as Native American music, American musical life, and the problematic lack of a systematic bibliography of American music.

Between 1899 and 1902 he traveled the eastern seaboard from the New England states as far south as South Carolina, searching out information on the musical life of the United States in the eighteenth century. By spending a great deal of time in libraries and methodically going through newspaper files, he compiled the first comprehensive treatment of American music in the colonial and revolutionary period. The results of his investigation were collected into a volume titled *Bibliography of Early Secular American Music*, which he offered to Herbert Putnam, the librarian of Congress, for publication. Though the publication was impossible—Sonneck finally had the book printed privately in 1905, at his own expense—Putnam realized that Sonneck had the background and the abilities to address the library's growing collection of music and books about music. On 1 August 1902 Sonneck was appointed the first chief of the Library of Congress's new Music Division. Sonneck married Marie Elisabeth Ames in Washington, D.C., in 1904; they did not have children.

Sonneck achieved a number of accomplishments during his fifteen-year tenure at the Library of Congress. In the beginning he stressed the acquisition of American publications, but he also amassed a collection of British imprints second only to the British Museum. Because the division did not have the resources to compete with the great European institutions in the field of early music manuscripts and printed partbooks, Sonneck concentrated his efforts on building excellence in the opera collection. Under his supervision, the library cultivated a superb collection of opera scores copied by hand from European manuscripts and acquired the Albert Schatz collection of opera librettos and related material, the purchase of which required a special congressional appropriation. Early on, he realized that there was no general index covering music periodicals in existence, so he commenced his own card-file index of the leading publications, in both current editions and back files. He invented the current Library of Congress classification system for musical scores and books (which improved on the previous Dewey Decimal system), and he played an active role in cataloging the thousands of items that came into the Music Division, partly through the copyright stipulation requiring deposit with the Library of Congress. In 1908 he inaugurated a series of music bibliographies that, by the time of his resignation, encompassed eight titles, all published by the Government Printing Office. His own contributions included studies of the first editions of American composers Edward MacDowell and Stephen Foster. Finally, he represented the United States at musical congresses held in Rome and London in 1911.

Sonneck continued his musicological research during his years in Washington as well. In 1905 he published *Francis Hopkinson, the First American Poet-Composer, and James Lyon, Patriot, Preacher, Psalmodist*, drawing partially on the background work done during his earlier travels along the East Coast. Several other historical works reflecting his interest in early American musical life followed, including two volumes of essays.

In 1915 Sonneck left Washington to take on the editorship of the *Musical Quarterly*, a scholarly journal newly established by the G. Schirmer publishing firm in New York City. From the lead article in its first issue, Waldo S. Pratt's "On Behalf of Musicology," the journal was unique in its time in the United States as a permanent record of the scientific and historical study of music—nonetheless readable by the layperson—rather than the more usual magazine reporting on current musical events. During the war years, when many of Europe's eminent musicologists were not reachable, Sonneck often filled out the *Musical Quarterly*'s pages with his own contributions written under an assumed name. His strong editorial hand shaped the publication until his death in New York City.

Though his interest in American music remained a constant throughout his life, in his later years he rediscovered his German heritage, especially in the person of Ludwig van Beethoven. In 1919 Sonneck and Harold Bauer founded the Beethoven Society of New York, a colloquium to foster the study, discussion, and performance of the great composer's works. In 1927 he represented the society as one of three American delegates to a conference held in Vienna on the centennial of Beethoven's death. During this time he published three works on the composer: *Beethoven: Impressions of Contemporaries* (1926), *The Riddle of the Immortal Beloved: A Supplement to Thayer's "Life of Beethoven"* (1927), and *Beethoven Letters in America* (1927), facsimiles of thirty-five then-extant letters with transcriptions of the texts, an English translation, and commentary by Sonneck.

• Sonneck's papers reside in the Library of Congress. He authored the definitive reference work on the opera libretto, *Catalogue of Opera Librettos Printed before 1800* (1914; repr. 1967). Of his historical writings, best known are *Bibliography of Early Secular American Music* (1905), *Early Concert-Life in America* (1907), and *Early Opera in America* (1915), although he also wrote definitive opinions on the history of "Yankee Doodle," "The Star-Spangled Banner," and other American tunes. Numerous articles have been written about Sonneck and his output, culminating in a 1983 Festschrift, *Oscar Sonneck and American Music*, ed. William Lichtenwanger, which includes essays on Sonneck as well as sixteen essays by Sonneck, some previously unpublished.

CHRISTINE HOFFMAN

SONNESCHEIN, Rosa (12 Mar. 1847–5 Mar. 1932), editor and Zionist, was born in Nagykansiza, Hungary, the daughter of Hirsch B. Fassel, a rabbi, and Fannie Sternfeld. She attained a high school education in Hungary and at a young age, in 1864, married Solomon Hirsch Sonneschein, a Reform rabbi; they had four children. In 1869 they immigrated to the United States and settled in St. Louis, Missouri. From the outset, their marriage was a disaster because they were wholly incompatible and because of her husband's alcoholism. During her tumultuous marriage, Sonneschein began a lifelong habit of smoking cigars after dinner, claiming that smoking helped alleviate the indigestion that resulted when she and her husband quarreled at the dinner table.

Finally, in 1891, after their children had grown up, Sonneschein left her husband, finalizing the divorce two years later. She moved to Chicago, Illinois, where she worked as a correspondent for German, American, and English periodicals, and published short stories. In 1895 she founded the *American Jewess*, the first periodical for American Jewish women. The journal tailored its message to middle-class Jewish women. Although many articles dealt with domestic concerns and with keeping the practice of Judaism alive in the home, Sonneschein also demanded a larger and more visible role for Jewish women within the Jewish community as well as in American society. In the April 1896 issue, she declared, "It will not be possible for the Jewess of the future to live the restricted life of her mother; she is a sharer in the universal broadening that has come to all womankind. It is the spirit of the times."

Sonneschein's journal also provided a forum for other Jewish women's spiritual and cultural concerns. The *American Jewess* was published during an era of progressive ferment in American Jewish women's lives, and the journal's pages reflected a growing debate over the religious roles of women in the American Jewish community and the changing nature of Jewish spirituality and observance. Some of the most innovative ideas for revitalizing Jewish worship and endowing Jewish women with greater religious authority and visibility found a home in the *American Jewess*.

Sonneschein, an ardent Zionist, also published articles by Theodor Herzl, the founder of the Zionist movement, and Max Nordau, another major Zionist thinker. In 1897 she was one of the few women delegates to attend the first World Zionist Congress in Basle, Switzerland. She also persuaded Temple Isaiah in Chicago to admit women to full membership without any restrictions—the first synagogue in the world to do so.

At its peak, Sonneschein's journal claimed a circulation of 29,000, but in 1899 financial problems forced her to stop publishing it. Perhaps also contributing to the journal's demise was Sonneschein's growing deafness; no longer could she conduct the sparkling verbal exchanges that had inspired her best thinking and writing. She lived mostly in anonymity and in pecunious circumstances until her death in St. Louis, Missouri.

• Little information is available on Sonneschein. The best source of information is the *American Jewess*, available on microfilm. Faith Rogow published a brief biographical essay in *European Immigrant Women in the United States* (1994), and Jack Nusan Porter, "Rosa Sonneschein and *The American Jewess* Revisited," *American Jewish Archives* 32 (1980), offers some additional information. See also the entry on Sonneschein in the *American Jewish Yearbook* 6 (1904/1905).

HARRIET SIGERMAN

SOPER, Fred Lowe (13 Dec. 1893–9 Feb. 1977), medical doctor and public health administrator, was born in Hutchinson, Kansas, the son of Socrates John Soper, a pharmacist, and Mary Ann Jordan, a schoolteacher. He attended the University of Kansas, earning a B.A. in 1914, and an M.S. in embryology one year later. After two years at the University of Illinois Medical School, he transferred to Rush Medical College at the University of Chicago, graduating with his M.D. in 1918. In addition, he earned a certificate in public health from Johns Hopkins University in 1923, eventually completing his doctorate in public health at that same institution in absentia two years later.

Soper was recruited to the Rockefeller Foundation (RF) while finishing his medical studies at Rush College. After his medical internship at Cook County Hospital in Chicago in 1919, he joined the staff of the RF's five-year-old International Health Board (IHB), whose directors were looking for young medical doctors to fulfill its mission to apply medical knowledge to practical problems of public health. He forsook the certainty of a clinical practice for a career in the emerging field of public health research and administration.

Soper married Juliet Snider in 1920; they had no children. Exactly one month later—and after a year of training with the IHB—he left with his wife for Rio de Janeiro, Brazil, to begin his first overseas assignment for the RF. He remained in Brazil for another 22 years, during which he worked together with the Brazilian government on hookworm, yellow fever, and malaria projects. His early yellow fever research provided the basis for his future emphasis on eradicating insect vectors and for his novel orientation to rural, rather than purely urban programs of disease control.

In the process of his medical research, Soper participated in the development of the South American nation's public health infrastructure, balancing the sometimes authoritarian aspects of disease control and eradication—typical of RF projects—with a commitment to eradication as a humanitarian project. While his oftentimes rigid approach to disease control was criticized by local authorities, Soper maintained throughout his career that the concept of disease eradication was fundamentally democratic, serving all populations and not favoring well-developed countries, regions, or neighborhoods.

The major achievement of Soper's time in Brazil was the successful eradication of the mosquito *Anopheles gambiae*, the malaria vector, by the end of 1940, the result of the radical strategy of confining the mosquito and fumigating its breeding places with the chemical Paris green. The success of the Brazilian malaria campaign—based in part on previous findings of Brazilian public health authorities—was noted by the RF as a turning point in the concept of disease control, bringing hope for success in disease eradication in other parts of the world. At the request of the Egyptian government, the RF sent Soper to North Africa in 1944 to stem the flow of *gambiae* at its source. Within a year, the mosquito had been eradicated. Soper then moved on to Naples, where he had quick success in controlling an epidemic of typhus, largely due to the invention by Soper's team of a blowing machine to quickly apply DDT powder to infected individuals. Soper himself noted in his memoirs that "Naples was a dramatic point in the history of man's battle against infectious diseases . . . The rapidity with which the Naples epidemic was controlled convinced even the most skeptical; overnight the mechanical dusting with DDT of fully clothed individuals became the standard method of typhus prevention" (p. 306).

During World War II, he was offered a job consulting on yellow fever and malaria for the U.S. Army, but he failed the physical exam; instead he spent the last three years of the war working on typhus prevention as a civilian member of the U.S. Typhus Commission in Egypt and Italy. After the war, Soper settled in Egypt, where he was to establish a regional office for RF activities in Africa and the Middle East, the foundation's largest region of activity. He remained less than a year, however, for in late 1946 the U.S. government appointed him director of the Pan American Sanitary Bureau (PASB, later PAHO). He took over that post on 1 February 1947. In leaving the RF Soper noted that while his years of service were happy ones, he had been increasingly disturbed by the RF's withdrawal from the field of public health. He saw his move to PAHO as a continuation of his work bridging medical knowledge and practical application to public health problems and made his first goal that of eradicating the urban yellow fever vector, *Aedes aegypti*, from the Americas. By 1977, however, *aegypti* still eluded public health officials, mainly because of the discovery of jungle yellow fever, a largely inaccessible source of reinfection in urban areas. Soper never wavered in his confidence, stating in his memoirs, "My faith in the eradication of *aegpyti* from the Americas is just as strong now as it was in 1967" (p. 357).

Soper retired from PAHO on 10 January 1959 and was named director emeritus. He continued publishing articles on public health problems and was a special consultant to the U.S. International Cooperation Administration and the U.S. Office of International Health. He also served as director of the Pakistan-Southeast Asia Treaty Organization Cholera Research Laboratory from 1960 to 1962. Soper received eight awards or medals, the most important of which were the Lasker Award (1946) and the Pan American Health Organization Gold Medal (1959). He was decorated by seven countries, including the United States (1944), Brazil (1942 and 1966), and Egypt (1947). He died in Wichita, Kansas.

In more than forty years in the field of public health, Soper championed pioneering work on disease control and eradication, especially for the diseases malaria, yellow fever, and typhus. His conviction that these diseases could be eradicated was controversial; before the early 1920s governments and public health agencies had previously concentrated their efforts on disease control, believing total eradication to be impossible to achieve. And while his approach was not universally welcomed by locals in the developing countries in which he worked, his admirers pointed to his advocacy of international cooperation on public health projects and for the democratic distribution of the benefits of disease eradication.

• Soper's papers, publications, diaries, and other memorabilia are in the Fred L. Soper Manuscripts Collection at the National Library of Medicine in Bethesda, Md. Documentation of his work from his tenure at the Rockefeller Foundation are in the Rockefeller Archive Center in Tarrytown, N.Y.; reports, letters, memoranda, and Soper's officer diaries are found mainly in record group 1.1 (project files) and record group 5 (International Health Board), and in the country files of the states in which he served. Soper wrote more than 123 articles on public health for English, Spanish, and Portuguese medical journals. Shortly before his death he published his memoirs, *Ventures in World Health: The Memoirs of Fred Lowe Soper*, ed. John Duffy (1977), and a collection of selected public health writings, *Building the Public Health Bridge: Selections from the Works of Fred L. Soper, M.D.*, ed. Austin J. Kerr (1970). Obituaries are in the *New York Times*, 11 Feb. 1977, and the *American Journal of Public Health* 67 (4 May 1977).

JULIA E. RODRIGUEZ

SOPHOCLES, Evangelinus Apostolides (1805 or 1807–17 Dec. 1883), professor of Greek, was born Evangelinus Apostolides in Tsangarada, Thessaly, Greece. His parents' names are unknown. Sophocles was from a leading Greek family, and he received an extraordinary education: first locally, then in Cairo, Egypt (where, after his father's untimely death, he followed his paternal uncle and first protector, the learned monk Constantius), and from 1820 to 1821 again in Greece (at the famous school at Mileès under the distinguished scholars Anthimos Gazès and Gregorios Constantas). It was Anthimos who used to call him "little Sophocles," in appreciation of the young pupil's unusual talent; later in life Evangelinus Apostolides adopted permanently the name of the ancient tragic poet. Returning to Cairo for a brief period, he worked as librarian in the Greek Orthodox monastery's library, learned Hebrew and Arabic, and read widely in ecclesiastical and Byzantine authors.

After the death of Constantius, Sophocles returned to the island of Syros, Greece, to take up a tutorship with his old teacher Anthimos. There, in 1827, he met the American missionary Josiah Brewer, who was assigned to Greece by the American Board of Commissioners for Foreign Missions of Boston; at Brewer's recommendation and with his support in 1826 Sophocles emigrated to the United States. In Boston he entered the Monson Academy to learn English and Latin and spent the academic year 1829–1830 studying at Amherst College. He spent ten difficult years, 1830 to 1840, as an instructor of Greek at the Mount Pleasant

Classical Institute (later the Amherst Academy); at the town grammar (high) school in Hartford, Connecticut; and at Yale College, where he taught from 1837 to 1842. In 1842 he established residence in Cambridge, Massachusetts, where he was to remain for the next forty years of his life. He joined the Harvard University faculty as "tutor" in 1842 and held that position until 1849. That year he was promoted to assistant professor and in 1860, after C. C. Felton's untimely death, to professor of ancient, Byzantine, and modern Greek. The Harvard period was the happiest and most productive part of his life, and Sophocles became intimately connected with one of the brilliant periods of that institution. His monumental learning placed him among the very few scholars able to teach all periods of Greek, ancient, Byzantine, and modern. A proponent of the positivistic approach of the "old philology" of the early nineteenth century, which sought objectivity and relief from the dogmatic hermeneutic presuppositions of the past, Sophocles was primarily, and above all, a grammarian and a lexicographer. For decades his manuals introduced American students to the study of the Greek language in a most clear, thorough, and systematic way. Thanks to him, the budding modern Greek scholarly tradition blended with the German-dominated American grammatical scholarship, then at its very peak. He was a member of the American Oriental Society and of the American Academy of Arts and Sciences. The legend of the eccentric and immensely learned professor of Greek survived long after his death. Longfellow wrote of him that "he made Diogenes a possibility." He used to read Greek authors to his chicken, which upon his call jumped on his shoulder and listened attentively, for it "loved Greek more than his own freshmen." His work in Greek grammar was continued at Harvard by William W. Goodwin, H. Weir Smyth, and Charles Burton Gulick.

His books in the sciences (astronomy, botany, mathematics), though well attested from abundant references to them in his correspondence, remain to this day unidentified despite his contemporaries' appreciation of them. He composed a grammar of modern Greek, *A Romaic Grammar, Accompanied by a Chrestomathy with a Vocabulary* (1842); the ground-breaking character of this twice-reprinted handbook was appreciated only many decades later. Much better known was his ancient Greek grammar, *A Greek Grammar for the Use of Learners* (1835), reprinted several times as *A Greek Grammar for the Use of Schools and Colleges*. Of all his publications this has been the most successful (according to Felton it was the best of all Greek grammars then in use in America). With his study *History of the Greek Alphabet with Remarks on Greek Orthography and Pronunciation* (1848), Sophocles contributed to one of the most hotly debated issues of the day, that of the true pronunciation of ancient Greek. His most important book, however, was the lexicon, to which he owes his scholarly renown: *Greek Lexicon of the Roman and Byzantine Periods, from B.C. 146 to A.D. 1100* 1870. Sophocles carried along from his home country the lexicographical wisdom of Anthimos Gazès, himself a compiler of a three-volume Greek lexicon (Sophocles's own copy of his teacher's lexicon is in the Harvard library). He died in Cambridge.

• A number of Sophocles's letters and other documents are preserved in the Harvard Archives, as is his will, wherein he bequeathed his books and his entire property to the "Constantius Fund" for the enrichment of the Harvard library. G. Soulis, "E. A. Sophocles," *Athena* 56 (1952): 125–41, includes a complete bibliography. Other significant biographies are those of William W. Goodwin in *Proceedings of the American Academy* 19 (1863–1884): 502 and C. L. Jackson in the *Harvard Alumni Bulletin* 25 (1923): 716–17. Two personal reminiscences of value are George H. Chase, *Tales Out of School* (1947), pp. 21–23, and George Herbert Palmer, "Reminiscences of Professor Sophocles," *Atlantic Monthly*, 1891, pp. 779–88. D. C. Hesseling evaluated his scholarship in "E. A. Sophocles, Neohelleniste," *Mededeelingen der Koninklijk Akademie* 59, no. 7 (1925): 3–11. His work receives significant mention in Frederick W. Danker, *A Century of Greco-Roman Philology* (1988), and John Edwyn Sandys, *A History of Classical Scholarship*, vol. 3 (1908; repr. 1967).

J. N. KAZAZIS

SORENSEN, Charles (27 Sept. 1881–13 Aug. 1968), automotive industry executive, was born in Copenhagen, Denmark, the son of Soren Sorensen, a wood craftsman and modelmaker, and Eva Christine Abrahamsen. His father immigrated to the United States in 1883 and settled in Erie, Pennsylvania; Charles and the rest of the family followed shortly thereafter. The family eventually settled in Buffalo, New York, and, after completing high school at the age of fourteen, Sorensen took a job there in 1896 as an apprentice pattern-maker at the Jewett Stove Works, working alongside his father. When his father relocated to Milwaukee, Wisconsin, Sorensen worked under his direction and also took correspondence courses in subjects such as drafting. When his father again moved (this time to Detroit, Mich.) in the following year, Sorensen, by now well trained as a pattern-maker, followed him and worked successively at the Art Stove Works, the Michigan Stove Works, and Bryant & Berry.

Tall and athletic, Sorensen was an enthusiastic fan of bicycling and soon became acquainted with Tom Cooper, a champion on the racing circuit. Interested in auto racing as well, Cooper was by 1902 in the process of developing racing cars in partnership with automotive pioneer Henry Ford. Cooper sought Sorensen's assistance in building a three-dimensional model of their car, and his efforts soon caught Ford's eye as well. The success enjoyed by the "999" racing car led to the formation of the Ford Motor Company in 1903, and by the spring of 1905 (accounts of the exact date vary) Sorensen was on the Ford payroll as a pattern-maker. In 1904 he married Helen E. Mitchell; the couple had one son.

Sorensen prospered at Ford Motor and soon expanded his pattern-making activities to include foundry work as well. Having earned the nickname "Cast-Iron Charlie" for his ruthless personality as much as for his industrial skills, Sorensen advanced within the company by consistently demonstrating a willingness to do whatever Ford, a notoriously tough taskmaster, required of him. Although he lacked a formal title for many years, Sorensen played a key role in the development of Ford products like the Model T and Model A. After becoming an assistant to production plant manager P. E. Martin in 1908, he assisted Ford in developing the techniques of mass production that made the company so successful. Although unfailingly loyal to Henry Ford, Sorensen later disputed the idea that Ford alone was responsible for the development of the assembly lines; in his autobiography, *My Forty Years with Ford* (1956), he claimed that "Henry Ford is generally regarded as the father of mass production. He was not. He was the sponsor of it."

With Model T production problems largely solved, Sorensen moved quickly to solidify his role in the Ford Motor Company. After the 1921 Ford takeover of the bankrupt Lincoln Motor Company, Sorensen brushed company founder Henry Leland aside and shortly thereafter drove him out of his own company. In the same year he also engineered the departure of William Knudsen, a brilliant executive who had become a Ford employee as a result of his own company's acquisition by Ford. Having succeeded Martin as chief of production by 1925, Sorensen successfully presided over Ford's massive new production facility at River Rouge. Although Ford's son Edsel had served as president of Ford since 1919, he was completely dominated by his father, and from 1925 onward Sorensen reigned as the company's de facto second in command.

Thus far content to remain in the background (Ford consistently displayed an intense dislike for those who outshone him), Sorensen clearly left his mark at Ford Motor. After finally convincing Ford to drop his beloved Model T in favor of the Model A in 1928, he demonstrated more resolve than tact in displacing many of the production staff that had made the Model T such a success. Having gotten (in his own words) "rid of all the Model T sons of bitches," he proceeded to ensure the success of the Model A; ironically, in producing the new car he utilized many of the ideas that his former rival Knudsen was using to such effect at competitor General Motors. He also demonstrated that his foundry skills remained untarnished with the development in 1932 of the Ford V-8 engine, which featured a block and crankcase cast as a single unit by means of an innovative new casting technique.

Sorensen soon faced a challenge to his authority in the form of Harry Herbert Bennett, an ex-navy fighter whom Ford initially hired as an artist in 1917. Bennett soon rose to a position of prominence within the company as the head of its so-called service department, which in reality functioned as his own personal security force. After being Sorensen's point man for a number of years, Bennett gained an increasing amount of influence over Ford by playing on the automobile magnate's fears of production interference (by Communists or unions) as well as the physical safety of his family (in the wake of the Lindbergh baby kidnapping in 1932). Although Sorensen's role in the notorious "Battle of the Overpass" in May 1937 (during which union organizers were beaten by Bennett's men, many of whom were mere thugs) remains unclear, he clearly shared Bennett's (and Ford's) antipathy towards organized labor. Sorensen and Bennett managed to work together for a number of years to prevent Ford's plant from becoming unionized, but the United Auto Workers finally succeeded in winning recognition at Ford in 1941 after a long and costly strike.

Sorensen, for his part, had already accepted additional responsibilities. With the threat of war looming, the federal government approached Ford Motor Company in December 1940 with a proposal to help produce the B-24 bomber. After an inspection visit at Consolidated Aircraft, the developer of the bomber, in San Diego, California, the following month, Sorensen developed a projected production schedule of one airplane per hour. Exceedingly ambitious in scope—Consolidated had anticipated production at a rate of one plane per day—Sorensen's plans were nevertheless accepted by the government, which soon began construction of a giant production facility at Willow Run, Michigan, some twenty miles west of Ford's River Rouge plant. In 1941 he overcame a long-held Ford idiosyncrasy by being named a vice president and director.

The war years proved difficult for both Sorensen and Ford Motor Company. While Sorensen remained preoccupied by a host of production problems at Willow Run that created a seemingly endless series of delays (the project soon became caustically known as "Will It Run?"), Ford Motor itself floundered as the aging leader of the firm became increasingly senile, and Bennett's machinations drove an increasingly deeper wedge between Henry Ford, his son Edsel, and Sorensen. Sorensen eventually managed to overcome the myriad of problems that he faced at Willow Run and achieved his production goals, yet his days at Ford Motor were numbered. Having already attracted (in the view of Ford) undue attention to himself, his position became vulnerable following Edsel Ford's death in 1943. Bennett, who was kept from becoming president of the firm, succeeded in having Henry Ford place him in a capacity that made him Sorensen's superior. After asking for his release in November 1943 without receiving an answer from Ford, Sorensen abruptly resigned in March 1944, allegedly having learned through a third party that Ford sought his departure.

Although the exact reasons for Sorensen's departure remain unclear, he wasted little time getting back on his feet. In June he accepted the presidency of Willys-Overland Motors, based in Toledo, Ohio, and helped the firm to successfully convert its wartime production of the popular four-wheel-drive Jeep to civilian models. After resigning as president in 1946, Sorensen stayed on as the firm's vice chairman until 1950, when he retired to Miami Beach. He divided his retirement between his home there and additional homes in the

Virgin Islands and Bethesda, Maryland, where he died following a long illness. He was survived by his second wife, Edith Thompson Montgomery, whom he had married in 1960 after the death of his first wife.

Though arguably one of the most successful executives in the history of the automobile industry, Sorensen ultimately fell victim to the same type of tactics that he had used with such effectiveness in his climb to the top of Ford Motor. During four decades at the firm, he exerted a force of character and powerful sense of organization that undoubtedly influenced the corporate culture there, in keeping with Henry Ford's own more prominent outlook on how to run a business. Sorensen embodied the kind of ruthlessness that very nearly fit the stereotype of the capitalist boss vilified by radical labor in the pre–World War II era. Yet his ambition and drive also are traits that have often been deemed virtues by American society.

• Sorensen's papers are divided between the National Automotive History Collection at the Detroit, Mich., Public Library and the Henry Ford Museum in Dearborn, Mich. His autobiography with Samuel T. Williamson, *My Forty Years With Ford* (1956), glosses over many important periods in Sorensen's life and should be used with caution. More insightful are Robert Lacey, *Ford: The Men and the Machine* (1986), and a trio of books by Allan Nevins and Frank Ernest Hill, *Ford: The Times, the Man, the Company* (1954), *Ford: Expansion and Challenge, 1915–1933* (1957), and *Ford: Decline and Rebirth, 1933–1962* (1963). An obituary is in the *New York Times*, 14 Aug. 1968.

EDWARD L. LACH, JR.

SORGE, Friedrich Adolph (9 Nov. 1828–26 Oct. 1906), political theorist and labor organizer, was born in Bethau bei Torgau, Saxony, the son of Georg Wilhelm Sorge, a pastor, and Hedwig Klothilde Lange. He fought alongside Friedrich Engels and other revolutionaries against the Prussian army in Baden in June 1849. Then, as a refugee in Geneva and London between 1849 and 1852, he came to know Wilhelm Liebknecht and other socialist pioneers, including Karl Marx himself. Unable to find work in London, he decided to emigrate to Australia, but due to illness was placed on the wrong ship and ended up in New York in June 1852. He soon moved to Hoboken, New Jersey, where he remained for the rest of his life, supporting himself as a music teacher. A few years after arriving in America, he married a young German immigrant named Mathilde (last name unknown), with whom he lived for more than fifty years. They had three children, only one of whom survived beyond childhood.

Sorge was at first a liberal and a labor sympathizer rather than a Marxist. In the 1850s he collected money for the German revolutionary cause and supported the abolitionist efforts of the Communist Club of New York (1857). He was converted to Marxism after the Civil War partly because of his ongoing interest in promoting the cause of revolution in Germany, and partly because he came to believe that the best way to advance the workers' cause was to build up the trade union movement, which was Marx's own view at that time. In doing so he rejected the thesis of Ferdinand Lassalle, the German revolutionary leader who believed that the "iron law of wages" doomed trade unions to fail, and who advocated political action and the establishment of worker-owned cooperatives as the only effective course of action. In June 1867 Sorge requested permission from Marx in London to establish what became Section 1 of the International Workingmen's Association (IWA, better known as the First International) in his hometown of Hoboken. From then until 1887, when he retired from public life, Sorge made tireless use of Section 1 of the IWA and of its successor organizations to promote the cause of trade unionism, not simply to raise wages, but also as a means of emancipating American workers from capitalism.

At first Sorge chose the National Labor Union (NLU) as the main target for Marxist propaganda. Founded in 1866 the NLU was the first attempt to establish a national American labor movement after the Civil War. Led by immigrant artisans like William Sylvis of the Iron Molders, the NLU accepted the internationalist outlook of the IWA, one of whose aims was to regulate what they saw as the exploitative flow of cheap immigrant workers into the United States from abroad. In return, the IWA upheld the NLU's efforts to coordinate the activities of regional and district trade unions. The NLU also supported currency reform and independent political action by the Equal Rights party. Sorge and the other leaders of the IWA dismissed the first of these objectives as irrelevant to working people, and the second as premature. In 1871 he withdrew Section 1 from the NLU and focused his efforts instead on a general campaign to promote the right to strike and the eight-hour day. Although its direct influence was limited to a few thousand German, French, and other immigrant workers, in New York and Chicago the IWA helped found national unions among cigarmakers and furniture workers, as well as in several other trades. Following the lead of the IWA in Europe, Sorge also opposed the rising influence of utopians, Proudhonian anarchists, and middle-class reformers in the socialist movement. He was particularly disturbed in 1872 when suffragists Victoria Woodhull and Tennessee Claflin, of New York Section 12, proposed an independent ticket for the presidency. Raised in a patriarchal culture, and fearful that feminist advocacy of free love would bring the IWA into disrepute among immigrant workingmen, Sorge went to the 1872 Hague Congress of the IWA to plead for Section 12's expulsion. Not only was Section 12 expelled, but Sorge was made general secretary of the First International as a whole. Sorge's hand was strengthened when Marx and his supporters transferred the headquarters of the declining organization from London to New York in hopes of keeping it out of the hands of the anarchists. But Sorge was unable either to revive the IWA in Europe or to extend its influence in America. Overcome by debt, ideological wrangling, and the impact of the 1873 depression, the

First International expired soon after Sorge resigned as secretary in September 1874.

In July 1876 Sorge played a major role in helping to found the Workingmen's party of the United States. This body, which united radicals from the East and the Midwest, represented approximately 3,000 organized socialists, 635 of whom originated in the IWA. Becoming the Socialist Labor party (SLP) one year later, this organization was to become the first really influential socialist party in American history. No sooner had the SLP been founded, however, than the old controversy of politics versus trade unionism broke out. Committed as he was to the primacy of trade union organizing, Sorge was unwilling to tolerate the influence of the Lassalleans in the SLP, so he quit the party. Sorge then threw his remaining influence behind the International Labor Union (ILU), which placed special emphasis on organizing unskilled factory workers. After 1887, frustrated by gout and the difficulties of labor organizing, Sorge spent his declining years in Hoboken collecting labor documents and corresponding with European Marxist leaders. In 1891–1895, at the suggestion of Friedrich Engels, he wrote a series of articles on the history of the American labor movement for *Die Neue Zeit*, the theoretical organ on the German Social Democratic party.

Sorge's death in Hoboken went largely unnoticed even in the American radical press. By that time the Forty-Eighter generation was largely dead, the Socialist Party of America under Eugene Debs had a significant native-born following, and the issue of political versus trade union action had long since been resolved. Sorge's heyday was in the 1870s and 1880s. Nevertheless, along with Joseph Weydemeyer, he played a significant role both in disseminating Marxist ideas among America's immigrant workers and in furthering the goal of socialist internationalism. He was rightly called "the father of American Marxism."

• There is no Sorge collection as such. But when the IWA was dissolved in 1876, he turned over the archives of the First International to the State Historical Society of Wisconsin, including quite a few of his own papers. Shortly before his death, Sorge also deposited with the New York Public Library the correspondence of Marx, Engels, and other Marxists with Americans (many of them letters to Sorge), together with his own library and collection of labor papers. References to Sorge's life can also be found in Samuel Bernstein, *The First International in America* (1965), David Herreshoff, *American Disciples of Marx: From the Age of Jackson to the Progressive Era* (1967), and in Stuart Bruce Kaufman, *Samuel Gompers and the Origins of the American Federation of Labor, 1848–1896* (1973). The most complete account is given in Philip S. Foner and Brewster Chamberlain, eds., *Friedrich A. Sorge's Labor Movement in the United States: A History of the American Working Class from Colonial Times to 1890* (1977). An obituary is in the socialist *New Yorker Volkszeitung*, 28 Oct. 1906.

JOHN LASLETT

SORIN, Edward Frederick (6 Feb. 1814–31 Oct. 1893), Roman Catholic priest and educator, was born in Ahuillé, France, the son of Julian Sorin de la Gaulter-ie, a gentleman farmer, and Marie Anne Louise Gresland de la Margalerie. In early childhood Sorin displayed a ready wit, firm decisiveness, and loyalty to his Breton family's Catholic faith. These traits remained with him for life. After a year of college in Laval, he opted for the priesthood and studied for a time at a small seminary in Precigné. From there he moved to the diocesan seminary in Le Mans, finishing his theological curriculum and receiving ordination in 1838. Two years prior to that, Simon Bruté, bishop of Vincennes, Indiana, visited Le Mans while touring the Continent and planted thoughts of missionary endeavor in the mind of the maturing seminarian. In 1840, after two years of work in the parish church of Parcé, Sorin joined the Congregation of the Holy Cross, a monastic order that had been recently formed by Basil Anthony Moreau, a professor at the seminary in Le Mans. That same year Bruté's successor, Celestine de la Hailandière, arrived to recruit volunteers for his diocese in the American Midwest. In 1841 Abbé Sorin and six lay brothers were sent to establish a congregation for service in Vincennes.

The first placement was in St. Peter's, nearly thirty miles from the bishopric, but by 1842 plans were afoot to begin work even farther away. St. Joseph County, in the northernmost part of Indiana, contained a parcel of land formerly owned by a Catholic missionary named Stephen T. Badin. This tract contained St. Mary's Lake and had been known for some time as Sainte Marie des Lacs. Bishop de la Hailandière granted this land to Sorin for the purpose of building a college. The priest took heart from the name of the county as well as the river that bisected it because St. Joseph was the patron saint of education. Arriving in November 1842, Father Sorin and his fellow monastics found that only three dilapidated log cabins graced this site near South Bend, Indiana. Within two years, though, he succeeded in erecting the first college edifice and obtained a state charter of incorporation for the University of Notre Dame du Lac. Within those same two years he also established, in addition to a Catholic men's college, a preparatory high school, an apprentice's vocational school, and a religious novitiate for his order.

Between 1844 and 1865 he served as the college's president, providing spiritual leadership and educational guidance with dogged persistence throughout the early years, which were troubled by financial stress, fires, and disease. These years also offered inspiring teaching opportunities.

In 1843 Sorin initiated another venture that eventually took on a momentum of its own. He introduced Sisters of the Holy Cross, also originally from Le Mans, for work at Notre Dame, housing them at nearby Bertrand, Michigan. In 1853 he persuaded Eliza Marie Gillespie to join the order and the following year secured a site for the motherhouse and academy near the university campus. After being trained in France, Gillespie took the name of Mother Angela; she led her order to rich achievements and institutional independence as a distinct religious community.

When Sorin stepped down from the college presidency in 1865 he founded the family magazine *Ave Maria* and thus gave impetus to another long-lived source of Catholic influence. Since the 1850s he had acted as provincial superior of his order, supervising missionary activities in northern Indiana, northeastern Illinois, and southern Michigan. In 1868 he was elected superior general of the entire congregation of the Holy Cross, and his duties became understandably much more inclusive, particularly regarding evangelical and educational work in Canada, France, and Bengal. When the third plenary council of Catholic bishops met in Baltimore in 1883, Sorin participated vigorously in considerations of the church's support for parochial schools and religiously sound education for people at all age levels. The same year, that of his golden jubilee, he suggested that the university begin the tradition of recognizing a Catholic layman for distinguished service to church and community. Since then annual awards of the Laetare Medal have been made on the fourth Sunday in Lent. In 1888 the French government recognized his lifelong efforts by conferring on him the insignia of Officer of Public Instruction. Sorin remained active until the end of a career that spanned more than a half century. He served as president of Notre Dame's board of trustees until his death, which occurred on the campus he had founded and nurtured so effectively.

• A journal and records titled "Missions Attended from Notre Dame" are housed in the archives of the University of Notre Dame, Notre Dame, Ind. Valuable information about his life can be gleaned from Arthur J. Hope, *Notre Dame, One Hundred Years* (1943).

HENRY WARNER BOWDEN

SOROKIN, Pitirim Aleksandrovich (21 Jan. 1889–10 Feb. 1968), sociologist, was born in Touria, Russia, the son of Aleksandr Prokopievtch Sorokin, an icon maker and craftsman, and Pelagia V. Rimskych. Sorokin's mother, a Komi peasant, died when he was three. He and his older brother traveled with their father, who died eight years later, throughout northern Russia earning a meager living working on village churches. The combination of Russian Orthodoxy and Komi mysticism deeply influenced Sorokin's personality and later scholarship.

Identified early as an exceptional student, Sorokin settled in St. Petersburg where he did advanced work first at the Psycho-Neurological Institute (1909–1910) and then at the University of St. Petersburg. There he received a first-class degree from the Faculty of Law in 1914, a magistrant of criminal law degree in 1916, and a doctorate in sociology in 1922. All work was completed for the last degree in 1917, but the Russian Revolution delayed its conferral.

In the interim Sorokin rose to prominence in the Social Revolutionary party and was elected the founding chair of the sociology department at the University of St. Petersburg (1919–1922). His political activities led to frequent imprisonments by the czar and later the

Bolsheviks, and after barely escaping execution he was banished with his wife, Elena Petrovna Baratynskaya Sorokin, in September 1922. He taught for a year at Charles University in Prague and then at the invitation of Edward A. Ross and Edward C. Hayes came to the United States to give a series of lectures on the Russian Revolution. The lectures and sponsorship of significant sociologists led to a job at the University of Minnesota where Sorokin stayed from 1924 to 1930. There he wrote six books, three of which, *Social Mobility* (1927), *Contemporary Sociological Theories* (1928), and *Principles of Rural–Urban Sociology* (1929), defined their fields at the time. These works brought Sorokin to the attention of Abbott Lawrence Lowell, who invited him to Harvard as founding chairman of its sociology department. There he attracted a group of graduate students who later had significant impact on the discipline. Among them were Robert K. Merton, Wilbert E. Moore, Kingsley Davis, Robert Bierstedt, and Robin Williams. Sorokin chaired the sociology department until April 1944 and continued as a member of the department of social relations until his retirement on 31 December 1959. He remained a productive scholar until his death at the family home in Winchester, Massachusetts.

Sorokin is known for many pioneering efforts in sociology. In Russia he advanced behaviorism in sociology and psychology, then shaped an inclusive approach to social phenomena in the *Sistema Soziologii* (2 vols., 1920). There he argued for sociology as an objective science, focused on human interaction and the systematic analysis of group structure and dynamics. His Minnesota works introduced many European social theorists to rank-and-file American sociologists and served as exemplars for empirical sociology. This was particularly the case for the works on social mobility and rural sociology. The reliance on cross-cultural data and comparative structural analysis stimulated a new, empirically grounded sociology of rural life and social stratification. At Harvard, however, his work moved him from the center to the periphery of the discipline. With the publication of *Social and Cultural Dynamics* (4 vols., 1937–1941) and his work on social and scientific criticism (1941–1948) and on altruism and social reconstruction (1950–1960), Sorokin became an outcast from the mainstream of empirically oriented, data-based, scientific sociology. For over two decades he wrote as a humanistic philosopher of history, concerned with the crisis of modernity and the emancipation of humanity. This phase of his career was increasingly dominated by his integralist philosophy, which fused into a unity the truths of God, science, art, ethics, and history.

Sorokin returned to prominence in his late career. The publication of two significant volumes on his work, Philip J. Allen's *Pitirim A. Sorokin in Review* (1963) and Edward A. Tiryakian's *Sociological Theory, Values and Sociocultural Change* (1963), combined with a grassroots write-in campaign that elected him president of the American Sociological Association in 1965 brought him back to the attention of mainstream sociologists.

Sorokin's contribution lies in breaking new ground and in his persistent, often combative and berative, criticisms of the sociological enterprise. He forced sociologists to rethink their models of society and the direction in which they would take the discipline. As a cacophonic and frequently scolding voice, he stimulated self-examination and invited controversy. It is for his contributions as an outcast and a pioneer that he is remembered in the discipline.

• Sorokin's personal papers, lecture notes, and draft manuscripts are in the archives at the University of Saskatchewan-Saskatoon, and his professional correspondence is at Pusey Library, Harvard University. Among Sorokin's other major works are *Sociology of Revolution* (1924); *A Systematic Source-Book in Rural Sociology*, with Carle C. Zimmerman and Charles J. Galpin (3 vols., 1930–1932); *Crisis of Our Age* (1941); *Society, Culture and Personality* (1947); *Reconstruction of Humanity* (1948); *Ways and Power of Love* (1954); *Fads and Foibles in Modern Sociology and Related Sciences* (1956); and *Sociological Theories of Today* (1966). Sorokin wrote two autobiographies, *Leaves from a Russian Diary* (1924) and *A Long Journey* (1963), and an overview of his intellectual development, "Sociology of My Mental Life," in *Pitirim A. Sorokin in Review*, ed. Philip J. Allen (1963), pp. 3–36. Shorter works analyzing his American career are Barry Johnston, "Pitirim Sorokin and the American Sociological Association: The Politics of a Professional Society," *Journal of the History of the Behavioral Sciences* 23 (1987): 103–22, and "Sorokin and Parsons at Harvard: Institutional Conflict and the Rise of a Hegemonic Tradition," *Journal of the History of the Behavioral Sciences* 22 (1986): 107–27; Lawrence T. Nichols, "Deviance and Social Science: The Instructive Historical Case of Pitirim Sorokin," *Journal of the History of the Behavioral Sciences* 25 (1989): 45–60; and Don Martindale, "Pitirim A. Sorokin: Soldier of Fortune," in *Sorokin and Sociology*, ed. G. C. Hallen and Rajeshwar Prasad (1972). An obituary is in *American Sociologist*, May 1968.

BARRY V. JOHNSTON

SOSS, Wilma Porter (13 Mar. 1900–10 Oct. 1986), women's economic rights activist, was born in San Francisco, California, the daughter of George Edison Porter, a photographer, and Clara (maiden name unknown). When she was six years old her parents divorced, after which Wilma and her mother went to live with her mother's parents in Brooklyn, New York, where her grandfather was a successful insurance man. Her mother soon remarried and returned to the West Coast, but Wilma remained in Brooklyn with her grandparents.

After Wilma graduated from high school in 1919, she entered the Journalism School of Columbia University and at the same time began working as a night reporter for the *Brooklyn Times*. In 1923 she left school to marry Joseph Albert Soss, who was in the advertising business. In 1925 she became a full-time movie reviewer for the *Brooklyn Times* and began writing a movie column called "Matinee Girl."

Two years later Soss became the assistant to Harry Reichenbach, a movie producer and publicist, an experience that gave her the background for her career as a publicist for a variety of industries. Between 1931 and 1934 she served as public relations consultant to three elite New York stores: Saks Fifth Avenue, Tailored Woman, and Shoecraft. Soss was soon reputed to be the highest-paid publicity woman on Fifth Avenue, earning $750 a week during the depression years. She went on to represent Alfred Dunhill of London, the International Silk Guild (1934–1941), and a number of railroad car manufacturers (1941–1947).

According to later accounts, Soss offered to represent a number of businessmen in their dealings with labor. They all refused, and it was then, she later said, that she decided that "the men of this country aren't what they used to be, and that it was up to the women to take over." Soss's view that businessmen were out of touch with their various constituencies was strengthened when she attended the 1947 U.S. Steel annual meeting. After gaining the floor, she asked that the board move the meeting from Hoboken, New Jersey, to Manhattan since women stockholders, who represented a major portion, if not the majority, of stockholders, would more readily attend a meeting in Manhattan, where many of them lived. Her proposal was resoundingly defeated.

The negative response strengthened Soss's conviction that women stockholders should have a voice in economic decisions. Business was the backbone of the United States, and stockholders, including women, required a voice. After 1947, Soss devoted herself as a full-time volunteer in promoting women's economic rights. She formed the Federation of Women Shareholders in American Business in 1947 and became a familiar face at annual meetings. As an experienced public relations person, she was also appalled at the obtuse language of annual reports and the unresponsiveness of board members to their shareholders. Soss rarely owned many shares in the companies whose meetings she attended, but through her effective publicity she rallied many women to her organization, and they gave her their proxies. As her efforts gained attention, so did her support. She owned only one share of U.S. Steel in 1947 for example, but by 1951 her voting strength had increased to over 10,000 shares.

In 1949 Soss appeared at the U.S. Steel meeting wearing a Gay Nineties costume, explaining that her outfit symbolized the old fashioned thinking of the corporation's board. In subsequent years she staged other dramatic appearances to gain publicity for her cause. At the 1960 CBS meeting, she arrived with mop and pail to "clean up everything." Soss always sat in the front row of meetings, frequently raised her hand to make motions, and always appeared polite. Indeed, she once told supporters while traveling to a New Jersey meeting: "Be very charming and very feminine today. After all, the men do have Mom complexes, you know."

Soss's motions to the boards of U.S. Steel, General Electric, CBS, the *New York Times*, and others included proposals to add women and minorities to the boards and challenges to the stock bonuses and high salaries of company executives. Throughout the

1950s, 1960s, and 1970s, she pressed her case for greater democracy and equal rights in U.S. corporations. She often joined forces with Lewis and John Gilbert, brothers who became known, with Soss, as "corporate gadflies."

As Soss's knowledge of the corporate world increased, her proposals became more sophisticated and challenging to management. In 1975, at the AT&T annual meeting, Soss suggested that Western Electric shares (owned by AT&T) be distributed to AT&T stockholders "instead of, in our opinion, a rip-off or sell-off of Western Electric" to outside interests. Soss argued that Western Electric was a "marvelous growth company" that would flourish if it were "untied from Ma Bell's apron strings and utility regulators." Though the resolution failed, it anticipated the greater activism that consumers in a variety of fields began to display in the late 1970s and 1980s.

Besides her regular participation in annual meetings, Soss provided commentaries on financial matters on the NBC Radio Network from 1955 to 1980, appearing in the regular features "Wilma Says" and "Pocketbook News."

Wilma Porter Soss considered herself an agitator for women's economic rights. Less than a month before she died in New York, she appeared at the *New York Times* annual meeting in her watchdog role. The title of "feminist" was often hurled at Soss as an insult by board members, but she accepted it proudly.

• No collections of Soss's papers are available, and there is no biography. Information must be gleaned from a variety of magazine and newspaper sources. Andy Logan's profile in the *New Yorker* entitled "Hoboken Must Go!," 17 Mar. 1951, pp. 34–51, provides the best early overview of her personality and activities. *Current Biography* (1965) updates her activities to that point. Various popular periodicals covered her attendance at annual meetings during the 1970s, most notably, *Business Week*, 17 Mar. 1975, p. 66, and Nancy L. Ross, "Gadflies Set to Buzz Shareholders' Meetings," *Washington Post*, 17 Apr. 1983. A comprehensive obituary is in the *New York Times*, 16 Oct. 1986.

JUNE SOCHEN

SOTHEL, Seth (?–c. 1694), proprietor and governor of Carolina, was born in England, but no details of his parentage or youth are known. By 1675 he possessed enough social status and wealth to be recommended to the proprietors of Carolina as a potential governor of their colony. At that time Anthony Ashley Cooper, earl of Shaftesbury, wrote to the governor of Carolina on behalf of Sothel, "a person of considerable estate in England," asking the governor to "Pray treat this gentleman as my friend." Sothel negotiated from the proprietors a manor in southern Carolina of 12,000 acres and made preparations to migrate to the colony. Before Sothel embarked he purchased in 1677 the earl of Clarendon's proprietary share in Carolina.

The same year that Sothel became a Lord Proprietor the colony of Albemarle County in northern Carolina was torn by the upheaval that would be known as Culpeper's Rebellion. In the course of deposing the acting governor, local rebels established control of the colony. Upon receiving conflicting reports of chaos in the Albemarle settlement, the proprietors prevailed upon Sothel to take the governor's post, authorizing him to investigate and punish those responsible for the rebellion.

Sothel left for Albemarle County in 1678, but his ship was intercepted off Gibraltar by North African pirates who took him to Algiers, where he was enslaved and held for ransom. Restrained with shackles and chains, Sothel was set to work on the city walls carrying mortar and stone for the masons. The Crown sought his release by offering to exchange two pirate captains, "Hadgamore" (Hadji Omar) and "Buffalo Ball." The pirates were taken to the Mediterranean to Vice Admiral Arthur Herbert, who was handling the hostage negotiation, but Sothel's release was stalled for another year by the pirates' demand for 6,000 pieces of eight. The ransom was bonded by one Wimbourne and Robert Cole, two Englishmen residing in Algiers, and Sothel was free by the summer of 1681. Sothel's harrowing experience in Algiers may account for the extraordinary efforts he subsequently made to increase his own wealth and power. When he returned to England, Sothel initially reneged on paying the ransom. It took the pressure of a court suit and the threat of debtor's prison to force him to pay on behalf of Wimbourne. When he left for Carolina, Sothel had still not paid the sum for Cole, who was seized and imprisoned in Algiers. The Crown ultimately secured Cole's freedom.

Sothel finally arrived in Albemarle County in 1682, finding a colony that had just barely returned to normal after several years of rebel government. The other proprietors still considered him a "very sober discreet gentleman" and had high expectations that he would solve the problems in the troublesome northern settlement. Sothel received vast land grants, a seigniory of 12,000 acres on Salmon Creek west of the Chowan River, and later another of the same size south of Albemarle Sound on the Pamlico River. As governor he controlled the Indian trade and was personally involved in the fur trade. Although Sothel was eventually accused of numerous crimes against settlers in Albemarle, there is evidence that he effectively governed for several years and also cooperated well with his fellow proprietor, the highly regarded Quaker John Archdale, who was present in the colony in this period.

Late in 1686 Sothel married a widow, Anna Willix, formerly from Exeter, New Hampshire. Her two previous husbands, Robert Risco, a merchant, and Captain James Blount, a planter, had left her considerable property. The Sothels had no children. They lived on the Salmon Creek plantation, where they raised tobacco, sheep, and hogs and from which he managed an extensive trade with the Indians.

If the charges against Sothel are to be believed, he became increasingly arbitrary in his governance of the colony, but his main crime appears to have been the illegal seizure of estates and the property of his political opponents. Within his first year as governor, complaints were lodged against him leading to a letter of reprimand from the other proprietors for failure to follow their instructions. The most serious of the questions raised by the proprietors were that Sothel had made unauthorized appointments to the council, that he had not established a special court concerning the recent rebellion, that he had misused public funds, and that he had wrongfully seized the property of an absentee owner. The colony received a respite from the governor for a brief period in 1685–1686 when he was in England, but after his return Sothel's abuses escalated. He was accused of taking the property of legitimate Barbadian traders in the course of branding them as pirates; imprisoning political opponents; accumulating through seizure plantations, slaves, and personal property; and taking bribes from felons and traitors. In the incident of the illegally detained Barbadian traders, one of them died during incarceration, whereupon Sothel confiscated his property and imprisoned the estate executor. Equally damaging was the charge that he seized the plantation of an orphaned child.

Since Sothel was never fairly tried for these alleged offenses, there is no way to determine the truth of these accusations. His chief antagonist, Thomas Pollock, whom he had arrested, finally moved against Sothel by force of arms in 1689, deposing and imprisoning him. Preparations were made to send Sothel to London for a hearing before the other proprietors, but he chose to be tried before the colony's assembly. He was found guilty, punished by a year's banishment, and forbidden ever to hold political office in the colony again. Colonel Philip Ludwell of Virginia, from whom Sothel had taken a 4,000-acre plantation, succeeded him as governor.

Always a survivor, Sothel went to southern Carolina, arriving in 1690 in Charles Town, which was in political turmoil. Governor James Colleton was under challenge by the powerful Goose Creek faction, a group of Barbadian-descended planters, and Sothel was greeted warmly as a potential ally of the government's opposition. As a proprietor Sothel legally claimed the governorship. Forging a political alliance with the Goose Creek men and the French Huguenot settlers, Sothel through a coup d'état became governor of southern Carolina. His first assembly passed a series of needed laws, including the colony's first slave code, but the proprietors disallowed them. It soon became apparent that Sothel's goals were self-aggrandizement and augmenting his wealth with land grants and a special tax on the fur trade for the governor's benefit. Upon receiving complaints from his enemies, the proprietors reacted strongly against Sothel by suspending him and replacing him with Colonel Philip Ludwell of Virginia in late 1691. Sothel briefly opposed Ludwell when the latter arrived in Charles Town in early 1692. His own misrule, however, had cost him his supporters, and he relinquished his commission, leaving the colony and returning to Albemarle in the fall of 1692. Sothel lived quietly the remaining two years of his life on his Salmon Creek plantation.

• Documents relating to Sothel's public and private life are published in W. Noel Sainsbury, ed., *Calendar of State Papers, Colonial Series: America and West Indies, 1677–1680* (1896) and *1685–1688* (1899); William L. Saunders, ed., *The Colonial Records of North Carolina*, vols. 1–2 (1886); Mattie E. E. Parker, ed., *North Carolina Higher-Court Records 1670–1696* (1968) and *1697–1701* (1971); and J. Bryan Grimes, ed., *North Carolina Wills and Inventories* (1912). Useful secondary sources are William S. Powell, *The Proprietors of Carolina* (1963); Lindley S. Butler, "The Governors of Albemarle County, 1663–1689," *North Carolina Historical Review* 46 (July 1969): 281–99; William R. Riddell, "From Slave to Governor," *Dalhousie Review* 9 (Jan. 1930): 475–80; Edward McReady, *South Carolina under Proprietary Government* (1897); and M. Eugene Sirmans, *Colonial South Carolina: A Political History, 1663–1763* (1966).

LINDLEY S. BUTLER

SOTHERN, Edward Askew (1 Apr. 1826–20 Jan. 1881), actor, was born in Liverpool, England, the son of John Sothern, a shipowner and merchant. (His mother's name is unknown.) Sothern studied medicine in London but quickly switched to theology, which occupied his attention for two or three years. He also participated in amateur theatricals in London, a pastime that culminated with his performance as Othello at the Theatre Royal, Island of Jersey.

Sothern's professional career began shortly thereafter. In the late 1840s he played a variety of major and minor roles at several provincial theaters. A series of false starts gradually gave way to successful appearances and recognition by fellow professionals of his promising abilities. A comparable series of engagements in the United States began in Boston, Massachusetts, in 1852. From 1854 to 1858, Sothern joined the company of distinguished tragedian and manager James Wallack in New York City. Still a journeyman, Sothern studied the acting of Wallack and others, and, at just the point at which Sothern had resolved to return to England, he was asked to play Armand Duval opposite actress Matilda Heron's Camille (22 Jan. 1857). He received good reviews from the critics, and Heron afterward engaged him to play Jason to her Medea, but he was not able to replicate the success of his prior role.

It was in comedy that Sothern was to make his first big mark and most lasting impression. He joined the company of the famed manager and actor Laura Keene, with whom he had worked briefly before he joined Wallack. Just one of many talented performers assembled by Keene, Sothern's stature rose dramatically when he appeared as Lord Dundreary in Tom Taylor's farce, *Our American Cousin*. Initially reluctant to play such a minor role—Dundreary had fewer than fifty lines—Sothern was allowed to "gag" the part with his own jokes, witticisms, gestures, mannerisms, and stage business. First presented 18 October 1858, the show was wildly successful and held the stage for almost the entire season. With each performance,

Sothern refined and expanded the role until it dominated the play entirely. Actor Joseph Jefferson III, also in the cast, noted that it was a "turning point" not only in Sothern's career but in the careers of Keene and himself as well. George C. D. Odell declared that *Our American Cousin* was "the outstanding feature of the year in the entire theatrical record for New York. Its long run set a new standard, and at last fixed New York as a metropolitan centre" (*Annals of the New York Stage*, vol. 7 [1931], p. 126). Sothern played Dundreary frequently in the months and years to follow, taking him to London's Haymarket Theatre on 11 November 1861 where he again held the stage for an entire season. In his *Journal of a London Playgoer*, Henry Morley wrote: "There is absolute vacuity in the head of Lord Dundreary. . . . He is polite and good-natured, although inane. . . . Mr. Sothern has overlaid it all with innumerable ludicrous touches of manner and by-play, and so imperturbably extravagant, that shouts of laughter follow almost every look and gesture." Sothern featured this character in other sketches and plays, most notably in the frequently presented *Dundreary Married and Settled*. In Sothern's hands, William Shakespeare's *Othello* was once even transformed into Dundreary for an 1868 benefit performance in London.

Sothern developed a series of featured roles to which he returned often. The first was in *Brother Sam*, introduced to London audiences during *Cousin's* first spectacular run. Sothern's next most successful role was David Garrick in the play by the same name. In it, Sothern cut a dashing profile and, to some observers, displayed a talent for nuance and emotion that extended the demands of his other roles. Sothern was popular in both the major cities and the countryside of the United States and England. In London, the Haymarket Theatre, a notable house of comedy under the management of J. B. Buckstone, was Sothern's regular venue.

All of Sothern's children played on the stage with varying degrees of success. The career of his first son, Lytton Edward, was cut short by an untimely demise in 1887. Edward Hugh Sothern was regarded as one of America's foremost Shakespearean players in the first two decades of the twentieth century. Two younger siblings, Eva and Sam, were also actors. Sothern was twice married. His second wife was the actress Fannie Stewart. Together they appeared many times on the stage. Still active and at the height of his career, Sothern became seriously ill in the spring of 1880 while on tour in the United States. He canceled his remaining engagements and returned to London, where he died.

Sothern was one of the most popular performers of his day. The American drama critic William Winter remembered Sothern as "the most whimsical of actors; but beneath his whimsicality there was a fine intelligence. He possessed a keen perception of character, a quick sense of humour, a potent faculty of imitation, combined with ample knowledge of human nature and of the social world" (Winter, p. 178). Lord Dundreary, the bewildered and bewhiskered eccentric mod-

eled on the "swells" of London and embraced by enthusiastic audiences on both sides of the Atlantic, is his lasting theatrical legacy.

• Sothern was described in many contemporaneous accounts including Brander Mathews and Laurence Hutton, eds., *Actors and Actresses of Great Britain and the United States* (1886); Montrose J. Moses, *Famous Actor Families in the United States* (1906); and William Winter, *Other Days* (1908). A book-length treatment published in London and New York shortly after his death is T. E. Pemberton, *Lord Dundreary: A Memoir of Edward Askew Sothern*.

MAARTEN REILINGH

SOTHERN, Edward Hugh (6 Dec. 1859–28 Oct. 1933), actor, was born in New Orleans, the son of Edward Askew (E. A.) Sothern and Fanny Stewart, English actors. His father had become famous the previous year as Lord Dundreary in *Our American Cousin* at Laura Keene's Theatre in New York. Sothern grew up in London. His father's playful nature and expansive acting style gave Sothern a life-long taste for a theater of romantic imagination.

Sothern attended school at Dunchurch Lodge, Warwickshire, and the Marylebone Grammar School in London. When he showed an inclination for drawing, his father apprenticed him to a scene painter. He was turned down for a scholarship to the Royal Academy and gave up his ambition to be a painter.

In 1879 Sothern went to New York to visit his father during one of his frequent American tours. His father asked him his plans, and Sothern suddenly announced that he wanted to be an actor. Despite reservations, his father gave him a small walk-on role in his production at the Park Theatre. At his first performance on 8 September the young actor froze and left the stage without saying his one line. His father sent him to the Boston Museum for three months to apprentice with William Warren and Mrs. J. R. Vincent (Mary Ann Farlow). He rejoined his father's company to play small parts in what was to be a final tour before E. A. Sothern's death in 1881.

Sothern spent the following season with John McCullough and Viola Allen in a repertory of thirteen plays that included Shakespeare and romantic dramas. "I did not play many important parts in that company," Sothern recalled, "but I studied all the plays, heard them spoken each night by very capable people, and always look back on that year as the most valuable training I ever had" (*Melancholy Tale*, p. 253). After a second season with McCullough, Sothern joined Daniel Frohman's company at the Lyceum Theatre. In 1885 he became a star in *The Highest Bidder*, which he adapted with the assistance of stage manager David Belasco from one of his father's old vehicles. He established himself as one of the country's foremost light comedians and romantic actors and remained at the Lyceum until 1898. In 1896 he married Virginia Harned, an actress in the company.

He enhanced his standing as a leading man by playing cloak-and-sword heroes in 1899 at the Knickerbocker Theatre: *The Song of the Sword, The Sunken*

Bell, and one of his most famous roles, D'Artagnan in *The King's Musketeers*. In 1900 he produced *Hamlet*, the first of the Shakespearean revivals with which he was identified for the rest of his career. "For years I worked at modern comedy and farce and melodrama and romantic drama," he said, "to save the money to produce 'Hamlet'" (*Melancholy Tale*, p. 390). He opened on 17 September at the Garden Theatre, with his wife as Ophelia. The *New York Times* (18 Sept. 1900) compared him favorably to Edwin Booth: "His clustering dark hair, his handsome, mournful eyes, his broad, pale brow, his fine profile are all reminders of the greatest of our Hamlets." Despite *Hamlet*'s critical and popular success, Sothern did not attempt other Shakespearean roles. He returned to his romantic repertoire in 1901 as François Villon in *If I Were King* and the King of Sicily in *The Proud Prince*. He revived *Hamlet* periodically, replacing Harned with Cissie Loftis in 1902 and casting a young Cecil B. deMille as Osric in 1903.

Julia Marlowe, a star actress who had been touring Shakespeare since 1887, saw Sothern's Hamlet that year. She was impressed with his respect for the text, his research, and his refined artistry. She proposed a joint tour under the management of Charles Frohman, brother and partner of Sothern's manager, Daniel. They opened at the Illinois Theatre in Chicago with *Romeo and Juliet* on 19 September 1904, followed a week later by *Much Ado About Nothing*, with *Hamlet* joining the repertory the third week. The Sothern-Marlowe combination was an important milestone in both actors' careers and in the history of Shakespearean production in America. It established Southern as a Shakespearean actor, freeing him from professional dependence on melodrama and comedy. It created an artistic partnership that was to endure and evolve into a personal relationship. It also demonstrated there was a national audience for Shakespeare.

The company opened in New York on 17 October at the Knickerbocker Theatre. The *Dramatic Mirror* called their *Romeo and Juliet* "one of the very best and most intelligent productions of a Shakespeare play that the local stage has known in recent seasons." For their second season Sothern and Marlowe presented *The Taming of the Shrew*, *The Merchant of Venice*, and *Twelfth Night*. For 1906–1907 they proposed including three costume dramas by contemporary authors: Gerhardt Hauptmann's *The Sunken Bell*, Hermann Sudermann's *John the Baptist*, and Percy Mackaye's *Joan of Arc*. The Frohmans opposed the non-Shakespearean additions and withdrew from management. Marlowe and Sothern negotiated a contract with the Shubert brothers that provided for a percentage of the net receipts rather than fixed salaries and a London engagement after their national tour.

During the 1907–1908 and 1908–1909 seasons Sothern returned to individual appearances in *A Fool Hath Said* (based on *Crime and Punishment*), *Don Quixote*, *Richelieu*, and his father's great success, *Our American Cousin*. Sothern and Marlowe reunited in 1908. The sponsors of the New Theatre in New York, an ambitious effort to create an endowed national repertory theater on the European model, invited the pair to inaugurate the project with *Antony and Cleopatra* on 6 November. The production was bedeviled with difficulties. Moreover, neither Sothern nor Marlowe received good reviews. Although they persevered through twelve weeks of twice-a-week performances, they withdrew at the end of their contract and returned to touring with their own company. To *Romeo, Merchant, Shrew*, and *Hamlet*, they added a new production, *As You Like It*, opening on 21 March at the Academy of Music in New York City. The critics were not favorable to Sothern's naturalistic elocution in his debut as Jaques, although by the next season the *Christian Science Monitor* in Boston found "every word . . . a pleasure to the ear and to the mind" and commended his "conversational tone."

For the season of 1910 Sothern and Marlowe developed their first *Macbeth*. Neither seemed suited in stature, temperament, or emotional power for the traditional conceptions of a warrior Macbeth and a villainous Lady Macbeth. Instead, they introduced a more poetic interpretation, with Macbeth akin to Hamlet in his introspection and sensitivity and Lady Macbeth Ophelia-like in her loneliness. They opened in New York on 5 December. As director, Sothern gave great attention to the play's scenic effects. Although staged with traditional nineteenth-century pictorial scenery, Sothern's *Macbeth* used mists and shadows and atmospheric lighting to emphasize mood over realism. The *Theatre* magazine (Jan. 1911) said "The Sothern-Marlowe *Macbeth* will be remembered as one of the most elaborate and satisfying the present generation has seen." After a record-setting New York run, the company played it for the rest of the season along with their other Shakespearean productions in a continental tour that included Baltimore, Washington, D.C., Pittsburgh, Cincinnati, Cleveland, Detroit, Chicago, St. Louis, Kansas City, Denver, San Francisco, and Los Angeles.

In October 1910 Sothern obtained a divorce from Virginia Harned. In August 1911 he and Marlowe were married in London. They toured regularly for three years, adding matinees of *Richelieu* and *If I Were King* to their Shakespearean repertory. In January 1914 Marlowe became ill, and Sothern finished the season by eliminating all Shakespeare except *Hamlet*, reviving *If I Were King*, *Richelieu*, and *Our American Cousin*, and introducing a new romantic history play, *Charlemagne*.

At the outset of World War I Sothern organized a tour of *If I Were King*, which ran until January 1914, and donated the receipts to the British Red Cross. When the United States entered the war, he went with Winthrop Ames to Europe to organize entertainment for the troops. During the winter of 1917–1918 he performed patriotic recitations and solo scenes at army camps at the front. Sothern and Marlowe resumed performing in New York and touring in 1919 and continued until 1924, when Marlowe's ill health forced her complete retirement.

During this period Sothern became interested in ideas that had developed in Europe for less representational scenery and more simplified staging for Shakespeare. For *Twelfth Night* in 1919–1920 he experimented with a single cutout background that could be varied with insets and lighting to suggest different locales with minimal changes of furniture. This allowed an uninterrupted flow of action and the use of more text in an acceptable three-hour-playing time. In his later productions he also abandoned the nineteenth-century practice of accompanying dramatic scenes with emotional music from a pit orchestra.

Sothern appeared under Belasco's management in new plays in 1925 and 1926. In 1928 he announced his retirement and gave a series of farewell lectures and solo recitations. He spoke in favor of a government-subsidized national theater and against the ascendancy of modern realistic drama. After his retirement, Sothern and Marlowe spent most of their time at their homes in Egypt and Switzerland and vacationing in England. He died in New York City.

• Sothern's *The Melancholy Tale of "Me": My Remembrances* (1916), recounts his childhood and some of his early professional accomplishments. Charles Edward Russell, *Julia Marlowe: Her Life and Art* (1926), is more useful on Sothern's career and personal life. A. Richard Sogliuzzo, "Edward H. Sothern and Julia Marlowe, Shakespearean Producers" (Ph.D. diss., Indiana Univ., 1967), is a comprehensive study of their artistic collaboration. Charles Shattuck discusses their work in the context of the history of Shakespearean staging in *Shakespeare on the American Stage* (1987). An obituary is in the *New York Times*, 30 Oct. 1933.

ARNOLD WENGROW

SOTO, Hernando de (1500?–21 May 1542), Spanish conquistador and explorer, was the son of Francisco Mendez de Soto, an important landowner in Jerez de los Caballeros, Badajoz Province, Spain, and Doña Leonor Arias Tinoco, a noblewoman from a family prominent in the city of Badajoz. De Soto usually gave his birthplace as Jerez de los Caballeros and considered it the seat of his family line.

At the age of fourteen, with at most a basic education, Hernando joined the 1514 expedition of Pedro Arias de Avila (Pedrárias) to Castilla del Oro, modern Panama. During the next nine years (1514–1523), de Soto rose to prominence and wealth by participating in raids on Indian villages thought to have food and gold. By 1517, he, Hernán Ponce de León, and Francisco Campañón had formed a company. Two years later, de Soto received land in the new town of Natá, Panama, governed by Campañón.

In 1523 de Soto served as a captain in Francisco Hernández de Cordoba's conquest of Nicaragua. His rewards, shared with Ponce, were real estate in León, Nicaragua, encomiendas (gangs of Indian laborers), Indian slaves, and interests in mines. By the late 1520s the partners (Campañón was dead) had diversified into the trade in Indian slaves and shipping and were two of the wealthier men in León.

De Soto, once a subordinate of Francisco Pizarro in Panama, became Pizarro's associate in the conquest of Peru in 1530 when Ponce and de Soto agreed to provide two ships, horsemen, and supplies for the venture in exchange for de Soto's appointment as the lieutenant governor of the principal town the Spaniards would found in Peru and a choice encomienda for Ponce.

De Soto and his party of 100 men and twenty-five horses joined the Pizarro expedition on Puna Island, Ecuador, on 1 December 1531. De Soto led the scouting parties as the army moved toward Cajamarca, where the Inca "emperor," Atahualpa, was camped. Sent to invite Atahualpa to the Spanish camp, de Soto put on a display of horsemanship that included charging his steed toward, and reining it in just short of, the seated Inca. This spontaneous act of intimidation, bravado, and infantile showmanship seems to have been very much in character. Although authors of romantic histories credit de Soto with objecting to the later execution of Atahualpa, the evidence suggests that he agreed with and participated in the decision. From Cajamarca, de Soto led the Spanish vanguard toward Cuzco during the last third of 1533.

Although his modest portion of Atahualpa's ransom (four of 217 shares) presaged a limited future in Pizarro's Peru, de Soto stayed for two more years, intent on gaining wealth and status equal to his ambitions. As agreed in 1530, on 27 July 1534 de Soto became lieutenant governor of Cuzco, a position he enjoyed until March 1535 when Diego de Almagro took control of the city during the first stage of his power struggle with Pizarro. Almagro rejected de Soto's subsequent bid to be his agent for the conquest of southern Chile. De Soto left Peru for Spain late in 1535.

De Soto reached Spain in the spring of 1536 with a fortune said to have been as much as 180,000 pesos de oro (several million dollars). Outfitting himself and his followers with stylish clothing and servants, de Soto became the darling of the queen and her ladies at court but failed to gain the government of any of the territories he requested, whether in South America or Guatemala. Eventually he was offered a contract to explore southeastern North America. Spanish expeditions there during the 1520s had reported the possibility of gems in unexplored inland mountains.

During this period of waiting, de Soto married Isabel de Bobadilla, the daughter of his late commander, Pedrárias. Their marriage in late 1536 or early 1537 was not the culmination of a lifelong romance as some writers have imagined but rather an alliance of families with properties in Central America entered into at a time when de Soto hoped to become governor of Guatemala. They never had any children.

De Soto's contract with the king was signed on 20 April 1537. He had five years to explore the territory from the Río de las Palmas (the modern Soto la Marina River) in Mexico to the cod fishery in Newfoundland before selecting 200 leagues (about 650 miles) of coast that would define the territory he could conquer. He was allowed to grant encomiendas of Indians and was given numerous economic benefits, including the governorship of Cuba, which he intended to make his supply base.

The de Soto expedition sailed from San Lucar on 6/7 April 1538 in ten ships. Recruitment of the 700 persons on board had been helped by the arrival of Alvar Núñez Cabeza de Vaca, who, having just returned from his famous walk across northern Mexico, hinted that great wealth might be found in the interior of North America, although he declined to join the expedition.

The fleet arrived at Santiago de Cuba on 9 June 1538. De Soto spent the time through the following spring accumulating supplies and sending Juan de Añasco to scout the west coast of Florida for a port to be used as a landing and supply point. (A west coast port avoided the lengthy and often difficult return voyage that a landing on the east coast of North America would have involved.)

De Soto sailed for Florida on 18 May 1539. After some difficulties due to weather and shallow waters in the bay that the expedition entered, approximately 600 men and 240 horses landed on 30 May. Most scholars place the landing on the south shore of Tampa Bay, perhaps at Rustin, but the documentary evidence is not so exact.

The de Soto expedition's precise route during the next four years is disputed, but its general track is not. From the landing, the army moved up the western side of the hilly core of peninsular Florida to make a winter camp at Anhica Apalachee, in or near modern Tallahassee. This route took de Soto through a part of Florida where Indians and their maize were abundant. To obtain bearers for his supplies, he routinely kidnapped chiefs and enslaved their subjects, fastening them together with neck chains to prevent escape.

During the course of 1540, the army moved north and then west. The first leg of the route was through modern Georgia to Cofitachequi, probably in the Camden-Columbia area of South Carolina. The second leg was up the drainage of the Wateree River into the mountains of North Carolina. Evidence collected by another Spanish explorer, Captain Juan Pardo, in 1566–1568 shows that de Soto probably passed through Swannanoa Gap and down the French Broad River into northwestern Georgia, to an Indian polity called Coosa. The survivors of the de Soto expedition later remembered Coosa as a populous garden of Eden, an image that helped to inspire the Tristan de Luna expedition (1559–1561). Freshwater pearls were found at Cofitachequi, but precious metals and gems were not found in the mountains.

From Coosa, de Soto pushed south and southwest to Mabilia, where a confederation of Indians laid a trap for him. In hard fighting, the Spaniards won the battle, although they lost some of their equipment when the town burned. From there de Soto marched to the northwest, up the Tombigbee River drainage, to a winter camp in northern Mississippi at Chicaza. The Indians attacked on 4 March 1541, burning what was left of the army's equipment.

From this winter camp, de Soto led his army to the northwest. On 8 May 1541 his scouts came to the Mississippi River. After building barges, the army crossed into Arkansas, where it spent the rest of the year. Exploration northward along the western bank of the Mississippi failed to reveal mineral resources, so the army went west into the Ozarks. Again disappointed in his search for gold, de Soto marched southeast, back to the Mississippi and a winter camp.

In the spring of 1542, de Soto explored more of southern Arkansas before dying from a fever at the Indian town of Guachoya. His body was sunk in the Mississippi, supposedly to keep the Indians from realizing he was a mortal human being rather than a demigod. The rest of the expedition spent another year trying to reach Mexico by an overland route, giving that up, returning to the Mississippi, and building boats in which it descended the Mississippi River and returned to Mexico.

De Soto is portrayed by many writers as more noble, gentle, and loving toward the Indians than other Spanish conquistadors. This portrayal is not borne out by his known actions in Central America, Peru, and the American Southeast. He was just as violent toward the Indians as were most of the leaders of the Spanish conquest of the Americas.

De Soto's expedition completed Spain's initial exploration of the American Southeast. It showed that the Appalachian mountains apparently did not contain precious metals and that the principal resources of the region were its peoples, soils, and forests.

• Hernando de Soto has no modern, book-length biography that is free from the romantic idealization of the man begun by Garcilaso de la Vega, El Inca, in his *La Florida del Inca* (1601). Typical of the genre is Miguel Albornoz, *Hernando de Soto: Knight of the Americas*, trans. Bruce Boeglin (1986). Short, critical biographies are James Lockhart, *The Men of Cajamarca* (1972), pp. 190–201, and Paul E. Hoffman, "Hernando de Soto, A Short Biography," in *The de Soto Chronicles*, ed. Lawrence A. Clayton, vol. 1 (1993), pp. 421–59. *The de Soto Chronicles* contains modern translations of all four accounts of de Soto's Florida expedition as well as some additional documents concerning it. The four accounts can also be found in Edward Gaylord Bourne, ed., *Narratives of the Career of Hernando de Soto* (1905). Other important sources are Antonio de Solar y Taboada and José de Rújula y de Ochotorena, *El adelantado Hernando de Soto* (1929), and José Hernández Díaz, *Expedición del adelantado Hernando de Soto a la Florida* (1938).

The expedition's history and route have been the objects of intensive study, notably John R. Swanton, *Final Report of the United States de Soto Expedition Commission*, repr. ed. (1985); Jerald T. Milanich and Charles Hudson, *Hernando de Soto and the Indians of Florida* (1993); and Charles Hudson et al., "Hernando de Soto's Expedition through the Southern United States," in *First Encounters: Spanish Explorations in the Caribbean and the United States, 1492–1570*, ed. Jerald T. Milanich (1989).

PAUL E. HOFFMAN

SOUCHON, Edmond (1 Dec. 1841–5 Aug. 1924), anatomist, surgeon, and public health educator, was born in Opelousas, St. Landry Parish, Louisiana, the son of

Eugene Souchon, a surgeon-dentist, and Caroline Pettit, both natives of France. His early education was acquired in private schools in St. Martinville, Louisiana, Mobile, Alabama, and New Orleans, except for a brief period when he attended a public school in New Orleans because of his father's ill health. Souchon later took pride in relating how he had to sell newspapers during this period to help the family finances.

As was true of other well-to-do Louisiana French, when the family fortunes revived, Souchon was sent to Paris to attend college. After college, in 1860 he enrolled in the school of medicine of the University of Paris. The outbreak of the American Civil War cut off his allowance, however, and he was forced to make his own way. He applied for an internship at Paris hospitals and on taking the rigorous examination ranked fourth of 350 contestants. He was assigned to Charité Hospital to work with one of France's outstanding surgeons, Alfred Armand Velpeau. In September 1861 James Marion Sims, a young Alabama physician gaining a reputation for his gynecological work, arrived in Paris. Velpeau asked him to perform at Charité his celebrated operation for vesicovaginal fistula. Designed to repair the resultant urinary and fecal incontinence following difficult childbirth, the operation was notable because Sims, after many years of experimenting on slave women, had discovered the knee-elbow (Sims) position, devised a special curved speculum (Sims's speculum), designed a new catheter to keep the bladder empty while the fistula healed, and finally learned to avoid infection by using silver sutures. Velpeau did not speak English, but Souchon was at hand to serve as Sims's interpreter. Sims was impressed with the young intern and, on learning of his financial problem, gave him an allowance to help finish his five-year course at Charité.

Although Souchon had not completed the requirements for a medical degree, when his father died shortly after the war he returned to New Orleans with a strong letter of recommendation from Sims to Tobias Gibson Richardson, the dean of the medical department of the University of Louisiana (now Tulane University). Richardson immediately provided Souchon with a room in one of the hospitals, helped him enroll in the medical school, and took the young man in as an assistant in his private practice. After his graduation in 1867 Souchon served as Richardson's prosector and later chief of clinic at Charity Hospital.

Souchon, who described himself as an "anatomist and artist," was employed by the university's medical department in 1867 to rebuild the school's medical museum, which had been destroyed during the Union occupation of New Orleans. In 1869 Souchon married Corinne Lavie of New Orleans, with whom he had three children. In 1871 he was appointed assistant demonstrator of anatomy, and from 1872 to 1876 he was demonstrator of anatomy. When the professor of anatomy and clinical surgery retired in 1885, Souchon was unanimously elected to the position. That same year he was a founder of the Louisiana Medical Library Association, an organization that laid the basis

for the state medical association's library. When funds became available for a new medical school building in 1891, he was appointed faculty representative to oversee the design and interior medical arrangements. In 1907 Souchon retired, the last professor in the school to hold the dual chair of anatomy and clinical surgery.

As a teacher Souchon was precise and exacting and organized every minute of his time. If a student, patient, or assistant kept him waiting, his temper would flare. He expected students to memorize the answers to his anatomical questions and was a terror to those who could not meet his exacting standards. Yet he was an excellent teacher who was among the first to use visual aids, developing many new and varied lab techniques, devising a pantograph, and using his graphic arts skills to enhance medical education exhibits. The class of 1904 resolved that his course in anatomy could not "be excelled," commending in particular his "clear and beautiful demonstrations, by means of the magic lantern." For students needing financial or other help, he was the soul of kindness. His colleagues considered him warm, voluble, and egotistical.

Souchon's artistic skill was demonstrated in his preparation of anatomical specimens using new methods of injection and coloration. One exhibit of his anatomical preparations won high praise from the president of the American Medical Association (AMA) in 1911, and another one in 1915 won him a medal at the Panama Exposition in San Francisco. His chief pride was his anatomical museum housed in the medical school.

As a surgeon Souchon was trained in the old school of anatomical surgery. In the preanesthetic period surgeons were rated by their manual dexterity and quickness. Until his retirement he amputated using a large amputating knife and a butcher saw, refusing to use the newer scalpels or saws. Yet he was an excellent surgeon and used his considerable mechanical aptitude to devise a number of devices for use in surgery, anesthesia, and anatomical work. His career coincided with the dawn of modern surgery, and he actively participated in it. Among his many surgical publications, his monographs on aneurisms and shoulder dislocations represent his best work.

Anatomy and surgery were only part of Souchon's interests. He published articles on topics such as education, public health, and care of the poor. In an essay entitled "The Duty of the Strong to the Weak Poor" he advocated a government sponsored system of clinics and hospitals to provide medical care for the poor. His most notable contribution was in public health. At a time when public health was emerging as a separate field of medicine, Souchon served as president of the Louisiana Board of Health from February 1898 to November 1905, holding the position under three governors. During his first year he played a leading role in the Atlanta Convention of southern states to standardize quarantine regulations against yellow fever. Locally he began systematizing the many public health laws and in 1899 published a 400-page sanitary code for Louisiana, the first of its kind in the nation. Recognizing the significance of the Reed Commission's discovery of the role the *Aedes egypti* mosquito played in yellow fever, Souchon in 1903 urged war on the mosquito population.

Souchon was active in medical associations, holding office in the AMA, the American Surgical Association, and the Southern Surgical and Gynecological Society. He was awarded honors by other anatomical and surgical associations and was a corresponding member of the Société Nationale de Chirurgie de Paris. He died at his home in New Orleans.

Souchon was a colorful individual with an original mind and widely diverse interests. His major contributions were in anatomy and surgery, but he also earned a place in the history of public health.

• The Howard-Tilton Library of Tulane University has the Edmond Souchon Collection, 1861–1953, which includes reprints and a volume of collected letters, largely requests for his reprints. The Rudolph Matas Medical Library in the Tulane Medical School also has a volume of his collected reprints and a folder containing miscellaneous material. The best short accounts of his life were written by two of his colleagues: Rudolph Matas, "Dr. Edmond Souchon, 1841–1924," *Transactions of the American Surgical Association* 43 (May 1925): 967–78, and Isidore Cohn, "Reflections on Edmond Souchon (1841–1924) by a Former Pupil," *New Orleans Medical and Surgical Journal* 93 (May 1941): 550–57. A more recent short biography is David W. Davis, Jr., "Edmond Souchon: Surgeon-Anatomist," *Bulletin of the Tulane University Medical Faculty* 23 (Aug. 1964): 273–81. Additional material on Souchon can be found in John Duffy, *The Tulane University Medical Center: One Hundred and Fifty Years of Medical Education* (1984), and Gordon H. Gillson, *Louisiana State Board of Health: The Progressive Years* (1976).

JOHN DUFFY

SOULE, Caroline Augusta White (3 Sept. 1824–6 Dec. 1903), minister and author, was born and raised in Albany, New York, the daughter of Nathaniel White, a mechanic, and Elizabeth Merselis. When she was twelve Soule entered the Albany Female Academy, from which she graduated in 1841. She was described at that time as being "so small, slender, timid and shrinking that she looked even younger" than seventeen. An excellent student, at graduation she was awarded one of the academy's gold medals for her essay on the "Goodness of God."

Soule's interest in and commitment to religion would define her life. Brought up in the Universalist faith of her father, she was invited after her graduation to teach at the Clinton Liberal Institute in Clinton, New York, a Universalist secondary school. Ill health, a condition that would plague her adult life, cut short her teaching career but not before she met her husband, the Universalist minister Henry Birdsall Soule, whom she married in 1843 and with whom she had five children. Until Henry Soule's death from smallpox in 1852, Caroline Soule's role was that of the dutiful minister's wife. She had sometimes helped him with his writing and editing projects, and after his death she turned to writing and teaching as a means of securing a livelihood.

Before the year was out Soule had written and published her first book, *The Memoir of Rev. H. B. Soule*, a hastily written and typically reverential account of her husband's life. Nonetheless, the book was favorably received within her denomination, and it launched her career as an author and editor. Writing under the names Aunt Carra and Caroline White Soule, she produced for the Universalist press numerous moral poems and stories for children and young adults. She also edited several Universalist journals, including for ten years (1856–1865) the *Ladies' Repository*, one of the earliest serials addressed to women on a serious level. Although the *Ladies' Repository* published its share of nineteenth-century sentimental offerings, it also emphasized ideas, literature, and the arts and was a proponent of women's rights.

In 1853, in order to reduce her expenses, Soule moved the family to a log cabin in the prairie town of Boonsboro, Iowa. She remained there until 1864, by which time her children were grown, and an eye problem forced her to seek treatment in the East. She never returned to Boonsboro except to visit her offspring still living there. Abel Tompkins, a Universalist publisher in Boston, issued the three novels that Soule wrote during this period, *Home Life* (1855), *The Pet of the Settlement* (1860), and *Wine or Water* (1862). Her style was heavily moralist and pedantic, and the religious values reflected in her stories appealed to her readers, who mostly were Universalist women.

The Universalist church's North American centennial, celebrated in 1870, shaped the next phrase of Soule's life. By then she was living in Fordham, outside of New York City, and in 1869 she had been one of the founders of the Woman's Centenary Aid Association (WCA), the purpose of which was to help the denomination raise $200,000 for the work of its second century. For the next year as the group's first president, and continuing for many years thereafter, Soule traveled extensively, speaking and working in behalf of her church. At the centennial gathering in Gloucester in 1870, she reported that the WCA had raised $36,000 and that 13,000 women had become members of the ad hoc association. The next year, buoyed by their success, the women made the WCA a permanent organization; the group operated under various names but was known finally as the Association of Universalist Women until 1961, when the Universalists and Unitarians merged into a single organization, the Unitarian Universalist Women's Federation. Soule was president of the group until 1880 and with a handful of other able women traveled, preached, wrote, distributed Universalist tracts, and raised funds from Maine to the Missouri River. The women's association was arguably the most effective organization in the Universalist church after 1870.

Soule's intense schedule further exacerbated her health condition and in 1875 forced a long trip to England for rest and relaxation. It was during this trip that she embarked upon the final phase of her life, as a Universalist missionary and minister in Scotland. The Universalist movement had never been strong in the

United Kingdom, and in 1874, when Universalists scattered throughout Scotland had asked the women's association for financial aid, they had been granted some funding. During her 1875 trip, Soule went to Scotland to meet with these Universalists. In the process, she helped them organize the Scottish Universalist Convention and dedicate their only church, at Stenhousmuir Larbert. She fell in love with the people and the land and in 1878 returned as the official missionary of the WCA. She preached in various Scottish communities, including Dunfermline, Larbert, Dundee, and Glasgow; she even preached in London, writing in an 1878 letter, "I have preached in London! I—an American woman." Few ordained women preachers existed in the United States at the time, but there were none at all in the Church of England. In 1879 Soule reorganized the Universalist church in Glasgow under a new name, St. Paul's Universalist Church. She was ordained by the Scottish convention in 1880 and served as pastor of St. Paul's, except for a three-year visit to the United States, until her retirement in 1892. She never returned to America and died in Glasgow.

In spite of ill health, Soule never tired of writing, traveling, preaching, and organizing on behalf of Universalism. Near the end of her life she declared that she had "written everything from a sermon to a song, and done everything from making sorghum molasses in a log-cabin on a prairie to preaching three times a Sunday in the city of London." If she was not a striking writer or an original religious thinker, she was a faithful worker in the vineyards of her faith and a fine example of an early public supporter of women's rights. Soule once described herself as "a most harmless woman, very simple in all my tastes and habits. All I desire from anybody is a warm welcome."

• The New York Public Library has a small collection of correspondence, clippings, and printed matter for the period 1875–1916, and the Andover-Harvard Theological Library of Harvard Divinity School holds many Soule items in the records of the Association of Universalist Women. Reliable short biographical accounts are Catherine F. Hitchings, "Caroline Augusta White Soule," *Journal of the Universalist Historical Society* 10 (1975): 134–36, and Russell E. Miller, *The Larger Hope*, vol. 2 (1985): 400–409. A longer study is Alan Seaburg, "Missionary to Scotland: Caroline Augusta Soule," *Transactions of the Unitarian Historical Society* 14 (1967): 28–41.

ALAN SEABURG

SOULE, Joshua (1 Aug. 1781–6 Mar. 1867), clergyman and bishop of the Methodist Episcopal Church, South, was born in Bristol, Maine, the son of George Soule, a farmer and community leader, and Mary Cushman. Although his parents were Presbyterians, Joshua joined a class of the Methodist Episcopal church in 1797 and one year later began to travel and preach with Joshua Taylor, the presiding elder (superintendent) of Methodist work in Maine, who presented Soule with his license to preach in 1798.

In 1799 Soule was admitted on trial to the New England Conference of the Methodist Episcopal church;

he was ordained a deacon in 1802 and an elder in 1803. From 1799 until 1803 he served churches in Maine and Massachusetts. In 1803 he married Sarah Allen; they had eleven children. He was appointed a presiding elder in Maine in 1804 and continued to supervise Methodist ministry in New England for the next twelve years. For at least part of this time his residence was Avon, Maine. He was elected as a delegate from the New England Conference to the 1812 and 1816 general conferences, the chief legislative body of the church.

Soule's leadership in Methodism reached beyond New England. He is considered the author of the constitution of the denomination. Adopted at the 1808 general conference, this document provided for a representative general conference with the geographical annual conferences sending ministerial delegates (formerly, all the traveling preachers were permitted to attend the general conference and vote). The constitution also stated six restrictive rules, which limited the legislative authority of the general conference and provided for the denomination's basic structure: local churches related to geographical annual conferences, which are under the authority of the general conference of the church. Further testimony to Soule's stature in the church came in 1816, when he was named its book agent in charge of managing its publishing work. When the church initiated a new periodical, *Methodist Magazine*, in 1818, Soule was chosen as its first editor. In 1819 he became a charter member and was elected treasurer of the Missionary and Bible Society of the Methodist Episcopal Church, one of Methodism's pioneer missionary organizations and the forerunner of its first official missionary body. Between 1816 and 1820 Soule was also active in the American Bible Society, founded in New York City in 1816 to distribute copies of the Bible around the world. From 1820 to 1824 he served churches in New York City and Baltimore.

Soule was at the center of controversy at the 1820 general conference. Until that time, the bishops appointed presiding elders to assist them in supervising the preachers and churches in each annual conference. Since many felt that the episcopal appointment of presiding elders was undemocratic and made them accountable to the bishops instead of to the preachers whom they served, the general conference approved legislation that provided that the annual conferences would elect the presiding elders. This same general conference elected Soule to the episcopacy. He refused to be consecrated, however, arguing that the election of presiding elders was unconstitutional, restricting the authority of the bishops to oversee the work of the church. Presiding elders, he held, must be appointed by their bishops and be directly responsible to them. Persuaded by Soule's position, the delegates suspended the election provision for the next four years. When the general conference convened in 1824 it adopted Soule's views, elected him again to the episcopacy, and rejoiced at his consecration.

The publication of Soule's sermon, "The Perfect Law of Liberty," preached before the South Carolina Annual Conference in 1827, created a second important dispute in which Soule was involved. Some alleged that the sermon contained unsound teaching in not clearly delineating the relationship of the Jewish law and the Christian faith. They felt, for example, that Soule's views left open the question as to the obligation of Christians to observe the Sabbath. At the 1828 general conference the Committee on Episcopacy found no inconsistencies between the doctrinal positions of the church and Soule's position.

A third controversy involving Soule occurred in 1844, when the general conference suspended Bishop James O. Andrew for his connection to slavery. Soule argued that this action violated the church's constitution. The general conference did not have the disciplinary authority to suspend a bishop on this matter. In the ensuing schism, which resulted in the formation of the Methodist Episcopal Church, South in 1845, Soule gave his approval to the new church, moved to Nashville, Tennessee, and became one of the active bishops of southern episcopal Methodism until his retirement in 1855. He was always opposed to slavery and was never a slaveholder. It may seem strange, therefore, that Soule, a northerner, cast his lot with Southern Methodism. Apparently he was convinced that traditional Methodist polity was more authentically preserved in the southern church than in the body from which it had separated.

Soule was one of the most important and recognized personalities in American Methodism in the first half of the nineteenth century. He was among its most capable preachers, administrators, and pastors. His work on the church's constitution, his leadership in the formation of the Methodist Episcopal Church, South, and his commitment to the authority of the episcopacy profoundly influenced its polity and ministry. Soule died in Nashville.

• A few of Soule's sermons were published, including *A Sermon on the Death of Francis Asbury* (1816), *The Substance of a Discourse Delivered in the New Methodist Meeting House in John Street, New York* (1818), and *Sermon on the Death of the Rev. William McKendree* (1836). His sermon "The Perfect Law of Liberty" was reprinted in William T. Smithson, *The Methodist Pulpit South* (1858). Biographical information is available in H. M. Du Bose, *Life of Joshua Soule* (1911); Theodore L. Flood and John W. Hamilton, *Lives of Methodist Bishops* (1882); and James Penn Pilkington, *The Methodist Publishing House: A History* (1968).

CHARLES YRIGOYEN, JR.

SOULÉ, Pierre (31 Aug. 1801–26 Mar. 1870), U.S. senator, jurist, and diplomat, was born at Castillon-en-Couserans in the French Pyrenees, the son of Joseph Soulé, a distinguished Napoleonic officer and a magistrate, and Jeanne Lacroix. Soulé spent his youth absorbing the republican spirit of revolutionary France and conversely enduring the strident discipline of a Jesuit seminary. He rejected the seminary and joined republican revolutionaries who opposed the Bourbon restoration. After a brief exile and pardon, he returned to Bordeaux, earned the degree of bachelor of letters in 1819, and went to Paris to study law. His admission to the bar in 1822 did not deter him from again plunging into the revolutionary movement against Charles X. Arrested and imprisoned, he managed to escape to England. After brief and unsatisfactory sojourns in Port-au-Prince, Baltimore, and New York, Soulé arrived in New Orleans, where many other Frenchmen had sought refuge.

Circumstances in 1826 provided a ripe atmosphere for the brash French exile. The turmoil surrounding the presidential election of 1828 was already in full swing, and the egalitarian rhetoric of the Jacksonians captivated Soulé, who joined the Democratic fold with characteristic aplomb. To improve his English, he decided to travel northward, where only English was spoken. He obtained letters of introduction to Andrew Jackson, visited him at "the Hermitage," and spent some time working as a gardener at the Dominican monastery in Bardstown, Kentucky. When he returned to New Orleans, he passed the bar examinations and began his legal practice under the tutelage of Moreau Lislet.

At the bar and from the hustings, Soulé's exceptional talents marked him for distinction. In the courtroom he attracted admiration, and Louisianans came to associate his name with the most celebrated criminal and civil cases. Aspiring lawyers sought to emulate his courtroom style for decades to come. Through his practice and real estate speculation, Soulé quickly amassed a fortune, and the city's clannish prominent families welcomed him into their homes, clubs, and continuous round of soirees. In 1828 he married Armantine Mercier, a young woman from one of the city's oldest families. They had one son.

Although Soulé always identified himself as a Democrat, he initially led the Foreign French faction in New Orleans. At a time when ethnic hostilities between the Gallic population and the Anglo-Americans were central to political divisions in Louisiana, Soulé championed everything French. As the fortunes of the Louisiana Democracy improved, Soulé campaigned for Democrats, and New Orleanians elected him a delegate to the state's constitutional convention in 1844. He served on the judiciary committee and supported an elective judiciary and fixed terms for judges. He led the fight to thwart the attempts of Anglo-Americans to place restrictions on the foreign-born that would have infringed upon their suffrage rights and barred them from the governorship.

In 1846 New Orleanians sent Soulé to the state senate, where he led the fight to abolish compulsory capital punishment, took an active part in debates to implement judicial reforms, fought to protect French interests, and pushed for a vigorous prosecution of the war with Mexico. When U.S. senator Alexander Barrow died in 1846, the legislature selected Soulé to fill the brief unexpired term. In the full-term election of 1848, the Whig majority in the legislature as well as a few dissident Democrats found Soulé to be less offensive than John Slidell and selected him as the state's full-term senator. Soulé's victory initiated a bitter and protracted struggle with Slidell for control of Louisiana's Democracy.

Soulé's senatorial career is difficult to assess. He took his seat in a Congress locked in acrimonious debates over slavery in the newly acquired territories, and he contributed to the impassioned atmosphere that allowed for little constructive statesmanship. His orations excited admiration and condemnation in equal measure. His advocacy of secession as the only solution for the South in 1850 prompted Louisianans to berate him as a southern extremist. Louisiana was the most Unionist state in the Deep South, and politicians had to maintain a careful balance between loyalty to the South and to the Union. Soulé had outdistanced his constituents, and he hastened to refute the charges and to accept compromise measures.

In questions of foreign policy, Soulé was aggressively expansionistic. He identified with the "Young American" movement and supported liberal republicanism around the globe. Strongly opposed to the policy of nonintervention in European affairs, he presented a resolution demanding American intervention with Turkey for the liberation of Lajos Kossuth, the Hungarian patriot, and advocated the annexation of Cuba. On the basis of his insistence that the United States seize Cuba, the Franklin Pierce administration offered him the post as minister to Spain in 1853, a decision that insulted Spain. Certain that he could bring Cuba to the United States, Soulé resigned his seat in the Senate and eagerly accepted the posting.

The unfortunate combination of an impetuous and imperious temperament and an obsession with acquiring Cuba drove Soulé's diplomatic career from one disaster to another. His arrogant manner insulted the queen of Spain and her ministers, accounted for two duels involving Soulé and his son, and effectively excluded him from court circles. Unchastened, he continued to contrive schemes to acquire Cuba that ranged from purchase to war. When Secretary of State William Marcy did order him to either purchase Cuba or to "detach" the island from Spain, Soulé used this authority to conspire overtly with republican revolutionaries in Spain and in France, prompting authorities in both countries to embarrass and harass him.

In August 1854 Marcy instructed Soulé to confer with James Buchanan, minister to Great Britain, and John Y. Mason, minister to France, on the matter of Cuba. With his diplomatic career in ruins and his ego badly battered, a petulant and belligerent Soulé went to the meetings at Ostend and Aix-la-Chapelle. He was the most forceful personality among the trio, and Spain was his responsibility. Although Buchanan wrote and tempered the document, the Ostend Manifesto was Soulé's work. The document recommended purchase and sanctioned wresting the island away from Spain.

Political expediency forced Marcy to reject the manifesto and to repudiate his own instructions. The Pierce administration had antagonized the North by forcing the Kansas-Nebraska Bill through Congress, and that success led to disastrous Democratic defeats in the North during the midterm elections of 1854. Expansion and slavery had become inextricably entwined in the northern mind. The plottings of the three ministers further enraged the antislavery North, and the Pierce administration backed away. Evidence of Soulé's involvement with revolutionary movements made it possible for the administration to absolve itself and to make Soulé the scapegoat. Abandoned by the administration, Soulé resigned his post on 17 December 1854, returned to Louisiana, and for a time thought about challenging Marcy to a duel.

Instead, Soulé sought to reestablish his law practice and his leadership in Louisiana's Democracy. Familiar accolades greeted his performances before the bar, but his political expectations were doomed when Buchanan rather than Stephen Douglas won the Democratic nomination and the presidential election of 1856. Buchanan gave his friend and confidant Slidell control of patronage, and Soulé was quickly deprived of all political substance. Desperate to regain power, Soulé split the Democracy and allied with old Whigs and Know Nothings to contest the state elections of 1859, a strategy that demonstrated his political impotence and confirmed the mastery of the victorious Slidell Democracy.

In the 1860 presidential election, Soulé's supporters rallied behind Douglas, who finished a poor third in the state. He led the cooperationists during the secession crisis not to support the Union but to oppose Slidell, who led the immediate secessionists. Soulé announced frequently and firmly that secession was inevitable and that he did not intend to be in the rear of that action. He admonished audiences, demanding that they recall his advocacy of secession in 1850 and that they remember repudiating his advice. Louisiana seceded, but the Confederacy had little to offer Soulé.

When Commodore David Farragut's fleet anchored before New Orleans on 24 April 1862, Soulé served as an adviser to Mayor John Monroe and as Confederate provost marshal. General Benjamin Butler saw Soulé as a threat in a hostile city. Soulé was arrested and charged with leading a secret society whose members opposed reconstruction of the Union and of being the primary supporter of the war in New Orleans. Paroled from Fort Lafayette in New York in November 1862, he fled to Havana and successfully ran the blockade to offer his services to the Confederacy at Richmond in September 1863. Jefferson Davis had disliked Soulé since their first meeting more than a decade before and would only offer him an honorary brigadier generalship. In 1865 he joined ex-senator William M. Gwin of California in an unsuccessful project to settle Confederate veterans in Sonora, Mexico.

By experience and temperament, Soulé was unsuited to the world of politics and diplomacy. He cut his political teeth on revolutionary movements in France, and he continued to think and speak in terms of principle and of his perception of right and wrong. He readily supported those perceptions whether with a dueling pistol in his private life or with recommendations for war against Spain or the antislavery North in his public life. Tact was simply beyond his purview.

In 1868 Soulé began to show signs of mental deterioration. He destroyed his private papers, and for some time before his death he was unable to recognize even family and friends. Several months before his death, the courts interdicted him. He died at his home in New Orleans.

• Soulé destroyed most of his papers in the last two years of his life. Still, important correspondence is in the Pierre Soulé Papers and the John Slidell Collection in the archives at Louisiana State University. The Stephen A. Douglas Papers in the University of Chicago Library also contain important letters, as does the William Marcy Collection in the Library of Congress. Arthur Freeman, "The Early Career of Pierre Soulé," *Louisiana Historical Quarterly* 25 (Oct. 1942), is a valuable study, as is James K. Greer, "Louisiana Politics, 1845–1861," *Louisiana Historical Quarterly* 12 (1929), 13 (1930). Leon Soulé, *Notice sur Pierre Soulé, Advocat à la Nouvelle Orléans, Senateur de la Louisiane à Washington* (1901), provides a sympathetic account of his career. Leon Soulé, *The Know Nothing Party in New Orleans: A Reappraisal* (1961), and Marius M. Carriere, "The Know Nothing Movement in Louisiana" (Ph.D. diss., Louisiana State Univ., 1977), provide important information detailing factional struggles in the La. Democracy. Soulé's diplomatic career is covered in J. A. Reinecke, Jr., "The Diplomatic Career of Pierre Soulé," *Louisiana Historical Quarterly* 15 (Apr. 1932), and Amos A. Ettinger, *The Mission to Spain of Pierre Soulé, 1853–1855, a Study in the Cuban Diplomacy of the United States* (1932).

CAROLYN E. DE LATTE

SOUSA, John Philip (6 Nov. 1854–6 Mar. 1932), composer, bandleader, and entertainer, was born in Washington, D.C., the son of John Antonio Sousa, a U.S. Marine Corps musician, and Maria Elisabeth Trinkaus. Sousa's musical training began at age seven, when he was enrolled in a Washington conservatory to study music theory, piano, violin, and various band instruments. When he was thirteen, his father enlisted him as an apprentice in the Marine Corps, where he served in the Marine Band and studied music. These years saw Sousa's first published compositions, including his first march, "The Review" (1873). By age twenty, when he left the Marine Corps, he was working as a violinist and occasionally as a conductor in several Washington theater orchestras. Sousa traveled for a time with a touring theatrical company and in 1876 settled in Philadelphia. Over the next few years he found employment as a violinist and conductor and was increasingly in demand as an arranger of music for theatrical productions. Sousa met his wife, Jane van Middlesworth Bellis, in Philadelphia early in 1879, and they were married later that year; the couple had three children. By age twenty-five he had already composed and published dozens of songs and instrumental works and had written the music for *Our Flirtations*, a successful touring variety show.

In 1880 Sousa, then on tour with *Our Flirtations*, received a telegram from the Marine Corps asking him to assume leadership of the Marine Band. Sousa accepted the offer by proxy through his father and returned to Washington by late September. At this time the Marine Band was primarily made up of European players, and its standard of performance was apparently quite low, but during his tenure as its director Sousa transformed this ensemble into the pride of Washington. Sousa imposed high standards of musicianship and professionalism and established a rigorous rehearsal schedule. There were several resignations among the bandsmen in the first few years of his tenure, but the ever-improving quality and reputation of the Marine Band allowed Sousa to attract some of the most talented musicians in the United States. Sousa was also instrumental in transforming the Marine Band's repertoire, replacing outdated and overused music, much of it from the Civil War era, with new arrangements of popular tunes and orchestral music and his own newly composed marches. While the Marine Band played concerts and performed for social functions at the White House, its primary function was as a marching band, performing ceremonial duties and leading military parades. The march gave the group its principal musical identity, and it was Sousa's marches that made the Marine Band stand out among all other military bands of the period. With popular marches such as "The Gladiator" and "The Rifle Regiment," both composed in 1886, Sousa gained national fame and recognition. "The Washington Post," commissioned in 1889 by the newspaper of the same name, was an international hit, based on sales of sheet music, and was quickly associated with a popular dance of the day, the two-step. Within a few years Sousa was universally known as the "March King." There was an enormous demand for Sousa's marches, both in their original band versions and in arrangements for every imaginable combination of instruments. Sousa's publisher during his years in Washington, Harry Coleman, became enormously wealthy on the strength of Sousa's popularity, but Sousa himself did not. Under the rather one-sided terms of their contract, Sousa was paid $35 per march but then surrendered all publishing rights to Coleman. Sousa also composed theatrical music during his years in Washington, achieving moderate success with his operetta *Désirée* (1883).

In 1892 Sousa resigned from the Marine Corps to form his own concert band. After nearly twelve years he seems to have chafed under the restrictions of military life, and he was particularly frustrated by the fact that, despite his fame, the Marine Corps never offered him commissioned rank. The main reasons for his decision, however, seem to have been a partnership offered by David Blakely and the opportunity to have complete artistic control over a band. Blakely, a promoter and businessman who had managed the successful band of Patrick Gilmore, guaranteed Sousa a salary four times that of his Marine Corps pay, and the two agreed to share profits and royalties on Sousa's published compositions. Soon thereafter, Sousa ended his publishing relationship with Coleman and made a much more profitable arrangement with John Church of Cincinnati. The newly formed Sousa Band was almost immediately recognized as one of the best ensembles of its kind in the United States. Sousa recruited many of the finest American and European instrumentalists, and the band included several true virtuosos, including cornet soloist Herbert L. Clarke and trombonist Arthur Pryor. As with the Marine Band, Sousa expected and received the very highest musical standards from the musicians of the Sousa Band.

Soon after its inaugural concert in Plainfield, New Jersey (26 Sep. 1892), Sousa took the band on tour, beginning nearly forty years of touring across America by rail. From the beginning, Sousa Band concerts were a mixture of orchestral transcriptions, works featuring Sousa's soloists, popular songs and dances, humorous novelty pieces, operatic arias, patriotic songs, and Sousa's own marches. Sousa fervently believed in giving audiences the sort of music they wanted, and he did his best to capture local color while on tour—the most famous example being his renditions of "Dixie" in southern states. He did his best to keep up with current musical styles, introducing ragtime pieces in the early 1900s and experimenting with jazz in the 1920s. After several enormously successful American tours in the 1890s, the Sousa Band embarked on its first European tour in 1900–1901, which included an extended stay in Paris, where Sousa represented the United States at the Paris Exposition. Three more European tours followed over the next five years, and in 1910–1911 the Sousa Band made a lengthy world tour. At the outbreak of World War I Sousa enlisted in the navy by special invitation and was commissioned as a lieutenant in the naval reserves. During the war years Sousa oversaw the training of hundreds of navy bandsmen at the Great Lakes Naval Training Station. After the war he returned to active touring with the Sousa Band and maintained a busy schedule throughout the 1920s. Sousa died in Reading, Pennsylvania, while on a guest conducting engagement.

Sousa's impact on musical life in America—particularly on the tradition of band music—is inestimable. In an age before widespread recordings and radio, his tireless touring brought his band to virtually every moderate-sized town in the United States. Millions of Americans heard his virtuoso performers, and for many of them the Sousa Band also provided their first exposure to classical styles. More than any other bandleader, Sousa changed the public's perception of band music from a predominantly military tradition to the concert band tradition that exists today. Sousa's 136 marches stand at the core of today's band repertoire, and his march "The Stars and Stripes Forever" (1896) remains the single most popular piece of band music. Much less well known today are the hundreds of other works he composed or arranged for the Marine Band and Sousa Band: overtures, novelty works, waltzes, and transcriptions of orchestral and operatic works. Sousa was also active as a composer of songs and stage works and was particularly successful with the operetta *El Capitan* (1895). Just as significant to succeeding generations of American musicians as Sousa's music were his efforts on behalf of securing the intellectual property rights of composers. Sousa was a charter member of the American Society of Composers, Authors, and Publishers, and he eventually served as ASCAP's vice president. He actively lobbied Congress on behalf of copyright reform prior to passage of the U.S. Copyright Law of 1909. In 1924 he appeared before Congress to fight for the right of composers to receive royalties from radio stations that broadcast their works.

• Sousa wrote copiously on musical and other subjects and wrote several autobiographical books and articles. The last of these, *Marching Along* (1928), was broadly fictionalized in the 1952 film *Stars and Stripes Forever*, starring Clifton Webb as Sousa. Paul E. Bierley is primarily responsible for detailing Sousa's life and works; he has produced both a definitive biography, *John Philip Sousa: American Phenomenon*, 2d rev. ed. (1986), and a catalog, *The Works of John Philip Sousa* (1984), which includes a complete list of Sousa's musical works and an annotated bibliography of his writings, as well as a list of secondary sources to c. 1983. A rather curious discography of Sousa's music, with particular emphasis on early recordings by the Sousa Band and others, is Walter Mitzinga, *The Sound of Sousa* (1986); see also James R. Smart, *The Sousa Band: A Discography* (1970). See also the entry on Sousa by H. Wiley Hitchcock in *The New Grove Dictionary of American Music* (1986) and Jon Newsom, ed., *Perspectives on John Philip Sousa* (1983).

J. MICHAEL ALLSEN

SOUTH, Lillian Herreld (31 Jan. 1879–14 Sept. 1966), physician, epidemiologist, and bacteriologist, was born near Bowling Green, Kentucky, the daughter of J. F. South, a physician, and Martha Bell Moore. She graduated from E. B. Potter College in Bowling Green in 1897. South studied at the Paterson (N.J.) General Hospital School of Nursing, earning an R.N. degree in 1899. She then enrolled at the Women's Medical College of Pennsylvania in Philadelphia, graduating with an M.D. in 1904. From 1906 to 1910 she practiced medicine in Bowling Green with partners J. N. and A. T. McCormack. During that period South and her associates founded St. Joseph's Hospital in Bowling Green, which opened in 1908 with forty-two beds.

Seeking advanced medical education, in 1910 South arranged to learn laboratory techniques from William H. Park, a pioneer in the application of bacteriology to public health. During that year she also expanded her knowledge of laboratory work at the Rockefeller Institute, the Mayo Clinic, and the Pasteur Institute in Paris. She then enrolled at Johns Hopkins University's School of Public Health, earning a master's degree. She was the first Kentuckian to receive a graduate diploma in public health.

In 1910 South was named director of the newly established Bureau of Bacteriology and Epidemiology within the Kentucky State Department of Health. She was responsible for the creation of the first bacteriology laboratory in the department and directed research there for thirty-nine years. She focused on improving and expanding laboratory services at the Kentucky State Health Department.

One of South's first projects as state bacteriologist was a 1912 survey of hookworm infestation in Kentucky. The Rockefeller Foundation endowed the Health Department with a $20,000 grant toward the eradication of this prevalent parasite. South determined that 106 Kentucky counties were infested. She promoted sanitary conditions and preventative measures, encouraging residents, for instance, to install screens on their windows and doors to minimize their contact with houseflies and other disease-carrying insects.

South also examined how houseflies spread hookworm, educating the public about this danger. She appraised the occurrence of poliomyelitis and leprosy in Kentucky. In the 1920s she lectured on bacteriology at the University of Louisville's School of Public Health. In 1930 she was appointed director of the university's School for Laboratory Technicians.

During her career South was active in state and national medical associations. She served as president and secretary-treasurer of the Association of Southern Medical Women and vice president of the Tri-County Medical Society, and she belonged to the Whitley County (Ky.) Medical Society. She served as business manager of the *Journal of the Kentucky Medical Association* from 1907 to 1943. She also was news editor for the periodical and assisted in its publication until 1951.

Perhaps South's most significant achievement was being the first woman elected as a vice president of the American Medical Association. In 1913 she was named third vice president of that association. She also was elected a fellow of the American Medical Association and certified as a diplomate of the American Board of Preventative Medicine in public health.

South married H. H. Tye, a judge, on 8 July 1926; they had no children. They lived in Williamsburg and Louisville, Kentucky, where South belonged to the Presbyterian church. Among her honors, South was named to the governor's staff and listed in directories of prominent scientists, including *Who Was Who in America*.

In 1950 South resigned from the laboratories she founded and directed. Suffering from chronic lymphatic leukemia, she died at the Pee Wee Valley (Ky.) Hospital. At the time of her death, South remained the only female physician to be chosen as a vice president of the American Medical Association.

• Biographical sketches of South appear in two obituaries: "Only Woman Vice.-Pres. of AMA Dr. South Dies at Age 91," *Journal of the Kentucky Medical Association* 64 (Oct. 1966): 890; and "South, Lillian Harreld," *Journal of the American Medical Association* 199 (30 Jan. 1967): 352.

ELIZABETH D. SCHAFER

SOUTHARD, Elmer Ernest (28 July 1876–8 Feb. 1920), psychiatrist, was born in Boston, Massachusetts, the son of Martin Southard, the manager of a small draying business, and Olive Wentworth Knowles. From a South Boston neighborhood he

characterized as "not far above the level of the slums," Southard attended the Boston Latin School and in 1897 was graduated with honors in philosophy from Harvard College. A brilliant student of Josiah Royce and William James, Southard also wrote poetry and short stories and was the Harvard chess champion from 1895 through 1900. After graduation he entered Harvard Medical School, from which he received an M.D. in 1901. Following a year's postgraduate study in Germany, Southard assumed a position as a pathologist at the Boston City Hospital, moving in 1906 to Danvers State Hospital. That same year he married Mabel Fletcher Austin, a graduate of Johns Hopkins Medical School and a lecturer at Wellesley College. They had three children. In 1909 Southard served on the Massachusetts Commission on Mental Diseases. Having joined the faculty of Harvard Medical School in 1904, in 1909 he was appointed Bullard Professor of Neuropathology, at that time the medical school's youngest full professor ever. In 1912 Southard assumed the first directorship of the Boston Psychopathic Hospital (now the Massachusetts Mental Health Center), a Harvard-affiliated state-run institution for the care of mild and incipient mental disorders.

It was for his pioneering work at the psychopathic hospital that Southard is recognized as one of the most significant and original psychiatric thinkers and practitioners of his time. He was a central participant in the early twentieth-century transformation of psychiatry from a marginal science focused primarily on the care of the insane into a powerful discipline concerned with everyday matters affecting everyone. The Boston Psychopathic Hospital, which Southard had helped to design, was a new kind of institution modeled on the German psychiatric clinic and the American general hospital. The institutional locus for psychiatry's transformation, the hospital represented a decisive break from the discipline's asylum-based past. Southard gathered together a group of young, talented physicians, among them Herman Adler, Karl Menninger, Abraham Myerson, and Harry C. Solomon. Many of them, like himself, were men of science from modest backgrounds who had been trained at elite institutions and were drawn to pathology, the postmortem study of diseased or defective brain tissue. The hospital, located in the midst of the city, was accessible to a wide range of patients, many of whom the hospital staff deemed not insane but nearly normal. Southard took several institutional and conceptual steps to accommodate these persons, who appeared to suffer more from difficulties rooted in everyday life (poor marital relations, for example) than from the symptoms of insanity. He established an outpatient clinic, one of the first in the United States for psychiatric cases.

In collaboration with Mary C. Jarrett, Southard set up a social service department that investigated patients' circumstances and provided follow-up supervision after discharge. He organized hospital-based apprenticeship programs that provided the impetus for the establishment, in 1918, of the Smith College Training School for Social Work, the first institution to train psychiatric social workers. Southard advocated that the conceptual distinction between the sane and the insane that had structured nineteenth-century practice be abandoned, and, as a corollary, he attempted to reorganize psychiatric knowledge around a metric concept of the normal. What Southard called "the happy inspiration of Binet" (Alfred Binet was the most important of the early psychometricians) prompted psychiatrists to envision all persons arrayed on a scale and to assess their variations from what they judged as normal. At the same time, Southard deemed certain everyday concerns—sex, marriage, manhood and womanhood; work, ambition, and worldly failure; habits, desires, and inclinations—as worthy of being incorporated into the psychiatrist's purview. An early exponent of industrial psychiatry, a committed eugenicist, and a tireless propagandist for his hospital and specialty, Southard crossed the country and traveled to Europe to deliver lectures. He fashioned a new psychiatry focused as much on normality as on insanity, a science applicable to everyone. This psychiatry of everyday life represented a major conceptual and institutional break from psychiatry's past.

A member of many (and president of several) scientific organizations and editorial boards, Southard was a prolific, sometimes idiosyncratic, and nearly always provocative writer, publishing nearly 200 papers. His publications range in subject matter from his early work in pathology to his later, more sociologically informed investigations and include a number of papers on eugenics and the feebleminded, as well as on philosophical topics. Southard also published three major casebooks: with Harry C. Solomon, *Neurosyphilis: Modern Systematic Diagnosis and Treatment* (1917), and *Shell-Shock and Other Neuropsychiatric Problems, Presented in Five Hundred and Eighty-nine Case Histories from the War Literature, 1914–1918* (1919); and, with Mary C. Jarrett, *The Kingdom of Evils: Psychiatric Social Work Presented in One Hundred Case Histories Together with a Classification of Social Divisions of Evil* (1922). The last is a fascinating, brilliant book in which Southard formulates the tenets of the new psychiatry. He died of pneumonia in New York City.

• Although scanty, the Southard papers at the Countway Library of Medicine in Boston contain some unpublished material, including a short, unfinished autobiography. Frederick P. Gay, *The Open Mind: Elmer Ernest Southard, 1876–1920* (1938), is a full, though dated, biography by a boyhood friend and fellow professor of medicine. *Bulletin of the Massachusetts Department of Mental Diseases* 4, no. 1 (1920), contains an annotated bibliography of Southard's works. Elizabeth Lunbeck, *The Psychiatric Persuasion: Knowledge, Gender, and Power in Modern America* (1994), based on Boston Psychopathic Hospital case records, is the fullest available treatment of Southard's thought and practice. An obituary is in the *Boston Transcript*, 9 Feb. 1920.

ELIZABETH LUNBECK

SOUTHARD, Samuel Lewis (9 June 1787–26 June 1842), attorney and politician, was born in Basking Ridge, New Jersey, the son of Henry Southard and Sarah Lewis, farmers. Southard's character and world view were shaped most significantly by his father, who preached and practiced the virtues of "republican simplicity," and the Reverend Robert Finley, a local Presbyterian clergyman who prepared Southard for college at Princeton. From his father, who by 1801 was serving in Congress, Southard was weaned on Jeffersonian precepts and a commitment to public service. For his part Finley planted in Southard a love of books and a commitment to such causes as promoting education and social reform.

Southard's interest in politics was reinforced following his graduation from Princeton in 1804 when he spent several years in Virginia's Northern Neck as a tutor in the household of Congressman John Taliaferro. In Virginia, Southard met future president James Monroe and other political notables. He read law and was admitted to the bar in Fredericksburg in 1810, and he married a Virginia woman, Rebecca Harrow, in 1812. Nonetheless Southard concluded that his future lay not in Virginia but closer to "my early acquaintance and college companions," as he put it in a letter to a Princeton classmate.

For several years Southard practiced law in Hunterdon County, New Jersey. He presided over a growing household that would include six children (three of whom reached adulthood) and spent much of his free time on politics. In 1814 he helped his father regain his seat in Congress and the following year ran successfully on his own for the state assembly. Openly ambitious, to an extent that irritated even his political friends, Southard consistently sought more lucrative and influential positions. He was throughout his life remarkably successful in achieving these goals, though it cannot be said that he ever achieved contentment.

By age twenty-eight Southard secured appointment to New Jersey's state supreme court, a position he relinquished in 1820. Despite his support for the admission of Missouri as a slave state, an unpopular position in New Jersey, Southard was elected to the U.S. Senate that year and participated on the select committee that forged the final Missouri Compromise. During his brief service in the Senate, Southard continually pressed for a cabinet appointment from President James Monroe. He was finally rewarded in 1823 when Secretary of the Navy Smith Thompson of New York accepted a position on the U.S. Supreme Court. Of all the notable positions he held, Southard most enjoyed his service in the Navy Department. Despite the everyday demands of directing naval operations across the globe and the frustrations of dealing with congressional leaders who opposed virtually all spending, Southard proved to be an effective and creative department head. In disciplining Commodore David Porter for the latter's unauthorized incursion at Foxardo in Puerto Rico in late 1824, Southard established an important precedent for civilian command of the military. He worked long hours planning a major expedition to Antarctica under Navy Department auspices but was stymied by Congress's failure to appropriate funds for the project. Nor was he successful in substantially enlarging the navy, given the strong pressures for economy exerted by Congress in the 1820s.

Remaining in his post through the term of Monroe's successor, John Quincy Adams, Southard was part of the inner circle of the administration, plotting policy and political moves. During this period he became increasingly friendly with Secretary of State Henry Clay. Once Adams was defeated for reelection in 1828, Southard worked tirelessly to advance Clay's political interests and his "American System" of protective tariffs and federally supported internal improvements. Southard agreed that "liberty is power" and that government had a significant role to play in shaping a dynamic economy. Consequently he rejected the strict construction precepts of older Jeffersonians and rising Jacksonian politicians and became a prominent force in the Whig party of the 1830s.

For nearly a quarter of a century Southard played a dominant role in New Jersey politics and government, maneuvering against a squadron of formidable Jacksonian leaders, among them Mahlon Dickerson, Garret D. Wall, Robert Stockton, and Peter D. Vroom. Serving as the state's attorney general beginning in 1829, he built a strong Whig organization and kept New Jersey Whigs competitive even during the height of Andrew Jackson's popularity. As governor during the winter of 1832–1833, Southard penned a strongly worded critique of secession, but he had little time to press for the Whig agenda on state issues. Elected again by the legislature to the U.S. Senate in March 1833, Southard was among the key figures in the Whig leadership. He was best known for his sharp criticism of Jacksonian banking policies, its administration of the Post Office, and its belligerence toward France.

Outside of politics Southard was active in the affairs of his alma mater and its sister institution, the Princeton Theological Seminary, both of which he served as a trustee. He was an active member of a half-dozen associations, ranging from seamen's aid societies to temperance, Bible, and colonization organizations at the local, state, and national levels. He frequently spoke to gatherings of these organizations and gave his share of Fourth of July addresses to various New Jersey audiences.

Southard's true love, however, remained politics. He spent hours coordinating Whig operations each election year; each fall saw him undertake an exhaustive speaking schedule. In 1840, when Southard's campaigning for William Henry Harrison included forays out of state as well as throughout New Jersey, he fully expected to be rewarded with a cabinet position. He was disappointed. When the new Congress convened in 1841 Southard accepted a consolation prize—president pro tempore of the U.S. Senate. As that body's chief presiding officer in 1841 and 1842, Southard made key rulings in the heated debates over recharter of a new national bank, tariff policy, and other controversies generated by President John Tyler's refusal to adhere to a party line dictated by Henry Clay.

Although Southard stood a heartbeat from the presidency for more than a year, he was less and less focused on politics. His finances were unhinged by several bad investments and an unfortunate liaison with the Morris Canal and Banking Company; his marriage was disintegrating; and his health broke. The main impact of Southard's final illness and death, of uremic poisoning, in Fredericksburg, Virginia, was to open a path for ambitious younger Whig politicians like future vice presidential candidate William L. Dayton and future House Speaker William Pennington. As a political figure, Southard was more a representative than a distinctive figure. His political journey from republican simplicity to the American System, for example, emblematized the impact of social and economic change on many Americans' values.

• Most of Southard's personal papers—roughly 20,000 items—are housed at the Firestone Library, Princeton University. Other useful collections of Southard material can be found in the New York Public Library and the Library of Congress. His voluminous official correspondence as navy secretary is in the National Archives. Significant secondary sources include Herbert Ershkowitz, "Samuel L. Southard: A Case Study of Whig Leadership in the Age of Jackson," *New Jersey History* 88 (Spring 1970): 5–24; Michael Birkner, "Samuel L. Southard and the Origins of *Gibbons v. Ogden*," *Princeton University Library Chronicle* 40 (Winter 1979): 171–82; Birkner, "The 'Foxardo Affair' Revisited: Porter, Pirates, and the Problem of Civilian Authority in the Early Republic," *The American Neptune* 42 (July 1982): 165–78; and Birkner, *Samuel L. Southard: Jeffersonian Whig* (1984).

MICHAEL J. BIRKNER

SOUTHWICK, Solomon (25 Dec. 1773–18 Nov. 1839), journalist and politician, was born in Newport, Rhode Island, the son of Solomon Southwick, a journalist, and Ann Gardner Carpenter. His father's newspaper, the *Newport Mercury*, supported the Revolution and was forced to suspend publication when the British occupied Newport in 1776. The family fled, lost its property to confiscation, and never recovered its prosperity after the war. As an adolescent, young Southwick worked on fishing and shipping vessels and was briefly a baker's apprentice. He was apprenticed to a printer in New York City and in 1791, as a journeyman, went to work at the *Albany (N.Y.) Register*, a leading anti-Federalist newspaper operated by the brothers Robert and John Barber. After Robert Barber withdrew from the concern, Southwick was given editorial duties and became a partner in 1792. In 1795 he married the Barbers' sister Jane Barber; they had nine children, of whom five grew to adulthood.

By 1800 Southwick's attention turned to party politics, and he relinquished his partnership in the newspaper while continuing to write its political essays. Fluent and persuasive as both a writer and a speaker, he rose swiftly in the Jeffersonian Republican (later Democratic) party. He was successively named clerk of the state assembly, clerk of the senate, and sheriff of Albany city and county. After John Barber's death in 1808, Southwick became sole proprietor of the *Regis-*

ter and made it the leading voice of the De Witt Clinton wing of the party. He was perceived to be "editorial lord-ascendant of the state" (*Albany Evening Journal*, 21 Nov. 1839), especially after the death in 1810 of the distinguished editorialist James Cheetham of New York. Southwick was named state printer, an enormously profitable position, especially after bankruptcy legislation in 1811 required printing a paid notice of each case in the official paper, the *Register*. He also became first president of the Farmers' and Mechanics' Bank of Albany, as well as a regent of the state university. As a later historian noted, he was "now in the zenith of his power and prosperity" and "all but worshipped by the republican members of the legislature" (Hammond, vol. 1, p. 290). It appeared that he was destined for high political office.

But as he prospered, Southwick overreached, believing that his popularity and plausibility would carry him to any objective. His career began to sour in 1812 when he was hired by the backers of the gigantic scheme to create a Bank of America to win approval for its charter in the legislature, despite his party's and his own previous opposition to bank charters. He was accused of setting spies on legislators and was ultimately tried for bribing the Speaker of the state assembly; he was acquitted, although the evidence against him was damaging. His party influence much weakened, he was stripped of the position of state printer in 1814. He soon was plunged deeply in debt from imprudent land speculation. In 1815 he turned his back on his oldest political ally, De Witt Clinton, and supported James Monroe for reelection as president. He was rewarded with the postmastership of Albany—an appointment his creditors supported in the hope that he could thereby pay his debts. In 1817 financial difficulties forced him to suspend publication of the *Register*, which was later revived by another owner.

None of Southwick's enterprises thereafter turned out well. In 1822 he was removed from his position as postmaster, purportedly for mishandling funds. Two ventures in journalism, *The Plough-Boy*, an agricultural weekly, and *The Christian Visitant*, soon failed. In 1822 he put himself forward as an independent candidate for governor, but he managed to win fewer than 3,000 votes. He later joined the anti-Masonic movement and supported it with a newspaper, the *National Observer*. In 1828 he ran as the candidate for governor of the Anti-Masonic party and won just enough votes to ensure the victory of Martin Van Buren. In his final years he became a lecturer, touring the state and trumpeting the virtues of Christianity and temperance. He died in Albany.

After his death, Southwick was recalled as one of the most ingratiating figures in his state's politics but incurably afflicted with poor judgment and unprincipled avidity for wealth and high office. As a political journalist, he was ranked with the best; the *Albany Evening Journal* of 21 November 1839, reprinting an article from the *New York Commercial Advertiser*, wrote: "If his style had less strength than that of Cheetham, it had equal boldness and more beauty; and there was a

time—say from 1800 to 1812—when few men in the state exerted a greater influence than Solomon Southwick."

• Solomon Southwick's writings include a long poem, *The Pleasures of Poverty* (1823), and *Five Lessons for Young Men; by a Man of Sixty* (1837). The American Antiquarian Society, Worcester, Mass., holds numerous books bearing his imprint. James Moore Caller and Mrs. M. A. Ober, *Genealogy of the Descendants of Lawrence and Cassandra Southwick of Salem, Mass.* (1881), reprints short biographical articles; additional information on the family is in Isaiah Thomas, *The History of Printing in America* (1812; repr. 1970), and Arthur M. Schlesinger, *Prelude to Independence* (1958). Clarence S. Brigham, *History and Bibliography of American Newspapers 1690–1820* (2 vols., 1947), contains details on Southwick's newspapers. His career as a journalist is summarized in Frederic Hudson, *Journalism in the United States* (1873). His political career is recounted in Jabez D. Hammond, *The History of Political Parties in the State of New York*, vol. 1, 4th ed. (1850); and DeAlva Stanwood Alexander, *A Political History of the State of New York*, vol. 1 (1906). Obituaries are in the *Albany Evening Journal*, 19 and 21 Nov. 1839, the latter reprinted from the *New York Commercial Advertiser*.

JAMES BOYLAN

SOUTHWORTH, Emma Dorothy Eliza Nevitte (26 Dec. 1819–30 June 1899), novelist, was born in Washington, D.C., the daughter of Charles LeCompte Nevitte, an Alexandria, Virginia, merchant, and his second wife, Suzanna George Wailes. Named Emma at birth, she was christened Emma Dorothy Eliza Nevitte in 1824 at the request of her dying father, thus giving her the initials E. D. E. N. by which she would be known as an author. Deeply troubled by her father's death, Emma found comfort in religious beliefs that would grow even stronger over time. Baptized a Roman Catholic but raised in the Episcopal church, she eventually embraced a nondoctrinal Christian outlook.

In 1826 Mrs. Nevitte married Joshua L. Henshaw of Boston, secretary to Daniel Webster. Emma Nevitte spent much of her childhood at her grandmother's home in St. Mary's County, Maryland. The background for her many stories associated with Maryland and Virginia would be developed and enriched as she traveled the countryside by horseback and listened keenly to the legends, ghost stories, and other tales told by the old people of the region. Indebted for her education to her stepfather, from whom she acquired her knowledge of the classics, she graduated in 1835 from the school for girls that Henshaw had established in Washington during the late 1820s.

She taught school until her marriage in 1840 to Frederick Hamilton Southworth, a Utica, New York, inventor. The following year the couple moved to a farm near Prairie du Chien, Wisconsin. Southworth taught in the public school of a neighboring town, Platteville, until she gave birth to a son, Richard. When she returned with her husband to Washington, D.C., in 1844 because of his unemployment, she was pregnant with her second child, Charlotte Emma. Abandoning the family to seek his fortune in South America, Frederick apparently never lived with his wife again. The Southworths were never formally divorced; reasons for their continued separation are unknown. Until his death in the early 1860s, Frederick tried periodically to get money from his wife or her publishers.

Southworth's family gave her little help during these hard times. She finally obtained a teaching job, but life continued to be a struggle on her meager salary of $250 a year. Her financial woes were aggravated further by her own ill health and that of her children. The difficulties of this period, which are reflected in her numerous stories of abandoned wives and in her continuing fear of poverty, would haunt Southworth for the rest of her life.

Late in 1845, in an effort to earn additional income, Southworth wrote her first short story, "The Irish Refugee," and submitted it to the *Baltimore Saturday Visitor*. Heartened by the $15 she earned from its publication, she soon placed her second story with Gamaliel Bailey's *National Era*. Bailey encouraged Southworth to continue writing. Her first novel, *Retribution* (1849), was serialized in fourteen weekly installments in the *National Era* before its publication in book form by Harper's. Its commercial success and the encouragement of John Greenleaf Whittier, then corresponding editor of the *National Era*, persuaded Southworth to become a fulltime writer. The home she purchased in Georgetown—in the early 1850s, overlooking the Potomac River—soon became a well-known literary meeting place.

Between 1849 and 1856 Southworth wrote regularly for the *National Era* and the *Saturday Evening Post*. Twelve of her novels appeared serially in their pages before publication in book form by Theophilus B. Peterson of Philadelphia, the major American publisher of inexpensive, sensational fiction. Each novel brought immoderate critical praise and increased sales to a rapidly growing reading public. After difficulties with Henry Peterson, editor of the *Saturday Evening Post*, Southworth became an exclusive contributor to Robert Bonner's *New York Ledger*, a family paper that published moral essays, fiction, and poetry. Her financial security was assured as she became the *Ledger*'s most popular writer. Eventually thirty of Southworth's novels appeared in serial form in the *Ledger*'s pages, contributing substantially to her considerable annual income of about $10,000 a year from her writing.

In 1859 Southworth traveled to England, where she spent the first two years of the Civil War. Though she generally wrote about the prewar South in positive terms, she was a staunch supporter of the Union upon her return home in 1862. Southworth's extraordinary literary output continued after the war. Acclaimed by the journal *Saturday Night* in the late 1860s as the "Queen of American Novelists," Southworth was perhaps the best writer and unquestionably the most popular of the multitude of mid-nineteenth-century sentimental novelists in the United States. Not until she was nearly seventy did she at last put down her pen. Her success was capped in 1877 when T. B. Peterson

published a forty-two volume uniform edition of her novels. Growing increasingly deaf in her last years, Southworth nevertheless remained busy until her death in Georgetown.

Despite her fame, Southworth seemed to have few pretensions regarding the merits of her novels. Although she implied that freedom from financial pressures might have given her the opportunity to write differently, she was evidently satisfied by having provided her hundreds of thousands of readers escape and instruction—both of which, she believed, were admirable accomplishments for any writer. Her Gothic plots are full of the sentimental and melodramatic conventions of the day, yet she made good use of authentic black speech and demonstrated an artful understanding of female psychology.

Southworth's most popular and most widely reprinted novel was *The Hidden Hand* (1859). Though afflicted by injustices that nineteenth-century women had to endure, its heroine bravely makes her own way in the world, turning the tables on men. While Southworth's heroines typically embody such conventional female values of her day as moral purity, religious faith, and domesticity, they do not exhibit an extreme female docility. Instead, her novels demonstrate that women can be self-reliant and not dependent on men to come to their aid.

• The standard work on Southworth's life and writings is Regis Louise Boyle, *Mrs. E. D. E. N. Southworth* (1939). Other helpful works include Herbert Ross Brown, *The Sentimental Novel in America, 1789–1860* (1940); Frank Luther Mott, *Golden Multitudes* (1947); Helen Waite Papashvily, *All the Happy Endings* (1956); Nina Baym, *Women's Fiction* (1978); Herbert F. Smith, *The Popular American Novel, 1865–1920* (1980); Alfred Habegger, "A Well Hidden Hand," *Novel* 14 (1981): 197–212; Nina Baym, *Novels, Readers, and Reviewers* (1984); and Susan Coultrap-McQuin, *Doing Literary Business: American Women Writers in the Nineteenth Century* (1990).

L. MOODY SIMMS, JR.

SOVINE, Red (7 July 1918–4 Apr. 1980), country musician, was born Woodrow Wilson Sovine near Charleston, West Virginia, the son of Alonzo C. Sovine, an equipment operator, and Rebecca Elizabeth Gray. Sovine grew up on a farm in Sugar Creek, West Virginia. Although the family had difficult times during the depression, Sovine described his childhood as a very happy one: "We would have had it a whole lot rougher . . . if it hadn't been for the farm. We had a cow, and we raised most of our food." Sovine began singing as soon as he began to talk. He loved the songs he heard at church and learned to sing all the familiar hymns. When he was twelve years old, his father gave him a twelve-dollar guitar for his birthday. Sovine taught himself to play the guitar and to accompany himself as he sang.

Winning an amateur contest in Charleston, West Virginia, during the early 1930s sparked Sovine's desire to perform on the radio. In 1935 he received his first radio assignment—singing duets with Johnnie

Bailes at WCHS, Charleston. The duo and their band, the Carolina Tar Heels, were invited to move to radio station WWVA, Wheeling, West Virginia, in 1936. Sovine performed with the band until 1939, at which time he decided to leave radio.

Sovine spent the next eight years (1939–1947) as a factory worker for the branch mill of the Gotham Hosiery Co. in Eleanor, West Virginia. He was eventually promoted to superintendent of the mill. In 1940 he married Norma Searls; they had four children. Though he spent much of his time with family and the mill during these years, Sovine continued to host a local radio program.

His tremendous love for singing prompted him to quit the business world in 1947 in order to resume his singing career. He returned to station WCHS, performing a solo program, and began to seek performing and recording opportunities. With encouragement from Bailes, Sovine organized his own band, the Echo Valley Boys, and moved to station KWKH, Shreveport, Louisiana. His program was a ten-minute slot at 5:05 A.M. Unfortunately, he had few listeners and no invitations for public appearances. Within three months Sovine was broke.

Sovine did not lack talent. He was a gifted country music singer, songwriter, and guitarist. He had a smooth, rich baritone voice, suited for singing as well as for public speaking. His style of singing and his vocal quality were often compared to that of Hank Williams. He had an easy, consistent manner in his singing and speaking. His songs included ballads, love songs, and gospel songs.

During the 1940s Hank Williams had become an important mentor, friend, and professional supporter of Sovine. Recognizing and admiring Sovine's talent, Williams recommended that Sovine become his replacement on WSFA radio in Montgomery, Alabama (c. 1948). Williams also helped Sovine secure a recording contract with MGM; his first session was in January 1949. Although he recorded twenty-eight songs for MGM during the next four years, Sovine did not have a major hit during that time. According to Sovine, "When my first record came out, I was so poor I didn't even have a record player to play it on. I had to take it over to Hank's mother's house to listen to it."

Sovine received his first major break into country music in June 1949. He was invited to become the replacement for Williams on the "Louisiana Hayride," one of the most popular country and bluegrass shows of that day. It aired on radio station KWKH every Saturday night. Sovine's popularity was also enhanced that year by his regular appearance on an early morning program sponsored by Johnny Fair Syrup. Sovine received an overwhelming response from the listeners, and because of his appearances on the show, sales of the syrup rose 280 percent in six months. As a result, *Broadcasters Magazine* featured a special article about Sovine and invited him to perform at the company's national sales convention that year. While in Louisiana Sovine met several people who had a tremendous influence on him. One such person was Webb Pierce,

another musician who was well established in country music. In 1951 he invited Sovine to be the introductory act for his road show. Sovine filled this role for approximately one and a half years; however, the two became lasting friends and performed together regularly until 1960.

In 1954 Sovine was invited to the Grand Ole Opry, and he and his family moved to Nashville, Tennessee. To Sovine, this invitation was the ultimate opportunity. In an interview (c. 1965) for the *Journal of Country Music*, Sovine said, "When they called me from the Grand Ole Opry and asked me if I'd like to join, I couldn't believe it. To me the Grand Ole Opry has always been the symbol of success in the Country Music business and I can't explain the feelings that were inside me the first time I stepped out on that stage and heard the applause." He continued to perform at the Opry the remainder of his life.

Sovine's first hit recordings occurred after he signed with Decca records in 1954. "Are You Mine?" (1955), a duet with Goldie Hill, was the first of several top-selling records. A duet with Webb Pierce, "Why Baby Why" (1955), was number one for four weeks on the Billboard charts and brought recognition to both performers. "Little Rosa," another duet with Pierce, reached number five the same year. Sovine continued to record and travel during the late 1950s and early 1960s. In 1961 and 1962 he recorded several singles on the Starday record label. With his tenth single release with Starday, he had his first solo hit for the label, "Dream House for Sale" (1964). In addition to single records, he recorded several albums during this time, such as *Country Boy–Country Girl* (1961), *Red Sovine* (1961), *Golden Country Ballads of the 1960s* (1965), and *Little Rosa* (1965).

Sovine was known for his beautiful singing voice; however, his speaking voice won him the reputation as "the greatest of all storytellers." Few musicians have made such an impact on audiences through narrative presentations. One of these recitations brought Sovine his first super hit. "Giddy-Up Go" (1965) was number one on the Billboard chart for six weeks and even crossed to the Pop Top 90 chart. Sovine seemed to have discovered the key to a successful recording career, as other recitations, such as "Phantom 309" (1968), brought similar record sales. His narrative ability produced equal results in 1976, when Sovine recorded "Teddy Bear," the story of a crippled little boy talking with a truck driver. Within five weeks after its release, the record was another number-one hit on the Billboard chart. It earned Sovine a gold record and 1976 award nominations from the Country Music Association for both single record and album. As late as June 1981, copies of "Teddy Bear" were rereleased in England. The record immediately became number four on England's pop charts.

Audiences loved Sovine, and he loved the audience. He performed in private clubs and restaurants, churches, and community centers and was a guest on many television shows. He spent six weeks in Vietnam, performing for and meeting the service men and women. He also toured in Canada, Germany, and other European countries.

While Sovine continued to perform on radio and in public, he devoted time to writing songs. Many of these songs were included in his shows and soon became popular with audiences and other performers. He received three BMI awards for his songwriting, for "Giddy-Up Go" (1965), "Missing You" (recorded by Webb Pierce in 1957), and "Little Rosa" (1956).

Although Sovine had difficult times, he worked hard throughout his life and always demonstrated determination and faith. While speaking of Sovine, Minnie Pearl (a longtime friend and coperformer at the Opry) said, "He was a real trouper. . . . He had dignity. . . . He loved to laugh and reminisce with people. . . . He made a wonderful contribution to country music." As stated by country music friend Ernest Tubb, "He was one of the finest people we had in country music. Red lived by my own philosophy: treat others as you would like to be treated. He was a sincere and dedicated man." Tributes such as these stated by his friends and fellow musicians for the *Tennessean* obituary show that they regarded him as a performer of great talent and presence, capable of expressing the deepest emotions through his singing and recitations.

His concern frequently resulted in directly helping others. In 1973 Sovine recorded "Take Time to Remember," a song written by Nita Lee about her nephew who died of cancer. The proceeds from this record were donated to the Cancer Society. This was one of the first recordings to be approved as a public service record bearing the society seal. On 6 September 1975 the governor of West Virginia presented Sovine with the key to the city and bestowed on him the honor of distinguished West Virginian for his many contributions and services to others. Sovine was also a strong supporter of the Easter Seal Society Crippled Children's Center and the Hank Snow Foundation for Prevention of Child Abuse.

Sovine's career was ended quickly when he suffered a heart attack while driving his car in Nashville. He died as a result of injuries suffered in the accident. Sovine's contributions to country music are numerous. He was one of the earliest country music performers to cross the lines to the pop charts while staying on the country chart. He was unique in his ability to deliver recitatives and was one of few country recording artists to be successful in this endeavor. He was also one of a limited number of performers to have a career spanning four decades, yet he was not forced to change his style. As a songwriter he penned many songs that have become standards for country music artists, and his songs retain a lyrical, flowing melody line that enhances the lyrics. He encouraged many other musicians, such as Charlie Pride and David Houston. Finally, Sovine's life is a testimony that goals may be reached through the combination of talent, determination, and hard work.

• William L. Sovine, a son of Red Sovine, supplied much information for this and is an important source for Sovine's biographical information. Few journal articles have been written about Sovine. Short biographical summaries are included in texts such as Barry McCloud, *Definitive Country* (1995). Recordings are listed in Joel Whitburn, *Top Country Singles, 1944–1993* (1994). Newspaper clippings (from the *Tennessean*, the *Cincinnati Enquirer*, the *Macon Telegraph*, and the *Detroit Free Press*); publicity announcements containing short biographical sketches; and record jackets are on file in the Country Music Association Library in Nashville. An obituary is in the *New York Times*, 5 Apr. 1980.

LINDA P. SHIPLEY

SOWER, Christopher, II (Sept. 1721–26 Aug. 1784), printer and publisher, was born in Laasphe, a village in Wittgenstein, Westphalia, in what is now Germany, the son of Christopher Sower and Maria Christina. The family emigrated to America in 1724 and settled first in Germantown, near Philadelphia, in Pennsylvania. Two years later, they moved inland to a farm in the Conestoga region. After Sower's mother joined Johann Conrad Beissel's Seventh Day Baptist community at Ephrata in 1731, father and son returned to Germantown. There the elder Sower became a printer and publisher best known for his newspaper, the *Pennsylvanische Berichte* (Pennsylvania Reporter). In 1751 he married Catharine Sharpnack with whom he had nine children. Christopher Sower II apparently enjoyed a happy family life.

Although the father never formally joined any religious group, the son was baptized by the German Baptist Brethren, popularly known as Dunkards, on 24 February 1737. After serving as deacon and elder, he was ordained a bishop on 10 June 1753. He continued to be active among the Dunkards throughout his adult life.

Like his father, Sower was a printer and publisher. Prior to his father's death in 1758, he was in charge of the bindery and the English language publications at the Sower establishment. After he inherited the business, he followed and expanded his father's basic policies in publishing the newspaper, almanacs, and religious materials, including a Schwenkfelder hymnal of 760 pages (1762), a second edition of the Lutheran and Reformed Marburg Hymn Book of 528 pages (1762), and a second (1763) and third (1776) edition of the German language Bible that his father first printed in 1743. In 1770, he published *Eine Einfältige und gründlich abgefasste Schul-Ordnung*, by the well-known Mennonite schoolmaster Christopher Dock whose school he had attended as a youth. In order to ensure an adequate supply of paper, he built a paper mill on the Schuylkill River in 1773. These achievements made Sower one of the wealthiest men in British America.

The Sowers, both father and son, participated by means of their publications in Pennsylvania's often lively politics as advocates of causes dictated by their religious beliefs. These included the election to the provincial legislature of Quaker candidates who would maintain the colony's separation of church and state, its pacifism, and its low taxes. Christopher Sower II also opposed the institution of slavery and castigated

German settlers who held slaves. Political and religious opponents, such as Benjamin Franklin and Henry Melchior Muhlenberg, attempted to undermine the Sowers' influence by establishing rival German language newspapers; these efforts were unsuccessful.

The American Revolution, however, devastated Christopher Sower II professionally and personally. Although he denounced British officials for passing the Stamp Act (1765), with its double taxation of the foreign language press, his belief in nonresistance and submission to existing political authority, characteristic of Quakers and German sectarians, prevented him from supporting the movement for independence from Great Britain. Consequently, in 1774 he withdrew from his business and turned over his printing enterprise to his son, Christopher Sower III, who became an active Loyalist. Shortly after the British occupation of Philadelphia in October 1777, Sower moved to the city to be with three of his children and to avoid the fate of other local pacifists whom the rebels had exiled to Virginia. Rather than leave with the British troops in May 1778 as did his son Christopher, he returned to Germantown. Rebel troops immediately took him into custody, the Sowers having been labeled traitors a few days earlier. Although state officials released Sower within a week, they confiscated his property and sold his house, lands, and other possessions.

Sower's last years were comparatively quiet and uneventful. After his wife died on 8 January 1777, he lived for nearly two years in Germantown with his brother-in-law, Henry Sharpnack, and then moved to nearby Methacton where he supported himself by bookbinding. He conducted an evangelistic tour in southeastern Pennsylvania in August 1780, and preached occasionally in the meetinghouses of the Brethren. He died of a stroke, probably in Methacton.

• Segments of the journal of Christopher Saur II are in the collections of the Schwenkfelder Library, Pennsburg, Pennsylvania, as are portions of his correspondence that were part of the Abraham H. Cassel Collection before its sale and dispersion. Cassel describes "Brother Cristopher Saur's Journal" in *The Brethen's Family Almanac* (1881). Donald F. Durnbaugh presents edited translations of significant Sower manuscripts, including portions of the journal and writings of Sower's contemporaries about him and his son, Christopher Sower III, in his *Brethren in Colonial America: A Source Book on the Translation and Development of the Church of the Brethren in the Eighteenth Century* (1967). The "Last Will of Christopher Saur, II, Printer in Germantown," appears in translation by Dieter Cunz in the *Pennsylvania Magazine of History and Biography* 69 (1945): 60–67. Although most secondary works on the Sowers emphasize Christopher Sower I, Oswald Seidensticker includes informative passages on Christopher Sower II in "Der jüngere Christopher Saur" and "Christopher Saur, der jüngere, and die Amerikanische Revolution" in his *Bilder aus der Deutsch-pennsylvanischen Geschichte* (1885), pp. 151–66. Martin G. Brumbaugh presents a passage on "The Second Sower, Elder of the Brethren Church," in his *History of the German Baptist Brethren in Europe and America* (1899), pp. 338–437, as does Edward Hocker in "Sower Printing House of Colonial Times," *Proceedings and Addresses of the Pennsylvania German Society* 53 (1948):

66–110. A more recent treatment appears in Stephen L. Longenecker, *The Christopher Sauers: Courageous Printers Who Defended Religious Freedom in Early America* (1981), pp. 23–148. A complete list of known Sower publications is interspersed in Karl J. R. Arndt and Reimer C. Eck, eds., and Gerd-J. Bötte and Werner Tannhof, comps., *The First Century of German Language Printing*, vol. 1 (1989).

JOHN B. FRANTZ

SOYER, Raphael (25 Dec. 1899–4 Nov. 1987), artist, was born Raphael Schoar in Borisoglebsk, Russia, the son of Avrohom Schoar, a Hebrew teacher, author, and amateur artist, and Bella Schneyer. Soyer's father encouraged his family to read fine literature and study art. Moses, Soyer's twin brother, and, Isaac, another brother born seven years later, both became artists, and Soyer's mother was creative as well, excelling in embroidery. Inspired by his parents and by the profound exploration of the human condition by authors such as Feodor Dostoevski and Anton Chekhov and artists such as Rembrandt Van Rijn, Francisco Goya, and Edgar Degas, Raphael Soyer began creating art in Borisoglebsk at an early age.

Denied a residency permit in 1912 as a result of the anti-Semitic government policies in their province, the Schoars traveled steerage class to the United States. They changed their name to Soyer and eventually settled in the Bronx. Soyer went to public school in New York City, but he dropped out of high school to help his family make ends meet. Beginning in 1915 he attended free art sessions at Cooper Union and the National Academy of Design, switching to the Art Students League five years later. Taking classes for two more years, he was encouraged by instructor Guy Pène du Bois to paint ordinary people and everyday life. He was affected even more profoundly by his visits to the Metropolitan Museum of Art and developed his distinctive style by the late 1920s. The subtle interplay of light and shadow and the sketchy application of paint evoke the emotional states of his subjects. Soyer had his first solo exhibition at the Daniel Gallery in 1929. Two years later Juliana Force, the director of the Whitney Studio Club (later known as the Whitney Museum of American Art), purchased five paintings and a drawing, his first works to enter into a public collection. That same year Soyer married Rebecca Letz, a friend of one of his sisters.

During the Great Depression Soyer exhibited widely, winning acclaim for haunting portraits and street scenes of New York's unemployed, painted in and around Union Square and the Bowery; a good example is *Transients*, an oil painting (c. 1936), in the James A. Michener Collection at the University of Texas at Austin. He also captured the changing face of the city's work force in images such as *Office Girls*, an oil created in 1936 (Whitney Museum of American Art). His sympathies for the working class were well known; however, Soyer never created art that was overtly political. He preferred instead to concentrate on character and context. He was an accomplished portraitist as well, his sitters including homeless acquaintances, professional models, artists, and performers. Characteristically, a Soyer portrait went beyond the public facade to reveal the inner person. Shown singly or in groups, his subjects are alert but seem alone and psychically vulnerable. These qualities are particularly striking in his self-portraits, such as the oil painting (c. 1927–1933) in the Phillips Collection, and in his group portraits of artists, such as *Homage to Thomas Eakins* (1964–1965, Hirshhorn Museum and Sculpture Garden). Honest in their appraisal of Soyer's appearance and character, these works are introspective. They convey the artist's ongoing curiosity about the effects of age and life's experiences. Soyer's many depictions of partly clothed or nude women, in contrast to erotic works by artists such as Titian, Goya, and Manet, make accessible the models' private moods while underscoring their vulnerability. Soyer also participated in New Deal art programs, including the graphic arts division of the Works Progress Administration's Federal Art Project. In 1939, along with his brother Moses, he painted murals for the post office in Kingsessing, Pennsylvania, his only major collaboration with one of his siblings.

Soyer first taught at the John Reed Club School of Art in 1930, and over the next thirty-seven years he taught in many places, including the Art Students League and the New School for Social Research. By the mid-1930s he was creating a significant body of work in etching and lithography. An advocate for artists' rights, he was active in the Artists Equity Association and the American Artists Congress.

Gaining prominence in the 1930s, at a time when realist art held sway in the United States, Soyer was associated with the Fourteenth Street School, a group of New York painters dedicated to honestly portraying urban life. In a career that spanned more than sixty years, he depicted people with compassion and dignity. With the ascendancy of abstraction in New York art by the late 1940s, Soyer fought for diversity and enduring human values, encouraging his peers to depict the human form, not to succumb to the temptation of following artistic fashions: "Let us artists, in forms adapted to our times, paint humanistically and intelligently, Man, and what Man touches, his aspirations and whatever happens to him in this eternal struggle for a better life" (quoted in "A Soyer Profile," *Art Digest* 25 [15 Apr. 1951]: 28). Along with Edward Hopper, Ben Shahn, and other prominent figurative artists, he founded *Reality: A Journal of Artists' Opinions*, published between 1953 and 1956, a public forum for artists choosing to work representationally. Soyer was elected an academician of the National Academy of Design in 1951 and to the American Academy of Arts and Letters in 1969. In his later years he devoted more time to writing, his books including *A Painter's Pilgrimage* (1962) and *Self-Revealment: A Memoir* (1969). Soyer died at his New York home.

Soyer was an important role model for those who chose not to conform to prevailing trends in American art, as he created and defended realist art well into his eighties. Perhaps the consistency of his contributions has kept his work relevant. As painter Alice Neel noted in *Art News* (Dec. 1979), "Raphael never cared about being or not being avant-garde. He deserves credit for sticking to figurative work, for remaining 100 percent what he was."

• Raphael Soyer's papers are in the Archives of American Art, Smithsonian Institution. Soyer also wrote *Homage to Thomas Eakins, Etc.* (1961). Lloyd Goodrich, *Raphael Soyer* (1972), is a comprehensive biography that is lavishly illustrated. Frank Gettings, *Raphael Soyer, Sixty-five Years of Printmaking* (1982), is an exhibition catalog created for the Hirshhorn Museum and Sculpture Garden and is the definitive study of the artist's graphic work. See also Norman L. Kleeblatt and Susan Chevlowe, eds., *Painting a Place in America: Jewish Artists in New York* (1991); Avis Berman, "Raphael Soyer at 80: 'Not Painting Would Be Like Not Breathing'," *Art News* 78 (Dec. 1979): 38–43.

RICHARD RUBENFELD

SPAATZ, Carl Andrew (28 June 1891–4 July 1974), first chief of staff of the U.S. Air Force, was born in Boyertown, Pennsylvania, the son of Charles Spatz, a state senator, newspaperman, and printshop owner, and Ann Muntz. Years later, Carl Spaatz added an *A* to his name to aid in pronunciation.

Spaatz graduated from the U.S. Military Academy at West Point in 1914. At the academy, he received the nickname "Tooey" because of his remarkable resemblance to an upperclassman named Toohey. The army first assigned Spaatz to Schofield Barracks, Hawaii, as an infantry officer. Excited by the growing interest among younger officers in the development of aviation, Spaatz secured transfer to the new flying field in San Diego. He was among the first twenty-five officers to qualify for the aviation branch of the Army Signal Corps and was dispatched for aviation duty along the Mexican border in 1916. In 1917 he married Ruth Harrison; they had three children. Also that year Spaatz accompanied the American Expeditionary Forces (AEF) to France, where he commanded an American flying school at Issoudun and slipped away from his ground assignment to fly with a British pursuit squadron, downing several German Fokkers during the St.-Mihiel and Meuse-Argonne offensives.

Returning to New York in 1918, Spaatz met Henry H. Arnold, then assistant director of military aeronautics, and the two aviators established an immediate bond that guided Spaatz's career for the next thirty years. Spaatz became Arnold's executive officer at Rockwell Field, San Diego, in December 1918 and stayed with Arnold at Fairfield Air Depot (now Patterson Field), Ohio, in 1929 and at March Field, California, in 1931. The Spaatz-Arnold team remained inseparable during the interwar era as part of a small band of army airmen who tried to keep the idea of air power and military aviation alive in a peacetime defense establishment that resisted such innovations. Both risked their careers in 1925 to testify in defense of William "Billy" Mitchell (1879–1936), the insubordinate crusader for an independent air force, during his court-martial. Spaatz also promoted aviation during this period by setting the record for continuous flight of 150 hours, 40 minutes, and 15 seconds in 1929 with Ira C. Eaker and several other army aviators. In 1939 Spaatz rejoined Arnold, recently appointed chief of the Army Air Corps, in Washington as assistant executive, serving variously in planning, matériel, and air staff positions in the office of the chief of the air corps.

Arnold dispatched Spaatz to London in 1940 as a special military observer to learn about German aerial tactics and British countermeasures during the battle of Britain. Spaatz contacted leading British airmen, preparing the way for successful coalition air warfare during the Second World War. Spaatz spent much of 1941 in Washington as Arnold's deputy commander, developing strategic bombing doctrine and pushing development of a huge new B-29 bomber. Arnold gave Spaatz the opportunity to implement strategic bombing doctrine as commander of the new Eighth Air Force, an armada of heavy B-17 and B-24 bombers based in Britain that launched during the summer of 1942 a massive bombardment of strategic German targets. Spaatz's coordination of the air offensive (and Arnold's support at home) led to Spaatz's appointment as Dwight D. Eisenhower's air commander for Operation Torch, the Allied invasion of North Africa, and in 1944 as air commander for Operation Overlord, the Normandy invasion. In each operation, Spaatz stressed precision bombing of vital strategic targets such as oil resources rather than the area bombing favored by Royal Air Force marshal Arthur Harris.

After the German surrender in May 1945 (attended by Spaatz), Arnold ordered Spaatz to command the strategic air offensive in the Far East that included the dropping of two atomic bombs on Japan. Spaatz attended the Japanese surrender aboard the battleship *Missouri*, making him the only American commander to be present at the surrenders of both Germany and Japan. By the time Spaatz replaced Arnold as commanding general, U.S. Army Air Force, on 2 February 1946, he was convinced that air power and strategic bombing had been the predominant weapon for the Allied victory. He headed the Spaatz Board in October 1945 that recommended the atomic bomb as the backbone for postwar American defense.

As U.S. Army Air Force commanding general, Spaatz confronted a major struggle with the U.S. Navy over whether seapower or airpower would provide the first line of American national defense in the postwar era. The conflict focused on the controversy over the structure of the postwar defense organization in the newly unified Defense Department. Spaatz recognized that air force autonomy and the chance of postwar emphasis on air power depended on the outcome of the unification debate. He formed an alliance with the assistant secretary of war for air, Stuart Symington, to fight behind the scenes and before the public and Congress to reorganize the air force, army, and navy as three autonomous services under the new single Department of Defense. Spaatz organized the Air Board under Hugh J. Knerr to design the army air force's program for unification and personally directed

a massive publicity campaign for air power. When the National Security Act of 1947 created a separate air force under a single military establishment, Spaatz became the U.S. Air Force's first chief of staff on 26 September 1947. He headed the U.S. Air Force until his retirement on 30 April 1948.

Spaatz continued to promote air power doctrine as chairman of the Civil Air Patrol and as military affairs columnist for *Newsweek* (1948–1961). He chaired the commission that chose Colorado as the site for an air force academy and was buried in the Air Force Academy cemetery after his death at Walter Reed Army Hospital in Washington, D.C.

Spaatz commanded the greatest air armada and bombing operation in history. He, Arnold, and Mitchell were the intellectual and organizational fathers of the U.S. Air Force.

• The Spaatz papers are deposited in the Manuscript Division of the Library of Congress, and Spaatz correspondence can be found in the Records of the Headquarters of the Army Air Force and of the U.S. Air Force in the National Archives. There is no good biography of Spaatz. The best work for Spaatz's contributions to the development of an American air force is Herman S. Wolk, *Planning and Organizing the Postwar Air Force, 1943–1947* (1984). Spaatz's relationship with Arnold is detailed in Thomas M. Coffey, *HAP, Military Aviator: The Story of the U.S. Air Force and the Man Who Built It, General Henry H. "Hap" Arnold* (1982). An analysis of Spaatz's role as military commander can be found in Alfred Goldberg, "General Carl A. Spaatz," in *The War Lords: Military Commanders of the Twentieth Century*, ed. Field Marshal Sir Michael Carver (1976). An obituary is in the *New York Times*, 15 July 1974.

JEFFERY M. DORWART

SPAETH, Sigmund (10 Apr. 1885–11 Nov. 1965), music critic, was born in Philadelphia, Pennsylvania, the son of Adolph Spaeth, a Lutheran minister, and Harriet Reynolds, a musician. He was brought up in a musical family, and all six of his siblings were part of the church choir, which was directed by their father. Spaeth received his Ph.D. from Princeton in 1910 in English, German, and philosophy with the thesis "Milton's Knowledge of Music." After a brief stint teaching English at the Asheville Academy in North Carolina, he moved to New York and began his career as a writer. Spaeth was the music critic for the *New York Evening Mail* from 1914 to 1918 and then a sports reporter for the *New York Times*. In 1917 he married Katherine Lane; they had no children. From 1920 to 1927 he served as the education director of the American Piano Company. It was in this period that he began to gain fame as the "Tune Detective."

Spaeth developed a vaudeville act based on his extensive knowledge of music. Wearing a Sherlock Holmes–style hat and smoking an oversized pipe, Spaeth would sit at a piano and play a few notes from a popular song of the day. He would then show how the same melody had origins in classical music or how several songs shared the same melody. Another popular routine was to sing the words to "Jack and Jill" in a variety of styles: hillbilly, Italian opera, or jazz, for example. As the "Tune Detective," he appeared on various radio stations, including KDKA as early as 1920. His ability to trace musical origins won him many fans and established Spaeth as a renowned expert on popular music. In 1928 the author of "Yes, We Have No Bananas" hired Spaeth as a defense witness in a plagiarism lawsuit, and he successfully argued that the melody of the song was based on Handel's *Messiah*, a song in the public domain.

While the fame of the "Tune Detective" grew, Spaeth was able to maintain a prolific output as writer. He published several books about music, including *Barber Shop Ballads* (1925), *Read 'em and Weep* (1926), and *Weep Some More, My Lady* (1927). During the 1930s he worked as an editor for a variety of magazines, including *McCalls*, *Esquire*, and *Literary Digest*. His radio career blossomed as well, and he had his own weekly show called "The Tune Detective" on NBC from 1931 to 1933. Spaeth used this moniker on numerous other radio programs and was also a frequent guest on variety shows. The fame of "The Tune Detective" soon drew him into the movie business, and he eventually made a series of film shorts for Paramount, Fox, and Warner Brothers.

Spaeth appreciated the historical significance of both popular songs and folk songs. In the introduction to *Weep Some More, My Lady*, he wrote that this collection of songs was a "fairly complete and impressively honest commentary on American manners and customs of the past." He was so dedicated to documenting and reviving performance styles of the past that he organized the Society for the Preservation of Barbershop Quartets Singing in America in 1933. This group remained active for more than twenty years, sponsoring performances in city parks.

In the 1940s, when television sets began to appear in America's living rooms, Spaeth jumped into the new medium. He hosted several television shows in the late 1940s and early 1950s, including "The Tune Detective" over New York station WPIX in 1948. The television show used the same format as his earlier radio show. Spaeth also appeared on many early variety shows, including those of Arthur Godfrey, Steve Allen, and Jack Paar.

During the 1940s and 1950s Spaeth served as an instructor or adviser for a variety of educational institutions, and in 1948 he published his biggest and most ambitious book, *A History of Popular Music in America*. Throughout the 1950s he also wrote a widely syndicated magazine column and was the editor of the *Music Journal* from 1955 to 1959. Spaeth died in his New York City home, a few months after his wife's death.

Spaeth was deeply involved with music his entire life but chose not to become a musician. He was instead a writer who devoted his life to encouraging the appreciation of music, both popular and classical. Spaeth believed that musical instruction was essential to a well-rounded education. By the time of his death, he had authored thirty-two books and countless magazine and newspaper articles, and his texts remain excellent sources of information about the history of popular music in America.

• A prolific author, Spaeth wrote little about himself. *Fifty Years with Music* (1959) contains one chapter titled "Mostly Autobiographical" that is little more than a list of his books. A special issue of the *Music Journal* (Apr.–May 1959) contains a good deal of biographical information about Spaeth; the issue was tied in with the publication of *Fifty Years with Music*. For a complete list of his publications see *Contemporary Authors* (1969).

NOAH ARCENEAUX

SPALDING, Albert Goodwill (2 Sept. 1850–9 Sept. 1915), baseball player and executive and sporting goods manufacturer, was born in Byron, Illinois, the son of James Lawrence Spalding and Harriet Irene Goodwill Wright. Although A. G., as he was most frequently known, was fond of the "rags-to-riches" description often applied to his life, his childhood was comfortably prosperous. His mother brought a large inheritance from a previous marriage, and his father managed a 320-acre estate, owned several rental homes, farmed, and trained horses. When his father died in 1858, Albert was sent to live with an aunt in Rockford, Illinois, where he attended public school and later the Rockford Commercial College. Before his mother and siblings joined him in Rockford, the twelve-year-old Albert spent much of his time at the town commons watching local boys play baseball. Too shy to ask the other boys to play, Albert earned an invitation to join the game by catching a fly ball hit beyond center field and hurling it to the catcher. Within a few years these informal games became a local schoolboy club, the Pioneers. In 1865, when Rockford businessmen formed a new baseball club, the Forest Citys, they asked Spalding to join as pitcher. In 1867 the Forest Citys defeated the Washington Nationals, reputed to be the best team in the United States; this established Spalding as a well-known pitcher. Many years later Spalding recalled that he was "never more proud of an accomplishment in baseball" (quoted in Levine, p. 8).

Spalding's rise to fame as a professional pitcher paralleled the transformation of baseball from its dual origins as either a gentlemen's club or a rowdy working-class pastime into a popular, commercial, and professional sport. When Spalding began to play, urban boosters and businessmen were just beginning to understand the role that teams could play as city symbols and profit makers; but baseball remained adamantly, if somewhat dishonestly, amateur. Player salaries were forbidden by the National Association of Baseball Players' rules, although clubs frequently employed players like Spalding in other jobs to support their play. Spalding was thus employed first not as a baseball player but as a clerk for one of the team's members. An early advocate for the forthright professionalization of the sport, Spalding questioned the duplicity of such practices, but in 1867 he accepted a pitching position with the Chicago Excelsiors and a job with an Excelsior supporter as a wholesale clerk. After only one game, his employer's business went under, and he was forced to return to the Forest Citys of Rockford. He quit high school and took a position at a local insurance company and a newspaper owned by the Forest Citys' vice president, the Rockford *Register*. In 1870 "Big Al," now 6′1″ and 170 pounds, became a professional player. He joined Harry Wright, the former manager of the Cincinnati Red Stockings, in Wright's newly created professional league, the National Association of Professional Baseball Players. With Spalding as captain and pitcher, Wright's Boston Red Stockings won four NAPBP championships from 1872 to 1875. In his five seasons with the Red Stockings, Spalding won 205 games as a pitcher and became known as "the champion pitcher of the world"; he also compiled a .324 batting average. While in Boston, Spalding married Sarah Josephine Keith, with whom he would have one son.

In 1876 prominent Chicago businessman and team president William Hulbert persuaded Spalding to leave Boston and become the pitcher and manager of the Chicago White Stockings. There Spalding made his most lasting contributions to the game. While building the White Stockings into one of the best teams in the United States, Spalding also aided in the transformation of baseball's public image and administration, making it into a respectable and popular pastime of middle-class America at the end of the century. In 1878 Spalding gave up pitching and devoted himself to team management and business full time. Under the presidency of Hulbert and management of Spalding, the White Stockings recruited the best talent in the nation and dominated baseball for nearly a decade. When Hulbert began organizing a new professional league, the National League of Professional Baseball Clubs, Spalding helped him draft the constitution and marshal support for the new organization. The National League standardized rules and created a bureaucracy of club owners and a board of directors to enforce rules, promote honest play, and govern the league. Seeking approval of the "better sort" of baseball's patrons, league bylaws forbade Sunday games, alcohol sales at the parks, and gambling—measures strongly endorsed by Spalding. Within the White Stockings' organization, such rules of personal conduct were applied even more stringently to players. After Hulbert's death in 1882, when Spalding became president of the Chicago team, he used censures, fines, the threat of dismissal, and Pinkerton detectives to enforce temperance and moral behavior among his players.

Spalding served as president until 1891 and remained an influential member of the league into the twentieth century. In business, as in baseball, he was a shrewd competitor, defeating attempts by other businessmen and even the players themselves to set up rivals to the National League. In 1901 he temporarily came out of retirement in order to serve as president of the league and to defeat attempts by other baseball businessmen to create a National League trust.

In addition to his baseball fame, Spalding was an enormously successful businessman who used his celebrity and baseball connections to build the largest sporting goods corporation in the country at the turn of the century. The same year that he moved to Chicago, Spalding and his younger brother James created the company A. G. Spalding and Brother to manufacture and sell baseball equipment. Building on his reputation as a star pitcher, A. G. handled publicity while his brother took charge of management, and his sister Mary served as the first bookkeeper. Mary's husband joined the firm in 1879, renamed A. G. Spalding and Brothers, and provided the capital for the brothers to buy the first Spalding factory to manufacture baseball bats. The company benefited from Spalding's influence in the National League, becoming the exclusive provider of baseballs for league play and the publisher of the *Official League Book*. These contracts undoubtedly added to the renown and commercial sales of the company's baseballs and of *Spalding's Official Baseball Guide*, an annual publication that Spalding himself edited from 1878 to 1880. However, Spalding never limited his concern to baseball exclusively. In keeping with his personal motto, "everything is possible to him who dares," the Spalding company created new markets, new products, and novel promotion schemes. His company had the additional distinction of being the first manufacturer of footballs, basketballs, golf balls, and golf clubs in the United States. The company also introduced innovations such as creating sporting goods boutiques in department stores, obtaining celebrity endorsements, and sponsoring teams.

Like his contemporary Theodore Roosevelt, Spalding believed that sports were an important means to build character. Both envisioned sport as a wholesome antidote to the late nineteenth century's urban industrial ills. To this end, Spalding used his celebrity, his forceful personality, and his considerable enthusiasm to promote baseball and athleticism generally. He represented American baseball and sports internationally, organizing trips around the world for his own team and American all-star teams. He also directed the American section on sports at the 1990 Olympic Games in Paris, which were held in conjunction with the World's Fair. This service earned him the rosette of the Legion of Honor from the nation of France.

In 1899 Spalding's wife suddenly died, and within two years Spalding married Elizabeth Mayer Churchill, a widow and childhood friend from Rockford. According to Spalding's biographer Peter Levine, Churchill and Spalding had carried on an affair for several years and had a son, Spalding Brown Spalding. When the couple married, Spalding renamed the boy Albert Goodwill Spalding, Jr. His wife was a follower of theosophy, a combination of Indian religion, social gospel, and the occult. Although Spalding always denied a belief in it, she persuaded him to move to California and join an idealistic community of theosophists in Point Loma. The couple built a home adjacent to the Point Loma compound, and Spalding became a prominent member and booster in nearby San Diego.

In 1910 Spalding's stature in the San Diego civic community earned him a nomination to run in the Republican primary for the U.S. Senate, but he lost by a slim margin. In keeping with his own philosophy of sport, Spalding credited baseball as having made him a worthy candidate of character and honesty. In 1911 he published a memoir and history of baseball.

In 1915 Spalding suffered a series of strokes, the second of which was fatal. He died in Point Loma and received an elaborate funeral at Point Loma's temple directed by prominent theosophers. Newspaper obituaries across the nation recognized Spalding, who had been a part of nearly every major event in baseball's history, as the father of what was now considered to be "America's game." In 1939 Spalding, who had been one of the greatest forces in promoting baseball and American sport generally, was inducted posthumously to the National Baseball Hall of Fame. A plaque commemorating his entry hailed him as the "organizational genius of baseball's pioneer days."

• Spalding's papers and correspondence are available in the Spalding papers at the National Baseball Library in Cooperstown, N.Y., and in the Spalding Collection at the New York City Public Library. Peter Levine, *A. G. Spalding and the Rise of Baseball: The Promise of American Sport* (1985), provides a thorough history of Spalding's baseball and business career, as well as a concise history of baseball. A second standard biography is Arthur Bartlett, *Baseball and Mr. Spalding: The History and Romance of Baseball* (1951); however, it is an undocumented and lightly written account of Spalding's life, based primarily on Spalding's own memoirs, *America's National Game* (1911). For information on Spalding's childhood and family background, see Harriet I. Spalding, *Reminiscenses of Harriet I. Spalding* (1910). For a general history of baseball during Spalding's era, see Harold Seymour, *Baseball: The Early Years* (1960).

MICHELLE BRATTAIN

SPALDING, Eliza Hart (11 Aug. 1807–7 Jan. 1851), pioneer and missionary, was born in Kennsington (now Berlin), Connecticut, the daughter of Levi Hart and Martha Hart, farmers who shared the same ancestor, Stephen Hart. When she was thirteen, the family moved to a farm near Holland Patent in Oneida County, New York. At home she learned the necessary crafts of spinning, weaving, and candle making. She attended Hamilton Oneida Academy and may have studied at Chipman Female Academy in Clinton, New York. Eliza was a serious and bright student. Slender and of medium height, she had dark brown hair and blue eyes and a "coarse voice." She was also very religious; baptized in August 1826, she joined the local Presbyterian church. For a while she also taught school. A friend of hers, known as Mrs. Jackson, suggested that she might wish to correspond with Henry Harmon Spalding of Prattsburg, New York, who had conveyed to Mrs. Jackson that he was looking for a woman who would "devote her life to educate the heathen." They began writing each other in 1830, and in the fall of 1831 they met.

Henry Spalding was a student at Western Reserve College in Hudson, Ohio, and Eliza moved there in 1832. In 1833 he graduated, and in October of that year they married; they had four children. Some years before, Henry Spalding had asked a woman named Narcissa Prentiss to marry him, but she rejected him. In an ironic twist, his bitterness and resentment over this rejection later complicated Eliza's and his missionary efforts. He was also virulently anti-Catholic, a feeling shared by Eliza, which later affected their efforts among the Indians. Their interest in religion bound them together, however, and her calm nature was a needed antidote to his contrary temperament.

After their marriage, the Spaldings moved to Cincinnati, Ohio; there Henry studied for the ministry at Lane Theological Seminary, where Lyman Beecher was president. While taking in students as boarders, Eliza studied at home from her husband's courses in scripture and theology. In 1835 Henry was ordained, and he and Eliza received appointments from the American Board of Commissioners for Foreign Missions (ABCFM), comprised of Congregational, Presbyterian, and Dutch Reformed churches. Their excursion west was delayed, however, while Eliza returned home to New York to give birth to a stillborn daughter.

In the meantime, in February 1835 Dr. Marcus Whitman and Rev. Samuel Parker had made an exploratory trip to present-day Idaho and Montana. Whitman, too, had applied for sponsorship from the ABCFM; he also married Narcissa Prentiss in early 1836. Whitman invited the Spaldings to join his expedition west, unaware that his wife had rejected Henry Spalding's marriage proposal years before. In March 1836 the two couples began an arduous trek west across the Rocky Mountains, through which Captain Benjamin Bonneville had taken wagons only recently. They stopped in St. Louis, Missouri, where the Spaldings (out of curiosity) visited the Catholic cathedral, and where, unbeknownst to them, two Nez Percé Indians were buried. They observed Mass being sung, which Eliza described as "heartless forms and ceremonies," and rejoiced that she and her husband had never embraced "such delusions."

Eliza was sick for most of the journey, and her husband was mortified that fate and their faith had brought them together with the woman who had spurned him. Along the way, they joined a caravan of the American Fur Company. The group later joined up with a convoy from the Hudson's Bay Company.

Having lost most of their possessions, the missionaries arrived at Fort Walla Walla on the Columbia River on 1 September 1836. The Whitmans founded their mission near there at Waiilatpu among the Cayuse Indians, who during this time were considered treacherous. The Spaldings, accompanied by 150 Nez Percé Indians, continued on to Lapwai, about 125 miles near present-day Lewiston, Idaho, on the southern tributary of the Clearwater River. There they established a mission among the Nez Percés, a nomadic tribe from the Cascades to the Rockies, part of the Inland Empire. The Nez Percés had been evangelized by Jesuit missionaries and had received their name from French explorers because they wore bits of decorative shells in their noses. Eliza Spalding and Narcissa Whitman were the first white women to cross the Rocky Mountains and the Continental Divide.

The Indians assisted the Spaldings in constructing buildings. Eliza quickly learned their language and opened a school in January 1837 for both children and adult Indians; the school eventually had 225 students. She taught English, spinning, weaving, knitting, and the Bible. She also painted water colors depicting biblical stories, which her husband used in preaching to the Indians.

Meanwhile, the tension between Henry Spalding and Narcissa Whitman intensified. The ABCFM had heard of the ongoing troubles and had decided to dismiss the Spaldings, rescinding its decision only after Marcus Whitman traveled east and assuaged the board's concern. In 1844 Eliza painted the *Protestant Ladder*, a diagrammatic painting showing the history of Christianity and depicting Martin Luther and John Calvin as vital links between Christ and heaven. A colorful and polemical work, it was designed to counteract the teaching of the Jesuits and is the only one of her paintings that was extant at the end of the twentieth century (Oregon Historical Society).

Around this time, relations with the Indians began to deteriorate. More and more whites were migrating to the area, disrupting the nomadic way of life of the Indians and bringing measles, for which the Indians had no immunity. White children survived, but not Indian. The Indians accused the missionaries of witchcraft. Attendance at Eliza's school ceased and she and her family were threatened.

Then on 29 November 1847 a band of Cayuse attacked the mission at Waiilatpu; the Whitmans and twelve others were massacred and forty-seven others were taken prisoner. Eliza Spalding, whose husband was away at the time, was informed of the tragedy and was urged to leave by friendly Nez Percés. She agreed but insisted on waiting until Monday, the day after the Sabbath. She and her family were spared, but the Whitman massacre marked the end of the two missions. Her husband rashly accused the "Romanists" and Jesuit missionaries of the killings; yet no subsequent historical data has given any credence to his charges.

In 1848 the U.S. Congress created the Oregon Territory and appointed a governor of the area, which eventually became the states of Washington and Oregon. Meanwhile, Eliza's health deteriorated. With the mission closed, she and her family moved to the Willamette Valley in late 1847. They settled on the Calapooya River, near present-day Brownsville, Oregon, where Eliza Spalding died, probably of tuberculosis.

Spalding was an example of the indomitable spirit of faith and determination that characterized the American concept of territorial expansion during the 1840s, known as Manifest Destiny. Her husband later returned to the Nez Percé Indians near Lapwai, where he died. In 1913 Eliza Spalding's body was disinterred and buried next to her husband near their old mission home. In 1968 the site was incorporated into the Nez Percé National Historical Park.

• The best sources of information are two works by Clifford M. Drury, *Henry Harmon Spalding* (1936) and *The First White Women over the Rockies* (3 vols., 1963–1966); volume one of the latter has much material on Eliza Spalding. See also Marvin M. Richardson, *The Whitman Mission* (1940), and Alvin M. Josephy, Jr., *The Nez Percé Indians and the Opening of the Northwest* (1965). Bernard De Voto, *Across the Wide Missouri* (1947), and LeRoy R. Hafen and Anne W. Hafen, eds., *To the Rockies and Oregon* (1955), offer a broader glimpse of the migration west. References to her painting is in Susan Larsen-Martin and Louis Robert Martin, *Pioneers in Paradise: Folk and Outsider Artists of the West Coast* (1984), and in George C. Groce, *The New-York Historical Society's Dictionary of Artists in America, 1564–1860* (1957). See also Deborah Lynn Dawson, "Laboring in My Savior's Vineyard: The Mission of Eliza Hart Spalding" (Ph.D. diss., Bowling Green State Univ., 1988).

GEOFFREY GNEUHS

SPALDING, Franklin Spencer (13 Mar. 1865–25 Sept. 1914), Episcopal bishop, was born in Erie, Pennsylvania, the son of John Franklin Spalding, an Episcopal priest and later the second bishop of Colorado, and Lavinia Deborah Spencer. His early years were spent in Erie, where his father was rector of St. Paul's Church, but in 1873 his father was elected missionary bishop of Colorado, and the family moved to Denver. In Denver, Spalding attended Jarvis Hall, a diocesan school to train boys for college. In 1883 he entered the College of New Jersey, Princeton, and graduated in 1887. At Princeton he was a successful debater and wrote for the *Princetonian*. When he graduated, Spalding had not reached a decision with regard to his future profession, so he taught for a year in the Princeton Preparatory School. There he learned quickly that teaching was not for him, and he thought about studying law. Gradually he reached the decision to enter the ministry, because in that profession he could serve both Christ and other people. He believed a person could do the most good as a clergyman. "It was not the saving of souls or the celebrating of the sacraments, but the opportunity which the ministry offered to a Christian man of doing good, strengthening the moral life and furthering the cause of righteousness in the world, that he believed called him" (Melish, *Franklin Spencer Spalding*, p. 33).

In the fall of 1888 Spalding entered the General Theological Seminary, New York, which at that time had rather low academic standards and was derisively referred to as a "theological boys' school." Spalding entered the seminary to become a missionary in the West, and while there he became the first president of the Western Missionary Club, which only those students who expected to go west of the Mississippi River could join. Each member promised to pray for the West each day and to use all means in his power to get men to spend at least three years in the mission field of the West. Seven graduates of the class of 1891 of General Seminary, including Spalding, went to Colorado as missionaries. On 3 June 1891 he was ordained to the diaconate by his father, the bishop of Colorado, and on the following Sunday began his ministry as pastor of All Saints' Church, North Denver. On 1 June 1892 he was ordained priest and immediately began his duties as headmaster of Jarvis Hall, where he remained until 1896.

In 1897 Spalding was called to be the rector of St. Paul's Church, Erie, Pennsylvania, where his father had served. He remained there until 1904. In 1898 he opened a parish house, which had a gymnasium with baths, an auditorium seating 500, rooms for classes and guilds, a large game room for boys, a reading room, and a kitchen and dining room. It was a parish house designed for service in the modern city and was in the tradition of the "institutional church" with "open church doors every day and all day." While at St. Paul's Spalding began to develop his approach to America's social problems. Shortly after going to Erie he spoke one Sunday afternoon to the prisoners in the penitentiary and noticed that a number of young boys were in the audience. He knew that young boys should not be placed with older criminals, and from that moment he became a social reformer. He became a prison reformer, joined pro-labor activities, and began reading the English Christian socialists, especially F. D. Maurice.

His ministry at St. Paul's brought him to the attention of the House of Bishops, and on 18 October 1904 they elected him missionary bishop of the District of Salt Lake (changed to the Missionary District of Utah on 10 Oct. 1907), which included all of Utah and parts of Colorado, Nevada, and Wyoming. He was consecrated on 14 December 1904 at St. Paul's Church in Erie and served until he was killed by an automobile in Salt Lake City. He had never married.

Because of his commitment to social and political issues, Spalding was known as the "socialist bishop." He believed that socialism would free the working class from its slavery to management and that socialism could help the Christian church bring meaning to the teachings of Jesus and achieve the society he envisioned. Christian socialism was the way to realize the Kingdom of God in America. He insisted that the church exists to save the human race and that material conditions must be made right. "Although a man cannot live by bread alone, he must have bread. . . . It is my duty to try to make the Church see that she must cease to be the almoner of the rich and become the champion of the poor" (*Christian Socialist*, Nov. 1914, p. 6). He was also a supporter of the ecumenical movement, especially the movement later called "Life and Work." In an article in the *Atlantic Monthly* (May 1913), he argued that the divisive influence of theology must be subject to the tolerant charity of religion. "Christian Unity will never come until the followers of Jesus Christ realize that his religion depends, not upon exact thinking, but upon Christlike living."

Spalding was a socialist Episcopal bishop in Utah, the center of Mormonism. It was said that he was the most dangerous enemy of Mormonism and was also the best friend of the Mormons. Friendly with many Mormon individuals, he was also a severe critic of Mormon theology. His deepest commitment was to apply Christianity to social conditions, especially the problems of the laborer. He was described as a modern Girolamo Savonarola, challenging his church to search its conscience and confess its shortcomings.

• Most of Spalding's papers are in the Archives of the Episcopal Church, Austin, Tex., and the Episcopal Diocese of Utah Papers, University of Utah, Marriott Library, Special Collections, Salt Lake City. Among Spalding's publications are "The District of Utah," *Spirit of Missions* 70 (Oct. 1905): 761–69; "The Church in the Mining Camp," *Spirit of Missions* 73 (Feb. 1908): 97–104; "Making New Friends in Utah," *Spirit of Missions* 77 (Oct. 1912): 762–67; "Doing Things Out West," *Spirit of Missions* 77 (Dec. 1912): 881–87; "The First Hospital among the Mountains: St. Mark's, Salt Lake City, Utah," *Spirit of Missions* 79 (Nov. 1914): 631–33; "What Is Left of Mormonism after Polygamy?" *Utah Survey* 1 (Nov. 1913): 1–8; "The Church at Work among Settlers in America," *Pan Anglican Congress, 1908*, vol. 6, sec. E, *The Church's Missions in Christendom: Speeches and Discussions Together with the Papers Published for the Consideration of the Congress* (1908): 4–6; "Christian Unity," *Atlantic Monthly*, May 1913, pp. 640–49; "Socialism and Christianity: Supplementary, Not Contradictory," *Christian Socialist* 8 (9 Nov. 1911): 1–3; "Christian Socialism," *Christian Socialist* 6 (1 Mar. 1909): 1–2; "The Bishop of Socialism and Trade Unionism," *Christian Socialist* 5 (1 Feb. 1908): 1–2; and *Joseph Smith, Jr., as a Translator* (1912). The major study of Spalding is John Howard Melish, *Franklin Spencer Spalding: Man and Bishop* (1917). Other studies are John R. Sillito, " 'Prove All Things, Hold Fast That Which Is Good'—Franklin Spencer Spalding: A Christian Socialist Dissenter from Capitalist Values," *Weber Studies* 1 (Spring 1984): 39–48; Sillito, "Franklin Spencer Spalding on Mormonism: A Documentary Approach," *Sunstone* 4 (July–Aug. 1979): 33–35; and Sillito and Martha Bradley, "Franklin Spencer Spalding: An Episcopal Observer of Mormonism," *Historical Magazine of the Protestant Episcopal Church* 54 (Dec. 1985): 339–49. Spalding is also treated in James W. Beless, Jr., "The Episcopal Church in Utah: Seven Bishops and One Hundred Years," *Utah Historical Quarterly* 36 (Winter 1968): 77–96. A number of obituaries noted his many accomplishments. Among them are "The Death of Bishop Spalding," *Spirit of Missions* 79 (Nov. 1914): 753–55; and Melish, "Rt. Rev. F. S. Spalding, D.D. An Appreciation," *Churchman* 110 (3 Oct. 1914): 432.

DONALD S. ARMENTROUT

SPALDING, John Lancaster (2 June 1840–25 Aug. 1916), Catholic bishop, was born in Lebanon, Kentucky, the son of Richard Spalding, a merchant and farmer, and Mary Jane Lancaster. Spalding was the scion of a union between two established American Catholic families, and in 1852 he went to St. Mary's College in Lebanon, where he excelled in oratory, was an active student leader, and served as an assistant teacher. In August 1857 Spalding entered Mount St. Mary's College in Emmitsburg, Maryland, the preeminent Catholic college in the country, but in January 1858, after an undetermined violation of the school's rather strict rules, the future bishop went home without completing his course of study. With the previous year's events behind him, Spalding entered Mount St. Mary's of the West in Cincinnati, Ohio, where he was immediately recognized as having leadership capabilities. Consequently, he gave an opening address to the college and graduated the following June with special honors.

Under the counsel of his uncle Martin John Spalding, the bishop of Louisville, the young Spalding then headed to the American College at the Catholic University of Louvain in Belgium. Influential in founding the American college, Bishop Spalding thought that a European education would benefit his young protégé and train him for future accomplishments. Spalding was eventually ordained a priest at the Cathedral of Malines in Belgium on 19 December 1863; he also received a licentiate of sacred theology in July of the following year. After his formal education at Louvain, Spalding followed the advice of his uncle (by then the premier American see as the archbishop of Baltimore) and traveled to Rome to informally study canon law.

Upon his return to the United States in the spring of 1865, Spalding became the secretary to Bishop Peter Lavialle of Louisville and was in charge of the cathedral school. This marked the beginning of Spalding's lifelong concern with the issue of Catholic education in the United States. Just a year after his return to the United States, the Second Plenary Council of Bishops at Baltimore was called, and Spalding was appointed personal theologian to Archbishop Francis Blanchet of Oregon City. The youngest priest in attendance, Spalding received the honor of being one of only three to address the council. Following the meeting, Spalding returned to Louisville and founded both a parish and school dedicated to the care of former slaves, a concern laid upon Spalding by the prefect of the American College at Louvain. After successfully establishing the church and school, Spalding was named chancellor of the diocese in 1871.

In February 1872 Spalding's uncle died, and at the request of Isaac Hecker, the holder of Martin Spalding's papers, Spalding moved to New York City to write his uncle's biography, *The Life of the Most Reverend Martin J. Spalding, D.D., Archbishop of Baltimore.* Following the publication of the book in 1873, Spalding stayed in New York and worked at St. Michael's parish, running the schools for boys and girls. While in New York, Spalding also wrote for the *Catholic World* and published a collection of essays entitled *Essays and Reviews* (1877). Through these and other writings, Spalding began to carve for himself a prominent niche in American Catholic literary life. His books include *Education and the Higher Life* (1890), *Things of the Mind* (1894), *Means and Ends of Education* (1895), *Thoughts and Theories of Life and Education* (1897), and *Religion, Agnosticism, and Education* (1902).

Following the creation of the diocese of Peoria, Spalding was named its first bishop and was consecrated in New York on 1 May 1877. The diocese of which Spalding took charge contained 45,000 parishioners, 50 priests, and 70 churches; twenty-five years after Spalding's consecration, the diocese had expanded to more than 120,000 parishioners, 181 priests, 214 churches, seven hospitals, and 61 schools. Spalding served Peoria for thirty-one years before retiring in 1908.

Allowing individual priests to manage their own affairs, Spalding took a distanced approach to managing the diocese and sought instead an active role for himself in civic and national affairs, particularly in what became known as the Americanist controversy. With an extensive American heritage, Spalding spoke out in favor of the fundamental compatibility of the American form of government and the Catholic faith. Emphasizing the importance of the choice of the individual and the freedom that America provided the church, Spalding verbally affirmed the positive nature of the American church-state relationship, even after Leo XIII's 1899 encyclical, *Testem Benevolentiae*, which condemned extreme expression of church and state separation.

Spalding also led efforts to emphasize the distinct contributions of Catholic education in the United States. Interested in preserving the uniqueness of Catholic education, Spalding unhesitatingly opposed Archbishop John Ireland of St. Paul's policy of leasing Catholic schools to the local school board, known as the Faribault/Stilwater plan. Spalding also vigorously and successfully fought the Edwards law in Illinois, which attacked private schools by strictly limiting foreign language instruction, maintaining that Catholic schools could train students to be Americans just as well as public schools.

Having received a graduate education in Europe, Spalding insisted upon the necessity of advanced theological training for American priests. Largely through Spalding's efforts, along with the generosity of his friend, the heiress Mary Gwendoline Caldwell, the Catholic University of America was founded in 1888. As an instrumental leader in Catholic education and a major force in motivating its founding, Spalding was offered the rectorship of the university but mysteriously turned it down. In 1902 Spalding's role as a national leader was further affirmed when President Theodore Roosevelt appointed him to the anthracite coal commission at the behest of the striking miners.

After many years of distinguished service on behalf of American Catholic education, Spalding's career ended in controversy. He was considered for the archbishopric of Chicago, but unsubstantiated rumors of a long-standing affair with the heiress Mary Caldwell prompted Catholic officials to withdraw the consideration. In 1905 he suffered the first of several strokes and in 1907 left the board of directors of the Catholic University of America. Spalding resigned from his bishopric in Peoria in 1908 and was made the titular archbishop of Scitopolis in 1909. Despite the controversy, Spalding was considered an outspoken proponent of Catholicism in America as it emerged from the shell of nativism, a sentiment voiced at Spalding's funeral by Archbishop J. J. Glennon of St. Louis, who said, "I have no fear in placing Archbishop Spalding as the one Catholic who has best understood the American mind. He has understood it because in all wherein it was best, it was his own." Spalding died in Peoria.

• Spalding's papers were destroyed upon his death. The most important biography is David Francis Sweeney, *The Life of John Lancaster Spalding* (1965). Another excellent source is John Tracy Ellis, *John Lancaster Spalding: First Bishop of Peoria, American Educator* (1961). For information on the Americanist controversy see Thomas T. McAvoy, *The Great Crisis in American Catholic History, 1895–1900* (1957), which was reprinted in paperback as *The Americanist Heresy in Roman Catholicism, 1895–1900* (1963). Lloyd P. Jorgenson, *The State and the Non-Public School, 1825–1925* (1987), discusses the issue of Catholic schools in America.

R. J. HEINIG

SPALDING, Lyman (5 June 1775–21 Oct. 1821), physician and teacher, was born in Cornish, New Hampshire, the son of Dyer Spalding, a farmer and soldier, and Elizabeth Cady Parkhurst. Spalding received a classical education at Charlestown Academy in New Hampshire, and in 1795 he began a three-year apprenticeship under Nathan Smith, the Spalding family doctor. In the winters during his apprenticeship, Spalding attended the medical school at Harvard, receiving a bachelor of medicine degree in 1797. The subject of his thesis was animal heat.

Soon after completing his medical studies at Harvard, Spalding moved to Hanover, New Hampshire, where he joined Smith in the medical school at Dartmouth, teaching courses in chemistry and materia medica and acting as demonstrator in anatomy. Not long after settling in Hanover, Spalding moved to Walpole, New Hampshire. After six months, however, he concluded that the town was too small to establish a successful medical practice and so moved to Portsmouth, the largest town in the state. Because of Portsmouth's distance from Hanover, Spalding was forced to relinquish his teaching duties at Dartmouth.

Spalding's sixteen years in Portsmouth were productive. It was there that he met Elizabeth Coues, whom he married in 1802; they had five children. His private practice became extensive, and he became a leading figure in the medical affairs of the town. As he had done in Hanover, Spalding founded a medical society in Portsmouth that later became the Eastern District Branch of the New Hampshire Medical Society, to which he was elected in 1801 and which he served as a censor, secretary, treasurer, librarian, and vice president. Spalding also established an anatomical museum in Portsmouth. Besides serving on Portsmouth's Board of Health, in 1801 he was appointed contract surgeon for U.S. military forts in Portsmouth harbor. It was during his residence in Portsmouth that Spalding received some of the first cowpox vaccine (used as a preventative for smallpox) imported into the United States and used it to vaccinate thirty patients.

In Portsmouth, Spalding originated and distributed bills of mortality for the town. Published from 1801 to 1811, his bills listed the number and causes of deaths for each month. Distributed to the medical leaders both of the United States—as well as the president—and Europe, the bills of mortality were an outgrowth of Spalding's interest in assessing the impact of tuberculosis on Portsmouth's health and of his curiosity about the longevity of the town's residents. These bills became the basis for annuity calculations for at least one insurance company (Estes and Goodman [1986]).

In 1807 Nathan Smith chose Spalding to act as demonstrator for the internationally eminent anatomist, the Scotsman Alexander Ramsay, who was at the time delivering a course of lectures at Dartmouth. Two years later Spalding was in Philadelphia attending lectures at the University of Pennsylvania. In 1810 Spalding attended lectures at the College of Physicians and Surgeons in New York and walked the wards of the New York Hospital with the rising young surgeon Valentine Mott. On returning to Portsmouth later that year, Spalding, who had become well known as a result of his work with Smith and Ramsay and the positive impression he had made in Philadelphia and New York, was invited to become professor of anatomy and surgery at the Fairfield Medical School, which was founded in 1803 at Fairfield, New York.

Because of his Fairfield appointment and his desire to obtain part of the medical practice of the late Edward Miller, Spalding moved his family to New York City in 1812. With the assistance of leading New York City physician Samuel Latham Mitchill, Spalding was introduced to New York society and built a successful practice. He served as secretary of the Medical Society of New York County, and, when Fairfield Medical School was incorporated as the College of Physicians and Surgeons of the Western District of New York in 1813, he was elected president of the school. Spalding resigned from this office as well as from the faculty four years later, in disillusionment with internal disputes among the trustees. In 1818, when Caspar Wistar died, Spalding made a serious effort to obtain the chair of anatomy at the University of Pennsylvania. He failed in this effort and failed again the next year when Philip Syng Physick switched chairs from surgery to anatomy.

Outside of a few pamphlets and articles in medical journals, Spalding wrote very little. When he was lecturing on chemistry at Dartmouth early in his career, he recognized the need for a manual on the nomenclature of the subject. This led him to prepare an English translation from the French edition of *A New Nomenclature of Chemistry*, which was published in 1799. He had planned to edit an American version of Robert Willan's *The Description and Treatment of Cutaneous Diseases* (1798–1808) but abandoned the project when he failed to arrange for reproduction of Willan's colored plates. Another project that never materialized was the publication of a textbook on the institutes of medicine. Spalding attempted to write the book when he was residing in New York City, but only the chapters on fever and yellow fever made it into print as pamphlets and articles.

Spalding is best known for his role in a book he did not write, *The Pharmacopoeia of the United States of America*. Spalding had expressed his dissatisfaction with the conflicting information found in the various state pharmacopoeias in 1808 at a meeting of the New Hampshire Medical Society. At an 1817 meeting of the New York County Medical Society he presented a plan for publishing a national pharmacopoeia that would set a national standard regarding substances used in medicines. The New York County Medical Society approved the suggestions, and a committee chaired by Spalding called on medical societies from four districts of the country to elect delegates to attend a convention in Washington, D.C. Only two districts, New England and the Middle States, sent delegates to the convention, which was held in January 1820. Spalding chaired the publication committee that issued *The Pharmacopoeia of the United States of America* in Boston in August 1820. Spalding's leading role in its publication won him the sobriquet "Father of the United States Pharmacopoeia."

Known as a skilled anatomist and surgeon, Spalding's anatomical preparations and dissections were admired by his colleagues. He was also an inventor. Spalding invented a galvanic battery for use in therapeutics, devised a process for manufacturing oxygen for inhalation, and invented a soda water fountain. Unfortunately for Spalding, he failed to obtain patents for his inventions, and as a result others gained not only the credit but the financial rewards for claiming these inventions as their own. A member of the American Philosophical Society, the American Antiquarian Society, the Preston (England) Literary and Philosophical Society, and the Societa Economica Agraria (Florence, Italy), Spalding was also a Mason, serving as grand lecturing master and grand secretary of the Grand Lodge of New Hampshire from 1801 to 1813.

In February 1821 Spalding, when walking along Pearl Street in New York City, was struck in the head by a box of rubbish that had fallen from a second-story window. He never recovered from the accident. Convinced that he had not long to live, Spalding wished to spend his last days close to his relatives. He gave up his medical practice and moved back to Portsmouth, where he died.

• Spalding's personal papers are in a number of institutions, including the Dartmouth College Archives, the New Hampshire Historical Society, the Herkimer County (N.Y.) Historical Society, the Massachusetts Historical Society, the Boston Medical Library of the Francis Countway Library of Medicine at Harvard Medical School, and the College of Physicians of Philadelphia. Besides those mentioned in the text, Spalding's other important publications include *A History of the Introduction and Use of Scutelaria Lateriflora (Scullcap) as a Remedy for Preventing and Curing Hydrophobia* (1819), *Reflections on Fever* (1818), and *Reflections on Yellow Fever* (1819). James Alfred Spalding, *Dr. Lyman Spalding: The Originator of the United States Pharmacopoeia* (1919), and Henry H. Hurd, "A Sketch of Dr. Lyman Spalding," *American Journal of Pharmacology* 91 (1919): 371–82, are useful accounts of Spalding's life and career. For specific aspects of his career, see Morris C. Leikind, "An Episode in the History of Small-pox Vaccination in New Hampshire," *Bulletin of the History of Medicine* 7 (1939): 671–83; J. Worth Estes and David M. Goodman, *The Changing Humors of Portsmouth: The Medical Biography of an American Town, 1623–1983* (1986); and Glenn Sonnedecker, "The Founding Period of the U.S. Pharmacopoeia. II: A National Movement Emerges," *Pharmacy in History* 36 (1994): 3–25.

THOMAS A. HORROCKS

SPALDING, Martin John (23 May 1810–7 Feb. 1872), second bishop of Louisville, seventh archbishop of Baltimore, and author, was born on the Rolling Fork River in present Marion County, Kentucky, the son of Richard Spalding, a prosperous farmer and merchant, and Henrietta Hamilton, both of Maryland Catholic stock. Educated at St. Mary's College, Marion County, and St. Joseph's Seminary, Bardstown, Kentucky, he was sent to the Urban College of the Propaganda in Rome to finish his theological studies for the diocese of Bardstown (later Louisville). After an impressive defense of 356 theses, he received his doctorate and was ordained in Rome on 13 August 1834.

Spalding served as pastor in Bardstown and Lexington, Kentucky, and as president of St. Joseph's College, Bardstown, before being chosen vicar general of the diocese of Louisville in 1844 and coadjutor of Bishop Benedict Joseph Flaget on 18 April 1848. Raised to episcopal rank 10 September 1848 in the cathedral of Louisville, he succeeded Flaget as bishop of Louisville upon the latter's death on 11 February 1850. A builder, Spalding provided his see city, then in its golden age, with a splendid cathedral and a large number of parishes and institutions that included a parochial school system. He was also, in 1857, the principal founder of the American College of Louvain in Belgium, which would send several talented priests to his diocese. In Louisville he attempted to restore calm when an outburst of nativist violence known as "Bloody Monday" was directed against Catholics on 6 August 1855.

Spalding was a prolific writer, most of his works being apologetical in nature. Besides an almost monthly essay for Catholic magazines for more than a decade, he published *Sketches of the Early Catholic Missions of Kentucky* (1844), *General Evidences of Catholicity* (1847), *Sketches of the Life, Times, and Character of the Rt. Rev. Benedict Joseph Flaget* (1852), *Miscellanea* (1855), and *A History of the Protestant Reformation* in two volumes (1860). He was also a noted orator and speaker, his most acclaimed effort being a series of lectures delivered at Tremont Temple in Boston, Cooper Union in New York, and the Smithsonian Institution in Washington, D.C., in 1860. After Orestes Brownson, he was the most influential American Catholic apologist of his day, his writings being particularly attuned to American audiences.

On 3 April 1864 Spalding was appointed archbishop of Baltimore, where he was installed on 31 August. It was the oldest and then most important Catholic see in the United States by reason of the preeminence accorded its archbishop. There he established more parishes and other institutions per year and introduced more religious orders than any other archbishop of Baltimore. Among the institutions was St. Mary's Industrial School, a home for the reclamation of wayward boys. Both in Louisville and Baltimore his principal efforts were directed, as his nephew and first biographer, John Lancaster Spalding, noted, "to the orphan, to the negro, to the sinful, to the outcast, to the aged, to all who suffered and had none to pity them." At an important point in the development of the American labor movement, Spalding was successful in deflecting a condemnation of labor unions as secret societies at the Second Plenary Council of 1866 and in allaying the fears of Rome and his fellow bishops concerning these unions. Essaying the role of leader of the American Catholic hierarchy, he persuaded his episcopal colleagues to provide an endowment for the American College in Rome and to oppose the recruitment of an American battalion to defend the Papal States, but he failed to avert a Roman condemnation of the Fenians, militant nationalists active in Ireland and the United States.

Spalding's most ambitious exercise of leadership was the Second Plenary Council of Baltimore of 1866. In contrast to the piecemeal approach of the earlier provincial and plenary councils of Baltimore in providing the peculiar legislation demanded by the Catholic church in the United States, Spalding produced a comprehensive code for the immigrant church, touching such matters as diocesan organization, sacraments, worship, education, pious and charitable associations, secret societies, and Catholic publications. Unwittingly he antagonized Archbishop Peter Richard Kenrick of St. Louis, who put himself in opposition to the council, and he failed to win the support of his fellow bishops for the three goals he had most at heart: a Catholic university, a uniform catechism, and concerted action on behalf of the freedmen, particularly the bishops' acceptance of a special ecclesiastic charged with the care of the latter.

In 1865 Spalding wrote a pastoral on *The Syllabus of Errors* of Pope Pius IX designed to assure Americans, Catholic and non-Catholic alike, that its condemnations did not encompass such American principles as freedom of conscience and the separation of church and state. Spalding sought to play a critical role at the First Vatican Council (1869–1870). When he perceived that the "inopportunists," those who would prevent a definition of papal infallibility, had failed, he submitted a compromise formula that embodied an implicit acceptance of the doctrine. His efforts as a compromiser, however, were frustrated by a dispute with Bishop Félix Dupanloup of Orléans, the leading opponent of a definition, which brought him into conflict also with a number of American bishops, most notably archbishops Kenrick of St. Louis and John Baptist Purcell of Cincinnati.

Spalding had an amazing capacity for work. He was a popular bishop both in Louisville and Baltimore but was strict in matters of dress, dancing, theatergoing, mixed marriages, and abortion. His opinions on American problems were highly valued by the Roman authorities, who on one occasion delegated him to resolve a serious crisis in episcopal authority in Chicago. Spalding was able to join an ardent patriotism with an undeviating loyalty to the papacy and to impart this dual allegiance to American Catholics generally. Though an old-stock American, he identified completely with the immigrant church. He died in Baltimore. To a greater degree, perhaps, than any other Catholic bishop at midcentury he had determined the character of the immigrant church by articulating its attitudes, modeling its institutions, and systematizing its discipline.

• Spalding's papers are in the archives of the archdiocese of Baltimore, but important material can also be found in the archives of the University of Notre Dame and the Congregation of the Propaganda Fide in Rome. His two principal biographies are J. L. Spalding, *The Life of the Most Rev. M. J. Spalding, D.D., Archbishop of Baltimore* (1873), and Thomas W. Spalding, *Martin John Spalding: American Churchman* (1973). See also Adam A. Micek, *The Apologetics of Martin John Spalding* (1951); Clyde F. Crews, *An American Holy Land: A History of the Archdiocese of Louisville* (1987); and Thomas W. Spalding, *The Premier See: A History of the Archdiocese of Baltimore, 1789–1989* (1989).

THOMAS W. SPALDING

SPANGENBERG, Augustus Gottlieb (15 July 1704–18 Sept. 1792), bishop of the Moravian church and its founder and organizer in North America, was born in Klettenberg, Germany, the son of Georg Spangenberg, a Lutheran pastor, and Dorothea Katharina Nese. Although orphaned at the age of nine, Spangenberg received a good education. While he was studying law at the University of Jena in 1722, he came under the influence of various strains within German Pietism. This religious movement sought the renewal of the church through deepening the piety of every Christian and encouraging practical application of their faith. Spangenberg was fascinated by their focus on the Bible and emotional experiences and changed the subject of his studies to theology. After receiving his M.A. in 1729, he became an assistant teacher in theology. He was also a leading member of a circle of Pietist students who were greatly influenced by Nikolaus, Count von Zinzendorf, and were in close contact with him and the Moravians who had settled on his estate at Herrnhut. In 1732 Spangenberg accepted a position at the University of Halle. Because of emerging differences between the Pietism at Halle and that of Herrnhut, especially over the importance of atonement versus God's grace for the redemption of a sinner, Spangenberg had to leave Halle in 1733. He moved to Herrnhut where he became Zinzendorf's personal assistant.

Spangenberg first went to North America in 1735. This trip was the beginning of more than twenty years of service in the American colonies, mostly in Pennsylvania. Even after his final return to Europe in 1762, he devoted most of his energy and time to the support of the Moravian church in North America. From 1735 to 1739 Spangenberg accompanied and assisted a number of Moravian colonists and Swiss and Schwenkfeldian emigrants who had temporarily found refuge on Zinzendorf's estate but continued on to North America to find a permanent place to practice their religious beliefs. After a short stay in Georgia, the Moravians finally settled in Pennsylvania and immediately began their missionary work among the Native Americans.

Back in Europe in 1739, Spangenberg organized the Moravian church in England and founded the Society for the Furtherance of the Gospel among the Heathen (1741). At the synod in 1744 Spangenberg was consecrated bishop and appointed the leader of the Moravian church in America. He went back to Pennsylvania at the end of that year and began to organize Bethlehem, north of Philadelphia, as the center of Moravian activity in North America. To be able to survive without financial help from Europe, Spangenberg developed a communal economy. The population of Bethlehem was divided into a "house" and a "pilgrim" congregation, the house congregation working under a communistic order to support the pilgrims, who worked as missionaries among the Native Americans or as pastors among the German-speaking settlers. Because of internal church politics and differences with Zinzendorf, for example, over the evolving new mysticism that had led to the use of extremely sentimental language, Spangenberg was removed from his office and had to return to Europe in 1749. He remained there until he was reinstated as leader of the American branch of the Moravian church in 1751. In the following year, he founded another settlement, the Wachovia in North Carolina (1752–1753), and under his guidance the Moravian church flourished. Besides the Wachovia and exclusively Moravian settlements like Bethlehem, other Moravian congregations, in several towns and rural areas in seven colonies, also prospered.

Another important part of Spangenberg's work was the supervision of mission activities. Although leadership was organized on a collegial basis, Spangenberg was very influential in this area as well. He visited mission settlements the Moravians had established mainly among the Mahicans and Delawares, and he organized and attended mission conferences and synods. The Moravians were very successful because of their unique missionary approach. Their purpose was not to civilize the Native Americans but to respect their way of life. Because the missionaries lived among the Native Americans, they understood their language and culture and tried to transfer Christian beliefs into this context. This close contact with Native Americans and the refusal of the Moravians to fight aroused suspicion among other white settlers about the position of the Moravians in the Seven Years War, a suspicion that ended only after eleven missionaries had been killed by Native Americans in 1755. Bethlehem became a refuge for the inhabitants of the countryside, but although the Moravians were ready to defend themselves, they did not get involved in the war.

The Moravian church in Europe suffered great financial trouble because the establishment of new settlements all over the world was expensive, and the Moravians had paid more attention to devotion than to economic endeavors. Spangenberg successfully reorganized the economic system in Bethlehem into a "family economy" to support the Europeans.

Spangenberg had visited Europe only once in this decade, in 1753–1754. Two years after Zinzendorf's death in 1760, Spangenberg permanently returned to Europe and became his successor. He was the leading figure in the governing body of elders and, among others, was responsible for mission and finances. He carried out visitations and presided at synods, and the church benefited greatly from his talents as theologian, financial adviser, administrator, and especially his spiritual leadership as bishop.

Spangenberg's writings were also very influential in gaining acceptance of the Moravian church and in standardizing its doctrine. He defended the positions of the Moravians in essays such as "Apologetische Schlußschrift" (1752). The Moravians had been accused of attacking orthodox theology as well as the positions of the sovereigns and the "Landstände." They, especially Zinzendorf, were also criticized as hypocrites, enthusiasts, extremists, and liars. Therefore, Spangenberg's biography, "Leben des Herrn Nikolaus Ludwig Grafen und Herrn von Zinzendorf" (1772–1775), was also an apologia. Most important, however, was Spangenberg's "Idea fidei fratrum" (1779), a statement of Moravian beliefs that organized Zinzendorf's radical thoughts and also toned them down. His experience in missionary work became obvious in his writings on mission (1754, 1782, 1784), where he developed Zinzendorf's ideas into realistic, concrete instructions. He also wrote about the history of the Moravian church (1774) and published sermons and theological essays.

Spangenberg was married twice. His first wife was the widow Eva Maria Ziegelbauer whom he married in 1740; she took on many responsibilities and was a great help to him in Bethlehem until she died in 1751. Three years later he married another widow, Martha Elisabeth Jaehne Miksch; she died in 1789. He had no children.

Spangenberg died at Berthelsdorf, Germany, and was buried at Herrnhut. Without his organizational and financial talents and his integrating qualities, the Moravians would not have been able to solve their many problems as well as they did. His theological opinions moderated their extreme positions and made the Moravian church acceptable to other Protestant churches.

• Spangenberg's personal papers are preserved in the Moravian Archives in Herrnhut, Germany, and Bethlehem, Pennsylvania. Copies of some of them can be found in the Library of Congress. Some of his works are available in English, including *An Exposition of Christian Doctrine* (1784) and *An Account of the Manner in Which the Protestant Church of the Unitas Fratrum, or United Brethren, Preach the Gospel and Carry on Their Mission among the Heathen* (1788). An abridged translation is *The Life of Nicholas Lewis Count Zinzendorf, Bishop and Ordinary of the Church of the United (or Moravian) Brethren* (1838).

The earliest biography of Spangenberg was written by Jeremias Risler, *Leben August Gottlieb Spangenbergs* (1794), but the best biography is by Gerhard Reichel, *August Gottlieb Spangenberg* (1906). A translation of the 1846 biography by K. F. Ledderhose was published under the title *The Life of Augustus Gottlieb Spangenberg* (1855). A good study of Spangenberg and the Moravian mission is Theodor Bechler, *August Gottlieb Spangenberg und die Mission* (1933).

CAROLA WESSEL

SPANIER, Muggsy (9 Nov. 1901–1 Feb. 1967), jazz cornetist and bandleader, was born Francis Joseph Spanier in Chicago, Illinois, the son of William Spanier, a certified public accountant, and Katherine Helen O'Reilly. Spanier's year of birth is widely given as 1906, but Bert Whyatt's research indicates 1901 as the correct year. Spanier's father was a semiprofessional classical pianist, and his mother played either accordion or concertina. They separated, and when his mother could not support the large family, Spanier was placed at the age of eight in a reform school. This was a brutal episode in his life, except for affording him the opportunity to learn to play drums and then cornet; when he was about age thirteen his father bought him his own cornet.

In his teenage years Spanier was a promising baseball pitcher, and his nickname derives from that of the famous manager of the New York Giants John "Muggsy" McGraw. The Chicago White Sox expressed interest, but Spanier's mother made him continue school. He devoted himself to the cornet. Studies with trumpeters Noah Tarantino of the Chicago Opera and Eddie Llewellyn of the Chicago Symphony continued after he later dropped out of school to work as a messenger boy and then in a record store.

In 1920 Spanier played in pianist Elmer Schoebel's Dixieland band, which included saxophonist Jack Pettis, trombonist George Brunies, and drummer Frank Snyder. In 1922 he joined Sig Meyer's Dixieland band, with which he remained for two years. During this time he often ended his nights listening to King Oliver's Creole Jazz Band, including Louis Armstrong. Spanier made his first recordings, "Mobile Blues" and "Someday Sweetheart," in 1924 as a member of the Bucktown Five and the following year recorded with the Stomp Six, both of these ad hoc studio groups including clarinetist Volly De Faut and pianist Mel Stitzel. Spanier played briefly in Husk O'Hare's Wolverines. He then joined a succession of little-known ensembles. These included Floyd Towne's Midway Gardens Band, in which he worked alongside pianist Jess Stacy, drummer George Wettling, and clarinetist Frank Teschemacher and broadcast on WNBA, and Charlie Pierce's band, with which he recorded "Bull Frog Blues" and "China Boy" (as Pierce's

Jungle Kings) and "Jazz Me Blues" and "Sister Kate" (as Pierce's Orchestra) in 1928. Sandwiched in between these dates was one with the Chicago Rhythm Kings (including singer Red McKenzie, Teschemacher, pianist Joe Sullivan, banjoist Eddie Condon, and drummer Gene Krupa), yielding versions of "There'll Be Some Changes Made" and "I've Found a New Baby." Another McKenzie and Condon date soon followed, as the Jungle Kings.

Early in 1929 Spanier traveled to San Francisco to join vaudeville and Dixieland clarinetist and singer Ted Lewis, whose band included Brunies and clarinetist Jimmy Dorsey. In Los Angeles they made the movie *Is Everybody Happy?* (1929), and the following year they toured Europe. In 1931, when Benny Goodman replaced Dorsey, Spanier made an important session apart from Lewis as a member of McKenzie's revived Mound City Blue Blowers, including tenor saxophonist Coleman Hawkins. Around 1934 he married Le Donne Clifford; they had no children and divorced in 1938. Spanier continued touring with Lewis and appeared with him in the movie *Here Comes the Band* (1935). He left Lewis in December 1936 to join Ben Pollack's orchestra as a replacement for Harry James. He remained with Pollack until early in 1938, when he suffered a perforated ulcer and nearly died.

After spending three months at the Touro Infirmary in New Orleans, and further months of convalescence in Chicago, Spanier founded his most important group: Muggsy Spanier's Ragtime Band. They opened in late April 1939 at the Panther Room of the Hotel Sherman, from which they broadcast nationally. Among his sidemen were Brunis, clarinetist Rod Cless, tenor saxophonist Nick Caiazza, and pianist Joe Bushkin. They later moved to the Off Beat Room in Chicago and then to Nick's in New York City, where they disbanded after a final recording session of mid-December 1939. Their recordings include "Big Butter and Egg Man," "At the Jazz Band Ball," "Relaxin' at the Touro," "At Sundown," and "(What Did I Do to Be So) Black and Blue."

After rejoining Lewis for a few months, Spanier returned to Chicago. He sat in with Bob Crosby's orchestra at the Blackhawk restaurant in May 1940 and soon joined it. They toured from Chicago to the West Coast and made the movie *Sis Hopkins* (1941). Spanier left Crosby in February 1941 and went to New York City to form a big band that proved to be only moderately successful. Modeled after Crosby's organization, Spanier's swing and Dixieland ensemble also presented an eight-piece band-within-the-band that at times included the leader, trombonist Vernon Brown, clarinetist Irving Fazola, and Ciazza, who are all heard on "Hesitating Blues" (1942). They held long engagements at the Arcadia Ballroom in New York but also took on a grueling touring schedule until Spanier was obliged to disband in September 1943 because of exhaustion.

Returning to Chicago, Spanier was involved in two serious car accidents. Once again he recovered and resumed playing in small bands, first in Chicago and from March 1944 in New York City, where he worked with pianist Art Hodes at Jimmy Ryan's club and with trombonist Miff Mole and clarinetist Pee Wee Russell at Nick's club, and participated in an all-star concert and recording session. He rejoined Lewis from May to August 1944 and then worked again mainly at Nick's. Russell left the band at the end of 1946 and Mole in April 1947, at which point Spanier took over its leadership. Early that same year he also participated in nine of the weekly broadcasts of Rudi Blesh's radio show "This Is Jazz."

In late November 1947 Spanier brought a band including Mole to Chicago for the opening of the Blue Note Club. Shuttling between cities, he returned to New York in February for engagements at Nick's and other venues. He was back in Chicago in October to work at the Blue Note and at Jazz Ltd (the latter engagement extending from early 1949 into 1950) but also appeared on Condon's television show in New York (Mar. 1949), at a concert in Hollywood (Oct. 1949), and with reed player Sidney Bechet in New York (Feb. 1950). On Valentine's Day 1950 Spanier married the widowed Ruth Marie Gluck O'Connell; they had no children.

As the revival of interest in New Orleans jazz gathered steam, Spanier began touring nationally with his own six-piece group, which early on included clarinetist Darnell Howard, pianist Floyd Bean, and bassist Truck Parham. Among their travels, too widespread to recount, were repeated engagements at the Club Hangover in San Francisco from 1950 onward. In 1957 Spanier disbanded and settled across the bay in Sausalito, California, while working for two years at the Hangover as a member of pianist Earl Hine's group. Beginning in October 1959 Spanier spent almost five years touring extensively with his own group. He also toured Europe as a soloist in the spring of 1960. Finally, after an appearance at the Newport Jazz Festival in July 1964, ill health forced his retirement. He died in Sausalito.

Whether delivered with its natural, open sound, or vocalized and muted, Spanier's cornet playing followed in the tradition of leading African-American New Orleans jazz cornetists, particularly Oliver and Armstrong, whom he deeply admired. As a bandmember or leader, he twice participated in historic developments in jazz. His numerous recording sessions of spring 1928, together with a contemporary session by McKenzie and Condon's Chicagoans (not including Spanier), are classics of Chicago jazz, a fervent offshoot of Dixieland jazz. Eleven years later his Ragtime Band struck a delightful balance between the predictability of arranged big band swing and the controlled chaos of improvised Dixieland; their widely imitated recordings are among the first to document the New Orleans jazz revival.

• The essential source is Bert Whyatt, *Muggsy Spanier: The Lonesome Road: A Biography and Discography* (1995), which corrects countless details of earlier publications on Spanier. Among these, interviews and briefer surveys include George Hoefer, "Muggsy Still a Driving, Communicative Jazzman," *Down Beat*, 4 May 1951, pp. 2–3, 8, 16; Max Jones, "Muggsy Flies in for 30 Minutes after 30 Years," *Melody Maker* 2 (Apr. 1960): 14; C. H. Garrigues, "Jazzman without a Home," *San Francisco Chronicle*, 13 Feb. 1961; Ian Crosbie, "The Big Band Muggsy Spanier," *Coda* 12 (Dec. 1974): 8–11; Albert McCarthy, *Big Band Jazz* (1974); and Alma Hubner, "Muggsy Spanier," and Dale Curran, "Hear That Ragtime Band," both in *Selections from the Gutter: Jazz Portraits from "The Jazz Record,"* ed. Art Hodes and Chadwick Hansen (1977). See also John Chilton, *Stomp Off, Let's Go!: The Story of Bob Crosby's Bob Cats & Big Band* (1983). For musical description, see Larry Gushee, "Muggsy Spanier," *Jazz Review* 1 (Dec. 1958): 40–41; Max Harrison, "Backlog 15: Muggsy Spannier [*sic*]," *Jazz Monthly* 10 (Apr. 1964): 6–7; and Digby Fairweather, "Muggsy Spanier," in *The Blackwell Guide to Recorded Jazz*, ed. Barry Kernfeld, 2d ed. (1995). Obituaries are in the *New York Times* and *San Francisco Chronicle*, both 13 Feb. 1967.

BARRY KERNFELD

SPANN, Otis (21 Mar. 1930–24 Apr. 1970), blues pianist and singer, was born in Jackson, Mississippi, the son of Frank Houston Spann, a farmer and preacher, and Josephine Erby. Spann was exposed to music as a young child. His mother had played blues guitar before renouncing blues as ungodly, and his father may have played piano. By Spann's own account, his father asked him at an early age if he wanted to be a bluesman and then, despite his mother's feelings about the music, bought him a piano.

Spann's Mississippi experiences alternated between Jackson and rural Belzoni. In Belzoni he was inspired and taught by a local pianist, Friday Ford, who was said by some musicians to have been Spann's biological father. Spann told researcher Paul Oliver many years later that Ford "was my daddy," but Oliver felt certain the statement was a musical reference. Whatever their relationship, Ford clearly took an interest in Spann, teaching him the piano's notes and chords while holding the young protégé on his lap. Spann is said to have played piano in his father's church at age five. By age eight, he supposedly had won a talent contest at a theater in Jackson. In an interview with Peter Guralnick shortly before his death, Spann recalled that the contest led to further employment: "Mr. Alamo, he used to send for me . . . to play for the vaudevilles. Man, I had a little tuxedo and a hat."

Jackson artists who served as early role models included Spann's longtime friend and mentor Little Brother Montgomery and an older cousin, Johnny Jones (who later recorded "Hoy Hoy"). Jones and Spann could each play harmonica as well as piano, and as teens, they teamed up to play house parties and juke joints in west central Mississippi. Spann attended Campbell Junior College in Jackson in the mid-1940s.

When Spann was around seventeen, his mother died, and his father sent him to Chicago to live with relatives. There he worked as a plasterer and kept in contact with other Mississippi musicians. He became acquainted with fellow pianists Big Maceo Merriwether—considered an important stylistic influence—

Memphis Slim, and Roosevelt Sykes. He also got to know Muddy Waters, who always referred to Spann as his "half brother," though the kinship was never corroborated.

In the mid-1940s Spann married Ola Marie (maiden name unknown), and they had three children. After a stint in the army between 1946 and 1951, Spann worked briefly with Chicago guitarist and harmonica player Louis Myers, then joined the Muddy Waters band in 1953. He recorded and toured with Waters for fifteen years in what proved to be an artistically fruitful collaboration, for it was the Waters blues band that brought the postwar "Chicago sound" to what may have been its most robust expression.

In addition to his work with Muddy Waters during the 1950s, Spann often recorded as a session pianist with harmonica virtuoso Little Walter and guitarist Jimmy Rogers—also members of the Waters band—blues rockers Chuck Berry and Bo Diddley, and urban blues icons Howlin' Wolf and Sonny Boy Williamson No. 2. A number of the records, issued on the Chess and Checker labels, are now considered classics: Waters's "Hoochie Coochie Man," Williamson's "Don't Start Me to Talkin'," and Wolf's "Back Door Man," among others.

In 1958 Spann accompanied Muddy Waters to England, where his piano and plaintive vocals made a deep impression on British audiences. On subsequent overseas tours with the Waters band and other groups, Spann continued to excite European audiences, especially members of the fledgling British blues-rock movement: Long John Baldry, Eric Clapton, the Yardbirds, the Animals, and Fleetwood Mac.

Starting in 1960 Spann's recordings, both as a featured artist and as a sideman, were targeted less to the well-established Chess/Checker black American audience and more to the burgeoning worldwide "blues revival" audience. Spann's credits during this prolific decade of recording included sessions in Europe and the United States for Candid, Storyville, Decca, Prestige, Vanguard, Bluesway, Arhoolie, Testament, and Spivey. In 1967 Spann married Mahalia Lucille Jenkins.

In late 1969 or early 1970 *Rolling Stone*, then America's premier rock magazine, sent blues writer Peter Guralnick to interview Spann. According to Guralnick, an editor at the magazine wanted to publish a tribute to Spann—altogether fitting in light of Spann's work on early rock classics. The tribute became a de facto obituary when Spann died of cancer in Chicago.

Spann was influential on three diverse musical fronts: as a key component in the most powerful blues band ever; as a major studio session player during the early days of rock 'n' roll and the golden age of Chess Records; and, finally, as a leader who influenced countless musicians and blues fans in the United States and Europe, effortlessly bridging the gap between down-home Delta blues and world rock.

Spann's piano style varied according to the situation. In the band format, where he preferred the harmonica to be the lead instrument, Spann contributed rhythmic bridges and underpinnings for the overall sound. When he soloed, he employed an expressive, syncopated style that he attributed, in part, to the shortness of his fingers. Willie Dixon, a former bandmate, paid him high tribute when he said Spann was a good musician because he knew how to make other musicians sound good.

In 1972 the site of the Ann Arbor Blues Festival was named Otis Spann Memorial Field. In 1980 Spann was elected to the Blues Foundation's Hall of Fame.

• For discographical information, see Mike Leadbitter and Neil Slaven, *Blues Records 1943–1966*, vol. 2 (1994); and Paul Oliver, ed., *The Blackwell Guide to Blues Records* (1989). For more historical information, see Peter Guralnick, *Lost Highway: Journeys & Arrivals of American Musicians* (1979); Sheldon Harris, *Blues Who's Who: A Biographical Dictionary of Blues Singers* (1979); David Evans, "Goin' Up the Country," in *Nothing but the Blues*, ed. Lawrence Cohn (1993); and Mike Rowe, *Chicago Breakdown* (1975). An obituary is in *Rolling Stone*, 11 June 1970.

BILL McCULLOCH
BARRY LEE PEARSON

SPARER, Edward V. (21 Mar. 1928–21 June 1983), founder of community legal services, was born in New York City, the son of Marcus Sparer, a retail merchant, and Ada Cohen. He graduated from Benjamin Franklin High School in New York City in 1946 and that year entered the City College of New York. While in college he joined the third-party presidential campaign of Henry Wallace and in 1947 went to the South to organize textile workers for Wallace. He encountered poverty, violence, racism, and suppression of free speech, which would motivate him for the rest of his life. Upon returning to City College he became interested in labor organizing. Sparer left school in 1949 without receiving a degree. The following year he married a classmate, Tanya Schecter; they had two daughters and a son.

After two years (1951–1953) in the U.S. Army, Sparer attended Brooklyn Law School, where he served as editor in chief of the law review. Upon graduating in 1959, he worked as a lawyer for the International Ladies Garment Worker's Union.

In the early 1960s the Ford Foundation began Mobilization for Youth (MFY), a program that sought to address problems of juvenile delinquency by organizing communities to create economic opportunities. Sparer, an institution builder, persuaded the foundation to create a legal services program. MFY Legal Services, founded in 1963 with Sparer as its first director, was the first neighborhood legal services program in the nation and became the model for the effective and controversial federal legal services program. In 1965 he founded the Columbia University Law School's Center on Social Welfare Policy and Law, the first of dozens of national support centers for legal services work.

As a lawyer, Sparer continued his early commitment to community organizing. In representing welfare clients he encouraged creation of local welfare rights organizations that, in 1964, led to the creation of the National Welfare Rights Organization. He served as general counsel to this group until his death.

In 1970 Sparer created the Health Law Project at the University of Pennsylvania School of Law. The project, under the guidance of a board of directors, included doctors and sociologists as well as lawyers and represented health care consumers seeking access to high quality, affordable health care. It conducted empirical research, produced books and studies, and trained students in law, medicine, and sociology.

Sparer understood that the law is fact-sensitive and moderately plastic. He developed theories to support claims that poor people have basic rights protected by the Social Security Act and the Constitution. *King v. Smith* (1968) struck down the common "man in the house" rules that denied aid to poor children whose mothers dated men. The U.S. Supreme Court held that states could not terminate aid to poor children because their mother had a boyfriend on the grounds that federal law defined "parent" as a person with a legal obligation to support children, and boyfriends are not legally obligated to support poor women and their children. Since then thousands of cases have required that states administer grant programs in accordance with the provisions of federal statutes.

The Court also accepted the arguments, initially developed by Sparer, that the right to aid should not be contingent upon the sacrifice of constitutionally protected liberties. *Shapiro v. Thompson* (1969) held that aid could not be denied to poor people who had exercised their constitutionally protected right to travel from state to state. The Court in *Goldberg v. Kelly* (1970) recognized the argument that aid could not be terminated without notice of the reasons and an opportunity to protest termination.

Sparer was a gifted teacher and organizer. He taught at Yale Law School from 1967 to 1969 and at the University of Pennsylvania Law School from 1969 until his death. In addition, he was a wise mentor to generations of lawyers, civil rights activists, social workers, doctors, nurses, midwives, and poor people seeking progressive social change. Sparer's legacy of institution building lives on in the Edward V. Sparer Public Interest Law Fellowship program at Brooklyn Law School, which provides opportunities and guidance to students seeking to do work in the Sparer tradition.

Sparer died at his family home in Woodstock, New York.

• Sparer published many articles and essays, including "Gordian Knots: The Situation of Health Care Advocacy for the Poor Today," *Clearinghouse Review* 15 (May 1981): 1–23, in which he discusses the difficulties in obtaining decent health care for the poor. In "Fundamental Human Rights, Legal Entitlements, and the Social Struggle: A Friendly Critique of the Critical Legal Studies Movement," *Stanford Law Review* 36 (Jan. 1984): 509–74, he synthesizes the critical critique of rights with efforts to obtain and enforce legal rights for vulnerable people. A comprehensive bibliography of Sparer's writings as well as several tributes written on the occasion of his death are in the *University of Pennsylvania Law Review*

132 (1984). Martha F. Davis, *Brutal Need: Lawyers and the Welfare Rights Movement, 1960–1973* (1993), provides a good account of Sparer's welfare rights work.

SYLVIA A. LAW

SPARGO, John (31 Jan. 1876–17 Aug. 1966), socialist reformer and writer, was born in Stithians, Cornwall, England, the son of Thomas Spargo, a stonemason, and Jane Hocking. As a child, Spargo worked in the Cornwall tin mines and subsequently joined the Social Democratic Federation, led by the Marxist Henry M. Hyndman. Although rising to a leadership position in the British labor movement, Spargo and his wife, Prudence Edwards, whom he married in 1901 and with whom he had one child, emigrated to the United States in 1901. His wife died in 1904, and the next year he married Mary Amelia Rose Bennetts. This second marriage resulted in three children.

Spargo became one of the American Socialist party's leading lecturers and writers, becoming particularly active between 1912 and 1917 in the Intercollegiate Socialist Society. He was elected a member of the party's national executive committee and worked closely with party leader Morris Hillquit. Spargo was associated with the center and right-wing elements of the party, his views a compound of socialism and reformist progressivism. He was strongly opposed to the militant class war position of the Industrial Workers of the World (IWW). Identifying the IWW as a syndicalist organization, Spargo insisted: "there is just as much danger to the Socialist movement in a compromise with Anarchism in its Syndicalist guise as in a compromise with capitalistic political parties." He saw the IWW as advocates of sabotage, and he declared sabotage to be the weapon of the lumpen proletariat. The IWW's strategy and tactics, he believed, were incompatible with the Socialist political program.

Spargo stressed the possibility of an evolutionary transition to socialism and defined revolution as the end result of a gradual process of change. He wrote in *Applied Socialism* (1912) that "we must reject the catastrophic theory of sudden transformations of the social organism as being not only incompatible with the fundamental philosophy of Marxian Socialism, but contrary to the whole movement of history." (In his later years he came to believe that "socialization" does not require public ownership.) At the same time, he was opposed to racist exclusion of immigrants, and before the 1917 American declaration of war he condemned militarism and "preparedness," taking stands on these issues at odds with those of the party's right wing. Also before 1917, Spargo adopted a favorable view of Woodrow Wilson when as New Jersey governor Wilson endorsed child labor legislation backed by the Socialist leader Florence Kelley.

Spargo's *The Bitter Cry of the Children* (1906) was his major contribution to a wider understanding of the oppressive conditions existing in American society. This book was triggered by his work in verifying the allegations of the number of underfed children in New York City contained in Robert Hunter's *Poverty,* a pioneering study of the American poor. Spargo accomplished his purpose of stating "the problem of poverty as it affects childhood." He wrote that the evils inflicted on children by poverty "are responsible for many of the worst features of that hideous phantasmagoria of hunger, disease, vice, crime and despair which we call the Social Problem." Spargo connected inadequate nutrition to the often poor classroom work of impoverished children. He affirmed the duty of society to assume the responsibility of caring for children. Sharply critical of opposition to child labor legislation, the book warned that in a society dominated by concern with profits there was need for unrelenting vigilance in protecting the welfare of children. Spargo emphasized that the problem of child labor was national and not merely regional, and he outlined a comprehensive program of remedial measures, including provision for free maternity hospitals and public health nursing, adoption of rigorous federal and state child labor legislation, and creation of a federal children's bureau. As historian Warren Trattner writes, "had all of Spargo's suggestions been implemented they would have brought about a pretty radical reconstruction of American society by nonradical means."

With U.S. entry into World War I, Spargo broke with the antiwar majority of the Socialist party and joined with such figures as Upton Sinclair, William English Walling, and Algie M. Simons in supporting the war effort. He wired President Wilson: "From now on, spiritually, I am clad in khaki." During the war he traveled to Europe to rally Socialists to support of the Allied cause, and at home he joined with George Creel of the government's Committee on Public Information and Samuel Gompers of the American Federation of Labor in forming the American Alliance for Labor and Democracy to counter the growing influence of the antiwar People's Council for Peace and Democracy. He accused the Socialist party of being "unneutral, un-American and pro-German" in opposing U.S. participation in the war. He also declared that the party should have accepted the war as a fact and sought to use the opportunities offered by wartime conditions to extend a collectivist program.

Spargo bitterly denounced the 1917 Bolshevik Revolution. He began issuing one study after another to argue the case that the Soviet leaders were immoral liars and autocrats set on defeat of the Allies. He characterized bolshevism as "a mad attempt by a brutal and degrading tyranny to carry out an impossible program," and he urged the crushing of bolshevism as "the supreme task of civilization." He described Lenin as "brutal, relentless, and unscrupulous, glorying in might, which is, for him, the only right." Seeing the Bolshevik movement as representing "the same brutality and the same faith that might is right which made Prussian militarism the menace it was to civilization," he contended that the Bolshevik "is the foe of progress and the ally of reaction."

In the wake of his rupture with the Socialist party and increasingly abandoning tenets of socialism, Spargo moved toward a position of endorsing labor-capital cooperation. He was appointed by Wilson as a "public" representative to the First Industrial Conference in 1919, to sit beside such business leaders as John D. Rockefeller, Jr., Bernard Baruch, and Judge Elbert Gary. Spargo pledged that he would not introduce into the conference "any socialist aim, or any socialist effort." What was required, Spargo believed, was that such persons as himself and Rockefeller unite in a common policy. He drafted the statement of the "public" representatives to the conference in collaboration with Rockefeller.

Trusted by President Wilson as an adviser on matters relating to the Socialist and labor movements, Spargo became a prime advocate of the official nonrecognition policy regarding the Soviet government. He urged support of anti-Bolshevik forces within Russia and forecast the early demise of Soviet rule, while he also opposed any design for the dismemberment of Russia on the grounds that such a policy would impede Russian economic development. When in August 1920 the Wilson administration made its most comprehensive statement on Russian policy, the document was largely based on a draft prepared by Spargo. The United States could not have friendly relations with Soviet Russia, it argued, for that government was based "upon the negation of every principle of honor and good faith . . ." There could be no official relations with "the agents of a government which is determined and bound to conspire against our institutions, whose diplomats will be the agitators of dangerous revolt." This statement outlined the main themes that would prevail in American policy toward Soviet Russia until Franklin D. Roosevelt's presidency.

In the remaining years of his life Spargo emerged as a political and cultural conservative who wrote of the potteries of Vermont and founded the Bennington Historical Museum. During 1925–1927 he headed the Vermont Sesquicentennial Commission. By the mid-1920s he had become a Republican, and about that time he wrote "that the Socialist philosophy is unsound, the Socialist program dangerous and reactionary, and the Socialist movement a mischievous illusion." In the 1930s he wrote articles attacking the New Deal and extolling private enterprise. In 1934, in an ironic comment on his own best-known work, he stridently opposed a child labor amendment on the ground that it would subjugate America's children "to a soulless bureaucracy."

After retiring as director and curator of the Bennington museum, he died in Old Bennington, Vermont.

• Spargo's papers are in the Wilbur Collection of the Bailey-Howe Library at the University of Vermont, Burlington. His other writings include *Applied Socialism: A Study of the Application of Socialistic Principles to the State* (1912), *Syndicalism, Industrial Unionism and Socialism* (1913), *Bolshevism: The Enemy of Political and Industrial Democracy* (1919), *The Jew and American Ideals* (1921), and *The Potters and Potteries of Bennington* (1926). Walter Trattner's introduction to the 1968 edition of *The Bitter Cry of the Children* is the only full account of Spargo's life. See also Ronald Radosh, "John Spargo and

Wilson's Foreign Policy, 1920," *Journal of American History* 52 (Dec. 1965): 548–65. An oral history memoir is in the Oral History Collection at Columbia University. An obituary is in the *New York Times*, 18 Aug. 1966.

HERBERT SHAPIRO

SPARKMAN, John Jackson (20 Dec. 1899–16 Nov. 1985), New Deal congressman and U.S. senator from Alabama, was born in Hartselle, Alabama, the son of Whitten Joseph Sparkman and Julia Mitchell Kent, sharecroppers. He attended rural Morgan County elementary and secondary schools, and in his last year at home he received a $75 bank loan from a cotton crop to pay tuition at the University of Alabama, where he enrolled in 1916. In 1918 he enlisted in the U.S. Army and later joined the Reserve Officers' Training Corps. Returning to school at Alabama, he earned a B.A. (1921), an LL.B. (1923), and an M.A. (1924) in history and political science. In 1923 he married Ivo Hall of Albertsville, Alabama; they had one child. Admitted to the Alabama bar in 1925, Sparkman established a law practice in Huntsville, Alabama.

First elected to the House of Representatives in 1936, Sparkman enthusiastically supported economic initiatives of the New Deal. He especially championed and monitored legislation concerning the Tennessee Valley Authority. As World War II approached, he endorsed President Franklin D. Roosevelt's Lend-Lease policy and the establishment of the military draft in 1941 and authored legislation that commissioned women to serve as physicians in the army and navy.

Backed by Alabama's Populist governor Jim Folsom and the labor unions, Sparkman won election to fill the vacant seat of Senator John H. Bankhead in 1946. Unlike many other southern senators, he supported President Harry S. Truman's Fair Deal, except his civil rights initiatives. Such support of the unpopular Truman did not hinder Sparkman's bid to gain a full Senate term. He was reelected in 1948 and continued to serve in the Senate until January 1979. His only real threat to reelection came in 1966 when Governor George C. Wallace considered opposing him, but family considerations prevented Wallace from running and allowed Sparkman to keep his post.

Sparkman became most prominent nationally in 1952. Representing Alabama at the Democratic National Convention that summer, he tried to ensure a civil rights platform that would appease both integrationists and segregationists. By navigating an acceptable moderate position and preventing a southern boycott of the party in 1952, Sparkman impressed Democratic powers such as Truman, Adlai Stevenson, and Sam Rayburn. Presidential nominee Stevenson offered Sparkman the vice presidential position and he accepted. He traveled over 36,000 miles and gave more than 400 speeches in the losing effort.

Although Sparkman campaigned arduously for Stevenson in 1952, his real forte lay in the halls of Congress. As a member and chair of the Banking and Currency Committee, the Housing Subcommittee, and the Urban Affairs Committee of the Senate, this rural Alabama senator significantly affected all housing and urban development legislation that emerged from Congress in the post–World War II era. In 1949 he pushed an omnibus housing bill through Congress that stimulated the housing boom of the 1950s. In 1958 he supported emergency housing legislation, but Senate Majority Leader Lyndon B. Johnson trimmed the appropriations for an even more radical urban renewal package offered in 1959. Under President John F. Kennedy, Sparkman maneuvered through Congress legislation that eventually funded most major cities' mass transit systems. When Johnson became president in 1963, Sparkman scrutinized all housing and urban renewal components of the Great Society.

Although Sparkman's support of federally subsidized housing reflected his dedication to some New Deal ideas, it was constantly tempered by the political realities of facing reelection in a Deep South state wracked by the upheavals of the civil rights movement. Never as rabid a segregationist as George Wallace, Sparkman, however, supported the white supremacist agenda when politically expedient. Opposition to President Truman's civil rights proposals drove him to the Dixiecrat party in 1948 and in 1956 he thought it necessary to sign the southern manifesto that lambasted *Brown v. Board of Education*. He also voted against the Civil Rights Act of 1964 and the Voting Rights Act of 1965.

Believing that economic aid to southern blacks and whites furthered the goals of the civil rights movement better than legislation, he channeled billions of dollars of federal patronage to Alabama. The Marshall Space Flight Center and Redstone Arsenal Missile Complex are testimonials to his congressional power. He supported labor unions, opposed overriding Truman's veto of the Taft-Hartley Act of 1947, and championed the Small Business Administration, which helped both blacks and whites establish their own enterprises. He believed, however, that Medicare and Medicaid would be too costly and opposed these Great Society measures.

As a member of the Senate Foreign Relations Committee for most of his Senate tenure, Sparkman consistently supported economic, military, and political means to contain Communism. Backing the Marshall Plan and NATO, he hoped the United States would not repeat the blunders made after World War I. Admiring the tough rhetoric of Secretary of State John Foster Dulles in the 1950s, he endorsed military ventures in Korea and Vietnam. Insisting that antiwar protesters in the 1960s treasonously thwarted the American military presence in Vietnam, he repeatedly urged Americans to wholeheartedly back the war effort. By the 1970s he had tempered his belief that American will and power could dominate the world, demonstrated by his support of the Panama Canal Treaty of 1978.

Having served in Congress for over four decades, John Sparkman decided to retire in 1978. He died in Huntsville, Alabama.

• Sparkman's papers are in the William Stanley Hoole Special Collection Library at the University of Alabama at Tuscaloosa. See *Journeys With the Senator* (1977) by Ivo Hall Sparkman. For insights into Alabama politics see William D. Barnard, *Dixiecrats and Democrats: Alabama Politics, 1942–1950* (1974); Dan Carter, *Politics of Rage* (1995); Paul T. David, *Presidential Nominating Politics in 1952* (1954); V. O. Key, *Southern Politics in State and Nation* (1950); and Porter McKeeves, *Adlai Stevenson: His Life and Legacy* (1989). Other accounts of Sparkman are in *Ralph Nader's Congress Project: Citizens Look at Congress* (1972); *U.S. News and World Report*, 22 Aug. 1952, pp. 24–39; *Time*, 28 May 1965, pp. 24–25; and *Newsweek*, 13 Nov. 1972, p. 36. Obituaries are in the *Atlanta Journal Constitution* and the *New York Times*, both 17 Nov. 1985.

RANDY FINLEY

SPARKS, Jared (10 May 1789–14 Mar. 1866), historian, editor, and clergyman, was born in Willington, Connecticut, the son of Eleanor Orcutt, who nine months later married Joseph Sparks, a farmer. His early life was somewhat unstable. In the mid-1790s he was sent to live with an aunt and uncle to relieve the burdens of the many children in the family, and with his adoptive family, he settled in 1800 in Camden, New York. In 1805 he moved home for a brief time and then went to live with another uncle in Tolland, Connecticut. There he apprenticed as carpenter and taught in local schools. Early on he displayed interests in literary and historical pursuits along with the more common interest in theology. While in Arlington, Vermont, he organized the Arlington Philosophical Society in 1808. He studied at the Philips Exeter Academy in New Hampshire, beginning in September 1809, the result of Sparks's early interests in the ministry and his receipt of a scholarship. There he met and became lifelong friends with another future New England historian, John Gorham Palfrey. At Philips Exeter he also wrote articles on such topics as education and astronomy for local newspapers. In 1811 entered Harvard College, from which he graduated in 1815 with the Bowdoin Prize for an essay on Isaac Newton. He then remained to study theology. Sparks had dropped out of college from May 1812 to June 1813 for financial reasons and tutored a family in Havre de Grace, Maryland. Witnessing there a British naval bombardment, he later published a firsthand account in the *North American Review*.

Following stints as a tutor in geometry, astronomy, and natural history from 1817 to 1819 and as editor of the *North American Review* from May 1817 to March 1818, as well as the receipt of a master's degree in theological studies from Harvard in 1819, Sparks accepted the call to the Unitarian ministry in Baltimore in 1819. Although serving as the chaplain of Congress in 1821, Sparks was never happy with his life in Baltimore and the District of Columbia. In 1823, with additional complications resulting from poor health, he returned to Boston, where, taking advantage of an opportunity, he purchased the *North American Review* and served as its editor until 1830. Sparks applied all his energies to the *Review*, and he made it the leading literary journal

in the United States. During his first tenure as its editor, a friend confided to Sparks that he had "heard it called . . . the first work of the kind in the United States," and Sparks continued to work to keep the *North American Review* on this level. Not until the 1820s when in his mid-thirties, did Sparks begin to discern his life work.

In the early 1820 Sparks was asked by a publisher to recommend an individual to edit and publish the writings and papers of George Washington. Sparks, who had visited Mount Vernon in 1815 after his graduation from Harvard, had long had an interest in and affection for Washington. Sparks took up this project and, after substantial negotiation, finally received permission in 1827 from Washington's nephew, Bushrod Washington, to examine the Washington manuscripts at Mount Vernon. This project started Sparks on a prodigious amount of editing and publication over the next three decades. While he was negotiating for the use of the Washington papers, Sparks traveled from New England to the South to examine the public records in those states concerning the revolutionary war period. In 1826 he published an important, groundbreaking essay, "Materials for American History," in the *North American Review*, arguing that before the history of the United States could be written, the historical manuscripts and archives had to be assembled and made more accessible; this essay captured his philosophy for his endeavors over the next few decades. "Sometimes the historian fails," Sparks wrote, "on account of his subject; at other times, for the want of materials." Sparks also made several trips to England and Europe to examine historical records concerning America, and his first trip in 1828–1829 established Sparks as one of the first American historians to use foreign sources. He was never found wanting for a lack of documentary sources.

Starting in the late 1820s, Sparks's name was on the title page of numerous volumes on American history. In 1829 and 1830 he brought out twelve volumes under the title *The Diplomatic Correspondence of the American Revolution*. In 1832 he was the author of the three-volume *Life of Gouverneur Morris*. Two years later, his major work, *The Life and Writings of George Washington*, began to appear, reaching twelve volumes when it was completed in 1837. Sparks's editorial work was later criticized for his changes in the Washington volumes. He "considered it a duty, appertaining to the functions of a faithful editor, to hazard such corrections as the construction of a sentence manifestly warranted, or a cool judgment dictated," and this aligned him with the philosophy of America's Romantic historians. Good taste, common sense, and even accuracy required that such changes be made. While Sparks labored on Washington, he started work on Benjamin Franklin, and between 1833 and 1840 he published ten volumes of *The Works of Benjamin Franklin; with Notes and a Life of the Author*. He also oversaw the publication of twenty-five volumes of *The Library of American Biography*, a pioneering biographical publication, between 1833 and 1849. Sparks's documentary works displayed his unbridled enthusiasm for his nation and the belief that the original documents could effectively tell the story of the country's development.

During the time that Sparks produced most of his major works, he was married twice: first in 1832 to Frances Anne Allen, with whom he had a child but who died in 1835; then in 1839 to Mary Crowninshield Silsbee, with whom he had five children, one of which did not survive infancy.

These publications made Sparks part of the leading constellation of mid-nineteenth-century American historians that included George Bancroft and William Prescott. He was appointed in 1838 the McLean Professor of Ancient and Modern History at Harvard College, teaching courses on such topics as the American Revolution. In 1849 he was named president of Harvard; in his three years as president he arranged and reclassified the early records of the school and published *The Correspondence of the American Revolution* (4 vols. 1853). Early in his career, Sparks wrote to Bancroft that his "absorbing passion is for books, knowledge, and thought, and I would not exchange it for all the wealth of all the Indies." His prodigious writing, editing, and mentoring of other scholars reflected these interests.

In 1853 Sparks retired from his professorship at Harvard. He traveled in Europe for a year (1857–1858) and continued to acquire material for a history of the American Revolution, a work he never finished.

A prolific historian of the mid-nineteenth century, Sparks was, more importantly, a pioneering documentary editor, publishing more than sixty volumes of historical writings over a thirty-year period. His career, composed of the diverse activities of a clergyman, literary journal editor, and educator, typifies historical practice in the first half of the nineteenth century, before the establishment of the professional discipline of historical scholarship by the end of the century. But while Sparks has the distinction of being the first college professor with responsibilities for teaching history, he has since been vilified by professional historians as a documentary editor who freely rewrote and revised original texts as his mood determined.

• Sparks's papers are located at Harvard University. Herbert Baxter Adams, *The Life and Writings of Jared Sparks* (1893), remains the fullest treatment of his life and work a century after its publication. More recent essays on aspects of Sparks's life and career include Galen Broeker, "Jared Sparks, Robert Peel and the State Paper Office," *American Quarterly* 13 (1961): 140–52, and Lester J. Cappon, "Jared Sparks: The Preparation of an Editor," *Proceedings of the Massachusetts Historical Society* 90 (1978): 3–21 and "American Historical Editors before Jared Sparks," *William and Mary Quarterly* 30 (1973): 375–400. Sparks also remains a subject of considerable discussion in general surveys of American historical writing, documentary editing, and archival development.

RICHARD J. COX

SPARKS, William Andrew Jackson (19 Nov. 1828–7 May 1904), congressman and commissioner of the General Land Office, was born near New Albany, Indiana,

the son of Baxter Sparks and Elizabeth Gwin, farmers. Sparks moved with his family to Macoupin County, Illinois, in 1836. He was orphaned, which threw the teenaged youth on his own resources and forced him to work on neighboring farms during the summers and study at public schools in the winter months. Eventually, Sparks taught school for a period of time, and he also secured an appointment as assistant clerk of the Illinois House of Representatives. In 1850 he graduated from McKendree College in Lebanon, Illinois. After reading law with Sidney Breese, a respected politician and jurist, Sparks gained admission to the bar in 1851 and opened his law practice in Carlyle, Illinois. He accepted an appointment by President Franklin Pierce in 1853 as U.S. land receiver for the Edwardsville land office, in which capacity he served three years. When an error of three dollars occurred in the account books, Sparks, a scrupulously precise person, traveled by stage to Washington, D.C., to prove that this alleged mistake was due to the miscalculation of a clerk in the nation's capital.

After resigning his position in Edwardsville, where in 1855 he married Julia E. Parker, Sparks resumed his law practice in Carlyle. The couple had no children. He was a presidential elector for James Buchanan in 1856. From 1856 to 1858 Sparks served in the Illinois House of Representatives, and in 1863 he succeeded to a vacant seat in the state senate. An active Democrat, he attended and presided at Democratic state conventions over the next several years and was a delegate from Illinois to the 1868 Democratic National Convention.

Sparks entered national politics in 1874 when the Democrats of the Sixteenth Congressional District, an agricultural area generally regarded as Republican territory, nominated him as their candidate for the U.S. House of Representatives. It was a particularly propitious time for Democrats. The economic collapse of 1873 had resulted in stagnation and insolvency for a number of businesses. Agricultural prices plummeted. The campaign of 1874 shaped up as a referendum on the economy as well as on the corruption and incompetence in the Ulysses S. Grant administration. Benefiting from the political and economic situation, Sparks rode a tidal wave of discontent that transcended politics and became a member of the first Democratic majority in the House in eighteen years. Once in office, Sparks, cautious and conciliatory, used the power of incumbency and his personality to solidify his hold on his constituents. A shrewd politician and pragmatist, he attracted support from both parties and was reelected three times.

Sparks offered his views on a number of issues and introduced various bills during his eight years in Congress. He sponsored legislation to remonetize silver and authorize the deposit of silver bullion in the Treasury, and he sought to provide for the organization of the Mississippi River Improvement Commission to construct and preserve levees and harbors. A Jacksonian Democrat who opposed high protective tariffs, he strongly advocated governmental regulation of railroads. Sparks chaired the House Committee on Public Lands and the Committee on Military Affairs and served on the Appropriations Committee.

Sparks spurned some of the unsavory aspects of his era's politics but remained a lively partisan. In a speech in 1876 he denounced the corruption, greed, and dishonesty of the post–Civil War era, insisting that an elected official's high station demanded "an entire abnegation of self" and that selfish influences must never take priority over the "untrammeled effort in all things to meet the demands of the people."

During the debate in Congress over the disputed presidential election of 1876, Sparks argued that the power to count and determine the electoral vote rested with the people under the Tenth Amendment and that members of the Democrat-dominated House, who directly represented the people, should tabulate votes and resolve the outcome. Nevertheless, he acquiesced to what he termed a stolen election that enabled Rutherford B. Hayes to become president. His partisanship resurfaced four years later in a heated debate over the 1880 presidential election. Sparks charged Representative James B. Weaver of Iowa, the 1880 presidential nominee of the Greenback party, with having indirectly aided Republicans during the campaign. The exchange took an ugly turn, nearly resulting in blows, when Sparks called Weaver "a scoundrel and a villain and a liar."

Because of the gerrymandering of his district, Sparks declined to seek another term in 1882 and returned to his law practice in Carlyle, where he earned a solid reputation as a good jury lawyer. Following the victory of Grover Cleveland in the 1884 presidential election, Sparks joined the Democratic administration as commissioner of the General Land Office, a division of the Interior Department, headed by Lucius Q. C. Lamar. On record as an opponent of powerful land schemers who wanted to plunder the public domain, Sparks endeavored to reform the land service. His goal was to preserve public lands for their appropriation by honest settlers looking for homesteads.

In his quest to uproot abuses in the land subsidy system, Sparks encountered stiff opposition from various groups, including railroad interests, cattle barons, land speculators, and some members of Congress. His zealous crusade ultimately cost him his job. The case that caused an irrevocable break with Lamar concerned the adjustment of the Chicago, St. Paul, Minneapolis, and Omaha Railroad's land grants. Despite Sparks's strenuous objection, Lamar certified 200,000 acres of land claimed by this railroad. When he finally concluded that powerful interests were obtaining more consideration from the Cleveland White House than they deserved, Sparks tendered his resignation in November 1887, delivering his letter personally to the president.

Sparks again returned to live a quiet life in Carlyle and practice law. Beginning in 1900 he spent winters in St. Louis. Involved with several financial institutions with heavy investments in various interests in the country, Sparks owned a considerable amount of real estate in his last years. He died at his St. Louis home.

Sparks was a man of absolute integrity whose reputation as a politician centered both in his devotion to the constitutional system and in his fluent appeal to his constituents and colleagues to believe in their institutions. A skillful lawyer and politician, he was chiefly motivated by his sympathy for the common man, whom he believed would be served best by reduced taxation, flexible currency, low tariffs, and the protection of public resources from the predations of railroads and other powerful corporations.

• Sparks left no personal papers. A number of his letters are in the Grover Cleveland Papers at the Library of Congress and in the manuscript collections of other contemporaries. His speeches appear in the *Congressional Record*. The *Annual Reports of the Commissioner of the General Land Office* (1885, 1886, 1887), Executive Documents, Department of the Interior, National Archives, are cogent analyses of land practices at the time and provide a wealth of information. An early article is John B. Rae, "Commissioner Sparks and the Railroad Land Grants," *Mississippi Valley Historical Review* 25 (1938): 211–30. The controversy with Lamar is presented briefly in James B. Murphy, *L. Q. C. Lamar: Pragmatic Patriot* (1973). See also *Copp's Land Owner, 1885–1887*. Sparks's letter of resignation as commissioner was published in the *New York Times*, 16 Nov. 1887. Obituaries are in the *Carlyle Union Banner* and the *Carlyle Constitution*, both 13 May 1904; the *St. Louis Daily Globe Democrat*, 8 May 1904; and the *St. Louis Post Dispatch*, 11 May 1904.

LEONARD SCHLUP

SPARKS, William Joseph (26 Feb. 1904–23 Oct. 1976), chemist and inventor, was born in Wilkinson, Indiana, the son of Charles Edward Sparks and Daisy McDaniel, farmers. Sparks was raised on the family farm, and when he was eighteen his father gave him the choice of a college education or a new Model T Ford. Sparks chose college and in 1922 entered Indiana University to major in history. On the advice of Professor Frank C. Mathers, he switched his major to chemistry at the end of his sophomore year. After receiving an A.B. with distinction in 1926, he worked as a chemist for the Sherwin-Williams Paint Company, switched to the Chrysler Corporation in 1928, and returned to Indiana University, from which he received an A.M. in 1929. He then worked for R&H Electrochemicals at Niagara Falls, where his co-worker was a former classmate from Indiana, Meredith Pleasant, whom he married in 1930; they had two sons and two daughters.

Sparks worked as a chemist for E. I. du Pont de Nemours from 1929 to 1934, when he and his wife began graduate work at the University of Illinois. There they worked under two of the United States's most prominent organic chemists—he under Carl Shipp ("Speed") Marvel, and she under Roger Adams. Sparks's interest in the economic importance of research led him to minor in economics. They both received a Ph.D. in 1936. After the children were grown, Meredith Sparks earned a law degree (1958), conducted a successful business as an attorney specializing in patents and technical matters, and served as president of the National Association of Women Lawyers (1981–1982). In 1934 Sparks received the first of his 145 patents. Twelve were issued to protect his postretirement inventions, and his last was issued in 1978, two years after his death.

In 1936 Sparks joined the Standard Oil Development Company (later Esso Research and Engineering Company, then Exxon) at Linden, New Jersey. In 1937, only one year after receiving his doctorate, he and his lifetime co-worker and close friend, Robert McKee Thomas, produced their first important invention, butyl rubber. Most synthetic rubber research at this time was strongly influenced by earlier research on natural rubber, which had shown that a diene (a hydrocarbon with two double bonds—isoprene obtained from natural rubber by pyrolysis or from turpentine) can be polymerized to produce rubbery products. Therefore most attempts to produce synthetic rubbers involved the polymerization of isoprene (2-methyl-1,3-butadiene), butadiene, and other dienes.

Sparks and Thomas were among the few investigators to defy convention by using starting materials other than dienes. They copolymerized a monoene (a hydrocarbon with only one double bond—in this case, isobutylene) with small amounts of a diene (usually less than 2 percent of isoprene) to obtain butyl rubber. This product contained enough double bonds for cross-linking but was more resistant to deterioration than natural rubber. Unlike diene rubbers, butyl rubber was substantially free of unsaturation (double bonds) after vulcanization and hence resistant to oxidation and weathering. Its low glass transition temperature (c. 70°C or 158°F), high impermeability to common gases including water vapor, and high hysteresis over a useful temperature range were also responsible for its commercial success.

At the time of its invention butyl rubber was unique not only because it was based on a monoene but also because of the severe and unusual conditions of its manufacture (continuous copolymerization in methyl chloride at −100° to −90°C [−140° to −130°F] using aluminum chloride as a catalyst). Before early experimental difficulties were solved, the new rubber was sometimes called "futile butyl." It was critically important during and after World War II, and by 1979 it was the third most widely produced synthetic rubber in the United States.

Sparks not only introduced a new and important material but also the new elastomeric concepts of marginal and controlled functionality (the number of reactive groups in a molecule) that were new to the study of rubbers. Fifty years later, much of the work done in rubber technology was still a direct outgrowth of his work. In 1963 the American Chemical Society's Division of Rubber Chemistry awarded Sparks its Charles Goodyear Medal in recognition of valuable contributions to the science or technology of rubber.

In 1939–1940 Sparks served as principal chemist at the U.S. Department of Agriculture's Northern Regional Research Laboratory, Peoria, Illinois, where he used his expertise on rubber and polymers to initiate work on dimer acids and polymers made from vegetable oils and high molecular-weight polyamide resins from drying oils, both of which have become important chemurgic products. Continuation of this work by NRRL scientists led to the development of the elastomer called Norepol. Yielding to an attractive offer, Sparks returned in 1940 to Esso, where he spent the remainder of his career. He became associate director of the Chemical Division in 1945, director in 1946, and scientific adviser, Esso's highest technical position, in 1958. During 1952 he was a student at the Harvard University School of Business Administration. Following his retirement in 1967 he continued to invent and serve the chemical profession. Although his professional activities left him little time for hobbies, he occasionally enjoyed golf and poker. After several years of ill health he died of heart failure at his home in Coral Gables, Florida.

Although best known as the coinventor of butyl rubber, Sparks applied his versatile and creative genius to a variety of subjects. During the 1930s he explored hydrogen peroxide chemistry and discovered its accelerating effect on the germination of seeds and its use as a leavening agent in baking. Among his commercially successful inventions or coinventions were styrene-isobutylene thermoplastic, film-forming copolymers as coatings for paper and paper milk cartons, a high styrene-isoprene emulsion copolymer that was the forerunner of artificial leather and shoe-sole resins, oxo alcohols, oxo ester plasticizers, plastics, corrosion-proof liners, stabilized polymers, rocket propellants, encapsulating oxidants, and food-wrapping films. All resulted in patents. In the fuel and lubricant areas that were Esso's main concern, he developed gasoline additives, diesel fuels, hydrocarbon refining processes, and alcohol-gasoline compositions. With Albert M. Gessler, Sparks held a number of patents on asphalts, including colored synthetic paving compositions.

Sparks was an active member of the American Chemical Society, serving on numerous committees and as ACS president in 1966. He received the society's highest award, the Priestley Medal, in 1965. In 1987 the Exxon Chemical Company established the annual Sparks-Thomas Scientific Award through the ACS Division of Rubber Chemistry. Sparks's service to science and technology also involved active participation in a number of other societies, including the American Institute of Chemists, from which he received a Gold Medal in 1954 and a Chemical Pioneer Award in 1970; the Scientific Research Society of America; American Institute of Chemical Engineers; National Academy of Engineering; Society of the Chemical Industry, from which he received the American Section's Perkin Medal in 1964; American Association for the Advancement of Science; Association of Research Directors; International Union of Pure and Applied Chemistry; and the National Academy of Sciences. He was chairman of the National Research Council's Division of Chemistry and Chemical Technology and an adviser to the U.S. State Department, Department of Agriculture, and the army.

According to biographer Charles Henry Fisher, though "usually soft-spoken, Sparks could become vehement when discussing the goals of science" (Fisher, "William Joseph Sparks," p. 263). Sparks, who believed that research should serve society and pay for itself, observed, "Science without a purpose is an art without responsibility" (Fisher, "William Joseph Sparks," p. 263), and "The image of science is going to suffer if people don't get any benefit from the money that is being spent on it" (Seymour, "William Joseph Sparks: Co-Inventor of Butyl Rubber," p. 185). He believed that basic research and engineering were receiving unprecedented attention while the art and science of invention were not given their due. Sparks was not only a great scientist and inventor, especially in the field of rubber chemistry and technology, but also a successful administrator, a statesman and spokesman for science, a valued consultant to various governmental agencies and educational institutions, and a lifelong dedicated servant of his profession.

• An autographed portrait and list of Sparks's publications and patents are in the Collection of Photographs of Famous Scientists of the Library of Congress. For Sparks's thoughts and concerns about the uses of research as well as the relationship between science and society, see his "Priestley Medal Address," *Chemical and Engineering News* 43, no. 16 (19 Apr. 1965): 110–13 (with cover portrait); "The 'Symbiotic Relationship'," *Chemical and Engineering News* 44, no. 11 (3 Jan. 1966): 7 (with cover portrait); "Good Chemists Never Quit," 38 (1961): 357–65; "Inventions Vital Third Dimension of Science," *The Chemist* 42 (1964): 107–8; and "Creativity, Competition, and Cooperation: The Combination to Prosperity," *The Chemist* 44 (1967): 65. Biographical articles include "Sparks Heads NRC Division of Chemistry," *Chemical and Engineering News* 31, no. 33 (17 Aug. 1953): 3382 (with cover portrait); Raymond B. Seymour and Charles Henry Fisher, "William Joseph Sparks," in their *Profiles of Eminent American Chemists* (1988), pp. 448–52 (with portrait); Seymour, "William Joseph Sparks: Co-Inventor of Butyl Rubber," in *Pioneers of Polymer Science*, ed. Seymour (1989), pp. 177–92; and Fisher, "William Joseph Sparks 1904–1976," in *American Chemists and Chemical Engineers*, ed. Wyndham D. Miles and Robert F. Gould, vol. 2 (1994), pp. 262–63.
An obituary is in *Chemical and Engineering News* 54, no. 45 (1 Nov. 1976): 6.

GEORGE B. KAUFFMAN

SPAULDING, Elbridge Gerry (24 Feb. 1809–5 May 1897), congressman and banker, was born in Summerhill, Cayuga County, New York, the son of Edward Spaulding and Mehitable Goodrich, farmers. Educated in nearby Auburn, Spaulding later read law in Batavia and Attica and by 1834 had been admitted to practice in Genesee County. That year he moved to Buffalo to clerk in the office of Potter & Babcock. He eventually became a partner, and when the firm dissolved in 1844, he took over its business, enjoying a thriving legal practice.

For all his success as an attorney, Spaulding increasingly turned his professional energies toward banking. In 1837 he had married Jane Antoinette Rich, whose father headed the Bank of Attica. They had no children. Spaulding served as the bank's counsel and became a major stockholder. At his urging, the bank was moved to Buffalo and transformed into the Buffalo Commercial Bank. Spaulding later lured the Farmers' & Mechanics' Bank of Batavia to Buffalo and became its president and chief investor. In the meantime, in 1841, his first wife had died and in 1842 he married Nancy Selden Strong, with whom he had three children. After his second wife's death in 1852, Spaulding married her sister, Delia Strong Robinson, in 1854.

Even as he built a career as a prominent Buffalo lawyer, banker, and businessman, Spaulding found time for politics. As early as 1836 he was city clerk, and by 1841 he was an alderman. A Whig, Spaulding was elected mayor of Buffalo in 1847. The next year he sat in the New York state assembly and was also elected to the U.S. House of Representatives. In Congress, Spaulding did little to advance sectional reconciliation and did not vote on any of the compromise measures of 1850 except to support the abolition of the slave trade in the District of Columbia. Returning to Buffalo in 1851, he two years later became state treasurer of New York. An ally of Whig boss Thurlow Weed, Spaulding nevertheless endeavored to secure the gubernatorial nomination in 1854 without Weed's blessing but came up empty-handed. As his party crumbled, Spaulding quickly made his way into the Republican ranks, sitting on the fledgling party's state committee by 1855. He returned to the House of Representatives in 1859. Moderate in his Republicanism, he made known to Congress his constituents' desire for compromise during the secession crisis.

Within a year of the Civil War commencing, Spaulding made his mark on the nation's history with a single piece of legislation. Amidst military and diplomatic reverses, both the Federal government and northern banks found themselves financially hamstrung by the end of 1861. Not surprisingly, the enormous costs of war far exceeded Federal receipts from tariffs and taxes. But existing laws mandated that, in borrowing the large sums it required, the government deal exclusively in gold or silver. This promised to exhaust the reserves that banks kept on hand to back their own operations. In meeting the revenue shortfall and credit and currency crunch, Secretary of the Treasury Salmon P. Chase yielded to Congress, especially to a Ways and Means subcommittee headed by Spaulding. Aided by Representative Samuel Hooper of Massachusetts, the Buffalo banker drew up a bill that flew in the face of many Americans' "hard money" prejudices as well as real constitutional doubts about the Federal government's authority to traffic in paper currency. The legislation proposed not only that the government be authorized to print money in the form of noninterest-bearing treasury notes but that creditors be given no choice but to accept the "greenbacks" as "legal tender for all debts, public and private" (by contrast, creditors could refuse the depreciated state bank notes then in circulation). Furthermore, this paper money would not be backed by the promise that greenbacks could be exchanged on demand for coin kept on reserve; instead, its worth was based simply on the government's credit. Spaulding defended this assault on financial orthodoxy as an admittedly extraordinary emergency measure by which Congress might carry out its power to support armies and the government might exercise its sovereign right to sustain itself. The proposal, Spaulding declared, was a matter "of *necessity* and not of choice" (*Congressional Globe*, 37th Cong., 2d sess., p. 523). In fact, Spaulding had made a choice, preferring "fiat money" to raising revenue through massive sales of U.S. bonds below their face value. Supported only reluctantly if at all by many prominent Republicans, including Secretary Chase, the Legal Tender Act made its way through Congress but only after being amended to require that import duties and interest on U.S. bonds continue to be paid in gold. As enacted in February 1862, the law authorized issuance of $150 million in legal tender notes that were interest free but exchangeable for Federal "5–20" bonds bearing 6 percent interest.

Most scholars would probably not go as far as Senator John Sherman did in declaring the Legal Tender Act "the turning point of our physical and financial history" (Sherman, vol. 1, p. 279). But the law was certainly enormously significant. It created a uniform national paper currency, placed the Federal government at the helm of the country's monetary system, and anticipated the day when the value of money would rest less upon gold than upon public faith and governmental authority. It represented, too, a notable episode in the wartime testing of constitutional boundaries and in the attendant development of more expansive notions of what the national government might do in the pursuit of goals deemed worthy by Congress or the executive. In more immediate terms, the issues of whether and how quickly—and, even, whether—Spaulding's greenbacks would be retired after the war ended and by what means the companion 5–20 bonds would be paid off would be central elements of the larger money question that became so prominent a feature of Gilded Age politics.

Spaulding played no conspicuous role in other significant legislation of the Thirty-seventh Congress, but he did support the issuance of $300 million more in greenbacks and spoke up for a national banking bill. Declining to run for reelection in 1862, he returned to private life in March 1863. The following year his Farmers' & Mechanics' Bank entered the war-spawned national bank system. Though jeered at by such worthies as Henry Adams and Francis Amasa Walker, Spaulding continued after Appomattox to defend the Legal Tender Act as a wartime necessity. The "father of the greenbacks" did not become a Greenbacker, however. Spaulding supported the gradual retirement of greenbacks from circulation and an early resumption of specie payments on the part of the federal government, and he insisted that he had intended that the

5–20 bonds be repaid in gold. He continued at the helm of the Farmers' & Mechanics' National Bank until his final years. Having helped turn the color of money from gold to green, Spaulding died in Buffalo.

• A collection of Spaulding papers is at the Buffalo and Erie County Historical Society in Buffalo, N.Y. Spaulding published his own account of the Legal Tender Act, *A Resource of War—The Credit of the Government Made Immediately Available. History of the Legal Tender Paper Money Issued during the Great Rebellion. Being a Loan without Interest and a National Currency* (1869). For scholarly assessments of his role in this legislation, see Bray Hammond, *Sovereignty and an Empty Purse: Banks and Politics in the Civil War* (1970), and Robert Sharkey, *Money, Class, and Party: An Economic Study of Civil War and Reconstruction* (1959). Adams and Walker's attack on Spaulding and the Legal Tender Act was reprinted in Henry Adams, *Historical Essays* (1891). Sherman's celebration of the act is in John Sherman, *Recollections of Forty Years in the House, Senate and Cabinet. An Autobiography* (1895). See also Leonard Curry, *Blueprint for Modern America: Nonmilitary Legislation of the First Civil War Congress* (1968), and Hendrik Booraem V, *The Formation of the Republican Party in New York: Politics and Conscience in the Antebellum North* (1983).

PATRICK G. WILLIAMS

SPEAKER, Tris (4 Apr. 1888–8 Dec. 1958), baseball player and manager, was born Tristram E. Speaker in Hubbard, Texas, the son of Archie Speaker, a carpenter, and Nancy Jane Poer. Speaker broke his right arm in a fall from a horse as a youngster and learned to bat and throw left-handed. Nicknamed "Tris" and "The Gray Eagle," the latter because of his prematurely graying hair and easy outfield style, he worked in his teens as a telegraph linesman and cowpuncher, and he was regarded as an excellent all-around athlete at Fort Worth Polytechnic Institute.

Speaker aspired to play professional baseball. Despite his mother's opposition to his being "sold into slavery," Speaker was signed in 1906 by Doak Roberts to pitch and play in the outfield for Cleburne of the North Texas League for $150 a month. In 1907 Speaker batted .314 for Houston of the Texas League, and that summer Boston Red Sox scout George Huff bought his contract for $750. But Speaker hit only .158 in seven games for Boston, and he was not offered a big league contract. In 1908, however, Speaker led the Southern Association in batting while playing for Little Rock and rejoined Boston in September.

Speaker played with the Red Sox from 1909 through 1915, starring both offensively and defensively. His .383 batting average in 1912 helped the Red Sox take the American League pennant and defeat the New York Giants in the World Series. As American League Most Valuable Player, Speaker received the Chalmers Award and an automobile, and a Boston jeweler gave him a sterling silver bat worth $500.

Next to Ty Cobb, Speaker ranked as the era's greatest all-around outfielder. Speaker usually battled Cobb for batting honors, frequently finishing second with averages that could have won titles in other years. Cobb outpaced Speaker by .410 to .385 in 1912 and

.390 to .365 in 1913. Speaker batted .338 in 1914 and .322 in 1915, helping the Red Sox defeat the Philadelphia Phillies in the 1915 World Series. Defensively, the center fielder anchored perhaps the greatest outfield ever, which included "Duffy" Lewis and Harry Hooper. Speaker played only seven full seasons with Boston but still ranks high among the Red Sox career leaders for triples (106), stolen bases (266), and batting (.339). He became the next highest paid American League player in 1914 when owner J. Joseph Lannin signed him to a two-year contract averaging $18,000 annually. Besides advertising Boston Gaiters, Speaker endorsed a $2 straw hat and other clothing.

Since Speaker had slumped offensively in 1915, Lannin suggested that his salary be cut to $9,000. When Speaker refused to sign, Boston traded him for two players and $50,000 to the Cleveland Indians. Speaker hit .386 in 1916, ending Cobb's incredible nine-year reign as American League batting champion. During the 11 seasons that Speaker played with Cleveland, he averaged .354, led the Indians in several offensive categories (batting average, hits, doubles, triples, runs batted in, stolen bases), and was the American League leader in doubles for four years in a row.

Although Speaker never attained another batting crown, he batted .388 and hit 50 doubles in leading Cleveland in 1920 to its first American League pennant and World Series championship. Speaker finished second to George Sisler in batting in 1920, third to Sisler and Cobb in 1922 with a .378 average, third to Harry Heilmann and Babe Ruth in 1923 at .380, and second to Heilmann in 1925 at .389.

Defensively, Speaker revolutionized center field play with his graceful style and his ability to cover ground, position himself well for hitters, and throw accurately. He exploited the dead ball era, frequently playing no more than 40 feet behind second base to prevent softly hit fly balls from falling in for hits, while his great speed frequently enabled him to catch balls hit over his head. He had the ability to judge the direction and distance of fly balls as soon as they were hit, and once he jumped a fence in Washington to make a remarkable catch. Speaker often slipped behind a runner on second base, took the throw from pitcher or catcher, and tagged out the startled base runner. Besides occasionally fielding ground balls near second base, he made unassisted double plays on short fly balls. As of the early 1990s, he was still the only outfielder to have made an unassisted double play in the World Series.

Speaker's career hitting and fielding statistics are impressive. No other major leaguer had as many career doubles (793), outfield assists (448), or outfield double plays (139). Thirty-five of his assists were made as a rookie in 1909. Speaker also led the American League in career outfield putouts (6,787). Besides batting over .375 six times and leading the American League eight times in doubles, he still ranks high on the all-time major league lists for hits (3,515), triples (233), batting average (.344), runs scored (1,881), extra base hits (1,133), and total bases (5,103).

Speaker succeeded Lee Fohl as Cleveland manager in July 1919, compiling a 616–520 won-lost mark (.542) through the 1926 season. Under Speaker, Cleveland finished second in 1919 and defeated Brooklyn five games to two in the 1920 World Series. In that fall classic, Speaker batted .320, fielded superbly, and handled his pitchers well.

In 1925 Speaker married Mary Frances Cudahy; they had no children. The following year a gambling scandal surfaced concerning a 1919 game between Cleveland and the Detroit Tigers. Because Speaker and Cobb were allegedly involved, American League president Ban Johnson persuaded both managers to resign. Speaker spent 1927 with the Washington Senators and closed out his American League career in 1928 as Cobb's teammate on the Philadelphia Athletics.

Speaker managed the Newark Bears of the International League in 1929 and 1930 and then broadcast Cleveland games. Later he worked in the wholesale liquor business in Cleveland, chaired the Cleveland boxing commission, and served briefly as part-owner and manager of the Kansas City club in the American Association. The Indians later employed him as a scout, batting instructor, and adviser. In 1937 he was the seventh player elected to the National Baseball Hall of Fame. His plaque there calls him "the greatest center fielder of his day." In 1952 an All-America Board of Baseball, consisting of twelve distinguished sportswriters and former manager Connie Mack, named Speaker and three other outfielders on an all-star team of greatest performers from 1900 to 1950. He died at Lake Whitney, Texas.

• There are no extensive collections of Speaker's papers, nor is there a full-length biography; but the National Baseball Library in Cooperstown, N.Y., houses material on Speaker's career. The Ellery Clark, Jr., Red Sox Analytical Letter Collection, in Annapolis, Md., includes correspondence of teammates "Duffy" Lewis and Harry Hooper. The Clark papers also contain interviews with Speaker and Lewis and Marty McManus under the title "A Closeup of Tris Speaker." Speaker's statistical accomplishments are detailed in *The Baseball Encyclopedia*, 9th ed. (1993); *Daguerreotypes*, 8th ed. (1990); and John Thorn and Pete Palmer, eds., *Total Baseball* (1989). For Speaker's roles with the Boston Red Sox and Cleveland Indians, see Frederick G. Lieb, *The Boston Red Sox* (1947); Ellery H. Clark, Jr., *Boston Red Sox: 75th Anniversary History* (1975); Franklin Lewis, *The Cleveland Indians* (1949); Tom Meany, *Baseball's Greatest Teams* (1949); and Lowell Reidenbaugh, *The Sporting News Selects Baseball's 25 Greatest Teams* (1988). An obituary is in the *New York Times*, 9 Dec. 1958.

DAVID L. PORTER

SPEAKS, Margaret (23 Oct. 1904–16 July 1977), soprano, was born in Columbus, Ohio, the daughter of General John Charles Speaks, a lumber and milling businessman, army officer, and U.S. congressman, and Edna Jane Lawyer. Both parents were musically gifted. Her father was a singer, her mother was a pianist, and the extended Speaks family boasted more than a dozen musicians of fine talent, including several professionals, most notable among them her composer-uncle, Oley Speaks.

Speaks began music lessons when she was three years old. Dance instruction followed shortly thereafter. The youngster's first public singing appearance probably took place in Memorial Hall in Columbus when she was only twelve years old. The *National Daily* of 23 October 1916 noted that "the little maiden had so recently come from Heaven, that perhaps the memory of the Angels' songs still lingers, for she sings like unto them."

She continued musical study, and after earning her high school diploma in three and a half years, she entered Ohio State University at age seventeen. There speaks pursued a variety of interests including sports, but she devoted most of her time to musical activities, studying voice privately with Samuel Richards Gaines, singing with and participating in various leadership roles with the Girls' Glee Club, and directing and performing in productions by her sorority, Kappa Kappa Gamma.

Shortly after her graduation from the university in 1925, Speaks was married briefly to Harold Cunningham, with whom she had her only child. The couple soon divorced, and she left for New York City and lived with her brother Charles and his wife until she could secure steady employment. By one account, Speaks performed for Jake Shubert in February 1926 at the Hartman Theatre in Columbus while he was in the Midwest with a touring production. This was perhaps a preliminary audition for her first job in the chorus of Sigmund Romberg's *Yo San* (1927; later christened *Cherry Blossoms*). The show enjoyed moderate success, and confident her career was secured, Speaks found a hall bedroom in Greenwich Village. She soon struck up a friendship with Leslie S. Pearl, a neighbor and successful advertising executive. They married in 1933.

Although she once commented that "she really didn't have to struggle for her career," the period immediately following *Cherry Blossoms* was lean indeed. Her next show, *Band Box Follies* (1927), was a dismal failure, but the *New American* (6 Sept. 1927) noted that "Miss Margaret Speaks . . . sings splendidly." Speaks rehearsed for a time with an Oscar Hammerstein show and even won a spot in the Ziegfeld *Follies*, but after consultation with her teacher and Uncle Oley she decided that for her "it was to be a concert and radio career or nothing." Thus she abandoned musical theater altogether.

Speaks began taking church and temple soloist and quartet positions in metropolitan New York, making appearances with choral organizations, and traveling on limited recital tours. She gave premiere performances of works by Mark Andrews, Ernest Charles, A. Walter Kramer, Frank La Forge, Clarence Olmstead, Oley Speaks, Harry R. Spier, and Victor Young. Early programs on which she appeared included performances by Marion Bauer, Ruth Crawford (Seeger), and Clara Edwards.

Speaks was also making sporadic radio appearances, including nonpaying performances over station WOR in New York, and a continuing series of programs on WRNY that secured the young singer her first representation with Judson Management, a division of Columbia Artists. Several months later, during a Hotel Commodore engagement, a representative of the Hoffman Beverage Company heard her and wanted "that voice on my program." It was on "The Hoffman Hour" that she first worked with Nelson Eddy. The two appeared from May through December 1932 with an orchestra led by William Merrigan Daly.

When "The Hoffman Hour" went off the air, she joined the Humming Birds Trio, which later teamed up with radio personality "Whispering Jack" Smith to do advertising spots. "Hoffman Hour" conductor Daly contacted her in June 1934 to perform with a quartet on "The Voice of Firestone." Within the year the quartet was disbanded, but Speaks agreed to stay on with the Firestone Chorus. Three months later she was singing duets with Richard Crooks and Gladys Swarthout.

In Speaks's first full year on "Firestone" (1934–1935), she was an assisting artist to Swarthout for twenty-seven broadcasts. By Speaks's second year her appearances increased to thirty-one, with twenty-two as a soloist, clearly indicating her increasing value to the Firestone company as a major radio personality. Shortly after accepting a permanent contract with Firestone in 1935, she made an extremely successful European tour, with appearances and live radio broadcasts that won audiences throughout the world.

In 1937 she was one of about a hundred artists, including Jack Benny, Eddie Cantor, Bing Crosby, Lawrence Tibbett, and Rudy Vallee, who formed a radio artists' union, the American Federation of Radio Artists (AFRA), which later became part of the American Guild of Musical Artists (AGMA). She eventually became a vice president of the union and was an active member until April 1954. AGMA later honored her as a "Founding Father" during its twentieth anniversary celebration in 1957.

Speaks maintained a practical attitude toward her career, commenting, "It's just a business, being a singer. It's no more important than any other business." In an interview she said:

No singer dares get temperamental today. You just step out to the footlights or microphone and watch the lights. And when the little green light goes on you sing and no monkey business about it. . . . In the days when two thousand persons was a tremendous audience, temperamental old girls used to dominate their audiences. Now audiences of millions of radio listeners dominate the singer. Any temperamental tricks by the singers and the audience just twirls the dial to something else. (*New York Herald Tribune* [Paris ed.], 15 Aug. 1936)

With such a practical attitude, it is not difficult to understand the steady growth of her popularity, climaxing from 1939 through 1941, when Speaks was voted the most popular classical female vocalist by polls in trade magazines *Motion Picture Daily*, *Radio Daily*, and *Radio Mirror*, an achievement she later said was the most rewarding in her career.

During World War II Speaks devoted much of her time to war efforts. With her brother, husband, and son in active duty, the conflict held a deeply personal threat for her. She made at least seventy appearances at canteens, war fund and bond drives, and Red Cross benefits. She also visited veterans' hospitals and participated in the presentation of defense awards to industries in the United States and Canada. Professional appearances increased dramatically, including performances at the White House, the Republican National Convention, the ASCAP "Cavalcade of American Music" at the New York World's Fair, Mayor Fiorello LaGuardia's "I am an American" celebration on Central Park Mall, two Town Hall recitals, and concerts with the Cleveland, Philadelphia, and National symphony orchestras.

Speaks's tremendous popularity did not delay her swift departure from "The Voice of Firestone" as featured soloist in 1943. At the time of her departure and replacement by tenor Richard Crooks, Speaks had appeared on a total of 280 broadcasts.

Early in 1944 she began overseeing funding, planning, and construction of a library to honor her uncle, composer Oley Speaks. Although the library was to feature a comprehensive collection of compositions by him, his niece also contacted dozens of American composers, their publishers, and agents requesting complimentary copies of their works for the library, accompanied by biographies and photographs. "I have always found the value of songs enhanced by knowing something about the composer," she wrote. "Somehow it seems to give the songs a background even if you don't happen to like the composer personally. Actually I can't think of one I have ever disliked." Dedicated in December 1949, the Oley Speaks Music Library featured a lending library with study area and a small recital hall housed in the high school of Canal Winchester, Ohio, his birthplace.

Speaks's professional retirement was at an alumni benefit recital at Ohio State University in 1954. However, she made benefit appearances for schools as late as the early 1970s, only a few years before her death. She died while on a summer holiday at the family's cottage in Blue Hill, Maine.

• Speaks wrote an article for a Campfire Girls publication, "The Singer," *Vocationally Yours*, Oct. 1948, pp. 29–36. Information for this article has been derived from a variety of contemporary periodicals, personal memorabilia, and the correspondence of Speaks herself. Articles of interest include "Memory Lane and Margaret," *New York Sun*, 20 June 1936; "One Way to Succeed as a Radio Singer," *New York Post*, 1 Feb. 1939; "Meet Your Neighbors," *Cue*, Westchester-Connecticut Section, 11 Oct. 1941; and "This Little Cape Codder," *American Home*, Oct. 1940, which is a pictorial spread on her home, complete with floor plans. A contemporary consideration of her is in David Ewen's *Living Musicians* (1940). An obituary is in the *New York Times*, 18 July 1977.

STEPHANIE TINGLER

SPEAKS, Oley (28 June 1874–27 Aug. 1948), song composer and singer, was born in Canal Winchester near Columbus, Ohio, the son of Charles William Speaks, a building contractor and grain merchant, and Sarah Ann Hesser. He was the youngest of eleven children, two of whom died in infancy. His father died when he was ten years of age. After Oley completed high school in his hometown, his family moved to Columbus, and Speaks found employment there as a clerk with the Cleveland, Akron and Columbus Railroad.

In addition to his railroad job in Columbus, Speaks held positions at various churches as a baritone soloist. He gained some notoriety as a singer—Josiah R. Smith described his voice in the *Columbus Dispatch* in 1891 as "singularly sweet and flexible, clear and melodious"—and made an initial foray into songwriting. Two of his songs, "In Maytime" and "When Mabel Sings," were published.

In 1898 Speaks continued his singing career in New York City as vocal soloist at the Universalist Church of the Divine Paternity and, four years later, at St. Thomas's Episcopal Church. While in New York, he studied voice with Carl Dufft, J. Armour Galloway, and Emma Thursby and composition with Max Spicker, a German-American composer and editor for the publisher G. Schirmer, and Will C. Macfarlane, organist at St. Thomas's and prominent sacred music composer. He returned to Columbus in 1906 to work in a church, but he returned to New York a few years later and remained there for the rest of his life.

It is as a composer rather than as a singer, however, that Speaks is best known. He wrote over 250 songs, although only 150 were published: 119 by G. Schirmer, Inc. (New York), and 31 by the John Church Company (Cincinnati). Speaks favored sacred and sentimental texts and set them in an uncomplicated manner. His songs were intended for amateur performers and audiences, and thus are readily accessible in all aspects of musical style. His melodies are generally stepwise, rhythms and harmonies are simple, and piano accompaniments are modest. In his songs, Speaks continued the tradition of the nineteenth-century parlor ballad—music for the artistic laity, the essence of which rests in the joy of music making. The intrinsic quality of Speaks's work has not been limited to amateur singers by any means; professional singers and teachers throughout the twentieth century were captivated by the essence and charm of the songs, and Speaks's melodies continued to be heard in concert halls and churches.

Of Speaks's voluminous output, three songs were especially popular: "On the Road to Mandalay" (text by Rudyard Kipling, 1907), "Morning (text by Frank L. Stanton, 1912), and "Sylvia" (text by Clinton Scollard, 1914). Each of these three songs sold more than one million copies. Other famous songs include "The

Bells of Youth," "To You," "The Secret," "Fuzzy Wuzzy," "Morning," "The Lord Is My Light," "The Prayer Perfect," "The Message," "In May Time," "Star Eyes," and "When the Boys Come Home." "When the Boys Come Home," published in 1911, was especially popular during World War I.

Speaks was not terribly critical about his choice of texts, and his lyrics came from a wide variety of sources. He set texts by such esteemed authors as Kipling and Emily Dickinson ("Charity," 1911) as well as by friends such as his former pastor, Washington Gladden ("Oh, Master Let Me Walk with Thee," 1917). Other texts came from hymns ("Hark! Hark, My Soul," 1923), Civil War poetry ("When the Boys Come Home," 1911), and the Bible ("Thou Wilt Keep Him in Perfect Peace," 1913, and "In the End of the Sabbath," 1918).

Speaks composed at a quick pace, often at a single sitting. He would memorize the text he was to set, then improvise at the piano until he completed the song. It is this spontaneity of the compositional process that was transferred and captured in his songs and helped to give them their quintessential charm.

As a writer of popular songs, Speaks was concerned about composers' rights and in 1924 joined the American Society of Composers, Authors, and Publishers (ASCAP). He served as a member of its board of directors from 1924 until poor health caused him to resign in 1943.

Speaks never married and was by nature shy and retiring, though not reclusive. His niece, Margaret Speaks, was a singer on radio and on stage. During the 1950s she recorded a number of her uncle's songs for MGM. Speaks died in New York City.

• Speaks's papers are in the Oley Speaks Music Library, Canal Winchester. A complete list of his published songs is in the pamphlet *The Oley Speaks Music Library* (1949). A particularly significant assessment of Speaks's life and work is Stephanie Kay Tingler, "Oley Speaks and the Oley Speaks Music Library Archive: A Legacy of the Twentieth Century American Art Song" (D.M.A. diss., Ohio State Univ., 1993). Other sources include *Oley Speaks*, a volume in G. Schirmer's *Course in Contemporary Musical Biography* (1919); the interview by Nelson H. Budd in the *Columbus Sunday Dispatch*, 7 July 1940; and an article on Speaks in David Ewen, *Popular American Composers* (1962). Obituaries are in the *New York Times*, 28 Aug. 1948, and in the *Canal Winchester Times*, 2 Sept. 1948.

WILLIAM A. EVERETT

SPECK, Frank Gouldsmith (8 Nov. 1881–6 Feb. 1950), ethnologist, was born in Brooklyn, New York, the son of Frank Gouldsmith Speck, a merchant, and Hattie L. Staniford. Speck was a fragile child and his health was precarious. His parents decided it would be to his benefit to remove him from his city home to a more rural environment until his health improved. In 1888 Speck was placed in the care of family friend Fidelia Fielding in Mohegan, Connecticut. The relationship between Speck's family and Fielding has never been entirely clear. The Specks had descended from Dutch settlers and the Mahican peoples of the area, which may explain a historical connection between the two families.

Fielding was a traditional Native American widow and one of the last native speakers of any Native American language in New England. She lived an isolated life close to nature and harbored a great love of natural history. Speck's whole career may be viewed as an expansion of the interests and perceptions he developed as a young man living in the woods of Connecticut with Fielding. In these formative years Speck was tutored by Fielding not only in natural life and history but in Mohegan and English writings as well. She instilled in him a great love and respect for native knowledge and the natural world that would color his research and scholarship for decades to come.

When Speck was fourteen he returned to live with his family in Hackensack, New Jersey. He entered Columbia University with no specific plans, but a career in the ministry seemed a possibility. While at Columbia he enrolled in a language course with John Dyneley Prince. Prince, an eminent linguist, was astonished to discover that Speck was able to provide firsthand details of Native American languages generally thought to be dead, such as Pequot-Mohegan and surviving remnants of Delaware-Mohican. By the time Speck graduated the two had coauthored three articles. More importantly, Prince introduced Speck to Franz Boas, whose influence on American anthropology at the beginning of the twentieth century was just developing and whose students would provide the foundation for the study of Native American language and culture. Both Prince and Boas encouraged the young Speck to enter a career in anthropological linguistics. Speck's relationship with Boas influenced his anthropological outlook profoundly and, subsequently, his choice of profession. Under Boas, Speck eventually undertook fieldwork in Oklahoma and Indian Territory that evolved into publications on Yuchi, Creek, Chickasaw and Osage tribes.

In 1904 Speck graduated from Columbia University and received his M.A. in 1905. Also in 1904 he began ethnographic fieldwork with the Yuchi Indians in Oklahoma, a tribe whose language belonged to an isolated linguistic stock, and that was formerly resident on the Savannah River in Georgia. Speck left Columbia for the University of Pennsylvania in 1908, where he was offered a George Leib Harrison Research Fellowship at the University Museum. He obtained his Ph.D. from Penn in 1908; his Yuchi fieldwork and research evolved into his doctoral dissertation, "Ethnology of the Yuchi Indians." This dissertation was published as the first volume and number of the newly established *Publications in Anthropology* of the University Museum. His doctoral research was also the basis for an article on the Yuchi that later appeared in Frederick Webb Hodge's *Handbook of American Indians* (1910). What made this research even more significant was the recording of social and ceremonial music on wax cylinders, subsequently transcribed by Jacob Sapir. Few of these recordings have survived, as Speck frequently reused the cylinders after transcription. This collaboration was published as the second number of the museum series (1911).

Speck remained in Philadelphia, making his winter home in Swarthmore, Pennsylvania. In 1910 he married Florence Insley; they had three children. Florence Speck participated fully in much of Speck's fieldwork.

Speck's professional life was devoted to research and teaching. His relationship to the University of Pennsylvania continued throughout his professional career. When Speck first arrived at the university there was no separate department of anthropology. Anthropology courses were taught in the University Museum, or as a subdivision of the Department of Religion. Speck's research fellowship was attached to the University Museum. In 1908 Speck was appointed instructor and assistant in general ethnology. He taught, worked in the museum, and traveled to Native American communities at every opportunity. He began work with the Penobscot in 1907. In 1910 Speck traveled to Labrador. Many publications came out of this fieldwork, including a major monograph, *Naskapi: Savage Hunters of the Labrador Peninsula* (1935).

In 1911 Speck was fired from the University Museum due to a conflict with the director of the museum, George Byron Gordon. Gordon wanted Speck to focus less on field research and more on the public and social functions necessary for museum fundraising. Gordon confiscated Speck's manuscript on the Penobscot, which had been submitted for publication to the museum. This manuscript was not recovered for many years. It was reworked by Speck in 1936 and published in 1940 as *Penobscot Man; or, the Life History of a Forest Tribe in Maine*. This work, despite its long delay, is considered one of Speck's most significant monographs. It has been heralded in subsequent studies of folklore, art, political organization, wampum, and shamanism. The discussion on material culture is considered particularly valuable, especially the sections on canoes, snowshoes, and other means of transportation.

Speck was immediately rehired by the university after his confrontation with Gordon and appointed assistant professor, filling the place of Daniel Garrison Brinton, who had taught anthropology through the Department of Religion. In 1913 Speck was appointed acting chairman of the newly formed Department of Anthropology; he became chairman in 1925. He was a senior member of the department for the rest of his life. While Brinton's influence on the study of language and culture at the University of Pennsylvania cannot be underestimated, a true Department of Anthropology, separate from the University Museum, began with Speck.

Speck was involved in several professional associations. He was the founder of the Philadelphia Anthropological Society. He served the American Anthropological Association as associate editor of *American Anthropologist* for more than a decade and as vice president in 1945–1946. Speck was very interested in the developing field of folklore as well. In the early twentieth century in the United States, anthropology and folklore shared a focus on the language and culture of Native American groups. Speck was a past president of the American Folklore Society and there are numerous titles dealing with topics of folkloric interest in his bibliography, including considerable material in the form of collected texts—a primary concern and interest of folklorists at the time. In regard to Algonkian groups alone, Speck recorded myths and tales from the Penobscot, Wawenok, Abenaki, Malecite, Micmac, Mohegan, Delaware, Montagnais-Naskapi, Timiskaming, and Timagami tribes.

Speck was a great and persistent fieldworker from his childhood to the moment of his death. His commitment to the field and to his informants was total. As his colleague William Fenton said, "No academic appointment, no learned gathering, no university functions took precedence over the visit of an Indian colleague, the summons to an Indian council, or the call to attend a ceremony. . . . He went to the field often, his trips were of short duration because of teaching duties, and back at the university he kept up a steady stream of correspondence with native Indian informants, usually on post cards" (Blankenship, pp. 9–13). His constant involvement with the field and his informants generated a wealth of articles over his lifetime on all aspects of Native American culture and society. Speck maintained close contacts with so many native communities over the decades that, even after his death, the mention of his name and acquaintance by subsequent fieldworkers was often the only invitation necessary.

After Speck's first years in Philadelphia he began to focus his interest on the Algonkians of the Eastern Woodlands. Over the years he paid at least one visit, and often many more, to nearly all native Algonkian communities, regardless of their level of acculturation. In the 1920s he turned his attention to salvaging the ethnology of extant tidewater Algonkians of Delaware and Virginia. These were mixed-blood remnants of the Delaware, Nanticoke, and Powhaten tribes.

His work with the Cherokee in the Southeast provided the bridge that led Speck to study Iroquois ceremonialism during his final years. Although much was known about the Iroquois in general, little had been studied of the diversity and local cultures of the several groups that made up the Six Nations. In 1931 Speck began intensive work on the ceremonial cycle of the Cayuga, publishing *Cayuga Midwinter Rites* in 1949. By this time Speck also had a strong core of his own students who had taken up his interest in Iroquoian culture and to whom he had imparted his dedication to the study of these tribes. With his colleague William Fenton, Speck began the Iroquois Conferences in 1945. Speck's last conference was the third (1947), when he was adopted by the Seneca and received his native name, *Gahehdago:wa* (Great Porcupine).

Speck's work on the Tidewater tribes and his earlier work on New England Algonkian language and culture are indicative of his strong commitment to the study and recording of dying languages and cultures. Unlike many who studied native culture in the early twentieth century as the last throes and remnants of a dying society, Speck felt a responsibility to record whatever could be attained of the traditional cultural forms and to study the changes in these forms as they continued to evolve. He considered the field of ethnology to be inexhaustible, not a static study of past cultures. From his point of view, every stage of culture change presented new challenges to the field of anthropology and new areas of culture for study. His interests covered the spectrum from collection and evocation of dying languages and customs to the study of the most Americanized aspects of native life.

According to William Fenton, Speck's rapport with his informants was so effective that he "could awaken dying speech patterns, arouse latent customs, and recall ritual that was well nigh forgotten and known but as hearsay in the minds of his informants" (Blankenship, p. 13). Another of Speck's students, Loren Eiseley, also remarked on Speck's commitment to the study of all aspects of culture, including those left for dead by other ethnologists: "A later generation of ethnologists will have to rely in large part upon Frank's records. He found and recorded customs still extant that other workers had assumed were extinct. He lovingly gathered up the broken bits of Algonkian tongues from speakers upon whose lips they were dying. He recorded the last details of their material culture. He worked mostly alone, before the day of big foundation grants" (Eiseley, p. 96).

Also playing a role in Speck's success as an anthropologist and fieldworker was his love and in-depth knowledge of natural history. His concern with several diverse fields of natural history remained vital, and he published a number of articles, based on original observations, in specialized journals. His knowledge of the natural world became closely integrated with ethnology, producing a variety of studies linking these two interests and providing some of the earliest work in the area of ethnoscience. This knowledge of natural history enabled Speck to discuss properties of plants and habits of animals with Native Americans. He elicited specialized vocabulary and reached an understanding of native natural history in a way few ethnologists were prepared to do.

Speck also maintained a genuine love for collecting material objects from his fieldwork. He was primarily interested in the pieces' cultural contexts. He sold most items to public museums, where they frequently arrived heavily annotated as to their context within their culture group. Much of Speck's collecting was motivated by specific problems in which he became occasionally interested. An example of this is his interest in the characteristic use of birch bark by the northern Algonkians, particularly the techniques of constructing bark vessels and the art styles that appeared on them. He successfully identified the double-curve as a fundamental motif in Algonkian design.

Speck's last years were spent combating a failing heart and kidney disease. He became critically ill in the field at the Allegheny reservation in Red House, New York. He was at the reservation as both an observer and participant in the Great Annual Renewal ceremony of the Seneca, and as a patient of the tribe's medicine men for his failing health. Speck died soon after at University Hospital in Philadelphia.

Perhaps because of his solitary childhood spent in the bush with Fidelia Fielding or because of the traditions of his ancestors in the seafaring community of the Atlantic coast, Speck believed in living simply and was most comfortable in primitive conditions. He was fiercely democratic and identified strongly with Native Americans and their values. Speck was totally lacking in pretension and, in the tradition of natural history, was a strong empiricist, more interested in recording new information than in theory. According to Fenton, although Speck was not adept at or interested in theoretical formulation, as was Boas, "he had a highly developed sense of problem. . . . No one who talked with Speck for long could doubt the wide range of his mind, his willingness to speculate in conversation, and his openness to new ideas. For him there was no orthodoxy" (Blankenship, p. 18).

• Speck's surviving field notes are held at the American Philosophical Society in Philadelphia. Other materials are in the archives of the University of Pennsylvania. His photographic negative files are at the Heye Foundation, Museum of the American Indian, New York City. Musical and language recordings that survive are housed in the Archives of Folk Music, Indiana University. Speck's experimental cinema reels are at the University Museum. A bibliography by John Witthoft is in *American Anthropologist* 53 (1951): 75–87. Speck has been lovingly and thoroughly remembered in Roy Blankenship, ed., *The Life and Times of Frank G. Speck* (1991), and in Loren Eiseley's autobiography *All the Strange Hours* (1975). An obituary by A. Irving Hallowell is in *American Anthropologist* 53 (1951): 67–75.

RIDIE WILSON GHEZZI

SPEED, James (11 Mar. 1812–25 June 1887), U.S. attorney general, was born in Jefferson County, Kentucky, the son of John Speed and Lucy Gilmer Fry, wealthy planters. He graduated in 1828 from St. Joseph's College in Bardstown, Kentucky, worked as a clerk for the county court for two years, then studied law at Transylvania University in Lexington. In 1833 he began a law practice in Louisville. Speed's family connections, gentlemanly demeanor, superior education, and dedication to his clients soon made him a highly successful lawyer. In 1840 he married Jane Cochran, with whom he had seven children.

Speed's political career was complicated by his and his family's long opposition to slavery. He was no radical, however; surrounded by business associates and friends who supported the institution, he was a gradualist who expected emancipation to come slowly, possibly in conjunction with colonization of African Americans abroad. He did not advertise his views either. In 1844 he quietly opposed Texas annexation for fear that it would enlarge the market for Kentucky slaves. Elected to the state legislature as a Whig in

1847, he worked diligently on constituents' requests but considered the work largely unimportant. In 1849 he ran as a delegate to the state constitutional convention, but his opponent forced him to discuss openly his support for gradual emancipation, and he lost. He served as a Louisville alderman, 1851–1854, and taught law at the University of Louisville from 1856 to 1858 and again from 1872 to 1879.

Speed detested the xenophobic American (Know Nothing) party that replaced the Whigs in Kentucky in the mid-1850s. Although long a friend of Abraham Lincoln, whom he had met through his brother Joshua Fry, Speed understood that a Republican could not carry a slave state like Kentucky. In the presidential contest of 1860, therefore, he served on a committee that united supporters of northern Democrat Stephen A. Douglas and Constitutional Unionist John Bell to defeat southern Democrat John Breckinridge in Kentucky. After the election, however, confident of Speed's loyalty to the Union, however, Lincoln made him mustering officer for Kentucky under his call for 75,000 volunteers at the outbreak of the Civil War. Until July, Speed was also commander of the Louisville Home Guard, which was responsible for seeing that arms forwarded to Kentucky did not fall into the wrong hands. Advising Lincoln on Kentucky politics, Speed acted on behalf of the administration, moving quickly, for example, to reassure Kentuckians that Lincoln did not support General John C. Frémont's assertion of military control over slave emancipation. Elected to the state senate as a Unionist (1861–1863), he saw at last the opportunity to strike a death blow at slavery. He was an eager but lonely supporter of Lincoln's proposal to offer federal support to loyal states that freed their slaves. In 1864 he, almost alone in the slaveholding section of Kentucky, vigorously promoted the proposed Thirteenth Amendment to abolish slavery.

In December 1864 Lincoln appointed Speed attorney general to replace Edward Bates, a border-state moderate increasingly at odds with radical Republicans, who had resigned. Winning the approval of radicals like Salmon P. Chase and Charles Sumner, Speed oversaw prosecutions under the Confiscation Acts, which seized the property, including slaves, of those in rebellion. However, he phased the program out with the end of the war. Speed recommended the trial by military authorities of those arrested for Lincoln's assassination, noting the extraordinary nature of the crime and the exigencies of wartime. His decision that Jefferson Davis had to be tried in federal district court in Virginia because military authorities did not have jurisdiction in peacetime was one reason Davis was never tried for treason.

At first, Speed, impressed by the numbers of ex-Confederates requesting pardons, was optimistic about Reconstruction. By November 1865, however, the passage of southern Black Codes limiting the rights of former slaves convinced him that former Confederates and Republicans had radically different conceptions of how to promote peace. In Speed's view,

President Andrew Johnson's failure to signal that discrimination was unacceptable made the Justice Department's efforts to protect freedmen almost impossible. Speed favored the Fourteenth Amendment proposed by Congress to assure equal protection of the laws. Disturbed by Johnson's defiance of Congress, he refused to join the National Union movement being organized by the president to unite Democrats and conservative Republicans in opposition to congressional reconstruction and resigned his office in July 1866. In September he presided over the southern loyalists' convention in Philadelphia, which was intended to demonstrate southern support for a more energetic reconstruction. Returning to Kentucky, Speed urged Kentucky Republicans to endorse giving the vote to African Americans.

The threat of racial change greatly strengthened conservative Democrats in Kentucky. Speed's support for African Americans made him virtually unelectable although he received symbolic Republican nominations for the U.S. Senate in 1867 and for Congress in 1870. Speed served as an attorney for the Freedmen's Bureau in Kentucky, directed a petition campaign against the state's poll tax, and advised clients on opposing discriminatory state legislation, but he was rarely successful. He served as a delegate to the Republican national conventions of 1872 and 1876, serving on the resolutions committee. In 1884, however, he supported Democrat Grover Cleveland against the allegedly dishonest James G. Blaine.

In his last years Speed became unwillingly involved in a public controversy with Joseph Holt, the judge advocate general during the Civil War who wanted Speed to testify that Andrew Johnson had seen petitions for mercy for accused Lincoln conspirator Mary Surratt. This presumably would have absolved Holt from the responsibility for her execution. Speed, citing the confidentiality of cabinet discussions, refused the request although he publicly praised Holt for his actions at the time. To the end Speed clung to his own sense of what was right. His last remarks on the controversy were published shortly after his death in Louisville.

• A few of Speed's letters may be found in collections of his correspondents, including Charles Sumner (Harvard University Library), Joseph Holt (Library of Congress), and Joseph Daveiss (Filson Club, Louisville). James Speed, *James Speed, a Personality* (1914), written by a grandson, is a biography. It reprints numerous letters and diary entries. See also *History of the Ohio Falls Cities and Their Counties* (1882) and *The Kentucky Encyclopedia*, ed. John E. Kleber (1992). An obituary is in the *New York Times*, 26 June 1887.

PHYLLIS F. FIELD

SPEER, Emory (3 Sept. 1848–13 Dec. 1918), jurist and congressman, was born in Culloden, Georgia, the son of the Reverend Eustace Willoughby Speer, an itinerant Methodist minister, and Anne King, the daughter of an Alabama clergyman. Named after a prominent Methodist bishop of Georgia, at age fifteen young Emory Speer ran off to join the Confederate cavalry and attached himself to Brigadier General J. H. Lewis's Kentucky brigade of mounted infantry. He saw his only military action in a vain attempt by Confederates to repel General William T. Sherman's march at Griswoldville, north of Macon, and remained with his unit until its dissolution at the war's end. Speer then enrolled in the University of Georgia, where he took an active part in the oratorical and debating club and graduated in 1869.

Under the tutelage of U.S. senator Benjamin H. Hill, Speer pursued a career in law and politics. After reading law with Hill, in 1870 Speer gained admission to the bar and set up a practice in Athens, Georgia. Over the next few years he became political editor of a local newspaper, helped organize a Democratic club that overthrew Republican control of the Athens city government, and served a brief term as state solicitor general. In 1877 Speer ran for Congress, but because his campaign failed to receive the backing of the Democratic party leadership, he ran as an Independent Democrat. He lost the race but ran again as an Independent the following year and won. In the process, however, Speer alienated the state's Democratic leaders, including his patron, Senator Hill, who actively campaigned against him. During this period of Democratic rule in the South, those who challenged the party's leadership did so at their own peril, and eventually Speer paid dearly for this decision.

Once in Washington, the Independent congressman warmed up to the Republican leadership, and by 1881 his persistent political maneuvering gained him important committee positions. When he ran for reelection in 1882, Speer received generous support from his district's Republican party. His open partisan leanings cost him the election, as Democrats successfully charged him with betraying his southern heritage and his race. Yet Speer made a number of friends within the ranks of his new party, and President Chester Arthur in 1883 appointed him U.S. attorney for the Northern District of Georgia. Speer continued to draw controversy in his new position. He succeeded in convincing a Georgia jury to convict nine Ku Klux Klansmen charged with interfering with the voting rights of African Americans, and the case was eventually appealed to the U.S. Supreme Court, where the justices upheld the conviction.

Speer emerged as a key figure in Republican circles and frequently advised the president on patronage decisions. When the federal judgeship for the Southern District of Georgia came open late in 1883, Speer recommended Henry P. Farrow, a former U.S. attorney and state Republican leader. President Arthur hesitated to appoint Farrow though, and when Speer himself expressed interest in the position, the president appointed him instead. Speer's nomination infuriated nearly every political leader in the state, including Republicans, who believed Farrow had been cheated out of the appointment, and southern Georgians, who viewed Speer, a northern Georgian, as an outsider. Still, after extensive debate, he won Senate confirmation in a close vote.

As a federal judge for the next thirty-three years, Speer steered a moderate course when it came to issues of economic regulation and antitrust. On the one hand he espoused the virtues of capitalistic economic development, and in cases like *Brewer v. Central of Georgia Railway* (1898) and *Central of Georgia Railway v. Macon* (1901) he refused to grant injunctions that would have hindered the expansion of railroads. On the other hand Speer desired to maintain a competitive economic environment and to preserve the public interest; thus, he broadly construed the Sherman Antitrust Act to apply to any restraints of trade, not just those deemed "unreasonable."

Speer's record on racial and civil rights issues was more controversial, as he actively sought to uphold the basic constitutional guarantees of African Americans. Most notably, in a series of peonage cases Speer pursued convictions with such zeal that some accused him of assuming the role of prosecutor. In *United States v. McClellan* (1904), for example, he stoutly defended the federal government's power to abolish peonage under both the Thirteenth Amendment's prohibition on involuntary servitude and a vaguely applicable 1867 statute. Nevertheless, Speer was no racial equalitarian; he firmly upheld the constitutionality of Georgia's antimiscegenation statute and frequently stated that only the "better elements" among the black population possessed a chance for social elevation. However paternalistic by modern standards, Speer's willingness to uphold the most fundamental civil rights of African Americans earned him the respect of black leaders and alienated him further from most white Georgians.

Over the course of his career, Speer made a number of enemies, but it was his decision to oppose President William H. Taft's 1912 reelection that proved the most disastrous. Largely for political reasons, the Department of Justice began to examine Speer's judicial conduct, and in August 1913 the House of Representatives authorized a subcommittee of the Judiciary Committee to conduct a formal investigation. Critics charged him with habitually misusing and exceeding his power as a judge. In 1914 the subcommittee held hearings in Macon and Savannah on the subject, but the inconclusive nature of most of the testimony, coupled with the Woodrow Wilson administration's unwillingness to push for impeachment, led to Speer's vindication. He remained on the bench, but the following year his opponents did succeed in dividing the Southern District of Georgia in two, thus cutting Speer's domain in half. Four years after the hearings he died in Macon, where he had lived since 1887. Speer was twice married—first in 1869 to Sallie Dearing, with whom he had five daughters before her death in 1879, and then in 1881 to Eleanora D. Morgan, with whom he had three children.

For more than three decades, Speer was a key figure in American politics and law. A frequent lecturer around the country, he served as dean of the Mercer University Law School from 1893 until his death and published several works, including *Removal of Causes from State to United States Courts* (1888), *Lectures on the Constitution of the United States* (1897), and *Lincoln, Lee, Grant, and Other Biographical Addresses* (1909).

A persistent theme throughout Speer's speeches and writings was his desire for the nation to heal the wounds of the Civil War and Reconstruction, and to a great extent he witnessed this development during his lifetime. A self-proclaimed disciple of Alexander Hamilton (1755–1804), Speer generally supported a strong federal government and viewed national loyalty as more important than regional ties or party affiliation. Unfortunately for him, Speer's unorthodox views, combined with his overbearing nature, often did not sit well with his fellow Georgians and made him one of the most controversial public figures of his day.

• No collection of Speer's papers exists, but letters from him do appear in the Henry Patillo Farrow Papers (Hargrett Rare Books and Manuscripts Library, University of Georgia), the Chester A. Arthur Papers, the Theodore Roosevelt Papers, and the William H. Taft Papers (all at the Library of Congress and available on microfilm). The University of Georgia Library contains most of Speer's speeches, while the Department of Justice files in the National Archives (Washington, D.C.) provide insightful information about Speer's dealings with peonage. His judicial decisions can be found throughout the *Federal Reporter* from 1884 to 1918. See also *Hearings before a Subcommittee of the Committee on the Judiciary, House of Representatives, Sixty-third Congress, on Conduct of Emory Speer . . .* , serial 19 (1914).

The most comprehensive and well-researched biographical treatment of Speer, with an extensive bibliography, is Mary Ann Hawkins, "He Drew the Lightning: Emory Speer, Federal Judge in Georgia, 1885–1918" (M.A. thesis, Georgia State Univ., 1984). See also Orville A. Park, "Judge Emory Speer, Biographical Sketch," *Report of the Thirty-sixth Annual Session of the Georgia Bar Association*, 1919, pp. 101–120. An obituary is in the *Atlanta Constitution*, 14 Dec. 1918.

TIMOTHY S. HUEBNER

SPEER, Robert Elliott (10 Sept. 1867–23 Nov. 1947), foreign missionary executive and ecumenical and Presbyterian leader, was born in Huntingdon, Pennsylvania, the second son of Robert Milton Speer and Martha Ellen McMurtrie. His father was a prominent lawyer, leader of the local Democratic party, and a two-term member of Congress (1871–1875), and Speer grew up as part of the social and economic elite of his community. He was raised in the Presbyterian tradition. He attended local schools; attended Phillips Academy, Andover, Massachusetts; and received a B.A. from the College of New Jersey (now Princeton University) in 1889.

He entered college determined to follow his father into the law, but representatives of the newly formed Student Volunteer Movement (SVM) helped him decide to become a missionary. He attended the Student Conference held by Dwight L. Moody at Northfield, Massachusetts, in 1887 and came under Moody's spell. He understood his new life direction to be a call of God and never wavered from it. He spent a year as traveling secretary of the SVM and enlisted over 1,100 students for Christian missions. He entered Princeton Theological Seminary in the fall of 1890 to prepare for ministry as a missionary. In the fall of Speer's second year Frank F. Ellinwood of the Board of Foreign Missions of the Presbyterian Church in the United States of America persuaded him to leave seminary and join the board as a missionary executive. He never returned to seminary and remained with the board for forty-six years, eventually becoming senior secretary and retiring in 1937.

He married Emma Doll Bailey in 1893; they had five children. Emma Bailey Speer volunteered with the YWCA American Committee for many years, and in 1915 she succeeded Grace Dodge as president of the National Board, a position she held until 1932.

Speer was a highly successful missionary executive, the most visible and forceful advocate for foreign missions in his generation. He teamed with Arthur J. Brown and made the Presbyterian board not only one of the largest denominational ones but also a model for others in its policies and procedures. In his administrative role he was a recruiter and counselor, a world traveler, and an effective interpreter and defender of foreign missions. He was a persuasive speaker; generations of students at SVM and Christian association summer conferences heard his appeal for missions, and so many responded that he was recognized as the greatest missionary recruiter of his day. He visited missionaries frequently, initially on a world trip in 1896–1897. The trips excited interests in missionary theory, and he subsequently published two important theoretical works: *Missionary Principles and Practice* (1902) and *Christianity and the Nations* (1910). He also encountered the non-Christian religions on their home grounds, and although he acknowledged their values in their cultural contexts, he became a widely recognized advocate for the absoluteness of Christianity. He challenged the religious syncretism proposed by the laymen's report, *Re-Thinking Missions* (1933). This report made the point that there was religious truth in all of the world's major religions, including Christianity, and suggested that there were many ways to reach that truth and that Christianity should become part of an evolving world religion. Speer's view, which he published in *The Finality of Jesus Christ* (1933), was that there was indeed truth to be found in all religions but that Christianity presented the final and ultimate truth, which encompassed and reached beyond that contained in other religions.

Speer eagerly participated in efforts to achieve greater Christian unity. He was a founding member of the Foreign Missions Conference of North America, a keynote speaker at the World Missionary Conference at Edinburgh in 1910, and one of the authors of the Jerusalem Message, issued by the International Missionary Council in 1928. This message was quickly recognized as one of the great missionary messages. It declared that Jesus Christ was "the final yet unfolding revelation of the God in whom we live and move and have our being," and also said to non-Christians, "We welcome every noble quality in non-Christian persons or systems as further proof that the Father, who sent his Son into the world, has nowhere left Himself without witness." He was the central figure in the effort to extend evangelical (Protestant) missions in Latin America and was chairman of the Committee on Co-operation in Latin America (1916–1936). He worked with the Federal Council of Churches from its earliest days, first as chairman of its Commission on Foreign Missions (1912–1916), then as chairman of the General War-Time Commission of the Churches (1917–1919), and finally as president (1920–1924). During his presidency he took the lead in raising the issue of racial justice and launched a Commission on the Church and Race Relations. This was the most visible form of his strong social gospel interests.

His own church called on Speer in matters other than foreign missions many times and elected him moderator in 1927. He was an early advocate of the full admission of women to the Presbyterian ministry. He was involved in several theological controversies in his church, including a major one with J. Gresham Machen in 1933 over the work of the Board of Foreign Missions. Machen took a fundamentalist position and charged that the board, and Speer as its leader, failed to represent the orthodox Christian message. The General Assembly of the Presbyterian Church supported Speer and the board. Machen withdrew and formed an Independent Board for Presbyterian Foreign Missions but failed to move the church his way. Speer emerged as the one person above all others who held his church together and to its traditional course during the fundamentalist era. He served as president of the Board of Trustees of Princeton Theological Seminary from 1937 until his death. The seminary library is named for him.

Speer wrote extensively on missionary, historical, and biblical topics, including twelve books about Jesus Christ. His aim was to challenge his readers to live the Christian faith. Although he wrote on theological topics, he did not associate himself with any particular theological group and considered himself to be simply an evangelical Christian. In all, he wrote more than seventy books and well over 1,000 articles. He preached regularly, and despite his status as a layman, he was widely hailed as one of the great preachers of his day. He spent his retirement speaking and writing and produced the popular devotional guide, *Five Minutes a Day* (1943). He died at Bryn Mawr, Pennsylvania.

• The Speer papers are in the Speer Library, Princeton Theological Seminary. The Speer family papers are in the Bryn Mawr College library. See also the papers of the Board of Foreign Missions, housed in the Presbyterian Historical Society, Philadelphia, Pa. Important other works not already cited include *Studies of the Man Christ Jesus* (1896), *Remember Jesus Christ* (1899), *Missions and Modern History* (2 vols., 1904), *The Christian Man, the Church, and the War* (1918), *The Unfinished Task of Foreign Missions* (1926), and *"Re-Thinking Missions" Examined* (1933). For biographical and interpretive material see: W. Reginald Wheeler, *A Man Sent from God: A Biography of Robert E. Speer* (1956); Bradley J.

Longfield, *The Presbyterian Controversy* (1991); essays in the *Princeton Seminary Bulletin* 42, no. 1 (Summer 1948); James A. Patterson, "Robert E. Speer and the Crisis of the American Protestant Missionary Movement, 1920–1937" (Ph.D. diss., Princeton Theological Seminary, 1980); Charles E. Harvey, "Speer Versus Rockefeller and Mott, 1910–1935," *Journal of Presbyterian History* 60, no. 4 (Winter 1982): 283–99; John F. Piper, Jr., *The American Churches in World War I* (1985); Piper, "Robert E. Speer on Christianity and Race," *Journal of Presbyterian History* 61, no. 2 (Summer 1983): 227–47; and Leon G. Rosenthal, "Christian Statesmanship in the First Missionary-Ecumenical Generation" (Ph.D. diss., Univ. of Chicago, 1989). An obituary is in the *New York Times*, 25 Nov. 1947.

JOHN F. PIPER, JR.

SPELLMAN, Francis Joseph (4 May 1889–2 Dec. 1967), Roman Catholic prelate, was born in Whitman, Massachusetts, the son of William Spellman, a grocer, and Ellen Conway, both the children of Irish immigrants. After attending public schools in Whitman, Spellman graduated from Fordham College in New York in 1911. He then entered the seminary for the Archdiocese of Boston and was sent to the North American College in Rome, where he studied at the Urban College of Propaganda. He received a doctorate in theology and was ordained a priest on 14 May 1916. At that time, the American hierarchy was becoming increasingly Romanized, and for an ambitious American student, study at the Urban College could be a stepping stone for ecclesiastical preferment because the professors there were predominantly Italian diocesan priests destined for service in the curia. Spellman wisely cultivated his professors, most notably Francesco Borgongini-Duca.

After he returned to Boston, Spellman was assigned by the archbishop, Cardinal William Henry O'Connell, first to pastoral work (1916–1918) and then to the staff of *The Pilot*, the diocesan newspaper, where he held a minor position. He was frequently at odds with the cardinal and the cardinal's nephew, Monsignor James P. E. O'Connell, the chancellor. (Secretly married, Monsignor O'Connell was ordered dismissed from the priesthood late in 1921.) In 1922 Spellman was assigned to the chancery staff and, in 1924, was named archivist of the archdiocese and given a part-time staff position on *The Pilot*. These were less than illustrious posts, but Spellman was undaunted. His English translations of two books by Borgongini-Duca greatly pleased Archbishop Giovanni Bonzano, the apostolic delegate to the U.S. hierarchy, and led Borgongini-Duca to recommend that Spellman be named a monsignor. O'Connell flatly rejected the recommendation, saying that his lowly status hardly warranted such consideration. This led him to seek advancement in the church hierarchy by enlisting the support of his connections in Rome.

In 1925 Spellman went with a group of Boston Catholics to Rome, where, in September, he was named director of the Knights of Columbus playgrounds in Rome and was also appointed an official of the congregation for the Extraordinary Affairs of the Church under the Vatican Secretariat of State—he was the first American to hold a curial position. During this stay in Rome Spellman made several valuable connections, both within the church and without, and he was also called upon to help the church publicize its stand against fascism. In 1931 Pius XI issued his condemnation of fascism in *Non Abbiamo Bisogno*. Because the church press had been suppressed by the fascist government, Eugenio Pacelli, one of Spellman's new friends who recently had become papal secretary of state, entrusted the letter to Spellman, who smuggled it to Paris where it was printed and distributed by the Associated Press and United Press.

In 1932 Spellman was named auxiliary bishop of Boston. He was consecrated on 8 September in St. Peter's Basilica by Cardinal Pacelli, assisted by Borgongini-Duca and Giuseppe Pizzardo. The consecration ceremony and the appointment were fraught with symbolic significance. Pius XI himself had given Spellman his motto, "Sequere Deum [to follow God]." The coat of arms that Borgongini-Duca had designed for him incorporated Columbus's ship the *Santa Maria*. Spellman wore the vestments that Pacelli had worn when he was consecrated by Benedict XV. Spellman thus symbolized a fusion of the Roman and American branches of the church.

Spellman's appointment to Boston was ironic. In 1905, though his name had not been on any canonical lists, O'Connell was named coadjutor archbishop of Boston. He owed his rise to his close friendship with Cardinal Raffaele Merry del Val, Pius X's secretary of state. Now he was receiving an auxiliary bishop, despite the fact that he had not asked for one, and to make matters worse, it was Spellman, whom he was not considering to be his successor. Before Spellman left Rome, moreover, Pius XI had assured the new bishop that he probably would succeed O'Connell.

Whether O'Connell suspected that Spellman had played a role in his nephew's dismissal or had heard of the pope's intention to name him coadjutor archbishop with right of succession or simply disliked his assistant, Spellman's seven years as auxiliary bishop in Boston were characterized by almost constant strain between him and the cardinal. O'Connell diminished the importance of his auxiliary in several ways, some of them petty. For one, O'Connell assigned Spellman to a parish in Newton Center, which was deemed less desirable than the one Spellman had requested, and he stressed that Spellman served only at his pleasure. Less ominously, the cardinal also frequently refused to publish Spellman's schedule for confirmations. The two were also at odds on several nonchurch issues. While Spellman was in the process of helping to draft a constitutional amendment to prohibit child labor, O'Connell publicly opposed it. Meanwhile, in contrast to the cardinal, who frequently was at odds with politician James Michael Curley, Spellman counted the mayor and sometime governor among his friends. The tension between Spellman and O'Connell was well known among the other U.S. bishops, but Spellman maintained a public silence. To his diary he once confided that the "Cardinal spoke to us and his most striking phrase was that even if a Bishop bought a bishopric he is still a bishop. And he might have added the same truth applies to a Cardinal." In this period he cultivated his Roman connections and built new American friendships, especially with Joseph P. Kennedy, through whom he came to know James Roosevelt and later his father, President Franklin D. Roosevelt. These associations would eventually enable Spellman to escape from Boston.

One of the key events of Spellman's tenure as auxiliary bishop was the visit of Cardinal Pacelli to the United States in the fall of 1936. Spellman hosted the cardinal at Newton Center and later accompanied him on his tour of the United States. The stated purpose of the trip was personal; he was to be the guest of Genevieve Brady, the wealthy widow of Nicholas Brady, friends of Spellman's since his years in Rome. The secret purpose was to meet with President Roosevelt to discuss the possibility of establishing formal diplomatic relations between the United States and the Holy See. Spellman was present at the meeting, which he arranged to take place at the president's boyhood home at Hyde Park, New York, on 5 November 1936, two days after his reelection to a second term.

After the death of Cardinal Patrick Hayes of New York on 4 September 1938, Spellman was not among those situated to be his replacement. Fate intervened, however, when, in the interim, Pius XI died. O'Connell, having missed the conclaves of 1914 and 1922, made certain that he arrived in Rome in time to participate in the 1939 conclave that elected Pacelli as Pius XII. Many other American prelates owed their advancements to their patrons in Rome, but Spellman now had the most powerful ally of them all, and on 15 April 1939 he was appointed archbishop of New York, the nation's principal diocese. His administrative abilities were immediately tested. During Pacelli's visit in 1936, Spellman had antagonized several members of the New York archdiocesan staff, and O'Connell and Archbishop Amleto Cicognani, the apostolic delegate, both urged him to make changes in the chancery office. Soon after Spellman's appointment, Monsignor James Francis McIntyre, the chancellor of New York, visited him in Newton Center and offered to resign. Spellman refused and subsequently built a strong relationship with McIntyre, naming him his auxiliary bishop in 1940 and his coadjutor in 1946.

Spellman was officially installed as archbishop on 23 May 1939 and directly set about to accomplish ten tasks assigned to him. Some pertained to financial matters involving the archdiocese and other institutions. Others were pastoral, an area in which Spellman was able to show great sensitivity, as for example when, after he paid a personal visit, he gained the restoration to the active ministry of Bishop Bonaventure Broderick, who had resigned as auxiliary bishop of Havana in 1905 under accusations of financial mismanagement and was then operating a gasoline station in the Archdiocese of New York. By May 1941 Spellman was able to report to Pius XII that he had accomplished all of the tasks assigned to him.

Of all his initial tasks, the one of greatest import was working to establish some type of diplomatic relationship between the United States and the Holy See. Spellman had been pursuing such a connection through private channels since 1935, but it now seemed especially necessary given the inevitability of war in Europe. Roosevelt had given an indication of potential support for the idea by sending Joseph Kennedy, then ambassador to the Court of St. James, to represent him at Pius XII's coronation. At home, the president presumably would have preferred to negotiate with the pope through his friend Cardinal George Mundelein of Chicago, but this avenue was closed to him with the cardinal's unexpected death on 2 October 1939, just weeks after war in Europe had begun. Spellman was now the American prelate with whom Roosevelt would have to deal, and the archbishop lost no time in seizing the initiative. On Christmas Eve, at Spellman's urging, Roosevelt named Myron C. Taylor as his personal representative to Pius XII, a pragmatic alternative to establishing formal diplomatic relations.

The Taylor appointment was one of Spellman's many successes with Roosevelt. That same month he was named vicar for U.S. armed forces and concomitantly had Father John O'Hara, C.S.C., president of the University of Notre Dame, appointed as his auxiliary bishop for the vicariate. As both archbishop of New York and military vicar Spellman became internationally as well as nationally respected, and he used his emerging renown to further ingratiate himself with the president. For example, he engaged in a bit of shuttle diplomacy between Roosevelt and Archbishop Samuel Stritch, Mundelein's successor in Chicago, and thus alleviated fears the president had had about the new archbishop.

Although both sets of grandparents had been Irish immigrants, Spellman always thought of himself as wholly American, an identification that became especially pronounced following U.S. entry into World War II. As the energetic mobilizer of the Catholic war effort, Spellman came to embody the image of the American Catholic as patriot. Indeed, his 1944 poem, *The Risen Soldier*, essentially linked the Allied war effort with redemption. But Spellman did far more than write patriotic poems. In February 1943, one month after the Casablanca Conference, he began a prolonged visit to U.S. troops—having first met with Roosevelt and received his full approval. Before his departure he received a request from Pope Pius XII that he come to Rome, and for this phase of the trip also he obtained the president's authorization. The tour's purpose was actually diplomatic as well as pastoral. In Spain he met with General Francisco Franco to relay U.S. assurances that its alliance with the Soviet Union was circumstantial and in no way a reflection of American sympathy with communism. Spellman then flew to Rome. During his ten-day visit there he met with Pius XII on several occasions, most likely to discuss efforts to negotiate a separate Italian surren-

der, though Spellman never revealed the precise nature of their conversations. From Rome he traveled to North Africa and afterward flew to London, where he attended the funeral of Cardinal Arthur Hinsley, archbishop of Westminster. While in London he met with Winston Churchill, and later, in Egypt, he gained the release of Italian priests and religious who had been interned there by the British. Then, on 14 May in Istanbul, he met for the first time Archbishop Angelo Roncalli, who was then the apostolic delegate to Turkey but who would later become Pope John XXIII. After Rome was bombed on 19 July, Spellman flew back to the United States to negotiate to have Rome declared an open city. In June 1944, after the liberation of Rome, he returned to see the pope and to advise him on American ecclesiastical matters, among which was the naming of Richard J. Cushing as successor to O'Connell, who had died earlier that year. While Spellman was in Rome, the pope offered him the position of papal secretary of state, which Spellman declined. Then, in 1946, Pius XII named him a cardinal.

Although Cardinal Spellman was generally thought to be the most powerful American prelate, his influence in the administration of national church bodies and the appointment of bishops was in fact limited, in particular by Archbishop Edward Mooney of Detroit and Archbishop Stritch of Chicago, both of whom were named cardinals at the same time as Spellman, as well as by Archbishop John T. McNicholas of Cincinnati. Outside the eastern United States, where he was the dominant force—securing such key appointments as Patrick J. O'Boyle as archbishop of Washington, D.C. (1947) and O'Hara as archbishop of Philadelphia (1950)—and once on the West Coast, where he obtained the appointment of McIntyre as archbishop of Los Angeles—Spellman had very little success in effecting appointments and affecting policy. Thus, despite the perception, he was not the sole force within the American church hierarchy.

As the century progressed Spellman, like other theological conservatives, became an outspoken and dogged opponent of communism—going so far as to have seminarians dig graves in Catholic cemeteries in New York after six weeks of a strike by union grave diggers affiliated with the Congress of Industrial Organizations. Spellman had accused the CIO leadership of having communist connections. The cardinal held firm, and the 1949 strike was resolved only after the grave diggers voted to sever their ties with the CIO and became affiliated instead with the American Federation of Labor (AFL). So unwavering was Spellman in his opposition to communism that he embraced the questionable political tactics of Wisconsin senator Joseph R. McCarthy.

After Roosevelt's death, Spellman continued to work for the establishment of full diplomatic relations between the United States and the Holy See, but his political clout was greatly diminished, and this would affect his relations with the Vatican as well as the White House. In 1950, after Myron Taylor resigned as the president's personal representative to the pope,

President Harry Truman did not submit a nomination for his replacement. Then, after Truman nominated General Mark Clark as ambassador to the Vatican in the fall of 1951 congressional opposition to the appointment grew so strong and the confirmation so controversial that in 1953 Spellman reported to Pius XII that the Senate would not confirm Clark or any other nominee, whereupon Giovanni Battista Montini, the pope's substitute secretary of state and (later Pope Paul VI), questioned whether American Catholics were doing their best to defend the Holy See against attacks being leveled against it by influential Americans. Later, when Catholic presidential candidate John F. Kennedy said he opposed the establishment of diplomatic relations with the Vatican because public opposition to the post would undermine any effectiveness that the ambassador might have, Spellman reacted strongly to the perceived betrayal by the son of his old friend Joseph Kennedy.

Spellman's influence with Roosevelt did not extend to his widow any more than it did to his successor. Responding to a series of articles that Eleanor Roosevelt wrote in 1949 in support of a bill being considered by the House of Representatives that would prohibit federal aid to parochial schools, the cardinal publicly charged the former first lady with anti-Catholic bias. Undeterred by controversy, Spellman, like prelates in the early part of the century, tried to put a check on American popular culture. In the late 1950s, for example, he called for Catholic boycotts of several motion pictures—in particular, *Baby Doll* (1956). It is possible that the resulting publicity influenced studio executives, but no doubt it also increased the popularity of the films he did not want people to see.

Spellman was a theological conservative at a time when the Catholic church was about to embark on theological and administrative changes that would put it at the forefront of progressive religious reform. Initially Spellman held back, as, for example, when Jesuit theologian John Courtney Murray began to speak out in favor of the separation of church and state and religious liberty. However, after Pius XII died in 1958 and was replaced by John XXIII, the new pope's new apostolic delegate, Archbishop Egidio Vagnozzi, soon began to meddle in the domestic affairs of the American bishops. This caused Spellman—suddenly the senior cardinal following the deaths that same year of Stritch and Mooney—to stand up to Vagnozzi. In the process, he become an agent for progressivism.

In 1961, after Vagnozzi criticized the use of higher criticism by some Catholic scholars, Spellman came to their defense. When the Second Vatican Council opened the following year, Spellman was elected one of the ten presidents. When he learned that Murray had been excluded from participation in the council by Vagnozzi and other Roman officials, he had the Jesuit named an official theologian in 1963. During the council's four sessions, Spellman made more interventions than any other American prelate. He also used his influence to make sure that the issue of religious liberty was addressed, when there was danger it might be omitted, and on 8 December 1965 the council issued its official declaration on religious liberty.

Spellman was not progressive, however, on the issue of American involvement in Vietnam, and his support for the war in light of growing opposition to it elicited criticism from many quarters, including the Vatican. In his 1965 address before the United Nations—the first ever by a pontiff—Pope Paul VI called for an end to war for all time. A few months later, making his traditional Christmas visit to U.S. troops, Spellman traveled to Vietnam. Upon his arrival, the insistent anticommunist and patriot uttered what would become, with slight modification, a slogan of support for the unpopular war: "My country right or wrong."

Cardinal Spellman died in New York City and was buried at St. Patrick's Cathedral. The most powerful American Catholic churchman in his day, he was a reflection of his time. A theological and political conservative, he nonetheless recognized the need for progress. Despite his exalted position in the American church hierarchy, he was an earnest defender of religious liberty, and he protected those under him from unwarranted attacks lodged by those above him. Spellman perhaps more than any other prelate of his era was able to bring Catholicism into prominence for the first time in U.S. history.

• Spellman's papers are in the Archives of the Archdiocese of New York at St. Joseph's Seminary, Dunwoodie, N.Y. The collection consists of his correspondence, his diary (a cursory account of events, which he kept up to 1948), and newspaper clippings. In addition to his bestselling novel, *The Foundling* (1951), Spellman wrote *The Road to Victory* (1942), *Risen Soldier* (1943), *Action This Day* (1943), *No Greater Love* (1945), *Prayers and Poems* (1946), *Heavenly Father of Children* (1947), *Cardinal Spellman's Prayerbook* (1952), and *What America Means to Me and Other Poems and Prayers* (1953). On his life and work, see Robert I. Gannon, S.J., *The Cardinal Spellman Story* (1962), an authorized study that is surprisingly honest, especially in regard to Spellman's relationship with O'Connell; Gerald P. Fogarty, S.J., *The Vatican and the American Hierarchy from 1870 to 1965* (1982), which concentrates on his role in national and international affairs; and John Cooney, *The American Pope* (1984), a highly negative evaluation that is based on interviews with many people who were close to Spellman. An obituary is in the *New York Times*, 3 Dec. 1967.

GERALD P. FOGARTY

SPENCE, Brent (24 Dec. 1874–18 Sept. 1967), U.S. congressman, was born in Newport, Kentucky, the son of Philip Spence, a commission merchant, Confederate army colonel, and postmaster, and Virginia Berry. He attended the University of Cincinnati, graduated from their law school in 1895, and was admitted to the Kentucky bar. Active in local and state politics, he served in the state senate from 1904 to 1908. He then served as vice president of a bank in Covington and as solicitor for Newport from 1916 to 1924. He married Ida Billerman in 1919; they had no children.

After being defeated for the Democratic nomination to the House of Representatives in 1926, Spence ran for Congress two years later but lost in the Republican landslide of 1928. Elected on the Democratic ticket to the Seventy-second Congress in 1930, he was reelected in 1932 as representative-at-large and in 1934 represented the newly created Fifth Congressional District of Kentucky. His district was primarily urban but had some agrarian areas. Spence was reelected to Congress thirteen consecutive times before his retirement in 1963. At that time he was one of the oldest members to ever serve in the House and had the longest congressional career of any Kentuckian. As a result of his poor speaking voice and eyesight, Spence was often underestimated by his colleagues, who judged him harshly because he had difficulty expressing his point of view. He was chairman of the powerful House Banking Committee from 1943 to 1963, except when the Republicans controlled Congress from 1947 to 1949 and from 1953 to 1955.

A quiet, gentle man, Spence was a strong supporter of the New Deal and the Fair Deal domestic policies, voting for such legislation as the Agricultural Adjustment Act (1933), National Industrial Recovery Act (1933), Social Security Act (1935), and authorization of the Reconstruction Finance Corporation (1933). In 1944 he was selected to attend the Bretton Woods Conference held at Bretton Woods, New Hampshire. Some thirty-three nations, including all of the major powers, attended this conference, which established the International Monetary Fund and the International Bank for Reconstruction and Development. The bank would provide stability in trade and loans to countries trying to recover from the war, while the fund facilitated world trade equitably. Throughout his congressional career Spence was an internationalist in foreign policy, voting for Lend-Lease (1941), the Bretton Woods Proposal (1944), the British Loan (1946), the Marshall Plan (1947), the Greek Turkish Aid Bill (1947), the Export Control Act (1949), the Defense Production Act (1950), and numerous other important pieces of foreign legislation. He supported the Truman Doctrine (1947) and the creation of the North Atlantic Treaty Organization (1949), and approved sending troops to Korea (1950). During the Korean War, he successfully pushed through the House a bill to freeze prices and wages.

Although his hearing and eyesight got progressively worse during the 1940s, Spence provided strong but impartial leadership on the Banking and Currency Committee. Because he was a poor speaker, he let others do the debating but provided the necessary skills to get crucial legislation passed. A former banker, Spence supported legislation that chartered the Export Import Bank and the Federal Deposit Insurance Act, which doubled insured savings from $5,000 to $10,000. While chairman of the Banking and Currency Committee, he opposed bank-holding companies and recommended that banks abandon real estate, insurance, and all nonbanking functions. A strong champion of locally owned banks, he successfully sponsored the Spence Robertson Holding Company Act of 1956 (the 1956 Banking Holding Company Act), which prevented great corporations from crossing state lines and buying local banks. Later he steered through Congress the Saving and Loan Holding Company Act (1959) and the Area Redevelopment Act (1961). Having established the Small Business Administration, Spence's committee provided legislation that made the agency permanent.

In addition to banking, Spence was interested in housing. He sponsored and successfully led the fight for passage of the Housing Act of 1949, which provided for construction of more than one million units of low-rent housing, as well as loans and grants to local communities to aid in slum clearance. In 1950 he led the fight for the passage of the administration's Rent Control Bill, and after its passage he served on the joint committee that reconciled the differences between House and Senate bills. Because of housing shortages and the Korean War, this bill was necessary to keep rents under control. Spence amended the Federal Housing Administration's regulations to insure mortgages on apartment houses in order to encourage permanent tenants. Mortgages "should be for permanent housing, not transient: anything else would be a prostitution of housing legislation," he said. Using all of his parliamentary skills, Spence blocked Republican attempts to cripple the Defense Housing and Community Services Act in 1951. This bill allowed the government to spend up to $50 million building houses in defense areas where the private sector had failed.

An early environmentalist, Spence was a strong supporter of antipollution measures. He was largely responsible for the Water Pollution Control Act of 1948, the first piece of federal legislation that dealt with this problem. Spence also secured funds for a pollution-control laboratory in Cincinnati.

U.S. News described Spence as a bulky, cordial Kentuckian, "one of those hard-working members of Congress who unpretentiously leave their imprint on national legislation" (July 1946, p. 73). Despite his poor eyesight and poor speaking ability, Spence was an effective legislator praised for firm and fair control of committee hearings. He was not, however, a powerful chairman outside the committee room as his bills were often altered and occasionally defeated on the House floor.

Despite his involvement in national issues, Spence was deeply concerned about his own district. He was largely responsible for the creation of the Greater Cincinnati Airport, Fort Thomas Veterans Hospital, and the Internal Revenue Data Processing Center in Covington. In addition, he was instrumental in the construction of local office buildings and flood walls and sponsored legislation that led to the completion of the Greenup Dam, located on the Ohio River, which connects Greenup, Kentucky, and Wheelsburg, Ohio. Failing health and state reapportionment forced the 87-year-old Kentuckian to retire from Congress in January 1963. He died in Fort Thomas, Kentucky.

• Spence's papers are in the Margaret I. King Library of the University of Kentucky in Lexington. See Richard Hedlund,

"Brent Spence and the Bretton Woods Legislation," *Register of the Kentucky Historical Society* 79 (Winter 1981): 40–56. An obituary is in the *New York Times*, 19 Sept. 1967.

RICHARD HEDLUND

SPENCE, Kenneth Wartinbee (6 May 1907–12 Jan. 1967), psychologist, was born in Chicago, Illinois, the son of William James Spence, an electrical engineer, and Mary E. Wartinbee. The family moved to Montreal, Quebec, Canada, where Spence was educated at West Hill High School and at McGill University, receiving a bachelor of arts degree in 1929 and a master of arts degree in 1930. He then undertook graduate study at Yale University, where he worked with the noted primatologist Robert M. Yerkes and the behavior theorist Clark L. Hull. After obtaining his Ph.D. in 1933, Spence was a National Research Council fellow and a research assistant at the Yale University Laboratories in primate biology. From 1937 to 1938 he was an assistant professor of psychology at the University of Virginia. In 1938 Spence moved to the State University of Iowa (now the University of Iowa) in Iowa City as an associate professor of psychology. In 1942 he was made professor of psychology and head of the psychology department, positions he held until 1964, when he became professor of psychology at the University of Texas.

Among the many awards and honors that Spence received during his career were the Wales Gold Medal in Mental Sciences (1929) and the Governor-General's Medal for Research (1930), both from McGill University. He was elected a member of the National Academy of Sciences and of the Society of Experimental Psychologists, and he was a fellow of the American Association for the Advancement of Science and of the American Psychological Association. Spence was awarded the Howard Crosby Warren Medal of the Society of Experimental Psychologists in 1953, was invited to present the prestigious Silliman Lectures at Yale University in 1955, and in 1956 received the first Distinguished Scientific Contribution Award of the American Psychological Association. He also served on the U.S. Air Force Committee on Human Resources and the Army Scientific Advisory Panel. His Silliman Lectures, published in 1956 under the title *Behavior Theory and Conditioning*, were, in effect, an integration and summary of much of his research and theorizing in the area of learning to that date. A number of his collected papers were published in 1960 as *Behavior Theory and Learning: Collected Papers*.

Spence's research interests ranged from discrimination learning in animals to classical conditioning in humans, the effects of anxiety on human motivation and learning, and factors involved in pilot aptitude. He extended and refined the research and theorizing that had been begun by Yale psychologist Clark L. Hull in an attempt to formulate an objective, mathematical theory of how learned behavior was acquired under carefully controlled conditions. Much of Spence's later research centered on the classical conditioning of the relatively simple and easily controlled blinking re-

sponse of the human eyelid and its relation to a number of factors, including the motivational effects of anxiety as measured by an anxiety scale developed by a former student, Janet A. Taylor, whom Spence subsequently married (date unknown; the marriage was childless). The general framework for his theorizing was provided by logical positivism, on which he worked with the philosopher of science Gustav Bergmann, and by a form of behaviorism that attempted to avoid the use of unobservable, mentalistic concepts. Spence understood psychology to be a natural science that, for a number of historical reasons, had developed more slowly than might have been expected. In *Behavior Theory and Conditioning* he concluded that "somehow psychologists and those interested in encouraging research in this field of knowledge must be made to see that the need for basic research that will lead to the discovery of general principles is even greater in this young, as yet undeveloped area than in the physical and biological sciences." He published analyses of operationism, of the nature of theory construction in psychology, and of the methods and postulates of behaviorism.

Spence was particularly interested in understanding and evaluating other approaches to many of the same problems with which he was working. Two possible alternatives to his own approach would have been the inclusion of unobservable but inferred mentalistic and cognitive variables and an emphasis on understanding the physiological mechanisms, including the genetic mechanisms, that underlie observed behavior. Given the state of development of psychological and physiological research at the time he was working, Spence believed that explicating the mathematical relationships between observable and measurable environmental variables and behavioral responses was the most fruitful approach to take. His method did not rule out the use of hypothetical variables intervening between the environment and the behavior, provided that those variables could be expressed in terms of mathematical relationships with what could be observed. For example, instead of theorizing about animal and human "expectations," Spence preferred to deal with theoretical learned anticipatory responses, such as the chewing and salivating responses that precede eating. These fractional anticipatory responses could be related both to the previous conditions under which learning had occurred and to the observed behavior at any given time. The goal was a theory of learned behavior in which pertinent, measurable variables would allow for the prediction of complex responses in both animals and humans.

Beginning in the 1960s, both behaviorism and positivism were generally questioned as approaches to the study of psychology and of science in general. Cognitive science, computer models of brain activity, and an increased understanding of the genetic bases of behavior as well as the physiological functioning of the central nervous system led to a movement away from Spence's behavioristic and mathematical approach to psychology. His influence continued more through the work of the seventy-five doctoral students he had guided than through reference to his own work. Spence died of cancer in Austin, Texas.

• Spence produced hundreds of technical papers in psychological journals, but the major thrust of his work can be understood from *Behavior Theory and Conditioning* (1956) and *Behavior Theory and Learning* (1960). An obituary and analysis of Spence's work is Howard H. Kendler, "Kenneth W. Spence 1907–1967," *Psychological Review* 74 (Sept. 1967): 335–41.

ROBERT G. WEYANT

SPENCER, Ambrose (13 Dec. 1765–13 Mar. 1848), politician and judge, was born in Salisbury, Connecticut, the son of Philip Spencer, a farmer and iron dealer, and Abigail Moore. After preparation with a Presbyterian minister in Canaan, Spencer entered Yale in 1779 but transferred to Harvard, from which he graduated in 1783. That year he began studying law in John Canfield's Sharon, Connecticut, office. In 1784 he eloped with Canfield's daughter Laura Canfield. They had eight children before Laura died in 1807. Later that year Spencer married DeWitt Clinton's widowed sister, Mary Clinton Norton, who died shortly thereafter, in 1808. The following year Spencer married her sister, Catharine Clinton Norton, who died in 1834. He had no children in his second or third marriage.

Spencer finished his three-year preparation for the bar by clerking for one year for John Bay in Claverack, New York, followed by two years in Hudson, New York, with Ezekiel Gilbert. Admitted to the bar in 1788, Spencer rose quickly to the top rank of Columbia County lawyers. He served as Hudson city clerk in the 1780s. In 1793 he was elected to the state assembly and to the state senate in 1796 through 1802. In 1798 Spencer switched his political affiliation from Federalist to Jeffersonian Republican, probably because of striking up what would be a lifelong friendship in 1797 with Republican John Armstrong.

Spencer's reputation as one of the most powerful figures in New York during the first two decades of the nineteenth century was in part owed to his skill in using the state's unique constitutional institutions. Appointing power was vested almost exclusively in the governor and four senators from designated districts who were chosen annually by the assembly. Appointed to this Council of Appointment twice, a rare occurrence, in 1797 and 1800, Spencer united with Clinton on his second tour in initiating the spoils system. The alliance with his future brother-in-law lasted until Clinton's death in 1828 and, save for a significant breach (1812–1816), was a major factor in both men's lives and in the state's politics. Control of the Council of Appointment remained a central objective for Spencer throughout its existence, an end he usually attained. As the governor lacked the sole appointing power, so he also lacked the veto power. The veto was exercised by the Council of Revision, which consisted of the governor, the chancellor, and the justices of the supreme court. Spencer was elevated to the Council of

Revision with his appointment in 1804 to the supreme court, and he was raised, pro forma, to chief justice in 1818. While it is a mistake to label Spencer a political boss in the modern sense of the term, he was the most effective New York political operative until replaced by Martin Van Buren around 1819.

Ironically for one who had switched parties, party regularity was for Spencer a lodestar. While the Jeffersonians were the majority party in the era, they were often fragmented, and Spencer was usually the leader of the dominant faction. An issue that served to split the party was legislative chartering of new banks, notably in 1804 and 1812. Spencer consistently opposed such measures as detrimental to investors in existing banks, including himself, and the question of the Bank of America's charter in 1812 was one of the reasons for his split with Clinton. After he helped keep Clinton in political exile until November 1816, Spencer became "convinced that my political fortunes are involved in Clinton's success" against the challenge to his hegemony by Van Buren, and he was instrumental in Clinton's successful gubernatorial run in 1817.

Despite his widespread political activity, Spencer played a significant role in developing the supreme court's jurisprudence during the formative era of American law. The court was uniformly concerned with maintaining a moral order, as represented in Spencer's opinion in *Jackson v. Gridley* (1820) invalidating a witness's testimony because he refused to take his oath on a Bible. Spencer wrote, "False swearing would expose him to punishment in the life to come." In addition the court was engaged in adjusting the law to fit burgeoning economic conditions, and Spencer's most notable contribution was his assertion in *Jackson v. Brownson* (1810) that the English law of waste (how much timber a tenant could cut) was "inapplicable to a new, unsettled country." While this was said in dissent and Spencer was ahead of contemporaries throughout the country, his position became the rule. Extracting a common thread of jurisprudence from Spencer's several hundred opinions is difficult, but the common sense demonstrated in his *Brownson* dissent was prevalent.

The constitutional convention of 1821 posed a threat to Spencer's political way of life, and despite his best efforts the threat became a reality. He and other members of the Council of Revision opposed calling the convention, but when the legislature overrode the council's objections, Spencer was elected to the convention. On the surface the convention seemed a disaster for Spencer. The Councils of Revision and Appointment were quickly eliminated, the suffrage was broadened despite his wailing and machinations, freedom of the press was extended to allow truth as a defense, he was "constitutionalized" out of office with the restructuring of the court system, and despite his argument that a bill of rights was superfluous, one was inserted. However, he joined moderates like his archfoe Van Buren in heading off more radical measures, such as a one-year gubernatorial term, and in denying the governor veto power. Similarly, he was with the majority in requiring special property requirements for black voters, and the new constitution indirectly made Christianity part of the law of the land, a measure he strenuously favored to promote order, by inclusion in the preamble.

The end of Spencer's judicial career was sealed in 1823, when the senate rejected his nomination to the new supreme court. Yet his political career was not over, although his optimism about being appointed to the U.S. Senate in 1824 was erroneous. He served as Albany's mayor (1824–1825), a term in the House of Representatives (1830–1832), and as presiding officer of the Whig National Convention in Baltimore in 1844. On entering Congress, Spencer disclaimed any party connection but quickly became a fierce opponent of Andrew Jackson, particularly on the question of Cherokee removal. Ironically, Spencer argued for the sovereignty of Native American people, while he had taken the opposite position as judge. His son John Canfield Spencer became secretary of war, and Ambrose Spencer was designated to negotiate with the Seneca at Buffalo Creek in 1842. Spencer also dabbled in silk culture in the 1830s. In 1839 he moved from Albany to Lyons, where he died.

• Spencer has been neglected, in part because of the paucity of his surviving manuscripts. Some of Spencer's letters are in the papers of John Armstrong at the New-York Historical Society and General Jacob Brown at the Massachusetts Historical Society. His court opinions are in William Johnson, *Reports of Cases . . . in the Supreme Court . . . in the State of New York*, vols. 1–20 (1807–1823), and George Caines, *New York Term Reports . . . in the Supreme Court of that State*, vols. 2 and 3 (1805–1806). For an understanding of Spencer's political activity, see Jabez D. Hammond, *The History of Political Parties in the State of New York* (2 vols., 1842). Spencer responded to Hammond in the *New World*, 19 Aug. 1843. See also Craig Hanyan, *De Witt Clinton and the Rise of the People's Men* (1996).

DONALD M. ROPER

SPENCER, Anna Garlin (17 Apr. 1851–12 Feb. 1931), minister, writer, and social reformer, was born in Attleboro, Massachusetts, the daughter of Francis W. Garlin, a city clerk, and Nancy Mason Carpenter, an active abolitionist, both of whom could trace their ancestry back to seventeenth-century New England. Reared in Providence, Rhode Island, and privately educated for the most part, Anna Garlin began her education and journalism career teaching in the Providence schools (1869–1871) and writing for the *Providence Daily Journal* (1869–1878). During this period, her religious thought grew increasingly liberal. In 1876 she withdrew from the Union Congregational Church of Providence because of theological differences. For the next two years she was loosely connected with the Free Religious Association, preaching occasionally for the local society and delivering a plenary address at the 1878 annual convention in Boston. Later that year, she married William Henry Spencer, a Unitarian minister and free religionist. She assisted her husband in ministry to several congregations in

Massachusetts and New York until his retirement in 1893. A son was born to the couple in 1879 but died shortly after birth; their daughter was born in 1884.

Like other prominent female clergy of her time, Anna Spencer entered public ministry in middle life. In 1891 at age thirty-eight she accepted the pastorate of Bell Street Chapel, an independent liberal congregation in Providence. The ethically based fellowship had been endowed by philanthropist James Eddy two years earlier and was dedicated "to God, to truth, and to all that ennobles humanity." An appointment of some distinction, Spencer was the first woman to be ordained in the state of Rhode Island. In *Bell Street Chapel Discourses* (1899), she described her ministry as one of "reverent, rational and ethical devotion" (p. viii). The free society, however, was broadly theistic in both creed and worship, eschewing both the "Christian badge" of the Unitarians and the abstractions of the free religionists. Public worship of this "one in All" was practiced in regular Sunday services with a Sunday school for ten months each year. The chapel's philanthropic mission was carried on through educational and social meetings held during the week and by Spencer's own participation in various social reform efforts.

In addition to pastoral work, Spencer also helped establish the Society for Organizing Charity in Providence and worked for the regulation of child labor and factory safety. As a board member of the State Home and School for Dependent Children, she chaired the International Congress of Charities, Correction and Philanthropy held as an auxiliary of the 1893 World's Columbian Exposition in Chicago and later edited the proceedings. After twelve successful years of ministry, she resigned from Bell Street in 1902 and moved her family to New York City to become an associate director and then lecturer (1903–1912) at the New York School of Philanthropy (later the Columbia University School of Social Work).

Spencer's social theology led to her involvement with the Ethical Culture movement, begun in 1876 by Felix Adler as a "non-religious" institution devoted to social reform and moral fellowship. In 1904, at the recommendation of Adler, who sought her help in promoting the "women's work" of the societies, Spencer was elected associate director of the New York Society for Ethical Culture. She organized and directed the Summer School of Ethics at Madison, Wisconsin (1908–1912), for the American Ethical Union and served for a time as executive secretary of that national federation of ethical societies. She was also among those of the union who signed a petition for the creation of the National Association for the Advancement of Colored People in 1909. Spencer's association with the Ethical Culture movement was short-lived, however. Adler apparently found her public demeanor "unwomanly" and also objected to her suffrage activities. Formal association with the movement ended in 1912, after which she embarked upon a distinguished academic career. From 1913 to 1918 she was a professor of sociology and ethics at the Meadville Theological

School, a Unitarian seminary in Pennsylvania, and followed that by a year at the University of Chicago. In 1920 she returned to Columbia University, where she remained a special lecturer in the social sciences until her death.

Spencer was a prolific author, writing more than seventy articles for both academic journals and general interest magazines. She was an eloquent advocate for the social and legal equality of women, working with her friend Susan B. Anthony in the National Woman Suffrage Association and the National Council of Women in the United States. Her most important essays on the concerns of women were brought together in the highly acclaimed *Woman's Share in Social Culture* (1913). Like fellow Unitarian and early feminist activist Charlotte Perkins Gilman, Spencer argued that a "comradeship of study, work, and social effort" would involve not only equality with men but also the development of entirely new ethical positions and social policies rooted in the unique experiences of women (p. 302). Those insights also led to her involvement in the Women's International League for Peace and Freedom and the founding of the Women's Peace Party in 1915. Active to the end, Spencer died of heart failure after collapsing during a dinner for the League of Nations Association in New York.

A woman of remarkable energy and an accomplished public speaker, Spencer was a tireless advocate for a multitude of reform causes including temperance, suffrage, world peace, and child welfare. Her commitment to these progressive programs were part of a broader moral philosophy rooted in a deeply held liberal religious faith. In his *Heralds of a Liberal Faith* (1952), Samuel A. Eliot praised Spencer as "one of the outstanding American women of her generation" (p. 58). Indeed, in an era when women remained on the margins of public power, she successfully lobbied for social reform from the pulpit and the lectern and in print. Few others, male or female, so embodied the progressive spirit characteristic of early twentieth-century liberalism.

• The Anna Garlin Spencer Papers are in the Swarthmore College Peace Collection. Spencer's *The History of the Bell Street Chapel Movement* (1903) chronicles her ministerial career there and is a valuable source on late Victorian liberalism. The piety and cultus of that religious faith can be found in her *Orders of Service for Public Worship* (1896) and in two later collections of devotional verse, *The Voice Within* (1910) and *O Soul of Man, Thou Must Arise* (1918). An important example of Spencer's early reform work can be found in *The Care of Dependent, Neglected and Wayward Children* (1894), edited with Charles W. Birtwell. See also her *Women and Regulation* (1896), an address before the American Purity Alliance on the legal status of women in India, and *Intemperance in Its Relation to Social Ills* (1891; repr. 1897). Her *The Family and Its Members* (1923) addressed specific domestic issues of the day such as divorce and education. Her final work, *The Council Idea* (1930), was an important reflection on the history, progress, and future of the National Council of Women in the United States. For important correspondence between Spencer and others involved in the Women's Peace Party, see its *Collected Records* (1914–1920). Sketches of her life can be found in two pamphlets, *Parting Words of Anna Garlin Spencer at Bell Street Chapel* (1902) and *Memorial: Anna Garlin Spencer* (1931). See also William Henry Spencer, *Spencer Family Record* (1907), and James G. Garland, *Garland Genealogy* (1897). For brief assessments of her contributions to Unitarianism and the Ethical Culture movement, see Dorothy Emerson, "Feminists and Religious Trailblazers," *World*, Mar./Apr. 1992, pp. 27–30, and Howard B. Radest, *Toward Common Ground: The Story of the Ethical Culture Societies in the United States* (1969). An obituary is in the *New York Times*, 13 Feb. 1931.

LAWRENCE W. SNYDER

SPENCER, Anne (6 Feb. 1882–27 July 1975), poet, librarian, and teacher, was born Annie Bethel Scales Bannister in Henry County, near Danville, Virginia, the daughter of Joel Cephus Bannister, a former slave and saloon owner, and Sarah Louise Scales. The only child of divorced parents, at the age of eleven Annie was sent to Virginia Seminary in Lynchburg, where she excelled in literature and languages. After graduating in 1899 she taught for two years, then in 1901 married fellow student Edward Spencer and lived the rest of her life in Lynchburg.

Outwardly it was a pleasant life that Spencer spent with her husband, a postal worker, and their three children in a comfortable house built in part by Edward. For twenty years (1925–1945) Anne Spencer was a librarian and part-time teacher of literature and language at the all-black Dunbar High School, named for the poet Paul Laurence Dunbar. The Spencers often entertained in their home well-known visitors to the city who, because of their race, were denied lodging in local hotels.

Their son Chauncey Spencer, who was born in 1906, remembered houseguests such as Langston Hughes, Paul Robeson, W. E. B. Du Bois, George Washington Carver, and Thurgood Marshall. Adjoining the house was "a beautiful garden tended by my mother," her son wrote. "As soon as mother, 'Miss Anne,' arrived home from her job as a librarian, she would head for the garden. . . . Either she was working with her flowers, which she cross-bred, or she'd be reading and writing in the garden house. This was my mother's world, the only world in which she felt comfortable" (Spencer, p. 42). The garden house, called "Edankraal," and the main house are maintained as historic sites.

A less tranquil side of Anne Spencer's life was her indignation toward racial and social injustice and her lifelong efforts to improve the lot of blacks. Her biographer, J. Lee Greene, records her successful campaign to replace the all-white faculty at a black high school with black teachers and "her outspoken opposition to tokenism when school integration came to Lynchburg" in the 1960s (Greene, p. 85). Her letters to newspaper editors and city officials, as well as her refusal to patronize segregated city buses and street cars, earned her grudging recognition as an uncompromising foe of Jim Crowism. "My mother was full of fire," her son recalled (Spencer, p. 17).

Anne Spencer had scribbled poems since school days, but her career as a poet began when she met James Weldon Johnson during his stay at the Spencer home in 1918 while he was helping to establish a local chapter of the National Association for the Advancement of Colored People. "He released my soul," she was to say (Greene, p. 78). Johnson recommended her to H. L. Mencken, and the two writers jointly sponsored the publication of her poem "Before the Feast of Shushan" in *Crisis: A Record of the Darker Races* (Feb. 1920). Based on the Book of Esther, the poem is a monologue by King Ahasuerus about his wife Vashti. Eleven Spencer poems were published between 1920 and 1931 in magazines such as *Crisis*, *Palms*, and *Opportunity*, which were associated with the Harlem Renaissance movement. Her poems have been frequently included in anthologies, beginning with Johnson's *The Book of American Negro Poetry* (1922, with five Spencer poems) and including *The Norton Anthology of Modern Poetry* (1973) and *Four Hundred Years of Virginia, An Anthology* (1985). Yet her poems published in her lifetime number less than thirty, and her biographer could account for only about fifty extant poems of the hundreds that Spencer remembered writing. Forty-two poems, including twenty-two previously unpublished, are printed in the appendix of the biography.

This slim surviving body of work has nonetheless established Anne Spencer as a significant American black poet of the twentieth century. Her themes are universal. She uses traditional forms: sonnets, epigrams in varied rhythm and rhyming schemes, and elegies such as "For Jim, Easter Eve," recalling Johnson. She published little poetry after his death in 1938. Most of Spencer's poems are short, with only "At the Carnival" (fifty lines) and "Before the Feast of Shushan" (forty-one lines) running much beyond twenty lines.

Spencer read widely and felt deeply. Her tribute to lost poets, "Dunbar," first published 1920, is in the voice of Paul Laurence Dunbar:

> Ah, how poets sing and die!
> Make one song and Heaven takes it;
> Have one heart and Beauty breaks it;
> Chatterton, Shelley, Keats and I—
> Ah, how poets sing and die!

In its four rhyming quatrains and concluding couplet "Life-long, Poor Browning Never Knew Virginia," published in 1927, sums up Browning's Italian exile, his pantheistic existence in nature after death, and his possible reunion with Elizabeth Barrett Browning. A touch of Gerard Manley Hopkins's sprung rhythm is in her description of a half-inch brown spider in "Po' Little Lib" (1977): "M O V E S thru the grass, O god / if it chance / For the drought driven air turns leaf into lance."

Greene indicates that "as a private poet, Anne Spencer did not see racial protest as her métier in poetry" (p. 138). An exception is "White Things," with its two intricate rhyming stanzas about a lynching.

Anne Spencer loved gardens, books, freedom, and the life of the mind—and when she died in Lynchburg she left a slender golden legacy in her poems and in her restored garden.

• Spencer's papers are in the archives at Alderman Library, University of Virginia. The basic source is J. Lee Greene's biography, *Time's Unfading Garden: Anne Spencer's Life and Poetry* (1977). Also helpful is Chauncey Spencer's autobiography, *Who Is Chauncey Spencer?* (1976). The Anne Spencer Memorial Foundation maintains her house, cottage, and garden and sponsors tours as described in [anon.], "This Was Anne Spencer," *Southern Living*, Apr. 1994, p. 26.

DORA JEAN ASHE

SPENCER, Archibald (1698?–13 Jan. 1760), Church of England minister and itinerant lecturer, first appears in historical records in the spring of 1743. Nothing is known of his parents or education. He joined Boston's St. John's Grand Lodge of Freemasons on 11 May 1743 and lectured on natural philosophy later that month. Benjamin Franklin (1706–1790) was in Boston at the time, met Spencer at the Freemasons' meetings, and attended his lectures. According to Franklin, Spencer first introduced him to the study of electricity. Franklin wrote in his *Autobiography* that he met "Dr. Spence [sic]" in Boston, "who was lately arrived from Scotland, and show'd me some electric Experiments. They were imperfectly perform'd, as he was not very expert; but being on a Subject quite new to me, they equally surpris'd and pleas'd me." The editors of *The Papers of Benjamin Franklin* (29 vols., 1959–) therefore theorized that Spencer might be one of the most influential persons in Franklin's life. But Spencer's lectures consisted of a general introduction to eighteenth-century science, focusing on Newton's discovery of the nature of color, Harvey's investigation of the circulation of blood, and the standard early eighteenth-century demonstrations of electricity from Francis Hauksbee's *Physico-Mechanical Experiments* (1719). Spencer's electrical knowledge did not include the use of the Leyden jar (the earliest capacitor), for the first experiments with it were just then taking place in Europe. The English publication of these experiments in April 1745 began Franklin on his electrical investigations.

Spencer lectured in Newport, New York, and Philadelphia through 1743 and 1744. Called "Dr." in his advertisements and in manuscript references, he was accepted as a medical doctor by all his contemporaries. In 1744 he attended a meeting of the fledgling American Philosophical Society. In 1745 he moved to Williamsburg, Virginia, where he lectured, and then to Fredericksburg, where he practiced medicine. During 1745 he often visited Mary Washington and, at the request of William Fairfax, who managed Lord Fairfax's great estate in Virginia, advised her to allow her son George Washington to go to sea.

In 1748 Spencer decided to become a minister. Learning of his intentions, the Reverend William Robinson of Virginia wrote Edmund Gibson, the bishop of London, on 27 July 1748, that Spencer was a deist and did not believe in the Scriptures. But Gibson died on 6 September 1748; Thomas Sherlock was appointed bishop of London on 1 October; and Robinson's charge was forgotten. In 1749 Spencer journeyed to London and took ministerial orders. Bishop Sherlock asked him what Americans thought concerning a bishop in America. Spencer wrote him on 12 June 1749 that he had talked with "several merchants and Gentlemen of Philadelphia and New York" who believed it would be "inconsistant with the Privileges of the People" and would "interfere with the Rights of the several Proprietaries." On 30 August he was licensed for Virginia and on 20 September 1749 received the royal bounty of £20 "to perform the Ministerial Office in Virginia." He arrived in Virginia in June 1750 but immediately left for Maryland.

In Annapolis he attended Tuesday Club meetings during the remainder of 1750. He constantly quarreled with and criticized other club members, trying to demonstrate his superiority. Consequently, in his *History of the Ancient and Honorable Tuesday Club*, Dr. Alexander Hamilton (1712–1756) labeled Spencer "Dr. Rhubarb" and commented that the club was disgusted with him "as an ostentatious pedant." Spencer delivered his last known lectures on natural philosophy in Annapolis in September 1750. Though Franklin also mentioned in his *Autobiography* that he bought all Spencer's apparatus, it seems unlikely that Spencer would have sold his apparatus while still giving lectures. It was probably not until late 1750 or afterward that Franklin bought his apparatus. Long before 1750 Spencer's electrical apparatus was undoubtedly far inferior to Franklin's. Franklin, however, was probably interested in Spencer's other equipment, such as his apparatus demonstrating the circulation of blood. Franklin had a machine for "exhibiting the circulation of the blood in the arteries and veins of the human body" in his collection on 13 July 1787, when Manasseh Cutler visited him.

In the fall of 1751 Spencer was awarded an appointment at All Hallows Parish, Anne Arundel County. In 1755 he joined the local gentry at the Ancient South River Club and for five shillings a year passed on to the club his copy of the *Pennsylvania Gazette* after reading it. He died in Annapolis. The *Maryland Gazette* obituary said he was "aged 62." His influence on Benjamin Franklin was insignificant.

• Spencer's few extant letters are in the Historical Society of Pennsylvania and in Lambeth Palace, London. For the latter, see William Wilson Manross, *The Fulham Papers in the Lambeth Palace Library* (1965). He appears in Dr. Alexander Hamilton's *Gentleman's Progress: The Itinerarium*, ed. Carl Bridenbaugh (1948), and especially in Hamilton's *The History of the Ancient and Honorable Tuesday Club*, ed. Robert Micklus (3 vols., 1990). *The Papers of Benjamin Franklin*, vol. 2 (1960), pp. 450–51, n. 6, mention him. In a biographical study, J. A. Leo Lemay established that Franklin's "Dr. Spence" was Archibald Spencer: "Franklin's 'Dr. Spence': The Reverend Archibald Spencer (1698?–1760), M.D.," *Maryland Historical Magazine* 59, no. 2 (1964): 199–216. For Spencer in Fredericksburg, see Douglas Southall Freeman, *George Washington*, vol. 1 (1948), pp. 194–95, 239. The best investigation of his scientific career is I. Bernard Cohen, "The Mysterious 'Dr. Spence,'" in Cohen's *Benjamin Franklin's Science* (1990), pp. 40–60. See also Lemay's review of Cohen in the *New England Quarterly* 64, no. 1 (1991): 166–69. An obituary is in the *Maryland Gazette*, 17 Jan. 1760.

J. A. Leo Lemay

SPENCER, Christopher Miner (20 June 1833–14 Jan. 1922), inventor and manufacturer, was born on his father's farm at Manchester, Connecticut, the son of Ogden Spencer, a farmer and dealer in wool, and Asenath Hollister. Parental ambitions seemed to destine him for the ministry, but when he went to live with his grandfather Hollister in 1845, supposedly to continue his education, he was introduced to mechanical arts and found a lifelong love of things mechanical. Two years later, he ended his formal education and went to work at the Cheney silk mill in South Manchester. During his spare time, Spencer built a working model of a steam engine, based on information he found in a book. In 1848 he entered an eight-month apprenticeship in the spinning and weaving machinery shop of Samuel Loomis of Manchester. He also attended Wilbraham Academy and in 1849 became a journeyman machinist. He returned for the next four years to the Cheney brothers, where he assisted Frank Cheney in the development of experimental machinery. In 1853 he moved to Rochester, New York, to work in the repair shops of the New York Central Railroad; soon afterward he was working in the armory of Nathan P. Ames at Chicopee Falls, Massachusetts, and in 1854 he moved to Hartford, Connecticut, and spent two years at the Colt armory helping to install new machinery. There he first became interested in the concept of a repeating rifle, and there he met his future partner, Charles E. Billings.

In 1856 Spencer returned to the Cheney firm as superintendent of the machine shop. Two years later, he invented an automatic silk-spooling machine, which eliminated the necessity of winding the silk by hand and which, Spencer later stated, foreshadowed his automatic turret lathe. The winder, as perfected by Hezekiah Conant, was later manufactured by Pratt & Whitney and marketed as the Willimantic Linen Winder.

Spencer continued to work on his repeating rifle. When he showed a crude wooden model to Richard Lawrence, a mechanical innovator formerly with the Robbins & Lawrence armory in Windsor, Vermont, and at the time master armorer at the Sharps Rifle Manufacturing Company, Lawrence urged him to build a working model. Spencer's repeater was a lever-action gun with a tubular magazine located in the stock and loaded through the butt. A spiral spring pushed the special rim-fire copper cartridges toward the breech, where the action of a rotating breech block placed them in the chamber. Seven shots could be fired in twelve seconds, and the magazine could be loaded in less than half the time needed to charge a muzzleloader. On 6 March 1860, Spencer received patent 27,393 for his repeating rifle.

The outbreak of the Civil War brought a demand for firearms and a willingness to consider innovative ideas. After testing, the United States adopted the rifle, and the Spencer Repeating Rifle Company was established to manufacture it. In May 1861 Spencer sold his rights to Charles Cheney, a company director, and had no further entrepreneurial interest in it, though he was to receive a royalty of $1 for each gun sold. Spencer was employed as superintendent of the works. Despite some hesitancy on the part of the military, during the war it procured some 94,000 carbines and 13,000 rifles, which performed admirably on the battlefield. Whereas an experienced soldier might get off three shots per minute with a muzzleloader, a Spencer-equipped soldier could fire fourteen to eighteen times; moreover, the weapon was effective to approximately 2,000 yards and seldom suffered mechanical failure. Spencer repeaters, said General Ulysses S. Grant, "are the best breech-loading arms now in the hands of troops."

In 1862 Spencer turned his attention to transportation and installed a steam engine, boiler, and steering mechanism on a buggy, thereby creating a horseless carriage. The chain-driven rear wheels were outfitted with a ratchet-and-pawl arrangement that allowed the outer wheel to turn faster while cornering. Spencer later recalled that the machine was able to keep up with the fastest trotting horses on a racetrack, but that rough surfaces prohibited speedy road travel. The machine also terrified horses, "so I turned to developments of useful nature and less destructive."

Returning to firearms, Spencer and fellow inventor Sylvester Roper invented the Spencer-Roper repeating shotgun and rifle and founded the Roper Repeating Arms Company at Amherst, Massachusetts, in 1866. Charles Billings joined the firm, and, after the firearms venture folded, in 1869 Billings and Spencer went to Hartford, Connecticut, and established a company, to manufacture drop forgings that in 1872 was named Billings & Spencer. The firm was both a technical and a financial success, in large part because of Billings's innovations.

At about this time, Spencer turned his attention to his greatest invention, the automatic turret lathe, or automatic screw machine. While experimenting with a machine to turn sewing machine bobbins automatically from bar stock, Spencer conceived of the automatic screw machine, which, with cams and levers, could be adjusted to perform several sequential operations on cylindrical parts without human intervention. He built his first model in secret and then demonstrated it to George Fairfield, president of the Weed Sewing Machine Company. On 30 September 1873 he obtained patent 143,306 for it. In 1874 he left Billings & Spencer; and, in 1876, he, together with Fairfield and others, organized the Hartford Machine Screw Company with Spencer as superintendent. This firm did not manufacture automatic screw machines for sale, but rather attempted to sell the machines' products, an

unwise strategy. Spencer's patent was faulty, and soon rival machines appeared. Eventually the "Spencer" automatic was put on the market under license by Pratt & Whitney.

Once again, Spencer was drawn to firearms. Together with Sylvester Roper, he invented the "pump," or slide-action, shotgun and rifle, and in 1882 they founded the Spencer Arms Company at Windsor, Connecticut. In 1883 he toured Europe with noted artist Albert Bierstadt, demonstrating his pump gun. Although the gun was a success, the company was not. When it failed, Spencer, who was treasurer, lost heavily.

In 1891, after several years of development, Spencer unveiled an automatic lathe that produced screws from a coil of wire. Two years later he organized the Spencer Automatic Machine Screw Company at Windsor, Connecticut. He remained with this company, improving their screw machines, while retaining a directorship of Billings & Spencer, until his retirement shortly before his death in Hartford. He also continued to invent and consult. The Spencer double-end automatic and Universal five-spindle automatic were improvements upon his earlier screw machines. He also worked with the New Britain Machine Company, perfecting, at age eighty, a six-spindle automatic screw machine.

Spencer married twice. In June 1860 he married Frances Theodora Peck, who died in 1881. On 3 July 1883 he married Georgette T. Rogers, and they had four children.

In 1916 Spencer fractured a hip when he fell on an icy pavement, but the indomitable inventor addressed a Hartford engineering meeting via loudspeaker while bedridden. Four years later, at eighty-seven, he took up aviation and made more than twenty flights. He was an active engineer until the week of his death.

Spencer was the embodiment of the Yankee inventor. In a long and incredibly active, diverse, and fruitful career, his far-ranging interest led to important developments in firearms, drop forging, and the evolution of machine tools. The development of American manufacturing in no small part rests upon Christopher Spencer's inventions.

• Small collections of Spencer papers are at the Connecticut Historical Society, Hartford, and the Windsor (Conn.) Historical Society. Other than entries in biographical dictionaries, few biographers have turned their attention to Spencer. A number of authors have examined his firearms and, in so doing, have touched upon other aspects of his remarkable career. Robert Barton, *Lincoln and the Yankee Gunsmith* (1942); Roy Martin Marcot, *Spencer Repeating Firearms* (1983); John C. McQueen, *Spencer: The First Effective and Widely Used Repeating Rifle and Its Use in the Western Theater of the Civil War* (1989); John D. McAulay, *Civil War Breechloading Rifles* (1987); and Noah Andre Trudeau, "That 'Unerring Volcanic Firearm,'" *MHQ: The Quarterly Journal of Military History* 7 (1995): 44–53, are examples. Of course, no history of machine tools would be complete without mention of Spencer's accomplishments. Such standards as L. T. C. Rolt, *A Short History of Machine Tools* (1965); Joseph M. Roe, *English and American Tool Builders* (1916); and Robert S. Woodbury, *Studies in the History of Machine Tools* (1972), include the automatic screw machine. His obituary is in the *New York Times*, 15 Jan. 1922.

CHRISTOPHER S. DUCKWORTH

SPENCER, Cornelia Phillips (20 Mar. 1825–11 Mar. 1908), writer and educational advocate, was born Cornelia Ann Phillips in Harlem, New York, the daughter of James Phillips, headmaster of a boys' school and later a mathematics professor and Presbyterian minister, and Judith "Julia" Vermeula, who later ran a girls' school, the Phillips Female Academy, in her home. James Phillips accepted a position as professor and chair of mathematics at the University of North Carolina (UNC) in 1826 and moved his family to rural Chapel Hill. Cornelia Phillips loved reading essays, biography, history, and books on English politics. She studied at home with her brothers but was not allowed to attend UNC, which did not accept women. She complained that she was allowed only the "crumbs that fell from the University's table," but she was a loyal supporter and later mounted a letter writing campaign that reopened the university, which had been closed during Reconstruction.

She married James Munroe "Magnus" Spencer, a lawyer, in 1855; they had one daughter. They lived in Clinton, Alabama, until his death in 1861. "Oh what a rich and full mind was his. What sweet companionship I have lost forever," she wrote. Heartbroken, she returned to Chapel Hill with her daughter and began writing and teaching. She also was a historian; a newspaper correspondent and editor; an essayist; a painter of china, wood, and canvas; and a botanist. She painted wild flowers that grew in the Chapel Hill area.

Spencer's essays in the *Watchman*, a New York magazine published by the Reverend Charles Deems, cofounder of the Church of Strangers in New York City, describe the final weeks of the Civil War in North Carolina. These articles became her first published book, *The Last Ninety Days of the War in North Carolina* (1866). Sources for this work, in addition to firsthand observations, included letters from friends, government officials, university officials, and Zebulon B. Vance, governor of North Carolina during the war. He called her "the smartest woman in North Carolina, and the smartest man too."

During the turbulent Reconstruction years, Spencer worked hard to improve educational standards. The Reconstruction government replaced the entire UNC faculty with political appointees, not scholars, but a boycott by students of the administration and faculty caused a financial crisis that forced the university to shut its doors in 1871. Spencer drafted letters to friends and people with influence and wrote newspaper articles. Her plan to restore the university invited the alumni to take charge. On her fiftieth birthday, she received a telegram with the news that the legislature had voted to reopen and fund the university.

President Frank P. Graham described her reaction in a speech to the board of trustees in 1930:

In the tragic era, Mrs. Cornelia Phillips Spencer, staunch champion of the public schools and the University, received March 20, 1875, a message from the committee in Raleigh that the University was to be opened again. For five years the bell had not rung in Chapel Hill. For five years she had worked and prayed for that day. She climbed the stairs to the Belfry and with her own hands rang the bell, which has never ceased to ring to this day. The people of North Carolina were on the march again. Under God, we will not turn back now!

In another letter-writing campaign, Spencer wanted to "induce the women of North Carolina to outfit the (university) scientific departments with new and improved apparatus."

From 1870 to 1876 Spencer wrote a weekly column for the *North Carolina Presbyterian*, earning $400 a year. Her pieces ran in the "Young Lady's Column" and offered advice to young women. She urged them to get an education and to strive for excellence. Additionally, she covered politics and social reform, particularly the women's movement. Spencer published *A School History of North Carolina* in 1887 and *First Steps in North Carolina History* in 1888. She helped establish UNC's Summer Normal School in 1877, the first summer school ever attempted by a state university. She obtained permission for women to attend classroom lectures and, along with her daughter and a niece, was allowed "to occupy rear seats and keep very quiet." She was instrumental in the founding of the Normal and Industrial School for Women, later the Women's College of the University of North Carolina at Greensboro. Both schools named buildings for her. She received an honorary doctorate in 1895 on the occasion of the university's 100th anniversary, two years before women were allowed to attend the university.

Phillips Russell, her great-nephew and author of *The Woman Who Rang the Bell*, wrote, "Whenever there was a task of such a nature to be done, requiring intelligence and energy, Cornelia was usually chosen as the burden-bearer." One of her tasks was to compile a list of alumni; another was to write names of graduates on parchment diplomas. She also wrote several hymns and poems for special occasions. Spencer took care of people throughout the community and was particularly kind to the workers who maintained the buildings and grounds. She also looked to one of her father's former slaves, Aunt Dilsey Craig, for comfort and advice.

Although she spent most of her life in Chapel Hill, she lived with her brother Charles, in Washington, D.C., for two years in the early 1880s. And in 1894 she moved into the Cambridge, Massachusetts, home of her daughter, who was married to James Lee Love, a mathematics professor at Harvard. Nearly deaf, she spent time in libraries and bookstores and continued writing to friends and family members. Spencer died in Cambridge and was buried in Chapel Hill, close to the university she helped save. A student in 1891–1892 described her this way: "I will never forget the esteem and almost sacred reverence in which she was held by the student body. . . . Her personality was most extraordinary. . . . She simply radiated something invisible and inspiring; a sort of magnetic field. She could furnish an empty room by simply sitting there."

• Spencer's diaries, journals, letters, and papers are in the Southern Historical Collection of the University of North Carolina. See also Phillips Russell, *The Woman Who Rang the Bell* (1949). Other sources include Hope S. Chamberlain, *Old Days in Chapel Hill* (1926); *Selected Papers of Cornelia Phillips Spencer*, ed. Louis R. Wilson (1953); Kemp P. Battle, *History of the University of North Carolina* (1907–1912); Rose H. Holder, *McIver of North Carolina* (1957); and Josephus Daniels, *Tar Heel Editor* (1939).

ELIZABETH B. DICKEY

SPENCER, George Eliphaz (1 Nov. 1836–19 Feb. 1893), U.S. senator, was born in Champion, New York, the son of Gordon P. Spencer, a physician, and Deborah Mallery. After attending McGill University in Montreal, Spencer read law and commenced practice at Newton, Iowa, in 1856. Attracted to the new Republican party, he served briefly in 1857–1858 as secretary of the state senate. He also speculated in land on the Iowa frontier (1857–1859) and scouted mining prospects in Colorado Territory before returning to Iowa in 1860.

During the Civil War Spencer initially served as sutler for the First Nebraska Regiment in the spring 1862 campaign up the Tennessee River and then joined the staff of Brigadier General Grenville M. Dodge, an Iowa friend in charge of Union forces at Corinth, Mississippi. Before beginning military service in the fall of 1862, Spencer married Bella Zilfa, a British-born author; they had no children. The war soon separated the couple as Spencer became Dodge's chief of staff and engaged in intelligence raids behind Confederate lines in southern Tennessee and northern Alabama. In July 1863 he was promoted to colonel and received permission to recruit Unionists from northern Alabama into the First Alabama Cavalry. Spencer led the unit as Union forces moved to Chattanooga, and then he commanded a vanguard cavalry brigade in William Tecumseh Sherman's march from Atlanta to Savannah and into the Carolinas. He was breveted brigadier general and mustered out in July 1865.

After the war, Spencer confided to Dodge that he was "strongly of the opinion that I should settle somewhere South, as I think the chances for making a fortune there the best." Through the last half of 1865, he crisscrossed Alabama purchasing cotton and preparing it for shipment to New York markets. He also lobbied unsuccessfully on behalf of Unionist friends for positions in Alabama's postwar government, but he soon became frustrated with the conservative direction of Reconstruction under President Andrew Johnson. By October 1865 Spencer was fully in the Radical Republican camp; he wrote Dodge that he favored "negro suffrage or reducing all these states to the position of territories & keeping them so for years to come." Disillusioned with the political situation in Alabama,

in June 1866 he headed west to speculate in mining stocks in San Francisco.

When Congress took control of Reconstruction in early 1867, Spencer returned to Alabama and secured an appointment as a register in bankruptcy. His wife joined him in July, and in addition to working the bankruptcy circuit, he labored to "carry Alabama and secure it permanently to the Republican party." Despite Bella's death from typhoid fever in August, he decided to remain "and help reconstruct this Godforsaken and miserable country. . . . since we have the colored men to help us we can out-vote [the conservatives] and I think if it becomes necessary, that we can out-fight them" (letter to Dodge). He campaigned aggressively for Republican candidates in the state elections of February 1868, and the new legislature rewarded him with a U.S. Senate seat. Reelected four years later, Spencer served from Alabama's readmission to the Union in July 1868 until 1879—well after conservative Democrats had "redeemed" the state from Republican rule in 1874. It was a turbulent tenure—conservatives immediately tagged him with the opprobrious epithet of "carpetbagger," and Spencer and other Republicans faced constant ostracism and intimidation from an overwhelming majority of white southerners.

A pivotal figure in Alabama politics during the 1870s, Spencer quickly emerged as a shrewd political infighter who used power and patronage to reward friends and punish enemies—both inside and outside his party. In Congress, Spencer acquired a reputation as a stalwart politician, a regular Grant Republican, yet his rhetoric and activity also reflected an idealistic concern for the welfare of the freedmen and a missionary belief in the necessity of southern "regeneration"—reshaping the region into a more progressive society. On economic measures, he energetically served constituent interests, especially as a member of the Senate Commerce Committee, where he steered federal funds to the South through the annual rivers and harbors appropriations. Although he continued to serve northern friends such as railroad entrepreneurs Grenville Dodge and Thomas A. Scott, he also fought for federal subsidies for southern railroads, currency expansion, and tariff and tax reform.

This diligent service mattered little to the Democrats because on Reconstruction issues, Spencer never wavered from the Radical line. He supported nationalization of black suffrage with the Fifteenth Amendment, opposed amnesty for unrepentant former Confederates, and pushed for civil rights legislation and enforcement measures to protect southern Republican candidates and voters from Democratic political violence. But declining northern support for Reconstruction increasingly isolated Spencer and a dwindling number of southern Radicals. Alabama conservative Democrats ousted the state's Republican regime in 1874 and promptly contested Spencer's 1872 reelection on the grounds of political corruption. The Republican Senate, however, rejected the case, and

Spencer served until the end of his term in March 1879.

Aware that he could never achieve reelection, Spencer began speculating in gold-mining operations in the Black Hills of Dakota Territory in 1876. In 1877 he married New York actress and author William Loring May Nunez, with whom he had one child. Shortly after he left the Senate, he sold his Black Hills property and moved the family to eastern Nevada, where he bought several silver mines. He became a commissioner for the Union Pacific Railroad in 1881, and his mining investments slowly went sour during the late 1880s. Financially strapped and in failing health, he returned to Washington to look for a patronage position. He died there of edema and a second stroke.

On balance, Spencer was clearly opportunistic, but his relentless pursuit of influence, power, and wealth was hardly rare among Gilded Age politicians and entrepreneurs. For their postwar effort to work the freedpeople into a more equitable position in American society, however, Spencer and other Republicans earned the enduring enmity of southern conservatives, and this negative historical image prevailed until the civil rights revolution of the 1960s.

• There is no central collection of Spencer papers, but he left a substantial correspondence in other collections, most notably the Grenville M. Dodge Papers at the Iowa State Historical Department. Scholarly work on Spencer is sparse. Focusing on his Alabama career is Sarah Van V. Woolfolk, "George E. Spencer: A Carpetbagger in Alabama," *Alabama Review* 19 (1966): 41–52, and Spencer is one of ten carpetbaggers profiled in Richard Nelson Current, *Those Terrible Carpetbaggers: A Reinterpretation* (1988). Useful for the broader political context is Sarah Woolfolk Wiggins, *The Scalawag in Alabama Politics* (1977). A full obituary is in the *New York Tribune*, 20 Feb. 1893.

TERRY L. SEIP

SPENCER, Ichabod Smith (23 Feb. 1798–23 Nov. 1854), clergyman, was born at Rupert, Vermont, the son of Phineas Spencer, an agriculturalist in comfortable circumstances, and Olive Sheldon. Soon after his father died in 1815, Spencer found work as a manual laborer in Granville, New York, and during a revival there professed his faith as a Christian. Relocating in nearby Salem, he found time to enter an academy, doing some teaching on the side. He saved enough to enter Union College in Schenectady as a sophomore, stood high in his class, and graduated in 1822. He then served as principal and teacher of the grammar school in that city for three years and also studied theology with Andrew Yates, professor of moral theology at the college. Continuing to serve in those capacities for another three years in an academy at Canandaigua, New York, he was also licensed to preach in 1826 by the nearby Presbytery of Geneva.

In 1828 he married Hannah Magoffin; they had four children. That same year he was called as colleague pastor of aged Solomon Williams at the Congregational church in Northampton, Massachusetts. Under Spencer's leadership a revival brought new life to the church once served by Jonathan Edwards. Four years later he was called to the pastorate of the Second Presbyterian Church of Brooklyn, New York, serving there until his death; the church was later renamed the Spencer Memorial Church.

Spencer preached solid, carefully prepared, biblically oriented, doctrinal sermons, which attracted a growing congregation. A few of his sermons were published in his lifetime, many later in posthumous collections. He preached from the perspective of the Calvinist evangelicalism of his time, informed by an emphasis on God's sovereignty and human depravity, unconditional election, and irresistible grace. He was a quiet, unostentatious man who traveled little and refused invitations to serve conspicuous pulpits. He focused his energies on his congregation, regularly making pastoral calls in homes, always busy seeking people out, deeply concerned with the plight of the poor; he was much loved by his parishioners.

Spencer was a founding member of the board of directors of Union Theological Seminary in New York City, remained active on that board for thirteen years, and taught biblical history there part-time from its opening in 1836 to 1840. The seminary defined itself as a Presbyterian institution; its faculty members were required to subscribe to the Calvinistic Westminster Confession. When the Presbyterian Church in the United States divided in 1837 over the proper interpretation of that confession, the Old School branch of the church, influenced especially by leaders of Scotch-Irish background and numerically strong in the Middle Atlantic states, insisted on a very strict position on the doctrines of predestination and original sin. The New School branch, with which most of Union's founders aligned themselves, held milder views of depravity and gave a larger place for human effort in seeking grace. This position was influenced by the Puritan traditions of old and New England to emphasize piety along with confessionalism and had growing numerical strength in New York and Ohio. Spencer was bound by conscience to the Old School yet was a mediator by temperament and continued his cooperation with Union, though his independent stance isolated him from some leaders on both sides. He was honored by a D.D. from Hamilton College in 1840, which at that time betokened significant recognition.

Spencer's most notable work was *A Pastor's Sketches; or, Conversations with Anxious Inquirers Respecting the Way of Salvation* (2 vols., 1851–1853). In this book he discussed in detail seventy-seven cases of what would later be called pastoral counseling, often involving persons struggling with anxiety problems. Apparently he had a remarkable verbal memory and reproduced much of a long conversation verbatim soon after a session was over. Concerned about the state of a person's soul, he could push hard at times. For example, he pressed one inquirer directly: "Will you attend to this matter of your salvation as well as you can, according to the word of God and with prayer, and endeavor to be saved? Will you do it, without any farther delay?" Nevertheless, though he did not at all anticipate twentieth-century trends toward nondirective approaches in pastoral guidance, he also displayed considerable patience and self-restraint. He followed the words above by adding, "If you do not wish me to say anything more to you about it; then, say so, and I will urge you no more: I shall be sorry, but I will be still. I am not going to annoy you, or treat you impolitely." He could be rigorously honest with himself when he realized he had made a mistake in his counseling. *A Pastor's Sketches* was widely read and was reprinted nearly a half-century later by the Presbyterian Board of Publication. More than a century after its original publication, Seward Hiltner, professor of theology and personality at Princeton Theological Seminary, wrote a *Preface to Pastoral Theology* (1958), devoting the bulk of the book to a careful analysis and criticism of Spencer's counseling, largely in a positive way. A modest, diffident man who disliked flattery and publicity, Spencer enjoyed good health until overtaken by what his biographer called "a most distressing disease" early in the last year of his life. He died in Brooklyn.

• For the Spencer family background, consult Nathaniel Goodwin, *Genealogical Notes* (1978), pp. 207–9. An informative biographical essay of more than 100 pages by James M. Sherwood prefaces the two-volume collection of Spencer's sermons he edited, *Sermons of Rev. Ichabod S. Spencer, D.D. . . . With a Sketch of His Life* (1855). The funeral oration was delivered by Gardiner Spring and published as a pamphlet, *Triumph in Suffering* (1855); Spring later introduced another collection of Spencer's sermons, *Discourses on Sacramental Occasions* (1861). Another posthumous work was a letter to a judge, *Evidences of Divine Revelation* (1865).

ROBERT T. HANDY

SPENCER, John Canfield (8 Jan. 1788–17 May 1855), lawyer, legislator, and cabinet member, was born in Hudson, New York, the son of Ambrose Spencer, a prominent lawyer and jurist, and Laura Canfield. He attended Williams College, then graduated from Union College in 1806. In 1807 he married Elizabeth Scott Smith, with whom he had four children. That same year he became the private secretary of Governor Daniel D. Tompkins and began to study the law, being admitted to the bar in 1809. After establishing his practice in Canandaigua, he was appointed postmaster there in 1814, and in the following year he became state district attorney for New York's five western counties. His growing reputation in the law was acknowledged in 1827 when he was appointed to a three-man commission that produced *The Revised Statutes of the State of New York* (1829), a major step in the modernizing of American law. His special contribution involved the revision of the statutes relating to state finance and to crimes and their punishments.

By this time, Spencer had also achieved prominence in politics. Earlier, he had been elected to one term in the House of Representatives (1817–1819), where he called for an investigation of the Second Bank of the United States to determine whether it had violated the conditions of its charter, and later he submitted a resolution for the removal of government deposits from it.

A prominent supporter of Governor DeWitt Clinton, he was the leading candidate in 1820 for election by the state legislature to the U.S. Senate but was defeated by Clinton's opponents. He served in the state assembly in 1820–1822 and in the state senate in 1825–1828, giving special attention to improving public education and abolishing imprisonment for debt.

Spencer's political career entered a new phase when he joined the Antimasonic movement, which after 1826 rapidly gained strength in western New York by promising to protect anxious Americans against what they feared were the secret conspiracies of the Masons. In 1829 he accepted an appointment from Governor Martin Van Buren as special prosecutor to investigate the alleged murder of William Morgan, which had excited popular anger against the Masonic order, but resigned a year later when he concluded that the state would not adequately support him. He was elected to the assembly in 1831 and 1833 by the Antimasons, who also made him president of their 1831 Baltimore convention, the first popular convention for the nomination of a presidential candidate. Spencer achieved prominence as an Antimasonic leader and as the author of an Antimasonic pamphlet, *A Portrait of Free Masonry* (1832), but the collapse of this movement after 1832 left him temporarily without a place in politics.

In 1837 he moved to Albany, where the next year he edited Henry Reeve's translation of Tocqueville's *Democracy in America*. By then he had joined the Whig party. In 1839 he became secretary of state under the new Whig governor, William H. Seward. As that office oversaw the state's education system, Spencer gave much attention both to improving the quality of teaching statewide and to the controversy that erupted in New York City when Roman Catholics protested Protestant dominance of that city's public schools. Rejecting Catholic demands for a share of public school money, he proposed that the more secular and more democratic state system be extended to the city. Although his bill to that end was defeated in 1841, his proposal was enacted into law the next year.

By that time Spencer's politics had carried him into the national cabinet of President John Tyler. Both as an Antimason and as a Whig, he had opposed the presidential ambitions of Henry Clay, and so he openly supported Tyler when America's first "president by accident" quarreled with Clay over public policy. Appointed secretary of war in 1841, he won Tyler's respect by his able management: "The great multitude of cases which had accumulated in the War Department," Tyler recalled, "melted away before his sleepless industry." During his two years in office, he worked to strengthen coastal defenses, expand frontier forts, improve navigation on western rivers, and promote the education of Native Americans. The Seminole War in Florida ended during his administration, leading him to urge that no new decision be made to force the removal of Indians westward: "It is hoped that the red man will then be suffered to rest in peace."

In 1842 Spencer's nineteen-year-old son, Philip, was hanged on the brig *Somers* for allegedly plotting a mutiny. Spencer issued an indignant public protest, leading the diarist Philip Hone to say that "a more dangerous opponent than John C. Spencer could not be found in the United States; stern, uncompromising, obstinate in temper, determined and energetic in action, and with talents equal to any effort which his feelings may prompt." After a lengthy trial, however, the captain of the *Somers*, Alexander MacKenzie, was exonerated.

In 1843 Spencer was nominated to the U.S. Supreme Court, but his identification with an unpopular president assured his defeat. In March of that year he left the War Department to become secretary of the treasury, where he administered the affairs of the department, said Whig political reporter Nathan Sargeant, "with an ability, assiduity, integrity and faithfulness seldom equaled since the days of Hamilton." In 1844 during the controversy over the annexation of Texas, however, he antagonized Tyler when he refused to deposit $100,000 in secret service money with a confidential agent, apparently to fit out a naval expedition against Mexico. When pressed by the president, he denounced such a transfer as illegal and resigned.

This action marked the end of his political career, as his connection with the unpopular Tyler administration left him with little political standing. He continued to have some prominence as a lawyer, in 1852 successfully defending Eliphalet Nott, the president of Union College, against charges of misappropriating money. An active member of the Episcopal church, Spencer was a trustee of Columbia College, where in 1854, against religious opposition, he unsuccessfully supported Oliver Wolcott Gibbs, a Unitarian, for a science faculty appointment. He also helped establish the Albany Hospital and the State Asylum for Idiots.

Spencer died in Albany. Once described as the "philosopher" of the New York bar, he made his most enduring contributions to the law and to the early development of public education in New York State.

• Aside from Spencer's Antimasonic pamphlet, *A Portrait of Free Masonry* (1832), his published works are scattered among several collections of state and national documents; various references to them can be found in *Niles' National Register*. Some of his papers are in the New-York Historical Society and the National Archives. The most extensive sketch of Spencer's life is in L. B. Proctor, *The Bench and Bar of New-York*, vol. 1 (1870). Useful supplements are W. A. Butler, *The Revision of the Statutes of the State of New York and the Revisers* (1889), and Elizabeth Bruchholz Haigh, "New York Antimasons, 1826–1833" (Ph.D. diss., Univ. of Rochester, 1980). Obituaries are in the New York *Evening Post*, 21 May 1855, and the *New York Daily Times*, 19 May 1855.

EDWARD K. SPANN

SPENCER, Joseph (3 Oct. 1714–13 Jan. 1789), revolutionary officer, was born in East Haddam, Connecticut, the son of Isaac Spencer and Mary Selden. The family's wealth and stature as farmer-merchants were firmly established for a half century in the community on both sides of the Connecticut River. After preparatory studies Spencer read law and was admitted to the bar. He was a farmer and a country merchant to supplement his dabbling in law. In 1738 he married his second cousin Martha Brainerd; the couple had five children. By 1753 he was appointed a judge of probate. In 1756, two years after his first wife's death, he and Hannah Brown Southmayd wed; they had eight children. From 1750 to 1766 he was elected a deputy to the Connecticut assembly, and after 1766 he served as an assistant in the upper house. Throughout his adulthood he was a pillar in the Millington Congregational Church.

In Millington and adjacent communities Spencer's multiple offices steered him also to military concerns of the provincial society. In the imperial struggle for North America in King George's War (1744–1748) he gained commission as a lieutenant in the locally raised company. He became a militia captain in 1752. In the climactic stage a decade later—the French and Indian War (1756–1763)—he was appointed major of the Twelfth Regiment of Connecticut on 13 October 1757, then became a lieutenant colonel in 1759 and colonel in 1766. He served in northern campaigns, including expeditions against Louisbourg, Ticonderoga, Crown Point, and Quebec. As Anglo-American hostilities escalated, Spencer was pushed to the foreground. In 1774 he moderated East Haddam's town meetings, which increasingly asserted American rights. When news of bloodshed at Boston hit Connecticut in 1775, Spencer and his recruits from Middlesex County formed the Second Connecticut Regiment. The sixty-year-old colonel marched his troops to Roxbury to join the siege around Boston. In April a special session of the legislature promoted him to brigadier general and placed him in charge of the defense of his home colony. That summer his unit was merged into the Continental service.

Despite such laurels the steady Spencer was perturbed. The traditional Connecticut penchant for hierarchy had been cast aside. On 2 June 1775 Spencer had been made a brigadier general by Congress, while Israel Putnam, junior to Spencer but a more flamboyant military figure, was jumped to major general. Spencer, nicknamed "Granny" by his troops, was so irritated that he left camp on 6 July without forewarning commander in chief George Washington. Washington then held the Connecticut line in low regard. Spencer headed to Lebanon, Connecticut, where Governor Jonathan Trumbull and the council of safety met. At Gray's Tavern council members Samuel Huntington and William Williams persuaded Spencer to return to his command under Putnam. Soon thereafter a remonstrance from Spencer's staff on his behalf alerted politicians at home that the new scheme "so far removes General Spencer from his former command, that he cannot and will not continue in the service under this arrangement . . . we apprehend the morals and good order and discipline of our troops will be greatly endangered under the present arrangement."

A Connecticut delegate to Congress, Silas Deane, reportedly called for Spencer's resignation. But the Connecticut assembly, through its other delegates, mollified Spencer and his cadre. Trumbull, Roger Sherman, and others not only praised his wisdom, prudence, integrity, and military skill, they also salved his ego. He returned to his troops around Boston, served for the duration of the successful siege, and in the spring of 1776 moved south to defend New York City.

When Washington established his line of defense around New York, Spencer (officially a major general as of 9 Aug.) was one of his counselors. He was placed in command of a third of the forces until Nathanael Greene recovered from illness. Spencer, George Clinton, and William Heath in September urged Washington to hold his ground south of Harlem. When this strategy proved ill advised, Alexander McDougall labeled the trio "a fool [Spencer], a knave, and an honest, obstinate man." As the Continentals scrambled in retreat from Harlem Heights and White Plains, and Washington regrouped, Spencer was dispatched to New England. He established his headquarters at Providence and again proved himself inert and ill starred. In September 1777 he called off an amphibious attack from Tiverton to Rhode Island, rightly fearing surprise had been lost. When pressured by Congress, Spencer demanded a court of inquiry and was pleased to be exonerated.

Spencer resigned his commission on 13 January 1778 to return home. Spencer reestablished his provincial political base, first as a member of the council of safety, as an assembly deputy in 1778, and as assistant in 1779. On 7 January and 14 October 1779 he was elected to Connecticut's congressional delegation. He seems to have attended Congress only 1 June through 17 September 1779 but was not active. For the following two years as the war wound down, Spencer served again on the council of safety. He died in East Haddam. Spencer, like Putnam and David Wooster, proved a disappointment as a tactician and strategist. Nonetheless the commitment of each to the revolutionary movement was crucial.

• Spencer's clashes with Congress and within the Continental army can be traced in the *Papers of the Continental Congress*, National Archives (available in microfilm). The *Militia Papers*, 2d ser., vol. 28, Connecticut State Archives, charts Spencer's colonial career. The nuances of colonial and revolutionary Conn. are in Christopher Collier, *Roger Sherman's Connecticut* (1971), and Joy Day Buel and Richard Buel, Jr., *The Way of Duty* (1984). The careers of Spencer, Putnam, and others are briefly sketched in North Callahan, *Connecticut's Revolutionary War Leaders* (1973). The most caustic criticism is found in Douglas S. Freeman, *George Washington* (1948–1957).

LOUIS W. POTTS

SPENCER, Lilly Martin (26 Nov. 1822–22 May 1902), painter, was born in Exeter, England, to the French émigrés Gilles Marie Martin, a teacher, and Angélique LePetit. Christened Angélique Marie, she was always known as Lilly (which she also spelled Lily and Lille). Her parents were deeply committed to social reform, working for temperance, abolition, and woman suffrage. Their liberal social beliefs, especially their concern with women's rights, laid the groundwork for their daughter's future success. In October 1830 the family immigrated to the United States, where Lilly Martin Spencer was to become one of the best-known female artists of her era.

The Martins first settled in New York City, but in 1832 a cholera epidemic drove them westward to Marietta, Ohio, where they purchased a farm. The four Martin children were educated at home, and it was at home, with the encouragement of her father, that Lilly Martin began to develop her artistic talents. In 1841 she held her first public exhibition at a local church rectory. Her subjects were those that would preoccupy her throughout her career: humorous domestic scenes, literary themes, and portraits.

In 1841 Martin's father left his wife in charge of the household and moved with his daughter to Cincinnati so that she could pursue her artistic education. During her seven years there, Martin devoted herself to improving her art, obtaining advice from the painters James Beard and John Williams. Cincinnati, she wrote her mother on 21 January 1842, "is literally full of portrait painters . . . but I shall beat them all, I hope, one day."

Lilly Martin had been in Cincinnati less than three years when in August 1844 she married Benjamin Rush Spencer. For most women of her era, marriage meant the end of any professional career, but this was not the case with Lilly Martin Spencer. In her husband she found a supportive and cooperative helpmate, who, like her father, encouraged her art. In fact, through the long years of their marriage, it was her art that supported the family while Benjamin helped his wife with her painting and domestic chores. Domestic tasks were particularly heavy in the Spencer household since Lilly gave birth to at least eight (and possibly as many as thirteen) children, seven of whom lived to adulthood. With so many children to care for, and the sales of Spencer's art often erratic and prices generally low, the family was always under financial strain.

In hopes of ameliorating their financial condition, as well as improving her art, Spencer and her family moved to New York City in 1848. Within two years of her arrival, however, discouragement had set in. She wrote to her mother on 29 March 1850, "When we came to New York, I found myself so inferior to most of the artists here. . . . I do not actually get half as well paid for my works than I did west, and however have to do ten times better work."

To correct deficiencies in drawing and coloring pointed out by many of her contemporaries (criticism that dogged her throughout her career), Spencer began to take evening drawing classes at the National Academy of Design. At the same time, at the urging of a friend, she increasingly turned to her own home life for subject matter. Humorous and sentimental images of domestic life, such as the kitchen scene *Peeling Onions* (c. 1852), became a mainstay of her art. This picture depicts a woman, a dead chicken at her elbow, pausing in the midst of slicing onions to wipe a tear from her eye. Spencer's ability to evoke such familiar moments became the basis for her popular reputation. Among her other noteworthy works are *Domestic Happiness* (1849), *Shake Hands?* (1854), *Fi! Fo! Fum!* (1858), and *War Spirit at Home* (1866).

By the 1850s many of Spencer's paintings were being reproduced in lithographic form, and numerous sanguine reviews were appearing in the press. The *Cosmopolitan Art Journal* wrote of her in September 1857, "No person is doing more than Mrs. Spencer to 'popularize' art, and for that people owe her a debt of gratitude."

In 1859 Elizabeth F. Ellet included an entry on Spencer in her *Women Artists in All Ages and Countries*. Yet such acclaim seems to have done little to boost the artist's sales, and in 1858, to ease their fiscal burdens, the Spencers moved their family to Newark, New Jersey. From then on, Spencer took on any artistic work that came her way, painting portraits and still lifes, producing engravings for *Godey's Lady's Book*, and even hand coloring photographs, something, she said, "I thought I never would stoop to do."

In the years after the Civil War as tastes turned increasingly toward European art, Spencer found selling her works more and more difficult. Yet, displaying the pluck and determination that characterized her throughout her career, she persevered. In the late 1860s, perhaps in an attempt to compete with the French academic works that were then flooding the New York market, she began work on the painting that many of her contemporaries considered her masterpiece, the large-scale allegorical work, *Truth Unveiling Falsehood* (1869). The picture was exhibited at the Women's Pavilion at the Philadelphia Centennial in 1876, where it was awarded a medal. Yet this did little to stem the downward slide of Spencer's career. In 1879 the family moved to Highland, New York, where they shifted residences several times.

In 1900, ten years after her husband's death, Spencer returned to New York City where she died, still struggling to make a living from her art. By this time her homespun subject matter and detailed style had long fallen from favor, but she continued to be revered as a pioneering figure in the arts. In January 1897 Candace Wheeler, in an article about women artists for *Outlook*, wrote of Spencer (with some hyperbole): "As far as I know, Mrs. Spencer was the only woman painter of the time—at least the only one—oh, tremendous achievement!—who painted in oils."

• Spencer's papers are available on microfilm through the Archives of American Art, Smithsonian Institution, Washington, D.C. A book-length treatment of the artist is the exhibition catalog by Robin Bolton-Smith and William H. Truettner, *Lilly Martin Spencer, 1822–1902: The Joys of Sentiment* (1973); it contains an extensive bibliography. David Lubin's *Picturing a Nation* (1994) includes a chapter on Spencer's domestic genre painting and its relation to the class and gender conflicts of the era. See also Elizabeth Johns, *American Genre Painting: The Politics of Everyday Life* (1991), on Spencer's place in American genre painting, and Helen S. Langa, "Lilly Martin Spencer: Genre, Aesthetics, and Gender in the Work of a Mid-Nineteenth-Century Woman Artist," *Athanor* 9 (1990): 37–41, on Spencer's career in the context of changing gender roles at mid-century. An obituary is in the *New York Times*, 23 May 1902.

REBECCA BEDELL

SPENCER, Matthew Lyle (7 July 1881–10 Feb. 1969), journalist and university president, was born in Batesville, Mississippi, the son of Flournoy Poindexter Spencer, a Methodist Episcopal minister, and Alice Eleanor Manes. During his youth the family moved around Mississippi, because of his father's duties as a circuit preacher. In 1893 the Spencers left the state for Georgia. For the next three years Spencer lived with his parents until family conflicts forced him to leave home.

At Kentucky Wesleyan College Spencer won distinction as a scholar, earning his A.B. in 1903 and his A.M. the following year. While completing these degrees, he worked part time as an instructor and later as a professor (1903–1904) in the college's English department. In 1905 he graduated from Northwestern University, earning a second A.M. The following year he accepted a position as assistant professor of English at Wofford College in Spartanburg, South Carolina. Much admired by his students and fellow faculty, he remained at the college for the next three years. While at Wofford, Spencer married Lois Hill of Anderson, South Carolina, in 1908. They later had one child, Lyle Manly Spencer, who became founder of Science Research Associates Reading Laboratories and later founder of the Spencer Foundation. This first marriage ended rather bitterly some years later, although the reasons remain a mystery because Spencer refused to discuss, even privately, his early life.

In 1905–1906 and again in 1909–1910, Spencer was fellow of English at the University of Chicago, earning his Ph.D. from the university in 1910. After completion of his doctorate, he was offered a full professorship at the Woman's College of Alabama.

Spencer remained only one year at Woman's College, assuming a post in 1911 as English professor at Lawrence College in Appleton, Wisconsin. He stayed at this position until 1918. In 1913 he also served as reporter and copyreader for the *Milwaukee Journal*; in 1917 he accepted the position of chief editorial writer of the *Journal*. This position was short-lived because he felt it his duty, as war raged in Europe, to enlist in the military.

During the later part of World War I in 1918, Spencer became a captain in Military Intelligence for the United States Army. After the war Spencer maintained Army ties and in 1929 was appointed lieutenant colonel in the special reserves. He retained this rank until his retirement some ten years later.

In September 1919, Spencer resumed teaching, accepting a position as director of the school of journalism at the University of Washington. A year later he married Helen McNaughton; they had three children. On 11 January 1926 Spencer was appointed dean of the School of Journalism. In September of the following year, he accepted the position as president of the university, the university's "political" climate having become so intolerable that then president Dr. Henry Suzzallo had been dismissed. Initially, the faculty and staff favored the new administration because more attention was given to salary increases and promotion opportunities. However, under Spencer's tenure the university began demanding higher academic performance for its students. Spencer advocated that admission requirements be stiffened and that elective and so-called "sop-courses" be dropped. He felt arts and sciences should be the heart of higher education, thereby greatly diminishing the role of technical and vocational training.

After a short time, opposition to Spencer's programs began to grow. One of the first groups expressing dissatisfaction was the Seattle High School Teachers' League. The league felt that the university, and especially the president, were biased toward the graduate school and were preventing new students from enrolling. The university's policy, according to league members, was discriminatory toward students who possessed "merely average ability." This was the beginning of a grass-roots movement showing opposition to the elitism of Spencer's administration.

In 1932 Clarence D. Martin was elected state governor. The election of a Democrat marked an important change in state politics. Also noticeable was a major restructuring of the university's administrative autonomy and admissions policy, allowing the enrollment to reflect a broader demographic range. With new direction in government and university policy, changes on the university's administrative level became necessary. For these reasons, Spencer resigned as president.

Leaving the university in April 1933, Spencer traveled to the University of Chicago, where he taught one year. In 1934 he organized the School of Journalism at Syracuse University, believing journalism was a specialized form of English deserving its own curriculum. That same year, he was appointed the university's first dean of the School of Journalism. Later, while on leave, Spencer traveled to Egypt in 1936 and again in 1945 becoming a visiting professor at the American University in Egypt. It was during his first five-month visit, that Spencer founded that university's Department of Journalism.

During the war years Spencer also established, and was made dean of, the War Service College at Syracuse University. The college provided core courses in math, science, and language for men about to enter service. During this time he was also instrumental in establishing propaganda as a specialized journalistic form. Working with the government, Spencer trained foreign journalists and radio correspondents in the art of propaganda, which was later incorporated by Radio Free Europe. He also provided valuable insight into the psychological ramification of this new journalistic form being used by Nazi Germany and Japan.

Before retiring from Syracuse in 1951 as emeritus dean, Spencer also lectured at Oriental Culture Summer College in Tokyo (1940), received the Columbia Scholastic Press Association's Gold Medal (1946), and Syracuse University's Distinguished Service Medal. Upon retirement, Spencer moved to Clearwater, Florida, where he later died.

During his professional career, Spencer published several works, including *Corpus Christi Pageants in England* (1911), *Practical English Punctuation* (1914), *News Writing* (1917), and *Editorial Writing: Ethics, Policy and Practice* (1924). He edited William Gilmore Simms's *The Yemassee* (1911).

Spencer was a man of strong convictions, which at times were perceived as egotism and arrogance by his colleagues. Among students, however, Spencer was well loved and admired. In his long teaching and administrative career, he instilled ethical and moral qualities that would follow his students into their professional careers. He condemned the "editorial writer who expects salary or recognition in return for daily utterances of silken sayings advocating measures he thinks his employer wants." According to Spencer, "Prostitution of editorial brains is the greatest curse of the newspaper profession." Known as the "Father of Television Journalism," Spencer taught and inspired many early television journalists who either attended his classes or read and admired his works.

• Spencer's early days as assistant professor at Wofford are noted in *The Bohemian* (1909); the *Wofford College Journal*, Oct. 1910, p. 45; and David D. Wallace, *History of Wofford College* (1951). An account of his marriage to Lois Hill, while at Wofford, appears in the *Wofford College Journal*, 1908 holiday number, p. 155, and the *Spartanburg Herald*, 23 Dec. 1908. A brief sketch of his earlier journalistic views is found in *Emory Magazine*, Nov.–Dec. 1970, p. 77. Spencer's presidency at the University of Washington is covered at length in Charles M. Gates, *The First Century at the University of Washington, 1861–1961* (1961). There is a personal interview conducted with Spencer's son (Col. Orton Spencer) at the Batesville Public Library, Batesville, Miss. An obituary is in the *New York Times*, 12 Feb. 1969.

C. E. LINDGREN

SPENCER, Niles (16 May 1893–15 May 1952), painter, was born in Pawtucket, Rhode Island, the son of Henry Lewin Spencer and Margaret Allen. The Spencer family business interests in Pawtucket were extensive and included banking and manufacturing, as well as the historically important Slater's Mill. Spencer received his education at the Rhode Island School of Design, where he was awarded a degree in 1915. Summers were spent studying with Charles Woodbury and later with the more avant-garde group surrounding Hamilton Easter Field in Ogunquit, Maine. In the fall of 1916 Spencer moved to New York to continue his studies. The lively intellectual milieu of Greenwich Village was in its heyday, and Spencer was exposed to many of the radical theoreticians and personalities of the time, who encouraged him to begin working in new directions. Deeply influenced by Cézanne's faceted explorations of landscape and still life, Spencer's paintings began to focus on the geometry of architectural shapes and how they related to their surroundings.

One hundred years before Niles Spencer's birth, Samuel Slater effectively launched the United States into the industrial revolution at Slater's Mill by introducing the English technology for water-powered manufacturing of cotton yarn. Thus it was no coincidence that Spencer chose to paint icons of the machine age: factories and industrial or urban architecture. Spencer's long association with industry was something of a birthright—the inheritance from his family's investments enabled him to paint without the burden of teaching or other employment, and it provided him with a subject he was to analyze and reinterpret throughout his life.

Spencer's work is often associated with a group of American classicist painters called the precisionists, a loosely knit group including Charles Sheeler, Charles Demuth, Louis Lozowick, George Ault, Elsie Driggs, and Ralston Crawford. The precisionists depicted the expanding American industrial landscape in spare, economic, and, ultimately, utopian terms. Clarity of image, unmodulated surface, and dynamic, architectonic compositions were characteristic of the style. Searching for a singular American subject, they embraced technology and man's creations as the only truly modern subject. Veneration of the machine and industry was not uniquely an American phenomenon; European artists and theoreticians between the two world wars were exploring similar ideas. The precisionists, however, epitomized a preoccupation that was uniquely American by combining a nostalgia for the past, which was quickly disappearing, with an exaltation of the industrial dynamism of the future.

During the 1920s Spencer produced a series of paintings using the architectural landscape of Provincetown, Massachusetts, as his focus. In a typical painting, the distinctive vernacular architecture of New England is silhouetted in an atmospheric light-gray wash, characteristic of an overcast day at the water's edge. Although in the winters Spencer returned to New York, where he rented studio apartments or rooms in the Lafayette Hotel, he preferred seaside towns such as Ogunquit; Bristol, Rhode Island; Sag Harbor, New York; Provincetown; and New London, Connecticut, in the warmer months. In the 1930s he turned from the light-filled landscapes of Provincetown to studies of New York City and of industry. A mural commissioned by the U.S. Treasury Department in 1937 for a post office in Aliquippa, Pennsylvania, resulted in many drawings and oil studies. This was a new vocabulary of forms for Spencer, and when he returned to Provincetown his leitmotives were the railroad, construction equipment, ice plants, and other industrial subjects.

Spencer's painting method was painstakingly slow. He revised and reworked his compositions until he ar-

rived at something that satisfied him. The surfaces of his paintings are loosely brushed layers of subtle, tonal changes of color. The palimpsest of each painting—the artist's process of distillation and decision-making—is visible through the many layers and changes of shape. His paintings are unique among the precisionists for precisely this process. Painterly brushwork, sophisticated tonalities of color, and evocation of mood combined to create a style that is sensitive and unique within the cold, hard precisionist canon. He never sought the easy facility or lightness of touch that characterized the work of some of the precisionists but rather chose to be guided by his feelings. Spencer's career can be divided into several distinct stylistic periods: the early Ogunquit paintings (1913–1922), which show the influence of Cézanne; the Provincetown paintings (1923–1930); the paintings of industry and New York (1931–1942); and the late geometric work (1943–1952), which shows Spencer's turn toward abstraction. During this last period, shapes became more two-dimensional and stylized and the subject less identifiable. Still-life paintings made throughout his life reflected these different stylistic concerns.

Spencer's output was relatively small, a result of his slow methodical working methods and his early death of a heart attack in Dingman's Ferry, Pennsylvania. During his lifetime he had only two one-person exhibitions, one at the Charles Daniel Gallery in 1925 and another, twenty-two years later, at the Downtown Gallery in 1947. However, he was asked to exhibit often in group exhibitions at the Whitney Studio Club; the Downtown Gallery; the Carnegie Institute; the Corcoran Gallery of Art (now Museum) in Washington, D.C.; the Pennsylvania Academy of the Fine Arts; Stedelijk Museum, Amsterdam, Holland; California Legion of Honor, San Francisco; the Museum of Modern Art; the Metropolitan Museum of Art and the Whitney Museum of American Art, New York; and the Venice Biennale (1948). His awards include an honorable mention at the Carnegie International in 1930; and a purchase prize from the Metropolitan Museum of Art in 1942. A memorial exhibition of his work was organized and circulated by the Museum of Modern Art in 1954, and another circulating exhibition of his work was organized by the University of Kentucky in 1965. In 1990 the Whitney Museum of American Art held a retrospective of his work.

Spencer married twice. His first marriage in 1917 to Betty Lockett ended in divorce in 1942, and in 1947 he married Catherine Brett. He had no children. Although widely known and respected by artists and museum curators, he was often described as reticent and introspective. Unwilling or unable to promote his work in an increasingly commercial environment, Spencer was often missing from the large survey shows of the period. The tireless work of his dealer at the Downtown Gallery, Edith Halpert, helped to ensure that Spencer's modest but important contribution to American art was not forgotten.

• Spencer's papers are in the Archives of American Art, Smithsonian Institution, and include studies for his mural commission as well as correspondence. Not many statements by Spencer about his work have survived, but those available can be found in Holger Cahill, "Paintings, Second List," *Newark Museum* (1926); a letter to the editor of *Art News* 43 (Sept. 1944); and the catalog for the exhibition *Niles Spencer*, Downtown Gallery (1947). Two monographs on Spencer's life and work, both illustrated exhibition catalogs, are Richard Freeman, *Niles Spencer* (1965), and Wendy Jeffers and Karal Ann Marling's essays in the Whitney Museum catalog, *Niles Spencer*, which includes more up-to-date findings on Spencer and his work. Articles on Spencer's work published during his lifetime or just after his death are Cahill, "Niles Spencer," *Magazine of Art*, Nov. 1952, pp. 313–15; Alonzo Lansford, "Niles Spencer Exhibits Anew after 19 Years," *Art Digest* (Nov. 1947); Marya Mannes, "Niles Spencer: Painter of Simplicities," *Creative Art* (July 1930): 59–60; Ernest W. Watson, "Niles Spencer," *American Artist* (Oct. 1944): 4–17; and Henry McBride, "An Elegant American Painter," *Art News* (Mar. 1954): 20–21, 61–62. Discussions of Spencer's work can be found in Martin Friedman's *The Precisionist View in American Art* (1960); Karen Tsujimoto, *Images of America: Precisionist Painting and Modern Photography* (1982); and Dorothy Miller, "Niles Spencer," in *New Art in America: Fifty Painters of the 20th Century*, ed. John I. H. Baur (1957), pp. 103–7. Obituaries are in the *New York Times* and the *New York Herald Tribune*, both 17 May 1952.

WENDY JEFFERS

SPENCER, Peter (Feb. 1782–July 1843), founder of the Union Church of Africans, was born a slave in Kent County, Maryland. Much of his early life is shrouded in obscurity. There is no record of his parents' names. Freed upon the death of his master, he moved to Wilmington, Delaware, sometime in the 1790s and received a basic education in a free African school supported by Quakers.

In Wilmington, Spencer soon established a reputation as a shrewd businessman with unblemished honesty. The 1814 *Wilmington Directory* listed him as "a labourer" residing at the corner of French and Chestnut streets, and his work as a mechanic resulted in strong business ties with both blacks and whites. The intelligence, sound practical sense, and great dignity of character he displayed in the business arena and as a property owner were matched only by his deep religious faith and personal piety.

Spencer joined the Asbury Methodist Episcopal Church, a predominantly white congregation in Wilmington. He quickly emerged as a class leader and lay preacher, devoting special attention to the African members of Asbury. As the African membership increased, tensions developed over segregated seating arrangements and the efforts of white Methodists to control the spiritual lives of Africans. Unwilling to accept an inferior status, Spencer and William Anderson led some of the Africans out in June 1805 and organized Ezion Methodist Episcopal Church. The new church, named for the port of Ezion-Geber, where Solomon kept a fleet of ships, was to function in connection with Asbury and the mostly white Methodist Episcopal Conference. When Spencer, Anderson, and their followers sought to choose their own pastors, they encountered strong opposition in December 1812 from James Bateman, a white elder from Philadelphia, Pennsylvania, who had been appointed at Ezion. The two sides appeared in a Wilmington court, but Spencer and the other charter members soon abandoned the case, left Ezion, and took steps toward complete ecclesiastical separation and independence.

Spencer became a staunch advocate of black religious freedom and of religious nationalism among his people. In July 1813 he and his followers purchased a lot from Quakers and organized the Union Church of Africans, a body also called the Union Church of African Members, the African Union church, the African Union Methodist church, and the Union Methodist Connexion. Incorporated under the Delaware law of 1787 that authorized free religious bodies, the Union Church of Africans drew up articles of association, dated 18 September 1813, four days after Spencer and Anderson were ordained as elder ministers. The document was signed by some forty charter members, six of whom were women. Spencer's wife, Annes, would later emerge as a significant force in the new church, a development not surprising in view of its acceptance of women as licensed preachers.

Spencer became the first pastor of the Union Church of Africans, and his personality gave it character and direction. The church soon expanded with the addition of congregations in Christiana, Delaware, and Kennett Square, Pennsylvania. In contrast to African Methodist leaders like Richard Allen and James Varick, Spencer rejected the Methodist Episcopal structure in favor of a more democratic arrangement. His church's structure consisted of one lay order, known as ruling, or lay, elders, which constituted the central policy-making board in each congregation. There were three orders of preachers—elder ministers, deacons, and licensed preachers. Also in contrast to other African Methodist leaders, Spencer rejected the itineracy in favor of the stationed pastorate and chose the loosely associated church system over the strong traditional Methodist connectional system. He was similar to other African Methodist leaders in retaining the doctrine of the Methodist Episcopal church as embodied in its general rules, articles of religion, and discipline.

Spencer combined strong pastoral leadership with a devotion to the educational, moral, social, and economic uplift of people of African descent. Under his guidance, the Union Church of Africans established a regional base with thirty-one congregations in Delaware, Maryland, Pennsylvania, New Jersey, and New York. A school was organized in connection with each congregation; Spencer taught the values of personal morality, the monogamous and stable family life, temperance and sobriety, economic self-sufficiency and cooperation, and Christian social responsibility. To further promote strong family life, black unity, and communal liberation, he inaugurated in 1813 the Big August Quarterly, a socioreligious festival of African

Union Methodists in Wilmington that was still occurring annually at the end of the twentieth century.

Spencer's involvement in the independent African Methodist movement extended beyond his own church. Between 1813 and 1816 he participated in a movement in Attleborough, Pennsylvania, that resulted in a separate African Methodist congregation. When Richard Allen called for a general meeting of African Methodists in Philadelphia in 1816, Spencer was among those invited. Disagreements with Allen concerning church polity and detailed matters of the discipline, however, prevented him from joining Allen's African Methodist Episcopal church. Besides, his own denomination was already organized, and he saw no need to unship matters a second time.

Spencer's name remains prominent in black church history and the black freedom movement. His strong stand against colonization and in favor of emancipation and the abolition of slavery stands as testimony to his significance as both a Christian leader and a proponent of equal rights and social justice. He stood tall among those imbued with a black nationalist consciousness in his time. His vision for his church and his people as a whole found expression in the 1822 and 1839 editions of his church's hymnal and in *The Doctrine and Discipline of the African Union Church* (1813).

Spencer died in Wilmington. Eight years after his death, a dispute erupted within the ranks of his church, resulting in a major schism in 1855–1856. Both the African Union Methodist Protestant church and the Union American Methodist Episcopal church claim Spencer as their founder.

• For information on Spencer's life, see Lewis V. Baldwin, *The Mark of a Man: Peter Spencer and the African Union Methodist Tradition* (1987); issues of the *Colored American*, 20 May 1837 and 21 Oct. 1837; Jacob F. Ramsey, *Father Spencer, Our Founder: His Work for the Church and the Race* (1914); Daniel J. Russell, Jr., *History of the African Union Methodist Protestant Church* (1920); and *The Discipline of the Union Church of Africans for the State of Delaware and Elsewhere*, 2d ed. (1841). An obituary is in the *Delaware State Journal*, 28 July 1843.

LEWIS V. BALDWIN

SPENCER, Platt Rogers (7 Nov. 1800–16 May 1864), penman and educator, was born in East Fishkill, New York, the son of Caleb Spencer and Jerusha Covell, farmers. After the death of Spencer's father in 1810, the family sought opportunity in the West and moved to Jefferson, Ohio. With a few brief exceptions, Spencer spent the rest of his life in this northeastern corner of Ohio. Spencer was unable to begin his formal education until he was twelve. But since paper was very expensive, he indulged his fondness for penmanship before and after on beds of sand, snowbanks, and any other surface he could find. His school training, though uneven, mirrored Americans' efforts to make educational opportunities universal. They placed strong emphasis on teaching students to read and write, thereby ensuring the perpetuation of their democratic ideals.

Penmanship was an important part of this process. Writing masters during the colonial period tended to maintain European traditions, passing along old techniques to a few promising students. It was an art form that required a certain degree of natural ability and considerable training. Such specialization did not fit well with the egalitarian goals of nineteenth-century educators. As a result, the first half of the century witnessed a relaxation of form and discipline in an effort to make writing skills accessible to everyone.

Technology also aided in this process. Quilled writing instruments, which eighteenth-century writing masters had to construct and maintain for their students, gave way to steel-tipped pens and lead pencils early in the century. In addition, engraving made it possible for each student to practice from individual copybooks. Together, these two developments freed instructors to teach classes of students instead of individuals.

Teaching in classes encouraged the adaptation of innovative European techniques designed to facilitate group learning. Johann Pestalozzi's theories taught uniform writing methods by using five horizontal lines, similar to the music staff. The Carstairs Method introduced an elaborate system of muscular exercises. They were "based on the unerring laws of nature as developed in the anatomy of the arms, hands, and fingers," wrote Benjamin F. Foster, who introduced this system to the country (quoted in Dougherty, p. 282).

By the mid-nineteenth century, Spencer emerged as the most popular synthesizer of the various techniques and theories. He adopted an elliptical style, which he attributed to the windblown flora he observed along the shores of Lake Erie in his youth. This story became mythologized over the years, until the Spencerian style was assumed to have a totally self-taught origin. More critical analysis led historian Ray Nash to conclude that Spencer, in fact, owed much to two earlier American chirographers, Benjamin F. Foster and Allison Wrifford.

Spencer opened a school on the family farm before he was twenty. To help meet expenses, he also found employment aboard Great Lakes cargo vessels and as a store clerk. Throughout this period he continued to perfect a style that incorporated elements of both efficiency and legibility, as well as being aesthetically pleasing.

Despite his rise to prominence in the 1850s, Spencer was not the only chirographer hoping to win favor with the public. Three elements came together to make Spencer's system a success. First, he formed a partnership with the influential Victor Moreau Rice, the superintendent of Public Instruction of the State of New York. Second, Spencer's marriage in 1828 to Persis Duty resulted in a family of six sons and five daughters. At one time they, their cousins, and in-laws—thirty-eight in all—taught the Spencerian System. Other influential penmen of the time joined with the family to popularize his style. Finally, Spencer incorporated his passion for poetry into the writing exercises in his stylebooks. Such verses as the following, printed in the 1857 *Compendium of Spencerian or Semi-Angular* copybook, taught his techniques at the same time they eliminated the drudgery of normally unimaginative writing exercises:

Let the pen glide like a gently rolling stream,
Restless but yet unwearied and serene;
Forming and blending forms with graceful ease,
Thus Letter, Word and Line are born to please. (p. 183)

Despite his later success, Spencer had a drinking problem in his twenties that forced him to abandon his goal of entering the ministry. With the assistance of his wife, he overcame his addiction to become an outspoken advocate of temperance by 1832. In addition, Spencer also became active in the abolitionist movement, being one of the founders of the Ashtabula County Anti-Slavery Society. He wrote and spoke out on these issues steadfastly throughout his life.

Spencer died at his home in Geneva, Ohio, never fully recovering from the death of his wife two years earlier. Technology has relegated Spencer and his fellow chirographers to the position of practitioners of a quaint form of communication from a less-hurried time. Today, speed and content have become paramount; form has become standardized and purely mechanical. Spencer's contributions to the art of penmanship gained popularity during the 1850s as the nation's educational system sought uniformity in instruction and grading. The wide acceptance of the Spencerian System meant that it would have a profound influence on penmanship forms well into the twentieth century.

• Spencer's papers are at the Newberry Library in Chicago. Copies of his stylebooks can be found at archives, museums, and bookstores across the country. For a bibliography of Spencerian copybooks, see Ray Nash, *American Penmanship, 1800–1850: A History of Writing and a Bibliography of Copybooks from Jenkins to Spencer* (1969). Mary L. Dougherty offers a brief discussion of Spencer in "History of the Teaching of Handwriting in America," *Elementary School Journal* 18 (Dec. 1917): 280–86. Spencer also has a somewhat fanciful entry in the Lewis Publishing Company's *Biographical History of Northeastern Ohio* (1893).

W. BRUCE BOWLUS

SPENCER, Robert Clossen, Jr. (13 Apr. 1864–9 Sept. 1953), architect, was born in Milwaukee, Wisconsin, the son of Robert C. Spencer, Sr., and Elizabeth Whiton King. Spencer's paternal grandfather, Platt R. Spencer, a vocal advocate of good penmanship and creator of the Spencerian hand, established a network of commercial schools, and R. C. Spencer, Sr., worked as the head of a Spencerian Business College.

In 1886 Spencer received a bachelor's degree in mechanical engineering from the University of Wisconsin. During his senior year, Spencer had befriended Frank Lloyd Wright, a nondegree student three years his junior. After drafting for a year for the Milwaukee architect Henry Koch, Spencer enrolled in the Massachusetts Institute of Technology in the fall of 1887, leaving after a year to work for the Boston firms of

Wheelwright & Haven (1888–1889) and Shepley, Rutan & Coolidge (1890–1891). In 1891 Spencer became the eighth recipient of the Rotch Traveling Fellowship, sketching in Italy, France, and England for two years and producing an impressive group of exquisite renderings. In 1893 he was sent to Shepley, Rutan & Coolidge's Chicago office to take charge of the interior decoration of the public library and the Art Institute of Chicago, both under construction. Spencer provided Renaissance-inspired designs for mosaics that were manufactured by Tiffany and installed in the library's many public spaces, while his scheme for the grand staircase of the Art Institute remained unexecuted.

In 1894 Spencer entered private practice in Chicago, forming a short-lived partnership with another draftsman from Shepley's, Robert R. Kendall. In March 1895 he took an office next to Frank Lloyd Wright's in Adler & Sullivan's Schiller Building. The two were soon inseparable; as Wright recalled, "Chicago conformists working in other offices, seeing us arm in arm down the street, would say in derision, 'There goes God-almighty with his Jesus Christ.'"

In 1897 Spencer and Wright joined Dwight H. Perkins and Myron Hunt in the loft of Perkins's newly completed Steinway Hall. Exchanging ideas and sharing draftsmen, the four architects attempted to answer Louis Sullivan's call for a modern American architecture that was free from the overt use of historic precedent. They formed the nucleus of a movement that eventually became known as the Prairie School.

In 1899 Spencer married Ernestine Elliott of Bath, Maine; they had three children. Moving to River Forest, Spencer established a flourishing domestic practice in Chicago's northern and western suburbs. He also received scores of commissions from small-town midwestern businessmen and designed occasional buildings for clients from all across the country. Several of his most important estates were landscaped by Jens Jensen, including the suburban mansion of August Magnus (Winnetka, Ill., 1904) and the country estates of Susan Denkman (Rock Island, Ill., 1909) and Fred Smith (near Terre Haute, Ind., 1909). Through Spencer's office passed numerous draftsmen who later established important Prairie School firms, including Walter Burley Griffin and Andrew Willatzen. In November 1905 Spencer took Horace S. Powers as his partner, forming the firm of Spencer & Powers.

Spencer's personal modern style first appeared in 1902 with the U. G. Orendorff house (Canton, Ill.). Fully formed by 1904, his style varied little thereafter. Consisting of simple geometric masses, often articulated with stained wooden boards that vaguely resembled medieval half-timbering and whose only decoration consisted of leaded windows of abstracted floral patterns, his buildings are related to but distinctly different from Wright's more complex and subtle Prairie designs.

By 1900, when he published the first major account of Wright's work in *Architectural Review (Boston)*, Spencer had embarked on a second career, writing architectural criticism for technical, professional, and popular journals. By 1915 he had penned more than seventy-five articles, mostly addressed to potential clients rather than colleagues. In addition to explaining the Chicago architects' goals of providing functional and practical designs that were aesthetically significant and original, Spencer often discussed contemporary architecture in England and Germany, bringing these foreign movements to the attention of his American audience.

The treatment of windows was of particular interest to Spencer. Leaded, stained-glass, casement windows grouped together under broad overhanging roofs were among the trademarks of the Prairie School. But casement windows presented a separate set of technical problems from the more common double-hung sash windows, as Spencer explained in "The Window Problem" (*House Beautiful*, May 1902). To remedy the situation, Spencer began inventing new window hardware and was awarded U.S. patents for a window lock in 1903 and casement adjusters in 1905 and 1908. In 1906 he organized the Casement Hardware Company and began manufacturing his inventions, which were eagerly sought out by his colleagues, including Wright and Griffin.

In 1909 Spencer was made a fellow in the American Institute of Architects. In 1917, by which time the office had completed nearly 275 projects, the firm was enlarged to Spencer, Powers and Martin with the addition of Edwin Martin, a graduate of Cornell University. Yet by then work had fallen off drastically, both because of World War I and because of a change of taste in favor of more conservative architectural styles among their midwestern clients that left many Prairie School architects unemployed. The partnership, which never recovered, was disbanded in 1923.

In 1928 Spencer emerged from semiretirement to accept a teaching position in the architecture department at Oklahoma College of Agriculture and Mining at Stillwater. Two years later he moved again, this time to Gainesville, Florida, where he taught at the University of Florida until 1933. At his wife's death in 1942, he moved to Tucson, Arizona, to spend his remaining years with his daughter. Spencer died in Tucson.

Spencer left a legacy of finely crafted Prairie School buildings in America's heartland. Of equal importance, his talent for explaining Chicago's turn-of-the-century modern architecture to the layman contributed greatly to the widespread, if brief, success of the Prairie School architects.

• Spencer's office papers have not been preserved, and very little documentary material remains. He donated the drawings he produced for the Rotch Traveling Fellowship to the Massachusetts Institute of Technology. The largest selection of his buildings to appear in a single article is William G. Purcell's "Spencer and Powers, Architects," *Western Architect* 20 (Apr. 1914): 35–39 and 24 unnumbered plates. The most complete investigation of the context of Spencer's career, as well as an evaluation of a handful of his buildings, is H. Allen Brooks's *The Prairie School* (1972). A sampling of Spencer's many articles includes "The Work of Frank Lloyd Wright," *Architectural Review (Boston)* 7 (June 1900): 61–72; "American Farmhouses," *Brickbuilder* 9 (Sept. 1900): 179–86; "Half-timber and Casements," *House Beautiful*, Dec. 1901, pp. 13–20; "Brick Architecture in and about Chicago," *Brickbuilder* 12 (Sept. and Nov. 1903): 178–87, 222–30, and 13 (Mar. 1904): 54–60; "Some New Ideas in Electric Lighting," *House Beautiful*, Mar. 1907, pp. 30–36; and "The Construction of the Stucco House," *Suburban Life*, Apr. 1912, pp. 244–47, 264–65.

PAUL KRUTY

SPENCER, Samuel (2 Mar. 1847–29 Nov. 1906), railroad president, was born in Columbus, Georgia, the son of Lambert Spencer, a planter and cotton merchant, and Vernona Mitchell. Spencer attended the elementary schools of Columbus and at the age of fifteen enrolled in the Georgia Military Institute at Marietta. He left the institute in 1863 to enlist as a private in Nelson's Rangers, a cavalry troop that included several other Columbus boys. Later Spencer served under General Nathan B. Forrest and also under General John B. Hood. After the war he spent a few months on his father's plantation before enrolling in the University of Georgia, from which he graduated with first honors in 1867. Even though his family hoped he would enter his father's cotton business, Spencer enrolled in the University of Virginia, receiving a civil engineering degree in 1869.

Spencer's first railroad employment was in 1869 as a rodman on the Savannah & Memphis Railroad, a short line in Alabama. He was promoted to higher posts and by 1872 was principal engineer. Spencer was married in 1872 to Louisa Vivien Benning, the daughter of Henry L. Benning, a judge of the Georgia Supreme Court. The couple had three children. In 1872 Spencer worked briefly on the New Jersey Southern Railroad. From 1872 to 1877 he was employed in both the traffic and transportation departments of the Baltimore & Ohio Railroad. After working for a short time on the Virginia Midland Railroad, Spencer became the superintendent of the Long Island Railroad in 1877. On the Long Island Spencer came to the attention of J. Pierpont Morgan, whose bank held some Long Island Railroad securities. Morgan was impressed with Spencer's tact and general knowledge of railroading.

In October 1879 Spencer returned to the Baltimore & Ohio as assistant to the president, John W. Garrett. In 1881 Spencer and Garrett went to Europe, where they secured a major loan for the B&O. On their return Spencer was appointed third vice president of the B&O. A year later he was elevated to second vice president. In 1884 he was made first vice president in charge of operations, when Robert Garrett became president upon the death of his father. During his years as president Robert Garrett depended heavily on the advice of Spencer. Garrett gave up the B&O presidency in the fall of 1887, and Spencer was elected president on 10 December 1887. Spencer was an active and forceful chief executive. He reduced the large B&O floating debt by selling the railroad's sleeping-car and telegraph services. Spencer believed that too much ancient rolling stock and certain rail securities were overvalued on the company books. The editors of the *Railroad Gazette* were pleased with the Spencer reforms as revealed in the B&O annual report. However, many members of the Baltimore & Ohio board were unhappy with the Spencer administration, and they also feared that the Drexel, Morgan & Company bank was trying to control the B&O through Spencer. Spencer resigned from the B&O presidency on 19 December 1888.

Spencer joined Drexel, Morgan & Company in March 1889 as a railway expert. By the end of 1890 he was made a partner in the firm. During the early 1890s the banking firm was very active in aiding and reorganizing several southern lines with financial problems. In 1892 the Richmond & Danville, which with its holding company, the Richmond Terminal Company, controlled a number of lines in six southern states, was facing receivership. In 1893 Drexel, Morgan & Company agreed to reorganize the Richmond & Danville and appointed Spencer one of the receivers for the troubled system. In the following reorganization several of the weaker lines were not included, but the new Southern Railway, a road of 4,600 miles, was established in June 1894, with Spencer as president.

Almost at once Spencer was seen to be an efficient and conservative manager of the new railroad. He grasped problems, paid great attention to detail, and was able to present his viewpoint clearly and directly. Since Spencer had risen through the ranks of railroad labor, he was popular with his employees. He directed his traffic officials to woo lumberyards, iron and steel mills, furniture manufacturers, and others who would use the southern states' rich natural resources. As early as 1901 Spencer was actively joining the "good roads" movement, which enabled farmers to move their crops to town. Spencer was seeking to make the South prosper as well as his Southern Railway. He urged the diversification of southern agriculture and also increased trade with Latin America. Spencer had earlier made an agreement with Milton H. Smith, president of the Louisville & Nashville, that neither road would promote or acquire new lines in the territory of the other without prior consultation. For several years these two major southern rail systems cooperated as they both expanded their mileage.

The Southern Railway greatly expanded its system in the decade after its creation. In 1895 Spencer gained control of the Alabama Great Southern and three years later acquired the Memphis & Charleston. Other smaller lines also were added. In the first dozen years the Southern Railway grew to a system of 7,500 miles with service to Washington, D.C., Richmond, Norfolk, Charleston, Atlanta, Chattanooga, Mobile, Memphis, Cincinnati, and St. Louis. In the same years freight and passenger traffic more than tripled, and annual earnings climbed from $17 million to $53 million. Spencer used most of the net income on road improvements and the purchase of equipment. The Southern Railway would pay no dividends on its common stock until after World War I. Instead Spencer was positioning his line for solid growth and continuing prosperity.

In the early years of the twentieth century Spencer was an ardent opponent of any further federal regulation of railroad rates. As spokesman for the railroads he vigorously opposed the Hepburn Act of 1906, which gave the Interstate Commerce Commission the power to set railroad rates under judicial review. Spencer died near Lynchburg, Virginia, in a rear-end collision of two of his own fast passenger trains. On the day of his funeral, in Washington, D.C., every Southern Railway train stood still for a five-minute observance. Samuel Spencer was a leading spokesman both for the railway industry and for the New South.

• Spencer's brief career with the Baltimore & Ohio Railroad is reviewed in John F. Stover, *History of the Baltimore & Ohio Railroad* (1987). Stuart Daggett, *Railroad Reorganization* (1908), gives details on the creation of the Southern Railway in the mid 1890s. For Spencer's dozen years with the Southern Railway, see Burke Davis, *The Southern Railway: Road of Innovators* (1985). Spencer's cooperation with the Louisville & Nashville Railroad is described in Maury Klein, *History of the Louisville & Nashville Railroad* (1972). An obituary is in the *New York Times*, 30 Nov. 1906.

JOHN F. STOVER

SPENGLER, Joseph John (19 Nov. 1902–2 Jan. 1991), economist and demographer, was born near Piqua, Ohio, the son of Joseph Otto Spengler and Philomena Schlosser, probably farmers. In 1927 he married Dorothy Marie Kress; they had no children. He received the A.B. in 1926, the M.A. in 1929, and the Ph.D. in economics in 1930, all from Ohio State University. His mentor at Ohio State was the well-known demographer Albert B. Wolfe.

While a graduate student at Ohio State in 1927–1930, Spengler held instructorship appointments there. He was also a research fellow of the Brookings Institution in 1928. After a brief period on the faculty of the University of Arizona in 1930–1932 and 1933–1934, he joined the faculty of Duke University in Durham, North Carolina, in 1934, having spent a visiting year there in 1932–1933. He was a member of the Duke economics faculty for the remainder of his career. From 1955 on, he was a James B. Duke Professor. Although he retired in 1972, he continued an active scholarly life at Duke for another decade.

Spengler's early interest in demography, as evidenced by his dissertation in the field, was maintained throughout his career. However, he never confined himself to that one field. In his first major work, *France Faces Depopulation* (1938), Spengler exhibited two professional interests in addition to the demographic—the history of thought and economic history—correlative interests that he would maintain throughout his career. Nevertheless, it was population problems that held center stage in that first major work. *France Faces Depopulation* argued that the recent history of French birth rates pointed to a significant future decline of the population with ominous implications for the future of France. In the 1930s a nation's military strength was often equated with the number of men of military-service age in the population. This, in turn, had important political implications for the nation's role in world affairs. As much as attention has been paid to population questions in the second half of the twentieth century by economists, in the period in which Spengler began his work in demography economists paid little attention to those questions. In his magisterial history of economic thought, written during and immediately after World War II, Joseph A. Schumpeter argued that major changes in economic theory around 1875, which decreased emphasis on long-run development of an economy and increased emphasis on short-run market effects, especially those coming from the buyers' side, led population economics to, as Schumpeter put it, "wilt."

What Schumpeter did not foresee was that two areas of economics—economic growth and economic development—would become of major importance to the profession in the second half of the twentieth century. In both of these areas population change, either directly or as reflected in labor force change, was a key element. In addition, the explosive growth of population in the world after World War II focused attention on demography and on related policy questions. *France Faces Depopulation* was republished in 1979, forty-one years after its first publication, perhaps the ultimate accolade for a scholar's work.

In 1940 Spengler published "Sociological Presuppositions of Economic Theory," an article that was a forerunner of still another lifelong interest—the philosophical and interdisciplinary aspects of economic thought. Four years after the publication of *France Faces Depopulation*, Spengler produced *French Predecessors of Malthus* (1942), a work that combined his interest in population problems with his interest in the history of economic ideas. There followed a brief fallow period of scholarly output; 1943 was the only year of his entire active career (1930–1980) when no scholarly publication by Spengler made an appearance. The reason for this was simple: he was engaged full time in 1942–1943 as regional price executive of Region 4 (Southeast U.S.) of the wartime Office of Price Administration. This experience seems to have reinforced his aversion to governmental bureaucracy and to bureaucrats generally.

In 1948 Spengler published a striking article, "The Problem of Order in Economic Affairs," which had been his 1947 presidential address to the Southern Economic Association. It evinces Spengler's insistence on keeping firm contact with the real world of economic life while generalizing and theorizing about the social phenomenon that an economic system represents. In this respect, as in several others, he might be classified as an institutional economist but not one of a doctrinaire type.

"The Problem of Order in Economic Affairs" is an example of Spengler's breadth of approach to large issues as well as to the erudition that illumined his papers written in this vein. The great challenge for the economic theorist is to provide an explanatory model of an economy in which the actions of millions of individuals result in an orderly production and exchange of goods and services. In the real world, each economic system, if it is to survive, must reconcile the autonomy of individuals with the necessity of their coordination in economic activity without significant interruption over time. Two general types predominate: the market economy and the state-directed economy. When Spengler wrote his presidential address in 1947, the contest between these two types, represented by the United States and the Soviet Union, was of worldwide importance. Spengler's article was a masterly exposition and evaluation of this contest, grounded in a remarkable survey of relevant economic and intellectual history. He headed the piece with an apt quotation from the philosopher A. N. Whitehead and then stated that "the problem of economic order is taking on the importance it had in classic Rome about the time Augustus substituted the principiate for the republic, and in Western Europe during the period of religious strife when Bodin [1530–1596] and others were searching for a means of unifying the community."

Later, in speaking of the particularization of social science in the modern period, he said, "With the differentiation of social science and social scientists, particular hypothetical subrealms of being have fallen under the dominion of particular groups of social scientists who have been implicitly charged, somewhat after the manner of priesthoods in ancient Egypt, to make their respective hypothetical subrealms of being adequately represent the corresponding and referent real subrealms of being." Such seemingly casual but penetrating analogies are often found in Spengler's more philosophical writings.

Spengler's analytical powers were truly impressive, at times approaching prescience. Speaking forty years before the Soviet Union began to crumble, he said in "Problem of Order" that "a centrally planned economy . . . almost certainly will neither maximize the rate of growth of per capita income nor bring about the particular kind of coordination most men want. For the entrepreneurial state lacks and probably will continue to lack the know-how, the moral integrity, the inventiveness, the capacity to give incentive, and the flexibility of economic behavior requisite in a dynamic world."

These three broad themes—demography, the history of economics, and the relationship of economics to other disciplines (especially philosophy and sociology)—were pursued by Spengler throughout his long professional career. In a period in which the discipline of economics became increasingly specialized and more and more isolated from other related areas of study, Spengler refused to narrow his interests. One important lesson of his career is that diverse but wisely chosen areas of study can reinforce one another. Thus he demonstrated that all scholarly productivity gains need not require increasing scholarly specialization.

Spengler's career was not a cloistered one. He was active in various professional organizations, a number of which honored him with an office or other distinction. He served as president not only of the Southern Economic Association (1947) but of the Population Association of America (1957), the American Economic Association (1965), and the Atlantic Economic Association (1976–1977) as well. His relationship with the History of Economics Society was a particularly close one; he was a founding member and a moving spirit in its birth in 1968. Later he served as its president and was honored as its distinguished fellow. He was also a key figure in the inauguration in 1968 of the *History of Political Economy* journal, published at Duke. These two initiatives revivified an important field of economics. Their continuing viability is testimony to the foresight of Spengler and a few colleagues at Duke.

A particularly fitting honor was Spengler's election in 1954 to the American Philosophical Society because the breadth of his intellectual interests exemplified the aims of that organization. He was also a recipient of the society's John F. Lewis Award. In very different arenas, he was a fellow of both the American Statistical Association, a recognition of his contributions to the mathematics of population change, and the American Association of Arts and Sciences. Finally, his individualistic political stance was reflected in his membership in the Mt. Pellerin Society, a conservative, libertarian group. He died in Durham.

In an assessment of Spengler's contribution for the American Philosophical Society, Allen Kelley, Spengler's colleague and close associate in his demographic work, said, "Professor Spengler's lifetime research program on the nexus of economics and demography represents his most important seminal contribution to the advancement of knowledge" (Kelley, p. 143). Spengler began his work in demography and economics when population questions were almost excluded from mainstream economics. More than anyone else of his generation of scholars, Spengler changed that situation. Indeed, at first he was almost alone in the endeavor, but Spengler never sought to march to someone else's drum. He possessed a kind of intellectual courage and independence rare in scholarly circles.

• For additional information on Spengler, including a bibliography of his demographic and other publications for the period 1929–1971, see Robert S. Smith et al., eds., *Population Economics: Selected Essays of Joseph J. Spengler* (1972), pp. 515–28. His later articles are indexed in American Economic Association, *Index of Economic Articles*, annual volumes for 1972–1980 and 1982–1984. Two of Spengler's later works are *Indian Economic Thought: Preface to Its History* (1971) and *Origins of Economic Thought and Justice* (1980). Spengler's own estimate, made late in life, was that he had published more than 250 articles. An assessment of his contributions to the field of demography is Allen C. Kelley, *Proceedings of the American Philosophical Society* 136 (1992): 142–47; a photograph accompanies this article. A similar assessment of Spengler's contributions to the history of economics is in Irving Sobel, "Joseph J. Spengler: The Institu-

tionalist Approach to the History of Economics," in *The Craft of the Historian of Economic Thought*, ed. Warren J. Samuels (1983). An evaluation by a former student is that of Leonard Silk in the *New York Times*, 4 Jan. 1991. An obituary is in the *New York Times*, 3 Jan. 1991.

ROYALL BRANDIS

SPERANZA, Gino Carlo (23 Apr. 1872–12 July 1927), immigration lawyer and author, was born in Bridgeport, Connecticut, the son of Carlo Leonardo Speranza, a professor of Italian literature at Yale and Columbia Universities, and Adele Capetti. His parents were both natives of Verona, Italy, and the family returned there frequently. Speranza received part of his early education in Verona as well as in the public schools of New York City. He then studied at City College of New York, receiving a B.S. (1892) and an M.S. degree (1895). Speranza took legal training at New York University Law School, earning an LL.B. in 1894 and joining the New York and federal bars in 1895. In 1909 he married Florence Colgate, a Barnard College graduate (1895) and settlement house activist. They did not have children.

International law was Speranza's specialty, and his interests focused on relations between the United States and Italy, particularly issues affecting Italian immigration. In 1897 he became legal counsel to the Italian consulate general in New York City. The Emigration Commission of the Italian government soon retained him to create a network of legal defense bureaus for Italian immigrants. In this capacity, he launched investigations of labor riots involving Italian-American workers in the West Virginia mining districts in 1906. This work induced the State Department to retain him for advice on immigration problems involving Italy and the United States. During his career, he intervened in the cases of hundreds of immigrants who encountered difficulties in the United States.

From 1900 to 1912 Speranza's legal talents earned him a variety of appointments and honors. He was a member of the Law Commission of the New York Prison Association and assisted in writing New York's probation laws. The Order of St. Christopher retained him as director of its training school for probation officers. In 1906, as a member of New York City's Intermunicipal Research Council, he helped write an extensive report on immigration that identified a host of problems but also proposed remedies. He served on the New York State Immigration Commission in 1910, and later he chaired the Commission on Crime and Immigration of the American Institute of Criminal Law. He also served on the executive council of Richmond Hill Settlement House in New York City.

In the same period, Speranza published many articles on Italian immigration in the nation's major popular and legal journals, including the *Outlook*, the *Journal of Criminal Law*, *Charities*, the *Nation*, and the *Survey*. Although he often discussed the positive aspects of Italian immigration and urged greater acceptance of cultural differences, he also covered the troubling dimensions of immigration. Speranza wrote with great insight on the crime, labor problems, "urban congestion," and various legal difficulties encountered by immigrants.

He was a founding member and secretary of the Society for the Protection of Italian Immigrants. Begun in 1901 by Sara Wool Moore, a New York City settlement house worker, this organization sought to "afford advice, information and protection of all kinds to Italian immigrants." Speranza spearheaded successful efforts to create a corps of uniformed guards, private employees of the society, to protect immigrants from confidence men who lurked at train stations and on Ellis Island. He also worked to establish an information bureau to provide advice on transportation and housing and to acquire quarters for lodging accommodations, loan libraries, an Italian theater, kindergartens, and dining facilities. Speranza initiated the society's most ambitious program in 1902, a labor bureau designed to counteract the influence of exploitive Italian labor agents, the padroni. The labor bureau attempted to find work for low standardized fees at approved job sites out of New York City. In conjunction with this project, Speranza published the results of his investigations into forced labor of immigrants in the South (especially West Virginia) in 1903.

When the society terminated the labor bureau in 1905, Speranza resigned and began two initiatives of his own with the backing of the Italian government. In 1906 he became director and chief investigating officer of the Investigating Bureau for Italian Immigrants, an agency designed to pursue cases of industrial safety negligence and fraud. He also established a Labor Information Office to provide services previously offered by the labor bureau.

In 1912 Speranza gave up his legal practice to concentrate on his writing career and to devote more time to volunteer activities. He became extensively involved with the School of Italian Industries, a venture his wife had begun in 1905. The school trained Italian immigrant women in the skills of making lace and embroidery as a means of providing livelihoods and preserving traditional crafts. Continuing until 1927, it may have been the longest-lived experiment of its kind in the United States.

When Italy entered World War I in 1915, Speranza went to the Italian front as a feature correspondent for the *New York Evening Post*, authoring more than sixty articles on the war. In April 1917 he volunteered to work with the American embassy and soon received an official appointment as attaché in the Political Intelligence Division. In this capacity, he traveled extensively throughout the military regions of Italy, writing a variety of reports. He remained in Italy after the armistice but suffered sharply from the anti-American backlash occasioned by President Woodrow Wilson's stand against Italian territorial claims. He returned to New York City in 1919 disillusioned by these negative reactions and determined to reconsider his positions on nationalism and immigration.

Speranza's earlier commitment to cultural pluralism and "soft assimilation" gave way to a conviction that

the United States was dangerously threatened by continued mass immigration. He brought these views together in *Race or Nation?: A Conflict of Divided Loyalties* (1925), a passionately argued work advocating a rigid program of Americanization. Speranza called for the cessation of immigration, the breakup of immigrant "colonies" in the United States, a twenty-year period for naturalization, and a constitutional amendment mandating use of a common, English language.

Ironically, during his last years he also actively worked on writing a comprehensive history of Italian contributions to the United States. In pursuit of this project, he had discovered and annotated the manuscripts of colonial American agent Philip Mazzei in Florence, Italy. Plagued by ill health throughout his life, Speranza died in a New York City hospital before finishing the project.

• The Gino Carlo Speranza and Florence Colgate Speranza Papers are in the Manuscripts Division, New York Public Library, and Speranza's papers from wartime Italy are in the Hoover Library at Stanford University. His *Diary of Gino Speranza: Italy, 1915–1919*, ed. Florence C. Speranza (2 vols., 1941), covers the war years and contains a partial bibliography of Speranza's writings. George E. Pozzetta, "Gino C. Speranza: Reform and the Immigrant," in *Reform and Reformers in the Progressive Era*, ed. D. R. Colburn and Pozzetta (1983), presents an overview of his life. Olga Peragallo, *Italian American Authors and Their Contribution to American Literature* (1949), provides a brief sketch of his literary career. An obituary is in the *New York Times*, 13 July 1927.

GEORGE E. POZZETTA

SPERRY, Charles Stillman (3 Sept. 1847–1 Feb. 1911), rear admiral in the U.S. Navy, was born in Brooklyn, New York, the son of Corydon Stillman Sperry and Catherine Elizabeth Leavenworth. He studied in Brooklyn and later at the Waterbury, Connecticut, high school. In 1862, at age fifteen, he gained admission to the U.S. Naval Academy. Sperry graduated tenth in his class of seventy-three in 1866, too late to see active service during the Civil War, but his youth at entry into the academy and his relatively high standing at graduation (the determinant of seniority within each Annapolis class) positioned him to outlast many of his classmates in the long, seniority-based climb to flag rank. Sperry's first sea assignment was to the 2,100-ton steam sloop USS *Sacramento*, on board of which he sailed to duty on the Asiatic Station. En route to a port call at Calcutta before reaching the Asiatic Station, the *Sacramento* went aground and was totally wrecked in the Godaveri River, India, on 19 June 1867. In 1868 Sperry married Edith Marcy, a granddaughter of the prominent governor William L. Marcy of New York. The couple had two sons.

Sperry's sea service for the next two decades mirrored that of many officers of the period: lengthy stays on distant stations manning sailing ships already eclipsed by technological developments. His sea service was broken three times (in 1874–1878, 1881–1884, and 1887–1891) by tours of duty at the Naval Academy, where he was reputed to be an outstanding mathematician. The war with Spain in 1898 found Sperry, now a senior commander, assigned to head the equipment department of the Brooklyn Navy Yard. It was a vital position, critical to the preparation of many ships for active war service, but it lacked the glamor attached to actual command. Following the war, Sperry was given command of the gunboat *Yorktown* and saw active service in the Philippine insurrection, supporting Major General Arthur MacArthur's northern Luzon campaign by blockading Lingayen Gulf, Luzon.

Sperry was promoted to captain in 1900 and given a second tour of duty on the Asiatic Station, principally in command of the cruiser *New Orleans*. During this period Sperry developed a close relationship with Rear Admiral Robley D. Evans, commander in chief of the Asiatic Station, an important connection for Sperry, who longed for the fame that had eluded him during the Spanish-American War. "I wish I had a few discreet newspaper friends to place my merits before the public," Sperry wrote to his wife in 1902. "The pies are few and the pieces small and I long for one big slice before I die." In the summer of 1904 Sperry attended the Naval War College at Newport as a student. Upon completion of the course, he was appointed president of the college, a position he held until May 1906, when he was promoted to rear admiral.

Sperry, during his tenure at the War College, developed an extensive knowledge of international law, which was put to use when he was assigned as a delegate to the International Conference to Revise Rules for Treatment of Sick and Wounded in Geneva (June through August 1906) and the Second Hague Conference on Prize Law (June to November 1907). Fortunately for Sperry, his chance at fame was soon to arrive. At the end of the Hague Conference he was ordered to assume command of the Fourth Division, U.S. Atlantic Fleet, just in time to take part in the famed world cruise of the "Great White Fleet," December 1907–February 1909. Shortly after the fleet's departure from the U.S. East Coast, Rear Admiral Evans, the fleet commander in chief, fell ill. While the second in command, Rear Admiral Charles M. Thomas, handled all of the social responsibilities of the fleet in foreign ports and Evans's chief of staff handled details at sea, the decision was made in Washington that Evans would be relieved upon the fleet's arrival on the West Coast.

A period of intense politicking followed, during which Sperry enlisted the assistance of General Horace Porter, an influential Republican and friend of President Theodore Roosevelt. This effort probably was unnecessary, for Evans had recommended Sperry for the position even before the fleet left its home port. Sperry was made commander in chief in May 1908. He led the fleet during its triumphal procession through New Zealand and Australia, where the fleet was extensively feted, and on to the Philippines and thence Japan, where Sperry was received by the emperor and his fleet given unprecedented tokens of Japanese hospitality. Part of the fleet then visited China, and after a period of gunnery practice in the Philip-

pines, the entire fleet returned to the U.S. East Coast via the Indian Ocean, Suez Canal, and various Mediterranean ports. The fleet's successful circumnavigation of the globe was marked by a presidential welcome by Roosevelt at Norfolk. Shortly afterward Sperry relinquished command of the fleet, participating in board duties in Washington until his retirement in September 1909. In those final months of his active service, Sperry saw one of his recommendations carried out. During the early stages of the world cruise he had strongly recommended that the fleet be painted at all times in war color, supplanting the white hull and buff superstructure scheme then the peacetime standard. His recommendation had been accepted, and after extensive testing, a slate gray shade, soon known as "battleship gray," was adopted. At the time of his death, Sperry had been ordered to Washington on special duty with the State Department to help perfect a translation from French of the Declaration of London, which set forth the principles of maritime law to be applied by the prize court at the Hague. There he contracted pneumonia and died after a short illness.

• His extensive correspondence is preserved in the Navy Historical Foundation's manuscript collection at the Library of Congress. For details of his participation in the world cruise, see James R. Reckner, *Teddy Roosevelt's Great White Fleet* (1988). His role in foreign policy and the impressions of many of his peers are in Richard H. Challener, *Admirals, Generals and American Foreign Policy, 1898–1914* (1973), and his role in the Second Hague Conference is outlined in Calvin DeArmond Davis, *The United States and the Second Hague Peace Conference* (1975). An obituary is in the *New York Times*, 2 Feb. 1911.

JAMES R. RECKNER

SPERRY, Elmer Ambrose (12 Oct. 1860–16 June 1930), engineer, inventor, and entrepreneur, was born in Cortland, New York, the son of Stephen Sperry, a farmer and carpenter, and Mary Burst, who died giving birth to him. Elmer was precocious mechanically and eagerly studied math and science at Cortland Normal School. His growing fascination for electrical technology and a visit to the Philadelphia Centennial Exhibition of 1876 helped ignite a lifelong drive to invent that would emphasize feedback control systems.

Following the advice of William A. Anthony of Cornell University, whose physics lectures he audited, Sperry invented a current regulator for arc-lighting in 1880. With the financial and technical support of the Cortland Wagon Company, Sperry developed a complete arc-lighting system, including a new arc lamp. Such success encouraged him to move to Chicago in 1882 to manufacture and market this innovation. He subsequently founded the Sperry Electric Light, Motor and Car Brake Company in February 1883. After receiving over $1 million in venture capital, he proceeded to install arc-lights throughout the Midwest, including an impressive illumination of Chicago's Board of Trade building. The Sperry Electric Light Company did not thrive, however, in part because of the competition from alternating-current and incandescent lighting; it went out of business in 1887. Sperry had also become dissatisfied with his heavy, yet routine, engineering responsibilities, which left little time for inventing.

Following his 1887 marriage to Zula Goodman, with whom he had four children, Sperry founded the Elmer A. Sperry Company in 1888 (purchased by the Sperry Electric Mining Machine Co. in 1891). The company reflected Sperry's desire to focus on invention and development projects that required simultaneous mechanical and electrical insight. To finance the operation, he planned to sell the resulting patent rights to manufacturing firms. For his most promising patents, however, he founded those firms himself. The first was the Sperry Electric Mining Machine Co. (Founded in 1889, and purchased by Thomson-Houston in 1892), it manufactured Sperry's electric pick and locomotive for mining applications. The second was a joint venture with Thomson-Houston: the Sperry Electric Railway Co., which was founded in 1892 and sold its patents to General Electric in 1895. Such cooperation gave Sperry the resources to develop his streetcar inventions that emphasized electric braking, power transmission, and speed control. A profitable enterprise, Sperry's brakes were especially successful until 1905, when Westinghouse's air brakes made them obsolete.

Resisting the trend to join General Electric's hierarchy, Sperry turned to the emerging automobile market. After fruitless negotiations to acquire George B. Selden's broad automobile patent of 1879, based on internal combustion, Sperry focused on electric cars. This reflected Sperry's tendency to innovate in areas that suited his previous experience and profits, but only to a point. His automotive patents included steering and braking mechanisms, but also battery power. With the help of his wife and daughter, Sperry studied enough chemistry to gain insight into the latter. After completing six prototype vehicles in 1898, he licensed the Cleveland Machine Screw Company to manufacture them. By 1900, the American Bicycle Company had purchased Sperry's automobile patents and formed the National Battery Company to develop his battery.

Sperry devoted most of the next decade to electrochemical processing in cooperation with Clinton Townsend, the inventor of the Townsend electrolytic process. He relied on Sperry's engineering and venture capital expertise to scale it up for the industrial production of chlorine and caustic soda. Although the partners suffered both engineering and marketing setbacks, they attracted the attention of financier Elon Huntington Hooker. After purchasing Sperry and Townsend's patents, he founded the successful Hooker Electrochemical Company in 1909. Sperry collaborated with Townsend again to remove iron from recycled tin powder with the American Can Company's financing. This followed Sperry's disappointing effort to produce paint pigments and palm oil. A series of patent infringement suits, the growing maturity of the detinning industry, and the profitable sale of his patents convinced Sperry to turn to a new technological domain: gyroscopic control systems.

In 1907 Sperry initiated a significant defense industry, albeit unexpectedly, when he began investigating the gyroscope's commercial potential. His first patent addressed automobile stability by employing a processing disk. After encountering the disdain of the automobile industry, however, Sperry turned to stabilizing ships. By 1908 he had achieved a major breakthrough: to a processing gyroscope he added a control system that used the ship's angular velocity as feedback. This increased dramatically the gyroscope's power to counteract the angular momentum of the rolling ship. Instead of attracting commercial shipping support, as expected, Sperry's patent caught the attention of Captain David Taylor of the U.S. Navy. Taylor grasped how such control could provide the stability necessary for long-range gunnery. In addition to providing Sperry with a mathematical analysis of his marine stabilizer, he helped arrange for full-scale testing.

This close association with Taylor also alerted Sperry to the enormous naval need to replace the magnetic compass with one capable of functioning within iron hulls. Both gunnery and navigational problems stimulated this demand. Although the gyrocompass's utility had already been demonstrated by Hermann Anschütz-Kaempfe, a German entrepreneur, Sperry began competing with his own design in 1909. He constrained a three-degree-of-freedom gyroscope with a suspended weight, which forced an alignment with the earth's spin axis. Sperry then corrected the errors resulting from the ship's acceleration and latitudinal changes with a feedback control system and an analog computer, respectively. By early 1911, the U.S. Navy began testing this device, including one in the powder magazine of the USS *Drayton*. Lucrative contracts soon followed, as well as invaluable data.

Sperry organized the Sperry Gyroscope Company in 1910 to support his work on the gyrostabilizer, the gyrocompass, and other new inventions. The company blossomed during World War I just as its future incarnation, Sperry-Rand, would thrive during the Cold War. For example, in December 1914 when Sperry Gyroscope was worth approximately $1 million, it received orders for gyrocompasses worth more than $800,000 from the British and Russian navies. Sperry subsequently engaged his invention and development department in increasing the performance of fire-control systems for battleships, searchlights for anti-aircraft and coastal-defense batteries, bomb and gunnery sights for aircraft, and anti-submarine weapons for the Atlantic convoys.

Sperry's humanitarian concerns remained, however, as his 1912 invention of a gyrostabilizer to improve aviation safety demonstrated. His son Lawrence and Glenn Curtis, pioneering aviators, provided an essential collaboration for that invention. Following Lawrence's dramatic demonstration of the device outside of Paris, the gyrostabilizer received a prize of 50,000 francs in 1914 for its contribution to aircraft safety. Nevertheless, the real payoff came from a navy contract for an aerial torpedo that would employ the gyro-stabilizer. A pioneering chapter in the history of guidance engineering, the project never overcame the accumulation of serious navigation errors in the automatic control system. Lawrence Sperry continued to develop the aerial torpedo after the war, with funding provided by the U.S. Army, where General William "Billy" Mitchell was an enthusiastic supporter. Lawrence's fatal plane crash in 1924, and subsequent army indifference, helped end that promising development. The German *Luftwaffe* resurrected it in World War II, however, with their V-1 flying bomb.

The Sperry Gyroscope Company adapted some of their military products for civilian use immediately after World War I. This included gyrocompasses and gyrostabilizers for the merchant marine, and light beacons for civilian airports. Sperry's enthusiasm for guidance engineering also manifested itself in the invention of an automatic pilot system for ships, which modeled kinematically the seemingly intuitive behavior of experienced pilots. He began such work in 1912 and successfully tested the system in 1922. Sperry Gyroscope's ability to remain profitable during this postwar transition encouraged Sperry to revive perhaps his most ambitious project: the compound diesel engine. Because a successful solution promised to open up enormous markets, he spent an estimated $1 million to increase significantly the power-to-weight ratio of diesel engines during the 1920s. Unlike entrepreneurs who devoted their senior years to maintaining the profitability of their youthful innovations, Sperry sought out increasingly greater challenges and influence until decisively defeated. Hence the significance of his diesel engine: although technically feasible, its excessive production cost doomed it commercially. It was Sperry's greatest failure, consequently, but hardly his Waterloo. In 1928 he brought his fault-detection system for railroads into commercial service. It measured both mechanical flaws and the misalignment of rails.

Sperry died in Brooklyn, the recipient of more than 400 patents and numerous international honors. He was a founding member of the American Institute of Electrical Engineers, a member of the Naval Consulting Board during World War I, a leader of the National Research Council and the Engineering Foundation, and president of the American Society of Mechanical Engineers (1928–1929). Sperry was politically conservative and a strong supporter of Herbert Hoover. After World War I, he fought hard to maintain U.S. relations with Japan. He was fascinated by Japanese culture and respected deeply the Imperial Navy's dedication to technological progress.

• Sperry's personal papers were collected and preserved by Elmer Sperry, Jr., and William Goodman, a nephew. Sperry's principle biography is Thomas P. Hughes, *Elmer Sperry: Inventor and Engineer* (1971), which contains detailed references and listings of Sperry's patents and publications. See also Hughes, "Elmer Sperry and Adrian Leverkuhn: A Comparison of Creative Styles," in *Springs of Scientific Creativity: Essays on Founders of Modern Science*, ed. Rutherford Aris et al (1983), and Hughes, *Science and the Instrument-Maker: Michelson, Sperry, and the Speed of Light* (1976). For additional insights into Sperry's character and personality, see William W. Davenport's biography of Lawrence Sperry, *Gyro!* (1978). For an overview of Sperry's technical accomplishments, see "The Engineering and Scientific Achievements of Ambrose Sperry," *Mechanical Engineering* 49, no. 2 (Feb. 1927): 101–17. Obituaries are in the *New York Times* and the *Herald Tribune*, 17 June 1930.

BRETT STEELE

SPERRY, Willard Learoyd (5 Apr. 1882–15 May 1954), Congregational minister and educator, was born in Peabody, Massachusetts, the son of William Gardner Sperry and Henrietta Learoyd. His father was a minister and later served as president of Olivet, a Congregational college in Michigan. Parsonage living bred austerity, and it is not surprising, therefore, that Sperry earned his undergraduate degree at his father's college (A.B., 1903). Deeply interested in science and literature as an undergraduate, he later wrote a study of William Wordsworth's last forty years, *Wordsworth's Anti-Climax*, which was published by Harvard University Press in 1935. Sperry saw in Wordsworth's more mature poems "the elemental genius of all religions"; and during the rest of his life, his sermons and essays reflected the insights he found in these poems.

The sudden suicide of a childhood friend during Sperry's his last year at Olivet reawakened his youthful religious speculations. It was during this crisis that he was elected Michigan's first Rhodes Scholar (1904) and registered in Queen's College, Oxford. These two unexpected events dramatically changed the direction of his life. At Queen's he was the student of its dean, the respected biblical scholar B. H. Streeter. He immediately took to the dean, found the Oxford tutorial system exhilarating, and wrote near the end of his life that the study of theology had given him "a sense of the continuity and stability of the Christian religion, as it has survived the vicissitudes of many centuries."

At Oxford he met and courted the sister of his closest friend, Charles Bennett, an Irishman from Dublin. His marriage in 1908 to the tempestuous Muriel Bennett, one of the first women to graduate from Trinity College, Dublin, proved challenging but enduring. They had one child.

Sperry's years at Oxford turned him into an anglophile and almost into an Anglican; he seriously considered the Episcopal priesthood before seeking Congregational ordination. His theology was always to be balanced between his strict Puritan heritage and his appreciation for the more formal but rich ceremonial style of the Church of England. Indeed, Harvard's Memorial Church, which was built while he was preacher, represents both of these Protestant traditions.

He returned home in 1907 with his Oxford M.A., studied for a year at the Yale Divinity School (M.A., 1908), was ordained, and served the First Congregational Church in Fall River, Massachusetts (1908–1914), and the Central Congregational Church in Boston (1914–1922) before becoming dean at the Harvard Divinity School in 1922. Soon he was also chair of the Board of Preachers to Harvard University, which made him effectively minister of the campus church. He was to hold both positions until his retirement in 1953 and was fondly termed by his colleagues as "the dean of Harvard deans."

Sperry led the Divinity School during a difficult period of its history. The school's affiliation with the more conservative Andover Theological Seminary, a union made in 1908 and filled with hopeful expectations, was challenged in 1922 in court by some of the Andover conservatives who felt that their faculty no longer subscribed to the Calvinistic creed, which was a requirement of their appointment. The court agreed, and the result was the dissolution of the affiliation. At this critical period it was the thoughtful and patient leadership of Sperry that enabled the school to reorganize and recruit in the 1930s talented faculty and students. But the school faced other difficulties. The 1929 depression negatively affected its financial base, and the minimum support given by the university during the presidency of James Conant (1933–1953), along with the problems created by the advent of the Second World War, hindered its best efforts to serve the church. Nevertheless, the accomplishments of its faculty and graduates were widely recognized and respected, providing a basis for the renewal of the school that took place in the 1950s.

Sperry was the author of several books of theology and two books of sermons. As a liberal and a modernist in the age of neo-orthodoxy, his ideas had a limited impact during his lifetime. Yet he was a fine writer, scholar, and preacher—effective, articulate, and reasonable. His volume of Lyman Beecher Lectures on preaching, *We Prophesy in Part* (1938), remains a masterpiece as does his study on public worship, *Reality in Worship* (1926). These books spell out his philosophy of ministry, which emphasized preaching, public prayer, and private meditation as the best ways to nourish the spiritual needs of parishioners.

He died in Cambridge shortly after retirement. His faith and the work of his life are described in words of St. Augustine that he often quoted: "O God, Thou has made us for Thyself and our hearts are restless until they find rest in Thee."

• Harvard University holds the extant Sperry papers. Its Andover-Harvard Theological Library has seven boxes of sermons and correspondence (especially helpful are his letters to his sister), and a special collection of pamphlets and articles by and about him. The University Archives at Pusey Library hold thirty-four boxes of personal and professional correspondence, manuscripts and notes, and documents relating to his work as dean. Two significant books by Sperry other than those discussed above are *The Disciplines of Liberty: The Faith and Conduct of the Christian Freeman* (1921), and *Strangers and Pilgrims: Studies in the Classics of Christian Devotion* (1939). There is no biography, but a chronology of his life can be found in William L. Fox, Jr., *Willard L. Sperry: The Quandaries of a Liberal Protestant Mind, 1914–1939*

(1991). See also Alan Seaburg, "A Learned Minister at Harvard, Willard Learoyd Sperry," *Harvard Theological Review* 80 (1987): 179–92.

ALAN SEABURG

SPERTI, George Speri (17 Jan. 1900–29 Apr. 1991), engineer, inventor, and educator, was born in Covington, Kentucky, the son of Italian Roman Catholic immigrants George Anthony Sperti and Caroline Speri. George was educated in public schools in Covington and received in 1923 an E.E. from the College of Engineering of the University of Cincinnati. He had pursued his studies as a co-op student with the Union Gas & Electric Company of Cincinnati, for whom he read meters in Cincinnati households and repaired defective meters in the shop. He soon discovered that the domestic meters were efficient, but that the company did not have a reliable industrial meter. Sperti set to work to construct a meter that would measure the great amount of electricity consumed by large industries. At the age of twenty-one, he built on his mother's breadboard a device he termed the kilo-volt ampere (KVA) meter, for use of which Westinghouse offered him a $50,000 long-term contract. He accepted a smaller sum of $23,000 and personally sold the European rights.

After receiving his engineering degree, Sperti turned down many higher-paying positions to stay on at the University of Cincinnati as a research assistant. Two years later he founded there the Basic Science Research Laboratory and became research professor and director.

Sperti became interested in cancer research after the death of a close friend. Working in conjunction with Leo G. Nutini, a cousin and physician, Sperti accepted the invitation of the Archbishop of Cincinnati, Most Rev. John T. McNicholas, to found a graduate school of scientific research as part of a federation of Catholic educational institutions, known as the Athenaeum of Ohio. Sperti left the university and created in 1935 in East Walnut Hills, Ohio, a suburb of Cincinnati, the Institutum Divi Thomae, named after St. Thomas Aquinas and later popularly called the St. Thomas Institute. It soon became one of the most prestigious small research centers in the United States. He also founded an auxiliary animal breeding farm and a marine biological laboratory in Palm Beach, Florida.

Sperti authored numerous scientific articles and held, with institute faculty, more than 150 patents; his experiments resulted in many discoveries beneficial to life. He invented the ultraviolet sun lamp and experimented successfully with irradiation to create vitamins, kill bacteria, and preserve processed foods such as orange juice. Discovering a cell-derivative he called biodyne (life-force), he found three different kinds: growth stimulators important to healing; respiration stimulators; and accelerators of cellular metabolism of sugar. Some well-known medicines made from biodynes were Sperti Ointment for burns, Preparation H, and Aspercreme. When the Japanese supply of agar-agar was cut off in World War II, Sperti developed an American substitute, a gelatinous product made from seaweed and used as the base for many products. He also discovered probiotics, which could combat certain kinds of infection. He received the first patent for fluorescent lights. The success of the first biodyne products led to the formation of Sperti Lamp Corporation, which produced not only the sun lamp, but in time, gunsights, oxygen equipment, astrocompasses, and other military and aviation instruments for the U.S. defense effort in World War II. In 1942 he was named a principal consultant of the War Production Board.

Sperti was the recipient of five honorary doctorates. He was one of six Americans appointed to the Pontifical Academy of Sciences by Pope Pius XI in 1936. He became a fellow of the Royal Society of Arts (London) in 1934 and received the Star of Solidarity of III Class from the Italian Republic in 1956 and the International University (Rome) Medal in 1958. Locally he received the William Howard Taft Medal for Notable Achievement in 1970 and was named the Cincinnati Scientist Engineer of the Year in 1970. He was admitted to the Northern Kentucky Leadership Hall of Fame in 1992. As Nutini wrote in his nomination of Sperti to this posthumous honor, "Dr. Sperti was known worldwide as a researcher, scientist, and educator. He put his research and desire to eliminate human suffering in front of personal recognition and gratification. In addition, he devoted his life to the education of future scientists and researchers in the hope that they would be able to carry on and fulfill his dreams" (*Souvenir Program Book to the Kentucky Bicentennial Celebration in Northern Kentucky 1792–1992* [1992], p. 19).

Sperti never married. In 1987 Mildred Sperti, his sister and secretary, who shared his home, died. The Institutum closed on 31 December 1987. The grounds and buildings and the Palm Beach laboratories were sold and the assets were divided between Mount St. Joseph College in Cincinnati and Thomas More College in Crestview Hills, Kentucky. Sperti died in Cincinnati.

• Conversations of the author with Leo G. Nutini, particularly a telephone interview of 12 July 1995, together with a partial listing of the writings of Sperti are in the Archives of Thomas More College, on whose board of overseers Sperti served from 1968 to 1977. Biographical accounts include "Genius in the Attic," *Cincinnati Alumnus* 42, no. 7 (July 1968): 3–11, and Mary Philip Trauth, " 'Pasteur of America': George Speri Sperti," *La Parola del Popolo* 68, no. 26 (Sept.–Oct. 1976): 62. Obituaries are in the *Kentucky Post* and the *Cincinnati Enquirer*, both 30 Apr. 1991.

MARY PHILIP TRAUTH

SPEWACK, Samuel (16 Sept. 1899–14 Oct. 1971), and **Bella Spewack** (25 Mar. 1899?–27 Apr. 1990), playwrights and journalists, were born, respectively, in Bachmut in the Ukraine and in Bucharest, Romania.

Samuel was the son of Noel Spewack, a small businessman, and Sema Zelavetski. Bella was the daughter of Adolph Loebel and Fanny Cohen.

Samuel's family left Russia when he was four years old. They settled in New York City, living modestly on Staten Island, where his father ran a laundry. Samuel attended public schools and went to Columbia University, where he majored in Russian studies. He left college in 1918, at the end of his junior year, to take a job as a police reporter on the *New York World*.

Bella had no memory of her father, and she used her mother's surname. When she was three years old her mother took her to New York City, where they lived in poverty on the Lower East Side. Her mother took in boarders to supplement her meager earnings as a seamstress and then married one of her boarders, named Noosan Lang, with whom she had two sons.

Bella was educated in the public school system. At Washington Irving High School she edited the school magazine and also won a bronze medal for an essay on Shakespeare. After graduation in 1917 she worked briefly for neighborhood papers before being hired by the *New York Call*. Over the next years she also wrote short stories and articles for magazines, and she acted as press agent for various organizations.

Samuel Spewack and Bella Cohen met when they were covering the same story for their respective newspapers. They married in 1922, and immediately after the wedding ceremony Samuel left for Italy to cover the Genoa Peace Conference. Bella soon joined him in Europe, and together they reported from Moscow (1922–1924) and Berlin (1924–1926). They had no children.

Their first play to be produced was *The Solitaire Man* (1927), a comedy-mystery set aboard an airplane and centered around a reformed jewel thief and a mid-air hijacking. It received favorable reviews when it opened in Boston, but it never reached Broadway. Their next effort was *The War Song* (1928), written in collaboration with comedian George Jessel, who also starred in the play as a Jewish soldier in World War I. The play struck critics as honest and convincing, and it marked the beginning of the Spewacks' long career on Broadway. Their *Poppa*, a comedy-drama set in New York's Lower East Side and directed by George Abbott, also opened in 1928. The plot concerns the efforts of a naive idealist to run for local office against a corrupt machine. The play was considered clumsy and contrived with a few amusing scenes.

Clear All Wires! (1932) was a reworking of the Spewacks' first joint effort, *Swing High Sweeney*, which had never been produced. Based on their experiences as correspondents in Moscow, the play is a high-spirited satire of Russian bureaucracy and the foreign press corps' efforts to get a "scoop." It was generally praised, in spite of its complicated plot and the questionable morality of the leading characters. The Spewacks next turned to solemn drama with *Spring Song* (1934), wherein a young woman impulsively seduces her sister's boyfriend whom she actually dislikes. She becomes pregnant and is forced to marry him and have the baby; predictably, she dies in childbirth. Critics found the play sentimental and "strangely unmoving."

The Spewacks went to Hollywood in 1930, where they wrote scripts for several films, including adaptations of their own plays (*The Solitaire Man* and *Clear All Wires!*). In 1935 they used their experiences to concoct a wild farce for Broadway, *Boy Meets Girl*, again directed by Abbott. The protagonists are two scriptwriters with a sure-fire plot formula: boy meets girl; boy loses girl; boy gets girl—or vice versa. The writers engineer a series of hilarious intrigues to help a young unwed mother who does, eventually, get the boy. The critics agreed that the situations were preposterous but continually laughable, being a near-perfect send-up of the idiocies of Hollywood, and "Boy Meets Girl" became a popular catch-phrase. The play ran for 669 performances and won the Roi Cooper Megrue Prize. It was included in Burns Mantle's *Best Plays* series, and the Spewacks adapted it into a successful film (1938) starring James Cagney and Pat O'Brien.

In 1938 they reworked *Clear All Wires!* into the book for a musical called *Leave It to Me!*, with music and lyrics by Cole Porter and direction by Spewack and George Smith. The production won general praise, especially for Mary Martin in her Broadway debut, singing "My Heart Belongs to Daddy" as she did a mock striptease at a Siberian railroad station. Gene Kelly also performed in the chorus in his first Broadway appearance. The musical ran for 291 performances and had a brief return engagement (sixteen performances) in 1939.

Their next three plays were failures. *Miss Swan Expects* (1939) and *Woman Bites Dog* (1946) ran for eight and five performances, respectively, and *Out West It's Different* (1940) never reached Broadway. However, the Spewacks continued to write film scripts, including *My Favorite Wife* (1940) and *Weekend at the Waldorf* (1945), which were box-office successes.

World War II changed the focus of their activities. Samuel was sent to London in 1942 as head of the Office of War Information's film unit. He wrote and produced *The World at War*, a documentary that made a powerful statement about the issues and the enemy. In 1943 he went to Moscow as press attaché to Ambassador W. Averell Harriman, an old friend. Bella became involved with the United Nations Relief and Rehabilitation Agency, and in 1946 she embarked on a tour of Eastern Europe for UNRRA.

In 1948 the Spewacks again teamed with Porter to write *Kiss Me, Kate*, which became the greatest success of their careers. The story is built around the off-stage relationship of two temperamental, divorced, but still-in-love actors who are playing the leads in *The Taming of the Shrew*, and additional complications are furnished by a farcical subplot. The production received rave reviews and earned a Page One Award and a Tony Award for the Spewacks. It played 1,077 performances on Broadway and toured extensively in the United States, and productions were mounted in more than twenty countries throughout the world. The Spewacks did not write the film version, but they did adapt the play for both American and British television.

The next three plays were written by Samuel alone. *Two Blind Mice* (1949), which he also directed, is a political satire involving two old ladies running a defunct Washington agency whose jobs are saved by a wisecracking newspaperman. It received mildly positive reviews. *The Golden State* (1950), which Samuel also wrote and directed, was produced by Bella. It concerns another slightly off-center old lady who runs a rooming house and thinks she has discovered gold in her backyard, but this play disappointed the critics. *Under the Sycamore Tree*, written and produced by Samuel, opened on London's West End in 1952. A fanciful comedy about an underground ant colony that is studying human beings, it starred Alec Guinness as an ant scientist. The play ran for 189 performances, but an off-Broadway production—the Spewacks' first venture off the main stem—in 1960 lasted only forty-one performances.

In 1953 the Spewacks wrote *My 3 Angels* [sic], based on a French comedy by Albert Husson, about a trio of kindly convicts (two murderers and an embezzler) in a tropical penal colony who use their skills to help a family solve its economic and personal problems. Critical reception was highly favorable, and the play ran for 344 performances. The Spewacks adapted it for television in 1960. A Hebrew version of the play was mounted in Tel Aviv in 1963, and a musical adaptation was produced in Toronto in 1985.

Their next stage vehicle was *Festival* (1955), a comic mixture of temperamental musicians and a conniving impresario, which failed to please. *Once There Was a Russian* (1961), which Samuel again wrote alone, was a satirical comedy set in the court of Catherine the Great. The play opened and closed on the same night, but undaunted he set to work on a musical version, with words and music by Frank Loesser. The result, called *Pleasures and Palaces*, did not survive its 1965 pre-Broadway tryout in Detroit.

Samuel also wrote short stories and four novels. In 1963 he received the Alumni Award from the Columbia School of Journalism. He died in New York. After Samuel's death, Bella concerned herself with negotiations for revivals of their plays. She died at her home in New York.

Samuel Spewack once said that the stage should not be a lecture platform but should be used to "entertain audiences and in the final sense move them." The Spewacks sought to do this through a mixture of knockabout farce and gentle satire built around outlandish characters. They often reached this modest goal in plays and films, and their skill won worldwide recognition with *Kiss Me, Kate*.

• Samuel and Bella Spewack's papers (approximately 75,000 items), consisting of correspondence and production files documenting their work in various entertainment media as well as drafts of novels, short stories, and articles, were donated to Columbia University in 1990. A major exhibition of the collection was mounted in Columbia's Rare Book and

Manuscript Library in 1993, accompanied by a catalog titled *From Russia to Kiss Me, Kate: The Careers of Sam and Bella Spewack*. The Billy Rose Theatre Collection of the New York Public Library for the Performing Arts at Lincoln Center has files of material on the authors and their works, including scripts, programs, photographs, posters, reviews, and other cuttings. See also "Those Writing Spewacks," *New York Times*, 15 Mar. 1936, and Bella Spewack, "My Life with Shakespeare," *Show*, Feb. 1944, pp. 70–71.

Samuel Spewack's four published novels are *Mon Paul* (1928), *The Skyscraper Murder* (1928), *Murder in the Gilded Cage* (1929), and *The Busy, Busy People* (1948). He wrote an eight-part series of articles on "The Broadway Revolution," *New York Telegram* (26 Dec. 1929–4 Jan. 1930). See also Bella Spewack's memorial tribute to her husband in *Dramatists Guild Quarterly* 8 (Winter 1972): 48–49. Her autobiography, *Streets: A Memoir of the Lower East Side*, written in 1922, was published in 1995. A biographical sketch of Bella Spewack, including a bibliography, is in Ann R. Shapiro, ed., *Jewish American Women Writers: A Bio-bibliographical and Critical Sourcebook* (1994). An obituary for Samuel Spewack is in the *New York Times*, 15 Oct. 1971, and an obituary for Bella Spewack is in the *New York Times*, 29 Apr. 1990.

DOROTHY L. SWERDLOVE

SPEYER, A. James (27 Dec. 1913–9 Nov. 1986), architect and museum curator, was born in Pittsburgh, Pennsylvania, the son of Alexander Crail Speyer, an investment banker, and Tillie Sunstein, a painter and sculptor. Born into a prominent Pittsburgh family that was actively involved in the arts, Speyer studied painting as a child but, at the urging of his pragmatic father, turned his artistic talents to the practice of architecture as a young adult. He attended Carnegie Institute of Technology in his home city, and received a bachelor of science degree in architecture in 1934. Afterward, Speyer continued his dual interest in architecture and painting, and from 1934 to 1937 he studied fine art at the Chelsea Polytechnic in London and at the Sorbonne in Paris.

Speyer considered the beaux-arts education that he received at Carnegie to be somewhat incomplete, and in the late 1930s he was privileged to become the first graduate student of the renowned German modern architect Ludwig Mies van der Rohe, who immigrated to Chicago in 1938. Mies revolutionized architectural education as director of the Department of Architecture at the Armour Institute of Technology (later Illinois Institute of Technology). Speyer later said it was the confrontation with Mies van der Rohe and his principles of architecture that led him to devote himself to architecture instead of painting. Speyer received a master's degree in architecture from IIT in 1941.

Immediately following graduate school, Speyer entered the U.S. Army, where he served from 1941 to 1946. He achieved the rank of major in the Army Intelligence Service, having served in the South Pacific. Initially, he was in charge of a chemical warfare intelligence team, and later, while stationed in Korea after the war ended, he was made an acting historic monuments inspector. His responsibility was to prevent damage to the historic temples by GI souvenir hunters.

Following his military service, Speyer continued the modernist teaching methods of Mies van der Rohe and taught senior architectural design at IIT from 1946 to 1961. Between 1957 and 1960 Speyer took a leave of absence from IIT to serve as a visiting Fulbright professor of architecture, by invitation of the Royal Government of Greece, at National University in Athens. His methods of teaching modern architectural design were highly influential upon an entire generation of Greek architects. Upon his return, Speyer taught graduate architectural design at IIT for one more year.

Concurrent with his teaching practice, Speyer had a thriving practice in residential design. Among the houses that he designed were the Zurcher house (1950) in Lake Forest, Illinois; the Jerome Apt house (1952–1953) in Pittsburgh, Pennsylvania; the Stanley G. Harris residence (1953) in Hubbard Woods, Illinois; the Rose residence (1956), for fabric designer Ben Rose, in Highland Park, Illinois; a penthouse for real estate developer Herbert Greenwald (1958) in Chicago; and a house for his mother (1961–1962) in Pittsburgh. His sleek and elegant buildings revealed the principles of modern design that he learned in his graduate studies at IIT. He also designed several renovations, including a house on Astor Street, in Chicago, for Suzette Davidson (1956–1957); and a house for Solomon B. Smith in the mid-1950s. Although intensely involved with teaching and an architectural practice, Speyer also maintained his interest in art and was a correspondent for *ArtNews* from 1955 to 1957. His articles, which appeared under the heading "News from Chicago," were reviews of exhibitions held at galleries and museums in Chicago.

In 1961 Speyer made a major career shift and accepted the position of curator of twentieth-century painting and sculpture at the Art Institute of Chicago, a position he held until his death in 1986. Although his lifelong interest in art prepared him well for such a career shift, Speyer claimed that it was a relatively impulsive move that compared to his conversion to modernist architecture under the tutelage of Mies van der Rohe. Speyer described his decision in a letter of 1982: "When offered the position of Curator of Twentieth Century Painting and Sculpture at The Art Institute of Chicago in 1960, I was galvanized by the potential and shocked into a realization of its appeal. This relatively impulsive decision to accept another change of direction within the arts has been of continuous aesthetic reward throughout the last twenty years."

Many of the first exhibitions that Speyer organized were decidedly architectural in their focus, including a Mies van der Rohe retrospective (1968), and Edifices and Monuments by Jean Dubuffet (1970–1971). As a curator Speyer was also responsible for organizing two important biennial exhibitions: one of works by Chicago and vicinity artists and the other an invitational exhibition of leading contemporary American artists. During his career, Speyer mounted exhibitions on subjects such as Henri Matisse, Edward Hopper, Picasso in Chicago, Dada and Surrealism, Constantin Brancusi, Georgia O'Keeffe, Georges Braque, Claes Oldenburg, Marcel Duchamp, Robert Rauschenberg, European Art in the Seventies, Sonia Delaunay, and many other leading twentieth-century artists and movements. At the time of his death, Speyer was co-curating with the Philadelphia Museum of Art the first U.S. retrospective of the German painter Anselm Kiefer.

Under Speyer's direction, the Art Institute's permanent collection of twentieth-century art grew to include outstanding works by artists of the 1950s to the 1980s, and he succeeded in developing one of the best collections of contemporary art in a U.S. museum. Among the significant gifts to come to the museum during his tenure was the Edwin and Lindy Bergman collection, containing a sizable collection of boxes and assemblages by the surrealist Joseph Cornell. During his twenty-five year tenure at the Art Institute of Chicago, Speyer became known as a dynamic force in the international contemporary art scene, counting among his friends such prominent collectors and artists as Jasper Johns, Frank Stella, Rauschenberg, O'Keeffe, Jean Dubuffet, and Chicago artists Leon Golub and Ed Paschke. Commenting on the contributions that Speyer made to both fields of art and architecture, Art Institute of Chicago director James N. Wood said, "Jim [Speyer] not only possessed the professionalism and skill of a first-rate curator, but he also represented for us in Chicago the ambitions of the entire modernist period. He was a product and a primary source of what we see as Modern, and he realized it as an architect, a curator, and in his lifestyle."

When asked how he would like to be remembered, in his 1986 oral history interview, Speyer replied, "I think I would like to be remembered for the quality of my own architecture and certainly for my accomplishments at the Art Institute. . . . Although I am often congratulated on architectural installations and presentations in the museum, which pleases me, of course, I think that I also have built a fine collection of paintings and sculpture for the permanent collection during the twenty-five years I've been here. I would like to be thought of in a kind of complete connection that way."

• The Department of Architecture at the Art Institute of Chicago is the largest repository of Speyer's architectural drawings and papers. Also, the Museum Archive at the Art Institute of Chicago has extensive information on the many exhibitions and acquisitions that Speyer oversaw. Speyer wrote numerous articles about his exhibitions and acquisitions in the institute's members' *Bulletin*. The most comprehensive study of Speyer's career as an architect and curator is a four-and-one-half-hour interview conducted in 1986. The 135-page interview was conducted by Pauline Saliga as part of the Architect's Oral History Program at the Art Institute of Chicago, and it is available in the institute's Ryerson and Burnham Libraries.

As an architect, Speyer's building designs were reviewed in *L'Architecture d'Aujourd'hui*, Nov. 1955, pp. 70–71, and Dec. 1958, pp. 74–75. Additional reviews were published in *Interiors*, June 1955, pp. 70–77, and *Architectural Record*, May 1956, pp. 157–61. In connection with his graduate work

with Mies van der Rohe, Speyer is mentioned in the following books, Rolf Achilles, *Mies van der Rohe: Architect as Educator* (1986); Franz Schulze, *Mies van der Rohe, a Critical Biography* (1985); Alfred Swenson, *Architectural Education at IIT 1938–78* (1980); John Zukowsky, *Mies Reconsidered: His Career, Legacy and Disciples* (1986); and Zukowsky, *Chicago Architects Design: A Century of Architectural Drawings from the Art Institute of Chicago* (1982).

Obituaries are in the *Chicago Tribune* and the *New York Times*, 11 Nov. 1986.

PAULINE SALIGA

SPEYER, Ellin Prince (14 Oct. 1849–23 Feb. 1921), philanthropist, was born Ellin Leslie Prince in Lowell, Massachusetts, the daughter of John Dyneley Prince, a chemist, and Mary Travers. Her parents died when she was young, and she was raised by her uncle William Riddell Travers, a prominent New York City lawyer, and his wife. Travers provided Speyer a private education through tutors. In October 1871 she married John A. Lowery, who died in 1892. They had no children.

Speyer began a career in social work in 1881 by contributing to the founding of the Hospital Saturday and Sunday Association (later the United Hospital Fund). Speyer served as secretary of the association and was treasurer of the Woman's Auxiliary Committee for forty years. The association was meant as a "single instrumentality broad enough to serve as a common channel of benevolence for every form and shade of religious or social opinion" (*New York Times*, 20 Apr. 1886). It distributed funds to Hahnemann Hospital in Philadelphia, the Home of Rest for Consumptives, Woman's Hospital, Home for Incurables, German Hospital, and other nonprofit institutions.

Speyer combined resources with Grace H. Dodge in 1883 to start the first Working Girls' Club in the United States (the "Irene Club") and maintained a commitment to the advancement of women throughout her life. She was treasurer and president of the Working Girls' Club for thirty years. In 1886 she helped establish the New York Skin and Cancer Hospital. At the start of the Spanish-American War, Speyer joined Elisabeth Mills Reid in answering the call of the American Red Cross Auxiliary No. 3 of New York for nurses to be trained for war duty. During World War I she chaired the mayor's committee on trained nurses for overseas work. Speyer was treasurer of the St. Mary's Free Hospital for Children and a member of the board of managers of the Loomis Sanatorium for Consumptives.

Four years after her first husband's death, Speyer opened a tea room in New York. She married for the second time on 11 November 1897 to James Speyer, president of Speyer & Co., a New York City international banking firm, and a school commissioner on the Board of Education. They had no children. From this point forward, Speyer had the opportunity to devote the remainder of her life to philanthropy. She was an active contributor to four settlement houses. In 1901 she and her husband donated $100,000 to Teachers

College of Columbia University for the establishment of an experimental training school and social settlement house named the Speyer School. The school was donated by the Speyers to provide a community resource center for local immigrant children and to inspire education and a democratic spirit. The school also offered training to recent high school graduates who were seeking permanent employment. The $70,000 building for the school included a gymnasium, baths, a kindergarten, offices, public libraries for children and adults, rooms for cooking, and a roof garden. In 1907 the Speyers donated funds for a gymnasium to the University Settlement Society, of which Speyer was the secretary.

Speyer continued her support of women after her marriage. In 1906 she opened her home to girls for the establishment of the Public Schools' Athletic League. She gave to the Working Girls' Vacation Society and in 1915 accepted the chair of Mayor John Mitchell's subcommittee on unemployment among women. She directed workshops that led to the employment of hundreds of women.

Speyer gave her largest contributions to animal-protection organizations. In 1910 she founded and served as president to the New York Women's League for Animals, formerly the Woman's Auxiliary to the American Society for the Prevention of Cruelty to Animals. Unlike the latter organization that focused on correction, the Women's League for Animals provided instruction to the poor, particularly children, on the proper treatment of animals. The first year lectures were given to youths at settlement houses. A free dispensary for animals and a rest farm for horses, Mountain Rest Farm at Fishkill, New York, were established. Speyer arranged an annual "Work Horse Parade" to award medals to New York City drivers who took good care of their horses. The idea caught on in other American cities and in Europe. Speyer found homes for horses no longer efficient for police duty and made sure that horses had nonslip shoes for icy surfaces. Within one year there were 600 active volunteer members. In 1913 Speyer helped raise funds to build the Lafayette Street Hospital. After her death her employees honored her by renaming it the Ellin Prince Speyer Hospital for Animals. In 1933 more than 16,000 sick animals received free care.

Speyer annually threw a Christmas Tree party at her Manhattan house on Madison Avenue for children of her friends, employees, and persons she met through the many organizations in which she was involved. She offered the children toys, candy, ice cream, and cake. She contributed to a number of other organizations: the Tuberculosis Preventorium for Children in Lakewood, New Jersey, the National Plant, Flower and Fruit Guild, the Children's Aid Society, the National League on Urban Conditions Among Negroes, the Lisa Day Nursery, and the Authors' League. She served as chair of the woman's committee of the Actors' Fund of America during World War I.

From the moment of her debut, New York high society marked Speyer to become a leading figure. The New York Times's praise of her wedding as "arranged with great care and taste" (12 Nov. 1897) was just the beginning of the public approbation she received for her social acumen. As a philanthropist, she was most committed to protecting animals from abuse. She bequeathed her largest donation of $50,000 to the New York Women's League for Animals. At her funeral, the famed violinist Fritz Kreisler played her favorite piece, Handel's *Largo*. She died at her home in New York City.

• For information on the first organization Speyer founded, see "Growing in Public Favor: Annual Report of the Hospital Saturday and Sunday Association," *New York Times*, 20 Apr. 1886. Details on Speyer's wedding are in "Commissioner Speyer to Wed," *New York Times*, 21 Oct. 1897, and in "Speyer-Lowery Nuptials," *New York Times*, 12 Nov. 1897. The Speyers' donation to Teachers College is described in "Speyer School Building: Specifications for a $50,000 Structure for the Teachers College," *New York Times*, 10 Aug. 1901; and "Speyer School Dedicated: Speakers Dwell on the Importance of the Experimental Institution Donated by Mr. and Mrs. Speyer," *New York Times*, 24 Apr. 1903. For information on Speyer's involvement with the fight against cruelty toward animals, see "For Relief of Animals: First Year's Report of Women's League Shows Remarkable Results," *New York Times*, 20 Apr. 1911; and "Protecting the Animals: Women's League Reports Large Increase in its Membership," *New York Times*, 19 Dec. 1911. See the *New York Times*, 31 Dec. 1912, for "Children with Mrs. Speyer: A Christmas Tree and a Party for 175 Little Ones She Knows." An obituary is in the *New York Times*, 23 Feb. 1921, an editorial of her funeral is in the *New York Times*, 26 Feb. 1921, and a description of her will is in the *New York Times*, 1 Mar. 1921.

BARBARA L. CICCARELLI

SPEYER, Leonora von Stosch (7 Nov. 1872–10 Feb. 1956), poet, was born in Washington, D.C., the daughter of Count Ferdinand von Stosch, a German nobleman who gave up his title to become an American citizen, and Julia Thompson. Leonora studied at the Brussels Conservatory and became a concert violinist at a young age. She toured the United States and Europe and in 1890, at age eighteen, made her debut with the Boston Symphony and played with the New York Philharmonic before she was twenty.

She married for the first time in 1893 and was subsequently divorced. In 1902 she married Sir Edgar Speyer, who also gave up his title to become a naturalized American citizen. She had four children. The Speyers lived abroad until 1915, then returned to the United States to live in New York.

Speyer's friendship with Amy Lowell and her interest in the imagist poets led her to write poetry. Her husband built her a little house near their home where she could write undisturbed. Each morning she played her violin until the music inspired her, and then she would write. "Music and poetry are so alike, really," she said, "the same glory of rhythm, of color, of sounds, notes and words clear-ringing, and above all the same dizzy heights of creation and vision."

When the onset of acute neuritis left her unable to play the violin, Speyer became immersed in reading and writing poetry. "By the time I was healed," she said, "I was not thinking of much else but verse. I was writing wildly, prolifically, and wholly happily." She said of her transference from music to poetry: "Having played the violin since my early youth, it seemed but another expression, perhaps a more subtle one, of the same art to find myself writing, studying, deep in the metrics of musical words" (*Twentieth-Century Authors*, p. 1319).

Scribner's Magazine, Century, Nation, Dial and other magazines published Speyer's poetry. She also translated and published poetry by Paul Verlaine and others. Her first book, *A Canopic Jar* (1921), received mixed reviews. Mark Van Doren called it "free verse that is not every day surpassed for decisive comment, clear conviction and unexceptional cadence" (*Nation*, 11 May 1921). In 1923 Speyer won the Charlestown Poetry Society's Blindman's Prize for "Obergammermu." She won the 1926 Poetry Prize from the *Nation* for her "Ballad of Old Doc Higgins." *Fiddler's Farewell* (1926), her second book, brought her the Pulitzer Prize for poetry in 1927.

Speyer's poetry is filled with the sounds and images of birds. In "Migration" she says, "The dawn is dizzy with birds." She speaks of larks, of "carrier-doves," of peacocks, of "thrushes' talk," and of the "gray stitches" that gulls make against the sky. In "Of Mountains" she says, "Only a bird would dare to break the stillness of this hour." In "Fiddler's Farewell" she calls her violin "my box of birds."

Speyer's other books of poetry are *Naked Heel* (1931), *Slow Wall: Poems New and Selected* (1939), and *Nor without Music* (published with *Slow Wall*, 1946). She was editor for *American Poets: An Anthology of Contemporary Verse* (1923).

In reviewing *Slow Wall*, Gladys Campbell spoke of Speyer's "virtuosity in creating melodious and rhythmical sound effects." Several of her poems were set to music, including "Rendezvous," music by H. H. A. Beach (1928); "Gulls," music by Ethel Glenn Hier (1940); and "Measure Me, Sky," music by Edmund F. Soule (1971).

Speyer's poetry was called feminine by some reviewers. L. G. Marshall said of it: "Her verse shows always, unmistakably, that it is by a woman. It is the poetry of a woman who knows her own littleness, but is never lowly" (*New York Herald Tribune*, 2 May 1926). Speyer wrote of women, but in new ways. She rewrote in verse the story of Eve, "The Story as I Understand It," and of Mary Magdalene, "One Version." She wrote of Sappho and of women from mythology. Of Speyer's later poems, simple melodic lyrics, W. B. C. Watkins said: "This is the kind of poetry which is for the most part taught in schools, and there is nothing here which anyone should fail to understand. This does not mean that Mrs. Speyer writes down to her public. She writes, with the genuine skill of long practice in traditional idiom, exactly what she

wants to write and what many will want to hear" (*New York Times*, 12 May 1946).

Speyer taught poetry workshops at Columbia University beginning in 1937. She was active in the Poetry Society of America for many years, holding the office of president from 1934 to 1936, the first woman to hold that position. In 1955 the society awarded her its Gold Medal for Distinctive Achievement. Speyer died in New York City.

• Biographical information can be found in Dorothea Lawrance Mann, "Anglo-American Poet: Lady Speyer," *Bellman*, 4 Jan. 1919, pp. 10–12. See also Edgar Speyer, *Leonora* (a biographical appreciation, in verse and drama, of his wife, written for the twenty-fifth anniversary of their marriage in 1926, 1927), and Dorothy Emerson, "Poetry Corner: Leonora Speyer," *Scholastic* 35 (16 Oct. 1939): 23e. A brief biography and some of her poetry is in *The World Split Open*, ed. Louise Bernikow (1974). The Pulitzer Prize announcement appears in the *New York Times*, 3 May 1927. For a discussion of her poetry, see Gladys Campbell, "A Singing Gallery," *Poetry*, July 1940, pp. 217–20. An obituary is in the *New York Times*, 11 Feb. 1956.

BLANCHE COX CLEGG

SPIEGEL, Sam (11 Nov. 1901–31 Dec. 1985), film producer, was born in Jaroslaw, Poland (then part of the Austrian empire), the son of Simon Spiegel, a tobacco merchant, and Regina (maiden name unknown). An undistinguished student at local schools, Spiegel frequented penny arcades and nickelodeons, though such entertainments were forbidden by his Orthodox Jewish parents. Although he spoke Yiddish at home, Spiegel also learned Russian, Polish, and German in the marketplace of Jaroslaw, a commercial center on the Russian border. In 1919 Spiegel moved with his family to Vienna. Soon after this he joined the Zionist Young Pioneer movement and immigrated to Palestine, where he lived on a kibbutz and worked as a manual laborer. In 1922 he married Rachel Agronovich, a Zionist settler from Canada, with whom he had a daughter. After abandoning the Young Pioneer movement in the mid-1920s, Spiegel found work as a cotton broker. He divorced his wife, broke off relations with his family (who had also immigrated to Palestine), and returned to Europe.

Spiegel immigrated to the United States in 1927, hoping to use his linguistic skills as a means of gaining entry to the burgeoning sound motion picture industry. He was first employed as a translator at Metro-Goldwyn-Mayer Pictures and later at Universal Pictures. In 1929 he was arrested for writing bad checks when he first arrived in the United States. After serving five months in jail, Spiegel was deported to Poland. The following year he was rehired by Universal Pictures to work for its European distribution office in Berlin. While employed by Universal, Spiegel began producing low-budget films independently. To escape Nazi persecution, Spiegel moved to Vienna in 1933 and later, after a brief time in Paris, to London, where he set up a film production company named the British and Continental Film Corporation Limited. The company's only film was the unsuccessful *An Old Spanish Custom* (1936), starring Buster Keaton. To finance the overbudget film, Spiegel again began passing bad checks. For this he was deported to France, where he remained for a short time before moving to Mexico in 1937. In Mexico he produced a variety stage show that was performed at the 1939 World's Fair in New York. A financial dispute with the Mexican government, which had backed the show, led to another brief imprisonment.

On his release from Mexican jail in 1939, Spiegel entered the United States illegally. He headed directly to Hollywood, where he had many European expatriate friends and contacts. In conjunction with 20th Century–Fox Pictures, Spiegel (using the assumed name S. P. Eagle) produced his first American film, *Tales of Manhattan* (1942), an episodic story of a coat that changes the lives of the various people who own it. The poorly financed and relatively unknown Spiegel used his extraordinary charm and persuasiveness to gather a star-studded cast for the film, including Henry Fonda, Ginger Rogers, and Charles Boyer. To be "spiegeled" or "spiegelized" eventually became Hollywood jargon for being cajoled or wheedled.

After establishing himself as a producer with *Tales of Manhattan*, Spiegel quickly became a leading figure on the Hollywood social scene. Despite a still precarious financial situation, the short and potbellied Spiegel gave lavish parties at his Beverly Hills home and freely indulged in gambling and womanizing. He was evasive about his shady past and falsely claimed to be a graduate of the University of Vienna and a former college professor. U.S. immigration authorities caught up with Spiegel in 1943, but his deportation was delayed because of World War II. In the meantime, the smooth-talking Spiegel managed to have his 1929 check fraud conviction overturned, which eliminated the threat of deportation. He became a U.S. citizen in 1947. The following year Spiegel married actress Lynn Baggett. The couple had no children, spent most of their married life apart, and divorced in 1955.

Though his social contacts enabled him to remain a popular figure in Hollywood, it took the flamboyant Spiegel nearly two decades to establish a reputation in the movie business. It was *The African Queen* (1951), a hit with both critics and audiences, that established Spiegel as a major producer. Based on a C. S. Forester novel, *The African Queen* starred Humphrey Bogart as a tough riverboat captain and Katharine Hepburn as an English missionary who find themselves traveling together down an African river during World War I. Spiegel financed the picture, which was filmed on location in Africa and at a London studio, with a combination of American and British funding. His success with *The African Queen* signaled the decline of the Hollywood studio system and the growing importance of the independent film producer working on an international scale.

Spiegel's next film, *Melba* (1953), a British-made biography of opera star Nellie Melba, was poorly received. Spiegel bounced back with the now classic *On the Waterfront* (1954), a hard-hitting drama of a young longshoreman's battle against labor union corruption. Spiegel's production values, including a score by Leonard Bernstein and the casting of major star Marlon Brando in the leading role, added prestige to the relatively low-budget, black-and-white film. *On the Waterfront*, the first film Spiegel produced under his own name, won the Academy Award for best picture.

In the mid-1950s Spiegel moved his base of operations to London. His productions of *The Bridge on the River Kwai* (1957), the story of British prisoners of war who are forced by their Japanese captors to build a bridge over a remote Burmese river, and *Lawrence of Arabia* (1962), based on the exploits of soldier-adventurer T. E. Lawrence, earned him two more Academy Awards for best picture. During this period Spiegel also produced two smaller scale films, *The Strange One* (1957), a military school drama, and *Suddenly, Last Summer* (1959), a screen version of a one-act play by Tennessee Williams. In 1957 Spiegel wed fashion model Betty Benson. The childless couple soon separated but remained legally married until Spiegel's death. An affair with British film production assistant Ann Pennington in the late 1960s gave Spiegel a son whom he acknowledged and supported.

Spiegel's greatest strength as a producer was his ability to recognize promising screen material and assemble the most talented and appropriate creative personnel to bring the movie to fruition. To keep his vast projects under control, Spiegel worked his objectives out in detail before production began. Many directors and screenwriters found him overbearing and demanding as a collaborator, but he was generous with funds and flexible with scheduling if more money or time would result in a better film.

Although a renowned voluptuary who enjoyed cruising the Mediterranean on his luxurious yacht with a bevy of young women, Spiegel deplored the sexually explicit, violent, and special effects–laden films that began appearing in the late 1960s and 1970s. "The truth is that the fun has been taken out of making pictures—it's all centered on the ambition to make money. But I made the most money when I went for the best in audiences," he maintained (Wolf, p. 62). None of Spiegel's later films—*The Chase* (1966), *The Night of the Generals* (1967), *The Swimmer* (1968), *Nicholas and Alexandra* (1971), *The Last Tycoon* (1977), and *Betrayal* (1983)—was a major success. Spiegel died while vacationing on the Caribbean island of St. Martin.

• The most thorough source of information on Spiegel is Andrew Sinclair, *Spiegel: The Man behind the Pictures* (1987). Katharine Hepburn mentions Spiegel frequently in her memoir *The Making of "The African Queen"* (1987). See also "Talk with a Moviemaker," *Newsweek*, 28 Dec. 1959, pp. 64–65; James F. Fixx, "The Spiegel Touch," *Saturday Review*, 29 Dec. 1962, pp. 13–15; "Hollywood: The Emperor," *Time*, 19 Apr. 1963, pp. 67–68; David Sterritt, "A Pinter Tale Told Backward with Laughs and Insights," *Christian Science Moni-*

tor, 17 Mar. 1983, p. 18; and William Wolf, "Doing It His Way," *New York,* 21 Feb. 1983, pp. 62–63. An obituary is in the *New York Times,* 1 Jan. 1986.

MARY C. KALFATOVIC

SPIER, Leslie (13 Dec. 1893–3 Dec. 1961), anthropologist, was born in New York City, the son of Simon P. Spier and Bertha Adler. Spier spent his childhood and early adult years in that city, attending the College of the City of New York and receiving a Bachelor of Science in engineering in 1915. His career as an anthropologist began even before he finished his degree, when Spier was assigned to the New Jersey Archaeological and Geological Survey as an assistant anthropologist in 1913. He also participated in surveys and excavations in New York and Delaware; this work resulted in a series of papers he wrote on the archaeology of the eastern United States.

Spier entered Columbia University in 1915 to study anthropology with Franz Boas. During his years in graduate school he was an assistant in the anthropology department at the American Museum of Natural History, where he worked under Clark Wissler and Robert H. Lowie, specialists in Native American cultures. He had begun graduate work with a strong interest in archaeology, but the influence of these mentors helped turn him increasingly toward physical anthropology and ethnology by the time he earned his doctorate in 1920. By the late 1920s he had moved away from physical anthropology, although he continued to be interested in the entire range of anthropology. Trained in a period before strict specialization became common, he continued to pursue research in many different areas.

Spier's dissertation, published as *The Sun Dance of the Plains Indians: Its Development and Diffusion* (1921), established the thrust of his professional work. He attempted to determine the origins of the Sun Dance, a religious ritual involving self-torture, by carefully comparing slight differences in its performance among neighboring Plains tribes. After examining modern performances of this ritual, Spier extrapolated its spread through the region at the time of its introduction. This work became a classic of the historical method of anthropology, applying ethnographic data to the reconstruction of unrecorded historic events, in this case tribal contacts. Contact and migration continued to interest Spier throughout his career.

In 1920 Spier moved to Seattle, Washington, where he was joined in 1921 by Erna Gunther, a fellow Columbia student and New York native whom he married that year. The couple taught at the University of Washington and did extensive fieldwork among the Coast Salish people of western Washington. In 1925 Spier founded a monograph series, *University of Washington Publications in Anthropology,* which he edited until 1931. He left the university when he and Gunther separated in 1927, formally resigning in 1930 when they divorced. During his years in Seattle Spier wrote his most admired work, *Havasupai Ethnography*

(1928); it further established his meticulousness and scrupulous regard for evidence.

Spier's work was usually rich in historical data and aimed to give a historical perspective and to place a culture, through limited comparison, in the context of surrounding cultures. While he continued to work on issues of historical reconstruction throughout his career, Spier was distressed by his colleagues' use of distributional data to recapture historical developments. He cautioned that scholars must not draw overly broad generalizations from this kind of data, and he was always wary of overarching theories. His own work was marked by understatement and extreme caution in interpretation.

Over twenty years, beginning in 1916, Spier worked in the field with many different Native American tribes of the Northwest Coast and the Southwest. However, he did no fieldwork after 1935, and ultimately his greatest influence stemmed from his work as a teacher and editor. He was instrumental in developing the anthropology departments of several institutions at a time when the field was continuing to shift its center from museums and government agencies to academia. In addition to his years at the University of Washington, Spier taught at Yale University (1933–1939) and the University of New Mexico (1939–1955), with shorter stints at the University of Oklahoma (1927–1929), the University of Chicago (1928 and 1930), and Harvard University (1939 and 1949). He also taught summer sessions at Columbia University during the 1920s and at the University of California (both Berkeley and Los Angeles) in the 1920s, 1930s, and 1940s. His long teaching career and his affiliation with so many institutions brought Spier in contact with an unusually large number of students. One of them, W. W. Hill, estimated in the late 1960s that Spier had influenced through direct personal contact at least half of the professional anthropologists working in America at that time. Spier's teaching focused on methodological approach (with stress on the use of empirical data), concern with cultural distributions, emphasis on cultural history, and analysis of cultural processes and growth.

Spier believed strongly that research needed to be written up and brought before the profession as speedily as possible. His own commitment to this was exemplified by his extensive activities as an editor. From 1934 to 1938 he edited *American Anthropologist;* in 1934 he founded *General Series in Anthropology;* two years later he founded *Yale University Publications in Anthropology,* which he edited until 1938. When he moved to the University of New Mexico in 1939 he continued this work, founding the *Southwestern Journal of Anthropology* (now *Journal of Anthropological Research*) and *University of New Mexico Publications in Anthropology* in 1944; he edited both until his death. Spier's prodigious editorial work helped to keep him abreast of research in all areas of the field.

Spier brought to both his teaching and his editing broad knowledge of the field and careful attention to detail. He was president of the American Anthropological Association in 1943; he was elected to the National Academy of Sciences (1946), the American Philosophical Society (1946), the Academy of Arts and Sciences (1953), and the California Academy of Sciences (1955); and he was awarded the Townsend Harris Medal (1946) and the Viking Fund Medal (1960). Despite these honors, he did not seek publicity and avoided professional politics. While a specialist in Native American culture, Spier was also dedicated to the essential unity of the entire field, as manifested in his work as an editor and his important role in establishing anthropology as an academic discipline in the United States. He died in Albuquerque, New Mexico.

• A collection of Spier's papers is in the Bancroft Library at the University of California, Berkeley. Other works by Spier include *An Outline of a Chronology of Zuni Ruins* (1917), *Klamath Ethnography* (1930), *Yuman Tribes of the Gila River* (1933), and *The Prophet Dance of the Northwest and Its Derivatives: The Source of the Ghost Dance* (1935). With A. I. Hallowell and S. S. Newman, Spier edited *Language, Culture, and Personality* (1941), a collection of essays in honor of Edward Sapir. An extensive professional obituary with bibliography is Harry W. Basehart and W. W. Hill, "Leslie Spier, 1893–1961," *American Anthropologist* 67 (1965). Hill's introduction to *American Historical Anthropology: Essays in Honor of Leslie Spier* ed. Carroll L. Riley and Walter W. Taylor (1967), also gives an overview of Spier's career.

BETHANY NEUBAUER

SPINGARN, Arthur Barnett (28 Mar. 1878–1 Dec. 1971), lawyer, was born in New York City, the son of Elias Spingarn and Sarah Barnett. He received an A.B. from Columbia University in 1897, as well as an A.M. in 1899 and an LL.B. in 1900. Spingarn also received an LL.D. from Howard University in 1941 and an L.H.D. from Long Island University in 1966. In 1918 he married Marion Mayer, a social worker; they had no children.

Admitted to the New York bar in 1900, Spingarn began private practice in New York City. He was soon associated with what later would be known as "civil rights" activism, both in and out of the courtroom. Consequently, in 1911 he was appointed vice president and chairman of the national legal committee of the National Association for the Advancement of Colored People (NAACP), a position he held until 1940. His work with the organization was interrupted by the First World War, during which Spingarn served as a captain in the U.S. Army Sanitary Corps (1917–1919). In 1940 he was elected president of the NAACP, succeeding his brother Joel E. Spingarn. He retained the presidency until his retirement in 1966.

From 1940 to 1957 Spingarn also served as the president of the NAACP Legal and Educational Fund, Inc. This organization was instrumental in laying the groundwork for the civil rights cases that culminated in the landmark *Brown v. Board of Education of Topeka, Kansas* (1954). Upon its conclusion, Spingarn and his associates turned their attention to other legal issues involving discrimination in the fields of housing and jobs. The NAACP under his leadership continued

to bring to the courts a series of cases designed to overturn longstanding discriminatory practices.

Spingarn and the NAACP were criticized at times because the president of the organization was a white Jewish man. U.S. representative Adam Clayton Powell, Jr., for example, was outspoken on this point, and Powell also objected to the strategy of working for change through use of the legal system. Spingarn stated that he understood the militant spirit for reform but rejected the Black Muslims' call for separateness between the races. The NAACP leadership continued to support Spingarn and his approach throughout his career and appointed him to the board of directors even after his retirement from the presidency.

Spingarn's other interests included collecting art and literature. He visited Europe regularly and acquired both artworks and rare books, many of which were auctioned off in the mid-1960s. His bar memberships included the American Bar Association and the New York City, County, and State bar associations. Spingarn served as the chair of the legal committee of the Social Hygiene division of the New York Tuberculosis and Health Association and of the same committee of the New York Probation Association. Literary and art interests led him to involvement and membership in the Bibliographic Society of London and the Peintres Graveurs of France.

Spingarn died at his home in New York City. He was lauded at his funeral service by a number of prominent lawyers and jurists, among them Roy Wilkins, executive director of the NAACP, and Associate Justice Thurgood Marshall of the U.S. Supreme Court. Justice Marshall remarked, "If it had not been for Arthur Spingarn, we would not have an NAACP today."

• Spingarn's collection of written materials chronicling the civil rights movement was donated to Howard University in 1948 as the Spingarn collection. He authored two books, *Laws Relating to Sex Morality in New York City* (1915; rev. ed., 1926) and *Legal and Protective Measures*, coauthored with J. Goldberg (1950). His involvement in the legal battles of the NAACP is chronicled in a large number of sources, including Jack Greenberg, *Crusaders in the Courts* (1994), and two books by Mark Tushnet, *Making Civil Rights Law: Thurgood Marshall and the Supreme Court, 1936–1961* and especially *The N.A.A.C.P.: Legal Strategy against Segregated Education, 1925–1950* (1987). An obituary is in the *New York Times*, 2 Dec. 1971, as is a description of his memorial service, 6 Dec. 1971.

BARRY RYAN

SPINGARN, Joel Elias (17 May 1875–26 July 1939), literary critic and social activist, was born in New York City, the son of Elias Spingarn and Sarah Barnett, Jewish immigrants from Austria and England. The senior Spingarn's success as a wholesale tobacco merchant enabled him to provide his family with the material comfort and security to which late nineteenth-century urban elite Americans were accustomed. After graduating from New York City's public school system, Joel Spingarn attended the Collegiate Institute of New York City and City College before enrolling in

Columbia College, from which he received a B.A. with honors in 1895. In December of that year he married Amy Einstein, sister of the scholar and diplomat Lewis Einstein; they had four children.

Following a year of graduate study in English and comparative literature at Harvard, Spingarn returned to Columbia, from which he received a Ph.D. in 1899. After working for four years as an assistant in the Department of Comparative Literature, he became an adjunct professor in 1904 and a professor in 1909. He disliked and was openly critical of what he considered the materialism and academic empire-building of Columbia under the leadership of President Nicholas Murray Butler. His opposition to the merger in 1910 of the English and comparative literature departments and his criticism of the firing of Harry Thurston Peck, a longtime member of Columbia's faculty, exacerbated difficulties between the young professor and the university administration and led to his dismissal in 1911, an action that ended his academic career. Thereafter he devoted his life to a variety of literary, reform, and horticultural interests.

Spingarn made his mark on American letters as a poet, editor, and critic. His poems appeared, among other places, in his *New Hesperides and Other Poems* (1911) and *Poems* (1924). He was one of the founders in 1919 of Harcourt, Brace and Company and for a number of years edited its European library series. It was, however, as a critic that he made his most significant contribution. His first book was *A History of Literary Criticism in the Renaissance* (1899). In 1911 he published *The New Criticism* followed in 1917 by *Creative Criticism*. The latter two volumes reveal the influence on his character and thought of the idealism and humanism of his Columbia mentor George Edward Woodberry and, more significantly, the impact on his critical theories of Italian philosopher Benedetto Croce. Spingarn contended that works of art are products of artistic inspiration or genius. They possess intrinsic value and are not subject to judgment by ordinary social, moral, or other criteria. Such notions contradicted the prevailing pragmatic and moralistic trends in contemporary American critical theory and exposed him to a barrage of criticism. Determining the character and extent of Spingarn's influence is problematic. Scholars have labeled him variously as a "patron of aesthetic radicalism," a "neohumanist," a "traditionalist," or even a "reactionary," but they generally agree that he occupies a significant place in the history of American criticism.

A man of deep conviction and a strong sense of public responsibility, Spingarn became active in reform politics in New York City and in 1908 ran unsuccessfully as a Republican candidate for Congress from the traditionally Democratic Eighteenth District of New York. An admirer of Theodore Roosevelt, he was a staunch supporter of the Progressive party and attended its conventions in both 1912 and 1916. It was not, however, in the arena of politics but in that of social reform that he made his most notable contribution to American life. Relatively orthodox in his economic views, Spingarn had some rather liberal and hence controversial attitudes toward the social problems of his day. He was atypical of many Progressive Era reformers in his commitment to racial justice, and he was among the cadre of liberals that constituted the early membership of the National Association for the Advancement of Colored People (NAACP). He joined the association and became a member of its executive committee in 1910, scarcely a year after its founding. In 1913 he established the Spingarn Medal, awarded annually to African Americans for outstanding contributions to their race. In 1914 Spingarn succeeded Oswald Garrison Villard as chairman of the NAACP's executive board. For the next quarter century he served the association as chairman of the board of directors, treasurer, and finally as president from 1930 until 1939. Following the death of Booker T. Washington in 1915, Spingarn and W. E. B. Du Bois sought to reconcile contending factions within the nation's divided African-American community. Their efforts resulted in the Amenia Conference of 1916 at which delegates agreed to work together for equal education, enfranchisement, an end to racial violence, and protection of African Americans' civil liberties. In 1917 Spingarn, who served as an intelligence officer and a major with the American Expeditionary Force in France, persuaded the War Department to sanction segregated officer training for able black troops, a move opposed by many blacks and whites alike. In 1918 he drafted an antilynching bill, introduced into the House of Representatives, to protect African-American draftees from white mobs, but the end of the war made the proposed legislation irrelevant.

During the 1920s Spingarn remained committed to the NAACP, but his literary endeavors, his responsibilities with Harcourt, Brace and Company, the expanding role of black leadership within the association, and his ill health diminished his participation in the NAACP's routine operations. As its president during the 1930s he sought to mediate factional disputes and help the association find direction amid the personal ideological and racial tensions that plagued the organization during the Great Depression.

Although he died at his home in Manhattan, during the last thirty years of his life Spingarn spent much of his time with his family at "Troutbeck," his country estate, in Amenia, Dutchess County, New York. There, in addition to his literary and reform pursuits, he studied and cultivated the clematis—the flowering vine on which he was an internationally recognized authority—and played the role of country squire, small-town newspaper publisher, and community patron.

• Spingarn's personal and professional papers are housed primarily in three collections, the Joel E. Spingarn Collection at the New York Public Library, the Joel E. Spingarn Papers at Howard University, and the Joel E. Spingarn Papers in the James Weldon Johnson Collection at Yale University. There are also useful Spingarn materials in the Arthur Spingarn Papers and the NAACP Papers at the Library of Congress. Marshall Van Deusen, *J. E. Spingarn* (1971), provides an illuminating study of Spingarn's thought and literary endeavors.

The most thorough examination of his work with the NAACP is Barbara Joyce Ross, *Joel E. Spingarn and the Rise of the NAACP, 1911–1939* (1972). Oswald Garrison Villard's remembrance of his friend, in the *Nation,* 12 Aug. 1939, p. 174, affords a contemporary's insight into Spingarn's personality and character. Spingarn's obituary in the *New York Times,* 27 July 1939, succinctly summarizes his rich and varied career.

ROBERT F. MARTIN

SPINK, J. G. Taylor (6 Nov. 1888–7 Dec. 1962), newspaper publisher, was born John George Taylor Spink in St. Louis, Missouri, the son of Charles Claude Spink, a newspaper publisher, and Marie Taylor, a bookkeeper. Two years before Spink's birth, his uncle Alfred Spink founded the *Sporting News,* a St. Louis-based sports and theatrical weekly that remained a family-owned business until 1977. Spink's parents worked relentlessly to transform the *Sporting News* from an uncertain business proposition into the preeminent publication of the baseball establishment. Spink soon followed their example, starting to work at the paper while he was in grammar school. Determined to instill stern work habits in his son, Spink's father gave him a sales route with a quota of four copies a week. The boy soon doubled this total while selling the *Saturday Evening Post* as well.

Distracted by his interest in the growing business, Spink finished eighth grade with some difficulty and had even more academic trouble in high school. He told his mother that he wanted to drop out after the tenth grade to work full time and asked her to intercede with his father. The elder Spink not only gave his consent, but he also found his son two jobs in succession, first as a stock boy for the Rawlings Sporting Goods Company in St. Louis and then as a copyboy for the *St. Louis Post-Dispatch.*

Within a year Spink had proved his mettle, and his father took him back into the family business as an office boy. Spink was expected to work seven days a week for the newspaper, which would soon be devoted exclusively to baseball.

When Spink was twenty-one, he launched a campaign to be appointed the American League's official scorer at the World Series. Many baseball writers coveted this assignment, but Spink won out after besieging league president Byron Bancroft Johnson, a friend of his father, with a barrage of telegrams. Spink's appeal was founded on the strong support that the *Sporting News* had given Johnson when he elevated the Western League into the American League in 1901. Spink held the scorer's position from 1910 until he resigned in 1920 after seeing the Cleveland Indians' Bill Wambsganss complete the only unassisted triple play in World Series history. After Johnson died in 1931, Spink remained devoted to his memory.

In 1914 Spink became publisher of the *Sporting News* and its allied publications, including the *Sporting Goods Dealer,* a highly successful trade monthly. That same year he married Blanche Keene of St. Louis; they had two children. Seven days after the wedding, Spink's father died. His first important editorial decision on his own was to announce the paper's support for the established American and National Leagues in their fight against the upstart Federal League. He contended that baseball had no room for a third major league, and he was instrumental in bringing about a "peace agreement" that put the Federals out of business after only two seasons.

Spink imbued the paper with new life by hiring a correspondent in each baseball city to provide original and fresh news, or "dope," as it was called. Circulation improved but soon was jeopardized by U.S. entry into World War I. When thousands of readers joined the armed forces and went overseas, they dropped their subscriptions. Taking a suggestion from Colonel Tillinghast L. Huston, co-owner of the New York Yankees, Spink proposed to Johnson that the American League send copies of the paper to the American Expeditionary Forces. Johnson agreed to buy 150,000 copies weekly, and individual teams purchased smaller quantities. As a result, the *Sporting News* prospered even as baseball played abbreviated seasons in 1918 and 1919.

Spink played a role in uncovering the "Black Sox" scandal, in which members of the Chicago White Sox were accused of conspiring with gamblers to throw the 1919 World Series. The *Sporting News* published stories that endorsed Johnson's work to expose those involved, and Spink personally investigated several St. Louis leads relating to the case.

During the 1920s the *Sporting News* earned its unofficial sobriquet, "The Bible of Baseball." The paper became an indispensable source for information, box scores, statistics, and records about the major and minor leagues. Spink worked his employees and reporters hard, prodding them at all hours with telegrams and telephone calls laced with impatience and salty language. Simultaneously, he promoted the *Sporting News* as the conscience of the game and the guardian of its integrity, much to the chagrin of Commissioner Kenesaw Mountain Landis, who had jealously staked out the same role for himself.

When both major leagues decided in 1929 to abandon their Most Valuable Player awards, Spink decided the honors were too important to be dropped and had the *Sporting News* create its own trophies. Later, he campaigned for separate awards for rookies, pitchers, and relief pitchers.

The Great Depression threatened baseball's economic viability, which thereby challenged the *Sporting News* to stay afloat. As several minor leagues folded, Spink embraced two controversial proposals to save the game: night baseball and radio play-by-play broadcasts. Both ideas were opposed by traditionalists, but both were adopted and proved successful.

The *Sporting News* rebounded only to be confronted by more serious difficulties when the United States became involved in World War II. Circulation declined again, and shortages of newsprint and other materials caused production problems. In 1943 Spink persuaded the War Department to authorize an overseas edition that proved to be the paper's salvation. Weekly distribution ran to a half million copies during the baseball season and ballooned to a million during the World Series.

To facilitate overseas shipping, Spink shrank the paper to a five-column tabloid featuring shorter, crisper stories. In addition, starting in 1942 the publication opened its pages to in-season coverage of football, basketball, and hockey. But for years these sports vanished when major league baseball players headed south for spring training.

Spink seized another opportunity in late 1941 when A. G. Spalding & Bros. decided to give up publication of its annual statistical baseball guides. Spink approached Landis and received permission to publish the 1942 edition of the official guide on very short notice. The book appeared, to good reviews, just before the season opened.

Spink earned Landis's enmity, however, when an overly flattering article about the publisher appeared in the *Saturday Evening Post* in June 1942. Landis, taking umbrage at writer Stanley Frank's depiction of Spink as "Mr. Baseball," announced that the commissioner's office would issue the official 1943 guide. Spink went ahead on his own, while the commissioner's guide did not appear until halfway through the season. The following year, Spink had the field to himself as the commissioner failed to publish a guide at all. After Landis died in late 1944, his successor, Albert B. Chandler, returned publishing rights for the official guide to the *Sporting News*. Three years later Spink published a laudatory biography, *Judge Landis and 25 Years of Baseball*, ghostwritten by sportswriter Fred Lieb.

After World War II Spink was joined in the family business by his son Charles Claude Johnson Spink, named for his grandfather and for Johnson. The younger Spink's indoctrination into the corporate culture of the *Sporting News* was as startling as his father's had been. He came to work in an expensive suit only to be ordered to clean up the stockroom. "You should have asked what to wear before leaving home," groused his father, who continued to work long hours and read almost every word in his paper. "He has never been concerned about the 40-hour week," said a speaker at a 1956 awards dinner. "He just wishes someone would invent the 40-hour day so that he could do all the things he'd like to do."

Spink also took an active interest in youth baseball and in the spread of the game to other countries. For years the *Sporting News* published special supplements on the American Legion's junior baseball program and supported other amateur organizations. In 1950 he made a trip to Japan to arrange an international semiprofessional tournament there.

Never content merely to report events, Spink was an early proponent of what later became known as advocacy journalism. Rather than simply publish stories about what baseball had just done, he strove to become an insider who could influence the shape of things before they happened. He editorialized against

the Brooklyn Dodgers' signing of Jackie Robinson in 1945, for example, but once Robinson had proved his ability, Spink declared that "the situation calls for tolerance and fair play on the part of players and fans."

Indefatigable until his last years, Spink remained absorbed by his job. He was a stickler for accuracy and a fanatic for getting the whole story and getting it right. "I am an opinionated man, but if the other fellow has a story, I am willing to listen to it and give it full coverage," he said.

The Baseball Writers' Association of America honored Spink in 1962 by creating an award in his name and making him its first recipient. The J. G. Taylor Spink Award for meritorious service to baseball and baseball writing is given each summer at the Baseball Hall of Fame in Cooperstown, New York.

Ill health forced Spink to begin a long winter vacation in Arizona in September 1961. After his return, he was generally confined to his home until his death in Clayton, Missouri.

• Spink's personal papers and business records are part of the corporate archives of the *Sporting News*, which also holds a considerable clipping file. C. C. Johnson Spink, *Taylor Spink: The Legend and the Man* (1973), is a collection of anecdotes about Spink. For background, see Fred Lieb, *Baseball as I Have Known It* (1977), and Eugene C. Murdock, *Ban Johnson: Czar of Baseball* (1982). Obituaries are in the *New York Times*, 8 Dec. 1962, and the *Sporting News*, 22 Dec. 1962.

STEVEN P. GIETSCHIER

SPINNER, Francis Elias (21 Jan. 1802–31 Dec. 1890), congressman and treasurer of the United States, was born in German Flats (now Mohawk), New York, the son of recent German immigrants, John Peter Spinner and Mary Brument. His father, a Roman Catholic priest who had renounced his church, was the pastor for two German-speaking congregations of the Dutch Reformed church in Herkimer and German Flats. Although his father was a university graduate, Spinner received only a common school education supplemented with what he could pick up through wide reading. Fascinated by accounting, Spinner longed to enter business, but his father wished him to learn a skilled trade and actually removed him from an apprenticeship to an Albany confectioner because he was being taught sales and bookkeeping. His father then apprenticed him to a saddlemaker in Amsterdam, New York.

At the age of twenty-two Spinner returned to Herkimer and became a merchant in partnership with Alexander Hackley. Two years later (1826) he married Caroline Caswell, with whom he had three children. In 1825 he helped to organize an artillery unit, in which he served as lieutenant, for the state militia. He quickly rose through the ranks in the largely ceremonial organization, achieving major general before he retired in 1835. His military "experience" won Spinner appointment as deputy sheriff in 1829, and in 1834 he was elected sheriff as a Democrat, serving a three-year term.

Earning a reputation for honesty, hard work, and a blunt, businesslike manner, Spinner seemed a logical choice in positions of public trust. In 1838 Democratic governor William Marcy named him one of the commissioners for overseeing the building of the state mental hospital in Utica. A subsequent politically motivated Whig investigation, despite heroic efforts, could find no financial wrongdoing in the enterprise. In 1839 the newly formed Mohawk Valley Bank invited Spinner to become its cashier, and in his twenty-year association with the institution he rose to be its president. During Democrat James K. Polk's presidential administration, he served as auditor and deputy naval officer at the Port of New York (1845–1849).

In 1854 antislavery Democrats upset over the passage of the Kansas–Nebraska Act elected the pugnacious Spinner to the Thirty-fourth Congress. He represented a district in north-central New York where Democratic factionalism on this issue and others had been simmering for a decade. Alone among those elected as Democrats, Spinner backed Nathaniel Banks in a long controversy over the House Speakership, thus identifying himself with the nascent Republican party. In 1856 he served on the special committee that investigated Representative Preston Brooks's caning of Senator Charles Sumner and on a conference committee that failed to agree on an army appropriations bill because of a disagreement over the army's use in Kansas. Spinner made his mark in committees, where he articulated principles and doggedly pursued them, rather than on the floor of the House, where he was seldom heard. Reelected in 1856 and 1858 as a Republican, Spinner rose to chair the Committee on Accounts.

Spinner strongly supported Salmon P. Chase, whose honesty he admired, as treasury secretary following Abraham Lincoln's election in 1860. Chase in turn recommended Spinner's appointment as U.S. treasurer in charge of the nation's accounts. Spinner, a strong nationalist, was an important adviser to Chase on matters such as the circulation of greenbacks (which bore Spinner's distinctive, hard-to-duplicate signature) and the creation of a national banking system. Because of the increased demands on his office due to the Civil War, Spinner presided over a vast increase in his workforce from fifteen clerks, copyists, and currency counters handling $8 million a month at the war's outset to hundreds of employees handling millions of dollars a day at the conflict's close. Feeling personally responsible for every dollar in his trust and lacking a suitable system to delegate authority, Spinner worked long days, often eating and sleeping in his office. At one point, fearing that the capital might fall to the Confederates, he had his employees pack up all the government's money in preparation for fleeing on a steamer down the Potomac. Needing large numbers of reliable employees not subject to military service, he was the first governmental administrator to turn to women. He vigorously defended their employment against critics, hired over one hundred, paid them well by the standards of the time, and insisted on their continued employment after the war. Other government bureaus soon followed his lead. This act is the one for which Spinner has been most remembered.

Spinner remained treasurer under Andrew Johnson and Ulysses S. Grant. When a new secretary of the treasury in 1875 assumed control over the appointment of clerks, however, Spinner feared that dishonest people might be hired and he would be held responsible. He resigned and moved to Jacksonville, Florida, where he enjoyed a vigorous outdoor life until his death in that city.

• Spinner's papers are at the Library of Congress. Some letters from his period as sheriff in Herkimer County are at the Cornell University Library. See also George A. Hardin, *History of Herkimer County, New York* (1893); Isaac S. Hartley, "General Francis E. Spinner the Financier," *Magazine of American History* 25 (1891): 185–200; A. L. Howell, "The Life and Public Services of Gen. Francis E. Spinner," *Papers Read before the Herkimer County Historical Society*, vol. 2 (1902). Brief recollections of Spinner occur in a number of memoirs, including most usefully Hugh McCulloch, *Men and Measures of Half a Century* (1888). An obituary is in the *New York Times*, 1 Jan. 1891.

PHYLLIS FIELD

SPINOLA, Francis Barretto (19 Mar. 1821–14 Apr. 1891), politician and congressman, was born in Stony Brook, Long Island, New York. His parents' background is obscure, although his mother's family, of Irish descent, were prominent in the American revolutionary cause. At age ten he attended Quaker Hill Academy in Dutchess County. Six years later he became a jeweler's apprentice in Brooklyn, then briefly a blacksmith, grocer, and carpenter. He also studied law and by 1844 was practicing in Brooklyn. But his life's work as an assiduous and faithful partisan activist had already begun. He started out a Whig but later joined the Democratic party. After serving in the Brooklyn city clerk's office in the early 1840s, he became an alderman on the Brooklyn Common Council in 1846, then was elected supervisor. In 1853 he entered the New York State legislature, serving first in the assembly and then in the state senate for four years from 1858. In these years he was clearly identified as a loyal follower of Augustus Schell and Daniel Sickles, leaders of the long-dominant Albany Regency of the state Democratic party. In 1860, he was a Douglas delegate to the interrupted Democratic National Convention, first in Charleston and then in Baltimore.

When the Civil War began, Spinola supported efforts to restore the Union but denounced the Republicans for pursuing the policies that had brought on secession. In 1862, he raised a brigade of volunteer troops in New York State ("Spinola's Empire Brigade") and was himself commissioned. He participated, as a Brigadier General of Volunteers, in the North Carolina coastal campaign in 1862–1863 as part of the 18th Army Corps and led his troops in Virginia during the Confederate retreat from Gettysburg. He was wounded twice in a battle with Lee's forces at the end of July 1863 and spent the rest of the war on recruiting duty in New York. His reputation as a soldier was not high: General Henry Halleck referred to him as "worthless" in an official dispatch. Further, Spinola was brought up on charges by an old political rival, General John A. Dix, concerning certain recruiting and financial improprieties that had provoked the troops in his command to riot; however, the charges were withdrawn.

In the years after the Civil War, Spinola returned to the New York Democracy's back rooms, this time as a loyal member of the Tammany Hall of John Kelly. While also active in the lucrative and patronage-driven insurance and banking business in New York City, he became renowned for his combative and menacing oratory against Republicans in the many election campaigns that filled up each year. He was a Tammany district leader in the 1870s and in 1876 was returned to the state assembly, serving two terms. He was an alternate delegate to the Democratic National Convention of 1884, and, while no advocate of anti-Tammany reformer Grover Cleveland, Spinola followed his loyalist dictates and party direction to support the New York governor in the presidential campaign that year. In 1886, he was rewarded by Tammany: he was nominated for Congress in the Tenth District of New York City and won a very close election to the Fiftieth Congress. In the House he served on the Military Affairs, Militia, and War Claims committees. He was reelected to the Fifty-first Congress in 1888 by a more comfortable margin. During his tenure in the House he became known both for his vituperative debating style and for his efforts to have Congress fund a memorial to those who had died on British prison ships during the Revolution.

Spinola was married but had no children. Although he and his wife lived separate lives for about twenty years, they were reconciled during the last five years of his life. At his seventieth birthday celebration, he announced that his goal in life was "to live to see the disruption of the Republican Party." He did not achieve it, dying in Washington, D.C., just after he had been reelected to the Fifty-second Congress in a massive electoral sweep. He left a fortune valued at between $500,000 and $1 million, much of it stock in street railways and in street lighting and heating companies. A colleague commemorated him in a speech on the House floor, saying that "no more thorough political partisan . . . ever breathed. He loved his party as he loved his country."

• There are no surviving Spinola papers nor any biography or scholarly articles about him. His life can be pieced together from his entry in the *Biographical Directory of the American Congress, 1774–1989*; his obituaries in the *New York Times*, 14 Apr. 1891, and the *New York World*, 15 Apr. 1891; and from the speeches of his colleagues on the House floor after his death in *Congressional Record*, 52d Cong., 2d Sess., pp. 2588–93, and *Appendix*, p. 215. His Civil War career can be traced in various entries in the *Official Records of the War of the Rebellion*.

JOEL H. SILBEY

SPITZKA, Edward Anthony (17 June 1876–4 Sept. 1922), anatomist and brain morphologist, was born in New York City, the only child of Edward Charles Spitzka, a neurologist, and Catherine Wacek. He received his early education in the public schools and, like his father, attended the College of the City of New York, from which he graduated in 1898. After college, Spitzka entered the College of Physicians and Surgeons of Columbia University and, on his graduation, with an M.D. in 1902, received the Harsen Clinical Prize and a fellowship in anatomy.

Already a medical student of exceptional ability, Spitzka chanced into an opportunity during the last year of his medical training that propelled him to a level of national notoriety that was well beyond his years. On 29 October 1901 at Aubrum Prison in New York, Spitzka, while still a medical student, conducted the autopsy on Leon Franz Czolgosz, the convicted assassin of U.S. president William McKinley. As other medical notables of some seniority were available, it is unclear why such a young and inexperienced individual was chosen, but four facts converging in the fall of 1901 form the likely explanation. First, during his last two years of medical school Spitzka had conducted an exhaustive series of studies on the human brain and published a total of eight papers, all of which appeared in print by September 1901. This productivity would have brought Spitzka significant local and national attention. Second, Spitzka was the son of Edward C. Spitzka, one of the founding members of the American Anthropometric Society and a neurologist prominent in state and national organizations. The stated goal of the AAS, to collect and study the brains of great and accomplished individuals, was also of particular interest to Edward A. Spitzka. Third, with a background in human brain anatomy and a rapidly growing number of publications, E. A. Spitzka contacted the AAS in the spring of 1901 and requested permission to conduct a detailed study of the brains in their collection. The boldness of this request would have brought him further attention. Fourth, New York, the state in which the assassination had taken place, may have overseen the appointment of the performer of this autopsy. Carlos F. MacDonald, a principal in the Czolgosz case, noted in the *New York Medical Journal* (1902) that it was "fortunate that the State was able to secure the services of so able a brain anatomist . . . as Mr. Spitzka." Spitzka reported a few very minor variations in gyri and sulci patterns in the brain of Czolgosz but concluded in an article in the *New York Medical Journal* (1902) that "nothing has been found in the brain of this assassin that would condone his crime." The autopsy not only propelled Spitzka into the national limelight but also reinforced his earlier studies on the anatomy of the human brain and formed the basis for his later studies on the potential link between brain morphology and behavior.

After receiving an M.D. in 1902, Spitzka remained at Columbia University for four years, first as a fellow in anatomy (1902–1904), then as demonstrator of anatomy (1904–1906). He was enormously productive during this period, publishing at least twenty-seven papers between 1902 and 1905. In 1906, at the age of twenty-nine, Spitzka was appointed professor and chair of general and descriptive anatomy at Thomas Jefferson University. On the death in 1913 of George McClellan, who had been the chair of applied and topographic anatomy at Jefferson, both chairs were consolidated under Spitzka's leadership. Spitzka published his detailed analysis of the brains in the AAS collection in 1907 and was coeditor, with J. C. DaCosta, of the seventeenth edition (1908) of the American version of *Gray's Anatomy*. The eighteenth (1910) and nineteenth (1913) editions of the American *Gray's Anatomy* were edited solely by Spitzka. These rather significant writing projects were completed by Spitzka by thirty-seven years of age. He continued to conduct research in brain anatomy and related topics and in September 1911 became the director of the newly opened Daniel Baugh Institute of Anatomy of Jefferson Medical College. This institute was, in its time, one of the most modern anatomy teaching and research facilities in the United States.

In his research Spitzka had a special interest in brain morphology, particularly that of famous and influential individuals (physicians, scientists, statesmen), of persons of different races (Eskimos, Asians, whites), and of individuals involved in criminal behavior (especially murderers). Begun at Columbia and continued at Jefferson, these investigations explored whether or not there were morphological features of the brain that might correlate with special talents or abilities or with behavior, be it good or antisocial. In the case of the brains of criminals, he not only attended many executions but also studied the brains of those executed and described the effect of electricity on brain tissue. Spitzka described the anatomy of the brains of numerous individuals, covering a range of society in at least thirty-two papers. While he described variations in brain structure in great detail, using many specimens (one paper used 100 brains), he was unable to ever offer convincing evidence that behavior, race, or intellectual prowess was reflected in gross brain structure. In spite of this ultimate outcome, Spitzka was considered a preeminent brain morphologist of his time.

Spitzka's responsibilities, and the resultant pressures, at Jefferson were significant. Not only was he the chair of anatomy and director of the Daniel Baugh Institute, but he was also the first at Jefferson to carry on an active basic science research program and the only member of the Department of Anatomy to receive a full-time salary from the university. By fall 1912 he was demonstrating paranoid behavior and excessive use of alcohol, and in November he was given a year's leave of absence by the board of trustees "on account of his health." Spitzka never returned and in April 1914 submitted his resignation to the board of trustees at Jefferson. He joined the Army Medical Corp in June 1917 and was honorably discharged, as a lieutenant colonel in January 1919. He was serving as chief medical referee with the Veterans Bureau when he had a cerebral hemorrhage and died, in New York. At the time of his death he was survived by his wife, Alice Pauline Spitzka and by his only child, a son, Edward J. Spitzka. Spitzka had earlier willed his body for scientific study.

• Sources on Spitzka's life and work include "Two New Professors for Jefferson," *Jeffersonian* 8 (1906): 156–57; C. M. Goss, *A Brief Account of Henry Gray F.R.S. and His Anatomy, Descriptive and Surgical* (1959), published by Lea & Gebinger of Philadelphia; F. B. Wagner, *Thomas Jefferson University: Tradition and Heritage* (1989), also published by Lea & Febiger; and D. E. Haines, "Spitzka and Spitzka on the Brains of the Assassins of Presidents," *Journal of the History of the Neurosciences* 4 (1995): 236–66.

DUANE E. HAINES

SPITZKA, Edward Charles (10 Nov. 1852–13 Jan. 1914), neurologist and psychiatrist, was born in New York City, the son of Charles A. Spitzka, a watchmaker, and Johanna Tag. After study at the College of the City of New York, Spitzka attended the Medical School of the University of New York, receiving the M.D. degree in 1873. As was customary in the period, Spitzka sought further training in Europe. From 1873 to 1876 he studied with notable scientists, serving for a time as assistant to the holder of the chair of embryology in Vienna. This period of intense academic pursuit, coupled with the European standard of scholarly excellence, greatly influenced Spitzka's subsequent thinking and attitude about his field and his peers. During his European stay he met and married (1875) Catherine Wacek; they had one child, a son, Edward Anthony Spitzka.

Spitzka returned to New York in 1876 and set up a practice that dealt primarily with diseases of the central nervous system. In addition to his clinical practice, he conducted research on the anatomy of the brains of humans and of animals as diverse as the iguana and porpoise; he also lectured on topics in embryology. Spitzka was especially vocal in his writings and in lectures about what he considered the inadequate and unenlightened treatment of the mentally ill patient in U.S. institutions. His criticism extended to issues of patient care, training of personnel, and the closed circle of administrators who ran such facilities. Spitzka's intense research activity in the period from 1876 to 1880 resulted in numerous publications and in a growing reputation as an expert witness in legal proceedings where mental state was an issue.

Spitzka was not one of the founding members of the American Neurological Association (ANA, founded 1875), but he joined it in 1877. He immediately immersed himself in the activities of the ANA, attending meetings, presenting the results of his research, and participating in the group's political functions. He was editor of the *American Journal of Neurology and Psychiatry* (1881–1884) and president of the ANA in 1890. Spitzka was also a member of the New York Neurological Association and served as its president (1883–1884). As described by his contemporaries, Spitzka had a domineering personality, was frequently opinionated and seemingly arrogant, and could be condescending to those he considered his intellectual inferiors. He was intolerant of poorly done science or clinical neurology and of archaic scientific views, and he was quick to press aggressively for the correctness of his own opinion. However, at the same time his peers acknowledged that he was well trained in the clinical and basic sciences and had great intellectual abilities and depth.

In December 1881 Spitzka was compelled, by order of the court, to testify for the defense at the trial of Charles Julius Guiteau, the assassin of President James A. Garfield. Spitzka was already well known in New York neurological circles and in the ANA; this unusual situation propelled him into the national limelight. Although he had previously formulated an opinion on the mental state of the assassin Guiteau (Garfield was shot on 2 July 1881 but lingered until 19 September), Spitzka had rejected requests by both sides to testify voluntarily. Once required to appear, however, he stated his views uncompromisingly. Based on his readings, Spitzka had earlier concluded in published opinions that Guiteau was insane. This view did not change after he personally examined Guiteau; if anything, it became even more dogmatic and unyielding. Of the nine individuals who examined the assassin, only Spitzka was asked a direct question concerning whether he thought Guiteau was or was not insane; the other witnesses were required to answer a hypothetical question. In Spitzka's view, Guiteau was insane when he shot Garfield and probably had been so for some time before. Spitzka tenaciously clung to this opinion in the face of aggressive and sometimes demeaning questions by the prosecution. He was the only defense witness who concluded, based on personal examination, that Guiteau was insane—an enormously unpopular view for which Spitzka was publicly ridiculed and his life threatened. The government's position was that a sane and calculating Guiteau had committed this crime, and the public wanted no part of a verdict that would allow him to suffer any punishment less than execution. Spitzka's opinion, although later vindicated, did not prevail; Guiteau was convicted and hanged.

Within two years of the Guiteau trial Spitzka published his text on mental diseases, *Insanity, Its Classification, Diagnosis and Treatment* (1883). This book was hailed as "the standard of psychiatric knowledge" at the time and went through two more editions. In it Spitzka defined various types of insanity (accompanied by examples), suggested causes or offered explanations for various mental illnesses, and attempted to view insane conditions in a broader biological perspective.

Although Spitzka's career flourished in his later years, the high point of his prominence was around the time of the Guiteau trial. In addition to holding elected offices in state and national professional organizations, he held clinical appointments at several New York hospitals, as well as academic appointments at the New York Post-Graduate School of Medicine and Columbia Veterinary College. Spitzka was also a founder

of the American Anthropometric Society (1889), and he received prizes for his scientific work. He published about 215 papers on diverse topics such as comparative brain anatomy, neurology, psychiatry, medicolegal topics, and general vertebrate anatomy, as well as reviews of books on embryology, zoology, and horse anatomy. Original discoveries made by Spitzka include optic structures in birds and in the iguana, auditory structures in whales, and the dorsolateral fasciculus ("marginal tract"). The marginal tract is the bundle of lightly myelinated nerve fibers located immediately external to the gray matter of the spinal cord dorsal horn; these fibers convey pain and thermal sensations. Sometimes called Spitzka's marginal tract, it was reportedly described by Spitzka a year before its discovery by Lissauer. Spitzka's scientific efforts stopped abruptly in 1903, and he later suffered from necrosis of the jaw. He died at his home in New York.

Spitzka made significant contributions to the fields of neuroanatomy and clinical neurology in the United States through his research, writings, and participation in professional organizations. He clearly viewed himself as a scholar neurologist, versed in science, as broadly defined, as well as in clinical medicine. Although many of his original observations have slipped into obscurity or have been upstaged by subsequent discoveries, his role in the trial of Guiteau secured him a place in medical history.

• Information on the life and contributions of Spitzka are in the obituaries "Edward Charles Spitzka," *Journal of Nervous and Mental Disease* 41 (1914): 209–19; "Edward Charles Spitzka of New York," *New York Medical Journal* 99 (1914): 134–35; and "Dr. Edward Charles Spitzka," *British Medical Journal* 1 (1914): 282. Personal and professional insights of his contemporaries are seen in N. E. Brill, "In Memoriam Dr. Edward Charles Spitzka," *New York Medical Journal* 99 (1914): 935–37, and in an article of the same title in *Journal of Nervous and Mental Disease* 41 (1914): 519–22. On his career see also C. L. Dana, "Early Neurology in the United States: The Hughlings Jackson Address," *Journal of the American Medical Association* 90 (1928): 1421–24; D. Denny-Brown et al., *Centennial Anniversary Volume of the American Neurological Association* (1975); and D. E. Haines, "Spitzka and Spitzka on the Brains of the Assassins of Presidents," *Journal of the History of Neurosciences* 4 (1995): 236–66. A most informative and valuable source is C. E. Rosenburg, *The Trial of the Assassin Guiteau* (1968).

DUANE E. HAINES

SPIVAK, Charlie (17 Feb. 1907–1 Mar. 1982), trumpet player and bandleader, was born Charles Spivak in Kiev, Ukraine. His parents' names are unknown. One of ten children, he immigrated to the United States as a three-year-old and was reared in New Haven, Connecticut. After initially studying the violin, he took up the trumpet at the age of ten and reportedly studied with George Hyer, a member of the New Haven Symphony. His early experience as an entertainer was gained in local bands and in a commercial orchestra led by violinist Paul Specht from 1924 to 1931.

Although he never acquired the improvisational skills to perform as a jazz artist, Spivak ironically found himself much sought after during the 1930s by prominent leaders of swing bands. As a result, he amassed illustrious credentials as a member of the trumpet section of several highly popular mainstream bands: Ben Pollack (1931–1934), the Dorsey Brothers (1934–1935), Ray Noble (1935), Bob Crosby (1937–1938), Tommy Dorsey (1938–1939), and as a partner of Jack Teagarden (1939). Whereas his early years with Specht had introduced him to the rigors demanded of a traveling instrumentalist, his affiliation with Pollack provided him with an enduring network of colleagues, such as Teagarden, Benny Goodman, Glenn Miller, and Harry James.

Spivak soon developed a national reputation. As a freelance artist in New York City between 1935 and 1937, he was heard on syndicated radio programs such as the "Ford Symphony Hour" and shows hosted by Kate Smith, Fred Allen, and Al Pearce. During the 1936–1937 season he ranked as the highest paid studio—and radio—musician in New York City. What set Spivak apart from his competitors were his sweetness of tone and its consistency across a wide range. This purity of sound, which Spivak himself characterized as a "velvet" or "plush" sound, was highly distinctive in the realm of jazz and jazz-related music because of the timbral variety and melodic inflections so important to African-American music-making. He was, in fact, often billed as "the man who played the sweetest horn in the world," a tag given him by Glenn Miller. Although capable of virtuoso effects, he was known for keeping gimmicks and tricks to a minimum. His trumpet-playing idol was his contemporary Bunny Berigan. Spivak's approach to his instrument was highly analytical, and he devoted considerable energy to studying the recordings of his peers as well as those of singers.

In the fall of 1939 Spivak set out on his own and formed his own band with the blessing and financial backing of Glenn Miller, a close friend of long standing. Miller helped find engagements for the new band, and in 1940 he even hired it with some regularity to stand as a proxy for his own band at New York's Hotel Pennsylvania. This enterprise proved short-lived, in part because of Spivak's inexperience and indecision and also because of his inability to create a marketable identity for the ensemble, musical or otherwise. Spivak was a jovial, unassuming individual who was well liked by his musicians, but he was uncomfortable projecting the show business persona that mesmerized audiences.

He tried again a year later with a group of Washington-based musicians, originally led by Bill Downer, and this time he achieved nationwide popularity. Spivak's second band, which flourished until 1956, owed its vitality to an expanded repertory—romantic ballads for the leader and jazz pieces for band members—and to the imaginative arrangements of new trombonist Nelson Riddle and former bandleader Sonny Burke. This band was featured in the 1944 films *Pin-Up Girl* and *Follow the Boys*, and it made a series of recordings. In addition to Riddle and Burke, notable alumni of his

ensemble include Willie Smith, Dave Tough, Les Elgart, Neal Hefti, and Sy Oliver. The first theme song associated with Spivak's band, "Night Is Ending," was superseded by "Stardreams," composed by Spivak and Burke and arranged by Burke.

In 1956 Spivak could no longer sustain the expense of keeping a big band together, and to take advantage of musical opportunities in the South he moved to Miami, Florida. He continued to perform, although with smaller groups, and began to hire local musicians to augment a nucleus of players for out-to-town engagements. In 1967 he took up residency in Greenville, South Carolina, where, as co-owner of Ye Olde Fireplace Inn, he led a band regularly for eleven years and maintained his own swing-era aesthetic in spite of changing tastes among the public. He was married three times; both his second wife, Irene Daye (whom he married in 1943), and his third wife, Dubby Hayes (whom he married in 1974), were singers in his band. His first wife's name was Fritzie (maiden name unknown). He died in Greenville.

Although Spivak is generally regarded as "one of the truly great lead trumpeters" (Simon, p. 426) of the swing era and as a "musician of great talent and integrity" (Schuller, p. 768), his acknowledged limitations as an improviser relegated him to a secondary position in artistic achievement, even when compared to other players such as Harry James and Ziggy Elman, who also lured audiences with a comparable "sweet" style. In fact, because of his inability to rival the popularity of Harry James, Spivak temporarily turned away from the standard of full-toned brilliance and, with the aid of a special mute reportedly suggested by Glenn Miller, offered solo playing of conspicuous delicacy and intimacy—similar to the trombone style of Tommy Dorsey—that was, according to Gunther Schuller, "too subtle for the average danceband fan." Nevertheless, Schuller observed that "with the help of a fine bassist, Jimmy Middleton, and drummer Davey Tough, as well as altoist Willie Smith (from Lunceford's band), Spivak's orchestra could swing with the best of them—especially when Spivak resorted to his beautiful-toned open-horn-playing" (p. 768).

• Spivak's career is assessed in George T. Simon, *The Big Bands*, 4th ed. (1981), and Gunther Schuller, *The Swing Era: The Development of Jazz, 1930–1945* (1978). An interview with Spivak is included in Zane Knauss, *Conversations with Jazz Musicians* (1977). Discographies appear in Brian Rust, *The American Dance Band Discography, 1917–1942*, vol. 2 (1975), and Charles Garrod, *Charlie Spivak and His Orchestra*, 2d ed. [pamphlet] (1986). An obituary is in the *New York Times*, 2 Mar. 1982.

MICHAEL J. BUDDS

SPIVAK, Lawrence (11 June 1900–9 Mar. 1994), publisher and producer of radio and television programs, was born Lawrence Edmund Spivak in New York City, the son of William Benjamin Spivak, a manufacturer of dresses and nurses' uniforms, and Sonja Bershad. Spivak's earliest experiences were mercantile as well as reportorial. After working for the *Brooklyn Ea-*

gle, he attended Harvard University and upon graduation in 1921 became business manager of *Antiques* magazine, while at the same time covering local stories for the *Boston American*. In 1924 Spivak married Charlotte Beir Ring, a psychologist. They had two children, a daughter, Judith Ring Frost, who died in 1962 and a son, Jonathan, who had a distinguished career as a reporter for the *Wall Street Journal*.

A stint on two sports magazines preceded Spivak's most important print connection, the *American Mercury*, the monthly founded in 1924 by H. L. Mencken and George Jean Nathan. In 1939, knowing that the magazine was losing money but attracted to its prominent place in American intellectual life, Spivak bought the publication from its owner, Paul Palmer. He served as both its editor and publisher from 1944 to 1950, during which period the iconoclasm about politics the *Mercury* had inherited from its founders hastened its eventual demise. (In 1936, in the pages of the *Mercury*, Mencken confidently predicted that "even a Chinaman could beat Roosevelt." FDR carried all but two states in the ensuing election.)

Always proud of the *American Mercury*, in 1944 Spivak with his *Mercury* colleague, the Jewish-American novelist Charles Angoff, edited the *American Mercury Reader*, a collection of articles, stories, reportage, poetry, and other writing from the periodical, aiming to give a representative selection of "something from every period in the magazine's life," rather than just the best-known or most widely reprinted articles. However, the losses from the *Mercury* continued to run at $100,000 a year, its prestige notwithstanding.

To pay for these, Spivak published Mercury Mystery Books in 1938, Bestseller Mystery Books in 1941, plus five broadly aimed pulp magazines, including several that persisted: *Ellery Queen's Mystery Magazine*, the *Magazine of Fantasy and Science Fiction*, and *Detective*. By this time, his broadcast interests had begun to crowd his publishing concerns; in 1950 Spivak sold the still unprofitable *Mercury* and in 1954 his interest in his remaining publications.

It was Spivak's interest in dramatizing stories in the *American Mercury* that led to his most notable achievement. In 1945, after discussions with radio producer Martha Roundtree, Spivak began the weekly radio program "Meet the Press." Its basic format, which has never changed, was established in the first broadcast: a moderator and four journalists of national stature question a well-known public figure, most often a politician, about current events. Spivak considered himself a "permanent panelist" rather than the moderator, a function initially performed by Roundtree.

Although the program began with the Mutual Broadcasting System, in 1955 Spivak sold the radio version of "Meet the Press" to the National Broadcasting Company, which began to televise it as well. Spivak saw the potential of the new medium to dramatize news and to expose a subject's character. "Television," he said, in a *Coronet* magazine interview in June 1955, "has an awesome faculty of showing up sincerity as well as insincerity. So if a man is honest and knows his stuff, he'll emerge with his proper stature. By the same token, so will a phoney."

The first guest to appear under video scrutiny was the former postmaster general and Democratic insider James A. Farley, in 1948. Subsequently, almost every major national figure as well as many international politicos and governors appeared on "Meet the Press," often at key moments in their careers: Presidents John F. Kennedy, Lyndon Johnson, Richard Nixon, Gerald Ford, and Jimmy Carter; Eleanor Roosevelt, Sir Anthony Eden, John Foster Dulles, Martin Luther King, Fidel Castro, Indira Gandhi, Golda Meir; and occasional literary figures such as Robert Frost. Senator Theodore Bilbo of Mississippi was driven to admit his membership in the Ku Klux Klan on the program, and with Soviet deputy premier Anastas Mikoyan, Spivak went on the attack, quipping, "Don't filibuster; we only have two minutes left." In 1965 "Meet the Press" struck new territory when it interviewed British prime minister Harold Wilson by satellite hookup.

Early programs often made the news themselves, as well as reporting and commenting on it. The program provided the country with one of its earliest exercises in investigating subversives in 1948 when on the air Whittaker Chambers accused Alger Hiss of being a communist. In later broadcasts, General Walter Bedell Smith announced that the Soviet Union had an atomic bomb, and in 1950 Governor Thomas E. Dewey announced that he would not run for president and exhorted voters to cast their ballots for Dwight Eisenhower. Adlai Stevenson announced that he was willing to run for president on "Meet the Press."

Spivak's questions left viewers with no clear sense of his own political preferences, a fact that identifies his style as an older one, with claims to objectivity that succeeding reporters would feel unable to assert. He was, however, similar to later reporters in his complex blend of persistence and politeness. His manner belied an acute consciousness of the power he wielded. "Men in public office live by the voters they attract," he said in the *Coronet* interview, "and it is therefore hard for a politician to refuse to appear on a program that attracts an audience of millions—and makes important news across the country next morning." To *Time* magazine in 1972 he explained, "I never try to catch a man. I will never try to trick him . . . [but] a man had better be prepared to justify or explain his changes of position."

Having moved permanently to Washington, D.C., Spivak retired from "Meet the Press" in 1975, after his program had been on radio for thirty years and on television for twenty-seven. By the time of his death in Washington, D.C., it had become the longest running program in the history of television and had spawned numerous rivals, such as "Face the Nation" and "Issues and Answers." In addition, during his early career, he produced two syndicated television shows about public affairs, "The Big Issue" and "Keep Posted."

From 1985 to 1993, with Julia Johnson White, he coproduced "The Annual Report Series," which featured conversations with former secretaries of state and defense and other cabinet officials. In addition on occasion he was a panelist on the program he created, "Meet the Press."

With his creation of the in-depth interview, the extended and relaxed examination of a single person, Spivak raised the level of television reporting at a time when the new medium was being defined. The format of "Meet the Press" was imitated, and in many cases the imitations were the equals of the original, although Spivak's persistence and courtliness continued to give his own productions a distinctly civilized tough-mindedness.

• After his death the bulk of Spivak's papers were deposited in the Library of Congress; those relating to his days at the *American Mercury* were sent to the Enoch Pratt Library in Baltimore, Md., which houses a large H. L. Mencken archive. They include numerous memorandums for the record written after Spivak's conversations with guests scheduled to appear on "Meet the Press" as well as with other figures from government. The *New York Times* and *Washington Post*, 10 Mar. 1994, published appreciations of his career.

ROGER LATHBURY

SPIVEY, Queen Victoria (15 Oct. 1906–3 Oct. 1976), classic blues singer and songwriter (on at least one recording known as Jane Lucas), was born Victoria Regina Spivey in Houston, Texas, the daughter of Grant Spivey, a straw boss on Texas wharfs and a string player, and Addie Smith, a nurse. She was one of eight children in a musical family. Her father and brothers were members of a local string band, and her three sisters, Addie "Sweet Peas," Elton "Za Zu," and Leona, also were singers. Spivey began playing piano at an early age and soon was performing with various local groups (including Henry "Lazy Daddy" Filmore's Blues-Jazz Band and L. C. Tolen's Band and Revue). There followed appearances in vaudeville houses and theaters throughout Texas, Missouri, and Michigan. As a teenager she worked at the Lincoln Theater (playing piano for silent movies) in Houston, Texas.

In 1926 Spivey went to St. Louis with the goal of meeting Jesse Johnson, a recording talent scout. After hearing her audition, Johnson awarded Spivey a contract to record four tunes for the OKeh label. One of them, "Black Snake Blues" (a Spivey original), established Spivey as a blues singer. Within the first month the record sold 150,000 copies, leading to a New York City recording date. Six Victoria Spivey discs were released in 1926 alone. Over the course of her career she would record on several other labels, including Victor, Vocalion, Decca, Bluesville, GHB, Folkways, and later in life, her own label, Spivey Records. Typical of Spivey's Texas singing style were off-tones, drops, moans, wails, and flat tones, which she used to great effect when performing as well as on collaborative recordings with stellar artists such as King Oliver, Louis Armstrong, Lonnie Johnson, Porter Grainger, Henry "Red" Allen, Eddie Durham, J. C. Higginbotham, Sidney DeParis, Lee Collins, Luis Russell, Albert Nicholas, Pops Foster, Zutty Singleton, Eddie Bare-

field, and "Memphis Minnie" (Minnie Douglas Lawless).

Returning to St. Louis in 1927, Spivey worked as a staff writer for the St. Louis Publishing Company. That same year she appeared in the musical revue *Hit Bits from Africana* in New York City. In 1929 she made her film debut in the King Vidor film *Hallelujah*. She appeared in two other musical revues in those early years, *4-11-44* in New York City in 1930 and, on tour in Texas and Oklahoma, *Dallas Tan Town Topics* in 1933.

Spivey is believed to have had four husbands among them, Reuben Floyd, whom she apparently married sometime around 1928 and with whom she remained until the early 1930s. However, her most significant marriage was to dancer William "Billy" Adams, whom she married sometime around 1934 and with whom she had a long professional association, until their relationship ended in 1951. Spivey and Adams performed in the highly successful Olsen and Johnson musical revue *Hellzapoppin* on Broadway in 1938–1939 and then on tour for an additional three and a half years. During the late thirties and the forties Spivey and Adams worked the vaudeville circuit and appeared at various exclusive clubs, lounges, and theaters in Chicago, Cleveland, St. Louis, and New York City (including the Apollo Theater).

Spivey was comparatively inactive during the 1950s, but in the 1960s her musical career revived, and the decade was filled with various artistic endeavors. She toured widely, both in the United States and abroad, appearing at blues festivals, on radio and television, and on college campuses, and as a blues historian she contributed to *Record Research* magazine. Her most noteworthy accomplishment of the period, however, was the establishment of her own record company, Spivey Records, which reissued many of her own recordings, brought out of retirement other classic blues singers (in particular, Lucille Hegamin and Alberta Hunter), and provided recording opportunities for a cadre of younger blues artists, with whom Spivey frequently shared recording sessions. Of the Spivey reissues, the most outstanding was *Victoria Spivey Recorded Legacy of the Blues* (1969), which features Spivey recordings made between 1927 and 1937 with the backing of trumpet greats such as King Oliver and Louis Armstrong.

Other highlights of Spivey's professional activity in the sixties and seventies included an appearance on "Lyrics and Legends" on New York television station WNET in 1963; at the American Folk-Blues Festival tour in England and Europe, also in 1963; at the Chicago Blues Festival in 1969; on the PBS show "Free Time" in 1971; and at the Philadelphia Folk Festival, broadcast on PBS in 1974. In the early 1970s she served as a blues adviser to the Conn Instrument Company of Chicago, and in 1976 she was featured in the BBC-TV documentary *The Devil's Music—A History of the Blues*.

A prolific songwriter (many of her songs were considered to be blues "tone poems"), Spivey contributed to the blues repertoire titles such as "Arkansas Road Blues," "Big Black Belt," "Blood Hound Blues," "Garter Snake Blues," "You're Going to Miss Me When I'm Gone," "No. 12, Let Me Roam," "Black Belt Blues," "Big Black Limousine," and "Organ Grinder Blues." According to one blues historian, "Spivey produced nearly 1,500 songs, many of them never credited to her" (Placksin, p. 33). During her final years, she was able to both inform and clarify for blues aficionados and researchers. She had lived through the various eras; she had heard and often performed with the legends; and her recall faculties were excellent. In 1970 Broadcast Music Incorporated (BMI) awarded Spivey a Commendation of Excellence "for long and outstanding contributions to the many worlds of music." She died at the Beekman-Downtown Hospital in New York City. According to her obituary in the *New York Times*, she was survived by two daughters.

• Excellent and extensive coverage of Spivey and her many careers appears in Daphne Duval Harrison, *Black Pearls: Blues Queens of the 1920s* (1988), and Sheldon Harris, *Blues Who's Who* (1979). The importance of her career in blues/jazz history is covered in Sally Placksin, *American Women in Jazz, 1900 to the Present: Their Words, Lives, and Music* (1982). In addition to her career as a blues singer and songwriter, her role as a blues historian is discussed in Derrick Stewart-Baxter, *Ma Rainey and the Classic Blues Singers* (1970). An obituary is in the *New York Times*, 7 Oct. 1976.

D. ANTOINETTE HANDY

SPOFFORD, Ainsworth Rand (12 Sept. 1825–11 Aug. 1908), sixth librarian of Congress, was born in Gilmanton, New Hampshire, the son of Rev. Luke Spofford, a Presbyterian pastor, and Greta Rand. Spofford was educated at home. As a youth he developed an insatiable appetite for reading and a love of books and served a brief apprenticeship as a bookbinder in Chilmark, Massachusetts, on Martha's Vineyard. Ill health prevented him from following his father and brother to Amherst College.

In 1845 Spofford migrated west to Cincinnati, where he found employment with bookseller and publisher Elizabeth D. Truman, widow of William T. Truman, an early publisher of the *McGuffey Readers*. Four years later he was the principal organizer of the Literary Club of Cincinnati, a group of young men who pledged themselves to debate the political and literary issues of the day. In 1851 he became a partner in the publishing business, and through his efforts Truman & Spofford became the city's leading importer of books by the New England Transcendentalists. Moreover, Spofford was responsible for arranging the lecture tours that brought Ralph Waldo Emerson, Theodore Parker, and Bronson Alcott west for the first time. On 15 September 1852 the young entrepreneur married Sarah Partridge, formerly of Franklin, Massachusetts. They had three children.

In 1859 Spofford became associate editor and chief editorial writer for the *Cincinnati Commercial*, the city's leading newspaper. He wrote partisan Republican editorials and indulged himself with lengthy observations about favorite topics, such as "The Art of Reading," in which he explained that "the true art is to read for ideas—not words." In 1861 the *Commercial* sent Spofford to Washington, D.C., to report on President Abraham Lincoln's inauguration. This trip led to his acceptance, in September 1861, of the position of assistant librarian of Congress. On 31 December 1864 President Lincoln promoted the knowledgeable and industrious assistant to the post of librarian of Congress.

Spofford believed that the Library of Congress, then located in the west front of the U.S. Capitol, should serve as the national library in spite of its small size and relative obscurity. For the next three decades, he used his talents as a skillful politician and an energetic librarian to convince congressmen and librarians that he was right. In promoting the legislation that rapidly established the Library of Congress as an institution of national importance, Spofford successfully combined nationalistic rhetoric ("the largest and most complete collection of books relating to America in the world is now gathered on the shelves of the British Museum") with sound, practical arguments. For example, he pointed out that the centralization of copyright activities at the library would save the government money and, through increased efficiency, benefit both authors and publishers. In building the library, Spofford took advantage of the post–Civil War expansion of the federal government and his personal friendships with Ohio congressmen.

Between 1865 and 1870, Librarian Spofford obtained the passage of several legislative acts that made the Library of Congress the largest library in the United States and ensured its future importance. He expanded the library's rooms in the Capitol; acquired the 40,000-volume library of the Smithsonian Institution; purchased in 1867 the unparalleled private library of collector and archivist Peter Force, which formed the foundation of the library's collections of Americana and incunabula (books printed before 1500); took advantage of new international exchange arrangements to expand the collections; and, most important of all, masterminded the centralization of all U.S. copyright registration and deposit activities at the library. Through the copyright law of 1870, the Library of Congress began receiving two copies of all copyrighted books, maps, prints, photographs, and pieces of music.

Spofford believed the American national library should be a permanent, comprehensive collection of the country's literature, "representing the complete product of the American mind in every department of science and literature." He made good progress in the first years of his administration. For example, in 1870 the educator Francis Lieber donated three volumes, inscribing them "To the National Library," and explained to Spofford: "It is not the official name, but I take the liberty. It is the name you have come to."

The dramatic expansion of the library's collections through copyright deposit soon created a space crisis, and Spofford outlined a plan for a separate building in 1873. He wanted a structure that would equal if not surpass the great national libraries of Europe. The building, however, was not authorized until 1886 and not completed for another decade. The delay caused severe overcrowding in the Capitol and nearly brought the library's operations to a halt. In 1897 the doors of the imposing and elaborately decorated new structure across the east plaza from the Capitol were opened to an admiring public. At the time it was the "largest, safest, and costliest" library building in the world and the object of great national pride. It is known today as the Jefferson Building of the Library of Congress.

In late 1896 the Joint Committee on the Library held hearings on the role and functions of the Library of Congress as it expanded into a separate building. Spofford was the principal witness, but his view of a national library as primarily an accumulation of the nation's literature was challenged by witnesses from the American Library Association. They believed it was time for the Library of Congress to begin emphasizing service and the use (not accumulation) of materials, that it should become a workshop for scholars, extending its purpose beyond the storehouse function that Spofford had developed. In particular, Melvil Dewey, librarian of the New York State Library, and Herbert Putnam, librarian of the Boston Public Library, argued that the institution should begin serving libraries and become a focal point for cooperative library activities.

The congressional hearings resulted in a major reorganization and expansion, effective 1 July 1897. The 72-year-old Spofford agreed to become chief assistant librarian under a new librarian of Congress, John Russell Young, and conscientiously and effectively continued in this position under Herbert Putnam, who became librarian of Congress in April 1899. Spofford served under Putnam until his death, in Holderness, New Hampshire. In the library's 1908 annual report, Putnam noted that Spofford's "most enduring service—the increase of the collections—continued to the last few weeks of his life, and continued with the enthusiasm, the devotion, the simple, patient, and arduous concentration that always distinguished it."

Spofford was a prolific essayist, editor, and compiler, an inveterate and almost compulsive popularizer of knowledge. The primary purpose of his many compilations was to select and summarize what he felt was the most useful information, whether it be statistical facts or literary essays. His reputation as a reliable source of information for official and unofficial Washington made him a well-known figure in the nation's capital.

Spofford provided his successors as librarian of Congress with four essential prerequisites for the development of an American national library: firm, bipartisan congressional support for the idea of the Library of Congress as both a legislative and a national institution; the beginnings of a comprehensive collection of Americana; a magnificent new building, itself a national monument; and a strong and independent office of librarian of Congress.

• Spofford's personal papers are in the Manuscript Division, Library of Congress, and his official correspondence is in the Library of Congress Archives, also in the Manuscript Division. Many of Spofford's writings are reprinted in John Y. Cole, ed., *Ainsworth Rand Spofford: Bookman and Librarian* (1975). Spofford's professional and personal interests are accurately described in the formidable title of his *A Book for All Readers, Designed as an Aid to the Collection, Use, and Preservation of Books and the Formation of Public and Private Libraries* (1900). A detailed account of his career is found in John Y. Cole, "Ainsworth Rand Spofford: The Valiant and Persistent Librarian of Congress," *Quarterly Journal of the Library of Congress* 33 (1976): 93–115. For his Cincinnati years, an important source is Carroll Hollis, "A New England Outpost: As Revealed in Some Unpublished Letters of Emerson, Parker, and Alcott to Ainsworth Spofford," *New England Quarterly* 38 (1965): 65–85. Herbert Putnam's "Ainsworth Rand Spofford: A Librarian Past: Ainsworth Rand Spofford—1825–1908," *The Independent*, 19 Nov. 1908, pp. 1149–55, is an insightful assessment. Seven presentations at a memorial service held at the Library of Congress on 12 Nov. 1908 illuminate aspects of Spofford's life and career. The 84-page volume, published by the District of Columbia Library Association under the title *Ainsworth Rand Spofford, 1825–1908* (1909), includes a list of Spofford's writings. An obituary is in the *New York Daily Tribune*, 13 Aug. 1908.

JOHN Y. COLE

SPOFFORD, Grace Harriet (21 Sept. 1887–5 June 1974), music educator and administrator, was born in Haverhill, Massachusetts, the daughter of Harry Hall Spofford, a clothing store clerk, and Sarah G. Hastings. Following her graduation with honors from Haverhill High School in 1905, Spofford attended Mount Holyoke College for a year to study with the renowned organist William Hammond Churchill. Because the college offered no credit for music performance studies and required domestic work of its students, she withdrew and transferred to Smith College, where she studied with the acclaimed composer-organist Henry Dike Sleeper and with pianist Edwin Bruce Story. After graduating from Smith in 1909, Spofford studied for a year in Boston with Richard Platt and gave lecture recitals for New England audiences. From 1910 to 1912 she taught music at Heidelberg University in Tiffin, Ohio. She then enrolled at the Peabody Conservatory of Music in Baltimore, where she received teacher's certificates in both piano and organ. She taught in the Preparatory Division at Peabody from 1913 to 1917 and subsequently became the executive secretary of the conservatory. She also contributed music criticism to the *Baltimore Evening Sun*. While at Peabody, she developed a close personal and professional relationship with her teaching colleague Elizabeth Coulson. The two women lived together in Baltimore, and in 1916 they coauthored *A Guide for Beginners in Piano Playing*.

In 1924 Spofford moved to Philadelphia to begin her duties as the first dean of the Curtis Institute of Music. At Curtis she contributed significantly to the charting of the institute's course, helping to establish a strong curriculum and instituting a program of international scholarships. Following a three-month tour of Europe in the summer of 1926, Spofford returned home eager to provide opportunities for foreign students to study at Curtis. "If we are ever to achieve international understanding," she declared, "I am sure it must come through mutual interchange of thought between artists."

In 1931 Spofford resigned from the Curtis Institute and moved to New York to pursue imaginative and innovative approaches to music education and the redefinition of the place of music in the new social order. There she held a variety of positions, opening a radio and music counselling service at a studio in the Steinway Building, becoming an executive secretary of Olga Samaroff's Layman's Music Courses, and lecturing in music at the Katharine Gibbs School. From 1934 to 1938 she served as associate director of the New York College of Music.

In 1935 Spofford was named director of the music school of the Henry Street Settlement, founded by Lillian Wald in 1927; this position proved to be Spofford's most notable achievement. Under her leadership, the Henry Street Music School made music available to the underprivileged. Besides serving as a center of neighborhood musical activities, the school's principal goal was the musical instruction of students who did not aspire to a professional musical career. Nonetheless, the school was prepared to educate those pursuing careers in music, and it trained students to perform as concertmasters and conductors of orchestras and to become teachers at leading conservatories. The faculty included internationally recognized musicians, many of whom were teachers from the Juilliard School of Music and the Curtis Institute.

After Spofford's arrival, the Henry Street Music School intensified its efforts to present new works by contemporary American composers. In 1936 Spofford commissioned faculty member Aaron Copland to write a stage work for the students of the school. The result was the play-opera *The Second Hurricane*, with a libretto by Edwin Denby. The work was premiered at the school's playhouse in 1937. Staged in a modern style by Orson Welles and conducted by Lehman Engel, the production received national and international critical acclaim. During Spofford's tenure as director, the school grew from about 300 to over 800 students, all the while stressing what Spofford called "the value of music as a common experience in living."

In 1953, one year before her retirement, Spofford traveled to Brussels, where she represented the U.S. Department of State at a conference that resulted in the founding of the International Society for Music Education, an organization that quickly became a vital force in music education circles throughout the world. Following her retirement, she continued to involve herself in noteworthy causes. As she once said to an interviewer, "one can retire from formal, paid work; but there is a responsibility to pass on one's ideas to younger people, and to make one's experience available to them, perhaps initiating new ways." Accordingly, she became a delegate to more than twenty international conferences in Europe and the Middle East on musicology, contemporary music, folk music, and education. From 1954 to 1963 she chaired the music committee of the International Council of Women, having been elected to the post at triennials in Helsinki, Montreal, and Istanbul. She served on the boards of directors of the "People to People" music committee of the United Nations Educational, Scientific, and Cultural Organization and of the International Relations Committee of the New York Federation of Music Clubs. From 1953 to 1964 she chaired the music commission of the National Council of Women of the United States.

In 1958 Spofford wrote to the poet Marianne Moore to request her cooperation in the composition of a musical work that would utilize radio to call the world to peace:

I conceive an oratorio or cantata based on positive forces for good, such as atomic energy for peace. If Schiller and Beethoven were living they might cooperate. But I believe we have creative spirits equal to the task. The oratorio could go by radio to all parts of the world. At the end there might be a simple chorus of seven lines to be sung—1 from Washington, 2 from Europe, 3 from Africa, 4 from South America, and 5 from Asia . . . I think a single syllable or sound meaning 'one' which all would sing or speak together might be a concluding idea.

She planned to have the peace oratorio performed for the seventy-fifth anniversary of the founding of the International Council for Women, scheduled for 1963. Her idea never reached fruition in her lifetime, though a modified version of her idea found expression in *Peace Cantata* (1986), a work commissioned by Regis College. Until her death in New York City, Spofford continued to work tirelessly to motivate the world's people to capitalize on music's time-honored potential for bringing about unity among groups. She never married and had no children.

A lifetime involvement in music, in which she had achieved international renown as an educator and administrator, had deepened Spofford's conviction that the proper use of music could further the cause of world peace. Her belief in music's power to bring people together earned her a reputation as an international ambassador of music.

• Most of Spofford's papers—including correspondence, diaries, and photographs—are in the Sophia Smith Collection at Smith College, Northampton, Mass. Clippings and other pertinent materials are in the Genealogical Division of the Haverhill Public Library, Haverhill, Mass. Information on the Henry Street Settlement school is contained in Spofford, "Music Schools in the Settlements," *Musical Digest*, Nov.–Dec. 1944. Also informative are Robert F. Egan, "History of the Music School of the Henry Street Settlement" (Ph.D. diss., NYU, 1967), and Myles H. Fellowes, "The 'Musical Lighthouse' of New York's East Side," *The Etude*, July 1939. Articles on Spofford include Arlette Phillipous, "Music as a Social Force," *Smith Alumnae Quarterly*, Feb. 1940, pp. 129–

32, and Hazel Nohavec Morgan, "Women in Music Education," *Triangle* of Mu Phi Epsilon, May 1962, pp. 6–8. Other pertinent articles are "Grace Spofford Honored by School," *Musical America*, June 1954, p. 29, and "Henry Street Music," *Newsweek*, 2 June 1952, p. 78. An obituary is in the *New York Times*, 7 June 1974.

S. MARGARET WILLIAM MCCARTHY

SPOFFORD, Harriet Elizabeth Prescott (3 Apr. 1835–14 Aug. 1921), fiction writer, poet, and essayist, was born in Calais, Maine, the daughter of Joseph Newmarch Prescott, a lawyer, entrepreneur, and politician, and Sarah Jane Bridges. Harriet, the oldest of seven children, two of whom died in infancy, grew up in a Calais household that, although burdened by her father's business troubles, encouraged her precocious intellectual development. By 1849 the family's finances had so deteriorated that her father left for Oregon City, Oregon, and Harriet, with her grandmother and an aunt, relocated to Newburyport, Massachusetts, where they lived in a boardinghouse run by another aunt. The move proved advantageous, however, for Harriet attended the prestigious Putnam Free School in Newburyport. When she was sixteen, a prizewinning composition on *Hamlet* so impressed Thomas Wentworth Higginson, one of the judges, that he became her mentor and lifelong friend. After graduation in 1852, Harriet joined her mother and siblings in Derry, New Hampshire, where she continued her education at Pinkerton Academy.

In 1855 or 1856 the family situation worsened. Her father returned, suffering from paralysis, and her mother's health failed. With both parents invalids and the family back in Newburyport, Harriet became the financial mainstay and worked up to fifteen hours a day writing fiction that she could sell quickly—though for small pay—to be published anonymously in the Boston story-papers. Her breakthrough came in 1858 when she sent "In a Cellar," a detective story set in Paris, to the *Atlantic Monthly*. Because of the story's sophistication, the editors doubted her authorship; Higginson recalls that he "had to be called in to satisfy them that a demure little Yankee girl could have written it" (*Letters*, p. 103). "In a Cellar," with other stories published in the *Atlantic* and collected in *The Amber Gods, and Other Stories* (1863), earned her popularity among general readers and respect and admiration from Boston's literary elite.

As a Romance writer of great power and originality, she favored tales with a supernatural twist and exotic settings and characters, particularly strong, unconventional women such as Yone, the unabashedly vain and immoral heroine of "The Amber Gods," or the inventive pioneer woman of "Circumstance," who sings to save her life when attacked by a forest beast. Harriet Prescott's tendency toward lush color and musicality in her early fiction is exemplified by Yone's recollections of the West Indies:

Everything there is an exaggeration. . . . When you see a white sky, a dome of colorless crystal, with purple swells of mountain heaving round you, and a wilder-

ness in golden greens royally languid below, while stretches of a scarlet blaze, enough to ruin a weak constitution, flaunt from the rank vines that lace every thicket—and the whole world, and you with it, seems breaking to blossom,—why then you know what light can do. [Bendixen, p. 53]

The cumulative effect of such charged description can be remarkably intense, so much so that Emily Dickinson admired "Circumstance" as "the only thing I ever saw in my life I did not think I could have written myself'" (St. Armand, p. 173). But Prescott still had a family to support and, from necessity, sometimes wrote so quickly and carelessly that, especially in her early novels, *Sir Rohan's Ghost* (1860) and *Azarian: An Episode* (1864), her descriptions can seem gratuitous and her plots too farfetched. Moreover, during the 1860s, American Romanticism was giving way to realism. *Azarian* was harshly reviewed by the young Henry James, who used the occasion to disparage what he called the Tennysonian "ideal descriptive style" (p. 269) and "exhort Miss Prescott to be *real*, to be true to something" (p. 276).

Harriet Prescott's financial constraints were eased somewhat when in 1865 she married Richard Spofford, an attorney supportive of her work. Because of his business and political interests, the couple spent winters in Washington, D.C., and summers in Newburyport, while providing financial sustenance for their families. In 1867 Harriet gave birth to their only child, a son, who died eight months later. In 1874 the Spoffords purchased Deer Island, on the Merrimack River between Newburyport and Amesbury, where their house became a cherished place for Harriet to work and a much-needed home for their extended families. In 1885 the Spoffords became legal guardians of Thomas and Marion Pierce, orphaned children of close friends. Marion became Harriet's companion, along with a niece, Katherine Prescott Moseley, after Richard's death in August 1888.

During the 1890s Harriet Prescott Spofford grew close to Annie Fields's Boston circle of women writers that included Louise Chandler Moulton, Rose Terry Cooke, Celia Thaxter, Gail Hamilton, and Sarah Orne Jewett, each of whom she memorialized in *A Little Book of Friends* (1917). Her association with the group reflects her commitment to making women's concerns major themes of her writing and portraying a wide range of complex women characters. From 1868 until her death on Deer Island, she was one of the most prolific, versatile, and popular American authors, publishing twenty-nine books, including short-story and poetry collections, novels, children's literature, studies of interior decoration and domestic management, and a fictionalized memoir of her Washington years. She also ceaselessly contributed short stories, poems, essays, and literary criticism to numerous magazines and appeared in several collaborative collections.

Although throughout her career she preferred to write poetry, over the years she also mastered the realistic depiction of New England life in local color stories, such as the interlocked narratives of her last collection, *The Elder's People* (1920). But even in many of her realistic stories she does not suppress her Romantic tendencies but, in psychologically accurate depictions of characters dominated by romantic illusions, creates a rich tension between the two styles. In a 1914 letter to literary critic Fred Pattee, she argues, "I cannot say that I am entirely in sympathy with any realism that excludes the poetic and romantic" (Bendixen, p. xix). Her achievement rests not only on the strength of her early, evocative Romantic tales, but also on her ability to develop as a short-story writer by juxtaposing the demands of realism against her undiminished gifts for Romantic description and characterization.

• Letters by Spofford are in the Barnard College Library; the Howe Library of the University of Florida, Gainesville; and among the Whittier papers at the Essex Institute in Salem, Mass., the William Conant Church Papers in the New York Public Library, and the Fred Lewis Pattee Papers at the Pennsylvania State University Library, University Park. Spofford published six collections of short stories; seven novels, many of which were originally serialized in magazines; five books of verse; four collections of essays; and several children's books. A long bibliography appears in Elizabeth K. Halbeisen, *Harriet Prescott Spofford: A Romantic Survival* (1935), a biography based on research that included interviews with friends who survived Spofford; Halbeisen also assesses stories and poems that appear only in magazines. Alfred Bendixen, in his introduction to *The Amber Gods, and Other Stories* (1989), surveys her life and work and quotes from unpublished letters. See also Rose Terry Cooke, *Our Famous Women* (1884); *Letters and Journals of Thomas Wentworth Higginson*, ed. Mary Thacher Higginson (1921); and William Dean Howells, *Literary Friends and Acquaintances* (1900). In the *North American Review*, Henry James favorably reviewed *The Amber Gods* (Oct. 1863, pp. 568–70) but attacked *Azarian* (Jan. 1865, pp. 268–77). Elizabeth Stuart Phelps, "Stories That Stay," *Century Magazine*, Nov. 1910, pp. 118–23, recalls "The Amber Gods" as one of her most memorable reading experiences, and Barton Levi St. Armand, *Emily Dickinson and Her Culture* (1984), details the influence of Spofford's fiction on Dickinson's poetry.

MEG SCHOERKE

SPOONER, John Coit (6 Jan. 1843–11 June 1919), U.S. senator, was born in Lawrenceburg, Indiana, the son of Philip Loring Spooner, a lawyer, and Lydia Lord Coit. At sixteen he moved to Madison, Wisconsin, where his father became reporter of the state supreme court. John attended the University of Wisconsin, which granted him a Ph.B. in 1864, although before the school's graduation ceremonies, he had enlisted in the Union army. He served one hundred days in the Fortieth Regiment of Wisconsin Volunteers and became a captain in the Fiftieth. Spooner saw action in Missouri in the last weeks of the Civil War before his regiment was ordered to Dakota Territory. Frontier duty left him time to begin reading law. He was mustered out in June 1866 and was made brevet major.

Back in Madison, Spooner took part in the Republican campaign of 1866. Governor Lucius Fairchild rewarded him by appointing Spooner his military secretary with the rank of colonel, an honorific title

Spooner retained for the remainder of his life. He continued his legal studies and was admitted to the bar in 1867. In 1868 he married Anna E. Main, a member of a prominent local family who had been pursuing a career as a professional singer; they had four children. The same year he was appointed assistant attorney general, and he also practiced law privately with his father. In 1870, striking out on his own, he moved to Hudson, a small town nestled in a rich timber valley in western Wisconsin.

At Hudson, Spooner took an immediate interest in Republican politics. In 1872, after a close election, he served a single term in the state assembly, where he backed railroad development in the western part of the state. Moreover, as chairman of the assembly's Committee on Education, he secured greatly increased funding for the state university. In the mid-1870s Spooner's legal career flourished as he emerged as a leading advocate for lumber and railroad interests. As a railroad lobbyist he resisted Granger-backed legislation for closer state regulation of transportation. In 1875, in the important test case *Schulenberg v. Harriman*, he successfully argued before the U.S. Supreme Court that, even though a federal land grant railroad had not completed construction before its time limit had expired, it did not lose its grant in the absence of a congressional enactment taking the land back.

In politics Spooner allied himself with lumber magnate Philetus Sawyer and Milwaukee postmaster and political wheelhorse Henry C. Payne. In 1881 Sawyer upset Republican state boss Elisha W. Keyes for a U.S. Senate seat, thereby sealing the threesome's domination of Wisconsin politics for two decades. Spooner became a fixture on the stump and in 1882 was appointed a regent of the University of Wisconsin. Three years later, with Sawyer's backing, he handily defeated his former employer Fairchild for the Republican caucus nomination for the U.S. Senate. Because the Republicans held a substantial majority in the legislature, Spooner easily won election. Twenty years after the fact, muckraker Lincoln Steffens charged that lumber interests had purchased the Senate seat for Spooner, but Steffens adduced no credible evidence to substantiate the charge.

Early in his Senate term Spooner took a balanced approach to the regulation of interstate commerce. In the name of competition, he favored a ban on railroad pooling, but because of the importance of inexpensive through traffic for the economy of the West, he opposed prohibiting rate discrimination between long and short hauls. He applauded the Interstate Commerce Act's ban against railroad passes and never accepted another pass after the legislation passed. Attentive to Wisconsin's dairy interests, Spooner supported the Oleomargarine Act of 1886, which taxed the manufacture and sale of the butter substitute.

Spooner stumped for presidential candidate Benjamin Harrison in 1888 and became a close unofficial adviser to the Hoosier president. Following custom, he sought appointive offices for Wisconsin Republicans, but he disliked patronage squabbles and stoutly defended the Civil Service Act. In the highly productive Fifty-first Congress, Spooner emerged as a legislative leader. Outraged at the suppression of black voting rights in the South, he fervently, albeit unsuccessfully, fought for a federal elections law as a remedy. In deliberations on the Sherman Antitrust Act, he added an important amendment that eased the initiation of federal court suits against combinations. When the McKinley tariff came before the Senate, Spooner advocated high duties for Wisconsin raw materials, such as lumber and tobacco, but showed less enthusiasm for highly protectionist rates on manufactures. He joined other Republicans in attaching to the bill a reciprocity provision designed to secure wider markets for American products.

After Wisconsin's Republican governor had pushed legislation requiring the use of the English language in public and parochial schools, German Lutherans abandoned the party in the 1890 elections. The Democrats carried the state legislature and elected one of their own to replace Spooner in the Senate in 1891. The next year Spooner made a sacrificial run as the Republican nominee for governor; although unsuccessful, he reduced the Democratic plurality.

Out of office, Spooner moved his family back to Madison. There he concentrated on his law practice, including service as counsel to the receivers of the Northern Pacific Railroad. He kept his hand in politics as well, both in organization and on the stump. After the panic of 1893 turned masses of voters away from the Democrats who held power in Washington, the Republicans regained control of the Wisconsin legislature and sent Spooner back to the U.S. Senate in 1897.

Spooner returned to Washington as an insider and joined Nelson Aldrich, William B. Allison, and Orville Platt in the Senate's dominant Republican clique known as "The Four." In the Fifty-fifth Congress he helped manage the protectionist Dingley Tariff to passage, although he failed in an attempt to amend the bill to create a commission to frame future tariffs. He backed bankruptcy legislation and the Erdman Act, calling for mediation of railway labor disputes. Before the end of the Fifty-fifth Congress, he became chairman of the Rules Committee and retained the post until his retirement.

In the winter and spring of 1898 Spooner stoutly defended President William McKinley's efforts to achieve a negotiated settlement of the war between Spain and its rebellious colony, Cuba. He reluctantly supported armed American intervention and warned against its becoming a war of conquest for the United States. After George Dewey's victory at Manila, Spooner broke with Republican party leaders and opposed annexation of Hawaii. When the Treaty of Paris offered the prospect of acquiring the Philippines, Puerto Rico, and Guam, Spooner defended the constitutionality and expediency of the move, but he made no secret of his opposition to permanent annexation of tropical regions with populations inexperienced in American ways. He considered these areas unfit for

eventual statehood and, therefore, argued against extending full constitutional rights to their inhabitants. As for Cuba, Spooner helped draft the Platt Amendment, less out of desire to perpetuate U.S. control of the island than to put its government on a secure footing to maintain its independence.

After McKinley's reelection in 1900, the president offered Spooner the post of attorney general, but he declined. When Theodore Roosevelt succeeded McKinley, Spooner soon became an intimate adviser of the new president, who was eager to build bridges to congressional leaders. In the Senate Spooner squired Roosevelt's Cuban reciprocity plan to passage. In the debate over a transisthmian canal, Spooner worked for a route through Panama rather than Nicaragua and weighed in with a legalistic defense of Roosevelt's questionable methods in procuring a canal treaty from the newly independent Panama.

In the meantime, factionalism began to plague Wisconsin Republicans. In 1902 Governor Robert La Follette, claiming the reform label, sought to derail Spooner's renomination, but the senator was so popular with the rank-and-file that he easily won renomination and reelection. Spooner believed that La Follette's favorite reform, the primary election, would destroy the party's infrastructure and reduce nominations to bitter personal fights. Nonetheless, by 1904 La Follette had taken possession of the state party apparatus. That year Spooner and his associates supported an alternative nominee for governor, but La Follette won the backing of President Roosevelt and the election.

In Washington, meanwhile, Spooner grew increasingly skeptical of some of the reform initiatives of the Roosevelt administration. Although he favored more effective railroad rate regulation and continued to defend the president on a variety of fronts, including foreign policy and conservation, Spooner objected to what he considered Roosevelt's unconstitutional aggrandizement of the executive at the expense of the legislative branch. In 1906 La Follette joined Spooner in the Senate and soon engaged him in bitter disputes over federal patronage. The next year, Spooner resigned his seat.

Upon leaving the Senate, Spooner moved to New York, where he practiced law, mostly corporate business, until his death there. Returning to the law suited his temperament. In the Senate he had quickly earned a reputation as that body's foremost legal and constitutional thinker. As a politician, he had little taste for intraparty machinations and squabbles, but he genuinely enjoyed the work of legislation and governing and was probably most satisfied when expounding a point of constitutional law on the Senate floor.

• A large collection of Spooner's papers is housed in the Manuscript Division of the Library of Congress. Spooner correspondence also appears in other collections, including the Theodore Roosevelt Papers (Library of Congress) and the Elisha W. Keyes Papers (Wisconsin State Historical Society). The *Congressional Record* is indispensable for any study of his career in the Senate. The only full-length biography is Dorothy Ganfield Fowler, *John Coit Spooner: Defender of Presi-*

dents (1961). James Richard Parker, "Senator John C. Spooner, 1897–1907" (Ph.D. diss., Univ. of Maryland, 1972), analyzes the latter portion of Spooner's congressional career. An obituary appears in the *New York Times*, 11 June 1919.

CHARLES W. CALHOUN

SPORN, Philip (25 Nov. 1896–23 Jan. 1978), electrical engineer and utility executive, was born in Folotwin, Austria, the son of Isak Sporn and Rachel Kolker. He emigrated with his family to the United States at age eleven and attended public schools in New York City. He became a U.S. citizen through his father's naturalization in 1907. He graduated with a degree in electrical engineering from Columbia University in 1918. While finishing the degree he took a position with the Crocker Wheeler Manufacturing Company, and in 1919 he became an electrical utility engineer with the Consumers Power Company in Michigan.

In 1920 Sporn took a position as protection engineer with the American Gas and Electric Power Company and remained with that firm until his retirement at age sixty-five. The firm provided power in Michigan, Indiana, Ohio, Kentucky, Tennessee, West Virginia, and Virginia. In 1923 Sporn married Sadie Posner; they had three children. Sporn rose through the company's ranks rapidly and, by the 1940s, was a nationally recognized figure in the field of electrical power. In the 1950s he emerged as a leader in the field of electrical power from nuclear energy. His clarity and originality of thinking and presentation brought him many invitations to serve in consulting, lecturing, advisory council, and congressional testimony settings.

Sporn became chief electrical engineer of American Gas and Electric in 1927, and from 1933 to 1947 he was chief engineer of the firm and its subsidiary companies. He was vice president of engineering in 1934, was elected a member of the board of directors in 1943, became executive vice president in 1945, and in 1947 became president and chief executive officer. His contributions as engineer and manager included his development in 1930 of a plan for fuller integration of the system and interconnection of the company's network with other utilities.

Under Sporn's leadership, American Gas and Electric pioneered in high-voltage transmission of power, moving first in 1947 to a 330,000-volt system. In 1954 the firm received the Charles A. Coffin Award for developing and demonstrating the first 345,000 volt transmission system. By every statistical measure, including mileage of lines, numbers of customers served, kilowatts generated and sold, and total revenues, the firm expanded greatly under Sporn's leadership. The company thrived under his leadership, and as a result of his planning, the firm engaged in a number of innovative developments and cooperative agreements. In 1956 Sporn developed a $7 million expansion plan to raise the company's kilowatt capacity by two-thirds in a five-year period. In 1958, in recognition that gas production was no longer part of the company's mission, the name was changed to American Electric Power.

Sporn made many contributions to the field of nuclear power. In 1952 he helped organize and then served as president of the Ohio Valley Electric Corporation, which was sponsored by fifteen utility companies in the Ohio Valley region to supply power to the Atomic Energy Commission's uranium-diffusion complex at Portsmouth, Ohio. OVEC built two large power plants with a total generating capacity of two million kilowatts. Sporn took a direct role in designing these plants. He also organized (in 1953) and served as president (beginning in 1955) of the Nuclear Power Group, Inc., a nonprofit research and development partnership, which planned and constructed the 180-megawatt Boiling Water Reactor plant at Dresden, Illinois, one of the first generation of on-line power reactors in the United States. He organized and chaired (1957–1967) the East Central Nuclear Group, which funded research into advanced reactor types, including High Temperature Gas-cooled Reactors and steam-cooled breeder reactors.

Meanwhile, at American Electric Power Company, Sporn continued to work on increasing the numbers of customers and the plant's capacity. In 1956 he convinced Kaiser Aluminum and Orlin Revere Metals (Ormet) Corporation to locate aluminum plants in the company's service region, guaranteeing full-time availability of 600,000 kilowatts to these plants. He also worked closely with electric cooperatives in Ohio, funded by the Rural Electrification Administration, forming a partnership between investor-owned and cooperatively owned companies for the supply of power. Sporn conceived of U.S. electrical power generating technology as part of the Cold War technological race with the Soviet Union, and in 1960 he announced that American Electric Power would cooperate with Westinghouse Electric Corporation in a joint venture. The new project was the construction of a 750,000-volt transmission line in West Virginia, which would outrank a world-record Soviet line of 500,000 volts.

On 1 December 1961 Sporn retired from American Electric Power and turned his attention more fully to his writing projects, to giving papers at conferences and lectures at special university programs, and to public service in areas related to power. He drew on his rich personal experience in high-voltage transmission innovation and in working with nuclear power to touch on subjects of wider contemporary interest, including the long history of systems analysis in the power industry; the interrelationship of economic considerations with engineering of systems; the relationship between different energy sources, such as coal and nuclear fuels and projections of energy need; the relationship between energy consumption and production in developing economies; the relationship of energy supply to the Cold War; and the use of power for desalinization of seawater in desert regions, particularly Israel.

In his published work, Sporn warned that while there is a clear correlation between energy production and consumption on the one hand and broader economic growth and progress on the other, the relationship is not one of cause and effect. Simply generating more power is no key to progress, which depends on a wide variety of factors including human resources, a vigorous and dynamic political structure, and environmental considerations such as topography, climate, and natural transportation routes. Furthermore, he did not see nuclear power as a panacea for energy supply problems and insisted that improved efficiencies in the use of conventional fossil fuels would be essential to supply the needs of an expanding economy. False hope had been placed in nuclear power, which he pointed out, could only go so far in meeting energy needs. He emphasized the fact that electrical energy represented less than one-fifth of the energy consumed in the United States. Direct usage of coal and petroleum, particularly in transportation, represented far more consumption, and thus, nuclear power (which could only be converted to electric power and ship-propulsion), would never be able to represent more than a small fraction of the energy consumed in the United States.

Sporn's clear and sophisticated analysis of such questions through the 1960s and 1970s in lectures at Columbia University, Massachusetts Institute of Technology and at conferences, made him a leading contributor to the active intellectual debates surrounding both systems thinking and the energy crisis in this era. Sporn's public service in areas related to power, engineering, resources, and nuclear questions, as well as his publication record in these areas won him a host of awards and national recognition from professional associations, universities, and governments. In World War II he was a consultant to the War Production Board; in 1947 he served as a consultant to the Oak Ridge nuclear facility; between 1953 and 1957 he served as a member of group of visiting advisors for the Brookhaven National Laboratory; he was a delegate to the first "Atoms for Peace" conference in Switzerland in 1953, and attended as an observer the second conference in 1955. From 1949 to 1951 he chaired an advisory committee on cooperation between the private power community and the Atomic Energy Commission. In 1959 he served on an ad hoc advisory committee on AEC reactor programs and policy. From 1947 to 1958 he served on the electric power committee of the National Security Resources Board.

Sporn was author or coauthor of eleven books and about 200 scientific papers and articles. As visiting lecturer or visiting professor, he taught at the Industrial College of the Armed Forces (1948–1957), at Cornell University's College of Engineering (1962 and 1965), and at MIT (1967, 1970). As a member of academic advisory councils, he served Cornell, MIT, Princeton, and Columbia.

Among Sporn's many awards were the American Society of Mechanical Engineers Medal (1962), the John Fritz Medal (1956), the Charles A. Coffin Award, the Edison Medal (1945), the Egleston Medal (1946), Columbia University's Medal of Excellence (1948), the Faraday Medal of the British Institution of Electrical Engineers, and chevalier of the French Legion of Honor. In addition, he was awarded honorary memberships in leading engineering professional associations, including the American Nuclear Society, the American Institute of Electrical and Electronic Engineers, and the American Society of Mechanical Engineers. He died in New York City.

• Among Sporn's works are *Heat Pumps*, with E. R. Ambrose (1947); *The Integrated Power System as the Basic Mechanism for Power Supply* (1950); *Energy: Its Production, Conversion and Use in the Service of Man* (1963); *Nuclear Power Economics: Analysis and Comments* (1964); *Foundations of Engineering* (1964); *Fresh Water from Saline Waters: The Political, Social, Engineering and Economic Aspects of Desalination* (1966); *Research in Electric Power* (1966); *Vistas in Electric Power* (3 vols., 1968), which includes many of his published and unpublished papers and articles, arranged by topic, over the period from 1925 to 1964; *Technology, Engineering, and Economics* (1969); *The Social Organization of Electric Power Supply in Modern Societies* (1971); and *Energy in an Age of Limited Availability and Delimited Applicability* (1976). An article on Sporn appeared in *Time*, 12 Mar. 1956. An obituary is in the *New York Times*, 24 Jan. 1978.

RODNEY P. CARLISLE

SPOTSWOOD, Alexander (1676–7 June 1740), lieutenant governor of Virginia and industrial entrepreneur, was born in northern Africa in the city of Tangier, the son of Robert Spotswood, a physician, and Catherine Elliott. The family was staunchly royalist. Alexander's father was personal physician to the first earl of Middleton, briefly the most powerful politician in Restoration Scotland, but later exiled as governor of Tangier. The earl's personal physician accompanied him and acted also as physician to the garrison. Alexander was first taken to England at the age of seven. His father died when he was eleven, just before the Glorious Revolution of 1688. After William III had displaced James II, Alexander did not follow the second earl of Middleton into Jacobitism and exile, but chose to make his first career in the British army created by William III to fight his wars against Louis XIV of France. He was commissioned ensign in the earl of Bath's foot regiment on 20 May 1693. Promoted lieutenant on 1 January 1696, he continued his military career under Queen Anne, fighting in the War of the Spanish Succession under the command of the duke of Marlborough. A captain before 1704, he was wounded at the battle of Blenheim in 1704 and captured at Oudenarde in 1708 but immediately exchanged. He was primarily active in army supply, particularly grain, being lieutenant quartermaster under Lord Cadogan, rising to lieutenant colonel.

In the course of his military service he became friendly with the Scots Whig general Lord George Hamilton, earl of Orkney and absentee governor of Virginia. Orkney appointed Spotswood his lieutenant governor from 1710, allowing him half the emoluments in exchange for performing the duties. This gave Spotswood an annual salary of £1200. Arriving in the Chesapeake on 20 June 1710, aboard HMS *Deptford*, Spotswood showed himself a firm but reasonable champion of imperial authority. He was in correspondence with William Blathwayt, surveyor and auditor general of royal revenues in America, who used his influence as supreme "imperial fixer" at Whitehall to secure the smooth acceptance of Spotswood's nomination as lieutenant governor (a royal office in its own right). Spotswood was soon writing to the Lords Commissioners of Trade and the Lords of the Admiralty about the need to suppress the shipment of Virginian tobacco to the Dutch Caribbean island of Curaçao and the Danish emporium on St. Thomas Island (in what are now the U.S. Virgin Islands), which violated the Acts of Navigation. He wanted a permanent Royal Navy patrol at the mouth of the Chesapeake to suppress enemy privateers and Virginian smugglers, and he labored to fortify the access to the Chesapeake against a French attack that never came. He sent 700 barrels of Virginia pork to Governor Robert Hunter (1666–1734) of New York in 1711 to help feed a proposed British amphibious attack on French Canada.

Spotswood had a strong bias against proprietary governments in the American colonies, especially that of North Carolina, with which Virginia had a boundary dispute. Spotswood saw the North Carolinians as wilfully ignoring "the plain Evidence of her Maj'ties Right to the Lands in dispute." When the Tuscarora Indians on the Carolina border unexpectedly rose in arms in 1711, Virginia joined New York and South Carolina in sending aid to North Carolina during the resulting Tuscarora War of 1711–1713, but Spotswood accused the North Carolina administration of provoking the Indians by misgovernment and pandering to pirates. He even banned the export of North Carolinian tobacco from Virginia's harbors at a time when North Carolina lacked both ships and a good port.

Pirates based in the Bahamas, a proprietary colony where the Lords Proprietors had virtually no authority, harassed trade between the Chesapeake and the West Indies. In 1717 Spotswood urged the London government to send forces to secure shipping "and particularly to the Bahamas to dislodge the Pyrates from thence." In 1718 Governor Woodes Rogers and a Royal Navy squadron installed a new royal regime in the Bahamas, and Captain Edward Teach (alias Blackbeard) fled from New Providence Island to North Carolina where he received a pardon and lurked in Bath. In Virginia Spotswood arrested and interrogated Blackbeard's former quartermaster. He then sent Captain Ellis Brand over the boundary with troops, and Lieutenant Robert Maynard of the Royal Navy with two sloops and a marine force to attack Bath from the sea. Teach died fighting in a vicious engagement in Ocracoke Inlet. Thirteen survivors from his crew were taken to Williamsburg, tried, and hanged. Governor Charles Eden of North Carolina subsequently pointed out that what Spotswood saw as a triumph of law and order was also a violent invasion of another jurisdiction.

The Virginia legislature had designated Williamsburg as the site of a new provincial capital to replace unhealthy Jamestown in 1699. Spotswood, as his friend Sir William Keith recorded, was an amateur of mathematics and architecture, and hoped to design Williamsburg as a showpiece for enlightened and rational imperial government. On the baroque plans of Governor Francis Nicholson, who had completed the capitol building in 1705, Spotswood imposed a neoclassical gridiron pattern. He deliberately built an octagonal magazine near the town center like the *praetorium*, or command post, of a Roman camp. He completed the governor's place, laying out falling Italianate gardens that were denounced as "imperial gardening" by local critics. From a new Bruton Parish church, to extensions to the jail, to the rebuilding of the College of William and Mary, which had been devastated by fire in 1705, Spotswood left his mark on the buildings and the ground plan of Williamsburg.

His relations with the planter oligarchy of Tidewater Virginia, and with the assembly they dominated, deteriorated over time. The planters objected to Spotswood's attempts to tighten quality controls on tobacco, since they used tobacco as currency to pay taxes. Equally controversial were his plans for controlling relations with the Indians, and creating a fund raised by subscription to pay for educating them, by restricting all Indian trade south of the James River to the post of Christanna and making it a monopoly of a Virginia Indian Company. By 1715 he faced a restive House of Burgesses. By 1719 he was at odds with both the House and the General Court. Planter oligarchs like Philip Ludwell and William Byrd II of Westover conspired against him with influential figures in London. By 1717 they had secured imperial disallowance of both his tobacco and his Indian trade measures. In 1722 his position was weak enough to be fatal when he clashed with the formidable commissary James Blair, minister of Bruton and head of the established Anglican church in Virginia. He was superseded by Governor Hugh Drysdale in September 1722.

Spotswood traveled many thousands of miles in Virginia on business. He knew the province and its resources well. In 1716 he led a party of sixty-three men on a trip to the headwaters of the Rapidan and then through Swift Run Gap across the Blue Ridge and down into the Shenandoah Valley, whence they turned back on 7 September. Rangers had already scouted the route, and the story that Spotswood gave the leading participants small golden horseshoes to mark them as Knights of the Golden Horseshoe is persistent but difficult to document. It does, however, capture the significance of the trip as a root of the notion of Manifest Destiny, as Spotswood did not just claim what he could see for George I on the Blue Ridge, but claimed America to the Mississippi.

Often by devious means, Spotswood had accumulated vast landholdings totalling 85,000 acres. He went to England in 1724 to lobby for the confirmation of his estate. There he met and married in that year Anne Butler Brayne, goddaughter of the duke of Ormonde, with whom he had four children. In 1730 he returned to Virginia to create an industrial empire on his properties. He had known about extensive iron ore deposits since 1710. An unlit blast furnace had been destroyed at Falling Creek in Virginia by the 1622 Indian rising, and an unsuccessful one operated at Saugus in Massachusetts from about 1646, but Spotswood's blast furnace complex was vast. His Tubal furnace, eight miles west of Fredericksburg, built about 1715, had a theoretical capacity of 1,000 tons p.a., and he rapidly became the biggest single iron producer in the British Empire. At first he employed skilled Germans settled at Germanna, near which Spotswood built a handsome house and gardens known sarcastically as "the enchanted castle." Later he used slave labor, water power, and charcoal from his extensive woods. An opponent of direct taxation of the colonies by Westminster, he was still a strong imperialist.

Spotswood served as deputy postmaster general of the American colonies after 1730, employing Benjamin Franklin (1706–1790) as his deputy in Philadelphia after 1737, and bringing a regular service down to Williamsburg. He had proposed the raising of an American regiment in 1727 during an Anglo-Spanish crisis, and when war with Spain came in 1739, he raised it. He was in Annapolis supervising its embarkation for the Caribbean to attack Catagena when he died. The greatest of Virginia's royal governors, he was a pioneer of concepts of Manifest Destiny and also of the American industrial revolution.

• Most of Spotswood's surviving personal manuscripts are in the custody of the Virginia Historical Society in Richmond. Many have been published in *Official Letters of Alexander Spotswood*, ed. R. A. Brock (2 vols., 1882–1885). His dealings with his council can be followed in *Executive Journals of the Council of Colonial Virginia*, vol. 3 (1928). His stormy relationship with the House of Burgesses can be traced in two volumes edited by H. R. McIlwaine: *Journals of the House of Burgesses, 1705–12* (1912) and *Journals of the House of Burgesses, 1712–1726* (1912).

There is important material on Spotswood in William Byrd of Westover's writings, especially *The Secret Diary of William Byrd of Westover 1709–1712*, ed. Louis B. Wright and Marion Tinling (1941) and *The London Diary, 1717–1721*, ed. Louis B. Wright and Marion Tinling (1958). Byrd's account "A Progress to the Mines in the Years 1732" is our only source for Spotswood's later life as an ironmaster in the eponymous Spotsylvania County. It is printed in *The Prose Works of William Byrd of Westover*, ed. Louis B. Wright (1966).

An account of the Swift Run Gap episode is in *The Journal of John Fontaine: An Irish Huguenot Son in Spain and Virginia 1710–19*, ed. Edward P. Alexander (1972). Spotswood is favorably depicted in Hugh Jones, *The Present State of Virginia*, ed. Richard L. Morton (1956). For his contribution to Williamsburg's architecture, see Marcus Whiffen, *The Public Buildings of Williamsburg* (1958). Spotswood's iron empire is partially described in his *Iron Works at Tuball* (repr., with historical introduction by Lester J. Cappon, 1945), and in more recent excavation reports of the Germanna site such as Douglas W. Sanford, "The Enchanted Castle in Context: Archaeological Research at Germanna," Archaeological Society of Virginia *Quarterly Bulletin*, 44, no. 3 (1989): 97–115.

There is an older biography by Leonidas Dodson, *Alexander Spotswood, Governor of Colonial Virginia 1710–1722* (1932), and a more recent one by Walter Havighurst, *Alexander Spotswood: Portrait of a Governor* (1967). A revisionist view can be found in Bruce P. Lenman, "Alexander Spotswood and the Business of Empire," *Colonial Williamsburg* 13, no. 1 (1990): 44–55.

BRUCE P. LENMAN

SPOTTED TAIL (1823–5 Aug. 1881), leader of the Brulé [Sican gu] Teton, was born in south-central South Dakota, the son of modest parents. (His name in his native tongue was Sinte Gleska.) At an early age, Spotted Tail sought a position of political leadership. As a young man he valiantly fought the Pawnee, earning his people's approval and becoming a praiseworthy man. This was his first step toward political leadership, and it enabled him to understand that political gain could be achieved by waging a successful military expedition.

Spotted Tail began to hone his diplomatic skills during the 1850s after the defeat of a Brulé band by the U.S. Army. He learned that the alternative to war was preserving peace through negotiation. The Brulé struggles against the United States became violent in the summer of 1854 when a Brulé band led by Brave Bear (also known as Conquering Bear) destroyed Lieutenant John Grattan's command east of Fort Laramie, Wyoming. That conflict cost Brave Bear his life. The following summer, on 3 September 1855, General William S. Harney commanded a punitive expedition against the Brulé. Harney descended on the Brulé band camped on Blue Water, in western Nebraska; this band was led by Brave Bear's successor, Little Thunder. Harney's soldiers killed eighty-five Brulé and captured seventy women and children.

After his success at Blue Water, Harney dictated peace terms to the Brulé. He ordered them to surrender those tribesmen who had killed several mail coach drivers in the fall of 1854. Spotted Tail had been a member of the party that had killed the drivers in an attempt to avenge Brave Bear's death. Placing the welfare of the group above that of individuals, ranking Brulé leaders requested that Spotted Tail and four of his companions surrender to military officials in 1855. The five men were imprisoned for four months at Fort Leavenworth, Kansas. While under "loose" arrest, Spotted Tail observed the U.S. military, and he became convinced that the Brulé could not win a general war against this army. Understanding that losing a war against the whites had limited political potential, Spotted Tail changed his resistance strategy from military encounters to nonviolent diplomatic defiance.

For the next ten years, Spotted Tail remained with the Brulé people and improved his political future. When Spotted Tail became the spokesman of his Brulé band in 1866, he continued to promote his beliefs so earnestly that his camp became known as a peace camp. Spotted Tail demonstrated his commitment to diplomacy by signing the 1868 Fort Laramie Treaty, which symbolized the U.S. government's peace policy toward the Tetons and was based on their eventual assimilation. Unlike Sitting Bull, Spotted Tail preferred negotiating to fighting; he believed statesmanship created more options than confrontation and that peace with the United States provided greater opportunities for him to gain prestige as well as to attain his people's goals and objectives.

In accordance with the 1868 treaty, Spotted Tail moved close to the Whetstone Agency, established on the Missouri River for the Brulé, but not into the agency. This act of resistance demonstrated his unwillingness to submit to the will of the United States; in addition it illustrated his active defiance of government policies through diplomacy. This nonmilitary opposition increased Spotted Tail's prominence with his own people but also led to disagreements with militant Teton, such as Sitting Bull, especially after Spotted Tail signed the Black Hills cession of 1876.

When rumors reached General George Crook that Crazy Horse was willing to discuss surrender, Crook convinced Spotted Tail to deliver peace terms. It was known that only a leader of Spotted Tail's stature could accomplish such a delicate task. In return for his cooperation, Spotted Tail demanded the removal of the agencies from the Missouri River; the government granted his request.

The chaotic times of the Sioux War of 1876–1877 and Spotted Tail's diplomatic tactics enabled him to avoid U.S. control. With the onset of peace, the United States forced Spotted Tail and his followers to settle at Rosebud Agency in south central South Dakota. In 1881 Spotted Tail made an unforgivable error by overstepping Teton boundaries of power. In council with others, Spotted Tail agreed to send children to the Carlisle Indian School in Pennsylvania. Then, without consulting subordinate leaders and the general population, Spotted Tail took the children from the school. He had made an important decision without community consent, and that hastened his fall. Several leaders lost faith in Spotted Tail, and Crow Dog, a subordinate Brulé leader and former tribal policeman, assassinated him.

• Letters describing Spotted Tail's career are found in the National Archives, Washington, D.C.: the Upper Platte Agency (1846–1870), the Whetstone Agency (1871–1874), and the Spotted Tail Agency (1875–1880), Letters Received by the Office of Indian Affairs, 1824–1880, Record Group 75; the Department of the West (1853–1861), Records of United States Army Continental Commands, 1821–1920, Record Group 393; and Records of the Adjutant General's Office, 1780–1917, Record Group 94. For Spotted Tail's biography, see George E. Hyde, *Spotted Tail's Folk: A History of the Brulé Sioux* (1961). See also, D. C. Poole, *Among the Sioux of Dakota: Eighteen Months' Experience as an Indian Agent* (1881; repr. 1988); Richmond L. Clow, "Sioux Response to Non-Indian Intrusion: Sitting Bull, Spotted Tail, and Crazy Horse," in *South Dakota Leaders: From Pierre Chouteau, Jr., to Oscar Howe,* ed. Herbert T. Hoover and Larry J. Zimmerman (1989); Donald E. Worcester, "Spotted Tail: Warrior Diplomat," *American West* 1, no. 4 (1964): 38–46; and Charles A. Eastman, *Indian Heroes and Great Chieftains* (1918).

RICHMOND L. CLOW

SPOTTSWOOD, Stephen Gill (18 July 1897–2 Dec. 1974), bishop of the African Methodist Episcopal Zion church and chairman of the National Association for the Advancement of Colored People, was born in Boston, Massachusetts, the only son of Abraham Lincoln Spottswood, a porter, and Mary Elizabeth Gram. The family was very religious. Spottswood received a B.A. from Albright College in Reading, Pennsylvania, in 1917 and a Th.B. from Gordon Divinity School in Boston in 1919; he attended Yale Divinity School in 1923–1924. In 1919 he married Viola Estelle Booker; they would have five children. That same year he joined the NAACP.

During the 1920s and 1930s Spottswood served as pastor of churches in Massachusetts, Maine, Connecticut, North Carolina, Indiana, and New York. During his tenure as pastor of John Wesley AME Zion Church in Washington, D.C. (1936–1952), he enlarged the congregation from 600 members to more than 3,000 and became increasingly prominent in denominational circles. From 1947 to 1952 Spottswood was head of the Washington, D.C., branch of the NAACP. He served as the head of the AME Zion Home Mission Department and in 1952 was elected bishop of the Tenth Episcopal District. In 1953 his wife was killed in a fire in Washington.

In 1954 Spottswood became a member of the board of directors of the NAACP, and in 1961 he was elected chairman, initially to complete the term of Robert Weaver. A moderate who emphasized economic betterment, Spottswood devoted many of his speeches and sermons to the need of building a better society based on legislation and voting. He participated in sit-ins and boycotts aimed at desegregating public accommodations.

In 1969 Spottswood married Mattie Brownita Johnson Elliott. He retired as bishop in 1972 though he continued in the top leadership post of the NAACP until his death. Widely respected for his dynamic, compassionate leadership, personal warmth, and commitment to the quest for freedom and equality, he was best known for his keynote speeches at the opening session of NAACP national conventions, especially for the one in Cincinnati in 1970 when he branded the Nixon administration as antiblack. He died at his home in Washington.

• The Stephen Gill Spottswood Papers are at the Amistad Research Center, Tulane University. See "Bishop Stephen Gill Spottswood," *Crisis,* Feb. 1975, p. 41. An obituary is in the *New York Times,* 3 Dec. 1974.

MILTON C. SERNETT

SPRAGUE, Achsa W. (17 Nov. 1827–6 July 1862), spiritualist and reformer, was born in Plymouth Notch, Vermont, the daughter of cousins Charles Sprague and Betsy Sprague, farmers. Her formal education was limited, yet Achsa was precocious and began teaching in the village school by the age of twelve. The Sprague family was considered quite intellectual for the small rural town, and their children were immersed in the classics. The Spragues also shared a predisposition to ill health; of the six siblings, three were considered mentally imbalanced. At the age of twenty, Achsa developed a severe case of arthritis that left her bedridden for over seven years. She considered herself healed through "angelic powers" and by 1854 began a career as a traveling lecturer and spiritualist.

Sprague's fame as a medium spread rapidly after her first appearance in the Union Church of South Reading, Vermont, and she eventually addressed audiences throughout North America. Although she struggled with her chronic disease, Sprague became a prominent leader in the public debate surrounding Spiritualism. Defined by Sprague as "the sublimated essence of all good," Spiritualism was criticized by some church members, including some clergy, on the grounds that it failed to profess faith in Jesus Christ and the immortality of the human soul. Yet large audiences appeared to hear Sprague, known as the "preaching woman." Although her reviews were mixed—some criticized her lack of formal organization—most agreed that she captivated her audiences with her personality and clever, if not intellectually superior, presentations.

Crowds were impressed by Sprague's ability to speak while in a trance for over an hour, with a strong voice, "a slightly swaggering gesture," and a "fair flow of ideas" (*Oswego Times*, 14 Dec. 1858). She eventually abandoned traditional medical practice, instead experimenting through seances, galvanic bands, and magnetizing processes. A supporter in the belief of the power of the mind in the healing process, Sprague emphasized the importance of religion in the quest toward wholeness. "If I could persuade you to read the Bible and be prepared it would be a great comfort to your mind," she wrote in 1858. "You have not sufficient power in religion" (Graham, Sprague Papers, Box 181). Sprague was paid for her lectures, but she eschewed business deals that would have appeared too commercial. "I would be instrumental in imparting Truth and doing good," she wrote. "If I cannot do this, I have no wish to do anything" (Graham, Sprague Papers, Box 181).

Sprague was a voluminous writer, capable of composing through what she called "automatic writing" as many as 4,600 lines in three days. She believed her writing was evidence of the power of God and wrote while in a trance through dictation. She was especially prolific in her later years, writing while in intense physical pain on themes of spiritual hope and despair as well as economic justice and social equality.

Sprague's social conscience was an outgrowth of her religious beliefs. As she traveled, Sprague observed the experience of the poor, and she grew acutely sensitive to societal oppression. An advocate for prisoners, she viewed them as "the victims of a bad social scheme" and worked for a more humane criminal justice system. Sprague considered alcoholic beverages to be the ultimate source of crime and objected to a society that allowed distillers to go free while it "imprisons the poor sufferer because it has fallen in the snare . . .

& take to the very bosom of society the very men that *made them what they are*" (Twynham, pp. 183–84).

Sprague further extended her work with the oppressed through antislavery efforts, bitterly resenting the institution that forced enslaved blacks "to fly like a hunted deer to the land of the Kings" (Canada) for rights denied them in their own country (Twynham, p. 182). Devoted also to the cause of woman's rights, Sprague petitioned the Vermont legislature for equal rights and became a sharp critic of women's role in society—and an even sharper critic of those women who accepted their lot:

When *woman herself*, through a false education which has bound her mind in chains, . . . *limits her own sphere*, . . . it is enough to bring the blush of shame upon every womans cheek who has soul enough or independence enough, to brave the scorn of the world in order to act, to do something for humanity. Woman must either be a slave or a butterfly, or at least she is so at the present time (Twynham, pp. 156–57).

A small portion of Sprague's work was published during her lifetime and shortly thereafter, most notably her poetry in *I Still Live, a Poem for the Times* (1862) and *The Poet and Other Poems* (1864). A number of magazines and journals, such as *The Blotter, The Spiritualist*, and *The Banner*, published her sermons and essays. Yet the vast majority of Sprague's work remained unpublished, including essays, journals, and correspondence. Sprague's correspondence with her family and numerous admirers attests to her popularity as a medium and the force of her personality. Although she was physically disfigured by her illness, Sprague's letters reveal that she received numerous proposals of marriage from both single and married men in her audiences. Sprague never married. Nevertheless, she was outspoken concerning women's rights in marriage, believing, for instance, that wives should have the right to limit their families and to leave their husbands in the event of an unhappy union (Sprague Papers, Box 181, no. 6, 17 July 1758; Twynham, p. 172).

Achsa Sprague died in Plymouth Notch, Vermont, at the age of thirty-four after a reoccurrence of her arthritis. At the time of her death her popularity as a lecturer and reformer was strong, bringing notoriety to her small hometown. While Sprague was alive pilgrims traveled great distances to reap the benefits of her spiritual gifts, and they continued to visit her home and grave after her death. Sprague's reputation suggests her importance to the Spiritualist movement, and the extent of her writing suggests her significance as a New England author. Moreover, although the importance of Spiritualism waned by the time of the Civil War, Sprague remained an important social reformer, often giving voice to issues before more popular leaders emerged.

• The Achsa Sprague Papers, including extensive correspondence, are in the Vermont Historical Society. In this collection is an interesting overview by Emma (Mrs. Theodore K.) Graham, including notes on letters not currently in the collection. Sprague's diaries, along with clippings and other papers, were last in the possession of the late historian Leonard Twynham (Twinem), but their location is now unknown; an extensive search of Vermont sources and Twynham's remaining family members has not revealed their location. Twynham did publish some excerpts from the diaries before his death; see "Selections from Achsa W. Sprague's Diary and Journal," *Proceedings of the Vermont Historical Society* 9, no. 3 (1941): 131–84. Twynham also published a biographical sketch on Sprague in the *Proceedings of the Vermont Historical Society* 9, no. 4 (1941): 271–78. The records of the state of Vermont contain "A Petition for Equal Rights" signed by Sprague in 1858. Her birth is recorded in vol. 6, p. 174 of Plymouth Land Records, Plymouth Notch, Vt. A death notice is in the *Rutland Weekly Herald*, 24 July 1862.

SHERYL A. KUJAWA

SPRAGUE, Frank Julian (25 July 1857–25 Oct. 1934), inventor and entrepreneur, was born in Milford, Connecticut, the son of David Sprague and Frances King. After finishing preparatory school, he was appointed to the U.S. Naval Academy. The excellent science faculty there included Albert Michelson, himself an Annapolis graduate, who was beginning the series of experiments that would win him America's first Nobel Prize in physics. Sprague's contemporaries at the naval academy included such future leaders of the electrical industry as Sidney Z. Mitchell, William Leroy Emmet, and S. Dana Green.

After graduation in 1878, Sprague was commissioned an ensign and spent two years at sea, where he found time to sketch out ideas for nearly sixty electrical devices, including a motor and a method of transmitting pictures by wire. The navy then assigned him to carrying out electrical experiments at the Newport Naval Station in Rhode Island. In order to view the more advanced European electrical scene, he secured orders to sail with the Mediterranean Squadron in 1882. On the way, he obtained the post of secretary to the awards jury of London's Crystal Palace Electrical Exhibition. There he met E. H. Johnson, a representative of Thomas Edison's electrical interests, who offered him a post with Edison. At this time, Edison was installing his first central power station, on Pearl Street in New York City. In 1883 Sprague joined Edison's construction department, where he worked on calculating the theoretical feasibility of circuit arrangements that Edison had developed. He quickly became a key member of the Edison team and helped to install Edison's "three wire" electric lighting systems in Sunbury, Pennsylvania, and Brockport, Massachusetts. He continued his inventive efforts, developing an electric motor that sparked less and ran at a more constant speed with varying load than its predecessors.

Sprague took a more optimistic view of the commercial possibilities of the electric motor than Edison did, and in 1884 he formed the Sprague Electric Railway and Motor Company, with Johnson as a partner and with Edison's factory as a manufacturing arm. In 1886 the first commercial Sprague motor began running a freight elevator in Boston. In 1887 more than 250 others went into use in stores, shops, and factories.

Sprague aimed his invention, however, primarily at another use: the propulsion of street railway cars, which were becoming pervasive in U.S. cities. Compared to the previous propulsion method—the horse—electric motors offered lower cost, higher speed, and greater cleanliness. When Sprague entered the business, other pioneers such as Edward M. Bentley and Walter H. Knight (Cleveland, Ohio), Charles J. Van Depoele (Indianapolis, Ind.), and E. Julien (New York City and elsewhere) had already made small electric street railway installations, which were typically less than five miles in length and served by fewer than ten cars. Such systems could demonstrate the speed and cleanliness of electricity. Since they did not distribute the cost of the expensive electric plan over very many passenger-miles of travel, however, they did not make money.

Sprague took on the challenge of proving electricity's commercial potential. Failing to interest the owners of New York's elevated railways, he targeted Richmond, Virginia. He contracted with the promoter of Richmond's trolley system to supply twelve miles of track to be served by thirty cars, which would climb hills and traverse curves yet also offer the affordable fares of a true mass transit system. He had not, however, developed in detail the technologies to make this vision a reality. Many of the inventions that came to serve as the basis for electric traction emerged by trial and error in the mud of Richmond. They included an overhead trolley, which was held on a swiveling stand, to take electricity off the wires; a three-point "wheelbarrow suspension" for mounting the electric motors under the car; single-reduction gearing for transmitting power to the driving wheels; and a series-parallel control for operating the motors in series when starting torque was needed, and in the more efficient parallel mode when the car was running. Having overcome many setbacks (including a bout with typhoid fever), Sprague delivered a system that met the contract requirements.

Sprague lost nearly $100,000 on the Richmond installation, but it positioned him for an early lead in repeating the triumph in cities across the nation. News that the operating costs of his system were only 40 percent of those with animal power propelled the United States into the electric trolley age. By 1889 the Sprague Company had installed sixty-seven electric railway systems, more than had any other company. About a hundred other systems were under construction in the United States by his company and its rivals. Also in 1889 he recapitalized the company at $800,000. Most of the new stock was purchased by the recently formed Edison General Electric Company, which merged with Sprague Company in that year. Sprague briefly accepted the post of consulting engineer but did not like some of the new company's technical decisions or its habit of referring to its electric railway product as the "Edison" system. He then launched another inventive effort that was aimed at control of elevators and street railway systems. In the mid-1890s he invented the "Multiple Unit" system, which permitted the assembling of street railway cars into trains, with each car having its own motor, controller, and individual control of the entire train. This system, which was first installed on Chicago's South Side Elevated in 1897, was the basis for modern elevated railway and subway systems. In 1902 he sold his second company, Sprague Electric, to General Electric for more than $1 million.

By this time, Sprague lived in New York City with his second wife, Harriet Chapman Jones, with whom he had three children. He and his first wife, Mary Keatinge, had one child. Still under fifty and a lean, intense, ambitious, daring, lone eagle inventor who was not yet ready for retirement, he was characteristically willing to commit to vast projects on the sketchiest of plans. He now addressed the challenge of the electrification of U.S. railways. Though the campaign included some notable triumphs, such as participation in the electrification of New York's Grand Central Terminal, it was not successful and cost him most of his fortune by the time of his death in New York City. His difficulties stemmed from a general slowdown in railroad innovation. The United States never embarked on a national policy of supporting the electrification of railroads to the degree that seemed imminent even as late as 1920. The Sprague Electric Company that later became successful in the U.S. electrical and electronics industry in the twentieth century was his son Robert's creation. With Frank Sprague, however, remains the credit for pioneering the commercial use of the electric motor, developing technology essential to modern subway systems, and demonstrating the large-scale practicality of the electric street railway, the shaper of U.S. cities and suburbs in the preautomobile era.

• Sprague's papers are in the Engineering Societies Library, New York City, and the New York Public Library. His published papers that contain useful historical insights include "Digging in the Mines of the Motors," *Journal of the American Institute of Electrical Engineers* 53 (May 1934): 712, and "Some Personal Notes on Electric Railways," *Electrical Review* 40 (15 Feb. 1902). The biography by Harriet Sprague, *Frank J. Sprague and the Edison Myth* (1942), though understandably partisan, contains valuable material. Harold Passer has detailed Sprague's business and technological contributions in *The Electrical Manufacturers* (1950) and in "Frank Julian Sprague," in *Men in Business*, ed. William Miller (1952). An obituary is in the *New York Times*, 26 Oct. 1934.

GEORGE WISE

SPRAGUE, Kate Chase (13 Aug. 1840–31 July 1899), political hostess, was born in Cincinnati, Ohio, the daughter of lawyer Salmon P. Chase and his second wife, Eliza Ann Smith. Named Catherine Jane Chase in honor of her father's first wife (the former Catherine Jane Garniss), she legally changed her name to Katharine Chase around 1860. She was known in the press and to her contemporaries as Kate. After her mother died when she was five years old, she and her father, who was becoming a prominent lawyer and antislavery spokesman, became very close. Intensely jealous when her father married for a third time in 1846, she was

sent to New York City to the fashionable and intellectually rigorous boarding school run by Henrietta Haines; she remained there for nine years, graduating in 1856. While in New York, she was exposed to the city's high society and developed refined and expensive tastes in music, furnishings, and fashion.

In 1849, while Kate Chase was at boarding school, her father was elected as a Free Soiler to the U.S. Senate. In 1856 he was elected governor of Ohio. A widower for a third time, Salmon Chase chose his sixteen-year-old daughter to be his official hostess at the governor's mansion in Columbus. While continuing to study languages and music at Lewis Heyl's seminary, Kate Chase also became her father's confidante, secretary, and partner in political ambition. The governor's mansion sparkled with fine food and excellent conversation as father and daughter courted a wide array of prominent politicians as part of their strategy to capture the 1860 Republican presidential nomination. To Kate Chase's intense disappointment, her father lost the nomination to Abraham Lincoln. She was only slightly mollified when Lincoln named Chase secretary of the Treasury. During the winter of 1861–1862, her first social season in the national capital, she outshone all other official hostesses—"la belle des belles" the press called her. Mary Todd Lincoln was openly envious of her youth and beauty, and Kate Chase, who bitterly resented what she considered the older woman's usurpation of the position rightfully hers, returned the venom.

Once in Washington, Kate Chase stepped up her expensive social campaign to gain the political support her father needed to sweep them both into the White House in 1864. Secretary Chase had little money, but his daughter's marriage in 1863 temporarily solved their fiscal problems. Having been courted by dozens of young men, Kate Chase chose newly elected Rhode Island senator William Sprague, who was ten years her senior and had made an estimated $25 million in textiles. It was widely believed that she accepted Sprague—rumored to frequent bars and brothels—for his money, which could, and did, underwrite her father's campaigns. While publicly disavowing an interest in the presidency, Salmon Chase continued to enlist his daughter's prodigious social skills, now enhanced by his son-in-law's wealth, to curry favor with politicians, editors, and financiers. As usual, Kate Chase Sprague was her father's antennae. At her parties, teas, and receptions, she picked up valuable inside information. Despite the Chases' best efforts, however, Lincoln was renominated in 1864.

After the Civil War, Kate Chase Sprague's social career flowered fully. Reporters covered her every move. She was compared to Madame de Staël and Dolley Madison. When her son, William, was born in the spring of 1865, newspapers carried stories of the new "prince of wealth" born to the "queen of society." In 1866 the first hints of marital discord between the Spragues surfaced, and there were rumors of divorce. Nevertheless, Salmon Chase and his daughter, known in the press as his "political priestess," trained their sights on the 1868 presidential campaign. When it was clear that the Republican nomination would go to Ulysses S. Grant, the pair worked feverishly behind the scenes to secure the Democratic nomination. Kate Chase Sprague even went to the party convention in New York to manage the floor fight from a nearby hotel room, a move her critics condemned as unladylike. Again, Salmon Chase lost the nomination. He was disappointed, but she was devastated. His only response to the news was, "How did Katie bear it?" (Phelps, p. 205).

When her father left the political arena after 1868, Kate Chase Sprague lost her purpose in life. Her daughter Ethel was born in 1869, but her marriage was openly unhappy. No amount of cajoling by her father could mend the rift for which he felt partially responsible. After Salmon Chase's death in 1873, Kate Chase Sprague abandoned all attempts to conceal her affair with New York senator Roscoe Conkling, known as "the Apollo of the Senate." Often in attendance in the Senate gallery when Conkling was expected to speak, she sent to his desk flowers that matched the color of her gown. Her fame began to turn to infamy. Oblique references to the affair began to appear in the press, and it was rumored that the daughters she bore in 1872 (Portia) and 1873 (Kitty) were not her husband's children. The most prominent men in public life, however, continued to travel to "Edgewood," her father's country house near Washington, D.C., where she lived apart from her husband, to enjoy her elegant dinner parties and seek her counsel. The women of official society made only those calls required by official protocol, and after William Sprague's Senate career ended in 1875, even these calls ceased.

Events in the summer of 1879 put an end to her marriage, her affair with Conkling, and her years as one of Washington's most prominent hostesses. Press accounts varied widely, but reporters agreed on the following: Kate Sprague and the children had joined William Sprague at "Canonchet," their enormous mansion at Narragansett Pier, Rhode Island. William Sprague left on business only to return without warning to find Conkling in his home. Drunk and enraged, Sprague drove Conkling off his property at gunpoint, pursued him into town, and threatened him in front of gaping townspeople. He then held his wife and children prisoner at Canonchet until Kate Sprague and her daughters escaped with the help of loyal servants.

In 1880 Kate Chase Sprague filed for divorce, demanding custody of the children, plus the right to use her maiden name. After two years of public wrangling, she was awarded custody of her daughters only and granted the right to be known as Mrs. Kate Chase. She took the girls to Europe and stayed there until their money ran out. They then returned to Washington, D.C., where she gradually sold off Edgewood's furnishings and her silver and then mortgaged the house again and again. Her two oldest daughters left to fend for themselves, leaving only Kitty, who was mentally retarded, and Kate Chase to struggle on alone. Wearing a matted blond wig, heavy makeup, and

cheap jewelry, Chase drove her rickety carriage from door to door selling eggs. In 1896 a group of her father's admirers raised the money to pay off the mortgage on Edgewood and set up a trust fund for her support. Kate Chase died at Edgewood of liver and kidney ailments just short of her fifty-ninth birthday. Once again she was in the news, as most of the nation's newspapers carried her obituary. Hers was a career, noted the *Cleveland Plain Dealer* (6 Aug. 1899), "filled with romance; a career of political influence, unequalled by any other American woman; a career of unprecedented splendor followed by bitter disappointment and closing in neglect and poverty." The U.S. government provided a special car to take her body to Cincinnati, where she was buried beside her father.

• Little but legend remains of Kate Chase Sprague. Most of her letters are preserved among those of her father at the Library of Congress. A few others are scattered in collections at the Rhode Island Historical Society and in the Jay Cooke Collection at the Historical Society of Pennsylvania. Her affair with Roscoe Conkling is discussed in David Jordan, *Roscoe Conkling of New York: Voice in the Senate* (1971). *So Fell the Angels* (1956), by Thomas and Marva Belden, tells the collective story of Salmon P. Chase, Kate Chase Sprague, William Sprague, and their children. There are two biographies about Kate Chase Sprague, Mary Merwin Phelps, *Kate Chase: Dominant Daughter* (1935), and Ishbel Ross, *Proud Kate: Portrait of an Ambitious Woman* (1953). One of the many obituaries is in the *New York Times*, 1 Aug. 1899.

KATHRYN ALLAMONG JACOB

SPRAGUE, William Buell (16 Oct. 1795–7 May 1876), pastor, collector, and biographer, was born in Andover, Connecticut, the son of Benjamin Sprague and Sibyl Buell. Nothing is known about what his parents did for a living. Sprague entered Yale College in 1811 and, despite a brief leave of absence due to eye problems, graduated with honors in 1815. Early in life Sprague expressed an interest in the ministry, but he delayed entering Princeton Theological Seminary until 1816 in order to tutor the children of Major Lawrence Lewis, a nephew of George Washington. Once at Princeton, Sprague studied under Samuel Miller (1769–1850), Archibald Alexander, and Ashbel Green. All three of these men were prominent educators and leaders in what would become known as Old School Presbyterianism, a conservative Calvinist theological position that emphasized God's sovereignty, sinful humanity's inability to save itself, and the need for a consistent practice of piety. In later years, Sprague remained relatively aloof from internecine Presbyterian theological conflict, preferring instead to focus on his passions for biography and history.

Sprague graduated from Princeton in 1819 and was ordained and installed as pastor of the Congregational church in West Springfield, Massachusetts, on 25 August. He became the congregation's sole pastor when his elderly colleague, the Reverend Dr. Joseph Lathrop, died on the last day of 1820.

Sprague was married three times. His first marriage to Charlotte Eaton in September 1820 ended less than a year later with her death. Sprague married again in 1824. His second wife, Mary Lathrop, died after thirteen years of marriage. In 1840 Sprague married Henrietta Burnett (Burritt, according to some sources) Lathrop, the younger sister of his second wife. Sprague had a total of ten children; the only child from his first marriage, three children from his second, and four from his third marriage survived to maturity.

Sprague remained in West Springfield for ten years. In 1828 he made his first voyage to France and England. During this trip and a visit to England, Scotland, and the Continent in 1836, Sprague developed relationships with numerous notable Europeans, like William Wilberforce and Hannah More, with whom he would maintain an extensive correspondence.

The Second Presbyterian Church called Sprague to Albany, New York, in 1829. In this congregation, Sprague pursued his ministry for forty years before retiring in September 1869. Following his retirement, Sprague moved to his son's home in Flushing, Long Island, where he died.

A prolific writer, Sprague began in 1847 his most notable publication, *The Annals of the American Pulpit* . . . (1857–1869). Sprague labored daily over a fifteen-year period on this nine-volume work in which he either edited the personal reminiscences or himself wrote biographies of hundreds of U.S. clergymen active in the years from 1629 to 1850. Magisterial in scope, these volumes remain a major source for information on the ministries of Congregationalist, Presbyterian, Episcopalian, Baptist, Methodist, Unitarian, Lutheran, Reformed, Quaker, Moravian, Swedenborgian, and Universalist leaders in colonial and antebellum America.

For his many literary achievements, Sprague received doctor of divinity degrees from Columbia College in 1828 and from Harvard in 1848 as well as a doctor of laws degree from Princeton College in 1869. Sprague's significant rhetorical skills coupled with his extensive use of biographical and historical anecdotes made him one of the most sought after and published preachers of his time. Sixty-eight of his sermons and sixty-six of his discourses or addresses were published in his lifetime.

Sprague's *Lectures on Revivals of Religion . . .* (1832) illustrates his relatively irenic approach in a period when controversy was rapidly hardening divisions within his church. While cautioning against the emotional excesses and theological speculation surrounding the revivals of the Second Great Awakening, he nevertheless acknowledged the place of revivals in the life of the church.

Sprague was also a noteworthy collector. Early in his career he was given a major portion of George Washington's original correspondence that had been used in Jared Sparks's publications of Washington's writings. This core collection Sprague supplemented with further acquisitions and important collections of historical autographs, Massachusetts election-day sermons, and pamphlets. These he gave to several libraries before his death. Princeton Theological Seminary in New Jersey and Union Theological Seminary in New York City received the majority of the religious materials, 1,000 bound volumes of pamphlets going to Princeton and eighty volumes of sermons to Union. Yale University was given a set of Massachusetts election-day sermons, and the New York State Library received pamphlets dealing with subjects outside of religion.

• Sprague's papers are available at the Yale University library. His major published works are *Letters on Practical Subjects, from a Clergyman of New-England to His Daughter* (1822), *Letters from Europe, in 1828* (1828), *Lectures to Young People, with an Introductory Address, by S. Miller, D.D.* (1830), *Hints Designed to Regulate the Intercourse of Christians* (1834), *Lectures Illustrating the Contrast between True Christianity and Various Other Systems* (1837), *Letters to Young Men, Founded on the History of Joseph* (1844), "Life of Timothy Dwight, President of Yale College," in *Library of American Biography*, 2d ser., vol. 4, ed. Jared Sparks (1845), *Visits to European Celebrities* (1855), *Memoirs of the Rev. John McDowell, D.D., and the Rev. William A. McDowell, D.D.* (1864), and *The Life of Jedidiah Morse, D.D.* (1874). For a brief biography and an extensive bibliography of Sprague's publications see Franklin B. Dexter, ed., *Biographical Sketches of the Graduates of Yale College*, vol. 6 (1912). See also Charles B. Moore, "Biographical Sketch of the Rev. William Buell Sprague, D.D., LL.D.," *New York Genealogical and Biographical Record* 8 (Jan. 1877): 1–8; W. V. Sprague, *Sprague Families in America* (1913); and Albert Welles, *The History of the Buell Family* (1881). An obituary and related articles are in the *Albany Evening Journal*, 9, 11, 12 May 1876.

MILTON J COALTER, JR.

SPRECKELS, Alma (24 Mar. 1881–7 Aug. 1968), museum builder and art collector, was born Alma de Bretteville in San Francisco, California, the daughter of Viggo de Bretteville, a farmer, and Mathilde Unserud. At age fourteen she was forced to quit school to go to work. At night she took art lessons at the Mark Hopkins Art Institute where, because of her beauty and statuesque figure (she was six feet tall), she also modeled for her instructors. One, the sculptor Robert Aitken, used her at age twenty-two to pose for a monument to commemorate Admiral George Dewey's victory at Manila Bay. Aitken's prize-winning statue of Alma, a bronze figure of a woman typifying the Republic, holding aloft a trident, stands on a granite pedestal atop San Francisco's Union Square.

The resulting publicity brought her to the attention of the sugar magnate and sportsman Adolph B. Spreckels. More than twice her age, he was still a bachelor. Alma, already notorious for having been involved in a scandalous breach-of-promise lawsuit against a gold miner from the Klondike, became Spreckels's mistress for four years until she succeeded in getting him to marry her in 1908; they had three children.

Urged on by her father, a descendant of French nobility, who instilled in the young woman the idea that she had an obligation to glorify the de Bretteville name, Alma felt that her destiny was to introduce

French culture to the West. For this she needed money, and Spreckels provided it for her. At her insistence, he built her a French mansion, the costliest and most beautiful residence in San Francisco. After the birth of their third child, she went alone to Paris in 1914 to find furniture for her home.

There she met Loie Fuller, an American expatriot, who once delighted Paris with her dancing at the Folies Bergère. "La Loie," as the French called her, was the self-appointed agent for Auguste Rodin and was determined to make Alma an important collector of his works. She introduced Alma to Rodin and also made her knowledgeable about antique furniture. Alma later wrote, "I used to be a student at the Mark Hopkins Art school [but] I knew nothing of art and imagined that all things antique were worth owning . . . [Loie] taught me that ugly things were also made in the old days and you had to learn to distinguish. One must admire furniture with beautiful lines and workmanship." She returned home the owner of two Rodins, with one of the original casts of *The Thinker* and *The Call to Arms*.

When the Panama-Pacific International Exposition opened in 1915 in San Francisco, where the French had built a replica of the Palace of the Legion of Honor for their exhibit with *The Thinker* brooding in the foreground, Alma knew that her destiny was to have the architect Henri Guillaume design for her a California Palace of the Legion of Honor and to place in it all the Rodins that had been exhibited at the fair. The California Palace of the Legion of Honor opened in 1924, six months after her husband, who financed the building, had died. Over the years, Alma filled the museum with a total of ninety-nine of Rodin's works as well as collections of French furniture, tapestry, porcelain, and French art. The French government presented her with the Cross of the Legion of Honor in 1924 at the dedication of her museum.

Spreckels was instrumental in the founding of Maryhill Museum in the state of Washington, where the eclectic collection contains Rodins and Indian basketry as well as the furniture and coronation gown of her friend, Queen Marie of Romania. She also helped to found the National Maritime Museum in San Francisco, which started with the nucleus of her model ship collection. Toward the end of her life she was working on a fourth museum, a Museum of the Dance for which she collected over two hundred pieces mostly pertaining to the Diaghilev era of the Ballets Russes.

Proud of the fact that she had been a working woman, in 1922 she prepared a report for President Warren Harding at his invitation on the condition of working women in Europe following World War I. She included suggestions for regulations for the betterment of American working women and concluded her report by stating, "I am sure you realize that the strength of our nation depends on the welfare of our women who are fast entering into the many fields of industry."

Spreckels was an irritation to San Francisco society, which considered her a woman of loose morals, uncouth and outrageous, who spoke in loud, gravel-voiced tones and drank martinis by the pitcherful. She cared little for their assessment and continued to work unceasingly for things she felt were important: the museums she founded, the gigantic fund drives for Red Cross, war orphans and widows in Belgium and France she spearheaded in the wake of two world wars, and the countless contributions of art she made to so many communities up and down the West Coast. She married Elmer Awl in 1939, but they were divorced in 1943.

Alma Spreckels achieved her ambition to bring French culture to the West. Through her efforts the works of Rodin, the beauty of French fine art, tapestry, furniture, and objets d'art were made available to anyone with the price of carfare to the beautiful museum that overlooks the Golden Gate. When she died in San Francisco, Mayor Joseph Alioto eulogized her as having "enhanced this city by her vision and artistic achievement. Generations of unborn will salute her memory for the splendor of all she bestowed."

• The correspondence between Alma Spreckels and Loie Fuller, which pertains to Alma's World War I fundraising for her California Legion of Honor Museum, can be found in the Loie Fuller Papers, Dance Collection, Lincoln Center, New York Public Library. Other material is available in the California Palace of the Legion of Honor archives; in the archives of Maryhill Museum, Goldendale, Wash.; in the Spreckels papers, Archives of American Art, Smithsonian Institution; and in the papers of Karl Kortum at the National Maritime Museum in San Francisco. Spreckels's report to President Harding on the conditions of working women in Europe can be found in the National Archives, Washington, D.C. For a biography of Alma Spreckels, see Bernice Scharlach, *Big Alma: San Francisco's Alma Spreckels* (1990). Her waning days are described in an article by Frances Moffet in the *New York Times*, 9 Oct. 1966. Obituaries are in the *San Francisco Examiner* and the *San Francisco Chronicle*, 8 Aug. 1968; the *New York Times*, 8 Aug. 1968; and *Newsweek*, 16 Aug. 1968.

BERNICE SCHARLACH

SPRECKELS, Claus (9 July 1828–26 Dec. 1908), manufacturer and capitalist, was born in Lamstedt, Hanover (in present-day Germany), the son of Diedrich Spreckels, and Gesche Baack, farmers. Growing up in relative poverty, he received a meager formal education and often worked for neighboring farmers for little more than bread and board. When revolutionary fervor swept the Germanic states during the 1840s, Spreckels decided to emigrate. After borrowing sufficient funds for steerage passage from a friend, he sailed from Bremen in 1846 and landed in Charleston, South Carolina, with little money and no firm prospects. He soon obtained work in a grocery store and within a few weeks had saved enough to pay off his debt. By working hard and accumulating savings, he was able to purchase the business upon the owner's retirement, paying off all his debts within a year.

By 1852 Spreckels had achieved considerable financial success. In that same year, he married a childhood sweetheart, Anna Christina Mangel, who had also immigrated to the United States and was working as a housemaid in New York City. The couple had thirteen children, five of whom reached adulthood. Seeking new opportunities, he sold his business in 1855 and moved to New York. There, he bought out the Samson Moore grocery store on West Broadway and was successful enough in both wholesale and retail operations to return with his entire family to Germany for a visit within a year.

Upon returning to New York, Spreckels made a decision that changed his life. Encouraged by his brother Bernard, a successful San Francisco grocer who regaled him with tales of the financial opportunities available on the West Coast, Spreckels decided to relocate. After selling the New York store to his brother-in-law, Spreckels purchased his brother's store and sailed for San Francisco. Arriving in July 1856, he was soon operating at a profit and in the following year added to his growing list of enterprises by opening a brewery.

Ever restless for new opportunities, Spreckels then entered the field in which he would achieve his greatest fame. In partnership with his brother Peter, his brother-in-law, and a few others, Spreckels in 1863 organized the Bay Sugar Refining Company in San Francisco. Ignorant of the sugar refining process, Spreckels returned to Germany and worked in a refinery there to obtain a working knowledge of the industry. A shrewd businessman who took advantage of opportunities when he found them, Spreckels also bought the equipment of the United States Refinery (then in bankruptcy proceedings) and shipped it to the West Coast for use in his own facility. The San Francisco operation proved immediately successful, and Spreckels sought to expand operations. However, when he was stymied in his attempts by the company directors, he sold out his interest in 1865 and traveled to Magdeburg, Germany, where he worked as a laborer for eight months in a sugar beet refinery.

Spreckels returned to California in 1867 and organized the California Sugar Refinery. Not yet willing to commit totally to sugar beets as a source of raw material because he feared excessive labor costs, Spreckels obtained cane sugar from Hawaii, the Philippines, Java, and China. He eagerly employed the latest technologies in his facility, patenting a faster refining method in 1868 and also patenting (on 28 July 1874) a method for producing hard or "loaf" sugar. His refining operations continued to expand, and production reached 250,000 pounds per day in 1871. In 1881 Spreckels constructed a new refinery, valued at $1,000,000, that was the most modern facility in the United States. By purchasing or merging with his competitors or driving them out of business by a price war, Spreckels held a near monopoly in West Coast sugar refining. He became known as the "Sugar King."

The growth of Spreckels's California operations was fueled in no small part by developments in the Hawaiian Islands. The 1876 passage of a reciprocity treaty with the United States allowed the duty-free importation of Hawaiian sugar to the United States; Spreckels, as always, was quick to take advantage of the new ar-

rangements. He arrived for his first visit to the islands on the ship that brought the news of the treaty's enactment. Spreckels immediately purchased more than half of the 1877 crop to beat the anticipated price increase. In addition to forming a partnership in 1880 with William G. Irwin, the leading sugar agent in the islands, Spreckels soon exercised, by virtue of his enormous wealth, tremendous political and economic influence in the kingdom of Hawaii. His financial support of King David Kalakaua gave him the leverage to obtain numerous concessions from the government, including the use of 40,000 acres of land at very favorable rates and the acquisition of water rights that facilitated the construction of two irrigation ditches. Spreckels formed the Hawaiian Commercial Company in 1878 to manage his varied local interests that later included banking operations and a steamship line. From his arrival in 1876 until 1886 he, along with King Kalakaua and Prime Minister Walter Murray Gibson, virtually ruled the kingdom of Hawaii, making and unmaking cabinets at will and incurring the wrath of many of his competitors. In 1886 the kingdom borrowed money in order to liquidate its indebtedness to Spreckels, and his political influence was largely eliminated.

With his position in Hawaii becoming less secure as time wore on, Spreckels renewed his old interest in sugar beets. He traveled to Germany in 1887 to further study beet processing technology and also purchased refining equipment that he shipped to California. After meeting with local farmers, he opened a refinery at Watsonville (the Western Beet Sugar Company) that began operations in 1888. The refinery was an immediate success, producing 700 tons of sugar a day by 1892. Encouraged by his success, Spreckels, following yet another fact-finding mission to Germany in 1896, began construction of a second facility, which was completed in 1899. The new facility, located five miles south of Salinas, California (the location was later named Spreckels), had a capacity of 3,000 tons a day, more than all other California beet sugar plants combined.

In the face of his many triumphs, Spreckels also endured numerous challenges. At the same time that his influence in Hawaiian affairs was coming under scrutiny, he also attracted unwanted attention from the so-called Sugar Trust in 1887. Composed of a number of East Coast firms operating under the control of the American Sugar Refining Company, the firm first attempted to enlist Spreckels through friendly persuasion. When that method failed, in an attempt to force Spreckels out of business the Trust purchased the American Sugar Refinery in San Francisco, one of the few remaining firms on the West Coast that was not under Spreckels's control. Spreckels responded by opening an East Coast refinery in Philadelphia in 1889. After a bitter two-year price war, a settlement that gave both parties an interest in each other's operation was reached. Although the conflict ended in a stalemate, Spreckels could feel satisfied, having initiated his fight against the Trust while at a ten-to-one disadvantage in capitalization.

Troubles within his own family, however, proved more difficult to subdue. With the increasing complexity of his varied operations in Hawaii, control of his sugar plantations passed in 1882 from the Hawaiian Commercial Company to the Hawaiian Commercial and Sugar Company. After the firm encountered financial difficulties in the early 1890s, a bitter family feud erupted, pitting Spreckels and his sons Adolph and John against his sons Rudolph and Claus A. "Gus" Spreckels. In 1893 Gus Spreckels filed a $2.5 million lawsuit against his father and in the following year gained control of the firm in an out-of-court settlement. The upstart brothers' triumph was short lived, however, for in 1898 a competing firm bought out the company and ousted the brothers from its management. Although Spreckels could not have been happy with the loss of his Hawaiian operations, he at least lived to see the family reconciled in 1905.

Spreckels's later years were busy ones. One of his interests was railroading, which he entered by financing the Pajaro Valley Railroad. Formed in order to facilitate the movement of his sugar to San Francisco, the road was opened in 1895 and completed by 1898. Responding to the complaints by San Francisco merchants regarding the high rates charged by the monopolistic Southern Pacific, in 1895 Spreckels helped finance and became president of the San Francisco & San Joaquin Valley Railroad. The railroad achieved its stated purpose and was sold to the Santa Fe Railroad around 1900. Also interested in commercial real estate, Spreckels built the Spreckels Building (later known as Central Tower) at the corner of Market and Third, the first skyscraper in San Francisco. Smoke emissions from San Francisco Gas and Electric generating plants smudged the building, and Spreckels's attempts to redress the grievance culminated in a social snub of Spreckels by the firm's president. In response Spreckels launched the Independent Electric Light and Power Company (1899) and the Independent Gas and Power Company (1901). A rate war ensued, and San Francisco Gas was forced to purchase the two firms in 1903, with Spreckels making a huge profit in the transaction.

Active until his death in San Francisco, Spreckels stands as yet another example of the contributions made by immigrants to the development of the United States. Arriving nearly penniless, he built a financial empire in several different enterprises and contributed greatly to the commercial development of both Hawaii and California.

• The papers of Claus Spreckels are divided between the Bancroft Library at the University of California, Berkeley, and the California Historical Society in San Francisco. For additional information see W. W. Cordray, "Claus Spreckels of California" (Ph.D. diss., Univ. of Southern California, 1955). A useful secondary source on his life and career is Jacob Adler, *Claus Spreckels: The Sugar King in Hawaii* (1966). Additional information pertaining to his struggles with the Sugar Trust can be found in Alfred S. Eichner, *The Emer-* *gence of Oligopoly: Sugar Refining as a Case Study* (1969). Obituaries are in the *San Francisco Chronicle* and the *New York Times*, 27 Dec. 1908.

EDWARD L. LACH, JR.

SPRING, Gardiner (24 Feb. 1785–18 Aug. 1873), Presbyterian clergyman, was born in Newburyport, Massachusetts, the son of Samuel Spring, a Congregational minister, and Hannah Hopkins. He entered Yale College and experienced a religious conversion during a revival at the school in 1802. After graduating in 1805, he began a five-year struggle to discover his true vocation. Although he entered a New Haven law office in order to study for a legal career in 1805, he moved to Bermuda at the end of the year and worked there for two years as a schoolteacher. He returned briefly to the United States to marry Susan Barney in May 1806; they had fifteen children. When he left Bermuda in late 1807, he resumed his law studies in New Haven and was admitted to the Connecticut bar in December 1808. He practiced law for another year but then chose to enter Andover Theological Seminary in Massachusetts in the fall of 1809.

Spring graduated from Andover after studying for one academic year and was ordained a Presbyterian minister and installed as pastor of the Brick Presbyterian Church in New York City in August 1810. He remained at the Brick Church for the next sixty-three years. Among the most notable achievements of his pastorate was the congregation's transfer from its original downtown location to a new building in midtown Manhattan in 1861. His evangelistic activities and involvement in various philanthropic enterprises gained him considerable notoriety in the city. He helped found the American Bible Society in 1816 and served on the interdenominational boards of the American Tract Society and the American Home Missionary Society. He also published a number of books and pamphlets, mainly collections of his sermons and addresses. These include *The Power of the Pulpit* (1848), *First Things* (2 vols., 1851), and *The Glory of Christ* (2 vols., 1852). His wife died in 1860, and in August 1861 he married Abba Grosvenor Williams.

While Spring was a doctrinal conservative and a staunch Calvinist, he sought to moderate the heated debates in his denomination over critical theological and political matters in the antebellum period. He identified himself with the traditionalist Old School party in the Presbyterian church but believed in maintaining fellowship with the revival-oriented, reform-minded New School faction. As a consequence, he invited the famous New School revivalist Charles G. Finney to speak at his church in 1827 and protested vigorously when his fellow Old School church members expelled the New School synods from the denomination in 1837. Moreover, during the controversy over slavery in the decades preceding the Civil War, Spring expressed sympathy for white southerners in his denomination and opposed attempts by abolitionists to harass them. He argued that, since the Constitution recognized the legality of slavery, Presbyterians had a responsibility to remain loyal to its provisions and respect the rights of slaveholders in their midst.

Following the secession of the southern states and the beginning of the Civil War, however, Spring used this same principle to condemn Presbyterians in the Confederacy who had entered into revolt against the United States. When the General Assembly, the central governing body of the denomination, assembled in May 1861 in Philadelphia, he introduced the famous "Spring Resolutions," proposals that called for the formation of a committee to consider the expediency of the church's expressing loyalty to the Union. Although conservatives argued that such an action would irrevocably split the Old School Presbyterian church along sectional lines, Spring's position was eventually adopted by the General Assembly after a heated debate. As a result, Old School Presbyterians went on record in support of the northern cause and declared that it was the Christian duty of all church members to help preserve the Union. The adoption of the Spring Resolutions led to the withdrawal of Presbyterians in the South from the denomination, and in December 1861 they organized their own Presbyterian Church of the Confederate States of America.

Despite the continuing division of the northern and southern branches of Old School Presbyterianism after the Civil War, Spring sought to heal the Old School–New School split in the North. His eloquent pleas on behalf of reunion at the 1869 General Assembly in New York led to the merger of the two northern Presbyterian denominations the following year. Growing infirm and suffering from deteriorating eyesight, he began in 1862 to share his ministry at the Brick Church with an associate. He died in New York.

• The principal source of information about Spring is his two-volume *Personal Reminiscences of the Life and Times of Gardiner Spring* (1866). In addition to the works mentioned above, Spring's books include *Essays on the Distinguishing Traits of Christian Character* (1813), *Obligations of the World to the Bible* (1839), and *The Attraction of the Cross* (1846). Lewis G. Vander Velde, *The Presbyterian Churches and the Federal Union, 1861–1869* (1932), discusses Spring's important role in his church's General Assembly. An obituary is in the *New York Times*, 20 Aug. 1873.

GARDINER H. SHATTUCK, JR.

SPRINGER, Reuben Runyan (16 Nov. 1800–11 Dec. 1884), businessman and philanthropist, was born in Frankfort, Kentucky, the son of Charles Springer, a farmer and postmaster, and Catherine Runyan. Educated in local schools until the age of thirteen, Springer then assisted his father in the Frankfort post office, becoming postmaster himself after his father's death in 1816. Two years later Springer became a clerk on the *George Madison*, a steamboat operating between Louisville and New Orleans. Several years later he secured a similar position on the *George Washington*, one of several boats owned by Kilgour, Taylor and Company, Cincinnati's leading wholesale grocery firm. In 1830 he married the daughter of a partner in the firm, Jane Kilgour, and joined his father-in-law as a third

partner. Ten years of diligent work led to both financial success and deteriorating health. In 1840 the firm dissolved, with the three partners retiring. Springer invested his not inconsiderable fortune in banking, railroads, and real estate, displaying a penchant for corner lots in rapidly growing Cincinnati. These conservative investments proved highly profitable, and his wealth expanded steadily.

Retirement gave Springer the opportunity to travel. He visited Europe on several occasions during the 1840s, gaining an appreciation for art and music, and he filled his house with eighteenth- and nineteenth-century French and German paintings. However, he is best remembered as a generous supporter of religious, charitable, and cultural institutions in his adopted city of Cincinnati. Although reared without strong religious beliefs, he found his wife's Roman Catholicism a source of strength, and he contributed heavily to various Catholic institutions. Beneficiaries of his generosity included St. Peter in Chains Cathedral, built only a block away from his modest home, the Convent of the Good Shepherd, and a home for wayward girls, as well as numerous hospitals and orphanages.

In the two decades after the Civil War, Cincinnati made great strides as a cultural center. These years witnessed the establishment of the Cincinnati Musical Festival (now known as the Cincinnati May Festival), the founding of the College of Music and the Cincinnati Art Museum, and the construction of Music Hall, one of the nation's first great concert halls. To all these Springer opened his purse. After the highly successful musical festivals of 1873 and 1875, he proposed that a building be constructed specifically for the great festivals, and he pledged $125,000 for that purpose. The pledge came with two stipulations, that the city provide the land free of taxes and that the citizens of Cincinnati match his contribution. Both the city and the citizens responded, although a heated debate divided the community over whether the building should be primarily a music hall or an industrial exposition center. "We are a mechanical people, not a race of fiddlers," angrily wrote one opponent. Springer stepped in to offer an additional $50,000, again to be matched, to construct buildings suitable for expositions adjacent to the hall. Eventually Springer's munificence reached about $200,000, with some going toward the purchase of a great organ. No sooner had the building opened, for the magnificent May Festival of 1878, than prominent citizens launched a movement to establish in the city a major music school, to be called the College of Music of Cincinnati. To that end they brought the musician and conductor Theodore Thomas from New York to head it, at an annual salary of $10,000. Although Thomas stayed only eighteen months, Springer's generosity made what is now the College Conservatory of Music of the University of Cincinnati a reality. During the next several years he contributed more than $200,000 to the college, including a permanent endowment of railroad bonds and a fund of $5,000 to supply gold medals for meritorious students.

He also made important contributions to the newly established art museum and to its affiliated art academy, and at his death much of his art collection went to the museum. Springer, who had no children, outlived the lifespan he predicted for himself by thirty years and his wife by sixteen years.

Springer was a quiet, dignified man whose modesty and reserve made him appear aloof to some. He brought to all phases of his life a sense of order and purpose. "He was the most methodical man I ever saw. He was systematic in everything," his friend and lawyer, General John H. Bates, described him (*Enquirer*, p. 4). Indeed, his financial success derived less from business acumen than from personal diligence and from the remarkable growth of Cincinnati during the pre–Civil War era. If his business career was less than remarkable, his philanthropy set him apart. It is fair to say that few cities had his equal. Even he did not know, or so he said once, how much he gave to various enterprises, but Cincinnati would have been a far less cultivated city without his generosity. While alive he refused to allow his name to be attached either to Music Hall or to the College of Music, and he sometimes modestly referred to himself as the city's "oldest steamboat clerk." At his death in Cincinnati, however, the city recognized his importance with a day of public mourning.

• The best assessment of Springer is Edward J. McGrath, "Reuben Springer, Cincinnatian, Businessman, Philanthropist," *Bulletin of the Cincinnati Historical Society* 13 (1955): 271–85. For a somewhat sentimental view, see "Reuben R. Springer" in Cincinnati Music Hall Association, *Golden Jubilee, 1878–1928* (1928). Entries in both the *Biographical Cyclopaedia and Portrait Gallery of the State of Ohio*, vol. 2, pp. 520–21 (1884) and *History of Cincinnati and Hamilton County* (1894) provide valuable but similar details. Zane Miller has provided an insightful essay on the history of Music Hall in *Cincinnati's Music Hall* (1978), and a general view of Cincinnati's rich cultural life may be found in Robert C. Vitz, *The Queen and the Arts: Cultural Life in Nineteenth-Century Cincinnati* (1989). Obituaries are in the *Cincinnati Enquirer* and the *Cincinnati Commercial*, 11 Dec. 1884.

ROBERT C. VITZ

SPRINGER, William McKendree (30 May 1836–4 Dec. 1903), lawyer, congressman, and judge, was born in New Lebanon, Indiana, the son of Thomas B. Springer and Katherine, who were probably farmers. In 1848 the family moved to Jacksonville, Illinois. After attending local schools in New Lebanon and Jacksonville, Springer studied further with Dr. Newton Bateman, a prominent educator in Illinois, and taught briefly in a Jacksonville school. In 1854 Springer entered Illinois College, an important local institution founded twenty-five years earlier by eastern New School Presbyterian missionaries. After attending the school for several years, Springer clashed with its cultural and political values. He was excluded from the school's oratorical contest in 1856, because his speech vigorously supported Stephen Douglas's Kansas-Nebraska policy. When he defended his right to partici-

pate, the faculty dismissed him from the school. He immediately transferred to Indiana University and graduated in 1858. He returned to Illinois and settled in Lincoln, where he published a Democratic newspaper and studied law. Admitted to the bar in 1859, he practiced law and continued as a journalist in Lincoln for the next two years. In 1859 Springer married Rebecca Ruter; they had one child. Between 1873 and 1899 Rebecca Springer published four novels, one volume of poetry, and many verses in magazines.

Springer's political career moved beyond advocacy in 1860, when he served as a member of the Democratic State Committee and was a losing candidate for state representative. Two years later he was elected to the state constitutional convention and was chosen as secretary by the convention. He advanced his political career considerably in 1861, when he moved to Springfield and began a law partnership with two prominent Democratic politicians, N. M. Broadwell and General John A. McClernand. The latter had served in both the state and federal legislatures and as a presidential elector in 1852, and from 1852 to 1856 he had resided in Jacksonville, where he and Springer probably first became acquainted. Broadwell was also a prominent Democrat and served as mayor of Springfield from 1867 to 1871. Although McClernand retired from the legal firm in 1865, Broadwell and Springer maintained the partnership for the next three decades. During the Civil War years, Springer was an associate editor of the *Illinois State Register*, and in editorials, speeches, and associations he demonstrated his essential opposition to the war.

From 1868 to 1870 Springer traveled in Europe with his wife, both for pleasure and for his wife's health. Returning to Springfield in 1870, he was elected to a term in the state house of representatives. In 1874 he was elected to the first of ten consecutive terms in the U.S. House, finally losing in 1894. Springer's service in the House was successful in that he attained certain leadership positions, he was a skillful parliamentarian, and he supported Democratic positions on key issues. However, his mobility and reputation were limited by his partisanship and his focus on small, often technical issues.

Throughout his congressional career Springer played a significant role in many investigations of corruption, especially in the 1870s. His most notable service was on the House committee that examined the frauds in the 1876 election. His stance on various policy issues fell within Democratic norms for the time, but some of them also changed over time. His position on the money question is the clearest instance of change. In 1878 he helped lead a bipartisan House caucus for soft money; in his 1891 run for the Speakership he took a position between the gold and bimetallist candidates for Speaker; in 1893 he supported repeal of the Sherman Silver Purchase Act; and in January 1895 he introduced President Grover Cleveland's bill to allow the sale of bonds backed with gold. Springer was a moderate on the tariff, favoring reduction but also accepting some protection. In 1888 he participated in the major tariff debate, and in 1891 he devised a strategy of introducing bills to reduce the tariffs on specific items rather than a single, comprehensive bill. As chairman of the Committee on Territories, he authored the bills organizing the Oklahoma Territory, creating a judicial system for the Indian Territory and granting statehood to Washington, Montana, North Dakota, and South Dakota.

As an articulate congressman with considerable seniority, Springer ascended to various leadership positions in the House and aspired to still more. In 1891 he sought the Speakership. In return for supporting Representative Charles Crisp, the eventual winner, he became chairman of the Ways and Means Committee, which carried with it the Democratic floor leadership. He also obtained a position on the committee for freshman congressman William Jennings Bryan, who had supported Springer in the Speakership contest and who, as a student at Illinois College a decade previously, had campaigned for him. In 1893, however, Speaker Crisp faced no opposition, and he appointed William Wilson to Ways and Means, while Springer was given the chairmanship of the lesser Banking Committee.

Throughout his congressional career, Springer spoke frequently, typically with considerable facts and often with partisan barbs. Republican leaders did not like him. Representative Joseph Cannon complained that Springer often sought the spotlight for his own benefit. Springer clashed frequently with Republican Speaker Thomas Reed, whose famous "rules" he vigorously and skillfully challenged. Reed was disdainful of Springer and frequently harassed him in debate. In the most notable episode, Springer repeated the words of Henry Clay, that he would rather be right than president. Reed interjected that he would never be either.

After Springer lost his race for reelection in 1894, President Cleveland appointed him to be judge of the Northern District of the Indian Territory and justice of the U.S. Court of Appeals for the entire territory. When his term expired in December 1899, Springer retired to Washington, D.C., where he practiced law for the next three years, until his death there.

• Springer left no personal papers. The *Congressional Record* is a convenient source for many of his speeches. Among the useful sketches of him are those in the *History of Sangamon County, Illinois* (1881); Joseph Wallace, *Past and Present of the City of Springfield and Sangamon County, Illinois* (1904); and John M. Palmer, *The Bench and Bar of Illinois* (1899). Arthur Wallace Dunn, *From Harrison to Harding: A Personal Narrative* (1922), contains useful information about Springer in Congress. See also Paolo E. Coletta, *William Jennings Bryan*, vol. 1, *Political Evangelist, 1860–1908* (1964); and Samuel Walker McCall, *Thomas Brackett Reed* (1914). Ernest L. Bogart and Charles M. Thompson, *The Industrial State 1870–1893* (1920), provides some insights into Ill. politics of this era. The best obituary is in the *Illinois State Register*, 5 Dec. 1903.

PHILIP R. VANDERMEER

SPROUL, Allan (9 Mar. 1896–9 Apr. 1978), banker, was born in San Francisco, California, the son of Robert Sproul, an immigrant from Scotland in the 1880s who worked as a freight auditor for the Southern Pacific Railroad, and Sarah Elizabeth Moore. He enlisted in the army air force when the United States entered World War I, but the armistice was signed before the second lieutenant flew any combat missions. Sproul resumed his education at the Berkeley campus of the University of California, receiving a B.S. in pomology in 1919. He was briefly employed by the California Packing Company and then as a bank agriculturist for the First National Banks of El Monte and Puente in southern California.

In 1920 Sproul joined the Federal Reserve Bank of San Francisco as head of the Division of Analysis and Research, gathering facts and figures about agricultural, business, and credit conditions in the Twelfth Federal Reserve District. In 1924 Chairman John Perrin appointed him secretary of the bank. Benjamin Strong, head of the Federal Reserve Bank of New York, invited Sproul to come east early in 1928. Strong's successor, George L. Harrison, renewed the offer, and in March 1930 Sproul joined the New York bank as secretary and assistant deputy governor.

As assistant deputy governor Sproul worked largely in the foreign function of the bank, developing an abiding interest in international monetary affairs. In 1934 he became Harrison's assistant, retaining the title of secretary. From April 1935 until 1937 he supervised the bank's foreign operations. He was named deputy governor in January 1936 and first vice president in March 1936. From September 1938 to November 1939 he was in charge of executing open market operations (the bank's trading in U.S. Treasury securities) and manager of the Federal Reserve System's Open Market Account. He was elected president of the Federal Reserve Bank of New York effective 1 January 1941. As ex officio vice chairman of the Federal Open Market Committee (FOMC), Sproul was a forceful advocate for positions sometimes at variance with those of the majority.

During World War II Sproul was among the Federal Reserve Bank presidents who wished to allow bank purchase of Treasury securities maturing in more than ten years and paying more than 2 percent, in opposition to Federal Reserve Board chairman Marriner S. Eccles, whose position prevailed. Federal Reserve Banks were purchasing Treasury bills for immediate credit to the seller. In September 1942 Sproul and two others on the FOMC dissented when the majority took the next step to make the bills the equivalent of cash. Banks selling bills to the Federal Reserve Banks at the posted rate could now repurchase them at their option for immediate delivery. Thus money could be invested in Treasury bills for even one day, with the assurance that it would earn .375 percent. At the January 1943 meeting Sproul and Alfred Williams of Philadelphia opposed direct purchase of bills from the Treasury to replace maturing Federal Reserve–owned bills, fearing this might create public concern about the government's credit. By March 1943 Sproul stood alone in reiterating this opposition.

In 1946 Sproul turned down the opportunity to be the first head of the International Bank for Reconstruction and Development (World Bank) in part because of his desire to participate in the Federal Reserve system during what he perceived as a period of "critical opportunity." From 1946 on Sproul was "one of the principals in the fight to free the Federal Reserve System from the pegging of prices of Government securities" (as he testified before the congressional Joint Committee on the Economic Report, Dec. 1954). He saw a need to change the wartime pattern of short-term rates if the Federal Reserve was to regain control over credit. Some unpredictability in the interest rate structure was introduced in August 1947 as the long-maintained .875 percent rate on one-year certificates of indebtedness was raised, narrowing the spread between short and long rates. Sproul continued thereafter to press for further narrowing. The long-term rate of 2.5 percent, he testified in May 1948, was "the anchor rate" that "should be continued for the foreseeable future."

By the summer of 1950 the Fed began to move in the direction of eliminating the World War II pegged prices on Treasury bonds. Secretary of the Treasury John W. Snyder was opposed. He thought that the August 1950 increase in the Federal Reserve discount rate from 1.5 percent to 1.75 percent was the result of pressure from Sproul and other New York bankers eager for the Fed to demonstrate real independence from the Treasury. The struggle culminated in the Accord of 4 March 1951, which made the Fed coequal: Treasury debt management would henceforth need to consider the Fed's "important responsibilities in the field of credit," as Sproul testified in 1952.

Sproul offered a classic clarification in a letter to the Joint Economic Committee (22 Apr. 1952): "independence of the Federal Reserve System . . . does not mean independence from the Government but independence within the Government." Congress intended the Federal Reserve Banks to be "allied to Government but not part of Government," he argued. The system "is protected both from narrow partisan influence and from selfish private interests." Sproul believed placing it under Civil Service and the General Accounting Office would undermine its independence and regional character.

On the second anniversary of the accord, a unanimous FOMC decided to confine operations to the short end of the market "under present conditions." However, on 11 June 1953 Sproul got four other Federal Reserve Bank presidents on the FOMC to join him in rescinding the March action; current and near term conditions called for greater flexibility. Board of Governors chairman William McChesney Martin and the three other governors present opposed the decision. At the September meeting Martin convinced three of the four other presidents to side with the governors in returning to "bills only" (or "bills preferably"), as the March 1953 policy was called. Only Sproul and President Oliver Powell of Minneapolis voted no.

Sproul disagreed with the doctrine expressed in the FOMC's December 1953 statement that except to correct disorderly markets, the sole purpose of open market transactions was to provide or absorb bank reserves. He also opposed the FOMC policy followed since March 1953 of desisting from open market purchases of maturing and "when issued" securities at a time of Treasury financing. Martin joined Sproul on 30 November 1955 in a decision to purchase securities in the forthcoming Treasury offering. Making an exception, the Fed bought $167 million of certificates in direct support of the Treasury refunding. At the March 1956 meeting—the last one he attended—Sproul remained the sole hold-out, opposing the FOMC's restrictive operating rules.

Sproul differed with others on the FOMC over techniques rather than general credit policies, as he emphasized in December 1954 in congressional testimony. "Bills only" might place the Fed in a straitjacket, he told the congressional committee investigating monetary policy since the accord. The market for longer-term securities had actually lost breadth, depth, and resiliency, he argued.

Some four years after he left the Fed, Sproul chaired a special committee on the balance of international payments appointed by President-elect John F. Kennedy. Its 18 January 1961 report expressed Sproul's long-held views:

[I]f, at times, long term rates are sticky, action should be taken to free them to move. Such intervention would not lessen the breadth of the market, nor deprive it of its ability to reflect underlying factors of capital demand and savings supply. Neither would it nor should it involve pegging of rates nor attempts to prescribe a pattern of rates extending throughout the rate structure. But it would mean nudging a sticky market in the directions indicated by the underlying factors in the market, and thus contribute to the effectiveness of monetary policy.

A month after Kennedy's inauguration the FOMC abandoned "bills only" because of a conflict between domestic and balance-of-payments goals. This ended what Sproul called "an eight-year aberration." He abhorred automatic rules or formulas: the world was too uncertain, the present too unclear, and our understanding of how monetary policy works too imperfect. Central bankers were "practitioners of an art, not a science." Sproul described "bills only" as a form of "norm addiction."

An ad hoc subcommittee set up in 1952 by Chairman Martin reflected Washington staff dissatisfaction with the New York Federal Reserve Bank's performance in managing the open market account for the Federal Reserve system. Sproul deeply resented the implication that he came to FOMC meetings "as a biased protagonist of the operating staff" of his bank and categorically denied that the Federal Reserve Banks were dominated by private banking or business influences.

The Banking Acts of 1933 and 1935 had diminished the position of the Federal Reserve Banks vis-à-vis the board. Harrison was annoyed by what he considered to be undue interference from Washington. During the 1940s Sproul had a gradually increasing role in policymaking, as the Treasury's borrowing requirements loomed large in credit policy. "Bills only" subsequently decreased the New York Federal Reserve Bank's discretion in carrying out Fed open market policies. The doctrine reflected Washington's dissatisfaction with what Sproul called "the power distribution involved in linkage between policy making by the Federal Open Market Committee . . . and the execution of policy by the New York Bank." Paul Volcker, a subsequent president, noted that Sproul "provided and preserved a leadership role for the Federal Reserve Bank of New York during a period when the balance of power was shifting to Washington."

Less than two months after Sproul began a fourth five-year term as president on 1 March 1956, he announced his resignation effective 30 June. Marriner Eccles had described Sproul as "a tower of strength" and "the ablest man in the System." His departure deprived the system of "its most distinguished and experienced executive" (*Economist*, 2 June 1956, p. 896) and increased the Washington board's control of the FOMC.

The Committee for Economic Development–sponsored Commission on Money and Credit recommended eliminating the FOMC in 1961. Sproul wrote to Representative Wright Patman that the 1935 law making the president of the Federal Reserve Bank of New York a continuing member of the FOMC recognized "the need for a living link between monetary policy and the money market." His presence, and that of four other reserve bank presidents on a rotating basis, made the FOMC "a unique contribution to the processes of democratic administration." Indeed, in December 1949 he had advocated shifting the Board of Governors' responsibility for rediscount rates and reserve requirements changes to the FOMC.

In 1956, after twenty-six years in New York, Sproul was eager to return to California and enjoy family life. He was married for fifty-two years to Marion Meredith Bogle, who died in 1973. They had three sons.

In October 1956 Sproul became a director, and later a consultant, to American Trust Company of San Francisco, continuing his association when it merged into Wells Fargo Bank. At the directors' meetings he gave monthly talks on monetary and financial issues until shortly before his death. He also served as director of Kaiser Aluminum and Chemical Corporation from 1957 to 1968. He died at his California home.

• Sproul's papers are in the archives of the Federal Reserve Bank of New York. For additional information see *Selected Papers of Allan Sproul*, ed. Lawrence S. Ritter (1980); *Current*

Biography, Dec. 1950, pp. 47–48; and Marriner Eccles, *Beckoning Frontiers* (1951). An obituary is in the *New York Times*, 11 Apr. 1978.

BENJAMIN J. KLEBANER

SPROUL, Robert Gordon (22 May 1891–10 Sept. 1975), university president, was born in San Francisco, California, the son of Robert Sproul, an auditor for the Southern Pacific Railroad, and Sarah Elizabeth Moore. After graduating from San Francisco's Mission High School in 1909, he enrolled at the University of California at Berkeley. A diligent student, Sproul was also active in Berkeley's collegiate life, being selected to academic honor societies, winning varsity letters as a member of the track squad, and serving as drum major for the marching band, president of the junior class, and president of the university YMCA. He earned his B.S. with a major in civil engineering in 1913. Sproul then worked for one year as an engineer with the city of Oakland's civil service board. In 1914 he resigned from that job to be cashier at Berkeley. On 6 September 1916 he married Ida Amelia Wittschen. They had three children. By 1920 he had become comptroller. Sproul's administrative and political skills led him to be named the university's vice president in 1925 and president in 1929, a position he held until he retired in 1958.

Sproul was unusual among major university presidents of the era in that he was a public high school graduate, held no advanced degrees, had never been a faculty member, and had no aspiration to a life of scholarship. He personified a new type of educational leader: one with professional expertise in institutional finance and bureaucracy along with an ability to explain budgets to the state legislature and civic groups. When named president in June 1929, he obtained a leave of absence from September 1929 to March 1930 to study the university's structure and governance. Because of the impact of the depression on the California economy and thus on university funding, he concentrated on state government relations and succeeded in restoring and eventually increasing state appropriations. A polished orator, Sproul pioneered the use of radio broadcasts and media relations to present the University of California's case to a statewide audience. He organized the order of the Golden Bear, an influential group of prominent Berkeley alumni whom Sproul mobilized on key legislative issues. His strategies worked so well for several decades that, according to *Time* magazine (6 Oct. 1947), he was known as the "symbol of the university to the state and the people, and the spearhead of the university's public relations."

During his presidency the University of California's total enrollment increased from 20,000 to more than 45,000. The university added three new undergraduate liberal arts colleges (Santa Barbara, Davis, and Riverside) to its comprehensive campuses at Berkeley and Los Angeles and its medical school in San Francisco, oceanography institute in La Jolla, and its observatory at Mount Hamilton. In addition to its physical expansion, the university gained academic stature for its graduate programs and research. In 1925 Berkeley was ranked ninth in quality of graduate departments; by 1957 it had risen to second. A measure of Sproul's pledge both to recruit and develop internationally eminent scholars was the number of University of California faculty who were named Nobel laureates while at Berkeley, a number that increased from none to six during his tenure. Sproul's commitment to building a strong faculty had a direct connection to the flourishing of "big science," as Berkeley became a leading campus for federally sponsored research and development in physics, chemistry, biology, engineering, and agriculture. During Sproul's presidency, faculty salaries at the University of California rose to be highest among all state universities in the nation. At the same time he managed to keep tuition low, so as to make the university affordable to all academically able applicants.

Robert Gordon Sproul represented a generation of university presidents who had to synchronize their own campus administration with the activities of numerous external commissions. Whereas some university leaders might have seen state commissions as an obstacle to institutional advancement, Sproul was especially skilled at using commission reports as a means to impede hasty decisions by the state legislature and eventually to get the results he sought. The first major test for Sproul's way of shaping policy came in 1931, when the issue of statewide planning for mass higher education arose. Sproul, as champion of the prestigious university, did not favor programs that would foster proliferation of new state colleges scattered throughout California. To offset the influence of local "booster" groups throughout the state, Sproul persuaded the state legislature to join the Carnegie Foundation for the Advancement of Teaching in an analysis of higher education planning in California. Although Sproul did not endorse all recommendations presented in the report, he successfully protected the primacy of his own institution, the University of California.

Throughout the remainder of Sproul's presidency, he was involved in numerous state commissions. The climax came with the 1957 Study for the Need for Additional Centers of Public Higher Education in California, an analysis that helped to develop the infrastructure for the current organizational leadership of higher education by the regents of the University of California, the trustees of the state colleges, and the Coordinating Council for Higher Education.

Despite Sproul's success in building an academically and financially strong university, he had to contend with the rivalry between Berkeley, located in northern California, and the new UCLA campus located in affluent, populous southern California, a rivalry that he feared could fragment his "one great university." This competition was part of a larger issue: how could public officials best reconcile mass higher education with excellence? Sproul's preference was for academically selective admission, but even this policy required expanded enrollments, given California's demographic growth. Sproul believed that undergraduates were better served by large classes taught by outstanding professors rather than small classes taught by mediocre faculty. Sproul eschewed the idea of university-built dormitories, favoring an arrangement whereby students fended for themselves in off-campus housing, fraternities and sororities, and cooperatives. His emphasis on student independence did not mean he was indifferent to student development. For Sproul, one key to fostering a coherent, memorable undergraduate experience was to provide a rich range of student activities. Nor did Sproul neglect instruction for undergraduates; at the same time that he attracted large-scale, sponsored research in the sciences to Berkeley, he devoted careful presidential attention to maintaining teaching excellence.

The University of California faculty was characterized by both outstanding scholarship and an unusually strong academic senate, leading Sproul to observe, "The faculty can't be driven. It can only be persuaded." The delicate balance of Sproul's faculty relations was jeopardized after World War II in the California loyalty oath controversy. Sproul aggravated matters in 1949 when he suggested adoption of a special oath, which he saw as a "harmless way to reaffirm the University's opposition to Communism." His proposal pleased neither those university regents who wanted a stronger requirement nor an equally determined faculty who resisted any such measure. In addition to perceiving the oath as an intrusion on the prerogatives of the academic senate, faculty resented Sproul's timing and mode of presentation, which they interpreted as saying, "sign or get out." Sproul later reversed his stand, agreeing with Governor Earl Warren that the proposed university oath was both ineffective and inappropriate. Sproul eventually recommended to the regents that thirty-nine members of the faculty senate who had not signed the oath be reappointed for the coming year on the basis of favorable endorsement by the university's Committee on Privilege and Tenure. Between 1949 and 1952 repeated attempts at compromise failed; during this period the regents fired thirty-one university faculty members. In 1952 a statewide employee oath was adopted, which had the effect of eliminating any provision that would single out university faculty; at the same time the faculty members who had been dismissed for refusing to sign the oath won their court case against the regents. Dissatisfaction with the state employee oath did not subside, and in 1967 the California Supreme Court declared invalid those provisions of the oath pertaining to membership in subversive organizations. In the meantime, however, the episode had rocked the university, as regents had been pitted against the faculty; there was some concern that as a result of this crisis Berkeley had slipped from the ranks of great national universities. Certainly it underscored the fragility of academic freedom and of the university's right to govern itself in an institutional environment subject to fluctuating moods of a state legislature.

Sproul was immensely popular with university undergraduates and alumni. When, for example, word spread that Sproul had been offered a prestigious university presidency elsewhere, Berkeley students organized a rally proclaiming, "Stick with Us, Bob!" The one strain in Sproul's relations with students came in 1936 over the issue of whether the highly organized and well-funded Associated Students of the University of California (ASUC) or the university president had ultimate power to hire and fire ASUC employees and to determine policies of such ASUC entities as the student newspaper or intercollegiate athletics teams. Sproul argued that ceding this power to ASUC would be administratively irresponsible and would forfeit the ASUC's nonprofit status, an administrative interpretation that prevailed at the time but was revisited by students and university officials for years to come.

For over four decades Sproul was active in the Republican party. At the 1948 Republican convention he nominated his longtime friend, Governor Earl Warren, as candidate for president of the United States. A joiner and booster who belonged to over 250 voluntary associations and civic groups, Sproul was especially active in environmental conservation. Between 1926 and 1958 he was awarded eighteen honorary degrees. He was named president emeritus of the University of California upon his retirement in 1958. He died in Berkeley.

Sproul stood out as the prototype of the academic leader of the mid-twentieth century by showing how an American university could achieve international stature in scholarship and research while also fulfilling local and state service obligations. As architect and catalyst for the great state university after World War I, he took to its limits the idea of the large flagship campus. At the same time, he fashioned the model for the multicampus state university system that broadened access to American higher education after World War II.

• Sproul's papers are in the Archives at the University of California, Berkeley. A comprehensive biography, with an anthology of selected speeches, is George A. Pettitt, *Twenty-Eight Years in the Life of a University President* (1966). The Carnegie Foundation for the Advancement of Teaching, "State Higher Education in California," *Twenty-Seventh Report of the President* (1932), gives a sense of Sproul's involvement in statewide planning for mass higher education. Verne A. Stadtman, *The University of California, 1868–1968* (1970), provides a thorough survey of Sproul's presidential tenure. "Big Man on Eight Campuses: California's Sproul: Is Everyone Entitled to a College Education?," *Time*, 6 Oct. 1947, pp. 69–76, is indicative of the national stature Sproul gained as real and symbolic leader of American higher education. An important source on the major governance controversy of his university administration is George R. Stewart, *The Year of the Oath: The Fight for Academic Freedom at the University of California* (1950). Ellen W. Schrecker, *No Ivory Tower: McCarthyism and the Universities* (1986), provides historical perspective and national context for the Berkeley loyalty oath controversy. A brief, intriguing glimpse of Sproul's Berkeley before the highly publicized student unrest of the 1960s is W. J. Rorabaugh, *Berkeley at War: The 1960s* (1989), pp. 9–22. An obituary is in the *New York Times*, 12 Sept. 1975.

JOHN R. THELIN

SPROULE, William (25 Nov. 1858–1 Jan. 1935), railroad president, was born in County Mayo, Ireland. His parents' names are unknown, although it is believed that he was tutored primarily by his father during his youth. At age eighteen he sailed to New York City, where he accepted a job with the American News Company. A few months later he moved west, where he clerked in the mercantile trade in San Francisco and Sacramento, California. In 1882 he began his forty-year career in the railroad industry as a clerk for the Southern Pacific Company.

Hard work and good fortune yielded a generous betterment in Sproule's circumstances. Within five years he was appointed an assistant general freight agent (solicitation or sales) for Southern Pacific at San Francisco. He was the company's youngest officer. In 1897 Sproule became a general freight agent, and a year later he was promoted to general traffic manager. He served in this capacity until 1906, when he became associated with the American Smelting and Refining Company and its affiliated interests as a traffic manager, a director, and a member of the company's executive committee in New York. He married Mary Louise Baird-Baldwin in 1905; they had no children, although she had two children from a previous marriage. In 1910 Sproule was named as the president of the Wells Fargo & Company, but he resigned in the latter part of the next year to become the director and president of Southern Pacific. Rarely did immigrants rise to presidential status of American corporations, but Sproule had become a leader of two such corporations in less than three decades following his immigration.

During World War I Sproule was the chairman of the Railroad War Board. In 1918, after the federal government assumed control of the railroads for war purposes, Sproule was named the district director for the Western Region of the United States Railroad Administration. Following the war, railroad carriers were returned to their owners and Sproule resumed his duties as president of Southern Pacific. Before and after the war, Sproule was beset by urgent difficulties at Southern Pacific. Continuing political unrest in Mexico, where Southern Pacific had significant investments, dashed hopes of increasing trade, and the opening of the Panama Canal drained the transcontinental traffic from railroads such as Southern Pacific. More significant, perhaps, were political developments at home, where Progressive Era legislation and litigation threatened the company's very being.

In 1912 Attorney General George W. Wickersham, at President William Howard Taft's direction, appealed to the Supreme Court seeking the division of Southern Pacific and Union Pacific—a union arranged more than a decade earlier by the late Edward H. Harriman. Shortly after 9 December 1912, joint sales offices were abolished, and Southern Pacific returned to an independent status. Union Pacific did not give up its aggressive posture toward Southern Pacific, nor did it end the federal government's curious devotion to the persecution of that company. After World War I the government filed suit, demanding the separation of Central Pacific—a crucially important subsidiary because of its ownership of the historic trackage from Ogden, Utah, to Oakland, California, along with important terminals and secondary routes—from Southern Pacific. The government then planned to give Central Pacific to Union Pacific. Southern Pacific would then be gutted and left with disconnected physical parts, while Union Pacific would gain by having its own route from Missouri River points to the San Francisco Bay. A spirited contest ensued in which Southern Pacific ultimately prevailed in 1923. Nevertheless, these legal battles sapped the company's funds and, more importantly, diverted its management's attention for more than a decade.

The company's spokesman on many matters, Sproule urged investors to look carefully and enthusiastically at opportunities in California and elsewhere in Southern Pacific's vast domain. He also took up the industry's causes, railing against antibusiness legislation and advocating a level playing field that would allow an adequate return on investment for the nation's railroads.

Although generally adept in public relations matters, Sproule was sometimes obtuse. In 1922 Southern Pacific purchased fifty locomotives from Baldwin Locomotive Works. Baldwin sought to advertise the purchase nationally by moving the entire shipment from near Philadelphia in a solid train that would be ballyhooed as the "Prosperity Special." Sproule was uneasy, however, protesting that Southern Pacific would be exposed to criticism if anything went wrong en route. Sproule's resistance was dimmed considerably after an onslaught of pleas from Baldwin, and he eventually acquiesed. He was astonished at the very positive public response to the unusual train. Thousands waited at trackside to see its passage, and thousands more inspected the train when it finally arrived for display at Exposition Park in Los Angeles. Even President Warren G. Harding took note, dispatching a telegram thanking Sproule for supporting national economic growth.

Sproule enjoyed a few personal diversions, and in addition to his duties at Southern Pacific he was active in various civic affairs. He played golf, but he favored walking as a means of staying physically fit. He served as the director of the Federal Reserve Bank and a member of the San Francisco Symphony Orchestra. He was a trustee for the Park Museum, the San Francisco Board of Park Commissioners, and the Palace of the Legion of Honor. He also served at one time as the president of the Bohemian Club and the Pacific Union Club. Sproule retired as the president of Southern Pacific in 1928, although he remained the president of the company's important Central Pacific subsidiary until his death at the family home in San Francisco.

Sproule was one of few immigrants who climbed the American corporate ladder in the early twentieth century. He had dogged determination, an innate sense of fairness, and considerable business savvy. Despite public censure over various railroad policies, Sproule ran a powerful organization, both in operations and traffic, whose considerable success continued unabated long after he retired.

• An abundance of Sproule's correspondence is at the Corporate Archives of the Southern Pacific Transportation Company in San Francisco, Calif. The best source of information on Sproule and the Southern Pacific is Don L. Hofsommer, *The Southern Pacific, 1901–1985* (1986). Other information can be found in *Railway Age Gazette*, 6 Oct. 1911, and *Overland*, Nov. 1915, pp. 410–15. A fairly useful obituary is in the *New York Times*, 2 Jan. 1935.

DON L. HOFSOMMER

SPRUANCE, Raymond Ames (3 July 1886–13 Dec. 1969), naval officer, was born in Baltimore, Maryland, the son of Alexander P. Spruance, a businessman, and Annie Ames Hiss, an editor for a publishing firm. Spruance was raised largely by his maternal grandparents and three aunts in East Orange, New Jersey, and attended the Stevens Preparatory School in Hoboken, New Jersey. In 1903 he was admitted to the U.S. Naval Academy, graduating in 1906.

Spruance was assigned initially to the battleship *Iowa*, and in 1907–1909 he participated in the global voyage of the "Great White Fleet" on the battleship *Minnesota*. He was commissioned an ensign in September 1908 and studied electrical engineering at the General Electric Company in Schenectady, New York. Spruance rose to the rank of lieutenant commander by 1917, serving successively on the battleship *Connecticut*, as senior engineer on the cruiser *Cincinnati*, as commander of the destroyer *Bainbridge*, as inspector of machinery at the Newport News Shipbuilding and Dry Dock Company, and on the battleship *Pennsylvania*. In 1914 he married Margaret Vance Dean; they had two children. In 1917–1918 he was assistant electrical officer of the New York Navy Yard. After the United States entered World War I, he was promoted to commander and made executive officer of the troop transport *Agamemnon*.

Between 1919 and 1940 Spruance established himself as an outstanding ship commander and naval strategist while rising to the rank of rear admiral. From 1919 to 1921 he commanded the destroyers *Aaron Ward* and *Percival*. He spent the next three years in the Bureau of Engineering, and from 1924 to 1926 he was assistant chief of staff to the commander, U.S. Naval Forces in Europe, and commanded the destroyer *Osborne*. In 1926–1927 Spruance was a student at the Naval War College, followed by tours in the Office of Naval Intelligence (1927–1929) and as executive officer of the battleship *Mississippi* (1929–1931). He returned to the Naval War College for two years in 1931 to supervise its correspondence courses, and from 1933 to 1935 he was chief of staff to the commander, Destroyers Scouting Force. By this time Spruance was recognized as one of the best intellects in the navy, leading to his assignment to the Naval War College for a third time in 1935. During the next three years he headed several departments at the college, enhancing his reputation as a keen student of the art of command

and strategic decision making. Following his tenure at the college, Spruance returned to the battleship *Mississippi* as its commander.

In February 1940 Spruance was appointed commandant of the Tenth Naval District, headquartered at San Juan, Puerto Rico, and in August 1941 he became commander of Cruiser Division Five. After the Japanese attack against Pearl Harbor in December 1941, Spruance's cruiser division was part of a carrier task force commanded by Vice Admiral William F. Halsey, Jr., that launched raids against the Gilbert and Marshall islands, Wake Island, Marcus Island, and the Japanese homeland. When Halsey became ill in May 1942, Spruance, a nonaviator, took over as commander of one of the two carrier task forces charged with repelling the Japanese advance on Midway Island.

During the battle of Midway (4–7 June 1942), Spruance, operating practically independently even though he was junior to the other task force commander, masterfully handled his two carriers and was the primary commander in this crucial American victory. Receptive to the advice he received from the air-oriented staff he inherited from Halsey and adhering to the orders of Admiral Chester Nimitz, commander of the Pacific Fleet, to avoid the exposure of his force "to attack by superior enemy forces without the prospect of inflicting . . . greater damage to the enemy," Spruance was at his best on 4 June, using his planes to hit the Japanese carriers when they were refueling planes on their decks, their most vulnerable condition, and then retiring to avoid a night encounter with the more powerful Japanese surface fleet. By the end of the battle the Americans had destroyed four Japanese carriers at the cost of one American carrier, and the initiative in the Pacific war now passed to the Americans.

Shortly afterward, Spruance was named chief of staff to Nimitz, and in September 1942 he was designated deputy commander in chief of the Pacific Fleet. Promoted to vice admiral in May 1943, he played a major role in planning Nimitz's Central Pacific offensive, which was designed to make the fullest use of the navy's rapidly growing carrier and amphibious forces along the most direct route to Japan. In August 1943 Spruance assumed command of the Central Pacific Force. In November 1943 he oversaw the capture of the Gilbert Islands and, in January and February 1944, the Marshall Islands.

In April 1944 Spruance, now an admiral, was designated commander of the Fifth Fleet. After directing raids against the Palau Islands, he was charged with invading the Mariana Islands, beginning with Saipan in June. The Japanese fleet came out in strength to oppose the American operation, resulting in the battle of the Philippine Sea (18–20 June 1944). Cautious by nature and fearful the Japanese might divide their force and use one part as a decoy while another made an end run to get at the transports, Spruance concluded that his principal mission was to protect the landing, and he adopted a defensive stance. To the chagrin of many of his airmen, he refused to sail west on the night of 18–19 June to close on the Japanese and instead waited for the Japanese, whose planes had greater range than his, to attack. When the Japanese attacked on 19 June, American pilots and gunners shot down hundreds of Japanese planes in the famous "Marianas Turkey Shoot." The Japanese also lost two carriers that day to American submarines. On 20 June, when the Japanese carriers were finally within range and it became clear the Japanese had not divided their force, Spruance struck with his air squadrons, sinking one carrier and damaging three others. As the Japanese retired in the night of 20–21 June, Spruance pursued but had to turn back because his fuel was running low.

The battle of the Philippine Sea, which permanently crippled Japanese naval air power, was a major victory for Spruance. But critics, mostly naval aviators who resented that a nonaviator controlled the carriers, were quick to criticize him for not annihilating the Japanese fleet. In their view he failed to use his carriers aggressively on 18–19 June to seek out the Japanese and hit them first and was too slow to attack on 20 June. Spruance's supporters discounted the criticism, arguing that he accomplished his mission of protecting the transports while destroying Japanese air groups and without losing any of his own ships. Many historians, however, agree with the critics, pointing out that Spruance could have sent his carriers west during the night of 18–19 June while still covering the landings.

Spruance relinquished command of the Fifth Fleet, renamed the Third Fleet, in August 1944 and took up station at Pearl Harbor to plan future operations. He resumed command of the fleet, again named the Fifth Fleet, in February 1945 and carried out the successful invasions of Iwo Jima and Okinawa. During the Okinawa operation the fleet came under fierce attack from Japanese suicide planes, one of which struck Spruance's flagship, the cruiser *Indianapolis*, forcing him to transfer to the battleship *New Mexico*. From June until the war's end in August 1945 Spruance was in Guam preparing for the invasion of Japan, and from November 1945 to February 1946 he was commander of the Pacific Fleet. Thereafter, he was president of the Naval War College until his retirement in 1948.

In January 1952 President Harry S. Truman appointed Spruance ambassador to the Philippines, then under the threat of the Hukbalahap (Huk) insurrection, which the Americans regarded as inspired and dominated by communists. His primary responsibility was to persuade Philippine president Elpidio Quirino to counter the Huks by reforming his regime, and, when that failed, to work for his defeat in the election of 1953. In the period before the election Spruance adopted an uncooperative and critical stance toward Quirino to undermine his regime, and in league with U.S. Air Force colonel Edward G. Lansdale, the top Central Intelligence Agency operative in the Philippines, he flagrantly intervened in the presidential campaign to help elect Ramon Magsaysay, who was thought to be a genuine reformer and strongly pro-American. Afterward, Spruance focused on the negotiations for a new treaty to expand America's existing military bases in the islands, but growing Philippine nationalism kept him from achieving a treaty before he retired in 1955.

Spruance was the outstanding American fleet commander of World War II, winning the two most significant naval battles in the Pacific war and successfully coordinating all the major amphibious operations in the Central Pacific as the United States pushed toward Japan. A master strategist, he was poised and decisive in battle. His orders were always precise, but once they were issued, he normally left the details to his subordinates. Aloof and unassuming, Spruance was publicity shy, and after the war he generally refused to respond to his critics. As a result, he did not receive the public credit and the rank of fleet admiral he justly deserved. He died in Pebble Beach, California.

• Spruance's papers are at the Naval War College at Newport, R.I. E. P. Forrestal, *Admiral Raymond A. Spruance* (1966), and Thomas B. Buell, *The Quiet Warrior* (1974), are capable biographies. Samuel Eliot Morison, *History of U.S. Naval Operations in World War II*, vols. 3 (1948), 4 (1950), 7 (1951), 8 (1953), and 14 (1960), praises Spruance's leadership and defends his controversial decisions. Clark G. Reynolds, *The Fast Carriers* (1968), while recognizing Spruance as the best American sea commander of the war, gives greater weight to his critics. Valuable references to Spruance's World War II service are also in E. B. Potter, *Nimitz* (1976), and Gordan W. Prange, *Miracle at Midway* (1982). Spruance's tenure as ambassador to the Philippines is discussed in Nick Cullather, *Illusions of Influence: The Political Economy of United States–Philippines Relations, 1942–1960* (1994). An obituary is in the *New York Times*, 14 Dec. 1969.

JOHN KENNEDY OHL

SPRUNT, James (9 June 1846–9 July 1924), entrepreneur, philanthropist, and author, was born in Glasgow, Scotland, the son of Alexander Sprunt, an exporter, and Jane Dalziel. Sprunt migrated with his parents to North Carolina in 1852, living first in Duplin County and then Wilmington, New Hanover County, where he attended school until age fourteen. During the Civil War he became a purser on a blockade-runner, but when the ship was captured in 1864, he was imprisoned only to make a daring escape to Halifax, Nova Scotia. He again became a ship's purser, returned to the South, and was shipwrecked off the coast of Florida. Avoiding Federal troops, he returned to Wilmington.

Following the war, with small profits from the sale of sugar he had previously managed to bring through the blockade, he purchased a few bales of cotton and established an exporting firm with his father called Alexander Sprunt and Son. Seeking markets for naval stores and later cotton, he journeyed to the North, Britain, Holland, Belgium, Switzerland, Italy, France, Germany, and Russia. In each of these places he made business connections, and within a few years, due in large measure to his untiring efforts, business acumen, and reputation for honesty, his business grew rapidly. When his father died in 1884, the company had more than fifty offices and agencies in foreign countries and was the largest cotton exporting firm in the United States. In 1902 Sprunt journeyed some 17,000 miles to establish new selling agencies for the cotton he shipped. In the years before he died, his company sold nearly 500,000 bales per year and boasted offices in various southern cities and European countries.

Deeply interested in history, Sprunt became president of the North Carolina Literary and Historical Association and president of the North Carolina Folk Lore Society. In 1900 he donated funds to the University of North Carolina to establish a series called James Sprunt Historical Monographs, later James Sprunt Historical Publications. By 1969 fifty-one volumes had been published in this series, including classics such as *The Negro in Mississippi* by Vernon Wharton. Sprunt himself was a writer of some ability and published several biographical and historical studies, including *Tales and Traditions of the Lower Cape Fear, 1661–1896* (1896) and *Chronicles of the Cape Fear River* (1914).

Sprunt was "the soul of hospitality," said his friend, historian James G. deRoulac Hamilton, and Sprunt's home in Wilmington and his Orton plantation in Brunswick County, North Carolina, on the Cape Fear River were "renown and loved by many." In 1883 he had married Luola Murchinson, and the couple had three children. At his Wilmington residence he maintained spacious gardens, and on the land in Brunswick County he established a working rice plantation. At both locations Sprunt entertained a number of guests. One visitor called him a "gifted conversationalist" and an "ideal host."

By the 1890s and early twentieth century, he was devoting himself to a wide variety of philanthropic and charitable activities. A Presbyterian and devout Christian, he attended church regularly, accepted positions of lay leadership, and contributed to the construction of several Presbyterial churches, including one at the University of North Carolina. He also established a loan fund at Davidson College in North Carolina, founded a lectureship at Union Theological Seminary in Richmond, Virginia, and financed several schools in China. His philanthropy also had a personal side. Crippled by an accident in his early manhood, he sent crippled mill children in his area to Baltimore for orthopedic treatment.

His success in business was matched by his growing renown, and in 1884 he succeeded his father as British vice consul, a post he held until his death in Greenville Sound (near Wilmington), North Carolina. He twice received commendations for his work from the British government. Between 1907 and 1912 he served as Imperial German consul.

• A significant correspondence detailing Sprunt's business, religious, and historical interests can be found in Alexander Sprunt and Son Records, Duke University Library, Durham, N.C.; especially important are files dated 1904–1910 and 1919–1921. Among Sprunt's writings are *A Colonial Apparition: A Story of the Cape Fear* (1898); *Derelicts: An*

Account of Ships Lost at Sea in General Commercial Traffic and a Brief History of Blockade Runners . . . (1920); and *In Memoriam: Mrs. James Sprunt* (1916). An obituary is in the *Wilmington Morning Star*, 10 July 1924.

LOREN SCHWENINGER

SPURR, Josiah Edward (1 Oct. 1870–12 Jan. 1950), geologist, was born in Gloucester, Massachusetts, the son of Alfred Sears Spurr, the owner of a fishing schooner, and Oratia Snow. Spurr entered Harvard on a scholarship in 1888, dropped out for a year, but, encouraged by Nathaniel Shaler, professor of paleontology and geology, returned to complete work for his B.A. in geology and graduated in 1893. He received the M.A. in absentia in 1894. During the summer of 1893 he took a job with the Minnesota geological survey, and his well-received professional report, "The Iron-Bearing Rocks of the Mesabi Range in Minnesota" (Minnesota Geological and Natural History Survey, Bull. No. 10, 1894), marked the beginning of a long career as a mining geologist. Election to membership in the Geological Society of America and the American Institute of Mining Engineers soon followed.

Taken on in 1894 as assistant to Samuel Franklin Emmons in the U.S. Geological Survey (USGS), Spurr mapped the mines at Leadville, Colorado, and described the geology of the Mecur mining district in Utah. In 1895, when mine owners petitioned the Geological Survey for a study of the Aspen mining district, Spurr, with assistant George Warren Tower, was given the assignment. *The Geology of the Aspen Mining District, Colorado* (1898) appeared as U.S. Geological Survey Monograph No. 31. In 1896, the USGS, under Director Charles Walcott, began to investigate Alaska's mineral resources, sending Spurr to do a reconnaissance of the Yukon region. With two assistants, he spent four months of arduous travel across the Chilcoot Pass and along the Yukon River, studying the geology, locating sources of placer deposits, and doing preliminary evaluation of the gold and other minerals. That August a miner named George Carmack discovered gold on the Klondike, setting off the gold rush to the Yukon in earnest. Spurr drew up a program of exploration for Alaska but did not return until 1898, when he did a more extensive reconnaissance of previously unexplored southwestern Alaska (USGS 20th Annual Report, Part 7) as part of the Survey's expanded investigation of the territory.

On leave from the Survey in 1897, Spurr was a delegate to the International Geological Congress in Russia. While in Europe he undertook graduate study at Friedrich Wilhelm University in Berlin. Dissatisfied with Prussian methods, he left for Paris to study briefly with Alfred Lacroix at the Sorbonne. Spurr never received a doctorate and lacked a thorough background in the physical sciences, which perhaps made him a bit defensive in his relations with academic geologists, who he felt did not appreciate the work of the mining geologist.

Spurr married Sophie Burchard in 1899 and, that same year, declined a position as geologist-in-charge of work in Alaska, apparently not wanting to be so far away from his new wife. Instead, taking her along, he accepted an assignment to do a survey of central and southern Nevada, including Death Valley, to fill in the lesser known parts of the Great Basin south of the 40th parallel for the geologic map of the United States. Spurr's reports on his fieldwork included a blunt attack on the views of Grove Karl Gilbert, who had been studying the Basin and Range region for many years. Spurr agreed with the interpretations of Walcott, Clarence King, and Frank Emmons, who believed that Basin and Range structure originated through the same processes of folding, faulting, and erosion that had formed the Appalachians. Gilbert, on the other hand, attributed its origin to block faulting. Spurr's attack angered Gilbert but stimulated him to pursue further work in the region; Gilbert's interpretation is today generally considered to be the correct one.

In April 1901, Spurr moved with his wife and infant son to Constantinople to become geologist and mining engineer to the sultan of Turkey. He studied gold deposits and served as a member of a commission to revise the mining laws. Returning to the United States in May 1902, Spurr rejoined the USGS, where he stayed until 1906, conducting a major study of the newly discovered mines of Tonopah, Nevada (USGS Professional Paper No. 42), as well as reporting on the ore deposits of Goldfield and Silver Peak, Nevada. During these years he also wrote several papers on the origin and genetic classification of ore deposits, indicating his interest in the more theoretical aspects of mining geology. In 1904 Spurr's *Geology Applied to Mining*, a concise and practical guide for the student and miner, was published (2d rev. ed., 1926).

In 1906, at a time when more and more mining companies were employing professional geologists, Spurr went to work for Daniel Guggenheim's American Smelting and Refining Company at a salary of $5,000 a year, no doubt feeling that private work could better support his growing family, which eventually included five sons. While investigating mines in Mexico for the company, Spurr met mining engineer W. Rowland Cox, and in 1908 he and Cox formed the consulting firm of Spurr & Cox, Inc. The partnership produced many reports on mines in Mexico and the western United States, and Spurr often served as a consultant in lawsuits. In January 1912 Spurr became vice president in charge of mining for the Tonopah Mining Company, for which he examined gold deposits in the Hudson Bay area and developed copper mines in Manitoba and Nicaragua.

During World War I Spurr lived in Washington, D.C., where, with his now wide experience with the mining industry, he served in various capacities as a government expert on mines and minerals. He was a member of the Committee on Mineral Imports, which, because of the shortage of ships, was charged with preparing a plan to reduce imports of raw materials. He then became the chief executive of the War Minerals Investigation Committee of the Bureau of Mines, directing a large team of volunteer technical experts who studied and advised on problems related to the supply of minerals for the war effort. After the war he was chief engineer of the War Minerals Relief Commission, investigating claims made by companies that had increased output of certain minerals at the government's request during the war and suffered losses when it was over. In this capacity Spurr was incorruptible but offended some with his uncompromising manner in dealing with claimants. Spurr's war experience made him aware of the need for a farsighted minerals policy and for an understanding of the political and economic factors involved in the control of mineral resources. For McGraw-Hill, he edited *Political and Commercial Geology and the World's Mineral Resources: A Series of Studies by Specialists* (1920) and *The Marketing of Metals and Minerals* (1925), coedited with Felix E. Wormser.

From 1919 until 1927, Spurr was editor of McGraw-Hill's influential *Engineering and Mining Journal*, which became the forum for his many editorials and articles, including one entitled "The Geologist as Engineer" (7 Feb. 1920), urging recognition of the "engineering geologist" as a professional whose practical knowledge had much to contribute to the more theoretical work of the general geologist. This concern for the status of the mining geologist had led Spurr to propose the publication of a new journal, *Economic Geology*, the first issue of which appeared in October 1905. He was also a moving force behind the founding of the Society of Economic Geologists in 1920 and served as its president in 1923. As the publishers of *Engineering and Mining Journal* remarked when he retired as editor, Spurr's intolerance of hypocrisy and wrongdoing at times led him into "undiplomatic expression." Nevertheless, in 1921, a poll of the deans of engineering schools listed Spurr among the top three "most highly esteemed" mining engineers in America.

Spurr's magnum opus was *The Ore Magmas: A Series of Essays on Ore Deposition* (1923), a two-volume work based on his previous studies of ore deposits. It is an opinionated book, a "scientific autobiography," as one reviewer called it, summarizing Spurr's belief that all ores and, indeed, all the structural features of the earth's crust have resulted from magmatic intrusion, with the various metals being deposited in sequence in a process of "magmatic differentiation" from the thick gelatinous magma that cooled as it forced its way upward through overlying rock. Most geologists of his day, who thought that ores were hydrothermal deposits from weak magmatic solutions, opposed Spurr's views, which were close to those of the eighteenth-century Scottish geologist James Hutton.

Also generally rejected by his fellow geologists were Spurr's ideas about the formation of the moon, which he thought had been marked by extensive volcanic action. In four privately published volumes of *Geology Applied to Selenology* (1944–1949), Spurr developed his theories not through astronomical research, but based on his study of a large photograph of the moon acquired from Mount Wilson Observatory and by comparing moon features with the earth's geology, with which he was so familiar. Although not generally accepted at the time, some of Spurr's ideas on ore deposition and selenology were later validated.

Although he taught undergraduate geology at Rollins College from 1930 to 1932, Spurr spent most of the last twenty years of his life in retirement, wintering in Winter Park, Florida, and spending the summers in East Alstead, New Hampshire. He died in Winter Park. Mount Spurr, in southwestern Alaska, and a mineral, spurrite, were named for him.

As a writer, editor, and government adviser, Spurr brought his own high standards of ethical conduct to bear on the mining business, where corruption and exploitation often occurred. Although many geologists of his day dismissed his theories on ore formation, the reports based on his accurate firsthand observations in the field have continued to be of service to later investigators. His recognition of the importance of economic geology helped to raise the level of research conducted by mining geologists, who usually worked for private companies rather than in universities where research was more commonly expected.

• Spurr's papers are at the American Heritage Center (formerly the Western History Research Center), University of Wyoming, Laramie. They include correspondence, notebooks, photographs, contracts, mining reports, and other material. In addition to his technical works, Spurr wrote two popular accounts of his explorations in Alaska, *Through the Yukon Gold Diggings* (1900) and "Into an Unknown Country: The Recollections and Journals of an Alaskan Expedition, 1898," a previously unpublished manuscript based on diaries he kept during his second USGS expedition and published in seven parts in *Alaska* (May–Nov. 1975). The best biography is the memorial by Jack Green in *Geological Society of America, Proceedings* (1968), pp. 259–72, which contains a full bibliography of over 100 published works. Other biographies include Harvard College, Class of 1893, *Twenty-Fifth Anniversary Report* (1918), and a sketch and portrait of Spurr as the new editor in *Engineering and Mining Journal* 108 (13 Sept. 1919): 474–76. An obituary is in the *New York Times*, 13 Jan. 1950.

MARGARET D. CHAMPLIN

SQUANTO. *See* Tisquantum.

SQUIBB, Edward Robinson (4 July 1819–25 Oct. 1900), physician, chemist, and manufacturing pharmacist, was born in Wilmington, Delaware, the son of James Robinson Squibb (occupation unknown) and Catherine Bonsall. After Squibb's mother died in 1831, the family moved to Philadelphia. In 1837 Edward became a pharmacist's apprentice. Five years later he entered Jefferson Medical College; he received his M.D. degree in 1845.

Squibb's Quaker upbringing instilled in him a desire to do good by reforming the practice of medicine and pharmacy. In 1845 Squibb established his own medical practice and served as an instructor and museum curator at his alma mater. Two years later he joined the U.S. navy as a surgeon. His local church disowned Squibb on the grounds that he had violated his pledge of pacifism by enlisting in the armed services. Yet Squibb saw no contradiction between his pacifism and his profession. As a medical doctor he would not have to engage in combat. Furthermore, Squibb believed he could alleviate suffering and help the navy eliminate the overseas slave trade."

For four years Squibb witnessed the sorry state of medicine and pharmacy as practiced on navy ships. The poor diet, hygiene, and living conditions of sailors left them subject to a variety of diseases. The navy purchased its pharmaceutical supplies from the lowest bidder, and manufacturers cut their costs by selling drugs mixed with sand, chalk, and other impurities. In 1851 Squibb reported on these conditions in the *American Journal of the Medical Sciences*. Such outspokenness became a hallmark of Squibb's career as a doctor and pharmacist. Also in 1851 Squibb convinced the navy to assign him to the Brooklyn Naval Hospital, where he set up a laboratory for the production of pharmaceuticals. He pioneered in anesthesia by developing a new way to distill ether. Squibb did not patent his process, however, because he believed that scientific knowledge should be available to all who were interested. Squibb married Caroline Cook in 1852; they had four children, three of whom survived infancy.

In 1857, after the navy refused him an increase in pay, Squibb left to become a partner in the Louisville Chemical Works. One year later he returned to Brooklyn, where he established a company to produce pharmaceuticals for the army. Tragedy struck in December 1858, when an employee accidentally set fire to Squibb's laboratory. In an attempt to save his papers from the fire, Squibb suffered disfiguring burns on his face and hands. Fortunately, friends and associates lent the promising young entrepreneur the funds needed to rebuild. His backers hoped that Squibb's drugs would supplant the "patent medicines" sold by unscrupulous manufacturers (these companies secured patents on their bottle designs, not the medicine itself, which frequently contained impurities and intoxicants, including opium).

The Civil War produced profits for Squibb's fledgling company. Military orders soared, and by the end of 1861 he had paid off his creditors. Meanwhile, Squibb continued to publish in leading scientific journals. He sat on the Committee for the Revision of the U.S. Pharmacopoeia, the reference work used by physicians and pharmacists to determine the safety and reliability of drugs. He succeeded in eliminating some of the impure drugs that had previously been listed in the pharmacopoeia. He tried unsuccessfully to convince the American Pharmaceutical Society and the American Medical Association (AMA) to campaign for stricter government regulation of the drug trade.

In the postwar years Squibb came close to financial ruin. Soon after completing construction of a large factory, the war ended and military orders for his supplies vanished. A general business depression affected his civilian sales. Difficulties in business did not distract Squibb from his reform efforts. He wrote articles on the dangers of patent medicines and helped customs officials detect unsafe imports. Occasionally his zealous campaign to eliminate impurities from the drug trade led him into conflict with some of the nation's largest pharmaceutical companies.

Disaster struck again in 1871, when fire destroyed one level of his laboratory. Despite this setback, business had revived enough so that Squibb could invest in a new enterprise, the National Chemical Wood Treatment Company. Here Squibb developed processes to distill acids, alcohol, and other chemical products from wood.

During the 1870s Squibb continued to spearhead the movement for pure drugs. He tried unsuccessfully to have the AMA take away control of the pharmacopoeia from the Pharmacopoeia Convention, a body of pharmacists that included patent-medicine manufacturers. In 1879 he led a successful drive for passage of a pure food and drug bill in New York. Two years later, an almost identical bill appeared in Congress but was defeated by a lobby of patent-medicine companies.

The 1880s brought unprecedented prosperity to Squibb's enterprises. The chemical wood company posted record profits while Squibb pharmaceuticals found their way into markets all over the world. The popularity of Squibb products drew fraudulent imitators, but Squibb still refused to secure a patent for his medicines, in part because he hoped to avoid any association with the patent-medicine trade. For the same reason Squibb opposed advertising, instead letting favorable word-of-mouth sell his pills and powders. Beginning in 1882 he published *An Ephemeris of the Materia Medica, Pharmacy, Therapeutics, and Collateral Information*, in which he reported the results of his consumer research, discussed the latest discoveries in pharmaceutical science, and attacked patent-medicine charlatans.

In 1892 Squibb's company became E. R. Squibb & Sons, as his two sons became partners. By this time Squibb's estate was valued at one-half million dollars. Although he announced his retirement, Squibb remained active in his laboratory and continued to edit *An Ephemeris*. Eight years later he died in his New York City home.

After his death, Squibb's business continued to grow. His sons sold the company to outside investors, who retained the family name. By 1957 E. R. Squibb & Sons employed 40,000 people and had earnings of three-quarter billion dollars. Squibb also left a legacy of reform that culminated with congressional passage of the Pure Food and Drug Act (1906), a law secured through the efforts of Dr. Harvey W. Wiley, one of Squibb's younger associates in the American Chemical Society. Thus Squibb the reform-minded scientist paved the way for government regulation of the industry he helped to build.

For additional information on Squibb's multifaceted career see *The Collected Papers of Edward Robinson Squibb, M.D., 1819–1900* (1988), a two-volume set that contains most of Squibb's journals, articles, and papers he presented at conferences. Note, however, that with the exception of two articles, this set does not contain material from *An Ephemeris*, which is available in many large university libraries. Squibb's early diary entries have been published in another two-volume work, *The Journal of Edward Robinson Squibb* (1930), which also includes a list of his published writings. For a full-length biography of Squibb, see Lawrence G. Blochman, *Doctor Squibb: The Life and Times of a Rugged Idealist* (1958). Squibb receives shorter treatment in William A. McGarry, *The Story of the House of Squibb* (1931); "Billion Dollar By-Product" in *The 50 Great Pioneers of American Industry*, comp. editors of *News Front* (1964), pp. 38–41; and Frederick J. Wulling, "Edward Robinson Squibb," chapter 2 in *Samuel W. Melendy Memorial Lectures: 1–4* (1946). John S. Haller, Jr., discusses Squibb's efforts to promote accurate prescription writing in "With a Spoonful of Sugar: The Art of Prescription Writing in the Late 19th and Early 20th Century," *Pharmacy in History* 26 (1984): 171–78. An obituary is in the *Brooklyn Daily Eagle*, 26 Oct. 1900.

JONATHAN J. BEAN

SQUIER, Ephraim George (17 June 1821–17 Apr. 1888), journalist and archaeologist, was born at Bethlehem, New York, the son of Joel Squier, a Methodist circuit rider, and Catherine Kilmer, who died when he was twelve. Because of his itinerant father's modest means, Ephraim had little formal education. He attended the Troy Conference Academy in West Poutney, Vermont, from 1836 to 1839.

In 1840 Squier tried his hand at poetry, launching the *Literary Pearl and Village Messenger* at Charlton, New York. The failure of the *Pearl* led him to move to Albany in 1841. There he founded the short-lived *Poet's Magazine* in 1842, of which only two numbers appeared. More important, Squier became an assistant editor of the *New York State Mechanic* (1841–1843), a publication devoted to the interests of laborers and the elimination of the system of state prison labor contracts. Squier also coauthored at least one of the reports of the New York State Mechanics' Association on the use of state prison labor and played a significant role in organizing local mechanics societies for political action. Squier's budding literary ambitions led him to edit George Tradescent Lay's *The Chinese As They Are* (1843).

Moving from social causes to politics, Squier became coeditor of the *Hartford* (Conn.) *Journal*. The partisan character of the *Journal* was made clear in its first number in November 1844: "Henry Clay, our first, last, and only choice." As coeditor, Squier entered into campaign journalism with an abandon that outraged his political opponents. He played an active role in organizing Clay Clubs, and he promoted political rallies throughout Connecticut. Squier's measures in the contest were considered instrumental in achieving a Whig victory in Connecticut. However, Clay's national defeat left Squier crestfallen.

Squier left Hartford after the election and sought his fortunes in Chillicothe, Ohio, as editor of the *Scioto Gazette*, but he devoted most of his time to his new-found interest: the prehistoric Indian mounds and earthworks of the Scioto Valley. In association with Edwin Hamilton Davis, from 1845 to 1847 he excavated two hundred mounds and surveyed roughly one hundred earthworks in Ohio. The results of these investigations were published by the newly established Smithsonian Institution as *Ancient Monuments of the Mississippi Valley* (1848), the first volume of the Smithsonian's *Contributions to Knowledge*. Squier and Davis's work was the first systematic survey of American antiquities.

Squier continued his archaeological investigations into the western counties of New York in the autumn and winter of 1848, under the joint auspices of the New-York Historical Society and the Smithsonian. The results of his fieldwork later appeared in *Aboriginal Monuments of the State of New York* (1851), which formed part of the second volume of the Smithsonian's *Contributions to Knowledge*.

Following the Whig presidential victory in 1848, Squier ardently sought a diplomatic appointment to Central America as the means to continue his archaeological research in that region. His application was supported by William Hickling Prescott and many other well-educated citizens. Squier became the first diplomatic appointee of the Zachary Taylor administration in April 1849, serving as chargé d'affaires to the Central American states. During his tenure, he negotiated commercial treaties with San Salvador, Honduras, and Nicaragua, and he was authorized to sign an agreement with Nicaragua for the construction of an interoceanic canal. Despite the failure of the Senate to ratify this agreement, deliberations on the issue strained Anglo-American relations, resulting in the Clayton-Bulwer Treaty. Squier's diplomatic duties left little time for research, but he did conduct two archaeological expeditions and made numerous ethnological observations of the region's peoples. Squier unearthed several stone idols that he deposited in the Smithsonian.

After returning to the United States in 1851, Squier completed work on the *The Serpent Symbol and the Reciprocal Principles of Nature* (1851) and published his two-volume *Nicaragua: Its People, Scenery, Monuments, and Proposed Interoceanic Canal* (1852). The publication of those works and Squier's earlier Smithsonian monographs established him as the leading authority on American antiquities and matters relating to Central America. It was then that he made his first tour of Europe, where he was feted and introduced to the principal ethnological and geographical societies of England, France, and Germany. He received a medal of recognition in 1856 from the Geographical Society of France for his Central America research and was elected an associate of the National Society of Antiquarians of France. That honor had previously been bestowed upon only one other American, Edward Everett.

Squier returned to Central America in 1853 as secretary and principal promoter of the Honduras Inter-

Oceanic Railway Company. With a corps of engineers, he made a preliminary survey of its projected route, negotiated the necessary concessions from Honduras, and organized at New York a company for implementing the project. Squier later returned to Europe to obtain the cooperation of English and French investors, along with guarantees of support from their respective governments. The final survey of the proposed railway was also conducted under Squier's direction, but the venture was never realized.

Squier's interest in Central America never faded. He promoted the American "rediscovery" of Central America occasioned by the acquisition of Oregon and California and championed its strategic importance for interoceanic communication. His scheme for immigration to Central America, its commercial development, and its political alignment with the United States were calculated to promote his own entrepreneurial interests as secretary of the Honduras railway company. Nonetheless, his writings on Central American antiquities, aboriginal peoples, geography, politics, economic productions, and commercial potential were significant contributions to knowledge. His *Notes on Central America* (1855) was followed by *Waikna, or Adventures on the Mosquito Shore* (1855), a romantic and largely autobiographical novel about the Mosquito Coast of Nicaragua, written under the pseudonym Samuel A. Bard. *The States of Central America* (1858) and *Monograph of Authors Who Have Written on the Languages of Central America* (1861) further attest to his lasting interest in the region.

Squier became increasingly involved with other matters after the failure of his railway scheme. His life took a decidedly different turn after his marriage to Miriam Florence Folline of New Orleans in 1857; they had no children. Thereafter Squier was busily engaged as chief editor of Frank Leslie's New York publishing firm and a member of New York's smart set.

In spite of his many undertakings, Squier was first and last a journalist. As editor of *Frank Leslie's Illustrated Newspaper*, he also wrote on myriad subjects other than archaeology, and he edited two volumes of *Frank Leslie's Pictorial History of the American Civil War* (1861–1862). Squier's association with Leslie was interrupted when he became a U.S. Claims Commissioner to Peru from 1863 to 1865. The primary reason he accepted that diplomatic appointment was to study Peruvian antiquities; most of his time there was spent surveying and photographing archaeological sites, much of it at his own expense.

Squier resumed his journalistic association with Leslie in 1865 and began preparing to publish his investigations. His progress in that work was slowed, however, by many other activities. He became consul general of Honduras at New York City in 1868. He also continued to pursue his archaeological and ethnological interests as the founder and president of the short-lived Anthropological Institute of New York in 1871.

Squier continued his association with Leslie and his archaeological and ethnological research until his divorce in 1873. When his ex-wife married Leslie a year later, Squier suffered a mental breakdown. His mental disorder remained for the rest of his life, limiting his once-inexhaustible capacity for research and writing. But with the assistance of his step-brother and keeper, Frank, he was able to oversee the completion of his long-awaited *Peru: Incidents and Explorations in the Land of the Incas* (1877). A much briefer volume, *Honduras and British Honduras* (1880), was his last. He died at his brother's home in Brooklyn.

Squier was credited with a cheerful disposition, an active intellect, and a ready wit. Driven by ambition, he possessed a talent to turn most situations to his advantage. He possessed far-ranging interests and his originality in research and writing broadened his accomplishments. Many of the greater and lesser scientific, literary, and political lights of nineteenth-century America passed through the ever-changing kaleidoscope of his career.

• An extensive collection of Squier's correspondence and manuscripts was deposited in the Library of Congress in 1908 by Frank Squier, Ephraim's younger step-brother and executor. The second largest collection of Squier correspondence, held by the New-York Historical Society, includes the Squier Family Papers. Other important collections of Squier letters and manuscript materials are located at the Huntington Library, San Marino, Calif.; the Western Reserve Historical Society in Cleveland; the Library of the Indiana Historical Society, Indianapolis; the Clements Library at the University of Michigan, Ann Arbor; and the Middle American Research Institute at Tulane University, New Orleans. Squier correspondence can also be found in the Smithsonian Institution Archives; the John Russell Bartlett Papers at the John Carter Brown Library, Providence, R.I.; the Samuel F. Haven Papers at the American Antiquarian Society, Worcester, Mass.; the Samuel George Morton Papers at the Historical Society of Pennsylvania; the Charles Eliot Norton Papers at the Houghton Library, Harvard University; and letters to Francis Parkman in the Massachusetts Historical Society.

Relevant secondary sources include Robert E. Bieder, *Science Encounters the Indian, 1820–1880: The Early Years of American Ethnology* (1986); William Stanton, *The Leopard's Spots: Scientific Attitudes toward Race in America, 1815–59* (1960); Thomas G. Tax, "E. George Squier and the Mounds, 1845–1850," in *Toward a Science of Man: Essays in the History of Anthropology*, ed. Timothy H. H. Thoresen (1975). An obituary is in the *New York Times*, 18 Apr. 1888.

TERRY A. BARNHART

SQUIER, George Owen (21 Mar. 1865–24 Mar. 1934), soldier and electrical engineer, was born in Dryden, Michigan, the son of Almon Justice Squier and Emily Gardner, occupations unknown. The family split up after his mother's death when Squier was seven. He went to live with his grandfather, while his only sister Mary was sent to live with family friends. Squier never married, and he remained devoted to his sister throughout his life. He won admission to West Point by competitive examination and graduated in 1887, seventh in his class (first in merit of discipline), with a commission in the Artillery Corps.

Assigned to Fort McHenry in Baltimore, Squier enrolled in the electrical engineering department at the

Johns Hopkins University with the conviction, as he later put it, that "military supremacy must be looked for primarily in the weapons and agencies provided by scientists and engineers" (Clark, 1974, p. 295). Despite resistance from conservative military superiors, he worked out a special arrangement with the secretary of war allowing him to pursue full-time graduate study at the university while fulfilling his military obligations on weekends and in the summers. With the completion, in 1892, of his doctoral thesis on the electrochemical effects of magnetization, supervised by distinguished physicist Henry Rowland, Squier became the first American army officer to earn an advanced technical degree (in physics in 1893). The next year he attended the International Electrical Congress at the World's Columbian Exposition in Chicago as an official U.S. Army representative and made important contacts there among leading European electrical engineers.

Detailed to Fort Monroe, Virginia, in 1894, Squier put his newly acquired scientific theory into practice. He set up an electrical engineering laboratory for the Artillery Corps. In collaboration with Albert Crehore, a Dartmouth College physicist he had met in graduate school, Squier invented electrical instruments for range finding and for studying high-speed projectiles. He also experimented with submarine telegraphy. He and Crehore took out several telegraphy patents (Squier eventually held sixty-five patents) and in 1899 cofounded the Crehore-Squier Intelligence Transmission Company to exploit these ideas commercially. Squier's telegraphic research brought him to the attention of Chief Signal Officer Adolphus Greely, who reassigned Squier to the Signal Corps during the Spanish-American War and later to cable-laying duty in the Philippines. Squier laid out and operated a network of thirty submarine telegraph cables from 1900 to 1903, gaining Squier an invaluable education in the military advantages of electrical communications.

Returning to the United States as a captain, Squier continued his electrical research, first as chief signal officer for the California district and later as head of the new Army Signal School at Fort Leavenworth, Kansas, where he climbed the ranks to major. In 1908 the Signal Corps, with a growing appreciation for the military significance of modern communication, appropriated $30,000 (ten times the entire Signal Corps budget on the eve of the Spanish-American War) for a new radiotelephony laboratory at the Bureau of Standards in Washington, D.C., and put Squier in charge. There he developed a new technique for transmitting radio signals by cable—"wired wireless," he called it—with important commercial (for multiplexing voice messages) and military (for secure communications) applications. He dedicated the invention to the public, a decision he would later regret.

Squier's career took a crucial turn in 1912 when he was appointed military attaché to the United States embassy in London, with orders to survey European military advances and assess their significance for American preparedness. The British high command, seeking to influence U.S. neutrality, gave Squier full access to its forces and arranged three exclusive tours of the front lines. What particularly impressed Squier was the role of combat aircraft. Squier had long been an advocate of air power. After promotion to assistant chief signal officer for the whole corps., he had supervised the first army trials of the Wright brothers airplane in 1908 and immediately appreciated its potential military implications. At a time when most professional soldiers still considered the airplane a curiosity, Squier was writing popular articles on the "Advantages of Aerial Craft in Military Warfare" and "What Mechanical Flight Means to the Army" (both 1908). As attaché, he compiled an influential secret report on allied military aviation.

In early 1917 Squier was promoted to chief signal officer (with the rank of brigadier general) and given responsibility for all army aviation and communication. Despite Squier's earlier advocacy, U.S. military aviation had fallen desperately far behind its European rivals, having only twenty-three trained pilots and fifty-five combat aircraft, most of them obsolete. In an attempt to catch up, Squier pushed through Congress a $640 million military aircraft procurement package, the largest single appropriations bill passed up to that point. Convinced that the key to success would be selecting a foreign aircraft design, modifying it appropriately, and then mass producing it with assembly-line techniques, Squier turned to automotive executives (thought to know the secrets of mass production) rather than to experienced aircraft designers. He and his "dollar a year" experts learned the hard way that making combat aircraft was considerably more difficult than making cars and never came close to achieving their stated production goals. Squier's failure to meet some admittedly unrealistic expectations led to several official investigations and ultimately to the creation, in April 1918, of a separate division of military aeronautics under another general.

Squier had better luck with his other wartime aeronautics projects. He oversaw the design and production of the famous Liberty Engine, a standardized aircraft powerplant that took better advantage of American automotive know-how. He also underwrote two of the most venturesome secret weapons programs of the war, Charles Kettering's Liberty Eagle, a self-guided aerial torpedo (or primitive cruise missile), and Robert Goddard's rockets. Neither saw action in World War I, but each anticipated deadly wonder weapons of the future.

Perhaps Squier's most important wartime legacy was making a place for science in the modern army. As chief signal officer he established the army's Radio Laboratories at Camp Alfred Vail (later Fort Monmouth, N.J.) in 1918. Renamed the Squier Signal Laboratory in 1935, this facility became the army's major center for defense electronics research and development. As the army's representative from 1916 to 1918 on the National Advisory Committee for Aeronautics (NACA), formed in 1915, Squier also played a key role in founding the Langley Aeronautical Laboratory in Langley, Virginia. It became the NACA's central aeronautics research facility in the postwar years, with close ties to army aviation. Realizing that research and development was just beginning, Squier worked closely with the corporate contractors who had to build military communications and aviation systems, often commissioning top industrial scientists and engineers as army officers to smooth the transition from laboratory to shop floor.

Squier retired in 1923 at the rank of major general. He spent his last years fighting AT&T over infringement on the "wired wireless" patents he had earlier dedicated to the public. He lost in court, but the case led to important reforms protecting the patent rights of federal employees. He received a number of professional awards and honors, including membership in the National Academy of Sciences and the Franklin Medal (1919). For his wartime achievements he was made a Knight Commander of the Order of Saint Michael and Saint George by Great Britain, Commander of the Legion of Honor by France, and Commander of the Order of the Crown by Italy (all 1919). Squier died in Washington, D.C.

Squier recognized, well before most of his army colleagues, that science and engineering would drastically change modern warfare. He dedicated his career to helping the U.S. Army exploit advanced technology, especially in communications and aviation, both through his own research and through the research of the laboratories he organized. He was among the first in the cadre of technically trained officers who would forge the modern military-industrial complex and in the process make the U.S. military virtually synonymous with high technology.

• Squier's papers are held by the National Archives (Office of the Chief Signal Officer, Record Group 111; Adjutant General Officer File, Record Group 94; Chief of Staff File, Record Group 165; National Advisory Committee for Aeronautics File, Record Group 255; National Bureau of Standards File, Record Group 167); the U.S. Air Force Academy Special Collections, Colorado Springs, Col.; the U.S. Army Historical Research Collection, U.S. Army War College, Carlisle, Pa.; the Army Signal Corps Museum, Fort Monmouth, N.J.; and the Historical Society of Michigan, Ann Arbor. The best biographical study is Paul Wilson Clark, "Major General George Owen Squier: Military Scientist" (Ph.D. diss., Case Western Reserve Univ., 1974), which includes a complete bibliography of Squier's writings and a list of archival sources. See also Clark, "Early Impacts of Communications on Military Doctrine," *Proceedings of the IEEE* (Sept. 1976): 1407–13, for an assessment of Squier's impact on military command and control technologies. Arthur E. Kennelly, "George Owen Squier," *National Academy of Sciences, Biographical Memoirs* 20 (1938): 151–59, provides a complete list of Squier's patents. Obituaries are in the *New York Times*, 25 Mar. 1934, and *Science*, 25 May 1934.

STUART W. LESLIE

STACY, Jess Alexandria (11 Aug. 1904–1 July 1995), jazz pianist, was born in Bird's Point, Missouri, the son of Fred Stacy, a railroad engineer, and Sarah Alexander. When he was ten the family moved to Malden, Missouri. Stacy's upbringing included some formal piano lessons, but his talent developed mainly from a self-taught reliance on his extraordinary ear. After graduating from high school in June 1920, he worked in riverboat bands, playing piano and calliope.

In 1924 Stacy married Helen Robinson; they had one child. He worked mainly in Chicago, Illinois, over the next decade, playing in obscure bands, including that of Floyd Towne, whose Midway Gardens Band included cornetist Muggsy Spanier and clarinetist Frank Teschemacher. In 1927 his marriage ended in divorce.

Stacy jumped to fame in July 1935 as a member of Benny Goodman's orchestra, though his relationship with the leader was always testy. Blues choruses near the start of "One O'Clock Jump" and a fleeting moment near the opening of "Topsy" (both recorded in 1938) are among his occasional brief solos with this big band; the sensational exception is a sensitive, beautifully constructed, lengthy solo in the midst of the otherwise bombastic rendition of "Sing Sing Sing," recorded at Goodman's Carnegie Hall concert of January 1938 in New York City. In March 1939 Stacy took over Teddy Wilson's role in Goodman's small group and thus had an opportunity to express himself as an improviser, but two months later Goodman hired Fletcher Henderson not only to continue supplying his magnificent arrangements to the big band, but also to play piano, even though his talents in this area were vastly inferior to Stacy's. Stacy quit Goodman in July 1939.

During this period he was featured on many recordings apart from Goodman. These include "Stomp" and "On the Sunny Side of the Street" (both 1937), among several sessions with vibraphonist Lionel Hampton; "Life Goes to a Party" (also 1937) from dates with trumpeter Harry James; "Beat to the Socks," "Carnegie Drag," and "Carnegie Jump" from the first and probably the finest of many sessions with guitarist and banjoist Eddie Condon; a number of titles with saxophonist Bud Freeman; and many solo recordings, including 78 RPM pairings of "In the Dark" and "Flashes" (1935) and "Candlelights" and "Ain't Goin' Nowhere" (1939).

In contrast to his service with Goodman, Stacy was much featured during his years with Bob Crosby's big band from September 1939 through 1942. He may also be heard as a soloist with the Bob Cats, Crosby's eight-piece band-within-the-band, on numerous titles, including "Spain" (1940) and "That Da Da Strain" (1942).

Stacy rejoined Goodman in December 1942. Near the start of this second engagement he served as accompanist to a guest singer, Frank Sinatra, who had just left Tommy Dorsey's band. This time Stacy was featured with Goodman's quartet and orchestra, both on record and in the movie *Sweet and Lowdown* (1944). He remained with Goodman until the leader disbanded in March of that year.

From December 1944 to June 1945 Stacy played a background role in trombonist Tommy Dorsey's "Big

Bertha" orchestra (as Stacy called it), including string sections of various sizes. Having married singer Lee Wiley in June 1943, he led his own big band, in which she was featured, from July 1945 to May 1946. They divorced in 1947. After working for three months with trumpeter Billy Butterfield's band at Nick's club in New York (some sources place this engagement in 1948 rather than 1946), Stacy returned for one last time to Goodman's band (November 1946 to mid-March 1947).

Stacy participated in a jam session in the movie *Sarge Goes to College* (1947). In California from May 1947 through February or April 1948 he once again attempted to lead a big band but failed. He married Patricia Peck in 1950. From the late 1940s to the early 1960s he played in piano bars, though he did appear with Crosby's Bob Cats again in several soundies (film shorts for video jukeboxes), including "March of the Bobcats," "Muskrat Ramble," "Panama," and "Who's Sorry Now?" (1951), and he was reunited with Goodman for performances in December 1959 and January 1960.

Finally Stacy could no longer stand the sleazy clubs in which he was working, and he left music to work as a mail clerk for Max Factor until he reached age sixty-five and retired. He performed at the Newport Jazz Festival at Carnegie Hall in New York City in early July 1974 and the following day recorded a solo album, *Stacy Still Swings*. He played at the Dixieland Jubilee in Sacramento, California, in 1974 and 1975 (or 1975 and 1976; accounts differ). His final performance was for the New Jersey Swing Club in 1979. He died in Los Angeles, California.

In published interviews Stacy came across as a delightfully perceptive and forthright man. He explained that he remained with Goodman not only because of the career opportunity it afforded, but also because it was so much fun to play with that first great Goodman band, despite his limited role in it and the leader's typically inconsiderate behavior. He belongs to a substantial group of players whom Goodman clashed with but could not do without. Hence, his subsequent returns to the fold, even after facing the indignity of being offered minimum union scale to recreate the "Sing, Sing, Sing" solo for *The Benny Goodman Story* during its filming in 1955; in this instance Stacy refused and walked off the set.

Stacy was an exceptionally talented, eclectic jazz pianist whose style is not easily summarized, ranging as it does from the audacious, bouyant, thick, two-handed contrapuntal playing heard on Hampton's "Stomp," where his approach recalls that of Earl Hines, to the spare and original motivic work heard on Condon's "Carnegie Jump," where Count Basie rather than Hines might come to mind. Many listeners feel that Stacy's contribution to the "live" version of "Sing, Sing, Sing" ranks among the greatest recorded jazz piano solos.

• Keith Keller gives a casual, loving account in *Oh, Jess!: A Jazz Life: The Jess Stacy Story* (1989); appendices offer a list of films and an exhaustive catalog of recordings. Complementing this book are essential surveys by Whitney Balliett, "Back from Valhalla," in *Improvising: Sixteen Jazz Musicians and Their Art* (1977); repr. in Balliett, *American Musicians: Fifty-six Portraits in Jazz* (1986). See also Bob Rusch, "Jess Stacy: Interview," *Cadence* 12 (May 1986): 8–19. Other useful sources include Richard Hadlock, "The Chicagoans," in *Jazz Masters of the Twenties* (1965; repr. 1985); Leonard Feather, "Piano Giants of Jazz: Jess Stacy," *Contemporary Keyboard* 5 (Mar. 1979): 68–69; John Chilton, *Stomp Off, Let's Go!: The Story of Bob Crosby's Bob Cats & Big Band* (1983); Derek Coller, "Jess Stacy: The Recent Past," *Mississippi Rag* 11 (July 1984): 16; Lowell D. Holmes and John W. Thomson, *Jazz Greats: Getting Better with Age* (1986); and D. Russell Connor, *Benny Goodman: Listen to His Legacy* (1988). An obituary is in the *New York Times*, 4 Jan. 1995.

BARRY KERNFELD

STADLER, Lewis John (6 July 1896–12 May 1954), geneticist, was born in St. Louis, Missouri, the son of Henry Louis Stadler, a banker, and Josephine Ehrman. The family strongly encouraged intellectual and cultural activities, but young Stadler had a lackluster academic record. He completed his primary and secondary school education in St. Louis, becoming interested in agriculture as a result of two summer vacations spent on farms. In 1913 he began to study agriculture at the University of Missouri, but he transferred to the University of Florida in 1915 when he decided to engage in citrus research. He received his B.S. in agriculture in 1917 and returned to the University of Missouri to begin graduate work in the department of field crops. Having earned an A.M. in 1918, Stadler then enlisted in the Field Artillery of the U.S. Army, where he was commissioned as a second lieutenant. The war ended before he was able to take overseas duty. Stadler returned to Missouri but left in 1919 to study biometry with H. H. Love and R. A. Emerson at Cornell University. Also in 1919 he married Cornelia Tuckerman; they had six children.

Despite his later prominence, Stadler's early career was erratic. At Cornell he failed to demonstrate the necessary talent for advanced graduate research and was discouraged from remaining in the graduate program, especially by Emerson. After a disappointing year he returned to the University of Missouri to continue his graduate research. He was to hold a lifelong affiliation with the school. He accepted an appointment as assistant in field crops in 1919 and became instructor in 1920. In 1921 he was promoted to assistant professor, finally earning his Ph.D. in field crops in 1922 on the basis of his agronomic research leading to the improvement of wheat yields. In 1925 he was promoted to associate professor and in 1937 to full professor.

The major intellectual stimulus in Stadler's career was his reading of Thomas Hunt Morgan's book, *The Physical Basis of Heredity* in 1920. Stadler was inspired to turn to genetics research. His first paper reflecting a genetics approach was "Variation in Linkage in Maize" (*American Naturalist* [1925]). Following this, Stadler embarked on a distinguished career as a geneticist, earning an international reputation as an expert on gene mutations and plant genetics. He spent the 1925–1926 year studying with the noted plant geneticist Edward Murray East at the Bussey Institution of Harvard University, doing so well that East subsequently claimed him as one of his own students.

During his long tenure with the University of Missouri Stadler helped create a successful center for agricultural genetics research. Although his career did not include extensive teaching, he inspired younger researchers to turn to questions of agricultural genetics. His international reputation attracted numerous research fellows to Missouri who followed his advice, especially on planning and executing critical genetics experiments.

Much of Stadler's mature research focused on the mutagenic effects of different forms of radiation, especially on economically important plants like maize and barley. Independently of geneticist H. J. Muller, Stadler began to study the mutagenic effects of X-rays on the germinal material in plants. In 1927, before the American Association for the Advancement of Science, Stadler confirmed Muller's report that had appeared only a few months earlier stating that X-rays could have mutagenic effects in *Drosophila*; Stadler's data was on the effects of ionizing radiation in barley and maize. He received some recognition for independently deriving similar conclusions at the same time as Muller, and the two became lifelong collaborators.

Stadler's subsequent research explored the different kinds of mutagenic effects induced by radiation and determined the extent to which the same kinds of effects occurred naturally in species like maize. Following large-scale experiments recognized by co-workers for their elegant design, Stadler concluded that irradiation with X-rays did not induce the kinds of mutations seen to arise spontaneously in maize. Instead, the effects of radiation were extragenic in nature. Stadler's mutagenic studies were extended to include the effects of ultraviolet (UV) radiation. In species like maize, he found that mutations induced with UV radiation were sometimes indistinguishable from naturally induced mutations. From other experiments, he was able to determine that UV radiation was effective in producing mutations at wavelengths usually absorbed by nucleic acids, pointing to the importance of nucleic acids in genetics well before these were recognized as hereditary material. In his later years, he turned to questions of evolution by focusing on the fate of mutations at specific gene loci in maize to determine if the mutagenic effects of X-rays could account for the kinds of mutations leading to evolutionarily significant changes. Following detailed long-term studies, he concluded that X-rays did not lead to the kinds of evolutionary changes that were due to true or subliminal changes that occurred naturally. Many of these studies were still in progress at the time of his death.

Though this work led Stadler to a distinguished and influential career, he produced only sixty-five publications. Nonetheless, his papers were hailed for their precision, logical presentation, and clarity of style. His experiments were so well designed that they rarely gave ambiguous results and proved highly influential on genetics research. Stadler was an acute critic who could ask probing, fundamental questions that would facilitate the execution of experiments.

Stadler was also a sociopolitical activist. In the 1930s he helped to assist European refugees fleeing from fascist regimes. He was a member of the American Committee to Save Anti-Fascist Refugees and the American Committee for Democracy and Intellectual Freedom. Working closely with the Rockefeller Foundation and the New School for Social Research, Stadler led efforts to bring refugee Emil Heitz to the United States from Europe. Stadler's political activism in the 1930s led to turbulence for him in the late 1940s, when his loyalty was called into question following the denial of a U.S. passport in 1948 to attend the Eighth International Congress of Genetics in Stockholm, Sweden. Ironically, it was the U.S. Department of Agriculture that had been responsible for denying him permission to travel. Stadler subsequently devoted significant energy and personal resources to clear himself of the charges.

Despite these troubles, Stadler held many administrative positions and received numerous academic honors. He was a member of the National Academy of Science, the American Philosophical Society, and the American Academy of Arts and Sciences. He became president of scientific societies, including the Genetics Society of America (1938), the American Society of Naturalists (1953), the American Association of University Professors (1932), and Sigma Xi (1953). He served on the Scientific Advisory Committee of the Selective Service System during World War II. He took short leaves from Missouri for year-long visits to Harvard and Cornell; he also visited Yale University and the California Institute of Technology for shorter intervals.

Stadler was especially known for his breadth of interests, which included cultural and intellectual activities involving literature and the arts. He was an articulate individual who gave engaging lectures and had a much-appreciated sense of humor. Colleagues frequently commented on his poise and calm, dignified demeanor. He died as a result of surgery in St. Louis, Missouri.

• Stadler's correspondence, notes, and manuscripts in the Western Historical Manuscripts Collection under the joint auspices of the University of Missouri, Columbia, and the State Historical Society. His published works include "Genetic Effects of X-Rays in Maize," *Proceedings of the National Academy of Sciences* 14 (1928): 69–75, and, with C. F. Swanson, "The Genetic Effects of Ultra-violet Radiations," in *Radiation Biology*, vol. 2, ed. A. Hollaender (1954). For biographical sketches see M. M. Rhoades, "Lewis John Stadler," *Genetics* 41 (1956): 1–3, and M. M. Rhoades, "Lewis John Stadler," National Academy of Sciences, *Biographical Memoirs* 30 (1957): 329–47.

VASSILIKI BETTY SMOCOVITIS

STAFFORD, Jean (1 July 1915–26 Mar. 1979), writer, was born in Covina, California, the daughter of John Richard Stafford and Mary Ethel McKillop. At the time of Stafford's birth, her father, an unsuccessful writer of westerns, was growing walnuts on land he had purchased in Covina, California, with money left to him by his father, a successful Texas cattle rancher. When Stafford was five, her father moved the family to San Diego, where he rapidly proceeded to lose the bulk of his inherited fortune on the stock exchange. The impoverished family then resettled first in Colorado Springs and soon afterward in Boulder, Colorado, the university town in the Rocky Mountains that Stafford called "Adams" in a number of her short stories. During the years when Stafford was attending public school and then the University of Colorado, her mother supported the family by operating a boardinghouse for female university students, while Stafford's misanthropic father worked sporadically on unpublishable manuscripts. Although Stafford felt marginal both within her own family and at the university, she excelled as a student, graduating with a B.A. and M.A. in 1936. Her college years were marked, however, by poverty as well as by the tragic suicide of her friend Lucy McKee Cooke, who shot herself in Stafford's presence.

A fellowship from the University of Heidelberg enabled Stafford to study philology abroad following her graduation. Describing her eagerness to leave behind her "tamed-down native grounds," she later wrote, "As soon as I could, I hotfooted it across the Rocky Mountains and across the Atlantic Ocean." Her stay in Germany during the time when Hitler's dictatorial powers were expanding provided her with material for several literary works, including her novella *A Winter's Tale* (1954).

Stafford returned from Europe in the spring of 1937 and took part in the Writer's Workshop in Boulder that summer. There she attracted the attention of poet/critic John Crowe Ransom and novelist Evelyn Scott, as well as the fledgling poet Robert Lowell. Following an unfulfilling year of teaching English at Stephens College in Missouri, Stafford briefly attended graduate school at the University of Iowa, but she soon fled to Cambridge, Massachusetts. She had been contemplating marriage to a Harvard graduate student of Chinese, James Robert Hightower, who had befriended her at the University of Colorado and who also was living in Heidelberg when they were students there. They never married, however, for by the time Stafford arrived in Cambridge, she already was infatuated with the brilliant, wealthy, but emotionally unstable Lowell. Despite being badly injured that autumn in a car accident that she blamed on Lowell's negligence and for which she subsequently sued him in order to pay her medical bills, she married Lowell in 1940 in New York City.

After a year in Baton Rouge, where Stafford worked as a secretary for the *Southern Review*, she and Lowell lived in New York, from which they departed to spend part of 1942–1943 with the writers Caroline Gordon and Allen Tate in Monteagle, Tennessee. When Lowell was jailed as a conscientious objector in 1943, Stafford rented an apartment in Black Rock, Connecticut, to be near him. During the year of Lowell's imprisonment, Stafford's female bildungsroman, *Boston Adventure*, was published. The novel, which critics compared to the novels of Marcel Proust and Henry James, was both a critical and commercial success. With the money she had earned from the book, Stafford purchased a house in Damariscotta Mills, Maine. She spent 1945–1946 refurbishing the house and working on her second novel, *The Mountain Lion*, a male-female double bildungsroman that many critics consider her finest literary achievement. Set in the West and written in the colloquial style of Mark Twain, the novel describes the coming of age of Ralph Fawcett and his troubled sister, Molly, who aspires to be a writer. By the time the novel was published, Stafford and Lowell had separated, and she had been admitted to Payne-Whitney Psychiatric Hospital in New York, where she would spend the better part of 1947–1948 being treated for depression and the alcoholism that would plague her for the remainder of her life.

A recipient of a Guggenheim Fellowship in 1948, the year that she divorced Lowell, Stafford rented an apartment in New York and worked on *In the Snowfall*, an autobiographical, never-to-be-completed novel about her friend's suicide; she also worked on the short stories that would be included in *Children Are Bored on Sunday* (1953). Already having begun to publish her beautifully crafted and psychologically penetrating short stories in *Partisan Review, Harper's, Sewanee Review*, and *Mademoiselle*, one of which, "The Hope Chest," received an O. Henry award in 1947, Stafford began a long and productive association with the *New Yorker* when "Children Are Bored on Sunday" was published in 1948. *New Yorker* editor Katharine S. White, to whom Stafford would later dedicate her *Collected Stories* (1969), not only became her mentor but a caring personal friend.

Stafford's short-lived second marriage, to *Life* editor Oliver Jensen in 1950, was terminated by Stafford in 1953, the year after her third novel, *The Catherine Wheel*, was published to mixed reviews. The novel combines the vernacular style of Twain and the elevated style of James. Describing a summer in Maine that Katharine Congreve and twelve-year-old Andrew Shipley spend together, the novel anatomizes the loss of innocence and the emotional turmoil of two character types that appear frequently in Stafford's fiction: a troubled adolescent and an introspective, disaffected older woman.

Stafford's third marriage, to *New Yorker* writer A. J. Liebling in 1959, brought her a modicum of personal happiness during a relatively unproductive period in her writing career. Following Liebling's death in 1963, Stafford settled into his house in the Springs, Long Island, where she supported herself by writing essays and book reviews. In 1966, after she had served as a Fellow at the Institute for Advanced Study of Wesleyan University, Stafford's *A Mother in History*, based on her interviews with the mother of John F. Kennedy's alleged assassin, Lee Harvey Oswald, was published. In 1970 Stafford received the Pulitzer Prize for fiction for her *Collected Stories* and was elected to the National Academy and Institute of Arts and Letters.

"Writing is agony but it also is life itself," Stafford told an interviewer in 1952. However, a stroke in 1976 virtually silenced the tongue and the pen of the witty, acerbic writer, whose work had been applauded for its ironic vision, lapidary style, psychological acumen, and sense of place. She died in White Plains, New York. At the time of her death, her long-awaited autobiographical novel, *The Parliament of Women*, remained unfinished. Stafford's novels and short stories, focusing primarily on the lives of female characters and often representing artful transmutations of her own experiences, are being discovered by a new generation of readers.

• The Collected Papers of Jean Stafford are in the Norlin Library, University of Colorado, Boulder. Her letters to Lowell are in the Houghton Library, Harvard University, and her letters to the author Peter Taylor are in the Vanderbilt University Library. For bibliographical material, see Wanda Avila, *Jean Stafford: A Comprehensive Bibliography* (1983). Biographies of Stafford include David Roberts, *Jean Stafford: A Biography* (1988); Charlotte Margolis Goodman, *Jean Stafford: The Savage Heart*, a feminist biography (1990); and Ann Hulbert, *The Interior Castle: The Art and Life of Jean Stafford* (1992). Critical studies include Mary Ellen Williams Walsh's *Jean Stafford* (Twayne 1985) and Maureen Ryan's *Innocence and Estrangement in the Fiction of Jean Stafford* (1987). Two articles dealing with *The Mountain Lion* are Blanche H. Gelfant's "Revolutionary Turnings: *The Mountain Lion* Reread" in her book, *Women Writing in America: Voices in Collage* (1984), and Charlotte Goodman, "The Lost Brother/the Twin: Women Novelists and the Male-Female Double Bildungsroman," *Novel: A Forum on Fiction* 17 (Fall 1983): 28–43.

CHARLOTTE GOODMAN

STAGER, Anson (20 Apr. 1825–26 Mar. 1885), telegraph pioneer, was born in Ontario County, New York, and raised in Rochester, New York. Information about his parents is sketchy. His father was probably Henry W. Stager, a prominent Rochester edgetool maker. His mother's identity is not known. Anson attended public schools in Rochester and at age sixteen was employed as a printer's devil by Henry O'Reilly of the Rochester *Daily Advertiser*. In 1846 O'Reilly built the first telegraph line between Philadelphia and Harrisburg and engaged Stager as an operator, first at Lancaster and Chambersburg and then at Pittsburgh as the lines were extended westward. By 1847 Stager, a self-taught telegraph operator, had achieved a reputation as the most skilled operator on the line and was appointed chief operator at Pittsburgh. That year he also married Rebecca Sprague of Buffalo; they had at least three children. The administrative skills he demonstrated at Pittsburgh led the following year to his appointment as chief operator of the Cincinnati office of the Pittsburgh, Cincinnati & Lou-

isville Telegraph Company. While at Cincinnati Stager made important improvements in the technical operation of the system. His major contribution was a method of operating a number of lines from a single battery, thus eliminating the costs of maintaining separate batteries for each line-wire. Between 1848 and 1850 Stager also served under Sears C. Walker of the U.S. Coast Survey, who developed a method of telegraphic determination of longitude.

In 1852 the Rochester-based directors of the newly formed New York and Mississippi Valley Printing Telegraph Company appointed Stager general superintendent of their lines; he continued to act in this capacity after the company was reorganized in 1854 and renamed Western Union Telegraph Company. Stager played a major role in Western Union's expansion into the states west of New York by working out a system of telegraphic coordination of railroad traffic that became standard on American roads. As the railroads adopted his system, Stager acquired exclusive rights-of-way and lines for Western Union, offering trained operators and priority service for railroad messages in exchange. Stager also made significant contributions to Western Union's administrative organization as the company grew to become the largest American company on the eve of the Civil War.

During the war Stager further demonstrated his administrative abilities as head of the Union military telegraph. Appointed superintendent of military telegraph lines in the West by General George B. McClellan (1826–1885), Stager was asked by Assistant Secretary of War Thomas A. Scott, whom he knew as superintendent of the Pennsylvania Railroad, to submit a plan for organizing the military telegraph system under a single manager. On 11 November 1861 Scott appointed Stager to this position with the rank of captain. In his 1865 annual report Stager noted that under his direction the military telegraph had greatly increased the mobility of the Union army through its efficient running of the military railroads and by accompanying the army into the field to provide communications in conjunction with the Signal Corps. Stager himself devised the telegraphic cipher system used by the military. When he retired from the military telegraph in 1866, Stager had achieved the rank of brigadier general.

Stager continued to serve as general superintendent of Western Union while heading the military telegraph, locating his headquarters at Cleveland in 1865. After the war he declined the general superintendency of the company, choosing instead to head the company's newly created Central Division. In 1878 Stager was also elected a Western Union vice president, but he resigned from the company in 1881. When Stager moved the headquarters of the Central Division from Cleveland to Chicago in 1869, he helped organize Western Electric Manufacturing Company and served as its president until 1884; this became a major manufacturing subsidiary for Western Union and later American Bell Telephone Company. In 1882 Stager also became president of Western Edison Electric

Light Company, a position he held until his death. Stager died in Chicago; three daughters survived him.

Anson Stager was an important figure in the early American telegraph industry. As superintendent of Western Union he was responsible for the company's expansion and its development of a nationwide network. In the process he helped create its system of railroad rights-of-way and its corporate organization. Although his role as superintendent of the Military Telegraph during the war created a conflict of interest that benefited Western Union, he further demonstrated his administrative ability by organizing an effective system of military telegraphs. Stager continued to be an important figure at Western Union for many years, but his later career is more notable for his activities as an entrepreneur within the electrical industry, as he founded Western Electric and Western Edison and built them into important companies.

• Letters and other documents by Stager are in National Archives Record Group 92, Records of the Office of the Quartermaster General, and Record Group 111, Records of the Office of the Chief Signal Officer; the John Dean Caton Papers, Library of Congress; and in Thomas E. Jeffrey et al., *Thomas A. Edison Papers: A Selective Microfilm Edition, Part II (1879–1886)* (1987). Information about Stager appears in William R. Plum, *The Military Telegraph during the Civil War in the United States* (3 vols., 1882); James D. Reid, *The Telegraph in America* (1879); Taliaferro P. Shaffner, *The Telegraph Manual* (1859); and Robert L. Thompson, *Wiring a Continent: The History of the Telegraph Industry in the United States 1832–1866* (1947). An obituary is in the *New York Times*, 23 Mar. 1885.

PAUL B. ISRAEL

STAGG, Amos Alonzo (16 Aug. 1862–17 Mar. 1965), intercollegiate football coach, was born in West Orange, New Jersey, the son of Amos L. Stagg, a shoemaker, and Eunice Pierson. During his high school years Lonnie, as he was called, decided he wanted to be a minister. When he graduated from high school he lacked the credits to attend Yale University, but he obtained a scholarship to the Phillips Exeter Academy, at which he excelled as a baseball player.

After graduating from Exeter and still determined to be a minister, Stagg entered Yale with the class of 1888. He played on the baseball team and pitched Yale to five consecutive "Big Three" championships, the competition being the annual rivalry between Harvard, Princeton, and Yale. Stagg also played football at Yale under the legendary Walter Camp. In 1889, his last year at Yale, he was named to Camp's first All-America team.

After receiving his B.A. Stagg began his studies at Yale Divinity School. (His instructor in biblical literature was William Rainey Harper.) But much to Stagg's disappointment he soon discovered that he was a poor speaker. He therefore abandoned the ministry and in 1890 decided to become a physical educator. He entered the Young Men's Christian Association (YMCA) Training School in Springfield, Massachusetts, as both a graduate student and a faculty member. He also coached the football and baseball teams and was a member of the group in Springfield that played the first game of basketball, the sport developed by his colleague James Naismith.

In 1892 Harper became president of the new University of Chicago and offered Stagg the position of associate professor and director of physical culture and athletics. Unlike many college presidents of the period, Harper felt that a winning football team would publicize the university. Stagg accepted the offer and thus became the first coach to be afforded academic status. (He was promoted to full professor in 1900.) Stagg married Stella Robertson of New York in 1894; they had three children.

Stagg coached football, as well as baseball and track, at the University of Chicago for forty years, until he was forced to retire at the age of seventy in 1932. His contributions to athletics in general and football in particular will probably never be matched. He was Chicago's faculty representative to the Big Ten for fifteen years and served on the first rules committee of the National Collegiate Athletic Association (NCAA). He was on every American Olympic committee from 1902 to 1932 and was a track coach for the 1924 Olympic team.

Stagg is unquestionably one of the great figures in the history of football. At Chicago he had 4 undefeated seasons and 7 Big Ten titles, won 255 games, and trained 11 All Americas. He was a prolific inventor of plays and a master strategist. His alleged innovations include the center snap, the man in motion, the onside kick, the T formation, the hidden ball trick, the place kick, the fake punt, the Statue of Liberty play, and various backfield shifts. He also designed the tackling dummy and was the first coach to have lights installed on the practice field. Moreover, he wrote the first book on football that used diagrams to outline plays. His other "firsts" include the implementation of wind sprints in practice, the use of hip pads in uniforms and numbers on players' jerseys, and the awarding of letters to outstanding performers. In addition, he designed troughs for the overflow of swimming pools and the indoor batting cage for baseball.

Stagg became a beloved legend at the University of Chicago. Early on the students began calling him "The Old Man" as a sign of affection. Later the adjective "Grand" was often added. In 1914, in response to a request by students and alumni, the trustees renamed the athletic field Stagg Field, thus making it the first field named in honor of a football coach.

Unwilling to retire from football after leaving Chicago, Stagg coached for the next fourteen years at the College of the Pacific in Stockton, California. He did so well there that in 1943 he was selected as Coach of the Year by his fellow coaches and Man of the Year by the Football Writers Association. In 1946 Stagg became assistant coach to his son Amos, Jr., at Susquehanna College in Pennsylvania. But after six years there his wife became ill, and the couple moved back to California because the warmer climate was better for her health. Nonetheless, Stagg kept on coaching, serving as the kicking coach at Stockton Junior College. He retired at the age of ninety-eight, after seventy-one years of coaching. His overall record was 314 wins, 181 losses, and 35 ties.

During his long career Stagg received many honors. In 1939 the Football Coaches Association created the Stagg Award, given each year to a person, group, or institution that advances football and "perpetuates the example and influence of Stagg." The next year the Touchdown Club of New York, which awards the Heisman Trophy, presented Stagg a special award for meritorious service. (The first Heisman Trophy was awarded to one of his former players, Jay Berwanger.) In 1958 he was inducted into the National Football Hall of Fame both as a coach and as a player, the first person ever honored in both categories.

For the last few years of his life Stagg lived in a nursing home. He died in Stockton, California.

Stagg probably contributed more to football than any other coach in history. Football coach Knute Rockne insisted that "all football comes from Stagg" (Wilson and Brondfield, p. 69). Stagg's most apparent and admirable trait was his commitment to honesty and fair play. Indeed, on his one hundredth birthday, the feature story in *Sports Illustrated* was titled "Amos Stagg: A Century of Honesty."

• The major sources of material on Stagg are Kenneth L. Wilson and Jerry Brondfield, *The Big Ten* (1967); John McCallum and Charles H. Pearson, *College Football U.S.A. 1869 . . . 1971* (1971); and Richard Whittingham, *Saturday Afternoon: College Football and the Men Who Made the Day* (1985). His early career at the University of Chicago is discussed in Thomas W. Goodspeed, *A History of the University of Chicago* (1916), and in Goodspeed, *The Founding of the First University of Chicago* (1919). Important magazine articles are in *Time*, 20 Oct. 1958; *Reader's Digest*, Dec. 1962; *Newsweek*, 13 Aug. 1962; and *Sports Illustrated*, 13 Aug. 1962. Obituaries are in the *New York Times*, 18 Mar. 1965, and in *Time*, 26 Mar. 1965.

JOANNA DAVENPORT

STAGGE, Jonathan. *See* Wheeler, Hugh Callingham.

STAHEL, Julius (5 Nov. 1825–4 Dec. 1912), soldier, journalist, and diplomat, was born Julius Stahel-Szamvald in Szeged, Hungary, the son of Andreas Stahel-Szamvald and Barbara Nagy. After receiving a classical education in Szeged and Budapest, he operated a bookstore in the latter city. In his early twenties he entered the Austrian army and rose to lieutenant. When Hungary waged a war for independence, Stahel joined the revolutionary forces of Louis Kossuth. The independence movement was suppressed in 1849, and he fled his native land, living in London and Berlin before coming to the United States in 1856.

For the next five years Stahel was employed as a journalist and teacher. When the Civil War broke out, he was on the staff of the *New York Illustrated News*. Quitting his job, he helped recruit the Eighth New York Volunteers, composed largely of European immigrants who elected him lieutenant colonel. During the first battle of Bull Run (Manassas), Stahel led the regiment, stationed south of Centreville, Virginia, in covering the retreat of the Union army to Washington, D.C.

On 11 August 1861 Stahel succeeded Louis Blanker as colonel of his outfit. On 12 November he was appointed a brigadier general of volunteers and given command of four regiments from New York and Pennsylvania. The following spring he served in the Shenandoah Valley under Major General John C. Frémont, who praised Stahel's "cool and effective" leadership on the "hottest part of the field" at Cross Keys on 8 June. Stahel was again cited for "coolness and bravery"—this time by Brigadier General Robert C. Schenck—at Second Bull Run (Second Manassas), where on 30 August he succeeded to the command of Schenck's First Division, First Corps, Army of Virginia.

Stahel's repeated commendations and the energetic expeditions he conducted between Bull Run and the Blue Ridge Mountains in the fall of 1862 won him command of the XI Corps, Army of the Potomac, following the battle of Fredericksburg. Only a week later, however, he was demoted to command of the cavalry attached to Major General Franz Sigel's Grand Reserve Division. In March 1863 Stahel was promoted to major general—probably owing as much to Abraham Lincoln's courtship of German voters as to Stahel's battlefield services—and was given command of the cavalry in Major General Samuel P. Heintzelman's Department of Washington.

From his headquarters at Fairfax Court House, Virginia, Stahel conducted numerous reconnaissances and raids through the spring of 1863. Despite the activity of his troops, however, he impressed some of his superiors as slow-moving and lazy. One of his most vociferous critics was Major General John F. Reynolds, to whose wing of the Army of the Potomac Stahel's division was attached at the outset of the Gettysburg campaign. Leading the pursuit of Robert E. Lee's Army of Northern Virginia, two of Stahel's regiments became the first Union troops to occupy the town of Gettysburg. A few days before the momentous battle, the War Department relieved Stahel of his command, integrated it into the Army of the Potomac, and sent him to Harrisburg, Pennsylvania, to command the mounted forces of Major General Darius N. Couch's Department of the Susquehanna. The transfer was clearly a demotion and marked the downturn of Stahel's career. While antiforeign prejudice may have played a role in Stahel's demotion, the action also reflected his record of under achievement and the lack of confidence he inspired in his troops.

The general held various commands and positions through the rest of the conflict. When President Lincoln delivered his address at Gettysburg on 19 November 1863, Stahel commanded the local guard of honor. Later that year he served on administrative boards in Washington, D.C. Early in 1864 he was sent to western Virginia to command the cavalry attached to the small army under Sigel. In the battle of New Market on 15 May, Stahel led 2,000 horsemen in a saber charge against the right flank of Major General John C. Breckinridge's Confederate army. The attack, begun too far from its target to produce a solid blow, ended in panic-stricken retreat and helped turn the tide against Sigel's forces. Three weeks later, however, Stahel conducted a more successful charge at Piedmont, Virginia, helping gain a victory for Sigel's successor, Major General David Hunter. For his service at Piedmont, where he was wounded, Stahel received the Congressional Medal of Honor in 1893.

When he recovered from his wound, Stahel performed court-martial duties in Washington and Baltimore. He resigned his commission on 8 February 1865. After the war he forged a distinguished career in the consular service, his most important postings being to Osaka, Japan (1866–1869, 1878–1884), and Shanghai, China (1884–1885). Upon returning to the United States in October 1885, he became a mining engineer and later owned mines in the West. At the time of his death in New York City, he was an executive of the Equitable Life Insurance Company. He was buried in Arlington National Cemetery. He never married.

Despite successful performances at Cross Keys, Second Bull Run, and Piedmont, Stahel was considered by many observers to be a poor combat leader and administrator. According to one of General Hunter's aides, Stahel "has never done anything in the field and never will." Hunter himself complained, "It would be impossible to exaggerate the inefficiency" of his cavalry leader. Even Stahel's friend and patron Sigel considered him "not . . . the right man" for a cavalry chief. "He is much too slow in all his doings." Some critics derided not only Stahel's ability but his appearance. One described him as "looking for all the world like a travelling clerk." Another called him "a dapper little Dutchman. . . . His appearance was that of a natty staff officer, and did not fill one's ideal of a major general."

As this last quote hints, Stahel encountered a certain amount of antiforeign prejudice from those who served with and under him, and such sentiment appears to have hobbled his career. Major General Alfred Pleasonton, commander of the cavalry of the Army of the Potomac, worked hard to bring about Stahel's relief during the Gettysburg campaign in order to add Stahel's horsemen to his own command. In letters to War Department officials, Pleasonton spoke for many native-born Americans by branding Stahel and other foreign-born soldiers as mercenaries: "I have no faith in foreigners saving our Government . . . in every instance foreigners have injured our cause."

• A small collection of Stahel's personal papers is in the Hungarian National Archives, Budapest. His campaign and battle reports and his wartime correspondence are in *The War of the Rebellion: A Compilation of the Official Records of the Union and Confederate Armies* (128 vols., 1880–1901). Biographical material is in Ella Lonn, *Foreigners in the Union Army and*

Navy (1951), and William C. Davis, *The Battle of New Market* (1975). The views of Union officers who had low opinions of Stahel are in Cecil D. Eby, Jr., ed., *A Virginia Yankee in the Civil War: The Diaries of David Hunter Strother* (1961), and James H. Kidd, *Personal Recollections of a Cavalryman with Custer's Michigan Cavalry Brigade in the Civil War* (1908). Edward G. Longacre, *The Cavalry at Gettysburg* (1986), examines Stahel's activities during the war's pivotal campaign. A substantial obituary is in the *New York Times*, 5 Dec. 1912.

EDWARD G. LONGACRE

STAKMAN, Elvin Charles (17 May 1885–22 Jan. 1979), agricultural scientist and educator, was born in Ahnapee (later Algoma), Wisconsin, the son of Frederick Stakman and Emelie Eberhardt, farmers. Soon after Stakman's birth, the family moved to Brownton, Minnesota. Stakman entered the University of Minnesota in 1902 and received his B.A. in botany in 1906 and his M.A. and Ph.D., both in plant pathology, in 1910 and 1913, respectively. He taught in the public schools from 1906 until 1909, when he accepted his first appointment as instructor in plant pathology at the University of Minnesota. In 1917 he married E. Louise Jensen; the couple did not have children.

As chair of the Department of Plant Pathology during the 1930s and 1940s, Stakman made the University of Minnesota an international center for education in plant pathology. With few interruptions, he continued at Minnesota until his retirement as professor in plant pathology in 1953. His wife died suddenly in 1962, and he never remarried. In retirement Stakman remained involved in the affairs of plant pathology until a serious illness in 1977. He died in Saint Paul, Minnesota.

Stakman had broad scientific knowledge and a charismatic personality that meshed with a changing set of circumstances in agriculture and foreign affairs. As a result, he became the major architect of two initiatives. First, he helped create an international network of research on crop diseases and continental-scale efforts to control them. Second, he was the lead scientist in designing an agricultural research program that eventually produced what became known as the green revolution, the development of high-yielding varieties of cereal grains.

Stakman's scientific reputation was built in the 1910s and 1920s, during the early days of professionalization of plant pathology. His Ph.D. work laid to rest a major theory of plant pathology, that a fungus not pathogenic to a cereal grain could acquire pathogenicity by growing in other species of cereal, known as "bridges." This bridging hypothesis, if true, reduced the possibility of producing cereal grains that were genetically resistant to fungal pathogens. Once Stakman's work laid the theory to rest, it made sense for plant pathologists to search for genetic variants of cereal grains that had in-born resistance to fungal diseases. Today's highly capitalized farm production practices, developed largely during Stakman's career, depended on the reliability of such resistant varieties.

In later work, Stakman made extensive collections of a group of pathogens known as "rusts." He and his students concluded that rusts came in many different physiological races and that new races could develop through genetic recombination when the rust reproduced sexually. The concept of physiological races in turn led to the concept that plant breeders must continually seek new disease-resistant varieties in a never-ending race against the evolutionary potential of the rusts. All modern efforts at plant breeding are based on these premises. Stakman also designed and promoted the "Barberry Eradication Campaign," in which the federal and state governments destroyed hundreds of millions of barberry plants all over the western United States. Barberry was a host of cereal rusts and the place where new physiological races of rust were created through sexual reproduction. In addition, Stakman outlined the ways in which fungal diseases were spread across the continent by wind. In recognition of his accomplishments in science, Stakman was elected to the National Academy of Sciences in 1933.

In 1941 Stakman was selected by the Rockefeller Foundation to lead a scientific delegation to Mexico to assess the needs for agricultural research in that country. This delegation was the direct result of recently improved relations between the United States and Mexico, fostered by Vice President–elect Henry A. Wallace's attendance at the inauguration of Mexico's president in 1940. Wallace wanted to provide technical assistance to Mexico, in part to keep Mexico close to the United States while Europe was collapsing in war. Stakman's delegation recommended a program of agricultural research, primarily for wheat and corn improvement. Mexico wanted to increase its agricultural production, and the joint Rockefeller-Mexican program began in 1943. By the late 1950s, program scientists had developed high-yielding varieties of wheat that sparked a green revolution all over the world. Rockefeller Foundation officials wanted Stakman to head the Mexican research program, but he declined and recommended instead two former students, J. George Harrar as head of the Mexican program and Norman E. Borlaug as chief wheat breeder. Harrar later became president of the Rockefeller Foundation, and Borlaug was awarded the Nobel Peace Prize in 1970 for creating the green revolution wheats.

Stakman conceived of agriculture in very broad terms, which undoubtedly were important in directing his many activities. In 1935, for example, he stated that "Agriculture is fundamental to human subsistence, an obvious fact too often ignored by our lawmakers, educators, and the general public. . . . [M]an is dependent on plant growth . . . for his very existence on earth" ("Science in the Service of Agriculture," *Scientific Monthly* 68 [1949]: 75).

• Stakman left important papers in two locations. The archives of the University of Minnesota and the library of the Department of Plant Pathology contain correspondence and memorabilia of his life. The archives of the Rockefeller Foundation contain a lengthy oral history, much correspondence, and many reports. Much of Stakman's philosophy can be found in *Campaigns against Hunger* (1967), written with Richard Bradfield and Paul Mangelsdorf. C. M. Christensen, *E. C. Stakman, Statesman of Science* (1984), provides an interesting biographical sketch by a colleague. Obituaries are in the National Academy of Sciences, *Biographical Memoirs* 61 (1992): 330–49, and (by Christensen) in *Phytopathology* 69, no. 3 (1979): 195.

JOHN H. PERKINS

STALLINGS, Laurence Tucker (24 Nov. 1894–28 Feb. 1968), writer and editor, was born in Macon, Georgia, the son of Larkin Tucker Stallings, a bank teller, and Aurora Brooks. He took to the craft of writing at a young age and read widely. After graduating from Wake Forest College in North Carolina in 1916, he became a reporter for the *Atlanta Journal*. In 1919 Stallings married Helen Poteat. They had two children.

Stallings volunteered to serve as a marine in the First World War, and this experience became the central theme in his work. Stallings himself believed that he had only one thing to say and did not make serious attempts at other subjects. The arguably most revealing work of Stallings's career is *Plumes* (1924), based on his combat experience. It is a largely autobiographical novel in which an idealistic young soldier loses his patriotism after losing a leg in a futile assault. Stallings's right leg was amputated in 1922 as a result of combat injuries that were exacerbated by a fall he suffered while a reporter for the *Washington Times*, a post he accepted in 1920. Like the hero of *Plumes*, Stallings joined the war out of a virile enthusiasm for the blood sport of soldiering—its pageantry and "plumes." Throughout the course of his career, Stallings attempted to reconcile this visceral response to the battlefield with the more reasoned knowledge that wars are fought by the poor on the ground in order to preserve the powerful afar.

Arriving in New York City in 1922 after a trip to Europe during which he wrote *Plumes*, Stallings began work as a copyeditor for the *New York World*. He met Maxwell Anderson, Alexander Woollcott, and other members of the Algonquin Round Table. Stallings was quickly promoted to drama reviewer. However, he was unable to attend performances around town easily and was given the post of book reviewer, publishing 400 articles in his first year. During this period Anderson and Stallings collaborated on the extremely successful play *What Price Glory?* (1924). This antiwar piece is remarkable for its use of raw colloquial speech as a dramatic device. In order to prepare audiences, the play was presented with a program note explaining, in part, that "*What Price Glory* is a play of war as it is, not as it has been presented theatrically for thousands of years." Regarding the use of language, "The audience is asked to bear with certain expletives . . . employed because the mood and truth of the play demand their employment." The tone is seen in a speech by a wounded sergeant: "They gave me ether so the stretcher bearers could steal a gold watch and eight hundred bucks off me. I certainly put up a squawk. . . . But a hell of a lot of good it did me. I went looking for the bird that got them . . . and I hung a shanty on the bimbo's eye." Because of the representation of military personnel, the Department of Justice, as well as representatives of the army and navy, unsuccessfully attempted to suppress the play. It was adapted as a motion picture in 1926, directed by Raoul Walsh. After this first success, Stallings and Anderson collaborated on *First Flight* (1925) and *The Buccaneer* (1925).

Stallings's most well-known short story, based on his war experiences, was "The Big Parade," which appeared in the *New Republic* (17 Sept. 1924). This story was adapted as the motion picture *The Big Parade* (1925), directed by King Vidor and starring John Gilbert and Renée Adorée. It was released to excellent reviews.

For the stage Stallings wrote the plays *Deep River* (1926) and *Rainbow* (1928). In 1928 Stallings collaborated with Oscar Hammerstein II on the musical *Rainbow* (1928), later produced on film as *Song of the West* (1930). He also wrote the stage adaptation of *A Farewell to Arms* (1930).

In 1931 Stallings became literary editor for the *New York Sun*. His story "Vale of Tears" appeared in that year, later included in *Men at War* (1942), a collection edited and introduced by Ernest Hemingway. "Gentleman in Blue" appeared in the *Saturday Evening Post* (20 Feb. 1932), and "Return to the Woods" came out in *Collier's* (5 Mar. 1932). Stallings edited and wrote an introduction and captions for *The First World War: A Photographic History* (1933), a collection of photographs from signal corps photographers, soldiers, war correspondents, and other eyewitnesses. He intentionally avoided a coherent narrative: "Here is the camera record of chaos, with the reader annoyed by only the briefest captions." From 1935 to 1936 Stallings was an editor for *American Mercury*.

From 1927 to 1938 Stallings was editor and manager for Fox Movietone News, in association with Truman Talley and Edmund Roach. In 1935 Stallings headed the "Fox Expedition," an operation whereby the Fox newsreel took its newly designed sound recording truck into Ethiopia in order to report on the movement of the Italian armies there. He contributed a series of articles to the *Saturday Evening Post* on this operation. In 1936 Stallings and his first wife were divorced. In 1937 he married Louise St. Leger Vance, with whom he had two children.

Throughout a portion of his career, Stallings also wrote screenplays for *Old Ironsides* (1926), *Too Hot to Handle* (1938), *Northwest Passage* (1940), and *The Jungle Book* (1942). While he did not like to write for movies because he felt that they were never realistic, he did it nonetheless, strictly for the money.

Stallings was drafted to return to military duty in April 1942, ostensibly in the public relations field, but some evidence suggests that he was involved in intelligence work. He left the service for the last time in June 1943. After the war he wrote a play, *The Streets Are Guarded* (1944), set in the context of World War II, and worked on the scripts for *A Miracle Can Happen* (1948), for King Vidor, and *She Wore a Yellow Ribbon* (1949), for Merian C. Cooper.

Stallings returned to his central theme—World War I—in his last published work, *The Doughboys* (1963). The book is an account of the work of the American Expeditionary Forces in Europe in the period 1917–1918. It is written in a lively and conversational style and is replete with historical detail.

In 1963, soon after the publication of *The Doughboys*, Stallings's other leg was amputated. He died at home in southern California.

• A file of Stallings's correspondence with Arthur Krock is at the Firestone Library at Princeton University. Joan T. Brittain, *Laurence Stallings* (1975), is a full-length biography of Stallings. Philo M. Buck, Jr., et al., *A Treasury of the Theatre*, vol. 1 (1940), contains the full text of *What Price Glory?* Adelaide Cumming, *A History of American Newsreels* (1967), discusses the management of the Fox Movietone newsreel, including the contribution of Stallings. Raymond Fielding, *The American Newsreel, 1911–1967* (1972), discusses the Fox Expedition, Stallings's role, and its contribution to motion picture journalism. King Vidor, *A Tree Is a Tree* (1953), discusses the collaboration between Vidor and Stallings in Hollywood, including numerous anecdotes about Stallings. Stallings was also the author of numerous newspaper and magazine articles, many of which are listed in Brittain. Obituaries are in *Variety*, 6 Mar. 1968, and in the *New York Times*, 29 Feb. 1968.

JANE COLLINGS

STALLO, Johann Bernhard (16 Mar. 1823–6 Jan. 1900), jurist and philosopher, was born in Seirhausen, Oldenburg, Germany, the son of Johann Heinrich Stallo, a schoolmaster, and Maria Adelheid Moormann. Under the tutelage of his father and grandfather, also a schoolmaster, Stallo gained a solid education, especially in mathematics, along with fluency in English, French, and the classical languages. At the age of thirteen he entered the Catholic normal school at Vechta, where he had his first exposure to German philosophy. Limited family resources precluded university study, and to avoid becoming a country schoolteacher, he immigrated to Cincinnati in 1839, following the path of an uncle who had succeeded as a printer in that city. The sixteen-year-old boy quickly secured a teaching position at a local parochial school. Recognizing a need for a German primer, in 1840 he wrote *ABC, Buchstabier- und Lesebuch, für die deutschen Schulen Amerikas*, which later he wryly described as his most brilliant literary success. A year later he joined the faculty of the newly founded St. Xavier College, where he also pursued his own studies in mathematics and the sciences. In 1844 he accepted a position as professor of chemistry, physics, and mathematics at St. John's College in Fordham, New York (now Fordham University). During his four years there he expanded his studies to include speculative philosophy and wrote in English his first major book, *General*

Principles of the Philosophy of Nature. Stallo hoped this work would introduce Americans to the main currents of German philosophy, especially Kant, Hegel, Fichte, Schelling, and Lorenz Oken. Although praised by American philosophers Ralph Waldo Emerson, Bronson Alcott, and William Torrey Harris, the book did not find a large audience, and years later Stallo regretted its publication, claiming he had written it while in his "intellectual infancy" and "under the spell of Hegel's ontological reveries" (*Concepts and Theories*, p. 6). In 1848, to ensure his economic future, Stallo returned to Cincinnati to take up the study of law. Admitted to the bar in 1849, his legal reputation, coupled with increasing political involvement, secured him an appointment in 1852 as judge in the Hamilton County Court of Common Pleas. His attraction to Jeffersonian liberalism led him to oppose slavery, nativism, and the temperance movement, and in the mid-1850s he shifted his political allegiance from the Democratic to the Republican party. About this same time he left the Roman Catholic church, and in 1855 he married Helene Zimmermann of Cincinnati, a Protestant. Although his seven children were all baptized in their mother's church, Stallo can be labeled most accurately a free thinker from this time on.

In politics Stallo served as an elector for John C. Frémont in 1856 and supported Abraham Lincoln in 1860. At the outbreak of the Civil War, Stallo enthusiastically called on Cincinnati's "freedom-loving Germans" to fight against despotism (Easton, p. 59). His impassioned plea, delivered at the local Turner Hall, led to the establishment of the Ninth Ohio Volunteer Infantry Regiment, under the command of his law partner, Robert S. McCook. Made up almost entirely of German Americans, "die Neuner" served with distinction during the great conflict. Disillusioned by the failure of Reconstruction and the corruption within the Ulysses S. Grant administration, Stallo supported the unsuccessful Liberal Republican move to nominate Charles Francis Adams in 1872; four years later his growing opposition to monopolies and high tariffs brought him back to the Democratic party. In 1885 President Grover Cleveland rewarded his support by appointing him minister to Italy. With the return of Republicans to power four years later, Stallo retired to a life of cultured leisure in Florence, Italy, where he died.

During his years of legal and political activism, Stallo continued to involve himself with educational matters. He served on the University of Cincinnati's Board of Curators, examined teaching candidates for the Cincinnati public schools, and lectured frequently on scientific subjects. In the 1850s he, along with August Willich, editor of the radical *Cincinnati Republikaner*, and Moncure Conway, a Unitarian minister, made up a trio of Hegelian thinkers who contributed significantly to Cincinnati's intellectual life. As a lawyer Stallo gained national recognition in 1870 for his defense of the Cincinnati School Board's decision to eliminate Bible reading and hymn singing as part of the daily curriculum. His wide-ranging interests are reflected in the collection of his writings published in 1893 under the title *Reden, Abhandlungen und Briefe.* Although his admiration for Hegelian ideas declined, he retained a deep interest in philosophy. *The Concepts and Theories of Modern Physics*, published in 1882 (with several later editions, including ones in German and French), remains his most important contribution to American thought. An epistemological study in which he criticized contemporary physical theory for its metaphysical assumptions, this well-reasoned volume presented views in some areas that paralleled those of the contemporary Austrian physicist and philosopher Ernst Mach. Despite the book's now obvious shortcomings, it remains one of the few American contributions to a philosophy of science, and it provides a clear view of the muddled state of physical theory in the late nineteenth century.

• A two-part article, "The Primary Concepts of Modern Physical Science," *Popular Science Monthly* 3 (Oct. 1873): 705–17, and 4 (Nov. 1873): 92–108, reveals the early development of Stallo's ideas later expressed in *The Concepts and Theories.* Two good introductions to Stallo's philosophical views are in *The Dictionary of Scientific Biography* (1975) and *The Encyclopedia of Philosophy* (1967). More extensive analyses are Stillman Drake, "J. B. Stallo and the Critique of Classical Physics," in *Men and Movements in the History of Science*, ed. H. M. Evans (1959); and Percy W. Bridgman's introduction to *The Concepts and Theories of Modern Physics* (1960). A somewhat dated but still useful doctoral dissertation is G. D. Wilkinson, "John B. Stallo's Criticism of Physical Science" (Columbia Univ., 1941). Loyd D. Easton, *Hegel's First American Followers* (1966), provides the most thorough view of his early life. Despite a few inaccuracies, the obituary in the *Cincinnati Enquirer*, 7 Jan. 1900, offers a warm personal assessment of his life.

ROBERT C. VITZ

STAMPS, V. O. (18 Sept. 1892–19 Aug. 1940), and **Frank Henry Stamps** (7 Oct. 1896–12 Feb. 1965), composers, singers, and music promoters, were born in Simpsonville, Upshur County, Texas, the sons of W. O. Stamps and Florence Corine Rosser, community leaders from Upshur County, where W. O. Stamps ran several sawmills and founded the community of Stamps. He later served two terms in the Texas legislature and for a time acted as head of the Texas prison system. Both V. O., born Virgil Oliver Stamps, and Frank Stamps, two of six brothers, were introduced to gospel music when their father hired a music teacher to conduct singing schools in the community. V. O. was fourteen at the time; Frank, six. Both brothers soon found they had an aptitude for the seven-shape note music taught in the school, a type of music that was widely popular in Texas at the time.

V. O. Stamps furthered his musical education by traveling to study at other rural singing schools, including one taught by R. M. Morgan in Texas (1907), and by 1911 he was conducting his own music schools in Upshur County. In 1909 he had married Addie Belle Culpepper; they had three children and later divorced. V. O. began to experiment with composing, and in 1914 he published his first song, "The Man behind the Plow." Soon thereafter he became a regional representative for the James D. Vaughan Music Company of Lawrenceburg, Tennessee. After living for a time at the company headquarters in Lawrenceburg, he returned to Texas to open a branch office at Jacksonville. By 1925 he had decided to found his own publishing company and that year compiled a songbook called *Harbor Bells*, named after one of his recent compositions. The book, which featured songs by numerous Texas composers, was extremely popular; it contained several songs for which V. O. had written the music, among them a few that would become gospel standards, for example, "Precious Memories."

In March 1926, after issuing two more songbooks, Stamps invited Alabama composer and singer J. R. Baxter to join the firm, and in 1927 the Stamps Publishing Company became the Stamps-Baxter Company. Relying on modern advertising and winning major recording contracts for the quartets it represented, Stamps-Baxter presented itself as a youth-oriented, "modern" gospel company, and through the 1920s it sold hundreds of thousands of songbooks. In 1929 the firm relocated to Dallas, where a printing plant was constructed. The firm established branch offices in Chattanooga, Tennessee, and Pangburn, Arkansas, and put out a monthly periodical called *Gospel Music News*. A school of music also was founded, and V. O.'s bass voice was featured in regular Stamps Quartet programs broadcast over powerful Dallas radio station KRLD. Although he was a Methodist in his personal life, Stamps sought to make his songbooks as nondenominational as possible in order to appeal to a wider audience. By the end of the 1930s, Stamps-Baxter had surpassed Vaughan's company, their primary competitor, as the major publisher of gospel music in the United States.

Frank Stamps attended high school at Gilmer, Texas, and then entered Pritchett Normal School in Texas. Although he admired his older brother V. O.'s ambition to become a gospel singer, Frank's first job after college was as an auditor for a Houston firm, which sent him overseas for a year. During World War I he served in the navy and afterward joined the Vaughan Music Company. In 1925, when V. O. left Vaughan to start the Stamps Publishing Company, Frank joined him and organized a quartet to travel the country publicizing the new firm. By 1927 he had organized Frank Stamps and His All-Star Quartet, one of the first widely known gospel quartets, and began to record for RCA Victor. Also in 1927, in Memphis, the group recorded "Give the World a Smile Each Day," which soon became a standard gospel number and a theme song for the Stamps-Baxter Company. By 1922 Frank had also begun to publish songs, such as "Reapers Be True" (1922), "Love Leads the Way" (1922), and "Mother's Bible" (1930). In 1931 he married Mary Naomi Marks, with whom he had a son, Robert Howard. By the late 1930s he was working for the rival Hartford Music Company and living in Greensboro, North Carolina.

In 1940, at the peak of the Stamps-Baxter success, V. O. died of a heart attack in Dallas (he had been married a second time, to Trueman Bussey). Frank moved to Dallas to take over V. O.'s famed Stamps Quartet and to help manage the business. In 1945, however, he and the members of the quartet broke from Stamps-Baxter and started a new publishing company, Stamps Quartet Music. Due in part to the popularity of the quartet's radio shows, the new company and its affiliated music school were immediate successes. Located in Dallas, by 1946 the school was attracting more than a thousand students. One of the innovative features of the new school was the All-Night Sing, a marathon concert featuring dozens of different quartets and singing groups. Begun by V. O. in 1940 and continued by Frank, the All-Night sing became popular throughout the South; by 1950 it was the single most-important performing venue for Anglo-American gospel music. By then, Frank was devoting most of his time to performing, to managing the quartet, and to traveling to various singing conventions. He died in Dallas.

• The best account of V. O. Stamps's life is the biographical sketch in *Precious Memories of Virgil O. Stamps*, Published by Stamps-Baxter (1941), pp. v–xi. A biographical account of Frank Stamps, written by his wife, appears in *Give the World a Smile* (1969), pp. 3–11. A survey of Stamps-Baxter is included in Lois S. Blackwell, *The Wings of the Dove: The Story of Gospel Music in America* (1978).

CHARLES K. WOLFE

STANBERY, Henry (20 Feb. 1803–26 June 1881), lawyer and politician, was born in New York City, the son of Jonas Stanbery, a physician, and Ann Lucy Seaman. When Stanbery was eleven, he and his family moved to Zanesville, Ohio. In 1815 he matriculated at Washington College in Pennsylvania. Graduating in 1819, he decided to pursue a career in law and began studying under Ebenezer Granger of Zanesville. When Granger died, Stanbery continued his studies under the direction of attorney Charles B. Goddard. When he reached the age of majority in 1824, Stanbery was admitted to the Ohio bar and began a distinguished legal career that commenced in a partnership with the illustrious Thomas Ewing of Lancaster, Ohio, the foster father of William Tecumseh Sherman and future attorney general of the United States and U.S. senator. In 1829 he married Frances Beecher, with whom he had five children before she died in 1840.

Stanbery remained in private practice until 1846, when he entered politics as a member of the Whig party. That year he was elected as Ohio's first attorney general, a recently created position. He also served as a delegate to the 1850 Ohio constitutional convention. Moving to Cincinnati in 1853, he spent the next thirteen years in private legal practice. During these years, Stanbery participated in important legal cases, including the 1854 *Piqua Branch of the State Bank of Ohio v. Knoop*. That case demonstrated his commitment to the sanctity of contract, a belief consistent with Whig political and legal philosophy. At issue was a law recently passed by the Ohio legislature that negated certain tax exemptions previously granted to the Piqua branch of the Ohio State Bank by an earlier session of the Ohio legislature. Stanbery argued successfully that the current law was unconstitutional because it was an infringement on a contractual obligation created between the state of Ohio and the Piqua bank.

When the tumultuous events of the 1850s brought an end to the Whig party, Stanbery joined the newly created Republican party. Although he undoubtedly embraced the central Republican tenet of stopping the spread of slavery into the western territories of the United States, he was never identified with the radical wing of the party. He was, for instance, a consistent opponent of black suffrage, a position that he maintained for most of his political career.

Despite his identification with the Republicans, Stanbery was highly regarded by members of both political parties. Part of this admiration was no doubt the result of an impressive physical presence and a demeanor that commanded respect. Stanbery's Lancaster neighbor, Democrat Samuel Cox, later described him as "symmetrical" in form, possessing a "rich" and "resonate" voice. "He moved with an air of dignity and respect" and "commanded attention wherever he appeared" (Cox, p. 588).

On 24 July 1866 Stanbery was drawn into the fray of partisan political controversy when he was appointed attorney general by President Andrew Johnson. After enjoying a brief honeymoon with congressional Republicans, Johnson alienated Radical Republicans by endorsing a conciliatory Reconstruction program toward the South with little regard for black civil rights. By the time Stanbery took office, Johnson had also angered many moderate and conservative Republicans, particularly with his veto of the Civil Rights Act of 1866. When Republicans scored solid victories in the fall 1866 elections, they moved quickly to undo Johnson's conciliatory Reconstruction program and replace it with a more radical version. Their principal legislative achievement was the Military Reconstruction Acts, a series of laws that imposed more demanding conditions on southern states, including the division of the southern states into five military districts subject to military authority instead of civilian rule and the disfranchisement of large numbers of southern voters.

Stanbery believed that the Military Reconstruction Acts were unconstitutional. Although his Whig background might have predisposed him toward a stronger central government, he believed these laws went too far in extending federal power at the expense of the states. To cabinet colleague Gideon Welles, Stanbery revealed that "he was clearly and unqualifiedly against the whole talk and theory of territorializing the States. Congress could not dismantle them. It had not the power" (Welles, vol. 3, pp. 11–12). Stanbery strengthened Johnson's resolve to thwart these acts by criticizing the laws in a series of opinions given to the entire cabinet in May 1867. According to Stanbery, U.S. army commanders could not legally remove officials from southern state governments or prevent southern citizens from voting if they had taken the previously prescribed loyalty oaths. When Johnson published Stanbery's opinion, thus signaling Congress of his intention to resist the laws, Congress responded by passing an additional Reconstruction act to overcome Stanbery's objections.

Stanbery was most prominent in national affairs during the impeachment proceedings against Johnson. Impeached primarily as a result of his violation of the Tenure of Office Act, Johnson was defended before Congress by a group of prominent lawyers headed by Stanbery. To avoid all appearance of impropriety, Stanbery resigned his office to conduct the defense. Worried about Johnson's loose tongue, Stanbery advised the president to refrain from talking with reporters lest he damage his case and "embarrass" Stanbery. Subsequent illness, however, prevented Stanbery from directing Johnson's defense, although he recovered enough to conduct admirably the defense's closing arguments.

After Johnson was narrowly acquitted by the Senate, he reappointed Stanbery to his old position of attorney general. Despite the respect Stanbery usually commanded, Radical Republicans could not forget the role he had played in defending Johnson. They, therefore, rejected his nomination, a rejection that cabinet members Welles and Orville Browning accurately characterized as motivated soley by the desire to punish Stanbery for defending Johnson.

His career in Washington over, Stanbery returned to Ohio and resumed his law practice in Cincinnati. He once again built up a flourishing practice before retiring in 1878 because of cataracts, a condition that eventually blinded him. In early 1880 he moved back to New York City, where he died. After the death of his first wife, Stanbery had married Cecelia Bond, who outlived him.

Although widely recognized as a man of integrity and principle, Stanbery was not adept at practicing the art of political compromise. Of conservative and somewhat inflexible temperment, his advice to Johnson encouraged the seventeenth president to become more recalcitrant in his attitude toward Congress. By encouraging this defiance through his interpretation of the Reconstruction Acts, Stanbery played a significant role in furthering conflict that resulted eventually in the first impeachment of a U.S. president.

• The Henry Stanbery Papers are in the Ohio Historical Society, Columbus, Ohio; the Thomas Ewing Papers, Library of Congress, Washington, D.C., include some correspondence. A number of contemporaries commented on Stanbery and his role as a member of Andrew Johnson's cabinet, including Samuel S. Cox, *Three Decades of Federal Legislation* (1885); Gideon Welles, *The Diary of Gideon Welles*, ed. John T. Morse (1911); and Orville Hickman Browning, *The Diary of Orville Hickman Browning*, ed. Theodore C. Pease and James G. Randall (1925). Works that provide useful information about Stanbery as attorney general and his role in several important Supreme Court cases include Albert Castel, *The Presidency of Andrew Johnson* (1979); Hans Trefousse, *Andrew*

Johnson (1989); and Charles Warren, *The Supreme Court in United States History* (1928). An obituary is in the *New York Times*, 27 June 1881.

BRUCE TAP

STANDING BEAR, Luther (Dec. 1868–19 Feb. 1939), Oglala Sioux chief, author, and actor, was born on the Sioux Pine reservation in South Dakota, the son of Standing Bear, a Sioux chief, and Pretty Face. Reared according to tribal tradition, Luther Standing Bear, named "Plenty Kills" at birth, learned the necessary skills of Plains Indian life. After a trip to Washington, D.C., and a meeting with President Rutherford B. Hayes, however, the elder Standing Bear questioned the Sioux ability to maintain their traditional culture in the face of U.S. expansion. His questions increased when the government tightened restrictions on the Sioux after General George Armstrong Custer's defeat at the battle of the Little Big Horn in 1876.

In 1879 Luther Standing Bear enrolled in Colonel Richard Pratt's experimental Indian school at Carlisle, Pennsylvania. Although the elder Standing Bear wanted his son exposed to European-American ways, the younger Standing Bear assented to the plan only to prove his bravery to his father and his people. "I was thinking of my father," Luther Standing Bear wrote in his autobiography *My People the Sioux* (1928), "and how he had many times said to me, 'Son, be brave! Die on the battle-field if necessary away from home.' The thought of going away with what was to us an enemy, to a place we knew nothing about, just suited me. My idea was that I was leaving the reservation to do some brave deed." Although Pratt's school was underfunded and ill prepared for boarding students, it did have a clear objective. Luther Standing Bear and his fellow classmates were, as he recalled in an *American Mercury* article, "to be made over into the likeness of the conqueror." Toward this end the school gave students European-American clothes, haircuts, and names—the latter selected at random from a list on the blackboard. When the young Standing Bear approached the board to choose his name, he later recalled, "I took the pointer and acted as if I were about to touch an enemy." The one he happened to touch was "Luther."

The Carlisle school implemented a single-minded curriculum. Introduced to the rudiments of a Western education, Indian students spent most of their time learning a semiskilled trade—Luther's was tinsmithing—and a market-oriented work ethic. During the summer the school assigned Indian students to live with whites to reinforce the discipline. Although Luther originally saw the school as an enemy, he quickly acclimated and became one of Pratt's success stories. In 1882, for example, Pratt sent Luther Standing Bear back to the latter's native Sioux on a recruiting trip for the Carlisle school. The next year Pratt promoted his school's success by arranging for Luther to work in John Wanamaker's famous department store in downtown Philadelphia.

After his experiences in Pennsylvania, in 1884 Luther Standing Bear returned to the Sioux reservation, where he became an assistant teacher, merchant, and substitute for the Episcopal missionary—having been baptized in the Episcopal church during his Carlisle years. Shortly after returning to the reservation Standing Bear also married Nellie DeCory, and in 1887 they had their first child, whom they named Luther. Although living on the reservation in 1890 at the height of the Ghost Dance movement, Luther and his immediate family remained interested but uninvolved observers. Nonetheless, after the massacre at Wounded Knee in December, his "blood boiled." "I was ready to go and fight then. There I was, doing my best to teach my people to follow in the white men's road—even trying to get them to believe in their religion—and this was my reward for it all! The very people I was following—and getting my people to follow—had no respect for motherhood, old age, or babyhood. Where was all their civilized training?" he asked. Despite his immediate anger, Luther continued to cooperate with whites, by overseeing the new government school, store, and post office, and serving as the assistant minister on the Pine Ridge reservation.

In 1902 Luther contracted to serve as the interpreter and chaperon for the Indians in Buffalo Bill's Wild West Show, which was scheduled to tour the British Isles. While in England, Luther not only enjoyed the major cities of England but also gained an audience with King Edward VII. It was also during this tour that Luther's daughter, Alexandra Birmingham Cody Standing Bear, was born. He agreed to continue as the show's interpreter the next season, but when the show's train wrecked in 1903, severely injuring Luther, he decided to end his touring duties.

Back on the reservation Luther's band made him chief in July 1905, but he chose not to remain with his people long after his appointment. Instead he hit the lecture circuit, "determining that if I could get the right sort of people interested, I might be able to do more for my own race off the reservation than to remain there under the iron rule of the white agent." He fought successfully in 1907 for an allotment of 640 acres and a fee patent that would allow him to sell the land, believing that these would give him the citizenship rights he desired. Also in 1907 he remarried. His new bride was May Splicer, of Mohawk dissent. After selling his land in Bennett County, South Dakota, Luther Standing Bear moved to Sioux City, Iowa, and later to Los Angeles, California, where in 1912 he became an actor.

In 1928 he published, with considerable editorial help from E. A. Brininstool, his autobiography *My People the Sioux*. Five years later he published a critique of American culture and U.S. Indian policy entitled *Land of the Spotted Eagle*. Also in 1933 he urged President Franklin D. Roosevelt to sponsor a bill requiring Native American history courses in all public schools. Three years later Luther Standing Bear and Jim Thorpe formed the Indian Actors Association to encourage Hollywood studios to hire more American

Indian actors and technical advisers. His efforts in the 1930s suggest that near the end of his life Luther Standing Bear became less accepting of European-American culture. "The white race today," he wrote in the *American Mercury*, "Is but half civilized and unable to order his life into ways of peace and righteousness." Thus he confessed, "I had tried to live a peaceful and happy life; tried to adapt myself and make readjustments to fit the white man's mode of existence. But I was unsuccessful. I developed into a chronic disturber. I was a bad Indian. I remained a hostile, even a savage, if you please. And I still am. I am incurable." Thus, Luther Standing Bear personified the American Indian struggle with the pressures of assimilation. In the end, his refusal to assimilate to the larger European-American culture became an inspiration to Native American movements later in the twentieth century. He died in Huntington Park, California, while working on the film *Union Pacific*.

• The Records of the Bureau of Indian Affairs include Luther Standing Bear's correspondence with government officials. In addition to his autobiographical pieces, *My People the Sioux*; "The Tragedy of the Sioux," *American Mercury*, Nov. 1931, pp. 273–78; and *Land of the Spotted Eagle*, Luther Standing Bear also published two titles for children: *My Indian Boyhood* (1931) and *Stories of the Sioux* (1934). L. G. Moses and Raymond Wilson, *Indian Lives: Essays on Nineteenth- and Twentieth-Century Native American Leaders* (1985), contains a biographical essay. For more information on the Carlisle school, see Richard H. Pratt, *Battlefield and Classroom: Four Decades with the American Indian, 1867–1904* (1964).

RICHARD C. GOODE

STANDISH, Burt L. *See* Patten, Gilbert.

STANDISH, Myles (1584?–3 Oct. 1656), Pilgrim military and political leader, was born in England, either on the Isle of Man or Lancashire, and may have been connected to the noted Catholic family Standish of Standish. Virtually nothing, however, is known of his early life or education until as a soldier in the Low Countries he became acquainted with the English Leiden separatist congregation from which many of the Mayflower passengers came. As the Pilgrims prepared to emigrate to America, Captain John Smith of Virginia fame offered his services as military officer, but the Pilgrim leaders preferred Standish even though at that time he was not a member of their congregation.

After the Mayflower's New England landfall in late 1620, Standish participated in the first explorations. He is credited with discovering an abandoned cache of corn in November 1620; the crop's production when planted the next spring may have saved the colony from extinction. He helped select the Plymouth site and as military officer designed its defenses. He also played a role in the initial negotiations with the neighboring Wampanoags and various other Indian groups around the Narragansett and Massachusetts bays. Now subject to annual election, he was regularly chosen captain of the militia and organized the band for training, watching, and patrolling early in 1621 when it appeared that relations with the Narragansetts might deteriorate into war. He was included in the informal council that first governed Plymouth Colony and then from 1624 he was formally elected to the colony's Court of Assistants (essentially a legislative upper house and judicial appellate court) virtually every year until his death.

During the first harsh winter in America, Standish's wife Rose (last name unknown) died, as did many of the original settlers. In 1624 he married Barbara (last name unknown), who had arrived the year before on the *Anne*. They had six children, four of whom survived infancy. There is no foundation for Henry Wadsworth Longfellow's "The Courtship of Myles Standish" (the surrogate courting of Priscilla Mullins) in this sparse evidence of Standish's family life.

The colony's survival assured by 1623, Standish was instrumental in defending Plymouth's authority against other Europeans, a role that remained important into the 1630s. In 1623 he led the rescue from starvation of the Wessagussett settlers near Massachusetts Bay who were employees of Thomas Weston, a "particular" holding rights in the region through the Council of New England but not legally subject to the Plymouth Company contract. In 1624 a dispute with John Oldham, another "particular," led Oldham to call Standish "a beggarly rascal" and threaten him with a knife. Standish disarmed him. Standish's most famous deed in enforcing Plymouth's sense of order came in 1628 with the suppression of Thomas Morton's rollicking trading post at Merry Mount, an incident that became embedded in New England myth and lore largely through Morton's scathingly sarcastic account in his *New English Canaan* published in Amsterdam in 1637. In that storied expedition Standish had the support of John Endecott and the newly established Puritan community of Salem, forerunner of the Massachusetts Bay Company. His last major effort was at Castine, Maine, in 1635 after a French party from Acadia seized a Plymouth trading post. Standish's expedition failed because of the incompetence of the captain of the vessel that the Plymouth authorities had hired to support the mission. Plymouth found itself unable to resolve this problem with the French Acadians without the concurrence of the recently founded Massachusetts Bay Colony. After 1635, in essence, Plymouth could not conduct foreign or Indian policy independent of its larger neighbor.

Standish garnered less fame but accomplished more of lasting significance from his role in the financial and economic development of Plymouth Colony. In 1625–1626, after Isaac Allerton and Edward Winslow had failed to renegotiate the Pilgrims' convoluted relationship with the parent companies, Standish returned to England. Standish also failed to negotiate a new agreement but successfully secured new loans and supplies. In 1627 he became one of the "Undertakers," eventually a dozen leading settlers, who personally assumed the colony's outstanding debts in exchange for local privileges in landholding and trading. In 1630 he was vested with power of attorney from the Council of

New England to oversee the transfer of that organization's land rights to Plymouth. Over the next several years he was elected treasurer six times in addition to his duties as assistant.

Beginning in 1631 Standish and John Alden began the development of what in 1637 officially became Duxbury, the first official new town in the Old Colony. The Duxbury Church, the first congregation separate from that of Plymouth town, was formed between 1634 and 1636. Standish lived there the rest of his life, farming and raising cattle. This initial dispersal of the first, original settlement was highly controversial because it was seen as potentially diluting the religious and social solidarity of the colony. Standish and others, in response, sought ways during 1637 to merge the Plymouth and Duxbury settlers by moving both to better lands. Both churches, however, vetoed the proposal, which then spurred the settlers of Duxbury to officially incorporate as a town. In 1638 Standish headed a committee of the General Court to lay out lands for Taunton, an act that confirmed the trend toward dispersal.

The process of town formation on the Massachusetts Bay pattern continued to cause problems of social and political control, however. In October 1639 for instance, Standish and Thomas Prence, as assistants, heard and resolved disputes over the establishment of Sandwich, involving charges that liberal land grants had been made to reputed unsavory characters. The assistants insisted that legal inhabitants had to be approved by the minister and church of the new town. In 1645 Standish and others laid out Duxbury New Plantation, which became Bridgewater in 1656. Thus Standish played a prominent role, along with the leaders of the Bay Colony, in forming and developing New England's characteristic settlement pattern.

Although fully committed to Plymouth's well-being, Standish was not a dedicated Separatist. In 1645 he initially supported William Vassall's petition to the General Court calling for religious toleration and political participation based only on good conduct. Winslow and William Bradford, in defeating the measure, persuaded Standish to change his mind. That year he performed his last military service by leading Plymouth's mobilization for a narrowly averted war with the Narragansetts.

Standish died in Duxbury, survived by his wife and four sons. His estate was valued in excess of £350, including one of the best farms in the colony. A cultivated man, Standish also left one of the largest and most diverse libraries in seventeenth-century English America. For nearly forty years Standish was not only Plymouth's chief military leader but also an important figure in the colony's political and economic life.

• Two essential primary sources making frequent mention of Standish are William Bradford, *Of Plymouth Plantation, 1620–1647,* ed. Samuel Eliot Morison (1952; repr. 1967), and Nathaniel B. Shurtleff and David Pulsifer, eds., *Records of the Colony of New Plymouth in New England* (12 vols., 1855–1861). The most convenient recent secondary source on Standish is Eugene Aubrey Stratton, *Plymouth Colony: Its History & People, 1620–1691* (1986). The best general history of the Old Colony is George D. Langdon, Jr., *Pilgrim Colony: A History of New Plymouth, 1620–1691* (1966).

RICHARD P. GILDRIE

STANDLEY, William Harrison (18 Dec. 1872–25 Oct. 1963), chief of naval operations and ambassador to the USSR, was born at Ukiah, California, the son of Jeremiah M. Standley, a sheriff of Mendocino County, and Sarah Jane Clay. He entered the U.S. Naval Academy in 1891, graduated in 1895, and earned an ensign's commission in 1897 after serving the requisite two years duty at sea. During the Spanish-American War and the Philippine Insurrection, Standley served with the Asiatic Fleet. He obtained his first command, a cruiser, in 1915 and took command of his first battleship four years later. He attended the Naval War College in 1920–1921. Known as a resolute leader, Captain Standley was boosted to flag rank ahead of several other captains who were higher on the selection list when he became rear admiral in 1927. He became vice admiral five years later.

In early 1933 Standley learned of plans to make him the next chief of naval operations, the navy's top post, succeeding William Veazie Pratt, who was scheduled to retire. To qualify him for the office, he was commissioned commander, Battle Force, U.S. Fleet, the navy's most prestigious and highest command afloat, on 8 June, which brought a fourth star dated from 20 May. About three weeks later, on 1 July, Admiral Standley became the sixth chief of naval operations and the first appointed by Franklin D. Roosevelt.

Over the better part of the next twelve years Roosevelt called on Standley to perform a variety of duties. He drafted the Vinson-Trammell Act, which provided the funds needed to expand the navy's number of ships and aircraft to the limits permitted by the Washington and London naval arms limitations treaties, and served as the U.S. delegate to the London Naval Conference in 1935–1936. During his tenure he often filled in for Secretary of the Navy Claude Swanson, when poor health kept Swanson from his duties. In September 1936, in part because of his failure to procure from Roosevelt the appointment of his assistant, Joseph K. Taussig, to command the U.S. Fleet, Standley decided to retire. Because full admirals could be extended beyond the statutory retirement age of sixty-four, Standley might have continued in his office, as the president requested, at least to complete a full four-year term as chief of naval operations. Standley stood firm and recommended William D. Leahy as his successor. He retired on 1 January 1937.

Standley left the navy for private business, working first at the 1939 World's Fair and later at Electric Boat Company. Recalled to active duty in 1941, he participated in defense planning with the Office of Production Management, supplying lend-lease material to the USSR with the Beaverbrook-Harriman Mission, investigating the attack on Pearl Harbor as a member of the Roberts Commission, and conducting public relations for the department.

Standley accepted the president's request that he become ambassador to the Soviet Union because, he later wrote, of a strong sense of duty and for fear of being assigned to tasks more monotonous than the previous year's. He assumed his post in April 1942. Standley was candid and often forceful with Soviet officials, habits that agitated the professional diplomats in the State Department. The admiral vigorously resisted their attempts to restrict the topics he might discuss with his hosts. In frustration Standley tendered his resignation in May 1943 and returned to the United States in October. He was recalled again to active naval service in March 1944 when Roosevelt assigned the admiral to the Planning Group of the Office of Strategic Services, where he remained until 31 August 1945, when he was relieved of all active duty.

In retirement he played golf and lectured on the threat the Soviet Union posed to the United States. He dabbled in Republican politics in California. In 1947 Governor Earl Warren named him to head a commission to investigate organized crime. The admiral also was an early supporter of Richard M. Nixon. Standley's memoir (with Arthur A. Ageton), *Admiral Ambassador to Russia*, appeared in 1955. He remained active in civic affairs in his later years. He died in San Diego. He was married to Evelyn Curtis, with whom he had five children. Their only son, William H. Standley, Jr., was a graduate of the U.S. Naval Academy and retired from the navy with the rank of rear admiral.

• Standley's papers are deposited in the Library of Congress and the University of Southern California. The Officer Biographies Files of the Operational Archives of the Naval Historical Center in Washington, D.C., hold a detailed resumé of Standley's life. In addition to his memoir, recollections of his experience in the Soviet Union are Standley and Rear Admiral Arthur A. Ageton, USN (Ret.), "The Cold War and Cultural Exchange," *United States Naval Institute Proceedings* 88 (Dec. 1962): 79–91. John C. Walter consulted Standley's papers for "William Harrison Standley," in *The Chiefs of Naval Operations*, ed. Robert William Love, Jr. (1980). An obituary is in the *New York Times*, 26 Oct. 1963.

RICHARD A. RUSSELL

STANFORD, Jane Eliza (25 Aug. 1825–28 Feb. 1905), philanthropist and collector, was born in Albany, New York, the daughter of Dyer Lathrop, a storekeeper and founder of the Albany Orphan Asylum, and Jane Anne Shields. Jane had some elementary schooling, followed by a year at the Albany Female Academy (established in 1814) when she was fifteen. In 1850 Jane married Leland Stanford, a lawyer from the neighboring town of Watervliet, New York, and they moved to Port Washington, Wisconsin. After fire destroyed the young lawyer's office, the couple returned to Albany.

Stanford remained in Albany to nurse her invalid father when her husband moved to California and, in 1852, opened a general store. After her father's death in 1855, Stanford moved to Sacramento, where her husband's business had flourished. In 1861 Leland Stanford was elected the first Republican governor of the state and, by the end of his term, was actively engaged in building the Central Pacific Railroad.

Jane Stanford led a traditional upper-class Victorian life, entertaining and becoming involved with philanthropic causes such as San Francisco kindergartens and a children's hospital in Albany. Leland Stanford, Jr., was born in 1868 to very proud parents. The boy, their only child, died of typhoid in Florence, Italy, at the age of fifteen.

To immortalize their son the Stanfords founded a university on their Palo Alto estate, south of San Francisco. Construction of the Leland Stanford Junior University began in 1885, and the school opened its doors in the fall of 1891. On the advice of Andrew D. White of Cornell University they hired David Starr Jordan, an eminent naturalist, to be its president. Despite their interest in the university, the Stanfords spent a considerable amount of time in Washington, D.C., during its construction because Leland Stanford was elected U.S. Senator for California in 1885 and again in 1891. He died at their home in Palo Alto in June 1893.

Leland Stanford's death, in the middle of the panic of 1893, forced Jane Stanford into an increasingly active role. Little had actually been willed to the university at the time of his death, except the land and two other farms (a bequest of $2 million was tied up with the rest of the estate). Their plan had been that, in the event of either spouse's death, the other should have the responsibility of creating the university to which both were so dedicated. Unfortunately, an intricate tangle of debts surrounded the estate, totaling $8 million; the estate was thus locked in probate. Stanford's lawyers advised her to close the university, as she had no money to maintain it.

Stanford refused to sacrifice the university, going to great lengths to keep it open. She was allocated an allowance from the estate for her own maintenance, so she listed all the professors as her personal servants to be able to pay them some salary. In 1897 Stanford took her jewels to London, hoping to sell them during Queen Victoria's Diamond Jubilee and thus gain some cash, but the market was not good, and she brought three-quarters of them back. The jewels were finally sold after her death, and the money, on her direction, provided a permanent endowment to the university's library.

Further financial problems arose in 1894 when the U.S. government filed suit against Leland Stanford's estate for $15 million. The partners of the Central Pacific had founded the Contract and Finance Company, which built the railroad at hugely inflated costs, creating a situation similar to the more famous Credit Mobilier scandal. Once again Stanford rose to the challenge. Fearing that a long court case would tie up funds long enough to force the university to close, she traveled to Washington, D.C., to talk to President Grover Cleveland and Attorney General Richard Olney. With their aid, the case was resolved in Stanford's favor by March 1896, being thrown out of the Supreme Court. Shortly after this Stanford gave the university a $2.5 million legacy, followed by $11 million in 1899 following the sale of the Central Pacific holdings.

Despite being solely responsible for the survival of Stanford University after her husband's death, Stanford created problems for the university. She idealized university life as quiet, studious, and idyllic, resenting anything that upset this vision. Stanford University had been coeducational from the beginning, a policy she approved of, feeling that women added a "refining influence" (Elliott, p. 135). However, when the percentage of women rose in 1899, she limited female enrollment to 500 at a time, without consulting anyone.

Stanford was very concerned with fulfilling the building program, laid out with her husband, at the expense of the educational aims of the school. While Jordan begged her for books and salary increases, Stanford toured the world searching for artifacts to adorn the university church and museum, even consulting with the Pope. This preoccupation proved to be shortsighted, not only because it jeopardized the university's credibility, but also because much of the building work was destroyed by the San Francisco earthquake in 1906. As Jordan wrote to Andrew White in 1906 after the earthquake, "These buildings . . . were put up by a tour de force, and the living organism of the University was almost starved in the process" (Elliott, p. 153).

The university's credibility was also jeopardized in 1900 when Jane Stanford forced the resignation of economics professor Edward Ross, a personal friend of Jordan's. Ross drew considerable public attention with his support of the 1894 railroad strike, and of the William Jennings Bryan presidential campaign of 1896, including writing a pamphlet supporting free silver. After the campaign Ross continued to speak at socialist clubs, airing commonly held views against Japanese immigration and predicting municipal ownership of utilities. Stanford heard of this behavior and made Jordan force Ross's resignation. Ross publicized the matter, resulting in a massive public outcry against a university that allowed its policy to be dictated by "an uncultured old woman" (Elliott, p. 354). Seven other members of the faculty resigned over the controversy, and there was talk of a boycott of the university in the academic community.

In 1903 Jane Stanford created a board of trustees for the university, retaining the position of president. She died of a heart attack brought on by strychnine poisoning in Honolulu, Territory of Hawaii. No investigation was ever made into her death.

Stanford showed strength and courage in maintaining the university in the face of great financial odds. However, her lack of real understanding of the nature of the institution threatened its academic credibility.

• A valuable collection of Stanford's letters is Gunther Nagel, *Iron Will: The Life and Letters of Jane Stanford* (1975). David Starr Jordan, *The Story of a Good Woman: Jane Lathrop Stanford* (1912), is a particularly useful biography as it quotes from original sources. Stanford's childhood and later travels are in the memoirs of her private secretary, Bertha Berner, *Mrs. Leland Stanford: An Intimate Account* (1935). A more critical look at her dealings with the university is in Orrin Elliott, *Stanford University: The First Twenty-Five Years* (1937). To understand Stanford fully it is necessary to understand her husband. A good basic biography is George T. Clark, *Leland Stanford: War Governor of California, Railroad Builder, and Founder of Stanford University* (1931). Carol Margot Osborne, *Museum Builders in the West: The Stanfords as Collectors and Patrons of Art 1870–1906* (1986), is also useful, as is David C. Frederick, "Railroads, Robber Barons, and the Saving of Stanford University," *Western Legal History* 4, no. 2 (Summer–Fall 1991): 225–56. The Ross case is discussed in Ross's autobiography, *Seventy Years of It* (1936), and James C. Mohr, "Academic Turmoil and Public Opinion: The Ross Case at Stanford," *Pacific History Review* (Feb. 1970): 39–61. Gary Ogle, "The Mysterious Death of Mrs. Leland Stanford," *Pacific Historian* (1981): 1–7, investigates her death by strychnine poisoning. An obituary is in the *Palo Alto Times*, 24 Mar. 1905.

CLAIRE STROM

STANFORD, Leland (9 Mar. 1824–21 June 1893), corporation head, governor of California, and U.S. senator, was born Amasa Leland Stanford in Watervliet, Upstate New York, the son of prosperous gentry parents Josiah Stanford and Elizabeth Phillips. Josiah Stanford was an innkeeper, landowner, and bridge and road contractor; he was also a strong supporter of the Erie Canal. Leland (he rarely used his first name) Stanford attended local schools until adolescence and then was educated at home under the tutelage of his mother. Legend has it that young Stanford was a voracious reader; books do not seem to have been of much interest to him in later life. In his late teens, Stanford attended the nearby Clinton Liberal Institute and, later, the Cazenovia Seminary. He read law with the Albany firm of Wheaton, Doolittle and Hadley and was admitted to the bar in 1848. That same year Stanford traveled to Port Washington, Wisconsin, to begin his legal practice. Stanford married Jane Lathrop in 1850. When Stanford's law office and a good portion of the entire town of Port Washington burned in 1852, he decided to join his five brothers in the new state of California, where they worked in a series of stores and mercantile establishments. Stanford went west alone (his wife's father apparently forbidding her to go until Stanford had established himself), sailing from New York and then opening a series of stores in the gold country towns near Sacramento.

By 1856, now joined by his wife, Stanford was in business with a brother in Sacramento, already making a great deal of money from his mercantile pursuits and forays into the local mining business. He had also started making inroads into local politics. Stanford rose with the infant Republican party. In 1857 he was the Republican candidate for state treasurer (he lost), and by 1859 he ran as the party's gubernatorial candidate (and lost again). With the outbreak of the Civil War and subsequent fracturing of the California Democratic party, Stanford found himself in the right place at the right time and became governor for a two-year term (1861–1863). While an undistinguished governor, Stanford was able to utilize the position to push forward a railroad project in which he himself was vitally interested.

In company with well-to-do Sacramento merchants Mark Hopkins, Charles Crocker, and Collis Huntington, Stanford had invested in a scheme by visionary engineer Theodore Judah to build a railroad east across the Sierras. The transcontinental railroad had long been an exciting idea in the minds of Americans eager to link the East with the West, but California's statehood in 1850 and the threatening clouds of disunion had pushed the scheme forward.

In 1863 ground was broken in Sacramento for the Central Pacific Railroad, a corporation jointly owned by Stanford and his business partners. Judah's death later that year robbed the company of its most important engineering figure, but the erstwhile merchants stepped in with the necessary capital to hire other skilled men. What is more, with Stanford in the governor's office, the massive, expensive project had an important, and certainly not disinterested, ally. As governor and, simultaneously, president of the Central Pacific, Stanford pushed forward legislation that resulted in public stock subscriptions to help fund rail construction across the Sierras.

Stanford's gubernatorial term expired in late 1863, and as he was not renominated, he turned his full energies to the railroad project. Six years later, at a lonely spot in northwestern Utah called Promontory, Stanford and his business partners celebrated the famed linkup between the eastbound Central Pacific and westbound Union Pacific. The Central Pacific would not have been built without a fortuitous combination of factors: the determination, even ruthlessness, of Stanford and his partners; the largess of the federal, state, and various local governments in the form of grants of funds and land; and the astounding labor of the railroad's mostly Chinese work force, many of whom were imported directly from China for the job.

The Big Four, as the major partners in the Central Pacific came to be known, divided their duties according to their particular strengths and proclivities. Crocker acted as construction boss, Hopkins helped to keep the books, and Huntington went east to raise money and engage in politics. Stanford was probably the weakest link in the chain, though his partners recognized his important role in California political affairs. Stanford, who always harbored hopes of national political success, spent much of his time meeting with political leaders, newspaper owners and editors, and other corporation figures. He also utilized his political and social connections to borrow money for the project. Much of the planning and carrying out of the Big Four's dynastic railroad plans was left to Huntington after Hopkins's death in the late 1870s.

By the mid-1870s Stanford owned a big share of a massive railroad empire, now consolidated as the Southern Pacific Railroad. Already well-off at the time of the Central Pacific groundbreaking, Stanford became fabulously wealthy as the railroad net expanded south into Los Angeles and east into the greater Southwest. The empire grew to include other transportation systems as well, such as steamship lines and interurban train networks. Money poured in, though the secrecy and complexity of the system's financial accounting has made it unlikely that a full picture of the origins and immensity of all the money will ever emerge. Stanford was not shy about ostentatious displays of wealth. His spending habits even worried his partners, who were concerned that Stanford was overextending himself based on projected railroad earnings. Two of Stanford's biggest purchases, bought in rapid succession, were a horse farm and vineyard on the San Francisco Peninsula and an immense art-filled mansion built atop San Francisco's Nob Hill. Stanford's farm, now the location of Stanford University, was the site at which photographer Eadweard Muybridge performed his famed studies of one of Stanford's racehorses at full gallop; the photographs, later published as *Horse in Motion* (1882), helped pioneer a version of photography that would eventually evolve into motion pictures.

Despite growing opposition to the political influence of the railroad empire, christened in print as the all-powerful "Octopus," Stanford and his partners never believed that the transportation network they had created was anything other than magnificent and beneficent. Political movements built precisely on railroad opposition, arguing that the Southern Pacific and its directors were simply too powerful and too rich for the public good, mystified and angered these men. They believed firmly that the transcontinental railroad project had been accomplished all to the greater glory of the nation, the West, and especially California, and any negative response was but personal jealousy or rank political opportunism. Such single-mindedness helped create a mixed legacy for men such as Stanford. Revered by many during his lifetime for his example of hard work and astounding success, Stanford nonetheless attracted his share of enmity, in part owing to his own lack of humility and his consequent misunderstanding of public perceptions regarding his fortune and his railroad.

The Stanfords had one child, Leland Stanford, Jr., born eighteen years into their marriage as the first transcontinental rail project neared completion in 1868. Leland, Jr., died of typhoid fever just shy of sixteen while on a grand European tour in 1884. His death shattered his parents, who had doted on the child. Grief at their son's untimely death nearly unnerved both parents. Stanford later recalled a vision he had the night following his son's death, in which the boy returned to encourage his father to use his fortune for the public good. Apparently Jane Lathrop Stanford helped break through her husband's grief to urge that a public memorial be created in honor of their only child. Leland Stanford, Junior, University was created on the Palo Alto land of Stanford's horse farm. Begun in 1885 and opened in 1891, the university was arguably the single greatest American philanthropic gift to date. The school, coeducational from the start, offered broad training in the arts and sciences and has since grown in prestige to the first rank of world universities.

In the later years of his life, Stanford focused much of his attention and energy upon the university. He did not, however, disengage himself completely from the public arena. He served, with little distinction, as U.S. senator from 1885 until his death. His senatorial tenure witnessed many important bills, including Chinese exclusion and the Interstate Commerce Act, but Stanford played a minor role and was in fact absent at several crucial roll calls. A stunted reach for the presidency in 1888 was little short of silly, and a flirtation with the Populist party as a presidential candidate in 1892 was outlandish. Stanford's few senatorial speeches or interviews characterize him as a fairly long-winded dispenser of bootstrap platitudes, though his ideas about race did mark him at least slightly as progressive. In a speech given in the U.S. Senate in 1890 regarding federal aid to public schools, Stanford argued that open education for all would eliminate what he termed "the race difficulty." In matters of labor and capital, Stanford tended toward the naive, arguing that it was unproductive for the two sides to oppose one another, that workers and management ought to work together since they were interdependent. In Stanford's words, labor and capital were as cause and effect and, as if scientifically ordained, there could be no antagonism between the two.

It was during this period, too, that the breach between Stanford and business partner Huntington grew most pronounced. Huntington, who had long expressed distaste for Stanford's political ambitions and ostentatious dilettantism, forced his way into the presidency of the Southern Pacific in 1890. The bitter struggle forever split what had been a long and immensely profitable business relationship. Plagued by ill health from his fifties onward, in part because of his great size, Stanford withdrew more and more from the public toward the end of his life. Many attempts were made to recover his once robust health through long excursions to various health spas in Europe. At his death in Palo Alto, California, various memorials and speeches in Washington and California testified to his success and fame. As yet, however, Stanford remains somewhat of a mystery, a man whose legacy and life await fuller explication.

• Manuscript material regarding the life of Stanford is quite rare, as many papers were intentionally or accidentally destroyed after his death. This may in part explain the relative dearth of scholarly investigation of this important figure's life and work. The largest collection of manuscript sources can be found in the Department of Special Collections and Archives of Stanford University, which has holdings for Jane Lathrop Stanford and Leland Stanford, Jr., as well. Stanford's speeches and gubernatorial addresses are preserved in special collections and government documents libraries. At the end of the century, the Southern Pacific Railroad published a set of books that compile the correspondence of the corporation figures over several decades. These books are rare; the Huntington Library of San Merino, Calif., owns a set. The Collis P. Huntington Papers at Syracuse University are also valuable. Norman E. Tutorow, *Leland Stanford: Man of Many Careers* (1971), is a full-length biography. David Lavender, *The Great Persuader* (1970), a life of Huntington, is an important source for information about Stanford. Oscar Lewis, *The Big Four* (1938), is informative but lacks scholarly apparatus. The most recent discussion of antirailroad thought and behavior in California is William Deverell, *Railroad Crossing* (1994).

WILLIAM DEVERELL

STANFORD, Sally (5 May 1903–1 Feb. 1982), San Francisco madam, mayor of Sausalito, California, and restaurant owner, was born Marcia Busby in Baker City, Oregon. (Some sources give her name at birth as Mabel Janice Busby, but in her autobiography she says Marcia is her given name.) Little is known of her parentage or early life, except that she grew up in poverty on an Oregon farm. Sally supplemented the family's income by caddying at a local golf course and working as a waitress.

At age sixteen Stanford eloped with Dan Goodan, grandson of a former governor of Colorado, who worked as the auditor of a local lumber company. Before their flight from Oregon, Goodan had taken $5,000 worth of company checks, for which he was arrested when the pair settled in Colorado. When Stanford went to the jail to visit her husband, she was also arrested for possessing stolen property, as Goodan had bought her an electric iron with the money he took. The local district attorney convinced her to plead guilty and spare the state a trial, for which she would get probation. She took his advice, but in July 1920 she was sentenced to two years in the Oregon State Penitentiary at Salem; parole was granted in September 1921. In her autobiography, *The Lady of the House* (1966), she said the experience changed her life. "It was there I also made up my mind never to be broke again. It seemed that only the poor were punished and the broke went to jail." Sources differ as to when Stanford and Goodan divorced. Accounts of her second and third marriages conflict, as one source indicates she was married to a Mr. Fansler from 1921 to 1927, while another says she married Ralph R. Bayham in 1925.

After her parole Stanford stayed with an uncle in southern California. Hearing of the money to be made in bootlegging during the Prohibition era, she started a one-woman business making and selling illegal liquor. She met her next husband, attorney Ernest Spagnoli, when she hired him to represent her in a traffic case in the Los Angeles court. The couple were married in 1927 and moved to San Francisco.

San Francisco in the 1920s and 1930s was home to speakeasies, nightclubs, gambling, and prostitution, and illegal industries of many varieties flourished. There was plenty of legal work for Stanford's husband, and she spent some time as a quiet housewife in one of San Francisco's new suburban neighborhoods. She and Ernest separated in 1929 (the marriage was annulled in 1933), at which time she decided to earn her living running a residential hotel in the district known as the Tenderloin. Also around this time Stanford adopted a child.

When a guest nearly died from a self-induced abortion, the police suspected that the hotel was a disorderly house and charged Stanford with pandering. Though she was not convicted, the experience signaled another major change in her life. Soon after her arrest, she decided to turn fiction into fact and open a brothel. To spare her prominent ex-husband any embarrassment should she be arrested again, she changed her name from Marcia Spagnoli to Sally Stanford; she chose the name from a newspaper headline that reported that Stanford had beaten California in a college football game. The name "Sally" came from a popular song of the day.

Over the next few years Stanford's innate intelligence and common sense helped her become one of San Francisco's most prominent madams. In 1942 she opened her most famous establishment, a magnificent mansion on Pine Street reportedly designed by New York architect Stanford White. Nicknamed "The Fortress," it was nearly impervious to raids and appeared outwardly respectable. Stanford did not live at the Pine Street house but had an equally elegant home on Clay Street not far away.

World War II changed the face of San Francisco forever, and the increased police presence near her establishment meant that Stanford would be watched (and arrested) with more frequency than in the past. Though she had been arrested seventeen times, she had been convicted only four times. She began to look for a new line of work and found it across San Francisco Bay in the little town of Sausalito, home to quaint shops, restaurants, coffeehouses, and stunning waterfront views of San Francisco and the surrounding area.

In 1948 Stanford bought and began the restoration of the Valhalla restaurant in this quiet bayside city. In the following year the Pine Street house was raided and shut down forever. Sally still retained ownership of the building, but she put her energy into Valhalla, which had a splashy opening in March 1950.

The next few years were happy and successful, and Stanford retained her ability to bounce back from adversity when her past occasionally caught up with her. In 1955 the California State Department of Alcoholic Beverage Control convened hearings to revoke her liquor license (based on her record as a madam), but she fought them for four years, eventually prevailing against the government.

In 1934 Stanford had married Louis Rapp, whom she divorced in 1941. In April 1951 San Francisco society was scandalized when she married Robert Gump, a member of the prominent family who had owned the city's most fashionable objet d'art shop since the nineteenth century. The two separated in December of the same year. In 1954 she married Robert Kenna.

Running a successful restaurant made Stanford aware of the many political currents in Sausalito. Most prominent was the conflict between those who benefit-ed from the many tourists that crowded city streets on the weekends and the wealthy owners of expensive hillside homes who resented this weekly invasion. Stanford felt that tourism was good for the town but that the accompanying uncontrolled growth was not.

When she had a disagreement with city officials about placing an electric sign above her restaurant, Stanford decided to enter local politics. Her first attempt was a run for city council in 1962. Her past, of course, was much discussed during the campaign, though distinguished personages such as Hillary Belloc, son of the English author, were strong supporters. She lost the election but continued to agitate for her concerns.

In 1966 her autobiography, *The Lady of the House*, was published. Though it carried her name as author, it was actually ghostwritten by a friend, newspaperman Bob Patterson. Its colorful language, unapologetic tone, and spicy subject matter made it a popular volume.

In 1972 Stanford was finally elected to the Sausalito city council. Significantly, she had used the name Marcia Owen—one of her aliases from the old days—instead of Sally Stanford (by now her legal name) during this, her fifth campaign. In 1976 she was elected mayor. Her platform included support for a ferry system to get people out of their cars and acquisition of waterfront property for public use.

In 1980 Stanford campaigned for reelection to the city council after her term as mayor had expired. She won the election and was named honorary vice mayor for life. Two years later she died in Greenbrae, California, of a heart attack, the last of a series of twelve coronary attacks during her life. Flags flew at half-mast throughout Sausalito, and local newspapers praised the woman who had risen from the back streets to the halls of government.

Sally Stanford's presence in California history reaffirms the rather loony image of the Golden State. Where else could a former madam change her life to become the mayor of a major tourist city? More seriously, her stance in favor of open, public spaces at a time of rampant development helped Sausalito retain its renowned beauty and charm.

• The Sausalito Historical Society has a large clipping file, as well as biographical files about Sally Stanford. Of the many books written about the history of San Francisco and Sausalito, only two cover Stanford's life in any detail. The first is her autobiography, *The Lady of the House* (1966). Also of interest is Curt Gentry, *The Madams of San Francisco* (1964). Newspapers that cover various aspects of her political life include the *Marin Independent Journal* and *Marinscope*. *Time* magazine, 22 Mar. 1976, discusses her political career as well. Obituaries are in the *New York Times*, 2 Feb. 1982; and *Newsweek* and *Time*, 15 Feb. 1982.

LYNN DOWNEY

STANKIEWICZ, Richard Peter (18 Oct. 1922–27 Mar. 1983), sculptor, was born in Philadelphia, Pennsylvania, the son of Anton Stankiewicz, a shoemaker and railroad worker, and Rozalia Petrociewicz. Anton

Stankiewicz was killed in a railroad accident when Richard Stankiewicz was two. His mother remarried, and in 1929 the family moved to Detroit, settling in a Polish neighborhood near railroad tracks and industrial dumping fields where Stankiewicz played as a child. He attended a Catholic middle school and was graduated from Cass Technical High School, which served Detroit's automotive industries. He studied mechanical drafting and engineering and was able to support himself through the 1950s and into the early 1960s as a patent draftsman with the skills he acquired at this time. He also studied art and music, and at graduation in 1940 he won a scholarship to the Cranbrook Academy of Art (in nearby Bloomfield Hills, Mich.), but family finances prevented him from accepting it.

After working in the Civilian Conservation Corps and at a Detroit tool and die shop where he drafted production machinery, Stankiewicz joined the U.S. Navy in July 1941. While serving in California, the Aleutian Islands, Washington, and Hawaii, he began to paint and to carve figures out of bone and wood. He also visited museums in San Francisco and Seattle, where he met artists in the community surrounding Mark Tobey and Morris Graves. He left the navy in 1947 and in 1948 moved to New York to study painting (on the G.I. Bill) with Hans Hofmann. Stankiewicz traveled to Paris with fellow Hofmann student Jean Follett in 1950, studying briefly with Fernand Léger and, more productively, with the sculptor Ossip Zadkine. He returned to New York in June 1951 a sculptor. His work from this period, insect forms produced out of plaster-encrusted wire, reveal the influence of Alberto Giacometti. Stankiewicz was a founding member of the Hansa Gallery (1951–1959), one of the earliest downtown artists' cooperatives, originally comprising twelve former Hofmann students. Other founding members included Jean Follett, John Gruen, Wolf Kahn, Allan Kaprow, Jan Müller, and Jane Wilson. From 1958 until 1965 Stankiewicz showed at the Stable Gallery; from 1971 on he was represented by the Virginia Zabriskie Gallery.

In 1953 Stankiewicz made his first welded metal sculpture. It employed detritus he had unearthed while preparing a garden in the backyard of his apartment house. Later he used junk found on city streets or purchased from a junk dealer on the Bowery. While the casually assembled, discarded materials conferred immediate shock value upon his work, Stankiewicz never denigrated these finds. Trying to explain why he used cast-off objects, Stankiewicz once asserted:

To pick up anything, to heft it, feel its surface, study its form and study it as a sculpture is an exciting exercise and an adventure that ought to be recommended. This close attention to things . . . makes one very much aware of how narrow is the esthetic of things in good taste—I'm thinking of the things that people acquire, what are supposed to be handsome things. They have a quite small range of texture and character after all. (artist's statement to the University of Minnesota Art Gallery, 5 Sept. 1955, Richard Stankiewicz Papers)

The critic and painter Fairfield Porter associated the mélange of machinery with Wallace Stevens's poem "The Man on the Dump," writing that just as Stevens connects "nouns and adjectives one would not naturally associate, so Stankiewicz associates a spring, a weight, and the casting from the top of a gas cooking stove to make a non-machine frozen into immobility by its own rust" (Friedman, p. 72).

In part because of its humble materials Stankiewicz's sculpture attracted attention in popular national magazines. In *Newsweek* (16 Jan. 1956, p. 52), for example, he was pictured alongside his *Secretary*, which was made out of an old boiler tank with a typewriter embedded in its belly. *Warrior*, another boiler tank in a precarious posture, was featured in *Time* (31 Dec. 1956, p. 50) under the headline "The Beauty of Junk." Stankiewicz's "junk sculpture" came to be associated with the urban scene celebrated by the Beat poets, and by 1958 his sculpture could be found in the collections of the Whitney Museum of American Art and the Museum of Modern Art, New York. He was included, with Jasper Johns, Robert Rauschenberg, Frank Stella, and Ellsworth Kelly, in the exhibition Sixteen Americans held at the Museum of Modern Art in 1959 and in New Forms—New Media I, a definitive exhibition in the history of "junk art," held at the Martha Jackson Gallery in New York in 1960. In 1961 Stankiewicz appeared with an international roster of artists in the Museum of Modern Art exhibition Assemblage, which traced the history of art comprising nonart materials from Picasso, Schwitters, and Duchamp to the present.

Stankiewicz had reached the apogee of his popularity by the early 1960s; his work was shown in Paris, where it influenced Jean Tinguely and the nouveau réalistes, French artists who incorporated mundane objects in their art. In 1961 Stankiewicz made a motorized sculpture, *The Apple*, for an exhibition of kinetic art shown in Amsterdam and Stockholm. His only motorized work, it remains in the collection of the Moderna Museet, Stockholm. Also in 1961 Stankiewicz married Patricia Doyle, a native of Australia and a secretary at the United Nations. In 1962 the couple left New York and settled in rural Worthington, Massachusetts, where they raised two sons. The marriage ended in divorce in 1977.

Although he appeared at the Guggenheim Museum in a public symposium on junk sculpture in 1962, Stankiewicz gradually withdrew from the New York art world in the 1960s. In 1967 he joined the art department at the State University of New York at Albany, where he established the sculpture program and taught until his retirement in 1981. A turning point in his career occurred in 1969 during a trip to Australia. Invited to work with the staff and facilities of a commercial fabricating plant in Sydney, he produced fifteen large-scale works of freshly milled industrial steel. The largest of these works, which is more than seventeen feet tall, is in the Australian National Gallery, Canberra. These new works exhibited some of the precarious postures of Stankiewicz's earlier, anthropomorphic works but essentially were geometric abstractions. By 1973, however, in some cylindrical configurations, Stankiewicz had reintroduced a human presence into his work. In the late 1970s he adopted an easel form, either free-standing or in relief, and embellished it with salvaged junk steel in a manner reminiscent both of his earliest work and of Hans Hofmann's "push pull" compositional strategy. The scale of his later work was generally larger than his sculpture of the 1950s. Although his later work was well received, Stankiewicz did not attain the degree of popular recognition he had enjoyed in the 1950s, when his innovative combination of surrealist fantasy, elegant composition, and derelict materials conferred on him the status of a trail blazer. He died at his home in Worthington, Massachusetts.

A member of the second generation of the New York School, Stankiewicz pioneered the incorporation of rusted metal machine parts in art, and his work may be seen as a precursor of assemblage, art created by the fusion of disparate parts into a meaningful whole. Although his sculpture frequently showed a high degree of humor, with figurative works bordering on caricature, Stankiewicz was intensely serious about his work, and for the duration of his career the cast-off quality of his materials was offset by elegantly calibrated compositions.

• The papers of Richard Stankiewicz, including correspondence, newspaper and magazine articles, financial records, and manuscripts of published statements and public addresses, are in the Archives of American Art, Smithsonian Institution, Washington, D.C. Also in the archives are texts of two important interviews with the artist, one by Richard Brown Baker in 1963, the other by Robert Brown in 1979. Stankiewicz described his art in "An Open Situation," *Contemporary Sculpture/Arts Yearbook* 8 (1965): 156–59, and in Philip Pearlstein, "The Private Myth," *Art News*, Sept. 1961, pp. 41–44, 61–62. Important works, in addition to those in collections already cited, are in the Albright-Knox Art Gallery, Buffalo; the Cleveland Museum of Art; the Solomon R. Guggenheim Museum, New York; the Israel Museum, Jerusalem; the Musée National d'Art Moderne, Georges Pompidou Center, Paris; the Philadelphia Museum of Art; and the Walker Art Center, Minneapolis. Catalogs of retrospective exhibitions were published by the University Art Gallery, State University of New York, Albany (1978), the Virginia Zabriskie Gallery, New York (1983 and 1987), and the Middlebury College Museum of Art, Middlebury, Vt. (1994). The most complete monograph on Stankiewicz is Maurene S. Donadio, *Transfigured Wasteland: The Sculpture of Richard Stankiewicz* (1996). See also B. H. Friedman, *The School of New York: Some Younger Artists* (1959). An obituary is in the *New York Times*, 29 Mar. 1983.

MAURENE S. DONADIO

STANLEY, Albert Augustus (25 May 1851–19 May 1932), educator, conductor, and composer, was born in the village of Cumberland, Rhode Island, the son of George Washington Stanley, a physician, and Augusta Adaline Jefferds. After formal schooling in Slatersville, Rhode Island, and experience as organist in local churches, Stanley was sent by his father in 1871 to the Leipzig Conservatory, where he studied piano and organ in addition to general musical subjects. Upon his return to America in 1875 he served for a year as head of the two-person music department at Ohio Wesleyan Female College in Delaware, Ohio. In October 1876 he became organist of Grace Church in Providence, where he played Saturday organ recitals that were well received. In Providence he attracted many organ pupils, and at the Friends School there he gave advanced piano lessons to Quaker students.

An organ recital in Albany, New York, in 1880 for the Music Teachers National Association enabled Stanley to broaden his horizons. Elected chairman of the executive committee for the 1881 meeting of the MTNA in Providence, he was likewise responsible for the highly successful 1882 meeting in New York. In 1883 he became secretary-treasurer, and in 1886 president, of the MTNA. Through the latter position he became known to Dr. James Burrell Angell, president of the University of Michigan, who in 1888 invited him to chair the music program at the university. Stanley spent the remainder of his career as director of the music school there until his retirement as professor emeritus in 1921.

Albert A. Stanley was a man of great energy and many enthusiasms, a fine organizer. He soon reorganized the hitherto private Ann Arbor School of Music as the University School of Music, which served as the academic music department of the University of Michigan, as well as the sponsor of an annual series of concerts together with the annual May Festival. As conductor of the Choral Union and the University Orchestra, he was responsible for their solid contributions to Ann Arbor's musical life. As director of the Choral Union series of concerts (1888–1921) and of the May Festivals (begun in 1894 with the Theodore Thomas Orchestra), he hired some of the world's top artists and helped choose the repertoire that they performed. He also wrote copious program notes for the Choral Union series of concerts. He was the administrator of the Stearns Collection of musical instruments, which was given to the School of Music in 1898 by Frederick Stearns. In 1918 he published a catalog of the instrument collection.

Apart from his activities at Ann Arbor, Stanley served as president of the Michigan Music Teachers Association in 1892 and was one of the founders in 1884 of the American College of Musicians and in 1896 of the American Guild of Organists. He was president (1906–1912) of the American Section of the International Music Society and was honorary vice president of the Musical Association in Great Britain.

As a composer Stanley was not a "modernist"; he refers repeatedly in his memoir to the "uglified music" of such composers as Alois Haba. However, he speaks there with pride of his own *Chorus Triumphalis* (1896) and his *Hymn of Consecration* (c. 1917). He was somewhat more inclined to voices than to instruments. He wrote two symphonies and a symphonic poem, *Attis*, but he composed many works for chorus. Among the latter are three works for chorus and orchestra: *A*

Psalm of Victory (1906), *Fair Land of Freedom* (1919), and *Laus Deo* (c. 1920). He was attracted to music with Greek associations; his *Greek Themes in Modern Musical Settings* was published in 1924 as volume fifteen of the *University of Michigan Studies, Humanistic Series.*

In December 1875 Stanley married his childhood sweetheart, Emma F. Bullock; they had one daughter. After the death of his first wife in 1911, Stanley married Dorothea Oestreicher in 1921. He died in Ann Arbor (where he was known to some as "Dad Stanley").

• Satisfactory published sources on Stanley are few, one being the article by Rosseter G. Cole in the *Dictionary of American Biography*, vol. 9 (1935–1936). This and other sources give the place of Stanley's birth as Manville, R.I., but in his memoir Stanley himself says it was Cumberland, a village near Manville. The unpublished memoir, "Echoes from a Busy Life," is held at the Michigan Historical Collections in Ann Arbor. Although it is short on biographic data, it contains surprisingly lavish descriptions of each annual concert of the Choral Union series and the May Festivals, even those known to Stanley only through letters and official reports. Appendix 1, "Condensed History of the University Musical Society" (1881–1925), is missing, but Appendix 2, "Detailed Repertoire of the Choral Union and Festival Series" (1881–1925), is present on twenty-two printed pages.

WILLIAM LICHTENWANGER

STANLEY, Carter (27 Aug. 1925–1 Dec. 1966), bluegrass musician, was born Carter Glen Stanley in McClure, Virginia, the son of Lee Stanley, a logger, and Lucy Smith Rake. The Stanley household included seven children from the couple's first marriages as well as Carter and his younger brother, Ralph. When Carter was a child, the family moved to Lucy Smith Stanley's birthplace on Clinch Mountain, where they had a small farm and ran a roadside grocery store. The farm was on a ridge with views into Tennessee and Kentucky; it later became a touchstone in Carter Stanley's music, and he often returned to the "Smith home place" during his adulthood.

Stanley's interest in music was fostered by his father's singing and his mother's banjo playing as well as by hymn singing at the McClure Primitive Baptist Church. The Stanleys were one of the few families in their area to own a radio during the 1930s, another early musical influence in Stanley's life. He got his first guitar from a mail-order catalog, and the mail carrier helped him learn to play. When Stanley was a teenager, his parents split up. During high school he joined his father in work at the sawmill; he and his younger brother, who played the banjo, also began performing with some friends at school dances and as an entr'acte at school plays. Lee Stanley did not appreciate having the boys practice at home; chased out of the house, they would play in the woods or the barn. As soon as he finished school, Carter Stanley joined the army, returning to Virginia in May 1946. He married Mary Magdalene Kiser, with whom he had five children.

During and after World War II, the popularity of country or "hillbilly" music spread as rural southerners moved into urban areas and brought their musical tastes to an expanding market. The creation of many new radio stations in the years following the war increased the demand for musicians to play on live shows, and Stanley was able to find steady radio work in the late 1940s. Upon his return from the war, Stanley joined Roy Sykes and the Blue Ridge Mountain Boys, playing a mixture of traditional mountain music and a new style being developed by Bill Monroe and the Blue Grass Boys (later dubbed "bluegrass" in recognition of their instrumental role in its formulation). When his brother Ralph returned from his tour in Germany in October 1946, Carter picked him up at the bus station in Bristol, Virginia, and took him directly to the studios of WNVA in Norton to play with Sykes. Ralph, who was not sure that he wanted to be a full-time musician, chafed at performing in someone else's band and soon convinced Carter that they should strike out on their own. In December 1946 their band, the Stanley Brothers and the Clinch Mountain Boys, found a home on WCYB in Bristol, where they played on a daily program called "Farm and Fun Time." The publicity generated by the radio show allowed the Stanley Brothers to book performances all over the area, and for several years they played in rural schoolhouses and small auditoriums in the tri-state area of southwest Virginia, western North Carolina, and eastern Tennessee.

The Stanley Brothers started out singing traditional ballads like "Man of Constant Sorrow" and covering Bill Monroe's compositions, but Carter began writing his own material around 1948. They signed their first record contract in 1947, with a small Johnson City, Tennessee, label called Rich-R-Tone, and had some success with "Little Glass of Wine" (1948), a song of fairly recent origin but with an archaic sound. They began recording for Columbia Records in 1948 and stayed with that label until 1952. The Stanley Brothers mixed high-spirited, raucous tunes with sweet, soft duets, with Carter usually taking the lead. Their distinct sound has often been described as having a "lonesome mountain" quality to it, and Carter's singing, which has been compared to revival testifying, was clearly reminiscent of his Baptist upbringing.

In 1951, despite their recent successes, the brothers stopped performing, probably out of exhaustion, and went to work briefly for the Ford Motor Company in Detroit. Then they parted ways for a time. After a few months, Carter began working with Monroe, recording "Get Down on Your Knees and Pray" (1951). Ralph considered returning to farming, but the Stanleys patched things up and returned to "Farm and Fun Time" together. The brothers seem to have had a somewhat tumultuous relationship, but family loyalty prevented their talking about this publicly. Carter, a natural performer who was always happy at the center of attention, tended to dominate his more reserved younger brother, and his looser, more experimental musical style guided the development of the band's music. This became more apparent after Carter's death, as Ralph carried on a career on his own but with a much more conservative sound.

In 1953 the Stanley Brothers signed with Mercury Records and recorded some of their best material, achieving a hotter, tighter sound than they had previously. Critics have described their initial work at Mercury, including gospel songs like "Cry from the Cross" (1956) as well as secular pieces like "Loving You Too Well" (1957) and "(Say) Won't You Be Mine?" (1953), as a high-water mark of early bluegrass music.

During the mid-1950s, the Stanley Brothers continued to perform in the South and Southeast, playing traditional and original compositions and entertaining their audiences with slapstick and blackface routines. However, the popularity of rockabilly during this period led the Stanleys to tinker with their sound, and they were pressured into playing boogie-woogie tunes that were unsuited to their style and unpopular with their longtime audience. With record sales down and Mercury dissatisfied with their work, the brothers left the company in 1958. That year the Stanleys moved to Live Oak, Florida, to join a television show, the "Suwanee River Jamboree," and they toured the Deep South with the sponsorship of the Jim Walter Homes Corporation, a producer of prefabricated houses. Also in 1958 the Stanley Brothers signed recording contracts with Starday and King. At Starday they recorded pieces that became part of the standard bluegrass repertoire, including "Carolina Mountain Home" (1959) and "Rank Stranger" (1960). At King Records, producer Syd Nathan pushed them to include more guitar and less banjo and mandolin, moving them slightly away from bluegrass's usual staccato sound.

In the early 1960s things looked bad for bluegrass generally and for the Stanley Brothers in particular. The locally produced radio shows that had supplied their audience were disappearing, and the rise of rock 'n' roll and commercialized country music was seducing away many of their fans. Money became tight, and the brothers could not afford to pay the salaries of their sidemen. Instead, they resorted to picking up musicians wherever they performed. Sometimes they were not able to pay for dinner or gas for the trip home until after they had been paid for their set. Joking about their financial plight, Carter commented, "I got all the money I need. I got enough to do me a lifetime—provided I die before breakfast tomorrow morning" (quoted in Wright, p. 168). The one bright spot was the growth of the folk music revival, which generated some interest in bluegrass among younger listeners who rejected the "establishment" sounds of rock 'n' roll and country. The Stanley Brothers were on the bill at folk festivals at Antioch College in 1960 and at the University of Chicago in 1961.

In the 1960s the Stanley Brothers continued to be based in northern Florida, and their performing schedule meant being away from home much of the time. They would play a grueling schedule of three or four daytime shows at schools, evening shows on weekends (at bars or drive-in theaters, sometimes using the roof of the concession stand as a stage), and at

parks on Sunday afternoons. Carter, the consummate showman, did not allow these circumstances to affect his work and seemed as happy as ever on stage; he kept Ralph going during the hardest times. However, by the mid-1960s Carter's health was failing, probably from alcohol abuse. Concerts of the period were described by some listeners as unmitigated disasters, and Carter did not always have the energy to stay on stage for a whole set. Ralph, previously always in the wings, was forced to take a more active role; Carter had been the creative half of the team, writing and arranging the music and doing most of the singing and talking to the audience. He became seriously ill in the spring of 1966, seemed to improve during a European tour that summer, then fell apart that fall. At his last performance, in October 1966, he had to leave the stage after only three songs. Carter insisted on being taken back to Smith Ridge, Virginia, where he spent the remaining months before his death. He was buried in the Smith family plot on a high ridge of Clinch Mountain. Ralph organized a series of bluegrass festivals in his brother's memory that were held near their childhood home.

Despite its roots in traditional music, bluegrass was still a fairly new musical form in 1966, and the Stanley Brothers were one of the bands that laid its foundations. While the form itself was named after Bill Monroe's band, some critics maintain that the Stanley Brothers, led by Carter, helped to established bluegrass as a musical style by forging it into a recognizable sound. Many of Carter's songs have been recorded by other country artists such as Emmylou Harris and Ricky Skaggs. Decades after his death, Carter Stanley's voice still is recalled as one of the most emotional and haunting that bluegrass has ever known.

• For additional information, see Bob Artis, *Bluegrass* (1975); Robert Cantwell, "The Lonesome Sound of Carter Stanley," *Bluegrass Unlimited* 10 (1976); Gary Reid, *Stanley Brothers: A Preliminary Discography* (1984); and Reid, "The Stanley Brothers in Florida," *Florida Bluegrass News* 1 (1985). While John Wright's oral history *Traveling the High Way Home* (1993) focuses largely on Ralph Stanley, there are many reminiscences of Carter as well. On the Stanleys' role in the early development of the bluegrass style, see Neil V. Rosenberg, "From Sound to Style: The Emergence of Bluegrass," *Journal of American Folklore* 80 (1967). See also Rosenberg, *Bluegrass: A History* (1987).

BETHANY NEUBAUER

STANLEY, David Sloane (1 June 1828–13 Mar. 1902), army officer, was born in Cedar Valley, Ohio, the son of John Bratton Stanley and Sarah Peterson, farmers. After a brief apprenticeship in medicine, Stanley entered the U.S. Military Academy in 1848, graduating ninth in a class of forty-three four years later. Commissioned a brevet second lieutenant in the Second Dragoons that fall, he received his regular appointment in September 1853. Stanley served as quartermaster and commissary for Lieutenant A. W. Whipple's railroad survey from Fort Smith, Arkansas, to Los Angeles, California. He was transferred to the First Cavalry

Regiment in March 1855 and was promoted to first lieutenant in 1861. In 1857, Stanley married Anna Maria Wright, daughter of an army surgeon, and participated under Colonel Edwin Vose Sumner in that year's campaigns against the Cheyenne Indians, including the battle of Solomon River, Kansas.

In March 1861, Stanley was promoted to captain. With the outbreak of the Civil War, he refused an offer of a colonelcy in a Confederate regiment to remain in the Union army. He fought in the battle of Wilson's Creek, Missouri, before receiving his appointment as brigadier general of volunteers in September 1861. A broken leg left him disabled until early 1862, when he assumed command of an infantry division in the Army of the Mississippi. Stanley fought in the campaigns for New Madrid, Island Number Ten, and Fort Pillow. Service at Iuka and Corinth brought additional acclaim, and on 29 November 1862, he was appointed major general of volunteers. Wanting to improve his mounted troops, William S. Rosecrans brought Stanley to his Army of the Cumberland as chief of cavalry. A good organizer, Stanley promptly began unifying scattered mounted units into a cavalry reserve, fighting at Stones River (for which he was brevetted to lieutenant colonel), Bradyville, Snow Hill, Franklin, Middleton, Shelbyville, and Elk River.

In November 1863, Stanley assumed command of the First Division, IV Corps. The following year, he took part in William T. Sherman's campaigns against Atlanta, winning brevet appointments to colonel and brigadier general in the regular army for his actions at Resaca and Ruff's Station, Georgia, respectively. On the recommendation of George H. Thomas, Stanley succeeded to command of IV Corps, and he had been detached with John M. Schofield's army to protect Sherman's rear when John Bell Hood moved north toward Nashville. He did well in an independent command at Spring Hill, then he took a bullet through his neck while leading a decisive assault at the battle of Franklin, for which he was promoted in 1865 to brevet major general and in 1893 awarded a Medal of Honor.

Following the close of the Civil War, Stanley and his IV Corps were sent to Texas, where they spent two months at Victoria as a demonstration against French involvement in Mexico. His corps was disbanded at San Antonio, but in July 1866, Stanley received the colonelcy of the Twenty-second Infantry Regiment in the reorganized army. In 1872, he led a 600-man escort for a railroad survey from Fort Rice toward the Powder River. Frequent skirmishing with the region's Hunkpapa Sioux culminated in a brisk fight near O'Fallon Creek. His most dramatic frontier service came the following year, when he led 1,900 men and 250 wagons in an armed reconnaissance into the Yellowstone River area. Accompanied by a team of scientists, a swarm of British noblemen, and the flamboyant Lieutenant Colonel George A. Custer, the Yellowstone expedition encountered armed Indian opposition but found much of scientific and economic interest.

Transferred with his regiment to Texas in 1879, Stanley was appointed brigadier general five years later. In that rank he also commanded the Department of Texas until his 1892 retirement from active duty. Stanley served as governor of the Soldiers' Home in Washington, D.C., from 1893 until 1898, after which he remained a resident of that city until his death there. He was survived by five of his seven children; his wife had died in 1895.

Like many of his officer peers, Stanley was disappointed that promotion in the regular army had not come more quickly. He remained a loyal supporter of Rosecrans during the post–Civil War era, when veterans fought and refought their wartime experiences in the popular press. Although Schofield had been instrumental in securing a general's star for Stanley, the latter labeled Schofield too ambitious and fearful of politicians. Sherman, however, criticized in his *Memoirs* the late arrival of Stanley's corps at the battle of Jonesboro. An acrimonious feud with William B. Hazen concerning Hazen's conduct at Shiloh and Missionary Ridge also marked Stanley's postwar career, but he saved his sharpest barbs for Jacob D. Cox, who allegedly misrepresented Stanley's actions at Franklin. "I could not stand him," wrote Stanley (*Personal Memoirs*, p. 138).

• Biographical material on Stanley may be found in Mark M. Boatner III, *Civil War Dictionary*, rev. ed. (1988); Francis B. Heitman, *Historical Register and Dictionary of the United States Army, from Its Organization . . . to 1903* (1903); Robert M. Utley, *Frontier Regulars: The United States Army and the Indian, 1866–1891* (1973); and Francis B. Robertson, "We Are Going to Have a Big Sioux War: Colonel David S. Stanley's Yellowstone Expedition, 1872," *Montana: The Magazine of Western History* 34 (Autumn 1984): 2–15. His intraarmy relations are discussed in Paul A. Hutton, *Phil Sheridan and His Army* (1985). Stanley's incomplete autobiography is *Personal Memoirs of Major-General D. S. Stanley, U.S.A.* (1917).

ROBERT WOOSTER

STANLEY, Francis Edgar (1 June 1849–31 July 1918), and his twin brother **Freelan Oscar Stanley** (1 June 1849–2 Oct. 1940), inventors and manufacturers, were born in Kingfield, Maine, the sons of Solomon Stanley and Apphia French, farmers. The brothers left home to attend the Farmington (Maine) State Normal and Training School, a teachers college. Graduating in 1871, Francis taught school at several towns in Maine. Freelan attended Bowdoin College before also starting a teaching career.

Discovering a talent for crayon portraiture, Francis gave up teaching in 1874 and settled on this new occupation in Lewiston, Maine, a major cotton textile center. To this successful business he soon added photography. Following the work of George Eastman and others, he developed a method of making photographic dry plates. Joined in 1884 by Freelan, who had been principal of a high school in nearby Mechanic Falls, Maine, the brothers established a shop in Lewiston in 1885 to manufacture dry plates.

In 1889 they sold the Lewiston operation and set up a new factory for the Stanley Dry Plate Company in Watertown, Massachusetts, a Boston suburb, although they used a Newton post office address. Their firm was not an important competitor of Eastman Kodak, but Kodak bought them out in January 1904.

The Stanleys had many interests, including the manufacture of violins and the conversion of gasoline to illuminating gas. Most important, the bearded brothers grew interested in motor carriages after seeing one, probably steam-powered, near Boston in 1896. They constructed several prototype steam cars in 1897, using their own lightweight copper boilers and other components made by specialists, including a small steam engine weighing just thirty-two pounds. Their 1898 car—weighing just 600 pounds—closely resembled those made by George Eli Whitney, another steam car pioneer in Boston.

The Stanley steamer at this point used a two-cylinder, 3½ horsepower engine with steam generated in a fourteen-inch boiler in which heat from a gasoline burner rose through 298 small copper tubes. The gasoline fuel was kept in a small copper tank, using a hand pump to keep it under about twenty pounds of pressure. The water tank could hold about fourteen gallons, enough for a fifteen-mile trip. A chain transmitted power from the engine to a differential on the split rear axle. Bicycle tubing formed the frame with elliptical springs and steering by a tiller. The wire-spoke bicycle wheels had two-inch tires.

At a demonstration of horseless vehicles—electric, gasoline, and steam—in Cambridge in November 1898, the Stanley car performed very well in the speed test, going one mile at 27.4 miles per hour and two miles at 22.2 miles per hour. It really sparkled in its attack on an eighty-foot wooden incline that rose to a maximum 36 percent gradient. Here it easily climbed to the top, its light weight giving it a strong advantage over the 1,200-pound Whitney steamer. The enthusiasm aroused by this demonstration led the Stanleys to turn their hobby into a business. In January 1899 they acquired a former bicycle factory adjacent to their dry plate operations in Watertown. They planned to assemble 100 steamers there to sell at $650 apiece. They had hardly begun when John Brisben Walker, the publisher of *Cosmopolitan* magazine, appeared at the factory in February 1899 and offered to buy a half-interest in it. Walker, who had been interested in horseless carriages for several years, had had his magazine sponsor a demonstration/race for them in New York City in 1896. The Stanleys at first refused to sell, but when Walker and his associate Amzi Lorenzo Barber, who had made a fortune in asphalt street paving, offered $250,000 for the entire business, they sold out.

The purchasers soon split into two companies, the Mobile headed by Walker, located in Tarrytown, New York, and the Locomobile by Barber, which soon moved from Watertown to Bridgeport, Connecticut. Barber enjoyed more success, making some 5,200 light steam cars on the Stanley design from 1899 through 1903. This is the first example of the quantity production of lightweight automobiles in the United States.

The early steamers of the Stanley type had many flaws. To achieve light weight, robustness had been sacrificed, so the chain, sprockets, and bearings frequently failed. Fuel economy was low as it burned more gasoline per mile to generate steam than was consumed by contemporary gasoline cars. To light the burner and heat the boiler when the water was cold was a complex process requiring thirty minutes. The driver had to watch in a mirror the water gauge on the boiler and change the rate of water feeding into the boiler when necessary. A failure to pay attention might lead to a burned-out boiler and expensive repairs. To keep the burner operating the driver had to pump air into the gasoline tank occasionally, and a stiff wind might blow it out. Fortunately the boilers did not explode, but sometimes the burners backfired and set the car afire. Steam cars could not be operated reliably in temperatures below freezing.

The Stanley's high consumption of water, about one gallon per mile, was a major problem. Drivers had to arrange for sources of water every few miles when planning a long trip. The solution to this was to use a closed system that condensed the steam for reuse, but a condenser was not feasible on the Stanley-type vehicle because the engine required lavish lubrication and the oil would foul the condenser and the boiler. A better steam car, made by the White company in Cleveland, employed a condenser from 1901 and a semi-flash boiler to generate steam quickly.

The Stanley brothers returned to the steam car business as the Stanley Motor Carriage Company in 1901, using their original factory, repurchased from Barber for just $20,000. In 1902 they dropped the chain drive, on which a crucial patent originally granted to Whitney was now held by the Locomobile company, in favor of a direct drive transmission. In 1903 they sold 300 vehicles. Soon they began using larger engines and the weight, comfort, and price of the cars gradually increased. In consequence, some of the problems of the lightweight cars were mitigated. Sales in most years totaled about 600 to 700 vehicles. The Stanleys soon had the steam market to themselves as the other producers shifted to gasoline engines, notably Locomobile in 1904 and White in 1910. Not until 1915 did the Stanley company adopt a condenser, but thereafter sales rose to a peak of 898 in 1918. In 1917, when they had reached the age of sixty-eight, the brothers sold their company. By the time it closed in the mid-1920s it had made a total of some 14,000 steamers.

The steam car has a romantic appeal in retrospect, with its silent movement, its apparent lack of pollution, and the great clouds of water vapor the uncondensed Stanley vehicles emitted on cool or damp days. But in reality no one associated with steam cars ever solved the problems of generating adequate steam at widely varying rates in different ambient temperatures and doing it simply enough for the average driver.

Francis Stanley married Augusta May Walker in 1870; they had three children. He died in Wenham,

Massachusetts, as the result of an accident while driving one of his cars. Freelan Stanley was married to Flora Tileston; the number of their children, if any, is unknown. After 1905 he spent much of his time in Colorado for health reasons and died in Newton, Massachusetts.

• The Stanley museum in Kingfield, Maine, holds archives and many items showing the wide-ranging interests of the brothers. The Stanley story must be pieced together from a variety of accounts. A good survey is George S. May, "Stanley Motor Carriage Company," *The Automobile Industry, 1896–1920* (1989), pp. 423–25, which is a volume in *The Encyclopedia of American Business History and Biography*. In the same volume see also James Laux, "Steam Cars," pp. 426–28. Thomas Derr, *The Modern Steam Car* (1942), contains some reminiscences of Freelan Stanley. Lord Montagu and Anthony Bird, *Steam Cars 1770–1970* (1971), is useful on the technology, as is Robert C. Sprague, Jr., "The Stanley Steam Cars," *Antique Automobile*, Jan.–Feb. 1977, pp. 30–41. The Stanley-Locomobile relationship is considered in L. J. A. Villalon and Laux, "Steaming through New England with Locomobile," *Journal of Transport History*, n.s., 5 (1979): 65–82, as well as Villalon, "The Birth of an Early Automobile Company," *Bulb Horn*, Apr.–June 1981, pp. 11–21, and Villalon, "The Locomobile Company of America," *Bulb Horn*, July–Sept. 1986, pp. 16–28, and Oct.–Dec. 1986, pp. 12–22. Useful, but not fully reliable, is Francis E. Stanley, "Stanley on Steam Patent Argument," *Motor Age*, 3 Jan. 1907, p. 27.

JAMES M. LAUX

STANLEY, Henry Morton (28 Jan. 1841–10 May 1904), journalist and African explorer, was born in Denbigh, Wales, the illegitimate son of Elizabeth Parry. He was named John Rowlands, perhaps the name of his father, and at an early age was sent to be educated in a workhouse, from which he fled in 1856. He worked his way on shipboard from Liverpool to New Orleans, where he was befriended by a merchant, Henry Morton Stanley, whose name he took as his own.

Stanley was working in a country store in Arkansas when the Civil War began, and he enlisted in a regiment of Arkansas infantry. Captured at the battle of Shiloh and imprisoned in Chicago, he changed sides to obtain his release, but, infected with a prison fever, he was soon discharged. In 1864 he enlisted in the U.S. Navy but deserted before the end of the war.

Stanley began to submit to newspapers articles, which, when accepted, were paid by the word, and he covered meetings of Indian leaders and American politicians and soldiers in the West. In 1867 he was employed by the *New York Herald* as a special correspondent to cover the Abyssinian campaign of British general Robert Napier. By chance, he was the first correspondent to file the story of the fall of Magdala, the release of the European prisoners, and the end of the war with the death of the Abyssinian king. Taken on as a regular reporter, he filed stories from Crete, Asia Minor, and the First Carlist War in Spain.

In October 1869 Stanley was summoned to Paris by James Gordon Bennett, the proprietor of the *Herald*, who instructed him to find David Livingstone, the fa-

mous African missionary believed to be lost in central Africa, but he was to begin the search only after completing a series of assignments in Egypt, Palestine, Turkey, and India. It was March 1871 before he left Zanzibar with a large expedition bound for Tanganyika (the two countries now form Tanzania) in East Africa. After suffering great hardships and surmounting obstacles and dangers, he found Livingstone at Ujiji. Raising his hat, he asked politely, "Dr. Livingstone, I presume?" (*How I Found Livingstone*, p. 78).

Together they explored the north end of Lake Tanganyika before Stanley emerged from the interior carrying letters and notebooks from the missionary, who had no wish to leave. His newspaper stories and his book, *How I Found Livingstone* (1872), brought him fame.

After covering the Ashanti campaign of General Garnet Wolseley in West Africa, Stanley led a second expedition to central Africa, this one jointly sponsored by the *Herald* and the *London Daily Telegraph*. Livingstone, seeking the source of the Nile, thought he had found it but died before he could prove his theory. Stanley's mission was to complete Livingstone's work. He left England in August 1874 for Tanganyika. There he trekked to Lake Victoria and circumnavigated it, the first known to do so. After exploring Lake Tanganyika, the expedition then set out in canoes down a river that flowed north, but it curved westward. It was the Congo, which he traced to the sea. Back in England he wrote the two-volume *Through the Dark Continent* (1878).

In 1879 Stanley returned to the Congo (now Zaire), and under the auspices of King Leopold of Belgium, he opened up new areas, established lines of communication, and founded the Congo Free State, a country owned personally by Leopold. Stanley remained there until 1884, when he attended the international congress on Africa in Berlin, at which European nations divided the continent among themselves. In 1885 he published *The Congo and the Founding of Its Free State*.

Stanley's final African expedition in 1887–1889 was his largest, most difficult, and most dangerous. Emin Pasha, an Austrian who had adopted Islam, was the governor of the southernmost province of the Sudan; he had been appointed when English general Charles "Chinese" Gordon, as governor general, ruled the country for Egypt. After the rebel armies of El Mahdi, the Islamic fundamentalist, expelled all Europeans and Egyptians and killed Gordon at Khartoum, it was learned that in this most remote province Emin still held out. An elaborate rescue was organized under Stanley, who selected British volunteers to serve as his officers.

With 650 men Stanley traveled up the Congo and then overland through the dense Ituri forest. Progress through the forest was so slow that Stanley decided to go ahead with a small force carrying rifles and ammunition for Emin. A rear column with half of the expedition was to be brought forward by his officers. After enduring near incredible hardships and suffering crippling losses of men and gear, Stanley met Emin on the shore of Lake Albert in April 1888. Weakened by privation and diseases, Stanley was more in need of rescuing than was Emin, who, quite content, was unwilling to be rescued. After waiting in vain for his rear column to appear, Stanley turned back to meet it, only to discover that the rear column had not moved. His officers had been unequal to the task; some had died. Stanley reorganized the men and supplies and brought them back through the dreaded forest to Lake Albert.

Then Stanley insisted that Emin leave with him, and he carried the reluctant Emin and many of his followers out of Africa by way of the east coast, becoming the first man ever known to traverse the width of Africa from coast to coast in both directions. Along the way he discovered Lake Edward and Mount Ruwenzori, the fabled "Mountains of the Moon." On reaching the safety of the coast the rescuer and the rescued were dined by German officers. Emin wandered out on a balcony, fell over it, and cracked his skull. When he recovered he went back into the interior, where he was killed by Arab slavers.

To protect his copyrights, Stanley had become a naturalized American citizen, but in 1892 he was repatriated as a British subject. In 1890 he married Dorothy Tennant, a socially prominent young artist; they had no children. Also in 1890 he wrote *In Darkest Africa*; in 1895 he served briefly as a member of Parliament; and in 1899 he was knighted. He died at his home "Furze Hill," near Pirbright in Surrey, England.

• Stanley's other writings include *Coomassie and Magdala* (1874) and *My Early Travels and Adventures in America and Asia* (2 vols., 1895). He also wrote the posthumously published *The Autobiography of Sir Henry Morton Stanley*, ed. Dorothy Stanley (1909). Biographies include John Bierman, *Dark Safari: The Life behind the Legend of Henry Morton Stanley* (1990); Byron Farwell, *The Man Who Presumed: A Biography of Henry M. Stanley* (1957); and the two-volume work by Frank McLynn, *Stanley: The Making of an African Explorer* (1989) and *Stanley: Sorcerer's Apprentice* (1991). An obituary is in *The Times* (London), 11 and 18 May 1904.

BYRON FARWELL

STANLEY, John Mix (17 Jan. 1814–10 Apr. 1872), painter, was born in Canandaigua, New York, the son of Seth Stanley, Jr., and Sally McKinney. Seth Stanley's occupation at the time of his son's birth is unknown, but after moving the family to Buffalo in 1815 he was employed as an innkeeper. John Stanley lived in Buffalo until he was apprenticed to a wagon maker in Naples, New York, in 1828. By 1832, however, he had returned to Buffalo as a professional sign painter. Stanley soon headed west, establishing himself in Detroit in 1834. There he made the acquaintance of John Bowman, an artist who apparently convinced Stanley to abandon sign painting in favor of portraiture. Bowman's assessment of the young artist's potential seems to have been justified, for Stanley continued to receive portrait commissions throughout his career.

Stanley opened a portrait studio in Troy, New York, in 1841. The following year he formed a partnership with Caleb Sumner Dickerman, intending to create a gallery that would document the Native American peoples then succumbing to European-American settlement. As Stanley later wrote, "These ancient possessors of the land are fast disappearing, and a few generations hence our descendants will have nothing, except such memorials, to remind them of the former existence of a race, which had made perhaps a more gallant and prolonged defense of their independence, than any recorded in the widespread annals of warfare between savage and civilized men" (*Congressional Globe*, 28 Dec. 1852, p. 158). The pair set out for the Oklahoma Territory in 1842 and spent three years traveling and painting in the region, Stanley recording Native Americans with a daguerreotype camera as well as a paintbrush. In 1845 the partners settled in Cincinnati, where Stanley finished portraits he had begun in the field, such as *Ko-rak-koo-kiss, a Towoccono Warrior* (1844). He also created new images such as *Osage Scalp Dance* (1845), which, though based on an actual practice, was a fictional narrative celebrating the triumph of virtue and civilization over savagery. As Stanley documented the "disappearing race" he also intended to communicate the fitness of its disappearance. The Indian Gallery opened to favorable criticism in January 1846 with eighty-three paintings and a catalog written by the artist.

In June Stanley headed for the Southwest, arriving in Santa Fe in August, just weeks after General Stephen Kearny's "Army of the West" occupied the city. Hired on as a topographical draftsman, Stanley accompanied Kearny on his fall campaign to San Diego. Lithographs of twenty-seven of his drawings were published as illustrations to Lieutenant William Emory's *Notes of a Military Reconnoissance* in 1848. Stanley left San Diego in December 1846, arriving in Oregon Territory the following spring. Based in Oregon City, he painted portraits of both Native Americans and local white settlers. In the fall he began an extended trip into present Washington State, where he stayed at the Waiilatpu Mission founded in 1836 by Marcus and Narcissa Whitman. Returning to Waiilatpu on 30 November 1847 from a trek north, Stanley discovered that he had missed by just one day the massacre of the Whitmans and others by the Cayuse.

Stanley continued to move west, arriving in Honolulu in August 1848. He spent more than a year on Oahu, painting leading Hawaiians, including King Kamehameha III and his queen, Kalama, to great acclaim. In 1850 Stanley returned to Troy to prepare the expanded Indian Gallery for a second tour. By the time the exhibition arrived at the Smithsonian Institution in 1852 it contained 152 paintings and was accompanied by a new catalog. In that year Stanley unsuccessfully petitioned Congress to purchase the gallery for the nation, but the Smithsonian offered exhibition space indefinitely. Stanley began his last trip west in May 1853 as the artist for the Northern Railroad Survey. Led by Isaac Stevens, governor of Washington Territory, the federal expedition was one of eight sent to survey possible routes for a transcontinental railroad. Stanley promoted the northern route by producing topographical views that portrayed a landscape favorable to development. Sixty of Stanley's images were ultimately published in the volume contributed by Stevens to the War Department's *Reports of Explorations and Surveys*. Although Stanley returned to Washington, D.C., early in 1854, his work on this twelfth volume of the *Reports* continued until its publication in 1860.

After his return to the capital Stanley married Alice English in May 1854; the following year the first of five children was born. In Washington Stanley's style was influenced by contemporary American genre and history painting as he depicted Native Americans in scenes of everyday life or high drama. These works synthesized historical documentation, popular appeal, and nationalistic sentiment, all presented in the most contemporary artistic languages. In 1854 Stanley painted an ambitious panorama, as concerned with drama as with reportage, based upon his survey travels. The coming of the Civil War inspired Stanley to create a panorama on that subject in 1862.

In 1863 Stanley moved from Washington to Detroit, where he achieved the greatest acclaim and prosperity of his career. Tragically, during these successful years, Stanley's Indian Gallery was destroyed in a fire at the Smithsonian on 14 January 1865; only five paintings survived the conflagration. Stanley continued to paint western scenes, but in images more idealized and dramatic than documentary. In 1867 he began to explore the new medium of chromolithography as a method of reproducing his works for a mass market. Among the paintings thus made available was one of Stanley's most popular, *The Trial of Red Jacket* (1863–1868). In 1872, as his reputation flourished Stanley died of heart failure in Detroit.

In a period of intense interest in the American West, John Mix Stanley traveled the region more extensively than any other single artist, participating in the annexation of northern Mexico and experiencing at first hand unrest in the newly settled Pacific Northwest. His varied oeuvre included work for the federal government, for private patrons, and for the nation itself in his lost Indian Gallery. Described by one critic as "the triumph of American genius fully employed in American subjects" (*Daily National Intelligencer*, 3 Mar. 1852, p. 3), the gallery documented Native American cultures while at the same time promoting the widely adopted notion that their disappearance before European-American settlement was inevitable and just. As an artist, Stanley participated in the development of the West while preserving images of what that development displaced.

• John Mix Stanley's papers are collected in the Smithsonian Institution Archives, the Archives of American Art, and the Artists' Files of the National Museum of Art/National Portrait Gallery Library. His own publications are limited to the two catalogs of the Indian Gallery, *Catalogue of Pictures in Stanley & Dickerman's North American Indian Gallery* (1846) and *Portraits of North American Indians with Sketches of Scenery, Etc.* (1852), and a "Memorial to the Honorable Senate and House of Representatives of the United States of America," *Congressional Globe*, 28 Dec. 1852 and 12 Jan. 1863, published in support of federal purchase of the gallery. Examples of Stanley's illustrative work can be found in Lieutenant William H. Emory, *Notes of a Military Reconnoissance, from Fort Leavenworth, in Missouri, to San Diego, in California* (1848), and in volumes 2 and 12 of the *Reports of Explorations and Surveys, to Ascertain the Most Practicable and Economical Route for a Railroad from the Mississippi River to the Pacific Ocean* (1855–1860). The most comprehensive modern assessment of Stanley's life and work is Julie Schimmel, "John Mix Stanley and Imagery of the West in Nineteenth-Century American Art" (Ph.D. diss., New York Univ., 1983), which includes a checklist of his known works and a comprehensive bibliography. Earlier biographies are found in Charles Richard Tuttle, *General History of the State of Michigan* (1873); W. Vernon Kinietz, *John Mix Stanley and His Indian Paintings* (1942); and Robert Taft, *Artists and Illustrators of the Old West, 1850–1900* (1952). Additionally, a catalog was published in 1970 to accompany the University of Michigan Museum of Art exhibition, "John Mix Stanley: A Traveller in the West."

ELIZABETH BECKENBACH LEAVY

STANLEY, Roba (1910–9 June 1986), country music singer and instrumentalist, was born near Dacula, in Gwinnett County, Georgia, the daughter of Rob (R. M.) Stanley, a popular local fiddler and singer. Rob Stanley's three brothers performed music, and the Stanley home was a gathering place for a number of local amateur musicians. Dacula was also the headquarters for the family of Gid Tanner, another well-known fiddler who went on to have an extensive recording career with the Skillet Lickers. Young Roba heard much of this music and, naturally, learned to play as well. She chose her brother's guitar, and by the time she was twelve she was accompanying her father as he traveled throughout the area playing at square dances. Roba's interest in music greatly pleased her father, who by now was around sixty-five years old, but it surprised residents who were unaccustomed to seeing a girl play this kind of old-time music.

The Stanleys' music began to professionalize somewhat in the early 1920s when Roba and Rob played for the political campaign of Sam Brown, who was running for the state House (Ninth District). Their exposure during the campaign, which included working in the Atlanta area, led to their appearance in 1924 on Atlanta radio station WSB, sponsored by a local furniture store. After several weeks of appearances, the furniture store owner contacted the General Phonograph Company, makers of OKeh label records, who had done several recording sessions in Atlanta and were planning another for 1924. Billed as the Stanley Trio (Roba, Rob, and a friend named William Patterson), the group made two records in a temporary studio in Atlanta in August 1924; one of the sides was "Whoa! Mule," which featured Roba's singing. Roba did two additional solo sides, accompanied by Patterson: "Devilish Mary," an old British ballad, and "Mr. Chicken," a comic vaudeville song. Though Roba did not think much of it at the time, her records earned her a place in the history of country music as the first woman soloist to record.

Roba Stanley's voice was clear and strong and well suited to the old acoustic recording process of the time. She also had a solid background in the traditional folk music of north Georgia. Ralph Peer, who had become the artists and repertoire director for OKeh, liked her sound enough to invite her, her father, and Patterson back to Atlanta in December 1924 for a second session. This session yielded three more sides, including the surprisingly rowdy "All Night Long." In 1925 Virginia singer Henry Whitter, a veteran recording artist who was trying to make a living singing country music, heard her and went to Atlanta to record with her. Together they did two OKeh sides, including Stanley's most famous song, "Single Life," with its well-known line, "I am single and no man's wife / And no man shall control me." Whitter wanted Stanley to go on a tour with him, but she did not trust that his motives were platonic and refused.

A few months after this session, Stanley met a young man from Miami, got married, and moved to Florida. "My husband didn't like for me to play out in public much," she recalled. She took her guitar with her but played very little after that. Her music career was effectively over by the time she was sixteen years old.

For decades Stanley forgot about her music and had no idea of her historic role in the genre. In 1976 she was rediscovered by folklorists Charles K. Wolfe and Peggy Bulger. Stanley had not even kept copies of her old records; she heard them for the first time in almost fifty years. A couple of years before her death, she finally began to reap some of the recognition due her; she was even saluted from the stage of the Grand Ole Opry.

Though Roba Stanley only had nine songs released in her short career, they were powerful and impressive statements of traditional singing and were surprisingly effective in reflecting a feminine perspective in what was at the time a man's music. Stanley died in Homestead, Florida.

• An interview published a year after Stanley's rediscovery is Charles K. Wolfe with Peggy Bulger and Gene Wiggins, "Roba Stanley: The First Country Sweetheart," *Old Time Music*, no. 26 (Autumn 1977): 13–19, which also contains the texts of six songs, as well as a discography. A more accessible, though far less detailed account appears in Mary A. Bufwack and Robert K. Oermann, *Finding Her Voice: The Saga of Women in Country Music* (1993).

CHARLES K. WOLFE

STANLEY, Sara G. (c. 1836–1918), African-American teacher of freedmen, was born in New Bern, North Carolina, the daughter of John Stuart Stanley and Frances Griffith, teachers, who ran an antebellum private school in New Bern patronized by free blacks throughout North Carolina. The Stanleys, free blacks related to a prominent slave-owning family of the same name, identified with their African-American community. As a youth, Sara Stanley would correct people

who mistook her for a white woman by explaining "I am a colored woman having a slight admixture of negro blood in my veins."

Stanley pioneered for her gender and race as an antebellum college student, studying at Oberlin College, Ohio, from 1852 to 1855. She left college before receiving her degree. Many North Carolina free blacks emigrated to Ohio at this time because of persecutions in the South, and this may have been why the entire Stanley family in New Bern emigrated to Cleveland in the late 1850s. With no income from their school, the family might have been unable to afford tuition for their daughter at Oberlin, or perhaps the family needed her to work as a teacher to provide income to the family.

Little is known about Stanley from the time she left college until the end of the Civil War. Sara G. Staley [*sic*] gave an antislavery speech at the Ladies Antislavery Society, an African-American association in Delaware, Ohio, in 1856, and the style of the extant speech suggests this may well have been Sara Stanley. She was one of the few black women in the country with a college education, and it would not be surprising if she were asked to speak, despite her youth. The speech addresses the hatred and prejudice against African Americans "fostered by religion and science united" that threatened to annihilate the race. "In view of these things, it is self-evident and above demonstration that we, as a people, have every incentive to labor for the redress of wrongs."

In 1862 she had a sufficiently important reputation as a writer within the African-American community to be asked to join the National Young [Black] Men's Literary Association. That same year the *Weekly Anglo-African*, a national periodical, published her critique of the poetry and the antislavery politics of John Greenleaf Whittier. Just as African-American literary critics of the twentieth century hold writers to a political as well as a literary standard, so did Stanley. "In the poetry of John G. Whittier, we find the nearest approximation to the distinctness of moral purpose, that earnest maintenance of universal freedom," she wrote approvingly.

It is not clear how she supported herself after she left college, but it seems likely she lived with her family in Cleveland and taught school. The first black woman teacher in the Cleveland public schools (late 1850s) was reputedly a well-educated woman named Stanley, although others have assumed this was Maria Stanley.

In 1864 Stanley was accepted as a teacher by the Protestant-based American Missionary Association (AMA) to teach newly freed people in Norfolk, Virginia. In her application she states her views on education and service:

I know that no thought of suffering and privation, nor even death, should deter me from making every effort possible for the moral and intellectual salvation of these ignorant and degraded people; children of a beneficent Father, and heirs of the kingdom of Heaven. And I feel, moreover, how much greater my own spiritual advancement will be, for while laboring for them, while living a life of daily toil, self-sacrifice, and denial, I can dwell nearer to God and my Savior.

In a second letter of application she explains further that she feels "bound to that ignorant, degraded, long-enslaved race by the ties of love and consanguinity; they are socially and politically 'my people.'"

While teaching in Norfolk, she spoke up against the AMA for maintaining racially segregated housing, as she believed the deepest principles of action within the association should be spiritual—that the son of God could be seen in the "person of a Negro" as well as in others. While she did not expect to be a social equal of whites in the North, she expected better of whites in the South on a spiritual mission.

The AMA reassigned her to a school in St. Louis, Missouri, in 1865 for personal reasons. (She was accused of having an affair with a married white male teacher in Norfolk, and had this been true, she would probably not have been retained as a teacher.) The first publicly elected school board in St. Louis (1865) refused to employ African-American teachers, so the AMA moved Stanley to a private school in Louisville, Kentucky, in 1866. Her letters and annual reports were frequently included in AMA publications, which was unusual and a recognition of her talent for writing and description. In one report to the AMA, Stanley described how her uneducated pupils bested a representative of the Freedmen's Bureau visiting her class. When he told them education accounted for their difference from whites, the children corrected him by saying money, not education, explained the difference. When he said, "Yes, but what enabled them to obtain it?" he expected they would give the answer he was looking for—education. "*How* did they get that money?" he asked. Stanley records, "A simultaneous shout burst forth, 'Got it off us; stole it off we all.'" Then she added her personal view: "A different answer might have been returned, but hardly a truer one as applied to the people of the South."

In 1868, when Stanley was teaching in Mobile, Alabama, she met and married Charles Woodward, a white Union veteran then managing the local freedmen's bank. The AMA urged that the interracial marriage take place in the North to avoid a possible violent reprisal by the Ku Klux Klan in Mobile. Stanley refused on principle. In 1869 her husband published a history of the Freedman's Bank, and Stanley, who assisted him as a cashier at times and was far better educated than he, may have assisted him in writing the book.

The Woodwards had only one child, who died in infancy, and the 1870 census for Mobile lists Stanley as a white woman. The determination of race was left to the census taker, who may have assumed she was white since she was married to a white man and since she had always appeared white to others who did not know of her African-American heritage. Perhaps she did not correct the census taker because this could have caused problems affecting her own happiness or because she was less idealistic than in her youth, when she sometimes would go out of her way to challenge racism by telling whites who mistook her for white that she was black.

Since the primary source on Stanley is her letters and writings to the AMA, when she ceased to be a teacher for them she became lost from historical view. The next source on her life is her application for a federal pension as a veteran's widow. There she mentions working as an engraver in Philadelphia, becoming a widow in 1885, and teaching at Lucy Lainey's new school in Georgia in the 1890s. The pension record lists her death as 1918 but does not indicate where she died.

Stanley was known and appreciated within the nineteenth-century African-American community as a speaker, writer, critic, and teacher. She was less prominent after her interracial marriage in 1870 until her death. Then, like many black women of achievement in the nineteenth century, she was lost to history until recent scholarly interest in the accomplishments of African-American women. Stanley pioneered for her gender and race by attending college before the Civil War and by teaching within the white-dominated American Missionary Association. Her Christian faith was central to her role as a pioneer in race relations.

• For Sara Stanley's unpublished letters c. 1864–1869, see the American Missionary Association Papers, Amistad Research Center, New Orleans. For published letters and reports, see the *American Missionary Magazine*, 1865–1867, and *Annual Reports of the A.M.A.*, nos. 19 and 20. See also the *Weekly Anglo-African*, 19 Apr. 1862, for her essay on Whittier. For a collection of the published and unpublished letters and speeches of Stanley, see Ellen Nickenzie Lawson, ed., *The Three Sarahs: Documents of Antebellum Black College Women* (1984), chapter 2, which also includes an extended biographical sketch of Stanley. For background on the Stanleys and New Bern, see *The Stanley Family and the Historic John Wright Stanley House* (1969); S. F. Miller, "Recollections of New Bern Fifty Years Ago," manuscript in Craven-Pamlico-Carteret Regional Library, New Bern, N.C.; and John Hope Franklin, *The Free Negro in North Carolina* (1943). See Henry L. Swint, *The Northern Teacher in the South, 1862–1870* (1941), pp. 88–89, and Gerda Lerner, comp., *Black Women in White America* (1972), p. 111, for references to Stanley's story about the visitor from the Freedmen's Bureau that do not cite her by name as the primary source.

ELLEN NICKENZIE LAWSON

STANLEY, Wendell Meredith (16 Aug. 1904–15 June 1971), Nobel Prize–winning scientist, was born in Ridgeville, Indiana, the son of James G. Stanley and Claire G. (maiden name unknown), the publishers of the local newspaper. Stanley attended public schools in the small town and after school assisted in the collection of news, in the printing shop, and in newspaper delivery. He attended the last two years of high school in Richmond, Indiana, and enrolled in Earlham College in that city in 1922. Stanley studied chemistry and mathematics and enjoyed a full social life. Although not a large young man, he played football throughout his college career and in his senior year was captain of a winning team. He was selected as an All-State end in a state noted for having several colleges with excellent sports programs. In addition to the acquisition of facts, Earlham College, formerly a Quaker school, emphasized the philosophical understanding of values and the importance of making moral and mental commitments. Stanley received a B.S. in 1926.

Though interested in a career coaching football, Stanley met a leading organic chemist, Roger Adams, on the campus of the University of Illinois in Urbana and entered that university as a graduate student in chemistry, with Adams serving as his preceptor. He received an M.S. in 1927 and elected to continue work toward the Ph.D., which was awarded to him in 1929. His research under Adams related to the chemistry of the biphenyls, and he also synthesized and studied some unusual fatty acids known to be bactericidal for the causal agent of leprosy. Some eleven papers on these subjects were published with Adams between 1927 and 1933.

Stanley met his wife, Marian S. Jay, among the group of students working in Adams's laboratory, and the three published together in 1929, the year in which Stanley and Jay were married. The couple had four children, one of whom became a professor of biochemistry at the University of California at Irvine.

In 1930 the young Ph.D. served as an instructor at Illinois and was granted a National Research Council Fellowship in chemistry. The couple lived in Munich, Germany, where Stanley worked with Heinrich Wieland on the sterols of yeast during the period 1930–1931. He returned to the United States to work in the Laboratory of General Physiology with W. J. V. Osterhout at the Rockefeller Institute for Medical Research in New York. Following Osterhout's interests, Stanley began studies on the biophysical and biochemical problem of the selective transport and accumulation of sodium and potassium ions in the giant plant cell, the alga *Valonia*. The organic chemist was thus initiated into a largely unfamiliar world of the biophysical chemistry of plant cells. He developed a useful model system for the study of ion transport and accumulation.

The Rockefeller Institute had created its Department of Animal and Plant Pathology, with laboratories in Princeton, New Jersey, in 1916. Headed initially by Theobald Smith, whose major interest was in veterinary diseases, the department eventually contained many major researchers. A branch of the Laboratory of General Physiology, comprised of John Northrop and Moses Kunitz, was transferred to the Princeton unit in 1926. Their successes in the late 1920s and 1930s at Princeton in the isolation and crystallization of enzyme proteins eventually pointed the way to Stanley's crystallization of a plant virus. The Laboratory of General Physiology in the institute in New York had been led from 1906 to 1924 by Jacques Loeb, who had stressed the importance of the study of the physical biochemistry of proteins in developing biological knowledge. After Loeb's death in 1924, Northrop led the Laboratory of General Physiology, in which Osterhout was a senior member and to which Stanley had been appointed as an assistant until his transfer to plant pathology in 1932.

In 1931 the institute in Princeton created its Division of Plant Pathology, led by Louis O. Kunkel, who was greatly interested in plant virus disease. In the next year, Kunkel brought Stanley to the division and asked him, as well as other members of the division, to work on the tobacco mosaic disease. The causative agent, the tobacco mosaic virus (TMV), had been detected in the 1890s in discoveries that marked the very beginning of virology. Members of the group in plant pathology developed assay systems for the virus, plant tissue cultures, and other knowledge important in the further study of the plant viruses.

In 1933 and 1934 Stanley, primarily an organic chemist and a novice in the field of plant virology, worked very hard to purify the virus from the juice of virus-infected tobacco plants. He used methods of isolation of large molecules developed in the previous decade, many of which had been explored by his colleagues at the Rockefeller Institute. By 1935 he had isolated an unusual crystalline form of the virus and had demonstrated and reported that it was a rather large protein. This could be dissolved and recrystallized without loss of infectivity, that is, the ability to cause a susceptible plant to produce a great deal more of the same type of infectious protein. In 1936 investigators in England confirmed Stanley's isolation and described the nature of the crystalline arrays of rodlike virus particles. They also reported the presence in the virus of a ribose nucleic acid, which was to be identified some twenty years later as the genetic and inheritable determinant of the virus.

Stanley, who was promoted within the Rockefeller Institute to the rank of associate in 1935 and to associate member in 1937, enlarged his laboratory in the next few years with physical chemists and protein chemists to explore many of the structural problems related to the nature of the tobacco mosaic virus and its genetically different virus strains, as well as the size and shape of other plant viruses. In 1940 Stanley was appointed a full member of the Rockefeller Institute. In the period from 1936 to 1941 his laboratory was also concerned with the structure and locus of the TMV nucleic acid.

Stanley's demonstration—that an isolable and chemically definable compound, comprised of protein and nucleic acid and little else, could serve as a pathogenic virus and embody the capabilities of compelling its exact duplication in suitable host cells—created a sensation in biological and chemical science. These capabilities, of compelling the formation of a protein coat and a genetically determining nucleic acid, were subsequently shown to reside in an infectious nucleic acid, which could be isolated from the virus. Later this virus nucleic acid would be synthesized by appropriate cell-free enzymes with the aid of a virus nucleic acid template. From 1936 to 1943 his important discoveries earned Stanley many significant medals and awards, including election to the American Philosophical Society and the National Academy of Sciences. These culminated in 1946 in a Nobel Prize, which was shared that year by James B. Sumner of Cornell University and John H. Northrop for their pioneering work on enzyme isolation and crystallization.

Prior to World War II Stanley's group had developed efficient methods of isolating large polymeric molecules. On the entrance of the United States into armed conflict, his laboratory became engaged in the concentration and purification of the influenza virus and the development of an influenza vaccine for the then-current virus. Stanley summarized these results on the occasion of his being awarded the Nichols Medal of the American Chemical Society in 1946. He became a consultant to the secretary of war and a member of the U.S. Army Commission on Influenza. For his services in the area of vaccine development, he received a Presidential Certificate of Merit in 1948.

Despite the many scientific successes at the Princeton laboratories, the trustees of the Rockefeller Institute decided to close this site, and in the period 1949–1957 many of the senior staff were compelled to commute or to move to the New York center. Some younger scientists scattered to various universities. In 1948 Stanley and Northrop elected to move to the University of California in Berkeley. In an optimistic period, anticipating major scientific growth and achievement, Stanley was asked to build the Virus Laboratory, an institute for virus research, and to chair a new Department of Biochemistry. After an arduous period of recruitment for both groups and of educational administration on the Berkeley campus, Stanley resigned from the chairmanship of the biochemistry department in 1953 and concentrated on running the virus lab.

In the mid 1950s his colleagues in the Virus Laboratory made several key observations of the virology of the time. F. L. Schaffer and G. E. Schwerdt crystallized the virus of poliomyelitis, and H. Fraenkel-Conrat and R. C. Williams separated the components of TMV and reassembled an infectious virus. The Virus Laboratory became the center of a new Department of Virology in 1958, and several of its members were recognized as world leaders in the various disciplines of this specialization. Stanley chaired this department until 1964; he was replaced by the physical chemist H. K. Schachman, who had worked for many years in Stanley's group at Princeton.

In the period of his official administrative positions at the University of California, Stanley was also embroiled in the campus storms around the growing atmosphere of McCarthyism and the imposition of loyalty oaths on faculty members. He served as chair of the University Senate Committee on Academic Freedom and publicly defended the rights of those who refused to sign. Although he signed the California oath himself, Stanley opposed the use of the oath as a condition of employment and welcomed a court decision declaring its unconstitutionality.

Between 1958 and 1964 Stanley was influential in the medically oriented scientific disciplines then growing within university and national structures. In addition to writing reviews and essays and editing books on viruses, he chaired the editorial board of the *Proceedings of the National Academy of Sciences* and served as director at large of the American Cancer Society and as a member of the Board of Scientific Counselors of the National Cancer Institute. After 1964 he was made a professor of molecular biology. In advisory committees of the National Institutes of Health, he actively promulgated the hypothesis that viruses were responsible for human cancer. Stanley served as president of the Tenth International Cancer Congress in 1970.

Stanley was often seriously ill in his later years but still traveled a good deal. He died in Spain after a scientific conference in which he had discussed tumor viruses. The institute and departments that he built in Berkeley are housed in the Wendell M. Stanley Hall on a hill on the university campus.

• Many of Stanley's original papers, as well as secondary literature evaluating his contributions, are listed in the bibliography following his biography in the *Supplement to the Dictionary of Scientific Biography* 18 (1990): 841–48. A biography written by John T. Edsall appears in the *American Philosophical Society Yearbook of 1971*. The *Rockefeller University Archives* contain a biographical note and a brief list of awards and memberships, as well as a collection of some administrative correspondence, 1931–1948, and three volumes of his collected reprints, 1927–1948.

SEYMOUR S. COHEN

STANLY, Edward (10 Jan. 1810–12 July 1872), U.S. congressman and military governor, was born in New Bern, North Carolina, the son of John Stanly, a prominent Federalist politician, and Elizabeth Franks. He attended the University of North Carolina in 1826 but left after his father suffered a debilitating stroke. In 1827 he enrolled in Alden Partridge's military school in Middletown, Connecticut, graduating in 1829. He studied law while serving as clerk of the Craven County Superior Court, was admitted to the bar in 1832, and moved to Washington, the seat of Beaufort County.

After serving for two years as solicitor of the Second Judicial District, Stanly was elected as a Whig to the U.S. Congress in 1837. He was reelected in 1839 and 1841. Sharing his father's nationalistic philosophy, he supported the Bank of the United States, protective tariffs, and federal aid to internal improvements. However, he achieved notoriety more for his intense partisanship and fiery temperament than for his abilities as a legislator. He engaged in numerous acrimonious exchanges with his fellow congressmen and in 1841 was involved in a well-publicized brawl with Henry Alexander Wise on the floor of the House. In 1843 the Democratic general assembly redrew the state's congressional districts, and he lost his bid for reelection.

Stanly took an active part in the campaign of 1844, representing his district as a delegate to the Whig National Convention and canvassing it on behalf of Henry Clay. That same year he won election to the House of Commons, where he served as Speaker. The even-handed manner in which he presided over the house helped dispel his image of impetuosity. He was re-elected to the Speakership in 1846 but resigned to accept an appointment as state attorney general.

Elected again to the House of Commons in 1848, Stanly led the movement to secure a charter and a state subsidy for the North Carolina Railroad, an east-west trunk line connecting Goldsboro with Charlotte. He also played a prominent role in the legislative debates over the status of slavery in the Mexican Cession. Although he owned a few slaves as house servants, Stanly was not strongly attached to the institution. One colleague in the general assembly later asserted that he was "always at heart an anti-slavery man" (Brown, p. 92). Stanly's nationalism also led him to the conclusions that Congress had exclusive jurisdiction over the territories, that the Wilmot Proviso was constitutional though impolitic, and that the people of North Carolina would stand by the Union even if the proviso should be adopted. While unable to prevent the passage of a series of strong proslavery resolutions, he did succeed in attaching an amendment affirming North Carolina's devotion to the Union and its abhorrence of secession.

The Whig-dominated general assembly having again redistricted the state, Stanly returned to the U.S. House of Representatives in 1849. He was one of the few southern Whigs to endorse Zachary Taylor's plan to admit California and New Mexico as free states. After Taylor's death, Stanly supported all of Clay's compromise proposals, including the abolition of the slave trade in the District of Columbia. In a controversial speech delivered on 6 March 1850, he denied that most northerners were hostile to slavery or that southerners had grievances of sufficient magnitude to justify disunion. "This Union cannot be, shall not be destroyed," he proclaimed. "Those whom God hath joined together, no man or set of men can put asunder."

Stanly's speech aroused resentment among southerners in both parties. One Whig congressman called it "unfortunate and foolish," complaining that "it would have been supposed almost, that he was a Northern and not a Southern representative" (Brown, p. 136). An angry exchange of words with Democrat Samuel W. Inge of Alabama led to a bloodless duel. In 1851 Stanly waged an aggressive campaign for reelection, defending his record in Congress, avowing his unswerving devotion to the Union, and even promising to send a fleet to South Carolina should that state attempt to secede. Although he represented a plantation district, in which slaves constituted a substantial proportion of the population, Stanly's success in pinning the disunion label on his Democratic opponent enabled him to win the election by a comfortable majority.

In the Thirty-second Congress (1851–1853), Stanly supported the presidential candidacy of Winfield Scott, working diligently but unsuccessfully to overcome suspicions on the part of southern Whigs that Scott was unsound on slavery. After the Democrats carried North Carolina in the state elections, they rearranged Stanly's district to give it a large Democratic majority. He did not seek reelection but moved to California and established a lucrative law practice in San Francisco.

Despite an avowal to retire from politics, Stanly soon found himself embroiled in partisan controversy. After the demise of the Whig party, his dislike of the Democrats and his aversion to the antiforeign and anti-Catholic principles of the American party led him to ally himself with the Republicans. He accepted the Republican nomination for governor in 1857, although he declined to commit himself fully to the party's antislavery platform. The decision of the Americans to nominate a separate ticket split the opposition vote and resulted in the election of the Democratic candidate. In the presidential election of 1860 he supported the Constitutional Union ticket but did not campaign actively for it.

Stanly remained loyal to the Union even after the secession of North Carolina. After the Federal army occupied the Albemarle and Pamlico Sound regions in 1862, he accepted an appointment as military governor of North Carolina. Arriving at his headquarters at New Bern on 26 May 1862, he found himself denounced as a traitor by his former friends and allies. Although he supported the policy of gradual and compensated emancipation that Abraham Lincoln had proposed at the beginning of the war, he opposed the Emancipation Proclamation of January 1863, believing that it would unnecessarily prolong the war and undercut his policy of promoting North Carolina's voluntary return to the Union. On 15 January 1863 he resigned the governorship in protest. He returned to California and endorsed Democrat George McClellan for president in 1864. After the war he supported Andrew Johnson's plan of Reconstruction and generally acted with the Democrats, although he never formally joined that party. He died in San Francisco. Stanly was twice married. In 1832 he married Julia Jones; she died in 1854. In 1859 he married Cornelia Baldwin. No children were born in either marriage.

Stanly's significance lay in his role as North Carolina's most outspoken Unionist. Although repeatedly denounced by his enemies as a southern man with northern principles, he sincerely believed that the interests of the South could best be protected from within the Union. That he was successful in all but one of his North Carolina campaigns indicates that a majority of his North Carolina constituents—at least until the Civil War—were receptive to that message.

• Stanly did not leave a collection of personal papers. However, numerous letters by him, as well as many references to him, are in Henry T. Shanks, ed., *The Papers of Willie Person Mangum* (5 vols., 1950–1956); and J. G. de Roulhac Hamilton and Max R. Williams, eds., *The Papers of William Alexander Graham* (8 vols., 1957–1992). Many letters by Stanly are also in the Pettigrew Family Papers, Southern Historical Collection, University of North Carolina Library; and in the Pettigrew papers, North Carolina Division of Archives and History. The most complete modern assessment of his career is Norman D. Brown, *Edward Stanly: Whiggery's Tarheel "Conqueror"* (1974). For his role during the sectional controversy of the 1850s, see also Joseph Carlyle Sitterson, *The Secession Movement in North Carolina* (1939), and Thomas E. Jeffrey, *State Parties and National Politics: North Carolina, 1815–1861* (1989). For his service as military governor of N.C., see Stanly's *A Military Governor among Abolitionists. A Letter from Edward Stanly to Charles Sumner* (1865); and William C. Harris, "Lincoln and Wartime Reconstruction in North Carolina, 1861–1863," *North Carolina Historical Review* 63 (1986): 149–68. An obituary is in the *San Francisco Daily Alta California*, 13 July 1872.

THOMAS E. JEFFREY

STANNARD, Henry (11 Dec. 1811–23 Mar. 1855), runner, was born in Killingworth, Connecticut, the son of Jacob Stannard and Jerusha Kelsey, farmers. As a youth, he engaged in farming and attended Amherst College for a brief period. Family tradition claims that he put his trunk on a stagecoach, then walked all the way to Amherst, Massachusetts. Stannard rose to fame after he won a ten-mile running race on 24 April 1835 sponsored by the Jockey Club at the Union Race Course on Long Island, New York, and thus became the first recognized champion runner in the United States. The race was reported to have resulted from a wager between John C. Stevens and Samuel L. Gouverneur that the former would find a runner who could run ten miles within one hour. Thus, in addition to the $1,000 winner's purse, an extra $300 would be awarded if the winner covered the distance in less than one hour. Stannard won the race in 59 minutes and 48 seconds to take both prizes. Within a year Stannard had won purses in twelve different states and had accumulated enough money to marry Polly Eliza Stephens and purchase a hotel in Killingworth, which he named the Pedestrian Hotel. His wife died in childbirth in 1837 and left one son. Stannard then married Polly Chadwick in 1838. They had one child. He also became the first American athlete to endorse a commercial product, promoting "Brooks Elastic Metallic Shank Boots" in advertisements printed in the *Spirit of the Times*.

Organized competition in running was in its infancy at this time. Most contests originated spontaneously as a result of wagers between individuals. In England organized pedestrian races had become quite popular. News of the athletic performances in these contests were read in the United States with much interest. In 1824 a program of running races was sponsored for the first time by the proprietors of the Orchard Race Course at Hoboken, New Jersey. Stannard was the leading runner in the United States until 1844, although he often had difficulty finding competitors. Since many of the purses in match races were contributed by the participants or their backers, few runners

were willing to risk their own funds in competing against the champion.

Stannard's last major victory was on 3 June 1844 in a ten-mile race sponsored by the proprietors of the Beacon Race Course at Hoboken. A purse of $300 was offered to the winner of the race, with an additional incentive of $200 if the winner covered a distance of 10¼ miles in less than one hour. Stannard won the race easily but required more than sixty-two minutes to cover the longer distance. The fact that the race had attracted 30,000 spectators encouraged the sponsors to schedule another series of races in October and November 1844. The arrival of three English professional runners in New York City shortly before the events added interest to the contest, which was billed as the first international running competition. Stannard remained the favorite of the seventeen runners who started in the final ten-mile race on 19 November 1844. Stannard ran the race in less than an hour but finished in sixth place behind the winner, John Gildersleeve of New York City, two of the Englishmen, and two other Americans. With this result Stannard's preeminence in American running came to an end.

Although Stannard appeared in a few more contests, the level of competition had picked up considerably, and he was no longer a winner. He soon faded into oblivion, but throughout the nineteenth century sporting journals from time to time recalled the memorable race when a human being first ran ten miles in less than an hour. Henry Stannard spent his last years in Killingworth, where he died.

• Copies of the Stannard Family Papers are in the Clarke Historical Library, Central Michigan University. The most complete account of the famous 1835 race is in the *New York Clipper*, 5 July 1958, which appears to be an unidentified reprint of an earlier account. Contemporary accounts of Stannard's races appeared in the *Spirit of the Times* (1844) and the *New York Post*. An account of the wager between John Stevens and Samuel Gouveneur is in Allan Nevins, ed., *The Diary of Philip Hone, 1828–1851* (1936). See also George Moss, "The Long-distance Runners in Ante-bellum America," *Journal of Popular Culture* 8 (1974): 370–82.

JOHN CUMMING

STANSBURY, Howard (8 Feb. 1806–18 Apr. 1863), soldier and explorer, was born in New York City, the son of Arthur Joseph Stansbury and Susanna Brown. In 1827 he married Helen Moody; they had two children. Stansbury was educated as a civil engineer and in October 1828 received his first significant assignment, which was to direct the series of surveys that were being undertaken with the goal of creating canals to link the Wabash River with Lake Erie and Lake Michigan. Between 1832 and 1835 he surveyed the route of what would become the Mad River and Lake Erie railroad, as well as the mouths of the Chagrin, Cumberland, and Vermilion rivers.

Stansbury surveyed the lower part of the James River in Virginia (1836) and surveyed rivers in Illinois in 1837. On 7 July 1838 he entered the U.S. Army as a lieutenant in the corps of topographical engineers.

Promoted to captain on 18 July 1840, Stansbury went on to conduct an extensive survey of the harbor of Portsmouth, New Hampshire (1842–1845). At the start of the Mexican War in 1846, Stansbury went to the Dry Tortugas, just west of Key West, Florida, where he surveyed the area for Fort Jefferson on Garden Key and made some of the original plans for its construction. In the same year, Stansbury directed the construction of an iron lighthouse on Carysfort reef, just east of Florida. When he returned to Philadelphia, Stansbury received the orders for the cornerstone of his career: the expedition to the Great Salt Lake in 1849–1850.

In the spring of 1849 Stansbury received his orders from John James Abert, head of the topographical corps. Stansbury was to march from Fort Leavenworth, Kansas, to the Mormon country around the Great Salt Lake, to survey that area and return by a more southerly route. On 31 May 1849 Stansbury left Fort Leavenworth with eighteen men, including Lieutenant John W. Gunnison, artist John Hudson, and Albert Carrington, a leading Mormon official. The company proceeded by way of South Pass in Wyoming to Fort Bridger, where Stansbury engaged Jim Bridger as a guide for the expedition. Dividing his men into two groups, Stansbury explored a new route to the Great Salt Lake by following a path between the Bear River and Echo Canyon trails. The expedition members spent the winter of 1849–1850 in Salt Lake City as guests of the Mormon population there. This, the most intricate part of Stansbury's mission, required diplomacy and tact. Since the Mormon state of Deseret (meaning "honeybee") was the only legally incorporated civil government in that area from 2 July 1849 through 5 February 1851, Stansbury and his men were to some extent visiting a foreign country.

Stansbury managed to placate Mormon leader Brigham Young. Stansbury's later recollections of the Mormon leader and of his people are noteworthy, since they showed some objectivity toward the Mormons. On Brigham Young himself, Stansbury wrote, "his personal reputation I believe to be above reproach" (Stansbury, p. 147). On the matter of polygamy, Stansbury asserted that "its practical operation was quite different from what I had anticipated. Peace, harmony, and cheerfulness seemed to prevail. . . . Confidence and sisterly affection among the different members of the family seemed pre-eminently conspicuous" (Stansbury, pp. 137–38). Stansbury went on to praise the ingenuity and resourcefulness of the Mormon people, while allowing that their beliefs would preclude them from living with any other Christian peoples without "constant collision, jealousy, and strife" (Stansbury, p. 138).

In the spring of 1850 Stansbury and his party of explorers made a complete circumnavigation of Great Salt Lake and surveyed the area. On their return journey, Stansbury sought to pioneer a new route that would go due east from Salt Lake City through the Wasatch Mountains. Stansbury located what became known as Cheyenne Pass and Bridger Pass; his return route would later be used by the Overland Stage and the Union Pacific Railroad. On 6 October 1850, as his exploration neared its end, Stansbury suffered an injury; he was brought by an ambulance to Fort Laramie, where he arrived on 12 October, concluding what had been a significant venture into the Great Basin area and the newly created land of the Mormon people.

Stansbury spent the next year and a half in Washington, D.C., where he wrote his classic report on the expedition. Originally printed as a government report, *An Expedition to the Valley of the Great Salt Lake* (1852) was printed commercially in the same year. The report brought both praise and denunciation; Stansbury's elegant prose did not prevent critics from attacking his fair-minded observations of the Mormon settlements. Stansbury's later career was anticlimactic. He took charge of the military roads in the Minnesota territory in 1858; he was promoted to major in the army after the start of the Civil War; he resigned from the military in September 1861, but he rejoined in 1862 and directed recruiting in the state of Wisconsin. He died in Madison, Wisconsin, of heart disease.

Stansbury was a calm, level-headed engineer and army officer. Although his exploration and surveys were in some respects as important as the more glamorous ones of John Wesley Powell and others, Stansbury lacked the quality of self-promotion that might have made him famous within his own lifetime. His report, a classic in terms of colorful description, objective observation, and reasoned analysis, stands as the best memorial to his life and career. In what was probably the most important assignment of his career—to establish relations with the Mormon leaders—Stansbury succeeded with aplomb. It was perhaps fortunate that the man who brought the American flag to the state of Deseret was not a traditional, West Point–schooled army officer. Although Stansbury's report of the expedition aroused fury among some easterners who despised the Mormons, the people who lived in the area of the Great Salt Lake praised it highly and esteemed the officer who had lived among them during the winter of 1849–1850.

• Stansbury's records and papers are in the National Archives. The best sources for an understanding of his life and career are Brigham D. Madsen, ed., *Exploring the Great Salt Lake: The Stansbury Expedition of 1849–1850* (1989); Madsen, "Stansbury's Expedition to the Great Salt Lake," *Utah Historical Quarterly* 56, no. 2 (1988): 148–59; Dale L. Morgan, *The Great Salt Lake* (1947; repr. 1995); and William H. Goetzmann, *Exploration and Empire: The Explorer and the Scientist in the Winning of the American West* (1966). Stansbury's own record of the expedition is indispensable for the student and historian.

SAMUEL WILLARD CROMPTON

STANTON, Edwin McMasters (19 Dec. 1814–24 Dec. 1869), U.S. attorney general and secretary of war, was born in Steubenville, Ohio, the son of David Stanton, a physician, and Lucy Norman. As a child, Stanton contracted a chronic asthmatic condition that plagued him throughout his life and may have contributed to the brusque irritability that characterized his temperament. Young Stanton attended local academies and, after his father's death in 1827, took a position as an apprentice in a Steubenville bookstore. In 1831 he entered Kenyon College, but his family's financial problems forced him to leave the following year. After working briefly at a bookstore in Columbus, Ohio, Stanton returned to Steubenville to study law in the office of his guardian, Daniel L. Collier. In 1836 he entered a partnership with Chauncey Dewey in Cadiz, Ohio. That year he married Mary A. Lamson, with whom he had two children.

In 1837 Stanton formed a second partnership with an old family friend, Judge Benjamin Tappan of Steubenville, though he continued to live in Cadiz and practice with Dewey. A prominent Democrat with antislavery inclinations, Tappan influenced the political beliefs of his young protégé. In 1837 Stanton was elected prosecuting attorney of Harrison County, and during the following year he promoted Tappan's successful campaign for the U.S. Senate. As a hard money Democrat, Stanton supported Martin Van Buren in the 1840 election, and from 1842 to 1845 he served as recorder of the Ohio Supreme Court in Columbus. Since his Kenyon stay, Stanton had harbored strong moral objections to slavery. He chose to keep his antislavery beliefs separate from his political stand, however, and he supported the James K. Polk administration during the Mexican War despite his misgivings about the expansion of slavery.

In 1844 Stanton's wife died, plunging him into a spell of deep depression. Nevertheless his legal career began to blossom. Dissolving his partnership with Tappan in 1845, apparently for personal reasons, he practiced with George W. McCook in Steubenville. In 1847 Stanton moved to Pittsburgh in search of more lucrative opportunities and, in partnership with Charles Shaler, soon developed an extensive practice in both Pennsylvania and Ohio. A tireless worker who relied on extensive case preparation, Stanton possessed a keenly logical mind and a forceful speaking style. He was also aggressive, even ruthless, in the courtroom, given to browbeating witnesses and treating with rude contempt opposing lawyers whom he considered his social or intellectual inferiors. In 1850–1851 he earned widespread recognition for successfully representing the state of Pennsylvania before the U.S. Supreme Court in a suit against a Virginia company that proposed building a bridge across the Ohio River at Wheeling, potentially restricting river traffic to Pittsburgh.

In 1856 Stanton married Ellen Hutchison, with whom he had four children. That year he moved to Washington, D.C., in hopes of developing his practice before the Supreme Court. Although he remained ostensibly aloof from politics, he formed a close friendship with Jeremiah S. Black, James Buchanan's attorney general, whom he had known when Black was chief justice of the Pennsylvania Supreme Court. In 1857 Black appointed Stanton special counsel to investigate the case of José Y. Limantour, who claimed title

to valuable California lands on the basis of alleged Mexican grants made prior to U.S. annexation. On his arrival in San Francisco in March 1858, Stanton compiled massive evidence to disprove Limantour's claims, and he exposed other fraudulent land claims as well, resulting in considerable savings for the federal government.

Stanton returned to Washington in early 1859 and resumed his law practice and close alliance with Black. When the Democratic party split on the sectional issue in 1860, Stanton followed Buchanan and Black in supporting John C. Breckinridge, the presidential nominee of the southern Democrats, because he considered Breckinridge the only candidate capable of preserving the Union. During a cabinet shake-up in December 1860, Black became secretary of state, and Buchanan appointed Stanton to replace him as attorney general. Throughout the closing months of Buchanan's term, Stanton strove forcefully to preserve the Union. In the cabinet, he and Black constantly pressured the vacillating president to adopt a strong position against secession and to retain control of Fort Sumter and other forts along the southern coastline. Moreover, Stanton secretly passed information on cabinet deliberations to Senator William H. Seward and other Republicans in Congress. During his brief tenure as attorney general, Stanton did as much as anyone in the administration to stiffen Buchanan's stand and resist the secessionist surge.

After Abraham Lincoln's inauguration in March 1861, Stanton remained in Washington, D.C., serving occasionally as a legal consultant to Secretary of War Simon Cameron. He also formed a close friendship with Major General George B. McClellan, the commander of the Department of the Potomac who became commanding general of the army in November, based on their shared Democratic loyalties and low estimate of the new administration. On the issue of slavery, however, Stanton quietly began to separate himself from the conservative Democrats. In December 1861 Cameron requested his advice on a section of his annual report that called for the recruitment of African Americans into the army. Acting on Stanton's recommendation, Cameron not only retained but strengthened the passage in the final draft, much to the consternation of President Lincoln, who feared its impact in the border states. On 13 January 1862 Cameron resigned as secretary of war, mainly because of exposés of mismanagement and corruption in the issuing of War Department contracts, and the following day the president appointed Stanton to take his place. Although Lincoln's motives are not entirely clear, the selection seems to have resulted from the influence of Secretary of State Seward, who considered Stanton a moderate, and of Secretary of the Treasury Salmon P. Chase, an old acquaintance from Ohio who recalled Stanton's antislavery views.

Stanton plunged into his new duties with energy and determination, and he proved to be a brilliant war manager. He developed close working relationships with congressional leaders of both parties, including the chairmen of key committees, which eased the passage of military bills. With congressional approval, he expanded the War Department office staff and rationalized its operations, spurring his subordinates to greater productivity through his driving, autocratic style and personal example of tireless work. He convinced Congress to pass a bill that led to the indirect regulation of the railroad system, and he concentrated the military telegraph in the War Department, thereby exerting tight censorship over the flow of war information. Although Stanton made no basic changes in the army's logistical departments, he formed their chiefs and other high-ranking officers at the capital into a temporary board of war, in effect an informal general staff that allowed him to draw upon professional military advice. Fiercely honest, the secretary strove to clean up the procurement scandals left from Cameron's administration, establishing regulations for War Department contracts that provided for open, competitive bidding and subjecting contractors to martial law. Stanton also followed a policy of rigid honesty and fairness in the granting of military commissions and other appointments.

As secretary of war, Stanton became increasingly disillusioned with his erstwhile friend McClellan, who had remained ensconced in the Washington defenses since the summer of 1861 and showed little inclination to take the offensive against the Confederate forces in Virginia. In March 1862 Stanton and other cabinet members convinced Lincoln to remove McClellan as commanding general of the entire army, though McClellan continued to command the Army of the Potomac. For several months in the spring and early summer of 1862, Lincoln and Stanton performed the role of commanding general. The two civilians pressured McClellan into launching his Peninsula campaign, personally directed the capture of Norfolk, and devised a nearly successful plan to trap Confederate general Thomas J. "Stonewall" Jackson's army in the Shenandoah Valley. In a controversial move, however, Stanton suspended recruiting in early April in order to reorganize the recruiting service—and in the apparent belief that the war would soon be over. Because of this step, as well as the administration's decision to detain Major General Irvin McDowell's corps as a shield for Washington, D.C., McClellan and his Democratic supporters claimed that the secretary of war had withheld essential reinforcements from the Peninsula offensive, contributing to its failure. While these charges were unfounded—McClellan's army strongly outnumbered the Confederates throughout the campaign—Stanton and McClellan remained bitter enemies, each calling for the removal of the other, until Lincoln finally relieved McClellan of command in November 1862.

In July 1862 Lincoln appointed Major General Henry W. Halleck to be commanding general of the army. However, Halleck was reluctant to take full responsibility for directing the military effort, an inclination reinforced by the ill-defined powers of his office, and Lincoln and Stanton continued to shoulder much of the burden. Throughout the middle stages of the conflict, the secretary of war played a central role in appointing and removing commanders, overseeing military operations, and even shaping strategy. After the Union defeat at Chickamauga in September 1863, he coordinated the rapid movement by railroad of more than 20,000 reinforcements from the Army of the Potomac to the beleaguered Union forces in Chattanooga, one of the most complex and dramatic logistical feats of the war. Stanton also promoted the trend toward a policy of "hard war" against the Confederacy. He supported the confiscation of the slaves and other property of active secessionists, and he pressed Lincoln to issue the Emancipation Proclamation and approve the enlistment of blacks.

Stanton's most controversial function was supervision of internal security, a duty that he assumed from Secretary of State Seward in March 1862. At first Stanton sought to restrict the exercise of martial law, and he ordered the release of most of the citizens interned under Seward. In response to the bitter controversies over conscription and the Emancipation Proclamation in 1862–1863, however, the administration broadened the suspension of habeas corpus, and the number of military arrests rose dramatically. In the Enrollment Act of March 1863, Congress established a militarized provost marshal general's bureau under Stanton's control—in effect a national police force—and the secretary employed this apparatus vigorously to enforce the draft and combat dissent. By midwar Stanton had transferred his loyalties fully to the Republican party, and he used his official powers to promote the Republican political cause, which he identified with preservation of the Union. In particular, his handling of soldier voting, including the mass furloughing of troops from key electoral states, contributed significantly to the Republican victory in 1864.

In March 1864 Lincoln appointed Ulysses S. Grant to supersede Halleck as commanding general of the army, retaining Halleck in the newly created position of chief of staff of the army. The result was an efficient command structure during the final year of the war: under Lincoln's overall direction, Grant and Halleck shaped strategy and oversaw operations, while Stanton focused on logistics and support, supplying the armies with manpower and the tools of war. While Stanton worked smoothly with Grant, his relationship was touchier with the chief Union commander in the western theater, William Tecumseh Sherman, whom the secretary considered hostile to the interests of the freedmen. After Appomattox, when Sherman overreached his authority by offering extremely generous surrender terms to Joseph E. Johnston's Confederate army, Stanton publicly overruled this agreement, leading to a bitter rift between the two men.

During the course of the war, Stanton's response to Lincoln evolved from disdain to respect and warm affection. While the two men often disagreed, the president was able to soften the war secretary's harsh demeanor and draw him out of his self-absorption, and they became close friends. Stanton was deeply shocked by Lincoln's assassination. He employed the powers of the War Department to hunt down the conspirators, pressed for a trial before a military commission, and personally participated in the prosecution. Stanton favored the death penalty for the convicted prisoners, including Mary Surratt, proprietor of the boardinghouse where plotting had transpired. However, the later charge that he conspired to withhold from President Andrew Johnson the court's recommendation of clemency in Surratt's case is almost certainly unfounded.

Stanton remained in the War Department after the war and oversaw the demobilization of the Union armies. Initially he supported Johnson's policies toward the South, even reversing his position to back the president's opposition to the immediate enfranchisement of the freedmen. During the summer of 1865, however, reports of violence against blacks and resistance to military rule in the southern states caused Stanton to shift toward the use of stronger measures. In particular, both he and General Grant were distressed by the growing number of lawsuits brought against army officers for enforcing martial law. Late in 1865 Joseph E. Maddox of Baltimore brought a suit against Stanton himself, charging that Maddox had been wrongly imprisoned for disloyalty during the war. If such cases were decided adversely, feared Stanton and Grant, officers would face financial ruin, and the army would be paralyzed in its ability to enforce Reconstruction in the South. Their concerns grew when, in April 1866, Johnson issued a proclamation declaring the rebellion at an end and the seceded states restored to the Union—a measure that appeared to remove the justification for military law.

Through 1866 and early 1867 Stanton played a difficult double role. Though he longed to resign, he remained in the cabinet in hopes of protecting the army and the fruits of victory, and he labored to alter Johnson's increasingly adamant opposition to congressional Reconstruction policies. Still professing moderation, Stanton avoided open commitment to the Radical Republicans. In March 1867, when Congress approved the Tenure of Office Act, intended in part to protect him from dismissal, Stanton actually supported the president in his unsuccessful veto. Behind the scenes, however, the secretary of war joined Grant in a campaign to bolster army commanders in the South and sustain martial law. In the process, the two leaders moved the army gradually from presidential control to an alignment with Congress. Stanton was the architect of the legislation passed in early 1867 that required the president to issue all orders to the army through the commanding general, and he supported the First and Second Reconstruction acts that established Republican-dominated governments in the former Confederacy, supervised by the federal military. By the summer of 1867 Stanton had given up his efforts at compromise and had moved into an alliance with the congressional Radicals. He and Grant drafted the Third Reconstruction Act that effectively removed the army in the South altogether from presidential control.

While Johnson had hitherto hesitated to dismiss Stanton for fear of an open breach in his administration, he now demanded the war secretary's resignation. Stanton refused, and on 11 August 1867 Johnson ordered him suspended from office and replaced by Grant as interim secretary of war. Bowing to "superior force," Stanton left office, but he awaited vindication in the next congressional session. In January 1868 the Senate ordered him restored to office on the basis of the Tenure of Office Act, which prohibited the dismissal of a cabinet official during the term of the president who had appointed him unless the Senate confirmed a successor. Much to Johnson's consternation, Grant quickly stepped down, and Stanton resumed his former position. In February the president tried again to oust Stanton, appointing Adjutant General Lorenzo Thomas as interim secretary. Urged on by the congressional Republicans, Stanton refused to acknowledge Thomas's appointment or physically vacate his office. The result was a constitutional impasse, and on 22 February the House of Representatives voted for the impeachment of Johnson on charges principally stemming from his dismissal of Stanton and violation of the Tenure of Office Act.

Stanton remained in the War Department day and night during most of the impeachment proceedings. Deeply disappointed by the Senate's failure to convict, the secretary resigned on 26 May 1868, and Johnson eventually replaced him with Brigadier General John M. Schofield. Stanton returned to private life exhausted, severely ill from chronic asthma, and virtually bankrupt from his years of public service. By the autumn of 1868 he had recovered sufficiently to conduct a speaking tour in support of Grant, the Republican presidential nominee. The exertion further weakened his health, however, and by 1869 he had become a semi-invalid, unable to resume his law practice and dependent on the financial support of his friends. Nevertheless, Stanton remained a hero to a great many Republicans, and in December 1869 President Grant appointed him to fill a vacancy on the U.S. Supreme Court. He died of chronic asthma in Washington, D.C., before he could assume the office.

Stanton was one of the central political figures of the Civil War era and one of the most controversial. His principal role was as chief manager under the president of the Union war effort—"Lincoln's Mars"—and his immense energy and organizational talent made possible the mobilization of the North's vast resources to achieve victory. In the process, he generated intense hostility, in part because of his abrasive personality and autocratic leadership style but more because his position as director of internal security inevitably made him a lightning rod for dissent. Stanton's strongest commitment was to preserve the Union, and his tenacious efforts during the early stages of Reconstruction to sustain the army and reverse President Johnson's policy of leniency toward the former Confederates did much to redeem the sacrifices of the war.

• The major collection of Stanton's personal papers is in the Library of Congress. A small collection is in the Henry E. Huntington Library, San Marino, Calif. Much of Stanton's official wartime correspondence is published in U.S. War Department, *The War of the Rebellion: A Compilation of the Official Records of the Union and Confederate Armies* (128 vols., 1880–1901). By far the most thorough and reliable biography is Benjamin P. Thomas and Harold M. Hyman, *Stanton: The Life and Times of Lincoln's Secretary of War* (1962). Other biographies include George C. Gorham, *The Life and Public Services of Edwin M. Stanton* (2 vols., 1899); Frank A. Flower, *Edwin McMasters Stanton: The Autocrat of Rebellion, Emancipation, and Reconstruction* (1905); and Fletcher Pratt, *Stanton: Lincoln's Secretary of War* (1953). Though he was a cabinet adversary of Stanton, Welles offers many insights into the war secretary's character and actions in *The Diary of Gideon Welles, Secretary of the Navy under Lincoln and Johnson* (3 vols., 1911), which also contains an introduction by John T. Morse, Jr. Assessments by men who worked under Stanton in the War Department include Charles A. Dana, *Recollections of the Civil War: With the Leaders at Washington and in the Field in the Sixties* (1898); Edward D. Townsend, *Anecdotes of the Civil War in the United States* (1884); and Charles F. Benjamin, "Secretary Stanton: The Man and His Work," *Journal of the Military Service Institution of the United States* 6 (1886): 239–56. For Stanton's relationship with Lincoln, see Burton J. Hendrick, *Lincoln's War Cabinet* (1946), and David H. Donald, *Lincoln* (1995). His role during Reconstruction is considered in Harold M. Hyman, "Johnson, Stanton, and Grant: A Reconsideration of the Army's Role in the Events Leading to Impeachment," *American Historical Review* 66 (Oct. 1960): 85–96; Brooks D. Simpson, *Let Us Have Peace: Ulysses S. Grant and the Politics of War and Reconstruction, 1861–1868* (1991); and Hans L. Trefousse, *Impeachment of a President: Andrew Johnson, the Blacks, and Reconstruction* (1975). William Hanchett demolishes the theory that Stanton was the center of the plot to assassinate Lincoln in *The Lincoln Murder Conspiracies* (1983).

WILLIAM B. SKELTON

STANTON, Elizabeth Cady (12 Nov. 1815–26 Oct. 1902), woman suffragist and writer, was born in Johnstown, New York, the daughter of Margaret Livingston and Daniel Cady, a distinguished lawyer, state assemblyman, and congressman. She received her education at the Johnstown Academy and Emma Willard's Troy Female Seminary and studied Greek with a local minister. Her knowledge of the law began at home, in conversations with her father, at dinners with New York's legal establishment, and in the social life of five Cady daughters and the stream of young men who came to Johnstown to study with Daniel Cady. The strict Scotch Presbyterianism and social conservatism of Elizabeth's upbringing were mitigated by the radicalism of her first cousin Gerrit Smith, an eccentric philanthropist, abolitionist, and religious critic, for whom Daniel Cady acted as lawyer and adviser. Back at home at the end of her schooling, Elizabeth occupied herself for several years with the family-centered duties of a wealthy daughter, including visits to relatives. A stay of several months with Gerrit Smith's family in the fall of 1839 introduced her to the prominent abolitionist orator Henry Brewster Stanton.

Elizabeth Cady married Henry Stanton in 1840, after the couple weathered the storm of Daniel Cady's disapproval. Henry Stanton had no means of support. He had cut short his professional training to work for immediate emancipation, loaned his savings to other antislavery agents, and worked for the financially troubled American Anti-Slavery Society without pay. After a wedding in Johnstown, the Stantons sailed to England to attend the World's Anti-Slavery Convention. Stanton later located the origins of the British and the American women rights movements in that convention's decision to bar American women, including Lucretia Mott, from taking their seats as delegates.

Marriage transformed Elizabeth's life in many ways. Henry agreed to complete his legal training with his father-in-law when the couple returned from abroad, but his preference for reform over his profession kept him poor and often away from home. Though Elizabeth Stanton lived a relatively prosperous life, she never attained the wealth that her parents and sisters enjoyed. Further, raising the seven children that she bore between 1842 and 1859 fell chiefly to her. Marriage, however, set in motion her metamorphosis into a reformer. Within months, she met all the leading women of the antislavery movement, who opened her mind to the puzzle of women's rights.

During the first seven years of her marriage Stanton lived variously in Johnstown and Albany with her parents and in Boston with her husband, while she deepened new friendships with Angelina Grimké, Sarah Grimké, Lucretia Mott, and members of the Boston and Philadelphia female antislavery societies. The lessons she learned were complex. In Boston she was drawn to the abolitionists who favored William Lloyd Garrison's moral absolutism; she hosted her husband's allies in the Liberty party who opposed Garrison; and she struggled to understand Theodore Parker's Transcendentalism. In Albany she dined with lawyers, judges, and legislators who debated legal reform and the property rights of married women and anticipated New York's constitutional convention of 1846. In correspondence with Mott and the Grimkés, she confronted religious questions as well as themes of women's individualism. Everyone who met her in the 1840s seemed taken with her charm and potential, and if she were to become a reformer, her friends expected her to reject orthodoxy and discover her own understanding of the divine will.

In 1847 the Stantons moved to Seneca Falls, New York, their home until 1862. A year later Elizabeth Cady Stanton initiated the call for a women's rights convention. From that meeting at Seneca Falls, on 19–20 July 1848, women issued the demand that their sacred right to the elective franchise be recognized. They wrote a Declaration of Sentiments and resolutions, arguing that consistency with the fundamental principles of the American Revolution required an end to women's taxation without representation and government without their consent. It accused men of usurping divine power and denying women their consciences by dictating the proper sphere of womankind. To illustrate women's disabilities under the law, the authors echoed attacks by legal reformers on English common law, particularly the principle that a woman lost her individual identity and rights when she married. The largest group at the 1848 meeting were antislavery Quakers from Rochester and Waterloo, New York, dissidents in the Society of Friends who were establishing the Congregational (later Progressive) Friends. Among them the convention's message found its strongest support, at a second convention in Rochester a few weeks later, in a modest petition campaign for woman suffrage late in 1848, and in the yearly meetings of Progressive Friends thereafter. Decades later Stanton wrote that advocacy of suffrage for women met resistance and that Frederick Douglass helped her to sway the crowd in its favor. Though nothing in the contemporary record confirms that story, the opposition of Friends and Garrisonians to voting could explain why participants doubted the importance of suffrage.

Women elsewhere took note of events in New York. Petitions for property rights and suffrage circulated in several states, and beginning in the spring of 1850 conventions of women's rights advocates became commonplace from Indiana to New England. This fledgling reform movement recognized Elizabeth Cady Stanton as one of its leaders, although her co-workers knew her principally by her writing until the Civil War. She wrote for Amelia Bloomer's *Lily* and Paulina Wright Davis's *Una*, and the letters, speeches, and resolutions she sent to most of the antebellum conventions were published in the antislavery and women's press. In her articles and public letters she embraced a wide range of changes that women of her generation were pursuing—entering medical schools, wearing short hair, experimenting with more rational dress, writing novels, and taking unusual jobs—and interpreted this cultural upheaval as part and parcel of her own pursuit of women's autonomy.

Stanton's goals were well defined (and controversial) before the Civil War. The right to vote measured how well society respected human rights, with disfranchisement signaling the refusal of white males to acknowledge equals. Women needed the vote because men could not represent them, she argued. She varied her explanations of why representation failed. When she indicted the laws of New York, she noted that the interests of men and women sometimes collided, in laws about child custody, for instance, and men legislated their own interests. At other times, especially but not exclusively after the war, she minimized conflict between the sexes to argue that neither men nor women could govern well alone, that a good society needed women's views to complement men's.

Stanton also developed early her demand that women's individualism be guaranteed within marriage. A married woman's right to property and wages should be inalienable, and her right to exit from an abusive or destructive marriage assured. Her right to decide with whom and when to bear children should be inviolate.

Criticism of Stanton's views of marriage and divorce came not only from angry clergymen defending a sacrament and men unwilling to yield their marital rights, but also from erstwhile allies such as Horace Greeley of the New York *Tribune*, who found her ideas too close to those of free lovers, and Caroline Dall of Boston, who wanted discussion of women's rights confined to education, jobs, and suffrage.

Though best known for exposing the legal and political bases of women's degradation, Stanton held churches accountable as well. When a local minister preached against the Seneca Falls convention in 1848, she boldly contested his interpretation of biblical passages and disputed his conviction that Christianity tolerated inequality. Like the radical abolitionists who demanded that churches condemn slavery, women, she believed, should renounce churches and ministers who proclaimed their inferiority. Until called to account by more cautious co-workers, she appealed to the women of New York to remember that constitutions and the words of St. Paul were mere parchments that should not limit their aspirations.

Stanton's participation in the women's rights movement intensified when, in 1851, she met Susan B. Anthony, an activist in the temperance movement and a friend of Rochester's women's rights advocates. Tied down by children and an absent husband, Stanton depended on Anthony's greater mobility and her willingness to build a movement for women's rights. Together they made New York a laboratory for agitation. In their first collaboration in 1852, Stanton joined Anthony's cause and presided over the Women's New York State Temperance Society until she was voted out of office because of her views on equal rights and her conviction that women needed the right to divorce. In 1854 they launched their first campaign to change specific laws regarding women, and while Anthony circulated petitions and tracts, organized meetings, and lobbied the legislature, Stanton crafted the arguments. From a sampling of laws regarding women, wives, mothers, and widows, she portrayed women caught in an unjust system that limited their custody of children, took their earnings, kept them at the mercy of dissolute husbands, and deprived them as widows of a home. Yearly until the Civil War Stanton and Anthony renewed their pressure on the legislature, extracting favorable reports in some years and mockery in others. In 1860, when Republicans controlled the legislature, they won a major revision in laws regarding the economic rights of married women, the custody rights of mothers, and equal rights for widows. When the war began, they were embarked on a similar campaign to rewrite New York's divorce law.

Stanton left Seneca Falls in 1862 to spend the next seven years in Brooklyn and New York City. When the Civil War brought women's rights meetings to a halt, she envisaged roles for women in the North's political mobilization. In 1863 she urged the loyal women of the North to prepare for the nation's reconstruction as a true republic and convened the Women's Loyal National League. Working with ladies' aid and antislavery societies as well as the league, Stanton and Anthony provided Massachusetts senator Charles Sumner with 400,000 signatures to petitions for the Thirteenth Amendment by the summer of 1864. Although the league copied women's earliest and least controversial antislavery activism as petitioners to Congress, its independence worried abolitionists. Rather than operating under the leadership of the American Anti-Slavery Society, the league pursued a strategy for emancipation that Garrison himself had not yet endorsed. Old alliances suffered further when Stanton identified the league with the presidential aspirations of John C. Frémont in 1864.

Beginning with the loyal league, Stanton gave new direction to the women's rights movement by making it a vehicle for expressing women's interests in politics, and during Reconstruction that new direction splintered the antebellum alliance of antislavery and women's rights forces. When Congress opened discussion of the Fourteenth Amendment at the end of 1865, Stanton joined the antislavery leadership in opposing educated suffrage or other restrictions on the voting rights to be granted to the former slaves. But when that leadership supported Republican proposals to enshrine manhood suffrage as the new standard of republican government, Stanton convened the American Equal Rights Association in the spring of 1866 to promote universal suffrage, competing directly with the American Anti-Slavery Society. In addition to petitioning Congress for universal suffrage, the association campaigned in most northern states where new suffrage requirements were under consideration. Stanton herself lectured in the campaigns of New York and Kansas. By the summer of 1867 abolitionists and Republican leaders openly opposed attempts to win woman suffrage in the states. A furious Stanton returned from Kansas in the company of the notorious George Francis Train, a Democrat and blatant racist, insisting that woman suffragists would find whatever allies they could and that no new voters should be added unless all citizens were given the right to vote. To make her point she lectured against the Fifteenth Amendment. This defiant political message shaped the *Revolution*, the newspaper she coedited with Parker Pillsbury from 1868 to 1870. It inspired the National Woman Suffrage Association (NWSA), founded in 1869. It informed her tour of the Midwest in 1869, when she raised fears that enfranchising black men endangered white women.

Stanton never stepped back to explain her decision to abandon the tradition of human rights, though she believed that her former allies preceded her in betrayal. In their effort to enfranchise freedmen in the South, they divided the rights of men from those of women, distinguished citizenship from voting rights, and refused to establish as constitutional law the principle that the federal government should protect voters. She also never retracted the attacks on African Americans that she leveled while mounting this fight. She did, however, stop herself. When time proved the Fourteenth and Fifteenth amendments inadequate

protection for blacks' voting rights in the South, she mounted the biggest suffrage campaign of her lifetime for "National Protection for National Citizens," arguing that the voting rights of all citizens were too important to be left to the states and should be guaranteed by constitutional amendment.

The national protection campaign, in which Stanton worked closely with Susan B. Anthony and Matilda Joslyn Gage and through the NWSA, began at the centennial celebrations of 1876. For eight years they mobilized women nationwide to petition Congress for a sixteenth, woman suffrage amendment, introduced in 1878 and voted down in 1887. So impressive was their progress that the rival American Woman Suffrage Association, under the leadership of Lucy Stone, which had focused on changing state laws, circulated the congressional petitions. The campaign also caught the attention of Frances Willard and the enormous Woman's Christian Temperance Union, whose work for woman suffrage dated from this same period.

At age sixty-five Stanton began to reduce her workload. She toured the country as a lecturer for the last time in 1880, after eleven years on the lyceum circuit. Never fond of meetings, she found more excuses to avoid them. She also closed the house in Tenafly, New Jersey, where she had moved in 1868, and resided chiefly with her children. From May 1882 through November 1883, from November 1886 to March 1888, and again from February 1890 to August 1891, she lived abroad with two children who had married and started families in Europe. Stanton was hardly idle. Between 1881 and her death, she published five books and hundreds of articles, and she still averaged three or four major speeches each year. Freed from lecturing, she completed the historical project that she and Anthony and Gage had started in the centennial year. Volumes one and two of the *History of Woman Suffrage* were published in 1881 and 1882. She worked on the third volume (published in 1886) in 1884 and 1885, when she resumed housekeeping to take care of her aging husband. (Henry Stanton died in 1887, after his wife returned to England.)

A more private life allowed Stanton to become a critic of the woman suffrage movement. Nominally president of the NWSA and its successor, the National American Woman Suffrage Association, until 1892, she was increasingly an outsider to a movement drawing adherents from evangelical churches, attracting believers in women's moral superiority and southerners who abhorred federal protection of voting rights, and empowering women who understood nothing of the lessons of human rights. Only Susan B. Anthony's insistence kept her in the association formed by merging the National and American suffrage associations, and she was defiant on its platform. At the first joint convention in 1890 she reaffirmed the importance of federal protection for voting rights, disputed the faith of Americans in state-by-state campaigning, and tied both to the growing disfranchisement of African Americans in southern states. The retreat from Reconstruction, she proclaimed, and the Supreme Court's declarations "that the United States has no voters and that citizenship does not carry with it the right of suffrage, not only have prolonged woman's disfranchisement but have undermined the status of the freedmen and opened the way for another war of races" (Anthony and Harper, vol. 4, p. 165). She lent her name to new, dissident suffrage societies carrying out the old goals of a secular movement for federal guarantees based on the argument of human equality. Her last appearance on the Washington stage came in 1892, when she addressed the House Judiciary Committee on "The Solitude of Self." Reprising themes of her speeches and articles since the 1850s, she spoke eloquently about woman's responsibility for herself and society's need to protect her individual rights.

In 1894 Stanton moved again off the center of universal suffrage. After a bitter defeat for woman suffrage in the New York State constitutional convention, she proposed educated suffrage as a reform more palatable to a generation of politicians who accepted Jim Crow in the South and dreaded the immigrant wave in the North. Educated suffrage, she argued, was fairer than existing standards, albeit a lowlier goal than universal suffrage. As many reformers had reasoned before her, she saw that education was not destiny, like gender or race, but a temporary status amenable to change.

What set Stanton apart most of all in her last decades was her conviction that the next great struggle would occur not against the state but against churches. In 1885 she tried to shepherd the NWSA into the fray and introduced resolutions "impeaching the Christian theology—as well as all other forms of religion, for their degrading teachings in regard to woman" (*Eighty Years and More*, p. 383). At about the same time she solicited contributors to a critical exegesis of the Bible. But when she published part one of the *Woman's Bible* in 1895, the suffrage association she had founded repudiated her ideas as damaging to the cause. Opposition from within the movement had no effect on her ambitions. In her mind critics of a struggle with orthodox religion simply echoed those who laughed at a woman's right to vote in 1848. By the 1890s Stanton's chief support came from the free thought movement. In 1898 she published parts one and two of the *Woman's Bible* and her autobiography, *Eighty Years and More*. They are in many respects companion volumes, the one containing commentaries on the Bible's treatment of women, the other casting Stanton's life and worldly work as a struggle against "the religious superstitions" that perpetuate women's "bondage more than all other adverse influences" (p. 471).

By her eightieth birthday Stanton could barely stand. Always plump, she had become fat, and arthritic knees could not hold her. She rarely left an apartment in New York City. Her eyesight faded, and by 1899 she was blind. She dictated articles and tried to revise her best-known speeches orally. She died at home in New York, leaving unmailed a letter to Theodore Roosevelt seeking his endorsement of woman suffrage.

Stanton's legacy is complicated by her inexcusable (and to her argument, unnecessary) assaults on the rights and reputations of black men during Reconstruction. She coined the language that would mar the woman suffrage movement long after her death, expressing outrage that white men would give preference in voting rights to all manner of men over their educated white mothers, wives, and sisters. But more quickly than most Americans, she recognized the dire consequences of turning back to the states the power to regulate the electorate. Throughout her life Stanton believed that rights mattered, in everyday life and over the lifetime of every person, and she worked hard as a writer and lecturer to expand the rights of individuals. She was a popular speaker with a sense of humor and a gift for connecting legal and political abstractions to their human consequences, both of which give her writing a timeless quality. Uncompromising and impatient as a reformer, and a democrat more in theory than in social practice, Stanton showed faulty judgment when she tried to set a political course.

• Stanton's papers, compiled from archives and printed sources, are microfilmed and indexed as the *Papers of Elizabeth Cady Stanton and Susan B. Anthony*, ed. Patricia G. Holland and Ann D. Gordon (1991). The first three volumes of the *History of Woman Suffrage* provide the best record of Stanton's political activity as well as her historical writing; vol. 4, by Susan B. Anthony and Ida Harper (1904), covers the late years of her suffragism. The autobiographical *Eighty Years and More: Reminiscences, 1815–1897* is very readable, and the *Woman's Bible* still attracts critical attention. The reprints of both books (1993) contain useful essays by Ellen C. DuBois, Ann D. Gordon, and Maureen McCarthy. Theodore Stanton and Harriot Stanton Blatch, eds., *Elizabeth Cady Stanton, As Revealed in Her Letters, Diary and Reminiscences* (2 vols., 1992), is heavily edited and unreliable. More valuable is the recent selection in DuBois, ed., *Elizabeth Cady Stanton, Susan B. Anthony: Correspondence Writings, Speeches*, rev. ed. (1992). Theodore Tilton wrote a charming biography of Stanton in *Eminent Women of the Age* (1868). The best modern biography is Alma Lutz, *Created Equal: A Biography of Elizabeth Cady Stanton, 1815–1902* (1940). Other useful biographies are Lois Banner, *Elizabeth Cady Stanton: A Radical for Woman's Rights* (1980), and Elisabeth Griffith, *In Her Own Right: The Life of Elizabeth Cady Stanton* (1984). For Stanton's early role in women's rights agitation, see two articles by Judith Wellman: "The Seneca Falls Women's Rights Convention: A Study of Social Networks," *Journal of Women's History* 3 (Spring 1991): 9–37, and "Women's Rights, Republicanism and Revolutionary Rhetoric in Antebellum New York State," *New York History* 69 (July 1988): 353–84. Stanton's home in Seneca Falls belongs to the National Park Service and is open to the public. Her role at the start of Reconstruction is explored in DuBois, *Feminism and Suffrage* (1978), a work that should be read in conjunction with Bettina Aptheker's critical essay in *Woman's Legacy: Essays on Race, Sex, and Class in American History* (1982).

ANN D. GORDON

STANTON, Frank Lebby (22 Feb. 1857–7 Jan. 1927), journalist and poet, was born in Charleston, South Carolina, the son of Valentine Stanton, a printer, and Catherine Rebecca Parry. In 1862 Stanton moved with his family to Savannah, Georgia, where he attended public school. His formal education ended soon after, interrupted by the Civil War, in which his father fought with the Confederate army. Stanton continued to study alone, however, reading extensively from Shakespeare and other classics.

When Stanton was eight his father died. Four years later, in 1869, he began his lifelong association with journalism when he started work as a copy boy and, later, printer's apprentice, at the *Savannah Morning News*, then edited by William Tappan Thompson. Stanton also began contributing poems to the newspaper, having written his first poem, "To Lizzie," at age eleven. This work caught the attention of Joel Chandler Harris, then the newspaper's associate editor, who encouraged Stanton to continue writing.

Stanton eventually became a reporter and feature writer for the newspaper but, as he told an interviewer in 1925, left his position to drift around Georgia as an itinerant printer for nearly a decade, until 1887. That year he moved to Smithville, Georgia, to write for the weekly *Smithville News*, and soon after he became the paper's owner and editor. Also in 1887, Stanton married Leona Jossey, who later became an inspiration for many of his poems. They had three children.

During Stanton's brief tenure, the *Smithville News* became a frequently cited source of witty commentary and humorous dialect verse and stories, many of which were reprinted in other newspapers throughout the state. In 1888 Stanton moved north to Rome, Georgia, where he became night editor of John Temple Graves's *Rome Daily Tribune*.

After only one year in Rome, Stanton accepted an offer in 1889 to join his former colleague, Harris, on the staff of the *Atlanta Constitution*, a position he held until his death. At first Stanton served as a reporter and feature writer, but within his first year he began his regular column, "Just from Georgia," one of the first newspaper columns in the United States. This daily feature, which soon became immensely popular, was a forum for Stanton's poems, songs, anecdotes, brief essays, and humorous sayings. The appeal of his writing lay in its homey, unpretentious quality, which conveyed a feeling of optimism and frequently relied on black and poor white "cracker" dialect. Despite the fact that the *Atlanta Constitution* saw itself as the voice of the New South, Stanton's "down home" writing nostalgically evoked the old, antebellum days where, as he once wrote, "We're doin' well in Georgy lan' / Down on the ol' plantation."

Some of the poems Stanton wrote in black dialect seem condescending, if not racist, by later standards. However, his contemporary readers saw such efforts as evidence of Stanton's sympathy and understanding. Indeed, Stanton was strongly against oppression of blacks and wrote two very serious poems denouncing lynching. One of these was inspired by his discovery in 1888 of the body of a black man, who had been hanged by a mob shortly before Stanton arrived. Yet the dominant motif in Stanton's verse is his essential cheerfulness, evidenced in such poems as "Keep

A-Goin'" and "This World," which concludes: "You git a thorn with every rose, / But *ain't* the roses *sweet!*"

Thus Stanton was not only widely read but, because of his use of dialect and the popular appeal of his work, was sometimes referred to as the James Whitcomb Riley of the South. He was honored by Governor Clifford Walker in 1925, on his sixty-eighth birthday, by being named Georgia's first poet laureate. After a brief illness, Stanton died at his home in Atlanta.

Stanton's daily column generated an enormous if uneven body of material, and he regularly collected these songs and verses in books, beginning with *Songs of a Day* (1892) and continuing through *Songs of the Soil* (1894), *Comes One with a Song* (1898), *Songs from Dixie Land* (1900), *Up from Georgia* (1902), *Little Folks Down South* (1904), and his posthumous *Just from Georgia* (1927). Two of Stanton's poems that others set to music became quite famous: "Jest A-Wearyin' fer You," by Carrie Jacobs Bond, and what became his most popular song, "Sweetes' Li'l Feller" (known as "Mighty Lak a Rose"), by the noted composer Ethelbert Nevin. These songs brought Stanton a nationwide audience and, had he copyrighted his writings, they would have also earned him a good deal in royalties.

Joel Chandler Harris states in his introduction to *Songs of the Soil* that Frank Stanton's verses "ring true to the ear because they come straight from the heart." That appeal, combined with Stanton's unabashed and, at times, sentimental optimism and love of Georgia lay at the core of an enormous contemporary popularity that reached not only throughout the South but across the nation.

• Stanton's papers are in the Beinecke Rare Book and Manuscript Library, Yale University; Butler Library, Columbia University; Henry E. Huntington Library, San Marino, Calif.; Margaret I. King Library, University of Kentucky; Lilly Library, Indiana University; Margaret Mitchell Memorial Library, Atlanta Historical Society; Newberry Library, Chicago; William R. Perkins Library, Duke University; University of California–San Diego Library; and Robert W. Woodruff Library, Emory University.

Bruce M. Swain wrote a biographical essay, with a bibliography, for the *Dictionary of Literary Biography*, vol. 25 (1977). In addition, Wightman F. Melton edited the pamphlet *Frank Lebby Stanton* (1938) for the Georgia Division of Information and Publications. Charles W. Hubner contributed a sketch of Stanton's life to the *Library of Southern Literature*, ed. E. A. Alderman and Joel Chandler Harris, vol. 11 (1908). See also Mildred Rutherford, *The South in History and Literature* (1906); Walter Chamber's interview with Stanton in *American Magazine* 19 (Feb. 1925): 118–26; "The Poet of Georgia," *Nation*, 19 Jan. 1927; and "A Columnist of the South," *Outlook*, 19 Jan. 1927. An obituary is in the *Atlanta Constitution*, 8 Jan. 1927.

FRANCIS J. BOSHA

STANWYCK, Barbara (16 July 1907–20 Jan. 1990), actress, was born Ruby Katherine Stevens in Brooklyn, New York, the daughter of Byron Stevens, a fisherman and construction worker, and Catherine McGee. Her mother died in a streetcar-related accident when

Stanwyck was three years old. Her father left the family and went to work on the Panama Canal, where he died. Stanwyck could not say for sure when she "officially" became an orphan but thought it may have been when she was "about five." She was raised by her older sister, Mildred, a show girl. When Mildred got a chorus job, Stanwyck was placed in foster homes, from which she often ran away. As a child she loved dancing, and after she quit school at age thirteen she worked and auditioned with Mildred for chorus spots.

At fifteen Stanwyck was hired into the Strand Roof chorus at $35 a week. Choreographer Earl Lindsay placed her in the chorus of a 1924 tour of the Ziegfeld *Follies*. The next year she was in the ensemble of the Broadway revue *Gay Paree*. Shortly after that show closed, she met producer Willard Mack, who was hiring for a play titled *The Noose*. He hired her and—inspired by program notes on veteran actress Jane Stanwyck in the play *Barbara Frietchie*—suggested a name change from Ruby Stevens to Barbara Stanwyck. In 1926 she appeared in *The Noose*, which starred matinee idol Rex Cherryman.

In 1927 Stanwyck did a screen test for Cosmopolitan Pictures and got a dance bit in the silent film *Broadway Nights*. Her first stage lead came in *Burlesque* (1927), which was blasted by the critics but netted her raves and became a hit. Through pianist and actor Oscar Levant Stanwyck met successful vaudeville star Frank Fay. Although they both claimed to have hated each other on sight, they became close after Stanwyck was hit hard by the untimely death in 1928 of Cherryman, with whom she had been romantically involved. Stanwyck and Fay married in August 1928 and within six months were Hollywood bound. Stanwyck was signed by United Artists for her first talkie, *The Locked Door* (1929).

Stanwyck's breakthrough came when Fay arranged for director Frank Capra to test her for *Ladies of Leisure* (1930). She and Capra clashed, and their interview ended with Stanwyck running out abruptly and Capra reporting to Columbia Pictures president Harry Cohn, "Forget Stanwyck. She's not an actress, she's a porcupine." Fay, however, convinced Capra to view a test Stanwyck had made for Warner Bros. of a scene from *The Noose*. Capra was moved to tears by the "emotional sincerity" of her acting, and he cast her in the lead. He captured a luminous performance from his star, who played a sardonic party girl who falls for a society artist. Two unusual traits of her acting style came to light: she always came prepared with the script committed to memory—the entire script, not just her own role—and she always did her best acting in the very first performance of a scene. Capra worked around the latter quality by excusing Stanwyck from rehearsals, while rehearsing the other actors more strenuously than usual, and filming the first take with multiple camera setups. He would direct her several more times; their films together included *The Miracle Woman* (1931), *Forbidden* (1932), and *The Bitter Tea of General Yen* (1933). The last film, an unusual love story with a dreamlike aesthetic quality, has been de-

scribed as Stanwyck's only art film. She later worked again with Capra on *Meet John Doe* (1941), starring opposite Gary Cooper.

In December 1932 the Fays adopted a ten-month-old boy they named Dion Anthony. But as Stanwyck's star rose, Fay's declined; Stanwyck claimed their relationship was the basis for the 1937 film *A Star Is Born*. Their marriage was further strained by Fay's heavy drinking and abusive behavior, and they divorced in 1935. Stanwyck retained custody of Dion but never became close to him, and he was permanently estranged from her as an adult.

Stanwyck became a disciplined, professional actress whose trademark was her raw voice. Her public appeal allowed her to move back and forth among the Hollywood studios. She is best remembered for her gritty screen performances, including the title role in King Vidor's *Stella Dallas* (1937), a hit tearjerker about a poor, crude woman whose daughter marries into society. Her portrayal, which drew from her working-class background and eschewed all glamour, earned her an Academy Award nomination, and she later remarked, "I poured my blood into that one." She also had leading roles in *The Mad Miss Manton* (1938), a screwball comedy costarring Henry Fonda; *Golden Boy* (1939), in which William Holden played his first starring role opposite her; and *The Lady Eve* (1941), a Preston Sturges comedy with Henry Fonda and Charles Coburn. Stanwyck, who had emerged as a talented comedienne in *The Mad Miss Manton*, handled Sturges's sparkling script as nimbly as her previous dramatic roles, and the film has become a classic. In 1942 she starred in Howard Hawks's *Ball of Fire* opposite Gary Cooper. Playing a stripper with a vivid vocabulary in this successful comedy brought her another Oscar nomination.

In May 1939 Stanwyck and screen heartthrob Robert Taylor eloped to San Diego for a civil ceremony; they had no children. She was devoted to Taylor and he dependent on her, but they began having marital problems in the late 1940s and were divorced in 1951.

Stanwyck's most famous film role came in 1944, that of the ruthless blonde Phyllis Dietrichson in Billy Wilder's *Double Indemnity*, a milestone film noir cowritten by Wilder and Raymond Chandler. Phyllis entices Fred MacMurray's insurance salesman Walter Neff into helping her kill her husband. Stanwyck brought a hard-boiled, predatory presence to the role, which has since become the standard against which femmes fatales are measured. She earned her third Academy Award nomination for best actress.

Throughout her career Stanwyck acted for some of Hollywood's most notable directors, including not only Capra, Vidor, Sturges, Hawks, and Wilder but also William Wellman, in *Night Nurse* (1931), *So Big* (1932), *The Great Man's Lady* (1942), and *Lady of Burlesque* (1943); George Stevens, in *Annie Oakley* (1935); John Ford, in *The Plough and the Stars* (1936); Cecil B. DeMille, in *Union Pacific* (1939); Anthony Mann, in *The Furies* (1950), a western; Fritz Lang, in *Clash by Night* (1952), based on the play by Clifford Odets;

Douglas Sirk, in *All I Desire* (1953) and *There's Always Tomorrow* (1956); Robert Wise, in *Executive Suite* (1954); Samuel Fuller, in *Forty Guns* (1957); and Edward Dmytryk, in *Walk on the Wild Side* (1962). Stanwyck's other notable films include *The Strange Love of Martha Ivers* (1946), a heated melodrama in which she again played a memorably ruthless bad girl, and *Sorry, Wrong Number* (1948), for which her portayal of a doomed wife opposite Burt Lancaster earned her a fourth Academy Award nomination. Stanwyck was highly respected among her peers for her work ethic: she was often the first person on the set in the morning and never arrived unprepared. She also displayed an interest in the technical processes of filmmaking and often insisted on performing her own stunts.

Stanwyck made her last film feature in 1965, but by then she had already made a successful transition to the small screen, beginning with her own 1960 NBC anthology series "The Barbara Stanwyck Show," for which she received an Emmy Award. On a 1968 television special Stanwyck explained her attraction to show business: "When I was a kid, I was so crazy about westerns. . . . Pearl White . . . was my idol. I swore when I became an actress—nobody told me, I just knew—that I was going to do that." Although she appeared in several film westerns, the one that made her millions of dollars was produced for television: she played Victoria Barkley, the no-nonsense ranch matriarch in the ABC series "The Big Valley" from 1965 to 1969, earning another Emmy Award. She worked for more than twenty years in television, receiving a third Emmy Award for her role in the popular miniseries "The Thorn Birds" (1983).

After having been denied four times, Stanwyck finally was given an Oscar in 1982, for lifetime achievement. In 1986 she was the recipient of the American Film Institute's Lifetime Achievement Award. Actor Walter Matthau observed, "She's played five gun molls, two burlesque queens, half a dozen adulteresses, and twice as many murderers. When she was good, she was very, very good. And when she was bad, she was terrific." A remarkably versatile actor, her technique was "so deceptively simple and elusive that she's the least mannered and pretentious of the major stars of her period" (Stephen Harvey, *Film Comment*, 1981). A "golden age" legend, she starred in many of Hollywood's top films in several genres, displaying notable stamina over a lengthy film and television career. She died in St. John's Hospital in Santa Monica, California.

• Research material is on file at the Academy of Motion Picture Arts and Sciences and the American Film Institute, both in Los Angeles. Many of Stanwyck's stellar performances are available on video. The definitive biography is Axel Madsen, *Stanwyck* (1994), which includes an excellent bibliography. Also useful is Homer Dickens, *The Films of Barbara Stanwyck* (1984), which contains a foreword by Frank Capra. Ella Smith's *Starring Miss Barbara Stanwyck* (1974) presents a picture-by-picture breakdown with comments from her peers, biographical information, and numerous photos. Other biographies include Jerry Vermilye, *Barbara Stanwyck* (1975); Al DiOrio, *Barbara Stanwyck: A Biography* (1983); and Jane Ellen Wayne, *Stanwyck* (1985). Bette Davis's autobiography (with Sanford Dody), *The Lonely Life* (1962), and such biographies as Lawrence J. Quirk's *Fasten Your Seat Belts: The Passionate Life of Bette Davis* (1990) and Whitney Stine's *Mother Goddam* (1974) have information of interest. Ava Gardner's autobiography, *Ava, My Story* (1990), has little on Stanwyck but much on Robert Taylor; also see Jane Ellen Wayne's *Robert Taylor* (1977) and her *Ava's Men* (1990). Frank Capra's autobiography, *The Name Above the Title* (1971), and Christina Crawford's *Mommie Dearest* (1978), a troubled memoir by the daughter of Joan Crawford, have significant information on Capra's and Crawford's careers and their personal relationships with Stanwyck. Anthologies, such as David Shipment, *Cinema, the First Hundred Years* (1993); Richard B. Jewell (with Vernon Harbin), *The RKO Story* (1982); John Douglas Eamse, *The MGM Story: The Complete History of Fifty Roaring Years* (1975); Richard Lawton, *A World of Movies: 70 Years of Film History* (1974); and especially *Hollywood, Sixty Great Years 1930–1990* (1992), featuring various contributors, have extensive photos and information. An obituary is in the *Los Angeles Times*, 21 Jan. 1990.

ELLIS NASSOUR
BETH A. SNOWBERGER

STAPLES, Waller Redd (24 Feb. 1826–20 Aug. 1897), Confederate congressman and post–Civil War jurist, was born at Stuart, Virginia, the son of Abram Staples, a member of the state legislature and clerk of court in Patrick County, and Mary Penn. He attended the University of North Carolina from 1842 to 1844 and the College of William and Mary for the next two years, graduating with honors in 1846. After law studies with Judge Norbonne Taliaferro in Franklin County, Virginia, he was admitted to the bar and began practice in 1848 as a junior associate of William Ballard Preston in Montgomery County. Preston's subsequent appointment as secretary of the navy by President Zachary Taylor not only enhanced young Staples's prestige but also compelled him to shoulder a large part of the firm's caseload.

Honing his courtroom skills in Virginia's Blue Ridge and Shenandoah Valley counties, Staples became increasingly prominent in Whig political circles as well. He represented Montgomery County in the lower house of the general assembly during the 1853–1854 legislative session and emerged as a champion of state aid for transportation and manufacturing interests. After the collapse of the Whig organization, he gained widespread notice by campaigning as a presidential elector for the Know Nothing (American) party in 1856 and the Constitutional Union party in 1860.

During the political crisis following Republican Abraham Lincoln's election to the presidency, Staples (who owned a substantial number of slaves) initially hoped that southern rights could be preserved within the Union; nevertheless, accepting political realities, he acquiesced in Virginia's April 1861 decision to secede. Shortly thereafter he was designated by the state secession convention to serve as one of Virginia's delegates to the provisional Confederate Congress (a position he held until February 1862). Meanwhile, he won the endorsement of home-district voters for a seat in the Confederate House of Representatives and, securing reelection in 1863, continued to serve in that body for the duration of the Civil War. Antagonism toward the South's arbitrary conscription laws led him to join the congressional opponents of President Jefferson Davis's administration in 1864.

With the collapse of the Confederacy, Staples resumed his law practice in Montgomery County. Hostile to Radical Reconstruction, he supported Virginia's white-supremacist Conservative party during the political struggles of the immediate post–Civil War years and was elected to a twelve-year term on the state Supreme Court of Appeals by the Conservative-dominated general assembly in 1870. Despite his anti-Republican biases and unapologetically nostalgic attitudes toward the Old South and slavery, Staples (together with his fellow justices) displayed a surprisingly equitable approach to the Commonwealth's recently freed black citizens in cases dealing with their inheritance, contractual, and procedural rights. He also established a reputation as a hard-working jurist whose opinions were characterized by commonsense reasoning and verbal clarity.

The case of *Antoni v. Wright* led to the most controversial episode in Staples's judicial tenure. This 1872 litigation arose from legislative efforts to deal with Virginia's public debt, a burdensome legacy from antebellum expenditures on railroads and other internal improvements. In the Funding Act of 1871 the general assembly had authorized Virginia's creditors to exchange prewar bonds for $30 million in new securities with interest coupons receivable for state taxes. Belatedly recognizing that these coupons might seriously reduce cash revenues for schools and other governmental services, the legislature had repealed the tax-receivable coupon feature in 1872. Predictably, the bondholders insisted that their contractual rights were being infringed. Contending that Virginia's financial integrity was at stake, a three-member majority of the state's supreme court justices upheld the claims of the creditor interests. Staples dissented. Echoing Jeffersonian themes, he argued that revenues pledged to public schools by the state constitution had been compromised by the Funding Act, that the provisions of the 1871 debt law were not perpetually binding on subsequent sessions of the legislature, and that the state possessed the sovereign power to manage its finances in accord with the popular will.

Staples had been outvoted, but his opinion gave encouragement to the ever-swelling number of Virginians who called for repeal of the Funding Act. Led by erstwhile railroad magnate William Mahone, this so-called "Readjuster movement" rallied support from public school advocates, political independents, dissident Conservatives, and black Republicans. Defeating the "Funder" (or debt-paying) Conservatives in the 1881 state elections, the Readjusters enacted their anticreditor information program into law the following year. Ironically, Staples himself soon became a victim of the political upheaval that he had helped to inspire.

Although he agreed with many Readjuster objectives, he opposed Mahone's increasingly close ties with Republicans at the state and national levels. Consequently, the Readjuster-controlled general assembly refused to reelect him to another term on the Supreme Court of Appeals in 1882.

Despite this setback, Staples's political eclipse proved to be short-lived. As the debt issue faded, the line between Funders and Readjusters rapidly blurred as well. Mahone and a significant number of his adherents became Republicans, while the great mass of one-time Conservatives rallied to the Democratic banner, enabling that party to emerge victorious in most Virginia elections after 1882. Staples, an ardent Democrat, successfully campaigned as a presidential elector for the party in 1884. That same year the general assembly appointed him to a three-member commission that prepared a revised version of the *Code of Virginia* (1887). Staples also received a gubernatorial appointment in 1886 to the rectorship of the board of visitors of the Virginia Agricultural and Mechanical College in Blacksburg. Holding that position until 1888, he conducted a purge of Readjuster-Republican administrators and faculty at the school.

Meanwhile, Staples reestablished himself in his old profession. A two-year stint as counsel for the Richmond and Danville Railroad during the mid-1880s was followed by an extended and lucrative partnership with Beverly B. Munford, another prominent lawyer, in Virginia's capital city. Now a respected elder statesman in the legal fraternity, Staples served as president of the Virginia State Bar Association in 1893–1894.

Never married, Staples lavished affection on a niece and several nephews and was a favorite among younger attorneys in Richmond for his skills as a raconteur. After several years of declining health, he died at his country home in Christiansburg, Montgomery County. Hailed throughout Virginia as one of the foremost legal minds of his generation, he had also played a significant role in the political life of the state.

• Letters written by Staples to various correspondents are extant in the Joseph Bryan Papers, the Guerrant papers, the Harvie papers, the Preston Family Papers, and the Tayloe Family Papers, all at the Virginia Historical Society in Richmond. See also the William Mahone Papers at the William R. Perkins Library, Duke University. Staples's numerous opinions as a judge are recorded in the *Virginia Reports*, vols. 61–76 (1870–1882). The retired justice provided extensive commentary on the Old Dominion's antebellum county court system in his presidential address to the state bar association in *Report of the Sixth Annual Meeting of the Virginia State Bar Association* (1894), pp. 127–56. For examples of contemporary assessments of Staples's personality and accomplishments, see Beverly B. Munford, *Random Recollections* (1905), and Rosewell Page, "Waller R. Staples," *Report of the Tenth Annual Meeting of the Virginia State Bar Association* (1898), pp. 113–19. Additional commentary on issues that confronted Staples during his judicial tenure may be found in William C. Pendleton, *Political History of Appalachian Virginia, 1776–1927* (1927); Samuel N. Pincus, *The Virginia Supreme Court, Blacks, and the Law, 1870–1902* (1990); and James Tice

Moore, *Two Paths to the New South: The Virginia Debt Controversy, 1870–1883* (1974). An obituary is in the *Richmond Dispatch*, 21 Aug. 1897.

JAMES TICE MOORE

STARBUCK, Edwin Diller (20 Feb. 1866–18 Nov. 1947), psychologist, was born Edwin Eli Starbuck in Guilford Township, Hendricks County, Indiana, the son of Samuel Starbuck and Luzena Jessup, farmers. He described his parents as devout Quakers who taught more by example than by instruction. In his intellectually formative years he developed an increasingly skeptical view of traditional Christian beliefs and dogma. This skepticism was accompanied by a keen interest in evolutionary theory, which led him to study philosophy at Indiana University where President David Starr Jordan was a known advocate of evolutionary theory. After his graduation in 1890, he recouped his finances by teaching for three years and then entered Harvard in 1893 because it offered the best graduate opportunity for the concurrent study of philosophy, religion, and psychology.

However, even at Harvard, "psychology of religion" did not yet exist as a course of study, and most of his research took place outside the bounds of his formal instruction. In addition, Starbuck developed question circulars independently of surveys later developed and refined at Clark University under the guidance of G. Stanley Hall. Starbuck had sent copies of his original questionnaires to Hall in 1894 and the spring of 1895 before enrolling for doctoral research at Clark in the fall of 1895 (the same year he received his M.A. from Harvard). In 1896 he married Anna Maria Diller, with whom he had eight children. He later honored her by changing his middle name to her maiden name.

At Harvard, Starbuck's independent work on question circulars regarding the topic of conversion caught the attention of William James. James supported Starbuck in the development and distribution of these questionnaires. Further, Starbuck's original survey responses were loaned to James in preparation for his 1901–1902 Gifford Lectures at the University of Edinburgh, and they were cited extensively in James's classic *The Varieties of Religious Experience*, the 1902 published version of the lectures. Starbuck's own presentation of these questionnaire responses was published as two articles in 1897, and it was later developed into a book, *Psychology of Religion* (1899). Many of Starbuck's original findings on and conceptualization of religious conversion have stood the test of subsequent empirical research and theoretical analyses. These psychological findings include the association between conversion and adolescence and the comparison between sudden, or involuntary, and gradual, or voluntary, conversion. Accordingly, although Starbuck's work is less well known than James's *Varieties*, his 1899 book is considered a classic within the field of psychology of religion.

While Starbuck was drawn to Hall because of his pioneering work on adolescence and to Clark University because of its openness to doctoral work in new areas of the young science of psychology, his personal and professional relationship with Hall became quite strained when Hall failed to acknowledge the primacy and independence of Starbuck's original questionnaire work on religious experience. Starbuck repeatedly tried to set the historical record straight, noting that his questionnaire work was initiated before his enrollment at Clark and before other similar work was begun by other Hall students at Clark, most notably James H. Leuba who published an article on conversion in 1896, one year before Starbuck's first published articles.

With the completion of Starbuck's doctoral studies at Clark University in 1897 came his first postdoctoral academic appointment as assistant professor of education at Leland Stanford Junior University, where he developed innovative college courses on psychology of religion, educational psychology, tests and measures, and character education. Stanford granted Starbuck a sabbatical leave in 1903, and he traveled to the University of Zurich to study with Ernst Meumann and conduct laboratory research on the relationship between physiological processes and changes in consciousness. Meumann was a student of Wilhelm Wundt and was a leader in the new field of educational psychology. This sabbatical research marked Starbuck's last major efforts in basic research. While his professional career was launched with the discovery of the empirical facts of individual religious experience through questionnaire research, the remainder of his professional career was dedicated to the application of the facts of the new science of psychology to religious education and to applied research on character education.

Starbuck accepted a short-lived position at Earlham College, directing a new school of education from 1904 to 1906, but when support for the program never materialized, he took a position in the combined division of philosophy and psychology at the University of Iowa in 1906. He began to write more about the implications of psychology of religion for religious education and was a frequent contributor to the meetings and publications of the Religious Education Association, organized in 1903. Beginning in 1912 Starbuck worked for two years as a consulting psychologist with the American Unitarian Association on the preparation of a new religious education curriculum. His research was based on a "child-centered" approach, emphasizing the indirect support of a child's moral development rather than the direct dissemination of doctrine and dogma via traditional religious instruction.

Starting in 1914 Starbuck directed most of his writing toward the topic of character education and later headed a nine-member committee that won a national contest in 1921. The contest, sponsored by the Character Education Institution in Washington, D.C., was for the best plan for character education in the public schools. Starbuck chaired the committee and was the primary author of the "Iowa Plan," which won. The contest prize of $20,000 funded in part the formation of the Research Station in Character Education and Religious Education in 1923 at the University of Iowa.

The name was later changed to the Institute for Character Research and received some support from state funds. Under Starbuck's direction, the institute produced publications such as *A Guide to Literature for Character Training* (1928) and *A Guide to Books for Character* (1930), which rated the potential of various pieces of children's literature to promote moral development. The success of his work on character education led to his recruitment by the University of Southern California to head another Institute of Character Research from 1930 until his retirement in 1943.

Starbuck is noted as a pioneer in the use of question circulars in the study of individual religious experiences in the early American psychology of religion. His later applied work in religious and character education, while ambitious in design and scope, did not directly produce further work on moral development or values education after his death. For example, the institutes at Iowa and USC did not survive past his respective tenures at each university. In sum, he helped to bring religion as a topic for empirical research to the emerging new science of psychology and to bring the findings of the new science of psychology to the religious and character education literature.

• Relevant correspondence on the conflict between Starbuck and G. Stanley Hall on questionnaires can be found in the archives of Clark University and of the University of Iowa. Bibliographies of Starbuck's published work can be found in Howard J. Booth, *Edwin Diller Starbuck: Pioneer in the Psychology of Religion* (1981), and in *Look to This Day: Selected Writings by Edwin Diller Starbuck* (1945), assembled and edited by the staff of the now defunct Institute of Character Research at the University of Southern California. Starbuck's autobiographical essay "Religion's Use of Me" was originally published in *Religion in Transition*, ed. Vergilius Ferm (1937), and is reprinted in *Look to This Day*. Appraisals of the historical significance of Starbuck's work in early American psychology begin with contemporary analyses such as James Bisset Pratt's review "The Psychology of Religion," *Harvard Theological Review* 1, no. 4 (Oct. 1908): 435–54, and extend to present-day secondary surveys of the field.

J. DAVID ARNOLD

STARBUCK, Mary Coffyn (20 Feb. 1646–13 Nov. 1717), Quaker minister, was born in Haverhill, Massachusetts, the daughter of Tristram Coffyn and Dionis Stevens, who had emigrated from Brixton in Devonshire in 1642. Generations of genealogical errors have made it virtually impossible to determine the Coffyns' social status in England, and Tristram Coffyn's religious views are uncertain. In Massachusetts he moved around a lot, living in Newbury and Salisbury as well as Haverhill, keeping an ordinary and running a ferry before, in 1659, heading the group that purchased Nantucket Island, where the family moved in 1660 or 1661. Tristram Coffyn served as a magistrate and was the island's most influential citizen until his death in 1681.

In 1662 Mary Coffyn married Nathaniel Starbuck, the son of Edward Starbuck; both father and son had been among Tristram Coffyn's associates in purchasing the island. Nathaniel Starbuck came to be one of the island's wealthiest citizens, a large landowner and active trader. The couple had ten children, eight of whom lived to marry. Starbuck's maternal status, and the fact that she became literate, are all that is known of her life before 1690. Thereafter, almost everything that is known comes from accounts left by three Quaker ministers who visited Nantucket between 1698 and 1704, Thomas Chalkley, Thomas Story, and John Richardson. They recorded that previously she had been part of a radical spiritist or "Electarian" sect, perhaps the group led by Peter Folger that bore certain similarities to the Calvinist Baptists. Both groups embraced adult baptism and opposed a professional clergy. She also had played an important role in keeping an established Congregationalist minister off the island. Richardson wrote of her in 1701 that "the Islanders esteemed [her] as a Judge among them." He thought Nathaniel Starbuck a capable man, but Mary Starbuck "so far exceeded him in soundness of Judgment, clearness of understanding, and an elegant way of expressing herself, and that not in an affected Strain, but very natural to her." Thomas Story agreed; in 1704 he described her as "a wise discreet woman, well read in the Scriptures . . . in great Reputation throughout the Island for her Knowledge in Matters of Religion, and an oracle among them on that Account, insomuch that they would not do anyThing without her Advice and Consent therein."

Given Starbuck's standing on the island, it was natural for the visiting Quakers to consider her a prize convert, and they apparently devoted considerable attention toward that end. She was resistant at first, but after hearing Richardson preach she began to weep and then "spoke tremblingly [that] all that ever we have been building and all that ever we have done is all pulled down this day." Story completed her conversion in 1704, and afterward the Starbuck home became the meeting place for the new Quaker group. Starbuck was its first recognized minister, and in 1708 she became the first clerk, or presiding officer, of the women's meeting. Under the leadership of Starbuck and her son Nathaniel, the number of Quakers on Nantucket grew until they became the dominant sect on the island.

"The Great Woman," as Richardson called Mary Starbuck, died on Nantucket and was buried next to the Quaker meetinghouse.

• Only one letter written by Mary Starbuck is known to have survived. Nathaniel and Mary Starbuck's account book is in the Peter Folger Museum and Library on Nantucket, as are the records of Nantucket Monthly Meeting of Friends. The only biography available is Roland L. Warren, *Mary Coffin Starbuck and the Early History of Nantucket* (1987). For information on the Starbuck and Coffin families, see Lydia S. Hinchman, comp., *Early Settlers of Nantucket* (1896), and Alexander Starbuck, *The History of Nantucket* (1924); Starbuck includes accounts by the Quaker ministers who visited the island. For an account of the tradition that Mary Starbuck began Nantucket's whaling activities, see Henry B. Worth, "The First Whaling Merchant of Nantucket," in *Nantucket*

Historical Association *Proceedings* (1915), pp. 26–34. The best general account of Nantucket's early history and Mary Starbuck's role in it is Edward Byers, "*The Nation of Nantucket*" (1987). Sydney V. James's biographical sketch in *Notable American Women*, vol. 3, (1971), pp. 347–49, is definitive.

THOMAS D. HAMM

STARK, Harold Raynsford (12 Nov. 1888–20 Aug. 1972), chief of naval operations, was born in Wilkes-Barre, Pennsylvania, the son of Benjamin Stark, a colonel and commander of the Ninth Pennsylvania Regiment, and Mary Frances Warner. Stark attended local schools and graduated with honors. He then entered the U.S. Naval Academy in Annapolis, Maryland, completing the academic portion in 1903. He made the required two-year cruise and was commissioned an ensign in February 1905. In 1907 he married Katherine Adele Rhodes; they had two children.

Stark's first assignment as a naval officer was aboard the USS *Minnesota*, which participated in the sailing of the Great White Fleet (1907–1909). Leaving the *Minnesota* in 1909, Stark successively commanded the torpedo boats *Porter* and *Stringham* and the destroyers *Lamson* and *Patterson*. He became the engineering officer aboard the USS *Brooklyn*, an armored cruiser based at the Boston Navy Yard. Transferring to the Asiatic Fleet in June 1917, he commanded the tender *Monterey* until November of that year.

When the United States entered World War I, Stark requested that his flotilla be assigned to the European theater to perform antisubmarine and escort duties. He took his flotilla from Manila to Gibraltar and put it to immediate use in the Mediterranean, a move that earned him his first Distinguished Service Medal. He spent the rest of the war on the staff of Admiral William S. Sims, who commanded U.S. naval forces in Europe, and he acquired valuable experience in arranging convoys and antisubmarine operations and, perhaps of greatest value to him later, in coordinating joint operations with the British admiralty.

At the conclusion of the war Stark returned to sea as executive officer of the USS *North Dakota*. After a period at the U.S. Naval Training Station in Norfolk, Virginia, he took the senior course at the Naval War College in Newport, Rhode Island, graduating in May 1923. Returning to sea that same year, he served as the executive officer of the USS *West Virginia* until 9 December 1923, when he became commanding officer of the USS *Nitro*. Returning to shore, he served as naval inspector of ordnance from 1925 to 1928 at the Naval Proving Grounds, Dahlgren, Virginia, and at the Naval Powder Factory, Indian Head, Maryland.

From October 1928 to October 1930 Stark, now a captain, served as chief of staff to the commander of the Destroyer Squadrons Battle Fleet. In November 1930 he was assigned as an aide to the secretary of the navy in Washington, D.C., serving under Charles Francis Adams (1930–1933) and Claude A. Swanson (1933). In December 1933 Stark assumed command of the USS *West Virginia*. Promoted to rear admiral, he

became chief of the Bureau of Ordnance, where he served from November 1934 until August 1937. In September 1937 he was given command of Cruiser Division Three, Battle Force, and in May 1938 he became commander, Cruisers, Battle Force. On 1 August 1939 President Franklin D. Roosevelt appointed Stark chief of naval operations (CNO), to succeed Admiral William Leahy, and promoted him to admiral.

Shortly after Stark's appointment as chief of naval operations, war broke out in Europe. The CNO, foreseeing the eventual involvement of the United States, began a modest but steady improvement in the navy's ability to fight a two-front war against either Germany or Japan or both of them. In the face of strong isolationist public opinion, Stark's ability to convince an otherwise skeptical Congress of the need for rearmament contributed to the emergence of a strong navy, which included all of the necessary supporting vessels and bases that would later be necessary to fight a two-ocean war. By the time the United States was drawn into the war in December 1941, the navy's state of readiness had been significantly enhanced.

Stark was committed to keeping Britain in the war and to defeating Germany first. He laid out those principles in his "Plan Dog Memorandum" to Secretary of the Navy Frank Knox and President Roosevelt in November 1940. Stark maintained that "if Britain wins decisively against Germany we could win everywhere; but . . . if she loses . . . we might, possibly, not win *anywhere*." To head off that possibility, Stark recommended that the United States "develop a strong offensive in the Atlantic as an ally of Britain and maintain a defensive in the Pacific." Roosevelt endorsed the general outlines of Stark's memorandum, and in January 1941 the U.S., Great Britain, and Canada began high-level military talks. The "Rainbow 5" war plan of spring 1941 embodied Stark's Europe-first strategy.

Stark's role in shaping that strategy was the high point of his tenure as CNO. The low point was the Japanese surprise attack on the U.S. Pacific Fleet at Pearl Harbor on 7 December 1941. Critics charged that Stark failed to keep the fleet's commander, Admiral Husband E. Kimmel, fully abreast of deteriorating U.S.-Japanese relations and thus bore partial responsibility for the lack of preparedness at Pearl Harbor. Stark was stripped of his command of the navy's operational forces a few weeks after the attack. But he retained his title as chief of naval operations until March 1942, when he was appointed commander of U.S. naval forces in Europe.

The new position, based in London, was largely an administrative one. Stark acted as liaison to the British Admiralty and to the French government-in-exile of Charles de Gaulle. In September 1943 he received the additional title of commander of the Twelfth Fleet, and oversaw logistical preparations for the cross-channel invasion of Europe the following year. In October 1944 General Dwight D. Eisenhower presented Stark with the army's Distinguished Service Medal for his "foresight and exceptional administrative ability, in planning and meeting the necessary personnel and material requirements" of the D day invasion. Stark officially stepped down from his posts in London in August 1945.

Meanwhile, controversy over the lack of U.S. preparedness at Pearl Harbor had reached a boiling point. In July 1944 the navy convened a court of inquiry to investigate events preceding the Japanese attack. In its official report, submitted to the secretary of the navy in October 1944, the court concluded that Stark had made a military error when he failed to transmit important information about the status of diplomatic relations to Admiral Kimmel. The report also faulted Kimmel, and Stark's successor as chief of naval operations, Admiral Ernest J. King, recommended that neither officer receive a position requiring the exercise of "superior judgment." The findings were made public in August 1945, shortly after Stark's return to Washington. Congress conducted its own investigation during late 1945 and early 1946. Some Republicans charged that Stark had conspired with President Roosevelt to leave the Pacific Fleet unguarded in order to invite a Japanese attack and draw the U.S. into the war. The committee's majority rejected those charges and, after reviewing evidence not available to the navy court of inquiry, concluded that Stark had kept Kimmel "fully informed . . . and amply warned of the imminence of war." In 1948 Admiral King retracted his harsh judgment of Stark's role and recommended him for another Distinguished Service Medal for his service in Europe.

Stark retired from active duty in April 1946. He resided in Washington and worked with the Navy Relief Society. Stark's family had a summer home in the mountains near Wilkes-Barre, Pennsylvania, and from 1959 to 1964 he served as chairman of the board of trustees of Wilkes College. He died in Washington. Although the final phase of Stark's career was overshadowed by the controversy over Pearl Harbor, he played an important role in preparing the United States for World War II—both by overseeing the build-up of naval forces and by helping determine the Europe-first strategy that guided U.S. conduct during the war.

• Stark's official and personal papers are at the Naval Historical Center, Washington Navy Yard, Washington, D.C. A thorough—and very sympathetic—account of Stark's career during World War II is B. Mitchell Simpson III, *Admiral Harold R. Stark: Architect of Victory, 1939–1945* (1989). Also useful are Clark G. Reynolds, *Famous American Admirals* (1978); Ray S. Cline, *The Washington Command Post: The Operations Division* (1951); and Samuel Eliot Morison, *History of U.S. Naval Operations in World War II* (15 vols., 1947–1962). On the Pearl Harbor controversy, see Joint Committee of the U.S. Congress, *Hearings on the Investigation of the Pearl Harbor Attack*, 79th Congress, 1st sess. 39 vols., 1946, and Gordon W. Prange, *At Dawn We Slept: The Untold Story of Pearl Harbor* (1981). An obituary is in the *New York Times*, 31 Aug. 1972.

THE EDITORS

STARK, John (28 Aug. 1728–8 May 1822), revolutionary war general, was born in Londonderry, New Hampshire, the son of Archibald Stark and Eleanor Nichols. His family had come from Ireland only eight years before. Stark grew up on the New England frontier, relishing the outdoor life and even serving as a guide for frontier expeditions.

Stark was naturally suited for service with Rogers' Rangers during the French and Indian War (1754–1763). In the service of the British, Rogers' Rangers led raids against the Indian allies of the French by adopting the Indian methods of woodcraft, ambush, and secret march. Stark displayed gallantry in action and rose to the rank of captain. He was present at the battle of Lake George in September 1755 and took part in the 1757 defense of Fort William Henry and in the unsuccessful attack on Fort Ticonderoga in July 1758. In the spring of 1759 he enlisted a new company and saw service at Crown Point and again at Ticonderoga. After the war Stark took up farming and milling and was one of the first settlers in Starkstown, later called Dunbarton. On 20 August 1758 he married Elizabeth Page; they would have five sons and six daughters.

A member of New Hampshire's Committee of Safety in 1774, Stark went to Cambridge, Massachusetts, immediately upon receiving word of the fighting at Concord and at Lexington in April 1775. He was appointed colonel of a newly formed New Hampshire regiment. Two months later he played an important role in the battle of Bunker Hill, deploying his men (by then consisting of two N.H. regiments) between Bunker Hill and Breed's Hill, in order to defend the patriots' left flank. His military experience served his side well, as he spotted several weak points in the American deployment and moved to fill them. One of Stark's best military qualities was the ability to size up a situation at a glance and to move quickly in order to maximize his position. His quote "Boys, aim at their waistbands" (Boatner, p. 1053) was excellent advice; it prevented their firing too early or too high, as might be expected from his inexperienced men. The American performance at Bunker Hill showed the British regular army that it should not take the developing Continental army lightly.

After the British evacuated Boston in March 1776, Stark, now a colonel in the Continental army, turned his attention to the defense of New York City. May 1776 saw him in Canada, retreating southward along with other American forces. By the end of the year, though, Stark and his men were back on the offensive. He led George Washington's advance in the battle of Trenton in December 1776 and took part in the battle of Princeton eight days later. Despite Stark's performance in battle, Congress passed over him for promotion. He resigned his commission in March 1777, returning home after telling colleagues that an officer who would not maintain his rank was unworthy to serve his country.

Stark's time as a civilian was short-lived. When British general John Burgoyne invaded New York, Vermont settlers realized that the fall of Fort Ticonderoga in early July 1777 had left them exposed. The government of New Hampshire received a plea for help from Vermont authorities; on 18 July the General Court (state legislature) of New Hampshire authorized the raising and equipping of a force. Selected to lead it and given the New Hampshire rank of brigadier general, Stark accepted on the condition that his command remain independent of congressional orders. Within twenty days Stark had formed a brigade of men, had marched them to Manchester, Vermont, and had them equipped for battle. Benjamin Lincoln, the Continental army general and one of the officers who had been promoted over Stark, had been sent to command the area. Stark refused to take orders from Lincoln, saying that his orders were from the people of New Hampshire. Stark outlined his plans, and Lincoln wisely acquiesced. Stark moved his brigade to Bennington on 8 August to protect the American supply depot there. Eight days later Burgoyne's troops, under British lieutenant colonel Friedrich Baum, arrived outside the town, intent on capturing the military supplies. An attack led by Stark left Baum dead and most of his 500-man force taken prisoner. Stark is supposed to have led his men with the cry, "There, my boys, are your enemies, the red-coats and Tories; you must beat them or my wife sleeps a widow tonight" (Caleb Stark, p. 60). Unfortunately for the British, the relief force of German soldiers under Colonel Heinrich Christoph von Breymann did not arrive until Stark's men had regrouped following their initial victory over Baum. Tired from their 25-mile march through hot, muggy weather, the Germans were driven back by the Americans.

The battle of Bennington was described by Washington as "the great stroke struck by General Stark near Bennington" (U.S. GPO, p. 38). Depriving Burgoyne of forces and equipment while boosting American morale, it helped force Burgoyne's surrender at Saratoga two months later. Stark was involved here as well, when his New Hampshire militia crossed the Hudson to take up a position in the British rear. It was then that Burgoyne requested surrender terms. Four days later, the British formally surrendered. In between the battles of Bennington and Saratoga, Congress had censured Stark for not following Lincoln's original orders, then thanked him shortly afterward for his performance at Bennington, and finally appointed him a brigadier general of the Continental army on 4 October 1777.

In the spring of 1778 Stark directed the northern department from its Albany, New York, headquarters. The following year he was stationed in Rhode Island but did not engage in combat. He was present at the battle of Springfield, New Jersey, in June 1780, conducted a body of volunteers to West Point, returned to New Jersey, then served (at West Point) on the board of general officers appointed to try Major John André, the British officer and spy, for his role in the treason of Benedict Arnold. Stark took charge of the northern department again in the spring of 1781, this time with its headquarters in Saratoga.

Stark received the brevet rank of major general on 30 September 1783 and retired soon thereafter. Returning to his home in Derryfield (now Manchester), New Hampshire, he resisted all pleas to enter public service and instead lived out his life tending to his farm. He died in Manchester. In 1894 New Hampshire selected Stark and Daniel Webster as its two representatives in National Statuary Hall in the U.S. Capitol, Washington, D.C. U.S. senator Jacob Gallinger declared that "the name of John Stark stands prominent, if not preeminent, among the greatest generals who fought under Washington."

Stark had a gift for being in the right place at the right time and then applying his military experience and leadership qualities to achieve success on the battlefield. His actions at Bunker Hill and Bennington turned the tide of the revolutionary war, as did his presence at Saratoga when he blocked Burgoyne's retreat.

• Stark's letters and papers are in the New Hampshire Historical Society and the New Hampshire State Archives. His grandson Caleb Stark published *Memoir and Official Correspondence of Gen. John Stark* (1860). His family history and his influence in his hometown are discussed in George Stark, *Origin of the Stark Family of New Hampshire and a List of Living Descendants of General John Stark* (1887); Roland Rowell, *Gen. John Stark's Home Farm* (1904); and C. E. Potter, *The History of Manchester* (1856). A twentieth-century biography is Howard P. Moore, *A Life of General John Stark of New Hampshire* (1949). For military matters see Herbert D. Foster, *Stark's Independent Command at Bennington* (1918). As to Stark's statue in National Statuary Hall, see U.S. Government Printing Office, *Proceedings in Congress upon the Acceptance of the Statutes of John Stark and Daniel Webster* (1895). For a thorough understanding of the larger contents of Stark's actions, see Mark Mayo Boatner III, *Encyclopedia of the American Revolution* (1966).

PHILIP H. VILES, JR.

STARK, John (11 Apr. 1841–20 Nov. 1927), music publisher, and his daughter, **Eleanor Stark** (May 1874–7 Apr. 1929), musician, were important promoters of ragtime. John Stark was born in Shelby County, Kentucky, and raised on a farm in Gosport, Indiana. He enlisted in the Indiana Heavy Artillery Volunteers during the Civil War, serving as a bugler. After the war he settled with his English-born wife in Missouri, engaging briefly in farming and then in selling ice cream from a wagon. He and his wife had three children. He opened a piano and organ dealership in Chillicothe and by 1882 moved his store to Sedalia, Missouri. Sedalia was a thriving town, and Stark did well despite competition from other stores.

In 1893 Stark issued his first sheet music publications, children's pieces written by Sedalia composers. Through the next few years he continued issuing music occasionally, but publishing remained a minor part of his business until he published Scott Joplin's masterpiece, "The Maple Leaf Rag," in August or September 1899. This event changed Stark's life, changed the life of Joplin, and affected the course of ragtime history.

Stark had moved to St. Louis by the time the music was published, but he used the address of his Sedalia store, operated by his son William, as the place of publication. Because of the unprecedented success of "The Maple Leaf Rag," Stark thereafter devoted himself to publishing music. He became an outspoken advocate of ragtime and prided himself on the quality of the music he issued, much of it composed by African Americans. He referred to his company as "The House of Classic Rags" and proclaimed in flamboyant advertisements the superiority of his ragtime publications, which he asserted were equal to the best classical music. For example, of Scott Joplin's *Easy Winners* he wrote: "Joplin calls them rags, Chopin would have called them something else. Bach might have called them inventions. But had either of the latter written them he would have added thirty-two candle power to his halo."

In 1905 Stark moved his office to New York, keeping his printing plant in St. Louis. Though the special quality of his piano ragtime publications was recognized by aficionados, it was overlooked by the larger, less discriminating mass public, and he never became a major publisher. In 1910 he gave up trying to compete in New York and returned to St. Louis. His publishing output decreased in the late 1910s with the growing popularity of jazz, to which he was adamantly opposed. His last publication was in 1923, although he continued reprinting music, and "The Maple Leaf Rag" remained his major source of income until the end of his life. He died in St. Louis, and the publishing house closed in the mid-1930s.

Stark's publishing catalog of more than 120 pieces was distinguished by some of the best ragtime created during the music's heyday, 1897–1917. In terms of quality, his list is headed by twenty-three compositions by Joplin, twenty-nine by James Scott, and twelve by Joseph F. Lamb. Other significant composers in his catalog were Arthur Marshall, Artie Matthews, Robert Hampton, and J. Russel Robinson. Stark also published several pieces of his own, as well as some by his son William's wife, Carrie Bruggeman Stark (who also used the pseudonym "Cy Perkins"). His son Etilmon J. Stark, a professional violinist and teacher, did arrangements and orchestrations for the firm and was a competent ragtime composer. His most successful composition was "Brain-Storm Rag" (1907), published under the pseudonym "Bud Manchester."

The family's foremost musician was Eleanor Stark. She was born in Maysville, Missouri, and as a child displayed considerable musical talent. In 1895, at around the age of eighteen, she went to Berlin, Germany, and then to Paris, France, to study piano with Moritz Moszkowski, a major composer and piano virtuoso. She ended her studies in the late spring of 1898 when, in response to her parents' fears over her safety during the Spanish-American War, she returned home.

Back in Missouri, she embarked upon a career as a concert pianist, giving solo recitals, accompanying singers, and playing in chamber ensembles. She first performed in smaller towns in Missouri, but within a few months she was appearing as a soloist at the St. Louis Musical Union and with the Carl Busch Philharmonic Orchestra in Kansas City.

Early in 1899 she moved to St. Louis, where she opened a teaching studio. Though she remained active in St. Louis musical life for the next few years, it was as an adviser to her father that she ultimately had her greatest impact. Her father made it clear in a letter to composer Arthur Marshall in 1906 that he relied upon her judgment in his publishing decisions. Through her father, she was able to exercise a taste otherwise unknown in popular music. It was on her urging that he published Joplin's song-ballet "The Ragtime Dance" in piano-vocal score in 1902, a work that Stark had previously refused because of its length. The picture of her seated at a grand piano on the covers of Artie Matthews's five "Pastime Rag" publications (1913–1920), pieces that are more like classical idealizations of ragtime than authentic rags, again reflects her advocacy of music for its inherent quality rather than its immediate public appeal. It is uncertain whether we will ever know the full extent of her influence on the "Classic Ragtime" concept, but her touch is there.

In 1905 she married James Stanley, a concert baritone who was to become a major recording artist with Victor Records in the 1920s. Through the 1910s, the two appeared together in recitals, and she also provided piano and organ accompaniments for his mixed vocal quartet (The Stanley Quartet, recorded around 1916 by Pathé Frères), and other vocal ensembles. During World War I she and her husband, on the personal request of General John Joseph Pershing, went to France to entertain American troops. She died childless in New York City after a short illness.

• John Stark's life, importance, and relationship to major ragtime composers are highlighted in Rudi Blesh and Harriet Janis, *They All Played Ragtime* (1950; rev. ed., 1971), the first history of ragtime and biography of Scott Joplin. Trebor Jay Tichenor, "John Stillwell Stark, Piano Ragtime Publisher: Readings from *The Intermezzo* and His Personal Ledgers, 1905–1908," *Black Music Research Journal* 9, no. 2 (Fall 1989): 193–204, uses Stark's personal papers and his publishing house newsletter to discuss Stark's ideals and aims. Edward A. Berlin, *King of Ragtime: Scott Joplin and His Era* (1994), uncovers considerable additional information on the Stark family and discusses the significance of Eleanor Stark.

EDWARD A. BERLIN

STARR, Belle (5 Feb. 1848–3 Feb. 1889), outlaw, was born Myra Belle Shirley in Carthage, Missouri, the daughter of John Shirley, a wealthy innkeeper, and Eliza Hatfield. In 1863 her brother, a Confederate guerrilla, was killed by Federal troops. In 1864 she moved with her family to Scycene, Texas (near Dallas), to avoid the turmoil of the border war in Missouri. She married Jim Reed, a former Confederate guerrilla from Missouri, in 1868; the couple had a daughter in 1869 and a son in 1871. Reed engaged in various criminal enterprises, including robbery and horse theft. The family fled to Los Angeles after Belle Starr's remaining brother was killed in a Texas gunfight and her husband murdered a man in Missouri. She returned with her family to Texas after federal agents in California began closing in on her husband's counterfeiting operations. In April 1874 Jim Reed robbed a stagecoach, and Belle Starr was charged as an accessory to the crime (although charges were later dropped). Jim Reed was killed by a deputy sheriff near Paris, Texas, on 6 August 1874.

In 1876 Starr sold her farm in Scycene and lived with various relatives for a while. In 1878 she moved to Youngers' Bend, Indian Territory (now Oklahoma), and for a time lived with Bruce Younger, a relative of the Missouri outlaw Cole Younger. This liaison probably helped perpetuate the myth that she carried on a lengthy affair with Cole Younger and had a child (Pearl) by him. On 5 June 1880 she married Samuel Starr, a Cherokee Indian. Belle and Sam Starr were found guilty of horse theft in 1883. Because it was the first conviction for both, they were given a lenient one-year sentence by Isaac "Hanging Judge" Parker at Fort Smith, Arkansas, but they served only nine months. After their release they presumably continued to rustle horses and engage in armed robbery. Starr was indicted several times but was never tried for the crimes. She was arrested again in 1886 for robbery but was released for lack of evidence. Her cabin in Indian Territory was reputedly a refuge for Jesse James and other noted regional outlaws, and she became a local celebrity because she consorted with lawbreakers. In a lengthy interview with the *Dallas Morning News* (7 June 1886) Starr denied that she dressed in male attire and "led a party of three men who robbed." But she did show the reporter a pair of revolvers and commented, "Next to a fine horse I admire a fine pistol." She concluded the interview by stating, "You can just say that I am a friend to any brave and gallant outlaw."

In December 1886 Sam Starr was killed in a gunfight. To hold onto her homestead in Indian Territory, Starr invited an Indian named Bill "Jim" July to live with her in 1887. She was shot and killed in ambush near her home in Youngers' Bend. The identity of her murderer was never determined, although speculation included her husband and even her son, James Edwin (Edward), with whom she was rumored to have an incestuous relationship.

Belle Starr's notoriety stemmed from her loose affiliation with other more famous Missouri outlaws, namely, members of the James-Younger gang, and the fact that she was a female engaged in criminal enterprises otherwise monopolized by males. Her national career was launched by the *National Police Gazette* in 1889 as part of its efforts to expose and capitalize on the popularity of western outlaws. Beginning in the late 1890s Starr became a biological "model" for popular criminology books, such as Richard Dugdale's *The Jukes* (1910) and Henry Goddard's *The Kallikak Family: A Study in the Heredity of Feeblemindedness* (1912), in which crime and other "social defects" were mapped out as hereditary and traced through highly entertaining family histories. The Italian physician Cesar Lombroso, often hailed as the "father" of modern criminology, featured Belle Starr in his work, *The Female Offender* (1895). She has been alternatively cast as a relative carrying the crime-ridden genes of other Missouri outlaws and as the mother of a "dynasty of outlaws." Her son, Edward, was a bootlegger who died in a saloon fight in 1896. Her daughter, Pearl, achieved notoriety as a prostitute in Fort Smith. According to legend, her genes eventually "yielded" the noted Oklahoma bandit Arthur "Pretty Boy" Floyd. More recently, she has been revived in popular culture as a nineteenth-century feminist figure.

• Much of the work done on Belle Starr is of dubious accuracy. Probably the best work is Glenn Shirley, *Belle Starr and Her Times* (1982), which contains a 25-page chapter that discusses books, poems, and movies about her. Richard Fox, *Bella Starr, the Bandit Queen* (1889), is the earliest biography. Samuel Harman, *Hell on the Border, He Hanged Eighty-Eight Men* (1898), also contains an account of Belle Starr and has been reprinted in various abridged versions. Another important source is *The Story of Cole Younger, by Himself* (1903), which debunks the often-held myth that Belle Starr had an illegitimate child by the famous outlaw. Burton Rascoe, *Belle Starr, "Bandit Queen"* (1941); Anton Booker, *Wildcats in Petticoats* (1945); Paul Wellman, *A Dynasty of Western Outlaws* (1961); and Carl Breihan and Charles Rosamond, *The Bandit Belle* (1970), are among the better biographies. Movies include *Belle Starr* (1941), starring Randolph Scott and Gene Tierney; *Belle Starr's Daughter* (1948); *Son of Belle Starr* (1953); and *The Long Riders* (1980). In 1980 *Belle Starr*, a television movie, featured Elizabeth Montgomery in the title role.

PAUL G. KOOISTRA

STARR, Ellen Gates (19 Mar. 1859–10 Feb. 1940), reformer and cofounder of Hull-House, was born in Laona, Illinois, the daughter of Caleb Allen Starr, a farmer and businessman, and Susan Gates Childs. Starr's father, through his grange activity, and her aunt Eliza Allen Starr, through her art and conversion to Catholicism, influenced Starr's early social, political, and religious development. In 1877 Starr enrolled at the Rockford Female Seminary but left after one year for lack of money. In the fall of 1878 she became a teacher at a country school in Mount Morris, Illinois, then accepted a position at Miss Kirkland's School for Girls in Chicago in 1879.

While at Rockford, Starr met Jane Addams, with whom she would later cofound Hull-House, the famous Chicago settlement. Both women had been experiencing periods of restlessness and believed their lives lacked purpose and direction. On an 1888 trip to Europe, Addams told Starr of her idea to create a settlement in Chicago similar to Toynbee Hall, the first settlement in London. Addams recalled that Starr embraced the idea with "vivacity, sincerity, and confidence." Addams and Starr stated that their purpose in creating a settlement was to "provide a center for higher civic and social life, to initiate and maintain educational and philanthropic enterprises and to investigate and improve the condition in the industrial districts of

Chicago" (Hull-House Association Statement of Purpose, Swarthmore College Peace Collection). In September 1889 Hull-House opened its doors to Chicago's poor.

The first successful endeavors of Hull-House were Starr's reading parties and art exhibits, which evolved into formal education programs and the establishment of the Butler Art Gallery. Combining her artistic and educational interests, Starr formed the Chicago Public School Art Society in 1894 for the purpose of placing works of art in classrooms to improve the decor and to educate and inspire the children. Starr served as the society's first president until 1897 when she left Chicago to learn bookbinding from T. J. Cobden-Sanderson in London. Influenced by John Ruskin, William Morris, and the arts and crafts movement, Starr began to see the disconnected relationship between industrialism and craftsmanship. She believed that handicrafts, such as bookbinding, should be taught to laborers to give them a renewed sense of purpose and pride in craftsmanship as well as a greater understanding of the industrial process. In 1898 Starr returned to Chicago and opened the Hull-House bookbindery, which attracted only a few students, forcing Starr to realize that the problem of lost craftsmanship in an industrialized society could not be solved easily.

Starr's exposure to the working-class neighborhood surrounding Hull-House and to the social philosophies of Ruskin and Morris influenced her involvement in Chicago's labor struggles. A quiet, petite, frail woman who was not hesitant to stand firm against injustice, she participated in labor strikes from 1895 to 1915. She collected milk funds to feed strikers' children, housed union members, picketed (for which she was often arrested), and wrote articles to promote public support and sympathy for the strikers. She campaigned against low wages, long hours, and unsafe working conditions, especially for women. Defending the actions of strikers, she declared, "If one must starve, there are compensations in starving in a fight for freedom that are not to be found in starving for an employer" (*New Republic*, 1 Jan. 1916, p. 219). In 1904 Starr helped found Chicago's branch of the Women's Trade Union League and became an honorary member of the Amalgamated Clothing Workers of America (ACWA) after supporting their 1915 strike. In conferring this honor on Starr, Sidney Hillman, ACWA president, described her as "one of the best little soldiers in the fight."

Starr's labor activities led to her participation in Chicago's Socialist party from 1911 until 1928. In 1916 she ran on the Socialist ticket for alderman of the Nineteenth Ward. Realizing that as a woman and a Socialist she had little chance of winning, Starr used the opportunity to raise public awareness of society's ills. She explained that she was a Socialist because she was a Christian. Starr condemned society for its lack of Christian values, believing that it was impossible to carry out the teachings of Christ under the existing capitalist system. She believed that the Christian religion taught that "all men are to be regarded as brothers" and that "no one should wish to profit by the loss or disadvantage of others." But Starr lost the race.

While fighting against the injustices of urban society, Starr simultaneously searched for a religion that would satisfy her intellectually, spiritually, and aesthetically. She came from a Unitarian background, but when she first began her religious quest she turned to Addams for advice. Addams was of little comfort, telling Starr that they should no longer discuss religion because they did not hold the same beliefs. Their divergent religious views created a rift in their friendship, which would later be compounded by disagreements over the running of Hull-House and Starr's labor activism. Mathematics professor Charles Wager, Starr's confidant for forty years, filled the void that was left by Addams's absence. Wager supported her every endeavor, including her religious pursuits. Starr drifted from one church to another until her 1920 conversion to Catholicism, believing ultimately that she had been "a Catholic at heart" for a good while.

Starr's later years were ones of decreasing public involvement and increasing physical infirmities. In 1929 she underwent surgery for a spinal abscess, but the operation left her paralyzed. Because Hull-House residents were unable to care for her, Starr moved into the Convent of the Holy Child in Suffern, New York. Here she spent her final years reading, painting, and corresponding with friends and family until her death.

Ellen Starr was a woman of unique qualities and vision, who marked a path for others to follow. Her life exemplifies how many women in the late nineteenth and early twentieth centuries struggled to define their lives amid the social, economic, and political reform impulses of the Progressive Era.

• Starr's papers are in the Sophia Smith Collection, Smith College, and include extensive notes by her niece Josephine Starr. Additional information regarding Starr can also be found in the Jane Addams Papers, Peace Collection, Swarthmore College; the Charles Henry Adams Wager Papers, Special Collections, Oberlin College; and the American Federation of Labor Records (Samuel Gompers Era), the Anita Blaine McCormick Papers, and the Henry Demarest Lloyd Papers, all of which are at the State Historical Society of Wisconsin, Madison. The most noteworthy articles written by Starr include "Hull House Bookbindery," *Commons*, June 1900, pp. 21–22; "The Renaissance of Handicraft," *International Socialist Review*, Feb. 1902, pp. 570–74; "Efforts to Standardize Chicago Restaurants—The Henrici Strike," *Survey*, May 1914, pp. 214–15; " 'Cheap Clothes and Nasty,' " *New Republic*, 1 Jan. 1916, pp. 217–19; "The Chicago Clothing Strike," *New Review*, Mar. 1916, pp. 62–64; "A Bypath into the Great Roadway," *Catholic World*, May and June 1924, pp. 3–44; and "A Few Trials of a Happy Convert," *Abbey Chronicle*, Mar. 1929, pp. 33–34. See also Jane Addams, *Twenty Years at Hull House* (1910) and "Art Work Done by Hull House," *Forum*, July 1895, pp. 614–17; Hull House Residents, *Hull House Maps and Papers* (1895); Vida Scudder Dutton, *On Journey* (1937); Jacob S. Potofsky, "Happy Birthday to Ellen Gates Starr," *Advance*, Apr. 1939, unpaged; and Eleanor Grace Clark, "Ellen Gates Starr O.S.B., 1859–1940: Life of the Co-Founder of Hull House," *Commonweal*, Mar. 1940, pp. 444–47. Notable secondary sources are Allen F. Davis, *Spearheads for Reform: The Social Settle-

ments and the Progressive Movement (1967); Allen F. Davis and Mary Lynn McCree, *Eighty Years at Hull House* (1973); and Eileen Boris, *Art and Labor* (1986). Obituaries are in the *New York Times* and the *Chicago Tribune*, 11 Feb. 1940.

JENNIFER L. BOSCH

STARR, Henry George (2 Dec. 1873–22 Feb. 1921), bank robber, was born near Fort Gibson in the Cherokee Nation, Indian Territory, the son of George Starr and Mary Scott, farmers. Henry Starr was the great-nephew of the noted "bandit queen" Belle Starr and the grandson of a regionally prominent outlaw, Tom Starr. Three-eighths Cherokee, Henry attended school from ages eight to eleven and proved to be intelligent and creative. In 1886 his father died; soon after his mother's remarriage, Henry left home and by age fifteen had become a working cowboy. His criminal career began in the forbidden whiskey trade.

In 1891 Starr was arrested for horse theft and was briefly confined at Fort Smith, Arkansas. He consistently claimed innocence and subsequently insisted that his mistreatment at the hands of officials led directly to a life of crime. He participated in the robbery of a railway agent in 1892 and later that year killed deputy federal marshal Floyd Wilson while resisting arrest near Lenapah, Indian Territory.

On 5 June 1893 Starr held up a bank in Bentonville, Arkansas, and promptly fled the region with seventeen-year-old Mary Morrison. They were apprehended in Colorado Springs, Colorado, and returned to Fort Smith. Starr spent the next four and a half years confined under terrible conditions. During this period he was tried and convicted for Wilson's murder and was sentenced to death. The U.S. Supreme Court reversed the conviction and remanded the case for a new trial. This resulted in a second death sentence, which was subsequently appealed and set aside.

While jailed, Starr performed an act of heroism, disarming another prisoner, the murderous Cherokee Bill (Crawford Goldsby) during an escape attempt and riot. In October 1897 Starr pleaded guilty to manslaughter in the Wilson case in return for a sentence of fifteen years to be served at Columbus, Ohio. President Theodore Roosevelt (1858–1919) commuted the term in January 1903 after obtaining a personal promise of good behavior from the colorful inmate.

Starr worked briefly in his mother's restaurant before entering the real estate business in Tulsa. In 1904 he married Ollie Griffin, a schoolteacher. A son born shortly thereafter was named Theodore Roosevelt Starr, after Henry's benefactor. Statehood for Oklahoma in 1907 allowed Arkansas to demand Starr's extradition for the 1893 Bentonville bank robbery, a procedure not recognized under laws for the Indian Territory. Probably as a consequence, Starr resumed his criminal ways.

Divorced by his wife, the robber struck in several states until arrested at Bosque, Arizona Territory, in May 1909. Starr was extradited to Colorado, convicted of holding up the bank at Amity, and sentenced to a term of twenty-five years. He served only until paroled

in 1913. A model inmate, Starr did roadwork, became an inmate-guard, and wrote *Thrilling Events: Life of Henry Starr*, published in 1914. The writer skillfully presented himself as a mistreated, unfortunate American Indian who reluctantly turned to crime but reformed in prison.

Starr soon violated the conditions of his release by departing the state with "Laura Williams," the wife of a Colorado merchant. Within five months a gang led by Starr had robbed fourteen small banks throughout Oklahoma. This remarkable crime spree ended on 27 March 1915 when Starr attempted to rob two banks in Stroud, Oklahoma, on the same day. The effort ended with Starr shot, crippled, and captured. By now a notorious bandit, Starr pleaded guilty and received a second sentence of twenty-five years. In prison he worked as a teacher and librarian, again proving adept at convincing Oklahoma authorities that the "Last Bad Indian" had finally become an honest citizen. He received a parole in only four years.

The imaginative and versatile Henry Starr then entered the embryonic silent movie business. He became part owner of Tulsa's Pan American Picture Company, producing and playing himself in *A Debtor to the Law* (1919). The film was a success, earning Starr the opportunity to move to California for a promising career in Hollywood. He declined the offer, however, perhaps in fear that leaving Oklahoma would result in prosecutions for crimes in other states.

In 1920, Starr married Hulda Starr (no direct relation). His deteriorating finances led to preparation of the *Story of Crime Life of Henry Starr*, first published posthumously in the *Wichita Eagle*. Perhaps his efforts to capitalize on years devoted to violent crimes and various prison terms, though initially well received, began to tire a sympathetic public because the pattern of misconduct resumed. An apparently desperate Starr and three companions tried to rob the People's National Bank of Harrison, Arkansas, on 18 February 1921. A former president of the institution resisted, shooting and paralyzing Starr, who lingered for four days. Just before dying, he made a claim that was possibly true, "I've robbed more banks than any man in America."

• In addition to Starr's autobiographical efforts, leading sources include Glenn Shirley, *Henry Starr: Last of the Real Badmen* (1965), and Paul Wellman, *A Dynasty of Western Outlaws* (1961).

FRANK R. PRASSEL

STARRETT, Paul (25 Nov. 1866–5 July 1957), building contractor, was born in Lawrence, Kansas, the son of William A. Starrett, a Presbyterian minister, farmer, and lawyer, and Helen Ekin, a Quaker teacher, journalist, and editor. Starrett attended Lake Forest University outside of Chicago in 1884–1885, but he quit when his father's health failed.

In 1888, after several years of entry-level jobs, Starrett entered the architectural firm of Daniel Burnham and John Wellborn Root in Chicago at his older brother Theodore's encouragement. He worked first as a tracer and stenographer, then as a draftsman. Burnham made Starrett superintendent on two buildings for the World's Columbian Exposition in 1893—Machinery Hall and the Mines and Mining Building. In the early 1890s Starrett had married Therese Hinman; they had two children. After the Columbian Exposition, Starrett moved with his family to Buffalo, New York, to oversee another Burnham project. This solo superintendence was a challenge to Starrett's negotiating skills: "[The builder] did his work so badly that my hands itched to take it over and do it myself" (Starrett and Waldron, p. 57).

In 1897 Starrett began work for the George A. Fuller Company of Chicago, already known for efficient construction of large commercial projects such as the Marquette Building (1895) in Chicago. After starting a Fuller Company office in Baltimore, Starrett was promoted in about 1900 to New York City, where the Fuller Company had just moved its head office. Starrett's first job in New York put him back on a Daniel Burnham design, the 21-story Flatiron Building (1902), which the Fuller Company financed, and into which they moved their headquarters. Harry S. Black, by now president of Fuller, placed Starrett in charge of all projects in Manhattan north of Fourteenth Street. Big jobs that required considerable negotiation among owners, subcontractors, and designers exercised his diplomatic skills constantly.

Black served as the finance man and Starrett, the construction man. Before 1905 Starrett was vice president of the Fuller Company, and then he became its president, a position he held for the next seventeen years (1905–1922). Meanwhile, Harry Black created a larger corporation, the United States Realty and Construction Company, which financed speculative real estate projects, and Black served as its president. During Starrett's tenure as president of Fuller, the firm built many of the biggest projects undertaken in the United States before the First World War: R. H. Macy's Department Store (1902), the Pennsylvania Station (1904–1910), and the Biltmore hotel (1913), for example, all in New York City. The Fuller Company also was involved in large industrial complexes like that of the Highland Park (Mich.) Ford plant and the ore docks for Ford's River Rouge plant, and well-known government monuments such as the Lincoln Memorial in Washington, D.C.

In pursuing jobs, Starrett at times competed with his four brothers, all of whom worked at different times for Fuller's chief rival, the Thompson-Starrett Company. Once he obtained a job, Starrett was determined to execute it swiftly and economically, and his money-saving efficiencies made his reputation. Starrett took many measures that ensured delivery of material on time: for example, during the building of Penn Station, the Fuller Company sent men to Italy so that the travertine stone used in construction arrived as needed.

During World War I Starrett went after and received contracts to build for the war effort. With private construction nearly halted by the war, the Fuller Company turned to building ships of steel in 1917: "Essentially, a ship was simply a steel building, built horizontally and not vertically, out in an open field" (Starrett and Waldron, p. 190). A Fuller subsidiary, the Carolina Shipbuilding Company, was established, and a shipyard was built on the Cape Fear River in North Carolina; it closed at the end of the war.

After the war Harry Black promoted Starrett to president of the U.S. Realty Company, an umbrella organization that included the Fuller Company. Starrett felt too removed from building, so in 1922 he and his brother William formed the Starrett Brothers, soon to be joined by Andrew Eken. This new firm landed very large building contracts, including Cass Gilbert's New York Life Insurance Building (1928), the (former) McGraw Hill Building (1931), and the triumph of Starrett's career, the Empire State Building (1931). In addition to large building jobs in the United States, firms with which Paul Starrett was affiliated built in Japan, Canada, and Cuba. By 1930 Starrett Brothers and Eken became Starrett Brothers Corporation, with the Starretts retaining controlling stock. This corporation included construction firms in New York and Chicago, a realty company, and an investing company.

Of the Empire State Building team, Starrett wrote: "I doubt if there was ever a more harmonious combination than that which existed on the Empire State, between owners, architects and builder" (Starrett and Waldron, p. 293). Still labor unions struck Starrett Brothers jobs in Newark and Cincinnati because the steel subcontractor on the Empire State Building did not hire union workers. After tense labor negotiations and the stress of building the Empire State Building at a record-setting pace, Paul suffered what he called a "rather severe nervous breakdown" (Starrett and Waldron, p. 308) and retired. Paul Starrett's first wife died in 1904; his second marriage (dates unknown) was to Elizabeth Root, with whom he had three children. Starrett died in Greenwich, Connecticut.

John Tauranac called Paul Starrett "a genius at negotiations and management" (Tauranac, p. 174), and Starrett proved his inimitability in that realm on the Empire State Building and many preceding jobs. The seventy-story Bank of Manhattan Building (1929–1930) at 40 Wall Street had been a key to his obtaining the Empire State job because construction speed was so important: the bank building went up in eleven months by starting the new foundations while the old buildings were still being demolished above.

Starrett worked with many well-known clients as well as architects, and the buildings that resulted changed the urban landscape in terms of appearance, density, and overall silhouette. The quantity of building for which Starrett was responsible seemed to be matched by quality, both in technique and in the respect with which subcontractors, labor leaders, owners, and architects were treated.

• The annual reports (1929–) of the Starrett Corporation are available at the corporation's office in New York City. The main source on Starrett's life, emphasizing his profession, is his own account written with Webb Waldron, *Changing the Skyline: An Autobiography* (1938). Raymond C. Daly, "75 Years of Construction Pioneering: George A. Fuller Company, 1882–1957," *Newcomen Society in North America* 24 (1957), summarizes the construction firm's contributions to speed and efficiency in building. A George A. Fuller Company publication illustrates many of the well-known buildings constructed under Starrett's leadership: *Fireproof Building Construction: Prominent Buildings Erected by the George A. Fuller Company* (1904; repr. 1910). More recent contributions about the Starrett brothers are John Tauranac, *The Empire State Building: The Making of a Landmark* (1995), and a brief sketch by Carol Willis in *Encyclopedia of New York City*, ed. Kenneth Jackson (1995). The architect William Gray Purcell wrote "A Note on the Starrett Family," a brief homage to the Starrett brothers and their mother, in *Northwest Architect* 13 (1949): 17. Paul Starrett's obituary is in the *New York Times*, 6 July 1957.

SHARON IRISH

STARRETT, William Aiken (14 June 1877–25 Mar. 1932), engineer, building contractor, and real-estate financier, was born in Lawrence, Kansas, the son of William A. Starrett, a Presbyterian minister, farmer, and lawyer, and Helen Martha Ekin, a Quaker teacher, journalist, and editor. He attended the University of Michigan for two years, then returned to graduate with a degree in civil engineering in 1917. In 1900 Starrett married Eloise Gedney of East Orange, New Jersey; they had two children.

In 1898 Starrett joined the just-opened New York office of the George A. Fuller Company, in which his brother Paul was a leader. By 1901 William Starrett had left that firm to work with his other brothers, Theodore, Goldwin, and Ralph, in their construction company, the Thompson-Starrett Company; William served as vice president. The Fuller Company and the Thompson-Starrett Company were leading rivals in the large-scale building industry in the early twentieth century, promoting speed and economy in construction. As an executive, Starrett can be credited with helping to streamline the organization of construction to make jobs proceed as quickly and efficiently as possible.

In 1913 Starrett left the construction firm to help his brother Goldwin in the architectural firm of Starrett and Van Vleck. During the time William was in the office, Starrett and Van Vleck designed straightforward commercial and office buildings in New York City, such as 8 West 40th Street (1916), into which the firm moved their offices.

During World War I Starrett served as chairman of the construction committee of the War Industries Board, which was in charge of all construction for the U.S. Army, including hospitals, housing, factories, roads, and utilities. As John Tauranac wrote, "The marvel of William Starrett's direction in the war effort was the speed with which he finished projects" (1995, p. 173). He gained the rank of colonel by the war's end. Starrett wrote about his cantonment work in *Building for Victory* (1919), an illustrated celebration of temporary military buildings.

At the end of the war Starrett returned to the Fuller Company (where his brother Paul was president) as vice president and worked in Japan, helping to design steel-framed, earthquake-resistant buildings in Tokyo. While Starrett traveled to and from Japan (1919–1921) for Fuller, he also served as the Republican mayor of Madison, New Jersey.

During the war Starrett began to write for a popular audience about his experiences in the construction industry and about the history of skyscraper-building. An article in *Scribner's* in 1923 told of the contrasts between Japan and the United States in building methods, illustrated with Starrett's own photographs.

The year 1922 found William and Paul Starrett leaving the Fuller Company and forming a new construction firm, Starrett Brothers and Eken. In the building boom of the 1920s the brothers flourished with their pooled experience, gaining a reputation for efficient and economical management of large building projects, primarily in the eastern United States. William Starrett excelled in the oversight of day-to-day building practice. The Starretts built the seventy-story Bank of Manhattan building (1929). They crowned their achievements with the construction of the Empire State Building in 1930 and 1931.

In 1929 William Starrett helped create the Starrett Brothers Corporation, a holding company that included the Starrett Brothers construction firm, Starrett Investing Company, and other real estate concerns. Starrett served as vice president of Starrett Brothers and Eken and as president of the Starrett Corporation, coordinating the activities of the various enterprises.

Starrett also built his reputation as a writer and speaker throughout the 1920s. A series of articles in the *Saturday Evening Post* detailed the growth of skyscrapers in urban areas for a general audience, as did his book *Skyscrapers and the Men Who Build Them* (1928). Of this book the noted commentator Lewis Mumford wrote, "It is good to have this bit of skyscraper history presented by an engineer who knew by experience and practice of what he spoke" (1952, p. 431). While Starrett distinguished between bad (usually overly decorated) and good, functional buildings, he generally promoted skyscrapers, "the accepted badge of cityhood . . . an intrinsically beautiful form" ("Mountains of Manhattan," p. 24).

Starrett died in Madison, New Jersey, after a series of strokes. In addition to his practical understanding of the building business, he was an excellent communicator, both within professional organizations and in the popular press. As a mark of his success, he was president of the Associated General Contractors of America in 1932, as well as a member of the American Society of Civil Engineers and the American Society of Mechanical Engineers. His broad interests in travel, politics, and history contributed to his discussions of buildings in an urban setting. His thirty-four years at the top of the construction industry helped transform those urban settings into cities with structures more crowded and taller than ever before.

• Starrett's brother Paul wrote a little about him in his memoir, *Changing the Skyline* (1938). His own series on the skyscraper appeared in the *Saturday Evening Post*: "Sky-high," 7 Apr. 1928, pp. 6–7 ff.; "The Mountains of Manhattan," 12 May 1928, pp. 24–25ff.; and "Building a Skyscraper," 9 June 1928, pp. 24–25ff. On the firms with which Starrett was involved, consult Paul Starrett (1938) on the Fuller Construction Company, and on the Thompson-Starrett Company, Louis Horowitz, *The Towers of New York: The Memoirs of a Master Builder* (1937). On the work of Starrett and Van Vleck, see John Taylor Boyd, Jr., "A New Emphasis in Skyscraper Design Exemplified in the Recent Work of Starrett and Van Vleck," *Architectural Record* 52 (Dec. 1922): 497–509. Starrett described his experiences in Japan in "New Construction in an Ancient Empire," *Scribner's* 74 (Sept. 1923): 273–87. Lewis Mumford, *Roots of Contemporary American Architecture* (1952), p. 431, gives a brief sketch of Starrett. John Tauranac, *The Empire State Building* (1995), mentions several of the Starrett brothers. Obituaries are in *Architectural Record* 71 (Apr. 1932): 275; *American Architect* 141 (May 1932): 94; and the *New York Times*, 27 Mar. 1932.

SHARON IRISH

STATLER, Ellsworth Milton (26 Oct. 1863–16 Apr. 1928), hotel founder, was born in Somerset County, Pennsylvania, the son of William Jackson Statler, a German Reformed pastor, and Mary McKinney. His father sought to supplement his meager income by farming and by selling handmade matches, with minimal success. The family moved to Bridgeport, Ohio, across the river from Wheeling, West Virginia, in 1868, where Reverend Statler purchased a general store while continuing his ministry. He died ten years later. In 1872 Statler joined two older brothers in securing employment at a Wheeling glass factory. He worked a twelve-hour shift firing furnaces as a "glory boy" for fifty cents a day.

When Statler turned thirteen, sheer persistence won him a job as a bellboy in Wheeling's McClure House, a bustling hotel catering to travelers and salesmen. He sought to refine his manners and speech, acquired bookkeeping skills, and learned the rudiments of hotel management. Promotions followed, to head bellboy at age fifteen, night desk clerk, and eventually day clerk. By age seventeen he displayed his entrepreneurial skills by leasing (and refurbishing on credit) the hotel's billiard room, and by installing a railroad discount ticket office in the lobby. Statler then purchased a private bowling club in Wheeling, where he added billiards, a barbershop, and a lunchroom. His enterprises earned him in 1894 an annual $10,000 income. Statler married Mary I. Manderback in 1895; they adopted four children.

Also in 1895 Statler expanded operations to Buffalo, New York, where he opened a 500-seat restaurant in the Ellicott Square Building. He found success only by shifting from an upscale to an economy meal format, supplemented by extensive advertisement and promotions. When Buffalo hosted the Pan American exposition in 1900 Statler built a 2,084-room tempo-

rary hotel, where he offered lodging and meals for a flat rate. Although bad weather and the assassination of President McKinley kept attendance low, Statler managed a small profit. More importantly, the experience led to the operation of a similar enterprise, the Inside Inn, on the Louisiana Purchase Exposition grounds in St. Louis in 1904. The temporary structure included 500 baths among its 2,200 rooms and employed 1,000. Despite suffering severe burns in an accident that nearly cost him his life, Statler continued to oversee operations and he cleared $361,000.

Statler participated in the hotel building boom of the early twentieth century by erecting the 300-room Hotel Statler (later renamed the Buffalo) in Buffalo in 1908, in which he took a very direct role in design and construction. It was the first hotel in the nation to have a bath and running cold water in each room. The Buffalo Statler served as a laboratory for other Hotel Statlers built in Cleveland (1912), Detroit (1914), and St. Louis (1917) and culminating in the 2,200-room Pennsylvania Hotel built in New York City in 1919. Although he built two other hotels later (a second hotel in Buffalo in 1923 and one in Boston in 1927), the Pennsylvania remained the jewel of the hotel chain.

After his first wife died in 1925, Statler married his secretary, Alice M. Seidler, in 1927. He died a year later in New York City, leaving an estate worth an estimated $15 million. His second wife assumed direction of the hotel company. The depression hit the hotel industry very hard, and Statler hotel operations following his death deteriorated until 1936, when Mrs. Statler added two personal advisers to the board of directors. Under their direction the Statler was the only one of the "Big Four" hotel chains to survive the depression. Mrs. Statler resigned from the board of directors in 1946.

As the founder of the first U.S. hotel chain owned by a single individual, Statler left his mark on the hotel industry in several ways. Unlike the other urban hoteliers of the pre-1917 building boom, who used European hotels as models, he consciously balanced an appeal to affluent guests with an emphasis on the traveling public—families, salesmen, and convention-goers—and sought to offer ambience and amenities at a reasonable price. He innovated constantly to offer comfort to his guests. In addition to being the first to offer a room with bath, Statler is credited with initiating such guest-room features as closets, full-length mirrors, medical and laundry services, free newspaper delivered to each room, and, ultimately, at the Boston Statler, a radio in each room. He stressed to his employees the importance of service—"The guest is always right"—and wrote a Statler Service Code that employees were to carry at all times. This focus on guest comfort and convenience stood in sharp contrast to the indifferent attention to guests characteristic of most nineteenth-century hotels.

Ellsworth Statler was a man of contrasts. A workaholic, he had high expectations of his subordinates. He paid above-industry-average wages and instituted a profit-sharing plan for his workers but opposed reducing their twelve-hour shift, fearing it would compromise the quality of service guests received. He was outspoken, competitive in business and leisure, and delegated authority only with great difficulty. Quick to innovate amenities, he was somewhat slow in adopting new management techniques. He lived ostentatiously but dressed inexpensively, and even purchased his reading glasses at Woolworth's. His emphasis on service while striving to reduce the number of employees serving hotel guests directly was a critical factor in his success.

• For detailed biographies see Floyd Miller, *Statler: America's Extraordinary Hotelman* (1968), published by the Statler Foundation, and Rufus Jarman, *Bed for the Night* (1952). The latter was excerpted serially before publication as "Headaches of a Hotelkeeper," *Saturday Evening Post*, 7, 14, and 21 October 1950. Jarman's focus is on the corporation after Statler's death. Articles about Statler can be found in M. Crowell, "Great Salesmen of Service," *American Magazine*, April 1917, pp. 18–21; "Golden Rules of Hotel Keeping," *American Magazine*, May 1917, p. 33ff; "How We Practice Business Good Manners," *System*, April 1917, pp. 369–77; "Hardest Job in Business," *System*, March 1922, pp. 270–72, E. E. Purinton, "Largest Hotel in the World; and Some Reasons for E. M. Statler's Success," *Independent*, 8 May 1920, pp. 202–3; "Details Make Our Big Problems," *Magazine of Business*, September 1927, p. 282; Walter Tittle, "Host to Millions," *World's Work*, November 1927, pp. 76–81; "50 Great Pioneers of American Industry," *New Front* (1964), pp. 138–40; and K. Nichols, "The Statlers," *Biography News*, May 1975, p. 473. An obituary is in the *New York Times*, 17 April 1928.

LLOYD SPONHOLTZ

STAUGHTON, William (4 Jan. 1770–12 Dec. 1829), Baptist minister and educator, was born in Coventry, Warwickshire, England, the son of Sutton Staughton and Kezia or Keziah (maiden name unknown). A gifted child, William received a plain education in Coventry and was apprenticed to a silversmith. At seventeen he experienced an evangelical conversion and went to Bristol to study at the Baptist academy there. By 1792 Staughton was preaching in Northamptonshire and managed to be present at the auspicious occasion when the Baptist Missionary Society was formed that year. The esteem of his friends, although he was young, was demonstrated in his election to the executive committee of the society.

In 1793 Staughton was invited to succeed the venerable John Ryland at Northampton Baptist Church, but he set his sights for the United States. John Rippon, Joseph Hinton, and Joseph Hughes, all prominent English Baptist clergy, recommended Staughton to Richard Furman in South Carolina; Staughton arrived in Georgetown, South Carolina, in 1793. He served a new congregation there but disliked both the climate and the practice of slavery.

He moved to New York in 1795 and contracted yellow fever. Called to the Baptist church at Bordentown, New Jersey, in 1797, he was also ordained there. In 1798 he settled in Burlington, New Jersey, where he and his schoolteacher wife, Maria Hanson, whom he

had married in 1794, kept an academy that qualified students for Princeton College. In Burlington he also organized a Baptist church. At the young age of twenty-eight, in recognition of his pastoral and educational efforts, including the editing of several classical texts, Princeton College conferred upon him the degree of doctor of divinity. During this period he developed a friendship with Thomas Paine and wrote apologetic materials against infidelity for the Christian community.

Following a tour of the West, Staughton settled in Philadelphia, Pennsylvania. In 1805 he became the pastor of the First Baptist Church in that city. His preaching increased the congregation greatly, partly because of his linguistic charm as an orator, and he moved into several voluntary Christian ventures. The church founded two significant mission churches during his pastorate, Third Baptist Church and First African Baptist Church. He preached four times each Sunday and was an active pastor, visiting the sick of the city.

In 1807 he began in his home what became the oldest theological school among American Baptists. He was mentor to important students of the next generation, including James E. Welch and John Mason Peck. He was one of the founders of the Philadelphia Female Bible Society, the first female Bible society in the United States (1807), and the Baptist Education Society of the Middle States (1812). In 1811 Staughton resigned his pastorate at First Baptist Church. Some members felt that he was overly British in his style, and Staughton feared that the congregation might split because of the rising anti-British sentiment of the city. He soon became the pastor of a newly organized congregation called Sansom Street Baptist Church in a new section of Philadelphia. He preached to ever-increasing crowds at Sansom Street, necessitating the erection of a new edifice that became a landmark of church architecture in the city. The building project cost $40,000, a large sum for this purpose in the Baptist community. The seating was designed in the round, with a baptistry located in the center of the plan. This unique architectural design was heralded throughout the urban Baptist community.

Staughton was described as a biblical preacher, able to mingle allusions from classical writers and contemporary youth themes. Theologically he was Calvinistic, preferring careful nurture of candidates for baptism to avoid hasty commitments. Examples of his sermons are reconstructed in his memoir.

Staughton rendered significant service to the American Baptist denomination. In 1814 he became the founding secretary of the General Convention of Baptists in the United States for Foreign Missions. For twelve years, he drew upon his considerable contacts in the missionary societies in Great Britain as well as friends in the southern and New England states. He was the principal correspondent with all of the early missionaries of the Baptist Board of Foreign Missions. He exhibited extensive knowledge of the foreign and domestic fields and gave much encouragement to the fledgling cause of Baptist missions.

When the Baptist Convention approved the founding of Columbian College in 1818, Staughton was unanimously chosen president. Embarking upon his official duties in 1822 in Washington, D.C., Staughton was installed as professor of general history, belles lettres, rhetoric, and moral philosophy in the classical department; he also served as professor of divinity and pulpit eloquence in the theological department at Columbian.

Staughton's career suffered calamities between 1823 and 1827. His resignation from his beloved Sansom Street Church in Philadelphia ultimately sent the debt-ridden congregation into bankruptcy. His wife died of typhus fever in 1823. Always dependent upon the unpredictable finances of the scattered Baptist congregations, Columbian College went into bankruptcy in 1826, and the Baptist General Convention officially withdrew its sponsorship.

Staughton returned to Philadelphia in 1827 and preached for several months at the New Market Street Baptist Church. In August 1829 he married Anna C. Peale of Philadelphia. Late in the summer that year, the trustees of the Georgetown Literary and Theological Institution in Kentucky invited Staughton to become the first president of the institution. The Baptists of Kentucky were anxious to have a leading educator design the plan of Georgetown, which became the oldest Baptist institution of higher education west of the Appalachian Mountains. In November 1829 the Staughtons commenced the trip to Kentucky, with Staughton weakened by a circulatory problem. He died in Washington, D.C., and was eventually buried in Philadelphia.

Staughton was well known as a preacher and scholar. The citizens of the nation's capital in 1826 requested that he deliver the eulogy for presidents Adams and Jefferson, both of whom had died on 4 July. In his teaching career he edited a Greek grammar, wrote a commentary on the Latin poet Virgil, and produced a revision of the works of the English Baptist theologian John Gill.

• There is a small collection of Staughton's manuscripts in the American Baptist Archives in Valley Forge, Penn., part of the official records of the Baptist Board of Foreign Missions. Staughton's works include *The Baptist Mission in India, Containing a Narrative of Its Rise, Progress, and Present Condition* (1811) and *The Works of Virgil* (1825). For biographical details, see S. W. Lynd, *Memoir of the Rev. William Staughton, D.D.* (1834), and Walter O. Lewis, "William Staughton," *Baptist Quarterly* (1942): 374–78.

WILLIAM H. BRACKNEY

ST. CLAIR, Arthur (23 Mar. 1737–31 Aug. 1818), politician and soldier, was born in Thurso, Caithness County, Scotland, probably the son of William Sinclair, a merchant, and Elizabeth Balfour. After a reported enrollment at the University of Edinburgh, St. Clair was apprenticed in 1756 to an eminent physician, Dr. William Hunter. He soon gave up anatomical studies, however, and obtained a commission in 1757 as ensign in the Sixtieth or Royal American Regiment of Foot. He served at Louisbourg (1758) and Quebec (1759), advancing to lieutenant.

In 1760 St. Clair married the wealthy Phoebe Bayard of Boston. He resigned his commission in 1762. His military allowance and her inheritance of £14,000 enabled the couple to settle, rich with 4,000 acres and soon prolific with seven children, in Pennsylvania's Ligonier Valley. He gained appointments as a colonial agent for the proprietary government in 1771 and, with the creation of Westmoreland County in 1773, as proprietary magistrate and a justice of the county court. While in these offices he challenged Virginia's claim to the Fort Pitt region, also claimed by Pennsylvania. He enlarged that dispute in 1774 with his failed attempt to arrest Dr. John Connolly, a Virginian who, to stake Virginia's claim, had seized and was restoring Fort Pitt (renamed Fort Dunmore to honor Virginia's governor).

The Revolution, however, engulfed that controversy. In 1775 St. Clair served as secretary to an embassy from the Continental Congress that drew up a treaty with Upper Ohio Valley Indians at Pittsburgh. Later that year he raised a regiment, which elected him colonel. Congress also commissioned him at that rank. He and his troops helped protect the defeated Americans' retreat from Canada in 1776. By February 1777, having served at Trenton (1776) and Princeton (1777), he had risen to major general, a rank he then shared with only four others. On 5 May St. Clair was ordered to Fort Ticonderoga, which was said to be impregnable but which, he noted on his arrival, was actually indefensible with the small force at his disposal. An overwhelming British force under John Burgoyne soon laid siege, on 5 July, occupying ground commanding the fort. St. Clair successfully withdrew. Congressional critics assailed the evacuation, suspending him from command. He demanded a formal court martial, which convened in September 1778 and exonerated him of the charged negligence. After Ticonderoga he held no major revolutionary battle commands, though he saw action as an aide-de-camp under General George Washington at Brandywine (1777) and Yorktown (1781). His finances, meanwhile, suffered greatly.

St. Clair, who early joined the Society of the Cincinnati and who presided over its Pennsylvania branch, stood with the anticonstitutionalists in the debate over the Pennsylvania Constitution of 1776, the most radically democratic in the thirteen states. Anticonstitutionalists sought to replace the powerful unicameral legislature with a bicameral body and a strong governor. A supporter of a stronger national government as well, St. Clair in December 1782 advised a delegation from the army to warn the Congress that "fatal consequences" would attend its failure to raise funds with which to pay the soldiers. This was on the eve of the Newburgh Conspiracy (1783), an effort on the part of General Horatio Gates, Major John Armstrong (1758–1843), and Gouverneur Morris to put the threat of military force behind efforts to strengthen the national government.

St. Clair served on his state's Council of Censors in 1783. Elected a delegate to Congress in November 1785, St. Clair became its president in February 1787 and was in that office when Congress passed the Northwest Ordinance. On 5 October, hoping to regain solvency, St. Clair reluctantly accepted congressional appointment as the first governor of the Northwest Territory. He had become, he joked in 1793, "a poor devil banished to another planet."

By 1788, when St. Clair established his territorial government, treaties containing Delaware, Shawnee, Wyandot, Ottawa, and Chippewa land cessions to the United States had been repudiated by large portions of the involved tribes. On the grounds that the Indian delegations had been unauthorized to make land cessions, militants from these tribes joined with like-minded Potawatomis, Miamis, Mingoes, and others to form a "Western Confederacy" (1786–1794). In 1789 St. Clair attempted at the Treaties of Fort Harmar—with the Six Nations, Wyandots, Delawares, Ottawas, Chippewas, Potawatomis, and Sauks—to defuse the explosive situation, but because he also treated with unrepresentative Indian parties (Shawnees, for example, were not represented at all) and because he would not disavow the previous cessions, Indian defiance continued. In 1790 Congress recognized that the territory faced full-scale war, and it authorized campaigns against militant Indian villages. In 1791 Major General St. Clair himself commanded a hastily organized and poorly supplied combined expedition of 1,400 regulars and militia. Some 1,000 Indians counterattacked and routed the Americans on 4 November 1791. The 630 Americans that were killed or captured, in addition to the many wounded, mark the battle as the deadliest ever for U.S. forces fighting Native Americans. Although a congressional committee and President George Washington exonerated St. Clair, he resigned his army commission.

As a Federalist territorial governor, St. Clair demonstrated his determination to preserve national authority, a determination that put him at odds with territorial inhabitants seeking self-government and statehood. His narrow interpretation of the Northwest Ordinance's provision that any territorial law must be adopted from a law on the books in one of the states set him against the territory's judges, who wanted more latitude in modifying other states' laws to fit local conditions. Claiming that only the governor had the authority to lay out counties, he set himself in 1799 against the first elected territorial legislature by vetoing a legislative plan for new counties and county seats. The legislature's hostility to the governor surfaced in its election that year of William Henry Harrison, rather than the governor's son, Arthur St. Clair, Jr., as a delegate to represent the Northwest Territory in Congress. As St. Clair came up for gubernatorial reappointment, petitions supporting him and opposing him reached President John Adams (1735–1826), who recommended St. Clair to the Senate, though he

attached to the recommendation the negative as well as the positive petitions. Still Federalist in February 1801, the Senate approved St. Clair's reappointment for a three-year term.

As the territory filled with U.S. citizens, St. Clair unsuccessfully sought to have the Congress subdivide it into three, rather than two, new territories. This was a transparent effort to delay statehood, and thus to maintain federal authority, by keeping each newly created territory's population below the 60,000 required by the Northwest Ordinance for statehood. St. Clair lost the struggle, and in 1800 the Northwest Territory was divided into the Indiana and Ohio territories. The Republican Congress's Enabling Act of 1802, moreover, allowed Ohio, despite its low population, to call a convention to prepare for statehood. Adamant that the people of the territory were not ready to govern themselves, the Federalist St. Clair, still governor, addressed the overwhelmingly Republican convention. Allowed the floor only as a private citizen, he scathingly attacked the Enabling Act and was, for that reason, insultingly dismissed by President Thomas Jefferson on 22 November.

Politically and financially bankrupt, St. Clair returned to the Ligonier Valley. He lost his property in 1810, having failed in his efforts to obtain remuneration from Congress for his past expenses and services. He retired, a poor man, to a log house on Chestnut Ridge, Pennsylvania, where he died after a carriage accident. A devoted officer who sacrificed his fortune raising troops for the Revolution and the Indian war in the Northwest Territory, St. Clair also represents an elitist persuasion, an aristocratic style, that became rapidly outmoded in the democratic aftermath of the American Revolution.

• Collections of St. Clair's papers are held by the Cincinnati Historical Society, Ohio Historical Society in Columbus, and Western Reserve Historical Society in Cleveland. Manuscripts can also be found in the Library of Congress. For a printed collection and detailed biography see William Henry Smith, ed., *The St. Clair Papers: The Life and Public Services of Arthur St. Clair* (2 vols., 1882). See also Ellis Beals, "Arthur St. Clair, Western Pennsylvania's Leading Citizen, 1764–1818," *Western Pennsylvania Historical Magazine* 12 (1929): 75–96, 141–96. For other biographies see Thomas A. McMullin and David Walker, eds., *Biographical Directory of American Territorial Governors* (1984), and Frazer Ells Wilson, *Arthur St. Clair, Rugged Ruler of the Old Northwest: An Epic of the American Frontier* (1944). For studies of the incidents in St. Clair's career and their relation to his society, see Randolph Chandler Downs, "Thomas Jefferson and the Removal of Governor St. Clair in 1802," *Ohio Archaeological and Historical Quarterly* 36 (1927): 62–67; Richard H. Kohn, *Eagle and Sword: The Federalists and the Creation of the Military Establishment in America, 1783–1802* (1975); [Arthur St. Clair], *A Narrative of the Manner in which the Campaign against the Indians, in the Year 1791, Was Conducted, under the Command of Major General St. Clair* (1812); Albert B. Sears, "The Political Philosophy of Arthur St. Clair," *Ohio State Archaeological and Historical Quarterly* 49 (1940): 41–57; and

Beverly Waugh Bond, *The Civilization of the Old Northwest: A Study of Political, Social, and Economic Development, 1788–1812* (1934).

GREGORY EVANS DOWD

ST. DENIS, Ruth (20 Jan. 1879–21 July 1968), dancer, choreographer, and teacher, was born Ruth Dennis in Newark, New Jersey, the daughter of Thomas Laban Dennis and Ruth Emma Hullo. Her mother, the second woman to receive a medical diploma from the University of Michigan Medical School, was an advocate of dress reform. Her father was a machinist by trade and an inventor by inclination. The pair had met at Eagleswood, a colony near Perth Amboy, New Jersey, where artists and freethinkers congregated. Their "marriage" was a matter of agreement, solemnized in a ceremony with neither clergyman nor justice of the peace officiating.

Because Ruth's mother was sickly and her father could neither keep a job nor achieve success with his inventions, Pin Oaks farm in Somerville, New Jersey, where the family moved in 1884, was turned into a boardinghouse. It drew a clientele with intellectual or artistic leanings. Through these paying guests little Ruth was exposed to Christian Science and to Theosophy, doctrines that were to influence how she lived and how she framed her dances. From her mother she learned physical exercises devised by American disciples of the French theoretician François Delsarte.

Delsarte, originally interested in freeing the voices of singers and orators and making them more expressive, related posture and gesture to corresponding emotions and thoughts. His American students systematized his theories into exercises that entered many areas of the culture, from acting schools to schoolchildren's recitations to classes promoting grace and good health among society women. Delsartean principles—also inspiring to St. Denis's contemporary Isadora Duncan—linked physical action with spiritual states and thus elevated dancing above its connotations of titillating entertainment. In her autobiography, *An Unfinished Life* (1939), St. Denis recalls the excitement she felt as a stagestruck thirteen-year-old on seeing a Delsarte matinee given by Genevieve Stebbins, one of the leading Delsarte teachers and theorists. Stebbins's beauty and grace gave St. Denis her first inkling that idealism and dance could be linked, and she commemorated the performance years later: "The image of her white Grecian figure became so indelibly printed on my mind that everything I subsequently did stemmed from this performance" (p. 16).

With her family's approval and support, Ruth Dennis made her debut at Worth's Dime Museum in Manhattan in 1894, performing dance routines of her own devising larded with splits and other mild acrobatics. She spent the next four years performing in revues and variety shows as one of many skirt dancers—making much of flourishing a skirt, kicking a shapely leg, or bending backward in flirtatious abandon—while finishing her high school education at Packer Collegiate Institute in Brooklyn. In 1898 she toured with a musical comedy and the following year was taken by the impresario Augustin Daly into one of the several casts of *A Runaway Girl*. It was in 1904, during a highly educational four-year stint dancing and acting in various plays (*Zaza, Madame DuBarry*, and *The Auctioneer*) mounted by the producer-director David Belasco, that she seized on the images and themes that guided her later career as an independent artist.

Stimulated by readings in Eastern philosophy and mysticism, by a mix of Christian Science and Theosophy, by manifestations of orientalism, and by a cigarette poster in a Buffalo drugstore that showed the goddess Isis serenely enthroned, Dennis premiered her first important solo dance in 1906. Belasco had urged her to change her name, and it was as Ruth St. Denis that she premiered *Radha* on the variety bill of a Sunday night smokers concert on 28 January 1906.

Despite the influence of the cigarette poster, *Radha* was set in India, not Egypt; but it incorporated some of St. Denis's plans for a more ambitious solo, *Egypta*, which was not presented until 1910. In *Radha*, St. Denis, a barefoot goddess in filmy veils, descended from her shrine to give her priests (hired extras) lessons in renunciation of the senses. Her alluring solos, to music from Léo Delibes's opera *Lakmé*, illustrated the charms of each sense before she returned, transfigured, to her niche. *Radha* baffled vaudeville critics by blending theatrical savvy and physical allure with spirituality. The performer's feet were bare, her attire flimsy, yet this was clearly no hootchy-kootch. Some found *Radha* too slow and serious for vaudeville.

St. Denis, beautiful, earnest, and high-minded, had already performed in salons of New York society, and she gave many interviews in which she preached the innate spirituality of dance. The year of her debut with *Radha*, the wives of prominent New York businessmen and artists launched her in a setting more dignified than that of a variety bill: a matinee of her own at the Hudson Theatre, featuring *Radha* and two new dances, *The Incense* and *Cobras*.

Some critics were still condescending: "Barefoot Wriggler Delights Society" was the headline of a review in the *New York World* on 23 March 1906. Yet many of the press and the public were able to see St. Denis as she wished to be seen. As her husband, Ted Shawn, wrote in 1920 in his *Ruth St. Denis: Pioneer and Prophet*, "But so intense in her concentration was Ruth St. Denis that she banished prudery from the mind of the beholder and he left the theatre conscious only of a revelation of great beauty and harmonious art, a pure intense fervor, and a profound peace" (p. v). Like Isadora Duncan, Ruth St. Denis pioneered the notion that dancing could reflect serious, even spiritual ideas.

Common themes emerge in the first dances of St. Denis as well as in those that she composed during her European appearances of 1907–1909 and for subsequent concert and vaudeville appearances throughout America. The dances were essentially solos—even when, as in the full-length dance drama *Egypta*, she was backed by supporting actors, dancers, and musicians. (St. Denis's younger brother, Brother, or Buzz, was often among them, using the stage name of René St. Denis.) Most of her dances dealt in some measure with transformation. In numbers like *Cobras* and *The Nautch* (1908), St. Denis simply assumed an exotic persona: in the first, she was a snake charmer, her gloved hands the snakes; in the second, she was an Indian street performer soliciting money. But in dances like *Radha, The Incense, Bakawali* (1913), and *O-mika* (1913), the heroine, whether mortal or a goddess, underwent purification or stripped off layers of mortality to discover and reveal her essential self. In *The Incense*, as an Indian woman, performing the ceremony of *puja*, St. Denis, swaying beatifically, rippled her remarkably flexible arms as if she had become one with the upward spirals of smoke. She knew little of Indian or Japanese dance but, fortified by her Delsartean training, drew her ideas from poetry, her postures and gestures from books of sculpture and painting. Her music was by Western composers working in the "à la orientale" mode. Very occasionally, as in *The Scherzo Waltz* (1914), she performed as herself, simply dancing to music in the manner of Isadora Duncan.

In 1914 St. Denis hired Ted Shawn and his partner to perform as a ballroom dance team on her programs. Shawn, who had begun as a student of theology and turned to dance as a way of reviving muscles disabled by diphtheria, made an immediate impression on St. Denis. Concerned with redefining dancing to a puritanical America as a "manly art," he could speak eloquently on the nobility of dance and its high status in antiquity. He soon became St. Denis's partner, and shortly thereafter they married and in 1915 established in Los Angeles a school, Denishawn, that attracted girls from "respectable" families as well as movie stars. A prospectus for 1918 lists courses in "basic technique, Delsarte, oriental dance, Egyptian dance, ballet, Greek dance, creative dance, music visualizations, plastique, geisha, piano, French, crafts, Red Cross."

Shawn was a shrewd businessman: for $50, a student could procure two dances, with sheet music and costume designs. He was also an enthusiastic teacher; St. Denis was, admittedly, better at inspiring. Both felt a sense of mission about Denishawn. They gave inspirational talks to the students and held classes out of doors to secure the uplifting effect of nature. Denishawn, St. Denis later wrote in her autobiography, was to be a "school of life" (p. 178). The school almost instantly spawned a company. Until 1929, with few breaks, St. Denis and Shawn toured the country (and, in 1925–1926, Asia) at the head of a group drawn from their students, among whom were Martha Graham, Doris Humphrey, and Charles Weidman. They performed items from the repertory on the vaudeville circuit as well as on more desirable concert tours where Denishawn was the sole attraction.

Shawn extended St. Denis's repertory of colorful locales to Siam, Java, Mexico, Spain, North Africa, and the American past. In Denishawn genre pieces like Shawn's *Ourieda—A Romance of the Desert* (1914) and *Cuadro Flamenco* (1923), St. Denis's *Ishtar of the Seven Gates* (1923), and the joint *The Garden of Kama* (1915), he played prince consort to his wife's queen, worshipper to her goddess, fiery wooer to her glamorous maiden. Both continued to perform solos, and Shawn set numbers on various of the company dancers.

Around 1917, St. Denis began to experiment with "music visualizations," inspired by Isadora Duncan and the ideas of the Swiss Emile Jaques-Dalcroze, which correlated movement not just with the rhythm of music but also with its pitch and instrumentation. In these, the dancers assumed no disguises and wore simple tunics or flowing dresses. Notable among these are her solos *Brahms Waltz* and *Liebestraum* (both 1922). Her protégée, Doris Humphrey, assisted her in some of these dances, collaborating on *Soaring* (1919), which featured Art Nouveau images of young women making an immense sheet of china silk billow above them or twist into a lily bud around the central figure. In 1919 and 1920, during a difficult period in the Shawn–St. Denis marriage, St. Denis toured a program of music visualizations on the concert circuit with an all-female group billed as the Ruth St. Denis Concert Dancers.

Although Shawn and St. Denis were reunited for subsequent tours—including a stint in 1927–1928 in which Denishawn was a featured attraction in the Ziegfeld Follies—the marriage (which was childless) finally fell apart in 1931, after a last duet tour in 1930. Shawn then began to tour with his successful Men Dancers and in 1941 turned "Jacob's Pillow," a farm he had bought in 1930 near Becket, Massachusetts, into a summer school and dance festival. However, he frequently invited St. Denis to perform at Jacob's Pillow, and both enjoyed presenting themselves to the press and the public as "great lovers."

Despite the success of Denishawn, bad luck and unwise financial management left St. Denis in straitened circumstances after the split. Compared to the powerful, austere, socially conscious dances being made by the "modern" dancers, St. Denis's work struck many as passé. During this last part of her career, she began dancing in Christian churches, adding the Virgin Mary and Mary Magdalene to her repertory of heroines with veils and spiritual transformations (e.g., *The Masque of Mary* [1934]). Connected to the Society of Spiritual Arts that she founded was a rhythmic choir to support her in church pageants. Almost up to her death her stamina was remarkable, her charisma indestructible. In her seventies, she was still radiant in the simple steps and fluid arm ripples of one of her first solos, *The Incense*. At the age of eighty-seven, she performed it one last time, at Orange Coast College in California, where she lived with her brother and his family. She died in Hollywood, California.

St. Denis was not a "modern dancer," but, as her major biographer, Suzanne Shelton, writes (*Divine Dancer* [1981], p. xv), she was "dedicated to the belief that behind each physical gesture was an emotional or spiritual motivation." That idea, as well as her sense of theater, her exploration of the female psyche, and the free body attitudes of her more abstract music visualizations, gave American modern dancers like Graham and Humphrey a base on which to develop their harsher, more contemporary work.

• Two hundred bound volumes of St. Denis's handwritten journals are located in the Ruth St. Denis Collection, Department of Special Collections, Research Library, University of California at Los Angeles. The same collection includes programs, letters, costumes, and other important items. Extensive archival material, including films, is also to be found in the Ruth St. Denis Collection and the Denishawn Collection, Dance Collection, New York Public Library for the Performing Arts. The major biography is Suzanne Shelton, *Divine Dancer: A Biography of Ruth St. Denis* (1981), which was reissued in paperback in 1990 as *Ruth St. Denis: A Biography of the Divine Dancer.* See also Christena L. Schlundt, *The Professional Appearances of Ruth St. Denis and Ted Shawn* (1962) and *Into the Mystic with Miss Ruth,* vol. 46 of Dance Perspectives (1971); and Jane Sherman, *The Drama of Denishawn Dance* (1979). A front-page obituary is in the *New York Times,* 22 July 1968.

DEBORAH JOWITT

STEARNES, Turkey (8 May 1901–4 Sept. 1979), Negro League baseball player, was born Norman Stearnes in Nashville, Tennessee, the son of Will S. Stearnes and Mary Everett. Although his daughter once said that he acquired his nickname because he flapped his elbows when he ran, Stearnes believed a protruding stomach during childhood was the reason. One of five children, he pitched for Pearl High School until "around 15 or 16 years old," when his father died. He then worked at any job he could find, including slopping pigs, driving wagons, delivering groceries, and general cleaning.

In 1921 Stearnes played professionally with the Montgomery, Alabama, Gray Sox in the Negro Southern League, a sort of black minor league. After playing for a year in Memphis, Tennessee, he was picked up by the Detroit Stars of the Negro National League, one of the two major black leagues. The Stars players worked in an automobile factory when they were not playing ball for Tenny Blount, who owned the numbers racket in Detroit. The team played black league games five days a week and semipro games against white teams in Michigan and Canada the other two days.

The Stars' home, Mack Park, had a high fence in right field, Stearnes recalled, and fell away to a deep center field. Despite the size of the ballpark, Stearnes hit 17 home runs, second in the league, and batted .365 during a sixty-game rookie season. (The Negro Leagues played 40 to 60 games a season, or about one-third as many as the white major leagues.) That fall the St. Louis Browns of the American League came to Detroit for a series against the Stars; it was quite unusual for a major league team to travel in order to play against a Negro League team. The Stars won two of the three games, with Stearnes batting .500 in twelve plate appearances. The following year he led the league in home runs with a relatively low total of 10 in 60 games, and he batted .358.

Physically, Stearnes was not a typical slugger. Weighing less than 170 pounds, he whipped his short, 35-inch bat from an odd left-handed stance, taking the toes of his right foot off the ground. "Yeah, Turkey had a funny stance, but he could get [his bat] around on you," sighed Satchel Paige. "He could hit it over the left field fence, or the center field fence, or over the right field fence. Turkey Stearnes was one of the greatest hitters we had. He was as good as anybody ever played baseball." Also a fast runner, he often batted leadoff and was a wide-ranging center fielder.

Stearnes let his bat talk—"he wasn't a good mixer," the players said, "he never popped off." Sometimes he talked to his bat and even took it to bed with him, it was said. When pitchers threw at his head, he told them, "You make it harder for you. If the ball comes across, I'm gonna hit that ball. You don't scare me."

For the rest of the 1920s, the glory years of black baseball, Stearnes kept his batting average well over .300 and remained among the leaders in home runs. His best power season was 1928, when he drove 24 over the wall, the second highest total ever in the history of the black leagues.

With the onset of the Great Depression, in 1930 Stearnes and other midwestern Negro League players went east to try to make more money. He briefly landed with the New York Lincoln Giants but found pickings were just as slim there and returned to Detroit by mid-1930. By then the Stars had moved to huge Hamtramck Park, which had a foul line 450 feet extending from home plate. Soon thereafter, Stearnes became the first player to hit a home run over the park's outfield fence. He arrived in time to help the Stars win the second-half pennant in the Negro National League that season. The Stars then lost to St. Louis, the first-half winner, in a seven-game playoff. Stearnes's St. Louis rival, George "Mule" Suttles, batted .357 in the series; Stearnes led all batters with a .467 average and knocked in 11 runs.

In 1931 Stearnes moved to Kansas City. Although he hit only 8 home runs that season, his record was good enough to lead the league for the fourth time. The next season he joined the Chicago American Giants, who played four blocks from the White Sox's Comiskey Park on the South Side. Even though home runs were hard to get in South Side Park, the Giants' huge ballpark, Stearnes led the league in doubles, triples, homers, and steals—a feat not equaled by any contemporary major leaguer.

When Suttles joined the Giants in 1933, the two great rivals became teammates. Suttles hit cleanup, while Stearnes led off. While Suttles's batting fell off in the new park, Stearnes flourished. He batted .342 in 1933 and .374 in 1934 to lead the American Giants to the pennant. They lost the Negro League World Series to Philadelphia in seven games. Finally, in 1935 Stearnes batted a rousing .434, one of the highest averages achieved in the Negro Leagues.

Stearnes played with the Philadelphia Stars in 1936, moved to Detroit, then came back to Chicago for two years before ending his career in Kansas City at the age of thirty-nine. He went out with a bang. In 1939 he led the league in batting with a .350 average and apparently in homers (no one else seems to have matched his 2 home runs). In 1940 he topped everyone again with 5 home runs, the first player to end his career as a league homerun champion. In 1946 Stearnes married Nettie Mae McArthur; they had two daughters.

After he left baseball, Stearnes said, "I went to work." He engaged in twenty-seven years of heavy labor, initially at $6 a day, on the rolling mills of the auto plants in Detroit, where he died.

During his career, Stearnes ranked first in the Negro League in triples, second in home runs and doubles, and fifth in batting average and stolen bases. He also won three batting crowns and six homerun championships. Against white big leaguers he batted .313 with 4 home runs in 14 games. Stearnes hit with consistency as well as power, with a lifetime batting average of .352. "I never counted my homers," he once said. "I hit so many, I never counted them." The black leagues did not keep careful records either, but later scholarship has determined that Stearnes was probably one of the two top black homerun hitters of his era, 1923 to 1940. Suttles narrowly outslugged him in total homers, 190 to 181, although the renowned Josh Gibson might well have been first if he had played more games. Reacting to the absence of Stearnes from the National Baseball Hall of Fame, James "Cool Papa" Bell said, "If they don't put Turkey Stearnes in the Hall of Fame, they shouldn't put *anybody* in!"

• For further reading, see Richard Bak, *Turkey Stearnes and the Detroit Stars* (1994); John B. Holway, *Blackball Stars* (1988), p. 248; and Dick Clark, "Norman 'Turkey' Stearnes," *The Ballplayers* (1990), pp. 1039–40. Stearnes's statistical record is found in *The Baseball Encyclopedia*, 9th ed. (1992), p. 2651. An obituary is in the *Detroit Free Press*, 6 Sept. 1979.

JOHN B. HOLWAY

STEARNS, Abel (9 Feb. 1798–23 Aug. 1871), California pioneer merchant and *ranchero*, was born in Lunenburg, Massachusetts, the son of Levi Stearns and Elizabeth Goodrich (occupations unknown). When his parents died within three months of each other in 1810, Stearns went to sea and rose from merchant sailor to supercargo before acquiring his own trading schooner in 1822. By then, a failed marriage to Persis (maiden name unknown) between 1817 and 1820 had resulted in the birth of a child in 1819. In the meantime, Stearns traveled to the East and West Indies, China, and South America before abandoning the sea, the United States, and apparently his own child in 1826. Settling in Mexico City, Stearns became a naturalized Mexican citizen in 1828 and moved to Monterey, California, the following year.

After spending two years in a failed attempt to secure a Central Valley land grant, Stearns moved to Los Angeles, where he opened a mercantile house in 1831. Three years later, he expanded his business by purchasing and enlarging the Casa de San Pedro, the only building then standing in the otherwise undeveloped "port" of Los Angeles. Possession of this warehouse gave Stearns a commanding role in the local hide and tallow trade that dominated the commercial economy of Mexican California. As the most important middleman in the southern half of the territory, Stearns did a brisk business purchasing and storing hides and tallow produced on the local *ranchos*, then selling or trading these items to American and British merchant vessels plying the coast. In exchange, Stearns received either cash or manufactured goods that he sold or traded to the local *rancheros*. Stearns quickly acquired an income that enabled him to branch out and become one of the few moneylenders in cash-poor California.

Stearns's success quickly placed him among the elite in *Californio* society. He became a close friend and partner of Don Juan Bandini of San Diego, one of California's preeminent *rancheros*. In 1835 Stearns won a seat on the Los Angeles *ayuntamiento* (town council), which he held for over a decade, and served briefly in 1836 as the pueblo's *síndico procurador*, an important office that combined the duties of city attorney, treasurer, and tax collector. Ten years later, Governor Pío Pico appointed Stearns provisional subprefect for the Los Angeles *partido*. In 1836 and again in 1844–1845 Stearns backed successful revolutions that expelled unpopular California governors appointed by Mexican authorities and replaced them with local favorites more sympathetic to his own interests. Stearns's prominence was such that when he was accused in 1840 of smuggling contraband through the Casa de San Pedro and avoiding tariff levies, he not only secured acquittal but was promptly appointed collector of customs.

Stearns was not always so fortunate, however. In 1835 a dispute with a Kentucky-born saloonkeeper named William Day resulted in a bloody brawl in which Day stabbed Stearns several times about the face, neck, and shoulders. Stearns recovered but was left with permanently impaired speech, and his face remained scarred for the rest of his life. These injuries further detracted from a homely appearance that had already earned for Stearns the unflattering moniker *Cara de Caballo* (horseface). Stearns's nickname and disfigurement did not, however, prevent him from successfully courting Juan Bandini's fourteen-year-old daughter Maria Francisca Paula Arcadia, whom he married in 1841. Though the couple had no children, their marriage was by all accounts a happy one that helped cement Stearns's ties to the *ranchero* elite. The couple's elegant home near the Los Angeles plaza, dubbed "El Palacio," quickly became one of the pueblo's most celebrated social centers.

In 1842 Stearns began his transition from merchant to *ranchero* when he purchased "Rancho Los Alamitos," a 26,000-acre estate on the Pacific coast immediately southeast of San Pedro. Three years later, he sold the Casa de San Pedro and used the proceeds to stock his land with cattle. Before the outbreak of the Mexican War put a temporary halt on further expansion,

Stearns acquired two more extensive properties in Baja California.

Stearns remained steadfastly neutral during the American conquest of California and carefully played both sides of the fence. He easily managed the transition from Mexican to American rule and retained all his property and prestige under the new regime. The federal land commission sent to investigate pre-1846 property claims in California quickly validated his titles, though Stearns spent a sizable sum warding off rival claimants to Los Alamitos. In 1847 he was again chosen *sindico* and two years later was elected as a delegate to the state constitutional convention at Monterey, where he helped draft and sign California's first organic law. Joining the Whig party, Stearns won a seat in the state assembly in 1850. An opponent of southern secession, Stearns became a Douglas Democrat after the collapse of the Whigs and was elected to a second term in the assembly in 1860. Following the outbreak of the Civil War, Stearns entered the Republican party and remained a member of the GOP until his death.

In the meantime, the end of the Mexican War had allowed Stearns to resume building his land and cattle empire. The onset of the gold rush sent California cattle prices soaring, and Stearns eagerly entered the booming new market for beef, which rapidly replaced the old hide and tallow trade.

Taking advantage of high prices, Stearns began to acquire the properties of *rancheros* tied down by legal entanglements before the land commission. Between 1850 and 1862, Stearns obtained title to at least ten *rancho* grants in Los Angeles, San Bernardino, and San Diego counties. When added to his original holdings, these comprised over 450,000 acres. Stearns also owned the Eagle Flour mill in Los Angeles and the Arcadia commercial building, which he built in 1858.

By the time he acquired these additional properties, however, Stearns's fortunes had already suffered a sharp reversal. A glutted market forced cattle prices steadily downward after 1856, while the disastrous floods of 1861–1862 and the prolonged drought of 1862–1865 wiped out thousands of cattle throughout southern California, driving many *rancheros* into bankruptcy. Stearns lost Los Alamitos to foreclosure and managed to stay in business only by mortgaging most of his remaining lands. To pay off these debts, Stearns and his creditors formed the so-called Robinson Trust in 1868 and began subdividing nearly 180,000 acres in Los Angeles and present-day Orange counties. With southern California on the eve of its first great real estate boom, the trust sold over 12,000 acres during its first year. Stearns was on his way to amassing a huge new fortune at the time of his death in San Francisco. An important transitional figure in the history and development of Los Angeles, Stearns, in the words of one biographer, personified "more than any other man of his generation . . . both the southern California of the Mexican tradition and the southern California of the [early] American period" (Cleland, p. 184).

• Stearns's papers are housed in the Henry Huntington Library in San Marino, Calif. The best published biography is "Abel Stearns: The Personification of an Age," in Robert Glass Cleland, *The Cattle on a Thousand Hills: Southern California, 1850–1880* (1941). The most recent and complete source is Philip Fedewa, "Abel Stearns in Transitional California, 1848–1871" (Ph.D. diss., Univ. of Missouri, 1970). See also Doris Marion Wright, *A Yankee in Mexican California: Abel Stearns, 1798–1848* (1977); John C. Hough, "Abel Stearns, 1848–1871" (Ph.D. diss., Univ. of California, Los Angeles, 1961); and Pearl Pauline Stamps, *Abel Stearns: California Pioneer, 1798–1871* (1926).

MICHAEL MAGLIARI

STEARNS, Frank Ballou (6 Nov. 1879–5 July 1955), automaker, was born in Berea, Ohio, the son of Frank McIntyre Stearns, a businessman, and Celia Ballou. Stearns's father was a pioneer in the stone-quarrying business in Berea and achieved wealth from this enterprise. The family moved to Cleveland, Ohio, when Stearns was a boy. When Stearns was fourteen years old he had a seminal experience when he visited the Chicago World's Fair with his father and was enthralled by the automobiles on display there.

After graduating from the University School in Cleveland in 1894, Stearns entered the Case School of Applied Science (now Case Western Reserve University), where his interest in internal combustion engines deepened. Much to his father's dismay, Stearns left Case after only one year and devoted himself to building a car, even though he had never driven one. Laboring night and day in the family's basement machine shop, Stearns completed his car in 1896. This car was notable not only because Stearns had constructed it in his basement, but also because it was the first car he had ever driven. The elder Stearns was so impressed with his son's vehicle that he advanced the young Stearns a $1,000 loan to convert the family barn behind their home into a machine shop for manufacturing cars. In 1898 Stearns formed a partnership with two brothers who were interested in cars, Ralph and Raymond Owen, and called the venture F. B. Stearns & Company. But the partnership was short-lived, as the Owen brothers left Stearns before the year was out.

In 1899 Stearns came out with his first production model Stearns car. He sold fifty cars that year and fifty more the following year. These early Stearns cars had a one-cylinder, two-stroke engine that gave eight horsepower. In 1901 Stearns began producing a heavier car with a huge one-cylinder (6¼-inch bore, 7-inch stroke) engine that produced eleven horsepower. This enormous cylinder capacity was unusual but made the car powerful. Called the Stearns gasoline surrey, this car carried five passengers and featured a steering wheel at a time when most cars still had tillers. Stearns increased his profile in Cleveland auto circles by helping to found the Cleveland Automobile Club in 1900; he later wrote for its publication, the *Cleveland Motorist*.

In 1902 Stearns married Maybelle Wilson, the daughter of Captain Thomas Wilson, founder of the

Wilson Marine Trust Company and the man who built the first iron boat on the Great Lakes. He had two daughters who survived him.

In 1902 Stearns reorganized his firm as the F. B. Stearns Company with himself as president, general manager, and treasurer, and his father as vice president and secretary. That year Stearns began producing two-cylinder as well as one-cylinder models, and by 1903 annual production was eighty cars. In 1904 Stearns decided to concentrate his attention on the manufacturing aspect of his company, leaving car sales and company management to R. M. York, who eventually became vice president. In 1906 Stearns introduced a four-cylinder car with four forward speeds. Two years later he unveiled a six-cylinder model that was capable of doing almost 100 miles per hour, although few roads in America at that time could accommodate such speed. In 1909 Stearns registered a distinctive white line around the radiator as a trademark for his car, and all of his cars thereafter bore this feature. (One of the company's advertising slogans was "The White Line Radiator Belongs to the Stearns.")

By the end of the first decade of production the Stearns car was becoming well known for a number of fine attributes. Speed was one: the Stearns was one of the fastest cars in America. Stearns cars won several hill climbs and road races, and Stearns himself drove one of his cars to victory in a Cleveland-to-Pittsburgh road race. In 1910 a Stearns car won the grueling 24-hour race on Coney Island's Brighton Beach, averaging 52.2 miles per hour over 1,253 miles. The Stearns car was also noted for its technical refinement, and combined with its speed and power it appealed to affluent motorists who wanted fun and excitement in their driving. Quality was one of the most important selling points of the Stearns car, a feature achieved partly by Stearns's innovative road tests. Stearns, who insisted that his cars should get rougher treatment at the factory than from their owners, initiated a searching test program unusual for its day: a Stearns car was loaded with bags of sand totaling 1,000 pounds and then driven to a checkpoint sixty miles from Cleveland and back. By 1910, impressed with the quality and performance of Stearns cars, cities such as Cleveland, New York, Chicago, and Buffalo were using Stearns cars as taxi cabs.

In 1910 Stearns took a significant step in the development of his car by adopting the Knight sleeve-valve engine. The British automaker Daimler had been using this engine since 1908, and in 1910 Stearns sent his chief engineer, James Sterling, to England to obtain the first license to build the engine in the United States. Whereas the conventional internal combustion engine employed poppet (mushroom-shaped) valves to allow the entry and exhaust of gases, the Knight engine (developed by Chicago newspaper man and mechanic Charles Y. Knight) used sliding sleeves to move up and down between the piston and the cylinder wall on a film of oil, allowing the intake of gases to take place through small port openings. With no poppet valves, springs, or camshaft, the Knight sleeve-valve engine was much quieter than conventional engines and was dubbed the "Silent Knight." The engine's disadvantages were slow acceleration, difficult starting, a high consumption of oil, and oily exhaust smoke. With the adoption of this engine in the 1911 models, the Stearns car became officially known as the Stearns-Knight. In 1912 the company produced 875 cars and also adopted an electrical starting system.

In 1915 Stearns introduced two notable additions to his product line. One was the L-4, a car he had been developing for three years; this was aimed at less affluent Americans, a spectrum of the public that entered the car market with the introduction of the Model T Ford in 1908. (Up to this time Stearns cars had been relatively expensive, selling at $3,000 or more.) The L-4 was designed as a low-priced quality car, its five-passenger touring version selling for $1,750. The car met with an enthusiastic reception and the Stearns company built a five-story addition to its plant to accommodate the demand for the car. In 1915 Stearns also introduced a five-ton truck, which was the first American-made truck to use the Knight sleeve-valve engine.

The years 1916 and 1917 represented the pinnacle of the Stearns company's production; it turned out 3,000 and 4,000 cars, respectively. But at the end of 1917, Stearns—only thirty-seven years old—announced his resignation from the company, partly because of a dispute over engineering policies, and partly because he wanted to conduct his own research. During Stearns's tenure at the helm, the company had produced a total of 10,000 cars. The company was reorganized and in 1918 annual production fell to 1,450 cars because of other production priorities during World War I. The company continued to manufacture Stearns-Knight cars but never again reached its prewar production. In 1925 John Willys, head of Willys-Overland of Toledo, Ohio (the only other major American auto manufacturer to use the Knight sleeve-valve engine), bought out the F. B. Stearns Company. The company struggled for the balance of the decade and ultimately fell victim to the Great Depression, ceasing production after December 1929 when stockholders dissolved the company. To the end the company stuck with the Knight engine, using it in the final production model. His company was gone but Stearns had established himself as a pioneer in Ohio's auto industry, and his car had a secure place as one of the highest quality cars of the first quarter-century of the American auto industry.

Even after leaving his corporation Stearns continued to serve as a consultant, but he devoted most of his time to a diesel engine that he had designed, tinkering with and making improvements on it in the machine shop at his home in Shaker Heights, Ohio, a suburb of Cleveland. He subsequently moved to a large estate in Chesterland (a suburb east of Cleveland) that he called "Stearnsington." He eventually obtained sixteen patents for his diesel engine and in 1935 sold it to the U.S. Navy. On the ample tract of land at his home, Stearns also engaged in organic farming and conducted soil and plant experiments. Stearns died at the University Hospital in Cleveland.

• Exhibits of Stearns cars and information on his work can be found at the Franklin Crawford Auto-Aviation Museum in Cleveland, Ohio. The National Automobile History Collection of the Detroit Public Library maintains a small file on Stearns. The Western Reserve Historical Society of Cleveland owns a Stearns diary from 1915. The most informative account of the Stearns auto company is Richard Wager, *Golden Wheels: The Story of the Automobiles Made in Cleveland and Northeastern Ohio, 1892–1932*, 2d ed. (1986). Obituaries are in the *Cleveland Plain-Dealer* and the *Cleveland Press*, both 6 July 1955, and the *New York Times*, 7 July 1955.

YANEK MIECZKOWSKI

STEARNS, George Luther (8 Jan. 1809–9 Apr. 1867), manufacturer and abolitionist, was born in Medford, outside of Boston, Massachusetts, the son of Luther Stearns, a physician, and Mary Hall. Stearns's formal education ended after his father's death in 1820. At the age of fifteen he moved to Brattleboro, Vermont, and worked for more than three years as a clerk in a relative's store. In 1827 he returned to Boston and found employment as a clerk in a ship chandlery firm. In this business Stearns learned the importance of reliable sources of supply, and in 1835, with financial support from his mother and his future father-in-law, he acted on his knowledge to establish himself in Medford as a manufacturer of linseed oil. Six years later Stearns entered into a partnership to purchase a patent for an improved method of manufacturing lead pipe. The pipe business produced a sizable fortune for Stearns, and he would draw from it liberally to support his reform interests.

A prominent member of the Medford Unitarian Church, Stearns was married twice. His first wife, Mary Ann Train, died in 1840, four years after they had wed. They had no children. In 1843 he married Mary Elizabeth Preston, a niece of the abolitionist (and close family friend) Lydia Maria Child; the couple had three children.

In the political struggle against slavery, Stearns took his stand with the Conscience Whigs and supported antislavery third-party candidates. He supported the Liberty party candidate James G. Birney in the presidential election of 1840 and provided substantial financial support for the Free Soil party campaign of 1848. A leading supporter of the antislavery coalition that resulted from this campaign, Stearns offered financial backing that helped to send Charles Sumner and, later, Henry Wilson to the U.S. Senate. In 1858 Stearns was invited to join the "Bird Club," an informal group of antislavery political activists assembled by the wealthy paper manufacturer Francis W. Bird. The group dined together regularly (on at least one occasion with John Brown) and played a central role in the formation of the Massachusetts Republican party. One of the club's members, John A. Andrew, served as the state's wartime governor.

By 1856 Stearns was deeply involved in the antislavery struggle in Kansas. As chair of the Kansas Committee of Massachusetts, Stearns raised money (much of it his own) to purchase Sharpe's rifles and other supplies to support the free state settlers in their fight against proslavery Missourians and a federally supported proslavery territorial government at Lecompton, Kansas. Deeply impressed with John Brown's call for retributive justice, Stearns became an important financial backer of the guerrilla chieftain in Kansas and joined the "Secret Six" in supporting and financing Brown's plans to extend his antislavery guerrilla war into Virginia.

After Brown's raid on the federal arsenal at Harpers Ferry, Stearns and a fellow conspirator, Samuel Gridley Howe, fled briefly to Montreal. But Stearns returned to defend his actions before a Senate committee investigating the role of "subversive organizations." He admitted that he supported Brown's efforts to "go into Virginia or some other state and relieve slaves," but he denied any knowledge of plans to commit treason against the United States. The committee uncovered no evidence to indicate that Stearns or anyone else outside Brown's raiding party had such knowledge.

During these years, Stearns entertained frequently at his Medford home. His regular dinner guests included luminaries of New England's reform culture such as Ralph Waldo Emerson, John Greenleaf Whittier, Wendell Phillips, Charles Sumner, Lydia Maria Child, Lucretia Mott, and Moncure Conway, a convert from Virginia who edited the *Commonwealth*, an antislavery newspaper financed by Stearns and his friends.

With the outbreak of the Civil War, Stearns joined in the abolitionist demand for emancipation as a federal war aim. He also agitated for the enrollment of black soldiers, and he actively recruited blacks in New York and Ohio to help fill the ranks of the country's first black military units, the Fifty-fourth and Fifty-fifth Massachusetts regiments. Stearns's recruitment of black troops soon became national in scope. Commissioned a major in the U.S. Army in June 1863, Stearns established a recruiting network headquartered first in Philadelphia and subsequently in Louisville, Kentucky, and Nashville, Tennessee.

Stearns opposed the Radical Republican challenge to Abraham Lincoln in 1864. But he found the president unyielding in his opposition to radical reform, and he predicted hopefully to Wendell Phillips in September 1864 that Lincoln's "party will fall to pieces as soon as the spoils are distributed—that will be our harvest." The harvest never came. Stearns's protests against the prejudicial and even brutal treatment of black troops and his demands for the creation of a black army commanded by an abolitionist general generated disagreements with Secretary of War Edwin Stanton that prompted Stearns's resignation in January 1865.

At the close of the war Stearns joined with J. Miller McKim and Charles Eliot Norton to establish the *Nation*. It was to be "a weekly newspaper," announced Stearns, "to advocate advanced opinions." Stearns, the single largest financial contributor to the new publication, initially supported E. L. Godkin as its editor. But Godkin's conservative views on black rights and on Reconstruction prompted Stearns to withdraw his financial support. In November 1865 he launched a rival weekly publication, the *Right Way*, and distributed more than 30,000 copies free of charge to support Negro suffrage and Radical Republican Reconstruction policies.

Although never a student of political economy, Stearns took a keen interest in currency and banking issues during the war. In 1864 he published a pamphlet warning against the dangers of speculation that he thought were inherent in the National Bank Act (1863). While headquartered in Philadelphia to recruit black troops, Stearns joined the weekly discussions of financial and political matters led by the influential political economist Henry C. Carey. At the close of the war Stearns warned against a sudden return to the gold standard and a rapid contraction of the currency. Stearns's financial affairs suffered badly after the war as the price of lead dropped precipitously. In March 1867, as his business declined further, the *Right Way* ceased publication. Frustrated by the need to retrench, Stearns died of pneumonia in New York City trying to stave off financial collapse. He did not live to see his goal of universal suffrage constitutionally secured.

• The George L. Stearns Papers, Kansas State Historical Society, Topeka, relate to the free state movement. See *U.S. Senate Committee Reports*, vol. 2 (1859–1860), pp. 1–25, for Stearns's role in the John Brown conspiracy. On wartime finance, see his *A Few Facts Pertaining to Currency and Banking, Adapted to the Present Position of Our Finances* (1864). On the recruitment of black troops, see Stearns's testimony before the American Freedmen's Inquiry Commission, RG 94, National Archives, Washington, D.C. A number of manuscript collections contain letters written by Stearns. See particularly the Charles Sumner Papers and the Wendell Phillips Papers, Houghton Library, Harvard University, Cambridge, Mass. Stearns's first biographer was the younger of his two sons, Frank Preston Stearns, *Life and Public Services of George Luther Stearns* (1907; repr. 1969); a modern biography, Charles E. Heller, *Portrait of an Abolitionist: A Biography of George Luther Stearns, 1809–1867* (1996), draws together much of Stearns's scattered correspondence. Stearns's efforts to destroy slavery and secure equal rights are treated in James M. McPherson, *The Struggle for Equality: Abolitionists and the Negro in the Civil War and Reconstruction* (1964), pp. 208–10 and passim; Stephen B. Oates, *To Purge this Land with Blood: A Biography of John Brown* (1970), pp. 232–34 and passim; William M. Armstrong, *E. L. Godkin: A Biography* (1978), pp. 76–91; and Richard H. Abbott, *Cotton and Capital: Boston Businessmen and Antislavery Reform, 1854–1868* (1991), pp. 119–23, 131–32, and passim.

LOUIS S. GERTEIS

STEARNS, Lewis French (10 Mar. 1847–9 Feb. 1892), theologian, was born in Newburyport, Massachusetts, to Jonathan French Stearns, a Presbyterian minister, and Anna S. Prentiss. After graduating in 1867 from the College of New Jersey (now Princeton University),

where his father was a member of the board of trustees, Stearns attended Columbia Law School for more than a year. Sensing a divine call to the ministry, he enrolled in Princeton Theological Seminary in 1869. At the time, Princeton was the leading seminary of Old School Presbyterianism, which taught a strict allegiance to the denomination's standards, the Westminster Confession of Faith. After studying at the Universities of Berlin and Leipzig in the 1870–1871 academic year, he returned to the United States and completed his preparation for the ministry at Union Theological Seminary in New York City. Though no less orthodox at that time, Union Seminary was nonetheless the center of New School Presbyterianism, which took a more liberal attitude toward subscription to the Westminster standards. Graduating in 1872, Stearns was ordained as pastor of a Presbyterian church in Norwood, New Jersey, the following year. In 1876 he became the professor of history and belles-lettres at Albion College in Michigan but was forced to resign in 1879 because of an eye illness. Troubled by the incompatibility of both Old and New School Calvinism to current trends in thought, Stearns found opportunity during his year of recuperation for theological reflection that led him away from traditional nineteenth-century orthodoxy. In 1882 he married Elizabeth Mann Benson; the number of their children, if any, is unknown.

Despite the protests of his father about his lack of spiritual and intellectual qualifications, Stearns had accepted a position as a professor of systematic divinity at Bangor Theological Seminary in Bangor, Maine, in 1880 and became a minister in the Congregational church. In his inaugural address, Stearns expressed his hope for reformulating the Protestant faith in accord with an emerging theological modernism, according to which theology should adapt itself to the spirit of the times. Stearns proposed a new christological starting point for theology. In the tradition of Reformed theology, most notably the Westminster Confession of Faith, the transcendence and immutable decrees of God shaped the entire theology. Stearns proposed the person of Jesus Christ as a more suitable theological starting point. In part, this proposal expanded the ideas of Henry Boynton Smith, the New School Presbyterian theologian with whom Stearns had studied at Union Seminary, but it also expounded the humanity of Jesus in a new way. Though he was careful not to deny the divinity of Christ, Stearns underscored the humanity of Jesus as the Christ, or the one in whom God dwelt. By making this shift Stearns, like other Protestant modernists, embraced the romantic theological tradition begun by Friedrich Schleiermacher as well as the philosophical idealism upon which it was grounded. Arguing against any sharp distinction between the secular and the sacred, advocates of this New Theology stressed divine immanence in history, humanity, and nature. They sought a theology that was not only compatible with modern science but was also impervious to scientific criticism. Stearns's articles in the *Andover Review*, the leading journal of what was called Progressive Orthodoxy, helped to shape the new theological movement. He publicized his ideas on an international stage as well in his lecture on theological trends within American Congregationalism, delivered at the International Congregational Council in London in 1891.

Despite an array of heresy trials, proponents of the New Theology after 1890 continued to reformulate the traditional faith while also defending the uniqueness of Christianity. Stearns contributed importantly to both endeavors. In 1890 he gave the prestigious Ely Lectures at Union Seminary in New York, later published as *The Evidence of Christian Experience* (1890), which as one colleague commented, earned Stearns "a wide and high reputation as a theologian" (*Andover Review*, p. 307). Stearns proposed that the truthfulness of Christianity could be defended, not by appeals to miracles or fulfilled prophecy, as in older orthodoxy, but by a new understanding of the doctrine of the atonement. Drawing from both H. R. Frank and Isaak A. Dorner, with whom he had studied at Berlin, Stearns grounded his new apologetic in the Christian experience of God's redemptive work through the crucifixion. This religious experience, which is above scientific examination, he argued, "presupposes . . . the great principles of that theistic philosophy which grows out of the common religious and moral experience of men." That same year, the trustees of Union Seminary unanimously elected Stearns to be W. G. T. Shedd's successor as professor of systematic theology. At the time, Union Seminary and the northern Presbyterian church were locked in a debate over proposals to revise the Westminster Confession of Faith or to replace it with a new confession. Although he shared Union Seminary's new commitment to modernism, Stearns declined the invitation because he could not conscientiously subscribe to the Westminster standards, as was then still required of all faculty members. He believed that the Westminster Confession wrongly placed salvation within the reach of only a part of humanity. Stearns's posthumous publication *Present-Day Theology* (1893) surveyed the major topics of the New Theology. After a brief, unknown illness, Stearns died in Bangor, Maine.

While the rise of historicism and Darwinism led many Protestants to reject traditional Christianity, Stearns sought to conform Protestant theology to modern thought. His contributions to modernist theology, though eventually eclipsed by both neo-orthodoxy and a resurgent evangelicalism, stood as a bulwark against agnosticism for many late nineteenth- and early twentieth-century Protestants.

• George L. Prentiss, "Biographical Sketch," in Lewis French Stearns, *Present-Day Theology* (1893), and "Lewis French Stearns," *Andover Review* 17 (1892): 307–8, provide the best, albeit brief, introductions to Stearns's life and thought. See also Daniel Day Williams, *The Andover Liberals* (1941), and William R. Hutchison, *The Modernist Impulse in American Protestantism* (1976), the latter on Stearns's theology and role within the modernist movement.

P. C. KEMENY

STEARNS, Lutie Eugenia (13 Sept. 1866–25 Dec. 1943), librarian and lecturer, was born in Stoughton, Massachusetts, the daughter of Isaac Holden Stearns, a doctor, and Catherine Guild. She was the youngest of eleven children. The family moved to Wisconsin in 1871, when her father became the superintendent of the Soldiers' Home in Wauwatosa, near Milwaukee, where he worked for five years, leaving to take up general practice in 1876 in Milwaukee. He later abandoned the family, divorced his wife, and returned to Massachusetts. Stearns attended Milwaukee State Normal School for two years, completed her training in 1886 (records of University of Wisconsin-Milwaukee suggest 1887), and taught fourth grade for two years in the Milwaukee public schools, working with the children of German immigrants. Dismayed by her students' lack of exposure to American culture and appalled by the lack of reading material available in her school, she remedied the situation by borrowing books from the Milwaukee Public Library. In 1888, during an era when librarians often perceived themselves as social reformers, she became head of the Circulation Department at the library and worked vigorously to increase circulation by outreach to schools, gradually boosting school circulation to 98,000 per year in 1894.

Stearns was active in the Wisconsin Library Association, which she served as secretary-treasurer in 1891, and in the American Library Association (ALA). She attended the ALA Conference of 1894 at Lake Placid, where she learned of the accomplishments of state library commissions in establishing both traveling libraries and free public libraries. Having collected copies of the legislation that established such commissions in Massachusetts and New Hampshire, she returned to Wisconsin and, with the assistance of Frank Hutchins, a founder of the Wisconsin Library Association, and state senator James H. Stout, began pressing for the establishment of the Wisconsin Free Library Commission. Supporting legislation was passed in 1895, and she was appointed the commission's secretary. Following a reorganization of the commission in 1897, Hutchins became its secretary and Stearns its first paid staff member. She threw herself with gusto into the work of developing libraries and library service in the small towns of Wisconsin, wearing out five fur coats in her travels over the next seventeen years. A lively and charismatic speaker, despite a serious stammer, Stearns traveled from one small town to another, drumming up interest in the establishment of local libraries. She organized a traveling library system, which sent collections of thirty to one hundred books to post offices or stores in towns too small to sustain their own libraries. Larger towns received advice and support in opening free public libraries. To assist local boards and librarians, Stearns wrote a manual, *Essentials in Library Administration* (1905), describing the process of building a library, arranging the collection, and selecting a librarian: "Save money in other ways, but never by employing a forceless man or woman as librarian."

In 1903 Stearns became the head of the Department of Traveling Libraries, but as Wisconsin's towns grew, the need for traveling libraries declined, and her position became increasingly routine. In 1914, following a serious illness succeeded by a nervous breakdown after the death of her mother and a sister, she resigned to begin work on the lecture circuit, speaking in thirty-eight states over the next eighteen years on peace, prohibition, women's rights, industrial reform, the League of Nations, and education. She campaigned vigorously for the Eighteenth Amendment and, always a feminist, traveled through Iowa, Missouri, Texas, and Wisconsin, advocating passage of the Nineteenth Amendment. Her activities included founding work in the Wisconsin Federation of Women's Clubs and membership in both the General Federation of Women's Clubs and the Women's International League for Peace and Freedom. Stearns was appointed a local regent for the State Normal School Board of Regents (1922–1927) and worked to expand the two-year course in normal schools to a four-year, degree-granting program. In 1928 she traveled to Europe with the American Seminar for International Relations and was present, in what she described as "the most momentous occasion of my life," at the signing of the Kellogg-Briand Pact. The depression ended her ability to make a living from her speaking engagements, and Stearns began to write a regular column, "As a Woman Sees It," in the *Milwaukee Journal*. From 1932 to 1935 her editors gave her "free rein, although I am a Dry, a Pacifist, and an Independent in politics." Ill health, rather than a dearth of opinions, led to her retirement in 1935. She died of cancer in Milwaukee, never having married.

Stearns was an idealist, though reality did not usually live up to her expectations, and her commentary often was tempered by a lively sense of humor. After women won the vote, she complained that they inherited their politics along with their religion and frequently voted "without knowing a plank in a platform from a planked whitefish" (*Wisconsin Magazine of History* [Summer 1959], p. 283). She observed that the General Federation of Women's Clubs failed to accomplish substantial goals because it assumed that the mere passage of a resolution would solve a problem. In an article in *Library Journal* titled "Tomorrow Is Just Another Day," she severely criticized the technical focus of training for librarianship: "The emphasis has always been laid largely on the technique of library administration—on the delicate and discriminating matters of classification and cataloging and . . . why *Tom Sawyer* should be and *Huckleberry Finn* should not be read by growing lads and how to find the name of Fannie Hurst's husband—as if even Fannie cared" (1 Nov. 1931, p. 894). The American public had been patient and accepting, but, she warned, "even a worm finally turns to save itself from death and some day the citizens are going to rise up and take the library situation into their own hands." She predicted that librarians would emerge from their hermitages and take on

their proper role of energetic outreach, education, and social reform.

• Stearns's professional publications include *The Child and the Small Library* (1898) and *Books of Interest and Consolation to Spinsters* (1904). The most complete biographic source is an autobiographical series, "My Seventy-five Years," *Wisconsin Magazine of History* 42 (Spring 1959): 211–18, (Summer 1959): 282–87, and 43 (Winter 1959–1960): 97–105. See also Earl Tannenbaum, "The Library Career of Lutie Eugenia Stearns," *Wisconsin Magazine of History* 39 (Spring 1956): 159–65; and "Lutie Stearns," *Wisconsin Clubwoman* (May/June 1940): 13, 33.

JODY L. CALDWELL

STEARNS, Marshall Winslow (18 Oct. 1908–18 Dec. 1966), jazz scholar and professor of English, was born in Cambridge, Massachusetts, the son of Harry Ney Stearns and Edith Winslow, occupations unknown. His father bought Stearns a set of drums when he was thirteen. After playing drums, guitar, and saxophone in the Cambridge area, he left aside performance to study at Harvard University (B.A., 1931) and Harvard Law School (1932–1934). Bored with the law, he instead took up medieval literature at Yale University, eventually earning a Ph.D. (1942) and serving a series of appointments on the English faculties of the University of Hawaii (1939–1941), Indiana University (1942–1946), Cornell University (1946–1949), New York University (1950–1951), and Hunter College, where he settled as a professor in 1951. His *Robert Henryson: A Biographical Study of the Fifteenth Century Scottish Poet* (1949) was not replaced as the standard work on the poet until after Stearns's death.

A still more illustrious second career had gotten underway during his years as a graduate student in English. He helped form the United Hot Clubs of America, a jazz appreciation society modeled along the lines of the Hot Club de France. His "Swing Stuff" was the first regular jazz-oriented column in *Variety*. Later he wrote a monthly column for *Saturday Review*, contributed to *Down Beat, Record Changer, Esquire, Harper's*, and *Life*, and edited articles on jazz for *Musical America*.

He won a Guggenheim Music Fellowship (1950–1951) and then a grant from the Ford Foundation (1951) to develop a basic course in jazz, first at NYU and then at Hunter. Through his tireless energy, his charming personality, and his extraordinary ability to funnel resources into a historically undersupported field, he founded the Institute of Jazz Studies at Hunter (1952) and served as its first director. Under its auspices he joined the music faculty at the New School for Social Research and, beginning in 1954, offered the first graduate course in jazz. The institute was transferred after Stearns's death to Rutgers, the State University of New Jersey. Now located on its Newark campus, it has become the foremost jazz archive in the world.

Stearns's work as a jazz writer, teacher, researcher, and archivist led to the publication of *The Story of Jazz* (1956). Despite subsequent developments in jazz style and jazz research, it was unsurpassed in its balanced and sensible presentation of the music's prehistory, history, social setting, musical elements, and international dissemination and remained the most widely used textbook in the field for about three decades. Also in 1956 an appointment as a special consultant to the State Department enabled him to tour the Near East with Dizzy Gillespie's big band. In 1958 he coordinated jazz events at the Brussels Exhibition and served as an adviser to the educational television series "The Subject Is Jazz." He taught at the School of Jazz in Lenox, Massachusetts, around 1958–1959.

Stearns had a daughter, Elizabeth Dixon, through a first marriage that ended in divorce. The name of his first wife and the date of their marriage are unknown. With his second wife, Jean Barnett, whom he married in 1959, he embarked on a third career in jazz dance (which had much more to do with American popular music than with jazz). Together with professional dancers, they gave entertaining demonstrations to enthusiasts. Eventually Marshall and Jean Stearns collaborated on a book that established a new field for scholarly study, *Jazz Dance: The Story of American Vernacular Dance* (1967). Using a comprehensive approach that wove together historical, biographical, and sociocultural commentary, while also offering technical description of dance steps, the authors traced jazz dance from its late nineteenth-century origins (in, for example, the cakewalk), to its decades of great popularity (manifested, for example, in national crazes for the foxtrot, the charleston, and the jitterbug), through to the gradual disappearance, during the 1950s and 1960s, of the art of tap dancing. *Jazz Dance* was published after Stearns's death from a heart attack in Key West, Florida, where he had been on leave from Hunter as a visiting lecturer at Key West Junior College.

• Stearns's career is summarized in obituaries: *New York Times*, 19 Dec. 1966; *Journal of American Folklore* 80 (1967): 300, by John F. Szwed, who gives a needlessly exaggerated and snobbish assessment of Stearns's place in jazz literature; and *Journal of Jazz Studies* 1, no. 1 (1973): 82–83, by J. R. Taylor, who gives a useful bibliography. This last journal also includes a fond and comparatively detailed portrait. See Robert Reisner, "Reminiscences of Marshall Stearns," *Journal of Jazz Studies* 1, no. 1 (1973): 84–89. A biographical essay by Richard Gehman appeared in *This Week* (July 1954); excerpts are in Eddie Condon and Gehman, eds., *Eddie Condon's Treasury of Jazz* (1957), pp. 205–8.

BARRY KERNFELD

STEARNS, Oliver (3 June 1807–18 July 1885), Unitarian clergyman and educator, was born in Lunenburg, Massachusetts, the son of Priscilla Cushing and Thomas Stearns, farmers. As a boy Stearns supplemented his lessons at district schools by reading privately with a local parson. In 1822 he entered Harvard College at the age of fifteen, a normal practice of the time and not necessarily a sign of extraordinary intellectual capacity. Still, he ranked second in his class and was invited to address the class of 1826 at its graduation ceremony. The following year he worked at a

private school in Jamaica Plain, but, under the genial influence of clergyman William E. Channing, he returned to Harvard in order to prepare for the ministry. While reading theology at the Divinity School he also tutored undergraduates in mathematics at the college. In 1830 Stearns graduated from seminary, was ordained, and became minister of the Second Congregational Society in Northampton, Massachusetts. Two years later he married Mary Blood, and the couple had eight children.

In 1830 Congregationalism was still officially supported by state law, but various churches had separated into conservative (Trinitarian) and liberal (Unitarian) factions while sharing the same denominational designation. Stearns identified with Unitarian institutions and training, embodying standard features of that orientation such as progressive religious thought and moral activism. He was a successful pastor in his first church until the spring of 1839 when poor health forced him to resign. Convalescing for a year rectified the situation, and in 1840 he accepted the invitation of the Third Congregational Society of Hingham, Massachusetts, to serve as its minister. There Stearns gradually acquired notice as a luminary in the pulpit, attracting attention for studious habits and thoughtful sermons that were full of erudition and earnest exhortation. Most of all, though, the preacher riveted audiences with his fiery opposition to slavery. Sometimes offended listeners would walk out of services, but Stearns refused to moderate his denunciations of the social and moral evil in deference to some people's tastes. One sermon of this sort, "The Gospel Applied to the Fugitive Slave Law," published in 1851, was one of the few pieces of his to appear in print.

In addition to concern for ethical standards and social practices Stearns was also interested in more general questions of intellectual development, probing in his sermons topics such as *Knowledge: Its Relation to the Progress of Mankind*, published as a pamphlet in 1852. Deliberations of that nature contributed to his being named in 1856 president of Meadville Theological School in Meadville, Pennsylvania. After acquitting himself well in that Unitarian academy he returned to Harvard Divinity School in 1863 to assume a professorship of pulpit eloquence and pastoral care. He also lectured regularly on the history of religious thought, instructing successive generations of ministerial candidates in his views regarding liberal thinking and moral progress. In 1870 Stearns became Parkman Professor of Theology, a post from which he taught systematics and ethics until his retirement in 1878. During those years he also served as dean of the Divinity School, and in this capacity he cooperated with president Charles W. Eliot in modernizing educational techniques at the nation's premier university. After almost four decades of marriage, his wife died in 1871, and Stearns married Augusta Hannah Cary Bailey the next year. They did not have children.

Stearns did not publish much, writing only a few articles for religious magazines. But he is credited with reaching an accommodating position between classical

Unitarian emphases and Transcendentalist tendencies, which appeared a generation later. As shown in essays such as "The Aim and Hope of Jesus," published in *Christianity and Modern Thought* (1872), it is clear that he based his reconciling views on an evolutionary model. He saw the historical development of Christian thought as the progressive movement of divine influence expressed in human experience. Stearns held that there was more to history than human processes; God's presence was manifest there too, for those discerning enough to perceive it. New experiences and expressions naturally created theological diversification, but they also drew strength from a single, holy inspiration and moved toward eventual harmony. As lecturer and occasional essayist he thus assured those in his denomination that there was room for Channing's dependence on biblical revelation and at the same time no real danger in Ralph Waldo Emerson's preference for the spiritual initiatives of private intuition. Many appreciated his perspective because it helped them reconcile an increasingly complex array of theological views during the latter half of the nineteenth century. Living in retirement for seven years Stearns died in Cambridge, Massachusetts.

• For additional information on Stearns's life and career, see A. S. Van Wagenen, *Genealogy and Memoirs of Isaac Stearns and His Descendants* (1901), A. D. Peabody, *Harvard Reminiscences* (1888), and S. A. Eliot, *Heralds of a Liberal Faith* (1910). Obituaries and related tributes are in the *Boston Transcript*, 20 and 22 July 1885.

HENRY WARNER BOWDEN

STEARNS, Robert Edwards Carter (1 Feb. 1827–27 July 1909), conchologist, was born in Boston, Massachusetts, the son of Charles Stearns, a bank clerk, and Sarah Carter. Stearns developed a love of natural history during his youth, an interest he shared with his father. After attending the Fort-hill School in Boston, he received mercantile training and followed in his father's footsteps.

For the first thirty years of his career, Stearns was employed in a variety of commercial, clerical, and farming enterprises. He was first employed as a bank clerk in Boston, but tiring of that work, in 1848 he painted and exhibited a 900′ by 8′ panorama of the Hudson River from the mouth of the Mohawk to Fort William. After his marriage in 1850 to his childhood friend Mary Ann Libby, he was employed by a Boston firm to evaluate the quality of coal and the ease of mining it in southern Indiana. He then served as a bookkeeper for a Boston firm until 1854, when he was appointed paymaster and general clerk for several Boston firms with copper-mining operations at Keeweenaw Point, Lake Superior, Michigan. He then returned to the Northeast, purchasing a farm in Dover, Massachusetts. He had learned about farming from his paternal uncle and maintained a lifelong interest in horticulture. However, he lost his assets in the crash of 1857 and, in 1858, left for San Francisco to join the

printing firm of Towne and Bacon, owned by his wife's relatives.

As acting editor of the *Pacific*, a Protestant weekly printed by that firm, he took a strong pro-Union position and became active in Republican politics in the years leading up to the Civil War. He is credited by historians with contributing substantially to the nonsecessionist movement in California through his role in the party and as editor of the *Pacific*. Based on these political activities, he served as deputy clerk for the California Supreme Court in 1862–1863 and as secretary to the California State Board of Harbor Commissioners from 1863 to 1868. Of delicate health since childhood, Stearns was forced to resign his position and return east for a rest in 1868.

From 1864 on Stearns had pursued his childhood love of natural history through affiliation with the California Academy of Sciences, located in San Francisco. He specialized in conchology, that is, the study of shells, and published his first scientific paper in the academy *Proceedings* in 1866. He served as the academy's vice president in 1866–1867 and was director of its museum in 1868, the year it suffered severe damage in an earthquake. Stearns staunchly supported efforts to rebuild, serving on the board of trustees from 1873 to 1885 and as corresponding secretary in 1874.

While on the East Coast in 1868–1869, he organized a natural history collecting expedition for the Smithsonian Institution to southwest Florida with Dr. William Stimpson and Colonel Ezekiel Jewett. After another brief stint at farming in Vineland, New Jersey, in 1870 Stearns returned to California, first to a farm in Sonoma County and then to San Francisco. He moved to Berkeley in 1874 when he was elected secretary of the University of California. In this capacity, he served as business executive under President Daniel Coit Gilman and, using his horticultural expertise, developed the grounds on the Berkeley campus. He also published a variety of papers on horticulture and gardening in California journals.

After his wife's death in 1879, Stearns's health deteriorated, and he resigned his university position in 1882. In recognition of his contributions to the university and the California Academy, he was awarded an honorary doctor of philosophy. Stearns then turned to his interests in science full time. In 1882 he conducted research in the Puget Sound region for the U.S. Fish Commission. In 1884 he moved to Washington, D.C., and was appointed assistant curator of the Department of Mollusks, U.S. National Museum (USNM), by Spencer F. Baird and paleontologist at the U.S. Geological Survey by Colonel John Wesley Powell. As assistant curator, Stearns oversaw the acquisition, arrangement, and description of the national collection of shells as well as the Smithsonian's publication of scientific papers on mollusks. The large shell collection that he amassed through fieldwork on the East Coast was purchased by the USNM and is listed as a "collection of scientific importance" in S. P. Dance's *History of Shell Collecting* (1986). While on the West Coast, Stearns published numerous descriptions of local recent and fossil mollusks in the *Proceedings of the California Academy of Sciences*. During his USNM tenure he continued to write on the systematics, variation, and geographic distribution of recent and fossil mollusks, especially of the Pacific Coast and Florida. He left a bibliography of some 156 scientific papers. In addition to his taxonomic studies, he wrote poems on natural history topics, a number of ethnological papers on the uses of shells in various cultures, and popular articles on shell collecting.

After retiring in 1892, Stearns was appointed an honorary associate of the National Museum. In 1895 he once again headed west, settling in Los Angeles with his only child, a daughter, for the remainder of his life. Despite the loss of most of his library in a fire, he continued his conchological studies and writing. He died in Los Angeles. Colleagues recalled Stearns as a hard worker with a lively sense of humor but subject to bouts of depression. His careers in politics and science allowed him to pursue his two favorite activities of "cussing and discussing." Ill health, from childhood on, motivated many of his career changes and moves to more congenial climates. An accomplished naturalist, his legacy resides largely in his shell collection and corpus of writings on the systematics, variation, and distribution of almost every group of mollusks.

• The Robert Edwards Carter Stearns Papers in the Smithsonian Archives contain correspondence documenting his conchological work, scrapbooks, and several autobiographical essays. Information about Stearns can also be found in official records and oral history interviews of S. Stillman Berry. At the archives of the Academy of Natural Sciences of Philadelphia, the Stearns papers consist of a small collection of letters and a poem; additional letters from Stearns can be found in other collections. *Smithsonian Miscellaneous Collections* 56, no. 18 (1911): 1–15, contains a bibliography of his scientific writings prepared by his daughter, Mary R. Stearns. Her privately printed obituary, "Robert Edwards Carter Stearns, 1827–1909," can be located at the California Academy of Sciences and Smithsonian's William Healey Dall Library. Dance's *History of Shell Collecting* does not address Stearns's work directly but is useful for placing his scientific career in context. An obituary is in the *Los Angeles Daily Times*, 29 July 1909. His colleague William H. Dall wrote obituaries in *Science* 30 (1909): 279–80 and *Nautilus* 23 (1909): 70–72.

PAMELA M. HENSON

STEARNS, Shubal (28 Jan. 1706–20 Nov. 1771), clergyman and evangelist, was born in Boston, Massachusetts, the son of Shubal Stearns and Rebecca Lairabee (or Lariby, or Larrabee). Stearns received little education, but he read widely. His family moved to Tolland, Connecticut, in 1715 and joined the local Congregational church. In 1727 Stearns married Sarah Johnson; they had no children. In 1745 Stearns heard George Whitefield preach. He adopted New Light views and urged his fellow believers in the Tolland church to form their own New Light congregation. Stearns pastored the church, which grew in size over the years. However, in 1751 the congregation was disrupted by an argument over the practice of infant baptism. Wait

Palmer, a Baptist preacher, convinced Stearns that the Bible taught that only adult believers could be baptized. Palmer soon baptized Stearns, who quickly organized a Separate Baptist church in Tolland. On 20 May 1751 Palmer and Joshua Morse ordained Stearns to the Baptist ministry, and he officially became pastor of the Tolland congregation, where he served until 1754.

By 1754 Stearns had become convinced that he was called to be an evangelist in the western part of the colonies. He and his family moved to Cacapon, Virginia, near present-day Winchester, along with the family of Daniel Marshall, Stearns's brother-in-law. They worked in western Virginia for a year but did not meet with great success. Feeling that he still was not where God intended for him to be, Stearns began to look for a new place of endeavor.

In November 1755 Stearns and Marshall and their families moved 200 miles south to the northern part of North Carolina, settling at Sandy Creek in Guilford County (present-day Randolph County). They organized the Sandy Creek Baptist Church with sixteen members, the first Separate Baptist congregation established in North Carolina. Stearns served as pastor with Marshall and Joseph Breed as assistants.

Stearns relocated to North Carolina because friends told him that people in the Piedmont region of the colony longed to hear the gospel preached. He found this report to be true, and his efforts produced an almost immediate response. Both Stearns and Marshall made preaching tours throughout the colony, seeking converts and organizing new churches. Within three years they founded two more churches, Abbott's Creek and Deep River, with over 900 members in their three churches. By the time of Stearns's death, Sandy Creek Church had produced forty-two churches and 125 ministers.

Because of the phenomenal growth among the Separate Baptists in the area, Stearns sought to organize their efforts in a more formal manner. In 1758 he led in the organization of the Sandy Creek Baptist Association. The first meeting, held in 1760, promoted cooperation and fellowship among the Separate Baptist churches in North Carolina and Virginia. The primary focus of the association was to appoint preachers to send out on mission efforts in other parts of the colonies. This association, the third oldest such organization in the United States and the first in the South, led the way in encouraging Baptist churches to pool their resources in evangelistic efforts.

After Stearns's death in Sandy Creek, North Carolina, the Sandy Creek Association and church declined. Although Stearns's death was the major blow, the church was also hurt by the scattering of the population in the area following the defeat of the Regulators at the battle of Alamance in 1770. Had Stearns lived, he probably would have been able to rebuild the church, but no one else had his ability and charisma.

Besides his strong position on believer's baptism, Stearns also emphasized the importance of living a Christian lifestyle and the need for a fellowship restricted only to like-minded believers. Combining a strong Calvinism with a fervent evangelicalism, he was well known for his animated and emotional preaching. Although short in stature, Stearns had a forceful personality. Some ranked him as second only to Whitefield in effectiveness. His preaching and that of other ministers inspired by him reached from Virginia through the Carolinas to Georgia. His emphasis on both Calvinism and evangelism helped pave the way for the union of the regular and Separate Baptists in the United States.

• For discussions of Stearns and his work, see Robert Baylor Semple, *A History of the Rise and Progress of the Baptists in Virginia* (1810); George Washington Paschal, ed., "Morgan Edwards' Materials towards a History of the Baptists in the Province of North Carolina," *North Carolina Historical Review* 7 (1930): 365–99; Paschal, *A History of North Carolina Baptists* (2 vols., 1930, 1955); David Benedict, *A General History of the Baptist Denomination in America and Other Parts of the World* (2 vols., 1813).

CAROL SUE HUMPHREY

STEBBINS, Genevieve (7 Mar. 1857–1914?), American Delsartean teacher and writer, was born in San Francisco, California, the daughter of James Cole Stebbins, a lawyer, and Henrietta Smith, who died when Genevieve was two years old. Stebbins was drawn to theatrical expression from an early age and performed pantomimes, songs, dances, and statue posing at family and public gatherings. In 1875 she moved to New York City to pursue a career in theater, first studying and touring with the actress Rose Eytinge. Stebbins's New York debut took place on 19 February 1877 in *Our Boys* at the New Broadway Theatre. Over the next eight years she appeared in several other plays.

In late 1876 or early 1877, Stebbins began a two-year study with the theater innovator James Steele Mackaye of the approach to dramatic expression initially developed by François Delsarte, a French theorist and teacher of acting, voice, and aesthetics. Through systematic observation of people in myriad situations, Delsarte had sought to understand how humans express character and emotion and how their instruments of expression (body, voice, and breath) actually function. From such research he developed a theoretical system of general principles that he believed applied universally to expression in any medium. Mackaye had incorporated into Delsarte's system his own "aesthetic" or "harmonic" gymnastics—exercises for relaxation, the controlled use of energy, and the expression of character traits, states of mind, and emotions. Midway through her studies with him, Mackaye engaged Stebbins to demonstrate for his Delsarte lectures at the Boston University School of Oratory, and eventually she was given full responsibility for the Delsarte program there. She also formed a partnership with Mary S. Thompson, the school's head assistant and vocal coach, with whom Stebbins opened two Delsarte schools, one in Boston and then another in New York. At their private schools, Stebbins taught an evolving version of the Delsarte system that included new elements she had developed as well as aspects of Mackaye's exercise program.

In February 1880 Stebbins and Thompson presented their first Delsarte matinee at the Madison Square Theatre in New York City. Attended mainly by fashionable women, these productions offered cultural entertainment and promoted the Delsarte system as a means to increase expressive powers in performance, oratory, or everyday life. In addition to readings, they included dance and quasi-dance genres performed by Stebbins—statue posing, pantomimes, dances, and dance-dramas. Such programs reflected an increasing emphasis among American Delsarteans on physical culture and bodily expression as the theory and practice was adapted for the general training of nonprofessionals, particularly middle- and upper-class women. Stebbins and Thompson were models for socially acceptable performance practice. The type of program they developed became popular across the United States as Delsarte exponents proliferated and spread the training and performance forms to ever widening circles of students.

In 1881 Stebbins traveled to Europe to prepare for a book on the Delsarte system. She contacted at least one of Delsarte's former pupils in Paris, the Abbé Delaumosne, and made an exhaustive study of classical sculpture in the museums to verify the Delsartean principles of expression to her own satisfaction. She also took acting lessons at the Paris Conservatory under François-Joseph Regnier.

From spring 1884 to spring 1885 Stebbins briefly returned to play a few roles in New York, but she then abandoned professional theater. She published her first book, *Delsarte System of Dramatic Expression*, in 1885. For the remainder of her career, she devoted herself exclusively to the theory and practice of expression that continued to evolve from both her Delsartean training and her independent studies in the sciences, the humanities, physical culture, and metaphysics. In 1886 she returned to Paris, where she met Delsarte's widow and obtained a Delsarte manuscript hitherto unknown in the United States. Stebbins's *Delsarte System of Expression* (as it was titled after the first edition) appeared in five subsequent editions. By the sixth, in 1902, the work had been considerably expanded and included the manuscript as well as additional material of her own. It became a key factor in the spread of the Americanized Delsarte system both across the United States and in Europe. Stebbins also published four other books and numerous articles on physical culture and expression.

By 1888 Stebbins had married Joseph A. Thompson, an attorney probably related to Mary Thompson. This marriage ended by October 1892, which also marked the end of Stebbins's joint teaching with her longtime partner. In April 1893—the same month as the last Stebbins-Thompson Delsarte matinee—Stebbins married Norman Astley, a journalist. There is no record of children from either marriage.

In 1893 Stebbins founded the New York School of Expression, located in Carnegie Music Hall, with Astley as its business manager. In 1894 F. Townsend Southwick, another noted Delsartean teacher, author, and performer, joined her as coprincipal until his death in 1903. Stebbins retired from the school in 1907, transferring the ownership to Charlotte Sulley Presby, a graduate of the school who had advanced from a teaching position to coadministrator with Stebbins.

Throughout the 1890s Stebbins's professional activities gained her increasing recognition on a national level. In 1892 she became a director on the board of the newly organized National Association of Elocutionists. In 1893 she served on the Advisory Council of Physical Culture for the upcoming Chicago World's Columbian Exposition, where she was also invited to demonstrate her work. She taught, lectured, and performed at colleges such as Wellesley and Ohio Wesleyan and in Boston, New Haven, Philadelphia, Cleveland, Buffalo, and Washington, D.C.

Stebbins continued to perform until at least 1903, with an increasing emphasis on dance as her primary expressive medium. Her programs included historical and national dances as well as her own original dances and dance-dramas. Her artistry inspired the great American dancer Ruth St. Denis, who has described Stebbins moving "in a series of plastiques . . . based upon her understanding of the laws of motion discovered by Delsarte" and performing the innovative *Dance of Day*, which depicted the progression from birth through life to death.

The last record of Stebbins is her editing and publication of *The Quest of the Spirit by a Pilgrim of the Way* (1914), the manuscript of a friend. Her death is a mystery, the only clue being the suggestion by a Dutch dance historian that she "disappeared without a trace during a field trip in India."

Stebbins's work contributed to the expansion of opportunities for late nineteenth-century American women to engage in physical culture and expression, particularly in the realm of dance and dancelike activities. She provided the means (teaching methodology), the rationale (her writings), and the model (her own and her students' performances) for what could be accepted as appropriate practices for middle- and upper-class ladies. By the 1890s there were hundreds of Delsarte teachers working throughout the United States, and Stebbins's methods and theory had also spread to Europe. The Delsarte system, as developed and taught by Mackaye, Stebbins, and their followers, created a context out of which the new "modern dance" would develop in the United States and Europe in the twentieth century.

• Stebbins's other works on physical expression and culture include *Dynamic Breathing and Harmonic Gymnastics; A Complete System of Physical, Aesthetic and Physical Culture* (1893); *Genevieve Stebbins's Drills* (1895); *The Genevieve Stebbins System of Physical Training* (1898; enl. ed., 1913); *Society Gymnastics and Voice Culture* (1888); and numerous articles,

particularly in the journal titled (at various times) *The Voice* (1879–1889); *Werner's Voice Magazine* (1889–1894); and *Werner's Magazine* (1894–1902). For Stebbins's professional life and significance, see Nancy Lee Chalfa Ruyter, *Reformers and Visionaries; The Americanization of the Art of Dance* (1979), and "The Intellectual World of Genevieve Stebbins," *Dance Chronicle* 11 (1988): 381–97; and Suzanne Shelton, "The Influence of Genevieve Stebbins on the Early Career of Ruth St. Denis," *Essays in Dance Research, Dance Research Annual IX* (1978), and *Divine Dancer; A Biography of Ruth St. Denis* (1981). Stebbins's influence on twentieth-century European physical culture and dance is demonstrated most notably in Hade Kallmeyer, *Harmonische Gymnastik* (*Harmonic Gymnastics*, 1910) and *Schönheit und Gesundheit des Weibes durch Gymnastik* (*Beauty and Health of the Woman through Gymnastics*, 1911), where she presents what she calls the "Stebbins-Kallmeyer" method. The influence on Kallmeyer and other Europeans is discussed in Eugenia Casini-Ropa, *La danza e l'agitprop* (*The Dance and Agitprop*, 1988).

NANCY LEE CHALFA RUYTER

STEBBINS, Horatio (8 Aug. 1821–8 Apr. 1902), minister, was born in South Wilbraham (present-day Hampden), Massachusetts, the son of Calvin Stebbins and Amelia Adams, farmers. He did not have an easy childhood. His mother died when he was six, and the financial needs of his family required him to help on the farm, which he remembered later consisted mostly of digging potatoes and husking corn. As a result, his initial schooling was erratic. Eventually, however, Stebbins was able to attend Phillips Academy in Exeter, New Hampshire, from which he graduated in 1846. He then attended Harvard, where he earned an A.B. in 1848 and, as a student in its divinity school, an A.M. in 1851. A story familiar to his friends told of how he had grown potatoes near Divinity Hall one summer, in addition to teaching, in order to earn his tuition at Harvard, a poignant vignette that attests to his difficult struggle to gain an education. Nevertheless, he completed his studies, and at age twenty-nine he was ready for the Unitarian ministry, which had been his goal for years.

Following his graduation, the First Parish Church in Fitchburg, Massachusetts, called Stebbins to their pulpit to be the colleague of their senior minister, Calvin Lincoln. He was ordained there in November and served until he became the associate of Ichabod Nichols at the First Parish in Portland, Maine, in 1855. Upon Nichols's death a few years later, Stebbins succeeded him as the pastor.

When Thomas Starr King, minister of the Unitarian church in San Francisco, California, died unexpectedly, Stebbins was called to that church upon the recommendation of Henry W. Bellows, one of the denomination's leading ministers. He accepted, moved to the West Coast, and remained there for thirty-five years until his health forced him to retire. He then returned to Cambridge, where he lived until his death.

Stebbins was married twice: on 3 June 1851 to Mary Ann Fisher, with whom he had three children before her death in 1875; and then to Lucy E. Ward, with whom he had two children.

Stebbins's long pastorate in San Francisco was a most significant ministry. The first years there had not been easy ones, for Starr King, as he was called, had been a highly esteemed minister, not only in his own church but throughout California. Indeed, King's uncompromising stand for the Union, expressed in hundreds of lectures, had played an important role in the state's decision to support Lincoln, and his leadership role on this issue had been deeply appreciated by the public. In time, however, Stebbins gained the confidence of his congregation, and through a long and successful ministry he was able to firmly establish the Unitarian movement on the West Coast.

During that ministry with Stebbins's active support, Unitarian churches were founded in Los Angeles, Santa Barbara, San Diego, and Portland, Oregon. In 1885 the Pacific Coast Unitarian Conference was also formed. As a historian of the San Francisco church noted at Stebbins's retirement, his years were "marked by the steady growth of a strong institution under the leadership of a wise and great-hearted minister" (Meserve, p. 34).

While his preaching was well received, it was also often controversial, for Stebbins believed in the freedom of the pulpit. When a committee from the Portland parish brought the complaint that certain conservative members objected to his bringing politics into his sermons, he replied, "Gentlemen, there is one person whose criticism troubles me more than that of all the rest of the parish; his name is Horatio Stebbins, and he is satisfied" (quoted in Seth Curtis Beach, obituary, Harvard University archives).

He also believed in speaking plainly to nonchurch members. In 1872 many in California from both political parties were in favor of excluding the Chinese. At a public gathering attended by the governor of one party and the former governor of the other, Stebbins called their policy to exclude the Chinese "absurd and ridiculous." Indeed, he added, "As a policy it is nonsense; as a principle it is nowhere" (quoted in Murdock, p. 60). Stebbins was also a firm believer in the right to vote for all, regardless of an individual's race or culture.

It was in the name of higher education, however, that Stebbins made his major contribution to the state of California. He served as a trustee and later as president of the Board of the College of California, which had extensive landing holdings but few funds. It was during his presidency and as a result of his urging that the college gave its land and buildings to help the new University of California, which had funds but no land to get started. Stebbins was also one of those who helped draft the legislation that established the charter of the university, ultimately serving for twenty-six years on its Board of Regents.

Stebbins was a trustee of Stanford University and an adviser to Senator Leland Stanford, its founder. In 1868 Stebbins wrote that the great task of education was "to augment the discourse of reason, intelligence, and faith, and to kindle the beacon fires of truth on all the summits of existence" (quoted in Jones, p. 35).

At Stebbins's death the president of Harvard, Charles W. Eliot, said, "In the presence of a growing and expanding soul like that of Dr. Stebbins, men feel that there is something in man independent of the body, not born to die" (*Christian Register* 81 [17 Apr. 1902]: 470). But it was Mark Twain who caught his character and ministry best when he declared, "Stebbins is a regular brick" (quoted in Meserve, p. 33).

• There is no general collection of Stebbins's manuscripts, but helpful items can be found at Harvard University, the Starr King School for the Ministry, the Bancroft Library of the University of California, and the Unitarian Church of San Francisco. Stebbins's only book was *Prayers* (1903), which was published after his death by family members for his friends and congregation. One of Stebbins's parishioners wrote an admiring biography with extracts from his writings; see Charles A. Murdock, *Horatio Stebbins, His Ministry and His Personality* (1921). For basic data, see Edward Hale, ed., *General Catalogue of the Divinity School of Harvard University* (1915), and the brief sketch in Samuel A. Eliot, *Heralds of a Liberal Faith* (1910). For background material on the Unitarian church in California, see Arnold Crompton, *Unitarianism on the Pacific Coast* (1957), and Henry C. Meserve, "The First Unitarian Society of San Francisco, 1850–1950," *Proceedings of the Unitarian Historical Society* 9 (1951): 24–44. For Stebbins's role in higher education, see William Carey Jones, *Illustrated History of the University of California* (1895).

ALAN SEABURG

STEBBINS, Joel (30 July 1878–16 Mar. 1966), astronomer, was born in Omaha, Nebraska, the son of Charles Sumner Stebbins, a Union Pacific Railroad accounting department supervisor, and Sara Ann Stubbs. In elementary school young Joel became interested in astronomy, and at the age of twelve he began reading all the books on the subject he could find in the Omaha public library. He made his own first telescope from a small lens and a rolled-up tube of newspapers; his parents encouraged his interest by buying an eyepiece and a larger lens for the much better telescope he completed in a high school manual training class. In 1895 Stebbins entered the University of Nebraska; his astronomy teacher there was Goodwin D. Swezey. After receiving a B.S. in 1899, Stebbins remained at Nebraska for one more year as a graduate student in astronomy, then spent another year at the University of Wisconsin under George C. Comstock, finishing his graduate work with two more years at the University of California, Berkeley, doing his thesis under W. Wallace Campbell at Lick Observatory on Mount Hamilton. He received a Ph.D. in astronomy in 1903.

Stebbins then became an instructor at the University of Illinois, where he taught mathematics as well as astronomy, and began a research program with its twelve-inch refracting telescope. He worked on photometry of stars, measuring their brightnesses by the traditional visual methods. In 1905 he married May Louise Prentiss, a classmate at Nebraska; they had two children.

In 1906 Stebbins, seeking a more accurate way of measuring the brightnesses (technically "magnitudes") of stars, made his first experiments in applying a quantitative, electrical method at the telescope. In collaboration with Fay C. Brown, a young physics instructor at Illinois, he designed and built a photometer based on measuring the current through a selenium cell, the resistance of which changes according to the amount of light falling on it. When they first tried their photometer, mounted at the focus of the twelve-inch telescope, it was not sensitive enough to respond even to the light of the bright planet Jupiter. Stebbins, an adaptable, creative scientist who was always eager to get results, took the photometer off the telescope and pointed it at the moon. It was more than bright enough, and within a few months they measured how the moon's brightness varies with phase (its "light curve"). Their results showed that the brightness depends not only on the illuminated area of the moon but also on the angle between the direction of sunlight to the moon and the direction of the sunlight reflected from the moon to the Earth. Stebbins correctly interpreted this as resulting from the irregular structure of the lunar highlands and mountains, riddled with tiny crevices that trap sunlight that is not shining straight down into them. By patient laboratory experimental work, Stebbins and Brown discovered that using a smaller selenium cell and cooling it with ice improved the sensitivity of their photometer. Soon Stebbins was making highly accurate measurements of the light curves of some of the brighter eclipsing double stars, yielding new quantitative results on their dimensions.

In 1911 Jakob Kunz, a physics professor at Illinois, suggested to Stebbins that a photocell in which an alkali-metal cathode emits electrons at a rate proportional to the amount of light falling on it would be more sensitive to the very faint radiation from stars. Kunz began making such cells experimentally, a delicate laboratory process, even before 1912–1913, when Stebbins went on sabbatical leave to Germany, where Paul Guthnick in Berlin and Hans Rosenberg in Tübingen were starting to do photoelectric photometry with cells of this type. On his return to Urbana Stebbins assembled a new photometer, built around one of the cells Kunz had made in the interim. Within a few years Stebbins was using it to measure variable stars with much greater accuracy than visual or photographic methods could achieve and at a fainter level of brightness than the selenium cell could reach. He was obtaining new physical information on eclipsing double stars and on intrinsic, regularly pulsating, variable single stars as well. He observed not only at Illinois but also as a visitor at Lick Observatory; his colleague Kunz continued to provide more and more sensitive photocells.

In 1922 Stebbins, who had moved rapidly up the academic ladder to full professor in 1913, left Illinois to succeed Comstock, his former teacher, as director of the University of Wisconsin's Washburn Observatory, with its fifteen-inch refracting telescope. With C. Morse Huffer, his former student at Illinois who had accompanied him to Wisconsin, Stebbins continued his photoelectric photometry research there. He depended on Kunz for cells and soon was measuring quantitatively the colors of stars (by measuring their magnitudes through color filters). This enabled Stebbins to study and map the absorption and scattering of the light from distant stars by interstellar dust particles in our galaxy.

In the summers of 1927 and 1928 Stebbins went back to Lick Observatory, taking his photoelectric photometer to measure accurately the magnitudes of Jupiter's four bright satellites and the planet Uranus. These measurements not only yielded physical information on these objects but also made it possible for him to set an upper limit to the possible light variations of the Sun, the source of illumination of all these bodies.

For many years Stebbins was practically the only astronomer doing photoelectric photometry in the United States, even though it was by far the most accurate method available. Most scientists considered it an esoteric specialty, but he had pioneered the subject and remained the undisputed master of it. In 1931 he became a research associate of the Carnegie Institution of Washington, which enabled him to use its sixty-inch and 100-inch telescopes at Mount Wilson Observatory in California on annual observing trips there. He worked increasingly on the colors and magnitudes of distant stars, clusters, and galaxies, pushing his measurements out to the boundaries of the observable part of the universe with what was then the largest telescope in the world. He brought the data back to Madison, where he reduced, analyzed, and interpreted it during the balance of the year.

In 1931 Albert E. Whitford, a graduate student at Wisconsin, began working with Stebbins and introduced an electronic amplifier into the photoelectric-photometry system, greatly increasing its sensitivity and making accurate measurements possible to even fainter light levels. Whitford stayed at Wisconsin as a faculty member and became Stebbins's collaborator in many astrophysical applications of their system to understanding the nature of the universe. They concentrated much of their photoelectric work on distant galaxies, the magnitudes of which Edwin Hubble and Milton L. Humason of the Mount Wilson staff needed for their observational studies of the expanding universe.

Stebbins and Whitford, now using photocells sensitive from the ultraviolet to the infrared spectral regions, began multicolor photometry of stars, clusters, and galaxies. This six-color photometry provided important new data on the temperatures of stars, the physical processes and the atoms and ions responsible for absorbing light in their outer layers, and the nature of the dust particles that interact with light in interstellar matter. After World War II, even more sensitive "multiplier" phototubes, in which the weak electron currents are internally amplified, became available. Stebbins immediately began using them to extend his measurements to still fainter objects.

An outstanding scientific leader, Stebbins had a friendly, outgoing manner and a keen, dry sense of humor. He possessed a rare blend of wit and wisdom and was frequently called on for after-dinner speeches at astronomical meetings. He was elected secretary of the American Astronomical Society for three terms, from 1918 to 1927, and served as its president from 1940 to 1943. In 1919 Stebbins was the secretary of the American delegation at the meeting in Brussels that organized the International Astronomical Union; in 1946 he was one of the three American delegates to the union's first postwar meeting in Copenhagen.

In 1948 Stebbins retired and moved to Menlo Park, California. He continued photoelectric observing at Lick Observatory, to which he commuted weekly from his new home. There Gerald E. Kron, who had been his student assistant at Wisconsin after Whitford and had then joined the Lick staff, collaborated with him.

When he finally retired completely from observational work at the age of eighty, Stebbins had been the prime mover in extending the accurate measurement of the brightnesses of celestial objects by a factor of ten billion, from his first measurements of Jupiter to the faintest stars measurable with the Palomar 200-inch reflector. At the end of his life he suffered from failing eyesight and then leukemia; he died in Palo Alto, California. His students, Whitford, Kron, and Olin J. Eggen, had by then become the leaders of the next generation of photoelectric photometrists, along with Harold L. Johnson, who had worked with Kron. Stebbins was an outstanding pioneer who opened a new field of observational astronomy and obtained important new data on every class of objects, from the sun and planets to distant galaxies.

• The most complete collections of Stebbins's letters are in the Department of Astronomy, College of Letters and Sciences Papers in the University of Wisconsin Archives, Memorial Library, University of Wisconsin, Madison. Many of his letters from his graduate student days to his post-retirement years are in the Mary Lea Shane Archives of the Lick Observatory, University Library, University of California, Santa Cruz. The best published source on his life and scientific career is the memorial biography by Albert E. Whitford, "Joel Stebbins 1878–1966," *National Academy of Sciences, Biographical Memoirs* 49 (1978): 293–316, which contains a complete bibliography of Stebbins's published scientific papers. In his later years Stebbins published several informal, semiautobiographical historical sketches on photoelectric photometry, three of which appeared in *Publications of the Astronomical Society of the Pacific*: "The Electrical Photometry of Stars," 52 (1940): 235–43; "Power from the Stars," 53 (1941): 84–97; and "Early Photometry at Illinois," 69 (1957): 506–10. All three articles contain valuable information on Stebbins's scientific career. He summarized much of his scientific work in general terms in "The Electrical Photometry of Stars and Nebulae," *Monthly Notices of the Royal Astronomical Society* 110 (1950): 416–28. An excellent obituary article, giving a vivid sketch of his personality, is Gerald E. Kron, "Joel Stebbins 1878–1966," *Publications of the Astronomical Society of the Pacific* 78 (1966): 214–22.

DONALD E. OSTERBROCK

STEBER, Eleanor (17 July 1914–3 Oct. 1990), operatic soprano, was born in Wheeling, West Virginia, the daughter of William Charles Steber, a bank cashier, and Ida A. Nolte. Her paternal grandfather had anglicized the German name Stuber into Steber. Her mother, who had displayed a strong voice in her youth but had been forced to drop out of high school to work in the family store, saw to the musical education of her daughter. Eleanor made her singing debut at age four in Wheeling's Trinity Lutheran Church, but she studied piano most seriously. In 1933 Steber enrolled in the New England Conservatory of Music, where she studied under William L. Whitney, the head of the voice department, whom she credited with instilling in her a solid bel canto technique. She graduated in 1938.

Steber's first performances were in Boston area churches and on the radio. In 1936 she appeared in a Work Progress Administration Opera Project in Boston in which she sang the role of Senta in an English-language production of Richard Wagner's *Der Fliegende Hollander*. After coming in second in the National Federation of Music Clubs' vocal competition in 1939, Steber moved to New York City and continued her vocal studies with Paul Althouse. In 1940 she won the Metropolitan Opera's radio Auditions of the Air. Her Metropolitan debut occurred the following season as Sophie in Richard Strauss's *Der Rosenkavalier*. She rapidly became a house stalwart, giving 404 performances in thirty-three different roles and once singing in two different operas in one day. A Mozart and Strauss specialist early in her career, she sang Constanze in an English-language version of Mozart's *Die Entführung aus dem Serail* in 1946 and played Arabella in the Metropolitan's first performance of the Richard Strauss opera in 1955. In 1958 she sang the title role in the world premiere of Samuel Barber's *Vanessa*. The following year she played Marie in the Metropolitan's first production of Alban Berg's *Wozzeck*. During the 1950s she experienced problems with her manager Rudolph Bing and sang fewer roles each passing season. Her last regularly scheduled performances were as Donna Anna in Mozart's *Don Giovanni* in 1962, during which time she quarreled with conductor Loren Maazel. Steber referred to her return in 1966, for a single performance as Minnie in Giacomo Puccini's *La Fanciulla del West*, as "the greatest single moment of my life" (Sloat, p. 240).

In addition to her New York performances Steber sang extensively with the San Francisco, Chicago, and Cincinnati opera companies. She only rarely went abroad. In 1947 she sang with the Glyndebourne Company in performances at the first Edinburgh Festival. In 1953 Steber sang Elsa in Wagner's *Lohengrin* at the Bayreuth Festival in Germany, and she performed the role of Minnie in *La Fanciulla* at the Maggio Musicale in Florence in 1954. Her interest in new American music led to her involvement in 1947 with Samuel Barber, whose *Knoxville: Summer of 1915* she premiered with Serge Koussevitzy and the Boston Symphony in 1948. She later made a recording of the piece and championed it throughout her career. Steber was also a popular figure on the "Voice of Firestone" radio and television programs, and she gave extensive concert tours, mostly in the United States.

As her operatic career declined Steber began teaching, first at the Cleveland Institute (1963–1972) and later at the Juilliard School in New York, at Brooklyn College, and privately at "Melodie Hill," her estate on Long Island. She founded the Eleanor Steber Music Foundation in 1973 to aid young singers.

As Steber candidly recounts in memoirs, her musical life was often disrupted by marital discord and alcohol. In 1938, while still a student, she married Edwin L. Bilby. The marriage ended in 1954. In 1957 she married Gordon Andrews. They were divorced in 1966. Steber had no children.

Steber failed to attain the highest level of stardom, perhaps because she was so versatile. Often taken for granted by audiences, she was gradually shunted aside by Bing, whom she believed discriminated against American artists. Some validity to this claim seems to exist, as Bing found cause to dismiss her despite continuing public adulation. A clear lyric soprano with excellent diction and technique, she was capable of handling Mozart and Strauss roles and also some of the more dramatic roles of Verdi and Puccini. However, her career was almost entirely American, causing her reputation to suffer. Steber died at the Attleboro Nursing Home in Langhorne, Pennsylvania.

• Steber's papers are housed in the Theater Collection of Harvard University. Just before her death she collaborated with Marcia Sloat on *Eleanor Steber; An Autobiography* (1992), in which she candidly sets forth many of the controversial aspects of her career, corrects the date of her birth, and explains the convoluted origins of *Knoxville: Summer of 1915*. The book includes an incomplete discography. She recorded extensively, beginning in 1941, when she was the anonymous soprano in a series of opera highlights recordings. Her complete opera recordings include Beethoven's *Fidelio* conducted by Arturo Toscanini in 1944, the 1953 *Lohengrin* from Bayreuth, and the 1958 recording of Barber's *Vanessa*. She also made numerous recordings of popular songs for RCA and Columbia. Her second husband founded a record company, ST/AND, that issued further collections from her repertoire. A private label issue of her 1954 production of *La Fanciulla del West* is particularly exciting. Also notable is her pioneering recording of Barber's *Knoxville: Summer of 1915*. Her video legacy includes operatic and song material from the "Voice of Firestone" programs. Her early Metropolitan career is treated in two works by Irving Kolodin, *The Story of the Metropolitan Opera, 1883–1950* (1953) and *The Metropolitan Opera, 1883–1966: A Candid History*, 4th ed. (1966). A useful appreciation is Albert Innaurato, "Those Demonic Divas," *Opera News* (Oct. 1992): 20–24, 37. An obituary is in the *New York Times*, 4 Oct. 1990.

MICHAEL B. DOUGAN

STEDMAN, Edmund Clarence (8 Oct. 1833–18 Jan. 1908), poet, critic, and stockbroker, was born in Hartford, Connecticut, the son of Edmund Burke Stedman, a lumber merchant, and Elizabeth Clementine Dodge, a poet. Stedman was two when his father died, forcing his mother to move with her two sons to the Plainfield, New Jersey, home of her parents. Her father, David Low Dodge, was reputedly the founder of the world's first peace society, but he ran his home with an iron fist. In 1839 "Ned" was sent to the Norwich, Connecticut, home of his great-uncle, James Stedman, a lawyer and classicist, who operated a boarding school in his home to supplement his income. Stedman desperately hoped that his mother's marriage in 1841 to William Burnet Kinney, editor of the *Newark Daily Advertiser*, would enable her to reunite the family, but Kinney rejected the plan. In 1875 Stedman wrote to Thomas Wentworth Higginson that he had grown up in the "Calvinistic back-country, where I was injured for *life*, and almost perished of repression and atrophy."

In 1850 the sight of his mother, Kinney, and two half sisters sailing for Italy, where Kinney would become chargé at Turin, brought deep pain to Stedman, who recalled in 1871 that when he returned for his sophomore year at Yale, "from utter loneliness, trouble, and inexperience I fell into the dissipation that drew me from my proper studies." Rusticated to Northampton, Massachusetts, he and a friend, billing themselves as "THE WELL-KNOWN TRAGEDIAN, ALFRED WILLOUGHBY, and his sister, Miss AGNES WILLOUGHBY," presented Shakespearean programs in Springfield, leading to Stedman's expulsion from Yale.

Supporting himself as editor-proprietor of several rural Connecticut newspapers, Stedman in 1853 eloped with Laura Woodworth, a seamstress; their marriage lasted until her death in 1905. Publishing the Tennysonian poem "Amavi" in *Putnam's* in 1854, Stedman moved to New York, where he worked in various businesses. The couple's two children were born at this time. In 1859 Stedman gained notoriety when he published the satirical "The Diamond Wedding" in the *Daily Tribune*. Becoming a journalist, he formed strong alliances with Bayard Taylor, Richard Henry Stoddard, Thomas Bailey Aldrich, and other young New York writers. In an 1885 letter to Aldrich, he recalled that Stoddard's *Songs of Summer* (1855) had initiated a movement among them of *"poetry for poetry's sake."* Rejecting what in *Poets of America* (1885) he called "the ethical and polemical fervor [of] . . . their predecessors," these poets "meditated the muse for simple love of beauty and song" (p. 439). In June 1860 *Harper's Monthly* commented that Stedman's *Poems, Lyrical and Idyllic* promised a "brilliant future" for a poet with a decided gift for the "expression of melody."

Early in the Civil War Stedman became a war correspondent for the New York *World*, but his doubts about the paper's financial health and disapproval of its Copperhead leanings prompted him in 1862 to accept a government clerkship in Washington, D.C. He returned to New York the next year to work for a bank and in 1864 opened his own brokerage firm, becoming the "Pan in Wall Street" of his 1867 *Atlantic Monthly* poem.

Discovering in himself a strong critical faculty, he explored in several essays the parallels between the contemporary British situation and that of the Alexandrian age, a time notable for learning but not artistic creativity. Their success led to a series on contemporary British poets for *Scribner's Monthly*. Influenced by the ideas of French critic Hippolyte Taine, Stedman brought a scientific rigor to American criticism. Praised in both England and America when it appeared in 1875, *Victorian Poets*, as Jerome Buckley wrote in *Victorian Poets: A Guide to Research* (1968), was the "first substantial critique [written] without special bias," one that related "Victorian poetry to the context of an analytical age and emphasize[d] a problem still too often neglected by the scholar: the problem of style."

The pressures of completing this book while working on Wall Street brought Stedman in 1874 to the verge of a nervous breakdown. A Caribbean vacation provided some respite, but the news that he had missed a market turn upset him. Forced to divide his time between business and art, Stedman's life was "consecrated to poetry, yet not devoted to it," to use a phrase from his essay on Bayard Taylor, whose premature death in 1878 prompted Stedman to begin a revaluation of American poetry in a series for *Scribner's*. He first recognized the achievements of Edgar Allan Poe and Walt Whitman, each then held in disrepute, and then wrote critical assessments of venerated figures such as Henry Wadsworth Longfellow and James Russell Lowell. The concluding "Twilight of the Poets" (1885) characterizes the age as a time "if not of decadence, at least a poetic interregnum." *Poets of America*, as Kermit Vanderbilt has written in *American Literature and the Academy* (1986), is a "milestone," the "first serious overview of American poetry."

In the early 1880s Stedman, with the aid of his elder son, Frederick, achieved substantial success on Wall Street, but in 1883 he learned that Frederick had embezzled large sums from the firm. Borrowing to avoid bankruptcy, Stedman redoubled his efforts in business and also undertook a succession of ambitious literary projects. The eleven-volume *Library of American Literature* (1888–1890), edited with Ellen M. Hutchinson, offered an inclusive definition of the national literature by incorporating travel writings, political documents, spirituals, sermons, folk sayings, and other vernacular writings. *The Nature and Elements of Poetry* (1892) defends poetry in an age of prose fiction. With George E. Woodberry, Stedman edited *The Works of Edgar Allan Poe* in ten volumes (1894–1895). Both *A Victorian Anthology* (1895) and *An American Anthology* (1900) were critical and commercial successes. The sale of his seat on the New York Stock Exchange in 1900 enabled Stedman to pay off his loans, but he had no source of income other than his pen.

Stedman regularly published lyrics in the leading magazines and was in demand as a poet for public occasions. His collections were greeted respectfully, but acute reviewers recognized that, as the *Nation* wrote on 1 April 1869, for all its "outward elegance of finish," his verse lacked depth: "It is not especially for coherent and forcible conception nor for strong thinking that we look to Mr. Stedman, but for . . . a pretty fancy, for an outward elegance of finish, and . . . an occasional delicate expression of genuine, common sympathies." Aware of his limitations, Stedman confessed in the 1897 "Proem to 'Poems Now First Collected'" that he had "strayed" from the muse, whom "I yet loved . . . most of all." But it was too late for him to take his own advice in *Poets of America* that to escape the poetic "twilight" poets should follow the lead of those novelists who portray "*Life* as it is, though rarely as yet in its intenser phases."

During a long career in which he came to be recognized as the leading critic of American poetry, the popular Stedman worked tirelessly to advance the cause of authorship, serving, for instance, as president of the American Copyright League. In 1904 the membership of the National Institute of Arts and Letters selected him, along with William Dean Howells, Augustus Saint-Gaudens, John Hay, John Lafarge, Edwin McDowell, and Mark Twain, as the first seven of the fifty-member American Academy of Arts and Letters, an organization whose creation Stedman had proposed. Termed by Harriet Monroe in *A Poet's Life* (1938) the "dean of American poets, the friend and helper of young aspirants," Stedman encouraged such younger poets as Edwin Arlington Robinson, William Vaughn Moody, and Percy MacKaye, who, he was confident, would lead the way out of the poetic twilight. MacKaye recalled that to spend time with Stedman, even in his seventies, "was to be reanimated with the vigor, the enthusiasm, the impressionable receptivity of a young man's vision of life." Stedman died in New York.

• The most important repository of Stedman materials is at Columbia University. Because he corresponded with virtually every important American writer during his long literary career, his letters are in numerous libraries, particularly the Houghton at Harvard. *The Life and Letters of Edmund Clarence Stedman*, ed. Laura Stedman and George M. Gould (2 vols., 1910), contains a complete primary bibliography and is an invaluable source. *The Poems of Edmund Clarence Stedman* (1908) is the standard collection. Since Stedman's editorial and critical works sold well, they are widely available. Margaret Fuller, *A New England Childhood* (1916), is an appreciative account of Stedman's early life in Norwich. The most complete modern treatment is Robert J. Scholnick, *Edmund Clarence Stedman* (1977). An obituary is in the *New York Times*, 19 Jan. 1908.

ROBERT J. SCHOLNICK

STEED, Thomas Jefferson (2 Mar. 1904–8 June 1983), U.S. representative, was born on a farm near Rising Star, Texas. His parents' names are unknown. His family, which he characterized as "tenant farmers, poor white trash," moved to Oklahoma when he was four, settling on a farm near Konowa. Though Steed was the most educated child in his family, he dropped out of high school after one semester. A voracious reader, chiefly of books about Thomas Jefferson, he later steeped himself in Capitol Hill history and lore. He more immediately furthered his education by working for the *Ada Evening News* and several other Oklahoma newspapers. In 1923 he married Hazel Bennett; they had two children. In the late 1930s he served four years as an administrative assistant to three Oklahoma Democratic congressmen.

Steed enlisted in 1942 as a private in antiaircraft artillery. He was released from active duty in May 1944 with the rank of second lieutenant and thereafter went overseas to join the Office of War Information, with whom he served in the China-Burma-India theater until December 1945. Traveling extensively throughout the vast subcontinent of India, Steed met Mahatma Gandhi, Jawaharlal Nehru, Louis Mountbatten, and Generals Joseph W. Stilwell and George E. Stratemeyer, among others. After managing an automobile agency in Holdenville, Oklahoma, in the first years after the war, he decided to run for Congress as a Democrat from the Fourth Congressional District in 1948. He won election to the Eighty-first Congress and to the fifteen succeeding ones, compiling at the time the longest tenure on Capitol Hill of anyone in Oklahoma's history.

During his thirty-two years, until his retirement at the end of the Ninety-sixth Congress in 1981, Steed gradually secured a reputation as a powerful force behind the scenes who rarely spoke in the House chamber, disliked ideologues, occasionally bombarded reporters with trenchant observations, and as an insider effectively channeled massive federal funding to his district. He also, thanks to his committee assignments, affected the course of legislation through the exertion of pressure on both the executive branch and on recalcitrant members of either party in Congress.

His first assignment on the Education and Labor Committee found him serving with two future presidents, Richard M. Nixon and John F. Kennedy. During his first term Steed coauthored a program granting federal funds to schools crowded with children of federal workers. With three military installations in his district, Steed opposed throughout his tenure all efforts to cut impact aid to these schools. As a member of the Public Works Committee, where he served five years, Steed played a key role in engineering a compromise in 1956 on legislation creating the $51 billion interstate highway system, at that time the largest peacetime public works measure in history. As a subcommittee chairman on the Small Business Committee, he conducted hearings on oil imports, providing testimony about the possible effect of a Middle East oil embargo.

It was as a member, beginning in the 1950s, of the Appropriations Committee, obtained through his friendship with the Speaker, Sam Rayburn, that Steed accumulated both power and influence. He successively chaired subcommittees on legislative activities and on Treasury, Postal Service, and General Government. He was instrumental in allocating funds for expanding the east front of the Capitol and in con-

structing the Rayburn Office Building, where he came to occupy a choice office.

In the 1950s Steed coauthored and perfected legislation that enormously benefited Oklahoma through a program of soil conservation and upstream flood control. With numerous tribes located in his district, Steed was also acutely interested in legislation protecting American Indian allotments. Though he could be sharp in some of his comments, members learned that his bark was usually worse than his bite. In August of his last year in Congress, House leaders scheduled time for a farewell to Steed, then seventy-six. Some 300 members appeared for the roll call on annual appropriations for the Treasury Department, Postal Service, and Executive Office for the President prepared by the subcommittee that Steed chaired. When action on the bill was completed, Republicans and Democrats alike rose, offering a standing ovation of farewell to a respected colleague. Steed's wife was a significant part of his life in Washington and was active among congressional wives.

A "work horse" more than a "show horse," Steed commented on the functions of a member of Congress stating that "he is not only a legislator but serves his constituents as an information service, a Chamber of Commerce in Washington and an errand boy." He died in Shawnee, Oklahoma.

• Steed's papers covering his congressional career from 1948 to 1980, comprising 549 boxes, are housed in the archives of the Carl Albert Center at the University of Oklahoma. An extensive interview with Steed was conducted by Frank Van Der Linden for the U.S. Capitol Historical Society in 1981. For the Ralph Nader Congress Project, Citizens Look at Congress, S. L. McElroy prepared an account of an extensive interview with Steed; these congressional interviews were published in 1972. From 8 June through 14 June 1983 numerous members of the House of Representatives paid their respects to Steed; their tributes appear in the *Congressional Record*. An obituary is in the *Daily Oklahoman*, 9 June 1983.

RICHARD LOWITT

STEEDMAN, James Blair (29 July 1817–18 Oct. 1883), army officer and politician, was born in Northumberland County, Pennsylvania, the son of Mellum Steedman and Margaret Blair. Steedman was orphaned at an early age and received little formal education. Instead, he took up the trade of printing and worked on newspapers in Lewisburg, Pennsylvania, and Louisville, Kentucky. He was a big, bluff, fearless man, fond of adventure and never intimidated. During the 1830s he served a stint as a volunteer in the army of the young Republic of Texas. Returning to the United States, he made his home in Ohio. In Napoleon, Ohio, in 1838, he married Miranda Stiles. During the 1840s he served two terms in the Ohio legislature.

The California gold rush once again aroused Steedman's adventurous streak, and he joined the hordes of forty-niners bound for the Pacific coast in that year. Riches eluded him on the banks of the Sacramento, and the next year found him back in Ohio, this time in

Toledo, where he finally settled down and returned to the newspaper business, publishing the *Toledo Times*. He again became active in Democratic party politics and was a strong backer of Illinois senator Stephen A. Douglas. In 1857 his involvement brought extra business, as he was appointed a public printer. In the crucial 1860 election year, Steedman was a delegate to the Democratic National Convention in Charleston, South Carolina. When that convention broke up in strife and another was called for Baltimore several weeks later to try to patch up the party, he was elected a delegate to it as well. That fall he ran for Congress on the Douglas Democrat ticket but lost.

After the fall of Fort Sumter, Steedman raised a regiment of his fellow Toledo residents (the Fourteenth Ohio) and on 27 April 1861 was officially mustered in as its colonel. The regiment became part of the original Army of the Ohio under General George B. McClellan (1826–1885) and participated in his victory at Philippi, Virginia (now W.Va.), on 3 June 1861. Steedman was ferocious in battle but was an atrocious officer at all other times—vain, unconcerned for the welfare of his troops, and conspicuous in drinking, gambling, and fornicating.

As one of the three-month militia regiments, the Fourteenth Ohio's term of enlistment ran out in August, but Steedman was able to persuade most of his men to reenlist for three years. The regiment retained its identity, was reorganized with Steedman still colonel, and became part of the command of General George H. Thomas, still part of the Army of the Ohio. On 19 January 1862 Steedman led his regiment successfully in the Union victory at Mill Springs, Kentucky. His combat record attracted notice, and on 1 March 1862 Abraham Lincoln submitted his name to the Senate for confirmation as brigadier general. Here problems arose. The *Toledo Times*, a staunchly Unionist paper, had run a series of articles considering the arguments for and against the right of secession. The series had concluded by roundly denying such a right, but the issue that had included the prosecession arguments was seized upon by congressional Republicans. Consequently Steedman's promotion was held up until 17 July.

On 8 October 1862 Steedman led his brigade at the battle of Perryville, Kentucky. After the Army of the Ohio was reorganized as the Army of the Cumberland, now under General William S. Rosecrans, Steedman continued to serve in Thomas's command in that army, which was designated the XIV Corps. On 31 December 1862 and 2 January 1863 he participated in the battle of Stones River in Tennessee, and the following summer he continued to command a brigade through the Tullahoma campaign, in which Confederate forces were maneuvered out of the state of Tennessee. On 15 August he was given command of one of the two divisions of a "Reserve Corps" under General Gordon Granger. Steedman's finest hour in uniform came that fall. With the rest of the Reserve Corps, he was stationed some miles north of the battlefield of Chickamauga while the fighting there raged through

19 September and the morning of 20 September. About midday, Granger decided on his own initiative to take Steedman and his division to reinforce Thomas. By the time they reached the field, the situation on the battlefield was critical and, but for their timely arrival, might have ended in complete disaster. Thomas directed Steedman to drive Confederates off of Horseshoe Ridge, where they threatened his right flank. Steedman did so with conspicuous gallantry, despite losing one-fifth of his men in twenty minutes of combat. His fiery courage, even carrying the colors of one faltering regiment, helped his largely inexperienced troops hold steady.

A month after the battle Steedman was transferred to rear-echelon duties in Chattanooga. In April 1864 he was promoted to major general but continued in command of the post of Chattanooga and later a district in northern Georgia. When, in the late fall of 1864, Thomas was sent north to Tennessee to organize garrison forces there into an army to oppose Confederate general John B. Hood's invasion, Steedman commanded a scratch division in this force, taking part in the Union victory at Nashville.

Steedman resigned from the army in August 1866 and became collector of customs for the Port of New Orleans. In 1869 he returned to Toledo and edited the *Northern Ohio Democrat*. He served in the state senate and, for the five months immediately preceding his death, was chief of police of Toledo. After the death of his first wife, he married Rose Barr, who also predeceased him; in 1878 he was married a third time, to Margaret Gildea. Steedman died in Toledo.

• For further information on Steedman see Peter Cozzens, *This Terrible Sound* (1992); U.S. War Department, *The War of the Rebellion: A Compilation of the Official Records of the Union and Confederate Armies* (128 vols., 1880–1901); and Ezra J. Warner, *Generals in Blue: The Lives of the Union Commanders* (1964).

STEVEN E. WOODWORTH

STEELE, Frederick (14 Jan. 1819–12 Jan. 1868), Union general, was born at Delhi, Delaware County, New York, the son of Nathaniel Steele. Appointed to the U.S. Military Academy, Steele was graduated in 1843, ranking thirtieth in a class of thirty-nine. He served in the Mexican War as a second lieutenant in the Second Infantry, earning brevet ranks of first lieutenant and captain for gallantry at the battles of Contreras and Churubusco. From 1848 to 1861 he served with the regiment at various posts in Minnesota, Nebraska, California, and Kansas. He was promoted to first lieutenant in June 1848 and to captain in February 1855.

Stationed at Fort Leavenworth, Kansas, at the outbreak of the Civil War, Steele was assigned to a battalion of regular troops and led them at the battle of Wilson's Creek, Missouri, on 10 August 1861. Several weeks later, on 23 September, he was appointed colonel of the Eighth Iowa. Promoted to brigadier general on 29 January 1862, Steele assumed command of the

District of Southwest Missouri and, in the spring, a division in Samuel Curtis's Army of the Southwest.

In December 1862 Steele commanded a division in William T. Sherman's operations against Chickasaw Bluffs above Vicksburg, Mississippi. His troops suffered heavy casualties in the fierce combat as the Confederates repulsed Sherman's assaults. Two weeks later, on 10–11 January 1863, Steele's division participated in the capture of Arkansas Post on the Arkansas River. For his competent performances in the operations, Steele received the rank of major general on 17 January, to date from 29 November 1862.

During Ulysses S. Grant's campaign against Vicksburg, May–July 1863, Steele served capably as a division commander in Sherman's XV Corps. After the capitulation of Vicksburg on 4 July, Steele assumed command of the Department of Arkansas or the VII Corps. Ordered to clear the state of Confederate forces, Steele advanced through Arkansas, capturing Little Rock in September. On 26 August he had been promoted to lieutenant colonel in the regular army.

In the spring of 1864 Steele was directed to advance southward across the state and cooperate with Nathaniel Banks's campaign up the Red River in Louisiana. Steele's command departed from Little Rock on this so-called Camden expedition on 23 March. Steele advanced southwestward, colliding with Confederate forces at Okolona on 3 April before turning eastward and fighting at Prairie d'Ane on 10–13 April and at Poison Spring on 18 April. The Federals occupied Camden for nearly a fortnight before beginning a retreat to Little Rock. At Jenkins Ferry on the Saline River on 30 April, Steele's troops repulsed the attacks of a numerically superior Confederate force, securing their retreat route to the state capital, which they reached on 3 May. Banks's operations along the Red River resulted in failure, but Steele was blameless as the Confederates mobilized troops to prevent his juncture with Banks.

Steele remained in Arkansas as department commander until the winter of 1865, when he commanded a division in Edward R. S. Canby's army in siege operations against Mobile, Alabama. At the close of hostilities, Federal authorities sent Steele to Texas, where he remained for nearly two years.

Mustered out as a major general of volunteers on 1 March 1867, Steele, with the rank of colonel in the regular army dating from 28 July 1866, assumed command of the Department of the Columbia in the Pacific Northwest. While on leave in San Mateo, California, he suffered an apoplectic stroke, which caused him to fall from a carriage; he died instantly.

• Accounts of Steele's life and Civil War career can be found in Edwin C. Bearss, *Steele's Retreat from Camden and the Battle of Jenkin's Ferry* (1967); Shelby Foote, *The Civil War: A Narrative* (1958, 1963, 1974); Samuel Carter, *The Final Fortress: The Campaign for Vicksburg, 1862–1863* (1980); Bearss, *The Vicksburg Campaign* (1985–1986); and *The War of the Rebellion: A Compilation of the Official Records of the Union and Confederate Armies* (128 vols., 1880–1901).

JEFFRY D. WERT

STEELE, Wilbur Daniel (17 Mar. 1886–26 May 1970), fiction writer, was born in Greensboro, North Carolina, the son of the Reverend Wilbur Fletcher Steele, a Methodist minister and scholar, and Rose Wood, an occasional writer. In 1892 the Steeles moved to Denver, Colorado, where Wilbur's father became professor of Bible at the University of Denver. In 1907 Steele received his B.A. from the University of Denver, majoring in history and economics, and soon enrolled in the Boston Museum School of Fine Arts. In 1908 he traveled to Paris to paint and in 1909 to Italy to etch. Later in 1909 he returned to the United States and settled briefly in Provincetown, Massachusetts, famous for its summer arts colony. Under the influence of several in the colony, he turned to the writing of short stories. At his father's insistence, in the fall of 1909, he briefly resumed his art studies, this time at the Arts Students' League in New York City. However, he continued his writing at night. "On the Ebb Tide," his first published story, appeared in the June 1910 issue of *Success Magazine*. After that, painting was strictly a spare-time activity.

In 1913 Steele married the painter Margaret Thurston and returned to Provincetown, where the couple spent several summers. They had two sons. The next year Harper published Steele's first novel, *Storm*. In the summer of 1915 Steele helped found the famous Provincetown Players company, which staged his plays *Contemporaries* (1915) and *Not Smart* (1916), both unpublished. Steele left the company in 1916, about the time that it moved to Greenwich Village. The Steeles stayed in Provincetown, where they had purchased a house. Steele avoided the service during World War I, instead making a trip to the Caribbean for *Harper's Magazine*. For some years the family lived comfortably, frequently traveling. Steele seemed incapable of settling down, and he would stay in Provincetown during the summer and move somewhere else for the winter.

Steele's first story collection, *Land's End and Other Stories*, appeared in 1918. Altogether from 1910 to 1920, he published approximately fifty-six short stories. In 1921 the O'Henry Memorial Award Committee of the Society of Arts and Sciences presented him a special award for the literary merit of his stories. Steele had stories published in the *Best Short Stories of America* nine times between 1915 and 1933. Its editor, Edward J. O'Brien, dedicated the volume for 1917 to Steele, but in the late 1920s, when fashions in story writing changed, O'Brien lost interest in him. During the 1920s Steele published three more novels, approximately fifty-four short stories, and four collections of stories.

Steele wrote in a variety of genres, including romances, mysteries, humor, sea stories, and westerns. Many of his stories take place in Africa, the Caribbean, or the South Seas. Most are melodramatic and complicated. Some are Freudian in content. He once said that, of all writers, O'Henry had most influenced him, and his stories have well-developed plots and, frequently, surprise endings. In fact he won several awards from the O'Henry Committee for his stories: first place in 1926, 1927, and 1931, and lesser awards in 1919, 1922, 1924, and 1929.

By 1930 editors of quality magazines began to reject traditional, densely plotted stories of romance or adventure, and Steele began to have trouble getting his stories published. He was not able to write the new more simple and less melodramatic stories wanted by these magazines—ones that had earlier printed him. With money problems, he turned to the popular weeklies and women's magazines, for example, the *Saturday Evening Post, Collier's, Ladies' Home Journal,* and *Woman's Home Companion.* He published at least twenty-five stories in the 1930s, most before 1935, and two novels. From 1940 to 1958 he published about six stories, all but one in the 1940s.

In 1931 Steele's wife Margaret died. The following year he married the actress-playwright Norma Mitchell in London. On their return to America, they settled in Hamburg, Connecticut. The Steeles moved to Hollywood for the winters of 1932–1933 and 1933–1934 for him to write film scripts, with little success. They were also there during the winter of 1939–1940. In 1934–1935 his mystery-comedy *Post Road* was a hit on Broadway. Under the name *Leaning on Letty* it was also a hit in Chicago in 1937–1938. He had *How Beautiful with Shoes* produced on Broadway in 1935, but it was not successful.

In 1945, with Steele's short-story writing about over, and, in effect as a tribute, Henry O'Neil edited an anthology, *The Best Stories of Wilbur Daniel Steele.* Unfortunately, Steele's last collection, *Full Cargo: More Stories* (1951), according to critics, was not his best. The aging Steele now concentrated on novels, publishing four from 1945 to 1955, none of them very memorable.

In 1956 the Steeles moved to Old Lyme, Connecticut, where both of them began to suffer failing health. In 1965 they were admitted to Highland Hall Convalescence Center in Essex, Connecticut, where they both died.

Although Steele is no longer celebrated, at the height of his career in the 1920s he was one of the most famous short-story writers in America. There was truly a revolution in fiction during the 1920s, and Steele and many others were left behind. Since he could not adapt to the changing style in short-story writing, he lost favor both of editors and critics. His novels and his plays have not proved to be of lasting importance. As he grew elderly, he had to give up writing and soon sank into obscurity. Nevertheless, some of his stories were among the best of his time.

• Steele's papers are in the Stanford University Library. The Steele Family Papers are in the University of Denver Archives. Steele's additional story collections are *The Shame Dance and Other Stories* (1923), *Urkey Island* (1926), *The Man Who Saw through Heaven and Other Stories* (1927), and *Tower of Sand and Other Stories* (1929). His additional novels are *Isles of the Blest* (1924), *Taboo* (1925), *Meat* (1928), *Undertow* (1930), *Sound of Rowlocks* (1938), *That Girl from Memphis* (1945), *Diamond Wedding* (1950), *Their Town* (1952), and

The Way to the Gold (1955). Steele wrote several plays, but only *Post Road* (1936) was published.

Little secondary material on Steele has appeared. Blanche Colton Williams in her collection of essays *Our Short Story Writers* (1925; repr. 1969) has a chapter on Steele. Also informative is Mary Heaton Vorse, *Time and the Town* (1942). There is one biography, brief to the point of incompleteness, Martin Bucco's volume in the Twain's United States Authors Series, *Wilbur Daniel Steele* (1972), which has an extensive bibliography. Another long listing of Steele's stories and other publications with a short bibliography of secondary works is contained in Mel Seesholtz, "William Daniel Steele" in *Dictionary of Literary Biography* 86 (1989): 264–71. An obituary is in the *New York Times,* 27 May 1970.

WALTER A. SUTTON

STEENDAM, Jacob (1616–c. 1672), merchant and poet, is believed to have been born in Enkhuizen, Holland, though his parentage is unknown. Much about his life is obscure. He grew up in Amsterdam and was a member of the Dutch Reformed church. In 1638 he was a member of the Segbloem, an institute of rhetoric, at Zegwaard, and much of his poetry reveals the influence of rhetorical training.

For fifteen years, beginning around 1637, Steendam was employed by the Dutch West India Company, leaving its employ upon his emigration to America. In 1641 he sailed to Guinea on the African Gold Coast as a merchant and remained there for the next eight years. During that time he composed a number of personal lyrics, which he gathered after his return to Amsterdam and published in 1649–1650 as *The Thistle Finch* (or *The Goldfinch,* depending on the translation). In these poems he recounts his early years, tracing his personal and spiritual maturation. In 1649 he married Sara de Rosschou, and they had one child.

Steendam is believed to have arrived in America around 4 April 1652. In that year, and again in 1660, he petitioned the Dutch West India Company to import African slaves and to trade on the Gold Coast. Records suggest that he prospered in the New World. He had extensive real estate holdings on Long Island and Manhattan, and in 1653 he was taxed 100 florins—his share for building a stockade in New Amsterdam. In 1655 he was one of four men recommended to serve as an orphan master, though he was not chosen, and in 1656 he was nominated for the honor of becoming a *schepen* (alderman), but again he was passed over.

For American audiences Steendam is best remembered for three poems he wrote about colonial New Netherland. His first of these, *The Complaint of New Amsterdam* (1659), was published in Amsterdam and is believed to have been the first poem written in the Dutch colony. As with each of his colonial poems, there is a strong polemical element. Steendam arrived in New Netherland at a time of political instability: the colony was threatened both by Native Americans and by the English. New Netherland was not a commercially profitable colony, and both the Dutch West India Company and the Dutch government paid scant attention to the plight of the colonists. Steendam wrote his poem as a plea for governmental protection and as a defense of the colony's commercial viability. He constructs the poem as a monologue by a daughter to her parent pleading for protection. The allegorical associations are unmistakable, with the child, "of Amsterdam . . . born, / Early of her breasts forlorn; / From her care so quickly weaned," representing the colony, and the parent representing Holland. Much of the poem is given over to ponderous mythical imagery, with the colony described as "a grandchild of the Gods," and the clear purpose is to emphasize the exalted origins and destiny of the colonial enterprise. The New World is depicted as a promised land, with "Milk and butter; fruits to eat / No one can enumerate; / Ev'ry vegetable known; / Grain the best that e'er was grown." However, the abundance and perfection are threatened by "the Swine [the English] / [who]Trample down these crops of mine."

A more ambitious work, the 300-line *The Praise of New Netherland* (1661), also published in Amsterdam, reveals a similar desire to cast the colony in the most favorable light, with the obvious purpose of encouraging more emigrants to join the colony. The poem begins by declaring "a nobler theme I sing. . . . New Netherland, thou noblest spot of earth, / Where bounteous Heaven ever poureth forth / the fulness of His gifts, of greatest worth, / Mankind to nourish." Steendam the rhetorician arranges the initial stanzas around the Aristotelian elements of air, fire, water, and earth, while in the later stanzas he settles in for a lengthy catalog of the fish, animals, natural resources, and plants. The poem ends with a divine invocation for a place where "Rule, doctrine; covenants, all in accord / With His pure word who is, of Lords the Lord."

In *Spurring Verses* (1662), Steendam again turned his efforts to political purposes, once more encouraging emigration to New Netherland. At this time there was an effort to colonize an area in Delaware with a group of Mennonites led by Peter Plockhoy, who published a pamphlet (which included Steendam's verses) in the hope of encouraging support for his endeavor. The early stanzas are essentially a reworking of material from Steendam's two earlier poems; however, the piece elucidates a new motive for emigration. After considering the "Fatherland" and its political arrangement, Steendam exhorts his audience: "Who would not, then, in such a formed community / Desire to be a freeman; and the rights decreed / To each and every one, by Amstel's burgher lords, / T'enjoy? and treat with honor what their rule awards?" Steendam believed that the suggestion of a democratic community and a sustained refutation of all the shortcomings of such an undertaking would persuade supporters. He ends praising "That land, which, *as I know*, no proper rival has" and emphasizing his firsthand knowledge of the virtues of his adopted home.

Perhaps because of the instability of the colony, Steendam returned to Amsterdam in 1660 and in 1666 set sail for Batavia. Details of this period in his life are sketchy. In 1667 he traveled to Bengal and then returned to Batavia in January 1668, where he became governor of the Orphans House. His final literary effort, *Moral Songs for Batavian Youth* (1671), published in Batavia, was another polemic designed to encourage youngsters to live a morally righteous life. Details of Steendam's last years are unknown, but he is believed to have died before September 1673, when records indicate that his widow died.

Steendam was by no means one of America's most accomplished poets, and certainly his importance is more historical than literary. However, his verse does reveal accomplishment, and in many ways his poems provide interesting thematic foreshadowings of writers such as Benjamin Franklin, Ralph Waldo Emerson, and Walt Whitman. In all his poems, Steendam reveals himself to be an enthusiastic, morally serious, and earnest man who devoted himself to the success of the grand social experiment of life in the New World.

• Some of Steendam's papers are in the John Carter-Brown Library in Providence, R.I.; the Lennox Library, New York; and the Royal Library at The Hague, the Netherlands. The first serious consideration of Steendam's works was Henry C. Murphy, *Jacob Steendam, Noch Vaster* (1861), a memoir containing translations of his three poems about New Netherland. The same material is reprinted in Murphy's *Anthology of New Netherland* (1865), along with considerations of Henricus Selyns and Nicasius de Sillè. The most complete modern assessment of his life and career can be found in Ellis Lawrence Raesly, *Portrait of New Netherland* (1945). See also William Loring Andrews, *Jacob Steendam, Noch Vaster: The First Poet of New Netherland* (1908); Mary L. D. Ferris, "A Note about Jacob Steendam," *De Halve Maen* (1976); and Henri and Barbara Van Der Zee, *A Sweet and Alien Land* (1978).

DAVID W. MADDEN

STEENROD, Norman Earl (22 Apr. 1910–14 Oct. 1971), mathematician, was born in Dayton, Ohio, the son of Earl Lindsay, a high-school teacher of manual training and drafting, and Sarah Rutledge. He attended public schools in Dayton. He graduated from high school at the age of fifteen, then worked for two years as a tool designer before attending Miami University in Ohio from 1927 to 1929. Owing to the economic difficulties of the Great Depression, the remainder of his undergraduate career was frequently disrupted. He received his B.A. in 1932 from the University of Michigan, where he was introduced to topology by Raymond L. Wilder. Receiving a fellowship in 1933, he went to Harvard and got his A.M. in 1934. He then went to Princeton, where in 1936 he received his Ph.D. with a dissertation, "Universal Homology Groups," written under the direction of Solomon Lefschetz. In 1938 Steenrod married Carolyn Witter in Petoskey, Michigan; they had two children.

Steenrod remained at Princeton as an instructor, (1936–1939) and then became an assistant professor first at the University of Chicago (1939–1942) and then at the University of Michigan (1942–1947). During 1944 he worked on flak analysis as a civilian attached to the navy at the Office of Scientific Research and Development. Following the war Steenrod returned to

Princeton as an associate professor; he was promoted to professor in 1952 and in 1968 was named Fine Professor, a chair he held until his death.

Apart from his dissertation, which involved several innovations in homology theory, Steenrod's mathematical research can be divided into three distinct periods of activity. The first concerned his work with Samuel Eilenberg on axiomatic homology theory. As algebraic topology developed in the twentieth century, there were a number of versions of homology, but nothing that could properly be called a general theory of homology. In a skillful analysis, Eilenberg and Steenrod examined the existing homology theories and, by extracting their common properties, produced a set of seven axioms defining the general theory ("Axiomatic Approach to Homology Theory," *Proceedings of the National Academy of Sciences*, 31 [1945]: 117–20). This system, now called the Eilenberg-Steenrod axioms, was also formulated for cohomology theory; it made explicit use of the algebraic structure that now forms the basis of modern algebraic topology. Notably, this included the use of commutative diagrams, exact sequences, and functorial properties. The entire theory was subsequently presented in their monograph, *Foundations of Algebraic Topology* (1952), which remains the classic account of the material.

The second aspect of Steenrod's career, which was roughly contemporaneous with the first, was concerned with the theory of fibre bundles. This theory originated in the mid-1930s and, like homology theory, existed in several different versions. Steenrod set about to give a standard account of the theory that reconciled the various approaches; in doing so he both popularized the theory and produced what became the standard theory for several generations of topologists. It involved his own contributions to the theories of cross-sections and of classifying spaces and was summarized in his book *The Topology of Fibre Bundles* (1951). In addition to the material on bundle theory, the book also contained valuable expositions of homotopy and obstruction theory. It has become a seminal work for both algebraic topologists and differential geometers.

Steenrod's third body of work began in 1947. During the years 1931 to 1941, various special cases of the classification of mappings of an m-complex into an n-sphere had been solved by an international galaxy of distinguished topologists; however, the case when $m = n + 1$, and $n \geq 3$, remained open and a particularly difficult challenge. Steenrod not only produced an ingenious solution (in 1947), but in doing so he also introduced a new kind of algebraic operation, which became known as "Steenrod squares." These proved to be extremely useful and led to a new class of cohomology operations, which included the so-called reduced Steenrod powers. Much of the activity from the early 1950s through the 1960s was devoted to the application of the techniques of the Steenrod algebra to a host of problems in algebraic topology. Many topologists regard this material as Steenrod's greatest contribution to the discipline. His lectures on this topic were written up and revised by David B. A. Epstein as *Cohomology Operations* (1962). Steenrod's final work was concerned with the Realization Problem and was left unfinished. He died in Princeton after a series of strokes.

In addition to his research, Steenrod was a gifted teacher who devoted great attention to his students. Three textbooks give evidence of his interest in pedagogical matters: *Advanced Calculus* (1959), written with Helen K. Nickerson and Donald C. Spencer; *First Concepts of Topology: The Geometry of Mappings of Segments, Curves, Circles, and Disks* (1966), written with William G. Chinn; and the *Homology of Cell Complexes* (1967), written by George E. Cooke and Ross L. Finney, based on Steenrod's lectures. The first was an experimental text intended to introduce the reader to a veritable panoply of modern mathematics, rather than a traditional exposition of advanced calculus. It was an unforgettable experience to have a course based on it, and it is regrettable that a final polished version of the text was never prepared. The second book was elementary and offered an engaging introduction to topological ideas by rigorously developing the preliminaries required for proving a pair of existence theorems that are of importance in calculus. The last book was a more or less standard rendition of the homology of cell complexes. One of Steenrod's last contributions to topology was his preparation of the two-volume *Reviews of Papers in Algebraic and Differential Topology, Topological Groups, and Homological Algebra* (1968), compiled and classified from contributions to *Mathematical Reviews*. This was an invaluable guide to the literature, and its success led the American Mathematical Society to prepare similar volumes in other areas of mathematics.

From 1948 to 1962 Steenrod was an editor of *Annals of Mathematics*. He was Colloquium Lecturer of the American Mathematical Society in 1957. He was elected a Member of the National Academy of Sciences in 1956.

• There is an appreciation of Steenrod's work in *The Steenrod Algebra and Its Applications: A Conference to Celebrate N. E. Steenrod's Sixtieth Birthday* (1970). Obituary notices are in National Academy of Sciences, *Biographical Memoirs* 55 (1985): 452–70, and in the *New York Times*, 16 Oct. 1971. The former contains a complete list of publications and a portrait.

JOSEPH D. ZUND

STEENWYCK, Cornelis Jacobsz (?–1685?), colonial merchant and public official, was born in Haarlem, the Netherlands. Nothing is known of his parents or his youth. He signed his name as van Steenwyck until 1654, and Steenwyck thereafter. He first appears in records of New Amsterdam in 1651, already well established. He rose rapidly to become one of the principal merchants of the city, owning several ships that traded to and from the Netherlands, Virginia, and the Caribbean. He owned property in New Amsterdam, Fort Orange (now Albany), and Fort Casimir (now

New Castle, Del.). In 1658 Steenwyck married Margareta de Riemer; they had seven children, none of whom survived to maturity. Steenwyck's portrait by Jan van Gooten, one of eleven pictures that decorated their elegantly furnished home, is at the New-York Historical Society.

Steenwyck assumed the civic responsibilities expected of a prominent merchant, serving as an orphan masters (a Dutch government officer charged with protecting the inheritance and other rights of minors when one or both of the parents have died) in 1653, from 1660 to 1663, and in 1671–1672, and as administrator of numerous estates. He was commissioned an ensign in the militia in 1654. He participated in government-sponsored policy meetings on a declining money exchange rate in 1657 and on financing military preparedness in 1663.

Steenwyck was often called to serve in diplomatic roles. On business trips to Holland, he communicated colonial concerns to the West India Company's directors in 1655 and 1658. He witnessed the peace treaty that ended the second Esopus War between settlers and Indians, and was one of the commissioners sent to Long Island in January 1664 to deal with English land claims there. The courts called him some forty-four times as arbitrator in civil suits, and when he served as *schepen* (alderman) he was often assigned to hold arbitration hearings.

He contributed generously toward repairing the city defenses in 1653 and 1655, and in 1664 he loaned a cannon to the blockhouse on Staten Island and 12,000 guilders to New Amsterdam. He was also a supplier to the city, providing planks and nails for the 1653 defenses, and later wainscoting for city hall and planks for a bridge, for all of which the city owed him 1,364 guilders in 1659.

He continued to serve the city government as a *schepen* in 1658 and 1660, and as a burgomaster in 1664 he was one of the commissioners who negotiated with Richard Nicolls, leader of the English invasion in 1664, and signed the articles of surrender. Following the English takeover, he continued to be active both in business, trading to both English and Dutch ports, and in public service. In 1665 he was reappointed as burgomaster and served as an alderman in 1666–1667. Typically, he responded with the largest contribution to a 1667 appeal to support the city's two Reformed church ministers.

Steenwyck accepted the fact of English rule and co-operated with English officials. He was appointed to two terms as the first Dutch mayor under the English, from 1668 to 1670, and then to the provincial council, on which he served from 1670 until the return of the Dutch in 1673. Governor Francis Lovelace, on departing for Delaware in the spring of 1672, left Councilors Steenwyck and John Delavall in charge of New York City and its environs. He also sent the two that summer to Albany to read the declaration of war between the Netherlands and England and to see that the fort and militia were fit, and he dispatched them in the fall to Elizabeth, New Jersey, to settle problems about

rents. Steenwyck also played a role in the colony's military affairs, helping to fortify the city in 1665 and contributing generously toward its defenses in 1672. He was promoted to captain and commissioned to raise a troop of cavalry on Manhattan. However, he proved equally cooperative with the Dutch military and naval force that reconquered the colony in 1673.

Steenwyck was among the representatives of the burghers chosen to meet with the Dutch commanders, who then reappointed him to the council, naming him a principal councilor to assist the new governor in "all cases relative to justice" and appointing him captain of the burgher guard. The new government sent him and other officers to force into submission the English inhabitants on eastern Long Island, but the mission withdrew in the face of strong opposition. He was also commissioned to determine the value of houses near the fort that were to be razed, to find rooms for refugees in New York, and to evaluate some lots. He was a tax commissioner in 1674, was assigned to find ships for military transport, and was one of three receivers appointed to close out the books of the West India Company in North America.

When English rule was reestablished late in 1674, Steenwyck and seven other Dutch leaders refused to take the oath of allegiance without assurances that rights guaranteed to the Dutch colonists in 1664 were still in effect. Governor Edmund Andros (Sir Edward Andros) responded by sending the eight leaders to prison and he threatened to confiscate their property until they agreed to take the oath. They eventually took it, but none was restored to the provincial government during Andros's administration.

Steenwyck was not, however, rendered insignificant. In a 1676 assessment, his worth was placed at £4,000, second in the city. That year he was invited to a meeting of provincial and local officials about fundraising, was on the committee to audit city accounts, and in 1679 participated as a principal merchant in two policy meetings, one about exporting wheat, the other about Iroquois relations. But it was not until Governor Thomas Dongan, who arrived in New York in 1683, appointed him as a judge on an admiralty court that he returned to office. Steenwyck served as an alderman briefly in 1683 and then was appointed to a third term as mayor in 1683–1684.

In 1684 he acquired from John Archer's estate, for which he was curator, the manor of "Fordham," his greatest land acquisition, which he bequeathed to the Reformed Church of New York. His will, written 20 November 1684 and probated 8 May 1685, establishes his approximate date of death. His estate was valued at £5,970. As one of the wealthiest merchants in a colony created for economic purposes, Cornelis Steenwyck financially supported, influenced, and participated in colonial government. He was pragmatic about changes in government as the Netherlands and England contended for power but in 1674 spoke out at great risk to protect colonists' rights. He gave freely of his time and wealth to improve the colony.

• There is no significant collection of Steenwyck's papers. References to him may be found throughout local and provincial records, including Berthold Fernow, ed., *The Records of New Amsterdam* (1896; repr. 1976), and the *New Netherland Documents* and *New York Historical Manuscripts* Series. Brief accounts of Steenwyck's life are in W. E. De Riemer, *The De Riemer Family* (1905), and I. N. P. Stokes, *The Iconography of Manhattan Island* (6 vols., 1915–1928). Bayrd Still, "New York's Mayoralty: The Formative Years," *New-York Historical Society Quarterly* 47 (1963): 239–55, reviews his career but praises him inappropriately for accomplishments in his third term as mayor that he hardly achieved alone, and some of which were actually realized during the term of his predecessor.

PETER R. CHRISTOPH

STEERE, Richard (c. 1643–20 June 1721), colonial merchant and religious poet, was born in Chertsey, England, the son of Richard Steere, a leather worker, and Annis Springall. Educated in Latin and literature at the Free Grammar School at Kingston-upon-Thames, he was apprenticed in 1658 as a cordwainer in the city of London. Granted the freedom of the Company of Cordwainers in 1666, he seems to have engaged in foreign trade with Barbados and the Americas as early as this period. In London, Steere became a member of the General Baptists, a group persecuted after the Restoration.

Although Steere was persecuted for his religious beliefs, his own poetry was never devoted to tolerance but to bigoted attacks on his image of a world-Catholic conspiracy. Steere's first public poetry was in response to "Absalom and Achitophel," John Dryden's poetic satire on the anti-Catholic earl of Shaftesbury and his plots to keep James II off the English throne. Steere's poem "The History of the Babylonish Cabals" (1682) improbably attempts to portray Shaftesbury as the biblical Daniel maintaining a pure conscience while his religious liberty and pure soul are harassed by ungodly enemies.

"A Message from Tory-Land to the Whig-Makers in Albian" (1682) employs a mock-Jesuit narrator and a burlesque meter with quadruple internal rhymes to reveal how Rome was the real power manipulating the Tory party in England:

> If you can't turn um, scorn um, burn um,
> Else with your sanctified Daggers adorn um,
> Bring to Perfection Destraction, and faction,
> The *Pope* will account it a glorious action.

A more serious effort is "Romes Thunder-Bolt; or, Antichrist Displaid" (1682), a pedestrian comparison of Catholicism to Antichrist and the Whore of Babylon. Lacking the crude humor of "A Message," this satire is marred by Steere's inability to handle the rhyming couplet with wit or a consistent meter.

After the Rye-House Plot—a Whig attempt to kill King Charles II and the duke of York (later James II)—a government persecution of Whigs and their printers, including Steere's, led the poet to flee to America in late 1682 or early the next year. Steere revisited London from Boston in December 1683. This almost fatal voyage was the inspiration for his maritime deliverance poem, "A Monumental Memorial of Marine Mercy" (1684). The escape from death increased his sense of the power of Providence in human life, as the poem clearly shows, and convinced him that his days as an Englishman were done. He remained in hiding while in London.

Returning to New England in 1684, Steere published his sea poem and became the clerk, acting lawyer, and trading agent for John Wheeler, a prospering trader of New London, Connecticut. Wheeler's death in 1691 left Steere free to aid and marry his widow Elizabeth about a year later and firmly establish himself in the American merchant community. It also made him the stepfather of six children at the age of fifty-two.

Steere traded and litigated his new possessions in relative peace until January 1695, when he joined three others in a suit against the city of New London for its prosecution of John Rogers for his deliberate disruption of Congregationalist meetings and his refusal to pay a tax for the minister's upkeep. Steere argued for religious liberty against the Congregationalists, whom he insisted on calling "Presbyterians," forcing Baptists and Quakers to pay for Congregationalist ministers. He lost and was fined five pounds. Yet the case highlighted the contradictions of forming a society based on dissenting religious ideals and then dealing with dissenters from those very ideals. Here Steere hypocritically demanded a latitude for action that he would certainly have denied Anglicans or Catholics.

Steere revised his early anti-Catholic works between 1688 and 1694. His "History of the Babylonish Cabals" was extensively rewritten and published as "The Daniel Catcher" with "Earth's Felicities," "Heaven's Allowances" and the acrostic "A Christian Alphabet" (1713). In the blank verse of "Earth's Felicities," the work of a mellowed old age spent in peace and plenty, Steere rediscovers St. Augustine's position that the earth is God's creation and is therefore good, if used correctly. Donald Wharton places two other poems included in this collection, "A Sea-Storm nigh the Coast" and a nativity ode influenced by John Milton (an oddity for a Baptist poet of this period), after 1693 but "well before" 1710, when "Earth's Felicities" seems to have been composed.

The Steeres moved to Long Island in 1710, and Elizabeth died there in 1712. In June 1712 Steere married Margaret Sylvester, a widow and the mother of four children. After she died in 1713, his last marriage was in March 1714 to Bethiah Mapes, a widow with five children. He died and was buried in Southold, New York, with provisions in his will for all his stepchildren. Steere's work is interesting as an example of religious polemic and as one vision of God's mercy in colonial America, but the poetry has had no discernible effect on other authors.

• See Donald Wharton's biography, *Richard Steere: Colonial Merchant Poet* (1979), for information on the poet and his prose, and George Littlefield, *The Early Massachusetts Press: 1638–1711* (1969), for the fullest selection of his poems. Wharton, *In the Trough of the Sea: Selected Sea-Deliverance Narratives* (1979), contains more information on "A Monumental Memorial of Maritime Mercy."

HENRY RUSSELL

STEFANSSON, Vilhjalmur (3 Nov. 1879–26 Aug. 1962), Arctic explorer, writer, and lecturer, was born in Arnes, Manitoba, Canada, the son of Johann Stefansson and Ingibjorg Johannesdottir, Icelanders who had arrived in Canada in 1877. In 1881 the family moved to North Dakota, where Vilhjalmur attended school and eventually the University of North Dakota, the University of Iowa (B.A. 1903), and Harvard, where he entered the divinity school before transferring to anthropology. In 1906 he left school without graduating to join the Anglo-American Polar Expedition as ethnologist. After failing to rendezvous with other expedition members, who had been shipwrecked, Stefansson wintered among the Eskimos of Tuktoyyaktut, adapting to the Eskimo way of life and learning their language.

In 1908 Stefansson, funded by the American Museum of Natural History, returned to the Arctic with Rudolph Anderson, a zoologist and former classmate at Iowa. The men wintered at Charles Brower's trade and whaling post near Barrow, Alaska, where Stefansson continued his studies of Eskimo language and culture. In 1909–1910 Stefansson traveled extensively along the coast on foot, over sea ice, and aboard coastal trading schooners. Eskimos helped him master their hunting and travel skills. In April 1910 Stefansson reached Victoria Island to investigate Eskimos who were said to rely on Stone Age technology and, more sensationally, to have strong Caucasian features. Although Stefansson's theory that the "Blond Eskimos," later known as the "Copper Eskimos," of Victoria Island might have been the descendants of Vikings has not been supported by other authorities, his discovery and study of an isolated, primitive people gave the young ethnologist his first international prominence. A book, *My Life with the Eskimo* (1913), describes Stefansson's 1911–1912 winter among these fascinating people.

Stefansson's well-publicized achievements, scientific honors, and talents as lecturer and writer attracted several sponsors. Stefansson accepted leadership of the Canadian Arctic Expedition to explore the Arctic Ocean for new lands and conduct geological research along the coast. It was the first large-scale scientific study of the Arctic supported by Canada. Officials divided the expedition into a southern party under Anderson and a northern party under Stefansson to facilitate Stefansson's exploration for new land, but the division allowed malcontents among the scientists to resist Stefansson's authority as field leader. Stefansson may have lacked the political skills necessary for leading a large party, particularly one isolated from his influence and angry about decisions made without consultation. Lacking Arctic experience, the Geological Survey scientists were unsure of their performance yet fearful that Stefansson, whom they considered to be more of a publicist than a scientist, would reap honors that they deserved. However justified their complaints were regarding his leadership, it is clear that the young geologists were mutinous in sentiment and encouraged Anderson, who envied his leader, to turn against him. Nonetheless, despite the discord and the tragic loss of *Karluk*, his intended base ship, Stefansson accomplished his goals, and the southern party completed its surveys, leaving the field in 1916.

The tragic loss of *Karluk* occurred after Captain Bob Bartlett, while trying to force a passage along the Alaskan coast, put the ship conveying the northern party into the ice. Stefansson was ashore hunting when the ship was swept eastward into the ice. Near Wrangel Island, Siberia, Bartlett abandoned ship and established a camp on Wrangel Island. Bartlett made a heroic sea ice crossing to get help, but several men starved before rescuers reached Wrangel, and others died trying to reach the mainland on their own.

Stefansson returned home in 1918 to devote the rest of his life to writing and lecturing about the Arctic, its peoples, and its economic prospects. He argued that the region was rich in resources that could be exploited for the benefit of the region and those nations willing to invest in development enterprises. His account of the Canadian Arctic Expedition in *The Friendly Arctic* (1921) is among the best books on the region; it encompasses an exploration narrative and considerable information on northern lands and peoples. Stefansson lived in New York until he married Evelyn Baird in 1941; they then moved to Vermont and, finally, to Hanover, New Hampshire, after his library was purchased for Dartmouth, and he and Evelyn joined the faculty. The couple had no children.

Americans continued to respect Stefansson's authority on northern matters and to support his literary projects, but his influence in Canada declined in the 1920s, after the failure of an attempt to raise reindeer on Baffin Island and his sponsorship of a Wrangel Island colony that ended with the loss of several lives. Stefansson's Canadian rival, Rudolph Anderson, and scientists of the Geological Survey zealously carried on the vendetta that started during the Canadian Arctic Expedition to the detriment of Stefansson's reputation.

Regardless of the controversies, Stefansson's work as an explorer gained him honors from governments and learned societies. He was the last explorer to discover new lands in the Arctic, and he fully credited the Eskimos who taught him how to hunt and travel in the region. As an explorer he sought knowledge rather than meaningless goals such as reaching the "farthest North" or achieving "the conquest of the pole." In this respect his career contrasts with those of famed explorers of his time such as Roald Amundsen and Robert Peary. With his persuasive advocacy of the need for government and private expenditures on economic development in the Arctic, Stefansson alerted the public to the strategic and economic importance of the region. As a scholar, explorer, visionary, and "prophet of the North," Stefansson made outstanding contributions to his chosen field of endeavor. He died in Hanover, New Hampshire.

• The largest collections of research material on Stefansson's career is in the Stefansson Collection, Baker Library, Dartmouth College, and the public archives of Canada, Ottawa. Works by Stefansson include his autobiography, *Discovery* (1964), and *The Northward Course of Empire* (1922). Recent biographical treatments include Richard J. Diubaldo, *Stefansson and the Canadian Arctic* (1978), a hostile view of Stefansson that reflects the animosity of the Canadian Geological Survey. For a sympathetic view of Stefansson's achievements, see William R. Hunt, *Stef: A Biography of Vilhjalmur Stefansson, Canadian Arctic Explorer* (1986). An obituary is in the *New York Times*, 27 Aug. 1962.

WILLIAM R. HUNT

STEFFENS, Lincoln (6 Apr. 1866–9 Aug. 1936), journalist, was born Joseph Lincoln Steffens in San Francisco, California, the son of Joseph Steffens, a banker, and Elizabeth Louisa Symes. In 1870 the Steffens family moved to Sacramento, where Steffens and his three sisters grew to adulthood in an upwardly mobile middle-class family.

After an undistinguished educational experience at the University of California at Berkeley, from which he graduated in 1889, Steffens traveled to Germany to continue his education. During 1889 and 1890 he studied ethics, philosophy, and art history at the Universities of Berlin and Heidelberg. The following year he explored psychology and fell in love with fellow American student Josephine Bontecou at Leipzig University. They moved to Paris in 1891 and studied at the Sorbonne. They secretly married in London in 1891 and returned to the United States in 1892.

Steffens launched a search for employment in New York City. Aided by an introduction provided by his father to Robert Underwood Johnson, associate editor of *Century Magazine*, he secured a position as a reporter with the *New York Evening Post*, where he worked on a number of different beats and learned firsthand how to investigate and craft newsworthy articles on local politics, economic conditions, and culture.

Steffens soon became the newspaper's first police reporter. Assigned to cover Rev. Charles H. Parkhurst's crusade against vice and the state legislature's Lexow Committee on police corruption, Steffens regularly prowled lower Manhattan's Mulberry Street, the nerve center of the police and detective forces. There, with the *New York Evening Sun*'s veteran police reporter Jacob Riis as his mentor, Steffens sharpened his skills as an investigative reporter and as a student of corruption, reform, and urban politics.

The investigations into police corruption resulted in the defeat of the Tammany political machine's mayor by a reform candidate, William L. Strong, in 1894. When he assumed the mayor's office in 1895, Strong appointed a board of police commissioners headed by Theodore Roosevelt. As part of his own education, Roosevelt gathered information from a variety of individuals, including Riis and Steffens. While covering Roosevelt's assault on corruption in the police department, Steffens used his column to champion police reform.

Roosevelt's departure in the spring of 1897 for Washington, D.C., and the return of the Tammany forces to city hall in the fall dampened the fires of reform and led Steffens to seek a new position where he could more fully utilize his European education, investigative skills, and reform politics. In 1897 Steffens left the *Evening Post* with a group of co-workers to resuscitate the *New York Commercial Advertiser*. As city editor, Steffens helped to transform the paper into a combined newspaper and news magazine. He recruited a dynamic group of writers, offering the opportunity to experiment and asking in return only that they write well and be willing to learn. During his tenure, the *Advertiser* attracted a number of men who either launched careers in journalism or honed their nascent journalistic skills. Guy Scull (war correspondent), Abraham Cahan (novelist and editor of the *Jewish Daily Forward*), Carl Hovey (editor of *Metropolitan Magazine*), and Norman Hapgood (editor of *Collier's Weekly*) all worked under Steffens.

Steffens also wrote a variety of pieces ranging from fiction to autobiographical sketches. His stories about ghetto life in New York City appeared in *Chap-Book* and the *Evening Post*'s Saturday supplements during 1896. The *Advertiser* published his "Roosevelt Stories," which explored Theodore Roosevelt's exploits and qualities. Another series of stories detailed his university experiences in Germany.

Steffens was offered the post of managing editor of *McClure's Magazine* in the spring of 1901, but he delayed taking the job until the fall. In the interim he and his wife took an extended vacation during which he attempted to write a novel. What he found, however, was that his years in journalism were not the prerequisite training for writing the great novel, as he had believed. Journalism was not just a way station on the road to somewhere else; it was his vocation.

Steffens began his new duties at *McClure's* in September 1901. Life behind a desk, however, brought with it too much administrative detail and too little time for writing. His creative energies were released when his editor, S. S. McClure, told him that he would never learn to edit a magazine by sitting in the office. Freed from his desk, Steffens took to the road in pursuit of news and material. Investigating, interviewing, writing, and editing on the go proved stimulating, and Steffens entered the most creative period of his career.

In 1902 Steffens became part of a movement that he was both influenced by and influential in shaping. His generation was attempting to make sense of the social and economic changes associated with industrialization, urbanization, and immigration. For many journalists, muckraking became the way to combine an examination of American life with a belief in the need for reform. Their goal was not just to expose but also to seek understanding and promote change. President

Theodore Roosevelt coined the term "muckraking" in 1906, but the movement had occupied a prominent place in American journalism since 1901. Muckrakers used words and images as a call to action for changes in political life, economic organization, race relations, and social injustice. Central to the dissemination of their findings were mass circulation magazines, such as *McClure's*, that drew on an expanding middle-class audience, employed the newest innovations in technology, and featured articles characterized by intensive research and graphic writing.

Steffens quickly earned the epithet of "muckraker" together with co-workers John S. Phillips, Ida M. Tarbell, and Ray Stannard Baker. Steffens's particular niche was the relationship between corruption and government and between knowledge and action. For the next decade he explored the way in which "the System," as he termed it, flourished whenever the proper mix of conditions existed. He concluded that the business community's self-interest and resources allowed it to pervert American traditions of representative government. The question, for Steffens, was whether or not "the people" would rally to regain control of their government once alerted to this fact.

Steffens concentrated first on urban government. He traveled from city to city talking with politicians, reformers, crooks, and editors. Based on his investigations, he crafted articles that combined the human interest approach to writing with the enthusiasm of the crusader and the purposefulness of the reformer. The compelling nature of his articles captured the reading public's interest. His articles on the battle between corruption and reform explored Chicago, Minneapolis, New York, Philadelphia, Pittsburgh, and St. Louis. Published separately in *McClure's* in 1902 and 1903, they appeared together as *The Shame of the Cities* in 1904. In many cases he was summarizing information already available to the public, yet Steffens revealed in a striking fashion the ubiquitous nature of municipal corruption and the equally widespread apathy on the part of the public.

Steffens's masterful manipulation of language and his grasp of the art of storytelling made his articles especially compelling. His thoughtful choice of words and their select repetition heightened the drama of his tale. For example, "The Shame of Minneapolis" is followed by "The Shamelessness of St. Louis" and "Pittsburgh: A City Ashamed." He personalized the stories of corruption and integrated his own visits into his account. Bosses and reformers had personalities, and Steffens made readers feel that they knew the actors. A sense of place and person, individual identification with the problem, and an urgent call to action gave *Shame of the Cities* its popular appeal.

By 1905 the reform impulse had begun to move from the municipal to the state level, and Steffens shifted his attention to the battle for good government in the nation's state capitals. A new series of his articles took shape and in 1906 became *The Struggle for Self-Government*. Steffens detailed the challenge posed by the ascendancy of business interests over the public interest. Just whom did state legislators represent? Were "the people" going to take back their governments?

Steffens continued to explore these issues after his departure from *McClure's* in 1906. Along with several other writers, Steffens purchased the *American Magazine*, and in less than a year it blossomed into a leading reform publication. Unhappy with editorial disputes, however, Steffens soon sold his share in the *American* and became a freelance writer. For the next two years he contributed articles to *Everybody's* and worked on a third volume of essays, *Upbuilders* (1909), which focused less on the dynamics of political life and more on individuals involved in the battle for reform. Steffens examined the impact of knowledge about graft on individual decisions to become reformers and analyzed the importance of moral leadership in mobilizing civic consciousness against the evils of corruption.

By 1909 the muckraking phase of Steffens's career was drawing to a close. At the invitation of Edward A. Filene, a Boston retailer and reformer, Steffens investigated Boston's government and developed specific proposals for reform. Rather than providing Steffens with an opportunity to draft a blueprint for change, the experience convinced him that it was harder to effect change than to write about the need for it. Although his proposals became part of the "Boston 1915" plan for civic rebirth, Steffens failed to complete his study of Boston and found himself less enthusiastic about the possibilities of changing conditions through journalistic revelations.

Disillusioned by the lack of change, frustrated by the failure of moral leadership to steer "the System" into responsible action, and saddened by his wife's death in 1911, Steffens channeled his activities into new directions. For the next twenty-five years Steffens lived on the go, traveling widely. He began to see his role as a mediator, helping to facilitate understanding between the old order and the new. He turned his attention to the revolutionary climate of the world outside the United States. During 1914 he traveled to Mexico to observe a revolution in the making. In a series of articles, he counseled the Mexicans to craft a constitution able to withstand corruption, interference, and exploitation from foreign countries such as the United States. Although angering many Americans with his anti-American stance, he worked with representatives of both governments to ease the volatile relations between the two nations.

Steffens continued in this mode when he journeyed to Russia in 1917 to observe and assess the nature of the revolution there. He believed that Americans had much to learn from the Bolsheviks' attempt to destroy "the System," but few Americans were interested. After World War I Steffens traveled again to Russia as part of an unofficial American diplomatic delegation headed by William C. Bullitt, but little came of his efforts to share what he saw as the promise of the Russian experience. Undeterred, he published *Moses in Red: The Revolt of Israel as a Typical Revolution* (1926), a novel in which he used the parable of the flight of the Israelites into Egypt to explain the Russian Revolution. Once again, he failed to engage the interest of the American public. In 1924 Steffens married Ella Winter, with whom he had a son, his only child. In 1927 the family settled in Carmel, California.

Steffens then devoted himself to the completion of his autobiography, which documents his interest in and frustration with reform and his fascination with the potential of revolutionary activities. Published in 1931, the two-volume *Autobiography* has been hailed as one of the best of its kind and has become a classic piece of literature. The *Autobiography* also revived interest in Steffens. His written work was in greater demand than it had been for many years, and he received numerous speaking engagements. While on a lecture tour during the fall of 1933, he had a heart attack. Not completely incapacitated, he continued his daily routine until his death at his home in Carmel. As his obituary in the *New York Times* suggested, Steffens's contribution rests on his work as a journalist. His investigative reporting style, his effective use of the human interest story, his quest for understanding, and his passionate belief in the potential of reform during his muckraking years ultimately influenced the shape of modern journalistic practice.

• Steffens's papers can be found in the Bancroft Library, the University of California at Berkeley, and at Columbia University. *The Letters of Lincoln Steffens*, ed. Ella Winter and Granville Hicks (1938), is also an important source. *The World of Lincoln Steffens*, ed. Ella Winter and Herbert Shapiro (1962), contains a representative sampling of Steffens's articles and covers his post-muckraking period particularly well. Justin Kaplan, *Lincoln Steffens: A Biography* (1974), is the only major biography of Steffens. Both Russell M. Horton, *Lincoln Steffens* (1974), and Patrick F. Palermo, *Lincoln Steffens* (1978), provide a good introduction to Steffens's career. Robert Stinson, *Lincoln Steffens* (1979), is an analysis of his writings. Irving Cheslaw, "An Intellectual Biography of Lincoln Steffens" (Ph.D. diss., Columbia Univ., 1952), contains a useful introduction to his intellectual world as well as an excellent bibliography. An obituary is in the *New York Times*, 10 Aug. 1936.

PATRICIA MOONEY-MELVIN

STEGNER, Wallace Earle (18 Feb. 1909–13 Apr. 1993), author and educator, was born in Lake Mills, Iowa, the son of George Stegner, a drifting, gambling worker, and Hilda Paulson. The itinerant family lived in Grand Forks, North Dakota, then Redmond and Bellingham, Washington, then East End, Saskatchewan, Canada, and then Great Falls, Montana, before settling in Salt Lake City, Utah, in 1921. After graduating from high school there, Stegner attended the University of Utah, where during his freshman year his contact with western writer-teacher Vardis Fisher stimulated his interest in creative writing. Awarded a B.A. from Utah in 1930, Stegner entered the University of Iowa as a graduate student in English and a part-time teacher. After receiving his M.A. in 1932, he briefly studied at the University of California, Berkeley, but soon returned to Salt Lake City to care for his mother, who died of cancer in 1933. He reentered the graduate program at Iowa in 1934, married fellow student Mary Stuart Page that year (they had one child), resumed teaching at Utah in 1935, and earned his Ph.D. from Iowa that same year. In 1936 Utah published a short version of his dissertation on the literary geologist Clarence Edward Dutton. Then Stegner began a renowned career combining scholarly and creative writing with equally successful teaching.

In 1937 Stegner won the Little, Brown novelette prize of $2,500 for *Remembering Laughter*, a compact tale of a virile husband, his frigid wife, and her vibrant sister in rural Iowa. That same year Stegner began teaching at the University of Wisconsin. He taught in 1939 (and later) at writers' conferences in Breadloaf, Vermont, where he met Bernard DeVoto and Robert Frost, among many other notable writer-teachers, then taught composition at Harvard from 1939 to 1944. Stegner's father committed suicide in 1940. Stegner continued to publish fiction long and short—some cast in Saskatchewan—nonfictional articles, and also *Mormon Country* (1942), a pro-Mormon history with fictional vignettes. In 1943 came *The Big Rock Candy Mountain*, his ranging, autobiographical family chronicle, in some 370,000 words. It dramatizes the repeated failures of the hero's footloose, paradoxical father as he and his home-loving wife migrate from one region to another, each scrupulously limned, in search of the American Dream, symbolized by the lovely western mountain of candy so celebrated in song; the mother's death by cancer and then the father's suicide; and finally the scarred hero's affirmation of life despite his uneasy memories. Stegner worked for *Look* magazine on articles regarding religious and racial intolerance, published as *One Nation* in 1945, and that year began to teach at Stanford University and to direct its writing program.

For the next twenty-six years Stegner combined distinguished teaching, impressive literary productivity, an enormous amount of traveling, and the garnering of a dozen or more fellowships, awards, and prizes, culminating in the Pulitzer Prize for fiction, which his *Angle of Repose* won in 1971, the year of his retirement from Stanford. He also excelled in biography, with *The Preacher and the Slave* (1950; retitled *Joe Hill: A Biographical Novel* [1969]), a fictionalized account of Joe Hill, the legendary labor union organizer executed in Salt Lake City in 1915 on a disputed charge of double murder. Better was Stegner's *Beyond the Hundredth Meridian: John Wesley Powell and the Second Opening of the West* (1954), which details Powell's trailblazing explorations and discusses his encouragement of government-sponsored scientific studies of the ecologically endangered West. Later came *The Uneasy Chair: A Biography of Bernard DeVoto* (1974). Stegner treats DeVoto with an objectivity warmed by collegiality: both men were westerners who taught in the East, criticized the liberal eastern establishment, liked rural parts of New England, and deplored the exploitation of the West. *The Sound of Mountain Water* (1969) is a collection of Stegner essays, letters, and lectures that lovingly praise nature and also comment on difficulties when one is labeled a "Western writer." Two collections of his short fiction, previously published in some of the most distinguished periodicals, are *The Women on the Wall* (1950) and *The City of the Living, and Other Stories* (1956), mostly about the pains of maturing and some echoing episodes in *The Big Rock Candy Mountain*. Stegner's *Wolf Willow* (1962) is a superb autobiography of his youth in Saskatchewan.

Among many other works, several stand out. His second book on Mormons, *The Gathering of Zion* (1964), is a well-researched trek document. *All the Little Live Things* (1967), a novel featuring characters and episodes introduced in earlier short stories, concerns an eastern literary agent retired among California hippies. Soon came *Angle of Repose*, easily Stegner's most complex masterpiece. It is based on the life of Mary Hallock, the real-life illustrator-writer who in 1876 married Arthur De Wint Foote, an engineer; left the East; and lived in the Far West with him. Stegner, who obtained Mary Hallock Foote's remarkable papers for the Stanford library, was long fascinated by them. He fictionalizes events in her troubled life by filtering them through an imagined grandson, an emeritus historian. He is the crippled victim of bone disease, abandoned by his wife and betrayed by their rebellious son, and studies his grandmother's papers to reconstruct her grief-stricken life in an effort to make sense of his own. Controversy arose concerning *Angle of Repose* when Foote's reminiscences were published in 1972 and critics began to see the great extent to which Stegner had quoted and paraphrased her voluminous journal entries and letters without any acknowledgment.

Stegner remained active following his retirement from teaching. As late as 1992 he published a group of essays titled *Where the Bluebird Sings to the Lemonade Springs: Living and Writing in the West*. The following year he went to Santa Fe to lecture, was badly injured in a traffic accident, and died there a few days later. He is universally regarded as one of the very finest writers of his era dealing with the personal challenges and the aesthetic rewards of life in the West. His is an eloquent voice pleading for familial understanding and respect for the land.

• Most of Stegner's papers are in the university libraries of Iowa, Mich., Pa., Stanford, and Utah. Other locations include the Ford Foundation in New York City and the Newberry Library in Chicago. Merrill Lewis and Lorene Lewis, *Wallace Stegner* (1972), concentrates on his western writings. Forrest G. Robinson and Margaret G. Robinson, *Wallace Stegner* (1977), is a critical biography. Anthony Arthur, *Critical Essays on Wallace Stegner* (1982), assembles reviews, articles, and essays by twenty-three critics, including Mary Ellen Williams Walsh, "*Angle of Repose* and the Writings of Mary Hallock Foote: A Source Study," pp. 184–209. Wallace Stegner and Richard W. Etulain, *Conversations with Wallace Stegner on Western History and Literature* (1983; rev. ed., 1990), has invaluable revelations and asides. Charles E. Rankin, ed., *Wallace Stegner: Man and Writer* (1996), assembles seventeen essays, fourteen of which are original. The main essay

in Elizabeth Cook-Lynn, *Why I Can't Read Wallace Stegner and Other Essays: A Tribal Voice* (1996), rebukes Stegner for "contribut[ing] to the politics of possession and dispossession" with respect to Native Americans. Obituaries are in the *Los Angeles Times*, 13 Apr. 1993; the *New York Times*, 15 Apr. 1993; and the *Times* (London), 21 Apr. 1993.

ROBERT L. GALE

STEICHEN, Edward (27 Mar. 1879–25 Mar. 1973), photographer and curator of museum exhibitions, was born Edouard Jean Steichen in Luxembourg, the son of Jean-Pierre Steichen, a copper miner, and Marie Kemp, a milliner. The family immigrated to Milwaukee in 1881. Edward Steichen began his distinguished career with an apprenticeship (1894–1898) at the Milwaukee American Fine Art Company, where he learned lithography and the basics of design. At the same time, with encouragement from his mother, he studied painting at the Milwaukee Art Students League.

In 1895, in the decade when photography was just beginning a long struggle to be accepted as equal to the fine arts, he began to teach himself photography, and that medium progressively dominated his practice. Yet his persona remained that of the painter. In one of his most famous early self-portraits (1901), Steichen's technically complex photograph poses him as a painter, with palette, brushes, and romantic costume. He did not abandon painting until 1922. During the first decade of the twentieth century, Steichen's extensive knowledge of European arts helped his friend and colleague Alfred Stieglitz introduce modern painting to American audiences.

In an observation calculated to surprise later critics who were unaware of his many years as a painter, Steichen wrote in his autobiography (1963), "Today, in retrospect, I believe my work as a photographer had a greater influence on my painting than my work as a painter had on my photography." Since his early photographs are characteristically "painterly" in their handling of chiaroscuro and texture, it is frustrating that he was not more detailed in his observation. What is even more frustrating is that he combined multiple negatives and mastered processes like gum bichromate, carbon printing, platinum, cyanotype, and gelatin silver, incorporating many of these into single prints. Even museum experts have difficulty determining how particular prints were achieved.

Though he had two prints accepted by the jury of the Second Philadelphia Photography Salon (1899), Steichen's most important early success came out of meeting the noted American photographer F. Holland Day during his first stay in Europe from 1900 to 1902. Day was so impressed by the younger man's pictures that he included thirty-five Steichen prints in his "New School of American Photography" exhibition in London and Paris (1901). As a result, Steichen was elected to the London-based Linked Ring Brotherhood, one of the most prestigious groups advocating "fine art photography."

Like many artists and photographers studying in Paris at the turn of the century, Steichen greatly admired the sculptor Rodin, whom he met in 1901. Rodin was delighted to pose for him and encouraged him to photograph his controversial sculpture of Balzac. Steichen's eloquent moonlit photographs of the Balzac (1908) revealed how sympathetically he interpreted Rodin's symbolic intent. Using multiple negatives, Steichen also created a mysterious portrait of Rodin with his sculpture of "Le Penseur." While in Paris, Steichen photographed Maurice Maeterlinck, whose metaphysical books *Treasure of the Humble* (1896) and *Wisdom and Destiny* (1898) were influential among many American artists.

In 1902 Steichen's first one-man show was held at La Maison des Artistes in Paris. Returning to New York City that year, he joined Stieglitz in founding the influential group called the Photo-Secession. This informal association included many of the most important American Pictorialists, photographers who believed in making pictures rather than simply taking them. The Pictorialists based their aesthetics on symbolism in painting and, like Steichen, pursued technical complexity as well as the ideals of fine art.

Steichen designed and decorated the "Little Galleries of the Photo-Secession" at 291 Fifth Avenue and hung the first exhibits for Stieglitz. Already famous as a photographer and editor, in his role as gallery owner Stieglitz made "291" the center of avant-garde art. Steichen's studio was just across the hall at "293." His work was exhibited at "291" regularly and his dark portraits, like that of J. Pierpont Morgan (1903), where the ponderous financier grips the knifelike handle of his chair, won him further recognition. Morgan so hated the portrait that he tore the first proof to shreds, but later he recanted and offered to buy a print of it. The same year Steichen married Clara E. Smith, with whom he had two children; the marriage ended in divorce in 1921.

To keep up with the exciting new modernist art movements, both Steichen and Stieglitz traveled frequently to Europe. It was Steichen, rather than his better-known colleague, who gained favor with avant-garde collectors like Gertrude and Leo Stein. He persuaded Stieglitz to publish reproductions of the works of Cezanne, Matisse, Rodin, Picasso, and John Marin in what became the single most admired photography journal, *Camera Work* (1903–1917). Steichen not only designed the cover for that publication but saw his own paintings and photographs reproduced therein over the years, culminating in a double issue (1913) featuring his work. His landscape photographs during these years favored twilight scenes whose mood matched that of the "Tonalist" painters. Steichen called his multiple methods "peinture à la lumière," painting with light.

During a trip to London and Paris in 1906–1907, the two colleagues encountered the new Lumière Autochrome process, which produced warmly luminescent color images on glass transparencies. The difficulty with the Autochromes was that they could not be exhibited as prints on walls, but they could be—and were—reproduced in color in *Camera Work*. Despite Stieglitz's objections, Steichen generously taught the process to Alvin Langdon Coburn, one of the most important members of the Photo-Secession.

In 1910 Stieglitz organized the "International Exhibition of Pictorial Photography" at Buffalo's Albright-Knox Museum, including thirty-one prints by Steichen. The show was later regarded as the swan song of Pictorialism.

The advent of World War I drastically altered Steichen's interests. When the liner *Lusitania* was sunk by the Germans in 1915, he decided he wanted to emulate Mathew Brady's group of Civil War photographers by recording the current conflict. Determined to serve as a photographer-reporter, he enlisted and was soon made commander of the photographic division of the U.S. Air Force. He remained with that branch for a year after the war in order to organize aerial reconnaissance photography, which was still in its infancy. For his efforts, France honored him as a Chevalier, Legion d'Honneur in 1919.

While living at Voulangis in France, Steichen destroyed his paintings to demonstrate his newly intensified devotion to photography. "I wanted to reach into the world to participate and communicate. . . . " He wanted to learn how to make photographs suitable for the printed page as a means of reaching larger audiences.

Although he was now pursuing realism in photography, Steichen also aimed at aesthetic excellence. He plunged into an intensive study of plane and solid geometry, becoming strongly influenced by Sir Theodore Andrea Cook's *The Curves of Life, Being an Account of Spiral Formations and Their Application to Growth in Nature* (1914). In 1921 Steichen went off to Venice, where he met the flamboyant modern dancer Isadora Duncan. Persuaded to travel with her troupe to Athens, Steichen took several stunning portraits of Duncan at the Parthenon.

Steichen had taken his first fashion photographs in Paris for *Art et Decoration* (1911). In 1923 he married Dana Desboro Glover, who died in 1957. The same year, back in New York City, he joined Conde Nast Publications as fashion photographer for *Vogue* magazine and portrait photographer for *Vanity Fair*. For the next fifteen years, Steichen produced remarkable portraits of stage and film stars such as Charles Chaplin, Marlene Dietrich, Gloria Swanson, John Barrymore, Katherine Cornell, Martha Graham, Paul Robeson, Fred Astaire, Maurice Chevalier, and Noël Coward, as well as likenesses of literati like H. L. Mencken, Alexander Wolcott, and his brother-in-law Carl Sandburg. Perhaps the most famous was his portrait of Greta Garbo dramatically framing her face with her hands. These portraits represented the height of Steichen's artistic powers, although his fashion pictures were just as striking. They were noted for their naturalism, allowing women to easily imagine themselves wearing the apparel depicted. The giant agency of J. Walter Thompson employed Steichen for advertising photography, where he also worked in a realistic style.

In 1928 Steichen became embroiled in a conflict with the U.S. government over his importation of Constantin Brancusi's sculpture "Bird in Space." Customs wanted to levy fees based on their opinion that the Brancusi was imported merchandise. He was successful in demonstrating that the bronze was a unique work of art and therefore not subject to customs duties. Steichen's efforts here were instrumental in gaining recognition for modernist art in all media.

In 1929, at fifty-nine, Steichen moved to a farm in Redding, Connecticut. There he devoted his spare time to breeding delphiniums, a horticultural practice begun before 1914. Ultimately, his flowers were so spectacular that he was given an exhibition of them at the Museum of Modern Art in New York in 1936. It was the first time that living flora had been exhibited as art by that institution.

Fashion and commercial photography gradually became "boring and repetitive" to him. In 1938 Steichen closed his New York studio to pursue a yearlong visit to Mexico, where he wanted to record native populations without their being aware that they were being photographed. Only small, handheld 35mm cameras could accomplish such a task. Steichen persuaded Carl Zeiss to provide him with a Contax camera whose finder disguised his activity. Steichen was not alone in this practice, as it was perhaps an inevitable outcome of the development of rapid small cameras and fast films, as well as the "candid" approach of journalists.

Despite his advancing age, Steichen was active during the Second World War as head of a unit of commissioned officers assigned to cover naval aviation. He was named director of the U.S. Naval Photographic Institute, commanded all combat photography, and ended as a captain in 1946. On board the USS *Lexington*, Steichen saw action in Pacific battles, experiences he described in his book *The Blue Ghost* (1947). He photographed the Marines at Kwajalein Island, and the U.S. Navy film "The Fighting Lady" was produced under his supervision.

Steichen's curatorial association with the Museum of Modern Art began when he organized two exhibitions during the war, "Road to Victory" and "Power in the Pacific." The Museum appointed him director of their Department of Photography, a post he kept from 1947 to 1962. In 1947 he gave up all his own commercial work to devote himself to curating nearly fifty exhibitions. The exhibition that guaranteed his international and enduring fame was "The Family of Man" (1955), which Steichen was convinced was "the most important undertaking" of his long career. It was a phenomenal success; its seemingly universal appeal lay in its thesis that all human experiences were similar despite cultural diversity. With 503 photographs representing sixty-eight countries, the exhibition traveled around the world under the auspices of the U.S. Information Agency. Nearly nine million people in thirty-seven countries saw it. Without question, it was the single most famous exhibition of photographs ever held. A book of the photographs, *The Family of Man*, sold two million copies in its original size; a smaller edition sold half a million copies; and paperback editions have been frequently reissued.

Revisionist critics have noted that Steichen did not always respect the integrity of the original prints, but cropped pictures to emphasize his points. Such a practice violated the new concept of the original photographic print as inviolable. The exhibition consisted of oversize blowups in a theatrical hanging that was impressive but later considered propagandistic.

Other Steichen exhibitions were influential, including "The Bitter Years: 1935–41" (1962), which featured pictures of depression era rural life taken largely by Farm Security Administration photographers. In 1961 Steichen was given a one-man retrospective at the Museum of Modern Art.

Among the many honors that Steichen received were the United States Distinguished Service Medal (1945), *U.S. Camera* Achievement Award (1949), the Cultural Achievement Prize of the Deutsche Gesellschaft für Photographie (1960), the first award granted to a non-Japanese by the Photographic Society of Japan (1961), the U.S. Presidential Medal of Freedom (1963), and his birthplace, Luxembourg, made him Commander of the Order of Merit (1966).

Steichen was married a third time to Joanna Taub in 1960. He died in West Redding, Connecticut. For a number of years he had been involved in color photography of a beloved tree on his land.

• Edward Steichen's photographs can be found in major museums and universities. The most important archives are at the Museum of Modern Art in New York and the International Museum of Photography at George Eastman House in Rochester, N.Y. (While he is mentioned frequently in the Archives of American Art, Washington, D.C., he does not have a separate entry.) Yale University's Beinecke Library owns 141 letters from Steichen to Stieglitz in the Alfred Stieglitz Archive. Steichen edited *U.S. Navy Photographs: Pearl Harbor to Tokyo* (1946). His autobiography, *A Life in Photography* (1963), offers a useful chronological survey of his experiences and opinions. Other sources include Weston Naef, *The Collection of Alfred Stieglitz* (1978), which discusses Steichen's prints at the Metropolitan Museum of Art, New York; Jonathan Green, ed., *Camera Work: A Critical Anthology* (1973); and Sadakichi Hartmann, "A Visit to Steichen's Studio," *Camera Work* no. 2 (Apr. 1903): 25–28, where the critic recognizes the poetry and symbolism of Steichen's landscapes and applauds the famous portraits of Rodin. Carl Sandburg wrote interesting introductions to *The Family of Man* and *Sandburg: Photographer's View* (1966).

ESTELLE JUSSIM

STEIN, Clarence Samuel (19 June 1882–7 Feb. 1975), architect and community planner, was born in Rochester, New York, the son of Leo Stein, a casket manufacturer, and Rose Rosenblat. In 1890, Leo Stein moved his company to New York City, where Clarence's reform-minded mother enrolled him in Felix Adler's Workingman's School of the Ethical Culture Society. Adler's school inspired Stein's lifelong commitment to work on social aspects of community life in architecture and urban design. The school and John Lovejoy Elliott's study groups shaped young Stein's progressive reform ideas and politics through observation and criticism of city life. This unusual education produced a sensitive young man who responded strongly to natural beauty, conceived new possibilities for urban beauty, and decried the social injustice, urban congestion, and slum environments of turn-of-the-century New York. Leaving school at sixteen, Stein worked several years in his father's business. He did not like it, nor did he like the study of architecture at Columbia University in 1904–1905.

In Paris from 1905 to 1911 he studied decorative arts and architecture at the École des Beaux-Arts. Paris, as much as the school, affected him profoundly. He experienced an apotheosis that influenced his urban designs, with their densely built structure juxtaposed to accessible natural green space. Paris's dense urban blocks, spacious parks, grand boulevards, human-scale neighborhoods, and joyous lifestyle inspired Stein to design communities that provided good lives for their residents. In his European travels Stein discovered the roots of Ebenezer Howard's Garden City movement in England at Bournemouth. The experience channeled much of his life's work into the design of new communities.

Returning to America, Stein worked from 1911 to 1917 for Bertram Grosvenor Goodhue on several large-scale projects: the 1912 San Diego Exposition, the copper mining town of Tyrone, New Mexico, San Diego Naval Air Station, and a number of Goodhue's architectural commissions, including St. Bartholomew Church. Stein also continued to explore urban social and political reform in the urban study groups of the Ethical Cultural Society, and he tried to achieve greater equity in housing for the people of New York. His collaboration with Henry and Belle Moskowitz in Al Smith's run for the New York governorship in 1918 led to his appointment as secretary of housing equity of Smith's Reconstruction Commission.

After a brief army enlistment in World War I, Stein left Goodhue's office to form an association with the New York architects Charles Butler and Robert D. Kohn, who had been principals in the Emergency Fleet Corporation of the U.S. Shipping Board's war worker housing projects. Stein also became associate editor for community planning of the *AIA* (American Institute of Architects) *Journal*. There he worked with its editor, Charles Whitaker, architect Frederick L. Ackerman, a student of British housing programs, and Lewis Mumford, a neophyte architectural historian. In 1923 Stein formed the Regional Planning Association of America (RPAA) with Whitaker, Ackerman, and Mumford, along with landscape architect Henry Wright, economist Stuart Chase, regionalist Benton MacKaye, housing economist Edith Elmer Wood, real estate investor Alexander Bing, and the editor of *Survey Graphic*, Robert Bruere. In 1931 housing reformer Catherine Bauer joined the group. During the next decade the RPAA became a creative and influential

force in American city and regional planning, as it put forth a vision of idealized urban growth: a system of cities and towns separated by open, green spaces connected by fast, efficient transportation. RPAA members wrote dozens of articles and books and developed one of the first major regional plans in America (for New York state). Stein and Wright worked with Bing and Ackerman to design and build several innovative residential communities—Sunnyside Gardens, Queens; Radburn, New Jersey; Chatham Village, Pittsburgh; Hillside Homes in the Bronx; and the Phipps Garden Apartments, Queens—and helped shape Greenbelt, Maryland, one of President Franklin Roosevelt's 1935 Greenbelt Towns. Roosevelt's New Deal did not, however, accept all of Stein's and RPAA's ideas for housing and "regional cities" with dispersed communities, or their more radical ideas for Tennessee Valley Authority regional planning.

In 1928, during the most creative period of his professional life, Stein married stage and film actress Aline MacMahon. They had no children. He worked mostly in New York City and she often in Hollywood. Their successful transcontinental marriage was an admirable model for career couples. They traveled frequently in Asia, Europe, and the Near East, and they entertained their friends extensively and graciously in their Central Park West apartment.

Stein's designs (especially Radburn) were models for major changes in traditional housing and community layout from 1930 to 1970. In the United States, the Radburn plan's green-centered, pedestrian-favoring superblocks were an urban design theme used in the layouts of residential areas in the rebuilding of American cities and the design of new towns and suburbs, for example, Reston, Virginia (1957), Columbia, Maryland (1964), Woodlands, Texas (1975), and hundreds of planned unit developments. After World War II this model influenced many European new town residential layouts, especially in Britain and Sweden, for example, Cumbernauld, Scotland (1955), and Vällingby (1950) outside Stockholm. The central feature of these superblocks was complete traffic segregation. Cars were parked on the periphery, while footpaths led into the clustered housing, schools, and stores. Interior spaces were often devoted to parkland and natural, open spaces.

Stein's long architectural practice also included other large housing projects, residences, and community buildings, some of which he designed in collaboration with others or as a consultant. These included Temple Beth-El in New York, the Ethical Culture School in Riverdale, New York, the Hudson Guild Camp buildings in Netcong, New Jersey, five public housing and defense housing projects in Los Angeles and Pittsburgh, Baldwin Hills Village in Los Angeles, and the new town center of Stevenage, England. Stein's urban design ideas are most thoroughly recorded in his volume *Toward New Towns for America* (1951) and in dozens of articles. In 1956 he was awarded the Gold Medal of the American Institute of Architects "for a lifetime of [architectural] practice . . . [which] early burst the limitations imposed on the design of an individual structure [to] embrace the wider aims of designing for mankind's environment." Stein, a community architect who lived well and worked in the service of society, died in his "sky parlor" apartment above Central Park West in New York City.

• Stein's papers, including correspondence with many key figures in the field of city planning from the 1920s to the 1960s, are in the Cornell University archives (Collection 3600). The most complete modern assessment of his contributions to western city and regional planning are in Lewis Mumford, "A Modest Man's Contribution to Urban and Regional Planning," *AIA Journal* (Dec. 1978): 18–29. Roy Lubove, *Community Planning in the 1920's: The Contribution of the Regional Planning Association of America* (1963), is an excellent discussion of the work of the group of urban planning intellectuals and professionals that Stein formed and led so productively from 1923 to 1933. The most recent evaluation of Stein's influence on modern city and regional planning is a series of articles by Kermit C. Parsons, including "Clarence Stein and the Greenbelt Towns—Settling for Less," *Journal of the American Planning Association* (Spring 1990): 161–83; "American Influence on Stockholm's Post World War II Suburban Expansion," *Planning History* (Spring 1992): 1–10; "British and American Community Planning: Clarence Stein's Manhattan Transfer, 1924–1974," *Planning Perspectives* (Apr. 1992): 181–210; and "Collaborative Genius: The Regional Planning Association of America," *Journal of the American Planning Association* (Autumn 1994): 462–82.

KERMIT C. PARSONS

STEIN, Gertrude (3 Feb. 1874–27 July 1946), author, was born in Allegheny, Pennsylvania, the daughter of Daniel Stein, a businessman, and Amelia Keyser. Stein spent her early years in Europe, where her parents were traveling; the family returned to America in 1879, settling the following year in Oakland, California, where Stein spent the rest of her youth. Of Oakland she was later to remark, "There is no there there." She countered the bland, suburban surroundings by reading voraciously: Shakespeare, Scott, Richardson, Fielding, Wordsworth.

After her parents had died, her mother in 1888 and her father in 1891, Stein's eldest brother, Michael, moved his siblings to San Francisco, where he had been directing a street railway company. Soon afterward, with her brother Leo and sister Bertha, Stein moved to Baltimore to live with an aunt. Leo Stein then decided to register at Harvard, and Gertrude followed, attending the Harvard Annex, precursor to Radcliffe College. She studied with William James, George Santayana, Josiah Royce, and Hugo Munsterburg, among others, and later cited James as the most significant influence of her college years. In 1897 she entered the Johns Hopkins University Medical School but quickly discovered that she was not enthusiastic about pursuing a career as a physician. Nevertheless, some of her experiences while studying medicine are reflected in her stories, most notably "Melanctha," in *Three Lives* (written 1905–1906).

Beginning in 1900, Gertrude and Leo Stein summered together in Europe. Leo decided to take up residence there, first in London (1902) and then in Paris (1903). Gertrude joined him in his flat at 27 rue de Fleurus, in the Montparnasse district of the city.

Although the Steins' expatriation was not unusual at the time—many artists, writers, and intellectuals found a more hospitable environment in Europe than in the United States—Gertrude sought in Paris a liberation from the strictures of American society that made her feel like an outcast. Her occasional writings during her undergraduate years reveal a troubled and depressed young woman, unable to envision herself fitting into such prescribed roles as wife and mother. Her "red deeps," as she termed her tumultuous feelings, became exacerbated at Johns Hopkins, where her acknowledged love for another woman was not reciprocated. This affair made its way into her first extended piece of fiction, *Things As They Are* (1903), which was published posthumously.

Stein's reputation as an avant-garde writer is based largely on her difficult, experimental, hermetic works, pieces that have been collected in eight volumes published by Yale University Press and in several other collections. Her large output, however, is not exclusively devoted to literary experimentation, but rather falls into four general categories: early autobiographical pieces, such as *The Making of Americans* (begun 1903, completed 1911) and *Things As They Are*, in which she focuses on difficult passages in her life; literary experiments—poetry, drama, and prose—in which she attempts to revive the meaning of words stripped of their cultural and emotional connotations; hermetic autobiographical pieces focusing on her relationship with Alice B. Toklas and their circle of friends and acquaintances; and memoirs, such as *The Autobiography of Alice B. Toklas* (1933) and *Everybody's Autobiography* (1937), written for a popular audience. Stein also published explanatory essays, such as "Composition as Explanation" and "What Are Masterpieces and Why Are There So Few of Them," many of which first were delivered as lectures at Oxford in 1926, and during an American tour in 1934–1935.

Stein's reputation as a cultural figure comes less from her writing than from her brilliant circle of friends. In the early 1900s, her brother Leo, with the advice of his friend Bernard Berenson and the art dealer Ambroise Vollard, began collecting art, including the work of Cézanne, Renoir, Daumier, Manet, Gauguin, Derain, Rousseau, and Matisse. The Steins' home became a meeting place for many accomplished and aspiring artists as well as writers, musicians, and a smattering of rich expatriates. Although when she first arrived in Europe, Stein was dominated by her outspoken brother, later, after Leo moved to Florence and Alice B. Toklas became Stein's companion, she became the center of one of the most important salons in Paris. She nurtured an intense relationship with Pablo Picasso, commemorated in his 1906 portrait of her, now at New York's Metropolitan Museum of Art. Among her other enthusiasms were F. Scott Fitzgerald, Sherwood Anderson, Thornton Wilder, Ernest Hemingway, Carl Van Vechten, the composer Virgil Thomson, and British painter Francis Rose. Her friendship with Hemingway was thwarted by Toklas's jealousy, as was her friendship with the heiress and literary impresario Mabel Dodge Luhan, who was instrumental in the early publication of Stein's work.

Stein and Toklas remained in their country home in Bilignin during World War II, despite their friends' urging that they flee to Switzerland for safety. After the war, they returned to Paris, where they were hosts to scores of young GIs who came to pay homage to Gertrude Stein, the literary legend. In the spring of 1946, Stein suddenly became ill; cancer was diagnosed and an emergency operation performed. She died in Paris.

Throughout her career, Stein flamboyantly denied her need for an audience. "I write for myself and strangers," she once commented, quickly modifying the statement to "I write for myself." "Reading Gertrude Stein at length," wrote Richard Bridgman, a patient scholar and one of her most astute critics, "is not unlike making one's way through an interminable and badly printed game book." Later readers have tended to agree, and Stein has been the subject of merciless parodies. The Beinecke Library at Yale, where her papers are housed, has collected, for example, a large number of humorous plays on Stein's famous, enigmatic remark: "Rose is a rose is a rose is a rose."

Privately, however, Stein longed for a readership that would acknowledge her contribution to modern literature. At times, her only sympathetic reader was Alice Toklas. She has been taken most seriously long after her death, when critics and scholars have applied feminist, structuralist, or deconstructionist theories in an attempt to explain, justify, or decode Stein's difficult works. It is important, in weighing these studies, to remember that Stein attempted not one experiment, but many and that the motivations for her hermetic writings—sometimes to veil her lesbian relationship with Toklas, sometimes to translate into prose the kind of experiments her colleagues were carrying out in art, sometimes to challenge her readers' preconceptions about language and narrative—do not make any single explanation viable for all of her works.

• The majority of Stein's manuscripts, letters, notebooks, and memorabilia is housed at the American Literature Collection of the Beinecke Library, Yale University. Eight volumes of the *Yale Edition of the Unpublished Writing of Gertrude Stein* appeared between 1951 and 1958, bringing into print most of Stein's short, experimental pieces. Other collections of her operas, plays, essays, and letters have been compiled by various editors.

In addition to the autobiographical volumes cited in the text above, Stein wrote *Wars I Have Seen* (1945). Letters to Stein were published as *Flowers of Friendship*, edited by Donald Gallup (1953); Stein's letters to Sherwood Anderson (1972) and Samuel Steward (1977) also have been published; a selection of her letters to Carl Van Vechten has been edited by Edward Burns (1986).

James Mellow, *Charmed Circle: Gertrude Stein and Company* (1974), is an informative biography. Other biographical studies include John Malcolm Brinnin, *The Third Rose: Gertrude Stein and Her World* (1959), and a volume published in conjunction with an exhibition at the Museum of Modern Art, New York, *Four Americans in Paris* (1970), which also focuses on Leo, Michael, and Sarah Stein. Extensive references to Stein's life appear in Linda Simon, *The Biography of Alice B. Toklas* (1977). Ray Lewis White, *Gertrude Stein and Alice B. Toklas: A Reference Guide* (1984), offers a comprehensive bibliography of the primary and secondary literature that supersedes earlier lists.

Richard Bridgman, *Gertrude Stein in Pieces* (1970), remains an indispensable source for scholars. Significant theoretical and feminist studies include Wendy Steiner, *Exact Resemblance to Exact Resemblance: The Literary Portraiture of Gertrude Stein* (1978); Marianne DeKoven, *A Different Language: Gertrude Stein's Experimental Writing* (1983); Jayne Walker, *The Making of a Modernist: Gertrude Stein from Three Lives to Tender Buttons* (1984); and Catherine Stimson, "The Mind, the Body and Gertrude Stein," *Critical Inquiry* 3, No. 3 (1977): 489–506.

LINDA SIMON

STEIN, Jules Caesar (26 Apr. 1896–29 Apr. 1981), entertainment executive and physician, was born in South Bend, Indiana, the son of Louis M. Stein and Rosa Cohen. His extraordinary achievements began in the classroom. A student at West Virginia University while still in his early teens, he graduated from the University of Chicago at the age of nineteen. His medical degree was earned at Rush Medical College, Chicago, in 1921. He acquired a specialty in ophthalmology at the Eye Clinic of the University of Vienna and first practiced this as chief resident in ophthalmology at Cook County Hospital in Chicago and subsequently in an affiliation with Dr. Harry Gradle, also of Chicago. His depth of knowledge is revealed in "Telescopic Spectacles and Magnifiers as Aids to Poor Vision" (1924), which quickly became the definitive manual in this specialty.

Stein married Doris Jones in 1928. They had two children. Although Stein's entry into show business with the founding of the Music Corporation of America (MCA) in 1924 would leave him little time to practice medicine, he never lost his devotion to helping individuals with diseases of the eye. His final years were spent financing, building, and equipping eye research centers at a number of medical institutions. The Jules Stein Eye Institute at the University of California, Los Angeles, benefited from both his financial largess and the time and talent that Stein and his wife brought to planning and developing this elaborately equipped facility.

In spite of Stein's earnest wish to be remembered for his philanthropy, it is as a show business entrepreneur and entertainment executive that he most affected lives by helping to shape popular culture in the twentieth century. Stein began in show business as an entertainer while still in college. His subsequent work as an agent evolved out of his inability to fulfill all the engagements offered to his band; he formed other bands, which provided him a fee for his services. His success in this endeavor, along with an early recognition that the music scene was changing with the spreading influence of jazz, encouraged him to join with William Goodheart in founding MCA, a talent agency, in 1924.

The collaboration was a fruitful one that affected the way live music and entertainment in general would be delivered to audiences for years to come. In the nascent days of MCA, Stein and Goodheart were content to organize and deliver bands to bookers for hotels and dance halls, taking a 10 percent agency fee. Bands in this era were characterized by stability in a single city, blandness of repertory, and anonymity beyond a small geographic area. Stein's innovations brought broad changes. Capitalizing on the growing popularity of jazz and the consequent migration of African-American bands from the South, MCA began to move bands on a weekly or even daily basis from one venue to another. The "one-night stand" increased business for the proprietor, enriched and encouraged entertainers, and made MCA an important intermediary in the entertainment process. In time, the dependence of all parties on MCA was such that Stein and Goodheart could demand, and were given, exclusive rights of representation. Bandleaders who agreed to deal with only their agency were guaranteed continuous work throughout the year. Similarly, bookers who signed on were assured of a better, and at times less expensive, flow of talent than would otherwise be available to them.

MCA's growing national success was assured with the addition of Guy Lombardo to its roster of stars under representation. By the mid-1930s Stein's organization represented more than half the nation's major bands, including those of Ted Weems, Isham Jones, and Benny Goodman.

Stein's interest in securing exclusive representation arrangements sometimes caused him to run afoul of his clients and the law. Some clients accused the firm of excessive control over their lives; others were more aggressive and took their complaints to the courts. An exclusive agreement in San Diego in 1946, for example, resulted in a competitor of one of MCA's clients suing MCA and winning an award for violation of restraint of trade under the Sherman Act.

In time, Stein saw Hollywood as the next opportunity for business and a larger arena for his commercial acumen. By 1937 the agency had amassed a large roster of film stars, including Bette Davis, Betty Grable, Joan Crawford, Greta Garbo, Eddie Cantor, Ingrid Bergman, Frank Sinatra, and Jack Benny. The firm was aggressive in acquiring additional stars by purchasing whole agencies. In the mid-1940s Stein and his colleagues bought out the agency business of CBS, and a deal for the Leland Haywood Agency gave MCA unquestioned influence in Hollywood.

By 1945 MCA was attracting much public attention and began to be called "the star-spangled octopus." It had everyone—stars, writers, musicians, directors, and producers. It controlled radio and packaged everyone from chorus members to stars.

Stein—along with Lew Wasserman, who replaced him as head of MCA in 1946—provided innovative approaches to structuring deals and tax strategies that would affect how movies were made and financed and how actors would be paid. Opting for a percentage of movie profits over fixed salaries for their clients gradually changed the balance of power in the industry from the studios to the stars.

An exclusively arrangement struck with the Screen Actors Guide in 1952, however, profoundly affected the future of the company. Ronald Reagan, then the head of the Screen Actors Guild, faced with growing unemployment of actors and recognizing the changing economics in the industry, provided MCA as agent the right to produce films, an opportunity long denied to them. This was a particularly attractive arrangement for Stein, Wasserman, and their colleagues. They had come to recognize the potential economic and cultural importance of television in the prosperous post–World War II era. Their production of popular television series during this period greatly enriched the company, which moved more aggressively into this area with the acquisition of Universal Pictures Co. in 1958–1959.

The growing influence of MCA as both agent and producer angered their competitors. A federal antitrust suit was brought against the company in 1962, and MCA withdrew from its worldwide talent agency business, releasing many stars from their contracts. Stein saw this event as the most difficult decision made in the company's history.

Stein's and his colleagues' effect on the development and delivery of popular culture cannot be overstated. The list of music, movie, and television stars under their representation and, more significantly, the financial and business arrangements made on their behalf, have had overarching consequences on Broadway, Hollywood, and the networks for much of the twentieth century.

Living in an era when multiple careers were uncommon, Stein enjoyed four—physician, ophthalmologist, agent, and chief executive of a major corporation. He also managed to fit into his busy life serious avocations in real estate, antiques, securities trading, and philanthropy, making important contributions in each of his endeavors. He died in Los Angeles.

• Stein was notable for avoiding publicity in his personal life. Significant information on Stein is in Michael Pye, *Moguls: Inside the Business of Show Business* (1980). An obituary in the *New York Times*, 30 Apr. 1981, is a valuable resource.

SYLVESTER A. MARINO

STEIN, William Howard (25 June 1911–2 Feb. 1980), biochemist, was born in New York City, the son of Fred M. Stein, a businessman, and Beatrice Borg. His father gave up work at an early age so he could donate his full time to the New York Tuberculosis and Health Association and other health agencies.

Stein's early education was at the Lincoln School at Teachers College, Columbia University. At age sixteen he transferred to Phillips Exeter Academy. Two years later he entered Harvard University, where chemistry became his major subject. After earning his B.S. in 1933, he remained at Harvard another year to pursue organic chemistry more extensively and then transferred to Columbia University to pursue biological chemistry in the College of Physicians and Surgeons. In 1937 he completed a Ph.D. thesis on the amino acids in elastin, a protein that gives muscles their elasticity.

Stein was married in 1936 to Phoebe Hockstader. They had three sons. In 1937 Stein joined the research group headed by Max Bergmann at the Rockefeller Institute for Medical Research, later Rockefeller University. Bergmann was a recent refugee from Nazi Germany whose biochemical studies over the years made him a welcome addition to the institute. He was quickly surrounded by a group of investigators who would become leaders in American studies on protein problems.

The Bergmann group was joined in 1939 by Stanford Moore, a Vanderbilt graduate who had recently finished a Ph.D. at the University of Wisconsin in biochemistry under Karl Paul Link. Moore and Stein quickly established a collaborative relationship that lasted until Stein's death. Bergmann suggested that Stein and Moore begin a study of solubility product methods for attacking amino acid problems in proteins. Within the next few years they were successful in developing a tedious procedure for studying amino acids that would later be abandoned for a more rapid approach.

By this time the United States became involved in World War II, and both chemists were drawn into separate research activities seeking therapeutic agents to neutralize the effects of mustard gas and of nitrogen mustards. Stein had some success in tracing the effects of mustard gases to reactive centers of peptides (strands of amino acids). Moore was involved with related problems in Washington, D.C.

In late 1944, as the war was entering its last year, Bergmann died. Stein and Moore wondered whether they would need to look for separate jobs when the war ended. However, Herbert Gasser, director of the Rockefeller Institute, assured them that there was still a place for their research at the institute. When the war ended, Stein and Moore returned to the institute to collaborate in their studies of proteins, polypeptides, and amino acids with the aid of younger colleagues. Some phases of their research were done separately, but they were each aware of the work of the other and usually published their work jointly.

Beginning with their return to protein studies, Stein and Moore needed to review the new approaches that had developed in recent years. Column chromatography (a method of separating substances from mixtures based on selective adsorption) and its various modifications were being used in some laboratories with modest success, while other investigators found these methods of little importance. Stein and Moore had confidence that they could be developed into a useful approach to protein chemistry. Meanwhile in England

Frederick Sanger was having success in establishing the sequence of the amino acids in the hormone insulin; he would soon establish the order of the thirty-one amino acid fragments that constituted the molecule, the two branches of which were joined at two positions by cystine molecules. Sanger's work was a major breakthrough in protein studies.

Stein, Moore, and Darrel Spackman substituted automated recording devices for individual fraction collectors. By the mid-1960s Stein and Moore utilized the innovations of their earlier years to carry out the structural analyses of two pancreatic enzymes—bovine pancreatic ribonuclease A and bovine pancreatic deoxyribonuclease A. The ribonuclease contained 124 amino acid units and four cys-cys bridges. The deoxyribonuclease contained 257 amino acid units but only two cys-cys bridges.

From 1958 onward Stein was involved with the publication of the *Journal of Biological Chemistry*, serving for six years on its editorial committee, three as chairman (1958–1961). In 1962 he was made a member of the editorial board of the *Journal*, serving as associate editor for four years (1964–1968). He became editor in 1968, but illness forced his resignation in 1971.

In 1972 Stein and Moore, together with Christian B. Anfinsen, were the recipients of the Nobel Prize in chemistry for their contributions to protein chemistry. Stein and Moore were also the recipients of numerous other honors and honorary degrees, both together and independently.

In 1969, while attending a symposium on enzymes in Copenhagen, Stein was stricken by paralysis, which was later diagnosed as Guillain-Barré syndrome. He was hospitalized for a year after returning to New York, and he returned to his apartment as a quadriplegic. His mind was still clear, but his legs gave him no support. Stein and his wife moved into an apartment near Rockefeller University so that he could visit the laboratory at frequent intervals in a wheelchair. He retained his interest in proteins and research in the laboratory even though he was unable to carry on physical work himself. Stein died in New York City.

• Stein's career is described fully by Stanford Moore in National Academy of Sciences, *Biographical Memoirs* 56 (1987): 414–40, which carries a full listing of his publications. Also see Moore, "Wm. H. Stein," *Journal of Biological Chemistry* 225 (1980): 9517–18, and Frederic M. Richards, "The 1972 Nobel Prize in Chemistry," *Science* 178 (1972): 492–93. The text of Moore and Stein's acceptance speech delivered in Norway in December 1972, "Chemical Structures of Pancreatic Ribonuclease and Deoxyribonuclease," appears in *Science* 180 (1973): 458–64. *Les Prix Nobel en 1972* also carries their acceptance speech. An obituary is in the *New York Times*, 3 Feb. 1980.

AARON J. IHDE

STEINBECK, John (27 Feb. 1902–20 Dec. 1968), author, was born John Ernst Steinbeck, Jr., in Salinas, California, the son of John Ernst Steinbeck, a businessman, accountant, and manager, and Olive Hamilton, a former teacher. As a child growing up in the fertile and sharply beautiful Salinas Valley—dubbed early in the century the "Salad Bowl of the Nation"—Steinbeck learned to appreciate his environment, not only the verdant hills surrounding Salinas, but also the nearby Pacific coast, where his family spent summer vacations. "I remember my childhood names for grasses and secret flowers," he wrote in the opening chapter of *East of Eden* (1952). "I remember where a toad may live and what time the birds awaken in the summer—and what trees and seasons smelled like." The observant, shy, but often mischievous only son had, for the most part, a happy childhood growing up with two older sisters, one adored younger sister, an assertive mother, and a quiet, self-contained father. Never wealthy, the family was nonetheless prominent in the small town of 3,000, for both parents engaged in community activities. Mr. Steinbeck was a Mason; Mrs. Steinbeck, a member of Eastern Star. Children of immigrants, the elder Steinbecks established their identities by sending deep roots into the community. Their son, on the other hand, was something of a rebel and a loner. Respectable Salinas circumscribed the restless and imaginative young man. Encouraged by his freshman English teacher, he decided at age fifteen that he wished to be a writer and spent hours as a teenager living in a world of his own making, writing stories and poems in his upstairs bedroom.

To please his parents, he enrolled at Stanford University in 1919; to please himself, he signed on only for courses that interested him: classical and British literature, creative writing, a smattering of science. The president of the English Club said that Steinbeck, who regularly attended meetings to read his stories aloud, "had no other interests or talents that I could make out. He was a writer, but he was that and nothing else" (Benson, p. 69). Writing was, indeed, his obsession. For five years the struggling author dropped in and out of the university, eventually taking off fall quarters to work for Spreckels Sugar in the factory near Salinas or on company ranches spread up and down the state. He worked closely with migrants and itinerants, and that association deepened his empathy for workers, the disenfranchised, the lonely, and the dislocated—an empathy that is a defining characteristic of his best work. Without taking a degree, he left Stanford for good in 1925, briefly tried construction work and newspaper reporting in New York City, and then returned to his native state in order to find leisure to hone his craft. During a three-year stint as a caretaker for a Lake Tahoe estate, he found the time both to write several drafts of his first novel, *Cup of Gold* (1929), and, at length, to woo a young woman vacationing at Lake Tahoe, Carol Henning, a San Jose native. After their marriage in 1930, he and Carol settled into the Steinbeck family's summer cottage in Pacific Grove, she to search for jobs to support them, he to continue writing.

During the 1930s Steinbeck wrote most of his best California fiction, from the stories composed in 1933–1934 and collected in *The Long Valley* (1938), to his recognized masterpieces: *Tortilla Flat* (1935), *In Dubious Battle* (1936), *Of Mice and Men* (1937), and *The Grapes of Wrath* (1939). But it took him the early years of the decade to test his stride, to polish his style, and to chart his fictional terrain. The prose in his first novel—the tale of Henry Morgan, pirate—is lush; the artist who loved words strikes exotic chords and burdens sentences with modifiers. In the other apprentice novels, *To a God Unknown* (1933) and *The Pastures of Heaven* (1932), Latinate phrases are trimmed, adjectives are struck, and the setting shifts to California. *To a God Unknown*, second written and third published, tells of patriarch Joseph Wayne's quest to tame and, at the same time, worship the land. Mystical and powerful, the novel testifies to Steinbeck's awareness of an essential bond between man and nature. In a journal entry kept while working on this novel—a practice he continued all his life—the young author wrote, "The trees and the muscled mountains are the world—but not the world apart from man—the world and man—the one inseparable unit man and his environment. Why they should ever have been understood as being separate I do not know." His conviction that characters must be seen in the context of their environments remained constant throughout his career. His was not a man-dominated universe but an interrelated whole, where species and the environment were seen to interact and where commensal bonds between people, among families, and with nature were acknowledged. The author observes life with a kind of scientific detachment, as *The Pastures of Heaven* demonstrates. Set in another tight California valley, this collection of loosely connected stories traces the lives of troubled, lonely, vulnerable farm families. By 1933 Steinbeck had found his terrain, had chiseled a prose style that was more naturalistic and far less strained, and had claimed his people—not the respectable, smug Salinas burghers, but those on the edges of polite society. Steinbeck's California fiction, from *To a God Unknown* to *East of Eden*, envisions the dreams and defeats of common people shaped by the environments they inhabit.

Undoubtedly Steinbeck's holistic vision was determined both by his early years roaming the Salinas hills and by his long and deep friendship with the remarkable Edward Flanders Ricketts, a marine biologist. Founder of Pacific Biological Laboratory, a marine lab eventually housed on Cannery Row in Monterey, Ricketts was a careful observer of intertidal life: "I grew to depend on his knowledge and on his patience in research," Steinbeck writes in "About Ed Ricketts," a lyrical tribute composed after his friend's 1948 death and used as the preface to *The Log from the Sea of Cortez* (1951). But Ricketts's influence on Steinbeck struck far deeper than the common chord of detached observation. Ricketts was a lover of Gregorian chant and Bach, Spengler and Krishnamurti, and Walt Whitman and Li Po. His acceptance of people as they were and of life as he found it was remarkable, articulated by what he called nonteleological or "is" thinking. Steinbeck adapted the term and the stance. His fiction examines "what is." The working title for *Of Mice and Men* was "Something That Happened." Several seminal "Doc" figures in Steinbeck's California fiction, all wise observers of life, epitomize the idealized stance: Doc Burton in *In Dubious Battle*, Slim in *Of Mice and Men*, Casy in *The Grapes of Wrath*, Lee in *East of Eden*, and of course Doc himself in *Cannery Row* (1945) and the sequel, the rollicking *Sweet Thursday* (1954). Ricketts, patient and thoughtful, a poet and a scientist, helped ground the author's ideas. He was Steinbeck's mentor, alter ego, and soul mate. Considering the depth of his eighteen-year friendship with Ricketts, it is hardly surprising that the bond acknowledged most frequently in Steinbeck's oeuvre is friendship between and among men.

Steinbeck's social consciousness of the 1930s was ignited by an equally compelling figure in his life, his wife Carol. She helped edit his prose, urged him to cut the Latinate phrases, typed his manuscripts, suggested titles, and offered ways to restructure. To write, Steinbeck needed buffers to keep the world at bay, and the gregarious and witty Carol willingly and eagerly fulfilled that role. In 1935, having finally published his first popular success with tales of Monterey's *paisanos*, *Tortilla Flat*, Steinbeck, goaded by Carol, attended a few meetings of nearby Carmel's John Reed Club. Although he found the group's zealotry distasteful, he, like so many intellectuals of the 1930s, found the communists' stance unassailable: workers suffered. Intending to write a "biography of a strikebreaker," he interviewed a fugitive organizer, and from the words of that hounded man came not a biography but one of the best strike novels written in the twentieth century, *In Dubious Battle*. Not a partisan novel, it dissects with a steady hand both the ruthless organizers and the grasping landowners. The author focuses not on who will win the struggle between organizers and farmers but on how profound is the effect on the workers trapped in between, manipulated by both interests.

At the height of his powers, Steinbeck followed this large canvas with two books that round out what might be called his labor trilogy. The tightly focused *Of Mice and Men* was one of the first in a long line of "experiments," a word he often used to identify a forthcoming project. This "play-novelette," a book that he intended to be both a novella and a script for a play, is a tightly drafted study of bindle stiffs whose dreams he intended to represent the universal longings for a home, "the earth longings of a Lennie who was not to represent insanity at all but the inarticulate and powerful yearning of all men," he wrote his agent. Both the text and the critically acclaimed 1937 Broadway play (which won the Drama Critics Circle Award for best play that year) made Steinbeck a household name, assuring his popularity and, for some, his infamy. (The book's language shocked many, and it is still listed with frequency on lists of "objectionable reading" or "banned books" for secondary school students.)

Steinbeck's next novel intensified popular debate about his gritty subjects, his uncompromising sympathy for the disenfranchised, and his "crass" language.

The Grapes of Wrath sold out an advance edition of 19,804 by mid-April 1939, was selling 10,000 copies a week by early May, and won the Pulitzer Prize for the year (1940). Published at the apex of the depression, the book about dispossessed farmers forced west captured the decade's angst as well as the nation's legacy of fierce individualism, visionary prosperity, and determined westward movement. It was, like the best of Steinbeck's novels, informed in part by documentary zeal and in part by Steinbeck's ability to trace mythic and biblical patterns. Lauded by critics nationwide for its scope and intensity, the book attracted an equally vociferous minority opinion. Oklahomans said that the story of the dispossessed Joads was a "dirty, lying, filthy manuscript," in the words of Congressman Lyle Boren. Californians claimed the novel was a scourge on the state's munificence, and an indignant Kern County, its migrant population burgeoning, banned the book well into World War II.

The author abandoned the field, exhausted from two years of research trips and personal commitment to the migrants' woes, from a five-month push to write the final version, from a deteriorating marriage to Carol, and from an unnamed physical malady. He retreated to Ricketts and science, announcing his intention to study seriously marine biology and to plan a collecting trip to the Sea of Cortez. The text Steinbeck and Ricketts published in 1941, *Sea of Cortez* (reissued in 1951 without Ricketts's catalog of species as *The Log from the Sea of Cortez*), tells the story of that expedition. It does more, however. The log portion that Steinbeck wrote (from Ricketts's notes) in 1941—after having worked on a film in Mexico, *The Forgotten Village* (1941), and struggling with a manuscript about Cannery Row bums, "God in the Pipes"—contains his and Ricketts's philosophical musings as well as keen observations on Mexican peasantry, hermit crabs, and "dryball" scientists. Quipped Lewis Gannett, there is "more of the whole man, John Steinbeck, than any of his novels."

With the exception of the knotty and underrated *Cannery Row*, composed immediately after he returned from a four-month stint overseas as a war correspondent in 1943, Steinbeck's work of the 1940s was less successful. His determination to shift directions was real enough. After writing *The Grapes of Wrath*, he declared that the novel was dead. He explored divergent paths: filmmaker, biologist, documentary historian (*Bombs Away: The Story of a Bomber Team* [1942]), and journalist. As war correspondent, he could make the commonplace intriguing (writing about the popularity of the song "Lilli Marlene" or his driver in London, Big Train Mulligan) and the uncommon riveting (as in his participation in a diversionary mission off the Italian coast). These columns were later collected in *Once There Was a War* (1958), and his postwar trip to Russia with Robert Capa in 1947 resulted in *A Russian Journal* (1948). During the 1940s Steinbeck published what many viewed as slight volumes, each a disappointment to critics who expected another tome to weigh in next to *The Grapes of Wrath*.

By far the most fulsomely reviewed and controversial book of the decade was his first novel after *Grapes*, *The Moon Is Down* (1942). Set in an unnamed Northern European village, this play/novelette (his second experiment with this form he had invented) tells of a town's resistance to what is obviously a Nazi invasion. The book, distributed by underground presses in occupied countries, inspired European readers and appalled many Americans. Two influential critics, James Thurber and Clifton Fadiman, declared in the nation's most prestigious circulars that Steinbeck was "soft" on Germans—his were too understandably human—and that his text in fact threatened the war effort because the author suggested that resistance meant a dogged belief in democratic ideals. Critics' barbs rankled the sensitive writer, as they had for years and would continue to throughout his career. Reviewers seemed either to misunderstand his biological naturalism or to expect him to compose another strident social critique like *The Grapes of Wrath*. Commonplace phrases such as "complete departure" or "unexpected" recurred in reviews of this and other "experimental" books of the 1950s and 1960s. A humorous text like *Cannery Row* struck many as fluff. In 1945 no reviewers recognized that the book's central metaphor, the tidepool, suggested a way to read this nonteleological novel that examined the "specimen" who lived on Monterey's Cannery Row, the street Steinbeck knew so well. Set in La Paz, Mexico, *The Pearl* (1947), a "folk tale . . . a black-white story like a parable," he wrote his agent, tells of a young man who finds an exquisite pearl, loses his freedom in protecting his wealth, and finally throws back into the sea the cause of his woes. Reviews noted this as another slim volume by a major author. *The Wayward Bus* (1947), a "cosmic Bus," sputtered as well.

Steinbeck faltered both professionally and personally in the 1940s. He divorced the loyal but volatile Carol in 1943. That same year he moved east with his second wife, Gwyndolyn Conger, a lovely and talented woman nearly twenty years his junior who ultimately resented his growing stature and felt that her own creativity as a singer had been stifled. With Gwyn, Steinbeck had two sons, but the marriage started falling apart shortly after the second son's birth and ended in divorce in 1948. That same year Steinbeck was numbed by Ed Ricketts's death. Only with concentrated work on a filmscript on the life of Emiliano Zapata for Elia Kazan's film *Viva Zapata!* (1952) would Steinbeck gradually chart a new course. In 1949 he met and in 1950 married his third wife, Elaine Scott, and with her he moved again to New York City, where he lived for the rest of his life. Much of the pain and reconciliation of the late 1940s was worked out in two subsequent novels: his third play/novelette *Burning Bright* (1950), a boldly experimental parable about a man's acceptance of his wife's child fathered by another man, and the largely autobiographical work he had contemplated since the early 1930s, *East of Eden*.

"It is what I have been practicing to write all of my life," he wrote to painter Bo Beskow early in 1948, when he first began research for a novel about his valley and his people (Steinbeck and Wallsten, p. 310). With *Viva Zapata!*, *East of Eden*, *Burning Bright*, and later *The Winter of Our Discontent* (1961), Steinbeck's fiction became less concerned with the behavior of groups—what he called in the 1930s "group man"—and more focused on an individual's moral responsibility to self and community. The detached perspective of the scientist gave way to a certain warmth; the ubiquitous "self-character" that he claimed appeared in all his novels to comment and observe was modeled less on Ed Ricketts and more on John Steinbeck himself. Certainly with his divorce from Gwyn, Steinbeck had endured dark nights of the soul, and *East of Eden* contains those turbulent emotions surrounding the subjects of wife, children, family, and fatherhood. "In a sense it will be two books," he wrote in his journal (posthumously published in 1969 as *Journal of a Novel: The "East of Eden" Letters*) as he began the final draft in 1951, "the story of my country and the story of me. And I shall keep these two separate." Many dismissed as incoherent the two-stranded story of the Hamiltons, his mother's family, and the Trasks, "symbol people" representing the story of Cain and Abel; more recently critics have come to recognize that the epic novel explores the role of the artist as creator, a concern, in fact, in many of Steinbeck's works.

Like *The Grapes of Wrath*, *East of Eden* was a defining point in Steinbeck's career. During the 1950s and 1960s the perpetually "restless" Steinbeck traveled extensively throughout the world with his beloved Elaine. With her, he became more social. Perhaps his writing suffered as a result; some claim that even *East of Eden*, his most ambitious post-*Grapes* novel, cannot stand shoulder to shoulder with his searing social novels of the 1930s. In the fiction of his last two decades, however, Steinbeck never ceased to take risks, to stretch his conception of the novel's structure, and to experiment with the sound and form of language. *Sweet Thursday*, the sequel to *Cannery Row*, was written as a musical comedy that would resolve Ricketts's loneliness by sending him off into the sunset with a true love, Suzy, a whore with a gilded heart. The musical version by Richard Rodgers and Oscar Hammerstein, *Pipe Dream*, was one of the team's few failures. In 1957 Steinbeck published the satiric *The Short Reign of Pippin IV*, a tale about the French monarchy gaining ascendancy. In 1961 he published his last work of fiction, the ambitious *The Winter of Our Discontent*, a novel about contemporary America set in a fictionalized Sag Harbor (where he and Elaine had a summer home). Increasingly disillusioned with American greed, waste, and spongy morality—his own sons seemed textbook cases—he wrote his jeremiad, a lament for an ailing populace. The following year, 1962, Steinbeck was awarded the Nobel Prize for literature; the day after the announcement, the *New York Times* ran an editorial, "Does a Writer with a Moral Vision of the 1930s Deserve the Nobel Prize?" by the influential Arthur Mizner. Wounded by the blindside attack, unwell, frustrated, and disillusioned, John Steinbeck wrote no more fiction.

But the writer John Steinbeck was not silenced. As always, he wrote reams of letters to his many friends and associates. In the 1950s and 1960s he published scores of journalistic pieces: "Making of a New Yorker," "I Go Back to Ireland," columns about the 1956 national conventions, and "letters to Alicia," a controversial series about a 1966 White House–approved trip to Vietnam, where his sons were stationed. In the late 1950s—and intermittently for the rest of his life—he worked diligently on a modern English translation of a book he had loved since childhood, Sir Thomas Malory's *Morte d'Arthur*; the unfinished project was published posthumously as *The Acts of King Arthur and his Noble Knights* (1976).

Immediately after completing *Winter*, the ailing novelist proposed "not a little trip of reporting," he wrote to his agent Elizabeth Otis, "but a frantic last attempt to save my life and the integrity of my creativity pulse" (Benson, p. 882). In a camper truck designed to his specification, he toured America in 1960. After his return, he published the highly praised "pungent potpourri of places and people" (Benson, p. 913), *Travels with Charley in Search of America* (1962), another book that both celebrates American individuals and decries American hypocrisy; the climax of his journey is his visit to the New Orleans "cheerleaders" who daily taunt black children newly registered in white schools. His disenchantment with American waste, greed, and immorality ran deep. His last published book, *America and Americans* (1966), reconsiders the American character, the land, the racial crisis, and the crumbling will. In these late years, in fact after his final move to New York in 1950, many accused him of increasing conservatism. It was true that with greater wealth came the chance to spend money more freely, and with status came political opportunities that seemed out of step for a "radical" of the 1930s. He initially defended Lyndon Johnson's views on the war with Vietnam (although Steinbeck died before he could, as he wished, qualify his initial responses), and he expressed intolerance for 1960s protesters whose zeal, in his eyes, was unfocused.

But the author who wrote *The Grapes of Wrath* never really retreated into conservatism. He lived in modest houses all his life, caring little for lavish displays of power or wealth. He preferred talking to ordinary citizens wherever he traveled, sympathizing always with the disenfranchised. He was a Stevenson Democrat in the 1950s; he was never a communist in the 1930s, and after three trips to Russia (1937, 1947, and 1963) he hated Soviet repression. In fact, neither during his life nor after has the paradoxical Steinbeck been an easy author to pigeonhole personally, politically, or artistically. As a man, he was an introvert and at the same time had a romantic streak, was impulsive, garrulous, a lover of jests and word play and practical jokes. As an artist, he was a ceaseless experimenter with words and form, and often critics did not "see" quite what he was up to. He claimed his books had "layers," yet

many claimed his symbolic touch was cumbersome. He loved humor and warmth, but some said he slopped over into sentimentalism. He was, and is now recognized as, an environmental writer. He was an intellectual, interested in inventions, jazz, politics, philosophies, history, and myth, quite a range for an author sometimes labeled simplistic by academe and the eastern critical establishment. Steinbeck died in New York City.

All said, Steinbeck remains one of America's most significant twentieth-century writers. His popularity spans the world, his range is impressive, and his output was prodigious: sixteen novels; a collection of short stories; four screenplays (*The Forgotten Village, The Red Pony, The Pearl*, and *Viva Zapata!*); a sheaf of journalistic essays, including four collections (*The Harvest Gypsies, Bombs Away, Once There Was a War*, and *America and Americans*); three travel narratives (*Sea of Cortez, A Russian Journal*, and *Travels with Charley*); a translation; and two journals. Three play/novelettes ran on Broadway—*Of Mice and Men, The Moon Is Down*, and *Burning Bright*—as well as one musical, *Pipe Dream*. Whatever his experiment in prose, he wrote with empathy, clarity, and perspicuity: "In every bit of honest writing in the world," he noted in a 1938 journal entry, "there is a base theme. Try to understand men, if you understand each other you will be kind to each other. Knowing a man well never leads to hate and nearly always leads to love."

• Steinbeck's papers are distributed in several major collections: Special Collections, Stanford University Libraries; the Humanities Research Center, University of Texas, Austin; the Center for Steinbeck Studies, San Jose State University; John Steinbeck Library, Salinas; the Bancroft Library, University of California, Berkeley; the Pierpont Morgan Library; and Special Collections, Columbia University. The most exhaustive biography is Jackson Benson, *The True Adventures of John Steinbeck, Writer* (1984). See also Jay Parini, *John Steinbeck, a Biography* (1995). Essential biographical sources are also *Steinbeck: A Life in Letters*, ed. with notes by Elaine Steinbeck and Robert Wallsten (1975), and Steinbeck's letters to his agent, *Letters to Elizabeth: A Selection of Letters from John Steinbeck to Elizabeth Otis*, ed. Florian J. Shasky and Susan F. Riggs (1978). The most complete bibliography of primary works is Adrian H. Goldstone and John R. Payne, *A Bibliographical Catalogue of the Adrian H. Goldstone Collection* (1974); bibliographies of secondary works are Robert DeMott, *John Steinbeck: A Checklist of Books by and About* (1987), and Warren French, "John Steinbeck," in *Sixteen Modern American Authors* (1989), pp. 582–622. Critical reviews of Steinbeck's work have been collected in *John Steinbeck: The Contemporary Reviews*, ed. Joseph R. McElrath, Jesse S. Crisler, and Susan Shillinglaw (1996). Good secondary studies of the writer are the pioneering works by Peter Lisca, *The Wide World of John Steinbeck* (1958), followed by *John Steinbeck: Nature and Myth* (1978). A solid and brief overview is Paul McCarthy, *John Steinbeck* (1980); a more extended analysis is Louis Owens, *John Steinbeck's Re-vision of America* (1985). Essential for an understanding of the Steinbeck/Ricketts relationship is Richard Astro, *John Steinbeck and Edward F. Ricketts: The Shaping of a Novelist* (1973), and essays in *Steinbeck and the Environment*, ed. Susan Beegel, Shillinglaw, and Wes Tiffney (1996). See Joseph R. Millichap, *Steinbeck and Film* (1983), for a solid introduction to the subject. An excellent collection of essays is Jackson J. Benson, ed., *The Short Novels of John Steinbeck: Critical Essays with a Checklist to Steinbeck Criticism* (1990).

SUSAN SHILLINGLAW

STEINBERG, Milton (26 Nov. 1903–20 Mar. 1950), rabbi and author, was born in Rochester, New York, the son of Samuel Steinberg, a peddler, and Fannie Sternberg. His Lithuanian-born father was religiously knowledgeable but, like many immigrants caught in the web of grinding poverty and social exclusion, had embraced both atheism and socialism. The young Steinberg excelled at school, winning numerous academic awards. When he was fifteen the family moved to New York City, where Milton continued his academic virtuosity and his study of Greek and Latin. A powerful speaker and logical thinker even as a youth, his views were constantly sought. He graduated summa cum laude and Phi Beta Kappa from the City College of New York in 1924.

In 1928 he received his rabbinic ordination from the Jewish Theological Seminary, where he was president of the student body. Steinberg had three teachers who profoundly influenced his subsequent career. Jacob Kohn, who emphasized the role of faith in the practice of Judaism, became Steinberg's rabbi and encouraged the young man to study for the rabbinate. The distinguished philosopher Morris Raphael Cohen, who stressed the primacy of a rational and critical approach, was Steinberg's teacher at City College. Mordecai M. Kaplan, founder of Reconstructionism, introduced to Steinberg the possibilities of reconceiving Judaism by eliminating its supernatural elements, thereby making it appropriate for contemporary needs.

Steinberg was an outstanding presence in the American rabbinate of his time. A charismatic figure, he devoted himself to metaphysical questions such as the nature of God, the chosenness of Israel, and the reality of evil. He began his pulpit career at Beth El Zedeck in Indianapolis in 1928. Dismayed by the meager Jewish knowledge of most congregants and appalled at the institutional weakness of American Judaism, Steinberg passionately devoted himself to adult education, lectures about Zionism, the need to combat anti-Semitism, and communal matters. Although many rabbis were involved in similar activities, Steinberg excelled at all of them and was indefatigable in his efforts to educate and elevate a variety of audiences both Jewish and non-Jewish. Steinberg married Edith Alpert in 1929. They had two children.

By 1933 he returned to New York to become rabbi of the Park Avenue Synagogue. One year later he published his first book, *The Making of the Modern Jew*, which was an account of Judaism's historical sojourn and revealed the author's passion for Jewish history. Steinberg's career was marked by his commitment to both the Hebraic and Hellenic dimensions of Judaism. From the former stemmed his passion for moral excellence and concern for justice. The Hellenic compo-

nent shaped Steinberg's philosophical thought. Yet Steinberg moved beyond the classical dichotomy of faith and reason by contending that the two are inextricably related. He dramatized this position in *As a Driven Leaf* (1939), his historical novel based on the life of the Talmudic heretic Elisha ben Abuyah. The protagonist declares, "There is no Truth without Faith. There is no Truth unless first there be a Faith on which it may be based."

Steinberg was initially persuaded by the teachings of Reconstructionism and in 1934–1935 was one of the founding members of its magazine, the *Reconstructionist*. He endorsed the Reconstructionist platform, which viewed Judaism through a sociological rather than a theological lens. Kaplan's call for the replacement of the synagogue by the Jewish community center as the focus of Jewish life appeared to strike a resonant chord in an America that did not ghettoize its Jewish citizens. Steinberg's *A Partisan Guide to the Jewish Problem* (1945) was an exposition of Judaism from a Reconstructionist point of view. But Steinberg, himself a theist, eventually critiqued Reconstructionism on theological grounds. He contended that Kaplan's movement lacked a concern for metaphysics and, consequently, offered no theological propositions concerning the meaning of God, the nature of the Torah, or the particular and universal meaning of Israel. He set forth his own view of Judaism's basic teachings in *Basic Judaism* (1947). Written for both Jews and Christians, the book contains a lucid formulation of the essentials of Jewish faith and ritual.

Steinberg was one of the very few rabbis of his generation intellectually equipped to address contemporary theological issues. At home in classical Jewish sources, he was trained as well in American and Continental philosophy, and he read extensively about Protestant theology. He subscribed to the task of theology as defined by his friend Will Herberg, who had called for a "revival of Jewish theology." This revival was to be based on a sensitive search for the word of God, regardless of where or how it is heard, in order to try to interpret it for contemporary times. This quest stood in stark contrast to the mainly pedestrian concerns of the American rabbinate. Near the end of his life, the Rabbinical Assembly of America invited Steinberg to deliver a series of lectures on contemporary theology whose purpose was to demonstrate the relationship between non-Jewish and Jewish thought. Published posthumously in 1960 as *Anatomy of Faith*, these lectures were a critique of the then contemporary intellectual currents of religious pragmatism and existentialism. Steinberg's lectures showed both points of contact and divergence between Jewish and Protestant theological thought. For example, in a critique of Liberal Judaism, which overemphasized innate human goodness, Steinberg, a practitioner of Conservative Judaism, aligned himself with the position of Reinhold Niebuhr, which emphasized humanity's narcissistic impulses. On the other hand, he criticized Niebuhr's position for stressing the evil nature of humanity. Although not a theologian in the formal sense of the term, Steinberg's philosophical skill and metaphysical passion were united in his own espousal of both modern culture and a love of Judaism.

Steinberg's sermons reflected his distinctive oratorical gifts. Passionately eloquent, he spoke on a wide range of topics. Two anthologies of selected sermons appeared posthumously: *From the Sermons of Milton Steinberg: High Holidays, Major Festivals* (1954) and *Only Human: The Eternal Alibi, from the Sermons of Rabbi Milton Steinberg: The Weekly Sidrah and General Themes* (1963). His best-known sermons were "To Hold with Open Arms" and "The Fall of Seraye." The first was delivered on Rosh Hashanah in 1944. In it Steinberg recalls his experience after being released from the hospital following his first heart attack. He urges his listeners to appreciate the blessings of the "ordinary" while simultaneously recognizing that these blessings belong "to the Universe and the God who stands behind it." His "Seraye" sermon, delivered the following day, is a powerfully moving eulogy for Jews who had been murdered in the Holocaust and an appeal to American Jews to remember their European brethren.

A man of tremendous energy, Steinberg was plagued by ill health and suffered from heart problems. His untimely death in New York City from a heart attack deprived American Jewry of a truly creative figure.

Milton Steinberg, it has been noted, was a "transitional thinker living in a transitional time" (Cohen, p. 220). He critiqued the regnant liberalism of his day for failing to take evil seriously. His later writings, while not abandoning the rational, anticipated the move from liberal to existential modes of thought in postwar Jewish expression despite his earlier critique of Søren Kierkegaard. Although seeking answers, he was intellectually comfortable in admitting that certain questions remained open. He insightfully analyzed the problem of Jewish identity in an open society. His strategy for combating anti-Semitism consisted of a program of Jewish self-acceptance based on knowledge of the tradition and indignation against anti-Semites. Recognizing the tenuous link between premodern and modern Judaism, Steinberg wrote about the "postmodern" long before that word became culturally fashionable. His listening for the word of God in midtwentieth-century America prefaced a movement that achieved maturity in American Jewish life during the 1970s and 1980s.

• Steinberg's posthumously published *A Believing Jew*, ed. Maurice Samuel (1951), is a collection of the author's reflections on various themes. The best source for the life and thought of Steinberg remains Simon Noveck, *Milton Steinberg: Portrait of a Rabbi* (1978). Noveck's "Milton Steinberg's Philosophy of Religion," *Judaism* 26 (1977): 35–45, contains a concise summary of the subject's belief that religion is a Weltanschauung. Alex J. Goldman's *Giants of Faith: Great American Rabbis* (1964), includes a biography of Steinberg with extensive citations from his sermons. Arthur A. Cohen, a disciple and student of Steinberg, includes two important essays about his teacher in his *The Natural and the Supernatu-*ral *Jew* (1963): "Introduction to *Anatomy of Faith*" and "Judaism in Transition: Milton Steinberg." See also Arnold Eisen, *The Chosen People in America* (1983), and Robert G. Goldy, *The Emergence of Jewish Theology in America* (1990). The Milton Steinberg Memorial Issue of the *Reconstructionist* 31 (1965) contains insightful articles by Eugene Borowitz, "Jewish Theology: Milton Steinberg and After" (pp. 7–14), and Jacob Neusner, "Milton Steinberg's Philosophy of Jewish Peoplehood" (pp. 15–22). An obituary is in the *New York Times*, 21 Mar. 1950.

ALAN L. BERGER

STEINBERG, William (1 Aug. 1899–16 May 1978), conductor, was born Hans Wilhelm Steinberg in Cologne, Germany, the son of Julius Steinberg and Bertha Matzdorf. Gifted as a pianist and violinist from an early age, he also wrote youthful compositions. He made his debut as a conductor at the age of thirteen, conducting one of his own works, and he gave his first public performance as a pianist at the age of fifteen. Steinberg studied piano, composition, and conducting at the Staatliche Hochschule für Musik, Cologne University, where his conducting teacher was Hermann Abendroth. He graduated in 1920 and was awarded the Wüllner prize for conducting. He was immediately engaged by Otto Klemperer as his assistant at the Cologne Opera; the two men became close collaborators, with Steinberg learning a great deal from his mentor. Serving as vocal coach, accompanist, rehearsal pianist, and assistant conductor, Steinberg was appointed principal conductor at the Cologne Opera in 1924.

Over the next few years Steinberg built up his experience and reputation at German-style opera houses. From 1925 to 1929 he was mainly based at the Neue Deutsches Theater in Prague, serving as music director in his two last seasons. In the late 1920s he was a frequent guest conductor at the Berlin Staatsoper. In 1929 he became music director of the Frankfurt Opera and also conducted the museum concerts there. His operatic programs in Frankfurt were progressive; they included the premieres of Arnold Schoenberg's *Von heute auf morgen* and George Antheil's *Transatlantic*, as well as an early performance of Kurt Weill's *The Rise and Fall of the City Mahagonny*. In 1933 Steinberg was abruptly dismissed by the Nazis from his post because he was a Jew. He stayed in Frankfurt and married Lotti Stern in 1934; they had two children.

Between 1934 and 1936 Steinberg formed an orchestra for the Jewish Culture League. This orchestra was comprised of musicians who had been hounded out of their jobs because they were Jews. The orchestra regularly performed in Berlin and Frankfurt, but when Nazi officials ordered its performances to be held only in secluded synagogues, Steinberg decided to emigrate. In 1936 he became cofounder, with the violinist Bronislaw Huberman, of the Palestine Symphony Orchestra, based in Tel Aviv. After an inaugural concert given by Arturo Toscanini, Steinberg became the first conductor of the orchestra and maintained connections with it for many years after it became the Israel Philharmonic Orchestra. Toscanini invited Steinberg to the United States in 1937 to conduct the newly formed NBC Symphony Orchestra. Among his performances with the orchestra was the world premiere of Aaron Copland's *Billy the Kid* ballet suite.

Steinberg based himself in the United States for the rest of his career, becoming an American citizen in 1944 and using William as his first name. He spent the 1943–1944 season in Cuba as conductor of the Havana Philharmonic Orchestra. His operatic debut in the United States came in October 1944 with a performance of Verdi's *Falstaff* at the San Francisco Opera, where he returned frequently over the next four years. But he mainly concentrated on orchestral conducting, holding significant appointments as music director of the Buffalo Philharmonic (1945–1952), the Pittsburgh Symphony (1952–1976), and the Boston Symphony Orchestra (1969–1972). He served as principal conductor of the London Philharmonic Orchestra (1958–1960) and made many guest appearances in Europe, Israel, and throughout the United States.

At Buffalo Steinberg enlarged the orchestra, extended the season, increased the annual budget, and developed the repertoire. His long tenure with the Pittsburgh Symphony marked his most substantial achievement as a conductor. He conducted a large repertory from baroque composers to the Second Viennese School (Schoenberg, Berg, Webern) and was a friend to contemporary American composers. With the composer Roy Harris, he organized the Pittsburgh International Contemporary Music Festival. He presented many premieres in Pittsburgh, including Ernst Toch's Symphony No. 3, Gardner Read's Symphony No. 3, Walter Piston's Violin Concerto No. 2, and George Rochberg's Violin Concerto. His skillful training helped the Pittsburgh Symphony become one of the half dozen best orchestras in the United States. Steinberg led the orchestra on a well-received tour of fourteen European and Middle Eastern countries in 1964. He also spread the orchestra's reputation through several tours in the United States and many recordings.

Steinberg's debut at the Metropolitan Opera came in 1965 with a performance of Verdi's *Aida*. He was principal guest conductor of the New York Philharmonic between 1966 and 1968 and led them in several premieres—Paul Creston's *Concerto for Saxophone and Orchestra*, Roberto Gerhard's Symphony No. 4, and Roger Sessions's Symphony No. 8. After a serious illness in 1972, he was forced to reduce his activities. After resigning his position in Pittsburgh in 1976, he was given the title conductor emeritus. He died in New York City.

Steinberg recorded extensively with the Pittsburgh Symphony Orchestra, his discs including a complete cycle of Beethoven symphonies and a performance of Brahms's Second Symphony on the Command label that won a Grammy for best classical album in 1961. He made some fine recordings with the Boston Symphony Orchestra for DGG, notably of music by Schubert, Bruckner, Richard Strauss, and Holst. He also recorded many pieces for Columbia, RCA Victor, EMI, Command, Everest, and for Pittsburgh's Festival of Contemporary Music label.

Steinberg was a fairly undemonstrative figure on the podium who eschewed attention-seeking pyrotechnics. "The more they dance, the quieter I stand," he once said of his conducting. Yet he had authority, vast experience, and great ability in training orchestras to play to a high standard. He was a straightforward, sometimes eloquent, interpreter of German orchestral music in particular, notably Beethoven, Brahms, and Richard Strauss, but he lacked any particular individuality. He presented scores literally without too much personality imposed on the music, and he considered it important to schedule contemporary music on some programs. Modest and self-critical yet proud of his many achievements, Steinberg did not regard himself as a great conductor. But he was sufficiently accomplished to become the first person to hold concurrently two directorships of major American orchestras, in Pittsburgh and Boston.

• Steinberg's personal letters, scores, and books are divided between his family and the Hillman Library at the University of Pittsburgh. The material deposited in the university library is split between three departments—special collections, music, and arts. One of Steinberg's few essays on music is "The Function of a Conductor" in *They Talk about Music*, ed. Robert Cumming (2 vols., 1971). Details of his career are given in Hope Stoddard, *Symphony Conductors of the U.S.A.* (1957), Gdal Saleski, *Famous Musicians of Jewish Origin* (1949), David Ewen, *Musicians since 1900: Performers in Concert and Opera* (1978), and Frederick Dorian and Judith Meibach, *A History of the Pittsburgh Symphony Orchestra* (1986). Steinberg's recordings are listed and discussed in John L. Holmes, *Conductors on Record* (1982).

KENNETH MORGAN

STEINDLER, Arthur (22 June 1878–23 July 1959), orthopedic surgeon, was born in Vienna, Austria, the son of Leopold Steindler, an attorney, and Caroline Goldberg. Steindler wanted to be a concert pianist, but his father convinced him to attend medical school. Steindler studied at the University of Prague from 1896 to 1898, completing his medical degree at the University of Vienna in 1902. He studied orthopedics with Edward Albert, Adolph Lorenz, and Carl Friedlander. Steindler was an assistant in Viennese hospitals and a lieutenant surgeon in the Austrian army.

Steindler emigrated to the United States in 1907, transferring European orthopedic methods. He assisted Dr. John Ridlon, who had urged him to move to the United States, at St. Luke's Hospital in Chicago, Illinois, and was an orthopedic surgeon at the Home for Crippled Children. In 1910 Steindler moved to Des Moines, Iowa, where he had a general practice, was professor of orthopedic surgery at the Drake University Medical School, and performed surgery at the Iowa Methodist and Iowa Lutheran hospitals.

In 1913 Steindler began commuting from Des Moines to the University of Iowa in Iowa City to practice and teach. He became a naturalized citizen the next year. By 1915 Steindler was appointed head of the

University of Iowa's Department of Orthopedics, where he developed a teaching and research program that gained international recognition. In 1914 he married Louise Junk; they had no children.

Steindler was a versatile surgeon: he performed plastic and reconstructive surgery and specialized in operative orthopedics, deformities and disabilities of the spine and thorax, and locomotion problems. He introduced a pioneer treatment for scoliosis known as the compensatory method and developed orthopedic operations for neuromuscular diseases and weakened and deformed limbs supplemented by occupational therapy. Steindler was interested in kinesiology and the biophysics of locomotion. He believed in "sound surgical inventiveness," utilizing basic principles and considering long-term results. He also explored the use of listening instruments to diagnose joint ailments.

Best known for teaching orthopedic surgeons, Steindler considered that his most important contribution. His Iowa City teaching hospital attracted many orthopedists. Every year Steindler selected physicians for an intense program of seminars and operations in orthopedics. He insisted that students have knowledge of current orthopedics technology and techniques. He accepted two or three students each year to undergo a three-year residency with him, consisting of a rigorous curriculum ranging from basic sciences to clinical orthopedics. Ruth Jackson, the first practicing female orthopedist, was Steindler's protégé. At least 250 doctors trained with him, and he proudly followed their careers. His students and colleagues established a research fund in his honor.

Steindler was intensely interested in his patients, believing that the doctor and hospital relationship with patients extended to their homes. He encouraged social work in the hospital and designed an ambulance service to ease patients' transportation to and from the hospital. He also arranged for a traveling clinic to examine patients in rural areas. During his career he offered hope for recovery to an estimated million patients, including those he treated directly, those who benefited from the procedures he developed, and those who were treated by physicians he trained.

Many crippled adults and children sought Steindler's help, having heard of his reputation for reshaping crippled bones and his humanitarian nature. "Doctor Steindler never permitted his acclaim to diminish his sympathy for the suffering," a peer wrote. "No detail ever was too small, no genuine desire of a patient too trivial to be overlooked or ignored." When Steindler arrived in Iowa City, only three orthopedists practiced in Iowa, and most patients were unable to receive treatment. The hospitals at Iowa City did not see many patients each year, because people either could not afford medical services or lived too far away from the town. At that time Iowa City's population was small, and medical students lacked sufficient practical experiences with patients.

Steindler lobbied for state medical support and wrote a proposal for indigent patients, primarily polio victims, to receive medical treatment. As a result of his efforts, the 1915 Perkins Act funded field clinics to evaluate children's health, and the 1919 Haskell-Klaus Act extended state-financed health care for adults. Steindler's devotion and foresight influenced the expansion of Iowa's system of indigent medical care.

The increase of patients enriched the growth of the University of Iowa's medical college. Steindler planned a hospital for his young patients, and more medical students and faculty were attracted to the city. Steindler directed the establishment of bone banks for grafting bone tissue in the hospital. As chief surgeon of the new Children's Hospital, he was dedicated to serving others. The hospital was the focus of his life; Steindler could often be found in the gymnasium or physical therapy and cast room, soothing and encouraging his patients.

Concerned with his patients' health and not his social or financial status, Steindler was outspoken about patients' rights. In 1937 he signed a "medical declaration of independence" written by leaders of the American Medical Association, protesting the federal government's refusal to assist the indigent to procure medical treatment. The statement reflected Steindler's creed that people's health is the government's concern.

Steindler was a prolific author of at least 200 research articles and eleven books. His *Orthopedic Operations: Indications, Technique and End Results* (1940) was considered a classic text with which all orthopedists were familiar. A lifelong student, he took engineering, physics, and mathematics classes to write *The Mechanics of Normal and Pathological Locomotion in Man* (1935). His publications revealed his ability to focus on individual cases and suggest corrective treatment or to view a procedure or condition in broader, historical context with other scientific and medical information. Most of his writing was intended to be instructive, although some tended to be more contemplative and philosophical about the role of orthopedics in medicine.

Named a fellow by the American Medical Association, Steindler reaped honors from foreign universities and medical societies, including the Royal College of Surgeons. In 1932 he was elected president of the American Orthopedic Association; he also was vice president of the International College of Surgeons. He was a diplomate of the Board of Orthopedic Surgery. The University of Iowa named him a distinguished service professor, and he served on the board of directors for the Iowa Society for Crippled Children and the Disabled. Steindler remained humble despite his professional and intellectual accomplishments and skillfully communicated with people representing all ages and socioeconomic classes.

Steindler was active in the university community, serving as a trustee for the School of Religion. Fluent in at least seven languages, which proved useful in translating lectures and publications, he studied history and music in his spare time. He and his wife hosted foreign students in their home, helping them to become self-sufficient. In World War I Steindler had been a contract surgeon for the U.S. Army Reserve Corps. During World War II he posted bond and helped his Jewish relatives to escape from Europe, and *Life* magazine pictured him demonstrating how to dress war wounds.

Steindler retired from the university in 1949 and accepted a position as head of the orthopedics department at Mercy Hospital in Iowa City. He continued healing patients and researching new orthopedics techniques. He died in his Iowa City home.

An *Iowa City Press-Citizen* editorial (23 July 1959) eulogized him: "Someone once wrote that all Dr. Arthur Steindler wanted to do was to help people get well. No finer tribute can be paid to any man." The premier issue of the *Iowa Orthopedic Journal* was a memorial to Steindler. The Iowa State Board of Regents renamed the University of Iowa's Children's Hospital the Steindler Building. An orthopedic clinic bearing his name operates in Iowa City, and the American Academy of Orthopaedic Surgeons sponsors an annual research award and lecture named in his honor.

• The University of Iowa Special Collections has a file on Steindler and several artifacts. Major books by Steindler not mentioned in the text are *Reconstructive Surgery of the Upper Extremity* (1923), *A Textbook of Operative Orthopedics* (1925), *Diseases and Deformities of the Spine and Thorax* (1929), *Postgraduate Lectures on Orthopedic Diagnosis and Indications* (4 vols., 1950–1952), and *Kinesiology of the Human Body under Normal and Pathological Conditions* (1955). A treatment of Steindler's life and career is Joseph A. Buckwalker, "Arthur Steindler: Founder of Iowa Orthopaedics," *Iowa Orthopedic Journal* 1 (Spring 1981): 5–12. An obituary is in the *Daily Iowan*, 25 July 1959.

ELIZABETH D. SCHAFER

STEINER, Edward Alfred (1 Nov. 1866–30 June 1956), Congregational minister and sociologist, was born near Bratislava in the Hungarian part of the Hapsburgs' Austro-Hungarian Empire, the son of Adolph Steiner, who died soon after his son's birth, and Jeanette Heller. The occupations of his parents are unknown. Young Steiner studied at public schools in Vienna and at a Gymnasium in Pilsen, Bohemia, before enrolling at the University of Heidelberg, from which he was graduated in 1885.

Sought by police for conspiracy because of his sympathy with the Slovak minority, Steiner emigrated to the United States. Initially, he worked as a tailor's apprentice in New York's garment district, as a New Jersey farm hand, and as a coal miner in Pennsylvania. As a result of a strike in the coal mines, he served six months in jail and then worked as a machinist in Chicago and as a deck hand on a Mississippi River boat. Born to Jewish parents, Steiner converted to Christianity in the early years after his immigration to the United States and enrolled at Oberlin College to study for the ministry. There he was influenced by the personalist theology of Henry Churchill King, which held that ultimate reality is personal. In 1891 Steiner received a B.D. from Oberlin, was ordained a Congrega-

tional minister, and in August married Sara W. Levy. They became the parents of three children.

After his ordination, Steiner served a small Congregational mission in St. Cloud, Minnesota, from 1891 to 1893, and a working-class immigrant congregation in St. Paul, Minnesota, from 1893 to 1896. From 1896 to 1899 he served a Congregational church in Springfield, Ohio, where he had difficulties with members of the congregation because of his interest in critical biblical studies and the social implications of the gospel, including a willingness to relate to African Americans as equals. Steiner served his last pastorate in Sandusky, Ohio, from 1899 to 1903. During four stormy years in this difficult parish, his Jewish background, his attacks on the summer resort's brothels and saloons, and his work with immigrants and industrial laborers during the week alienated some members of Steiner's congregation. Influential Congregationalists in Ohio such as Washington Gladden and King advised him to prepare for a teaching career. Subsequently, Steiner did graduate study at the universities of Berlin and Göttingen.

A popular weekly magazine, the *Outlook*, commissioned Steiner to travel to Russia to prepare a biography of Leo Tolstoy in 1903. Tolstoy gained his lasting admiration by rising above racial and national barriers "to meet all human beings upon a high and common level." The Russian writer instilled in Steiner a difficult precept, he said: "Give everything and ask nothing in return." Although others might not treat him as a brother, he was intent on treating others as such. "When one has finally yielded himself to all men of all races and classes, when one can be unconscious of hampering barriers between, when one does not feel anything but pity for the tainted, a desire to include the halt and the halting rather than to exclude them," said Steiner, "then one has reached the highest point of spiritual experience." That was the goal toward which Tolstoy pointed him. "Young man, you can't make this world right, unless *you* are right," the world-famous novelist said as Steiner prepared to depart. "The Kingdom of God must be within *you*, if you want to hasten its coming into the world" (Steiner, *Against the Current*, p. 213).

In 1903, while he was doing research at Tolstoy's Russian estate "Yasnaya Polyana," Steiner was invited to become professor of applied Christianity at Grinnell College in Iowa. There, he lectured and published widely on ethnicity, immigration, and race relations. Human unity—without appeal to class, race, or religious prejudice—became his central theme. "I teach one religious doctrine with a scientific dogmatism and one scientific doctrine with a religious zeal: that underneath all the differences in races and classes, humanity is essentially one" (Steiner, *From Alien to Citizen*, p. 321).

Through his studies of immigration, Steiner contradicted the belief that the influx of various ethnic groups would result in a degeneration of the populace; he challenged equally the notion that an American super race might be created instead. Racially mixed children were more or less normal, he said. In his view, every immigrant group contributed its distinctive experience to the American "melting pot"; few racial traits were immutable, and the benign nature of the country's conditioning influences would infuse the American spirit in the new settlers. "I came here with the same blood as theirs and the same heritage of good or ill, bequeathed by my race," he observed, "yet I feel myself completely at one with all which this country possesses that is worth living for and dying for" (Steiner, *On the Trail of the Immigrant*, p. 308). Yet, race prejudice continued to be deeply ingrained in the United States, said Steiner. He made a personalist's argument against such "primitive" and "contagious" prejudice and devoted his life to overcoming it. "We need to have created in us the spirit of reverence for the human soul, no matter how encased in crude flesh," said Steiner. A person may be "crude, illiterate, ill-kept and unkempt; yet he is a brother man struggling upward. Whoever, whatever he is, he deserves our respect, if only for the spark of the divine flame within him" (Steiner, "What to Do for the Immigrant," in Mrs. Delphine Bartholomew Wells et al., *Conservation of National Ideals* [1911], pp. 64–65).

During World War I, Steiner later recalled, he was shunned by some people in Grinnell, Iowa, because of his pacifism. The college's academic freedom protected his position, however, and he lived to teach 4,000 to 5,000 Grinnell students, including Harry L. Hopkins, who became President Franklin D. Roosevelt's closest political adviser. After the death of Steiner's first wife in January 1940, he retired from the Grinnell College faculty in 1941. In October 1941 Steiner married Clara Elizabeth Perry. In retirement, he lived and died in Claremont, California.

• There is a small collection of Edward A. Steiner Papers at Grinnell College. His autobiographical works are *Against the Current: Simple Chapters from a Complex Life* (1910), *The Eternal Hunger: Vivid Moments in Personnel Experience* (1911), and *From Alien to Citizen: The Story of My Life in America* (1914). The most important of Steiner's other books include *Tolstoy the Man* (1903), *On the Trail of the Immigrant* (1906), *The Immigrant Tide: Its Ebb and Flow* (1909), *The Broken Wall: Stories of the Mingling Folk* (1911), and *The Making of a Great Race* (1919). There has been little scholarly interest in Steiner's career and thought, but see Ralph E. Luker, *The Social Gospel in Black and White: American Racial Reform, 1885–1912* (1991). For obituaries, see the *Des Moines Register* and the *New York Times*, both 2 July 1956.

RALPH E. LUKER

STEINER, Lewis Henry (4 May 1827–18 Feb. 1892), physician, state senator, and librarian, was born in Frederick, Maryland, the son of Christian Steiner, a merchant, and Rebecca Weltzheimer. Steiner studied at the Frederick Academy and in 1846 graduated from Marshall College in Mercersburg, Pennsylvania, where he was considered a particularly gifted student of chemistry. He went on to study medicine at the University of Pennsylvania, from which he received his M.D. in 1849. Returning home, he established a medical practice in Frederick. In 1852 he moved to Baltimore and thereafter devoted himself to teaching chemistry in relation to medicine.

Between 1853 and 1859 Steiner was a professor of chemistry and natural history at Columbian College (now George Washington University) and a professor of chemistry and pharmacy at the National Medical College, both in Washington, D.C. From 1854 to 1859 he taught chemistry and physics at the College of St. James in Hagerstown, Maryland, and in 1855–1856 he lectured on applied chemistry at the Maryland Medical Institute in Baltimore. From 1856 to 1861 and again in 1864–1865 Steiner was professor of chemistry at the Maryland College of Pharmacy, also in Baltimore. Among his several published works on these subjects are *The Utility of Colleges of Pharmacy: Address to the Maryland College of Pharmacy* (1856) and *Report on the Recent Contributions of Chemistry to the Medical Profession* (1857). In 1855 he translated, with Daniel Breed, *Heinrich Will's Outlines of Chemical Analysis, Prepared for the Chemistry Laboratory at Giessen [Germany]*. He was assistant editor of the *American Medical Monthly*, published in New York, from 1859 to 1861.

Steiner contributed numerous articles on scientific topics to the *Mercersburg Review*, largely in the 1850s, which were simultaneously published in pamphlet form, and to the *Maryland Review* and the *Southern Quarterly*. In addition, as an elder of the German Reformed church in Frederick and a member of the Potomac Synod of the church, he compiled, in collaboration with Henry Schwing, *Cantate Domino: A Collection of Chants, Hymns and Tunes, Adapted to Church Service* (1859). In 1869 he translated for the synod's publishing house a number of popular German children's stories written by Fritz Hoffmann.

At the start of the Civil War, Steiner returned to Frederick and joined the U.S. Sanitary Commission, a volunteer civilian organization concerned with the health and care of those serving in the Union army and navy. Appointed chief inspector with the Army of the Potomac, he issued, in 1862, an official *Report . . . Containing a Diary Kept during the Rebel Occupation of Frederick, Md., and an Account of the Operations of the U.S. Sanitary Commission during the Campaign in Maryland, September, 1862* and, in 1866, *A Sketch of the History, Plan of Organization, and Operations of the U.S. Sanitary Commission*. With the end of the war, Steiner returned to Frederick. In 1866 he married Sarah Spencer Smyth (or Smith according to some sources); they had six children.

For the next two decades Steiner devoted himself principally to various forms of public service. In 1865 he was elected president of the Frederick County School Board, where he served until 1868, concerning himself especially with the education of black children. From 1871 to 1883 he was active in politics as a Republican Maryland state senator, and over these same years he wrote on politics for the *Frederick Examiner*. In 1876 he was a delegate to the Republican National Convention that nominated Rutherford B.

Hayes for the presidency. Steiner remained active in medical organizations as a member of the American Medical Association, a founding member (1876) and later president (1879) of the American Academy of Medicine, and a member of the American Public Health Association, of which he was vice president in 1876–1877.

Steiner's career took yet another direction when in 1884 he was appointed the first head of Baltimore's new municipal public library, built and endowed by his friend, philanthropist Enoch Pratt. Pratt wrote to his board of trustees on 1 October 1884, "In my opinion, much depends on the selection of a Librarian to organize a proper system" (Castagna, p. 118). In Steiner he found a person of proven administrative ability in wartime with a commitment to public education and wide scholarly interests. The Enoch Pratt Free Library, which became one of the country's great libraries, opened to the public in 1886, and Steiner served as its director until his death. Under his scholarly leadership and that of his son, historian Bernard Christian Steiner, who succeeded him, the library's branch system was expanded and the book holdings substantially increased. Its collections were "probably more broadly based than those of many public libraries of the time" (Castagna, p. 119).

Steiner was a trustee of several colleges and a member of the American Association for the Advancement of Science, the Maryland Academy of Science, and the Philadelphia Academy of Natural Science. Memberships in the Maryland Historical Society and the New Haven (Conn.) Colony Historical Society attest to his interest in regional history and genealogy. Steiner died at his home in Baltimore.

• The Rare Books and Manuscripts Division of the New York Public Library has correspondence from 1861 to 1864 regarding Steiner's service with the U.S. Sanitary Commission. The Historical Society of Frederick Country (Md.), Inc., in Frederick, and the Maryland Department of the Enoch Pratt Free Library in Baltimore have some archival material on Steiner and his family. His scientific papers published between 1853 and 1891 are available in the general collection of the Library of Congress. A descendant of a German family that had settled in Frederick County in the early eighteenth century, he compiled *Genealogy of the Steiner Family: Especially of the Descendants of Jacob Steiner* (1896), published posthumously. He edited Ralph Dunning Smith's *The History of Guilford, Connecticut, from Its First Settlement in 1639* (1877), written by his father-in-law. His brief historical sketch, *The Enoch Pratt Free Library,* was published in the Johns Hopkins University Studies in Historical and Political Science series (1890). Wyndham Miles, "Lewis Henry Steiner," *Capital Chemist* 19 (Nov. 1969): 229–30, elucidates Steiner's career as a teacher of medical chemistry. His role as librarian is touched on in the article on the Enoch Pratt Free Library by Edwin Castagna in the *Encyclopedia of Library and Information Science,* vol. 8 (1972). An obituary is in the *Baltimore Morning Sun,* 19 Feb. 1892.

ELEANOR F. WEDGE

STEINER, Max R. (10 May 1888–28 Dec. 1971), composer and conductor, was born Maximillian Raoul Walter Steiner in Vienna, Austria, the son of Gabor Steiner, a theatrical producer, and Maria Hollman, a restaurant operator. A gifted and precocious child raised in a musical family, he rose rapidly through Vienna's prestigious Imperial Academy of Music, which he entered in 1901, and at the age of fourteen composed a musical comedy, *The Beautiful Greek Girl,* which played in Vienna for two years. As a teenager he studied under Gustav Mahler and Robert Fuchs and toured abroad. In 1912 Steiner married a woman named Beatrice whose maiden name is unknown. They had no children, and the marriage ended in divorce. Steiner arrived in the United States at age twenty-six, by way of England, having been declared an enemy alien with the outbreak of World War I. Over the next fifteen years he became Broadway's best-known orchestrator and most successful conductor, collaborating with George Gershwin, Jerome Kern, Florenz Ziegfeld, Victor Herbert, and George White in some of the best-known musicals of the jazz age. Steiner married Audrey Van Liew, a singer, in 1912. They had no children and eventually divorced.

Steiner had made his reputation in arranging other men's music. His only original composition was "Peaches," which died on Broadway after only two weeks, and it was as an orchestrator that he originally came to Hollywood. In 1929 Steiner orchestrated Harry Tierney's *Rio Rita* for RKO as he had on Broadway and was given a one-year contract at the studio. At first, RKO executives were unsure how to use Steiner. They feared audiences, new to sound films, would wonder where the music was coming from. So his initial assignments involved writing music for the film's opening titles and closing credits. Then he was asked to pad the soundtrack for studio films dubbed into Spanish. It was not until Steiner wrote his first complete score for the Academy Award-winning film *Cimarron* (1930) that moviegoers and studio heads began to recognize the dramatic possibilities of background scoring.

Two years and nineteen films later Steiner wrote the complete score for the film *Symphony of Six Million* (1932), produced by David O. Selznick. It was the first film to use music under dialogue, and years afterward Steiner observed that the movie "opened up the art of underscoring" and launched his career as a film composer. Steiner's talent at illuminating action with sound brought critical praise in *Bird of Paradise* (1932), *The Most Dangerous Game* (1932), and the classic *King Kong* (1933), another Selznick-Steiner collaboration that brought the art of movie orchestration to a new level.

Steiner's great gift for original melody and adaptation was governed by a determination "to subordinate myself to the picture." He came to feel that when movie music became "too decorative" it lost its "emotional appeal." That was why a good film score never called attention to itself. It furthered the action of the film, the emotion of the moment, or the qualities of a character, often through the use of leitmotifs that expanded the immediacy of the film's conversation with its audience.

Steiner's ideas have rarely been better illustrated than in *The Informer* (1935), a brooding John Ford film about the Irish rebellion that won Steiner his first Oscar. Toward the end of the film the informer, played by Victor McLaglen, is imprisoned. He has betrayed his best friend for a mere twenty pounds. His isolation is deepened by the constant drip of water into his cell. Steiner wanted to catch each of these drops musically and worked with the property man to regulate the dripping so that it occurred in tempo. The result is a musical phrase that captures the informer's hopelessness, examines his remorse, and anticipates his violent end.

Steiner's inventive mastery of what came to be known as the "classic" Hollywood narrative involved pushing the limits of the new medium. For Selznick's *The Garden of Allah* (1936), Steiner helped develop the "push-pull track" that gave a stereo sound to mono recordings, greatly widening the possibilities of orchestration. For *The Charge of the Light Brigade* (1936), his first film at Warner Brothers (WB), the effect furthers the audience's anxiety as the British army valiantly rides to certain death. The film's director, Michael Curtiz, shared Steiner's sense of how central scoring had become in Hollywood storytelling. Their teaming in *Kid Galahad* (WB, 1937), *Four Daughters* (WB, 1938); *Angels with Dirty Faces* (WB, 1938), *Dodge City* (WB, 1939), *Daughters Courageous* (WB, 1939), *Virginia City* (WB, 1940), *Santa Fe Trail* (WB, 1940), and *Casablanca* (WB, 1942) made for big box office and a distinctive Warner Brothers sound that commanded an audience's attention.

Steiner's most memorable work is his scoring of the nearly four-hour *Gone with the Wind* (Selznick, 1939). In a characteristic fit of creativity, Steiner wrote nearly three hours of music in little more than two weeks, working, by his own estimation, fifty-six hours without sleep so the picture could make its booking date. Steiner labored on eleven other films in that year and received Oscars in 1942 and 1944 for *Now, Voyager* (WB) and *Since You Went Away* (Selznick). The fecundity took its toll on his personal life. He was divorced from Louise Klos, whom he had married in 1936 and with whom he had one child, in 1945. Two years later his son committed suicide. Steiner married Leonette Ball in 1947.

The collapse of the studio system after World War II greatly curtailed the number of films Hollywood produced but not Steiner's indomitable enthusiasm for the projects that came his way. His scores for *Mildred Pierce* (WB, 1945), *Life with Father* (WB, 1947), *The Big Sleep* (WB, 1946), *The Treasure of Sierra Madre* (WB, 1948), *Key Largo* (WB, 1948), *Johnny Belinda* (WB, 1948), and *White Heat* (WB, 1949) are classics of their kind. His work on *The Caine Mutiny* (Columbia, 1954), *The Searchers* (WB, 1956), and *A Summer Place* (WB, 1959) showed that even in his seventies the Steiner magic remained.

Slowed by illness and failing sight, Steiner continued working. *Two on a Guillotine*, a pedestrian 1965 Warner Brothers release, showed the old master still

up to his old tricks, frightening audiences in a haunted house as he had thirty-two years before when King Kong first lumbered out of the primeval forest. In the intervening era, Hollywood's classic cinema had developed into a worldwide crowd pleaser. And no one defined the sound of that cinema more than Steiner. He died in Hollywood, California. One of Hollywood's most prolific composers, Steiner worked on more than 300 film productions in a 36-year career that set a pioneering standard for excellence in the film industry. His three Oscars and eighteen total Academy Award nominations testify to his unique place in the art of composing film scores.

• Steiner's papers as well as many of his scores and soundtrack recordings are held at Brigham Young University's Harold B. Lee Library. Steiner's discussion of his craft can be found in Nancy Naumburg, *We Make the Movies* (1937); Roger Manvell and John Huntley, *The Technique of Film Music* (1957); and Tony Thomas, *Film Score: The Art and Craft of Movie Music* (1991), which uses significant sections of Steiner's unpublished autobiography. Steiner's work within the Hollywood studio system is described in Rudy Behlmer, *Memo from David O. Selznick* (1972), and Ted Sennett, *Warner Brothers Presents* (1972). Steiner's significance in the evolution of movie music is analyzed in Irwin Bazelon, *Knowing the Score: Notes on Film Music* (1975); Mark Evans, *The Music of the Movies* (1975); Randall D. Larson, *Musique Fantastique: A Survey of Film Music in the Fantastic Cinema* (1985); William Darby and Jack Du Bois, *American Film Music: Major Composers, Techniques, Trends, 1915–1990* (1990); Christopher Palmer, *The Composer in Hollywood* (1990); Caryl Flinn, *Strains of Utopia: Gender, Nostalgia, and Hollywood Film Music* (1992); Royal S. Brown, *Overtones and Undertones: Reading Film Music* (1994); and George Burt, *The Art of Film Music* (1994). An obituary is in the *New York Times*, 29 Dec. 1971.

BRUCE J. EVENSEN

STEINHARDT, Laurence Adolph (6 Oct. 1892–28 Mar. 1950), diplomat and corporate lawyer, was born in New York City, the son of Adolph Max Steinhardt, a successful steel-enameling manufacturer, and Addie Untermyer, the sister of Samuel Untermyer, an influential New York lawyer and crusader for Jewish rights. Both parents were of German-Jewish ancestry. Steinhardt attended Columbia University, earning his B.A. in 1913 and his M.A. and LL.B. two years later, and he was admitted in 1916 to the New York bar. In 1920, after serving in the field artillery in World War I and on the staff of the provost marshal general as a sergeant, he became associated with his uncle's prominent law firm, Guggenheimer, Untermyer and Marshall. In 1923 Steinhardt married Dulcie Yates Hofmann; they had one child, a daughter.

During the 1920s Steinhardt, a shrewd, ambitious, energetic, and wealthy lawyer with political connections, became involved with the Democratic party in New York through which he met another young lawyer, Franklin D. Roosevelt. In 1932 Steinhardt, seeking to enhance his political career, became a major contributor to Roosevelt's preconvention campaign, the "Before Chicago Club." After Roosevelt's election,

Steinhardt declined an assistant secretary of state position. The president then named him minister to Sweden, making Steinhardt at age forty the youngest chief of a mission and launching him on a significant diplomatic career.

In Stockholm, Steinhardt, always industrious, demonstrated that he was a careful worker who gave attention even to minute details, and he successfully negotiated one of the country's first reciprocal trade agreements. He enjoyed diplomatic life and, desiring to become an ambassador, he told Roosevelt in 1936 that he would not return to Sweden. Meanwhile, he advised the president on New York politics, conferred with his college classmate and newspaper publisher Arthur Hays Sulzberger to ensure support from the *New York Times*, and contributed generously to the Democratic National Campaign Committee. In 1937 he received the ambassadorship to Peru, where he focused on cultural and trade issues and played an important role in the successful Lima Pan-American Conference.

In 1939 President Roosevelt, who considered Steinhardt "a good fixer and hoss trader," transferred him to Moscow and ordered that a copy of the ambassador's cables to the State Department be sent also to the White House for his direct information. Arriving in the USSR just before the stunning Nazi-Soviet Non-Aggression Pact, Steinhardt had an excellent staff and provided his government with highly informed assessments of the situation. Following the start of the European war with Germany's and then Russia's invasion of Poland, he foresaw an extended period of Russo-German cooperation, contrary to the president's hopes. He argued for a hard-line, quid pro quo policy toward the Kremlin, even if it sometimes meant using his country's full diplomatic influence on rather minor ends. After the Soviet attack on Finland, starting the winter war of 1939–1940, many in the United States demanded his recall or a diplomatic break with the USSR. Steinhardt insisted, however, that it was foolish to think that Russia would respond to only a gesture, and he continued to report that Russia and Germany had to cooperate with each other for a while. When Washington offered concessions to the Kremlin later in 1940 to win Stalin's friendship, because of the growing power of Germany and Japan, Steinhardt disliked the policy and thought that it weakened the American position. Soviet-American relations did not improve. He failed to interpret correctly reliable information concerning an imminent Nazi invasion of Russia, and following the June 1941 attack he initially anticipated the fall of Moscow. He soon recognized, however, the Soviet resolve to fight, and the subsequent American decision to aid the USSR changed the nature of the relations between the two countries. Steinhardt's usefulness in Moscow, consequently, came to an end as the U.S. pursued a more conciliatory policy toward the Kremlin. Soon after the United States entered World War II Roosevelt appointed him to neutral Turkey. Nevertheless, Steinhardt had, according to Soviet expert Loy Henderson of the State Department, done "an outstanding job in difficult circumstances."

Steinhardt's assignment to the strategically located Turkey with its important raw materials, such as chrome, illustrated his reputation as an experienced diplomat, especially given that over the years Ankara had objected to the sending of ethnic Jewish ambassadors from America. Both the Allied and Axis powers sought more active Turkish support in the war, but Germany's influence was strong, and the Turks feared Russian intentions and were fearful of being used for British interests in the eastern Mediterranean. The ambassador recognized Turkey's delicate situation and its economic dependence on Germany. He advocated a policy of mutual respect, not financial threats, and he conducted a successful preemptive buying program by the Allies to keep strategic items from the Germans. While he had played a controversial role in Moscow in limiting the flow of Jewish refugees to the United States, by 1944 Steinhardt was using his influence to aid the passage of Jewish refugees from the Balkans to Palestine. He also persuaded Ankara to free American flyers who had been interned, and he received the Legion of Merit for his efforts. Thus, although Turkey did not break diplomatic relations with Germany until the summer of 1944, Steinhardt had good reason to be pleased with his performance.

Roosevelt appointed Steinhardt to Czechoslovakia in late 1944. By the time he arrived in 1945, the Soviet position there appeared dominant because the Central European country had been liberated by the Red Army. The new ambassador, nonetheless, saw an opportunity to prevent Soviet control. As Czech national elections approached in 1946, he remained confident even though Washington seemed not to recognize and support his arguments that Czechoslovakia was a pivotal country. In the election the Communists did much better than Steinhardt had predicted; although they did not win a majority, they controlled the coalition cabinet. Still optimistic, he argued that cultural and economic agreements with Prague could gain support for the liberal democratic groups. The State Department, though, gave little attention to Prague and seemed to concede Czechoslovakia's withdrawal from the Marshall Plan Conference. Then, during Steinhardt's leave for an illness, Washington decided to withhold financial credits from the Czechs and possibly missed an opportunity. The absent Steinhardt apparently acquiesced in the decision, although earlier in Ankara he had actively opposed similar policies on the part of England. The Communist coup d'état in February 1948 destroyed his hopes for reintegrating the nation into the Western orbit. His "able leadership," historian Walter Ullman has argued, had tried "to make Washington realize that new forces" in the postwar world were "making former United States diplomatic and political conceptions largely obsolete."

Following the coup, President Harry S. Truman sent Steinhardt to Ottawa, and the Canadians welcomed the experienced ambassador. They welcomed, also, his positive attitude toward Canadian-American relations; meanwhile, he again entertained hopes for a political career and election to one of New York's top offices. But in 1950, at the age of fifty-seven, he died in a plane crash near Ottawa, on his way to a political dinner in New York. Funeral services were held in Ottawa and New York City's Temple Emanu-El; Steinhardt was buried in the family mausoleum at Brooklyn's Washington Cemetery.

Few political appointees can match Steinhardt's remarkable diplomatic career; he became, according to diplomat George V. Allen, an "unusually effective ambassador," though he was never regarded as a career diplomat. Conscientious, diligent, and willing to express his recommendations, he was a well-informed reporter who usually worked closely with his staff and did not bypass normal State Department channels by going directly to the president. He was controversial, however, and his personality provoked strong reactions among many of his subordinates. Steinhardt grew, nonetheless, with his significant responsibilities, and on his death the *New York Times* praised him as "the most widely experienced diplomat in the service of the American people." He had ably held challenging and sensitive assignments for seventeen consecutive years during a turbulent period of the twentieth century.

• The Steinhardt papers are in the Library of Congress and should be supplemented with State Department records at the National Archives and the appropriate volumes in the Foreign Relations of the United States series. Two unpublished Ph.D. dissertations are Ralph R. Stackman, "Laurence A. Steinhardt: New Deal Diplomat, 1935–1945" (Michigan State Univ., 1967), and Joseph O'Connor, "Laurence A. Steinhardt and American Policy toward the Soviet Union, 1939–1941" (Univ. of Virginia, 1968). See also Travis Beal Jacobs, *America and the Winter War, 1939–1940* (1981); Barry Rubin, "Ambassador Laurence A. Steinhardt: The Perils of a Jewish Diplomat, 1940–1945," *American Jewish History* 70, no. 3 (1981): 331–46; David J. Alvarez, "The Embassy of Laurence A. Steinhardt: Aspects of Allied-Turkish Relations, 1942–1945," *East European Quarterly* 9, no. 1 (1975): 39–52; and Walter Ullman, "Czechoslovakia's Crucial Years, 1945–1948: An American View," *East European Quarterly* 1, no. 3 (1967): 217–30. See the obituaries, editorials, and photographs in the *New York Times* and *Washington Post*, both 29 Mar. 1950.

TRAVIS BEAL JACOBS

STEINHAUS, Edward Arthur (7 Nov. 1914–20 Oct. 1969), insect pathologist, was born in Max, North Dakota, the son of Arthur Alfred Steinhaus, a storekeeper and farmer, and Alice Blanche Rhinehart, an elementary school teacher. Steinhaus grew up in Max, North Dakota, and Faribault, Minnesota. Before college Steinhaus worked at a printshop and developed a lifelong interest in writing, editing, and publication. In 1932 Steinhaus entered North Dakota Agricultural College (now North Dakota State University), from which he graduated with a B.S. in bacteriology in 1936. In 1939 Steinhaus received a Ph.D. in bacteriology with a minor in entomology from Ohio State University. He then spent one year as a research postdoctorate working on insect microbiology at Ohio State University, supported by a Muelhaupt Fellowship.

In 1940 Steinhaus was hired as a bacteriologist by the U.S. Public Health Service Rocky Mountain Laboratory in Hamilton, Montana. In 1944 he became a lecturer in the Department of Bacteriology at the University of California, Berkeley. Soon after, he transferred to the College of Agriculture and Agricultural Experiment Station at Berkeley, as an assistant professor of insect pathology. He was promoted to professor of insect pathology in 1954. Between 1945 and 1960 Steinhaus organized and administered the world's first laboratory of insect pathology, at Berkeley. He continued to serve as laboratory director after it became the Department of Insect Pathology in 1960 and then the Division of Invertebrate Pathology in 1963. Steinhaus was a Guggenheim Fellow in 1960–1961. In 1963 Steinhaus was elected president of the Entomological Society of America and presented the principal address at the Second International Congress of Insect Pathology, in Paris. That same year he was made a fellow of the American Academy of Microbiology and became the first dean of the School of Biological Sciences, University of California, Irvine. At his death, he held the titles of professor of pathobiology and director of the Center for Pathobiology at the University of California, Irvine.

Steinhaus was highly regarded internationally and was elected to the All-Union Entomological Society of the U.S.S.R. in 1968. During 1968, he also presided over the Insect Pathology Section at the Thirteenth International Congress of Entomology, in Moscow; was nominated by the Entomological Society of America for the National Medal of Science; and was elected to the National Academy of Sciences. Steinhaus's enormous stature and impact on science was recognized in 1959 when he was selected by the Entomological Society of America to give one of its first Founder's Memorial Lectures, the highest award given by this society for outstanding research accomplishment.

Steinhaus was unquestionably the most distinguished insect pathologist in the world and one of the most accomplished biologists of the twentieth century. His broad interdisciplinary training in microbiology and entomology, combined with his notable abilities at writing, editing, and administration, were important components of his life's research. In seventeen years he made the University of California, Berkeley, the world center for insect pathology research and graduate training. He was considered an excellent, patient teacher and trained students from around the world, many of whom went on to become eminent scientists. They in turn established laboratories modeled after that of Steinhaus. He authored the basic reference books *Insect Microbiology* (1946), *Principles of Insect Pathology* (1949), and, with Mauro E. Martignoni, *Laboratory Exercises in Insect Microbiology and Insect Pathology* (1961), the first laboratory manual on this topic. He was author of approximately 200 research papers on the subjects of viral, bacterial, protozoan, and fungal infections of insects. He edited and contributed to the two-volume *Insect Pathology: An Advanced Treatise* (1963). His book on the history of insect pathology, *Disease in a Minor Chord* (1975), was published posthumously.

In 1959 Steinhaus founded the *Journal of Insect Pathology* (now *Journal of Invertebrate Pathology*) and served as its editor for many years. He founded and organized the Society for Invertebrate Pathology, serving as its first president in 1967–1968. In addition to his groundbreaking efforts on behalf of insect pathology, he had a profound influence on the field of entomology in general. He was instrumental in founding the *Annual Review of Entomology* in 1955, and served as coeditor for its first seven volumes. As a result of his editorial skills, the *Annual Review of Entomology* reached a high level of excellence and became the world's most important serial publication in entomology.

Much of Steinhaus's research was on viral diseases of insects. He was one of the first to describe granulosis and noninclusion viruses of insects, which he studied by means of electron microscopy. He described or recorded nearly fifty new viruses from insects. He worked with the International Committee of Nomenclature and Classification of Insect Viruses to standardize terminology. He was the first to demonstrate the practical potential of using insect nuclear polyhedrosis viruses to control field crop pests. In 1942 Steinhaus was instrumental in developing interest in and promoting the use of *Bacillus thuringiensis* after it had been neglected for decades. He demonstrated this bacterium's effectiveness against pest caterpillars, studied its properties and the insecticidal action of its crystalline endotoxin, and developed methods for its mass production. He was concerned with the safety of microorganisms used in biological control and conducted many tests to demonstrate their harmlessness to nontarget organisms and proposed methods for standardizing such tests.

When Steinhaus united the disciplines of microbiology, pathology, and entomology in his attempts to understand the underlying causes of disease in insects, he gave form to the new discipline of invertebrate pathology. Thus, he is commonly regarded as the "founder of modern insect pathology." From both the research and teaching standpoint, Steinhaus was a giant in creating this modern discipline. He applied his research to practical uses of controlling insect pests with microorganisms. Insect pathogens have subsequently become a major area of research for modern pharmaceutical and chemical firms. The successful use of *B. thuringiensis* toxins as microbial insecticides and in transgenic cotton, corn, potatoes, and other plants is a direct outgrowth of Steinhaus's pioneering research. Current research on baculoviruses for insect pest control and genetically engineered baculoviruses for pharmaceutical production can also be traced back to Steinhaus.

Steinhaus had married in 1940 Mabry Clark, who held an M.S. in bacteriology from Ohio State University and briefly taught at North Dakota State University; they had two daughters and a son. In addition to being a homemaker, his wife provided encouragement and scientific assistance to Steinhaus throughout his career.

A Congregationalist, Steinhaus was a religious man who believed that there was no conflict between a belief in God and the concepts of science. He stated "that invertebrate pathology and invertebrate pathologists, as do other sciences and scientists, have a responsibility and role to fill in the general betterment of society and man's lot on earth" (quoted in Briggs, p. v). In a relatively short life of fifty-four years, Steinhaus accomplished a great deal, in spite of severe congenital health defects that he kept secret from nearly everyone. Among other abnormalities, his left hypothalamus was nonfunctional, he was missing a kidney, and he had an inverted stomach. After his death, in Irvine, California, his colleagues and physicians marveled that he could have accomplished all that he did and admired his courage.

Steinhaus was a visionary scientist who nurtured a new biological discipline, insect pathology, that has benefited and will increasingly benefit humanity by providing environmentally safe, biologically based alternatives to chemical pesticides. Biologist, educator, author, entomologist, administrator, editor, bacteriologist, virologist, Steinhaus was one of the most productive scientists of his time and trained many of the most important living scientists in this discipline.

• The E. A. Steinhaus Papers are housed in the Department of Special Collections at the University of California, Irvine Library. Important sources are John D. Briggs, "Edward A. Steinhaus," *Journal of Invertebrate Pathology* 14 (1969): iii–v; an anonymous biography, *Vision, Courage, Accomplishment: The Life of Edward A. Steinhaus* (1970), Miscellaneous Publication No. 2, Center for Pathobiology, University of California, Irvine; E. Gorton Linsley and Ray R. Smith, "Edward Arthur Steinhaus," *Journal of Economic Entomology* 63 (1970): 689–91; and E. F Knipling, "Edward Arthur Steinhaus, 1914–1969," National Academy of Sciences, *Biographical Memoirs*, 44 (1974): 303–327, which includes a bibliography of Steinhaus's papers. An obituary is in the *New York Times*, 21 Oct. 1969.

DONALD CURTISS STEINKRAUS

STEINIGER, Anna. *See* Clark, Frederic Horace, and Anna Steiniger.

STEINITZ, William (17 May 1836–12 Aug. 1900), chess player, was born Wilhelm Steinitz into a poor Jewish family in Prague, the son of Josef Salamon Steinitz, an iron worker, and Anna Torshová. His parents wanted Steinitz to become a rabbi, and he therefore received a good early education in both religious and general fields, tutored privately by rabbis. Steinitz left home at age nineteen, possibly in part because his mother had died and his father had remarried. After moving first to Strakonici (now in the Czech Republic) in 1855, Steinitz went in 1858 to Vienna, where he entered the Polytechnic Institute to study mathematics. He supported himself by tutoring, working as a tailor, and playing chess for money in cafés. Steinitz completed only the first year of his degree; he spent much of his time playing chess and was soon dismissed for lack of progress and refusal to take exams.

Steinitz then devoted himself to chess, winning the Vienna Championship in 1861–1862. He made his international debut at a tournament in London soon afterward, finishing in sixth place. Settling in England in 1862, Steinitz began a relationship with a woman named Caroline Golder. Although he and Caroline would live together for twenty-seven years, until her death, they apparently were never officially married. Golder gave birth to a daughter in August 1866. The space for the father's name was left blank on the birth certificate, but the child's last name was recorded as "Steinetz." Steinitz won a small tournament in Ireland in 1865.

In 1866 Steinitz claimed the title of world champion after his surprising defeat of Adolf Anderssen, widely considered the strongest player in the world, in a match in London, 8–6. However, no governing organization existed that could officially confer the title of world champion; hence Steinitz's claim remained in dispute until 1886, when he defeated Johannes Zukertort 12.5–7.5, in a match held jointly in New York, St. Louis, and New Orleans. He successfully defended the title against Mikhail Chigorin in 1889 in Havana, winning 10.5–7.5; in 1890–1891 in New York against Isidor Gunsberg, winning 10.5–8.5; and again in Havana against Chigorin in 1892, this time winning 12.5–10.5. He finally lost the title to 25-year-old Emanuel Lasker in 1894 in New York, by a margin of 12–7 and lost the return match in 1896–1897 in Moscow, 12.5–4.5. His other match victories include defeating Harry Bird in 1866 and Joseph Blackburne in 1876. Steinitz also had notable tournament successes, capturing first prize in premier international tournaments in London in 1872 and Vienna in 1873 and 1882, placing second in London in 1883, and winning in New York in 1894.

A British citizen for most of his life, Steinitz emigrated to the United States in 1884 because of the nationalistic prejudice he continued to encounter in British chess circles and because America seemed to offer greater economic opportunities for the professional chess player. Following Caroline's death in 1892, Steinitz became involved with an American woman named Elizabeth (last name unknown). No marriage certificate is on record. She had two children while living with Steinitz, but it is doubtful that he fathered the second child, since he was playing in Europe when she would have been conceived. Following the psychological strain of losing the bitterly contested matches to Lasker and a dismal performance in London in 1899, Steinitz, by this time economically destitute, began to collapse psychologically. He died a charity patient at the East River Sanitarium on Ward's Island, New York.

The first official world chess champion and the first player to articulate a systematic theory of positional chess strategy, Steinitz is considered the "father of modern chess." He is chiefly remembered today as the first major modern theoretician of the game. Drawing on the ideas of the German player Louis Paulsen, he contended that chess should be understood not as a struggle between two players but as a theoretical system. At the beginning of the game, all forces exist in perfect equilibrium, but as play commences, different types of unbalance unfold. Space, time, and force are the dimensions in which imbalances become most significant. The violent, romantic, swashbuckling attacks that had, until Steinitz, been popular at all levels of chess, could not, according to his arguments, work in the absence of a previously existing positional superiority. This superiority could exist as a transitory advantage, an advantage in time, or as a permanent advantage in either space or force. The phrase most closely associated with Steinitz's theory is "the accumulation of small advantages." Steinitz's theory also dealt with the importance of strong pawn centers, not just the classical two-pawn center but alternative strong positions—of isolated pawns, queen side pawn majorities, "bad" bishops, the advantage of two bishops, and the importance of weak squares. He developed new strategic ideas in the theory of the Dutch Indian and Ruy Lopez openings.

Dubbed as well the "father of modern annotation," Steinitz also changed the way chess games are described. As chess editor of the *Field* from 1873 to 1882 and editor and proprietor of the *International Chess Magazine* from January 1885 to December 1891, Steinitz gained a reputation as a superior commentator. Unlike the early writers who had merely said which side was winning, Steinitz was careful to point out where each side had erred and exactly what constituted the winning side's advantage. Always a controversial figure in chess, Steinitz used his columns, especially in the *International Chess Magazine* to scathingly attack his political enemies. His other writings include the instructional chess books, *The Modern Chess Instructor* (2 vols., 1889) and *The Book of the Sixth American Chess Congress* (1891), which became a valuable collector's item.

• The most comprehensive guides to Steinitz's life and games are Ludwig Bachmann, *Schachmeister Steinitz* (4 vols., 1910–1921), which contains a biography and more than 1,000 games; and J. Gilchrist and David Hooper, *Weltgeschichte des Schachs: Steinitz* (1968), with 575 games. The best English language source is Karl Landsberger, *William Steinitz, Chess Champion: A Biography of the Bohemian Caesar* (1993). Also see Charles Devidé, *A Memorial to William Steinitz* (1901), reprinted as *William Steinitz, Selected Games* (1974). Max Euwe's excellent book, *The Development of Chess Style* (1968), traces the development of chess theory and devotes a third of its pages to Steinitz's strategic ideas. Articles on Steinitz can be found in Hooper and Kenneth Whyld, *The Oxford Companion to Chess* (1984); Harry Golombek, *Golombek's Encyclopedia of Chess* (1977); and E. G. Winter, ed., *World Chess Champions* (1981). An obituary is in the *New York Tribune*, 14 Aug. 1900.

ELIZABETH ZOE VICARY

STEINMAN, David Barnard (11 Jun. 1886–21 Aug. 1960), consulting engineer, was born in New York City, the son of Louis Kelvin Steinman, a factory worker, and Eva Scollard. Steinman graduated from the City College of New York in 1906 and went on to study engineering at Columbia University. Throughout this period he worked as a part-time instructor in the New York City public schools. Having completed his graduate course work at Columbia in 1910, he was hired as an instructor of civil engineering at the University of Idaho. With the publication of his thesis on suspension and cantilever bridges in 1911, he received a Ph.D. in engineering. At Idaho he advanced to the position of professor, and by the time he resigned in 1914 to return to New York, his expertise as a civil engineer had enabled him to make a number of physical improvements to the campus. In 1915 he married Irene Stella Hoffman; they had one daughter and two sons.

Steinman's return to New York City was prompted by a request from Gustav Lindenthal, one of the nation's leading bridge engineers. Their association began at Columbia when Steinman was a student of the elder engineer. In this new role Steinman was a special assistant in the design and construction of two notable bridges—both completed in 1917—the massive Hell Gate arch bridge over the East River in New York and the continuous truss Sciotoville railroad bridge that linked Ohio and Kentucky. He briefly served as principal assistant engineer in 1917 just before Lindenthal's dissolution of the office. In that same year Steinman joined the newly established New York office of prominent engineer J. A. L. Waddell. So successful was Steinman in attracting new work that Waddell, whose primary office had been in Kansas City, moved east. His year with Waddell gave Steinman useful new experience in the business aspects of engineering.

In 1918 Steinman took the position of evening instructor at the City College of New York. When CCNY established an engineering school that same year, he accepted the position of associate professor and advanced quickly to become professor in charge of civil and mechanical engineering, responsible for all aspects of developing and implementing the engineering program. In addition to traditional subject areas, he expanded the curriculum to include the study of aeronautics and automotive technology, fields so new that he found it necessary to devise his own instructional material.

In 1920 Holton Robinson, a bridge engineer who specialized in structural steel work, asked Steinman to join him in designing a suspension bridge for Florianópolis, Brazil. It took three years to raise the necessary funding, but when the bridge was completed in 1926, it was the longest eye-bar suspension bridge in the world. In 1923 Steinman was introduced to cable spinning and steel erection when he and Robinson worked on the Rondout Bridge in New York State. This was a brief experience, however, as Steinman was never put on the payroll and after two months was let go. He then spent a six-month stint with the New York

Central Railroad, where among other things he checked bridge designs, devised methods for strengthening existing bridges, and prepared new designs.

Steinman opened his own one-desk office in March 1921 in space rented from another engineer. Despite having the skill to design all types of bridges, he specialized in suspension bridges. The talents that he and Robinson brought to the loose partnership they formed in 1923 made them leaders in the field of suspension bridge design and construction. This productive association lasted until Robinson's death in 1945.

One of the first projects that came to the new office was the Steubenville bridge across the Ohio River. The bridge had been built in 1904, but its deck and truss unexpectedly buckled under heavy loading in 1923. Steinman was called in to examine the damage and make recommendations for repairs, which were completed the following year.

Steinman was retained in 1923 as the designing engineer on the board of engineers for the planned Carquinez Strait highway bridge in California. Although he proposed to cross the waterway that drained California's Central Valley with a suspension bridge, he prepared plans for a cantilever type bridge according to the board's wishes. Steinman took into account California's unstable geological conditions, and the bridge, which opened in 1927, was one of the first designed to resist earthquakes.

When, in 1923, the government of New South Wales decided to bridge Sydney Harbor, an international competition was held for designs and bids. One of the entrants, the English Electric Company of Australia, hired Steinman to produce the plans for a monumental suspension bridge. His growing reputation had led the company to believe his work would be successful, but despite a lengthy visit to Australia during which he promoted his vision, plans for a less expensive metal arch bridge were chosen.

Always setting the highest standards for himself and the conduct of his practice, Steinman served in 1924–1925 on the National Commission on Ethics and Practice of the American Association of Engineers. While on the commission, he helped write an engineer's code of ethics: Specific Principles of Good Professional Conduct. In 1925 he was elected president of the AAE, and in 1929 he was appointed to the New York State Board of Examiners for Professional Engineers.

In addition to the dozens of small projects carried out by Steinman during the 1920s, he worked on the Mount Hope suspension bridge across Narragansett Bay in Rhode Island. The Mount Hope Bridge Commission planned to build a cantilever bridge, but the state legislature balked at the price and refused to fund the project. As a result the commission located bankers willing to back a less expensive suspension bridge project to be financed by tolls. Begun in 1927, it was completed in 1929. A notable aspect of the project concerned the individual parallel cable wires that had to be replaced during installation. Always the astute engineer and businessman, Steinman was aware of possible difficulties with a new type of wire that was being used. To protect his reputation, he wisely obtained guarantees from the manufacturer to cover the cost of possible replacement.

Between 1928 and 1931 Steinman designed and supervised the construction of the St. Johns suspension bridge over the Willamette River near Portland, Oregon. In making the cables, Steinman experimented with a new technique using prestressed wire rope strands rather than parallel wires in the cables. His fondness for John Roebling's Brooklyn Bridge may have influenced his use of great Gothic arches in the design of the St. Johns bridge towers.

Steinman's artistic sense played a major role in much of his work, and biographer William Ratigan said that he was as temperamental as any artist. He was one of the first engineers to use paint and light to emphasize the beauty of a bridge's lines. Designed to become part of their surroundings, his bridges were painted shades of green. At night, floodlights illuminated their towers, while smaller lights were often strung along the decks and the entire length of their great arcing cables.

Constructed over the Penobscot River between 1929 and 1931, the Waldo-Hancock Bridge in Maine was the first long suspension bridge built in that state. In 1932 Steinman received the Artistic Bridge Award for his design of this span. Because of the savings realized during its construction, the state was in a position to offer Steinman the opportunity to design a second structure, the Verona Island Bridge. His attention to the details of cost and his knack for completing projects under budget made him an extremely popular engineer during the difficult years of the depression. In an era when much of the economy was without work, Steinman and Company had a number of projects running concurrently.

Although seemingly out of character, the towering Skyride at Chicago's Century of Progress Exposition in 1933 and 1934 was also the work of Steinman. Its two steel towers and cable-mounted moving passenger cars amounted to a modified version of a transporter bridge and its 1,800-foot span nearly equaled that of the recently opened Ambassador Bridge in Detroit. When they were built, the towers, standing at over 600 feet, were the tallest structures west of Manhattan.

In 1934 Steinman was given the job of designing the Marine Parkway Bridge that would connect Brooklyn and Rockaway on Long Island. His first choice was a suspension bridge, but he was forced to develop a vertical lift bridge for the site. Politicians feared that suspension bridge towers would be a danger to aircraft at nearby Floyd Bennett Field.

Steinman won the contract for designing and overseeing the construction of the Henry Hudson Bridge, which, built between 1934 and 1938, spanned the area where the Hudson and Harlem rivers converged at the north end of Manhattan. In 1908 the city's plan had featured a monumental masonry arch, but funding was not available. Similar financial problems dogged the Henry Hudson Bridge Authority in the 1930s, when it sought public funding. Ultimately, private financing was arranged, and Steinman was able to build the metal arch bridge he had envisioned in his 1909 C.E. thesis at Columbia. Fears that the bridge's toll would discourage traffic were unfounded, and because its use was so great, Steinman was immediately commissioned to build the second deck that was part of his original design.

In the late 1930s Steinman produced the designs for both the tiny 350-foot Sullivan-Huttonsville Bridge between Indiana and Illinois and the 8½-mile-long series of bridges that made up the Thousand Islands Bridge across the St. Lawrence River between the United States and Canada. When it was discovered that the Thousand Islands suspension span was unstable in windy conditions, Steinman alleviated the problem by adding diagonal cable stays. This occasion prompted him to begin a nearly fifteen-year study of suspension bridge aerodynamics. Where many of his contemporaries believed that bridges needed to be more flexible, Steinman's investigations led him to conclude that suspension bridges could be made better only by making them more rigid.

It was not until 1948 that the first steps were taken to adapt the Brooklyn Bridge, which had been completed in 1883, to twentieth-century traffic needs. Much to his delight, Steinman was engaged to reconstruct and widen the bridge, with his primary plans calling for a complete alteration of its appearance in order to make it usable. But, in an awakening of preservation instincts, his plans were modified to conserve the bridge's original appearance and atmosphere. Steinman removed trolley and elevated railroad tracks, widened the single-lane roadways to three lanes each, and replaced all the decking of both the roadways and promenade. The project was completed in 1952.

The upper and lower peninsulas of Michigan are separated by the five-mile-wide Straits of Mackinac. This gulf was an impediment to the state's commerce and economic development as the waterway could be traversed only by ferry whose operation depended on weather conditions. Climatically, the locale was treacherous, with especially brutal winters. Great masses of ice from Lake Huron forced their way through the narrow channel as they moved toward Lake Michigan, and gale force winds were not unknown in the area. Steinman had first considered the possibility of bridging the waterway after a 1914 visit, and he conducted his first studies in 1934. But it was not until the 1950s that he won the contract, and in 1954 work finally began. Steinman's knowledge of bridge design and long study of aerodynamics bore fruit as he was able to design a structure able to withstand the extreme forces nature imposed on the area. The bridge opened to traffic in 1957.

One of Steinman's final domestic efforts involved his design for a long-span suspension bridge across Verrazanno Narrows at New York City. As early as 1926 he had considered such a project and over the years prepared designs to promote the idea. His gateway bridge to the United States would be called the

Liberty Bridge, and until the decision was finally made to build the bridge in the late 1950s, it seemed as if Steinman would be chosen to do it. He was disappointed when, despite his best efforts, the design contract went to fellow suspension bridge expert Othmar Ammann.

Steinman's position as one of the world's leading experts on suspension bridges made him an international figure and in the late 1950s brought additional engagements when several foreign governments sought his services. Iraq in 1956 commissioned him to design a bridge across the Tigris River at Baghdad. In a daring move in 1956 to unite the European and Asian continents, the Turkish government commissioned him to design a suspension bridge across the Bosporus at Istanbul.

Steinman was an extremely prolific engineer and writer. In addition to designing bridges, he wrote about them and the people who built them. Along with Sara Ruth Watson, he coauthored *Bridges and Their Builders* (1941). It was well received, and in 1945 he wrote about the Brooklyn Bridge in *The Builders of the Bridge, the Story of John Roebling and His Son*. It is estimated that he designed more than 450 bridges and authored some twenty books and 600 professional papers. Ever the renaissance man, his many interests included writing poetry. At least 150 of his poems, filled with bridge symbolism, were published.

Steinman was a tireless worker, organizer, and joiner who always sought to better the engineering profession. Throughout his career he lectured on bridge design at colleges and universities and earned no less than nineteen honorary degrees. Among the many professional organizations to which he belonged were the American Society of Civil Engineers, American Railway Engineering Association, American Association of Engineers, Society of Automotive Engineers, and New York State Society of Professional Engineers, and in 1934 he was the founder and first president of the National Society of Professional Engineers. He also belonged to the Columbia University Club and the Engineers of New York. Among the countless honors Steinman received during his life were twelve medals he received for scholarship while at the City College of New York. The ASCE presented him with its Croes Medal in 1919 for his paper on the Hell Gate Arch Bridge, the Norman Medal in 1923 for a paper on locomotive loadings for railway bridges, and the Thomas Fitch Rowland Prize in 1929. His designs were recognized for their beauty, and between 1930 and 1942 he received six artistic bridge awards. Steinman died at his residence in Manhattan.

• A good summation of Steinman's attitude regarding the engineer as artist is found in his article "Bridges—From Dream to Realization" written for *The Transit of Chi Epsilon* 25, no. 2 (1953). Information on specific bridges for which he was responsible can be found in the *Engineering News-Record* and in the huge volume of reports and articles Steinman authored. These appeared in journals such as *American Engineer*, *Consulting Engineer*, *Civil Engineering*, *American Institute of Steel Construction News*, *Journal of the American Concrete Institute*, *Professional Engineer*, and *Military Engineer*. William Ratigan, *Highways Over Broad Waters* (1959), is an extremely laudatory biography of Steinman. Despite being hagiographic, it contains details not found elsewhere. An obituary is in the *New York Times*, 23 Aug. 1960.

WILLIAM E. WORTHINGTON, JR.

STEINMETZ, Charles Proteus (9 Apr. 1865–26 Oct. 1923), electrical engineer, was born Karl August Rudolf Steinmetz in Breslau, Germany, the son of Karl Heinrich Steinmetz, a lithographer in the government railway service, and Caroline Neubert. Like his father and grandfather, he was afflicted at birth with the physical deformity of being a hunchback, and as an adult he was scarcely four feet tall. He attended the St. John's Gymnasium in Breslau and graduated at the head of his class in 1882; he was even exempted from the final oral examination that was required of Gymnasium graduates.

In 1883 Steinmetz matriculated at the University of Breslau. Although his primary area of specialty was pure mathematics (geometry), he also pursued an unusually broad course of studies, including astronomy, biology, chemistry, electricity, physics, and political economy. In 1888 he completed his doctoral studies with a dissertation on algebraic geometry concerning the spatial involutions defined by a net of nth order surfaces ("Ueber die durch ein lineares Flächen-systeme n^{ter} Ordnung definierten mehrdeutigen involutorischen Raumverwandtschaften"), directed by Heinrich Schröter. During his university years (at least since 1884) Steinmetz was active in the student Socialist group and served as ghost editor of their newspaper, the *People's Voice*. This increasingly attracted the disfavor of German government authorities, until finally a series of his articles led to the discovery of his identity and an order for his arrest. Steinmetz immediately fled the country, and his doctoral degree was not granted.

After a brief sojourn in Austria, Steinmetz spent six months of the academic year 1888–1889 in Zürich at the *Eidgenösse Technische Hochschule* (the Swiss Federal Institute of Technology). There he studied engineering, which offered the possibility of commercial employment, although he would have preferred to continue his career in mathematics. His studies in this area, however, had only the prospect of a teaching position, which was precluded by his political activities (all German universities available to him at the time were government controlled). Likewise, it was impossible to stay indefinitely in Switzerland, and so he decided to immigrate to the United States.

Steinmetz arrived in New York City on 1 June 1889. Immediately after his arrival he began learning English, and he applied for citizenship on 10 June 1889. At this time he changed his name to Charles Proteus Steinmetz. The name "Proteus" was a nickname that had been bestowed on him by his university classmates in Breslau to honor his abilities and versatility. With a letter of introduction he obtained a position as a draftsman in the Eickemeyer and Osterfeld Manufacturing Company in Yonkers, New York. The company made electrical equipment, and since Steinmetz had an interest in electricity, his skills were recognized and he was given a laboratory in which to work. In 1892 the General Electric (GE) Company bought out the Eickemeyer company (ostensibly to obtain their patents but also to acquire Steinmetz, who out of loyalty to Eickemeyer had declined to leave). In early 1893 he was transferred to the GE facility in Lynn, Massachusetts, but in 1894 he relocated to Schenectady, New York, which became his permanent home; that same year he became a naturalized U.S. citizen. Steinmetz was appointed Head of the GE Calculating Department, which did the routine engineering work, and in 1901 he was named chief consulting engineer. By this time his work had become sufficiently recognized that he was awarded an honorary A.M. by Harvard (1902), and an honorary Ph.D. by Union College (1903). Both these honors were significant because he had not received a university degree in Germany; they also came relatively early in his career, indicating a real appreciation of his accomplishments by the academic community. In 1902 he joined the faculty of Union College as head of the electrical engineering department and professor of electrical engineering; he remained in this position until 1913, working strictly on a gratis basis. During this time he was charged with setting up an electrical engineer program (of his own design) at Union.

Steinmetz's reputation in 1911 was such that, as chief consulting engineer, his yearly salary from GE was $18,000, which made him one of the highest-paid engineers in the United States. He continued to teach on a part-time basis at Union until the creation of a separate Consulting Engineering Department at GE demanded his full attention. This department was designed to handle non-routine engineering problems, and his new title suggested nothing less than a full-time employment with GE. In reality, Steinmetz was asked to step in whenever a difficult problem arose, but otherwise he was given complete freedom to pursue whatever research was of interest to him. This included a personal laboratory with virtually any equipment and staff he needed. He subsequently became professor of electrophysics (1913–1923) at Union, where he gave a few lectures on special occasions. He served as president of the American Institute of Electrical Engineers (AIEE) from 1901 to 1902 and as president of the Illuminating Engineers Society from 1915 to 1916. In 1903, in a poll conducted by *American Men of Science* of the leaders of science in America, he was rated twelfth (out of 150) in physics and fifty-first (out of eighty) in mathematics. He was awarded the Elliott Cresson Medal, the highest award of the Franklin Institute, in 1913.

Steinmetz was a born expositor; while still a student he had contributed popular scientific articles to newspapers. In Zürich a publisher had approached him about collecting this material into his first book, "Astronomy, Meteorology, and Cosmogony" (1888); and before coming to the United States, having written technical electrical papers for the journal *Electrotechnische Zeitschrift*, he was hired as their American correspondent. One of his first engineering assignments with the Eickemeyer Company was to improve on the design of an alternating single-phase motor; this led him to discover his power law of hysteresis (1891), which was a major achievement. Announced at the New York meeting of the AIEE, the discovery immediately established his national reputation. In 1893, at a meeting of the International Electrical Congress in Chicago, he presented his symbolic method (the use of complex numbers) for the computation of alternating current phenomena; this essentially revolutionized the field and attracted worldwide attention. Steinmetz presented his first complete treatment of the symbolic method in his book *Theory and Calculation of Alternating Current Phenomena* (1897), written with Ernest J. Berg; it was subsequently improved in the books *Theory and Calculation of Transient Electrical Phenomena* (1909), *Theory and Calculation of Electric Circuits* (1917), and *Theory and Calculation of Electrical Apparatus* (1917). Such material required a more mathematical and scientific approach to electrical engineering problems, which was addressed in his other textbooks: *Theoretical Elements of Electrical Engineering* (1901), *General Lectures on Electrical Engineering* (1908), *Radiation, Light, and Illumination* (1909), *Engineering Mathematics* (1911), and *Elementary Lectures on Electrical Discharges, Waves and Impulses and Other Transients* (1911). These went through many editions, educating his contemporaries and influencing several generations of readers. In 1907 Steinmetz had begun to seriously consider electrical transients—electrical phenomena of a short duration—such as lightning. This investigation took a new turn in the summer of 1920, when his vacation cabin at Camp Mohawk was hit by lightning. This led him to devise lightning arrestors to protect transmission lines as well as to consider the laboratory generation of lightning. In 1921 he constructed a generator capable of producing a discharge of 100,000 volts (roughly one million horse power) for one hundred-thousandth of a second. This captured the imagination of the public, and at the time of his death he had been nearing completion of an even more powerful generator.

Steinmetz had some two hundred patents, including ones for a magnetite arc generator; induction, polyphase, and various motors; generators; dynamos; transformers; and equipment related to long distance transmission lines. During his latter years he participated in numerous public affairs activities, including membership at the Board of Education (1912–1923) and service president of the Common Council (1916–1923) and chairman of the City Planning and Park Commission (1913–1923). In all of these activities he remained true to his socialist views, which he expressed in his book *America and the New Epoch* (1916). His final book, *Four Lectures on Relativity and Space* (1923), was of a purely expository character and was based on public lectures.

Steinmetz never married, but in 1903 he formally adopted one of his assistants, Joseph LeRoy Hayden, as his son. Hayden and his wife, and ultimately their three children, came to live with him in his home/laboratory on Wendell Avenue in Schenectady. Steinmetz had a great love for children and delighted in his relations with the public. As a consequence he was much beloved, and numerous stories circulated about his omnipresent cigar, his fondness for practical jokes, and his hobbies (which included a conservatory stocked with cacti, a Gila monster, and a half-dozen alligators). His charm was irresistible, as illustrated by his first meeting with Thomas Alva Edison. Upon realizing that Edison was deaf, Steinmetz "conversed" with him by tapping on Edison's knee in Morse code! Steinmetz died unexpectedly of a heart attack in Schenectady, following a strenuous six-week cross-country lecture tour.

Steinmetz must be regarded as one of the fathers of electrical engineering, and his work symbolizes the fruitful interaction between mathematics, science, and practical engineering. He made outstanding contributions to the field, and his influence was transmitted not only by his discoveries and inventions, but also by his writings. Much of the methodology of modern circuit theory was developed and became widely known through his textbooks. His successful experience with GE encouraged other companies to become involved in basic research, which was a new departure in American industrial thinking. Finally, his was a true "rags to riches" story that has been an inspiration to immigrants, to those affected with a physical disability, and to those whom society would dismiss as "non-conformists."

• Steinmetz's papers are in the Hall of History Foundation of the General Electric Research and Development Center in Schenectady, N.Y. A selection of Steinmetz's writings is in *Steinmetz: The Philosopher*, ed. Ernest Caldecott and Philip L. Alger (1965). His textbooks, which went through numerous editions, were finally reissued as *Electrical Engineering Library* (9 vols., 1921). Steinmetz's own estimate of his work, found in his papers after his death, was reprinted as Chapter 5 of *Recollections of Steinmetz: A Visit to the Workshops of Dr. Charles Proteus Steinmetz*, ed. Emil J. Remscheid (1977). Steinmetz's essay, "Science and Religion," *Harper's Monthly Magazine*, Feb. 1923, pp. 296–302, furnishes an excellent example of his expository skill. Early biographies of Steinmetz, about a half-dozen in number, are all of a decidedly popular character; most of them tend to establish the "Steinmetz myth" rather than give an accurate picture of the man and his work. A definitive biography that does much to remedy the situation is Ronald R. Kline, *Steinmetz: Engineer and Socialist* (1992). George Wise, *Willis R. Whitney, General Electric and the Origins of U.S. Industrial Research* (1985), gives a valuable overview of Steinmetz's relationship with General Electric. An editorial and obituary are in the *New York Times*, 27 Oct. 1923; obituaries are also in *Science*, 16 Nov. 1923, pp. 388–90; *Journal of the Institute of Electrical Engineers* 42 (Nov. 1923): 1224–25; the *General Electric Review*, Dec. 1923, pp. 793–801; and the British *Journal of the Institution of Electrical Engineers* 62 (1924): 984–85.

JOSEPH D. ZUND

STEINWAY, Christian Friedrich Theodore (6 Nov. 1825–26 Mar. 1889), piano manufacturer, was born in Seesen, in the duchy of Brunswick (central Germany), the son of Heinrich (Henry) Engelhard Steinweg (later Steinway), a piano manufacturer, and Julianne Thiemer. He attended Jacobsohn College in Seesen, where he excelled in the sciences, especially acoustics. He was also an accomplished pianist, and in 1839, at age fourteen, he demonstrated his father's pianos at the Brunswick State Fair, where they won first prize and a gold medal. After completing his college education, he went to work making pianos in his father's workshop in Seesen. When the Steinway family left Brunswick for America in 1850, C. F. Theodore (originally Theodor) remained in Seesen, where in 1852 he married Josephine Luederman. The couple had one child. Seeking to expand his piano business, he moved to Wolfenbüttel in 1853 and to Brunswick in 1860. Friederich Grotrian became his partner in 1856; the piano firm would later be known as Grotrian-Steinweg. After the tragic deaths of his two brothers Charles and Henry, Jr., in 1865, Theodore sold his business to his partners, Grotrian, Helfferich, and Schulz, and left for America to help his aging father and younger brothers carry on their business.

He arrived in New York on 26 October 1865 and immediately became responsible for the scientific and technical aspects of making pianos at the firm, while his younger brother William devoted himself to the selling and marketing of them. Theodore was a brilliant engineer, and under his direction, the twentieth-century piano took shape. Building on the groundwork laid by his brother Henry, Jr., Theodore applied his knowledge of acoustics and other scientific principles to the construction of pianos, revolutionizing piano design. In the twenty years he was in America, he was responsible for 41 of the firm's 101 patents. Among the most important were the duplex scale, which increased the richness of tone by allowing portions of the string that had been previously dampened to sound ("a more liquid singing tone than I could imagine," wrote Hermann von Helmholtz, a Berlin acoustician and collaborator of Steinway's); a cupola iron frame, designed to increase the strength of the piano frame to withstand thirty-five tons of tension; an improved action, which gave the player great control over the heavy hammer as it hit the key; overstringing, the utilization of longer strings and the repositioning of the bridge to the center of the soundboard, which gave the piano greater resonance; and a one-piece rim, made of eighteen laminated layers, designed to strengthen the case of the piano. "There was nothing in the realm of science having any bearing on piano construction which was overlooked," wrote Steinway's colleague, the piano historian Alfred Dolge.

By the end of the century these improvements and innovations had resulted in a piano of unsurpassed power, sensitivity, and tonal beauty; an instrument enthusiastically endorsed by Liszt, Wagner, Gounod, Rubinstein, and other leading musicians of the day. Theodore also anticipated the demand in America for the upright piano and was responsible for the large-scale production of that instrument, which by 1895 accounted for 95 percent of all piano sales in America. Theodore Steinway, in contrast to his genial and extroverted brother William, was described as intense, introverted, brilliant, and irascible. Trained as an engineer, he was a perfectionist in his attention to mechanical detail. After twenty years in America, he returned in 1885 to Germany where he felt more at home and where he could be near his colleague and friend von Helmholtz. In describing Steinway's accomplishments, Helmholtz had written in 1871, "With such a perfect instrument as yours—I must modify many of my former expressed views regarding pianos." Steinway remained actively involved in the firm's Hamburg and London operations and continued making improvements on the piano until his death in Brunswick. He was honored by both scientists and artists. He was a member of the Royal Prussian Academy of Fine Arts in Berlin and an honorary member of the Academy of Fine Arts in Stockholm and the Societé des Beaux-Arts in Paris. A trained scientist and a brilliant engineer, Steinway's application of scientific principles to the building of pianos was his greatest contribution. Dolge, who knew Theodore well, described him as a man who "aimed to create a piano which would respond to the demands of the modern dynamic compositions of Liszt, Wagner or Rubenstein, and would orchestra-like, fill the large concert hall to its remotest corners. . . . [Steinway] revolutionized piano making and all other auxiliary industries by forcing the acceptance of scientific methods upon all who desired to stay in the progressive march."

• Frederick Allen, "Steinway," *Invention and Technology* (Fall 1993): 34–43, has a detailed description of the technology of the modern Steinway, for which Theodore was largely responsible. See also Alfred Dolge, *Pianos and Their Makers* (1911; repr. 1972), for a biographical sketch of Steinway by a colleague who knew him well. Information has also been supplied by Henry Ziegler Steinway, Steinway's grandnephew. An obituary is in the *New York Tribune*, 27 and 31 Mar. 1889.

MARGARET MORELAND STATHOS

STEINWAY, Henry Engelhard (15 Feb. 1797–7 Feb. 1871), piano manufacturer, was born Heinrich Engelhard Steinweg in Wolfshagen, in the duchy of Brunswick (central Germany), the son of Heinrich Zacharias Steinweg and Elizabeth Rosine. As a youth he was forced to overcome seemingly insurmountable hardship and tragedy. When Napoleon's troops invaded Germany, they killed several of his brothers and burned the Steinway home. At age fifteen a tragic accident killed his father and remaining brothers. In 1815, at age eighteen, he joined the army and is said to have fought in von Blucher's army at the battle of Waterloo, where he won a medal for "bugling in the face of the enemy." As a youth he was interested in musical instruments and, although lacking formal musical training, made a zither or a dulcimer while in the army. He also had a natural talent for working with

wood and, after leaving the service, was apprenticed to a cabinet-maker in Goslar. In 1820 he settled in the nearby town of Seesen, where he worked in the shop of an organ builder and where in 1825 he married Julianne Thiemer. Nine children were born to the Steinways: Christian Friederich Theodore (C. F. Theodore), Doretta, Charles, Henry, William, Albert, Anna, Hermann, and Wilhelmine.

By 1800 the piano had replaced the harpsichord in Europe as the preferred keyboard instrument. Steinway, according to family legend, made his first piano in the kitchen of his home in 1825 in Seesen. In 1839 he exhibited a grand and two square pianos at the Brunswick State Fair and was awarded first prize and a gold medal. This achievement enhanced Steinway's reputation as a master piano maker. In 1848–1849 the revolutions and uprisings throughout central Europe brought political and economic unrest to Germany, and although Steinway had prospered in business, he made the decision at age fifty-three to emigrate to America, where his son Charles had already gone to seek out new opportunities for the family. With his wife, his three daughters, and four of his six sons, he embarked from Hamburg on the SS *Helene Sloman* and arrived in New York on 9 June 1850. Steinway and his sons worked for other established piano makers for about two years in order to learn the English language and American business methods. During this period Steinway worked for a firm called Lausch making soundboard for pianos, for which he received six dollars a week.

On 5 March 1853, after anglicizing their name, the Steinways established themselves in business as Steinway & Sons in a rented loft at 85 Varick Street in lower Manhattan, where they produced square pianos at the rate of one per week. Their first piano, a six-octave square, sold for $500. Within a year they were obliged to move to larger quarters at 82–88 Walker Street. After only one year in business, they won a prize at the Metropolitan Fair in Washington, D.C. In 1855 they won a gold medal at the American Institute Fair at New York's Crystal Palace for their innovative seven-octave piano, which combined a one-piece castiron frame (patented by Alpheus Babcock in 1825) with overstringing, a design in which the bass strings cross the treble strings in a diagonal pattern. The result was an instrument of great power and tonal beauty, which caused a sensation. After this success, they were obliged to move again in 1860, to a larger factory on Fourth Avenue that Steinway had planned and supervised. For the first time in the history of the firm, steam-driven machinery was installed. By the end of the Civil War, the firm was producing 2,000 pianos each year. The firm built its first grands in 1856 and its first upright in 1862. In 1859 Henry, Jr.,'s decision to apply overstringing to a grand piano with a one-piece castiron frame proved to be epoch making in the development of the piano, as it resulted in an instrument capable of tonal and dynamic subtleties unimagined at the time.

Tragedy struck in 1865 when two of Steinway's sons and coworkers, Henry, Jr., and Charles, died within three weeks of each other: Henry, Jr., of tuberculosis and Charles of typhoid fever. Grief-stricken, the father asked his eldest son to sell his piano business in Germany and come to America to help carry on the family business. C. F. Theodore Steinway arrived in New York in October 1865 and immediately became the head of the technical and scientific departments of the New York factory as well as a partner. In 1866 Steinway Hall, which Steinway had planned and supervised, opened in New York and soon became one of the most important cultural centers in the city. Through the firm's sponsorship of many great European artists, including Teresa Carreno, Rafael Joseffy, and Anton Rubinstein, the Steinways demonstrated to the public the brilliance, power, and tonal beauty of their instruments.

A Steinway piano won first prize and a gold medal at the great Paris Exposition of 1867, establishing the firm's international reputation. The basic Steinway design—the "American system," as it was called—with its one-piece castiron frame and overstringing, revolutionized piano making and was soon adopted by all important piano manufacturers in Europe.

After Steinway's death in New York City, his son William became president of the company. From 1870 to 1910 the firm moved its plant and operations to Astoria, Long Island, where William had bought land. During World War II the firm made components for gliders for the U.S. Army Air Force. By 1988 the firm had built a half million pianos. Four generations of Steinways ran the business with unparalleled success until 1972, when the family sold Steinway & Sons to the Columbia Broadcasting Company, Inc. In 1985 the Birmingham brothers of Boston purchased the company from CBS. "The Steinways' rise to a position of world leadership in the industry was meteoric," wrote social historian Cyril Ehrlich. "Within two decades, the Steinway family emigrated to America, transformed the instrument's technology, established the essential features of the piano we use today, assumed leadership of the American industry and then returned to conquer Europe."

• The Steinway archives are located at La Guardia Community College, Long Island City, N.Y. The best history of the rise of Steinway & Sons is in Henry E. Steinway, *People and Pianos* (1953). See also Ronald Ratcliff, *Steinway & Sons* (1989), for a history of the firm that includes an account of Henry E. Steinway's early years in Germany. Alfred Dolge, *Pianos and Their Makers* (1911; repr. 1972), provides excellent biographical sketches of Steinway family members who Dolge knew personally. Cyril Ehrlich, *The Piano: A History* (1976; repr. 1990), gives a detailed account of the 1867 Paris International Exhibition at which Steinway & Sons won first prize and international acclaim. Daniel Spillane, *History of the American Pianoforte* (1890; repr. 1969), is a history of the piano industry in America. Cynthia Hoover, *The Steinways and Their Pianos in the Nineteenth Century* (1981), describes the impact of the industrial revolution on piano builders in both America and Europe. Michael Lenehan, "Building the Steinway Grand K 257," *Atlantic Monthly*, Aug. 1982, pp.

32–58, has a step-by-step description of the making of a Steinway piano at the factory on Long Island. Arthur Loesser, *Men, Women and Pianos*, is a brilliant and witty social history of the piano and its place in society. Information has also been provided by Henry Ziegler Steinway, William Steinway's grandson. An obituary is in the *New York Tribune*, 8 Feb. 1871.

MARGARET MORELAND STATHOS

STEINWAY, William (5 Mar. 1835–30 Nov. 1896), piano manufacturer, was born Wilhelm Steinweg in Seesen, in the duchy of Brunswick (central Germany), the son of Heinrich Engelhard Steinweg (Henry Steinway), a piano manufacturer, and Julianne Thiemer. He attended the Jacobsohn Hochschule in Seesen, where he majored in music and languages. He is said to have played the piano well and to have had such a good ear that he could tune a three-stringed grand piano to perfection. Although too young to have worked with his father and brothers in the piano-making business in Seesen, he grew up in an atmosphere that helped prepare him for his future work in the family company.

William was fifteen when he arrived in New York with his family on 9 June 1850. As he had a decided talent for music, he was offered the choice of either studying music or learning the profession of making pianos. He chose the latter and was apprenticed to the firm of William Nunn & Company in New York.

When the firm of Steinway & Sons was founded on 5 March 1853, he joined his father and brothers making pianos in a rented loft at 85 Varick Street. He started work as a bellyman installing soundboards but before long was involved in the marketing of the pianos. In 1865 a tragedy occurred in the family when two of his brothers, Charles and Henry, Jr., died within three weeks of each other. This left his grieving father with the overwhelming task of running the business without his two most experienced partners. To avert a crisis, Henry Steinway asked his eldest son, C. F. Theodore Steinway, to sell his piano business in Brunswick and come to America. Theodore arrived in New York on 26 October 1865 and immediately became head of the scientific and technical departments, leaving William, at age thirty, in charge of the marketing and commercial aspects of the business. In the decades to come, the scale of William's marketing and promotional techniques in both America and Europe reached proportions hitherto unknown in the piano trade.

To create an interest in the Steinway piano and to stimulate the public's interest in concert music, Steinway oversaw the building of Steinway Hall in New York, which his father had planned. The hall, seating 2,000, formally opened in 1866 and quickly became one of the leading cultural centers in New York. Acting as concert manager, Steinway introduced Americans to the great artists of the day, including Teresa Carreno, Leopold Damrosch, Rafael Joseffy, and Anton Seidl. The firm also sponsored the American tours of the celebrated pianists Anton Rubinstein in 1872 and Ignaz Paderewski in 1892, for whom they provided their best pianos. Steinway also sought recognition at the important international piano exhibitions. After the Steinway piano won first prize and a gold medal at the great Paris Exhibition in 1867—a triumph for the "Steinway system"—William aggressively sought and received endorsements from leading artists and royalty including Berlioz, Liszt, Rossini, Wagner Gounod, Saint-Saëns, and Queen Victoria.

Seeking to further expand the business, Steinway, who had become president of the company after his father's death in 1871, opened a sales office in London in 1877 and a second piano factory in Hamburg, Germany, in 1880. In 1870 he had purchased 400 acres of land in Astoria, New York, and established the village of Steinway, Long Island City, where since 1910 the entire firm of Steinway & Sons has been located.

William, described in company publications as urbane, warm-hearted, and imaginative, was also very active in civic and philanthropic affairs. He was chair of the Rapid Transit Commission, which laid the first subway lines in New York City; a delegate to the Democratic National Convention in 1888; and a lifelong friend of President Grover Cleveland. He was also president of the Liederkranz Society, the foremost German singing society of its day, for fourteen years. In 1861 he had married Regina Roos; they had two children before their divorce. In 1880 he had married Elizabeth Ranft in Dresden, Germany; they had three children. He died in New York City.

William Steinway's extraordinary entrepreneurial and marketing skills were vital to the growth and success of the Steinway company, both nationally and internationally, in the post–Civil War era. While his brother Theodore designed and made the pianos, William sold them. Besides successfully marketing the Steinway piano with techniques that were considered revolutionary at the time, he was responsible for developing the dealer network in America and a system of agents for the Steinway piano throughout the world.

• For additional information on William Steinway, see "Alfred Dolge's Tribute to William Steinway," *American Art Journal* 12 (1896): 135. Michael Lenehan, "Building the Steinway Grand K 257," *Atlantic Monthly*, Aug. 1982, pp. 32–58, has a biographical portrait of William by his grandson, Henry Ziegler Steinway, who also supplied information for this article. An obituary is in the *New York Times*, 1 Dec. 1896.

MARGARET MORELAND STATHOS

STEJNEGER, Leonhard Hess (30 Oct. 1851–28 Feb. 1943), ornithologist, herpetologist, and museum curator, was born in Bergen, Norway, the son of Peter Stamer Steineger, a merchant, and Ingeborg Catharina Hess. Born with the German surname Steineger, he took its Norwegian spelling after 1870. At the age of sixteen Stejneger showed an interest in zoology—especially birds—and kept extensive notes and sketches from field observations. In 1871 he published in *Journal für Ornithologie* lists and notes on birds he observed during his family's frequent visits to Meran in southern Tyrol (then part of Austria). After early

schooling at the Smith Theological School and the Bergen Latin School and later with a private tutor at Meran, Stejneger entered the University of Kristiania in Oslo, Norway. Although he studied medicine at the behest of his family for two years, Stejneger graduated in 1875 with a degree in law from Royal Frederic's University, Kristiania (later the University of Oslo), and immediately entered his father's business, continuing his scientific investigations in his free time. After the failure of his father's business in 1881, Stejneger departed for the United States to pursue a career in ornithology. He left behind, and later divorced, his wife Anna Normann, a schoolteacher whom he had married in 1876. They had no children.

In October 1881 Stejneger arrived in Washington D.C., and sought out Spencer Fullerton Baird, the secretary of the Smithsonian Institution and a fellow ornithologist, with whom Stejneger had actively corresponded for several years. In 1878 Stejneger had named his first newly discovered bird species, *Lanius bairdi*, in Baird's honor. Baird invited Stejneger to continue his research in the bird collection of the Smithsonian's National Museum of Natural History. This association led to his employment with the U.S. Signal Service for a meteorological expedition to the Commander Islands from March 1882 to October 1883. During this expedition Stejneger collected bird specimens, including bones of the recently extinct Pallas's cormorant and Steller's sea cow. In July 1884 he became an assistant in the bird collection of the Smithsonian's National Museum of Natural History and prepared an ornithological exhibit for the 1885 World's Industrial and Cotton Centennial Expositions in New Orleans, Louisiana. Later that year Stejneger became an assistant curator of birds and conducted research on arctic bird species of the Pacific Rim, especially the islands of Russia, the United States, and Japan. From 1884 to 1888 he published ninety-three articles, book chapters, notes, and obituaries, including more than 360 pages of text for the *Natural History of Birds* in J. S. Kingsley's popular series *The Standard Natural History*. On 5 February 1887 he received U.S. citizenship.

In March 1889 the National Museum of Natural History appointed Stejneger as its first full-time curator of reptiles and batrachians. Although he had no previous training in herpetology—the study of reptiles and amphibians—he quickly became one of the field's foremost authorities. Stejneger continued to publish occasional ornithological works, especially on Japanese birds, while devoting most of his remaining professional career to reptiles and amphibians. His initial exertion in reorganizing and improving the museum's herpetological collections led to such exhaustion and deterioration of his health that he left Washington for two months in late 1889. During that time Stejneger collected reptiles and amphibians with C. Hart Merriam in the Grand Canyon and the San Francisco Mountain region of Arizona. In 1893 he prepared an exhibition of poisonous snakes and turtles for the World's Columbian Exposition in Chicago and published *The*

Poisonous Snakes of North America in 1895. In 1892 Stejneger had married Helene Maria Reiners; they adopted a daughter in 1907.

Between 1895 and 1922 Stejneger participated in numerous expeditions to monitor the decline in fur seal populations and distributions in the northern Pacific. During his 1883–1884 trip to the Commander Islands, Stejneger had first observed the detrimental effects of seal hunting. In 1895 Stejneger returned to the Pribilof and Commander islands on assignment of the U.S. Fish Commission to document the subsequent population decline. In 1896 and 1897 U.S. president Grover Cleveland named him to the International Fur Seal Commission, under which he traveled extensively around the Pacific Rim. His authoritative writings on the fur seal question earned a gold medal at the Paris Exposition in 1900. Reflecting his long-term interest in the region, Stejneger published in 1936 a biography of Georg Wilhelm Steller, whose 1750 travel diary had served as inspiration and guide during his first northern Pacific expedition.

Stejneger continued his studies of amphibians and reptiles and in 1900 traveled to Puerto Rico to collect reptiles and amphibians for the Pan-American Exposition, held in Buffalo, New York. In 1917 he published, with Thomas Barbour of Harvard University, the first *Check-list of North American Amphibians and Reptiles*, with subsequent editions published in 1923 and 1943. Stejneger's herpetological research was slowed after he assumed greater administrative duties at the Smithsonian's National Museum of Natural History. In 1903 he briefly served as the acting head curator of the Department of Biology and in 1911 became head curator of biology, a position from which he was exempted indefinitely from retirement by executive order of President Herbert Hoover in 1921. Stejneger actively directed biological research at the museum until his death in Washington, D.C.

Stejneger devoted more than sixty years to the Smithsonian Institution and his adopted country. He had a productive research career, publishing more than 400 articles, largely on herpetology and ornithology, and an influential administrative career, implementing Baird's vision of developing the National Museum of Natural History through international exploration and cooperative research. He was an active member of the International Committee on Zoological Nomenclature from 1898 to his death and a member of the Permanent Committees of the International Zoological Congress and the International Ornithological Congresses. He was made a knight of the first class of the Royal Norwegian Order of St. Olaf in 1906 and a commander of that order in 1939. Stejneger was elected to membership in the National Academy of Sciences in 1923 and held honorary or corresponding memberships in many other societies. On his eightieth birthday in 1931 he was elected honorary president for life of the American Society of Ichthyologists and Herpetologists, who dedicated to him an issue of the society's journal, *Copeia*.

• The Smithsonian Institution Archive, Washington, D.C., holds the personal correspondence, diaries, manuscripts, notes, papers, and photographs of Stejneger in Record Unit 7074. His official correspondence is filed with the records of the Division of Reptiles and Amphibians, 1873–1968 (Record Unit 161), the Department of Biology, 1897–1943 (242), the Departments of Biology and Zoology, 1901–1954 (143), and the Baird Ornithological Club of Washington, D.C., 1922–1949 (7110). Reminiscences of Stejneger are included in the Lucile Quarry Mann Interviews, 1977 (9513). Robert V. Bruce, *The Launching of Modern American Science, 1846–1876* (1987), discusses the development of the National Museum of Natural History at the Smithsonian Institution in which Stejneger played a significant role but does not treat the career of Stejneger. A biographical account is by Alexander Wetmore in the National Academy of Sciences, *Biographical Memoirs* 24 (1947): 142–95. An obituary is in the *Evening Star* (Washington, D.C.), 1 Mar. 1943.

PAULA DePRIEST

STELLA, Joseph (13 June 1877–5 Nov. 1946), painter, was born in Muro Lucano, Italy, the son of Michele Stella, an attorney, and Vincenza Cerone. Stella's father was financially able to send his children to the Liceo Umberto I in Naples, where they studied French and English as well as classical and modern literature. Joseph Stella received his diploma from the Liceo in 1895.

Following his graduation from the Liceo, Stella went to the United States, arriving in New York City in 1896. At the urging of his older brother Antonio, a doctor who had been in America for a few years, young Stella began studies for a medical degree. While he remained in medical and pharmacological school through the spring of 1898, by 1897 he also was attending the Art Students League in New York. In 1898 Stella enrolled in the New York School of Art, where he studied for three years. About 1902 he married Mary Geraldine Walter French, who was from Barbados. The couple were together for only a few years in the early part of the century, and the date of their parting is unknown, although they lived with each other again in the 1930s. They had no children.

Stella's early images resembled the realistic style of the Old Masters, especially the fifteenth- and sixteenth-century Flemish and German artists, whom he not only admired as a child in Italy but studied at the Metropolitan Museum of Art in New York as well. The exceptional technical quality of his early drawings marked his abilities: his images of workers and factories and of newly arrived immigrants demonstrated his ability to work in black and white, and it was in the medium of graphite and charcoal that his work excelled in these years. In 1906 Stella's art was exhibited for the first time when it appeared in the Society of American Artists' annual exhibition—he showed *Old Man* (c. 1905, private collection). Because of his critical reputation as a competent illustrator (he had begun working for the social reform publication *Outlook* in 1905), Stella was commissioned by the welfare and reform journal *Charities and the Commons* (later the *Survey*) to depict a mine disaster in Monongah, West Virginia, in 1907. This was followed by work the next year on *Charities and the Commons'* noted series "The Pittsburgh Survey," which addressed issues of Pittsburgh industry. Stella continued to work for the *Survey* sporadically throughout the teens.

Stella returned to Europe in 1909, visiting France and Italy. He remained on the Continent for almost four years. It was on a trip to Paris in 1911–1912 that he became impressed by the Italian futurists (who were enamored with a new, fast-moving society) and began to paint in a more colorful and dynamic manner that echoed the quick-paced visions of artists such as Gino Severini and Umberto Boccioni. Stella's palette turned away from the black and white of his earlier graphite and charcoal drawings and became a medley of bright hues. At the same time his style ceased to resemble the Old Masters but instead, like the futurists, echoed a new preoccupation with depicting images in an abstracted manner that reflected not only the form of a subject but its emotional ambience as well. *Battle of Lights, Coney Island, Mardi Gras* (1913–1914, Yale University Art Gallery) was painted in this style. The bright jarring colors and the explosive shapes recall the frenzied atmosphere of a densely packed amusement park.

Arriving back in the United States in December 1912, Stella spent most of the remainder of the decade in New York, exhibiting two paintings in the International Exhibition of Modern Art (the Armory Show) in February 1913. By the late 1910s he was painting in a more symbolist, mystical manner as exemplified by *Prestidigitator* (1916, Whitney Museum of American Art, New York City). His works during this period were the most abstracted of his career. The mysterious imagery of *Prestidigitator*, which eludes a logical or rational explanation (save that, owing to the definition of prestidigitate as "a sleight of hand," it may vaguely represent a magician's arena), is similar to the cryptic works that were done by others associated (as Stella was) with the Arensberg circle, a group of prominent avant-garde artists whose sarcastic attitude of questioning the form and significance of art was their hallmark. One of Stella's means of support during this period was the work that he did for the *Survey*, which was conducting investigative studies of urban and industrial sites. He traveled to Bethlehem, Pennsylvania, in 1918 to make illustrations of steelworkers for the publication.

Concurrently, but continuing into the early 1920s, Stella continued to paint images that were influenced by the futurist art that he had seen in Europe. The works for which he is best known are his many versions of the Brooklyn Bridge and *New York Interpreted (The Voice of the City)* (1920–1922, Newark Museum, Newark, N.J.). Stella's dazzling scenes of bridges, factories, and other structures symbolized the optimism that characterized America's industrial sector in the 1920s. This was a buoyant era in Stella's life as well. In 1923 he began living with Helen Walser and her children, although the two never married. In August 1923 Stella became a U.S. citizen.

Typical during several periods of Stella's career, disparate themes competed with one another in his art in the early 1920s. He turned toward America to paint his commanding architectural images and turned toward Italy to create his delicate botanical silverpoints and floral creations in oil. After another trip to Italy, Stella was painting Madonnas in Neopolitan landscapes by the mid-1920s. His dual allegiance was best expressed by his friend Charmion von Wiegand when she wrote that he "is rooted in the soil of Italy as no other living painter in America. . . . [he] sees life intensely with a modern eye, but he records his vision in the pure color and form of Southern Italy. Yet, no painter has understood the lyric beauty of Manhattan better than Stella has" (*New York Times*, 23 Feb. 1941). In 1920 Stella's association with the Arensberg circle resulted in his appointment to the exhibition committee of Katherine Dreier's Société Anonyme. He participated in the first (1920) and subsequent exhibitions of the Société.

In 1926 Stella returned to Europe, where he resided until 1934. Most of this time was spent in Paris, although he made trips to Italy and New York throughout this period. His paintings were distinguished by flamboyant, strong colors particularly evident in his still-life and landscape paintings and by a primitive simplicity, especially in the figural images, that bordered on Italian folk art but also looked to Renaissance masterpieces for inspiration. Stella exhibited in Paris, Rome, and Naples throughout these years.

On account of the increasingly poor economic and political situation in Europe, Stella finally relocated to New York in 1934 but never really reestablished himself successfully on the American scene. Throughout these years until his death in New York City, he did collages (which he had begun to produce in the 1920s), painted for the Works Progress Administration, and, most consequential for his art, visited Barbados for a short time in 1938. The results of this trip were images that reflected, in color and depiction, the joyous feeling that enveloped him in the tropical environment. Ironically, this optimism did not describe his state of mind in the last years of his life, spent alone in New York where he was physically and emotionally ailing. Critics, while heralding the earlier precisionist, industrial images, could not seriously accept the brashness of color and form that was present in his later work. They dismissed it as, in the words of one writer, "occultist indulgence in posturish picture-making" (*Art Digest*, 15 Jan. 1941, p. 18). Although a retrospective of his work was held in 1939 at the Newark Museum, Stella lamented that he could not "induce anyone living in New York to see my pictures. . . . The N.Y. press kept silent." He died never having enjoyed a critical acceptance of the entire range of his work. Finally, of a 1994 retrospective at the Whitney Museum of American Art, prominent critic Hilton Kramer wrote that viewers "are never in any doubt that you are in the presence of a prodigious talent" (*New York Observer*, 2 May 1994). That enthusiasm for Joseph Stella's work continues to be supported by other critics, scholars, and the viewing public.

• The most important repository for Stella's papers, which includes his published and unpublished writings on life and art as well as relevant letters, is the Joseph Stella Papers at the Archives of American Art, Smithsonian Institution. Other important collections include the Paul Kellogg Papers, Social Welfare History Archives, University of Minnesota Libraries, Minneapolis; the Bernard Rabin Papers, Cranberry, N.J.; and the Carl Weeks Papers, Iowa State Education Association, Des Moines. The most comprehensive monograph, which includes English translations of some of his writings as well as an extensive bibliography and exhibition history is Barbara Haskell, *Joseph Stella* (1994). See also Irma Jaffe, *Joseph Stella* (1970), for Stella's writings in the original Italian; Joann Moser, *Visual Poetry: The Drawings of Joseph Stella* (1990), for Stella's works on paper; Judith Zilczer, *Joseph Stella* (1983); and John I. H. Baur, *Joseph Stella* (1971). For important contemporary accounts of Stella see Thomas Craven, "Joseph Stella," *Shadowland* (Jan. 1923): 11, 78; Hamilton Easter Field, "Joseph Stella," *Arts* (Oct. 1921): 24–27; and Carlo de Fornaro, "A Forceful Figure in American Art," *Arts & Decoration* (Aug. 1923): 17, 60–61.

MARILYN S. KUSHNER

STELZLE, Charles (4 June 1869–27 Feb. 1941), clergyman, labor advocate, and writer, was born in New York City, the son of the German immigrant John Stelzle, a small brewer, and Doretta Uhlendorf. Stelzle grew up in poverty on the Lower East Side, and after the death of his father he worked at age eight as a tobacco stripper for fifty cents a week. He joined a street gang and was arrested twice, but his mother sent him to Sunday school at the Presbyterian Hope Chapel. He changed his ways, learned the trade of a machinist, and, stirred by the desire to help, began theological studies.

Stelzle was ordained a Presbyterian minister in 1900. He preached at Hope Chapel in Minneapolis from 1895 until 1897, Hope Chapel in New York City from 1897 until 1899, and at Markham Memorial Chapel in St. Louis until 1903. In all three, he organized outreach activities to attract urban workers. Noticing Stelzle's energy and effectiveness, Charles L. Thompson, president of the Presbyterian Board of Home Missions, suggested to the church's leaders that Stelzle was the right man to reach out to immigrant urban workers. Thompson belonged to the Social Gospel, also called Social Christianity, which was part of the Progressive reform movement. The Social Gospel tried to attract urban workers to the Protestant churches, notably by supporting industrial reform legislation.

In 1903 Stelzle moved back to New York City and became superintendent of the Presbyterian Department of Church and Labor. During 1908–1910 he also directed its Department of Immigration, worked closely with the new Federal Council of the Churches of Christ, and in 1910 founded the East Side Labor Temple as a forum for ministers and workers. A member of the International Association of Machinists, he also was a delegate at American Federation of Labor conventions from 1905 to 1915, where he met many labor leaders. During these years, he published *The Workingman and Social Problems* (1903), *Boys of the Street* (1904), *Messages to Workingmen* (1906), *Principles of Successful Church Advertising* (1909), and *Church and Labor* (1910), and he contributed to newspapers such as the *Christian Socialist* and the *Philadelphia North American*. He was among the most effective spokesmen from the Protestant church to industrial labor.

Stelzle saw no conflict between labor politics and the Gospel. As he stressed in *The Gospel of Labor* (1912), "the healthy Christian life is lived in the world among men . . . in the primary and in the labor union . . . in the shop and in the office." This was the modern meaning of the teachings of "Christ the toiler," he argued, and not "absolute acceptance of the inspiration of the Bible." When in 1910 workers struck against a twelve-hour, seven-day work week at the Bethlehem Steel Works in Pennsylvania, he braved middle-class opinion by supporting the strikers. Having seen much abuse of alcohol during his youth, Stelzle also was a prohibitionist. In 1914–1915 he directed a large-scale study of the effects of drinking and published *Why Prohibition?* (1918). But, to his sorrow, he did not convince many workers.

Stelzle's stance angered conservative Presbyterians. In 1913 they forced him to resign from the Department of Church and Labor and charged that he was a socialist. The Presbyterian General Assembly cleared him in May 1915, but he was unable to resume his work. Stelzle then directed the New York City Committee on Unemployment in the winter of 1914–1915, became field secretary of the Federal Council of Churches of Christ, 1916–1918, and was a publicity director for the American Red Cross, 1917–1919. In order not to jeopardize his work for labor during World War I, Stelzle avoided taking sides publicly, but he did not promote in his sermons and writings the official view that the war was a "crusade for democracy" against a uniquely wicked Germany. His anger broke through in September 1918, when he scandalized superpatriots by gleefully asserting in a sermon that the end of the war would not bring the victory of bourgeois capitalism. Instead, "when the war ends, there will be an industrial revolution. The workers are going to rule this country and every other country in the world."

After the war, Stelzle became a well-known freelance writer and syndicated columnist on social issues, and he wrote an autobiography, *A Son of the Bowery* (1926). During the Great Depression, he tried to convince churches to tax members for local unemployment relief and defended the New Deal against critics. From 1937 to 1939 he was executive manager of the Good Neighbor League, founded at the request of Franklin D. Roosevelt to prevent social tensions from being exploited by political extremists.

In 1889 Stelzle married Louise Rothmayer of New York. She died in 1890, and in 1899 he married Louise Ingersoll, who survived him. He had one child with his first wife and two with his second. Little is known about his family, and even his autobiography contains little about his personal life. Stelzle died in New York City.

Stelzle left no immediate legacy. In the 1900s and early 1910s he was probably the American Protestant clergyman most listened to by urban workers. Yet in the end he failed to win over many workers. He also failed to alter the character of the Presbyterian Church, which for many decades remained focused on the individual sinner and rather unconcerned with the society that may have made him sin. But his writings, and the example set by his activism, may have influenced Protestant ministers who strove for a more community-oriented and politically active pastoral service in the 1960s and afterwards.

• The archives of the Presbyterian church in Philadelphia, especially its holdings on the Federal Council of the Churches of Christ, contain much about Stelzle. An activist rather than a thinker, he has not attracted the attention of historians partly because of the collapse of the Social Gospel after World War I. He receives cursory mention in Henry F. May, *Protestant Churches and Industrial America* (1949); Robert T. Handy, *The Social Gospel in America, 1870–1920* (1966); and Robert Nichols, *Presbyterianism in New York State* (1963). He is given more lengthy attention in Charles Howard Hopkins, *The Rise of the Social Gospel in American Protestantism, 1865–1915* (1940); Hopkins and Ronald C. White, *The Social Gospel: Religion and Reform in Changing America* (1976); and James S. Armstrong, "The Labor Temple, 1910–1957: A Social Gospel in Action" (Ph.D. diss., Univ. of Wisconsin, 1974).

THOMAS REIMER

STENGEL, Alfred (3 Nov. 1869–10 Apr. 1939), physician, was born in Pittsburgh, Pennsylvania, the son of Gottfried Stengel, a civil engineer, and Frederica Suzan Hertle. Stengel attended public schools and enjoyed some private tutoring before entering the University of Pennsylvania in 1886. As a class officer during his tenure at the university, Stengel was able to pose for Thomas Eakin's famous painting *The Agnew Clinic*. Stengel can be seen sitting among the bearded officers of 1889, 1890, and 1891, his head resting on the shoulder of a neighbor. While in school, he turned his attention to medicine, and after graduating from Pennsylvania's medical school in 1889, he interned for eighteen months at the Philadelphia General Hospital.

In 1891, following his internship, Stengel was both offered a position at the University of Texas in Galveston and nominated by his friend pathologist Allen Smith to serve as quiz master in pathology at the University of Pennsylvania Medical School. Accepting Smith's offer, Stengel gained exposure at the University of Pennsylvania Medical School, which probably led to his election as pathologist at the German Hospital (now Lankenau) in 1892. In 1893 Stengel became assistant to William Pepper, professor of medicine and provost of the University of Pennsylvania. He taught clinical medicine in this position for three years and, thereafter, quickly rose to prominence.

Between 1896 and 1898 Stengel served as professor of clinical medicine at the Woman's Medical College of Pennsylvania while maintaining his connection with the university, where he eventually became full professor in 1911. In 1898 Stengel accepted the editorship of the *American Journal of Medical Sciences* and commenced his prolific medical writing career. Between 1898 and 1924 Stengel made significant contributions to medical writing. He married Martha Otis Pepper, a niece of William Pepper, in February 1909; they had three children.

Stengel also served as editor of the American edition of Hermann Nothnagel's *Cyclopedia of Medicine* (1901), and he authored "Diseases of the Blood" in volume seven (1896) and "Diseases of the Spleen" in volume nine (1897) of Thomas Lathrop Stedman's *Twentieth Century Practice* (21 vols., 1895–1903). Stengel wrote *A Textbook in Pathology* (1898), which went through nine editions, and in his lifetime contributed more than 200 articles to medical journals, concentrating mainly on diseases of the blood, kidneys, and metabolism.

When William Pepper died in 1898, his son William (future dean of the medical school) invited Stengel to share his father's practice with him. This Stengel did until 1911, when he became full professor at the medical school. Considered an excellent teacher and administrator, Stengel belonged to a generation of physicians that concentrated on anatomy and physiology, although he encouraged fundamental sciences and original investigations in other fields. He became interested in therapeutic procedures and advocated developments in industrial clinics and government participation in medical care. His success as a teacher stemmed directly from his skill as a pathologist and his ability to unfold clinical problems simply and succinctly.

During Stengel's presidency of the American College of Physicians from 1925 to 1927, he oversaw the merging of the American Congress on Internal Medicine with the college, revamping the entire organization into the leading organization of internists in the United States. In 1931 he became vice president of the university in charge of medical affairs, in which position he created an unparalleled medical facility. Determined to stimulate an interest in research, he coordinated the programs of the graduate medical and veterinary and the undergraduate medical school, producing a well-functioning medical center. He retained his position of vice president until his death.

Professionally active, Stengel served as president of the College of Physicians of Philadelphia (1934–1937) and, until his death, as president of the Wistar Institute of Anatomy and Biology. He was also a member of the Association of American Physicians, the Philadelphia Pathological Society, and the National Advisory Health Council. During World War I he was a major in the U.S. Army Reserve Corps and was in charge of the U.S. Public Health Services, investigating munitions industries in eastern Pennsylvania.

Considered modest and somewhat shy, Stengel was nevertheless an eloquent and intelligent speaker. Although he regretted that his education lacked a more classical and mathematical bent, he possessed a fierce intelligence, a thorough knowledge of human nature, and an unwavering dedication to medicine. He died at his home in Philadelphia.

Dr. Stengel's greatest contribution to medicine stemmed from his ability to apply physics to medical problems. His founding of the Department of Medical Physics ultimately led to the development of numerous electronic instruments, important in clinical diagnosis as well as in monitoring the physiological function of patients. A leading medical authority in the United States, Stengel was instrumental in devising a medical center for the University of Pennsylvania. Immensely respected by his colleagues, William Pepper III wrote of him in his memoirs, "The penurious Stengel came to Philadelphia without friends or relations and . . . by his own efforts, brains and native intelligence rose to a commanding position in medicine."

• Many of Stengel's writings, scattered among different medical journals, can be found at the University of Pennsylvania's Medical Library. Biographical accounts include William Pepper's article in *Transactions and Studies of the College of Physicians of Philadelphia* 4 (1939): 242–44, and T. Grier Miller, "Alfred Stengel 1869–1939," *Transactions of the Association of American Physicians* 64 (1939): 15–16. For useful information on Stengel's relationship to Pepper and his laboratory, see Donald Young et al., *The William Pepper Laboratory and Laboratory Medicine of the University of Pennsylvania: An Integrated History* (1995), pp. 29–30, 47–48. For information on Stengel's Department of Medical Physics, see David Cooper, "The Johnson Foundation for Medical Physics— The First Department of Medical Physics and Biophysics," *Transactions and Studies of the College of Physicians of Philadelphia* 6, ser. 4 (1984): 113–24. An obituary is the *New York Times*, 11 Apr. 1939.

DAVID Y. COOPER
MICHELLE E. OSBORN

STENGEL, Casey (30 July 1890–29 Sept. 1975), baseball player and manager, was born Charles Dillon Stengel in Kansas City, Missouri, the son of Louis Stengel, an insurance agent and later a street sprinkler company owner, and Jennie Jordan. The youngest of three children, Stengel grew up in a middle-class family and graduated from the Garfield Grammar School in 1906. A versatile athlete, the left-handed Stengel played basketball, football, and baseball at Central High School, and he was a pitcher on the baseball team that won the 1909 Missouri state high school championship.

The following spring the 19-year-old Stengel quit high school to play professional baseball with the Kansas City Blues of the American Association. The Blues converted Stengel to outfield play and assigned him in 1910 to Kankakee, Illinois, of the Northern Association, then to Shelbyville, Kentucky, then to the Maysville, Kentucky, team of the lower-class Blue Grass League, where he batted an unimpressive .233. (Overall, his batting average with the three clubs was .236.) That winter Stengel entered the Western Dental College of Kansas City, but in the spring of 1911 he joined the Aurora, Illinois, team of the Wisconsin-Illinois League and led the league in batting and stolen bases. That impressive performance moved the Brooklyn Dodgers of the National League to purchase Stengel's contract and to assign him to the Montgomery, Alabama, team of the Southern Association. After batting .290 with Montgomery, Stengel joined the Dodgers late in the 1912 season, and in an auspicious debut he struck four hits and stole two bases in his first game and finished the season with a .316 batting average in 17 games.

As a fledgling major leaguer in 1913, the 5′8½″, 175-pound Stengel, who was nicknamed "Casey" for his Kansas City origin, demanded and received a $2,100 contract. That season Stengel hit the first home run at Brooklyn's new Ebbets Field and batted .272 overall. Over the next four seasons his batting, fielding, and colorful antics made Stengel a local favorite. Stengel's "baseball instincts" also drew praise from sportswriters, one commenting that he was "spectacular even when doing nothing in particular." In 1914 Stengel batted .316 and led the league with a .404 on-base percentage. Two years later his enthusiastic leadership and clutch hitting helped Brooklyn win a close race and land its first National League pennant since 1900; Stengel's .364 batting also led Brooklyn's losing effort in the 1916 World Series.

After the 1917 season, in which he batted .257 and led the Dodgers in runs scored and runs batted in, Stengel was traded to the Pittsburgh Pirates. He played only 39 games for the Pirates in 1918 before joining the U.S. Navy and spending the rest of the year directing the baseball program at the Brooklyn Navy Yard. Rejoining the Pirates in 1919, Stengel was batting .293 after 89 games when he was traded to the Philadelphia Phillies. Hampered by leg and back ailments, Stengel postponed his debut with the Phillies until 1920 when he batted .292 in 129 games. The following season, after batting .305 in 24 games, Stengel was traded to the New York Giants.

Still hobbled by sore legs, the 31-year-old Stengel appeared in only 18 games with the 1921 Giants, but he gained valuable insights by observing manager John McGraw's tactics that included platooning his players and scouting rival players. As a platooned outfielder, Stengel played fewer than 200 games over the 1922 and 1923 seasons, but he notched his best offensive marks by batting .368 and .339 with an on-base percentage of better than .400. Stengel's hitting during those seasons helped the Giants win two league championships, and his .400 hitting contributed to the Giants' victory in the 1922 World Series.

Traded to the Boston Braves in November 1923, Stengel batted .280 in 131 games. In August of that year he married Edna Lawson, a film actress and daughter of a California banker and building contractor. The next season, after he batted only .077 through May, Stengel's 14-year major league playing career ended. Stengel played in 1,277 games, batted .284, scored 575 runs, drove in 535 runs, and fielded .964. In three World Series appearances Stengel batted an overall .393.

Stengel's more illustrious career as a baseball manager began in 1925 when he served as playing manager of the Worcester, Massachusetts, team of the Eastern League. In 1926 his mentor McGraw helped him become manager of the Toledo, Ohio, club of the American Association. For six seasons Stengel managed Toledo, during which time his team won the 1927 American Association title and he gained a reputation as an effective leader and colorful crowd pleaser.

In 1932 Stengel's reputation led to his appointment as a coach with the Dodgers. After coaching for two seasons, he succeeded Max Carey as the team manager. But Stengel's first stint as a major league manager proved inauspicious; from 1934 to 1936 his team won just 208 games while losing 251. Notwithstanding his crowd-pleasing antics and his effective development of young players, Stengel was fired and was actually paid not to manage in 1937. Stengel's second managerial stint, a six-year term with the Boston Bees that began in 1938 after Stengel invested $43,000 in that financially straitened team, was also ineffective. After posting a winning season in 1938, Stengel's team recorded five consecutive losing seasons. In 1943 a new Boston owner purchased Stengel's stock shares and dismissed him as team manager.

During the years 1944–1948 Stengel successfully managed the Milwaukee and Kansas City teams of the American Association and the Oakland, California, team of the Pacific Coast League. A turning point in Stengel's fortunes came in 1948 when his Oakland team won the league championship and his success in developing young players prompted George Weiss, the general manager of the American League's New York Yankees, to appoint Stengel as the team's manager.

The appointment of the 58-year old Stengel as manager of baseball's most famous team drew criticism from many observers, but an Oakland writer predicted that he would be an excellent bench manager. For his part Stengel declared, "I've never had so many good players before. . . . I've been hired to win, and I think I will." During the 1949 season Stengel's adroit platooning of players overcame a rash of injuries as he drove the Yankees to a one-game victory in the American League pennant race and to a World Series victory. For his achievement Stengel was voted manager of the year by the Baseball Writers Association.

During the years 1950–1953 Stengel's Yankees won four more league championships and World Series titles, making Stengel the first to manage five consecutive World Series winners. In praising his rival, Cleveland manager Al Lopez cited Stengel's platooning tactics and his innovative use of a preseason instructional school for developing young players.

In 1954 Lopez's Cleveland team ended Stengel's victory skein, but Stengel's Yankees rebounded to win the next four American League pennants and added

World Series victories in 1956 and 1958. By then Stengel, who was dubbed "the Old Professor" by reporters, was a national celebrity, with stories of his "legend" appearing in books and major magazines. In 1958 Stengel embellished his legend when he appeared before a congressional subcommittee that was probing major league baseball's antitrust exemption. He regaled the panel with one of his humorous, rambling discourses that reporters had taken to calling "Stengelese."

After the Yankees lost the 1959 pennant race, Stengel again led the team to victory in 1960 but lost a seven-game World Series struggle to Pittsburgh. Five days after that loss, Yankees owner Dan Topping staged a "resignation" ceremony in which Stengel was dismissed and awarded a $160,000 bonus. With 10 American League championships and seven World Series victories in his 12 seasons as Yankee manager, the 70-year-old Stengel's reputation in major league baseball was assured. But after returning to California and working at his wife's bank, Stengel accepted an offer from George Weiss, who had become general manager of the National League's expansion New York Mets, to become the new team's manager.

In 1962 Stengel managed the Mets, a team of castoffs and rookies, to a 40–120 record, the worst performance by a National League team since 1899. Over the next two seasons the Mets also finished last, but Stengel's charisma and the very ineptitude of his team enabled the 1964 Mets, playing at their newly established Shea Stadium, to outdraw the champion Yankees by more than 400,000 fans. The following year, after breaking a hip in a fall, Stengel announced his final retirement at an elaborate ceremony.

In retirement Stengel functioned as a baseball ambassador. From 1966 to 1974 he attended every World Series and every Mets' spring training camp, and he frequently delivered speeches in his inimitable "Stengelese" style. In 1966 he was voted into the National Baseball Hall of Fame, which he described as "an amazing thing." Stengel died at Memorial Hospital in Glendale. An elaborate funeral followed, and it was announced that he left an estate of $807,000. When his wife died in 1978, she left an estate of $3 million. The couple had no children.

• The National Baseball Library, Cooperstown, N.Y., has extensive clipping files on Stengel's life. His autobiography is *Casey at the Bat: The Story of My Life in Baseball*, with Harry T. Paxton (1962). Among several biographies of Stengel, Robert Creamer, *Stengel: His Life and Times* (1984), is outstanding. Others include Joseph Durso, *Casey: The life and Legend of Charles Dillon Stengel* (1967); Frank Graham, Jr., *Casey Stengel: His Half Century in Baseball* (1958); Norman MacLean, *Casey Stengel: A Biography* (1971); and Charles S. Verral, *Casey Stengel: Baseball's Greatest Manager* (1978). Stengel's managerial career is included with other baseball managers in Charles B. Cleveland, *Baseball's Greatest Managers* (1950); William Heuman, *Famous Coaches* (1968); Tom Meany, *The Magnificent Yankees* (1957); Edwin Pope, *Baseball's Greatest Managers* (1960); Ray Robinson, *Baseball's Most Colorful Managers* (1970); and Harold Rosenthal, *Base-*

ball's Best Managers (1961). Stengel's personality is depicted in Frederick G. Lieb, *Comedians and Pranksters of Baseball* (1958); and Harold Liss, *Baseball's Zaniest Stars* (1971). Stengel's place in the history of major league baseball is in David Q. Voigt, *American Baseball* vols. 2 and 3 (1983); and his records as player and manager are in John Thorn and Pete Palmer, eds., *Total Baseball*, 3d ed. (1993). Among the best articles on Stengel's life are Arthur Daley, "The Philosophy of Casey Stengel," *New York Times Magazine*, 26 July 1953, pp. 14ff; J. K. Hutchins, "Casey at the Bat," *Saturday Review of Literature*, 15 Apr. 1967, pp. 29ff; Gilbert Millstein, "Musings of a Dugout Socrates," *New York Times Magazine*, 26 Aug. 1962, pp. 17ff; "That Man," *Time*, 3 Oct. 1956, pp. 58–62; "Stengelese Sampler," *Sports Illustrated*, 23 Dec. 1974, pp. 54–55. An obituary is in the *New York Times*, 1 Oct. 1975.

DAVID Q. VOIGT

STENNIS, John Cornelius (3 Aug. 1901–23 Apr. 1995), senator, was born in Kemper County, Mississippi, the son of Howell Stennis and Cornelia Adams, farmers. One of the leading families in that rural county, the Stennises were mostly professional people—doctors, lawyers, teachers, and legislators. A 1923 graduate of Mississippi State University, Stennis earned his law degree from the University of Virginia four years later. In 1928, just a year out of law school, he won election to the Mississippi legislature. Local voters next elected him prosecuting attorney and then circuit judge. In 1931 Stennis married Coy Hines; they had two children.

After securing his status in local politics, Stennis ran for the position opened by the death of longtime Mississippi senator Theodore Bilbo. In the 1947 special election, Stennis defeated his five Democratic opponents, capturing 27 percent of the vote. He ran as the dignified conservative candidate, and he avoided demagoguery on the race question. Running strongest in the eastern Mississippi counties in which he had served as a judge, he won 94 percent of his home county's vote.

As a junior senator, Stennis came under the tutelage of Richard B. Russell of Georgia, who had been in the Senate since 1933 and was arguably its most influential operator. At Russell's behest Stennis was appointed to the Armed Services Committee in 1951, and he eventually rose to chairman of that committee in 1969. He also was a member of the powerful Appropriations Committee.

Stennis first emerged as a leader in the Senate during the inquiry into the actions of Senator Joseph McCarthy of Wisconsin in 1954. Stennis was the first Democrat to speak out in the Senate against his GOP colleague. Known for his personal rectitude, he was named by his colleagues to the committee that investigated McCarthy.

At this time Stennis also began to assume a more prominent role in foreign affairs. In 1954 he warned President Dwight Eisenhower about intervening in Vietnam. Moreover, he opposed the president's New Look foreign policy of reducing military spending and relying on nuclear weapons. He favored conventional forces as the bulwark of a strong defense and believed that budgetary concerns should be secondary to national security issues.

Throughout the 1950s Stennis opposed cuts to the Department of Defense budgets. At the same time he tried to define limits to the use of force. Although he was a firm cold warrior, he believed that the United States should not bear any burden to fight global communism, arguing that the United States should only go it alone on foreign policy matters in Europe and Latin America, not Asia.

In 1962 Stennis, a firm supporter of the Department of Defense as well as a senator valued for his integrity and work habits, led an investigation into accusations that the Pentagon had muzzled officers who wanted to speak up against communism. That same year Stennis also became the chairman of the Armed Services Committee's Preparedness Investigating Subcommittee, the Senate watchdog of the Defense Department.

Despite Stennis's initial concern about U.S. actions in Vietnam, during the 1960s he emerged as an important ally for Democratic presidents John F. Kennedy and Lyndon B. Johnson as they escalated the U.S. presence in the Asian nation. Stennis was a strong supporter of the Tonkin Gulf resolution, which broadened the president's power to commit U.S. forces in Vietnam. During the debate over the resolution, he maintained, "Our honor, our safety, and our security are at stake. . . . We dare not run away, certainly not while we are under attack" (Downs, pp. 94–95). If Stennis had earlier opposed a go-it-alone policy in Asia, he nonetheless believed the United States had an obligation to protect its troops and defend its flag once under attack.

After congressional approval of the Tonkin Gulf Resolution, Stennis supported President Johnson's troop requests of 1965–1968 without question. In 1966 Stennis said that to win the battle in Vietnam the United States should call up the reserves, increase taxes, enforce economic controls, and institute rationing. He predicted that as many as 600,000 American troops might be needed to defeat the North Vietnamese. In fact, in 1967 Stennis held subcommittee hearings that called for escalation and continued bombing of North Vietnam. Also in 1967, Stennis returned to his ongoing role as conscience of the Senate, chairing an investigation of Senator Christopher Dodd of Connecticut that led to Dodd's censure for misuse of congressional funds and a new code of ethics for the Senate.

In 1968 the Tet Offensive shook Stennis's confidence about the American mission in Vietnam. He no longer believed that he could support additional troops unless the United States adopted a new policy. The next year, as the slow American de-escalation began, Stennis became the chairman of the Armed Forces Committee.

Despite shifts in his views about Vietnam, Stennis remained a confidant of the American presidents on foreign policy. When President Richard M. Nixon decided to expand the bombing to Cambodia, he secretly informed Senators Russell and Stennis, who gave Nixon their consent. Stennis often defended Nixon's execution of the war and his defense budgets against opposition from his Democratic senatorial colleagues. Yet over time, Stennis came to regret that the president had usurped much of the Senate's role in foreign policy. In 1971 he sought to strengthen the Senate's position, introducing Senate Joint Resolution 95, the forerunner to the War Powers Act (1973), which limited the power of the president to commit U.S. troops into military combat without the consent of Congress.

In 1973 President Nixon tried to exploit Stennis's reputation for fairness to save his own political skin during the Watergate crisis. Instead of turning over his Watergate tapes to the special prosecutor, Nixon proposed to allow Stennis to authenticate the White House's transcripts of the tapes. At first Stennis agreed, but later the Stennis compromise collapsed as the attorney general and others opposed it.

Throughout this entire period, Stennis rarely faced serious challenges in his bids for reelection to the Senate. In 1970, for example, he faced no opposition. During his tenure in the Senate, he avoided the race baiting that many of his southern Democratic colleagues in the Senate favored. Despite his more dignified tone, he opposed racial equality. Beginning with his opposition in 1948 to the elimination of the poll tax to his 1983 opposition to the Martin Luther King, Jr., holiday, he constantly voted against civil rights legislation.

During his lengthy Senate tenure, Stennis also rose to a position of prominence on the Appropriations Committee, which he used to bring significant federal funds to his home state of Mississippi. In 1972, for example, Mississippi received $1,158 per capita in federal spending, higher than any other southern state except Virginia.

On 30 January 1973 two muggers shot the 71-year-old senator as he walked home from a dinner given in his honor by the National Guard Association. One bullet entered his left thigh, and the second ripped through his stomach, pancreas, and colon. Eight surgeons operated for six hours to save his life. The wounded senator did not return to Congress until September.

In 1982 Stennis faced his first serious challenger to the Senate seat he had held since 1947. Haley Barbour, a 35-year-old Republican, outspent Stennis in his effort to unseat the incumbent. Barbour ran a tough campaign, contending that Mississippi needed a senator for the '80s, a not so veiled reference to the fact that Stennis was in his 80s. Stennis countered with advertisements that showed him hard at work late at night in his Senate office. Despite the challenge, Stennis easily retained his seat, winning 63.9 percent of the vote. Ironically, Stennis, the longtime opponent of civil rights legislation, ran stronger with the state's black voters than its white voters. But times had indeed changed. In 1982 and again in 1984 Stennis campaigned for a black Democratic candidate in the state's Second Congressional District.

In the 1980s Stennis continued to advocate a strong defense, but increasingly he concentrated his efforts on delivering federal largesse to his home state. He fought hard and ultimately successfully for the $2 billion Tennessee–Tombigbee River Waterway. He battled railroad interests, environmentalists, and budget-conscious senators, and the river project opened to barge traffic in 1985. Also, in 1987 Stennis secured $17.1 million for a naval homeport in Pascagoula.

In September 1987 Stennis announced that he would not seek an eighth term in the Senate. When he left office on 3 January 1989, only one man, Carl Hayden of Arizona, had served longer than Stennis's Senate tour of 41 years, 1 month, and 29 days. Upon leaving the Senate, Stennis returned to Starkville, Mississippi, taking up residence at the John C. Stennis Institute of Government and the John C. Stennis Center for Public Services at Mississippi State University. His name dotted the state, bearing witness to his ability to send home federal dollars. For instance, the John C. Stennis Space Center tests rocket motors at the National Aeronautics and Space Administration (NASA) laboratory near Bay St. Louis, Mississippi.

When Stennis left the Senate he also retired a tradition, the dominance of the southern Democrats in that chamber. Much of their power had come from their long tenures in office and one-party politics in their home states. But that had begun to change, and while Stennis, who remained a Democrat even though he had much in common with Mississippi whites fleeing to the GOP and the GOP's presidential candidates, delayed the transition to two-party politics in Mississippi, his political career could not stop the rise of the GOP in the South. He died in Jackson, Mississippi.

• Stennis's papers are at the University of Mississippi. Information about Stennis's political career is in Alexander Lamis, *The Two-Party South* (1990), and Dale Krane and Stephen Shaffer, *Mississippi Government and Politics: Modernizers versus Traditionalists* (1992). V. O. Key, Jr., *Southern Politics in State and Nation* (1949), tells about Stennis's first race. See also Jack Bass and Walter DeVries, *The Transformation of Southern Politics* (1976). The Stennis record on foreign policy is in Michael S. Downs, "Advise and Consent: John Stennis and the Vietnam War, 1954–1973," *Journal of Mississippi History* (1993): 87–114. An obituary is in the *New York Times*, 24 Apr. 1995.

CHRISTOPHER MACGREGOR SCRIBNER

STEPHEN, Adam (c. 1721–16 July 1791), revolutionary war general, was born in the parish of Rhynie, Aberdeenshire, Scotland. The identities of his parents are unknown. Stephen probably attended a parish school and a grammar school. In 1736 he entered King's College of the University of Aberdeen, receiving a master of arts degree on 27 March 1740. Stephen then studied in the medical program at the University of Edinburgh and probably obtained a degree in medicine. After leaving Edinburgh, Stephen became a naval surgeon. He participated in the siege of Port l'Orient, France, May–September 1746; on one occasion he took charge of his ship's gunnery. Forgoing further British military service, Stephen came to America in 1748 and established a physician's practice at Fredericksburg, Virginia, earning a reputation as a skilled surgeon. Finding income too limited and competition from other physicians, Stephen decided to also fulfill an ambition of becoming a great planter. By 1753 he had settled on his 2,000 acre "Bower" plantation, along Opequon Creek in Frederick County, Virginia (now Jefferson County, W.Va.).

As war was about to erupt with France in 1754, Stephen joined the colony's militia regiment as a captain. Thus Stephen began a long, often rivalrous, association with George Washington. During much of the French and Indian War, Stephen was acting commander of the Virginia troops in place of the absent Washington. The two men fought together at Great Meadows on 27 May 1754 and at the surrender of Fort Necessity to the French on 4 July 1754. During the latter part of 1754 Stephen was promoted to major and then lieutenant colonel. Stephen, with the temporary British rank of captain, fought in the ill-fated battle on the Monongahela on 9 July 1755 as a member of Edward Braddock's expeditionary force; he subsequently penned a slashing critique of the effectiveness of the British soldiery that made the rounds of the British ministry. The earl of Holdernaise, the British secretary of state, praised the clarity of Stephen's account of the battle. For the remainder of the French and Indian War, in Pennsylvania, Stephen commanded road building operations and also troops in the field, being in charge of the garrison at Fort Ligonier, which in July 1759 repelled the French in the last battle of the war on the Pennsylvania frontier. Stephen led the Virginia expedition against the Cherokees in 1761–1762 that resulted in peace rather than bloodshed.

In between wars Stephen applied himself to his farming, livestock raising, and plantation industries as well as to giving medical attention to his neighbors in the Shenandoah Valley. He unsuccessfully challenged Washington for a burgess seat from Frederick County in 1761, an election so heated that Washington thereafter ran for burgess from Fairfax County. Stephen did not run again for a seat in the House of Burgesses. He did hold local offices in Frederick and then in Berkeley County as justice of the peace, sheriff, and county lieutenant. He commanded one of the two Virginia militia forces during "Lord Dunmore's War" of 1774, but was not present at the battle of Point Pleasant. In 1775 he chaired the Berkeley County committee of safety, served as an Indian commissioner at Fort Pitt, and was elected to the Third Virginia Convention (though he was disqualified because of accusations of rigging the election).

Stephen joined the Continental army in May 1776 as colonel of the Fourth Virginia regiment, and Congress elected him brigadier general on 4 September 1776. He entered Washington's army in November 1776 as it retreated through New Jersey. Stephen distinguished himself at the battle of Trenton by capturing Hessians trying to escape by way of the Princeton Road. During January–June 1777 Stephen had charge of much of the forward troops while the main army encamped at Morristown; on 19 February 1777 he was appointed major general and commander of a division. His soldiers frequently engaged British detachments. Stephen earned Washington's censure for bringing on an ill-fated battle at Piscataway, New Jersey, on 10 May 1777. Stephen and Washington differed as to employment of troops: Stephen favored driving the British out of all New Jersey, while Washington contended that such a course would overtask his limited manpower and resources.

Stephen fought bravely at Brandywine and Germantown. At the latter battle on 4 October 1777, however, he shouldered much of the blame for the confusion among the American forces. He was the first to give the order for retreat; more damaging was the charge that he failed to rally his troops after the battle and for a while was not with them. The failure at Germantown called for a scapegoat. Stephen, much older than the other officers, brusque in manner, and known as a heavy drinker, was the ideal candidate. Stephen called for a court of inquiry, which led to a court-martial. He was convicted for "unofficerlike behaviour" in the retreat from Germantown and for being "frequently intoxicated," though not in battle. The sentence was "dismission" from the army. Lafayette, on his own solicitation, was given Stephen's division. Stephen blamed Washington for what he deemed his unjustifiable dismissal but refrained from publicly challenging the verdict when it became evident that he lacked support in Congress.

Oddly, Stephen did not suffer opprobrium among his neighbors in Virginia for his ouster from the Continental army. He represented Berkeley County in the House of Delegates from 1780 to 1784. He prospered on his valley farm and greatly expanded his real estate holdings. During the revolutionary war he had established an arms manufactory. One charge that followed Stephen during both wars was conflict of interest, as many thought he had profited unduly from sale of his livestock, grain, and whiskey to the army.

Stephen founded the town of Martinsburg, Virginia (now West Virginia), on his property and built a home there to which he moved in the 1780s; the edifice is maintained by the General Adam Stephen Memorial Association and is listed in the National Register of Historical Places. Stephen served in the Virginia ratifying convention of June 1788, at which he gave two speeches. He ardently supported adoption of the Constitution and sought to have the nation's capital located along the Potomac. Stephen never married but had a common-law relationship with his housekeeper, Phoebe Seaman, with whom he had one child, a daughter. Stephen died at his Martinsburg home.

• The George Washington Papers, Library of Congress, are a major source for Stephen's military career in both the French and Indian War and the revolutionary war. Letters are found in the many collections of papers of military figures of the time. Small but important collections of Stephen papers are found at the Library of Congress and the Darlington Memorial Library, University of Pittsburgh. Virginia county (Frederick and Berkeley) and legislative records pertain to Stephen's civic activities. Sylvester K. Stevens et al., eds., *The Papers of Henry Bouquet*, vols. 2–5 (1951–1984), contain a wealth of detail on Stephen's role during the French and Indian War. For the only biography, see Harry M. Ward, *Major General Adam Stephen and the Cause of American Liberty* (1989). Short articles on Stephen include Mary V. Mish, "General Adam Stephen, Founder of Martinsburg, West Virginia," *West Virginia History* 22 (1961): 63–75, and Thomas E. Van Metre, "Adam Stephen—The Man," *Berkeley Journal* 2 (1970): 12–21. Obituaries are in the *New-York Magazine; or Literary Repository*, 1 Aug. 1791; the *Virginia Herald* and *Fredericksburg Advertiser* of 4 Aug. 1791; and the *Virginia Gazette and General Advertiser* (Richmond), 10 Aug. 1791.

HARRY M. WARD

STEPHENS, Alexander Hamilton (11 Feb. 1812–4 Mar. 1883), congressman and Confederate vice president, was born on a piedmont farm near Washington, Georgia, the son of Andrew Stephens and Margaret Grier. A few months after his birth, his mother died. Within a year, his father remarried. When Aleck was fourteen, calamity struck again when his father died of pneumonia, to be followed a few weeks later by his stepmother from the same virus.

Stephens had admired his father tremendously. A serious, religious man, he ran the local school and was Aleck's first teacher. After his death, the Stephens children were split up and taken in by relatives, Aleck and an older brother going to live with their uncle Aaron Grier and his wife in nearby Raytown. In 1828 Stephens entered Franklin College (later the University of Georgia). He graduated first in his class, earned a considerable reputation in debating societies, and briefly seemed quite happy and contented. After graduation, he taught school and then studied law on his own. He passed the bar exam in 1834, and two years later he ran for the state assembly. Aligning himself with the George M. Troup faction in opposition to the pro-Jackson group, he won easily. He served five years in the House and one in the Senate.

Stephens seemed an unlikely prospect for the demanding, grueling life of a politician. He was painfully small, usually weighing around ninety pounds, with a sallow complexion, a sunken bony face, a huge head, and a scrawny body. "A malformed ill-shaped half finished thing," he once described himself. He was also sickly, suffering throughout his life from headaches, stomach pains, diarrhea, arthritis, and colitis. His emaciated form and shrill powerful voice were a combination so strange as to compel attention. Still, his weak physique as well as his lowly origins contributed to his prickly sensitivity to perceived criticism. On at least five occasions, Stephens responded to such insults by issuing challenges to duels in order to avenge his honor. Among his antagonists were William L. Yancey in 1846, Herschel V. Johnson in 1846, and Benjamin H. Hill in 1856. In no instance was his reckless dare taken up, although he was involved in a brawl with Judge Francis N. Cone in 1848 during which he sustained serious injuries. Accompanying this acute

sense of honor was an unrelenting conviction of his own rectitude from which arose his practice of presenting his views as axioms and principles rather than as personal beliefs. His were the politics of a fierce ideal.

Stephens developed an intense, somewhat paternal, relationship with his younger stepbrother Linton. He also had an enduring friendship with Robert Toombs, his antithesis in temperament and physique. And he was unfailingly generous to relatives in need as well as to countless young people whose education he supported financially. But he never married and never had a serious romantic relationship, and he never could shake his deep melancholy.

In his half-decade in the Georgia legislature, Stephens concentrated on economic issues. He strongly favored state aid for internal improvements, such as the building of the Atlantic and Western Railroad, and he usually voted for river and road projects. But he adamantly opposed loaning the state's credit to banks, even to provide relief after the panic of 1837. When the Troup faction began to merge with the Whigs, despite reservations about the protective tariff provision in Henry Clay's American System, Stephens concurred. Having learned parliamentary skills and gained a public reputation in the state legislature, he ran for Congress in 1843. That year, the Whigs swept the state, so he won easily.

Stephens's characteristic first act on entering Congress was to protest his own election. With his usual punctilio, he pointed out that he had been elected on a statewide ticket, not in a district as the Constitution required. His objection overruled, he then settled into life in the capital and identified himself with the Whig party, now even endorsing the protective tariff and its advocate, Henry Clay, who was to be the party's presidential nominee in 1844. But the overriding issue of Stephens's first term was the annexation of Texas. Like Clay, Stephens opposed annexation. He rejected John C. Calhoun's view that Texas was vital to the protection and expansion of slavery. Instead, he thought annexation "a miserable humbug," calculated by the Democrats to divide the Whigs in the South as well as nationally. Yet southern opinion was so strongly favorable that Stephens felt compelled to shift ground. Accordingly, he helped Milton Brown of Tennessee draft the successful House resolution for admission.

The expansionist plans of President James K. Polk, whom Stephens soon came to detest, were in his view, detrimental to the South. The war with Mexico especially could cause unnecessary friction over the status of slavery in a Mexican territory taken in war. While Stephens reluctantly voted for war supplies, he tried continually to get Congress to forbid acquisition of any territory as a result of the conflict. After the treaty of Guadalupe Hidalgo was ratified, Stephens believed slavery could still be kept out of the Mexican territories because Mexico had abolished slavery in 1829, so neither popular sovereignty nor the Supreme Court could decide the matter. With the disposition of these newly acquired lands now at stake, Stephens believed that the South needed a sympathetic Whig in the White House, and he was a founder-member of the Young Indian Club in Congress in 1847 (Abraham Lincoln was another) that worked to develop the candidacy of Zachary Taylor, the Mexican war hero and Louisiana slaveholder.

The events surrounding the Compromise of 1850 produced a crisis in Stephens's political career. First, President Taylor fell under the influence of northern Whigs who encouraged him to urge the immediate admission of California and New Mexico as free states. Appalled, Stephens and Toombs pressured the Whig caucus to adopt a resolution forbidding Congress from passing any law against slavery in the territories or against the slave trade in the District of Columbia. When the caucus voted against this, both men resigned from the party. Nevertheless, they also resisted the simultaneous efforts of Calhoun to form an exclusively southern party. Instead, Stephens cooperated with Clay, and later Stephen A. Douglas, in passing the measures that comprised the compromise, ensuring throughout that a condition for the passage of the California statehood bill was some degree of compensation and protection for the South.

Back in Georgia, former Whigs Stephens and Toombs and a Democrat, Howell Cobb, cooperated to form a new Constitutional Union party, which was intended to face down an emergent Southern Rights party that threatened secession. Pledging to uphold the compromise as a final settlement of sectional differences as long as slavery was not interfered with anywhere (the Georgia Platform, as it was called), the party won control of the legislature in 1850 and, a year later, elected Cobb governor and sent Toombs to the U.S. Senate. But the Constitutional Unionists did not exist outside Georgia, Alabama, and Mississippi; Cobb soon returned to the Democrats; and Stephens hovered on the margins of the Whig party, hoping to play a role in the realignment of parties that he believed imminent.

Instead of a realignment, the Whigs simply disintegrated after 1852. Stephens then joined the Democrats. Soon, he became a leading figure in the national party. First, he played a pivotal role in the passage of the fateful Kansas-Nebraska Act of 1854. Through several speeches, notably one on 17 February 1854, he rallied southern support for the bill, claiming that it was consistent with the compromise and simply asserted a traditional principle of congressional nonintervention in territorial matters. When the bill seemed to be buried in May, Stephens brought it to a vote by employing a complex parliamentary maneuver. After its speedy passage, Stephens remarked with pride: "I feel as if the *Mission* of my life was performed."

But the status of Kansas itself had still to be determined. So he threw himself into the struggle to bring Kansas into the Union as a slave state or, failing that, to keep it out. He actively supported the admission of Kansas under the pro-slavery Lecompton constitution, and when that failed, he resorted to the subterfuge embodied in the English bill to keep the territory out. This bill reformulated the conditions for Kansas's admission in terms the inhabitants could not possibly accept, a maneuver that Stephens fully acknowledged to be fraudulent.

Stephens was at the height of his power in 1858. Yet, amazingly, he announced his intention to retire from politics. In a farewell speech on 2 July 1859, he predicted that, since the constitutional principle of state equality had been sustained, there was "no cause of danger, either to the Union, or to southern security in it." And he dismissed the worries of southern extremists who were insisting on congressional protection for slavery in the territories, because he did not think slavery either could or would go into those areas.

In the 1860 election extremists, like his friend Robert Toombs, worked hard to break up the Democratic party, but Stephens only entered the campaign after he had been selected, without his approval, as a Douglas elector. In the wake of Lincoln's election, he did hasten to reassure Georgians that the new president was no threat. Along with several other leading politicians, he addressed the legislature on the situation. In his 14 November 1860 speech, he said that the Union protected slavery, that no unconstitutional or hostile act had been taken to justify secession, and that a state convention should be called, along with a regional conference of all the southern states. This brilliant speech, temporarily slowing the movement to secession, provoked a famous exchange with President-elect Lincoln, in one letter of which Lincoln made the often-quoted comment: "You think slavery is *right*, and ought to be extended; while we think it is *wrong*, and ought to be restricted."

Privately, however, Stephens seems to have been convinced that secession was unavoidable after Lincoln's election. Indeed, he and the state's antisecessionist leaders did little to influence the election of a secession convention or its members once it was called. Had they done so, the outcome might conceivably have been different, since the resolution to oppose immediate secession failed in the convention by only thirty-six votes, 166–130.

A few months later, the formation of the Confederate government drew Stephens back into public life. He was one of Georgia's delegates to the Provisional Congress in Montgomery. Serving on the rules committee and on the committee to devise a constitution for the Confederacy, he urged the retention in its essentials of the U.S. Constitution he so admired. Soon he was being considered for vice president, since a representative from a large state like Georgia, especially one that had opposed secession, would complement the more radical Jefferson Davis, who was expected to be chosen president. Although apprehensive about the future of the Confederacy, Stephens accepted the post.

On 21 March the new vice president gave a dramatic speech in Savannah, in which he announced that the cause of the Confederacy was not the defense of states' rights or of endangered interests, but rather "its foundations are laid, its cornerstone rests upon the great truth, that the negro is not the equal to the white man; that slavery—subordination to the superior race—is his natural and normal condition." Although immediately disavowed by President Davis, the "cornerstone speech" almost certainly represented Stephens's own view. Despite occasional expressions of uneasiness about slavery as a viable institution in the modern world and as a status for the "poor African," he had come to assume that it was an unalterable reality that provided not only better conditions than Africa had but also the sole means for blacks and whites to coexist. Stephens was a benign master as well as an orthodox supporter of slavery. His half-dozen slaves were mainly house servants, and they were leniently treated and never sold. Most of them stayed with him after emancipation.

Stephens's record as vice president was unusual and, not surprisingly, was much criticized. After his election, he was active as a Confederate commissioner to urge Virginia to secede, as a propagandist for the government's produce loan, and as president of the Senate in Richmond. But soon he became distressed at how the war was being run, and by winter 1861–1862 Davis no longer consulted him. So he returned to Crawfordville where he remained until the fall of 1864. But he did not retreat into passive silence or wage a destructive campaign against Davis, as has often been claimed. Rather, he publicly criticized administration policies in the hope that they might be improved. His main targets were the Confederate reliance on loans rather than taxation to finance the war; the use of conscription; the unfair method of impressment of provisions at below market prices; and most important, the suspension of habeas corpus, resulting in arbitrary arrests. At Davis's request, Stephens even undertook a mission to Washington in June 1863, aimed at negotiating a prisoner exchange that the vice president hoped might become the basis for discussion of peace and recognition of southern independence. But after the Union victories at Vicksburg and Gettysburg, Stephens returned empty-handed.

Stephens's criticism of the administration became open opposition in early 1864. Davis had interpreted the peace mission as proof that negotiation was futile. Then, Governor Joseph E. Brown of Georgia began to challenge the Confederacy frontally for its "usurpation" and "tyranny." Stephens joined him, condemning the Confederate government for what he considered its foolish priority of "independence first and liberty afterward." Stephens was further annoyed by Davis's refusal to encourage or even consider peace sentiment in the Union during the 1864 election. Unlike Davis, Stephens never embraced the idea of total war and the assumption that the South could only bring the war to an end on the battlefield. In November 1864 he returned to Richmond to try to prevent further damage. He presided over the Senate and urged alternative policies to revive the Confederacy's sagging morale. Another peace mission was his final contribution. He met with General Ulysses S. Grant at City Point and then with Lincoln at Hampton Roads (3 Feb. 1865), but no armistice was concluded.

After the war, the vice president was arrested and imprisoned briefly at Fort Warren in Boston harbor. In October 1865 President Andrew Johnson released him on parole, hoping that he would use his influence and his past record as an opponent of secession to moderate sentiment in the South. Despite Johnson's dissuasion, Stephens then allowed himself to be chosen U.S. senator by the Georgia legislature. The selection of the unpardoned vice president of the Confederacy was one of the most telling indications persuading the U.S. Congress that the southern delegations elected under Johnson's restoration policy should not be readmitted. Nevertheless, in a widely praised speech to the Georgia legislature and in testimony before the Joint Committee on Reconstruction in early 1866, Stephens urged southerners to accept the end of slavery, be conciliatory toward the North, and grant the freedmen the legal and civil rights of citizenship. But, a few months later, he insisted that the Georgia Assembly reject the Fourteenth Amendment that Congress was demanding because, he said, "terms precedent to the restoration of all their rights" should not be required of equal states in the Union. Then, he turned his energies to writing *A Constitutional View of the Late War between the States* (1868–1870), a two-volume apologia for the southern separatist movement. The book claimed that "the conflict in principle arose from different and opposing ideas as to the nature of what is known as the General Government," rival principles that he saw as "Federation" and "Centralism." Slavery was merely "the question" on which this dispute ultimately turned. The first of many constitutional explanations of the Civil War and the source of the erroneous term "War between the States," the book sold quite well, though dry and prolix. Stephen answered his critics in a sequel titled *The Reviewers Reviewed* (1872).

With the onset of Reconstruction in 1867–1868, Stephens became still more gloomy and despairing. He advised fellow Georgians not to comply with the Reconstruction Act but to let it go into operation, as he felt it was certain to do anyway, without stultifying themselves by giving their assent. Thereafter, Stephens maintained a stance of noninvolvement, repudiating even the leadership of his state's Democratic party, which soon accepted black suffrage, competed electorally with the new Republican party, and tried to accommodate to postwar economic and social reality. Stephens repudiated this "New Departure" policy and refused to support the Democratic presidential nominee in 1872, Horace Greeley. Instead, he backed the abortive Straight Democratic candidacy of Charles O'Connor of New York, after earlier buying a share in the Atlanta *Southern Sun* as a vehicle for propagating his purist states' rights views that he now called "Jeffersonian democracy."

In 1873, after losing a bid for the U.S. Senate to the state's leading New Departure Democrat, John B. Gordon, he ran for Congress from his old Eighth District. He was elected, partly as a result of support from leading Republicans in the state. This unlikely Republican backing for the South's leading Bourbon and out-and-out opponent of Reconstruction arose because Stephens and local Republicans had begun to collaborate against the ruling New Departure Democrats. This collaboration would expand to the national level in 1874 when Congressman Stephens endorsed President Grant for a third term. Stephens acknowledged a personal admiration for Grant that had its origin in their 1865 meeting at City Point. So he aligned himself with the Grant administration following his return to the House by voting for the "salary grab" and for Grant's policy in Louisiana of sustaining the Reconstruction government of William P. Kellogg. To cover himself in his district, he also played a conspicuous role in opposition to the Civil Rights bill that placed him, on one occasion, in a dramatic confrontation debating against Robert B. Elliott, the leading African-American Republican from South Carolina. When the third-term scheme fizzled out, Stephens still maintained links with local Georgia Republicans. He was reelected to the House in 1874 after surviving 111 ballots for the nomination and again in 1876 and 1878 without a Republican challenge. But he played no significant role in Congress; indeed, he seemed barely alive. Seeing him in 1876, a Washington newspaperman wondered "how anything so small and sick and sorrowful could get all the way from Georgia. . . . If he were to draw his last breath at any instant you would not be surprised."

The sickly political veteran had still one more card to play. In 1882 he was elected governor of Georgia, piling up a massive 60,000-vote majority and carrying all but seven counties. This climactic victory was evidence of Stephens's remarkable influence and endurance, both personal and political. But, after a busy four months in office, his increasingly precarious health finally gave out, and he died in Atlanta.

• The private papers of Stephens are voluminous. The largest single collection is in the Division of Manuscripts at the Library of Congress. The archives at the Manhattanville College of the Sacred Heart at Purchase, N.Y. contain the extensive correspondence between Stephens and his younger stepbrother Linton. Other collections are in the manuscripts departments at Duke University, Emory University, the University of Georgia at Athens, and the Historical Society of Pennsylvania. Many wartime and postwar letters from Stephens are in the Herschel V. Johnson Papers at Duke University. See also Ulrich B. Phillips, ed., "The Correspondence of Robert Toombs, Alexander H. Stephens and Howell Cobb," *Annual Report of the American Historical Association for 1911* (1913). There is also Myrta Lockett Avary, ed., *Recollection of Alexander H. Stephens: His Diary When a Prisoner at Fort Warren, Boston Harbor, 1865* (1910). A Georgia political friend, Henry Cleveland, published a collection of his speeches, with a eulogistic sketch; *Alexander H. Stephens in Public and Private* (1866). Also published during his lifetime was Richard M. Johnston and William H. Browne, *Life of Alexander H. Stephens* (1878). Thomas E. Schott, *Alexander H. Stephens of Georgia: A Biography* (1988), is a fine recent study that replaces Rudolph von Abele, *Alexander H.*

Stephens: A Biography (1946), as the best available. Several earlier lives of Stephens are either too old to be useful or lack scholarly credibility.

On Stephens before the war, see Daniel Walker Howe, *The Political Culture of American Whigs* (1979), and Michael P. Johnson, *Toward a Patriarchal Republic: The Secession of Georgia* (1977). On Stephens's Confederate period, see John R. Brumgardt, "The Confederate Career of Alexander H. Stephens," *Civil War History* 27 (Mar. 1981): 64–81; and the long discussion in Edmund Wilson, *Patriotic Gore: Studies in the Literature of the American Civil War* (1962). For Stephens after the war, see Alan Conway, *The Reconstruction of Georgia* (1966); Michael Perman, *The Road to Redemption: Southern Politics, 1869–1879* (1984); and C. Vann Woodward, *Tom Watson: Agrarian Rebel* (1938), where his political course can be followed.

Stephens's speeches in Congress can, of course, be found in the *Congressional Globe* and the *Congressional Record*. His speech on secession is featured in William W. Freehling and Craig M. Simpson, eds., *Secession Debated: Georgia's Showdown in 1860* (1992). A lengthy obituary is in the *Atlanta Constitution*, 4 and 5 Mar. 1883.

MICHAEL PERMAN

STEPHENS, Ann Sophia Winterbotham (30 Mar. 1810–20 Aug. 1886), fiction writer, was born in Humphreysville, Connecticut, the daughter of John Winterbotham, a wool merchant, and Ann Wrigley. At her mother's untimely death, her father married his sister-in-law Rachel, who raised Ann. Ann attended Abby Punderson's dame school and was also informally educated by the poet-patriot Colonel David Humphreys, owner of the wool manufactory of which her father was partner.

In 1831 she married Edward Stephens, merchant of West India goods, and moved with him to Portland, Maine. There he published the *Portland Magazine* (first issue, 1 Oct. 1834), which she edited and for which she wrote her frequently anthologized poem "The Polish Boy." In addition Ann Stephens compiled a regional anthology, the *Portland Sketch Book* (1836).

After a journey west through the Wyoming Valley of Pennsylvania and Ohio, the couple settled in New York City in 1837. Edward Stephens was employed in the Custom House, and Ann became associate editor of the *Ladies' Companion*. After a study of Native American languages she contributed to that periodical two stories of Native American life: "Mary Derwent" (1838) and "Malaeska" (1839). Between 1839 and the end of her life her output was continuous and prolific, scarcely interrupted by the birth of her two children. In her New York home on Cottage Place she enjoyed an active social life, becoming a chatelaine of New York's literary society. In December 1841 Ann Stephens joined the editorial staff of *Graham's Magazine* issued by George Rex Graham of Philadelphia. In addition she contributed to a variety of periodicals, including some with which her husband was associated: *New York Express, Sunday Morning News, Brother Jonathan,* and the *Columbian Lady's and Gentleman's Magazine,* for which she wrote a serial, "Romance of the Real," based on the Myra Clark Gaines lawsuit. (Gaines was a litigant in a will contest that lasted half a century.) She edited Frank Leslie's first periodical, *Frank Leslie's Ladies Gazette of Fashion* (1854–1856), and in 1856 *Mrs. Stephens' Illustrated New Monthly*, published by her husband. In 1858 this was merged with *Peterson's Magazine.*

Stephens's connection with *Peterson's Magazine* and with its publisher, Charles J. Peterson of Philadelphia, was important, lucrative, and long lasting. For some forty years she contributed to its pages serials later published in book form by Peterson's brother T. B. Peterson, a Philadelphia publisher of romantic fiction. The resulting succession of novels included *Fashion and Famine* (1854), *The Old Homestead* (1855), *Mary Derwent* (1858), *The Rejected Wife* (1863), *The Wife's Secret* (1864), *Mabel's Mistake* (1868), and *The Curse of Gold* (1869). Stephens's melodramatic narratives, historical romances, and domestic novels of city life skillfully combined sensationalism with high morality. As early as 1846, in "The Literati," Edgar Allan Poe wrote of her work: "She is fond of the bold, striking, trenchant—in a word, of the melo-dramatic; has a quick appreciation of the picturesque, and is not unskilful in delineations of character. . . . Her style is what the critics usually term 'powerful,' but lacks real power through its verboseness and floridity. . . . Her faults . . . belong to the effervescence of high talent."

Between April 1850 and November 1851 Stephens took a much publicized European tour in the course of which she received attentions from Charles Dickens, William Makepeace Thackeray, Alexander von Humboldt, and Louis-Adolphe Thiers. In 1858 when the first Atlantic cable was laid, she was invited to write odes to celebrate the event. She also dabbled in politics, and her circle included several political friends, among them Mirabeau B. Lamar, president of the republic of Texas, and President James Buchanan. In April 1861 she reported an assassination plot on Abraham Lincoln's life but was not heeded. After her husband's death in 1862 she spent several winters in Washington, D.C.

In 1869 T. B. Peterson & Brothers published a fourteen-volume uniform edition of her works, an edition enlarged in time by her later novels: *Married in Haste* (1870), *A Noble Woman* (1871), *The Reigning Belle* (1872), *Lord Hope's Choice* (1873), and *Bertha's Engagement* (1875).

In 1860, when her reputation was unquestioned and her popularity at its height, the newly founded firm of Irwin P. Beadle projected a series of dime novels and decided to begin the series with a Stephens serial originally published in the *Ladies' Companion* in 1839. The firm paid her $250 for the right to reprint and in June 1860 issued *Malaeska: The Indian Wife of the White Hunter* as Beadle's Dime Novel Number One. *Malaeska*, the only Stephens novel that was destined for survival, launched a widely circulated series and sold about a half-million copies in its various reprints. A graphic delineation of Native-American life, the story also had strong feminist interest. Between 1860 and 1864 the Beadle firm published additional Stephens narratives: *Myra, the Child of Adoption. A Romance of*

Real Life (1860), *Sybil Chase; or, The Valley Ranche. A Tale of California Life* (1861), *Esther. A Story of the Oregon Trail* (1862), *Ahmo's Plot; or, The Governor's Indian Child* (1863), *Mahaska, the Indian Princess* (1863), and *The Indian Queen* (1864).

Stephens died in Newport, Rhode Island, during a visit to Charles Peterson. A new 23-volume edition of her works was in press, and her serials were still running in *Peterson's Magazine*. The prolific and highly professional writer had provided romances for three generations of readers; she also had authored the first Beadle dime novel for mass production, a book that, according to the *Chicago Tribune* in 1929, had "a more important effect on the reading habits of its generation than any other publication of its time."

• Scattered letters of Ann Stephens are deposited in the Connecticut Historical Society, the Historical Society of Pennsylvania, the New-York Historical Society, the Boston Public Library, the Huntington Library, and the Brown University Library. The New York Public Library's Manuscript Division has a manuscript scrapbook relating to Stephens, and the library also has a scrapbook of clippings and obituaries. Stephens's death record (city clerk, Newport, R.I.) establishes her birthdate, since it states that at her death on 20 Aug. 1886 her age was 76 years, 4 months, and 21 days. (Most sources cite her birthdate erroneously.) For biographical details, see James A. Eastman, "Ann Sophia Stephens" (master's thesis, Columbia Univ., 1952), and Madeleine B. Stern, *We the Women: Career Firsts of Nineteenth-Century America* (1994). Obituary notices are in the *New York Tribune*, 21 Aug. 1886; the *Sun*, 21 Aug. 1886; and *Publishers Weekly*, 28 Aug. 1886.

MADELEINE B. STERN

STEPHENS, Linton (1 July 1823–14 July 1872), lawyer and politician, was born in Crawfordville, Georgia, the son of Andrew Stephens, a farmer and school teacher, and Matilda Lindsey. Both parents died of malaria in 1826, and Linton was raised by maternal relatives until 1837, when his half-brother, Alexander Hamilton Stephens, thirteen years older and already a prominent lawyer and politician, assumed guardianship. The elder Stephens saw to it that Linton received as good an education as he had been given, sending him to Franklin College (later the University of Georgia) in Athens, 1839–1843, from which he graduated with first honors. He went to Washington and listened to congressional debates and attended sessions of the U.S. Supreme Court during the winter of 1843–1844 and worked in the law office of Robert Augustus Toombs, a friend and political ally of both brothers. Stephens took a law degree at the University of Virginia (1844–1845) and attended Joseph Story's lectures at the Harvard Law School.

He returned to Georgia, passed the bar in 1846, and began his practice. Stephens was elected to the Georgia legislature as a Whig from Taliaferro County, 1849–1852, until his marriage and move to nearby Sparta, in adjacent Hancock County, which he represented from 1853–1855. He was one of the chief organizers of the Constitutional Union party, a short-lived coalition of unionist Whigs and Democrats created in the crisis over the Compromise of 1850, but drifted back to the Whigs and followed his brother into the Democratic party by 1857. Defeated for the legislature in the Know Nothing fever in 1855, Linton never enjoyed the electoral success or the hold on voters of his brother, "who was always less combustible and far the better politician" (Schott, p. 234). He suffered two more defeats by Know Nothings for congressional seats, in 1855 when he ran as an independent and as a Democrat in 1857.

In 1852 he married a wealthy widow, Emmeline (Thomas) Bell, daughter of James Thomas, a prominent judge and planter and a friend of his brother's. He moved to Sparta, his home for the remainder of his life, and entered a law partnership with Richard M. Johnston. He had three daughters with his first wife, who died in childbirth in 1857. Maddened by grief, and blaming himself for her death, he was "never . . . quite normal" thereafter. His loss accentuated his always highstrung emotional state and fondness for alcohol. In 1867 he married Mary W. Salter, daughter of R. H. and A. W. Salter. He had known her mother in Washington on the eve of the Civil War and met her again with her daughter in 1865, while visiting his brother, who was being held as a prisoner of war at Fort Warren in Boston Harbor. There were three children by this marriage.

When the Democratic convention deadlocked in 1857 over their choice for governor, Stephens nominated as a compromise candidate Joseph E. Brown, which was "probably the most momentous act of his political career" (Schott, p. 233) because Brown, a virtual political unknown at the time, would remain a power in the state's politics until the 1890s. Governor Brown reciprocated by appointing him to the Georgia Supreme Court in 1859, from which Stephens resigned in 1860 for health reasons after barely a year. Linton Stephens opposed disunion and cosponsored with his brother a resolution in the Georgia secession convention calling on the southern states to attend an Atlanta conference, but the delegates voted it down. Unionist to the last, Stephens nevertheless volunteered for the Confederate army in May, was elected captain of his company, and served from 16 July 1861 as lieutenant colonel of the Fifteenth Georgia Infantry in a brigade commanded by General Robert Toombs. He resigned 19 December 1861, frustrated with military life. He was an early and increasingly bitter critic of the administration of Confederate president Jefferson Davis, opposing the conscription act of 1862, suspension of habeas corpus, and imposition of martial law. Stephens worked against the Richmond government as a member of the Georgia legislature and was a strong ally of Governor Brown and Alexander Stephens, who had become vice president of the Confederacy. Linton sponsored a peace resolution that was controversial because of bitter disagreements between its supporters and the friends of Jefferson Davis over military and diplomatic strategy. He also served as a lieutenant colonel, Seventh Georgia Battalion, States Guard Cavalry of the state militia, 1863–1864, during William T. Sherman's Atlanta campaign, but he saw no action.

After the war Stephens was the spokesman for his disfranchised brother, who could not vote as a former top Confederate official, and he fought Republican forces controlling Georgia during Reconstruction. In the state election of 1870 Stephens had black voters who had failed to pay their poll tax arrested, along with the election officials who accepted their ballots, and was himself arrested by Governor Rufus Bullock in 1871. The matter was dropped soon after he presented his own case before a federal commission. He resisted the attempt of some Democrats to fuse with Liberal Republicans supporting Horace Greeley's candidacy against President Ulysses S. Grant in 1872. Stephens died in Sparta, Georgia, from "a congestion of the bowels and lungs," probably brought on by the exertions of this campaign and his efforts as an investigator for the state into the abuses of the Bullock regime, though like his brother his health was never strong.

Stephens was nearly always in the shadow of his diminutive brother but played an important role in Georgia politics. He is remembered almost entirely because he was the alter ego and emotional mainstay of his far more important sibling, who was elected to Congress before and after the war as a representative and senator and was Georgia's governor at the time of his death. Alexander Stephens never married; a biographer said "Linton was his wife." It is impossible to quantify the intensity of their relationship, or fully explain it, but it was passionate and affectionate. Its importance, particularly to the older man, should not be discounted. For thirty-four years they carried on an extensive correspondence when separated, as they often were. Their closeness and dependence on each other when together was often noted. They apparently never differed on any important matter, arriving at the same positions even before conferring, though Linton's marriages (especially the first) caused his brother some pain and sense of loss. Linton Stephens was without question the most important individual in the adult life and career of Alexander H. Stephens.

• Many of the papers of Linton Stephens can be found in manuscript collections devoted primarily to Alexander H. Stephens. The most important are at the University of Georgia and the Georgia Department of Archives and History, as well as at Duke University, Emory University, the Library of Congress, and the National Archives. James D. Waddell, *A Biographical Sketch of Linton Stephens* (1877), consists primarily of letters from Linton to his brother, with little of value from the Civil War years. The chief published sources on Linton continue to be the several biographies of his brother. Eudora Ramsay Richardson, *Little Aleck: A Life of Alexander H. Stephens* (1932), is written for the general reader in an interesting but overly sentimental and emotional manner and lacks any documentation, though it was based on a close reading of basic published sources listed in the bibliography. Rudolph Von Abele, *Alexander H. Stephens: A Biography* (1946), is a scholarly treatment by a careful historian, who criticized Richardson's work for "its amiability . . . exceeded only by its fatuousness." Yet both authors had insights into the relationship between the brothers. Thomas E. Schott, *Alexander H. Stephens of Georgia* (1988), is a massive work and in turn critical of Von Abele. It lacks some of the literary grace of the two previous titles but relies heavily on them and their basic interpretations, supported by the author's own work in primary sources. An obituary is in the *Atlanta Daily Sun*, 16 July 1872.

MICHAEL B. CHESSON

STEPHENS, Uriah Smith (3 Aug. 1821–13 Feb. 1882), labor leader, was born near Cape May, New Jersey. His parents' names and occupations are not recorded, but it is known that his father's financial losses during the panic of 1837 forced Stephens to give up his studies for the Baptist ministry and apprentice himself to a tailor. Upon the completion of his training, Stephens worked briefly as a schoolteacher in New Jersey and then in 1846 moved to Philadelphia, where he established himself as a tailor. Seven years later he left the city and, after traveling through the Caribbean and Central America, lived for nearly five years in California.

Stephens had developed an interest in economics as a young apprentice, and during his California years he became a dedicated reformer and abolitionist, campaigning for Republicans—John Frémont and Abraham Lincoln—in the presidential elections of 1856 and 1860. When he returned to Philadelphia in 1858, he began to participate in the labor movement. In February 1861 he attended the first national labor assembly of the decade; it focused, not on economic goals, but on an effort to preserve the Union without going to war. Concluding that workers would make better legislators than the men currently in power, the convention elected a Committee of Thirty-Four to promote the election of labor candidates. Stephens was one of those elected, but the project ended when war broke out in April.

In 1862 Stephens helped organize a tailors' union, the Garment Cutters' Association. The organization soon floundered, but Stephens believed that it could have survived if it had maintained a policy of secrecy like various fraternal orders to which he belonged. Secrecy would protect union members against employers' reprisals and at the same time build a sense of seriousness and solidarity within the organization. Anticipating the collapse of the Garment Cutters, he said, "When the dissolution takes place, I shall make an effort to get some good men together and originate something different from what we have ever had." The Garment Cutters disbanded in 1869, and a few weeks later Stephens and eight other former members organized a new union, the Noble Order of the Knights of Labor. The members elected Stephens to the top position, master workman. Shortly thereafter, Stephens and another founder of the Knights, Robert Macauley, opened their own tailor shop, which functioned as a kind of headquarters for the new order.

For the next ten years, Stephens's ideas played a dominant role in shaping the practices and philosophy of the Knights of Labor. First came the dedication to secrecy and ritual. Both were to be found in other unions of the time, but they were rarely practiced with such enthusiasm as among the Knights. Second came Stephens's conviction that, while it was important in the short run to improve conditions for wage laborers, the Knights' future lay in replacing wage labor with cooperatives. This system, he believed, would bring about "the complete emancipation of wealth producers from the thralldom and loss of wage slavery." Besides secrecy and cooperation, Stephens stressed a third principle: education. Workers should be taught to recognize the common interests of all labor, to understand that "an injury to one is an injury to all." In addition, they should become informed and active citizens. Although Stephens was dedicated to improving the lives of workingmen, he believed that they had many interests in common with capital. For this reason, he supported the use of the boycott, in which members acted as citizens and consumers, rather than strikes, in which they asserted their distinct claims as members of the working class.

Few of Stephens's ideas were uniquely his, but his conviction, his organizing skill, and the coherence of his thought provided a compelling vision for the union during its early years. In some ways, his philosophy went beyond what his fellow union members were prepared to accept. For instance, he was convinced that it was no longer sufficient to organize by trade and to deal only with skilled white males. "I can see ahead of me an organization that will cover the globe," he told his followers. "It will include men and women of every craft, creed and color; it will cover every race worth saving." This effort to reject the divisions that had weakened many earlier organizing efforts was not immediately embraced by the Knights; during their early years they remained craft-based and did not admit women until 1882. Nevertheless, the vision that Stephens articulated paved the way for the Knights' unusually inclusive policies in later years.

Throughout the Knights' first decade Stephens led the organization as master workman of District Assembly 1, which controlled the organization's General Assembly. In 1878 he was elevated to the position of grand master workman. He resigned later that year in order to run for Congress on the Greenback-Labor ticket. After his defeat in November he was reelected grand master workman and served for another year. But by this time many of his key ideas were facing mounting opposition. Class antagonisms had been heightened by the bitter strikes of the 1870s; in addition, many members felt that in order to grow, the Knights must abandon their commitment to secrecy. This policy was drawing attack both from socialists and, more harmfully, from the Catholic church; a prominent Catholic member of the Knights, Terence V. Powderly, headed a growing antisecrecy and antiritual faction within the order.

In part because of these disagreements and in part because of ill health, Stephens resigned his office in 1879. Shortly thereafter, Powderly and his followers won control of the General Assembly. Stephens continued to contest Powderly's policies, but after a final break between the two in 1881 the Knights formally abandoned the principle of secrecy. Stephens died the following year in Philadelphia. In 1886 the Knights granted a $10,000 pension to his family.

As Stephens's opponents had predicted, the organization soared in membership once his rules of secrecy were abandoned; a number of successful strikes (opposed even by Powderly) brought in still more members. Yet Stephens's intellectual and organizational contribution remains central to the story of the Knights of Labor and therefore to the history of the American labor movement. As his obituary in *Journal of United Labor*, a Knights of Labor publication, observed, "All through our rituals and laws will be found the impress of his brain, and inspiration of his keen insight into the great problems of the present hour."

• Stephens does not appear to have left any personal papers. For information about his career, see John R. Commons et al., *History of Labour in the United States*, vol. 2 (1918); David Montgomery, *Beyond Equality: Labor and the Radical Republicans, 1862–1872* (1967); Gerald N. Grob, *Workers and Utopia: A Study of Ideological Conflict in the American Labor Movement, 1865–1900* (1967); Terence V. Powderly, *Thirty Years of Labor, 1859–1889* (1889); Norman J. Ware, *The Labor Movement in the United States, 1860–1895* (1929); Philip S. Foner, *History of the Labor Movement in the United States*, vol. 1 (1947); and Richard Oestreicher, "Terence Powderly, the Knights of Labor, and Artisanal Republicanism," in *Labor Leaders in America*, ed. Melvyn Dubofsky and Warren Van Tine (1987). An obituary is in the *Journal of United Labor*, 15 Feb. 1882.

SANDRA OPDYCKE

STEPHENS, William (28 Jan. 1671–Aug. 1753), British colonial official, was born at Bowcombe Manor, Isle of Wight, the eldest son of Sir William Stephens, a baronet and former lieutenant governor of the Isle of Wight, and Elizabeth (maiden name unknown). Young William first attended school at Winchester before entering King's College, Cambridge, where he was awarded the A.B. degree in 1684 and the M.A. four years later. He studied law at the Middle Temple but was never called to the bar. In 1696 Stephens married Mary Newdigate, daughter of Sir Richard Newdigate; they had seven sons and two daughters.

In 1697 Stephens was elected to Parliament, an office he held for twenty-five years. During this time he also served as a militia officer and justice of the peace. He was appointed commissioner of the victualing forces in 1712, a position that he subsequently mismanaged. After he squandered his inheritance and failed to win reelection to Parliament in 1727, he sold the family estate. Disgraced and in debt, he was befriended by Colonel Samuel Horsey, an officer of the York Building Company, who gave him a position with the company in Scotland in 1729; after five years Stephens, penniless and forlorn, returned to London. Colonel Horsey again rescued Stephens when he employed him to survey a barony of land in South Carolina. Stephens sailed for Charleston in 1736, accompanied by his son Thomas. While there he visited Savannah, Georgia; there he met General James E. Oglethorpe, with whom he returned to London.

Colonel Horsey again intervened for Stephens when he recommended him to Oglethorpe for the position of secretary for the colony of Georgia. Since Oglethorpe failed to submit regular reports, the trustees of the colony decided to appoint an officer in Savannah to keep them apprised of conditions in the colony. Stephens, now sixty-six years old, accepted the position for six years at fifty pounds per annum. He arrived in Savannah on 1 November 1737. As an officer, adviser, and observer to the trustees, he was instructed to report on all matters of interest concerning colonial activity. Initially, he resided in Savannah, but in 1739 the trustees awarded him a 500-acre grant at the mouth of the Vernon River about twelve miles south of Savannah that was popularly called "Bewlie."

The colony of Georgia, founded for philanthropic, military, and mercantile reasons, had not flourished as the trustees had intended. Their restrictions on landholding, along with a misguided devotion to silk production, prohibitions on slavery and rum, and their failure to provide for either a governor or elected assembly, caused the colony to languish and its settlers to become defiant and factious. Many Georgians envied the prosperous plantation-slave system that thrived in neighboring South Carolina.

From the outset Stephens was received cordially as he mingled with the local inhabitants. He was critical of both the doctrine and ritual of the religious services conducted by the Wesley brothers and the Reverend George Whitefield. After the removal of Thomas Causton for mismanagement of public funds, Stephens was appointed keeper of the public stores. Ostensibly opposed to free ownership of land and the introduction of slavery, he reported to the trustees that most of the settlers who left the colony on this account were shiftless or lazy. A year later, however, he acknowledged dissatisfaction over land restrictions and slavery. In 1783 the "malcontents" began making formal complaints to the trustees.

In 1740 Stephens issued "A State of the province of Georgia . . ." to show the superior advantages of Georgia and its resources. The "malcontents," led by Patrick Tailfer, the chief of a Scottish club that opposed the trustees' regulations against slavery and landholding and their prohibition of rum, charged that Stephens had misrepresented conditions in Georgia when he declared against slavery. Stephens was further embrassed when his son Thomas became associated with the "malcontents." In 1741 Thomas was selected to present a petition to the king and Parliament from the disaffected faction that charged the trustees had mismanaged the colony. After conducting an investigation that vindicated the trustees, in 1742 the trustees lifted the ban on rum, but not on slavery. Thomas Stephens was publicly reprimanded before the British House of Commons for making scandalous and malicious charges against the trustees. Angered by his son's campaign against the trustees, Stephens disinherited his unrepentant son. In 1759 Thomas wrote a biography of his father, attempting in the process to justify his own role as the agent of the "malcontents."

The trustees divided the colony into two counties in 1741; Stephens became president at Savannah, while Oglethorpe presided at Frederica. Although Stephens held an impressive title and received eighty pounds per year for his expanded duties, Oglethorpe still exercised civil and military authority over the entire colony. When Oglethorpe left Georgia in 1743, the trustees consolidated the two counties and made Stephens president of the colony.

During his presidency Stephens prevented a threatened Indian uprising when Mary Musgrove and her spouse Thomas Bosomworth unsuccessfully demanded compensation for Musgrove's services as an interpreter to Oglethorpe. To protect the interests of the colony, Stephens ordered the arrest of several South Carolinians who refused to purchase licenses to trade with Indians in Georgia. In 1743 the trustees provided for fee simple ownership of land, and in 1749 they finally withdrew the prohibition on slavery. Stephens's most enduring achievement was the remarkable journal that he kept from his arrival in Savannah in 1737 until September 1749. Generations of historians have been indebted to him for recording details about life and conditions in colonial Georgia.

By 1750 Stephens, feeble and incapacitated, was persuaded to allow Vice President Henry Parker to administer the colony. Stephens retired in April 1751 to his home at "Bewlie" that had been managed by his third son Newdigate since 1742. There he lapsed into a coma in mid-August 1753 and died the next day.

Stephens's thirteen years of public service in Georgia were marked by unwavering loyalty to authority and a sincere interest in the welfare of the colony. He was a staunch conservative in politics and religion. Since he lacked business acumen, he relied on privileged connections for patronage. He seemed to have a broad and sympathetic understanding of people, but his advanced age and upper-class background made it difficult for him to comprehend the needs of the remote and backward colony of Georgia.

• "William Stephens' Journal, 1737–1740" was published in Allen D. Candler, *Colonial Records of Georgia*, vol. 4 (1906) and supp. (1906); for later years, see E. Merton Coulter, ed., *The Journal of William Stephens, 1743–1745* (2 vols., 1958, 1959). The earliest biography of Stephens was written by his son Thomas Stephens, *The Castle Builders, or the History of William Stephens of the Isle of Wight, Esq., Lately Deceased* (1759). Among the best secondary sources of Stephens's career in Georgia are Kenneth Coleman, *Colonial Georgia, a History* (1976); James R. McCain, *Georgia as a Proprietary Province* (1917); Trevor R. Reese, "Introduction," *The Clamorous Malcontents: Criticisms and Defenses of the Colony of Georgia, 1741–1743* (1973); Reese, *Colonial Georgia: A Study in British Imperial Policy in the Eighteenth Century* (1963); Betty Wood, *Slavery in Colonial Georgia, 1730–1775* (1984); and Natalie F. Bocock, "William Stephens," *Georgia Historical Society* 17 (Dec. 1933): 243–58. Also see Carole Watterson, "William Stephens, Georgia Secretary, 1737–1741" (M.A. thesis, Univ. of North Carolina, 1966).

R. FRANK SAUNDERS, JR.

STERETT, Andrew (27 Jan. 1778–9 Jan. 1807), American naval officer, was born in Baltimore, Maryland, the son of John Sterett, a shipping merchant, iron manufacturer, and officer during the Revolution, and Deborah Ridgley, the sister of General Charles Ridgley, a Maryland shipowner and officer in the Revolution. Sterett apparently went to sea in the merchant service, but with the creation of the Department of the Navy in 1798 his interests turned there. Thanks to his family's influence as prominent Federalists, Sterett was able to obtain a commission as third lieutenant aboard the frigate *Constellation*. His commission, dated 25 March 1798, arrived in time for him to join the frigate on its first cruise on 24 June 1798.

The *Constellation* began its voyage by first going down the bay from Baltimore to Norfolk, where it spent several weeks fitting out. Early in September it cleared the Capes, ordered to cruise from there to Florida in search of French privateers as part of the navy's Quasi War operations. In December 1798 the frigate was ordered to cruise the waters in the West Indies between St. Kitts and Puerto Rico; Sterett was in command of the frigate's third division.

On 9 February 1799 the *Constellation*, which was at that time off the island of Nevis, came within sight of the French frigate *L'Insurgente*. The frigates closed, and in a hard-fought battle the *Constellation* captured *L'Insurgente*. The *Constellation* suffered only two men killed and three wounded while the French frigate had twenty-nine killed and forty-one wounded. In a letter written to his brother nearly one week after the battle Sterett made an extraordinary claim. According to him one of the Americans killed, Neal Harvey, was a "fellow I was obliged to run through the body with my sword, and so put an end to a *coward*. You must not think this strange, for we would put a man to death for even looking pale on board *this* ship." The substance of the letter is uncorroborated and may indicate more about Sterett's bravado than conditions aboard the *Constellation*.

In July the *Constellation* returned to New York, where Thomas Truxtun, captain of the frigate, submitted his resignation from the navy in a dispute over rank. Samuel Barron took command, and Sterett sailed with him back to the West Indies. By December 1799, however, Truxtun had returned to service and once more commanded his old frigate. Sterett, promoted to first lieutenant, sailed with him again to the West Indies.

On the morning of 1 February 1800, off St. Kitts the *Constellation* encountered the larger French frigate *La Vengeance* and gave chase. Sterett commanded the bow gun and was the first to open fire. After closing with the enemy, the *Constellation* managed to get the best of the battle, but in darkness *La Vengeance* slipped away, denying Truxtun and his men their final moment of glory.

Sterett returned once more with Truxtun to New York and in August 1800 sailed with him as first lieutenant aboard the frigate *President*. On 25 October Truxtun detached Sterett to command the schooner *Enterprise*. Two months later, while sailing off St. Kitts, Sterett captured the French privateer *L'Amour de la Patrie*.

On 1 June 1801, following the conclusion of the Quasi War, *Enterprise*, with Sterett in command, sailed for the Mediterranean from Baltimore. On the first of August he captured a Tripolitan cruiser. For this gallant action Congress offered its thanks and voted to present him with a sword as a symbol of its appreciation. He came back to the United States in November, then returned to the Mediterranean in February 1802. He spent the next several months in routine patrol protecting American commerce and making port visits. On 17 January the *Enterprise* captured a Tripolitan vessel, *Paulina*. Sterett left the *Enterprise* on 6 April when he went aboard the frigate *Chesapeake*, homeward bound.

Later in 1802 Sterett returned to his home in Baltimore, where he undertook to direct the final stages of the construction of the schooner *Vixen*, which was launched at the end of June. Sterett requested and was granted leave to make a merchant voyage; while away in the East Indies Sterett was promoted to the rank of master commandant.

When Sterett returned to the United States in May 1805 he was offered command of the brig *Hornet*. Although anxious to return to service, Sterett was angry that he had never received the sword promised to him by Congress for his capture of the Tripolitan vessel. Added to this was an even more serious source of resentment. Rank meant everything to Sterett and his fellow officers. Stephen Decatur, although junior to Sterett in rank, had been promoted over him to captain as a result of Decatur's exploits in Tripoli harbor leading an expedition to destroy the captured frigate *Philadelphia*. Whatever the merits of the case, Sterett was furious, and in his anger he resigned from the service. Sterett returned to service in the merchant marine and within a few months of his resignation sailed on a trading voyage to Latin America. He died in Lima, Peru, presumably of disease.

• Very little has been published about Sterett. Sources include records in the Naval History Division, United States Navy; *Naval Documents Related to the Quasi War between the United States and France* (7 vols., 1935–1938); *Naval Documents Related to the United States Wars with the Barbary Powers* (6 vols., 1939–1944); William M. Fowler, Jr., *Jack Tars and Commodores: The American Navy, 1783–1815* (1980); and Christopher McKee, *A Gentlemanly and Honorable Profession: The Creation of the U.S. Naval Officer Corps, 1794–1815* (1991).

WILLIAM M. FOWLER

STERLING, George (1 Dec. 1869–17 Nov. 1926), poet, was born in Sag Harbor, New York, the son of George Ansel Sterling, a medical doctor, and Mary Parker Havens. Sterling's development as a poet came relatively late. His parents destined him for the priesthood and in 1886 sent him to St. Charles College in Ellicott City, Maryland, where he was strongly impressed by the lectures of the poet Father John Bannister Tabb. After three years of college, Sterling refused further study and moved to San Francisco, where he worked for his uncle, Frank C. Havens, a wealthy real estate agent. In San Francisco Sterling fell under the influence of poet Joaquin Miller. Later, under the tutelage of Ambrose Bierce, he began to write poetry while continuing to work competently, if unenthusiastically, for his uncle. In 1896 he married Caroline Rand, a sister of his uncle's wife, but he did not accept the restrictions of monogamy and disliked the pressure for financial success.

Sterling's first literary success was "Memorial Day Ode," published in the *San Francisco Examiner* through Bierce's influence in 1901. His next major work, the title poem in his first collection, *The Testimony of the Suns and Other Poems*, published in San Francisco in 1903, is a statement of cosmic pessimism based on the then-common theory that the universe is eternal and spatially infinite. Thus the whole process of evolution is pointless; life anywhere will eventually die and begin again:

How oft, O Life, on worlds forgot,
  Hast thou, in thine unnumbered forms,
  Gone forth to Time's transmuting storms,
And fought till storm and stress were not!

How oft hast striven, hoped, and died,
  And, dying, fared to gracious rest,
  The Night's inevitable guest,
In alien realms unverified!

Although "The Testimony of the Suns" has magnitude, a degree of power, and the "sidereal" chill ascribed to it by critic Harriet Monroe in 1916, it is more often merely bombastic. Sterling's natural inclination was toward heavy ornamentation, a style that won him a turn-of-the-century audience—he was hailed as a great poet by Bierce, Upton Sinclair, Jack London, and Theodore Dreiser—but alienated later generations of readers.

"A Wine of Wizardry," published through Bierce's influence in William R. Hearst's *Cosmopolitan* in September 1907, brought Sterling widespread attention. The shifting, colored imagery of the poem owes something to the poet's experiments with hashish and quite possibly something to Oscar Wilde's *The Sphinx*. Bierce proclaimed the poem as "great" and asserted that Sterling was the country's greatest living poet. When other critics disagreed, Bierce refuted them, in the magazine's December issue. As a result, Sterling became nationally known and a frequent contributor to magazines with a national circulation.

In 1905 Sterling moved to Carmel, then a new real estate development, which quickly turned into a leading art colony. Widely known as "the King of Carmel," he became thoroughly identified with the spirit of the place, acting as host for writers, as he did for later visitors to San Francisco. Sterling made many literary friends and left a voluminous correspondence that provides a picture of his era and probably is more valuable than his poetry. His correspondents included Edwin Markham, H. L. Mencken, and Robinson Jeffers.

Sterling's reputation continued to grow over the next half dozen years. His "Ode on the Centenary of the Birth of Robert Browning" took one of two second prizes (one of the three cash awards) in the 1912 *Lyric Year* contest, which later became famous for relegating Edna St. Vincent Millay's "Renascence" to fourth place. Sterling's fortunes began to turn in 1914. He had been unfaithful from the early years of his marriage, and in 1914 he and his wife were divorced. He then made a traumatically unsuccessful attempt at establishing himself as a poet in New York City.

After returning to San Francisco in 1915, Sterling spent the rest of his life trying to reconcile himself to being the city's unofficial poet laureate. Rapidly changing tastes in poetry made it difficult for him to place his poems in good magazines. Harriet Monroe's lacerating review of his work in *Poetry* (Mar. 1916) represents a view that, unfortunately for Sterling, was gaining precedence: "The truth is, this sort of pomposity has died the death. . . . When Mr. Sterling learns to avoid the 'luscious tongue' and the 'honeyed wine', he may become the poet he was meant to be" (p. 311). Long a heavy drinker, and now beset with guilt over the suicide of his ex-wife, he became an alcoholic. Even so, he continued to write prolifically, with some success. In 1923 his *Selected Poems* was published by Holt, Sterling's first national publisher. His finest work, the dramatic poem *Lilith*, was published locally in 1919 and in a revised form by Macmillan in 1926. The bitter adventures of its hero, Tancred, reflect an internalized pessimism. Although the poem occasionally slips into cliché and is rather self-consciously evil, it has moments of genuine lyricism.

Late that same year Sterling took cyanide in the free room he kept at the Bohemian Club in San Francisco. His reputation, which by that time had declined sharply, has since been totally eclipsed. His poetry seems destined to remain obscure. If Sterling is remembered as a poet, it likely will be for *Lilith*. Probably he will be better remembered for his correspondence and as a literary man whose life touched those of his more celebrated contemporaries.

• Major collections of Sterling's papers are at the Henry E. Huntington Library and Art Gallery, San Marino, Calif.; the New York Public Library; the University of California at Berkeley; and Indiana University. Smaller collections are at St. John's Seminary, Camarillo, Calif., and at the libraries of Dartmouth, Harvard, the University of Kansas, Mills College, Middlebury College, the University of Pennsylvania, Scripps College, Stanford, the University of Chicago, the University of California at Los Angeles, the University of Texas, the University of Virginia, and Wagner College. In addition to those already mentioned, the most important volumes of Sterling's poetry are *A Wine of Wizardry and Other Poems* (1909), *The House of Orchids and Other Poems* (1911), *The Caged Eagle and other Poems* (1916), *The Binding of the Beast and Other War Verse* (1917), *Rosamund: A Dramatic Poem* (1920), *Sails and Mirage and Other Poems* (1921), *Selected Poems* (1923), and *After Sunset* (1939). A thorough list appears in Cecil Johnson's *A Bibliography of the Writings of George Sterling* (1931). Most of Sterling's letters appear in Dalton Gross, "The Letters of George Sterling" (Ph.D. diss., Southern Illinois Univ., 1968). The biographical introduction to Gross's dissertation is published as "George Sterling: King of Carmel," *American Book Collector*, Oct. 1970, pp. 8–15. A full length biography, in the Twayne's United States Authors Series, is Thomas Benediktsson, *George Sterling* (1980).

DALTON GROSS
MARYJEAN GROSS

STERLING, James (1701–10 Nov. 1763), Anglican minister and poet, was born in Downrass, King's County, Ireland, the son of James Sterling, a captain in the British army, and Patience Hansard. He graduated from Trinity College, Dublin, in 1720. His poetic drama, *The Rival Generals*, was performed at Dublin's Theatre-Royal and published in three editions in 1722. He married Nancy Lyddal, an actress, who played in *The Rival Generals*. In 1723 the couple went to London, where she acted in numerous roles in Lincoln's Inn Fields. Three of Sterling's poems appeared in *Miscellaneous Poems* (1724), edited by Matthew Concanen. Sterling's play, *The Parracide*, though published in 1736, was written and performed in the mid-1720s. His translation of Musaeus, *The Loves of Hero and Leander* (1728), was reprinted several times. Throughout the late 1720s, Nancy Sterling continually developed as an actress, but as her health gradually failed, she returned to Dublin's Smock Alley Theater, where she gave her farewell performance on 22 May 1732 in a favorite role as Polly Peachum in John Gay's *Beggar's Opera* (1728), reciting James Sterling's poignant epilogue at the end.

After his wife's death, Sterling took an M.A. from Trinity (1733) and became a minister. While serving as chaplain to His Majesty's "own Royal Regiment of Foot," Sterling published *The Poetical Works of the Rev. James Sterling*, volume 1 (1734). No second volume appeared.

Sterling decided in 1736 to emigrate to America, planning at first to sail for Boston, where he hoped to become the minister at King's Chapel. But a number of Boston Anglicans wanted no part of a minister who was a playwright and had been married to an actress. He received the royal bounty for going abroad as a missionary on 16 September 1737. Two months later, on 16 November, he became the minister at All Hallows Parish, Anne Arundel County, Maryland, where he remained until his resignation on 18 July 1739, when he was appointed rector of St. Anne's, Annapolis, by Governor Samuel Ogle. When the great revivalist minister George Whitefield visited Annapolis, he condemned Sterling for tolerating what are "falsely called *innocent* entertainments of the polite part of the world; for women are as much enslaved to their fashionable diversions, as men are to their bottle and their hounds."

On 26 August 1740 Sterling resigned from St. Anne's to accept the more lucrative parish of St. Paul's, Kent County, Maryland, where he lived in Chestertown. On 19 September 1743 he married Rebecca Holt, widow of Rev. Arthur Holt. Their daughter, Rebecca, was born on 22 November 1744. The date of his second wife's death is unknown, but on 7 September 1749 he married his third wife, Mary Smith. Several incidental glimpses of Sterling turn up in Charles Peale's letterbook. Sterling baptized Peale's son Charles Willson Peale and suggested the name St. George for another of Charles Peale's sons, who was born on 23 April 1745, St. George's Day. Peale also describes Sterling's vicious attack on Whitefield, when the itinerant was visiting Sterling's church in June 1746.

In Maryland, Sterling wrote several poems, including *An Epistle to the Hon. Arthur Dobbs*. He sent it to London for publication in 1749, but the messenger died on the voyage. Sterling himself left for Ireland and England in the fall of 1751. He published the *Epistle to Dobbs* (1752) in Dublin, and it was reprinted in London. He went on to London, where he and a group of merchants (including John Hanbury) appeared before the Lords Commissioners of Trade on 16 April 1752 seeking "a grant for an exclusive trade upon that coast [Labrador], which Mr. Sterling . . . informed them that a very valuable trade for furs, whale fins, fish and masts might be opened there." Because of the Hudson's Bay Company's rival claims, the Board of Trade rejected Sterling's petition. Sterling also drew up a memorial creating a new Maryland customs district, presented it to the Lords of Treasury, and was appointed on 12 May 1752 to the collectorship at the salary of £80 a year. Although numerous influential American and Englishmen objected to Sterling's collectorship, they were unable to have it rescinded.

On 20 April 1752 Sterling asked the bishop of London for financial help to return to Maryland, and received for a second time the royal bounty for going abroad as a missionary. He left London in early June and arrived in Annapolis on 7 August 1752 on his way back to Chestertown. Visiting Annapolis the next year, on 21 August 1753, he entered into the Tuesday Club's typical humor with a conversation on "the prodigies of nature," telling "Stories of Great Irish Bulls with two heads, monsters as yet unheard of, of monkies that could discourse Intelligibly, Salamanders that could drink punch and Rum, Camelions that lived at Court upon mere air, and often Changed their Color, wearing an artificial Skin, Cockatrices that killed with a look, etc." He had come to Annapolis for a meeting of the clergy and joined Rev. Thomas Bacon in preparing the address to the governor. Over a year later, when Governor Horatio Sharpe called a special meeting of the assembly because of the outbreak of hostilities on the frontier, he asked Sterling to preach a sermon on the occasion, 13 December 1754. The assembly paid for printing 300 copies of the dynamic sermon, which was reprinted in London. Sterling published essays and poems in the *Maryland Gazette* and sent off a number of poems to the Reverend William Smith's *American Magazine* (1757–1758). His poem "Verses Occasioned by the Success of the British Arms in the Year 1759" (*Maryland Gazette*, 3 Jan. 1760), contains a section describing the progress of civilization in America, giving the poet a chance to lament the destruction of the wilderness as the woods were cleared for farmland:

> The Trees now prostrate, all their Glories fade,
> Their branching Honours, once a grateful Shade,
> Laid low on Earth, a dreary Thicket gloom
> No more to rise, and ne'er again to bloom.
> The Parent Birds forsake their downy Nests,
> Their Cares all flutt'ring in their little Breasts,
> Pearch on the neighb'ring Trees, or wing the Skies,
> Bemoan their helpless Young, in doleful Cries.

Sterling died in Kent County, survived by his third wife and his daughter, Rebecca.

• A few of Sterling's letters are extant in Lambeth Palace, London. See William Wilson Manross, *The Fulham Papers in the Lambeth Palace Library* (1965). A host of information is gathered in Lawrence C. Wroth, "James Sterling: Poet, Priest, and Prophet of Empire," *Proceedings of the American Antiquarian Society* 41 (1931): 3–54. A number of additional poems are identified as Sterling's in J. A. Leo Lemay, *A Calendar of American Poetry in the Colonial Newspapers and Magazines* (1972). Two of his English poems appear in David F. Foxon, *English Verse, 1701–1750* (1975). For his appearance at the Tuesday Club, see Dr. Alexander Hamilton, *The History of the Ancient and Honorable Tuesday Club*, ed. Robert Micklus (3 vols., 1990). A biographical and critical study of Sterling, together with a primary and secondary bibliography, is in J. A. Leo Lemay, *Men of Letters in Colonial Maryland* (1972). A long obituary is in the *Maryland Gazette*, 17 Nov. 1763.

J. A. LEO LEMAY

STERLING, John Whalen (17 July 1816–9 Mar. 1885), educator, was born in Wyoming County, Pennsylvania, the son of Daniel Sterling, a lumberman and government contractor, and Rachel Brooks. After preparing at academies in Hamilton and Homer, New York, and reading law for two years at a Wilkes-Barre, Pennsylvania, law office, Sterling entered the College of New Jersey (later Princeton) as a sophomore in 1837. Three years later he graduated with honors and returned to Wilkes-Barre to serve as principal of Wilkes-Barre Academy. From 1841 to 1844 he combined studies at Princeton Theological Seminary with work as a tutor at the College of New Jersey. Sterling spent the next year as a Presbyterian preacher in Tunkhannock, Pennsylvania, near his boyhood home. Although an active member of the Presbyterian church for the rest of his life, he never again served as a full-time preacher.

In 1846 Sterling moved to Wisconsin, where he remained a dedicated educator for nearly four decades. He spent two years in Waukesha, first as a mathematics professor at Carroll College and then as the head of a private school. In 1848 he moved permanently to Madison with the encouragement of Eleazer Root, a regent of the University of Wisconsin, which at the time existed only on paper. Sterling was the infant institution's first and, for a short time, only professor. His task was to prepare a group of students for university-level study; in February 1849 he opened the university's preparatory department in a room at the Madison Female Academy while the first university building was under construction. After Sterling's first class of twenty male pupils completed its preparation, the first college class was under way in 1850. Sterling married Harriet Dean in 1851; as they raised three children of their own, they also counseled and assisted countless university students. Sterling was instrumental in organizing the Athenaen, the first student literary society on campus, in 1850. He was personally interested in his students and always willing to meet with them outside of class. The Sterlings assisted needy students and nursed those who were sick. After a residential facility was completed in 1855, they lived in one of its faculty apartments and supervised the dining hall. And when the university made the controversial decision to admit female students beginning in 1863, the Sterlings did what they could to make women students comfortable on campus.

During the 1850s Sterling was the university's professor of mathematics, natural philosophy (which included physics and chemistry), and astronomy, and he continued to teach mathematics in the preparatory department. As the faculty grew gradually and underwent periodic reorganizations during the next few decades, Sterling continued to teach as many as five classes per day. He was professor of natural philosophy and astronomy from 1867 to 1874, and, following a brief leave to recover from ill health, professor of mathematics from 1874 until he became professor emeritus after his retirement in 1883. Although Sterling's three and a half decades at the University of Wisconsin witnessed the beginnings of a focus on research, he concentrated on teaching a fixed body of knowledge that was consistent with his belief in the Scriptures. Virtually the only exception to his old-style approach to scholarship was a paper he delivered on lightning and lightning rods in 1874. As a professor, he was conscientious, caring, and always thorough.

Throughout his association with the University of Wisconsin, Sterling was an administrator and an adviser to students as well as a professor. In the early years the university staff was so small that all of the faculty members carried out administrative tasks; Sterling took a turn as librarian, for example. When the board of regents appointed Henry Barnard to replace resigning chancellor John Lathrop in 1858, it also looked to Sterling to oversee university operations during Barnard's many expected absences from campus. In 1861, when the board accepted Barnard's resignation, it named Sterling dean of the faculty; he remained the university's chief administrative officer until Paul Chadbourne took over as president in 1867. During this six-year period, Sterling oversaw buildings and grounds maintenance, assembled university

catalogs, collected tuition, and conferred degrees, in addition to teaching. The board changed his title to vice chancellor in 1865, and he continued in that role after Chadbourne arrived. After Chadbourne resigned in 1870 and before John Twombly took over as president in 1871, Sterling was again the temporary head of the university. By that time, his title was vice president, which he retained until his retirement. In 1881 the Sterlings moved from a private home to Ladies Hall to serve as resident advisers for the women students who lived there.

Many people honored Sterling, during his life as well as after his death in Madison. The caption beneath his portrait sums up the high regard he had earned at the university: "Father of the University." In 1921 the University of Wisconsin regents named a building in his honor; Sterling Hall became the home of the physics and astronomy departments.

• Sterling's papers are in the University Archives, Memorial Library, University of Wisconsin, Madison. The collection consists mainly of account books and a small number of personal letters. Merle Curti and Vernon Carstensen, *The University of Wisconsin: A History, 1848–1925* (1949), contains some background on Sterling and detailed accounts of his many roles at the University of Wisconsin. See also Reuben Gold Thwaites, ed., *The University of Wisconsin: Its History and Its Alumni* (1900), and the unattributed "Prof. Sterling, a Jubilee Memory," *Wisconsin Alumni Magazine* 5 (June–July 1904): 303–7. An obituary and an account of Sterling's funeral are in the *Wisconsin State Journal*, 9 and 11 Mar. 1885.

CHRISTINE A. OGREN

STERLING, Ross Shaw (11 Feb. 1875–25 Mar. 1949), oilman and politician, was born near Anahuac, Chambers County, Texas, the son of Benjamin Franklin Sterling, a storekeeper and farmer, and Mary Jane Bryan. He attended local public schools until 1887, dropping out after his mother's death. Sterling then worked with his father, becoming store manager by his seventeenth birthday. In 1896 he struck out on his own, freighting produce across Galveston Bay to the city of Galveston. He married schoolteacher Maud Abbie Gage in October 1898; the couple had five children.

After opening a second store in Chambers County shortly after his marriage, Sterling saw even greater potential profits in the nearby oil fields that were rapidly developing in wake of the boom set off by the Spindletop discovery of 1901. Having disposed of his other stores, Sterling opened a chain of feed stores in 1903 in Saratoga, Sour Lake, Humble, and Dayton, Texas. Hardworking and quick to take advantage of opportunities, he supplied the teamsters that were busy hauling supplies to the oil fields and soon held a near monopoly in the feed trade. He shortly acquired an interest in the Dayton Lumber Company as well, supplying construction lumber for oil storage tanks.

Sterling relocated to Houston in 1906, and after the panic of 1907 he entered still another field—banking—when he acquired four local banks at distress prices. Using his various enterprises to finance each other, he entered the venture in which he would enjoy his greatest success—oil production—in 1909 with the purchase of two wells in the Humble field. Immediately successful, he added additional wells and in early 1911 combined forces with a number of other independent producers to form the Humble Oil Company. Capitalized at $150,000, Sterling served as the new firm's first president. By plowing company profits into the acquisition of additional oil leases, he enabled the firm's holdings to enjoy continuous growth, and within a few years they were valued at between $1 and $4 million.

Although Sterling initially resisted efforts to introduce multifunction firms in the region (serving as president of the Texas Oil Producers and Landowners Association in 1915), economic realities soon dictated that his own firm join their ranks. Along with several other noted independent producers, he formed the Humble Oil and Refining Company in June 1917 and served as president. The new firm began operations capitalized at $4 million and soon moved into retail sales and refining. Continued expansion required the continual purchasing of new oil leases in order for the firm to remain competitive, and financial resources were soon strained. In a move that benefited both firms, Humble sold 50 percent of its stock to Standard Oil (New Jersey) in 1919 for $17 million. Standard Oil acquired a badly needed source of crude oil, and Humble obtained capital needed for expansion, while largely retaining local control of operations. Eager to explore new opportunities, Sterling relinquished the presidency to William Stamps Farrish in 1922, retaining the position of chairman of the board.

Sterling entered the newspaper business in 1923 by purchasing the financially feeble *Houston Dispatch*. He acquired the *Houston Post* in the following year and combined the two as the *Houston Post-Dispatch*. He also made outside investments in real estate but found his attention drawn increasingly toward politics. An advocate of Prohibition and a firm believer in honest government, Sterling was revolted by the corruption of former Democratic governor James Ferguson and his wife Miriam "Ma" Ferguson. Sterling threw his support to the Republican gubernatorial candidate in 1924, only to see Ma Ferguson elected as her husband's stand-in. After successfully supporting anti-Ferguson candidate Dan Moody for the post in 1926, however, Sterling was rewarded with the chairmanship of the Texas Highway Commission. Sterling successfully removed partisan politics from the commission and conducted an honest administration. His proposed highway construction plan of May 1928 would have greatly increased construction in the state, but the state legislature, committed to funding highways out of current revenue, balked at issuing bonds backed by a gasoline tax for financing the project. Eager to see his proposed plan implemented and chagrined at the prospect of another Ferguson in the governor's mansion, Sterling ran for the office himself in 1930 and was easily elected.

Conservative politically and personally, Sterling held a narrow view of his gubernatorial powers. Refus-

ing to campaign in the legislature for causes dear to his heart, he even sent clerks to read most of his messages to the body. As Texas increasingly felt the onset of the depression, he took limited measures—attempting to cut government waste coupled with modest tax increases—to combat declining state revenues. Although Sterling did establish a state child welfare department and a commission for unemployment relief, his sole effort to increase employment was a modest "speed-up" of existing public works projects.

Sterling's greatest crisis came when the oil market collapsed in the summer of 1931. Although he succeeded in forcing the passage of a limited conservation bill through the legislature, overproduction and waste still threatened the East Texas oil fields. Sterling responded by invoking martial law in Gregg, Rusk, Upshur, and Smith counties on 17 August 1931. The National Guard shut down all wells, although the field reopened on 5 September with a 225 barrel per day limit. Sterling's action was overturned by a federal district court on 18 February 1932, and although the U.S. Supreme Court eventually upheld Sterling in 1940, the final decision came too late to vindicate the governor. Again facing Ma Ferguson in the 1932 Democratic primary, Sterling (a notoriously poor public speaker) was a victim of his own overconfidence, the depression, and voter fraud, and he lost the runoff primary by 3,300 votes. An embittered Sterling returned to private life and spent the balance of his life attempting to recoup his personal fortune, which had largely evaporated in the early stages of the depression. Successful enough to donate $100,000 to Texas Christian University, he died in Fort Worth, Texas.

A man of vision and drive in business, Sterling was unable to transfer that success to the public sector. Nevertheless, he was an important figure in the early days of the Texas oil fields and a major force in the creation of Humble Oil (now a part of Exxon Corporation).

• The papers of Ross Shaw Sterling are held at the Texas State Library in Austin. He was also the subject of Warner E. Mills, Jr., "The Public Career of a Texas Conservative: A Biography of Ross Shaw Sterling" (Ph.D. diss., Johns Hopkins Univ., 1956). The best secondary source of information on Sterling remains Henrietta M. Larson and Kenneth W. Porter, *History of Humble Oil and Refining Company: A Study in Industrial Growth* (1959). Also useful are Ralph W. Steen, *Twentieth Century Texas: An Economic and Social History* (1942), and Warner E. Mills, *Martial Law in East Texas* (1960). An obituary is in the *Houston Post*, 26 Mar. 1949.

EDWARD L. LACH, JR.

STERN, Bill. *See* Stern, William.

STERN, Curt (30 Aug. 1902–23 Oct. 1981), geneticist, was born in Hamburg, Germany, the son of Barned Stern, a dental supplies salesman, and Anna Liebrecht, a schoolteacher. Stern's youthful interest in natural history led him to study biology at the University of Berlin, where he received his Ph.D. in 1923 at the early age of twenty-one for work on mitosis (cell division) and the physiology of freshwater unicellular organisms. He became a scientific investigator in Richard Goldschmidt's department of the Kaiser Wilhelm Institute in Berlin (1923–1933). Fascinated by genetics, he wrote a manuscript arguing against Goldschmidt's interpretation of "crossing over," a rare phenomenon in which the offspring of certain matings exhibited specific unusual combinations of traits that were expected to co-occur as a group. Stern supported the view held by T. H. Morgan of Columbia University that this phenomenon is caused by the interchange of genetic material between the two members of a pair of chromosomes. Such interchange had the consequence that certain genes were no longer on the same chromosome, and thus their associated traits occurred independently of each other. Perhaps in consequence, Goldschmidt arranged an International Board of Education (Rockefeller Foundation) grant for Stern to work under Morgan on fruit fly (*Drosophila*) genetics from 1924 to 1926. At Columbia Stern specialized in correlating genetic changes with visible chromosomal changes.

He soon discovered that the Y chromosome, which contains genes that determine sex and is normally found only in males, contains other genes. The unusual behavior of those genes led Stern into a long series of investigations of the effects of gene dosage and the mechanics of "dosage compensation," which protects against the effects of extra copies of a gene.

Returning to Germany in 1926, he finally obtained one of the first clearcut cytological proofs that crossing over involves the exchange of chromosome segments (1931); Barbara McClintock and Harriet Creighton, using maize, supplied a parallel demonstration the same year. During this period Stern served as an important advocate of Morgan's interpretation of Mendelian genetics. His major review articles, widely appreciated on both sides of the Atlantic, marshaled the evidence with great clarity.

In 1931 Stern married an American, Evelyn Sommerfeld; they had three daughters. Stern in 1932 obtained another Rockefeller grant to work with Morgan's group, by then at the California Institute of Technology, and he attended the Sixth International Congress of Genetics in Ithaca, New York, en route to Pasadena. Hitler's takeover in Germany occurred before the completion of his fellowship in 1933. Being Jewish, Stern feared the dangers posed by the Nazis. Accordingly, his wife traveled to Germany to explore the situation. On the advice of Stern's German colleagues, the family remained in the United States. Stern became a U.S. citizen in 1939.

After taking a temporary position at Western Reserve University, Stern moved to the University of Rochester, where he was a research associate (1933–1935), assistant professor of zoology (1935–1937), associate professor (1937–1941), and professor and head of the Department of Zoology and of the Division of Biology (1941–1947). A major finding of his Rochester years was that crossing over can occur in somatic cells as well as in germ cells, yielding organisms with patches of genetically aberrant tissue. Working with *Drosophila*, Stern developed this unusual condition into a major tool for exploring the control of development: if a patch of tissue of an unusual genetic constitution occurs at a particular place, will it behave in accordance with some preestablished pattern determined by the organism or will it behave "autonomously," according to its own genetic constitution?

During the war he headed a group that studied the biological effects of low doses of radiation. The results indicated that there is no "safe" threshold below which radiation is not harmful. This finding proved important in postwar debates about nuclear safety and earned Stern membership on an Atomic Energy Commission advisory committee regarding the biological effects of radiation (1950–1953).

In consequence of a long-standing interest, he published an extremely influential textbook, *Principles of Human Genetics*. Its three editions (1949, 1960, 1973) sold more than 62,000 copies and were translated into at least seven languages. From 1947 on a substantial part of Stern's work aimed at synthesizing the knowledge of human genetics and training investigators in that field. He was also a pioneer in providing genetic counseling on the basis of modern knowledge.

From 1947 to 1970 Stern was professor of zoology (and, from 1958, of genetics) at the University of California, Berkeley. Although he was increasingly occupied with human genetics, he concentrated his experimental research on *Drosophila* because of the difficulty of conducting appropriate experiments on humans. He was able to show that some sort of "prepattern" controls many features of organismal development. If a cell has the right genes to manifest a certain property (e.g., to grow a bristle), it still must be at the right place at the right time as determined by the prepattern, or it will not express that property. He devoted many studies to analyzing the sources of prepatterns and the effects they could call forth in cells that had different combinations of genes. The underlying problems are both important and difficult; Stern's work in this domain was continued in the 1980s and 1990s by his collaborators, students, and intellectual descendants.

Stern was an extraordinarily clear expositor and teacher whose high standards of clarity and of scientific proof were tempered by personal modesty. These traits help explain his wide influence over the next generation of geneticists, especially when combined with his publication of more than 200 scientific articles, supervision of some thirty doctoral students, editorship of *Genetics* (1947–1951), high offices (president of the Genetics Society of America, the American Society of Human Genetics, the American Society of Zoologists, and the Thirteenth International Congress of Genetics), and his interests in human genetics, genetic counseling, and the history of genetics. Ironically, after retirement he was afflicted with Parkinson's disease, a condition the genetic basis of which had long been of interest to human geneticists. He died in Sacramento, California.

• Stern's papers, including voluminous correspondence, manuscripts, and reprints, are at the American Philosophical Society, Philadelphia, and are described in B. Glass, *A Guide to the Genetics Collections of the American Philosophical Society* (1988). A biography and scientific bibliography can be found in James V. Neel, "Curt Stern," National Academy of Sciences, *Biographical Memoirs* (1987). Two autobiographical essays describe his scientific work: "A Geneticist's Journey," in *Chromosomes and Cancer*, ed. J. German (1974), and "From Crossing Over to Developmental Genetics," *Stadler Genetics Symposia* 1–2 (1971). The cytological proof of crossing over appears in "Zytologisch-genetische Untersuchungen als Beweise für die Morgansche Theorie des Faktorenaustausches" (Cytological-genetic investigations as proofs of Morgan's theory of factor exchange), *Biologisches Zentralblatt* 51 (1931): 547–87. In addition to his *Principles of Human Genetics*, he published two other books in English: *Genetic Mosaics and Other Essays* (1968) and, with Eva Sherwood, *The Origin of Genetics* (1966), which contains translations and reprints of Mendel's original papers and related papers in the history of genetics. Among his essays for a wider audience are "The Journey, Not the Goal," *Scientific Monthly* 58 (1944): 96–100; "In Praise of Diversity," *American Zoologist* 2 (1962): 575–79; "Genes and People," *Perspective on Biology and Medicine* 10 (1967): 520–23; and "The Continuity of Genetics," *Daedelus* 99 (1970): 882–908.

RICHARD M. BURIAN

STERN, Edith Rosenwald (31 May 1895–11 Sept. 1980), philanthropist and social reformer, was born in Chicago, Illinois, the daughter of Julius Rosenwald, a wealthy business executive and philanthropist, and Augusta Nusbaum, also of German Jewish descent. Edith Rosenwald grew up during the years when her father, as head of Sears, Roebuck and Co., amassed an enormous personal fortune, which he used to endow numerous educational institutions, including many for African Americans, and other philanthropic endeavors. Her father's efforts on behalf of those who were less fortunate, coupled with his religiously inspired beliefs in justice and sharing, inculcated in Edith, the middle of five children, a lifelong sense of social purpose and commitment.

After attending the progressive Chicago University Elementary School, Edith entered a local high school until age fifteen, when she was sent for a year to a girls' boarding school in Dresden, Germany. After returning to the United States, she married Germon F. Sulzberger in 1913. Divorced from Sulzberger in September 1920, she married Edgar Bloom Stern, a prominent New Orleans businessman, in June 1921 and moved with him to New Orleans.

Within six years the couple had three children, and in her self-defining role as Mrs. Edgar Stern, Edith began to pursue socially minded pursuits related to children. In 1926, for example, when their oldest child, Edgar, Jr., was ready to begin nursery school, she leased a building adjacent to the campus of Newcomb College, hired graduate students to supervise her child as well as the children of about a dozen friends, and thus founded the New Orleans Nursery School. In addition to providing financial support, Stern, as president of the board, played an active role in overseeing operations at the facility, which, in 1939–1940, was incorporated into the college as the Newcomb Nursery School.

In 1929, when Stern's oldest son was ready to begin elementary school, she established Metairie Park Country Day School, a progressive coeducational school in what was then a rural area of greater New Orleans. In addition to giving money for the purchase of fourteen acres of land, Stern participated in the search for a headmaster. The school, which opened with fifty-six pupils, is still in operation.

As president of the New Orleans Cotton Exchange and of the New Orleans Community Chest, as well as a trustee of Tuskegee University and a member of the board of directors of the United States Chamber of Commerce, Edgar Stern was a highly respected New Orleanian, and in 1930 he was made planning chairman of the fundraising drive to merge two local African-American schools, Straight College and New Orleans College, into Dillard University. At the university's founding, he became the first president of its board of directors, a post that Edith Stern filled after his death in 1959.

In addition to civic concerns, Stern also participated in local politics. In January 1946, on the Saturday night before the mayoral election in which reform candidate deLesseps Story "Chep" Morrison faced a seemingly impossible challenge against incumbent Robert S. Maestri, Stern helped lead a highly successful women's political event called the March of Brooms. Hundreds of women, each shouldering a household broom (Stern had secured hundreds from Sears), marched shoulder to shoulder for several blocks to the theme "A Clean Sweep for Morrison" before arriving at a massive rally at the Jerusalem Temple. After Morrison's phenomenal win, the new mayor appointed Stern to the New Orleans Parkway and Park Commission and named her executive secretary of the public housing projects in the city. Her political work was nationally recognized in 1951, when she was named as Louisiana's representative to a 48-woman commission formed to advise the Defense Department on issues related to women in the armed forces.

Also in the early 1950s, Stern, along with several friends and a small paid staff, worked as the Voters' Registration League to purge the voter registration rolls of ineligible voters, that is, persons who had long been dead, or had moved away, or had never existed. Their efforts were widely reported by the local press in late November, early December 1951, when Stern, as league treasurer, alleged that Registrar of Voters William S. Farrell (a member of the Old Regulars political machine) had eliminated opponents of the Old Regulars from the voting lists and designated able-bodied, literate voters as disabled or illiterate so that poll workers could "assist" them and thereby influence their votes. It was a struggle for the league to secure the voting rolls, but once they had them the women were able to challenge the "disabled" status of many persons listed on them, and that same year the number of voters registered as disabled or illiterate was reduced from nearly 10,000 to 4,075. To benefit the campaigns of candidates who were not politically affiliated, the league compiled and sold lists of registered voters, information that would be hard to come by otherwise. League members also encouraged greater participation in the democratic process by contacting voters and urging them to vote.

As president of the New Orleans Garden Study Club and as a member of the Conservation Committee of the Garden Clubs of America, Stern was well suited to the Parkway and Park Commission post, itself a reflection of perhaps her greatest legacy, the beautiful public gardens at the Sterns' magnificent home, "Longue Vue," named for the Hudson River inn where the couple had become engaged. Edith Stern later willed Longue Vue, along with $5 million to maintain it, to the city.

Through the Stern Fund the Sterns contributed millions to various progressive causes, among them the work of consumer advocate Ralph Nader and of biologist and later Citizens Party presidential candidate Barry Commoner as well as the Fund for Investigative Journalism. Yet Edith Stern's personal convictions were manifested in private ways as well. In 1930, for example, she gave a private dinner party at which a few dozen guests were treated to the gorgeous contralto voice of Marian Anderson, whom Stern had earlier heard singing at her cook's black Baptist church. Years later, after District Attorney Jim Garrison had arrested local businessman Clay Shaw in connection with the assassination of President John Kennedy, Stern publicly befriended him—a particularly bold act given that she had been a big supporter of the slain president and had entertained him in her home when he was still a U.S. senator. Many prominent people were feted at Longue Vue, among them Adlai Stevenson, Eleanor Roosevelt, Chaim Herzog, and, in the entertainment field, Jack Benny and Ethel Merman, among others.

The arts was another area of interest for the Sterns, who in 1957 bolstered the struggling New Orleans Symphony with a gift of $300,000. Edith Stern was also a major supporter of the New Orleans Museum of Art (also known as the Delgado Museum) and served on its board of trustees. In addition to contributing several major works from her private collection and bequeathing Longue Vue to the museum, she financed a new wing and, with New Orleans architect Arthur Q. Davis, secured for the museum a collection of colonial period paintings from the Cuzco school. In 1961 President Kennedy named her to the National Cultural Center Advisory Committee on the Arts.

A financial backer of Jewish organizations and a supporter of the state of Israel, in 1971 Stern received the Hannah Solomon Award from the National Council of Jewish Women. In recognition of her civic service, she also received the Weiss Brotherhood Award from the National Conference of Christians and Jews. In its 26 January 1968 issue, *Life* magazine featured her, photographed in full color at Longue Vue, as one of the "Grandes Dames Who Grace America," and in

its centennial issue in June 1977, the New Orleans *States-Item* referred to the Sterns as the city's outstanding philanthropists in the newspaper's first century of existence. Stern was most proud, however, of the *Times-Picayune* Loving Cup, the city's most prestigious civic honor, which she received in 1964. It was especially meaningful because Edgar Stern had been the recipient in 1930, and the Sterns thus became the only couple in the city to receive the cup individually.

Like her father before her, Edith Stern used her good fortune to become a significant force for culture, art, philanthropy, and progressive political ideals. Intelligent with an organizational bent, she found ways of developing her personal contributions into established cultural institutions maintained by her adopted city. After her death, in New Orleans, she was buried beside her husband at Longue Vue.

• For more information on Stern's life and family, see Gerda Weissmann Klein, *A Passion for Sharing: The Life of Edith Rosenwald Stern* (1984). A portrait of Stern can be found in Edwin Adams Davis, *The Story of Louisiana*, vol. 2 (1960), p. 14. For local press coverage of her activities with the Voters' Registration League, see the *Times-Picayune*, 29 Nov. 1951, pp. 1 and 5, and 4 Dec. 1951, pp. 1 and 2; the *Item*, 29 Nov. 1951, p. 15; and the *States*, 29 Nov. 1951, p. 8, and 19 Dec. 1951, p. 4. An obituary and related editorial are in the *Times-Picayune/States-Item*, 12 Sept. 1980.

EDGAR LEON NEWMAN

STERN, Elizabeth Gertrude (14 Feb. 1889?–9 Jan. 1954), social worker and writer, was raised in Pittsburgh, Pennsylvania, as the daughter of Aaron Kleine Levin, a cantor and rabbinical assistant, and his wife, Sarah Rubenstein. The particulars of Stern's birth, however, remain uncertain. Although she consistently maintained that she was born in Königsberg, Prussia, and came to the United States with her parents, the Levins, in 1892, her oldest son revealed in 1988 that his mother was actually born in Pittsburgh to Christian Limburg, a merchant and store owner, and Elizabeth Morgan. Like her husband, Leon Stern, whom she married in 1911, Elizabeth Stern apparently was born out of wedlock, raised by Jewish foster parents, and claimed to be Jewish in order to hide her true, illegitimate origins. Although it may be impossible to ever establish with certainty the true circumstances surrounding Stern's birth, if her eldest son's story is even partly true, it sheds new light not only on Stern's literary representations of Jewish women, but also on her own self-representation as an Eastern European immigrant born into a devoutly religious Jewish family.

After attending local public schools in Pittsburgh, she became a student at the University of Pittsburgh, graduating in 1910. She subsequently moved to New York and enrolled in the New York School of Philanthropy (later renamed the New York School of Social Work) where she met her future husband, fellow student Leon Stern. In the years immediately following their marriage, they worked together on a number of projects. In Galveston, Texas, during 1912–1913, they assisted in Jacob Schiff's efforts to reroute American Jewish immigration from New York to the Southwest. A decade later they coauthored *A Friend at Court* (1923), a "casebook" of a female probation officer based on actual cases with which they were familiar.

The mother of two, Stern actively pursued her interests in both social work and writing. In addition to her work in Galveston, she served as assistant to the director of the Yorkville Community East Side House Settlement in New York (1911), director of welfare work for the John Wanamaker store in Philadelphia (1918–1919), director of welfare work at the Temple Israel Community Center in New York (1923), and executive director of the Council House in New York (1924). In recognition of her achievements as a social worker, she earned an honorary master's degree from the University of Pittsburgh in 1918.

Elizabeth Stern began writing for local newspapers as early as 1908. By 1914 she had become a feature writer for the *Philadelphia Sunday Press* and soon after a columnist for the *Philadelphia Sunday Record*. From 1924 through 1926 she published several feature articles in the *New York Times*, and by 1926 she was writing for the *New York Evening World* as well as for the *Philadelphia Public Ledger*, for which she assumed the pen name Eleanor Morton. After 1926 almost all of her nonfiction works were written under this name, including her 1933–1937 column for the *Philadelphia Inquirer*, her collection of essays, *Not All Laughter* (1937), and her three biographies: *Memories: The Life of Margaret McAvoy Scott* (1943), an American businesswoman who, like Stern, successfully combined a career with motherhood and marriage; *Josiah White: Prince of Pioneers* (1947), a Quaker inventor; and *The Women Behind Mahatma Gandhi* (1954), a study of Gandhi's wife and his many female disciples. At the same time, she wrote short stories for various magazines and newspapers (including the *Ladies' Home Journal* and the *American Hebrew*) as well as several novels, either under her own name (*This Ecstasy* [1927]; *A Marriage Was Made* [1928]; and *Gambler's Wife* [1931]) or, as with *When Love Comes to Woman* (1929), under the name of Leah Morton.

Stern first adopted the pen name of Leah Morton in 1926 with the publication of her most popular and critically acclaimed work, *I Am a Woman—and a Jew*. Claiming to be the autobiography of an Eastern European Jewish immigrant who comes to the United States as a child and spends her youth in the Jewish section of a small city situated along the Ohio River, *I Am a Woman—and a Jew* focuses on its author's struggle to meet the demands placed on her as a social worker, wife, mother, and writer. It examines her struggle to come to terms with her Jewishness, discovering, after years of soul-searching, what being a Jew actually means to her. Although contemporary reviewers assumed that *I Am a Woman—and a Jew* was, as it claimed to be, the autobiography of its author, soon unmasked as Elizabeth Stern, it was in fact an autobiographical novel. Though many of the particulars of the novel were drawn from Stern's own life (or, at least her

life with the Levins and later with Leon Stern), the novel's two central dramas—the heroine's struggle to establish a career, despite her husband's skepticism and at times resistance, and the internal and familial conflicts that her marrying a non-Jew created—were fictional in nature. *I Am a Woman—and a Jew* is a rare and valuable record of a woman's struggle to come to terms with Jewish self-identity. Like Stern's other autobiographical novel, *My Mother and I*, it was first published as an anonymous piece in the *Ladies' Home Journal*, in 1916, and expanded and published in book form a year later with the author identified as E. G. Stern. *I Am a Woman—and a Jew* details an odyssey that continues to reflect both the spiritual journey of many modern Jews, especially women, and the generational tensions inherent in any immigrant group's struggle to become part of American society.

The extent to which Stern found religious meaning in Judaism either in her childhood or as an adult remains unclear, but by 1928 she had joined the Philadelphia Ethical Society, a branch of Ethical Culture. She later became a member of the Religious Society of Friends, devoting much of her time and energy to various Quaker organizations. Elizabeth Stern died in Philadelphia. The author of thirteen books that received much popular and critical attention, her greatest legacy remains her writings.

• Stern's papers can be found in the Quaker Collection at the Haverford College Library. No book-length critical study of her or her work has yet been written but see T. Noel Stern, *Secret Family* (privately published, 1988), and Ellen M. Umansky, "Representations of Jewish Women in the Works and Life of Elizabeth Stern," *Modern Judaism* 13 (1993): 165–76. A critical analysis of *I Am a Woman—and a Jew* can be found in Ellen M. Umansky's introduction to the 1986 reprint of Leah Morton (pseud.), *I Am a Woman—and a Jew* (1926; repr. 1986). Obituaries are in the *Friends' Intelligencer*, 23 Jan. 1954; the (Philadelphia) *Friend* 127 (1954): 248; and the *New York Times*, 10 Jan. 1954.

ELLEN M. UMANSKY

STERN, Otto (17 Feb. 1888–17 Aug. 1969), physicist, was born in Sohrau, Germany, the son of Oskar Stern, a miller and grain merchant, and Eugenie Rosenthal. In 1892 the family moved to Breslau, where Stern completed his early education. He attended the universities of Freiburg in Breisgau, Munich, and Breslau as an undergraduate, and received a Ph.D. in physical chemistry from the University of Breslau in 1912. As a postdoctoral associate of the eminent physicist Albert Einstein at the University of Prague in 1912 and the University of Zurich in 1913, he gained his first exposure to the emerging theories of contemporary physics that would coalesce into quantum mechanics in the next decade. In 1913 he and Einstein coauthored a theoretical paper concerning the vibrational energy retained in a diatomic hydrogen molecule when its temperature reaches absolute zero. That same year, he published an ingenious paper on the theoretical calculation of the entropy constant of the perfect monatomic gas. By combining classical statistical mechanics with some of the new quantum concepts being advanced by Einstein and others, he was able to lend support to the theoretical conclusions of the German physicist Otto Sackur, whose strict reliance on poorly understood quantum concepts alone had left him on shaky ground.

In 1914 Stern became an unsalaried lecturer at the University of Frankfurt but was soon drafted into the German army as a private and sent to the Russian front as a meteorologist. He was later a noncommissioned officer and spent some time in France before finishing out World War I doing military research in a War Department laboratory in Berlin. Throughout the war, Stern's military duties left him with enough research time that he was able to publish two theoretical papers immediately after the war ended concerning the validity of the Nernst Heat Theorem (in essence the third law of thermodynamics) in solid solutions and mixed crystals. In 1918 he returned to Frankfurt as the assistant director of the Institute for Theoretical Physics.

In 1919 Stern began the first of many experiments utilizing the molecular beam. Invented by the French physicist Louis Dunoyer in 1911, the molecular beam was of little use until Stern grasped its potential to shed light on molecular behavior. Previously, Stern's interest in physics had been strictly theoretical, but upon learning of Dunoyer's invention he determined to use it to test various theories that had never been proved or disproved experimentally. By evaporating silver atoms in an oven, then releasing them in a gaseous stream through a narrow orifice so that they entered a large vacuum in the configuration of a thin beam, he found that he could observe the atoms' behavior in a free, or noncolliding, state and make measurements using macroscopic tools. His first experiment with the beam was to verify the theoretical calculations of the nineteenth-century Scottish physicist James Clerk Maxwell concerning the velocity of gas molecules. By placing two rotating toothed wheels in the path of the beam and then making a few simple calculations regarding the atoms that passed through gaps in both wheels, he was able to determine the velocity of these atoms. The results of this experiment, published in 1920, proved that Maxwell had been correct.

Stern next used the molecular beam to investigate the magnetic moment, or the strength and direction of magnetism, of atoms. Whereas classical physics posited that the magnetic moment could potentially take any direction, a new theory derived from the work of the Danish physicist Niels Bohr and the German physicist Arnold Sommerfeld known as space quantization suggested that the magnetic moment could have only two directions, either the same as or opposite to the direction of the magnetic field. With the assistance of a Frankfurt colleague, Walther Gerlach, Stern devised a way to prove once and for all which theory was correct. By beaming silver atoms between the poles of a nonuniform magnet, Stern reasoned that the beam would either become much broader (the classical prediction) or split into two narrower beams (the space quantization prediction). The so-called Stern-Gerlach experiment, in actuality a number of experiments conducted between 1920 and 1922 whose results were published in five separate papers, resulted in a split beam. By offering further evidence that classical physics could not properly explain atomic behavior, the experiment gave further momentum to the development of quantum mechanics.

In 1921 Stern accepted a position as associate professor of theoretical physics at the University of Rostock but left two years later to become both a full professor of physical chemistry at the University of Hamburg and the director of its as-yet-unfinished Institute of Physical Chemistry. He organized a laboratory dedicated to magnetic beam research and devoted much time and attention to developing an apparatus that could produce a very narrow beam of high intensity. He used this new facility and equipment to evaluate the premise of the French physicist Louis de Broglie, who in 1924 suggested that atomic particles had wave properties and then calculated theoretically what the wavelengths were. When Stern passed a beam of helium gas through the rotating toothed wheels onto a lithium fluoride crystal, the beam diffracted around the crystal in a wavelike pattern. He was able to calculate the wavelength by determining the velocity, as in the Stern-Gerlach experiment, and by plotting the spacing between the helium atoms on the crystal. The results of the experiment, published in 1931, attested to the correctness of Broglie's prediction.

Stern's most important experiments with the molecular beam determined the magnetic moment of the proton and the rotational magnetic moment of the hydrogen molecule, and estimated the magnetic moment of the deuteron, a positively charged particle consisting of a proton and a neutron. The English physicist Paul Dirac had postulated that the ratio of the proton's moment to that of the electron was equal to the inverse ratio of their masses; however, Stern showed that the proton's moment was more than twice as strong as Dirac had predicted it to be. He also demonstrated that theoretical predictions of the moments of the hydrogen molecule and the deuteron were wide of the mark. Stern published the findings of all three experiments in 1933. On the basis of these experiments with the molecular beam, particularly those concerning the magnetic moment of the proton, he was awarded the Nobel Prize in physics for 1943.

In 1933 Germany's Nazi government began dismissing Jewish faculty members, including a number of Stern's colleagues, from German universities. Although Stern was exempted temporarily because of his prior military service, he resigned from both the University of Hamburg and the Institute of Physical Chemistry in protest. He immigrated to the United States that same year, became affiliated with the Carnegie Institute of Technology in Pittsburgh, Pennsylvania, as a research professor of physics, and organized another molecular beam laboratory. Unfortunately, despite the generous support of the Buhl Foundation, the shortage of funds for research during the Great Depression prevented Stern from achieving in the United States the same kind of experimental success he had enjoyed in Germany. He became a naturalized U.S. citizen in 1939 and served as a consultant to the War Department during World War II. He was elected to membership in the Royal Danish Academy in 1936 and the National Academy of Sciences in 1945. In 1946 the confirmed bachelor retired to Berkeley, California, where two of his sisters lived and where he had taught as a visiting professor in 1930. He continued to experiment and publish until a few years before his death there.

Emilio Segrè, the Italian-born physicist who won the Nobel Prize in physics for 1959, described Stern as "one of the greatest physicists of [the twentieth] century." Having developed the molecular beam as a tool for investigating the nature and properties of atomic particles, Stern contributed greatly to the emergence of quantum mechanics in the 1920s by providing experimental data to either prove or disprove several theories related to molecular, atomic, and subatomic behavior.

• Stern's papers are in the archives of the American Physical Society. An autobiographical tape dictated by Stern is located in the archives of the Eidgenossische Technische Hochschule in Zurich, Switzerland. His biography and a complete bibliography of his scholarly work appear in Emilio Segrè, "Otto Stern," National Academy of Sciences, *Biographical Memoirs* 43 (1973): 215–36. Many details concerning his days at the University of Hamburg are included in Immanuel Estermann, ed., *Recent Research in Molecular Beams: A Collection of Papers Dedicated to Otto Stern on the Occasion of his Seventieth Birthday* (1959). An obituary is in the *New York Times*, 19 Aug. 1969.

CHARLES W. CAREY, JR.

STERN, William (1 July 1907–19 Nov. 1971), sportscaster, was born in Rochester, New York, the son of Isaac Stern, a wealthy clothing manufacturer and merchant, and Lena Reis. Bill Stern, who was spoiled by his father, attended public school in Rochester and Hackley Preparatory School in Tarrytown, New York, from which he was expelled for being a truant. After completing his education at Casadilla Preparatory School in Ithaca, New York, he attended the Pennsylvania Military College in Chester, Pennsylvania. Following his graduation in 1930, Stern went to work in his father's retail clothing business. An interest in the theater brought him to New York, where he worked from 1931 until 1935 as a stage manager at the Japanese Gardens, the Roxy theater, and Radio City Music Hall.

While working at Radio City, Stern got his first career break. Self-confident and brash, in 1934 he talked his way into narrating two minutes of the Navy–William and Mary football game with NBC's renowned sportscaster Graham McNamee. Though the reviews were favorable, NBC released Stern after only a few games because of his arrogance and conceit. Unable to find further work in radio, in June 1935 he joined Stein's Stores, a chain of men's clothiers that had expressed interest in sponsoring college football broad-

casts. Stein's sent Stern to Shreveport, Louisiana, where he went to work announcing Centenary College games with Jack Gelzer for station KWKH.

Stern's broadcasting stint there ended in October 1935, following an accident that irrevocably altered his life. Returning to Shreveport following the Centenary–University of Texas game in Austin, he was involved in a head-on automobile collision that cost him his left leg. The amputation required a lengthy recovery period that involved therapy with morphine and other painkillers as well as sleeping pills. Over the next twenty years Stern's real and psychosomatic pain, both from the accident and a recurrent kidney ailment, prompted him to seek relief in narcotics until he became addicted to morphine, Demerol, and sleeping pills.

During this period, Stern became engaged to a distant cousin, Harriet May, who encouraged him to return to sportscasting. In 1936, NBC once again hired him to join their sportscasting team of McNamee, Bill Slater, and Don Wilson. Stern's addiction did not affect his sportscasting abilities for some years. Nor did it disrupt his plans for his marriage, which took place in April 1937; the Sterns had three children. By 1939 Stern's deep voice and engaging on-air personality brought him stardom at NBC.

For thirteen consecutive years, from 1940 until 1952, *Radio Daily* named Stern the most popular radio announcer. In 1939 he broadcast his first Rose Bowl after the bowl committee overcame its objection to having a Jew broadcast the game. That same year he announced the first live televised sporting event ever broadcast, a baseball game between Princeton and Columbia on 17 May. In 1939 he also began hosting the weekly "Colgate Sports Newsreel," a position that he held until the sponsor dropped the show in 1951. Stern's guests included personalities such as Eleanor Roosevelt and Mickey Rooney, as well as Babe Ruth and Jack Dempsey. The fifteen-minute program consisted of interviews and vignettes with dramatic, often fictionalized, twists, such as Stern's account of Abner Doubleday inventing baseball because of Abraham Lincoln's deathbed request, or Thomas Edison's deafness resulting from a beaning by Jesse James. Stern defended his fanciful stories by claiming that his was not a sports show: "it's entertainment for the same kind of people who listen to Jack Benny." With Stern as host, "Sports Newsreel" became the first successful national sports radio show. At the time Stern was earning more than $200,000 per year.

Stern also enhanced his celebrity status by appearing as himself in brief roles in such motion pictures as *The Pride of the Yankees* (1942), *Stage Door Canteen* (1943), and *West Point Story* (1950). Stern organized NBC's sports division in 1940 and served as its director from then until 1952. In 1951 he earned an Emmy for his radio work.

In the 1950s Stern's drug addiction began to seriously interfere with his radio broadcasting. After NBC removed him as sports director in 1952 and relegated him solely to the radio booth, Stern left NBC for a lucrative three-year contract with the ABC network in 1953. Although his addiction had affected his work at NBC, August Busch, president of Anheuser-Busch Brewing Company, convinced ABC to hire Stern for a daily sports show that the brewery would sponsor. In return, Anheuser-Busch paid Stern $125,000 a year on top of the $55,000 the network would pay. Success, though, did not dampen the insecurity and fear of failure that had plagued him from his earliest days in radio. He repeatedly sought relief in narcotics.

Finally, on 2 January 1956, a date he later referred to as his "personal Armeggedon," a drugged Stern arrived late for the broadcast of the Sugar Bowl. When he took the microphone he stumbled over his words and finally froze. He had to be helped from the broadcast booth. After a few months ABC permitted Stern to return to radio as host of a daily fifteen-minute sports show. His drug problem remained, however, and in June, at his wife's insistence, he checked himself into the Institute of Living in Hartford, Connecticut. In December he walked out of the institute free of his dependence on drugs. Stern's account of his addiction and comeback is told in his autobiography, *The Taste of Ashes* (1959).

Stern again returned to radio in the spring of 1957, and that fall he began a nightly sports show for the Mutual Radio Network that he hosted until shortly before his death in Rye, New York. In 1984 Stern became a charter member of the American Sportscasters Association Hall of Fame. His wit and nimble mind enabled him to quickly cover on-air mistakes and endeared him to his fans. In one incident, he was calling an apparent touchdown run by Army's fullback Doc Blanchard when he realized that halfback Glenn Davis was the actual ball carrier. He quickly invented a lateral from Blanchard to Davis just shy of the goal line. Stern earned a reputation as one of the country's best-known and most capable radio sportscasters with a style that often blurred the line between fact and fiction.

• Sources of information on Stern include "More Lateral than Literal," *Time*, 6 June 1949, p. 79, and "Bill Stern," *Collier's*, 29 April 1959, p. 78. An obituary is in the *New York Times*, 21 Nov. 1971.

BRIAN S. BUTLER

STERNBERG, George Miller (8 June 1838–3 Nov. 1915), physician and bacteriologist, was born at Hartwick Seminary in Otsego County, New York, the son of Levi Sternberg, a Lutheran minister, and Margaret Levering Miller, a linguist and theologian. He received his early schooling at Hartwick Seminary, operated by the Evangelical Lutheran church. Beginning at age sixteen he taught in rural schools for three years to help support his family. Sternberg then returned to teach science and mathematics at Hartwick Seminary and began to study medicine with Horace Lathrop, a doctor from Cooperstown, New York. Following a course of medical lectures in Buffalo, he entered the College of Physicians and Surgeons in New York City. He received his M.D. in 1860.

When the Civil War began Sternberg was commissioned on 28 May 1861 as an assistant surgeon in the U.S. Army and assigned to the command of General George Sykes in the Army of the Potomac. At the battle of Bull Run, Confederate soldiers captured him when the Union army retreated. Allowed enough freedom to care for sick prisoners, Sternberg escaped and rejoined his unit. He remained under General Sykes's command until a bout with typhoid fever sent him north to convalesce. For the rest of the Civil War he held positions as executive officer of the U.S. General Hospital at Portsmouth Grove, Rhode Island; assistant to the medical director of the Department of the Gulf in New Orleans; assistant medical director at Columbus, Ohio; and director of the U.S. General Hospital at Cleveland, Ohio.

After the Civil War the army sent Sternberg to the western frontier, first to Jefferson Barracks, Missouri, and then to Fort Harker, Kansas. Sternberg encountered the first of many epidemics in July 1867 when cholera swept through Fort Harker. It claimed among its victims his wife of less than two years, Louisa Russell of Cooperstown, New York; they had no children. During his stint as post surgeon at Fort Riley, Kansas, Sternberg was breveted captain and then major for duty under fire against the Arapaho and Cheyenne in 1868. He married Martha L. Pattison of Indianapolis in September 1869. She often helped with his research; they had no children.

As an army surgeon Sternberg moved frequently from post to post. Wherever the army stationed him, he made natural history observations and sent Indian artifacts, fossils, and geological and biological specimens to the Army Medical Museum and the Smithsonian Institution and to respected naturalists like Joseph Leidy and Edward D. Cope, both of Philadelphia. At some posts he had enough leisure to engage in private practice and to pursue his scientific interests from makeshift home laboratories. At Fort Riley he improved the anemometer for recording wind speed and direction, and in 1870 he patented a thermoregulator that maintained even temperatures in hospital wards.

Sternberg is best known for his work on yellow fever, which he began in 1870 during an epidemic at Governor's Island in New York harbor. While stationed at Fort Barrancas, Florida, from 1872 to 1875, he encountered two yellow fever epidemics, nearly dying of the disease himself in 1875. As a result he acquired permanent immunity. The first of his many scientific articles on the disease, "An Inquiry into the Modus Operandi of the Yellow Fever Poison," appeared in the *New Orleans Medical and Surgical Journal* (n.s., 3 [1875]: 1–23).

In 1876, after recuperating in Europe for six months, Sternberg was assigned to Fort Walla Walla (now Washington). He saw action during the war with the Nez Perce Indians at the battle on the Clearwater in 1877 and was breveted lieutenant colonel. In Walla Walla he began his pioneering career in bacteriology with a study of surgical disinfectants. He mastered French and translated Antoine Magnin's *Bacteria* (1880), the first comprehensive text on bacteriology published in the United States. He supplemented the second edition of the translation (1884) with his own photomicrographs and accounts of his original work. Although self-taught, Sternberg's careful research on disinfectants earned him respect and gave credibility to the emerging science of bacteriology.

The army assigned Sternberg to the National Board of Health, first appointing him to the Havana Yellow Fever Commission in 1879. He found no causative agent in a microscopic search of specimens from more than 100 yellow fever patients. Over the next decade his methodical research discredited several proposed microbial candidates. His *Report on the Etiology and Prevention of Yellow Fever* (1890) quieted similar premature claims for years. In New Orleans in 1880 he began investigations of malaria that challenged the claims of Edwin Klebs and Caddero Tommasi-Crudeli to have found a malaria bacillus. In 1885 he was the first American to demonstrate in a case of malaria the protozoan that French army physician Alphonse Laveran had identified as its cause.

Sternberg continually pressed the army for his own research facilities. Whenever he was stationed near Washington, D.C., he had laboratory privileges at Johns Hopkins University in Baltimore and was an active member of its vibrant research community. Sternberg maintained a tireless pace and exacting standards, but he never hurried. His Johns Hopkins colleagues praised his modesty and sought his advice. He completed a major study of antiseptics and disinfectants there for the National Board of Health, work that won the Lomb Prize from the American Public Health Association in 1885. In 1881 he and Louis Pasteur separately discovered an organism in human saliva that caused septicemia in rabbits; Carl Friedlander later found it to be the pathogenic agent of pneumonia. Sternberg modestly downplayed his own role in its identification and named the bacterium *Micrococcus pasteuri*.

In August 1881 the army sent Sternberg to Fort Mason in San Francisco for nearly three years, despite his desire to be curator of the Army Medical Museum. He was returned to Baltimore in 1884 as examiner of recruits. Always hoping for his own laboratory, in 1886 he accepted the directorship of the new Hoagland Laboratory that was to open in 1888 at Long Island Medical College in Brooklyn. He gambled that in the interval the army would transfer him to New York; instead, yellow fever investigations sent him to Brazil, Mexico, and Havana. For two years he directed the Hoagland laboratory by correspondence from his post in San Francisco, where he wrote his 886-page *A Manual of Bacteriology* (1892). His book instantly became the standard reference in bacteriology. At last, in 1892, he got the coveted post in New York City. He established a research program at the Hoagland Laboratory to im-

prove methods for smallpox immunization. He was in the vanguard of thinking about immunity, having theorized about the role of phagocytic white blood cells several years before Elie Metchnikoff published his theory of phagocytosis in 1884. He later wrote two books on immunology: *Immunity, Protective Inoculations in Infectious Diseases and Serum Therapy* (1895) and *Infection and Immunity, with Special Reference to the Prevention of Infectious Diseases* (1903).

In May 1893 the president appointed Sternberg the army surgeon general. During his nine-year tenure he modernized the Army Medical Department and gave military physicians the educational opportunities and research facilities that he had long sought. Within a month he established the Army Medical School in Washington, D.C., to provide a laboratory-based curriculum in military medicine, surgery, and hygiene. He installed up-to-date operating rooms and laboratories in army hospitals and established a tuberculosis sanitarium at Fort Bayard, New Mexico.

In the summer of 1898 typhoid fever epidemics swept through army camps in the United States, killing thousands of volunteers who were mustering for the Spanish-American War. Sternberg and the Army Medical Corps came under severe criticism, despite their heroic efforts to provide temporary hospitals, supplies, medical personnel, and improved sanitation. President William McKinley appointed a commission chaired by Major General Grenville M. Dodge to investigate. The Dodge Commission absolved Sternberg of blame, pointing to the failure of Congress to provide funds for physician training or advance preparations and to inadequate transport for supplies. The commission's report led Congress to pass legislation that helped Sternberg reorganize the Army Medical Department and form the Medical Reserve Corps, the Army Nurse Corps, and the Corps of Dental Surgeons.

Sternberg's astute use of scientific boards sent trained bacteriologists into the field, with extraordinary results for preventive medicine. In 1898 he asked Major Walter Reed and two surgeons of the U.S. Volunteers, Edwin Shakespeare and Victor C. Vaughan, to form a Typhoid Fever Board to study the epidemic among the troops. Their report demonstrated the importance of human contact and flies in transmitting typhoid fever. In 1900 Sternberg again appointed Reed to head a Yellow Fever Commission, composed of Aristides Agramonte, James Carroll, and Jesse W. Lazear, to investigate the transmission of yellow fever after a devastating outbreak in Cuba. Their legendary experiment identified *Aedes aegypti* as its mosquito vector, a theory first suggested to Sternberg by Carlos Finlay in 1879. The result brought fame to Reed and immense satisfaction to Sternberg.

Sternberg became prominent in the medical profession as president of the American Public Health Association (1886), the American Medical Association (1897), and the Association of Military Surgeons (1900). As a member of the Washington scientific elite, he was president of the Cosmos Club, the Philosophical Society, the Biological Society, and, for twenty years, the Audubon Naturalist Society. After his retirement in 1902 he worked to provide sanatorium care for indigent tuberculosis patients and housing for the poor. He presided over the Citizens' Relief Association, and in 1907 he served on the President's Homes Commission at the request of Theodore Roosevelt.

Sternberg died in Washington, D.C., and was buried at Arlington National Cemetery in Virginia beneath a large monument dedicated to his memory. Although not the most renowned bacteriologist, Sternberg was the most important figure in American bacteriology in the 1880s, helping to codify the field in its infancy. As surgeon general he presided over the transition to a scientifically trained Army Medical Corps.

• A small collection of Sternberg correspondence is at the National Library of Medicine in Bethesda, Md. The National Archives, RG 112, contains the records of the Office of the Surgeon General. In addition to many scientific articles, Sternberg's other important works include *Photo-Micrographs and How to Make Them* (1883), *Malaria and Malarial Diseases* (1884), *A Textbook of Bacteriology* (1896; 2d rev. ed., 1901), and *Sanitary Lessons of the War and Other Papers* (1912). A biography by his wife, Martha L. Sternberg, *George Miller Sternberg: A Biography* (1920), includes his bibliography. See also John M. Gibson, *Soldier in White: The Life of General George Miller Sternberg* (1958). George Miller Sternberg, *Collected Papers* (3 vols., 1925), includes biographical sketches by various authors. Indispensable for understanding the life of a post surgeon and Sternberg's work as army surgeon general is Mary C. Gillett, *The Army Medical Department, 1865–1917* (1995). Alfred I. Tauber, "The Birth of Immunology. III: The Fate of the Phagocytosis Theory," *Cellular Immunology* 139 (1992): 505–30, assesses Sternberg's theories of immunity. Margaret Warner provides context for his research on yellow fever in "Hunting the Yellow Fever Germ: The Principle and Practice of Etiological Proof in Late Nineteenth-century America," *Bulletin of the History of Medicine* 59 (1985): 361–82.

PATRICIA PECK GOSSEL

STERNBERG, Josef von (29 May 1894–22 Dec. 1969), film director, was born Jonas Sternberg in Vienna, Austria, the son of Moses Sternberg and Serafin Singer. Little is known of Sternberg's childhood beyond a few pages of his memoirs, where he describes his family's poverty, his father's brutality, and his impressions of life in fin-de-siècle Vienna. Eventually, after traveling across the Atlantic four times, the family settled in New York City.

Sternberg left school at fifteen and worked at various jobs until joining the World Film Company as a film cutter in 1914. After wartime service with the army signal corps, he began his Hollywood career, acquiring a credit as "Josef von Sternberg" for one of the films he worked on before his first directorial effort, *The Salvation Hunters* (1924). That independent film impressed Hollywood's luminaries with its somber artistic aspirations and gained him a contract with Metro-Goldwyn-Mayer. At MGM he completed *The Exquisite Sinner* (1926), which the studio considered so commercially flawed that it had the picture reshot by another director and released under a different title. Although after seeing *A Woman of the Sea* (1926), one critic at the time placed Sternberg among America's most innovative filmmakers, the film's producer, Charlie Chaplin, was so displeased with it that he had the negative destroyed.

Sternberg's career breakthrough came at Paramount with *Underworld* (1927), a triumph of visual kinetics over pulp-magazine material. Sternberg created such bravura scenes as a light-streaked one in which a gangster's hideout is shot to pieces around him.

In 1926 he married Riza Royce; they divorced five years later.

The Last Command (1928) confirmed Sternberg's status: he directed Emil Jannings as a Russian general reduced by the revolution to playing bit parts in Hollywood spectacles. A respected, profit-earning director by 1929, Sternberg went to Berlin to direct Jannings's first talkie, *The Blue Angel* (1930). Marlene Dietrich's seductive presence in that film announced the most productive phase of Sternberg's career.

By 1935 Sternberg and Dietrich had made seven films together. She submitted herself to his exacting direction, enduring take after take while he sought the lighting effect, the angle, the gesture that turned her face into a fascinating, unfathomable icon of sexual allure. All but one of their films were set in highly romanticized locales from Morocco to China. When *Blonde Venus* (1932), Sternberg's attempt to portray middle-class American sexuality, was thwarted by studio censors, he turned to eighteenth-century Russia and Seville during carnival as hallucinatory settings for his most baroque, sardonic treatments of power and desire: *The Scarlet Empress* (1934) and *The Devil Is a Woman* (1935).

While Sternberg's productive pace slackened after he left Paramount in 1935, his creativity hardly faltered. *Crime and Punishment* (1935), one of two films he made at Columbia, is an interesting exercise in style rather than a satisfying adaptation of Dostoevsky, but the operetta *The King Steps Out* (1936) reveals an unexpectedly deft comic touch. The surviving shreds of *I, Claudius* (1937) show Sternberg working in top form before the English production was shut down. A return to MGM resulted, again, in only one film, *Sergeant Madden* (1939); Sternberg was too much his own man to work happily in Louis B. Mayer's tightly controlled organization and it was only with *The Shanghai Gesture*, released by United Artists in 1941, that he again completed a film with the bite of his earlier work.

In 1943 he married Jeanne Annette MacBride, although they were divorced two years later. About this time he made a film for the Office of War Information: *The Town*, a twelve-minute documentary on the typically American small town of Madison, Indiana.

After this, Sternberg sold his Neutra-designed California home and moved to a site on the Hudson River. Here he immersed himself in writing, sculpting, and—he claimed—Chinese philately. He was married for a third time, to Meri Ottis Wilner, in 1948; they had one son. After returning to Hollywood to make *Jet Pilot* (1950; released 1957) and *Macao* (1952) at RKO, Sternberg evidently decided that he could no longer tolerate the studio system. In 1953, invited to make a film in Japan, he undertook his most remarkable work. *The Saga of Anatahan* was based on the experiences of a group of Japanese shipwrecked during the war on a Pacific island but, as in his films with Dietrich, the exotic setting simply provides the elements for a realm where emotional complexity is reduplicated in intricate screen imagery.

In his last years, finally settled in Los Angeles, Sternberg worked on his memoirs, taught classes at UCLA, and traveled to film festivals around the world, attending retrospectives of his work and serving on juries. He died in Los Angeles with a secure reputation as one of the greatest of American film directors.

• Letters from Sternberg to film scholar Herman Weinberg (1948–1969) are in the Herman G. Weinberg Collection of the New York Public Library. Unpublished scripts for some of his films are in the MGM Archive of the University of Southern California and the Paramount Collection of the Margaret Herrick Library, Academy of Motion Picture Arts and Sciences, in Los Angeles. Sternberg's book of memoirs is *Fun in a Chinese Laundry* (1965). For biographical and critical treatment, film credits, and bibliographies, see Herman G. Weinberg, *Josef von Sternberg* (1967); Andrew Sarris, *The Films of Josef von Sternberg* (1966); John Baxter, *The Cinema of Josef von Sternberg* (1971); Peter Baxter, ed., *Sternberg* (1980); Gaylyn Studlar, *In the Realm of Pleasure* (1988); Carole Zucker, *The Idea of the Image* (1988); and Peter Baxter, *Just Watch!* (1993). An obituary is in the *New York Times*, 23 Dec. 1969.

PETER BAXTER

STERNE, Simon (23 July 1839–22 Sept. 1901), attorney and political reformer, was born in Philadelphia, Pennsylvania, the son of Henry Sterne, a storekeeper, and Regina (maiden name unknown). Educated in the public schools of Philadelphia, Sterne briefly attended the University of Heidelberg, then returned to his city of birth to read law. He received his legal degree from the University of Pennsylvania in 1859 and joined the bar that same year.

Migrating to New York City in 1860, Sterne promptly gained admission to the bar, lectured on the science of government and political economy at Cooper Union (1863), wrote for the New York *Commercial Advertiser* (1863–1864), and edited the *New York Social Science Review* (1865). A Democrat with broadening contacts, Sterne was among those retained as counsel for former Confederate president Jefferson Davis during the early stages of Davis's post–Civil War legal ordeal. In 1870 Sterne married Mathilde Elsberg. They had one child.

Publicly involved during a period in which urban political party organizations, "machines" led by "bosses," gained political power in New York City and elsewhere at the expense of the commercial and professional elites that had dominated municipal politics,

Sterne fought for fully one-third of a century against the new political order. Believing in minority or proportional representation in municipal and even state legislatures, Sterne was a founder and the first secretary of the Personal Representation Society (1866). He and his allies sought without success to provide for minority representation in New York City charter revisions during 1872–1873 and 1897 and during the New York State constitutional conventions of 1867 and 1894. Basically, the reform envisioned multimember legislative districts with voters entitled to cast as many votes as there were legislators to be elected therefrom and free to distribute these as they wished, even to cast all for one candidate. Advocates saw the reform as a means to two ends. First, it would strengthen the opposition political party. More significantly, it would foster the election, ostensibly by disinterested voters, of independent candidates, thus weakening the pernicious grip of political parties and parochial local party organizations on legislative nominations and elections. (Between 1874 and 1882, New York City did provide for minority party representation on its board of aldermen, but without the provisions, cumulative voting, for example, that made proportional representation attractive to reformers.) As early as the mid-1880s, Sterne argued for functional representation in municipal government, with citywide economic interest groups, rather than district-based political organizations, central to governance. In this he anticipated elements of early twentieth-century urban progressivism.

From the 1870s through the 1890s, Sterne participated in a number of municipal reform campaigns, most famously and successfully as the secretary of the Executive Committee of Citizens and Taxpayers for the Financial Reform of the City of New York, the so-called Committee of Seventy, which contributed to the overthrow of "Boss" William Marcy Tweed and the Tweed Ring during 1871–1872. More controversial was Sterne's involvement with the blue ribbon Commission to Devise a Plan for the Government of Cities in the State of New York, appointed by Governor Samuel J. Tilden in 1875. The body's 1877 report revealed the concerns of businessmen and professionals over the state of municipal affairs. In their most sweeping recommendation, the commissioners called for the creation of elective boards of finance in cities to oversee spending, taxing, and borrowing, with board membership and the electorate restricted in large cities to property taxpayers and rent payers above cutoff levels. No member of the commission was more outspoken than Sterne in questioning universal adult male suffrage in urban settings; to him, mass electorates mobilized by professional political organizations posed a serious threat to taxpayers in cities. The commission's proposed amendments to the state constitution passed the state legislature once, in 1877, but died there the next year without being put to a necessary second test.

Sterne's closeness to New York City merchants also made him increasingly aware of the effects of the transportation revolution on the fortunes of the metropolis's mercantile community. In particular, anticompetitive practices, such as pooling by trunk railroad lines linking Atlantic coast cities and the Midwest, reduced New York's commercial advantages over rival seaports. Initially a believer in laissez-faire, Sterne came to support governmental regulation of railroads. Representing New York City commercial organizations, he conducted the state legislature's Hepburn Committee investigation of the New York Central and Erie railroads (1879); three years later he prepared legislation establishing the New York Railroad Commission. Sterne subsequently was consulted by the United States Senate Select Committee on Interstate Commerce, chaired by Senator Shelby Cullom, and was involved in the drafting of legislation creating the Interstate Commerce Commission, following which he reported personally to President Grover Cleveland on government-railroad relations in Europe (1887).

Sterne died in New York City. His historical significance lies in his early involvement in issues of political reform and economic regulation that would dominate politics in the Progressive Era.

• The New York Public Library houses a disappointing collection of Sterne's papers. John Foord, *The Life and Public Services of Simon Sterne* (1903), remains useful, though it is uncritical and dated. It provides a listing of Sterne's important publications, but see also Simon Sterne, *Railways in the United States* (1912), a posthumous collection of essays. Iver Bernstein, *The New York City Draft Riots: Their Significance for American Society and Politics in the Age of the Civil War* (1990), and David C. Hammack, *Power and Society: Greater New York at the Turn of the Century* (1982), offer sophisticated analyses and comment on Sterne. Lee Benson, *Merchants, Farmers, & Railroads: Railroad Regulation and New York Politics, 1850–1887* (1955), is indispensable. Stephen Skowronek, *Building a New American State: The Expansion of National Administrative Capacities, 1877–1920* (1982), refers briefly and perceptively to Sterne and places him in context. An obituary is in the *New York Times*, 23 Sept. 1901.

SAMUEL T. McSEVENEY

STERNE, Stuart. *See* Bloede, Gertrude.

STETSON, Augusta Emma Simmons (12 Oct. 1842–12 Oct. 1928), Christian Science practitioner, teacher, and founder of the First Church of Christ Scientist, New York City, was born in Waldoboro, Maine, the daughter of Peabody Simmons, a carpenter and architect, and Salome Sprague. During her childhood in Damariscotta, Maine, Stetson developed her considerable musical talent, which she put to use as an organist at the Methodist church in which her parents were active. She attended the Lincoln Academy, New Castle, Maine, after high school. Her marriage to shipbuilder Frederick Stetson in 1864 took her to England, India, and Burma, but his ill health required that he leave the family business, and the couple, who had no children, returned to live with her family in Boston. To earn a living, Stetson chose to develop her already acknowledged talent for public speaking by attending the Blish School of Oratory in Boston in 1882.

Stetson's more public life began in the spring of 1884 when she attended a lecture by Mary Baker Eddy, the founder of Christian Science. Stetson later described this encounter as having alleviated the intense feelings of grief and physical weakness brought on by nursing her invalid husband (1913). After the lecture, Eddy asked Stetson to visit her, indicating that Stetson had a future in Christian Science. By the fall of 1884 Stetson was enrolled at Eddy's Massachusetts Metaphysical College, relieved by Eddy of the burden of paying the $300 tuition. She professed to be not very interested in Christian Science at first but at the end of twelve sessions felt ready to attempt healing. Reluctant to try and fail among those who knew her best, Stetson spent four weeks at Skowhegan, Maine, where she reported effecting numerous healings. She gave her patients Eddy's *Science and Health with Key to the Scriptures* to read along with instructions on how to apply Christian Science principles. In 1885 Eddy summoned Stetson back to Boston where she served as one of five Christian Science preachers at Chickering Hall in addition to giving other lectures on Christian Science.

In 1886 Eddy asked Stetson to move to New York City, where for a year teachers had been establishing small Christian Science teaching institutes. Stetson worked to shape them into a single organization, and in 1888 seventeen Christian Scientists incorporated as the First Church of Christ, Scientist, New York City, with Stetson as their elected official preacher. In 1890 Stetson was ordained pastor of First Church. Her increasing following, the establishment of a Sunday School and a Reading Room, and the need for space for practitioners required several moves to more spacious quarters. The Christian Scientist enterprise in New York City prospered in large part because Stetson was so successful at attracting the support of the wealthy.

In spite of outward success, by 1891 there was enough tension among members of First Church that six, all of them Eddy's former students, left the congregation to start Second Church. Stetson responded by organizing the New York City Christian Science Institute peopled by her supporters. The cornerstone was laid in 1899 for an elaborate structure for First Church—larger than the mother church in Boston—at Ninety-sixth Street and Central Park West. The cost was over $1 million, but by the time the building was dedicated in 1903 it was paid for, along with a $100,000 residence for Stetson next door.

Stetson's success generated both admiration and apprehension in Boston. Her obvious ambition began to concern Eddy and the board of directors of the mother church by the late 1890s, and some of her activities caused unfavorable publicity for Christian Science. In 1901 Stetson's husband died in the midst of a widely publicized trial over the contested will of Helen C. Brush, a woman who had sought healing from Stetson and had left money to First Church. Stetson and First Church won the lawsuit, but there was testimony questioning the efficacy of Christian Science healing and why Stetson had not been able to heal her husband or Brush. Stetson's teachings were also of concern, in part because of her emphasis on material prosperity as a demonstration of Christian Science. One student quoted her as saying, "We need health and strength and peace, and for these we look to God. But let us not forget that we also need *things*" (Swihart, p. 43). Rumors that Stetson expected to succeed Eddy as head of Christian Science were frequent (as were her denials), and there was speculation that Eddy's 1902 limiting of First Reader's terms to three years was prompted by Stetson. She had assumed this position after an 1895 bylaw prohibiting personal preaching and ordaining the Bible and *Science and Health with Key to the Scriptures* as the pastor of Christian Science was inserted by Eddy into the *Manual of the Mother Church.* Stetson stepped down but not without consulting a lawyer about whether First Church could secede from Christian Science. In 1908 Stetson began plans for a branch of First Church, contrary to the *Manual*'s limitation of branch churches to the mother church. After a meeting with Eddy, in which declarations of mutual respect and affection were made, Stetson changed her mind.

Stetson's public declaration of loyalty did not sufficiently reassure Eddy and the board of directors, and an investigation into her teachings began in 1909. First Church practitioners revealed what the board considered errors, among them, denigration of sexuality, directing destructive thoughts against rivals and enemies, lying under oath by distinguishing the "spiritual" from the "material" self, and invoking her relationship with Eddy as unique. Stetson's license as a Christian Science teacher and practitioner was revoked in September 1909, she was dropped from membership in the mother church, and her resignation from First Church was accepted after a letter from Eddy convinced the divided congregation that this was the best course.

Stetson spent the last eighteen years of her life declaring her loyalty to Eddy, teaching her own version of Christian Science, and criticizing the Christian Science Board of Directors as having strayed from Eddy's true teachings. She interpreted her ouster as a test of loyalty and a sign that she would lead the "Church Triumphant" away from material organization. She remained in her home next to First Church, founded a Christian Science choral society with members who remained loyal to her, and participated in newspaper and radio efforts to preach Nordic supremacy and the Protestant principle as the foundation of America. With the exception of *Poems Written on the Journey from Sense to Soul* (1901), her major writings were collected and published during these years: *Reminiscences, Sermons and Correspondence 1884–1913* (1913), *Vital Issues in Christian Science with Facsimile Letters of Mary Baker Eddy* (1914), which gives details of the 1909 controversy with the board of directors, and *Sermons Which Spiritually Interpret the Scriptures and Other Writings on Christian Science* (1924). Stetson died on her eighty-sixth birthday in Rochester, New York.

Her cremated remains were buried at Damariscotta, Maine.

Stetson's career is evidence that women in American religious history have been more likely to attain success as spiritual leaders in traditions outside the mainstream. Christian Science, with its woman founder and openness to women as practitioners and teachers, gave Stetson an arena in which to exercise her talent for preaching, leadership, music, and fundraising. Her relationship with Christian Science and her acrimonious departure from the Christian Science organization can best be understood within the context of that movement's process of setting boundaries over polity and doctrine.

• There is only one biography of Stetson, half of the volume *Since Mrs. Eddy* by Altman K. Swihart (1931). Swihart includes an extensive bibliography along with a description of the contents of "twenty-six large portfolio volumes of clippings, letters, and programs" gathered by Stetson's students and covering the years from 1895 to 1930 at Union Theological Seminary, New York City. The Huntington Library (San Marino, Calif.) holds letters about Christian Science by Stetson to James Henry and Florence Belle Donnelly Hayes as well as personal papers and correspondence regarding Stetson's relationship with Mary Baker Eddy and First Church, New York. Also included are Stetson's teaching materials and writings and letters by Eddy addressed chiefly to Stetson. Chapter ten of the third volume of Robert Peel's biography, "Quod Erat Demonstrandum," *Mary Baker Eddy: The Years of Authority* (1977), tells the story of Stetson's dismissal from Christian Science from the Christian Science perspective. Peel's documentation refers to letters and other writings from and about Stetson in the Archives of the Mother Church, Boston, but these are not easily accessible to scholars. An obituary is in the *New York Times*, 13 Oct. 1928.

MARY FARRELL BEDNAROWSKI

STETSON, John Batterson (5 May 1830–18 Feb. 1906), hat manufacturer and philanthropist, was born in Orange, New Jersey, the son of Stephen Stetson, a hatter, and Susan Batterson. Like several of his brothers, Stetson learned the hat trade at an early age as an apprentice in his father's shop. The long hours necessary to acquire and perfect the craft kept Stetson from receiving much formal education, but his mother taught him to read and write using the Bible and newspapers.

Over the years Stetson became a fine hatmaker, but because his older brothers were already involved in his father's operation, he saw little opportunity in his family's small business. Anxious for advancement, the frail and nervous young man struck out on his own. Nearing thirty, he moved to Philadelphia and established his own hat business. There he made and repaired hats as well as shaped wooden forms for other hatters. But Stetson contracted tuberculosis (a fairly common illness for hatters at the time because of the damp, closed-in work areas) and was not expected to live more than a few months. Because drier, warmer climes were recommended for those with lung problems, Stetson sold his business and attempted to regain his health by traveling West.

In 1860 he took a train to Illinois but soon settled in St. Joseph, Missouri—one of several teeming staging areas for those venturing to the Far West. There he took a job in a brickyard, advanced rapidly to the position of manager, and became a partner in the firm. The following year, however, the Missouri River flooded, destroying the business, and Stetson was left looking for work. At loose ends, he joined a group of adventurers in 1862 heading for the gold fields in Colorado.

His long hike to the Rocky Mountains restored his health and made him aware of a very different way of life than he had known in the East. More important, Stetson noticed that hats used in the rugged West needed to protect their wearers from the elements. Not finding his fortune in gold-mining, he returned to Philadelphia in 1865 and established another hat shop. Initially he manufactured and sold a few hats in the standard styles of the day. Not satisfied, Stetson then innovated. He developed a hat for use in the West with a wider brim to protect its wearer from sun and rain and a high crown to keep the head cooler. He sent samples of this hat—"The Boss of the Plains"—to dealers throughout the West, and orders started pouring into his Philadelphia shop. This hat, soon nicknamed the "Stetson," became standard headgear in the western United States.

With demand increasing, Stetson expanded his factory, but when even greater space was needed he took his operation out of the city's business district and built a larger plant in the suburbs. Because of his own bout with tuberculosis, Stetson constructed his new six-story facility with workers' health in mind; the fireproof building was designed to allow in light and to permit fresh air to circulate. His interest in his employees manifested itself in other ways as well. The factory had an auditorium for free concerts and Sunday school lessons, a library, and ultimately a hospital that provided workers with free health care. Stetson offered other employee benefits including a profit-sharing plan, annual Christmas bonuses, and a building and loan association to encourage workers to save money. These programs appeared to be benevolent, but Stetson, like many other employers of the era, used them in an attempt to mold a reliable work force and to keep unions out of his firm. Stetson and these paternalistic practices were opposed by the American Federation of Labor.

By the 1880s, Stetson had turned to philanthropic pursuits. A longtime monetary supporter of the Baptist church, he became aware that a small Baptist school, De Land Academy, near his winter home in Florida needed financial support. Stetson gave so generously to the institution—erecting several buildings and providing it with a $1 million endowment—that it changed its name to Stetson University, and he was made president of the renamed school's board of trustees.

Stetson was married twice; with his first wife (name unknown) he had one child, and with his second, Sarah Elizabeth Shindler, he had two children. He died in De Land, Florida, leaving to his family an estate estimated to be worth between $5 million and $10 million. At the time of his death, the John B. Stetson Company employed more than 3,500 people and annually manufactured two million hats that were distributed worldwide.

By providing an innovative new style of hat that met the needs and demands of the western frontier, John Stetson created and then successfully filled a huge new market. The actor John Wayne immortalized the hatmaker by referring to the "Stetson" as the "hat that won the West."

• Information on Stetson and his firm can be found in Elbert Hubbard, *Little Journeys to the Homes of Great Business Men: John B. Stetson* (1911); Lyman M. Nash, "The Hat That Crowned the West," *Coronet* (Aug. 1961): 54–56; John O'Rourke, "John Batterson Stetson: His Felt Hat Turned to Gold," *The American West* 20 (Jan.–Feb. 1983): 22–23; and Ralph Richmond, *The Stetson Century: 1865–1965* (1965). Mary Blout Christian, *Hats Off to John Stetson* (1992), is a children's book. An obituary is in the *New York Times*, 19 Feb. 1906.

WILLIAM B. FRIEDRICKS

STETTHEIMER, Florine (19 Aug. 1871–11 May 1944), painter, designer, and salon hostess, was born in Rochester, New York, the daughter of Joseph Stettheimer, a dry goods merchant, and Rosetta Walter, a member of a prominent German-Jewish family. Stettheimer and her four siblings spent much of their childhoods living in Europe, particularly in Stuttgart, Munich, and Paris. Their father abandoned the family when Stettheimer was a child, and as a result of his disappearance, close emotional bonds were formed among the three youngest sisters (Carrie, Florine, and Ettie) and their mother, and so Stettheimer grew up in a largely matriarchal environment. (The two older siblings, Stella and Walter, both married and moved to northern California.)

Educated largely in Europe, Stettheimer showed early promise as an artist and worked with a variety of tutors. From 1892 to 1895 she attended the Art Students League (ASL) in New York (the only art school in the country where women students were allowed to paint from live models) and studied with Kenyon Cox, Carroll Beckwith, and H. Siddons Mowbray. In 1895 she was elected to the governing body of the ASL. After graduating, Stettheimer returned, with her mother and two sisters, to Europe, where she continued her studies in Munich, Berlin, and Paris while maintaining a studio in New York. A pivotal experience for was seeing Vaslav Nijinsky dance with the Ballets Russes in Paris in 1912. This led Stettheimer to conceive of her own ballet based on the Parisian art students' Quatre Arts Ball. She designed sets and costumes for the never-produced ballet using a variety of innovative materials, including cellophane. Concurrently in her paintings, Stettheimer worked through numerous European postimpressionist and modernist styles, including symbolism, fauvism, and pointillism, and she designed neorococo furniture in gesso and gold leaf.

In 1914, following the outbreak of World War I in Europe, the four Stettheimer women returned and settled permanently in New York City. Their townhouse on the city's Upper West Side and their summer rental estates in Westchester quickly became the sites for an informal salon where the Stettheimers entertained famous and infamous members of the avant-garde in arts, music, letters, and philosophy. Among the celebrated guests and friends were artists Marcel Duchamp, Elie Nadelman, and Georgia O'Keeffe; writers Carl Van Vechten, H. L. Mencken, Avery Hopwood, Sherwood Anderson, and Joseph Hergesheimer; photographers Edward Steichen, Alfred Stieglitz, Cecil Beaton, and Arnold Genthe; and art critics Henry McBride, Leo Stein, and Paul Rosenfeld.

Determined to create a new American style of painting to suit the new century, Stettheimer initially adapted beloved compositions by favorite artists such as Manet, Velasquez, and Titian and synthesized the styles of Matisse and Van Gogh. In 1916, while her new style was still developing, her friend Marie Sterner offered Stettheimer her first solo exhibition, which was held on the top floor of Knoedler's Gallery in New York. Determining that her works would best be viewed as an "installation," Stettheimer draped the walls with white muslin, and in the gallery alongside her paintings she included a reproduction of her canopy bed, gilded with her intertwined initials. Although it was moderately well received by critics, the exhibition resulted in no sales, and thereafter Stettheimer chose to exhibit only in group shows.

By 1917 Stettheimer—borrowing pure color, flat fields, and diminishing sizes of compositional elements from Persian miniatures—had developed the mature style in which she would work, with slight variations, for the next twenty-five years. Within her compositions she occasionally experimented with time as the fourth dimension—a prevalent concept she discussed with Duchamp, among other artist friends—and thereby offered a variation on the cubist sense of time and space as relative and constantly changing. Disregarding the classical Renaissance "frozen moment," she instead developed a form of narrative painting that recalled medieval Sienese panel painting in which a single figure is depicted several times within the same composition to represent the passage of time. To this revival of pre-Renaissance composition Stettheimer added her strong European decorative tradition and interest in theater, creating contemporary "conversation piece paintings" in which she, her family, and friends are depicted in identifiable settings.

During the 1920s Stettheimer began a series of portraits of family and close friends, including Van Vechten (Beinecke Library, Yale), McBride (Smith College Museum of Art), Stieglitz (Fisk University Museum), and Duchamp (private collection). Conceived as a minibiography, each portrait recorded the sitter's physiognomy (which the artist altered to suit her fancy) and also included references and visual clues to particular events and situations from the subject's life story, personality, vocations, and avocations. Stettheimer's portraits are nonnarrative and layered with meaning. Complex images encoded in all aspects of their subject matter, handling, design, and intention are integral to the meaning in her paintings. By inviting viewers to recognize individual motifs and references in the work, she was able to prolong its temporality. Just as Marcel Proust constructed narratives using detail and nonsequential time, Stettheimer presented continuously unfolding biographies wherein themes of personal memory and family intimacy were superimposed over a few chronological anchors.

Another important facet of Stettheimer's work after 1920 was her incorporation of aspects of popular culture into her painted compositions and designs. Although she was never a social realist—generally avoiding the depiction of pressing contemporary concerns, such as war and poverty—Stettheimer's mature paintings are distinguished by their inclusion of respectful and imaginative images of African and Native Americans, women, and homosexuals, all of whom are shown as self-confident and presented with humor but without the usual exploitation related to sexual or racial stereotyping. Her highly experimental compositions, including *Asbury Park South* (Fisk University Museum), *Natatorium Undine* (Vassar College Art Collection), and *Spring Sale at Bendel's* (Philadelphia Museum of Art), incorporated numerous colors and varied subject matter as well as the influences of jazz, African-American and folk cultures, contemporary philosophies, and technological breakthroughs in photography and film. Stettheimer's final creative output comprised more than 150 paintings that are bold, ironic, inventive, and among the most interesting produced in the early decades of the twentieth century, offering an intimate perspective on the private and public relationships shared by many influential figures in the art world between the two world wars. During her lifetime numerous art critics referred to Stettheimer as one of the "few important women painters in the history of art." She sent individual paintings to virtually every important art exhibition of her time in New York, Chicago, Washington, D.C., Philadelphia, and Paris; when it was shown, her work was invariably singled out for praise.

In addition to painting, Stettheimer wrote bitingly ironic modernist poetry and designed neorococo furniture and picture frames. She also designed the sets and costumes for the opera *Four Saints in Three Acts*, composed by Virgil Thomson with a libretto by Gertrude Stein. In 1928–1929 Stettheimer invited the young composer to visit her studio and to play the score of the opera, which was based on the lives of about a dozen Spanish baroque saints. The decoration of Stettheimer's beaux-arts studio—her idiosyncratic aesthetic was evident throughout: huge cellophane curtains framing the dining room, Nottingham lace trimming the putti-bounded bedroom, and gilded and white furniture designed by the artist to complement the individualized frames of her paintings—convinced Thomson to ask her to undertake the project. She agreed and threw herself into it, first making tiny maquettes of each act and figure, much as she had done decades earlier in designing her ballet. The opera opened with an all-black cast in Hartford, Connecticut, in 1934. The reviews of the music and the libretto were mixed, but Stettheimer's designs were universally applauded. The collaboration represented the first time that a significant American artist had designed the stage and costumes for an American theatrical production. Stettheimer's highly individualized designs featuring cellophane, feathers, crystal, and lace marked a pivotal point in future stage decoration; it was the first time that an established fine artist had created stage design and costumes as a significant artistic aspect of a production.

Rosetta Stettheimer died in 1937 after years of ill health. Stettheimer shocked her sisters by moving out of their townhouse and moving into her beaux-arts studio. It was the first time in sixty-six years that she had lived on her own, and the move resulted in ill will between her and her sisters. Stettheimer continued to entertain members of various art and literary circles and also began to work on a series of definitive *Cathedral* paintings in which she presented an ironic view of various aspects of urban New York life: Times Square with the advent of talking motion pictures, Wall Street and the financial district, Fifth Avenue and its socioeconomic connotations, and the New York art scene. Stettheimer's final work, *Cathedrals of Art*, in which she directed ironic barbs against the three major New York art museums, the Metropolitan Museum, the Museum of Modern Art, and the Whitney Museum of American Art, was unfinished at the time of her death in a New York hospital. Although she pointedly asked her lawyer, Joseph Solomon, to destroy all of her paintings after her death, her final request was ignored both by Solomon and by her sister Ettie (Carrie having died six weeks after Florine). Instead they donated the most significant paintings to museum collections across the country (all four *Cathedral* paintings are at the Metropolitan Museum of Art) and the early works, as well as her correspondence, archives, and furniture, to Columbia University.

In 1946 McBride, Duchamp, Kirk Askew, and Monroe Wheeler organized a retrospective of Stettheimer's work that opened at the Museum of Modern Art and later traveled to Chicago and San Francisco. Her work subsequently disappeared into museum basements for several decades until it was rediscovered by feminist artists and art historians in the late 1970s. Over the next two decades, Stettheimer's work was included in several group exhibitions and small shows at the Institute of Contemporary Art in Boston, the Katonah Museum in New York, and other venues, and she became a cult figure among contemporary artists such as Andy Warhol and Kiki Smith. In 1995 a second major retrospective of Stettheimer was organized at the Whitney Museum of American Art in New York. It attracted large crowds and generated renewed interest in the artist and her work.

Stettheimer was an archetypal modernist artist. She was unfettered by financial or domestic responsibilities and lived on the fringes of the first generation of the modern jazz age. She was an astute social historian who provided a unique, alternative perspective from which to view the period between the world wars. As Carl Van Vechten noted after her death, "She was both the historian and the critic of her period and she goes a long way toward telling us how some of New York lived in those strange years after the First World War, telling us in brilliant colors and assured designs, telling us in painting that has few rivals in her day or ours" (p. 356).

• Stettheimer's extant diaries and correspondence are located in the Beinecke Rare Book and Manuscript Library at Yale University. Her early scrapbooks and many early works are stored in the Rare Book Room of the Avery Library at Columbia University in New York City. For an early evaluation, see Henry McBride, *Florine Stettheimer* (exhibition catalog, Museum of Modern Art; 1946). Also useful are Parker Tyler, *Florine Stettheimer: A Life in Art* (1963), and Carl Van Vechten, "The World of Florine Stettheimer," *Harper's Bazaar*, Oct. 1946. The revival of interest in Stettheimer in the late 1970s was led by Linda Nochlin; see her "Florine Stettheimer: Rococo Subversive," *Art in America*, Sept. 1980, pp. 65–83. See also Barbara Bloemink, *Friends and Family: Portraiture in the Work of Florine Stettheimer* (exhibition catalog, Katonah Museum of Art; 1993); Bloemink and Elizabeth Sussman, *Florine Stettheimer: Manhattan Fantastica* (exhibition catalog, Whitney Museum of American Art; 1995); and Bloemink, *The Life and Art of Florine Stettheimer* (1995).

BARBARA J. BLOEMINK

STETTINIUS, Edward Reilly (15 Feb. 1865–3 Sept. 1925), businessman and second assistant secretary of war, was born in Chicago, Illinois, but grew up in St. Louis, Missouri, the son of Joseph Stettinius, a wholesale grocer, and Isabel Reilly Gorman. Edward was an excellent student who had to drop out of St. Louis University in 1881 at age sixteen to take care of his mother and chronically ill brother, his father having died years earlier. He held a number of clerical jobs over the next seven years. In the late 1880s he became involved in stock brokering with several firms. He speculated heavily and lost a great deal of money. After his mother's death in 1891, Stettinius left for Chicago where he lost even more money on the stock market.

In 1892 Stettinius took a job, probably as bookkeeper, with a company that manufactured steam boilers. He rose rapidly in the firm, having caught the eye of its president, O. C. Barber. In 1894 he married Judith Carrington; they had four children, one of whom, Edward R. Stettinius (1900–1949), became secretary of state.

Through his own abilities and his continued association with Barber, Stettinius became a top executive in the steam boiler firm and at the same time in the Diamond Match Company, which Barber also headed. As the executive offices of both companies were located in

New York City, Stettinius moved to Staten Island in 1905. He later became president of the match company, leading it to prominence in the field. He also made a notable contribution to industrial safety. Matches at that time were made with white phosphorus, a substance that often caused serious illness among workers. After Diamond Match acquired a patent on a nonpoisonous match compound, Stettinius persuaded his board of directors to share the patent with competitors.

When World War I broke out, J. P. Morgan & Co. became the largest purchasing agent for the Allied forces. The Morgan firm hired Stettinius to oversee munitions procurement, first on a part-time basis, then as head of the export department of the Morgan firm. This unit came to oversee enormous expenditures. Not only did it negotiate contracts with suppliers in behalf of the Allied governments, it supervised every aspect of a transaction up to, and including, delivery. Stettinius earned a reputation as a hard-driving though considerate manager who surrounded himself with very able people. He also earned large amounts of money because for a time he was paid a percentage of the sales. On 1 January 1916 he became a partner in the Morgan firm.

Ironically, Stettinius's importance declined after the United States entered the war. His connection with the Morgan company, widely criticized for war profiteering, and his identification with the Republican party made him a pariah to influential members of Woodrow Wilson's administration. Although named first as surveyor general of supplies and then as second assistant secretary of war, he did not receive responsibilities commensurate with his abilities. In the former case his duties never were specifically defined; in the latter his most important roles were to serve on the Inter-Allied Munitions Council and to facilitate purchases made by the Allied Expeditionary Forces in France. Those responsibilities he did receive he carried out with his usual efficiency, earning the respect of those with whom he worked, such as General John J. Pershing.

After the war, Stettinius continued to be a valued member of the Morgan firm, helping to restructure several large companies such as General Motors and the Guaranty Trust Company. In the fall of 1922 he suffered the first of a series of stomach ailments that led to an operation the following March for what was described at the time as a deep-seated abdominal abscess. He never fully recovered from the surgery and in August 1925 began showing signs of heart failure. He died at his home in Locust Valley, Long Island.

• Some correspondence and scrapbooks of the senior Stettinius are in the Stettinius papers in the Alderman Library of the University of Virginia, although the bulk of the collection is devoted to Edward R. Stettinius, Jr. The only biography is John Douglas Forbes, *Stettinius, Sr.: Portrait of a Morgan Partner* (1974). Forbes had access to several privately printed accounts of Stettinius's service during the war and has interviewed people who knew and worked with him. An obituary is in the *New York Times*, 4 Sept. 1925.

ROBERT JAMES MADDOX

STETTINIUS, Edward Reilly, Jr. (22 Oct. 1900–31 Oct. 1949), business executive, U.S. secretary of state, and U.S. delegate to the United Nations, was born in Chicago, Illinois, the son of Edward Reilly Stettinius, Sr., a J. P. Morgan and Company partner and assistant secretary of war during World War I, and Judith Carrington. Some members of his family used the spelling Rilley or Riley. Stettinius grew up in Chicago and New York City. He graduated from the Pomfret School in Connecticut and attended the University of Virginia for four years. However, he left in 1924 with only six of the sixty credits necessary for graduation. He spent much of his college time ministering to poor Appalachian hill families and working with employment agencies trying to assist poor students at the university. He missed many classes and was frequently away from campus. Because he avoided alcohol and fraternity parties, his classmates called him "Abstemious Stettinius." He considered becoming an Episcopal minister upon leaving school, but a trip to Europe as a traveling companion to philosophy instructor William S. A. Pott changed his mind. Upon his return, feeling he could best help society through industry, he took a position as a stockroom attendant in the Hyatt Roller Bearing Company offered to him by General Motors vice president and family acquaintance John Lee Pratt. Pratt was a University of Virginia alumnus who had learned of Stettinius's social work by reading his alma mater's publications. By 1926 Stettinius became Pratt's assistant and implemented innovative employee benefit programs. In 1924 he married Virginia Gordon Wallace; they had three sons.

In 1931 Stettinius was named General Motors vice president in charge of industrial and public relations. Meanwhile, he continued his social work by volunteering with unemployment projects. Through this work he met Franklin Roosevelt, who involved Stettinius in the New Deal's National Recovery Administration. Stettinius served as a liaison officer between the National Industrial Recovery Administration in Washington and the Industrial Advisory Board. Business success brought Stettinius to the attention of the chairman of the board of United States Steel, Myron Taylor, who offered him a position as vice chairman of the company's finance committee. Accepting the position in 1934, Stettinius quickly implemented a reorganization program that improved employee welfare, plant production, and public relations. In 1936 he became director and chairman of the finance committee. When Taylor retired in 1938, he named Stettinius, then only thirty-eight years old, as his replacement. Vigorous, handsome, and personable, Stettinius rose rapidly in the business world, earning the nickname "the White-Haired Boy," an allusion to his prematurely white hair.

Stettinius's business acumen and progressive social views again brought him to the attention of President Roosevelt in 1939. Asked to chair the War Resources Board, Stettinius left United States Steel in 1940 and placed his corporate assets in a blind trust. In 1941 he entered government service full-time as director of priorities in the Office of Production Management, where he urged the advancement of the program to develop synthetic rubber. In 1942 he was named administrator in charge of the Lend-Lease Administration, which was created to oversee the implementation of the Lend-Lease Act. This act allowed the United States to provide to Britain and eventually other allies war material for which they were unable to pay but nonetheless sorely needed to stave off German conquest of Europe. Stettinius quickly streamlined the organization to support with greater efficiency the Allied war effort, befriending many Allied diplomats in the process. He was particularly helpful in winning support for lend-lease from a hesitant U.S. Congress. The Lend-Lease Administration offered, in Stettinius's view, a pattern for international cooperation, which he wrote about in *Lend-Lease: Weapon for Victory* (1944).

Stettinius replaced Sumner Welles as under secretary of state in 1943. Both Roosevelt and Secretary of State Cordell Hull intended for Stettinius to use his skills to reorganize the State Department, which was suffering from lack of policy coordination and a poor public image. Stettinius concentrated on the reorganization of the State Department, integration of State Department policy with other executive offices involved in foreign relations, implementation of a public relations program, and creation of an international security organization.

Stettinius's first overseas mission of consequence was a visit to Britain in the spring of 1944 to discuss with Winston Churchill and the British Foreign Office postwar economic principles and to lay the groundwork for a world security organization. At the meeting the British agreed to an August 1944 conference on the international organization in Washington, D.C., and Stettinius established a close relationship with British under secretary of state for foreign affairs, Sir Alexander Cadogan. The conference on the world security organization convened in August 1944 at Dumberton Oaks in Washington, D.C., and Stettinius was named to head the U.S. delegation. The conference delegates elected him chairman, and he worked closely with Cadogan and the Soviet delegate Andrei Gromyko to create the framework for the United Nations (UN), establishing the General Assembly, the Security Council, the International Court, and the Economic and Social Council.

Soon after the Dumberton Oaks Conference, Secretary Hull's health began to fail, and Stettinius was named acting secretary of state. In November 1944 Hull's poor health forced him to resign, and President Roosevelt quickly nominated Stettinius to replace him. Stettinius was easily confirmed by the Senate on 30 November 1944, a popular choice despite some concerns about his lack of international and diplomatic experience. He expanded the reorganization of the State Department and released all of Hull's assistants except for Dean Acheson, the assistant for congressional relations. His department rapidly took on a more businesslike look as he made Joseph Grew his under secretary, William Clayton his assistant for for-

eign economics, and Nelson Rockefeller his assistant for inter-American affairs. Confirmation of these appointments met considerable opposition in the Senate and required Roosevelt's personal intervention to ensure Democratic support. Stettinius placed emphasis on improving cooperation with other government departments and agencies, the president's cabinet, and the Pentagon. He sought to improve the department's relations with the public by publicizing department policies and initiating a series of radio shows explaining the department's functions. His public popularity grew to the point that his name was mentioned as a possible 1948 presidential candidate.

In February 1945 Stettinius accompanied Roosevelt to the Yalta Conference and was instrumental in developing the U.S. proposals for the conference, among them the Declaration on Liberated Europe and UN Security Council voting procedures. He personally presented the latter proposal and persuaded both Churchill and Stalin to accept the American formula. The Yalta Conference set a meeting for the spring of 1945 in San Francisco to prepare the United Nations Charter and established many policies that outlined postwar cooperation among the victorious Allies. Immediately after the Yalta Conference, Stettinius attended the Mexico City Conference to line up support among Central and South American representatives for the United Nations. He also sought to strengthen the joint stand among the nations of the Western Hemisphere against pro-Axis Argentina. The negotiations culminated in the Declaration of Chapultepec, which affirmed a joint American stand on the United Nations with concessions by the United States to strengthen regional alliances.

Stettinius returned to Washington, D.C., and was named by the president to head the U.S. delegation to the United Nations Conference on International Organization in San Francisco, which included Democratic senator Tom Connally and Senator Arthur Vandenburg, an influential Republican who had abandoned isolationism in favor of a more internationalistic foreign policy. During the preparations for the conference, President Roosevelt died, and the new president, Harry S. Truman, asked Stettinius to continue his preparations as instructed by Roosevelt. Truman, however, believed Stettinius to be soft in his dealings with the Soviets, particularly as the Russians proceeded to take advantage of the accords negotiated at the Yalta Conference. Truman was determined to appoint James Byrnes to replace Stettinius as soon as the San Francisco Conference concluded, though he publicly supported Stettinius and did not inform the secretary of his decision until the conference had concluded. As Stettinius led the U.S. delegation at the San Francisco Conference in April and June 1945, a substantial rift was already apparent in Soviet relations with the United States. In this difficult atmosphere, Stettinius struggled to achieve consensus among all the delegates, often meeting Russian delegate Gromyko and Allied delegates in his private quarters to negotiate particularly difficult issues. A disagreement with the

Soviets over the Security Council veto was not settled until Stettinius, with Truman's approval, sent a telegram to Truman's envoy to Stalin, Harry Hopkins, who then convinced Stalin to allow Gromyko to agree on the veto issue. Owing in large part to Stettinius's tireless efforts, confident negotiating style, and persuasive personality, the UN Charter was finally approved by all members of the conference on 26 June 1945. As the conference closed, Truman notified Stettinius of his intention to nominate Byrnes as his secretary of state and offered Stettinius the position of the first U.S. representative to the UN General Assembly. Stettinius accepted the position of U.S. representative to the UN and resigned as secretary of state on 27 June 1945. He went to London to begin his new duties in September 1945.

Stettinius soon grew disillusioned with the development of the Cold War and the widening rift between the West and the Soviet Union. He resigned in June 1946, frustrated with the Truman administration's refusal to use the UN to pursue its Cold War diplomacy. Stettinius had anticipated being an integral figure in Truman's postwar foreign policy but found that he was being largely ignored. Returning to his country home, "The Horseshoe," on the Rapidan River in Virginia, he accepted an appointment as rector of the University of Virginia. He was active in raising funds for the university's Woodrow Wilson School of Foreign Affairs; established the Liberian Company, a corporation that promoted American investment in Liberia and became a forerunner of the American foreign-aid program to Liberia; and traveled frequently. He authored *Roosevelt and the Russians: The Yalta Conference* (1949), which he based on his own meticulous notes and which defended the actions taken by Roosevelt.

In February 1949 Stettinius suffered his first heart attack. He died at the home of his sister in Greenwich, Connecticut.

• Stettinius's papers are in the Alderman Library of the University of Virginia. Also see *The Diaries of Edward R. Stettinius, Jr., 1943–1946,* ed. Thomas M. Campbell and George C. Herring (1975); Richard L. Walker, "E. R. Stettinius, Jr.," in *The American Secretaries of State and Their Diplomacy,* vol. 14, ed. Robert H. Ferrell (1965); and Walter Johnson, "Edward R. Stettinius, Jr.," in *An Uncertain Tradition: American Secretaries of State in the Twentieth Century,* ed. Norman A. Grabner (1961). An obituary is in the *New York Times,* 1 Nov. 1949.

MICHAEL J. DEVINE
NATHAN GILES

STEUBEN, Friedrich Wilhelm von (17 Sept. 1730–28 Nov. 1794), inspector general of the Continental army, was born in Magdeburg, Germany, the son of Wilhelm Augustin von Steuben, a Prussian army officer, and Maria Justina Dorothea von Jagow. Baptized as Friedrich Wilhelm Ludolf Gerhard Augustin von Steuben, he usually called himself Frederick William von Steuben in America and signed his letters "Steuben." He spent most of his early childhood in Russia, where his father was a military engineer. In 1742 the family settled in Breslau, Silesia, where Steuben was tutored in mathematics by Jesuits. In 1746 Steuben became a lance corporal in the Lestwitz Infantry Regiment at Breslau and in 1749 was commissioned an ensign in that regiment. He was promoted to second lieutenant in 1752.

Steuben undoubtedly was well schooled in the harsh, unforgiving discipline and machinelike drill associated with Frederick the Great's military system. During the Seven Years' War (1756–1763) Steuben was principally a staff officer. By 1758 he was serving as adjutant of a Prussian volunteer corps, and in 1759 he became adjutant of a brigade. By 1761 he was promoted to captain and transferred to the Prussian general headquarters as an assistant quartermaster in charge of both matters of supply and various administrative duties in the field.

When Frederick the Great ruthlessly downsized his army at the end of the Seven Years' War, Steuben was among the many officers discharged. In 1764, after several months of job hunting, Steuben became chamberlain for Prince Joseph Friedrich Wilhelm of Hohenzollern-Hechigen in southern Germany. In 1769 another south German prince, the margrave of Baden, made Steuben a knight of the aristocratic Order of Fidelity based on an erroneous lineage prepared by Steuben's father. That year Steuben also annexed the title of baron to his name, probably justifying the usage with the same spurious lineage.

Steuben's comfortable life at Hohenzollern-Hechigen ended in late 1776 amid stories of his alleged homosexuality and accusations of his having taken improper liberties with young boys. Steuben's sexual orientation cannot be determined from the scant evidence about his personal life that has survived. He never married, but his many acquaintances in America never thought him anything other than a confirmed bachelor. True or false, the rumors drove Steuben to seek new employment. After efforts in Austria and Baden failed, Steuben went to Paris in June 1777 to seek a position in the French army or the army of the United States, whose diplomatic representatives were based there.

Through a small network of contacts, Steuben was introduced to the U.S. representatives Benjamin Franklin and Silas Deane. Although impressed by Steuben's credentials, Franklin refused to engage Steuben's services, because he and Deane were instructed by the Continental Congress to discourage foreign officers who could not speak English, and Steuben spoke only German and French. Steuben returned to Germany, but an offer of free passage to the United States brought him back to Paris several weeks later. Franklin and Deane subsequently gave Steuben letters of introduction to George Washington and Robert Morris with the understanding that he would be a volunteer without rank or pay.

Steuben sailed from Marseilles in September 1777 and arrived at Portsmouth, New Hampshire, on 1 December. On 5 February 1778 he reached York, Pennsylvania, where Congress was sitting. Learning that Congress had accepted his volunteer services and had directed him to join the Continental army at Valley Forge, Steuben nevertheless made known his intention of serving as a volunteer only for a short time. If after a reasonable trial period his military talents were deemed useful by Washington, Steuben told the congressmen, he would expect respectable rank and pay.

Steuben arrived at Valley Forge in late February. Although his first meeting with Washington was hampered by the necessity of language translation, Washington was impressed by Steuben's gentlemanly demeanor and military knowledge, and he readily agreed to the trial period that Steuben requested.

In March, Washington asked Steuben to serve temporarily as inspector general and to begin his duties by instructing the soldiers in the long-neglected subjects of discipline and drill. To the amazement of the Americans, who were unaccustomed to officers acting as drillmasters, Steuben initially formed a model company, which he personally instructed with the aid of a translator. By April, Steuben had acquired four assistant inspectors and had extended drill instruction to the whole army. Lacking adequate drill manuals, Steuben wrote daily lessons in which he greatly simplified and softened Prussian methods to fit the immediate needs and free-spirited ways of the American soldiers. Washington's aide-de-camp John Laurens wrote his father on 28 February 1778 that Steuben "seems to understand what our Soldiers are capable of, and is not so starch a Systematist as to be averse from adapting established forms to stubborn Circumstances" (Hamer et al., vol. 12, pp. 483–84).

The transformation that Steuben wrought in the training of the Continental army greatly impressed Washington and other observers. In May 1778 Congress, acting at Washington's recommendation, officially appointed Steuben inspector general of the army with the rank and pay of major general. Congress, however, failed to delimit the inspector general's authority and responsibilities. Thus over the next several months Steuben, despite his repeated assurances to the contrary, lobbied hard to annex broad command and administrative power to his new office. His request for broader control was curbed by the Continental Congress on the advice of Washington.

Washington nevertheless continued to value Steuben's efforts to improve the Continental army, particularly with regard to the military manual that Steuben wrote during the winter of 1778–1779. Entitled *Regulations for the Order and Discipline of the Troops of the United States*, it included a revision of the drill instructions that Steuben had composed at Valley Forge and a new section on general administrative procedures. The manual became an indispensable guide for the Continental army and remained in active use by U.S. soldiers until the War of 1812, going through more than seventy editions. During ensuing campaigns, Steuben devoted more of his knowledge and energy to arranging the Continental army and inspecting its men, equipment, and administrative records.

Steuben's efforts to introduce the rudiments of military organization and efficiency met with success nearly everywhere but Virginia, where in November 1780 he became the senior Continental officer with orders to mobilize the state's resources and to forward men and supplies as rapidly as possible to General Nathanael Greene's army opposing Lord Cornwallis in the Carolinas. Steuben's carefully laid plans were frustrated by Virginia's exhausted condition after more than five years of war, the slow response of its public officials, and repeated British incursions up the state's broad rivers.

On 25 April 1781, during an advance up the James River by General William Phillips, Steuben made a respectable stand with a small militia force at Blandford, Virginia, before being obliged to retreat. The British subsequently destroyed large quantities of tobacco at Petersburg and burned the barracks at Chesterfield Court House, where Steuben had tried to assemble reinforcements for Greene. Steuben bitterly blamed these military disasters on state officials, unable to comprehend the reluctance of Governor Thomas Jefferson and the general assembly to disrupt the lives of thousands of private citizens by drafting them into long-term militia service to build and man fortifications.

At the end of April 1781 General Lafayette replaced Steuben as Continental commander in Virginia, freeing Steuben to gather his reinforcements and join Greene's army. Steuben decided to leave Virginia as soon as possible, but the arrival of Cornwallis's army prevented him from doing so. Although Steuben regarded Cornwallis's presence in Virginia as only a temporary incursion, and he remained single-mindedly determined to execute outdated orders from Greene to march to South Carolina with a 500-man detachment of Continental recruits, he yielded to pressure from state authorities to postpone his departure in order to guard a large stock of military stores fifty miles from Richmond. On 5 June, however, Steuben decided that his force was insufficient to defend the stores, and he withdrew his men five miles to the south, leaving most of the stores to be destroyed by Loyalist rangers. The next morning Steuben began marching toward Carolina. He reached the Roanoke River, about thirty miles from the state line, before public criticism and an apparent mutiny by his men brought him to his senses on 11 June. Finally convinced that Cornwallis did not intend to return to the Carolinas, Steuben began retracing his steps the next day, and one week later he joined Lafayette in Hanover County, Virginia.

Refusing to admit wrongdoing, Steuben went to Charlottesville to supervise recruiting efforts, but he soon retreated to a nearby country house to recover from fatigue of body and mind and the oppressive Virginia summer heat. By the end of August Steuben regained his physical and emotional health, and public anger about his misdeeds subsided amid excitement over the news that Cornwallis's army had been besieged at Yorktown. Steuben arrived at Williamsburg on 13 September, and as one of the three senior Continental major generals present during the ensuing siege, he was permitted by Washington to command a division. Steuben's division was on duty in the American trenches on 17 October, when Cornwallis's offer of surrender was received. Steuben invoked the rules of European military etiquette to obtain the honor of remaining in the lines until the final capitulation occurred two days later.

After the Yorktown victory, Steuben continued as Washington's inspector general, uncovering deficiencies in discipline and administration, and during the spring of 1783 he assisted in making plans for a postwar American military establishment. He also played a prominent role in forming the Society of Cincinnati, an association of Continental officers that became controversial largely because of a provision for hereditary membership, which egalitarians such as Jefferson decried as a means of introducing aristocratic distinctions into the American republic. After Washington took leave of his officers in New York City on 4 December 1783, Steuben accompanied him to Annapolis, where on 23 December the commander in chief resigned before Congress and, as one of his last official acts, wrote a letter of commendation for Steuben, acknowledging his "faithful & meritorious Services" (RG 46, entry 7, National Archives).

Steuben resigned his commission in March 1784. Having no prospects of European employment or reward, he remained in the United States and leased the "Louvre," a large estate on the east side of Manhattan Island. There he planned to live a genteel life on the large compensations that he confidently expected to receive from Congress. However, in September 1785 Congress allowed him only a fraction of his inflated expense claims and no pension. By the fall of 1787 Steuben had to move from the Louvre to a boardinghouse on Wall Street, and by the end of 1788 he was so deep in debt that two wartime friends, Benjamin Walker and Alexander Hamilton, took over his finances. Hamilton's appointment the following year as secretary of the Treasury in the new federal government was fortunate for Steuben. With the support of Secretary Hamilton and President Washington, Steuben submitted his war claims to the U.S. Congress in August 1789. The annual pension of $2,500 that Congress granted Steuben in May 1790 was much less than he expected, but it was enough to allow Walker and Hamilton to restore order to his finances. Forced to live more frugally, Steuben spent the summers between 1790 and 1794 in a log cabin on land near Utica, New York, that the state had given him in 1786. In May 1794 Steuben moved permanently to his cabin, where he died.

An unremarkable figure on the European stage for the first three-quarters of his life, Steuben became a prominent actor in the American Revolution through good luck, professional skill, hard work, and energetic self-promotion. The patent falsity of the many tales that Steuben felt compelled to tell Americans of high European distinctions do not alter the fact that he had impeccable credentials as a soldier. Having received advanced training in military administration, he understood completely how a professional army should operate. His principal shortcoming was that, although he learned to speak English passably well within a year of his arrival in the United States, he never fully mastered American political discourse. A plain-spoken, apolitical soldier with rather simplistic authoritarian values, Steuben never troubled his mind much with the complexities of republican government or democratic society. Americans who penetrated Steuben's stern, often blustering, drill-field demeanor found him to be a charming, generous, good-humored man with whom it was difficult to remain angry for long.

A stout man of medium height with strong facial features, Steuben engaged the attention and imagination of American officers and soldiers through the force of his personality. He was unrivaled among the citizens of the new nation as an expert on military affairs. His introduction of European military concepts to the Continental army marks the beginning of a truly professional military tradition in the United States.

• The principal collection of Steuben's papers is at the New-York Historical Society. Smaller collections are at the Historical Society of Pennsylvania, at the Chicago Historical Society, at the Oneida County Historical Society, Utica, N.Y., in the George Washington Papers at the Library of Congress, and in the Papers of the Continental Congress at the National Archives. Edith von Zemenszky and Robert J. Schulmann compiled documents from those and other repositories in a seven-reel microfilm edition, *The Papers of General Friedrich Wilhelm von Steuben, 1777–1794* (1984), which includes only occasional transcriptions, no annotation, and a limited index. For printed documentary sources, see W. W. Abbot et al., eds., *The Papers of George Washington* (1983–); Richard K. Showman et al., eds., *The Papers of General Nathanael Greene* (1976–); Stanley J. Idzerda et al., eds., *Lafayette in the Age of the American Revolution, Selected Letters and Papers, 1776–1790* (1977–); Julian P. Boyd et al., eds., *The Papers of Thomas Jefferson* (1950–), in which Boyd strongly criticizes Steuben's actions in Virginia in an editorial note, "The Conduct of General Steuben," in vol. 6, pp. 619–39; and Philip M. Hamer, et al., eds., *The Papers of Henry Laurens* (1968–). Biographies include John McAuley Palmer, *General von Steuben* (1937), and Philander D. Chase, "Baron von Steuben in the War of Independence" (Ph.D. diss., Duke Univ., 1972). For an account of Steuben's role as inspector general, see David A. Clary and Joseph W. A. Whitehorne, *The Inspectors General of the United States Army, 1777–1903* (1987).

PHILANDER D. CHASE

STEVENS, Abel (19 Jan. 1815–11 Sept. 1897), Methodist Episcopal minister and editor, was born in Philadelphia, Pennsylvania, the son of Samuel Stevens, printer, and Mary Hochenmeller. Some sources place his birth date as 17 January. Stevens completed undergraduate studies at Wesleyan University, Middletown, Connecticut, in 1834, the year in which the New England Conference admitted him to the Methodist ministry. He served churches in Boston and Rhode Island, advancing from trial status to deacon in 1836 and to elder in 1838. After a scholarly tour of Europe in 1837, he married Marguerite Otheman in 1838; they had six children. Stevens continued his ministry and received an M.A. from Brown University in 1839.

In 1840 conference bishops appointed Stevens editor of the Methodist paper *Zion's Herald*, published in Boston. He held this post for twelve years, resigning in 1853 to accept leadership of a new denominational publication, the *National Magazine*, in New York. As a writer and editor, Stevens favored moderate positions in support of compromise during an era of controversy and schism. Regarding the slavery debate, for example, he avoided the strong abolitionist stance of some other Methodists and editors in the North. Instead, Stevens's editorials in the *Zion's Herald* gradually developed an antislavery stance that acknowledged the ills of slaveholding but tried to reconcile factions and prevent absolute fragmentation among Methodist churches. He lamented the schism of 1844–1845 when the southern churches withdrew to form the Methodist Episcopal Church, South.

After the division, some vocal northern Methodists continued to condemn slavery, focusing their attention on the membership of slaveholders in the border states who remained under the northern church's administration. Stevens favored compromise, supporting the position of northern bishops that slaveholders could remain members of the denomination. In 1856 he received appointment as editor of the New York denominational paper, *Christian Advocate and Journal*, a post he had declined in 1848. In his new office he began sparring with abolitionists. By 1860 his moderation appealed to few in the polarized nation and denomination, and he was not reappointed editor. He continued to present his position, however, by helping to found a new paper, *The Methodist*, to rival the *Christian Advocate*. After the Civil War, Stevens hoped to reunite the denomination by allowing southern churches easy readmission; many fellow northerners opposed this, however, and alienation on both sides kept the regional denominations divided. Stevens retired in 1865 but contributed to newspapers occasionally as associate editor and continued to write.

Stevens had begun in the mid-1840s to write memoirs, biographies, and histories. His *Sketches and Incidents; or, A Budget from the Saddle-bags of a Superannuated Itinerant*, first published in 1843 and reprinted in several subsequent editions, presented a series of stories that celebrated Methodist piety and the traveling preacher. In the 1850s he turned to histories, publishing *Memorial of the Early Progress of Methodism in the Eastern States* (1851–1852) and *The History of the Religious Movement of the Eighteenth Century, Called Methodism* (1858–1861), works that laid a foundation for several additional histories and editions in the following decades, including the four-volume *History of the Methodist Episcopal Church in the United States of America* (1864–1867). In his accounts he continued to advocate moderation, trying to resolve the disputes of his day. Stevens defined Methodism as ecumenical religion, even though southern and northern churches had split and controversies about authority, holiness,

personal religious experience, and doctrine flared after the Civil War. During this period, he compiled material for the Methodists' centenary celebration in 1866, and he published several biographies in the same decade, commemorating Nathan Bangs and notable Methodist women. His *The Women of Methodism* (1866) contained sketches of Susanna Wesley, the countess of Huntingdon, and Barbara Heck, all important supporters and leaders of early Methodist groups.

After retiring in 1865, Stevens moved to Europe, settling in Geneva, Switzerland, where he wrote his biography of Madame de Staël, whom he presented as an example of propriety during the French Revolution. In 1869 he married Amelia Dayton; she soon died, and he married Frances C. Greenough in 1871. The couple moved in 1888 to San José, California, where Stevens died. He had no children.

In a lifetime of writing and editing, Stevens tried to steer the Methodist Episcopal church away from divisions, and he shaped a historical legacy that celebrated Methodist unity and its influence in American culture.

• Stevens's papers are in the United Methodist Church Archives at Drew University in Madison, N.J. The newspapers Stevens edited, especially *Zion's Herald* and *Christian Advocate and Journal* are the best compilations of his opinions on the issues of his day, and his editorial stances are summarized in Edward D. Jervey, "*Zion's Herald*: The Independent Voice of American Methodism," *Methodist History* 25 (1987): 91–110. Stevens's books reflect his evaluations of Methodist history and Christian character. Although not precise in historical details, *Sketches and Incidents; or, A Budget from the Saddle-bags of a Superannuated Itinerant* (1843) contains anecdotes about Stevens's ministry. For the context of Methodist history, see Emory Stevens Bucke, ed., *The History of American Methodism* (3 vols., 1964). The *Methodist Union Catalog* (preliminary ed., 1967) contains a full list of Stevens's publications.

PHILIP N. MULDER

STEVENS, Alzina Ann Parsons (27 May 1849–3 June 1900), printer, labor organizer, journalist, and settlement worker, was born in Parsonsfield, Maine, the daughter of Enoch Parsons, a farmer and carpenter, and Louisa Page. While Alzina Parsons was still young, her father gave up farming and settled the family in the mill town of Somersworth, New Hampshire, where she attended high school. A lifetime of self-supporting work began after her father's death in 1864, when she took a job in a textile mill.

Parsons left New England about 1871 to learn a trade in Chicago. After a year of knocking on doors, she was hired to learn the printer's craft in a small, nonunion book and job firm. She first came to public attention as president of Working Women's Union No. 1 at its founding in 1878. The goal of this union, brainchild of the Chicago Council of Trades and Labor Unions and the Socialist Labor party, was to organize "the unorganized masses" of women to affiliate with trade unions, and Stevens obtained financial help from the powerful Chicago Typographical Union for this purpose.

In speeches to the Working Women's Union, Stevens presented a well-developed argument about woman's right to work, through which she tried to counter those in the labor movement who wanted to reduce competition for jobs by driving women from the labor force. She insisted that the days of female dependency were done, that women were obliged to support themselves, and that their right to work equaled men's. Moreover, she asserted, the strength of the working class would be determined by men's adaptation to these new circumstances and their solidarity with women. Stevens herself obtained membership in the Chicago Typographical Union in 1879 through an amnesty program for nonunion printers that the union paired with an endorsement of membership regardless of sex.

Alzina Parsons married a Mr. Stevens in 1876 or 1877 but soon moved without him to Toledo, Ohio, presenting the traveling card of a journeyman printer to the typographical union in 1881. Over the next decade she transformed herself from printer to journalist while remaining active in the labor movement. She worked first as a proofreader and copyeditor for H. H. Hardesty, publisher of local histories and atlases; while working for Hardesty, she also wrote a *Military History of Ohio* (1887). Her articles began to appear in the labor press, notably in *John Swinton's Paper*, and her union membership changed to an honorary one by 1888. In 1890 she was writing for the Democratic daily, the *Toledo Bee*.

Stevens had joined the Knights of Labor in 1883 through a trade assembly for printers; seven years later she headed the order's district assembly of northwestern Ohio. Service on a committee to foster cooperation between the Knights and the Federation of Labor in Toledo suggests how fully integrated into the labor movement she had become. Her growing prominence in the movement also reflected her leadership among wage-earning women whose interest in the Knights climbed despite an exodus of men into craft unions. Stevens led the Joan of Arc Assembly, one of Toledo's two assemblies for women, and organized women in surrounding towns. Knights master workman Terence Powderly deemed her "thoroughly versed on all subjects pertaining to woman's work and wages" (to Mrs. Alexander Sullivan, 27 Jan. 1892). Stevens declined an offer to succeed Leonora Barry as the order's general investigator of women's work in 1890.

Stevens also emerged as a strong advocate of political action by labor to offset the power of economic concentration. Writing in *John Swinton's Paper* in support of Henry George's candidacy for mayor of New York City, she favored voting "class against class" (31 Oct. 1886) but modified her stance in the next few years to favor alliances between the working class and middle-class reformers against the trusts. She pressed the Knights of Labor to join discussions leading to the formation of the People's party, and after the party's founding convention at St. Louis in 1892, Stevens accepted an offer to coedit a Populist newspaper, the *Vanguard*, published weekly in Chicago.

Before Stevens left Ohio, Powderly appointed her to represent the Knights on the Women's Labor Committee of the World's Congress Auxiliary, a body charged with planning labor meetings at the World's Columbian Exposition to be held in Chicago in 1893. The assignment reintroduced her to the city's activists and a new generation of prominent women, most notably Jane Addams of Hull-House and Corinne S. Brown of the Illinois Woman's Alliance. Her standing among them was soon evident when the head of the congress auxiliary rejected the labor committee's proposed program in favor of one deemed by Stevens to be too neutral to interest the laboring classes, and she led the committee to resign in protest.

Stevens had returned to Chicago as women's groups and labor were campaigning against sweatshops and in favor of passage of the Illinois Factory and Workshop Inspection Act. The *Vanguard* became a voice in the reformers' campaign until the newspaper collapsed, victim of a bank's failure, just as the Inspection Act became law in 1893. Governor John P. Altgeld appointed Stevens to be assistant factory inspector under Florence Kelley, posts they held until 1897. From an office at Hull-House the inspectors monitored sanitary conditions in sweatshops, enforced the law's provisions limiting child labor and the hours of women's work, and lobbied for further legislation to protect children.

In the last years of her life, Stevens moved into Hull-House. The list of her duties indicates a willingness to pitch in wherever necessary, but she continued to devise ways of resisting the exploitation of wage-earning women and children. She established unions in women's trades and fought to integrate them into the citywide labor movement. She headed the Dorcas Federal Labor Union and worked with the Council of Women's Trade Unions of Chicago, both based at the settlement. She also presided over the Hull-House Women's Club. She is best known, however, for the projects she pursued to protect children: lobbying for better compulsory education laws and creation of the Juvenile Court of Cook County and improvising a model for the work of juvenile probation officers. She became the court's first probation officer in 1899.

Always self-supporting, Stevens defied the odds against women's occupational mobility in her generation. Throughout the 1880s she was optimistic that her experience might spread and transform not only women's work but also the working class. "[T]he labor question can never be settled, *never*, without [women's] intelligent and hearty co-operation," she wrote in *John Swinton's Paper* (21 Feb. 1886); but working conditions worsened, and craft unions failed to match the promise of the Knights of Labor as vehicles for women's economic power. Without abandoning hope for working-class solidarity, she allied with middle-class reformers to gain protective legislation. Stevens died of diabetes at Hull-House.

• Stevens's name and work recur in manuscript records of the Chicago Typographical Union, Chicago Historical Society, and in publications of the Knights of Labor. The only substantial body of her correspondence survives in the Terence V. Powderly Papers, Catholic University of America. A few letters exist in the Henry Demarest Lloyd Papers, State Historical Society of Wisconsin. The same library owns all but the last issue of the *Vanguard*. Hardesty included her *Military History of Ohio* as a section of his local histories as early as 1884. In addition to annual reports on their investigations, Stevens and Kelley coauthored the essay on wage-earning children in *Hull-House Maps and Papers* (1895); articles based on her investigations include "The Tenement House Curse: Some Chicago Tenement Houses," *Arena* 9 (Apr. 1894): 662–68, and "Child Slavery in America: The Child, the Factory, and the State," *Arena* 10 (June 1894): 117–35; also see her "Life in a Social Settlement—Hull House, Chicago," *Self-Culture* 9 (Mar. 1899): 42–51. For her family's history, see Henry Parsons, *Parsons Family: Descendants of Cornet Joseph Parsons*, vol. 2 (1920), p. 207, though she and her siblings are not traced there. The best sources on her employment are her newspaper articles about women's labor. Meetings of the Working Women's Union were covered by both the *Socialist* (Chicago) and the *Chicago Tribune*. Two biographical sketches appeared in her lifetime, in the *Journal of United Labor*, 16 Aug. 1888, and in Frances E. Willard and Mary A. Livermore, eds., *A Woman of the Century* (1893). The only modern, published study is the entry by Allen F. Davis in *Notable American Women*. Immortalized in Jane Addams, *Twenty Years at Hull House* (1910), Stevens crosses the pages of most major works on Chicago reformers in the late nineteenth century, notably Ray Ginger, *Altgeld's America* (1958); Dorothy R. Blumberg, *Florence Kelley* (1966); and Meredith Tax, *The Rising of the Women* (1980). Useful references to her work in the 1870s are found in Carolyn Ashbaugh, *Lucy Parsons* (1976), and Mari Jo Buhle, *Women and American Socialism* (1981). Brief but insightful comments on Stevens's life are in Florence Kelley, "Industrial Democracy: Women in the Trade Unions," *Outlook* 84 (15 Dec. 1906): 926–31. Obituaries are in the *Chicago Tribune*, the *Toledo Bee*, and the *New York Times*, all 4 June 1900.

ANN D. GORDON

STEVENS, Ashton (11 Aug. 1872–11 July 1951), theater critic, was born in San Francisco, California, the son of James William Stevens and Hannah Laura Thompson. Educated in public schools in Oakland, California, he studied in a law office in Salina, Kansas, for one year, after which family circumstances forced him to return to San Francisco to earn money giving banjo lessons (he remained passionate about the instrument throughout his life).

Two chance meetings with publishers quickly propelled Stevens into a career as a critic. One of his banjo students was Frederick Marriott, publisher of the *News Letter*, a literary weekly. Stevens so impressed Marriott with his comments following a concert in 1894 that he hired him, first to write about music and then theater. This led to a job covering theater for the *San Francisco Morning Call* in 1896, and, in 1897, to a job editing the *News Letter* and the *Overland Monthly*. The second fortuitous meeting was with William Randolph Hearst in 1898 on the ferry between Oakland and San Francisco; this meeting led to Hearst's hiring Stevens to cover theater for his flagship newspaper,

the *San Francisco Examiner*. In 1900 Stevens married Aleece Uhlhorn; they had no children and remained married until her death in 1926. The following year Stevens married Florence Katherine Krug; they had no children.

Stevens devoted the rest of his career to reviewing theater for Hearst papers. Following ten years at the *Examiner* (1898–1908), he worked for two years at the *New York Evening Journal* (1908–1910) before spending the final forty-odd years of his career with Hearst's ever-shifting foothold in Chicago—first with the *Chicago Examiner* in 1910, and continuing with the *Herald and Examiner* (1910–1932) and the *Herald-American* (1932–1951).

Stevens worked in an era when reviewers could hobnob with performers and still command authority in print. He was close friends with John Barrymore, the great actor who spent his waning years losing his battle with alcohol on Chicago stages. In his 1944 biography of Barrymore titled *Good Night, Sweet Prince*, Gene Fowler referred to Stevens as the "sagacious dean of the drama critics," and pointed out Stevens's hallmark ability to write criticism that was tough but never mean: "Although Mr. Stevens never coddled an inferior performance, he smeared no poison on his critical darts. He brought a gay creativeness to his task, a voice clearly heard, yet so unlike the iconoclastic snarls of those who grow violently wise after a last night's event." It was this ability to leaven his judgments that earned Stevens the sobriquet "the mercy killer."

Stage and screen writer Ben Hecht echoed this view when he took a look back at the theater critics who had been active when he was a journalist in Chicago in the 1910s. In his article "Wistfully Yours" (*Theatre Arts*, July 1951), Hecht described the Chicago of his salad days as being both dramatically and journalistically backward, "But, oddly enough, we had the finest group of drama critics I have ever known." He put Stevens at the top of the list: "He was (and is) indeed of that rare tribe of witty men that the French once produced—de Gourmont and Anatole France—who found more pleasure in using their wit to brighten praise than to sharpen malice."

Stevens was the only critic in Chicago whose headlines frequently featured his own name: This may have been an example of the bombastic editorial style of Hearst, but Stevens usually managed to justify the fanfare, sprinkling his writing with witty turns of phrase.

In San Francisco, Stevens befriended one of the greats of the time by writing that "dull people don't like Mrs. Fiske's acting." In Chicago he predicted the success of the bright fifteen-year-old boy who lived across the street, Orson Welles. But he was not the kind of gadfly who cozied up to every star: he carried on a protracted feud with actor-manager Richard Mansfield. He could also dismiss a play with a sharp remark. In one review of a particularly bad play, he remarked that on his way out he had passed a murdered gangster on the sidewalk. Returning to the subject of the play and its playwright, he suggested that the wrong man had been killed.

Stevens died in his Chicago apartment. The lasting historical significance of a career such as Stevens's is not easy to gauge. He was not the kind of critic who defines movements. He did not champion playwrights of significance. His career in Chicago paralleled a steady decline in the theatrical vitality of that city. And yet he was perhaps the supreme exemplar of the rare reviewer who manages to convey an optimistic love of the theater even when panning a performance. He rendered his judgments honestly, with wit, wisdom, and heart. He could not save a theater community that was losing battles against technology in the form of radio and film, and against New York City, which in his time cemented its position as America's theater capital. But Stevens informed and entertained his many avid readers, and he perhaps helped to keep alive the hope for a theater that could—and eventually did—do better.

• Some of Stevens's reviews are on microfilm at the Harold Washington Library in Chicago. Many of his interviews with actors were collected in 1923 under the title *Actorviews*. Stevens wrote one play, *Mary's Way Out*, in collaboration with Charles Michelson. For a thorough profile of Stevens see Bill Doll, "Ashton Stevens," *Theatre Arts*, July 1951. Obituaries are in the *New York Times*, 13 July 1951, and *Newsweek*, 23 July 1951.

SCOTT FOSDICK

STEVENS, Doris Caroline (26 Oct. 1888–22 Mar. 1963), suffragist and feminist activist, was born in Omaha, Nebraska, the daughter of Henry Hendebourck Stevens, a small businessman, and Caroline Koopman. After graduating from Oberlin College in 1911, Stevens did settlement work in Cleveland, Ohio, taught high school for two years, and then abandoned regular employment to become a full-time organizer for the Congressional Union, the militant suffrage organization. In 1914 she caught the eye of Alva Belmont, the dictatorial millionaire patron of militant suffragism. Working under the direction of Belmont and Alice Paul, the founder and driving force behind the Congressional Union and its successor, the National Woman's party (NWP), Stevens opened headquarters, organized meetings, and spoke for suffrage throughout the country. When the CU began to picket the White House in an attempt to force President Woodrow Wilson to support the suffrage amendment, Stevens was one of the suffragists arrested. In 1917 she was sentenced to sixty days in prison for picketing on Bastille Day with a banner that proclaimed, "Liberty, Equality, Fraternity." Defended by Dudley Field Malone, her future husband, collector of the port of New York, and a close friend of and avid campaigner for Wilson, Stevens received a presidential pardon after three days. Malone attracted public attention by resigning his position in protest against the government's failure to enfranchise women.

Stevens celebrated the suffrage victory in 1920 by writing the history of militance, *Jailed for Freedom* (1920), and then married Malone in 1921. They moved to Paris, where Malone built a lucrative law practice winning French divorces for wealthy Americans. Stevens became a kind of personal companion and right-hand woman to Alva Belmont, who had settled in France after the suffrage victory and turned her attention to international feminism. Steven's marriage to Malone quickly proved troubled. He drank excessively, spent time with other women, and, on at least a few occasions, physically abused Stevens. In 1923 she met and began an intimate relationship with Jonathan E. Mitchell, a journalist whom she married in 1935 after her 1929 divorce from Malone. She had no children in either marriage.

Throughout this period, Stevens moved in the bohemian circle of Greenwich Village through her part-time residence in Croton-on-Hudson, a "country" enclave of radical artists and intellectuals, and experienced as well the expatriate community in Paris and on the Riviera. Immersed in the sexual revolution of the 1910s and 1920s, she served as a symbol of "New Womanhood." With a reputation as a beautiful and vivacious feminist, she emphasized cooperation with men. In a 1927 speech she concluded that "the only fun in life is where men and women play together, and men and women work together."

Throughout the 1920s and 1930s Stevens devoted herself to international feminist activities in Europe and the Americas. The NWP turned its attention after 1920 to passage of an equal rights amendment. Stymied at home by widespread opposition from other women's organizations concerned about the impact of equal rights legislation on protective labor laws for women, the NWP turned to the international arena, working for an equal rights treaty. Stevens lobbied at the League of Nations; helped to found and served as the first chairman of the Inter-American Commission of Women, created in 1928 at the Havana meeting of the Pan-American Conference; and that same year attracted international attention when she was arrested outside the French president's summer palace, where she and a small group of women sought support from the signers of the Kellogg-Briand treaty for the principle of equal rights for women. She studied international law at Columbia in preparation for her work on behalf of independent nationality for married women (that is, a wife's nationality not automatically following that of her husband) at the First World Conference for Codification of International Law at The Hague in 1930, and she served from 1931 to 1936 on the League of Nations' Women's Consultative Committee on Nationality. She chaired the Inter-American Commission of Women until 1939, when she was removed by the U.S. government in what she bitterly described as a left-wing coup engineered by Eleanor Roosevelt. In the course of her international work, she adopted for herself the title "youngest international feminist leader."

By the 1930s Stevens had moved from her vaguely socialist politics of the 1910s in a decidedly rightward direction. Her second husband, Mitchell, wrote for

William F. Buckley's *National Review*, and in the 1950s Stevens and Mitchell supported the anti-Communist crusade of Senator Joseph R. McCarthy.

Stevens also changed her feminist affiliations in later years. When Alva Belmont died in 1933, Stevens learned that the older woman, who had promised her a legacy in return for her years of personal service, had revoked her bequest to Stevens and directed the money to the NWP instead. Although Stevens undertook legal action and eventually received a settlement from the estate, she continued to resent Alice Paul, whom she suspected of turning Belmont against her. This controversy set the stage for Steven's break with the NWP in 1947, in the aftermath of an acrimonious lawsuit over the leadership and resources of the organization.

After leaving the NWP, Stevens channeled her feminist efforts into the Lucy Stone League, a New York group that carried the feminist legacy into the 1960s by advocating equal rights and seeking to attract younger women to the cause. She also took up songwriting, and her sentimental ballads based on childhood memories of Nebraska, such as "Red Peony," met with a measure of success in the entertainment industry. But Stevens never turned away from the women's cause, and her obituary headline in the *Washington Star* labeled her a "famous feminist." In 1986, twenty-three years after her death in New York City, her desire to help make feminism a recognized area of study within the university came to fruition when Princeton University announced that her estate had endowed a chair in women's studies. As a militant suffragist, a symbol of emancipated womanhood, a staunch advocate of equal rights, and a champion of international feminism, Stevens left her mark on American society.

• Stevens's voluminous papers, which include correspondence, speeches, organizational papers, diaries, accounts of dreams, transcriptions of the taped reminiscences of Jonathan Mitchell, and unpublished drafts of short stories, plays, and novel chapters, are in the Schlesinger Library at Radcliffe College. The National Woman's Party Papers, housed at the Library of Congress, are available on microfilm from the Microfilming Corporation of America. See Leila J. Rupp, "Feminism and the Sexual Revolution in the Early Twentieth Century: The Case of Doris Stevens," *Feminist Studies* 15, no. 2 (1989): 289–309. Useful discussions of the militant suffrage movement include Linda G. Ford, *Iron-Jawed Angels: The Suffrage Militancy of the National Woman's Party, 1912–1920* (1991), and Christine A. Lunardini, *From Equal Suffrage to Equal Rights: Alice Paul and the National Woman's Party, 1910–1928* (1986). On the post-1920s movement, see Susan D. Becker, *The Origins of the Equal Rights Amendment: American Feminism between the Wars* (1981); Nancy F. Cott, *The Grounding of Modern Feminism* (1987); and Leila J. Rupp and Verta Taylor, *Survival in the Doldrums: The American Women's Rights Movement, 1945 to the 1960s* (1987). A short obituary is in the *New York Times*, 25 Mar. 1963.

LEILA J. RUPP

STEVENS, Edwin Augustus (29 July 1795–8 Aug. 1868), railroad company executive, was born in Hoboken, New Jersey, the son of John Stevens, an inventor and entrepreneur, and Rachel Cox. Stevens was educated by private tutors, and in 1812 he began assisting his father and elder brother Robert in the management of family-owned ferryboat lines that provided service across the Delaware River between Philadelphia and Trenton and Camden, New Jersey.

In 1825 Stevens and his family extended their transport operations by acquiring control of the Union Line, which consisted of stagecoach service between Trenton and New Brunswick, New Jersey, and ferry boat service from New Brunswick and South Amboy, New Jersey, to New York City.

The Stevens family also initiated the first railroad operations in New Jersey. In 1826 John Stevens constructed a small railroad line on his property in Hoboken, which he used to demonstrate the feasibility of the new technology to legislators and potential investors. In 1830 the New Jersey legislature granted Edwin and his brother a corporate charter for the Camden and Amboy Railroad Corporation. Robert became the railroad's president and Edwin became the treasurer and manager.

In 1831 the state legislature merged the operations of the railroad with the Delaware and Raritan Canal Company, owned by prominent politician Robert Stockton, to create the United Companies. The state granted the United Companies a thirty-year monopoly on all railway and canal transport between New York and Philadelphia in exchange for payment of $200,000 in stock, a guaranteed annual dividend of $30,000, and a payment of a transit duty levied on all interstate traffic along the route.

The Camden and Amboy Railroad completed construction between South Amboy and Camden in 1834. The Stevenses initially used English locomotives, which were transported across the Atlantic and reassembled by company employees. The family later established locomotive works at Belleville, New Jersey, where they constructed the first locomotives made in the United States, and at Bordentown, New Jersey, where they also manufactured locomotives for other railroads.

Holding a monopoly over one of the most heavily traveled routes in the country, the Camden and Amboy became fabulously wealthy. Every railroad from the South and the West seeking to transport freight or passengers to New York City either had to pay duties and use the Camden and Amboy (plus the Stevens ferry line across the Hudson River) or else take a more circuitous route across New York State. Stevens's railroad was able to pay a 12 percent dividend every year, even during recessions that bankrupted other railroads.

Stevens's railroad protected its monopoly by extensive political activity, which included lavish parties and contributions to New Jersey politicians and candidates at every level of government. In his *History of the Railroads and Canals of the United States of America* (1860), Henry Varnum Poor, founder of Standard & Poor's, noted that "the Company is the paramount authority in the State dictating the legislation upon all subjects in which it has a real or fancied interest." Poor estimated that the United Companies had paid more than $2.5 million to the state of New Jersey by 1860 and provided the major sources of funding of the state government operations. Journalist William Edgar Sackett, in *Modern Battles of Trenton* (1895), declared, "Such a thing as a [political] candidate announcing his opposition to the railroad company and surviving the election was almost unheard of in State politics. . . . So absolute was its [Camden and Amboy's] control of all departments of the State government that the State itself came to be known derisively among the people of other States as the State of Camden and Amboy."

In 1836 the United Companies acquired the Philadelphia and Trenton Railroad, which controlled a busy Pennsylvania route and owned rights to a bridge over the Delaware River. The United Companies later acquired control of the New Jersey Railroad and Transportation Company, which ran between New Brunswick and Jersey City, and also the Morris and Essex Railroad, which connected Newark to Dover and Hackettstown.

In 1854 the United Companies persuaded the New Jersey legislature to enact new legislation that continued its monopoly rights (set to expire in 1865) until 1869. When Robert Stevens died in 1856, Edwin succeeded him as president of the Camden and Amboy.

In 1863 Stevens negotiated and approved an agreement with the Pennsylvania Railroad under which the latter leased certain United Companies' properties to obtain a direct route to New York City. Edwin retired from the presidency of the Camden and Amboy Railroad in 1867 and was succeeded by William Gantzer. The Pennsylvania Railroad later acquired full control over the United Companies' properties in 1871.

The Stevenses' steamship operations had also led to an interest in naval warfare technology. Robert and Edwin conducted experiments on, and designed percussion shells for, guns on warships and were early proponents of the development of ironclad warships. The U.S. Navy Department contracted with them to begin construction of a large prototype armored vessel, the *Stevens Battery*, in 1842 but then failed to provide funding to complete its construction. After the outbreak of the Civil War, Edwin constructed a much smaller version, the *Naugatuck*, which joined in the attack on the *Merrimac*. He also loaned several of his company's ferryboats to the navy for use in the naval blockade of the southern coast.

In 1836 Stevens had married Mary B. Picton of West Point, New York, with whom he had two children before her death in 1841. His second wife was Martha Bayard Dod of Princeton, New Jersey, whom he wed in 1854, and with whom he had seven children.

When Stevens died in Paris, he left an estate worth $18 million. Stevens, like his father, was interested in promoting the development of engineering education. In his will he left extensive land holdings in Hoboken and nearly $1 million to be used to set up the Stevens Institute of Technology, which opened in 1870 on the former family estate, "Castle Point," in Hoboken.

• The Stevens Family Papers are located at the New Jersey Historical Society, Newark, which has published Miriam Studley et al., eds., *Guide to the Microfilm Edition of the Stevens Family Papers* (1968). See also James Elfreth Watkins, *Sketches of John Stevens, Robert L. Stevens, Edwin A. Stevens* (1892). Information about Stevens and his family's role in New Jersey politics can be found in Wheaton Lane, *From Indian Trail to Iron Horse: A History of Transportation in New Jersey* (1939); George L. A. Reilly, *The Camden and Amboy Railroad in New Jersey Politics, 1830–1871* (1951); and George H. Burgess and Miles C. Kennedy, *Centennial History of the Pennsylvania Railroad Company 1846–1946* (1949). Information on Stevens's work on armored ships is contained in James P. Baxter III, *The Introduction of the Ironclad Warship* (1933). An obituary is in the *New York Times*, 11 Aug. 1868.

STEPHEN G. MARSHALL

STEVENS, Emily (27 Feb. 1882–2 Jan. 1928), actress, was born in New York City, the daughter of Robert E. Stevens, a stage manager, and Emma Maddern, an actress. Although her parents had been on the road during most of their adult lives, they settled into a house in the country at Larchmont, New York, during Emily's early childhood. There they were often joined by Minnie Maddern (later Mrs. Fiske), the daughter of Emma's sister, who was to become the premier actress of the American stage. Although many sources refer to Emily Stevens as a niece of Mrs. Fiske, they actually were cousins.

Stevens was educated at two convent schools, the Institute of the Holy Angels at Fort Lee (N.J.) on the Hudson and St. Mary's Hall in Burlington, New Jersey. A golden-haired beauty with a quick wit, she had suffered a nervous breakdown in childhood, and her face tended to look sad in repose. At eighteen, she was invited by her cousin Minnie to play a maid in *Becky Sharp*. Stevens made her debut on 8 October 1900 in Bridgeport, Connecticut, and remained with Mrs. Fiske's company for eight years. Five weeks after her debut came her first speaking role, that of the title character's younger sister in *Tess of the D'Urbervilles*, at the Grand Opera House in Chicago. After the death of her mother in 1903, Stevens grew even closer to her cousin Minnie and to Minnie's husband, Harrison Grey Fiske, who nicknamed her "the Whiffet." The two women sailed together to Europe in the summer of 1903, visiting Germany and Switzerland.

In New York again, Stevens attracted critical attention for the emotional depth she packed into the one-word reaction "Ah!" in *Leah Kleshna*, which opened 12 December 1904 at the Manhattan Theatre. The strain of touring several productions over the next few years took a toll on Stevens's relationship with her older cousin. While Mrs. Fiske continued to take her popular hits on the road, Harrison Fiske gave Stevens a New York engagement and her first starring role, playing opposite George Arliss in *Septimus* at the Hackett Theatre in 1909. She won both critical and popular acclaim as, in Mrs. Fiske's description, an "emotional ingenue." Of her performance in *The Boss* at the Astor Theatre in 1911, *Life* magazine noted: "Miss Emily Stevens is harvesting the fruits of her considerable apprenticeship with Mrs. Fiske. Her teaching is shown a little by imitation of mannerisms of speech, but more creditably in freedom from conventional pose and movement." At Chicago's Princess Theatre in 1912, Stevens played a triumphant 100-performance engagement as Mary Turner in *Within the Law*. By 1914 Stevens had emerged as one of America's most popular young actresses, but signs of nervous exhaustion prompted Mrs. Fiske to take her cousin to New England for a restful summer vacation.

By 1916 Stevens could afford to live in an apartment at the Brevoort Hotel in Manhattan, where she attracted such interesting New Yorkers as Alexander Woollcott to her lively salons, but she broke off all relations with both of the Fiskes. As if to demonstrate her independence from Mrs. Fiske, she took on one of her cousin's great roles, Hedda Gabler, in a 1926 New York revival; and she refused to go on the road as was expected of stage stars of the day. She found her greatest role in Louis K. Anspacher's *The Unchastened Woman*, which opened at the 39th Street Theatre on 9 October 1915 and ran 193 performances. Walter Prichard Eaton described her portrayal of the bored, neurotic wife: "The charm of the woman, the vampire allure, the worldly ease, the ready wit, the restless, neurasthenic vacancy of life, the selfish cruelty, are all indicated surely, easily and vividly." Indeed, during the peak years of her career, Stevens made a specialty of playing "modern" women—attractively feminine yet imperiously self-contained. Other such parts included leading roles in *The Fugitive* (1917), *The Gentile Wife* (1918), and *Fata Morgana* (1924). She also proved herself a gifted comedienne in *Sophie* (1920). Having found success on her own, Stevens became less insistent about her kinship with Mrs. Fiske and allowed journalists to perpetuate the mistaken impression that she was a niece rather than a cousin.

In her last year Stevens was under the care of a neurologist. When he was unavailable during the Christmas holidays of 1927, Dr. Milton J. Wilson treated her nervous condition by administering a sedative. On the morning of New Year's Day 1928, Stevens's maid found her unconscious in the living room of her apartment at 50 West Sixty-seventh Street, the windows wide open. She was taken to a hospital and died there without regaining consciousness. The cause of death was variously reported as pneumonia or a drug overdose.

A *New York Times* editorial (4 Jan. 1928) commented on Stevens's long apprenticeship to Mrs. Fiske: "The young woman who is willing to give ten years to unimportant parts for the sake of bringing out her own best qualities seems rare today. To such, Miss Stevens's career is worth considering." Perhaps the most fitting assessment of her contribution came in a letter to the editor of the *New York Times* Dramatic Mail Bag

(15 Jan. 1928): "One must be grateful for so beautiful a talent, but one must regret that it was adequately and worthily displayed so seldom. Miss Stevens could be charming, but her best roles were disagreeable; it seems to be the fate of actresses who bear evidence of high mental gifts to portray in modern drama women of unpleasant disposition."

• The Billy Rose Theatre Collection at the Lincoln Center Library has a clippings file on Emily Stevens. The best general source of biographical material is Archie Binns, *Mrs. Fiske and the American Theatre* (1955). A three-column obituary with photograph is in the *New York Times*, 3 Jan. 1928.

FELICIA HARDISON LONDRÉ

STEVENS, George (18 Dec. 1904–8 Mar. 1975), film director, was born George Cooper Stevens in Oakland, California, the son of Landers Stevens and Georgia Cooper, performer/managers of a San Francisco theater troupe. Stevens worked intermittently as a child actor, making his stage debut at age five at San Francisco's Alcazar Theatre. After one year at Valley Union High School in Sonoma, California, Stevens moved with his family to Los Angeles, where his father sought work in the burgeoning movie industry. The younger Stevens embarked on a career behind the camera, beginning in 1921 with a job as a still photographer at a shop in Glendale, California.

While still in his teens Stevens was hired as an assistant cameraman by the Hal Roach studios and was sent to Utah to work with master cameraman Fred Jackman on the "Rex, the King of Wild Horses" series. Staying with the Hal Roach studios for several years, he worked as a cameraman and gag writer on numerous short comedy films with Stan Laurel and Oliver Hardy and eventually began directing comedy shorts. Moving to Universal studios in 1932, Stevens made an inauspicious debut as a director of feature-length films with the little-noticed comedy *The Cohens and Kellys in Trouble* (1933). Stevens moved on again, this time to RKO, the studio for which he worked exclusively over the next seven years.

Stevens's initial films for RKO were more undistinguished, low-budget efforts. When finally given the chance to direct an "A-picture"—a screen version of Booth Tarkington's novel *Alice Adams*—thirty-year-old Stevens rose to the challenge. A well-cast Katharine Hepburn played the title character, a resourceful girl from the lower middle class who aspires to be part of her small midwestern city's beau monde. The commercial and critical success of *Alice Adams* (1935) promoted Stevens to the ranks of major directors. Thereafter, RKO assigned Stevens to a wide variety of projects. The most notable were *Annie Oakley* (1935), with Barbara Stanwyck and Melvyn Douglas; *Swing Time* (1936), often called the best of the Fred Astaire–Ginger Rogers pairings; *Vivacious Lady* (1938), with Ginger Rogers and newcomer James Stewart; and a screen adaptation of Rudyard Kipling's portrayal of the raj, the adventure classic *Gunga Din* (1939), with Cary Grant, Victor McLaglen, and Douglas Fairbanks, Jr. Less successful were *Quality Street* (1937), a poorly received second collaboration with Katherine Hepburn; *A Damsel in Distress* (1937), with Fred Astaire and Joan Fontaine; and *Vigil in the Night* (1940), with Carole Lombard.

Leaving RKO, Stevens made the popular romantic comedy *Penny Serenade* (1941), with Irene Dunne and Cary Grant, for Columbia Pictures and worked for a third time with Katharine Hepburn on MGM's *Woman of the Year* (1942), the first pairing of Hepburn with Spencer Tracy. Stevens made two successful comedies with Columbia studios' leading actress, Jean Arthur: *Talk of the Town* (1942), which also starred Cary Grant and Ronald Colman, and *The More the Merrier* (1943), a humorous look at the wartime housing shortage, co-starring Joel McCrea.

Stevens then volunteered for the U.S. Army Signal Corps, spending two and half years heading the film unit. Among the events he recorded were the D-Day invasion, the liberation of Paris, and the opening of the Dachau concentration camp.

After mustering out as a lieutenant colonel, Stevens returned to Hollywood determined to make movies that said something about the human condition. Working for RKO for one last time, Stevens made *I Remember Mama* (1948), the story of a struggling Norwegian immigrant family in San Francisco presided over by a wise and forbearing matriarch played by Irene Dunne. Based on John Van Druten's popular stage play, this drama offered many comedic touches and stands as a transitional work in Stevens's career.

It was with *A Place in the Sun* (1951; Paramount), starring a photogenic young Montgomery Clift and Elizabeth Taylor, that the mature George Stevens fully emerged. Stevens won the Academy Award for best director for this updated version of Theodore Dreiser's novel *An American Tragedy*. His next effort was a quickly forgotten melodrama, *Something to Live For* (1952; Paramount), with Joan Fontaine and Ray Milland. Stevens bounced back with the landmark western *Shane* (1953; Paramount), featuring Alan Ladd as a gunslinger who comes to the defense of homesteaders. The film symbolized the lawless, independent Old West giving way to an orderly New West of farmers and ranchers. This theme was followed into the twentieth century with *Giant* (1956; Warner Bros.), in which a wealthy Texas cattleman (Rock Hudson) is forced into competition with his former hired hand (James Dean) who has struck oil, ushering in an even newer West. Stevens won a second Academy Award for best director for *Giant*. *A Place in the Sun*, *Shane*, and *Giant* comprise what has been called Stevens's American Trilogy. The critical acclaim and popular success of these big-budget "prestige" pictures made George Stevens one of the most highly regarded directors of the 1950s.

Stevens had a clear sense of what he wanted from his actors and a polite but no-nonsense style of conveying his wishes. Some performers, especially those uncertain of their own talent, blossomed under his precise direction. Elizabeth Taylor gave two of her finest per-

formances in Stevens's *A Place in the Sun* and *Giant*. Others, such as Carole Lombard, Montgomery Clift, and James Dean, chafed at the bit. The reserved Stevens gave an unnerving "silent treatment" to uncooperative performers and avoided working with them again.

Stevens's directorial skill was, perhaps, put to its greatest test with his screen version of *The Diary of Anne Frank* (1959; 20th Century–Fox). Critics praised Stevens for making a visually interesting film out of a story that takes place in an attic and for avoiding cheap sentiment. *The Diary of Anne Frank*, however, was not a box-office success. George Stevens devoted the next five years to an even more ambitious work, *The Greatest Story Ever Told* (1965; United Artists), a retelling of the Gospels, with Swedish actor Max Von Sydow as Jesus and a gallery of international stars in cameo roles, including John Wayne as a centurion. Critical opinion was divided, and audiences, with other large-scale attractions from which to choose, such as *The Sound of Music* and *My Fair Lady*, stayed away. Undaunted, the still-versatile Stevens made the relatively short, small-scale, "contemporary" comedy-drama *The Only Game in Town* (1970; 20th Century–Fox), a character study of an aging Las Vegas chorus girl and a compulsive gambler, played by Elizabeth Taylor and Warren Beatty. This modest effort garnered some favorable reviews but drew little attention. It was Stevens's last film. He died in Lancaster, California.

George Stevens photographed scenes from a number of angles, which enabled him in the editing process to further shape the story and sharpen performances. He also produced most of his major films, and this gave him greater control over the finished picture than most directors who operated under the constraints of the Hollywood studio system and the Production Code. An overview of his career reveals a number of consistencies such as sympathy with the social outcasts that were so frequently his protagonists and admiration for strong, loyal women. Stevens made heavy use of long takes and carefully positioned actors in framing devices such as windows, doorways, and pillars to provide a badly needed third dimension.

A serious man with a wry sense of humor, Stevens took little interest in the Hollywood social scene and felt that too many people in the movie industry were inspired by what they saw on the screen in other movies rather than by real life. He was married twice—to Yvonne Shevlin from 1930 to 1947 ("I was tired of playing Mary Todd to his Lincoln," she said of their amicable divorce) and to Joan McTavish from 1969 until his death. His only child, award-winning television producer George Stevens, Jr., founded the American Film Institute and served as its director from 1967 to 1980. He has done much to restore his father's reputation, most significantly with the well-received 1984 documentary *George Stevens: A Filmmaker's Journey*, which he directed and produced.

• The papers of George Stevens are in the George Stevens Collection at the library of the Academy of Motion Picture

Arts and Sciences, Beverly Hills, Calif. Bruce Humleker Petri, *A Theory of American Film: The Films and Techniques of George Stevens* (1987), offers a thorough, film-by-film analysis of Stevens's directorial techniques. Donald Richie, *George Stevens: An American Romantic* (1970), is an interesting, if brief, analysis of Stevens's career. Articles of interest are Pete Martin, "The Man Who Made the Hit Called *Shane*," *Saturday Evening Post*, 8 Aug. 1953, pp. 32–33, 46, 48, 53, which provides a rare glimpse into the director's personality and private life; and Douglas McVay, "George Stevens Films from 1923 to the Present Day," *Films and Filming*, Apr. 1965, pp. 10–14, and May 1965, pp. 16–19, a rambling, two-part article examining the virtues and flaws in Stevens's work, with emphasis on the big films of the 1950s. See also Roger Alan Miller, "George Stevens: Profile of a Film Director" (M.A. thesis, Univ. of California, 1966), and the American Film Institute's *Dialogue on Film*, no. 1, 1972 (an entire Stevens issue). An obituary is in the *New York Times*, 10 Mar. 1975.

MARY C. KALFATOVIC

STEVENS, Isaac Ingalls (25 Mar. 1818–1 Sept. 1862), military leader and politician, was born in North Andover, Massachusetts, the son of Isaac Stevens and Hannah Cummings, moderately well-to-do farmers. After attending local schools and Phillips Academy, Stevens received appointment to the U.S. Military Academy in 1835, from which he graduated first in his class in 1839.

Stevens was commissioned as a second lieutenant in the Army Corps of Engineers and oversaw construction at various sites along the New England Coast. During his first assignment at Fort Adams in Newport, Rhode Island, in 1841 he married Margaret Lyman Hazard; they had five children. In the Mexican War, Stevens served on the staff of General Winfield Scott during the campaign from Veracruz to Mexico City. He contributed greatly to the reconnaissances of geography, fortifications, and enemy numbers, and was wounded at Mexico City.

Stevens returned to coastal fortification work until 1849, when he was detailed to the U.S. Coast Survey as the second in command to director Alexander Dallas Bache. He published *Campaigns of the Rio Grande and of Mexico* in 1851 and in 1852 campaigned for Franklin Pierce. On Pierce's election, Stevens sought and received appointment as governor of the newly created Washington Territory in March 1853. Stevens saw the relatively minor position as an opportunity to be in the forefront of what he believed would become the fastest growing section of the nation as well as the entry port to the markets of China and Japan. To foster his plans, Stevens also garnered appointment to head the northern railway survey, one of several sanctioned by Congress to determine the most feasible route for a transcontinental railway.

Primarily as a result of Stevens's energy and persistence, the northern survey turned out to be exceedingly thorough and comprehensive. He took issue with prevailing views that most of the region between Minnesota and the Pacific Coast was arid and sterile. He noted many fertile valleys suitable for agriculture and pointed to additional vast regions valuable for grazing purposes.

As governor and ex officio superintendent of Indian affairs, Stevens proved to be energetic and able. In his four years as governor (1853–1857), followed by an equal period as territorial delegate to Congress (1857–1861), Stevens fought, usually successfully, for roads, mail service, lighthouses, and the final settlement of Hudson's Bay Company claims left over from the 1846 boundary settlement. A major disappointment was his inability to secure a northern transcontinental railroad, the consequence of increased sectional divisions in Congress.

Of greatest concern to the new territory was the settlement of Indian title. Although later criticized for acting in haste, Stevens consulted at length with federal officials. He and his associates met with the tribes over a period of eighteen months before negotiating nine treaties at eight councils in 1854–1855. These treaties generally established temporary reservations, where the tribes or bands would be trained in agriculture and mechanical arts, attend schools, receive instruction in Christianity, and be partially supported by annuities for twenty years. At the end of that time, or earlier if possible, the treaties allowed for the division of reservation lands in severalty. One unusual feature added by Stevens was to allow fishing, hunting, gathering, and pasturing in common with citizens on open and unclaimed lands. Although these provisions subsequently generated legal disputes that continue to the present day, the original intent was to allow these activities as a temporary subsistence measure until the country was settled or allotment took place.

Despite the treaties, an Indian war (usually termed the Yakima War) broke out in 1855–1856 in response to increased pressures from miners and agrarian settlers. Stevens organized territorial volunteers to mount an aggressive campaign and quarreled with the regular army, believing it was not protecting the lives and property of settlers. Stevens declared martial law in Pierce and Thurston counties based on his conviction that half-breed settlers (many of them former Hudson's Bay Company men with Indian wives) were obstructing the territory's war effort. When the civil courts refused to act, Stevens ordered the volunteers to arrest territorial justice Edward Lander, who for a short time was jailed. Stevens was reprimanded by President Pierce and arrested for contempt of court.

Stevens was, however, supported by his constituents, who elected him to Congress as a delegate in 1857. A lifelong Democrat and a supporter of the South's constitutional right to slavery, Stevens became the national campaign manager for John C. Breckinridge in the 1860 presidential campaign. As a result, Stevens, though an ardent Unionist, received a relatively minor appointment as colonel (soon thereafter brigadier general) of the Seventy-ninth Regiment of New York Volunteers after the firing on Fort Sumter. He served in the successful campaign to take the Sea Islands of South Carolina in the fall of 1861 and fought at Second Bull Run (Second Manassas) in late August

1862. Stevens was killed leading his troops at Chantilly, Virginia, and was posthumously promoted to major general.

Stevens was dubbed by his peers as a "regular go-ahead man." He was part of the expansionist "Young America" movement of the 1850s that viewed American institutions as supreme and as destined to expand across the continent. He was able to secure great loyalty from those who shared his goals but was less successful with subordinates or constituents, who did not give unflinching devotion to his objectives. Stevens's reputation as a military leader has remained high, but his political career, particularly his martial law declaration, and his efforts as a treaty negotiator have come under attack in recent years.

• Stevens's papers are at a number of repositories, including the University of Washington, the Washington State Library (Olympia), and the Washington State Historical Society. His official correspondence is contained within various record groups at the National Archives. His son, Hazard Stevens, wrote a pietistic biography, *Life of Isaac Ingalls Stevens* (1900). A modern biography is Kent D. Richards, *Isaac I. Stevens* (1979; repr. 1993). See also Richards, "Isaac I. Stevens and the Federal Military Power in Washington Territory," *Pacific Northwest Quarterly* 63 (1972): 81–86; and Richards, "Historical Antecedents to the Boldt Decision," *Western Legal History* 4 (1991): 69–84. An excellent article is D. W. Meinig, "Isaac Stevens, Practical Geographer of the Early Northwest," *Geographical Review* 45 (1955): 542–58.

KENT D. RICHARDS

STEVENS, John (1749–6 Mar. 1838), engineer and inventor, was born in New York City, the son of John Stevens, a shipowner and merchant, and Elizabeth Alexander. In later years Stevens's father entered politics, serving as treasurer of New Jersey and as president of the New Jersey convention that ratified the U.S. Constitution. In 1766 Stevens entered King's College, now Columbia, and graduated in 1768. He studied law for three years but never practiced it; instead, he joined his father in New Jersey politics and served as a special aide to Governor William Franklin, the son of Benjamin Franklin. Upon the outbreak of the Revolution he was commissioned a captain by General George Washington and for the duration of the war served as treasurer of New Jersey and for one year as surveyor-general for the state's eastern division. From 1784 to 1787, having bought at auction a large tract of land in New Jersey, he devoted his energies to developing the estate and building a home for his young wife, Rachel Cox, whom he had married in 1782. The couple had seven children.

Witnessing the historic experiments that occurred in 1787 and the following year on the Delaware River changed Stevens's whole life. On two occasions the ill-fated Connecticut inventor, John Fitch, launched the first steamboat, the first time propelled by steam-driven oars and the second by paddles. *Perseverance*, as his vessel was called, in the summer of 1788 made a successful run from Philadelphia to Burlington, New Jersey. Stevens was enthralled, and from that moment

until his death he devoted himself and his fortune to the advancement of steam-propelled transportation both on water and on land. Immersing himself in the science of steam, he designed boilers and engines on paper. His influence with Congress helped pass the first U.S. patent law in 1790, and he received one of the first patents. He improved the design of the vertical steam boiler and invented a Savery-type steam engine, both conceived with steamboats in mind. He also applied steam to the working of bellows.

Though Stevens's father's death in 1792 and the administration of his vast estate occupied much of Stevens's time, he was able over the next five years to continue his experiments. His greatest obstacle was finding workshops with competent mechanics until he met Nicholas J. Roosevelt, who operated a foundry in Belleville, New Jersey. Enlisting the backing of his wealthy brother-in-law, Chancellor Robert R. Livingston of Clermont, New York, he formed a partnership with Roosevelt. In 1798 Livingston succeeded in having John Fitch's lapsed grant for the exclusive privilege of steamboat operation on the waters of New York State transferred to him, and with this incentive the partners concentrated on developing a steamboat that would surpass the pioneering work of Fitch. After their first effort, the *Polacca*, proved to be a failure, they tried other designs and methods, but Livingston's appointment as minister to France in 1801 terminated his participation.

Stevens then became consulting engineer for the Manhattan Company, organized to provide an adequate water supply for the city. He convinced the directors that steam pumping should be used, but the engines of his own design proved inefficient. Determined to promote transportation in general, the inventor turned to educating the public and in 1802 became president of the Bergen Turnpike Company, formed to construct roads across Bergen County in New Jersey.

Refusing to give up on steamboating, Stevens continued to work with Roosevelt and in 1803 obtained a patent for a multitubular boiler. The next year his small vessel *Little Juliana*, operated by twin screw propellers, successfully crossed and recrossed the Hudson River several times, and he redoubled his efforts. His vision was to establish a ferry system between Hoboken and New York and to provide regular steamboat service between New York and Albany. In 1806 he began planning a 100-foot steamboat, the *Phoenix*, with a screw propeller, but before its completion Fulton's *Clermont*, in 1807, won the honor of making a round trip to Albany and back. Fulton's success was primarily due to the adoption of side paddle wheels, an idea that Roosevelt had tried earlier. The blow to Stevens's pride was matched by his anger over the fact that the trip was made under a monopoly granted to his former partner, Livingston, who had met Fulton in France, observed his trials on the Seine, and financed the *Clermont*. Though he was subsequently offered the chance to join them, he declined because of his agreement with Roosevelt and his determination to go his own way.

Frustrated by the Livingston and Fulton monopoly, the inventor had his fill of steamboating, and leaving the field to them and two of his sons, Robert and Augustus, who continued running the *Phoenix* on the Delaware, he turned to adapting the steam engine for the railroad. He proposed building a railway from Albany to Lake Erie rather than a canal. "Let a railway of timber," he wrote, "be formed between Lake Erie and Albany. The angle of elevation in no part to exceed one degree. . . . The carriage wheels of cast iron, the rims flat with projecting flanges to fit the surface. . . . The moving power to be a steam engine, nearly similar to one on board the *Juliana*." Thus, like a prophet ahead of his time, he laid down the essentials of railroading; but not until years later did anyone take him seriously. Even his former backer, Robert Livingston, considered his proposal impractical. Stevens petitioned the legislatures of several states, and finally in 1815 New Jersey formed a company to erect a line between Trenton and New Brunswick, the first American railway act. The Pennsylvania legislature followed suit in 1823 and granted Stevens the right to operate on it. In neither case, however, was money appropriated. To convince officials of the feasibility of steam locomotives, the doughty old inventor, at the age of seventy-six, designed and built on his Hoboken estate a model of a steam-powered engine and ran it on a circular track. This, the last of his innovations that brought his active career to an end, took place the same year as the Erie Canal was opened. Nevertheless, he lived to see his vision realized. His sons Robert L. and Edwin A. in 1830 became president and treasurer of the railroad company chartered by the New Jersey legislature and given a monopoly between New York and Philadelphia.

Like most keen inventors, John Stevens conceived imaginative yet practical ideas that were never carried out in his lifetime—an armored navy, a bridge across the Hudson, a vehicular tunnel under the Hudson, and an elevated railway system for New York. He died in Hoboken, New Jersey.

• The Library of the Stevens Institute of Technology in Hoboken, N.J., has a collection of Stevens's papers and letters. The standard biography is A. D. Turnbull, *John Stevens: An American Record* (1928). The family's involvement with early American railroading is covered by R. H. Thurston, "The Messrs. Stevens of Hoboken," *Journal of the Franklin Institute*, Oct. 1874, and J. E. Watkins, *Biographical Sketches of John, Robert L. and Edwin A. Stevens* (1892). Stevens's work receives extensive treatment in John H. Morrison, *History of American Steam Navigation* (1958), and Oliver Jensen, *Railroads in America* (1975). An obituary is in the *New York Morning Herald*, 8 Mar. 1938.

ELLSWORTH S. GRANT

STEVENS, John Cox (24 Sept. 1785–10 June 1857), yachtsman, was born in Hoboken, New Jersey, the son of John Stevens, an attorney and locomotive inventor, and Rachel Cox. Stevens grew up with his ten siblings on the Stevens family estate in Hoboken. After graduating from Columbia College in 1803, Stevens invested in the development of steam-propelled water vessels. In 1809 he married Maria C. Livingston, a member of the wealthy and prominent Livingston family of New Jersey. Stevens and his wife divided their time between the Hoboken property owned by the Stevens family, a mansion in Manhattan, and a large farmhouse on the western end of Long Island. In 1827 he and his brother Robert started the first dayline of steamboats that traveled on the Hudson River from New York City to the eastern terminus of the newly built Erie Canal in Troy, New York. He was also involved with the construction of several steam craft at a shipyard on the Stevens family property in Hoboken. The property included Elysian Fields, a spot popular among the New York and New Jersey elites for picnicking and sporting events.

Steven was a leading figure in New York's emerging bourgeois culture in the early nineteenth century. He was an original member of the Union Club, a social organization representing New York City's oldest families founded in 1836, and was president of the horse racing Jockey Club for many years. He was one of the most prominent sportsmen in New York, sponsoring various events at his Hoboken property, including the first organized baseball game, which took place on the Knickerbocker Base Ball Grounds at Elysian Fields on 19 June 1846. Stevens also owned a successful racehorse named Eclipse (after the famous English racehorse of the same name), which won a highly publicized match race on Long Island in 1823 against Sir Henry, a leading racehorse in the South. Another of Stevens's racehorses, Black Maria, won thirteen of twenty-five races between 1829 and 1835.

Above all Stevens was an avid yachtsman, owning and sailing a number of racing and passenger vessels throughout his life. In 1844 he and eight fellow yachtsmen met aboard his schooner *Gimcrack* anchored off the southern tip of Manhattan and formed the New York Yacht Club. Stevens was named commodore of the club, a position he held until 1855, and the club's headquarters were originally housed at Elysian Fields.

In 1851 Stevens headed a syndicate that bought the schooner *America* and sailed it to Cowes, England, a popular meeting place for English yachtsmen. At Cowes, Stevens issued a challenge to race any English vessel for a stake of ten thousand guineas. Probably because the English held little respect for American yachting, no one took his offer. Stevens then entered the Squadron Cup on 22 August, a race around the Isle of Wight against fourteen British yachts. The *America* won the race, finishing twenty-eight minutes ahead of the closest competitor, and returned to the United States considered the world champion. The cup won in the race was transferred to the New York Yacht Club. Beginning in 1870 the club sponsored a regular race called the America's Cup, named after the victorious schooner, held between American and European yachts for possession of the cup won by Stevens in the Squadron Cup.

Following his victory in the Squadron Cup, Stevens's activities in yachting declined. In his last years he spent most of his time at the family estate. Stevens died in Hoboken.

• John Dizikes, *Sportsmen and Gamesmen* (1981), devotes a chapter to the life and career of Stevens. For an exhaustive history of the New York Yacht Club and extensive biographical information on Stevens, see John Parkinson, Jr., *The History of the New York Yacht Club* (1975). See also Melvin Adelman, *A Sporting Time* (1986). Archibald Turnbull, *John Stevens: An American Record* (1928), contains a complete history of the Stevens clan through the nineteenth century.

THADDEUS RUSSELL

STEVENS, John Frank (25 Apr. 1853–2 June 1943), civil engineer, was born in West Gardiner, Maine, the son of John Stevens, a tanner and farmer, and Harriet Leslie French. Stevens attended Maine State Normal School for two years in preparation for a teaching career. At the conclusion of his schooling in 1873, bleak economic conditions held little promise of a job, and he chose to go west. Entry into the field of civil engineering evolved from his experience in the Minneapolis city engineer's office. For two years he carried out a variety of engineering tasks and at the same time gained experience and an understanding of the subject. He became a practical engineer, self-taught and driven by a self-described "bull-dog tenacity of purpose." In 1878 Stevens married Harriet T. O'Brien. They had five children, two of whom died in infancy.

Stevens's first professional position was in Texas as assistant engineer with the then-expanding Denver & Rio Grande Railroad. From there he went to Canada, where between 1881 and 1885 the Canadian Pacific Railway sought to complete a transcontinental rail system linking Montreal and the Pacific coast. Stevens was hired to scout a location for the route west of Winnipeg in the Rocky Mountains, and ultimately he was involved in locating and constructing that section and also those through the Selkirk and the Gold Range mountains.

In 1886 Stevens was engaged by the Chicago, Milwaukee and St. Paul Railroad as a field engineer for the construction of a route between Sioux City and Manila, Iowa. That same year he went to northern Michigan and served as principal assistant engineer charged with locating and building lines for the newly formed Duluth, South Shore & Atlantic Railroad. Although a large part of his work involved surveying, he assisted in all phases of railroading—reconnaissance, locating, organizing, and construction. Between 1889 and 1895 he worked for James J. Hill, owner of the Great Northern Railway, during the period when that line was to be extended from Havre, Montana, through the Rocky Mountains and on to Puget Sound.

Although it was possible to get through the mountains, of the two existing routes, one was far to the south at the bottom of the state of Montana, and the other was well above the Canadian border. A middle passage was believed to exist but was not discovered until December 1889 when Stevens located Marias

Pass. It was the lowest, shortest, and most direct route across the continental divide and the one that had been sought for decades. The Great Northern was so appreciative of Stevens's work that in 1925 the company honored him with a bronze statue at Marias Pass.

Stevens excelled in the role of pathfinder. The Great Northern called on him again in 1890 to find the best route for the line between Spokane and Puget Sound. The passage he discovered through the Cascade Mountain range would eventually be named Stevens Pass. He was chief engineer of the railroad when the Cascade Tunnel was bored through the range at the pass. In 1902 he was also appointed to the position of general manager of the Great Northern.

By the early twentieth century Stevens was considered by many to be the world's foremost railroad civil engineer. The Chicago, Rock Island and Pacific Railway had hired him in 1903 as its chief engineer, and he soon became the vice president in charge of operations. He left that position in 1905 and accepted the job of chief engineer of the Panama Canal, then being constructed by the U.S. government. The project had languished for decades while the area was under French ownership, and conditions had changed little even after the United States assumed control in 1904. When Chief Engineer John F. Wallace resigned in June 1905, Hill suggested that President Theodore Roosevelt hire his friend Stevens for the position.

Stevens saw the work basically as a railroading project, for its success hinged on the ability to move huge amounts of excavated material—something at which railroads could excel. He accepted the assignment even without knowing exactly what type of canal was to be built. A decision as to whether it would be dug entirely at sea level or with a series of locks had yet to be made. Contrary to the recommendations of an international commission for a sea-level waterway, Stevens held that a lock canal was the only rational solution. His arguments were persuasive enough to convince the president and Congress, which had the final approval.

Digging the actual waterway was only part of the monumental undertaking. The organization of a physical plant was nearly as daunting as the excavation itself. Stevens gave a free hand to his medical staff members in the eradication of yellow fever and supplied them with the materials needed to improve sanitation. Not only did he establish the lines for steady sources of all types of workers, but he also saw to it that a constant supply of wholesome food was maintained for them and that extensive worker housing was built along with warehouses and repair shops. He made sure that the best and strongest construction equipment possible was brought into use. His skillful organization of the entire undertaking ensured its completion, although that did not happen until 1914. Unexpectedly, in 1907 he resigned as both chief engineer and chairman of the Isthmian Canal Commission. He claimed his departure was strictly for personal reasons. He was succeeded by Colonel George W. Goethals who, along with his staff, was detached from the U.S. Army for duty in the Canal Zone.

Immediately after he returned to the United States, Stevens was engaged by the New York, New Haven and Hartford Railroad to conduct a detailed valuation of the company's assets in anticipation of upgrading the entire system. As vice president in charge of operations, he worked on this project for two years. In 1909 he again went west, where he was put in charge of finding a route through central Oregon for the Great Northern and Northern Pacific railroads. After the successful completion of this project, he established an office in New York City and from 1911 to 1917 was engaged as a consulting engineer.

Following the collapse of czarist Russia in 1917, leaders of the provisional government appealed to President Woodrow Wilson for help with their transportation systems. Stevens was selected to chair a board of prominent U.S. railroad experts sent to Russia to rationalize and manage a system that was in disarray. After the overthrow of the provisional government, the board's work ceased. Stevens remained in Allied-occupied Manchuria and in 1919 headed the Inter-Allied Technical Board charged with the administration and operation of the Chinese Eastern and Siberian railways. He remained in an advisory capacity until occupying Allied troops were withdrawn; he finally left in 1923. After his return to the United States Stevens continued to work as a consulting engineer, ending his career in Baltimore in the early 1930s. He then retired to Southern Pines, North Carolina.

Stevens's career coincided with railroading's most expansive era and the time when the technology changed dramatically. Not only did the volume of traffic expand, but increases in speed and in the weight of equipment also necessitated improvements and changes in the rights-of-way. Stevens's final contribution to engineering occurred in 1935 when he wrote a brief autobiography that closed with a chapter addressed to young engineers. In it he set forth his values, based on his long and successful career, and gave advice to those who would follow. An extremely talented, and restless, engineer, he tended to stay in a position no longer than the time it took to complete the task at hand. He rarely remained in situations more than two years, regardless of their importance. Honesty and a modest, self-effacing manner brought about loyalty in those who worked for him.

Stevens received a number of honors during his long career. In addition to the Distinguished Service Medal of the United States, he was decorated by the governments of France, China, Japan, and Czechoslovakia. He received the John Fritz Medal in 1925 in recognition of his great achievements in civil engineering. The Hoover Gold Medal of the American Society of Civil Engineers was presented to him in 1938. A long-time member of the ASCE, he was made an honorary member in 1922 and served as the organization's president in 1927. He was elected to honorary membership of the Western Society of Engineers in 1935. He died in Southern Pines.

• A small and varied collection (eighty items) of Stevens's papers in the Manuscript Division of the Library of Congress sheds light on his later life covering the period 1914–1942. His autobiography, *An Engineer's Recollections* (1936), is the best source for details about his life and first appeared as a series of articles in *Engineering News-Record* (1935). A detailed "Memoir of John Frank Stevens" appeared in the *Transactions of the American Society of Civil Engineers* (1944). An obituary is in the *New York Times*, 3 June 1943.

WILLIAM E. WORTHINGTON, JR.

STEVENS, John Harrington (13 June 1820–28 May 1900), Minnesota pioneer and founder of Minneapolis, was born to Gardner Stevens and Deborah Harrington when they were living temporarily in Brompton Falls, Lower Canada, near the Vermont border. He was reared mainly in Vermont, where he attended common schools before leaving home at age fifteen to join an older brother in Wisconsin's lead mining region. In 1840, when serving in the Wisconsin territorial militia during the removal of the Winnebago west of the Mississippi River, he became acquainted with territorial governor Henry Dodge, a fellow Democrat. With Dodge's aid he was appointed a captain in the army's quartermaster department when the United States went to war against Mexico in 1846. During the war he participated in the campaigns in both northern Mexico and the Veracruz–Mexico City region. After his discharge in 1848 he intended to move to southeastern Texas, where he had made a land claim near the Rio Grande, but a chance meeting with John Catlin, the last secretary of Wisconsin Territory, turned his attention to the upper Mississippi area, where the formation of Minnesota Territory was imminent. Catlin, who had visited the region near the Falls of St. Anthony on the Mississippi River, persuaded Stevens, who suffered from a pulmonary affliction, that he would benefit from its acclaimed salubrious climate.

In 1849, when Stevens moved to the newly created Minnesota Territory, he again displayed his knack for cultivating the goodwill of prominent people. He met and then worked for Franklin Steele, the Fort Snelling sutler and erstwhile developer of the land adjoining the east side of the Falls of St. Anthony. At Steele's instigation Stevens staked out the first land claim on the west side of the river near the falls. This 160-acre claim where downtown Minneapolis developed caused Stevens to be generally considered the "Father of Minneapolis." In 1850, soon after his marriage to Frances Helen Miller of Westmoreland, New York, with whom he would have six children, he began farming part of his claim and selling lots to settlers. Stevens appeared to have had a rare opportunity to become wealthy by subdividing and selling some of Minnesota's most coveted ground, but, perhaps because of a prearrangement, he relinquished much of the land to Steele.

He then turned his attention to farming and the promotion of agriculture. He brought milk cows from Iowa to his claim in 1850 and three years later augmented his small herd with full-blooded Devon cattle.

As Minnesota's foremost proponent and practitioner of scientific agriculture, he was a cofounder of the Hennepin County Agricultural Society in 1853 and the next year, with the assistance of Oliver H. Kelley of Elk River, was a key organizer of the Minnesota Territorial Agricultural Society. In 1860, while serving in the state senate, he introduced the legislation that created the State Agricultural Society. As the first secretary of that organization, he promoted fairs and the goals of improved livestock and crop yields.

In 1856 Stevens moved to Glencoe Township, McLeod County, an area of new settlement on Minnesota's prairie near the western edge of the Big Woods. Although he claimed land there and evidently intended to farm, he was soon drawn into other activities in Glencoe, the township's main village. In 1858 he became one of the owners and the editor of the *Glencoe Register*. He edited that Democratic newspaper until 1863, when he returned with his family to Minneapolis. Stevens represented the Glencoe area in the first state house of representatives (1857–1858), in the state senate (1859–1860), and again in the house (1862). He was named a brigadier general in the state militia in 1859 by Democrat Henry Hastings Sibley, Minnesota's first state governor. In his first legislative term, Stevens successfully sponsored legislation calling for the establishment of a state agricultural college at Glencoe, but the state's failure to fund its construction doomed the enterprise. In 1862, during Minnesota's short-lived but violent conflict with the Dakota, he was the military commander of a portion of the frontier that included Glencoe, but he saw no action. In the fall of 1863, before returning to Minneapolis, which became his permanent home, Stevens served as one of the state's commissioners to collect the votes of Minnesota soldiers serving in the Virginia theater of the Civil War.

In Minneapolis he edited various newspapers and periodicals, including the *Minneapolis Chronicle, Farmer and Gardener, Farmers' Tribune,* and *Farm, Stock and Home.* Late in life he established his reputation as a local historian. His *Personal Recollections of Minnesota and Its People and Early History of Minneapolis* (1890) contains a wealth of biographical information about pioneer Minneapolitans. In 1895 he and another former newspaper editor, Isaac Atwater, coedited the *History of Minneapolis and Hennepin County.* Throughout his career in editing and writing Stevens maintained his interest in stimulating Minnesota agriculture. After serving on the executive committee of the State Agricultural Society for many years, he was chosen the organization's president in 1893 and 1894. He was a Democratic member of the state house of representatives in 1876 but refused to launch a reelection bid.

Although he never held a major political office and did not achieve much success in business, Stevens attained great popularity. Throughout his late Minneapolis career he was fondly called "Colonel" Stevens and hailed as the city's most important link to its frontier beginnings. The romantic view of him as a noble pioneer endeared him to Minneapolis schoolchildren, who helped preserve the house Stevens had built in 1849–1850. In 1896 some ten thousand children, working in relays, ceremoniously towed Minneapolis's pioneer home to its permanent location in Hiawatha Park near the celebrated Hiawatha Falls. Stevens, who evidently had a stroke during the emotional house moving, was in failing health the remainder of his life. Suffering from pneumonia, he died shortly after observing his golden wedding anniversary.

• The Stevens papers are in the Minnesota Historical Society, St. Paul. Although Stevens dealt primarily with others in his *Personal Recollections,* it nonetheless contains much information about aspects of his life. For Stevens's roles in founding Minneapolis and other enterprises, see Isaac Atwater and John H. Stevens, eds., *History of Minneapolis and Hennepin County* (1895); William Watts Folwell, *A History of Minnesota* (4 vols., 1921–1930); and a lengthy biographical sketch in the *Minneapolis Times,* 28 Dec. 1898. For his interest in agriculture, see Darwin S. Hall and R. I. Holcombe, *History of the Minnesota State Agricultural Society* (1910), and Karal Ann Marling, *Blue Ribbon: A Social and Pictorial History of the Minnesota State Fair* (1990). For his newspaper career in Glencoe, see Daniel S. B. Johnston, "Minnesota Journalism in the Territorial Period," *Collections of the Minnesota Historical Society* 10, pt. 1 (1905): 247–351. On the preservation of the Stevens House, see June Drenning Holmquist and Jean A. Brookins, *Minnesota's Major Historic Sites: A Guide,* 2d ed. (1972). The most complete obituary is in the *Minneapolis Times,* 29 May 1900.

WILLIAM E. LASS

STEVENS, John Leavitt (1 Aug. 1820–8 Feb. 1895), journalist and diplomat, was born in Mount Vernon, Maine, the son of John Stevens and Charlotte Lyford, farmers. His education in the local public schools was followed by study at the Waterville Liberal Institute and the Maine Wesleyan Seminary. In 1845 he married Mary Lowell Smith; they had one child. Stevens also that year embarked upon a career as a Universalist minister.

Stevens became attracted to the antislavery crusade and in 1855 left the ministry to become part owner, with James G. Blaine, of the *Kennebec Journal* in Augusta, Maine. Although Blaine left the paper in 1858, Stevens stayed on as editor and owner until 1869 and continued to write for the paper in the intervals between his diplomatic assignments. His writings were described as high-toned, direct, and often brilliant. Identifying with the antislavery crusade, Stevens was among the founders of the Republican party in Maine, serving as state party chairman from 1855 to 1860. He was a state delegate to the Republican party's 1860 convention in Chicago, where he supported William H. Seward's nomination for the presidency. From 1865 to 1870 Stevens served three years in the Maine House of Representatives and two in the Maine Senate.

As an active Republican, Stevens was appointed minister to Uruguay and Paraguay in 1870 by Secretary of State Hamilton Fish. In South America, Stevens found himself in the midst of one of the civil conflicts that marred the Rio de Plata region at that time. The War of the Triple Alliance pitted Argentina, Brazil, and Uruguay against Paraguay. Stevens unsuccessfully attempted to mediate the conflict, which ended only with the utter destruction of Paraguay. Otherwise he worked successfully to protect U.S. private business interests in the region.

Stevens returned to Maine in 1873 and for the next four years pursued his literary and journalistic interests. In 1877 President Rutherford B. Hayes appointed him minister to Norway and Sweden. While diplomatic events proved uneventful during his six-year stay in Stockholm, Stevens wrote the *History of Gustavus Adolphus* (1884), which was for some time thereafter considered by the critics as the seminal work on the period of the Thirty Years' War, 1618–1648. In 1883 Stevens returned to Maine, where he again pursued his writing interests.

In 1889 President Benjamin Harrison appointed Stevens minister to the Hawaiian kingdom, where the corrupt administration of King Kalakaua was confronted by a small group of prosperous Americans who dominated the island's sugar industry. Between 1875 and 1890 this group benefited from a trade treaty that permitted Hawaiian sugar easy access to the United States. When Congress eliminated that privilege in 1890, this small group of white elite landowners conspired to abolish the monarchy and seek annexation to the United States in order to preserve their privileged position.

Tensions increased for two years following the 1891 ascension to the throne of Queen Liliuokalani, as she sought to tighten her control over the government. The white American elite appealed to Stevens for assistance, because he was a proponent of Hawaiian annexation. In January 1893 Stevens directed the landing of 150 marines from the USS *Boston*, anchored in Honolulu Harbor, to protect American lives and property. In reality the landing was designed to intimidate Queen Liliuokalani. Acting on his own, Stevens quickly accorded recognition to the provisional government headed by the U.S. sugar magnate Sanford P. Dole. With Stevens's approval, Dole's provisional government dispatched a commission to Washington to negotiate annexation.

In Washington the outgoing Harrison administration did not have the political will to push for annexation of the Hawaiian Islands, and the new president, Grover Cleveland, who did not favor annexation, withdrew the treaty from Senate consideration. Cleveland also withdrew recognition of the Dole government, ordered the recall of Minister Stevens, and paved the way for the restoration of Queen Liliuokalani.

Despite contemporary opinion, Stevens's role in the Dole conspiracy has been open to debate. President Cleveland sent James H. Blount, a devout antiexpansionist, to Hawaii to investigate the matter. Blount concluded that indeed Stevens had entered into the revolutionary plot, but his report was flawed by the fact that he only interviewed persons associated with the Hawaiian monarchy. Subsequently, a U.S. Senate investigatory committee, which heard sworn testimony from the conspirators themselves, concluded in 1894 that Stevens had not been part of their plan.

After returning to the United States, Stevens resided in Augusta, Maine, where he died.

• Stevens's account of the situation in Hawaii is in his "A Plea for Annexation," *North American Review* 157, no. 445 (Dec. 1893): 736–45. An authoritative account of Stevens's career is in *Representative Citizens of the State of Maine* (1903). an excellent analysis of U.S. imperialist sentiment in the late nineteenth century is in Michael J. Divine, *John W. Foster: Politics and Diplomacy in the Imperial Era, 1873–1917* (1980). Stevens's assignment to Latin America is the subject of José B. Fernández, "Relations on the Periphery: Paraguay," in *United States and Latin America, 1850–1903: Establishing a Relationship*, ed. Thomas M. Leonard (1997). An analysis of Stevens's activities in Hawaii is in William A. Russ, Jr., *The Hawaiian Revolution, 1893–1894* (1959). Among the most significant works on the U.S. acquisition of Hawaii is Julius W. Pratt, *Expansionists of 1898: The Acquisition of Hawaii and the Spanish Islands* (1936). The Senate committee investigation of the Hawaiian revolution is in U.S. Senate, *Hawaiian Islands: Report of the Committee on Foreign Relations*, 2 vols., 53d Cong., 1894, S. Rept. 227.

THOMAS M. LEONARD

STEVENS, Leith (13 Sept. 1909–23 July 1970), composer and conductor, was born in Mt. Moriah, Missouri, the son of Andrew Stevens, a piano teacher, and Elizabeth S. Wooderson, also a piano teacher. Stevens had three sisters, and the family moved to Kansas City when he was two years old. He was a precocious youth and began taking piano lessons as soon as he was big enough to sit on the piano bench. His parents encouraged his musical endeavors, and he made rapid progress. By age eleven he was accompanying singers in the Kansas City area, and at sixteen he entered the Horner Institute of Music (now part of the University of Missouri–Kansas City), where he made his conducting debut the same year. During his time there he was the piano student of John Thompson and also had the opportunity to accompany the acclaimed vocalist Ernestine Schumann-Heinck and her students. Madame Schumann-Heinck was so taken with the young pianist that she invited him to tour with her, and he spent the summer of 1928 in preparation as her house guest in Coronado Beach, California. While there he met another of her guests, Laura Townsley (Mary) McCoy, who later became his wife. Unfortunately, the proposed tour with Schumann-Heinck never occurred.

That summer Stevens was awarded a fellowship (full tuition) at the prestigious Juilliard School of Music in New York City. His acceptance effectively took him away from Kansas City permanently. He studied there for three years, from October 1928 through May 1931. A year before leaving Juilliard he accepted a position as vocal arranger for the Columbia Broadcasting System radio network. In 1931 he married Mary McCoy, and in 1933 he became a staff conductor at CBS. Stevens excelled in his work and quickly established a solid reputation as a fine young composer, arranger, and conductor on such series as "The Columbia Workshop," "Studebaker Champions" with Helen Morgan, "The Heinz Magazine of the Air," "The Chevrolet Program for General Motors," and "The Star Shoe Program." In 1935 he began a two-year course of study with the noted composition teacher Joseph Schillinger, and in June 1937 he joined the very popular CBS radio show "The Saturday Night Swing Club." A year later he was named head of the music department for CBS.

In 1939 he left New York City for Hollywood, where he composed and conducted for the radio series "Big Town," which starred Edward G. Robinson. This was followed through the years by other radio series—the "Ford Summer Hour" (1940), "Free Company" (1941), "Lionel Barrymore" (1942), "Abbott and Costello" (1942), "Dr. Fights" (1945), "Request Performance" (1945), "Academy Award" (1946), "Dick Powell" (1946)—and composing for the cinema. Stevens's first film score, *Syncopation*, was written in 1941 for the RKO studio.

With the advent of World War II, Stevens became radio director of the Southwest Pacific Area for the Office of War Information, after which he joined the U.S. Army. From 1942 to 1945 he was director of Radio Sydney, Australia, and during this time he divorced his wife, Mary, on 13 December 1945. Upon his release from the military, Stevens resumed civilian life in Hollywood as a composer and conductor, and on 15 December 1945 he married the Australian-born Peggy Joan McCartney. His skills suited him well for working in the film industry, and he accepted more and more film assignments.

In 1950 he contributed an impressive score for the George Pal film *Destination Moon*, the first of a series of science-fiction film scores that he composed, which also included *When Worlds Collide* (1951), *The Atomic City* (1952), and *The War of the Worlds* (1953). His work in this genre is noteworthy. Concurrently, he began writing innovative film scores that included jazz elements. He was among the first cinema composers to utilize the jazz idiom for film scores and was the first to build a score around jazz elements exclusively, in the film *Private Hell 36* (1954). Other films using jazz include *Eight Iron Men* (1952), *The Glass Wall* (1953), and *The Wild One* (1954).

On 13 December 1955, exactly ten years after his first divorce, Stevens divorced his second spouse, Peggy, and married Elizabeth Struan Hughes two days later. She was the great-granddaughter of the former prime minister of Australia, Sir John Robertson.

During his long career Stevens composed music for over sixty films and received three Academy Award nominations, although he never won an Oscar. His nominations came in 1956, for the song "Julie," from the film of the same name; in 1959, for his film score *The Five Pennies*; and in 1963, for his music for the movie *A New Kind of Love*. He was a founding member of the Composers and Lyricists Guild of America, serving as that organization's first president from 1954

to 1962, and he taught film composition as an adjunct professor for the University of California, beginning in 1960.

Stevens composed music for early network television programs and continued to do so throughout the remainder of his career, scoring over two hundred shows for the television departments of CBS, Metro-Goldwyn-Mayer, 20th Century–Fox, and Paramount. He began writing television music in 1950 with the "Burns and Allen" show and through the years composed and conducted for many additional series— "Ann Southern," "Michael Shane," "Dante," and "Mr. Novak"—as well as individual episodes of other series, including "Hotel de Paree," "Cheyenne," "Twilight Zone," "Have Gun Will Travel," "Dick Powell Theatre," "Empire," "The Untouchables," "Rawhide," "Daniel Boone," "Lost in Space," "Voyage to the Bottom of the Sea," "Long Hot Summer," "Jesse James," "Lancer," "Custer," "Land of the Giants," and "Judd for the Defense." In April 1969 he was named music director for Paramount Television, a position he held until his death.

Just past noon on 23 July 1970, Stevens received word at his office that his wife had been killed that morning in a one-car accident in the Santa Rosa Mountains near Palm Springs, California. He received the news calmly and made several telephone calls to get more information about the accident and inform people of her death. Minutes later he collapsed and died of a heart attack.

Stevens is held in high esteem by those who worked with him. His friend and fellow composer David Raksin recalled, "Leith Stevens was one of my favorite colleagues. He was not only a fine composer of music for films but also a charming person—stylish, humorous and exceptionally able in all endeavors. I admired his film scores, and especially his way of handling himself in the exasperating situations so typical of our profession."

Stevens was a talented musician who was equally at home in classical, jazz, and commercial musical realms. He exerted a profound influence on other composers who wrote for the radio, cinema, and television through his innovative ideas, solid body of work, and the powerful position he held in the Hollywood film community. Thus, he helped to shape the style of this type of music and to direct its course in the second half of the twentieth century.

• Stevens's papers and original scores are at the University Archives, University of Missouri–Kansas City. See James Hamilton's "Leith Stevens: A Critical Analysis of His Works" (Ph.D. diss., Univ. of Missouri–Kansas City, 1976), and Alfred W. Cochran's "Leith Stevens and the Jazz Film Score: *The Wild One* and *Private Hell 36*," *IAJE: Jazz Research Papers* 10 (1990). Articles about Stevens include Fran Kelley, "Leith Stevens: Unsung Hero," *Metronome* 71 (Sept. 1955): 20, 27; "Leith Stevens Files 50G Suit vs. Shorty Rogers," *Down Beat*, 3 Oct. 1956; "Leith Stevens," *Film Music Notes* 16 (Winter 1956); "Partial Settlement," *Down Beat*, 9 Jan. 1958; "Blessings from the Avant Garde," *Down Beat*, 12 Mar. 1964; and "Don't Abuse, Stevens Warns on Electronic

Synthesizer," *Billboard*, 29 Mar. 1969. Articles about specific film scores include J. Starr's "Destination Moon," *Life with Music* 3 (May–June 1950); "The Wild One," *Film Music Notes* 13 (Jan.–Feb. 1954): 3–7; and "A Score for Five Pennies," *Down Beat*, 9 July 1959. An obituary is in the *New York Times*, 24 July 1970.

ALFRED W. COCHRAN

STEVENS, Nettie Maria (7 July 1861–4 May 1912), cytologist, was born in Cavendish, Vermont, the daughter of Ephraim Stevens, a carpenter, and Julia Adams. Stevens's mother died in 1863, and her father remarried two years later. She was educated in the public schools of Westford, Massachusetts, and graduated from the Westfield, Massachusetts, Normal School in 1883. To earn money to continue her education, Stevens taught Latin, English, mathematics, physiology, and zoology at a high school in Lebanon, New Hampshire; worked as a librarian at the Chelmsford, Massachusetts, Free Public Library; and taught at the Howe School, Billerica, Massachusetts.

By 1896 Stevens had saved enough money to go to Stanford University, attracted by the school's reputation as a youthful, innovative institution offering students the chance to pursue their own scholastic interests. She began as a special student in September 1896, was awarded regular freshman standing in January 1897, and three months later was admitted to advanced standing. She originally had planned to major in physiology, but she concentrated increasingly on histology. Stevens received her bachelor's degree in 1899 and remained at Stanford as a graduate student. She received the master's degree in 1900, and her thesis, "Studies on Ciliate Infusoria," was published in the *Proceedings of the California Academy of Sciences* in 1901. During her four years at Stanford Stevens spent her summer vacations at the Hopkins Seaside Laboratory at Pacific Grove, California, pursuing histological and cytological research.

Armed with an M.A. degree, Stevens returned to the East to study at Bryn Mawr College and pursue a Ph.D. degree. Her first work there was with Joseph Weatherland Warren on the physiology of frog contractions, but very shortly thereafter she began to work with the geneticist Thomas Hunt Morgan. At this time, Morgan's major interests were in cytology and regeneration, and it was later that he accepted a chromosomal theory of heredity. After six months at Bryn Mawr, Stevens was given a fellowship to study abroad. This European experience (1901–1902 and a return trip in 1908–1909) at the Naples Zoological Station and at the Zoological Institute of the University of Würzburg, Germany, under the cytologist/embryologist Theodor Boveri, greatly expanded her research experience.

Her letters written during these years stress her scholarly preoccupations, but they also suggest an anxiety about financial matters. Because she alone was responsible for her support, she was constantly concerned about finances. None of the available material suggests any kind of a romantic attachment.

Stevens was awarded the Ph.D. degree by Bryn Mawr in 1903, and her dissertation was published that same year. She retained an affiliation with the university for the rest of her life, beginning as a research fellow in biology from 1902 to 1904 (her research from 1903 to 1904 was funded by a Carnegie Institution grant). In 1904–1905 she was a reader in experimental morphology, and from 1905 to 1912 she was an associate in experimental morphology. Although the trustees of Bryn Mawr eventually created a research professorship for her, she died of breast cancer before she could occupy it.

During the eleven years between 1901, when she published her first paper, and her death, she published at least thirty-eight papers. Although most of her work was in cytology, she was concerned with experimental physiology as well. Most of these studies were carefully conceived and superbly executed, but one set of observations and interpretations was especially important. Stevens, during the years of her Carnegie Foundation grant work, demonstrated that sex is determined by a particular chromosome. During the period of Stevens's research, other investigators also were exploring the relationship between the chromosomes and heredity. The behavior of the chromosomes during cell division had been described, but speculations about their relationship to Mendelian heredity had not been experimentally confirmed. No trait had been traced from the chromosomes of the parent to those of the offspring; neither had a specific chromosome been linked with a specific characteristic. Hints that the inheritance of sex might be related to a morphologically distinct chromosome suggested the possibility of such a connection. If sex were shown to be inherited in a Mendelian fashion, then a chromosomal basis for heredity would be supported.

Stevens apparently had become interested in the problem of chromosomes and sex determination by 1903. That year she applied to the Carnegie Institution for a grant and described one of her research interests as "the histological side of the problems of heredity connected with Mendel's Law." Another important cytologist, Columbia University professor Edmund Beecher Wilson, was working on the same problem at the same time. Since both Wilson and Stevens concluded that sex was determined by a specific chromosome, the question of priority is sometimes raised. Until recently usually Wilson was credited with the discovery. However, it is apparent that the two arrived at their corresponding discoveries quite independently.

The important breakthrough described by Stevens in her paper, published by the Carnegie Institution in 1905, included her study of the common meal worm, *Tenebrio molitor*. She had studied spermatogenesis in five insect species from four different groups and observed that two species had an extra or "accessory" chromosome in the male. The meal worm was especially interesting because the size of one chromosome was different in males and females. In 1905 she established that male meal worms have nineteen large chromosomes and one small one and that females have twenty large ones. She cautiously concluded that this situation represented a case of sex determination by the particular pair of differently sized chromosomes. Postulating that the spermatozoa containing the small chromosome determine the male sex and that those containing ten large chromosomes determine the female sex, she suggested that sex may in some cases be determined by a difference in the amount or quality of the chromatin (the substance of which chromosomes are composed). Since the results in other species were so variable, Stevens, like Wilson, hesitated to make an unequivocal statement. Yet she clearly recognized the significance of her discovery and investigated spermatogenesis in a number of different species to try to determine a pattern. Although biologists at the time were skeptical of her theory, and she herself constantly questioned her assumption of a Mendelian basis for the inheritance of sex, her work was vitally important in providing observational evidence for the importance of the chromosomes in heredity.

Stevens's accomplishments were recognized by many of her colleagues, yet she failed to attain a level of professional success commensurate with her achievements. She remained on a low rung of the academic ladder at Bryn Mawr College, and her achievements have not yet received full credit, partly because of gender bias and partly because of Wilson's more extensive contributions to biology in general. Stevens was one of the first American women to make a significant theoretical contribution to biology.

• There are no large collections of Stevens's papers, but the Carnegie Institution and the American Philosophical Society possess some letters. Some of her more important works are: "Further Studies on the Ciliate Infusoria, Licnophora and Boveria," *Archiv fuer Protistenkunde* 3 (1904): 1–43; "A Study of the Germ Cells of *Aphis rosae* and *Aphis oenetherae*," *The Journal of Experimental Zoology* 2 (1905): 313–33; "Studies in Spermatogenesis with Especial Reference to the 'Accessory Chromosome'", *Carnegie Institution of Washington Publication*, no. 36, pt. 1 (1905); "Studies in Spermatogenesis. A Comparative Study of the Heterochromosomes in Certain Species of Coleoptera, Hemiptera and Lepidoptera, with Especial Reference to Sex Determination," *Carnegie Institution of Washington Publication*, no. 36, pt. 2 (1906); "Studies on the Germ Cells of Aphids," *Carnegie Institution of Washington Publication*, no. 51 (1906). For a bibliography of Stevens's work see Marilyn Bailey Ogilvie and Clifford J. Choquette, "Nettie Maria Stevens (1861–1912): Her Life and Contributions to Cytogenetics," *Proceedings of the American Philosophical Society* 125 (1981): 292–311. For biographical material, see the same, as well as Stephen Brush, "Nettie M. Stevens and the Discovery of Sex Determination by Chromosomes," *Isis* 69 (1978): 163–72. Thomas Hunt Morgan wrote an evaluative obituary, "The Scientific Work of Miss N. M. Stevens," *Science* 36 (1912): 468–70.

MARILYN BAILEY OGILVIE

STEVENS, Robert Livingston (18 Oct. 1787–20 Apr. 1856), engineer, inventor, and naval architect, was born on his father's estate, "Castle Point," in Hoboken, New Jersey, the son of John Stevens, an inventor, and Rachel Cox. His name reflected the close association between his father and Chancellor Robert Livingston of New York. Privately tutored, Stevens became interested in steamboating while assisting his father, who was engaged in experiments on steam engines. At the age of seventeen, Stevens operated across the Hudson River the steamboat *Little Juliana*, which his father had built to demonstrate the feasibility of a ferry service. Four years later he helped in the design and construction of the *Phoenix*, suggesting her concave water line and, under Captain Moses Rogers, was master on her pioneer ocean voyage, the first ever from New York to Philadelphia, in 1809. For at least fifteen years thereafter, with headquarters in Trenton, he managed the operation of the *Phoenix* on regular runs between Philadelphia and Trenton on the Delaware River. The collaboration with his father culminated in the completion of *Juliana* in 1811 and her entry into service between New York and Hoboken, the world's first steam ferry system.

Stevens devoted the rest of his life to naval architecture. As a widely acclaimed leader in that profession, he designed and had built nearly twenty steamboats and ferries that incorporated his successive inventions. These included a method for installing knees of wood and iron inside the ship's frame, a cutoff for steam engines, and balanced poppet valves. He replaced the cast iron walking beam with one of wrought iron, shortened its length, and added a gallows frame. He improved the steam engine by a forced-draft firing system under the boiler, by making the boiler strong enough to carry pressures of fifty pounds per square inch, and by perfecting a marine tubular boiler. He also introduced the split paddle wheel, "hog framing" for boats (which prevents bending at the boat's center), and the present type of ferry slip.

Stevens did not confine his inventiveness to steamboating. He made important contributions to railroading, naval armament, and yacht racing. Upon the formation of the Camden & Amboy Railroad & Transportation Company in 1830 (later the Pennsylvania Railroad), Stevens was elected president and chief engineer. That same year he traveled to England to study English locomotives and en route designed the T-rail, which became the standard section on all American railroads. At the same time he invented the hook-headed spike and the "iron tongue" (now the fish plate) as well as the fastenings used to complete a rail joint, all of which improved the strength of rails. Returning with the Stephenson-style locomotive *John Bull*, he inaugurated the first railway service in New Jersey on a trial trip at Bordentown, New Jersey, on 12 November 1831, with himself at the throttle. The Camden & Amboy line prospered, furnishing service between Camden and Amboy in seven hours for three dollars. For the next fifteen years he divided his time between railroading and steam navigation.

Earlier, near the end of the War of 1812, Stevens had perfected for naval use a bomb that could be fired from a cannon and a percussion shell, which the U.S. government bought in large quantities. This work had led him, his father, and brothers to the development of armor-plated warships. After submitting their plans to Congress, they waited thirty years for authorization to construct a steamer "shot and shell proof." Then in a newly built drydock in Hoboken, Stevens began its construction but died before the ship could be finished.

Stevens's fourth major interest, stimulated by his elder brother John Cox Stevens, was the gentleman's new sport of sailing. The New York Yacht Club was founded aboard John Cox's schooner *Gimcrack* in 1844, and John Cox served as its commodore for eleven years. He and his brothers made innovations in yacht design, rig, ballasting, and fittings that had a great impact on racing technology. In 1845 Robert designed the 92-foot-long centerboard sloop *Maria*, for some years the fastest yacht in the NYYC fleet. In 1851 she raced as a trial horse for the famous *America* and beat her easily a few months before the latter won the historic race in England that established the America's Cup. A bachelor all his life, Stevens resided mostly in Hoboken and New York. He died in Hoboken.

• A collection of Stevens's papers and letters is in the Library of the Stevens Institute of Technology in Hoboken, N.J. Biographical accounts include A. D. Turnbull, *John Stevens, an American Record* (1928); R. H. Thurston, "The Messrs. Stevens of Hoboken," *Journal of Franklin Institute* (Oct. 1874); and J. E. Watkins, "Biographical Sketches of John, Robert L. and Edwin A. Stevens" (1892). See also John H. Morrison, *History of American Steam Navigation* (1958); Oliver Jensen, *Railroads in America* (1975); James Phinney Baxter III, *The Introduction of the Ironclad Warship* (1933); and William H. Taylor and Stanley Rosenfeld, *The Story of American Yachting* (1958). An obituary is in the *New York Tribune*, 22 Apr. 1856.

ELLSWORTH S. GRANT

STEVENS, Stanley Smith (4 Nov. 1906–18 Jan. 1973), psychologist, was born in Ogden, Utah, the son of Stanley Stevens, operator of an electrical business, and Adeline Smith. Both his parents, who were members of the Church of Jesus Christ of Latter-day Saints, died in 1924, and he worked for a while running his father's business before spending three years in Europe as a missionary for the church. He then studied various topics at the University of Utah and Stanford University before moving in 1832 to Harvard, where, partly as a result of discussions with E. G. Boring and B. F. Skinner, for whom he served as a research assistant from 1932 to 1934, he decided to study psychology. It was also at this time that he was struck by the disparity between empirical science and revelatory religion (including his own Mormonism). Out of this intellectual dissonance emerged his lifelong interest in the philosophy of science, a topic widely discussed in the 1930s. He received his Ph.D. from Harvard in 1934.

Stevens remained at Harvard after his graduation, studying physiology with Hallowell Davis on a research fellowship (1934–1935), studying physics on another fellowship (1935–1936), and then rising

through the ranks. He became an instructor (1936–1938), an assistant professor (1938–1944), an associate professor (1944–1946), and a professor of psychology (1946–1962). He married Maxine Leonard in 1930; they had one son. Following their divorce, he married Geraldine Stone in 1963; they had no children.

Stevens preferred to be called a "psychophysicist"—he even had his title changed to professor of psychophysics in 1962—because his mission was to find the scientific laws relating events in the external world (events described by physics) to events in mental experience (events described by psychology). The word psychophysics had been invented in 1860 by G. T. Fechner; today the term seems somewhat ambiguous because in its strictest sense it refers only to a science that relates the intensities of mental sensations to the intensities of the physical stimuli that evoke those sensations. In a loose sense it has also come to refer to those aspects of sensory science that involve psychological as well as physiological issues.

Stevens's early career at Harvard was devoted to research on auditory sensation, a topic on which he and Davis wrote the textbook *Hearing: Its Psychology and Physiology* (1938), and on which he later wrote the popular book *Sound and Hearing* (1965). With Davis and M. H. Lurie he wrote a paper demonstrating that damage to particular regions of a guinea pig cochlea causes hearing loss for tones of particular frequencies (*Journal of General Psychology* 13 [1935]: 297–315). This paper did much to support the "place theory" of hearing originally put forward by H. von Helmholtz in his book *On the Sensations of Tone* (1863). Stevens also showed that the perceived pitch of high tones increases with intensity while the pitch of low tones decreases with intensity (*Journal of the Acoustical Society of America* 6 [1935]: 150–54), and he separately measured what earlier researchers had called tonal "volume" and tonal "density." Tonal volume referred to the apparent "bigness" of a tone (for example, the tones of a tuba sound "bigger" than those of a piccolo), and tonal density referred to the apparent "compactness" of a tone (a bugle blast seems to be hard and compact and to have a luster that is lacking in the more diffuse sound of an organ). These examples are drawn from a review by J. C. R. Licklider of the physical and psychological correlates of auditory stimuli, contributed to the famous *Handbook of Experimental Psychology* (1951), which was edited by Stevens.

Eventually, with M. Guirao and A. W. Slawson, Stevens was able to relate perceived volume and density to perceived loudness in their paper "Loudness: A Product of Volume Times Density." His early studies of this last variable involved asking subjects to listen to a tone and produce a tone that seemed to them a certain percentage as loud; his results indicated that perceived loudness did not grow linearly as the tone intensity increased logarithmically, whereas Fechner had suggested that it would. Later, after conducting various experiments in the 1950s, Stevens concluded that the perceived loudness of tones itself also increases logarithmically as the tone intensity increases logarithmically. Such a pattern is consistent with a "psychophysical power law" (sometimes called Stevens's Law), according to which the perceived intensity of a sensation is believed to increase as a power of the stimulus intensity. Stevens's scale of loudness, measured in "sones" (one sone is defined as the loudness of a 1,000-cycles/sec. tone that is 40 decibels above the listener's threshold heard binaurally) was made the basis of the loudness scale adopted by the International Standards Organization in the 1950s, but Stevens later suggested an emendation to that scale. He also developed a procedure for calculating the overall loudness of complex noise, a procedure that also became part of an international standard.

In collaboration with many colleagues from approximately 1955 to 1973, Stevens showed that the psychophysical power applies not only to the sensory dimension of perceived loudness but to other perceptions as well, including perceived lightness (grayness), brightness, warmth and cold, voice level, tonal volume, tonal density, viscosity, visual length, visual area, coffee odor, tactile roughness, tactile hardness, perceived heaviness, perceived vibration intensity, perceived pressure on the skin, and perceived electric shock intensity. He invented the technique of "cross-modality matching," whereby the subject matched a given perceived brightness by exerting pressure on a hand grip or by adjusting the volume of a sound to match the intensity of brightness. Each sensory dimension was associated with a particular value of the power (exponent) in the power law. For example, perceived loudness was predicted by the tone intensity raised to a power of 0.67, implying that doubling the physical intensity of an auditory stimulus would not necessarily double its perceived loudness. Later Stevens suggested that each could be expressed as a fraction comprising only rather low whole digits (for example, the exponent 0.67 is the fraction ⅔) and published a list of these exponents in "Neural Events and the Psychophysical Law" (*Science* 170 [1970]: 1043–50). Stevens discussed the relationship between the power law and Fechner's logarithmic law in "On the Psychophysical Law" (*Psychological Review* 64 [1957]: 153–81) and in his book *Psychophysics* (1975), which was edited by G. Stone.

Stevens was also well known for his application of so-called "operationism" to psychophysics and psychology in general. Writings by physicist P. W. Bridgman and by members of the Vienna Circle such as R. Carnap influenced Stevens's belief that the communication of science demanded not only that scientific assertions be true but also that they be clearly defined for other scientists. Such definitions had to be "operational," that is, meaningful within a particular experimental context using particular measurements clearly understandable to those encountering them for the first time. Stevens used operational definitions in psychophysics to reconcile his nonbehaviorist conviction that mental experience was an acceptable topic for scientific investigation with his preference for behaviorist methodology and its emphasis on observable behav-

ior. In later years he became particularly concerned with the definition and statistical analysis of measurements both of physical stimuli and of mental sensations.

Stevens's other research included the demonstration in 1940, with John Volkmann and Edwin B. Newman, that perceived sensations of pitch do not increase linearly as tone frequency increases. This clarified an issue that had been disputed by famous pioneers of sensory science such as Wilhelm Wundt and Carl Stumpf. In 1941, with Clifford T. Morgan and Volkmann, Stevens proposed a "neural quantum theory" of sensory processing. In the 1940s he also became well known for his classification of psychophysical methods, which in turn depended on his classification of the different scales used in measurement, and he assisted W. H. Sheldon in devising and validating rating scales for measuring components of human physique and temperament. Stevens died while attending a conference in Vail, Colorado.

• Stevens's short autobiography is in G. Lindzey, ed., *A History of Psychology in Autobiography*, vol. 6 (1974), pp. 393–420. A summary of Stevens's early views on operationism, which were influenced by discussions with E. G. Boring, is "Psychology and the Science of Science," *Psychological Bulletin* 36 (1939): 221–63. His later opinions on psychophysical measurement and on behaviorism are in "Measurement, Statistics, and the Schemapiric View," *Science* 161 (1968): 849–56, and "Issues in Psychological Measurement," *Psychological Review* 78 (1971): 426–50. See also his "Theory of the Neural Quantum in the Discrimination of Loudness and Pitch," *American Journal of Psychology* 54 (1941): 315–35; "The Relation of Pitch to Frequency: A Revised Scale," *American Journal of Psychology* 53 (1940): 329–53; and "On the Theory of Scales of Measurement," *Science* 103 (1946): 677–80. See also Stevens et al., *Varieties of Human Physique* (1940), and Stevens and W. H. Sheldon, *The Varieties of Temperament* (1942). An obituary and a complete bibliography of Stevens's publications are in G. A. Miller, National Academy of Sciences, *Biographical Memoirs* 47 (1975): 424–59.

DAVID J. MURRAY

STEVENS, Thaddeus (4 Apr. 1792–11 Aug. 1868), congressman, was born in Danville, Vermont, the son of Joshua Stevens, a cobbler and land surveyor, and Sarah Morrill. Born into a poor frontier family and abandoned by his father, Stevens also had a clubfoot, leading him to channel his energies into academic work and to develop a lifelong sympathy for the disadvantaged. Around 1807 Sarah Stevens moved her family to nearby Peacham, Vermont, where she worked at odd jobs to pay the town's small school tuition for her children. "My mother was a very extraordinary woman," Stevens later remarked, expressing an affection that bordered on reverence. "She worked day and night to educate me. I was feeble and lame in youth, and as I could not work on the farm, she concluded to give me an education" (*Congressional Globe*, 40th Cong., 3d sess., pp. 129–30). Although nonobservant in his adulthood, Stevens remained influenced by Sarah's moral example and staunch Baptist faith. "I never regard anyone as a Christian who does not come up to my mother's standard," he noted on another occasion (Stevens papers, n.d.).

The cultural environment of late eighteenth-century Vermont—with its emphasis on religion, personal austerity, social deference, and self-improvement—formed the bedrock of Stevens's political convictions. At home, school, and church he acquired his earliest understanding of the hybrid social philosophy he would spend a lifetime defending. He articulated this ideology in a fashion owing to the Revolution-era "republican" language of civic virtue and social organicism, but he wedded this older political idiom to the increasingly pervasive liberal value system that defined antebellum America.

On 9 July 1814, in a Dartmouth College commencement speech replete with references to classical republics, Stevens provided an early demonstration of this ideological synthesis by bemoaning the invidious effects of "party spirit" and "vice" while also maintaining that personal enterprise "draws Christianity on its train that banished barbarism [and] superstition from a great portion of the globe." He argued that intellectual and material ambition were imperative to the sustainment of an orderly and harmonious society. "If the lofty mansion sometimes becomes the habitation of costly excess," he warned, "the hovel and the cabin are as frequently polluted by the gratification of baser passions" (Palmer, ed., *Thaddeus Stevens Papers*). Throughout a long public career, Stevens dedicated himself to widening channels for individual improvement and to defending his notion of progress as consistent with the larger interests of society.

After graduating from Dartmouth College in August 1814, Stevens began his meteoric rise from what he termed "the rough paths of indigent obscurity." The following year he moved to York, Pennsylvania, to take a teaching job and to read law with a local attorney. Upon passing the bar he moved to Gettysburg. There he was soon recognized as the leader of the county legal profession, commanding hefty fees for his work and accumulating significant land and business holdings. His election to five terms on the Gettysburg Council between 1822 and 1831 marked his newfound status as a community leader.

In the late 1820s Stevens became active in Pennsylvania's Antimason party, an organization whose dual messages of anticonspiracy and antiexclusivity hearkened back to the preoccupation with social organicism he learned as a youth. Through their alliance with the Whig party on such issues as education reform, banking, and internal improvements, Antimasons like Stevens forwarded their vision of a society at once orderly and deferential, fluid and forward-looking.

Stevens was elected to the Pennsylvania House of Representatives in 1833. In the spring of 1835 he delivered a rousing and emotional speech opposing the nullification of the state's first public education statute. Defying the legislature's widely anticipated capitulation to the electorate's recent antitax revolt, Stevens labeled the proposed repeal bill "an act for branding and marking the poor" and argued that public education preserved channels for self-improvement. In response to his address, the legislature unexpectedly rejected the repeal and passed a substitute strengthening the existing school mandate.

Stevens also spearheaded a successful effort to charter the Second Bank of the United States for Pennsylvania and chaired a special committee to investigate Masonry. His overzealous and abrasive approach prompted the press to label him "the Arch Priest of Antimasonry." His constituents agreed, and in 1836 he lost in his bid for a fourth term.

Although Stevens was reelected to the legislature in 1837, the following year saw his premature political demise in Pennsylvania's so-called Buckshot War. When the Whig-Antimason coalition found its assembly majority hinging on a handful of contested districts, Stevens and his lieutenants maneuvered unsuccessfully to organize the lower house. A mob of armed Democratic loyalists soon flocked to Harrisburg, prompting the commander of the state militia to instruct his men to assemble with a specified quantity of buckshot in hand. In the ensuing chaos, Stevens was forced to crawl out of a back window at the state capitol to flee the hostile crowd. Although reelected to the legislature two more times (1839 and 1841), he found his influence markedly diminished. In 1842, politically and financially bankrupt, he left Gettysburg for the larger city of Lancaster to resume the practice of law and recoup his losses.

During his absence from the assembly in 1837, Stevens served as a delegate to the Pennsylvania constitutional convention, where he opposed Democratic efforts to loosen general electoral qualifications and to disfranchise the state's free black population. Although he spent most of his time supporting internal improvements and central banking, he was most remembered for his advanced position on race issues. He denounced statutory inequities, called for new protections for free blacks against southern slave hunters, and ultimately refused to sign the new constitution because it categorically disfranchised black citizens.

The dissolution of the Antimasons in the late 1830s left Stevens without a political party. As slavery commanded increasing public attention, he found himself ideologically isolated from the conservatism of the Whig party—the only major organization he might logically have joined. His thwarted bid for a cabinet position in the William Henry Harrison administration further embittered him toward the party's leadership. Yet in the 1848 elections, building on his early political antislavery activity, he and a small group of insurgents successfully captured the Lancaster County Whig organization. Stevens headed the local ticket and was elected to the U.S. House of Representatives.

In his first two congressional terms, Stevens became a leading opponent of the "Slave Power." He delivered several well-attended speeches against the Compromise of 1850, arguing, "It is a principle of the common law . . . that by the *general* law man is not the subject of property . . . and that, wherever the slave is beyond the jurisdiction of such local law, no matter how he gets there, he is free" (*Congressional Globe*, 31st Cong., 1st sess., app., p. 766). Adopting the most radical version of the antiextensionist position, he suggested that the federal government had no right to foster or protect slavery outside of the states in which it existed. Although Stevens's radicalism alienated his more conservative constituents, the evaporation in 1850 of his once-substantial electoral margin did not temper his course. In defiance of the stringent new Fugitive Slave Act, he gave legal and illegal assistance to runaway slaves. His role as co-defense counsel in the sensational 1852 Christiana Slave Riot case also accentuated his estrangement from the regular party. Stevens's clients were charged with treason for harboring a runaway slave, killing one of his would-be captors and wounding two others. The defendants were acquitted, and later that year Stevens was denied renomination to Congress.

After brief membership in the Know Nothing party, Stevens helped found the Pennsylvania Republican party, under which banner he was reelected to Congress in 1858. In the wake of the turbulent events of the 1860–1861 secession crisis, he was tapped to chair the Ways and Means Committee, the plum of congressional appointments, since its chairman controlled all budgetary matters and acted as his party's floor manager. Already known for his uncommon parliamentary skills, Stevens soon earned recognition as an effective, even domineering majority leader. His misanthropic personality provided an aura of invincibility, but nothing so enhanced his position as his widely feared wit. Potential adversaries avoided confrontation with him for fear of falling victim to his notoriously ruthless barbs.

Aside from his outspoken advocacy of abolition and civil rights, Stevens provided a strong voice for traditionally Whig positions on fiscal and budgetary matters. A consistent supporter of internal improvements and paper money, he generally used his position as Ways and Means chairman to enlarge the federal government's role in the economy. Like most Pennsylvanians, he was a confirmed protectionist. His ownership of an ironworks outside of Gettysburg exposed Stevens to a barrage of attacks from his opponents, who claimed that his support for higher tariffs was a product of personal interest. However legitimate such claims may have been, it is certain that Stevens's Caledonia Ironworks never contributed to his wealth. Even as it continued to run deficits, he refused to close the plant. One former employee recalled, "Mr. Stevens used to call it his sinking fund, and only kept it running to give the people work" (*Philadelphia Times*, 14 July 1895).

Although his personal relationship with Abraham Lincoln bordered on antagonistic, Stevens lent important congressional support to the administration. Railroading entire military appropriations bills through the House with as little as five minutes of debate, he also managed legislation creating the greenback and imposing the first federal income tax. Moreover, he secured passage of conscription laws and successfully proposed blanket congressional authorization of presidential suspensions of the writ of habeus corpus. However, Stevens and his fellow Radicals were disheartened by the slow pace of the war effort. The president's reluctance to endorse revolutionary means and ends—emancipation, the enlistment of black soldiers, and the extension of civil liberties to free blacks—earned him the enmity of "ultras" like Stevens. Still, in 1864, after the Radicals failed to find an alternative candidate, Stevens campaigned energetically for Lincoln's reelection. In turn, the president privately acknowledged that, though the Radicals were "the unhandiest devils in the world to deal with, their faces [were] set Zionwards" (28 Oct. 1863, *Lincoln and the Civil War Diaries and Letters of John Hay*, ed. Tyler Dennett [1939], p. 108).

The end of the war presented the Republican party with several distinct policy options, the most radical of which was pioneered by Stevens. Arguing that the southern states were conquered territories, outside of the Union, without constitutional protections, and subject to direct congressional governance, he proposed a wide-reaching land redistribution program aimed at breaking the economic and political influence of the planter elite and creating an independent black yeomanry. Like most of his contemporaries, he understood civil rights as entailing equality under the law and equal opportunity for self-advancement, but he viewed the enfranchisement of freedmen as a privilege and not a right, beyond congressional authority and secondary in importance to the socioeconomic restructuring of the South.

In 1866 and 1867 Stevens found himself forced to juggle dual roles as House leader and Radical chieftain. He forged a precarious balance between compromise and principle. When his land redistribution program was defeated in February 1866, he accepted the party's moderate course and defended the Freedmen's Bureau and civil rights bills against presidential opposition. Later that year he shepherded the relatively moderate Fourteenth Amendment, parts of which he had authored, through the House. Although he viewed these measures as incomplete, he counseled his fellow Radicals to "take what we can get now and hope for better things in further legislation" (*Congressional Globe*, 39th Cong., 1st sess., p. 3148).

As a member of the Joint Committee on Reconstruction, Stevens found himself pinched between his ideological allegiance to the Radical wing of the Republican party and pressures exerted by moderate party members to temper the course of Reconstruction. Following the 1866 Republican landslide, he attempted once more to secure passage of a radical program, only to find Republicans in and out of the committee still determined to pursue a moderate course. The 1867 Military Reconstruction Act, although widely associated with Stevens, was actually a mainstream measure that enjoyed only the lukewarm approval of the Radical minority. It made no provision for land reform, opting instead to place the southern states under temporary military occupation pending their creation of "republican" constitutions allowing for impartial suffrage and civil liberties. However insufficient he judged the bill in its final form, Stevens maneuvered it through the House with characteristic determination.

Stevens has been viewed as an uncompromising ideologue and, in the words of a fellow congressman, "the radical leader, if not dictator, of the House." His flair for rhetorical stagecraft and strong-arm tactics obscured what one moderate congressman, John Sherman, noted in retrospect—that Stevens was more effective in the full House than in the Joint Committee. In the larger body he acted as Republican leader and forcefully drove through measures he had opposed as too moderate in committee. Occasionally he attempted, without success, to amend such legislation in the full House. Habitually pragmatic, he accepted his defeats and resumed support of the party's moderate policies. Thus the contemporary journal *Galaxy* called him in July 1866 the "boldest and coarsest of the great managers of Congress," while the Boston *Advertiser* remarked on 13 August 1868 that "no man was oftner outvoted." Both were correct. Stevens pushed his fellow Republicans as far as they were willing to move and then worked with ruthless energy to clear moderate legislation past wavering party members and the Democratic minority.

Although Stevens is best remembered for his role in the 1868 impeachment of Andrew Johnson, he was by then so near death that younger members of the House played a far more active role in the prosecution. Stevens's most notable contribution to the effort was his authorship of the eleventh article of impeachment, an omnibus charge universally acknowledged to stand the best chance of securing a conviction. Although chosen as one of the impeachment managers, he was too weak to finish his principal remarks and had to hand his speech to another colleague for completion. After Johnson's acquittal on 16 May, Stevens grew increasingly disillusioned and spent his final weeks in a hopeless, last-ditch effort to reimpeach the president.

A measure of Stevens's complexity, his personal life has been a constant source of speculation among his contemporaries and historians alike. In the late 1840s he adopted two teenage nephews, toward whom he was as demanding as he was devoted, sparking an often turbulent relationship. Although he never married, he shared his home and parental responsibilities with his mulatto housekeeper of twenty years, Lydia Hamilton Smith. Little evidence exists to support or refute the common assumption that they were romantically involved, but Smith was clearly a companion and partner in a unique domestic relationship more indicative of Stevens's personal acceptance of social integration than a motive for his radicalism.

Stevens died at his Washington, D.C., home. His body lay in state at the U.S. Capitol and was returned to Lancaster for burial in a small, interracial cemetery. Upon his request, his tombstone read,

I repose in this quiet and secluded spot,
not from any natural preference for solitude
But, finding other Cemeteries limited as to Race,
by Charter Rules,
I have chosen this that I might illustrate
in my death,
the Principles which I advocated
Through a long life:
EQUALITY OF MAN BEFORE HIS CREATOR.

For nearly a century after his death, Stevens was saddled with the blame for the failures of Reconstruction. As historians began to reevaluate the troubled legacy of the postwar era, Stevens reemerged as a figure whose grasp on the Republican party was often more apparent than actual. He staked out an advanced position on race issues, but in forging a course between principle and pragmatism; he failed to achieve his most extensive goals. Steadfastly committed to the hybrid political ideology he learned in his youth, Stevens advanced the cause of equal opportunity throughout a long life of public service.

• The largest compilation of Stevens's papers is housed at the Library of Congress in both the Thaddeus Stevens and Edward McPherson collections. A comprehensive microfilm edition of his papers, drawing on dozens of manuscript collections, government publications, and newspapers, is Beverly Wilson Palmer, ed., *The Thaddeus Stevens Papers* (1994). Important correspondence and speeches are in Palmer and Holly Byers Ochoa, eds., *Selected Papers of Thaddeus Stevens* (2 vols., 1997). The first complete, modern biography is Richard N. Current, *Old Thad Stevens: A Story of Ambition* (1942). A more sympathetic examination is Fawn M. Brodie, *Thaddeus Stevens: Scourge of the South* (1959). Both are well researched and have extensive if dated bibliographies. The most balanced and comprehensive modern biography is Hans L. Trefousse, *Thaddeus Stevens: Nineteenth Century Egalitarian* (1997). An important article on Stevens's role during Reconstruction is Eric Foner, "Thaddeus Stevens, Confiscation, and Reconstruction," in *The Hofstadter Aegis*, ed. Stanley Elkins and Eric McKitrick (1974). The best historiographical overview is provided by James A. Jolly, "The Historical Reputation of Thaddeus Stevens," *Lancaster County Historical Society Papers* 74, no. 2 (1970): 34–63. For obituaries and reminiscences by Stevens's congressional colleagues see the *Congressional Globe*, 40th Cong., 3d sess., 1868, pp. 129–50.

JOSH ZEITZ

STEVENS, Thomas Holdup (22 Feb. 1795–21 Jan. 1841), naval officer, was born Thomas Holdup in Charleston, South Carolina. As a young child he was orphaned but was adopted by General Daniel Stevens of Charleston. In recognition of his adoption Holdup petitioned the South Carolina legislature in 1815 to change his name to Thomas Holdup Stevens. He was educated at home.

Thanks to the influence of the general and other prominent Charlestonians, Stevens received a midshipman's appointment early in 1809. He reported for duty aboard the brig *Hornet* on 4 February at Charleston. In December he was ordered to the frigate *Constitution*, then in Boston undergoing repairs. He remained in Boston aboard *Constitution* until June 1810, when he transferred to the frigate *President* at New York, on which he cruised briefly but was furloughed on 2 October.

Stevens returned to Charleston, where on 26 November 1810 he reported for duty aboard the frigate *John Adams*, which had recently been brought out of ordinary at New York. After outfitting, the frigate spent several months cruising American waters. At the outbreak of the War of 1812 the *John Adams*, which was in Boston, was ordered to New York to be fitted for sea. Fearing that the refitting would take several months, Stevens volunteered for service aboard the *Constitution*, knowing that ship would get to sea sooner. He was instead dispatched to serve under Commodore Isaac Chauncey on the Great Lakes.

Shortly after arriving Stevens participated in a successful night assault against enemy forces at Black Rock on the Niagara River. He commanded boat number three in the attack. Stevens, who received a relatively minor wound, was highly commended by his commanding officer, Lieutenant Samuel Angus. In January 1813 he was appointed acting lieutenant (later confirmed by the Congress to date from 24 July 1813).

In April Stevens was sent to Erie, Pennsylvania, to join Lieutenant Oliver Hazard Perry, who was involved in building a squadron to defend Lake Erie. Stevens took command of the sloop *Trippe*, a small merchant vessel purchased at Niagara and armed with a single 32-pound cannon. In August *Trippe* and several other vessels sailed for the western end of the lake.

Perry established his base at Put In Bay, an excellent location from which to cover the British squadron under Commodore Robert Barclay operating out of the Detroit River. On 10 September the two squadrons met in battle. *Trippe* took a position near the end of the American line and fought a long-range duel with *Little Belt* and *Lady Prevost*, which received considerable damage. As the battle turned decisively in the Americans' favor, *Little Belt* and another British vessel *Chippeway* attempted to escape. *Trippe* and the schooner *Scorpion* chased and captured them. While Stevens served well in the battle of Lake Erie he was not mentioned in dispatches. This may have been a result of his friendship and support for Jesse Duncan Elliott. After the battle Perry and Elliott, along with their respective supporters, engaged in a long-running and vicious debate about Elliott's conduct at the battle.

Stevens remained at the Erie station until early December 1814, when he was detached and ordered to report to the frigate *Java*. Apparently in ill health, he never joined *Java* but was instead furloughed to Middletown, Connecticut. In 1815 Stevens married Elizabeth Read Sage, daughter of a wealthy Middletown, Connecticut, merchant. The couple had six children; their eldest son, Thomas Holdup, became a well-known naval officer.

Stevens returned to active duty in May 1816, serving from then until January 1823 at a variety of shore stations. In January 1823 Stevens took command of the schooner *Jackal* and joined Captain David Porter's West Indian Squadron that was chasing down pirates. *Jackal* patroled off the northwestern coast of Cuba. Together with other vessels of the squadron they managed to capture several pirates. After a short visit in the states, Stevens returned to the West Indies in command of the schooner *Shark*.

Shark returned to New York on 13 May 1824, and shortly thereafter Stevens was granted a three-month leave. He was promoted to master commandant on 3 March 1823, again serving at shore stations in Baltimore, New York, and Washington. He did not go to sea again until 22 August 1829, when he sailed in command of *Ontario*, bound for the Mediterranean Station, where Stevens remained for two years.

After returning to the United States he was posted to the navy yard at Charlestown (Boston), Massachusetts. In 1836 he was promoted to captain. From 15 March 1836 to 29 February 1840 Stevens was detached from duty and remained in the status "awaiting orders." On 29 February he was appointed to command the Washington Navy Yard. He died suddenly in this post the next year.

• Manuscript sources are in the Naval Records Collection of the Office of Naval Records and Library. Although biased, James Fenimore Cooper, *The History of the Navy of the United States* (2 vols., 1839), is useful for additional information on Stevens. See also William M. Fowler, Jr., *Jack Tars and Commodores: The American Navy, 1789–1815* (1984). Two Department of the Navy publications are also useful, *Dictionary of American Naval Fighting Ships* (9 vols., 1959–1981), and William S. Dudley, ed., *The Naval War of 1812: A Documentary History* (1984).

WILLIAM M. FOWLER, JR.

STEVENS, Wallace (2 Oct. 1879–2 Aug. 1955), poet, was born in Reading, Pennsylvania, the son of Garrett Barcalow Stevens, an attorney and businessman, and Margaretha Catherine Zeller, a former schoolteacher. The second of five children, Wallace grew up with two brothers and two sisters in a home where their thrifty, politically active father was a respected member of the community and "mother just kept house and ran the family." This included reading a chapter from the Bible to the children every night and on Sundays playing and singing hymns at the piano—activities echoed in the "choirs" and "chorales" of the later lyrics. Books were another source of pleasure in the Stevens household and a way to indulge the family disposition for personal privacy. Stevens later observed, "At home, our house was rather a curious place, with all of us in different parts of it, reading" (Holly Stevens, *Souvenirs*, p. 4).

In the summer the Stevens children spent time in the Pennsylvania countryside at their grandfather's farm in Feasterville and later at a resort in nearby Ephrata, which occasioned newsy, style-conscious letters from a teenage Wallace to his mother. These rural summers were a prelude to the young poet's climbs in the Pennsylvania mountains and to his Whitmanesque forty-mile tramps over the New Jersey palisades. They fostered an enduring affinity for the American landscape.

The Stevens family belonged to the Dutch Reformed church through their paternal background but regularly attended the First Presbyterian Church in Reading, where Stevens's mother was a member and where his parents had married. The three boys received their primary education at Evangelical Lutheran church schools, and Wallace was sent to live for a year with an uncle, the minister of a Lutheran congregation in Brooklyn, New York, where he attended the parochial school attached to the church. In the fall of 1892 Stevens entered Reading Boys' High School, taking the classical curriculum, which required Greek and Latin as well as the usual liberal arts courses. A classmate described Stevens at this time as "a whimsical, unpredictable young enthusiast, who lampooned Dido's tear-stained adventures in the cave, or wrote enigmatic sonnets to gazelles" (Holly Stevens, *Souvenirs*, p. 11), singling out both the gift for parody and the incipient skepticism that flourished during the poet's years at Harvard. Stevens already possessed a marked gift for language as well as a lawyerly aptitude for persuasive rhetoric, for he won several prizes for oratory in his junior and senior years of high school. Intending to become a writer, he enrolled at Harvard University in 1897 as a special student, undertaking a non-degree-bearing, three-year course of studies.

Harvard provided Stevens with an "anchorage of thought," as he put it. College life broadened his experience and offered sophisticated new perspectives. The period between September 1897 and June 1900 was distinguished by intense conversations with fellow students about literature, aesthetics, and social values and by bursts of original poetry. They were years punctuated by letters from his father full of instruction and advice. Stevens's choice of courses included French and German literatures, English poetry, medieval and Renaissance fine arts, and American constitutional and political history, while annotated texts from those years show that he independently studied Italian. He participated energetically in the literary life of the college, contributing poetry and essays to its undergraduate magazines and becoming an editor and then president of the *Harvard Advocate*. A colleague on the staff of the *Advocate* remembered Stevens at age twenty as a large, handsome, healthy person with curly hair, a modest, engaging manner, and a friendly smile, who was tolerant and kindly toward both colleagues and contributors of manuscripts (Holly Stevens, *Souvenirs*, p. 37). This description of a friendly, tactful, and, above all, sociable young man suggests a portrait singularly at odds with the remote, nearly unapproachable Stevens of the later years. At the same time the student who in high school had lampooned Virgil's Dido now turned out "The Ballad of the Pink Parasol," a lively parody of *ubi sunt* elegiacs and an irreverent comment on the then-current fashion in English poetry for lyrics modeled on old French verse forms.

The Cambridge years shaped Stevens's aesthetics, thinking, and personal tastes to a significant extent. At this time the hot subjects in literature were the French *symboliste* and Parnassian poets. In nearby Boston the Museum of Fine Arts was stimulating widespread interest in Oriental poetry, philosophy, and art with its Ernest Francisco Fenollosa Collection, while Fenollosa's lectures and translations were igniting what would become the imagist movement in American poetry. On campus Charles Eliot Norton was teaching a newly translated Dante; William James was exploring religious experience and expanding Charles Sanders Peirce's philosophy of pragmatism; and Henri Bergson's theories of creative evolution and a collective élan vital were being discussed and contrasted with scientific materialism and philosophic positivism. Not least, from Stevens's point of view, a young George Santayana was writing about Beauty and lecturing on Lucretius, Dante, and Goethe as "philosophical poets." Stevens gained the older man's notice in informal discussion groups, and Santayana famously responded to Stevens's early sonnet "Cathedrals Are Not Built along the Sea" with a sonnet of his own. Stevens continued all his life to regard Santayana as a valued mentor. Biographer Milton J. Bates observed, "If Santayana and Garrett Stevens could not be one man, they could still be—and were—cobegetters of the poet who spent a lifetime trying to restore these halves to their first integrity" (*Wallace Stevens: A Mythology of Self* [1985], p. 35).

By the time Stevens had completed his three years at Harvard, he had tentatively settled on journalism as the path to a literary career. In June 1900 he moved to New York City, where he remained for sixteen years. He worked as a reporter for the *Tribune* and then as an assistant editor on a monthly magazine, *World's Work*. Separated from family, friends, and university life, he ranged over "this electric town," gradually coming to enjoy its variety and sophistication and attempting to capture in words the busy life of the river along the West Street wharves. Apart from vacations spent in Reading, his social life was confined to occasional visits from former classmates. He attended Stephen Crane's funeral, spent hours reading in the Astor Library and at the Harvard Club, sat in the dark vault of St. Patrick's Cathedral, haunted art galleries and the Morgan Library, went to the theater, experienced strong feelings of wanderlust, questioned his vocation, and on weekends indulged in solitary hikes along the Jersey side of the Hudson River.

By 1901, finding himself remote from the productive literary life he had envisioned, Stevens acceded to his father's urging and enrolled at New York Law School. He graduated on 10 June 1903 after two years of study, including an apprentice year as a legal clerk, and was admitted to the New York bar the following June. That same summer, on a trip to Reading, he met Elsie Viola Moll, whom he courted for five years over the strenuous objections of his father. His choice of a marriage partner from the wrong side of the tracks, who not only gave piano lessons but worked as a shop-girl, precipitated an irreparable split with the elder Stevens. After one abortive attempt to introduce the young woman to his family, Stevens refused to visit his home until after his father's death in 1911.

The pair were married in 1909, and Stevens brought "the prettiest girl in Reading" back to New York to live on West Twenty-first Street until their final move to Connecticut in 1916, when Stevens joined the Hartford Accident and Indemnity Company, the firm with which he would remain until his death. These were highly productive years for Stevens. Not only was he quickly gaining experience in his profession, beginning to specialize in bond claims and insurance law, but as a member of the group that gathered around his Harvard classmate Walter Arensberg, he was initiated into the avant-garde life of the city. The Arensberg salon included Alfred Kreymborg, Donald Evans, and the enfant terrible of French art, Marcel Duchamp. Stevens was exposed to the new postimpressionist art—cubism, surrealism, and New York dada—that formed the basis for his mature appreciation of Paul Klee and Piet Mondrian.

Elsie Stevens did not care for New York or feel at ease with her husband's avant-garde friends; she returned to her family and friends in Reading for prolonged stays. Wallace Stevens was invited to contribute to "little magazines" such as *Others*, the *Dial*, and *Poetry*. He became one of a circle of kindred literary spirits, venturesome editors, and gifted poets—most significantly William Carlos Williams, Marianne Moore, and Harriet Monroe (then the editor of *Poetry*)—who, unlike the expatriated T. S. Eliot, Ezra Pound, and Gertrude Stein, remained on native ground. Stevens's own poetry was fast developing the irreverent enigmatic style, the turn of wit, the surprising linguistic gestures, the elegance, the flamboyance, the chastity, the rich coloration, the aesthetic purity—in short, the idiom—that distinguishes his work.

Between 1913 and the appearance of *Harmonium*, his first book, in 1923, Stevens published approximately 100 poems and a pair of plays, beginning with "Carnet de Voyage," a set of eight poems, in the September 1914 issue of *Trend*. The reception was mixed. Louis Untermeyer, who responded sympathetically to the poetry of Robert Frost, objected to Stevens's "too-intellectual involutions" (Serio, p. 5); other critics dismissed the poet as an aesthete, a dandy, or an ironist "more clever than true" (Serio, p. 5). In 1922 Yvor Winters hailed Stevens as a "cool master" and the "greatest of living and of American poets," although after the appearance of *Harmonium* he took sharp exception to Stevens's "hedonism" (Serio, p. 8).

Included in *Harmonium* were poems that have since become part of the American literary tradition: "Sunday Morning" (1915), "Thirteen Ways of Looking at a Blackbird" (1917), "Anecdote of the Jar" (1919), "The Snow Man" (1921), "The Emperor of Ice-Cream" (1922), and the long, quasi-autobiographical, lexically dazzling "Comedian as the Letter C" (1922). The book received appreciative reviews in the *Dial*, *Poetry*, the *Nation*, and *New Republic* from readers such as Marianne Moore, John Gould Fletcher, Harriet Monroe, and Mark Van Doren. Stevens was a "superb virtuoso" (Serio, p. 9) and his imagination a "riot of gorgeousness" (Serio, p. 10). He was an aesthete whose poems provided "an escape into a sphere of finer harmony between instinct and intelligence" (Serio, p. 9), but the book did not sell. T. S. Eliot's *The Waste Land*, published the year before, was hailed as the most significant poetic achievement of the century; *Harmonium* was remaindered at eleven cents a copy.

In 1924 Stevens and his wife sailed to California by way of Havana and the Panama Canal and cruised along the Gulf of Tehuantepec, memorialized in the enchanting "Sea Surface Full of Clouds." Their only child, Holly, who was born that year, eventually became the primary "Stevens scholar," editing first the *Letters of Wallace Stevens* (1966), then a carefully dated selection of the poetry and a play (*The Palm at the End of the Mind* [1971]), and finally *Souvenirs and Prophecies: The Young Wallace Stevens* (1977), all of which continue to be essential sources of information. *Harmonium* was reissued by Knopf in 1931 with the addition of fourteen poems, but from 1924 to 1932 Stevens concentrated on insurance claims and his growing daughter and wrote no verses. His legal work—the adjudication of bond claims—necessitated travels to various parts of the country, but his vacations were spent at Key West, the tropical locale of many of the "Florida poems."

In 1932 Wallace and Elsie bought a large house on Westerly Terrace in Hartford near Elizabeth Park, and in 1934 Stevens became a vice president of the Hartford Accident and Indemnity Company. He indulged his passion for well-made books, fine catalogs, good food, good wine, and exotic teas. He added prints and scrolls to collections acquired in the course of a far-flung correspondence, and he picked up the occasional *objet* or artifact, such as the small jade Buddha he asked Dutch plantation owner Leonard van Geyzel to send him from Ceylon. In the "Adagia" of *Opus Posthumous*, among a wealth of epigrams having to do with poetry and the creative life, one also finds a reference to "Bombay Duck," a recipe for "Parfait Martinique," and the quizzical observation, "Money is a kind of poetry." However, the large, well-dressed businessman—Stevens stood over six feet tall and weighed more than 200 pounds—continued to make forays into New York City, to various galleries, to a favorite bakery, to bohemian Greenwich Village, and to the Museum of Modern Art. Although he was becoming more and more protective of his personal privacy, Stevens was careful to preserve communication with the generation of poets and writers who gathered at the Gotham Book Store during the 1930s and early 1940s. By 1935 he had broken a silence of more than eight years with the publication of *Ideas of Order*, containing the celebrated "Idea of Order at Key West," and in the next decade he published the poems and composed the essays that constitute his fertile middle period.

"Owl's Clover," Stevens's most overtly "political" poem, appeared in 1936, followed in 1937 by the rhythmic, asymmetrical, Picasso-inspired "The Man with the Blue Guitar," which successfully combined social interrogation with aesthetic brilliance. Stevens's poetry has been construed as both "pure" and "abstract," but, like Picasso's *Guernica*, the verses that focus on violent destruction in "The Man with the Blue Guitar" addressed the impending world war. In September 1939 Stevens wrote to his friend in Ceylon about "this unbelievable catastrophe," "As the news . . . of the war comes in, I feel a horror of it: a horror of the fact that such a thing could occur" (*Letters*, pp. 342–43). But happenings in the "actual world" served to stimulate Stevens's imagination and to mature his art. By 1942, well into the war, Stevens had published in quick succession *Parts of a World*—a collection of sixty-three poems including "Poems of Our Climate," "Connoisseur of Chaos," and that ineluctable poem of the mind, "Of Modern Poetry"—and the central poem of the middle period, "Notes toward a Supreme Fiction," dedicated to his closest friend, Henry Church. The three sections of "Notes"—"It must be abstract," "It must change," and "It must give pleasure"—spell out Stevens's theory of poetry, which is also, as he pointed out some years later, a philosophy of life. His Baudelairean anatomy of pain, "Esthétique du Mal," composed in 1944, explores the satanic aspects of human existence with a certain irony but also celebrates the miracle of survival in a physical world. His standing as a major poet had grown with each publication, and Stevens was now in a position to support valued contemporaries such as Marianne Moore and Allen Tate and to encourage younger poets, among them Delmore Schwartz, E. E. Cummings, and Richard Eberhart.

The last decade of Stevens's life was a time of increasing public recognition. He was inducted into the National Institute of Arts and Letters in 1946. Between 1947 and 1951 he was asked to lecture at distinguished universities and at the Museum of Modern Art in New York; he read his poetry at the famous Ninety-second Street YMHA (Young Men's Hebrew Association) and at the Connecticut Academy of Arts and Sciences. These talks are collected with earlier essays in *The Necessary Angel: Essays on Reality and the Imagination* (1951) and in *Opus Posthumous*; the YMHA reading is recorded. He received the Bollingen Prize in poetry in 1950, the Gold Medal of the Poetry Society of America in 1951, and the National Book Award in 1951 and again in 1955. In 1954 Knopf published *The Collected Poems of Wallace Stevens*; that same year Stevens was offered, and declined, the Charles Eliot Norton Chair of Poetry at Harvard. The following year the *Collected Poems* won the Pulitzer Prize in poetry. Most striking of all, perhaps, this decade was the period of the late great poems. "The Auroras of Autumn" (1947) and "An Ordinary Evening in New Haven" (1949) are notable among the longer poems. *The Rock*, the concluding section of the *Collected Poems*, contains the elegy for Santayana, "To an Old

Philosopher in Rome," the near-hallucinatory "World as Meditation," and the luminous "Final Soliloquy of the Interior Paramour," with its utterly simple language and terminus of profound composure. Stevens died in Hartford, Connecticut, and is buried there. A plaque bearing his name has been placed at the Cathedral of St. John the Divine in New York City, in the Poet's Corner honoring the greatest American poets.

Stevens's reputation has steadily grown over the years. As his work continues to influence contemporary writing, thinking, and aesthetics, his poetry has become virtually a sounding board for critical theory. He has been called a "pure poet," a "philosophical poet," and an enigmatic "poet's poet." The Stevens canon has been approached by way of the New Criticism, phenomenology, structuralist and formalist theories, Freudian psychology, and Jungian symbolism. Stevens's "gaiety of language" has been explored from various linguistic perspective from R. P. Blackmur's early study, "Examples of Wallace Stevens," in *Hound and Horn* (5 [1932]), to Ludwig Wittgenstein's language games and Mikhail Mikhailovitch Bakhtin's dialogics in the 1980s and 1990s. He has been compared with Dante and François Villon, Walt Whitman and Emily Dickinson, Stéphane Mallarmé and Paul Verlaine. J. Hillis Miller introduced deconstruction and Jacques Derrida to American literary theory with "Stevens's 'Rock' and Criticism as Cure," in the *Georgia Review* (30 [1976]), while postmodern approaches to the poetry have variously employed Marxist, feminist, neo-Freudian, and neohistoricist critiques.

Wallace Stevens is the quintessential American poet. Like T. S. Eliot and Ezra Pound, he drew deeply on European art, music, and philosophy, transmuting Old World values into a singularly individual poetic style. More deliberately, with William Carlos Williams, Robert Frost, and Marianne Moore, Stevens's "shaping spirit" has illuminated the native landscape and energized the native idiom. While not a regional poet, as Babette Deutsch pointed out, Stevens "was immensely concerned with the indigenous and the local." His poetry expresses the independence, the experimental direction, and the quirky originality of American thought. Phrases from Stevens have become part of contemporary language; his poems have been set to music, quoted in books on biology and mathematics, given titles to ballets and newspaper articles. Like Walt Whitman and Emily Dickinson, he has deeply influenced generations of younger poets. Stevens's riddling, meditative, cryptic, lyric poems appear to have easily outdistanced his critics, interpreters, and theorists, which is perhaps the index of their greatness.

• The Wallace Stevens Archive at the Henry E. Huntington Library, San Marino, Calif., contains the majority of Stevens's notebooks, journals, manuscripts, books from his library, photographs, drawings, and more than 1,000 letters to him. Other collections are at Dartmouth College, Harvard University, the University of Buffalo, and the University of Massachusetts at Amherst. Apart from the biographical material provided by Holly Stevens in *Letters* and *Souvenirs*, Peter Brazeau's invaluable *Parts of a World: Wallace Stevens Remembered: An Oral Biography* (1983), records interviews with Stevens's colleagues, acquaintances, and family members. Joan Richardson's two-volume study *Wallace Stevens: The Early Years, 1879–1923* (1986) and *Wallace Stevens: The Later Years, 1923–1955* (1988) is the most comprehensive biography to date. Major collections of critical essays include Roy Harvey Pearce and J. Hillis Miller, eds., *The Act of the Mind: Essays on the Poetry of Wallace Stevens* (1965); Frank Doggett and Robert Buttel, eds., *Wallace Stevens: A Celebration* (1980); and Albert Gelpi, ed., *Wallace Stevens: The Poetics of Modernism* (1985).

The criticism on Stevens is immense. Among important early approaches to the poetry are Yvor Winters, "Wallace Stevens; or, The Hedonist's Progress," in Winters's *The Anatomy of Nonsense* (1943); R. P. Blackmur, "Examples of Wallace Stevens," in Blackmur's *Language as Gesture: Essays in Poetry* (1954); Joseph N. Riddel, *The Clairvoyant Eye: The Poetry and Poetics of Wallace Stevens* (1965); Doggett, *Stevens' Poetry of Thought* (1966); James Baird, *The Dome and the Rock: Structure in the Poetry of Wallace Stevens* (1968); and Helen Hennessy Vendler, *On Extended Wings: Wallace Stevens' Longer Poems* (1969), as well as her later *Words Chosen Out of Desire* (1984). Some useful studies are A. Walton Litz, *Introspective Voyager: The Poetic Development of Wallace Stevens* (1972); Adalaide Kirby Morris, *Wallace Stevens: Imagination and Faith* (1974); Harold Bloom, *Wallace Stevens: The Poems of Our Climate* (1977); Glen MacLeod, *Wallace Stevens and Company: The "Harmonium" Years, 1913–1923* (1983); Eleanor Cook, *Poetry, Word-Play, and Word-War in Wallace Stevens* (1988); Barbara M. Fisher, *Wallace Stevens: The Intensest Rendezvous* (1990); and Alan Filreis, *Wallace Stevens and the Actual World* (1991). Melita Schaum, *Wallace Stevens and the Critical Schools* (1988), provides a succinct overview of the critical history through the 1980s; John N. Serio, *Wallace Stevens: An Annotated Secondary Bibliography* (1994), presents a detailed and comprehensive survey of the criticism from 1916 through 1990. Obituaries are by Delmore Schwartz in the *New Republic*, 22 Aug. 1955; John Ciardi in the *Nation*, 22 Oct. 1955; William Carlos Williams in *Poetry*, Jan. 1956; and Babette Deutsch in *Poetry: London–New York* (Winter 1956).

BARBARA M. FISHER

STEVENS, Will Henry (28 Nov. 1881–25 Aug. 1949), painter and teacher, was born in Vevay, Indiana, the son of Edward Montgomery Stevens, a pharmaceutical chemist, and Ella Dimock. Interested in art from childhood, Stevens was privately tutored in drawing from the age of ten. After graduating from high school he attended Wabash College in Crawfordsville, Indiana, for a year. In 1901 Stevens became a student at the Cincinnati Art Academy. However, he disliked the teaching of Cincinnati's luminary artist Frank Duveneck, who was known for his dark, heavy Germanic style of painting, and he preferred the more ethereal style of Connecticut impressionist John H. Twachtman. Having won a design competition sponsored by Rookwood Pottery in 1904, Stevens went to work for one of America's leading manufacturers of fine arts ceramics. At Rookwood, Stevens produced designs for fireplace tiles and participated in the decoration of the Wall Street and Fulton Street stations of the New York subway system, the first subway in the United States.

In 1906 Stevens continued his art training at the Art Students League in New York, where he studied with William Merritt Chase and became friends with realist painters Jonas Lie and Van Dearing Perrine. Absorbed with painting landscapes, Stevens explored the outlying rural areas of New Jersey in search of pastoral scenes to paint, ignoring the bustling city that inspired the modernists of the era. He adopted the still-popular style of impressionism espoused by his teacher Chase, whose theatrical behavior in the classroom was abrasive to the modest and self-effacing Stevens.

Stevens's friendships with Lie and Perrine in New York led to his first solo exhibition of pastels in 1907 at the New Gallery on West Thirtieth Street. His paintings were featured in the exhibit Paintings by Americans there the following year, and in 1908 he was given a second one-man exhibition that included several oil paintings in addition to a series of his new pastels. After Stevens's early success in New York, however, he returned to the Midwest, and his exhibition activities were redirected away from the major center of critical attention in Manhattan. Stevens participated in numerous exhibitions throughout the Midwest and later throughout the South that provided him with a large audience for his work but little serious national critical attention. Although he exhibited his work frequently, he was out of the national spotlight and did not participate in the major exhibitions that made prominent careers for innovative artists of his generation. Yet Stevens made annual visits to New York and was familiar with contemporary art trends. At Rookwood, Stevens had met designer Grace Hall. They married in 1910 and had one child.

In 1921 Stevens was hired to teach art at Sophie Newcomb College, the women's division of Tulane University in New Orleans, where he taught drawing and painting for twenty-seven years until his retirement in 1948. The following year he became the director of the summer school at Natchitoches, Louisiana. Always a rambler in search of quiet and peaceful scenic vistas, Stevens painted the bayou regions of Louisiana during his early years in New Orleans.

By 1923 Stevens had exhibited at the National Academy of Design, the Pennsylvania Academy of the Fine Arts, the Philadelphia Art Institute, the Art Institute of Chicago, the City Art Museum of St. Louis (now the St. Louis Art Museum) and the Isaac Delgado Museum of Art in New Orleans (now the New Orleans Museum of Art), as well as at galleries in New York, Cincinnati, Cleveland, Pittsburgh, and Indianapolis, through which he attained a significant regional reputation. A turning point for Stevens's career came in 1926, when he was introduced to the abstractions of Wassily Kandinsky and Paul Klee featured in the Brooklyn Museum exhibition sponsored by the Société Anonyme, later shown in an abbreviated version at the Anderson Galleries in Manhattan. From this exposure, Stevens began to examine the realm of abstraction; however, he never abandoned painting and exhibiting landscapes and genre scenes. Concurrently he developed a formula for making his own non-smudging pastels, which he worked with other materials to create a distinctive mixed-media technique of rich and unusual surface textures.

Stevens first exhibited his innovative symbol paintings, free-form abstractions inspired by Kandinsky and Klee, at the Isaac Delgado Museum of Art in December 1931. Two months later he was included in an exhibition organized by the Arts and Crafts Club of New Orleans at the Montross Gallery in New York. An unidentified critic for the *New York Sun* singled out Stevens's work for praise. Throughout the 1930s Stevens continued to exhibit his more traditional work in the South and Midwest. He was accorded one-man exhibitions at the Mint Museum in Charlotte, North Carolina, and the Cincinnati Art Museum and the Washington County Museum of Fine Arts in Hagerstown, Maryland, in 1938, and his work *Painting No. 1* was included in the contemporary art section of the 1939 New York World's Fair.

National attention increased when Stevens's work was shown in a solo exhibition at New York's Kleemann Galleries in 1941. The exhibition was favorably reviewed in the *New York Times* and *Art Digest*, and the Boston Museum of Fine Arts purchased *Pinnacles* and *Winged Form* from the show for the museum's permanent collection. Later in 1941 Stevens staged pendant exhibitions at the Kleemann Galleries—where he showed landscapes and regional genre scenes of the rural South—and at the Willard Gallery—which featured his lyrical abstractions. Although this proved to be Stevens's last show in New York, he held a solo show at Black Mountain College in 1944. Black Mountain professor Joseph Albers, formerly of Germany's Bauhaus, encouraged Stevens to join the nationally acclaimed Abstract American Artists group, but Stevens never took Albers's recommendation. In 1946 Stevens organized his final solo exhibition at the Isaac Delgado Museum. He left New Orleans two years later to retire in the city of his birth. After only one year of retirement, during which time he was unable to paint very much due to illness, he died in Vevay, Indiana.

Well-respected during his lifetime and frequently exhibited, Will Henry Stevens's reputation languished for almost forty years after his death. Although highly regarded in the South as a regionalist artist, he was little known outside the region, and his works were not included in major texts on American art. His works began to attract more widespread recognition after a series of exhibitions featuring his inventive abstractions were held during the late 1980s and early 1990s, and more of his works began to enter major museum collections. Stevens is presently acknowledged as one of the enlightened painters of abstraction in the United States working just prior to the advent of abstract expressionism in the 1950s.

• Stevens's friend Bernard Lemann interviewed the artist in 1947–1948 for a memoir, "Will Henry's Nature: The Pictorial Ideas of W. H. Stevens," an unpublished typescript in the collection of the Howard Tilton Memorial Library, Tulane University. Other archival material on Stevens is in the Archives of American Art, Smithsonian Institution. The most extensive research on Stevens has been done by Jessie Poesch, *Will Henry Stevens* (1987), but still much basic information about the artist needs to be clarified. Blue Spiral 1 Gallery in Asheville, N.C., sponsored a series of Stevens exhibitions accompanied by catalogs and brochures, including Paul Grootkerk, *Picturesque Regionalism: The Agrarian Paintings of Will Henry Stevens* (n.d.); Marianne Lorenz, *Abstract Landscapes and Non-Objectives: Mature Work 1938–1949* (1992); Percy North, *Beyond Appearances: Abstractions by Will Henry Stevens* (1993); Estill Curtis Pennington, *Will Henry Stevens from the Mountains to the Sea* (1994); and Poesch, *Will Henry Stevens: The Oriental Influence* (1996). See also Gail Levin and Marianne Lorenz, *Theme and Improvisation: Kandinsky and the American Avant-Garde* (1992); North, *Visions of an Inner Life: Abstractions by Will Henry Stevens* (1988); and North, "Nature's Spirit in the Late Abstractions of Will Henry Stevens," *Southeastern College Art Conference Review* 11 (Spring 1989): 295–300.

PERCY NORTH

STEVENS, William Oliver (7 Oct. 1878–15 Jan. 1955), writer and educator, was born in Rangoon, Burma, the son of the Reverend Edward Oliver Stevens and Harriet Calista Mason, American Baptist missionaries. Both the Stevens and the Mason families had labored in the Burmese missions for two generations; Stevens's maternal grandfather, Francis Mason, was a noted linguist who translated the Bible into the Karen language. In 1887 William Stevens sailed to the United States to pursue his education in American schools. He was graduated from Colby College in Waterville, Maine, as a member of Phi Beta Kappa in 1899. After teaching English for a year at Colby, Stevens proceeded to graduate school at Yale University, where he took his Ph.D. in English in 1903. His dissertation, *The Cross in the Life and Literature of the Anglo-Saxons*, was published in the Yale Studies in English series the following year.

In September 1903 Stevens was hired as an instructor in English at the United States Naval Academy in Annapolis, Maryland. During a decade of rapid expansion Stevens played a critical role in modernizing the academic curriculum and in building a department that would produce the next generation of American naval historians. His marriage in 1904 to Claudia Wilson Miles, the niece and ward of Rear Admiral Hugo Osterhaus, gained him entry into high-ranking naval circles; they had two children. During his early years at the academy, Stevens made a reputation for himself as a satirist and cartoonist with his *Annapolis Alphabets*, collections of limericks and drawings that poked fun at Maryland politics and the naval establishment. He also published extensively in local and national periodicals, including the *Baltimore Sun* and *St. Nicholas*, and in the process formed close friendships with the Baltimore newspaper magnate Charles Grasty, the cartoonist McKee Barclay, and the aspiring iconoclast H. L. Mencken. Stevens soon achieved a reputation as one of the leading young literary figures of Maryland; in 1909 the *Baltimore Sun* dubbed him "the Lewis Carroll of Annapolis."

In the years between 1909 and 1924 Stevens turned increasingly to writing naval history, which at that time fell within the purview of the academy's English department. Troubled by the lack of textbooks that would keep midshipmen and officers abreast of the latest developments in naval history and theory, Stevens inspired the English department to publish *The Navy, 1775–1909* (1910) to remedy the problem. Stevens followed this work with *The Story of Our Navy* (1914); *Composition for Naval Officers* (1918), a rhetoric and guide to naval correspondence; and his masterpiece, *A History of Seapower* (1920), coauthored with a younger colleague, Allan Westcott. Each of these textbooks marked a step away from the traditional hagiographical treatment of naval history toward a modern emphasis on the role of politics and technology in warfare at sea. Stevens's most important innovation was to update the work of Alfred Thayer Mahan, stressing the growing importance of communications and the enormous potential that the airplane offered for navies of the future. This modern outlook brought Stevens to the attention of Josephus Daniels, Woodrow Wilson's reform-minded secretary of the navy, who commissioned him to design an educational program for enlisted men that was later implemented in the fleet.

During the First World War Stevens published extensively in periodicals such as the *New York Times*, the *Yale Review*, and *Atlantic Monthly*, and he soon gained a reputation as the leading American civilian authority on naval issues. In the postwar years Stevens's unabashed advocacy of submarine and air power and his opposition to the Washington Naval Treaty of 1922 brought him into conflict with the "battleship" admirals who still dominated the postwar navy. Henry B. Wilson, superintendent of the naval academy from 1921 to 1925, was one of these admirals; when Stevens's teaching contract expired in 1924, Wilson refused to renew it. Stevens protested his dismissal to Secretary of the Navy Edwin Denby (1870–1929) but with no success. In a parting shot, Stevens published a scathing indictment of Wilson's tenure at the naval academy in the *New York World* on 2 August 1925; the article, illustrated with caricatures of the superintendent, soured his relationship with the navy for the remainder of his life.

After leaving the naval academy Stevens turned to a career in secondary education, a field that provided him more scope to experiment with interdisciplinary programs and to implement his theories about pedagogy. In a March 1920 article in the *Educational Review* entitled "Mark Hopkins or the Ph.D.?" Stevens had decried the influence of the German university, with its emphasis on research, as ultimately harmful to American college and secondary school teaching. His own record of scholarship notwithstanding, Stevens maintained that publishing was merely a "fruit" of teaching and that ultimately the study must take second place to the classroom. In autumn 1924 Stevens became the headmaster of the Roger Ascham School in White Plains, New York; the following year he moved to Bloomfield Hills, Michigan, to serve as the

first headmaster of the Cranbrook School. Working with the school's founders, George Booth and Ellen Scripps Booth, Stevens played a major role in fostering Cranbrook's innovative integration of the arts into the preparatory school curriculum.

In 1935 Stevens left Cranbrook; after a one-year stint as head of the Department of English and Journalism at Oglethorpe University in Atlanta, Georgia, he turned to writing full time. In the late 1930s he published an influential series of American travel books, beginning with *Nantucket, the Far-Away Island* (1936) and *Annapolis, Anne Arundel's Town* (1937); both prominently featured Stevens's pen-and-ink illustrations. From 1937 Stevens made his permanent residence in Nantucket and in New York City, where he was a member of the Century Association.

In the course of the next two decades Stevens published over twenty books. Several titles explored spiritualism, a topic that attracted Stevens's attention after the death of his younger son, William Mason, in the South Pacific in 1942. Stevens's studies led him to join the American Society for Psychical Research, and he served as a trustee of the organization in the late 1940s. The birth of two children to his elder son Hugo rekindled his interest in juvenile literature, and in his final years he worked with the publishers Dodd & Mead on a series of biographies of famous Americans for children. Stevens died in New York City.

Stevens revolutionized the teaching of naval history in the United States; his *A History of Seapower* was used to train all naval officers between 1920 and 1955. More than any other individual he adapted the theories of Mahan to the realities of twentieth-century warfare. Stevens's modernization of the humanities curriculum at the naval academy would later serve as a model for other colleges. In the 1920s and 1930s he brought the same penchant for experiment to secondary education in his integration of the arts into the curriculum of the Cranbrook School. Perhaps Stevens's most influential contribution was as a popularizer of new ideas in the arts and sciences. Master of a lucid prose style, Stevens introduced the literate public to current thought on a wide range of topics through his numerous books and essays in leading periodicals.

• The major collection of Stevens's papers is located at the U.S. Naval Academy, divided between the Archives and the Special Collections Branch of Nimitz Library. During his fifty-year career as a writer Stevens published forty-seven books and over one hundred periodical articles. In addition to those already mentioned, the most important on naval issues include "Democracy in the Navy," *Atlantic Monthly* 122 (1918): 672–76; "The Submarine," *Yale Review* 7 (1918): 465–78; "What Won the War?" *Atlantic Monthly* 123 (1919): 374–80; "The Fate of the Dreadnought," *United States Naval Institute Proceedings* 47 (Feb. 1921): 191–200; "Scrapping Mahan," *Yale Review* 12 (1923): 528–42; and "Our Yes-Man Navy," *Forum* 100 (1938): 211–15. Two volumes lay out the fruits of Stevens's psychical investigations: *Beyond the Sunset: New Vistas to Immortality* (1944) and *Unbidden Guests* (1945). The best published sources of information on Stevens are *The Drummer-Boy of Burma* (1943), a largely autobiographical account of his boyhood in the 1880s; the *New York Times* obituary of 16 Jan. 1955; and Michael P. Parker, "Alphabetical (Dis-)Order: The Annapolis Satires of William Oliver Stevens," *Maryland Historical Magazine* 85 (Spring 1990): 15–43.

MICHAEL P. PARKER

STEVENSON, Adlai Ewing (23 Oct. 1835–14 June 1914), vice president of the United States, was born in Christian County, Kentucky, the son of John Turner Stevenson, a tobacco farmer, and Eliza Ann Ewing. In 1852 he moved with his family to Bloomington, Illinois, where he worked in his father's sawmill and taught school to earn money to attend Illinois Wesleyan and then Centre College in Danville, Kentucky. His father's death in 1857 compelled Stevenson to return home to care for his mother and younger brothers. He read law under Robert E. Williams and opened an office in Metamora, Illinois, in 1858.

Stevenson developed an interest in politics in 1858 when he heard the Lincoln-Douglas debates in Illinois. His first position was that of master in chancery of the Circuit Court of Woodford County, which he held during the four years of the Civil War. A "War Democrat" opposed to secession and committed to the suppression of the southern rebellion by force, Stevenson helped to organize the 108th Regiment Illinois Volunteer Infantry. A presidential elector for George B. McClellan in 1864, Stevenson won election as prosecuting attorney for the Twenty-third Judicial District, serving from 1865 to 1869. He married Letitia Barbour Green in 1866; they had four children.

In 1869 Stevenson returned to Bloomington to open a law partnership with his double cousin, James Stevenson Ewing. Stevenson also served as president of the McLean County Coal Company, a family enterprise that became Bloomington's second largest industry. With a home on Franklin Square and a successful law firm and business, he became a respected member of the community.

Stevenson's beginning in national politics was in 1874, when he defeated the Republican incumbent for a seat in the U.S. House of Representatives. Two years later he lost his bid for reelection, but he regained the seat in 1878. Serving in Congress for two nonconsecutive terms while representing a rural Republican constituency, Stevenson in large measure managed to succeed because of his persuasive skills, political instincts, and numerous local connections. He made politics out of the issue of nonpartisanship, learned to work with people holding opposing political viewpoints, adopted a cautious approach in handling divisive issues, and mixed ambition with anxiety. During his four years in Congress, Stevenson favored soft money, low tariffs, and electoral college reform to provide for a more direct way of electing a president.

A turning point in Stevenson's career occurred in 1884 with the presidential election of Grover Cleveland, who in 1885 selected Stevenson as first assistant postmaster general. Stevenson relished this assignment, but he earned the wrath of civil service reformers for removing thousands of Republican postmas-

ters. In 1888 he attempted to become Cleveland's running mate but eventually withdrew his name from consideration. Following his defeat for reelection in 1888, Cleveland sent Stevenson's name to the Senate for confirmation as associate justice of the Supreme Court for the District of Columbia. Because Republicans controlled the upper chamber, they blocked the nomination in order to allow the new chief executive, Benjamin Harrison, to fill the vacancy.

Chairman of the Illinois delegation, Stevenson played an important role at the 1892 Democratic National Convention in Chicago. He worked to collect votes for Cleveland and persuaded the Illinois delegates to vote unanimously for the former chief executive. Stevenson emerged as the party's vice presidential nominee. His attractiveness stemmed from several factors. A political moderate and man of temperate disposition, he did not antagonize the diverse interests of the delegates and found himself in the advantageous position of being a compromise choice. He especially appeased southern delegates upset with Cleveland's stand on currency and also added geographical balance to the Democratic ticket headed by a New Yorker.

Stevenson concentrated much of his 1892 campaign in the South, a region where farmers distrusted Cleveland's hard-money views. He replied to the complaints of dissatisfied southern Democrats with assurances of federal investment in the region, locally controlled elections, tariff reductions, and party patronage with Cleveland's election. A dedicated campaigner, he contributed to the Democratic victory and helped to carry the South and Illinois.

Vice President Stevenson held office during a troubling time. A severe depression gripped the nation, contributing to social unrest and political protest, while Democrats divided on the money issue. Stevenson supported the president's efforts to lower the tariff, and he also endorsed the administration's foreign policy. Stevenson approved of the administration's handling of the Venezuelan boundary dispute with Great Britain, the Olney corollary to the Monroe Doctrine, and the withdrawal from the Senate of the Hawaiian annexation treaty. His foreign policy views were a mixture of anti-imperialism, moralism, nationalism, isolationism, and patriotism. During his four years in office from 1893 to 1897, Stevenson traveled widely, made numerous friends on Capitol Hill, and acquired the respect of senators for his impartiality and courtesy while presiding over the Senate.

In 1896 Stevenson belatedly sought the Democratic presidential nomination, counting on a deadlocked convention. Highly divisive issues, such as the coinage argument, defied compromise, and Stevenson, a skilled neutralist and bimetallist, lost the nomination to the more militant silverite William Jennings Bryan. Upon the close of the Cleveland administration, Stevenson resumed his law practice. President William McKinley appointed him in 1897 to serve on the Bimetallic Monetary Commission, a group that sought unsuccessfully to convince European leaders to accept international bimetallism at an established ratio between silver and gold. Stevenson backed McKinley's decision to ask Congress for a declaration of war against Spain in order to end Spanish oppression in Cuba. He said: "Had our ears remained deaf to the cry of the stricken and starving at our doors, we would not have been guiltless in the high court of conscience, and before the dread judgment seat of history."

Stevenson won the Democratic vice presidential nomination in 1900 on the ticket headed by Bryan because he was the most available man to provide harmony. Nominated in 1892 to balance a slate led by a conservative, Stevenson obtained his second nomination in 1900 as an elder conservative statesman to equipoise a ticket headed by a progressive. His talents to survive in both the Cleveland and Bryan camps in the same decade gave him a rare political distinction. Republican governor Joseph W. Fifer of Illinois recognized this trait when he described Stevenson as a brilliant observer of people and one of the ablest and most discreet statesmen of his time.

During the 1900 campaign, Stevenson embarked upon a formal crusade against the growth of trusts and imperialism, which he defined as the paramount issue. He presented a number of objections to overseas expansion, insisting that a republic should have no subjects, but he failed to propose a constructive alternative or offer a blueprint for new realities in American foreign policy.

After the defeat of the Democratic ticket in 1900, Stevenson returned to Bloomington. Eight years later he ran a close race for governor of Illinois, basing his campaign on the issues of civil service reform and the management of the state's charitable institutions. He promised to serve one term and conduct the gubernatorial office in a businesslike fashion. Stevenson lost to the Republican incumbent, Charles S. Deneen. In 1912 Stevenson supported Woodrow Wilson for the presidency and introduced the candidate to a Bloomington crowd. Stevenson died in a Chicago hospital.

A cautious centrist and coalition Democrat, Stevenson sought harmony in an era of change and intense partisanship, offered soothing words to heal internal dissension, and refused to indulge in personal vendettas. A formidable raconteur, he was the quintessential gentleman who reportedly never made a personal enemy of a political adversary. He was also a party regular who preached the politics of accommodation. As vice president, he served as a transitional figure between the conservative tradition of Democracy under Cleveland and the progressive brand under Bryan and Wilson. In the end, however, Stevenson's most lasting contribution to American politics might be the founding of a political dynasty. A grandson of the same name ran as the Democratic presidential nominee in 1952 and 1956, and Adlai E. Stevenson III served as a U.S. senator.

• Stevenson's papers are in the Illinois State Historical Library at Springfield. Adlai E. Stevenson, *Something of Men I Have Known* (1909), is his published book of reminiscences.

The major work on Stevenson is Leonard Schlup, "The Political Career of the First Adlai E. Stevenson" (Ph.D. diss., Univ. of Illinois at Urbana-Champaign, 1973). See also Schlup, "Democratic Talleyrand: Adlai E. Stevenson and Politics in the Gilded Age and Progressive Era," *South Atlantic Quarterly* 78 (1979): 182–94; Schlup, "Gilded Age Politician: Adlai E. Stevenson of Illinois and His Times," *Illinois Historical Journal* 82 (1989); 219–30; Schlup, "The American Chameleon: Adlai E. Stevenson and the Quest for the Vice Presidency in Gilded Age Politics," *Presidential Studies Quarterly* 21 (1991); 511–29; James S. Ewing, "Mr. Stevenson, The Democratic Candidate for Vice-President," *American Monthly Review of Reviews* 22 (1900): 420–24; Francis E. Leupp, "Mr. Bryan's Running Mate," *Independent* 52 (1900): 2139–42; and John W. Cook, "Life and Labors of Hon. Adlai Ewing Stevenson," *Journal of the Illinois State Historical Society* 8 (1915): 209–37. Obituaries are in the *New York Times*, 16 June 1914, and the *Bloomington Daily Pantagraph*, 17 June 1914.

LEONARD SCHLUP

STEVENSON, Adlai Ewing, II (5 Feb. 1900–14 July 1965), governor, diplomat, and two-time candidate for president, was born in Los Angeles, California, the son of Lewis Green Stevenson, a businessman, and Helen Louise Davis. He was named after his grandfather, an Illinois Democrat who was Grover Cleveland's vice president in 1893–1897 and William Jennings Bryan's running mate in 1900.

Stevenson's parents moved back to Bloomington, Illinois, when he was six. An otherwise placid midwestern small-town childhood was marred by a tragedy at a children's party in December 1912 when a .22 rifle in his hands accidentally discharged and killed a young girl. A bright boy but an indifferent student, young Stevenson moved on from Illinois public schools to Choate and then to Princeton, class of 1922. His father insisted that he go to Harvard Law School, but Stevenson, liking neither the school nor the law, flunked out after his second year.

After an enjoyable interlude in journalism, Stevenson in 1925 entered Northwestern Law School where he worked hard and did well. He then joined Cutting, Moore & Sidley, an old and respected Chicago firm. On 1 December 1928 he married Ellen Borden, a glamorous but self-centered and unstable young debutante with artistic aspirations. In 1937 he bought a farm in Libertyville on the North Shore, his home for the rest of his life. The Stevensons had three sons, one of whom, Adlai III, later became senator from Illinois (1970–1981). Ellen Stevenson grew to resent her husband's increasing social and political prominence, and they were divorced in 1949.

Loyal to the family tradition in Democratic politics, Stevenson joined the migration of young lawyers to Franklin Roosevelt's Washington in 1933. More a faithful Democrat than an ideological New Dealer, he returned in 1935 to his Chicago law practice. With a lively interest in foreign affairs nourished by regular European travel, he soon became president of the Chicago Council on Foreign Relations and, after war broke out in Europe, chairman of the Chicago chapter of William Allen White's interventionist Committee to Defend America by Aiding the Allies. In isolationist Chicago, dominated by Colonel Robert R. McCormick's hectoring *Tribune*, the great debate of 1940–1941 grew especially bitter. Stevenson's eloquent and thoughtful speeches won the admiration of the interventionist publisher of the *Chicago Daily News*, Colonel Frank Knox; after Knox became secretary of the navy, he asked Stevenson to serve as his special assistant.

In Washington Stevenson found himself involved in labor mediation, inspection of naval facilities, contract-drafting, speech-writing and race relations. In the winter of 1943–1944 he led a Foreign Economic Administration mission to survey economic needs in liberated Italy. After Knox's death in April 1944, Stevenson, disappointed in the expectation of the undersecretaryship, returned briefly to Chicago, but soon went to Europe for the United States Strategic Bombing Survey.

In 1945 the State Department asked Stevenson to organize public support for the embryonic United Nations. His deft handling of the press at the founding conference in San Francisco led to his appointment as deputy chief of the U.S. delegation to the UN Preparatory Commission. The illness of Edward Stettinius, the nominal chief, enabled Stevenson to play a central part in shaping the UN's structure. He served as senior adviser to the U.S. delegation at the first session of the General Assembly and as alternate delegate to the New York sessions in 1946 and 1947.

While Stevenson found foreign affairs especially fulfilling, he did not neglect Illinois politics. The shrewd Chicago boss Jacob Arvey, hoping to improve party prospects by presenting respectable candidates, urged him to run for governor in 1948. Chronically indecisive when faced with career choices, Stevenson acceded to Arvey's request only at the last minute. But he turned out to be an effective and even joyous campaigner, denouncing Republican corruption and winning 57 percent of the vote, the largest plurality in the state's history.

As governor, Stevenson found great satisfaction in tackling state issues, cleaning up state government, and exposing ties between politics, gambling, and the mob. Surrounding himself with able young men, many of whom went on to high executive and judicial positions, he won national attention as a civil libertarian by a ringing veto of the Broyles loyalty-oath bill.

He intended to seek reelection as governor in 1952. When President Harry S. Truman, having chosen not to run, turned to him as a possible presidential candidate, Stevenson displayed his customary self-deprecation and indecisiveness. Friends nevertheless organized a draft movement. The success of Senator Estes Kefauver in the primaries prompted city bosses, alarmed by Kefauver's Senate investigations into organized crime, to look for an alternative. Stevenson's welcoming speech to the delegates electrified the Chicago convention in July, and he won the nomination

on the fourth ballot. He selected Senator John Sparkman of Alabama as his running mate.

Vowing to "talk sense to the American people," Stevenson was a compelling candidate. His literate speeches, drafted by accomplished writers in his Springfield headquarters and polished, often up to the moment of delivery, by the candidate himself, astonished voters with their elegance and wit. Republicans dismissed his admirers as "eggheads," and thoughtful critics found more rhetoric than substance in his oratory. Stevenson was still a conservative Democrat, uneasy with organized labor, reluctant to appeal to minorities, and on prickly terms with President Truman.

His fate was to run against a national hero in General Dwight D. Eisenhower and to do so at a time when the political cycle was undergoing one of its periodic shifts. The Republicans used the themes of corruption, communism, and the unpopular Korean War to telling effect. Eisenhower took 55.1 percent of the popular vote and won by 442–89 in the electoral college.

During the next four years, Stevenson was the preeminent Democratic spokesman, defending civil liberties against McCarthyism and indicting the Republican administration as controlled by business. In November 1955 he announced his candidacy for the presidency. After beating off a challenge from Kefauver in the primaries, he was nominated on the first ballot. The convention chose Kefauver as vice presidential candidate.

His 1956 campaign was more substantive and more liberal than 1952 but less arresting to the electorate. As Stevenson wryly put it, "You can only be a virgin once." His advocacy of a nuclear test ban and of the abolition of the draft was ahead of its time and unavailing against a military authority in the White House. Eisenhower took 57.7 percent of the popular vote and won the electoral college by 457 to 73.

As 1960 approached, Stevenson declined to become an active candidate but once again permitted friends to organize a draft movement. At the Los Angeles convention, he came in fourth when Senator John F. Kennedy was nominated on the first ballot. Moved both by contempt for Richard M. Nixon, the Republican candidate, and by the hope of becoming secretary of state, Stevenson gave nearly a hundred speeches in the fall campaign. Introducing Kennedy to a California audience, Stevenson drew a contrast with typical grace and insight: "In classical times when Cicero had finished speaking, the people said, 'How well he spoke'—but when Demosthenes had finished speaking, the people said, 'Let us march.'"

The victorious Kennedy, though a Stevenson supporter in 1952 and 1956, had been exasperated by Stevenson's candidacy in 1960 and did not want a senior man of independent mind and constituency heading the State Department. He offered Stevenson the ambassadorship to the United Nations—an offer that Stevenson rather glumly accepted.

At the UN Stevenson exerted considerable influence through his stature, intelligence, and charm. He had less influence in Washington. His exchanges with Dean Rusk, a secretary of state wedded to the Cold War, were frustrating. Although Kennedy declared Stevenson "indispensable" at the UN, gaps in age and temperament more than on issues gave their relationship a formal cast.

While accepting the premises of the Cold War, Stevenson preferred negotiation to confrontation and argued for more attention to the Third World. The failure of Washington to brief him fully on the Central Intelligence Agency–sponsored Bay of Pigs invasion of Cuba in April 1961 led him to endorse a CIA cover story before the UN—an incident that caused him much distress. During the missile crisis in October 1962, Stevenson's advocacy of early concessions as a means of getting the missiles out won him a reputation as a "dove" in a nest of "hawks," though he redeemed himself in Kennedy's eyes by his nervy performance in the UN debate. The crisis was finally resolved along much the lines Stevenson had urged by the United States withdrawing American missiles from Turkey in exchange for the withdrawal of Soviet missiles from Cuba.

With Kennedy's assassination in November 1963, Stevenson hoped for a larger role in shaping foreign policy, but he was to have less influence with President Lyndon Johnson than with Kennedy. By 1965 he was dubious about Johnson's escalation in Vietnam, favoring instead a political settlement. He was even more dubious about Johnson's unilateral despatch of troops to the Dominican Republic in face of an alleged but unproven communist uprising. "If we did so badly in the Dominican Republic," he wrote privately, "I now wonder about our policy in Vietnam."

His frenetic life of work, speeches, parties, and travel was wearing him down. He was overweight, smoked too much, suffered from arteriosclerosis and hypertension, and disdained the advice of doctors. While walking down a London street, he suffered a massive fatal heart attack.

Stevenson's great impact came from his revitalization of the Democratic party in the 1950s. His lofty conception of politics, his impatience with liberal (and conservative) clichés, his call for new ideas, and his belief that history offered no easy answers set the tone for a new political era. He not only redefined the party mission but brought a new generation of idealists and activists into politics and thereby prepared the way for the Kennedy presidency. More than either of them recognized or admitted, Kennedy was the heir and executor of the Stevenson revolution.

• The main body of Stevenson's papers is at Princeton University; his gubernatorial papers are at the Illinois State Historical Library. Important letters and other documents are published in Walter Johnson, ed., *The Papers of Adlai E. Stevenson* (8 vols., 1972–1979). His own books, mostly collections of speeches, include *Major Campaign Speeches* (1953), *Call to Greatness* (1954), *What I Think* (1956), *The New America* (1957), *Friends and Enemies* (1959), *Putting First Things First* (1960), and *Looking Outward: Years of Crisis at the United Nations* (1963); also see Michael Maher, ed., *An Illinois Legacy: Gubernatorial Addresses of Adlai E. Stevenson, 1949–1952* (1985).

The major biography, thorough, sympathetic, illuminating, and unworshipful, is by a close Stevenson friend, John Bartlow Martin, *Adlai Stevenson of Illinois* (1976) and *Adlai Stevenson and the World* (1977). Shorter biographies include Kenneth S. Davis, *The Politics of Honor: A Biography of Adlai Stevenson* (1967), based in part on personal interviews; Porter McKeever, *Adlai Stevenson: His Life and Legacy* (1989), by a longtime associate; and Jeff Broadwater, *Adlai Stevenson and American Politics* (1994), informed and incisive. "Adlai Stevenson: The Man from Libertyville" (1990) is an excellent television documentary, produced and written by Andrew B. Schlesinger.

Personal glimpses are provided in Elizabeth Stevenson Ives, *My Brother Adlai* (1956), and Edward P. Doyle, ed., *As We Knew Adlai: The Stevenson Story by Twenty-two Friends* (1966). The Columbia Oral History Office's Stevenson project, undertaken shortly after his death, contains interviews with close associates. See also published memoirs of Harry Ashmore, William Attwood, Lauren Bacall, George W. Ball, Chester Bowles, Alistair Cooke, Paul H. Douglas, John Kenneth Galbraith, Hubert Humphrey, John Bartlow Martin, T. S. Mathews, George S. McGovern, James Reston, Wilson Wyatt, and Charles Yost.

On Stevenson's governorship, see Patricia Harris, *Adlai: The Springfield Years* (1975). The 1952, 1956, and 1960 elections are covered in the chapters by Barton J. Bernstein, Malcolm Moos, and Theodore C. Sorensen in *History of American Presidential Elections, 1789–1968*, ed. Arthur M. Schlesinger, Jr., and Fred L. Israel, vol. 4, *1940–1968* (1971), and by Alonzo Hamby, George Gallup, Jr., and Alex Gallup and Gil Troy in *Running for President: The Candidates and Their Images*, ed. Schlesinger et al., vol. 2 (1994). For the UN years, see Richard J. Walton, *The Remnants of Power: The Tragic Last Years of Adlai Stevenson* (1968), and the chapter on Stevenson in Seymour Maxwell Finger, *Your Man at the UN* (1980).

ARTHUR M. SCHLESINGER, JR.

STEVENSON, Andrew (23 Mar. 1785–18 Jan. 1857), Speaker of the House of Representatives and American minister to Great Britain, was born in St. Mark's Parish, Culpeper County, Virginia, the son of the Reverend James Stevenson and Frances Arnett Littlepage. Educated at the College of William and Mary, he became an assistant to the clerk of the Henrico County court in 1800 and three years later qualified as deputy clerk of the hustings court in Richmond. He was admitted to the bar in the autumn of 1805.

In April 1809 Stevenson was elected to represent Richmond in the Virginia House of Delegates, in which he served from 1809 to 1816 and from 1819 to 1821. There he was instrumental in establishing the Literary Fund to provide money for public schools. The War of 1812 imposed many demands on Stevenson's time and talents. He served as Speaker of the House of Delegates during the years 1812–1816 and as a member of Richmond's city council during the years 1812–1814. In 1813 he raised and equipped a company of light artillery. He participated in operations along the Potomac and in Norfolk but was unsuccessful in winning a commission in the U.S. Army.

Although Stevenson was generally supportive of internal improvements, he was suspicious of the role of the federal government.

He opposed rechartering the first Bank of the United States, and after the War of 1812 he raised his voice against the expansion of judicial powers by the Supreme Court of John Marshall. Stevenson introduced resolutions denouncing the court's decisions in *McCulloch v. Maryland* (1819) and *Cohens v. Virginia* (1821) and spoke out against Congress's right to restrict slavery as a prerequisite for Missouri's admission to the Union.

In February 1809 Stevenson had married Mary Page White of King and Queen County. She died in 1812 while giving birth to their only child, and in 1816 Stevenson took as his second wife Sarah Coles of "Enniscorthy" in Albemarle County. This second marriage, which also produced one child, brought Stevenson important political connections. Sarah Coles was a cousin of Dolley Madison, her brother Isaac had been secretary to Thomas Jefferson, and her brother Edward was James Madison's secretary.

Twice defeated by John Tyler, Jr., for election to the House of Representatives, Stevenson was sent to Congress by voters in Hanover, Henrico, New Kent, and Charles City counties and Richmond City in April 1821. Six years later he was chosen Speaker by the anti-Adams forces and retained his position in three successive elections. During this time he strongly supported the policies of the Jackson administration. To this end he advocated Indian removal, he took a Unionist position during the nullification crisis, and he joined the war to kill the second Bank of the United States.

To reward Stevenson's faithful backing, Jackson in May 1834 nominated him as minister to Great Britain. Anticipating confirmation and fighting ill health, Stevenson resigned from the House the next month. Nullifiers and supporters of the bank, however, joined forces in the Senate to reject the nomination, twenty-three to twenty-two. The next year he chaired the Democratic party convention in Baltimore that nominated Martin Van Buren for the presidency. Jackson again named Stevenson as minister to the Court of St. James's, and in March 1836, despite a recommendation from Henry Clay's Committee on Foreign Affairs that Stevenson again be rejected, the Senate confirmed the appointment, twenty-six to nineteen.

Stevenson's stint in London was a turbulent one. He negotiated most-favored nation status for American vessels trading with Singapore, aided in securing the Smithson legacy that led to the founding of the Smithsonian Institution, won indemnification for slaves seized from three American brigs and freed by British authorities in the Bahamas during the years 1831–35, sought reduction of British tariffs on American tobacco and rice, and worked toward a settlement of the dispute over the northeast boundary of the United States. Nevertheless, his successes were overshadowed by several political slips. He was chagrined when the *New York Sunday Morning News* reported that he hoped

Britain would undergo a democratic revolution and repeal the act of union with Ireland in the wake of financial collapse. According to the paper, Stevenson believed the Van Buren administration could help the course of revolution by discouraging the removal of American specie to England in the aftermath of the panic of 1837. His Whig enemies in Congress used these statements, as well as remarks about the probable failure of attempts to cripple the Bank of United States, to make it appear he had reversed his earlier positions. This justified their demands for his recall and their attempts to factionalize the Democratic party. More embarrassing was a contretemps with Irish leader Daniel O'Connell, who delivered an address decrying slave breeding in the United States and suggesting that the American minister "trafficks in blood, and . . . is a disgrace to human nature" (quoted in Wayland, p. 184). Stevenson sent a note to O'Connell asking for an explanation and hinting that if honor were not satisfied, he intended to challenge him to a duel. John Quincy Adams asked for a committee of inquiry to consider impeaching Stevenson, but his motion was tabled.

After the Whig presidential victory in 1840, Stevenson requested to be recalled. His subsequent public career proved abortive. In 1842 he missed by one vote being elected governor of Virginia. Four years later he successfully defended editor Thomas Ritchie, Jr., the son of his political ally, on a murder charge resulting from the death of rival editor John Hampden Pleasants in a duel. In May 1848 Stevenson presided over the Democratic convention in Baltimore that nominated Lewis Cass for president. During the sectional crisis following the Mexican cession, he advocated defending slave owners' property rights by any means, including secession, although he ultimately endorsed the Compromise of 1850. In 1852 he was mentioned as a possible vice-presidential candidate for Cass. Active in the colonization movement since the 1830s, he became a vice president of the Virginia Colonization Society in February 1855. The following May he succeeded Joseph Carrington Cabell as rector of the University of Virginia.

In addition to politics, Stevenson pursued interests in agricultural reform. An early member of the Agricultural Society of Albemarle, he was elected to the Royal Society while in London. Throughout the 1850s he continued to be a favorite orator at agricultural fairs.

Stevenson's wife died in October 1848. The next year he married Mary Schaaf of Georgetown, D.C.; they had one child. Stevenson died at "Blenheim," an 895-acre estate in Albemarle County, Virginia, that he had purchased in 1846.

• The Library of Congress holds the bulk of Stevenson's extant papers, including nine letterbooks covering the period of his diplomatic service. The Records of the State Department at the National Archives include his instructions and dispatches. A series of Sarah Coles Stevenson's letters from London, collected by William L. Royall and published in *Century*

Illustrated Monthly Magazine 78 (1908–1909): 453–63, 508–18, 733–41, shed light on her husband's career at the Court of St. James's.

Francis Fry Wayland, *Andrew Stevenson: Democrat and Diplomat, 1785–1857* (1949), is a full-length biography. Essays by Charles Francis Adams, Eugene Norfleet Gardner, and Howard Temperley provide discussion of several incidents in greater detail. See Adams, "John Quincy Adams and Speaker Andrew Stevenson of Virginia: An Episode of the Twenty-Second Congress (1832)," *Proceedings of the Massachusetts Historical Society* 2d ser., 19 (1906): 504–53; Gardner, "Andrew Stevenson," *Richmond College Historical Papers* 1 (June 1916): 257–308; and Temperley, "The O'Connell-Stevenson Contretemps: A Reflection of the Anglo-American Slavery Issue," *Journal of Negro History* 47 (Oct. 1962): 217–33.

SARA B. BEARSS

STEVENSON, Carter Littlepage (21 Sept. 1817–15 Aug. 1888), Confederate general, was born near Fredericksburg, Virginia, the son of Carter Littlepage Stevenson and Jane Herndon, occupations unknown. He was the nephew of Andrew Stevenson, who served as Speaker of the House of Representatives from 1827 to 1834. As a young man, Stevenson developed an interest in engineering, which, combined with a traditional respect for the military, led him to seek an appointment to the U.S. Military Academy at West Point. Through his family's political connections, he received the coveted appointment and entered the Corps of Cadets on 1 July 1834. His career at West Point, however, was lackluster, and at graduation in 1838 he stood forty-second in a class of forty-five cadets and was commissioned a second lieutenant in the Fifth Infantry. Two years later, on 22 September 1840 he was elevated to first lieutenant. Stevenson was stationed at Fort Winnebago, Wisconsin (1838–1840), saw action against the American Indians in Florida (1840–1841), and served in garrison at Detroit Barracks, Michigan (1841–1844). He was later stationed at Fort Wilkins (1844–1845) on Lake Superior at Copper Mine Harbor. In 1842, while stationed in Michigan, he married Martha Silvery Griswold. They had five children, most of whom died in infancy.

At the outbreak of the war with Mexico, the Fifth Infantry was sent to Texas, and in the early days of the conflict, Stevenson saw action at Palo Alto on 8 May 1846 and the following day at Resaca de la Palma. He later served as aide-de-camp to Brigadier General Hugh Brady. Stevenson's service in Mexico earned him the rank of captain on 30 June 1847. He then served on the frontier at Fort Gibson in the Indian Territory (present-day Oklahoma) and at Fort Belknap, Texas (1851–1852). From 1855 to 1856 he escorted John Pope's expedition to explore routes for the Pacific railroad, during which he had a skirmish with Apache Indians near the mouth of Delaware Creek in New Mexico Territory on 13 June 1856. Stevenson again saw action during the Second Seminole War (1856–1857) at Big Cypress Swamp on 5–6 March 1857 and near Bowleg's Town on 13 March 1857. He participated in the Mormon (or Utah) Expedition in

1858 and continued to serve on the frontier at Fort Stanton and at Fort Union in New Mexico Territory until the outbreak of the Civil War.

On 6 June 1861 Stevenson submitted his resignation from the army and departed on a leave of absence, but the resignation was not forwarded by his superiors. He was later dismissed from the service, "it having been ascertained, to the satisfaction of the War Department, that he had entertained and expressed treasonable designs against the Government of the United States." Following Virginia into the Confederacy, Stevenson was appointed a major of infantry in the provisional army. In July 1861 he was named colonel of the Fifty-third Virginia Infantry and was stationed with his regiment in western Virginia and later along the Weldon Railroad in southeastern Virginia. On the recommendation of General P. G. T. Beauregard, he was appointed a brigadier general to rank from 27 February 1862 and assumed command of a brigade in East Tennessee. In August, when Major General Edmund Kirby Smith invaded Kentucky, Stevenson was left behind in East Tennessee and led the force that compelled the Federal withdrawal from Cumberland Gap in September. Elevated to division command, he was promoted to major general to rank from 10 October and continued to serve in the Department of East Tennessee until 18 December 1862.

Sent with his division to Mississippi, Stevenson arrived at Vicksburg on 30 December in time to witness the Federal withdrawal following their repulse at Chickasaw Bayou, and for a time he commanded the Vicksburg defenses. He led his division throughout the Vicksburg campaign of 1863, during which his command was shattered at Champion Hill on 16 May. During the siege, his division occupied the fortifications from Railroad Redoubt on the left to South Fort, overlooking the Mississippi River, on the right. Upon the fall of Vicksburg (4 July 1863), Stevenson was exchanged and went on to serve as a division commander in the Army of Tennessee. He saw action in the battles around Chattanooga and throughout the Atlanta campaign. In the latter campaign, he particularly distinguished himself in the actions at Resaca (15 May 1864) and Kennesaw Mountain (27 June 1864). When John Bell Hood assumed command of the army, Stevenson temporarily commanded a corps until replaced by Lieutenant General Stephen D. Lee. Stevenson then led his division during Hood's invasion of Tennessee and fought at Nashville, in which engagement he stubbornly defended the center of the Confederate line at Overton Hill. He led what was left of his division through the dismal campaign in the Carolinas and was engaged for the final time at Bentonville on 19 March 1865. Unlike other Confederate division commanders, who were less aggressive in the field, his service during the Civil War led a noted historian to refer to Stevenson as "one of the fighting division commanders of the Confederate army of the West."

Paroled at Greensboro, North Carolina, on 1 May 1865, Stevenson returned to Virginia, where he worked as a civil and mining engineer until his death in Caroline County. In February 1914 the federal government erected a bronze likeness of Stevenson on the grounds of Vicksburg National Military Park.

• For additional information see *The War of the Rebellion: A Compilation of the Official Records of the Union and Confederate Armies*, ser. 1, vols. 17, 24, 31, 38 (128 vols., 1880–1901); Ezra J. Warner, *Generals in Gray* (1959); Stewart Sifakis, *Who Was Who in the Confederacy* (1988); William C. Davis, ed., *The Confederate General*, vol. 6 (1991); and Francis B. Heitman, *Historical Register and Dictionary of the United States Army, From Its Organization, September 29, 1789, to March 2, 1903*, vol. 1 (1903).

TERRENCE J. WINSCHEL

STEVENSON, James (24 Dec. 1840–25 July 1888), naturalist and ethnologist, was born probably in Maysville, Kentucky. Nothing is known of his parents or his early life. On 22 April 1856 Lieutenant Gouveneur K. Warren of the U.S. Army Corps of Topographical Engineers hired him in St. Joseph, Missouri, to accompany his expedition that summer. Stevenson became assistant to the party's geologist and naturalist, F. V. Hayden, thus commencing a close relationship that endured for more than twenty-two years.

Hayden and Stevenson worked for Lieutenant Warren in 1856 and 1857. During the first season they ascended the Missouri River to the mouth of the Yellowstone and then explored the lower Yellowstone to the vicinity of Terry, Montana (then in Nebraska Territory). The next summer the party left the Missouri south of present-day Omaha to find a route to Fort Laramie, exploring the Platte, Loup, and Niobrara rivers and the Sand Hills region of Nebraska along the way. On the return trip they circled the Black Hills and visited the White River Badlands.

Hayden was twelve years older than Stevenson and already an experienced naturalist when the two met. In their early years together Stevenson was strictly Hayden's apprentice; he helped gather the fossils, rocks, and animals that were part of the vast collection of natural history specimens Hayden dragged back from the West. Stevenson took no interest in the scholarly aspects of this work, and Hayden rarely mentioned him as more than a collector. Apparently their relationship was close, however, for there are hints that Stevenson spent the winter of 1856–1857 in Washington, D.C., where presumably Hayden employed him in odd jobs.

The only evidence that Stevenson continued with Hayden during the next several seasons are two later statements of Hayden. In his *Fifth Annual Report* (1872) Hayden hailed Stevenson "for over twelve years of unremitting toil as my assistant." In his *Sixth Annual Report* (1873) he mentioned Stevenson as "my principal assistant . . . in this wild life for sixteen years." Hayden could be careless about the details of his recollections, but both statements associate Stevenson with Hayden during the years 1858–1860. During that time Hayden and Fielding B. Meek gathered samples in Kansas in 1858, and then for fifteen months beginning in May 1859 Hayden and Stevenson joined Captain

William F. Raynolds for further explorations of the upper Missouri and Yellowstone rivers.

Hayden finished his pre–Civil War explorations during the autumn of 1860; he did not return to the field again until August 1866. Stevenson enlisted in the Union army with the Thirteenth Regiment of New York Volunteers, supposedly in 1861; there is confirmation of his enlistment in a letter of Hayden (Dec. 1862) to a colleague, describing Stevenson as a lieutenant with that regiment, at the time stationed in Washington, D.C. According to an unconfirmed report, Stevenson participated in the second battle of Bull Run (Manassas). Hayden mentioned Stevenson on two other occasions in his correspondence: in March 1863, noting he was with the Army of the Potomac, then two months later saying he had mustered out of the service. At that point Hayden hoped Stevenson would join him in Beaufort, South Carolina, to help collect natural history specimens (which Hayden was able to do while serving as a surgeon and hospital administrator), but he did not. Stevenson's whereabouts over the next three years cannot be determined.

For three months in the summer and autumn of 1866 Hayden returned to explore and collect in the Badlands and other regions of South Dakota. Stevenson accompanied him and presumably returned with him to Washington, D.C., that winter. From the spring of 1867 through the summer of 1878 Stevenson took part in every summer's work with Hayden, exploring parts of modern Nebraska, Colorado, Wyoming, Utah, Idaho, Montana, New Mexico, and Arizona. The essential work of Hayden's Survey of the Territories was to make maps, prepare inventories of the resources encountered, and collect and describe samples of the natural history. Probably Stevenson returned to Washington each winter as an employee of Hayden's survey, but whether he lived or traveled elsewhere during the off seasons, or how often he held other jobs, is unknown. During March 1875 he tried some other work, but he was back in harness with Hayden by that summer.

In 1867 Stevenson was one of six members of Hayden's professional staff in the field, holding the position of assistant geologist. In 1869 he was "managing director and general assistant," implying that he was no longer helping to collect specimens but was now coordinating the many nonprofessional details of fieldwork, such as food, campsites, routes, rendezvous points, transportation, and communications between staff members, who were often widely dispersed within their assigned locations. Stevenson was known as one of Hayden's most effective advocates, and during the 1870s he was helpful in lobbying Congress for a steadily increasing appropriation for the survey. Between 1873 and 1878 he was executive officer of the survey with broad supervisory duties over the several field divisions. This was an improvement on an experiment Hayden tried in 1872, when he organized two divisions and named himself and Stevenson to head them. During the summer of 1872 Stevenson and Nathaniel P. Langford claimed a first ascent of the Grand

Teton in Wyoming. Later climbers disputed their claim, but a careful appraisal of the evidence has recently concluded that Stevenson and Langford probably did what they said.

After the 1878 season Congress decided to reorganize the several scientific groups then working in the West. The result was the creation in 1879 of two new institutions: the U.S. Geological Survey (USGS) and the Bureau of Ethnology. Though he gained a position with the new USGS, Hayden was disappointed not to have been chosen to head that agency. He retired to Philadelphia, thereby ending a long association with Stevenson. Stevenson was appointed a temporary general assistant at the USGS in 1881—not executive officer, as was reported in his obituaries. John Wesley Powell, the head of the Bureau of Ethnology, hired Stevenson in August 1879 to lead an exploring and collecting party to New Mexico and Arizona that would study ethnology and archaeology at several pueblo ruins. Thus began a new venture for Stevenson that would fascinate him to the end of his life. He worked among the Navajo, Hopi, Jicarilla Apaches, and especially the Zuñi, as well as most of the Rio Grande pueblos, and he visited the Mission Indians of California. He studied ancient cliff dweller settlements, notably at Canyon de Chelly and Cochiti.

He collected numerous artifacts of historic and living cultures (now at the Smithsonian), the importance of which has never been properly assessed. He published little, but his wife, Matilda Coxe Evans Stevenson, whom he had married in 1872, made use of his extensive notes in her several publications. The Stevensons had no children. He died in New York City of what contemporaries called "mountain fever," a generic description for a variety of unrelated diseases.

• Stevenson's papers were never systematically collected and may now be lost. A few of his letters and scattered references to him are found among Hayden's papers, RG 57 at the National Archives; S. F. Baird's papers at the Smithsonian Archives; in the National Anthropological Archives (which also holds some of his wife's papers); and in the James D. Butler Papers at the Wisconsin Historical Society.

He published only one article with the Hayden survey, "A List of Mammals and Birds Collected in Wyoming Territory," *Fourth Annual Report* (1871), pp. 461–67. Illustrated catalogs of his collections, an article on a Navajo healing ceremony, and references to other papers he read (on pictographs, pottery, and sand paintings) appeared in annual reports of the Bureau of Ethnology during the 1880s, especially the second (1883), third (1884), and eighth (1891).

The outline of Stevenson's life known to the public derives from several obituaries, the fullest of which appears in *Science*, 10 Aug. 1888; it contains errors of fact and is based on unsubstantiated assumptions. Though similarly flawed, the article in the *Dictionary of American Biography* (1935) still deserves attention because it was written by William Henry Holmes, a longtime colleague. On the Teton climb, see William M. Bueler, *The Teton Controversy: Who First Climbed the Grand?* (1981).

MIKE F. FOSTER

STEVENSON, John White (4 May 1812–10 Aug. 1886), governor of Kentucky and U.S. senator, was born in Richmond, Virginia, the son of Andrew Stevenson and Mary Page White. His father was a leading Virginia politician who served as Speaker of the House of Representatives and U.S. minister to Great Britain.

Stevenson received his education from private tutors in Richmond and in Washington, D.C. He attended Hampden-Sydney College (1828–1829) and graduated from the University of Virginia in 1832. After graduation Stevenson studied law in the Westmoreland County, Virginia, office of his cousin, Willoughby Newton. Stevenson briefly practiced law in Charlottesville, Virginia, before moving to Vicksburg, Mississippi. In 1841 he moved to Covington, Kentucky, and two years later he married Sibella Winston. The couple had five children.

Stevenson became involved in local politics, and in 1845 he was elected to the Kentucky legislature as a representative from Kenton County. He served three successive terms in the legislature. Stevenson also served as a delegate to the Kentucky constitutional convention of 1849. In 1848, 1852, and 1856 he was a delegate to the Democratic National Convention, and in 1854 he aided in the publication of the *Code of Practice in Civil and Criminal Cases* for Kentucky. By 1857 Stevenson was well known in the Democratic party, and he was elected to two terms in the national House of Representatives (1857–1861), where he contended for the admission of Kansas to the Union under the Lecompton constitution. In his principal speech in Congress, Stevenson spoke for the preservation of the Union but noted the right of the slave states to defend their interests. He was defeated in a bid for reelection in 1860.

Stevenson supported the efforts of fellow Kentuckian John J. Crittenden to preserve the Union. However, Stevenson was prosouthern in his political sympathies. In 1865 he was a delegate to the National Union Convention, which supported President Andrew Johnson's Reconstruction policies. In 1867 Stevenson was elected lieutenant governor on a pro-Johnson ticket with gubernatorial candidate John Helm, who was gravely ill at the time of his election. Helm died five days after his inauguration, whereupon Stevenson became governor. In 1868 he won a special election over Republican R. Tarvin Baker to fill out the remaining three years of Helm's term.

During his term as governor, Stevenson faced numerous difficulties. The continuation of unchecked violence and lawlessness by bands of outlaws and former guerrillas in some sections of Kentucky in the years following the Civil War forced him to send the state militia into several counties to restore order. He also warned his fellow Kentuckians not to interfere with the civil rights of former slaves. While he verbally supported the extension of their civil rights, Stevenson relied on local authorities to protect black Kentuckians from racial violence.

As governor, Stevenson worked for the promotion of education in Kentucky, supporting a tax to aid the public school system in the commonwealth and establishing a state bureau of education. He also implemented reforms regarding more humane treatment of inmates in Kentucky's prisons and mental institutions. In fiscal matters, Stevenson was a conservative, urging the state to cease issuing bonds to cover short-term debts. To improve the commonwealth's economy, Stevenson created a state bureau of immigration to attract people to settle in Kentucky, and he ordered a study of the state's financial status. Credited with several innovative ideas, Stevenson easily ranks as one of the better governors of nineteenth-century Kentucky.

In 1871 Stevenson resigned the governor's office and became a U.S. senator from Kentucky, defeating the incumbent, Thomas C. McCreery of Owensboro, and Thomas L. Jones of Newport. While in the Senate, Stevenson followed a very conservative political course. He believed in a strict interpretation of the U.S. Constitution and opposed federal interference in the governments of the states. He also opposed the spending of federal monies on internal improvements.

In 1877 Stevenson left the Senate and resumed his legal practice in Covington, Kentucky. He served as chief legal counsel to the Kentucky Central Railroad and became one of the railroad's major stockholders. He also taught criminal law and contracts in the Cincinnati Law School. In 1880 he was chosen chairman of the Democratic National Convention scheduled to meet in Cincinnati. Four years later he was elected president of the American Bar Association. Stevenson died in Covington, Kentucky, and was buried in Cincinnati, Ohio.

• The papers of Stevenson are located in the Library of Congress and the library of the University of Kentucky. Stevenson's papers as governor of Kentucky are located in the collections of the Kentucky State Library and Archives and the Kentucky Historical Society. A book-length biography of Stevenson has yet to be published, but numerous references to his term as governor are in E. Merton Coulter, *The Civil War and Readjustment in Kentucky* (1926), and George Lee Willis, Sr., *Kentucky Democracy* (3 vols., 1935). An excellent article on Stevenson is in Lowell H. Harrison, ed., *Kentucky's Governors 1792–1985* (1985). For a biographical sketch of Stevenson, see Jennie Chinn Morton, "Governor John W. Stephenson [sic]," *Register of the Kentucky Historical Society* 5 (May 1907): 13–15.

RON D. BRYANT

STEVENSON, Matilda Coxe Evans (12 May 1849–24 June 1915), ethnologist, geologist, and explorer, was born in San Augustine, Texas, the daughter of Alexander Hamilton Evans, a lawyer, writer, and journalist from Virginia, and Maria Coxe of New Jersey. Stevenson grew up in a privileged, middle-class household in Washington, D.C. Following her education in a girl's finishing school and seminary, she defied convention and studied law as well as served an apprenticeship in chemistry and geology at the Army Medical School. Even though there were no opportunities for college or advanced degrees or employment in the sciences for women at the time, Stevenson decided to become a mineralogist and geological explorer. She was able to pursue these goals through her marriage, in 1872, to geologist and naturalist Colonel James Stevenson.

Following a distinguished career in the Civil War, James Stevenson became the executive officer of Hayden's United States Geological Survey of the Territories and later the Bureau of American Ethnology (BAE) and the U.S. Geological Survey. During the 1870s the Stevensons traveled to Colorado, Idaho, Wyoming, and Utah and created world-famous fossil and ornithological collections now housed in the Smithsonian Institution. Their most famous contribution to geology was their scientific discovery and study of Yellowstone's geysers in 1878.

In 1879 the BAE was formed by Major John Wesley Powell, and the BAE's first expedition was a collecting and research trip to Indian communities in New Mexico and Arizona. Stevenson, the first American woman to participate in a government-sponsored scientific expedition, was called "volunteer coadjutor in ethnology," that is, an unpaid assistant to her husband, the expedition's leader. The Stevensons spent six months at Zuñi and Hopi collecting ethnographic objects and amassing information on cultural and social aspects of Puebloan life. Resulting from this fieldwork was Stevenson's earliest known publication, a booklet called "Zuñi and the Zuñians," which presented the first scientific description of Puebloan life. Unfortunately, many people in the late nineteenth century considered women incapable of scientific work and assumed that "Zuñi and the Zuñians" was penned by James. In fact, the opposite was true. As secretary of the Smithsonian Institution Spencer Baird noted in 1882, all reports, articles, and catalogs of collections that had been attributed solely to James Stevenson were actually coauthored by Matilda Stevenson, even though her name never appeared on a title page. The conventions of the day meant that works written by women were ignored and unrecognized. The result was that it was several years before Matilda Stevenson's early geological and anthropological contributions were officially acknowledged and appreciated.

The Stevensons conducted research as the first husband-wife team in anthropology. Throughout the 1880s they traveled yearly throughout the southwestern United States, residing among the Zuñi, Hopi, and Navajo and at various Rio Grande Pueblos. They surveyed archaeological sites and mapped geological features in the Southwest and California. Matilda became noted for her skill in collecting ethnographic data. By 1884 she was internationally recognized for her objectivity and reliability, skills that scholars continue to appreciate. After her husband's death in 1888, Stevenson continued their work at the BAE, this time as the first woman government anthropologist. She was paid a salary and thereby became the first professionally employed woman anthropologist in the world.

Stevenson was not a prolific writer, but the works she produced in the BAE Annual Reports, *Science*, and the *American Anthropologist* are considered classics of Victorian anthropology. Her BAE annual reports include *The Religious Life of the Zuñi Child* (1887), the first work to analyze child-rearing and religious practices surrounding childbirth in a non-Western culture; *The Sia* (1894), the first ethnography of a Rio Grande Pueblo; *The Zuñi Indians: Their Mythology, Esoteric Fraternities, and Ceremonies* (1904), still considered the major reference work on Zuñi religion; and *Ethnobotany of the Zuñi Indians* (1915), which helped define the field of ethnobotany; Stevenson also published articles on Pueblo religion, games, clothing, costume, and material culture and gave numerous public and professional lectures.

Stevenson, also a pioneer in women's rights, was founder and first president of the Women's Anthropological Society of America in 1885. This was the first professional scientific society to be organized by women, who because of their gender were barred from membership in intellectual societies. Stevenson spent a great deal of time and energy demonstrating that women were competent scientists and scholars. She fought diligently and unceasingly to break down barriers to women's participation in the scientific community. Stevenson was eventually made a member of the Anthropological Society of Washington, the American Association for the Advancement of Science, the Archaeological Institute of America, the National Society of the Fine Arts, and the Washington Academy of Sciences. She also worked tirelessly for the preservation of America's cultural heritage; with Alice Fletcher she introduced the first federal legislation to preserve archaeological sites.

Stevenson felt that her task as an anthropologist was to record every phase of Indian life before it was irretrievably lost. As she wrote to Powell, "I want to do a comparatively complete and connected history of an aboriginal people whose thoughts are not our thoughts, weaving all the threads into an intelligent and satisfactory whole for the civilized students. It is my wish to erect a foundation upon which students may build" (23 May 1900). In this she accomplished her task; her works are still used as the basis for anthropological work in the area. She set standards in long-term fieldwork. Stevenson spent more than twenty-five years at Zuñi—evidence of a commitment to understand the deeper meanings of a single society—and eleven years with the Rio Grande Pueblos, establishing a strong foundation for comparative methodology that is a hallmark of anthropology. Until her death in Oxon Hills, Maryland, after several years of heart problems, Stevenson spent the greater part of each year in New Mexico gathering information for a monumental work, a comparison of all Pueblo religions. So vast in scope was this project that it took anthropologist Elsie Clews Parsons twenty-four years to complete and publish *Pueblo Indian Religion* (2 vols., 1939), a magnum opus on the subject.

• Stevenson's papers, including unpublished manuscripts and fieldnotes, are housed in the National Anthropological Archives, Smithsonian Institution. Some of her papers will be found in the materials of John P. Harrington. The most detailed accounts of Stevenson's works are Nancy O. Lurie, "Women in Early American Anthropology," in *Pioneers of American Anthropology*, ed. June Helm (1967), and "Matilda Coxe Evans Stevenson," in *Notable American Women, 1607–1950*, vol. 3 (1971). See also Nancy Parezo, "Matilda Coxe Stevenson: Ethnologist," in *Hidden Scholars*, ed. Parezo (1993); "Matilda Coxe Stevenson" in *Women Anthropologists: A Biographical Dictionary*, ed. Ute Gacs et al. (1988); and Margaret Mead and Ruth Bunzel, eds., *The Golden Age of American Anthropology* (1960).

NANCY J. PAREZO

STEVENSON, Robert Louis (13 Nov. 1850–3 Dec. 1894), writer, was born in Edinburgh, Scotland, the son of Thomas Stevenson, a civil engineer, and Margaret Isabella Balfour. An only child, Stevenson was chronically ill throughout his childhood. His nurse Alison Cunningham, to whom he dedicated *A Child's Garden of Verses* (1885), both entertained and frightened him with stories of Scottish martyrs that left him with a lifelong fascination with folklore and diablerie. Stevenson's family was famous for lighting the coastline of Scotland (his grandfather Robert built the Bell Rock lighthouse), and he himself spent time as a young man of nineteen on Earraid, off Mull ("Memoirs of an Islet," 1887), where his father supervised the construction of the Dhu Heartach lighthouse (*Records of a Family of Engineers*, 1896). Earraid was the model island for a stunning story of the sea, "The Merry Men" (1882), and the island later reappeared as the site of David Balfour's marooning in *Kidnapped* (1886). Although Stevenson was bound to study engineering on entering Edinburgh University in 1867, he quickly separated himself from the family tradition. To appease his father he agreed to study law, and in 1875 he passed the bar and became an advocate. Although he never practiced, he still made immeasurable use of his legal scholarship.

Stevenson was destined to be a writer. He was a voracious reader of everything from French police novels to Jacobite history to Covenanters' memoirs and correspondence ("If you care to get a box of books . . . let them be *solid*"). Everywhere he went he carried a pocket notebook. Fluent in French and Latin, proficient in German, adept at Scots, he set himself the task of learning to write and in a famous phrase, often misunderstood, played the "sedulous ape" to a host of English and American authors from Sir Thomas Browne to Henry David Thoreau. No contemporary writer worked harder at studying the masters, and none could match his own style for clarity, concision, and elegance.

Were Stevenson not a writer, he would have been known as a traveler. Apart from Scotland, he toured Germany, Belgium, Italy, Switzerland, France—culturally and intellectually his second home—and the United States. In France in 1876, in the artists' colony of Grez ("Fontainebleau," 1884), Stevenson met and fell in love with Fanny Osbourne, an exotic looking American woman with a talent for painting, at least ten years his senior, and with two children and a husband in the San Francisco Bay area. In 1879, after learning that Osbourne was in ill health in California, Stevenson booked passage in steerage for the Atlantic journey and then crossed the continental United States in an "emigrant" train. Although the purpose of the trip was a reunion with Osbourne, who planned to divorce her husband, the class of travel was partly for the experience and partly a consequence of Stevenson's limited funds. Through these years he never earned enough from his writing to support himself fully, and he was still financially dependent on his father. If the hardship of the travel very nearly killed him, it nonetheless provided him with an abundance of graphic material. Although he would have disdained any comparison with Emile Zola, in reality he was the journalist-reporter who recorded the language and represented the customs and character of the people and places he encountered in his travels. The result was *The Amateur Emigrant* (1883), one of the most authentic accounts of American life as seen through the eyes of a transcontinental traveler.

In California, and seriously ill, probably with tuberculosis, Stevenson lived first in Monterey ("The Old Pacific Capital," 1880), cared for by an expatriate Frenchman, and later in a comfortable, furnished room in San Francisco ("A Modern Cosmopolis," 1882). His essays on both places demonstrate his quick yet sympathetic study of the young nation and his recognition of how emigrants such as those he encountered on the train were part of the economic and cultural forces forming one of the great cities of the world, the "new" Pacific capital. Years later, in *The Wrecker* (1892), the novelist re-created the San Francisco he had remembered, the city where he first met Charles Warren Stoddard, who had been to the Pacific and had fired his imagination with tales of the South Seas. Stevenson and Osbourne married in San Francisco in May 1880 and, for a honeymoon, moved up to Calistoga and camped out in an abandoned mining cabin. They had no children together, but she had the two from her first marriage. *The Silverado Squatters* (1883), although barely noticed at the time of its publication, is a California classic, one of the most subtle descriptions of the beauty of the landscape, the charm of a life already past, and the harbinger of one struggling to be born.

Stevenson returned to Europe in 1880, and for the next four years, after moving between England and France and finally settling in Bournemouth (1884), he proceeded to write in the variety of forms (essays, short stories, travel, poetry, and novels) that were already becoming his hallmark. By 1886, with the publication of *Kidnapped* and *The Strange Case of Dr. Jekyll and Mr. Hyde*, he achieved worldwide fame. After the death of his father a year later, he left England in search of a better climate for his health. He never returned. He sailed to New York City, where *Jekyll and Hyde* was a sensation on the stage, and then he moved upstate to Saranac Lake in the Adirondacks, where E. L. Trudeau treated him at his tuberculosis sanatorium. During this stay on the East Coast Stevenson so-

lidified the connections that were crucial to his U.S. publishing career. In 1885 Will Low, an American artist whom Stevenson had met ten years earlier in Paris, had arranged for *A Child's Garden* to be published by Scribner's. They were subsequently authorized to publish *Kidnapped* and *Jekyll and Hyde*. Stevenson was now visited by E. L. Burlingame, the editor of *Scribner's Magazine*, who persuaded the novelist to contribute twelve monthly articles ("as long or as short as I please . . . and on any mortal subject"), and who returned to New York City with power over all of Stevenson's books in the United States. In *Scribner's* Stevenson published his most enduring essays, including "A Christmas Sermon," "Pulvis et Umbra," "A Chapter on Dreams," and "The Lantern-Bearers."

Samuel Sidney McClure, the newspaper syndicator, also visited Stevenson at Saranac Lake and made him an offer the novelist could hardly refuse: $10,000 for a series of "letters" from the South Seas, a fee substantial enough for Stevenson to charter the *Casco* in Oakland (June 1888) and begin his first cruise through the Pacific (the letters were initially published in 1891 in the *New York Sun* under the title *The South Seas*). Stevenson's travels through the Pacific constitute one of the most exciting periods of his life. He landed first in the Marquesas, spent time in Tahiti, and in January 1889 settled for six months in Honolulu. He was taken in by the royal family and became an intimate of King Kalakaua. Hawaii was the source for an important body of work, including the chapters on the eight islands printed in the *Sun* but omitted from the posthumously published *In the South Seas* (1896). A visit to the leper colony on Molokai was the background for his public defense of the Belgian priest, *Father Damien* (1890), who was accused of contracting leprosy by sleeping with lepers, while a trip to the Big Island inspired the transplantation to the islands of a European folktale, "The Bottle Imp" (1891). Sailing from Honolulu in midsummer 1889, Stevenson eventually settled with his family in Samoa, on the island of Upolu, and built "Vailima," his plantation home in the hills above Apia.

Enjoying the best health of his life, he worked at an astonishing pace, producing at a level that surpassed all but the best of his earlier performances. He drew on his American experience for *The Wrecker* (1892), with its thinly veiled portrait of S. S. McClure, and for the brilliant novella, *The Beach of Falesá* (1892). *The Ebb-Tide* (1894) extended the graphic depiction of South Sea rogue life that was introduced in *Falesá*. Stevenson continued to write historical fiction, completing *David Balfour* (1893), the reflective and elegiac sequel to *Kidnapped*, and beginning *Weir of Hermiston* (1896), the truncated masterpiece of law and retribution that he was writing on the day he suffered a cerebral hemorrhage and died at Vailima. Stevenson was one of the great letter writers of the century, and his last long pages to Sidney Colvin (*Vailima Letters*, 1895) capture the splendor of a bright new place and the portrait of an artist at work and in repose, the self-styled "exile of Samoa."

American culture had a profound impact on Stevenson. He was drawn first to the writers of the Renaissance, particularly Walt Whitman, whose passion for freedom he found exhilarating, and Nathaniel Hawthorne, whose fables of conscience demonstrated the enormous potential and versatility of the short story. Like his good friend Henry James (1843–1916), Stevenson was committed to both the art of fiction and the artist's freedom, and like James he was both psychologist and realist. But if Stevenson was invigorated and challenged by American life and art, he in turn left his own mark on the new culture. With nothing more than the initials "R. L. S." to go on, his work was enthusiastically received on that side of the Atlantic. The *New York Times* reprinted "A Lodging for the Night" (1877), his first short story, within a month of its publication in England and proceeded to lift three more stories from the English magazines over the next few years. Subsequently Stevenson (writing under his own name) was reviewed regularly in the U.S. press. At his death, the New York and San Francisco newspapers printed extensive retrospectives that rivaled the English and Scottish obituaries. Stevenson had become identified in the public mind with America. His wife, Fanny, who drew him across the plains to California; his openness to the diversity of peoples, an attitude he shared with another admiring writer, Mark Twain; and his adaptation of the American language all conjoined to give him the mark of a native son, although everyone knew he was first and last a Scotsman. The spell he exercised over the new land survives in the physical legacy he left behind. His books, manuscripts, and correspondence were bought by major U.S. collectors of the twentieth century—Harry Elkins Widener, Henry Huntington, Edwin Beinecke, and Morris Parrish—and form the core of the Stevenson collections at various university libraries. There are museums and historical memorials in Saranac Lake, Monterey, St. Helena, and San Francisco. Stevenson was painted and sculpted by American artists: the most prominent portrait is by John Singer Sargent (now in the Whitney Museum); the most significant sculpture is by Augustus Saint-Gaudens (St. Giles Church, Edinburgh); and the best-known illustrations of his most famous books, *Treasure Island* (1883) and *Kidnapped*, are by Newell Convers Wyeth.

For Americans, as for others, Stevenson represented that rare combination of artist and philosopher; no story failed to delight, and no text was without ethical meaning. He was the bridge between two worlds, the last of the Victorians and the first of the moderns. His modernity resided in an unwavering devotion to a lean and muscular art, an unadorned yet unforgettable style, pitched to an age that demanded an image of its quickened pace but knew it not. He was modern, too, in his subjects: the nature of evil, duality in human personality, and ambiguity as an inalterable condition of existence. Even those values that seemed most tied to the past—loyalty, courage, and pride—had a modernist's edge, especially when they were associated with the stoicism that underlay them all.

• Stevenson's manuscripts and correspondence are largely distributed among five research libraries: the Beinecke at Yale, the Houghton at Harvard, the Huntington in San Marino, Calif., the Firestone at Princeton, and the National Library of Scotland in Edinburgh. Among the numerous editions of Stevenson's collected writings, the most important are the Edinburgh (1894–1898), Pentland (1906–1907), Vailima (1922–1923), Tusitala (1924), and South Seas (1925). One-volume editions are Janet Adam Smith, ed., *Henry James and Robert Louis Stevenson: A Record of Friendship* (1948), and DeLancey Ferguson and Marshall Waingrow, eds., *RLS: Stevenson's Letters to Charles Baxter* (1956). For a collection of his correspondence, see Bradford A. Booth and Ernest Mehew, eds., *The Letters of Robert Louis Stevenson* (4 vols., 1994). Two essential texts for Stevenson studies are bibliographical: George McKay, *A Stevenson Library* (1951–1964), a six-volume catalog of the Beinecke collection; and Roger Swearingen, *The Prose Writings of Robert Louis Stevenson* (1980), a meticulous account of the contextual history of every known prose composition. Although the biographies are beyond counting, the following are informative: Graham Balfour, *The Life of Robert Louis Stevenson* (1901); Joseph Furnas, *Voyage to Windward* (1951); Jenni Calder, *Robert Louis Stevenson: A Life Study* (1980); and Frank McLynn, *Robert Louis Stevenson* (1993). David Daiches presents a useful critical introduction in *Robert Louis Stevenson* (1947), and Paul Maixner compiles a broad selection of nineteenth-century criticism in *Robert Louis Stevenson: The Critical Heritage* (1981). Calder in *Stevenson and Victorian Scotland* (1981) and Andrew Noble in *Robert Louis Stevenson* (1983) collect essays by contemporary critics. Edwin Eigner in *Robert Louis Stevenson and the Romantic Tradition* (1966) and Robert Kiely in *Robert Louis Stevenson and the Fiction of Adventure* (1974) both work with novelistic traditions, while Barry Menikoff focuses on textual and contextual history in *Robert Louis Stevenson and "The Beach of Falesá": A Study in Victorian Publishing* (1984), and modernism and the short story in *Robert Louis Stevenson: Tales from the Prince of Storytellers* (1993). Some of the newspaper articles published after his death are the *New York Daily Tribune*, 18, 23, and 30 Dec. 1894; the *San Francisco Chronicle*, 17 and 18 Dec. 1894; and the *New York Times*, 18 Dec. 1894.

BARRY MENIKOFF

STEWARD, Austin (1793–1865), antislavery reformer, was born in Virginia, the son of Robert Steward and Susan (maiden name unknown), slaves. About 1800 a well-to-do planter, William Helm, purchased the family. Escaping business reverses and debts, Helm moved to Sodus Bay on New York's Lake Ontario frontier and shortly thereafter, in 1803, to Bath, New York, taking young Austin with him. Hired out for wages, Steward entered the employ of a Mr. Tower in Lyons, New York, where he worked until 1812. Escaping, he went to Canandaigua, where he worked for local farmers and attended an academy in Farmington. While thus employed, Steward learned of New York's 1785 law banning the sale of slaves brought into the state subsequent to that date. Drawing upon the state's 1799 gradual emancipation statute as well as an 1800 court decision, *Fisher v. Fisher*, which ruled that hiring out a slave constituted an intentional and fraudulent violation of the 1785 law, he openly asserted his freedom and continued to hire his labor in his own name, despite challenges from Helm.

Sometime between 1817 and 1820 Steward moved to Rochester. In 1825 he married a Miss B—of Rochester, the youngest daughter of a close friend, who bore him eight children and, overcoming white opposition, ran a successful grocery business. During these prosperous years, he became an activist on behalf of other northern blacks, both de jure and de facto free, who were subject to prejudice and treated as second-class citizens. From 1827 to 1829 he was an agent for *Freedom's Journal* and the *Rights of All*, both black newspapers. In 1830 he served as vice president of the first Annual Convention for the Improvement of Colored People, held in Philadelphia.

Steward and his family moved to Upper Canada (now western Ontario) in 1831, where they joined a group of African Americans who had fled Cincinnati after the race riots of 1829. There, they had established, under the leadership of their agent Israel Lewis, an organized black community called Wilberforce. Steward invested the savings from his grocery in the project and undertook a major role in its proceedings, replacing Lewis as its principal leader until the community collapsed six years later. His career there, however, was beset with ill fortune. He soon fought with Lewis over the handling of the community's finances and other matters until in 1836 Lewis was dropped as the community's principal agent. The brothers Benjamin Paul and Nathaniel Paul, who replaced him, proved equally unsatisfactory, the latter, who was sent to England to raise funds, never rendering a satisfactory account of his mission. By 1837 Wilberforce, wracked by internal dissension, had virtually ceased to exist, and Steward, his savings gone and his reform efforts blasted, returned to Rochester with his family.

Reestablishing himself in the grocery business, Steward prospered for a season, but the aftershocks of the 1837 panic and a disastrous fire finally destroyed the enterprise. Steward moved back to Canandaigua about 1842, where he taught school and continued his antislavery work as an agent for the *National Anti-Slavery Standard*. Although he gradually faded into obscurity, he was active for a while in the then-emerging political antislavery movement. He served as president of the New York Convention of Colored Men in 1840, 1841, and 1845 and lobbied for black male suffrage on equal terms as white suffrage.

Steward, like most other black activists, remained on the periphery of the antislavery movement, whose inner circles kept even noted abolitionist Frederick Douglass at a distance. Moreover, by the 1840s, Steward, tainted by his association with the failed Canadian settlement and lacking a personal following, was pushed from the black national convention limelight by younger, more aggressive black leaders such as Henry Highland Garnet, James McCune Smith, and Charles B. Ray.

Steward is best remembered for his autobiography, *Twenty-Two Years a Slave and Forty Years a Freeman*, published in 1857. It provides only a sketchy outline of his life and addresses his understanding of the evils of slavery, but it testifies primarily to the vicissitudes that African Americans experienced even in the North in its depiction of the struggle of one exceptional black man against social and economic discrimination and exclusion from the full political and legal privileges that white citizens enjoyed.

Steward pressed to achieve full citizenship for himself and others like him. For example, he attempted, unsuccessfully, to enlist in the Steuben County militia during the War of 1812, embraced the popular temperance reform of the 1830s, and served a term as clerk of Biddulph Township during his years in Canada. In the end, however, he always remained a marginal figure. His autobiography was his most effective undertaking; his strongest message was a plea to "those who have the power" to "have the magnanimity to strike off the chains from the enslaved, and bid him stand up, a Freeman and a Brother!" He died in Rochester, New York.

• There is very little primary or secondary material on Steward. Primary material on Steward can be gleaned from scattered references in antislavery manuscript collections. The introduction to the 1969 edition of his autobiography, *Twenty-Two Years a Slave*, written by Jane H. Pease and William H. Pease, provides an overview of his career in the antislavery and black freedom movements. For an elaboration of the Wilberforce settlement, see Pease and Pease, *Black Utopia: Negro Communal Experiments in America* (1963). Robin Winks, *The Blacks in Canada* (1971), provides a broad context for the black experience in Canada, and Pease and Pease, *They Who Would Be Free: Blacks' Search for Freedom, 1830–1861* (1974; repr. 1990), discusses the free black experience in the antebellum northern states; each contains an extended bibliography. C. Peter Ripley, ed., *The Black Abolitionist Papers* (5 vols., 1985–1992), esp. vol. 3, provides not only an extensive documentary context but also the most recent survey of sources pertaining to Steward.

WILLIAM H. PEASE
JANE H. PEASE

STEWARD, Ira (10 Mar. 1831–13 Mar. 1883), labor leader, was born in New London, Connecticut. Very little is known about Steward's childhood and personal life. Even while he was alive, friends commented on how little they knew of his background and family. Steward's friend and physician E. E. Spencer, for example, "knew him closely for ten years" but did not know where he was born or the names of his parents. Steward was raised in Boston but at nineteen moved to Providence, Rhode Island, where he apprenticed as a machinist. Within a year he was fired from the Draper Machine Company because of his "peculiar views."

As a young man, Steward became steeped in the radical antislavery movement of antebellum New England. Unconfirmed rumors that he fought alongside John Brown in Kansas swirled around him for the duration of his life. As a resident of Boston during the years of Reconstruction, Steward became a central figure in an alliance of middle-class abolitionists, such as William Lloyd Garrison, Charles Sumner, and Wendell Phillips, with labor opponents of slavery. As historian David Roediger notes, this unique alliance "stressed simultaneously the eight-hour day for Northern workers and Radical Republican measures for black civil rights in the south." Long after the Civil War, Steward argued that the legacy of the antislavery movement was to complete the unfinished task of liberating the American worker. Steward believed this process had to begin with a legislatively enforced shortened workday. By the early 1860s he became a leading figure in the International Union of Machinists and Blacksmiths of North America, where as a delegate in 1863 he obtained passage of a declaration that for the first time called for a law requiring an eight-hour workday. Also in 1863, as a result of his work with the machinists, he founded and became the leader of the Boston eight-hour movement. Steward spent most of the last twenty years of his life publicizing the eight-hour movement through actions as a labor activist, pamphleteer, and lobbyist. He served as president of both the Boston Eight-Hour League and the National Ten-Hour League.

Steward condemned the wage system that, he believed, deprived workers of the civic and economic freedom to which they were entitled. From his earliest known writings in 1851 (a letter to the *Weekly Mirror*) until his death, he, along with many other labor leaders, argued that wage labor turned laborers into commodities, making it difficult if not impossible for them also to be citizens. Steward believed that shorter hours and higher wages provided workers with a way out of this form of industrial "slavery." He wrote that increased wages and decreased hours would allow "every man" to be a "capitalist," by which he meant a self-employed or cooperatively employed citizen-worker. This would lead, he argued, to "a republicanization of labor, as well as a republicanization of government." For Steward, in other words, economic independence was a necessary precondition for political independence.

To this end, Steward was one of the first labor leaders to look to the state for assistance in the process of freeing the American worker. Steward regularly lobbied the Massachusetts legislature and worked with the Massachusetts Bureau of Labor Statistics (the first such bureau in the country, founded in 1869), to promote shorter-hour legislation. In 1874 Massachusetts became the first state to pass an effective ten-hour law for women and children.

Steward opposed separate labor parties as well as Greenbackism, a movement popular among workers and farmers that called for the government to abandon the gold standard, and was considered an eight-hour monomaniac by many leaders of the mainstream labor movement as a result. Nonetheless, his activism brought him into close association with some of the country's most important labor reformers and radicals of the post–Civil War years, including Phillips, F. A. Sorge, George E. McNeill, and George Gunton. Despite Steward's prickly personality, the latter two considered Steward to be a mentor; both continued to work in the eight-hour movement after Steward's death. Another important collaborator was his first wife, Mary B. Steward, who composed the short poem that became nationally known during the late nineteenth-century struggle for the shorter workday: "Whether you work by the piece or work by the day, / Decreasing the hours increases the pay." Mary Steward's death in 1878 left Ira Steward "completely unnerved," according to historian William Edlin (*Comrade*, pp. 65–66). In 1880 Steward married his cousin Jane Steward Henning and moved to Plano, Illinois.

Along with his activism, Steward spent much of his time attempting to write a book titled "The Political Economy of Eight Hours." The book was never published, although George Gunton's *Wealth and Progress* (1887) was based largely on Steward's notes. Steward's manuscript contains many fascinating insights about workers and the nature of the economy. In "The Political Economy of Eight Hours," the self-taught Steward proposed, albeit in what historian David Montgomery has aptly called "crude and unsophisticated" prose, a working-class alternative to mainstream political economy, which Steward labeled a "social economy."

Steward's social economy was far ahead of its time, for it emphasized working-class consumption as the key to economic growth and political democracy. He argued that the key to increasing workers' standards of living was to increase their "habits and wants." By working fewer hours at higher wages, Steward believed, workers would be able to cultivate their needs as consumers. As he wrote in the essay "A Reduction of Hours an Increase of Wages" in *Fincher's Trades Review* in 1865, "those who labor moderately have time to cultivate tastes and create wants." This, in turn, would redound to the benefit of other workers, as increased demand led to more jobs and higher wages. Steward suggested that consumption represented the fulcrum of the economy; it was what set off the cycle of jobs, wealth, and growth.

Steward drew a sharp dichotomy between "civilized" workers, who consumed well, lived comfortably, and maintained republican political institutions, and "savages," who, either through poverty or ignorance, had not learned the importance of consumption. Therefore, Steward believed that it was absolutely necessary that the standard of living of all workers be raised. Given the rise of international markets that served to "bring the most remote parts of the world into buying and selling relations with each other," any solution to the problem of what Steward called "wage slavery" had to include not just skilled American workers but unskilled workers from around the globe. At times, Steward argued that the internationalization of the world economy made it necessary for workers to extend their notions of solidarity beyond their craft and even their nation. On other occasions, however, he echoed other nineteenth-century American labor leaders in condemning the low standard of living of foreign workers as well as unskilled American workers, in effect, blaming them for their plight. Nevertheless, his suggestion that working-class participation in democratic government depended on high wages, leisure, and consumption was a lasting legacy to the American labor movement.

Exhausted by the labors on his uncompleted manuscript, Steward died in Plano. An obituary in the *Chicago Tribune* noted that Steward was "known to the nation" for his work on behalf of the eight-hour day.

• Steward's manuscript "The Political Economy of Eight Hours" and many of his letters are held at the State Historical Society of Wisconsin. His published works include "Poverty," in Massachusetts Bureau of Statistics of Labor, *Fourth Annual Report* (1873), pp. 411–39; and "A Second Declaration of Independence" (1879) in *We the Other People: Alternative Declarations of Independence by Labor Groups, Farmers, Woman's Rights Advocates, Socialists, and Blacks, 1829–1975,* ed. Philip Foner (1976). His famous pamphlets *A Reduction of Hours an Increase of Wages* and *The Power of the Cheaper over the Dearer,* both chapters in his uncompleted magnum opus, were published in *A Documentary History of American Industrial Society,* ed. John R. Commons et al., vol. 9 (1958). The most complete examination of Steward's life and ideas appears in David Montgomery, *Beyond Equality: Labor and the Radical Republicans, 1862–1872* (1981), pp. 249–60. Helpful articles include William Edlin, "The Life and Work of Ira Steward," *The Comrade* 1 (Dec. 1901): 65–66; Dorothy Douglas, "Ira Steward on Consumption and Unemployment," *Journal of Political Economy* 40 (Aug. 1932): 532–43; Hyman Kuritz, "Ira Steward and the Eight Hour Day," *Science and Society* 20, no. 2 (Spring 1956): 118–34; Alexander Yard, "Albert Parsons and the Tragedy of Economic Empire," in *The Haymarket Scrapbook,* ed. Dave Roediger and Franklin Rosemont (1986); Kenneth Fones-Wolf, "Boston Eight Hour Men, New York Marxists and the Emergence of the International Labor Union: Prelude to the AFL," *Historical Journal of Massachusetts* 9 (1981): 47–59; Roediger, "Ira Steward and the Anti-Slavery Origins of American Eight-Hour Theory," *Labor History* 27, no. 3 (Summer 1986): 410–26; and James Green and Hugh C. Donahue, *Boston's Workers: A Labor History* (1979). See also the obituary in the *Chicago Tribune,* 14 Mar. 1883, and the reminiscence of a friend, E. E. Spencer, "Ira Steward," a lecture given 13 Nov. 1895, which is held at the State Historical Society of Wisconsin.

LAWRENCE GLICKMAN

STEWARD, Julian Haynes (31 Jan. 1902–6 Feb. 1972), anthropologist, was born in Washington, D.C., the son of Thomas G. Steward, chief of the Board of Examiners of the U.S. Patent Office, and Grace Garriot. Steward once remarked that nothing in his family background or in his early education accounted for his later interest in anthropology.

In 1918 Steward was admitted to the newly established Deep Springs Preparatory School (now Deep Springs College) near Death Valley. There he was exposed to the lifeways of the local Paiute and Shoshone Indians, an experience that was enhanced when in his freshman year at the University of California at Berkeley he discovered academic anthropology in a course given jointly by Alfred Kroeber, Robert Lowie, and Edward Gifford. The following year he transferred to Cornell University, where, in the absence of an anthropology faculty, he completed his undergraduate training in geology and zoology. Livingston Farrand,

then president of Cornell and himself an anthropologist, nurtured Steward's continuing interest in anthropology and urged him to return to Berkeley to take his doctorate in anthropology, which he received in 1929.

In 1928 Steward began to teach at the University of Michigan, where he gave the university's first course in anthropology. In 1930 he moved to the University of Utah and did archaeological research on puebloid cultures. Accompanied by his wife, Jane Cannon, whom he had married in 1933 and with whom he would have two children, he spent 1934 on field research in Owens Valley, Death Valley, and northward through Nevada to Idaho and Oregon. In 1935 he became associate anthropologist in the Bureau of American Ethnology (BAE) of the Smithsonian Institution, where he remained until 1946. On loan to the Bureau of Indian Affairs (BIA) in 1935, he assisted in the creation of programs for the reform of the BIA, which resulted in a transformation that is usually referred to as the New Deal for American Indians. At the BIA Steward observed firsthand the relation between subcultures and the larger society that occupied his teaching, research, and writing for the remainder of his life.

While at the BAE Steward founded the Institute of Social Anthropology and chaired a committee that reorganized the American Anthropological Association. He helped establish the National Science Foundation and was instrumental in helping create the Committee for the Recovery of Archaeological Remains, subsequently the nation's River Basin Archaeological Surveys Program, often referred to as the model and stimulus for salvage archaeology in the United States. In partnership with Wendell Bennett, he established the Virú Valley Project in Peru, a research program that contributed significantly to the archaeology of South America.

Steward's outstanding achievement at the BAE was his management and editorship of the six-volume *Handbook of South American Indians.* In this major work Steward identified links between what he saw as culture types and the evolutionary schema toward which his research had clearly inclined him, a model he called "multilinear evolution" that paid special attention to the varieties of ecological, technological, and historical circumstances exposed by expanding global research. It is, in his words, "essentially a methodology based on the assumption that significant regularities in culture change occur, and it is concerned with the determination of cultural laws."

Although Steward has always been identified as a cultural anthropologist, he maintained that the line between archaeology and cultural anthropology was largely artificial, referring to the data of archaeology as ethnohistory on (or in) the ground. He believed that archaeology was more than potsherds and monuments, test pits and stratigraphy.

Throughout his professional life Steward carried on his search for cross-culturally valid regularities. In effect he saw his anthropological mission as a search for causes. And while he was appropriately cautious about spelling out laws or ineluctable causes, he was not immune from the criticism of those who dismissed the search for cultural regularities, citing diffusion as an argument against Steward's evolutionary propositions. He responded by drawing attention to the force of cultural and ecological factors in determining when, where, how, and if diffusion of cultural items or artifacts could take place, thus making diffusion an aspect of cultural evolution, a dependent rather than an independent variable.

According to Robert Murphy, Steward "minimally hoped that anthropologists would accept the position that culture is an orderly domain in which causality operates, and [its] operation is accessible through scientific method. Given the complexity of our subject matter, this may have been a naive expectation, but to Steward these were the unstated premises which underlay the rest of his theories" ("Introduction," p. 10).

In 1946 Steward accepted a professorship at Columbia University, starting at a time when the influence of Franz Boas still dominated the anthropology program. During his years at Columbia he supervised some thirty-five doctoral dissertations. Steward also planned and supervised the preparation, fieldwork, and write-up activities of five graduate students in the department's first attempt to study the culture of an entire area—in this instance, Puerto Rico. Publication of *The People of Puerto Rico*, the team enterprise, was delayed until 1956; it is still considered one of the significant contributions that mark Steward's eminence among anthropologists.

Steward had left Columbia in 1952 to become university professor at the University of Illinois. There he mounted an even more ambitious research effort to document "the processes of change in peasant agricultural systems that have been exposed to outside markets and wage labor" (Murphy, p. 12). To this end he established a program called Studies in Cultural Regularities. The work was carried on between 1957 and 1959, and the results were published in 1967 under the title *Contemporary Change in Traditional Societies*.

In 1952 Steward was awarded the Viking Fund Medal in General Anthropology, and in 1954 he became one of the first scholars outside the hard sciences to be elected to the National Academy of Sciences. In 1969 graduate students in the University of Illinois's anthropology department launched a twice-yearly journal, the *Steward Anthropological Society Journal*.

In his research Steward combined induction with deduction, moving from hunches stimulated by reading and observation and advanced by certain "logical inferences" to create a hypothesis. He did not see the field as a place where one went to record as carefully as possible a general description of a culture. He was guided by a firm set of deductive hypotheses to be tested by documentary and archival resources and by the careful collection of data in the field.

Steward's significance in the history of anthropology derives from a number of innovative ideas and practices. Other anthropologists had dealt with the shaping force of environmental factors, but Steward emphasized the importance of culture and its effects on the environment. He was impatient with anthropologists who used the terms environment and ecology interchangeably. His cultural ecology postulated a relationship among the resources of a particular environment, the tools and knowledge available to exploit those resources, and the patterns of work designed to bring them to bear upon the resources. Despite his devotion to the search for causes and regularities Steward remained generally indifferent to the premises of applied anthropology because he fully understood the differences in values, theories, and claims for social action that permeated the discipline. He persuaded many anthropologists to replace the stultifying "culture area" concept with the concept of "culture type." And he participated in a revolt against the restrictions of historical particularism and cultural relativism. He saw anthropology as a search for explanation rather than the hopeless pursuit of immutable truths.

Because Steward was diligent in the use of empirical data in his theoretical formulations, a few critics have labeled his results inductive or empirical generalizations. Although he was uncommonly sensitive at times, he considered these charges vacuous, remarking that it was self-evident that no theory springs full-blown out of a dataless vacuum. In short, he said, he could construct theory in the only way possible—by affirming the inescapable value of facts but not binding the scope of explanation exclusively to those facts.

Steward died in Urbana, Illinois.

• Steward's papers, including copies of an extensive correspondence (1926–1973), are in the university archives of the University of Illinois. A complete bibliography of his work is in an appendix to an obituary by Robert A. Manners and Jane C. Steward in *American Anthropologist* 75 (June 1973): 886–903. For treatments of Steward's life and work, see *International Encyclopedia of the Social Sciences*, vol. 18 (1979); Gordon R. Willey, *Portraits in American Archaeology: Remembrance of Some Distinguished Americanists* (1988); Robert A. Manners, ed., *Process and Pattern in Culture: Essays in Honor of Julian Steward* (1964); and Robert Murphy, "Introduction: The Anthropological Theories of Julian H. Steward," in Julian Steward, *Evolution and Ecology: Essays on Social Transformation*, ed. Jane C. Steward and Robert T. Murphy (1977). This posthumous publication and Steward's *A Theory of Culture Change* (1955) together contain some of Steward's more noteworthy essays.

ROBERT A. MANNERS

STEWARD, Susan Maria Smith McKinney (1847–7 Mar. 1918), physician, was born in Brooklyn, New York, the daughter of Sylvanus Smith, a pork merchant, and Ann Springstead. She grew up in a farming community with her large, prosperous family. As a teenager she learned to play the organ, studying under two prominent New York city organists, John Zundel and Henry Eyre Brown. She became an accomplished organist, but she had other goals. The deaths of two of her brothers during the Civil War and the high death rates from a cholera epidemic in Brooklyn in 1866 may have influenced her choice of a medical career. Her versatile mind and disciplined approach earned her an M.D. in 1870 from the New York Medical College for Women. She thus became the first African-American woman to graduate from a medical school in the state of New York and only the third in the United States.

In 1874 Susan Smith married the Reverend William G. McKinney and then practiced under the name of Dr. Susan Smith McKinney. Two children were born of this marriage before her husband's death in 1892. Dr. McKinney conducted a private general practice at 205 DeKalb Avenue in Brooklyn from 1870 to 1895. Serving both white and black patients, she had another office in Manhattan. During the period of her medical practice in Brooklyn, she also served as the organist and choir director at the Bridge Street African Methodist Episcopal (AME) Church near her office.

In 1881 McKinney cofounded the Brooklyn Women's Homeopathic Hospital and Dispensary (later renamed Memorial Hospital for Women and Children), a hospital for African Americans, where she served as a staff physician until 1896. During 1887 and 1888 she was engaged in postgraduate study at the Long Island Medical College Hospital in Brooklyn. She was also on the staff of the New York Medical College and Hospital for Women in Manhattan from 1892 to 1896. From 1892 to 1895 she was one of two female physicians at the Brooklyn Home for Aged Colored People and served as a member of its board of directors. McKinney was an active member of the Kings County Medical Society and the New York State Homeopathic Medical Society.

In 1896 the widowed McKinney married the Reverend Theophilus G. Steward, a U.S. Army chaplain with the Twenty-fifth U.S. Colored Infantry. She accompanied him for two years on tours of duty in Montana and Wyoming, where she gained medical licenses and practiced. In 1898, shortly before her husband's retirement from the army, she became a faculty member, teaching health and nutrition, and a resident physician at Wilberforce University, Wilberforce, Ohio, a school supported by the African Methodist Episcopal church. She held both positions for twenty-two years until her death. Rev. Steward joined his wife at Wilberforce and became a member of the history faculty.

In 1911 Steward and her husband participated as delegates of the AME church at the First Universal Races Congress at the University of London. She addressed the interracial group of delegates with a presentation entitled "Colored Women in America." In 1914 she presented a paper, "Women in Medicine," before the National Association of Colored Women's Clubs in Wilberforce, Ohio; it included a nearly complete list of African-American women who had completed medical school and practiced in America up until that time.

With forty-eight years in the medical profession, Steward was a leading woman physician as well as a musician, public speaker, and devoted church-woman. The Susan Smith McKinney Steward Medical Society, the first organization of African-American female physicians, founded in 1976 in the greater New York area, took the name of this pioneer. Steward died at her home on the campus of Wilberforce University.

• Information on Steward is in Leslie L. Alexander, "Early Medical Heroes: Susan Smith McKinney-Steward, M.D. 1847–1918," *The Crisis* (Jan. 1980): 21–23; Alexander, "Susan Smith McKinney, M.D. 1847–1918," *Journal of the National Medical Association* (Mar. 1975): 173–75; and William Seraile, "Susan McKinney Steward: New York State's First African-American Woman Physician," *Afro-Americans in New York Life and History,* July 1985. She is also mentioned in Hallie Q. Brown, *Homespun Heroines and Other Women of Distinction* (1988), p. 248.

ROBERT C. HAYDEN

STEWARD, Theophilus Gould (17 Apr. 1843–11 Jan. 1924), author, clergyman, and educator, was born in Gouldtown, New Jersey, the son of James Steward, a mechanic who had fled to Gouldtown as an indentured child servant, and Rebecca Gould, a descendant of the seventeenth-century proprietor of West Jersey, John Fenwick. His family's interest in history and literature supplemented his elementary school education in Bridgeton, and his mother encouraged him to challenge "established truths." He began preaching in 1862, was licensed to preach by the African Methodist Episcopal (AME) church in 1863, and was appointed to serve a congregation in South Camden, New Jersey, in 1864.

In May 1865 Steward accompanied AME bishop Daniel A. Payne and others on a mission to South Carolina, where they reestablished the denomination, which had been banned from the state after the Denmark Vesey slave rebellion conspiracy of 1822. From 1865 to 1868, Steward nurtured new AME congregations in South Carolina. In 1866 he married Elizabeth Gadsden; before her death in 1893, they had eight children.

From 1868 to 1871, Steward was the pastor of the AME congregation in Macon, Georgia, which was later renamed Steward Chapel AME Church in his honor. From his base in Macon, Steward actively participated in the business and politics of Reconstruction. He worked as a cashier for the Freedmen's Bank in Macon and speculated in cotton futures. He helped to write the platform of Georgia's Republican party in 1868 and served as an election registrar in Stewart County, Georgia. He organized a successful protest by freed slaves in Americus, Georgia, against compulsory labor contracts and attacked the practice of limiting jury service to white males.

Leaving Georgia in 1871, Steward spent the next twenty years as the pastor of AME congregations in Brooklyn, New York; Philadelphia, Pennsylvania; Wilmington, Delaware; and Washington, D.C. In 1873 he undertook a mission to Haiti, establishing an AME congregation in Port-au-Prince, and in 1877 he completed his first book, *Memoirs of Mrs. Rebecca Steward* (1877). From 1878 to 1880, he studied at Philadelphia's Protestant Episcopal Church Divinity School.

In the subsequent decade, Steward published two theological works, *Genesis Re-read* (1885) and *The End of the World* (1888). In these two books, he undertook Christian reinterpretations of the first and the last things—the doctrines of creation and of the eschaton. *Genesis Re-read* offered a liberal evangelical's assimilation of Darwinian evolutionary theory into Christian doctrine by arguing that evolution took place within a divine plan. *The End of the World* contested Anglo-Saxon triumphalism by contending that a final clash of nations would purge Christianity of its bondage to racism and give birth to "new nations," borne out of darkness to walk "in the light of the one great God, with whom there are no superior races and no inferior races."

Defeated in a bid for the presidency of the AME denomination's Wilberforce University in 1884 and at odds with its bishops because of repeated challenges to their authority, Steward won an appointment as chaplain to the Twenty-fifth U.S. Colored Infantry Regiment in 1891. His wife died in 1893, and three years later, in 1896, he married Susan Maria Smith McKinney, a widow and physician; they had no children. After service at Fort Missoula, Montana, and Chickamauga, Georgia, Steward and his regiment were sent to Cuba in 1898 at the beginning of the Spanish-American War. On his return to Brooklyn later that year, he addressed a celebration of the war's conclusion.

Steward wrote a novel, *A Charleston Love Story*, in 1899, but his main interest was military history. In addition to two pamphlets, *Active Service; or, Gospel Work Among the U.S. Soldiers* (1897) and *How the Black St. Domingo Legion Saved the Patriot Army in the Siege of Savannah in 1779* (1899), he published *The Colored Regulars in the U.S. Army* (1899), a vindication of the service of African-American soldiers in the Spanish-American War.

Sent to the Philippines in 1900, Steward was stationed in Manila, where he served as superintendent of schools for Luzon province. In 1902 he was transferred back to the United States with the Twenty-fifth Infantry Regiment and stationed at Fort Niobrara, Nebraska, and Fort Brown near Brownsville, Texas. In August 1906 white residents reported that soldiers from Steward's regiment had briefly roamed through Brownsville's streets, freely shooting up its cafes and dance halls, killing a civilian and injuring a police officer. The soldiers maintained their innocence and implicated no one, but President Theodore Roosevelt dismissed them from service without honor and barred them from future government service. Steward, who had retired from the army in 1907, did not join in the African-American community's outcry against Roosevelt's arbitrary action. But in his autobiography he wrote, "I have yet to find one officer who was connected with that regiment who expresses the belief that our men were guilty."

In 1907, Theophilus and Susan Steward moved to Ohio, where he became vice president, chaplain, and professor of French, history, and logic and she became the college physician at Wilberforce University. Active in fundraising efforts for Wilberforce, Theophilus Steward advocated military training for African-American men as preparatory to their struggle for freedom. In 1911 the Stewards were the AME delegates to London's Universal Races Congress.

An active contributor to such newspapers as the *Cleveland Gazette* and the *Indianapolis Freeman*, Steward returned to familiar territory in his last books: family history in *Gouldtown, a Very Remarkable Settlement of Ancient Date* (1913), and military history in *The Haitian Revolution, 1791 to 1804* (1914). He published his autobiography, *From 1864 to 1914: Fifty Years in the Gospel Ministry*, in 1921.

• Steward's papers are in the New York Public Library's Schomburg Center for Research in Black Culture. For biographies see William Seraile, *Voice of Dissent: Theophilus Gould Steward (1843–1924) and Black America* (1991), and Albert George Miller, "Theophilus Gould Steward, 1843–1924" (Ph.D. diss., Princeton Univ., 1994). On the intellectual context and several phases of Steward's career, see August Meier, *Negro Thought in America, 1880–1915* (1963); Ralph E. Luker, *The Social Gospel in Black and White* (1991); Clarence E. Walker, *A Rock in a Weary Land: The African Methodist Episcopal Church during the Civil War and Reconstruction* (1981); John M. Carroll, *The Black Military Experience in the American West* (1971); John D. Weaver, *The Brownsville Raid* (1970); Ann J. Lane, *The Brownsville Affair* (1971); and Garna L. Christian, *Black Soldiers in Jim Crow Texas, 1899–1917* (1995).

RALPH E. LUKER

STEWART, Alexander Peter (2 Oct. 1821–30 Aug. 1908), soldier, educator, and park commissioner, was born at Rogersville, Tennessee, the son of William Stewart and Elizabeth Decherd. He entered the U.S. Military Academy on 1 July 1838 and in 1842 graduated twelfth in a class of fifty-six. While at West Point, he roomed for two years with future Union general John Pope and for a time with future Confederate general James Longstreet. He was commissioned a second lieutenant in the Third Artillery and ordered to Fort Macon, North Carolina. After one year's service at the coastal fort, he returned to West Point to become an assistant professor of mathematics. On 31 May 1845 he resigned his commission and in August married Hattie Bryon Chase; they had three children. From 1845 until 1861 he was an academic, holding professorships of mathematics and mental and moral philosophy first at Cumberland University, Lebanon, Tennessee, and then at Nashville University.

A Whig in politics, he supported John Bell for the presidency in 1860, and although opposed to secession, on 17 May 1861 he was commissioned a major in the Artillery Corps of the Provisional Army of Tennessee. His initial duty stations were on the Mississippi River. In late May he was at Fort Randolph instructing newly organized companies in artillery drill; next it was Fort Pillow; and in mid-August he went to Island Number 10 with a three-company battalion of heavy artillerists. Stewart and his battalion fired their first shots in anger from big guns emplaced in the Columbus, Kentucky, water batteries on 7 November during the battle of Belmont.

On 16 November 1861 Stewart was made a brigadier general and assigned to command a Tennessee infantry brigade in Major General Leonidas Polk's command. As a brigade commander in B. Franklin Cheatham's division, he fought at Shiloh (6–7 Apr. 1862), at the siege of Corinth (28 Apr.–30 May), in Braxton Bragg's invasion of Kentucky (Aug.–Oct.), at Perryville (8 Oct.), and at Stones River (31 Dec. 1862–2 Jan. 1863). At Shiloh he led his brigade in repeated charges against the Hornets' Nest, where Union soldiers held the Confederates at bay for more than eight hours. At Perryville he and his troops first hammered and then crushed Brigadier General James S. Jackson's division, and at Stones River, on 31 December, he battled Philip Sheridan's division in the cedars.

Stewart was promoted to major general to rank from 3 June 1863 and assumed command of a division in Lieutenant General William J. Hardee's corps of the Army of Tennessee. He saw his first combat as a division commander in defense of Hoover Gap during the Tullahoma campaign (23 June–7 July). At Chickamauga, on 19 September, he and his Little Giant Division shattered four Union brigades and in the two-day battle suffered 1,733 casualties out of the 4,000 engaged. Although wounded, Stewart remained in the saddle throughout the battle. He experienced bitter defeat at Missionary Ridge (25 Nov.) when his division, along with other units holding the army's center, gave way in face of the Army of the Cumberland's charge up the steep slopes.

The 1864 Atlanta campaign found Stewart and his division in John Bell Hood's corps. He saw action at Rocky Face and Resaca and hammered the Twentieth Corps at New Hope Church on 25 May. At Resaca he had three horses shot from under him. On 7 July Stewart assumed command of the corps formerly led by Polk and was promoted to lieutenant general to rank from 23 June.

Hood now superseded Joseph E. Johnston as commander of the Army of Tennessee, and there was a radical change in Confederate strategy. Johnston had held to a policy of yielding space for time in hopes of taking advantage of a Union blunder. Hood's strategy was to seize the initiative, lashing out of the Federal columns as they closed on Atlanta. This change in strategy, with the advantage that earthworks gave the defenders, had grim repercussions for Stewart and his corps. On 20 July at Peachtree Creek and at Ezra Church on the 28th, Stewart led his corps in savage fighting. In the latter battle, he was wounded in the head and was out of action until mid-August. He was present at the evacuation of Atlanta (1 Sept.) and marched with Hood into Middle Tennessee. He and his corps were mauled at bloody Franklin (30 Nov.), were battered at Nashville (15–16 Dec.), and suffered on the retreat to Tupelo, where Hood resigned his command. On 16 March 1865 Stewart was named to command the Army of Tennessee following its transfer to North Carolina and led this once mighty army in its final battle at Bentonville (19–21 Mar.).

Paroled at Greensboro, North Carolina, 2 May 1865, Stewart returned to life as an academic and held a professorship at Cumberland University until 1870. He next tried his hand in the business world, becoming secretary of the St. Louis Mutual Life Insurance Company. In 1874 he became chancellor of the University of Mississippi at Oxford. He brought to the position experience as a teacher, leadership, respect honed on many battlefields, and an unimpeachable character. All these were needed, because the university, buffeted by the economics of the Reconstruction years, was hard-pressed to survive. He was equal to the challenge, and when he resigned in 1886, the university again had a bright future. At "Ole Miss" the students in private called him "Old Straight," his wartime nom de guerre, given him by his soldiers because of his military bearing and character.

In 1890 President Benjamin Harrison signed into law a bill creating Chickamauga and Chattanooga National Military Park. Stewart was named by the president as one of the three commissioners to oversee the nation's first national military park. Elected by his two colleagues, both former Union soldiers, as resident commissioner, Stewart relocated from St. Louis to Chattanooga to give on-site leadership to all facets of development of the park—overseeing road construction, meeting with state commissions, and encouraging placement of monuments. The park was formally dedicated and opened to the public by Vice President Adlai Stevenson in September 1895. In 1906, because of failing health, Stewart moved to Biloxi, Mississippi, from where he continued to perform his duties as park commissioner by correspondence. He died in Biloxi and was buried in Bellefontaine Cemetery in St. Louis.

Stewart, unlike too many people, learned from his errors. A lackluster performance at Shiloh was followed by a series of successes and increased responsibilities that climaxed at Chickamauga. His leadership of a division in the Atlanta campaign was recognized and he was given a corps, but by then it was too late for the Confederacy to capitalize on his talents as a combat commander.

• Biographical information on Stewart is in George W. Cullum, *Biographical Register of the Officers and Graduates of the U.S. Military Academy, at West Point, NY* (1891); F. B. Heitman, *Historical Register of the United States Army, from Its Organization September 29, 1789, to March 2, 1903* (1903); and articles in *Confederate Veteran*, Sept. 1908 and Jan. 1909. For his military career see Clement A. Evans, ed., *Confederate Military History—Extended Edition*, vol. 1 (1987), and *The War of the Rebellion: A Compilation of the Official Records of the Union and Confederate Armies* (128 vols., 1880–1901). Obituaries are in the *New Orleans Times Democrat*, *St. Louis Globe Democrat*, and *Chattanooga News*, 31 Aug. 1908.

E. C. BEARSS

STEWART, Alexander Turney (12 Oct. 1803–10 Apr. 1876), dry-goods merchant, was born in Lisburn, County Antrim, Ireland, the son of Alexander Stewart and Margaret Turney. His father died when Stewart was a young boy, at which time he was sent to live with his maternal grandfather. His grandfather planned for Stewart to enter the ministry and, in furtherance of that goal, secured his attendance at Belfast College. However, the sudden death of the grandfather, coupled with Stewart's lack of interest in the religious life, ended the plan. After receiving his education, Stewart headed for the United States, landing in New York City in 1818.

Upon first arriving, Stewart worked as a tutor in a private school run by Isaac F. Bragg. After only a short time, he returned to Ireland to pick up an inheritance of approximately $5,000 and intended to remain there, investing the money in his native land. However, at the urging of a friend from the United States, Stewart came back to New York to go into business. In 1823 he opened up a small shop trafficking in Irish laces. It was also in that year that Stewart married Cornelia Mitchell Clinch; the couple would have no children.

Stewart demonstrated a remarkable aptitude for commerce and introduced a number of then-radical innovations to his business. He was an early pioneer in the concept of "one retail price for all" and also permitted exchanges of merchandise for either cash or different products. Stewart insisted that customers be treated with consideration and honesty, and his stores offered "free entrance" (allowing customers to browse without being constantly monitored by a store patron). He also was one of the first to extensively utilize mail order sales (using a variety of newspapers nationwide to market his products). An astute businessman and manager, he insisted on strict discipline among his employees and always took only the best men for business partners. His firm belief in cash-based transactions paid off handsomely during the business panic of the mid-1830s, and by 1837 he was able to buy up the inventories of his competitors at deep discounts because of his ready access to cash. He soon turned a handsome profit on the merchandise for himself, and his success allowed him, in 1846, to purchase for the sum of $65,000 the property at the northeast corner of Broadway and Chambers Street, on which he built a marble structure that would house his first retail and wholesale dry-goods business. Widely known as the "Marble Palace," it was the first commercial structure to feature a marble facade and was also noted for its domed atrium, extravagant fixtures, and mahogany cabinets. As the business flourished, Stewart was able to undertake the first of his many charitable endeavors: in 1847, during the famine in Ireland, he chartered a ship, loaded it with supplies, and sent it to Belfast with the expressed order to give a free ride back to any upstanding men and women who sought a better life in America. Many took him up on the offer, and Stewart found gainful employment for most of them.

Stewart's dry-goods establishment became the largest such enterprise in New York City when, in 1850, he expanded the building to Reade Street. In 1862 he erected an eight-story building at the corner of Broad-

way and Tenth Street for the cost of $2.75 million; at the time it was the largest retail store in the world. Known as the "Iron Palace," it featured a cast-iron front and eventually occupied an entire city block. (Stewart's wholesale trade remained at the old location.)

The business soon began to extend beyond the confines of New York. Stewart opened up offices and warehouses in Boston, Philadelphia, Paris, Lyons, Manchester, Belfast, Glasgow, and Berlin, as well as in other cities. He also established a number of mills in New Jersey and throughout New England that manufactured goods such as cotton, silk, blankets, carpets, ribbons, and thread, exclusively under the name of A. T. Stewart & Co.

The success of Stewart's vast enterprise can best be attributed to the foresight and shrewdness he displayed at times when it was lacking in other businessmen of the day. For example, at the onset of the Civil War, cotton would surely become scarce with southern supplies cut off. Stewart predicted an inevitable rise in the demand for cotton; thus, he made it a point to buy up large amounts of the material and was, therefore, able to corner the cotton market. Additionally, at the start of the war, when the government was having trouble clothing soldiers who needed to be sent to the front quickly, he purchased the entire output of several woolen mills and manufactured uniforms and flannel underwear for the troops, which he sold in large quantities to the government at reasonable prices.

An additional challenge for Stewart during the war years came in the form of the first lady. Enormously fond of shopping, Mary Todd Lincoln visited Stewart's store on many trips to New York and ran up a considerable debt to the merchant. While Stewart no doubt found the first lady's attention gratifying, he was less enthusiastic regarding her payment habits and on at least one occasion contemplated suing her for payment of past due debts.

By this time Stewart's annual income was said to be around $2 million. With this increase in wealth, his philanthropy increased as well. In 1862 he donated $10,000 to the relief effort designed to aid operatives in Lancashire, England, who were out of work on account of the cotton famine. During the Civil War he contributed $100,000 to the U.S. Sanitary Commission. In 1871 he gave $50,000 to the city of Chicago to help those harmed by the great fire there. Perhaps Stewart's greatest act of charity was the purchase of the Hempstead Plains on Long Island, where he constructed the "model town" of Garden City, designed to supply working-class people with comfortable homes at the lowest cost feasible. While Garden City never became a haven for working-class folks, it did become a successful community.

Stewart was a close friend of Ulysses S. Grant, and when Grant became president in 1879 he named Stewart to the post of secretary of the treasury. Federal law, however, prohibited any person engaged in business from holding that position. Stewart attempted to turn his business over to trustees, but this measure was considered insufficient. He would never hold public office.

Stewart died in New York City. On 6 November 1878 the coffin containing his remains was stolen and held for ransom. The money was paid in 1879, and, according to the uncorroborated memoirs of New York City police superintendent George W. Walling, the body was returned. That story remains unconfirmed, however.

• Most of Stewart's personal correspondence was destroyed, but a small collection apparently exists in the Rare Book and Manuscript Division of the New York Public Library. For biographical information, see the *New York Times*, 6–12 Mar. 1869 and 26 Oct. 1886; *Harper's Weekly*, 29 Apr. 1876; *Harper's New Monthly Magazine*, Mar. 1867; I. N. Phelps Stokes, *The Iconography of Manhattan Island*, vols. 5–6 (1918–1928); C. H. Haswell, *Reminiscences of an Octogenarian of the City of New York* (1896); M. H. Smith, *Sunshine and Shadow in New York* (1868); Stephen N. Elias, *Alexander T. Stewart: Forgotten Merchant Prince* (1992); and Harry E. Resseguie, "A. T. Stewart's Marble Palace, the Cradle of the Department Store," *New York State Historical Society Quarterly* 48 (1964): 131–62. Obituaries and editorials at the time of Stewart's death are in the *New York Times*, 11–14 Apr. 1876; the *New York Evening Post*, 10–11, 13 Apr. 1876; and the *New York Sun*, 11–14 Apr. 1876.

FRANCESCO L. NEPA

STEWART, Alvan (1 Sept. 1790–1 May 1849), lawyer and abolitionist, was born in South Granville, New York, the son of Uriel Stewart, a farmer. His mother's name is unknown. In 1795 the family moved to Westford, Vermont, where Alvan attended common school and at age seventeen began studying anatomy and medicine. He then attended the University of Vermont, teaching school during the winters to support himself. In 1811 he went to Canada to teach, but when anti-American sentiment increased and the War of 1812 began, he returned to the United States. Stewart graduated from college in 1813, taught common school for a short period of time, and then began the private study of law in Cherry Valley, New York. After completing his studies, he practiced there for sixteen years.

Though his parents had been farmers of very moderate means, Alvan accumulated considerable property in the course of his practice and at the age of thirty-one was elected mayor of Cherry Valley. He married Keziah Holt of Cherry Valley; they had five children. He was a popular speaker and successful lawyer. G. C. Saxton, a former law partner of Stewart, said of him: "It was proverbial of Stewart as a lawyer that he always succeeded in every suit commenced by himself. From 1826 to 1836 I do not remember an exception to this rule; embracing more than one hundred suits." Abolitionist Theodore Dwight Weld recalled Stewart's "batteries of wit, irony and sarcasm" and his "power with the *reductio ad absurdum* in argument, in which he had no peer."

Stewart, originally a Democrat, became a supporter of the Whig party as a result of the debate over tariffs during the presidency of Andrew Jackson. Stewart argued for the necessity of protective duties to protect northern manufacturing, whereas such tariffs angered the cotton producers of the South and most Jacksonians who resented federal intrusions on states' rights. Stewart also advocated other anti-Jackson measures such as a national banking system, federal financing of internal improvements, and a public education system.

Influenced by the religious revivals in central New York that had been sparked by the preaching of Charles G. Finney, Stewart began in 1832 to dedicate himself to the temperance and antislavery campaigns. He moved to Utica, New York, the site of an important Finney revival in 1826 and near Oneida Institute, a center for abolitionist activity under the leadership of Beriah Green. After joining the American Anti-Slavery Society in 1834, Stewart gave up his legal practice in order to travel throughout the "burned-over district" central and western New York, organizing antislavery and temperance societies, gathering money, and making speeches. The "burned-over district," which had been swept by fires of the spirit during the 1820s and early 1830s when Finney was planting his fervent religiosity in community after community, was fertile soil for Stewart's labors. Contemporaries knew him as a compelling orator with a keen mind and sharp wit.

Stewart played an important role in the organization of the New York State Anti-Slavery Society. In 1835 he issued a call for a state antislavery convention. Nearly 600 supporters converged upon Utica on 21 October 1835 for a meeting at Bleecker Street Presbyterian Church. An antiabolitionist mob broke up the meeting and forced those in attendance to retire to the home of Gerrit Smith in Peterboro. Here the New York State Anti-Slavery Society was officially organized. Stewart was made a member of the society's executive board and was elected president.

Stewart's leadership of the New York State Anti-Slavery Society was controversial. He drew the fire of Beriah Green because of his failure to support Oneida Institute. Some fellow abolitionists resented Stewart because of his wealth, while others thought he promoted the state society more than the national antislavery cause. Stewart had argued that agents of the national antislavery body be kept out of the state and that funds raised in the state be used for local purposes rather than being forwarded to the national body.

Stewart was an early advocate of going beyond the moral suasion means associated with William Lloyd Garrison and the New England abolitionists who were founders of the American Anti-Slavery Society in 1833. The Garrisonians wrote and lectured against slavery but shunned politics or legal tactics as too corrupt. Stewart helped establish the rival American and Foreign Anti-Slavery Society in 1840 in part because he believed that moral suasion alone would not bring an end to slavery. In 1840 he joined Myron Holley of

Rochester, New York, in calling for the formation of a third party with the single platform of abolitionism. Dedicated to the "One Idea" of immediate emancipation, the Liberty party ran Stewart for governor of New York State in 1840 and in 1844, but without success. When a faction of the Liberty party attempted to expand its platform to include positions on issues other than slavery, Stewart allied himself with the Liberty League in 1847 in order to maintain the original mission of the Liberty party.

The Garrisonians dismissed the U.S. Constitution as a proslavery document. Stewart, however, along with William Goodell, another member of the Gerrit Smith circle, developed an antislavery argument based in part on the Constitution's due process clause. Stewart believed that positive law afforded a basis to deny the legitimacy of slavery. He urged legislation to guarantee a jury trial for fugitive slaves, and he insisted that Congress had the power to abolish slavery in the District of Columbia. In 1845 he argued that slavery was contrary to the New Jersey state constitution of 1844 before the New Jersey Supreme Court, but his arguments were not upheld in the New Jersey legal system. Though Stewart and his coadjutors lost the case, his articulation of an antislavery argument based on the Constitution was an important weapon in the arsenal of the abolitionists. Stewart's advocacy of political means to end slavery also included his opposition to the internal slave trade and the gag laws passed by Congress to prohibit the introduction of antislavery petitions.

Though Stewart became disenchanted with politics because many abolitionists were drifting over to the Free-Soil party, organized in 1848 while the Liberty League remained small and ineffectual, he did not abandon his principles. In 1849, though weakened by illness, Stewart wrote his sister, "You must know that in six months I have traveled not less than 6,000 miles in running to and fro on the earth, pleading for the slave. I have done four times more labor for him this year, than in any previous one." Stewart died in New York City.

• Manuscript material can be found in the Alvan Stewart Papers, New York State Historical Association Library, Cooperstown, and in the Alvan Stewart Correspondence, New-York Historical Society, New York City. Stewart's son-in-law Luther R. Marsh compiled *Writings and Speeches of Alvan Stewart on Slavery* (1860). Stewart awaits a biographer, but a brief sketch of his life is in Gerald Sorin, *The New York Abolitionists* (1971). On Stewart's constitutional views, see Daniel R. Ernst, "Legal Positivism, Abolitionist Litigation, and the New Jersey Slave Case of 1845," *Law and History Review* 5 (1986): 337–65, and William M. Wiecek, *The Sources of Antislavery Constitutionalism in America, 1760–1848* (1977).

MILTON C. SERNETT

STEWART, Anthony (1738–1791?), merchant, was born in Aberdeen, Scotland, the son of James Stewart, an attorney, and his wife, whose name is unknown. Anthony Stewart immigrated to America in 1753 and by 1764 was a merchant in Annapolis, Maryland. In that year he married Jean Dick, whose father, James Dick, had emigrated from Edinburgh, Scotland, in 1734 and become a prosperous merchant in Londontown, a few miles from Annapolis. Anthony and Jean Stewart had three sons and four daughters.

James Dick took his son-in-law into partnership, and the firm of Dick and Stewart became one of Maryland's most successful. The firm was the Maryland agent for John Buchanan and Son, a major London company in the Chesapeake tobacco trade. Dick and Stewart also owned a ropewalk and retail stores in Annapolis, Londontown, Baltimore, and Frederick and traded with the West Indies, Europe, and Madeira. Profits from the business enabled Stewart to invest in nearly 1,800 acres of land and to purchase a large brick mansion in Annapolis.

Colonial protest against the Townshend Duties of 1767 reached Maryland in 1769, when Baltimore merchants acceded to pressure from their Philadelphia competitors and signed a nonimportation agreement. Stewart and Dick joined two other local merchants in calling a meeting in May 1769 to discuss whether Annapolis and Anne Arundel County should also embrace nonimportation. Stewart and Dick were not patriot enthusiasts. Instead, they hoped to shape a weak nonimportation agreement for Anne Arundel County that would cause minimal disruptions to trade. Anne Arundel County did adopt a weak nonimportation agreement, but Stewart considered it too restrictive and refused to sign it.

Stewart's first brush with the local patriots committee came in January 1770, when the brigantine *Good Intent* arrived in the port of Annapolis. The ship carried cargo consigned to Dick and Stewart and to other merchants in the area. Stewart and his father-in-law argued that they had ordered the goods before Anne Arundel County merchants adopted a nonimportation agreement. However, the merchants committee decided that Dick and Stewart could not unload the ship and ordered it back to Britain.

As political unrest grew in Maryland in the early 1770s, patriots increasingly viewed Stewart with distrust. When Stewart stood as a candidate for a seat in the Maryland General Assembly in May 1773, voters proved suspicious of his political sympathies and connections and elected his opponent by a landslide. His opposition to a general assembly resolution adopted in May 1774 that called on lawyers to stop prosecuting cases for British creditors confirmed his loyalism in the minds of many Maryland patriots.

In 1773 Dick and Stewart's London firm, John Buchanan and Son, unexpectedly went bankrupt. Dick and Stewart was one of the Buchanan firm's largest debtors, and the bankrupt company's trustees pressed the Maryland company for payment. Dick and Stewart had little success collecting debts owed to the firm and therefore was unable to pay what it owed Buchanan. Also that year the British Parliament passed the Tea Act. The act triggered the Boston Tea Party, to which Parliament responded by closing Boston's port;

as a result, tea became a powerful symbol of British oppression.

In 1773 Stewart purchased a small ship, which he named the *Peggy Stewart* after his eldest daughter. After one profitable voyage to Madeira, he dispatched the vessel to England with orders to its captain to sell it. When the captain could not get Stewart's asking price, he advertised for cargo to ship back to the colonies. Among the freight collected for the voyage were seventeen packages consigned to the Annapolis firm of Thomas Charles Williams and Company. The packages contained 2,320 pounds of tea. Stewart did not learn of the contraband aboard the *Peggy Stewart* until the ship reached Annapolis in October 1774. His own interest in the ship's cargo was limited to fifty-three servants. The ship's captain urged Stewart to off-load the ship quickly, since the vessel was "leaky" and the servants had already spent nearly three months on board. Stewart tried to pay the entry duty on the servants and the rest of the ship's cargo except the tea. British law required duty on the entire contents of a ship, however, and the customs collector refused to accept partial payment. Stewart finally paid the duty on the ship's whole cargo.

Word that tea was aboard the *Peggy Stewart* spread quickly. Annapolis patriots held a meeting, as did the county committee. Stewart tried to explain his actions, but nothing could assuage the outrage at his payment of the duty on the tea. Groups of radical patriots from Baltimore and western Anne Arundel County demanded harsh penalties. Some suggested that Stewart be tarred and feathered, while others demanded the destruction of his ship and its cargo. On 19 October 1774 the patriots held a final outdoor meeting. Stewart would have satisfied most who attended if he had publicly apologized and burned the tea. A radical minority, however, continued to insist on the destruction of the *Peggy Stewart* as well.

Stewart feared for his safety and that of his family and property. The recent birth of their sixth child kept his wife confined to bed at their house in Annapolis, and James Dick urged Stewart to do what the radicals demanded. When the radical patriots refused at the 19 October meeting to budge from their demands, Stewart realized that nothing less would satisfy them. He therefore boarded the *Peggy Stewart*, ordered it run aground off Windmill Point in Annapolis Harbor, and set fire to the vessel. Within a few hours, the ship burned to the waterline.

Stewart's burning of the *Peggy Stewart* did not placate the radical patriots. They continued to threaten and harass him, even burning him in effigy. The boycott against British goods, the failure of their English partner, and the "tide of popular clamor" against them following the *Peggy Stewart* affair made it impossible for Dick and Stewart's firm to continue. The partnership dissolved, and Stewart fled to England in 1775, leaving his family behind.

Stewart returned to America in 1777 with a letter recommending him for a position with the British occupying New York. He eventually became an evaluator of losses claimed by Loyalists and one of ten directors of the Associated Loyalists, a group formed in New York to coordinate the activities of Loyalists in America. Stewart's wife and family joined him in New York in 1781. The Maryland General Court indicted Stewart for outlawry in 1781 but later dropped the charge. The same year the state confiscated 1,513 acres of Stewart's land (the state allowed his wife to sell their Annapolis home), pledging the proceeds from its sale to support a new currency emission.

After the war, Stewart petitioned the British government for compensation for his losses, which included land, his various business interests, and the value of the *Peggy Stewart* and its cargo. He received an annual pension of £200, a pittance compared with his losses. In September 1783 Stewart and his family immigrated to Nova Scotia, where he became a merchant in Halifax. In 1788 Stewart petitioned the British government for an increase in his pension. He wrote that he had suffered "a Sudden Stroke of the Palsey," which had left him "entirely deprived of the use of the right side." Stewart claimed that the stroke had rendered him incapable of carrying on his business. The *Halifax Weekly Chronicle* reported on 14 May 1791 that Anthony Stewart, Esq., "late of this place," had died "at Annapolis in Maryland."

• In 1905 Richard D. Fisher of Baltimore attempted to find materials relating to Stewart in Britain and Nova Scotia. From Britain he received eighty-six pages of transcripts from the Public Record Office detailing Stewart's claim for losses from the burning of the *Peggy Stewart* and the confiscation of his Md. property during the war. The *Baltimore News* printed some of these materials in 1905 and 1906, and affidavits relating to the *Peggy Stewart* affair are in "The Burning of the *Peggy Stewart*," *Maryland Historical Magazine* 5 (1910): 235–45. The materials gathered by Fisher are in the Fisher Transcripts, Maryland Historical Society, Baltimore. Other biographical information, including a copy of a letter to Fisher from Stewart's great-grandson Douglas Stewart of Dartmouth, Nova Scotia, and a letter from Mrs. A. Sprague Coolidge, another descendant, detailing Stewart's genealogy, is in topic file G 1456-810 at the Maryland State Archives, Annapolis. This file also contains references to relevant materials in the Public Archives of Nova Scotia. Douglas Stewart, writing in 1905, stated that he did not know the death date of his great-grandfather but that there was "no doubt" that he was buried in St. Paul's Anglican churchyard in Halifax. Church records show that Stewart's wife and several other family members are buried at St. Paul's, but no mention of Stewart's interment was found. The best secondary source on Stewart is George A. Gipe, "The Day They Burned the *Peggy Stewart*," *Maryland Magazine* 5 (Summer 1973): 12–15, although the article has no references and little information regarding Stewart's post-Md. career. Richard A. Overfield, "The Loyalists of Maryland during the American Revolution" (Ph.D. diss., Univ. of Maryland, 1968), has a few references to Stewart and helps put his Loyalist activities during the war in context.

GREGORY A. STIVERSON

STEWART, Bennett McVey (6 Aug. 1912–29 Apr. 1988), politician, was born in Huntsville, Alabama, the son of Bennett Stewart and Cathleen Jones. After attending local public schools in Huntsville and Birmingham, he entered Miles College in Birmingham, where he earned a bachelor of arts in 1936. After serving as assistant principal of Irondale High School in Birmingham from 1936 to 1938, he became associate professor of sociology at Miles College. In 1938 Stewart married Pattye Crittenden; they had three children. Leaving teaching in 1940 to sell insurance, he eventually became an executive of the Atlanta Life Insurance Company and in 1950 was sent to Chicago to open an office there. Stewart remained in the insurance business for the next eighteen years and then embarked upon a career in city politics. He was first employed as a city building inspector and concurrently served as a rehabilitation specialist for the city's Department of Urban Renewal. In 1971 Stewart was elected to the Chicago City Council as an alderman for the Twenty-first Ward, and in 1972 he held the dual office as Democratic committeeman; he remained in these posts until 1978.

As a member of the city council, Stewart was involved in the power struggle that ensued following the death of Mayor Richard J. Daley in December 1976. Daley, considered the last of the old-time big city political bosses, ruled Illinois Democratic politics virtually single-handedly until his death. Stewart, a Daley "machine loyalist," first supported Alderman Wilson Frost to succeed Daley, but when Frost was pressured to take himself out of the running Stewart seconded the nomination of Alderman Michael Bilandic, who was chosen interim mayor.

Stewart's own rise to higher political office came in October 1978 following the death of Representative Ralph Metcalfe. He was tapped as his party's candidate to succeed Metcalfe by the ten Democratic ward committeemen from the First Congressional District. Though Stewart was an African American, his candidacy sparked controversy within the black community because of his loyalist ties to Daley and his successor. Daley was often criticized for perfecting the instruments of racial suppression and repressing civil liberties through the police force. *Chicago Tribune* columnist Vernon Jarrett wrote that City Hall's choice of Stewart defied "political logic" and would "unnecessarily agitate the black community." "[Tom] Donovan [patronage boss at City Hall] and the other remnants of the Daley machine," he wrote, "are not only thumbing their noses at the black community, they are trying to deliver a message to even the most respected black leaders of their own party" (*Chicago Tribune*, 20 Oct. 1978).

Nonetheless, in the general election that followed three weeks after Stewart's nomination, the Democratic candidate was victorious, defeating Republican A. A. "Sammy" Rayner by a wide margin. He became a member of Congress on 3 January 1979 and served on the House Appropriations Committee, where he voted in favor of the massive financial bailout of the Chrysler Motor Corporation, which had employed more than 1,500 of his constituents from the First District. In addition, he became a champion of his dis-

trict's low-income citizens and received national recognition for his advocacy of emergency appropriations to provide low-income families with home heating assistance.

Despite his successes in Congress, Stewart was accused by his political opponents of financial mismanagement during his tenure with the Chicago Housing Authority (CHA). In response to this criticism, he sought and received a study of the city agency by the U.S. General Accounting Office. The investigation cleared his name and concluded that poor management and bookkeeping, not actions attributable to Stewart, had caused the agency's near collapse.

With the CHA business behind him, Stewart focused his attention on fighting a proposed constitutional amendment prohibiting school busing. He attacked the proposal as "a subversion to the Fourteenth Amendment and an attempt to reestablish segregation in the United States" (Ragsdale and Treese, p. 140). His efforts helped defeat House approval of the proposed amendment. He also succeeded in securing congressional approval of a bill (originally introduced by his predecessor, Metcalfe) designating February as Black History Month to honor African Americans who had contributed to the growth and history of the United States.

Stewart served only one term in Congress, being defeated in the 1980 primary by anti-machine Democrat Harold Washington. Returning to Chicago, he resumed his career in local politics, serving from 1981 to 1983 as an interim director of the Chicago Department of inter-Governmental Affairs, to which position he had been appointed by Mayor Jane Byrne. He also served as one of Byrne's administrative assistants.

A skilled ward politician, Stewart did not really distinguish himself until he went to Congress and became a champion for families on public assistance and other disadvantaged poor who could not help themselves. He assumed a leadership role in the House opposing those seeking to "turn the clock back" to the segregated pre-1960s. Nonetheless, it was difficult for Stewart to shake his ties to the Daley machine, and he was considered by some critics to be nothing more than a "party hack." Perhaps his greatest recognition came as the man Harold Washington defeated, which was an important step in Washington's advancement toward becoming Chicago's first black mayor in 1983. Stewart died in Chicago.

• Background information on Stewart can be found in *The Biographical Directory of the United States Congress 1774–1989: Bicentennial Edition* (1989) and in Bruce A. Ragsdale and Joel D. Treese, *Black Americans in Congress, 1870–1989* (1990). On Stewart's nomination to succeed Metcalfe and his ultimate victory, see Vernon Jarrett, "City Hall Displays More Than Racism," *Chicago Tribune*, 20 Oct. 1978, and "A Tuesday Night on the South Side," *Chicago Tribune*, 10 Nov. 1978. An obituary is in the *Chicago Tribune*, 28 Apr. 1988.

LEO J. DAUGHERTY III

STEWART, Charles (28 July 1778–6 Nov. 1869), naval officer, was born in Philadelphia, Pennsylvania, the son of Charles Stewart, a ship master, and Sarah Ford,

Irish immigrants. His father died when Stewart was two, and his mother married a Captain Britton (full name unknown). Enamored of the sea, Stewart entered the merchant service at the age of thirteen. Displaying considerable skill, he rose from cabin boy to mate, and in 1797 he commanded the yearly "Black Ship," the only European vessel allowed to trade with Japan at that time. The start of the naval war with France in 1798 altered Stewart's fortunes; he left the merchant marine and was commissioned as a lieutenant in the young U.S. Navy on 9 March 1798.

Commanding the schooner *Enterprise* (1800–1801), Stewart captured two French privateers. Transferred to the USS *Constellation*, he served as the ship's first lieutenant. He served in the Mediterranean during the Tripolitan War, both aboard the *Constellation* and as commander of the brig *Siren*. He provided cover for his colleague Stephen Decatur's burning of the USS *Philadelphia* in the harbor at Tripoli, so the Tripolitans could not use the ship against the United States, and generally won praise for his wartime efforts. Promoted to captain on 22 April 1806, Stewart supervised the construction of naval gunboats at the New York Navy Yard (1806–1807) and then took a leave of absence from the naval service, during which time he returned to the merchant marine.

The start of the War of 1812 brought Stewart back to active duty. He commanded the USS *Constellation*, which was blockaded in the harbor of Norfolk, Virginia. Despite his efforts, Stewart was unable to pierce the British blockade. In the summer of 1813 he was transferred to command of the 44-gun USS *Constitution*, which was being refitted in Boston harbor. On 25 November 1813 he married Delia Tudor, a sister of both the essayist William Tudor and Frederic Tudor, the "Ice King." The couple had two children. Their grandson, Charles Stewart Parnell, would be a pivotal figure in Anglo-Irish debates over the question of Irish home rule.

On 31 December 1813 Stewart led the *Constitution* out of Boston harbor and commenced a cruise that lasted until April 1814. He destroyed a number of British vessels and made his way to harbor in Marblehead, Massachusetts, just ahead of pursuing British warships. Soon afterward, he returned to Boston harbor and again found himself blockaded. The blockade remained in effect through most of 1814.

During the night of 17 December 1814 Stewart led his ship out of port and evaded the British blockaders. At this point he was the only American naval captain on the high seas, and he determined to make his cruise a memorable one. Unaware of the Treaty of Ghent, signed on 24 December 1814, which formally ended the war, Stewart, on 20 February 1815, encountered and fought two British ships off Madeira: the 34-gun *Cyane* and the 21-gun *Levant*. Stewart maneuvered his ship brilliantly and managed to rake both of his opponents without once exposing his own bow or stern to enemy broadsides. Both British ships surrendered to Stewart. He had accomplished something that no enemy of the British navy had done since 1697. The victo-

ry was noteworthy and praiseworthy, but Stewart and other chroniclers tended to exaggerate the odds of fighting against two smaller ships. On his return voyage, Stewart was pursued by British ships, which recaptured the *Levant*, but the *Constitution* escaped with its larger prize. Stewart entered New York harbor on 15 May 1815 to a hero's welcome; he received a gold medal and the Thanks of Congress. Although he never attained the type of popular fame of his friend and colleague Decatur, Stewart was from this point on often referred to by the nickname of "Old Ironsides."

Stewart commanded the European Squadron (1816–1820) and the Pacific Squadron (1820–1824). He was court-martialed for unknown reasons on his return to the United States in 1824, but the charges against him were changed to commendations by the court-martial. He was a member of the Board of Naval Commissioners (1830–1832), and he commanded the Home Squadron (1842–1843) and the Philadelphia Navy Yard (1838–1841, 1846, 1854–1861). He was made the senior flag officer of the navy in March 1859. Placed on the retired list on 21 December 1861, he nevertheless received the high honor of being made rear admiral on the retired list on 16 July 1862. His career in the navy began with being commissioned by President John Adams and concluded with being honored by President Abraham Lincoln. Stewart died at Bordentown, New Jersey.

Stewart's naval career was both splendid and uneven, with the bulk of his wartime service coming before he reached the age of forty. He lived long enough to see the changes from sail to steam power and from wooden ships to iron ones. He witnessed the conclusion of the Civil War, a conflict that would have been almost unthinkable to the gallant band of U.S. naval officers who led the navy to its victories during the War of 1812. As commander of the USS *Constitution* during its final war cruise, Stewart gained and has held a place of honor and praise in the annals of the U.S. Navy. For longevity of service, coolness and courage under fire, and gallantry in his personal dealings, Stewart had few rivals in the early history of the navy.

• There are no known collections of Stewart manuscripts. The most comprehensive study of Stewart and his colleagues is Christopher McKee, *A Gentlemanly and Honorable Profession: The Creation of the U.S. Naval Corps, 1794–1815* (1991). Other sources for Stewart's life and career are Leonard F. Guttridge and Jay D. Smith, *The Commodores: The U.S. Navy in the Age of Sail* (1969), and Edward L. Beach, *The United States Navy: A 200-Year History* (1986). For the specifics of Stewart's service in the War of 1812, Theodore Roosevelt, *The Naval War of 1812* (1882), and Alfred T. Mahan, *Sea Power in Its Relations to the War of 1812* (1905), remain valuable. See also Lynn W. Turner, "The Last War Cruise of Old Ironsides," *American Heritage* 6 (Apr. 1955): 56–61; and Tyrone G. Martin, *A Most Fortunate Ship* (1980). For a look at the connection between Stewart and his grandson and namesake in Ireland, see F. S. L. Lyons, *Charles Stewart Parnell* (1977), and Jane Cote, "The Tudors and the Stewarts: American Ancestors of Charles Stewart Parnell," *Eire-Ireland* 27 (1992): 7–19. An obituary is in the *Philadelphia Public Ledger*, 8 Nov. 1869.

SAMUEL WILLARD CROMPTON

STEWART, Donald Ogden (30 Nov. 1894–2 Aug. 1980), writer, was born in Columbus, Ohio, the son of Gilbert Holland Stewart, a lawyer and circuit court judge, and Clara Ogden. Young Donald was a bookish social outcast growing up in Ohio, and at the age of fourteen he persuaded his parents to send him to Phillips Exeter Academy in New Hampshire for his secondary education. Stewart thrived at Exeter, but after graduating in 1912 he returned to Columbus that summer to find himself again in adverse circumstances: his father had been arrested for stealing library books and later died in the midst of intense publicity about the case before it came to trial. His mother had become an alcoholic requiring constant care, and his older brother died. With the help of loans and a scholarship and with the intervention of other family members and friends, he nevertheless was able to enter Yale that fall.

Majoring in English, he wrote for the college newspaper and developed a strong interest in literature and music. The former social outsider, who had now developed the affable personality that became his trademark, was also granted admission to Yale's elite Skull and Bones Society. Financial need directed him toward business rather than a literary career, and after graduating in 1916 he joined the managerial staff of American Telephone and Telegraph (AT&T).

During the next two years Stewart worked successively in Birmingham, Pittsburgh, and Chicago. He took a temporary leave of absence from AT&T in the spring of 1918 when he was drafted into military service. He was sent to the Naval Officers Training School in Chicago, but poor eyesight kept him from combat, and he remained at the school for the duration of the war as an instructor. After the war ended, he was assigned to an AT&T division in Minneapolis, Minnesota, where he met F. Scott Fitzgerald. Stewart's blossoming friendship with Fitzgerald rekindled his interest in literature, and he began to plan a literary career for himself.

Stewart left AT&T in the spring of 1920 and spent the summer at a manufacturing company in Dayton, Ohio. At last feeling financially secure enough to try his luck as a writer, he moved to Greenwich Village in New York City, then the center of avant-garde culture in America and the home base of Fitzgerald and other rising literary stars. Through Fitzgerald, Stewart met Edmund Wilson, who was then assistant editor of *Vanity Fair*. Stewart began contributing to the magazine parodies of contemporary writers that were well received and soon afterward were published in book form as *A Parody Outline of History* (1921). Finding his niche as a writer of light satire, Stewart quickly wrote another book in the same vein, *Perfect Behavior* (1922), a spoof of etiquette manuals.

In late 1922 Stewart traveled abroad for several months. He was especially captivated by Paris and its colony of U.S. writers, among them Ernest Hemingway, who was then at the very beginning of his literary career. The serious mood among the literati there, informed more by the gloom of T. S. Eliot's "Waste Land" than the speakeasy atmosphere of the Village,

turned Stewart's satirical eye and pen away from superficial subjects. The result of this redirection was his novel *Aunt Polly's Story of Mankind* (1923), but this dark send-up of American greed and hypocrisy was rejected by the reading public.

In later life Stewart claimed that he was proudest of *Aunt Polly*, but in the wake of its failure he concluded that his appeal lay in his gift for lighter satire. He returned successfully to that format in his next book, *Mr. and Mrs. Haddock Abroad* (1924), a humorous account of American tourists in Europe. During Stewart's own second trip abroad in the summer of 1924 and his third visit the following summer, he traveled with Hemingway to Spain to attend the bullfights and festival in Pamplona, events that Hemingway later immortalized in *The Sun Also Rises* (1926). Stewart appears in Hemingway's novel as Bill Gorton, the glib, wisecracking friend of Jake Barnes, the book's protagonist.

Back in the United States, Stewart helped Hemingway's career, arranging for the first U.S. publication of his short story collection *In Our Time* in 1925, the same year that Stewart published another novel, *The Crazy Fool*. Stewart was not flattered by his portrayal in *The Sun Also Rises*, although he acknowledged that some of the character's quips were his own. He dismissed the book as lightweight and without lasting significance, although his critical judgment was likely impaired by the recognition that with its publication Hemingway had permanently eclipsed him. In any event, their friendship ended for good in the fall of 1926, after Stewart criticized Hemingway for reading what he viewed as a tasteless parody of Dorothy Parker's verse at a social gathering.

By this time Stewart had been working for a year as a screenwriter for Metro-Goldwyn-Mayer, spending months at a time in Hollywood while he also completed another novel, *Mr. and Mrs. Haddock in Paris, France* (1926). In the summer of 1926 he married Beatrice Ames. They settled in New York City; the couple eventually had two children. For the next few years Stewart supported his family by writing a weekly column for the *Chicago Tribune* and contributing humorous sketches to the *New Yorker* while he tried to establish a new career as a playwright.

Stewart's first play, *Los Angelos* (1928), written with Max Mercin and produced by George M. Cohan, folded on Broadway after two weeks. He was more successful with his second, *Rebound* (1929), written after he had experienced the theater firsthand as a supporting actor in Philip Barry's play *Holiday* in 1928. In 1929 Stewart published his last novel, *Father William*, a gentle satire of a businessman. Further success at playwriting eluded him, however, and Stewart moved to Hollywood in 1930 so that he could work full-time as a screenwriter.

Stewart successfully adapted to this role, turning out scripts—alone or in collaboration with other writers—for numerous films that provided American audiences with temporary relief from depression-era gloom and the anxieties of the world war that followed. They included such classics as *Dinner at Eight* (1933); *Kitty Foyle* (1940); *The Philadelphia Story* (1940), an adaptation of a Philip Barry play for which he won an Academy Award; *Keeper of the Flame* (1942); and *Life with Father* (1947).

Stewart and his first wife were divorced in 1938, and the following year he married Ella Winter Steffens, the widow of journalist Lincoln Steffens; they had no children. Beginning in the late 1930s Stewart became a prominent critic of fascism as an active member and officer of several professional organizations, including the Screen Writers Guild and the League of American Writers. He also served as president of the Hollywood Anti-Nazi League during the war.

Stewart's liberalism was viewed with increasing suspicion in the Cold War climate of the late 1940s, and by 1950 he found himself blacklisted for his refusal to cooperate with investigations by the House Committee on Un-American Activities of alleged Communist infiltration in Hollywood. No longer able to find employment in America, he moved to London in 1951 and lived there until his death. He did little professionally in England beyond creating English dialogue for dubbing in European movies. In 1975 his autobiography, *By a Stroke of Luck!*, was published.

Stewart's most enduring legacy is his body of work for film, but he is also remembered for his association with the Hemingway-Fitzgerald Paris circle of the 1920s. He may have been privately dismayed at being only a minor participant in that "moveable feast" and at his own inability to create great literature, but in old age he voiced contentment with "a hell of a happy, lucky life."

• The best source of biographical information on Stewart is *By a Stroke of Luck!*, his 1975 autobiography. Memoirs and biographies of Stewart's contemporaries also include accounts of his life and activities; see especially John Dos Passos, *The Best Times* (1966); Carlos Baker, *Ernest Hemingway: A Life Story* (1969); and Kenneth S. Lynn, *Hemingway* (1987). An obituary is in the *New York Times*, 3 Aug. 1980.

ANN T. KEENE

STEWART, George Rippey (31 May 1895–22 Aug. 1980), writer and professor, was born in Sewickley, Pennsylvania, the son of George Rippey Stewart, a businessman, and Ella May Wilson. He learned to read at home and in the public school in his mother's home town of Indiana, Pennsylvania, becoming a voracious reader of Rudyard Kipling, Robert Louis Stevenson, and, especially, the adventure stories of G. A. Henty. A bout of pneumonia led his father to move the family to the more benign climate of Azusa, a citrus grove town in southern California, by 1908. There the bookish, shy George belatedly fell in love with the outdoors, bicycling and hiking in the Sierra Madre and the canyon of the San Gabriel River and camping in the San Bernardino Mountains. (He became in time, and remained for all of his days, a dedicated trout fly fisherman.) After successfully investing in Ontario and Anaheim orange groves, George's father moved

the family in 1911 to Pasadena, where the youngster completed the last two years of high school. After private tutoring, he attended Princeton (1913–1917), taking literature courses and deciding to teach. After his A.B., he served two years of World War I (1917–1919) in the U.S. Army Ambulance Service but did not go overseas. Like his father, he caught pneumonia, which damaged his lungs and bothered him for the remainder of his life.

Stewart's stint of graduate work (1919–1920) at the University of California, Berkeley, was the turning point in his career. Chauncey Wells taught him to love both literature and creative writing, and Herbert E. Bolton of the history department made an incipient westerner out of the Pennsylvanian. Stewart wrote his M.A. thesis (1920) on "Robert Louis Stevenson in California." He took his Ph.D. at Columbia (1922), writing his doctoral dissertation on technical aspects of the meter of ballads. He was an instructor of English at the University of Michigan in 1922 and at the University of California, Berkeley, in 1923. In 1924 he married Theodosia "Ted" Burton and in 1925 was promoted to assistant professor. They had two children.

The seed planted by Bolton soon germinated. Stewart began to write and teach in the field of western Americana, starting with articles on Bret Harte, then an edition of Harte's stories and poems, and finally a definitive biography, *Bret Harte, Argonaut and Exile* (1931). In 1936 he published a solid popular book, *Ordeal by Hunger*, which is still the basic source of information on the Donner party tragedy. It read like fiction, although it was fact, and it became a favorite with readers. So Stewart, although he remained a scholarly professor, developed a sort of dual personality, writing at the same time more trade books, both fiction and nonfiction.

Stewart remained at "Cal" for the rest of his academic career, retiring in 1962 as a professor emeritus. He taught summer sessions at the University of Michigan and Duke University (1926, 1939), was a resident fellow in creative writing at Princeton (1942–1943), and served as a Fulbright professor at the University of Athens in 1952–1953. During World War II he received a special appointment as a U.S. Navy civilian technician, writing on a submarine project at Pearl Harbor, and also was an editor for the University of California's Division of War Research.

Stewart's two bestsellers were the novels *Storm* (1941) and *Fire* (1948). His *Earth Abides* (1949) was science fiction. *Names on the Land* (1945), a minor classic in the field of onomastics, or onomatology (the science or study of names) demonstrated his expertise in nomenclature, especially place names. A founder of the American Name Society, he served as chair of an advisory commission of the California Place-Names Project (1944–1947). In 1970, 1975, and 1979 he published *American Place Names*, *Names on the Globe*, and *American Given Names*. His interest in history and geography led to the novel *Sheep Rock* and the nonfiction *U.S. 40* (1953) and *The California Trail* (1962). Although the latter was "written to order" for the American Trails Series, it is one of his best books, perhaps the best single volume on the westward movement to California. Stewart studied San Francisco's vigilantes of 1851 in his *Committee of Vigilance* (1964), and in his Plutarchian *Good Lives* (1967) he collected honorable westerners, such as General John Bidwell, to contrast them with stereotypical reckless and lawless men of western legend.

A member of the California Historical Society, Phi Beta Kappa, Modern Language Association, American Name Society, and San Francisco's Bohemian Club, Stewart won excellent reviews in scholarly journals as well as general publications. Yet he has been given little critical attention, perhaps because his field, the West, was considered superficial by many academics. His shyness was another factor. Moreover, his very productivity, versatility in both fiction and nonfiction, and popularity made his work somehow suspect on campus. He did apply fictional techniques in his nonfiction "long narratives," but he never abused Clio by taking liberties with historical facts. Some of his interpretations of the Donner party, however, have been questioned by revisionist historians. But Stewart always insisted that all good regional writing, including his own thirty-eight books and approximately eighty-five articles and reviews, must meet stringent criteria, particularly that of a sense of place. The narrative must be true in its history and geography and in the relationship of its people to the land.

The Commonwealth Club of California gave Stewart its Silver Medal for literature in 1936 for *Ordeal* and its Gold Medal in 1938 for *East of the Giants*, his first novel. *Storm* and *Fire* were both Book-of-the-Month Club selections, and *Earth Abides* received the first International Fantasy Award. In 1960 the California Historical Society made him a fellow. In 1968 the University of California presented him with its Centennial Citation and made him a Berkeley fellow. *Not So Rich as You Think* (1968), an early-warning ecology book, won the Sidney Hillman Award. In 1972 the California Historical Society awarded Stewart its prestigious Henry R. Wagner Medal. In 1980 he was given an Honors Award by the Association of American Geographers. Although afflicted with Parkinson's disease, he continued to write until his death in San Francisco.

• Stewart's papers are in the Bancroft Library, University of California, Berkeley. There is also an unpublished autobiography there, along with extended interviews in that library's Regional Oral History Office. There is a pamphlet in Boise State University's Western Writers Series, John Caldwell's *George R. Stewart* (1981). There are sketches in *Who's Who in California* (1942–1943); *Who's Who on the Pacific Coast* (1949); *Who Was Who in America*, vol. 7 (1981); and Fred Erisman and Richard W. Etulain, eds., *Fifty Western Writers* (1982). See also vol. 36 (1979) of the *Bulletin of Bibliography*. Two of his colleagues have written useful appreciations of Stewart: Ferol Egan, "In a World of Creation," *Westways*, July 1980, pp. 16–19, 80, and Wallace Stegner, "George R. Stewart, Western Writer," *American West*, Mar.–Apr. 1982, pp. 64, 67–69. Irving Stone, ed., *There Was Light* (1970), contains a reminiscence of Stewart's graduate year at Berkeley, and a sketch of his career is in the *San Francisco Examiner-Chronicle*'s Scene section, 12 Aug. 1979. An obituary is in the *New York Times*, 26 Aug. 1980.

RICHARD H. DILLON

STEWART, John George (2 June 1890–24 May 1970), congressman and architect of the U.S. Capitol, was born in Wilmington, Delaware, the son of Hamilton Stewart, a stonecutter turned successful contractor, and Marie Schaefer. Stewart studied civil engineering at the University of Delaware, leaving during his third year of study in 1911 to assume a clerkship in his father's contracting firm, Stewart and Donahue, and to marry Helen Tabor Ferry of Norristown, Pennsylvania. As Stewart rose through the ranks of the company, achieving a partnership in 1919 and the presidency in 1929, the firm grew to be one of the largest of its type on the East Coast. Under his direction Stewart's company obtained numerous federal and commercial contracts for the construction of roads, bridges, and factories. The firm's restoration of the original Du Pont black powder plant at Hagley, Delaware, led to commissions to supervise construction of the Henry F. du Pont residence at Winterthur (now the Winterthur Museum of American Decorative Arts) and to extend the elaborate formal gardens of Alfred I. du Pont at Nemours, also in Delaware. Stewart's contacts with the du Pont family had a definitive influence on his career. Through the du Ponts, Stewart acquired entrée into Delaware state politics as well as a lifelong preference for traditional and classical modes of architectural design over the European modernism that dominated midcentury practice.

Stewart's political career began with his appointment as the governor of Delaware's Emergency Relief Commission in 1931. By 1934 he campaigned successfully as a Republican for the U.S. House of Representatives, serving one term from 1935 to 1937. During this term Stewart's wife died. Failing in his bid for a second term, Stewart married Rae Dickerson Lauritsen in 1937 and returned to the construction company, which he had inherited upon his father's death in 1933. Stewart chose to sell the company in 1942 and to pursue a career that would lead him back to Washington. From 1942 until 1947 Stewart worked in sales, negotiating major government contracts for the Hercules Powder Corporation of Delaware and the Pennsylvania Engineering Company. His expertise as an engineering contractor and his government experience helped Stewart to gain the position of chief clerk of the Senate Committee for the District of Columbia in 1947. In spite of his openly Republican partisan allegiance, Stewart remained a federal staff member through the Democratic 1949–1951 congressional term, rising to director of the Speaker's Bureau in 1953. On 1 October 1954 Stewart was appointed architect of the U.S. Capitol by Republican president Dwight D. Eisenhower. The eighth man to hold the office of architect of the Capitol since its creation in

1793, Stewart was also, perhaps, the most controversial.

As architect of the Capitol, the officer in charge of the maintenance, administration, and construction of all the structures and grounds comprising the 134-acre U.S. Capitol complex, Stewart presided over several extensive and widely publicized building projects. Most notably, Stewart's administration oversaw the construction of the "New" Senate Office Building (1955–1958; now known as the Dirksen Office Building), the Rayburn House Office Building (1955–1965), the extension of the east front of the original Capitol Building (1958), and a comprehensive remodeling of the Longworth Office Building (1966–1968), as well as the preliminary planning and design selection for the James Madison Building of the Library of Congress (completed 1982). Stewart received much criticism in the architectural press for his adherence to classically derived forms, rich materials, and art deco–like sculptural programs in the buildings produced under his aegis. Critics of the period, who generally favored "International Style" modernism, attributed the conservative style of building during Stewart's tenure to his lack of professional design training and desire to monumentalize the ambitions of his congressional patrons at the expense of contemporary aesthetic dogma. Stewart's projects were attacked as reminiscent of "the Hitler era," "Mussolini modern," and as "monstrosities" conveying "a double impression of extravagance and parsimony." Stewart chose not to respond publicly to such vituperation, instead concentrating on keeping his powerful supporters such as Speaker of the House Samuel Rayburn (D.-Tex.), Senate Majority Leader and later President Lyndon Baines Johnson (D.-Tex.), Senator Hubert Humphrey (D-Minn.), and House Minority Leader and later President Gerald R. Ford (R.-Mich.) pleased with the work produced under the mantle of the office of the architect of the Capitol. In spite of several pointed criticisms of his work, the American Institute of Architects granted Stewart an honorary membership in 1957, followed in 1958 by an honorary degree in engineering from his alma mater, the University of Delaware. Stewart's architectural advisory committee may have been loaded with the most conservative practitioners of the era, but the results of his administration satisfied congressional leaders and allowed Stewart to retain his office until his death, in Washington, D.C.

The buildings produced under John George Stewart during his sixteen years as architect of the U.S. Capitol may not have made the revolutionary stylistic statement many leaders in the architectural profession desired, but in projects like the Rayburn Office Building Stewart succeeded in maintaining the hallmark classical matrix of U.S. government design through the heyday of the modernist movement in American architecture.

• Documents and drawings relating to Stewart's tenure as architect of the Capitol, as well as standard biographical information, are held by the Office of the Architect of the Capitol.

Representative critiques of his work include "The Emperor of Capitol Hill," *Architectural Forum* 129 (Sept. 1968): 80–85; Douglas Haskell, "Saying Nothing, Going Nowhere," *Architectural Forum* 111 (Aug. 1959): 134ff.; and Hunter Lewis, "Capitol Hill's Ugliness Club," *Atlantic Monthly* (Feb. 1967): 60–66. For a summary of the history, duties, and projects of the architects of the Capitol, see *Official Congressional Directory 1987–8*, 100th Cong., U.S. Government Printing Office (1987): 737–45. Obituaries are in major newspapers such as the *New York Times*, the *Washington Post*, and the *Washington Star*, all 25 May 1970.

J. LAURIE OSSMAN

STEWART, Maria W. (1803–17 Dec. 1879), writer, black activist, and teacher, was born Maria Miller in Hartford, Connecticut (information about her date of birth and parentage is not known). Orphaned at five years old and indentured to a clergyman's family until she was fifteen, Maria Miller supported herself as a domestic servant and gained a rudimentary education by attending "Sabbath schools." Miller's marriage on 10 August 1826 to James W. Stewart, a Boston shipping agent, placed her in the small and vibrant free black Boston community that had established organizations and institutions in the late eighteenth and early nineteenth centuries for northern blacks coming out of bondage. Stewart's brief period of financial security ended when unscrupulous executors cheated the young widow out of her inheritance following the death of her husband in 1829.

Lacking family and funds, Stewart, who had no children, was forced to rely again on her own resources. In late 1820s the second series of evangelical revivals was sweeping across the country converting thousands of Americans to a more fervent and active Christian experience. Like many of her age, Stewart became "a humble instrument in the hands of God" to win "some poor souls to Christ." She was also influenced by the increasingly aggressive activism of many Boston blacks who had organized, in 1826, the Massachusetts General Colored Association, an antislavery society that advocated the immediate abolition of slavery and supported the first black newspaper, *Freedom's Journal*, published in New York City. David Walker, an outspoken member of the association, published a passionate manifesto called *David Walker's Appeal* in September 1829. Walker's call for African Americans, slave and free, to engage in the struggle against slavery and racism was combined with warnings to whites about the inevitability of a slave insurrection if slavery persisted. The *Appeal* greatly influenced Stewart. So, too, did Walker's death six months after the demise of Stewart's husband. Coupled with a conversion experience, it contributed to her belief that she was a divinely chosen advocate for the human rights of African Americans. Instilled with divine courage, she felt compelled to "sacrifice" her life "for the cause of God and my brethren."

In 1831 Stewart began writing and in 1832 began giving public lectures to black Bostonians about their critical role in the movement for the abolition of slavery and racism. These political critiques complemented her religious writings, which stressed the importance of spirituality in the individual and the community. Her first essay, *Religion and the Pure Principles of Morality* (1831), as well as most of her other writings and speeches that followed, were published as pamphlets by white abolitionist William Lloyd Garrison or appeared in *The Liberator*, Garrison's antislavery newspaper. In 1832 she published *Meditations from the Pen of Mrs. Maria W. Stewart*, a collection of her religious meditations, and in 1835 *Productions of Mrs. Maria W. Stewart*, a compilation of her religious meditations and political essays.

Stewart's religious writings revealed the degree to which she was immersed in the larger national and international evangelical community and showed the influence of developing traditions in black evangelicalism. Stewart stressed an immanent God engaged in the affairs of humankind. Also, like other evangelicals, she consistently noted her conversion as the signal event in her life and expressed her sense of "duty" to help convert nation and the world. She borrowed heavily from the Bible, as did other evangelicals of her era, sometimes using language almost verbatim from the King James version.

Unlike white Christians, Stewart reiterated a developing tradition within black Christianity that stressed an omnipotent God who was concerned about divine justice as much, if not more than, divine love. She conflated temporal and spiritual deliverance from the bondage of sin and slavery; the "cause of Christ" was the elimination of sin and the destruction of "the chains of slavery and ignorance." Like so many African-American Christians, Stewart emphasized biblical evidence of human equality. She thanked God, for instance, that "thou art no respecter of persons" (*Productions*, 46). Thus, in discrete ways, Stewart's sacred works were as political as they were religious.

Stewart's political writings and speeches were a constant blend of the sacred and the secular. Indeed, she believed that Christianity was the foundation of political, social, and economic change; abolition, equal rights, and black unity depended upon African-American commitment to divine direction. While recognizing exceptions to her claims, she argued that men came under particular scrutiny because they were falling short in their decreed role as fathers, husbands, and community leaders. At the same time, Stewart reflected nineteenth-century gender roles in her admonitions to wives and mothers to ensure "moral worth and intellectual improvement" in the rising generation through exemplary piety and education. Knowledge equaled power, Stewart claimed, and was deeply intertwined with spiritual growth. Her stress on education expressed resentment and dismay about her own and other black children's, especially young girls', limited opportunities in the antebellum North. Restrictions on black education were analogous to limited employment opportunities. Stewart condemned whites in general for exploiting black labor (particularly domestic labor) because of self-interest.

Stewart consistently argued that black unity was critical in the struggle for abolition and equality. Troubled by what she perceived as "prejudices and animosities" among blacks, she insisted that blacks would never eradicate slavery, poverty, and ignorance until "we become united as one." She advocated not only the establishment of black schools and churches but also separate black businesses. She urged African Americans to "unite and build a store" of their own and to "promote and patronize each other." As the first American woman to deliver a public lecture about political subjects to both men and women, Stewart confronted strident opposition. Her passionate, and, at times, abrasive language, in so many ways similar to Walker's, was unacceptable from a woman. While her widowhood allowed her a degree of autonomy that a single or married woman in the early nineteenth century lacked, Stewart was confronted with prevailing sexual proscriptions that relegated women to subordinate positions politically, economically, and socially. And prohibitions against women lecturing to men, especially about political and social issues, existed as much in the black community as in the dominant society. The negative responses to her often blunt directives to black audiences led to another "first." She was the first African-American woman to deliver a lecture in defense of women's rights.

Because of the increasing opposition against her and perhaps because of limited opportunities, Stewart moved to New York City. Before leaving Boston, she delivered a "Farewell Address" in 1833 in which she defended the right of women to play prominent roles in society. Citing biblical as well as historical examples, Stewart asserted that "women . . . in all ages . . . have had a voice in moral, religious and political subjects" (Richardson, p. 68). Having been called of God, she was merely fulfilling her divine duty: "What if I am a woman; is not the God of ancient times the God of these modern days?" (Richardson, p. 68). New York afforded Stewart the opportunity for more advanced education through her membership in the New York City black women's Female Literary Society. While records show that she attended the Women's Anti-Slavery Convention in 1837 and in 1850 was mentioned in the *North Star* as a member of the Committee of Arrangements to benefit the paper, Stewart dedicated most of the rest of her life to teaching. Beginning in the mid-1830s to the 1870s, she taught in New York, Brooklyn, Baltimore, and Washington, D.C., public and private schools. In the early 1870s she combined teaching and work as matron of the Freedmen's Hospital in Washington, D.C.

In 1879 Stewart filed and won her claim for a widow's pension from the U.S. Navy for her husband's service. She used the money to publish a new edition of her writings and speeches to which she added an autobiographical account of her experiences during the Civil War. *Meditations by Mrs. Maria W. Stewart* appeared just eight months before she died in Washington, D.C.

Both as a writer and speaker, Stewart reflected and established the parameters, along with David Walker, of a developing tradition within black protest that persisted, in several ways, into the late twentieth century. The themes of unity, separate and collective action, community development, and an understanding of politics within an evangelical context were echoed by prominent nineteenth- and twentieth-century activists. Stewart's rejection of the inferior status of black women and her assertion that black women must have a prominent role in the movement toward equality became fundamental in late nineteenth- and twentieth-century black feminist theory. As the forerunner of nineteenth-century black feminists like Anna Julia Cooper and Ida B. Wells, Stewart located the distinctiveness of black women's oppression at the nexus of race and gender.

• For Stewart's political writings and speeches see *Maria W. Stewart, America's First Black Woman Political Writer: Essays and Speeches*, ed. Marilyn Richardson (1987); Richardson's introductory essay is a thorough biographical sketch and literary analysis. Stewart's religious writings are in *Spiritual Narratives*, ed. Sue E. Houchins (1988). Patricia Hill Collins, *Black Feminist Thought: Knowledge, Consciousness, and the Politics of Empowerment* (1990), provides a contemporary critique of Stewart as a feminist.

RITA ROBERTS

STEWART, Potter (23 Jan. 1915–7 Dec. 1985), U.S. Supreme Court justice, was born in Jackson, Michigan, the son of James Garfield Stewart, a chief justice of the Ohio Supreme Court, and Harriet Loomis Potter. Stewart was chairman of the undergraduate newspaper at Yale University, where he received a bachelor's degree in 1937 and a law degree in 1941. After serving during the Second World War as a naval officer and attaining the rank of lieutenant junior grade, he entered private practice and local politics in Cincinnati, Ohio. In 1943 he married Mary Anne Bertles, with whom he had three children.

In 1954, when Stewart was only thirty-nine, he was appointed to the U.S. Court of Appeals for the Sixth Circuit. In 1958, President Dwight D. Eisenhower appointed him to the U.S. Supreme Court, where he served until his retirement in 1981. Although he had a background in Ohio Republican politics and was appointed to the Supreme Court by a Republican president known for his antipathy to judicial liberalism, Stewart was not a conservative justice. Rather, he followed a moderate, pragmatic approach that defied easy categorization. He favored First Amendment rights of free speech and religion and the Equal Protection rights of blacks and other insular minorities, while also supporting state criminal law-enforcement efforts. He tended to search for middle-of-the-road solutions and to embrace procedural grounds in order to defer the making of difficult substantive decisions. He believed that he should approach each case on its merits, without striving to further an ideological agenda. Over time, his practical approach marked him as a

centrist who adhered to no particular wing of the Court.

Stewart's 23-year tenure on the Supreme Court roughly coincided with the eras of Chief Justices Earl Warren and Warren Burger. On the Warren Court, Stewart frequently stood outside the prevailing liberal consensus, particularly on matters concerning state criminal law enforcement. His centrist inclinations meant, however, that he also declined to align himself with the Burger Court's occasionally aggressive pursuit of politically conservative causes.

Stewart's gift for aphorism yielded a memorable opinion in *Jacobellis v. Ohio* (1964), which, to his chagrin, survived as his most widely quoted judicial utterance: "I shall not today attempt further to define the kinds of material I understand to be embraced within [the term 'hard-core pornography,' to which the justice believed that state criminal laws in the area of obscenity were constitutionally limited]; and perhaps I could never succeed in intelligibly doing so. But I know it when I see it, and the motion picture involved in this case is not that."

When, in *Braunfeld v. Brown* (1961), the Court sustained the constitutionality of a Sunday-closing statute, Stewart's brief but forceful dissent reflected his common-sense dedication to individual liberty: "Pennsylvania has passed a law which compels an Orthodox Jew to choose between his religious faith and his economic survival. That is a cruel choice. It is a choice which I think no State can constitutionally demand. For me this is not something that can be swept under the rug and forgotten in the interest of enforced Sunday togetherness." On the question of the constitutionality of the death penalty (which was ultimately answered in the affirmative), he insisted on scrupulous adherence to fair procedure and wrote that certain death sentences before the Court were "cruel and unusual in the same way that being struck by lightning is cruel and unusual" (*Furman v. Georgia* [1972]).

In 1968, when Warren announced his intention to retire, Stewart removed himself from consideration for the position of chief justice, mindful of the internal dissension that had been generated when members of the Court previously had sought the position. He later played a significant role in formulating the Court's unanimous opinion in *Nixon v. United States* (1974), which ordered President Nixon to surrender to the special prosecutor the tape recordings whose disclosure later led Nixon to resign.

Stewart retired from the Court at the relatively junior age of sixty-six. He continued to sit for several years as a judge on federal courts of appeals. He also made recordings for the sight-impaired and served as co-narrator of a popular television series about the Constitution (1984). He died in Hanover, New Hampshire.

• Stewart's papers are held at Yale University. Neither a formal biography of Stewart nor a comprehensive assessment of his judicial work has appeared. For brief accounts, see Jerald H. Israel, "Potter Stewart," in *The Justices of the United States*

Supreme Court, 1789–1969, ed. Leon Friedman and Fred Israel, vol. 4 (1969); Leon Friedman, "Potter Stewart," in *The Justices of the United States Supreme Court: Their Lives and Major Opinions*, ed. Leon Friedman and Fred L. Israel, 2d ed. (1978); and Barnett Meresman, "A Lawyer's Lawyer, A Judge's Judge: Justice Potter Stewart and the Fourth Amendment," *University of Chicago Law Review* 51 (1982): 509–44. For an example of Stewart's view of the law, see Potter Stewart, "Or of the Press," *Hastings Law Journal* 26 (1975): 631–37. An obituary is in the *New York Times*, 8 Dec. 1985.

LEONARD H. BECKER

STEWART, Rex William (22 Feb. 1907–7 Sept. 1967), jazz cornetist, was born in Philadelphia, Pennsylvania, the son of Rex Stewart, a violinist and singer, and Jane Johnson, a pianist, who taught him music from the age of four. In 1914 he started playing alto horn and then cornet in a boys' band in Washington, D.C., where his parents had settled sometime earlier. After three years' experience with this group, he played on the Potomac riverboats and then in 1920 joined Ollie Blackwell's Jazz Clowns to tour with Rosa Henderson's blues revue, *Go-Get-It*. When the show folded in Philadelphia, he found work with the Musical Spillers, a family vaudeville act whose code of behavior Stewart violated so often that he was dismissed in 1923. Instead of returning home, though, he stayed in New York City to freelance in dozens of small Harlem clubs.

In the fall of 1924, after an engagement with Billy Paige's Broadway Syncopators, Stewart joined banjoist Elmer Snowden's band at the Balconnades, where he played with such talented young jazzmen as trombonist Jimmy Harrison and reedman Prince Robinson. When his idol Louis Armstrong left the Fletcher Henderson Orchestra in early November 1925 he recommended Stewart as his replacement. It took much coaxing from Snowden, but the younger cornetist finally agreed to join Henderson at the Roseland Ballroom the following May, only to believe himself still inadequate to the task nine months later, when he quit to join younger brother Horace Henderson's Collegians at Wilberforce University in Ohio. In October 1928 Stewart returned to New York and resumed his place in the elder Henderson's band for another year or so. After a brief stint with Alex Jackson around 1930 he joined McKinney's Cotton Pickers in Detroit and stayed with them from August 1931 to early 1932, when he once again returned to Fletcher Henderson. From June 1933 until August 1934, Stewart led a twelve-piece band at the Empire Ballroom opposite the Roseland on Broadway, but he eventually left because of poor business. With further opportunities for leadership of his own band diminishing, Stewart worked for a few months with Luis Russell's band before joining Duke Ellington in December 1934.

With the exception of a brief period between April and October 1943, during which time he worked with Benny Carter and formed his own band in Los Angeles, Stewart remained with Ellington until December 1945. After almost two decades of national exposure on both records and radio broadcasts and in theaters and ballrooms, Stewart attempted once again to go out on his own. In early 1946 he formed a seven-piece group, the Rextet, and worked in New York at the Three Deuces and Kelly's Stable on Fifty-second Street and the Savoy Ballroom and the Apollo Theater in Harlem as well as at the Savoy Cafe in Boston. He next went on tour for a few months with Norman Granz's Jazz at the Philharmonic and in October 1947 reassembled his Rextet for a European tour booked by the Hot Club of France; in June 1948 he disbanded the group and worked as a soloist with local jazz bands in Germany. Enjoying his newfound fame in Europe as a visiting jazz star, Stewart also took time to indulge another passion; he studied gourmet cooking at Le Cordon Bleu, ultimately earning a certificate of proficiency in December 1949. In the summer of that year he also had gone on a successful tour of Australia with Graeme Bell's traditional jazz band.

After securing a divorce from his first wife, Margie Slaughter, with whom he had at least three children, Stewart married Ruth Hansen around 1950. From 1950 to 1952 he worked sporadically in Philadelphia, New York, and Boston, using a farm he had bought near Troy, New York, as a home base. He also had a radio show on WROW and lectured on jazz at Dartmouth and Bennington College. In the spring of 1953 he formed a group starring clarinetist Albert Nicholas to work at the Savoy in Boston, after which he spent a few more years freelancing. In the summer of 1957 Stewart was asked to assemble and direct a big band of Fletcher Henderson alumni to appear at the Great South Bay Festival on Long Island. Recorded in November and December, the music of the seventeen-piece Henderson All Stars featured Stewart with Buster Bailey, J. C. Higginbotham, Coleman Hawkins, Ben Webster, and other stars of the Swing Era. Also in December, along with Red Allen, Vic Dickenson, Pee Wee Russell, and Hawkins, he appeared on the historic telecast "The Sound of Jazz." The next year Stewart restaged the Great South Bay Festival concert with slightly different personnel, and recordings were made in August 1958 shortly after his July appearance at the Newport Jazz Festival as leader of the Ellington Alumni All Stars.

From early 1958 through the summer of 1959 Stewart worked regularly at Eddie Condon's in New York City, and in 1960 he moved to Los Angeles to be close to his now-adult children. He found very little work there, however, and once again accepted a job hosting shows on the all-jazz station KNOB. Always highly literate, despite a limited formal education, and a lively raconteur, Stewart also began writing his autobiography as well as articles on jazz for *Down Beat*, *Playboy*, *Evergreen Review*, *Melody Maker*, and *Jazz Journal*. In his later years he planned to complete the account of his career in music, but two European tours in 1966 and a few concerts in California occupied most of his time before his sudden death from a heart attack in Santa Barbara.

Although Stewart had been initially impressed by Johnny Dunn and Bubber Miley, it was Louis Armstrong's brilliant solos with King Oliver, Clarence Williams, Fletcher Henderson, and his own recording groups that served as the younger player's major inspiration. His own best early work can be heard on "The Stampede" (1926) and a number of other Henderson titles from 1928 to 1931, including "My Gal Sal," "Sugar Foot Stomp," "Clarinet Marmalade," and "Singin' the Blues"; the latter two were especially notable for his emulation of white cornetist Bix Beiderbecke. Stewart also can be heard to advantage on McKinney's Cotton Pickers' "Rocky Road," "Never Swat a Fly," and "Do You Believe in Love at Sight?" where his heated, rhythmic style offers direct contrast to the sober lyricism of lead trumpeter Doc Cheatham. By the time he joined Ellington, Stewart was a highly individualized stylist with an intense, hard-punching delivery increasingly characterized by the use of artfully controlled "off-notes" produced by the partial lowering of the cornet's valves. Although not featured nearly as much as Cootie Williams, Ellington's star trumpeter, Stewart nevertheless contributed greatly to the varied texture that was the Ellington trademark. Among his many showcase performances, "Trumpet in Spades," "Braggin' in Brass," "Tootin' Through the Roof," "Boy Meets Horn," "Morning Glory," and "John Hardy's Wife" are the most strikingly indicative of his powers, while his own small-band records during the same prewar period offer equally exceptional performances. In addition to the several films he appeared in as a member of the Ellington orchestra, Stewart also had an acting role in *Syncopation* (1942), in which he portrayed a fictitious New Orleans trumpeter.

• A primary source of biographical data is Rex Stewart, *Boy Meets Horn*, ed. Claire P. Gordon (1991), a posthumously published first-person account of his early life and career to about 1950. His *Jazz Masters of the Thirties* (1972) is a collection of twenty previously published essays about some of the colleagues he most admired. See also an interview with John Dengler in J. Lee Anderson, "A Bringer of Joy," *Mississippi Rag*, Feb. 1994, pp. 1–8. For a more general background of his professional associations, see Walter C. Allen, *Hendersonia: The Music of Fletcher Henderson and His Musicians* (1973); Stanley Dance, *The World of Duke Ellington* (1970) and *The World of Swing* (1974); Mark Tucker, ed., *The Duke Ellington Reader* (1993); and Albert J. McCarthy, *Big Band Jazz* (1974). Stewart's recording career is thoroughly documented in Brian Rust, *Jazz Records, 1897–1942* (1982), and Walter Bruyninckx, *Swing Discography, 1920–1988* (12 vols., 1985–1989); abbreviated biographical entries can be found in John Chilton, *Who's Who of Jazz* (1972), and Roger D. Kinkle, *The Complete Encyclopedia of Popular Music and Jazz*, vol. 3, *L–Z* (1974).

JACK SOHMER

STEWART, Slam (21 Sept. 1914–10 Dec. 1987), jazz string bassist, bandleader, and educator, was born in Englewood, New Jersey. Nothing is known of his parents or his real name. He was raised as Leroy Elliott Stewart, but he said, without offering details, that a different name is on his birth certificate. His adopted father was a caretaker and gardener. Stewart started on violin at age six or seven and switched to string bass while in high school in Englewood.

His father worked for Dwight Morrow, an affluent man whose daughter Anne married Charles Lindbergh. After Stewart graduated, Morrow helped send him to the Boston Conservatory of Music, where he studied string bass for one year while playing in local bands. At this time he began to imitate Ray Perry, who hummed in unison with violin bowing; Stewart's humming, situated an octave above his bowed bass, became his overused musical signature.

In 1936 he joined trumpeter Peanuts Holland's band in Buffalo, New York. He returned to New Jersey and then started playing in New York City clubs. Around 1937 he met guitarist and singer Slim Gaillard at a jam session at an after-hours club in Harlem. The next day they played together on Gaillard's radio show on WMEW in New York. Martin Block, host of "The Make Believe Ballroom" on that same station, volunteered to manage the new duo, Slim and Slam, in which Stewart acquired his lasting nickname. They toured theaters nationally and had a huge hit with the nonsense song "The Flat Foot Floogie (with the Floy, Floy)"; at the next World's Fair a copy of this disc was buried in a time capsule, together with a recording of John Philip Sousa's "Washington Post March."

Stewart also worked with the Spirits of Rhythm (spring 1939), Van Alexander's dance orchestra (1940), and his own trio at Kelly's Stable in New York (late 1940). Slim and Slam performed in the comedy film *Hellzapoppin'* (1941), but the duo broke up the next year, when Gaillard was inducted into the armed forces. Stewart played in Fats Waller's group in the film *Stormy Weather* (1943), and while in California, guitarist Tiny Grimes took Gaillard's place. A successful jam session with pianist Art Tatum led to their joining Tatum in a trio from 1943 to 1944. Stewart had perfect pitch and was able to keep up with Tatum's impetuous habit of reharmonizing popular songs, playing them in different keys, or changing keys in the course of a tune. "He never did get me," Stewart told interviewer Doug Long. "I was able to follow him right straight through."

Tatum's trio played at the Three Deuces in New York. Apart from Tatum, Stewart recorded "Afternoon of a Basieite" and "Sometimes I'm Happy" at a session with saxophonist Lester Young in December 1943, and during 1944 he also worked at the Three Deuces with pianist Johnny Guarnieri's trio, and he played in Grimes's quartet.

Late in 1944 Tatum went to Los Angeles, California, and Stewart took over the trio, with Erroll Garner serving as its pianist. The Three Deuces remained his home base, but he also toured extensively. Concurrently from late January to November 1945 Stewart was a member of clarinetist Benny Goodman's quintet and sextet. During this same year he recorded "Groovin' High" and "All the Things You Are" with Dizzy Gillespie's amalgamated swing and bop group (February), two magnificently energetic duos with tenor saxophonist Don Byas, "Indiana" and "I Got Rhythm," in a concert at Town Hall (9 June); "Slam Slam Blues" with vibraphonist Red Norvo (also June); and "Three O'Clock in the Morning" with Byas's quartet, including Garner (August).

In January 1946, after Garner had a hit record, "Laura," and went out on the road as a leader, Billy Taylor took Garner's place in Stewart's trio; they also worked as a quartet with drummer Doc West. Stewart worked with Tatum again that spring. His trio continued with John Collins replacing Grimes in 1946 and Mary Lou Williams taking over the piano chair by the time of the movie *Boy! What a Girl* (1947).

After performing with Garner in France in May 1948, Stewart moved to Los Angeles and played on and off with Tatum during the late 1940s and early 1950s, with Everett Barksdale serving as their guitarist. Stewart worked in trumpeter Roy Eldridge's quartet (1953), continued leading a trio with Beryl Booker as his pianist from 1953 to 1955, and then toured as accompanist to singer and pianist Rose Murphy from around 1956 into the 1960s. He was reunited with Gaillard for a performance at the Great South Bay Jazz Festival in summer 1958.

In the mid-1960s Stewart settled permanently in Binghamton, New York. After retiring temporarily due to illness, he led his own trio in New York City late in 1968 and for work in Binghamton television studios. He rejoined Gaillard one last time for a quartet performance at the Monterey Jazz Festival with organist Milt Buckner and drummer Jo Jones in 1970. He then toured Europe with Buckner and Jones in April 1971. While performing in San Francisco, California, with Tatum in 1951, Stewart had met a singer and pianist, Claire (maiden name unknown). They married around 1970 and had two children.

From the early 1970s onward, Stewart taught at the State University of New York in Binghamton, gave programs on jazz history at Binghamton area schools, and produced jazz concerts at the Roberson Center in Binghamton. He rejoined Goodman in June 1973 for the Newport Jazz Festival in New York and then toured steadily with the clarinetist until March 1976, including a trip to Europe in 1974. In February 1977 Stewart suffered a heart attack, followed by a stroke. He recovered to play at the Grand Parade du Jazz in Nice, France, in July 1977, and that same year he played at Hopper's in New York in a duo with guitarist Bucky Pizzarelli. The duo performed regularly on the *Today* show on NBC during 1978.

Stewart rejoined Goodman occasionally in 1979 and for a last time as a guest soloist in June 1985. He toured internationally with saxophonist Illinois Jacquet (c. 1980–1981). In May 1984 he was awarded an honorary doctorate in music from SUNY Binghamton. He died in Binghamton. The date is given incorrectly as 9 December in the *New York Times* obituary; the funeral home confirmed the correct date, 10 December.

Having discovered a coarse, humorous sound, Stewart relentlessly hummed and bowed his solos through half a century of jazz. Unfortunately, a little of this gimmick goes a very long way. It seems a shame that Stewart never tried to make his solos beautiful, deep toned, and heady, along the lines of an Oscar Pettiford. Otherwise, in his principal role as an accompanist, plucking the instrument in a conventional jazz manner to keep rhythm and harmony in place, he ranks with any of the finest jazz bassists.

• Oral histories of Stewart are at Yale University and at the Institute of Jazz Studies, Newark, N.J.; see also the recollections of Stewart in Grimes's oral history, at the same institute. Published surveys and interviews include Jim Burns, "Slim & Slam," *Jazz Journal* 21 (Sept. 1968): 4–5; Les Tomkins: "How My Bass Started Singing," *Crescendo International* 13 (Nov. 1974): 17; John S. Wilson, "Slam Is Back, Fit As a Bass Fiddle," *New York Times*, 8 Sept. 1977; Doug Long, "Slam Stewart: Interview," *Cadence* 8 (Sept. 1982): 8–10, (Nov. 1982): 8–10; John Chilton, *Who's Who of Jazz: Storyville to Swing Street*, 4th. ed. (1985); James M. Doran, *Erroll Garner: The Most Happy Piano* (1985): 59–65; and Max Jones, *Talking Jazz* (1987), 228–32. See also Arnold Shaw, *The Street That Never Slept* (1971; repr. as *52nd Street: The Street of Jazz*, 1977); D. Russell Connor, *Benny Goodman: Listen to His Legacy* (1988); and Laurie Wright, *"Fats" in Fact* (1992). An obituary is in the *New York Times*, 11 Dec. 1987.

BARRY KERNFELD

STEWART, William Morris (9 Aug. 1825?–23 Apr. 1909), lawyer and U.S. senator, was born near Lyons, New York, the son of Frederick Augustus Stewart and Miranda Morris, farmers who soon moved the family to Trumbull County, Ohio. William left home at fourteen and worked as a laborer and schoolteacher to pay his way through preparatory schools in Ohio and in Lyons, New York. A Lyons attorney introduced Stewart to legal studies and in 1848 loaned him funds to enter Yale University. Stewart left Yale after three terms to seek his fortune in the gold fields around Nevada City, California. By 1852 he had earned enough to resume reading law.

Stewart entered politics as a Whig and attended the 1852 Whig National Convention. Most of his early political experience, however, came as a Democrat under the auspices of his legal mentor, John R. McConnell, district attorney of Nevada County and an influential mining lawyer. When McConnell won election as California attorney general in 1852, Stewart, only just admitted to the bar, was appointed county district attorney in his place. When McConnell took a leave of absence in June 1854, Stewart was appointed the state's acting attorney general. After his six-month term as acting attorney general expired in December 1854, Stewart joined a San Francisco law practice that included former Mississippi governor and U.S. senator Henry S. Foote, whose daughter, Annie Elizabeth Foote, Stewart married in 1855. The couple had three daughters. In 1855 former senator Foote attempted to use the new American, or "Know Nothing," party to revive his political career, and Stewart likewise tried to win the nomination for attorney general at the Know Nothings' 1855 state convention. When that effort failed, he returned to Nevada City, reformed his partnership with McConnell, and rejoined the Democrats, with whom he stayed until the Civil War, when pro-Union sentiments led him into the Republicans.

Stewart was meanwhile building a reputation as a formidable mining lawyer. In 1852 he chaired a famous "miners' meeting" in Nevada City that set precedents regarding claims and titles that Stewart would eventually write into federal statute. Between 1855 and 1859 a flourishing practice in Nevada and Sierra counties, California, increased his familiarity with the legal problems and personalities of western mining. The 1859 discovery of Nevada's Comstock Lode drew him to Virginia City, where he emerged as the leading attorney handling the tangled litigation stemming from competing claims. As Stewart believed that mineral development required large-scale enterprise, he identified with his clients, who were generally mining corporations who sought to exclude independent prospectors. Huge in stature and brash and intimidating in the courtroom, Stewart combined expertise and careful research with, in a contemporary's words, a "known determination to win at any cost" (Elliott, p. 20). In his 1908 *Reminiscences*, Stewart acknowledged his part in the audacious manipulation frequent in Comstock courts.

A heavy-handed campaign to unseat territorial justice John Wesley North, whose rulings favored small-scale operators, nearly derailed Stewart's political career. In January 1864 Nevadans defeated a proposed state constitution by a 4–1 margin, in part because they perceived the document, in whose drafting Stewart had been prominent, as a scheme by the "Great Lawyer" and his San Francisco backers to dominate the new state. A regional depression attributed to speculation and wildcat mining soon reconciled many Nevadans to systematic development by California capitalists and redeemed the corporations' inveterate proponent. When Nevada entered the Union in the autumn of 1864, Stewart gained a seat in the U.S. Senate as a Union Republican.

Stewart arrived in Congress during debate over regularizing the West's disparate rules governing access to minerals on public lands. Placed on the Committee on Mines and Mining, Stewart and California Republican John Conness drafted the National Mining Law of 1866, a momentous measure for its embrace of "free mining," which promoted rapid private development with minimal governmental supervision. One of the Republican moderates driven into alliance with the Radicals by President Andrew Johnson's intransigence over Reconstruction, Stewart supported Johnson's impeachment, drafted the Senate version of the Fifteenth Amendment, and sat on the conference committee that decided the amendment's ultimate wording.

In early 1868 Stewart hired Samuel Clemens, an acquaintance from Virginia City, for the botched clerkship immortalized in Mark Twain's "My Late Senatorial Secretaryship" (1868). Stewart played a strategic role in the Gilded Age drive to embellish Washington, D.C., as a staunch backer of Alexander R. Shepherd's 1871–1874 public works program and as a conduit for funds from West Coast investors into District of Columbia real estate, an activity that culminated in the 1890s with his part in the founding of Francis G. Newlands's Chevy Chase Land Development Company.

Difficulties mounted during Stewart's second term. Though ample, his income from the law and investments never kept pace with his expensive life, exemplified by his ornate Dupont Circle mansion known in Washington as "Stewart's Castle." Indebtedness enhanced the penchant for sharp practice that gained Stewart international notoriety in the Emma Mine scandal in which the Nevada senator helped to entice the U.S. minister to Great Britain, Robert C. Schenck, into a scheme to market worthless mining stock to British investors. When the powerful Bank of California official William P. Sharon signaled his ambition for a Nevada Senate seat, the Central Pacific Railroad, a major financial backer of Stewart, withdrew support, despite Stewart's friendship with railroad official Collis P. Huntington. Lacking adequate funds for his reelection fight against Sharon, Stewart withdrew from the 1874 race.

Out of office, Stewart continued to garner healthy attorney's fees, only to lose them in mining promotions. The embarrassing U.S. Senate performances of Sharon and his successor, James G. Fair, another of the mining tycoons known as "Bonanza Kings" who used new wealth to dabble in politics, reconciled old supporters such as the Central Pacific with Stewart. The railroad provided the essential financial and practical support that enabled Stewart to return to the Senate in 1887 after a twelve-year absence.

After his comeback, Stewart displayed his flair for developmental politics. For example, he campaigned to open the resource-rich Walker River Indian Reservation, and he thwarted geologist John Wesley Powell's proposed moratorium on settlement of western lands pending a comprehensive irrigation survey. The hesitant dedication to black suffrage Stewart showed at the time of the Fifteenth Amendment had dissipated by 1890–1891, when he became one of the handful of Republican senators whose defection helped to kill the measure to protect African-American voting in the South known as the Force Bill.

Yet the currency debate dominated Stewart's later career. The Republican equivocation on unlimited coinage of silver was unpopular in mine-dependent Nevada, and Stewart secured reelection in 1893 by aligning with the Nevada Silver party. Despite his ties to the Pacific railroads, he briefly labeled himself a Populist. Stewart tried to overcome such incongruities through polemical speeches and writings that tested Senate colleagues' patience and gained him a reputation as a crank. In 1896 he supported William Jennings Bryan.

In 1899 Congressman Francis G. Newlands, an erstwhile protégé less embroiled in the silver debate, nearly unseated Stewart in an election tainted by charges of corruption. In 1900 Stewart rejoined the Republicans and tried to detach himself from the fading silver issue, but his inability to block Newlands's 1902 Senate election dramatized his declining power. Amid these troubles, Stewart achieved a legal triumph as senior counsel for California's Catholic hierarchy in the Pious Fund case, the first dispute resolved by the Permanent Court of Arbitration in the Hague. His wife died in 1902 in the San Francisco area's first fatal car accident. A year later he married a Georgia widow, May Agnes Atchison Cone.

Nearly eighty when his fifth term ended in 1905, Stewart hoped to resume law practice in Rhyolite, Nevada, but he retired to Washington and was there only a year before he died.

Stewart's career focused on contentious problems of western resource allocation, but he also supported higher education, especially the University of Nevada and Stanford University, of which he was a founding trustee. A memorable, boisterous personality, Stewart symbolized the Far West's advent into national politics.

• Stewart's papers in the Nevada Historical Society, Reno, begin in 1886, omitting the influential early phase of his legal and political career. George Rothwell Brown, ed., *Reminiscences of Senator William M. Stewart of Nevada* (1908), vividly captures this brash character, including his tendency toward amenable interpretations of events. Biographies include Russell R. Elliott's evocative *Servant of Power: A Political Biography of Senator William M. Stewart* (1983). David A. Johnson clarifies Stewart's place in Nevada's push for statehood in essays such as "A Case of Mistaken Identity: William M. Stewart and the Rejection of Nevada's First Constitution," *Nevada Historical Society Quarterly* 22, no. 9 (Fall 1979): 186–98, and "The Courts and the Comstock Lode: The Travail of John Wesley North," *Pacific Historian* 27 (1983): 31–46. William Gillette, *The Right to Vote: Politics and the Passage of the Fifteenth Amendment* (1969), explains Stewart's part in that episode. Alan Lessoff, *The Nation and Its City* (1994), and Kathryn A. Jacob, *Capital Elites* (1995), reveal Stewart's importance to Gilded Age Washington. On Stewart's entanglement with the currency issue, see Mary Ellen Glass, *Silver and Politics in Nevada; 1892–1902* (1969). An obituary is in the *San Francisco Chronicle*, 24 Apr. 1909.

ALAN LESSOFF

ST. GEORGE, Katharine Delano Price Collier (12 July 1894–2 May 1983), congresswoman, was born in Bridgnorth, England, the daughter of Price Collier, an editor, and Katharine Delano. Growing up in the wealthy atmosphere of Tuxedo Park, New York, one of America's first havens for millionaires, Katharine Price Collier knew and enjoyed the advantages of a private education both in the United States and in schools in England, France, Germany, and Switzerland. (Fluent in French, she would later lend her early acquired language skills to the Voice of America during the 1950s.) Upon the death of her father in November 1913, Katharine returned to the United States to complete her schooling. In April 1917 she married

George Baker St. George, who in 1919 became the owner of a coal brokerage firm; the couple had one daughter.

From 1917 to her election to Congress in 1946, St. George raised her daughter and served as a vice president of her husband's business. With her daughter she raised championship English setters and pointers. She also became active in local civic affairs. Beginning in 1926 she was an officer of the local Red Cross chapter and sat on Tuxedo Park's board of education, which repeatedly elected her as president from 1930 to 1946.

Although she was a first cousin of Franklin D. Roosevelt, St. George came from a family that had been Republican for generations. Elected in 1931 to the Tuxedo Park Town Board, she parlayed this assignment into a leadership role in the party as president of the Tuxedo Republican Club and governor of the Woman's National Republican Club. Dropping out of Republican politics during Roosevelt's first two terms as president, St. George believed that family connections transcended politics; however, her cousin's decision to seek a third term spurred St. George's reentry into the political arena, where she remained for the rest of her life. Between 1940 and 1948 St. George served successively as treasurer, vice chairperson, and finally chairperson of the Orange County Republican Committee and was also a delegate to the 1944 Republican National Convention.

In 1944 Hamilton Fish, a longtime friend of the St. Georges, who had represented New York's Twenty-ninth Congressional District for nearly a quarter of a century, lost his seat to Augustus W. Bennet. Soon after Bennet's election, St. George decided to challenge Bennet in the 1946 Republican primary, which she won after campaigning tirelessly for fourteen months. Entertaining small dinner groups and giving countless speeches, St. George mixed easily with both farmers and factory workers, quickly laying to rest any concerns that she understood only the lives of the wealthy. With the Republican establishment behind her, St. George readily defeated her Democratic opponent that fall. Successfully renominated in 1948, she went on to serve nine terms until her defeat in 1964.

St. George was one of only six women sworn in when the Eightieth Congress began its first session in January 1947. A member of the New York State Agricultural Society, she initially hoped to serve on the House Committee on Agriculture because of the prominence of dairy farming in her district. The Military Affairs Committee was also a logical place for St. George since West Point was one of her constituencies, but instead she was appointed to the Post Office and Civil Service Committee. Although not her first choice, she enjoyed her work there, remaining a member for eight of her nine terms. Despite her zealous efforts and previous successes, in 1953 she failed to persuade her colleagues to pass legislation that would have granted the postmaster general, rather than Congress, the authority to increase postal rates.

Other committee appointments for St. George included one term on the Committee on Government

Operations (1953–1955), two terms on the Committee on Armed Services (1957–1961), and finally two terms on the House Rules Committee (1961–1964), where she had the distinction of being the first woman named to that pivotal committee. Such a prestigious appointment was a reward for laboring quietly and effectively in the trenches for seven previous terms.

In addition to her committee service, St. George was always interested in foreign affairs, having spent much time traveling throughout her life. Still she knew her district did not share the same enthusiasm; therefore, at the outset of her congressional career, St. George maintained a staunchly noninterventionist position. As the years passed, however, she steadily took a more active role in international affairs and in her last years in Congress served as president of the bipartisan U.S. Group of the Inter-Parliamentary Union, which sought to improve intergovernmental relations.

During the eighteen years she served in Congress, St. George sponsored numerous pieces of legislation. In deference to her rural constituents, she offered a bill in 1954 to authorize the Defense Department to use surplus butter in military rations and to limit reductions in dairy price supports. During the 1950s St. George proposed bills to establish a federal safety division in the Labor Department, provide a code of ethics for government service, and prohibit Veterans' Administration payments to anyone advocating the overthrow of the U.S. government. Reflecting her conservative Republican views, she also scorned President John F. Kennedy's creation of the Peace Corps by executive decision, an act she declared unconstitutional. On another occasion she declined to support a pay increase for federal workers that was enacted in 1964, believing the federal budget was already large enough.

In general, St. George acted in accordance with her firmly held conservative, pro-business principles. Yet in one area she parted company with many of her stalwart Republican colleagues: equal rights for women. She believed that equal pay was essential to women's successful participation in modern American society. Consequently, in 1950 she crafted a bill that would guarantee equal pay for women. St. George's initial efforts met with little success among her male counterparts, but she managed to keep the issue alive for the rest of her congressional career, and in 1963 the Eighty-eighth Congress finally passed a bill that promised equal pay for women.

In 1964 St. George sought reelection for a tenth term but was defeated when Barry Goldwater's crushing defeat at the polls brought down a host of other Republicans, including a significant portion of the New York congressional delegation. St. George lost by a little more than 6,000 votes to John G. Dow, a liberal Democrat who up until then had not held public office. At age sixty-eight, St. George retired to her home, where she continued to dabble in local politics as chair of the local Republican committee. She remained active in community affairs until her death at home in Tuxedo Park.

The increased activism of women in politics during World War II led to a renewed interest in public service, especially for women of means like St. George who acted on feelings of noblesse oblige. Growing up in a Republican culture, St. George relied on its core beliefs of personal responsibility, limited government, and fiscal austerity as her political compass. For eighteen years she thrived in Congress's male-dominated environment, eventually gaining the trust and admiration of most of her male colleagues.

• St. George's papers are in the Cornell University Archives. For biographical information see Edward B. Lockett, "F. D. R.'s Republican Cousin in Congress," *Collier's*, 19 Aug. 1950, pp. 27, 40, 42, and Alice Fraser, "Two New but Not Too New," *Independent Woman*, Jan. 1947, pp. 2–3. Brief summaries of St. George's career can be found in secondary works. See, for example, Office of the Historian, U.S. House of Representatives, *Women in Congress, 1917–1990* (1991); Rudolf Engelbarts, *Women in the United States Congress, 1917–1972: Their Accomplishments; with Bibliographies* (1974); and Hope Chamberlin, *A Minority of Members: Women in the U.S. Congress* (1973). A brief obituary is in the *New York Times*, 5 May 1983.

EDWARD A. GOEDEKEN

STICKLEY, Gustav (9 Mar. 1858–21 Apr. 1942), cabinetmaker, house designer, and editor, was born in Osceola, Wisconsin, the son of Leopold Stoeckel and Barbara Schlaegel, farmers. Leopold, whose German parents immigrated to Wisconsin early in the nineteenth century, changed the family's name to Stickley. Young Stickley spent most of his childhood on the family farm near Osceola. He did not like the life of a farmer at the time, but he later advocated agrarian ideals, which he felt should be the basis of American family life. In 1870 Stickley's father moved the family to Stillwater, Minnesota, where he took up the trade of stonemason. He apprenticed Gustav to a stonemason, but at age twelve the young boy found the work even more distasteful than farming. Shaping stone, however, did lead Stickley to an appreciation of wood and the ease with which it could be shaped.

Leopold Stickley suddenly abandoned his family sometime in the early 1870s, leaving Gustav to support his mother and ten brothers and sisters. Gustav continued to work for a while as a stonemason but soon got a new job at a sawmill. In 1873 his uncle, Jacob Schlaegel, offered to move the family to Laynesboro, Pennsylvania, and to employ Stickley and his brothers at his chair factory in nearby Brandt. Another Schlaegel uncle, a minister, promised to tutor the Stickley children in the arts and letters, philosophy and religion. Gustav proved particularly good at his studies and especially liked Ralph Waldo Emerson, Henry David Thoreau, and Walt Whitman, all of whom emphasized individual will and the beauty of the natural world. The works of John Ruskin, Thomas Carlyle, and William Morris were most influential on Stickley. Ruskin identified a connection between design and values and developed a political and economic philosophy, emphasizing that the unique character of individual craft labor was more fulfilling than the anonymity of mass-produced goods by assembly workers. Carlyle asserted society's obligation to help the poor and believed that the upper classes must attend to those less fortunate if society were to remain stable and just. Morris was perhaps the most radical in his philosophy. He believed that socialism was the only ethical option left to those who were dismayed by the inequalities and indignities of industrial capitalism. Morris, more than any other designer, sought to forge a moral union between society and the goods it produced by advocating handmade products. Stickley eventually incorporated many of the ideas of all three men into his own philosophy.

Equally important to Stickley's development was the time he spent in his uncle's chair factory learning the art of woodworking. Stickley delighted in this work, finally finding a manual labor that suited his disposition and his creative impulses. He was a talented woodworker and a good if sometimes imperious manager. In four short years he moved from assembly worker to foreman of the company.

In 1883 Stickley married Eda Ann Simmons; they had five daughters and one son. In 1884 Stickley moved the family to Binghamton, New York, where he opened a chair factory in partnership with his brothers. In 1888 Stickley left his brothers and took a job with the city of Binghamton in developing an electric railway system. In 1890 he became vice president of the Binghamton Street Railway but left soon afterward to begin a furniture manufacturing company with Elgin A. Simonds in Auburn, New York. Stickley also worked as director of manufacturing operations at the New York State Prison in Auburn between 1892 and 1894 in order to raise more capital for the Stickley and Simonds Company. It was at this job that Stickley had the dubious distinction of designing the state's first chair used in the electrical execution of inmates. In 1892 the Stickley and Simonds Company moved to Eastwood, New York, and began making reproductions of Chippendale and Louis XIV style furniture. Stickley traveled to Syracuse frequently on business, and in 1894 he and his family settled in that city. Stickley never forgot the simple lines and hand production of the furniture he saw in the Shaker community of New Lebanon, New York. Influenced by Morris's writings, Stickley traveled to Europe in 1898 to meet with the artists working there in the Arts and Crafts movement.

Stickley returned to the United States determined to change the way Americans ordered their domestic lives. Like Morris, he was convinced that good design executed with hand labor would be morally uplifting and instructing. Stickley took as his model the English Arts and Crafts movement, including Morris's spiritual group and its commercial component, Morris, Marshall and Company. Other parallel arts and crafts schools, including the Pre-Raphaelite Brotherhood, the Century Guild, the Art Workers Guild, and the Handicraft Guild, also shaped Stickley's views about the nature of art and its place in society. Stickley began designing and producing what he called Craftsman furniture, which stood in stark contrast to the Victorian furniture still in vogue. Craftsman furniture had rectangular lines, simple finishes, and utilitarian fabrics. In 1900 he exhibited the Craftsman line at a furniture exhibition in Grand Rapids, Michigan. The new style quickly became popular, and Stickley expanded his Eastwood factory to produce handmade metal work, textiles, leather, and other home furnishings. He called the Eastwood complex the Craftsman Workshop and promoted its products as the result of his design philosophy.

Stickley's philosophy gained expression in his magazine, the *Craftsman*, which he first published in October 1901. The first issue of the *Craftsman* was devoted to Morris, "the patron saint of 'integral education' from the different points of view of art, socialism, business affairs and friendship." Stickley later summed up his vision for the *Craftsman* when he said, "Through these articles it was hoped to combat the spirit of commercialism which is the worst peril of our prosperous new century."

Stickley's ambition for reforming the way Americans lived and worked led him to form the Craftsman Home Builder's Club, which provided free information on "well-built, democratic, well-planned homes." Mail-order firms such as Sears, Roebuck and Company, helped popularize the Craftsman Home by selling complete house kits to do-it-yourself home builders. Stickley published two volumes of house plans, *Craftsman Homes* (1909) and *More Craftsman Homes* (1912).

Stickley's ideas were closely allied with those of the early twentieth-century progressives who worked for reforms in business and society to promote healthy working and living environments for families. In keeping with the progressive mindset, Stickley sought to establish a profit-sharing collective of all furniture manufacturers, which he called United Crafts. This union would have fulfilled the economic and political implications of his early design philosophy, but several deals he struck to accomplish this goal came to naught. Instead, Stickley took more control over his increasingly popular furniture business, eventually overextending himself. In March 1915 he filed for bankruptcy, and the *Craftsman* merged with the Art Society of America's *Art World*, which emphasized antique, European designs.

The world that Stickley envisioned was doomed by technological advances in the early twentieth century that radically changed the way Americans lived. The harnessing of electricity in particular offered unprecedented opportunities for new home designs and furnishings. This new wave of industrialism carried a buoyant optimism in its wake. No longer nostalgic for a simpler past, Americans were ready to plunge into a new century confident in the belief that industrial capitalism offered an easier life for everyone. Stickley was not prepared for these changes.

By the early 1920s Stickley and Craftsman were no longer household words. Stickley receded into obscurity and died at his daughter's home in Syracuse, New York. By all accounts Stickley was a warm, personable man with a missionary's zeal for his beliefs. If his actions or business dealings seemed contradictory to his writings, it was because his philosophy was and always would be profoundly at odds with modern capitalism.

Stickley was the most important proponent of American Arts and Crafts. His dedication to his craftsmanship garnered respect and trust among colleagues as well as customers. His prominence cannot be underestimated when considering the Arts and Crafts movement in the United States. Stickley and his designs enjoyed a revival during the late 1970s and early 1980s as Americans, disillusioned with modern synthetic materials, turned once again to the simple lines and natural materials of the craftsman style. However, this revival carried none of the philosophical underpinnings that Stickley emphasized as fundamental to his aesthetic, and therefore it should not be seen as a continuation of the Arts and Crafts tradition. Renewed interest in Stickley caused the republication of the *Craftsman, Craftsman Homes*, and Stickley's catalogs, all of which led scholars to reconsider Stickley and his legacy.

• A collection of Stickley's furniture and some papers are at the Henry Ford Museum, Dearborn, Mich. Some Stickley papers are at the Winterthur Museum, Winterthur, Del. Stickley's early life is a source of some speculation, with many of the details coming from reminiscences of family members. A critical biography is Barry Sanders, *A Complex Fate: Gustav Stickley and the Craftsman Movement* (1996). See also Wendy Kaplan, *"The Art That is Life": The Arts and Crafts Movement in America, 1875–1920* (1987); Mary Ann Smith, *Gustav Stickley, the Craftsman* (1983); Joseph Bavaro and Thomas Mossman, *The Furniture of Gustav Stickley: History, Techniques, Projects* (1982); and John Crosby Freeman, *The Forgotten Rebel: Gustav Stickley and His Craftsman Mission Furniture* (1966). An obituary is in the *New York Times*, 22 Apr. 1942.

CLIFTON C. ELLIS

STICKNEY, Alpheus Beede (27 June 1840–9 Aug. 1916), lawyer and railroad executive, was born in Wilton, Franklin County, Maine, the son of Daniel Stickney, a farmer and occasional Universalist preacher, and Ursula Maria Beede. Stickney's childhood was marred by poverty. His father relocated the family twice before 1850, only to abandon them. Stickney was forced to assist his mother in factory piecework in order to make ends meet. At the instigation of an uncle, his mother relocated with her children to Carroll County, New Hampshire, in 1850, and for the following six years "A.B.," as he insisted on being called, alternated factory work with intermittent sessions at local public schools. In 1856 he began attending a Freewill Baptist academy in New Hampshire, occasionally interrupting his education with teaching stints in local schools to support himself. After returning to Maine in 1858, he attended another academy, taught some more, and eventually began legal studies in the office of Josiah Crosby in Dexter, Maine.

Finding only limited prospects for advancement in Maine, Stickney followed the lead of a brother and relocated in Minnesota in June 1861. Possessing little in the way of financial resources and still searching for a suitable career, he settled in the St. Croix River community of Stillwater and worked briefly as a postal clerk before taking a teaching position in the local public schools. Stickney gained admittance to the Washington County, Minnesota, bar in 1862, and after a brief and unhappy stint as the editor of the *Stillwater Messenger*, he turned his attention toward law and land speculation. With prospects brightening in 1863, he married Kate W. H. Hall; they had seven children.

Sensing greater opportunities in the state capital, Stickney moved to St. Paul in 1869. In 1871 he entered the field in which he would make his greatest mark, railroading, by assisting in the organization of the North Wisconsin Railway Company. Although the small line never proved profitable and Stickney disposed of his holdings in 1873, his experience with the line convinced him that vast profits were to be made in railroading. In 1872 he became vice president, general manager, and chief counsel of the newly formed St. Paul, Stillwater & Taylor's Falls Railroad Company and deepened his commitment to local railroad construction by organizing the St. Croix Railway & Improvement Company in the same year.

Stickney's career as a railroad builder entered a new realm when he accepted an invitation from James J. Hill, the leading railroad figure in the upper Midwest, to serve as construction superintendent of the St. Paul, Minneapolis & Manitoba Railway in 1879. The following year he added the duties of general superintendent of the western division of the Canadian Pacific Railroad, another of Hill's projects. While employed by the Canadian Pacific, Stickney became involved in a controversy over a conflict of interest regarding land speculation along the route. Although accused of improperly taking advantage of real estate transactions for personal profit, he managed to maintain his position after convincing Hill of his innocence.

No doubt eager to leave the controversy behind him, Stickney returned to St. Paul as the vice president of the Minneapolis & St. Louis Railway Company in 1881. His duties there were broad and included supervision of a subsidiary line, the Minnesota Central, but Stickney yearned to run his own railroad. In 1883 he resigned from the Minneapolis & St. Louis, and in the fall of that year he became president of the Minnesota & Northwestern Railroad. Backed by a group of English and American investors, the line connected St. Paul with Chicago and soon extended its operations to St. Joseph and Kansas City, Missouri, by way of acquisitions—the Wisconsin, Iowa & Nebraska Railway, which operated between Waterloo and Des Moines, Iowa—as well as new construction and the leasing of existing properties. After the assets of the Minnesota & Northwestern were transferred to the new Chicago, St. Paul & Kansas City Railway in 1887, Stickney served as president of that line as well.

Stickney headed the Chicago, St. Paul & Kansas City until 1892, when following another reorganization he became the chairman of the board of the Chicago Great Western Railway. Becoming president of the line in 1894, he made his greatest mark in the railroad business at its helm. He made effective use of construction syndicates, most notably the Minnesota Loan & Debenture Company, to expand the Chicago Great Western's lines and maintain company profitability. A warm and loving husband and father, he extended this facet of his personality into relations with his employees. With a paternalistic approach to labor relations, he instituted a profit-sharing plan for workers in the 1890s that was years ahead of its time, and he maintained an ongoing concern for safety in the workplace. Stickney underwrote the construction of Liberty Hall, a recreational center at the Chicago Great Western's new machine shop complex in Oelwein, Iowa, in 1898, noting at the time, "It is better to have men reading and talking than drinking and whoring." His efforts at employee relations paid off. The line suffered little work disruption, and workers often referred to their workplace as "the Stickney."

Stickney's efforts to ensure traffic for his line extended beyond internal operations. Recognizing the need to maintain agricultural shipping, he tirelessly promoted scientific agriculture in the region and encouraged additional settlers to relocate to the upper Midwest. He was also a leading figure in establishing the St. Paul stockyards in 1882 and the Omaha Grain Exchange, which soon helped make Omaha the nation's fourth largest grain market.

While respected by his peers as a shrewd and forceful operator, Stickney was best known for his differences with other railroad men in terms of public policy. Interested in statistical data and its applications to business, he made extensive use of business records in developing operational and maintenance policies at Chicago Great Western. Again ahead of his time, he often faced internal opposition to his policies. He argued against the current practice of raising capital through bond sales and for the expansion of railroad capital through stock sales. Stickney's most controversial stance was his endorsement of federal railroad regulation. In *The Railway Problem* (1891), he urged the implementation of a national rate schedule based on the type of commodity being shipped and average terminal and line-haul expenses. While his plea for a rate schedule that was fair to both shippers and stockholders played well with reformers at the dawn of the Progressive Era, rival railroad owners suspected him of seeking an edge for his highly competitive route between Chicago and the Twin Cities. Even his old associate Hill, who bitterly opposed federal intervention, told him, "If you had my railroad [the massive Great Northern], I would expect you to have my thoughts."

Controversy continued to dog Stickney in his later years. He resigned the presidency of the Chicago Great Western in 1900 but remained chairman of the board until 1908. In the wake of the panic of 1907, the line was forced into receivership, and Stickney served as a coreceiver of the railroad for a few months before retiring to his summer residence in White Bear Lake, Minnesota. In 1909 he charged that the industry had reverted to its old and ruinous practice of issuing extensive rebates to favored shippers, leading to an investigation by the Interstate Commerce Commission. Stickney presented a proposal before the commission for rate law reforms that would have made such practices impossible and outlined his ideas in *Railway Rates* (1909).

Stickney's first wife died in December 1899. In 1901 he married Mary Crosby, the daughter of his old law preceptor. They had no children. In addition to his business activities, he served for many years on the St. Paul Park Commission and was a founder of the St. Paul Metropolitan Opera House. He died at his home in St. Paul.

Stickney rose from a childhood of poverty to the status of self-made millionaire by hard work and opportunistic risk taking. He made notable achievements in upbuilding several railroads and the upper Midwest, and he pioneered the use of hard historical data in business planning and development, which became commonplace. He was often at odds with fellow railroad men regarding the issues of government regulation and competition, but many of his ideas later proved valuable in an industry increasingly forced to deal with federal regulation of its operations.

• Stickney's papers are at the Minnesota Historical Society, St. Paul, Minn. In addition to the texts mentioned previously, Stickney also authored *The Economic Problems Involved in the Election of 1896* (1896), *The Defects of the Interstate Commerce Law* (1905), and *Shall Theoretical and Practical Agriculture and the Physical Development of Childhood Be Added to the Curriculum of the City Public Schools?* (1910). The best secondary scholarship on Stickney is H. Roger Grant, *The Corn Belt Route: A History of the Great Western Railroad Company* (1984) and "A. B. Stickney and James J. Hill: The Railroad Relationship," *Railroad History* 146 (Spring 1982): 9–22. Obituaries are in the *St. Paul Dispatch*, 9 Aug. 1916, and the *New York Times*, 10 Aug. 1916.

EDWARD L. LACH, JR.

STICKNEY, Trumbull (20 June 1874–11 Oct. 1904), poet, was born Joseph Trumbull Stickney in Geneva, Switzerland, the son of Austin Stickney, a classics scholar, and Harriet Champion Trumbull. Apart from periods spent in New York City or Connecticut (Hartford was the family home) in 1879–1881, 1886–1888, and 1890–1891, the family lived in various locations in Europe throughout Stickney's childhood. The pattern of incessantly moving instilled in Stickney a sense of rootlessness, though it also allowed him splendid educational opportunities. According to most sources, his father educated him at home; but his biographer, Sean Haldane, documents the role of various governesses during his childhood.

In September 1891 Stickney entered Harvard College, where he studied the classics and began to learn Sanskrit (initiating a lifelong interest in Indian philosophy). He acted in student plays and contributed poetry, essays, and short stories to the *Harvard Monthly*, a student literary magazine. Friends included aspiring poets William Vaughn Moody and George Cabot

Lodge. Stickney graduated in June 1895 with honors and the following fall enrolled at the University of Paris.

Stickney lived in Paris for the next eight years. He distressed his family by what they suspected to be a wild lifestyle; however, despite evidence of various romantic relationships, in particular with Elizabeth Cameron, friend and beloved of Henry Adams, he seems to have lived circumspectly as he pursued classical studies at the University of Paris. In 1902 he published *Dramatic Verses* in a limited edition. In 1903 he earned the first doctorate in literature ever granted by the Sorbonne to an American. For this degree he wrote a short thesis in Latin and a long thesis in French, "Les Sentences dans la Poésie Grecque d'Homère à Euripides."

During the summer of 1903 Stickney traveled in Greece, then returned to the United States in September to become an instructor of Greek at Harvard. In early 1904 he began to develop headaches and other symptoms of what proved to be a tumor of the brain. Stickney, who had once remarked to Moody that he cared for "nothing but poetry," continued to work on poems during his last months, even after he became blind. He died in Boston and was buried in Hartford.

Stickney's quietly charismatic personality attracted a range of friends from Henry Adams and George Santayana to contemporaries such as Lodge and Moody and those younger than himself, such as his Harvard students and Shane Leslie. Some of his friends were concerned by his tendency toward depression. "Joe has become and is terribly, cynically hopeless," Lodge commented in a letter he wrote in 1896 (quoted in Haldane, p. 71); and Moody's memorial essay referred to Stickney's sense of "a nameless oppression, a sense of the futility of the worldly outcome" (p. 1018). Santayana believed that although Stickney's decision to return to the United States in 1903 indicated a shift in "allegiance from classic antiquity . . . closer to the groping mind of our day, to the common people, and to the problem of America," life in the United States was a shock to him, and the change of cultural climate bred the brain tumor that killed him (quoted in Haldane, pp. 175–76).

However that may be, Stickney's poetry is strongly colored by the struggle against despair:

Leave him now quiet by the way
To rest apart.
I know what draws him to the dust alway
And churns him in the builder's lime:
He has the fright of time.

I heard it knocking in his breast
A minute since;
His human eyes did wince,
He stubborned like the massive slaughter beast
And as a thing o'erwhelmed with sound
Stood bolted to the ground. (*Poems*, p. 167)

The sonnet "Near Helikon" describes an idyllic landscape, which then reminds the poet of his own life:

To me my troubled life doth now appear
Like scarce distinguishable summits hung
Around the blue horizon: places where
Not even a traveller purposeth to steer,—
Whereof a migrant bird in passing sung,
And the girl closed her window not to hear.
(*Poems*, p. 171)

His final illness may have deepened, but it did not cause this tendency to despair. Several of his later poems, nevertheless, refer precisely to a turmoil in his mind, most notably the following fragment:

Sir, say no more.
Within me 't is as if
The green and climbing eyesight of a cat
Crawled near my mind's poor birds. (*Poems*, p. 264)

Stickney was virtually unknown during his lifetime. The memorial volume edited by Lodge, Moody, and John Ellerton Lodge in 1905 did not generate public enthusiasm, and Stickney's poetry was largely ignored until Conrad Aiken included him in his 1929 anthology *American Poetry 1671–1928*, announcing that in doing so he was trying to "disturb prevailing notions . . . and set in motion a revaluation of American poetry" (p. vii). Stickney has often been anthologized since but remains on the edge of the American literary canon.

Stickney's interest in drama led him to write verse plays, play fragments, and dramatic monologues. Friends like Moody valued the dramatic poems highly, but most readers have preferred his shorter lyrics. The general though not unanimous critical opinion is that Stickney wrote magnificent passages but few successful whole poems. Two more recent poets have in effect supported this view by writing poems, deeply felt acts of homage, which take their inspiration from brief passages of Stickney's poems and build their own structures on the fragments: James Dickey's "Exchanges: Being in the Form of a Dialogue with Joseph Trumbull Stickney" (1971) and John Hollander's "Variations on a Fragment by Trumbull Stickney" in his *Tesserae and Other Poems* (1993).

Stickney remains a significant force in American literary culture. His membership in the "lost generation" of the 1890s (writers who died young, such as Lodge and Moody, Stephen Crane, and Frank Norris) accounts for some of the interest in him. But he did leave a substantial group of powerful if uneven poems, and what he accomplished in his thirty years fully explains the response of Edwin Arlington Robinson upon hearing of his death: "We could not afford to lose him" (quoted in Whittle, *Trumbull Stickney*, p. 34).

• Manuscript drafts of *Dramatic Verses* are at the Houghton Library at Harvard; Stickney manuscripts, relevant letters by George Cabot Lodge, and an unpublished memoir by Lodge are in the Lodge papers at the Massachusetts Historical Society. The most complete and accessible volume of Stickney's poetry is *The Poems of Trumbull Stickney*, ed. Amberys R. Whittle (1972); this volume, based mainly on the 1905 *Poems of Trumbull Stickney*, contains a foreword by Edmund Wilson that reprints Wilson's influential essay "The Country I Remember," *New Republic*, 14 Oct. 1940, pp. 529–30. The fullest anthology collection is John Hollander, ed., *American Poetry: The Nineteenth Century*, vol. 2 (1993). A full-length biography is Sean Haldane, *The Fright of Time: Joseph Trumbull Stickney 1874–1904* (1970), which relies heavily on Stickney's letters to his favorite sister, Lucy; the chapter "Stickney's Poetry, 1905–1970" reviews critical commentaries and selections in anthologies. A full-length critical study is Whittle, *Trumbull Stickney* (1973); arguing that Stickney is not a representative poet of his time, Whittle emphasizes his use of landscape and the theme of time. This study includes a bibliography of works by and about Stickney, to which should be added A. H. Griffing, "The Achievement of Trumbull Stickney," *New England Quarterly* 46 (1973): 106–12, and Ross C. Murfin, "The Poetry of Trumbull Stickney," *New England Quarterly* 48 (1975): 540–55. Accounts by those who knew him include William Vaughn Moody, "The Poems of Trumbull Stickney," *North American Review* 183 (1906): 1005–18, and Henry Adams, *The Life of George Cabot Lodge* (1911).

DAVID BARBER

STIEGEL, Henry William (13 May 1729–10 Jan. 1785), glassmaker and iron founder, was born in Cologne, Germany, the son of John Frederick Stiegel and Dorothea Elizabeth (maiden name unknown). After the death of his father, Stiegel came to America with his mother and a younger brother, arriving on 31 August 1750 in Philadelphia. Stiegel married Elizabeth Huber in 1752. She was the daughter of Jacob Huber, owner of the Elizabeth Furnace in Lancaster, Pennsylvania, one of the most significant and long-standing iron foundries in eighteenth-century America. Stiegel apparently learned the ironmaking trade from his father-in-law and took over management of the operation in 1757. Henry and Elizabeth had two children before her death in February 1758. He married Elizabeth Hölz in October 1758; they had one child.

Into the 1770s Stiegel ran Elizabeth Furnace and pursued other ironmaking interests as well. Although tradition often refers to him as "Baron Stiegel," perhaps because it has been asserted (probably apocryphally) that some of his iron stoves bear the cast inscription "Baron Stiegel ist der Mann / Der die Oefen giessen kann" (Baron Stiegel is the cove / That can cast your iron stove), there is no evidence that Stiegel was of noble or aristocratic birth. In the *Pennsylvania Chronicle* for 27 March 1769, he advertised "Iron Castings, Of all dimensions and sizes, such as kettles or boilers for pot-ash works, soap-boilers pans, pots from a barrel to 300 gallons, ship cabooses, kachels and sugar-house stoves, with cast funnels of any height for refining sugars, weights of all sizes, grate bars, and other castings for sugar works in the West Indies, &c." While many of his products were of a strictly functional nature, his stoves are among the masterpieces of the rococo style in America.

Stiegel's glassmaking ventures began in 1763, when he was a principal proprietor in the settlement of the town of Manheim, Pennsylvania, in conjunction with Charles and Alexander Stedman, merchants from Philadelphia who had helped Stiegel purchase Elizabeth Furnace earlier. Stiegel hired away several glassblowers, including Martin Greiner, an experienced craftsman who had been working in New York, Christian Nassel, who worked for Caspar Wistar, Christian Gratinger, and Jacob Halder, and glassmaking began in the fall of 1764. The *Pennsylvania Gazette* for 7 February 1765 noted that "the Glass-house, . . . erected in the Town of Manheim, is now compleatly finished, and the Business of Glass-making in it carried on; where all Persons may be suited in the best Manner, with any Sort of Glass, according to their Order."

Stiegel produced wares in the Germanic tradition, such as green glass bottles, window glass, tablewares, and chemical wares, during the first five years of operation. After the passage of the Townshend Acts and the resulting nonimportation agreements by American merchants, Stiegel expanded his production, modified his wares to suit the Anglo-American taste, and fashioned more sophisticated tablewares of better quality in order to take advantage of the expanded colonial market. He built a new factory, the American Flint Glass Manufactory, in 1769, hired English glassblowers and decorators, and produced colorful engraved and pattern-molded wares of lead and soda-lime glass. He argued in the *Pennsylvania Journal* for 5 July 1770, "As the proprietors have been at an immense expence in erecting said works, and engaging some of the most ingenious artists in said manufacture, which is now arrived at great perfection, and above all, at this crisis it is the indispensable duty, as well as interest of every real well wisher of America, to promote and encourage manufactures amongst ourselves, . . . which they expect to merit a continuance of, by selling their goods on much lower terms, than such imported from Europe are usually sold." By 1772 Stiegel was selling, in common, enameled, and other forms, an extensive variety of decanters, tumblers, wine glasses, syllabub cups, jellies, smelling bottles, salts, cruets, creampots, inkstands, flowerpots, candlesticks, and a "great variety of glasses, too tedious" to mention (*Pennsylvania Gazette*, 4 June 1772).

Despite a vigorous marketing effort, promoted by a wide advertising campaign in Pennsylvania, New York, Massachusetts, and Maryland and encouraged by Stiegel's influential friend John Dickinson, Stiegel became overextended financially and ultimately failed. His glass factory closed on 5 May 1774, and he was sent to debtor's prison in Philadelphia.

Stiegel's last years are not well documented. Once freed from prison, he was virtually destitute and traveled from place to place in eastern Pennsylvania, working at various jobs in Reading Furnaces, Schaefferstown, and elsewhere. He eventually was taken in by his relative George Ege in Charming Forge, an ironmaking operation once owned by Stiegel, where he died.

An immigrant of apocryphal aristocratic lineage and an energetic self-promoter, Stiegel lived a rags-to-riches-to-rags life that has made him, with the help of his biographers, one of the most colorful and romantic figures in the annals of American craftsmen. As one of the three principal glass manufacturers in eighteenth-century America (Wistar and John Frederick Amelung being the other two) and the first to produce sophisticated tablewares nearly equal to English glass in quality and style, and as a manufacturer of ornate cast-iron wares in the rococo taste, Stiegel had great importance in the rise of American manufacturing. He imported technological skills and design influences from abroad and participated in the proliferation of domestic wares that made up what historians increasingly call the consumer revolution of the eighteenth century. Stiegel's glass was very similar in material and appearance to contemporary English and European glass, and the process of identifying Stiegel glass has occupied scholars for much of this century. Much painted glass in the Germanic (or "Pennsylvania Dutch") style, for example, was once attributed to Stiegel, but it is now known that Stiegel did not produce objects of this type. Despite his successes, Stiegel's difficulties with raw materials for his glass and wood for his kilns, and his customers' abiding preference for English wares, ultimately doomed his efforts to failure.

• Fifteen volumes of Stiegel's accounts are in the Historical Society of Pennsylvania, Philadelphia, and, along with his many newspaper advertisements and surviving works, are the basis of scholarship on his life and work. Many authors reprint one or more of Stiegel's newspaper advertisements; several of them are conveniently collected in Alfred Coxe Prime, comp., *The Arts and Crafts in Philadelphia, Maryland, and South Carolina, 1721–1785* (1929). The classic study of Stiegel, now seriously outdated but nevertheless essential, is Frederick William Hunter, *Stiegel Glass* (1914; repr. 1950). This work remains useful from a biographical and historiographical standpoint and contains a helpful chronological bibliography of early works on Stiegel, but its analysis of Stiegel's glassmaking and glass needs to be understood in the light of more recent scholarship and connoisseurship, which has backed away from some of Hunter's more over-ambitious attributions. Particularly helpful are George S. McKearin and Helen McKearin, *American Glass* (1941), who coined the term "Stiegel-type" to more accurately reflect the situation, and the same authors' *Two Hundred Years of American Blown Glass* (1950). The most sophisticated work on Stiegel is by Arlene Palmer: see her "Pennsylvania German Glass," in *Arts of the Pennsylvania Germans*, ed. Catherine E. Hutchins (1983), pp. 200–210; "'To the Good of the Province and Country': Henry William Stiegel and American Flint Glass," in *The American Craftsman and the European Tradition, 1620–1820*, ed. Francis J. Puig and Michael Conforti (1989); and the relevant sections of her *Glass in Early America* (1993). See also Henry Chapman Mercer, *The Bible in Iron: Pictured Stoves and Stoveplates of the Pennsylvania Germans*, 3d ed. (1961), and Morrison H. Heckscher and Leslie Greene Bowman, *American Rococo, 1750–1775: Elegance in Ornament* (1992). Stiegel glass and iron is included in many collections, including that of the Winterthur Museum, Winterthur, Del., and the Metropolitan Museum of Art, New York City.

GERALD W. R. WARD

STIEGLITZ, Alfred (1 Jan. 1864–13 July 1946), photographer and editor, was born in Hoboken, New Jersey, the son of Edward (originally Ephraim) Stieglitz, a German-born wool merchant, and Hedwig Werner. Stieglitz grew up in an affluent, cultured family who felt at home on two continents. After his family moved to New York City, Alfred was educated at the Charlier Institute, Townsend Harris High School, and the City College of New York, where he was ranked consistently as one of the top ten students in his class. By 1881 his father, a Civil War veteran, had made a fortune that enabled him to retire and take his family to Europe, where he provided his children the best possible continental education.

In the fall of 1881 Stieglitz enrolled at the Realgymnasium in Karlsruhe, Germany, and in October 1882 he entered the Berlin Royal Technical High School, or Königliche Technische Hochschule, to study mechanical engineering, also auditing a physics course at the University of Berlin. An indifferent engineering student except for his flair for mathematics, Stieglitz much preferred music, literature, and art to what he considered the dull, incomprehensible lectures in science and technology.

Sometime after October 1882 and before the academic year of 1885 (his own accounts vary about the exact date), Stieglitz started experimenting with his first camera. He soon began to study photography and photochemistry with Hermann Vogel, a member of the faculty at the Technische Hochschule and an international expert on the technical aspects and scientific applications of photography. Stieglitz quickly became Vogel's laboratory assistant, helping his professor carry out his pioneering experiments with night photography, color photography, and other potential innovations. Under Vogel's direction, Stieglitz was immediately enthralled, and photography dominated his interest, his education, and his life from that point onward. Now science and engineering courses served a compelling purpose—to help him understand and manipulate the camera and the darkroom so that he could create beautiful photographs.

Stieglitz carried his camera everywhere, and during summer vacations he took walking tours of Europe, photographing landscapes and people at every turn. By 1885 he had withdrawn as a full-time student to concentrate on his own experiments in photography, and he began to write articles for German photography journals. In 1887, when Stieglitz was twenty-three, he won the first of his more than 150 prizes in photography, this initial medal in a competition sponsored by the prestigious London *Amateur Photographer*. Soon afterward, journals of photography in England and Germany began to publish his photographic prints.

Stieglitz was deeply influenced by a journey in 1889 to an international photography exhibition in Vienna, where he first encountered the work of leading nineteenth-century photographers such as William Henry Fox Talbot, Louis-Jacques-Mandé Daguerre, and Julia Margaret Cameron. He began what would be a lifelong crusade, as he himself described it, "for the recognition of photography as a new medium of expression, to be respected in its own right, on the same basis as any other art form" (Norman, p. 6). His father, however, had other plans for his son. Although Edward Stieglitz loved art and was an amateur painter as well as a serious collector and patron of art, he viewed it as an avocation, not a profession. In 1890 the elder Stieglitz summoned his son home from Europe; it was time for him to settle down, take a responsible job, and begin to look for a wife.

Subsidized by his father, Stieglitz went into business with two friends, buying a photoengraving firm in New York and converting it into the Photochrome Engraving Company. But he was a halfhearted businessman, devoting most of his prodigious energy to his own photography instead. In 1893 Stieglitz become an editor of *American Amateur Photographer*. By the time he was thirty, he had become the most visible American proponent of photography as an art form, and not only had he staged exhibitions of avant-garde photography but he was also called on to organize overseas exhibitions of American photography.

In 1893 Stieglitz fulfilled his parents' hopes that he would settle down to family life by marrying Emmeline Obermeyer, the sister of his wealthy business partner Joseph Obermeyer, whose family fortune grew out of their brewery business. The union proved fortuitous because Edward Stieglitz lost a major part of his own fortune in the panic of 1893 and ensuing depression. By 1895 Stieglitz had retired from the Photochrome Engraving Company, no longer able to draw on his father's financial support for the faltering business. From this time on, largely supported by his wife's income, he devoted his full energy to photography.

In 1896 Stieglitz gave up his editorial role at *American Amateur Photographer* and helped to merge the memberships of the Society of Amateur Photographers of New York and the New York Camera Club into the new Camera Club of New York, of which he quickly became a leader. Intensely interested in faithfully reproducing artistic photographs, Stieglitz founded *Camera Notes* in 1897 as the official publication of the Camera Club of New York. He edited the landmark quarterly journal until 1902, in the process frequently provoking contention and controversy as well as the enmity of more conservative members of the club. *Camera Notes* served as Stieglitz's personal podium in his campaign to establish pictorial photography as a legitimate art form.

In the first issue, Stieglitz articulated his mission to recognize "what is going on in the photographic world at large, to review new processes and consider new instruments and agents as they come into notice; in short, to keep our members in touch with everything connected with the progress and elevation of photography" (*Camera Notes*, July 1897). Stieglitz was a demanding and masterful editor, filling his pages with beautiful photogravure and halftone reproductions of images by the era's greatest photographers, including J. Craig Annan, Fred Holland Day, Rudolf Eickemeyer, Jr., Frank Eugene, Gertrude Käsebier, Clarence H. White, Eduard (later Edward) Steichen, and Stieglitz himself. He also published lively, intelligent reviews and essays on photography by critics such as Sa-

dakichi Hartmann, Charles H. Caffin, Dallett Fuguet, William M. Murray, and Joseph T. Keiley.

Stieglitz's only child, Katharine, was born in 1898, but by then his home life was relegated to a distant second place behind his photography. In addition to his work on *Camera Notes*, Stieglitz continued to produce his own photographs, unmatched in their technical purity. In 1899 a one-man show of eighty-seven prints at the Camera Club of New York displayed the range of the work he had achieved since 1885. By the turn of the century Stieglitz was probably the best-known, most-honored photographer in the world, hailed in the United States and in Europe for innovations such as his successful experiments in night photography and glycerine-platinum printing, especially in his striking portraiture and his luminous Manhattan cityscapes.

Almost belligerently self-assured, Stieglitz grew even more authoritative and demanding as his success grew; furthermore, he seemed to thrive on controversy. In 1902, after a long series of conflicts with members of the Camera Club of New York, Stieglitz resigned from *Camera Notes*. (Expelled from the Camera Club in 1908, he won reinstatement later, then resigned permanently.) At the same time he orchestrated an exhibition, American Pictorial Photography, held at the National Arts Club of New York and announced that it presented the works of the Photo-Secession, a term inspired by the secessionist groups of artists in Europe who broke away from conventional art movements. In 1903 he and the young photographer and painter Edward Steichen and a few others began to lay plans for what would become the full-fledged Photo-Secession group of photographers. An essential component of their plan was a permanent gallery where advanced photographers could display their work and where modern paintings, drawings, and sculpture might also be exhibited.

The Photo-Secession needed a journal and a home, Stieglitz believed. The journal that he christened *Camera Work* first appeared in January 1903, beginning where *Camera Notes* had ended but quickly surpassing that periodical with its excellent reproductions of photographs, drawings, and paintings and its provocative essays and reviews. Over the years *Camera Work* published images by Stieglitz, Steichen, Auguste Rodin, Henri Matisse, Pablo Picasso, and a host of other photographers, painters, and artists. George Bernard Shaw wrote for the journal, as did Rodin, Maurice Maeterlinck, H. G. Wells, and Gertrude Stein, in her first publication in the United States. Stieglitz edited, produced, and often paid for the publication of *Camera Work* from the first issue in 1903 until the last one in 1917.

Stieglitz and Steichen found their headquarters in 1905 at 291 Fifth Avenue on the top floor of a brownstone where Steichen had his first studio in New York. There they established the historic small gallery that came to be known as the Little Galleries of the Photo-Secession, or simply as "291." The Stieglitz-Steichen collaboration gave some of the major modern artists of Europe and the United States their first exhibitions in

New York. Steichen, who lived and worked in France from 1906 to 1914, introduced Stieglitz to some of the leading artists of the day, including Picasso, Matisse, sculptor Constantin Brancusi, and the American painters Max Weber, John Marin, Alfred Maurer, and Arthur Carles. He also introduced Stieglitz to the drawings of Rodin and the impressionist paintings of Paul Cézanne. At 291, Stieglitz and Steichen mounted the first American exhibitions of Rodin's drawings (1908); Matisse's watercolors, drawings, and etchings (1908); Marin's watercolors (1909); Henri de Toulouse-Lautrec's lithographs (1909); Jean-Jacques Rousseau's oils and drawings (1910); Cézanne's watercolors (1911); Picasso's drawings and watercolors (1911); and Matisse's sculptures—his first sculpture exhibition anywhere (1912).

This farsighted affirmation of modern art filled the walls of the Little Galleries of the Photo-Secession as much as five years before the International Exhibition of Modern Art in 1913—the celebrated Armory Show that has traditionally been credited with introducing the work of the European avant-garde to the American public. With Steichen's help, Stieglitz proved to be a pathfinder in modern painting as well as modern photography, whose cause he had greatly advanced in 1910 when he successfully organized the massive International Exhibition of Pictorial Photography at the Albright Art Gallery in Buffalo, New York. There he put together the most extensive display of American photography in history, augmented by the best work of photographers from Europe. Although Stieglitz served as an honorary vice president of the Armory Show, he had little involvement in it, but he did simultaneously offer a retrospective exhibition of his photographs at 291—the only one-man show he ever granted himself in his own gallery.

In 1915–1916 Stieglitz lent his name, money, and expertise to another experimental journal of the arts. Titled 291, it was the brainchild of his friends and associates Agnes Ernst Meyer, Paul Haviland, and Marius De Zayas. Another new artist turned up at 291 in 1916—a quiet, dour young woman dressed austerely in black. Her name was Georgia O'Keeffe. A friend of O'Keeffe's had earlier brought Stieglitz a bundle of her paintings, which he included in a group exhibition at 291 in 1916. Awed as she was by the great Stieglitz, O'Keeffe was "startled and shocked" to have her private work displayed for public view. She went to 291 Fifth Avenue to argue with Stieglitz about it, but in the end she left the work hanging on his gallery walls.

The entry of the United States into World War I in 1917 marked the end of an era for Stieglitz, for he published his final issue of *Camera Work* that year and closed the doors of 291. The final show was O'Keeffe's first solo exhibition anywhere. During the war years Stieglitz concentrated on promoting the work of painters who interested him—O'Keeffe first of all, Marsden Hartley, John Marin, Abraham Walkowitz. When O'Keeffe gave up teaching art in Canyon, Texas, to come to New York to paint, Stieglitz found an absorbing new subject. He photographed her intimately and obsessively over the years.

In 1918 Stieglitz, then fifty-four, left his wife of twenty-five years and moved into a small apartment in Manhattan with O'Keeffe, then thirty-one and a painter whose great promise Stieglitz eagerly set out to fulfill. He devoted much of his energy for the rest of his life to guiding and promoting O'Keeffe's development as an artist—sometimes to her dismay and to the detriment of her health. For the first few years of their romance, Stieglitz and O'Keeffe spent part of each year at Oaklawn, the Stieglitz country estate at Lake George, New York, the environs of which Stieglitz, O'Keeffe, and their friends captured in photography and paintings.

Photography and publishing once more engrossed Stieglitz's attention by 1922, when he edited and published *MSS Magazine* with the help of novelist and critic Paul Rosenfeld and critic and poet Herbert J. Seligmann. A one-man show of 116 recent Stieglitz photographs (1918–1923) attracted critical attention in New York in 1923, as did O'Keeffe's exhibition of one hundred watercolors, pastels, and oils. In the following year Stieglitz and O'Keeffe gave a joint exhibition of sixty-one of his recent prints and fifty-one of her paintings.

In 1924, after six years of conflict, Stieglitz and his wife were divorced. That same year O'Keeffe and Stieglitz were married and soon settled into a suite at the Shelton Hotel in New York. Except for his summer respites at Lake George, Stieglitz lived in a succession of apartments and hotels all his life, usually developing his photographs in a makeshift darkroom in the bathroom.

Beginning in 1925 Stieglitz opened the Intimate Gallery at the Anderson Galleries on Park Avenue, where he exhibited work by O'Keeffe, Marin, Hartley, Arthur Dove, and his new protégé, photographer Paul Strand. This gallery was soon followed by another, An American Place, located at 509 Madison Avenue. There Stieglitz put the spotlight on new photographers such as Ansel Adams and Eliot Porter, and on the painters he watched over—primarily O'Keeffe, Marin, Hartley, and Dove. He had brokered artistic careers from the earliest days of his 291 gallery, and he continued to do so through nearly seventy-five shows before An American Place, his last gallery, closed its doors in 1946. One of its finest exhibitions had been Stieglitz's retrospective one-man show in 1932, an exhibit of 127 prints produced from 1892 onward. In 1933, approaching his seventieth birthday, Stieglitz gave to the Metropolitan Museum of Art a collection of 1,000 photographs, drawings, and paintings, works of art representing more than a hundred photographers and painters.

In 1934 Stieglitz gave what would be his last one-man exhibition at An American Place, this time showing not only recent photographs but images he had made as early as 1884. In celebration of his birthday that year, a group of his friends published *America and Alfred Stieglitz: A Collective Portrait* (1934), a book-length tribute from colleagues and admirers, including William Carlos Williams, John Marin, Marsden Hartley, Harold Clurman, Gertrude Stein, Paul Strand, Jean Toomer, and Sherwood Anderson.

As far as can be determined, Stieglitz made his final photographs in 1937 and then put his camera down for good. As the years wore on and his health deteriorated, O'Keeffe spent more and more of her time painting in Abiquiu, New Mexico. He stayed at home by choice. "I never knew him to make a trip anywhere to photograph," O'Keeffe remembered. "His eye was in him, and he used it on anything that was nearby. Maybe that way he was always photographing himself" (O'Keeffe, *Georgia O'Keeffe: A Portrait by Alfred Stieglitz* [1978]).

Edward Steichen remembered in his autobiography, *A Life in Photography* (1963), the "prodigious amount of work" accomplished by Stieglitz. Yet he could often be found in the center of the galleries that constituted his universe, "talking, talking, talking," Steichen recalled, "talking in parables, arguing, explaining. He was a philosopher, a preacher, a teacher, and a father-confessor." Caricaturist Marius De Zayas saw Stieglitz as a midwife who brought "new ideas into the world" (Norman, p. 123). Through his prescient embrace of the modernist spirit, Alfred Stieglitz empowered the work of other artists and helped to shape an American century. But he was first and last a photographer, and his "greatest legacy to the world," in Steichen's words, "is his photographs."

• The Alfred Stieglitz Archives is part of the Collection of American Literature in the Beinecke Library at Yale University. Photographs and other relevant papers may be found in the Archives of American Art and the National Gallery in Washington, D.C., the Museum of Modern Art in New York, the Royal Photographic Society in London, and the Metropolitan Museum of Art in New York. Helpful overviews and excerpts of Stieglitz's writings are in Christian A. Peterson, *Alfred Stieglitz's Camera Notes* (1993), and Jonathan Green, ed., *Camera Work: A Critical Anthology* (1973). See also Sarah Greenough and Juan Hamilton, eds., *Alfred Stieglitz: Photographs and Writings* (1983). Interviews with Stieglitz are in Herbert J. Seligmann, *Alfred Stieglitz Talking, 1925–1931* (1966). An excellent illustrated, technical reference on Stieglitz the photographer and the collector is Weston J. Naef, *The Collection of Alfred Stieglitz: Fifty Pioneers of Modern Photography* (1978). An authoritative biography is Richard Whelan, *Alfred Stieglitz: A Biography* (1995), and a balanced and well-documented study written by Stieglitz's niece Sue Davidson Lowe is *Stieglitz: A Memoir/Biography* (1983). For an intimate personal portrait, see Dorothy Norman, *Alfred Stieglitz: An American Seer* (1973). Despite its adulatory purpose, helpful information found nowhere else is in Waldo Frank et al., eds., *America and Alfred Stieglitz* (1934). A commendable study of the Stieglitz-O'Keeffe relationship is Benita Eisler, *O'Keeffe and Stieglitz: An American Romance* (1991). For a look at Stieglitz in his milieu, consult Edward Abrahams, *The Lyrical Left: Randolph Bourne, Alfred Stieglitz, and the Origins of Cultural Radicalism in America* (1986), and Robert M. Crunden, *American Salons: Encounters with European Modernism, 1885–1917* (1993). See also William Innes Homer, *Alfred Stieglitz and the American Avant-Garde* (1977) and *Alfred Stieglitz and*

the Photo-Secession (1983), and Roxana Robinson, *Georgia O'Keeffe: A Life* (1989). Penelope Niven, *Steichen: A Biography* (1997), offers a full account of the Stieglitz-Steichen relationship. An obituary is in the *New York Times*, 14 July 1946.

PENELOPE NIVEN

STIEGLITZ, Julius (26 May 1867–10 Jan. 1937), chemist, was born in Hoboken, New Jersey, the son of Edward Stieglitz, a merchant, and Hedwig Werner. His father, a German immigrant who accumulated considerable wealth as an importer of woolen goods, prospered after moving to New York in 1871 and becoming a supplier to the city's major department stores. Julius, his identical twin Leopold, and his older brother Alfred, the renowned photographer, attended New York public schools, where the twins ranked at the top of every class. In 1881 the three brothers enrolled in the Realgymnasium in Karlsruhe, Germany, for a rigorous German education. Graduating in 1886 at the top of the class, the twins decided to pursue different vocations. In 1889 Leopold received an M.D. from the University of Heidelberg and Julius a Ph.D. in chemistry from the University of Berlin, each with highest honors. The twins maintained a lifelong devotion to each other, a closeness reflected in their marriages to the Stieffel sisters of Karlsruhe. Julius married Anna Maria Stieffel in 1891; they had three children. Widowed in 1932, he married Mary Meda Rising in 1934. She was his 1920 Ph.D. student and fellow faculty member at the University of Chicago; they had an adopted child.

Stieglitz returned to the United States in 1890. He held positions at Clark University and the Parke, Davis Company before joining the new University of Chicago in 1892 as a docent, an unsalaried position that gave him the opportunity to lecture, for which he collected a part of the student registration fees. Financial aid from his father enabled him to support his family until he obtained a salaried position. He became an instructor of chemistry in 1894, rose through the faculty ranks to full professor in 1905, and served as department chairman from 1915 to his 1933 retirement. Acknowledged by chemists as one of the premier teachers of chemistry in the United States, he guided more students through their doctoral degrees than anyone else at Chicago. The university welcomed women graduate students, and twenty-five women received their doctorates under his direction.

Stieglitz was internationally known for his *Elements of Qualitative Chemical Analysis* (1911). He revolutionized the teaching of the subject through this book, which was based on the new branch of physical chemistry, in contrast to existing texts, which were little more than a set of instructions to follow without any reasoning or explanation.

Stieglitz accomplished most of his research between 1892 and 1917, during which period he became a founder of physical organic chemistry. Self-taught in physical chemistry, he offered such novel courses as Physical Chemistry Applied to Organic Problems and Physico-Organic Research. He applied physical chemistry to organic reactions and proposed mechanisms involving a variety of novel, transient entities to account for the rearrangements and final products of addition, catalytic, and other organic reactions and for such phenomena as the color changes of indicators. The most far-reaching of his contributions was his 1899 concept of the carbonium ion intermediate, a carbon atom having only six electrons and bearing a positive charge. This concept subsequently gave rise to more experimental work than any other in American chemistry.

After 1917, when Stieglitz's productive years of research were over, physical organic chemistry underwent a transformation with the new electronic theories of the chemical bond of Gilbert N. Lewis and Linus Pauling. Stieglitz's student Howard Lucas, at the California Institute of Technology, was a key figure in the rapid development of the new field from the late 1920s. Stieglitz, however, was left behind in this transformation. He did not accept Lewis's idea of the shared electron pair bond, having adopted earlier a purely electropolar view of valence. His last published statement on the subject was a 1922 review article on bonding theories of the twentieth century, in which he again rejected electron pair bonding. There is, however, evidence in the form of correspondence that he eventually accepted Lewis's claims. Charles W. Porter, in preparing his *Molecular Rearrangements* (1928), wrote to him for his thoughts on several rearrangement reactions. Stieglitz responded by acknowledging the electron pair bond, now seeing how it was possible for such bonds also to have the polar characteristics necessary to understand rearrangements by the unequal sharing of electrons between atoms.

In the latter half of his career Stieglitz engaged in science policy, public affairs, and the relation of chemistry to medicine and industry. In 1901 he was a member of the University of Chicago committee seeking a union with the Rush Medical College and was central to the working out of the financial arrangements for the successful union. His efforts led to a relationship with the American Medical Association, and in 1905 the AMA appointed him to its Council of Chemistry and Pharmacy, a position he held until 1924. During World War I he was chairman of the Committee on Synthetic Drugs, which had the duty of recommending government licenses for pharmaceutical companies to manufacture certain needed drugs following the disruption of the import of German synthetics. As chairman he decided what drugs had to be made and which companies were to make them, and he continued to help guide the development of U.S. drug production after the war. During the war he also served as advisor to the Federal Trade Commission and played a major role in overcoming the American dependence on European imports of synthetic chemicals. As advisor to the Chemical Foundation after the war, he was a persuasive advocate for the development of strong American synthetic drug, dye, and other fine chemical industries.

In 1928 Stieglitz served as the editor of *Chemistry and Medicine*, a wide-ranging survey on the applications of chemistry to medicine. He was also on the board of editors of the American Chemical Society Monograph Series from its inception in 1919 to his death. Honors include the presidency of the ACS in 1917 and election to the National Academy of Sciences in 1911. In 1940 Chicago established the Stieglitz Lectures in his memory. He had a lifelong love of music and was an expert cellist. He expressed through outdoor photography his sensitivity to the beauty of nature, his prints bearing characteristics of the professional. A relaxed, calm, unhurried person, he was in good health all of his life until a heart attack late in 1936. A second, more severe attack resulted in his death in Chicago.

Stieglitz was an influential figure in American chemistry during the first third of the twentieth century, both for his advocacy of the importance of chemistry to medicine and industry and for his attempt to unite physical and organic chemistry, his work serving as an early model for the latter, embryonic field.

• The archives of the University of Chicago holds a small amount of Stieglitz material, consisting of class notes, biographical material written on the occasion of his death, and some correspondence. Detailed accounts of his life and career are by Herbert N. McCoy, "Julius Stieglitz, May 26, 1867–Jan. 10, 1937," *Journal of the American Chemical Society* 60 (Nov. 1938): 3–21, and William Albert Noyes, "Julius Stieglitz, 1867–1937," National Academy of Sciences, *Biographical Memoirs* 21 (1941): 275–314; both authors include a bibliography of his publications. Hermann I. Schlesinger, a Chicago colleague, provides a brief portrait in "American Contemporaries," *Industrial and Engineering Chemistry* 24 (May 1932): 587–88. His grandniece, Sue Davidson Lowe, describes his relationship with his parents and brothers in her biography of his older brother, *Stieglitz: A Memoir/Biography* (1983). For his contributions to physical organic chemistry, see Dean Stanley Tarbell and Ann Tracy Tarbell, *Essays on the History of Organic Chemistry in the United States* (1986). An obituary is in the *New York Times*, 11 Jan. 1937.

ALBERT B. COSTA

STIGLER, George J. (17 Jan. 1911–1 Dec. 1991), economist, was born in Renton, Washington, the son of Joseph Stigler, a brewer, longshoreman, and real estate developer, and Elizabeth Hungler. He attended public schools in Seattle. Like many young boys he joined the Boy Scouts and spent a great deal of time outdoors. He later attended the University of Washington at Seattle, graduating in 1931 with a B.A. in business administration, with the intention of going into business. However, because the Great Depression made it difficult to find employment, Stigler chose to get an M.B.A. at Northwestern University. During his year there he came into contact with an inspiring teacher, Coleman Woodbury, who stirred his interest in academics. After a year back at the University of Washington, Stigler returned to Chicago, studying economics from 1933 at the University of Chicago.

The University of Chicago had an outstanding economics department in the 1930s with a faculty and a student body that included Frank Knight (Stigler's dissertation adviser), Jacob Viner, Milton Friedman, Allen Wallis, and Paul Samuelson. A number of these people had an enormous impact on his life. In 1936 he married Margaret Louise Mack, a graduate student in anthropology; they had three sons. Also in 1936 he accepted a teaching appointment at Iowa State University, receiving one of only two teaching positions available in economics. Two years later he moved to the University of Minnesota, where he stayed for eight years. From there he moved briefly to Brown University (1946–1947) and then to Columbia University (1947–1958). In 1958 he returned to the University of Chicago as the first Charles Walgreen Professor and remained there until his death. In 1964 he was elected president of the American Economic Association, and he served as president of the History of Economics Society in 1977.

Stigler became a major intellectual force behind one of the most influential schools of thought in economics, known as the Chicago School. This movement, which began at Chicago and included figures such as Friedman, Theodore W. Schultz, Ronald Coase, Gary Becker, and Robert Lucas (all of whom became Nobel Prize winners in economics) breathed new life into the classic works of Adam Smith and some of his contemporaries. This neoclassical tradition soon spread to other graduate programs, including those at Minnesota, Columbia, and Carnegie-Mellon.

Stigler's own work was in the field of microeconomics, the study of how individuals and firms act and react in various situations, but his great passion was the study of the intellectual history of economics. He was a master at tracing the evolution of economic ideas. His Ph.D. dissertation, *Production and Distribution Theories* (1940), analyzed the development of the marginal productivity concept in the theory of production. In addition, he later wrote a well-received study of one of the major underpinnings of microeconomics, "The Development of Utility Theory" (*Journal of Political Economy* 58 [Aug. 1950]: 373–96).

Stigler's primary area of research within microeconomics was industrial organization, the study of the behavior of firms in various industries, with special emphasis on regulation. Within that field, he was concerned with industry concentration, that is, the number of firms in particular industries. Early in his career he favored an activist antitrust policy, including extensive restrictions on mergers and the breaking up of companies found to have significant monopoly power in order to promote more competitive behavior. However, in the 1960s he began to have a change of opinion. Researchers were finding that government officials and political appointees in charge of antitrust enforcement often responded to political pressures rather than using sound economic judgment in their decisions regarding breaking up businesses. Because of these reports, Stigler began to champion a minimalist antitrust policy that would allow practically all business practices except conspiracies to raise prices and divide up markets. He believed monopolies

should be prevented by encouraging domestic and foreign competition, not through government regulation. This view of antitrust policy is often associated with the Chicago School and influenced the Justice Department during the administration of Ronald Reagan.

Stigler himself believed that his greatest scientific contribution was in the area of the economics of information. Prior to his work, little analysis had been done on how agents in an economy acquired information. In "The Economics of Information" (*Journal of Political Economy* 69 [June 1961]: 213–25), he developed a theory of how agents acquire information when it is difficult or costly to do so. Because searching for information—about the best price for a car, for example—is costly because of the time and effort it takes, a rational person will search only until the value of additional information just equals the cost of searching for it. This relatively simple and intuitive result spawned an enormous number of studies in areas ranging from labor economics to the economics of advertising.

Beyond these areas, Stigler contributed to many other fields of economics. For instance, in one short study, "The Cost of Subsistence" (*Journal of Farm Economics* 27 [May 1945]: 303–14), he found that the adult minimum dietary requirements could be obtained at very little cost, just over $400 in 1996 prices. Because most countries in the world have per capita incomes above that number, he concluded that the prevalence of malnutrition around the world was due more to political causes than to poverty. He also argued that Americans spend far above this number because they are paying for palatability of foods, variety of diet, prestige of various foods, and other cultural aspects of consumption.

As a result of his vast body of work, Stigler was a highly honored member of his profession. From 1972 to 1991 he was the editor of the *Journal of Political Economy*, one of the most prestigious academic journals in economics. He was awarded the Nobel Prize in economics in 1982 and the National Medal of Science in 1987. He retired from teaching at the University of Chicago in 1981 but remained an active member of the economics department and of the profession until his death in Chicago.

• Stigler wrote or edited nearly 30 books and more than 100 articles. His autobiography, *Memoirs of an Unregulated Economist* (1988), is a vivid and wonderfully written account of both his personal and professional life. He published a number of collected essays that are accessible to the layperson but are substantive and reflective of his more technical work. His most widely read collections include *The Citizen and the State: Essays on Regulation* (1975) and *The Economist as Preacher, and Other Essays* (1982). At his death, the *Journal of Political Economy* published a special edition (101, no. 5 [Oct. 1993]) to honor him. The volume contains essays about his life and about the many contributions he made to the field of economics as well as a complete bibliography of his writings.

KYLE D. KAUFFMAN

STILES, Charles Wardell (15 May 1867–24 Jan. 1941), zoologist and public health official, was born in Spring Valley, New York, the son of Samuel Martin Stiles, a

Methodist minister, and Elizabeth White. Raised in an atmosphere of religious severity, Stiles was torn between his father's drive for him to become a minister and his own desire to become a scientist. To satisfy his family's observance of the Sabbath, Stiles turned his religious studies into a game by mastering reading the Bible in French, German, Italian, and Greek, an exercise that greatly expanded his linguistic abilities. After finishing high school in Hartford, Connecticut, Stiles gave in to family pressures and enrolled at Wesleyan College in Middletown, Connecticut. Since Stiles had no intention of giving in to his father's desires for him to become a minister, he led a carousing and revolutionary life that tested the bounds of Wesleyan discipline. Stiles's strife to obtain high marks, the tension with his father, and the recurrence of debilitating headaches culminated in a case of neurasthenia, which caused him to abruptly leave college. Stiles's neurasthenia and headaches dramatically improved after he was fitted with glasses and his father surrendered to his son's desire to become a scientist.

On recovering his health, Stiles went to Europe with the goal of studying science with many of the best-known scientists of the world and there spent the first year in general studies with a Catholic brotherhood, Freres Chretiens, in Paris and in Göttingen, Germany. Having acclimated himself to European life for a year, Stiles began his scientific studies by enrolling in the University of Berlin, where he studied under H. W. G. Waldeyer, Hermann von Helmholtz, and Emil Heinrich duBois-Reymond. After two years in Berlin, Stiles continued his studies under the zoologist Rudolph Lukhardt in Leipzig. Stiles completed his European studies by spending brief periods at Robert Koch's Institute in Berlin, the Austria Zoological Station in Trieste, and the Pasteur Institute in Paris. With this training in biology, Stiles returned to the United States in 1891 and became consulting zoologist at the Bureau of Animal Industry of the Department of Agriculture, where he would study the parasites that plagued farm animals.

One of Stiles's first projects at the bureau was to systematize the nomenclature of helminths, or parasitic worms. On examining the specimens in the collection of American parasites, he noted with surprise that it did not include samples of hookworm. From his European studies, Stiles knew that eating dirt put one at risk for hookworm and that this diet practice was common in the southern United States. In his lectures to the medical students at the Johns Hopkins Medical School, beginning in 1897, Stiles repeatedly told the students that if they encountered anemia and dirt-eating in a tropical or subtropical climate they should suspect patients of having hookworm and examine their stools for hookworm eggs. Stiles's lectures paid off: a student, Bailey K. Ashford, while serving as an army surgeon stationed in Puerto Rico, examined the stool of one of his anemic patients and found hookworm eggs.

Ashford took these specimens to Stiles for examination, but at that time his former teacher was in Eu-

rope. Stiles's knowledge of trichinosis, a disease contracted from uncooked pork, had led to his being selected in the late 1890s as scientific attaché at the American embassy in Germany to investigate that nation's allegation that American pork was unhealthy; he found that an outbreak of trichinosis in Germany was not due to pork products from the United States. Just as Stiles returned to the United States, he received another hookworm sample from Allen J. Smith, pathologist at the University of Texas at Galveston. On examining the Texas fecal sample, Stiles found that the parasites it contained differed from the European hookworm, *Ancylostoma duodenale*. Stiles now examined the specimen Ashford had brought to Washington and found that it was identical to the parasite that Smith had found. These findings showed that the American hookworm was not the same species as that found in Europe. Stiles named the American hookworm *Uncinata americanus* (*Necator americanus*).

In the period between 1893 and 1902, while the hookworm work was in progress, Stiles participated in organizing American scientists at the Zoological Station in Naples, Italy, and in introducing medical zoology through lectures and presentations at a number of American medical schools in the East. These health-related interests drew attention to Stiles and resulted in his transfer to the U.S. Public Health Service, where he was professor of zoology from 1902 to 1930.

Once Stiles had established in 1902 that *Uncinata americanus* was the cause of American hookworm disease, he began a campaign to eradicate the disease. Stiles was aware that the anemia could be relieved and the disease cured by ridding the body of the parasites by administering thymol followed by a cathartic; the disease could be prevented by wearing shoes—hookworm is transferred frequently to barefooted individuals who walk through areas contaminated with feces—and installing sanitation measures, namely properly constructed privies and toilets attached to sewers or septic tanks. Stiles did not meet with any great success in his early campaign against hookworm until he met the southern publisher (and later ambassador to the Court of St. James), Walter Hines Page, who brought him into contact with the General Education Board, one of the John D. Rockefeller's philanthropies. Stiles's presentation to the General Education Board, concerning the need for studies of the disease and measures to prevent its spread, resulted in the organization of the Rockefeller Sanitary Commission. With the appointment of Wickliff Rose as director and Stiles's continued pressure, progress was made in controlling hookworm in the South. The disease was not finally brought under control until modern bathrooms attached to sewers and septic tanks were installed throughout the southern United States.

At the Public Health Service's Hygiene Laboratory, Stiles continued his scientific work on parasites. In the course of this work he rearranged the American helminth collection and identified several new species of parasites. In 1895 he was elected to the International Commission on Zoological Nomenclature and served as its secretary from 1898 to 1936. His most significant academic contribution, the monumental *Index-Catalogue of Medical and Veterinary Zoology* coauthored with Albert Hassall, with its associated catalogs of insects, parasites, protozooa, crustacea, and arachnids, was an ongoing project from the 1890s until the mid-1930s.

Stiles married Virginia Baker in June 1897; they had one daughter. Stiles died at the Marine Hospital in Baltimore, Maryland.

• Relatively few of Stiles's personal papers have been found. Manuscripts pertaining to various parts of his life are in the collections of the Smithsonian Institution. There are some papers in the U.S. National Archives (Department of State Archives). A great deal of Stiles's work is contained in reports or other publications of the Bureau of Animal Industry, the Public Health Service and the Archives of the Rockefeller Foundation in North Tarrytown, N.Y. Biographical articles include Benjamin Schwartz, "Early History, in Part Esoteric, of Hookworm," *Journal of Parasitology* 25 (1930): 283–308; F. G. Brooks, "Charles Wardell Stiles," *Bios* 18 (1947): 139–69; and Mark Sullivan, *Our Times* 3 (1930): 290–332. Information about various phases of Stiles's career are in James H. Cassedy, "'The Germ of Laziness' in the South, 1900–1915: Charles Wardell Stiles and the Progressive Paradox," *Bulletin of History of Medicine* 45 (1971): 159–69, and "Applied Microscopy and American Pork Diplomacy: Charles Wardell Stiles in Germany, 1898–1899," *Isis* 62 (1971): 4–20; Schwartz, "A Brief Résumé of Dr. Stiles's Contributions to Parasitology," *Journal of Parasitology* 19 (1933): 257–61; John Ettling, *"The Germ of Laziness": Rockefeller Philanthropy and Public Health in the South* (1981); and Greer Williams, *The Plague Killers* (1969). An obituary is in the *New York Times*, 25 Jan. 1941.

DAVID Y. COOPER

STILES, Ezra (29 Nov. 1727–12 May 1795), Congregational minister and president of Yale College, was born in North Haven, Connecticut, the son of Isaac Stiles, the local minister, and Kezia Taylor, daughter of the poet Edward Taylor. His mother died in bearing him, and within a year his father married Esther Hooker, great granddaughter of Thomas Hooker, the founder of Connecticut.

Ezra Stiles's public career was that of a prominent Congregational minister. Graduating from Yale in the class of 1746, he stayed on to study theology, receiving his master's degree in 1749 and serving as tutor in the college from 1749 until 1755. In that year he was called to the pastorship of the Second Congregational Church of Newport, Rhode Island. Two years later he married Elizabeth Hubbard of New Haven, with whom he had eight children. He and the family remained in Newport until British occupation of the town drove them out in 1776. In 1777 he accepted the ministry of the church in Portsmouth, New Hampshire, which had just lost its pastor, Samuel Langdon, to the presidency of Harvard College. The church lost Stiles to the Yale presidency the following year. He remained in that office until his death.

As president Stiles brought to Yale a badly needed political, financial, and intellectual success. An earlier president, Thomas Clap, had begun a quarrel with the Connecticut legislative assembly in the 1750s over ecclesiastical issues, and the governing corporation of clergymen had done little since then to end it. The college was thereby deprived of crucial financial support from the state. It took most of Stiles's tenure as president to heal the rift and to win, in 1792, a legislative act restoring state funding. He was able to do so, despite an uncooperative corporation, by making Yale so respectable intellectually that students flocked to it in record numbers, reaching a high of more than 250 students in the early 1780s, by far the largest enrollment of any American college. Tuition payments were not sufficient to expand the teaching staff in the way that Stiles wished, and he was obliged to take on most of the advanced instruction himself. In doing so he modernized the curriculum by the introduction of new texts and new subjects (history and belles lettres) and by instituting examinations for graduation that were more than perfunctory. Stiles was one of the most learned men of his time in America, and his reputation served to add luster to that of Yale.

But what Stiles did as pastor in Newport or as tutor and president of Yale is less significant than the record his papers furnish of a highly articulate and self-conscious American grappling with the intellectual problems that confronted other Americans and the rest of the world in the second half of the eighteenth century. Stiles early acquired the habit of writing down what he was thinking, not only in letters to friends (of which he generally kept copies) but also in diaries and notebooks and on scraps of paper, which he preserved in extraordinary quantities.

Stiles's intellectual odyssey began in the Yale library, where he encountered English writers like Shaftesbury, Pope, and Samuel Clarke, who challenged his commitment to the Puritan theology that had guided New Englanders for more than a century. For a time he was tempted by Arminian notions of free will and even by deism. But before he came to the point of avowing his heresies publicly, he worked his way through them to an evangelical faith in the revealed word of God and the Calvinist doctrines that the seventeenth-century Puritans had found in it. What he retained was a confidence that the only way to the truths he now cherished was through the free exchange of ideas in the open market. After his departure from Yale for Newport, President Clap withdrew the infectious writings of Samuel Clarke from the library. Stiles wrote to him pleading for a "generous and equal Liberty" in ideas. The only way to conquer error, he argued, was "to come forth into the open field and dispute the matter on an even footing."

Stiles adhered to this belief in freedom—religious, civil, and political—throughout his life, coupling with it an intellectual curiosity that knew no bounds. He was curious about climate and for thirty-two years (1763–1795) kept a daily record of maximum and minimum temperatures, using a thermometer furnished him by Benjamin Franklin (1706–1790). He was curious about demography and gathered population figures—births, marriages, deaths—from every available source, including midwives (Malthus later used some of his data). He interrupted his sleep regularly to peer for hours through a telescope to chart the course of comets and to ascertain the dimensions of the aurora borealis. He visited settlements of Indians to ask the inhabitants the kinds of questions that later anthropologists would pursue. At Newport he took advantage of the presence of a Jewish community to learn Hebrew and undertake studies of the Kabala. While still a tutor at Yale he began an extensive scholarly correspondence with scientists and savants in Britain and Europe. Although he never brought his lifelong investigations of a multitude of subjects to fruition in published books and never traveled far from New England, he became so well known abroad that the University of Edinburgh awarded him an honorary doctorate in 1765.

While pursuing his ideas in encyclopedic fashion, Stiles kept religion at the center of his life; he was devoted to his church and adored by its members. His belief in religious freedom included a conviction that Christ had sanctioned no particular form of church organization and a suspicion of governmental attempts to impose one. He was particularly fearful that the Episcopal church, abetted by the British government, would attempt to subject other denominations in America to an Anglican bishop. To forestall any such attempt, he took a leading role in 1766 in uniting Presbyterian and Congregational churches. But as the union matured (resulting in a convention that met annually in the late 1760s and early 1770s) he characteristically drew back from participation. The religious and intellectual freedom he cherished seemed to him to require not only restraining the state from interference in religion but also the self-restraint of ministers from any kind of activity in politics.

For Stiles this form of self-denial may have been dictated as much by temperament as by principle. After 1765, as Americans resisted British attempts to impose taxation and other unwanted regulations, Stiles rejoiced in their courage but kept his distance. "I am a Friend to American Liberty, of the final prevalence of which I have not the least doubt," he wrote in 1773. But he could not himself join in the thrilling defense of it: "I am a Spectator indeed of Events, but intermeddle not with Politics. We [ministers] . . . cannot become the Dupes of Politicians without Alliances, Concessions and Connexions dangerous to evangelical Truth and spiritual Liberty."

When American liberty, as he saw it, finally triumphed, Stiles allowed himself to preach a sermon, *The United States Elevated to Glory and Honor* (1783), in which he foresaw the spread of liberty throughout the continent. The French Revolution confirmed his confidence that old tyrannies could not stand before the freedom unleashed by American independence. In his early years he had identified himself with the seventeenth-century Puritans who had resisted the efforts of Charles I and Archbishop Laud to dictate their religion. At his graduation from Yale he had publicly de-

fended the proposition that the authority of hereditary kings is not derived from divine right. At that time, like other American colonists, he took pride in a British constitution that protected subjects from their rulers. But when the British constitution failed them and they moved to independence, Stiles moved with them and perhaps a little beyond most in placing his confidence not so much in laws and constitutions as in the people themselves. When the French did to their king what the English had done to Charles I, many Americans were shocked, but Stiles wrote passionately in defense of regicide and declared his conviction that the "common people will generally judge right, when duly informed. The general liberty is safe and secure in their hands."

Stiles remained a spectator, but a cheering one. His belief in liberty had grown to a belief in democracy, and he had recorded his thoughts about it at every stage. In that record of one man's progression from subject to citizen, much of it still in manuscript, lies his principal legacy. He died in New Haven.

• The Stiles papers are at the Yale University Library, which has published a microfilm edition of them in twenty-two reels, with Harold Selesky, *A Guide* (1978). The most important of Stiles's publications in his own lifetime were *A Discourse on the Christian Union* (1761), *The United States Elevated to Glory and Honor* (1783), and *A History of Three of the Judges of King Charles I* (1794). See also *The Literary Diary of Ezra Stiles* (3 vols., 1901) and *Extracts from the Itineraries and Other Miscellanies of Ezra Stiles* (1916), both edited by Franklin B. Dexter. Abiel Holmes, Stiles's son-in-law, published *The Life of Ezra Stiles* (1798). The only modern biography is Edmund S. Morgan, *The Gentle Puritan: A Life of Ezra Stiles* (1962).

EDMUND S. MORGAN

STILL, Andrew Taylor (6 Aug. 1828–12 Dec. 1917), physician and founder of osteopathy, was born in Jonesville, Virginia, the son of Abraham Still, a Methodist minister and physician, and Martha Poage Moore. Still's father held various church appointments on the western frontier, and the family eventually settled in Baldwin, Kansas. Still's early education was interrupted by these moves, but he received some formal schooling in classrooms and through tutors until the age of twenty. Although he subsequently studied medicine with his father, he never attended a medical school before starting his practice as a physician in the 1850s. In 1849 he met and married Mary Margaret Vaughan; they had five children.

In the Kansas Territory Still became involved in the antislavery struggle and in 1857 was elected to the quasi-legal Free Kansas legislature. In 1859 his first wife died, and the following year he married Mary Elvira Turner, with whom he had seven children. In 1861, Still enlisted in the Union army and was assigned to the Ninth Kansas Cavalry, Company F, as hospital steward. In 1862 he returned home, organized his own command, and was commissioned captain. Later he was transferred to the Twenty-first Kansas Militia with the rank of major. After the war he resumed his career as a physician.

In 1864 three of his children died of meningitis in spite of the efforts of local regular physicians. This tragedy made him question orthodox medical practices. He investigated the principles of the rival sectarian "schools" of homeopathy and eclecticism, which challenged the use of venesection (bloodletting) and mineral drugs, such as mercury, and substituted other drug remedies. However, he found these systems as wanting as orthodox medicine. Furthermore, as a Methodist, he concluded that if drinking alcohol was sinful, taking other drugs into the body might also be against God's will. After investigating various drugless approaches he ultimately adopted some principles and practices of "magnetic healing," a number of whose practitioners had begun "rubbing" the spine as a means of restoring the proper balance of energy to dysfunctional parts of the body. Still's abandonment of orthodoxy led to his being "read out" of the local Methodist church. In 1875 he and his family moved to Kirksville, Missouri, where he advertised himself as "A. T. Still, Magnetic Healer." In the 1870s he also became interested in the unorthodox practices of bonesetters, who in addition to reducing dislocations also manipulated painful and diseased joints, including those of the spine. Still found that manipulating vertebrae to "put them into the proper place" benefited not only structural problems, but also other seemingly unrelated conditions, such as asthma. He concluded that most diseases were the result of an obstructed blood supply that was brought about by misplaced vertebrae. Correct the misalignment, he reasoned, and symptoms elsewhere in the body would disappear.

In the 1880s he traveled around Missouri as "the lightning bonesetter," sometimes effecting spectacular cures in front of large crowds. By 1889 he established a permanent clinic in Kirksville, where he treated chronically ill patients from all across the Midwest. At about this time Still began to call his discovery "osteopathy." In 1892 he founded the American School of Osteopathy (ASO) in Kirksville, and its enrollment grew rapidly. The original four-month curriculum was expanded to two years in 1896, three years in 1905, and four years in 1916, by which time it incorporated all of the subjects offered in an orthodox medical school except pharmacology and materia medica. Meanwhile, graduates of the ASO, who were designated as doctors of osteopathy (D.O.s), founded other colleges, eventually making osteopathy the largest sectarian group of licensed "physicians and surgeons" to challenge orthodox medicine in the United States during the twentieth century.

Still spent his later years trying to keep the movement doctrinally pure. Although he once noted that he believed "but little of the germ theory and care much less," a number of early osteopaths tried to reconcile osteopathic principles with medical science. And though Still wanted to produce general practitioners who could handle ordinary surgical and obstetrical cases and sanctioned the use of anesthetics, antiseptics, and antidotes, he rejected vaccines, serums, and other drugs that a few osteopathic schools were incorporating into their curricula. By 1910, the year of his second wife's death, Still had retired from college affairs, and the following year the ASO catalog noted that the school was teaching the use of vaccines and serums in one of its courses. In 1914 Still suffered a stroke, which impaired his speech. He nevertheless sent a message to the annual meeting of the American Osteopathic Association in 1915 supporting the retention of the rule that no college that taught the complete range of drug therapeutics could be considered a reputable osteopathic school. The association, however, repealed this provision, which ultimately led to the full teaching of materia medica in osteopathic colleges and the current licensing of D.O.s as qualified physicians and surgeons in every state. Still died in Kirksville.

Still's medical contribution was to focus new attention on the role that the musculoskeletal system may play in disease and the potential value that spinal manipulative therapy may have in overall patient management. In the process he launched a new health profession, which, in the late twentieth century, boasted thousands of practitioners and provided for the health care needs of more than twenty-five million Americans.

• Still was the author of four books: *Autobiography* (1897), *Philosophy of Osteopathy* (1899), *Philosophy and Mechanical Principles of Osteopathy* (1902), and *Osteopathy: Research and Practice* (1910). Uncritical biographies by followers and supporters that nevertheless contain much useful information include E. R. Booth, *History of Osteopathy and Twentieth Century Medicine* (1924); Arthur G. Hildreth, *The Lengthening Shadow of Andrew Taylor Still* (1938); and Carol Trowbridge, *Andrew Taylor Still, 1828–1917* (1991). For a general history of the osteopathic profession, see Norman Gevitz, *The D.O.'s: Osteopathic Medicine in America* (1982).

NORMAN GEVITZ

STILL, Clyfford (30 Nov. 1904–23 June 1980), painter, was born in Grandin, North Dakota. The names of his parents are not known, although his father is known to have been an accountant. The year after his birth Still's family moved to Spokane, Washington. In 1910 his father sought work in Bow Island near Alberta, Canada. For the remainder of his school years, Still traveled between Alberta and Spokane, where the family kept a residence. He attended the Edison Grammar School and the Spokane University Preparatory School.

Still's early interest in drawing and painting culminated in 1925 with a trip to New York City, where he visited the Metropolitan Museum of Art and enrolled in the Art Students League. His independent attitude and aloofness caused him to resign from the league on the same day: "The exercises and results I observed I had already explored for myself some years before and had rejected most of them as a waste of time" (quoted in O'Neill, p. 177).

Returning to Spokane, Still attended Spokane University, from which he graduated in 1933. After college Still took a position as a teaching fellow at Washington State College, Pullman, moving up to instructor and then assistant professor by 1941. On the recommendation of portrait painter Sidney E. Dickenson, who had seen his work in Pullman, he spent the summers of 1934 and 1935 at the Trask Foundation (Yaddo) in Saratoga Springs, New York, where he devoted his full attention to painting.

In 1935 Still exhibited at the National Academy of Design in New York, one of the last times he submitted work to a juried exhibition. Despite being urged to stay in New York by others at Yaddo, Still returned to Washington State College. There he received a master's degree in 1935, writing his thesis on Cézanne.

Still's work throughout the 1930s, wrote Thomas Albright in an *ARTNews* article after Still's death (Sept. 1980), "ran parallel, in subject and darkly brooding palette, to Regionalism or American Scene Painting." Examples of Still's regionalist work include *Row of Elevators* (c. 1928–1929, National Museum of American Art), a vivid depiction of stark white grain elevators reaching into the sky. Though Still's early work is in the figurative tradition of the regionalists, by 1937 he had moved to the sharp abstraction that characterized his later work, as in *1937–8–A* (1937, Albright-Knox Art Gallery, Buffalo, N.Y.). His *Self-Portrait* (1940, private collection) is among his last purely representational works.

Still left Washington State College in the spring of 1941 and moved to northern California. Taking employment in the burgeoning war industries, Still worked in the ship-building yards and aircraft factories of the San Francisco Bay area through the summer of 1943, painting in his free time. He had a solo exhibition at the San Francisco Museum of Art in March 1943.

Returning to academia in the fall of 1943, Still took a position at the Richmond Professional Institute in Virginia. In addition to his teaching load, Still completed many paintings and began using the large canvases that he would use for the rest of his career. Paintings such as *1943–J* (1943, San Francisco Museum of Modern Art) and *1944–G* (1944, San Francisco Museum of Modern Art) illustrate how Still's use of bold colors applied in a jagged, thick impasto style was codified at this time. These and other works from this period were painted on the huge canvases, often more than six feet tall, that became the hallmark of abstract expressionism.

Still resigned from the Richmond Professional Institute in 1945 and moved to New York. There he was introduced to art collector and gallery owner Peggy Guggenheim by fellow painter Mark Rothko. Guggenheim gave Still a one-man show at her Art of This Century Gallery in February 1946.

Though beginning to achieve recognition in New York, Still returned to San Francisco in the fall of 1946 to take a position at the California School of Fine Arts (CSFA), where he remained until 1950. He did not, however, cut himself off from the New York art world. With regular correspondence he maintained close contact with Rothko and other artists. Solo exhibitions at the Betty Parsons Gallery (Apr. 1947) and the California Palace of the Legion of Honor (San Francisco, July 1947) further enhanced his reputation. This latter exhibition included the work *January 1947* (1947, Albright-Knox Art Gallery, Buffalo, N.Y.), which was composed of swirling patches of white and black on a brown background.

In the summer of 1948 Still resigned from the CSFA, went to New York, and with Rothko began planning for a school of art that would employ a number of working artists, including Rothko, William Baziotes, Robert Motherwell, and David Hare, as instructors. Planning for the school bogged down in endless theorizing, and the idea was postponed for a year. Still returned to the CSFA that fall. Eventually opening in October 1948, the school, called "The Subject of the Artist," which Still later commented was a "completely absurd name" (quoted in O'Neill, p. 187), quickly closed.

In 1950 Still resigned from the CSFA and moved once again to New York. The subject of one-man shows at the Betty Parsons Gallery (Apr. 1950 and Jan. 1951), which included the painting *1947–S* (San Francisco Museum of Modern Art), Still was also represented at the 15 Americans exhibition at the Museum of Modern Art in 1952. Refusing an offer to exhibit at the 1957 Venice Biennale, Still did not publicly exhibit his art again until the retrospective at Buffalo's Albright Art Gallery in 1959.

Wishing to avoid the associative connotations of titles, Still initiated his system of coding his works with a system of dates, letters, and numerals around the time of the Buffalo retrospective. Still taught at Hunter College (1951) and Brooklyn College (1952–1953), then spent much of 1954 traveling throughout the West, stopping to work in San Francisco and Tucson. In 1960 he served as visiting artist at the University of Colorado, Boulder; this was his last teaching assignment.

The Albright Art Gallery retrospective of 1959 brought together seventy-two of Still's canvases executed between 1937 and 1957. In a brief introductory statement published to accompany the show, Still expounded on his artistic theories and explained that, for the artist, it was "necessary not to remain trapped in the banal concepts of space and time nor yield to the morbidity of 'the objective position'; nor to permit one's courage to be perverted by authoritarian devices for social control."

Now in his mid-fifties, Still made a major change in his life. Purchasing a 22-acre farm in Carroll County, Maryland, Still converted some of the farm's structures into studio space. He lived at the farm until 1966 when he purchased a house in nearby New Windsor, retaining the farm and its studio space.

Building on his relationship with the Albright Art Gallery, in 1964 Still gave thirty-one paintings spanning nearly his entire career (1937–1963) to the now-renamed Albright-Knox Art Gallery. In 1966 the gallery exhibited the thirty-one works, plus two it had purchased earlier, and dedicated a room in the museum to Still.

In a move parallel to his earlier donation to the Albright-Knox Art Gallery, in 1975 Still presented the San Francisco Museum of Modern Art with twenty-eight works, again spanning his career (1934–1974). As was the case in Buffalo, an exhibition of the gift, plus two the museum already owned and three lent by Still, was held the following year. Upon the completion of the museum's new building in 1995, a large gallery was devoted to Still's gift.

In 1979 seventy-nine paintings were exhibited at the Metropolitan Museum of Art in a retrospective that was the largest ever given by the museum to a living artist.

Still carefully controlled his public persona. He personally authorized biographical sketches for early exhibition catalogs; and, particularly after his withdrawal from the New York art world, his contact with fellow artists, critics, and galleries was minimal. Tall and thin, with a full shock of white hair in his later years, Still was captured by a number of photographers, including Hans Namuth, Lord Snowdon, Still's wife, Patricia (maiden name and date of marriage unknown), and their daughter Sandra. These photographs show Still's piercing gaze and meticulous person, looking, as Thomas Albright termed him in *ARTNews* (Sept. 1980), like a "combination of Savonarola, Zarathustra and Captain Ahab."

A plethora of awards was showered on Still in his later career. He received the Award of Merit Medal for painting from the American Academy of Arts and Letters (1972) and in 1978 was elected a member of the academy.

Still was hailed as one of America's most important painters of the twentieth century by the same art establishment that he once reviled as a "fraudulent arena of poltroon politicians and charlatan hucksters who pretend they love art" (*Newsweek*, 22 Dec. 1969). As a teacher Still had a strong influence on the emerging artists of the San Francisco Bay area; additionally, the work of Mark Rothko and Barnett Newman was affected by Still's powerful aesthetic. Still died in Baltimore.

Still kept tight control over his work. At his death fewer than a third of his more than 750 canvases had ever been exhibited. His testament stipulated that the works remaining in the estate should go to an American city that would provide them with a suitable museum.

• Major collections of Still's work are held by the Albright-Knox Art Gallery, Buffalo, N.Y., and the San Francisco Museum of Art. Other significant works are in the National Gallery of Art, Washington, D.C., the Baltimore Museum of Art, the Museum of Modern Art, the Whitney Museum of American Art, New York City, and the Hirshhorn Museum and Sculpture Garden at the Smithsonian Institution. Still's letters to Barnett and Annalee Newman are in the Archives of American Art at the Smithsonian. A biographical profile by Katharine Kuh, "Still, the Enigma," is in *Vogue*, 1 Feb. 1970, pp. 180–83, 218–20. An important article on Still is E. C. Goossen, "Painting as Confrontation: Clyfford Still," *Art International* 4, no. 1 (1960): 39–43. The exhibition catalog *Clyfford Still, 1904–1980: The Buffalo and San Francisco Collections* (1992) includes substantial biographical material and reproduces a large selection of his works in color. See also John P. O'Neill, *Clyfford Still* (1979), the exhibition catalog from the Metropolitan Museum of Art. Obituaries are in the *Baltimore Sun*, 6 July 1980, and the *New York Times*, 25 June 1980.

MARTIN R. KALFATOVIC

STILL, William (7 Oct. 1821–14 July 1902), abolitionist and businessman, was born near Medford in Burlington County, New Jersey, the youngest of the eighteen children of Levin Still, a farmer, and Charity (maiden name unknown). Still's father, a Maryland slave, purchased his own freedom and changed his name from Steel to Still. His mother escaped from slavery and changed her given name from Cidney to Charity. With a minimum of formal schooling, William studied on his own, reading whatever was available to him. He left home at age twenty to work at odd jobs and as a farmhand. In 1844 he moved to Philadelphia where he found employment as a handyman, and in 1847 he married Letitia George. They had four children.

In 1847 the Pennsylvania Society for the Abolition of Slavery hired Still as a clerk, and he soon began assisting fugitives from slavery who passed through the city. After the passage of the Fugitive Slave Act of 1850, the society revived its Vigilance Committee to aid and support fugitive slaves and made Still chairman. One of the fugitives he helped was Peter Still, his own brother who had been left in slavery when his mother escaped. Finding Peter after a forty-year separation inspired Still to keep careful records of the former slaves, and those records later provided source material for his book on the Underground Railroad.

While with the Vigilance Committee, Still helped hundreds of fugitive slaves, and several times he nearly went to prison for his efforts. In 1855, when former slaves in Canada were being maligned in the press, he and his brother traveled there to investigate for themselves. His reports were much more positive and optimistic than the others and helped counteract rumors that former slaves were lazy and lawless. Five years later he cited cases of successful former slaves in Canada in a newspaper article that argued for freeing all the slaves.

Although Still had not approved of John Brown's (1800–1859) raid on Harpers Ferry, afterward Brown's wife stayed with the Stills for a time, as did several of Brown's accomplices. Still's work in the antislavery office ended in 1861, but he remained active in the society, which turned to working for African-American civil rights. He served as the society's vice president for eight years and as president from 1896 to 1901.

Still's book, *The Underground Railroad* (1872), was unique. The only work on that subject written by an

African American, it was also the only day-by-day record of the workings of a vigilance committee. While he gave credit to "the grand little army of abolitionists," he put the spotlight on the fugitives themselves, saying "the race had no more eloquent advocates than its own self-emancipated champions." Besides recording their courageous deeds, Still hoped that the book would demonstrate the intellectual ability of his race. Along with the records of slave escapes he included excerpts from newspapers, legal documents, correspondence of abolitionists and former slaves, and some biographical sketches. He published the book himself and sent out agents to sell it. The book went into three editions and was exhibited at the Philadelphia Centennial Exposition in 1876.

Although he had not suffered personally under slavery, Still faced discrimination throughout his life and was determined to work for improved race relations. His concern about civil rights in the North led him in 1859 to write a letter to the press, which started a campaign to end racial discrimination on Philadelphia streetcars, where African Americans were permitted only on the unsheltered platforms. Eight years later the campaign met success when the Pennsylvania legislature enacted a law making such discrimination illegal. In 1861 he helped organize and finance the Pennsylvania Civil, Social, and Statistical Association to collect data about the freed slaves and to press for universal suffrage.

Still was a skilled businessman as well as an effective antislavery agent. He began purchasing real estate while working for the antislavery society. After leaving that position he opened a store where he sold new and used stoves and coal. In 1861 he opened a coal yard, a highly successful business that led to his being named to the Philadelphia Board of Trade. In 1864 he was appointed post sutler at Camp William Penn, where black soldiers were stationed.

Still's independent nature was illustrated in 1874 when he repudiated the Republican candidate for mayor of Philadelphia and supported instead a reform candidate. He explained his position at a public meeting and later in a pamphlet entitled *An Address on Voting and Laboring* (1874). He was also a lifelong temperance advocate, and as a member of the Presbyterian church he established a Mission Sabbath School. His other civic activities included membership in the Freedmen's Aid Commission, organizing around 1880 one of the first YMCAs for black youth, and helping to manage homes for the aged and for destitute black children and an orphan asylum for children of black soldiers and sailors. Poor health forced him to retire from his business affairs six years before his death at his home in Philadelphia.

• Part of William Still's journal of the Philadelphia Vigilance Committee, along with some personal correspondence, is in the Historical Society of Pennsylvania in Philadelphia. His *A Brief Narrative of the Struggle for the Rights of the Colored People of Philadelphia in the City Railway Cars* (1867) tells the history of that campaign. Alberta S. Norwood, "Negro Welfare Work in Philadelphia Especially as Illustrated by the Career of William Still, . . . " (M.A. thesis, Univ. of Penn., 1931), includes some of Still's correspondence. *Still's Underground Rail Road Records* (1883), the third, revised edition of his book, contains a biographical sketch by James P. Boyd; also see Larry Gara, "William Still and the Underground Railroad," *Pennsylvania History* 28 (Jan. 1961): 33–44. His obituary appeared in the *Philadelphia Public Ledger*, 15 July 1902.

LARRY GARA

STILL, William Grant (11 May 1895–3 Dec. 1978), composer, orchestrator and arranger, and musician, once called the "Dean of Afro-American Composers," was born in Woodville, Mississippi, the son of William Grant Still, a music teacher and bandmaster, and Carrie Lena Fambro, a schoolteacher. His father died during Still's infancy. Still and his mother moved to Little Rock, Arkansas, where she taught school and in 1909 or 1910 married Charles Shepperson, a railway postal clerk, who strongly supported his stepson's musical interests. Still graduated from high school at sixteen, valedictorian of his class, and went to Wilberforce University.

Still's mother had wanted him to become a doctor, but music became his primary interest. He taught himself to play the oboe and clarinet, formed a string quartet in which he played violin, arranged music for his college band, and began composing; a concert of his music was presented at the school. In 1915, just a few months shy of graduation, Still dropped out of Wilberforce in order to become a professional musician, playing in various dance bands, including one led by W. C. Handy, "the Father of the Blues." That year he married Grace Bundy, with whom he had four children. They divorced in the late 1920s.

A small legacy from his father, which Still inherited on his twenty-first birthday, allowed him to resume his musical studies in 1917, this time at Oberlin College's conservatory. World War I interrupted Still's studies, and he spent it in the segregated U.S. Navy as a mess attendant and as a violinist in an officers' mess. After being discharged in 1919 Still returned to the world of popular music. He had a strong commitment to serious music and received further formal training during a short stay in 1922 at the New England Conservatory. From 1923 to 1925 he studied, as a private scholarship pupil, with the noted French "ultra-modernist" composer Edgard Varèse, whose influence can be heard in the dissonant passages found in Still's early serious work.

Still managed to make his way both in the world of popular entertainment and as a serious composer. He worked successfully into the 1940s in the entertainment world as a musician, arranger, orchestrator, and conductor. As an arranger and orchestrator, he worked on a variety of Broadway shows, including the fifth edition of Earl Carroll's *Vanities*. He also worked with a wide variety of entertainers, including Paul Whiteman, Sophie Tucker, and Artie Shaw. Still arranged Shaw's "Frenesi," which became one of the bestselling "singles" of all time. He also conducted on the radio for all three networks and was active in early television.

Despite his many commercial activities, Still also produced more serious efforts. Initially these works, such as *From the Land of Dreams* (written in 1924 and first performed a year later) and *Darker America* (also written in 1924 and first performed two years later), were described by critics as being "decidedly in the ultra-modern idiom." He soon moved into a simpler harmonic milieu, often drawing on jazz themes, as in *From the Black Belt* (written in 1926 and first performed in 1927), a seven movement suite for orchestra.

Still's most successful and best-known work, *Afro-American Symphony* (completed in 1930 and first performed a year later), draws heavily on the blues idiom; Still said he wanted "to demonstrate how the blues, so often considered a lowly expression, could be elevated to the highest musical level." To some extent the symphony is "programmatic," since after its completion Still added verses by black poet Paul Laurence Dunbar that precede each movement. Still believed that his symphony was probably the first to make use of the banjo. The work was well received and has continued to be played in the United States and overseas.

Still was a prodigious worker. His oeuvre includes symphonies, folk suites, tone poems, works for band, organ, piano, and violin, and operas, most of which focus on racial themes. His first opera, *Blue Steel* (completed in 1935), addresses the conflict between African voodooism and modern American values; its main protagonist is a black worker in Birmingham, Alabama. Still's first staged opera, *Troubled Island* (completed in 1938), which premiered at the New York City Opera in March 1949, centers around the character of Jean Jacques Dessalines, the first emperor of Haiti. The libretto, begun by the black poet Langston Hughes and completed by Verna Arvey, depicts the Haitian leader's stirring rise and tragic fall. Still married Arvey in 1939; the couple had two children. Arvey was to provide libretti for a number of Still's operas and choral works.

Among Still's other notable works are *And They Lynched Him on a Tree* (1940), a plea for brotherhood and tolerance presented by an orchestra, a white chorus, a black chorus, a narrator, and a soloist; *Festive Overture* (1944), a rousing piece based on "American themes"; *Lenox Avenue*, a ballet, with scenario by Arvey, commissioned by CBS and first performed on radio in 1937; *Highway 1, USA* (1962), a short opera, with libretto by Arvey, dealing with an incident in the life of an American family and set just off the highway in a gas station.

Still received many awards. Recognition had come relatively early to him—in 1928 the Harmon Foundation honored him with its second annual award, given to the person judged that year to have made the "most significant contribution to Negro culture in America." He won successive Guggenheim Fellowships in 1934 and 1935 and was awarded a Rosenwald Fellowship in 1939.

Still's early compositions were in an avant-garde idiom, but he soon turned to more conventional melodic and harmonic methods, in what he later described as "an attempt to elevate the folk idiom into symphonic form." This transition may have made his serious work more accessible, but for much of his career he sustained himself and his family by pursuing more commercially successful endeavors.

Still dismissed the black militants who criticized his serious music as "Eur-American music," insisting that his goal had been "to elevate Negro musical idioms to a position of dignity and effectiveness in the fields of symphonic and operatic music." And at a 1969 Indiana University seminar on black music he asserted, "I made this decision of my own free will. . . . I have stuck to this decision, and I've not been sorry."

During his lifetime Still broke many racial barriers. He was heralded as the first black man to have a major orchestral work played before an American audience, the first to conduct a major symphony orchestra (the Los Angeles Philharmonic) in an evening of his own compositions (at the Hollywood Bowl in 1936), and the first to conduct a major all-white orchestra in the Deep South (the New Orleans Philharmonic in 1955 at Southern University). He is also credited with being the first black man to have an opera performed by a "significant" American company (the New York City Opera in 1949). He composed into his late seventies; the Fisk Jubilee Singers performed a piece by him at the Fisk University Centennial Celebration in 1971. He died in Los Angeles.

• Verna Arvey, *William Grant Still* (1939), is a concise biography. He is also treated in R. B. Haas, ed., *William Grant Still and the Fusion of Cultures in American Music* (1972), and in David Ewen, *American Composers: A Biographical Dictionary* (1982). See also *Who's Who in Colored America, 1938–1940* (1940). An article on Still's life and work may be found in *Current Biography* (1941), pp. 829–30.

DANIEL J. LEAB

STILLÉ, Alfred (30 Oct. 1813–24 Sept. 1900), medical professor, was born in Philadelphia, Pennsylvania, the son of John Stillé, a merchant, and Maria Wagner. Expelled from Yale in 1830 in his sophomore year for participating in a student rebellion, Stillé transferred to the University of Pennsylvania, where he graduated from the college in 1832 and from the medical school in 1836.

By 1835 Stillé had become house physician at the Philadelphia Hospital (later Philadelphia General Hospital), where he studied physiology and pathological anatomy under William Wood Gerhard and Caspar Wistar Pennock. Both Gerhard and Pennock had studied in Paris with Pierre-Charles-Alexandre Louis, who, in his investigation of disease, emphasized, first, the correlation of disease symptoms in the patient with postmortem examination and, second, the importance of observation and medical statistics. The typhus epidemic of 1836 in Philadelphia provided Gerhard, Pennock, and Stillé with an opportunity to put Louis's method into practice, and their study of 120 patients resulted in Gerhard's classic paper in the *American Journal of the Medical Sciences* on the distinction between typhus and typhoid fever. The episode was crucially significant for Stillé's later career: in 1836 he left for Paris to study medical diagnostics with Louis and returned to Philadelphia in 1839 a zealous advocate of the French medical philosophy.

No greater contrast could then be found between the extensive training given to a French physician and that experienced by his American counterpart. Medical schools in the United States required attendance for only two years; even this requirement was less than it seemed, for the curriculum rarely included opportunities for dissection, the lectures in the second year were invariably the same as those in the first, and only those students willing to pay private teachers were able to learn the medical specialties. Admission standards were nonexistent, the thesis requirement was usually waived, and the degree was awarded after a perfunctory oral examination. Any attempt at reform was invariably stymied by the apprehension that if any one medical school raised its standards, students would desert it for another. Thus in 1847 when the University of Pennsylvania took the unprecedented step of lengthening the annual course from four months to five and a half months, student enrollment dropped, and the attempt was soon abandoned.

Stillé returned from France with the conviction that reform was nevertheless necessary if the United States were to keep pace with European developments. His subsequent career in Philadelphia conflated his advocacy of curricular reform with the search for professional advancement; his leadership of the reform movement and its subsequent success culminated in a chair at the University of Pennsylvania, then the leading center of medical education in the United States.

From 1839 to 1841 Stillé served as a resident physician at the Pennsylvania Hospital, a traditional first step on the road to medical advancement, but it was not until 1845, after he had built up a modest private practice, that he obtained his first teaching position: an appointment as lecturer on pathology and the practice of medicine at the Philadelphia Association for Medical Instruction, a medical college that offered instruction only during the summer. Stillé won greater prominence, however, as a leading member of the reform movement that resulted in the establishment of the American Medical Association (AMA) in Philadelphia in 1847. The success of the AMA depended on winning the support of the Philadelphia medical schools—if the University of Pennsylvania Medical School and Jefferson Medical College continued to stand aloof, the campaign for improved medical education would be stillborn, and the AMA itself would die a quick death. Thus Stillé's role in Philadelphia as a propagandist for reform and his position as secretary of the organizing committee were crucial to the AMA's early success, and in recognition of his services, Stillé

was unanimously elected secretary of the AMA at its first meeting.

In 1848 he published *Elements of General Pathology*, a textbook that focused on the description of disease lesions. In 1849 Stillé was appointed visiting physician at St. Joseph's Hospital, and in 1850 he resigned his position at the Philadelphia Association on account of ill health. In 1854 he received his first major appointment: professor of the theory and practice of medicine at the medical department of Pennsylvania College. His positions as president of the Pathological Society of Philadelphia (1859–1862) and president of the Philadelphia County Medical Society in 1862, as well as the publication of *Therapeutics and Materia Medica* (1860) contributed to his appointment as professor of the theory and practice of medicine at the University of Pennsylvania in 1864.

Stillé's appointment at Penn coincided with a renaissance in the fortunes of the university medical school, which—challenged by a host of competitors, located in a part of the city that Penn's provost was to describe as "vile . . . and growing viler every day," and damaged by the abrupt exodus of its students from the southern states—was no longer the country's leading medical school. In 1865 the medical curriculum was expanded through the creation of an auxiliary medical faculty in the sciences. In 1874 the university moved to a more salubrious site west of Philadelphia where a new university hospital was added to the medical school. In 1876 the course of study was extended from two to three years, the term was lengthened from four to five months, a progressive curriculum was installed, and the professors were put on a fixed salary. Stillé, who had sounded the clarion for curricular reform in a speech in March 1873, could reflect in 1877 that, despite resistance from a substantial section of the medical professoriate, nearly everything he and the new provost William Pepper had demanded four years earlier had been achieved. Penn stood with the University of Michigan and Harvard in the vanguard of the reform movement of American medical education.

Throughout the decade Stillé won the highest honors—the presidency of the AMA was conferred in 1871, and in 1876 he was appointed vice president of the Centennial Medical Commission—yet the tide was already turning against him. Stillé's edition of the *United States Dispensatory* (1879), written with John Maisch, was warmly received, but other works from this period, most notably *Cholera* (1885), revealed that Stillé rejected the germ theory of disease as mere theoretical speculation. The new science of bacteriology, according to Stillé, consisted only of "German speculation on pathology and therapeutics." Stillé, whose teaching and research consistently advocated clinical observation, medical statistics, and hospital practice, was unwilling to accept laboratory medicine. According to Charles Burr, a student during Stillé's last year at Penn (1884), Stillé was a suitably remote figure from a past that was fast disappearing: "His personal influence upon us was small. His lectures were carefully prepared and carefully read. His clinical descriptions were clear, his points in differential diagnosis well put; his pathology was that which had been dominant at the more active period of his life. . . . He looked even then like a patriarch . . . with a great mass of snow-white hair, long beard and clear, healthy skin." Stillé's first wife, Caroline Barnett, whom he had married in 1841 and with whom he had his only three children, had suffered mental illness for many years. In 1899, shortly after her death, Stillé married Katherine Blackiston. Stillé died in Philadelphia.

• Letters to and from Stillé are in the Isaac Hays Papers at the American Philosophical Society and at the Horace Howard Furness Memorial Library at the University of Pennsylvania. Lecture notes and transcripts of his lectures are in the Alfred Stillé Papers at the College of Physicians of Philadelphia. Stillé's writings on medical reform and medical education are contained in valedictory lectures before students at the medical schools with which he was associated during his career, most notably *Medical Education in the United States* (1846). Excerpts from Stillé's writings and thoughts on religion, politics, literature, and other subjects are in Katherine Blackiston Stillé, *Fragments: Being a Sketch of Dr. Alfred Stillé* (1901). The most reliable memorial is Charles W. Burr, "A Sketch of Dr. Alfred Stillé," *University Medical Magazine* 13 (Jan. 1901): 759–65. An intimate and lively appreciation of Stillé is William Osler, "Alfred Stillé," *University of Pennsylvania Medical Bulletin* 15 (June 1902): 126–32; Osler refrains from evaluating Stillé's later medical writing except in a positive light, and his account is not always accurate. The best account of the meaning of the Parisian medical experience for the members of Stillé's generation is John Harley Warner, "Remembering Paris: Memory and the American Disciples of French Medicine in the Nineteenth Century," *Bulletin of the History of Medicine* 65 (1991): 301–25. The transfer of French medicine to the United States is analyzed in John Harley Warner, "The Selective Transport of Medical Knowledge: Antebellum American Physicians and Parisian Medical Therapeutics," *Bulletin of the History of Medicine* 59 (1985): 213–31, and Russell M. Jones, "American Doctors and the Parisian Medical World," *Bulletin of the History of Medicine* 47 (1973): 40–65, 177–204. The most sophisticated account of the institutional context provided by Philadelphia medicine for clinical diagnosis and postmortem examination in the hospital is Charles Rosenberg, "From Almshouse to Hospital: The Shaping of Philadelphia General Hospital," *Milbank Quarterly* 60 (1982): 108–54. The Penn professoriate initiated curricular reform as early as the 1830s; an authoritative account that reveals that reform at Penn was impeded only by financial constraints is Thomas Huddle, "Competition and Reform at the Medical Department of the University of Pennsylvania, 1847–1877," *Journal of the History of Medicine* 51 (1996): 251–92. An obituary is in the *Philadelphia Public Ledger*, 25 Sept. 1900.

SIMON BAATZ

STILLMAN, James (9 June 1850–15 Mar. 1918), banker, was born in Brownsville, Texas, the son of Charles Stillman, a cotton broker of New England origins, and Elizabeth Pamela Goodrich. Before he was six years old, Stillman's father moved the family away from the unsettled frontier conditions of Texas to New York City. There he attended private schools and a military academy at Ossining, New York. At age sixteen he went to work in the cotton brokerage firm of Smith,

Woodward & Stillman, where his father was a partner. As his father's health declined, Stillman took over many of the elder's responsibilities. At age twenty-one he received full power of attorney from his father, and in 1872 he became a partner in the reorganized firm of Woodward and Stillman. The year before he was made a partner he had married Sarah Elizabeth Rumrill, with whom he had five children.

William Woodward tended to the cotton interests of the firm while Stillman explored financial opportunities in Texas land and railroads, both for the firm and for the estate left by his father worth more than $1 million. His activities brought him to the attention of Moses Taylor, president of the National City Bank in New York, who aided some of his enterprises. In 1884 Stillman joined the board of directors of the bank, and on the death of Taylor's successor in 1891, he was elected president.

Stillman continued his predecessors' policy of maintaining large reserves, much greater than required by law, to reassure depositors, while beginning a process of great expansion. He moved the bank into underwriting industrial securities and providing call loan money for Wall Street. The solidity of the bank attracted deposits from the country's leading industrialists, who in turn became both buyers of the securities he offered and sources of yet more offerings. Stillman formed alliances with many of these magnates, inviting them to sit on the bank's board. The most important was William Rockefeller, president of Standard Oil of New York, who became a close friend. Both of Stillman's daughters married sons of Rockefeller. The National City Bank became the main Standard Oil bank, handling large deposits and aiding the leaders of Standard Oil in investing the immense dividends the oil monopoly produced.

Rockefeller, Stillman, and Henry H. Rogers became known as the "Standard Oil Gang," whose manipulative exploits in the stock market aroused both fear and envy. The stock of the Amalgamated Copper Company—floated by the National City Bank in 1899 for a highly inflated $75 million and earmarked to form the basis for a copper monopoly—moved up and down violently in the market in a pattern that provided great opportunities for men with inside knowledge. In the mines of Butte, Montana, employees fought with dynamite and steam hoses against opponents of Amalgamated Copper. Their other speculative operations in utility and railroad securities added to the notoriety of the "Gang."

Stillman transformed the bank, making it by 1907 the largest bank in the United States with a network of correspondent banks across the country and around the world ready to provide payment and collection services, loans, and foreign-trade financing for expanding American industry. When the panic of 1907 erupted, J. P. Morgan overcame his personal dislike of Stillman and worked closely with him to stop the run on New York's trust companies that threatened to bring down the entire financial structure of the country.

Stillman spoke seldom and gave a general impression of cold arrogance. He ran his bank autocratically. Despite that his board of directors included millionaires who were major figures in the industrial and financial world, none ever disagreed with him or debated his pronouncements at board meetings. He encouraged the bank's employees to bring him information on the activities of their fellows. While he could be severe with transgressors, "Mr. Stillman was a man who never praised" (Vanderlip, p. 119). In 1909 Stillman entered into semiretirement, taking the post of chairman of the board of directors and selecting Frank A. Vanderlip as president. For the next few years he spent most of his time in France, keeping a close rein on his successor through a steady flow of coded cables and letters instructing Vanderlip how to run the bank. From 1915 on Stillman was in poor health with circulatory problems but maintained his ties with his bank, returning to the United States in 1917 to take over when Vanderlip entered government service during World War I.

While in France, Stillman added works by Titian and Rembrandt to an art collection that he had begun in a small way while a schoolboy and that now filled his Paris mansion. Still, he ruefully admitted "that when he looked at his own paintings, in spite of anything he might do, he could see in plain figures on the canvas the annual interest figured upon the cost of the picture" (Vanderlip, p. 223). In 1894 Stillman had separated from his wife, whom he considered mentally unbalanced, and forbade her to communicate with him or the children, and when he died in New York City he left an estate estimated at between $40 million and $50 million to his children. He made no bequests to charity.

The bank Stillman took over in 1891 primarily served the financial interests of members of the Taylor family and their companies. The financial institution he left at his death was the foremost commercial bank in the country offering to big business, Wall Street, and other banks across the country a source of ready money and the comprehensive financial services needed as the United States expanded its role in the global economy.

• The Stillman papers are in the Rare Book and Manuscript Library, Columbia University. Anna Robeson Burr, *The Portrait of a Banker: James Stillman, 1850–1918* (1917), is admiring, while John K. Winkler, *The First Billion: The Stillmans and the National City Bank* (1934), is very critical. The relevant chapters in Harold van B. Cleveland et al., *Citibank, 1812–1970* (1985), describe the bank's activities in detail. Stillman is the dominating figure in Frank Vanderlip's autobiography, *From Farm Boy to Financier* (1935). Contemporary opinion on Stillman's financial operation can be sampled in Edwin Lefèvre, "Captains of Industry: James Stillman," *Cosmopolitan* 35 (1903): 333–36; John Moody, *The Truth about Trusts* (1904); and Thomas W. Lawson, *Frenzied Finance* (1905). On Stillman and the panic of 1907, see Herbert L. Satterlee, *J. Pierpont Morgan: An Intimate Portrait* (1939); on the "Standard Oil Gang," see John T. Flynn, *God's Gold: The Story of Rockefeller and His Times* (1932), and Allan Nevins, *John D. Rockefeller: The Heroic Age of American Enter-*

prise, vol. 2 (1940); on the Amalgamated Copper Company, see Michael P. Malone, *The Battle for Butte* (1981). An obituary is in the *New York Times*, 16 Mar. 1918; his will is discussed in the newspaper six days later.

MILTON BERMAN

STILLMAN, Samuel (27 Feb. 1737–12 Mar. 1807), Baptist clergyman, was born in Philadelphia, Pennsylvania; his parents' names are not known. His family soon moved to Charleston, South Carolina, where he received a rudimentary classical education at Rind's Academy and was converted under the ministry of Oliver Hart, a Baptist pastor with whom he later studied theology. In 1759 Stillman was ordained as an evangelist at First Baptist Church in Charleston. While traveling to Philadelphia later that year, he married Hannah Morgan; the couple had fourteen children.

Stillman's pastoral labors began in 1759 in James Island, South Carolina, where he served until he suffered a pulmonary illness in 1761. The illness led him to a better climate in Bordentown, New Jersey, where he served two congregations. In 1764 he became an assistant minister to James Bound at Second Baptist in Boston, Massachusetts, and one year later he was installed as pastor at First Baptist Church in Boston, where he served for forty years, restoring the congregation's reputation as an evangelical church after years of accusations of formalism and liberalism.

Stillman was active in numerous charitable and educational ventures. He helped incorporate Rhode Island College (later Brown University) in 1764 and remained one of its chief promoters in the Baptist community, also serving as a fellow and a trustee of the institution. In Massachusetts he worked with the Humane Society, the Charitable Fire Society, and the Female Asylum. Stillman was also an organizer and officer of the Massachusetts Baptist Missionary Society, the first of its kind in the United States. A devotee of the English Baptist missionary, William Carey, Stillman believed that the Christian faith could produce social transformation and that revivals spawned missionary growth.

Stillman valued the social and political thoughts of John Locke, especially Locke's distinctions between civil and spiritual "societies." He also accepted the position of Isaac Backus on the separation of church and state. He thought that colonists who demanded certain liberties from Great Britain should also demand total emancipation of African slaves as well if they were to be consistent. An ardent patriot during the Revolution, he urged the army to fight well so that diplomats could construct an honorable peace. In 1775, during the British occupancy of Boston, he and his family fled to Philadelphia. He returned in 1776 and was said to be the only clergyman to hold public services throughout the duration of the war. Stillman continued to voice his concern for liberty and, in an election sermon in Boston in 1779, advocated limits on the powers of magistrates and a bill guaranteeing individual rights. In 1788 Stillman was elected as a representative from Boston to the Constitutional Convention, where he served as one of fifteen clergymen, though apparently without distinction.

A popular preacher, Stillman frequently gave eulogies for prominent persons and preached ordination sermons for Baptist ministers in the area. He also published over thirty sermons and addresses and in 1799 was invited to preach the eulogy in Boston for George Washington.

Stillman's theology may be described as evangelical Calvinism: he held to typical Calivinist principles but also emphasized human initiative in religious organizations and revivals to enhance individual spirituality. Following Locke's religious philosophy, Stillman urged the General Court of Massachusetts in 1779 to adopt principles of complete religious freedom and bring an end to establishment religious bodies. As a Baptist minister, he practiced "closed communion" but was also active in numerous ecumenical activities with other Boston ministers. In 1794 he extolled the democratic impulse of the French Revolution because it secured freedom from the oppressive establishment of religion, but he abhorred the excesses of the Jacobins and the Reign of Terror.

Stillman died in Boston. In concert with his friend and longtime colleague, the Reverend Thomas Baldwin, he made Boston the focal point of Baptist life in New England.

• Some of Stillman's letters are at the American Baptist Historical Society, Rochester, N.Y. For biographical details, consult William Buell Sprague, *Annals of the American Pulpit*, vol. 6, *Baptists* (1860). *A Biographical Sketch of the Author's life in Select Sermons on Doctrinal and Practical Subjects* (1808) and *A Discourse Preached in Boston Before the Massachusetts Baptist Missionary Society, May 25, 1803* (1803). Of his more than thirty published sermons, the following are notable: *A Sermon Preached Before the Honorable Council and the Honorable House of Representatives of the State of Massachusetts Bay in New England at Boston May 26 1779 Being the Anniversary for the Election of the Honorable Council* (1779); *Charity, Considered in a Sermon* (1785); *Thoughts on the French Revolution* (1794); and *Select Sermons on Doctrinal and Practical Subjects* (1808). An obituary is Thomas Baldwin, *The Peaceful Reflections and Glorious Prospects of the Departing Saint. A Discourse preached in the First Baptist Church in Boston, March 16, 1807 at the interment of Rev. Samuel Stillman* (1807).

WILLIAM H. BRACKNEY

STILLMAN, William James (1 June 1828–6 July 1901), journalist, artist, and diplomat, was born in Schenectady, New York, the son of Joseph Stillman, a machinist, and Eliza Ward Maxson. Enduring a strict, impoverished childhood, he retained an intense love of nature and an abiding religious faith. Potentially a brilliant student, and with some financial help from some of his older brothers, he graduated from Union College in Schenectady in 1848 after three years, regretting that he had not studied art.

Stillman studied painting briefly under Frederick Church in 1848–1849. He sold his first landscape in the fall of 1849, and he then sailed to England arriving in January 1850. There he met Joseph Turner, John Ruskin, and the pre-Raphaelites. He studied art under Adolphe Yvon in Paris, where he was impressed by Henri Rousseau, Eugène Delacroix, and Jean-François Millet. Returning to the United States, Stillman was a disciple of Ruskin, and his faithful landscapes earned him the sobriquet "the American pre-Raphaelite" and an associateship in the Academy of Design. In 1855 he founded and edited the short-lived weekly, *Crayon: A Journal Devoted to the Graphic Arts and the Literature Related to Them*, for art essays and poetry. Around 1856 he organized the Adirondacks Club so he could spend his summers with his literary companions, including Henry Wadsworth Longfellow, Ralph Waldo Emerson, James Russell Lowell, and Louis Agassiz, the zoologist and founder of the Boston Comparative Zoology Museum. Stillman taught himself photography while wintering in Florida in 1857. He lived briefly with Ruskin, and although they eventually disagreed fundamentally on art, Stillman named his eldest son after Ruskin. In 1860 he married Laura Mack; they had three children.

During the Civil War, from December 1861 to the spring of 1865, Stillman was appointed American consul to Rome, then under papal jurisdiction. In 1865 he became American consul at Khaniá (Canea) in Crete, then under Ottoman rule and on the verge of savage civil strife. Stillman's reports on the events, especially the Cretans' self-annihilation rather than surrender at the monastery of Arkadi, were instrumental in persuading the great powers to send ships to rescue the noncombatants. His reports and his book, *The Cretan Insurrection of 1866–7–8* (written in 1869–1871 but not published until 1874), constitute the primary sources for historians of this period. Under the stress of making the besieged consulate a haven for refugees, his wife, who apparently suffered from depression, committed suicide in 1868, after the birth of their daughter. Lacking the support of the new American government, Stillman resigned and began photographing sites in Crete, Athens, and Aigina. He published and sold his photographs as *The Acropolis of Athens* (1870) to pay off some of his debts, but he no longer felt able to paint landscapes.

In 1869 Stillman moved to England and lived briefly with Dante Rossetti. In 1871 he married Marie Spartali, the daughter of the Greek consul general in London; they had three children. He began contributing to various English newspapers and was the Balkans correspondent for the *London Times* after 1875. His compassionate though objective reports from Turkish-occupied Bosnia brought Montenegro to British public attention, raised money for the refugees, and forced the British government to take the principality and its aspirations into account. His letters and those of Arthur Evans, Balkan correspondent for the *Manchester Guardian*, were exploited by the former prime minister William Gladstone and the Liberal Opposition. Having given a telescope to the Slavic rebels, allowing them to see enemy locations and numbers, Stillman was instrumental in enabling them to defeat 20,000 Turks and capture a fortified citadel. He recounted these events in *Herzogovina and the Late Uprising* (1877).

On a commission from Scribner's in 1879, Stillman sailed from Ithaca to the Aegean and Crete and published his account as *On the Track of Ulysses* (1888). Asked by the Archaeological Institute of America to investigate excavation opportunities in Crete, he examined some recently exposed walls from the palace at Knossos. Although this project was rejected by both the Cretans and the Turks, his drawings of the walls and their inscribed masons' marks were the first records of Minoan architecture and are still central in scholarly arguments about what Evans later found at the site. Stillman took more photos of Athens, which he sold to Sir Lawrence Alma-Tadema for use in his classically based paintings.

As the *London Times* correspondent in Greece, Stillman was offered a bribe by government officials, which he refused, not to disclose governmental corruption to his readers. While there, he was invited to accompany the commission to establish a new boundary along northern Greece, but he was too ill with cholera to take part. Later, when Greece was blockaded by England in May 1886, he helped the Greek prime minister call a cease-fire.

In January 1885 the American Numismatic and Archaeological Society requested that Stillman report on the authenticity and merits of the massive Cypriot collections sold by Luigi Palma di Cesnola to the New York Metropolitan Museum. He concluded that their usefulness was seriously diminished by a reckless attribution of provenances, repairs and alterations of items, and the nonexistence of the single deposit of the so-called treasure of Curium. After the published opinions of many art experts in the preceding years, Stillman's report stands out for its intelligence and archaeological insight. From 1886 to 1890, when Americans hoped to acquire the claim to excavate at Delphi, he pointed out in a series of letters to the *Nation* that the Greek authorities were exploiting the Americans while negotiating with the French, who had a prior claim to the site.

Asked by the *London Times* in 1889 to choose between Athens or Rome as a base, he chose Rome for family reasons, despite preferring Athens himself. In Italy he was a close observer of the premier, Francesco Crispi, who in January 1891 publicly honored Stillman for his help in negotiations with the English. He informed Crispi of a political conspiracy against him and exposed an Italian banking crisis before it became obvious to everyone. Crispi consulted him about political appointments and the events in Abyssinia. Stillman wrote a biography, *Francesco Crispi, Insurgent, Exile, Revolutionist, and Statesman* (1899). In 1898 he retired to Frimley Green, Surrey, England, where he wrote his autobiography before his death there. Of his portrait in volume 1, sketched in 1856, Lowell said, "You have nothing to do for the rest of your life but to try to look like it." The portrait in volume 2, sketched by his daughter in 1900, reveals his priorities were otherwise.

Stillman earned his living and reputation through his literary skills. His extensive writings reveal his compassion, objectivity, and humanity as well as the diversity of his talents. He gave assistance both to besieged refugees and to consulting English, Greek, and Italian politicians. As a *London Times* foreign correspondent, he was one of the earliest of the powerful journalists with political influence. Although frustrated as an artist through lack of training, he was an articulate art critic. He was intimately familiar with the American literary establishment and leading painters of the time, of whom he left noteworthy impressions. Exhibiting naiveté and faith, he acted without any thought of the consequences to himself, possibly taking after his father in this regard. Indeed, his apparent lack of concern for the needs of his first family may have mellowed with the death of his son in 1874, because he considered the wishes of his second family when choosing to live in Rome. Without being rich or elected to office, he made a difference in art, literary circles, Crete, Montenegro, Greece, and Italy.

• Stillman's consular dispatches are in the National Archives in Washington, D.C. A few were published by George G. Arnakis, "Consul Stillman and the Cretan Revolution of 1866," in the *Transactions of the Second International Cretological Congress of 1966* (1969). In addition to innumerable published letters, essays, articles, and two manuals on photography, Stillman wrote *Venus and Apollo in Paintings and Sculpture* (1897); *Billy and Hans, My Squirrel Friends: A True History* (1897), a delightful and humane account of two squirrels he adopted; *Little Bertha* (1898); *The Union of Italy, 1815–1895* (1898); and *The Old Rome and the New and Other Stories* (1898), a collection of essays. His *Autobiography of a Journalist* (1901) is candid and full of reminiscences of some of the eminent people he encountered but somewhat vague on the chronology of events. Obituaries are in the *New York Evening Post*, 8 July 1901, and the *London Times*, 9 July 1901.

D. J. Ian Begg

STILWELL, Arthur Edward (21 Oct. 1859–26 Sept. 1928), railroad builder and urban promoter, was born in Rochester, New York, the son of Charles Herbert Stilwell, a merchant, and Mary Augusta Pierson. At age sixteen, following his father's failure in business, Arthur Stilwell ran away from home to become a traveling salesman. With only a few years of formal education and tutoring at home, Stilwell's drive and ambition surmounted his lack of training as he sold advertising in railroad timetables. In 1879, while in Virginia, he met and married Jennie A. Wood, and they moved to Kansas City, where he operated briefly a printing shop. Following a short stint as an insurance salesman for Travelers Insurance Company in Chicago, he returned to Kansas City in 1886 and embarked on a career as a railroad and urban promoter.

Stilwell employed the small amount of capital he had accumulated to form a trust company; then, backed by investors from Kansas City, Philadelphia, and St. Louis, he created a myriad of companies to construct a belt railway, erect a hotel, and build an office building, grain elevators, and a union passenger station. With an extraordinary talent for raising venture capital, he formed the Kansas City, Pittsburg & Gulf Railroad in 1892 to construct a line from Kansas City to the Gulf of Mexico. Linking Kansas City with the Gulf was not an original idea, as midwesterners had long sought such a railway to expedite the export of grain and other agricultural products. Stilwell originally planned to establish a Gulf terminal at Sabine Pass, Texas, but later founded a new townsite, Port Arthur, on Sabine Lake. Between 1892 and 1897 Stilwell sold securities, issued construction contracts, established townsites, and pushed the KCP&G southward. Winning considerable support from Dutch investors, he created Mena and De Queen, Arkansas; De Ridder and De Quincy, Louisiana; and Nederland, Texas, along the route—towns named in recognition of his investors. Enormous costs and construction difficulties delayed opening a canal from Port Arthur to the Gulf, and traffic on the railroad failed to meet expectations. Attempting to secure more business for the line in the Midwest, Stilwell formed yet another carrier running north and east from Kansas City to Omaha, Nebraska, and Quincy, Illinois. Overextended, the rail empire collapsed in 1899 as John W. Gates and E. H. Harriman took over the Kansas City, Pittsburg & Gulf, which became the Kansas City Southern Railway. Completion of the canal that year, and the discovery of oil at Spindletop near Port Arthur in 1901, helped make the KCS a profitable railroad and Port Arthur a major center for petroleum refining.

Undaunted by his losses, Stilwell formed another major rail project in 1901, the Kansas City, Mexico and Orient Railway, and a trust company to finance it. This scheme proposed to construct a line from Kansas City southwest across Kansas, Oklahoma Territory, and Texas to the Rio Grande and then across northern Mexico to Topolobampo on the Gulf of California. Stilwell hoped that Topolobampo, the Pacific port closest to Kansas City, would come to rival San Francisco and Los Angeles as a major port of entry. This, too, was not an original idea, but one promoted by others as early as the 1870s. Over the next decade Stilwell raised capital in England and in the Northeast and constructed lines south from Wichita, Kansas, and in three locations in Mexico. Using his flare for publicity, Stilwell placed stories about the "Orient" in leading magazines and newspapers. He brought investors west to see the completed sections and trumpeted the scheme in Mexico and Europe. Aided in Mexico by the government of President Porfirio Diaz, Stilwell sought to complete the line from the Rio Grande to the Gulf of California, but construction difficulties in the Sierra Madres and the Mexican Revolution precluded finishing the project. Faced with huge financial losses and depredations by revolutionists in Mexico, the KCM&O failed in 1912. Stilwell was ousted as president, and the line entered receivership until 1928. The Atchison, Topeka and Santa Fe Railway purchased the KCM&O and then sold the operations in Mexico to the Mexican government in 1940. Under government ownership, the project in Mexico was completed as the Ferrocarril de Chihuahua al Pacifico in 1961.

After the loss of the KCM&O, Stilwell and his wife moved to France where he wrote books attacking the "Cannibals of Wall Street" who had stripped him of his enterprises. He published books and poems pleading for peace after World War I erupted, but by the 1920s he was writing books of fiction and nonfiction about spiritualism. Stilwell claimed that his railroads and urban promotion schemes were products of dreams, "fairies," and "brownies." Influenced by Robert Louis Stevenson and Sir Arthur Conan Doyle, who claimed that their writings were the result of "dreams" or "the little people," the publicity-seeking Stilwell used his revelations to attract notoriety and to enhance the sale of his books. His memoirs appeared serially in the *Saturday Evening Post*. As early as 1922 the Stilwells returned to New York City, where he died. Thirteen days after his death, Jennie Stilwell took her own life.

Stilwell possessed a commanding presence and an engaging personality. About six feet tall and weighing almost two hundred pounds, he presented a handsome and athletic appearance. Always elegantly dressed and carrying a gold headed cane, he affected the mannerisms of an English duke. A devout Christian Scientist and ardent Republican, Stilwell conveyed to all his enthusiasm for life and eternal optimism. He made major contributions to the development of transportation in the south central states, and some of his urban promotions also proved successful. He committed gross errors of judgment concerning the economic viability of his schemes but nevertheless raised tens of millions of dollars in capital for them.

• No substantial body of Stilwell papers exists. Minute books of Stilwell's Kansas City projects are located at the offices of the Kansas City Southern Railway in Kansas City, and some materials concerning the Kansas City, Mexico and Orient Railway are in the Baylor University Library in Waco, Tex. Stilwell's autobiography, "I Had a Hunch," with James R. Crowell, appeared serially in the *Saturday Evening Post* (1927–1928). See also Stilwell's *Cannibals of Finance: Fifteen Years' Contest with the Money Trust* (1912) and *Forty Years of Business Life* (1926). A biography of Stilwell is Keith L. Bryant, Jr., *Arthur E. Stilwell, Promoter with a Hunch* (1971). Additional information can be found in David Pletcher, *Rails, Mines and Progress: Seven American Promoters in Mexico, 1867–1911* (1958), and John Leeds Kerr and Frank Donovan, *Destination Topolobampo: The Kansas City, Mexico and Orient Railway* (1968). On Stilwell's Port Arthur scheme see Keith L. Bryant, Jr., "Arthur E. Stilwell and the Founding of Port Arthur: A Case of Entrepreneurial Error," *Southwestern Historical Quarterly* 75 (1971): 19–40.

KEITH L. BRYANT, JR.

STILWELL, Joseph Warren (19 Mar. 1883–12 Oct. 1946), army officer, was the son of Benjamin W. Stilwell and Mary A. Peene. He was born near Palatka, Florida, where his father, a man of many parts, was attempting, unsuccessfully, to start a lumber business. Benjamin Stilwell subsequently moved his family back to his home town of Yonkers, New York, and settled down to become an executive with an electric utilities company. Stilwell was educated in Yonkers schools and graduated from the U.S. Military Academy in 1904. Following an assignment (1904–1906) with the Twelfth Infantry on Cebu in the Philippine Islands, where the army was engaged in pacifying rebellious tribes, Stilwell returned to the Military Academy (1906–1910) to teach French and Spanish. In 1910 he married Winifred Smith; they had five children.

Between 1911 and 1917 Stilwell again served with the Twelfth Infantry in the Philippines (1911–1912) and at the Presidio of Monterey, California (1912–1913), and he had another tour at West Point (1913–1917), where he taught in the Department of English and History and then the Department of Modern Languages while also coaching football and basketball. He was promoted to captain in 1916. In August 1917 he was assigned as brigade adjutant to the Eightieth Division at Camp Lee, Virginia, and in December was ordered to France to become chief intelligence officer of IV Corps. Except for periods of detached duty with the British and the French, Stilwell stayed with the corps for the duration of the war. For several months in 1919 he was at Cochem, Germany, while IV Corps was stationed in the area on occupation duty. He won promotions, all temporary, to major in 1917, to lieutenant colonel in 1918, and to colonel in 1919.

Stilwell quickly grew dissatisfied with the monotonous routine of the peacetime army and in 1920 requested assignment to a new program organized by the Military Intelligence Division to train officers in an Asiatic language. Since the slots in Japanese had already been filled, Stilwell was assigned to the University of California in Berkeley to learn Chinese for a year, after which he continued his studies in Peking (Beijing), China. He arranged to travel extensively in China once he realized how dull life in a legation compound could be and in the process learned far more about the country and its people than most foreigners did. Stilwell's expertise in Chinese affairs shaped the remainder of his career. He concluded his tour in China in 1923 but returned twice more. From 1926 to 1929 in Tientsin (Tianjin) with the Fifteenth Infantry, which was stationed in China under the terms of the Boxer Protocol, he served first as a battalion commander and later as the regiment's executive officer. From 1935 to 1939 Stilwell was assigned to China as military attaché. Although he rated the Chinese soldier as potentially the equal of any, if only competent leadership could be found, Stilwell was not impressed by the ability of Chiang Kai-shek's (Jiang Jieshi) Kuomintang (Nationalist) government to harness China's military potential in the conflict with Japan that began in 1937. Poor leadership, corruption among the political and military elite, and the persistence of regional loyalties all undermined China's cause, he believed.

Following his second tour in China, Stilwell also established his credentials as one of the peacetime army's ablest tacticians. He had already attended both the Infantry School at Fort Benning, Georgia (1923–1924) and the Command and General Staff School at Fort Leavenworth (1924–1925), and between 1929 and 1933 he headed the Infantry School's tactical section. It was there that he earned the nickname of "Vinegar Joe" for the acerbic way he criticized those whose competence and intelligence did not measure up to the high standards to which he held himself. Three times Stilwell's immediate superior, Colonel George Marshall, had to fend off demands by the post commander for Stilwell's transfer. Marshall, who had first come to know Stilwell when both men were serving in Tientsin, understood both Stilwell's difficult temperament and his uncommon abilities. When Marshall became chief of staff of the army in 1939, he placed a premium on ability and quickly promoted Stilwell to brigadier general. (Stilwell had reverted to his prewar rank of captain in 1919 and had since earned promotions to major, lieutenant colonel, and colonel.) Stilwell also received increased responsibilities: command of a brigade at Fort Sam Houston (Sept. 1939), of the Seventh Division at Fort Ord (July 1940), and of III Corps (July 1941), which had its headquarters at the Presidio. By the time the United States entered World War II, Stilwell, who consistently distinguished himself on maneuvers, was recognized as the army's ablest corps commander and was selected to lead its first overseas initiative, the occupation of Dakar in French West Africa. However, the operation was postponed, and in the meantime (Feb. 1942) a commander was needed for the newly created China-Burma-India (CBI) theater. Assignment to this theater, which he reluctantly accepted as his duty, mired Stilwell in the sort of politics he dreaded. Not only would he command the theater, where most American units would not consist of the infantry he understood but of aviation, logistics, and engineering personnel, but he was also named chief of staff to Generalissimo Chiang of China and coordinator of lend-lease in the vast but remote area. The far-reaching authority that Stilwell required to perform his mission threatened the Kuomintang leadership, for Chiang and his subordinates feared that giving Stilwell such power might cost them their personally profitable control of their armies and ultimately of China itself. Instead, Chiang practiced the politics of delay.

Stilwell faced a crisis as soon as he arrived in the region, for Japanese forces had already invaded the British colony of Burma, then the only route still in Allied control through which supplies could be delivered by land to nonoccupied portions of China. No U.S. ground personnel were available to defend Burma, and so Stilwell had to urge the British and the Chinese to do more there. Their forces could not hold, and Stilwell, who declined a chance to be flown out of northern Burma, led about 100 people (many of them civilian medical personnel) on a difficult retreat, carried out mainly on foot, from northern Burma across mountainous terrain to India. Once in India, Stilwell told the press that the defenders of Burma had taken a "hell of a beating." He thereafter dedicated himself to regaining Burma, but to do so he needed the commitment of the British, who placed a much higher priority on their Mediterranean campaigns, and of the Chinese Kuomintang, whose leadership preferred to subordinate operations against the Japanese in order to strengthen their hand in the on-again, off-again civil war against the Chinese Communists. Stilwell declined to have direct contact with top Communist leaders but through U.S. embassy personnel and other sources came to think highly of Communist military capabilities and wished to bring their forces into a common effort against Japan.

Realizing that he would not receive any substantial number of U.S. infantrymen (he eventually got one regiment), Stilwell sought Chiang's cooperation in employing American personnel to supervise the training of Chinese troops, some at Ramgahr, India, and the bulk in southwestern China. Stilwell's efforts led to vexatious bickering with British authorities, with Chiang, and with Major General Claire Chennault, the commander of U.S. air forces in China. Chennault differed with Stilwell on the allocation of supplies and other issues, and he did not hesitate to use his independent access to Chinese leaders to undermine Stilwell's credibility. Until northern Burma could be regained and a new road from India constructed, such supplies as were available had to be flown across the Himalayas from India to China.

Stilwell's tasks were further complicated in 1943, when a new Allied command structure was established, the Southeast Asia Command (SEAC). In addition to retaining the positions he had held since 1942, Stilwell was named deputy supreme commander of SEAC. His immediate superior in SEAC was the glamorous Lord Louis Mountbatten, still another of the British officers Stilwell came to dislike. As Stilwell's biographer, Barbara Tuchman, put it, "The interlocking and overlapping areas of command, geographically, operationally and nationally under these arrangements, were of such tangled complexity that no one then or since has been able to sort them into a logical pattern" (Tuchman, p. 383).

When the successful effort to retake Burma began in late 1943, Stilwell temporarily took refuge in the field in the hope that his presence would spur Nationalist generals to fight more aggressively. His critics sarcastically asked why a lieutenant general preferred to act as if he were a company commander, a captain's task. On Stilwell's return to Chungking (Chongqing), the wartime capital of China, Washington, worried by a successful new Japanese offensive in eastern China, demanded that he be made commander of the Chinese armed forces, Chiang refused to do so and countered by insisting Stilwell be recalled. The United States yielded in October 1944 and also split CBI itself into two more manageable commands.

Stilwell spent early 1945 at a desk in Washington, where he served as chief of Army Ground Forces, a position that oversaw training throughout the United States. He chafed at his desk job and was pleased when he was ordered to Okinawa in June 1945 to take command of the Tenth Army. By this time the fighting there had been concluded save for mopping up action,

but Stilwell had to oversee the construction of base facilities and hoped he might win a place for the Tenth Army and himself in the invasion of Japan then being planned. The war ended before the invasion took place, and Stilwell's final assignment took him to San Francisco, where he commanded the Sixth Army and the Western Defense Command. He was scheduled to retire at the end of 1946, but in September he was found to have an advanced case of stomach cancer. He died in San Francisco.

Stilwell's reputation in the Second World War was based on his status as the ranking U.S. officer in the China-Burma-India theater. His unmatched knowledge of Chinese affairs made him an obvious choice for the assignment and cost him the one he relished, command of American ground troops. Throughout his tenure he tried to prod the Kuomintang leadership into doing more to contribute to the Allied war effort in Asia, but for Chinese armies to fight effectively, Chiang would have had to submit to American demands and allow Stilwell to take charge of their modernization and their deployment. Given the almost impossible array of tasks he was assigned, Stilwell's recall was not the product of personal failings but instead illustrated that, as Tuchman observed at the time of the American war in Vietnam, the power of the United States to influence events in Asia was limited.

• Stilwell's diaries and papers are at the Hoover Institution Archives, Stanford, Calif. Excerpts from Stilwell's wartime diaries and correspondence are in Theodore H. White, ed., *The Stilwell Papers* (1958). Among the secondary sources on Stilwell are Barbara W. Tuchman, *Stilwell and the American Experience in China, 1911–1945* (1970), a deservedly praised biography; Jack Belden, *Retreat with Stilwell* (1943); and Frank Dorn, *Walkout: With Stilwell in Burma* (1971). Essential are three exhaustively researched volumes by Charles Romanus and Riley Sunderland, *Stilwell's Mission to China* (1953); *Stilwell's Command Problems* (1956); and *Time Runs Out in CBI* (1959). An obituary is in the *New York Times*, 13 Oct. 1946.

LLOYD J. GRAYBAR

STILWELL, Simpson Everett (25 Aug. 1849–17 Feb. 1903), army scout, was born in Tennessee, the son of William Stilwell and Clara (maiden name unknown), farmers. He was a brother of Frank C. Stilwell, a western outlaw. The family moved to Kansas, where in 1863 his parents divorced. Soon afterward Stilwell, whose nickname was "Jack," left home and found various means of employment along the Santa Fe Trail.

In March 1867 Stilwell enlisted as a laborer at Fort Dodge, Kansas. By June he had become a scout and in September was assigned to the Forsyth Scouts under the command of General George A. Forsyth. Among the youngest in the group, he was nonetheless considered quite capable. A contemporary recalled that he was a "reckless, harum-scarum fellow, full of fight and fun." Forsyth remembered him as "a handsome boy of about nineteen, with all the pluck and enthusiasm of an American frontier lad."

Stilwell achieved military fame during the battle of Beecher Island in September 1868. While on patrol in northeast Colorado, Forsyth and his command encountered a superior force of Indians. At Stilwell's suggestion, Forsyth moved his forces onto Beecher Island in the Arikaree River. Despite his good defensive position, Forsyth quickly realized that only reinforcements could save him and his men. He then asked for volunteers to break through the Indian lines and relate his dire situation to the authorities at Fort Wallace, Kansas. Stilwell was the first scout to volunteer. His exuberance had an uplifting affect on the other men. Of the rest, Forsyth selected Pierre Trudeau to accompany Stilwell. Forsyth knew that Trudeau was more experienced than Stilwell but considered Stilwell the more intelligent and resourceful of the two men.

The effect of Stilwell's enthusiasm was short-lived. Two days later, Forsyth and his men, believing that Stilwell and Trudeau had been killed, sent Jack Donovan and J. J. Pliley to Fort Wallace. However, four days after leaving Beecher Island, Stilwell and Trudeau arrived at Fort Wallace ahead of Donovan and Pliley. Although Donovan would accompany forces from Fort Wallace back to Beecher Island on 25 September to drive away the Indians and to escort Forsyth's group back to Fort Wallace, Stilwell was acclaimed as the hero of Beecher Island for alerting military officials about Forsyth's plight. The one casualty was Trudeau, who, for all his years of experience, found the intense experience too much to handle and nearly suffered a nervous breakdown before reaching Fort Wallace.

At the end of 1868 Stilwell was discharged from the Forsyth Scouts but continued to serve as an army scout under various commanders, including George Custer, Philip Sheridan, and Ranald S. McKenzie. His scouting and fighting abilities against the Indians in the southern plains were praised by his superiors. In 1881 Stilwell's military career drew to a close. Succumbing to chronic rheumatism, Stilwell knew he could no longer fully carry out his duties and submitted his resignation.

After leaving the army Stilwell settled in El Reno, Oklahoma, near the Kiowa Agency. For a time he was a deputy U.S. marshal and a police justice. He studied law and was admitted to the bar in the early 1890s. Through his military and political connections he was appointed U.S. commissioner in Anadarko, Oklahoma, in 1894 and was reappointed in 1897.

Stilwell's new life was not confined entirely to judicial matters. He kept in contact with military leaders and former Forsyth scouts. As a public official, he took a personal interest in the social and commercial life of El Reno. By the early 1890s he had become a good friend of William F. "Buffalo Bill" Cody. In 1895 he married Esther Hannah White in Braddock, Pennsylvania; the couple had no children.

In 1898, due to failing health and at the insistence of Buffalo Bill, Stilwell moved to northwest Wyoming. Not content with a life of leisure, he continued to practice law, rented a farm near Marquette, and received an appointment as a U.S. commissioner. Known as Judge Stilwell, he quickly became a respected member within his newly adopted community. He died of pneumonia in Cody, Wyoming.

During his life Stilwell witnessed a variety of transitions in the West. But his epitaph had long been inscribed in the minds of friends and military leaders. Although age had taken its physical toll, he was still remembered fondly as the gallant youth among Forsyth's Scouts at Beecher Island.

• Glimpses into Stilwell's life on the Kiowa Agency in Oklahoma can be found in Works Projects Administration interviews and Record Group 75, Kiowa, Comanche, Apache, and Wichita Agency Records, Oklahoma Historical Society. A good book about primary sources on Stilwell is Orvel A. Criqui, *Fifty Fearless Men: The Forsyth Scouts & Beecher Island* (1993). For reminiscences about Stilwell at Beecher Island see *The Beecher Island Annual* (1904–1963) and the George A. Forsyth Papers, Colorado Historical Society. For scholarly accounts about Beecher Island, see John H. Monnett, *The Battle of Beecher Island: The Indian War of 1867–1869* (1992), and David Dixon, *Hero of Beecher Island: The Life and Military Career of George A. Forsyth* (1994). Obituaries are in the *Wyoming Stockgrower and Farmer*, 24 Feb. 1903, and the *Big Horn County News and Courier*, 21 Feb. 1903.

CARL V. HALLBERG

STIMPSON, William (14 Feb. 1832–26 May 1872), marine zoologist and museum administrator, was born in Roxbury, Massachusetts, the son of Herbert Hathorne Stimpson, an inventor and successful stove merchant, and Mary Ann Devereau Brewer. He was educated in the public schools of Cambridge, Massachusetts. His interest in natural history was piqued when he saw a copy of Augustus A. Gould's *Report on the Invertebrata of Massachusetts* (1841), and while still in high school Stimpson sought out Gould and secured a copy of the treasured volume. Gould introduced Stimpson to several other naturalists, including William G. Binney and Louis Agassiz. In 1849 Stimpson published his first scientific paper, a description of a new species of land snail.

He persisted in his studies of nature despite the strong opposition of his father, who wanted him to become an engineer. The elder Stimpson relented when William became a student of the celebrated Louis Agassiz in October 1850. During two and a half years with Agassiz, Stimpson studied all classes of marine invertebrates and systematically dredged the Atlantic from Boston to Maine. Within two years Stimpson emerged as America's foremost practitioner of scientific dredging. He published papers on a variety of marine creatures, particularly the mollusks, in the *Proceedings of the Boston Society of Natural History*, and in 1851 he published a book on molluscan nomenclature entitled *A Revision of the Synonymy of the Testaceous Mollusks of New England*.

In late 1852 Gould and Agassiz recommended their young student for the post of naturalist on the United States North Pacific Exploring Expedition (1853–1856), and Stimpson received the appointment in November 1852. While on this little-known expedition, which followed close on the heels of Commodore Matthew Perry's epochal journey to Japan, Stimpson became one of the first western naturalists to collect in and around Japanese waters. Stimpson's proficiency with the dredge enabled him to amass over 10,000 specimens of marine invertebrates on the voyage, many of which he described (in elegant Latin) in a series of papers in the *Proceedings of the Academy of Natural Sciences of Philadelphia.*

On his return from the expedition Stimpson accompanied the specimens to the Smithsonian Institution in Washington, D.C., where he spent the next nine years working up reports of the expedition. As a result of his investigations, he was soon recognized as one of the world's authorities on marine crustacea. He also continued to publish descriptions of mollusks, annelids, and echinoderms. In 1860 Columbian University (now George Washington University) awarded Stimpson an honorary M.D. in recognition of his accomplishments, the only degree he ever received. While based in Washington, Stimpson organized several informal scientific clubs, the most prominent of which were the Potomac Side Naturalists Club and the Megatherium Club. Stimpson's jovial personality put him at the center of these club's social activities.

From 1858 to 1863 Stimpson contributed zoological reviews to the *American Journal of Science,* where he was a conspicuous advocate of American scientific efforts. His reviews also reveal his lifelong interest in the subject of classification and scientific nomenclature, and he championed the cause of rigorous and exacting standards in describing new species.

In July 1864 Stimpson married Annie Gordon of Ilchester, Maryland. Soon thereafter Robert Kennicott, an Illinois naturalist and director of the Chicago Academy of Sciences, asked Stimpson to oversee operations at the newly reorganized museum in Chicago while Kennicott was exploring in Alaska. In December 1864 Stimpson agreed to the temporary appointment. A fire in June 1866 destroyed much of the Academy's collection, and in October of that year word reached Chicago that Kennicott had died in May. In January 1867 Stimpson was appointed director and secretary of the Chicago Academy of Sciences.

The Academy moved into a new "fireproof" building in January 1868, and a few months later Stimpson was elected to the National Academy of Sciences. Working energetically to build up the Chicago Academy's collections, Stimpson donated his own personal cabinet of mollusks and acquired the state of Illinois's insect collection. He also called upon the Smithsonian Institution for assistance, and by June 1869 he had secured on permanent loan the Smithsonian's collection of crustacea. Within another year Stimpson had assembled a large and invaluable collection, particularly rich in marine invertebrates. All of these materials were brought together very quickly, and the scientific community was largely unaware of the quality and quantity of specimens housed at the Academy.

In addition to his responsibilities at the Academy, Stimpson continued his own research. In the spring of 1870 he was among the earliest naturalists to systematically dredge and report on the deep-water fauna of Lake Michigan. During the summer of 1871, suffering from an advanced case of tuberculosis, he traveled to Cambridge, Massachusetts, and to Washington, D.C., to gather up all of his scattered scientific manuscripts and notes. For twenty years he had been working on a massive monograph that included descriptions and illustrations of every mollusk known to inhabit America's Atlantic coast. Other unpublished papers included the zoological report of the North Pacific Exploring Expedition, a report on the crustacea of North America, and a series of papers on dredging.

On 8 October 1871 a fire broke out on the West Side of Chicago, and thirty-six hours later most of the city was laid to waste, including the Chicago Academy of Sciences and all of its collections and manuscripts. The loss proved too much for Stimpson to bear. Despondent over the destruction of his life's work, he ignored his doctor's orders to rest for the winter and instead traveled to Florida in an attempt to recoup some of what had been lost. Unfortunately, Stimpson's rapidly deteriorating condition forced him to abandon his plans. He had a brief reunion with his family before he died of tuberculosis at Ilchester, Maryland. He was survived by his wife and two of their three children.

• The most important repository for Stimpson's letters is the Smithsonian Institution Archives. A number of letters written to Stimpson are in the Chicago Academy of Sciences Archives. Among the more important of Stimpson's scientific papers are "Synopsis of the Marine Invertebrata of Grand Manan; or, The Region about the Mouth of the Bay of Fundy, New Brunswick," *Smithsonian Contributions to Knowledge* 6, no. 5 (1854): 1–60; "Prodromus Descriptionis Animalium Evertebratorum in Expeditione ad Oceanum Pacificum Septentrionalem missa, C. Ringgold et Johanne Rodgers, ducibus, observatorum et descriptorum," in eight separate parts, *Proceedings of the Academy of Natural Sciences of Philadelphia* 9 (1857): 19–31, 159–66, 216–21; 10 (1858): 31–40, 93–110, 159–63, 225–52; 12 (1860): 22–47; "The Crustacea and Echinodermata of the Pacific Shores of North America," *Journal of the Boston Society of Natural History* 6 (1857): 444–532; and "Researches upon the Hydrobiinae and Allied Forms," *Smithsonian Miscellaneous Collections* 7, no. 4 (1866): 1–57.
Works about Stimpson include A. G. Mayer, "Biographical Memoir of William Stimpson," *Biographical Memoirs National Academy of Sciences* 8 (1918): 419–33, and W. H. Dall, "Some American Conchologists," *Proceedings of the Biological Society of Washington* 4 (1888): 129–33. An obituary is in the *Chicago Tribune,* 12 June 1872.

RONALD S. VASILE

STIMSON, Henry Lewis (21 Sept. 1867–20 Oct. 1950), cabinet member and statesman, was born in New York City, the son of Lewis Atterbury Stimson, a stockbroker, and Candace Wheeler. In 1871 Stimson's father sold his seat on the New York Stock Exchange and took his family to Europe, where for the next three years he studied to become a physician. Following the family's return to the United States, Stimson's mother died, and young Henry was sent to live with his grandparents. At the age of thirteen Stimson went off to Phillips Academy in Andover, Massachusetts. He continued his education at Yale, receiving his bachelor's degree in 1888. While at Yale, he was elected to Skull and Bones, a secret society that afforded him with important contacts for the rest of his life.

Stimson then attended Harvard Law School, graduating in 1890 with a master of arts degree. Returning to New York, he was admitted to the bar and joined the law firm of Root and Clark in 1891, becoming a partner two years later. The firm's senior member, Elihu Root, a future secretary of war and secretary of state, became a key influence and role model for Stimson. In 1893 Stimson married Mabel White, to whom he had been engaged since his senior year at Yale. The couple remained childless during their 57-year marriage.

While establishing himself as a successful Wall Street lawyer, Stimson also became involved in local Republican politics. In 1906 President Theodore Roosevelt, a fellow member of the Boone and Crockett hunting club, named Stimson United States attorney for the Southern District of New York. During his three years in that office, Stimson's most noteworthy cases involved antitrust and fraud charges against the American Sugar Refining Company and Charles W. Morse of the Bank of North America. By this time, Stimson had become closely associated with Theodore Roosevelt's brand of progressivism. When he ran for governor of New York in 1910, he was widely perceived as Roosevelt's handpicked candidate. While Stimson had built a reputation as an effective lawyer and public servant, his austere manner and aloof personality made him an ineffective campaigner. In the only run for elective office in his career, he was defeated convincingly by the Democratic candidate, John A. Dix, Jr.

In 1911 President William Howard Taft, in a move intended in part to defuse Theodore Roosevelt's growing opposition, appointed Stimson secretary of war. As a member of Taft's cabinet, Stimson unsuccessfully urged the president to support legislation specifically enumerating unfair business practices and establishing a federal agency to regulate corporations involved in interstate commerce. As head of the War Department, Stimson sought to build on the reforms initiated by Root during the McKinley and Roosevelt administrations that sought to strengthen the powers of the secretary of war and the general staff and to modernize the department's bureaucracy.

At the end of the Taft administration, Stimson resumed his law practice in New York. He became a central figure in the New York State Constitutional Convention of 1915, pressing for the adoption of an executive budget system. Although he helped to win support for a greatly strengthened executive in the convention, the voters of New York subsequently rejected the constitution he had been so instrumental in drafting.

With the outbreak of war in Europe in 1914, Stimson became an outspoken advocate of military preparedness. When the United States entered the war, Stimson, who was then forty-nine years old, volunteered for service in the army. He became an artillery officer and saw active duty in France. Stimson left the service shortly after the armistice, having attained the rank of colonel, and once again took up the practice of law. As a corporation lawyer on Wall Street during the 1920s, Stimson enjoyed a substantial income of about $50,000 a year, but he did not find the private practice of law entirely fulfilling. He therefore responded favorably in 1927 to President Calvin Coolidge's request that he take on a diplomatic mission in Nicaragua. Between 1912 and 1925, American marines had helped to keep Nicaragua's Conservative party in power. Following the withdrawal of American forces, civil war broke out in the country between supporters of the Conservative and Liberal parties. Coolidge sent Stimson to Nicaragua to mediate a settlement of the conflict. During his month-long stay in Nicaragua, Stimson worked out an agreement between the leaders of the contending sides that called for American supervision of an election in 1928 and for the creation of a national constabulary to be trained by Americans. Although Stimson's efforts were hailed as a success at the time, one rebel general, Augusto Sandino, rejected the settlement and continued to wage war against the American-backed government for the next several years. By the early 1930s, following the departure of the last American marines, Anastasio Somoza Garcia, a man whom Stimson judged to be a "very frank, friendly, likeable young liberal" (Hodgson, p. 112), had begun to build a family dictatorship that would last for nearly a half century.

Stimson's apparent success in Nicaragua led President Coolidge to name him governor general of the Philippines in 1928. Stimson accepted the notion of the "white man's burden," once stating that "three hundred years of Spain worked a wonderful operation on the Malay race even if it killed a lot of them in doing it" (Gerber, p. 357), and he opposed independence for the Philippines. Nevertheless, his emphasis on economic development and his willingness to treat the leaders of Filipino society with respect made him a popular figure in the islands. His stay lasted only one year, however, because Herbert Hoover called him back to Washington, D.C., in 1929 to become secretary of state.

In that capacity Stimson headed the American delegation to the three-month-long London Naval Conference in 1930. Stimson supported limiting the arms race in ships not covered by the 1922 Washington Naval Treaty—cruisers, destroyers, and submarines—not because of a philosophical commitment to disarmament but rather as a means of defusing growing tensions between the United States and Britain. The conference produced an agreement among the United States, Britain, and Japan to establish a 10:10:7 ratio in destroyers and cruisers, to limit submarines, and to maintain a moratorium on the construction of capital ships, but Stimson was unsuccessful in convincing France and Italy to join in the treaty. Within a few years, moreover, Japan would renounce the treaty's restrictions.

Japan's invasion and takeover of Manchuria in 1931 posed the greatest challenge to Stimson's diplomacy during his tenure as secretary of state. Although, like many other Westerners, he was initially more favorably disposed toward Japan than China and hoped that moderates in the Japanese government would be able to restrain the excesses of the military, he soon concluded that a strong response by the United States to Japanese aggression was necessary. Because public opinion and President Hoover opposed forceful action, Stimson formulated an American response that was ultimately more symbolic than substantive. In January 1932 the secretary of state proclaimed what came to be known as the Stimson Doctrine, which stated that the United States would not "recognize any situation, treaty or agreement" brought about by aggressive threats or acts of war. While incurring the hostility of Japan, the Stimson Doctrine had no direct effect on events in China.

Stimson was also a central figure in negotiations in 1931 that led to a one-year moratorium on the payment of all intergovernmental debts growing out of World War I. The moratorium was intended as a means of averting a collapse of the world banking system. When the moratorium expired in 1932, Stimson unsuccessfully urged Hoover to adopt a policy that would allow for the permanent cancellation of most debt payments owed to the U.S. government as an incentive for the British and French to renounce their claims for continued reparations from Germany.

When Hoover left office in 1933, Stimson went back to his law firm. As the world moved toward war in the late 1930s, he publicly supported the idea of collective security and the need for a strong American military. In 1940 Franklin D. Roosevelt invited Stimson to join his cabinet as secretary of war. Roosevelt believed that his appointment of such a prominent Republican (along with the naming of former Republican vice presidential candidate Frank Knox to the position of secretary of the navy) would help to deflect partisan criticisms of his efforts to prepare for the possibility of war.

One of Stimson's first actions as secretary of war was to press for the adoption of a selective service system. Believing that the defeat of Britain would be disastrous for the United States, Stimson also became a leading spokesperson in favor of lend-lease and other forms of military aid for Britain in the period before the Japanese attack on Pearl Harbor. Once the United States entered the war, Stimson and the army chief of staff, General George C. Marshall, with whom the secretary established a close working relationship, supported establishing a second front through a cross-channel invasion as quickly as possible. Stimson was disappointed that Winston Churchill convinced Roosevelt to delay such a campaign until 1944.

Although Stimson was not himself involved on a day-to-day basis with the War Department's organization of war production, he assembled a team of subordinates, including Robert Patterson, John J. McCloy, Robert Lovett, and Harvey Bundy, which proved very effective in mobilizing the nation's resources for the war effort. Stimson did play a central role in approving the decision to intern the more than 100,000 people of Japanese descent living on the West Coast. Responding to exaggerated claims from officials in California about the threat these individuals posed to national security, Stimson's own racial prejudices were undoubtedly a factor in his decision to recommend to President Roosevelt the most massive U.S. violation of civil liberties of the war.

One critical responsibility Stimson assumed during the war was general oversight of the Manhattan Project, the top-secret program to develop an atomic bomb. Work on the bomb was such a closely guarded secret that following Roosevelt's death in April 1945, Stimson had to inform the new president, Harry S. Truman, about the existence of the bomb project. Stimson then was a major influence on Truman's decision to use the bomb on Japan. Stimson himself appointed and chaired a special advisory body, the Interim Committee, to make recommendations to the president concerning the use of the bomb. Stimson, like most members of the committee, had assumed from the outset that if the bomb became operational before the war ended, it would be used. While heavily influenced by a desire to end the war as quickly as possible and to avoid an invasion of the Japanese home islands, Stimson also sensed that use of the bomb might strengthen America's position in postwar negotiations with the Soviet Union and that a demonstration of the bomb's unprecedented power might also make the postwar control of atomic energy more likely.

By the time Stimson was ready to step down as secretary of war the month after the Japanese surrender, he had reconsidered his position on the potential impact of the atomic bomb on postwar diplomacy. In a final memo to Truman, Stimson warned that relations with the Soviets might be "irretrievably embittered . . . if we fail to approach them now and merely continue to negotiate with them, having this weapon rather ostentatiously on our hip." In a sentence that has since been widely quoted, Stimson advised Truman: "The chief lesson I have learned in a long life is that the only way you can make a man trustworthy is to trust him; and the surest way to make him untrustworthy is to distrust him and show your distrust" (Stimson and Bundy, p. 644). Stimson's final plea for a bilateral approach to the Soviets on the issue of atomic energy was not adopted.

In his final year as secretary of war, Stimson also played an important role in discussions within the Roosevelt and Truman administrations concerning the postwar treatment of Germany. In the fall of 1944 Secretary of the Treasury Henry Morgenthau, Jr., proposed a plan that received tentative support from

President Roosevelt for Germany to be partitioned and deindustrialized to prevent it from ever again having the capacity to threaten the peace of the world. Stimson lobbied hard against what came to be called the Morgenthau Plan, arguing that destroying Germany's industrial base would weaken the postwar economy of all of Europe and that such a punitive policy would fly in the face of all the lessons learned from the aftermath of World War I. His arguments helped persuade Roosevelt to back down from any commitment to the Morgenthau Plan and later reinforced Truman's final rejection of the proposal.

Following his retirement on his seventy-eighth birthday, Stimson returned to his estate on Long Island, where he lived with his wife until his death there. In retirement he worked with McGeorge Bundy on his memoirs, which were published in 1948 under the title *On Active Service in Peace and War*.

Henry Stimson was a distinguished public servant who during his long career enjoyed the respect of a wide spectrum of people in official Washington. In the years after he left government service in 1945, Stimson became a hero and inspiration to what some have called the "foreign policy establishment." Many of the men who shaped American foreign policy through the first decades of the Cold War, including Robert Patterson, John J. McCloy, Robert Lovett, and McGeorge Bundy, were Stimson protégés who shared with him a common social and educational background, having ties to Yale or Harvard and Wall Street. They also shared Stimson's commitment to an internationalist conception of collective security and an unshakable belief in the rectitude of American purposes.

Stimson's last act as a government official was to warn against the dangers of adopting too harsh an approach to the Soviet Union, but his principal legacy for subsequent policymakers during the Cold War was his affirmation of the necessity of the United States assuming a position of global leadership in which American disinterestedness was taken for granted. Stimson's own integrity and high-mindedness were unquestionable. He was, nonetheless, also a man whose vision was limited by racial and class bias. While he was always correct in his dealings with individuals, throughout his career he was unable to overcome the racial and ethnic prejudices that had been prevalent in Victorian America. Not only did these prejudices affect his views on American relations with non-European nations, they also contributed to his willingness to maintain second-class citizenship for African Americans serving in the military. Similarly, Stimson constantly emphasized the importance of individual "character" in judging a man. However, he inevitably found it much easier to see "character" in a fellow Yale or Harvard man than in an individual who lacked the advantages of a privileged upbringing.

• Stimson's papers, including his extensive diaries, are in the Yale University Library and are also available on microfilm. Stimson's own writings, in addition to his memoir, include *American Policy in Nicaragua* (1927), *Democracy and Nationalism in Europe* (1934), *The Far Eastern Crisis: Recollections and Observations* (1936), and "The Decision to Use the Atomic Bomb," *Harper's Magazine*, Feb. 1947, pp. 97–107. The significance of the latter article is discussed in Barton J. Bernstein, "Seizing the Contested Terrain of Early Nuclear History: Stimson, Conant, and Their Allies Explain the Decision to Use the Atomic Bomb," *Diplomatic History* 17 (Winter 1993): 35–72. A prominent biography is Godfrey Hodgson, *The Colonel: The Life and Wars of Henry Stimson, 1867–1950* (1990). See also Elting E. Morison, *Turmoil and Tradition: A Study of the Life and Times of Henry L. Stimson* (1960), and Richard Current, *Secretary Stimson: A Study in Statecraft* (1954). Other works that concentrate on Stimson's diplomatic career include Robert H. Ferrell, *American Diplomacy in the Great Depression: Hoover-Stimson Foreign Policy, 1929–1933* (1957), and Armin Rappaport, *Henry L. Stimson and Japan, 1931–33* (1963). For a study that focuses on Stimson's views on domestic issues, see Larry G. Gerber, *The Limits of Liberalism: Josephus Daniels, Henry Stimson, Bernard Baruch, Donald Richberg, Felix Frankfurter and the Development of the Modern American Political Economy* (1983). An obituary is in the *New York Times*, 21 Oct. 1950.

LARRY G. GERBER

STIMSON, Julia Catherine (26 May 1881–29 Sept. 1948), nursing leader and superintendent of the U.S. Army Nurse Corps, was born in Worcester, Massachusetts, the daughter of Henry Albert Stimson, a prominent Congregational minister, and Alice Wheaton Bartlett, a civic leader. Both parents were descendants of long-established New England families with a strong tradition of public service and professional achievement that their seven children would continue. Parental expectations were as high for their daughters as for their sons. At a time when only 3 percent of American women went to college, all four Stimson daughters were sent to Vassar College, and three of them obtained graduate degrees.

In 1886, when Julia was five, her father took a pastorate at Pilgrim Congregational Church in St. Louis, Missouri. He moved in 1893 to New York, where Julia attended the Brearley School until she entered Vassar in 1897 at the age of sixteen. On graduating in 1901 Stimson confronted the problem of how to use her energy, education, and intelligence. She wanted to become a physician, but her parents forbade this idea. Her uncle, Lewis Atterbury Stimson, a distinguished surgeon on the faculty of Cornell University Medical College, also discouraged her. It is of interest to note that her brother Philip and her youngest sister, Barbara (born when Julia was seventeen) both became doctors. By the time their last child grew to young adulthood, the senior Stimsons accepted the idea of sending a daughter to medical school.

In August 1901 Stimson received a scholarship to attend a summer course at the Marine Biological Laboratory in Woods Hole, Massachusetts. The following fall she won a fellowship for graduate studies in zoology at Columbia University. After two years there she worked in the medical illustration department of Cornell University Medical College.

Stimson was a striking woman of great vitality, nearly six feet tall, with penetrating blue eyes. Yet this physical vigor masked a surprising fragility. From her teens Stimson suffered from a skin ailment that progressed in severity from inflammation to necrosis requiring skin grafts. In 1903 she had an attack severe enough to require hospitalization. Still unsure about her future career, Stimson traveled abroad in the summer of 1904. During this trip she met Annie Warburton Goodrich, the inspiring superintendent of the New York Hospital Training School for Nurses.

This fortunate encounter certainly influenced Stimson's decision to begin her nursing studies there in the fall of 1904. The program was demanding, both academically and physically. In addition to courses, student nurses' ward work often totaled twelve hours daily. During this time Stimson's skin disorder became so severe that she took two leaves of absence amounting to nearly a year. Despite this, she graduated from the New York Training School in 1908. Goodrich, who recognized Stimson's high intelligence and serious commitment to a professional career, recommended her for the position of superintendent of nurses at the newly established Harlem Hospital. In three years at Harlem, she not only fulfilled her nursing and administrative responsibilities but compiled a handbook of drugs and solutions for nurses, which was published in 1910. She also helped a colleague create an innovative social service department to help underprivileged patients and their families.

By 1911 Stimson was ready for a fresh challenge. She accepted an offer to head the newly established Social Service Department at St. Louis Children's Hospital. Employing paid medical social workers to educate, supervise, and help patients understand doctors' orders was still a new idea at this time. The Children's Hospital managers insisted that social workers be fully accepted as part of the medical team. No patient was to be discharged from the ward until a social worker had made sure that the parents understood what was necessary to care for the child's health.

For Stimson, going to St. Louis in October 1911 meant returning to a city she had known when her father was a pastor there. Prominent St. Louis women had founded the Children's Hospital in 1879 and decided to affiliate their institution with Washington University School of Medicine in 1910. Despite this association, women managers continued the tradition of independent leadership within their sphere of influence. They raised their own funds to establish a social work department that same year.

Like many pioneer social workers, Stimson drew on her nursing experience to develop medical social work as a distinct yet cooperative service that would complement doctors' and nurses' efforts to restore patients to health, or to help them and their parents cope better with illness and disability. However, unlike many early social workers, Stimson never lost her primary professional identity as a nurse. Her executive ability, compelling personality, and extensive social contacts among influential St. Louisans were helpful in gaining both financial support and professional credibility for the new department. As head of social service, she served both Children's Hospital and the other Washington University–affiliated teaching institution, Barnes Hospital.

By 1913 Stimson had become superintendent of nurses at both teaching hospitals. Under her energetic leadership, nursing and social work flourished. Beyond her professional responsibilities, Stimson also found time to complete a master's degree in sociology, with a thesis supporting the need for national health insurance. After she left St. Louis in May 1917 for wartime service in France, the degree was awarded to her in absentia.

In 1909 Stimson had become a Red Cross nurse, and in 1913 she organized St. Louis nurses to work in an emergency hospital during the Ohio Valley flood. By 1914 she had joined the National Committee on Red Cross Nursing. When the United States entered World War I in 1917, the Red Cross organized base hospital units across the country, and Stimson became chief nurse for Washington University Medical School's Base Hospital 21. Its medical staff was drawn from Barnes and Children's hospitals. Her group joined the British Expeditionary Forces near Rouen, France, at a hospital that treated up to a thousand sick and wounded each day. In 1918 her father published Stimson's vivid letters home as a book, *Finding Themselves*. Her narrative captured the heroic spirit of wartime nursing and the personal qualities of courage, enthusiasm, and professional good judgment that made her such an effective leader.

Stimson's military superiors soon recognized her superb leadership and administrative skills. By April 1918 she had been promoted to chief nurse of the American Red Cross in France, responsible for organizing American Red Cross nurses throughout the country. Her dual status as a nurse for both the Red Cross and the army helped her with the delicate task of working effectively within and between both organizations to coordinate nursing care. In meeting this administrative challenge, Stimson showed both flexibility and resolve when each was appropriate—breaking red tape and placing her nursing units exactly where they were needed at the right time. She insisted that nurses report directly to physicians and be obeyed next after them. Despite great administrative authority, she never forgot the individual nurse or patient and the pressures war brought to bear on them. Warmhearted and compassionate by nature, Stimson retained her essential humanity, humor, and sensitivity even under the most difficult battlefield conditions. No experience in civilian nursing could have prepared her for coping with patients blinded and burned by poison gas. Yet her responses were both practical and deeply humane. She once lent her cherished violin to cheer a wounded soldier suffering from shell shock.

As the war ended Stimson was appointed director of the American Expeditionary Force's Nursing Service, where she oversaw the demobilization of some 10,000 nurses throughout Europe. She received many honors for her wartime work, including the Distinguished Service Medal from General John J. Pershing. Typically, her most treasured war mementos were gifts from the doctors and nurses who had been her colleagues in the field.

Stimson returned to Washington, D.C., in July 1919 as dean of the Army School of Nursing and acting superintendent of the Army Nurse Corps. In December the latter position was made permanent, and Congress enlarged its responsibility by an act establishing veterans' hospitals. Stimson became the first woman to hold the rank of major in 1920. Yet despite army nurses' heroic wartime work, Congress granted them only "relative" rank at that time, denying them the privileges and salaries of commissioned officers. During the fourteen years Stimson worked in Washington, she improved army nurses' morale by seeing that they were given new opportunities for postgraduate study, improved housing conditions, and retirement privileges for longevity and disability. She retired from the Army School of Nursing in 1933 and resigned as superintendent of the Army Nurse Corps in 1937 to spend time with her mother, who died that same year. A devoted daughter, sister, aunt, and colleague, Stimson never married or had children. In recognition of her leadership in nursing education, she was awarded the Florence Nightingale Medal of the International Red Cross in 1929.

After her mother's death, Stimson sought renewed activity and was elected president of the American Nurses' Association in April 1938. This position allowed her to return to a demanding schedule of speeches and meetings. Reelected to a second term as president, Stimson organized the Nursing Council on National Defense in 1940. From this position, she led a national drive to encourage a new generation of women to enter army nursing and directed the first American census of registered nurses. Stimson herself returned to active service in 1942–1943 and used her speaking skills to recruit nurses for the army in twenty-three cities. Congress finally granted army nurses full commissioned rank in 1948. Stimson was promoted to colonel on the retired list in August of that year, just six weeks before her death in Poughkeepsie, New York.

• Stimson's personal papers are on indefinite loan to the Cornell University Medical College Archives in New York City and include early letters, diaries, photographs, and scrapbooks. Her official papers are in the files of the Army Nurse Corps, Army Medical Department, Washington, D.C. Information about her career as a medical social worker is in the Washington University Medical School Archives, St. Louis, Mo. A contemporary view of her wartime work appears in Lavinia Dock et al., *American Red Cross Nursing* (1922). An obituary and editorial are in the *American Journal of Nursing* 28, no. 11 (Nov. 1948): 675–76, 732.

MARION HUNT

STINE, Charles Milton Atland (18 Oct. 1882–28 May 1954), research chemist, was born in Norwich, Connecticut, the son of Milton Henry Stine, a clergyman and author, and Mary Jane Atland. Stine spent most of his early life in Harrisburg and Lebanon, Pennsylvania, except for three years in Los Angeles (1892–1895). In 1897 he entered Gettysburg College and over the next decade earned three degrees in science and art there, culminating with a Ph.D. in chemistry from Johns Hopkins in 1907. After graduating he joined the Du Pont Company of Wilmington, Delaware, as a research chemist in its Eastern Laboratory (founded in 1902), one of the pioneer industrial research laboratories in the United States. In 1912 he married Martha Molly; they had two daughters. From 1907 to 1916 Stine worked on improving explosives and the processes used to make them. Included were the new high-explosive compounds trinitrotoluene (TNT) and tetryl, which were used in artillery shells in World War I. This research led to nineteen patents. In the course of this work, he built the first small-scale "pilot plant" at Du Pont and became involved in the chemical engineering necessary to scale up processes from small to large plants. This early experience convinced Stine of the importance of chemical engineering, a discipline he strongly supported in later years. Under his leadership Du Pont would become one of the few centers of chemical engineering research in the United States in the 1920s and 1930s.

In 1916 Stine became involved in Du Pont's research initiative in synthetic dyestuffs. Before World War I the Germans had dominated the American market for dyestuffs. Wartime interruption of commerce left the United States with inadequate supplies of dyestuffs for everything from clothing to postage stamps. For several years Stine was in charge of chemical research in connection with the development and manufacture of chemicals needed to make dyestuffs.

In 1919 Stine was promoted to assistant director of Du Pont's large and diverse Chemical Department. Beginning in 1910 Du Pont had diversified its product line into nitrocellulose plastics, including celluloid, dyestuffs, and paints. Problems in managing these varied products led the Du Pont management in 1921 to reorganize into a number of divisions, each of which was responsible for a product line. At this time the centralized Chemical Department was also broken up and each division given its own research laboratory. Stine was left with a small group of chemists in the old Chemical Department. For the next several years he struggled to find a mission for a central research laboratory in a decentralized corporation. In 1924 he was promoted to chemical director, which put him in charge of the Chemical Department and also gave him informal oversight of all the company's research programs. Most of the research that the Chemical Department performed was at the behest and at the expense of the product divisions, but Stine had conceived of a unique mission for his laboratory.

Stine became convinced that chemical technology was advancing so rapidly that the fundamental scientific understanding of the technology was inadequate. He believed that the investigation of the basic chemical principles underlying the new technologies would inevitably lead to improved products and processes. In December 1926 he put forward a proposal to the company's executive committee, now headed by the new company president, Lammot du Pont. In the memorandum "Pure Science Work," Stine proposed what he called a "radical departure" for Du Pont into university-style research. To bolster his argument he cited an article by Secretary of Commerce Herbert Hoover, "The Vital Need for Greater Financial Support to Pure Science Research." The interested but still skeptical Du Pont executives asked Stine for a more concrete proposal, which he submitted several months later. He now referred to the work he wanted to do as fundamental research that had the goal of discovering the general chemical principles underlying chemical technology. He suggested several areas that appeared to be critical to Du Pont: colloid chemistry, catalysis, chemical engineering, organic chemical synthesis, and polymerization. Du Pont should do this work, Stine asserted, because the universities were not doing enough or in some cases not doing anything at all.

The executive committee approved the program in March 1927 and was prepared to fund it at the very generous level of $300,000 per year. The budget granted Stine enough money to hire some of the most prominent academic chemists in the United States, but soon he discovered that they were not interested in participating in his experiment. He turned to newly minted Ph.D.s. Over the next two years Stine hired about fifteen young men, some with outstanding scientific credentials. Most of them went on to develop long and distinguished careers with Du Pont; one became a senior vice president, and one of them, Wallace H. Carothers, was responsible for the most important innovation in the company's long history, nylon.

In 1927 Carothers was teaching chemistry at Harvard. He was recommended to Stine by Carothers's Ph.D. adviser at the University of Illinois, Roger Adams, an eminent organic chemist and Du Pont consultant. In several meetings and exchanges of correspondence, Stine emphasized that the area of polymers, or long-chain molecules, was largely unexplored scientifically. During the 1920s Du Pont introduced three important new products made from the natural polymer cellulose: Duco lacquers, rayon fibers, and cellophane films. Duco lacquers revolutionized automobile painting and made a rainbow of colors possible; rayon took the fashion business by storm; and cellophane changed packaging forever. By the late 1920s Du Pont had a huge stake in polymer-based products, and Stine wanted to understand them in a more fundamental manner. Joining Du Pont in February 1928, Carothers began a series of classic investigations into polymers that established the scientific underpinning for the new discipline. In the course of this work, in April 1930 Carothers's associates discovered two synthetic polymers that had rubberlike and fiberlike characteristics. Over the next several years these discoveries led to neoprene synthetic rubber and nylon fibers. In subsequent decades Du Pont chemists made countless other innovations in polymeric materials.

Nylon and polymers made Du Pont one of the most successful American corporations in the twentieth century.

The early successes of the fundamental research program helped Stine earn a promotion in 1930 onto Du Pont's executive committee. He also was elected to the board of directors. For the next fifteen years Stine strongly supported scientific research at Du Pont. He also spread the gospel of science through numerous speeches and publications aimed at industry and the general public. In 1940 he was awarded the prestigious Perkin Medal of the American Section of the Society of Chemical Industry for valuable work in applied chemistry. After his retirement in 1945, he became increasingly interested in the application of science to medicine and agriculture. He owned and operated a scientifically controlled dairy farm in Wilmington with his wife. His greatest accomplishment was the establishment of basic scientific research as a permanent aspect of Du Pont's highly regarded research enterprise in the twentieth century.

• There are extensive manuscript collections of Stine papers, biographical materials, and bibliographies of his publications in many of the Du Pont Company accessions in the Hagley Museum and Library in Wilmington, Del. Among his numerous publications are "Chemical Engineering in Modern Industry," *Transactions of the American Institute of Chemical Engineers* 21 (1928): 45–54; "Industrial Chemistry," in *A Century of Industrial Progress*, ed. Frederic William Wile (1928); "Structure of an Industrial Research Organization," *Industrial and Engineering Chemistry* 21 (1929): 657–59; "Chemical Research: A Factor of Prime Importance in American Industry," *Journal of Chemical Education* 9 (1932): 2032–39; "Coordination of Laboratory and Plant Effort," *Industrial and Engineering Chemistry* 24 (1932): 191–93; "Fundamental and Applied Chemical Research," in *Profitable Practice in Industrial Research*, ed. Malcolm Ross (1932); "Relation of Chemical to Other Industry," *Industrial and Engineering Chemistry* 25 (1933): 487–95; "Approach to Chemical Research Based on a Specific Example," *Journal of the Franklin Institute* 218 (1934): 397–410; and "The Place of Fundamental Research in an Industrial Research Organization," *Transactions of the American Institute of Chemical Engineers* 32 (1936): 127–37. His career is discussed in David A. Hounshell and John Kenly Smith, Jr., *Science and Corporate Strategy: DuPont R&D, 1902–1980* (1988). Another biographical source is "Perkin Medal," *Industrial and Engineering Chemistry* 32 (Feb. 1940): 137.

JOHN KENLY SMITH

STINSON, Katherine (14 Feb. 1891–8 July 1977), aviation pioneer, was born in Fort Payne, Alabama, the daughter of Edward Anderson Stinson and Emma Beavers, farmers. An enthusiast of aviation early in life, Stinson learned to fly from pioneering flyer Max Lillie at Cicero Field near Chicago, obtaining the fourth pilot's license issued to a woman on 19 July 1912. Her younger siblings—Marjorie, who ran a flying school; Eddie, who founded the Stinson Aviation Company; and Jack, an aircraft technician—followed her aviation dreams and also achieved fame in the profession.

Stinson started to make a name for herself as an aviator in 1913 when she began appearing in airshows throughout the United States. Billed as the "flying schoolgirl," she excited the public with her exploits. Pretty, petite, and frail looking, Stinson emphasized her femininity while participating in a heavily male profession. "I weigh only about 101 pounds," she said. "I'm very particular about that one pound." Because of her size most Americans had difficulty believing that Stinson could control an aircraft. Her obvious success as a pilot brought her great popularity.

Stinson's aeronautical exhibitions led to her establishing several aviation records. She was the first woman to carry the U.S. mail, making a flight at Helena, Montana, on 23–27 September 1913. Stinson also claimed this distinction for Canada by flying the mail from Calgary to Edmonton on 9 July 1918. She was the first woman to perform an aerial loop-the-loop, in Chicago on 18 July 1915, a feat that she repeated many times thereafter. She was also the first woman to skywrite, using fireworks for the purpose in Los Angeles on 17 December 1915.

In December 1916 Stinson traveled with an entourage to Asia for an exhibition tour. She was a great hit in Japan, where her first appearance at Tokyo's Aoyama Parade Ground in January 1917 drew 25,000 people. The Japanese were of course thrilled by her aerobatic flying, but her small size and the fact that she was a woman performing these feats in a severely gender-restricted society caused much of the excitement. She wrote at the time, "The women have simply overwhelmed me with attention and seem to regard me as their emancipator." She added, "The women were wild with enthusiasm," but curiously, "the men were not far behind." Stinson's exploits sparked the organization of several women's flying clubs in Japan and applications to a Tokyo flying school by several local women. One woman, Komatsu Imai, was inspired to become a pilot by Stinson and spent several years as a barnstormer. In addition to exhibitions in Japan, Stinson also went to China for several airshows, returning to the United States only in May 1917.

By the time of her return the United States had entered World War I. Turned down when she tried to enlist as a pilot in the army, Stinson began flying with the Red Cross on humanitarian ventures associated with the war. She also traveled and performed aerobatics to boost morale during the war. In that regard she set nonstop speed and duration records: she flew from San Diego to San Francisco, 610 miles, in nine hours and ten minutes on 11 December 1917; and she flew from Chicago to Binghamton, New York, 601.763 miles, in ten hours and ten minutes on 23 May 1918. She also helped out at the Stinson Flying School in San Antonio, Texas, which had been founded by her brother, her sister, and her in 1915 and was now being employed by the Aviation Section of the Army Signal Corps to train military pilots.

The stress of the war effort took its toll, however, and while assisting the Red Cross on one trip she contracted tuberculosis. The illness effectively ended Stinson's flying career, as she took several years to recover. In the process of convalescence Stinson went to the arid, warm climate of New Mexico, where she recuperated and lived off her business investments. In 1928 she met and married Miquel A. Otero, a World War I aviator and the son of a former territorial governor. The two decided that the life of a gypsy flyer was not appropriate for their marriage, and both effectively retired. Thereafter she lived in Santa Fe, worked with the local Red Cross, raised two daughters, and became a successful interior designer. In 1962 Stinson suffered a stroke and went into a coma from which she never recovered. She died in Santa Fe.

Katherine Stinson's flying career was relatively short, but significant. She was one of the first women to gain fame as a flyer, establishing in the 1910s that women, no matter how small, could handle aircraft. As such, she was a forerunner of the women flyers of a later era.

• There is no formal collection of Stinson's papers. Material by and about her can be found in scattered collections at the Evans Memorial Library, Aberdeen, Miss., and the National Air and Space Museum, Smithsonian Institution. Short sketches of her career can be found in the various editions of *Who's Who in American Aviation;* John W. Underwood, *The Stinsons: The Exciting Chronicle of a Flying Family and the Planes that Enhanced Their Fame* (1969); Claudia M. Oakes, *United States Women in Aviation through World War I* (1978); and Valerie Moolman, *Women Aloft* (1981). An obituary is in the *New York Times,* 11 July 1977.

ROGER D. LAUNIUS

STIRLING, Lord. *See* Alexander, William.

STITT, Edward Rhodes (22 July 1867–13 Nov. 1948), naval surgeon and author, was born in Charlotte, North Carolina, the son of William Edward Stitt, a merchant and former Confederate army officer, and Mary Rhodes. Stitt's mother died in 1870, and Stitt was brought up by an aunt in Rock Hill, South Carolina. He attended a private school before enrolling in the University of South Carolina, from which he graduated with a Bachelor of Arts in 1885. He attended the Philadelphia College of Pharmacy, earning a Ph.C. in 1887, then received an M.D. from the University of Pennsylvania in 1889. He had already been accepted into the U.S. Navy Medical Corps and was commissioned an assistant surgeon.

Beginning his naval career in 1890, Stitt put his extensive education to use. Serving in the Atlantic and the Mediterranean, he became interested in the transmission of tropical diseases. He was one of the first navy surgeons to diagnose using a microscope to identify microorganisms as opposed to relying on the nature of a patient's symptoms. Among traditionalists, who felt challenged, Stitt's practice was somewhat controversial. In 1892 he married Emma W. Scott; they had three children.

Stitt's expertise in tropical diseases landed him positions on medical boards and commissions in the United States to study the possibility of constructing a Central American canal linking the Atlantic and Pacific oceans. In 1895 Stitt favored a route through Nicaragua. Later, when yellow fever and malaria were proven to be transmitted via mosquitos, he opted for the Panama site. Between 1895 and 1905 he studied at George Washington University, Brooklyn's Hoagland Laboratory, and the London School of Tropical Medicine. Additionally, he worked with the famous Walter Reed and James Carroll team at the Army Medical School.

The navy put Stitt's expertise, education, and professional contacts to good use. In 1902 he became the head of the Departments of bacteriology, chemistry, and tropical medicine at the Navy Medical School in Washington, D.C. This stint of duty was interrupted only by two short tours in the Philippines, where Stitt made on-site medical investigations. During this phase of his career, he produced two well-accepted books, *Practical Bacteriology, Hematology and Animal Parasitology* (1908) and *Diagnostics and Treatment of Tropical Diseases* (1914). The first was reprinted many times, eventually numbering ten editions, and the second was revised and reprinted seven times over a forty-year period. In 1916 he became the commanding officer of the Navy Medical School, and promoted to rear admiral in 1917, he was awarded the Navy Cross for his service during World War I.

When Surgeon General W. C. Braisted resigned for reasons of ill health in 1920, Stitt was selected as his replacement. He held this position for eight years, serving as the medical consultant to three U.S. presidents, Woodrow Wilson, Warren G. Harding, and Calvin Coolidge. During this period, he returned to the Navy Medical School as a lecturer and also lectured at several civilian medical schools.

After serving two terms as surgeon general, Stitt returned to the navy as inspector general, medical activities, West Coast. On 1 August 1931 Admiral Stitt retired from active duty. However, he was a regular visitor to the Navy Medical School and was a valued consultant through World War II. In 1933 Stitt's first wife died, and in 1935 he married Laura A. Carter. They had no children, and their marriage ended with Laura's suicide. In 1937 he married Helen Bennett Newton. They had no children.

Stitt was a small man, an easy conversationalist, and a skilled raconteur of navy "sea stories." He kept a goatee and was a member of the choir of Washington's St. Matthew's Episcopal Church. Stitt's chief contribution to his country was in the field of tropical medicine. Because of his fine work, thousands of Americans were able to survive the trials of the Asian campaigns of World War II. He died in Bethesda, Maryland.

• The record of Stitt's achievements in the navy are in the National Archives and Records Administration, Navy Department Files, Bureau of Medicine and Surgery. Stitt's career is also traced in the *Annual Reports of the Surgeon General* (1920–1931). Obituaries are in *Annals of Internal Medicine* 30 (1949): 233–34; *Journal of the American Medical Association* 138 (1948): 1051; *Military Surgeon* (1949): 71–72; and *Washington Academy of Science Journal* 39 (1949): 381–82.

ROD PASCHALL

STITT, Sonny (2 Feb. 1924–22 July 1982), jazz alto and tenor saxophonist, was born in Boston, Massachusetts, the son of Edward H. S. Boatner, a music professor, and Claudine Tibou, who played and taught piano and organ; she later married Robert Stitt. Raised in Saginaw, Michigan, Sonny, whose given name was Edward, took up piano at age seven before turning to clarinet and alto saxophone. He received informal lessons from local saxophonist "Big Nick" Nicholas and saxophonist Wardell Gray, who slept and practiced in Stitt's room when in Saginaw, there being no hotel for African Americans in the town.

During summer vacation from high school Stitt led a band and toured Michigan with Nicholas and trumpeter Thad Jones. As members of Cornelius Cornell's band, they ranged as far as Tennessee. Stitt declined an offer to join bandleader Ernie Fields when his mother threw a fit about his not finishing school. After a stint with the band of Claude and Clifford Trenier, he graduated. Stitt worked in Boston with Sabby Lewis's big band (c. 1942), and in Detroit he joined the 'Bama State Collegians (1942), touring to New York in 1943. During this period Stitt was deeply influenced by Charlie Parker's alto sax playing, heard on recordings with pianist Jay McShann's big band. In New York, Stitt participated in bop jam sessions in clubs on Fifty-second Street and in Harlem. In July 1943 he joined Tiny Bradshaw's big band in New York and toured to St. Louis and Kansas City, where he met and briefly rehearsed with Parker, who said, "You sound too much like me."

Stitt first recorded in 1944 as a sideman with Bradshaw. Late in April 1945 he joined Billy Eckstine's bop big band, in which saxophonists John Jackson, Dexter Gordon, Leo Parker, and he were known as the unholy four, for their wild behavior. Stitt recorded with Eckstine in May and probably went on the orchestra's ensuing tour of the Northeast and South, but he had left Eckstine by the fall. In March 1946 he joined Dizzy Gillespie's big band, which performed in New York from April to June. Not the orchestra's main alto soloist, Stitt served in effect as Charlie Parker's replacement in a bop sextet drawn from the big band, Parker and Gillespie having parted company. In this setting Stitt made his first significant recordings, including "Oop Bop Sh'Bam," on 15 May 1946. Three days earlier he had participated in an all-star Bebop Jam Session at Lincoln Square Center, and in June he left Gillespie to lead his own groups. He made further seminal bop recordings that year: with trumpeter Kenny Dorham as co-leader of the Bebop Boys; playing alongside trumpeter Fats Navarro in drummer Kenny Clarke's group; and the following day as a member of Navarro and Gil Fuller's Modernists, who recorded two-sided 78 rpm versions of "Boppin' a Riff," "Fat Boy," "Everything's Cool," and "Webb

City," affording Stitt ample opportunity to show his talent as an improvising alto saxophonist.

Owing to troubles stemming from an addiction to narcotics, Stitt lost his New York City police cabaret card sometime in the mid- to late 1940s and was unable to take nightclub work in the city until the card was reauthorized, in around 1950. Late in 1946 or early in 1947 he went to Chicago, where he played with trumpeter Miles Davis and tenor saxophonist Gene Ammons in jam sessions and with tenor saxophonist Johnny Griffin at ballroom dances. He led bands at the Twin Terrace Café and the Strode Hotel Lounge, employing trumpeter Freddy Webster for the latter engagement. In the summer he moved to Detroit, and later that year he played in jam sessions with Gillespie, Davis, and Parker at the El Sino Club. Stitt returned to New York at the beginning of 1948.

Having taken up tenor saxophone as a means of getting away from the overwhelming influence of Parker's alto playing, Stitt made his first recordings on tenor with trombonist J. J. Johnson's Boppers on 17 October 1949. There followed on 11 December an outstanding session under his own name with pianist Bud Powell, bassist Curley Russell, and drummer Max Roach as his sidemen; they recorded versions of "All God's Chillun Got Rhythm," "Sonny Side," "Bud's Blues," and "Sunset" (actually the ballad "These Foolish Things"). This quartet expanded to include Davis, trombonist Benny Green, and baritone saxophonist Serge Chaloff for a Stars of Jazz concert at Carnegie Hall on 24 December.

That same fall, 1949, Ammons and Stitt formed a quintet that worked mainly at Birdland in New York from 1950 to 1951. Their finest recordings, made under Ammons's leadership in 1950, present the tenor saxophonists in improvisational battles on two takes of "You Can Depend on Me" and three of "Blues Up and Down." Stitt also briefly tested the idea of playing baritone saxophone, featured on Ammons's 1950 recordings of "Chabootie" and "Seven Eleven," and he continued to play the alto instrument, notably on his own quartet recording of "Imagination."

Stitt worked with Ammons intermittently to 1955. He rejoined Gillespie for three months early in 1958, and he toured Britain with Jazz at the Philharmonic in 1958 and 1959. By this time, perhaps years earlier, a first marriage had failed; details are unknown. In 1960 he married Pamela W. Gilmore; they had two children. Stitt was the second in a succession of unsatisfactory replacements for saxophonist John Coltrane in Davis's quintet, which he joined in September 1960 for a European tour. He left Davis by early 1961. Ammons and Stitt performed in Chicago from late 1961 into February 1962. He toured Japan in a sextet with Johnson and trumpeter Clark Terry in 1964. He played in Europe the same year and in Scandinavia in 1966 and 1967. As a member of the Giants of Jazz he toured with Gillespie, trombonist Kai Winding, pianist Thelonius Monk, bassist Al McKibbon, and drummer Art Blakey in 1971 to 1972. In 1974 he performed

in *The Musical Life of Charlie Parker* at the Newport Jazz Festival-New York.

Throughout these years and continuing through the last decade of his life, Stitt mainly worked on his own as a leader and soloist, often employing whatever local accompanists were available, rather than trying to maintain a group, and sometimes simply showing up at other people's jobs. In the company of other saxophonists he was almost fearsome. Extremely competitive, he delighted in devastating the competition as much as he delighted in making music. Alto saxophonist Art Pepper described Stitt sitting in at the Blackhawk in San Francisco while working with Jazz at the Philharmonic and challenging Pepper to a lightning-fast head-to-head duel on "Cherokee": "It's a communion. It's a battle. It's an ego trip. It's a testing ground." In addition to Ammons and Pepper, Stitt's worthy opponents included tenor saxophonists Eddie "Lockjaw" Davis, Sonny Rollins, Paul Gonsalves, Zoot Sims, Ricky Ford, and Red Holloway.

Stitt recorded prolifically under his own name. Few saxophonists have had their career so thoroughly documented, and large portions of his work for the Roost and Verve labels in the late 1950s to early 1960s are sometimes dismissed critically as representing a workmanlike, uncaring Stitt. But the merely average mid-career Stitt session seems powerfully substantial by comparison with much of the saxophone playing associated with a revival of bop from the mid-1970s onward. Among many highlights are the albums *Sonny Side Up*, co-led with Gillespie and Rollins for Verve (1957) and including on "The Eternal Triangle" (another of the countless retitlings of "I Got Rhythm") a tenor battle with Rollins in which the two men are even more closely matched in timbre and melody than in the earlier Ammons and Stitt duels; *Personal Appearance* (1957); *Boss Tenors*, co-led with Ammons (1961); *Sonny Stitt Plays Bird* (1963); and *Salt and Pepper*, co-led with Gonsalves (1963). His work during these years is also preserved in the documentary *Jazz on a Summer's Day* (1960), filmed at the 1958 Newport Jazz Festival. On the LP *What's New!!! Sonny Stitt Plays the Varitone* (1966), he explored a then-new device for the electronic modification of saxophone pitch and timbre, but unlike his contemporary Eddie Harris, Stitt soon lost interest in this area of saxophone sound. Generally speaking, his playing on his last fifty or sixty albums is perhaps a notch below his earlier productions, but there are a sufficient number of inspired exceptions, including *Tune-Up! Constellation*, and *12!* (all from 1972), *In Walked Sonny* (1975), and *Good Life* (1980).

By the 1970s international travel had become a part of Stitt's working routine. He visited Europe many times, including an appearance at the 1974 Umbria Jazz Festival captured in the film *Jazz in piazza* and a trip to England for duels with Holloway in December 1980. He also performed and recorded in Japan, and he played in Israel and Brazil. Stitt replaced Pepper, who had just died, at the Kool Jazz Festival in New

York in July 1982, shortly before his own death of lung cancer in Washington, D.C.

Michael James has noted that Stitt's alto saxophone recordings of 1946 raise a fundamental question about jazz criticism, in which individuality and original creativity are typically valued above all other considerations. Certainly Stitt was Parker's closest imitator, but he was also the most talented and well-rounded of the early alto saxophonists influenced by Parker. He understood both the erudite side of Parker's playing and his deep connection to the blues, and the mid- to late 1940s efforts of such contemporaries as John Jackson, Sonny Criss, and Ernie Henry seem halting by comparison with Stitt's work. At such moments as the burst of notes in his solo during the opening theme of "Everything's Cool," his approach to improvisation is every bit as complex and swinging as Parker's, and to the question of imitation, one is tempted to respond, "Who cares?" Without modifying his interest in improvising harmonically rich melodies with tremendous technical facility, Stitt in any event moved away from Parker upon taking up tenor saxophone. Apart from the obvious but crucial difference in instrumental timbre, one hears in Stitt's tenor improvisations—and also in his subsequent work on alto—a greater tendency to spin out long lines, evidently with the aim of maintaining a hard-driving rhythmic flow.

• Interviews with Stitt include David B. Bittan, "Don't Call Me Bird!: The Problems of Sonny Stitt," *Down Beat*, 14 May 1959, pp. 19–20; Les Tomkins, "Sonny Stitt Says There's No Succesor to Bird," *Melody Maker*, 16 May 1959, p. 6; Ronnie Scott, "But This Time, My Prince Has Come," *Melody Maker*, 9 May 1964, p. 10; Brian Case, "How Stitt Lost His Bottle," *Melody Maker*, 15 Aug. 1981, pp. 20–21; Al Levitt, "Le nouveau style de Stitt," *Jazz magazine*, no. 304 (Feb. 1982): 16–19, 48; and Wayne Enstice and Paul Rubin, *Jazz Spoken Here: Conversations with Twenty-two Musicians* (1992). J. A. Mitchell prepared a photo essay, "Gallery: Sonny Stitt," *Jazz Magazine 2*, no. 4 (1978): 25–27. Assessments of his work are in Michael James, "Stitt, Parker, and the Question of Influence," *Jazz Monthly* 5 (Jan. 1960): 9–10, 30; Barry McRae, *The Jazz Cataclysm* (1967; repr. 1985); Jim Burns, "Early Stitt," *Jazz Journal* 22 (Oct. 1969): 6–8; and Thomas Owens, *Bebop: The Music and Its Players* (1995). Catalogs of his recordings include "Sonny Stitt," *Swing Journal* 36 (Mar. 1982): 240–47; and Dieter Salemann et al., *Sonny Stitt: Solography, Discographical Informations* [sic], *Band Routes, Engagements in Chronological Order* (1986). See also Martin Williams, "Sonny Stitt in the Studio," *Jazz Journal* 16 (Aug. 1963): 12–13; Art Pepper and Laurie Pepper, *Straight Life: The Story of Art Pepper* (1979); and Jack Chambers, *Milestones 2: The Music and Times of Miles Davis Since 1960* (1985). Obituaries are in the *Los Angeles Times*, 23 July 1982; the *New York Times*, 24 July 1982; and *Village Vanguard*, 10 Aug. 1982.

BARRY KERNFELD

ST. JOHN, Charles Edward (15 Mar. 1857–26 Apr. 1935), astronomer and educator, was born in Allen, Michigan, the son of Hiram Abiff St. John, a millwright, and Lois Amanda Bacon. His mother was the intellectual force in the family, and it was from her that St. John received the support and encouragement to complete his education in the face of illnesses and economic difficulties.

In 1876 St. John graduated from the Michigan State Normal School (now Eastern Michigan University), but the effort drained him physically and mentally, and he spent nine years rebuilding his strength. Of this period in his life a colleague later wrote, "It is probable, however, that these were the years in which he built up the philosophy of life which he followed throughout his career" (Adams, p. 286). Needing to work, he became an instructor in physics (1885–1892) at the Normal College. He also resumed his studies at the Michigan Agricultural College (later Michigan State University), from which he earned a B.S. in 1887. Following two years (1890–1892) of graduate work in electricity and magnetism at the University of Michigan, he entered Harvard University, where his instructors included John Trowbridge and Benjamin Peirce. He earned his A.M. in 1893 and was awarded the John Tyndall Fellowship, which included a year of graduate work abroad. St. John spent the following year at the Universities of Berlin and Heidelberg and then returned to Harvard, where he received his Ph.D. in physics in 1896.

At Harvard St. John took up experimental and theoretical problems in electrical conduction and self-induction, light, and magnetic permeability in a curriculum that emphasized the laboratory method of teaching physics and original research work. "Wavelengths of Electricity on Iron Wires," based on experiments he carried out in the Jefferson Physical Laboratory, appeared in the *American Journal of Science* in 1894. The following year the *Annalen der Physik und Chemie* published the results of St. John's earlier work in Berlin on black-body radiation.

Doctorate in hand, St. John returned for one year to the University of Michigan as an instructor in physics. In 1897 he was invited to join the faculty of Oberlin College as associate professor of physics and astronomy. "I anticipate a good deal of pleasure and satisfaction in it," he wrote back. He remained at Oberlin for eleven years, rising to professor in 1899 and dean of the College of Arts and Sciences in 1906. Plunging into his new academic position with characteristic enthusiasm and energy, he chaired the college's athletic committee for many years, served on the town's waterworks board, and headed the Second Congregational Church's board of trustees. He also left an indelible mark in the classroom, saving his best performance for advanced and graduate courses. A former student remembered, "His mathematical presentation possessed a remarkable clarity and his laboratory demonstrations were thoroughly prepared and beautifully carried out. In his lectures he often closed his eyes for considerable periods of time in order to concentrate upon the subject." An avid outdoorsman, St. John often spent the summer months exploring the Far West, tramping through British Columbia and Alaska, hiking and camping in the high Sierras, and visiting Yellowstone National Park.

St. John's association with Oberlin and his career as an educator ended in 1908 when he moved to Pasadena, California, to become a staff member of the Carnegie Institution's Mount Wilson Observatory, founded by George Ellery Hale in 1904. At Hale's invitation he had spent several summers, starting in 1898, at the Yerkes Observatory at Williams Bay, Wisconsin, helping Ernest F. Nichols measure the relative heats of fixed stars. Out of that work and his association there with other staff members came the opportunity to start afresh, at age fifty-one, as a research scientist.

At Mount Wilson St. John worked mainly in solar physics. Early on he investigated the H and K lines of ionized calcium in the solar spectrum. He began by measuring the absolute wavelengths of these lines in terrestrial sources in the laboratory and then compared them with the corresponding emission and absorption lines in the solar spectrum, paying special attention to the spectral lines over sunspots and flocculi (calcium and hydrogen clouds in the solar atmosphere). Spurred on by John Evershed's 1909 discovery of differential velocity displacements of Fraunhofer lines in the penumbras of sunspots, St. John carried out between 1910 and 1912 an extensive series of measurements involving hundreds of lines of different elements. From his study of the flow of gases at different levels in sunspots, he concluded that ionized calcium is present at the highest level in the solar atmosphere, followed by hydrogen, with the heavy and rare elements restricted to the lower portions. As a final check, he compared his results with those of spectrums observed by S. A. Mitchell during solar eclipses; there proved to be a high degree of correlation, which gave him much satisfaction. In 1916 he disputed W. H. Julius's ideas about the importance of anomalous dispersion for the displacements in the spectral lines.

As a research scientist, St. John's reputation rests in part on his work on the revision of Henry Rowland's wavelength tables for the solar spectrum, completed and published in 1928. In this massive work St. John, in collaboration with Charlotte Moore, Louise Ware, Edward Adams, and Harold Babcock, corrected and standardized to the international system the wavelengths of 22,000 lines. Their revisions, based on separate measurements made with both grating spectrographs and an interferometer, included many new identifications, the intensities of the lines in sunspots as well as in the solar disk, temperature and pressure classifications, and excitation potentials. An active member of the International Astronomical Union, St. John served as the president of the Union's Solar Physics Commission from 1919 to 1924.

Between 1917 and 1928 St. John measured the gravitational redshift of spectral lines, as predicted by Einstein's theory of general relativity. On the basis of forty lines, he reported negative results in 1917; in 1923, he reversed himself and announced that he was satisfied that the gravitational displacement of the Sun's Fraunhofer spectrum was detectable. His final publication, in 1928, using 1,537 lines, gave the same re-

sults. Referring to his original forty lines reported on in 1917, he wrote, "In view of later work on the complete band, these lines might be called the "Forty Thieves.""

In 1930 St. John retired, having published eighty papers. Following retirement he was appointed as a research associate. A lifelong bachelor, he died in Pasadena.

• The George Ellery Hale Papers in the California Institute of Technology Archives, Pasadena, contain a small amount of St. John's correspondence, as do the Harlow Shapley Papers in the Harvard University Archives. The Oberlin College Archives also have some manuscript material. A survey of his career is provided by Walter S. Adams, National Academy of Sciences, *Biographical Memoirs* 18 (1937): 285–304, with portrait and bibliography. Details about his early career are in obituaries by Alfred H. Joy, *Popular Astronomy* 43 (1935): 611–17; C. G. Abbot, *Astrophysical Journal* 82 (1935): 273–83; and Harold D. Babcock, *Publications of the Astronomical Society of the Pacific* 47 (1935): 115–20. See also Klaus Hentschel, "The Conversion of St. John: A Case Study on the Interplay of Theory and Experiment," *Science in Context* 6 (1993): 137–94. An obituary is in the *New York Times*, 27 Apr. 1935.

JUDITH R. GOODSTEIN

ST. JOHN, Isaac Munroe (19 Nov. 1827–7 Apr. 1880), soldier and engineer, was born in Augusta, Georgia, the son of Isaac Richards St. John, a businessman, and Abigail Richardson Munroe. St. John graduated from Yale in 1845, the youngest member of his class. He briefly studied law and worked as assistant editor of the *Baltimore Patriot* before turning to civil engineering in 1848. He was active in railroad expansion until the Civil War, first on the engineering staff of the Baltimore and Ohio Railroad until 1855 and for the next five years as head of the construction division of the Blue Ridge Railroad in Georgia and South Carolina.

St. John entered Confederate service as a volunteer private but transferred for engineering duty to General John B. Magruder's Army of the Peninsula. He was commissioned captain in the Corps of Engineers in February 1862. On 18 April of the same year he was promoted to major and made chief of the new Nitre Corps of the Ordnance Department.

Josiah Gorgas, the head of the Confederate Ordnance Department, knowing of St. John's reputation as an efficient and energetic organizer, chose him for the most crucial task in ordnance supply, the supply of nitre, the basic component of gunpowder. The Confederacy entered the war with, according to historians' greatly varied estimates, between a one-month and one-year supply of gunpowder. With very little capacity to produce more, the future of Confederate arms depended on supply through the blockade. On Gorgas's recommendation, an act of the Confederate Congress on 11 April 1862 created the Nitre Corps and charged it with the responsibility of extracting nitre from the caves of the South and with the development of artificial nitre beds.

The Confederate Congress extended the authority of the Nitre Corps over all mining and mineral development, including the crucial development for military use of iron, lead, and copper. One instance of how St. John used this authority was his emergency organization of sulphuric and nitric acid production to make fulminate of mercury for the supply of percussion caps. St. John also had authority over all iron output, making Confederate railroads dependent on him to provide and repair track and rolling stock. Within the Ordnance Department, St. John's advice to Gorgas was influential on a range of issues beyond his specific responsibilities.

St. John was the most spectacular of Gorgas's managers in his new Ordnance Department. Unlike other established bureaus, such as the Quartermaster Department, the new Ordnance Department came into being with no restricting organizational structure and an open mandate to organize ordnance supply. Gorgas established and coordinated the organization while giving his subordinates broad discretionary powers. The organizational heads of his department formulated plans, while Gorgas decided on their feasibility against bureau priorities and available resources. The Ordnance Department survived its foundling year as the least successful bureau to become the most successful and efficient of the Confederate supply departments. Much of Gorgas's success came from his ability to select exceptional organizers for his bureau, and St. John was the most noteworthy of a distinguished group. The Confederate Congress acknowledged the importance of his contribution, when on 22 April 1863 it elevated the Nitre Corps to the separate and independent Nitre and Mining Bureau with the status of other war departments. The authority of the new bureau was extended to the control of civilian contracts for the manufacture of iron and the setting of priorities for its use.

The Nitre and Mining Bureau achieved what was possible within the limitations of Confederate supply. Despite its efficiency, it produced only about half the nitrates needed, though it made up the deficiency through import. Owing to the complementary efficiency of George Washington Rains in organizing gunpowder production, the Confederacy met its powder needs. In the crucial area of iron production, the Nitre and Mining Bureau, despite its exceptional efforts, did not meet all of the Confederacy's needs.

St. John left the Nitre and Mining Bureau, when on 16 February 1865 he became commissary general with the rank of brigadier general, succeeding the controversial but maligned Lucius B. Northrop. Again he employed his balance of organizational skill and diplomacy to achieve impressive short-term improvement in supply. However, as St. John anticipated, the same failures in transportation, importation, and funding that frustrated Northrop eventually undermined his efforts.

Near the end of the war, on 28 February 1865, St. John married Ella J. Carrington, with whom he had six children. Following the war St. John returned to civil engineering, first as chief engineer of the Louisville, Cincinnati, and Lexington Railroad from 1866 to 1869 and then for the next two years as chief engineer of Louisville, Kentucky. He subsequently worked as a consulting engineer and head of the Mining and Engineering Department for the Chesapeake & Ohio Railroad and in 1873 served as chief engineer for the Elizabeth, Lexington & Big Sandy Railroad. St. John died of apoplexy in White Sulphur Springs, West Virginia.

• St. John's Civil War career is well covered and placed in the broader context of the Ordnance Bureau in Frank E. Vandiver's superb *Ploughshares into Swords: Josiah Gorgas and Confederate Ordnance* (1952). Richard D. Goff's equally distinguished *Confederate Supply* (1969) places St. John in the overall context of Confederate supply. Vandiver's study includes an indispensable annotated bibliography of manuscript sources, of which the most important are the Records of the Confederate Ordnance Bureau, 154 vols., National Archives, and the accompanying Nitre and Mining Bureau File Box. See also Vandiver, ed., *The Civil War Diary of General Josiah Gorgas* (1947), and George Washington Rains, *History of the Confederate Powder Works* (1882), a study of the powder works by the person who built and ran it and who organizationally overlapped with St. John.

EDWARD HAGERMAN

ST. JOHN, John Pierce (25 Feb. 1833–31 Aug. 1916), governor of Kansas and Prohibitionist, was born in Brookville, Indiana, the son of Samuel St. John and Sophia Snell, farmers. He attended country schools in Indiana, receiving a rudimentary education. Owing to his father's fondness for alcohol, the family suffered economically, and during his teens he was forced to support himself by working in a store. Later in life St. John recalled, "Boy as I was, I hated the demon, Drink, that had made such a change in my father, had broken my mother's heart, and darkened my boyhood's home" (Headley, pp. 776–77). In 1847 he moved with his parents to Olney, Illinois, where at the age of nineteen he married Mary Jane Brewer. Two months after the marriage St. John left his wife and departed for California. This marriage produced one child and ended in divorce in 1859.

In California St. John took any available job. He mined, cut wood, clerked in a store, fought Indians, and worked on a steamboat. After seven years in California, St. John returned to Illinois, where he studied law in an attorney's office and was admitted to the bar in 1860. That same year he married Susan J. Parker; they had three children.

During the Civil War St. John joined the Illinois Volunteer Infantry, rising to the rank of lieutenant colonel. In 1869 he moved to Olathe, Kansas, where he practiced law and embarked on a political career. In 1872 he was elected to the Kansas Senate, but after one term he refused renomination. Meanwhile, he was earning a statewide reputation as a foe of alcohol. In 1878 he was chosen president of the Kansas State Temperance Union. Moreover, that same year he was the successful Republican candidate for governor, carrying the staunchly Republican state by a large margin.

Prohibition of alcohol was the dominant political issue in Kansas throughout St. John's four years as governor. In his 1879 message to the legislature, St. John said of liquor, "Could we but dry up this one great evil that consumes annually so much wealth, and destroys the physical, moral and mental usefulness of its victims, we would hardly need prisons, poorhouses, or police" (Pickering, p. 382). With the governor's active support, the legislature drafted a Prohibition amendment to the state constitution and submitted it to the electorate in the 1880 election. St. John campaigned for adoption of the proposed amendment while running for a second term as governor. On election day both St. John and Prohibition triumphed. In the 1850s Kansas had been an early battlefield in the war against slavery, and according to the idealistic governor in the 1880s it was in the vanguard of the fight against an equally pernicious foe. "We have now determined upon a second emancipation, which shall free not only the body but the soul of man," St. John proclaimed in his 1881 message to the legislature (Andreas, vol. 1, p. 288).

During his administration St. John also had to confront the consequences of the first emancipation. In 1879–1880 Kansas was the destination for an estimated 15,000 to 20,000 African Americans escaping from economic exploitation and political persecution in the South. As head of the Kansas Freedmen's Relief Association, Governor St. John led the effort to provide food, shelter, and employment for these so-called Exodusters. He solicited relief funds from throughout the country and won nationwide recognition for his humanitarian crusade.

After four years in office, St. John was not ready to lay down the burdens of office. Contrary to the state's two-term tradition, in 1882 St. John accepted the Republican gubernatorial nomination for a third time and ran on a platform dedicated to rigid enforcement of Prohibition and woman suffrage. An ardent advocate of women's right to vote, he believed that politically empowered females would line up solidly behind the cause of Prohibition.

The third time, however, was not lucky for St. John. He was the first Republican gubernatorial candidate to suffer defeat in the state's history. St. John's violation of the two-term precedent alienated some voters, whereas others were offended by his Prohibition stance and his support for woman suffrage.

Defeat did not cause St. John to moderate his views. Instead, in 1884 he left the GOP when the party's national convention refused to endorse Prohibition. He then accepted the Prohibition party nomination for president. The Prohibition party platform and its presidential candidate not only urged the outlawing of liquor but also espoused woman suffrage. Moreover, St. John attacked the federal government's racially discriminatory policy toward Chinese immigrants. On this issue he claimed to represent "the old Republican spirit" of equality, "which that party in its greed to

catch the vote of the Pacific states now repudiates" (Jutkins, pp. 86–87).

In the presidential campaign of 1884, Republicans bitterly attacked St. John, regarding him as a traitor who lured teetotaling voters from the GOP fold. Across the nation irate Republicans burned him in effigy more than 500 times, and he was shot at twice. Unharmed, he conducted a vigorous campaign, focusing much of his effort on the pivotal state of New York. On election day he won 150,000 votes, almost fifteen times the number garnered by previous Prohibition presidential candidates. Moreover, his 25,000 votes in New York were sufficient to deny Republican James G. Blaine that state's key electoral votes and to ensure victory for Democrat Grover Cleveland.

Following his break with the Republican party, St. John continued to speak out, backing the Populist cause in the late 1890s and supporting Democratic candidate William Jennings Bryan in the presidential race of 1900. As late as 1912 he toured Kansas on behalf of woman suffrage, and two years later, at the age of eighty-one, he stumped the East in support of Prohibition. During his life he reportedly traveled more than 350,000 miles and gave more than 4,500 speeches for the Prohibition cause. After suffering heat prostration on a speaking tour, he died in Olathe, Kansas.

When St. John won his third nomination for governor, he called it "a victory for principle, and principle is everything." This summed up his philosophy of life. Principle was all important, and when faced with the choice of remaining safely in the Republican fold or embracing the Prohibitionists, St. John did not hesitate in choosing sobriety over party fidelity. Condemned as a Judas by practical politicians who could not comprehend his idealism, he became a political pariah. Yet to the end of his life he dedicated himself to those causes he deemed vital to the emancipation of humanity.

• St. John's papers are in the Kansas State Historical Society. Biographical sketches are in Frank W. Blackmar, ed., *Kansas: A Cyclopedia of State History* (1912); William E. Connelley, *History of Kansas—State and People* (1928); P. C. Headley, *Public Men of To-day* (1882); A. T. Andreas, *History of the State of Kansas* (1883); Isaac O. Pickering, "The Administration of John P. St. John," *Transactions of the Kansas State Historical Society* 9 (1905–1906): 378–94; and Homer E. Socolofsky, *Kansas Governors* (1990). See Robert G. Athearn, *In Search of Canaan: Black Migration to Kansas 1879–80* (1978), for St. John's role in the Exoduster movement, and Robert Smith Bader, *Prohibition in Kansas* (1986), for his fight against alcohol. On St. John's presidential campaign, see D. Leigh Colvin, *Prohibition in the United States* (1926), and A. J. Jutkins, *Hand-Book of Prohibition* (1885). An obituary is in the *New York Times*, 1 Sept. 1916.

JON C. TEAFORD

ST. JOHN, Lynn Wilbur (18 Nov. 1876–30 Sept. 1950), college athletics coach and administrator, was born in Union City, Pennsylvania. His parents' names are unknown. His family moved to Monroe, Ohio, where he began his athletic career by playing sports in high school. After graduating in 1896 he began teaching school in Barberton, Ohio, although his career goal was to become a doctor. In 1900 he enrolled at Ohio State University in Columbus and played varsity football, but he left after one year to teach and coach at Fostoria (Ohio) High School because of a death in his family. A year later he was able to return to college, this time at the College of Wooster in Wooster, Ohio, where he also coached the major sports and served as athletic director.

In 1903 St. John married Barbara Floy Leader; they had two children. He remained at Wooster after graduating in 1906, adding the teaching of biology to his athletic duties. In 1909 St. John became basketball and football coach and athletic director at Ohio Wesleyan College in Delaware, Ohio. He arranged his schedule to attend morning classes at Starling-Ohio Medical College in Columbus. In 1912 Ohio State appointed him business manager of athletics, head baseball and basketball coach, and football line coach.

St. John intended to continue his medical studies, but in 1913 athletic director John R. Richards suddenly resigned. St. John inherited Richards's duties, informally at first, and arranged for Ohio State's admission into the Western (later Big Ten) Conference. In 1915 he was named athletic director and head of the physical education department. St. John remained as basketball coach until 1919 and as baseball coach until 1928. As an assistant to head football coach John W. Wilce until 1922, he helped Ohio State become a national power. When the team's popularity outstripped the 18,000-seat capacity of Ohio Field, St. John oversaw construction of Ohio Stadium, a horseshoe-shaped facility that sat 66,210 when it opened in 1922.

Ohio State's growing prominence in intercollegiate athletics led to other building projects, including a men's gymnasium and natatorium, a women's physical education building, and two 18-hole golf courses designed by the famous golf course architect Alister Mackenzie. Despite receiving public criticism for the golf courses, St. John acquired the land for the courses just before the Great Depression was at its worst and modified the contract to allow reduced mortgage payments when necessary.

By the time St. John gave up his last coaching position, he was an acknowledged leader in the Western Conference and influential in the basketball affairs of the National Collegiate Athletic Association (NCAA). He had been appointed to the NCAA Basketball Rules Committee in 1911 while he was still at Ohio Wesleyan, and he was reappointed after moving to Ohio State. He served continuously until 1937 and chaired the committee from 1919 to 1937. Kenneth S. Wilson, later commissioner of the Big Ten Conference, said that "St. John, by his diligence and unswerving devotion to the sport, was able to bring order out of a chaotic situation."

In 1917 St. John had also become a member of the Joint Basketball Committee, designed to coordinate the sport among high schools, colleges, the YMCA, the Amateur Athletic Union, and the Canadian Amateur Basketball Association. He chaired the committee from 1927 to 1932 and was responsible for reducing conflict between its constituents. After resisting an effort by collegiate officials to exclude all other groups from its ranks, he remade the organization into the National Basketball Committee of the United States and Canada. Reelected as chair in 1936, he served until 1937. A member of the U.S. Olympic Committee, he also helped organize the first Olympic basketball competition in 1936.

Known throughout the basketball community as "Saint," St. John retired from Ohio State in 1947. At that time plans were being formulated to construct a basketball field house, which was named in his honor when it opened in 1956. In his retirement he served as a scout for the Pittsburgh Pirates baseball club and worked on compiling a history of Ohio State athletics. He died in Columbus after suffering a stroke, and in 1962 he was elected posthumously to the Naismith Memorial Basketball Hall of Fame.

• Clipping files on St. John are in the Naismith Memorial Basketball Hall of Fame, Springfield, Mass., and the Ohio State University Archive, Columbus. Obituaries are in the *New York Times*, 1 Oct. 1950, and the *Sporting News*, 11 Oct. 1950.

STEVEN P. GIETSCHIER

ST. JOHNS, Adela Rogers (20 May 1894–10 Aug. 1988), journalist, author, and screenwriter, was born in Los Angeles, California, the daughter of Earl Rogers, a noted criminal defense lawyer, and Harriet Belle Greene. From an early age, Earl Rogers exerted an important influence on his daughter's life. After her parents' divorce, when Adela was eight, the young girl chose to remain with him. She later described their life together and her father's courtroom triumphs in her adoring biography, *Final Verdict* (1962).

Earl and Adela Rogers could seldom claim a permanent address; he frequently changed residences to be closer to his clients, and "home" was a shifting series of fancy hotel suites in cities throughout the West. Their constant moves disrupted Adela's schooling. As her contemporary Ishbel Ross noted in the first general overview of women in journalism, *Ladies of the Press* (1936), "She failed to graduate from grammar school but went to high school. She failed to graduate from high school but went to college." Her college career ended after a few weeks. Although Adela's classroom education was uneven and episodic, she gained another kind of education through observing the people in her father's courtrooms and law offices. "Now and then I learned from going to school," she recalled in her autobiography, *The Honeycomb* (1969). "When I didn't, I had learned from pimps, professional prostitutes, gamblers, bank robbers, poets, newspapermen, jury bribers, millionaire dipsomaniacs, and murderers." These experiences provided an ideal training for a woman who would gain fame as a crime reporter—the first woman to be assigned to a regular, big city police beat.

Aided by her father's introduction, Adela Rogers began her newspaper career in 1913 as a cub reporter for William Randolph Hearst's *San Francisco Examiner*. In the following year, Hearst transferred her to his newly acquired Los Angeles paper, the *Herald*, where she further developed her skill as a journalist. Her beats included the police department, city hall, the hotels, society, and even sports, and she was able to parlay her youthfulness, femininity, and charm into a number of exclusive stories. She also attracted the attention of the *Herald*'s chief copyeditor, William Ivan "Ike" St. Johns, whom she married in 1914.

Adela Rogers St. Johns's connection with the Hearst newspaper chain spanned more than half a century. Besides reporting for the *Examiner* and the *Herald*, she worked out of the city rooms of Hearst papers in Chicago, New York, and Washington, D.C., and her stories were also distributed through Hearst's International News Service. Her assignments included many of the leading stories of the day: the murder trial of Leopold and Loeb (1925); the trial and execution of Bruno Richard Hauptmann, accused of kidnapping and killing the Lindberghs' baby (1935); the rise and assassination of Louisiana's Senator Huey "Kingfish" Long (1935); the love affair between Edward VIII and Wallis Simpson and the king's abdication (1936); and the long-count prizefight between Jack Dempsey and Gene Tunney (1927). Although she officially ended her career as a reporter in 1948, her longstanding loyalties to the family of her old employer brought her out of retirement, at age eighty-two, to cover the bank robbery and conspiracy trial of his granddaughter, Patricia Hearst, for the *San Francisco Examiner*.

St. Johns followed a style of journalism that was deeply subjective, bristling with personal indignation, and laden with sentiment. Observers called the practitioners of this kind of writing "sob sisters," and St. Johns proudly accepted that appellation. "I had trouble being an objective unprejudiced reporter, being born a rooter for or against something or somebody," she confessed in her autobiography. Her goal was to empathize and to guide her readers' own emotional responses, to "unpack" her "heart." "The idea of a sob sister, unlike that of the objective reporter, was to walk right into the experience," she commented. "To reach hearts, you have to do more than report facts. Get under the skin, become part of another life, *let* your heart beat with another's heart." A clear example of the blazing personal emotion she invested in her stories is her report of the jury's verdict in the Hauptmann case:

Keep Your Hands Off Our Children
The Lindbergh jury didn't say Guilty, though that is the technical verdict they brought in. . . .
They didn't only say Put to Death. What they really said was
Keep Your Hands Off Our Children
Leave Our Children ALONE
Keep the Bloody Hands of Crime Off Our Babies

This is what we tell you now. You Can Never Get Away with It. We will always send you to Die in the Chair *if you touch our children.*

The same kind of personal involvement with her subject that characterized St. Johns's reporting also shaped her other writing. She arrived in Los Angeles at the moment that Hollywood was becoming the motion picture capital of the world, and she quickly made a name for herself as a Hollywood insider. She went nightclubbing with Mabel Normand, helped Gary Cooper buy his first dinner jacket, sewed up the seat of Rudolph Valentino's only pair of pants when he ripped them on his car door, and dished up stories about these exploits to a star-struck public. Billed as the "Mother Confessor of Hollywood," she wrote celebrity profiles and interviews for *Photoplay*, another arm of the Hearst publishing empire and the first movie fan magazine. She collected and expanded a number of these pieces for *Love, Laughter, and Tears: My Hollywood Story* (1978).

St. Johns developed a parallel career as a writer of fiction, drawing on her experiences as a crime reporter and Hollywood insider and fashioning them into short stories and longer works. Most of her short fiction, aimed especially at a female audience, appeared in Hearst publications such as *Good Housekeeping*, *Cosmopolitan*, and *American Magazine*. She was also responsible for several full-length novels and screenplays and a book titled *How to Write a Short Story and Sell It* (1956).

Late in life St. Johns became more interested in religious concerns, and her writings took a new turn. *Affirmative Prayer in Action* (1957) was an examination of "new thought" beliefs; her bestselling novel, *Tell No Man* (1966), similarly reflected her interest in spiritual matters. Her last published volume was *No Good-byes: My Search into Life beyond Death* (1981). She became a minister in the Church of Religious Science and was at work on a book called "The Missing Years of Jesus" at the time of her death.

President Richard Nixon commemorated her lifetime of accomplishments in publishing (and her earnest support of his political career) in 1970 by bestowing on her the Medal of Freedom, the nation's highest award for civilians. He lauded her for her "exceptional ability to reveal the human story behind the news."

An ongoing theme in much of St. Johns's writing was the difficulty that women faced when they attempted to balance marriage, motherhood, and a career. This was a dilemma with particular relevance for her own life. Each of her three marriages, to "Ike" St. Johns (1914–1927), to Stanford football star Richard Hyland (1928–1934), and to airline executive F. Patrick O'Toole (1936–1942), ended in divorce. She was the mother of four children: two from her first marriage, one from her second, and a fourth adopted child. Reflecting the importance of the family claim on her, St. Johns frequently boasted about her expanding network of descendants. Her obituary in the *Los Angeles Times* counted "9 grandchildren, 19 great-grandchildren and 8 great-great-grandchildren." She died in Arroyo Grande, California, and was buried, along with many of the Hollywood celebrities whose lives she had chronicled, in Forest Lawn.

The passage of time has not been kind to Adela Rogers St. Johns's reputation. Her writing style, with its sentimental stream-of-consciousness, its excessive verbiage, and its generous use of the pronoun "I," received increasingly harsh reviews as tastes changed. One critic dismissed *Love, Laughter, and Tears* as "a series of gushy clichés" and attacked St. Johns as "a total reactionary." "Her moralizing and funeral-wreath sentimentality continue to the last soggy page," he added (*Library Journal*, July 1978). Once touted as "the Greatest Girl Reporter in the World," St. Johns had become, by the 1960s and 1970s, a living relic of early Hollywood and Hearst's heyday, which she memorialized on television talk shows. Furthermore, even when it was first awarded, the accolade of "World's Greatest Girl Reporter" had been somewhat misleading (and not only because St. Johns was already thirty-nine years old and a grandmother). The title was created and kept alive by the vast power of the Hearst publishing empire. A St. Johns publicity stunt for one newspaper became "news" in the rest of the chain, and other Hearst magazines kept up the drumbeat of favorable reviews. Nevertheless, Adela Rogers St. Johns possessed an uncanny ability to be in the right place at the right time and to get stories where her competitors failed. She covered the top news stories of her generation, and she numbered among her friends, her confidants, and her best sources many of the cultural icons of the era.

• Adela Rogers St. Johns does not seem to have left a collection of her personal papers. Sketches of her life are in *Current Biography 1976* and *Editor and Publisher*, 17 Aug. 1957, p. 57, and 29 Nov. 1969, pp. 15, 38, 40. Supplementary material is most crucial for filling in information about chronology, which St. Johns kept deliberately vague in her own writing. Her prodigious outpouring of writing appears in the Hearst newspapers (*San Francisco Examiner, Los Angeles Herald, Chicago American, New York Journal*) and in magazines such as *Photoplay* (sometimes under a number of pseudonyms), *Good Housekeeping, Collier's, Saturday Evening Post, Ladies' Home Journal, McCall's, American Magazine*, and *Reader's Digest*. Some of her favorite short stories were collected in *Never Again and Other Stories* (1949). She makes a number of cameo appearances in W. A. Swanberg, *Citizen Hearst* (1961), but she is not the focus of that account. Two works that begin to explore the impact of women on the world of journalism are Phyllis Leslie Abramson, *Sob Sister Journalism* (1990), and Maurine H. Beasley and Sheila J. Gibbons, *Taking Their Place: A Documentary History of Women and Journalism* (1993). The most accurate and detailed obituary is in the *Los Angeles Times*, 11 Aug. 1988.

BARBARA LOOMIS

ST. LEON, Count de. *See* Randolph, Paschal Beverly.

STOCK, Frederick August (11 Nov. 1872–20 Oct. 1942), orchestra conductor, was born in Jülich, near Cologne, Germany, the son of Friedrich Karl Stock, a military bandmaster, and Louise Leiner. His father gave him his first musical instruction. At the age of fourteen he entered the Cologne Conservatory, where he studied the violin with Georg Japha and composition with Engelbert Humperdinck, the composer of the opera *Hänsel und Gretel*. Upon completion of his studies, Stock became in 1891 a violinist in the Gürzenich Orchestra (named for the hall in which it played) of Cologne. There Theodore Thomas, the conductor of the Chicago Symphony Orchestra, which he had founded in 1891, heard Stock play and engaged him as a member of the American orchestra beginning in the autumn of 1895. When Stock arrived in Chicago in October of that year, Thomas informed him that there were no openings in the violin section of the orchestra and assigned him to the first desk of the violas. Stock, who had never played viola, survived this rather harrowing initiation, and remained the assistant principal violist of the orchestra until 1905. In 1899 Thomas began to allow Stock to conduct some rehearsals and occasional concerts on tour. He formalized this arrangement in 1903 by naming Stock assistant conductor of the orchestra.

Upon the sudden death of Theodore Thomas in January 1905, the Chicago Symphony's board of trustees appointed Stock interim conductor. During the next three months the trustees cast about for some well-known European conductor to take over the orchestra. Hans Richter and Felix Mottl, both former associates of the composer Richard Wagner, were seriously considered, as was the somewhat younger Felix von Weingartner. In April 1905 the board voted unanimously to elect Stock, then only thirty-two, as permanent conductor. Thus began Stock's tenure of thirty-seven years as conductor of the Chicago Symphony, which ended only with his death—a span that was to be exceeded only by Eugene Ormandy's forty-four years with the Philadelphia Orchestra. At the time the permanent conductor was expected to conduct most of the concerts of his ensemble, and Stock did so, being spelled only very occasionally by an assistant or guest conductor, or by a composer conducting his own works.

The only interruption in Stock's long relationship with the Chicago Symphony occurred during World War I, when anti-German feeling was running high in the United States. He had applied for American citizenship immediately on his arrival in 1895 but he had failed to take out his second papers within the required time and, hence, became technically an enemy alien when the United States declared war on Germany in 1917. He came to believe that his continued presence on the podium under the circumstances was injurious to the orchestra, and in August 1918 he requested the orchestra's trustees to grant him a leave of absence until such time as he could secure full American citizenship. The trustees reluctantly granted his request in October. By early February 1919 Stock's reapplication for citizenship was so far advanced that the trustees invited him to take up his duties anew, and he did so at a concert later that month, receiving an ovation from both audience and orchestra. He became a citizen of the United States on 22 May 1919.

Stock was responsible for several new initiatives in the Chicago Symphony during his years as director. He persuaded the board of trustees to establish a pension fund for members of the orchestra. He began regular series of popular concerts, with low-priced tickets, and of children's concerts, conducting many of the performances himself. Because in the aftermath of World War I it no longer seemed feasible to import musicians from abroad, he encouraged the trustees in 1920 to form the Chicago Civic Orchestra to train young musicians in the orchestral repertoire and to drill them into skilled orchestra players, with a view toward bringing the best of them into the Chicago Symphony and other professional orchestras. Stock was also the chief conductor of this ensemble.

Although Stock was most comfortable conducting the great romantic composers from Beethoven through Wagner and Brahms, he performed Mahler's vast Symphony No. 8 in 1917, only a year after its American premier by Leopold Stokowski and the Philadelphia Orchestra. Stock also conducted the world premier of Prokofiev's Third Piano Concerto in 1921, with the composer as soloist. The American composer and educator, Howard Hanson, in a 1938 survey of performances of American compositions by American orchestras in the preceding twenty years, found that Stock and his orchestra had played more than any other ensemble: 272 compositions by 85 composers. Stock himself composed numerous works, especially orchestral compositions. They were generally played only by the Chicago Symphony under Stock's baton during his lifetime and have since been totally forgotten.

Stock married Elizabeth Muskulus in Milwaukee, Wisconsin, in 1896; they had one daughter. He died in Chicago of a heart attack, just after conducting the opening concerts of the 1942–1943 winter season.

Stock's career is difficult to evaluate. He seems to have been, for a conductor of a major symphony orchestra, a remarkably self-effacing man. Unlike his glamorous contemporaries, Serge Koussevitsky, Leopold Stokowski, and Arturo Toscanini, he had little or no interest in self-promotion. Though he toured frequently with the Chicago Symphony through the Midwest and the South, he only rarely brought the orchestra to the music centers of the eastern United States, and he guest-conducted the New York Philharmonic and the Philadelphia Orchestra only once or twice during the 1920s. He made a number of recordings, the first as early as 1916, but the only ones available with any regularity in the second half of the century were those of the Beethoven's Fourth and Fifth Piano Concertos, made in the early 1940s with Artur Schnabel as soloist. Yet there can be no doubt that he both preserved and enhanced the fine orchestra that he had inherited from Theodore Thomas and that he served both it

and his adopted home city of Chicago with a devotion rare both then and since.

• There are some papers of Frederick Stock in the Newberry Library in Chicago. Articles on Stock appear in the *Chicago Tribune*, 25 Oct. and 1, 8, and 15 Nov. 1942, and in the *New York Times*, 12 Apr. 1905, 15 and 25 Aug. 1918, 23 and 26 Jan. 1921, 21 and 23 Nov. 1940, and 25 Oct. 1942. The standard source for the early history of the Chicago Symphony is Philo Adams Otis, *The Chicago Symphony Orchestra: Its Organization, Growth and Development, 1891–1924* (1924). See also Howard Hanson, "Report of Committee on American Music," in *Proceedings of the Music Teachers' National Association . . . 1938* (1938), and Ezra Schabas, *Theodore Thomas: America's Conductor and Builder of Orchestras, 1835–1905* (1989). Obituaries are in the *Chicago Tribune* and the *New York Times*, both 21 Oct. 1942.

JOHN E. LITTLE

STOCKARD, Charles Rupert (27 Feb. 1879–7 Apr. 1939), biologist and anatomist, was born in Stoneville, Mississippi, the son of Richard Rupert Stockard, a physician, and Ella Hyde Fowlkes. Stockard received a B.S. in 1899 from the Mississippi Agricultural and Mechanical College, at which he had served as a commandant and acting professor of military science and tactics for the last two years of his undergraduate education. In 1901 he received a medical degree from the same institution. Following graduation, Stockard taught military science at Jefferson Military College in Natchez, Mississippi, until 1903, after which he began graduate work in zoology at Columbia University under Thomas Hunt Morgan.

As a graduate student, Stockard was most intrigued by abnormal embryology. He studied the relative effects of environmental and hereditary conditions by monitoring the development of fish eggs treated with toxic chemicals at different stages of maturity. Stockard's summers were spent doing research at the Marine Biological Laboratory in Woods Hole, Massachusetts, the Carnegie Institution Laboratory for Tropical Biology in Dry Tortugas, Florida, the Naples Zoological Station, and other biological stations in the United States and Europe. Stockard received a Ph.D. from Columbia in 1907 and joined the faculty of Cornell University Medical College as an assistant in embryology and histology later that same year.

During his first few years at Cornell Stockard served as an instructor in comparative morphology, an assistant professor of embryology and histology, and a volunteer instructor of surgical anatomy for medical corps officers. In 1911 he was appointed professor of anatomy and head of the Cornell anatomical laboratories. Soon after this appointment, Stockard and his fellow researcher George Nicholas Papanicolaou observed that the reproductive cycle of female guinea pigs could be characterized by cellular changes in the vagina. This discovery prompted the development of several noninvasive techniques to determine the reproductive status of female research animals, which proved integral to the identification of ovarian hormones. Later, Papanicolaou developed innovative diagnostic procedures for cancers of the respiratory and reproductive tracts based on the observations he and Stockard had made. In 1912 Stockard married Mercedes Mueller of Munich, Germany. They had two children.

In 1922 Stockard earned an M.D. from the University of Wurzburg in Germany following a single summer of preparation. His research on the effects of alcohol and anesthetics on patterns of animal growth and maturation enabled him to identify crucial points of development during which a fetus is particularly sensitive to environmental stimuli.

Stockard's vigorous and animated speaking style was well known within the American scientific community, and his distinguished career included appointments as the DeLamar Lecturer at the Johns Hopkins University (1925), Harrington Lecturer at the University of Buffalo (1926), Beaumont Foundation Lecturer at the University of Detroit (1927), Lane Lecturer at Stanford University (1930), Potter Memorial Lecturer at Jefferson Medical College (1934), and Joseph Collins Research Lecturer at the New York Academy of Medicine (1937). In addition, Stockard served as editor of *American Anatomical Memoirs, American Journal of Anatomy* (1921–1939), *Biological Generalia*, and *Journal of Experimental Zoology*. He presided over the American Association of Anatomists (1928–1930), the American Society of Zoologists (1925), and the board of scientific directors at the Rockefeller Institute for Medical Research (1935–1939). In 1933 Stockard became vice president of the American Association for the Advancement of Science and served as a trustee of the Marine Biological Laboratory at Woods Hole, the Long Island Biological Association, and the Bermuda Biological Station. He belonged to many organizations, including the American Association for Cancer Research, American Philosophical Society, American Society of Naturalists, National Academy of Sciences, New York Academy of Medicine, New York Zoological Society, Society of Experimental Medicine and Biology, Sigma Xi, Nu Sigma Nu, and Alpha Omega Alpha.

Charles Stockard published more than 150 works on cytology, endocrinology, embryology, genetics, medicine, and education. Noted most readily for his studies of abnormal morphology and the experimental production of monstrosities during fetal development, Stockard's most memorable works include *An Experimental Analysis on the Origin of the Blood and Vascular Development* (1915), *Hormones and Structural Development* (Beaumont Foundation Lectures, 1927), and *The Physical Basis of Personality* (1931). Stockard worked as a biomedical researcher and anatomist at Cornell University Medical College and the Huntington Fund for Cancer Research until his first bout with lung cancer, six months before he died of heart disease in New York City.

• No formal collection of Stockard's papers exists, but the details of his life have been described in F. P. Mall, "Reorganization of the Department of Anatomy at Cornell University Medical College," *Anatomical Record*, Aug. 1911, and D. J. Edwards, *American Philosophical Society Yearbook* (1939). An obituary is in the *New York Times*, 8 Apr. 1939.

KRISTIN M. BUNIN

STOCKBRIDGE, Horace Edward (19 May 1857–30 Oct. 1930), agricultural chemist and editor, was born in Hadley, Massachusetts, the son of Levi Stockbridge and Joanna Smith. He grew up on the college farm of the Massachusetts Agricultural College (now part of the University of Massachusetts at Amherst), where his father was president and a prominent leader in American agricultural education. In 1878 Horace earned a B.S. degree from Massachusetts Agricultural College in a joint program with Boston University. In 1882 he traveled to Göttingen, Germany, where he earned his Ph.D. in agricultural chemistry under Wilhelm Henneberg in 1884. Upon his return to the United States, Stockbridge was married in 1885 to Arabella "Belle" Lamar, member of a prominent political family from Sumter County, Georgia. The couple eventually had eight children, only four of whom survived to adulthood.

Stockbridge moved to Japan in 1885, accepting a post at the Imperial College of Agriculture and Engineering in Sapporo. Subsequently, he received additional appointments as a chief chemist and geologist for the imperial Japanese government. During this period Stockbridge published *Rocks and Soils* (1888), a textbook that went through multiple editions. After the death of an infant child in Japan, he returned to the United States, accepting a position as director of the Indiana Experiment Station in Lafayette.

The next year, Stockbridge was offered a job as both head of the North Dakota Experiment Station and president of North Dakota Agricultural College in Fargo. In North Dakota, he soon found himself in the middle of a dramatic political controversy between the governor, who was associated with populism and the Farmer's Alliance, and the Republican party appointees who sat on the college's board of directors. After accusing members of the board of various shoddy and possibly corrupt practices, Stockbridge was dismissed in May 1893.

Stockbridge then moved to Georgia, where he spent some time managing a 1,000-acre farm near his wife's family. He moved again in 1897, to Florida, where he served as dean of Florida Agricultural College and as agriculturist at the Florida Agricultural Experiment Station. In Florida he researched the southern livestock industry, while becoming increasingly active in publicizing agricultural science through state fairs, farmers' institutes, and popular writing.

From 1906 to 1919 Stockbridge served as editor of a major agricultural journal, the *Southern Ruralist*. During Stockbridge's tenure, the Atlanta-based periodical became one of the most aggressive promoters of scientific agriculture and crop diversification in the South. Stockbridge's editorials also revealed a willingness to frankly address major political and economic topics that went beyond agricultural issues. His editorials encouraged immigration from Italy as a solution to southern rural labor shortages, exposed political meddling at agricultural experiment stations, and attacked German Americans who were lukewarm about U.S. involvement in World War I. In 1915 the paper published a special issue titled "Farmers and Socialism," in which Stockbridge seemed skeptical about the promises of any radical reform, but frequently endorsed "home market clubs" and farmers' cooperatives. Stockbridge's importance in agricultural political issues also grew through the Farmers' National Congress, an organization that he headed in 1916 and 1917. In 1917 Stockbridge questioned the Liberty Bond program because he assumed that Treasury Secretary William McAdoo favored legislation that would have permitted an increase in second-class postage rates, thus hurting the agricultural press and its readers. McAdoo responded with a harsh telegram, aired publicly in the press, denying that he supported any such legislation and attacking Stockbridge's commitment to American service personnel. Other leaders in the Farmers' National Congress repudiated Stockbridge's tactics, but the charges concerning his patriotism were groundless (his son Basil was a much-decorated World War I veteran). Nevertheless, the issue embarrassed Stockbridge and the National Farmers' Congress on the national stage. Evidently, such disputes concerning the political nature of Stockbridge's editorials contributed to his resignation from the *Southern Ruralist* in 1919. In the 1920s Stockbridge continued to write for agricultural papers and managed the family farm in Georgia. His politics had varied somewhat over his career, though by the 1920s he was prominent in Georgia's fledgling Republican party. He was active in the Episcopal church and had served as a trustee of the University of the South. He died in Atlanta.

Stockbridge's peripatetic career reflects the opportunities and pitfalls for agricultural scientists in the late nineteenth and early twentieth centuries, an era when many Americans looked hopefully toward agricultural science for a quick fix to rural problems. The supply of skilled scientists was inadequate for the demand, however, creating frequently changing opportunities for men like Stockbridge. He also came into conflict with the administrators of agricultural colleges and experiment stations in disputes over the political value of such institutions.

Significantly, Stockbridge's research, predating the split of the field into its various specialties, bridged several of the agricultural sciences. His research projects touched such disparate topics as fertilizing the hops crop in Japan, developing fungicides for the potato scab in Indiana, responding to locusts and wheat rust in North Dakota, promoting livestock industry and new feed crops in Florida, and distilling petroleum from shale. Perhaps his most significant work was as an editor. Stockbridge's repeated efforts to popularize agricultural science and promote crop diversification played an important role in the agricultural history of the American South.

• Papers relating to Stockbridge's career with experiment stations and agricultural colleges are in the appropriate college archives in Florida, Indiana, and North Dakota. The Office of Experiment Station Records at the National Archives also holds official correspondence. The Sapporo Agricultural College in Japan holds a collection of over 100 Stockbridge documents. The University of Massachusetts at Amherst holds Stockbridge family materials, including a journal that his wife kept during their four years in Japan. Stockbridge's editorials in the *Southern Ruralist* are the best sources for his political views; see also the published reports of the annual meetings of the Farmers' National Congress of the United States. David B. Danbom discusses Stockbridge's career in North Dakota in "The North Dakota Agricultural College Controversy of 1893," *North Dakota History* 53 (Winter 1986), and *"Our Purpose Is to Serve:" The First Century of the North Dakota Agricultural Experiment Station* (1990). Manuscript material related to this episode may be found at the State Historical Society of North Dakota, Bismarck, and at the North Dakota Institute for Regional Studies, Fargo.

MARK R. FINLAY

STOCKTON, Annis Boudinot (1 July 1736–6 Feb. 1801), poet and state host, was born in Darby, Pennsylvania, the daughter of Elias Boudinot, a merchant and silversmith, and Catherine Williams. Even as a young woman, Annis Boudinot was known to the local Princeton, New Jersey, elite as—in the words of her friend Esther Edwards Burr—"a pretty, discreet, well-behaved girl. She has good sense and can talk very handsomely on almost any subject." Given this characterization of her, Annis Boudinot Stockton clearly experienced the advantages afforded to white women from elite families in the eighteenth century. Her family prospered from her father's far-flung business activities—from the mercantile and silversmithing business in Philadelphia to attempts at copper mining in northern New Jersey to trading as an innkeeper and serving as postmaster in Princeton. At a time when few women, even of her class, received much education, Annis Boudinot evidently received training in reading, writing, rudimentary ciphering, and the arts of sewing and dancing.

In 1753 her father moved the family to Princeton, where Annis could circulate among Princeton's favored families, especially those, like the Burrs, attached to the College of New Jersey (now Princeton University). Annis Boudinot's marriage to Richard Stockton during the winter of 1757–1758 brought her into one of the oldest landed elite families of Princeton. Prior to the Revolution, her husband's royal appointments (political appointments made in the colony by the British crown) created for Annis Stockton a high-profile life of social engagements. She bore six children but found time for writing nonetheless, even though she managed a large estate, by herself, during her husband's frequent absences in Philadelphia and New York. The family owned a few slaves and used other workers at "Morven," the Stocktons' Princeton estate.

Like many of the landed families of that area and era, the Stocktons stood to lose a good deal during the revolutionary war. It should come as no surprise, then, that Richard Stockton was, at first, reticent to declare a position about the growing conflict between the colonies and Britain. Once he declared his purpose to side with the colonists, Richard Stockton lost his royal appointments, and he seems to have been singled out for particular abuse when the British troops were in New Jersey. The family left their estate hurriedly in 1776, and Richard was soon after taken prisoner by the British. While Annis Stockton was in hiding with five of her six children (son Richard stayed behind with a trusted household servant), the estate was ransacked by Cornwallis and his troops, who used Morven as a central headquarters. Richard Stockton died in 1781, less than four years after the family returned to Morven.

During the years when Richard was alive, Annis Stockton wrote prolifically on many issues having to do with state affairs and matters of family and friendship. As a widow, Annis Stockton hosted some of the fetes held by Congress when it met in Princeton in 1783, under the presidency of her brother, Elias Boudinot. She frequently entertained George and Martha Washington, and, over the course of several years, she hosted a number of members of the French, Italian, and Polish nobility, along with key American officials. Annis Stockton was proud of her family, and she worked hard to establish for herself and her children a set of social circumstances that would reflect her own favoring of high social class.

In addition to being a well-known woman of state affairs, Annis Stockton was a member of a writing circle that at various times included Elizabeth Graeme Fergusson, Francis Hopkinson, John Dickinson, Philip Freneau, and Anna Young Smith. Her earliest poems, written when she was perhaps fifteen or sixteen, reveal wide reading in the poetry, history, and philosophy of her day. She wrote in the most common poetic forms of the eighteenth century—odes, hymns, epithalamia, epitaphs, songs, sonnets—on themes of friendship, the "battle" of the sexes, affairs of state, death, and religious beauty and belief. As a woman of an elite group, Annis Stockton wrote poetry that indicated her firm attitudes about what was then considered good sense, decorum, and rationality modified by an appropriate amount of sensibility. In holding these attitudes, she was in line with a central philosophy promoted in Scotland, England, and the British colonies (especially the middle Atlantic colonies); the "school" of "Common Sense" featured benevolence in moral philosophy and a hopeful democratic tolerance in civic affairs.

As a woman writer, Stockton was faced with the troubling problem of writing on issues related to sentiment (that is, a recognition of the emotional life and its relationship to friendship and poetic inspiration) without being discounted as too emotional and irrational and thus being excluded from serious consideration by intellectuals. Like many women writers of her day, Stockton employed a common formula in her poems; she would begin by reflecting upon her presumed "lowly" status as a woman even as she adopted (and transformed) a well-known and "decorous" topic or theme as her text. In one of her many poems to George Washington, for instance, written after the end of the revolutionary war, Stockton begins:

> Say, can a female voice an audience gain
> And Stop a moment thy triumphal Car
> And will thou listen to a peaceful Strain:
> Unskill'd to paint the horrid Scenes of war.

In writing in this way, Stockton at once showed her knowledge of the neoclassical epic tradition, acknowledged (as was expected of a woman writer) a weakness before her subject, and through her expertise with words justified her writing of poems.

Her expertise was rewarded again and again in that she saw her poems published more frequently than perhaps any other woman of her century; indeed, she was sometimes credited with having written poems that were published anonymously on "patriotic" themes, even when the poems were not hers. She received personal reward, as well, when Washington would visit her or write letters indicating his admiration of her genius. In July 1782, in one of the many letters he wrote to her, Washington praised Stockton's poetic abilities:

Your favor [letter] of the 17th conveying to me your Pastoral on the subject of Lord Cornwallis's capture has given me great satisfaction. Had you known the pleasure it would have communicated, I flatter myself your diffidence would not have delayed it to this time. Amidst all the compliments which have been made on this occasion, be assured, Madam, that the agreeable manner and the very pleasing sentiments in which yours is conveyed have affected my mind with the most lively sensations of joy and satisfaction. This address from a person of your refined taste and elegance of expression affords a pleasure beyond my powers of utterance; and I have only to lament that the hero of your pastoral is not more deserving of your pen; but the circumstance shall be placed among the happiest events of my life.

Her family connections and her poetic abilities brought Annis Boudinot Stockton a public renown exceptional for a woman of her day. She drew the attention of significant statesmen in North America and Europe, and she published poems in some of the most important newspapers and magazines of her era, including the *New American Magazine, New York Mercury, Pennsylvania Chronicle, Pennsylvania Magazine, New Jersey Gazette, Columbian Magazine, American Museum, Christian's, Scholar's,* and *Farmer's Magazine,* and the *Gazette of the United States.* Having written throughout her life, Stockton collected an oeuvre that numbers into the hundreds. Twenty-one of her poems were published during her lifetime, from 1758 through 1793, sometimes under the initials "A. S." or under the pseudonym "Emilia" or "Amelia." Stockton was clearly an accomplished writer whose energy and ability found in the highly stylized form of eighteenth-century poetry an appropriate medium for the display of her versatile talents. She gained a favorable reputation in her own day, and she encouraged others, especially women, to write poetry. Indeed, in terms of the sisterhood of eighteenth-century women with whom she associated, Annis Stockton was highly influential. She died in the Princeton area, probably at the home of a daughter.

• Stockton's manuscripts are located in a number of places in the middle Atlantic area. Until 1985 the Boudinot-Stockton family papers at the Princeton University Library, the Stockton family papers at the Historical Society of Princeton (housed at the Mudd Library, Princeton University), the Stockton and Rush papers at the Historical Society of Pennsylvania, and the George Washington papers at the University of Virginia were the primary collections that held Annis Stockton's materials. In 1985 the New Jersey Historical Society received from a descendant a manuscript copybook of Stockton's poetry, revealing that Stockton wrote more than ninety poems in addition to those housed at other locations. In 1994 several Stockton letters and one poem were catalogued and made available by the Rosenbach Museum and Library, Philadelphia.

A good source for general information about the Stockton family is Alfred Hoyt Bill, *A House Called Morven: Its Role in History*, revised by Constance Greiff (1978). On Annis Stockton particularly see also Lyman H. Butterfield, "Morven: A Colonial Outpost of Sensibility. With Some Hitherto Unpublished Poems by Annis Boudinot Stockton," *Princeton University Library Chronicle* 6 (1944): 1–16, and Butterfield, "Annis and the General: Mrs. Stockton's Poetic Eulogies of George Washington," *Princeton University Library Chronicle* 7 (1945): 19–39. The most accurate accounts of Stockton's life and writing appear in Carla J. Mulford, "Annis Boudinot Stockton and Benjamin Young Prime: A Poetical Correspondence, and More," *Princeton University Library Chronicle* 52 (1991): 231–66, and Mulford, *"Only for the Eye of a Friend": The Poetry of Annis Boudinot Stockton* (1995).

CARLA J. MULFORD

STOCKTON, Betsey (c. 1798–24 Oct. 1865), educator, was born in slavery of unrecorded parentage. As a child Betsey was given by her owner, Robert Stockton, as a wedding gift to his daughter when she married Reverend Ashbel Green, the president of the College of New Jersey. Most of Betsey Stockton's early life was passed as a slave domestic in the Green home at Princeton, except for four years that she spent with Green's nephew Nathaniel Todd when she was an adolescent. At Todd's she underwent a period of training intended to instill more piety in her demeanor, which had not been developed in the affectionate, indulgent Green household. Stockton returned to the Green home in 1816 and was baptized in the Presbyterian church at Princeton in 1817 or 1818, having given evidence through speech and deportment of her conversion to Christian ways. At the time of her baptism Stockton was formally emancipated from slavery, the Greens being reform-minded people who supported the abolition of slavery and believed she was prepared for freedom. Stockton became very well educated through their tutoring and the use of their enormous private library. So competent did Stockton become

that the Greens finally placed her in charge of their entire household, and she remained as a paid domestic and family member.

Stockton often spoke to Green about her wish to journey abroad, possibly to Africa, on a Christian mission. Green introduced her to Charles S. Stewart, a young missionary, newly ordained in 1821, who was about to be sent by the American Board of Commissioners for Foreign Missions (ABCFM) to Hawaii. The ABCFM made special concessions to allow Stockton to join the mission because of her piety and interest in traveling and missionary work. Michael Osborn of the theological seminary at Princeton wrote a recommendation for Stockton, stating that she had a full and complete knowledge of all the Scriptures, the Jewish antiquities, the geography of the holy lands, and the larger catechism in addition to a keen understanding of English composition, literature, and mathematics. In short, she was well qualified for missionary endeavors. Through a special agreement between Green, the Stewarts, and the ABCFM, she joined the mission both as a domestic in the Stewart household and as a missionary. The agreement stated that although she was to assist Harriet Stewart domestically, Stockton was not to be called upon for menial work "more than any other member of the mission, or this might manifestly render her life servile, and prevent her being employed as a teacher of a school, for which it is hoped that she will be found qualified."

Stockton arrived in Hawaii in April 1823. She was part of the second company of Congregational missionaries sent to the islands to convert Hawaiians to Christianity. Upon their arrival in Honolulu, the company was greeted by an African from Schenectady, Anthony Allen, who was living in Hawaii. Allen presented the new arrivals, possibly because of the presence of Stockton, with gifts of food, including a whole goat for their trip to Lahaina, Maui, where they were stationed.

Stockton distinguished herself in Lahaina by offering education to the common people instead of erecting schools only for the alii (chiefs, or nobility). In the past, the Hawaiian chiefs had not allowed the missionaries to teach the commoners. By August 1824, however, the chiefs had determined that the missionaries could teach the lower levels of Hawaiian society as well. Charles Stewart's journal reveals the chiefs' new attitude:

Indeed, till within a few weeks, they (alii) have themselves claimed the exclusive benefit of our instructions. But now they expressly declared their intentions to have all their subjects enlightened by the palapala (letters or learning), and have accordingly made applications for books to distribute among them. In consequence of this spirit, we have today been permitted to establish a large and regular school among their domestics and dependents.

Stockton's school was formed upon special request from commoners in Lahaina, as Stewart's journal entry of 20 August 1824 revealed:

Now the chiefs have expressed their determination to have instruction in reading and writing extended to the whole population and have only been waiting for books, and an increase in the number of suitably qualified native teachers, to put the resolution, as far as practical, into effect. A knowledge of this having reached some of the makaainana, or farmers of Lahaina . . . including the tenants of our own plantation, application was made by them to us for books and slates, and an instructor; and the first school, consisting of about thirty individuals, ever formed among that class of people, has, within a few days, been established in our enclosure, under the superintendence of B-(Betsey), who is quite familiar with the native tongue.

The missionaries, including Stockton, believed that education among the common people would prove, as it had among the chiefs, "the most effectual means," as Stewart wrote, "of withdrawing them from their idle and vicious habits and of bringing them under the influence of our own teachings in morality and religion." Stewart praised Stockton's efforts: "B-(Betsey) is engaged in a fine school kept by her every afternoon in the chapel adjoining our yard," and she took part in all the social activities of the mission settlement.

In 1825, over 78,000 spelling books had issued from the mission presses, and by 1826, 8,000 Hawaiians had received instruction on Maui. Stockton's efforts to educate the commoners had borne fruit, and the missionary efforts combated drunkenness, adultery, infanticide, gambling, theft, deceit, treachery, death, and what Stewart called "every amusement of dissipation." The missionary and educational efforts that Stockton extended to the masses also had a democratizing effect on the Hawaiians, as, while the chiefly class taxed off most of the food the commoners produced, they could not take away promised salvation. As Stewart remarked of the commoners, "Their only birthright is slavery. . . . Surely to such, the message of salvation must prove indeed 'glad tidings of great joy.'"

If, after the shortest and most perfect tuition, many are capable of composing neat and intelligent letters to each other, now, almost daily passing from island to island, and from district to district; so far from judging them not susceptible of attainments in the common branches of education, we need not fear to encourage a belief, that some may yet rejoice in the more abstruse researches of philosophy and science. They can be civilized, they can be made to partake, with missions of their fellow-beings, in all the advantages of letters and the arts. Nor is there more doubt, that they can be converted to Christianity.

The Stewarts decided to return to Cooperstown, New York, after two and a half years because of Harriet Stewart's poor health. Stockton accompanied them, leaving native Hawaiian teachers she had trained to take her place. She ran the Stewart household and assisted Harriet Stewart with her children until Harriet Stewart's death in 1830. Stockton continued to care for the Stewart children, perhaps until Charles Stewart

remarried in 1835. Venturing forth on her own, she taught at an infant school in Philadelphia, journeyed to Canada where she established a school for Indians along the same lines as the school she had started in Hawaii, and then returned to Princeton to set up a school, which later became the Witherspoon Street Colored School, the culmination of her life's work. She labored there, supported by northern blacks and whites and was committed to abolition in the area, until her death.

She was a strong role model for blacks and the less fortunate at every institution she established and administered. At her death, the *Freedom's Journal* of Cooperstown observed, "The superintendent and visitors of the public schools unhestantly state that, in their inspections, they found no school better trained, better instructed, or with evidence of greater success than hers." Stockton was buried with the Stewart family at Lakewood, and her tombstone attests to that family's kinship with her: "Of African blood and born in slavery she became fitted by education and divine grace, for a life of great usefulness, for many years was a valued missionary at the Sandwich Islands in the family of Rev. C. S. Stewart, and afterwards till her death, a popular and able Principal of Public schools in Philadelphia & Princeton honored and beloved by a large circle of Christian Friends." Betsey Stockton had overcome bondage to distinguish herself as an educator of the disadvantaged and underprivileged.

• The Hawaiian Mission Children's Society (HMCS) in Honolulu, Hawaii, contains the journal of Charles S. Stewart that describes Stockton's capable role in Lahaina, Maui. The HMCS collection also includes letters from contemporaries and diaries with references to her contributions, such as the letter from Michael Osborn to Jeremiah Evarts, 6 Sept. 1821, recommending Stockton to the ABCFM for a missionary appointment to Hawaii and the agreement signed by Betsey Stockton, C. S. Stewart, and Ashbel Green sent to Levi Chamberlain, 18 Nov. 1822. Thomas French, *The Missionary Whaleship* (1961), contains the letter from Ashbel Green to Jeremiah Evarts, 3 Sept. 1821, recommending Betsey Stockton for missionary service.

BARBARA BENNETT PETERSON

STOCKTON, Charles Herbert (13 Oct. 1845–31 May 1924), naval officer and author, was born in Philadelphia, Pennsylvania, the son of William Rodgers Stockton, an Episcopalian clergyman, and Emma Trout Gross. After attending the Germantown Academy and the Freeland Academy in Collegeville, Pennsylvania, Stockton was appointed to the U.S. Naval Academy in 1861. Because of the proximity of Confederate Forces during the Civil War, the academy was temporarily relocated to Newport, Rhode Island.

Stockton's first combat action was as a midshipman on the U.S.A. *Macedonian* in 1864, when that vessel was attempting to intercept the Confederate steamers *Florida* and *Tallahassee*. He graduated from the U.S. Naval Academy the next year. In 1866 he was promoted to ensign and served aboard the *Dacotah*. Subsequently, he was assigned to the *Chattanooga*, then he reported to the *Mohican* and cruised the Pacific Ocean for three years. He was promoted to lieutenant in 1869.

Stockton spent almost all of the 1870s at sea. In 1870 he was aboard the *Congress*, sailing in the West Indies, to Greenland, and to the Mediterranean. During 1874–1875 he joined the *Swatara* and circumnavigated the world. While in Asian waters, he assisted in the observations of Venus to develop new navigational techniques. In 1875 he was assigned to the Hydrographic Office in Washington, D.C., and was there for about one year. In 1875 he married Cornelia A. Carter; they had one daughter. In 1876 he went back to sea on the *Plymouth* of the North Atlantic Squadron, where he remained for four years. On 1 July 1876 Cornelia died. Subsequently, he was posted to the New York Naval Yard, and in the summer of 1880 he was assigned to the Torpedo Station at Newport, Rhode Island.

Also in 1880 Stockton married Pauline Lentilhon King; they had a son and a daughter. He was promoted to lieutenant commander in November of that year. He returned to sea from 1882 until 1885 as the executive officer aboard the *Iroquois* in the Pacific. During that stint of duty, he participated in the suppression of a Panamanian riot, serving as the commander of a battalion of U.S. sailors.

In the late 1880s Stockton began to write and lecture, mostly on legal subjects. While attached to the U.S. Navy's Bureau of Yards and Docks, he published a pamphlet, *Origin, History, Laws and Regulations of the United States Naval Asylum* (1886). In the summer of 1887 and 1888 he began a lecturing career, first speaking at the Naval War College in Newport, Rhode Island. In 1888 Stockton was part of a commission that studied the need for a navy yard in the state of Washington. In 1891 the Puget Sound Navy Yard was established near Bremerton, Washington. In 1889 he commanded the *Thetis*, accompanying an American whaling fleet to the Bering Sea and Arctic Ocean.

On his return from the northern climes in 1892, Stockton resumed his more scholarly work and was promoted to commander. Assigned to special duty with the Naval War College, he began an intensified study of the law of the sea and began to lecture on the subject. In 1895 he was at sea again as the commander of the *Yorktown* on the Asiatic Station. He returned to academic duties in 1897. In 1898 he became the president of the Naval War College and published a book, *International Law: A Manual Based upon Lectures Delivered at the Naval War College by Freeman Snow*. In 1899 he was promoted to captain, and during 1901–1903 he returned to Asian waters as the skipper of the battleship *Kentucky*. From 1903 to 1906 he was naval attaché in London. In 1904 he published a paper, "United States Naval War Code," and a book, *International Law: Recent Supreme Court Decisions and Other Opinions and Precedents*.

On 7 January 1906 Stockton was promoted to rear admiral. During 1906–1907 he was the president of a Board of Inspection and Survey and was posted to examination and retirement boards. In addition he was dispatched on special duty to Bordeaux, France, for the Maritime Exposition in that city. He retired from active service on 13 October 1907.

Upon his retirement from the navy, Stockton accepted the presidency of George Washington University. During his tenure the university was physically moved to a new location, the system of finances was revised, and the number of students doubled. He produced his final book, *Outlines of International Law*, in 1914, and he stepped down from heading the university in 1918. Stockton died in Washington, D.C.

Stockton contributed to the development of international law when the United States was becoming a leading world power. Combining considerable practical experience with scholarly work, he added to the literature on international standards of conduct and on the vital subject of resolving disputes peacefully.

• Stockton's career is traced in the U.S. Navy Registers, 1862–1907, a list of officers, with summaries of their navy service. A biography of Stockton is Marcus Benjamin, *Charles Herbert Stockton: An Eminent Churchman* (1925). The Stockton family history is in T. C. Stockton, *The Stockton Family of New Jersey* (1911). Stockton's obituaries are in the *Army and Navy Journal*, 14 June 1924, and the *Washington Evening Star*, 1 June 1924.

ROD PASCHALL

STOCKTON, Frank Richard (5 Apr. 1834–20 Apr. 1902), novelist, was born in Philadelphia, Pennsylvania, the son of William Smith Stockton, a Methodist minister and pamphleteer, and his second wife, Emily Hepsibeth Drean. After graduating from Philadelphia's Central High School in 1852, Stockton wanted to be a writer, but, following his father's insistence that he select a more practical trade, he became a wood engraver. He established an office in New York in 1860 after his marriage in April of that year to Mary Ann (also known as Marian) Edwards Tuttle from Georgetown, South Carolina; the couple did not have children. His wife, a former literature teacher in his mother's school, collaborated with him on some of his nonfiction books, including *The Home: Where It Should Be and What to Put in It*, published in 1873. In that same year, Mary Mapes Dodge, with whom Stockton had worked at *Hearth and Home* in 1868, invited Stockton to join her staff of *St. Nicholas Magazine*. She also admired his first book, *Ting-a-ling* (1870), an ironic fairy tale. Stockton abandoned engraving to become her assistant editor until 1878, when he quit in order to write full time. Over the next twenty-four years, he wrote realism and fantasy, science fiction and detective stories, children's literature, and adult romances. He wrote about capitalists, pirates, clergymen, recluses, and women of almost every age and class. Gradually he became one of the most popular writers in late nineteenth-century America, and his books were respected by critics, librarians, and reviewers.

Stockton's success was predicated on the rise of a literate middle class who signaled their social status by the amount of leisure they could enjoy. The new reading phenomenon of the late nineteenth century enabled hundreds of writers to flourish whose literary productions were clever and witty and united by one main goal: they meant to amuse. They mentioned universal themes such as frustration and delusion, they cited current social issues ranging from courtship and house buying to caste and feminism, but they always returned to a happy ending, "happy" in the sense not only of good humor but also in the sense that a restoration of traditional values had been achieved.

As a window upon this kind of reading phenomenon, Stockton's fictions do more to reveal the tastes, aspirations, and anxieties of his lower-middle-class readership than they do to contribute to purely literary developments of his era. His model reader is generally like his character Pomona: a maidservant who rises to the middle class in a series of stories beginning with the novel *Rudder Grange* (1879), she describes herself as socially "nigh the crack" between the workers and the bourgeoisie. At the other class limit, his readership is represented by Mr. Tolman, the title character of the 1880 *Harper's Monthly* story that William Dean Howells said was his favorite because of its realistic technique. A successful businessman whose corporation can function without him, Tolman finds fulfillment in purchasing a cozy little bookshop. That is, Tolman is most comfortable when stepping down to the lower middle class to which Pomona has risen. Even in an adventure novel like *Kate Bonnet* (1902), where the main character rebels against his stultifying life as a plantation manager by becoming a pirate, the magnet of class pulls hard: instead of pillaging towns and sinking ships, he ends up merely as Blackbeard's bookkeeper.

The phenomenon of class readership explains why Stockton said his favorite novel was *Ardis Claverden* (1890), whereas readers preferred his other books, such as *The Casting Away of Mrs. Lecks and Mrs. Aleshine* (1886), a humorous romp of old-fashioned housewives; *The Adventures of Captain Horn* (1895), an action-oriented bestseller; *What Might Have Been Expected* (1874), a precursor of *Tom Sawyer*; *The Great War Syndicate* (1889), a futuristic novel reminiscent of Edward Bellamy's *Looking Backward*; and *The Great Stone of Sardis* (1898), a science-fiction novel; as well as his children's literature, such as the short stories "The Griffin and the Minor Canon" and "The Bee-Man of Orn" (both 1887). In one sense, *Ardis* is part of the era's fixation on the New American Woman and complements other Stockton stories on the same theme, as with the obvious symbolism of "The Great Staircase at Landover Hall" (1898), where a woman trips over a child's toy and falls down a staircase to her death, her unfulfilled spirit haunting the house thereafter. In a more realistic venue, a woman in *The Late Mrs. Null* (1886) discovers that she can achieve the greatest independence and freedom only by pretending to be married; she announces that her nonexistent husband, a "null," is the best spouse a woman could have.

However, *Ardis Claverden* won Stockton's fondness also because the novel's heroine encoded Stockton's frustration as an author with the audience that had allowed him to prosper first as an editor for *St. Nicholas Magazine* and as a writer. Ardis was smart, handsome, rich, extremely able, and mature, yet adventurous. She is far more interesting and talented than any man or woman in her middle-class town. The more others recognize her merits, the more she is distrusted. The more others acknowledge her superiority, the more she is misunderstood or abused.

Clearly Stockton's self-reflexive meaning is as transparent as his symbolism in "The Great Staircase." As successful as he was as a genteel humorist and as a civilized writer, he naturally felt great frustration at the limits imposed by his bourgeois readership. He felt that his every literary effort had to entertain; he wrote in tepid dread that his readerly queen, the genteel reader, might whisper "we are not amused." Thus several of his stories center on the necessity of hiding talent and invention. Thus he wrote several critical essays insisting that his type of writing was *all right, really!* (See "The Pilgrim's Packets" [1873] or "Plain Fishing" [1888].) Thus a subtext of his "Mark Twain and His Recent Works" (1893) marvels at how Twain is able to manage social criticism while gaining popularity and critical esteem. Thus, on 5 November 1900, less than two years before his death in Washington, D.C., Stockton wrote to his publisher about a recent dream; his beloved home had burned down, leaving him with nothing but the clothes he wore, homeless with nowhere to go.

A prolific author who commanded international popularity and critical respect during his writing career, Stockton would fast become virtually unknown after his death. Contemporaries like Rudyard Kipling, William Dean Howells, Robert Browning, and Robert Louis Stevenson praised his works. In more recent times, his stories have suited only special purposes, such as the literary historian interested in America's first science-fiction novelist or reinterpreters such as Maurice Sendak, who selected two of Stockton's children's stories to illustrate in the 1960s. In the 1880s Stockton's name was as famous as Mark Twain's, but it would be forgotten a century later even to some who had read his stories, such as "The Lady, or the Tiger?" In short, Stockton was both a model and a victim of his times, an era that prided itself on the amount of attention it could devote to reading for leisure.

In what may be Stockton's best story, "Our Archery Club" (1879), the two best archers do not earn the club's admiration. The first archer, though he wins the prize, shoots accurately but mechanically, without any style. The other is unorthodox, shooting arrows from below his belt, causing gentlefolk to exchange disapproving glances. Stockton was not a formulaic hack writer, nor was he shockingly original, a Kate Chopin or a Theodore Dreiser. When a choice had to be made, he subjugated any literary urges to his reading club's tastes. Like the first archer in "Our Archery Club," he won many hearts and many prizes during his career. However, he depicted his archer dreaming of eagles but settling for targets filled with straw.

• Stockton's letters and papers are at the Pierpont Morgan Library in New York City, the Princeton University Library, and the Clifton Waller Barrett Library at the University of Virginia. His fiction is collected in the 23-volume Shenandoah Edition *The Novels and Stories of Frank R. Stockton* (1899–1904), and his science fiction is in *The Science Fiction of Frank R. Stockton*, ed. Richard Gid Powers (1976). The standard biographies are Henry Golemba, *Frank Stockton* (1981), and Martin I. J. Griffin, *Frank Stockton: A Critical Biography* (1939).

HENRY GOLEMBA

STOCKTON, John Potter (2 Aug. 1826–22 Jan. 1900), lawyer, senator, and New Jersey attorney general, was born in Princeton, New Jersey, the son of Robert Field Stockton, a naval officer, and Harriet Maria Potter. Like the Adamses of Massachusetts and the Jays of New York, the Stocktons of New Jersey were prominent in public affairs for over two centuries. Stockton graduated from the College of New Jersey (later Princeton University) in 1843. He read law in the office of his cousin Richard Stockton Field and was admitted to the bar in 1850. Stockton then practiced law in Princeton and Trenton. He married Sarah Marks, with whom he had three children.

Family connections aided Stockton's political career, which extended to the end of the century. Soon after Stockton's admission to the bar, the New Jersey legislature appointed him a commissioner to revise and simplify the practices and proceedings in the state courts. From 1852 to 1858 he was reporter to the Court of Chancery, publishing the decisions of the courts of chancery and appeals as *Equity Reports* (3 vols., 1856–1860). In 1858 President James Buchanan appointed Stockton U.S. minister resident to the Papal States, a post he held until 1861, when he requested his own recall.

During the Civil War, Stockton practiced law in Trenton. As a Democrat, he entered into the politics of a state with a unique attitude on national issues. The historian Charles Merriam Knapp wrote, "Of all the states that did not secede from the Union, New Jersey officially was the most outspoken in defence of the doctrine of state sovereignty and in opposition to the war and its conduct" (p. iii). The state remained Democratic during the Civil War and opposed Republican postwar Reconstruction policies, maintaining a states' rights tradition it had held since the Constitutional Convention of 1787.

At the state Democratic convention in 1862, Stockton reported the platform for the committee on resolutions, stating the views of New Jersey Democrats, including Stockton, concerning the war. While they supported the national administration in suppressing the rebellion by all constitutional means, they objected to the administration's suspension of the writ of habeas corpus, and to its restrictions of speech and the press. The resolutions also expressed opposition to the emancipation of slaves. Furthermore, the New Jersey Democrats contended, powers reserved to the people by the Constitution were being assumed by the government in Washington. Thus, in 1862 they formally supported President Abraham Lincoln's waging war to supress rebellion, but with strong reservations.

By 1864 New Jersey War Democrats and Copperheads (Northern Democrats sympathizing with the South and seeking to end the war) joined to support General George McClellan as a candidate for the presidency. At the Democratic National Convention, Stockton nominated McClellan. The general won New Jersey's electoral votes, but in the lower house of the state legislature, Democrats lost several seats to the Union-Republicans. This set the stage for a complicated senatorial contest, with Stockton the central character.

Stockton was elected U.S. senator on 15 March 1865 by a joint session of the state legislature. The legislature was so closely divided between Democrats and Union-Republicans, however, that it could elect a senator only after changing its traditional rule from requiring a majority vote to requiring simply a plurality. Stockton had received a plurality of forty votes; but the Union-Republican candidate received thirty-seven, and four others received one vote each. The Union-Republicans in the New Jersey legislature protested officially to the U.S. Senate that the election was irregular because Stockton had not received as many votes as were cast, in total, for the other candidates. Nevertheless, the Senate seated Stockton and forwarded his credentials to the Committee on the Judiciary. The committee report upheld Stockton's election by a vote of twenty-two to twenty-one and noted that New Jersey statutes provided that senators be chosen by a joint session, without any reference to a majority or plurality vote. Stockton, on the Senate floor, pointed out, "Senators are not always elected . . . in any state . . . in precisely the same way." The dignified senator went on, "It is a very unpleasant thing to have any one believe that a gentleman would claim a seat to which he was not clearly entitled" (quoted in Byrd, vol. 1, p. 391).

The debate in the Senate reflected post–Civil War animosities and emotional partisanship, within the context of the struggle between the Congress and President Andrew Johnson. It also reflected jealousy between Congress and state legislatures over control of election procedures. A vote of the full Senate on 23 March 1866 upheld the Judiciary Committee's favorable report on Stockton; however, in acrimonious debate it was challenged by Senator Charles Sumner of Massachusetts because Stockton, as a member of the committee, had been one of those voting on the report. Sumner proposed a reconsideration of the vote of 23 March. In reply to this challenge, Stockton withdrew his vote. The Senate then voted that Stockton was not entitled to his seat. This occurred on 27 March 1866, after he had been serving in the Senate for a year.

The case of Stockton's Senate seat attracted nationwide attention. There was speculation that had the Democrat Stockton retained his seat, President Andrew Johnson's veto of the Civil Rights Act might not have been overridden. The New Jersey legislature, displeased over a presumed infringement of its sovereignty, tried to withdraw its ratification of the Fourteenth Amendment; it did not succeed. Stockton presented the Senate with a state-by-state analysis of senatorial election procedures, proving they were a "snarl of inconsistencies and mismanagement" (Byrd, vol. 1, p. 392). In July 1866 Congress passed a law to regulate the time and procedure for electing senators, the first step toward reform of senatorial election procedures. In New Jersey, the Union-Republicans, in special legislative session, elected Alexander H. Cattell to the Senate. He took his seat on 19 September 1866.

Stockton was elected again to the Senate in 1869 and this time was seated without a problem. He served on the Committees on Foreign Affairs, the Navy, Appropriations, Patents, and Public Buildings and Grounds. He participated in debates on Reconstruction and international law and was instrumental in establishing much needed life-saving stations along the coast and appropriating funds to maintain them. Stockton was not returned to the Senate in 1875.

In 1877 Stockton was elected attorney general of New Jersey, a post he held for the next twenty years. After his last term as attorney general, he continued to practice law. His lifetime of public service upheld his family tradition and earned him continued respect. He died at the Hotel Hanover in New York City, where he was living with his daughter and son-in-law.

• The Stockton family papers are at Princeton University. Thomas Coates Stockton, *The Stockton Family of New Jersey, and Other Stocktons* (1911), includes essential biographical information. Charles Merriam Knapp, *New Jersey Politics during the Period of the Civil War and Reconstruction* (1924), is essential for an understanding of attitudes in New Jersey and Stockton's role in its complicated politics, including the contest over the Senate seat. Eric L. McKitrick, *Andrew Johnson and Reconstruction* (1960), addresses the political context of the unseating of Senator Stockton. Robert C. Byrd, *The Senate 1789–1989: Addresses on the History of the United States Senate*, vol. 1 (1988), pp. 391–93, clarifies the Senate's procedure in unseating Stockton. An obituary is in the *New York Times*, 23 Jan. 1900.

SYLVIA B. LARSON

STOCKTON, Richard (1 Oct. 1730–28 Feb. 1781), lawyer and signer of the Declaration of Independence, was born in Princeton, New Jersey, at his family's mansion "Morven," which became the state governor's residence in 1956, the son of John Stockton, a Somerset County Court justice, and Abigail Phillips. The family was prominent among the landowning gentry, but their political reputation did not extend beyond their own neighborhood. Richard's father, a Presbyterian convert from Quakerism, enrolled him at the College of New Jersey (now Princeton University) in 1746.

After graduating in 1748, Stockton practiced law. In 1755 he married Annis Boudinot; they had six children. At age twenty-seven, he inherited Morven and

began to acquire extensive properties with the proceeds of his lucrative law business. In June 1766 he began a fifteen-month sojourn in Great Britain. Stockton arrived in London with two entrées that would gain him access to some of the capital's most powerful men: a letter of introduction from New Jersey governor William Franklin and an address to George III from the College of New Jersey's trustees. He presented the address at an audience with the king, visited the marquis of Rockingham (then prime minister) at his home, met many prominent parliamentary leaders, and received an honorary citizenship from the city of Edinburgh. Stockton was chiefly responsible for persuading John Witherspoon, a Scottish Presbyterian minister who would later sign the Declaration of Independence, to become president of the College of New Jersey.

Stockton's influence soared after his return to colonial America. Having previously performed little public service—save as trustee for the College of New Jersey in 1757 and as justice of the peace in 1765—he was rapidly promoted to high office by Governor William Franklin, whose father, Benjamin Franklin (1706–1790), then a colonial agent, had befriended him in London. Stockton became a royal councilor in 1768, a judge of common pleas in 1772, and a supreme court justice in 1774.

While accepting that Americans owed allegiance to the Crown, Stockton consistently opposed Parliament's taxes on the colonists because his legal training had imbued him with the conviction that no levies could be imposed on communities not entitled to elect representatives to the House of Commons. He maintained this principle even while holding high office under the Crown, although his role in opposing unconstitutional measures was minor. On 22 June 1776, New Jersey's provincial congress appointed him to the Second Continental Congress. Stockton took his seat on 1 July and voted for independence the next day.

When New Jersey's revolutionary legislature chose a governor in August, it deadlocked between Stockton and William Livingston before finally electing Livingston by one vote. The legislators then offered Stockton the chief justiceship, which he declined. He instead resumed his seat in Congress.

Stockton's home lay in the path of British troops invading New Jersey in pursuit of George Washington's army, and he evacuated his family to a friend's house in Monmouth County. Tories discovered Stockton's presence, arrested him on 30 November 1776, and imprisoned him in New York. Reports of deliberate mistreatment led Congress to issue a formal protest to British authorities in January 1777. Stockton's health, which had been poor since the 1760s, broke under the strain of his purposefully harsh confinement. The Declaration's only signer to be captured, he became the sole signer to repudiate independence when, about March, he swore allegiance to the king in exchange for his freedom. He nevertheless gave no assistance to the British and took an oath of loyalty to New Jersey in December 1777. Otherwise he ceased all political activity. He died after a three-year struggle with cancer at Morven, which he had been attempting to rebuild after its destruction by British raiding parties in late 1775.

• Correspondence by Stockton is located in the Green Manuscripts at Princeton University Library and the Reed Manuscripts at the New-York Historical Society. Documents concerning Stockton's public career are in William A. Whitehead et al., eds., *Archives of the State of New Jersey*, vol. 10 (1886). See also James McLachlan, *Princetonians, 1748–1768: A Biographical Dictionary* (1976), and Henry Bill, *A House Called Morven, 1701–1954* (1954).

THOMAS L. PURVIS

STOCKTON, Robert Field (20 Aug. 1795–7 Oct. 1866), naval officer and entrepreneur, was born in Princeton, New Jersey, the son of Richard Stockton (1764–1828), a prominent lawyer, and Mary Field. Beginning with Robert Stockton's grandfather, Richard Stockton (1730–1781), a signer of the Declaration of Independence, members of four successive generations of the wealthy and influential family served in the Continental Congress or the United States Congress.

Robert F. Stockton first distinguished himself in the U.S. Navy. Withdrawing from the College of New Jersey (now Princeton University) at age sixteen, he accepted appointment as a midshipman in the United States Navy. Before and during the War of 1812, he served under the command of Commodore John Rodgers (1773–1838). Promoted to lieutenant in 1812, Stockton was later mentioned in dispatches for his services, including the defenses of Washington, D.C., and Baltimore, Maryland (1814). Stockton also saw action against Algiers (1815), whose pirates had preyed on Americans, then served a four-year tour of duty with the navy's powerful Mediterranean Squadron.

Stockton's naval career next took him to the west coast of Africa and then to the Caribbean. Sympathetic to the American Colonization Society, he escorted an agent of that organization to Africa and negotiated with natives a treaty (1821) that yielded a tract of land at Cape Mesurado, which became Liberia, to colonize freed slaves from the United States. (Stockton later helped found and served as president of the New Jersey Colonization Society.) While on duty off Africa, Stockton captured several French slave ships and a Portuguese letter of marque. The latter seizure resulted in litigation that carried to the U.S. Supreme Court, which upheld his action. During 1822, he took part in a naval expedition against pirates in the West Indies.

In 1823 Stockton married Harriet Maria Potter of Charleston, South Carolina, who bore him nine children, including John Potter Stockton, a prominent lawyer and politician. From 1828, when he inherited holdings of his father upon the latter's death, until 1838, Robert F. Stockton remained on inactive naval duty and devoted himself to business affairs and to his family. Stockton's enterprises in New Jersey were the Delaware & Raritan Canal and the Camden & Amboy Railroad, which, as the Joint Companies, were legally separate but financially unified. Ownership was concentrated in a small group, including Stockton, John Potter (Stockton's father-in-law), Robert L. Stevens, Edwin A. Stevens, and John Jacob Astor (1763–1848). The waterway, which ran between Bordentown and New Brunswick, New Jersey, was one of the important "anthracite canals," so named because they transported coal from eastern Pennsylvania to tidewater, in this case with access to the harbor of New York City. The railroad linked terminals on the Delaware River and Raritan Bay, also within striking distance of New York City's harbor. The canal and railroad companies were chartered by the New Jersey state legislature, which also granted them monopoly privileges between Philadelphia and New York City and approved creation of the Joint Companies (1830–1831). In return, the state received a lucrative financial interest in the companies and the right to purchase them when their charters expired. The Camden & Amboy provided free passes to politicians and subsidies in the form of advertising to newspapers to protect its position at the expense of potential competitors and shippers along the route.

Stockton returned to naval duty as a captain in 1838, serving briefly in the Mediterranean and in Europe. Earlier a backer of John Quincy Adams and then of Andrew Jackson, Stockton took leave to campaign for William Henry Harrison for president in 1840. He next supported John Tyler (1790–1862), who had succeeded to the presidency on Harrison's death (1841). Rejecting Tyler's offer of the navy secretaryship, Stockton secured administration support for the construction of a screw propeller-and-sail warship, its screw the idea of John Ericsson, who later designed and built the famous *Monitor*. Stockton helped oversee building of the USS *Princeton*, named for his hometown, then assumed command of the vessel. The bursting of one of the warship's largest guns, designed by Stockton, which killed, among others, the secretary of state and the secretary of the navy, almost sank his naval career (1844). An official inquiry, however, cleared him of responsibility for the mishap.

During the crisis of 1845–1846 with Mexico over Texas, Stockton, now a commodore, was assigned first to the Gulf of Mexico, then to the Pacific, arriving off California after the outbreak of war with Mexico. During July 1846, he succeeded Commodore John D. Sloat in command of the Pacific Squadron. Sloat's forces had already captured Monterey and San Francisco; their commander had, without authority, proclaimed the annexation of California. Stockton added to his navy forces Americans who had revolted against Mexican rule, created the short-lived Bear Flag Republic, and, under Lieutenant Colonel John C. Frémont, formed a California battalion. In imperious language that fairly assured resistance by Californians, Stockton also declared the annexation of California. Frémont occupied San Diego, and Stockton took Los Angeles, following which Stockton improperly declared the creation of a civilian territorial government.

A September revolt of Californians retook Los Angeles and most of southern California. Stockton, joined by Brigadier General Stephen W. Kearney and his small command, which had arrived overland from New Mexico, recaptured Los Angeles in January 1847. Fighting in southern California ended that same month. Conflict between Stockton and Kearney regarding governance in California was resolved soon after the arrival of Commodore W. Branford Shubrick, who as senior officer assumed command and divided authority with Kearney.

Retiring from the navy in 1850, Stockton again turned to family, business, and political concerns, settling the estate of his father-in-law, serving (as a Democrat) in the U.S. Senate (1851–1853), and holding the presidency of the Delaware & Raritan Canal (1853–1866). He joined the nativistic American (Know-Nothing) party, belonging to the faction that rejected unification with the Republican party. During the secession crisis of 1860–1861, he was a New Jersey delegate to the ill-fated Washington Peace Conference of February 1861. The venerable warrior was called to the colors one final time when Governor Joel Parker (1816–1888) designated him to command New Jersey's militia during Confederate General Robert E. Lee's 1863 invasion of Pennsylvania. Stockton died in Princeton.

• No collection of Stockton's papers has been located. Thomas C. Stockton, *The Stockton Family of New Jersey and Other Stocktons* (1911), provides rich information on the large and remarkable family. George Rogers Taylor, *The Transportation Revolution, 1815–1860* (1951); Philip C. Davis, "The Persistence of Partisan Alignment: Issues, Leaders, and Votes in New Jersey, 1840–1860" (Ph.D. diss., Washington Univ., 1978); and William E. Gienapp, *The Origins of the Republican Party 1852–1856* (1987), refer to Stockton's business and political activities. K. Jack Bauer, *The Mexican War, 1846–1848* (1974), and Neal Harlow, *California Conquered: War and Peace on the Pacific, 1846–1850* (1982), focus on his 1846–1847 military role. Bauer credits Stockton with energy and sound strategy but faults his diplomacy and tactics. Obituaries are in the *New York Times* and the *New York Tribune*, 9 Oct. 1866.

SAMUEL T. MCSEVENEY

STODDARD, Charles Warren (7 Aug. 1843–23 Apr. 1909), author and educator, was born in Rochester, New York, the son of Samuel Burr Stoddard and Harriet Abigail Freeman. Samuel Stoddard failed in 1851 as a paper manufacturer in Rochester, whereupon he relocated as an importer-exporter and a merchandise broker in San Francisco and called for his wife and family to join him three years later. Charles Stoddard reluctantly returned to school near Rochester in 1857, but two years later he was happily back in San Francisco, where he worked in a bookstore, attended the theater, and published some poetry in the *Golden Era*. He took a few college classes in Oakland, enjoyed literary and theatrical friendships, and then bummed through the Hawaiian Islands in 1864. He published a book of poems edited by Bret Harte, became a Roman Catholic convert in 1867 after considerable spiritual unrest, returned to Maui, and wrote splendid travel letters for various newspapers.

During two decades of restless travel, Stoddard uneasily combined overt Catholic Christianity and usually covert homosexuality. The latter he mainly practiced with Hawaiian lads. His allusions in this regard are always oblique, even in personal letters. A summer in Tahiti in 1870 resulted in *South-Sea Idyls* (1873). He toured Europe and the Middle East from 1873 to 1877; met Ambrose Bierce, Joaquin Miller, Mark Twain (who hired Stoddard as his witty, live-in secretary and paid companion in London from 1873 to 1874), and other celebrities abroad; sampled Munich bohemianism; and sent travel columns for $15 a week to the *San Francisco Chronicle*.

The year 1878 was pivotal for Stoddard, who, returning home, might well have become a major writer if he had focused his intellect and stylistic virtuosity. He might have capitalized on the popularity of his *South-Sea Idyls*, which was published in England as *Summer Cruising in the South Seas* in 1881, and was sufficiently popular in the United States to warrant a revised edition in 1892, with an introduction by William Dean Howells, who lauds the author's "mustang humor." But instead of buckling down, Stoddard chose to dawdle and drift for months and years, edit the *Saturday Press* in Honolulu and cuddle his native "kids," teach English literature at Notre Dame from 1885 to 1886, and return to Europe as the paid companion of a widow and her son. He taught literature at the Catholic University of America, in Washington, D.C., from 1889 to 1902. During this period he most enjoyed summer excursions, travel-letter writing, and literary friendships with luminaries such as Henry Adams, Hamlin Garland, John Hay, Rudyard Kipling, and Robert Louis Stevenson—all of whom found him charming, kind, gentle, knowledgeable, and brilliantly articulate, but also shy, aloof, and dangerously overweight. All preferred his friendship to his writing.

In his declining years, Stoddard freelanced, sponged on friends, and returned to California, settling at last in Monterey. Despite being plagued by inflammatory rheumatism, he wrote new essays and tried to assemble autobiographical fragments but suddenly suffered a fatal heart attack in Monterey.

Stoddard wrote travel books, religious items, and miscellaneous works. *South-Sea Idyls* collects loosely related autobiographical and travel essays, one of which, "Chumming with a Savage," sketches an intimate native friend who dies because he is not Christian enough to be serene but is too Christian to revert to joyous paganism. *A Trip to Hawaii* (1885) is a pleasant guidebook for would-be travelers but is marred by the inclusion of passages plagiarized from *South-Sea Idyls*. *The Lepers of Molokai* (1885, 1908) is a hasty, graphic account of Stoddard's visits to two Hawaiian leper colonies. His minor classic is *Hawaiian Life: Being Lazy Letters from Low Latitudes* (1894), a group of local-color essays on old Hawaii from the late 1860s to the mid-1880s. *The Island of Tranquil Delights* (1904), spotty but often sparkling, contains his last Pacific-area travel essays and also a bit of fiction. Meanwhile, Stoddard had also written about the Middle East, first in *Mashallah! A Flight into Egypt* (1881), which is exciting and fun-loving, and then in *A Cruise under the Crescent: From Suez to San Marco* (1898), somewhat prolix and wearisome. *Over the Rocky Mountains to Alaska* (1899) is a charming, observant little travelogue.

Stoddard's religious books show great versatility. *A Troubled Heart and How It Was Comforted at Last* (1885) is his tender, touching *Apologia pro Vita Sua*. In it, Stoddard never intellectualizes but chooses instead to dramatize the ineffable comfort he found in his church. *The Wonder-Worker of Padua* (1896) is a sincere but simplistic biography of St. Anthony of Padua. *In the Footprints of the Padres* (1902) details the history of California missions, includes a brilliant essay on San Francisco's Chinatown, and proved popular enough to merit a revised edition (1911).

Stoddard's miscellaneous works are among his best. *Father Damien: The Martyr of Molokai* (1901) is Stoddard's stark account of his self-sacrificial friend's work with lepers. (Stoddard's *Diary of a Visit to Molokai in 1884*, posthumously published in 1933, is more detailed.) *Exits and Entrances* (1903) is a potpourri of biographical and travel essays, bohemian pieces, and half-fictional personal narratives. *For the Pleasure of His Company: An Affair of the Misty City: Thrice Told* (1903) is a weird, half-autobiographical novel about life in San Francisco's art colony, and parades many of Stoddard's literary, artistic, theatrical, and journalistic acquaintances—and the author himself—as roman à clef characters. The issue of homosexual conduct is handled so indirectly that it was missed by most contemporary readers.

Stoddard had a soft and melancholy but often effective poetic voice, as evidenced by *Poems* (1867), which concern nature, are occasionally idyllic, and display astonishing versatility in handling oddly accented lines, unusual rhyme schemes, and elaborate stanzaic forms. His finest poem is "The Two Cleopatras," in lush, highly metaphorical blank verse and with this refrain: "Night is the shadow of that Ethiop queen." "The Cocoa Tree" has this poignant line: "Into the thankless sea I cast my fruit." After Stoddard's death, his friend Ina Coolbrith, the California poet, assembled *Apostrophe to the Skylark* (1909), a collection of his best verse.

Charles Warren Stoddard possessed superb descriptive powers, was comically egocentric, had a genuine poetic talent, and might have reached literary eminence if he had only written a frank autobiography with vignettes of his admiring, indulgent friends.

• Manuscript materials concerning Stoddard are in almost fifty places, mainly in repositories in California, Hawaii, Indiana, Massachusetts, New York, and Washington, D.C. See J. Albert Robbins, ed., *American Literary Manuscripts*, 2d ed. (1977). The best contemporary criticism is Théodore Bentzon (Marie Thérèse Blanc), "Un Loti amèricain: Charles Warren Stoddard," *Revue des Deux Mondes* 138, no. 4 (1 Dec. 1896): 615–44. The most thorough critical treatment is Carl

G. Stroven, "A Life of Charles Warren Stoddard" (Ph.D. diss., Duke Univ., 1939). Franklin Walker, *San Francisco's Literary Frontier* (1939), presents the artistic milieu. M. E. Grenander, "Ambrose Bierce and Charles Warren Stoddard: Some Unpublished Correspondence," *Huntington Library Quarterly* 23 (1960): 261–92, is of great interest. A reliable survey of Stoddard's life and works is Robert L. Gale, *Charles Warren Stoddard* (1977). Roger Austen, "Stoddard's Little Tricks in *South Sea Idyls*," *Journal of Homosexuality* 8 (1983): 73–83, is informative, as is Austen's distinguished *Genteel Pagan: The Double Life of Charles Warren Stoddard*, ed. John W. Crowley (1991).

ROBERT L. GALE

STODDARD, Cora Frances (17 Sept. 1872–13 May 1936), temperance educator and writer, was born in Irvington, Nebraska, the daughter of Emerson Hathaway Stoddard and Julia Frances Miller, farmers. Her parents moved the family from their farm in Nebraska to their native East when Cora was a child. In East Brookfield, Massachusetts, her mother and father joined the temperance movement, and Julia Stoddard soon rose in prominence to become the president of the local Woman's Christian Temperance Union (WCTU). Her mother's dedication to temperance, coupled with her writing and editing skills, served as a model for Stoddard's activism in the temperance movement and her writing proficiency. Stoddard received a public school education and then went on to receive her bachelor's degree from Wellesley College in 1896. She taught high school for one year in Middletown, Connecticut, then was employed for two years in the business field.

In 1899 Stoddard moved to Boston, taking employment as a private secretary to Mary H. Hunt, director of the Department of Scientific Temperance Instruction for the National WCTU (NWCTU). Stoddard played a pivotal role in the compulsory temperance education program that was instituted in public schools in a number of states following a successful nonpartisan political campaign by the NWCTU. Using textbooks, Stoddard educated teachers, administrators, and students about the dangers of alcohol. She evaluated textbooks already published on the subject and prepared texts of her own for use in classrooms. Although the NWCTU stopped emphasizing the program after 1907, Stoddard's skill in putting together appropriate classroom material helped to influence young people who as adults were to support passage of the Eighteenth Amendment outlawing the production, distribution, and marketing of liquor.

Illness forced Stoddard to resign from her position in 1904, and she left for Cortland, New York, to take an administrative job at a local normal school. She returned to Boston two years later to found the Scientific Temperance Federation, an organization that rejuvenated the work of the then deceased Hunt. Stoddard spent the next thirty years gathering information and statistics on the social and physiological effects of alcohol and writing a number of articles and pamphlets on the subject. The results were compiled and published in the *Scientific Temperance Journal*, distributed by the

Anti-Saloon League beginning in 1913. As editor of the journal, Stoddard soon became a leading figure in the Boston Temperance Movement.

Feeling as other reformers did that alcoholism resulted from moral weakness in an individual, Stoddard involved herself in state and national campaigns advocating constitutional amendments that would end the availability of liquor—and thus would inhibit the temptation to drink. As an American representative to the Twelfth International Congress against Alcoholism in London in 1909, she read a paper titled "The Relation of Juvenile Temperance Teaching to National Progress." At the International Hygiene Congress in Washington, D.C., in 1912, she put on exhibit the newest evidence of alcohol's effects on public health. The exhibit was so well received that it went on display across the country for the next eight years.

In her pamphlet *Alcohol's Ledger in Industry* (1914), Stoddard documented how liquor created a loss of "industrial efficiency and safety" among workers. Her *Handbook of Modern Facts about Alcohol* (1914) appeared in both English and Spanish; focused on the social and personal aspects of alcoholism, the handbook targeted immigrant communities and urban life as the circumstances most conducive to chronic drinking and most afflicted by its consequences. Although she admitted in a letter that the evidence was "not proof-positive," she believed that for "millions of people . . . drink was a matter-of-fact part of their daily life" and that therefore alcohol consumption had increased.

Stoddard accepted the directorship of the Bureau of Scientific Temperance Investigation in 1918. When passage of the Eighteenth Amendment in 1919 fulfilled her political mission, she nevertheless continued to write and speak on the detriments of alcohol and began an investigation into the effects of Prohibition. By 1922 Stoddard assumed the duties of director of the Department of Scientific Temperance Instruction in schools for the NWCTU, and in 1925 her directorship was extended to the World WCTU. In this capacity she conducted surveys and issued reports to disprove claims that Prohibition had increased drug addictions, an argument also made in her book *Wet and Dry Years in a Decade of Massachusetts Public Records* (1922). Stoddard's *History of Scientific Temperance Instruction* (n.d.) attributed the passage of the Eighteenth Amendment to the effort to educate a generation of youth in temperance. She served as an associate editor of the *Standard Encyclopedia of the Alcohol Problem* (6 vols., 1925–1930), sponsored by the Anti-Saloon League.

Stricken with crippling arthritis, Stoddard resigned from her posts with the WCTU in 1933 but remained active in the Scientific Temperance Federation until her death in Oxford, Connecticut. She had never married. Although Prohibition's end occurred as her health was failing, she remained resolute on her stand for temperance. Stoddard's dedication to ending the problems associated with alcohol took her to such countries as Chile, Finland, and Latvia. Remembered by those who knew her as a genial woman, she impressed temperance leaders and workers at home and abroad. Keeping current with new techniques and studies, Stoddard tirelessly crusaded to prevent what she believed were the detrimental physical and neurological effects of alcohol.

• Some biographical details on Stoddard are found in Ernest H. Cherrington, ed., *Standard Encyclopedia of the Alcohol Problem*, vols. 5–6 (1929–1930), and the *Scientific Temperance Journal* (Summer 1936). In addition to those mentioned above, Stoddard's writings dealing with the issues of alcohol in Massachusetts include *More Massachusetts Records and Prohibition* (1925), and, with Amy Woods, *Fifteen Years of the Drink Question in Massachusetts* (1929). A prolific writer, she also wrote *Science and Human Life in the Alcohol Problem* (1925); with Aubra D. Williams, *Scientist Experiments with Alcohol* (1935); and the pamphlets *Alcohol in Every Day Life* (1913); *The World's New Day and Alcohol* (1929); *Alcohol in Experience and Experiment* (1934); and *Some Practical Aspects of the Alcohol Question*. Stoddard's views are also found in Irving Fisher, *The Noble Experiment* (1930). She was a contributing editor to the *American Issue*. Information on the temperance movement can be obtained in Norton Mezvinsky, "The White-Ribbon Reform, 1874–1920" (Ph.D. diss., Univ. of Wisconsin, 1959); Ruth Bordin, *Woman and Temperance: The Quest for Power and Liberty, 1873–1900* (1981); and Jack S. Blocker, *American Temperance Movements: Cycles of Reform* (1989). Stoddard's death certificate is on file at the Conn. State Dept. of Health, Hartford.

MARILYN ELIZABETH PERRY

STODDARD, Elizabeth Drew Barstow (6 May 1823–1 Aug. 1902), writer, was born in Mattapoisett, Massachusetts, the daughter of Wilson Barstow, a shipbuilder, and Betsy Drew. Although the Barstow name was prominent in Mattapoisett, the family's upper-class status was tenuous because of Wilson Barstow's periodic business failures. Elizabeth Barstow studied for two terms (summer 1837 and winter 1840–1841) at Wheaton Female Seminary in Norton, Massachusetts. In 1852 she married Richard Henry Stoddard, a poet who made a living as a hack writer and—because of Nathaniel Hawthorne's influence—as a New York City Custom House officer (1853–1870). The financially straitened couple had three children, but only one lived beyond early childhood; they lived in New York City, where Elizabeth Stoddard died.

Stoddard's writing was first published in 1852, when the *Literary World* accepted her work "Phases." But her biggest career opportunity came from the position of "Lady Correspondent" for the *Daily Alta California*, a San Francisco newspaper. Stoddard later recalled the bold circumstances of her employment with the California publication: she arranged a meeting with the newspaper's editor, Charles Washburn, and persuaded him to hire her "to write New York letters" for the *Alta* (*Saturday Evening Post*, 30 June 1900, p. 1223). Consequently, from 1854 to 1858 the outspoken and witty "E. D. B." wrote semimonthly columns, numbering seventy-five in all and consisting of social and literary commentary. Stoddard's self-proclaimed "irreverent pen" covered a wide variety of topics, including New England life, English and American literature, temperance, slavery, and the women's rights movement.

The *Alta* columns provide important clues to Stoddard's literary likes and dislikes. She wrote in praise of Charlotte and Emily Brontë, Ralph Waldo Emerson, Edgar Allan Poe, and George Sand, among others. Although Stoddard confessed to a "curious infatuation" with their formulaic plots and commercial success, she lamented a lack of quality in popular novels written by American women during her day. Significantly, she rejected morally didactic, sentimental novels whose female characters fit the mold of domesticity and "true womanhood": "In reading such books I am reminded of what I have thought my mission was: a crusade against Duty . . . which is cut and fashioned for us by minds totally ignorant of our idiosyncrasies and necessities" (Buell and Zagarell, p. 326).

In addition to her blatant disregard for the image of the pious and pure Victorian woman, Stoddard's pronounced secularism ("sinner that I am, I confess to secular habits entirely") and bold treatment of sexuality were unorthodox for her time. A work of short fiction, "My Own Story" (1860), was approved by James Russell Lowell for the *Atlantic Monthly* only after Stoddard agreed to tame its sexual frankness. Not surprisingly, then, Stoddard's bold voice sparked charges of immorality from some of her contemporaries.

Although Stoddard's tendency to make caustic comments disrupted several friendships over the years, her sharp tongue and keen insight also drew people to her. One acquaintance observed, "On every variety of subject she talked with originality and ready wit; with impassioned speech expressing an individuality and insight most unusual and rare" (quoted in Buell and Zagarell, p. xii). Stoddard boldly asserted her "impassioned" individuality in her first novel, *The Morgesons* (1862). This loosely autobiographical novel traces the growth of Cassandra Morgeson from a mischievous child to a strong-willed woman. Despite its conventional love-and-marriage ending, *The Morgesons* makes a strong bid for female independence and social equality. In his review for the *New York Tribune*, George Ripley commented, "The story will be read as a development of powerful, erratic, individual passion" (19 July 1862).

During the 1860s, Stoddard's most prolific decade, she wrote two novels in addition to *The Morgesons: Two Men* (1865) and *Temple House* (1867). While all three novels received critical praise upon initial publication, none gained wide popularity. In addition to her novels, Stoddard published a dozen short stories in *Harper's* during the 1860s. Throughout this decade of intense writing, the Stoddards' Manhattan home served as a literary salon for various lesser-known writers, among them Elizabeth Akers Allen, George Henry Boker, Edmund Clarence Stedman, and Bayard Taylor.

Other than a children's book for adults, *Lolly Dinks's Doings* (1874), Stoddard did not publish much during the 1870s. A brief tide of good reviews during the late 1880s, however, led to the reprinting of her novels and inspired her to resume writing stories, essays, and poems for magazine publication. Notably, William Dean Howells's public praise for her writing helped revitalize interest in her work and contributed to the publishing of her collection *Poems* (1895). Overall, Stoddard's later work is not as strong. The scholars Lawrence Buell and Sandra A. Zagarell attribute this decline in literary merit to a lack of confidence because of commercial failure and the "conventionalizing" influence of her literary associates (pp. xx–xxi).

One of the most unconventional aspects of Stoddard's writing derives from her keen eye for the details of New England life. In *Literary Friends and Acquaintance* (1900), Howells celebrates Stoddard for providing a "foretaste of realism": "In a time when most of us had to write like Tennyson, or Longfellow, or Browning, she would never write like any one but herself." Stoddard's portraits of social and geographic landscapes—modeled after her seaport hometown—anticipated American regionalism, a strain of realism characterized by careful attention to people's habits and customs in a specific geographical location. Stoddard herself, however, rejected the "realist" label and preferred to call herself a romantic (Buell and Zagarell, p. xxii). In fact, Stoddard's work offers a unique blend of literary genres, including Victorian social realism, American regional realism, and Gothic romance.

A significant forerunner of American realism, Stoddard is also a transitional figure with respect to narrative technique. *The Morgesons*, with its sparing use of transitions and of third-person narration in dialogue ("she/he said"), is an important precursor to modern fiction.

Only moderately heralded during her own time, Stoddard's work remains in virtual obscurity even among specialists in nineteenth-century American literature. Nevertheless, for her unconventional views on society in general and on women in particular, as well as for her innovative approach to literary forms, Elizabeth Barstow Stoddard deserves recognition.

• Many of Stoddard's manuscripts are in the collected Edmund Clarence Stedman Papers, Butler Library, Columbia University. An important critical study and useful bibliographic source is Lawrence Buell and Sandra A. Zagarell's selection of Stoddard's works: *The Morgesons and Other Writings, Published and Unpublished* (1984). James Matlack's biographical overview, "The Literary Career of Elizabeth Barstow Stoddard" (Ph.D. diss., Yale Univ., 1967), contains a comprehensive, annotated bibliography of Stoddard's work. Richard Foster's introduction to *The Morgesons* (1971) provides a good bibliography of secondary sources. An obituary is in the *New York Times*, 2 Aug. 1902.

KARI BLOEDEL

STODDARD, George Dinsmore (8 Oct. 1897–28 Dec. 1981), psychologist, was born in Carbondale, Pennsylvania, the son of Eugene Anson Stoddard and Charlotte Dinsmore. Stoddard served as an officer in the

Field Artillery of the Army Reserve Corps from 1918 until 1923 and took an A.B. in chemistry from the Pennsylvania State College in 1921. He then studied psychology with Theodore Simon at the University of Paris, in France, from which he received a *diplôme*, or certificate for completing a course of study, in 1923. Simon had collaborated with Alfred Binet in developing the famous Binet-Simon Measuring Scale of Intelligence of a generation earlier. From the work of Simon and Binet Stoddard learned to view mental measurement as a yardstick of potential, not of fixed mental ability, as most American mental testers believed. In 1923 Stoddard entered the State University of Iowa, where he completed his doctorate in two years; he specialized in mental testing and educational evaluation. In 1925 he married Margaret Trautwein; they had five children. Stoddard remained at Iowa City until 1942, where he became a major figure and, indeed, a center of controversy in the new interdisciplinary field of child development.

At Iowa Stoddard rapidly rose through faculty ranks; appointed assistant in psychology and education in 1925, he served as assistant professor of psychology from 1926 to 1928 and as associate professor in 1928–1929, attained the rank of full professor in 1929, and later served as both head of psychology and dean of the Graduate College. By 1929 Stoddard had published fifteen major research articles and had coauthored a study on academic tests for high school students. He was also one of the architects of the Iowa Placement Tests, completed in 1928, which became nationally recognized as early attempts to measure what students at various elementary and secondary levels had learned. His main area of research interest was measurement of academic achievement, as distinct from the measurement of the intelligence quotient. The Iowa Placement Tests, one of his great legacies, proved seminal to its whole field, inspiring virtually all such tests for decades to come. In 1929 Stoddard became interim director of the Iowa Child Welfare Research Station (ICWRS) and permanent director the next year. Because of the ICWRS's distinction in its field, this appointment made him one of the most powerful members of the Iowa faculty.

The ICWRS, founded in 1917, was North America's first research institute devoted to scientific research on children, and it remained, in the 1930s, the leading institute in its kind in the western world. Before Stoddard's arrival, ICWRS research, like that done elsewhere in the field, was normative. Researchers measured all aspects of the normal child, normal in this sense meaning both typical and belonging to a group. Child scientists believed that normal children belonged to a particular group whose development was regular, symmetrical, and linear. They also assumed that all children in a particular group were interchangeable in that they could represent one another in various statistical measurements. In that sense child researchers usually denied the individuality of any child, for they assumed that children could be placed in groups or categories, that such group membership

was permanent, and that each individual in each group could vary in his or her traits only from the mean for the group at large. Such assumptions were profoundly deterministic, regardless of whether they were formulated as "hereditarian" or "environmentalist," because they assumed that the individual could not change group membership from one group or social class to another.

As ICWRS director Stoddard encouraged his colleagues to challenge this mainstream group determinism in the various fields in which they worked, such as Howard V. Meredith in physical growth, nutrition, physiological development; Beth L. Wellman and Harold M. Skeels in learning and cognition; and Ruth Updegraff and Kurt Lewin (among others) in social psychology. The ICWRS's most controversial work during Stoddard's tenure attacked the era's group determinism in two fields: mental measurement and individual psychology. In the late 1930s and early 1940s Wellman and Skeels, working under Stoddard's guidance in developing theories of mental measurement, challenged psychologists' conventional wisdom that the IQ was fixed at birth by arguing that when the IQs of children under the age of six were systematically retested, about 40 percent changed up or down at least one standard deviation (that is, fifteen IQ points or more). In one famous, three-year orphanage study, Skeels and his associates discovered that the orphanage's poor social environment was having a deleterious effect on normal children whose mean IQs had declined dramatically, from borderline normal (about 83 points) to feebleminded (less than 60 points). This work was the subject of enormous controversy; the critics of the Iowa position prevailed until the 1960s, when Head Start began as a federal program in early childhood intervention, and psychometric studies, begun in the late 1950s and running into the 1970s, which were done to justify Head Start, coincidentally helped rehabilitate the Iowa work on IQ variance.

The other high-profile work at the ICWRS was that of the German Jewish refugee scientist Kurt Lewin and his students, who tried in various ways to create a psychological science of American democracy by conducting experiments in social psychology that would identify the principles of democratic, as distinct from authoritarian, leadership. Lewin and Stoddard were intellectually attuned to one another; hence theirs was a full partnership in social psychology, whereas Stoddard had given the ICWRS's psychometricians their fundamental ideas and questions. Stoddard insisted that individuals were the products of psychological rather than biosocial forces, and this assumption permeated the Iowa work, no matter what its topic. Along with a small number of left-liberal intellectuals, such as anthropologist Margaret Mead and philosopher Horace Kallen, the Iowa scientists insisted that the individual, not the group, was the locus of concern in psychological science, thus departing from their science's mainstream dogmas. At the same time, however, Stoddard and his colleagues thought that normal children were truly interchangeable and, therefore, that their individuality was symmetrical, which paradoxically undercut the researchers' ability to proclaim the individual's autonomy from group membership. In this sense the Iowa researchers remained in fundamental agreement with the basic assumption of the interwar era, that the individual could not exist apart from the larger whole to which he or she "belonged." In that important way they did not anticipate the later focus on individualism and individuation, which produced many movements and reforms after the 1950s, such as Head Start.

An enthusiastic New Deal liberal, Stoddard was a confidante of such liberal figures of the age as social worker Harry Hopkins and artist Grant Wood. In 1942 he became commissioner of education of the state of New York and president of the University of the State of New York (later the State University of New York). This appointment gave him a platform from which to promote his liberal agenda, in which he linked the goals of a democratic society and the hows and whys of educational science's ability to create a just social order. In particular he continued to promote preschool and junior college education, and even adult continuing education. In 1946 he contributed to peace. He advised General Douglas MacArthur in Japan about education there, and later in the year he served in the first American delegation to the new United Nations Economic, Social, and Cultural Organization (UNESCO) meeting in Paris, France.

In 1946 too he left New York to become president of the University of Illinois in Urbana-Champaign. His politics generated conservative opposition from the start. His autocratic style, not uncommon in academic administrators in the 1930s, was slightly off-putting by the transitional 1950s. In 1953 the university trustees summarily dismissed him after he supported the American Medical Association's ban on research and use of an alleged cancer cure, Krebiozen, which was produced from cattle or horse serum. Andrew Ivy, vice president in charge of the university's health sciences campuses in Chicago, supported the full development of the drug, which Stevan Durovic, a Yugoslav immigrant with a colorful past, had developed. Krebiozen's efficacy as a cancer cure was never fully established. The opposition of the traditional academic and medical establishment to the drug had animated Stoddard to fight it as well. The controversy was emblematic of other controversies of the post-1950s era, in which traditional experts or professionals lost ground to champions of popular interests—the end of uncritical popular reverence for expertise.

Stoddard published more than one hundred articles, many of them of a popular or political character, and several books. In probably his most important scientific book, *The Meaning of Intelligence* (1943), he defended his then-controversial ideas on the IQ and its flexibility. In *Child Psychology* (1934), which he wrote with Beth L. Wellman, he outlined the parameters of the new science of child development. In such earlier works as *Iowa Placement Examinations* (1925) and *Study Manual in Elementary Statistics* (1929), which he

prepared with E. F. Lindquist, a leading statistician of the day, Stoddard showed his mettle as a theorist of mental measurement. He defended his actions in the Krebiozen controversy in "*Krebiozen,*" *The Great Cancer Mystery* (1953).

In 1954 Stoddard left Illinois for New York University, where he headed a major institutional self-study. In 1956 he became dean of the school of education and in 1960 chancellor and executive vice president at the university. He retired from New York University in 1964 and then served as vice chancellor of Long Island University until 1969, when he retired. His career never again had the tempestuousness that it had before. He died at his home in Manhattan.

His life symbolized the actions and attitudes of the liberal intellectual of the middle decades of the twentieth century, the quintessential New Deal liberal who believed in the promises of professionalism and positivistic science but went a step further than most of his liberal colleagues and argued that the individual can be an autonomous person. In that sense he was very much the disciple of John Dewey. He was always interested in applying science to expanding the opportunities for any and all individuals in democratic society.

• Stoddard's surviving correspondence is chiefly located in the records of the University of Iowa, the University of Illinois, and New York University; Stoddard correspondence is also in the records of the Laura Spelman Rockefeller Memorial and, especially, of the General Education Board, Rockefeller Archive Center, Tarrytown, N.Y. An oral history interview of Stoddard with Milton J. E. Senn is in Senn's massive oral histories of child development and child guidance, Historical Division, National Library of Medicine, Bethesda, Md. A good bibliography of his work while ICWRS director is Charles C. Spiker, comp., *The Institute of Child Behavior and Development* (1967).

Hamilton Cravens, *The Triumph of Evolution* (1978; repr. 1988), and Dorothy Ross, *G. Stanley Hall* (1972), provide an overview for the history of psychology. Joseph McVicker Hunt, *Intelligence and Experience* (1961), and Robert R. Sears, *Your Ancients Revisited* (1975), offer an insider's view of the rise of child development. Cravens, *Before Head Start* (1993), covers Stoddard's career in child development at the ICWRS. Patricia Spain Ward, " 'Who Will Bell the Cat?' Andrew C. Ivy and Krebiozen," *Bulletin of the History of Medicine* 58 (1984): 28–52, discusses the history of the Krebiozen controversy and has numerous bibliographical leads. On the character of post-1950s debates over expertise in American culture, see Alan I Marcus, *Cancer from Beef* (1994). Obituaries are in the *New York Times*, 29 Dec. 1981, and the *Des Moines Register*, 30 Dec. 1981.

HAMILTON CRAVENS

STODDARD, Richard Henry (2 July 1825–12 May 1903), poet, critic, and editor, was born in Hingham, Massachusetts, the son of Reuben Stoddard and Sophia Gurney. In 1828 his father, the master and part owner of a ship, was lost at sea. Stoddard and his mother lived briefly with her puritanical in-laws and then in squalor with her own improvident relatives in mill towns. When she married another sailor, the three lived in New York City beginning in 1835. Stoddard went to school, read voraciously from 1840, but then went to work to help support the family. He was an errand boy, an office boy, a scrivener, a bookkeeper, and—from 1843 to 1845—an apprentice iron molder.

Although his mother and stepfather were poor and unsympathetic, Stoddard found and read good books, began to write poetry, and in 1848 met established writers George Henry Boker and Bayard Taylor. Gaining confidence, he sought advice from editors and publishers and was soon publishing in respectable journals such as *Godey's Lady's Book*, the *Home Journal*, the *Knickerbocker*, the *Southern Literary Messenger*, and the *Union Magazine*. Stoddard, Boker, and Taylor were dubbed "the Trinity" in the *Knickerbocker*. In 1849 Stoddard financed the publication of his own book of poems titled *Foot-Prints*, but he soon realized that his imitations of works by John Keats were so dreadful that he burned every copy except one (now in the Library of Congress).

In 1852 Stoddard published *Poems*, which was favorably reviewed and sold well. In 1852 he married Elizabeth Drew Barstow, a bright and liberal woman from Mattapoisett, Massachusetts, whom he encouraged to write. He later said that whereas she had genius, he had more talent. In 1853, through the considerable political influence of James T. Fields, the distinguished Boston publisher, and Nathaniel Hawthorne, popular author of *The Scarlet Letter* and *The House of the Seven Gables*, Stoddard was appointed an inspector in the New York Custom House, a position he held until 1870. He was also a literary reviewer for the *New York World* from 1860 to 1870. During these years, while he wrote steadily, his wife published three novels of her own, which because of their honest New England naturalism were more forward looking than anything he ever produced. Beginning about 1870, the Stoddards presided over an influential literary salon at their home on East Fifteenth Street. Habitués included Thomas Bailey Aldrich and Edmund Clarence Stedman. Although Stoddard and Herman Melville worked in similar positions on the New York docks, they never became close friends; however, Melville did visit the Stoddards' salon a few times.

Stoddard acted as ex–Civil War general George Brinton McClellan's confidential secretary in the New York Department of Docks from 1870 to 1873. He was records librarian for New York City from 1877 to 1879. In 1880 Stoddard became the literary editor of the *New York Mail and Express*, holding this position until his death. He also did much other editorial work for other publications, including the *Aldine* (1871–1875), and became an astute and encouraging—though always conservative—judge of poetry sent to him by younger writers.

Over the years he produced anthologies such as *The Late English Poets* (1865) and *Poets and Poetry of America* (1874) and edited standard coffee-table items such as *The Loves and Heroines of the Poets* (1861) and *Readings and Recitations from Modern Authors, Being Pearls Gathered from the Fields of Poetry and Romance* (1884,

coedited with his wife). Although Stoddard deplored and inveighed against the advent of bohemianism in literature, he was, oddly enough, an often vulgar conversationalist in private.

Stoddard regarded himself first and foremost as a poet. After his 1852 *Poems*, he published *Songs of Summer* (1857), *The King's Bell* (1863), *Abraham Lincoln: An Horatian Ode* (1865), *The Book of the East, and Other Poems* (1871), a "complete edition" in 1880, and *The Lion's Cub; with Other Verse* (1890). His poetry strikes the rare reader today as effete, mechanically melodious, derivative and clichéd, and thinly didactic. "Arcadian Hymn to Flora" and "Ode," both in his 1851 collection, begin thus, respectively: "Come, all ye virgins fair, in kirtles white," and "Pale in her fading bowers the Summer stands, / Like a new Niobe with claspèd hands." Several of his poems are cast in exotic locales—which Stoddard, who never traveled abroad, had only read about. He also wrote poetry for juvenile readers on Little Red Riding Hood and General Israel Putnam, among other subjects. Better than any of his versifying are his anecdotal prose treatments of various authors he knew and admired. These included *Poets' Homes* (1877), *Nathaniel Hawthorne* (1879), *The Homes and Haunts of Our Elder Poets* (1881), and *The Life of Washington Irving* (1883).

Stoddard was a devoted bibliophile. He edited books by other authors and generous selections from the works of still others, usually with informative prefaces. Figures so treated include Elizabeth Barrett Browning, William Cullen Bryant, Lord Byron, Charles Dickens, William Hazlitt, Charles Lamb, Henry Wadsworth Longfellow, Nathanael Lyon, Prosper Mérimée, Edgar Allan Poe, Thomas Mayne Reid, Percy Bysshe Shelley, Algernon Charles Swinburne, William Makepeace Thackeray (whom he once met), and William Wordsworth.

Stoddard had an opportunity to write a significant autobiography, because he was at a center of the country's genteel tradition as it evolved in New York City and resisted realistic and naturalistic literary advances. But his *Recollections, Personal and Literary* (1903) is disappointing because of its egocentric, anecdotal, and superficial contents. He remains, however, a figure to be both admired for his assiduity and pitied. His childhood was little better than a long horror. Later he must have known that his brilliant wife was aware of his intellectual limitations. Of their three children, one was born deformed and soon died, another died in early childhood, and a third, a talented young playwright, predeceased him, as did his wife. Stoddard died in his New York City home.

• Many of Stoddard's voluminous manuscripts and papers are in libraries at Columbia, Cornell, Harvard, and Yale Universities. Others are in the American Antiquarian Society at Worcester, Mass.; the Buffalo and Erie County Historical Society, Buffalo, N.Y.; the Huntington Library, San Marino, Calif.; and the New-York Historical Society. Frank Luther Mott in both *A History of American Magazines 1865–1885* (1938) and *A History of American Magazines 1885–1905* (1957) mentions Stoddard's work frequently. John Tomsich,

A Genteel Endeavor: American Culture and Politics in the Gilded Age (1971), puts Stoddard in context with his friends and fellow conservatives Thomas Bailey Aldrich, George Henry Boker, George William Curtis, Richard Watson Gilder, Charles Eliot Norton, Edmund Clarence Stedman, and Bayard Taylor. Sybil Weir, "*The Morgesons*: A Neglected Feminine *Bildungsroman*," *New England Quarterly* 49 (Sept. 1976): 427–39, analyzes and praises Elizabeth Stoddard's best novel. An obituary is in the *New York Times*, 13 May 1903.

ROBERT L. GALE

STODDARD, Solomon (bap. 1 Oct. 1643–11 Feb. 1729), Congregational pastor and theologian, was born in Boston, Massachusetts, the son of Anthony Stoddard, a prominent merchant, and Mary Downing, a niece of Governor John Winthrop (1588–1649) and sister of the wife of Governor Simon Bradstreet. Solomon graduated from Harvard College in 1662, was appointed a fellow or tutor at the college in 1666, and served as its first librarian. He then spent two years as a chaplain in Barbados. He was allegedly about to embark for England in 1669 when a delegation from Northampton, Massachusetts, persuaded him to succeed their recently deceased young pastor, Eleazar Mather. Perhaps lacking the conversion experience that was a necessary condition of full church membership for ministers as well as laymen, he was not officially installed as pastor until September 1672. In March 1670 he married his predecessor's widow, Esther, a daughter of the eminent Reverend John Warham of Windsor, Connecticut. They reared twelve children, three of them Eleazar Mather's, in the parsonage.

During the sixty years of Stoddard's pastorate, Northampton grew from a frontier outpost to a prosperous agricultural community and county seat. The town was blessed with excellent farmland in the Connecticut River floodplain and a strategic location at the crossroads of New England's major inland travel routes. Delegates from Northampton became spokesmen for the western region in the Massachusetts General Court, and Solomon Stoddard's son John (b. 1682, Harvard 1701) became the region's most prominent land speculator, magistrate, and military commander.

Northampton's greatest claim to fame from the 1670s to the 1730s, however, was Solomon Stoddard's success as a preacher. Stoddard's church became renowned for periodic revivals of piety, and his ecclesiology articulated the third phase of the Puritan experiment in New England communities. It appeared to Stoddard and many of his contemporaries that the children of the intensely religious founders were faltering in spiritual intensity. The third generation of religious leaders, coming to power in the 1670s and 1680s, labored inexhaustibly to recall their flocks to anxiety about eternal salvation. They revived the Calvinist program of discounting even highly moral "good works" and trusted only in Christ as the purchaser of God's saving grace for humankind. Impassioned denunciations of the sins of complacency have been labeled "jeremiads" by historians, a favorite sermon technique that linked the contemporary crises of the New England colonies (King Philip's War in 1675–1676, earthquakes and hurricanes, and the 1684–1685 revocation of their charters by King Charles II and King James II) with the abandonment of their forefathers' spiritual mission. Stoddard excelled at the jeremiad—from his country outpost he especially castigated urban fashions in attitude and costume—but he also provided a remarkably popular alternative vision of individual and communal spiritual commitment. He preached God's love as well as God's wrath, and he exhorted all who found in their hearts any ground of hope for salvation to come into the church. This was a shocking breach with the rules of earlier generations, for it dismissed not only testimony of experienced grace as the criterion for full church membership, but also the second generation's compromise of an additional "half-way" membership status for those who consented to be governed by Christian rules but lacked the "born-again" experience. After years of argument, Stoddard persuaded his church to open the Lord's Supper to all who were not openly sinful in life and to embrace that sacrament as a possible means of receiving God's saving grace. Denounced by traditionalists, especially the Reverend Increase Mather of Boston, for taking Congregationalism too far toward Presbyterianism and thereby losing the distinction between the church as a body of sanctified persons and the secular community, Stoddard was nevertheless widely followed by ministers and churches in western Massachusetts and Connecticut. He also spread his influence through the Connecticut ministry of his eldest son, Anthony, and the five pastors who married his daughters. Through these daughters, the Stoddard-Williams-Dwight clan became the socioreligious elite of western New England in the first half of the eighteenth century. When Stoddard died he was eulogized in his home region and even in once-hostile Boston as a fallen patriarch.

Stoddard published vigorous arguments for his doctrinal innovations in two thematic clusters that reflect the two sides of his professional personality. One motif was evangelical: he exhorted laymen to trust in Christ's mercy and advised ministers to find Christ within their hearts, not just scholarship in their heads. The most significant publications in this vein were *The Safety of Appearing at the Day of Judgment in the Righteousness of Christ* (1687); *An Appeal to the Learned* (1709); *A Guide to Christ* (1714); and *The Defects of Preachers Reproved* (1724). The second motif, Stoddard's attraction to hierarchical church governance and his disdain for laymen's presumptuousness as judges of souls, is evident in *The Doctrine of Instituted Churches* (1700) and *An Examination of the Power of the Fraternity* (1718).

Stoddard's increasing emphasis on the governing power of the minister and elders within the congregation earned him the epithet "Pope" of the whole Connecticut River Valley. Some churches refused to join the regional bandwagon and adhered instead to the more democratic 1648 Cambridge Platform, which gave lay members great control over church admissions and discipline of alleged sinners. One of the clearest quarrels over these policies came from East Windsor, Connecticut, where Stoddard's son-in-law Timothy Edwards tirelessly advocated Stoddard's system, in is Connecticut manifestation as the Saybrook Platform, against a resistant congregation. It was in this environment that Jonathan Edwards (1703–1758) grew up, and after his education at Yale he arrived in Northampton in 1726 to become copastor and presumptive successor to his grandfather. He continued Stoddardean church practice and theological assumptions through the great revivals of 1735 and 1740–1742, then rejected both for producing neither authentic spiritual regeneration nor godly behavior. Edwards was dismissed in 1750 by the congregation, which still embraced Stoddardean principles.

After midcentury, however, the term "Stoddardean" fell out of use, although many of its elements survived under other doctrinal labels. As a strategy of trying to maintain the old Puritan double goal of a gathered and regenerate church that still embraced the whole community, it was appropriate to its time. Later generations found that secularized institutions served better as a societal adhesive, and particular churches tended to become either doctrinally bland and welcoming to the whole neighborhood or tightly interknit clans of the spiritually intense who maintained no ambitions to govern the town as a political jurisdiction. The unquestioned linkage of Calvinist church and intrusive state that was particularly Puritan in America ended with the reign of "Pope" Stoddard in Northampton.

• No collection of Stoddard's personal papers or manuscript versions of his published writings exists; scattered items can be found in the Mather papers at the Massachusetts Historical Society in Boston and in the Forbes Library in Northampton. Most of the extant documents are listed in the notes to Ralph J. Coffman's *Solomon Stoddard* (1978). Stoddard's writings, most of which have not been republished since their first appearance, can be found in microprint in Clifford K. Shipton, ed., *Early American Imprints, 1639–1800* (1955–1963). The Coffman work is the sole book-length biography and critical study, but it has received overwhelmingly negative assessment by other scholars. We still, therefore, must rely on John L. Sibley, *Biographical Sketches of Graduates of Harvard University*, vol. 2 (1881), pp. 111–22. Serious students must still consult Perry Miller's seminal article, "Solomon Stoddard, 1643–1729," *Harvard Theological Review* 34 (1941): 277–320, although the historiographical tide has turned against his "frontier" interpretation. The best analysis of Stoddard the theologian is Thomas A. Schafer, "Solomon Stoddard and the Theology of the Revival," in *A Miscellany of American Christianity: Essays in Honor of H. Shelton Smith*, ed. Stuart C. Henry (1963), pp. 328–61. See also the discussion of Stoddard's principles and career and an update of the critical bibliography in Patricia J. Tracy, *Jonathan Edwards, Pastor: Religion and Society in Eighteenth-Century Northampton* (1980).

PATRICIA J. TRACY

STODDARD, Theodore Lothrop (29 June 1883–1 May 1950), political philosopher and nativist advocate, was born in Brookline, Massachusetts, the son of John Lawson Stoddard, a lecturer and writer, and Mary Hammond Brown. Stoddard grew up in Massachusetts. His parents separated in 1888; his mother raised him, but Stoddard's father sustained a close relationship, including extensive travel both domestic and abroad. Stoddard graduated magna cum laude from Harvard College in 1905; he then studied law at Boston University until his admission to the Massachusetts bar in 1908. That year he traveled extensively in Europe, a trip that greatly impressed him with the burgeoning complexity and difficulties of European politics at the turn of the century. He became convinced of both the imminence of a massive European war and the naiveté of American political leadership. On his return to the United States he enrolled in Harvard, studying political science and earning the Master of Arts in 1910 and the Doctor of Philosophy in 1914.

Stoddard's sensitivities about race and world politics had been forged under the tutelage of Madison Grant, and his doctoral dissertation's treatment of the lingering aftereffects of the French Revolution anticipated the political intricacies that fueled World War I. His successful anticipation of the scope of the war allowed Stoddard to gain a reputation as a lecturer and political philosopher. His first book, *Present-Day Europe* (1917), earned him a position with the magazine *World's Work* as director of the foreign affairs department (1918–1920). This position provided a limited audience; however, Stoddard's most successful book, *The Rising Tide of Color against the White-World-Supremacy* (1920), offered him major recognition from a paradoxically broad yet elitist readership. *Rising Tide* sought to expose the pervasive dangers that powerful ethnic minorities posed to the dominant Anglo-Saxon culture that had been weakened during the unstable years following World War I. Many of Stoddard's ideas were syntheses of old theories about genetics and Anglo-Saxon cultural superiority, but he extended these theories to a broader public open to such ideas during the uncertain political times of the 1920s. He believed in the ultimate superiority of Anglo-Saxon culture and argued that it would be corrupted by intermingling, either genetically or politically, with non-Nordic races. He opposed large-scale immigration and championed anti-immigration laws and acts. The rise of nonwhite political forces, he reasoned, would lead to chaos on a global scale. Stoddard produced an average of one book a year, many concerned with different aspects of the race question, but none met with the success of *Rising Tide*. His final books on this issue were *Reforging America* (1927) and *Clashing Tides of Color* (1935).

Stoddard married Elizabeth Guildford Bates in 1926; she died in 1940. They had two children. He married Zoya Klementinovskaya in 1944.

Despite lackluster sales during the Great Depression, Stoddard continued writing on other subjects, including a history of childhood in various eras, a collection of sayings about luck, a biography of Richard Croker (a Tammany Hall boss), travel books, and works on global economics. His continuing interest in politics caused him to move to Washington, D.C., in the early 1930s, but he continued to maintain a residence on Cape Cod.

The rise of Nazism in Germany provided Stoddard a new outlet for his theories, and in 1939 he served as a special correspondent to Germany for the North American Newspaper Alliance. *Into the Darkness* (1940) appraised Hitler's early regime; while not endorsing Hitler, it admitted some appreciation of Hitler's eugenics experiments. From 1940 to 1945 Stoddard served as a foreign policy expert for the Washington *Evening Star*. His reputation as a political theorist was virtually destroyed by the horrors of Nazi Germany and modern science's debunking of his theories concerning eugenics and racial superiority. His disgrace meant that his death from cancer in Washington, D.C., was barely noted in the public press, though an obituary appears in the *New York Times*. Stoddard held memberships in the Unitarian Church, the Republican party, and learned societies in many of areas relevant to his pursuits, including history, political science, sociology, and genetics.

Although Stoddard's theories have fallen on the ashheap of history's other morally-corrupt philosophies, his place as an important molder of white supremacist and nativist thought during the 1920s cannot be disputed. F. Scott Fitzgerald castigated his work in *The Great Gatsby* (1925) and included a thinly-veiled passage from *Rising Tide*.

• Some of Stoddard's papers are in the Harvard University Library. For retrospective critiques of Stoddard's ideas and his influence on his era, see John Higham, *Strangers in the Land* (1963), and Thomas F. Gossett, *Race: The History of the Idea in America* (1963).

GENE C. FANT, JR.

STODDART, James Henry (13 Oct. 1827–9 Dec. 1907), actor, was born in Barnsley, Yorkshire, England, the son of James Henry Stoddart, a Scottish provincial actor, and Mary Pierce, an actress before her marriage. James and his four brothers began acting while their father was employed at the Theatre Royal in Glasgow. James made his debut at the age of five, playing Martin Haywood in Douglas Jerrold's *The Rent Day*. At seventeen he and his brother Robert joined the Theatre Royal company in Aberdeen. Characteristically, even at that young age, James specialized in old men's parts, for which his angular appearance and his reserved acting style, conveying a maturity beyond his years, were well suited. James moved on to theaters in Yorkshire and Liverpool, where he supported many star performers of the London stage. In 1854 James followed his brother George to the United States. He was immediately hired by James W. Wallack, initiating an American career that extended over fifty years. His first New York performance came on 7 September as Mr. Sowerby in *A Phe-*

nomenon in a Smock Frock. In 1855 Stoddart married the actress Matilda Phillips; they had three children, one of whom died in infancy. The following year he enlisted with Laura Keene's new company operating in Philadelphia and Baltimore. For the 1857–1858 season he and his wife joined a company in Alabama. The following year he moved to John T. Ford's company in Baltimore, where he appeared in *Richard III* with Edwin Booth and John Wilkes Booth. He also worked with Dion Boucicault and his wife, Agnes Robertson. Although Boucicault criticized Stoddart for lack of variety—"Stoddart is always Stoddart"—he hired Stoddart and his wife for his new Winter Garden company in New York. Stoddart stayed two years, working with Boucicault, Booth, Joseph Jefferson, and Charlotte Cushman.

In the mid-1860s Stoddart joined Mrs. John Woods's Olympic Theatre company, where he created one of his first major characterizations, the lawyer Mr. Moneypenny in Boucicault's *The Long Strike*. In 1867 Stoddart rejoined Wallack's company, where for seven seasons he played eccentric parts such as the bumpkin suitor, Bob Acres, in Richard Sheridan's *The Rivals* and the vociferous fraud Doctor Ollapod in George Colman the Younger's *The Poor Gentleman*. In 1873 Stoddart embarked on an ill-fated starring tour, despite his misgivings that he was not a star "gifted with ability far beyond other fellows." His attempt the following season to tour with his brother George was similarly unsuccessful. For the 1875–1876 season A. M. Palmer hired Stoddart for his Union Square Theatre. On 23 November Stoddart scored one of his biggest successes, starring as the conniving innkeeper Pierre Michel in *Rose Michel*. Stoddart enjoyed successful runs with *Miss Moulton* (1876), *The Banker's Daughter* (1878), and the farcical *French Flats* (1879), in which Stoddart produced gales of laughter when he entered disheveled after an encounter with a jealous opera singer. In the 1881 production of *The Lights o' London* Stoddart played the villain, who is thrown from London Bridge into the Thames in the climactic scene. In 1884 Palmer assumed management of the Madison Square Theatre, where Stoddart played minister Jacob Fletcher in the prosperous run of *Saints and Sinners*. Another success was *Captain Swift* (1888), in which Stoddart co-starred with Maurice Barrymore.

Recalling his fond memories as a stock actor in Alabama, Stoddart in 1891 created the distinguished southern gentleman Colonel Preston—one of his finest achievements—in Augustus Thomas's *Alabama*. *Alabama* traveled to Seattle and Portland, returned to New York, and then toured for another two years. The frequent national tours (including two to California) Stoddart made during his twenty-year association with Palmer made him a well-known figure throughout the country. After Palmer's retirement, Stoddart moved to Charles Frohman's management in 1894, when he played Joe Aylmer in *The Sporting Duchess*, which ran in New York and toured for nearly three seasons. Stoddart followed that in 1901 with a characterization regarded as the capstone of his career, playing the religious fanatic Lachlan Campbell in *Beside the Bonnie Briar Bush*, based on writings of Ian Maclaren. William Winter hailed his portrait of the stern Scottish father as "extraordinary for sincerity, elemental power, and overwhelming pathos." He praised Stoddart's "delicate exaggeration, which produces the perfect effect of nature."

Stoddart was tall and thin, with a large mouth and wide-set eyes. He usually played older men and character roles, just as he had begun doing at age seventeen. He joked that he made his career playing fathers weeping over wayward daughters. He had a fondness for wigs and boasted that one season he bought a wig every week to enhance his collection. Stoddart confessed to a "nervous temperament," and on several occasions he sought reassurances from Palmer that he could handle a particularly challenging role. While rehearsing for *The Parisian Romance* in 1883 he abandoned the lead role of Baron Chevrial, leaving it to Richard Mansfield, for whose career it provided a tremendous boost. Stoddart expressed satisfaction that he enjoyed a lengthy career playing primarily in New York and working with the best managers and the best companies. He prided himself on the "sincerity of purpose" he brought to his work, and Winter praised his "unpretending worth, unfailing geniality, sweetness of temperament, gentleness of bearing, probity of conduct, and patient and thorough performance of duty."

Stoddart felt a kinship with land and at one time tried to develop a commercial pear orchard. For about twenty years he lived at "Avenel," a small farm near Rahway, New Jersey. In the late 1880s he moved to Sewaren, New Jersey, where he maintained a garden. He was playing Lachlan Campbell in Galt, Ontario, in 1905 when he was stricken with paralysis. He died at his New Jersey home.

• Helpful information on Stoddart is in the Billy Rose Theatre Collection of the New York Public Library for the Performing Arts at Lincoln Center and in the Harvard University Theatre Collection. Stoddart's autobiography, *Recollections of a Player* (1902), also is informative, as are articles in the *New York Tribune*, 28 and 31 Jan. 1896. Obituaries are in the *New York Times*, 10 Dec. 1907, and the *New York Dramatic Mirror*, 21 Dec. 1907.

ROGER A. HALL

STODDERT, Benjamin (1751–17 Dec. 1813), first secretary of the Naval Department, was born in Charles County, Maryland, the son of Thomas Stoddert, a tobacco planter, and Sarah Marshall, daughter of a prominent family in the same colony. Nothing is known of his early education, but as a young man he served an apprenticeship in the merchant community of Philadelphia, where his friends included the young James Wilkinson, later a general in the Continental army. During the American Revolution, Stoddert adopted "Canada" as a temporary middle name to show his support for an enlarged confederation. In 1777 Wilkinson helped him obtain a captaincy in Thomas Hartley's Pennsylvania Regiment. Stoddert fought in the battle of Brandywine, receiving a wound that would afflict him for the rest of his life, and he later won praise for his service in fighting Indians on the upper Susquehanna River. He resigned his commission in April 1779 because the merging of his unit with the Pennsylvania Line would have placed him lower in rank than other officers with less seniority.

Through his connection with Wilkinson and his proximity to the Continental Congress at Philadelphia and York, Stoddert met many important men. These contacts led to his appointment as deputy forage master to the Continental army, a civilian appointment that was equivalent to the rank of major, a title by which he was later known. Beginning 1 September 1779 he became secretary to the Board of War and served in that status until his resignation on 1 February 1781. In 1781 he married Rebecca Lowndes, daughter of the Lowndeses of "Bostock House" in Bladensburg, Maryland, with whom he would have eight children prior to her death in 1800.

Stoddert prospered for a time as a civilian, forming a commercial partnership with Uriah Forrest and John Murdock and trading in tobacco out of Georgetown, where he built a fine home. He also bought and sold land in the Georgetown area, and he aided President George Washington by purchasing acreage that was later ceded to the government to become part of the District of Columbia. In January 1794 he incorporated the Bank of Columbia to assist in these activities. The downfall of Robert Morris in 1797, however, hurt Stoddert's financial affairs and weakened the value of his land holdings at the same time that commerce in general and the Potomac tobacco trade in particular were also falling off. Meanwhile, on 30 April 1798 Congress created a separate Naval Department to be headed by a cabinet-level officer. When George Cabot refused an appointment to that position, Secretary of State Timothy Pickering suggested Stoddert, whom he knew to be a staunch Federalist and a capable administrator. President John Adams approved, and Stoddert accepted.

Stoddert accepted nomination as the first secretary of the navy on 28 May 1798, inheriting a woefully small and mismanaged force. His staff of about ten people operated out of a two-room office in Philadelphia. Acting with diligence and vigor, he moved ships rapidly out to sea, began the construction of new vessels, and created a system by which naval forces could be supplied and repaired. He also decentralized the procurement process to make it more efficient, giving more authority to naval agents in various ports. He purchased permanent naval yards, among them installations at Washington, D.C., Norfolk, Boston, Portsmouth, New York City, and Philadelphia. Stoddert's vision was of an American navy that would make "the most powerful nations desire our friendship" (Jones, p. 62), and his first report to Congress called for the construction of a dozen 74-gun ships of the line, in addition to twelve frigates and twenty or thirty smaller vessels. Almost all of the work, he believed, could be done in the United States.

Several months into Stoddert's tenure, the United States became involved in an undeclared naval war with France that involved a considerable amount of ship-to-ship combat, most of it against French privateers in the West Indies. This Quasi-War was in many respects, as Michael A. Palmer has suggested, Stoddert's war, since the secretary put together and deployed the U.S. naval force consisting of some fifty ships, 1,044 guns, and 7,600 men. He must receive considerable credit for the remarkable achievement of American arms, demonstrated in the capture of eighty-four French vessels and the freeing of more than 150 American merchant ships. Stoddert demanded that his captains be aggressive: "I had rather burn all our ships than have them commanded by indifferent men" (Carrigg, p. 72). He dismissed Captain Isaac Phillips for allowing a British ship of the line to search the *Baltimore*, he found a shore position for Captain Sam Nicholson who was not doing enough with the *Constitution*, and he supported Captain Thomas Truxtun, whose capture of the French naval frigate *Insurgente* demonstrated the skill, valor, and aggressive patriotism that the secretary espoused.

President Adams was deeply interested in naval affairs, but he allowed Stoddert a great deal of latitude, especially in the deployment of U.S. ships. The president did overrule the secretary once, siding with Captain Silas Talbot in a dispute with Truxton over seniority. Moreover, the president was less than enthusiastic about Stoddert's emphasis on building ships of the line. In general, however, Adams appreciated Stoddert's abilities. For his part, Stoddert was the one member of the cabinet who was more loyal to the president than to Alexander Hamilton and who supported Adams in sending ministers to France to end the Quasi-War. When he left office, Adams sent Stoddert a farewell letter acknowledging their friendship.

In January 1801, with the war over and the Republicans coming into power, Stoddert called for a smaller navy consisting of frigates and ships of the line. The Republican administration would move in a different direction, but President Thomas Jefferson asked Stoddert to stay on nonetheless. He resigned early in the new administration, however, in part because he simply did not like public service. After leaving government service, he returned to business but without great success, and died heavily in debt.

Stoddert was an effective administrator who played an important role in creating the U.S. Navy and in assisting it to gain a tradition of martial success. He is also credited with being the "first naval theorist of the United States Navy" (Jones, p. 69). The navy that Stoddert built languished for a time, but many of the ships and officers of the Quasi-War went on to bring glory to the United States in the War of 1812.

• Stoddert's papers are held among the Continental Congress Papers and the Washington papers and in the Stoddert Collection in the Library of Congress. The best account of Stoddert's life and career is in Michael A. Palmer, *Stoddert's War: Naval Operations during the Quasi-War with France* (1987).

For other perspectives on Stoddert and the navy, see John J. Carrigg, "Benjamin Stoddert," in *American Secretaries of the Navy*, ed. Paolo E. Coletta (1980), and three articles in the *American Neptune*: Robert L. Scheina, "Benjamin Stoddert, Politics, and the Navy," 36 (1976): 54–68; William G. Anderson, "John Adams, the Navy, and the Quasi-War with France," 30 (1970): 117–32; and Robert F. Jones, "The Naval Thought and Policy of Benjamin Stoddert, First Secretary of the Navy, 1798–1801," 24 (1964): 61–69. There is also an interesting and appreciative account of Stoddert's work in Stanley Elkins and Eric McKitrick, *The Age of Federalism* (1993). An obituary is in the Washington, D.C., *National Intelligencer*, 24 Dec. 1813.

S. CHARLES BOLTON

STOESSEL, Albert Frederic (11 Oct. 1894–12 May 1943), conductor, violinist, and composer, was born in St. Louis, Missouri, the son of Albert John Stoessel, a theater musician, and Alfreda Wiedmann. Studying violin first with his father and then with Hugo Olk, a former student of Joseph Joachim in Berlin and concertmaster of the St. Louis Orchestra, the musical prodigy's public education ended with the eighth grade. A precocious talent sharpened by family nurturing and community support, fifteen-year-old Albert entered the Berlin Hochschule für Musik, studying violin with Emanuel Wirth and Willy Hess (boy wonder soloist with Theodore Thomas's Orchestra in the United States, 1868–1872, and later concertmaster of the Boston Symphony Orchestra), and theory and composition with Hermann Kretzschmar. He and classmate Arthur Fiedler of Boston studied violin and chamber music with Professor Gustav Axner.

In 1913 Stoessel began his professional career touring Germany, Switzerland, and Holland as second violinist with the Hess String Quartet. He made his solo debut performing three concerti in one evening with the Blüthner Orchestra in Berlin, a city where he occasionally played chamber music with pianist Artur Schnabel. He performed as soloist in London and Paris before returning to the United States in 1915, making his home near Boston in Auburndale, Massachusetts. That fall Stoessel made his American debut with the St. Louis Symphony. He played the Henri Vieuxtemps A Minor (Fifth) Concerto, utilizing his own orchestrated score. His younger sister, Edna (who also trained at the Berlin Hochschule), performed as pianist with Stoessel in his recitals throughout his career.

At the Berlin Hochschule he was awarded a teaching assistantship, and in that capacity he fell in love with his student Julia Pickard. They were married in her native Auburndale, Massachusetts, in 1917; they had three children.

Shortly after being appointed concertmaster of the St. Louis Symphony in August 1917, he was drafted into the U.S. Army. Soon he was commissioned a second lieutenant in the infantry and later was appointed bandmaster of the 301st Infantry Band ("Boston's Own"). He was the first commissioned officer bandmaster in World War I. His army career ended as director of the Allied Expeditionary Forces (AEF) Bandmasters' and Musicians' School located near General

John J. Pershing's headquarters in Chaumont, France. It was there that an association began with the AEF School's consultant, the famed New York Symphony conductor Walter Damrosch. French conductor and composer André Caplet, a key AEF School faculty member to whom Stoessel's Violin Sonata is dedicated, provided Stoessel with significant conducting and composing influence after just four months' association.

He returned to the United States in June 1919, accepting from Damrosch a position with the New York Oratorio Society. This experience led to a career change from violinist to conductor but did not exclude his soloing with major U.S. orchestras (e.g., Boston and Cleveland) and assisting world-famous tenor Enrico Caruso on his last tour in 1920.

While holding the prestigious positions as conductor of the New York Oratorio Society, music director of the Chautauqua (N.Y.) Institution, and director of the Worcester (Mass.) Festival, he amplified his AEF School pedagogy notes to publish a textbook, *The Technique of the Baton* (1920). The monograph provides several photographs of Maestro Stoessel. Among his other pedagogical books, *Essentials of Violin Mastery* (1925) had popular appeal.

At this time his music compositions, dating even from childhood, were often published and performed. The *St. Louis Centennial March and Two-Step* (1909), inspired by the local world's fair, was his earliest published work. Most notable among his mature violin, orchestral, and choral works are Suite Antique for two violins and piano or chamber orchestra (1922); *Cyrano de Bergerac* (1922), a symphonic poem; Concerto Grosso for Piano and Orchestra (1936); and *Beat! Beat! Drums* (1921), scored for mixed voices, trumpets, and drums. Stoessel's musical style is often neoclassical, displaying a thorough command of orchestration and a good sense for textual setting in his several vocal solo, choral, and choral and orchestral works. He was the editor of choral, chamber ensemble, and orchestra collections and made numerous orchestral transcriptions of works popular with recital and concert audiences in the early twentieth century. Important publishers of his music included J. Fischer, C. Fischer, Birchard, and Boston.

In 1923 Stoessel was the founder and chairman of the New York University (NYU) Department of Music, resigning in 1930. He founded the Juilliard Graduate School's orchestra and opera programs in 1927 and directed their activities until 1943. Philip James, whom he met at the AEF Bandmasters' School and who became a lifelong friend, ably assisted him at NYU and later served as chairman of the Department of Music for twenty years.

Throughout his educational activities Stoessel continued to perform as a solo and chamber ensemble violinist and violist and as a guest conductor. His immense talent, well-deserved successes, and James's recommendations led to consideration of Stoessel for the positions of music director of the Metropolitan Opera and the Cleveland Orchestra. (Both positions were awarded to European-born conductors.) Many of his students progressed to professional opera and conducting careers in the United States (see McNaughton for listings).

Stoessel suffered from heart disease, although active in sports, including tennis, swimming, and golf. He died suddenly in New York City before a distinguished audience while conducting the premiere of Damrosch's *Dunkirk* for the awards ceremony of the American Academy of Arts and Letters and the National Institute of Arts and Letters.

Following his death, the *Worcester Evening Gazette* provided an illuminating obituary: "Mr. Stoessel had a genius for applying all his attributes to his musical leadership. His attractive personality, his sense of organization, his industry, his intense interest in young artists and composers, his desire to please and inspire audience [*sic*], his skill as a public speaker, his loyalty to friends—these all went into his work. Those who worked for him admired him and were glad to do his bidding." John Tasker Howard summarizes Stoessel's stature in *Our American Music* (1946): "The sudden death of Albert Stoessel (1894–1943) brought to a close one of the most brilliant careers in the history of American Music" (p. 482). In 1927 Stoessel had conducted the first complete performance in New York City of J. S. Bach's Mass in B Minor. In 1944 the Oratorio Society of New York dedicated its eighteenth performance of this work to the memory of Stoessel.

• A comprehensive discussion of Stoessel's career is found in Charles D. McNaughton, "Albert Stoessel, American Musician" (Ph.D. diss., New York Univ., 1958). Stoessel wrote to the *New York Times*, 21 Feb. 1937, regarding his opera, *Garrick*, and Olin Downes reviewed the dramatic work in the *Times*, 25 Feb. 1937.

Stoessel's lecture, "Capacities of the Stringed Instruments," delivered at Carnegie Hall in 1941, is published in Robert E. Simon, ed., *Be Your Own Music Critic* (1941). John Erskine's program notes for a Concert by the Orchestra of the Juilliard School of Music (In Memory of Albert Stoessel), 12 Nov. 1943, provide collegial insights into the person and musician. An obituary is in the *New York Times*, 13 May 1943.

D. ROYCE BOYER

STOKES, Anson Phelps (13 Apr. 1874–13 Aug. 1958), clergyman, educator, and historian, was born in New Brighton, Staten Island, New York, the son of Anson Phelps Stokes, a banker, and Helen Louisa Phelps. He graduated from Yale with a B.A. degree in 1896 and, having inherited a large fortune from his maternal grandfather, Isaac Newton Phelps, spent the following year traveling abroad, mostly in East Asia. Upon his return, he enrolled in the Episcopal Theological School in Cambridge, Massachusetts, to study for the Episcopal ministry. Before his graduation, however, Arthur Twining Hadley, Yale's new president, prevailed on him to take the post of secretary of the university. He nevertheless received the bachelor of divinity degree in 1900, as well as an M.A. from Yale, and also was ordained a deacon in the Episcopal church. In 1903 Stokes married Caroline Green Mitchell; they had three children. Anson Phelps Stokes, Jr., followed his father into the Episcopal ministry, serving as bishop of Massachusetts from 1956 to 1970.

Stokes had a remarkable career as Yale's secretary, serving from 1899 to 1921. During that time he built up what had been a minor clerical office into the second most powerful position in the university, acting as Hadley's right-hand man and often making the hard decisions that the more easygoing Hadley was likely to defer. He played a major role in moving Yale from provincial college to leading university by promoting the graduate and professional schools, organizing the alumni, raising endowment funds, and providing the driving force for new building projects.

When Hadley retired as president of Yale in 1921, Stokes, then a vigorous and able forty-six year-old, was widely regarded as the natural successor. He was Hadley's candidate and had considerable support among faculty and alumni, but his forcefulness and decisiveness had made him many enemies. Some influential trustees and alumni questioned his opposition to military preparedness before 1917, though his later service in planning for the army's educational work during the war tended to offset that criticism. More importantly, Yale had become secularized to such an extent that Stokes's clerical status was an obstacle for many. As a result, he was ultimately passed over in favor of an outsider, James Rowland Angell. Although deeply hurt by his rejection, Stokes accepted the decision graciously and met with Angell to provide information and advice to smooth the transition. Then in 1921 he resigned, sold his home to Yale to be used as a faculty club, and left New Haven.

While serving as Yale's secretary, Stokes maintained his clerical status by serving from 1900 to 1918 as assistant minister at St. Paul's Church in New Haven, where he engaged in social and charitable enterprises. At a meeting held at Stokes's home in New Haven early in the century, Clifford W. Beers organized a committee that was later credited with initiating the mental hygiene movement in the United States. At Yale, Stokes took part in promoting the religious activities of Dwight Hall, a campus ministry center. Stokes was also instrumental in the founding of Yale-in-China, the University's missionary enterprise.

Stokes embarked on a full-time ministerial career in 1925 when he accepted appointment as canon residentiary at the Washington Cathedral (National Cathedral) and was ordained to the priesthood by Bishop James E. Freeman of Washington. His position at the cathedral gave Stokes the opportunity to engage in charitable and educational activities. He promoted urban renewal projects in the city and interfaith cooperation in the religious community. He was, at various times, president of the Washington Housing Association and the Family Services Association. In 1916 he was one of three men who proposed the founding of the Institute for Government Research, the first unit of what later became the Brookings Institution. He

was also active in the Social Welfare Department of the Episcopal Diocese of Washington.

At the cathedral, he served as chairman of the committees on St. Albans School, the College of Preachers, and the Cathedral Library as well as Ways and Means. He retired from his position as canon residentiary in 1939, when he reached the age of sixty-five, though he remained a member of the Cathedral Chapter until 1942. At his retirement the *Washington Post* said of Stokes that "finely sympathetic, broadly generous, he has worked with Jew, Catholic, and Protestant, black and white, and has been their loyal comrade in every worthy endeavor." Leaving Washington, he spent the rest of his life at what had been his summer home in Lenox, Massachusetts, where he died.

Throughout his life, Stokes maintained a lively interest in the welfare of black Americans. As president of the Phelps Stokes Fund, a charitable trust founded by his two aunts, he actively supported black educational projects, serving for a time as a trustee of Tuskegee Institute. He wrote a brief biography of Booker T. Washington and an essay in celebration of Tuskegee's fiftieth anniversary. He also argued in favor of Marian Anderson's appearance at Constitution Hall before the Daughters of the American Revolution in 1939 and published his statement to the DAR as a pamphlet entitled *Art and the Color Line* published by the Phelps Stokes Fund.

When Stokes retired, he told friends that he wanted to devote himself to writing two major historical works: "A History of Universities from Their Origin in the Twelfth Century to the Present," of which he had already completed more than a million words, and "Church and State in the United States 1789–1939," which he deemed to be ready for publication within a year. It was only in 1950, however, long after his retirement, that Canon Stokes published the latter work, by then a three-volume study, *Church and State in the United States*, an annotated compilation of the major documents in church-state relations since American independence. The work has been commended by scholars as complete, balanced, and reliable and is regarded as an indispensable resource for historians of American religion.

At his death, the *New York Times* wrote, "To the life of the American spirit, he made one of the great contributions of his time."

• The papers of Anson Phelps Stokes are in the Yale library; papers relating to his work as secretary are in the university archives, and his unpublished "History" is in the manuscript division. His ministry in Washington is recorded in the archives of Washington Cathedral as well as in the cathedral's publication *Cathedral Age*. Among Stokes's many publications, mostly pamphlets published by the Phelps Stokes Fund, are *Christ and Man's Latent Divinity* (1910), *Memorials of Eminent Yale Men* (1914), *Tuskegee Institute: The First Fifty Years* (1931), and *Negro Status and Race Relations in the United States, 1911–1946: A Thirty-Five Year Report* (1948). His work at Yale and the controversy over presidential succession are treated in George W. Pierson, *Yale: College and University, 1871–1937* (2 vols., 1952, 1955). An obituary and editorial are in the *New York Times*, 15 and 16 Aug. 1958.

EARL H. BRILL

STOKES, Caroline Phelps. *See* Stokes, Olivia Egleston Phelps, and Caroline Phelps Stokes.

STOKES, Isaac Newton Phelps (11 Apr. 1867–18 Dec. 1944), architect and historian, was born in New York City, the son of Anson Phelps Stokes, a banker, and Helen Louisa Phelps. His education was interrupted by episodes of ill health, but he entered Harvard University in 1887 and graduated in 1891. Stokes worked briefly in banking before he began to study at the School of Architecture of Columbia University from 1893 to 1894. He left without taking a degree and went to Paris to study housing design at the École des Beaux Arts. Improved tenement housing was to be a lifelong interest of his. In 1895 he married Edith Minturn. They had an adopted daughter.

With a Harvard classmate, John Mead Howells (son of the novelist William Dean Howells), Stokes entered a competition for the design of a settlement project in New York, and after winning they returned to New York. In 1897 they established the architectural firm of Howells and Stokes, which continued until 1917. The firm designed many prominent buildings, including the Baltimore Stock Exchange; the headquarters of the American Geographical Society at 156th Street and Broadway in New York City; Bonwit Teller's department store at Fifty-eighth Street and Fifth Avenue in New York City; Woodbridge Hall at Yale University; and at Harvard University, the Dudley Memorial Gate and the Music Building (renamed Paine Hall). St. Paul's Chapel at Columbia University is perhaps one of their most distinctive designs. With its solid masonry construction and Guastavino tiles, it remains a conspicuous architectural presence at the Morningside Heights campus of Columbia.

Stokes's interest in tenement housing prompted him to criticize the "dumbbell" floor plan (so-called from the shape of the buildings), which was generally used in New York City and was designed for multiple-dwelling buildings that conformed to the 25-by-100-foot city lots that had originally been laid out for one-family town houses. Stokes agreed with Ernest Flagg—an architect who in 1894 published in *Scribner's* magazine an influential article on tenement housing—that larger building lots were essential to the design of comfortable, healthful, attractive tenement housing.

The firm of Howells and Stokes designed the Tuskegee (built in 1901), a tenement building at 213–215 West Sixty-second Street, in which the apartments were designated for occupancy by African-American tenants. The project was financed by members of Stokes's family, who before the Civil War had been active in the abolitionist cause and who continued to support improved living conditions for African Americans through private investments and philanthropic

grants of the Phelps-Stokes Fund. Stokes was an officer of the fund and from 1911 to 1937 was chairman of its Housing Committee. Stokes helped draft the New York Tenement House Law of 1901, and in later years he participated in a number of model tenement designs, such as the Dudley Homes (1910) on East Thirty-second Street. He was a supporter of the City and Suburban Homes Company, which built notable apartment complexes, such as those at York Avenue (formerly Avenue A) between Seventy-eighth and Seventy-ninth streets. Stokes believed in private initiative and capital investment for urban improvement; but from the 1930s onward, federal, state, and city governments dominated housing reform.

In 1908 Stokes, while visiting a friend, was struck by the sight of an engraving of a view of New York harbor, drawn in 1794 by Saint-Mémin. Stokes later wrote: "Something in the aspect of the little group of houses clustering along the river bank . . . combined with something in the attitude of the two figures in the foreground and in the appearance of the coach hurrying along the road in the middle distance, suggested to me the idea of writing a book on the history of New York prints." From this random incident grew Stokes's passion for collecting prints, drawings, maps, and images of all kinds relating to New York. He eventually donated his unparalleled collection to the New York Public Library.

Out of Stokes's interest in collecting historic views of New York developed his interest in the history of the city. In 1915 he began publication of his monumental historical work, *The Iconography of Manhattan Island, 1498–1909*, which grew to six thick quarto volumes (completed in 1928), lavishly illustrated and filled with the results of extensive scholarly research, including a detailed chronology of the history of the city and a carefully compiled index that gives ready access to a wealth of information. He also published *New York Past and Present—Its History and Landmarks* (1939) and collaborated on other historical works.

Stokes was a supporter of many institutions: the Phelps-Stokes Fund, the New York Public Library (trustee 1916–1938), the New-York Historical Society (medal award, 1925), and others. He served on the Art Commission of the City of New York from 1911 to 1939. Stokes died in Charleston, South Carolina, where he was visiting his sister and brother-in-law.

Stokes's designs for such buildings as St. Paul's Chapel at Columbia University secure for him an enduring place as an architect. His work on housing reform and tenement design persists in such buildings as the landmarked City and Suburban Homes complex at Seventy-ninth Street and York Avenue, which remains a model for urban development. His *Iconography* is an essential source for New York history. His work in urban housing exemplifies the successful efforts of private initiative in active amelioration of public issues.

• Major collections of manuscript material relating to Stokes are at the New-York Historical Society (letterbooks containing thousands of pages of correspondence), the New York Public Library (materials relating to his *Iconography*), the Schomberg Center of the New York Public Library (materials relating to the Phelps-Stokes Fund), the office of the Phelps-Stokes Fund in New York, the New York Genealogical and Biographical Society (materials on family history), and the Yale University Library (papers of Anson Phelps Stokes). Stokes wrote an autobiographical memoir, *Random Recollections of a Happy Life* (1941), which was published in a limited edition; copies are at the New York Public Library, the New-York Historical Society, and Avery Library of Columbia University. Architectural drawings by Stokes for St. Paul's Chapel are at Avery Library. Other drawings are at Yale, Harvard, Berea College, and at other institutions for which Stokes's firm designed projects. For additional references, see the citations given by Deborah S. Gardner in "Practical Philanthropy: The Phelps-Stokes Fund and Housing," *Prospects: An Annual of American Cultural Studies* 15 (1996): 359–411. See also Roy Lubove, "I. N. Phelps Stokes: Tenement Architect, Economist, Planner," *Journal of the Society of Architectural Historians* 23 (May 1964): 75–87. The view by Saint-Mémin is reproduced in John A. Kouwenhoven, *The Columbia Historical Portrait of New York* (1953). At the New-York Historical Society is a portrait by De Witt M. Lockman, and at the Metropolitan Museum of Art is a portrait by John Singer Sargeant, *Mr. and Mrs. I. N. Phelps Stokes* (1897). Obituaries are in *The New-York Historical Society Bulletin* 29 (Jan. 1945): 41–42; *New York History* 26 (1945): 263–64; the *New York Herald Tribune*, 19 Dec. 1944; and the *New York Times*, 19 Dec. 1944.

F. J. SYPHER

STOKES, Joseph, Jr. (22 Feb. 1896–9 Mar. 1972), pediatrician, was born in Moorstown, New Jersey, the son of Joseph Stokes, Sr., a physician, and Mary Emlen. Born into a medical family, Stokes attended Haverford College, majored in English literature, and graduated in 1916. He then attended the University of Pennsylvania medical school, graduating in 1920. For two years he interned at the Massachusetts General Hospital, working under George Minot, and spent another two years serving on the staffs of the Pennsylvania and Children's hospitals. In 1921 he married Frances Elkington; they had four children.

Licensed to practice in Pennsylvania, Stokes accepted several families for treatment on a contract basis. Limiting his practice to pediatrics in 1924, he joined the faculty of the University of Pennsylvania medical school and became a staff member at the Children's Hospital of Philadelphia. He soon was appointed acting chairman of pediatrics at Children's Hospital, taking charge of pediatric service. In 1939 Stokes was appointed the Bennett Professor of Pediatrics, chairman of the Department of Pediatrics, and physician in chief to the Children's Hospital of Philadelphia. Possessing excellent administrative abilities, Stokes as chief of Children's Hospital gathered an outstanding staff and organized a pediatric research department. Among the scientists he brought to Children's Hospital were Werner Henle and Gertrude Henle in virology; Zvee Harris and Rebecca Harris in microbiology; Seymour Cohen, Robert McAllister, and Lewis Coriell in cancer

research; and Alfred Bongiovanni in endocrinology, all outstanding physicians in their fields.

Unlike so many medical leaders, Stokes was a master clinician. It was once said of him that he could hear more through a stethoscope than any other teacher at the University of Pennsylvania. Concerned with overpopulation and unwanted children, Stokes pioneered in the 1920s an effort to found a maternal health center for population control. Because of the unpopularity of such a facility in a small community, Stokes housed the center in a building that was half in Delaware County and half in Philadelphia County, so that if the police threatened in either county, the organization could easily move to the other county. Stokes's clinic was a prototype for later family planning clinics. He also helped prepare a small book under the auspices of the Friends Service Committee, *Who Shall Live?* Stokes was a founder of the Philadelphia Marriage Council, and he arranged for Emily Mudd to be its first director.

Stokes's main scientific effort was his studies of infectious diseases in children. In the 1930s he pointed out the dangers of the polio vaccines developed by Brodie and Kolmer. Also he was a pioneer in carrying out field studies of human influenza vaccines and in the use of ultraviolet light to control respiratory infections. Stokes and Geoffrey Rake were the first to attempt vaccination against measles with attenuated virus vaccines. They met with some success. In 1954 Stokes and his colleagues were the first to feed the attenuated polio virus vaccine, developed by Hilary Kaprosky, to infants.

During World War II Stokes directed a program to control infectious hepatitis by administrating gamma globulin, which proved effective in preventing the disease. President Harry S. Truman awarded Stokes the Certificate of Merit of the U.S. Army, the highest military honor that can be awarded to a civilian. The first to introduce a viral diagnostic laboratory, Stokes also was the first to appoint a professor of virology, Werner Henle. Stokes was active in a number of field trials for vaccines and was credited with developing theories for mumps and rubella. A member of the American Friends Service Committee, Stokes was also the last surviving member of the Armed Forces Epidemiological Board. Stokes died at his home in Chestnut Hill, Pennsylvania.

Through his use of gamma globulin to prevent and treat hepatitis, Stokes realized the importance of a supply of the immune serum from which to prepare gamma globulin. He then founded the serum bank at the Children's Hospital of Philadelphia. A gifted pediatrician and physician with an avid interest in research, Stokes was in part responsible for widespread inoculation against polio, mumps, rubella, hepatitis, and measles. Without his dedication, immunization would not be nearly so advanced today.

• Stokes's papers, including a large collection of letters, manuscripts, papers, lectures, and speeches, are preserved at the American Philosophical Society in Philadelphia. Treatments of Stokes can be found in Alfred M. Bongiovanni, "Letter to the Editor—Joseph Stokes, Jr.," *Pediatrics* 50 (1972): 163–64; and Horace L. Hode, "Presentation of the John Howland Medal and Award to Dr. Joseph Stokes, Jr.," *American Journal of the Diseases of Children* 104 (1962): 440–42. See also Jonathan Rhoads, "Joseph Stokes, Jr. (1896–1972)," *Year Book of the American Philosophical Society* (1972). An obituary is in the *New York Times*, 12 May 1972.

DAVID Y. COOPER
MICHELLE E. OSBORN

STOKES, Montfort (12 Mar. 1762–4 Nov. 1842), U.S. senator, North Carolina governor, and Indian commissioner, was born in Lunenburg County, Virginia, the son of David Stokes, a planter, magistrate, and vestryman, and Sarah Montfort of Halifax County, North Carolina, the scion of a prominent, wealthy family. Little is known of Stokes's early life, but he claimed to have sailed as a boy on a merchantman out of Edenton and to have served in the Continental navy under Commodore Stephen Decatur as a fourteen year old. Reportedly he was captured and endured seven hard months aboard the prison ship *Jersey* in New York harbor. He also claimed to have served against the British after his return to North Carolina, but there is no corroborating evidence to verify his revolutionary service. Nevertheless, Stokes built a public career on his contention that he had fought in the patriot cause.

In the 1780s Stokes settled in Salisbury, Rowan County, North Carolina, where he read law with his distinguished brother John Stokes, a bona fide revolutionary hero for whom Stokes County was named. There he formed a lifelong friendship with Andrew Jackson and gained his first public office. In 1790 he was elected militia captain and clerk of the Rowan County Superior Court. Stokes married Mary Irwin in 1790. They had one child before her death in 1791. In 1796 he married Rachel Montgomery, a daughter of Hugh Montgomery. Rachel Stokes inherited several thousand acres in Wilkes County, and the family settled there about 1812. They built a large plantation house named "Monte Rouge" at Brown's Ford, four miles west of Wilkesboro. Located on a knoll overlooking the Yadkin River, the mansion afforded a beautiful view of the valley.

From 1799 to 1816 Stokes was clerk of the North Carolina Senate. During this time he declined election to the U.S. Senate (1804) and was a Democratic-Republican presidential elector in 1804 and 1812. In 1804 he was also appointed major general of the state militia, a post he held at the beginning of the War of 1812; however, he saw no active duty. From 1805 to 1838 Stokes was a University of North Carolina trustee, and from 1802 to 1807 he was deputy grand master of the state Masonic order. He was a Mason for fifty-eight years.

Stokes resigned his North Carolina Senate clerkship in 1816 after his election to the U.S. Senate. He served in Washington from December 1816 to March 1823, when the legislature elected a successor. He sat on the District of Columbia and Military Affairs committees and chaired the Post Office Committee. Politically aligned with the Democratic-Republicans, he initially affiliated with the Crawfordites; then he fell under John C. Calhoun's influence before becoming an ardent Jacksonian. He was a Jacksonian presidential elector in 1824 and 1828.

During the Missouri debates, Stokes grew increasingly fearful that the slavery issue would divide the United States irrevocably. He thought that the majority of northerners in Congress, in keeping with growing sentiment among their constituents, had decided to prevent slavery's expansion in all of the Louisiana Purchase territory. He urged acceptance of the Missouri Compromise thusly: "All that we from the slave-holding States can do at present, is to rescue from the rapacious grasp of these misguided fanatics a considerable portion of the Louisiana Purchase . . . by consenting that slavery be prohibited in the Northern portion . . . by this prudent and proper concession, we shall quiet the minds of many people" (*Raleigh Register*, 17 Mar. 1820).

Stokes's procompromise stance proved unsatisfactory to North Carolina legislators and cost him his seat. After his return to his home in Wilkes County, he resumed the life of planter. But his political ambitions had not been sated. He represented Wilkes County in the North Carolina Senate, 1826–1827, and in the House of Commons, 1829–1831. Subsequently he served two terms as governor, an office filled by legislative election. His election signaled the continued dissatisfaction of western North Carolinians with the state constitution of 1776, which determined that easterners would have inordinate power in the legislature. Stokes had long championed the constitutional movement that culminated in the more equable amendments of 1835.

As governor, Stokes maintained tradition by calling for internal improvements and public education; however, his administration is best remembered for a series of dramatic events: the burning of the capitol building; reactions to the Nat Turner insurrection; the breakup of Jackson's cabinet, and the nullification controversy. His strongest response came in support of President Jackson's South Carolina policy. A consistent Unionist, Stokes denounced "the measures recommended by an excited portion of the Southern people . . . and hoped that we shall cling to the Union of the States as now connected" (*N.C. House Journal* [1832]: 143). Stokes vigorously supported the reelection of Jackson, noting: "We are at peace with the world, and our national debt nearly paid off. Secure in such inestimable advantages, I would ask, for what purpose are we urged to change an administration, that has been so beneficially employed for our common welfare?" (*N.C. House Journal* [1831]: 149).

It is not surprising that Jackson would reward his old friend's loyalty. The president appointed Stokes one of three commissioners to investigate conditions in the Indian territory that was being created west of Missouri. Stokes resigned his governorship in December

1832 to accept the appointment, and by February 1833 he had settled near Fort Gibson in Indian territory. He remained in the West for the next ten years, returning only once to visit his wife and family in North Carolina. Stokes's second marriage lasted some forty-six years and produced five sons and five daughters, but it was not congenial. Rachel Stokes had refused to accompany her husband to Oklahoma, and they were effectively separated for the last ten years of the marriage.

It is curious that a man of seventy years would embrace the arduous frontier. Life was rugged, even primitive, at western frontier outposts, and the accommodations and pay were miserable. In 1837 Stokes was appointed agent to the Cherokee, a post President John Tyler refused to continue in 1841. For the last few months of his life, he was subagent to the Seneca, Shawnee, and Quapaws. Stokes frequently complained about the treatment of the Indians and the malignant influence of missionaries among them. Impoverished and virtually friendless, Stokes died and was buried near Fort Gibson in what is now Oklahoma.

No doubt Stokes was well connected socially and politically. At one time he was arguably the foremost political leader in western North Carolina. He held numerous high offices successfully, but his fortunes—both personal and political—waned over time. To understand his enigmatic public and family life, one must consider his demeanor and character. He was hot-tempered and rash, particularly in stressful situations and under the influence of drink. Often personally charming and congenial, he was also profane and addicted to gambling. These traits may well account for his estrangement from family and his political decline.

• The North Carolina State Archives, Division of Archives and History, Raleigh, holds a small collection of Stokes's personal papers and his gubernatorial papers. See also the *Annals of Congress*, 16th Cong.–18th Cong.; the *Raleigh Register*, 17 Mar. 1820; and the *Little Rock Arkansas State Gazette*, 7 Dec. 1842. The best secondary sources are William Omer Foster, "The Career of Montfort Stokes in North Carolina," *North Carolina Historical Review* 16 (July 1939), and Grant Foreman, "The Life of Montfort Stokes in the Indian Territory," *North Carolina Historical Review* 16 (Oct. 1939).

MAX R. WILLIAMS

STOKES, Olivia Egleston Phelps (11 Jan. 1847–14 Dec. 1927), and **Caroline Phelps Stokes** (4 Dec. 1854–26 Apr. 1909), philanthropists, were born in New York City, the daughters of James Boulter Stokes, a banker, and Caroline Phelps. Both were educated at home in an atmosphere of Christian piety and civic service, although Caroline spent several happy years at Miss Porter's School in Farmington, Connecticut. Their ancestors were of English Puritan stock: Thomas Stokes, who came to America in 1789, was a founder of the American Bible Society and the New York Peace Society. Their maternal grandfather, Anson Greene Phelps, was a successful businessman, entrepreneur, civic leader, and philanthropist who, as a founder of the New York Colonization Society, had helped to establish the Republic of Liberia in West Africa.

The two sisters were similar in personality and outlook. Both were reverent Christians of independent means whose lives were informed by an abiding concern for the underprivileged and oppressed. They believed deeply that the human soul is eternal, that all human beings are the children of God, and that "not one must be lost"—irrespective of color, nationality, or station. In a composition, "The Poor," written when she was eleven years old, Caroline wrote: "The poor people suffer much. . . . I think the tenement houses are dreadful places, almost as bad as prisons." As an adult, she was known for her keen intelligence, decisiveness, and delicate sense of humor and was described as "a woman whose personality combined the spiritual and practical enriched by world-wide travel." Similarly, Olivia was widely respected for her intelligence, dignity of character, excellent judgment, and "practical philanthropy."

Following the death of their parents after 1881, Olivia and Caroline traveled widely in the United States, Europe, and Palestine, making a pilgrimage to Jerusalem. In 1896–1897, with their brother James, they took a trip around the world, which included extensive travels in India among the poor and downtrodden. The events of this trip Caroline later chronicled in the form of an anonymously published (by "A.B.") novel titled *Travels of a Lady's Maid*. Olivia also published several volumes of writings, including *Pine and Cedar: Bible Verses* (1885), *Forward in the Better Life* (1915), *Saturday Nights in Lent* (1922), and *The Story of Caroline Phelps Stokes* (1927).

The Stokes sisters, who never married, are among America's first women of independent means who, as a result of inheritance, were philanthropists in their own right. Their philanthropic interests included advancing the Christian religion, the cause of women and American minorities (especially American blacks and American Indians), education, and improving housing for the poor. Caroline served on the Improved Dwellings Council in New York. Olivia was the first secretary of the Young Women's Christian Association (YWCA) in the United States, and the sisters gave major support to both the YWCA and the YMCA during their lifetimes. Their philanthropies, undertaken both jointly and individually, include such religious benefactions as St. Paul's Chapel at Columbia University, the open-air pulpit at the Cathedral of St. John the Divine in New York City, and chapels at Berea College (Kentucky), Tuskegee Institute (Alabama), and Yale-in-China; support for education, such as Woodbridge Hall at Yale University, a gymnasium for Woman's College in Constantinople, Dorothy Hall at Tuskegee Institute, and public libraries at Ansonia, Connecticut, and Redlands, California; and social causes, such as the Caroline Cottage at the New York Colored Orphans Asylum and a building to house the Peabody Home for Aged and Infirm Women (also in Ansonia). Their special interest in housing led them, with the advice of their nephew, Isaac Newton Phelps Stokes, to finance the construction of model tenement housing for black families in New York City and to underwrite the work of the City and Suburban Homes Company in New York.

When Caroline died from an infection after a lengthy illness (in Redlands, Calif.), her bequests continued this legacy. Her sympathies for the cause of American blacks and Indians led her to make significant bequests to southern institutions such as Tuskegee, Hampton (endowing scholarships for "Negro and Indian students"), and Calhoun Colored School. Additionally, Caroline left nearly $1 million to endow and establish the Phelps-Stokes Fund, specifying that the income be used "for the creation and improvement of tenement housing in New York City" and "for educational purposes in the education of Negroes both in Africa and the United States, North American Indians and needy and deserving white students." Olivia had been involved with her sister in the planning of the Fund and gave to it in 1915 two improved model tenements she had built for black families on land adjoining her grandfather's estate in Manhattan. Olivia left a further bequest to the Fund to "found a school in Liberia similar to the Tuskegee . . . Institute"—the Booker Washington Agricultural and Industrial Institute, established at Kakata, Liberia, in 1929. She died in Washington, D.C., naming Barnard College as her residuary legatee. She was buried near Caroline at Redlands.

• Letters by Olivia and Caroline Phelps Stokes are in the manuscript collections of the Schlesinger Library at Radcliffe College, the Phelps-Stokes papers in the Sterling Library at Yale University, and the Archives of the Phelps-Stokes Fund, held by the Schomburg Center for Research in Black Culture of the New York Public Library. Brief biographical sketches may be found in the 1920, 1930, and 1946 *Reports of the Phelps-Stokes Fund*. A full-length biography of Caroline, *The Story of Caroline Phelps Stokes* (1927), written by Olivia, is available in typescript in the Phelps-Stokes Fund Archives. For information on the Phelps and Stokes families, see Anna Bartlett Warner, *Some Memories of James Stokes and Caroline Phelps Stokes* (privately printed, 1892); Oliver S. Phelps and Andrew T. Servin, *The Phelps Family of America and Their English Ancestors* (1899); Anson Phelps Stokes, *Stokes Records* (1910); Isaac Newton Phelps Stokes, *Random Recollections of a Happy Life* (typescript, 1932); Anson Phelps Stokes, *Reminiscences of Anson Phelps Stokes* (privately printed, 1956); and Phyllis B. Dodge, *Tales of the Phelps-Dodge Family: A Chronicle of Five Generations* (1987). Caroline's obituary was published in the *New York Times*, 28 Apr. 1909. Olivia's appeared in the *New York Times*, 15 Dec. 1927 and the *New York Herald Tribune* 15 Dec. 1927; an article on her will was printed in the *New York Times*, 25 Dec. 1927.

RONALD AUSTIN WELLS

STOKES, Rose Pastor (18 July 1879–20 June 1933), political radical, was born Rose Harriet Wieslander in Augustow, Russian Poland, the daughter of Hindl Lewin and Jacob Wieslander, a fisherman. Stokes, a member of the Socialist party and, later, the Communist Party USA, acquired her radical politics from the poverty and hardship of her early years.

After a brief, idyllic early childhood in the shtetl, with magical days spent fishing with her grandfather, she and her mother moved to a dreary tenement apartment in London several years after Hindl and her husband had separated. They lived in extreme poverty, and Hindl became a strike leader in the garment factory where she worked. Eventually she remarried, and her second husband, Israel Pastor, a peddler, moved the family to Cleveland, Ohio. But times were hard, and eleven-year-old Rose went to work in a cigar factory and soon became the family's sole breadwinner. Over the next thirteen years she rolled stogies in various cigar sweatshops, snatching whatever education she could by borrowing books from coworkers and the public library. She learned about socialism by attending lectures and studying its precepts on her own and with coworkers. She also participated in an effort to organize several cigar factories. But, gradually, she drifted out of the socialist fold in Cleveland.

In 1900, after writing a whimsical letter to the English-language page of the *Yidisher Tageblatt*, an Orthodox Jewish newspaper, Rose Pastor joined the paper as a columnist. Initially she stayed in Cleveland and wrote from afar while continuing to work in the cigar sweatshop, then moved to New York City in 1903. She wrote a variety of pieces for the *Tageblatt*—poetry, slice-of-life observations, short stories, and her regular column, "Just Between Ourselves, Girls." Using the pseudonym "Zelda," she offered advice to young Jewish working-class women on the manifold responsibilities of being proper, bourgeois Jewish women. Suppressing whatever socialist leanings she had developed in the cigar factories, she urged her readers to be industrious, cooperative, and "indispensable" to their employers. She also interviewed celebrated figures such as settlement-house leader Lillian Wald and James Graham Phelps Stokes, son of a wealthy prominent New York family and another leader in the settlement-house movement.

Meeting Graham Stokes was a turning point in Rose Pastor's life. With him, she crossed the threshold into marriage (1905) and political activism, first as his partner and then as his enemy. For the first twelve years of their childless marriage, they worked as compatriots in the socialist struggle. She became an effective thinker and speaker for causes such as the shirtwaist makers' strike of 1909, the New York hotel waiters' strike of 1912, and the birth control movement. She also wrote proletarian plays and traveled as a representative for the Intercollegiate Socialist Society (ISS), bringing the message of socialism to college campuses throughout the Northeast, South, and Midwest.

Rose Pastor Stokes was an effective publicist for socialism. She spoke before a variety of groups—Jews, non-Jews, workers, students, white-collar professionals, and women's groups—and packaged her socialist message in a palatable fashion for her audiences. Her socialism steadily evolved from a vague and somewhat utopian philosophy of love and equality to a rigorously doctrinaire Marxist ideology. But her message always retained a personal and visionary quality. In her speeches she spoke convincingly of her impoverished early years and of her hopes that socialism would obliterate such suffering for future generations. Her audiences loved her. She spoke forthrightly and eloquently, and genuinely tried to reach out to her listeners more as a "chum than an agitator." A slender woman with thick auburn hair, usually braided around her head, she often flashed a warm, gentle smile as she spoke.

In speeches she claimed that her political consciousness was aroused only after she had left the class of the have-nots, or the "makers of wealth," as she called this class, and entered the class of the haves, "the takers of wealth." She viewed herself both as a parasite of the existing system and, as she wrote in a poem, as a comrade of the "joyous workers yet to be" in the abolition of that system.

World War I proved to be a watershed in her marriage to Graham Stokes. Both supported U.S. entry into the war and, in 1917, even severed their ties with the Socialist party over its strong antiwar sentiment. But the victory of the Bolshevik Revolution brought Rose Pastor Stokes back into the socialist fold. Shortly after returning to the party in 1918, she was charged with espionage for accusing the federal government of colluding with war profiteers. Her husband's uncle, W. E. D. Stokes, assisted the government in making a case against her by spying and informing on her. But her conviction was subsequently overturned on appeal.

From then on, as Stokes noted in a letter, she and her husband lived as "friendly enemies" because of their growing political differences. Their marriage stumbled along for seven more years before a final eruption ended in divorce in 1925. Meanwhile, Stokes had steadily moved into the hierarchy of the nascent Communist party. In December 1919 she was nominated as a representative to the U.S. Congress on the newly formed Communist party ticket. The young party was a male bastion, and she was one of the few women elected to the executive committee. In November 1922 she attended the fourth Congress of the Communist International as a delegate of the American party and reported on the congress's special Negro Commission for the *Worker*.

After her divorce—from which she walked away financially unprotected—she struggled to make a living from her writing and continued her party work as best she could. Two years later she married Isaac Romaine, a young functionary in the party. They had no children together, but Romaine had a son from a previous marriage whom Stokes loved as her own child. Their marriage was loving despite daunting poverty and personal problems. In 1929 Stokes underwent a mastectomy for a malignant tumor. She devoted her energies to battling her illness and finishing her autobiography, although she longed to rejoin the political struggle. She traveled to Germany three times for special radia-

tion treatment but, after a long and valiant struggle, quietly passed away in a hospital in Frankfurt, Germany.

Dedicating her life to revolutionary social change, Rose Pastor Stokes came to her radicalism through her class and ethnic background. Her mother's activism in the garment sweatshops of London profoundly influenced her; similarly, in the cigar factories of Cleveland, working among politically conscious Jews, and on the Lower East Side, she received a vivid education in human misery. Still, only after Stokes left her working-class status could she consciously align herself with her working-class brothers and sisters and devote all of her energies to struggling against such "pain and sorrow." She courageously chose to remain in this struggle rather than follow her gentile, and genteel, husband back onto the path of respectability after World War I. In doing so, she took the political road paved with risks and hardships, yet one congenial with her values and her cultural and familial upbringing.

• Rose Pastor Stokes's papers are housed at Sterling Library, Yale University, and are also available on microfilm. The Socialist Collections of the Tamiment Library, New York University, includes additional papers, mostly correspondence and newspaper clippings. Correspondence between Rose Pastor Stokes and Graham Stokes is included in the James Graham Phelps Stokes Collection, Columbia University. Rose Pastor Stokes's autobiography, *I Belong to the Working Class* (1992), offers a vivid, if doctrinaire, account of her radical development. See also Pearl Zipser and Arthur Zipser, *Fire and Grace: The Life of Rose Pastor Stokes* (1989), for a graceful, informative narrative of her life. Patrick Renshaw, "Rose of the World: The Pastor-Stokes Marriage and the American Left, 1905–1925," *New York History* 62 (Oct. 1981): 415–38, explores the tensions and complexities of the Pastor-Stokes marriage. See also two dissertations, available on University Microfilms: Kathleen Ann Sharp, "Rose Pastor Stokes: Radical Champion of the American Working Class, 1879–1933" (Duke Univ., 1979), and Harriet Sigerman, "Daughters of the Book: A Study of Gender and Ethnicity in the Lives of Three American Jewish Women" (Univ. of Mass., Amherst, 1992).

HARRIET SIGERMAN

STOKOWSKI, Leopold Anthony (18 Apr. 1882–13 Sept. 1977), conductor, was born in the Marylebone district of greater London, Middlesex County, England, the son of Joseph Boleslaw Kopernik Stokowski, a cabinetmaker of Scottish and Polish extraction, and Anne (Annie) Marion Moore, the daughter of an Irish bootmaker. Although he grew up in a nonmusical family, young Leopold was musically precocious, learning to play the violin, piano, and organ while still a child. With little more than a grade school education Stokowski began conducting at the age of twelve and in 1896, at thirteen, was accepted as a student at the Royal College of Music. There he studied piano, organ, composition, and counterpoint, becoming a member of the Royal College of Organists at age sixteen and a fellow of the College of Organists when he was eighteen.

Stokowski's professional career began in 1900, when he became organist and choirmaster for St. Mary's Anglican Church on Charing Cross Road in London. Two years later he moved to a like position at the more prestigious St. James Church, Picadilly. While there Stokowski studied at Queen's College, Oxford, earning his bachelor of music degree in November 1903.

It was at St. James Church that the Reverend Leighton Parks, rector of the eminent St. Bartholomew's Church in New York City, first heard Stokowski play. Reverend Parks had come to England in 1905 seeking an organist and choirmaster for St. Bart's; with Stokowski his search ended.

Moving to the United States in 1905, Stokowski stayed at St. Bart's until 1908. His official position broadened to include regular recitals of organ music, spiced with his own romantic organ transcriptions of orchestral music by Tchaikovsky, Beethoven, Wagner, and others. He dreamed of conducting, however, and with the help of concert pianist Olga Samaroff (Lucie Hickenlooper) he auditioned for and won the conductorship of the Cincinnati Symphony Orchestra in 1909. He and Samaroff were married in 1911; they would have one child. Stokowski's three seasons with the Cincinnati Symphony Orchestra (1909–1912) were a prelude to his move to Philadelphia and his quarter-century association with the Philadelphia Orchestra.

Arriving in Philadelphia to conduct the 1912–1913 season, Stokowski gave primacy to rebuilding the orchestra. By 1921 only five players of the 1912 group were left. Stokowski developed a larger ensemble whose flexibility, precision, and ability to project beautiful sound and orchestral color led composer Sergei Rachmaninoff, among others, to call it the finest orchestra in the world. For Stokowski, a dramatist and storyteller in music, the ensemble was an ideal instrument, as both live concerts and Victor recordings attested. Free breathing for his brasses and winds, free bowing for the strings, and reseating of his players to match the acoustical possibilities of the music played and the concert hall played in all contributed to the intensity, flexible phrasing, and sonority on which the "Stokowski Sound," as it became known, was based. In order to balance and to project orchestral sound Stokowski devised a series of baffles, sound reflectors, and resonators that immensely improved concert hall sound and clarity while enhancing the beauty and power of his Philadelphia recordings in the late twenties and thirties.

Stokowski was a driving force behind the founding of the Curtis Institute of Music in 1924. In 1926, having divorced Samaroff in 1923, he married Evangeline Brewster Johnson, with whom he would have two children. This union also ended in divorce, in 1937.

By the late twenties and early thirties Stokowski had become a key figure in an effort to unite theater, music, dance, and drama with lighting and design worthy of this new multimedia approach. Exemplary were the American premiere productions of Stravinsky's *Les noces* (1928); Stravinsky's ballet *Le sacre du printemps*,

with Martha Graham dancing the sacrificial maiden (1930); Schoenberg's *Die Glückliche Hand* (1930); Berg's *Wozzeck* (1931); Stravinsky's *Oedipus Rex* (1931); Prokofiev's *Le pas d'acier* (1931); Schoenberg's *Pierrot lunaire* (1932); and Carlos Chavez's ballet *H.P.*, with costumes and sets by Diego Rivera (1932). Concurrently Stokowski studied the electronics of recording and radio broadcast performance, which led to 1931–1932 experiments that paired Stokowski and his orchestra with the scientists of the Bell Telephone Laboratories, experiments important for the future of electrical transcription, FM radio, and stereophonic sound.

Such untraditional concerns on the part of Stokowski were criticized by a growing number of traditionalist critics. Stokowski's penchant for playing contemporary and avant-garde music—such as that of Stravinsky, Schoenberg, Varèse, Berg, and Cowell—in addition to his own orchestral transcriptions of works by Bach, Debussy, Chopin, Mussorgsky, and over thirty other composers served to intensify the hostile reaction from critics and musical academics. Then too Stokowski's lifestyle was as unconventional in matters of personal values and philosophy as were many of his musical interpretations. Coupled with his idiosyncratic personality such differences further antagonized many influential critics, as they confronted a musician who failed to conform to their more traditional conception of a conductor.

Stokowski resigned as music director of the Philadelphia Orchestra in 1936. Although he guest conducted the orchestra for several years after that, his work on three motion pictures, *The Big Broadcast of 1937, One Hundred Men and a Girl* (1937), and the path-breaking *Fantasia* (1940) further alienated the critics. But his reputation among musicians, particularly those who worked with him, and his popularity with the public were unharmed by his unorthodoxy and personal eccentricity. By the time he left Philadelphia in his late fifties opinion of him and his work was divided. To some he was a mere showman in sound; to others, a musical genius, but no one denied that he was a maverick.

After his work on *Fantasia* was completed Stokowski, who had always enjoyed the company of young people, expressed a desire to found a young musicians' orchestra drawing on the wealth of youthful American talent he had observed. After fifteen hundred auditions—one thousand of which he conducted himself—Stokowski formed the All American Youth Orchestra (AAYO) in 1940. The members, whose ages ranged from fourteen to twenty-five, were led by eighteen Philadelphia Orchestra musicians as section leaders. With financial backing from Columbia Records and the encouragement of the U.S. State Department, the orchestra spent the season touring twenty-six Latin American cities, with Stokowski serving as conductor without pay. The tour was an immense success and was followed by thirteen recordings for Columbia. The 1941 AAYO season included performances in fifty-four U.S. cities as well as Toronto, Canada, and Tijuana, Mexico. Stokowski himself assumed all responsibility for tour expenses. The orchestra was warmly received across the country and ended its season by making several more recordings for Columbia Masterworks. The orchestra then disbanded.

World War II cost Stokowski his dream of making the orchestra a permanent part of the American musical scene. Wishing to lure Stokowski back to the RCA recording fold, David Sarnoff, president of RCA, asked him to conduct the NBC Symphony Orchestra on network radio, while making recordings with the orchestra for RCA. Stokowski accepted and in 1942 became coconductor with Arturo Toscanini. By 1944 the venture failed because of Toscanini's personal antipathy and the criticism from corporate sponsors that Stokowski programmed too much contemporary music.

Stokowski spent one season, in 1944–1945, as founder-conductor of the New York City Symphony, two summer seasons (1945 and 1946) as music director of the Hollywood Bowl Symphony Orchestra, and three seasons (1947–1950) as coconductor, with Dmitri Mitropoulos, of the New York Philharmonic Orchestra. In 1945 Stokowski married Gloria Laura Vanderbilt, with whom he had two children. Like his previous marriages, this third and final one ended in divorce, in 1955.

The early fifties were the nadir of Stokowski's career. Although he made many guest appearances and notable recordings, appeared on the CBS series "Twentieth Century Music Hall," and worked actively with the American Composer's Alliance for new music, Stokowski lacked the kind of musical home base that Philadelphia had provided for him in the twenties and thirties. Although Stokowski was at that time interested in assuming a post as permanent conductor of a major orchestra, his experimental tendencies and his penchant for performing new music worked against him. Orchestral board members were less impressed by Stokowski's skills than they were fearful of his experimental approach to music.

The trough of the wandering years was reached coincidentally with a new beginning in 1955–1956. RCA canceled Stokowski's recording contract, ending a music-making relationship of almost forty years, mainly because he had no first-rank orchestra of his own and thus no built-in urban sales base for his recordings. At the time RCA viewed the 74-year-old Stokowski as a musical has-been. However, a representative of the second-rank Houston Symphony Orchestra, seeking an established conductor, approached Stokowski and offered him the position. He accepted and was given a three-year contract. While the union of Stokowski and Houston seemed unlikely, it worked well for five seasons (1955–1960). Stokowski enjoyed stability and recording contracts with EMI and Everest. Houston received beautiful music making and a sense of musical eminence, since its orchestra made records and played with a new level of intensity and sensitivity.

With his work in Houston as springboard, Stokowski's buoyancy and optimism returned. Renewed American interest in his work was exceeded by Europe's "rediscovery" of him in the late fifties and sixties. As a result he made numerous European recordings and played to packed houses there until well into the seventies. Stokowski also toured the Soviet Union in 1958, playing ten concerts with three Soviet orchestras—the first American conductor to do so since the onset of the Cold War.

During the late fifties and sixties Stokowski was asked to conduct all over the world; his engagements included his first return to Philadelphia in nineteen years. This 1960 engagement was followed by yearly appearances with the Philadelphia Orchestra until 1967. He conducted two operas for the New York City Opera Company and Puccini's *Turandot* for the Metropolitan, and he made orchestral recordings for EMI, Everest, Vanguard, Decca, London, United Artists, Columbia, CRI, MK records, and RCA. Pressed by the volume and variety of his commitments, Stokowski left Houston in the fall of 1960 even as Houstonians, growing weary of Stokowski's penchant for programming knotty twentieth-century works, wanted to move backward to Beethoven and Brahms by moving forward with Sir John Barbirolli.

In the spring of 1962 Stokowski announced the formation of a new New York–based symphony orchestra. The American Symphony Orchestra was to be built on the model of the earlier AAYO; gifted teenagers and young adults would constitute the bulk of orchestra members, with older professionals serving as section leaders. Stokowski conducted all of the auditions himself, and in November 1962 the new orchestra gave its first concert in Carnegie Hall, a typically Stokowskian blend of Gabrieli, Bach, Shostakovich, and Beethoven.

From then until the spring of 1972 Stokowski served as music director of the orchestra, receiving no pay and reimbursing a portion of each season's deficit out of his own pocket. Even though there was a constant turnover of personnel as Stokowski's protégés moved on to established orchestras, Stokowski kept the orchestra's sections filled and its performance caliber high. The ensemble was notable for its mix of ethnic and racial minorities and its relatively large number of women players.

Commenting on the orchestra in performance, critic Winthrop Sargeant noted that he had once believed that the unique style and performance sound evoked by Stokowski was actually the product of the great Philadelphia orchestra that he had created. Yet here, more than twenty years after leaving Philadelphia, was the same intensity, sonority, range of color, and spontaneity. Clearly, concluded Sargeant, the phenomenon expressed was the "Stokowski Sound," which the conductor was able to draw from any orchestra he conducted. For ten seasons the orchestra provided New Yorkers with surprises. Old music, new music, and premieres, such as the first performance of Charles Ives's Fourth Symphony, alternated with more standard fare. Stokowski recorded with the orchestra on several labels.

During this period Stokowski's accomplishments were recognized by France, Poland, and Rumania. He received a Grammy for his recording of Ives's Fourth Symphony, *High Fidelity*'s Musician of the Year Award for 1967, and the first International Montreux Award in 1968 for his contributions to music and to the recording industry. Also in 1968 Stokowski was given the Golden Baton Award of the American Symphony Orchestra League. In 1972 he was awarded the Howland Medal by Yale University.

Throughout the sixties Stokowski conducted in New York during the fall and winter. He spent the spring and summer in Europe conducting and recording for EMI and, from 1964 to 1972, for English Decca (London) in the new multichannel "Phase Four" process. This period produced some of the finest recordings of his career.

By 1972 Stokowski had grown weary of the administrative duties he carried as music director in New York, and he resigned his position with the American Symphony Orchestra. He returned to England, bought a home in Nether Wallop, outside London, and devoted his remaining years to performing and to recording on a number of labels. On the day of his death, at his home in Nether Wallop at age ninety-five, he was scheduled to begin recording rehearsals of Rachmaninoff's Second Symphony for Columbia Records.

• There is no collection of Stokowski's correspondence and papers, since the cargo container holding his personal effects was washed overboard on its journey from Britain to the United States following Stokowski's death. The largest collection of Stokowskiana, including papers, music scores, orchestral transcriptions, recordings, and memorabilia, is housed in the Stokowski Collection, Curtis Institute of Music in Philadelphia. Also there is a collection of more than one hundred letters from Stokowski to his personal assistant and confidant from 1929 to 1945, Sylvan Levin, as well as Oliver Daniel's voluminous collection of notes, documents, and interviews, which provided the basis for his *Stokowski: A Counterpoint of View* (1982), the most thorough and detailed account of Stokowski's career. Many radio and television interviews are available from Classical Recordings Archive in El Cerrito, Calif. Published works include Stokowski's *Music for All of Us* (1943), an account of what he considered most important in music and in the art of making music. Biographical studies of Stokowski other than Daniel's include William Ander Smith, *The Mystery of Leopold Stokowski* (1990), which provides insight into his personality, philosophy, and way with the orchestra. Also important are Abram Chasins, *Stokowski: A Profile* (1979), which focuses on the contradictions and paradoxes of Stokowski's behavior, and Preben Opperby, *Leopold Stokowski* (1982), which is particularly good on his early years in Philadelphia. Other works of importance include Edward Johnson, ed., *Stokowski: Essays in Analysis of His Art* (1973); Herbert Kupferberg, *Those Fabulous Philadelphians* (1969); Frances A. Wister, *Twenty-Five Years of the Philadelphia Orchestra* (1925); Charles O'Connell, "Leopold Stokowski," in *The Other Side of the Record* (1949); and Robert E. McGinn, "Stokowski and the Bell Telephone Laboratories: Collaboration in the Development of High-Fidelity Sound Reproduction," *Technology and Culture*, 24 Jan. 1983, pp. 38–75.

WILLIAM ANDER SMITH

STOLBERG, Benjamin (30 Nov. 1891–21 Jan. 1951), journalist and reformer, was born in Munich, Germany, of unknown parentage. He was adopted by Michael and Rada Stolberg, Russian immigrants to Germany, who had built a successful chocolate business. His adopted parents provided him with an excellent education, culminating in his graduation from the Realgymnasium in Munich in 1908, the year he immigrated to the United States.

After arriving in the United States, Stolberg enrolled in Washington University in St. Louis to study medicine. Within a year, however, he dropped out of school, and between 1909 and 1914 he roamed the country, supporting himself by working as a casual laborer and saving on expenses by boarding in settlement houses. Somehow he amassed enough money to matriculate in 1914 at Harvard University, from which he received a B.A. in philosophy in 1917, a year ahead of his class. Stolberg then did graduate study at the University of Chicago, where in 1919 he earned an M.A. in sociology. While a graduate student at Chicago he lived at Hull-House. Between 1919 and 1921 he lectured on sociology and social work at the Universities of Oklahoma and Kansas. In 1921 he returned to Chicago to serve as head of vocational placement for the city's public school system.

In 1922 Stolberg resigned his position to become acting editor of the *Journal of the Brotherhood of Locomotive Firemen*, a job he held until 1923. While editing the union newspaper, Stolberg also did freelance writing for the *Chicago Tribune*, the *New York Evening Post*, the *Nation*, and the *New Republic*. Having developed a real talent for writing newspaper and magazine articles on contemporary social, economic, and political subjects, Stolberg moved to New York City in 1923 in order to situate himself better for a career as a full-time freelance journalist. He continued to write regularly for the *Evening Post* and other newspapers and for many liberal and left-leaning journals of opinion. In January 1925 Stolberg married Mary Malvina Fox, with whom he had one child and whom he divorced in 1929. For two years, 1928–1929, he served as associate editor of the *Bookman*.

During the 1920s Stolberg considered himself to be a reformist socialist sympathetic to the Socialist Party of America (SPA). Between 1925 and 1927 he acted as chair of the New York branch of the League for Industrial Democracy, an affiliate of the SPA. Stolberg, together with many other socialists, opposed bolshevism because they perceived the emerging Leninist system as too statist, insufficiently democratic, and a threat to basic human rights. Yet Stolberg also criticized the American Federation of Labor (AFL) as timid and conservative. His published writings reflected Stolberg's iconoclastic politics and antipathy toward both communism and conservative unionism. Indeed, his idiosyncratic politics carried over into the decade of the Great Depression and the New Deal. While most socialists found themselves attracted to Franklin D. Roosevelt and the New Deal, and the majority of SPA members in New York moved into the Roosevelt coalition in 1936 through the American Labor party, the same beliefs that earlier led Stolberg to reject communism turned him against the New Deal. In his eyes, New Dealers had let themselves be led astray by communists and communist sympathizers into creating a more coercive state. The more statist the New Deal appeared to grow, the more conservative Stolberg turned.

In 1935 Stolberg published *The Economic Consequences of the New Deal*, a book that criticized Roosevelt's reforms. Yet, simultaneously, he lauded the leaders in the labor movement, especially John L. Lewis, who split from the AFL in order to create the Congress of Industrial Organizations (CIO). In February 1937 in an article in the *Nation*, Stolberg acclaimed Lewis and the CIO for "profoundly affecting our two major political parties . . . [and] transforming the relationship of government to industry . . . [making the CIO] the most progressive and vital force in American life today." Later in 1937 Stolberg served on John Dewey's special commission of inquiry to investigate Joseph Stalin's charges against Leon Trotsky, then living in exile in Mexico. As part of the commission inquiry, Stolberg visited Trotsky, who convinced the commission members that Stalin's charges were false. It is likely that Stolberg's experience in this case strengthened his distaste for communism and Soviet Union.

Less than a year after visiting Trotsky, Stolberg changed his opinion of the CIO and began to write for more conservative publications. Whereas once he wrote articles for the *Nation* extolling labor militancy and industrial unionism, in January 1938 Stolberg began to write for the Scripps-Howard newspaper chain. In a special series on the CIO, Stolberg asserted that the Communist party had infiltrated both the labor organization and the agencies in the Roosevelt administration that dealt with labor affairs. Whereas once Stolberg envisioned the CIO as the most progressive social movement in the United States, he now saw it as the Trojan horse of bolshevism, subverting the labor movement, the New Deal, and the nation. He expanded his newspaper articles on the CIO into a book, *The Story of the CIO* (1938), the sad tale of a labor movement gone bad as a result of communist influence. By then he also condemned the New Deal for promoting "bureaucratic liberalism" and "state capitalism."

Increasingly conservative in his politics, Stolberg during the 1940s began to write for the archconservative *American Mercury* and to support the anti–New Deal and "Fortress America" Republicanism of Herbert Hoover and Robert A. Taft. Always the political maverick, however, Stolberg remained loyal to those trade unionists who identified communism and the Soviet Union as the enemy. Thus in 1944 he published *Tailor's Progress*, a history of trade unionism among Jewish immigrant workers in the clothing industry, which extolled the anticommunist president of the International Ladies' Garment Workers' Union, David Dubinsky, and castigated the less overtly anticommunist leader of the men's clothing workers, Sidney Hillman. No longer a major figure in American journalism or the author of articles that shaped people's perceptions of social reality, Stolberg died at home in New York City a relatively obscure person.

Neither an individual who altered the course of politics nor a person who reshaped journalism, Stolberg retains significance as the author of articles and essays that distill the social and political ambience of the 1920s and 1930s. His post-1938 articles and books, moreover, disclosed the anticommunist sensibilities that underlay the Cold War "red scare."

• Some Stolberg papers and a transcribed oral history interview are at the Columbia University Library. A book-length biography of Stolberg has yet to be published. An obituary is in the *New York Times*, 22 Jan. 1951.

MELVYN DUBOFSKY

STONE, Abraham (30 Oct. 1890–3 July 1959), and **Hannah Mayer Stone** (15 Oct. 1893–10 July 1941), physicians and marriage counselors, were born, respectively, in Russia and New York City. Abraham was the son of Miron Stone, a merchant, and Amelia Chamers. Hannah was the daughter of Max Mayer, a pharmacist, and Golda Rinaldo. At a time when the discussion of sexuality, fertility, and reproduction was highly controversial—even in the context of marriage—the Stones were leaders in the movement to educate adult Americans on these matters, and they wrote a modern marriage manual that remained authoritative for several generations.

From early childhood Abraham Stone wanted to become a physician, and his parents sent him to live with an uncle in New York City in 1905. He received his medical degree from New York University and Bellevue Medical College in 1912, served as intern and resident at Knickerbocker and St. Mark's hospitals from 1912 to 1915, and became a U.S. citizen in 1915, the year he began the private practice of urology in New York City. His dedication to learning is reflected in the fact that he continued general education during medical training and received the bachelor of science degree in 1916 from New York University. Hannah Mayer earned the pharmacy degree from Brooklyn College in 1912 and worked at Bellevue Hospital until she married Abraham in 1917. While he served as a lieutenant in the army medical corps during World War I, she attended New York Medical College. After his discharge from the army and her graduation from medical school in 1920, they began a private practice of medicine in New York City that provided their principal source of income for the rest of their lives. They had one child, a daughter who also became a physician.

The lives of the young medical couple were changed through their relationship with Margaret Sanger, the leader of the birth control movement in the United States. In 1921 they attended an international conference that Sanger had organized to promote her cause, in part to participate in a session for physicians on contraceptive methods. They later participated in a meeting of physicians that Sanger called for the purpose of discussing the opening of a birth control clinic in New York City. When the first medical director of Sanger's Clinical Research Bureau proved unsatisfactory, Hannah Stone replaced her in 1925 and won recognition as the clinical expert on contraception. Although her work at the Sanger clinic was unpaid, it placed her in the center of a rapidly developing area of medical practice, sexual and marital counseling. In 1928 she published "Therapeutic Contraception," a careful study of clinical records that definitively disproved the claims of some leading physicians that safe and effective contraceptive practice was impossible.

In 1929 the Clinical Research Bureau was raided, Hannah was arrested, and patient records were seized, but this attempt to suppress the birth control clinic failed as local medical groups rallied behind the issue of confidentiality of patient records, and the judge threw the case out of court because the police informant had pathological conditions that justified the medical care she was given. Hannah, now a heroine to civil libertarians, became a principal in another key birth control court case the following year, this one involving her right to import contraceptive devices. Her victory in *United States v. One Package* (1936) established an exemption for physicians from federal restrictions on the possession and distribution of contraceptive information and materials. The Stones trained a large number of the physicians who were beginning to offer birth control services; they wrote many important articles on their clinical experience with contraception, sex counseling, and the treatment of infertility; and as authors, editors, speakers, and litigants in court cases that challenged the Comstock laws (prohibiting the mailing of obscene materials, which then included birth control information), they remained at the center of the political struggle to promote reproductive autonomy for women.

The Stones' clinical experience revealed a great need for preventive sex education. In 1929 Abraham began lecturing on marriage at the Labor Temple, and in 1931 the Stones established the first marriage counseling service under medical direction in the United States at the Community Church. They were pioneers in the use of group therapy for marital sexual dysfunction. Their most influential work was *A Marriage Manual* (1935), which survived several battles with censors over advertising and was rejected by the major book clubs because it was considered too explicit but won critical praise and generations of buyers as the most authoritative work of its kind. Organized as a series of hypothetical counseling sessions between young couples and their medical counselor, *A Marriage Manual* promoted the ideal of perfect mutuality and spiritualized erotic fulfillment, symbolized by synchronized mutual orgasm in coitus.

When Hannah died of a heart attack in New York City, Abraham, who never remarried, replaced her as medical director of the Clinical Research Bureau and continued their work as editor of the *Journal of Contraception* (1935–1940) and *Human Fertility* (1940–1948) and as a member of the editorial board of *Fertility and Sterility* (1949–1959). He was a founder and president (1942) of the American Association of Marriage Counselors and in 1947 received the Albert and Mary Lasker Award of the Planned Parenthood Federation of America. Also in 1947 he represented the National Research Council at the world conference on family and population in Paris and was elected vice chair of the International Union of Family Organizations. A vice president of both the Planned Parenthood Federation of America and the International Planned Parenthood Federation, in 1951 he served the World Health Organization of the United Nations as an adviser to India on population control. He died in New York City while still actively engaged in medical practice and consulting.

Among their professional associates, the Stones were prized as consensus builders who were able to work with potential allies from the sometimes competing disciplines of medicine, social work, nursing, and the law as well as with lay activists in the birth control movement. Hannah was revered by patients and feminist allies as the "Madonna of the Clinic" whose kindness and quiet competence encouraged a generation of genital-shy women to become interested in and to assume control of their bodies. Although the Stones published a great deal, both were discriminated against by more traditional medical organizations, probably because of their reputations as sexual reformers. Hannah was denied membership in the New York County Medical Society, and although Abraham held adjunct academic appointments, he never received the clinical professorship in marital counseling that his contributions to the field might have merited. A short man with a large mustache whose speeches and publications exhibited a love of classical literature as well as science, Stone brought professionalism and a serene idealism to all his affairs.

• Abraham Stone's papers are in the Countway Library of Medicine, Boston, Mass. Hannah Stone's work is documented in the Margaret Sanger Papers in the Library of Congress, Washington, D.C., and in the Sophia Smith Collection, Northampton, Mass. Her "Therapeutic Contraception" appeared in *Medical Journal and Record* 6 (21 Mar. 1928): 8–17. Abraham collaborated with Norman Himes on *Practical Birth-Control Methods* (1948; revised as *Planned Parenthood: A Practical Guide to Birth-Control Methods* [1951]) and with Lena Levine on *The Premarital Consultation: A Manual for Physicians* (1956). Some important works, such as the Margaret Sanger Clinical Research Bureau's pamphlet on the rhythm method of contraception, were published anonymously, but most of their articles can be located through *Index Medicus*. Substantial discussions of the Stones' work are provided in Ellen Chesler, *Woman of Valor: Margaret Sanger and the Birth Control Movement in America* (1992), and in the oral history of Emily H. Mudd in the Schlesinger Library, Cambridge, Mass. Obituaries for Hannah are in the *New*

York Times and New York Herald Tribune, both 11 July 1941, and in Human Fertility 6 (Aug. 1941): 108–13. Alan F. Guttmacher's obituary on Abraham is in Fertility and Sterility 10, no. 5 (Sept.–Oct. 1959): 421–23, and short notices are in the New York Times, 4 July 1959 and the Journal of the American Medical Association 171 (26 Sept. 1959): 449.

JAMES W. REED

STONE, Arthur John (26 Sept. 1847–6 Feb. 1938), silversmith, was born in Sheffield, England, the son of Joseph Stones (the *s* was dropped later) and Ann Mills. Stone's father, a prospector who was fatally injured while hunting for gold in Australia, died when Arthur was only seven. As a result, Stone was forced to go to work and terminate his early education in church schools. In 1861 he was apprenticed to Edwin Eagle of Sheffield, a master silversmith who still practiced traditional handcraft methods. At the completion of his training in 1868 Stone practiced his craft in Edinburgh for a year before returning to Sheffield, where he eventually landed a position with James Dixon and Sons. In the fall of 1884 Stone set out for America, seeking greater opportunity in the New World.

On his arrival in the United States, Stone worked briefly as a silversmith for the William B. Durgin Company in Concord, New Hampshire, before accepting a job with the Frank W. Smith Company of Gardner, Massachusetts, in 1887. In 1895 Stone left the Smith Company to become a partner with J. P. Howard in New York City. These experiences with commercial silver manufacturers, combined with his training in traditional methods, provided Stone with a wide range of experience and skills that, when united with his natural talents for draftsmanship and intellectual interest in the history of art and design, would serve him well in later life.

A propitious marriage in 1896 to Elizabeth Bent Eaton, the widow of a wealthy Gardner businessman, marked a turning point in Stone's life. The couple had no children. By 1897 he left Howard and Company and returned to Gardner, where he first practiced as a designer, often working in copper. These transition years ended in 1901, when, bolstered by the capital provided by his wife, Stone was able to realize his ambition to open his own silversmithing shop. In that same year he also joined the Society of Arts and Crafts of Boston, in which he would attain medalist and master craftsman status. For more than three decades Stone operated his shop, employing specialist craftsmen and other workers and producing substantial quantities of flatware and hollowware. In time the Stone shop became recognized as one of the leading makers of traditional, substantial, handwrought silver in the arts and crafts mode. Rejecting the mass-production methods and elaborate ornament typical of the nineteenth century and adhering largely to the tenets of the English arts and crafts aesthetic, Stone designed and made silver with sleek, pure lines and restrained, often floral or naturalistic decoration. His idealistic goal was to reunite design and production in a small shop, emphasizing hand craftsmanship and producing high-quality works of art.

Over the years Stone employed at least thirty-nine craftsmen at various times between 1901 and 1938, working with as many as a dozen at any one time. Following the arts and crafts ideal, Stone shared profits and allowed many of his craftsmen to add their own surname initial mark to the shop mark on pieces they worked on. While Stone himself was active in all phases of production in his shop's early years, as time passed and the volume of business increased he devoted more time to designing, ornamenting, and chasing. His wife kept meticulous records of shop activity, photographed each work, handled public relations and marketing, and served as the general business manager. Stone suffered a stroke in the fall of 1926, but his faculties remained intact, and he was able to supervise and inspect the work of the shop until his retirement in September 1937. He died in Gardner, Massachusetts.

Stone received many important ecclesiastical, collegiate (especially from Harvard and Yale), corporate, and business commissions, and he filled many private orders for domestic plate such as bowls, vases, tea-wares, plates, mugs, and tankards. Much of his shop's work was relatively simple and elegant, and his objects in the colonial revival mode seemed to resonate especially well with his New England clients. Among his most important pieces are a gold pyx-monstrance-ciborium of 1909 designed by architect Frank E. Cleveland and made for the Church of the Advent in Boston; an altar set designed by Bertram Grosvenor Goodhue and made in 1913 for the Cathedral Church of St. James (Episcopal) in Chicago, which contains ivory reliefs carved by Johannes Kirchmayer; and several loving cups made for Harvard University. Collector and arts and crafts advocate George G. Booth of Detroit was one of Stone's most important patrons; actress Julia Marlowe and George Dudley Seymour of Yale were also among his best customers. Stone's silver is represented in many public and private collections, and his position as a leading figure in the New England arts and crafts movement is secure.

• Stone's papers are in the Museum of Fine Arts, Boston; the Archives of American Art, Smithsonian Institution; the Brooklyn Museum, Brooklyn, N.Y.; and Worcester Art Museum, Worcester, Mass. The archives of the Society of Arts and Crafts, Boston, in the Boston Public Library are also useful. The MFA collection of Stone material includes books from his working art library, a short film demonstrating silversmithing, and a significant collection of Stone's silver. A biography is Elenita C. Chickering with Sarah Morgan Ross, Arthur J. Stone, 1847–1938, Silversmith and Designer (1994). See also the following works by Chickering: Arthur J. Stone, Handwrought Silver, 1901–1937 (1981), the catalog of an exhibition at the Boston Athenaeum; "Arthur J. Stone's Presentation Silver," Decorative Arts Society Newsletter 11, no. 5 (Mar. 1985): 1–6; "Arthur J. Stone, Silversmith," Antiques 129, no. 1 (Jan. 1986): 274–83; and "Arthur J. Stone's Silver Flatware, 1901–1937," Silver 19, no. 1 (Jan.–Feb. 1986): 10–19.

GERALD W. R. WARD

STONE, Barton Warren (24 Dec. 1772–9 Nov. 1844), evangelist, educator, and speculative theologian, was born near Port Tobacco, Maryland, the son of John Stone and Mary Warren, farmers. Reared in Pittsylvania County, Virginia, he moved in 1790 to North Carolina to study law at Guilford Academy. His career plans changed when he was converted to an aggressive form of evangelical Protestantism under the influence of James McGready, a "New School," or revivalist, Presbyterian renowned for emotional preaching. Stone abandoned his Anglican baptism and by 1793 was a candidate for ministry in the Presbyterian church, studying under the Reverend William Hodge.

Stone found it difficult, however, to believe all the doctrines required for ordination, particularly such traditionally Calvinist points of theology as predestination. After a stint in Georgia teaching languages at a small Methodist seminary, he returned to North Carolina, where in 1796 the Orange Presbytery licensed him after he hesitantly assured them that he accepted the church's doctrine so far as it corresponded to the Bible's teachings. He served as an itinerant frontier preacher in Tennessee before his placement by the presbytery as minister at Cane Ridge in Bourbon County, Kentucky, in 1798. Three years later he married Elizabeth Campbell; they had five children before her death in 1810.

Cane Ridge became a lightning rod for theological debate. Frontier revivals forced to the fore issues that threatened to divide several Protestant denominations—namely, whether Christian conversion meant an emotional experience or an ordered, moral life; whether sinners had a measure of free will; and whether ministers should be highly educated. Already deeply affected by McGready's style and message, Stone visited Logan County, Kentucky, in the spring of 1801 to watch his mentor's emotional services. He returned to Cane Ridge determined to replicate what he had seen, only on a much larger scale. With like-minded ministers across the Protestant spectrum, he cleared a large area, set up a tent to hold less formal services, and sent word that meetings would begin on 8 August 1801. An estimated 20,000 people attended a weeklong revival that saw overwrought believers shouting, barking, and dancing "in the Spirit." The week ended with a communion service open to all Christians.

The Cane Ridge revival spawned similar camp meetings throughout the state, and these meetings in turn intensified the debate. The battles escalated to the point that Stone and four other ministers withdrew from the Kentucky Synod to form the independent Springfield Presbytery in 1803. Within a year, however, they decided that the Bible gave no credence to ecclesiastical institutions, and they disbanded the organization. Seeking a return to a unified "primitive" Christian church as described in the New Testament, Stone and his followers refused denominational affiliation and referred to themselves simply as "Christians."

Stone became a leader of this rural movement to restore Christianity to its "original" state. The movement expressed itself in such then-radical forms as the Church of Jesus Christ of Latter-Day Saints (Mormons) and the United Society of Believers in Christ's Second Appearance (Shakers). Elias Smith in Massachusetts, James O'Kelly in Virginia, and Alexander Campbell in the Kentucky region joined Stone as more traditional restorationists who continued to accentuate the sole authority of the Bible. Convinced that Protestant denominations were unbiblical, they swore off all descriptive labels except the ones found in the Bible, namely "Christian" and "disciple." The movement underscored the growth of a Jeffersonian frontier democracy that wanted to overthrow established hierarchies and creeds for a simple gospel that could be understood by any Bible reader.

After his wife's death, Stone moved to Tennessee in 1812. That year he married his first wife's cousin, Celia Wilson Bowen; they had six children. In 1815 he settled in Lexington, Kentucky. Fearing the growing strife over slavery, he released both his slaves and began to support publicly the establishment of a black colony in West Africa. He continued to lead the loosely affiliated congregations who adhered to his vision of Christian unity. Stone taught school and in 1826 founded the *Christian Messenger*, a paper that called for ecumenical evangelicalism and the end of denominational rivalry.

In 1824 Stone met Campbell, leader of the Disciples of Christ restorationists. Although not in full accord with Campbell theologically, Stone proposed cooperation. On 1 January 1831 they agreed to work together in moving beyond denominational affiliations, hoping to restore New Testament Christian unity. Stone even shared editorial duties at the *Christian Messenger* with the Disciple minister John Johnson.

Prone to theological speculation, Stone wrote a series of controversial pamphlets in the early 1820s that led Thomas Cleland, a Presbyterian minister, to charge him with retreating from Trinitarian doctrine and becoming a Unitarian. For over a decade the two figures carried on a doctrinal war, as Cleland attacked Stone's writings and Stone defended his right to go beyond denominational interpretations, insisting that the Bible did not use the traditional Trinitarian language of the church.

Aged and worn from years of itinerant ministry, Stone moved to Jacksonville, Illinois, in 1834. He continued to edit the *Christian Messenger* and even conducted several revivals. In 1841 he suffered a stroke, which severely hampered his physical strength. He died in Hannibal, Missouri, at the home of his son-in-law, Captain S. A. Bowen.

Stone's legacy remains in the aggressive evangelical style that characterized much of American Christianity throughout the nineteenth and twentieth centuries. Camp meetings that Stone helped to popularize offered a sense of community on the frontier. His rejection of institutional orthodoxies accentuated a widespread nineteenth-century faith in the average believer's common sense, a trait that still characterizes American evangelicalism.

• A collection of Stone's papers was published as *Works of Elder B. W. Stone, to Which Is Added a Few Discourses and Sermons by Elder James M. Mathes*, vol. 1 (1859). Stone's pamphlets include *An Address to the Christian Churches in Kentucky, Tennessee, and Ohio on Several Important Doctrines of Religion* (1821) and *Letters to James Blythe, D.D., Designed as a Reply to the Arguments of Thomas Cleland, D.D.* (1824); Cleland's reaction to these writings include *The Socini-Arian Detected: A Series of Letters to Barton W. Stone, on Some Important Subjects of Theological Discussion* (1815) and *Letters to Barton W. Stone, Containing a Vindication Principally of the Doctrines of the Trinity, the Divinity, and Atonement of the Saviour, Against His Recent Attack in a Second Edition of His "Address"* (1822).

Stone's posthumously published *The Biography of Elder Barton Warren Stone, Written by Himself* (1847) offers a helpful but biased chronology. See also William Garrett West, *Barton Warren Stone: Early American Advocate of Christian Unity* (1954). Rhodes Thompson, *Voices from Cane Ridge* (1954), was once the standard work. Recent investigations by John Boles, *The Great Revival, 1787–1805* (1972) and *Religion in Antebellum Kentucky* (1976), have clarified Stone's part in the frontier revival. Anthony L. Dunnavant, ed., *Cane Ridge in Context: Perspectives on Barton W. Stone and the Revival* (1992), and Paul Conkin, *Cane Ridge, America's Pentecost* (1990), link Stone to the several religious cultures that he ingeniously integrated to create a distinctively American tradition.

PHILIP K. GOFF

STONE, Bentley (1907–10 Feb. 1984), dancer, choreographer, and teacher, was born in Plankinton, South Dakota, the son of Robert S. Stone, a mining engineer, and Maggie Marshall. Stone's early childhood was spent in South Dakota. When he was of school age the Stone family moved to Milwaukee, where his academic education went as far as two years at Marquette University. In his adolescence he had shown talent in a local dance school, and he was fired with the ambition to be a dancer. He left college and went to New York to pursue further training and a career in musical theater. He studied ballet with Luigi Albertieri, tap dancing with Johnny Boyle, and an eclectic type of dancing with Margaret Severn, a concert dancer. He appeared with Severn in concerts, partnering her in *Frenzy* to music by Wilckens and *In the Hall of the Mountain King* to music by Grieg. He also performed a solo, *Fool's Dance*.

Tall, handsome, and a dedicated worker, he was selected for the ensemble of a touring company of the musical *Hit the Deck*. On returning to New York he joined the cast of *The Street Singer* as the dancing partner of the star, Queenie Smith. This was followed in 1929 by a season in Hoboken, New Jersey, performing the Agnes de Mille dances in a spoof of the nineteenth-century extravaganza *The Black Crook*.

A successful audition for the ballet contingent of the Chicago Civic Opera brought Stone to Chicago in 1929, and Chicago was home to him thereafter. As a member of the opera ballet he danced in the Laurent Novikoff–directed dance episodes of a large opera repertoire as well as in special ballet events. Among the works in which Stone appeared were the Novikoff-choreographed *Chopiniana, Coq d'Or, Prince Igor*, and *Punchinello*. He performed with the opera ballet until the mid-1930s, working under Vecheslav Swoboda, Edward Caton, Muriel Stuart, and Ruth Page. As his opera ballet career progressed, around 1932 Stone choreographed some of the episodes demanding classical dancing, such as the "Dance of the Hours" in *La Gioconda* and the ballet in *La Juive*.

Stone was interested in the possibilities of American themes for dances, and when Walter Camryn, a member of the opera ballet who shared that interest, became involved in presenting such dances for avant-garde concerts in the early 1930s, Stone choreographed two solos for him, *Turkey in the Straw* and *Casey at the Bat*, the latter enduringly popular.

In the summer of 1933, in a project connected with Chicago's Century of Progress Exposition, Michel Fokine was invited to Chicago to stage the ballet *Coppélia*; Stone danced the leading male role. In 1934 Ruth Page, *première danseuse* of the opera ballet, selected Stone as lead dancer and her partner. Together they created and performed short dances and entire ballets for two decades. The important item on an all-ballet program presented by the opera in the fall of 1934 was the premiere of the one-act ballet *Hear Ye! Hear Ye!* choreographed by Ruth Page to the commissioned score by Aaron Copland. Stone partnered Page as the male member of the cabaret dance team whose murder was the center of the trial, the subject of the piece. That season Stone also danced leads in Page's *Love Song* (Schubert), *Iberian Monotone* (Ravel), and *The Gold Standard* (Ibert).

Although he was a virtuoso ballet dancer, Stone did not choreograph in that genre for himself. He avoided showy *batterie* and pirouettes, instead inventing expressive movements to give point to his dances. Page sometimes included a group of dancers from the opera ballet corps in post-opera tours, and Stone assisted her in choreographing group dances and short ballets such as *Hicks at the Country Fair*, to music by Stravinsky. They also collaborated on a large-scale piece, *Americans in Paris*, to the George Gershwin score (the added "s" in the title to justify the large cast).

In the summer of 1937 Stone went to England to study with Marie Rambert. She was preparing her company for a tour of the Continent and took him into her company as a principal dancer. With the troupe he danced the leads in *Spectre de la Rose, Les Sylphides, Swan Lake*, and *Death and the Maiden*. Stone choreographed for the company *Pavane pour une infante défunte* (Ravel).

For the 1937 and 1938 seasons dancers of the Chicago opera ballet corps participated in the New Deal's Federal Theater. Page and Stone were appointed directors of the project, which included dancers, a theater, and the services of a composer and designers. They collaborated on a lusty bit of Americana, a ballet based on the popular barroom ballad "Frankie and Johnny," with Page as the vengeful Frankie and Stone as two-timing Johnny. It was a smash hit, frequently restaged for American companies, including the

Dance Theatre of Harlem. A performance by Page's Chicago Ballet was televised in 1976.

The Federal Theater came to an end in 1939, and with a nucleus of the opera ballet corps and Federal Theater dancers, the Page-Stone Ballet, a company of some thirty dancers, was formed. For almost a decade it toured the United States and South America. In 1950 Page and Stone took a company made up of recruits from major ballet troupes, plus several from the now defunct Page-Stone Ballet, to Paris in a repertoire featuring *Frankie and Johnny* and *Americans in Paris*. From his first years in Chicago, Stone was also involved in teaching. For a number of years he taught several classes a week in Oak Park, a Chicago suburb. But he found the school's grossly commercial point of view distasteful and, joining forces with Walter Camryn, in 1941 founded the Stone-Camryn Ballet School.

When the United States entered World War II, Stone was drafted and served two and a half years in the air force as a staff sergeant. After the war there were a few short tours with the Page-Stone Ballet. In the summer of 1948 he performed at the annual Jacob's Pillow Dance Festival and also served as an instructor in the Jacob's Pillow summer school. From the 1950s to the end of his career, Stone devoted himself full time to teaching, and the Stone-Camryn school attracted talented pupils from many states.

Concerned with training professionally oriented students, Stone realized that dance as a theatrical art required that students have theatrical experiences. Together with Camryn he founded the Stone-Camryn Ballet, which presented programs with advanced students and professionals in pieces choreographed by their mentors. Stone made ballets to music by Mozart and Boccherini and a ballet based on Hans Christian Anderson's *The Little Match Girl*, set to music by Gluck. A poetic ballet, geared to young children, was *A Friend Is Someone Who Likes You*. Stone seldom appeared on these programs.

In 1963 Stone, touched by a news account of the suicide of a young girl fished out of the Seine in Paris, created a ballet pervaded by the ambiance of postwar life. The ballet, *L'Inconnue*, set to music by Poulenc, was performed by the Stone-Camryn Ballet with American Ballet Theatre principals John Kriza and Ruth Ann Koesun, alumni of the Stone-Camryn school, as guest artists.

In the 1970s and early 1980s the Stone-Camryn school attained national prominence and respect. Although artists of every kind were scrambling for government and foundation subsidies, Stone and Camryn turned their backs on grants, yet gave innumerable scholarships to talented youngsters. Many successful dancers owed their training to them.

Stone brought intellectuality to teaching ballet. He analyzed the physical elements and the aesthetics of positions and movements. Although he championed simplicity and abhorred flamboyance, his own dancing was brilliant, and the combinations of steps he presented were intricate and often choreographic.

The Stone-Camryn Ballet School was closed in 1981, but the precepts of classic simplicity and the importance of American themes in dance continued to be carried on by a generation of young teachers brought up in the school. Stone died in Chicago, never having married.

• Bentley Stone's papers and some archival films are in the Dance Archives of the Newberry Library in Chicago. Many references to Stone and his work with Ruth Page are in John Martin, *Ruth Page: An Intimate Biography* (1977). A number of photographs of and references to Stone are in Ruth Page, *Page by Page* (1978), particularly in the sections on the South American tour of the Page-Stone Ballet and the experience of Les Ballets Americains in Paris. Page, *Class* (1984), contains descriptions of dance classes Ruth Page took with many masters in various places and includes descriptions of and comments on classes with Stone. Additional material on Stone is in Andrew Mark Wentink, "The Ruth Page Collection: An Introduction and Guide to Manuscript Materials through 1970," *Bulletin of Research in the Humanities* 83 (Spring 1980): 67–162.

ANN BARZEL

STONE, Charles Augustus (16 Jan. 1867–25 Feb. 1941), and **Edwin Sibley Webster** (26 Aug. 1867–10 May 1950), electrical engineers, were born, respectively, in Newton and Roxbury, Massachusetts. Stone was the son of Charles Hobart Stone, a wholesale butter merchant, and Mary Augusta Greene. Webster was the son of Frank G. Webster and Mary Fidelia Messenger. Webster's father was a banker who eventually became a senior partner in the Boston firm of Kidder, Peabody & Company. These solidly upper-middle-class origins provided connections with Boston business and banking interests that endured throughout Stone and Webster's personal and professional lives.

Stone and Webster first met in 1884 while taking the entrance examination for the Massachusetts Institute of Technology. Possessing similar backgrounds and interests, they quickly became such inseparable friends that fellow students at MIT began referring to them collectively as Stone and Webster rather than as individuals. As engineering students they chose to concentrate on the relatively new field of electrical engineering. United in this interest, they persuaded their professors to allow them to write a joint senior thesis examining the efficiency of a Westinghouse alternating-current generator, and they planned to go into partnership following graduation in 1888. However, Charles R. Cross, the department head in electrical engineering, advised them against this plan. At the time the engineering community remained dubious about the future of electrical power and its applications in industry, and Cross did not believe that sufficient demand existed in the Boston area to support both Stone and Webster as independent consulting engineers. Briefly discouraged, Stone accepted a position as Elihu Thomson's assistant at the Thomson Electric Welding Company. Webster left on a tour of Europe that lasted for several months. When he returned to Boston, Webster went to work for Kidder, Peabody &

Company. The idea of an independent consulting firm refused to die, however, and in November 1889 Stone and Webster decided to pursue their dream. Using $2,600 borrowed from their parents, the pair founded the Massachusetts Electrical Engineering Company. They hired a recent MIT graduate to manage the office while they searched for clients. Webster took on a full-time position with their new firm in January 1890, and Stone joined him a few months later.

Success with their first major project, the design and construction of a 400-horsepower hydroelectric plant on the Presumpscot River in Maine for S. D. Warren and Company, led to additional contracts. Over the next three years the firm of Stone & Webster continued to expand as they built small power plants throughout New England. By 1893 their reputation for technical expertise combined with their connections to Boston banking interests led to Stone & Webster being hired to evaluate light and power company securities for the Street Railway and Illuminating Properties Trustees. Banks had obtained these securities in lieu of cash payments from manufacturers such as Westinghouse following a financial panic. With the electric power industry still in its infancy, the securities were almost unsalable. The firm of Stone & Webster was asked to examine various properties around the nation.

Stone and Webster had ventured into electrical engineering as technical consultants, not as financial managers, but their work for the trustees provided them with experience that they would put to good use. That is, their original intention was to advise clients as to the most cost-effective methods to employ in developing electric light and power plants. As engineering consultants, they made recommendations to clients regarding site selection and mechanical equipment as well as overseeing the actual construction process. Their firm initially did not take any financial interest in the actual power plants beyond the usual consulting fees. This changed after the depression of 1893. They invested in the Nashville Electric Light and Power Company, a utility company that they saw as being one of the most promising of the ones they had researched. They gained a controlling interest and oversaw the expansion of the company and then sold their interest at a tremendous profit. The young entrepreneurs moved quickly from this first investment into a large portfolio of investments in power, lighting, and transportation companies.

As the business of Stone & Webster grew, their individual identities remained blurred within the company, although their personal lives were distinctly separate. Webster married Jane de Peyster Hovey in June 1893 and had four children. Stone married Mary Adams Leonard, nine years later, in June 1902 and also had four children. At work, however, they continued to share an office, sitting at desks side by side, and signed correspondence as "Stone & Webster," a practice they continued even after business interests required the establishment of separate offices in New York and Boston. In 1905 the two partners invited ad-ditional partners into the firm, beginning with an MIT classmate, Russell Robb. By 1912 Stone & Webster had seven full partners, employed approximately 600 people, and occupied an eight-story building. In addition to providing traditional engineering consulting services, Stone & Webster contracted with thirty-five electric and railway companies to serve as their business managers. Each utility company remained an independent entity until 1925. At that time Stone & Webster organized a holding company, the Engineers Public Service Company, which acquired control of the local utilities that they had managed. Stone & Webster relinquished control of these utilities following passage of the Public Utility Holding Company Act of 1935, which prohibited many formerly legal utility management practices.

While the financial acumen of Stone & Webster contributed to the firm's involvement in managing numerous electric utilities throughout the United States, their technical expertise remained undisputed. After a few years of designing power plants for other contractors to build, the firm formed a construction division and performed all aspects of construction itself. Stone & Webster quickly became noted for state of the art turn-key projects. That is, the client would provide the firm with its specifications and Stone & Webster would undertake every phase of a project's completion, from the initial site selection and design process to the final construction. Many of the projects completed by Stone & Webster included features that set records, such as the Big Creek transmission system in California. Its 241 miles of 150 kilovolt lines formed the highest voltage being carried over the longest distance attempted up to that time. By 1930 Stone & Webster had been responsible for building facilities that generated one-tenth of the nation's electrical power, as well as playing a prominent role in other areas of construction and industrial engineering.

Following World War I the partners in Stone & Webster incorporated the firm as Stone & Webster, Inc. Webster became president and Stone was named chairman of the board. Various subsidiary firms were established to handle different aspects of the old firm's business, such as Stone, Webster & Blodget, which dealt in securities. Separate offices had been established in 1915, when Stone moved his office to New York, but the partners retained the custom of maintaining side by side desks in both cities. Following Stone's death in New York City, Webster succeeded him as vice chairman, a position he retained until his own death in Newton, Massachusetts.

• David N. Keller, *Stone & Webster 1889–1989: A Century of Integrity and Service* (1989), provides an official company history of the firm, its growth into myriad engineering interests, and its founders. Many of the individual power companies founded or managed by Stone & Webster have also published histories, such as Robert C. Wing, *A Century of Service: The Puget Power Story* (1987), which includes biographies of Stone and Webster and provides detail on their actions in individual situations. Thomas P. Hughes, *Networks of Power: Electrification in Western Society, 1880–1930* (1983), includes a detailed analysis of Stone & Webster's activities within the overall context of the growth of the electric utility industry in the United States. Obituaries for Stone & Webster are in the *New York Times*, 26 Feb. 1941 and 11 May 1950, respectively.

NANCY FARM MANNIKKO

STONE, Charles Pomeroy (30 Sept. 1824–24 Jan. 1887), soldier and civil engineer, was born in Greenfield, Massachusetts, the son of Alpheus Fletcher Stone, a physician, and Fanny Cushing. An 1845 graduate of West Point, he served as an ordnance officer throughout the Mexican War, winning brevets for "gallant and meritorious conduct" at Molino del Rey and Chapultepec. In 1853 he married Maria Louisa Clary, with whom he had one child.

By 1856 Stone had risen only to first lieutenant; that November he left the army for private life. As a member of a commission to evaluate northern Mexico for commercial development (1857–1859), he made an extensive tour of Sonora. Later he was acting U.S. consul at Guaymas. On the eve of the Civil War Stone published a well-received travelogue, *Notes on the State of Sonora* (1861).

On 16 April 1861 Stone reentered military service, the first of many thousands of northerners to join the volunteer army. As a colonel in the inspector general's office, he commanded the volunteer defense forces of Washington, D.C., including those who guarded President-elect Abraham Lincoln. Following Lincoln's inauguration, Stone rounded up spies in the capital and foiled attempts to capture arsenals and supply depots for the Confederacy. In July he rejoined the Regular Army as commander of the newly organized Fourteenth Infantry. The following month he returned to the volunteers as a brigadier general, one of the first Regular officers to win such an appointment.

Although Stone appeared well qualified for high command, his career was in jeopardy almost from the moment he took the field. His martinetish habits alienated many of his volunteer troops and generated adverse publicity. Government officials took exception to his conservative politics, his vocal opposition to abolitionism, and his friendships with old army colleagues now in Confederate service. Stone partook liberally of the hospitality of Virginia secessionists, was solicitous of their property, and returned slaves who sought refuge in his camps. Critics alleged that spies passed easily through his lines and that he frequently conferred with enemy officers under flags of truce.

Stone might have risen above these controversies had he proven to be a successful field commander. Instead, he accomplished little of tactical or strategic value. In June and July 1861 he led 2,500 volunteers toward Leesburg, Virginia, to cover the upper Potomac against enemy incursions, to stop the flow of rebel supplies from Baltimore and Virginia, and to open the obstructed Chesapeake & Ohio Canal. When within sight of Leesburg, however, reports of an enemy advance caused him to abort the mission short of its most important objectives.

Disaster struck in late October 1861, when Stone, commanding a division on the Maryland side of the Potomac, failed to support a reconnaissance in force toward Dranesville, Virginia. His tardy movement ended when one of his brigades, under former Republican senator Edward D. Baker of Oregon, was surrounded and decimated atop an eminence known as Ball's Bluff. In the wake of the debacle, some critics accused Stone of sending Baker, a close friend of Lincoln, to his death along with hundreds of his men.

Ball's Bluff prompted Congress to form an investigating panel, the Joint Committee on the Conduct of the War. Its zealous chairman, Radical Republican senator Benjamin F. Wade of Ohio, compelled Stone to appear before the tribunal in early January 1862. In reply to accusations that he had mishandled operations along the Potomac, Stone blamed Baker for the defeat, a tactic that alienated the committee members. Much of Stone's testimony was rebutted by other witnesses, including subordinates with grievances against him, some of whom also impugned Stone's loyalty. When Senator Wade publicized his own doubts about Stone, rumors began to circulate that the latter was guilty of what English journalist William Howard Russell called "treason—a common crime of unlucky generals."

Stone paid little attention to the rumors. Only when recalled by the committee on 31 January did he realize the danger he was in. At once he asked to see any charges that had been drawn up against him, but he was rebuffed. He was also denied the right to cross-examine witnesses who had testified against him. When Stone made an impassioned plea of innocence, the committee played deaf.

Following this latest round of questioning, Secretary of War Edwin M. Stanton, who had come to view Stone as a traitor, drew up an order for his arrest. Stone's superior and friend, Major General George B. McClellan, commander of the Army of the Potomac, risked censure by suspending the order. Early in February, however, a refugee from Leesburg entered McClellan's lines with new information about clandestine meetings between Stone and enemy officers. According to the informant, the Confederates had expressed "great cordiality" toward and "confidence" in the brigadier. Learning of the allegations, Secretary Stanton demanded Stone's arrest, and this time McClellan assented.

On 9 February 1862 Stone was taken into custody in Washington and conveyed to New York Harbor, where he was imprisoned in Fort Lafayette, a holding pen for political and military prisoners. Without displaying an arrest warrant, the jailer placed Stone in solitary confinement and permitted him no contact with lawyers or even with relatives.

For almost two months Stone was held in solitary confinement in New York, a victim of Lincoln's suspension of habeas corpus along the eastern seaboard. Repeatedly he petitioned the government for a copy of the charges against him, but every request was denied. On 4 July he wrote directly to Lincoln, asserting his innocence and seeking leniency; the president did not reply. Even letters to Stone's old patron, McClellan, went unanswered. Not until 16 August, after Congress passed a resolution prohibiting Federal prisoners from being held without charges for more than thirty days, was Stone released.

After spending some weeks with his family, the general made the rounds of official Washington to learn who had ordered his arrest and on what grounds. President Lincoln, Secretary Stanton, and every other official he interviewed denied involvement or pleaded ignorance of the case. Stone's subsequent request for a court of inquiry was denied, although he was granted a third appearance before the Committee on the Conduct of the War. At last apprised of the evidence against him, he refuted it to the satisfaction of every panel member, including Senator Wade. After his first marriage ended, in 1863 he married Annie Jeannie Granier, with whom he had five children.

His reputation only partially restored, Stone returned to active duty, briefly serving as chief of staff to Major General Nathaniel P. Banks, a former Democratic congressman. Reverting to his Regular Army colonelcy in April 1864, he was assigned an infantry brigade in the V Corps, Army of the Potomac. For some months he tolerated the rigors of field campaigning, but on 13 September ill health—the result of his imprisonment—and the suspicion of some of his colleagues drove him to resign his commission.

For the remaining years of his life Stone worked as a mining, canal, and construction engineer while seeking redress for the damage done to his career. In 1870 he went to Egypt at the invitation of the khedive and rose to chief of staff of that country's army. Returning home in 1883, he resumed his effort to clear his name. Four years' worth of appeals to government officials, however, failed to gain the court of inquiry he deserved or the vindication he so desperately desired. Ironically, the disgraced soldier closed out his public life by constructing the foundation of one of the symbols of American freedom, the Statue of Liberty. Stone died in New York City.

Stone was the most celebrated example of a high-ranking Democrat who ran afoul of the administration that supervised the Union war effort. His relations with the White House and the Congress, initially strong, were quickly weakened by his imperious demeanor, his disdain of volunteer troops, his impolitic associations with the enemies of his government, and a rather cavalier attitude toward his civilian superiors. For all that, Stone appears to have been a conscientious soldier dedicated to preserving the Union. Certainly the government's decision to hold him for six months without charges and upon evidence too flimsy to withstand legal scrutiny was not only unconscionable but unsustainable under either the Constitution or the Articles of War.

• Samples of Stone's wartime and postwar correspondence repose in the William T. Sherman Papers and the Alexander Macomb Mason Papers at the Library of Congress and in the Minor Family Papers at the Virginia Historical Society. The Louis G. Cowan Papers in the Columbia University Libraries include an unpublished account of Stone's work on the Statue of Liberty. Reports and correspondence covering the general's war service are in *The War of the Rebellion: A Compilation of the Official Records of the Union and Confederate Armies* (128 vols., 1880–1901). For testimony in the government's investigation of Stone, see pt. 2 of *Report of the Joint Committee on the Conduct of the War*, 37th Cong., 3d sess., 1863–1868, Rept. 108. Other contemporary sources on his troubles in the aftermath of Ball's Bluff include John D. Baltz, *Hon. Edward D. Baker* (1888), and Richard B. Irwin, "Ball's Bluff and the Arrest of General Stone," *Battles and Leaders of the Civil War*, vol. 2, ed. Robert U. Johnson and Clarence C. Buel (4 vols., 1887–1888). His postwar service in Egypt receives attention in William B. Hesseltine and Hazel C. Wolf, *The Blue and the Gray on the Nile* (1961). An informative obituary is in the *New York Times*, 25 Jan. 1887, but it omits details of Stone's trial and incarceration.

EDWARD G. LONGACRE

STONE, David (17 Feb. 1770–7 Oct. 1818), governor, congressman, and jurist, was born at "Hope Plantation" near Windsor in Bertie County, North Carolina, the son of Zedekiah Stone and Elizabeth Shivers Hobson. Zedekiah Stone established a plantation in Bertie County prior to 1769 and was an active patriot in the political arena during the American Revolution. A man of financial substance, he was determined to provide young David with an excellent education. After preparatory studies at Windsor Academy, Stone graduated from the College of New Jersey (now Princeton University) in 1788 with first honors. Subsequently he read law with William R. Davie and was admitted to the state bar in 1790. In 1793 Stone married Hannah Turner; the couple had six children who survived infancy.

Stone's public service career began at age nineteen when he represented Bertie County in the Fayetteville convention of 1789 that ratified the federal Constitution. With few interruptions he held offices of trust until late 1814. In 1790 he was elected to the first of five terms in the state house of commons, the lower house of the North Carolina General Assembly; there he manifested Federalist principles, supporting internal improvements and education. From 1795 to 1798 he was a superior court judge, a post he resigned after his election to the U.S. House of Representatives. He changed political parties about this time and voted for Thomas Jefferson in the 1800–1801 presidential imbroglio. He was a member of the first standing House Ways and Means Committee. He resigned on 25 January 1801, before the Sixth Congress ended, in order to assume a seat in the U.S. Senate. Although Stone spoke rarely and was no legislative leader, he generally supported the Jefferson administration. In 1806 the North Carolina General Assembly retired Senator Stone, who refused to resign until 17 February 1807, but elected him to a second tenure as superior court judge. He served as judge for two years before his election as governor in 1808 and 1809.

Perhaps the clearest exposition of Stone's policies as governor was in his message to the general assembly on 22 November 1809. He advocated economic development in both agriculture and industry. Of industry he noted: "If, therefore, the native ingenuity and enterprize of our citizens can be properly aided, there can exist no doubt but they will by the manufacture of our own materials . . . soon render the state completely independent of supplies derived from foreign countries." Stone also recognized the vital importance of improved transportation: he advocated "opening and improving our roads, removing obstructions to the navigation of our rivers, cutting canals, and so forth." Proposing that North Carolina should provide excellent public and higher education, Stone stated that among other purposes education would promote the inculcation of American institutions and pride in country so necessary in moving citizens away from alien manners, governments, and institutions. In advocating higher salaries for judges, he characterized courts as "those sacred temples from which the laws extend their protection to the lives, the liberties, the fortunes, and characters of the citizens" (*N.C. House Journal*, 22 Nov. 1809, pp. 4–7).

In 1810 Stone declined reelection although he had been a popular governor. He was returned to the house of commons in 1811 and to the U.S. Senate in 1812. This Senate tenure was controversial as he deserted President James Madison, joining the Federalists in opposing measures to prosecute the war with Great Britain. He stood against embargoes, direct taxation, and the appointment of Secretary of the Treasury Albert Gallatin to the peace commission.

In his opposition to Madisonian war policies, Stone had rejoined the Federalists. His stance was abhorrent to the Jeffersonian Democrats who controlled the North Carolina legislature. He had not complied with the legislature's instruction, and in December 1813 the general assembly censured him by a narrow majority. He waited until 24 December 1814 to resign and made a spirited defense of a senator's right to follow the dictates of conscience rather than those of political party.

Having resigned in disgrace, Stone's political career was concluded. He took up residence in Wake County, resumed his legal practice, and supervised his agricultural holdings in Wake and Bertie counties. Hannah Stone died in April 1816; a year later he married Sarah Dashiell of Washington, D.C. There were no offspring of this union. In May 1818 he was elected president of the Neuse River Navigation Company. To a degree, this election repaired his public reputation and enabled him to promote internal improvements. Six months later Stone died unexpectedly at "Restdale Plantation," Wake County, on the Neuse River six miles east of Raleigh.

Tall and impressive in bearing and a man of considerable personal charm, Stone was long a favorite of North Carolina. His political career was characterized by attention to duty and personal integrity. He served his state well, but changes in his political affiliations besmirched his reputation.

• There are sixty items in the collection of Stone's private manuscripts held by the North Carolina State Archives, Division of Archives and History, Raleigh; his gubernatorial and legislative papers are held by the same repository. See also the *Annals of Congress* and his obituary in the *Raleigh Register*, 9 Oct. 1818. There are few secondary works to consult aside from D. H. Gilpatrick, *Jeffersonian Democracy in North Carolina, 1789–1816* (1931).

MAX R. WILLIAMS

STONE, Edward Durell (9 Mar. 1902–6 Aug. 1978), architect, was born in Fayetteville, Arkansas, the son of Benjamin Hicks Stone, a landowner, and Ruth Johnson, an English instructor at the University of Arkansas. He spent his early years in Fayetteville, the "Athens of the Ozarks." His family was socially distinguished by ancestry and inherited wealth. Both of his parents valued education and the arts, and Stone continued this tradition by enrolling at age eighteen in the University of Arkansas, where he demonstrated a talent for illustration.

In 1923, at the urging of his brother, James Hicks Stone, an architect, he left Fayetteville. He joined his brother in Boston, committed to studying and practicing architecture. His academic training in architecture occurred at the Boston Architectural Club, followed by one-year sessions at Harvard University (1925–1926) and the Massachusetts Institute of Technology (1926–1927). Stone never completed his academic programs and never received an academic degree. In 1923, Henry R. Shepley, of the Boston firm Coolidge, Shepley, Bulfinch and Abbott, had offered Stone his first job. Shepley, whom Stone described as his "first patron," guided his early progress as an architect, and along with Jacques Carlu at MIT introduced him to European theories of modern design.

In 1927 Stone successfully competed for the Rotch Traveling Scholarship. He spent the following two years in Europe, returning in 1929 to begin a career in New York City. His first major opportunity came in 1930, when the team of architects working on Rockefeller Center appointed him chief designer for the shells of two theaters: Radio City Music Hall (1932) and the Center Theater (1932). In 1933 Stone was the first American-born architect to design an International Style house in the northeastern United States, the Richard H. Mandel house (1935) in Mt. Kisco, New York, a project designed in collaboration with Donald Deskey. Popular interest in the Mandel House drew clients to Stone, and, in 1936, after working briefly for Wallace K. Harrison, he organized his own firm. Among his early clients were A. Conger Goodyear, Henry R. Luce, and George P. Marshall. In 1938 Stone and Philip Goodwin were selected to design the Museum of Modern Art (1939), "one of New York's great International Style structures" (Goldberger, *City Observed*, p. 173). With Goodwin, Stone also designed the Food Building for the 1939 World's Fair in New York.

Beginning in 1940 Stone's work veered away from literal interpretations of the International Style. Exhibiting a growing appreciation for natural materials, he explored new design treatments, such as laminated wood surfaces for interior walls, and generally favored wood-constructed ranch-style houses with broad sloping roofs, large expanses of glass, and masonry walls. During World War II, he headed the Department of Planning and Design for the U.S. Army. Following his military service, he taught intermittently both at Yale (1946–1952) and at New York University (1946–1952). In the late 1940s Stone received commissions to design hotels in Panama and Lebanon. In the ensuing years his practice extended to eight countries on three continents, and he joined Louis Kahn, Mies van der Rohe, and the firm of Skidmore, Owings and Merrill in pioneering a postwar worldwide practice.

His encounters, in the late 1940s and early 1950s, with the architectural traditions of India, Spain, and the Middle East transformed his work. He appropriated exotic historical elements into his work and intermingled them with International Style forms to produce a "personal style that was lush and highly decorative" (*New York Times*, 7 Aug. 1978). Described, variously, as "new romanticism," "harem classical," or "international tropical," his new work introduced open floor plans, reflecting pools, textured decorative surfaces, patterned light, and overhanging flat roofs with colonnades to a receptive international audience. His designs, in 1954, for the U.S. Embassy in New Delhi fulfilled his new vision of architecture. The embassy complex was the most celebrated achievement of his career. Its "grace and serenity" generated unprecedented acclaim for a work of contemporary architecture and riveted public attention on Stone's work. His first American iteration of "international tropical" was the Stuart Company building (begun in 1956) in Pasadena, a work patterned after the embassy. A third interpretation of his style was the U.S. pavilion at the Brussels Worlds Fair (1958). In 1958 he was also selected in a competition to design the John F. Kennedy Center for the Performing Arts in Washington, D.C.

In the 1960s Stone presided over one of the largest and most successful architectural practices in the world. In 1966 his firm had commissions of $1 billion on the drawing boards. Many of these commissions were for academic institutions (State University of New York campus in Albany, 1968), museums (Ponce, Puerto Rico, 1962; Stuhr Museum of the Prairie Pioneer, Grand Island, Nebr., 1967), civic buildings (Presidential Palace, Islamabad, Pakistan, 1961; City Hall, Paducah, Ky., 1965), and a sports stadium (Busch Stadium, St. Louis, 1966). He received a Gold Medal from the American Institute of Architects in 1955, and in 1960 he became a Fellow of the American Institute of Architects. Through these years Stone deepened his alienation from the modern movement. He emerged as one of the most outspoken dissenters against what he described as the "hygienic austerity" of architecture. Critical of buildings executed in glass

and aluminum, he challenged the architectural profession to design works that would endure as permanent symbols of their time.

His notions of permanence gravitated toward large-scaled buildings executed with rich materials. Widespread disfavor greeted works such as the General Motors buildings in New York (designed with Emery Roth & Sons and completed in 1968) and the Kennedy Center. Critics of architecture disparaged his Neo-Formalist, marble-clad buildings as banal and pompous. For the balance of his career he was labeled a reactionary, along with his contemporary, the Japanese-American Minoru Yamasaki (1913–1986), whose work over three decades closely paralleled Stone's. His final project, in partnership with his son, Edward Durell Stone, Jr., was the Florida State Capitol in Tallahassee (1973–1977). He died in New York City.

A courtly and genial man who collected pre-Columbian pottery, Stone was married three times. His first two marriages, in 1931 to Orlean Vandiver and in 1954 to Maria Elena Torch, ended in divorce. His third wife, Violet Campbell Moffat, whom he married in 1972, and their daughter survived him as did his four children from his previous marriages.

Stone occupies an influential position within American architecture of the twentieth century. His early embrace of European modernism elevated him to the forefront of American architects working in that idiom. His subsequent drift away from modernism led to a brief but creative period during which he reconciled traditional values with modern design and reawakened the architectural profession to the possibilities of ornamentation. His designs for major buildings introduced such features as filigree terrazzo screens, reflecting pools, and colonnades that became familiar sights on hospitals, hotels, libraries, factories, and civic buildings throughout the world.

• The most comprehensive collection of drawings, correspondence, and recorded and filmed interviews is the Edward Durell Stone Papers in the University Library, University of Arkansas. Stone published two books, *The Evolution of an Architect* (1962), a semiautobiographical account, and *Edward Durell Stone, Recent and Future Architecture* (1967). Noteworthy examples of his quarrel with modernism are his essay "The Case against the Tailfin Age," *New York Times Magazine*, 18 Oct. 1959, and an interview, "Are Most Cities Too Ugly to Save?: Interview with Famed Architect Edward Durell Stone," *U.S. News and World Report*, 30 Nov. 1964. Biographical sketches that review his career only through the late 1950s are Winthrop Sargeant, "Profiles from Sassafras Branches, Edward D. Stone," *New Yorker*, 3 Jan. 1959, and a cover story, "More Than Modern," *Time*, 31 Mar. 1958. From the same period, an insightful commentary on his influence is Robin Boyd, "The Counter-Revolution in Architecture," *Harper's*, Sept. 1959. From about 1935 to 1975 both *Architectural Record* and *Architectural Forum* include many articles on Stone's work; see, for example, "A Final Look at Brussels," *Architectural Forum* 109 (Oct. 1958): 104–9, and "The Work of Edward Durell Stone," *Architectural Record* 125 (Mar. 1959): 157–72. For an overview of his work in California see Allan Temko, "The Legacy of Edward Stone," *San Francisco Chronicle*, 21 Aug. 1978. Obituaries appear in the *New York Times*, 7 Aug. and 8 Aug. 1978.

JEFFREY CRONIN

STONE, George Washington (24 Oct. 1811–11 Mar. 1894), jurist, was born in Bedford County, Virginia, the son of Micajah Stone, a planter, and Sarah Leftwich. As the nation grew in the early nineteenth century, the Stones migrated westward in search of fresh land and new opportunities, and in 1818 they settled in Lincoln County, Tennessee, along the Alabama border. There Stone, one of ten children, received his education in the area's common schools. On the death of his father in 1827, Stone engaged briefly in some commercial pursuits before reading law with James Fulton, a Fayetteville, Tennessee, lawyer. Stone never attended college, but in 1834 he earned his license to practice law, married Mary Gillespie, and moved to Talladega County, Alabama. The couple had one child. Two years later Stone and the small but talented cadre of lawyers who had settled in the area assembled for the first meeting of the county bar association. Of the eleven members of this group, three—including Stone—later went on to serve as chief justices of the state.

Stone's contact with such an able contingent of attorneys paid handsome dividends when it came to career advancement, and during the next few years the ambitious Stone made every effort to elevate his professional status. In 1839 he gained admission to the bar of the Alabama Supreme Court and became acquainted with some of the leaders of the state's legal community, including William P. Chilton, with whom he entered into a partnership later that year. In 1843 Stone lost a bid for a circuit judgeship, but six months later he was appointed to the very same judicial post when the veteran judge who had defeated him died. While Stone later won reelection to the position, he served only a single six-year term as circuit judge. The heavy workload and poor compensation, coupled with his wife's death in 1848, prompted Stone to resign in 1849. He moved to Hayneville, in Lowndes County, to return to the practice of law, and his name was mentioned later that year as the Democratic nominee for governor. At about the same time he married Emily Moore, the daughter of a wealthy and influential Lowndes County planter; they had four children.

Stone practiced law in Lowndes County for the next seven years, during which time he made an unsuccessful run for the state supreme court in 1853 and nearly engaged in a duel in 1855 before resolving the dispute peacefully. A lifelong Presbyterian, Stone dutifully submitted to the discipline of the church for his involvement in the near-duel, and the Alabama legislature subsequently made an exception to the anti-duelling oath sworn by public officials, permitting him to hold office again despite the indiscretion. In 1856 the legislature elected him to the supreme court. Although known neither for his oratorical skills nor his personal magnetism, Stone's reputation as a competent, hard-

working lawyer had catapulted him to the state's highest judicial body.

Stone's ascension to the bench coincided with the sectional crisis and Civil War, events that had a tremendous impact on his life and work over the next few decades. Like most southern state judges, Stone placed loyalty to the Confederacy over the power of individual states, and in a series of cases he upheld the constitutionality of the Confederate military draft. After the war, Alabama's provisional government, made up of antebellum Unionists, declared that the members of the supreme court held their positions illegally, and Stone lost his judicial position. His reputation as a competent legal professional, however, remained intact, even among Unionists. In 1865 the same legislature that had denied him his seat asked Stone to prepare a revised penal code for the state. After completing the task, he married Mary E. Wright in 1866 (his second wife had died four years before) and moved to Montgomery to resume the practice of law. The couple had no children.

When the political climate changed, Stone rode the rising tide of conservatism back onto the supreme court. In 1876 Alabama's "Redeemer" Democratic governor reappointed him to the bench, where he cooperated in reversing the constitutional and legal changes wrought by Reconstruction. Stone and his judicial colleagues narrowly defined the scope of legal protections guaranteed to former slaves under the Fourteenth Amendment of the U.S. Constitution. In *Green v. State* (1882), for example, a case involving the murder trial of an African American, Stone held that local government officials' efforts to select an all-white grand jury did not violate the amendment. Moreover, in a series of cases the court held that the Fourteenth Amendment's civil rights guarantees had no bearing on Alabama's antimiscegenation law. On economic and regulatory matters, meanwhile, Stone's record was a mixed one. He held corporations to be persons under the Fourteenth Amendment, generally made it difficult for individuals to sue railroad companies for damages in injury suits, and yet strictly upheld legislatively imposed regulation of railroad rates.

By far Stone's most significant contribution to Alabama's legal development lay in the area of criminal law. Over the course of his twenty-seven years on the supreme court, Stone waged a multifaceted campaign against the rampant violence that plagued much of the nineteenth-century South. In *McManus v. State* (1860), a case where an assailant beat his victim in the head with a brick, Stone upheld the lower court's conviction for voluntary manslaughter and criticized Alabamians for allowing "notions of chivalry or personal prowess" to govern the nature of their disputes. Most important, in *McManus* he invoked the spirit of the English common law by ruling that self-defense involved an individual's "duty to retreat" from a dangerous encounter before taking violent action. In another line of decisions during the 1870s and 1880s, Stone worked to change the law of concealed weapons, both by narrowing the legal loopholes that allowed gun-toters to carry their arms and by encouraging the legislature to remove all such exceptions to the prohibition on carrying concealed weapons. Finally, in another series of cases, most notably *Parsons v. State* (1886), Stone carefully scrutinized the insanity defense and other forms of legal excuse and sought to increase the burden placed on defendants to prove their insanity. In all these ways Stone sought to reform his state's criminal justice system to prevent the spread of lawlessness and violence.

Stone was one of the longest-serving and most important jurists in his state's history. Near the end of his career he frequently spoke out in favor of judicial reforms such as the merging of law and equity and the simplification of pleading in civil suits. Although he briefly returned to the political fray by engaging in President Grover Cleveland's 1892 campaign in Alabama, Stone's significance lay in his nearly 2,500 written opinions spread over a half-century of judicial service. Appointed chief justice of the Alabama Supreme Court in 1884 and in 1886 and 1892 reelected to that position, Stone was truly one of the architects of his state's highest court. His learned and well-reasoned decisions earned him national recognition and helped build the court's reputation in the aftermath of the Civil War. He served as chief justice until he died in Montgomery.

• A small collection of Stone papers is at the State of Alabama Department of Archives and History, but they contain only a few letters to Stone praising his judicial service and are of little value. The best primary sources available are Stone's judicial opinions, which constitute the bulk of the *Alabama Reports* from 1856 to 1865 and 1876 to 1894. William H. Brantley, *Chief Justice Stone of Alabama* (1943), is more a narrative of Alabama politics with occasional references to Stone than a full-fledged biography of the judge. The best overall biographical sketch of Stone's life and career is Francis Gordon Caffey, "George Washington Stone, 1811–1894," in *Great American Lawyers*, ed. William Draper Lewis, vol. 6 (1909), pp. 165–93. Richard Maxwell Brown, "Southern Violence—Regional Problem or National Nemesis? Legal Attitudes toward Southern Homicide in Historical Perspective," *Vanderbilt Law Review* 32 (Jan. 1979): 225–50, is a valuable discussion of Stone's accomplishments in the area of criminal law, as is Janis Faye Adkinson, "George Washington Stone and Alabama Criminal Law: A Battle against the Southern Legal Tradition" (master's thesis, Univ. of Florida, 1991).

TIMOTHY S. HUEBNER

STONE, Harlan Fiske (11 Oct. 1872–22 Apr. 1946), chief justice of the United States, was born in Chesterfield, New Hampshire, the son of Frederick Lauson Stone, a farmer, and Anne Butler, a former schoolteacher. Two years after his birth, the Stones moved to Mill Valley, near Amherst, Massachusetts, to provide greater educational opportunities for their four children.

Stone entered the Massachusetts Agricultural College in 1888 at the end of his sophomore year in high school, intending to study science. A prank, however, led to his expulsion. In 1890 he was accepted at Amherst College, where his intellectual and public speaking skills flourished. Upon graduation in 1894, he taught for a year in Newburyport, Massachusetts. A growing interest in the law led him to enroll in Columbia Law School in 1895, which at the time was adopting the case method of teaching under the leadership of Dean William A. Keener.

Stone graduated in 1898 and clerked for a year in the firm of Sullivan & Cromwell. He then joined the firm of Wilmer & Canfield on a partial basis, devoting the balance of his time to teaching equity and trusts at Columbia. On 7 September 1899 he married his childhood sweetheart, Agnes Harvey; they had two children.

Because of temperamental and policy differences with the new, authoritarian president of Columbia, Nicholas Murray Butler, as well as the inadequate salary at the law school, Stone resigned his professorship in 1905 and became a full partner in the firm, now called Wilmer, Canfield & Stone. However, the lure of teaching was strong, and despite stormy relations with Butler, Stone returned to Columbia in 1910 as professor of law and dean of the law school. In 1915 he was named Kent Professor of Law; he stayed at Columbia until 1923.

Stone proved an inspiring and effective teacher, and in later years he considered his work as a teacher of far greater value than his accomplishments as a judge. William O. Douglas, a student of his and later a colleague on the Supreme Court, wrote that Stone "was an excellent teacher in this [case] method; no one was better at it than he. He never made an affirmative statement as to what the law was. . . . All he did was question, question, question. Finally, one caught on." Other students testified not only to his pedagogical skills, but to his caring about them as well. Henry Clay Greenberg recalled that after Dean Stone refused him a tuition loan of $180, he called Greenberg back into his office and informed him that he had just discovered a "dormant" scholarship fund of $180. Greenberg later learned that Stone had paid the money out of his own pocket, and he had "no doubt that my case was not unique."

While Stone was dean, Columbia became a center for the new school of jurisprudence known as legal realism, which rejected formalism and static legal rules and instead searched for the experiential and role of human idiosyncracy in the development of the law. Although he played a pivotal role in upgrading the school's admission requirements and setting high standards of scholarship for the faculty, conditions that allowed the realists to pursue their nontraditional studies, Stone was condemned by President Butler for not moving fast enough. Butler accused Stone of intellectual conservatism and charged that legal education at Columbia had "fallen into the ruts."

All evidence indicates that Stone fostered the new scholarship and that his own exalted views of the value of a legal education dovetailed rather than conflicted with new ideas. Butler, who could not tolerate independence from his deans, also may have resented Stone's support of faculty dissenters during the First

World War. Although an Anglophile and interventionist, Stone understood and respected divergent views: During the war he served on a board that examined claims of conscientious objectors, and shortly after the Armistice he wrote an essay, "The Conscientious Objector," that some people consider a classic in its defense of nonconformism.

The growing conflict with Butler, a dislike for administrative work, and the lure of a higher income in private practice led Stone to resign as dean on 21 February 1923. The outpouring of respect and affection from former students and colleagues must have assured Stone that his years there had not been a waste, but he had no regrets about leaving. "Long tenure as the head of any institution," he wrote, "tends to emphasize [an individual's] faults and minimize his strong points, and in that situation a change is good both for the individual and the institution."

Stone had little chance to enjoy his lucrative salary as head of the litigation department at Sullivan & Cromwell. The various scandals that broke out shortly after President Warren G. Harding's death soon tarred the attorney general, Harry M. Daugherty, and forced his resignation. President Calvin Coolidge needed someone who would not only oversee the various investigations, but would also be perceived by the public as above reproach. Although Stone was at that time not well known outside legal and academic circles, Coolidge had met him and wanted him for the job. On 1 April 1924 Stone left Wall Street to become attorney general of the United States.

He realized his first priority would be dismissing the hacks that Daugherty had appointed and replacing them with men of integrity. He ousted the notorious William J. Burns and then named the young J. Edgar Hoover as head of the Federal Bureau of Investigation (FBI). Aware of the threat that any federal police agency posed to a democratic society, Stone wanted the FBI to model itself on Scotland Yard, and he identified three key principles: the FBI had to be law-abiding, all appointees should be men of intelligence and some education, and agents should be thoroughly trained for their work.

The attorney general found his department confronted with a huge backlog of cases dating from various war measures, with little indication of which cases were current, in default, or resolved. Setting an example for his staff, Stone took an active role in the agency, including arguing cases in the federal courts.

Stone appreciated the free hand the president gave him to run the Justice Department and reciprocated in the fall of 1924 by campaigning for Coolidge's reelection. He had nothing against the Democratic candidate, former solicitor general John W. Davis (1873–1955), but considered the Progressive party candidate, Robert M. La Follette (1855–1925) of Wisconsin, a radical whose election would "disrupt the fundamental organization and administration of many of the national institutions." La Follette's proposal to allow Congress to reenact a law that the Supreme Court had declared unconstitutional appalled the basically con-

servative Stone, who saw the idea as threatening the integrity of the judiciary as well as the separation of powers. Although he did not care for politics, he told his sons, the campaign had been worthwhile, and if Coolidge wanted him to stay at the Justice Department, he would do so.

Shortly after the election, Associate Justice Joseph McKenna informed Coolidge of his desire to retire from the Court, and on 5 January 1925 the president sent Stone's name to the Senate. The nomination was greeted with near-universal approval, although at the Senate hearings some objections were raised that his connection to Wall Street would make him a judicial tool of Corporate interests. Stone appeared briefly before the Judiciary Committee, the first nominee ever to do so, to defend his record as attorney general. On 5 February the Senate confirmed him by a vote of 71 to 6. Stone took the oath of associate justice of the U.S. Supreme Court on 2 March 1925.

Although in a speech delivered less than a year earlier, Stone had declared, "I make no pretense to being an authority on the Constitution," his work as a teacher and lawyer had on occasion involved questions of constitutional law. Aware of the ferment that had led La Follette to suggest a legislative override of judicial invalidation of a law, Stone believed the answer to lie in judicial self-restraint. He had, in fact, spelled out some of his ideas on the proper role of courts in a free society in a series of lectures given a decade earlier and then published as *Law and Its Administration* (1915). He felt that legislation should be given every presumption of constitutionality and wrote that "it is a salutary principle that the burden of establishing the unconstitutionality of a statute rests on him who assails it" (*Metropolitan Casualty Insurance Co. v. Brownell* [1935]).

Although it often takes a few years for new members of the Court to adjust and begin pulling their own weight, Stone settled in comfortably in a short period of time. Justice Louis D. Brandeis wrote approvingly of Stone's work within three months after the latter had taken his seat. In many ways, the work of an appellate judge fulfilled Stone as teaching had years earlier; it involved a search, not for a fixed rule of law, but for guiding principles. Like Brandeis, Stone was willing to look at nontraditional sources for information, a process that the realists had advocated when he had been dean at Columbia. In an address he gave to the American Bar Association in 1928, he said:

The questions which come to us are rooted in history and in the social and economic development of the nation. To grasp their significance our study must be extended beyond the examination of precedents and legal formulas, by reading and research in fields extra-legal, which nevertheless have an intimate relation to the genesis of legal rules we pronounce.

Once on the bench, despite fears that he would be just another conservative defending corporate interests, Stone allied himself with Brandeis and Oliver Wendell Holmes (1841–1935). Together, they constituted the Court's liberal faction that called for judicial restraint and deference to the legislative will in policy making. In fact, by 1929, Chief Justice William H. Taft somewhat rued his earlier enthusiasm for Stone. "He is a learned lawyer in many ways," Taft wrote, "but his judgments I do not altogether consider safe. He definitely has ranged himself with Brandeis and Holmes in a good many of our constitutional differences."

It would, however, be misleading to label Stone a liberal. He had, for example, little of the skepticism of Holmes, who deferred to majority will out of belief that reform could not succeed. Stone took legislation seriously and believed that the Court's proper role was to review statutes within the constitutional system. Neither did he have the passion for reform that often marked Brandeis's opinions. Stone, for example, refused to go along with either the majority in striking down a Florida tax that deliberately discriminated against chain stores or with Brandeis's dissent defending the tax (*Liggett v. Lee* [1933]). "I think you are too much an advocate of this particular legislation," Stone told his colleague. "I think our dissents are more effective if we take the attitude that we are concerned with power and not with the merits of its exercise." He then concurred with Justice Benjamin N. Cardozo's dissenting opinion, which condemned both the majority's flouting of the legislative prerogative as well as Brandeis's defense of the statute.

It was Stone's commitment to judicial restraint, not his political views, that made him increasingly uncomfortable in the 1930s as the "Four Horsemen"—Justices Pierce Butler (1866–1939), James C. McReynolds, George Sutherland and Willis Van Devanter—consistently attacked New Deal legislation because they disagreed with its wisdom. While federal and state governments attempted to cope with the unprecedented challenges of the depression, the Court's conservative bloc refused to even acknowledge the existence of economic distress, much less allow the government flexibility to meet the crisis. When the Court struck down the Agricultural Administration Act in 1936 (*United States v. Butler*), an impassioned Stone dissented, charging the majority with reading its own views into law, ignoring the wisdom of the legislature, and "torturing" the Constitution. He did not care for Franklin D. Roosevelt's Court-packing plan, but he well understood why the president suggested such a drastic measure.

In some ways Stone was a transitional figure in the modern Court. He believed in judicial restraint but also recognized the difference between economic policies and civil liberties. In cases involving economic legislation, absent a clear constitutional bar, he maintained that the courts should defer to the legislature. But when individual rights were at issue, the courts should play a protective role. In his opinion in *United States v. Carolene Products Co.* (1938), Stone noted that henceforth the Court would take a limited role in reviewing economic regulation. Yet he wrote in his famous Footnote 4 that "there may be a narrower scope

for operation of this presumption of constitutionality when legislation appears on its face to be within a specific prohibition of the Constitution, such as those of the first ten Amendments, which are deemed equally specific when held to be embraced within the 14th." In other words, the courts would not presume constitutionality when legislatures curtailed free speech, impeded the political process, or impinged upon the rights of the accused.

If any doubts remained as to Stone's commitment to protecting individual liberties, they should have been laid to rest by his dissent in *Minersville School District v. Gobitis* (1940). The majority, speaking through Justice Felix Frankfurter, upheld a Pennsylvania law mandating that public school students salute the flag. Frankfurter dismissed the First Amendment claim by the Jehovah's Witnesses and, citing judicial restraint, said the courts should not second-guess the legislature. Stone wrote a powerful dissent, one that within a few years would be endorsed by a majority of the Court when it reversed the *Gobitis* decision (*West Virginia State Board of Education v. Barnette* [1943]).

On 2 June 1941 Chief Justice Charles B. Hughes retired, and President Roosevelt named Stone to succeed him. Some people thought the appointment a reward for his defense of New Deal measures, but as the justice himself noted, "Washington is under no illusion that I am a New Dealer." In fact, Felix Frankfurter and others had argued that, with war approaching, it would be a gesture of national unity if the Democratic Roosevelt appointed the Republican Stone to the center chair. When the Senate gathered to vote on the nomination on 27 June 1941, Senator George William Norris, who had opposed Stone's initial appointment to the Court sixteen years earlier, rose to admit his error and to praise him, urging quick confirmation. The Senate unanimously agreed.

Despite expectations that Stone would make a great chief justice, his record is disappointing. This is all the more ironic because Roosevelt soon filled the bench with men who nominally shared Stone's views on judicial restraint and deference to the legislature. Stone had differed from his conservative, property-oriented colleagues in the 1920s and 1930s because he had seen the judicial role as neutral, with careful adherence to craft and precision in framing opinions. He had no more approved of some of the reform legislation than they, but he rejected the view of the judiciary as a superlegislature "correcting" the errors of the elected branch.

Now his colleagues on the left, inspired in part by Stone's own Footnote 4 and his *Gobitis* dissent, wanted to charge forward and use the power of the judiciary to protect individual liberties from legislative interference. However, while Stone believed that individual rights deserved greater judicial protection than property rights, he did not consider them absolute. He viewed law as an evolutionary process, changing in the orderly manner embodied by the common law. Stone had come to accept social justice as a legitimate factor in appellate judging, but even with a more socially aware law one had to move carefully, allowing the processes of the law to make delicate adjustments between competing values. He would allow the courts and judges great flexibility but not unbounded use of power. Narrow holdings, allowing incremental advances, struck him as the best way to accommodate changing needs.

These views had not sat well with the Four Horsemen; neither did they sit well with the activist wing of the Roosevelt court—Hugo Black, William O. Douglas, and Frank Murphy. In the five years that Stone occupied the center chair, the Court lost any sense of unity; split votes, with multiple opinions, became the norm. He did manage to impose some unity on war-related issues, such as Japanese internment (*Hirabayashi v. United States* [1943]) and sabotage (*Ex parte Quirin* [1942]), but he never seemed to be able to "mass the Court" as chief justices Taft and Hughes had done. Stone had objected to Hughes's tight control of the conference, which had precluded much discussion on individual cases; so as chief Stone allowed almost unlimited discussion, which soon had the justices bogged down in what one described as endless talk.

The demands of the job, as well as the constant refereeing among the justices, took their toll. In early June 1945 he described himself as "tied to my oar like a galley slave and pulling for dear life to keep from going down with the stream," but he denied rumors of retirement. In his dissent in *Girouard v. United States* (1946), regarding the power of Congress to deny citizenship to conscientious objectors, he concluded, "It is not the function of this Court to disregard the will of Congress in the exercise of its constitutional power." A few minutes after reading this opinion, Stone suffered a stroke; he died later that day from a massive cerebral hemorrhage.

• The Stone papers are in the Manuscript Division of the Library of Congress. Stone's articles and speeches are in numerous law reviews, but of especial significance regarding his jurisprudential views, in addition to *Law and Its Administration*, are "Fifty Years' Work of the Supreme Court," *American Bar Association Journal* 53 (1928): 259–81, and "The Common Law in the United States," *Harvard Law Review* 50 (1936): 4–26. Stone authorized a biography, Alpheus T. Mason, *Harlan Fiske Stone: Pillar of the Law* (1956). See also Samuel J. Konefsky, *Chief Justice Stone and the Supreme Court* (1945). Among the many articles about him, see Noel T. Dowling, "The Methods of Mr. Justice Stone in Constitutional Cases," *Columbia Law Review* 41 (1941): 1160–89; Richard A. Givens, "Chief Justice Stone and the Developing Function of Judicial Review," *Virginia Law Review* 47 (1961): 1321–65; and Herbert Wechsler, "Stone and the Constitution," *Columbia Law Review* 45 (1946): 764–800. A front-page obituary is in the *New York Times*, 23 Apr. 1946.
MELVIN I. UROFSKY

STONE, Horatio (25 Dec. 1808–25 Aug. 1875), sculptor and lecturer, was born in Jackson, Washington County, New York, the son of Reuben Stone and Nancy Fairchild, farmers. He began wood sculpting at an early age, but his father preferred him to be about his farm chores. As a result Stone left home abruptly and didn't communicate with his parents for many years. He studied and practiced medicine in New York between 1841 and 1847. Little else is known about his formal education.

Stone moved to Washington, D.C., in 1848, not to pursue medicine, but to make his living as a sculptor. While in the city, he accepted sculpture commissions and taught art. Stone had several studios, including a room in the basement of the U.S. Capitol. He was instrumental in organizing the Washington Art Association and served as the only president during its four-year existence in the 1850s, often speaking or lecturing on the group's goals. The association was instrumental in persuading artists to petition Congress to recognize and support American artists, and it was successful in ending the rule of Captain Montgomery C. Meigs over the selection of artists. The association's efforts resulted in President James Buchanan's appointment of a Federal Art Commission in 1859 and the incorporation of a National Gallery of Art the following year.

During the American Civil War Stone served as a contract surgeon for the Union forces beginning in September 1862 and ending three years later. He was assigned to Washington, Baltimore, New York, and a fort in Delaware during this period.

Stone's first commercial success with sculpture had been his busts. His bust of Chief Justice Roger B. Taney (1854), now in the U.S. Supreme Court building, and his bust of Thomas Hart Benton, the Missouri senator, won the medal of the Maryland Institute in 1857. In August 1856 Congress had authorized Stone to proceed with a seven-foot-high model of a full-length statue of John Hancock, *President of Congress*, for which he was to be paid $500. The model was satisfactory, and in late January 1857 the appropriate congressional committee proposed "$5,500 to Dr. Stone for his statue." Payments were made to Stone between 1857 and 1861; the statue was completed in 1861. Today the Hancock statue stands at the foot of the grand staircase on the west side of the Capitol's Senate wing.

Congress paid Stone $10,000 for a full-length statue of Alexander Hamilton, first secretary of the treasury. From 1866 to 1868 Stone worked in Italy, completing the pedestal in Rome in 1868; it was engraved with an allegorical theme. The Hamilton statue now stands in the Rotunda of the Capitol, placed there in 1868.

In 1871 Stone produced three bronze vases, titled *Republic*, *Freedom*, and *Ecce Homo*. He published a booklet in 1874 describing these last two, which had been exhibited in the U.S. Capitol since 1871; Stone hoped to attract buyers for them.

Stone's statue of Edward Dickinson Baker, the Oregon senator killed at Balls Bluff, Virginia, in 1861 while serving as a major general in the Union army, is in the Capitol's Hall of Columns. Its purchase was authorized by Congress in 1873, notwithstanding an unfavorable report from the Joint Committee on the Library, which had jurisdiction over such matters. The report did not question Senator Baker's qualities or criticize the model, but it suggested that once Congress started memorializing its members in sculpture or painting, it would be difficult to discontinue the practice. Congress, however, overruled the committee. This statue also cost $10,000.

Stone had always had grand plans and visions, frequently making models for significant projects. He made models of Samuel F. B. Morse for a proposed (but never built) *National Telegraph Memorial Monument* for the city of Washington, D.C., and he also made models for statues of Admiral Farragut (the commission instead went to Vinnie Ream Hoxie) and of Doctor William Harvey (for New York's Central Park).

In April 1875 Stone made an overland journey from Washington to California to speak before the California Academy of Sciences in San Francisco. He was elected a member of the academy at that meeting, and this discourse was published in San Francisco the same year. He returned to Washington and sailed again for Italy in May 1875. On his arrival he set to work on the Baker statue. Stone had been involved with the project since 1861, when it was first proposed, and he had executed a statuette as early as 1867. He died three months after his arrival in Carrara, Italy, and was buried there. He had never married. The statue of Baker arrived in Washington, D.C., a year later.

In *Ten Years in Washington* (1873), Mary C. Ames characterized Stone as "a pale, dissatisfied, restless man, whose hands were busy with uncongenial tasks, but whose brain was haunted with noble ideals, to which he was powerless to give form or substance. Opportunity, the ultimate test of all power, came to him" in the form of the *Hamilton* commission. Stone is remembered primarily for the *Alexander Hamilton* statue in the U.S. Capitol Rotunda, seen by several million visitors each year. His activities with the Washington Art Association changed the composition of the Capitol's art, and the fruits of his work in establishing the National Gallery of Art are enjoyed by patrons to this day.

• Stone's estate papers are in the National Archives under Record Group 21-7688-0 Series. Stone wrote several volumes, including *Freedom* (1864), a small collection of poems. One of the poems from that volume, "Eleutheria," was set to music. In 1857 he published his *Inaugural Address . . . and an Address on National Art* upon assuming the presidency of the Washington Art Association. *Addresses before the Washington Art Association* (1858) contains the lectures delivered at that group's annual meeting. *Ecce Homo and Freedom* (1874) was a pamphlet describing two of his bronze vases. *Unity of the Arts* (1875) is the speech Stone delivered before the California Academy of Sciences. Charles E. Fairman, *Art and Artists of the Capitol of the United States of America* (1927), is also a good source. There is a Charles Loring Elliott portrait (1845) of Stone, owned by the Corcoran Gallery of Art. An important source is Martha Morris, "Horatio Stone (1808–1875), Nineteenth Century American Sculptor" (master's thesis, George Washington Univ., 1966), which includes the best available list of Stone's work. Obituaries are in the *New York Times*, 22 Sept. 1875 and 24 Sept. 1875.

PHILIP H. VILES, JR.

STONE, I. F. (24 Dec. 1907–18 June 1989), journalist, was born Isidor Feinstein in Philadelphia, Pennsylvania, the son of Bernard Feinstein, a storekeeper, and Katherine Novak. In 1914 the Feinsteins moved to Haddonfield, New Jersey, where at the age of fourteen Stone singlehandedly produced *The Progress*, a short-lived newspaper championing the League of Nations while opposing racism and intolerant religious fundamentalism.

Before leaving high school, through voracious reading, Stone had discovered his "scouts of civilization"—independent, inquiring minds such as Socrates, Aristotle, Copernicus, Descartes, Spencer, Darwin, and Woodrow Wilson. By the time he enrolled at the University of Pennsylvania in 1925, Stone, whose birth language was Yiddish, had acquired Hebrew and Latin, as well as an enthusiasm for Jefferson, Marx, and Kropotkin.

When Stone left the university in 1927 he had a semester of Greek and a conviction that reading the sources in the original was the best road to truth. He had also written for two Philadelphia papers, the *Inquirer* and the *Record*, the latter owned by J. David Stern, a believer in investigative journalism who became Stone's sponsor. Joining Stern's *Camden (N.J.) Evening Courier*, Stone took up editorial writing.

In 1929 Stone married Esther Roisman; they had three children. In 1931 Stern made him an editorial writer for the *Philadelphia Record*. In his editorials Stone, then a socialist, argued that conventional liberalism was too weak-willed to save the depression-racked nation. Though advocating central planning and control, he criticized Franklin D. Roosevelt's "fascist" tendencies. In 1933 Stone became chief editorial writer for Stern's strongly pro-Roosevelt *New York Post*, eventually concluding that Franklin Roosevelt was America's best defense against runaway capitalism.

Stone remained at the *Post* for five years. Worried by the anti-Semitism flowing into the United States from Nazi Germany (and having written for radical publications as Geoffrey or Abelard Stone), in 1937 he changed his name legally to I. F. Stone. His first book, *The Court Disposes* (1937), supported Roosevelt's unsuccessful plan for enlarging the Supreme Court to counteract its "reactionary" core.

In 1938 Stone became associate editor of *The Nation*; in 1940 he moved to Washington, D.C., as its capitol editor, remaining in that post until 1946. His second book, *Business as Usual* (1941), argued that American military unpreparedness was engineered by contractors who arranged scarcities to increase their profits. Details that emerged after the war tended to support Stone's conclusions.

While still at *The Nation*, in 1942 Stone became a reporter and columnist for Ralph Ingersoll's liberal New York newspaper *PM*. *Underground to Palestine* (1946; rev. ed., 1978) expanded a *PM* series based on Stone's travels from the "ghost town" of Vienna through the British naval blockade of Palestine with 1,015 "illegal" Jewish immigrants, death-camp survivors from Eastern Europe. He concluded, "If those ships were illegal, so was the Boston Tea Party." In 1948 followed *This Is Israel*, another pro-Zionist book. Yet by 1967 Stone was enraging the American "Israel lobby" by asserting the need for a separate Arab Palestine.

After *PM* closed, in 1949 Stone joined the liberal *New York Daily Compass*. Upon its demise in 1952 in an era he described as "haunted" by the twin specters of Cold War abroad and suppression of dissent at home, Stone, financed by a small pension, his savings, a small loan, and (at first) 5,000 subscribers at $5 yearly, began *I. F. Stone's Weekly*, a four-page newsletter entirely written by Stone. His wife handled most of the publication's business.

Stone was grateful for constitutional guarantees of free speech through continued second-class mailing privileges during such an era. He dubbed himself "an anachronism, an independent capitalist" in that he paid his bills promptly, "just like a bourgeois" and was even one up on Benjamin Franklin—"I do not accept advertising."

The *Weekly*, eventually claiming a circulation of 66,000, was Stone's passport to journalistic fame. His subscribers, mostly journalists and other opinion-makers, came to rely on the conclusions reached by Stone's eclectic mind, conclusions based on the information he mined from the ten newspapers and countless official documents he read daily. He wrote, "All the information is available to the public if you know where to look."

Stone's methods derived in part from his near-deafness. Often unsure what speakers and witnesses had said, he had come to rely on transcripts. Standing apart from official Washington and its press conferences—he noted that bureaucracy hated independent journalists—Stone compared data, uncovered inconsistencies, and sought the truth behind them.

In *The Hidden History of the Korean War* (1952; rev. ed., 1969) Stone argued, largely from Commerce Department documents (he said bureaucracies published so much that the truth was bound to leak through somewhere), that the war had been engineered by the United States, South Korea, and nationalist China for their mutual benefit.

Stone's *Weekly* attacked politicians who abused power, in March 1953 accusing the Red-hunting senator Joseph McCarthy of wanting "to create a kind of dictatorship for himself within the framework of established government." Stone fought the era's surge toward loyalty oaths and restrictive immigration laws, as well as the excesses of the Federal Bureau of Investigation and the Central Intelligence Agency, yet his publications were never officially challenged. He later remarked that in an era of blacklisting he had been too small to blacklist.

The Truman Era (1953) was the first of Stone's books based on *Weekly* articles; five subsequent books of compilations underlined what James Newman called "the positive contribution he made to an understanding of history . . . while it was unfolding." In

1956 Stone, who had never made a secret of his support for causes favored by the prewar Communist-led Popular Front, visited the Soviet Union. His conclusion that "this is not a good society, and it is not led by honest men" cost him 400 left-leaning subscribers.

In 1957–1958 Stone caught the U.S. government lying about the range of detectability of atomic testing, one of many causes of international distrust during the Cold War. In 1964 he uncovered enough inconsistencies in testimony regarding the Tonkin Gulf incident, which brought the United States into the Vietnam War, to undermine government claims of communist provocation. His circulation widened, and his discoveries accelerated internal opposition to the war. Stone's 1964 speech to the radical Students for a Democratic Society (SDS) was called by the SDS leader the cause of the 1965 pro–civil rights, antiwar march on Washington.

In 1965, nearly blind, Stone underwent eye surgery. After a first heart attack, his newsletter became biweekly in 1968. Continuing pain forced him to close it in 1971. Another operation improved his hearing. Stone continued to write for *The Nation* and the *New York Review of Books*.

In 1972 Stone received the A. J. Liebling award for "unrelenting investigation of governmental power." A 1973 documentary film by Jerry Bruck, Jr., *I. F. Stone's Weekly*, was praised at the Cannes Film Festival and gained wide circulation in universities and colleges. In 1974, the year investigative reporting by the *Washington Post* helped end Richard Nixon's presidency, Stone was resident scholar at American University. In 1975 he received the Eleanor Roosevelt Peace Award and, finally, his B.A. from the University of Pennsylvania.

The Trial of Socrates (1988), part of a projected series on the history of free speech, was Stone's last and most financially rewarding work. Stone taught himself classical Greek so that he could read the original sources and "tell the Athenian side of the story." Calling Plato's dialogues on Socrates tragic drama, Stone charged the gadfly Socrates with being an elitist who contrived his own death: he "needed the hemlock as Jesus needed the Crucifixion, to fulfill a mission." Stone died in Boston.

Stone believed in the fundamental power of truth. He agreed with James Madison and Thomas Jefferson that a free press was the corrective, and if necessary, the scourge of government. Biographer Robert C. Cottrell concluded that Stone's life proved that "the journalist could stand as an intellectual, the intellectual as a political activist, and that the political activist could act as the conscience of his chosen profession."

• Stone's papers and other original source material relating to Stone can be found at Boston University, Harvard University, Radcliffe College, the New York Public Library, the State Historical Society of Wisconsin, and Yale University, and in the presidential libraries of Harry Truman, Dwight Eisenhower, John F. Kennedy, and Lyndon Johnson. Andrew Patner, *I. F. Stone: A Portrait* (1988), is a series of wide-ranging interviews with Stone. Other books compiled from

Stone's *Weekly* articles are *The Haunted Fifties* (1963), *In a Time of Torment* (1968), *Polemics and Prophecies* (1970), *The Killings at Kent State* (1971), and Neil Middleton, ed., *I. F. Stone's Weekly* (1973). A useful biography is Robert C. Cottrell, *Izzy: A Biography* (1992). Useful obituaries are in *The Guardian* (London), 19 June 1989, and *The New York Times*, 19 June 1989, followed for the next several days by a series of appreciations.

JAMES ROSS MOORE

STONE, Irving (14 July 1903–26 Aug. 1989), author, was born in San Francisco, California, the son of Charles Tannenbaum (sometimes spelled Tennenbaum), a store clerk, and Pauline Rosenberg. His parents divorced when he was seven, and by his senior year in high school his mother had remarried. Stone legally changed his surname to that of his stepfather. Stone said that his passion for reading derived from his mother, who instilled in him early the idea that education was the way to advance in life. As a young man Stone fulfilled a promise to his mother to attend the University of California at Berkeley. Supporting himself by playing the saxophone at dances, picnics, and parties, he majored in political science and economics, earning his B.A. in 1923.

After completing an M.A. in economics at the University of Southern California (1924), Stone returned to Berkeley (1924–1926) and finished most of the work for a Ph.D. in economics before losing interest in and abandoning his dissertation. Having been a lecturer at both schools while pursuing his graduate work, Stone decided to become a playwright, going off to Paris to write plays, none of which was successful. During this time, however, Stone was introduced to the paintings of Vincent Van Gogh, who then was little known, and finding them strikingly fresh, he decided to make Van Gogh the subject of a book. Stone first wrote several detective novels, using the proceeds to finance research on Van Gogh for six months in several European countries.

In the early 1930s he returned to the United States, settling in New York's Greenwich Village, where over the course of six months he wrote four drafts of *Lust for Life*, a novel based on the life of Van Gogh. Stone hoped to appeal to a wide audience by writing what he would later call a "bio-history," a biographical novel rather than a traditional biography. His book, however, was rejected by seventeen publishers. Jean Factor, his future wife, helped him prune the long book, and Longmans Green and Company accepted it in 1934. *Lust for Life* immediately appeared on most bestseller lists. Both the new career and his 1934 marriage that grew out of this project lasted for the rest of his life. Jean Factor also remained his permanent editor. The couple had two children.

During the rest of the 1930s and 1940s Stone wrote both nonfiction works and more biographical novels. In 1941 Doubleday, which became Stone's permanent publisher, published the nonfiction biography *Clarence Darrow for the Defense*, about the famous attorney who fought legal battles on behalf of unpopular causes

and clients. One of Stone's most successful books of the 1940s, on the *New York Times* bestseller list for thirteen months, was the biographical novel *Immortal Wife* (1944), his first effort to focus on the life of a woman, Jessie Benton Frémont, the wife of nineteenth-century explorer John Charles Frémont.

Among the works that Stone produced in the 1950s were the biographical novel *The President's Lady* (1951), about Andrew Jackson and his wife Rachel, and the biographical novel *Love Is Eternal* (1954), about Mary Todd and Abraham Lincoln. After four-and-a-half years of research and writing, Stone's biographical novel *The Agony and the Ecstasy* appeared in 1961. Its subject was Michelangelo Buonarroti, the Renaissance painter, sculptor, and architect, and it was one of the more popular books of Stone's career.

In the 1970s and 1980s Stone turned his attention to two men he believed to be pivotal, along with Karl Marx and Albert Einstein, in shaping the modern world. *The Passions of the Mind*, a biographical novel about Sigmund Freud, appeared in 1971. *The Origin* was published in 1980 and was a biographical novel focusing on Charles Darwin, his voyage on the *Beagle*, and what evolved thereafter. In *Depths of Glory* (1985) Stone returned to an interest with which he began his career as an author of biographical novels, focusing on another artist, Camille Pissaro.

Some of Stone's books reached even wider audiences through movie adaptations. In 1953 Charlton Heston and Susan Hayward starred as Andrew Jackson and his wife in *The President's Lady*. The 1956 movie *Lust for Life* starred Kirk Douglas, as Van Gogh, and Anthony Quinn, who won an Academy Award portraying Gauguin. In 1965 Charlton Heston and Rex Harrison appeared in *The Agony and the Ecstasy*.

Throughout his career Stone believed in careful research, and for his biographical novels he attempted to immerse himself as deeply as possible in information about his subjects and identify closely with them in order to achieve an accurate blend of fiction and fact. For his research into Michelangelo, for example, Stone worked as a sculptor's apprentice and at a quarry at Carrara as Michelangelo had done.

In addition to writing, Stone lectured at several universities, including Indiana University, Bloomington, in 1948 (as visiting lecturer in creative writing), the University of Washington, Seattle, in 1961 (as visiting lecturer in creative writing), the University of Southern California in 1966 (as lecturer in writing biography and biographical novels), and California State Colleges in 1966 (as lecturer). Although he never completed his Ph.D. dissertation, Stone was awarded several honorary doctorates, including one from the University of California at Berkeley (1968). He was involved in a variety of arts groups and was the founder of the Academy of American Poets (1962).

Criticism of Stone's work has not been universally enthusiastic. Most reviewers agree that his research is thorough and careful, but some feel also that the result is neither good history nor good fiction. Some find the amount of historical detail woven into his books a bit dull. Another concern has been that Stone's intense identification with his heroes may interfere with his objectivity and that he seems to idealize his subjects.

While it may not be clear yet how permanent Stone's literary contribution will be, there is no doubt that he has so far remained popular with a worldwide general audience always eager to buy his books, which have been translated into more than thirty languages. And he has been credited with making details about significant historical and cultural figures such as Van Gogh, Freud, Darwin, and others accessible to large numbers of readers. Irving Stone died in Los Angeles.

• Stone's personal papers and manuscripts are to be housed at the Bancroft Library University of California, Berkeley. Important nonfiction works not mentioned above are *Dear Theo: The Autobiography of Vincent Van Gogh* (1937), Van Gogh's letters to his brother edited by Stone and his wife; *They Also Ran: The Story of the Men Who Were Defeated for the Presidency* (1945); *We Speak for Ourselves: A Self-Portrait of America* (1950), a collection of autobiographical excerpts written by famous Americans; *Lincoln: A Contemporary Portrait* (1962), edited with Allan Nevins; and, *I, Michelangelo, Sculptor* (1962), letters edited by Stone and his wife. Important biographical novels not included above are *Sailor on Horseback* (1938), about Jack London; *Adversary in the House* (1947), about Eugene V. Debs; *Those Who Love* (1965), about Abigail and John Adams; and *The Greek Treasure* (1975), about Henry and Sophia Schliemann's search for ancient Troy. In addition, *The Irving Stone Reader* was published in 1963, and *Irving Stone: Three Complete Novels* (*Lust for Life, The Agony and the Ecstasy,* and *The President's Lady*) appeared in 1981. Lewis Stieg, *Irving Stone: A Bibliography* (1973), provides a thorough list of Stone's writings up to the early 1970s. Information about Stone can be found in Joseph Henry Jackson's introduction to *The Irving Stone Reader* (1963); Roy Newquist, *Counterpoint* (1964); and Stone's long, colorful biographical sketch in *Contemporary Authors Autobiography Series*, vol. 3 (1986). Obituaries are in the *Chicago Tribune*, the *Los Angeles Times*, the *New York Times*, and the *Washington Post*, all 28 Aug. 1989, and the *Times* (London), 29 Aug. 1989.

ALAN KELLY

STONE, John Augustus (15 Dec. 1800–29 May 1834), actor and playwright, was born in Concord, Massachusetts, the son of Joshua Stone, a cabinetmaker, and Sarah Avery. Little is known of Stone's childhood, but by the time he was twenty he had begun a career as an actor, making his debut in the popular melodrama *Douglas* at the Washington Garden Theatre in Boston. The role he played in that production was Old Norval, an odd choice for a young man, but it was in the roles of eccentric comics and old men that Stone made his mark as an actor. Although he never attained star status, he was regularly employed and apparently quite popular as a character actor, first in Boston, after 1822 in New York, and by 1831 in Philadelphia. Early in his acting career, in 1821 he married the actress Amelia (Greene) Legge, who from that time on was known on stage as Mrs. Stone. The couple had two boys, Christopher Lucius and Henry, both of whom followed their parents into acting careers.

Stone's work as an actor was overshadowed by his skill as a dramatist. He commenced writing for the stage in 1824, when his first play, *Restoration; or, The Diamond Cross*, was performed at the Chatham Garden Theatre, New York, on 4 November. He published *Tancred; or, The Siege of Antioch* in 1827, but apparently the play, which was set in 1097 during the first crusade, was never produced. *Metamora; or, The Last of the Wampanoags*, the play on which Stone's reputation is based, was produced two years later. Stone wrote *Metamora* in response to the first playwriting contest offered in the United States, by the nation's leading star, Edwin Forrest, who was looking specifically for an American Indian role. Fourteen plays were entered and judged by a committee of distinguished American literati chaired by William Cullen Bryant, and Stone was proclaimed the winner. The play, based on King Philip's War in 1675–1676, opened on 15 December 1829 at the Park Theatre. Although reviews were mixed, Forrest's powerful performance as the fierce, yet sensitive and just "noble savage" and Stone's well-structured mix of action, pathos, and spectacle left the audience overwhelmed. The last lines of the play, Metamora's dying curse, display the mixture of poetry and pathos in the hero: "May your graves and the graves of your children be in the path the red man shall trace! And may the wolf and panther howl o'er your fleshless bones, fit banquet for the destroyers! Spirits of the grave, I come! But the curse of Metamora stays with the white man! I die! My wife! My Queen! My Nahmeokee!" (Moody, *Dramas*, p. 226). *Metamora* remained in Forrest's repertoire for forty years as one of his most popular and lucrative vehicles. Ironically, this play, which earned thousands for Forrest (in one week it grossed $3,928 for six performances), secured only the contest prize of $500 for Stone. It ensured its author a place in the history of American drama, however, because of its immense popularity, because it inspired a host of other Indian plays during the antebellum years, and because it was a cut above its kind.

Metamora marked the summit of Stone's career as a playwright, but he wrote several dramas after it. In 1831 three of his works were produced. *Tancred, King of Sicily; or, The Archives of Palermo* was performed at the Park Theatre, New York, on 16 March 1831. Diarist Philip Hone found the play "eloquent in language and interesting in action" (Nevins, vol. 1, p. 39). *The Demoniac; or, The Prophet's Bride* played the Bowery Theatre, New York, on 12 April 1831. Neither of these pieces has survived, but Stone's extensive revision of James Kirke Paulding's *The Lion of the West* opened at the Park Theatre on 14 November 1831. James Henry Hackett, the popular comic actor, wanted the central role of Colonel Nimrod Wildfire (a character styled after Davy Crockett) beefed up, and Stone obliged. This version of the play was performed successfully by Hackett during the next two years. In 1833, however, the actor commissioned British playwright W. B. Bernard to do yet another revision, called *The Kentuckian*, which Hackett used for the next twenty years. In 1833 Stone entered and won another of Forrest's play contests with *The Ancient Briton*, the historical tragedy of Brigantius, who, in league with Queen Boadicea, subjugates Britain to avenge his wife's death. The "rugged bosom" and "sinewy arms" of the hero would seem to have made the play a fine vehicle for Forrest's muscular acting style, but it received only one performance.

Stone's next play, *The Knight of the Golden Fleece; or, The Yankee in Spain*, was also a vehicle, this time for George Handel Hill, a very different kind of actor from Forrest. Also known as "Yankee" Hill, this actor was perhaps the most popular in a long line of players who interpreted the Yankee character, a comic American bumpkin who was not usually successful with women but who often had a shrewd business sense and who could be instrumental, intentionally or not, in unraveling the plot. Stone's play opened at the Park Theatre on 10 September 1834, was repeated several times during its first season, and held the stage for fifteen years after, largely because of the popularity of its star.

Stone wrote two other plays, which were performed in Charleston, South Carolina, *Fauntleroy; or, The Fatal Forgery* and *La Roque, the Regicide*, but little is known of the subject matter or the dates of performance of either one. Still another play, *Toureton*, has been attributed to Stone, but no more is known than the title. Stone probably wrote eleven plays, two of which won the prestigious Forrest contest, and two others of which were requested by other stars. Despite this honorable record, however, Walter Meserve points out that the author, like most antebellum playwrights, did not fare well in the theater. It was customary and perfectly legal at the time for actors to buy scripts outright. While Forrest's contests undoubtedly encouraged writers like Stone, the prizes hardly rewarded the playwrights. As a result, Stone, who made only a journeyman's wages as an actor, earned far less as a writer. This lack of reward certainly kept him in poverty and could have contributed to the ill health, despondence, and, as James Rees noted, "incipient insanity" (p. 98) that caused him to take his own life in 1834 by jumping from the Spruce Street Wharf in Philadelphia into the Schuylkill River. Newspapers reported the suicide and mourned his death, and Forrest, who had often bought Stone clothes and paid his bills during his life, also erected a stone on his grave, which read: "To the Memory of John Augustus Stone, Author of Metamora, by His Friend Edwin Forrest." Stone is remembered for that single play, which, although subjected to burlesque in John Brougham's 1847 *Met-a-Mora; or, The Last of the Pollywogs* and again in 1990 as a portion of Richard Nelson's play *Two Shakespearean Actors*, has retained an important position in the history of American drama.

• Sketchy details of Stone's life appear in the biographies of Edwin Forrest by James Rees, *The Life of Edwin Forrest* (1874); William Rounseville Alger, *Life of Edwin Forrest, the American Tragedian* (1877); and Richard Moody, *Edwin Forrest, First Star of the American Stage* (1960). Moody combines biographical information with critical comment in his introduction to *Metamora* in *Dramas from the American Theatre, 1762–1909* (1966). Other critical assessments of Stone's work can be found in Arthur Hobson Quinn, *A History of American Drama from the Beginning to the Civil War* (1923), and Walter Meserve, *An Emerging Entertainment: The Drama of the American People to 1828* (1977) and *Heralds of Promise: The Drama of the American People during the Age of Jackson, 1829–1849* (1986). Production information is provided in J. S. Ireland, *Records of the New York Stage*, vol. 1 (1867); G. C. D. Odell, *Annals of the New York Stage*, vol. 3 (1928); and Allan Nevins, ed., *The Diary of Philip Hone* (2 vols., 1927). Moody discusses the gradual discovery of the complete text of *Metamora* in "Lost and Found: The Fourth Act of *Metamora*," *American Literature* 34 (1963): 353–64. Stone's plays *Tancred* and *Metamora* are available on microprint in *Three Centuries of Drama: American* and in volume 14 of *America's Lost Plays* (1941).

JACK HRKACH

STONE, John Marshall (30 Apr. 1830–26 Mar. 1900), soldier and governor of Mississippi, was born in Milan, Gibson County, Tennessee, the son of Asher Stone and Judith Royall. When John was eleven, his father died, leaving his mother to support nine children. Stone's education was limited to only common schools as a consequence of the family's financial situation. He first worked as a teacher, then as a clerk on a Tennessee River steamboat that ran between the Ohio River and Eastport, Mississippi. In 1855 he settled in Eastport and was engaged with a business house. Four years later he moved to neighboring Iuka, where he served as station agent for the Memphis and Charleston Railroad.

At the outbreak of the Civil War, Stone helped raise a company of troops and was elected captain of the Iuka Rifles, which became Company K of the Second Mississippi Infantry. Stone led his company into battle at First Manassas, where, in their first test under fire, both captain and company acquitted themselves with courage. The Mississippians held their line against great odds but finally yielded to overwhelming numbers and rallied behind Thomas "Stonewall" Jackson's fresh troops. In April 1862, when the regiment was reorganized, Stone was elected colonel. He led the regiment in the Seven Days' battles and earned praise from his division commander for the manner in which he "skillfully handled" his troops. Colonel Stone continued his creditable performance at Second Manassas, South Mountain, and Antietam. On the bloody field at Antietam he was severely wounded in action near Dunker Church. The following year, on the first day of battle at Gettysburg, he was wounded in the side by a piece of shell.

In the spring of 1864 Colonel Stone commanded the brigade in the battle of the Wilderness, during which action his troops heroically staved off disaster by holding firm against overwhelming numbers. Fighting again at Spotsylvania and Cold Harbor, he led his regiment in several actions around Petersburg and during the siege of that city. In January 1865 he returned home on furlough. On 12 April, the same day Robert

E. Lee's army stacked its arms at Appomattox Court House, while returning to his regiment, Stone was taken prisoner by Union cavalry near Salisbury, North Carolina. Sent to Camp Chase near Columbus, Ohio, he was later transferred to the prison on Johnson's Island in Lake Erie, where he remained until 25 July 1865.

As a soldier, Stone had exhibited great personal bravery and was known by those in the ranks as a "modest, unpretending man" who was "gallant and lionhearted." One Mississippian wrote, "Col. Stone's stainless blade flashed like a meteor in the fore front [sic] of battle, and he wrote his name upon his soldier's hearts as the bravest of the brave." Another member of the regiment echoed those sentiments, writing, "The thunders of battle never disturbed his equanimity, or brought the pallor of fear to his bronzed and bearded cheeks, but facing with dauntless heart the horrors of a hundred battle-fields, he nobly won his scars, with his face and front to the foe."

Upon his release, Stone returned to Iuka and railroad work. Entering politics in 1866, he was the first elected mayor of Iuka, then treasurer of Tishomingo County. In 1869 he was one of only a few Democratic candidates elected to the state senate, and he was reelected in 1873. In 1872 he married Mary Gilliam Coman. Their two children died in infancy, so the couple adopted three of Stone's nieces.

In 1876 Stone was chosen president pro tempore of the senate by acclamation. He became acting governor on 27 March of that year after the forced removal and resignation of Governor Adelbert Ames, a former Union general, and the impeachment of the black lieutenant governor, Alexander K. Davis. Elected to a four-year term as governor in 1877 by a vote of 97,727 to 47, Stone worked to return control of the state to the white population by abolishing the voting restrictions on former Confederate soldiers enacted by the Reconstruction government. He was an advocate of affordable education, and the Mississippi Agricultural and Mechanical College (now Mississippi State University), which he later served as president, was founded during Stone's administration in 1878. A state board of health was also established during his first term as governor.

Defeated for reelection, Stone returned to Iuka and agricultural pursuits but remained active in public life. In 1884 his successor as governor named him chairman of the state commission to regulate the railroad industry. He also supervised construction of the Tishomingo County Courthouse.

Elected again to the governorship in 1889 by a vote of 84,929 to 16 (showing the dominance of the Democratic party in the postwar South), Stone served from 1890 to 1896. He followed a hard money policy and worked to reduce taxes, cut state expenditures, and encourage railroad development. His policy of rigid economy helped to greatly reduce the state's debt. He also supported calling a state convention that drafted the enduring constitution of 1890. One contemporary wrote, "Among the governors of Mississippi there has been none more popular with the people, who stood higher in their confidence and esteem, or who was more able, zealous and conscientious in the discharge of official duties than the present incumbent, John M. Stone."

Governor Stone was also active in veterans' affairs. In 1895 he became one of the directors of the Vicksburg National Military Park Association, which secured the establishment of a national military park at Vicksburg in 1899. Nine months prior to his death he was named president of Mississippi Agricultural and Mechanical College. He died in Holly Springs.

• A small collection of Stone's papers is in the Mississippi Department of Archives and History. See also "John Marshall Stone," *Biographical and Historical Memoirs of Mississippi*, vol. 2 (1891); Dunbar Rowland, *Military History of Mississippi* (1908); Rowland, *Mississippi* (1907); and J. S. McNeily, "Climax and Collapse of Reconstruction in Mississippi, 1874–1896," *Publications of the Mississippi Historical Society* 12 (1912).

TERRENCE J. WINSCHEL

STONE, John Stone (24 Sept. 1869–20 May 1943), engineer and inventor, was born in Dover, Goochland County, Virginia, the only son of Charles Pomeroy Stone, a former brigadier general of volunteers in the Union army, and Annie Jeanie Stone. His parents gave the son both family names. In 1870 Stone's father accepted an appointment as chief of staff to Khedive Ismail in Egypt, where Stone received his early education. Private tutoring was supplemented by travel in Europe and the Middle East. In 1883, when Great Britain took over the administration of Egypt, Stone's family returned to the United States. Stone attended Columbia Grammar School in New York City for three years and between 1886 and 1888 was an undergraduate at the Columbia University School of Mines. From 1888 to 1890 he was a student at the Johns Hopkins University, where he specialized in mathematics and physics under Professor Henry A. Rowland but did not take a degree. During this period he became interested in the work of the English physicist and mathematician Oliver Heaviside and particularly in the application of Heaviside's ideas and methods to the problems of wired telephony. Stone left the university in 1890 and took a position with the mechanical department of the Bell Telephone Company in Boston, which was searching for solutions to the problems of long-distance telephone service, especially the attenuation and distortion that became evident when voice signals were transmitted over distances of more than a few hundred miles. Heaviside had made important contributions to the theoretical solution of these problems, and Stone's first significant work for Bell involved applying Heaviside's theories and techniques to the company's New York–Chicago line. This work was reflected in Stone's early patents, nos. 469,475 and 487,102, which were assigned to the Bell Telephone Company.

At the same time, Stone had also become interested in high frequency circuits, in the phenomenon of electrical resonance, and in the demonstration by Heinrich Hertz in 1887–1888 that electromagnetic waves could be transmitted through space without wires. These emerging interests encouraged him to resign from Bell in 1899 and enter business as an independent consultant. (Retained by the telephone company as an "advisory expert," he never cut his ties with telephone engineers and executives.) Work for a client on a radio direction-finding system encouraged Stone to develop his own system of wireless telegraphy. He took out an important patent on tuning (no. 714,756) on 2 December 1902, eighteen months before the granting of Marconi's famous "four-circuit" tuning patent (no. 763,772). Conflict between these two patents was finally decided in Stone's favor by the U.S. Supreme Court in 1943, shortly after Stone's death.

To advance his radio experiments and develop the hardware that would enable him to bid for contracts, in December 1900 Stone formed the Stone Wireless Telegraph Syndicate and set up experimental stations on the Charles River embankment in Cambridge, Massachusetts. From this grew the Stone Telegraph and Telephone Company, incorporated in July 1902 and financed by Boston venture capital. In establishing his radio system, Stone attempted to obtain precise tuning of both transmitter and receiver so that only a single wave was emitted and detected, which was difficult with the spark transmitters of the day. Stone placed his faith in multiple tuned circuits, two in the transmitter and two in the receiver, and stipulated that there should be "loose coupling" between each pair of such circuits. Other radio systems, such as the Marconi system, he believed, tried to radiate as much power as possible from the antenna. With this goal in view, these systems coupled tuned circuits tightly together with the result that each transmitter radiated, and each receiver received, not one signal but several. In particular, tight coupling resulted in a two-humped curve of resonance. Stone sought single-frequency tuning, not maximum power output, and a resonance curve with only one, not two, peaks.

Despite several tests and demonstrations of his system, Stone's company failed to win contracts from the U.S. Navy, then the principal purchaser of such equipment, and the company was dissolved in 1913. His roughly 100 radio patents were sold to Lee de Forest. Stone settled in New York City as an independent consultant on radio and telephone matters and rendered a valuable service by bringing de Forest's audion, or triode vacuum tube, to the attention of telephone engineers. Stone emphasized that the audion could serve not only as an amplifier or relay—the function originally of interest to the telephone company—but also as a generator of continuous waves and therefore as the basis for a new generation of radio transmitters. He married Sibyl Wilbur, a writer from Elmira, New York, in 1918; they had no children, and the marriage ended in divorce. In 1919 Stone moved to San Diego, California, where he continued to serve AT&T as a consulting engineer and to experiment with radio, particularly with short wave transmission and directional antennas.

Stone was active in the professional engineering societies of his day and in 1907 founded the Society of Wireless Telegraph Engineers, a predecessor of the Institute of Electrical and Electronics Engineers. He served as president of the Institute of Radio Engineers in 1914–1915 and was awarded its Medal of Honor in 1923. He died in San Diego.

Throughout his life Stone inspired loyalty in his employees and won the respect and affection of his professional colleagues. His close friend Lee de Forest noted his "quiet humor" and "somewhat Rabelesian [sic] spirit" and called attention to the elegant and precise language of his patent applications (de Forest, pp. 521–22). Stone's importance in his chosen field of communications engineering derives from his early insistence on the importance of tuning and selectivity, his use of advanced mathematical methods and insistence on precise measurements, and the fact that he was a valuable link between two communities of engineers: the older group that had grown up around telephone technology, and the newer group that formed around radio. An active member of both communities, he contributed to both technologies.

• The location of Stone's personal papers, if any have survived, is not known. A comprehensive if laudatory account of his life and work is George H. Clark, *The Life of John Stone Stone: Mathematician, Physicist, Electrical Engineer and Great Inventor* (1946), which also contains a list of his patents. A short account is in Orrin E. Dunlap, Jr., *Radio's 100 Men of Science* (1944), pp. 149–53. A thorough analysis of Stone's key patent on tuning is contained in U.S. Supreme Court, Cases Adjudged at October Term, 1942, *Marconi Wireless Telegraph Company of America v. United States* (decided 21 June 1943), especially the majority opinion written by Chief Justice Harlan Fiske Stone. An early account of the Stone wireless system is Louis Duncan, "The Stone Wireless Telegraph System," *Electrical World and Engineer*, 24 Oct. 1903, pp. 675–76. Stone's attempts to win contracts from the U.S. Navy are described in L. S. Howeth, *History of Communications-Electronics in the United States Navy* (1963); his role in diffusing knowledge of de Forest's audion is analyzed in Hugh G. J. Aitken, *The Continuous Wave: Technology and American Radio, 1900–1932* (1985). Obituaries by Lloyd Espenschied, Lee de Forest, and George H. Clark are in the *Proceedings of the Institute of Radio Engineers* 31 (1943): 463, 521–23.

HUGH G. J. AITKEN

STONE, John Timothy (7 Sept. 1868–27 June 1954), Presbyterian pastor and educator, was born in Stowe, Massachusetts, the son of Timothy Dwight Porter Stone, a Congregationalist minister, and Susan Margaret Dickson. He graduated from Amherst College in 1891. Following graduation from Auburn Theological Seminary in 1894, he served at the Olivet Presbyterian Church, Utica, New York, from 1894 to 1896. In 1895 he married Bessie Parsons; they had three daughters. He then was pastor at the Presbyterian Church in

Cortland, New York (1896–1900), and at Brown Memorial Presbyterian Church in Baltimore, Maryland (1900–1909).

Stone's major pastoral ministry was at Fourth Presbyterian Church in Chicago, Illinois, from 1909 to 1930. At Fourth Church, Stone concentrated on evangelism and increasing church membership. His strategy included sending out thirty or forty young businessmen to invite other young men in the neighborhood to become involved in the life and work of Fourth Church. Within five years after his arrival in Chicago, the membership of Fourth Church had increased from around 630 to about 1,300. Under his leadership, the congregation also built an edifice comparable to major cathedrals throughout the world. Gothic in design, the sanctuary provided seating for 1,400. The impressive complex also included a Sunday school building, a manse, a courtyard featuring a fountain, and a clubhouse equipped with a gymnasium, classrooms, and a dining hall. The building project was completed in May 1914 at a cost of around $740,000. In the same years that witnessed the construction of a new Fourth Presbyterian Church, Stone led his congregation to support the construction of two other church buildings, one for the Persian mission on West Huron Street and the other for the Bohemian mission in Lawndale.

During his tenure at Fourth Church, Stone served on various local and national boards including the Chicago Tract Society, the Presbyterian Hospital, and the Men and Religion Forward Movement. He also frequently spoke at colleges and universities across the nation. In 1913 the General Assembly of the Presbyterian Church in the United States of America elected Stone to serve as moderator. During the early 1920s, he guided the reorganization and consolidation of the boards of the Presbyterian denomination.

Stone continued his pastorate at Fourth Church for two years after accepting a call to the presidency of Chicago's McCormick Theological Seminary in 1928. As president, Stone announced an ambitious building program with a price tag of $3 million. The fiscal exigencies of the Great Depression forced curtailment of the construction plans, but Stone kept the seminary on a solid fiscal basis during the 1930s. He also raised academic standards, accomplished an affiliation with Lane Theological Seminary, and instituted policies that benefited faculty such as providing sabbatical leaves. He married Marie Briggs in June 1932; they had two sons. Following his retirement from McCormick in 1940 Stone served interim pastorates. He enjoyed fishing and camping with his family and friends in the Estes Park region of the Rocky Mountains and spent time in Coral Gables, Florida. He died in Chicago.

During the first part of the twentieth century, Stone emerged as a premier Presbyterian pastor and educator. He espoused a conservative but not a fundamentalist theology. During the fierce fundamentalist controversy, Stone, like many other midwestern large-church pastors, remained in the moderate wing of the Presbyterian church, flanked on the left by the liberal evangelicals, or inclusivists, and on the right by the fundamentalists, or exclusivists. The moderate party worked for a united denomination committed to mission. In his preaching, Stone sought primarily to call people to serve Jesus Christ. He regularly cited the words of William Carey, the early nineteenth-century missionary to India, "Expect great things from God. Attempt great things for God." Close friends and colleagues noted his genuine love of all people, his genial personality, and his powerful commitment to evangelism and mission. In a tribute offered a few days after his death, Harold A. Dalzell, vice president of the College of Wooster, referred to Stone as "truly a great man of God."

• The archives of Fourth Presbyterian Church contain a variety of informative sources: official church records; *The Fourth Church*, a monthly publication with news about the congregation and texts of Stone's sermons and addresses; and some of Stone's books including *Everyday Religion: A Book of Applied Christianity* (1927) and *Christianity in Action* (1930). Other papers of Stone, including an anecdotal autobiography, are privately held. For scholarly treatments of Stone's career at Fourth Church, consult Marilee Munger Scroggs, *A Light in the City: The Fourth Presbyterian Church of Chicago* (1990), and Scroggs, "Making a Difference: Fourth Presbyterian Church of Chicago," in *American Congregations*, vol. 1, *Portraits of Twelve Religious Communities*, ed. James P. Wind and James W. Lewis (1994). For a summary of Stone's presidency, see Ovid R. Sellers, *The Fifth Quarter Century of McCormick: The Story of the Years 1929–1954* (1955). Memorial tributes to Stone are in *McCormick Speaking* (Oct. 1954).

CHARLES E. QUIRK

STONE, Lucinda Hinsdale (30 Sept. 1814–14 Mar. 1900), educational reformer, was born in Hinesburg, Vermont, the daughter of Lucinda Mitchell and Aaron Hinsdale, and cousin to two other educational pioneers, Emma Willard and astronomer Maria Mitchell. Her father, a freethinking renegade from the local Congregational church who owned a woolen mill on 260 acres, died before Lucinda's second birthday. Lucinda was shaped both by the family's intellectual and political progressivism and by her mother's deep regret for her own lack of educational opportunity. At age three Lucinda was sent to the district school, and at thirteen she entered the coeducational Hinesburg Academy. She was introduced to her future profession when, at fifteen, she was asked to teach a summer school. She briefly attended Mrs. Cook's Female Seminary in Middlebury but, rapidly disenchanted by its traditional female curriculum, returned to the academy an adamant advocate of coeducation: "I felt I knew things in a different way from that in which the seminary girls knew them. I had been better, more thoroughly and broadly taught in our academy with young men and young women in the same classes" ("Club Talks," 1891). At once the beneficiary and a sharp critic of the best education available to an American girl of her era, she took from the academy "an irrepressible desire for the higher, more thorough, college education for women, which should cure the affectation and pettiness of school girls,—in short, give them something worthy to live for and to do for others" (Perry, p. 30).

During her last years at the academy its principal was James Andrus Blinn Stone, a Middlebury College graduate, Baptist minister, and abolitionist, who appreciated her passion for learning, especially for Greek, a study forbidden to women. In 1836 they parted temporarily—he to teach at Andover Theological Seminary and she at the Burlington Academy. Soon she went south as a governess on a Natchez, Mississippi, plantation, where a firsthand glimpse of slavery confirmed her own abolitionism, while James took a church in Gloucester, Massachusetts. In 1840 they were married at the home of Lucinda's sister in Grand Rapids, Michigan. The first of their three sons was born in Gloucester the following year. In 1843 James was offered the principalship of the Kalamazoo branch of the University of Michigan, which had recently absorbed the Michigan and Huron Institute operated by the local Baptist church. The couple moved west for good, in time for the birth of their second son.

When the Michigan legislature created eight such branches to feed the incipient state university at Ann Arbor, it had also mandated affiliated female seminaries. Kalamazoo's female seminary needed a principal, and Lucinda Stone took the post. From the first, the branch (which had been renamed the Kalamazoo Literary Institute in 1835) was "coeducational in fact but not in theory" (Goodsell and Dunbar, p. 43) by reason partly of spatial constraints, partly of the Stones' educational views. In the next twelve years the Stones jointly led the burgeoning institution, whose enrollment tripled while its reputation thrived. In 1855, under the first private charter issued by the state legislature, the institute became Kalamazoo College, with James Stone as president and Lucinda Stone as principal of its Female Collegiate Institute and instructor of moral and intellectual philosophy and English literature. She gained a reputation for academic excellence, pedagogical brilliance, intellectual progressivism, and personal charisma. For twenty years the Stones presided over a rich academic community, fostering progressive ideas and hosting a pantheon of illustrious visitors that included Ralph Waldo Emerson, Frederick Douglass, Elizabeth Cady Stanton, and William Lloyd Garrison.

In 1863, under the shadow of financial crisis and wartime enrollment decline, the conservative Baptist trustees, increasingly disgruntled by the Stones' iconoclasm, engineered their ouster. Lucinda Stone's feminism and teaching of contemporary authors incurred specific opprobrium. Three-quarters of the student body withdrew in protest, though many returned the following year. In a trial that shook the community, the Stones were excommunicated from the Baptist church.

The major projects of the last half of Lucinda Stone's life expanded her fundamental commitment to women's education. She operated her own female seminary, and between 1867 and 1875 she took eight groups of young women on study tours of Europe. From 1855 on she and James Stone lobbied the state legislature to open the University of Michigan to women, and in 1870 her student Madelon Stockwell became the first woman admitted. In 1890, as only the second woman awarded an honorary doctorate by the university, she proposed raising funds to endow a professorship for a woman, arguing, with her usual uncompromising conviction, "It is very certain that if young women are to be educated in any school there should be women on the faculty" (letter, 1890). She traveled, wrote, and lobbied tirelessly on behalf of municipal suffrage for women.

The project that brought Lucinda Stone national recognition began much earlier. In 1852 she was one of eight Kalamazoo women who founded the Ladies' Library Association, the first lending library in the city and only the third such women's club in the nation. She saw these clubs as "'post-graduate' courses of study . . . which, more than Vassar, and Smith, and Wellesley Colleges, are the real institutions at present educating American women" ("Club Talks," 1883). She saw their power to break through women's isolation within their homes, their social groups, their educational deprivations, their prejudices. Fostering clubs all over the state, she became known as the "mother of Michigan women's clubs," and in her last years she was active in the General Federation of Women's Clubs, working with many feminist luminaries of the day. She wrote a column, "Club Talks," for several Michigan newspapers as well as articles for the *Woman's Journal*, and she became a charter member of the Michigan Women's Press Association. On Stone's eightieth birthday Susan B. Anthony wrote that "not only Michigan women, but the women of the nation and the world owe her very much for her persistent efforts to secure the perfect equalities of educational opportunities for girls" (Perry, p. 160). She died in Kalamazoo.

• Lucinda Stone's papers, including an autobiographical sketch, letters, and many of her "Club Talks" columns, are in a collection at the Kalamazoo Public Library. Her account of the events surrounding her exile from the college, "An Episode in the History of Kalamazoo College: A Letter to Hon. J. M. Gregory, L.L.D" (1868), is in the Upjohn Library archives at Kalamazoo College. Also in the college's archives is Charles T. Goodsell and Willis F. Dunbar, *A Centennial History of Kalamazoo College* (1933), which recounts the official history of the Stones' Kalamazoo College years, and the invaluable *Reunion of Former Pupils of Rev. J. A. B. Stone, D.D., and Mrs. L. H. Stone*, ed. Julia Gilbert Elder (1886). Stone's "History of Coeducation in the University of Michigan" is in the Michigan Pioneer and Historical Collections at Waldo Library, Western Michigan University, along with a short biographical sketch of her by Mary M. Hoyt, titled "Mrs. L. H. Stone," and an account of "Attending the Branch at Kalamazoo in 1843" by A. D. P. Van Buren. This collection also houses the records of the Kalamazoo Ladies' Library Association, whose history is compiled in Grace J. Potts, *Women with a Vision* (1979). Stone contributed an essay on coeducation to Anna Brackett, ed., *The Education of*

American Girls (1874). See also Charles R. Starring, "Lucinda Hinsdale Stone," *Michigan History* 42 (Mar. 1958): 85–97; and Gail B. Griffin, "Lucinda Hinsdale Stone: Champion of Women's Education," in *Historic Women of Michigan: A Sesquicentennial Celebration*, ed. Rosalie Troester (1987). Two biographies are Belle M. Perry, *Lucinda Hinsdale Stone: Her Life Story and Reminiscences* (1902), mostly a tribute that does not document sources, and Griffin, "'Heretic': Lucinda Hinsdale Stone," in *Emancipated Spirits: Portraits of Kalamazoo College Women*, ed. Griffin et al. (1983).

GAIL B. GRIFFIN

STONE, Lucy (13 Aug. 1818–18 Oct. 1893), abolitionist and woman's rights activist, was born in West Brookfield, Massachusetts, the daughter of Francis Stone and Hannah Matthews, farmers. Her hard-working parents transmitted to their daughter—one of nine children—both their abolitionist commitment and their Congregationalist faith. Young Lucy retained their radical antislavery stance but found herself increasingly distant from the Congregationalist church after its leaders criticized abolitionists Sarah Moore Grimké and Angelina Emily Grimké for unfeminine behavior in speaking to mixed audiences in churches during their 1837 tour of Massachusetts. Stone also broke with her parents in pursuit of higher education. At the age of sixteen, after completing local schools, she taught and saved money for advanced study. She attended nearby Mount Holyoke Seminary for one term in 1839, returning home to attend to the illness of a sister. Stone waited until 1843 to enroll at the Oberlin Collegiate Institute (later Oberlin College); with her graduation in 1847, she became the first Massachusetts woman to earn a bachelor's degree.

Confirmed in both her abolitionist and feminist beliefs during her years at Oberlin, Stone gave her first public talk on woman's rights from her brother's pulpit in Gardner, Massachusetts, in December 1847. She was then hired as an agent for the Garrisonian Massachusetts Anti-Slavery Society the following year. Admonished by her employers to cease her practice of mixing the two controversial topics in the lectures they sponsored, Stone responded, "I was a woman before I was an abolitionist" (*Woman's Journal*, 15 Apr. 1893). She then proceeded to arrange to speak for the society on weekends, while reserving her weekdays for lectures on woman's rights. A popular orator, Stone garnered praise from William Lloyd Garrison's paper, the *Liberator*, for her "conversational tone. . . . She is always earnest, but never boisterous, and her manner no less than her speech is marked by a gentleness and refinement which puts prejudice to flight" (25 Aug. 1848). In addition, she played a leading role in the burgeoning woman's rights movement, serving as an organizer for its first national convention in Worcester, Massachusetts, in 1850.

Until 1855 Stone was in perpetual motion, lecturing across the country for feminism and abolitionism and related reforms, including temperance, dress reform, and married women's access to property rights and to divorce. Her own marriage in 1855 to Cincinnati hardware merchant Henry B. Blackwell, however, slowed her pace. A fellow abolitionist and the brother of pioneer women doctors Elizabeth Blackwell and Emily Blackwell, Henry Blackwell joined with Stone in celebrating their union with a protest against the legal inequalities of husband and wife. He also supported Stone in her decision later that year to reclaim her birth name as her legal signature. In 1856 Stone's family network was further augmented when her dear friend and Oberlin classmate, Antoinette Brown (Antoinette L. B. Blackwell), the first woman ordained in a regular Protestant denomination, married Henry Blackwell's brother Samuel Charles Blackwell. While Stone maintained visibility within the abolitionist and woman's rights conventions, she also devoted considerable energy to her husband's struggle to establish himself, first in Chicago as a publisher's representative, then in northern New Jersey, and to her only child, Alice Stone Blackwell, who was born in 1857. Despite her family responsibilities, Stone nonetheless protested her disfranchisement in 1858 by allowing the seizure of her household goods at her Orange, New Jersey, home rather than pay taxes levied by a government in which she could not participate.

During the Civil War, Stone joined other feminist-abolitionists to found the Woman's National Loyal League, an organization committed to the full emancipation and enfranchisement of African Americans. When Reconstruction began, Stone became a founder of the American Equal Rights Association (AERA), a union of woman's rights and abolition supporters determined to support the extension of voting rights irrespective of both race and sex. Under its auspices, Stone made an extended tour of Kansas in 1867, campaigning for state constitutional recognition of equal rights for both women and African Americans. But federal congressional action, first on the Fourteenth Amendment, which provided civil rights for freed slaves while ensuring voter protection only for men, and then on the Fifteenth Amendment, which guaranteed equal rights without regard to color while pointedly neglecting the issue of sex, angered many woman's rights supporters. Stone ultimately resigned herself to the provision of voting rights for African-American men without concomitant enfranchisement of white or black women. Declaring "I will be thankful in my soul if *any* body can get out of the terrible pit" quoted in Elizabeth Cady Stanton et al., eds., *History of Woman Suffrage*, vol. 2 [1881], p. 384), she continued to support the Republican party. Susan B. Anthony and Elizabeth Cady Stanton felt differently, and in May 1869 they led an exodus from the AERA to form the National Woman Suffrage Association (NWSA). The new organization refused to support constitutional changes that did not at the same time enfranchise women. Later that year, Stone, her husband, Mary Livermore, Julia Ward Howe, and others held a convention in Cleveland, at which they founded the rival American Woman Suffrage Association (AWSA) dedicated to achieving woman suffrage, especially through state-level legislation, while refusing to undermine achievements in African-American civil rights.

Also in 1867, Stone and Blackwell relocated their household to Dorchester, Massachusetts, and raised capital for a newspaper to be called the *Woman's Journal* by selling shares in a joint stock company to Boston supporters. Livermore agreed to merge her Chicago-based reform paper, *The Agitator*, into the new publication, now issued from the Boston headquarters of the American Woman Suffrage Association, and remained editor in chief from the debut of the paper on 1 January 1870 until 1872, when Stone assumed primary responsibility for the weekly appearance of this official organ of the AWSA with assistance from her husband and, after 1882, their daughter, Alice.

Stone remained in demand as a suffrage speaker, addressing state legislatures, women's clubs, collegiate alumnae, and political conventions from Colorado to Vermont, but increasingly she focused her attention on the paper, which she likened to "a big baby which never grew up, and always had to be fed." "Devoted to the interests of woman, to her educational, industrial, legal and political equality, and especially to her right of suffrage," the *Woman's Journal*, and particularly Stone's writing, covered a vast array of events, history, and personalities. Ironically, Stone's principles blocked her one attempt to exercise her own right to suffrage; in 1879 she registered under the new Massachusetts law permitting women to vote in school elections, but her name was erased by officials who refused to accept her enrollment under her own, not her husband's, surname.

For many years, Stone maintained a virulent (and reciprocated) animosity toward Stanton, Anthony, and the NWSA, yet she ultimately became convinced that reunification of the suffrage movement was in the best interest of all. In 1890 she assisted the merger of the NWSA and the AWSA into the National American Woman Suffrage Association, becoming the chair of its executive committee, but her failing health kept her close to home except for occasions that honored her pioneering suffrage activism. Her last public appearance took her to the Congress of Representative Women at the Chicago World's Columbian Exposition in May 1893. After she died at her home in Dorchester, Stone's was the first body cremated in New England.

Lucy Stone was a key figure in the American woman's rights movement for nearly a half century, bringing it from tutelage within the abolitionist movement to full organizational autonomy. Firmly committed to natural rights irrespective of sex, Stone maintained a distance from more controversial gender issues, such as divorce and free love. Instead, she worked tirelessly as lecturer, organizer, publisher, and tactician in pursuit of full legal equality, particularly the enfranchisement of women.

• Major collections of Stone's papers are held as part of the Blackwell Family Papers at both the Library of Congress and at the Schlesinger Library, Radcliffe College, Harvard University. Additional correspondence can be found in Patricia G. Holland and Ann D. Gordon, eds., *Papers of Elizabeth Cady Stanton and Susan B. Anthony* (1991), microfilm. Two published volumes include selected letters and helpful commentary: Leslie Wheeler, ed., *Loving Warriors: Selected Letters of Lucy Stone and Henry B. Blackwell, 1853 to 1893* (1981), and Carol Lasser and Marlene Deahl Merrill, *Friends and Sisters: Letters between Lucy Stone and Antoinette Brown Blackwell, 1846–1893* (1987). Alice Stone Blackwell's *Lucy Stone* (1930) is a daughter's appreciative biography; Elinor Rice Hays, *Morning Star: A Biography of Lucy Stone* (1961), strikes the same tone. Ellen C. DuBois, *Feminism and Suffrage: The Emergence of an Independent Women's Movement in America, 1848–1869* (1978), provides an excellent account of Stone in the context of the Reconstruction schism in the woman's rights movement. Andrea Moore Kerr, *Lucy Stone: Speaking Out for Equality* (1992), provides a speculative interpretation of Stone's personal relations. Obituaries and tributes are in *Woman's Journal*, 28 Oct. 1893.

CAROL LASSER

STONE, Marshall Harvey (8 Apr. 1903–9 Jan. 1989), mathematician, was born in New York City, the son of Harlan Fiske Stone and Agnes Harvey. The elder Stone was a prominent jurist who subsequently served on the U.S. Supreme Court from 1925 to 1942 as an associate justice and from 1942 to 1946 as chief justice. The younger Stone attended public schools in Englewood, New Jersey, before entering in 1919 Harvard University, where it was assumed that he would study law.

Stone became interested, however, in mathematics and received an A.B. in 1922 from Harvard in this subject. In order to ascertain whether he liked teaching, he became a part-time instructor during 1922–1923. When this experience was a success, he proceeded to earn an A.M. in 1924 and began working on his doctoral studies. He spent 1924–1925 studying mathematics in Paris, and with his research well under way, he taught at Columbia University as an instructor from 1925 to 1927. His Ph.D. was awarded in 1926, with the dissertation "Ordinary Linear Differential Systems of Order n and the Related Expansion Problems," supervised by George D. Birkhoff.

Stone returned to Harvard as an instructor of mathematics in 1927–1928 and as assistant professor from 1928 to 1931. He then moved to Yale University as an associate professor but returned to Harvard as an associate professor in 1933. There he became a professor in 1937 and served as chair of the mathematics department from 1942 to 1946. During World War II he was a civilian attached to the Office of the Chief of Naval Operations in 1942–1943 and the Office of the Chief of Staff of the War Department in 1944–1945, with overseas service in the China-Burma-India and European theaters.

In 1946 Stone became the Andrew Macleish Distinguished Service Professor at the University of Chicago, where from 1946 to 1952 he served as chair of the mathematics department. In the latter capacity he was instrumental in modernizing and revitalizing the Chicago program and making it one of world-class stature. As a token of homage and respect, colleagues have referred to Stone's chairmanship as "the Stone Age" at Chicago. Upon his retirement in 1968, he accepted the newly created George David Birkhoff Professorship of Mathematics at the University of Massachusetts in Amherst. He occupied this position full time until 1973 and half time until his second retirement in 1980. In addition to these positions, Stone was an inveterate traveler and a visiting professor at almost two dozen universities in a dozen different countries.

Stone's initial research, between 1925 and 1928, was devoted to classical analysis and centered on orthogonal expansions of eigenfunctions of linear differential operators, a favorite topic of his mentor Birkhoff. In 1929, however, Stone's interests abruptly changed to the abstract theory of linear operators, or transformations in Hilbert space. This theory was already being developed by John von Neumann in Germany, and it is a tribute to Stone's great power as a mathematician that, virtually unaided, he was able to successfully compete with von Neumann in this area. His first results appeared in brief announcements in the *Proceedings of the National Academy of Sciences* (1929–1930), and by 1932 he had produced a 600-page volume, *Linear Transformations in Hilbert Space and Their Applications to Analysis*, which has been hailed as one of the classics of twentieth-century mathematics. Much of his work in this area was independent of that of von Neumann and had a distinctly different character, involving new proofs of the Great Spectral Theorem, the Stone Representation Theorem for one-parameter groups of unitary groups (1932)—which was too late to be included in his book—and the Stone–von Neumann Uniqueness Theorem for irreducible solutions of the canonical commutation relations in quantum mechanics (1932).

In the mid-1930s Stone's interests, like those of von Neumann, took a new turn that was directed to the general structure of algebras of operators on an abstract space. Whereas such considerations led von Neumann to his theory of continuous geometry, in Stone's hands it developed into a general theory of Boolean algebras and their applications to general topology, as well as the theory of rings and ideals. This was treated in a pair of lengthy papers in the *Transactions of the American Mathematical Society* (1937), and was masterfully summarized in his survey paper "The Representation of Boolean Algebras" (1938), which included the Stone Representation Theorem for boolean algebras; the Čech-Stone Compactification Theorem; and the Stone-Weierstrass Approximation Theorem. The latter was subsequently discussed, in an elementary manner, in his paper "Generalized Weierstrass Approximation Theorem" (1948). These papers not only stress the fecundity of abstract reasoning but also the power of topological methods in modern analysis, and they also have important applications in logic and topology. See for example Russell C. Walker's *The Stone-Čech Compactification* (1974) and Peter T. Johnstone's *Stone Spaces* (1982). Moreover, Stone's ideas have been credited with influencing the origins of category theory (see *Functional Analysis and Related Fields* [1970], which was the proceedings of a conference in his honor, ed. Felix E. Browder). While Stone's mathematical activity continued following the war, much of his energy was devoted to administrative duties. Many of his postwar publications were of an expository character or of work done before the war.

Stone was much honored in his lifetime and was widely regarded as one of the senior statesmen of American mathematics. He was elected a member of the National Academy of Sciences in 1938, at the early age of thirty-five. He was colloquium lecturer of the American Mathematical Society in 1939, its president in 1943–1944, and the Gibbs Lecturer in 1956. He served on the AMS Council (1936–1938), was an editor of the *Transactions of the American Mathematical Society*, the *Annals of Mathematics*, and the *American Journal of Mathematics*, and edited *Mathematical Reviews* (1945–1950). He was president of the International Mathematical Union (1952–1954) and the International Committee on Mathematical Instruction (1961–1972). In 1982 he was awarded the National Medal of Science.

In 1927 Stone married Emmy Portman; they had three children. They were divorced in 1962, and he subsequently married Ravijojla Kostic and adopted her daughter. Following his Amherst retirement Stone continued to travel and be in demand as a visiting lecturer. He died quite suddenly (apparently of a stroke) at the age of eighty-five, while on a visit to a music festival in Madras, India.

• An autobiographical sketch is in *McGraw Hill Modern Scientists and Engineers*, vol. 3 (1980), pp. 164–66. Stone was a gifted writer, and two of his best expository articles are "The Revolution in Mathematics," *American Mathematical Monthly* 68 (Oct. 1961): 715–34, and his Gibbs Lecture, "Mathematics and the Future of Science," *Bulletin of the American Mathematical Society* 63 (Mar. 1967): 61–76. Stone's contributions are briefly discussed in Jean Dieudonné, *History of Functional Analysis* (1981). Obituaries appear in the *Notices of the American Mathematical Society* 36 (Mar. 1989): 221–23, and the *New York Times*, 11 Jan. 1989.

JOSEPH D. ZUND

STONE, Melville Elijah (22 Aug. 1848–15 Feb. 1929), journalist, was born in Hudson, Illinois, the son of Elijah Stone, a Methodist minister, and Sophia Louisa Creighton. In 1860 Stone's family moved to Chicago, where he attended Chicago High School for one year. He began his career as a reporter in 1864 on the *Chicago Tribune*, then worked on the *Chicago Republican* (later *Inter Ocean*) and the *Chicago Post and Mail*. He married Martha Jameson McFarland in 1869; they had two sons and a daughter.

In 1869 Stone acquired an iron foundry, which was destroyed in the great Chicago fire of 1871. After the fire Stone served as a director of relief, an experience that shaped his understanding of the communal nature of urban life and the public duty of private citizens. Throughout his career he held leadership positions in civic organizations, including the Chicago Citizen's Association, the Civil Service Reform League, and the

Union League Club. He served as treasurer of the Chicago Drainage Canal and as a member of the Chicago Board of Education. In politics he was a Lincoln Republican and later a mugwump, which he described as a "Republican with a conscience."

Stone's first major enterprise was the *Chicago Daily News*, which he and two partners, Percy Meggy and William Dougherty, founded in 1875. Meggy was the money man, Dougherty the reporter, and Stone the editor. In July 1876 Victor F. Lawson bought out Meggy and Dougherty and began a long career as publisher of the *Daily News*. On the editorial side, Stone assembled a splendid staff of writers, including George Ade, Bill Nye, and Eugene Field. Stone's own specialty was what he called "detective journalism." For Stone, this usually meant the exposure of official corruption and the punishment of "public plunderers," though in 1886 Stone also played an active role in bringing the Chicago Haymarket conspirators to trial and, in the case of four of them, to execution.

Although Stone believed, as he wrote in his autobiography, that "to print the news" was the highest duty of journalism, he created a remarkable editorial page as well. In editorials, the *Daily News* portrayed Chicago as a single community, or one large family. While most newspapers of the time supported individual private enterprise, the *Daily News* called for government-sponsored public works and social welfare. Stone even argued that the city should provide jobs for the poor in hard times. Such a plan would be costly, he admitted, but in a larger sense "nothing would be lost, but simply capital would be removed from one pocket to another, to be circulated for the good of the community." He believed that no class in society can afford to ignore another . . . we are far too interdependent."

The *Daily News* quickly became the most popular newspaper in Chicago with a circulation of 100,000 by 1885. Although Stone declared his newspaper "wholly divorced from any private or unworthy purpose," it was an enterprise that made Stone a wealthy man by age forty. In 1888 he unexpectedly retired, sold his interest in the firm to Lawson, and set off for Europe with his family to live a life of leisure on Lake Geneva. In 1890 they returned to Chicago, where Stone worked on civic projects and became president of the Globe National Bank.

In December 1892 several Midwestern newspapermen, members of the Western Associated Press, organized a news service called the Associated Press of Illinois. This new organization was designed to compete with the old Associated Press of New York, which the Midwestern publishers denounced as a selfish monopoly in collusion with the United Press and Western Union Telegraph. Stone became general manager of the Associated Press of Illinois in 1893, and the new AP quickly became a formidable national force in newsgathering.

Unlike earlier news services, the Associated Press of Illinois was a cooperative, nonprofit enterprise owned by member newspapers who shared, rather than bought and sold, the news. Stone believed that the co-operative character of the new AP was its singular virtue. Membership control made it possible and necessary for the AP to be impartial and unbiased, Stone believed. In a speech in 1916 he proclaimed the AP "in form at least, an ideal news-gathering association" and an essential democratic resource, through which the news is "automatically truthful and fair."

Although Stone imagined the new Associated Press to be an institution clothed in the public interest, he insisted that it was in law a private business. This distinction became crucial in 1900 when the Supreme Court of Illinois declared it to be a common carrier, obligated to provide its news to any applicant. This ruling was intolerable to leading members, who insisted on the right to control the prerogatives of membership. They immediately abandoned the Illinois corporation and reorganized the Associated Press in New York. Once again Stone became general manager, a position he held until his retirement in 1921. This is the version of the AP that survived, although the U.S. Supreme Court ruled in 1945 (*Associated Press v. United States*) that the AP, while not a common carrier, must open its membership to all legitimate applicants.

As general manager Stone greatly expanded the foreign service, while also making the AP the dominant domestic news service—a beneficent public servant in the eyes of its members, an ironfisted private monopoly in the eyes of nonmembers. Under Stone's leadership, the AP adopted the most advanced telegraph, cable, and wireless technologies. Through his frequent travels and business negotiations, Stone became friends with dozens of world leaders. Because of his personal friendship with the leading diplomats of Japan and Russia, for example, Stone was able to play an important behind-the-scenes role in the Portsmouth, New Hampshire, conference that ended the Russo-Japanese War of 1904–1905.

In a tribute to Stone in 1918, Adolph Ochs, publisher of the *New York Times*, wrote: "The success of the Associated Press is Melville E. Stone's success. The association is stamped all over with Stone's handiwork, his thought, his ideals, his abilities, and his sense of public service. It is his monument." The monument that Ochs eulogized was built upon Stone's belief that the AP could be simultaneously a public service and a private enterprise. In 1918 Stone helped to secure a U.S. Supreme Court decision that declared the AP news report to be a commodity in which the association held private property rights. On the one hand, Stone insisted that the AP was a purely private business and "the output of the Associated Press is not the news; it is its own story of the news." On the other hand, he deemed his Associated Press to be one of the great public institutions of the new century.

This easy blending of public and private lay at the heart of Stone's philosophy of journalism. And it is his legacy, for the dictum that private enterprise is automatically the best guarantor of honesty, impartiality, and public service became the quintessentially American doctrine of journalism in the twentieth century. Stone died in New York City.

• The best source on Stone's life is his autobiography, *Fifty Years a Journalist* (1921). Stone also wrote a revealing series of articles titled "The Associated Press" in *Century Magazine*, Apr. 1905, pp. 888–95; May 1905, pp. 143–51; June 1905, pp. 299–310; July 1905, pp. 379–86; and Aug. 1905, pp. 504–10. Stone's role in founding the *Daily News* and the AP is described in Charles H. Dennis, *Victor Lawson: His Time and His Work* (1935). Useful for personal details is *"M. E. S.," His Book: A Tribute and a Souvenir of the Twenty-five Years, 1893–1918, of the Service of Melville E. Stone as General Manager of the Associated Press* (1918). Studies of Stone's *Chicago Daily News* include David Paul Nord, "The Public Community: The Urbanization of Journalism in Chicago," *Journal of Urban History* 11 (1985): 411–41, and Donald J. Abramoske, "The Founding of the *Chicago Daily News*," *Journal of the Illinois State Historical Society* 59 (1966): 341–53. The most detailed studies of the newspaper during the Stone years are two unpublished dissertations: Donald J. Abramoske, "The *Chicago Daily News*: A Business History, 1875–1901" (Ph.D. diss., Univ. of Chicago, 1963), and Royal J. Schmidt, "The *Chicago Daily News* and Illinois Politics, 1876–1920" (Ph.D. diss., Univ. of Chicago, 1957). The best history of the Associated Press during the Stone era is Richard A. Schwarzlose, *The Nation's Newsbrokers*, vol. 2: *The Rush to Institution from 1865 to 1920* (1990). Two opposite assessments of Stone's AP are offered by Oliver Gramling's laudatory history, *AP: The Story of News* (1940), and Upton Sinclair's scathing critique, *The Brass Check: A Study of American Journalism* (1920). Stone's obituary was carried on the front page of the *New York Times*, 16 Feb. 1929.

DAVID PAUL NORD

STONE, Ormand (14 Jan. 1847–11 Jan. 1933), astronomer, was born in Pekin, Illinois, the son of Elijah Stone, a Methodist minister, and Sophia Louise Creighton. Stone was educated in various schools in towns where his father preached until the family settled in Chicago in 1859. He exhibited an early enthusiasm and talent for mathematics and, before finishing high school, took private lessons in mathematics and astronomy from Truman H. Safford, the director of the Dearborn Observatory. He entered the original University of Chicago in 1866 and was associated with that institution until 1870. In the meantime he taught as an instructor at Racine College in Wisconsin (1867–1868) and at the Northwestern Female College in Illinois (1869). He became an assistant in 1870 at the U.S. Naval Observatory, where until 1875 he was associated with mathematical astronomer Simon Newcomb. In 1875 he was awarded an A.M. in astronomy by the University of Chicago, and in the same year he became the director of the Cincinnati Observatory. On the recommendation of Newcomb in 1882, Stone was appointed professor of astronomy and director of the Leander McCormick Observatory at the University of Virginia. He held this position until 1912, when he retired on the Carnegie Foundation. In 1871 he married Catherine Flager, who died in 1914. He then married in 1915 Mary Florence Brennan. There were no children of either marriage.

Stone's contribution and reputation rest on three major areas of activity. First, although much of his interest was mathematical, he was an accomplished and skilled astronomer. Participating in the observation of three solar eclipses, he witnessed the eclipse of 1869 in Iowa and led the Naval Observatory expedition to Colorado in 1878 and the McCormick expedition to South Carolina in 1900. In addition, he made noteworthy visual observations of double stars (1877–1882), which led to new star lists; of nebulae, particularly the nebula in Orion (1896); various comets; and the satellites of Saturn (1895–1897). These observations were well received and among the best done in their time. While at Cincinnati, Stone was also involved in the adoption of standard time zones by the railroads, who put them in place in November 1883. They were adopted nationwide only by an Act of Congress in March 1918.

Stone's second contribution was his remarkable ability to judge and foster talent in young people. At Cincinnati he discovered and encouraged the pursuit of mathematics by a high school student, Eliakim H. Moore, who subsequently became one of the great figures in American mathematics and the founder of a distinguished mathematical school at the University of Chicago. At the University of Virginia, Stone trained some thirty Vanderbilt fellows, who later assumed prominent administrative and educational positions in the United States. These included two college presidents, five professional astronomers, six professors of mathematics, two professors of physics, and a dean of an engineering department, among others. Stone also took an active interest in the development and improvement of secondary education in the state of Virginia.

Stone's greatest contribution to mathematics was his founding of a new journal, *Annals of Mathematics*, in 1884. At the time only two other major mathematical journals existed in America: the *Analyst*, founded by J. E. Hendricks in 1872, and the *American Journal of Mathematics*, founded by J. J. Sylvester in 1878. The former was of an intermediate level and much of it was accessible to undergraduates, while the latter was becoming an internationally known research journal. Unfortunately, after completing ten volumes, the *American Journal of Mathematics* ceased publication in 1883. Although there was general agreement among American mathematicians that it had served a useful purpose and should be continued, no one had stepped forward with the energy or resources to revive it. At this point Stone proposed the new journal, which he would personally finance and edit in cooperation with his numerous mathematical friends. The *Annals* proved to be popular and quickly surpassed the *Analyst* in both the quality and quantity of the material published in it. However, it was costly, and although the University of Virginia helped support it during its last two years, in 1899 Stone had to relinquish control of the journal to Harvard. Ultimately it found a permanent home at Princeton, where it grew into a prestigious world-class research journal.

While Stone was editor in chief of the *Annals*, he contributed eight papers dealing with celestial mechanics—primarily on the orbits of comets and the motion of Hyperion (one of the larger satellites of Saturn). After the moves to Harvard and Princeton, he remained an editor until 1924, then served as an associate editor until 1932. He remained in good health in his later years and enjoyed the success achieved by his former students, whom he affectionately called his "old boys." He was killed instantly when hit by an automobile while walking along a road near his home near Fairfax, Virginia.

Stone belongs to the triumvirate of mathematical astronomers—together with George W. Hill and Newcomb—that loomed large on the American scene at the turn of the century. While he was clearly the lesser member and failed to receive either the others' acclamation or honors, nevertheless his contributions were of widespread value to the fledgling astronomical and mathematical communities at large. In 1903, in a poll conducted by *American Men of Science* of the leaders in science in the United States, he was rated fifteenth of fifty in astronomy and forty-third of eighty in mathematics. Stone was among those scientists whose devotion, enthusiasm, and giving of himself to the astronomical and mathematical communities were sorely needed in his day, and he merits our recognition.

• A list of Stone's scientific publications up to 1900 can be found in the *Catalogue of Scientific Papers*, 3d and 4th ser., comp. Royal Society of London (1896–1923). A choice example of his writing, which reveals much about his personality and views, is his obituary notice of Simon Newcomb in *Astrophysical Journal* 30 (Oct. 1909). Obituaries are in the *Bulletin of the American Mathematical Society* 39 (May 1933): 318–19, *Science* 77 (27 Jan. 1933): 107–8, and *Popular Astronomy* 41 (June–July 1933): 295–98, which contains a detailed listing of his students at the University of Virginia.

JOSEPH D. ZUND

STONE, Roy (16 Oct. 1836–6 Aug. 1905), civil engineer and military officer, was born in Steuben County, New York, the son of Ithiel V. Stone, a prosperous farmer, and Sarah (maiden name unknown). In 1854 he enrolled at Union College in Schenectady, a school that in 1845 had become the first liberal arts institution in the country to offer engineering courses. Stone studied civil engineering for at least two semesters and received an honorary A.B. in 1857. He settled in Warren County, Pennsylvania, where his father owned property. In 1861 he married Mary Elizabeth Marker; they had two children.

When the Civil War broke out, Stone volunteered for action in June 1861 and became a major in the Thirteenth Pennsylvania Reserves. He spent most of the war in Virginia in the Army of the Potomac, though he also served in Pennsylvania and Illinois. Stone was involved in intelligence gathering by means of a surveillance balloon at Fairfax Courthouse in March 1862. Promoted to corporal, in April and May 1862 he fought at the battle of Seven Pines in Virginia and in June and July in the Seven Days' battles. Detailed on recruiting service, he raised an entire regiment by the end of August and participated in the defense of Washington, D.C., until December 1862. As a colonel he led the 149th Pennsylvania Volunteers in the Peninsular campaign in late 1862 and early 1863. He commanded the Army of the Potomac's Second Brigade, Third Division, First Corps in the Union's loss at Chancellorsville in April and May 1863 and the Third Brigade, Fourth Division, Fifth Corps at Gettysburg. Severely wounded in fighting near McPherson's Barn on the first day of the battle of Gettysburg, he was captured and held for a time by Confederates. Promoted to brevet brigadier general after Gettysburg, he was wounded again in May 1864 when his horse fell on him in the second day of fighting in the Wilderness campaign. From September to December 1864 he commanded the volunteer depot at Camp Curtin, near Harrisburg, Pennsylvania. He concluded his Civil War service in command of a military prison and post at Alton, Illinois.

Stone's experiences in the Civil War convinced him that the United States needed better roads. After the war, in the capacities of both a civil engineer and an information officer, he promoted various kinds of transportation developments, including harbor and road improvements in New York and New Jersey. Together with Albert A. Pope, Stone led the Good Roads movement in America. At the 1893 Columbian Exposition in Chicago, Stone organized the National League for Good Roads. Also in 1893, Pope convinced Congress to establish a Bureau of Public Roads and Office of Road Inquiry in the Department of Agriculture. Agriculture secretary Julius S. Morton appointed Stone to investigate the nation's public roads and report on whether the federal government should take greater responsibility for them.

For nearly ten years, much of Stone's work in the Good Roads movement took place within the Department of Agriculture, where he served as special agent and engineer in the Office of Road Inquiry (1893–1896), which he directed in 1897 and again in 1899. He wished for that office to be the locus of advocacy as well as expertise. Between 1893 and 1903 he published various reports, addresses, and essays on road building, most of them in annual yearbooks and other publications of the Department of Agriculture. Among his writings were *New Roads and Road Laws in the United States* (1894), "Road Building in the United States" (1895), "Notes on the Employment of Convicts in Connection with Road Building" (1895), "Road Improvement in Governors' Messages" (1899), "Necessity of Congressional Action in Road Improvement" (1902), and "Good Roads and How to Get Them" (1903).

In June 1898, after the United States declared war on Spain, Stone took a leave of absence from the Agriculture Department to rejoin the army as chief of engineers and a brigadier general in the volunteers. When the United States widened the war to expel the Spanish from Puerto Rico, he participated in an expedition there in July and August under the command of General Nelson A. Miles. Miles's force, which sailed from Guantanamo, Cuba, on 21 July, included two companies of engineers and 3,400 infantry and artillery. Stone assisted the operation in road building and intelligence gathering. He later published two essays that derived from his experiences and continuing interest in the island, "Agriculture in Puerto Rico" (U.S. Department of Agriculture, *Yearbook*, 1898 [1899]) and "Our Failure in Porto Rico" (*North American Review* 181 [1905]). After the war he worked in the Agriculture Department until at least 1901.

Stone exemplified the nineteenth-century combination of civil engineering and military leadership. Though he participated as a young man in the Civil War and as an old man in the Spanish-American War, his major significance lies in his advocacy of transportation improvements at the dawn of the age of the automobile. He died in Mendham, New Jersey.

• Limited materials relating to Stone are in the Schaffer Library at Union College in Schenectady, N.Y. Many of his publications are at the National Agricultural Library in Green Belt, Md. His correspondence related to the Bureau of the Public Roads is at the National Archives in Suitland, Md. Biographical information is on his memorial at Arlington National Cemetery. Highlights of his public life are in *The War of the Rebellion: A Compilation of the Official Records of the Union and Confederate Armies* (128 vols., 1880–1901); Bruce E. Seely, *Building the American Highway System: Engineers as Policy Makers* (1987); and David F. Trask, *The War with Spain in 1898* (1981). Obituaries are in the *Washington Post* and the *New York Times*, 7 Aug. 1905.

PETER WALLENSTEIN

STONE, Samuel (1602–20 July 1663), Puritan religious leader and early settler of Hartford, Connecticut, was born in Hertford, England, the son of John Stone, a freeholder. Although his mother's name is unknown, his baptism was recorded at All Saints Church on 30 July 1602. He may have received part of his early education at Hale's Grammar School, established in Hertford in 1617, and in 1620 he matriculated at Emmanuel College, Cambridge, as a pensioner (a scholarship student). At least by the time he received his B.A. in 1623 he had become sympathetic to the evangelical religion of the Puritans, since he went on to study divinity with Richard Blackerby of Ashen, Essex, who had refused to subscribe to the Thirty-nine Articles of the Church of England. In Essex he entered a circle of Puritan ministers that included Thomas Shepard and Thomas Hooker, among others. After receiving his M.A. in 1627, he became the curate of Stisted in that county but was suspended for nonconformity on 13 September 1630. Shepard recommended him for a lectureship in Towcester, Northamptonshire, and he lived there before emigrating to New England in 1633 as the associate of Thomas Hooker. With Hooker as pastor, Stone became on 11 October 1633 the first teacher (the minister responsible for doctrinal and scriptural instruction) in the church at Newtown (later Cambridge), Massachusetts. When Shepard arrived in New England, Stone, noted for the "pleasancy in his conversation" according to Cotton Mather, entertained him in his home and took part in the negotiations to sell the town of Newtown to Shepard's group of immigrants.

When the Newtown group emigrated once again in 1636, they named Hartford, their new settlement in Connecticut, after Stone's birthplace. In 1637 Stone was the chaplain to Captain John Mason's troops in the Pequot War, accompanying them on the bloody attack on the Pequot fort and assisting them, as Mason said, by spending the preceding night "with the Lord alone wrestling with Him by Faith and Prayer." In the same year he was one of the representatives of his church to the synod called to deal with the supposed antinomian threat of Anne Hutchinson, and he later represented his church in the meetings and synods of 1643 and 1646–1648, which were called to answer the presbyterianizing Westminster Assembly's challenge to New England's congregational church order. Stone's senior colleague, Hooker, included in his subsequent defense of the congregational New England way a critique of the English presbyterian Samuel Hudson's argument that the visible church was the integral whole made up of individual churches. Hudson's reply appeared three years after Hooker's death in 1647, and Stone, now the sole minister of the Hartford church, produced *A Congregational Church Is a Catholike Visible Church* (1652) as "an office of love to [Hooker] and truth." He gave a relentlessly logical form to Hooker's contention that the church was visible only in particular congregations that were individual species of the universal "Church Catholike" considered as a genus. In later years Stone defended the congregational way from attacks from the left by writing a confutation of the English antinomians John Saltmarsh and Tobias Crisp, but this unpublished manuscript has disappeared.

Stone expanded on Hooker's comparatively generous conditions for accepting applicants to church membership by speaking against the demand for a relation of the time and manner of their conversion. He supported in his church and in the synod of 1657 the baptism of those who could only claim church membership through their grandparents, the basis of the later Half-Way Covenant. He also took a stronger line than Hooker on the necessary authority of the ministry, calling it "a speaking aristocracy in the face of a silent democracy" of church members. This last attitude embroiled him in controversy when he refused in 1653 to allow his church to vote on whether to call poet Michael Wigglesworth as his associate. The quarrel dragged on for six years during which Stone resigned his office, was reinstated, refused to celebrate the Lord's Supper, withdrew to Boston, and returned to Hartford. All of this involved heated exchanges of letters, a council of Connecticut churches, appeals to the General Court, and the mediation of ministers from Massachusetts. Stone's triumph came at the cost of a permanent division in the church when a number of dissenters moved to Hadley, Massachusetts, under the leadership of William Goodwin, the lay ruling elder.

Stone had married his first wife, whose name is unknown, probably before he left England. She died in 1640, "having smoked out her days in the darkness of melancholy" according to Hooker, and in the following year Stone married Elizabeth Allen, who shared his ensuing years in Hartford. They had at least five children, and Stone's patriarchal role as instructor in his family reverberated in his activities in the larger community. As the teacher in his church, he prepared *A Short Catechism Drawn Out of the Word of God* (1684), which was used in manuscript and appeared in print two decades after his death. He supervised in his home the preparation of several young men for the ministry, including John Minor, a Pequot missionary-interpreter, and John Cotton, Jr., the son of Massachusetts's most important minister. He left also in manuscript a "Body of Divinity," which according to Cotton Mather "has often been transcribed by the vast pains of our candidates for the ministry, and it has *made* some of our most considerable divines." In his final years he was troubled with a number of ailments and in 1657 made one of the conditions of his return to Hartford the settling of "some able phisitian" in the town. After 1660 he shared the increasing burden of his pastoral duties with the Reverend John Whiting. He died at Hartford of his infirmities, widely respected among the New England ministry for his mastery of logical argument, his learning, and his ready wit. Appropriately, the contents of his study accounted for nearly a quarter of the property listed in his will.

• Comparatively little has been written on Stone. Cotton Mather's "Doctor Irrefragibilis: The Life of Mr. Samuel Stone" appears in his *Magnalia Christi Americana* (1702). Useful information also appears in the introduction to *Samuel Stone's Cathechism, Reissued* (1899). The anonymously edited "Papers Relating to the Controversy in the Church of Hartford, 1656–1659," in *Collections of the Historical Society of Connecticut* 2 (1870): 51–125, prints documents pertaining to the quarrels between Stone and members of his congregation in the 1650s. George Leon Walker, *History of the First Church in Hartford* (1884), prints Stone's will and gives a good account of the controversies, while Paul R. Lucas puts them in a larger context in *Valley of Discord: Church and Society along the Connecticut* (1976).

FRANK SHUFFELTON

STONE, Wilbur Fisk (28 Dec. 1833–27 Dec. 1920), judge, was born in Litchfield, Connecticut, the son of Homer Bishop Stone and Lucy Linsley, farmers. When Wilbur Stone was six, his family migrated to farms in New York and Michigan, then settled in Indiana in 1840. After four years the family made its final trek to Iowa Territory. Stone worked on the farm, and at eighteen he returned to Indiana for schooling. He studied at an academy at Rushville, then entered Asbury University (now De Pauw), studying classics and supporting himself by teaching. In his senior year, he participated in a student rebellion and was suspended for refusing to take an official pledge. With others, he joined the senior class at Indiana University, graduating with an A.B. in 1857. He continued his studies at Indiana to earn an LL.B. in 1858 and an A.M. (date unknown), supporting himself as a tutor in classics.

Stone often wrote for newspapers, and after finishing his degrees he became editor of the *Evansville Dai-ly Enquirer*. He also began to practice law and became active in politics as a Democrat. In 1859 he went to Omaha, where he became editor of the *Nebraskan*, dazzling the locals with his knowledge of shorthand. In Omaha, Stone met settlers from Jefferson Territory, now Colorado. In the spring of 1860 he joined an ox-team party, reaching Denver in six weeks. Catching mining fever, he became a prospector at Tarryall in South Park. The next winter, he helped establish a "Claims Club" and local government at Canon City. After returning to South Park, he was elected to Colorado's first territorial legislature, which assembled in Colorado City in 1862, and he was reelected in 1864. He was also appointed assistant U.S. attorney in 1862, serving until 1866.

In 1863 Stone made an arrest right out of the movies. At a mining camp outside Breckenridge, he rescued his man from a lynch mob. He talked his way in, removed the noose, showed pistols, forced his and the prisoner's horses through the crowd, and galloped away to Denver.

Late in 1865 Stone went back to Indiana and married Sarah J. "Sallie" Sadler of Bloomington the following March. They returned to Colorado and settled in Pueblo. The marriage lasted until Sarah's death in 1910; the couple had two children, both sons. Also in 1865 Stone was appointed the first district attorney at Pueblo. He was elected to continue in 1868, the same year he became the first editor of the *Chieftain*, Pueblo's first newspaper. He served commercial and civic organizations and was president of both the Pueblo School Board and the first town board. Because his work often involved Hispanic citizens of Pueblo, he learned Spanish and much of the history of the area. In 1871 Stone became a promoter of the new Denver and Rio Grande Railroad and served as its general counsel from 1872 to 1877.

In 1875 Stone was elected to the Colorado constitutional convention, representing Pueblo. He was leader of the minority Democrats, chaired the judiciary committee, and served on several other committees. The following year Stone was nominated by the Democrats to stand for a seat on the supreme court of the new state. The Republicans swept the election, but the winner, Justice Ebenezer Wells, soon resigned to return to private practice. The state bar held a special meeting and, with concurrence of both parties, nominated Stone as the sole candidate to fill the vacancy.

Stone served on the Colorado Supreme Court for the remaining eight years of the Wells term, but in 1885 he was defeated for reelection. During Stone's tenure on the court it rendered many basic decisions to accommodate the common law to the unique conditions of Colorado. The most notable of these concerned irrigation. Stone wrote the court's first opinion that recognized the prior appropriation system of water law, and in 1882 he participated in the court's most famous water law decision, *Coffin v. Left Hand Ditch Co.*, which rejected a direct, constitutional challenge to the prior appropriation system.

After his term expired in 1886, Stone returned to private law practice, appearing as counsel before the supreme court. He served two years as a judge on the criminal court for Arapahoe County.

In 1891 Congress established the Court of Private Land Claims to adjudicate claims against the federal government arising from Spanish and Mexican land grants in the Southwest. President Benjamin Harrison appointed Stone as one of five judges on the new court. He was both the only judge from the region and the only judge who spoke Spanish. Stone served on the court until its business was completed in 1904.

The most interesting matter to come before the Court of Private Land Claims was the Peralta claim asserted by James Reavis, who claimed to own 12.5 million acres between Silver City, New Mexico, and Phoenix, Arizona, based on a grant from the Spanish Crown to Don Miguel de Peralta in 1748. The claim was made through his wife, Doña Sofia Micaela de Peralta Reavis, who was said to be the sole heir of Don Miguel. The claim was an elaborate fraud, involving forged documents planted in official records in Madrid and Seville, Spain; Guadalajara, Mexico; and California. Stone helped unravel the fraud, spending several months in Spain in the winter of 1895.

After completion of the court's work, Stone returned to law practice in Denver, serving as president of the state bar in 1908–1909. He was a lecturer at Denver Law School and held numerous charitable posts. In 1915 he was appointed U.S. commissioner for the federal district court in Denver. There, he conducted his last hearing sitting up in bed three days before he died.

Stone was the editor and an author of *History of Colorado*, a four-volume work published in 1918. He also wrote short histories of the Colorado bench and bar and numerous articles and essays. In addition to his command of college Greek and Latin, he was fluent in Spanish and spoke French, German, and some Italian. He was active in the Episcopal church, serving twenty-five years as lawyer for the diocese of Colorado. At the end of his life, however, Stone turned to Christian Science. The quintessential pioneer, he went to frontier Colorado at age twenty-six and worked there through sixty years and a half-dozen occupations. Stone was never wealthy but lived a comfortable life, able to travel abroad often and send his sons to Harvard.

• Stone has a brief file at the Colorado Historical Society in Denver. The longest published biography is five pages in vol. 2 of Jerome C. Smiley, *Semi-Centennial History of the State of Colorado* (1913). Stone's opinions for the Colorado Supreme Court are in vols. 3–8 of the *Colorado Reports*. His opinions for the Court of Private Land Claims are in the papers of Thomas Benton Catron, University of New Mexico Library, and on microfilm in the New Mexico State Archives and the Arizona State Library and Archives. His histories of the Colorado judiciary are in vol. 34 of the *Colorado Reports* (1906) and in vol. 1 of Smiley. Two unpublished essays are in the Bancroft papers, Western History Collection, University of Colorado at Boulder library. Stone is prominent in the Ph.D.

dissertation of Donald Wayne Hensel, "A History of the Colorado Constitution in the Nineteenth Century" (Univ. of Colorado at Boulder, 1957). Richard Wells Bradfute, *The Court of Private Land Claims* (1975), is the best source on that court, and it cites other sources about the Peralta case. There are mentions of Stone in many articles in *Colorado Magazine*. An obituary is in the *Rocky Mountain News*, 28 Dec. 1920.

RICHARD B. COLLINS

STONE, William (c. 1603–c. 1660), third proprietary governor of colonial Maryland, was born in England, probably in Northamptonshire. Little is known about his family, except that he had four brothers. The names of his parents are not known.

Stone migrated to Virginia by 1628 and served as an agent of his uncle Thomas Stone, a London merchant active in the Chesapeake tobacco trade. By 1642 Stone had amassed a landed estate of over 5,000 acres in Virginia and had assumed a prominent role in the counties of Accomack and Northampton on the Eastern Shore, including service as a sheriff, burgess, and vestryman in Accomack. Stone's strong ties to influential Protestants, particularly Puritans, in both England and the New World, as well as his mercantile connections, brought him to the attention of Cecilius Calvert, second Lord Baltimore. Lord Baltimore was struggling to contain religious tensions in Maryland and to find an effective successor as governor to his younger brother Leonard Calvert, who had died in 1647. He chose Thomas Greene, but the new governor was too aggressive in promoting Catholic interests and aroused the fears of the Protestant majority.

Lord Baltimore persuaded Stone to assist him in charting a less confrontational course for the colony, and through a commission issued in August 1648, Stone became the new governor of Maryland. By early 1649 he had moved to the province with his wife Verlinda Graves and four of their children among a total retinue of thirty-three persons. At Calvert's behest, Stone also encouraged other Virginians to resettle in Maryland. In the ensuing months, some 400 to 600 people migrated northward to populate what first became Providence Hundred and then, by 1650, part of a new county named Anne Arundel. Stone's commission required that he swear he would not harass anyone who believed in Jesus Christ, including Roman Catholics. Stone proceeded to implement Calvert's vision of a colony tolerant of all Christians. Lord Baltimore had already added several Protestants to the council, and at his direction Stone placed the colony under the primary authority of non-Catholics who headed the militia and judiciary in the various counties. These officeholders were also required to swear not to oppress Catholics.

Stone convened his first assembly on 2 April 1649 and his second the following April. These two legislatures are notable for enacting the colony's first substantial body of permanent statutes. While the acts consisted primarily of bills Calvert had dispatched from England, the delegates revised them and introduced a few new laws. The most celebrated statute was the 1649 Act Concerning Religion, which legislated the guarantees of religious toleration earlier extended through the oaths required of officers. Stone's clarification of the bases for assembly membership also firmly established elected representation, and in 1650 the assembly officially became bicameral.

Stone's leadership and the proprietor's policies were continuously threatened from within by zealous Catholics like former governor Greene, who pressed the assembly to recognize Charles II as the rightful monarch in England, and by more militant Protestants, who adamantly opposed any Catholic participation in politics. The latter were encouraged by parliamentary commissioners Richard Bennett and William Claiborne, long enemies of the Calverts, who ventured to Maryland in March of 1652 after first subduing Virginia for the new authorities in England. Bennett, Claiborne, and their adherents proclaimed a new government that initially excluded Stone and many other proprietary officers. Stone, swearing loyalty to the commonwealth, reached some accommodation with the victorious Virginians and was reinstated as governor on 28 June 1652, although he ceased for a while to issue writs in Lord Baltimore's name. The proprietor's vigorous lobbying in London brought assurances that he would retain control of Maryland, and accordingly he urged Stone to become more assertive of the Calverts' rights. By early March 1654, Stone had ended his collaboration with the parliamentary commissioners while still professing loyalty to the commonwealth itself. He attempted to restructure the government with new commissions and new oaths of loyalty, but he was forced to capitulate a second time in July. Six months later, in January 1655, under orders from Lord Baltimore, Stone resumed leadership of proprietary adherents most concentrated in the lower western shore counties and marched on Patuxent and Anne Arundel, areas of settlement overwhelmingly Protestant and strongly committed to the parliamentary commissioners. Stone and his army were decisively defeated in a battle at the Severn River on 25 March 1655. The former governor was captured and sentenced to death, but a petition in his behalf from soldiers in the opposition army prevented his execution. He remained imprisoned for an uncertain period of time. Over the next three years, while the parliamentary commissioners held sway, Stone had no public presence.

The authorities in England eventually reconfirmed Lord Baltimore's claims, but when the proprietor issued a new commission in 1656 he demoted Stone, a rebuke no doubt for being insufficiently aggressive on Calvert's behalf earlier in the decade. Stone's former subordinate, Josias Fendall, was designated the new governor. After the successful reestablishment of Lord Baltimore's authority within the province in 1658, Stone served almost two years as a member of the council and the provincial court. He did not attend the assembly in 1658 and died in Charles County before the next legislature convened.

Stone probably sold his lands in Virginia in the early 1650s but acquired a comparable 5,000 acres in Maryland, including "Poynton Manor," which he was given in 1654 for his services to Calvert. He was survived by his wife and six children.

• The documentary evidence for Stone's career is found primarily in the *Archives of Maryland*, vols. 1 (1883), 3 (1885), 4 (1887), and 10 (1891), and in Clayton Colman Hall, ed., *Narratives of Early Maryland, 1633–1684* (1910). Critical secondary sources include Bernard C. Steiner, *Maryland during the English Civil Wars* (1906–1907) and *Maryland under the Commonwealth: A Chronicle of the Years 1649–1658* (1911); and Harry Wright Newman, *The Stones of Poynton Manor* (1937). Edward C. Papenfuse et al., eds., *A Biographical Dictionary of the Maryland Legislature, 1635–1789* (2 vols., 1985), has the most authoritative summary on Stone.

DAVID W. JORDAN

STONE, William Joel (7 May 1848–14 Apr. 1918), U.S. representative, governor of Missouri, and U.S. senator, was born in Madison County, Kentucky, the son of William Stone and Mildred Phelps, farmers. Stone left home in 1863 and traveled to Columbia, Missouri, to the home of his sister and her husband, an attorney. He lived with them, attended the University of Missouri (1863–1868), and then read law in the office of his brother-in-law. In 1869 Stone was admitted to the bar and opened a practice in Nevada in southwestern Missouri. In 1874 he married Sarah Louise Winston of Jefferson City; they had three children.

Stone, a Democrat, served three terms in the house (1884–1890). In 1890 he began a campaign for the governorship; he was elected in 1892. In this capacity he exhibited tendencies that were termed "progressive" after 1900. Stone called for an employers' liability law to make it easier for workers and their dependents to obtain damages for injury or death in work-related accidents. This proposal won the support of organized labor, support he enjoyed for the remainder of his career. The railroads, the most hazardous industry of the time, used their powerful lobbyists to block passage of the bill. After the bill's defeat, Stone tried to pressure the legislature to pass a law to regulate lobbying. He addressed a letter to each legislator and made it public to rally popular support. The lobbyists not only prevented the antilobby law, but they also mounted an attack on Stone after his term as governor ended. Stone had made himself vulnerable to such attacks by representing, in his capacity as a lawyer, certain firms chiefly interested in political influence.

In 1895–1896 Stone gained national recognition as one of the leaders in the move by which supporters of silver coinage took control of the Democratic party. As the panic of 1893 produced a severe depression, Stone concluded that the country needed "good money and plenty of it," as he said in a speech in 1893 before the New York Board of Trade and Transportation. Stone was one of a group of five, including three senators and two governors, who masterminded the strategy used to take control of the party in time for the national convention of 1896. In the midst of this struggle the

St. Louis Republic, owned by former governor David R. Francis, a gold Democrat, charged in an editorial that Stone's way of "tiptoeing" into a community to "fix a little scheme" without attracting attention "had won for him the sobriquet of 'Gum-Shoe' Bill" (26 Mar. 1896). Stone's followers adopted the nickname and used it to stress his skill in mediating conflicts within the party and achieving harmony. Stone exemplified this trait throughout his career.

Stone's support of labor legislation, work against lobbying, and leadership in the silver cause came back to haunt him after 1900 as he campaigned for a seat in the U.S. Senate. Gold Democrats and the major railroad lobbyists waged a furious battle against him. They did not stop at accusing him of lobbying but tried to tie him to the sensational charges of bribery and corruption that were racking the Missouri legislature. Two grand juries investigating all aspects of the scandal indicted the lieutenant governor and several legislators but found Stone guilty of no wrong. He had acted as lawyer for several important Missouri corporations. Perhaps he should have been more careful about a few, but he had not engaged in lobbying, much less bribery. However, these unsubstantiated charges continued to surface from time to time during his senatorial career.

In January 1903 the Missouri legislature elected Stone to the Senate and reelected him in 1909. By 1914 the Seventeenth Amendment required popular election of U.S. senators, and Stone won a third term easily. In his first term Stone attracted little notice as one of a small minority of Democrats in an overwhelmingly Republican Senate. He utilized his time to study issues he believed would be important when the Democrats would be back in power, as he confidently anticipated. The matters particularly capturing his attention were foreign trade, which was tied to the tariff; banking and currency; and problems growing out of the new position of the nation as a world power. He had no intention of remaining tagged as an agrarian silverite.

In Stone's second term increased Democratic membership combined with his greater seniority allowed better committee assignments. He became a member of both the Finance and Foreign Relations committees. As progressives in both parties struggled to reduce the tariff, Stone became a leader of reform Democrats and often cooperated with like-minded Republicans. Stone had become so well informed on details of foreign trade that progressive Republicans deferred to him to answer questions raised by opponents of tariff cuts.

Stone played a pivotal role, albeit a rather devious one, in the national convention of 1912. As manager for the campaign of fellow Missourian Champ Clark, Stone tried to effect compromises to gain the necessary two-thirds majority for the nomination. William Jennings Bryan's efforts to block Clark caused Stone to conclude that Bryan sought a fourth nomination. Convinced by then that neither Clark nor Bryan could become president if nominated, Stone turned to Woodrow Wilson in the belief that, once nominated, Wilson could hold Democrats and win enough progressive Republicans to be elected. Stone quietly arranged an adjournment that gave Wilson's managers time to make the necessary deals to gain the nomination. Adjournment also prevented Clark from reaching the convention hall to confront Bryan.

Stone became an ardent admirer of President Wilson early in his first term, and Wilson reciprocated with respect and kind feelings. He relied on Stone to use his mediation skills, knowledge of the caucus, and adroit recommendations on appointments to hold the slim Democratic majority in line. Seniority made Stone the ranking member on both the Finance and Foreign Relations committees. He chaired a subcommittee of the former that was responsible for many detailed schedules of the Underwood-Simmons Tariff of 1913, which sharply reduced import taxes. In March 1914, when Augustus O. Bacon of Georgia, chair of the Foreign Relations Committee, died, Stone took his place.

The outbreak of World War I made Stone one of the chief figures in the administration. Although his position on some issues was somewhat enigmatic, he was viewed as Wilson's spokesman in the Senate on foreign affairs, and leading journals did profiles on him. Stone did not entirely agree with Wilson's insistence that Germany abide by the old rules of blockade while using a new weapon, the submarine. Stone doubted that the United States should become the guardian of international law, and he feared that Wilson's course would lead the nation into a war in which it had, according to Stone, no vital interest. At the same time, his admiration for and confidence in the president kept Stone from doing more than urging Wilson not to take an irrevocable position. Stone wrote to the president, "I want . . . to stand by you, and I mean to do so up to the last limit" (24 Feb. 1916). Although the letter was phrased in a conciliatory vein, there was a guarded warning in the word "limit."

That limit was reached when Wilson, in response to German resumption of submarine attacks on neutral shipping in February 1917, demanded that Congress authorize him to arm merchant vessels. Stone argued that the measure was an unconstitutional executive usurpation of the congressional power to decide the issue of war or peace. With almost a premonition of events to come, Stone asserted that such action created a dangerous precedent.

Wilson reacted angrily and declared that he was "through with Stone." Stone had correctly anticipated that the metropolitan press would vilify him, but he was deeply hurt by Wilson's attitude. Stone completed his alienation from the president by voting against the war resolution. Nonetheless, he averred that if Congress declared war, he would support it fully; as he said in his brief speech against the resolution on 4 April 1917, printed in the *Congressional Record* (65th Cong., 1st sess., p. 210), "In war there can be no divided patriotism." He was true to his pledge and used his still considerable influence on behalf of all administration war measures. Although Missouri had a large German-American population that opposed the war, Stone was not their spokesman, for they were overwhelmingly Republican. Nor was Stone a true isolationist, because he supported the concept of a league of nations and, on behalf of Wilson, made certain that the Democratic platform of 1916 endorsed such a league. Stone had become a convert to the Wilsonian view of a "peace without victory," and when Wilson abandoned such a peace program, Stone felt betrayed.

On his way to the Senate on 11 April 1918 Stone suffered a stroke; he died in Washington, D.C. He had been a national leader for so long that people reacted almost in disbelief when they learned of his death. Major papers ran long stories about his death, summaries of his career, and editorials reflecting on both. Wilson forgot his pique, recalled Stone's loyal support on many occasions, sent a huge wreath of flowers, wrote a sympathetic note of condolence to Stone's widow, and ordered that the presidential railroad car carry Stone's body, the family, and distinguished guests to Missouri for Stone's burial.

Stone is to be remembered chiefly for his efforts throughout his long career to get Democrats to unite on major issues. In the Wilson administration he played a principal role in shaping the final version of the 1913 tariff. He worked strenuously behind the scenes to mediate conflicts over details of the Federal Reserve Act of 1913. As a long-time friend of labor, Stone gave needed support for the clause in the Clayton Act of 1914 that exempted labor unions from antitrust statutes, and he pushed an act through the Senate to exclude convict-made goods from interstate commerce. Although occasionally journalists reversed earlier opinions of him and termed him a progressive, more often they continued to call him a bourbon Democrat. His record does not warrant that label, but it is hard to categorize him as either liberal or conservative, for he was less concerned with ideology than with accomplishment.

With regard to foreign affairs, Stone's position evolved from simple anti-imperialism in 1900 to the Wilsonian vision of a world order of peace and justice for all peoples. Ironically, this led to his refusal to support armed intervention in 1917. Stone believed that U.S. participation in the war destroyed the hope for lasting peace. Stone wrote an article titled "Effect of Preparedness upon America's Influence and Power" for the July 1916 issue of the *Annals of the American Academy of Political and Social Science* (66:125–29), in which he said, "This country has a mission to perform." In respect to the war, he meant that the United States should wait until the warring powers, once their resources were exhausted, accepted Wilson's mediation.

• Stone's papers are housed in the Western Manuscripts Collection, University of Missouri, Columbia. They represent only certain topics but offer significant insights. Indispensable are Stone's letters to and from Wilson and Joseph P. Tumulty in the Woodrow Wilson Papers, Library of Congress. Scattered letters can be found in other collections in the same library. The *Congressional Record* gives remarks, votes, and complete speeches that Stone made in the Senate, 1903–1918. Ruth Warner Towne, *Senator William J. Stone and the Politics of Compromise* (1979), is a full-length biography, and it contains an extended, annotated bibliography. For an interesting, although not altogether reliable, profile of Stone, consult *Nation*, vol. 100, p. 624. Obituaries are in the *New York Times*, the *St. Louis Republic*, and the *St. Louis Post-Dispatch*, all 15 Apr. 1918.

RUTH WARNER TOWNE

STONE, William Leete (20 Apr. 1792–15 Aug. 1844), editor and historian, was born in New Paltz, New York, the son of William Stone, a minister and conservative Federalist, and Tamson Graves. Shortly after Stone's birth, his family moved to the Susquehanna River Valley, where his father preached among several congregations in the vicinity of Cooperstown and where Stone developed an interest in Indian lore. At age seventeen Stone left his father's farm to apprentice at the *Cooperstown Federalist* with editor John Prentiss. In 1813 he purchased a Federalist newspaper in nearby Herkimer, the *Herkimer American*, which had formerly been run by Prentiss. He sold it in 1814 and moved to Hudson, New York. In 1817 he married Susannah Pritchard Wayland, a sister of the president of Brown University. They had one child and also adopted a young nephew of Stone. Stone and his wife moved to Albany and bought the *Albany Daily Advertiser*. Unfortunately, Stone later found that its debtors had gone bankrupt, depriving him of an expected $6,000 in income. He moved in 1819 to Hartford, Connecticut, to edit the *Hartford Mirror*, a historically Federalist paper, which he directed toward a more literary focus. During his two years in Hartford he also established a literary club that published a magazine, the *Knights of the Round Table*.

In 1821 Stone moved to New York City and became editor and coproprietor of the *New York Commercial Advertiser*, which he continued to edit until his death. During his long career at the *Advertiser* he was known for his pronounced dislike for the person and policies of Andrew Jackson. Although he proclaimed his Federalism long into the 1830s, Stone was a close friend and political ally of Governor DeWitt Clinton and earned the honorary title of colonel from Clinton's administration for his support of the Erie Canal project. As an editor Stone openly advanced his own opinions, including early support for Greek independence, ridicule of Frances Wright's views on the women's movement, advocacy of the federal emancipation of slaves, and urging more humane treatment of Native Americans. A voice for obedience to the law, justice, and factual accuracy, he was remembered by fellow Whig editor Horace Greeley as a man of honest and fearless opinions.

Stone also published several pamphlets on current events during the 1830s. *Letters on Masonry and Anti-Masonry* (1832) sought to quell anti-Masonic fever by arguing that while Masonry had outlived its use, it was a harmless organization. *Complete Refutation of Maria Monk's Atrocious Plot* (1836), republished under a variety of titles, was based on Stone's own visit to the Montreal nunnery where Monk claimed she had been impregnated by a priest. After authoritatively prying into every closet and trapdoor of the abbey, he pronounced Monk an imposter. While Stone was probably correct in his conclusions, his self-confidence was lampooned in a biting poetic satire on his Montreal trip, Laughton Osborn's *The Vision of Rubeta* (1838). Osborn's satire seems all the more accurate in view of Stone's *Letter to Doctor A. Brigham on Animal Magnetism* (1837), which described Stone's trip to Providence, Rhode Island, to investigate the effects of mesmerism on Loraina Brackett. Confident in the truth of his own perceptions but probably the victim of a clever hoax, Stone came away from the interview convinced that Brackett could see the paintings in his private study 200 miles away in New York City.

Among Stone's most valuable accomplishments were his histories, which continue to be useful for their reliance on primary materials and factually corroborated interviews. In 1834 he devoted himself to writing a complete history of the Iroquois. Finding the New York state archives inadequate for his purposes, he lobbied from 1834 to 1838 to get state legislative action for the retrieval of documents on American history from European archives. Stone's first history, the two-volume *Life of Joseph Brant—Thayendanegea, and Also Containing Border Wars of the American Revolution* (1838), was noteworthy for its impartiality toward both white and Native American conduct. Stone also exonerated Brant from his alleged involvement in the Wyoming Massacre, a claim he supported with additional evidence in *Poetry and History of Wyoming* (1841). Though quick to affirm the norms of his own society, Stone sought to redeem Native Americans from charges of savagery. The *Life of Brant* was criticized in the *North American Review* for being hastily assembled and lacking sustained focus on either its protagonist or the Border Wars. Perhaps conceding this criticism, Stone revised the work slightly and reissued the text as *Border Wars of the American Revolution* (1843).

Of lasting value in Stone's histories was his deliberate decision to reprint as many speeches and original documents as possible. As he remarked in the *Life of Brant*, future generations would prefer to interpret the meaning of past events from actual documents rather than from the opinions of a historian. His next history, *Life and Times of Red Jacket* (1841), was both a perceptive study of the orator's life and the most complete collection of Red Jacket's speeches. Stone developed a complex, respectful portrait of the orator that included his skills at political intrigue, his sarcasm, his faith to his people, and his intemperate drinking. Particularly in explaining Red Jacket's opposition to Christian missionaries and Indian land sales after 1805, Stone described an evolving character, and though gradually overtaken by drunkenness, a leader who understood the complicated position of the Senecas at the time.

In 1840 Stone's paper published a review of James Fenimore Cooper's *History of the Navy* that complained that Cooper slighted the accomplishments of Oliver Hazard Perry. Cooper sued Stone for libel and won a financial award. When Stone later editorialized that Cooper would not need a locksmith to get the money (alluding to Cooper's once inducing a magistrate to pry open a creditor's trunk), Cooper sued again, but the court eventually vindicated Stone after his death.

Stone had written only seven chapters of his next Iroquois history, *The Life and Times of Sir William Johnson*, when he died from natural causes at his father-in-law's home in Saratoga Springs. His son, William Stone, Jr., who attributed his father's death to overwork, finished the *Johnson* history. Stone also wrote short local-color sketches and historical fiction, based on his memories of pioneer life around Cooperstown, his acquaintance with New York society, and his interest in American history. Toward the end of his life Stone was active in philantrophical causes, working on behalf of the New York Institute for the Deaf and Dumb and serving as superintendent of the common schools from 1843 to 1844.

• A ninety-page biography of Stone by his son, William Stone, Jr., appeared in the 1866 edition of *Life of Red Jacket*; a shorter version is in William Stone, Jr., *The Family of John Stone* (1888). See the *North American Review*, Oct. 1839, Oct. 1841, and Jan. 1842 for reviews of *Brant*, *Wyoming*, and *Red Jacket*. Stone's other publications include *Narrative History of the Great Albany Constitutional Convention* (1821), *History of the Grand Erie Canal Celebration* (1825), *Matthias and His Impostures* (1833), *Tales and Sketches* (1834), *The Mysterious Bridal* (date unknown), *Mercy Disborough: A Tale of New England Witchcraft* (1844), *Lectures and Addresses on Social and Literary Topics* (date unknown), *Ups and Downs in the Life of a Distressed Gentleman* (1836), and *Uncas and Miantonomoh* (1842). Obituaries are in the *New York Commercial Advertiser*, 16 Aug. 1844, and the *New York Tribune*, 17 Aug. 1844.

GRANVILLE GANTER

STONE, Witmer (22 Sept. 1866–23 May 1939), naturalist and science historian, was born in Philadelphia, Pennsylvania, the son of Frederick Dawson Stone, a businessman and librarian of the Historical Society of Pennsylvania, and Anne Evelina Witmer. His family was of Quaker and Pennsylvania-German origin. Stone's attraction to natural history began during early childhood; and at the age of sixteen, he organized the "Wilson Natural Science Association" in collaboration with his brother Frederick D. Stone, Jr., and their young friends, Stewardson and Amos P. Brown. The goals of this amateur club were to study and collect samples of the geology, flora, and fauna of the region around Germantown. In later years, Stone recalled that the association provided the boys with an "admirable basis" for their future careers as scientists, reflected in the broad range of their professional scholarly activities. After six years at Germantown Academy,

Stone enrolled at the University of Pennsylvania, where he received an A.B. in 1887 and an A.M. in 1891.

In March 1888 Stone was appointed a Jessup Fund Student at the Academy of Natural Sciences of Philadelphia, one of the leading natural history research centers and museums in the United States. His subsequent association with the academy spanned more than fifty years and included positions as conservator of the ornithological section (1891–1918), assistant curator (1893–1908), curator (1908–1918), executive curator (1918–1925), curator of vertebrates (1918–1936), honorary curator of birds (1938–1939), director (1925–1929), emeritus director (1929–1939), and vice president (1927–1939). At the time of his death, the Academy Council noted that Stone's "life became so merged with that of the Academy that for many years it was difficult to think of them apart." Stone married Lillie May Lafferty in 1904; they had no children.

Perhaps Stone's most important contribution at the academy was to salvage and preserve the irreplaceable zoological specimens that formed the core of the institute's collections. For some twenty or so years before Stone's arrival at the academy, many important specimens had been stored under "deplorable conditions" and their historical value largely ignored. Stone undertook the tedious labor of restoring and properly cataloging thousands of study skins and bottled specimens. Through his efforts, more than 600 type specimens were located and saved from the deteriorating collections of John J. Audubon, John Cassin, John Gould, and John K. Townsend. Stone also rehabilitated the enormous herpetology collection of Edward D. Cope as well as mammal collections and mammal type specimens.

Stone's contributions to American natural science extended far beyond his activities with the academy, however, as he assumed leadership roles in a number of scientific organizations. Most notable was his work with the American Ornithologists' Union, to which he was elected an associate in 1885 and a fellow in 1892. Stone served the AOU as a member of its council (1898–1939), its Committee on Bird Protection, and its Committee on Nomenclature and Classification, which he chaired from 1919 to 1931. As chairman of the latter committee, he was largely responsible for producing the fourth edition of the AOU *Check-list of North American Birds* (1931), at that time the definitive reference on nomenclature, taxonomy, and geographic distribution of North American birds. He was vice president (1914–1920) and president (1920–1923) of the AOU and editor of the organization's scientific journal the *Auk* (1912–1936), in which he critiqued many thousands of scientific publications. His own technical papers, published mainly in the *Auk* and in the various publications of the Academy of Natural Sciences, covered a broad array of geographical regions and topics, including taxonomic revisions, regional faunas, plumage, molt, color variation, and migration.

Stone published a number of major works, including his classic, the two-volume *Bird Studies at Old Cape May* (1937), for which he received the Brewster Memorial Medal posthumously in 1939 from the American Ornithologists' Union. Based on decades of fieldwork in southern New Jersey, this opus reveals "Stone at his best, both as a naturalist and a writer" (Rehn, pp. 307–8). In it he combines his skillfully crafted and engaging literary style with an extensive scientific data base to produce a "delightful account" of the region's bird life. Perhaps equally well known is his *The Plants of Southern New Jersey, with Special Reference to the Flora of the Pine Barrens and the Geographic Distribution of the Species* (1911), an 800-page study regarded in its day as one of the most important regional floristic studies of eastern North America. Other valuable contributions by Stone included *The Mammals of New Jersey* (1908), *American Animals* (1902), and *The Birds of New Jersey, Their Nests and Eggs* (1908, 1909).

Stone's father was an authority on Pennsylvania history, a fact that may have contributed to Stone's interest in the history of American natural science. Stone's voluminous production of studies and biographies, most of which appeared in *Cassinia*, *Auk*, or *Leading American Men of Science*, included biographical sketches of Audubon, Alexander Wilson, Titian R. Peale, John Cassin, John K. Townsend, William Bartram, and George Ord. Stone was particularly interested in the early period of western exploration, the discovery and naming of new bird species, and the details of bibliographic documentation.

Among the many honors accrued by Stone, the most noteworthy included vice president and president of the American Society of Mammalogists, fellow of the American Association for the Advancement of Science, member of the American Philosophical Society, and honorary memberships in the Linnaean Society of New York, the British Ornithologists' Union, and numerous national and local zoological societies. In 1931 he received the Otto Hermann Medal for his studies of bird migration, including particularly his *Graphic Representation of Bird Migration* (1889). Stone received the Alumni Award of Merit from the University of Pennsylvania in 1937. His surname is commemorated in the scientific names of a gentian and a grasshopper, both of which are native to the New Jersey pine barrens.

Stone was highly respected as a scholar and revered as a mentor and colleague by his associates. Biographer James A. G. Rehn recalled that Stone was "ever ready to give of his time and knowledge to help others" and that, despite a somewhat reserved personality, he possessed a "lighter side, a merry twinkle of the eye, a touch of delicate whimsey, or a hearty laugh, to show that beneath all the serious thought there was a buoyant spirit, keenly alive to the world about" (pp. 312–13). Although Stone's major field was ornithology, he also produced valuable contributions to the fields of botany, entomology, mammalogy, herpetology, invertebrate zoology, history, and biography. One of the last of the "old school" general naturalists, Stone remains best known for his work as a writer, historian, and conservator. He died in Philadelphia, Pennsylvania.

• Principal collections of Stone's papers are at the University of Pennsylvania archives and at the Library of the Academy of Natural Sciences in Philadelphia, although his extensive correspondence is found in archival papers of many zoologists who were his contemporaries. Most of his zoological and botanical specimens are at the Academy of Natural Sciences in Philadelphia. Major sketches of Stone include James A. G. Rehn, "In Memoriam: Witmer Stone," *Auk* 58 (1941): 299–313, which includes a portrait; Cornelius Weygandt, *Philadelphia Folks* (1838), pp. 266–69; Francis W. Pennell, "The Botanical Work of Witmer Stone," *Bartonia* 20 (1938–1939): 33–37, which contains a partial list of Stone's botanical publications; and Wharton Huber, "Witmer Stone," *Journal of Mammalogy* 21 (1940): 1–4, containing a partial bibliography of Stone's mammalogy publications. Most of Stone's technical papers were published in the *Auk*, *Journal of Mammalogy*, *Proceedings of the Academy of Natural Sciences*, and *Cassinia*. For his botanical collections and publications, see Frans A. Stafleu and Richard S. Cowan, *Taxonomic Literature* 6 (1986): 24–25.

MARCUS B. SIMPSON, JR.

STONEHAM, Horace Charles (27 Apr. 1903–7 Jan. 1990), major league baseball owner, was born in Newark, New Jersey, the son of Charles A. Stoneham, stockbroker and principal owner of the New York Giants baseball club, and Hannah McGoldrick. Stoneham's father was a gambler and entrepreneur of dubious reputation who made his fortune in the manipulation of the New York Stock Exchange. In 1919 the elder Stoneham bought controlling interest in the syndicate that purchased the New York Giants franchise. In this environment, Stoneham developed an abiding interest in the business and sport of major league baseball, and while still in his teenage years he gathered valuable experience working as a ticketseller, a groundskeeper and a junior executive in the Giants' front office.

After graduating from Fordham University, Stoneham drifted west and briefly worked in a California copper mine before returning to New York City. In 1924 he married Valleda Pyke; the couple had three children. In 1929 Stoneham became a full-time administrator in the Giants' organization, astutely advising his father to replace the aging manager, John J. McGraw, with popular Giants' first baseman, Bill Terry. When his father died in 1936, Stoneham inherited part of the Giants' franchise, was elected president, and at age thirty-two became the youngest team owner in major league baseball history.

Almost from the beginning of his tenure as owner of the Giants, Stoneham developed the reputation of being so intimately involved with the day-to-day operation of the ballclub that his emotional investment in the team was more important than his financial investment. Too often he seemed to allow sentiment to cloud his good business judgment. As a consequence, the organization was in financial difficulty during much of

the time he was in control. Throughout his career Stoneham was extremely loyal to his players, managers, and staff, and he agonized over trading players whom he liked even when such moves were of obvious benefit to the club.

Stoneham made two decisions of major importance during his first dozen years as owner of the Giants. The first was his reluctant move to reassign his faltering manager Terry to the club's farm system and replace him with another Giant hero, Mel Ott, as player-manager after the 1941 season. Ott's uninspired leadership kept the Giants mired in the second division during the war years, and in the middle of the 1948 season Stoneham was forced into the painful decision of firing Ott and replacing him with the controversial Leo Durocher, manager of the Giants' arch rival Brooklyn Dodgers. This move hit the baseball world like a bombshell, but it proved fortunate for Stoneham and the Giants. While still with the Dodgers, Durocher had publicly insulted the Giants in general and Ott in particular with his famous phrase, "Nice guys finish last." In fact, the Giants under Stoneham and Ott were made up of decent men, and in 1947 they did finish last. Under the leadership of the fiery Durocher, however, the Giants became a different team. Durocher and Stoneham argued vigorously over the ballclub's personnel for the remainder of the 1948 season. Finally Durocher convinced the hesitant owner to completely rebuild the team. They fired Ott's entire coaching staff, benched slugger Johnny Mize, and traded Stoneham favorites Sid Gordon, Willard Marshall, and Buddy Kerr to the Boston Braves for shortstop Alvin Dark and second baseman Eddie Stanky, forming the double play combination that Durocher coveted.

These wholesale changes devastated Stoneham, but within two years Durocher had led the Giants to the miracle finish of 1951: in the final seven weeks of that season they erased a 13½ game Brooklyn lead and won the final playoff game against the Dodgers, culminating with Bobby Thomson's dramatic home run in the bottom of the ninth inning that gave Stoneham's franchise its first pennant in fourteen years. By 1954, featuring the spectacular center fielder Willie Mays as their young superstar, the Giants won a second pennant and swept the Cleveland Indians in that year's World Series.

Within two years of the triumphant 1954 season, Stoneham and the Giants were in the throes of major financial problems. The venerable Polo Grounds, scene of many of the great moments in baseball for three-quarters of a century, was crumbling, street crime in the vicinity of Coogan's Bluff was increasing, and parking was becoming a serious concern. By early 1957 Stoneham was on the verge of moving his franchise to Minneapolis when Brooklyn Dodgers' owner Walter O'Malley convinced him to relocate to San Francisco at the same time the Dodgers moved to Los Angeles, thus ensuring the continuation of the traditional rivalry between the New York teams on the West Coast.

This dual move shocked the baseball world in 1958, but it proved beneficial for both teams. In the lucrative Los Angeles market, the Dodgers became one of the richest franchises in baseball. The Giants were also revitalized financially, averaging 1.5 million customers for their first decade at Candlestick Park adjacent to San Francisco Bay. In 1962, with Alvin Dark as manager, the club won its last National League pennant under Stoneham. By 1967, however, attendance began to slip at Candlestick, where thick fogs and icy Pacific winds dampened fans' enthusiasm for the novelty of major league baseball. In 1968 Charles O. Finley moved his Kansas City Athletics to Oakland, across the bay from San Francisco. The Bay Area was hard pressed to support two major league teams, and Stoneham soon began to experience the same heavy financial losses he had suffered in New York.

In order to avoid bankruptcy, Stoneham began selling his minor league franchises, and to reduce his bloated payroll he traded popular players like Mays, Willie McCovey, and Juan Marichal, thus further alienating fans. By the close of the 1975 season the Giants drew only slightly more than half a million customers, the lowest attendance of any major league team that year. In 1976 Stoneham sold his beloved Giants for $8 million to real estate developer Bob Lurie and meatpacker Arthur Herseth and retired from the business world. He died in Scottsdale, Arizona.

Throughout his forty-year career as president of the Giants, Stoneham developed the reputation of being a baseball purist, taking a childlike pleasure in the game. He was one of the last of the independent club owners who relied solely on the success of his baseball team for his livelihood. He was hard-drinking, sentimental to a fault, and was thought by many baseball operators to be an easy mark, especially when he had had too much Scotch. (Durocher once wrote, "To say that Horace can drink is like saying Sinatra can sing.") Stoneham's achievements as an executive, however, indicate that he was a shrewd judge of talent and a good businessman (he was named *The Sporting News*'s executive of the year in 1954). Fellow owner Bill Veeck, in a perceptive article in *Sports Illustrated* (31 May 1965), characterized Stoneham as being "helpless as a fox" with a "remarkable ability to simultaneously outdrink and outtrade the opposition." Bowie Kuhn, in his *Hardball: The Education of a Baseball Commissioner* (1987), said that Stoneham "may well have been the best-liked owner in baseball over the years I observed the game." Although he preferred to work quietly behind the scenes, Stoneham was at the forefront of progressive owners who brought African-American and Latino players to the major leagues. Through the years he presided over five National League pennant winners, including the 1951 "Miracle at Coogan's Bluff," and one World Series championship. He orchestrated many productive trades and managerial changes, and probably saved the franchise with its transplantation to the West Coast. His association with the Giants organization spanned the careers of legendary figures like Christy Mathewson, John McGraw,

Carl Hubbell, Durocher, and Mays, who wrote in *My Life In and Out of Baseball* (1966), "No one I know reacts more generously or loyally than Horace Stoneham."

• Stoneham is mentioned prominently in two books devoted exclusively to the history of the Giants in New York: Frank Graham, *The New York Giants* (1952), and Noel Hynd, *The Giants of the Polo Grounds* (1988). He is also covered in Russ Hodges's *My Giants* (1963), an account of the history of the Giants organization, including their early years in San Francisco. For Stoneham's position as an owner-businessman, see Don Kowet, *The Rich Who Own Sports* (1977), and Harold Parrott, *The Lords of Baseball* (1975). Stoneham's part in the much-publicized move of the Giants and Dodgers to the West Coast is the subject of part of John Helyar, *Lords of the Realm: The Real History of Baseball* (1994). In his biography of Durocher, *The Lip* (1993), Gerald Eskenazi reviewed the infamous Hollywood banquet in which entertainer Danny Kaye did an imitation of a drunken Stoneham staggering around the dais. He is mentioned with more respect in Alvin Dark, *When in Doubt, Fire the Manager* (1980), and in Willie Mays, *Say Hey* (1988). An obituary is in the *New York Times*, 9 Jan. 1990.

BRUCE L. JANOFF

STONEMAN, Ernest V. (25 May 1893–14 June 1968), country music singer and instrumentalist, was born Ernest Van Stoneman in Monarat (Iron Ridge), Carroll County, in southwestern Virginia, the son of Elisha C. Stoneman, a farmer and Baptist lay preacher, and Rebecca Bowers. His mother died when Ernest was three, and he was reared by his father and three cousins (Burton, George, and Bertha Stoneman), all of whom participated in the rich folk music tradition of the Blue Ridge Mountains. As a boy he learned folk ballads in a traditional manner from family and friends but also discovered songbooks, sheet music, and even scholarly collections of ballads, and added those to his sources. He also learned how to play the autoharp, an unusual instrument that was being imported into the mountains through such avenues as Sears Roebuck and Montgomery Ward catalog sales. He soon developed a unique style in which he was able to play lead melodies in addition to using the instrument as accompaniment.

Stoneman's formal education ended in the seventh grade. As a young man he worked at a variety of jobs, including carpentry, and like many of his friends, he made music informally at evening dances and on weekends. In November 1918 he married Hattie Frost from nearby Rockbridge County and found himself a part of another deeply musical family. He began enjoying music with his new in-laws, and he and Hattie began a family that would grow to fifteen children. In later years most of these children would take up music and become part of the performing Stoneman family.

In 1924, while working as a carpenter in Bluefield, West Virginia, Stoneman heard a Victrola record by an old friend of his, Henry Whitter, of Fries, Virginia, near where Stoneman had grown up. Whitter was singing a local ballad, but Stoneman was amazed that the company had recorded him and was convinced that he could sing the same kind of song much better. After writing to two major record companies in New York, he was invited to come up and record. He did so, securing a contract with the OKeh label (General Phonograph Company) and recording two mountain songs, "The Titanic" and "The Face That Never Returned" (OKeh 40288), released in May 1925. Both records sold well, and the commercial record companies, who were just beginning to record what would later be called country music, beat a path to Stoneman's door. At first the companies offered him a flat rate of $50 a side for his work, but later Stoneman was able to negotiate lucrative royalties.

From 1925 to 1934 Stoneman emerged as probably the most prolific record-maker in the field of old-time country music. In addition to OKeh, his labels included Edison, Gennett (with its subsidiaries Champion, Challenge, Supertone, and Silvertone), Victor, Plaza/Pathe, Paramount, and American Record Corporation (Vocalion). His total prewar discography appears to total more than 260 sides. Some of these were done with just his own guitar, autoharp, and harmonica accompaniment, but others were done with full string bands that included his in-laws Bolen and Irma Frost, his wife Hattie, and his cousins George and Willie. Other significant musicians from the Galax area on these sides were Frank and Oscar Jenkins, humorist Eck Dunford, Herbert and Earl Sweet, and fiddler Kahle Brewer. Recording names included the Dixie Mountaineers, the Blue Ridge Cornshuckers, and the Pilot Mountaineers, in addition to simply Ernest V. Stoneman.

The depression all but destroyed Stoneman's recording career, and by 1932 he had lost his home and most of his possessions in the Galax area. The family relocated to Washington, D.C.; there they struggled in poverty for several years and Stoneman found what work he could as a carpenter. (At one time he did finishing work on President Franklin D. Roosevelt's yacht.) By 1947 Stoneman had trained many of his children in his musical style and began to revive his musical career under the aegis of the Stoneman Family. They soon became a fixture in the District of Columbia country music scene and gained even more fame in 1956 when "Pop" (as Stoneman was now known) won a large cash prize on an NBC network television quiz show. A contingent of the family also started a band called the Bluegrass Champs that had a national following on Arthur Godfrey's television show.

In the 1960s the Stoneman Family rode the surge of folk music's popularity with a series of chart hits, a number of long-play records, an affiliation with Walt Disney's theme park, and their own syndicated TV show, some episodes of which featured Stoneman playing the autoharp and singing. Folk music collector Mike Seeger began interviews with Stoneman and recorded his unique autoharp playing on a series of Folkways LPs that had a major influence on younger folk musicians. But by 1968 Stoneman's health began

to fail and soon he was hospitalized. He died in Nashville, Tennessee.

• The definitive study of Ernest Stoneman and his family is Ivan M. Tribe, *The Stonemans: An Appalachian Family and the Music That Shaped Their Lives* (1993), which includes a discography. Obituaries are in the *New York Times* and the (Nashville) *Tennessean*, both 15 June 1968, and *Cash Box*, 29 June 1968.

CHARLES K. WOLFE

STONEMAN, George (8 Aug. 1822–5 Sept. 1894), soldier and governor of California, was born in the western New York village of Busti, the son of George Stoneman and Catherine Cheney. After attending a Jamestown, New York, academy, he received an appointment in 1842 to West Point, from which he graduated four years later. Commissioned a second lieutenant in the First Dragoons, during the Mexican War he served as quartermaster for the "Mormon Battalion" in Brigadier General Stephen Watts Kearny's expedition to California. Following the war he was stationed at various army posts in the Southwest, rising to the rank of captain in the Second Cavalry.

In April 1861, while commanding Fort Brown, Texas, Stoneman refused a surrender demand from his departmental commander, Brigadier General David E. Twiggs, who had gone over to the Confederates, and then managed to escape with his company to New York City by means of a steamboat that he seized. After remounting his company at Carlisle Barracks, Pennsylvania, he took it to Washington, D.C., the first cavalry to reach the capital after the outbreak of the Civil War. Promoted to major, he served on the staff of his West Point classmate General George B. McClellan (1826–1885), during the latter's campaign in western Virginia in the early summer of 1861. After McClellan received command of all Union forces in the Virginia theater, Stoneman became a brigadier general and chief of cavalry of what would become known as the Army of the Potomac. During the Peninsular campaign (Apr.-July 1862), however, he accomplished little owing to McClellan's practice of attaching the mounted forces to infantry corps instead of employing them as a consolidated unit. Perhaps for this reason Stoneman in the fall of 1862 transferred to the infantry, where at first he headed a division in the III Corps. On being promoted in November 1862 to major general, he commanded that corps at the battle of Fredericksburg, Virginia (13 Dec. 1862), winning promotion to the brevet rank of colonel in the regular army for gallantry in action.

Early in 1863 Major General Joseph Hooker assumed command of the Army of the Potomac and proceeded to organize its cavalry into a separate corps headed by Stoneman. Next he gave Stoneman a key role in the Chancellorsville campaign (28 Apr.-5 May 1863), namely to cut the railroads between General Robert E. Lee's forces and Richmond prior to an offensive by the rest of the Union army. Unfortunately for the success of this plan, after being delayed by uncrossable rivers and muddy roads, Stoneman's troopers failed to inflict any serious damage on the railroads; in the words of one of them, "Our only accomplishments were the burning of a few canal boats on the upper James River, some bridges, hen roosts, and tobacco houses." On the other hand, contrary to the view expounded by many historians, it is unlikely that the absence of Stoneman's raiding force was a major factor in Hooker's defeat at Chancellorsville: cavalry that remained with Hooker's army unavailingly detected the Confederate flanking march that led to the defeat, and even if Stoneman had been at Chancellorsville with his full strength he would not have necessarily been in the right position or possessed the means to alter the course of events.

Nevertheless, Hooker blamed Stoneman, along with various other of his generals, for his failure and therefore relieved him of command on 7 June 1863. From August 1863 to January 1864 Stoneman held the basically administrative post of chief of the Cavalry Bureau in Washington. In 1864 he went to Tennessee, where he briefly commanded the XXIII Corps, then was placed in charge of a cavalry division attached to the Army of the Ohio. In this capacity he served in William T. Sherman's Atlanta campaign (May-Sept. 1864), during which he persistently sought to perform a brilliant feat that would restore his military reputation, only to experience repeated frustration. Finally, in late July, Sherman assigned Stoneman, at his behest, a mission that held the promise of making him a hero in the North. According to Sherman's formal orders, he was to join with Brigadier General Edward McCook's cavalry division in cutting a railroad south of Atlanta; then, if he deemed it practicable, he was to attempt to liberate Union officer prisoners being held at Macon, Georgia, and the nearly 30,000 Federal enlisted men imprisoned at Andersonville, Georgia. Instead, and perhaps with Sherman's informal or tacit sanction, he did not link up with McCook (whose force was virtually destroyed) but headed straight for Macon, where on 30 July his troopers made a feeble attack that the Confederate defenders easily repulsed. He thereupon started back toward Sherman's army but on the following day was intercepted by Confederate cavalry near Sunshine Church and compelled to surrender along with 500 of his men. Quite understandably, following his capture he sat on a log and wept.

Bolstering the surmise that Stoneman had Sherman's unofficial permission to strike directly for Macon and Andersonville, in October 1864 Sherman arranged for Stoneman's release by means of an exchange and, instead of court-martialing him for disobedience of orders, put him in command of all cavalry in northeast Tennessee. From there, in December 1864, Stoneman conducted a raid that resulted in the destruction of the vital Confederate saltworks at Saltville, Virginia, and in March-April 1865 he concluded his Civil War career with a foray through southwestern Virginia and western North Carolina. Although these operations did little to restore his reputation,

they did win him promotion to brevet major general in the regular army.

For nearly four years following the war Stoneman served as commandant of the Richmond-Petersburg District in Virginia, during which period he married Mary Oliver Hardisty of Baltimore, by whom he had four children. In 1869 he became colonel of the Twenty-first Infantry and headed the Department of Arizona until August 1871, when he was retired from the army for disability. Moving to an estate near Los Angeles called "Los Robles," he became a California railroad commissioner in 1879 and in 1882 won election as a Democrat to the governorship of that state by a large majority. As governor (1883–1887) he championed stricter regulation and taxation of railroads and the subsidizing of irrigation projects, policies that brought him into conflict with the legislature, which, despite his twice calling it into special session, ultimately blocked them. Upon completing his term as governor he retired from public life. He died in Buffalo, New York, and was buried with full military honors on the shores of Lake Chautauqua not far from his birthplace.

Stoneman was handsome, brave, and enterprising. These qualities, however, were offset by arrogance, poor judgment, and above all by what Napoleon considered to be the worse deficiency in any general: the lack of good luck. Consequently, he was one of those generals whose performance fell short of both his own aspirations and the expectations of others.

• The main primary source of information about Stoneman and his activities during the Civil War is *The War of the Rebellion: A Compilation of the Official Records of the Union and Confederate Armies* (128 vols., 1880–1901), with his correspondence and the reports of those officers who served under him being the most revealing documents. The best, as well as most accessible, secondary source on his role in the Civil War is Stephen Z. Starr, *The Union Cavalry in the Civil War* (3 vols., 1979–1985). Ernest B. Furguson, *Chancellorsville 1863: The Souls of the Brave* (1992), describes and analyzes Stoneman's part in the Chancellorsville campaign, and Albert Castel, *Decision in the West: The Atlanta Campaign of 1864* (1992), does the same for his role in the Atlanta campaign. Despite its age, the best readily available account of Stoneman's tenure as governor of California appears in Hubert Howe Bancroft, *History of California*, vol. 7 (1890).

ALBERT CASTEL

STONOROV, Oskar Gregory (2 Dec. 1905–9 May 1970), architect, was born at Frankfurt-am-Main, Germany, the son of Gregor Stonorov, a bridge engineer, and Helene Traub. He grew up at Karlsruhe, where he studied piano in contemplation of a career in music. In 1924 he studied anatomy and mathematics at the University of Florence and spent some months as an apprentice to sculptor Aristide Maillol at Banguls-sur-Mer, France.

In 1925 Stonorov entered the Eidgenössische Technische Hochschule in Zurich, where he studied architecture with Karl Moser and became interested in the work of Frank Lloyd Wright through Moser's son,

Werner, who had studied at Taliesin. However, he was dissatisfied with the curriculum and did not complete his degree.

In 1928 he joined the office of André Lurcat in Paris as a student assistant. There he learned the practicalities of architectural practice and the latest developments in the discipline. Lurcat introduced him to the artistic community of Paris. At the suggestion of Christian Zervos, the editor of *Cahiers d'Art*, Stonorov and architect Willy Boesiger prepared a volume on Le Corbusier that was published in a format designed by Le Corbusier himself, the first of its distinguished series *Oeuvres complètes* (1937, 1946).

About this time Stonorov began his first major independent design project, a hospital intended to be built in Karlsruhe. He visualized a structure that would create a therapeutic environment that could contribute to a patient's healing. The concept was based on eliminating the traditional wards and airless corridors in favor of a series of cubical units with improved light and ventilation. He developed a broad spectrum of support for his undertaking, including the mayor of Karlsruhe, a board of leading German physicians, and Albert Einstein, but the building was never realized.

In 1929, when Stonorov emigrated to the United States, he was ambitious, learned, and possessed of a vision of architecture in the service of humanity that was to set the pattern for his subsequent career. He worked in various New York architectural firms. Interested by architectural developments in socialist societies, Stonorov, together with Boesiger, entered a competition to design a theater in Kharkov, in the Soviet Union, to be used by the community at large rather than as a gilded palace for the local elite. Although his design did not win, in 1931 he collaborated with Alfred Kastner, the winner of the Kharkov competition, on an entry for a major Soviet government structure, the Palace of the Soviets. Their design took second prize, ahead of entries by Le Corbusier and Gropius, but the winner was Ioneff, a suitor of Stalin's daughter Svetlana.

Stonorov and Kastner were dismissed from their New York architectural firms because of the political unpopularity of the Soviet regime in the United States, so they moved to Philadelphia, using the $6,000 prize to establish a firm there. Their first client was a hosiery workers union interested in constructing housing. Stonorov and his coworkers saw labor unions as a potent constituency for improving the living conditions of workers and their families. They imagined a better community environment than dreary rows of company houses but understood that if American cities were to be remade, the community and local politicians had to be involved directly in the process. An immediate result was the first housing project of the New Deal era, the Carl Mackley houses in Philadelphia (1932). The rooms of its 282 units were spacious; there were communal nurseries, laundries, and recreational facilities, as well as provision for the automobile, which Stonorov recognized as an essential appurtenance of American working-class life. These were then new concepts for public housing. A further innovation was a detailed survey of the potential residents about their needs, resources, and perceptions of desirable housing, the results of which substantially influenced the planning. The undertaking was technologically innovative through its pioneering use of reinforced concrete for dwelling units.

In the process, Stonorov rapidly acquired a political education and a circle of influential supporters. He was a founder of the Labor Housing Conference, which lobbied for a federal housing program. This led to the creation of the U.S. Housing Authority. Stonorov set the goals and provided resources and office space to give the conference impetus. He gained a brilliant collaborator in Catherine Bauer, the author of *Modern Housing* (1934).

Throughout the 1930s Stonorov strove to gain wider professional acceptance for American modern architecture, drawing on native tradition, as expressed by the work of Frank Lloyd Wright, for example, and enriched by the ideas of successive emigrants from Europe. The result was that by 1939 the American "modern movement" had become more than a peripheral version of developments in France and Germany and could be so viewed by professionals on both sides of the Atlantic. In 1938 Stonorov married Elizabeth Foster, the daughter of a Philadelphia industrialist. They had four children.

In 1941 Stonorov joined George Howe and Louis Kahn to create a new firm. Its first significant postwar project was Cherokee Village (1949), a mixture of cluster housing and individual dwellings on a wooded site in suburban Philadelphia. Stonorov's main idea was a design for family living in an agreeable, almost bucolic, setting. He also undertook the renovation of traditional Pennsylvania fieldstone farmhouses, preserving the masonry shell but creating within spacious areas for entertainment and family living, often using nontraditional materials such as chrome and steel.

Stonorov's various interests came together in 1947 for a city planning exposition, "Philadelphia Panorama," developed in collaboration with Edmund Bacon of the City Planning Commission. This offered a program for the city's future that was remarkable for its vision of broad community participation. In the years that followed, Philadelphia was widely regarded as a pioneering example of urban renewal, with Stonorov active in all aspects of the work.

He made other important public exhibitions for the 1939 New York World's Fair, a 1950 exhibit at the Corcoran Gallery, and the Government of India Pavilion for the 1964 New York World's Fair. Particularly noteworthy was the exhibition "Sixty Years of Living Architecture: The Work of Frank Lloyd Wright," which opened at the Palazzo Strozzi in Florence and traveled throughout Europe and the Americas (1951–1954).

During the last decades of his life, Stonorov returned to some of his earlier interests, among them sculpture (he made portrait busts of Indira Ghandi, Rudolf Serkin, and others) and large urban sculptural projects, including municipal fountains and abstract works. In this way architecture, the arts, and his views on the city and the family flowed together. His work in his last firm, Stonorov and Haws (founded 1953), followed this pattern.

Stonorov's interest in urban projects continued until the end of his life, although the national housing movement never achieved its original goals. Stonorov gave up on a national enterprise in favor of local undertakings, especially in the Philadelphia area (Schuylkill Falls, 1954–1955; Washington Square East, 1958; Southwark Plaza, 1962). The postwar housing boom favored isolated single-family dwellings in suburban areas, so, with public housing inceasingly restricted to cheaply built complexes for the urban poor, Stonorov redirected his ideas for sophisticated community construction to apartment complexes, especially in the Philadelphia area (Hopkins House, 1962; Plaza Apartments, 1965; Casa Fermi, 1966).

Stonorov was impatient with the vanity and individualism of many of his colleagues. "Architects have not learned to cooperate; they have no passion for anonymity. But Urbanism is greatly dependent on the culture of building, not the technology of building. We have zoos of technologies. But we are far from the Art of Togetherness which is total Architecture. . . . Today almost every architect is a tuba player" (*Architettura* 200: 75).

Stonorov's continental manner, distinctive accent in four languages, ready opinions, and broad cultural frame of reference sometimes seemed out of place in his adopted city and led some to deem him a poseur. But his genius, persuasiveness, creativity, and vivid personality soon broke through others' reserve and incredulity.

Through his work on the Detroit Redevelopment Project (1955), Stonorov began a close collaboration with Walter Reuther, head of the United Automobile Workers, who shared his belief that American labor unions, having gained economic goals, were lapsing into complacency, even corruption. New agendas were needed, such as education, housing, medical care, retirement, and recreational programs. This led to Stonorov's last major undertaking, the UAW (later the Walter and Mary Reuther Memorial) Family Education Center (1970) at Onoway, Michigan, a kind of union campus, learning center, and recreation area. Architect and union chief worked together, even collaborating on cabinetry and lighting fixtures.

Stonorov and Reuther were killed in the crash of Reuther's private plane at Pellston, Michigan.

• Stonorov's papers are in the Archive of Contemporary History, University of Wyoming, Cheyenne. Published essays include "Theaters and Places of Entertainment," in *New Architecture and City Planning*, ed. Paul Zucker (1944), pp. 99–107. Two booklets written jointly with his partner, Louis Kahn, are *You and Your Neighborhood* (1945) and *Why City Planning Is Your Responsibility* (1945). The major source for Stonorov's professional career is a biographical essay by Frederick Gutheim in a special issue of *Architettura* (Milan) devoted to Stonorov, vol. 18, no. 2 (whole no. 200) (1972).

This also contains a detailed listing of Stonorov's projects and appreciations by Edmund Bacon, Bruno Zevi, Otto E. Reichert-Facilides, and Louis Kahn; a list of Stonorov's major works and a biographical sketch by Jan Schall appears in the *Macmillan Encyclopedia of Architects*, vol. 4 (1982), pp. 134–35. Biographical sketches, portraits, and reminiscences appear in "The Importance of Being Oskar," *Greater Philadelphia Magazine*, Nov. 1962; the *New Yorker*, 5 Aug. 1967, pp. 45–50; and Peter Blake, *No Place Like Utopia: Modern Architecture and the Company We Kept* (1993), pp. 31–37. For Stonorov's role in public housing, see Ursula Cliff, "Oskar Stonorov: Public Housing Pioneer," *Design and Environment* 2, no. 7 (Fall 1971): 50–57, particularly for the Carl Mackley houses.

BENJAMIN R. FOSTER

STORER, Arthur (Feb. 1645–c. 1687), merchant and astronomer, was probably born in Buckminster, Leichestershire, England, the son of Edward Storer and Katherine Babington. He was baptized on 20 February 1645. Arthur's father died before his birth, and in 1647 his mother married William Clarke, an apothecary. By the time Arthur Storer was of school age, his family was living in Grantham, where Arthur and his brother attended King's School, along with Isaac Newton. The Storer brothers' mother was a close friend of Newton's mother. Since the Newtons lived several miles from Grantham, they arranged for Isaac to live with the Clarkes during the four years or so that he attended King's School.

Dr. Joseph Clarke, the brother of Storer's stepfather, taught mathematics at King's School and later practiced medicine in Grantham. Clarke has been credited with stimulating the budding genius in the young Newton, and Storer may also have gained from his step-uncle an early appreciation of mathematics and the physical sciences. Storer's uncle on his mother's side, Humphrey Babington, was a senior fellow at Trinity College, Cambridge. Storer's formal education appears to have ended at King's School, but his uncle Babington arranged for Newton to be admitted to Cambridge, where he later became a distinguished faculty member.

Nothing is known about Storer's adult years until 1672, when he appeared as a witness to the will of his brother-in-law James Truman. Truman died in Calvert County, Maryland, shortly after he and his wife had immigrated to Maryland with their children and several servants. Storer may have accompanied them, or he may have preceded them to Maryland.

In 1678, when he was back in England on a visit, Storer initiated correspondence with Newton through his uncle Babington. Storer asked Babington to have Newton check the figures in two tables he had constructed. One table gave the altitude of Polaris above or below the celestial pole, and the other showed the azimuth of Polaris from true north, both calculated at hourly intervals for different latitudes. Storer claimed that he had used a new method of calculation that enabled him to determine the azimuth directly without first finding the altitude, and he solicited Newton's opinion of his work.

Storer wrote Newton three more times from London while awaiting a ship to take him back to Maryland, and he received two letters in response. Storer sent Newton a new table showing the hourly azimuth of the sun and explained the methodology he had followed in creating the astronomical tables.

Storer's most important astronomical observations came after his return to Maryland. In the fall of 1680 a comet, described as one of the "most spectacular" of the seventeenth century, attracted the attention of astronomers around the world. The science of mathematical astronomy was in its infancy, and leading astronomers throughout Europe tracked the comet in an effort to explain its motion and changing appearance. Newton discussed the comet of 1680 in detail in *Principia* (1687). Using data on the position of the comet between November 1680 and February 1681 supplied by observers in England, Europe, and overseas, Newton successfully explained the motion of the comet through the winter sky. Among the data Newton had at his disposal were two sets of observations from North American astronomers—from Thomas Brattle at Harvard College in Cambridge, Massachusetts, and from Storer, in Calvert County, Maryland. Although Newton cited the Massachusetts observations in *Principia*, he did not specifically name Brattle as the source; he used Storer's figures more extensively and credited him by name.

In April 1683 Storer wrote his last letter to Newton. In it he included observations he had made of another comet that had appeared over Calvert County in August and September 1682. This chart of data was for the comet named Halley's, after Edmond Halley, who used his own observations of the 1682 comet to chart its course and to establish that it was a periodic comet that would return approximately every seventy-six years.

A modern scholar has termed Storer's data on the comet of 1682 "far superior to those made by Halley himself" and noted that although the astronomical instruments Storer used were few and crude, the accuracy of his observations "was exceeded by very few observers anywhere" (Broughton, pp. 91–92). The only astronomical instruments Storer is known to have used were a "pocket piece" (perhaps a small telescope or astrolab), a prospective glass (a mariner's "spy glass"), a homemade quadrant, a bow, and a forestaff.

Storer's observations of the comets of 1680 and 1682 were made "at the River Patuxent near Hunting Creek, Maryland," where his widowed sister, Ann Truman, and her second husband, Robert Skinner lived. Storer probably lived with the Skinners, because his estate inventory, taken after his death, lacks most of the items necessary for housekeeping.

Arthur Storer died in Calvert County, Maryland. He never married and left no children. He called himself a merchant in his will, but his estate inventory suggests that his mercantile activities were small scale. Storer appears to have specialized in importing apothecary and medicinal goods. Several legacies mentioned in his will were to be paid out of money he had on account with Samuel Taylor, a London druggist, and the most valuable item in his inventory was a new shipment of "physical means," or medicinal items. Having been raised in the house of an apothecary, Storer had apparently acquired the knowledge and sources of supply in London he needed to support himself in Maryland by importing and dispensing medicines.

Storer's inventory includes "a parcell of mathematical Instruments," probably the astronomical apparatus he used to make his observations. He also had a library of fifty-two books, a large library for the day, especially given his modest means.

Storer's life in England and in Maryland was unexceptionable except for his penchant for astronomy. His careful calculations and systematic observations of the nighttime sky from the banks of the Patuxent River in Calvert County, Maryland, advanced the science of astronomy and earned him a place among the handful of astronomers operating in British North America in the seventeenth century.

• Storer's estate papers are at the Maryland State Archives in Annapolis. Virtually the only other primary sources relating to him are the six letters he wrote to Isaac Newton, either directly or through his uncle Humphrey Babington. The letters are printed in Sir Isaac Newton, *Correspondence*, ed. H. W. Turnbull et al., vol. 2 (7 vols., 1959–1977), pp. 269–85, 368–72, 387–93. Storer's life and astronomical observations are detailed in Lou Rose and Michael Marti, *Arthur Storer of Lincolnshire, England, and Calvert County, Maryland: Newton's Friend, Star Gazer, and Forgotten Man of Science in Seventeenth-Century Maryland* (1984). Peter Broughton, "Arthur Storer of Maryland: His Astronomical Work and His Family Ties with Newton," *Journal for the History of Astronomy* 19 (1988): 77–96, provides important genealogical information on Storer and corrects some errors and unsubstantiated claims in the Rose and Marti biography. In addition, Broughton checked the accuracy of Storer's observations by computer and provides an assessment of their accuracy as compared to other seventeenth-century data.

GREGORY A. STIVERSON

STORER, David Humphreys (26 Mar. 1804–10 Sept. 1891), physician and naturalist, was born in Portland, Maine, the son of Woodbury Storer, a merchant, shipowner, and chief justice of common pleas, and Margaret Boyd. He received an A.B. degree from Bowdoin College in 1822, after which he took up the study of medicine and graduated from the Harvard Medical School in 1825. Having apprenticed to Dr. John Collins Warren (1778–1856), Storer established a practice in Boston, where he remained throughout his career, coming to specialize in obstetrics. Like some others of his generation and community, Storer combined active interests in both medicine and science. His bibliography lists more than 100 works, which are nearly evenly divided between medicine and natural history. The two subjects characterize certain periods of his life; most of his medical contributions appeared around 1850–1855, especially in the *American Journal of the Medical Sciences*.

Though Storer was keenly interested in zoology, and those activities largely sustain his historical reputation, there is no indication that he sought to replace his medical career with science. His commitment not only to medical practice, but to its improvement was demonstrated in 1838 when, in cooperation with Jacob Bigelow, Oliver Wendell Holmes (1809–1894), and Edward Reynolds, he helped to establish the private Tremont Street Medical School in Boston. The school's instruction was offered during times when Harvard was on a vacation schedule and further supplemented that institution by its clinical approach when such teaching methods were little used in the university. Storer took charge of obstetrics. Among his advanced educational practices was the use of manikins and the assignment of students to attend labor as a means of promoting clinical observation and experience. From 1849 to 1858 he was visiting physician at the Massachusetts General Hospital and from 1854 to 1868 was obstetrician at the Boston Lying-In Hospital. During the years 1854–1868 he was professor of obstetrics and medical jurisprudence in the Harvard Medical School and from 1855 to 1864 was its dean. For some thirty-five years he was a medical examiner for Mutual Benefit Life Insurance Company of New Jersey. Storer is not credited with any notable contributions to medical knowledge, but through his teaching and his strong and fostering personality he influenced the professional outlook of his students and colleagues. In 1866 he served as president of the American Medical Association and in 1876 was a founder of the American Gynecological Society. In the latter year Bowdoin College honored Storer with the LL.D. degree.

Storer's interest in science was apparent during his undergraduate years when he showed particular interest in mineralogy, entomology, and ornithology. He was an original member (1830) and vice president (1843–1860) of the Boston Society of Natural History, and it was through that body and the American Academy of Arts and Sciences that he projected his scientific interests. Initially he was most concerned with mollusks, and in 1837 he published a translation (from French) of L. C. Kiener's *General Species and Iconography of Recent Shells*.

Storer's attention was turned to the study of fishes in 1837 when he was appointed a commissioner to the Zoological and Botanical Survey of Massachusetts and was assigned the study of reptiles and fish. His disciplined schedule brought him to the collections of the Boston Society of Natural History in the early morning hours, and his affability and enthusiasm won him support and cooperation when he visited the wharves and fish markets to collect specimens and information. His state report appeared in 1839, but this was only a prelude to many years of independent work that resulted in his "History of the Fishes of Massachusetts," which was serially published in the *Memoirs of the American Academy* in 1853 and 1867. In the latter year it was published as a separate work. Storer included species descriptions (especially of saltwater fishes) and histories and discussed the economic significance of the fish. In 1845 he prepared a compilation on North

American fishes, which was published the following year by the American Academy. Storer's ichthyological works were largely catalogues of individual species. These he described and also gave miscellaneous information on distribution, behavior, and commercial considerations. He was largely dependent on others for specimens and information, although physical descriptions generally were his own. Economic interests were an important motivation for his work, and he demonstrated little interest in larger issues of taxonomy and relations of zoological forms.

Storer was a friend of Louis Agassiz and brother-in-law to ornithologist Thomas M. Brewer. In 1829 he married Abby Jane Brewer, who died in 1885. Of their five children, Francis Humphreys Storer became a chemist, and Horatio Robinson Storer became an obstetrician and gynecologist. Storer was much admired in both the medical and scientific communities, and his name was assigned to several zoological specimens. He was a man of empathy, impetuous and of strong feelings and actions in regard to matters of right and justice. D. Humphreys Storer, as he sometimes is called, died in Boston, Massachusetts, the city's oldest physician.

• Storer's papers are at the Countway Library of the Harvard Medical School and in the Boston Museum of Science. His chief published works are "Reports on the Ichthyology and Herpetology of Massachusetts," in Storer and William B. O. Peabody, *Report on Fishes, Reptiles and Birds of Massachusetts* (1839); "Synopsis of the Fishes of North America," *Memoirs of the American Academy of Arts and Sciences*, n.s., 2 (1846): 253–550; and *A History of the Fishes of Massachusetts* (1867). A bibliography of his publications is in Bowdoin College Library, *Bibliographical Contributions* 2 (Aug. 1892): 72–78. Biographical sketches include *Journal of the American Medical Association* 17 (3 Oct. 1891): 533–34; Samuel H. Scudder, *Proceedings of the American Academy of Arts and Sciences* 27 (1891–1892): 388–91; Samuel Garman, "Dr. D. H. Storer's Work on Fishes," *Proceedings of the Boston Society of Natural History* 25 (1890–1892): 354–57; W. L. Bierring, "David Humphreys Storer, M.D.," in Morris Fishbein et al., *History of the American Medical Association, 1847–1947* (1947); and George E. Gifford, Jr., "The Ichthyological Dean," *Harvard Medical Alumni Bulletin* 39 (1964): 22–27.

CLARK A. ELLIOTT

STORER, Horatio Robinson (27 Feb. 1830–18 Sept. 1922), pioneer gynecologist and anti-abortion crusader, was born in Boston, Massachusetts, the son of David Humphreys Storer, a prominent naturalist and medical professor, and Abby Jane Brewer. His father had written on the fishes of Massachusetts and North America, helped establish the Tremont Street Medical School in Boston, and eventually taught obstetrics and medical jurisprudence at Harvard Medical School. Storer followed remarkably similar professional interests.

Storer graduated in 1850 from Harvard College, where he had studied with his father's friends zoologist Jean Louis Rodolphe Agassiz and botanist Asa Gray. After completing a report on the fishes of Labrador and Nova Scotia for the Boston Society of Natural

History, Storer began the study of medicine under his father at Tremont. He also enrolled at Harvard Medical School, where he completed an M.D. in 1853. During two years of postgraduate observation and training in Europe, he served for a period as assistant to Sir James Y. Simpson, who taught Storer the use of chloroform in childbirth and surgery. Storer, who subsequently coedited Simpson's *Obstetrical Memoirs* (2 vols., 1855–1856), brought the anesthetic technique back to Boston, where he established a specialty practice in obstetrics and gynecological surgery, one of the first such specialty practices in the nation.

In 1857 Storer began the professional activity for which he is best remembered: a crusade against abortion. Widely practiced in the United States at that time, abortion was openly advertised in the popular press and generally not illegal, as long as the pregnancy was terminated prior to "quickening" (the perception of fetal movement by the mother), which usually occurred in the fourth or fifth month of gestation. Storer argued, as had his father and many others before him, that gestation was a continuous process; to interrupt it before quickening was no different from interrupting it after quickening. Working through the new American Medical Association (founded in 1847), Storer appears also to have been motivated by a strong desire to rid his field of irregular healers, who were alleged to be performing many of the nation's abortions, and by a rather blatant streak of antifeminism.

From Boston, Storer coordinated efforts around the country by individual physicians and local medical societies affiliated with the AMA to press their state legislatures for statutes banning abortion at any point in gestation. Toward that end he also published voluminously on the subject in medical journals, wrote books for fellow physicians, and wrote popular tracts for the general public, including *Why Not? A Book for Every Woman* (1866) and *Is It I? A Book for Every Man* (1867). After studying for a time at Harvard Law School, he coauthored with the legal scholar Franklin Fiske Heard his most substantial work, *Criminal Abortion: Its Nature, Its Evidence, and Its Law* (1868). Between the late 1860s and the early 1890s this crusade was largely successful, as state after state moved for the first time in American history to proscribe abortion at any point in gestation.

Storer was also involved in a number of other professional controversies and innovations during his career. According to one historian of obstetrics, Storer "kept things stirred up wherever he was" (Thoms, p. 150). He developed new procedures in gynecological surgery, became an early champion of the medical use of rubber gloves, and agitated the cause of municipal sanitation. In an open dispute with his Harvard colleagues in 1865 he championed chloroform over ether then bolted Boston just ahead of his formal expulsion from the Harvard faculty in order to become professor of obstetrics and medical jurisprudence at the Berkshire Medical College in Pittsfield, Massachusetts. He recemented his professional relations in Boston two years later, when the Berkshire Medical Col-

lege folded. Storer is generally regarded as one of the founders of gynecology as a separate medical field and in 1869 helped launch and edit the *Journal of the Gynecological Society of Boston*. He was one of five surgeons who "came to monopolize the ovariotomies of the United States and Canada" (Toner, p. 5).

Storer married Emily Elvira Gilmore in 1853; the couple had four children. After Emily's death in 1872, Storer married her sister, Augusta Caroline Gilmore, that same year. Also in 1872 Storer retired from active practice, having failed to recover fully from an operation, and moved to Italy to restore his own health. After Augusta's death in Italy two years later, Storer returned in 1876 to semi-retirement in Newport, Rhode Island. Later that year he married Frances S. Mackenzie, a founder of Saint Elizabeth's Hospital in Boston. With this third marriage, Storer became a fervent Roman Catholic and later left portions of his estate to various Catholic agencies. He gave the Boston Medical Library his impressive collection of medals of medical interest.

When Storer died in Newport at the age of ninety-two, the press paid less attention to his career as a medico-legal activist, health-care professionalizer, and pioneering gynecologist than to the fact that he had been Harvard's oldest living graduate. He is now remembered, however, as having significantly influenced the evolution of U.S. abortion law in the nineteenth century.

• Storer's personal papers, including key correspondence from his campaign against abortion, are in the Countway Library, Harvard Medical School. In addition to the works already mentioned, Storer published at least eighty other items of substance (mostly in medical journals) and probably an equal number of letters, comments, reports, or observations. While the bulk of his publications dealt with technical aspects of gynecology and gynecological surgery, Storer also addressed subjects such as nymphomania, female alcoholism, and insanity in women in "The Unfitness of Women for Medical Practitioners," *Boston Medical and Surgical Journal* 75, no. 9 (1866): 191–92. Joseph M. Toner, *A Sketch of the Life of Horatio R. Storer, M.D.* (1878), covers Storer's early career and lists most of Storer's published works to that point. Herbert Thoms, *Chapters in American Obstetrics* (1933), contains a fine assessment of Storer's career. James C. Mohr, *Abortion in America: The Origins and Evolution of National Policy, 1800–1900* (1978), tells the story of Storer's successful crusade to criminalize the practice of abortion. The *New York Times*, 19 Sept. 1922, published an obituary, as did virtually all of the Newport and Boston papers; the *Times*, 28 Nov. 1922, p. 21, also noted the disposition of Storer's estate.

JAMES C. MOHR

STOREY, Wilbur Fiske (18 Dec. 1819–27 Oct. 1884), journalist, was born near Salisbury, Vermont, the son of Jesse Storey and Elizabeth Pierce, farmers. He spent one term at the village academy in Middlebury, Vermont, and then apprenticed to a printer. He moved to New York City in 1836 as a printer on David Hale's *Journal of Commerce*. He was influenced by

Hale's racism, antiabolitionism, and Jacksonianism and became familiar with James Gordon Bennett's new sensationalist New York *Herald*.

Storey stayed in New York until he could save enough money to move west. From 1838 to 1841 he published two partisan Democratic papers, the *La Porte Herald* in South Bend, Indiana, where a sister lived, and the *Mishawaka (Ind.) Tocsin*. He moved in 1842 to Jackson, Michigan, where another sister lived, and read law for two years. Jackson was a growing city with a new state prison and no Democratic newspaper, so before the 1844 presidential election Storey began the weekly *Jackson Patriot*. For his services he was appointed postmaster by the new president, James K. Polk. In 1847 Storey married Maria Parsons Isham, a Congregational minister's daughter, but after Polk's term was over he lost his postmaster's job and his marriage began to deteriorate. In Jackson he was a consistent Democrat, supporting Polk and the Mexican War, attacking antislavery, and helping Michigan Democratic leader Lewis Cass. He was elected to the state constitutional convention in 1850 and was responsible for the clause that no mechanical trade be taught to convicts at the state prison.

The state party organ, the *Detroit Free Press*, ran into financial difficulty in 1853, and Storey was offered a half interest for only $3,000. He bought out his partner and assumed complete control. Storey was a genius at typography, and he remade the paper's format, added a city news department, and started a Sunday edition. He made the *Free Press* the most popular paper in Detroit with a formula of sensationalism and complete news coverage. With its focus on murder, rape, and seduction, under shocking column heads, the paper became the dirtiest in the Midwest. Storey spent all day at the paper, putting his personal stamp on everything that appeared. He warred continuously with the typographical union, was frequently sued for libel, and had a long feud with Henry Tappan, president of the University of Michigan.

In politics Storey was a rabid Negrophobe, and he believed that slavery was no concern of the federal government. Antislavery fanaticism would lead to a breakup of the union, he believed. Storey supported Stephen A. Douglas and popular sovereignty, continental expansionism, and the annexation of Cuba. He was a passionate opponent of Prohibition and defended Catholics and immigrants against the Know Nothings. His editorials were widely reprinted.

When the Republican party was organized at Jackson in 1854, Storey denounced it as sectional and permeated with nativism. He was a delegate to the 1856 Democratic convention that nominated James Buchanan, but he followed Douglas in his break with the president over the Lecompton Constitution. Storey backed Douglas for the 1860 nomination and blamed Buchanan for the election of Abraham Lincoln. But he attacked secession as unconstitutional and supported early attempts to suppress it.

In May 1861 Storey bought the *Daily Chicago Times* from Cyrus McCormick. It was a weak Douglas paper

with a circulation of less than 1,000. Chicago had become the leading city of the Midwest and needed a strong Democratic paper to rally the region behind Douglas for 1864. Another factor in the move was the final dissolution of his marriage. His last editorial in the *Free Press* announced the death of Douglas.

Storey remade the *Chicago Times* in the image of the *Free Press*, improving its typography with new presses and type, adding a page of local news, and emphasizing sensationalism. Until September 1862, when the Emancipation Proclamation was announced, he had supported the war effort and the Lincoln administration. Now he became one of the president's most relentless critics. The unconstitutional action of "Czar Abraham," Storey screamed, had turned the war into an extended John Brown raid and would flood the Midwest with blacks. Not a day passed without an attack on Lincoln as the *Times* became the leading Copperhead paper in the country. On 3 June 1863 the army seized the *Times*'s offices on orders of General Ambrose Burnside. But Chicago was a Democratic city and there were threats of a riot, so Burnside was forced to revoke his order, and the *Times* reappeared on 5 June. Storey had not crossed the line to treason and had consistently opposed secret societies such as the Knights of the Golden Circle. After Lincoln's reelection in 1864 and with the end of the war in sight, Storey moderated his attacks on the president.

Despite its extreme politics, the *Times* left all of its midwestern rivals behind in its coverage of war news. Its war correspondent Sylvannus Cadwallader, had a special relationship with General Ulysses S. Grant that he used to advantage. When the war ended, the *Times* was the most widely circulating paper in the Midwest.

For the next twenty years the *Times* was the undisputed circulation leader of midwestern journalism. It was politically independent with extensive news coverage. In 1866 it went to an eight-page, six-column format and in 1873 to twelve pages. The Sunday edition was sixteen pages of entertainment, expanded to twenty-four by 1881, when Storey printed in one issue the entire revised version of the New Testament. Franc Wilkie, his chief assistant since 1865, headed an extensive network of foreign correspondents from London in the 1870s, and the *Times* had its own correspondent to cover the Indian wars.

Indecent sensationalism was its outstanding characteristic, used to appeal to its working-class audience. Storey's headline of a hanging, "JERKED TO JESUS," is an example. In 1870 Storey was horse-whipped by burlesque dancers he had attacked. He remained antiunion and set up a typographical school for women to train as strike-breakers. His relationships with women often earned public notice and influenced his career. Storey had been frequenting prostitutes since his move to Chicago and in 1863 had contracted paresis, a brain disease caused by syphilis. He grew increasingly erratic by the 1870s as the *Times* crucified politicians, the medical profession, lawyers, and judges and disregarded private reputations. Having divorced his wife in 1867, he married Harriet

Dodge in 1868. When she died of pneumonia in early 1873 he was inconsolable; he set out to ruin her doctor and turned to spiritualism to contact her through seances. Eureka Pearson became his third wife in 1874 after she agreed in a prenuptial contract to give up any inheritance from Storey. He had no children.

In 1874 Storey began a broadside attack on city politicians that resulted in at least twenty libel suits but no final judgments. He was a millionaire by this time and increasingly reactionary. Storey had always believed in small government, low taxes, and individual enterprise, and that city government should abandon social services and be cut to the bone.

By 1876 Storey was experiencing the symptoms of paretic dementia, periodic attacks of dizziness, and in 1878 he had a paralytic stroke. In 1879 his wife persuaded him to change his will to leave his entire estate to her. In May 1882 a third stroke left him paralyzed. He died in Chicago. There followed a long contest between Storey's siblings and his widow over the will, which left the *Times* without effective direction, and it ceased publication on 3 March 1895.

• None of Storey's papers survives. The standard biography is Justin E. Walsh, *To Print the News and Raise Hell! A Biography of Wilbur F. Storey* (1968). The best interpretation of Storey's place in Chicago journalism is David Paul Nord, "The Public Community: The Urbanization of Journalism in Chicago," *Journal of Urban History* 11 (1985): 411–41. A different focus is in Gunther Barth, *City People: The Rise of Modern City Culture in Nineteenth-century America* (1980), chapter 3. Much valuable information is offered by Storey's longtime assistant, Franc C. Wilkie, *Personal Reminiscences of Thirty-five Years in Journalism* (1891). Obituaries are in the *Chicago Times* and the *Chicago Tribune*, 28 Oct. 1884.

JAMES L. CROUTHAMEL

STORM, Hans Otto (29 July 1895–11 Dec. 1941), writer and radio telegraph engineer, was born in Bloomington, California, the son of Joachim Otto Storm, a bank teller, and Marie Rehwoldt. His parents both came from Germany and met in the United States. Storm grew up in Anaheim, California. After graduating from public high school, he worked for a year in the electrician's trade. In 1917 he was conscripted into the army, but he spent most of the war in hospitals on account of illness. Afterward Storm was frequently ill, and he was never robust.

In 1920 Storm received a B.A. in engineering from Stanford University and went to work as a radio engineer in radio telegraphy with the Federal Telegraph Company in Palo Alto, California. He married Grace Cleone Camp in 1921 and was subsequently employed in radio telegraphy with Mackay Radio from 1925 to 1930. From 1931 to 1932 he took a job with All-American Cables in Nicaragua and Peru, then returned to Mackay Radio for two more years. His last job was designing and installing radio equipment for Globe Wireless, Ltd., in San Francisco, where he was chief engineer. During his professional career, Storm was responsible for a number of technological achievements, such as developing the arc converter electrode,

a terminal through which electricity is discharged, and introducing novel methods to remotely control radio transmitters and receivers.

As a fiction writer, Storm produced mostly novelettes and short stories. Self-taught in literature, he devoured a great number of classics but was particularly attracted to the work of Jack London and then of Joseph Conrad. The greatest intellectual influence on Storm was the work of Thorstein Veblen, especially *The Theory of the Leisure Class* (1899) and *The Engineers and the Price System* (1921). Veblen analyzed the psychological bases of social and economic institutions, with a special focus on the part played by technicians in contemporary society. Storm's distinctly clipped literary style and incisive analysis both reflected his intellectual training as an engineer.

Storm's first book, *Full Measure* (1929), treated an idealistic young engineer on the staff of an organization involved in the transmission of wireless communications. Set in Central America, Los Angeles, and China, the work was poorly received. However, Storm's fortune reversed itself with *Pity the Tyrant* (1937), which won the Gold Medal of the Commonwealth Club of California. The tale centers around an unnamed German-American engineer working for a power company in Lima, Peru. While observing strikes of bus drivers and telephone workers, he becomes acutely conscious of the exploitation of Peruvian workers at the hands of both native and foreign employers. He is eventually fired and forced to leave Lima because he tries to defend one of the strikers, refusing to serve as a strikebreaker.

Pity the Tyrant was hailed as a provocatively radical novelette. The authorities of Peru were so incensed by the book that, when Storm returned to Lima in 1939 on a communications system installation job, he was immediately expelled from the country. In an autobiographical statement, he described his political views as advocating a three-fold outlook: "The distribution of the world's goods and powers on a broad popular base, with some favoritism toward productive workers; the discouragement of aggressiveness; [and] as far as is compatible with these values, the greatest freedom to the individual in his private life." He claimed that he became a radical by reading the *Los Angeles Times* at home. In 1935 Storm was elected to the executive committee of the Communist-led League of American Writers. The critic Edmund Wilson characterized Storm's left-wing ideas as distinctly predepression; he found Storm linked to the tradition of the Germans who fled to the United States after the 1848 revolution.

In 1939 Storm published *Made in U.S.A.*, a social fable. The novelette narrates, in objective style, the story of the passengers on board the *India*, a 12,000-ton steamer, on a cruise around the world. The ship's owner has pressured the captain to run the *India* to pieces in order to get the insurance. When the *India* goes aground near an island supposedly populated by cannibals, the true pettiness of the passengers is revealed.

Storm's last published works were also markedly political. *Count Ten* (1940), Storm's only full-length novel, treats the wandering life of a young radical. At the outset the protagonist is jailed for resisting the draft in World War I, and at the conclusion he is incarcerated again as a consequence of his work for a left-wing social movement modeled on the End Poverty in California campaign of Upton Sinclair. "The Two Deaths of Kaspar Rausch," which appeared in *O'Brien's Best Stories* (1940), treats a journalist who dies fighting in the Spanish Civil War.

A year later Storm, in a hurried effort to complete a large radio transmitter located in San Francisco for the U.S. Army, was killed accidentally by an electrical shock while testing the transpacific transmission equipment. In 1948 David Greenhood, an editor and friend of Storm's, published a memorial collection, *Of Good Family: Stories and Observations about Spanish America*. The volume contains *Pity the Tyrant*, as well as stories, essays and notebook entries about Peru and neighboring countries.

• A substantial appreciation of Storm is in Edmund Wilson, *The Boys in the Back Room: Notes on California Novelists* (1941). Autobiographical quotations appear in the entry on Storm in *Twentieth Century Authors*, ed. Stanley J. Kunitz and Howard Haycraft (1942).

ALAN M. WALD

STORROW, Charles Storer (25 Mar. 1809–30 Apr. 1904), civil engineer, was born in Montreal, Quebec, Canada, the son of Thomas Wentworth Storrow, a merchant, and Sarah Phipps Brown. Storrow's father was a successful Boston merchant who, before Storrow's birth, moved his family to Montreal in 1808 for business reasons and then back to Boston in 1812. Storrow spent his early youth in the Boston area and in 1818 sailed with his family to France, where his father set up an import-export business in Paris. For the next six years Charles attended French private schools. In 1824 he returned to Massachusetts to continue his education, spending the next two years at the Round Hill School, a progressive preparatory school in Northampton. He entered Harvard College as a sophomore in 1826 and profited especially from the school's recently strengthened science curriculum.

In his senior year, faced with deciding on a profession and distressed over the recent collapse of his father's business, he turned for advice to engineer Laommi Baldwin II, a family friend. From that time until Baldwin's death in 1838 the two men corresponded frequently, with Baldwin serving as Storrow's mentor during his years of engineering training and early practice. After graduating at the top of his class in 1829, Storrow returned to Paris to live with his family and embark on an engineering program at the École des Ponts et Chaussées, one of the few Americans to do so in the antebellum period. During the next two years (1830–1832) he studied under leading French engineers and scientists such as Louis-Marie-Henri Navier, the founder of structural analysis, attended public lectures in the applied sciences at the Conservatoire des Arts et Métiers, met prominent scientists at the Académie des Sciences (including its president, Pierre-Simon Girard, an important hydraulic engineer and theorist), and purchased French engineering books both for himself and for shipment to Baldwin. He frequented the Tuesday soirées at the Paris home of the marquis de Lafayette, a family friend, where he was introduced to distinguished scientists like Alexander Humboldt and Georges Cuvier and political figures. He put his two summers abroad to good use by inspecting engineering works in and around Paris (1830) and in Britain (1831). In July 1830 he was an eyewitness to the revolution that overthrew Charles X and brought Louis-Philippe to power.

Although worried that his lack of engineering experience would seriously hurt his chances for employment, Storrow was hired only days after his return to the United States in 1832 as an assistant engineer on the construction of the Boston and Lowell Railroad. He was named chief engineer and agent, or general manager, of the completed line in 1836. That year he married Lydia Cabot Jackson, the daughter of Dr. James Jackson of Boston; they had seven children. A year earlier, he had published *A Treatise on Water-Works*, a milestone scientific study that drew heavily on recent advances in European and especially French hydraulic theory, in particular the work of Marie Riche de Prony, R. Génieys, and Jean-Baptiste Bélanger. Widely utilized by a generation of hydraulic engineers in the building of canals and waterworks, his study was instrumental in introducing scientific methods to American engineering practice. In 1841–1842 he participated with engineers James F. Baldwin and George Whistler in water measurement experiments on the Lowell power canals, directing the trials and writing the reports. The experiments marked the beginning of the classic age of New England hydraulic experimentation, whose contributors included James B. Francis, Uriah Boyden, John R. Freeman, and Hiram Mills. In 1845 he was hired by the Boston Associates as chief engineer, agent, and treasurer of the newly formed Essex Company to build the industrial city of Lawrence, Massachusetts, on the north bank of the Merrimack River. In the next three years he drew up the city's plan, laid out its streets, supervised the construction of its factories and boardinghouses, and designed and constructed its North Canal and Great Stone Dam, thereby creating a waterpower of 10,000 horsepower. The dam, a massive granite structure standing 32 feet high and 900 feet long (1,600 feet counting wing walls) that he designed using mathematical theory, is considered a monument of nineteenth-century American engineering. In the 1860s he built another canal and laid out streets and factory sites at Lawrence on the south bank of the Merrimack River. For the first fifteen years of the town's existence he played a prominent role in the Lawrence community: he was president of its first two banks, chaired its early school and finance committees, and was elected as its first mayor (1853). When the city's Pemberton Mill collapsed in 1860, killing more than eighty workers and injuring many more, he was named treasurer of the relief committee set up to help the victims and their families. He served as the Essex Company's chief engineer until 1869 and as its agent and treasurer until 1882, when he assumed the largely titular position of president. He retired from the company in 1889, at the age of eighty.

Though most of his professional life was devoted to the construction of Lawrence and the management of its waterpower, from time to time he took on other engineering assignments. In 1861 he conducted a hydraulic survey of the Concord and Sudbury river basins for the commonwealth of Massachusetts, and in 1862 he was appointed by the governor as an engineering consultant to the long-stalled Hoosac Tunnel project in the western part of the state. In the latter capacity he traveled to France to inspect French tunneling techniques, including the use of compressed-air drills, at Mont Cenis in the Alps. Following his return he submitted a report to the Massachusetts Senate. In 1876–1879 he served as a park commissioner of the city of Boston.

Storrow and his wife lived in Boston all their married life except for the fifteen years (1846–1860) they resided in Lawrence. Storrow was known as a gentle, kindly man who possessed a scholar's love of books and an engineer's attention to detail and insistence on accuracy. At the time of his death (in Boston at his home on Beacon Street), an anonymous fellow engineer remarked, "Mr. Storrow came nearer the ideal of the perfect gentleman than any man I have ever known" (*Engineering News* 51 [1904]: 423).

Storrow contributed significantly both to the theory and the practice of civil engineering. In an age when American engineering was largely taught and practiced empirically, he was trained in advanced European theory and served as a major agent of transfer of that theory to the United States by means of his *Treatise on Water-Works*. His principal accomplishments as a practicing engineer are his design and construction of the textile city of Lawrence and especially its Great Stone Dam, whose mathematically modeled profile was much copied in later structures.

• Many of Storrow's personal papers, including an autobiographical sketch written in 1829, are privately held by his descendants, the Charles S. Denny family of New London, N.H. His undergraduate theses are in the Harvard University Archives. His correspondence during his Paris years (1830–1832) and other letters are in the Samuel Storrow Collection of the Massachusetts Historical Society. His business papers relating to the Essex Company are deposited in the Museum of American Textile History in Lowell and the Immigrant City Archives in Lawrence. For an assessment of the influence of his overseas training on American engineering practice, see Peter A. Ford, "Charles S. Storrow, Civil Engineer: A Case Study of European Training and Technological Transfer in the Antebellum Period," *Technology and Culture* 34 (1993): 271–99. The definitive study of the Great Stone Dam is Peter M. Molloy, "Nineteenth-Century Hydropower: Design and Construction of Lawrence Dam, 1845–1848," *Winterthur Portfolio* 15 (1980): 315–43. See also Peter A.

Ford, "An American in Paris: Charles S. Storrow and the 1830 Revolution," *Proceedings of the Massachusetts Historical Society* 104 (1992): 21–41, on his firsthand observation of the July Revolution; and Duncan E. Hay, "Building 'The New City on the Merrimack': The Essex Company and Its Role in the Creation of Lawrence, Massachusetts" (Ph.D. diss., Univ. of Delaware, 1986), on his management of the Essex Company. Shortly after Storrow's death, his friend and fellow engineer Hiram F. Mills contributed a short biography and an assessment of his career to the *Proceedings of the American Academy of Arts and Sciences* 40 (1904–1905): 769–73.

PETER A. FORD

STORY, Joseph (18 Sept. 1779–10 Sept. 1845), U.S. Supreme Court justice, legal scholar, law professor, and congressman, was born in Marblehead, Massachusetts, the son of Elisha Story, a prominent physician and surgeon, and Mehitable Pedrick, the daughter of a wealthy Loyalist merchant who lost most of his fortune during the Revolution. Story's father was an early patriot and a member of the Sons of Liberty. He participated in the Boston Tea Party and later served at Lexington, Concord, Bunker Hill, Long Island, White Plains, and Trenton. Growing up in the aftermath of the Revolution, Joseph absorbed from both of his parents republican values, Unitarian theology, a heritage of Puritan idealism, a fierce sense of nationalism, and an unbending dedication to public service.

Story studied at the Marblehead Academy until the fall of 1794 when his father withdrew him from school because the schoolmaster, William Harris (later president of Columbia University), beat Story with a ruler for some minor offense. Harvard refused to admit the fifteen-year-old Story because he lacked sufficient education. Crestfallen, Story studied at home and by January was sufficiently prepared to enter the university. At Harvard he thrived on studying and scholarship and neither drank nor caroused in any other noticeable way. He graduated in 1798, second in his class. After college Story returned to Marblehead to read law with Samuel Sewell, then a congressman and later chief justice of Massachusetts. He later read law with Samuel Putnam in Salem.

Story gained admission to the bar in 1801 and began practicing in Salem, in Essex County, a Federalist stronghold. Story gravitated to the Jeffersonian Republicans, working closely with the powerful Crowninshield family. Their patronage helped him gain a seat in the Massachusetts House of Representatives (1805–1808), and when Jacob Crowninshield died Story finished his term in Congress, serving from late 1808 to 3 March 1809. Although a Republican, Story opposed the embargo President Thomas Jefferson had imposed on American exports to warring powers in Europe. This opposition earned Story the unrelenting enmity of the notoriously thin-skinned Jefferson. In 1810 Story returned to Washington where he successfully argued the Yazoo land case, *Fletcher v. Peck*, on behalf of New England investors. In 1811 Story once again served in the Massachusetts House of Representatives, where he was elected Speaker. On 15 November 1811 President James Madison nominated Story to the U.S. Supreme Court to replace the late Justice William Cushing. Story was Madison's fourth choice, in part because Jefferson was so opposed to him. But, fortunately for Story, Levi Lincoln and John Quincy Adams declined the post, even though the Senate confirmed both, and the Senate refused to confirm Alexander Wolcott. At just barely thirty-two years old, Story was the youngest person ever nominated to the Court. The Senate confirmed both Story and Gabriel Duvall on 18 November 1811, and Story took his seat on 3 February 1812. He remained in that office until his death.

Jefferson's instincts about Story were essentially correct. After joining the Court, Story quickly became an ally of John Marshall, a powerful supporter of judicial nationalism and a proponent of an expansive reading of the Constitution. Like Marshall, Story opposed states' rights and found implied powers throughout the Constitution. While riding circuit, Story declared, in *United States v. Bainbridge* (1816), that "whenever a general power to do a thing is given, every particular power necessary for doing it is included."

On the Court, Story persistently argued for expansive federal powers. Throughout his career Story attempted to create a federal common law for criminal, civil, and admiralty jurisdictions. This would have allowed federal judges to adopt rules, procedures, and interpretations of the law that would have been applied nationally in all federal courts. For example, Story wanted the Supreme Court to interpret the Constitution to include a federal common law of crimes. Had the Court done this, the national government could have prosecuted people under the common law, rather than needing a statute passed by Congress, giving the federal government enormous legal power. Because of his views on this issue, Story silently dissented in *United States v. Hudson and Goodwin* (1812), where a bare majority of the Court found that the national government could not enforce the common law of crimes. A year later, in *United States v. Coolidge* (1813), Story, acting as a circuit justice, deftly avoided *Hudson and Goodwin* in creating a federal common law in admiralty cases. On appeal the full Court reversed Story's circuit court decision in *Coolidge*, on the basis of *Hudson and Goodwin*.

After *Hudson and Goodwin*, Story urged Congress to pass legislation to "give the Judicial Courts of the United States power to punish all crimes and offenses against the Government, as at common law." In 1812 Story sent a draft of such legislation to the attorney general and in 1818 sent a similar proposal to Senator David Daggett of Connecticut. In 1825 Congress amended the federal criminal code, based on a draft that Story provided. In 1842 he wrote Senator John Macpherson Berrien urging a recodification of all federal criminal law and the extension of the common law to all federal jurisdiction. In addition to lobbying for federal criminal law legislation Story helped draft the Reporter's Act of 1817, which provided an annual salary for the official reporter of the Supreme Court, and

the federal bankruptcy statute of 1841, something for which he had lobbyied for two decades.

Story's behind-the-scenes support for expanded federal jurisdiction and his attempts at creating a federal common law of crimes paralleled his efforts in creating a federal common law for commercial cases. In *Van Reimsdyk v. Kane* (1812), while riding circuit, Story applied general common law to a diversity case. Thirty years later, in *Swift v. Tyson* (1842), Story would gain the support of the Court to create a general federal common law for civil procedure. *Swift* allowed all entrepreneurs in the nation to be more confident in their assumptions about how contracts and commercial notes would be interpreted in the federal courts. The case remained good law until 1938.

Just as he sought to strengthen the federal government, Story opposed states' rights. Story's first nationalist assault on states' rights was in his opinion in *Fairfax's Devisee v. Hunter's Lessee* (1813), in which he reversed a decision by the Virginia courts that upheld the confiscation, during the Revolution, of land owned by British subjects. Story found that these seizures violated the peace treaty of 1783 and the Jay Treaty of 1794. His opinion was an unequivocal endorsement of the supremacy clause of the Constitution in the face of state common law. The Virginia courts denied the constitutionality of the Supreme Court's jurisdiction in the case, which then came back to the Court as *Martin v. Hunter's Lessee* (1816). In *Martin*, Story presented his greatest statement of federal supremacy, arguing that under Section 25 of the Judiciary Act of 1789 the Supreme Court was the final authority in disputes between the states and the federal government. Story used the occasion to denounce concepts of states' rights, pointing out that the Constitution was not created "by the states in their sovereign capacities, but emphatically, as the preamble of the constitution declared, by 'the people of the United States.'" In a powerful and logically irrefutable opinion, Story asserted that the people (through the federal government) were sovereign, not the states. He reminded Virginia and the nation that the Constitution was "to endure through a long lapse of ages, the events of which were locked up in the inscrutable purposes of Providence," and therefore the Constitution had to be interpreted with flexibility to provide for the "exigencies of the future." Story argued that not only did Congress have the constitutional power to give the Supreme Court appellate review of state decisions but that, without such final authority resting in the Supreme Court, the nation's legal system could not function. According to Story, such review was not merely constitutionally permissible but absolutely necessary for the welfare of the nation. *Martin* was, as his best biographer notes, "Story's constitutional tour de force" and "possibly . . . the ablest and most impressive piece of constitutional analysis to be found in the Supreme Court's reports" (Newmyer, p. 111). *Martin* led Virginia to the brink of nullification, with Jefferson himself working behind the scenes to undermine the Supreme Court's power. *Martin* also set the stage for Chief Justice Marshall's overwhelmingly nationalist decisions in *Sturgis v. Crowninshield* (1819), *Dartmouth College v. Woodward* (1819), *M'Culloch v. Maryland* (1819), and *Cohens v. Virginia* (1821).

Despite *Martin*, and some notable opinions involving civil procedure, trusts and estates, private property, admiralty, and international law, the importance of Story's jurisprudence is not fully reflected in his Supreme Court opinions. In addition to his numerous circuit court opinions, Story wrote 268 majority opinions for the Supreme Court. This is small by modern standards but significant for his era. Marshall, however, wrote twice that many. But, despite the number, Story rarely wrote opinions in the most important cases.

Throughout his career Story served under two very strong chief justices, Marshall and Roger B. Taney. Marshall usually assigned the most significant cases to himself, leaving the less politically important cases to others. Story was able to write the opinion in *Martin v. Hunter's Lessee* (1816)—the most significant in his early court career—only because Marshall had an economic interest in the case. Under Taney, Story's most important opinions were *Prigg v. Pennsylvania* (1842) and *Swift v. Tyson*.

Story also authored twenty-three separate opinions, statements, and dissents, but most of these were in obscure cases, often involving technical subjects such as admiralty law, banking, or property. His most important concurring opinion was in *Dartmouth College v. Woodward*, in which he provided extra intellectual support for Marshall's opinion. Here Story also articulated modern notions of the role of corporations and their relationship to the government. He also joined (and probably helped write) Marshall's dissent in *Ogden v. Saunders* (1827). Under Marshall he wrote a few other dissents and dissented without opinion in a number of important cases, including *Cherokee Nation v. Georgia* (1831). Unlike Marshall, Story believed Cherokee land should be considered a foreign nation for purposes of federal lawsuits.

In 1837, under Taney, Story wrote three major dissents. Taney's chief justiceship also limited Story's opportunity to write key opinions. President Andrew Jackson appointed Taney in 1836 to lead the Court away from Marshall's (and Story's) judicial nationalism. By 1837 the Jacksonian majority was fully in place, and Story was the last remaining nationalist justice from the Marshall era. He was surely uncomfortable with the undoing of what he had helped create. Thus, between 1837 and 1839 Story wrote five dissents, three in the landmark cases *Briscoe v. Bank of the Commonwealth of Kentucky* (1837), *Mayor of New York v. Miln* (1837), and *Charles River Bridge v. Warren Bridge* (1837), that altered or overturned key precedents of the Marshall Court. In these cases Story resisted the Jacksonian counterattack on the nationalist jurisprudence on the Marshall Court. In *Charles River Bridge* Story also argued for the perpetuation of vested interests and existing businesses, at the expense of economic development. One of the largest stockholders in

the Bridge Company was Harvard University, where Story was on the board of overseers (since 1819), a fellow of the Harvard Corporation (since 1825), and a professor. This apparent conflict of interest did not prevent him from participating in the case.

That Story's flurry of dissents ended by 1839 suggests how much he was, through most of his career, able to help shape decisions that he could support. His major dissents all came in a three-year period after Taney became chief justice. By 1839 Story was once again exerting enormous influence on the Court. Thus, Story spoke for a unanimous Court in his extremely important decision in *Swift v. Tyson*, which created a federal common law for commercial litigation. This was a major victory for Story, who had throughout his career been trying to nationalize law. The fact that the court was unanimous in *Swift*, with even the extreme states' rights advocate Peter V. Daniel supporting Story's decision, suggests his intellectual power and ability to convince his colleagues to follow his lead.

In the difficult jurisprudential area of slavery, Story's nationalism outweighed his personal dislike for the institution. Sometimes the two dovetailed. Story's nationalism, as well as his personal distaste for slavery, also led him to vigorously enforce federal laws for the suppression of the African slave trade. In a number of charges to New England grand juries (which were subsequently published) Story vigorously denounced the illegal trade. In *United States v. the Amistad* (1841) Story interpreted a treaty and international law to free a boatload of Africans who had been illegally taken to Cuba. While on a ship taking them from one part of Cuba to another, the "Amistads," as these Africans were known, revolted. Eventually their ship ended up in Long Island Sound, where it was towed to Connecticut. Story found that the Amistads were free because they had been illegally taken to Cuba in violation of laws and treaties prohibiting the African slave trade. However, Story refused to order the United States to assist in returning the Africans to their homeland. Thus they languished in the United States for years, until abolitionists raised enough money for their eventual transportation to Africa.

A year later Story wrote the opinion of the Court in *Prigg v. Pennsylvania*, which upheld the constitutionality of the Fugitive Slave Law of 1793. Speaking for a sharply divided Court (in addition to Story's opinion there were five concurrences and one dissent), Story also created a common law right of recaption for masters seeking fugitive slaves. Although personally opposed to slavery, Story wrote this overwhelmingly proslavery decision in *Prigg* in order to nationalize power over fugitive slave rendition. Story's support for the fugitive slave law, which he enforced on circuit, fit with his desire to strengthen the national government at the expense of states' rights. In striking down Pennsylvania's personal liberty law in *Prigg*, Story hoped to prevent free states from interfering with the return of fugitive slaves, which he feared would then lead to southern hostility toward the Union. To achieve these goals Story was willing to accept the possibility that some free blacks might be illegally enslaved under the 1793 law or under the common law right of recaption that he found in the Constitution. In *Prigg*, he spoke for a more divided Court in his overarching nationalist approach to fugitive slave renditions.

Story retained an active career off the bench. He was a close confidant of the Massachusetts politician Daniel Webster and helped him write a speech denouncing President Andrew Jackson's veto of the recharter of the Second Bank of the United States. When Webster became secretary of state, he relied on Story's expert knowledge of international law as well as his sage advice when negotiating what became the Webster-Ashburton Treaty. In what seems to be a breach of ethics, even by the standards of the early nineteenth century, Story colluded with Webster in developing a strategy for bringing *Dartmouth College v. Woodward* to the Supreme Court and "circulated Webster's argument among professional friends with an imprimatur of approval" (Newmyer, p. 177). Story lobbied for the appointment of friends and protégés to judgeships and other offices and was in constant contact with members of Congress, often writing them to suggest legislation. His draft of a federal criminal law became the basis for the Federal Crimes Act of 1825. After *Prigg v. Pennsylvania*, Story wrote Georgia senator John M. Berrien, outlining a procedure for federal enforcement of the Constitution's fugitive slave clause. In the Fugitive Slave Law of 1850 Congress adopted similar concepts. While service on the bench normally precludes political activity, in 1820 Story won election to the Massachusetts Constitutional Convention, and in 1836–1837 he served on a state commission to consider a codification of Massachusetts law. From 1819 until his death he was on the governing boards of Harvard University. He never considered that these activities might create a conflict of interest.

Story also remained active in other ways. From 1815 to 1835 he served as president of the Merchant's Bank of Salem, which was a branch of the Bank of the United States after 1816, and accordingly he "repeatedly attempted to use his influence with Treasury Department officials to secure large bank deposits in the branch bank of which he was President" (White, *American Judicial Tradition*, p. 41). From 1818 to 1830 he was also vice president of the Salem Savings Bank. Despite this connection to a bank affiliated with the Bank of the United States, he participated in *M'Culloch v. Maryland*, in which Marshall upheld the constitutionality of the Second Bank of the United States.

Story was not content to be only a justice, a banker, a university trustee, an adviser to politicians, and a part-time lobbyist with Congress. Story's boundless energy led him to two other parallel careers, which alone would have made him a major figure in American legal history. While serving on the bench, Story was also the nation's most important and prolific legal scholar and the major professor at Harvard Law School, where he helped train a generation of new lawyers.

Throughout his life, Story was a scholar and a writer. Before his court years he published a poem, *The Power of Solitude* (1802). Critics had little good to say about this mundane effort, which ended Story's hopes of achievement in the literary world. His first legal work, *A Selection of Pleadings in Civil Actions* (1805), was more successful and presaged his extraordinary lifelong contribution to legal scholarship. In 1809 he published an edition of Joseph Chitty's *Practical Treatise on Bills of Exchange*, which included American as well as British cases. This was the beginning of Story's leadership in Americanizing English law. A year later Story edited Charles Abbott's *Treatise of the Law Relative to Merchant Ships and Seamen* (1810). Thus, as he went to the Supreme Court, Story was not only a successful attorney but was also one of the nation's experts in two key areas of commercial law. Initially Story did not continue his scholarly endeavors on the bench. He published little until 1829, when he simultaneously accepted the Dane Professorship at Harvard Law School and embarked on his career as a legal scholar. This second, parallel career, is tied to changes in American politics.

In 1828 Story worked hard for the reelection of John Quincy Adams. Andrew Jackson's victory disturbed Story; Jackson's attacks on the Bank of the United States, his Supreme Court appointments, and his policy of American Indian removal, which was a direct refutation of the Court's opinion in *Worcester v. Georgia* (1832), confirmed that Story's fears were justified. Jacksonian Democracy meant a new order, one that clashed with Story's values of nationalism, the rule of law, and respect for property rights.

On the eve of the Jacksonian revolution, Story embarked on his second career as a professor at Harvard Law School and legal scholar. By training lawyers and writing legal treatises that argued for constitutional nationalism and the perpetuation of conservative legal and economic values, Story clearly hoped to counter Jacksonian democracy, the rise of states' rights southern politicians, and the antinationalist sentiments of the president and his followers.

Story's presence at Harvard Law School permanently altered the institution. In 1828 only one student registered for the university's law program. The following fall Story helped attract twenty-eight new students. By 1844 the school had 156 students from twenty-one states. Harvard, under Story, became the premier law school in the nation and one that was truly national in its student body and in the law it taught. Story used his professor's podium to instill a sense of constitutional nationalism in his students.

Story's students included Charles Sumner, the U.S. senator and champion of civil rights; Wendell Phillips, the greatest abolitionist orator of the age; Richard Henry Dana, Jr., the author and antislavery lawyer; John Wentworth, who migrated to Chicago, where he edited the city's first newspaper and helped to create the Republican Party; and future president Rutherford B. Hayes. Supreme Court justices John McLean, Thomas Todd, and Henry Baldwin sent their sons to study under Story. Story taught Benjamin R. Curtis, who went on to the Supreme Court, as well as six future federal judges, two future attorneys generals, and at least thirty-nine state judges, including five state chief justices. Six future senators, nine future congressmen, and some sixty others who went into state or national politics or public service learned their constitutional law from Story.

When he first started teaching at Harvard in 1829, Story prepared a series of lectures on the Constitution that eventually led to his most important book, the three-volume *Commentaries on the Constitution* (1833). By then Story had already published *Commentaries on the Law of Bailments* (1832). In quick order he published the politically significant *Commentaries on Conflicts of Laws* (1834), *Commentaries on Equity Jurisprudence* (2 vols., 1836), *Commentaries on Equity Pleadings* (1838), *Commentaries on the Law of Agency* (1839), *Commentaries on the Law of Partnership* (1841), *Commentaries on Bills of Exchange* (1843), and *Commentaries on the Law of Promissory Notes and Guarantee of Notes* (1845). In 1840 he also published a one-volume edition of his *Commentaries on the Constitution*, under the title *A Familiar Exposition of the Constitution*. Story also wrote law review articles, encyclopedia entries, essays in popular magazines, and *A Discourse on the Past History, Present State, and Future Prospects of Law*, published in Edinburgh in 1835. His publications became the basis for many private law libraries. Attorneys throughout the nation, unable to get recent reports of cases, relied on Story's *Commentaries* for their understanding of the law. In his writings, even more than in his court opinions, Story shaped the development of American law. He also found financial success, although that was hardly his motivation. By 1844 his royalties were more than twice his annual salary as a justice.

Story gained more pleasure from teaching and writing than any other activity. His love for his students and his heavy workload may have been the result of his somewhat tragic family life. His first wife, Mary Lynde Oliver, died in June 1805, shortly after their marriage. His father had died two months earlier, and Story responded to these combined losses by burying himself in work. Later in 1805 he married Sarah Waldo Wetmore, the daughter of Judge William Wetmore of the Boston Court of Common Pleas. Sarah Story became an invalid after the death of their third surviving child in 1831. Altogether they had seven children, but only two, Mary and William Wetmore, survived to adulthood. William Wetmore Story became a lawyer, wrote an important treatise on the law of contracts, and published an edition of his father's letters in which he edited out some embarrassing correspondence concerning Story's suggestions on how to adopt a new fugitive slave law.

In 1843 Story was so ill that for the only time in his judicial career he did not sit with the Court. The Court felt his absence. By this time Taney not only respected Story's legal brilliance but also had come to rely on him as the in-house scholar, the lawyers' lawyer, on the Court. Story returned for the 1844 term but was ill and unhappy. He planned to resign as soon as a successor could be named, but before he could resign he died in Cambridge, Massachusetts.

• Major collections of Story papers are at Harvard, the Library of Congress, the University of Texas, Yale, and the Massachusetts Historical Society. Many of his letters are found in collections of others, scattered throughout the United States and in Europe. A published collection of his papers is *The Life and Letters of Joseph Story*, ed. William Wetmore Story (2 vols., 1851), an edition that omits embarrassing correspondence about slavery. Story's Supreme Court opinions are found in vols. 11–44 of *United States Reports*. His circuit court opinions are reported in the *Federal Cases [1789–1880]* (30 vols., 1894–1897). Story wrote at least thirteen major books. The most important of his writings for the development of the United States, as well as for understanding Story's thinking, was his three-volume *Commentaries on the Constitution of the United States* (1833). Story also published scores of articles, charges to juries, and speeches. The best list is in the bibliography of the premier biography of Story, R. Kent Newmyer, *Supreme Court Justice Joseph Story: Statesman of the Old Republic* (1985). Other helpful biographies are Gerald T. Dunne, *Justice Joseph Story and the Rise of the Supreme Court* (1970), and James McClellan, *Joseph Story and the American Constitution* (1971). G. Edward White, *The American Judicial Tradition* (1976; repr. 1988), provides a very fine short sketch of Story. Also useful are George L. Haskins and Herbert A. Johnson, *Foundations of Power: John Marshall, 1801–1815* (1981); G. Edward White, *The Marshall Court and Cultural Change, 1815–1835* (1988); Carl B. Swisher, *The Taney Period, 1836–64* (1974); Stanley I. Kutler, *Privilege and Creative Destruction: The Charles River Bridge Case* (1971); Robert Stevens, *Law School: Legal Education in America from the 1850s to the 1980s* (1983); Charles Warren, *History of Harvard Law School and of Early Legal Conditions in America* (3 vols., 1908); Alan Watson, *The Comity of Errors* (1992); Harold M. Hyman and William M. Wiecek, *Equal Justice under Law* (1982); Robert Cover, *Justice Accused: Antislavery and the Judicial Process* (1975); Roscoe Pound, "The Place of Judge Story in the Making of American Law," *American Law Review* 48 (1914): 676–97; Paul Finkelman, "Story Telling on the Supreme Court: *Prigg v. Pennsylvania* and Justice Joseph Story's Judicial Nationalism," *Supreme Court Review* 1994 (1995): 247–94; and William R. Leslie, "The Influence of Joseph Story's Theory of Conflict of Laws on Constitutional Nationalism," *Mississippi Valley Historical Review* 35 (1948): 203–20. An obituary is in the *Boston Daily Advertiser*, 12 Sept. 1845.

PAUL FINKELMAN

STORY, William Edward (29 Apr. 1850–10 Apr. 1930), mathematician and educator, was born in Boston, Massachusetts, the son of Isaac Story, a lawyer, and Elizabeth Bowen Woodberry. Story entered Harvard College in 1867 and was one of the first to graduate with honors (in 1871), a year after the honors program was instituted. After graduation he went to Germany for further study. In Berlin he attended lectures of the noted mathematicians Karl Weierstrass and Ernst Kummer as well as of the physicist Hermann von Helmholtz. Story also took courses under the mathematician and theoretical physicist Carl Neumann in Leipzig, where Story received a Ph.D. in 1875 for his dissertation titled "On the Algebraic Relations Existing between the Polars of Binary Quantic." On his return to the United States in 1875 he became a tutor at Harvard. This position enabled him to renew his acquaintance with the family of Harvard mathematician and astronomer Benjamin Peirce (1809–1880) and exerted a decisive influence on his subsequent career. By good fortune, while he was abroad a suitable outlet for his talents had been established in the United States, with the founding of the Johns Hopkins University in Baltimore in 1876. To ensure that mathematics was conducted on a suitably high level in the new institution, President Daniel Coit Gilman hired one of the most distinguished of European mathematicians, the British algebraist James J. Sylvester, in 1876. Sylvester was acquainted with the Peirce family and, based on their recommendation, agreed that Story should be hired as his associate. Soon after arriving in Baltimore to take up his position at Johns Hopkins, Story met Mary Deborah Harrison. They were married in 1878; the couple had one child.

While at Johns Hopkins, Story worked hard to bring the level of mathematical activity closer to the standard he had known in Germany by founding the University Mathematical Society. (The American Mathematical Society—originally the New York Mathematical Society—was founded only in 1888.) He also collaborated with Sylvester in founding and editing the first American mathematical research journal whose contents were comparable to European journals of this period, the *American Journal of Mathematics*. Unfortunately he and Sylvester quarreled over certain editorial judgments made by Story in Sylvester's absence; relations between them were strained thereafter, and this quarrel ended Story's association with the *Journal* around 1884. It is not surprising then that some years later Story was pleased to accept an invitation from another new institution, Clark University in Worcester, Massachusetts, which opened in 1889 and intended, like Johns Hopkins, to be a graduate research institute.

Story was able to bring with him to Clark his best student from Johns Hopkins, Henry Taber. Together they continued research into algebra and invariant theory. In this early period Story wrote two papers on the covariants of a system of quantics, one published in the *Proceedings of the London Mathematical Society* (1892), the other in *Mathematische Annalen* (1893). Of the other three faculty hired at Clark—Henry Seely White, Oskar Bolza, and Joseph Perott—White and Bolza left during a period of strife in 1891–1892 to take positions at Northwestern University and the University of Chicago, respectively. From 1892 until the Ph.D. program in mathematics was closed in 1921, Story, Taber, and Perott were the only faculty. Despite this shortage of fresh talent, Story worked hard to keep mathematical research alive. In 1893 he was elected president of what has been called the "zeroth" International Congress of Mathematicians, held in

conjunction with the World's Columbian Exposition in Chicago. Subsequently he published a very short-lived journal of mathematics called the *Mathematical Review* (1896–1897). He accrued many academic honors, among them election to the National Academy of Sciences in 1908.

It is perhaps through his graduate students at Clark that Story's influence can most clearly be seen. In its quarter-century of existence the program at Clark granted twenty-five Ph.D.s, of which at least sixteen dissertations were written under Story's direction. The most distinguished of these doctoral students was Solomon Lefschetz, who came to Clark in 1910. In his first year at Clark, under Story's direction, Lefschetz wrote a dissertation titled "On the Existence of Loci with Given Singularities." Lefschetz's contributions to algebraic topology later gained him worldwide fame and eventually a position at Princeton that he held for thirty years.

When the graduate programs at Clark University were closed in 1921 because of financial exigency, Story was forcibly retired. Before retirement he seems to have acquired an interest in the history of mathematics, as he wrote the pamphlet *Omar Khayyam as a Mathematician*, which was published in 1919. After retiring, he became president of the Omar Khayyam Club of America (1924–1927). He also compiled one of the world's largest bibliographies of mathematical literature on thousands of note cards stored in several dozen boxes. These interests kept him active until his death in Worcester a few weeks before his eightieth birthday.

• Correspondence between Sylvester and Story, and between Sylvester and Gilman concerning the editorial controversy at the *American Journal of Mathematics* are in the papers of Sylvester and Gilman in the Milton S. Eisenhower Library at the Johns Hopkins University. Documents connected with Story's service at Clark University are in the archives of Clark University. Story's articles in the *American Journal of Mathematics* are concerned with elliptic functions ("The Addition-Theorem for Elliptic Functions," 7 [1885]: 364–75) and geometry ("A New Method in Analytic Geometry," 9 [1887]: 38–44), but his major interest for most of his life was in the theory of quantics, for which his best paper, "On the Covariants of a System of Quantics," appeared in *Mathematische Annalen* 41 (1893): 265–72. His bibliography of mathematics is stored in the archives of the American Mathematical Society in Providence, R.I. A discussion of his career in the context of the development of mathematics in the United States is the article by Roger Cooke and V. Fred Rickey, "W. E. Story of Hopkins and Clark" in *A Century of Mathematics in America*, pt. 3, ed. Peter Duven (1989), pp. 29–76.

ROGER COOKE

STORY, William Wetmore (12 Feb. 1819–7 Oct. 1895), sculptor and writer, was born in Salem, Massachusetts, the son of Joseph Story, a justice of the U.S. Supreme Court and Harvard law professor, and Sarah Waldo Wetmore, the daughter of a prominent Boston judge. During his formative years spent in Cambridge, Massachusetts, Story was exposed to the vibrant intellectual communities of Harvard College (now University) and antebellum Boston, and he pursued a variety of creative pastimes while simultaneously preparing to enter the family profession of law. Upon graduating from Harvard in 1838 and Harvard Law School in 1840, he was admitted to the bar and proceeded to distinguish himself as a Boston attorney. He also served as a reporter to the U.S. Circuit Court and published important treatises on the laws of contracts (1844) and personal property sales (1847). In 1843 he married Emelyn Eldredge of Boston, a childhood acquaintance. Artistic ambitions earlier awakened continued to occupy Story, however, and despite the pressures of his legal practice he managed to participate in local artist associations, contribute verse and criticism to some of the day's bolder opinion journals, and develop a modest reputation as an amateur painter and clay modeler.

The death of his father in 1845 was the catalyst for Story's rise to celebrity as a sculptor, an occupation relatively new for American practitioners when Story chose to cultivate that career and exit the predictable course of success he had been treading as a lawyer and occasional author. A memorial statue, destined for Mount Auburn Cemetery, was planned to honor Joseph Story, and the commission for its execution rather unexpectedly went to William Story, whom the organizing committee had approached initially for aesthetic advice. He accepted with the proviso that he first be permitted several years study abroad to acquire the necessary technical proficiency, and accordingly he left Boston in 1847 for a three-year excursion through Europe that resulted in completed designs for his father's monument and an intense immersion in Rome's international colony of sculptors. Although he returned twice to Boston in the 1850s to gain committee approval for the *Joseph Story* memorial and to supervise its installation, Story had become disengaged from American life, which he now perceived as provincial and limiting to his talents. In 1856 he resolved to commit himself to sculpture as his principal profession and settle permanently in Rome. He secured handsome quarters for his family in the venerable Palazzo Barberini, where he proceeded to entertain an urbane, affluent circle of fellow expatriates and cosmopolitan literati who came to function as an invaluable source of commissions.

Story's efforts to perfect an original idiom within the language of idealized neoclassicism then fashionable for sculpture consumed him through the remainder of the 1850s. He experimented with many different stylistic shadings of figural classicism, and he interpreted subjects as diverse as the mythological *Hero* (1857), *Marguerite* (1858) from Goethe's *Faust*, and the nursery conceit of *Little Red Riding Hood* (c. 1853). Few of these compositions sold, however, and he grew despondent over the failure of critics to pay serious attention to this work. The American press, while curious about his self-exile from Boston and familiarity with foreign-born notables, often emphasized Story's literary productions, which were ongoing and included poetry—some imitative of the novel dramatic mono-

logues being written by Robert Browning, a close friend of Story's in Italy—art theory (*Proportions of the Human Figure According to a New Canon for Practical Use* [1866]), political commentary, and the acclaimed *Roba di Roma* (1862), a travel account of contemporary Rome.

Story's sculpture in the so-called ideal or imaginative, narrative vein, eventually attracted wide and excited notice in 1862 at the London International Exposition, where the public encountered his mysteriously meditative seated figures of the Egyptian queen *Cleopatra* (1858, Los Angeles County Art Museum) and the legendary *Libyan Sibyl* (1861, Metropolitan Museum of Art). Curiously, these marbles, which dramatized decisive moments in the imagined psychological existence of their subjects, were not grouped with the American art on display but included in the modern Roman pavilion, their transport costs to London having been furnished by Pope Pius IX. Advance curiosity about Story's *Cleopatra* also had been fueled by American novelist Nathaniel Hawthorne, who had seen the clay model for this imposing figure in Story's studio in Rome and appropriated it as the masterpiece of his romanticized sculptor, Kenyon, in *The Marble Faun* (1860), which profiled Italy's modern art community. The combination of papal imprimatur, fictional publicity, and original staging of the familiar female themes these statues personified catapulted Story into the front ranks of contemporary sculpture, where he remained until neoclassicism itself had exhausted its aesthetic reign by the 1890s.

For more than a quarter of a century Story repeated and refined the formula that had earned him recognition in London. Enjoying a vigorous business in original commissions and copy orders, he produced a progression of critically praised compositions, most depicting ancient personalities in pensive attitudes drawn from myth, the Old and New Testaments, Shakespeare, and the ancient Greek playwrights. Characteristic of these probing, heroic-scaled works—mostly carved in marble—are his studies of *Medea, Contemplating the Murder of Her Children* (1864; 1868 replica, the Metropolitan Museum of Art), *Sappho*, planning her suicide (1863, Museum of Fine Arts, Boston), and *Saul, When the Evil Spirit Was Upon Him* (1863; revised version, the Fine Arts Museum of San Francisco). Story's gravitation to such themes prompted his biographer, Henry James, to observe that "it was in their dangerous phases that the passions most appealed to him" (*William Wetmore Story and his Friends*, vol. 1 [1903], p. 194).

Story's exploitation of acutely observed archaeological accessories, his exploration of the physiognomy of subconscious thought and transitional states of mind, and his facility at manipulating marble surfaces to belie the stone's cold inelasticity secured his renown as an innovative sculptor within the classical figural tradition he assiduously respected. His base of patrons spanned from European nobility and the British peerage to moneyed Americans and municipal and government agencies, and aspiring sculptors of various nationalities sought him out for counsel and to survey his success when they visited or began their training in Rome. Story's busy studio—located on the via San Nicolo Tolentino through the mid-1870s and thereafter operating from custom-designed quarters at #7 via San Martino a Macao—was a popular tourist destination often noted in period guidebooks.

Throughout his career Story avowed disdain for portraiture, which he considered a lesser branch of sculpture. Financial comfort allowed him to accept only those portrait commissions of personal interest, exampled by his tender bust of the poet *Elizabeth Barrett Browning* (1866, Boston Athenaeum), or those of great public prestige. Memorable among this limited group of "grand-manner" portrait memorials are his monuments to the revolutionary war hero *Colonel William Prescott* (1880, Bunker Hill, Charlestown, Mass.), *Chief Justice John Marshall* (1883, U.S. Supreme Court, Washington, D.C.), the recumbent tomb sculpture of financier and philanthropist *Ezra Cornell* (1884, Sage Chapel, Cornell University), and the colossal commemorative sculpture honoring "The Star-Spangled Banner" author *Francis Scott Key* (1886) installed in a temple-like structure in San Francisco's Golden Gate Park.

Story accrued a wide range of awards in his later life, including the U.S. fine arts commissionership at the 1878 Universal Exposition held in Paris, election to the French Legion of Honor, and a professorship at Rome's Academy of St. Cecelia in acknowledgment of his musical prowess.

By the 1880s Story shifted increasing responsibilities for his studio operations to his son, Thomas Waldo, himself a promising sculptor. Although Story conceived several new ideal figures in these later years, he devoted much of his time to travel and to writing. Dating from this fertile publishing period are his novel *Fiammetta* (1886), several stage tragedies, additional volumes of original poetry, and the critical essays *Conversations in a Studio* (1890) and *Excursions in Arts and Letters* (1891). Although he twice paid return visits to the United States on lecture invitations, he preferred Europe and built a leisure residence in the resort village of St. Moritz. The 1893 death of his wife eroded Story's enthusiasm for work, and his health quickly declined. His final energies were diverted to the creation of Emelyn Story's elegiac grave monument titled *Angel of Grief Weeping Bitterly over the Dismantled Altar of His Life* (1894, Protestant Cemetery, Rome). Story subsequently retired to the Tuscan country villa of his married daughter, the Marchesa Edith Peruzzi, in Vallombrosa, where he died. He was interred with his wife at the Protestant Cemetery in Rome.

A flattering posthumous monograph by Mary E. Phillips, *Reminiscences of William Wetmore Story, the American Sculptor and Author*, appeared in 1897, as did numerous obituaries and memorial tributes summarizing his sprawling accomplishments as an artist and renaissance personality. Story's modern reputation is rooted largely in Henry James's two-volume biography of 1903, *William Wetmore Story and His Friends*,

commissioned by the sculptor's surviving children. A project assumed by James to offset his financial strains of that time, the book dodged the question of Story's enduring merits as a sculptor and focused instead on the price and rewards of his expatriate identity and eclectic talents. Only with the reclamation of critical appreciation of American neoclassical sculpture beginning in the 1970s have Story's psychological inventiveness and technical versatility in this chosen craft been accepted into permanent record by art historians.

• Although Story never bequeathed his papers to any single archive, the two main repositories of manuscript material illuminating his career and friendships are Houghton Library at Harvard University and the Harry E. Ransom Humanities Center at the University of Texas at Austin. In addition to those titles cited in the entry, other notable works written by Story include *The Life and Letters of Joseph Story* (1851), *Poems* (1847 and 1856), *Graffiti d'Italia* (1868), *A Roman Lawyer in Jerusalem* (1870), *He and She; or, A Poet's Portfolio* (1883), and *Poems and Lyrics—Parchments and Portraits* (1886). His famous statue of Cleopatra was the focus of special analysis in Albert Ten Eyck Gardner, "William Story and Cleopatra," *Metropolitan Museum of Art Bulletin*, n.s., 2 (1943). Useful critical assessments include William H. Gerdts, "William Wetmore Story," *American Art Journal* 4 (1972); Frank R. DiFederico and Julia Markus, "The Influence of Robert Browning on the Art of William Wetmore Story," *Browning Institute Studies* 1 (1973); and Jan Seidler (Ramirez), "A Critical Reappraisal of the Career of William Wetmore Story, American Sculptor and Man of Letters" (Ph.D. diss., Boston Univ., 1985). An obituary is in the *New York Times*, 8 Oct. 1895.

JAN SEIDLER RAMIREZ

STOTESBURY, Edward Townsend (26 Feb. 1849–16 May 1938), business executive and financier, was born in Philadelphia, the son of Thomas P. Stotesbury, a partner in a sugar refinery, and Martha Parker, a staunch Pennsylvania Quaker. Stotesbury attended Friends Central School in Philadelphia and graduated in 1865. He began working at age sixteen in a wholesale grocery firm as a clerk and then took a job in his father's sugar refinery, Harris and Stotesbury. His father arranged for Edward to work for the banking firm of Drexel and Co. in 1866 at a salary of $200 per annum. This entry position involved such mundane chores as cleaning inkwells, sweeping the office, and running errands. However, young Stotesbury seemed to possess a natural aptitude for banking, and by observation and dedication to the work he soon became proficient in reading balance sheets and became well informed on "commercial paper."

The Drexel firm needed a New York connection in order to continue its growth and so in 1871 formed Drexel, Morgan & Co. At that time, renowned New York banker J. Pierpont Morgan noted, "One of the brightest and most promising young men in the Philadelphia office is Edward T. Stotesbury." In 1875 Stotesbury was given an interest in the firm, and in 1883 he was taken in as full partner.

Meanwhile, in 1873 Stotesbury married the beautiful and charming Fannie Butcher. They established a home at 1515 Vernon Street and started a family of two daughters. The couple planned to build a new home on Stotesbury family land in Chelton Hills, then a suburb of Philadelphia, but in 1881 the young wife died suddenly.

Stotesbury reacted by immersing himself in his work, which expanded to become international in scope and brought him greater financial success. A significant example was his participation in floating the International Chinese Loan of 1909, which required several trips abroad during the protracted negotiations. He also remained involved locally. In 1910 he accepted the position of chairman of the board of the Philadelphia public transit system. He quickly brought in Thomas E. Mitten, a renowned transit manager, to head up the reorganized company. Financing was secured, and within a few years the service, which had been widely criticized, gained a reputation as a soundly run system. However, in 1920 there was a split between the Mitten faction and the Stotesbury group over the issue of the fares to be charged. Stotesbury believed that fares should be raised as required to maintain the hard-won fiscal condition of the company, while Mitten believed that fares should be kept as low as possible to maximize ridership. Mitten petitioned the State Public Service Commission for a reduction in rates without consulting Stotesbury or his associates. The resulting rift was a severe one. Later, when the issue was brought to a vote of the full board of directors, the Philadelphia Rapid Transit Company's executive committee sided with Mitten's proposal. Stotesbury and his two associate directors resigned.

In the interim Stotesbury was active in various Liberty Loan drives to help finance the war effort, in particular the Red Cross War Fund in 1917, in which he was personally influential in obtaining subscriptions of nearly $3.5 million. For this he received special recognition from the Red Cross, as well as from the French government in the form of a cross of a chevalier of the Legion of Honor.

Stotesbury was one of the original backers of the movement to celebrate the 150th anniversary of the Declaration of Independence, when the sesquicentennial was proposed in 1918. However, he changed his mind and resigned from the enterprise's board of direction in 1923, insisting that the "World Fair idea" had become outgrown with an increasingly constricted modern life and that the effort would be a failure. Yet, when it became evident that the city administration was completely committed to hosting the sesquicentennial celebration, Stotesbury put aside his personal beliefs and agreed to help raise some $3 million in sesquicentennial Participation Certificates.

Stotesbury married Mrs. Oliver Eaton Cromwell, the former Lucretia Roberts of Chicago, in January 1912. The event took place at the bride's home in Washington, D.C., and was a highlight of the capital's social season. The second Mrs. Stotesbury was a glittering socialite, and the couple's "town house" at Twentieth and Walnut was the scene of many impressive gatherings. In 1916, on the fiftieth anniversary of

his employment with Drexel, Stotesbury began construction of "Whitemarsh Hall" on a 250-acre site in Chesnut Hill. It took five years and $2 million to complete the 145-room mansion, exclusive of furnishings.

For many years, Stotesbury's principal diversion was the rearing of thoroughbred horses. He served as president of the National Horse Show of America, Inc., and was American representative of the International Horse Show at the Olympic meet in London in 1908. In later years, he strenuously and successfully opposed the opening of the bridle paths in Fairmont Park to motorists. He was also a patron of the arts, and his collection of paintings, tapestries, furniture, and porcelains was on display for several months in 1932 at the Pennsylvania Museum of Art while he was on an extended overseas trip.

Stotesbury was a life member of the board of trustees of the University of Pennsylvania and an honorary member of the managing board of the University of Pennsylvania Fund. He also served on the board of trustees of Drexel Institute for a time.

Although, contrary to persistent legend, Stotesbury had not served as a drummer boy in the Civil War, he had a lifelong interest in playing the snare drum and would often bring his drum along to speeches and other occasions to give an energetic impromptu performance.

Stotesbury was active in the affairs of Drexel & Co. until his death; indeed he had been in his Philadelphia office and had dropped by the Reading Co. offices, where he served as finance chairman, on the day he died suddenly.

• Articles addressing details of Stotesbury's life and career can be found in the *Philadelphia Inquirer*, 9 Oct. 1969 and 25 Feb. 1973; in the *Philadelphia Public Ledger*, 12 Apr. 1916; and in the *Philadelphia Evening Bulletin*, 10 July, 7 Sept., 12 Sept., and 8 Oct. 1969. Various issues of the *Electric Railway Journal* in 1910 contain references to Stotesbury and Mitten, while issues in the spring and summer of 1920 cover the battle for the Philadelphia Rapid Transit Board allegiance and Stotesbury's defeat and resignation. Obituaries are in the *Philadelphia Inquirer*, 16, 17, and 19 May 1938.

JAMES H. GRAEBNER

STOTHART, Herbert Pope (11 Sept. 1885–1 Feb. 1949), composer, was born in Milwaukee, Wisconsin, the son of Paul N. Stothart, a social worker, and Henrietta Weidner. Stothart's childhood was spent in Wisconsin. He was a choirboy in the Episcopal church, where he earned medals for his singing ability. With plans to be a teacher, he graduated with a degree in education from the Milwaukee Normal School. In 1909 Stothart accepted a position as assistant professor of music at the University of Wisconsin. During the six years he was there, he wrote and directed shows for the Haresfoot Society, the university musical theater club. Some of the musical themes were used later in his film scores. One of the musicals, *The Manicure Shop*, received special attention and was staged in Chicago.

In 1915 Stothart left Wisconsin to realize his new dream: to work in professional theater. He worked a short time in Chicago theater and later moved to New York with a letter of introduction to the great producer Arthur Hammerstein. Impressed by Stothart's abilities, Hammerstein hired him to conduct the touring company of Rudolf Friml's musical *High Jinks*. Stothart traveled with the show throughout Europe and England. At the end of his travels in 1919 he married Dorothy Wolfe, a young woman from New York whose family was involved in theater. They had a daughter. The marriage ended four years later with Dorothy's premature death.

A break came for Stothart when he met Arthur Hammerstein's nephew Oscar Hammerstein and collaborated with the young lyricist on a show called *Tickle Me*. The show ran for sixty-six performances in 1920. The next decade was devoted to musical theater in New York, collaborating with greats such as Vincent Youmans (*Wildflower*, 1923) and George Gershwin (*Song of the Flame*, 1925). Stothart's collaboration with Friml and Otto Harbach in 1924 resulted in the hit musical *Rose Marie*, which traveled to England and Europe under Stothart's baton after a successful run in the United States. Metro-Goldwyn-Mayer bought the rights to *Rose Marie* and made it into a silent film in 1927 starring Joan Crawford. The film was remade in 1935, starring Jeanette Macdonald and Nelson Eddy, with musical score composed by Stothart.

Stothart's first experience composing film music came in 1928, when Arthur Hammerstein was interested in a silent Russian film called *The End of St. Petersburg*. Hammerstein asked Stothart to write music to accompany the film and presented it in some of his theaters. Stothart enjoyed the experience, and by the end of the decade, when it was becoming evident that sound pictures were the wave of the future, he accepted a contract with Louis B. Mayer to score motion pictures for MGM. During the last few years Stothart had grown close to his first wife's sister Mary Vernon Wolfe, who helped raise his daughter. He married her in 1929 and with some reluctance left New York and moved with his bride and daughter to California, where he began a new life. This second marriage produced two children.

The Hollywood studios were eager to exploit the new use of sound in films and for the first few years produced numerous musicals. Stothart was a natural choice at MGM to serve as musical director and conductor on these films. His first project was *The Rogue Song* (1930), featuring opera star Lawrence Tibbett. Then followed ten more musical pictures, with songs and musical direction by Stothart and background score by William Axt. When interest in musical films waned, Stothart turned his talents to writing dramatic music for films. Along with Max Steiner and Alfred Newman, Stothart pioneered the new craft of composing film music. He essentially created the MGM "sound," which differed somewhat from that of the other studios because of its more subtle and introspective nature. He liked using folk songs, patriotic music,

and songs of the story's locale. He often employed wordless choruses for an angelic and sentimental effect. He incorporated classical music when appropriate and believed the movie theater was a fine place to present good music to the public. His use of strings became a Stothart trademark. He worked with the string section of the orchestra to produce a soft, muted tone with heavy use of portamento, a gliding from one note to the next on the strings. His music is often sentimental, and his manuscripts are marked with performance instructions such as "exquisite" and "with extreme tenderness." He believed the music should support the drama but not draw attention to itself. In Stothart's words, "The sincere musician in motion pictures does not mind the fact that the public does not realise his music's importance. On the contrary. If an audience is conscious of music where it should be conscious only of drama, then the musician has gone wrong. We can let the audience hear the music where music naturally would be heard, but in dramatic moments it must be subordinated" ("Film Music," *Behind the Screen: How Films Are Made* [1938], pp. 143–44).

The Squaw Man (1931) was Stothart's first film in which he composed the entire, if sparse, dramatic score. He went on to score most of MGM's literary classics during the 1930s, including *Treasure Island*, *David Copperfield*, *A Tale of Two Cities*, *Anna Karenina*, *Romeo and Juliet*, *The Good Earth*, *Mutiny on the Bounty*, and *The Wizard of Oz*. During the 1940s Stothart scored the now-classic films *Waterloo Bridge*, *Mrs. Miniver*, *Random Harvest*, *The Human Comedy*, *Madame Curie*, *Thirty Seconds over Tokyo*, *National Velvet*, *The Valley of Decision*, *The Yearling*, and many others. He won an Academy Award in 1939 for the musical score of *The Wizard of Oz*, with songs by Harold Arlen and E. Y. Harburg.

Stothart died in Los Angeles. He collaborated with the most celebrated names of the musical theater in the 1920s. His twenty-year career in film music was devoted to one studio, MGM. His years there coincided with what is considered the "Golden Age" of Hollywood, approximately 1930 to 1950. He is considered one of the pioneers of the art and craft of film scoring.

• Research materials on Stothart can be found at the library of the Academy of Motion Picture Arts and Sciences, Los Angeles. Stothart contributed essays to several publications, including "The Orchestra—Hollywood's Most Versatile Actor," *Film Music Notes* 3, no. 5 (Feb. 1944); "Telling History with Music," *Lions Roar* 3, no. 5 (Dec. 1944); and "Film Music," in *Behind the Screen: How Films Are Made*, ed. Stephen Watts (1938), pp. 138–44. See also Tony Thomas, "The Film Music of Herbert Stothart," liner notes of special issue LP. For a complete listing of Stothart's film scores, see Stephen Smith, *Film Composers Guide* (1990), pp. 215–16. A brief survey of Stothart's career appears in four issues of the *Max Steiner Annual* (1973, 1974, 1979, 1980), and Aljean Harmetz describes Stothart's music for *The Wizard of Oz* in *The Making of the Wizard of Oz* (1977). An obituary is in *Variety*, 2 Feb. 1949.

LINDA DANLY

STOUFFER, Samuel Andrew (6 June 1900–24 Aug. 1960), sociologist, was born in Sac City, Iowa, the son of Samuel M. Stouffer, an editor of the *Sac City Sun*, and Irene Holmes. He attended Morningside College in Iowa, receiving a B.A. in 1921. After he received an M.A. in English literature from Harvard in 1923, he spent three years as editor of the *Sac City Sun* before undertaking graduate study at the University of Chicago, where he earned a Ph.D. in sociology in 1930. In 1931–1932 he did postdoctorate work at the University of London. In 1924 he married Ruth McBurney; they had three children.

Stouffer pursued an academic career in several major research universities interspersed with research appointments in the federal government. He was an instructor in sociology at the University of Chicago in 1930–1931 and later was appointed as professor, serving in that capacity from 1935 to 1946. From 1931 to 1935 he was assistant professor at the University of Wisconsin, being promoted to professor there in 1935. From 1946 until his death, he was professor of social relations at Harvard University, where he was also founder and director of the Laboratory of Social Relations. In the federal service, he served as a staff member of the Central Statistical Board in the 1930s and was head of the Research Branch, Information and Education Division of the War Department from 1941 to 1946. He also worked as a member of the team of social scientists assembled by Gunnar Myrdal, whose efforts resulted in *An American Dilemma: The Negro Problem and Modern Democracy* (1944), and as executive secretary of a Social Science Research Council committee studying the social effects of the Great Depression.

Stouffer was a major figure in an influential generation of young American sociologists who led the transformation of American sociology from a mainly armchair discipline into a social science firmly grounded in empirical social research. The transformation was made possible in the main by the development of sample survey methods, data-collection procedures through which valid data generalizable to large populations could be collected. The sample survey made it possible for sociologists to test their theories by confronting their ideas with empirical observations. Sample surveys also became a major device used by the federal government to collect information rapidly and economically about a wide variety of topics, from unemployment to consumer purchases. Much of his work built upon the training in social statistics he had received at Chicago under William F. Ogburn and at the University of London under Karl Pearson and Ronald A. Fisher. His contributions to statistical theory included an elaboration of partial correlation and causal interpretation of survey data.

Although Stouffer played an important part in the development of the intellectual foundations of sample surveys, his main contribution was through his leadership of the Research Branch at the War Department during World War II. The Research Branch conducted hundreds of sample surveys of soldiers and airmen on a wide-ranging set of topics, including soldier morale, attitudes toward the fairness of military service, and acceptable grounds for discharge. These surveys along with others conducted for the State Department and the Department of Agriculture provided sufficient evidence on the policy utility of sample surveys to establish this methodology as a permanent feature of social data gathering in the federal government. *The American Soldier*, the first two volumes of the four-volume work *Studies in Social Psychology in World War II* (1949–1950), of which Stouffer was the senior author of three, extracted the major social science and technical findings of the work done by the Research Branch. In addition to vast amounts of information concerning how soldiers in World War II reacted to military service, the volumes also made strong technical contributions to measurement theory. *Studies in Social Psychology* is also cited frequently as among the best examples of the contributions that excellent social research can make to public policy.

In the mid-1950s, Stouffer conducted a national sample survey on the American public's tolerance for dissent, the results of which were published in *Communism, Conformity and Civil Liberties: A Cross-section of the Nation Speaks Its Mind* (1955; repr. 1992). The study was undertaken partly in reaction to the federal obsession in the early 1950s with security and other forms of "McCarthyism." It was likely also a reaction to a painful incident in which Stouffer's security clearance was suspended (but later restored) after the War Department received a spiteful accusation concerning his alleged association with "communist friends." According to the study, Americans were much more tolerant of dissenters than was thought to be the case. Furthermore, better educated persons were even more tolerant, as were community leaders. Stouffer's survey did much to bring the McCarthy period to a close. His own political views tended toward the liberal wing of the Republican party. He was a strong defender of civil rights and firmly believed in the necessity for toleration of dissent.

Stouffer also wrote on topics that were somewhat remote from public policy concerns. His studies of migration patterns within and between cities continue to constitute one of the few examples of rigorous sociological theory being confronted with data. In the 1950s he conducted research on conformity with norms, showing that conflicting loyalties were a source of nonconformity in individual behavior.

Stouffer's early training in English literature and journalism apparently served him in good stead. He had the ability to present complex ideas clearly and plainly, undoubtedly a great aid to getting his work in the military accepted and used. Although he was an excellent administrator, Stouffer preferred to work alone and accordingly had few research assistants or graduate students working closely with him. His influence on the field of sociology has been more through his writings than as a mentor.

In recognition of his contributions to sociology, Stouffer was elected president of the American Sociological Association in 1952 and president of the American Association for Public Opinion Research in 1953. He was also an elected Fellow of the American Academy of Arts and Sciences and of the American Statistical Association. Stouffer died in Cambridge, Massachusetts.

• A selection of Stouffer's writings appears in his book *Social Research to Test Ideas* (1962), compiled shortly before his death. A short biography by M. Brewster Smith appears in the *International Encyclopedia of the Social Sciences*, vol. 18 (1979), pp. 277–80.

PETER H. ROSSI

STOUGHTON, William (30 Sept. 1631–7 July 1701), colonial politician and lieutenant governor of Massachusetts, was born, probably in England, the son of Israel Stoughton and Elizabeth Clarke. The family soon immigrated to Dorchester, Massachusetts, where Stoughton's father became a large landowner and outspoken politician before returning to England in 1644 to enlist in the parliamentary army. Stoughton followed him after graduating from Harvard in 1650. He studied at Oxford, becoming a fellow of New College and receiving an M.A. on 30 June 1653. He was appointed minister of the Sussex parish of Rumboldswycke near Chichester in 1659 but lost his Oxford fellowship following the restoration of Charles II and returned to Massachusetts in 1662. There he continued to preach, as in a famous election sermon of 1668 delivered before the Massachusetts General Court in which he proclaimed that "God sifted a whole Nation that he might send choice Grain over into this Wilderness" (*New-England's True Interest*, p. 19). But he declined repeated offers to minister to the Dorchester or Cambridge churches.

Instead, Stoughton, who never married, turned to a life as Dorchester farmer and Massachusetts magistrate. Admitted to freemanship in 1665, he rose exceptionally quickly to the ranks of the colony's assistants in 1671 and was annually reelected until 1686. He served as a commissioner of the United Colonies from 1674 to 1676 during the troubled times of King Philip's War and again from 1680 to 1686. His most onerous duty, however, lay in representing Massachusetts in England between 1677 and 1679. With his fellow "messenger" Peter Bulkeley he found himself starved of money and authority with which to negotiate and unable to bring his own government to recognize the seriousness of the Crown's hostility to the Puritans of Massachusetts. After his return he refused further invitations to act as agent; instead, with Bulkeley and another longtime political ally, Joseph Dudley, he assumed leadership of the political faction in Massachusetts urging accommodation to English regulation. Another bond uniting these moderates was participation in several speculative land companies seeking title to former Indian lands in the Merrimack River Valley and the Nipmuck country of south central Massachusetts. Dudley and Stoughton, for example, joined with several English investors in 1683 to become the absentee proprietors of the town of Oxford that they then settled with refugee French Protestants.

England's revocation of the Massachusetts charter opened the way for these moderates to come to power, and in May 1686 Stoughton became deputy president under Dudley of the Crown-imposed Dominion of New England. He continued in office after the arrival of royal governor Sir Edmund Andros in December, serving as councilor and associate judge. Unlike Dudley, however, he never committed himself so completely to the unpopular new regime as to be dragged down by its fall; when rebellion erupted in Boston in April 1689 upon news of England's Glorious Revolution, Stoughton stood among those who demanded Andros's surrender and shared in the temporary government that followed. He joined four other former dominion councilors in publishing an account of Andros's arbitrary rule. But only in May 1691 did he accept reelection as assistant in a restored charter government.

Stoughton's reputation as a scrupulous and politically dexterous moderate recommended him to the group of agents negotiating in London for a new government for Massachusetts. In the royal charter brought to Boston in May 1692, he was named lieutenant governor, an office he held, with the added position of chief justice, until his death. Almost immediately his appointment as chief judge of the juryless special court established to deal with the witchcraft accusations centering on Salem Village plunged him into the episode that has most damaged his reputation. Convinced of the admissibility of testimony by witnesses of their being tormented by specters of the accused, Stoughton pressed the early proceedings so ardently that only eight days separated the start of the first victim's trial and her public hanging. Later, when an uneasy governor Sir William Phips stayed a further round of executions in the fall of 1692, Stoughton angrily left the court, convinced that witches still remained to be purged from the land. He refused to follow his fellow judge, the diarist Samuel Sewall, in expressing public remorse for his role in the affair.

But Massachusetts continued to look to Stoughton for leadership. He quietly helped gather evidence for the charges of maladministration that prompted Phips's recall to London in November 1694. Thereafter until his death he acted as the effective head of the Boston government, except between May 1699 and July 1700 when Phips's successor as governor, Richard Coote, earl of Bellomont, left his principal government of New York to reside in Boston. Through these years Stoughton's self-effacing concern to restore the tradition of consensus rule disrupted by Andros and Phips did much to defuse political tensions within Massachusetts. A further incentive for unity was the need to raise men and money to defend the province's frontiers against a succession of destructive French and Indian attacks, a task Stoughton assumed with resolution but only limited success.

Historians have deplored Stoughton's shifting political allegiances, multiple officeholding, and merciless rigor during the Salem trials. Contemporaries, however, saw these as the fruits of a stern sense of duty and an overriding dedication to preserving the essentials of New England's godly heritage at a time of bewildering change. They cherished his old-fashioned austerity—in 1697 Sewall found his lieutenant governor "Carting Ears of Corn from the Upper Barn"—and noted his benefactions to Puritan institutions, such as the huge gift of nearly £1,000 in 1698 used to build Stoughton College at Harvard, forerunner of the modern Stoughton Hall. His lifelong commitment to being, in Cotton Mather's phrase, "a real friend to New-England," explains both his past high and his present dour reputation.

• Stoughton's letters are scattered through the Massachusetts Archives; the Mather papers in the Massachusetts Historical Society; volume 5 of the Blathwayt papers in Colonial Williamsburg; and Colonial Office Papers, class 5, vols. 857–861, in England's Public Record Office. Printed writings are *New-England's True Interest* (1670) and *A Narrative of the Proceedings of Sir Edmund Androsse and His Complices* (1691) in *The Andros Tracts*, ed. W. H. Whitmore, vol. 1 (1868). Biographical sketches are in John L. Sibley, *Biographical Sketches of Graduates of Harvard University*, vol. 1 (1873), and J. W. Deane, "William Stoughton," *New-England Historical and Genealogical Register*, vol. 50 (1896). See also Thomas Hutchinson, *History of the Colony and Province of Massachusetts-Bay*, with a memoir and additional notes by L. S. Mayo (1936); Charles W. Upham, *Salem Witchcraft* (1867); Richard R. Johnson, *Adjustment to Empire: The New England Colonies, 1675–1715* (1981); and Robert E. Moody and Richard C. Simmons, eds., *The Glorious Revolution in Massachusetts: Selected Documents, 1689–1692* (1988).

RICHARD R. JOHNSON

STOUT, Gardner Dominick (21 Apr. 1903–16 Jan. 1984), investment banker, museum president, and naturalist, was born in New York City, the son of Andrew Varick Stout, a stockbroker, and Ethel Dominick. As a small boy, visits to the American Museum of Natural History first aroused Stout's interest, he said, "in natural history and the world of animate things." While vacationing with his family at a summer home in Rumson, he wandered along the Jersey shore, exploring the natural world and observing the behaviors of the shorebirds. Stout's interest in nature was balanced by his commitment to the family business, and he graduated cum laude from Yale University in 1926. Later that year he joined the Wall Street banking firm of Dominick and Dominick, which had been founded in 1870 by his grandfather Bayard Dominick. In 1928 Stout purchased a seat on the New York Stock Exchange for $335,000, which was at the time the highest price ever paid for a seat. That same year he became a general partner in Dominick and Dominick. In 1930 he married Clare Kellogg, who shared his enthusiasm for travel and nature. They had three sons.

In 1942 Stout temporarily set aside his business career and entered the U.S. Navy as a lieutenant (junior grade); he saw action in the Atlantic and Pacific theaters during World War II. By 1946, the year of his discharge, Stout had achieved the rank of commander,

having served as an operations officer on the staff of Admiral Thomas Kinkaid, commander of the Seventh Fleet.

After the war Stout resumed his duties with Dominick and Dominick. In 1964 he was named president of the firm. Three years later he became executive board chairman, and in 1968 he retired from the Wall Street house.

Throughout his life Stout's commitment to his career as a banker was counter balanced by his love of the American wilderness, of wild places the world over, and of the flora and fauna of these regions. He loved in particular to view birds in their natural habitats. He visited Cape Cod and the Outer Banks off the Carolinas. Later still, he journeyed to the Great Barrier Reef in Australia and to Central America and Africa. He realized, though, that nature studies did not have to involve extensive travel. "You don't need to go that far," he observed. "You can go to the Jamaica Bay wildlife reserve, which is a New York City park—I drive out there at 7 in the morning and walk around seeing thousands of ducks and geese, with the Empire State Building on the horizon."

Stout's lifelong interest in nature and in birds led to his election as chairman of the executive committee of the National Audubon Society, an office he held from 1946 to 1958. In 1959 he was chosen a trustee of the American Museum of Natural History. And in 1968, after his retirement from Wall Street, he became the seventh president of the museum, succeeding Alexander M. White in the unsalaried, full-time post.

As he assumed the president's chair, Stout described himself as "excited and stimulated by the opportunities" the museum offered. He considered the American Museum as the "greatest museum of natural history in the world," both in its exhibits and in the research pursued by the scientific and curatorial staff. In fact, as Stout pointed out, the two were linked, since it was the "research people whose work" made possible the "marvelous displays and habitat groups."

During his seven years as president, Stout had a marked effect on many aspects of the museum. Older halls were renovated and new ones opened. These latter included the Peoples of the Pacific (conceived and completed under the supervision of the anthropologist Margaret Mead) and the Hall of Mexico and Central America. Also established were the People Center, the Alexander M. White Science Center, and the Hall of Mollusks (opened not long after Stout retired from the presidency). The Frick Paleontological Building, which housed the largest collection of fossil mammals in the world, and the Perkin Wing of the Hayden Planetarium were added to the museum's facilities during Stout's tenure.

Eager to demonstrate the museum's relevance to the contemporary world, Stout supervised its involvement in the environmental movement. He was a prime mover behind an exhibit titled "Can Man Survive?" which opened in 1969. "Because the Museum has such large and varied collections, and because many of the species represented in our collections are now extinct," he explained in an annual report to the museum's trustees, "we occupy a very special position in assessing the threat that man has posed to all living things, including himself." And Stout added that the role the museum "should play in the environmental crises should be as scientific adviser and counsel," showing people "how they can best adapt themselves and their life standards to produce a sound environment."

Stout also took the lead in fundraising. In connection with the museum's centennial in 1969, he presided over an ambitious campaign that by the time of his retirement had collected $22 million for the institution.

In 1975 Stout stepped down as museum president. In recognition of his accomplishments, Mayor Abraham Beame awarded Stout New York City's highest civic award, the Bronze Medallion. "The American Museum of Natural History is one of the City's greatest assets," observed the Mayor, "and Gardner Stout has been one of the Museum's most valuable treasures." In 1980 he was honored further with the opening of the Gardner D. Stout Hall of the Asian Peoples, the museum's largest permanent anthropological exhibition.

Stout also sponsored and served as the editor of the *Shorebirds of North America* (1967). This sumptuously produced volume was well received, and it was praised by Peter Farb in the *Saturday Review* (25 Nov. 1967) as "among the finest nature books ever to come off the presses in this country."

Stout died at a convalescent home in Stanford, Connecticut.

• The American Museum of Natural History has a small collection of Stout's administrative files, including material dealing with the museum's centennial in 1969. For biographical information on Stout, consult the file maintained on him at the American Museum of Natural History. Additional sources include Frank Graham, *The Audubon Ark: A History of the National Audubon Society*, with Carl W. Buchheister (1990); Geoffrey Hellman, *Bankers, Bones and Beetles: The First Century of the American Museum of Natural History* (1969); and Lyle Rexer and Rachel Klein, *American Museum of Natural History: 125 Years of Expedition and Discovery* (1995). Also useful is an article on Stout in the *New York Times*, 29 Oct. 1968. Obituaries are in the *New Canaan Advertiser*, 19 Jan. 1984, and the *New York Times*, 17 Jan. 1984.

RICHARD HARMOND

STOUT, Rex (1 Dec. 1886–27 Oct. 1975), mystery writer, was born Rex Todhunter Stout in Noblesville, Indiana, the son of John Wallace Stout, a newspaper editor and school superintendent, and Lucetta Todhunter. In 1887 the Stouts moved to Kansas, where Rex and his eight siblings spent their youth. Stout was a brilliant child. According to his primary biographer, John McAleer, Stout had read the Bible twice by the time he was five years old, read his father's library of more than a thousand books by age of eleven, and was a mathematical prodigy. In 1903, after graduating from high school at sixteen, he left for the University of Kansas in Lawrence. Despite his talents, Stout was unable to pay tuition and found no support at the university.

He went to Topeka and took jobs as an usher and a bookkeeper for the next two years. In 1904 he sold his first work, a poem that was never published, to *Smart Set* for $12.

In 1905 Stout joined the navy and worked on President Theodore Roosevelt's yacht, the *Mayflower*, as pay-yeoman until 1907. He then bought his discharge for $80 and wandered the country working odd jobs, commonly bookkeeping. Between 1907 and 1911 Stout was essentially rootless. He lived in twelve states in as many months, and his most notable literary achievement was the sale of three more poems to *Smart Set* and two stories to *Short Stories*. Stout's travels, however, roused his interest in a writing career.

In 1912 Stout moved to New York and began a remarkably productive period. In the next five years he turned out four novels, all published in periodicals, and thirty more short stories. The period ended in 1916 when he married Fay Kennedy and joined his brother Bob Stout in business. Stout would not again write for publication until 1929.

Stout's brother had conceived the idea of a school banking system that would arrange savings programs for schoolchildren. In exchange for one-third ownership, Stout created and implemented a method of operating his brother's system. In 1926 he secured financial independence by selling his share of the business to his brother, which left him free to pursue his interests in the publishing industry and continue his writing.

Stout's second career as a novelist began in Europe. He and Fay spent 1927 to 1929 in Paris, where *How like a God*, Stout's first novel published in book form, was finished. The two then returned to the United States and built a home, "High Meadow," in Connecticut near Brewster, New York. At High Meadow Stout led an orderly, focused life and mostly engaged in writing and gardening. Fay, however, was not content with country life and continued to live in the city where she could maintain her social affairs. The childless marriage ended in divorce in 1931. Stout married Pola Hoffmann in 1932, and the couple had two daughters.

Between 1929 and 1934 Stout produced four more novels: *Seed on the Wind* (1930), *Golden Remedy* (1931), *Forest Fire* (1933), and *The President Vanishes* (1934). These novels, along with *How like a God*, received mixed reviews in the United States and England. While critics claimed that the novels attempted to compete with William Faulkner, Ernest Hemingway, and Joseph Conrad and were known as Stout's "serious fiction" (Anderson, p. 6), they were neither popularly nor critically successful. *Fer-de-Lance* (1934), the first Nero Wolfe detective story, marked the beginning of Stout's fame.

During the next forty years Stout wrote thirty-three Nero Wolfe novels, ending the series with *A Family Affair* in 1975, the year of his death at High Meadow.

These books "reconciled the formal detective story with the hard-boiled detective story" (Townsend, p. xxv). In doing so, Stout expanded the range of crime fiction. Indeed, the Nero Wolfe mysteries combine the refined elements of Sherlock Holmes with an American rusticity. While Stout's plots are soundly mysterious and his settings are perfectly constructed, the mysteries reached fame through the relationship between the great detective Nero Wolfe and his rough-and-tumble partner Archie Goodwin. Wolfe is brilliant, ponderous, and unpredictable. He solves a mystery through logic and carefully planned interrogation, invariably without leaving the privacy and comfort of his home. The handsome and sophisticated Archie Goodwin, on the other hand, prefers the action of the streets and is often frustrated by Wolfe's lack of disclosure. To use one of McAleer's analogies, Wolfe's wryness is a "whetstone" for Archie's drollery. Neither Wolfe nor Archie can do without the other, and together, critics agree, the pair is unequaled. The Nero Wolfe mysteries rapidly attracted a worldwide following. ABC aired a Nero Wolfe radio series periodically from 1943 to 1950; Stout was translated into twenty-six languages; and by 1975 a hundred million books had been sold.

As World War II enveloped America, Stout became an active propagandist for the war effort and democracy. In 1941 he helped to sponsor the Fight for Freedom Committee and Freedom House, was elected president of Friends of Democracy in 1942, and helped form the Society for the Prevention of World War III in 1944. As chairman of the Writers' War Board, Stout hosted the radio series "Victory Volunteers" and created and conducted the CBS weekly radio series "Our Secret Weapon."

After the war, Stout fought for writers' economic rights. He had served as president of Vanguard Press (1925–1928) and had helped bring out leftist books otherwise not likely to be published. He again followed his interest in helping writers and in 1945 became president of the Authors' Guild, a position that helped him increase the royalties paid by paperback publishers. He was also a founder of the Writers' Board for World Government (1949), was elected president of the Authors' League in 1951, and was appointed president of Mystery Writers of America in 1958.

His ongoing commitment to democracy and his outspoken anticommunist attitude refute a 1950 accusation by Merwin Hart to the House's Select Committee to Investigate Lobbying Activities that Stout was a communist. An affiliation with the *New Masses*—a liberal-arts magazine that later adopted a communist agenda—was cited as evidence of Stout's misconduct. In turn, he initiated an attack on McCarthyism through his position as president of the Authors' League.

Rex Stout, civil libertarian, politician, and writer, received international accolades. His admirers included Oliver Wendell Holmes, Franklin D. Roosevelt, Hubert Humphrey, John Wayne, John Steinbeck, Marlene Dietrich, and the Maharajah of Indore. P. G. Wodehouse wrote, "His narrative and dialogue could not be improved, and he passes the supreme test of being rereadable" (McAleer, foreword). Readers find much more to the Nero Wolfe stories than the usual crime fiction and find much more to Stout than the writer of mysteries.

• The Burns Library at Boston College has a substantial collection of Stout's correspondence and manuscripts, especially relating to the end of Stout's career. Syracuse University Library contains some Rex Stout correspondence in the papers of Egmont Arens, Phyliss McGinley, and Dorothy Thompson. The Schlesinger Library on the History of Women in America at Radcliffe College holds Rex Stout correspondence in the papers of Adelaide Frank. The Nero Wolfe mysteries have been published both in singular and collected form. Collections include *Black Orchids* (1942), *Not Quite Dead Enough* (1944), and *Three at Wolfe's Door* (1960). Stout's short stories "Excess Baggage" (*Short Stories*, Oct. 1912, pp. 26–32) and "The Pay Yeoman" (*All-Story Magazine*, Jan. 1914, pp. 186–92) are noteworthy examples of his early style. Stout commented on writing in "A Good Character for a Novel," *New Masses*, 15 Dec. 1936, pp. 17–18; "What to Do about a Watson," in *The Mystery Writer's Handbook* (1956); and "The Mystery Novel," in *The Writer's Book*, ed. Helen Hull (1969). Examples of Stout's political writing during World War II are "Where They'll Find the Strength of Our Country," *Philadelphia Inquirer*, 29 June 1941; "We Shall Hate, or We Shall Fail," *New York Times Magazine*, 17 Jan. 1943; and "Sense or Sentiment," *Prevent World War III*, May 1944, p. 3. John McAleer, *Rex Stout: A Biography* (1977), exhaustively surveys Stout's life and includes a complete list of his voluminous work. Guy M. Townsend, *Rex Stout: An Annotated Primary and Secondary Bibliography* (1980), is the best bibliographical source and also concisely discusses Stout's career. For an account of Stout's popularity, see David R. Anderson, *Rex Stout* (1984). Anderson also critiques popular Nero Wolfe novels and novellas including *Fer-de-Lance* (1934), *Some Buried Caesar* (1939), *Over My Dead Body* (1940), *Before Midnight* (1955), *A Right to Die* (1964), and *Please Pass the Guilt* (1973).

SCOTT W. ERICKSON

STOVEY, Harry Duffield (20 Dec. 1856–20 Sept. 1937), baseball player, was born Harry Duffield Stow in Philadelphia, Pennsylvania, the son of John P. Stow, a watchman, and Lizzie (maiden name unknown). Forbidden by his mother to play professional baseball because players were known as hard-drinking rowdies, he had his name put in the newspapers as "Stovey" instead of Stow. He was the great-grandson of Charles Stow, of the famous Philadelphia bellmakers Pass and Stow, who recast the original Liberty Bell after it was cracked in 1752.

Stovey left school after the eighth grade and worked sporadically as a laborer, watchman, and boilermaker while spending most of his time playing amateur baseball. In 1876 he pitched for the Defiance Club of Philadelphia, supposedly an amateur team though some players were paid, and led the club to the amateur championship of Philadelphia. He started the 1877 season with Defiance, then played briefly at Williamsport, Pennsylvania, as a pitcher, first baseman, and second baseman. In September he signed as a pitcher with the Philadelphia Athletics, a professional team that along with New York had been expelled from the National League after the 1876 season for not fulfilling its game commitments. The Athletics, however, played National League teams in 1877, and Stovey beat Chicago in his professional debut.

In 1878 Stovey signed with the New Bedford, Massachusetts, Clam-Eaters (International Association) as a substitute first baseman at $60 a month. Why he abandoned pitching is a matter of conjecture. During the two years in New Bedford, he became the star of the team. In 1879 he married Mary L. Walker, with whom he had three daughters, and made his permanent home in New Bedford.

In 1880 Stovey reached the major leagues with Worcester, Massachusetts, of the National League. In his first season, the 5'11½", 180-pound ballplayer, who threw and batted right-handed, led the league in triples and home runs.

When the Worcester team folded in 1882, several teams sought to sign him. He elected to join the Philadelphia Athletics of the American Association, the rival of the National League, and in his seven years with the Athletics became one of baseball's outstanding players. He hit both with power and for average, had a strong throwing arm, covered a great deal of ground in the outfield, and ran the bases with speed. The first player to wear sliding pads, he was referred to as "the father of the base slide." He led the Athletics, who had chosen him captain, to the league championship in 1883.

During his years in Philadelphia, Stovey led the league in runs scored and home runs four times and in slugging average in 1884. In 1888 he showed his powerful arm in a distance-throwing contest sponsored by the *Cincinnati Enquirer*, finishing second to Ned Williamson of Chicago (National League) with a throw of 123 yards, 2 inches.

In 1890, when the short-lived Players' League was formed, Stovey jumped to its Boston club. In helping Boston win the pennant that season, Stovey led the league in stolen bases (97) and finished second in home runs (11). When the Players' League collapsed after one season, a quarrel ensued between the National League and the financially weak American Association over the ownership of Stovey and Louis Bierbauer. The fight led to the folding of the American Association, the formation of a twelve-team National League, which included four teams from the former American Association, and the ruling of the Board of Control that the National League team in Boston owned the rights to Stovey. In 1891 he signed with Boston for $4,200, "a whole lot in those days" as Stovey remarked later. The Boston team won the pennant that year, but the club's financial problems and Stovey's fading skills led to his release the following June. He played for Baltimore until August 1893; he then signed with Brooklyn, where he ended his major-league career.

In 1894 Stovey played briefly for Allentown, Pennsylvania (Pennsylvania State League), before leaving to join New Bedford (New England League) as manager and captain. Rather than accept a cut in salary the next year, he left baseball for good and joined the New Bedford police force. In 1901, while walking his beat along the waterfront, he dove fully uniformed between two wharves to rescue a seven-year-old boy who had fallen between them. Stovey rose to captain in the force in 1915, a position he held until his retirement in 1923. Afterward he led a quiet but active life marked by games of bocce and summers in a cottage owned by a daughter in the Methodist Camp Ground on Martha's Vineyard. The last three years of his life he was an invalid because of hip problems that stemmed from his frequent sliding into bases as a player. He died at his home in New Bedford and was buried in Oak Grove Cemetery.

The statistics contained in baseball encyclopedias differ in presenting Stovey's record, but they agree that he led in home runs five times and in runs scored four times and that he hit 19 homers in 1889, a remarkable achievement in the dead-ball era. He was the first player to hit more than 20 triples in a season, with either 23 or 25 in 1884. He led in triples three or four times. He hit a total of 122 home runs. His career batting average as recorded in various sources ranges from a low of .288 to a high of .307. Most sources credit him with 441 stolen bases, though two give him 774. The reason for the discrepancy is that, during much of Stovey's career, a stolen base was credited for each base runner advanced by his own volition (that is, if the runner advanced from first to third on a single, he was credited with having stolen third base). Though some sources credit him with 156 stolen bases in 130 games in 1888, most revise the figure to 87. He played the outfield in 945 games and first base in 550.

All agree, however, on Stovey's baserunning ability. He allegedly circled the bases in just over 14 seconds in 1891, and one writer noted that when it came to daring, Stovey "would take more chances than a sailor at a turkey raffle."

One of nineteenth-century baseball's star players, Stovey was the first to combine speed with both power and batting average, and he was excellent defensively, especially as an outfielder. He played on championship teams in three major leagues: the American Association, the Players' League, and the National League. In addition, he was respected for his honesty and model behavior on and off the field. A brief sketch of Stovey's early career written in 1880 states, "He is a strictly temperate, honest, and ambitious young man, and in every respect a model professional player." Although Stovey did not win election to the National Baseball Hall of Fame even long after his death, he remains highly regarded by students of nineteenth-century baseball.

• The National Baseball Hall of Fame Library in Cooperstown, N.Y., has a small clipping file on Stovey. His major-league records may be found in *The Baseball Encyclopedia*, 10th ed. (1996); *Total Baseball*, 3d ed. (1993); *The Sports Encyclopedia: Baseball*, 14th ed. (1996); and Gene Karst and

Martin J. James, Jr., *Who's Who in Professional Baseball* (1973), with the first two sources probably the most accurate. A brief sketch of Stovey's career appears in the Society for American Baseball Research, *Nineteenth Century Stars* (1989). The *New York Clipper*, 7 Aug. 1880, contains a woodcut portrait of Stovey and a sketch of his early baseball career. George V. Tuohey, *A History of the Boston Baseball Club* (1897), includes some little-known facts about Stovey as well as an account of the Boston championship team on which he played. David Q. Voight, *American Baseball from Gentleman's Sport to the Commissioner System* (1966), and Harold Seymour, *Baseball: The Early Years* (1960), present the historical background. The *New Bedford Standard-Times*, 1 Oct. 1982, contains a column urging Stovey's election to the Baseball Hall of Fame. Obituaries are in the *New Bedford Standard-Times*, 20 Sept. 1937, and the *New York Times*, 21 Sept. 1937.

RALPH S. GRABER

STOWE, Calvin Ellis (26 Apr. 1802–22 Aug. 1886), biblical scholar, promoter of common schools, and husband of Harriet Beecher Stowe, was born in Natick, Massachusetts, the son of Samuel Stow, a baker, and Hephzibah Bigelow, a seamstress and practical nurse. His father died in 1808, reducing a family of already limited means to near penury. At the age of twelve he began working in a paper mill. A local patron paid for his attendance at Bradford Academy. His academic performance attracted the attention of additional benefactors, who agreed to finance further education on condition that he prepare for the ministry.

Following a stint at Gorham Academy, Stowe enrolled in Bowdoin College, where fellow students included Franklin Pierce, Nathaniel Hawthorne, and Henry Wadsworth Longfellow. Graduating in 1824 at the head of his class, Stowe remained at Bowdoin for one year as librarian and instructor. It was at this point that his surname first acquired the final *e*. Stowe attended Andover Theological Seminary between 1825 and 1828. While at Andover he completed two works of biblical scholarship, *Jahn's History of the Hebrew Commonwealth* (1828), a translation from the German of Johann Jahn, and an annotated edition of Robert Lowth's *Lectures on the Sacred Poetry of the Hebrews* (1829). In 1830 he was named editor of the *Boston Recorder*, one of the nation's oldest and most prestigious religious periodicals.

Stowe went to Dartmouth College in 1831 as a professor of Latin and Greek. While at Dartmouth, in 1832, he married Eliza Tyler and was ordained as a Congregational minister; The couple had no children. Stowe left Dartmouth in 1833 at the request of Lyman Beecher, accepting the chair of biblical literature in Beecher's newly established Lane Theological Seminary in Cincinnati, Ohio.

While in Cincinnati, Stowe added to his growing fame as a biblical scholar two additional distinctions that would eventually eclipse the former. Following the death of his wife in 1834, Stowe married, in 1836, Lyman Beecher's daughter and future novelist Harriet Elizabeth Beecher, with whom he had seven children. In that same year he was sent to Europe on a dual commission: to purchase books for the Lane Seminary library and to prepare a report on education for the benefit of the state legislature.

From the beginning of his tenure at Lane, Stowe was a staunch supporter of public education. His work with seminarians seems to have convinced him that rigorous professional education and scholarship in the new western states ultimately depended on the quality of elementary and secondary education available. Stowe was an active member, along with Lyman Beecher, William Holmes McGuffey, and Samuel Lewis, in the Western Literary Institute and College of Professional Teachers, an organization dedicated to the support and improvement of public schools. Stowe spoke at a convention of the Western Literary Institute in 1835 on the Prussian schools, a topical subject in the wake of Victor Cousin's report on the same, published in New York that year. When Stowe's plans for European travel on behalf of the Lane Seminary library were announced, his colleagues in the institute prevailed on the Ohio legislature to charge Stowe with a study of European, particularly Prussian, schools.

Stowe's *Report on Elementary Public Instruction in Europe Made to the Thirty-sixth General Assembly of Ohio* (1837) was delivered at a propitious moment, at a point when concern for American education was reaching a new peak and when individual states were creating new bureaucratic structures to systematize schooling. The legislature in Ohio ordered 8,500 copies of Stowe's report to be printed and sent to every school district in the state. The report was further reprinted by order of the legislatures in Massachusetts, Michigan, Pennsylvania, and other states. Legislation in Ohio (1838) and elsewhere concerning the funding and supervision of common schools reflected standards described and advocated in Stowe's report.

In 1850 Stowe accepted the chair of religion at Bowdoin College only to accept two years later the position of his retiring mentor, Moses Stuart, at Andover Seminary. Meanwhile his wife had achieved almost instantaneous fame as the author of *Uncle Tom's Cabin* (1852). Subsequently, Stowe accompanied his wife on European tours in 1853, 1856, and 1859, serving as Harriet's public spokesman. From the beginning of their marriage Stowe, a noted storyteller and stylist in his own right, had encouraged Harriet's literary aspirations. Harriet Stowe's *Oldtown Folks* (1869) is, according to the couple's son Charles, particularly indebted to Calvin Stowe's boyhood experience.

Stowe retired from Andover in 1864, moving to Hartford, Connecticut. His wife's earnings allowed the purchase of a winter home in Mandarin, Florida. The author of numerous theological books and articles throughout his career, Stowe published his major and bestselling work in retirement. *The Origin and History of the Books of the Bible* (1867) addressed the question of the New Testament's inspiration. Informed by contemporary German scholarship, the work reflected nonetheless a relatively conservative Protestant interpretation of the Scriptures and was accessible to the general reader.

Having established a name for himself in theological and educational circles, Stowe was sought out from early in his career for his services as a speaker, writer, and professor. He was proficient in a remarkable number of ancient and modern languages. Proud of his wife's accomplishments, he resented nevertheless, in later years, being addressed as "Mrs. H. B. Stowe's husband." He died in Hartford after a long decline.

• Stowe's papers connected to his work at Lane Theological Seminary are in the Jesuit-Krauss-McCormick Library in Chicago and the Presbyterian Historical Society in Philadelphia. Correspondence is also in a number of Beecher collections, including the Stowe-Day Library (Hartford) and the Schlesinger Library of Radcliffe College. The most complete work on Stowe is John Stanley Harker, "The Life and Contributions of Calvin Ellis Stowe" (Ph.D. diss., Univ. of Pittsburgh, 1951). Earle Hilgert, "Calvin Ellis Stowe: Pioneer Librarian of the Old West," *Library Quarterly* 50 (1980): 324–351 is also useful.

Many biographies of Harriet Beecher Stowe offer insight on Calvin Stowe. See especially their son C. E. Stowe's *Life of Harriet Beecher Stowe* (1889) and Joan D. Hedrick, *Harriet Beecher Stowe: A Life* (1994). Edward Wagenknecht, *Harriet Beecher Stowe: The Known and the Unknown* (1965), includes a useful chapter on the couple's relationship. There are obituaries in the *Congregationalist*, 26 Aug. 1886, and the *New York Times*, 23 Aug. 1886.

ANDREW D. MULLEN

STOWE, Harriet Beecher (14 June 1811–1 July 1896), author, was born in Litchfield, Connecticut, the daughter of Lyman Beecher, a clergyman, and Roxana Foote. Her father, one of the most popular evangelical preachers of the pre–Civil War era, was determined to have a role in shaping the culture of the new nation. Her mother, from a cosmopolitan, novel-reading, Episcopalian family, studied painting and executed portraits on ivory. After bearing nine children, she died when Stowe was five. Stowe's father quickly remarried, but from this point, Stowe's sister Catharine Beecher became the strongest female influence in her life.

A precocious child with a quick memory, Stowe stood out even within the remarkable Beecher family. Observing her oddity and "genius," her father said he would give $100 if she were a boy and her brother Henry Ward Beecher a girl. At age eight she entered the Litchfield Female Academy, an excellent school founded to "vindicate the equality of female intellect"; there the strongest influence on her was John Brace, whose methods of teaching composition she later imitated. She was an eager writer in what Brace called this "literary loving school." Her first assignment was an essay on "The Difference between the Natural and Moral Sublime"—a topic, Stowe noted, "not trashy or sentimental, such as are often supposed to be the style for female schools." At age nine she volunteered to write weekly essays; at age thirteen she won the honor of having her composition read aloud at the annual school exhibit, where it made her father sit up and ask who the author was. When the answer came, "Your daughter, sir," Stowe experienced what she later

called "the proudest moment of my life" (Cross, vol. 1, p. 399).

In 1824 Stowe entered Catharine Beecher's Hartford Female Seminary, where she studied the most difficult subjects in the male college curriculum, including Latin and moral philosophy, and aspired to become an artist like her mother. Although she painted throughout her life and left some remarkably accomplished canvases, her true vocation was to paint with words. From 1829 to 1832 she taught composition at the Hartford Female Seminary and at age nineteen wrote to her brother George, who like all of her brothers entered the ministry, "It is as much my vocation to preach on paper as it is that of my brothers to preach viva voce."

In 1832 she moved with her family to Cincinnati, Ohio, where her father had accepted the presidency of Lane Seminary. While her father campaigned to "save the West" from the influences of infidelism and Roman Catholicism, Stowe observed new customs and relished the dialects spoken at the Cincinnati landing. Her literary career blossomed. She published a widely adopted *Primary Geography* (1833) that won the praise of the bishop of Cincinnati for her tolerant views of Catholics, taught in Catharine Beecher's Western Female Academy, and participated in the social and literary gatherings of the Semi-Colon Club, for which she wrote many of her early essays and stories, pioneering the use of dialect and reflecting on customs in her native New England. Many of these writings were published in the *Western Monthly Magazine* and were collected in her first book of fiction, *The Mayflower* (1843).

In 1836 she married Calvin Ellis Stowe, a biblical scholar and professor at Lane Seminary. With his encouragement she became "a literary woman," regularly adding to their slender finances by contributing sermons and temperance tales to the *New-York Evangelist* and writing stories for *Godey's Lady's Book* and various gift books. During their fifty-year-long union Calvin Stowe remained a judicious adviser and staunch supporter of Harriet Beecher Stowe's literary career, but their domestic life was made difficult by their temperamental differences, seven children, money problems, Calvin's hypochondria, and Harriet's haphazard domestic management.

In 1843, moved by the millennial spirit of the times and by the suicide of her brother George, Stowe experienced a deepening of her faith, a "second birth" more meaningful than her first conversion experience at age fourteen. Her profound identification with Christ as a man of sorrows and lover of the lowly helped her through years of poverty, ill health, and domestic difficulty and informed her most famous fiction. In 1849 their eighteen-month-old son, Samuel Charles, died in a cholera epidemic that swept Cincinnati. "It was at *his* dying bed and at *his* grave," Stowe wrote of Charley, "that I learnt what a poor slave mother may feel when her child is torn away from her." When the passage of the Fugitive Slave Law the following year implicated the North in just such family separations, Stowe began writing *Uncle Tom's Cabin*. Serialized in the *National Era* between 5 June 1851 and 1 April 1852, the story had a huge following and sold more than 300,000 copies in the United States during the first year after it was published in book form by J. P. Jewett in 1852. Drawing on the familiar genre of the slave narrative but casting it in a fiction bristling with regional types and racy slang, Stowe wrote what was recognized at the time as a great American novel.

Uncle Tom's Cabin follows the fortunes of Tom, a faithful slave who is sold away from his family, and Eliza and George Harris, who flee their bondage in Kentucky. As the Harrises make their way toward Canada and freedom—Eliza by heroically crossing the ice of the Ohio River with her child, George by impersonating a white man—Tom is sent deeper into slavery. He is purchased by August St. Clare at the behest of his young daughter, Evangeline (Eva), who on her deathbed urges her father to free Tom, but St. Clare is killed in a tavern brawl, and Tom is sold again. Under the tyrannical power of Simon Legree on a plantation on the Red River in Louisiana, Tom dies from a beating. The story was immediately put on stage, translated into dozens of languages, and embodied in popular culture in the form of songs, toys, and figurines. The impact of *Uncle Tom's Cabin* on the conscience of the nation, already tender from the outrages of the Fugitive Slave Law, was such that when Stowe came to the White House in 1862, Abraham Lincoln is said to have greeted her with the words, "So you're the little woman who wrote the book that started this great war" (Charles Edward Stowe and Lyman Beecher Stowe, *Harriet Beecher Stowe: The Story of Her Life* [1911], p. 203).

The success of *Uncle Tom's Cabin* made Stowe an international celebrity and a focus of antislavery sentiment. In 1853 she published *A Key to Uncle Tom's Cabin*, an antislavery polemic written to answer critics who complained that her novel had exaggerated the brutalities of slavery. At the invitation of two Scottish antislavery societies she undertook a tour of the British Isles. As she recounted in *Sunny Memories of Foreign Lands* (1854), she was met by large crowds, feted at antislavery soirees, showered with money for the cause, and presented with a petition from more than half a million British women urging their American sisters to end slavery. She used money given her to free slaves, distribute antislavery literature, and support antislavery lectures, but her most powerful antislavery weapon remained her pen. In 1854, when Congress was debating the Kansas-Nebraska Act, Stowe published in the *Independent* "An Appeal to Women of the Free States of America, on the Present Crisis on Our Country" and circulated petitions to defeat the bill. When it passed, opening the possibility of slavery in the new territories, Stowe wrote her second antislavery novel, *Dred: A Tale of the Great Dismal Swamp* (1856). In contrast to the Christian pacifism of Tom in *Uncle Tom's Cabin*, her hero Dred is presented as the son of Denmark Vesey, the historical figure hanged in South Carolina for fomenting rebellion among the slaves.

The following year her nineteen-year-old son, Henry Ellis, a freshman at Dartmouth College, died while attempting to swim the Connecticut River. Struggling with the probability that he had died "unregenerate," Stowe wrote *The Minister's Wooing* (1859), the first of her New England novels and a liberal reworking of the Calvinist theology of her upbringing. It was serialized in the *Atlantic Monthly*, a prestigious new journal Stowe helped to found. Based in part on materials from her mother's life, *The Minister's Wooing* participated in the mythification of New England that was central to the *Atlantic Monthly*'s cultural mission.

During the Civil War as opportunities to make money through authorship multiplied, Stowe was foremost among professional writers. In 1862 she published *Agnes of Sorrento* (inspired by her trip to Italy on her third tour of Europe in 1859–1860) and *The Pearl of Orr's Island* (the second of her New England novels) and continued to write occasional columns for the *Independent*. In 1864 she instituted in the *Atlantic* a monthly column on household topics—rightly gauging the pulse of the nation during the Civil War. "The public mind," she wrote her editor, James T. Fields, "is troubled, unsettled, burdened with the *real*. . . . *Home* is the thing we must strike for now." After her husband retired in 1863, Stowe became the sole support of her large family. She continued her domestic columns in the *Atlantic* for three years, wrote children's stories, a volume of poetry titled *Religious Poems* (1867), and a collection of biographies called *Men of Our Times* (1868). She also bought a home in Mandarin, on the St. Johns River, becoming one of the first northerners to winter annually in Florida. The weight of these commitments and various domestic difficulties, such as the alcoholism of her son Frederick, who was wounded in the Civil War, delayed work on her third New England novel, *Oldtown Folks* (1869). A compendium of New England life and lore, it was based in part on her husband's recollections of life in Natick, Massachusetts. With Donald G. Mitchell ("Ik Marvell") she was coeditor of *Hearth and Home* in 1868 but resigned in 1869 to write *Lady Byron Vindicated* (1870), the story of Lord Byron's incestuous relationship with his half-sister, Augusta Leigh.

This strange chapter in Stowe's career can best be understood in the context of the politics of Reconstruction America, when the push for civil rights for black men was fanning into popular sentiment similar goals for women. Stowe herself embraced woman suffrage at this time and briefly entertained the possibility of an alliance with Susan B. Anthony and Elizabeth Cady Stanton, who tried in 1869 to recruit her to write for their paper, the *Revolution*, and who were calling attention to the sexual double standard by highly publicized public meetings on sexual scandals. Stowe, who all her life had used the cloak of male power and the posture of true womanhood to pursue her sometimes quite radical goals, balked at this overt alliance on women's issues. However, she used her acquaintance with Lady Byron to write what she may have intended to be the *Uncle Tom's Cabin* of women's sexual slavery. It was a miscalculation. Bravely mentioning incest but narrowly defending the honor of an aristocratic Englishwoman's pure and Christian life, Stowe succeeded only in provoking a torrent of abuse in the press. Burned by this incident, Stowe never again attempted direct speech on sexual matters. However, in her society novels—*Pink and White Tyranny* (1871), *My Wife and I* (1871), and *We and Our Neighbors* (1875)—Stowe used a loosely plotted journalistic fiction to comment on women's roles, reform, and domestic politics. She brought her literary career to a close with *Poganuc People* (1878), fictionalized reminiscences of growing up in Litchfield. She died in Hartford.

Throughout her career Stowe used literature as her father used his pulpit: to shape public opinion. Rooted in common sense, democratic values, and her own experience as a woman and a mother, her views mirrored and appealed to those of the "plain average." She urged the nation to civil disobedience, challenged religious orthodoxy, and dared to discuss incest—all in the name of motherhood, Christianity, and democracy. Writing at a time when women were denied the vote and had no representation in Congress, she used literature to have a political voice, without betraying her socialization as a "true woman." Speaking nationally to an increasingly heterogeneous public and paying attention to dialects, racial differences, and regional customs, Stowe contributed to the elaboration of a national culture and to what Ellen Moers called "the American Real." Always controversial, Stowe fell into disrepute in the latter half of the nineteenth century. When literature became professionalized and more formal, aesthetic standards of art prevailed, and Stowe's passion and finely honed rhetoric were judged "melodramatic" and "sentimental." Her strongly marked characters, particularly Uncle Tom, were seen as stereotypes, an impression increased by the minstrel darkies of the "Tom shows" that continued into the twentieth century. Her reputation rose again in the wake of the the women's movement of the 1970s. *Uncle Tom's Cabin* continues to be read around the world for its principled defense of the lowly and oppressed.

• The largest collections of Stowe's papers are at the Harriet Beecher Stowe Center in Hartford, Conn., and at the Schlesinger Library in Cambridge, Mass. The Sterling Library and Beinecke Library at Yale University hold smaller collections, as does the University of Virginia. Correspondence with her editor, James T. Fields, and his wife, Annie Adams Fields, is in the Huntington Library, San Marino, Calif. Correspondence with William Lloyd Garrison is in the Boston Public Library; with George Eliot, in the New York Public Library. C. E. Stowe, *Life of Harriet Beecher Stowe, Compiled from Her Journals and Letters* (1889), contains some letters not available elsewhere. Barbara M. Cross, ed., *The Autobiography of Lyman Beecher* (1961), contains some first-person reminiscences by Stowe and her siblings. The standard biographies are Joan D. Hedrick, *Harriet Beecher Stowe: A Life* (1994), and Forrest Wilson, *Crusader in Crinoline: The Life of Harriet*

Beecher Stowe (1941). See also Charles H. Foster, *The Rungless Ladder: Harriet Beecher Stowe and New England Puritanism* (1954), and Marie Caskey, *Chariot of Fire: Religion and the Beecher Family* (1978), on Stowe's religious ideas, and Jeanne Boydston et al., eds., *The Limits of Sisterhood: The Beecher Sisters on Women's Rights and Woman's Sphere* (1988), for writings on the "woman question." Margaret Holbrook Hildreth, *Harriet Beecher Stowe: A Bibliography* (1976), is an accurate guide to Stowe's writings. On *Uncle Tom's Cabin*, see E. Bruce Kirkham, *The Building of Uncle Tom's Cabin* (1977), Thomas F. Gossett, *"Uncle Tom's Cabin" and American Culture* (1985), and the following influential evaluations: James Baldwin, "Everybody's Protest Novel," *Partisan Review* 16 (1949): 578–85; Edmund Wilson's essay on Stowe in *Patriotic Gore: Studies in the Literature of the American Civil War* (1962); Ellen Moers, *Harriet Beecher Stowe and American Literature* (1978); and Jane Tompkins, "Sentimental Power: *Uncle Tom's Cabin* and the Politics of Literary History," *Glyph* 8 (1981): 79–102. Alice Crozier, *The Novels of Harriet Beecher Stowe* (1969), provides interpretations of her major works. Elizabeth Ammons, ed., *Critical Essays on Harriet Beecher Stowe* (1980), includes key nineteenth-century reviews as well as twentieth-century evaluations.

JOAN D. HEDRICK

STRACHEY, William (1572–1621), historian and secretary of the Virginia Company, was born in Lesnes, England, the son of William Strachey, a draper, and Mary Cooke. He spent his early years in Saffron Walden, Essex. Strachey's father was a member of an ambitious yeoman family that owned substantial town property. In 1587 he was granted a coat-of-arms, making him a gentleman, a status inherited by his son. His mother came from a family of well-off London merchants. Strachey attended Emmanuel College, Cambridge, in 1588, and in 1605 he was a member of Gray's Inn, though he apparently neither took a degree nor practiced law. In 1595 he married Frances Forster; they had two children. After the death of his father's second wife in 1602 he came into the family property; it was much encumbered and never quite supported him in the life of a gentleman.

In London he traveled in literary company and was at least acquainted with Ben Jonson, Thomas Campion, and John Marston. He published a sonnet commending Jonson's *Se janus*, and Campion thought enough of Strachey to dedicate an epigram in his name, *Ad Gulielmum Stracheum*. He invested money in the Blackfrier's Theater, which he frequently attended.

In 1606 Strachey left England for Constantinople to assume the position of secretary to Sir Thomas Glover, who had been appointed the new ambassador and agent of the Levant Company, one of the major English trading companies. Strachey's career in the Mediterranean proved to be a disaster. He fell afoul of Glover by establishing a friendship with Hugh Holland, an English recusant and scholar traveling in the East, and then by allying himself with Henry Lello, the previous ambassador; both men were enemies of Glover. Dismissed by the ambassador, Strachey returned to London in 1608.

Strachey found employment with the Virginia Company, which was organizing a relief expedition for the Jamestown colony. He invested 25 pounds in two shares of the company and in May 1609 sailed for Virginia on the *Sea Venture* with Sir Thomas Gates and Sir George Somers. A hurricane struck the fleet seven or eight days from the Virginia capes. The ships scattered but eventually reached Jamestown, all except the *Sea Venture*, which ran aground on Bermuda. The ship's company spent nine months on the island, coping with discontent among the settlers and with the needs of survival. They built two ships and reached the James River in May 1610 only to find the colony on the verge of collapse. Gates took charge and soon determined that the only hope of survival lay in abandonment of the colony, but Jamestown was saved by the timely arrival of a fleet under Lord De la Warr. Strachey became secretary of the colony and in July 1610 sent to England a copy of his letter to a "noble lady" that described the shipwreck and the perilous state of the colony. Shakespeare may have used his narrative of the wreck in writing *The Tempest*, but the company was unprepared to publicize such a candid account. Strachey's piece remained unpublished until 1625 when Samuel Purchas printed it as *A true reportoire. . . .* Strachey returned to England in the fall of 1611 and immediately took up a writing career. Early in 1612 he published a copy of the colony's *Lawes devine, morall, and martiall*, and he began a longer history of colonization. He never succeeded in finishing this work, but he did produce a shorter version, *The Historie of Travaile into Virginia Britannia*, which was not published until the mid-nineteenth century. Strachey lived his last years in London, for a time at Blackfriers; was married a second time, to Dorothy (maiden name unknown), sometime after the death of his first wife in 1615; and died unsung in Camberwell, a suburb of London. He was buried at St. Giles, Camberwell.

In keeping with the practice of the time, Strachey's work was largely derivative. In the *Lawes*, Strachey did little more than compile the work of Sir Thomas Gates and Lord De la Warr. *The Historie* drew heavily on the work of Richard Hakluyt and John Smith, though the sections on the Indians contain original material. It was in *A true reportorie* that Strachey proved himself an original and imaginative writer. His account of the storm at sea, the wreck, and the experience on Bermuda demonstrated a sharp eye and a lively pen.

• *A true reportorie of the wracke and redemption of Sir Thomas Gates, Knight*, originally published in *Hakluytus Posthumus or Purchas His Pilgrimes* (1625), can be found in *A Voyage to Virginia in 1609*, ed. Louis B. Wright (1964). David H. Flaherty has edited *For the colony in Virginea Britannia: lawes devine, morall, and martiall, etc.* (1969). *The Historie* exists in three manuscripts: the Percy manuscript at Princeton, the Ashmole manuscript in the Bodleian Library, Oxford, and the Sloane manuscript in the British Museum. R. H. Major edited the Sloane manuscript for the Hakluyt Society, *The Historie of Travaile into Virginia Britannia . . .* (1849). The Percy manuscript was published for the Hakluyt Society, Louis B. Wright and Virginia Freund, eds., as *The Historie of Travell into Virginia Britania (1612)* (1953). The most recent biography is S. G. Culliford, *William Strachey, 1572–1621* (1965).

BERNARD W. SHEEHAN

STRAIGHT, Dorothy Payne Whitney (23 Jan. 1887–13 Dec. 1968), publisher, educator, and philanthropist, was born in Washington, D.C., the daughter of Flora Payne and William C. Whitney, then secretary of the navy. Her father had added a fortune made in urban railways to his wife's dowry and with other socially prominent New Yorkers founded the Metropolitan Opera. Dorothy therefore enjoyed a materially and culturally rich childhood, whose comfort was marred by the death of her mother when Dorothy was six and of her father when she was seventeen. She then came into her own fortune and the temporary custody of her brother Harry and his wife Gertrude Vanderbilt, who sponsored Dorothy's debut but otherwise left her mainly to herself. For part of each year she traveled in Europe with a governess and a companion, visiting cathedrals and reading books. When she was in Manhattan, she filled her free time with meetings of women's clubs and charitable societies. After graduating from the Spence School, she took classes at Columbia University. She also saw suitors but took few of them seriously. As an orphan with her own money she enjoyed greater freedom than her peers. Little pressured to marry, she took up a variety of political causes, some traditional (like charities for children) and some less so (like woman suffrage). As an officer of the New York Junior League (a charitable society of women) she guided members toward greater community involvement, leading the society to provide clean tenement housing for working single women.

In 1905 she met Willard Straight at the house of her friend and his love-interest, Mary Harriman. Mary's father, E. H. Harriman, the railroad magnate, and Straight, a sometime diplomat and representative of American commercial interests, were working to build railroads in China. Straight came from Oswego, New York, went to Cornell, and was on his way up in Wall Street by virtue of his energy and intelligence, but he was not of the social class of Harrimans or Whitneys. Harriman kept him as a business agent but rejected him as a son-in-law. In 1909 Straight began courting Dorothy Whitney, who, unlike Mary Harriman, had no parents to keep her from him. In 1911 they married amid whispers that Straight was a fortune hunter.

As it turned out Dorothy Whitney Straight was fortunate in being able to make her own decision. Willard Straight was a good husband who shared her interests. Both were friends of once and would-be future president Theodore Roosevelt, and both supported him on the Progressive ticket in 1912. She continued to work for woman suffrage, sharing platforms with Carrie Chapman Catt and marching in parades. She persuaded her husband to speak for woman suffrage at the all-women Colony Club.

After reading Herbert Croly's 1909 book *The Promise of American Life*, the Straights invited him to visit them. They shared his belief that reformers must continuously press for political and social change that would tend toward more democratic government and more even distribution of wealth. Believing that a national journal could mobilize its readers to push politicians toward reforms of labor, commercial, industrial, and foreign policies, Dorothy Straight offered to underwrite such a magazine edited by Croly. The *New Republic* began appearing in 1914, featuring articles by Croly, Walter Lippmann, John Dewey, Learned Hand, Randolph Bourne, and Charles Beard. Willard Straight played the role of publisher and attended editorial meetings, but Dorothy Straight critiqued each issue as it appeared and suggested comments her husband might make. At least once when the magazine was ignoring an issue on which she felt strongly—in this case a campaign of slander against the New York City commissioner of charities, whom she supported—she asked Croly to lunch and persuaded him to cover the matter. As the *New Republic* matured, it became more independent of the Straights, but they stood by it even when Theodore Roosevelt attacked it for its radicalism.

When the United States entered the First World War, both Straights volunteered to serve. Dorothy became chair of several committees, chief among them the Council of Women's Organizations, a clearinghouse meant to coordinate the activities of women's volunteer groups. Willard became a major in the army. He survived the war, but not the peace: he died in the influenza epidemic of 1919 while attached to the U.S. delegation at Versailles.

Bereft, Dorothy slowly returned to her life. She reared her three children and attended to reform projects, including the New School for Social Research, which grew out of the *New Republic*, extending the magazine's project to, in one ally's words, "educate the educated." She helped to organize a national association of Junior Leagues and served as its first president. She continued to push Junior Leaguers toward more political activities, like disarmament. She drew criticism from some league members who, like many Americans in the postwar era, had tired of reform.

In 1925 she married an Englishman, Leonard Elmhirst, an agricultural economist whom she met at Cornell while planning a memorial for her husband. Like Willard Straight, Elmhirst had energy and big ideas (he was a friend of Indian reformer Rabindranath Tagore) and was slightly below her class: he thought her "too damnably rich." They moved to England and bought Dartington Hall, a Devonshire castle, which they transformed into an experimental school. The curriculum would grow from students' interests. Pupils would learn by doing and would be citizens of a self-governing and, with farming and handiwork, partly self-sustaining community.

The Elmhirsts ran the school themselves, teaching and administering until 1930, when they brought in a headmaster who made the school a little less experimental and significantly more prosperous. They had by then two children of their own. Dartington became, under the Elmhirsts' supervision, a thriving arts community. Dorothy continued to publish the *New Republic* until she gave up her U.S. citizenship in 1936 and put money for the journal in trust. She saw her lifelong reform efforts not as political maneuvering but as work, as she put it, "to make of our social life the rich product of a work of art." The institutions she built became important parts of the liberal political communities in the United States and Britain. She remained active in the affairs of the school she created. She died at Dartington Hall.

• The bulk of Dorothy Whitney Straight Elmhirst's papers are in the Kroch Library of Cornell University, along with those of her husband Willard and her son Michael. The Willard and Dorothy Straight Papers are available on microfilm. Many papers relating to her later life are at Dartington Hall. The New York Public Library contains a run of the *Junior League Bulletin*. W. A. Swanberg, *Whitney Father, Whitney Heiress* (1980), discusses her earlier life in relation to her father. Michael Young, *Elmhirsts of Dartington Hall* (1982), focuses on her later life. Leonard Knight Elmhirst's little memoir *The Straight and Its Origin* (1975) is useful, as is Michael Straight's *After Long Silence* (1983). Louis Auchincloss, *The Vanderbilt Era* (1989), considers her first marriage in relation to the arranged marriages of her peers. Alvin Johnson's autobiography *Pioneer's Progress* (1952) is a participant's account of the early years at the *New Republic* and the New School for Social Research.

ERIC RAUCHWAY

STRAIGHT, Willard Dickerman (31 Jan. 1880–1 Dec. 1918), diplomat and business executive, was born in Oswego, New York, the son of Henry H. Straight and Emma May Dickerman, both teachers. After his father's death in 1886, Willard spent two years in Japan, where his mother taught at the Girls' Normal School in Tokyo. Orphaned in 1890, he was adopted jointly by Dr. Elvire Rainier and Laura Newkirk, friends of his parents in Oswego. In 1897 he entered Cornell University, where he earned the bachelor's degree in architecture in 1901. It was at Cornell that he developed a strong interest in Asia under the tutelage of Professor of History Henry Morse Stephens.

In his senior year at Cornell, Straight accepted an invitation from Sir Robert Hart of the Chinese Imperial Customs Service to enter the service upon graduation. Since the 1850s, customs in China had been administered by foreigners of several nationalities. During the Taiping Rebellion, the Imperial Maritime Customs, headed by Englishmen, was created to ensure honesty and efficiency in the collection of customs duties. Straight worked for the customs service until 1904, when he went to Korea and Manchuria as a correspondent for Reuters News Service during the Russo-Japanese War. Straight's work as a journalist brought him to the attention of the U.S. State Department. After the war, he was appointed private secretary to the new American minister to Korea, Edwin V. Morgan, with the additional responsibility of vice consul general. His experience in Korea sparked a new interest in opportunities for American economic expansion in Asia. Following the establishment of the Japanese protectorate in Korea, Straight returned to the United States. His connection with Morgan then resulted in his appointment as secretary of legation in Havana when Morgan was sent to Cuba as minister. After diplomatic service in Korea and Cuba, he returned to China in 1906 as U.S. consul general at Mukden. His formal diplomatic career reached a climax when he returned to Washington, D.C., in 1908 as acting chief of the Division of Far Eastern Affairs.

Like many Western diplomats in Asia, Straight concluded that politics and business were inseparable and that American policy in the Far East should reflect that mutuality of interest. He was determined to establish an American sphere of influence in China similar to those already established by the European powers. Moreover, he believed that American capital, as well as trade, deserved an equal opportunity in Manchuria and other areas of China. His commitment to the Open Door policy (that all nations should have equal commercial rights in China) was strengthened by a growing conviction that Japan constituted a threat to American economic interests in China.

Even before he assumed his new duties in Washington, Straight had engaged in an active correspondence with railway magnate Edward Harriman, who shared his commitment to a bold American policy in China. Once he arrived in Washington, Straight was authorized by the State Department to enter formal discussions with Harriman concerning a stronger American investment program in China, including a worldwide railroad network. Following the formation in 1909 of a new American banking group to participate in a proposed international banking consortium, Straight returned to China as the representative first of the American group and then the international consortium that sought to pool its resources for the development of China's infrastructure, particularly railroads in Manchuria. Straight viewed the Four-Power Consortium created in 1910 as a counterbalance against both Japan and Russia in Manchuria. However, following the Chinese Revolution of 1911, these two countries forced their way into the consortium, thus dampening the enthusiasm of American investors for the project, which eventually failed in 1913 when President Woodrow Wilson withdrew support.

Shortly after his marriage in 1911 to Dorothy Whitney, daughter of Wall Street financier William C. Whitney, with whom he would have one child, Straight entered the Wall Street firm of J. P. Morgan and Company as Far Eastern analyst. Returning from China in 1912, he continued to promote the Far East, first by assuming the presidency of the American Asiatic Association in 1913 and later by helping to establish *Asia* magazine, a popular monthly that developed out of the more narrowly business-oriented *Journal of the American Asiatic Association*. Straight and his wife also participated in planning and establishing the political and cultural journal the *New Republic* in 1914,

which reflected his continuing interest in political issues. The *New Republic* initiative was an expression of Straight's desire to elevate the level of political discourse with a lively journal of liberal thought and opinion. It also reflected his close association with Herbert Croly, who became its editor.

Straight emerged from the consortium venture with valuable experience and new ideas as well as a wide circle of contacts in the international banking community and among European government officials. Wilson's withdrawal of government support for the American banking group also persuaded him that, because of the uncertainties of the American political system, the State Department could not be counted on as a dependable ally. As a result, he encouraged the Morgan firm to participate in international loan programs for China but to do so without direct government involvement.

The outbreak of World War I afforded Straight and other American bankers an opportunity to position American capital for the future battle for overseas investment and markets. In 1915 Straight resigned from the house of Morgan to pursue his own interest in law and international trade. A proponent of American intervention on the Allied side, he was also active in the "preparedness movement." Most significant, however, was his association with Frank Vanderlip and the National City Bank in the formation of the American International Corporation (AIC) in late 1915.

The AIC was founded for the expressed purpose of promoting American investment and foreign commerce on a worldwide scale. Its officers and leaders were determined to fill the gap left by the withdrawal of European capital from the investment markets of the world under the pressure of the financial requirements of the war. Arguing for an aggressive investment program in Asia and Latin America, Straight urged American capitalists to seize the opportunity to capture markets and hold them after the war, while also pursuing a new level of cooperation with European financial interests. By the time of Straight's resignation from the AIC to join the army in 1917, American bankers and the government were in the process of redefining their policies along the lines he had suggested.

When the United States entered World War I in 1917, Straight was commissioned a major assigned to the adjutant general's office. He was placed in charge of the War Risk Insurance Bureau's overseas program, after which he attended the Army War College in France and became a liaison officer. Assigned to the American peace mission at the war's end, he was preparing for the new responsibility when stricken by influenza and pneumonia. Straight died in Paris two weeks after the armistice.

Straight was catholic in his interests and achievements. Diplomat, businessman, military officer, Asian expert, and sometime artist, he compiled a record of significant accomplishment in both finance and diplomacy. Although his work as a diplomat was substantial, his most important contribution to American economic and political life lay in his long-term vision of an active and systematic program of worldwide investment and market expansion. Straight's conception of a dynamic investment program, linked to the expansion of foreign markets and reinforced by government policy, became the foreign economic policy of the years that followed. His career and ideas bridged the gap between the Open Door market expansionism of the early twentieth century and the mature finance capitalism embraced by American business in the postwar era.

• The Willard Dickerman Straight Papers are housed at Cornell University Library in the Regional History Collection. For a detailed description see Patricia Gaffney, ed., *The Willard Straight Papers at Cornell University: Guide to the Microfilm Edition* (1974). The most complete biographical study is Herbert Croly, *Willard Straight* (1924). The standard work on Straight's diplomatic and business activities is Charles Vevier, *The United States and China, 1906–1913: A Study of Finance and Diplomacy* (1955). However, the later stages of his business career are best analyzed in Harry N. Scheiber, "World War I as Entrepreneurial Opportunity: Willard Straight and the American International Corporation," *Political Science Quarterly* 84 (Sept. 1969): 486–511. See also Helen Dodson Kahn, "The Great Game of Empire: Willard D. Straight and American Far Eastern Policy" (Ph.D. diss., Cornell Univ., 1968); Louis Graves, with nine illustrations by Straight, *Willard Straight in the Orient* (1922), reprinted from "An American in Asia," *Asia*, Sept. 1920–May 1921; George Marvin, "Willard Straight," *Japan* 13 (Nov.-Dec. 1924): 67–89; "Major Willard Straight," *Bulletin of the American Asiatic Association* 1 (15 Dec. 1918): 33–35; "Willard Straight," *New Republic*, 7 Dec. 1918: 163–64; and Raymond A. Esthus, *Theodore Roosevelt and Japan* (1966). A trenchant, critical, and revisionist account of Straight is in Michael Hunt, *Frontier Defense and the Open Door: Manchuria in Chinese-American Relations, 1895–1911* (1973). An obituary is in the *New York Times*, 2 Dec. 1918.

JAMES J. LORENCE

STRAIN, Isaac G. (4 Mar. 1821–14 May 1857), explorer and naval officer, was born in Roxbury, Pennsylvania, the son of Robert Strain and Eliza Geddes. His middle name was probably Geddes, although this has never been confirmed. Little is known about his early life, but he received sufficient education to enter the U.S. Navy as a midshipman in December 1837. After nearly five years of service in the West Indies and along the coast of Brazil, Strain was assigned to a naval school in Philadelphia in 1842 and remained there for nearly one year.

Strain's experiences off the Brazilian coast had piqued his interest in the largely unexplored country, and in 1843, with assistance from the Academy of Natural Sciences in Philadelphia, he organized an expedition to the interior of Brazil. Taking a leave of absence from the navy, he journeyed to South America with fellow expedition members, but their attempts to explore the dense, forbidding Brazilian jungles were unsuccessful. Sometime in 1844 Strain returned to the navy as a lieutenant aboard the USS *Constitution* when

it docked in Rio de Janeiro and served on that ship for the next few years, primarily in the East Indies.

In 1848 Strain left the *Constitution* to serve on the USS *Ohio*, which had been assigned to patrol the waters off the west coast of Mexico during the Mexican War. When the war ended that summer, Strain left the ship at anchor in La Paz, Mexico, to explore the peninsula of Lower California. Late in 1848 he headed for New York on the USS *Lexington*, but as it headed down the South American coast he saw another opportunity to pursue his interest in exploration and received permission to go ashore in Valparaiso. He then proceeded across the continent to Buenos Aires, recording his observations of the nearly year-long journey. They were later published in book form as *Cordillera and Pampa, Mountain and Plain: Sketches of a Journey in Chili and the Argentine Provinces in 1849* (1853).

In January 1850 Strain was appointed by the Interior Department as a member of the Mexican Boundary Commission and served in that post until 1853. That year he volunteered to lead an expedition to explore the Isthmus of Darien (later renamed the Isthmus of Panama) on behalf of the U.S. government to determine whether a ship canal could be built linking Caledonia Bay on the Caribbean to the Gulf of San Miguel on the Pacific Ocean. Strain and his fellow explorers endured numerous hardships for almost a year, and the expedition attracted wide notice. He was commended by the navy for his heroism in completing the difficult undertaking, which claimed nine lives. His conclusion, expressed in a report issued by the secretary of the navy in 1854, was that an isthmus canal using that route would be impossible to build.

Strain's last activity as an explorer occurred in the summer of 1853, when he joined members of an expedition aboard the USS *Arctic* seeking to determine the feasibility of an underwater telegraph cable between the United States and Great Britain. He spent his final years in declining health, a consequence of the Darien expedition, and died in Aspinwall, Colombia (now Colón, Panama), a year after the publication of his only other known written work, *A Paper on the History and Prospects of Interoceanic Communication by the American Isthmus* (1856).

In addition to membership in the Academy of Natural Sciences, Strain was also active in the American Ethnological Society of New York and the Historical and Geographical Institute of Brazil. Despite his ambitions, his short life precluded his playing a major role in the annals of South American exploration, and his 1853 account of his transcontinental journey is now more a curiosity—only one of a number of accounts written by travelers to that continent in the nineteenth century—than a document of historical interest. However, as a participant in early efforts that led to the building of the Panama Canal and the laying of the transatlantic cable, Strain deserves mention as a figure of minor significance in American history.

• Biographical information on Strain is limited. See Nathan Crosby, *Annual Obituary Notices of Eminent Persons 1857* (1858); *Proceedings of the Academy of Natural Sciences of Philadelphia*, vol. 2 (1846); and J. T. Headley, *Darien Exploring Expedition under the Command of Lieutenant Isaac G. Strain* (1885). See also U.S. Navy Department Registers, 1837–1857, for a record of Strain's naval service.

ANN T. KEENE

STRAKOSCH, Maurice (15? Jan. 1825–9 Oct. 1887), and **Max Strakosch** (27 Sept. 1835–17 Mar. 1892), opera and concert impresarios, were born in Gross-Seelowitz (now Zidlochovice), near Brünn, Moravia (now Brno, Czechoslovakia), the sons of a liquor distiller and his wife. Maurice was also a pianist and a composer. Max and Maurice's brother Ferdinand also worked as an impresario, and their sister Louise performed as a singer under the name Madame Fischoff.

When Maurice was three years old, the Strakosch family moved, evidently temporarily, to Germany. He made his debut as a prodigy at the age of eleven, performing a Hummel concerto in Brno. He then spent several years traveling around and performing in Germany, against the wishes of his father. He eventually made his way to Vienna, where he studied composition with the theorist and composer Simon Sechter. A meeting with Franz Liszt in 1840 convinced Strakosch of his own limitations as a pianist, and he subsequently studied voice. He sang for a year in Zagreb, then left for Italy with a letter of introduction to Giuditta Pasta, with whom he studied for three years; she encouraged him both to study voice and to remain a pianist. In the early 1840s he performed widely as a piano virtuoso and as a singer throughout Europe. During this time he appeared in concert with Giovanni Bottesini (bass) and Luigi Arditi (violin), two musicians with whom he would later be associated in the United States; he also met Gioacchino Rossini (in Florence) and Salvatore Patti (in Venice). As a result of the 1848 revolution, Strakosch left Paris, where he was employed as a pianist, and traveled to New York City, where he was hired by Patti, then the manager of Palmo's Opera House. During that year Strakosch gave several concerts in New York, performing on the piano and assisted by various singers and other instrumentalists. Following standard practice, he included many of his own compositions in his concerts. In late 1848 he and the soprano Amalia Patti (sister of sopranos Carlotta and the famous Adelina Patti) organized a concert troupe that undertook a two-year tour of the United States. In early 1851 he organized the Strakosch Grand Concert Company, a troupe that featured several singers, including Amalia Patti and Teresa Parodi, the violinist Miska Hauser, Strakosch, and, somewhat later, Ole Bull; the troupe toured intermittently until at least 1856. In November 1851 Strakosch managed the debut of the eight-year-old Adelina Patti in New York City. He solidified his fortuitous relationship with the Patti family in 1852 with his marriage to Amalia. The couple raised two children; their son Robert also became an impresario.

While Maurice was establishing himself as a performer, composer, and impresario, his younger brother Max was being schooled in Germany; he also undertook training as a businessman in the later 1840s and after the revolution went into business with his father. He immigrated to the United States in 1853 and at first lived with his brother. He worked in the New York dry-goods business until 1855, when he became an agent for Maurice's concert and opera troupes.

Maurice Strakosch's activities as a performer and manager meanwhile had continued apace. According to an article in *Leslie's Illustrated Journal* (10 Jan. 1857), between 1848 and 1857 Strakosch gave some 1,755 concerts in front of audiences totaling 900,000. During this period Strakosch toured widely as a pianist, composer, and the manager of both opera companies and operatic concert troupes. In 1855 he entered into a short-lived partnership with Max Maretzek and Ole Bull to manage the Academy of Music Opera Company; in early 1857 he directed the company himself. That same year he and Bernard Ullman jointly managed Sigismond Thalberg's first tour of the American West, an eleven-week expedition that included some sixty concerts given in thirty cities in the Midwest and Canada. During 1857–1858 he and Ullman jointly managed the Ullman and Strakosch Opera Company, a troupe based at the Academy of Music in New York and financially backed by Thalberg. This company toured the United States extensively until early 1860 and was saved from near disaster in its final (1859–1860) season by Adelina Patti's operatic debut (on 24 Nov. 1859, in *Lucia di Lammermoor*); Max Strakosch acted as the troupe's business manager in 1859. After the company disbanded, Maurice and Adelina Patti attempted a concert tour that was interrupted by the outbreak of the Civil War. Subsequently, Maurice Strakosch and the Patti family returned to Europe, where Strakosch spent most of the next seven years managing the soprano's very successful career. In 1868 Adelina Patti married the marquis de Caux, who assumed her professional management.

After Maurice returned to Europe, Max ran the U.S. end of their managerial business; he also worked closely with Jacob Grau, another impresario with whom Maurice had become acquainted when he was managing Thalberg. Max also served as manager to the pianist Louis Moreau Gottschalk from 1862 to 1864, first in partnership with Grau and later by himself. Throughout the 1860s Max was associated with a variety of opera companies, and in 1868 he managed the American soprano Clara Louise Kellogg in concerts and in an operatic venture with Max Maretzek. In 1868 and 1869 Strakosch sought to manage Gottschalk again, but the pianist died in the latter year, before the relationship resumed. In 1869 Max brought Carlotta Patti from Europe to the United States, where she gave concerts and opera peformances.

In Europe in 1870 Maurice Strakosch convinced the Swedish soprano Christine Nilsson to undertake an American tour jointly managed by him and his brother. She agreed, and her two spectacularly successful seasons in the United States made the Strakosch brothers wealthy. While in Europe, Nilsson was managed by Maurice's son Robert; in the United States her affairs were seen to by Max and Maurice. In 1874 she returned to America for a third acclaimed season.

Throughout the 1870s Max continued to oversee the American activities of various opera troupes, some of them more successful than others. In 1877 he joined forces with Henry Mapleson (son of James Mapleson) to organize an American tour by a troupe dubbed by the press "The Three Graces," which featured singers Marie Roze, Clara Louise Kellogg, and Annie Louise Cary. Max subsequently organized the Max Strakosch English Opera Company, which included these three singers in addition to numerous others; the company toured and performed widely in the United States for several years. Also in 1877 Max married Kate B. Nielson of New York City; they had four children.

In 1873 Maurice managed concerts by Carlotta Patti and toured with her in both Europe and America. The following year, back in Paris, Maurice—along with his brother Ferdinand and Eugenio Merelli—assumed management of the Theatre Italien. Finances at the house were not secure, however, and Strakosch's eventual resignation provoked some controversy. In 1877 he and Ole Bull formed a concert troupe that also included Emma Thursby and Minnie Hauk; this company toured America and Europe until Bull's death in 1880. During this period Maurice also acted as manager for the German violinist August Wilhelmj during his American tour. Maurice returned to Europe in June 1880; he remained active there for the rest of his life, maintaining close contact with the United States through his brother.

Throughout his entire career, Maurice Strakosch was an active performer and composer as well as an impresario. He wrote numerous compositions for the piano, mostly showy salon pieces, études, dances, and variations on operatic themes or popular tunes. He also composed at least one opera, *Giovanna Prima di Napoli*, which was premiered in New York by Maretzek's Astor Place Opera Company in January 1851. It was more as an impresario than as a composer or performer, however, that Strakosch exerted his significant influence on the development of American musical culture. As Harrison Fiske wrote of him in 1888, Maurice Strakosch was "the greatest speculator and opera and concert manager of his day . . . A detailed biography would be nothing short of a history of Italian opera and the musical world for the past century. He either brought out or knew personally, with but few exceptions, the prominent members of every branch of the musical profession." In addition to his formidable organizational abilities, Maurice Strakosch also was known for both character and integrity. As the bass Karl Formes remembered in 1891, "Maurice Strakosch was a good man, an honest, enterprising impresario, and a gentleman in one word. He was the only manager I ever had of whom I could say all this." Maurice Strakosch died suddenly in Paris.

Max Strakosch, in contrast with Maurice, was not a performing musician. His influence on American musical life during the second half of the nineteenth century, however, was no less significant or far-reaching than his brother's. Max was a skillful negotiator, a shrewd businessman, and one of the most popular and financially successful impresarios active in the United States. According to his obituary, he left his wife and children in "comfortable circumstances" at the time of his death. Like his brother, he managed many of the most important musicians who appeared in the United States during the second half of the century. According to the *New York Times*, Strakosch's success "was due to the happy faculty which he possessed of making friends and of conciliating enemies." The *New York Clipper* reported that he "believed in Italian opera to the last, and often expressed his regret that he could not reenter the field against the Wagnerian hosts." Max Strakosch remained active in the managerial business until 1888, when he was diagnosed with a brain tumor that paralyzed both his legs. For the next four years he spent his winters at the Home for Incurables in New York City and the summers at his home in Bellport, Long Island. He died of pneumonia at the Home for Incurables.

• Maurice Strakosch published his memoirs, *Souvenirs d'un Impresario*, in 1887. An abridged translation of the memoirs is "Strakosch and Patti," *Musical Courier*, 24 Oct. 1900. Primary sources on the Strakosches are scanty; there are scrapbooks and some correspondence in the Metropolitan Opera Archives in New York. According to Laurence Lerner, in 1970 the Max Strakosch Papers were in the collection of Mrs. John Elliott of New York; by the mid-1980s, however, these materials could not be located. Information about the Strakosches can be gleaned from a variety of primary and secondary sources, including Sara Bull, *Ole Bull: A Memoir* (1883); Louis Moreau Gottschalk, *Notes of a Pianist* (1881); Max Maretzek, *Crotchets and Quavers; or, Revelations of an Opera Manager in America* (1855) and *Sharps and Flats: A Sequel to Crotchets and Quavers* (1890), published jointly in a modern edition under the title *Revelations of an Opera Manager in 19th Century America* (1968); Clara Louise Kellogg, *Memoirs of an American Prima Donna* (1913); Karl Formes, *My Memoirs: Autobiography of Karl Formes* (in German, 1888; English trans., 1891); and Harrison Grey Fiske, *The New York Mirror Annual and Directory of the Theatrical Profession for 1888*. Mary Ellis Peltz, "Romance a Hundred Years Ago," *Opera News* (22 Feb. 1964): 12–15, focuses on extant love letters a young Adelina Patti wrote to Max Strakosch. Relatively recent works that are useful include Laurence Lerner, "The Rise of the Impresario: Bernard Ullman and the Transformation of Musical Culture in Nineteenth-Century America (Ph.D. diss., Univ. of Wisconsin, 1980), and Allen Lott's more reliable "The American Concert Tours of Leopold De Meyer, Henri Herz, and Sigismond Thalberg" (Ph.D. diss., City Univ. of New York, 1986). Obituaries for Maurice Strakosch are in the *New York Clipper*, 15 Oct. 1887, and the *New York Times*, 11 Oct. 1887. Those for Max appeared in the *New York Times*, 18 Mar. 1892, and the *New York Clipper*, 26 Mar. 1892 and 2 Apr. 1892.

KATHERINE K. PRESTON

STRANAHAN, James Samuel Thomas (25 Apr. 1808–3 Sept. 1898), capitalist and civic leader, was born in Peterboro, Madison County, New York, the son of Samuel Stranahan and Lynda Josselyn, farmers. As a child he attended local district schools and worked on the family farm. Following the death of his father when James was eight, his mother remarried another farmer, John Downer, and James spent the final years of his youth on his stepfather's farm. Although the details of his next few years are uncertain, it is known that he taught in local schools and spent a year in study at Cazenovia Seminary. After gaining some knowledge of land surveying, he worked in that occupation for a period of time. Following an abortive 1828 trip to Michigan, where he attempted to enter the fur-trading business, Stranahan returned to New York and entered the wool business in Albany.

In 1832, at the behest of fellow Peterboro resident and noted abolitionist Gerritt Smith, he assisted in founding the manufacturing town of Florence in Oneida County. Stranahan served his new community as postmaster and also engaged in the lumber business. In 1837 he married Marianne Fitch of Westmoreland, New York; they would have three children. Elected to the New York Assembly as a Whig in 1838, he served one term before relocating to Newark, New Jersey, in 1840. Changing occupations yet again, he entered the railroad construction business. By taking a large portion of his compensation in company stock, he was able to secure the basis of his personal fortune.

Never reluctant to pursue opportunity, Stranahan relocated in 1844 to Brooklyn, New York, where he would achieve his greatest fame and accomplishments. He organized and served as manager and president of the Atlantic Dock Company, which developed a forty-acre basin with surrounding warehouses in the Red Hook section of the city. Able to accommodate at least 130 ships at a time and often referred to as "the depositing end of the Erie Canal," the facility provided Brooklyn with a distinct advantage in the often fierce competition for business among eastern ports. Stranahan also served as both president and manager of the Union Ferry Company, which held the franchise for service between Brooklyn and the neighboring island of Manhattan.

Unable to resist the lure of politics in his new surroundings, Stranahan was elected to the city board of aldermen in 1848. Although he was defeated in a bid for the mayor's office in 1850, his growing popularity resulted in his election to the U.S. House of Representatives in 1854. His reelection attempt in 1856 failed, but Stranahan was not out of the public eye for long. Appointed to the first Metropolitan Police Commission on 1 January 1857, he soon locked horns with New York City mayor Fernando Wood, who, as a member of Tammany Hall, resented the attempt by upstate politicians to usurp his control over the police forces of New York, Staten Island, and Brooklyn. Although his elective political career ended with his 1856 defeat, Stranahan remained politically active. Joining the Republican party, he attended the conventions of 1860 and 1864 and later served as a presidential elector for Benjamin Harrison in 1888.

With his fortune secure and possessed of a growing reputation in civic circles, Stranahan became president of the Prospect Park Commission in 1860. Following the acquisition of part of the 526-acre site that year, Stranahan worked tirelessly to ensure its completion. At his direction Calvert Vaux submitted a preliminary sketch of the grounds in February 1865; by the following year a comprehensive development plan was submitted for approval by Vaux and Frederick Law Olmstead. Stranahan served on the commission until 1882. In recognition of his efforts he received a statue in the park, designed by Frederick William MacMonnies and dedicated on 6 June 1891. The statue bore the inscription "Reader, if you seek my monument, look about you."

Stranahan spent the Civil War as president of the War Fund Committee; with the assistance of his wife, who served as president of the Women's Relief Association, they raised $400,000 for the benefit of Union soldiers. Following her death in 1866 he married Clara Cornelia Harrison in 1870. They had no children. In 1869 Stranahan had undertaken his second great effort on behalf of Brooklyn, the construction of the Brooklyn Bridge. Named to the executive committee of the New York Bridge Company in the fall of 1869, he helped to restore public confidence in the project after the fall of the "Tweed Ring" in 1872. By replacing William "Boss" Tweed and three of his compatriots—all of whom had been involved with the bridge company—with noted reformers (including Abram S. Hewitt, who later became mayor of New York), Stranahan did much to ensure that the project would proceed as planned. Likewise, his support of chief engineer William A. Roebling was critical during a period in which questions concerning the long-time invalid's health threatened to remove him from the project. After surviving the various controversies, Stranahan presided over the dedication of the bridge on 24 May 1883.

The growing movement to consolidate Brooklyn into a "Greater New York" led Stranahan into his final service on behalf of Brooklyn. Arguing that the consolidation would lead to improved transportation facilities, more efficient government, and lower taxes, Stranahan helped to overcome the resistance of groups such as the Loyal League of Brooklyn. Following the passage of a nonbinding referendum in 1894, the present-day boundaries of New York City became effective on 1 January 1898. Stranahan died that same year in Saratoga, New York, where he habitually spent his summers.

Stranahan is an example of the type of ambitious man who traveled widely in search of economic opportunity in mid-nineteenth-century America. Having made his fortune in his adopted community, he in turn provided leadership on three critical projects that helped to shape modern-day Brooklyn.

• No collection of Stranahan's papers appears to have survived. His career receives attention in David C. Hammack,

Power and Society: Greater New York at the Turn of the Century (1982), David McCullough, *The Great Bridge* (1972), and William Lee Younger, *Old Brooklyn in Early Photographs, 1865–1929* (1978). His obituary is in the *Brooklyn Eagle*, 3 Sept. 1898.

EDWARD L. LACH, JR.

STRAND, Paul (16 Oct. 1890–31 Mar. 1976), photographer, was born in New York City, the son of Jacob Strand, a salesman, and Matilda Arnstein. Strand enrolled at the Ethical Culture School in 1904, studying photography under Lewis Hine and art appreciation with Charles Caffin before graduating in 1909. In 1907 a visit to the photographer Alfred Stieglitz's Little Galleries of the Photo-Secession with Hine's class induced Strand to become an artistic photographer. After high school graduation, while making his living as a freelance commercial photographer, he spent his free time making luminous soft-focus platinum photographs then popular in artistic circles. However, in 1915, influenced by Post-Impressionist and Cubist art and persuaded by Stieglitz's call to take a less romantic look at his immediate surroundings, Strand produced a series of New York portraits and street studies that combined the angularity of Cubist composition with evocations of the harsh reality of contemporary urban life. These works, including *Wall Street* and *Blind Woman*, remain some of his best-known and most influential photographs. Stieglitz immediately proclaimed them in his journal *Camera Work* as "rooted in the best traditions of photography," providing a brutal directness that marked "the direct expression of today." Stieglitz's acclaim brought Strand instant renown. Almost immediately, other photographers started creating angular views of contemporary subjects.

In 1918 Strand enlisted in the U.S. Army, serving until 1919 as an X-ray technician at Fort Snelling, Rochester, Minnesota. While there he started making medical films, and in 1920 he joined photographer-painter Charles Sheeler to make *Manhatta*, an impressionistic and angular eight-minute film portrait of the skyscraper culture of lower Manhattan. This short movie is widely considered to be the first avant-garde film made in America.

Through the late 1910s and 1920s Strand made his living as a freelance motion picture camera operator shooting short documentaries, scenes for Hollywood productions, and sporting events. However, he devoted his free time to writing art criticism and photographing. During this period he also remained under Stieglitz's strong influence, allowing his photographs to be exhibited only at Stieglitz-sanctioned exhibitions. In 1922, when Strand married a fellow Ethical Culture School graduate, Rebecca Salsbury, he even created a multiple photograph portrait of her similar to one Stieglitz was creating of his own lover and future wife, painter Georgia O'Keeffe.

Like Stieglitz, Strand was disillusioned with the moral compromises he saw encompassing modern urban life. In response, by the late 1920s, he began pro-

ducing elegant close-up photographs of plants, driftwood, rocks, and forest scenes, eventually raising his camera to encompass the broader rural landscape. In 1930 he vacationed at Mabel Dodge Luhan's Taos, New Mexico, artists' resort, returning there in 1931 and 1932 to photograph the surrounding desert and the remains of long-deserted Colorado mining towns.

However, by 1932 Strand's life seemed to be disintegrating. His friendship with Stieglitz was deteriorating because of mutual jealousy, his film business had succumbed to new technologies, and his marriage was breaking up over Rebecca Salsbury's demands for more independence. In response, Strand traveled to Mexico, drawn in part by sympathy for that country's leftist politics and governmental celebration of its indigenous cultures. After photographing church santos and peasants living in Oaxaca and Michoacán, and exhibiting his own photographs in a Mexico City streetside arcade, Strand remained in Mexico to help establish and run a government film program. He created *Redes* (The Wave) (1936) as the program's first production. Reflecting his new adherence to Marxism, this feature-length tale told of a successful uprising of a peasant fishing community to fight the exploitation of a corrupt middleman.

Now enraptured by the concept of community-produced political cinema, Strand returned to New York in late 1934 and immediately started attending meetings of the Group Theater repertory company and the leftist film group Nykino. The following year, he traveled to the Soviet Union to meet influential film and theater directors, including Sergei Eisenstein and Alexander Dovchenko, and upon his return to the United States, he joined Ralph Steiner and Leo Hurwitz to film Pare Lorentz's *The Plow that Broke the Plains*, released in 1936. That same year Strand married Group Theater actress Virginia Stevens and helped to organize and head Frontier Films, an independent leftist film cooperative modeled on the Group Theater. Under Frontier Films' auspices, he helped edit *Heart of Spain* (1937) in support of the Republican cause and directed an innovative, though commercially unsuccessful civil liberties feature, *Native Land* (1942).

Frontier Films dissolved with America's entry into World War II, leading Strand to start shooting government propaganda films, including *It's Up to You* (1943). However, his interests already were returning to still photography. After publishing *Photographs of Mexico*, a twenty-print photogravure portfolio of his Mexican photographs in 1940, he traveled to Vermont to photograph back-country farmers and their surroundings. The resulting luminously printed, classically humanistic photographs, along with Strand's reputation as a major force in photographic modernism, induced Museum of Modern Art Acting Curator of Photographs, Nancy Newhall, to give Strand that museum's first retrospective presenting the work of a living photographer. Following that successful exhibition, she then collaborated with Strand to create the book *Time in New England* (1950), a patriotic celebration of that region's politically assertive past. Although commercially unsuccessful, this book, comprising the artist's photographs interspersed with colorful texts that Newhall had drawn from the region's historical figures, offered some of Strand's finest plant studies from the 1920s, including *Toadstool and Grasses, Georgetown, Maine* (1928); compelling portraits of small-town citizens and farmers such as *Mr. Bennett, Vermont* (1944); and strikingly framed patriotic symbols like *Town Hall, Vermont* (1946).

A year before completing *Time in New England* Strand divorced Virginia Stevens and started dating Hazel Kingsbury, assistant to fashion photographer Louise Dahl-Wolf. By 1950 he and Kingsbury had taken up residence in France, driven into self-exile, Strand later would suggest, by the repressive anti-Communist climate in America. In France, Strand married Kingsbury in 1951. He completed *La France de Profil* (1952), a portrait of postwar, small-town French life, in which he interspersed his photographs with texts written and designed by the poet Claude Roy. From his home in Orgeval, just outside Paris, Strand would spend the rest of his life assembling and completing similar book portraits celebrating primarily rural cultures. In each case, an associate familiar with the history and concerns of that place would provide the text. Gradually, Strand completed books on Italy, the Outer Hebrides, Egypt, and Ghana. He also photographed extensively in Morocco and Romania. These projects led him to create such masterful portraits as *Young Boy, Gondeville, Charente, France* (1951) and *Family, Luzzara, Italy* (1953).

Many established photographers, from Walker Evans to Eliot Porter, have admitted to having been strongly influenced by Strand's impeccably rich and detailed prints, concern for formal relationships, respect for his subjects, and ability to distill the essence of his subjects. However, through much of the 1950s and 1960s his reputation fell into eclipse. His dedication to view cameras and fine printing, his largely frontal compositions, and his devotion to creating politically motivated celebrations of traditional, largely rural cultures did not fit an artistic world fascinated with the hand camera and the constant change of contemporary life. By the late 1960s, however, Strand received renewed acclaim first through European exhibitions and then by means of a retrospective exhibition sponsored by the Philadelphia Museum of Art (1971). This support induced Strand to publish a new edition of his Mexican photographs (1967) and to support the creation of two new portfolios, *On My Doorstep* and *The Garden*, both published shortly after his death in Orgeval, France.

• Strand's photographic archive is owned by Aperture Foundation, Inc., and is in Lakeville, Conn. Additional prints and manuscript materials are at the Center for Creative Photography, University of Arizona, Tucson. The National Gallery of Art, Washington, D.C., and the J. Paul Getty Museum, Malibu, Calif., also own substantial collections of Strand photographs. Strand's significant articles include "Photography," *Seven Arts* 2 (Aug. 1917): 524–25; "The Art Motive in Photography," *British Journal of Photography* 70 (5 Oct.

1923): 613–15; "Photography and the Other Arts," a lecture delivered at the Museum of Modern Art in 1945 and published in *Paul Strand Archive: Guide Series Number Two* (1980); and "Realism: A Personal View," *Sight and Sound* 18 (Jan. 1950): 23–26. Besides the works mentioned above, Strand published the following: *Un Pease*, with text by Cesare Zavatini (1955); *Tir a'Mhurain*, with text by Basil Davidson (1962); *Living Egypt*, with text by James Aldridge (1969); *The Garden* (1976); *Ghana: An African Portrait*, with text by Basil Davidson (1976); and *On My Doorstep* (1976). Strand's work is presented in numerous catalogs, including Catherine Duncan, *Paul Strand: The World at My Doorstep, 1950–1976* (1994); Sarah Greenough, *Paul Strand: An American Vision* (1990), which presents the most comprehensive bibliography of his work; *Paul Strand: A Retrospective Monograph, 1915–1968* (1970); and Nancy Newhall, *Paul Strand: Photographs, 1915–1945* (1945). Critical analysis of his photographs, films, and achievements are in numerous books and essays, most significantly Maren Strange, ed., *Paul Strand: His Life and Work* (1991); and John B. Rohrbach, "Paul Strand: Art for Society's Sake" (Ph.D. diss., Univ. of Delaware, 1993). An obituary is in the *New York Times*, 2 Apr. 1976.

JOHN B. ROHRBACH

STRANG, James Jesse (21 Mar. 1813–9 July 1856), schismatic Mormon prophet, was born in Scipio, New York, the son of Clement Strang and Abigail James, farmers. Intellectually precocious and largely self-educated, Strang early on displayed a complex and passionate combination of idealism and ambition that would characterize his life and that can be seen most clearly in the diary he wrote between the ages of eighteen and twenty-three. As a young adult, Strang worked briefly as a teacher, lawyer, postmaster, and newspaper editor before moving to Burlington, Wisconsin, in 1843 to settle close to the relatives of his wife of seven years, Mary Perce. In February 1844 he visited the Mormon headquarters in Nauvoo, Illinois, met Joseph Smith (1805–1844), converted to Mormonism, and suggested that the beleaguered Mormons consider moving to Wisconsin.

Within a month of Smith's assassination on 27 June 1844, Strang produced a letter, allegedly from Smith, shortly before his death. Of controversial authenticity, the letter instructed Strang to set up a Mormon colony at Voree, Wisconsin (just west of Burlington), and appeared to appoint Strang as Smith's prophetic successor. Strang also announced that upon Smith's death he had received an angelic ordination. As evidence of the legitimacy of his claims, Strang began to deliver revelations in Smith's "Thus saith the Lord" oratorical style. He also denounced polygamy as an abomination and called for Mormons to gather at Voree rather than undertake what he claimed would be a foolhardy migration westward with Brigham Young. In September 1845, in the presence of four witnesses, Strang dug up and then "translated" a set of three small brass plates. He would later "translate" an extension of and commentary on Mosaic Law, which he called *The Book of the Law of the Lord*. Strang's non-Mormon biographer Milo Quaife described the work as "a complete framework of government . . . applicable to any population, however great, and laying down regulations for the most important relations of human society" (p. 138).

As Joseph Smith's only immediate successor to claim direct charismatic authority to lead the Mormons, Strang soon attracted most of the leading dissenters from the policies of Brigham Young and the larger group of Mormons, who moved to Utah in 1846–1847. Among his followers were many who subsequently helped found the Reorganized Church of Jesus Christ of Latter Day Saints and other early Mormon factions, including groups led by James C. Brewster, Joseph Smith's brother William, and other individuals critical of polygamy. Strang's successful missionary trip to the eastern United States in the summer of 1846 threatened to undercut support for the Mormon migration west, but internal conflicts at Voree soon began to threaten the cohesion of Strang's own movement. Particularly divisive was John Cook Bennett, an opportunistic adventurer who, between 1840 and 1842, had become Joseph Smith's chief assistant until he was expelled from the community for alleged acts of immorality. In 1846, when Strang was vying against Brigham Young, Bennett joined Strang's group and soon rose to second in command, only to be expelled from Strang's church for "apostasy" and "various immoralities"; before he left, Bennett had sowed dissention in the group by helping to introduce the controversial Order of the Illuminati, an oath-bound secret society.

Beginning in 1847, Strang made plans to move with his followers to Beaver Island in Lake Michigan, where he set up his City of James. In 1849 he privately reversed his position on polygamy by secretly marrying nineteen-year-old Elvira Field, the first of four plural wives. Also in 1850, he had himself crowned king in a ceremony attested to by 234 witnesses. Over the next six years, Strang and his followers sought and gained control of local government positions, and in 1852 and 1854 Strang was elected to the Michigan legislature, where he served with distinction. Conflict between Mormons and non-Mormons continued to fester, however, leading to violence and lawsuits, most notably suits in May and June 1851 (which resulted in acquittal) that charged Strang and his associates with counterfeiting, robbing the mails, and trespassing on federal lands.

Although Strang eventually attracted some 500 followers to his Beaver Island "kingdom," his movement continued to be plagued by poverty and by tensions between his followers and the nearby non-Mormon populations. These tensions culminated in the shooting of Strang by disgruntled former followers on 16 June 1856, followed by his death three weeks later and the expulsion of his supporters from Beaver Island by non-Mormon mobs. Although Strang remained conscious until shortly before he died, he never appointed a successor. A small remnant of his church, with some 200 members, continues to survive in Wisconsin and other states.

James J. Strang was the most brilliant and capable of the claimants to leadership of the Mormon movement who challenged the power of Brigham Young and the Council of the Twelve Apostles immediately after Joseph Smith's death. His career, at least on the surface, seems strikingly similar to Smith's own, with visions, revelations, "translations" of plates, "gathering" of followers to Zion, association and eventual break with John C. Bennett as second in command, introduction of secret societies and polygamy, coronation as "king," and internal and external tensions contributing to eventual martyrdom. One of the most accomplished debaters in the early Mormon movement, unsurpassed as both journalist and polemicist, Strang could well have been successful in any number of different fields of endeavor. As husband to his plural wives, he has been described as firm yet loving. The motivation of this enigmatic genius, who may have fabricated his prophetic credentials in order to garner the power to create a community that would embody his humane ideals, still remains to be untangled.

• The most extensive manuscript materials on Strang's complex and conflicted career are found in the James J. Strang Papers in the Coe Collection of the Beinecke Library at Yale University, comprising 544 lots, with a detailed summary description by Dale L. Morgan. Particularly revealing primary publications are Strang's *The Diamond* (1848), *Ancient and Modern Michilimackinac* (1854), *The Prophetic Controversy* (1856?), the expanded edition of his *Book of the Law of the Lord* (1856), his *Diary*, edited by Mark A. Strang (1961), and his newspapers, the *Voree Herald* and the *Northern Islander*. For Strang's extensive publications and the polemical literature associated with his movement, see Dale L. Morgan, "A Bibliography of the Church of Jesus Christ of Latter Day Saints [Strangite]," *Western Humanities Review* 5 (Winter 1950–1951): 42–114. The standard scholarly biography by Milo M. Quaife, *Kingdom of Saint James* (1930), has been qualified but not superseded by Roger Van Noord's journalistic account, *King of Beaver Island* (1988), which focuses primarily on Strang's political role in Michigan. For Strang's motives, see Lawrence Foster, "James J. Strang: The Prophet Who Failed," in his *Women, Family, and Utopia: Communal Experiments of the Shakers, the Oneida Community, and the Mormons* (1991), pp. 170–81. Strangite polygamy is analyzed in John Quist, "Polygamy among James Strang and His Followers," *John Whitmer Historical Association Journal* 9 (1989): 31–48.

LAWRENCE FOSTER

STRANG, Ruth May (3 Apr. 1895–3 Jan. 1971), educator, was born in Chatham, New Jersey, the daughter of Charles Garrett Strang and Anna Bergen, farmers. Strang's family moved to Jamaica, Long Island, when her father inherited a farm there. Later the family went to Phoenix, Arizona, when her father was ill with bronchitis. Much younger than her two brothers, Strang later recalled being anxious and lonely for much of her childhood. In 1909 the Strangs sold the farm and settled on Lafayette Street in Brooklyn.

Strang enrolled at Adelphi Academy, a coeducational private school on Lafayette Street, where she joined the debating, German, and walking clubs, played on the basketball team, and became captain of the hockey team. Active in the Lafayette Avenue Presbyterian Church, Strang's ambition and her sense of mission were fueled in part by its ministers, Cleland B. McAfee and Charles Albertson. Her later writings on the importance of extracurricular activities and group work reflected her enjoyment of these associations.

At the time of her graduation in 1914, Strang hoped to attend Wellesley College, but her father objected, wishing her to stay home and take care of the family. Instead, she matriculated at the Pratt Institute, two blocks from her home. In 1916 she completed a normal program in household science and embarked on a career in interior decorating. Her mother's illness forced her to leave work temporarily, but she took a second job in 1917 teaching home economics in a New York City public school. She also taught Sunday school and volunteered at a settlement house for Italian boys. Strang delighted in the children and remained grateful to them, later insisting that "from these children I learned much more than they learned from me" (Havighurst, p. 370).

Strang resigned from school-teaching in 1920. Though the school principal, her parents, and her brother Benjamin, who had earned a B.A. at Columbia College and an M.A. at Teachers College, Columbia University, opposed the change, Strang enrolled at Teachers College, where she earned a B.S. in 1922 and a Ph.D. in 1926. She studied reading and psychology with Professor Arthur I. Gates and nutrition with Mary Schwartz Rose, subjects she continued to research during her career. At Rose's urging, Strang taught in the Department of Health Education at Teachers College and for two years supervised health education at the Horace Mann School. She relished the challenge of teaching and worked hard to prepare original material.

Strang turned her attention to education in guidance counseling when she spent three summers (1926–1928) as the head of a residence hall at the University of North Carolina College for Women. In 1926 she became a research fellow at Teachers College, one of the first institutions in the United States to offer training programs for women deans who were struggling to advise women students in high schools and colleges. Teachers College professor Sarah Sturtevant encouraged Strang to study guidance education and introduced her to the writings of social workers such as Mary E. Richmond, whose studies supported Strang's conviction that students' difficulties needed to be addressed on a case-by-case basis. Believing that most teachers also served as guidance counselors to their students, Strang urged that they be trained accordingly.

From the late 1920s through the 1930s Strang focused on guidance education and produced several seminal works in the field. With Sturtevant as coauthor, she published two studies on women deans in high schools and colleges in the late 1920s. She wrote two influential books in the 1930s, *The Role of the Teacher in Personnel Work* (1932) and *Counseling Technics in College and Secondary School* (1937). As a leader in the guidance field Strang was editor from 1938 to 1960 of the journal of the National Association of Deans of Women (today the National Association for Women in Education).

Despite her advocacy of guidance, Strang admitted that few high school or college guidance programs could provide the in-service education of teachers, case conferences, counseling, patience, and tact that was needed to ensure that all students reached their potential. Nevertheless, she continued to campaign for the ideal guidance program. Viewing education as the keystone of democracy, Strang argued that school activities such as classes and clubs provided a laboratory "in which to work out the problems of the democratic way of life" (Strang, *Group Activities in College and Secondary School* [1941], p. 1).

In addition to guidance, Strang contributed to the fields of child development and reading education. Her *Introduction to Child Study* (1930) remained in print for thirty years, and she wrote several books on reading, *Problems in the Improvement of Reading in Secondary Schools* (1938) and *Explorations in Reading Patterns* (1942), as well as many volumes of juvenile literature for teenage readers. Strang was a member of the International Reading Association, the American Association for Gifted Children, and the National Association of Deans of Women; was a fellow in the American Public Health Association; and served on the boards of many organizations, including the Girl Scouts of America and the National Society for the Study of Education.

Despite her prolific research (thirty books by 1960 and more than 300 articles), Strang rose slowly through the ranks at Teachers College, owing, she believed, to gender discrimination. She was assistant professor from 1929 to 1936, associate professor from 1936 to 1940, and full professor from 1940 to 1960. Her social life revolved around Teachers College and her students, but her activities were limited by family responsibilities. Following the death of her parents in the late 1920s, Strang, who never married, continued to live at home, caring for her brothers until the late 1930s, when she moved to her own apartment near Columbia University. Even after moving away from home she cared for her brothers, visiting Benjamin twice daily in his final illness. Strang retired from Columbia in 1960 and took a position at the University of California at Berkeley that summer. From fall 1960 to 1968 she was a professor of education and the director of the reading development program at the University of Arizona in Tucson. From 1968 to 1969 she was a visiting professor at the Ontario Institute for Studies in Education. She then retired to Amityville, New York, where she died.

Devoted to the ideal of developing every individual's potential, Strang served as the primary adviser to more than 100 doctoral candidates in the field of education. She was an exemplary mentor who attended to the social, intellectual, emotional, and even financial needs of her students. Their success, she insisted, was her greatest reward.

• Special Collections, Milbank Memorial Library, Teachers College, Columbia University, has correspondence between Strang and Dean William Russell. Also see the papers of William F. Russell, Officers Records. Adelphia Academy in Brooklyn has Strang's yearbook. The two best sources are "Ruth M. Strang: An Autobiographical Sketch," and Charles Burgess, "Ruth Strang: A Biographical Sketch," both in *Leaders in Education: The Seventeenth Yearbook of the National Society for the Study of Education*, ed. Robert J. Havighurst, pt. 2 (National Society for the Study of Education, 1971). Also useful is Frederick D. Kershner, Jr.'s entry on Strang in *Notable American Women*; Kershner created a unique portrait from his interviews with Strang's colleagues. Two studies that put Strang's contribution in perspective are Lawrence A. Cremin et al., *A History of Teachers College, Columbia University* (1954), and Ruth E. Barry and Beverly Wolf, "A History of the Guidance—Personnel Movement in Education" (Ed.D., Teachers College, Columbia Univ., 1955). For a bibliography see Amelia Melnik, "The Writings of Ruth Strang," *Teachers College Record* 61, no. 8 (May 1960). *The Journal of the National Association of Women Deans and Counselors* is also an excellent source, particularly vol. 24, no. 2 (Jan. 1961), which is dedicated to Strang at the time of her retirement; entitled "Glimpses of Guidance," the issue includes statements from thirty-two of Strang's doctoral students. See also C. D. Rogers, "Ruth Strang's Diagnostic Legacy," paper presented at the annual meeting of the California Reading Association, Nov. 1981, ERIC no. ED215300. An obituary is in the *New York Times*, 5 Jan. 1971.

SARAH HENRY LEDERMAN

STRASBERG, Lee (17 Nov. 1901–17 Feb. 1982), acting teacher, was born Israel Strassberg in Budanov, Austria-Hungary (now Russia), the son of Baruch Meyer Strasberg, a garment worker, and Ida Diner. Strasberg's father and older siblings immigrated to the United States in 1904; the rest of the family followed in 1908 and settled on the Lower East Side of New York City. Lee's participation in theater began as a child when he performed with the Progressive Dramatic Club, an amateur Yiddish theater group. He dropped out of high school after his sophomore year when his younger brother died of influenza. To help support the family, Lee took a job as a clerk with a wig manufacturing company, eventually becoming a partner in the firm.

In 1923 the Moscow Art Theater spent a season in New York, and Strasberg attended their performances with fascination. The next year he enrolled at the Clare Tree Major School of the Theatre and studied for three months. He continued his studies at the American Laboratory Theatre in New York, working with Richard Boleslavsky, who had been a student of Russian actor Konstantin Stanislavsky. Although he only spent one semester with Boleslavsky, Strasberg absorbed Stanislavsky's system of acting, which he would elaborate in his teaching and directing for the rest of his life. Most significant to him was the concept of "affective memory"—using an actor's personal experience to create a living emotion on stage. Strasberg later returned to the American Laboratory for a special five-month course for directors. He also read extensively in

theatrical history and theory, collecting books on the subject for the rest of his life.

Strasberg took the theoretical principles he had learned to the Chrystie Street Settlement House, where he directed plays between 1924 and 1931. It was there that he met Nora Krecaun, whom he married in 1926 (They had no children, and she died in 1929.) He made his professional acting debut on Broadway in 1925 in *Processional*. That year he also met Harold Clurman, the stage manager for *Garrick Gaieties of 1925*, in which Strasberg was appearing. The two young men became quick friends and spent hours discussing ideas for a new kind of theater. In 1931, with Cheryl Crawford, they founded the Group Theatre, a theatrical collective that stressed a unified approach to performance based on the principles of Stanislavsky's system. The company of twenty-eight actors included Stella Adler, Franchot Tone, and Robert Lewis. Strasberg left the Group Theatre in 1937, disgusted by its infighting and power struggles. He also had bitter disagreements with colleagues over the correct interpretation of Stanislavsky's ideas, most notably with Adler. Adler, who had studied with Stanislavsky in 1934, insisted that Strasberg misused affective memory in ways that were disruptive and potentially damaging to actors. In 1934 Strasberg married his second wife, Paula Miller, an actress with the Group Theatre; they had two children. After leaving the Group Theatre, Strasberg worked to establish his professional directing career; he directed sixteen plays between 1938 and 1951. While most of his stagings were less than successful, the best, like Ernest Hemingway's *The Fifth Column* (1940) and Clifford Odets's *The Big Knife* (1949), exemplified his gift for portraying complex emotional layers, his acute sensitivity to rhythm, and his solid ensemble directing. Strasberg moved to Hollywood in 1944 and stayed for three years, directing screen tests and learning the film business. In addition to directing, Strasberg gave private acting lessons. He worked on developing an American version of Stanislavsky's system, which he described in the influential article "Acting and the Training of the Actor" (*Producing the Play*, ed. John Gassner [1941], pp. 128–62). He urged actors to prepare for roles by delving into the character's prehistory, sometimes going back to childhood to understand the character's behavior. The play then became the public climax of the character's private existence.

Strasberg was not initially involved in the institution that would shape most of his professional life. The Actors Studio was founded by Elia Kazan, Crawford, and Lewis in 1947. Strasberg was probably not asked to help organize the school because he and Kazan differed in their approach to teaching. For his part, Strasberg was not sure he wanted to get involved with the Actors Studio because it was not planning to develop a theater, an outlet he coveted to practice stage direction. However, he began teaching there in 1948 and became the artistic director in 1951. The poor reviews Strasberg's *Peer Gynt* received that year may have made a greater commitment to the Actors Studio appealing. As Kazan became more and more involved in directing, Strasberg took over more of the teaching, and it was at the studio that he really developed his famous "Method."

The studio was intended to be a place where actors could perform noncommercial roles, working against type and expanding their repertoire. In principle all actors, even if they were currently performing on Broadway, were required to audition, although there were some exceptions. Actors Studio members included Maureen Stapleton, Anne Bancroft, Eva Marie Saint, Ben Gazzara, Sidney Poitier, Shelley Winters, and Sally Field. Neophytes and stars were thrown together in a democratic process that sometimes grated on the more experienced actors. In workshops, scenes were prepared and performed for groups of fellow actors, and the criticisms, while generally welcomed, were notoriously harsh. With time, standards were somewhat relaxed. Strasberg himself was often accused of courting stars to the neglect of the rank-and-file membership. His relationship with Marilyn Monroe drew particular criticism. Monroe became very close to Strasberg, sometimes staying with his family. She came to classes at the studio regularly, but she never auditioned and performed only once (to a less-than-honest response, according to many). Strasberg was the principal beneficiary in Monroe's will, receiving all her personal effects and delivering the eulogy at her funeral.

Strasberg remained the focus of controversy and criticism throughout the Actors Studio heyday in the 1950s and early 1960s. He was extremely shy and socially awkward. While he could not stand criticism, he was given to temperamental outbursts and violent criticism of others. Despite his loquaciousness, he had difficulty communicating clearly with his colleagues. He complained that the cumulative work that was at the heart of the Actors Studio was lost on casual visitors, leading to misunderstanding of his teaching and misrepresentation in the press. There were also criticisms of the Method itself. In the public mind, Marlon Brando and James Dean, both Strasberg students, were archetypal Method actors: intense, instinctive, and rebellious. Critics claimed that actors from the studio were excessively mannered in their search for naturalism, mumbled their lines, needed to know their "motivation" for the smallest action performed onstage, and were unprepared to perform the classics. Strasberg defended the basis of the Method, saying it was "really a summation of what actors have always done unconsciously whenever they acted well" (Steven Hager, "Lee Strasberg," *Horizon*, Jan. 1980, p. 23). He had staunch supporters as well as committed enemies, but even those actors who disliked him generally conceded that he was an effective teacher.

In the early 1960s Kazan and Strasberg struggled over the studio's mission. Kazan believed it should remain a studio, while Strasberg felt it was time to develop an ensemble theater in which the techniques of the Method could be brought to the stage under the best possible circumstances. Strasberg hoped to establish a

national theater, and the creation of the Lincoln Center seemed the moment for this to come to fruition. But Kazan was asked to organize a separate ensemble for the Lincoln Center, and Strasberg felt betrayed by his colleague and former student. The studio went ahead on its own, however, establishing the Actors Studio Theatre in 1962. This was to be a "floating" company, with actors committing five months at a time to the ensemble, allowing stars who did not want to participate full time to pursue their careers on Broadway or in Hollywood. Some members felt this was contrary to the original spirit of the studio, a feeling that was exacerbated when stars were allowed to make commitments of less than five full months when their schedules did not allow it.

Unfortunately, mismanagement and a lack of clear direction plagued the Studio Theatre from the outset. Strasberg, in his high-handed way, made decisions without consulting others. The ensemble's first production, *Strange Interlude*, was staged in 1963 to mixed reviews. Many felt it was a vehicle for its star, Geraldine Page, rather than a true ensemble piece. Even supporters of the studio admitted that the performance was not worthy of the Actors Studio's promise and training. The next two productions were mediocre to miserable; *Baby Want a Kiss*, the only real commercial success of the Actors Studio Theatre, received bad reviews but was popular because Paul Newman and Joanne Woodward starred in it. The biggest disappointment was the 1964 staging of Anton Chekhov's *The Three Sisters*. This had long been one of Strasberg's favorite plays, and he directed the production, which he dedicated to Monroe's memory. Although he purportedly had trouble controlling its leading actresses, Page and Kim Stanley, the play was very well received in New York. But when *Three Sisters* and *Blues for Mister Charlie* (both with several cast changes) were taken to a festival in London in 1964, they were universally panned. The Actors Studio Theatre never recovered, and many of the studio's important actors departed, never to return.

Despite the difficulties with the Actors Studio Theatre, Strasberg's acting workshops continued to be popular. He expanded his teaching commitments with the founding of the Actors Studio West in Los Angeles in 1966 and the Lee Strasberg Theatre Institute in New York and Los Angeles in 1968. Strasberg's second wife died in 1966, and he married Anna Mizrahi two years later; they had two children. Strasberg began to divide his time between New York and Hollywood and taught a whole new crop of stars, including Robert DeNiro and Al Pacino. Strasberg returned to acting in 1974 with a role in *The Godfather Part Two*, for which he received an Academy Award nomination for best supporting actor. He performed in several more films, including *Boardwalk* and *Going in Style* (both 1979). Strasberg died in New York City.

Strasberg taught several generations of actors, and his Method has had a profound effect on acting and directing in American theater and movies. Many actors credited him as the principal motivating force in their choice of career. Tennessee Williams observed that Actors Studio members had an especially intense and honest style of acting, and it was this naturalism that Strasberg introduced and fostered in American theater.

• For more information on Strasberg contact in writing the Lee Strasberg Theatre Institute, 115 East Fifteenth Street, New York, N.Y. 10003. Works by Strasberg not mentioned in the text include an introduction to Tony Cole's *Acting: A Handbook of the Stanislavski Method* (1947); "Working with Live Material," *Tulane Drama Review* (Fall 1964); and "Looking Back," *Educational Theatre Journal* (Dec. 1976), a reminiscence of his years with the Group Theatre. He edited and wrote an introduction to *Famous American Plays of the 1950s* (1964). His autobiography is *A Dream of Passion: The Development of the Method* (1987). A full-length biography of Strasberg is Cindy Adams, *Lee Strasberg: The Imperfect Genius of the Actors Studio* (1980). Robert H. Hethmon, ed., *Strasberg at the Actors Studio* (1965), is based on tape recordings made during sessions at the Actors Studio. See also Harold Clurman, *The Fervent Years: The Group Theatre and the 30s* (1945); David Garfield, *A Player's Place: The Story of the Actors Studio* (1980); Susan Strasberg (Strasberg's daughter), *Bittersweet* (1980); and Elia Kazan, *Elia Kazan: A Life* (1988). An obituary is in the *New York Times*, 18 Feb. 1982.

BETHANY NEUBAUER

STRATEMEYER, Edward (4 Oct. 1862–10 May 1930), writer, creator of popular juvenile series, and founder of the Stratemeyer Syndicate, was born in Elizabeth, New Jersey, the son of German immigrants Henry Julius Stratemeyer, a tobacconist, and Anna Siegal. The youngest of six children, Stratemeyer worked in his brother's tobacco store after completing high school. Even as an adolescent, Stratemeyer experimented with writing and distributing stories; a 31-page pamphlet, "The Tale of a Lumberman (as Told by Himself)," from 1878 is the earliest example of his amateur printing efforts. Five years later he published an amateur—and short-lived—boy's story paper, *Our American Boys*, filled with his own fiction. In 1888 he became assistant editor of the *Young American* and more significantly, sold an 18,000-word story, "Victor Horton's Idea," to *Golden Days*, a children's story paper. The latter event marked the start of his professional writing career.

Stratemeyer moved to Newark, New Jersey, in 1890; there he owned and operated a newspaper and stationery store, supplementing his income by writing popular fiction. He married Magdalene Van Camp in 1891; their first child was born in 1892. By then Stratemeyer was already demonstrating the speed and versatility that would prove so crucial to his writing success. Under various pseudonyms, he penned mystery, western, and sporting dime novels for Street & Smith's *Nick Carter Library, New York Five Cent Library,* and *Log Cabin Library;* detective dime novels for Munro's *Old Cap Collier Library;* boys' serials for at least three boys' story papers, *Golden Days, Argosy,* and *Good News;* and short stories for the *Newark Sunday Call.* He also began editing *Good News* in 1893.

Continuing to utilize new forms and genres, Stratemeyer sold his first romance (written under the shared pseudonym Julia Edwards) to the *New York Weekly* and published his first book in 1894. *Richard Dare's Venture,* part of the Bound to Succeed series, traced the rising fortunes of a small-town boy who moves to New York City and manages a stationery store; like many of Stratemeyer's early boys' stories, it was loosely modeled on Horatio Alger's success formula. Similar titles soon followed, most revisions of his story paper serials.

The Stratemeyers' second and last child was born in 1895, the year that he began editing *Young Sports of America* (later renamed *Young People of America*). He started his own story paper, *Bright Days,* in 1896 but discontinued it in February 1897.

His first major writing success came in 1898 with *Under Dewey at Manila,* the initial volume in the Old Glory series. Timely historical fiction about the Spanish-American War, *Under Dewey* quickly went through several editions and helped establish Stratemeyer's reputation as an author for boys. In 1899 he created the Rover Boys, which became one of the most popular series of its time and a prototype for later series. A departure from the Alger formula, the Rover Boys used active, affluent contemporary boys as protagonists and combined several popular types of plots, including school adventures, travel, athletics, and mysteries, into one series.

Most of Stratemeyer's books appeared under his own name and two pseudonyms, Captain Ralph Bonehill and Arthur M. Winfield. Stratemeyer frequently explained that his mother had suggested the latter name: Arthur because of its similarity to "author"; Winfield so that he might "win in the field." The M—his own invention—stood for thousands, indicating the thousands of books he hoped to sell. By the early 1900s he was already accomplishing this goal: he had created almost two dozen series in only ten years. These included historical fiction such as the Flag of Freedom, Mexican War, and Colonial series; hunting and outdoor stories in the Young Hunters and Young Sportsman's series; travel adventures via the Pan-American series; Alger-like success stories in the Working Upward series and the Bound to Win reprint series; and school tales in the Putnam Hall series. Indeed, in later interviews, Stratemeyer actually altered part of the Winfield anecdote so that M stood for millions—more accurately reflecting his sales.

An astute businessman, Stratemeyer established the Stratemeyer Literary Syndicate about 1904 or 1905 as a means of increasing book production. He recruited journalists and other writers to complete manuscripts from his ideas or outlines, paying a flat rate per manuscript and purchasing all rights. About 1906 Stratemeyer also negotiated an agreement with one of his publishers, Cupples & Leon, to lower the price of his series books to fifty cents. He has thus been called "the father of the fifty-center," for other publishers soon followed suit, and the lower prices coincide with—and probably caused—a boom in series book sales.

With the syndicate in place and sales rising, Stratemeyer devoted more effort to developing new series, outlining plots for annual additions to ongoing series, hiring writers and illustrators, editing incoming manuscripts and galley proofs, and dealing with publishers. Syndicate series developed by Stratemeyer included the Air Service Boys, Baseball Joe, Bomba the Jungle Boy, Bunny Brown and His Sister Sue, Great Marvel, Kneetime Animal Stories, the Motor Boys, the Motor Girls, the Radio Boys, Ruth Fielding, the Saddle Boys, and the X Bar X Boys. He also acted as a literary agent of sorts; he purchased the rights to series and stories created and written by other writers and then either marketed the series to publishers or used the stories as the basis for syndicate books.

As he increased the syndicate's production, Stratemeyer decreased his own writing, ending his favorite series—the Rover Boys—in 1926. Four years later, with the syndicate producing approximately thirty volumes annually, Stratemeyer died in Newark, New Jersey. His two daughters, Harriet Stratemeyer Adams and Edna Camilla Stratemeyer, took over management of the syndicate, continuing his work.

During the years that he ran the Stratemeyer Syndicate, Stratemeyer developed more than eighty-five series, including the syndicate's four best-known offerings: the Bobbsey Twins, Tom Swift, the Hardy Boys, and Nancy Drew. Before and during his syndicate days, he wrote approximately 200 books and stories; as head of the syndicate, he planned or outlined about 700 more. In 1927 one newspaper account estimated sales of Stratemeyer and syndicate books at close to 20 million copies; sixty years after Stratemeyer's death, sales were estimated at almost ten times that amount, most stemming from series or offspring of series he had created.

• A small collection of papers pertaining to the Stratemeyer Syndicate's history is at the Beinecke Rare Book and Manuscript Library, Yale University; the Stratemeyer Syndicate Archives are at the New York Public Library but are uncataloged and thus unavailable to researchers. For a full bibliography of Stratemeyer's work, see Deidre Johnson, *Stratemeyer Pseudonyms and Series Books: An Annotated Checklist of Stratemeyer and Stratemeyer Syndicate Publications* (1982); newer discoveries are found in Peter C. Walther, "Edward Stratemeyer and the Old Cap Collier Library," *Newsboy* 26, no. 6 (1987): 86–87; Johnson, "Early and Miscellaneous Stratemeyer Writings," *Dime Novel Round-Up* 57 (1988): 60–62; James D. Keeline, "The Secret of Box MSS 107; or, What the Nancy Axelrad Papers Revealed," *Newsboy* 32, no. 1 (1994): 11–18, and 32, no. 2 (1994): 11–16; and Johnson, "Stratemeyer Syndicate Archives Box 7856; or, What the NYPL Archives Revealed," *Dime Novel Round-Up* 65 (1996). Stratemeyer's works are discussed in Carol Billman, *The Secret of the Stratemeyer Syndicate: Nancy Drew, the Hardy Boys, and the Million Dollar Fiction Factory* (1986), which focuses on five key series; John T. Dizer, *Tom Swift and Company* (1982), which concentrates on boys' fiction; Bobbie Ann Mason, *The Girl Sleuth: A Feminist Guide* (1975), which examines series for girls; Arthur Prager, *Rascals at Large; or, The Clue in the Old Nostalgia* (1971), a nostalgic overview of series in general; and Johnson, *Edward Stratemeyer and the Stratemeyer Syndicate* (1993). Three syndicate ghostwriters have published accounts of their connection with Stratemeyer: Roger Garis, *My Father Was Uncle Wiggily* (1966); Leslie McFarlane, *Ghost of the Hardy Boys* (1976); and Mildred Wirt Benson, "The Ghost of Ladora," *Books at Iowa* 19 (Nov. 1973): 24–29. Additional secondary sources are listed in David Farah and Ilana Nash, *Series Books and the Media; or, This Isn't All!: An Annotated Bibliography of Secondary Sources* (1996). An obituary is in the *New York Times*, 12 May 1930.

DEIDRE A. JOHNSON

STRATEMEYER, George Edward (24 Nov. 1890–9 Aug. 1969), air force officer, was born in Cincinnati, Ohio, the son of George Stratemeyer, an army officer, and Belle Retig. After spending most of his youth in Peru, Indiana, Stratemeyer entered the U.S. Military Academy at West Point, New York, in March 1910. He graduated in June 1915 and was commissioned a second lieutenant in the infantry, initially assigned to the Seventh Infantry Regiment. After brief service with the Thirty-fourth Infantry Regiment, he transferred to the Aviation Section of the Signal Corps in September 1916 and learned to fly at Rockwell Field in San Diego, California. In 1916, now a first lieutenant, he married Annalee Rix; they had no children. Stratemeyer was promoted to captain in May 1917. During and immediately after World War I he served as the organizer and commanding officer of the School of Military Aeronautics at Ohio State University and as a test pilot and later commander at the Air Service Mechanics School at Kelly Field in Texas.

During the interwar period Stratemeyer gradually rose in rank to brigadier general, earning a reputation as an able administrator and an officer of mature judgment. Following a tour at the Air Service Mechanics School at Chanute Field, Illinois, in 1921, he was stationed in Hawaii for three years and then taught tactics at West Point from 1924 to 1929. In 1929–1930 Stratemeyer attended the Air Corps Tactical School at Langley Field, Virginia, and from 1930 to 1936 he was a student and later an instructor at the Command and General Staff School at Fort Leavenworth, Kansas. Between 1936 and 1938 Stratemeyer was commanding officer of the Seventh Bombardment Group at Hamilton Field, California, and in 1938–1939 he attended the Army War College in Washington, D.C. Thereafter, until the United States entered World War II in December 1941, he served in Washington as executive officer to the chief of Air Corps and then as head of the Training and Operations Section in the Office of the Chief of Air Corps.

After briefly commanding the Southeast Air Corps Training Center at Maxwell Field, Alabama, Stratemeyer, now a major general, was named in June 1942 as chief of the Air Staff at the Army Air Forces (AAF) headquarters in Washington, D.C. A year later he was sent to the China-Burma-India theater (CBI), where he initially served as commanding general of AAF operations in the India-Burma sector. He was responsible for the supply and maintenance of the Fourteenth

Air Force in China, air operations over Burma and protection of the air route to China, the coordination of the Air Transport Command's operations in the CBI, and the training of Chinese and American personnel. Stratemeyer also served as air adviser to Lieutenant General Joseph W. Stilwell, commander of the CBI, a post that taxed his considerable diplomatic skills as he tried to resolve the many personal and strategic disputes between Stilwell and Major General Claire Chennault, commander of the Fourteenth Air Force.

At the end of 1943 Stratemeyer was given command of the Eastern Air Command, an integrated AAF–Royal Air Force command that was part of the Southeast Asia Command. During the next year and a half his forces won air superiority over Burma, supported ground operations in Burma and India, and ferried large quantities of supplies from India to China. In July 1945 Stratemeyer, with the rank of lieutenant general, went to China as commanding general of the AAF in China and deputy commander of U.S. Forces China theater. After the Japanese surrendered in August, he supervised the air redeployment of more than 200,000 Chinese Nationalist troops from western to eastern China.

Stratemeyer returned to the United States in early 1946 to head the newly created Air Defense Command, which was responsible for the organization of the air defense of the United States. Two years later he was appointed head of the Continental Air Command, a combined authority consisting of the Air Defense Command and the Tactical Air Command. After a year's tenure in this assignment, he was appointed commander of the Far East Air Forces (FEAF), headquartered in Tokyo, Japan. In this post he introduced an innovative training program, developed challenging unit exercises, maintained a high state of readiness, and replaced many of the FEAF's obsolete propeller-driven fighters with F-80 and F-86 jet fighters.

After the United States entered the Korean War in late June 1950, Stratemeyer's forces, in conjunction with the navy's carrier-based planes, quickly won air superiority over South and North Korea and played a major role in repelling the North Korean invaders from South Korea by providing close ground support for the United Nations (UN) forces and interdicting enemy supply lines. They also engaged in some strategic bombing, and by the end of August 1950 they had knocked out most of the enemy's major military and industrial installations in North Korea.

During the fall of 1950 Stratemeyer's FEAF supported the UN forces as they crossed the thirty-eighth parallel and pushed north through North Korea toward the Yalu River, the boundary between North Korea and China. When the Chinese entered the war in strength in November 1950, the FEAF inflicted heavy casualties on them while the UN forces retreated from North Korea. In early 1951 the FEAF checked the growth of Chinese air power in Korea so that the Chinese ground offensives in the spring of 1951 had little air support. Despite a considerable effort, however, the FEAF was unable to cripple the Chinese logistical system.

Believing that an expanded strategy would bring victory, Stratemeyer favored an extension of the war beyond Korea, including the bombing of Chinese territory. However, for institutional and constitutional reasons, he was careful not to get involved in the controversy over the war's strategy between President Harry S. Truman and the UN commander, General Douglas MacArthur. While an admirer of MacArthur, who advocated bombing China and publicly questioned Truman's decision to confine the war to Korea, Stratemeyer stated in a press release in March 1951 that any decision to send bombers beyond Korea should be made at the governmental or UN level, not by field commanders. In May 1951 Stratemeyer suffered a heart attack, and after a long hospitalization he retired in November 1952.

Following the end of the Korean War, Stratemeyer criticized Truman's strategy, telling a Senate committee in 1954, "We were required to lose the war. We weren't allowed to win it." He also argued that the FEAF's ability to destroy enemy forces in Korea demonstrated that air power was the most economical means of waging war and protecting the free world against Communist aggression, particularly if the air force were authorized to employ nuclear weapons. An able administrator and strategist in two wars and a fervent proponent of air power, Stratemeyer died in Orlando, Florida.

• Stratemeyer's papers are at the U.S. Air Force Historical Research Agency, Air University, Maxwell Air Force Base, Ala. His career is summarized in *Biographical Register of the Officers and Graduates of the U.S. Military Academy*, vols. 6–9 (1921, 1931, 1941, 1951). References to Stratemeyer's service during World War II are in Wesley Frank Craven and James Lea Cate, eds., *The Army Air Forces in World War II*, vol. 4: *The Pacific: Guadalcanal to Saipan, August 1942 to July 1944* (1950) and vol. 5: *The Pacific: Matterhorn to Nagasaki* (1953); and Charles F. Romanus and Riley Sunderland, *Stilwell's Command Problems* (1956) and *Time Runs out in CBI* (1959), both in the *U.S. Army in World War II* series. Stratemeyer's service during the Korean War is discussed in Robert F. Futrell, *The United States Air Force in Korea, 1950–1953* (1983); and D. Clayton James, *The Years of MacArthur*, vol. 3: *Triumph and Disaster, 1945–1964* (1985). An obituary is in the *New York Times*, 11 Aug. 1969.

JOHN KENNEDY OHL